Encyclopedia of
Social Work

19th
Edition

Encyclopedia of Social Work

19th Edition

Editorial Board

Richard L. Edwards, *Editor-in-Chief*
June Gary Hopps, *Associate Editor-in-Chief*

L. Diane Bernard
Diana M. DiNitto
Patricia L. Ewalt
Michael Frumkin
Alejandro Garcia
Jesse J. Harris

Martha N. Ozawa
Rosemary C. Sarri
Elfriede G. Schlesinger
Fredrick W. Seidl
Constance W. Williams

Linda Beebe, *Executive Editor*
Nancy A. Winchester, *Managing Editor*

NASW PRESS

National Association of Social Workers
Washington, DC

Executive Editor	Linda Beebe
Managing Editor	Nancy A. Winchester
Senior Editor	Fran Pflieger
Editorial Secretary	Sarah Lowman

Copy Editors

Wendy Almeleh

Stephen D. Pazdan

Laurel J. Rumpl

Kendall W. Sterling

Samuel Allen	Annette Hansen
Ida Audeh	K. Hyde Loomis
Donna L. Brodsky	Jack C. Neal
Greg Edmondson	Chhaya M. Rao
Kathleen A. Elinskas	Stephanie Selice

Wolf Publications, Inc.

Proofreaders

Susan J. Harris

Editorial Experts, Inc.	Vivian Mason
Marcie Fenster	Stella D. Matalas
Louise Goines	

Indexer

Bernice Eisen

Word Processor

Donna Rambler

Copyright © 1995 by the NASW Press

Library of Congress Cataloging-in-Publication Data
Encyclopedia of social work.   19th edition, 1995
Washington, DC, National Association of Social Workers.
v. 25 cm.
Decennial, 1977–
The 18th updated with a supplement, 1990
Continues: Social work year book.
ISSN 0071-0237 = Encyclopedia of social work.

Social service—Yearbooks.   I. National Association of Social Workers.
II. Supplement to the Encyclopedia of social work.
DNLM: HV 35 E56

HV35.S6	361'.003	30-30948
ISBN 0-87101-255-3 hardcover		MARC-S
0-87101-256-1 softcover		
0-87101-258-8 CD-ROM		

Printed in the United States of America
Cover and interior design by Quinn Information Design

Contents

Preface **xv**

How to Use the Encyclopedia **xix**

List of Reader's Guides **xxii**

Biographies   2569

Appendixes

Index   I-1
(Full index appears in all three volumes.)

P

Pacific Islanders
Noreen Mokuau

The thousands of islands in the Pacific Ocean have collectively become known as Polynesia, Micronesia, and Melanesia. These islands are spread across 64 million square miles and exhibit a variety of physical settings and climatic extremes ranging from snowcapped mountains (New Guinea–Melanesia) to rain-soaked forests (Kauai–Polynesia) to sweltering equatorial heat (Marshall Islands–Micronesia) (Oliver, 1988). Although the physical environment does not necessarily shape culture, the variation in geography of the Pacific Islands hints at the cultural diversity of its inhabitants. Islanders from Hawaii, Samoa, Tonga, New Zealand, and the Cook Islands (Polynesia); from the Federated States of Micronesia, the Northern Mariana Islands, Guam, Palau, the Marshall Islands, and Nauru (Micronesia); and from New Guinea, New Caledonia, Fiji, and the Solomon Islands (Melanesia) constitute a sampling of the many cultural groups that are part of the Pacific Basin region.

The United States maintains formal political relationships with certain peoples from Polynesia and Micronesia, but not with Melanesia. People in the Polynesian islands of Hawaii and American Samoa are affiliated through statehood and territorial status, respectively. People in five Micronesian entities—Guam, the Federated States of Micronesia, the Republic of the Marshall Islands, the Northern Mariana Islands, and the Republic of Palau—are associated with the United States through territorial status, commonwealth status, or free association status.

This entry describes two sets of Pacific Islander peoples: (1) those with the largest population census in the United States and (2) those who do not reside in the United States but who maintain political affiliations with the country. The descriptive overview of Pacific peoples includes information on general characteristics, cultural values and traditions, and psychosocial problems and issues. Such an overview has broad implications for the profession of social work in its consideration of culturally competent practice with Pacific Islander peoples.

PACIFIC ISLANDERS IN THE UNITED STATES
Pacific Islanders with the largest population census in the United States in 1990 were Hawaiians (211,014), Samoans (62,964), Chamorros (49,345), Tongans (17,606), and Fijians (7,036) (Harrison, 1991). This section presents major descriptive characteristics of the three largest Pacific Islander groups in the United States.

Hawaiians
Most Hawaiians (138,742) reside in their indigenous homeland, Hawaii. They constitute only 13 percent of the total state population of 1,108,229 (Asian/Pacific Islander Data Consortium, 1992). A large number of Hawaiians (34,447) also reside in California (Harrison, 1991).

An important population characteristic for Hawaiians relates to blood quantum. Hawaiians who are of mixed (part-Hawaiian) ancestry account for 96 percent of the population. Various factors such as interracial marriages and high death rates have contributed to a tremendous decline in the numbers of pure-blood Hawaiians. The major concern generated from this decline relates to the depopulation of Hawaiians as an indigenous people. Hawaiians, therefore, give greater emphasis to the perpetuation of their culture through its values and traditions.

Cultural values and traditions. The values that infuse Hawaiian culture reflect the importance of relationships (Mokuau, in press). Relationships define the reciprocal energy that binds the individual, the family, the environment, and the spiritual world. Hawaiians, like other Pacific Islander groups, emphasize collective affiliation rather than individualism and promote a worldview of people in harmony with each other, the environment, and the spiritual world.

Kanahele (1986) identified multiple values in Hawaiian culture that reflect the importance of affiliation: humility, spirituality, generosity, graciousness, keeping promises, intelligence, cleanliness, and helpfulness. Perhaps the one value that captures the essence of affiliation is "aloha." *Aloha* has many different meanings, such as "hello" and "goodbye," but it also refers to a love and caring for people and the environment. Aloha refers to the common bond of humanity and to the interrelatedness of all things in this world and the spiritual world.

Biopsychosocial problems and issues.
Although values of relationships and affiliation have endured in Hawaiian culture in contemporary times, they have not insulated Hawaiian people from an array of health and psychosocial problems. Hawaiians fare poorly on major indexes of health and wellness. They have a life expectancy rate that is five years shorter than that of other groups in Hawaii (Johnson, 1989b) and a high mortality rate from cardiovascular disease (Wegner, 1989a), cancer (Le Marchand & Kolonel, 1989), and diabetes (Johnson, 1989a; U.S. Congress, 1987).

Social indicators reflect the impoverished status of Hawaiians. Hawaiians are disproportionately represented in lower-income brackets and are underrepresented in the higher education system. Nineteen percent of Hawaiian families in Hawaii earn less than $15,000 per year as compared with 13 percent of families in other ethnic groups (Papa Ola Lōkahi, 1992). Their underrepresentation in higher education is noted through enrollment census (9 percent) and graduation rates (2 percent) (Alu Like, 1988), which are not proportionate to their population size in Hawaii (13 percent). In addition to low income and poor educational achievement, a litany of psychosocial problems confronts Hawaiians. These problems include high rates of domestic violence, incarceration in adult and juvenile facilities, substance abuse, and teenage pregnancy (Blaisdell & Mokuau, 1991).

An understanding of the problems among Hawaiians originates in an understanding of oppression and racism and of the effect of such forces on the life of a people. Historical accounts indicate that institutional oppression against the Hawaiian people (see historical reviews in Cooper & Daws, 1985; Dougherty, 1992; Kameeleihiwa, 1992) has resulted in an erosion of an indigenous culture and has manifested itself in an array of health and psychosocial problems.

Samoans
Samoans are indigenous to American Samoa and Western Samoa; however, many Samoans who reside in the United States are from the territory of American Samoa. Samoans from American Samoa travel easily throughout the United States because of their status as American nationals. They reside primarily in California (31,917) and Hawaii (15,034) (Harrison, 1991). The migration of

Samoans to the United States, which started in the 1950s, is attributed to three major factors: (1) the transfer of naval base personnel with the closing of the U.S. naval base in American Samoa in 1951, (2) increased opportunities for education and employment in the United States, and (3) the increase in population and the concomitant lack of employment and economic opportunities in American Samoa (California Department of Mental Health, 1981).

Cultural values and traditions.
As in the Hawaiian culture, the values in Samoan culture revolve around relationships. "Dominant values ... in Samoan culture focus on the family, communal relationships and the church" (Mokuau & Chang, 1991, p. 159). The well-being of the collective unit takes precedence over the interests of individual family members, and thus behaviors and practices are guided by values of reciprocity, cooperation, and interdependence (Mokuau & Tauiliili, 1992).

Fa'a Samoa, the Samoan way of life, emphasizes kinship ties and the recognition that all who are related by birth or adoption belong to one family. The unity of the family is illustrated by large donations of money on the request of a family chief (matai) for other members of the family (Fiatoa & Palafox, 1980). It is an expectation that family members help others with expenses such as weddings, funerals, and moving (Calkins, 1962). The structure and responsibilities of the family are affirmed by the church; the church, in turn, is supported by contributions from the families.

Psychosocial problems and issues.
Samoans in the United States experience problems related to cultural adjustment. The contrast of Samoan values (collectivism) with mainstream American culture (individualism) often leads to conflict for Samoans. For example, the competitive spirit needed to succeed in higher education is often viewed as secondary by many Samoans who "value religion and family unity ... more highly than a western-style education" (Rose, 1990, p. 6). A typical result is poor performance in educational achievement, disenchantment, and loss of motivation to succeed (Rose, 1990).

Another set of problems may occur because of intergenerational conflicts, which may arise between older Samoan parents and grandparents who want their children to retain cultural values and traditions and younger Samoans who struggle to be Samoan and still fit into American society. Illustrative conflicts that may emerge include younger Samoans not wanting to attend church as often and demonstrating greater reluctance to donate salaries to the family.

The difficulties of cultural adjustment are manifested in many other psychosocial problems. In Hawaii 27 percent of Samoans live below the poverty line (Brewer & Hosek, 1987) and less than 1 percent of the University of Hawaii population are Samoans ("Hawaii's Samoans Fail," 1987). Samoans also have the highest rate of child abuse in Hawaii (Hawaii Department of Human Services, 1988), are overrepresented in prison populations (Iyechad, 1992), and have a high rate of alcoholism (Whitney & Hanipale, 1991).

The polarities in value systems between Samoan culture and mainstream American culture have led to problems of adjustment. As with other minority groups of color, Samoans struggle with the preservation of their indigenous ways and survival in a Western-oriented society.

Chamorros

Chamorros in the United States are natives of Guam and other Mariana Islands. Referred to as Guamanian in U.S. census reports, they reside primarily in California (25,059), with some residing in Hawaii (2,120) (Harrison, 1991). The native people of Guam prefer, for cultural and political reasons, to be recognized as Chamorros rather than Guamanians (Cristobal, 1990; Untalan, 1991), and there are continuing efforts to clarify the distinction. Guam, the largest and southernmost island of the Marianas, is a territory of the United States, and its people are considered to be American nationals, with opportunities to travel freely in the country. Many Chamorros who move to California and Hawaii are motivated by reasons of education and employment, as well as by military commitment.

Cultural values and traditions. Chamorros share the emphasis on family life values and traditions with other Pacific Islander peoples. The foundation for Chamorro culture is group cohesion and interdependence.

> The family is the cornerstone of a Chamorro's personal life from birth to death. An individual's personal identity, social status and responsibility, all revolve around the family. The Chamorro family consists of an entire network of social, cultural and economic relationships among kinsmen. (Untalan, 1990, p. 5)

Within the family hierarchy, traditional Chamorro values highlight a reverence for the elders. Reverence for elders is demonstrated by the symbolic bow (nginge) and smelling of the elder's right hand (Jose et al., 1980). Grandparents assume a role of teaching and caring for grandchildren as well as children.

For Chamorros in the United States, the maintenance of the family support system provides assistance in finding homes and job referral and also provides emotional security, initial guidance, and advice on how to survive in a Western culture (Shimizu, 1982). Individual responsibilities exist but are viewed in the context of achieving social and familial obligations.

Psychosocial problems and issues. Many of the problems confronting Chamorros in the United States relate to cultural transition and change, including the differences in value systems between Chamorro culture and mainstream American culture. Although Chamorro values are still evident in Chamorro American culture, some members of the younger generation are challenging and diffusing the traditional foundation (Shimizu, 1982). Shimizu noted that much of this challenge has developed because the younger generation has more options and opportunities for greater individual freedom of choice and lifestyles.

Psychosocial problems for Chamorros in the United States are difficult to assess because this population is dispersed and the data describing their circumstances are limited. However, available information suggests that the breakdown of cultural values and the deterioration of cultural identity are due to two major factors (Untalan, 1991): (1) the geographic isolation of Chamorros from family members and (2) the pervasive influence of Western values and norms on Chamorros in the United States. Although problems of mental health do not appear to be significantly different from those of members of the larger American society, Chamorro people with mental health needs do not readily use mental health services (Shimizu, 1982).

PACIFIC ISLANDERS IN U.S.-ASSOCIATED JURISDICTIONS

The United States maintains political relationships with several Pacific Island jurisdictions. The population censuses for these groups in their island homelands are varied: American Samoa (46,773), Guam (133,152), Federated States of Micronesia (101,108), Republic of the Marshall Islands (46,020), Commonwealth of the Northern Mariana Islands (43,345), and Republic of Palau (15,122) (U.S. Bureau of the Census, 1991a, 1991b, 1991c, 1991d; University of Hawaii School of Public Health, 1991). Although there is great diversity among these peoples, shared values and psychosocial problems exist.

Cultural Values and Traditions

One traditional value is pronounced in Pacific Island cultures: the primacy of the family–collective unit. The extended family and communalism are fundamental to cultures of the Pacific Islands (Finau, 1989). In American Samoa and Guam, the concept of family often extends beyond the nuclear family to include other members related by blood, marriage, or adoption. In the majority of ' Micronesian islands, the traditional extended family unit is based on the matrilineage group (Hezel, 1989). Lineage traditions dictate that all normal resources coming from the land (food and other products) are shared and distributed through the entire matrilineage group. This type of communal kin-based organization fosters family solidarity.

Psychosocial Problems and Issues

The traditional lineal family structure in the Pacific Islands has changed considerably with Western influence. Within the past two decades, the lineal family and the emphasis on the nuclear family have deteriorated. Changes in the family structure have precipitated a variety of psychosocial problems and issues.

Problems of suicide, child abuse, substance abuse, and increasing rates of mental illness are emerging as a result of rapid social change and modernization. Since 1960 the suicide rate for young Micronesian males has reached epidemic proportions (Rubinstein, 1985). For those at highest risk, males 15 to 24 years old, the average annual rate in the 1980s ranged from 70 per 100,000 in the Republic of Palau to 206 per 100,000 in Chuuk, one of the states of the Federated States of Micronesia (Hezel, 1989).

Child abuse is becoming more evident with the disruption of the traditional family structure. The majority (69 percent) of child abuse cases noted in the Republic of Palau as well as in Chuuk, Pohnpei, and Yap (three states in the Federated States of Micronesia) are due to neglect (defined as the absence of physical amenities and physical necessities for life as well as the deprivation of emotional support and attention). Some cases are attributed to physical abuse (20 percent) and sexual abuse (11 percent) (Marcus, 1991).

Substance abuse, particularly the use of alcohol, is increasingly becoming a part of Micronesian lifestyle. Alcohol has been incorporated into major community events in Yap, of the Federated States of Micronesia; the Republic of Palau; and, to a lesser extent, the Marshall Islands (Hezel, no date). On other islands, such as Kosrae and Pohnpei of the Federated States of Micronesia, a native substance, sakau, is the alcoholic drink of choice (Takeuchi, 1989). Pacific health authorities recognize substance abuse as a priority health issue and possibly the leading health problem in the Pacific (University of Hawaii School of Public Health, 1991).

SOCIAL WORK PRACTICE WITH PACIFIC ISLANDERS

The social work profession is founded on a commitment to help oppressed peoples. Background information reveals that many Pacific Islanders are impoverished and are experiencing an array of problems attributed to social change, cultural adjustment, and modernization. Social work practice with Pacific Islanders in the United States and in U.S.-associated jurisdictions requires an understanding of the various cultures to develop and implement culturally competent services.

Culturally competent social work practice refers to a body of knowledge and skills that compassionately responds to the needs and issues of culturally diverse populations. The design, implementation, and evaluation of culturally competent services can be guided by several premises that focus on an appreciation of diversity and the uniqueness of different groups of people. For the various groups of Pacific Islanders, culturally competent practice begins with the awareness that traditional Pacific Islander values and traditions are different from Western values and traditions. Such an awareness generates the understanding that mainstream social work services may not be appropriate because of their basis in Western theories and norms, and it produces an appreciation of the cultural strengths and richness inherent in the values and traditions of various cultural groups. Thus, culturally competent practice provides services to Pacific Islanders that are congruent with their worldviews, values, and traditions and addresses their problems in ways that empower the group.

Social workers can demonstrate cultural competence with Pacific Islander populations in different ways. For example, social workers can advocate for policy changes that require increased attention and responsiveness to Pacific Islander peoples. They can provide culturally compatible services to individuals and their families. They can conduct research that increases an understanding of assessment and intervention protocols that are appropriate for Pacific Islanders. The following sections build on previous information on cultural values and psychosocial problems and provides brief practice illustrations with Hawaiians, Samoans, Chamorros, and other Micronesian groups in U.S.-associated jurisdictions.

Health Care Services for Hawaiians

Hawaiians experience poor health on a variety of indicators (Wegner, 1989b), yet mainstream health care services have been underused, primarily because the services are inaccessible to this population. Many Hawaiians in Hawaii reside in rural areas where services are not readily available. Most of the health care services are located in urban areas on the island of Oahu; therefore, those Hawaiians who reside in rural areas on Oahu and especially on neighboring islands are excluded from health care services. The cost in terms of travel time and finances, especially from neighboring islands to Oahu, precludes many Hawaiians from making the hospital and clinic visits vital to treatment and prevention.

The involvement of social workers in health care for Hawaiians relates to advocacy efforts to develop and deliver services in high-density Hawaiian communities. These efforts may require organizing and mobilizing Hawaiian communities to identify their needs and to confront government and health care officials on the provision of services to high-risk populations. They also require an insight on the part of social workers to invite and encourage the participation of Hawaiian people in decision making related to advocacy; community mobilization; and, ultimately, the development and delivery of services.

Samoan Family-Centered Program

Substance abuse, particularly, alcoholism, is one of the problems noted in Samoan culture. Whitney and Hanipale (1991) stated that in 1986, 100,000 gallons of beer were sold in American Samoa. With an adult population of about 18,000 at that time, the computations show consumption of nearly 22 gallons per year per capita (C. Keener, personal communication, as cited in Whitney & Hanipale, 1991). Samoans in Hawaii and California also demonstrate a high risk for alcoholism (Lindo, 1989; Pleadwell, 1992). Furthermore, Samoans do not readily use drug rehabilitation clinics and programs (Lindo, 1989).

One way for social workers to deal with alcoholism in the Samoan population is to become involved with the family, for example, by designing a family-centered prevention program that is compatible with traditional Samoan values and that promotes the participation of members. An integral part of the family-centered approach is the education of family members; prevention or reduction of alcohol use may depend on family members' being familiar with the symptoms, behavioral patterns, and consequences of alcoholism and monitoring its use. Involvement of the head of the

Samoan household, possibly the chief (matai), or the pastor of a church may also facilitate the participation of family members and influence the prevention or reduction of high-risk behaviors.

Chamorro Cultural Identity

As the third largest Pacific Islander group in the United States, Chamorros from Guam are still relatively unknown because of their small numbers. They are often misidentified as another Pacific Islander group or as Hispanics. For Chamorros in the United States, adjusting to a new set of values, combined with having others impose different cultural identities on them, leads to problems of cultural alienation and identity conflict. For Chamorros residing in Guam, the situation of identity conflict and deterioration of cultural values still exists because of the pervasive influence of American culture and rapid social change.

It is instructive for social workers practicing with Chamorros in the United States or in Guam to acknowledge the importance of the cultural identity that many Chamorros ascribe to themselves. According to Cristobal (1990), "Despite academic evidence to the contrary and, more importantly, despite the sheer tenacity of a group of people who ... defiantly proclaim themselves to be Chamorro, many refuse to acknowledge the existence of the Chamorro people" (p. 11).

The focus on group identity and cultural values is appropriate for Chamorro people and facilitates work on other psychosocial problems and issues that result from rapid social change. A broader social work effort would be to assist in advocacy efforts for legislation that would promote political recognition of Chamorros and other Pacific Islander groups.

Suicide among Micronesian Males

The epidemic proportions of suicide among young Micronesian males in their island homelands (Hezel, 1989) must be addressed. The suicide rates have been attributed to changes in the structure of the family and the difficulties of Pacific Islanders to respond to social changes (Hezel, 1989; Rubinstein, 1985). The increasing influence of American culture in Micronesian communities has contributed to institutional changes such as the conversion of a subsistence economy to a cash economy and the adoption of a Western government structure. These factors have further influenced the breakup of the traditional Micronesian family.

The challenge for social workers practicing with people in their indigenous homelands is to develop a partnership for action. The partnership would require the participation of indigenous Pacific Islander peoples and the American government in planning and implementing any agenda for change. Opportunities for collaboration should increase the likelihood that changes are culturally appropriate and responsive to the needs of the people. With problems such as suicide, prevention and treatment programs emphasizing cultural identity directed at the family are central to utilization by high-risk Pacific Islander groups. On many Pacific islands, it is too late to erase some of the problems resulting from rapid social change; however, it is never too late to recognize the fallacy of imposing one culture on another.

There is a need for social work research on policy and practice issues relevant to all Pacific Islander populations. The limited information available on these populations indicates an increasing scope of problems and a need for culturally competent services. Research endeavors focusing on the incidence and prevalence of problems, as well as on solutions to problems that have a basis in cultural competence, are essential.

CONCLUSION

Several broad descriptions for culturally competent social work practice with Pacific Islanders can be drawn.

1. Social workers need an understanding of the origins of problems in Islander populations, and they must possess a familiarity with the influence of oppression on values, behaviors, and lifestyle practices. (For example, they should understand the effects of rapid, and imposed, social change on populations in their indigenous homelands.)
2. Cultural values and traditions that are central to these populations should be incorporated in the design and delivery of services (for example, family-directed services).
3. Social workers should advocate for educational opportunities and economic justice.
4. In delivering services, social workers should encourage Pacific Islanders' participation in decision making around problem identification and resolution.
5. Services must be accessible in terms of both location and cost.
6. Service delivery must include respect for, and more important, encouragement of cultural affiliation and identity as a way to empower the individual and his or her family. (People vary in their identification with their indigenous culture and Western culture, and promotion of the self/group-ascribed identity is important.)

Pacific Islanders often have been overlooked in the social work literature because of their small population and the limited information about them. Their population in the United States and in the U.S.-associated jurisdictions is small compared to other population groups. Their story is compelling because the demise of cultural values and norms and the increase of psychosocial problems indicate a greater tragedy—the extinction of a small, unique, and diverse population. Social work can assume a central role in advocating for the empowerment of Pacific Islanders and designing culturally compatible services.

REFERENCES

Alu Like. (1988). *Native Hawaiian students at the University of Hawaii: Implications for vocational and higher education.* Honolulu: Author.

Asian/Pacific Islander Data Consortium. (1992). *Asian and Pacific Islander American profile series 1A: Hawaii.* San Francisco: Author.

Blaisdell, K., & Mokuau, N. (1991). Kānaka maoli: Indigenous Hawaiians. In N. Mokuau (Ed.), *Handbook of social services for Asian and Pacific islanders* (pp. 131–154). Westport, CT: Greenwood Press.

Brewer, N., & Hosek, L. (1987, July 14). Samoans' budget woes erode the old traditions. *Honolulu Star Bulletin,* pp. A-1, A-10.

California Department of Mental Health. (1981). *Samoans in America.* Oakland, CA: Author.

Calkins, F. G. (1962). *My Samoan chief.* Honolulu: University of Hawaii Press.

Cooper, G., & Daws, G. (1985). *Land and power in Hawaii.* Honolulu: Benchmark Books.

Cristobal, H. A. (1990, February). The organization of people for indigenous rights: A commitment towards self-determination. *Pacific Ties,* pp. 10–11, 14.

Dougherty, M. (1992). *To steal a kingdom: Probing Hawaiian history.* Waimanalo, HI: Island Press.

Fiatoa, L., & Palafox, N. (1980). The Samoans. In N. Palafox & A. Warren (Eds.), *Cross cultural caring: A handbook for health care professionals in Hawaii* (pp. 250–271). Honolulu: University of Hawaii John A. Burns School of Medicine.

Finau, S. A. (1989). *Health care in the Pacific: Who would bell the cat?* Paper presented at the Public Health Association Conference, University of Melbourne, Victoria, Australia.

Harrison, R. J. (1991). *Key findings from the 1990 census. (Presentation for the meeting of the Minority Advisory Committee on the Asian and Pacific Islander population).* Washington, DC: U.S. Department of Commerce, Bureau of the Census.

Hawaii Department of Human Services. (1988). *A statistical report on child abuse and neglect in Hawaii 1980-87.* Honolulu: Program Development, Family and Adult Services Division and Planning Office.

Hawaii's Samoans fail to excel in school. (1987, July 13). *Honolulu Star Bulletin,* p. A-4.

Hezel, F. X. (1989). Suicide and the Micronesian family. *The Contemporary Pacific, 1*(1–2), 43–74.

Hezel, F. X. (no date). Why and how alcohol is a problem. *Micronesian seminar.* Ponape: Federated States of Micronesia.

Iyechad, G. L. (1992, March 8). Many Samoans here find adjustments difficult and stereotypes binding. *Honolulu Star Bulletin & Advertiser*, pp. F-1, F-5.

Johnson, D.B. (1989a). Diabetes: Epidemiology and disability. *Social Process in Hawaii. 32,* 104-112.

Johnson, D. B. (1989b). An overview of ethnicity and health in Hawaii. *Social Process in Hawaii, 32,* 67–86.

Jose, M., Jr., M., Waki, L., Lizarra, V., Santos, A., Sablan, O., Garrido, J., Leon-Guerrero, R., & Demapan, M. (1980). The Chamorros. In N. Palafox & A. Warren (Eds.), *Cross-cultural caring: A handbook for health care professionals in Hawaii* (pp. 8–25). Honolulu: University of Hawaii John A. Burns School of Medicine.

Kameeleihiwa. L. (1992). *Native land and foreign desires: Pehea lā e pono ai?* Honolulu: Bishop Museum Press.

Kanahele, G. H. S. (1986). *Kū kanaka: Stand tall.* Honolulu: University of Hawaii Press and Waiaha Foundation.

Le Marchand, L. L., & Kolonel, L. N. (1989). Cancer: Epidemiology and prevention. *Social Process in Hawaii. 32,* 134–148.

Lindo, J. K. (1989). *Pacific Island resource.* Oakland, CA: Association of Asian/Pacific Community Health Organizations.

Marcus, M. N. (1991, May 5). Abuse and neglect. *Islander,* pp. 6–9.

Mokuau, N. (in press). Hawaiians. *Asian American encyclopedia.* Pasadena, CA: Salem Press.

Mokuau, N., & Chang, N. (1991). Samoans. In N. Mokuau (Ed.), *Handbook of social services for Asian and Pacific Islanders* (pp. 155–169). Westport, CT: Greenwood Press.

Mokuau, N., & Tauiliili, P. (1992). Families with native Hawaiian and Pacific Island roots. In E. W. Lynch & M. J. Hanson (Eds.), *Developing cross-cultural competence* (pp. 301–318). Baltimore: Paul H. Brookes.

Oliver, D. L. (1988). *The Pacific Islands.* Honolulu: University of Hawaii Press.

Papa Ola Lōkahi. (1992). *Native Hawaiian health data book.* Honolulu: Author.

Pleadwell, B. A. (Ed.). (1992, Fall). Substance abuse report concerns health officials. *Hawaii Health Messenger,* p. 3.

Rose, J. S. (1990, February). Samoans in higher education: Moving towards assimilation or equalization? *Pacific Ties,* p. 6.

Rubinstein, D. H. (1985). Suicide in Micronesia. In *Culture, youth and suicide in the Pacific: Papers from an East–West Center conference* (pp. 88–111). Honolulu: University of Hawaii, Center for Asian and Pacific Studies.

Shimizu, D.L.G. (1982). *Mental health needs assessment: The Guamanians in California.* San Francisco: Pacific Asian Mental Health Research Project.

Takeuchi, F. K. (1989, November 6). Sakau's an elixir of choice, culture. *Honolulu Star Bulletin,* p. A-6.

University of Hawaii School of Public Health. (1991). *Pacific Island mental health and substance abuse: A supplement to a reevaluation of health services in U.S.-associated Pacific Island jurisdictions.* Honolulu: Author.

Untalan, F. M. (1990, February). American policy: Its insidious effects on Pacific Island families. *Pacific Ties,* pp. 5, 7, 16, 23.

Untalan, F. M. (1991). Chamorros. In N. Mokuau (Ed.), *Handbook of social services for Asian and Pacific Islanders* (pp. 171–182). Westport, CT: Greenwood Press.

U.S. Bureau of the Census. (1991a). *Census bureau releases 1990 census population counts for American Samoa.* Washington, DC: U.S. Government Printing Office.

U.S. Bureau of the Census. (1991b). *Census bureau releases 1990 census population counts for the Commonwealth of the Northern Mariana Islands.* Washington, DC: U.S. Government Printing Office.

U.S. Bureau of the Census. (1991c). *Census bureau releases 1990 census population counts for the Commonwealth of the Republic of Palau.* Washington, DC: U.S. Government Printing Office.

U.S. Bureau of the Census. (1991d). *Census bureau releases 1990 census population counts for Guam.* Washington, DC: U.S. Government Printing Office.

U.S. Congress, Office of Technology Assessment. (1987). *Current health status and population projections of Native Hawaiians living in Hawaii.* Washington, DC: U.S. Government Printing Office.

Wegner, E. L. (1989a). Hypertension and heart disease. *Social Process in Hawaii, 32,* 113–133.

Wegner, E. L. (Ed.). (1989b). *Social Process in Hawaii: Volume 32. The health of native Hawaiians: A selective report on health status and health care in the 1980s.* Honolulu: University of Hawaii Department of Sociology.

Whitney, S., & Hanipale, F. (1991). *Feeling strong: Themes in Samoan drinking and recovery.* Unpublished manuscript. Pago Pago: American Samoa.

FURTHER READING

Alailima, F. (1988). *Aggie Grey: A Samoan saga.* Honolulu: Mutual Publishing Company.

Dudley, M. K., & Agard, K. K. (1990). *A call for Hawaiian sovereignty.* Honolulu: Na Kane O Ka Malo Press.

Liliuokalani. (1989). *Hawaii's story by Hawaii's queen.* Rutland, VT: Charles E. Tuttle Company.

Robillard, A. B., & Marsella, A. J. (Eds.). (1987). *Contemporary issues in mental health research in the Pacific Islands.* Honolulu: University of Hawaii Social Science Research Institute.

Stannard, D. E. (1989). *Before the horror: The population of Hawaii on the eve of western contact.* Honolulu: University of Hawaii Social Science Research Institute.

Noreen Mokuau, DSW, is professor, University of Hawaii, School of Social Work, 2500 Campus Road, Honolulu, HI 96822.

For further information see

Alaska Natives; Asian Americans Overview; Civil Rights; Community Needs Assessment; Ethnic-Sensitive Practice; Families Overview; Human Rights; Social Development; Social Welfare Policy.

Key Words

culturally competent practice	diversity
	Pacific Islanders

Pagan de Colon, Petroamerica

See Biographies section, Volume 3

Parole

See Probation and Parole

Partners

See Marriage/Partners

Patient Rights

Ruth Irelan Knee
Betsy S. Vourlekis

Efforts to articulate and enforce key elements of rights of individuals as they enter and interact with the health and mental health care system evolve constantly. Currently these efforts take place in the context of heightened national concern over escalating health care expenditures and a dramatically reconfiguring system of health care delivery and financing. As many customary health care structures and organizations change, a fundamental understanding of basic patient rights and their application across health care and mental health care settings is needed.

Patients' rights in health care continue to undergo changes in scope and complexity with each decade. In addition to protecting the basic constitutional rights of the individual patient as a citizen, health care providers must be concerned with preserving important humanistic components in the health care delivery system, including personal autonomy, dignity, and privacy. Certain rights of the individual patient as consumer in the health care system have been defined through laws, court decisions, professional standards, and public attitudes. The "patients' rights movement" has expanded rapidly since the mid-1960s and has contributed to increased public and professional awareness of how systematic abuses of rights may occur in health care programs.

HISTORICAL DEVELOPMENTS AND INFLUENCES

Prominent developments in and influences on evolving concepts of patient rights include the following:

- Federal equal health opportunity regulations based on requirements of Title VI of the Civil Rights Act of 1964 established procedures to ensure equal access to treatment regardless of race or ethnicity, and forced integration of general hospitals, nursing homes, and institutions for the mentally ill and mentally retarded. The principle of nondiscrimination in access to care and treatment was later generalized and applied to other groups.

- Civil rights and civil libertarian litigation related to abuses of constitutional rights within health care facilities and programs led to the requirements of informed consent and due process safeguards for activities such as medical experimentation (Katz, 1993) and involuntary commitment to a mental hospital (*O'Connor v. Donaldson*, 1975).
- In the early 1970s several class action lawsuits heard in federal courts established the right to liberty and the concept of "least-restrictive alternative" of care for nondangerous mentally ill and mentally retarded individuals, and for the first time set standards of care for such individuals who continue to reside in institutions (*Wyatt v. Stickney*, 1971, 1972). These decisions brought about significant changes in public institutions and programs for mentally disabled people and gave impetus to the deinstitutionalization movement.
- The landmark 1973 U.S. Supreme Court decision *Roe v. Wade* recognized a woman's right to control her own body and, within appropriate time limits, to decide about an abortion with her physician. Although legal challenges and regulatory restrictions continue to be mounted with respect to abortion, the articulation of a right to choice and self-determination has had implications in other areas of health care.
- Patient rights monitoring and advocacy structures have heightened awareness and adherence. Beginning in 1975, state agencies on aging established under the Older Americans Act of 1965 received federal funds to establish a nursing home ombudsman program to monitor the implementation of regulations protecting patients' rights in nursing homes and to receive and investigate complaints.
- Consumerism and consumer activists have increasingly questioned the safety, quality, and price of products, including health care and therapies. Patients, as consumers, have demanded information and asserted their right to be active participants in treatment and in the definitions and assurance of its quality.
- Medical technology's capacity to prolong life beyond the individual's ability to function as a person forced reexamination of the ethics relating to the provision of lifesaving measures for terminally ill people. Complex issues surrounding these decisions and others (for example, allocation of scarce life-sustaining technology and resources) gave rise to the bioethics movement and the increasing participation of professional ethicists in health care decisions.

Efforts to define aspects of patients' rights and to resolve related ethical issues have involved health care providers and their professional organizations, consumer groups, regulatory agencies, courts, and state and federal legislatures. Concepts of specific rights are established and maintained through a variety of processes such as class action suits leading to court decisions; political organizing and advocacy to influence legislation and accompanying regulations; professional standard setting for institutions and practitioners; and informal processes of changing norms, values, and customs.

These processes have resulted in important and influential statements of patient rights. For example, the Joint Commission on Accreditation of Healthcare Organizations (JCAHO) reviews hospitals' compliance with a specific set of patients' rights as a part of its accreditation process (JCAHO, 1993). Specific standards refer to the individual's right to (1) respectful, individualized care; (2) information about his or her condition, including any experimentation or research projects affecting care and treatment; (3) involvement in making decisions regarding this care; and (4) personal privacy and confidentiality of information.

Another important declaration of patient rights is a result of federal legislation. Regulations promulgated in response to nursing home reform legislation under the Omnibus Budget Reconciliation Act of 1987 detail facility responsibilities to ensure specific resident rights as a requirement of participation in the Medicare and Medicaid programs. Among the many rights are (1) nondiscrimination in admission and care regardless of source of payment; (2) freedom from unnecessary physical and chemical restraints; (3) the right to be informed about all care and to participate in care planning; (4) freedom from verbal, sexual, physical and mental abuse, corporal punishment, and involuntary seclusion; and (5) the right to personal property, access to the telephone and privacy of mail, and the right to share a room with a spouse who is also a resident of the facility.

A number of states have passed legislation that provides a "bill of rights" for patients in mental hospitals and institutions for the mentally retarded. The basic concepts contained in this legislation were reinforced through the Developmentally Disabled Assistance and Bill of Rights Act of 1975 and the Mental Health Systems Act of 1980. (Although the Mental Health Systems Act was repealed by the Omnibus Budget Reconciliation Act of 1981, Section 501, or the Patients' Bill of Rights, was retained.)

Although currently there is no single codification of "patients' rights" to guide patients and practitioners, there are basic categories of rights about which there is considerable agreement, derived from both formal and informal sanctions.

MAJOR CATEGORIES OF PATIENTS' RIGHTS

Major categories of rights apply broadly across patient populations and illnesses, although the specific issues of concern may vary. The five categories discussed in the sections that follow are potentially applicable to all health care and mental health care settings and involve all health care providers.

Nondiscrimination

Federal civil rights legislation made it illegal to deny access based on race or ethnicity to health care facilities receiving federal funds. More recent efforts to ensure patient rights have focused on differential access and care associated with gender, source of payment, type of illness, or disability status of the patient.

In spite of antidiscrimination laws and requirements, there is no universal right of access to health care in practice. Health care providers may refuse service because of the source of payment (for example, Medicare or Medicaid) or the lack of ability to pay. Patients with limited means and no insurance frequently forgo routine medical care altogether and may be subjected to discrimination in the form of "dumping" when they seek emergency care (Ansell & Schiff, 1987).

The acquired immune deficiency syndrome (AIDS) epidemic has challenged all segments of the health care system with respect to nondiscrimination in care. Early in the epidemic, refusal to treat or care for AIDS patients by both institutions and health care professionals was fueled by insufficient information, by legitimate public health concerns, and by fear of the disease and stigmatization of those who suffered from it. Currently all major health care provider organizations, including NASW (1993), have adopted ethical position statements concerning the professional's duty to treat. Furthermore, since the passage of the Americans with Disabilities Act of 1990 (ADA), refusal to treat based on a patient's human immunodeficiency virus (HIV) status or diagnosis of AIDS is illegal. ADA extended the concept of nondiscrimination to include the right to mainstream living for disabled individuals. ADA was designed to protect people with physical and mental disabilities from discrimination because of their disability in private employment, public accommodation, public transportation, telecommunications, and other public services.

ADA provisions relate to an individual's right to health care in several additional ways. Disabled people are guaranteed access to the broad range of services and establishments that most Americans take for granted, including physicians' offices, clinics, health spas, and other places of exercise or recreation. A physician may not refuse to see a patient for a physical problem because he or she believes the individual has or had a mental illness. Furthermore, aids such as interpreters or readers must be available to allow people with hearing or visual impairments to participate in health services. The law prohibits the use of preemployment medical examinations and inquiries except in those circumstances when all applicants for a specific position may be asked how they would perform in job-related functions (Milstein, Rubenstein, & Cyr, 1991).

Least-Restrictive Environment

The right of the individual to treatment or care in the least-restrictive environment applies to protection from unnecessary institutionalized care. Originally, movement of mentally ill or developmentally disabled people from hospitals and "training schools" into community placements, family homes, or their own homes was designed to allow them a freer lifestyle and to contribute to their rehabilitation/habilitation process. The ensuing negative consequences of what came to be known as "deinstitutionalization" were frequently related to a lack of both individualized and programmatic planning and to inadequate community resources, resulting in patient dumping and unmet needs. Philosophical debates continue about public policies that in effect make a homeless shelter "less restrictive" than a mental hospital (Bachrach, 1992; Belcher, 1988; Mikva, Minow, & Wald, 1993).

Statutory limitations on the use of involuntary hospitalization (along with due process guarantees for individuals when this occurs) ensure that people are hospitalized (institutionalized) against their wishes only if they are judged to be dangerous to themselves or others. Such admissions typically involve two independent assessments by physicians and are time-limited, with periodic judicial review. People who do not meet the criteria and who do not agree to voluntary hospitalization cannot be detained in the institution. Although this right is frequently confused with the right to refuse treatment, careful adherence to the principles of "least-restrictive environment" in situations of potential involuntary hospitalization should lead to vigorous pursuit of appropriate alternative treatment resources to the extent possible. This process requires time and communication.

Nursing home reform legislation under the Omnibus Budget Reconciliation Act of 1987 contained provisions that also limited the use of these facilities for certain individuals. In Medicare- and Medicaid- approved facilities, patients must be screened so that those in need of specialized care because of either mental illness or developmental disability will not be put in a nursing home unless they require care for a physical disability.

Choice and Self-Determination

Specific applications of a patient's general right to an active role in decision making about aspects of his or her own care, including the right to choose not to receive any treatment, are in the forefront of the evolving societal conceptions of proper care. Fundamental to any ability to choose and control care is access to essential information. Reinforcing such access are the concepts of informed consent, the right to review one's medical records, and the right to participate in one's own treatment planning.

Informed consent. The concept of informed consent came into being in large part through the realization that the human rights of subjects of medical research had not been taken seriously enough. Disclosures concerning radiation studies undertaken by the federal government in the 1940s and 1950s reinforced public understanding of the importance of this issue ("Nuclear Guinea Pigs," 1994). However, it was revelations in the 1970s about the disregard of the rights of human subjects involved in the Tuskegee Syphilis Study that led funders of research, particularly the federal government, to mandate institutional review board approval of all federally funded research with human subjects. Each institution doing this type of research must establish an institutional review board or bioethics committee to prevent abuses (Caplan, Edgar, King, & Jones, 1992; Federal Policy for the Protection of Human Subjects, 1991; Thomas & Quinn, 1991; Tuskegee Syphilis Study Ad Hoc Advisory Panel, 1973).

Current standards of practice require individuals participating in research protocols to sign informed consent documents. This type of document is also required by hospitals and other medical care providers before surgery or other medical procedures in which the patient may be at risk. This is done for both nonexperimental and experimental treatments. Informed consent assumes that there

has been adequate communication between the physician–researcher and the patient so that the patient understands the procedure, the risks, and the anticipated results before agreeing to it. In many situations it is also important for family members to have the same understanding.

Access to medical records. Patients have a generally accepted right to request information from their own medical records. This right is subject to certain limitations and is governed by state statutes, which differ from state to state. The right to participate to the fullest extent possible in planning processes related to treatment and care is reinforced by federal regulations and standards for those patient groups most vulnerable to its abuse—that is, people who are mentally ill or developmentally disabled and those who are residents of nursing homes.

Right to refuse treatment. An important component of patient self-determination is the right to refuse (or forgo) treatment. Some applications of this right are fraught with controversy, whereas others have gained widespread societal acceptance. Competent adults have the right to refuse treatment even though such treatment might prevent later serious disabilities or death. However, when applied to people with mental illness, the right to refuse medication or other forms of treatment, including hospitalization, except in instances of extreme emergency, generates controversy (Bentley, 1993; Mizrahi, 1992; Rosenson, 1993).

Other issues center around decision making for a minor child. To a large extent parents determine what health care a child is to receive. However, state laws concerning parental notification when a teenage girl plans to have an abortion exemplify the controversy that surrounds the exercise of these rights in some circumstances. In other instances the hospital or other health authority may require health care interventions such as vaccinations, blood transfusions, or surgical procedures even when these go against parental wishes or religious beliefs.

The right of a competent adult to refuse life-sustaining treatment when the illness is terminal is currently widely accepted in health care, whereas the right to actively induce one's death (assisted or unassisted) is not (Brock, 1992). Many discussions of the so-called right to die fail to distinguish adequately between the two circumstances. The current issues complicating the right to refuse treatment have to do with finding appropriate mechanisms to ensure that an individual's choices are articulated and upheld or determining who can articulate the patient's wishes if the patient can no longer do so. Differentiating between comfort measures and treatment can also be difficult, as can distinguishing between prolonging life and prolonging the onset of death.

Advance directives. Advance directives are methods to better ensure that an individual can decide what should happen—that is, can make and express choices about the use of technology or "heroic measures" at the end of life—when there is the possibility that the person may not be competent to make this decision when the time comes. In the absence of clear directives, courts may be called on to make decisions. State laws vary with respect to living wills and designation of power of attorney, two important forms of advance directives (Soskis & Kerson, 1992).

The importance of advance directives has been emphasized by both state and U.S. Supreme Court decisions (*Cruzan v. Director, Missouri Department of Health,* 1990; *In the Matter of Claire Conroy,* 1985; *In the Matter of Karen Quinlan,* 1976). In the 1970s states began to pass laws concerning the content of these directives and the process of decision making when a person is in a terminal state and has made no directive. Currently all states have such laws. Congress passed the Patient Self-Determination Act as part of the Omnibus Budget Reconciliation Act of 1990 to stimulate the use of advance directives. Specifically, the law requires all Medicare and Medicaid providers to give each patient written information on the patient's right, according to applicable state law, (1) to accept or refuse life-sustaining treatment in the event of terminal illness and (2) to formulate an advance directive if one so chooses. If a patient has made an advance directive, this must be documented in the patient's permanent medical record.

Freedom from Harm and Abuse

The general concept of a patient's right to be free from harm and abuse has a number of important applications. For example, people receiving care in institutional settings currently must be paid for any work they do, even when such work is considered "therapeutic." Use of restraints as a part of care, treatment, or behavior control (including chemical restraints, locked seclusion or "quiet rooms," and commonly used restraint devices such as "gerry chairs" or wrist ties) is subject to explicit standards. Typically, standards require documentation of the circumstances necessitating restraint and a time-limited physician's order (JCAHO, 1993). Documentation is subject to review by surveying and accrediting personnel. In the case of nursing home residents, federal standards explicitly prohibit the use of restraints for the purpose of discipline or staff convenience. Several states have made it a prosecutable offense to restrain nursing home residents improperly, and the National Citizens Coalition for Nursing Home Reform has an ongoing campaign to achieve restraint-free nursing homes throughout the country (Burger, 1993).

In a development with major implications for social work, the concept of ensuring no harm was extended to the patient's immediate return to the community. In the mid-1980s, concerns increased about harm to patients from premature or inadequately planned discharges that might result from the shift in financial incentives to hospitals under the Prospective Payment System and misuse of its diagnosis-related groups reimbursement system. Consumer advocacy efforts led to congressional hearings, a somewhat strengthened Office of Beneficiary Services within the Health Care Financing Administration, and specific requirements in revised federal regulations addressing discharge planning for all Medicare and Medicaid patients.

Confidentiality, Privacy, and Personhood

The concept of the patient's ethical right to confidentiality of his or her medical record and privacy concerning the information it contains applies across all health care settings. Nevertheless, in most states unauthorized disclosure of information from medical records is not illegal. By standards of good practice, professionals must obtain signed patient consent before releasing or requesting information from the record. Discussion of the patient's medical condition should be limited to those who are directly involved in treating the individual. This means having the patient's permission to speak with family members or caretakers. In settings such as psychiatric hospitals or drug treatment programs, standards may require that the consent be put in writing. The AIDS epidemic has raised important dilemmas for society and health care professionals in balancing individual rights to confidentiality and privacy with public health and individual concerns for safety and well-being. The health care professional's foremost responsibility to maintain confidentiality and protect patient privacy applies equally to people who have tested positive for HIV or have AIDS. Therefore, potential limits to client confidentiality posed by the professional's "duty to protect" must proceed from an understanding of the well-established ethical obligations with respect to maintaining or breaching confidentiality (Reamer, 1991). Currently legal decisions are emerging to guide professionals in the complex circumstances that may limit confidentiality (for example, a patient with HIV who continues to be sexually active with an uninformed partner) (Harding, Gray, & Neal, 1993).

Particularly for those living in institutions, privacy and personhood also involve practical matters such as the right to wear one's own clothing and have certain personal belongings, to have and spend one's own money, and to cohabit with one's spouse. Regardless of setting, this concept includes the right to be examined in private and to be addressed and treated with respect and dignity.

Professionals increasingly face threats to patient confidentiality and privacy of information that are not completely within the individual practitioner's direct control. The growing use of computerized records, which afford easier and wider access to patient data, and the interpretation of information by nonclinical personnel such as case managers and claims reviewers require careful institutional safeguards. With standardized record keeping under national health care reform, federal legislation is needed to protect the privacy of medical records (Alpert, 1993).

MECHANISMS FOR ENSURING RIGHTS

Rights and responsibilities of patients, families (next of kin), health care providers, and payers of health care are monitored and enforced through a number of mechanisms. The nursing home ombudsman program, mandated nationwide by federal law under the Older Americans Act, is an example of an approach to monitoring. Each state must have laws that ensure the ombudsman access to facilities, residents, and records for reporting and processing complaints. The 1987 nursing home reform legislation contained provisions to ensure that ombudsmen are asked to participate in nursing home survey and certification processes. In 1992 reauthorization of the Older Americans Act under Title VII further strengthened the program, calling for coordination with programs for prevention of elder abuse, neglect, and exploitation.

The Civil Rights of Institutionalized Persons Act of 1980 gave the U.S. Department of Justice the right to sue states to protect the rights of those confined in state institutions, including prisons and facilities for people with mental illness or mental retardation. The Protection and Advocacy for Mentally Ill Individuals Act of 1986 created a national network of protection and advocacy agencies to protect the rights of mentally ill people, both inside and outside state institutions. When this legislation was reauthorized in 1991, the scope was broadened to support advocacy on behalf of

people in jails and prisons, board-and-care facilities, homeless shelters, and federal facilities such as Veterans Administration hospitals. The Senate report accompanying the 1991 legislation highlighted the special problems and cultural barriers faced by racial and ethnic minorities in obtaining protection for their legal rights in mental health care systems (U.S. Senate, 1991).

At times processes to implement the rights of children under 18 years of age may override parental control and decision making. In the case of severely handicapped infants, hospital infant care review committees (established by the Child Abuse Prevention and Treatment Act Amendments of 1984, known as the "Baby Jane Doe" amendments) have the responsibility of deciding when and whether to withhold treatment from such newborns. Decisions must be based on the anticipated effectiveness or futility of treatment for survival of the infant. There have been instances of litigation in situations in which the hospital committee recommended stopping any life supports, but the parents wanted them continued even though the infant had no hope of independent existence. Public health or public safety and child abuse laws may enter into the decisions made to disregard parental wishes. In some cases a guardian is appointed to represent the interests of the child or fetus.

Quality assurance measures related to the implementation and enforcement of patients' rights requirements increasingly are aspects of good health provider management practices. Although objective measures exist for some rights, appropriate implementation of many rights depends on attitudes, relationships, and value judgments. Evaluation of implementation can sometimes be obscured by professional and provider traditions. Educational approaches, including on-the-job training, make an essential contribution to sensitizing health care practitioners to constitutional, legal, and ethical aspects of patients' rights. The growth of ethics institutes has resulted in advances in specialized educational curricula and readily available professional training and educational resource materials. Public and consumer education helps people understand both their rights and their responsibilities, leading to a less-passive stance with respect to health care and empowering patients and their families to demand their rights or to translate requirements into practical solutions.

DEBATES AND DILEMMAS

A full understanding of patient rights includes confronting the ethical complexity of competing values and balancing of needs; this is part of any consideration of individual rights in a social context, including the rights of families and society. Current debates about rights often reflect this reality. Excessive focus on the patient's interests, without acknowledging and balancing the interests and needs of family members who are clearly affected, can result in decisions that are untenable and damaging to family well-being. Yet, individualistic approaches to patient's rights frequently overlook the moral and practical claims of families (Nelson, 1992). One individual's rights may conflict with those of another. The controversy over whether health care professionals have a responsibility to reveal their HIV status pits the patient's right to be protected from harm against the health care professional's right to confidentiality, privacy, and nondiscrimination. Appropriate resolution of such dilemmas requires thoughtful consideration of many dimensions of rights, a well-informed approach to determining competing risks, and the courage to resist emotional appeals that are one-sided (Daniels, 1992).

Financial Consideration

Given the reality of limited resources, health care decisions are frequently made with reference to financial or other resource considerations, and not solely on need. The types of choices that must be made are particularly apparent in the use of highly complicated technology or in selection of recipients for organ transplantation. Although Medicare currently pays for dialysis and transplants for all people with end-stage renal disease, such condition-specific universal coverage is unique. Furthermore, most policymakers question the fiscal capability of a publicly supported program to eventually cover all such high-technology treatment for all potential conditions. Availability of third-party or public funds for many complex or "exotic" procedures varies widely, and many families resort to media appeals and public fundraising to support anticipated life-saving surgery.

Organ Donation

Selling of organs for transplantation was prohibited by the National Organ Transplant Act of 1984. Later, the Omnibus Budget Reconciliation Act of 1986 (P.L. 99-509) required all hospitals with transplantation programs to join a national organ-sharing network and mandates organ-distribution procedures that consider such factors as medical need, waiting time, and quality of donor–recipient organ tissue match. Although they are not supposed to be major criteria, issues of age, life expectancy, and social worth often become aspects of decision making. P.L. 99-509 also requires all Medicare and Medicaid participating

hospitals to have protocols for identifying potential organ donors. Many donors are young people who have been killed in accidents or by gunshot. There is some concern among professionals and advocacy groups that the pressure to harvest viable organs overrides consideration of the victim's family and makes investigation of the causes of death impossible.

Lifestyle Factors

Growing evidence supports the contribution of lifestyle choices (for example, substance abuse, smoking, diet, lack of exercise, and sexual promiscuity) to many illnesses and premature death. Questions are raised about whether individuals who make poor lifestyle choices should have the same access to scarce health resources as persons with a healthier lifestyle.

Right to Die

How far should society go with the "right to die"? In the past the movement to promote this right was primarily concerned with how an individual can make known his or her wish to avoid heroic measures; promotion of suicide was not an objective. The escalating national controversy over medically assisted suicide has brought to the fore the many concerns about euthanasia, prompting some states to pass laws prohibiting assisted suicides. Under such laws a mentally competent patient may choose to refuse treatment, thus hastening the inevitable outcome of a terminal condition, but may not ask for assistance in medically terminating her or his life. Proponents of this right argue for patient self-determination (including not incurring often extensive medical debts), humanity, and dignity to avoid needless suffering and die peacefully. Health professionals are reexamining their ethical principles in relation to this dilemma (NASW, 1993).

SOCIAL WORK ROLES

Social workers perform clinical, organizational, and social action roles in the ongoing definition and implementation of patients' rights. To meet these responsibilities, social workers must be knowledgeable about the specific policies, standards, and state laws that are currently applicable to their health care setting. When so informed, they are able to educate and counsel patients and families and interpret pertinent policies, procedures, research protocols, responsibilities, risks, or alternative choices. Professionals also must be aware of the types of circumstances, and specific state laws addressing them, in which their legal duty to ensure the safety and protection of others may outweigh an individual's rights. Social workers frequently mediate between patient and family members and other health care professionals, promoting communication and exchange of information that can assist in upholding patients' wishes or resolving painful disagreements over conflicting wishes and views. Psychosocial data and assessments are essential to many clinical decisions involving high-risk treatments, organ transplants, or termination of care and provide crucial information to guide many aspects of care when patients are not able to speak for themselves.

At the organizational level social workers should contribute to the development and revision of facility policies that operationalize abstract rights concepts such as choice, confidentiality, and personhood on the practical level. They may organize and facilitate patient and resident councils, which also can monitor and speak to patients' concerns and needs. In many programs social workers are assigned or seek rights-related responsibilities as members of bioethics, patient care, or other decision-making committees. Case and cause advocacy may well be called for to ensure that a patient or group of patients is not denied access to medically necessary care when moving from facility to facility or from one community to another. In addition, social workers must recognize and seek to influence the wider social context within which all such rights are either bolstered or challenged.

REFERENCES

Alpert, S. (1993). Smart card, smarter policy: Medical record, privacy and health care reform. *Hastings Center Report, 23*, 13–23.

Americans with Disabilities Act of 1990. P.L. 101-336, 104 Stat. 327.

Ansell, D. A., & Schiff, R. L. (1987). Patient dumping. *Journal of the American Medical Association, 257*(11), 1500–1502.

Bachrach, L. (1992). What we know about homelessness among mentally ill persons: An analytical review and comments. *Hospital and Community Psychiatry, 43*, 453–464.

Belcher, J. R. (1988). Are jails replacing the mental health system for the homeless mentally ill? *Hospital and Community Psychiatry, 24*, 185–195.

Bentley, K. J. (1993). The right of psychiatric patients to refuse medication: Where should social workers stand? *Social Work, 38*, 101–106.

Brock, D. W. (1992). Voluntary active euthanasia. *Hastings Center Report, 22*, 10–22.

Burger, S. G. (1993). *Avoiding physical restraint use.* Washington, DC: National Citizens Coalition for Nursing Home Reform.

Caplan, A. L., Edgar, H., King, P. A., & Jones, J. H. (1992). Twenty years after, the legacy of the Tuskegee Syphilis Study. *Hastings Center Report, 22*(6), 29–40.

Child Abuse Prevention and Treatment Act Amendments of 1984. P.L. 98-457, 98 Stat. 205.

Civil Rights Act of 1964. P.L. 88-352, 78 Stat. 241.

Civil Rights of Institutionalized Persons Act of 1980. P.L. 96-247, 94 Stat. 349.

Cruzan v. Director, Missouri Department of Health, 110 S. Ct. 2841 (1990).

Daniels, N. (1992). HIV-infected health care professionals: Public threat or public sacrifice? *Milbank Quarterly, 70*, 3–42.

Developmentally Disabled Assistance and Bill of Rights Act of 1975. P.L. 94-103, 89 Stat. 486.

Federal Policy for the Protection of Human Subjects: Notices and Rules. (1991). *Federal Register, 56*(117), 28002–28032.

Harding, A. K., Gray, L. A., & Neal, M. (1993). Confidentiality limits with clients who have HIV: A review of ethical and legal guidelines and professional policies. *Journal of Counseling and Development, 71*, 297–305.

In the Matter of Claire Conroy, 486 A.2d 1209 (N.J. 1985).

In the Matter of Karen Quinlan, 335 A.2d 647 (N.J. 1976).

Joint Commission on Accreditation of Healthcare Organizations. (1993). *Accreditation manual for hospitals.* Oak Bridge, IL: Author.

Katz, J. (1993). Ethics and clinical research revisited: A tribute to Henry K. Beecher. *Hastings Center Report, 23*(5), 31–39.

Mental Health Systems Act of 1980. P.L. 96-398, 94 Stat. 1564.

Mikva, A. J., Minow, M., & Wald, P. M. (1993). Tribute to the legacy of Judge David L. Bazelon. *Georgetown Law Journal, 81*, 1–26.

Milstein, B., Rubenstein, L., & Cyr, R. (1991, March). The Americans with Disabilities Act: A breathtaking promise for people with mental disabilities. *Clearinghouse Review,* pp. 1240–1249.

Mizrahi, T. (1992). The right to treatment and the treatment of mentally ill people. *Health & Social Work, 17*, 7–11.

National Association of Social Workers. (1993). *Social work speaks: NASW policy statements* (3rd ed.). Washington, DC: NASW Press.

National Organ Transplant Act of 1984. P.L. 98-507, 98 Stat. 2339.

Nelson, J. L. (1992). Taking families seriously. *Hastings Center Report, 4*, 6–12.

Nuclear guinea pigs—Human radiation experiments 1940–1970. (1994, January 5). *New York Times,* p. 10.

O'Connor v. Donaldson, 422 U.S. 563 (1975).

Older Americans Act of 1965. P.L. 89-73, 79 Stat. 218.

Omnibus Budget Reconciliation Act of 1981. P.L. 97-35, 95 Stat. 357.

Omnibus Budget Reconciliation Act of 1986. P.L. 99-509, 100 Stat. 1874.

Omnibus Budget Reconciliation Act of 1987. P.L. 100-203, 101 Stat. 1330.

Omnibus Budget Reconciliation Act of 1990. P.L. 101-508, 104 Stat. 1388.

Protection and Advocacy for Mentally Ill Individuals Act of 1986. P.L. 99-319, 100 Stat. 478.

Reamer, F. G. (1991). AIDS, social work, and the "duty to protect." *Social Work, 36*, 56–60.

Roe v. Wade, 410 U.S. 113 (1973).

Rosenson, M. K. (1993). Social work and the right of psychiatric patients to refuse medication: A family advocate's response. *Social Work, 38*, 107–112.

Soskis, C. W., & Kerson, T. S. (1992). The Patient Self-Determination Act: Opportunity knocks again. *Social Work in Health Care, 16*(4), 1–18.

Thomas, S. B., & Quinn, S. C. (1991). Tuskegee Syphilis Study, 1932–1972: Implications for HIV education and AIDS risk education programs in the black community. *American Journal of Public Health, 81*(11), 1498–1505.

Tuskegee Syphilis Study Ad Hoc Advisory Panel. (1973). *Final report of the Tuskegee Syphilis Study Ad Hoc Advisory Panel.* Washington, DC: U.S. Government Printing Office.

U.S. Senate. (1991). *Report on Senate Bill S14-75 "Protection and Advocacy for Mentally Ill Individuals Amendments of 1991."* Washington, DC: U.S. Government Printing Office.

Wyatt v. Stickney, 325 F. Supp. 781 (M.D. Ala. 1971).

Wyatt v. Stickney, 334 F. Supp. 373 (M.D. Ala. 1972).

FURTHER READING

Annas, G. (1989). *The rights of patients.* Carbondale: Southern Illinois University Press.

Buchanan, A. E., & Brock, D. W. (1989). *Deciding for others: The ethics of surrogate decision making.* New York: Cambridge University Press.

Faden, R. R., & Beauchamp, T. I. (1986). *A history and theory of informed consent.* New York: Oxford University Press.

Kane, R. A., & Caplan, A. L. (Eds.). (1989). *Everyday ethics: Resolving dilemmas in nursing home life.* New York: Springer.

Sabitino, C. P. (1991). *Patient Self-Determination Act: State law guide.* Washington, DC: American Bar Association, Commission on Legal Problems of the Elderly.

ADDITIONAL RESOURCES

Bazelon Center for Mental Health Law
1101 15th Street, NW, Suite 1212
Washington, DC 20005

Choice in Dying, Inc.
200 Varick Street
New York, NY 10014

The Hastings Center
255 Elm Road
Briarcliffe Manor, NY 10510

Kennedy Institute of Ethics
Georgetown University
Washington, DC 20057

National Citizens Coalition for Nursing Home Reform
1424 16th Street, NW
Washington, DC 20036

Ruth Irelan Knee, MSSA, ACSW, is a consultant in long-term/mental health care, 8809 Arlington Boulevard, Fairfax, VA 22031. **Betsy S. Vourlekis, PhD, ACSW, LCSW,** is associate professor, University of Maryland at Baltimore County, Department of Social Work, Catonsville, MD 21228.

For further information see

Abortion; Advocacy; Bioethical Issues; Children's Rights; Civil Rights; Deinstitutionalization; End-of-Life Decisions; Ethics and Values; Families Overview; Health Care: Direct Practice; Hospice; Hospital Social Work; Human Rights; Legal Issues: Confidentiality and Privileged Communication; Professional Conduct; Professional Liability and Malpractice; Quality Assurance; Suicide.

Key Words	
advance directives	patient rights
confidentiality	self-determination
informed consent	

Peace and Social Justice

Dorothy Van Soest

Although there has been much talk about the ending of the Cold War and of the new peace possibilities that would follow, the actuality of war and violence both globally and domestically continues to be a critical concern. During the 1980s there was evidence of an increased sense of professional social work responsibility to address the serious effects of militarization, social injustice, violence, and the nuclear threat (Gil, 1989; Goldberg, 1984; Greenwald & Zeitlin, 1987; Iatridis, 1988; Korotkin, 1985; Rice & Mary, 1989; Schachter, 1986; Schaffner Goldberg & Rosen, 1992; Sewell & Kelly, 1988; Stenzel & Baeck, 1983; White, 1986; Williams, 1987; Zealley, 1987). The purpose of this entry is to provide a framework for peacemaking as an integral aspect of professional practice by presenting an overview of peace and social justice concerns that have implications for social work.

KEY CONCEPTS AND DEFINITIONS

Peace: Positive and Negative Concepts

The concept of peace is operationalized in the peace literature in two ways: (1) peace as a "negative" concept, meaning the absence of war, and (2) peace as a "positive" concept, which contends that violence is present whenever people are being influenced in such a way that they are not being allowed to reach their full potential (Boulding, 1977; Galtung, 1969). The positive peace concept unites the struggle for peace with the social work profession's commitment to social justice and the elimination of racism, sexism, heterosexism, and other forms of oppression. A view of peace as being incompatible with malnutrition and hunger, poverty, and the denial of people's rights to self-determination (Brock-Utne, 1985) is consistent with social work's traditional concern about people who are poor and oppressed.

Violence

Violence can be defined as any act or situation that injures the health and well-being of others; it is discerned within the context of oppression, with manifestations at the personal, institutional, and structural levels (Bulhan, 1985). Gandhi (1960) conceptualized two distinct aspects of violence: physical and passive, with passive violence—in the form of discrimination, oppression, and exploitation—giving rise to physical violence. Whereas personal, physical violence is obvious and widely acknowledged, structural and institutional violence is subtle and often unnoticed; it is "the violence not seen as such" (Galtung, 1969; Keefe & Roberts, 1991). A working definition of violence thus includes both personal and physical violence and institutional and structural violence, such as war and the threat of war, poverty, patterns of inequity that are built into the structure of systems in the form of institutionalized racism and sexism, and the nuclear threat. Garcia's (1981) definition of peace envisioned not only the absence of war but also the absence of violence in this broad sense:

> By peace we mean the absence of violence in any given society, both internal and external, direct and indirect. We further mean the nonviolent results of equality of rights, by which every member of that society, through nonviolent means, participates equally in decisional power which regulates it, and the distribution of resources which sustain it. (p. 165)

Social Justice

Three contemporary views of social justice that are based on major philosophical theories or worldviews include

1. legal justice, which is concerned with what a person owes to society and often involves a debate about retribution versus restitution
2. commutative justice, which is concerned with what people owe each other and is related to interpersonal equity issues
3. distributive justice, which is concerned with what society owes a person.

Although distributive injustice does not minimize the effects of oppressive characteristics of all three types of justice, it can be seen as an underlying cause of the inequalities in legal and commutative forms. Distributive justice claims involve decisions about the allocation of resources such as food, clothing, and shelter—decisions that require the setting of parameters. Three concep-

tions of distributive justice hold divergent views about how such parameters should be set.

Libertarian view. The libertarian view of justice, which was particularly popular in the 1980s, is primarily concerned with liberty, which gives individuals freedom from coercion to share what they have rightfully acquired and the liberty to voluntarily dispose of possessions as they choose. Libertarians strongly oppose welfare rights, as well as any coercive mechanisms imposed by governments to get some citizens to aid others or to intentionally redistribute resources (Hayek, 1960; Nozick, 1974). Libertarians believe that the only appropriate role of government is to protect people from aggression in the community (the police) and the society from outside aggression (Hospers, 1992). Thus, libertarians support the need for a strong military, as long as it does not go beyond the limited role of government to protect its citizens from outside aggression and does not interfere with the free market economy.

Utilitarian view. Whereas libertarians focus on rights, utilitarians approach justice by weighing the relative benefits and harms and determining what maximizes the greatest good for the greatest number. The utilitarian view has been used to justify the redistribution of resources and to justify unequal distribution of resources and benefits, both in the interests of the common good. The "common good" is open to definition, and the definition determines the parameters within which to make a social justice claim; for example, the "greatest good" can be defined as a strong security through military strength, or it can be defined as a healthy, educated, and productive citizenry.

Egalitarian view. Rawls (1971) developed two egalitarian principles that prohibit the justification of inequalities on the grounds that the hardships of some people are offset by a greater common good:

1. Basic liberties must be equal, because citizens of a just society are to have the same basic rights.
2. There should be a fair equality of opportunity and inequalities in power, wealth, income, and other resources must not exist except insofar as they work to the absolute benefit of the worst-off members of society (Dworkin, 1992).

Egalitarianism, which makes redistribution of resources a moral obligation, is the most consistent of the three perspectives with a social work peace and social justice agenda. To summarize in a very general and simple form, then, social justice can be understood as including economic, social, and political equality that is based on egalitarian principles. A primary concern related to peace and social justice is with the oppressive characteristics of injustice, in other words, with the forms of violence used to perpetuate inequality.

Peace and Social Justice, Development, and Human Rights: Inseparable Concepts

Cowgar (1989) maintained that peace is not possible without justice, and thus advocacy for justice is seen as the most important peace work. However, although issues such as equality may be inseparable from peace, Sewell and Kelly (1988) pointed out the dangers of believing that working for justice is the same as working for peace. Although the slogan "If you want peace, work for justice" reflects the interconnectedness of the issues and serves as a useful tool for coalition building and organizing, one should not make the assumption that working for justice automatically means working for peace. For example, working to eliminate homelessness does not automatically translate into reductions in the military budget or in military interventions. Thus, a positive notion of peace involves making the peace and social justice linkages explicit.

Social justice, human rights, and development cannot be separated from peace. Human rights provide the grounding for social justice claims, and social justice is a precursor to peace. According to the preamble of the *Universal Declaration of Human Rights,* adopted by the United Nations in 1948, "Recognition of the inherent dignity and of the equal and inalienable rights of all members of the human family is the foundation of freedom, justice, and peace in the world" (United Nations, 1988). Development—defined as a process of improving a society's capabilities to meet social and economic demands aimed at the liberation and fulfillment of individuals, beginning with the eradication of poverty (Agere, 1986; Omer, 1979)—is a means of ensuring human rights, eliminating injustice, and promoting peace.

CONSEQUENCES OF WAR, VIOLENCE, AND SOCIAL INJUSTICE

From the advent of the Cold War to the beginning of the 1990s, militarism grew to the point of taking over the world economy. From 1960 to 1987, world military expenditures totaled $17 trillion (in 1986 U.S. dollars), and in 1990 alone nearly $900 billion was spent worldwide on weapons. In 30 years, military expenditures grew faster than the world's economic product per capita (Sivard, 1991). The production and sale of arms has become a lucrative business for many countries, most notably the former Soviet Union and the United States. Development of sophisticated nuclear weapons changed the nature of war and profoundly influenced economic, social, psychological, and political processes. These realities have monumental consequences in relation to loss of human life because of wars, the social and economic influence of increased militarization, and the dangers of the nuclear threat.

Impact on Human Lives

The loss of human lives is the ultimate reality of militarism and war. From 1500 to 1990, there have been an estimated 141,901,000 war-related deaths in the world; more than half of all those killed were civilians. However, during the 1980s, 75 percent of all people killed in wars were civilians (Sivard, 1991). Between the end of World War II and the early 1980s, there were between 140 and 160 conflicts in which perhaps 10 million people were killed (Edwards, 1986; Lefever & Hunt, 1982).

Social and Economic Impacts

Although popular opinion continues to espouse the belief that military spending is good for the economy, there are convincing arguments that it may actually be destructive to the economic health of society (Barnet, 1981; Bluestone & Harrison, 1982; Galbraith, 1981; Mahony, 1982; Russett, 1970; Sivard, 1991). It has been contended that excessive military spending tends to deflect expenditures for social welfare needs, such as health and education, endangering the welfare of society in the long run (Dumas, 1986; Iatridis, 1988; Korotkin, 1985; Russett, 1970). For example, a comparison ranking of 142 countries revealed that the 12 countries with the largest military expenditures in 1987 all made a poorer showing in economic–social standing than in military power (Sivard, 1991). The United States, which ranked at the top in military power, ranked number 18 in infant mortality rate and number 22 in the under-age-five mortality rate. Additional social indicators reveal a deleterious effect of militarism in relation to poverty rates, inadequate housing, hunger, and inadequate education. The least-well-off members of society—particularly female heads of households—were most affected by domestic budget cuts during the 1980s. The middle class also suffered from the combined effects of social disinvestments and military spending (Gioseffi, 1988; Iatridis, 1988).

Impact of the Nuclear Threat

Although millions of people have suffered and died as a result of conventional wars, nuclear weapons have changed the nature and risks of war in un-imaginable ways. The United States has used small nuclear weapons twice, with catastrophic consequences for the people of Japan. Current nuclear arsenals are lethal beyond imagination, and the possibility that nuclear weapons could be used again remains a reality. The United States and the former Soviet Union's combined 1990 inventory of 52,000 nuclear weapons embodied an explosive force 1,600 times that of the firepower released in World War II, Korea, and Vietnam combined, which killed 44 million people (Sivard, 1991). Although it is expected that the number of U.S. and Russian strategic weapons will be reduced by the year 2003 to the lowest level since 1969, two dangerous and unresolved dilemmas compel worldwide attention:

1. No safe, environmentally benign, or economically feasible method exists for disposing of the tons of plutonium, the most lethal substance on earth, from dismantled warheads.
2. Nuclear proliferation continues: In 1990 there were six known nuclear powers, with the expectation by military analysts that 31 countries would be able to produce nuclear weapons by the year 2000 (Harris & Markusen, 1986; Sivard, 1991).

Psychological denial, or psychic numbing, is a common response to the potential of nuclear weapons to unleash unparalleled cataclysm. However, facing the nuclear threat brings an appropriate urgency to the way militarism is viewed. Studies have suggested that a full-scale nuclear war could kill between 300 million and 1 billion people initially, with more to follow, and that firestorms would cover much of the earth for months with sooty smoke, threatening the survival of the human species (Edwards, 1986; Sagan, 1984).

ALTERNATIVE STRATEGIES FOR PEACE AND SOCIAL JUSTICE

Although there may be general agreement that peace and social justice are desirable, there is a wide divergence of opinion about how to prevent nuclear war and the appropriate role of militarism. Three types of strategies represent an overview of the range of alternatives: commonly espoused military solutions, alternative self-defense strategies, and economic conversion.

Commonly Espoused Military Solutions

Nuclear deterrence, combined with the idea that a limited nuclear war is a feasible tactic, has been the official long-term U.S. strategy. It is based on the idea that when nuclear weapons are aimed at other nations, the risk of war is lessened (Krauthammer, 1982). When each nuclear power has the ability to incinerate the defenseless population of the other many times over, a "balance of terror" is maintained. Fear of retaliation, which would be tantamount to suicide, thus keeps each side from attacking.

Strategic defense against a nuclear attack is needed if deterrence fails; thus the strategic defense initiative (SDI) aims to move the arms race to defensive weaponry. The Star Wars imagery of a protective shield against nuclear weapons appeals to a need for security. However, the United States would continue to maintain offensive nuclear weapons along with SDI (Dyson, 1984). Although serious criticisms were leveled at the program even from within the U.S. Department of Defense and cuts were made in defense spending, SDI continued with ambiguous support at the beginning of the 1990s.

Another approach is peace through strength and a new world order. The U.S. Department of Defense's (1983) approach to peace is to gain security through military buildup by modernizing strategic nuclear forces and improving the readiness of conventional forces. Combined with the motivation to be secure from enemy attack is a defensive strategy labeled "coercive diplomacy," which involves threatening an opponent with dire consequences if an aggressive action is not abandoned. With the collapse of the Soviet Union and political discussions about cuts in the defense budget, new threat-based arguments emerged to sustain the need for a strong defense. Some proponents of this strategy go beyond the fear-based defense argument to an emphasis on identifying opportunities to influence a new world order (George, 1992).

Alternative Self-Defense Strategies

Non-nuclear resistance advocates (Dyson, 1984) propose complete unilateral nuclear disarmament combined with vigorous deployment of non-nuclear weapons and a willingness to use them.

Nonviolent resistance, on the other hand, requires an active pacifism that prohibits the shedding of any person's blood except one's own, disobedience to unjust laws, and a refusal to collaborate with unjust authorities. Proponents of pacifism point to its long and honorable history and suggest that the abolition of nuclear weapons is a task of the same magnitude as the abolition of slavery (Dyson, 1984).

Civilian-based defense is a national defense against internal usurpations and foreign invasions by prepared nonviolent noncooperation and defiance by the society's population and institutions (Sharp, 1985). Its aim is to enable a country to deny attackers their objectives, to become politically unrulable by would-be tyrants, and to subvert the attackers' troops and functionaries to unreliability and even mutiny.

Economic Conversion: A Swords-into-Plowshares Alternative

This alternative proposes the dismantling of a large portion of the world's war-making capabilities and the transferring of resources from military to civilian purposes through a planned process that would not cause social and economic dislocation. In the United States, five economic conversion bills have been introduced since 1963, four in the House and one in the Senate. The most comprehensive of these is the Defense Economic Adjustment Act (H.R. 101), introduced in 1977, which became a model for conversion proponents and attracted growing legislative support during the early 1990s. Since 1980 there has been considerable grassroots conversion activity in the United States, Great Britain, West Germany, Sweden, and Italy (Renner, 1990). Major issues related to economic conversion include the adaptation of research, production, and management practices in arms-producing factories to civilian needs and criteria; the retraining of employees; the refashioning of production equipment; and the finding of civilian uses for military bases and personnel (Renner, 1990).

ROLE OF SOCIAL WORK

Social workers are diverse in their ideological, personal, and professional perspectives about the myriad problems and alternative solutions related to peace and social justice issues (Van Soest, Johnston, & Sullivan, 1987). The purpose of the following discussion is to contribute to the development of a framework for peacemaking as an integral part of professional commitment and practice. Advocacy for peace and social justice is promoted by making linkages with professional values, traditions, and commitment to oppressed populations and by suggesting roles in the areas of social policy, direct practice, and education.

Social Work Values, Traditions, and Practice Experience

Promoting peace and social justice and resisting nuclear war are consistent with the central values of the social work profession, which stress self-determination, human rights, and social equity. The profession has a tradition of reform- and peace-related activities that are based on a commitment to human dignity and improvement of social conditions. Social workers of the Settlement House era expressed a moral indignation about the violence of war and understood that poor and powerless people are victims of a violent world. The only two women from the United States ever to have won the Nobel Peace Prize for their contributions to peace were Emily Greene Balch, who worked at the Dennison Settlement House in Boston and was a cofounder of the Women's International League for Peace and Freedom, and Jane Addams, who presided over the Women's Peace Conference at The Hague. Lillian Wald, who was part of the first group of social workers to speak out against World War I, wrote a Peace Manifesto and went to the Peace Conference at The Hague (Addams, 1906, 1922/1983; Sullivan, 1993). Mary Church Terrell and Ida B. Wells-Barnett organized for world peace before and during World War I and were deeply involved in the social justice struggles of the late 19th and early 20th centuries. The collective work of early social workers with a variety of immigrants led to a distinctive understanding about the interrelatedness between war and an unjust social order.

Social workers, through their work with both victims and perpetrators, have experienced firsthand the tragic consequences of violence. Social workers serve military personnel and their families and work to ensure that the military establishment responds adequately to their needs. During the 1980s, social workers served victims of unemployment, homelessness, hunger, farm foreclosures, and other human problems related to political and economic priorities dedicated to war and war readiness. The profession's 25-year history of struggling with ways to promote social justice for oppressed populations, which began in the 1960s, demonstrates a developing commitment to people of color, women, gay men and lesbians, and other vulnerable groups. The social work profession is uniquely equipped to promote peace and social justice given such a rich history of practice experience, an accrued range of knowledge, and collective understanding of economic, political, and social issues.

Social Policy Role

The basic debate about a warfare state versus a welfare state is of critical concern to social work, particularly when military allocations deplete resources to the extent that society cannot provide for the social welfare needs of its citizens. Institutional violence—which is born of political and economic deprivation, inequitable resource allocations, and oppressive elements of social policy and services—is thus directly linked with militarism. Several peace and social welfare policy positions taken by the social work profession recognize this linkage. NASW adopted an official policy statement on peace and social welfare in 1987 and established a national Office of Peace and International Affairs in 1989. The NASW Delegate Assemblies adopted peace as a social policy priority goal in 1982, 1986, and 1990, and NASW's Board of Directors has taken several policy positions on military interventions. The International Federation of Social Workers adopted an International Policy on Peace and Disarmament in 1988.

Thus, there is support and recognition by national and international associations for professional responsibility to promote peace and social justice, and specific policies provide guidelines for alternative strategies. Professional opposition to nuclear deterrence is endorsed, and the existence of nuclear and other weapons of mass destruction is seen as antithetical to social work. Nonviolent approaches to conflict resolution and self-defense are consistent with official policy, social work values, and practice wisdom. Economic conversion to a peacetime economy frees up resources to meet people's needs and to restore the economy in a way that has the potential of creating community among people.

A critical analysis of the economic and social impact of militarism on employment rates, welfare of children and families, homelessness, and so on is essential to effective social justice advocacy. With a clear understanding of the effect of the arms race on the economy and the impact of budget priorities on oppressed populations, social workers are in a position to advocate for legislation aimed at economic conversion, the transferring of funds from military to human service programs, and nuclear disarmament and other weapons reductions. To fulfill their role as peacemakers, social workers can engage in a variety of strategies, such as lobbying, educating, organizing, forming coalitions, and policy advocacy.

Direct Practice Role
Practice issues related to the nuclear threat and militarism are not necessarily atypical or peculiar in social work practice, although they might not be readily comprehended. The core conditions of the helping relationship that form a constellation of skills and attitudes for social work—genuineness, caring or unconditional positive regard, empathic understanding—are the same characteristics that are required of peacemakers. A framework for promoting peace consists of practice approaches that support caring and heal relationships, rather than separating people from each

other and perpetuating violence. Social work skills, such as empathic communication and active listening, are antidotes to violence and are essential ingredients for successful nonviolent resolution of conflicts.

The professional social work role includes the responsibility to respond to the potential impact of the nuclear threat on individuals, families, and groups in practice. Thus, social workers must understand, from a psychosocial perspective, how the nuclear threat affects mental and emotional health, the normal development of children, intergenerational relationships, and a family's ability to master various stages of the life cycle (Greenwald & Zeitlin, 1987). This role requires that social workers first face their own denial, psychic numbness, and sense of powerlessness. Although social workers must be careful not to impose their own concerns about the nuclear threat on clients, they also must not collude with clients' possible fears and helplessness, which inhibit social workers' ability to care, to feel effective in the world, and to engage in the change process.

Clinical social work practice involves assessment and intervention related to psychological and cultural aspects of violence, the common roots of personal and political violence, and nonviolent change strategies. Awareness of violence in social services delivery systems requires discernment of how social work colludes with structural injustice through the use of social control practice strategies. Practitioners can play a role in promoting peace and social justice in all practice settings through the use of nonviolent skills and strategies. For example, school social workers use nonviolent conflict-resolution strategies to resolve disputes between children and adolescents; family therapists use the same skills and promote nonviolent communication among family members; similarly, occupational social workers help resolve work and employee–employer disputes.

Role of Social Work Education
Education is one of society's institutions that can stimulate positive change in the direction of improving the human condition and reducing global and personal violence. The social work profession, which is by nature interdisciplinary, is in a position to capitalize on the proliferation of peace studies programs and concentrations within a variety of disciplines on many college and university campuses (Thomas & Klare, 1989; Wein, 1984). Social work educators can help translate social work students' broad concern for individuals and society into a more profound understanding of peace and social justice issues. The overall

goal of education for peace and social justice is essentially to develop students' capacity for peacemaking, which is defined as "conceiving, gestating, and nurturing those conditions in which all can develop their good qualities, their capacity to be fully human" (Reardon, 1988, p. 54). Peacemaking requires human qualities that parallel the personal qualities and skills that social work educators hope to develop in students, suggesting a natural fit between peace education and social work education.

To help prepare students for their peacemaking role, social work educational programs, faculty–student relations, and teaching strategies should be nonviolent in nature. The practice methods that are taught in the classroom must themselves be egalitarian and nonviolent; that is, they must involve respect for client self-determination, emphasize empowerment rather than social control, and entail positive influence efforts that are noncoercive (Klein, 1987). Peace and social justice content can be infused into the social work curriculum or can be organized into separate elective courses. Available curriculum resources include a peace studies book that is written from a social work perspective (Keefe & Roberts, 1991) and a curriculum guide for incorporating peace and social justice issues into social work education, published under the auspices of the NASW Peace and Social Justice Committee (Van Soest, 1992).

Conclusion

Since the beginning of the social work profession, there has been discussion about the role and responsibility of social work to promote peace and social justice. Although it is generally accepted that peace and social justice are important to people's collective well-being, there is a wide diversity of opinion about what the concepts mean and about the conditions and strategies for achieving them. The intent of this entry is to encourage ongoing dialogue by synthesizing the key concepts and presenting a framework that is consistent with social work values, knowledge, skills, and tradition.

References

Addams, J. (1906). *Newer ideals of peace.* New York: Macmillan.

Addams, J. (1983). *Peace and bread in time of war.* Silver Spring, MD: National Association of Social Workers. (Original work published 1922)

Agere, S. (1986). Participation in social development and integration in sub-Saharan Africa. *Journal of Social Development in Africa, 1*(1), 93–110.

Barnet, R. (1981). *Real security: Restoring American power in a dangerous decade.* New York: Atheneum.

Bluestone, B., & Harrison, B. (1982). *The deindustrialization of America.* New York: Basic Books.

Boulding, K. E. (1977). Twelve friendly quarrels with Johan Galtung. *Journal of Peace Research, 16*(1), 75–86.

Brock-Utne, B. (1985). *Educating for peace: A feminist perspective.* Tarrytown, NY: Pergamon Press.

Bulhan, H. A. (1985). *Frantz Fanon and the psychology of oppression.* New York: Plenum Press.

Cowgar, C. D. (1989). Dilemmas of peace and justice. In D. Sanders & J. Matsuoka (Eds.), *Peace and development* (pp. 79–87). Honolulu: University of Hawaii Press.

Dumas, L. J. (1986). The military albatross: How arms spending is destroying the economy. In J. Wallace (Ed.), *Waging peace: A handbook for the struggle to abolish nuclear weapons* (pp. 100–105). New York: Harper & Row.

Dworkin, R. (1992). Hypothetical contracts and rights. In J. P. Sterba (Ed.), *Justice: Alternative political perspectives* (pp. 145–157). Belmont, CA: Wadsworth.

Dyson, F. (1984). *Weapons and hope.* New York: Harper & Row.

Edwards, A.J.C. (1986). *Nuclear weapons: The balance of terror, the quest for peace.* Albany: State University of New York Press.

Galbraith, J. K. (1981, June–July). The economics of the arms race—And after. *The Bulletin of Atomic Scientists,* pp. 13–16.

Galtung, J. (1969). Violence, peace, and peace research. *Journal of Peace Research, 10*(3), 167–191.

Gandhi, M. (1960). *All men are brothers: Life and thoughts of Mahatma Gandhi, as told in his own words.* Ahmedabad, India: Navajivan Publishing House.

Garcia, C. (1981). Adrogyny and peace education. *Bulletin of Peace Proposals, 2,* 163–178.

George, A. I. (1992). *Forceful persuasion: Coercive diplomacy as an alternative to war.* Washington, DC: U.S. Institute of Peace Press.

Gil, D. G. (1989). Work, violence, injustice and war. *Journal of Sociology and Social Welfare, 16*(1), 39–53.

Gioseffi, D. (Ed.). (1988). *Women on war: Essential voices for the nuclear age.* New York: Touchstone.

Goldberg, G. S. (1984). Adding the arms race to the psychological equation. *Social Work, 29,* 481–483.

Greenwald, D., & Zeitlin, S. (1987). *No reason to talk about it: Families confront the nuclear taboo.* New York: W. W. Norton.

Harris, J. B., & Markusen, E. (Eds.). (1986). *Nuclear weapons and the threat of nuclear war.* New York: Harcourt Brace Jovanovich.

Hayek, F. A. (1960). *The constitution of liberty.* Chicago: University of Chicago Press.

Hospers, J. (1992). The libertarian manifesto. In J. P. Sterba (Ed.), *Justice: Alternative political perspectives* (pp. 41–53). Belmont, CA: Wadsworth.

Iatridis, D. S. (1988). New social deficit: Neoconservatism's policy of social underdevelopment. *Social Work, 33,* 11–15.

Keefe, T., & Roberts, R. E. (1991). *Realizing peace: An introduction to peace studies.* Ames: Iowa State University Press.

Klein, R. (1987, March). *Integrating peace and nonviolence in social work education and social work practice.* Paper presented at the Annual Program Meeting of the Council on Social Work Education, St. Louis, MO.

Korotkin, A. (1985). Impact of military spending on the nation's quality of life. *Social Work, 30,* 369.

Krauthammer, C. (1982). In defense of deterrence. In E. W. Lefever & E. S. Hunt (Eds.), *The apocalyptic premise* (pp. 69–81). Washington, DC: Ethics and Public Policy Center.

Lefever, E. W., & Hunt, E. S. (Eds.). (1982). *The apocalyptic premise: Nuclear arms debated.* Washington, DC: Ethics and Public Policy Center.

Mahony, B. R. (1982). The case for nuclear pacifism. In E. W. Lefever & E. S. Hunt (Eds.), *The apocalyptic premise: Nuclear arms debated.* (pp. 279–293). Washington, DC: Ethics and Public Policy Center.

Nozick, R. (1974). *Anarchy, state and utopia.* New York: Basic Books.

Omer, S. (1979). Social development. *International Social Work, 22*(3), 12.

Rawls, J. (1971). *A theory of justice.* Cambridge, MA: Harvard University Press.

Reardon, B. A. (1988). *Comprehensive peace education: Educating for global responsibility.* New York: Teachers College Press.

Renner, M. (1990, June). *Swords into plowshares: Converting to a peace economy* (Worldwatch Paper No. 96). Washington, DC: Worldwatch Institute.

Rice, S., & Mary, N. L. (1989). Beyond war: A new perspective for social work. *Social Work, 34,* 175–178.

Russett, B. M. (1970). *What price vigilance? The burdens of national defense.* New Haven, CT: Yale University Press.

Sagan, C. (1984). Nuclear war and climatic catastrophe. *Foreign Affairs, 62,* 257–292.

Schachter, B. (1986). Growing up under the mushroom cloud. *Social Work, 31,* 187–192.

Schaffner Goldberg, G., & Rosen, S. (1992). Disengulfing the peace dividend. *Social Work, 37,* 87–93.

Sewell, S., & Kelly, A. (1988). *Professions in the nuclear age.* Brisbane, Queensland, Australia: Boolarong Publications.

Sharp, G. (1985). *National security through civilian-based defense.* Omaha, NE: Association for Transarmament Studies.

Sivard, R. L. (1991). *World military and social expenditures.* Washington, DC: World Priorities.

Stenzel, A. K., & Baeck, A. (1983). Social work and human survival in the nuclear age: A call for action. *Social Work, 28,* 399–401.

Sullivan, M. (1993). Social work's legacy of peace. *Social Work, 38,* 513–520.

Thomas, D., & Klare, M. (Eds.). (1989). *Peace and world order studies: A curriculum guide.* Boulder, CO: Westview Press.

United Nations. (1988). *The international bill of human rights.* Geneva: United Nations.

U.S. Department of Defense. (1983). *Soviet military power.* Washington, DC: Author.

Van Soest, D. (1992). *Incorporating peace and social justice into the social work curriculum.* Washington, DC: National Association of Social Workers.

Van Soest, D., Johnston, N., & Sullivan, M. (1987). Orientation to peace and justice in professional social work education in the United States. *Social Development Issues, 10*(3), 81–99.

Wein, B. J. (Ed.). (1984). *Peace and world order studies: A curriculum guide.* New York: World Policy Institute.

White, R. K. (Ed.). (1986). *Psychology and the prevention of nuclear war.* New York: New York University Press.

Williams, L. F. (1987). Under the nuclear umbrella. *Social Work, 32,* 246–249.

Zealley, H. (1987). Professional voices. In H. Davis (Ed.), *Ethics and defence: Power and responsibility in the nuclear age* (pp. 226–240). New York: Basil Blackwell.

FURTHER READING

Bok, S. (1990). *A strategy for peace: Human values and the threat of war.* New York: Vintage Books.

Caldicott, H. (1986). *Missile envy: The arms race and nuclear war.* New York: Bantam Books.

Carlson, D., & Comstock, C. (Eds.). (1986). *Securing our planet: How to succeed when threats are too risky and there's really no defense.* Los Angeles: Jeremy P. Tarcher.

Glossop, R. J. (1987). *Confronting war: An examination of humanity's most pressing problem.* Jefferson, NC: MacFarland and Company.

Macy, J. R. (1983). *Despair and personal power in the nuclear age.* Philadelphia: New Society Publishers.

Northwood, L. K. (1977, January–March). Warfare or welfare—Which direction for America? [Special issue]. *Journal of Sociology and Social Welfare, 4,* 3–4.

Reardon, B. A. (1985). *Sexism and the war system.* New York: Teachers College Press.

Ruddick, S. (1989). *Maternal thinking: Toward politics of peace.* New York: Ballantine Books.

Schmookler, A. B. (1988). *Out of weakness: Healing the wounds that drive us to war.* New York: Bantam Books.

Sivard, R. (1994). *World military and social expenditures 1994.* Washington, DC: World Priorities.

Yoder, J. H. (1984). *When war is unjust: Being honest in just-war thinking.* Minneapolis: Augsburg.

Dorothy Van Soest, DSW, is project director, Violence and Development Project, Office of Peace and International Affairs, National Association of Social Workers, 750 First Street, NE, Suite 700, Washington, DC 20002, and visiting associate professor, The Catholic University of America, Washington, DC.

For further information see

Advocacy; Civil Rights; Community Organization; Disasters and Disaster Aid; Ethics and Values; Gang Violence; Homicide; Human Rights; International and Comparative Social Welfare; Policy Analysis; Poverty; Primary Prevention Overview; Social Justice in Social Agencies; Social Planning; Social Welfare Policy; Social Work Profession Overview; Social Workers in Politics; Victims of Torture and Trauma; Violence Overview.

Key Words

development	social justice
human rights	violence
peace	

Pediatric AIDS

See HIV/AIDS: Pediatric

Pension Programs

See Retirement and Pension Programs

Perkins, Frances

See Biographies section, Volume 3

Permanency Planning

See Adoption; Child Foster Care; Child Welfare Overview

Person-in-Environment

James M. Karls
Karin E. Wandrei

P*erson-in-environment (PIE)* is a system for describing, classifying, and coding the problems of social functioning of the adult clients of social workers. Developed under a grant from NASW, PIE uses the organizing construct of person-in-environment to provide a system of brief, uniform descriptions of a client's interpersonal, environmental, mental, and physical health problems. The system also includes an assessment of the client's ability to deal with these problems.

PIE balances client problems and strengths. For each of the client's interpersonal problems, the social worker can note the extent of the disruption caused by the problem and the strength of the client to deal with the problem. PIE is not a behav- ior theory-based diagnostic system producing a formal diagnosis, but rather a system for identifying, describing, and classifying the common problems brought to the social worker. Problems are viewed not as existing in the person only but in the total person-in-environment complex. PIE is intended for use in all fields of social work practice and by practitioners of varying theoretical orientations.

NEED FOR CLASSIFICATION SYSTEM UNIQUE TO SOCIAL WORK

The social work profession has long struggled to assert its independence and uniqueness among the human services professions. For lack of a common system of communication, social work has had to rely on the systems of other professions such as medicine, psychiatry, and law to describe its clientele. An important step in its struggle for autonomy is for social work to acquire its own language, its own nomenclature, for the kinds of problems with which it uniquely deals.

Lourie (1978), writing on social work's role in case management, stated:

First we need uniform definitions of the problems families and individuals have which are universally understandable and acceptable for use and which all concerned would be willing to apply. Perhaps, as with concepts of dependency and neglect, we need to mandate these if they are to work. We need to recognize that present diagnostic, legal and social labels do not describe how people function. They are labels more comforting to the professionals than useful for clients' care and treatment. (p. 161)

In this same vein Meyer (1987) wrote:

It is important [for social work] to find a unifying perspective that will provide greater cohesiveness to social work practice. Such a perspective would have to reflect the person-in-environment focus that has become central to the purpose of social work practice. Furthermore, to capture the multiple strands of practice, it should not espouse any particular approach or theory; ideally, it should allow for an eclectic approach to case phenomena. Finally such a perspective would have to address the complexity that characterizes the case situations dealt with in social work practice. The purpose of a perspective on practice is to bind together social workers who are all doing different things to carry out the same purposes. (p. 414)

The "Working Statement on the Purpose of Social Work" (Minahan, 1981) added to the rationale for developing a classification system using the person-in-environment construct: "The purpose of social work is to promote or restore a mutually beneficial interaction between individuals and society in order to improve the quality of life for everyone" (p. 6). It went on to state:

Social workers focus on person-and-environment *in interaction*. To carry out their purpose, they work with people to achieve the following objectives.

- Facilitate interaction between individuals and others in their environment.
- Help people enlarge their competence and increase their problem solving and coping abilities.
- Influence social and environmental policy. (p. 6)

The NASW definition of clinical social work (NASW, 1984) lends further support to the PIE construct and its focus on problems of social functioning:

Clinical social work shares with all social work practice the goal of enhancement and maintenance of psychosocial functioning of individuals, families and groups. . . . Clinical social work practice is the professional application of social work theory and methods to the treatment and prevention of psychosocial dysfunction, disability, or impairment including emotional and mental disorders. The perspective of person-in-situation is central to clinical social work practice. Clinical social work includes interventions directed at interpersonal interactions, intrapsychic dynamics, and life-support and management issues. (p. 4)

PIE is constructed to help demonstrate the unique way social workers go about their work. By providing uniform descriptions of the common problems of social work's clientele both in their interactions with others and with the social institutions in their communities, PIE provides a mechanism for communicating complex case phenomena in terms that clients, other social work practitioners, and other human services professionals can understand. It also serves as a means for planning and testing social work interventions and offers

- a common language for all social work practitioners in all settings for describing their clients' problems in social functioning
- a common, concise description of social phenomena that could facilitate treatment or amelioration of the problems presented by clients
- a basis for gathering data required to measure the need for services and to design human services programs and evaluate effectiveness
- a mechanism for clearer communication among social work practitioners and between practitioners and administrators and researchers
- a basis for clarifying the domain of social work in the human services field.

HISTORY OF CLASSIFICATION SYSTEMS

Social work has had a love-hate relationship with classification and diagnostic systems, being particularly opposed to systems that label individuals as deviant or that otherwise stigmatize or stereotype. Nonetheless, social workers have been aware of the usefulness of identifying categories of psychosocial problems. Since the early 1980s the field of social work has been moving toward a more scientific approach to testing its theories and interventions, and many social workers support the classification of problems as a means toward conscious and deliberate planning of social work interventions. Objections to the use of classifications are raised more because of classification's misuse rather than the classification itself. The client and the social worker each can see that a clear description of psychosocial problems will aid the client's well-being.

The PIE system is not the first attempt by human services professionals to classify and codify the problems of clients. Earlier efforts include the work of the Committee on Psychosocial Diagnosis and Classification sponsored by the American Orthopsychiatric Association in 1982, which reaffirmed the need for a standard classification system but failed to complete one because of the lack of an acceptable theoretical framework (personal communication with G. Allison, American Orthopsychiatric Association Committee on Psychosocial Diagnosis and Classification, 1982).

The *International Classifications of Health Problems in Primary Care* (Committee on Professional and Hospital Activities, 1979) and *Developing Codes and Classifications for Social Workers in Health Care* (Henk, 1985) list psychosocial codes that are relevant to general social work practice but that were designed to identify problems unique to the primary health care setting. More widely used in medical settings is the *International Classifications of Disease* (Commission of Professional and Hospital Activities, 1980), which lists psychosocial problems also relevant to social work. The *Classification and Codes for Children and Youth,* by Minnesota Systems Research (1977), classifies common problems of social functioning that occur in those populations.

The most significant system currently used by social workers is the fourth edition of the *Diagnostic and Statistical Manual of Mental Disorders* (American Psychiatric Association [APA], 1994), known as DSM-IV. Although DSM is a disease-oriented system, previous editions (DSM-III and DSM-III-R; APA, 1980, 1987) recognized the presence of social stressors as contributory to the mental diseases in its Axis IV. However, the system did not allow the social worker to systematically identify and record psychosocial functioning factors. The editors of DSM-IV, with input from the

PIE task force, have modified Axis IV. Its title has been changed from "Psychosocial Stressors" to "Psychosocial and Environmental Problems," and it lists eight general areas that may be considered. Although an improvement over DSM-III-R, this listing has overlapping categories and remains much too simplistic for social work practice. It does encourage the non–social work practitioner to consider interpersonal and environmental factors that might otherwise be ignored. But, in keeping with the medical model, the major emphasis of both DSM-III-R and DSM-IV is still on classification of mental disorders. DSM perceives problems as residing in the individual rather than in the relationship between the individual and other people or society. Thus, DSM remains essentially antithetical to social work philosophy and the generally accepted role of social work as promoting the interaction between individuals and their environment for the betterment of both.

HISTORY OF PERSON-IN-ENVIRONMENT SYSTEM

PIE originated as a response to the long-held construct in social work of person-in-environment and to two developments in the 1980s: the introduction of DSM-III and the incorporation of constructs from system, ecological, and holistic theories into social work practice theories.

DSM-III, DSM-III-R, and DSM-IV describe human behavior problems primarily in terms of mental disease as befits the medical profession. Except for those social work practitioners who identify strongly with psychiatry, social work as a profession has diligently resisted a medical disease–oriented model for describing and classifying client problems. The profession has a general disdain for narrowing the focus on human problems to the individual's psychopathology and ignoring social or environmental conditions or the client's strengths. However, to communicate with other professionals and to document individual and societal disequilibrium, social workers have had to use the diagnostic, descriptive language of non–social work origins, such as psychiatry, law, and medicine. Social workers, particularly those in psychiatric settings, found themselves adopting the disease model of psychiatry and using a descriptive system that had little relevance to the work for which they had been trained.

The incorporation of system, ecological, and holistic theories of human behavior into social work practice theory also influenced the construction of the PIE system. Social work historically has advocated a holistic approach in its concern for both person and environment but, for lack of a way to bridge the two, has alternated its practice focus from one to the other, focusing for a while on psychological issues and for a while on environmental matters. It became clear that a system that isolated and described the person and environment factors could serve as a bridge, allowing the practitioner to analyze the problem complex (biological, psychological, social, and environmental aspects) in a more efficient manner and to plan, execute, and test interventions in an orderly way.

In this climate PIE was conceived, and in 1981 NASW funded a two-year project to develop a system for classifying the problems of social functioning experienced by social work clients. A 12-member task force of prominent social workers, both practitioners and academicians, formulated the issues and content of the system. The task force's goal was to develop a way to give a clear and concise picture of what was going on in the life of a client. The task force hoped to develop a system that was sufficiently comprehensive to encompass the full range of client problems but that was succinct and brief enough to be used in everyday practice. Such a descriptive system would provide a common language for communicating the problems experienced by social work clients (a problem classification system) and a mechanism for implementing and testing the range of interventions used in practice. The task force was aware of the imprecision inherent in establishing classes or categories in any of the sciences, especially the social sciences. It was also aware of the limits of such a system in describing the dynamic interaction among the factors that might be described. Recognition of the difficulties did not change the imperative that social work must develop at least a rudimentary classification system if it was ever to establish itself as a major profession.

CONCEPTUAL AND THEORETICAL FOUNDATIONS

The task force reviewed an array of relevant concepts and theories from the behavioral and social sciences before formulating the design for the PIE system. The resulting system was influenced by concepts and constructs from sociology, psychology, psychiatry, and social work. It is perhaps best described as an "integrated practice model" (Parsons, Hernandez, & Jorgensen, 1988) in which the target of intervention is the whole problem complex. It also reflects systems theory concepts, as it adapts the micro and macro framework of Anderson (1981) and the life model of Germain and Gitterman (1980). The system also uses concepts of prevention in mental health proposed by Parad (1965) and Bloom (1979) that emphasize concern for precipitating factors and the linking of inter-

ventions with stressful life events. Also influencing the discussion were the ideas of Clare and Cairns (1978), Erickson (1957), Fitzgerald (1978), Germain and Gitterman (1980), Gordon (1981), Hollis (1981), Janicak and Andriukaitis (1980), Katz (1984), Klein (1980), Lourie (1978), Perlman (1957), Reid and Epstein (1972), Richmond (1917), Rosenfeld (1983), and Siporin (1983).

The PIE system describes the problems of adult clients of social workers. In focusing on adults the task force did not overlook the need to eventually establish similar systems for children and families, but this endeavor was beyond the scope of this task force. The PIE system can be used to deal with the problems of families and children by assessing the problems of individual adults in the case situation.

To avoid the consensus difficulties that the American Orthopsychiatric Association encountered, the task force opted to develop a system that would be as atheoretical and as simple as possible without compromising depth of problem description. In this vein it also opted for a system that was primarily *descriptive* of the client's problem rather than *explanatory*, leaving the task of explaining the problems and their causes to individual practitioners, who have their own particular theoretical orientations.

The development of the "social role functioning" factor was influenced by Sarbin (1954), Thomas and Feldman (1967), and Turner (1954). The descriptors for social role functioning problems were derived from the direct experience of practitioner members of the task force. These descriptors reflected to some extent the various social work models and behavior theories, notably those of Hollis (1981), Perlman (1957), and Reid and Epstein (1972), and psychodynamic and ego psychology concepts that task force members had incorporated into their practice.

Although the PIE system focuses on social functioning problems or social dysfunction (situations in which there is clearly a non-optimal balance between individual and environment), it remains compatible with the "nature" metaphor in social work philosophy that calls for viewing the individual in terms of growth. The PIE system addresses an individual's problems of living with the goal of producing an optimal balance between the person and the environment, thus enhancing the individual's growth.

The concept of "environment" was operationalized on Warren's (1963) model of community. As Warren stated, "Its focus is less on a particular geographic area as the focus of analysis than on the types of systemic relationships into which people and social organizations come by virtue of their clustering together in the same location" (p. vii). The PIE task force adopted the Warren model to formulate a six-element descriptor covering the social institutions and organizations found in most communities to facilitate the individual's social well-being and social functioning. The category of "environment" in PIE was further construed to describe the interaction problems between the individual and a community's social institutions, that is, the interaction between the client and the health, safety, social services, judicial, and educational systems. The problems in the environment are the factors that prevent the person's access to the needed institution.

The person-in-environment (also referred to as "person-in-situation" and "person:environment") construct developed and elaborated upon by various theorists such as Germain and Gitterman (1980), Richmond (1917), and Siporin (1983) was key to the development of the PIE system. And, although not explicit, concepts from systems theory are clearly apparent in the interactional model that PIE projects.

THE SYSTEM'S STRUCTURE

PIE is a four-factor system. Each factor describes a feature of the client's problem situation. The first two factors constitute the core of social work practice and are discussed here in detail; the other two factors complete the description of the problem complex.

- **Factor I** identifies and describes the client's *problems in social functioning*. It describes the problems, their severity and duration, and the client's capacity to resolve them.
- **Factor II** describes *problems emanating from the environment* that affect the client's social role functioning. Like Factor I, it also describes the problem and its severity and duration.
- **Factor III** describes the *mental health problems* the client may be experiencing.
- **Factor IV** provides a statement of the client's *physical health problems*.

Factor I

Factor I describes problems in social role functioning, defined as the performance of activities of daily living required by the culture or the community for the individual's age or stage of life. A description of the client's problem in Factor I includes five components:

1. a statement of the social interaction area in which the problem is occurring (Table 1)
2. a descriptor for the type of problem (Table 2)

TABLE 1
Social Roles and PIE Codes

Role	Code
Familial	1000.xxx
Parent	1100.xxx
Spouse	1200.xxx
Child	1300.xxx
Sibling	1400.xxx
Other family	1500.xxx
Significant other	1600.xxx
Other interpersonal	2000.xxx
Lover	2100.xxx
Friend	2200.xxx
Neighbor	2300.xxx
Member	2400.xxx
Other (specify)	2500.xxx
Occupational	3000.xxx
Worker (paid economy)	3100.xxx
Worker (home)	3200.xxx
Worker (volunteer)	3300.xxx
Student	3400.xxx
Other (specify)	3500.xxx
Special life situation	4000.xxx
Consumer	4100.xxx
Inpatient/client	4200.xxx
Outpatient/client	4300.xxx
Probationer/parolee	4400.xxx
Prisoner	4500.xxx
Immigrant (legal)	4600.xxx
Immigrant (undocumented)	4700.xxx
Immigrant (refugee)	4800.xxx
Other (specify)	4900.xxx

3. an indication of the problem's severity (Table 3)
4. an indication of how long the problem has been present (Table 4)
5. an estimate of the client's physical, mental, and psychological strength (Table 5).

TABLE 2
Social Role Problems and PIE Codes

Problem	Code
Power	xx10.xxx
Ambivalence	xx20.xxx
Responsibility	xx30.xxx
Dependence	xx40.xxx
Loss	xx50.xxx
Isolation	xx60.xxx
Victimization	xx70.xxx
Mixed	xx80.xxx
Other (specify)	xx90.xxx

TABLE 3
Severity of Problems and PIE Codes

Severity	Code
Catastrophic	5
Very high	4
High	3
Moderate	2
Low	1
No problem	0

TABLE 4
Duration of Problems and PIE Codes

Time since Onset	Code
2 weeks or less	5
2–4 weeks	4
1–6 months	3
6 months to 1 year	2
1–5 years	1
More than 5 years	0

TABLE 5
Coping Skills and PIE Codes

Coping Skills Level	Code
No coping skills	5
Inadequate	4
Somewhat inadequate	3
Adequate	2
Above average	1
Outstanding	0

To record assessment findings and to facilitate research, a numerical code is used to identify the problems found in Factor I. The system also includes succinct written descriptions for each problem. The PIE system allows practitioners to note as many social functioning problems as can be identified.

Factor II

Factor II describes the problems in the client's environment as they affect the client's social functioning. In PIE the environment includes both the physical and social contexts in which people live. Factor II identifies problems in the social institutions that exist in most communities to facilitate an individual's well-being and development. It also notes the absence of necessary institutions. A description of a client's problem in Factor II includes the following three components:

1. an identification of the social system in which a problem related to the client's problem in social functioning is located (Table 6)
2. a statement of the severity of each problem (Table 3)
3. a judgment on the length of time the problem in the social institution has existed (Table 4).

As in Factor I, the findings can be noted using a numerical system or succinct written statements. The PIE system allows for noting as many environmental problems as can be identified.

CODING

The coding system that has been developed for recording PIE statements is described in detail in Karls and Wandrei (1994). For Factor I a seven-digit code is used. For example, the code 1130.213

TABLE 6
Environmental Problems and PIE Codes

Problem[a]	Code
Economic/basic needs system	5000.xx
Food/nutrition	5100.xx
Shelter	5200.xx
Employment	5300.xx
Economic resources	5400.xx
Transportation	5500.xx
Discrimination	5600.xx
Education/training system	6000.xx
Education/training	6100.xx
Discrimination	6200.xx
Judicial/legal system	7000.xx
Justice	7100.xx
Discrimination	7200.xx
Health, welfare, and safety system	8000.xx
Health/mental health	8100.xx
Safety	8200.xx
Social services	8300.xx
Discrimination	8400.xx
Voluntary associaton system	9000.xx
Religion	9100.xx
Community groups	9200.xx
Discrimination	9300.xx
Affectional support system	10000.xx
Affectional support	10100.xx
Discriminiation	10200.xx

[a]Each type of environmental problem contains three to 11 subtypes. For example, 5101.xx is a food/nutrition problem: lack of a food supply on regular basis; 8201.xx is a safety problem: violence or crime in the neighborhood; 5301.xx is unemployment: employment not available in the community.

describes a person who for three years has experienced moderate problems with parenting responsibilities and whose coping skills are somewhat inadequate. In Factor II, the six-digit code 5401.21 describes the environment of a client who for two years has experienced moderate economic problems (Figure 1).

CASE EXAMPLES

Child Welfare

The teacher of a five-year-old child suspects that the child is being sexually molested by her mother's live-in boyfriend. The situation is reported to Child Protective Services (CPS). On investigation the CPS worker finds that the mother has been using crack cocaine heavily for the past six months and that, because she has been able to find only part-time work at minimum wage, she has not been paying rent and is about to be evicted. She complains of health problems, reporting that she was recently diagnosed as having diabetes. She confides to the CPS worker that she was sexually molested as a child by her stepfather. Her boyfriend was supposed to help financially, but he recently lost his job and has no money. The couple has been fighting a lot recently, and the woman is

FIGURE 1

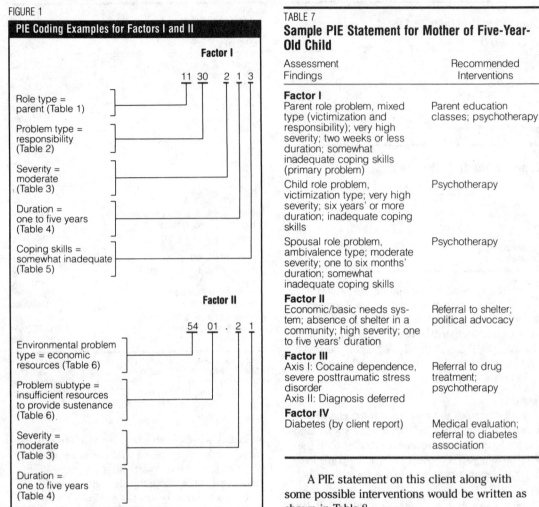

PIE Coding Examples for Factors I and II

Factor I

11 30 2 1 3

Role type = parent (Table 1)

Problem type = responsibility (Table 2)

Severity = moderate (Table 3)

Duration = one to five years (Table 4)

Coping skills = somewhat inadequate (Table 5)

Factor II

54 01 . 2 1

Environmental problem type = economic resources (Table 6)

Problem subtype = insufficient resources to provide sustenance (Table 6)

Severity = moderate (Table 3)

Duration = one to five years (Table 4)

TABLE 7
Sample PIE Statement for Mother of Five-Year-Old Child

Assessment Findings	Recommended Interventions
Factor I	
Parent role problem, mixed type (victimization and responsibility); very high severity; two weeks or less duration; somewhat inadequate coping skills (primary problem)	Parent education classes; psychotherapy
Child role problem, victimization type; very high severity; six years' or more duration; inadequate coping skills	Psychotherapy
Spousal role problem, ambivalence type; moderate severity; one to six months' duration; somewhat inadequate coping skills	Psychotherapy
Factor II	
Economic/basic needs system; absence of shelter in a community; high severity; one to five years' duration	Referral to shelter; political advocacy
Factor III	
Axis I: Cocaine dependence, severe posttraumatic stress disorder Axis II: Diagnosis deferred	Referral to drug treatment; psychotherapy
Factor IV	
Diabetes (by client report)	Medical evaluation; referral to diabetes association

A PIE statement on this client along with some possible interventions would be written as shown in Table 8.

VALIDITY AND RELIABILITY

Important steps in establishing the usefulness of a classification system are the systematic assessment of its acceptability, feasibility, coverage, reliability, and validity. Acceptability concerns whether users agree that the categories and their definitions have "face validity," that is, that they encompass the language and ideas of the profession. Feasibility indicates whether the system is understandable and easily applied. Coverage is achieved to the extent that there is a fit of the system in practice and that few clients fall in the categories of "unspecified" or "other." Reliability indicates how well practitioners agree with each other on the identification of categories. Validity is a measure of usefulness and reflects how well the system measures what it is supposed to measure.

In 1984, a nationwide pilot test of PIE was conducted. Two chapters from each NASW region were selected, and five members from each chap-

ambivalent about staying in the relationship. Because there is little affordable housing in her community, she is also concerned that she will become homeless.

Because the PIE system focuses on the adult, a PIE statement in this situation with some possible interventions would read as shown in Table 7.

Older Adult
A 77-year-old woman, widowed two years ago, is referred to the senior services center by her physician, who has been treating her for severe arthritis. She is very depressed, cries frequently, seems unable to leave her house, and has withdrawn from her former activities and associations. Her children all live out of the area, and her only close friend died five weeks ago. The social worker at the center has learned that state funding for the center is about to be cut drastically and that services for this kind of client are to be eliminated.

TABLE 8
Sample PIE Statement for 77-Year-Old Woman

Assessment Findings	Recommended Interventions
Factor I	
Spousal role problem, loss type; high severity; one to five years' duration; somewhat inadequate coping skills	Psychotherapy; widows support group
Friend role problem, loss type; high severity; one to six months' duration; somewhat inadequate coping skills	Psychotherapy
Factor II	
Health, safety and social services system; Other social service problem (threatened elimination of services); high severity; two to four weeks' duration	Political organizing
Factor III	
Axis I: Major depression, single episode	Psychotherapy
Axis II: No diagnosis	Medication referral
Factor IV	
Arthritis (by client report)	Consultation with physician; arthritis support group

ter representing differing theoretical orientations, direct practice settings, and length of time in practice were asked to use the system with two clients and then complete a questionnaire about their experience. Feedback on the use of the system was generally positive. Most respondents indicated that they were able to use the system with a minimum of difficulty to describe their clients. Three-fourths (76 percent) of the respondents thought the manual was clear and that it described the client's situation clearly and concisely. Eighty-two percent agreed that it helped them identify when social work interventions were needed. Sixty-five percent said it would help them communicate with other practitioners and that it provided a basis for gathering data to measure the need for services.

A pilot reliability study funded by NASW was conducted in 1989 at four sites: United Charities of Chicago, the Los Angeles–University of Southern California County General Hospital, the Social Work Department of the New York State Psychiatric Institute, and the Massachusetts Department of Mental Health. Videotaped cases were examined, and a total of 197 social workers rated 16 videotapes, with four to 30 raters per tape. Although this study was too small for any definitive conclusions about reliability to be made, the findings were generally positive in that there was a high level of agreement on the identification of the PIE categories in the types of problems tested.

A grant has been approved and is awaiting funding from the National Institute of Mental Health to conduct a large, multisite national field test of the PIE system's reliability across a variety of cases representing the range of social work practice. Further evidence of the system's impact is found in a proposal to include some of its features in DSM-IV's Axis IV, which focuses on social supports and environmental resources. Informal tests of PIE in Italy, the Netherlands, Japan, Canada, and Australia have yielded positive responses.

This preliminary testing suggests that the PIE system has likely acceptability and feasibility in practice, and likely reliability. Further testing for interrater reliability and validity is anticipated with funding from the National Institute of Mental Health.

APPLICATIONS

PIE helps sort out the often complex array of problems that the client brings to the social work practitioner. It permits a nonjudgmental description of the problems the client is experiencing. A uniform method of describing client problems allows social workers to plan actions and interventions more responsibly. Instead of social work assessment following the methodological expertise of the practitioner, PIE enables a social worker in a family service agency to describe a client's problems in a way that will be understood by a colleague in a child welfare or mental health setting. Also important, the client should be able to understand the problem assessment and participate more fully in problem resolution or reduction.

As a teaching tool the PIE system is eminently useful in helping the student learning casework to understand the domain of social work practice and to develop an assessment and treatment plan that is clear and understandable. Because this system is essentially atheoretical, it permits the instructor to use whatever casework model or behavior theory has been adopted and apply it to the individual case. For researchers and administrators PIE serves as a database to aid the collection, classification, and analysis of social conditions and social interactional problems in which social workers intervene. In the future it could be used to collect data routinely on client problems and community conditions. Such data could facilitate both social program and social policy development.

FUTURE OF PIE

For social work to gain parity with professions like medicine/psychiatry, law, and the ministry, it must adopt a nomenclature for identifying its area of expertise. The future of PIE is linked to the willingness of social work practitioners, administrators, and educators to learn and implement a new way of identifying client problems. Few occupational groups are willing to pay the costs of transforming themselves, regardless of the benefits. The medical profession's efforts to raise educational standards in the early 20th century required great expenditures of money, power, and friendship; the effort changed the image of medicine dramatically in one generation. Psychiatry's DSM-III and the profession's effort to promote DSM as a universal classification system cost millions of dollars and a great expenditure of energy, as well as the defection of numerous practitioners. But the effort resulted in nearly universal usage among mental health workers and has greatly enhanced the status of psychiatry.

Inherent in the development of a new system is the risk of intraprofession conflicts between those who are either content with the state of things or at least not open to radical change and those who seek to upgrade the field. And there is a risk that splits in the profession could occur. But the change could both increase the professional status of social work and meet the ideals and values of social work by improving the quality of care.

The current version of PIE is an early model of a vehicle for describing the problems of social functioning of social work clients. It works. It helps unravel the problem complex brought to the social worker and leads to better intervention planning. As a developing system PIE will need ongoing testing and refinement. The language for describing some problems is still awkward, and the categories need refinement and perhaps expansion. But this is the first step in a journey of a thousand miles, and the continued development of the PIE system can lead social work to a new clarity and understanding of its domain. By unraveling the problem complex, it can help social work fulfill its mission of reducing to the barest minimum the common problems clients bring.

With the increasing importance in the United States of case management and managed care, and with the advent of a national health policy that will demand more accountability, PIE, with its uniform, succinct descriptors of social problems, could provide data useful to those wanting hard data on the services social workers provide. Should the third-party reimbursement system become less oriented to the disease model, it is possible that social work practitioners could be reimbursed for services to ameliorate problems in social functioning and to reduce environmental problems. A computerized version of PIE, currently in development, could help expedite the assessment process and produce uniform data about the human condition that could benefit the consumer of social work services, practitioners, administrators, program planners, and researchers alike.

REFERENCES

American Psychiatric Association. (1980). *Diagnostic and statistical manual of mental disorders* (3rd ed.). Washington, DC: Author.

American Psychiatric Association. (1987). *Diagnostic and statistical manual of mental disorders* (3rd ed., rev.). Washington, DC: Author.

American Psychiatric Association. (1994). *Diagnostic and statistical manual of mental disorders* (4th ed.). Washington, DC: Author.

Anderson, J. (1981). *Social work methods and processes.* Belmont, CA: Wadsworth.

Bloom, B. (1979). Prevention of mental disorders: Recent advances in theory and practice. *Community Mental Health Journal, 15,* 179–191.

Clare, A. W., & Cairns, V. (1978). Design, development and use of a standardized interview to assess social maladjustment and dysfunction in community studies. *Psychological Medicine, 8,* 589–604.

Commission of Professional and Hospital Activities. (1980). *International classifications of diseases, ninth revision, clinical modifications* (ICD-9-CM). Ann Arbor, MI: Author.

Committee on Professional and Hospital Activities (Ed.). (1979). *International classification of health problems in primary care* (2nd ed.). Oxford, England: Oxford University Press.

Erickson, E. (1957). *Childhood and society.* New York: Basic Books.

Fitzgerald, R. (1978). Classification and recording of social problems. *Social Science and Medicine, 12,* 255–268.

Germain, C., & Gitterman, A. (1980). *Life model of social work practice.* New York: Columbia University Press.

Gordon, W. E. (1981). A natural classification system for social work literature and knowledge. *Social Work, 26,* 134–138.

Henk, M. (1985). *Developing codes and classifications for social workers in health care.* Available from Public Health Service, 601 East 12th Street, Kansas City, MO 64106.

Hollis, F. M. (1981). *Casework: A psychosocial therapy.* (3rd ed.). New York: Random House.

Janicak, P., & Andriukaitis, S. N. (1980). DSM-III: Seeing the forest through the trees. *Psychiatric Annals, 10,* 284–297.

Karls J. M., & Wandrei, K. E. (1994). *The PIE manual.* Washington, DC: NASW Press.

Katz, A. (1984). Reflections on an elusive vision: Social work in health. *Journal of Public Health, 5,* 410–422.

Klein, R. (1980). Doctors and social workers. *British Medical Journal, 12,* 1–7.

Lourie, N. (1978). Case management. In J. Talbott (Ed.). *The chronic mental patient: Problems, solutions and recommendations for a public policy* (pp. 155–172). Washington, DC: American Psychiatric Association.

Meyer, C. H. (1987). Direct practice in social work: Overview. In A. Minahan (Ed.-in-Chief), *Encyclopedia of social work* (18th ed., Vol. 1, pp. 409–422). Silver Spring, MD: National Association of Social Workers.

Minahan, A. (1981). Purpose and objectives of social work revisited. *Social Work, 26*, 5–6.

Minnesota Systems Research, Inc. (1977). *Classification and codes for children and youth (social work)*. Minneapolis: Author.

National Association of Social Workers. (1984). *NASW standards for the practice of clinical social work*. Silver Spring, MD: Author.

Parad, H. (Ed.). (1965). *Crisis intervention*. New York: Family Service Association of America.

Parsons, R. J., Hernandez, S. H., & Jorgensen, J. D. (1988). Integrated practice: A framework for problem solving. *Social Work, 33*, 417–421.

Perlman, H. H. (1957). *Social casework: A problem solving process*. Chicago: University of Chicago Press.

Reid, W. J., & Epstein, L. (1972). *Task centered casework*. New York: Columbia University Press.

Richmond, M. E. (1917) *Social diagnosis*. New York: Russell Sage Foundation.

Rosenfeld, J. M. (1983). The domain and expertise of social work: A conceptualization. *Social Work, 28*, 186–191.

Sarbin, T. (1954). Role theory. In G. Lindzay (Ed.), *Handbook of social psychology* (pp. 546–552). Cambridge, MA: Addison-Wesley.

Siporin, M. (1983). The therapeutic process in clinical social work. *Social Work, 28*, 193–198.

Thomas, E., & Feldman, R. (1967). *Behavioral science for social workers*. New York. Free Press.

Turner, R. (1954). Role: Sociological aspects. In G. Lindzay (Ed.), *Handbook of social psychology* (pp. 546–557). Cambridge, MA: Addison-Wesley.

Warren, R. (1963). *The community in America*. Chicago: Rand McNally.

Williams, J.B.W., Karls, J., & Wandrei, K. (1989). The person-in-environment (PIE) system for describing problems of social functioning. *Hospital and Community Psychiatry, 40*, 1125–1126.

FURTHER READING

Gordon, W. E. (1969). Basic constructs for an integrative and generative conception of social work. In G. Hearn (Ed.), *The general systems approach* (pp. 5–11). New York: Council on Social Work Education.

Gordon, W. E. (1981). A natural classification system for social work literature and knowledge. *Social Work, 26*, 134–138.

Karls, J. M., & Wandrei, K. E. (1992). PIE: A new language for social work. *Social Work, 37*, 80–85.

Karls, J. M., & Wandrei, K. E. (1992). The person-in-environment system for classifying client problems. *Journal of Case Management, 1*(3), 90–95.

Karls, J. M., & Wandrei, K. E. (1994). *Person-in-environment system: The PIE classification system for social functioning problems.* Washington, DC: NASW Press.

Kirk, S., Saporin, M., & Kutchins, H. (1989). The prognosis for social work diagnosis. *Social Casework, 68*(5), 295–304.

Mattaini, M., & Kirk, S. (1992). Assessing assessment in social work. *Social Work, 36*, 260–266.

James M. Karls, DSW, LCSW, ACSW, is a faculty member, San Francisco State University, School of Social Work, 1600 Holloway Avenue, San Francisco, CA 94132. **Karin E. Wandrei, DSW, LCSW, BCD,** is deputy regional director, FamiliesFirst, Hercules, CA, and a private practitioner, 669 Alma Avenue, #201, Oakland, CA 94610.

For further information see

Assessment; Diagnostic and Statistical Manual of Mental Disorders; Direct Practice Overview; Goal Setting and Intervention Planning; Mental Health Overview; Social Work Practice: Theoretical Base; Social Work Profession Overview.

Key Words

assessment · person-in-environment · diagnosis · environmental stress

Personnel Management
Peter J. Pecora

In the human services, line staff and supervisors constitute one of the most important resources for maximizing agency productivity and effectiveness. Personnel management in social work agencies involves key functions that must be performed to develop and maintain a group of skilled, productive, and satisfied employees:

- recruiting, screening, and selecting social work and other personnel
- specifying and allocating job tasks to design position descriptions and staffing patterns
- designing and conducting performance appraisals
- orienting, training, and developing staff
- supervising and coaching ongoing task performance
- handling employee performance problems
- enforcing employee sanctions and, when necessary, dismissing workers.

A host of issues and tasks are associated with these key personnel management functions, such as job classification and wage setting, support of work teams, promotion of worker motivation and productivity, employee health and safety, labor–management relations, quality assurance, personnel administration law, and merit system reform. Personnel management overlaps greatly with supervision of staff in that many supervisory responsibilities include functions such as promoting teamwork, setting unit goals, promoting and supporting ethnic and cultural diversity, negotiating organizational demands, and managing conflict.

PERSONNEL POLICIES

Personnel *policies* specify the rights and privileges as well as responsibilities an employer expects of a worker and what a worker can expect from an employer. Personnel *practices* consist of how personnel policies are put into operation or administered. The articulation of goals or objectives for sound personnel policies and practices are expressed in personnel *standards*. (Trader, 1978, pp. 1025–1026)

Personnel policies can aid morale by providing a framework for consistent treatment of staff (Cox, 1984). If they are carefully reviewed with new employees and updated with current staff, personnel policies help staff understand their responsibilities, options, and fringe benefits. To comply with legal mandates and agency accreditation standards, personnel policies must be reviewed periodically by the agency's board of directors or the public civil service commission. For example, NASW (1990) has agency accreditation standards relating to the classification of social work personnel.

Personnel policies vary according to the type of social welfare agency, such as a private non-profit agency, a private for-profit agency, or a public agency operating under civil service regulations. Table 1 presents a typical table of contents for a personnel manual for a nonprofit private or voluntary social welfare organization. In addition to the sections listed in Table 1, such manuals should also specify the ways in which the agency's policies are modified or new ones are established.

Generally, personnel policies are developed by a board of directors and agency administrator with assistance from supervisory and line staff. In certain cases, a civil service commission, personnel committee, the agency's board, an executive, or a joint board–staff committee may design the personnel policies (Cox, 1984). However they are developed, the total set of personnel policies must be approved by the agency's board of directors, the civil service commission, or the governing body that has responsibility for agency policy in this area.

RECRUITING AND SELECTING EFFECTIVE EMPLOYEES

Recruiting and screening potential staff members are important components of personnel management. Task-based job descriptions must be developed and essential worker "competencies" (knowledge, skills, abilities, and attitudes) must be identified. Careful planning and interpersonal skills are required for interviewing job candidates in a courteous and professional manner.

Recruitment is an important step in providing the agency with an adequate number of applicants. Selection involves reviewing the qualifications of job applicants and interviewing them to

TABLE 1
Typical Table of Contents for a Social Services Agency Personnel Manual

Introduction
  Organization philosophy and mission
  Major organizational goals and objectives
  Organizational programs or types of services
1. Employment
  Hiring authority
  Nondiscrimination and affirmative action policies
    and safeguards (includes safeguards as
    mandated by the Equal Employment Opportunity
    Commission, affirmative action, and the
    Americans with Disabilities Act)
  Types of employment (full-time, part-time,
    temporary, volunteer)
  Probationary period procedures
  Maintenance and access to personnel records
2. Working hours and conditions
  Work schedule and office hours
  Flexible time
  Overtime or compensatory time
  Types of absence and reports
3. Salaries and wages
  Wages and salary structure and rationale
  Paydays
  Deductions
  Raises (merit and cost of living) guidelines and
    rationale
  Compensation for work-related expenses
  Employee access to current salary schedule
4. Employee benefits
  Leaves and absences
    Vacations
    Holidays
    Sick days
    Personal days
    Maternity leave
    Paternity leave
    Leave of absence
    Other excused absences
  Insurance
    Social security
    Medical insurance

Life insurance
Disability insurance
Unemployment insurance
Workers' compensation
Pension or retirement plans
5. Employee rights and responsibilities
  Employee responsibilities
  Employee rights
  Grievance procedures
6. Performance and salary review
  Procedures
  Timing
  Use of probation periods or suspension
  Promotion policies and procedures
7. Staff development
  Orientation of new employees
  Planning process for in-service training and
    related activities
  Educational programs and conferences
8. General policies and procedures
  Outside employment
  Office opening and closing
  Telephone
  Travel
  Personal property
9. General Office Practices and Procedures
  Office coverage
  Smoking
  Use and care of equipment
10. Termination
  Grounds of dismissal
  Resignation
  Retirement
  Release
  Reduction in force
Appendixes
  Organizational chart
  Salary ranges by position
  Equal opportunity guidelines on sexual harassment
  Conflict of interest policies
  Personnel evaluation procedures and forms

SOURCE: Adapted from Cox, F. M. (1984). Guidelines for preparing personnel policies. In F. M. Cox, J. L. Erlich, J. Rothman, & J. E. Tropman (Eds.), *Tactics and techniques of community practice* (2nd ed., p. 275). Itasca, IL: F. E. Peacock; and Wolfe, T. (1984). *The nonprofit organization: An operating manual* (pp. 63–64). Englewood Cliffs, NJ: Prentice Hall.

decide who should be offered the position. Placement involves assigning the new employee to the position and orienting the person properly so that he or she can begin working (Shafritz, Hyde, & Rosenbloom, 1986).

The five major steps involved in recruitment and selection include

1. developing a job description that outlines information regarding the minimum requisite qualifications for the position in terms of education, experience, and skills
2. recruiting employees by posting position announcements, by advertising, and by other outreach

3. screening job applicants using application forms, resume reviews, references or criminal background checks, and tests (if appropriate)
4. conducting screening interviews
5. selecting the person and notifying other applicants.

The employment selection process is an important investment of administrative time. If this process is not carried out properly, supervisory staff and managers will spend valuable time and energy overcoming marginal work performance, increased organizational conflict, and the stress involved in transferring or terminating the staff person (Goodale, 1989; Janz, 1989). Although many local, state, and federal laws affect recruitment, three major sets of law and policy help shape what is effective and legal practice in this area: (1) affirmative action; (2) equal employment opportunity; and (3) the Americans with Disabilities Act.

Affirmative Action and the Equal Employment Opportunity Commission (EEOC)

Legislation for equal employment opportunity and affirmative action, primarily Executive Order No. 11246, continues to affect the recruitment, screening, and selection of employees in both business and social welfare organizations. The distinctive components of EEOC laws are based on Title VII of the Civil Rights Act of 1964 (P.L. 88-352). A number of laws also support equal opportunity in relation to such factors as age (Age Discrimination in Employment Act of 1967, as amended); handicap status (sections 503 and 504 of the Rehabilitation Act of 1973, as amended); veteran status (Vietnam Era Veterans' Readjustment Assistance Act of 1974); and equal pay (Equal Pay Act of 1963).

Klingner and Nalbandian (1985) noted that

with few exceptions, Title VII [equal employment opportunity] prohibits employers, labor organizations, and employment agencies from making employee or applicant personnel decisions based on race, color, religion, sex, or national origin. Although it originally applied only to private employers, the concern of [equal employment opportunity] was extended to local and state governments by 1972 amendments to the 1964 Civil Rights Act. (p. 64)

Equal opportunity laws reflect a management approach to reducing employee discrimination by ensuring that equal opportunity is implemented in all employment actions. Executive Order No. 11246 and other laws require nondiscrimination, which involves the elimination of all existing discriminatory conditions, whether purposeful or inadvertent. In 1967 Executive Order No. 11246 was amended to include gender protection to be in alignment with Title VII.

Employers with 15 or more employees, employment agencies, labor unions, state and local government, educational institutions, and federal contractors (with contracts of more than $50,000 and 25 or more employees) must carefully and systematically examine their employment policies to be sure that they do not operate to the detriment of any person on the grounds of race; color; religion; national origin; sex; age; or status as a disabled individual, disabled veteran, or veteran of the Vietnam era. Administrators must also ensure that the practices of those responsible in matters

of employment, including all supervisors, are nondiscriminatory. Employment discrimination based on sexual orientation is not covered under this set of policies.

One response to the requirements of EEOC laws and executive orders is the development of affirmative action plans. Affirmative action involves taking steps to ensure proportional recruitment, selection, and promotion of qualified members of groups formerly excluded, such as ethnic groups and women. Many types of employers, unions, and employment agencies are required to plan and document through written affirmative action programs (AAPs) the steps they are taking to reduce underrepresentation of various groups. Most public and private organizations that provide goods and services to the federal government and their subcontractors must comply with the provisions of affirmative action as described in Executive Order No. 11246 (Ivancevich, 1992).

Although both equal employment opportunity and affirmative action seek to eliminate employment discrimination, the safeguards and improvements mandated by these guidelines vary in relation to specific employee recruitment, screening, selection, and promotion practices. For example, a mental health agency may develop a specific recruitment campaign to recruit and hire more female supervisors to increase the proportion of female administrators in the agency as part of its plan to comply with affirmative action regulations. In contrast, EEOC guidelines cover such areas as the type of questions that can be asked on an employment application or in an interview (for instance, criminal record, marital status, number of children, ethnicity) and emphasize the use of screening or interviewing committees composed of a mix of males, females, and ethnic group members.

There are a number of differences between EEOC and affirmative action that should be noted:

- Equal opportunity is a legal obligation; affirmative action is voluntary.
- Equal opportunity is neutral with respect to protected characteristics; affirmative action gives preference to individuals, based on protected characteristics.
- Equal opportunity is prohibitory; affirmative action is promotional in the sense of preferring members of protected groups.
- Equal opportunity is a permanent obligation; affirmative action, by its nature, is a temporary remedy (Panaro, 1990).

In addition to banning certain types of application or interview questions, EEOC guidelines require that the selection process for candidates not have an "adverse impact" on any social, ethnic, or sex group unless the procedure is validated through job analysis or employee selection research (EEOC, 1978). *Adverse impact* is indicated when an employee selection rate for any race, sex, or ethnic group is less than 80 percent of the rate of the group with the highest rate of selection. However, greater differences in selection rate may not constitute adverse impact when the differences are based on small numbers (EEOC, 1978). Proscriptions against discrimination in employment mandate that any requirement (education or experience) used as a standard for employment decisions must have a manifest relationship to the employment in question (Meritt-Haston & Weyley, 1983).

Americans with Disabilities Act

The Americans with Disabilities Act (P.L. 101-336) was enacted July 26, 1990. It extends broad civil rights protection to the many Americans with disabilities and contains four major sections: (1) employment (Title I), (2) state and local government services (Title II), (3) public accommodations provided by private entities (Title III), and (4) telecommunications (Title IV). The act is neither preemptive nor exclusive; stricter requirements of state or federal law will continue to apply. The purposes of the act are

1. to provide a clear and comprehensive national mandate for the elimination of discrimination against individuals with disabilities
2. to provide clear, strong, consistent, enforceable standards addressing discrimination against individuals with disabilities
3. to insure that the federal government plays a central role in enforcing the standards established in this Act on behalf of individuals with disabilities
4. to invoke the sweep of congressional authority, including the power to enforce the 14th Amendment and to regulate commerce in order to address the major areas of discrimination faced day-to-day by people with disabilities. (Davis, Wright, & Tremaine Law Firm, 1992, p. 1)

The effective date for compliance with specific sections of the Americans with Disabilities Act varies by topic and by the size of the corporation or entity. The employment provisions became effective July 26, 1992, for employers with 25 or more employees, and July 26, 1994, for employers with 15 to 24 employees. The public accommodations provisions were in place by the end of 1992.

The act is not an affirmative action law; it is, however, an EEO law in that it addresses discrimination in three major areas: (1) hiring; (2) accommodation of a disabled person on the job; and (3) access of disabled persons to public and private facilities. A person with a disability also must be qualified under the act. A qualified individual with a disability is one who, with or without "reasonable accommodation," can perform the "essential functions" of the job that the person holds or desires. Qualification is a two-step process involving an analysis to determine the essential functions of the job and an evaluation of whether the individual can perform the functions with or without a reasonable accommodation (EEOC, 1991).

The act includes a provision that requires organizations to have "reasonable accommodations" for all consumers and employees. The concept of reasonable accommodation is the new, unique distinguishing characteristic of employment practices under the Americans with Disabilities Act. The concept is not, however, well defined in the act. Essentially, a *reasonable accommodation* is an action by the employer that assists a disabled person to perform the essential job functions. To determine whether a disabled individual is qualified for a position, he or she must be evaluated assuming all reasonable accommodations will be provided. If the disabled individual is then not qualified for the position, the candidate may be rejected (EEOC, 1991; Perry, 1993).

Recent and ongoing court cases may alter what is permissible under EEOC, affirmative action, and Americans with Disabilities Act guidelines. Government updates and legal consultations are important resources for assessing the adequacy of organizational procedures.

SPECIFYING JOB TASKS AND POSITION DESCRIPTIONS

One of the key components of excellence in human services agencies is attention to the details of human services work. One of the basic tools necessary for clarifying or modifying job responsibilities is an accurate job description. Experienced supervisors who have used job analysis skills to develop position descriptions in their work unit have identified many benefits of the position description, including the following four: (1) It serves as a basis for clarifying job expectations with workers, because prior job descriptions are often vague and incomplete; (2) it facilitates worker performance reviews, because there is specific information about job tasks and competencies necessary for assessing outcome; (3) it serves as an information base for assessing staffing needs and for requesting additional staff support based on tasks performed in the unit; and (4) it serves as a tool for monitoring the relationship between the work performed by staff and the goals and objectives of the agency (Pecora & Austin, 1987).

ORIENTING, TRAINING, AND DEVELOPING STAFF

The induction process is critically important to the new worker and deserves considerable attention by the organization. First impressions of the agency are lasting ones, and it is to the agency's benefit that orientation programs be positive experiences. The basic purpose of orientation is to introduce the new worker to the organization, its policies and procedures, the worker's colleagues, his or her role and responsibilities, and the authority structure. The basic components of such an orientation are usually completed over several working days, followed by additional on-the-job orientation that may include providing documentation on policy, agency history, social case history procedures, and sample case studies.

The induction process of a new worker should include a complete description of the agency's structure with lines of authority and communication, personnel procedures, and career opportunities. New workers need a full explanation of the purpose, goals, and objectives of the agency. Because most human services agencies are part of a larger network of services, it is important to supply a brief description of the role of the agency in this network, including an identification of relevant policies and regulations pertaining to state and federal regulations or agency bylaws. Copies of the organizational chart should be made available along with an updated personnel handbook.

Staff development programs can be viewed from many different vantage points. A program can be a single workshop or a six-month series of in-service training events. Several programs might be the major components of an agency's annual staff development plan. A staff development plan provides workers with opportunities to improve skills and gain new knowledge away from the job and provides supervisors with an opportunity to improve their own knowledge and skills.

For some administrators, agency staff development programs may be viewed as costly enterprises and only justifiable in terms of disseminating new policies and procedures. For other administrators, staff training is one of the essential strategies for preventing employee obsolescence because of technological, cultural, or social change (Odiorne, 1984). From the perspective of service recipients, staff development programs are essential if clients are to be served by staff who

are knowledgeable about the latest treatment or service delivery approaches.

SUPERVISING ONGOING TASK PERFORMANCE

Supervision encompasses a broad range of tasks, including helping staff set work priorities, establishing work unit goals, monitoring and evaluating employee performance, and providing supportive and education-oriented supervision (see Austin, 1981; Kadushin 1992; Middleman & Rhodes, 1985; Munson, 1993; Shulman, 1982).

Designing and Conducting Performance Appraisals

Worker performance appraisal is concerned with systematically assessing how well agency staff members perform their jobs over a specified period. Performance evaluations are designed to measure the extent to which the worker is achieving the requirements of his or her position and should be based on clearly specified, realistic, and achievable criteria reflecting agency standards (Kadushin, 1992). Superior performance appraisal methods encourage supervisors and workers to set realistic and measurable goals for job performance. Measurable evaluation criteria also help motivate, direct, and integrate worker learning and provide staff with examples of how they can evaluate their own performance.

The inability of staff members to meet certain performance standards may be a result of dysfunctional or unclear agency policies, a shortage of critical resources, inadequate supervisory feedback, or other administrative shortcomings. Sound performance evaluations help supervisors and managers to distinguish agency-related problems—that should be corrected through organizational change—from worker-related performance difficulties that may be corrected by in-service training or formal staff development programs (Mager & Pipe, 1970). Quality improvement efforts have shown that a substantial number of service delivery problems are the result of organizational problems (Deming, 1986).

Evaluating staff on at least an annual basis is important for determining pay raises, promotability, future assignments, and the need for discipline. Sound performance appraisal systems help agencies meet EEO requirements in the areas of promotion or discipline (Jensen, 1980; Odiorne, 1984). Finally, given the amount of autonomy and discretion of most social services agency staff, consumers have a right to expect a minimum amount of staff supervision and monitoring as part of agency quality control. As a result of performance evaluations, consumers are more likely to be assured of effective service and protected from continuation of inadequate service (Kadushin, 1992).

Challenges in evaluation. Despite the many advantages of performance evaluation, human services and other organizations continue to struggle with two primary challenges. First, which performance standards or criteria should be used to judge a worker's job performance? Second, once the criteria have been identified, how and to what extent can they be measured (Howell & Dipboye, 1982)?

Human services agencies use a variety of process or outcome criteria to evaluate worker performance. Most performance criteria fall into the following general categories: output quality, output quantity, work habits and attitudes, accident rates, learning ability, and judgment or problem-solving ability (Howell & Dipboye, 1982). However, many performance evaluations concentrate too much on subjective personality traits or on the peripheral aspects of the worker's performance (attitude, punctuality, orientation to managers) and not enough on the degree to which the employee has attained specific outcome criteria.

Categories of standards. Performance appraisal methods can be categorized into two groups: (1) objective or "absolute standards" and (2) subjective or "comparative standards" (Cummings & Schwab, 1973). Objective methods examine the use of certain key skills, performance of essential practice functions, and concrete outputs such as provision of therapy that improves client skills in certain areas. Other objective standards might be decreasing payment error rates, improving the number of foster homes recruited, or increasing the number of children reunified with parents. Subjective performance evaluation methods use one of the three following approaches to measurement: (1) comparing an individual's performance in relationship to other individuals by using group norms; (2) assessing individual performance on the basis of relatively fixed, independently determined standards; and (3) judging individual performance by carefully observing what people do (Howell & Dipboye, 1982; Odiorne, 1984).

Handling Employee Performance Problems
Developing accurate job descriptions, hiring the most qualified personnel, using measurable job-related performance criteria, and conducting effective performance appraisal interviews provide a solid foundation for analyzing and dealing with a variety of employee performance problems. Employee performance problems can be minimized and more easily handled if the personnel functions described in the preceding sections have been adequately addressed.

It is important to distinguish between worker and agency performance problems. Employee "performance problems" are often viewed as evidence of a lack of worker knowledge or skill (training need), poor attitudes (a lack of commitment to the job), need for more supervision, or poor use of time. However, employee performance difficulties may also be a result of a host of nonworker factors such as unclear agency policies, resource limitations, vague work priorities or performance standards, poor supervision, excessive caseload demands, and assignment of inappropriate cases. Supervisors and managers need to look closely at both worker and agency factors before deciding on a course of action.

Handling worker performance problems requires that certain employee regulations and grievance-handling procedures have been specified in the agency's personnel policies (Odiorne, 1984). Using personnel policies, standard operating procedures, supervision principles, and the job analysis process, the supervisor can assess the match between worker competencies and the job requisites, seek continuously to clarify performance standards, and remove obstacles to employee success.

Supervisors also provide access to training, monitor performance, and provide feedback and favorable consequences for effective work behaviors (Odiorne, 1984). In addition, managers should be sensitive to the possibility that personal factors may be contributing to poor performance. These factors might be a worker's health problems; stress or other emotional difficulties; family pressures; or poor work habits, such as carelessness; or poor time management.

Employee termination. Discharging staff can be one of the most difficult and unpleasant tasks in managing personnel. Supervisors and personnel managers are often given this responsibility without sufficient information and training to plan and carry out employee terminations. A variety of references provide excellent information and guidelines for handling employee terminations (see Coulson, 1981; Jensen, 1981; Morin & Yorks, 1982; Roseman, 1982).

Clear job specifications and performance standards are essential to evaluate employee performance. Because employee termination can occur for reasons beyond poor performance or misconduct, agencies must develop explicit policies that describe the conditions under which an employee can be terminated. Written policies provide the operational guidelines for termination, protect staff from arbitrary actions, and help ensure that termination decisions are legal and fair. A host of legal issues surround termination, and nearly all groups of employees have some type of protection under the law that is enforced by local courts, state human rights agencies, the EEOC, and in the case of unions, the National Labor Relations Board (Ewing, 1983; Lopatka, 1984).

Sexual harassment. Sexual harassment is one of the most egregious violations of a person's civil rights, and it has become recognized in recent years as a type of performance problem with significant potential for worker grievance. As with racial harassment, sexual harassment is increasingly recognized as one of the most sensitive employee issues to handle. Agency supervisors and managers, as well as the organization, have been held liable by local and federal courts.

Sexual harassment involves unwelcome sexual advances, requests for sexual favors, and other verbal or physical conduct of a sexual nature. Harassment can be verbal, visual, or physical. For example, visual harassment involves leering, suggestive ogling, offensive signs and gestures, or open display of pornographic and other offensive materials. Verbal harassment includes sexually explicit jokes, sexual suggestions, highly personal innuendos, and explicit propositions. Examples of physical harassment are brushing up against the body, patting, squeezing, pinching, kissing, fondling, forced sexual assault, and rape.

The incidence of sexual harassment is much higher than commonly thought. In 1980 the Federal Merit System conducted a survey of 23,000 randomly selected male and female civilian employees; the return rate was 85 percent. Employees were asked if between May 1978 and May 1980 they had received "any forms of uninvited and unwanted sexual attention" from a person or persons with whom they worked (Merit Systems Protection Board, 1981, pp. 26–37). The forms of behavior identified were

- actual or attempted rape or sexual assault
- pressure for sexual favors
- deliberate touching, leaning over, cornering, or pinching
- sexually suggestive looks or gestures
- letters, phone calls, or materials of a sexual nature
- pressure for dates
- sexual teasing, jokes, remarks, or questions.

Approximately 42 percent of the women and 15 percent of the men reported being sexually harassed during this period. Only 1 percent of men and women reported the severest form of harassment (actual or attempted rape or sexual assault). But if that 1 percent is projected to the total 1,875,000 federal employees at that time, then about 18,750 federal employees were victimized during this period.

Less severe sexual harassment such as letters, phone calls, pressure, and touching was reported by 16 percent of the respondents, projected to be about 300,000 workers. Sexual teasing, jokes, and suggestive gestures were reported by 8 percent of the respondents, or about 150,000 workers. Sexual harassment appears to occur more than once for each victim. These types of findings were also found in studies reported in the popular press and business journals (Collins & Blodgett, 1981; Crull, 1979; Safran, 1976).

The overall findings from these surveys are that sexual harassment is widespread and occurs regardless of a person's age, marital status, appearance, ethnicity, occupation, or salary. These studies show that many women are treated unequally, discriminated against, and abused (Neugarten & Miller-Spellman, 1983). The courts are continuing to defend victims' rights in proving their case as reflected by a 1993 Supreme Court ruling (*Harris v. Forklift Systems*) that workers suing their employers need not show that they suffered psychological injury (Greenhouse, 1993). Therefore, explicit personnel policies must be developed, carefully prepared training should be provided to all staff members, and incidents must be handled fairly and promptly.

OUTLOOK FOR THE PROFESSION

Personnel management functions must be refined as part of an approach to practice that emphasizes organizational effectiveness and customer-focused refinement of services (Rapp & Poertner, 1987). To accomplish this, social work administrators must begin addressing key personnel management functions in new ways. Performance standards must be clarified and strengthened, moving from a focus on process to a more balanced focus on outcomes and process.

Many supervisors and midlevel social work administrators need skills-based supervisory training to supplement the clinical skills and experience they bring to their positions. This need is reflected in the growing number of administrators enrolling in social work post-master's management certificate programs, public administration training, and other related degree programs.

Social welfare organizations will experience pressures similar to those in the for-profit sector in the years ahead. For example, in anticipation of technological change and reorganization of services under "managed care," unions are placing greater emphasis on job security and on improving the skills of the work force through training. Personnel in social welfare agencies may also demand more attention to training and staff development as the prospect of minimal salary increases looms even larger in the coming years. In both the for-profit and nonprofit sectors, management is recognizing the importance of involving the work force more actively in the decision-making processes of the organization. Staff quality-improvement teams are being organized to provide ideas for improving agency productivity and working conditions on an ongoing basis. These quality teams and other managerial innovations should provide the foundation for building organizational mechanisms that foster improved communication, reward creativity, and promote worker-sensitive procedures for handling organizational change.

REFERENCES

Age Discrimination in Employment Act of 1967. P.L. 90-202, 81 Stat. 602.

Americans with Disabilities Act. P.L. 101-336, 104 Stat. 327.

Austin, M. J. (1981). *Supervisory management for the human services.* Englewood Cliffs, NJ: Prentice Hall.

Civil Rights Act of 1964. P.L. 88-352, 78 Stat. 241.

Collins, E. G., & Blodgett, T. B. (1981). Sexual harassment . . . some see it . . . some won't. *Harvard Business Review, 59,* 76–95.

Coulson, R. (1981). *The termination handbook.* New York: Free Press.

Cox, F. M. (1984). Guidelines for preparing personnel policies. In F. M. Cox, J. L. Erlich, J. Rothman, & J. E. Tropman (Eds.), *Tactics and techniques of community practice* (2nd ed., pp. 274–289). Itasca, IL: F. E. Peacock.

Crull, P. (1979). *The implications of sexual harassment on the job: A profile of the experience of 92 women* (Research Series Report No. 3). New York: Working Women's Institute.

Cummings, L. L., & Schwab, D. P. (1973). *Performance in organizations: Determinants and appraisal.* Glenview, IL: Scott, Foresman.

Davis, Wright, and Tremaine Law Firm. (1992). *Special summary of the Americans with Disabilities Act prepared for The Casey Family Program* [Mimeograph]. Seattle: Author.

Deming, W. E. (1986). *Out of crisis.* Cambridge: Massachusetts Institute of Technology Center for Advanced Engineering Study.

Equal Employment Opportunity Commission, U.S. Department of Justice, U.S. Department of Labor. (1978). Uniform guidelines on employee selection procedures. *Federal Register, 43,* 38920-39315.

Equal Employment Opportunity Commission, U.S. Department of Justice, U.S. Department of Labor. (1991). *The Americans with Disabilities Act: Your responsiblities as an employer.* Washington, DC: Author.

Equal Pay Act of 1963. P.L. 88-38, 77 Stat. 56.

Ewing, D. W. (1983). Your right to fire. *Harvard Business Review, 61*(2), 32–34, 38, 40–42.

Goodale, J. G. (1989). Effective employment interviewing. In R. W. Eder & G. R. Ferris (Eds.), *The employment interview—Theory, research and practice* (pp. 307–324). Newbury Park, CA: Sage Publications.

Greenhouse, L. (1993, November 10). Court, 9–0, makes sexual harassment easier to prove. *New York Times,* p. A-15.

Howell, W. C., & Dipboye, R. L. (1982). *Essentials of industrial and organizational psychology.* Homewood, IL: Dorsey.

Ivancevich, J. M. (1992). *Human resource management* (5th ed.). Homewood, IL: Richard D. Irwin.

Janz, T. (1989). The patterned behavior description interview: The best prophet of the future is the past. In R. W. Eder & G. R. Ferris (Eds.), *The employment interview—Theory, research and practice* (pp. 158–168). Newbury Park, CA: Sage Publications.

Jensen, J. (1980). Employee evaluation: It's a dirty job but somebody's got to do it. *Grantsmanship Center News, 8*(4), 36–45.

Jensen, J. (1981). Letting go: The difficult art of firing. *Grantsmanship Center News, 9*(5), 37–43.

Kadushin, A. (1992). *Supervision in social work* (4th ed.). New York: Columbia University Press.

Klingner, D. E., & Nalbandian, J. (1985). *Public personnel management: Contexts and strategies.* Englewood Cliffs, NJ: Prentice Hall.

Lopatka, K. T. (1984). The emerging law of wrongful discharge: A quadrennial assessment of the labor law issue of the 80's. *Business Lawyer, 40*(1), 1–32.

Mager, R. F., & Pipe, P. (1970). *Analyzing performance problems.* Belmont, CA: Fearson Pitman.

Merit Systems Protection Board. (1981). *Sexual harassment in the federal workplace: Is it a problem?* Washington, DC: U.S. Government Printing Office.

Meritt-Haston, R., & Weyley, K. N. (1983). Educational requirements: Legality and validity. *Personnel Psychology, 36*(4), 743–753.

Middleman, R., & Rhodes, G. (1985). *Competent supervision: Making imaginative judgements.* Englewood Cliffs, NJ: Prentice Hall.

Morin, W. J., & Yorks, L. (1982). *Outplacement techniques: A positive approach to terminating employees.* New York: AMACOM.

Munson, C. E. (1993). *Clinical social work supervision* (2nd ed.). New York: Haworth Press.

National Association of Social Workers. (1990). *NASW standards for social work personnel practices.* Silver Spring, MD: Author.

Neugarten, D. A., & Miller-Spellman, M. (1983). Sexual harassment in public employment. In S. W. Hays & R. C. Kearney (Eds.), *Public personnel administration: Problems and prospects.* Englewood Cliffs, NJ: Prentice Hall.

Odiorne, G. S. (1984). *Strategic management of human resources.* San Francisco: Jossey-Bass.

Panaro, G. P. (1990). *Employment law manual.* Boston: Warren, Gorham, & Lamont.

Pecora, P. J., & Austin, M. J. (1987). *Managing human services personnel.* Newbury Park, CA: Sage Publications.

Perry, P. M. (1993, January–February). Avoiding charges of discrimination against the handicapped. *Law Practice Management,* pp. 34, 35–38.

Rapp, C., & Poertner, J. (1987). Moving clients center stage through the use of client outcomes. *Administration in Social Work, 11*(3–4), 23–40.

Rehabilitation Act of 1973. P.L. 93-112, 87 Stat. 355.

Roseman, E. (1982). *Managing the problem employee.* New York: AMACOM.

Safran, C. (1976, November). What men do to women on the job: A shocking look at sexual harassment. *Redbook,* pp. 149, 217–224.

Shafritz, J. M., Hyde, A. C., & Rosenbloom, D. H. (1986). *Personnel management in government: Politics and process* (3rd ed.). New York: Marcel Dekker.

Shulman, L. (1982). *Skills of supervision and staff management.* Itasca, IL: F. E. Peacock.

Trader, H. P. (1978). Personnel procedures in social work. In J. B. Turner (Ed.-in-Chief), *Encyclopedia of social work* (17th ed., pp. 1025–1029). Washington, DC: National Association of Social Workers.

Vietnam Era Veterans' Readjustment Assistance Act of 1974. P.L. 93-508, 88 Stat. 1578.

FURTHER READING

Edwards, R. L., & Yankey, J. A. (Eds.). (1991). *Skills for effective human services management.* Silver Spring, MD: NASW Press.

Fisher, R., & Ury, W. (1983). *Getting to yes: Negotiating agreement without giving in.* New York: Penguin Books.

Hasenfeld, Y. (Ed.). (1992). *Human services as complex organizations.* Newbury Park, CA: Sage Publications.

Hays, S. W., & Kearney, R. C. (Eds.). (1983). *Public personnel administration: Problems and prospects.* Englewood Cliffs, NJ: Prentice Hall.

Jensen, J. (1981). How to hire the right person for the job. *Grantsmanship Center News, 9*(3), 21–31.

Keys, P. R., & Ginsberg, L. H. (Eds.). (1988). *New management in human services.* Silver Spring, MD: National Association of Social Work.

Rapp, C., & Poertner, J. (1992). *Social administration: A client-centered approach.* White Plains, NY: Longman.

Slavin, S. (Ed.). (1985). *Managing finances, personnel, and information in human services.* New York: Haworth Press.

Peter J. Pecora, PhD, is manager of research, The Casey Family Program, and associate professor, University of Washington, School of Social Work, 1300 Dexter Avenue North, Suite 400, Seattle, WA 98109.

The author wishes to thank Stacy Radley and Gloria Rendon of the University of Utah for technical advice regarding affirmative action and equal employment opportunity regulations.

For further information see

Civil Rights; Disability; Employee Assistance Programs; Ethics and Values; Management Overview; Management: Diverse Workplaces; Occupational Social Work; Professional Conduct; Quality Assurance; Sexual Harassment.

Key Words

administration
affirmative action
equal employment opportunity
management
personnel management

Pharmacology

See Psychotropic Medications

PIE

See Person-in-Environment

READER'S GUIDE

Planning

The following entries contain information on this general topic:

Family Planning
Goal Setting and Intervention Planning
Health Planning
Management Overview
Planning and Management Professions
Social Planning
Strategic Planning
Volunteer Management

Planning and Management Professions
Richard T. Crow

Planning and management professionals typically interact with social workers who occupy planning or management positions in human services organizations. Although it has long been common for social workers to move into managerial and planning positions after having worked in a human services organization for a number of years, it is increasingly common for human services organizations to employ non–social workers in such positions. This entry discusses the philosophical, theoretical, and technical orientation of professionals from non–social work backgrounds who occupy these positions, emphasizing differences and similarities with social work training.

The planning and management professions discussed here are business administration, public administration, urban planning, health administration and planning, and educational administration. These professions have either an accrediting or a certifying body that mandates specific content for the profession's educational program. In many respects the educational programs leading to degrees in these professions use identical sources and content. The material used is also similar to that included in graduate social work programs that prepare students to assume managerial and planning positions. Nonetheless, distinctive aspects can be identified, primarily in the philosophical and technical orientations of the programs.

BUSINESS ADMINISTRATION

Colleges and universities offer degrees in business, business administration, and management. There are 274 institutions that offer a bachelor's degree, 60 that offer a master's degree, and six that offer a doctorate in business (*The College Blue Book*, 1991). There are 731 institutions that offer a bachelor's degree in business administration, 405 that offer a master's degree, and 71 that offer a doctorate. And 404 institutions offer a bachelor's degree, 109 a master's degree, and 29 a doctorate in management.

The accrediting agency for business administration programs, the American Assembly of Collegiate Schools of Business (1991), stated that "management education must prepare students to contribute to their organizations and the larger society and to grow personally and professionally throughout their careers. The objective of management education accreditation is to assist programs in meeting these challenges" (p. 2). The accredited undergraduate program must meet the following standards:

- [The curriculum] should provide an understanding of perspectives that form the context for business. Coverage should include ethical and global issues; the influence of political, social, legal and regulatory, environmental, and technological issues; and the impact of demographic diversity on organizations.
- [The] curriculum should have a general education component that normally constitutes at least 50 percent of the student's four-year program.
- The curriculum should include foundation knowledge for business in the following areas: accounting, behavioral science, economics, and mathematics and statistics.
- The business curriculum should include written and oral communication as an important characteristic.
- The school should state additional requirements for completion of the undergraduate business degree consistent with its mission. Majors or specializations should be consistent with the institutional mission and the availability of resources. (American Assembly, 1991, pp. 19–20)

Accredited master's degree programs in business must also meet specific standards:

- The curriculum should include instruction in the following core areas: financial reporting, analysis, and markets; domestic and global economic environments of organizations; creation and distribution of goods and services; and human behavior in organizations.
- The MBA curriculum normally should require a minimum of 30 semester hours beyond the MBA core areas. A minimum of 18 hours is required in courses outside the area of specialization, if any.
- Basic skills in written and oral communication, quantitative analysis, and computer usage should be achieved either by prior experience and education or as a part of the MBA curriculum.
- Each school's curriculum planning process should set additional requirements consistent with its mission and goals. The program should allow adequate elective material for reasonable breadth.
- The curriculum should integrate the core areas and apply cross-functional approaches to organizational issues. (American Assembly, 1991, pp. 21–22)

Although the underlying philosophical orientation of business is influenced by the profit motive, capitalism, and the free enterprise system, there is recognition that other perspectives must be understood. This perspective is reflected in the standard that states that both the undergraduate- and graduate-level curricula should include content on ethical, global, political, social, legal, regulatory, environmental, and technological issues, as well as an awareness of demographic diversity within organizations (American Assembly, 1991). Although such an orientation can be at cross-purposes with the basic tenets of social work, it does not have to be. However, an overemphasis on such issues as cost-effectiveness, productivity, and quantifiable results can influence how an individual with such an orientation manages. There have been efforts to adopt a more businesslike posture in the management of human services organizations; such a focus must be balanced, however, by a value system that recognizes the dignity of the individual, the right to self-determination, the need to accept individuals as they are, and the need to avoid imposing judgment.

The number of graduates holding bachelor's and MBA degrees continues to increase and, as opportunities in the private sector continue to decrease, more of these graduates may turn to human services and nonprofit organizations for employment. Such individuals are more likely to work in large bureaucratic organizations than in small voluntary agencies. State departments of public welfare and mental health have continued to hire business graduates, especially MBAs. Social workers and social work managers need to be able to work with these people without compromising their values.

The primary professional organization for business school graduates is the American Management Association. Other professional organizations are specific to certain areas of practice, such as the American Marketing Association, American Finance Association, and Society of Certified Public Accountants, or to a geographic region, such as the Southern Marketing Association and Southern Management Association. The Association of MBA Executives is exclusively for those with master of business administration degrees.

Although graduates might join one or more of these organizations, membership is not required. There is no certification process except for certified public accountants, who must pass a rigorous examination in the state in which they seek to practice. In other areas of business, the master of business administration degree is the only credential required.

PUBLIC ADMINISTRATION

There are 129 colleges and universities that offer a bachelor's degree in public administration, 181 that offer a master's degree, and 24 that offer a doctorate (*The College Blue Book*, 1991). Other degree programs in the field use a number of designations, including public administration and planning, public administration and policy, public administration and public service, public affairs, public affairs and administration, public affairs management, public agency administration, public and environmental affairs, public and social services, public management, public planning and management, public policy administration, public services, public services administration, and public systems management (*The College Blue Book*, 1991).

Only graduate programs in public administration are accredited by the National Association of Schools of Public Affairs and Administration (NASPAA). Opinions are mixed as to the value of accreditation, and several of the better-known programs are not accredited. Whether or not an individual graduates from an accredited program does not influence employment. Accredited programs require students with limited educational background or professional experience to devote the equivalent of two academic years to full-time study. Those with a strong undergraduate background or significant managerial activities can have some requirements waived or reduced (NASPAA, 1993). Accreditation guidelines for the public administration curriculum state that the curriculum purpose is

to prepare students for professional leadership in public service.... The curriculum components are designed to produce professionals capable of intelligent, creative analysis and communication, and action in the public service.... The common curriculum components shall enhance the student's values, knowledge, and skills to act ethically and effectively:

- in the management of Public Service Organizations, the components of which include: human resources, budgeting and financial processes, information, including computer literacy and applications
- in the application of quantitative and qualitative techniques of analysis, the components of which include: policy and program formulation, implementation and evaluation, decision-making and problem-solving
- with an understanding of the public policy and organizational environment, the components of which include: political and legal institutions and processes, economic and social institutions and

processes, organization and management concepts and behavior. (NASPAA, 1993, pp. 3–4)

In addition to this common core, accredited programs may offer areas of specialization or concentration so long as they are consistent with the program's mission (NASPAA, 1993). A final component of the accredited program is an internship that "shall be made available by the program, and students who lack a significant professional work background shall be strongly encouraged to take advantage of it" (NASPAA, 1993, p. 5).

The philosophical orientation of public administration is influenced by the organizational context of the public sector, a situation similar to what social workers encounter in a public human services agency. Although public administration places greater emphasis on the role and function of government than does social work, both social work and public administration graduates are prepared for an environment that must be responsive to external pressures from the public, politicians, and special interest groups. Further similarities between the two professions concern ethical issues and functioning in an environment in which employees are protected by a merit system. In addition, in the 1960s and 1970s, citizen participation significantly influenced the planning process in both the human services and public administration. The need to hold public hearings and allow for citizen input brought both these professions under closer public scrutiny.

The primary difference in the preparation of students in public administration and social work is that public administration places greater emphasis on budgeting and financial knowledge and skill and on the role and function of government. The degree of emphasis depends in part on the institutional placement of the program. Some are freestanding, autonomous programs in public administration, others are housed in departments of political science, and a few are components of business administration programs. Regardless of the program's placement, however, it must meet the standards noted earlier if it is to be certified.

Public administrators participate mainly in two professional organizations: the American Society of Public Administration and the International City Management Association. Membership is not mandated, but it is encouraged. Neither organization has any responsibility for setting binding standards or guidelines for professional practice. There is no nationally recognized certification or licensing of public administrators, and although some states encourage management personnel to become certified through one of the several certification programs available in the country, no sanctions are imposed if an individual does not become certified.

EDUCATIONAL ADMINISTRATION

There are 17 colleges and universities that offer a bachelor's degree in educational administration, 215 that offer a master's degree, and 92 that offer a doctorate (*The College Blue Book*, 1991). In addition, six institutions offer a bachelor's degree in educational administration and supervision, 82 a master's degree, and 26 a doctorate (*The College Blue Book*, 1991). The National Council for Accreditation of Teacher Education (NCATE) is the accrediting agency for programs in education. In its most recent revision of accreditation standards, NCATE no longer accredits specific programs. Instead it accredits an entire unit (a college, school, or department of education within an educational institution). Therefore, in accrediting a unit the council considers both undergraduate and graduate programs. The education profession has a unique graduate program—the educational specialist—that requires graduate work beyond the master's degree, typically 30 semester hours or its quarter-hour equivalent. Each program must be accredited by the national accrediting agency and by the respective state department of education. Although NCATE does not set specific curriculum standards for programs in supervision or administration, the following standards must be met for all professional studies:

- The professional studies component(s) is a well-planned sequence of courses and experiences that includes knowledge about professional education and relates it to the realities of practice in schools and classrooms.
- The unit ensures that each course and experience of the professional studies component(s) is built upon and reflects defensible knowledge bases.
- The professional studies component(s) includes knowledge about the social, historical, and philosophical foundations of education; theories of human development and learning; research and experience-based principles of effective practice; impact of technology and societal changes on schools; evaluation, inquiry, and research; and educational policy.
- Courses and experiences support the development of independent thinking, effective communications, the making of relevant judgments, professional collaboration, effective participation in the educational system, the discrimination of values in the educational arena, and professional ethics.
- The unit provides for study and experiences that help education students understand and apply

appropriate strategies for individual learning needs, especially for culturally diverse and exceptional populations.

- The curriculum for professional studies component(s) incorporates multicultural and global perspectives. (NCATE, 1992, pp. 49–50)

Typical course work for graduate students in educational administration includes leadership, decision making, communication, law, personnel, planning, management information systems, finances, and collective bargaining.

The philosophical orientation of educational administration is rooted in the behavioral sciences and has a humanistic perspective. Thus, social work managers and planners should find this approach complementary to their practice. Just as social work managers or planners are often called on to work with school principals and superintendents on issues of mutual concern, individuals with advanced degrees in educational administration are found in a variety of human services organizations, especially in managerial or planning roles in large public agencies.

The primary professional association is the National Education Association (NEA), and each state has an NEA affiliate that acts as a labor union on behalf of teachers. This organization, along with the American Federation of Teachers, has been active in legislation that affects teachers.

An individual who serves in an administrative or supervisory capacity in an elementary or secondary school must be certified by the state department of education. There are no examinations, but to be certified an individual must have the appropriate advanced degree.

URBAN PLANNING

There are eight institutions that offer a bachelor's degree in urban planning, 21 that offer a master's degree, and seven that award a doctorate. Twelve offer a bachelor's degree, 15 a master's degree, and six a doctorate in urban and regional planning; 18 offer a bachelor's degree, seven a master's degree, and one a doctorate in urban affairs; four offer a bachelor's degree, nine a master's degree, and two a doctorate in urban design; and 105 offer a bachelor's degree, 25 a master's degree, and six a doctorate in urban studies (*The College Blue Book*, 1991). In 1989, the Planning Accreditation Board was recognized as the accrediting agency for urban planning programs and accreditation standards were developed. The board's planning accreditation program "is intended to foster high standards for professional education in planning"

(Planning Accreditation Board, 1989, p. 1). In the board's accreditation document, criteria for the urban planning curriculum are described:

> Planning is future-oriented and comprehensive. It seeks to link knowledge and action in ways which improve the quality of public and private development decisions affecting people and places. Because [of] its future orientation, planning embraces visionary and utopian thinking, yet also recognizes that the implementation of plans requires the reconciliation of present realities to future states. To become effective and ethical practitioners, students must develop a comprehensive understanding of cities and regions, and of the theory and practice of planning. They must also be able to use a variety of important methods in their practice. They must become sensitive to the ways in which planning affects individual and community values, and must be aware of their own roles in this process. (Planning Accreditation Board, 1989, p. 15)

The curriculum for urban planning studies must include the following:

- Knowledge components: structure and functions of urban settlements; history and theory of planning processes and practices; administrative, legal, and political aspects of plan-making and policy implementation; and familiarity with at least one area of specialized knowledge of a particular subject or set of issues
- Skills components: problem formulation, research skills, and data gathering; quantitative analysis and computers; written, oral, and graphic communications; collaborative problem solving, plan-making, and program design; and synthesis and application of knowledge to practice
- Value components: issues of equity, social justice, economic welfare, and efficiency in the use of resources; the role of government and citizen participation in a democratic society and in the balancing of individual and collective rights and interests; respect for diversity of views and ideologies; the conservation of natural resources and of the significant social and cultural heritages imbedded in the built environment; and the ethics of professional practice and behavior, including the relationship to clients and the public, and the role of citizens in democratic participation. (Planning Accreditation Board, 1989, pp. 15–18)

The course content included in urban planning programs reflects the philosophical and technical orientation of the urban planner. Courses typically have a strong emphasis on physical planning, such as urban site design, population and economic analysis, zoning, housing, recreation, transportation, and cartography. In the 1960s and early 1970s, there began an emphasis on social planning along with physical planning that continues today. Included in this emphasis is concern for the environmental impact of planning decisions.

A primary distinction between planners trained in schools of social work and those trained in urban planning programs involves the relationship between product and process. Urban planners possess a high degree of technical skill and are able to produce technically sound and sophisticated products, but they have not been introduced to the process of achieving consensus that characterizes the social work planner. Although some urban planners specialize in human services planning, their expertise tends to be of a technical nature. Social workers and urban planners can complement one another. Typically schools of social work do not emphasize the technically sophisticated skills and knowledge base of urban planning, and expertise in these areas can be beneficial in the planning process.

Urban planners are most often found in state, regional, and municipal planning departments or agencies, and social work managers and planners often work with urban planners in planning activities that affect individuals, groups, and communities. A vital role of social workers in such situations is to influence plans for the benefit of these client groups.

The professional association that planners most often affiliate with is the American Planning Association. To be recognized as a planner, an individual should be certified by the American Institute of Certified Planners, which requires meeting certain education and experience requirements and passing a written examination.

HEALTH ADMINISTRATION AND PLANNING

Various degree programs are available in health administration and planning, with 40 schools offering a bachelor's degree, 25 a master's degree, and three a doctorate in health care administration (*The College Blue Book*, 1991). Other degree programs use such designations as health care management, health administration, health services administration, and hospital administration (*The College Blue Book*, 1991).

The Accrediting Commission on Education for Health Services Administration (ACEHSA) accredits only graduate programs, which must provide curriculum content in the following eight areas:

- Assessment and understanding of the health status of populations; determinants of health and illness; and factors influencing the use of health services

- Understanding of the organization, financing, and delivery of health services, drawing on the social science disciplines (broadly defined to include economics, law, political science, psychology, sociology, and related disciplines)
- Understanding of, and development of skills in, economic, financial, policy, and quantitative analysis
- Understanding of the values and ethical issues associated with the practice of health services administration and the development of skills in ethical analysis
- Understanding of, and development of skills in, positioning organizations favorably in the environment and managing these organizations for continued effectiveness
- Provision of opportunities for development of leadership potential, including stimulating creativity and interpersonal and communication skills development
- Understanding of, and development of skills in, the management of human, capital, and information resources
- Understanding of, and development of skills in, assessing organizational performance and, in particular, methods to assure continuous improvement in the quality of services provided. (ACEHSA, 1992, pp. 5–6)

The curriculum of undergraduate programs, which hold membership in the Association of University Programs in Health Administration (AUPHA), must focus on the following content areas:

- The liberally educated health services manager with content in: communication (written and oral); computational skills (mathematics and quantification); critical thinking (ability to analyze problems); and, societal context (historical, philosophical, social, economic, political, and scientific foundations)
- Conceptual and technical competency in management: theories of management; functional areas of management; and managerial skills
- Conceptual and technical competencies in health services: determinants and measurement of health and disease; health services organization and delivery; and, the unique characteristics of the economic, legal, managerial, political, and social aspects of health services organization and delivery
- Applications to health services management: faculty supervised practicum/internship and integrative exercises. (AUPHA, 1989, pp. 4–5)

Individuals who earn graduate or undergraduate degrees in health administration are exposed to some of the same course content as individuals in the other degree programs discussed in this entry, but the emphasis here is on the application of knowledge and skill in the health care context.

The philosophical orientation of the health care profession has been influenced by its move into a competitive market and by the growing number of proprietary health care facilities. Further, there has been an increase in the number of nonprofit health care facilities and programs. Health care has become more of a business, and the social work manager and planner must recognize that this shift requires administrators to be sensitive to the balance between profit, efficiency, and service. Educational programs housed in schools of business are likely to give stronger philosophical and technical emphasis to the profitability of services; programs housed in public health programs or schools of allied health science tend to emphasize service, as do freestanding, autonomous programs. The technical skills that students acquire in these programs are more sophisticated than those typically found in social work programs.

Health administration programs emphasize the health-related dimensions unique to the health care profession. Individuals in these programs gain an understanding of disease, individual patterns of disease, epidemiology, and the relationship of advanced technology to disease. Further, the management of health care systems is influenced by the relationship between medical and administrative staffs and their respective concerns.

Although most states mandate a planning function requiring, for example, a certificate of need for expansion or development, the emphasis on free enterprise and competitiveness has minimized the role and function of planning. Many decisions affecting health care are politically motivated, further reducing the role of planning.

Graduates from health care programs work primarily in hospitals. Other employment settings include medical group practices, health maintenance organizations, nursing homes, and, increasingly, home health agencies. Social workers affiliated with the health care system need to influence health administrators to be mindful of the service component of health care as the system continues to move toward profitability and efficiency. This is true for social workers in direct practice and in management or planning positions.

Health care administrators affiliate with several professional organizations, including the American Hospital Association, the Medical Group Management Association, and the American College of Hospital Administrators. Membership in the latter organization is granted on the basis of an examination and the publication of papers relevant to the profession.

SUMMARY

Although there are clearly differences among the professions discussed in this entry, there are also similarities in educational preparation. Some of the differences are related to philosophical orientation, whereas others are a matter of emphasis. For example, it would be expected that a program in business administration would focus more on profit. Similarly, a public administration curriculum would emphasize government.

The similarities between these management professions and social work include an understanding of organizational and management concepts, the social and political environments, and concepts of budgeting. Similarities between social workers and urban planners include an understanding of the planning environment, the techniques of developing a plan, and the ability to write a comprehensive plan.

The philosophical orientation of a profession is evident in the accreditation requirements for its schools. Each set of accreditation standards reflects a particular orientation, but there is also a great deal of similarity between standards. For example, there is evidence that attention must be given to ethical and environmental issues. And there is a need to recognize that organizations do not function within a vacuum but operate within a global framework.

Social workers interact with the planning and management professions within the context of traditional agencies, but there is a growing number of nonprofit human services organizations. It has been suggested that nonprofit organizations "are central to American society and are indeed its most distinguishing feature" (Drucker, 1990, p. xiii). This realization is also evident in the development of programs that emphasize the nonprofit sector at various universities; the Mandel School of Applied Social Sciences at Case Western Reserve University offers a joint degree with the university's nonprofit program.

The natural affiliation between social work and the management professions has led some schools of social work to offer joint or dual degree programs. Five schools currently offer a joint degree program with public administration or public affairs; eight offer a joint degree program with business administration; 10 offer a joint degree program with public health; seven offer joint degree programs with urban planning or urban studies; and three schools offer a joint degree program with education (Council on Social Work Education, 1992).

REFERENCES

Accrediting Commission on Education for Health Services Administration. (1992). *Criteria for accreditation.* Alexandria, VA: Author.
American Assembly of Collegiate Schools of Business. (1991). *Achieving quality and continuous improvement through self-evaluation and peer review: Standards for business and accounting accreditation.* St. Louis: Author.
Association of University Programs in Health Administration. (1989). *Full undergraduate membership criteria.* Arlington, VA: Author.
The college blue book: Degrees offered by college and subject (23rd ed.). (1991). New York: Macmillan.
Council on Social Work Education. (1992). *Summary information on master of social work programs: 1991–92.* Washington, DC: Author.
Drucker, P. F. (1990). *Managing the non-profit organization: Practices and principles.* New York: HarperCollins.
National Association of Schools of Public Affairs and Administration. (1993). *Standards for professional master's degree programs in public affairs and administration.* Washington, DC: Author.
National Council for Accreditation of Teacher Education. (1992). *Standards, procedures, and policies for the accreditation of professional education units.* Washington, DC: Author.
Planning Accreditation Board. (1989). *The accreditation document: Procedures and standards of the planning accreditation program.* Washington, DC: Author.

FURTHER READING

Crow, R. T., & Odewahn, C. A. (1987). *Management for human services.* Englewood Cliffs, NJ: Prentice Hall.

Odiorne, G. S. (1990). *The human side of management: Management by integration and self-control.* New York: Free Press.
Rosen, E. D. (1993). *Improving public sector productivity: Concept and practice.* Thousand Oaks, CA: Sage Publications.
Slavin, S. (Ed.). (1985). *An introduction to human service management.* New York: Haworth Press.
Slavin, S. (Ed.). (1985). *Managing finances, personnel, and information in human services.* New York: Haworth Press.
Weinbach, R. W. (1990). *The social worker as manager: Theory and service agencies.* New York: Longman.
Weiner, M. E. (1990). *Human service management: Analysis and applications* (2nd ed.). Homewood, IL: Dorsey Press.

Richard T. Crow, PhD, ACSW, is associate dean and professor, University of Alabama, School of Social Work, Tuscaloosa, AL 35487.

For further information see

Case Management; Citizen Participation; Community Organization; Health Care: Direct Practice; Health Planning; Interdisciplinary and Interorganizational Collaboration; Licensing, Regulation and Certification; Managed Care; Nonprofit Management Issues; Organizations: Context for Social Services Delivery; Public Services Management; Sectarian Agencies; Social Planning; Strategic Planning; Volunteer Management.

Key Words
administration
nonprofit
  organizations
professional education
social planning

Police Social Work
Harvey Treger

Social work has a history of working cooperatively with other professions: medicine, psychiatry, law, education, architecture, nursing, the military, and so forth. As a result of their experiences, social workers have developed knowledge and skills as enablers to other professions. For example, physician Richard C. Cabot recognized around the turn of the century that the information he gleaned from social workers who visited the homes of his patients contributed to his understanding of family and environmental factors, which enabled him to diagnose and treat children more effectively (Rossen, 1987). Social work, in turn, can benefit from Cabot's experience by examining how other professions can enable social work practice. A recent area of social work specialty is police social work. Police social work provides social work services to citizens—including victims, offenders, and other people and their families—referred by the police. Social workers work in police departments or outside police departments in social work or mental health agencies and in private practice. Such interprofessional cooperation with the police can produce insights into the planning, implementation, and evaluation processes of interprofessional programs and can stimulate issues such as turf and areas of cooperation, communication, and decision making for the entire social work profession.

BUILDING A SOCIAL WORKER–POLICE RELATIONSHIP

The police sometimes perceive themselves as the social agency of last resort. Citizens often get an immediate response from the police in the evenings and on weekends when social agencies are closed and a personal, family, or community crisis or dispute arises. It is estimated that the police spend from 50 percent to 90 percent of their time in social services–type situations (Treger, 1987).

The literature reveals that police experience with social workers and social agencies has been unsatisfactory, in part because the police have not been trained in the referral process. Police prefer not to refer citizens to social agencies for several reasons (Bard, 1970). For one, the police perceive social workers as unavailable when needed. Furthermore, the police believe social workers are reluctant to serve those clients the police have referred and to inform the police about the assessment and referrals' cooperation (Treger, 1975). Social workers perhaps are reluctant to accept police referrals for services because they may not fully appreciate the community's need for protection as well as the opportunity to initiate early intervention with clients who are referred under external pressure.

For cooperation to develop, both the police and social workers must recognize their mutual goal—to protect and serve the community—and must share an interest in working together. A positive personal relationship is a necessary first step toward developing cooperation. The social work profession needs only to draw on its rich experience with individuals, families, and groups and use that experience to guide new initiatives. The relationship will develop as both the police and social workers work together on common problems toward a common goal.

Initiating Contact

Police social work programs have developed outside of the police departments under either private mental health and family services agency auspices or under city human services departments. Social workers and police can resolve or solidify the conflicts and misperceptions that often exist between them through ongoing experiences and relationships. For interprofessional cooperation to begin, the opportunity to communicate must exist, and social workers and police must develop positive interpersonal relationships and be of service to each other in their respective professional roles, at the same time serving the community. It is easier to initiate contact, for example, over coffee, lunch, or at the water cooler if the social workers work in the same building. Making contact takes more imagination and initiative if social workers work in a social agency police social work program or in private practice in another building.

Contracting. One working arrangement involves contracting for private practice social worker services to police departments. In this arrangement, cost is based on population—contract costs change as population increases. In addition, the social workers pay all overhead costs, including office space, telephone and telephone service pagers, secretarial assistance, and liability insurance. Moreover, police officers, their families, or city employees receive services at no additional cost (Treger, 1989). Police must accompany social workers on all crisis calls. Furthermore, the social workers conduct their assessments of all juveniles in the police department. The social workers, upon request, also will provide police training or community education. The contract specifies that social workers provide 24-hour availability and a response time of no more than 10 minutes when contacted by phone and no more than one hour when requested in person. Social workers will refer all citizens for ongoing services to public and private practitioners based on the citizens' ability to pay.

Understanding Each Other's Roles

In building a relationship, it is useful to emphasize commonalities rather than differences; parties can address their differences after they have established a positive relationship. Social workers should be aware of their role in police social work, the police officers' role, the decisions both parties make, and the differential areas of authority. Social workers also must understand that the police consider dependability, availability, and response time high-priority factors. Furthermore, patrol officers tend to be concrete in their thinking: they view a person as either a member of the police department or as external to the police. Police also tend to view themselves as an embattled profession—not always understood and appreciated by the public. As in other professions, the police have a subculture of their own.

The police may represent many things to many people, depending on people's life experiences. Citizens may feel uncomfortable coming to a police department for social services, whereas others, especially if their behavior is out of control, may be comforted by the limits and control the police agency represents. Most families, though, have reacted positively toward receiving social work services in a police department, according to a preliminary study in two upper-middle class communities of parents with children younger than age 18 who were referred to a police social work program (Curtis & Lutkus, 1976). Furthermore, the study found that most parents whose children became involved with the police did not perceive the referral process to be coercive. The study concluded that "the environment of a police department does not impede parents' willingness to accept social work services but may actually enhance the social worker's acceptability as a helping agent" (Curtis & Lutkus, 1976, p. 11). However, "experience indicates that those who refuse service associated with the police department are unlikely to use service elsewhere" (Treger, 1987, p. 264).

Resolving Power and Control Issues
Professionals can come into conflict with other professionals when they have not resolved their own issues of power and control. Both police and social workers are fearful of co-optation of each other's roles. Officers who work with youths and their families may be especially sensitive about social workers because they work with the same people, and there is some overlap with social work tasks. Authority and discretion flow from knowledge and skill. Social workers can avoid conflict with police if they are clear about what kinds of problems they will be working on, what decisions they are trained to make, and what intervention skills they can use in the process. Police most likely will respect other professionals who know who they are, what they do, and how they can be useful. A police chief once asked another police chief, "Why are you interested in those guys [social workers]?" The first police chief replied, "Because they are looking at us." The police become interested in social workers when social workers are interested in the police and the roles the police perform.

Police who participate in contracting-for-services arrangements may be concerned with control issues (Treger, 1989). Social workers who start to make the decisions about who should be referred for social work services—a police responsibility—will be invading police turf and conflict likely will ensue. Social workers should be aware that the police have the authority to arrest, detain, and make a disposition. The police also can use their authority to encourage citizens who are in danger of hurting themselves or others and are reluctant to seek interventive services to try social services. Social workers need to consider protection of the community as primary and should accept the fact that, in some instances, the authority of the police can be a useful assist to

engaging citizens in social work services. The police also may make court referrals so that the court may later mandate the citizen to accept social services or face incarceration.

In new programs, as in any new relationship, the parties will test each other. For example, a police sergeant who wanted to test a social worker suggested the social worker decide who should be referred to the police. Knowing that a social work referral is considered a police disposition, the social worker declined. If social workers want to help police officers understand social work, they could perhaps have police officers accompany them on visits to a social agency or invite officers to an assessment of a client with a mental health crisis. In addition, to minimize officer resistance to using social work services, social workers might make periodic presentations during police departmental meetings of the services they offer and describe the outcomes in cases the police had referred to the social workers. Social workers can address police concerns about control by demonstrating availability and effective service provision.

However, some gray areas will arise because of cooperation; confidentiality may be one. Both social work and law enforcement have codes of ethics on sharing information (Treger et al., 1985). In Germany, confidentiality between police social workers and the police is not a problem. German law specifically forbids social workers to share client information with the police. However, social workers may accept information from the police. The *Law Enforcement Code of Ethics* for police officers in the United States states, "Whatever I see or hear of a confidential nature or that which is confided to me in my official capacity will be kept ever secret unless revelation is necessary in the performance of my duty" (Treger et al., p. 86). Social workers are also committed to responsibly use information gained in a professional relationship.

In many American police social work programs, social workers share a social assessment and service plan with police only with the client's written consent. Development of such a policy usually involves legal consultation so that social workers will conform to state law and professional standards. Social workers inform clients that their discussions with a social worker are confidential unless a client's behavior violates a law or is injurious to the client or others, in which case social workers will encourage the client to inform the police. Social workers who conceal law-violative behaviors may place themselves in the position of an accomplice, do not protect the community, and defeat the goal of developing more socially responsible behavior. Furthermore, concealment may prevent a client from accepting the consequences of his or her behavior (Treger, 1975). Schools of social work and professional associations must discuss and illuminate the issue of loss of confidentiality in police agencies.

CHARACTERISTICS OF AN EFFECTIVE POLICE SOCIAL WORK PROGRAM

Atmosphere of Cooperation

Arrangements for social work cooperation with the police is an ongoing process that will change over time and experience following the unique characteristics and resources of a particular community and police agency. It is the author's experience that most police social work programs exist in communities with populations between 30,000 and 100,000; however, there is no documented evidence to support this. Police and social workers define behaviors differently depending on the community and neighborhood. Where there is a lack of money or services, a social problem may be defined as a police problem; as a result, there will be differential dispositions. For example, in Bureau County, Illinois, large numbers of juveniles were sentenced to the state correctional facility. On investigation, researchers learned that the judge sentenced so many youths to the correctional facility because there were no resources in the county (personal communication with H. McKay, sociologist, Institute for Juvenile Research, Chicago, 1975). Citizens must organize and demand social services. In communities with a low tax base and a multitude of needs, social work services in a police department may be nonexistent. It should be possible for states to assist poorer communities with special appropriations to initiate or share programs with neighboring communities. This is an area for social planning (Treger, 1980).

Police agencies and social work agencies are organized differently. The police generally are highly authoritarian, bureaucratic, and oriented to crisis situations and immediate action. Social workers generally are more self-directed, more process oriented, less bureaucratic, and more oriented to resolving problems in a longer time frame. Police deal mostly with people's actions in terms of whether those actions violated a law. Social workers are mostly concerned with why people behave as they do and what intervention is indicated and desired. These differences sometimes create strain but can be alleviated, if not eliminated, through improved communication and an atmosphere of cooperation. Social work services do not supplant police services but comple-

ment them. Requests for funds for a police social work program, then, should not be for a police officer *or* a social worker but, rather, a police officer *and* a social worker. If police are to accept social work services, those services should fit easily into a police organization. Such services frequently fall under the investigation division because they provide an external service along with youth services.

Adequate Salary and Skills

On the basis of the author's experience, the question of salary for a social worker is often closely related to acceptance of the social worker by the police department. However, once the social worker has demonstrated expertise and usefulness, the police are much less interested in the social worker's salary (Treger, 1981). A social worker in a police department should have three to five years of postgraduate (master of social work) experience in mental health, family service, child welfare, or criminal justice. The social worker must be skilled in dealing with crisis situations, confident and secure in his or her identity and professional role, and comfortable working with the police. In addition, a social worker who is action oriented and has a good sense of humor may find quick acceptance in a police agency.

Effective Staffing Patterns

Staffing patterns of police social work programs should reflect the diversity of the community and the kinds of predicaments to which the police respond. Situations come to the attention of the police for at least three reasons: (1) They are mandated by law, (2) alternative resources are unavailable, and (3) citizens may define their situations as a law enforcement problem. As a result of contact with a police social worker, citizens may redefine their situations and seek social work services rather than police services.

In beginning programs, it is important for social workers to offer services in areas in which police are asking for input and that are within social work practice, such as family disputes and parent–child conflicts. Both the police and social workers may need to be flexible, however. For example, rather than having the police take action, social workers may identify issues in a neighborhood dispute and meet with people on the block to resolve a problem. Sometimes police may seek guidance and consultation about how to begin a social work program. Staffing patterns will be related to program design. Assessment and referral programs or longer term social work programs will require different arrangements. The availability of both financial and social welfare resources as well as police department interest also will affect staffing patterns. If there is an abundance of services in a community, an assessment and referral program may avoid duplication of services and be cost-effective.

Timely and Appropriate Consultation

It is an acceptable and recommended practice that police social workers with two years of postgraduate (master's) experience obtain professional consultation as needed from police, legal, social work, medical, or psychiatric professionals (NASW, 1990). Experience indicates that inputs from other professions may increase the quality and support for the service. Furthermore, timely consultation will enable social workers to maintain service quality, will increase support for the service, will help social workers ensure community protection, and will further the training and education of the social work staff (Treger, 1993). For example, the Association of Police Social Workers in Illinois— approximately 40 police social workers—meet quarterly to discuss areas of concern such as suicide, debriefing, family violence, and police training. Between meetings, social workers may meet in groups to provide support and consultation. Program planning should provide an adequate budget for consultations.

Effective Victim and Witness Programs

During the 1960s, victim and witness assistance programs began independent of police social work programs. Sometimes these programs were incorporated into police social work services. Victim and witness programs initially were designed to assist victims and witnesses involved in criminal episodes and were based on the belief that offenders and their rights receive too much attention, whereas the rights and social and psychological needs of the victims are neglected. Through the cooperation of victims and witnesses, the police and prosecutors also believed they were getting more convictions without additional time and expense. Initially in the early police social work demonstration projects, police referred victims of rape and marital disputes (Treger, 1975). Later, some police social work programs offered services to other victims and witnesses.

Staffing in present victim and witness programs, which are under the auspices of district attorney, city manager, and law enforcement agencies, differ from police social work programs. Most police social work programs are staffed by social workers with a master's degree, a few with bachelor degrees in social work or allied professions such as psychology or counseling. Most of the victim and witness programs are staffed by few paid

members and a large group of volunteers. Furthermore, current victim and witness programs are funded largely through the U.S. Department of Justice and from offender fines collected by the state under victim compensation laws (Kadish, 1983).

The services in police social work programs and victim and witness programs also differ. Police social work programs typically provide crisis intervention; assessment; and ongoing individual, group, and family intervention as well as referrals to other agencies or professions. Victim and witness programs usually offer short-term counseling and referrals to agencies that provide specialized services and, by monitoring court calendars and keeping in touch with victims, attempt to reduce the time victims spend waiting for hearings and trials. Staff also serve as victim advocates and strive to obtain separate and secure waiting rooms. Most victim and witness programs educate the community about their plight and need for services. As crime rates rise, there are more victims who collectively can represent a powerful voting bloc, thus receiving increased attention from public policymakers. However, because of cost cutting and downsizing, some victim and witness and police social work programs have been trimmed or eliminated. Demonstrated effectiveness will be critical to their ongoing survival.

Proper Training

When different professions work together, they are involved in informal, unplanned training. A police chief once told another chief that the police social worker was "all right" because the chief had changed his thinking. He quickly turned to the social worker and asked, "Or have I changed?" Actually they both had changed. As a result of their working relationship, they respected their human qualities and differential skills in facilitating each other's work. It would be useful for social workers in police agencies and police to do an experience survey to identify issues in their relationship that could be incorporated into training sessions.

A recent survey (Treger, 1993) of 39 Illinois police social work programs (a 70 percent response rate) found that social workers were concerned with training in legal issues—liability, mental health, domestic violence, and stalking. They were also interested in issues involved in their relationship with the police, such as confidentiality, police understanding of the social work role, acceptance of social work in police agencies, and police understanding of social work treatment. Other training needs related to practice issues such as program implementation and development;

trauma debriefing; and how to deal with violence, sexual assault cases, community disasters, suicide, domestic and neighbor disputes, and elder abuse. In addition to these issues, training might address program maintenance and change and knowledge and skills to deliver services.

The survey also found that 67 percent of the programs had relationships with colleges and universities for training students. A market exists for universities to sponsor institutes, conferences, and short courses for police social workers and police. Police social work programs have expanded; there are more services available to a wider range of people. Programs have expanded from serving citizens referred by the police to providing personal services to police and their families and government employees as well as providing training for police officers. Rather than casting a broader net to bring more people into the justice system, police social work programs are diverting juveniles and adults from the justice system into the more appropriate social services system. It is a measure of confidence in the usefulness of social work that communities continue to support police social work programs.

CHALLENGES

The social work profession faces several challenges in police social work programs. For one, the profession needs to plan national and state police social work conferences that involve schools of social work and state and national police organizations. In addition, social workers must plan a national clearinghouse to deal with inquiries and disseminate information.

Furthermore, social workers need to design research and special projects programs, appointing committees to provide encouragement, and to stimulate research, resource development, and consultation in developing new police social work programs. Finally, the social work profession needs to identify the common elements in its rich experience with other professions and illuminate these elements in social work education for interprofessional cooperation.

REFERENCES

Bard, M. (1970). *Training police as specialists in family crisis intervention.* Washington, DC: U.S. Government Printing Office.
Curtis, P., & Lutkus, A. M. (1976, November). *Attitudes toward police social work.* Paper presented at the 28th annual meeting of the American Association of Psychiatric Services for Children, San Francisco.
Kadish, S. H. (1983). Victim and witness assistance programs. In S. H. Kadish (Ed.), *Encyclopedia of crime and justice* (Vol. 4, pp. 1600–1604). New York: Free Press.
National Association of Social Workers. (1990). *NASW standards for social work personnel practices.* Silver Spring, MD: Author.
Rossen, S. (1987). Hospital social work. In A. Minahan (Ed.-in-Chief), *Encyclopedia of social work* (18th ed., Vol. 1, pp. 816–821). Silver Spring, MD: National Association of Social Workers.
Treger, H., in cooperation with Thomson, D., Collier, J., Michaels, R., Quinn, P., & Cousins, J. (1975). *The police–social work team.* Springfield, IL: Charles C Thomas.
Treger, H. (1980, September). Guidelines for community work in police social work diversion. *Federal Probation,* pp. 3–8.
Treger, H. (1981). Police–social work cooperation: Problems and issues. *Social Work, 26,* 426–433.
Treger, H. (1987). Police social work. In A. Minahan (Ed.-in-Chief), *Encyclopedia of social work* (18th ed., Vol. 2, pp. 263–268). Silver Spring, MD: National Association of Social Workers.
Treger, H. (1989). The police social work team. In W. G. Bailey (Ed.), *The encyclopedia of police science* (pp. 480–486). New York: Garland.
Treger, H. (1993). [Survey of Illinois police social work programs]. Unpublished raw data.
Treger, H., Cousins, J., Silavin, S., Risdon, K., & Emrickson, C. (1985, November). [Panel discussion]. In H. Treger (Chair), *Public safety and the individual: Social work practice and the police.* Symposium conducted at the meeting of the National Association of Social Workers, Chicago.

Harvey Treger, MA, is emeritus professor of social work, Jane Addams College of Social Work and Department of Criminal Justice, University of Illinois at Chicago, 1040 West Harrison Street, Chicago, IL 60607.

For further information see

Adult Corrections; Citizen Participation; Civil Rights; Community Practice Models; Community-Based Corrections; Criminal Justice Overview; Criminal Justice: Social Work Roles; Domestic Violence: Legal Issues; Ethnic-Sensitive Practice; Family Views in Correctional Programs; Gang Violence; Homicide; Interdisciplinary and Interorganizational Collaboration; Juvenile Corrections; Legal Issues: Confidentiality and Privileged Communication; Probation and Parole; Rehabilitation of Criminal Offenders; Runaways and Homeless Youths; Substance Abuse: Legal Issues; Suicide; Victim Services and Victim/Witness Assistance Programs; Violence Overview.

Key Words

corrections   police social work
criminal justice

Policy Analysis
Susan D. Einbinder

Nearly everyone has an opinion about policies and the political processes that produce them. This, however, does not a policy analyst make. Policy analysis, an emerging interdisciplinary specialty, falls under the umbrella of general social sciences as well as within the disciplines of economics, political science, and sociology. As another form of knowledge development, policy analysis requires systematic forms of inquiry and evaluation. Some of the most prevalent tools include needs assessment, cost–benefit analysis, cost-effectiveness analysis, outcome studies, case studies, and meta-analysis. Policy analysis is done in a variety of settings, by a wide range of people from diverse backgrounds with increasingly sophisticated research skills, knowledge bases, and informational technologies. Policy analysis is opinion-making raised to professional status.

This entry is a brief overview of policy analysis and its relationship to social policy, its intellectual roots, and an indication of its major research methodologies. It reviews who does policy analysis and where its products can be found.

Policy analysts create opinions; their advice is used to influence policies. Bona fide policy analysts are knowledgeable about the policy realm and usually have quantitative methodological skills. In addition, policy analysts often are well versed in substantive issues that policies address. The tools of policy analysis are applied to substantive issues and policies in a particular arena. People who are involved in influencing and making policy use advice from policy analysts to choose among many possible policy alternatives. The products of policy analysis are among the many factors used to create, influence, stymie, reform, alter, revise, or change policies at all levels of government and in the private sector.

Policy analysts usually focus on formal written policies that emanate from government institutions—in short, they focus on public policy. Although many policy arenas, such as industrial or transportation policies, affect social welfare, the focus of this entry is social policy, which itself has broad and flexible borders (DiNitto, 1991; Jansson, 1994; Prigmore & Atherton, 1986; Trattner, 1989). Social policy can be viewed as attempts by government to guarantee some minimum standard of living for citizens in domains such as social insurance, public aid, health and mental health care, education, housing, and personal social services (DiNitto; Kahn, 1964; Prigmore & Atherton).

Policy analysis has increasingly involved the use of social sciences methodologies to describe and perhaps to prescribe the processes and content of policies (McCall & Weber, 1983). Although policy analysis involves the use of some fundamental social sciences research methodologies, the more technical or quantitative methodologies (that is, multiple regression, cost–benefit analysis, and trend analysis) require specialized knowledge to understand and use and are rarely covered in the training of most master's-level social workers.

The ethical dimensions of giving advice to people in power who can actually use it to wield change is a valid consideration of those engaged in policy analysis. Some policy analysts believe that the products of their labors can be purely objective; others adopt the values of the person soliciting their opinions, and still others apply specific values to the issue at hand (Jenkins-Smith, 1982). Policy analysis is, after all, a political activity (Weimer & Vining, 1992). Determining the relative desirability of policies and their implications is rarely an empirical matter; such decisions are more often ethical or ideological (Wright, 1992). Hagen and Davis (1992) pointed out that policy analysts highlight the importance of policy initiatives fitting into existing societal values. The explication of values becomes increasingly important in choosing among competing options (Caputo, 1989).

Policy analysis is carried out by people from many disciplinary and professional backgrounds and falls under the umbrella of general social sciences as well as within the disciplines of economics, political science, and sociology. It is encompassed by an intellectual undertaking dubbed the "policy sciences" (Lerner & Lasswell, 1951). Perhaps because of the multitude of academic and disciplinary backgrounds of its adherents, policy analysis is developing into an integrated, interdisciplinary enterprise (Croston, Fellin, & Churchill, 1987; Cunningham & Dunn, 1987). As a result, its disciplinary boundaries are becoming obscure, and its methodologies and knowledge bases are merging. These developments simultaneously enrich policy analysis and make its precise definition difficult. Policy analysis even has its own jargon; the media refer to those who practice it as policy "wonks." Within the emerging field of policy analysis, even jack-of-all-trade policy analysts disagree about the boundaries of this slippery term. Another source of imprecision is that the object of policy analysis—that is, policy—is also a dynamic, constantly changing phenomenon.

Considering the practical consequences of policy changes on social work and its clients, social workers should be well represented among policy analysts; surprisingly, they are not. Relatively few social workers identify themselves as policy analysts. In 1991 fewer than 1 percent of NASW members reported having such jobs (Gibelman & Schervish, 1993); even fewer identified themselves as involved in planning.

POLICY ANALYSIS AND SOCIAL POLICY

In general, policies mediate relationships within and among three main arenas of modern life: (1) the government, (2) the economy, and (3) private life. Each of these institutions is complicated, multilayered, and dynamic. Government expands and contracts, what transpires in the market changes over time, and the boundaries of private life are in constant flux. Because the boundaries overlap, some aspects of life fall into more than one arena. Which aspects of life fall under the institutional reach of government, the marketplace, or private life are constantly shifting. Policies can structure the relationships within and among each arena. The recent federal parental-leave legislation is a cogent example. This policy allows parents to take time off to care for a new baby in their family, enhancing their ability to balance work (that is, the market) with family (private life) through government intervention (creation, implementation, and eventual evaluation of the legislation). The passage of this legislation was accomplished through extensive policy analysis.

When boundaries among government, the market, and private life are debated, the functions and structures of policy are redrawn and revised. Unintended consequences of policies are recognized; old policies are examined and reevaluated; bad ones are revoked; and new policy solutions are formulated, tested, and compared. The products of policy analysis help illuminate which policies should change and how these changes might reverberate throughout all aspects of modern life. By showing "what if," "how," or "why," policy analysis sheds light on the foreseeable consequences.

DISCIPLINARY ROOTS OF POLICY ANALYSIS

Weimer and Vining (1992) defined *policy analysis* as "client-oriented advice relevant to public deci-

sions and informed by social values" (p. 1). Offering policy advice is as much art as craft (Wildavsky, 1987), and the timing of the effort can be crucial to its success (Kingdon, 1984). Policy analysis refers both to a set of technical skills used to describe, assess, and influence social policies and to a perspective about what government should do that is based on an assessment of the circumstances and potential for interventions to make things better.

Policy analysis, therefore, requires both knowledge and skills. Among them are the ability to gather, organize, and communicate information when time and access are limited; a perspective about government's role in private affairs; technical skills, primarily in economics and statistics, to assemble and interpret data; working knowledge of political activities and organizational capacities in the policy realm; and an ethical framework to guide one's relationship to the policy analysis client (Weimer & Vining, 1992). Policy analysis knowledge and skills can be used in all stages of policy process, from policy formulation (Michel, 1991) and implementation (Bardach, 1977; Castellani, 1992; Nakamura & Smallwood, 1980) to policy evaluation (Haugh & Claxton, 1993; Haveman, 1987–1988; Rochefort, 1993).

Social planning requires some policy analysis (Faludi, 1973; Friedmann, 1987; Kahn, 1969; Mayer, 1985). Whereas policy analysis tends to be a pragmatic adjunct to policy-making—professional advice given to decision makers—social planning usually is more comprehensive than policy analysis; it covers the entire cycle of problem definition, proposal development, decision making, planning and program design, and evaluation (Tropman, 1987). Policy analysis skills can be used by planners at each stage of a planning procedure, making the line between social planner and policy analyst difficult to draw.

The field of policy analysis has its intellectual roots in a number of social sciences disciplines. Economists view social policies predominantly from the market perspective. They are concerned with allocation of resources—usually money—among the government, the market, and private life. They might analyze tax revenues and transfers in efforts to make these aspects of policy as efficient and equitable as possible (for example, see Garfinkel, 1982).

Political scientists view policies predominantly from the government realm because they are interested in how government operates at various levels and how government policies affect the market and private life. Few policy analysts today fail to recognize the influence of the political context on the development and implementation of public policy (Gummer, 1990; Kaufman, 1981; Lipsky, 1980; Wilson, 1989).

Some sociologists explore how social policies influence social institutions and social behavior. The subfield of political sociology explores the link between government and society. Social policies serve as one important link in this relationship (Demerath, Larsen, & Schuesser, 1975). Sociologists have been particularly active in developing methodologies to evaluate the effectiveness and impact of social policies and programs (Rossi & Freeman, 1993).

Other people from diverse backgrounds also engage in policy analysis. Historians have been adept at identifying the broad cultural and contextual factors that influence policies. People who are concerned about children have given extended attention to family and health policy (National Commission on Children, 1991). Because social policies are promulgated through laws, regulations, and guidelines, they often entail legal analysis and challenge (Cooper, 1988; Glendon, 1989; Minow, 1990; Stein, 1978).

METHODS OF POLICY ANALYSIS

Because policy analysis covers such a broad array of skills and foci and has evolved from diverse disciplinary bases, there are many methods of doing it, each with its own focus and purpose. Almost every method of social scientific inquiry has been used to describe, explain, and analyze social welfare policies and their effects. In a sense, policy analysis has no epistemology or methodology of its own; it is a hybrid field, defined by the objects of study rather than by any theory or method of inquiry. Consequently, any list of policy analysis methods will be incomplete.

Policy analysis can explore one policy, compare two or more policies with each other, or model the future implications of a variety of different policy changes (Singer & Manton, 1993). Policy analysis can examine one stage in policy development or can look across all stages of policy, from design to implementation and evaluation. Sometimes policy experiments are possible. The experimental designs, which strengthen the internal validity of the research, allow policy analysts to more confidently determine whether differences found between policies occurred by chance rather than by intention. Other designs, such as quasi-experimental or nonexperimental studies, are the only way to find out which policy option is the "best." The following is a review of the most prominent methodologies used in policy analysis to describe, analyze, and compare policies.

Needs Assessment

Social policies address problems. First, to address problems sensibly or to assess the outcome of ameliorative efforts, the policy analyst identifies the nature, scope, and extent of the problems. He or she accomplishes an assessment of the extent of need in a variety of ways, through different methodologies (Rossi & Freeman, 1993). He or she may document the nature of the problem through analysis of existing information found in the published and unpublished literature, databases such as the U.S. Census or the Current Population Survey, agency records, specially conducted social surveys of individuals or households, or interviews with key experts. The policy analyst can use such information to describe the current state of need and to forecast likely needs (Rossi & Freeman, 1993).

Cost–Benefit Analysis

Cost–benefit analysis, developed largely by economists, is an approach that attempts to relate the direct and indirect costs of social policies and programs to the direct and indirect benefits of those policies (Weimer & Vining, 1992). Cost–benefit analysis requires that both the costs and the benefits of policies and programs be calculated in monetary form. This is frequently difficult to do, because policy analysts are often unable to give a precise dollar figure for saving a life, strengthening a family, or helping a child feel less depressed. The ethics of quantifying such aspects of life are another aspect of this methodology that has been receiving attention (Buxbaum, 1981; Copp, 1985; Zerbe, 1991). Research examples can be found (Weisbrod, 1982), as well as guidance on the how-tos (Gramlich, 1990).

Cost-Effectiveness Analysis

Cost-effectiveness analysis looks at the costs of different policies in achieving the desired policy results (Weimer & Vining, 1992). Unlike cost–benefit analysis, this methodology does not require the monetization of the benefits of each policy. Although policy analysts may not know the dollar value of certain benefits, they can compare which policy or program costs less to achieve the same desired outcome, regardless of monetary value of the expected benefits.

Outcome Studies

One can assess the effectiveness of a policy without knowing the policy's cost or monetizing the benefits. Outcome studies can document the comparative effectiveness of different policy alternatives. Using conventional quasi-experimental and experimental research designs, policy analysts are able to assess the extent to which some policy intervention has had the intended impact on the social problem it was designed to address. Outcomes can be measured in many different ways, including through the use of psychological and social measures of individuals; the examination of trends in social indicators, such as the poverty thresholds, crime, or mortality rates of a given population or area; or the study of the behavior of groups and organizations.

Case Studies

Many studies of social policy can be described as case studies or as comparative case studies (Yin, 1993). Case studies involve the systematic and detailed description and analysis of the formation, implementation, and evaluation of specific social policies. Examples include analyses of the War on Poverty initiative (Moynihan, 1970), federal revenue sharing (Terrell, 1976), comparative efforts of Western nations to care for children and families (Kamerman & Kahn, 1991), and the impact of crime policy on inner-city drug markets (Reuter & MacCoun, 1992).

Meta-analysis

Meta-analysis is a quantitative method of summarizing the results of existing outcome research. Rather than being a method of gathering new information, meta-analysis involves a systematic way of collating and analyzing existing research literature and findings. It is commonly used to summarize an extensive literature on the effectiveness of psychotherapeutic interventions and is useful whenever an extensive group of quantitative studies of the outcome of policy or program interventions must be examined (Light & Pillemer, 1984; Wachter & Straf, 1990). Meta-analysis can provide guidance to policymakers in the early phases of policy development by summarizing existing quantitative studies and can assist them after a series of policy outcome studies have been conducted (see, for example, Miller & Miller, 1992).

A variety of other sophisticated approaches are used to study policy, including microsimulation techniques (Garasky & Barnow, 1992) and multiple regression (Elliot & Krivo, 1991; Gormley, 1991). As with any methodology, the quality of the results is only as good as the data being used. Quantification may obscure poor data and mislead those who do not possess the increasingly technologically challenging skills needed to understand the products of policy analysis.

WHO DOES POLICY ANALYSIS?

There are no standard eligibility requirements, certification exams, or required specific sequences of courses to become a policy analyst. That is not to say that no skills and experience are necessary. Most professionals who do policy analysis have backgrounds in the social sciences and have a particular interest in some substantive policy area (McCall & Weber, 1983). Policy analysts include economists, political scientists, historians, education specialists, psychologists, urban planners, sociologists, and social workers. Other practitioners of policy analysis have advanced degrees specifically in public policy from university graduate programs that focus on the field. Other professionals, including social work managers, planners, and supervisors, public interest lawyers, legislative assistants, and journalists, conduct policy analysis as part of their work.

Because it has no single disciplinary base or accrediting institution, the field of policy analysis is truly interdisciplinary in origin and practice. Policy analysts borrow, import, synthesize, and create techniques and methodologies from a variety of fields. Because of this rich diversity, policy analysis as a field continues to evolve. Although social policy, social planning, and policy analysis are not exclusive social work arenas, social workers have contributed to the growth and development of each, albeit on a limited basis.

Policy analysts are employed by many types of organizations: universities, private think tanks, advocacy organizations, social services institutions, government agencies, and political offices. Among the private nonprofit organizations that conduct policy analysis relevant to social welfare are the Urban Institute, Brookings Institution, American Heritage Foundation, Rand Corporation, Institute for Research on Poverty, Children's Defense Fund, the National Center for Children in Poverty, Child Trends Inc., Economic Policy Institute, and Center for the Study of Social Policy. The policy analyses that many of these organizations sponsor are funded by grants from private foundations and from government grants and contracts.

Other private nonprofit organizations carry out policy analysis on an occasional basis when a particular issue is of special importance to their membership. For example, organizations such as NASW, the American Medical Association, and the Urban League will conduct policy analyses so that they can influence the course of legislation in areas of their concern. Many other smaller organizations hire private consultants to assist them in collecting, organizing, and analyzing information regarding the impact of policies on their constituents.

The federal government is a major producer of policy analysis. Elected and appointed officials constantly call on government agencies to describe and justify what the officials do and how they might be able to do it better. Among the important government agencies that engage in policy analyses are the Congressional Budget Office, which functions as the policy analysis arm of Congress, and the General Accounting Office, which provides policy analyses on areas of interest as requested by various government officials. In addition, each federal department has its own policy analysis group ready to assist the staff in gathering and analyzing information to evaluate, implement, reform, or develop policies. Since 1946 the president has had an economic and monetary policy analysis group: the Council of Economic Advisors. State and local governments also hire policy analysts and conduct policy analyses to assist their own departments, although not as extensively as the federal government.

WHERE TO FIND POLICY ANALYSES

The products of policy analysis are contained in private and public reports, journal articles, and books. Public reports can usually be obtained from the sponsoring agency or department, often for a modest fee.

More than 30 professional journals are geared toward policy analysis (Wright, 1992). Some of the ones that regularly publish reports relevant to social policy are *Policy Sciences, Journal of Human Resources, Administrative Science Quarterly, Public Administration Review, Journal of Public Policy,* and *American Journal of Public Health.* Many consider the *Journal of Policy Analysis and Management* to be the preeminent journal in this evolving field; the Association for Public Policy Analysis and Management sponsors it, and membership reflects the interdisciplinary nature of policy analysis. Although these journals frequently include analyses of social policy, one can find useful articles in many other more specialized journals that cover substantive fields, such as health, children, criminal justice, housing, employment, and education. Articles that include policy analysis appear regularly in many social work journals, especially in *Social Work, Social Work Research, Social Service Review,* and *Children and Youth Services Review.*

ROLE FOR SOCIAL WORKERS

Social workers are involved in social policy and policy analysis, albeit usually indirectly. At each step in the social policy process (as summarized by Tropman, 1987), social workers and their professional organizations may be involved in assembling information relevant to these policy processes and in attempting to influence the course of events. Unlike those based primarily in academic disciplines, social workers often see firsthand what services are needed, and they see the intended and unanticipated consequences of existing social policies on their clients. Social workers can influence social policy in their roles as policy experts, researchers, advocates, lobbyists, managers, community organizers, planners, and clinicians. Some social workers contribute to this emerging interdisciplinary field; others work on developing a unique social work approach to social policy and policy analysis, referred to as "policy practice" (Jansson, 1984, 1994; Wyers, 1991). Social workers can develop their own approach, but they risk being ignored by policymakers. Fortunately, there is a lot of middle ground between these two approaches, ground that is important for the future of the social work profession. It is certainly an area worth exploring.

Policy analysis is a tool that social workers can wield to improve social policies. It is one important way they can make their voices and the voices of their clients heard among the din of others with professional opinions.

REFERENCES

Bardach, E. (1977). *The implementation game: What happens after a bill becomes law.* Cambridge, MA: MIT Press.

Buxbaum, C. B. (1981). Cost–benefit analysis: The mystique versus the reality. *Social Service Review, 55,* 453–471.

Caputo, R. K. (1989). Integrating values and norms in the evaluation of social policy: A conceptual framework. *Journal of Teaching in Social Work, 3*(2), 115–131.

Castellani, P. J. (1992). Closing institutions in New York State: Implementation and management lessons. *Journal of Policy Analysis and Management, 11*(4), 593–611.

Cooper, P. J. (1988). *Hard judicial choices: Federal district court judges and state and local officials.* New York: Oxford University Press.

Copp, D. (1985). Morality, reason and management science: The rationale of cost–benefit analysis. *Social Philosophy and Policy, 2*(2), 128–151.

Croston, T. A., Fellin, P., & Churchill, S. R. (1987). Teaching policy analysis and development: Interdisciplinary perspectives. *Journal of Teaching in Social Work, 1*(2), 97–111.

Cunningham, L. L., & Dunn, V. B. (1987). Interprofessional policy analysis: An aid to public policy formation. *Theory into Practice, 26*(2), 129–133.

Demerath, N., Larsen, O., & Schuesser, K. (Eds.). (1975). *Social policy and sociology.* New York: Academic Press.

DiNitto, D. M. (1991). *Social welfare: Politics and public policy* (3rd ed.). Englewood Cliffs, NJ: Prentice Hall.

Elliot, M., & Krivo, L. J. (1991). Structural determinants of homelessness in the United States. *Social Problems, 38*(1), 113–131.

Faludi, A. (1973). *Planning theory.* Tarrytown, NY: Pergamon Press.

Friedmann, J. (1987). *Planning in the public domain: From knowledge to action.* Princeton, NJ: Princeton University Press.

Garasky, S., & Barnow, B. S. (1992). Demonstration evaluations and cost neutrality: Using caseload models to determine the federal cost neutrality of New Jersey's REACH demonstration. *Journal of Policy Analysis and Management, 11*(4), 624–636.

Garfinkel, I. (Ed.). (1982). *Income-tested transfer programs: The case for and against.* San Diego: Academic Press.

Gibelman, M., & Schervish, P. H. (1993). *Who we are: The social work labor force as reflected in the NASW membership.* Washington, DC: NASW Press.

Glendon, M. A. (1989). *The transformation of family law.* Chicago: University of Chicago Press.

Gormley, W. T., Jr. (1991). State regulations and the availability of child care services. *Journal of Policy Analysis and Management, 10*(1), 78–95.

Gramlich, E. M. (1990). *Benefit–cost analysis for government programs.* Englewood Cliffs, NJ: Prentice Hall.

Gummer, G. (1990). *The politics of social administration: Managing organizational politics in social agencies.* Englewood Cliffs, NJ: Prentice Hall.

Hagen, J., & Davis, L. V. (1992). Working with women: Building a policy and practice agenda. *Social Work, 37,* 495–502.

Haugh, K. H., & Claxton, G. J. (1993). Guaranteeing coverage with multiple insurers: Closing gaps and easing transitions. *The Future of Children: Health Care Reform, 3*(2), 123–141.

Haveman, R. H. (1987–1988). Policy analysis and evaluation research after twenty years. *Policy Studies Journal, 16*(2), 191–218.

Jansson, B. C. (1984). *Theory and practice of social welfare policy: Analysis, processes, and current issues.* Belmont, CA: Wadsworth.

Jansson, B. C. (1994). *Social policy: From theory to practice* (2nd ed.). Monterey, CA: Brooks/Cole.

Jenkins-Smith, H. (1982). Professional roles for policy analysts: A critical assessment. *Journal of Policy Analysis and Management, 2*(1), 88–100.

Kahn, A. J. (1964). *Social policy and social services.* New York: Random House.

Kahn, A. J. (1969). *Theory and practice of social planning.* New York: Russell Sage Foundation.

Kamerman, S. B., & Kahn, A. J. (1991). *Child care, parental leave and the under 3's.* New York: Auburn House.

Kaufman, H. (1981). *The administrative behavior of federal bureau chiefs.* Washington, DC: Brookings Institution.

Kingdon, J. W. (1984). *Agendas, alternatives and public policies.* New York: Harper College.

Lerner, D., & Lasswell, H. D. (Eds.). (1951). *The policy sciences.* Stanford, CA: Stanford University Press.

Light, R., & Pillemer, D. (1984). *Summing up: The science of reviewing research.* Cambridge, MA: Harvard University Press.

Lipsky, M. (1980). *Street-level bureaucracy.* New York: Russell Sage Foundation.

Mayer, R. (1985). *Policy and program planning.* Englewood Cliffs, NJ: Prentice Hall.

McCall, G. J., & Weber, G. H. (1983). Policy analysis across academic disciplines. In S. Nagal (Ed.), *Encyclo-pedia of policy studies* (pp. 201–221). New York: Marcel Dekker.

Michel, R. C. (1991). Economic growth and income equality since the 1982 recession. *Journal of Policy Analysis and Management, 10*(2), 181–203.

Miller, T. I., & Miller, M. A. (1992). Assessing excellence poorly: The bottom line in local government. *Journal of Policy Analysis and Management, 11*(4), 612–623.

Minow, M. (1990). *Making all the difference: Inclusion, exclusion and American law.* Ithaca, NY: Cornell University Press.

Moynihan, D. P. (1970). *Maximum feasible misunderstanding.* New York: Free Press.

Nakamura, R., & Smallwood, F. (1980). *The politics of policy implementation.* Harrisburg, PA: St. Martin's Press.

National Commission on Children. (1991). *Beyond rhetoric: A new American agenda for children and families.* Washington, DC: Author.

Prigmore, C. S., & Atherton, C. R. (1986). *Social welfare policy: Analysis and formulation* (2nd ed.). Lexington, MA: D. C. Heath.

Reuter, P. H., & MacCoun, R. J. (1992). Street drug markets in inner-city neighborhoods: Matching policy to reality. In J. B. Steinberg, D. W. Lyon, & M. E. Vaiana (Eds.), *Urban America: Policy choices for Los Angeles and the nation* (pp. 227–251). Santa Monica, CA: Rand Corporation.

Rochefort, D. A. (1993). *From poorhouses to homelessness: Policy analysis and mental health care.* Westport, CT: Auburn House.

Rossi, P., & Freeman, H. (1993). *Evaluation: A systematic approach.* Newbury Park, CA: Sage Publications.

Singer, B. H., & Manton, K. G. (1993). How many elderly in the next generation? *Focus, 15*(2), 1–10.

Stein, T. (1978). *Children in foster homes: Achieving continuity of care.* New York: Praeger.

Terrell, P. (1976). *The social impact of revenue sharing: Planning, participation, and the purchase of service.* New York: Praeger.

Trattner, W. (1989). *From poor law to welfare state: A history of social welfare in America.* New York: Free Press.

Tropman, J. (1987). Policy analysis: Methods and techniques. In A. Minahan (Ed.-in-Chief), *Encyclopedia of social work* (18th ed., Vol. 2, pp. 268–283). Silver Spring, MD: National Association of Social Workers.

Wachter, K., & Straf, M. (Eds.). (1990). *The future of meta-analysis.* New York: Russell Sage Foundation.

Weimer, D. L., & Vining, A. R. (1992). *Policy analysis: Concepts and practice* (2nd ed.). Englewood Cliffs, NJ: Prentice Hall.

Weisbrod, B. A. (1982). A guide to benefit–cost analysis, as seen through a controlled experiment in treating the mentally ill. *Journal of Health Politics, Policy and Law, 7,* 808–845.

Wildavsky, A. (1987). *Speaking truth to power: The art and craft of policy analysis* (2nd ed.). New Brunswick, NJ: Transaction Books.

Wilson, J. Q. (1989). *Bureaucracy.* New York: Basic Books.

Wright, J. D. (1992). Public policy analysis. In E. F. Borgatta & M. L. Borgatta (Eds.), *Encyclopedia of sociology* (Vol. 3, pp. 1571–1576). New York: Macmillan.

Wyers, N. L. (1991). Policy-practice in social work: Models and issues. *Journal of Social Work Education, 27,* 241–250.

Yin, R. K. (1993). *Case study research.* Newbury Park, CA: Sage Publications.

Zerbe, R. (1991). Comment: Does benefit cost analysis stand alone? Rights and standing. *Journal of Policy Analysis and Management, 10*(1), 96–104.

Susan D. Einbinder, PhD, is assistant professor, University of Southern California, School of Social Work, Los Angeles, CA 90089.

For further information see

Advocacy; Community Needs Assessment; Economic Analysis; Federal and Administrative Rule Making; Planning and Management Professions; Policy Practice; Public Social Services; Research Overview; Social Planning; Social Welfare Policy; Social Work Profession Overview.

Key Words

policy analysis	social planning
policy-making	social policy
policy research	

Policy Practice

Demetrius S. Iatridis

Until the 1980s social policy in social work was mainly concerned with the history of social welfare and the typology of its services. In other words, social policy was regarded as a field rather than a problem-solving process. Thus, throughout the 20th century, for example, courses on social welfare history, programs, and services have not usually included information on the formulation and implementation of social policy or on theories and practice skills. In short, social workers in social policy positions have not usually been trained for social policy practice. This perspective, however, is rapidly changing.

SOCIAL POLICY: FIELD AND PROCESS

Social policy, according to an evolving view, is both a field and a process. As a field, social policy focuses on the interests and development of society as a whole and on measures to help individuals, including poor people and other powerless individuals. As a process, it involves a series of related steps, an orderly, systematic procedure (Bartlett, 1958) that is designed to formulate and implement policies to solve social problems.

The issue of hunger illustrates the dual nature of social policy as a field and a process. International officials relate famine to ineffective methods of producing and distributing food; misguided trade policies; and poor-quality sanitation, roads, schools, and health care. These social conditions delineate the field of social policy and the parameters of the social policy problem. Ending hunger, however, requires much more than understanding the nature of the problem or providing generous donations of humanitarian aid and direct social services. Instead, social workers recognize that it is necessary to develop and implement antihunger policies and measures in several domains of the social system to reduce and prevent hunger. In short, what is also required is a problem-solving process. Thus, the evolving view suggests that social policy is also a problem-solving, interventive method of social work that is based on a systematic body of knowledge, methods, and practice skills. Social workers need social policy methods in the context of professional practice.

Theory and Practice

The field and process of social policy, incorporating cybernetic advances and effective technological tools, currently focus on both theoretical models and practice skills. Social workers plan social policy interventions through projects to change policies and social action to reform social conditions. They also guide the implementation of social policy projects. Current social work curricula and practice approaches do not just describe social welfare trends and programs in the field of social policy; they also prescribe how to analyze social policies systematically, identify alternative policies, and design and implement social services programs. In the health care field, for example, social workers who support social change and reform of the health care system analyze and determine which policy is most effective and just: a single-payer approach to health care or the employer–employee model proposed by President Clinton. They also must design plans, programs, and guidelines to implement the selected health policy.

Thus, the social policy context of social work practice is being transformed from strictly descriptive, historical, and conceptual orientations that exclude practice realities to a prescriptive, problem-solving, action- and practice-oriented interventive method for social policy reform (Iatridis, 1994; Jansson, 1994; McInnis-Dittrich, 1994). Helping people by formulating and implementing social policy is the core of this development.

Development of Social Policy

Although social work has been concerned about social welfare policy and services throughout its existence (Wenocur & Reisch, 1989), it was not until the 1980s that social policy theory and its practice component began to crystallize in the profession. During this period social policy in social work was influenced by technological advances in the general field of policy development that were successfully applied to several societal domains and functions, including economic policy, defense policy, ecological policy, foreign policy, and public decision making. The formulation and implementation of public policy gradually developed after World War II into a major and crucial discipline and activity in both the public and private sectors. The investment of billions of dollars of public funds now depends on the formulation, implementation, and evaluation of policies that are designed to justify what was and what will be spent by local, state, and national governments and international organizations.

Social policy (that is, policy applied to the social domains of society) is a relative newcomer in modern societies that use policy formulation and implementation as a crucial approach and tool of government and private-sector decision making (Frey, 1987; Iatridis, 1983; Neugeboren, 1983; Nulman, 1983; Sosin & Caulum, 1983). Social work began to incorporate social policy theory and practice technology into social work practice in the 1980s. It thus developed and refined social policy theories and practice skills for social work practice (Dear, Briar, & Van Ry, 1986; Figueira-McDonough, 1993; Jansson, 1984; Pierce, 1984; Wyers, 1991).

In this context, social policy in social work practice provides social workers—including those in direct services, counseling, community organization, planning, and administration—with theory and practice approaches to developing or changing social policies. Social policy planners in social work formulate interventions—social policies, programs, and projects for change and societal reform—and guide their implementation (Haynes & Mickelson, 1986). The aim of these interventions is to prevent, solve, resolve, or dissolve agency, community, and societal problems that affect the behavior of individuals and their families and to improve community resources and social services (Briar & Briar, 1982; Dolgoff, 1981; Frey, 1988; Gilbert, Specht, & Terrel, 1993; Hagen & Davis, 1992; Iatridis, 1988).

VALUES THAT GUIDE INTERVENTIONS

The road to social policy practice was paved by developing policy values, theories, and practice skills. Social policy is planned from the perspective of a set of values and an ideology. Policies to reform health care, for example, depend on the values that drive them. Thus, a concern about the costs and organizational efficiency of health care results in policies to reduce costs and to increase efficiency, whereas a concern with social justice and equality results in policies for universal coverage and access for all Americans.

Values are major dimensions of social policy practice that convey legitimacy, public commitment, and loyalties and that help structure the behavior of individuals, groups, and communities. Social justice, equality, democratic processes, and empowerment of disadvantaged and powerless people are crucial social policy values in social work practice.

Values are embedded in theory and practice. As a set of related propositions, theory explains and predicts phenomena in the field and guides the interpretation of variables. Theory and practice interact: Theory is informed and shaped by practice, and vice versa. Social workers apply theory to interpret professional behavior and control activities as a test of practice and to understand and explain situations in their work (Bisman, 1994; McInnis-Dittrich, 1994).

Social and Distributive Justice

Social work values, described in the profession's code of ethics (National Association of Social Workers, 1994; Sheafor, Horejsi, & Horejsi, 1991), drive all social policy interventions in social work, including social policy practice. Prevailing concepts of distributive justice and equality, however, underlie and justify social policy practice more specifically. Society's distribution of resources, including wealth, power, knowledge, and human services—major concerns of social policy practice—is associated with social justice and equality. The core issue is who gets what, when, how, and why. Distributive justice demands that public policy allocate resources in a particular democratic and participatory way. Fairness and equality demand that social policy and the distribution of goods and services not be left to random selection, to the needs of those in power, or to economic mechanisms that offend moral commitments and social work values or exclude active participation in decision making by those who are affected by the decisions.

Four major models of justice have emerged in the literature: (1) the utilitarian model, based on early classical liberalism (Galston, 1980); (2) the market model, based on Adam Smith's variation of utilitarianism and on economic individualism incorporated into capitalism (Friedman & Friedman, 1980; Nozick, 1974); (3) the fairness model, based on social contract theory and Rawls's (1971) perspective; and (4) the socialist–Marxist model, based on Marxist theory (Heilbroner, 1980). In the context of the social work profession's code of ethics, social workers usually opt for the fairness model in social policy practice. For Rawls, the leading modern commentator on this view, the primary concern of justice is the basic structure of society (that is, the way social institutions distribute fundamental rights and duties and the manner in which the advantages arising from social cooperation are distributed). In this justice model of policy practice, all people have equal rights to basic liberties, and rational beings can accept inequalities only if the inequalities work to the advantage of those who are least well off. Social workers in social policy practice are committed to social change and the redistribution of goods and services to improve social justice and equality for all people, particularly the powerless and disadvantaged ones. In the justice model, social policies ensure that all people have access to the resources, services, and opportunities they require.

Self-Determination

Social policy practice in social work is based on the achievement of freedom and egalitarianism, including self-determination, self-actualization, democratic self-government, and full participation of citizens in policies that affect their lives. Participatory democracy is a holistic ideal in which the participation of all in decision making is essential to protect individuals' private interests. It requires the establishment of an extended and comprehensive social services system as a human right for all people, to allow them, through active participation, to refine their own humanity and to reach their highest potential. Social workers are keenly aware that helping clients be active participants in making decisions about their future is key to the success of social work practice (McInnis-Dittrich, 1994).

SCOPE OF SOCIAL POLICY

Leaders of different countries, the general public, and professional commentators perceive the nature, scope, and methods of social policy practice in different ways. For example, some commentators prefer broad policy perspectives that focus on the interests of society as a whole and on the well-being of all citizens and communities, not only on those of poor people (Iatridis, 1994; Jones, 1986). Others view social policy in a narrow perspective that equates social policy practice with social welfare measures for poor people (Tropman, Dluhy, Lind, Vasey, & Croxton, 1976). Some authors focus on social policy as a field and emphasize only its philosophical nature and theoretical component (Axinn & Levin, 1993; Johnson & Schwartz, 1994); others see social policy as a technical interventive process of problem solving and emphasize its practice component (Patton & Sawicki, 1986; Stokey & Zeckhauser, 1978), whereas some perceive it as both a field and a process (Iatridis, 1994; Jansson, 1994; Netting, Kettner, & McMurtry, 1993). Finally, social policy is sometimes used as a synonym for other terms, such as "social welfare," "social planning," or "policy analysis" (Mayer, 1985).The term "social policy planning" as used here includes both policy analysis–formulation and policy implementation.

Goals and Objectives

Whereas clinical social work practice focuses mainly on behavioral changes in small systems, including individuals, families, and small groups, policy practice in social work is concerned mainly with policy changes in large systems—organizations, communities, institutions, and societies—for the benefit of individuals and their families. Social policy planners in social work, for example, analyze existing or proposed policies of organizations that provide services (such as schools and social services, and housing and health agencies), communities that are planning their development (for example, inner-city, rural, and suburban communities or regions), and social institutions (such as educational, health care, religious, and social welfare institutions and the economic market) that influence the well-being of individuals and families. Thus, social policy planners analyze social policies and priorities; formulate and recommend alternative policies for social development and the efficient use of scarce resources; design programs, plans, and projects to implement policies; and organize, manage, monitor, and evaluate social work interventions in organizations, communities, and institutions.

Approaches and Roles of
Social Policy Planners

Within this context, social policy practitioners use an extensive repertoire of social work approaches and perform several roles according to the phases of the policy-planning process. For example, in formulating policy and programs, they assume the role of analyst–planner, analyzing and providing technical information and defining a framework of values. In implementing projects or programs, they frequently take on the role of administrator, using organizational and managerial skills and knowledge. In evaluating outcomes of policy interventions, they play the role of researcher, providing scientific knowledge and methodology (Iatridis, 1994; Patton & Sawicki, 1986).

Social policy practitioners also perform various roles, including laissez-faire, rational, normative, and advocacy roles, according to the policy situations they encounter. Laissez-faire approaches and roles call for the social work practitioner to do little or nothing, expecting that in due time the forces inherent in a system will become active and that problems will gradually disappear. In such cases policy planners may promote inaction and recommend that an intervention not be undertaken at a given time.

Rational approaches and roles are characterized by logic and scientific reasoning, emphasizing the important benefits derived from objective procedures and from quantifying and measuring concepts. For example, policy planners may use a technical scientific method for analyzing and implementing a policy based on technical analytic tools, including input–output and cost–benefit approaches.

Normative approaches and roles are based on value concepts and principles that are dominant in a community without necessarily rejecting rational approaches. Values, rather than empirical, technical concerns, define the role of the social work practitioner.

Advocacy and social action approaches and roles are characterized by the deliberate promotion of specific goals and interests of clients. The practitioner's role is to empower specific groups, including poor people, children, women, elderly individuals, communities, groups, or consumers, rather than promote common interests. Although social action is necessary in most policy changes, it is especially emphasized in advocacy (NASW, 1994).

INTERVENTIONS

Levels of Intervention

Social policy practice usually consists of macro-level interventions, but policy changes may take place at one or more administrative and geographic level: local, state, regional, national, international, or global. The points of policy inter-

vention—the levels at which action and change will take place—frequently include a combination of levels. For example, the policies and operations of community mental health facilities may also depend on actions at the federal and state levels. Likewise, actions at the local level to change patterns of segregation may also require judicial decisions at higher levels (for example, the U.S. Supreme Court) and federal executive regulations.

Types of Intervention

Within this context, policy practitioners usually engage in one or more types of projects—legislative, administrative, or judicial—that are designed to change undesirable social conditions. All three types of projects, or a combination, may be required in any given social policy intervention (for an in-depth discussion of these tasks and projects, see Copley and O'Leary, 1988).

Legislative tasks and projects establish guidelines to be followed by members of society. For example, a law against gender discrimination may be intended to achieve equal pay for women and men who hold similar jobs and have similar qualifications. A law raising the drinking age from 19 to 21 or requiring an investigation before a person buys a handgun is intended to reduce crime and violence and to stop people ages 19 to 21 from consuming alcoholic beverages or unreliable people from possessing handguns.

Administrative projects, tasks, and actions are what organizations and governments do to put laws into practice. For example, administrative regulations or actions in the hiring and firing of employees in organizations are usually necessary to comply with gender-discrimination laws. In addition, traffic police take administrative action to enforce speed limits or restrictions against driving while intoxicated. Administrative regulations may also include such actions as mailing social security checks and regulations about the forms to be completed by social welfare recipients.

Judicial projects and decisions take place when courts apply the law to a specific situation. For example, existing laws or practices may be declared unconstitutional, as has been the case with school segregation, racial discrimination, and antiabortion protests that block access to clinics.

Central Issues

Although social policy practitioners deal with various policy problems and issues, three fundamental and directly related policy issues—the desired society, organization of resources, and distribution of goods and services—invariably challenge social policy practice, explicitly or implicitly, covertly or overtly. (See Iatridis, 1994, for further discussion of these issues.)

The desired society. What kind of society, community, or organization is sought? What kind of social relations should be achieved? A society's social policies usually conform to the kind of society visualized and desired by its members. For example, social policies in a democratic society are usually democratic, whereas in an authoritarian society, community, or organization, they are usually authoritarian and oppressive. In social policy practice, policy planners analyze existing and proposed policies in relation to the kind of society, community, or organization that is desired; their analysis provides normative criteria for policy formulation. For example, the policies and programs of a nonprofit agency usually conform to the agency's nonprofit mission, whereas those of a child welfare agency are child oriented.

Organization of resources. How should societal, community, organizational, or institutional forces be structured, and how should physical and human resources be used? Societies, communities, and agencies organize their structure and allocate their human and physical resources to achieve their mission and goals. Institutional and group relations, priorities, and activities that produce required goods and services follow the images that societies, communities, and organizations have of themselves. For example, in Western urbanized industrial societies, educational institutions, not the family, are assigned the responsibility of formal education. Social classes may be rigidly separated, as in caste societies, or flexibly stratified, as in modern societies. Voluntary labor, not slavery or coercion, is used to motivate citizens and the labor force to produce in a free society. Whether mothers of young children in single-parent families should be encouraged to work at home for family preservation or to join the labor force is usually a matter of how communities want to organize themselves and allocate their labor force and what priorities they set. (The same holds true for welfare policies that require mothers who receive Aid to Families with Dependent Children to work for their welfare benefits.) The role of government or the private sector in providing assistance and human services to poor people also depends on how society sees itself and how it organizes its resources. Usually policy issues are seen in the context of social organization and the allocation of rights, resources, and responsibilities.

Distribution of goods and services. What share of the produced goods and services in a society, community, or organization should be allocated to individuals, groups, and social classes? How should power and social services be distributed? What are the appropriate criteria for distributive justice?

Societies, communities, and organizations establish principles for the distribution of power in decision making and for the goods and services they produce. For example, the wages and salaries of workers and employees may be determined in various ways: according to need, according to merit, or according to an individual's contribution to the production process. Criteria for social justice and equality are directly associated with the ways in which goods and services are distributed. Wealth and poverty, power and powerlessness, and education and illiteracy are frequent outcomes of rules regarding the distribution of goods and services. Policy issues of social welfare, social services, or facilities for social development are usually seen in the light of established distributive rules. Solutions to these problems also depend on dominant patterns of distribution.

Whether explicit or implicit, these three policy questions challenge social policy practice and underlie the improvement of social conditions. In this context, social policy practice is concerned with how societies, communities, organizations, and institutions formulate, determine, resolve, implement, and evaluate these three related issues.

Social policies for social development are driven by answers to and a consensus about these questions. Because social needs, including income, food, housing, health, and education, are socially constructed, social policies to meet these needs depend on the answers to the three policy questions. In this sense, social policy formulation involves and implies normative criteria and negotiations for priorities among competing needs and goals, community and group interests, ethical and cultural values, and unequal access to resources.

Institutional Base of Policy Practice

Social policy emanates from a society's institutional structure, which reflects the society's values and norms. Hence, social policy can be better understood in the context of a system of interdependent political, economic, and social institutions. The policy model in Figure 1 depicts the institutional context of social policy practice.

Social policy practice is centrally concerned with the formulation of policy guidelines for society's institutions, such as the government, the educational system, the welfare state and its organizations, the economic market, religion, and the

FIGURE 1

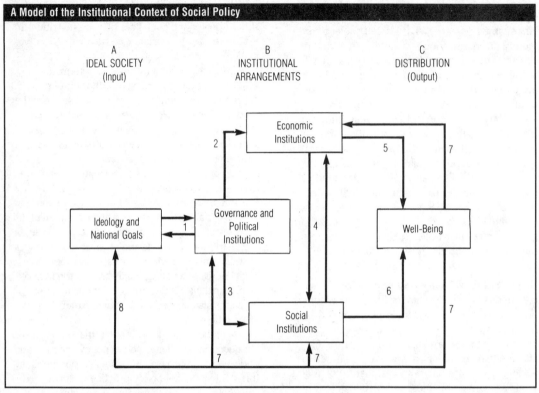

A Model of the Institutional Context of Social Policy

SOURCE: latridis, D. (1994). *Social policy: Institutional context of social development and human services* (p. 21). Copyright © 1994 by Wadsworth, Inc. Reprinted by permission of Brooks/Cole Publishing Company, Pacific Grove, CA.

family. However, three major types of institutions are conventionally identified. Political institutions, including the U.S. Congress, political parties, and the electoral system, regulate the use of and access to power. Economic institutions, such as the market, produce and distribute goods and services. Social institutions, including the family, the educational system, and religions, produce patterns of human relations.

In policy practice, social workers divide each category of institutions into subunits. For example, social institutions include stratification institutions, which determine the distribution of positions and resources; kinship institutions, which deal with marriage, the family, child protection, and socialization of young people; and cultural institutions, which are concerned with religious, scientific, and artistic activities. Moreover, welfare state institutional policies may be divided into specializations, or subunits, that represent specific functional areas of policy practice (see Figure 2).

It is through policy changes that institutions adapt and evolve and additional institutions emerge to meet new human needs. As institutional policies change, they mold the behavior of individ-

uals, groups, organizations, and communities—the clients of social work practice.

STAGES OF SOCIAL POLICY PROCESS

Social workers recognize that the process of clinical and policy interventions is characterized by several stages, beginning with the referral of a client and ending with the termination of services. Among the various stages of the social policy process, two are usually considered to be the most significant: policy analysis–formulation, which requires mainly cognitive skills, and implementation planning, which primarily has an organizational and administrative orientation. These two stages correspond to the diagnosis and treatment stages of the clinical social work process. Policy planners may focus on one or both stages in practice.

Policy Analysis–Formulation Stage

Social policy planners usually start with formulations of the client's problem and analyses of the socioeconomic conditions in which the problem is embedded (see Figure 3). In clinical practice, social workers begin this stage with formulations

FIGURE 2

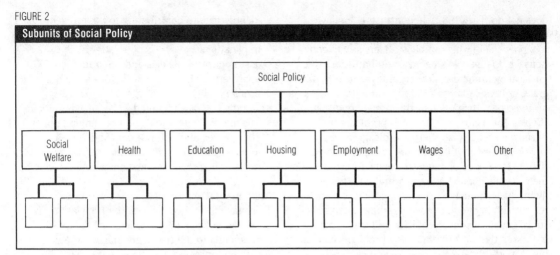

Subunits of Social Policy

Source: Iatridis, D. (1994). *Social policy: Institutional context of social development and human services* (p. 15). Copyright © 1994 by Wadsworth, Inc. Reprinted by permission of Brooks/Cole Publishing Company, Pacific Grove, CA.

FIGURE 3

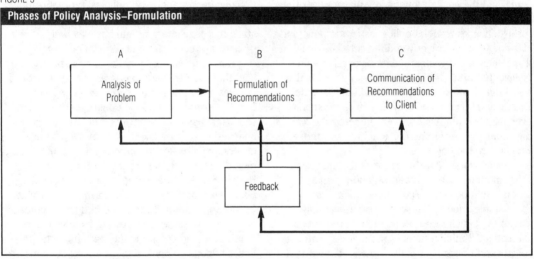

Phases of Policy Analysis–Formulation

Source: Iatridis, D. (1994). *Social policy: Institutional context of social development and human services* (p. 44). Copyright © 1994 by Wadsworth, Inc. Reprinted by permission of Brooks/Cole Publishing Company, Pacific Grove, CA.

of the individual's clinical problem and a diagnostic study of the client's environment, including family, work, significant relationships, and behavioral patterns. This stage is usually referred to as "diagnosis" in clinical work, whereas in policy practice it is called "analysis of the problem."

In social policy practice, social workers identify the policy problem or issue and conduct a diagnostic study of its socioeconomic, political, and organizational environment. This environment includes the key players who are involved—the individuals, groups, organizations, and institutions that attempt to shape the policy (that is, elected or appointed officials, organized groups, and commu-

nity leaders). For example, the policy players in the debate over national health insurance include federal government officials, legislators in the U.S. Congress, and the special advisory council on health care. The American Medical Association, insurance companies, employers, health care providers, and pharmaceutical and medical equipment corporations, all of which may support or oppose the policy, also qualify as players, as do various consumer groups, including poor people, women, and elderly people.

Social workers usually distinguish between a policy and a policy problem or issue. For example, "public policy" is anything a government does or does not do (Dye, 1987). In contrast, a "policy problem" or "issue" exists when at least two factors prevail: (1) when a policy affects social conditions (that is, people's behavior and attitudes, the physical environment, poverty, hunger, health, illiteracy, or homelessness) and (2) when the players disagree over the policy or the social conditions (Copley & O'Leary, 1988). Policy problems frequently arise because there are disagreements among players about either the goals and objectives of the policy or the best means to achieve them. In this context, policy formulation necessarily involves an analysis of social conditions and the resolution of conflict. For example, analyses of social conditions involve social and economic indicators that describe a policy problem, such as infant mortality and its etiology, and require a consensus about the tolerable rate of the problem.

Policy planners identify social conditions surrounding the policy problem, its impact on well-being, and the conflict among key players over the policy or the social conditions associated with it. For instance, as a social policy issue, the policy of allowing time for prayer in public schools involves disagreement between students or parents who believe that time for prayer violates their constitutional rights and school officials who allow time for prayer. The issue also involves disagreement over social conditions between citizens who fear the country is becoming too religious and those who believe the opposite.

Social workers at this stage of the process study, monitor, explain, forecast, and evaluate social conditions and recommend social policy. For example, monitoring social conditions may lead to the conclusion that in 1990 there were an estimated 2.2 million homeless people; explaining social conditions may result in the statement that decreases in funding for food stamps, welfare benefits, and housing subsidies have made housing unaffordable for people; forecasting social conditions may involve the prediction that the number of homeless people will increase by 10 percent annually over the ensuing three years; evaluation may lead to the conclusion that too many homeless people die from exposure and lack of proper medical care; and recommendations may suggest that the amount of federal funds allocated annually to low-income housing programs should be increased by 50 percent.

During this stage, social policy planners perform various tasks. They

- ascertain the existence of a policy problem or issue
- define the nature of the policy problem and its socioeconomic environment

- identify factors contributing to the problem
- recognize key policy issues and their implications
- assess current policies and programs
- analyze the history of efforts to resolve the problem
- identify key players and decision-making bodies
- identify, evaluate, rank, and recommend policy alternatives and outline costs and benefits
- forecast the effect of recommended policies
- make policy recommendations to clients.

Implementation Stage

This stage is concerned with the translation of approved policies into practice (see Figure 4). It corresponds to the treatment stage of the clinical social work process, the stage that follows the completion of the clinical diagnostic study.

Policy social workers at the implementation stage organize, monitor, and evaluate the operationalization of approved policies in organizations, communities, institutions, or societies. It is at this stage that legislative, administrative, and judicial policies are converted into legislation, organizational directives, decisions, programs, projects, or acts that are designed to operationalize approved policies and change targeted social conditions.

For example, suppose Congress passes a bill requiring a system of universal health coverage financed mostly by taxes. The government agencies responsible for the implementation of the law, including the U.S. Department of Health and Human Services, design appropriate guidelines, plans, programs, procedures, forms, and services. In addition, administrative and budgetary guidelines are issued; procedures are established for monitoring and enforcing the law's implementation; budgetary appropriations and allocations are made; and trained staff, offices, and equipment are obtained. Finally, the U.S. Supreme Court upholds the constitutionality of the law.

In this context, policy social workers operationally describe the policy to be implemented and the necessary human and material resources; define the levels at which the policy will be implemented (local, state, federal, or international); outline and analyze legislative, administrative, and judicial considerations; develop political strategies; and establish monitoring methods and criteria for evaluating critical junctions of the implementation process. They also monitor and evaluate outcomes or results achieved and recommend the continuation or discontinuation of the intervention. In brief, they devise projects, programs, legislation, plans, administrative regulations, and actions to operationalize approved policy; monitor implementation

FIGURE 4

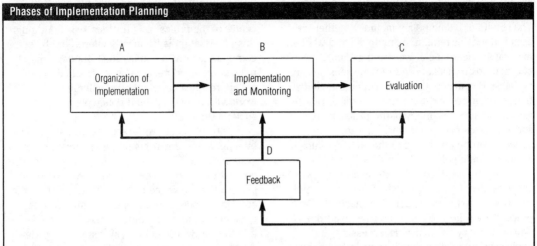

Phases of Implementation Planning

activities and their progress; evaluate outcomes; and recommend adjustments to, or discontinuation of, the intervention.

The social work literature treats the stages of policy practice and its tasks in different ways. For example, Gilbert and Specht (1987), Jansson (1994), and Patton and Sawicki (1986) have all suggested terms for describing the stages. McInnis-Dittrich (1994) proposed a model called ANALYSIS:

A *approach:* including the methods used and the values expressed in the policy

N *need:* what needs are addressed?

A *assessment:* what are the policy's strengths and weaknesses?

L *logic:* the connection between the need and a means of solving the problem

Y *your reaction:* your experience with the policy

S *support:* the financial support for the policy

I *innovation:* provisions for changing the program

S *social justice:* important issues of social justice.

Iatridis (1994) suggested a model called SCIENCE:

S *sociopolitical environments:* the societal context of the problem, its ideological frameworks, and its social justice–equality implications

C *causes of the problem:* a literature review of the etiology, a model of how the problem develops, and major policy questions

I *interventive approaches:* present policies and needs that are being met, alternative policies, and their impact

E *establishment and ranking of recommendations:* list of recommendations by importance, their pros and cons, connection with needs, and support and resistance expected

N *narrative of programs for implementation:* list and explanation of programs and plans to convert policy into action, resources needed, and criteria to evaluate success

C *characteristics of implementation:* cost, prerequisites, problems anticipated, training required, monitoring of performance

E *evaluation of outcome:* assessing whether goals and objectives have been achieved and determining whether the intervention should be continued.

IMPLICATIONS FOR SOCIAL WORK PRACTICE AND EDUCATION

The incorporation of social policy methods into social work practice highlights several related issues.

Effects of Social Policy

The first issue is the realization that social policy affects the parameters of what happens in society—that public policies affect who gets what in society and how, and determine what goods and services are available and who pays or benefits. The results of public policy include whether citizens find jobs or remain unemployed and whether medical services, social welfare benefits, unemployment insurance, and retirement pensions are available. Because policies determine the allocation of resources and the nature of social programs and services, many of the problems that social workers encounter when providing direct services can be attributed to the shortcomings of socioeconomic policy.

In this context, social work as a public profession operates, to a great extent, under social policy. To be a part of these decision-making processes, social workers need to expand the skills necessary for analyzing, assessing, and implementing public policy in a systematic and well-informed way.

Linking Direct Services to Social Reform
The second issue is that social policy links two major components of social work practice: direct services to individuals and reforms of societal institutions that influence the individuals' well-being; that is, social policy connects individuals with the systems of society. Social workers link people with systems that provide them with resources, services, and opportunities and promote effective and humane operations (Pincus & Minahan, 1973) using several different intervention methods, rather than only one approach (Johnson, 1989; Sheafor & Landon, 1987).

Even before the turn of this century, social work was confronted with these two approaches. The profession's dual vision of itself included, on the one hand, social activism for policies to change socioeconomic environments and, on the other hand, direct services and counseling to individuals and their families. Those who espoused social activism included Jane Addams, the founders of the Chicago School of Civics and Philanthropy (later the School of Social Service Administration of the University of Chicago), Grace and Edith Abbott, participants in the settlement house movement, and Marion Hathway. They argued for making social change and policy reform the epicenter of the profession (Wenocur & Reisch, 1989).

Those who advocated direct services included the Charity Organization Societies of the late 1800s, the founders of social casework, Mary Richmond, and the New York School of Philanthropy (later the Graduate School of Social Work at Columbia University). They contended that

direct work with individuals and the development of a scientific helping method should be the epicenter of the profession (Trattner, 1989). Although this polarization is frequently interpreted by some commentators as a conflict in methods, it mainly reflects the need in social work practice for multiple approaches and methods, including direct work with individuals and policy planning for societal reform.

Current social work practice is characterized by a person-in-environment perspective and by systems theory, both of which highlight the policy context of practice. The person-in-environment perspective views the individual client within the context of societal policies and regulations, the community and its resources, and the organization that provides services; systems theory views the client as a member of various systems, including the family and the community. It is unrealistic to practice social work without attending to conditions in the community and to social forces and policies that affect an individual's adjustment.

Thus, social work practice is charged with adjustments of both the individual and society. It is not content merely with the adjustments of individuals, particularly when such adjustments require adaptations to dysfunctional societal mechanisms. Without attention to social dysfunctions, social work's clients remain subjected to the overwhelming power of harmful social conditions. Freedom from powerlessness, alienation, and mental illness, as well as from one's economic and social configuration, must be associated with changes in social policy. It is through social policy that social work can legitimate and improve social services to individuals and their families and alleviate harmful social conditions and social problems such as hunger, poverty, child abuse, physical and mental illness, migration, homelessness, acquired immune deficiency syndrome (AIDS), and substance abuse. In a context of mutuality, both clinical and policy components of social work practice help people's social functioning.

Social workers know that some types of environments and social organization are better suited to satisfying human needs than are others. The choice of optimal social policies and organizational patterns that increase the quality of life is crucial for the well-being of social work clients. It is through social policy practice that social work can balance its strong component of individualism with its social component. Social work curricula have begun to reflect social policy developments and to provide students with opportunities to engage in social policy practice.

Organizational and Public Policies

The third issue is that policies of organizations that provide social services set the parameters of social workers' activities. For example, policies of organizations that provide services set priorities and govern what social workers do, whom they serve, when and how they serve, and how they are paid. Agency goals, authority, and regulations determine programs, projects, and fees for services to clients.

Participation in Public Policy-Making

The fourth issue is that through social policy practice, social work can relate to public policy decisions that have direct implications for citizens' access to resources, allocation of services, individual freedom, and well-being. Social policy in social work addresses contemporary governmental concerns about the implications of rapid urbanization, modernization, and globalization for individual and community behavior. These are among the forces that generate the persistent problems of inadequate incomes; unemployment; inequality of income, wealth, education, and political power; housing; economic and political powerlessness; crime; and behavioral dysfunctions of individuals and groups.

Improving Social Justice

The fifth issue is that social policy practice provides social work with approaches to improve social justice, fairness, and equality. By formulating national or communitywide policies and large-scale projects to increase fairness, equality, and human rights (the foundation of American society and its institutions), social workers can affect societal parameters of well-being for the overwhelming majority of citizens. Social justice demands that the distribution of goods and services not be left to random selection, to the needs of those in power, or to economic mechanisms that offend moral commitments. It is in this sense that social policies for distributive justice become a fundamental prerequisite in social work practice. Social policies that empower powerless individuals and stimulate development bring about the changes in people's environments that are necessary to improve their social functioning.

Social work practice is constantly evolving. It is not static and does not take place in a vacuum. Instead, it constantly adjusts, transforms, and expands its progressive knowledge and practice base (Kirst-Ashman & Hull, 1993). Social policy methods in social work practice reflect this principle; they reflect changes and developments, different ideological climates, the constant interaction of people with various systems around them, and the conditions of the social economy. Practice horizons have been expanded beyond interpersonal transactions by, for example, popular demands for civil and human rights of African Americans, women, and other groups; the rediscovery of poverty in the 1960s; the urban crisis and riots; AIDS; and the popular demand to improve the health care and welfare systems. Social injustice and conditions of social economy pressure social work to expand beyond the realm of the individual and include social policy reform of the environment. By responding to these forces, social work practice theory becomes directly relevant to the real societal arena, linking people with their environment and improving people's social functioning.

To discharge these responsibilities, social policy practice in social work requires more effective investments in knowledge building and research-informed practice (Hopps, 1985). Such investments are likely to increase the profession's practice effectiveness, evaluation capability, and range of interventive methods to meet the challenges of modern society.

REFERENCES

Axinn, J., & Levin, H. (1993). *Social welfare* (3rd ed.). New York: Longman.

Bartlett, H. M. (1958). Toward clarification and improvement of social work practice. *Social Work, 3,* 3–9.

Bisman, C. (1994). *Social work practice.* Monterey, CA: Brooks/Cole.

Briar, K. H., & Briar, S. (1982). Clinical social work and public policies. In M. Mahaffey & J. Hanks (Eds.), *Practical politics: Social work and political responsibility* (pp. 45–54). Silver Spring, MD: National Association of Social Workers.

Copley, W. D., & O'Leary, M. K. (1988). *Public policy skills.* Croton-on-Hudson, NY: Policy Studies Associates.

Dear, R. B., Briar, K. H., & Van Ry, A. (1986, March). *Policy practice: A "new" method coming of age.* Paper presented at the Annual Program Meeting, Council on Social Work Education, Miami, FL.

Dolgoff, R. L. (1981). Clinicians as social policy makers. *Social Casework, 62,* 284–292.

Dye, T. R. (1987). *Understanding public policy.* Englewood Cliffs, NJ: Prentice Hall.

Figueira-McDonough, J. (1993). Policy practice: The neglected side of social work intervention. *Social Work, 38,* 179–188.

Frey, G. A. (1987, March). *Toward a conceptual framework for policy-related social work practice.* Paper presented at the Community Organization and Social Administration Symposium, Council on Social Work Education, St. Louis, MO.

Frey, G. A. (1988). *A framework for policy-related practice.* Unpublished manuscript. School of Social Work, Portland State University, Portland, OR.

Friedman, M., & Friedman, R. (1980). *Free to choose*. San Diego: Harcourt Brace Jovanovich.

Galston, W. A. (1980). *Justice and the human good*. Chicago: University of Chicago Press.

Gilbert, N., & Specht, H. (1987). Social planning in the public sector. In A. Minahan (Ed.-in-Chief), *Encyclopedia of social work* (18th ed., Vol. 2, pp. 602–619). Silver Spring, MD: National Association of Social Workers.

Gilbert, N., Specht, H., & Terrel, P. (1993). *Dimensions of social welfare policy* (3rd ed.). Englewood Cliffs, NJ: Prentice Hall.

Hagen, J. L., & Davis, L. V. (1992). Working with women: Building a policy and practice agenda. *Social Work, 37,* 495–502.

Haynes, K. S., & Mickelson, J. S. (1986). *Affecting change: Social workers in the political arena*. New York: Longman.

Heilbroner, R. (1980). *Marxism: For and against*. New York: W. W. Norton.

Hopps, J. G. (1985). Effectiveness and human worth [Editorial]. *Social Work, 30,* 467.

Iatridis, D. (1983). Neoconservatism reviewed. *Social Work, 28,* 101–107.

Iatridis, D. (1988). New social deficit: Neoconservatism's policy of social underdevelopment. *Social Work, 33,* 11–15.

Iatridis, D. (1994). *Social policy: Institutional context of social development and human services*. Monterey, CA: Brooks/Cole.

Jansson, B. (1984). *Theory and practice of social welfare policy: Analysis, processes, and current issues*. Belmont, CA: Wadsworth.

Jansson, B. (1994). *Social policy: From theory to practice* (2nd ed.). Monterey, CA: Brooks/Cole.

Johnson, L. C. (1989). *Social work practice: A generalist approach* (3rd ed.). Boston: Allyn & Bacon.

Johnson, L. C., & Schwartz, C. L. (1994). *Social welfare* (3rd ed.). Needham Heights, MA: Allyn & Bacon.

Jones, C. (1986). *Patterns of social policy: An introduction to comparative analysis*. London: Tavistock.

Kirst-Ashman, K. K., & Hull, G. H., Jr. (1993). *Understanding generalist practice*. Chicago: Nelson-Hall.

Mayer, R. R. (1985). *Policy and program planning: A developmental perspective*. Englewood Cliffs, NJ: Prentice Hall.

McInnis-Dittrich, K. (1994). *Integrating social welfare policy and social work practice*. Monterey, CA: Brooks/Cole.

National Association of Social Workers. (1994). *NASW code of ethics*. Washington, DC: Author.

Netting, E. F., Kettner, P. M., & McMurtry, S. L. (1993). *Social work macro practice*. New York: Longman.

Neugeboren, B. (1983). *Organization, policy, and practice in the human services*. New York: Longman.

Nozick, R. (1974). *Anarchy, state and utopia*. New York: Basic Books.

Nulman, E. (1983). Family therapy and advocacy: Directions for the future. *Social Work, 28,* 19–22.

Patton, C. V., & Sawicki, D. S. (1986). *Basic methods of policy analysis and planning*. Englewood Cliffs, NJ: Prentice Hall.

Pierce, D. (1984). *Policy for the social work practitioner*. New York: Longman.

Pincus, A., & Minahan, A. (1973). *Social work practice: Models and method*. Itasca, IL: F. E. Peacock.

Rawls, J. (1971). *A theory of justice*. Cambridge, MA: Harvard University Press.

Sheafor, B. W., Horejsi, C., & Horejsi, G. (1991). *Techniques and guidelines for social work practice*. Needham Heights, MA: Allyn & Bacon.

Sheafor, B. W., & Landon, P. C. (1987). Generalist perspective. In A. Minahan (Ed.-in-Chief), *Encyclopedia of Social Work* (18th ed., Vol. 1, pp. 660–669). Silver Spring, MD: National Association of Social Workers.

Sosin, M., & Caulum, S. (1983). Advocacy: A conceptualization for social work practice. *Social Work, 28,* 12–17.

Stokey, E., & Zeckhauser, R. (1978). *A primer for policy analysis*. New York: W. W. Norton.

Trattner, W. I. (1989). *From poor law to welfare state*. New York: Free Press.

Tropman, J. E., Dluhy, M., Lind, R., Vasey, W., & Croxton, T. A. (1976). *Strategic perspectives on social policy*. New York: Pergamon Press.

Wenocur, S., & Reisch, M. (1989). *From charity to enterprise: The development of American social work in a market economy*. Chicago: University of Illinois Press.

Wyers, N. L. (1991). Policy-practice in social work: Models and issues. *Journal of Social Work Education, 27,* 241–250.

FURTHER READING

Hart, A. F. (1989). Teaching policy to the clinical master's student: A historical perspective. *Journal of Teaching in Social Work, 3,* 35–43.

Reamer, F. G. (1993). *The philosophical foundations of social work practice*. New York: Columbia University Press.

Rottman, G. C. (1985). *Philanthropists, therapists, and activists: A century of ideological conflict in social work*. Cambridge, MA: Schenbaum.

Specht, H., & Courtney, M. (1994). *Unfaithful angels: How social work has abandoned its mission*. New York: Free Press.

Ward, G. C., & Middleman, R. R. (1989). *The structural approach to direct practice in social work*. New York: Columbia University Press.

Zastrow, C. (1987). *Understanding human behavior in the social environment*. New York: Macmillan.

Demetrius S. Iatridis, PhD, is professor and chair, Social Policy, Boston College, Graduate School of Social Work, Chestnut Hill, MA 02167.

For further information see

Advocacy; Citizen Participation; Civil Rights; Community; Community Organization; Community Practice Models; Federal and Administrative Rulemaking; Federal Social Legislation from 1961 to 1994; Human Rights; Interdisciplinary and Interorganizational Collaboration; Mass Media; Peace and Social Justice; Policy Analysis; Social Planning; Social Welfare History; Social Work Practice: History and Evolution; Social Workers in Politics; Welfare Employment Programs: Evaluation.

Key Words	
advocacy	social policy
policy practice	social welfare

Politics

See Social Workers in Politics

Poverty

Claudia J. Coulton
Julian Chow

Poverty is generally thought of as material deprivation. However, the operational definition of poverty currently used in the United States is restricted to money income. Poverty is defined by the federal government as a range of income thresholds adjusted for the size of the family, the age of the householder, and the number of children under age 18 in the family. The absolute money-income thresholds are updated yearly on the basis of the Consumer Price Index.

Money income is defined as the sum of gross pre-taxed money; wages and salary; net income from self-employment; any other form of cash income, including interest and dividends; and cash transfer payments, such as pensions, social security, public assistance, and unemployment compensation. Money income does not include capital gains, the value of assets, or any noncash benefits from either private or public sources (U.S. Bureau of the Census, 1992). A given household (family or individual) is considered poor if its money income for a year falls below the threshold.

MEASURE OF POVERTY

It was not until the mid-1960s that the United States developed an "official" measure of poverty, developed by the Social Security Administration in 1964 and revised in 1969 and 1981. When it was created in the 1960s, the poverty measure used the price of the U.S. Department of Agriculture's Economy Food Plan as the base for determining

the amount of income needed for subsistence living. At that time, a typical family spent one-third of its total expenditures on food. Therefore, the poverty line was set at three times the cost of the minimal food budget for the household of a particular size. Since then, the federal government has adapted and the poverty thresholds are updated yearly and adjusted for inflation according to the reported income from the Current Population Survey.

Purposes

A standard measure of poverty serves two purposes. First, it provides a basis for comparing the differences in poverty levels across types of households, age groups, regions, and time (Ruggles, 1990). The poverty measure allows for an understanding of the economic well-being of various groups in the society. Because the comparison is based on a fixed level of income resources, it represents an absolute measure of poverty.

Second, a poverty measure allows policymakers and program developers to target a population and to plan interventions for those who have limited economic resources once they know the income conditions of various groups at a given time and across time. In fact, it was for this programmatic purpose that Orshansky (1965a, 1965b) developed the original concept of the poverty measure.

Limitations

The federal measure of poverty has several limitations. One major limitation is that the arbitrary measure does not take changing patterns of consumption into account. Over the years, the costs of other necessities, such as housing and medical care, have risen more rapidly than the cost of food. As a result, food now accounts for only about one-fifth of an average family budget. If the poverty line were adjusted to reflect this current consumption pattern, the poverty-income thresholds would be approximately 50 percent higher than they are today (Ruggles, 1990; Schwarz & Volgy, 1992).

Another limitation is that the poverty measure focuses narrowly on money income and excludes the value of taxes, capital gains, and noncash benefits from public sources, such as housing assistance and food stamps, and from private sources, such as fringe benefits and health insurance. Since the mid-1980s, the U.S. Bureau of the Census has studied the value of noncash benefits and the effects of taxes on poverty. It found, for example, that when all tax and noncash benefits were taken into account, the poverty rate in 1992 fell from 14.5 percent to 10.4 percent (U.S. Bureau of the Census, 1993a).

An additional limitation of the poverty measure is that it does not adequately reflect the full spectrum of material need. If poverty is interpreted as the situation in which one's minimal needs are not met, then the experience of material hardships, such as poor housing and inadequate medical care, ought to be taken into account as well. Research suggests that the relationship between money income, as used in the official poverty measure, and material hardships is relatively weak; for example, income explained only a small percentage of the variance in material hardships in Mayer and Jencks's (1989) study. What is more important is the lack of basic necessities that determines the experience of being poor.

A final limitation in the current approach to measuring poverty is the failure to consider assets, even when income is low, which may make some poor persons materially better off than they would appear to be on the basis of their income (Sherraden, 1991). Research has shown, however, that assets held by low-income households, particularly those that are in long-term poverty, are so low that they would not affect the overall level of poverty if assets were taken into account (Ruggles, 1990).

Unlike the fixed poverty standard in the United States, European countries often use a relative measure in which poverty is defined as a proportion (for example, less than half) of the nation's median income. A relative standard rises and falls as the overall standard of living shifts and avoids some of the difficulties that a fixed standard encounters as patterns of consumption change.

Income Inequality

A poverty measure should not be confused with a measure of income inequality. Although the poverty measure provides information on the population below certain income thresholds, it does not measure the distribution of income. The Gini-index of income concentration and the proportion of aggregate income received by households in different quintiles are two common measures of income inequality (U.S. Bureau of the Census, 1991b). The income distribution has indeed become more unequal since the 1970s. The share of income received by the highest quintile of households was 46.5 percent in 1991, 44.4 percent in 1981, and 43.5 percent in 1971 (U.S. Bureau of the Census, 1993b). Although poverty has often been the target of public policy in the United States, inequality has received little direct attention from policymakers.

TRENDS IN POVERTY IN THE UNITED STATES

Overall Trends

According to the official governmental poverty figures available since the 1960s, the proportion of the population in poverty has fluctuated from year to year, with the peak in the early 1960s. During the 1970s, the poverty rate declined gradually, reaching a record low of 11.1 percent in 1973. The 1980s marked the rebound of poverty, despite overall economic growth during that period. Since 1989, the number of persons below the official poverty level and the poverty rate have risen consecutively. In 1991, 36.8 million people, representing 14.5 percent of the nation's population, were living below the official poverty level (U.S. Bureau of the Census, 1993c).

Figure 1 presents the trends in poverty for selected years from 1959 to 1992. As can be seen, the poverty rate has tended to rise during recessionary periods (the shaded areas on the figure).

FIGURE 1

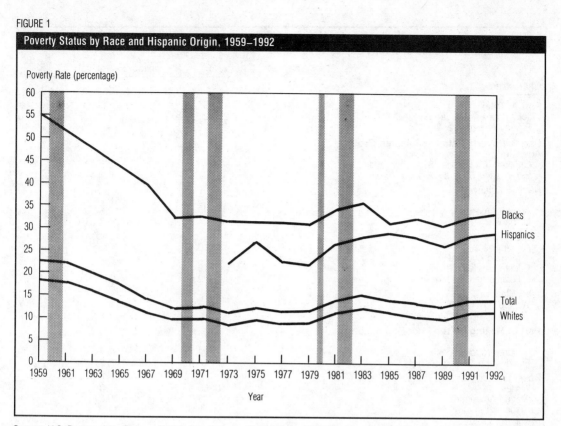

Poverty Status by Race and Hispanic Origin, 1959–1992

SOURCE: U.S. Bureau of the Census. (1993). *Poverty in the United States: 1992*. Washington, DC: U.S. Government Printing Office.
NOTE: The shaded area represents the recessionary period.

However, the experience in the 1980s showed that the poverty rate did not fall to the prerecessionary level. This pattern suggests that the determinants of poverty are structural as well as cyclical (Sawhill, 1988).

Differences across Groups
The chance that individuals will be poor differs markedly across various groups within the population. Table 1, Part B, displays the poverty rates for people in selected categories. Part C indicates the proportion of all poor people who fall into various categories.

Age is an important determinant of poverty status. Children make up a sizable proportion of the population in poverty. In 1992, over 40 percent of the nation's poor were children under 18 years, and more than one-fifth (21.9 percent) of all the nation's children lived in poverty.

Since the mid-1970s, the poverty rate for children has been higher than for other age groups, whereas before that time, elderly (people age 65 and over) had the highest poverty rate of any age group. Elders, however, have benefited from governmental antipoverty programs, such as social

security and Medicare, to the extent that the proportion of elderly people in poverty declined from about one-fourth in 1969 to about one-ninth in 1992 (U.S. Bureau of the Census, 1993a).

Poverty rates also differ among various racial groups. Although the majority of poor people in this country were white in 1992, the poverty rates in most racial minority groups exceeded the rates for whites in that year (see Figure 1). African Americans, with a poverty rate of 33.3 percent, were three times as likely to be poor as were whites, whose poverty rate was 11.6 percent. Persons classified as Hispanic Americans (who may be of any race) had a poverty rate of 29.3 percent, and the rate for Asian Americans was 12.5 percent in 1992 (U.S. Bureau of the Census, 1993c).

The recent trends in poverty have not affected only racial and ethnic groups, however. Since the late 1980s, nonelderly non-Hispanic white people, particularly white families with children, have fallen into poverty at a more rapid rate than have black people (Shapiro, 1992). Family structure also defines subgroups that differ markedly in their poverty rates. Thus, whereas the overall poverty rate for families was 11.7 percent

TABLE 1
Selected Characteristics of Poor People, 1970–1992

Characteristic	United States Total		
	1970	1980	1992
Part A: Total			
Total poor (in thousands)	25,420	29,272	36,880
Poverty rate (percentage)	12.6	13.0	14.5
Part B: Poverty Rates in Selected Groups			
Age Group			
Children (under age 18)	15.1	18.3	21.9
Elderly (age 65 and over)	24.6	15.7	12.9
Race–Ethnicity			
Whites	9.9	10.2	11.6
African Americans	33.5	32.5	33.3
Hispanics[a]	24.3	25.7	29.3
Family Type[b]			
All families	10.1	10.3	11.7
Married couples[c]	5.3	6.2	6.2
Male-headed families[c]	10.7	11.0	15.6
Female-headed families	32.5	32.7	34.9
Work Status:			
Worked[d]	—	6.7	7.0
Worked year-round full-time	—	3.9	2.6
Part C: Making Up the Poor Population			
Age Groups			
Children (under age 18)	41.1	39.4	39.6
Elderly (age 65 and over)	18.9	13.2	10.8
Race–Ethnicity			
Whites	68.8	67.3	66.5
African Americans	29.7	29.3	28.8
Hispanics[a]	8.6	11.9	18.0
Family Type[b]			
Married couples[c]	51.4	48.8	41.7
Male-headed families[c]	3.2	3.4	5.9
Female-headed families	37.1	47.8	52.4
Work Status[e]			
Worked	—	40.6	40.3
Worked year-round full-time	—	8.7	9.2

SOURCES: U.S. Bureau of the Census. (1982). *Characteristics of the population below the poverty level: 1980*. Washington, DC: U.S. Government Printing Office; U.S. Bureau of the Census. (1993c). *Poverty in the United States: 1992*. Washington, DC: U.S. Government Printing Office.
[a]Hispanics may be of any race.
[b]The term *family* refers to a group of two or more related persons who live together.
[c]1973 is the reporting year for data on married couples and male-headed families.
[d]1980 data refer to persons aged 15 and over; 1992 data refer to persons aged 16 and over.
[e]This proportion is based on the number of poor people ages 16 and over.

in 1992, the rate for married-couple families was 6.2 percent (the lowest poverty rate), and the rate for female-headed households was 34.9 percent (the highest). In other words, female-headed families represented the largest proportion (52.4 percent) of all poor families in 1992 (U.S. Bureau of the Census, 1993c).

Poverty has largely been an urban phenomenon because poor people, like most of the U.S. population, tend to live in urban areas. In 1992 the majority (74.2 percent) of poor people resided in metropolitan areas. However, although public attention has often focused on the urban poor, poverty rates are somewhat higher in rural areas. For example, the poverty rate was 13.9 percent in metropolitan areas but 16.8 percent in nonmetro-

politan areas in 1992 (U.S. Bureau of the Census, 1993c). Studies have shown that the metropolitan and rural poor differ somewhat (see, for example, Dudenhefer, 1993). For instance, poor people in rural areas are more likely to work and to be persistently poor than are their urban counterparts.

Work and Poverty
Despite the public view that poor people do not work, a relatively large proportion of them are, indeed, employed. In 1992, for example, 40.3 percent of poor individuals (ages 16 and over) worked, and 9.2 percent worked in year-round full-time jobs (U.S. Bureau of the Census, 1993c). Although the poverty rate among individuals who work has been relatively low (7.0 percent in 1992),

TABLE 2
Working Status of Poor Families in 1992

| | Below Poverty Level | |
Status	Number (in thousands)	Percentage
All family types	7,960	11.7
With no workers	3,268	31.6
With one or more workers	4,692	8.1
One	3,368	17.6
Two or more	1,324	3.4
With year-round full-time workers	1,464	3.2
One	1,339	4.6
Two or more	125	0.7
With part-time workers	3,228	27.9

SOURCE: U.S. Bureau of the Census. (1993c). *Poverty in the United States: 1992*. Washington, DC: U.S. Government Printing Office.

many workers cannot earn enough to keep their families above the poverty threshold.

To keep themselves above the poverty line today, most families need to have more than one member who is employed. Table 2 presents the poverty rates for families, depending on the labor force participation of their members. Families with two full-time workers have the lowest poverty rates.

PERSISTENCE OF POVERTY

Although poverty has typically been viewed as a temporary shortfall of resources, there has been a recurrent concern among policymakers and researchers about the permanence of poverty. The intent is to understand both the extent to which poor people remain poor for an extended period and whether there is an intergenerational pattern of poverty. Most efforts to understand longitudinal aspects of poverty have relied on data from the Panel Study of Income Dynamics (PSID), conducted by the Survey Research Center of the University of Michigan, or the Survey of Income and Program Participation (SIPP), conducted by the U.S. Bureau of the Census.

In its 1992 report on poverty from the Current Population Survey, the U.S. Bureau of the Census (1993c) included the year-to-year transitions into and out of poverty by analyzing the longitudinal data available from the SIPP. On the basis of interviews with people in all seven waves of the 1987 panel over a two-year period (1987 and 1988), the Census Bureau reported that 74.3 percent of those who were poor in 1987 remained poor in 1988. Minority or elderly status, nonmetropolitan residence, a change in family status from married couple to another family type, and a decrease in

the number of workers in the family were the major characteristics of those who could not exit poverty.

It is important to distinguish between two ways of looking at the length of time people spend in poverty: beginning spells of poverty or spells in progress. Studies that have used the PSID to examine a sample of completed spells have found that about 60 percent to 80 percent of the poverty spells last only one year (Gottschalk, McLanahan, & Sandefur, 1992; Ruggles, 1990). However, this finding does not mean that at any given time most poor people will have a short spell.

To address the permanent condition of poverty, it is important to look at spells in progress as well. An analysis of the PSID according to this perspective indicates that although approximately two-fifths of those who become poor in a given year will exit poverty within that year, over half the nonelderly individuals who are poor at any time are in the midst of a spell of poverty lasting more than nine years (Bane & Ellwood, 1986).

Long-term poverty is not evenly distributed among poor people; some are at a higher risk than are others of being persistently poor. The highest rates of persistent poverty have been found among black people (especially black children), members of female-headed households, individuals with low levels of education, and disabled people (Adams, Duncan, & Rogers, 1988; Duncan, Coe, & Hill, 1984; Hill, 1985; Hill, Hill, & Morgan, 1981).

The extent to which poverty persists through generations is not clear. There is some evidence that a slight majority of those who grew up in poor families escaped poverty as adults (Hill, 1985), and across the income spectrum there appear to be only moderate correlations between parents' and children's incomes (Behrman & Taubman, 1990; Solon, 1992). Nevertheless, children who grow up in families that have been poor for a long time have a significantly higher risk of having lower educational levels and lower incomes and of being dependent on welfare as adults than do children from families that never experience poverty or do so only for a short time (Duncan, Hill, & Hoffman, 1988; Duncan & Rogers, 1991; McLanahan, 1985).

MACROSTRUCTURAL FACTORS

Poverty and Labor Market Conditions
A number of forces in the economy have contributed to the increase in poverty since the 1980s and to its concentration among racial and ethnic groups and families with children in inner cities. These forces include a decline in the manufacturing sector; falling real wages; and decreasing labor

force participation, especially among racial and ethnic men of prime working age.

The mix of jobs in the United States has been shifting gradually from those in goods-producing industries to those in the service sector (Harrison & Bluestone, 1988; Murphy & Welch, 1991). The manufacturing sector had traditionally been the location for relatively high-wage work that can be done by workers without higher education. In the service sector, low-skill jobs generally pay low wages, and higher-wage jobs demand training beyond a high school diploma. As manufacturing has declined, low-skill workers have shifted to service industries with lower wages. The magnitude of these effects has been most severe in northern industrial cities with high concentrations of blue-collar workers and neighborhoods that grew around factories as a base of employment (Kasarda, 1989).

Average wages rose steadily after World War II but have been falling since 1973 (Mishel & Frankel, 1991). By 1990 they had fallen nearly 20 percent (Peterson, 1991). Low-skill workers have borne most of the decline in wages. In fact, within industries, the gap in wages between high school and college graduates nearly doubled in the 1980s (Murphy & Welch, 1993, p. 107). This widened gap in wages reflects the overall increase in the demand for high-skill workers and the severe slackening of the demand for those without post-secondary education (Blackburn, Bloom, & Free-man, 1990).

Further evidence of the falling demand for low-skill workers can be seen in the labor force participation of men with low skills. Whereas the unemployment rates of male college graduates stayed the same from the mid-1970s to the end of the 1980s, they more than doubled for men with a high school education or less (Blackburn, Bloom, & Freeman, 1990). For minority men without a high school education, the proportion who were not working more than doubled over the same period, reaching almost 50 percent by the late 1980s (Kasarda, 1989).

Thus, the combination of the loss of blue-collar jobs, falling wages among low-skill workers, and the declining employment of men has contributed to the growth of both the working and the nonworking poor. These powerful economic forces are important factors in explaining the overall growth in the number of poor people in the 1980s. They also help explain why young minority families in urban areas have been most severely affected; the industrial jobs were concentrated in the older central cities of the north-central and northeast regions, workers from racial and ethnic

groups have disproportionately held low-skill jobs, and youths entering the labor market in the 1980s were caught in a time of rapid industrial restructuring.

Poverty and Family Structure

A sizable portion of the increased poverty rates among children since the mid-1970s can be attributed to the increasing proportion of families with children that are headed by women (Mishel & Frankel, 1991; Smith, 1989). The proportion of all families with children headed by women grew from 10 percent in 1970 to 18 percent in 1980 and to 22 percent by 1992 (Rawlings, 1993; U.S. Bureau of the Census, 1992). However, the decline in the average number of children in families across the economic spectrum softened the adverse economic impact of this change in family structure to an important degree (Gottschalk & Danziger, 1993). Poverty rates among children would have risen even more if the typical family size had not decreased over the same period.

Female-headed families with children have extremely high rates of poverty for several reasons. Only about 38 percent of mothers with children under 18 in these families work full-time all year (U.S. Bureau of the Census, 1993c). Even when they do work, women earn hourly wages that are about 66 percent of men's wages (Mishel & Frankel, 1991). Women with children have household duties that often limit the amount of time that they work. Furthermore, child care is expensive; poor working women who head families pay approximately 25 percent of their income for child care (U.S. Bureau of the Census, 1991a), and only about 30 percent of them receive child support from the noncustodial fathers (Garfinkel & McLanahan, 1986).

The female-headed family is disadvantaged economically when compared with the two-parent family because the majority of married women with children work today. Whereas only 26 percent of married women with children worked at least part-time in 1960, by the end of the 1980s, 62 percent did so (Mishel & Frankel, 1991). As wages for low-skill workers have fallen, it has become necessary for a family with relatively low educational attainment to have two breadwinners to earn enough income to stay above the poverty line.

Female-headed families with children are created through divorce and separation, widowhood, and the birth of children to never-married women. Today, growth in the number of female-headed families with children is due largely to unmarried women giving birth, rather than to divorce or the death of a spouse—factors that were predominant in the past. Declining rates of marriage among parents with low educational attainment have been attributed, in part, to the declining employment prospects of men with low skills (Wilson, 1987). In many low-income communities, there is now an undersupply of men with jobs to marry the women who are there (Wilson & Neckerman, 1986). However, economic factors alone cannot explain the rapidly declining rates of marriage that, among African Americans, have fallen at similar rates among white people and among the affluent (Mare & Winship, 1991). For African American couples in particular, a secure economic future, represented by the employment of both mothers and fathers, appears to be a more important prerequisite for marriage than it was in the past (Testa, Astone, Krogh, & Neckerman, 1989).

Racial Discrimination

Racial discrimination has played a role in the higher poverty rates experienced by some groups—notably African Americans and Hispanic Americans—and in the rising level of poverty caused by the failure to invest in and build the human resources of a growing subgroup of the population. The factor that is most directly related to poverty is the discrimination that continues to be a barrier to employment. Studies pairing African American, Latino, and white applicants for entry-level jobs have shown that white applicants are preferred (Cross, Kenney, Mell, & Zimmermann, 1990; Turner, Fix, & Struyk, 1991). Surveys have demonstrated that employers do not consider some groups to be employable and favor young African American men the least (Kirschenman & Neckerman, 1991).

The systematic underinvestment in selected racial or ethnic groups has contributed to the rising level of poverty as these groups have increased as a proportion of the population. The inequality of educational opportunities for people in racial and ethnic groups at the elementary, secondary, and college levels has persisted, despite the growing expenditures for public education in disadvantaged communities (Orfield & Ashkinaze, 1991). Discrimination in housing has also led to the segregation of groups in less desirable locations with fewer resources to support their economic development (Massey & Denton, 1993).

POVERTY, COMMUNITY, AND QUALITY OF LIFE

The urban neighborhoods that house a large number of poor people have received increasing attention since the early 1980s. Particularly in northern industrial cities, a higher portion of poor people now live in neighborhoods in which more than 40 percent of their neighbors are also poor (Coulton & Chow, 1993; Coulton, Pandey, & Chow, 1990; Jargowsky & Bane, 1991). The outmigration of the middle class during the 1970s left only poor people behind, so entire neighborhoods became homogeneously low income (Jargowsky & Bane, 1991). As formerly nonpoor families joined the ranks of the poor in the 1980s because of falling wages and employment, underemployment and unemployment, combined with the continued but slower exodus of the middle class from the cities, created even more impoverished neighborhoods (Coulton et al., 1990). The size of the low-income populations in poor areas also declined (Littman, 1991), but the outmigration of low-income people took place at a slower rate.

Three factors have been linked to the concentration of poverty in inner cities: racial segregation, the suburbanization of jobs, and city–suburban inequality. The highly segregated nature of northern cities (Massey & Denton, 1989) has led to concentrated poverty because racial groups have higher poverty rates, having been hardest hit by changes in the urban labor markets and having been victims of discrimination (Massey, 1990; Massey & Eggers, 1990). This segregation, which persists because of racism and housing discrimination, further disadvantages residents of inner-city poor neighborhoods because of the resulting social and geographic isolation they experience. (Galster, 1992; Massey & Denton, 1993).

The movement of jobs, especially manufacturing jobs, to the suburbs would be expected to place low-skill residents of inner-city neighborhoods at even greater disadvantage than in the past. However, although jobs have clearly been suburbanized, especially in northern industrial cities (Hughes, 1990; Kasarda, 1989), there has been considerable debate about its net impact on low-skill and those in racial and ethnic populations (Jencks & Meyer, 1990). Rosenbaum and Popkin (1991) found that in one city the employment status of inner-city residents who moved to the suburbs improved compared to that of a control group who remained in the inner city. Also, suburban employers often have negative expectations of workers simply because these workers live in inner cities (Kirschenman & Neckerman, 1991). Transportation patterns that run mainly into the central cities rather than across regions limit inner-city workers' access to jobs (Hughes, 1991). Nevertheless, it appears that there is considerable variation among metropolitan areas in the particular mix of suburban jobs and the distance between the jobs and the workers who live in the central cities (Johnson & Oliver, 1991), making it difficult to generalize about the geographic and attitudinal barriers to the employment of inner-city workers in the suburbs.

Ironically, growing disparities between impoverished central cities and affluent suburbs appear to limit economic opportunities not only for poor people, but for the regions in general (Ledebur & Barnes, 1992; Nathan & Adams, 1989; Rusk, 1993). Just as the 1970s saw an increasing concentration of poverty, the 1980s saw an increasing concentration of affluence at the outskirts of many metropolitan areas. More and more people began living in homogeneous enclaves at one extreme or the other of the economic spectrum (Coulton & Chow, 1993), raising concerns about the growing economic divide in this society (Reich, 1991).

EFFECTS OF IMPOVERISHED COMMUNITIES

The publication of *The Truly Disadvantaged* (Wilson, 1987) touched off a debate and lines of research that have altered the thinking about poverty in recent years. Wilson argued that macrostructural forces, including deindustrialization and suburbanization, had transformed poor inner-city neighborhoods into isolated enclaves. These communities fostered further poverty because they were cut off from mainstream influences, such as information about jobs, health, and resources, and because they contained few role models for success. Institutions that had previously provided avenues out of poverty, for example, churches and schools, had crumbled through disinvestment and the lack of leadership. Behaviors that are inconsistent with economic success, such as dropping out of school and teenage pregnancy, had become the norm.

This provocative argument, which was made more controversial by its revival of the term *underclass,* had several effects. For one, it reactivated the discussion of the behavior and attitudes of poor people that before its publication had been equated with blaming the victim (Jencks, 1992; Katz, 1993). But it now placed this discussion within the context of structural and community change.

Another result was the stimulation of research to determine how and why conditions had changed in poor communities and whether living in such communities indeed had negative effects on the residents. This research, which is still in progress, ranges from ethnographic studies of individual communities (see, for example, Anderson, 1991) to tests of epidemiological models of behavioral transmission (Crane, 1991). Although conditions have worsened in many poor communi-

ties, the processes are still not well understood. There is beginning evidence that living in concentrated poverty puts families and children at risk of a variety of undesirable outcomes (Coulton, Korbin, Su, & Chow, 1993), but it has been difficult to disentangle the effects of neighborhoods from individual and family differences (Jencks & Mayer, 1990; Tienda, 1991).

APPROACHES TO ALLEVIATING POVERTY

Although poverty means that a household has too few material resources to meet its needs, many strategies for reducing poverty are aimed at the fundamental causes of this situation, rather than being restricted to the provision of direct material supports. This section presents an overview of the various types of antipoverty approaches.

Income and Material Support

Means-tested and universal income-transfer programs, such as Aid to Families with Dependent Children (AFDC) and social security benefits, have an antipoverty effect in that they move some families whose pretransfer income was below the poverty line to a point at or above the poverty threshold. In recent years, the antipoverty effects of transfers for the elderly have been much larger than have those for families with children partly because of the failure of public assistance payments to keep up with inflation (Danziger, Haveman, & Plotnick, 1986; Lav, Lazere, Greenstein, & Gold, 1992).

The tax system is also used, to some degree, to reduce poverty. The earned-income tax credit (EITC) is the most notable example of this approach. With the EITC, families whose income is below a designated level receive a payment that supplements their low wages. Although this program has achieved only a modest reduction in poverty among working poor people (Ellwood, 1988), its expansion is part of the current effort to "make work pay."

In recent years attention has turned to the potential role of income support from noncustodial parents in reducing poverty and dependence on welfare among families with children. Although many states' child support initiatives focus on the AFDC population (Garfinkel, 1992), better enforcement of child support can also reduce poverty among the working poor.

Labor Market Strategies

Because not working or working for low wages is the most direct cause of poverty in families with young children and individuals of prime working age, both the supply of labor and the demand for labor have been the targets of antipoverty strategies. On the supply side are all the many and varied programs that address the skills, attitudes, knowledge, and limitations of low-income people with respect to work. Beginning with the Work Incentive (WIN) program in 1967 and including the Job Opportunities and Basic Skills Training Program (JOBS) of the Family Support Act of 1988, these types of training and job placement programs have moved many of the participants out of poverty, although other participants have left welfare but earned poverty-level wages (Gueron & Pauly, 1991). Yet the overall antipoverty impact of such programs is limited by the small number of participants relative to the large number of working and welfare poor in the states (Hagen & Lurie, 1992).

Although the industrial restructuring of the past two decades has led to a rapid decline in the number of available low-skill jobs, antipoverty programs have done little to increase the demand for labor. Public service employment, which was a cornerstone of the New Deal of the 1930s, has been controversial in recent years (Levitan & Gallo, 1992). Today, public service employment is a minor portion of what are generally thought of as training programs, such as the Job Corps and the Job Training and Partnership Act (JTPA), and is typically viewed as work experience, rather than public works (Bassi & Ashenfelter, 1986). Efforts to create new employment opportunities for poor workers in the private sector are gaining increasing attention, though. Usually implemented as community–business partnerships or entrepreneurial support programs, they operate on a small scale at the neighborhood or municipal level.

Early Intervention

The recognition that poor children suffer a variety of disadvantages that put them at risk of becoming poor adults has led to the development of various early intervention programs that have an antipoverty focus. Among the best known of these are birth-to-school projects, compensatory education programs, and two-generation programs.

Birth-to-school programs target children from birth to school age and may include outreach, developmental assessment, parenting education, at-home and preschool developmental programs, parent-to-parent networks, and a variety of other components. There is as yet little uniformity among these efforts, which are operated by states, counties, local agencies, and neighborhood groups. Evaluations are just beginning to show some positive effects on child development, but the long-term, antipoverty effects will be difficult to determine (Weiss & Jacobs, 1988).

Compensatory education programs have attempted to raise poor children's educational attainment by providing special funds to public schools. As with the birth-to-school projects, researchers have not been able to link the modest gains in outcomes for children to reductions in poverty (Glazer, 1986).

Two-generation programs are a recent development that explicitly ties early intervention to support child development with employment training for parents who are poor (Smith, Blank, & Collins, 1992). These programs integrate public programs that are intended for children, such as the Early and Periodic Screening, Diagnosis and Treatment Program and Head Start, with human-resource-development programs for adults, such as JOBS and JTPA.

Community-Building Initiatives

As evidence that conditions in poor communities may themselves be a barrier to reducing poverty mounts, attention has turned to the antipoverty effects of community-building strategies. Community-building projects are generally tailored to individual neighborhoods or subsections of a municipality. These projects have several common elements, although all the elements are not present to the same degree (*Building Strong Communities,* 1992). The Atlanta Project, the Dudley Street Neighborhood Initiative in Boston, and the Community Building Partnership in the Sandtown–Winchester area of Baltimore are well-known examples of such projects.

Leadership for community building usually comes from partnerships both within the neighborhood and with external stakeholders and resources. Many projects have been stimulated by an external resource, such as a foundation or governmental agency, but have quickly been taken over by local residents as workers and decision makers.

Community-building initiatives are comprehensive in their view of what must be changed to restore poor communities to a level of functioning that can support healthy and self-sufficient families. Thus, economic development, human resource development, housing, family support, health care, and education are all targeted for investment or reform.

These initiatives rest on a foundation of local institutions, organizations, and individuals whose assets are used to their fullest and are complemented by the introduction of new resources and skills. Collaboration, coordination, and integration are key elements. Because an identified area and population are the focus, existing programs can be monitored to see how they can work together better to achieve common goals.

Community-building initiatives have already succeeded in improving some of the conditions in poor neighborhoods. Whether they will also be able to decrease poverty in these neighborhoods remains to be seen.

ROLES FOR SOCIAL WORKERS

Social workers were historically the predominant profession working with and on behalf of poor people. When public assistance was combined with social services, most recipients received social work services along with financial support. Today the role of social workers with respect to poverty is not as pervasive or well defined. Although many of the clients of mental health, family service, and child welfare agencies are indeed poor, alleviating poverty is not typically the focus of social work practice within these settings. New conceptions of social work roles are needed given the complexity, growing persistence, and geographic concentration of poverty.

One role that deserves increased attention is community development. Community development requires skills in community analysis, social planning, community organizing, and social action, all within the traditional repertoire of social work practice. Moreover, community development requires the ability to foster economic opportunities for area residents through work on industrial retention, local business development, job training, and placement. Social workers with these skills and experience can fill an important function within community development where professionals are needed to help rebuild poor communities.

Another role for social work is community practice. Poverty involves a complex set of interactions between personal characteristics and a community's resources and opportunities. Community practice combines work with individuals and families with community work. The focus becomes enhancing resources and opportunities along with personal capacities to take advantage of these. As individuals develop so do communities, and the two become mutually reinforcing. This is an emerging role for social work and a type of practice that is responsive to our current understanding of poverty as a community phenomenon.

REFERENCES

Adams, T., Duncan, G., & Rogers, W. (1988). *Persistent urban poverty: Prevalence, correlates and trends.* Ann Arbor, MI: Survey Research Center.

Anderson, E. (1991). Neighborhood effects on teenage pregnancy. In C. Jencks & P. E. Peterson (Eds.), *The urban underclass* (pp. 375–398). Washington, DC: Brookings Institution.

Bane, M., & Ellwood, D. (1986). Slipping into and out of poverty: The dynamics of spells. *Journal of Human Resources, 21,* 1–23.

Bassi, L. J., & Ashenfelter, O. (1986). The effect of direct job creation and training programs on low-skilled workers. In S. H. Danziger & D. H. Weinberg (Eds.), *Fighting poverty: What works and what doesn't* (pp. 133–151). Cambridge, MA: Harvard University Press.

Behrman, J., & Taubman, P. (1990). The intergenerational correlation between children's adult earnings and their parents' income: Results from the Michigan panel survey of income dynamics. *Review of Income and Wealth, 36*(2), 115–127.

Blackburn, M. L., Bloom, D. E., & Freeman, R. B. (1990). The declining economic position of less skilled American men. In G. Burtless (Ed.), *A future of lousy jobs: The changing structure of U.S. wages* (pp. 31–76). Washington, DC: Brookings Institution.

Building strong communities: Strategies for urban change. (1992, May). Report of a conference sponsored by the Annie E. Casey, Ford, and Rockefeller Foundations, Cleveland.

Coulton, C., & Chow, J. (1993). *Concentration of poverty and affluence.* Cleveland: Case Western Reserve University, Center for Urban Poverty and Social Change.

Coulton, C., Korbin, J., Su, M., & Chow, T. (1993). *Community level factors and child maltreatment rates.* Cleveland, OH: Case Western Reserve University, Center for Urban Poverty and Social Change.

Coulton, C., Pandey, S., & Chow, J. (1990). Concentration of poverty and the changing ecology of low-income, urban neighborhoods: An analysis of the Cleveland area. *Social Work Research & Abstracts, 26*(4), 5–16.

Crane, J. (1991). Effects of neighborhoods on dropping out of school and teenage childbearing. In C. Jencks & P. E. Peterson (Eds.), *The urban underclass* (pp. 299–320). Washington, DC: Brookings Institution.

Cross, H., Kenney, G., Mell, J., & Zimmermann, W. (1990). *Employer hiring practices: Differential treatment of Hispanic and Anglo job seekers.* Lanham, MD: University Press of America.

Danziger, S. H., Haveman, R. H., & Plotnick, R. D. (1986). Antipoverty policy: Effects on the poor and the nonpoor. In S. H. Danziger & D. H. Weinberg (Eds.), *Fighting poverty: What works and what doesn't* (pp. 50–77). Cambridge, MA: Harvard University Press.

Dudenhefer, P. (1993). Poverty in the rural U.S. *Focus, 15*(1), 37–46.

Duncan, G., Coe, R., & Hill, M. (1984). The dynamics of poverty. In G. Duncan (Ed.), *Years of poverty, years of plenty* (pp. 33–70). Ann Arbor: University of Michigan, Institute for Social Research.

Duncan, G., Hill, M., & Hoffman, S. (1988). Welfare dependence within and across generations. *Science, 239,* 467–471.

Duncan, G., & Rogers, W. (1991). Has children's poverty become more persistent? *American Sociological Review, 56,* 538–550.

Ellwood, D. T. (1988). *Poor support: Poverty in the American family.* New York: Basic Books.

Family Support Act of 1988. P.L. 100-485, 102 Stat. 2343.

Galster, G. (1992). Housing discrimination and urban poverty of African-Americans. *Journal of Housing Research, 2,* 87–122.

Garfinkel, I. (1992). *Assuring child support: An extension of social security.* New York: Russell Sage Foundation.

Garfinkel, I., & McLanahan, S. S. (1986). *Single mothers and their children: A new American dilemma.* Washington, DC: Urban Institute Press.

Glazer, N. (1986). Education and training programs and poverty. In S. H. Danziger & D. H. Weinberg (Eds.), *Fighting poverty: What works and what doesn't* (pp. 152–179). Cambridge, MA: Harvard University Press.

Gottschalk, P., & Danziger, S. (1993). Family structure, family size, and family income: Accounting for changes in the economic well-being of children, 1968–1986. In S. Danziger & P. Gottschalk (Eds.), *Uneven tides: Rising inequality in America* (pp. 167–193). New York: Russell Sage Foundation.

Gottschalk, P., McLanahan, S., & Sandefur, G. (1992, May 28–30). *The dynamics and intergenerational transmission of poverty and welfare participation.* Paper presented at the conference on Poverty and Public Policy, Madison, WI.

Gueron, J. M., & Pauly, E. (1991). *From welfare to work.* New York: Russell Sage Foundation.

Hagen, J. L., & Lurie, I. (1992). How 10 states implemented JOBS: A study looks at states' choices during the initial stages. *Public Welfare, 50,* 13–21, 56.

Harrison, B., & Bluestone, B. (1988). *The great U-turn: Corporate restructuring in and the polarizing of America.* New York: Basic Books.

Hill, M. (1985). The changing nature of poverty. *The Annals, 479,* 31–47.

Hill, M., Hill, D., & Morgan, J. (Eds.). (1981). *Five thousand American families.* Ann Arbor: University of Michigan, Institute for Social Research.

Hughes, M. A. (1990). Formation of the impacted ghetto: Evidence from large metropolitan areas, 1970–1980. *Urban Geography, 11,* 265–284.

Hughes, M. A. (1991). Employment decentralization and accessibility. *Journal of the American Planning Association, 57,* 288–298.

Jargowsky, P. A., & Bane, M. (1991). Ghetto poverty in the United States, 1970–1980. In C. Jencks & P. E. Peterson (Eds.), *The urban underclass* (pp. 235–273). Washington, DC: Brookings Institution.

Jencks, C. (1992). *Rethinking social policy: Race, poverty, and the underclass.* Cambridge, MA: Harvard University Press.

Jencks, C., & Mayer, S. E. (1990). The social consequences of growing up in a poor neighborhood. In L. E. Lynn & M. G. H. McGeary (Eds.), *Inner-city poverty in the United States* (pp. 111–186). Washington, DC: National Academy Press.

Johnson, J. H., & Oliver, M. L. (1991). *Empowering community based organizations serving concentrated poverty areas in Los Angeles.* Los Angeles: University of California, Center for the Study of Urban Poverty.

Kasarda, J. D. (1989). Urban industrial transition and the underclass. *Annals of the American Academy, 501,* 26–47.

Katz, M. B. (1993). The urban "underclass" as a metaphor of social transformation. In M. B. Katz (Ed.), *The*

"underclass" debate: Views from history (pp. 3–23). Princeton, NJ: Princeton University Press.

Kirschenman, J., & Neckerman, K. M. (1991). "We'd love to hire them, but ...": The meaning of race for employers. In C. Jencks & P. E. Peterson (Eds.), *The urban underclass* (pp. 203–233). Washington, DC: Brookings Institution.

Lav, I., Lazere, E., Greenstein, R., & Gold, S. D. (1992). *The states and the poor: Budget decisions hurt low income people in 1992.* Washington, DC: Center on Budget and Policy Priorities.

Ledebur, L. C., & Barnes, W. R. (1992). *Metropolitan disparities and economic growth: City distress and the need for a federal local growth package.* Washington, DC: National League of Cities.

Levitan, S. A., & Gallo, F. (1992). *Spending to save: Expanding employment opportunities.* Washington, DC: George Washington University, Center for Social Policy Studies.

Littman, M. S. (1991, March). Poverty areas and the "underclass": Untangling the web. *Monthly Labor Review, 114,* 19–32.

Mare, R. D., & Winship, C. (1991). *Socioeconomic change and the decline of marriage for blacks and whites.* Madison: University of Wisconsin, Institute for Research on Poverty.

Massey, D. S. (1990). American apartheid: Segregation and the making of the underclass. *American Journal of Sociology, 96,* 329–357.

Massey, D. S., & Denton, N. A. (1989). Hypersegregation in U.S. metropolitan areas: Black and Hispanic segregation along five dimensions. *Demography, 26,* 373–391.

Massey, D. S., & Denton, N. A. (1993). *American apartheid: Segregation and the making of the underclass.* Cambridge, MA: Harvard University Press.

Massey, D. S., & Eggers, M. L. (1990). The ecology of inequality: Minorities and the concentration of poverty, 1970–1980. *American Journal of Sociology, 95,* 1153–1188.

Mayer, S., & Jencks, C. (1989). Poverty and the distribution of material hardship. *Journal of Human Resources, 24,* 88–113.

McLanahan, S. (1985). Family structure and the reproduction of poverty. *American Journal of Sociology, 90,* 873–901.

Mishel, L., & Frankel, D. M. (1991). *The state of working America.* Armonk, NY: M. E. Sharpe.

Murphy, K. M., & Welch, F. (1991). The role of international trade in wage differentials. In M. H. Kosters (Eds.), *Workers and their wages: Changing patterns in the United States* (pp. 39–76). Washington, DC: American Enterprise Institute Press.

Murphy, K. M., & Welch, F. (1993). Industrial change and the rising importance of skill. In S. Danziger & P. Gottschalk (Eds.), *Uneven tides: Rising inequality in America* (pp. 101–132). New York: Russell Sage Foundaton.

Nathan, R. P., & Adams, C. F. (1989). Four perspectives on urban hardship. *Political Science Quarterly, 104,* 483–508.

Orfield, G., & Ashkinaze, C. (1991). *The closing door: Conservative policy and black opportunity.* Chicago: University of Chicago Press.

Orshansky, M. (1965a, January). Counting the poor: Another look at the poverty profile. *Social Security Bulletin, 28,* 3–29.

Orshansky, M. (1965b). Measuring poverty. In *Social Welfare Forum, 1965* (pp. 211–223). New York: Columbia University Press.

Peterson, W. C. (1991). The silent depression. *Challenge, 34*(4), 29–34.

Rawlings, S. W. (1993). *Household and family characteristics: March 1992.* Washington, DC: U.S. Government Printing Office.

Reich, R. B. (1991). *The work of nations: Preparing ourselves for the 21st century.* New York: Alfred A. Knopf.

Rosenbaum, J. E., & Popkin, S. J. (1991). Employment and earnings of low-income blacks who move to middle-class suburbs. In C. Jencks & P. E. Peterson (Eds.), *The urban underclass* (pp. 342–356). Washington, DC: Brookings Institute.

Ruggles, P. (1990). *Drawing the line.* Washington, DC: Urban Institute.

Rusk, D. (1993). *Cities without suburbs.* Baltimore: Johns Hopkins University Press.

Sawhill, I. (1988). Poverty in the U.S.: Why is it so persistent? *Journal of Economic Literature, 26,* 1073–1119.

Schwarz, J., & Volgy, T. (1992). *The forgotten Americans.* New York: W. W. Norton.

Shapiro, I. (1992). *White poverty in America.* Washington, DC: Center on Budget and Policy Priorities.

Sherraden, M. (1991). *Assets and the poor: A new American welfare policy.* Armonk, NY: M. E. Sharpe.

Smith, J. P. (1989). Children among the poor. *Demography, 26,* 235–248.

Smith, S., Blank, S., & Collins, R. (1992). *Pathways to self-sufficiency for two generations: Designing welfare-to-work programs that strengthen families and benefit children.* New York: Foundation for Child Development.

Solon, G. (1992). Intergenerational income mobility in the United States. *American Economic Review, 82,* 393–408.

Testa, M., Astone, N. M., Krogh, M., & Neckerman, K. M. (1989). Employment and marriage among inner-city fathers. *Annals, 501,* 79–91.

Tienda, M. (1991). Poor people and poor places: Deciphering neighborhood effects on poverty outcomes. In J. Huber (Ed.), *Macro-micro linkages in sociology* (pp. 244–262). Newbury Park, CA: Sage Publications.

Turner, M., Fix, M., & Struyk, R. (1991). *Opportunities denied, opportunities diminished.* Lanham, MD: University Press of America.

U.S. Bureau of the Census. (1982). *Characteristics of the population below the poverty level: 1980.* Washington, DC: U.S. Government Printing Office.

U.S. Bureau of the Census. (1991a). *Population profile of the United States: 1991.* Washington, DC: U.S. Government Printing Office.

U.S. Bureau of the Census. (1991b). *Trends in relative income: 1964 to 1989.* Washington, DC: U.S. Government Printing Office.

U.S. Bureau of the Census. (1992). *Statistical abstract of the United States: 1992* (112th ed.). Washington, DC: U.S. Government Printing Office.

U.S. Bureau of the Census. (1993a). *Measuring the effect of benefits and taxes on income and poverty: 1992.* Washington, DC: U.S. Government Printing Office.

U.S. Bureau of the Census. (1993b). *Population profile of the United States: 1993.* Washington, DC: U.S. Government Printing Office.

U.S. Bureau of the Census. (1993c). *Poverty in the United States: 1992.* Washington, DC: U.S. Government Printing Office.

Weiss, H. B., & Jacobs, F. H. (1988). *Evaluating family programs.* New York: Aldine De Gruyter.

Wilson, W. J. (1987). *The truly disadvantaged: The inner city, the underclass, and public policy.* Chicago: University of Chicago Press.

Wilson, W. J., & Neckerman, K. M. (1986). Poverty and family structure: The widening gap between evidence and public policy issues. In S. H. Danziger & D. H. Weinberg (Eds.), *Fighting poverty: What works and what doesn't* (pp. 232–259). Cambridge, MA: Harvard University Press.

FURTHER READING

Cottingham, P., & Ellwood, D. (Eds.). (1989). *Welfare policy for the 1990s.* Cambridge, MA: Harvard University Press.

Jencks, C., & Peterson, P. (Eds.). (1991). *The urban underclass.* Washington, DC: Brookings Institution.

Peterson, P., & Rom, M. (1990). *Welfare magnets: A new case for a national standard.* Washington, DC: Brookings Institution.

Wilson, W. J. (Ed.). (1993). *The ghetto underclass: Social science perspectives.* Newbury Park, CA: Sage Publications.

Claudia J. Coulton, PhD, LISW, ACSW, is professor, Mandel School of Applied Social Sciences, Case Western Reserve University, 10900 Euclid Avenue, Cleveland, OH 44106. **Julian Chow, PhD, LISW,** is assistant director, Center for Urban Poverty and Social Change, Case Western Reserve University, 10900 Euclid Avenue, Cleveland, OH 44106.

For further information see

Aid to Families with Dependent Children; Childhood; Community Needs Assessment; Families Overview; Families: Demographic Shifts; Employment and Unemployment Measurement; Federal Social Legislation from 1961 to 1994; Homelessness; Housing; Hunger, Nutrition, and Food Programs; Income Distribution; Income Security Overview; Jobs and Earnings; JOBS Program; Mutual Aid Societies; Primary Prevention Overview; Public Social Services; Rural Poverty; Sectarian Agencies; Social Security; Social Welfare History; Welfare Employment Programs: Evaluation; Women Overview.

Key Words

income inequality	unemployment
income maintenance	welfare
minority groups	

Pray, Kenneth

See Biographies section, Volume 3

Prevention and Wellness
Neil Bracht

Since the 1980s a plethora of innovative community-based health promotion and disease prevention programs have been successfully implemented both nationally and internationally (Bracht, 1990). The health promotion and wellness movement is expanding, affecting thousands of people and influencing social environments and lifestyles. The rapid proliferation of no-smoking policies in public places and work sites is but one example. Although community demonstration projects initially focused on risk factors associated with heart disease, cancer, and stroke, newer preventive programs and research efforts have been targeted at the complex social–health issues of alcohol and drug abuse (Pentz et al., 1989), teenage pregnancy (Vincent, Clearie, & Schuchter, 1987), acquired immune deficiency syndrome (AIDS) (Leukefeld & Battjes, 1991), and a wide range of interventions to enhance social supports and self-esteem (Gilchrist, Schinke, & Blythe, 1979). This broadened focus offers increased opportunities for social workers and professionals in other behavioral disciplines to collaborate with citizens' and consumers' groups to improve health and to shape policy decisions that will improve people's day-to-day social and work environments.

In 1986 Canada hosted the First International Conference on Health Promotion. The Ottawa Charter, which was developed at the conference, has become a benchmark for developing standards and approaches to health and ecological improvement. The establishment of the Healthy Cities movement in the World Health Organization was a tangible outcome of the Ottawa conference. In the United States, the Year 2000 Health Objectives for the Nation set national goals for promoting and improving the health status of Americans. Healthy Cities programs in the United States are also increasing. Partnership arrangements among governments, foundations, industry, communities, and voluntary citizen and health groups have forged new approaches to community-based programs, services, and research (Badura & Kickbusch, 1991; Thompson, Wallack, Lichtenstein, & Pechacek, 1991; Wallack, 1990).

This emerging health promotion paradigm recognizes the strong relationship between health, lifestyle, and social norms. Although more recent preventive approaches have not abandoned the role and responsibility of individuals in changing their lifestyles, they have emphasized local empowerment and policy changes as opposed to solely behavioral or educational approaches (Jenkins, 1991; Milio, 1980). The wide use of community organization strategies in community-based programs supports community empowerment strategies and recognizes the historical contributions of social work to this field of study and application (Bracht & Kingsbury, 1990). Most of the

large community-based research and demonstration projects from 1970 to 1990 incorporated principles of community organization, emphasizing local agenda setting, interorganizational cooperation, and active citizen involvement (Carlaw, Mittelmark, & Bracht, 1984; Elder et al., 1986; Maccoby & Solomon, 1981; McAllister, Puska, Koskela, Pallonen, & Maccoby, 1980; Puska, Salonen, Tuomilehto, Nissinen, & Kottke, 1983; Stunkard, Felix, Yop, & Cohen, 1985).

Community efforts typically involve the formation of partnerships between communities and sponsoring agencies or foundations in a framework of community organization strategies that lead to eventual community ownership of programs and interventions (Goodman & Steckler, 1989). Health care professionals and related medical or social systems are important resources for facilitating this new health promotion movement, but community empowerment is the emerging approach (Fahlberg, Poulin, Girdano, & Dusek, 1991). Grassroots efforts in advocacy for and protection of children, crime prevention in neighborhoods, and the prevention of violence are important parallel developments in coalition building.

SCIENTIFIC DEVELOPMENT IN DISEASE PREVENTION

Epidemiology provides a perspective on the distribution and determinants of disease and social problems in populations. For example, approximately 80 percent of all deaths, and a higher proportion of preventable deaths in the United States, are attributable to a few conditions (Colvez & Blanchet, 1981). The major causes of mortality, morbidity, and disability are (1) circulatory disease, (2) neoplasms, (3) trauma, (4) respiratory disease, (5) musculoskeletal disabilities, and (6) mental illness. Therefore, it is not surprising that these conditions take up the largest share of U.S. medical costs. Data from the National Health Survey and social security analyses support the impact of these six conditions (Colvez & Blanchet, 1981). Common risk factors are associated with many of these conditions. Preventive programs that are aimed at modifying dietary or smoking habits may decrease the risk of several kinds of illnesses (heart disease, hypertension, and cancer). Likewise, attempts to prevent drug and alcohol abuse by teenagers will have a related impact on trauma, mental illness, and possibly future heart disease.

Milio (1980) identified eight specific risk factors (cigarette smoking, air pollution, dietary excesses, dietary deficits, hazardous work sites, alcohol abuse, non-medical drug abuse, and hypertension) that she estimated contribute to 33 percent of acute illnesses, 36 percent of acute disabilities, and 65 percent of chronic illnesses. Today, one must include the great additional burden to individuals and families of deaths related to AIDS, as well as the alarming increase in the deaths of teenagers and adults from gun-related homicides and drunk driving.

The notion of clustering risk factors is fundamental to the development of population-based intervention strategies. Broad public health intervention programs, rather than programs aimed only at high-risk groups, may be both more effective and more cost-efficient. Community multisectoral approaches (integrating preventive activities, such as smoking cessation, with a person's work site, church, and recreational or educational organizations) have been shown to be effective in a wide variety of studies (Shea & Basch, 1985). The European and North American Healthy Cities projects emphasize multisectoral approaches, along with considerations of social equity. Calls for the modification of the formal medical, public health, and allied health care curricula to produce health care practitioners who are oriented toward prevention, as well as toward treatment, and toward the whole person and his or her psychology are increasingly being heard.

Chronic diseases, including heart disease, cancer, diabetes, obesity, sexually transmitted diseases, emphysema, hypertension, liver ailments, and mental illness, represent the social epidemics of advanced industrial societies. These diseases,

which have some genetic predisposition, are clearly susceptible to the control of risk factors that are substantially behavioral and social in origin (Bellock & Breslow, 1972). New and recurring infectious diseases, such as AIDS and other sexually transmitted diseases, tuberculosis, and measles, add to the growing burden of chronic disease. Several large-scale experiments at the community level, as well as numerous individual clinical studies, are providing evidence that lifestyles can be altered, risk factors can be reduced, and environments can be protected (Farquhar et al., 1985; Shea & Basch, 1985). School-based health education programs, when combined with community-wide interventions, have been effective in reducing the onset of cigarette smoking (Perry, Kelder, Murray, & Klepp, 1992) and alcohol and drug use (Pentz et al., 1989; Wagenaar & Wolfson, 1993).

National health education campaigns are increasing people's awareness of the importance of reducing risks to health. Americans are exercising more and are changing their diet to lower their blood cholesterol level. If lung cancer in both men and women could be reduced, there would most likely be a decline in the overall death rates from cancer or at least a leveling off. It is now widely believed that many cancers are caused by factors that are primarily behavioral (for example, smoking, overall diet, heavy alcohol consumption, and excessive exposure to the sun).

Although scientific discussion and debate naturally continue on the interpretation of recent clinical and preventive studies, many public health officials are moving to expand programs to accelerate health promotion and to prevent illness. Current projects sponsored by the National Cancer Institute's Office of Cancer Prevention have targeted thousands of citizens around the country. The American Stop Smoking Trial (ASSIST), an expansion of the Community Intervention Trial for Smoking Cessation and described by Thompson et al. (1991), is being conducted in 17 states and focuses on advocacy of a change in policy to control smoking.

Parallel with scientific breakthroughs in epidemiological and biomedical arenas has been the substantial progress in social and behavioral science research related to successful methods for changing lifestyles, reducing stress, and educating people about the risk of disease (Hamburg, Elliott, & Parron, 1982; Jessor, 1984; Kobasa, Maddi, & Puccetti, 1982). Social workers have become more active in prevention work and have contributed to this expanding knowledge base (Bracht, 1990; Coulton, 1978). Meyer (1984) suggested that it is time to apply social work knowledge, values, and skills to an epidemiological orientation.

COMMUNITYWIDE HEALTH PROMOTION PROGRAMS

Green (1990) summarized recent national and international developments in health promotion. Earlier, Wittman (1978) illustrated how preventive epidemiological approaches could be applied to mental health problems. Kemper and Mettler (1990) applied the community approach to a population of elderly people in Idaho. Kane (1985) discussed the wider health policy issues and contributions that challenge social workers. Coordinated efforts focused on the total population may provide the best opportunities for the kind of societal changes required to promote the public's health. Brody (1983) noted that these studies, unlike previous costly ones that concentrated on persons already at high risk of cardiovascular disease, are relatively inexpensive efforts that promote communitywide prevention by creating an awareness of heart healthy living habits and increasing the opportunities to pursue these habits. In these studies, special task forces staffed by influential people devise the programs that help individuals improve their eating and exercise habits.

Cooperative Models

Communitywide programs require the active involvement of citizens in health and rely on proved strategies of community analysis (Bracht, 1988) and citizen participation. Health education efforts are promoted through sophisticated communications and media channels and are conducted through locally based neighborhoods, groups, and organizations. Such approaches offer models for the long-term ownership and incorporation of health promotion efforts by the public (Winett, King, & Altman, 1989). A significant advantage of a communitywide approach is the ability to reinforce changes in individual lifestyles through organized community support programs and environmental changes. In the Minnesota Heart Health Program (Mittelmark, 1986), some local restaurants in the three communities participating in the study provided "hearted" menu items that supported dietary changes started in the home; this practice is now common in many restaurants in these communities. In addition, grocery stores used colored labels to indicate low-salt foods, and church groups sponsored "exercise Sundays," when parishioners were urged to walk or ride bikes to church. (Lassater, 1991, described other church-sponsored health projects.)

Also, special health education curricula were developed for school-age children, and industry groups combined their resources to promote physical exercise and no-smoking policies throughout their community. These multiple support networks increased the public's awareness of health and demonstrated the community's competence in promoting health and coordinating preventive programs. Five years after the withdrawal of federal funds from the Minnesota Heart Health Program, 14 of the original 25 intervention programs were still being sponsored by the three communities involved in the study. This empowerment factor is central to citizen participation models described by Bracht and Tsouros (1990).

An original model of cooperation by citizens and professionals was tested in Finland during the North Karelia heart disease prevention study. At the time of the study (the 1970s), Finland had one of the highest rates of heart attack in the world. Reporting on the changes that occurred during 10 years of a community intervention program, Puska et al. (1983) reported that the program effectively reduced the population mean values of the major risk factors for coronary heart disease. The 10-year follow-up for people age 30 to 50 showed that among the men and the women, respectively, the estimated reductions were 25 percent and 14 percent for smoking, 3 percent and 1 percent for mean concentrations of serum cholesterol, 3 percent and 5 percent for mean systolic blood pressure, and 1 percent and 2 percent for mean diastolic blood pressure. Similar positive results have been found in studies of heart disease in Stanford, California (Farquhar et al., 1985), and Pawtucket, Rhode Island (Elder et al., 1986).

Workplace Programs

Although individuals must assume the ultimate responsibility for their health, positive changes in lifestyles to promote wellness require support from and changes in policies in the workplace and social settings. Concern over burnout and other psychosocial stressors has led to research on effective preventive psychological techniques. An experiment conducted at one manufacturing firm (Peters, 1977) examined the effects of daily relaxation breaks on five self-reported measures of health performance and well-being. For 12 weeks, 126 office workers voluntarily filled out daily records and reported biweekly for daily additional measurements. After four weeks of baseline monitoring, the subjects were randomly divided into three groups. Group A was taught techniques for producing a relaxation response, Group B was instructed to sit quietly, and Group C received no instruction. Groups A and B were asked to take two 15-minute relaxation breaks daily. After eight weeks, it was found that the greatest improvement on every index occurred in Group A. The investigation demonstrated that it is feasible for office workers to incorporate relaxation breaks into their daily routine and that doing so may be associated with improvement in their perceptions of their health and in self-satisfaction. In another study (Blair, Smith, & Collingwood, 1984) a random sample of 170 teachers in three public schools and one control school, who participated in a 10-week health-promotion program that emphasized exercise, stress management, and nutrition, increased their participation in vigorous exercise, improved their physical fitness, lost weight, and lowered their blood pressure. The teachers reported a higher level of general well-being and were better able to handle the stress of their job.

Organized approaches through the workplace, although effective in most instances, are deficient in that they reach only people who are employed and typically only those employed by larger corporations that can afford the initial investment in promoting health. As was suggested earlier, communitywide programs may be the most comprehensive approach to effecting improvements throughout the population and to reaching underserved and underemployed groups. Bracht (1990) discussed the applications of health promotion programs for special populations, such as black and Hispanic people.

Organization-Sponsored Programs
Many institutions and organizations in the community conduct or sponsor health promotion programs. Weisbrod (1991) described the status of health promotion programs in a survey of four midwestern cities. As Table 1 shows, a variety of institutional sectors sponsor such programs: church groups (Lassater, 1991), schools (Perry et al., 1992), and work sites (Sorenson, 1990), as well as public health departments and some hospital and health care centers. The National Cancer Institute's ASSIST project, in a seven-year intervention study (1992–1998) in partnership with the American Cancer Society, contracts with 17 state health departments to reduce cigarette smoking. Typically, health promotion programs deal with a wide range of areas: exercise; nutrition; smoking cessation; education about and screening for heart disease or cancer; personal, home, and driver safety; weight management; alcohol and drug abuse; stress management; and AIDS education. Although exercise and smoking-cessation programs are the most popular, there are also many

TABLE 1
Primary Sponsorship of Health-Promotion Programs, by Community Sector, Four Midwestern Cities, 1986–1987

Sponsor	Number	Percentage
Government units	161	7
Medical organizations	232	10
Schools	564	23
Nonprofit organizations	208	9
Commercial health-promotion organizations	179	7
Churches	79	3
Work sites	980	41
Total	2,403	100

SOURCE: Weisbrod, R. (1991). Current status of health promotion activities in four midwest cities. *Public Health Reports, 106*, 310–318.

programs for stress management and drug or alcohol abuse that often involve social workers. R. Black (1984) saw considerable potential for the involvement of social workers in this expanding field:

> Social work must strive to redirect health policy and programs toward a true emphasis on health promotion and disease prevention in the community.... At the level of clinical services it is critical that social workers become actively involved in those programs directed toward educating people about the potential threats to health that accompany certain choices in behavior and lifestyle. (pp. 91, 92)

NEW CHALLENGES FOR SOCIAL WORKERS
The need for health and social service professionals to engage in collaborative campaigns of public health awareness has never been more apparent or more of a challenge. Smoking and behaviors related to drug abuse remain a critical focus of health-promotion efforts, as does AIDS education. Weick (1984) carefully analyzed the pitfalls involved in attempts to emphasize only an individual's responsibility for changing his or her lifestyle.

Cigarette Smoking
In the area of smoking, for example, high priority must be given to advocacy projects to offset targeted marketing (for example, to young men and women and to black people) by the tobacco industry. Although many Americans have stopped smoking, the absolute number of smokers has increased, as has the proportion of heavy smokers among those who smoke. Young women are smoking more and, if pregnant, are putting their fetuses at a higher risk of low birthweight.

A study of health beliefs and smoking patterns in heart patients and their wives is instructive (Croog & Richards, 1977). Men who survived heart attacks stopped smoking at a very high rate and held steady in this respect for eight or nine years, depending on when they were interviewed in this longitudinal study. Their brush with death and the advice of their physicians apparently conspired to bring about behavioral change and greatly increased their survival rates. However, their wives showed no change in their smoking behavior, despite the life-threatening heart attacks their husbands had suffered. With social workers' focus on family dynamics, educational strategies aimed at other family members could add to social work's important role in the health field. For social workers, the U.S. Environmental Protection Agency's 1993 report on the dangers of passive smoking provides new opportunities to discuss smoking risks with pregnant women and related family members. Human services agencies and staff should take the lead in enforcing no-smoking policies at their work sites.

Professional/Community Partnerships

Communitywide health campaigns require the active involvement of health professionals with citizen groups and community organizations. Such professional–community partnerships (Bracht & Gleason, 1990) provide rich opportunities for the special community organization and group work skills of social workers. Historically, social workers have been concerned with the broader aspects of health and social betterment (wellness). Jane Addams hired the first woman graduate of Johns Hopkins Medical School to come to Chicago's steaming tenements in 1893 to open the country's initial well-baby and pediatric clinic, and the Cincinnati Social Experiment (a neighborhood health center) was originally conceived and carried out by a group of social workers who stressed neighborhood and environmental health (Bracht, 1978). As Rosen (1974), the public health historian, noted "the roots of social medicine are to be found in organized social work. It was here that medicine and social science found a common ground for action in the prevention of tuberculosis, securing better housing and work conditions" (p. 113). Social work skills and resources were an important part of the battle to conquer the infectious diseases that decimated earlier generations.

However, even though those early experiments in prevention were important models for action, there was no rigorous scientific measurement of benefits, as there is today, nor was there the expanded range of new media and policy interventions that have been found to be effective.

Education and Epidemiology

Today, several schools of social work (at Columbia University, the University of Minnesota, and the University of Pittsburgh, for example) offer dual-degree programs that provide training in both social work and public health. Such graduate programs prepare professionals for the challenges of what Terris (1983) called the "second epidemiological revolution"—the fight against chronic diseases. Most chronic diseases are related to social and lifestyle factors, requiring interdisciplinary approaches for solution. The recognition that social support (Schafer, 1981) is an important preventive tool has particular significance for current social work practice. Specialized training in preventive techniques and epidemiological approaches are critical if preventive programs that are aimed at such communitywide problems as drug abuse, child and spouse abuse, and the increasing rate of teenage pregnancies are to succeed. The use of coalition-building skills and strategies in implementing communitywide demonstration projects (Bracht & Gleason, 1990; Dluhy, 1990; Feighery, Rogers, & Bracht, 1990; Mizrahi & Rosenthal, 1992) will continue to be social workers' important contribution to health promotion efforts.

In addition, social workers can effectively use counseling skills to help individuals change unhealthy habits. A national study of some 1,200 social workers in Cancer Care (Faibair, 1984) found that group counseling was prevalent: Thirty percent of the social workers were conducting groups for stress reduction and relaxation, 29 percent were leading active education groups, and 14 percent were facilitating self-support groups. This focus on group and educational efforts is a good starting point for a greater focus on epidemiology and education. As Faibair stated:

Our social work role is rapidly developing in a medical field where the information from science is also shifting, at times bursting or exploding with new possibilities for prevention and control of disease. Historically, early interventions with cancer patients sought to utilize and integrate mental health theory, focusing on the individual in analytically oriented clinical work. Today's current work increasingly flows from an understanding of the natural history of the disease process and of the importance of social support systems, and from research results and assessment of patient concerns. From public health concepts we have learned that using the planning process has had the effect of larger numbers of patient viewpoints influencing the direction of interventions chosen for implementation. Although our feet are firmly planted in social case work process, adding the patient's viewpoint is moving many of us towards incorporating adaption of innovations from other fields such as educational or behavioral techniques. (p. 11)

Other Functions

The traditional functions of social workers in prevention and community health work are still important. For example, participation with other team members in case finding and planning outreach services to clients in maternal and child health programs, family planning programs, suicide-prevention programs in schools, and programs to prevent physical and sexual abuse in families are critical areas of preventive work. Social workers continue to lead health discussion groups and to organize self-support groups for patients to promote better health and the empowerment of clients. They should also continue to function in advocacy roles with community health groups to establish policies to protect the environment and to improve people's access to services.

FUTURE PROSPECTS FOR SOCIAL WORKERS

What are some implications for social work practice in the areas of prevention? First, professionals need to be alert to pitfalls in the current enthusiasm over changing people's lifestyles. Continuing efforts to blame only victims for deleterious health behaviors are a ploy for doing nothing. Strong social reforms must accompany individual or group actions (for example, the enormous expenditures for cigarette advertising cannot be ignored). Second, social workers need to guard against the excursions or manipulations of the government into the private lives and habits of citizens (Faden, 1987).

Efforts to promote health and to prevent disease must be seen in the light of other larger health care reforms. For example, the encouraging increases in prevention activities discussed here are inconsistent with the shockingly large number of people who have no access to health care because they have no insurance or have limited health insurance benefits. Furthermore, the minimal preventive efforts are eroded because of the preoccupation with cost containment that denies or limits basic benefits for primary mental health care. In addition, investments in social welfare programs, such as Head Start and job retraining, must be expanded in efforts to improve health and mental health because education and income are two of the most critical determinants of health status (U.S. Public Health Service, 1988).

Academic preparation for health promotion work will require professional schools to move

aggressively to increase their faculties' expertise in both behavioral strategies to modify lifestyles and community-policy strategies. Selected field practicum opportunities for community education and organizing should be developed further. A number of health promotion guides and tools for assessing community programs are available to assist professional and lay leaders (see, for example, Linney & Wandersman, 1991); the Stanford Health Promotion Resource in Palo Alto, California, distributes one of the most comprehensive arrays of materials. In addition, the Centers for Disease Control use PATCH (Planned Approach to Community Health) (Green & Kreuter, 1992). Several coalition-building guides (T. Black, 1983; Feighery et al., 1990; Mizrahi & Rosenthal, 1992; Roberts-DeGennaro, 1987) and *The Community Collaboration Manual* of the National Assembly of Health and Social Welfare Organizations (1991) are also useful.

Concepts of organized community action to promote health and to prevent disease have a long tradition in public health and social work practice. Early efforts to control tuberculosis and other infectious diseases through citizen and community involvement have been reported in the literature (Bracht, 1978). Today the contributions of behavioral epidemiology, biomedical research, and alternative forms of healing are clarifying the relationship between lifestyle risk factors and the development of disease. The approach to community intervention is becoming increasingly interdisciplinary. As Dubos (1980) noted, "The health field is no longer the monopoly of the medical professions; it requires the services of all sorts of other skills. Collaboration will become increasingly urgent as the community demands steps be taken not only to treat its diseases, but also to protect its health" (p. 43).

Improved applications of community organization theory and methods are contributing to the generally successful community interventions reported nationally and internationally. At the core of these community approaches is a process of community engagement and participation that is used to facilitate and support the interventions. The community itself (in partnership with professionals) becomes the agent of change for improved health. Social workers traditionally have been concerned with the social aspect of illness and have facilitated community groups to exercise their own problem-solving skills to maximize health. This focus on helping to equip people to become active partners in the management of their own health affairs is a continuing priority.

REFERENCES

Badura, B., & Kickbusch, I. (1991). *Health promotion research: Towards a new social epidemiology* (World Health Organization Regional Publications, European Series #37). Copenhagen: World Health Organization.

Bellock, N., & Breslow, L. (1972). The relationship of physical health status and health practices. *Preventive Medicine, 1,* 409–421.

Black, R. (1984). Looking ahead: Social work as a core health profession. *Health & Social Work, 9,* 85–95.

Black, T. (1983). Coalition building—Some suggestions. *Child Welfare, 62,* 263–268.

Blair, J., Smith, M., & Collingwood, T. (1984). Health promotion for educators: Impact on health behaviors, satisfaction and general well being. *American Journal of Public Health, 74,* 147–151.

Bracht, N. (1978). Public health social work. In N. Bracht (Ed.), *Social work in health care: A guide to professional practice* (pp. 243–260). New York: Haworth Press.

Bracht, N. (1988). Use of community analysis methods in community programs. *Scandinavian Journal of Health Care, 1,* 23–30.

Bracht, N. (1990). Applications to special populations—Case studies. In N. Bracht (Ed.), *Health promotion at the community level* (pp. 253–256). Newbury Park, CA: Sage Publications.

Bracht, N., & Gleason, J. (1990). Strategies and structures for citizen partnerships. In N. Bracht (Ed.), *Health promotion at the community level* (pp. 109–124). Newbury Park, CA: Sage Publications.

Bracht, N., & Kingsbury, L. (1990). Community organization principles in health promotion: A five-phase model. In N. Bracht (Ed.), *Health promotion at the community level* (pp. 66–88). Newbury Park, CA: Sage Publications.

Bracht, N., & Tsouros, A. (1990). Principles and strategies of effective community participation. *Health Promotion International, 5,* 199–208.

Brody, J. (1983, September 6). Whole cities organize to fight heart disease. *New York Times,* p. 22.

Carlaw, R., Mittelmark, M., & Bracht, N. (1984). Organization for a community cardiovascular health program: Experiences from the Minnesota Heart Health Program. *Health Education Quarterly, 11,* 243–252.

Colvez, A., & Blanchet, M. (1981). Disability trends in the United States population. *American Journal of Public Health, 71,* 464–471.

Coulton, C. (1978). Factors related to preventive health behavior: Implication for social work intervention. *Social Work in Health Care 3,* 297–310.

Croog, S., & Richards, S. (1977). Health beliefs and smoking patterns in heart patients and their wives. *American Journal of Public Health, 66,* 921–930.

Dluhy, M. (1990). *Building coalitions in the human services: Guidelines for Practice.* Newbury Park, CA: Sage Publications.

Dubos, R. (1980). *Man adapting.* New Haven, CT: Yale University Press.

Elder, J. P., McGraw, S. A., Abrams, D. B., Ferreira, A., Lasater, T. M., Longpre, H., Peterson, G. S., Schwartfeger, R., & Carleton, R. A. (1986). Organization and community approaches to community-wide prevention of heart disease: The first two years of the Pawtucket Health Program. *Preventive Medicine, 15,* 107–117.

Faden, R. (1987). Ethical issues in government-sponsored public health campaigns. *Health Education Quarterly, 14*(1), 27–37.

Fahlberg, L. L., Poulin, A. L., Girdano, D. A., & Dusek, D. E. (1991). Empowerment as an emerging approach in health education. *Journal of Health Education, 22,* 185–193.

Faibair, P. (1984, March). Trends in social work interventions. In *Proceedings: National conference on practice, education, and research in oncology social work* (pp. 10–11). American Cancer Society, New York.

Farquhar, J., Fortmann, S., Maccoby, N., Haskell, W., Williams, P., Flora, J., Taylor, C. B., Brown, B. W., Solomon, D. S., & Hulley, S. (1985). The Stanford Five-City project: Design and methods. *American Journal of Epidemiology, 122,* 323–334.

Feighery, E., Rogers, T., & Bracht, N. (1990). *Building and maintaining effective coalitions* (How-To Guide on Community Health Promotion, No. 12). Palo Alto, CA: Stanford Health Promotion Resource Center.

Gilchrist, L. P., Schinke, S., & Blythe, B. (1979). Primary prevention services for children and youth. *Children and Youth Services Review, 1,* 379–391.

Goodman, R. M., & Steckler, A. (1989). A model for the institutionalization of health promotion programs. *Family and Community Health, 11,* 63–78.

Green, L. (1990). Contemporary developments in health promotion. In N. Bracht (Ed.), *Health promotion at the community level* (pp. 29–44). Newbury Park, CA: Sage Publications.

Green, L. W., & Kreuter, M. W. (1992). CDC's planned approach to community health as an application of PRECEED and an inspiration for PROCEED. *Health Education, 23,* 140–144.

Hamburg, D., Elliott, G., & Parron, D. (1982). *Health and behavior: Frontiers of research in the biobehavioral sciences.* Washington, DC: National Academy Press.

Jenkins, S. (1991). Community wellness: A group empowerment model for rural America. *Journal of Health Care for the Poor, 1,* 388–404.

Jessor, R. (1984). Adolescent development and behavioral health. In J. D. Matarazzo, S. M. Weiss, J. A. Herd, & N. E. Miller (Eds.), *Behavioral health: A handbook of health enhancement and disease prevention* (pp. 69–90). New York: John Wiley & Sons.

Kane, R. (1985). Health policy and social workers in health, past, present and future. *Health & Social Work, 10,* 258–270.

Kemper, D., & Mettler, M. (1990). Building a positive image of aging: The experience of a small American city. In N. Bracht (Ed.), *Health promotion at the community level* (pp. 304–314). Newbury Park, CA: Sage Publications.

Kobasa, S. C., Maddi, S. R., & Puccetti, M. C. (1982). Personality and exercise as buffers in the stress–illness relationship. *Journal of Behavioral Medicine, 5,* 391–404.

Lassater, T. (1991). Religious organizations and large-scale health and related lifestyle change programs. *Journal of Health Education, 22,* 233–239.

Leukefeld, C., & Battjes, R. (1991). Preventing the spread of HIV [Special issue]. *Journal of Primary Prevention, 12,* 3–7.

Linney, J. A., & Wandersman, A. (1991). *Prevention Plus, III. Assisting alcohol and other drug prevention programs at the school and community level: A four-step guide to useful program assessment.* Rockville, MD: U.S. Department of Health and Human Services, Office for Substance Abuse Prevention.

Maccoby, N., & Solomon, D. S. (1981). Heart disease prevention: Community studies. In R. Rice & W. Paisley (Eds.), *Public communication campaigns* (pp. 105–126). Beverly Hills, CA: Sage Publications.

McAllister, A., Puska, P., Koskela, K., Pallonen, U., & Maccoby, N. (1980). Psychology in action: Mass communication and community organization for public health education. *American Psychologist, 35,* 375–379.

Meyer, C. (1984). Perils and promise of the health practice domain. *Social Work in Health Care, 10,* 3–11.

Milio, N. (1980). *Promoting health through public policy.* Philadelphia: F. A. Davis.

Mittelmark, M. (1986). Community-wide prevention of cardiovascular disease: Education strategies of the Minnesota Heart Health Program. *Preventive Medicine, 15,* 1–17.

Mizrahi, T., & Rosenthal, B. (1992). Managing dynamic tensions in social change coalitions. In T. Mizrahi & J. Morrison (Eds.), *Community organization and social administration: Advances, trends, and emerging principles* (pp. 11–25). Haworth Press.

National Assembly of National Health and Social Welfare Organizations. (1991). *The community collaboration manual.* Washington, DC: Author.

Pentz, M. A., Dwyer, J. H., MacKinnon, D. P., Flay, B. R., Hansen, W. B., Wang, E.Y.I., & Johnson, C. A. (1989). A multi-community trial for primary prevention of adolescent drug abuse: Effects on drug use prevalence. *Journal of the American Medical Association, 261,* 3259–3266.

Perry, C. L., Kelder, S. H., Murray, D. M., & Klepp, K. (1992). Community wide smoking prevention: Long-term outcomes of the Minnesota Heart Health Program and the Class of 1989 Study. *American Journal of Public Health, 82,* 1210–1216.

Peters, R. (1977). Daily relaxation response breaks in a working population. I and II: Effects on self-reported measures of health, performance and well-being. *American Journal of Public Health, 67,* 946–959.

Puska, P., Salonen, J. T., Tuomilehto, J., Nissinen, A., & Kottke, T. E. (1983). Evaluating community-based preventive cardiovascular programs: Problems and experiences from the North Karelia project. *Journal of Community Health, 9,* 49–63.

Roberts-DeGennaro, M. (1987). Patterns of exchange relationships in building a coalition. *Administration in Social Work, 11,* 59–67.

Rosen, G. (1974). *Medical police to social medicine.* New York: Science History Publications.

Schafer, C., (1981). The health related function of social support. *Journal of Behavioral Medicine, 4,* 281.

Shea, S., & Basch, C. (1985). A review of five major community-based cardiovascular disease prevention programs (Part 1). *American Journal of Health Promotion, 4,* 203–211.

Sorenson, G. (1990). Involving worksites and other organizations. In N. Bracht (Ed.), *Health promotion at the community level* (pp. 158–180). Newbury Park, CA: Sage Publications.

Stunkard, A., Felix, M., Yop, P., & Cohen, R. Y. (1985). Mobilizing a community to promote health: The Pennsylvania County Health Improvement Program (CHIP). In J. Rosen & L. Solomon (Eds.), *Prevention in health psychology* (pp. 143–190). Hanover, NH: University Press of New England.

Terris, M. (1983). A cost-effective national health program. *Journal of Public Health Policy, 5,* 233.

Thompson, B., Wallack, L., Lichtenstein, E., & Pechacek, T. (1991). Principles of community organization and partnership for smoking cessation in the Community Intervention Trial for Smoking Cessation (COMMIT). *International Quarterly of Community Health Education, 11,* 187–203.

U.S. Environmental Protection Agency. (1993). *Respiratory health effects of passive smoking, lung cancer, and other disorders.* Washington, DC: U.S. Government Printing Office.

U.S. Public Health Service, Office of Health Promotion. (1988). *Disease prevention and health promotion: The facts.* Washington, DC: U.S. Government Printing Office.

Vincent, M., Clearie, A., & Schuchter, M. (1987). Reducing adolescent pregnancy through school-based education. *Journal of the American Medical Association, 257,* 3382–3386.

Wagenaar, A. C., & Wolfson, M. (1993). Trade-offs between science and practice in the design of a randomized community trial. In T. K. Greenfield & R. Zimmerman (Eds.), *Community action projects: New research in the prevention of alcohol and other drug problems* (pp. 119–127). Washington, DC: U.S. Department of Health and Human Services.

Wallack, L. (1990). Improving health promotion: Media advocacy and social marketing approaches. In C. Atkin & L. Wallack (Eds.), *Mass communication and public health: Complexities and conflicts* (pp. 147–163). Newbury Park, CA: Sage Publications.

Weick, A. (1984). The concept of responsibility in a health model of social work. *Social Work in Health Care, 10,* 13–26.

Weisbrod, R. (1991). Current status of health promotion activities in four midwest cities. *Public Health Reports, 106,* 310–318.

Winett, R. A., King, A. C., & Altman, D. G. (1989). *Health psychology and public health: An integrative approach.* New York: Pergamon Press.

Wittman, M. (1978). Application of knowledge about prevention to health and mental health practice. In N. Bracht (Ed.), *Social work practice in health care* (pp. 201–210). New York: Haworth Press.

Neil Bracht, MSW, MPH, is professor, University of Minnesota, School of Social Work and School of Public Health, 224 Church Street, SE, Minneapolis, MN 55455.

For further information see

Alcohol Abuse; Citizen Participation; Drug Abuse; Employee Assistance Programs; Health Services Systems

Policy; International and Comparative Social Welfare; Managed Care; Maternal and Child Health; Natural Helping Networks; Occupational Social Work; Organizations: Context for Social Services Delivery; Primary Prevention Overview; Public Health Services; Self-Help Groups; Social Planning; Social Welfare Policy; Substance Abuse: Direct Practice.

Key Words

health behavior   prevention
health promotion

Primary Health Care

Julianne S. Oktay

Primary health care—care that is comprehensive, coordinated, accessible, accountable, and continuous (Institute of Medicine, 1978)—is one of the three sectors into which health care services are divided: primary, secondary, and tertiary. Primary care is distinguished from secondary and tertiary care in that it deals with common problems that are treated in community settings and includes prevention. Primary care is often referred to as "first-contact care" because patients have direct access to primary care providers, unlike specialized care, for which they often have to obtain referrals. It is sometimes said that from the physician's point of view, in primary care the patients stay the same while the problems change, whereas in specialized care, the problems stay the same while the patients change.

Primary health care received increased attention throughout the world when the International Conference on Primary Health Care of the World Health Organization (WHO, 1978) identified it as the key to attaining health care for all people by the year 2000. The assembly encouraged member countries to move away from centralized, specialist facilities and toward family- and community-based care provided by nonspecialized general health providers; emphasized the promotion of health, the prevention of disease, and the integration of mental and physical health services; and advocated a holistic approach that includes the physical, mental, and social aspects of health. In addition, it adopted the following definition of primary care:

Essential health care based on practical, scientifically sound and socially acceptable methods and technology made universally accessible to individuals and families in the community by means acceptable to them and at a cost that the community and the country can afford to maintain at every stage of their development in a spirit of self-reliance and self-determination. . . . It is the first level of contact of individuals, the family and the community with the national health system, bringing health care as close as possible to where people live and work and constitutes the first element of a continuing health care process. (WHO, 1978, p. 25)

In the United States, primary health care services are provided in a wide variety of settings, such as physicians' offices, health maintenance organizations, public health clinics, and community health centers. Primary care physicians in the United States are family practitioners (formerly called "general practitioners"); specialists in internal medicine (often called "internists"); pediatricians; and, in some classifications, obstetricians–gynecologists. New types of health practitioners, such as nurse practitioners and physicians' assistants, also provide primary care services. In many poor urban neighborhoods, emergency rooms of hospitals have become major providers of primary care because the residents do not have access to traditional forms of primary care.

Primary care is a much more central component of health care in many countries than it is in the United States. In developing countries, where specialists are prohibitively expensive, a concept called "community-oriented primary care," or COPC, is gaining popularity. Although most primary care in the United States is provided on a one-on-one basis to individual patients, in COPC, the community is seen as the patient, community health needs are defined with epidemiological methods, and programs are developed for the benefit of entire communities. COPC physicians often live in the community, where they integrate clinical and population-based methods (Institute of Medicine, 1982).

HISTORICAL PERSPECTIVES

In the early years of medicine in the United States, primary care practitioners provided the majority of health care. Many of the current specialty areas were developed in the 1930s, and by 1950 more than 15 boards were certifying specialists. The proportion of generalist physicians fell from 75 percent in 1935 to 45 percent in 1957. By the 1960s some health planners began to recognize that there was an imbalance between the health care needs of the population and the types of medical providers being trained (Rogers, 1973). Although most health problems could be well cared for by primary care practitioners, most physicians were going into specialized areas. At that time, initiatives were undertaken to increase the number of primary care providers, including the creation of a board specialty in family practice in 1969. In the 1970s, federal assistance was provided to support the training of primary care providers. In addition, the National Health Service Corps Revitalization Amendments (P.L. 101-597) provided scholarships and loans for medical education and required recipients to serve in primary care centers after graduation.

In the same period, the federal government provided support to primary care health care in underserved areas, particularly inner cities (neighborhood health centers, community health centers, health maintenance organizations) and rural areas (migrant health centers, Appalachian health services, and area health education centers). Other federal funding of primary care programs was provided through maternal and child health services, and later through homeless health care programs. In the 1980s, federal funds to recruit primary care physicians dropped significantly, as did federal funding for primary care services for underserved people. Grants to family practice residencies fell 25 percent between 1980 and 1988, so that by the late 1980s less than 30 percent of medical school seniors were selecting primary care residencies (Institute of Medicine, 1989). Today, despite the Council of Graduate Medical Education's goal that half the nation's medical providers should be in primary care, most medical students still specialize (Adler, Boyce, Chesney, Folkman, & Syme, 1993). One major obstacle to the increase in the number of primary care physicians is that the salaries of specialists continue to be about double those of primary care physicians. Primary care physicians also complain about their long working hours, lack of respect in the medical community, and the growing population of chronically ill, aged patients. President Clinton's 1994 health care proposal included incentives for medical schools to train more primary care physicians.

PRIMARY HEALTH CARE SETTINGS

Few health care settings in the United States provide true primary care, although many use the term to describe their services. Most first-contact settings do not provide care that is comprehensive, coordinated, and continuous. The settings that come closest to the primary health care model, such as health maintenance organizations, family medicine residencies, maternal and child health programs, and community health centers, are in the minority. The health care delivery system is changing rapidly and may be changed further if health care reform is instituted.

Major Settings

Health maintenance organizations. Health maintenance organizations (HMOs) are prepaid plans that combine health insurance and the delivery of health care services. Members (or employers or both) pay a fixed monthly payment and receive a wide range of health services, including primary care. The first HMOs—Kaiser Permanente in California and Health Insurance Plan in New York—were started in the 1950s. HMOs did not serve a substantial portion of the U.S. population until the 1970s, when they began to expand rapidly. By 1990 their growth had slowed considerably, as other models of care, such as preferred provider organizations, became more widely available. In 1992 about 15 percent of the U.S. population was enrolled in more than 500 HMOs, and 21 states had more than 10 HMOs (Gold, 1991). Because HMOs have an incentive to keep people healthy and to avoid high-cost services, they often emphasize preventive services and primary care.

Federally funded primary care settings. Community health centers, migrant health centers, and homeless health care programs are designed to serve people in medically underserved regions and communities, such as rural areas and inner cities. They are staffed mainly by physicians who are paying back obligations for loans and scholarships under the National Health Services Corps Act.

Community and migrant health centers began in 1962 with a small program for migrant farm laborers. Shortly thereafter, two neighborhood health centers were established, one in rural Mississippi and one in a housing project in Boston. In 1964, health centers were established as part of the Economic Opportunity Act (P.L. 88-452) to offer comprehensive health care and to promote economic development in their communities. In 1975 the economic development goal was dropped, and funding for community and migrant health centers was placed under the Public Health Service Act (P.L. 99-660). In 1990, 547 community, migrant, and homeless health centers were serving 6 million people, or about one-quarter of the nation's medically indigent (National Association of Community Health Centers, 1993; Zuvedas, 1990).

Other government funded primary care programs are funded through the Maternal and Child Health Block Grant programs, which provide such services as prenatal care, adolescent pregnancy programs, and genetics services. State and local public health departments also provide primary care services, including pre- and postnatal services, well-child care, immunization programs, and screening programs. Although these programs do not usually offer comprehensive services, they are often part of broader primary care programs.

Family medicine residencies. Family medicine has been defined as "the field of study that emphasizes the provision of comprehensive health care for people of both sexes and all ages, continuously over time and in the context of their personal social support groups in the communities where they live" (Parkerson, 1982, p. 107). Residency programs in family medicine often provide primary health care services in addition to training physicians. Family medicine evolved from general practice and became a board-certified specialty in 1969. Training is provided in pediatrics, internal medicine, and obstetrics–gynecology. Family medicine specialists are also trained in the psychosocial aspects of health care, especially aspects relating to families, and social workers often have important roles in providing this training (Grooper, 1992; Hess, 1985; Zayas, 1992).

Other Settings

Outpatient departments. Outpatient services have historically been provided only at teaching hospitals or hospitals in inner cities. However, ever since Medicare adopted the system of diagnosis-related groups, many hospitals have moved services from inpatient settings to more lucrative outpatient settings. From 1985 to 1990, the proportion of community hospitals with outpatient departments jumped from one-half to more than three-fourths (Weiss & Lonngvist, 1994). Although much of the outpatient care that hospitals provide is not continuous or comprehensive, some outpatient departments are providing primary health care.

Private physicians' offices. Most first-contact care occurs in physicians' offices. Emergency rooms also provide first-contact care for common problems, especially in inner cities where resources are limited and most of the population does not have adequate health insurance. This care does not usually meet the definition of true primary care because it is not comprehensive or continuous.

PSYCHOLOGICAL AND SOCIAL FACTORS

It is increasingly recognized that psychological and social factors are of special importance in primary health care.

Mental Disorders

It has been recognized for some time that only a small proportion of people who suffer from mental disorders are seen in mental health facilities or receive care from mental health practitioners. Community surveys conducted in the 1960s found that the majority of persons with mental disorders did not receive *any* specialized care. Early surveys done of general practices in England and of HMOs in the United States showed that people with mental disorders were more likely to go to their family physicians with such complaints as headaches, backaches, and other generalized somatizations than to mental health centers or providers (Hankin & Oktay, 1979). More recent data from the National Institute of Mental Health Epidemiologic Catchment Area Program (Regier et al., 1993) found that only 6.4 percent of the U.S. population sought mental health services from general medical physicians. Only 28.5 percent of those with a mental health disorder received any services for mental health problems or addictions (Regier et al.). However, 5 percent to 10 percent of the patients in primary care settings have been diagnosed with major depression, and two to three times that many have mild depressive symptoms (Katon & Schulberg, 1992). Data from the Medical Outcomes Study, collected from 11,242 outpatient visits, indicated that patients with depression had worse perceived health and greater bodily pain than did other patients (Wells, Stewart, et al., 1989).

Many people with mental disorders do not get adequate treatment in primary health care settings. Primary care physicians do not recognize mental disorders in many of their patients (Wells, Hays, et al., 1989), and even when they do, the disorders are often not treated (Morlock, 1989). Major barriers to treatment include the practitioners' lack of training in this area, providers' and patients' negative attitudes toward mental health services, and constraints on the way medical care is delivered, such as the short amount of time that primary care practitioners spend with their patients (Hankin & Oktay, 1979).

The high prevalence of patients with some form of depression in primary care settings is due partly to the fact that patients with depression tend to be high users of medical services (Katon, 1987) and partly to the fact that chronic illnesses, such as heart disease and cancer, act as stressors that often lead to depression, anxiety, and other mental health problems. Researchers are beginning to identify interventions, such as health education, meditation, counseling, hypnosis, stress management, cognitive behavior therapy, and groups, that can reduce the prevalence of mental disorders associated with chronic illnesses (Hill, Kelleher, & Shumaker, 1992). The implications of this research for primary health care are important because many patients who have heart disease or cancer are followed on an ongoing basis in a primary health care center.

As attention turns to the prevention of mental disorders (Mrazek & Haggerty, 1994; National Institute of Mental Health Steering Committee on Prevention, 1993), and not just to their treatment, patients in primary health care centers who have chronic illnesses should increasingly be recognized as an at-risk population who can benefit from preventive mental health services. Some research also has shown that people with mental disorders are likely to have social problems. In one study (Clare, 1982), half the patients in a primary care setting who had a mental disorder also had a social problem, such as a marital, housing, or employment problem. These findings have important implications for social work in primary health care.

Prevention and Treatment of Diseases

To the extent that patients who are most at risk for heart disease, cancer, and other chronic illnesses can be identified in the primary health care sector, interventions that improve their lifestyles and psychological health will also be important in preventing physical and psychological morbidity. In the 1980s, great advances were made in the field of immunology, and there was increased recognition of the connection between the mind and the immune system (Locke & Colligan, 1986). Ader (Ader, Felton, & Cohen, 1990), who taught rats to suppress their immune functioning with behavioral conditioning, coined the term *psychoneuroimmunology*.

Research has begun to show how specific psychosocial events directly influence the immune system's ability to protect the body from diseases (Pert, Ruff, Weber, & Herkenham, 1986). For example, spousal caregivers of Alzheimer's disease patients show a decrease in immune function over time (Kiecolt-Glaser & Glaser, 1992). Research has also shown that group support can improve immune functioning in cancer patients (Fawzy et al., 1990, 1993). As a result of this type of research, social work interventions may be increasingly used in programs to prevent and treat diseases (Moyers, 1993).

Physical Illness

Perhaps because of the mind–immune system connection, stress and social support have emerged as important predictors of health problems and have been shown to relate to recovery from illness. There is evidence that social support acts as a buffer to stress, and that because people with strong social support systems are often able to cope with stress better, they are less likely to become ill (Ell, Nishimoto, Mediansky, Mantell, & Hamovitch, 1992).

Chronic disease. The pattern of disease in the United States has changed from mainly infectious, acute diseases to predominantly chronic diseases. As the population of older people rapidly expands, the prevention and management of chronic disease will become a central focus of primary care. The successful treatment of chronic diseases depends largely on patients' compliance with treatment regimens. Common diseases, such as heart disease, hypertension, diabetes, and arthritis, are treated largely with a combination of drugs and behavioral changes like diet, exercise, and smoking cessation. Because most chronic diseases are not curable, patients must learn to manage their diseases over long periods. Unfortunately, rates of compliance with medical regimens in chronic illness are notoriously low (Grilli & Lomas, 1994). Because patients' and their families' beliefs about health, lifestyles, health practices, and cultural patterns all play a role in patients' compliance with treatment, it is important for practitioners to have good communication skills and knowledge of their patients' cultures to encourage patients to comply with treatment and to prevent chronic illness through effective health education.

Cultural and social factors. Different cultures think about health and health care in different ways. Not only do they hold different explanatory models of illness, but they have different expectations about health care and health providers and different value systems (Kleinman, 1988). All types of health behaviors are closely related to these cultural factors. With the rapid growth of minority groups in the population, the United States is fast becoming a multicultural society. In the coming years, the understanding of cultural factors and their contribution to health care will become increasingly important to the delivery of effective health care in this country.

Poverty and marginal social status have long been recognized as important factors in health care. In the United States, the health status of poor people and of racial and ethnic groups lags behind that of the rest of the country (Adler,

Boyce, Chesney, Folkman, & Syme, 1993; Pappas, Queen, Hadden, & Fisher, 1993). Mortality and morbidity in these groups are higher than those of the total population, partly because poor people face more stressors and partly because they are less likely to receive adequate health care services, including preventive care (U.S. Public Health Service, 1991).

SOCIAL WORK IN PRIMARY HEALTH CARE

Social work has a long history in primary health care. In 1905 the physician and educator Dr. Richard C. Cabot included social workers as home visitors in his clinic at Massachusetts General Hospital and, in effect, started the first social work department in a U.S. hospital. In 1916 social workers were integrated into child welfare centers, and the Social Security Act of 1935 brought social workers into primary care programs nationally through the Maternal and Child Health and Crippled Children's programs. In the 1960s and 1970s, social workers were part of the community and neighborhood health centers that were sponsored by the antipoverty programs. Social workers were mandated staff at the first federal HMOs and in the early family medicine residency programs. As social work departments expanded in hospitals in the 1970s and 1980s, they began to provide services in outpatient programs and emergency rooms. In the late 1980s the Division of Maternal and Child Health of the U.S. Department of Health and Human Services began to support the training of social workers in public health concepts (Henk, 1989). The National Institute of Mental Health has been working with the new Institute for the Advancement of Social Work Research (sponsored by NASW, the Council on Social Work Education, and other social work education groups) to encourage research on social work in primary health settings to prevent and treat mental disorders.

Role of Social Work

It has often been pointed out that social work has an important contribution to make to primary health care. Morton (1985) stated that

> social workers know better than any other health discipline the impact of social conditions on the health status of mothers and children. They are familiar with the policies and legislation regarding social welfare systems and agencies. They should use this knowledge to effect social change and not abdicate this responsibility to other disciplines. (p. 48)

Public health and social work have highly compatible worldviews. Both have broad, multicausal frameworks; both focus on the community, as

well as on the individual; and both recognize the importance of prevention (Siefert, 1986). Descriptions of the role of social workers in both public health activities and primary care often emphasize the community organization and administration components of the role and discuss such activities as assessing health needs in the community; administering programs; planning and evaluating health services; participating in primary prevention campaigns, such as basic health education, smoking prevention, education about acquired immunodeficiency syndrome (AIDS), and drug abuse prevention; developing public policy statements; and advocating for the health needs of the community (Miller, 1987; Morton, 1985). However, most social workers in primary care are in direct service roles, providing counseling and acting as liaisons to community services (Greene & Kulper, 1990; Oktay, 1984). Many social workers in primary care work with patients who are anxious or depressed (Azzarto, 1993; Diamond, Detweiller, & Noce, 1987; Huxley & Fitzpatrick, 1985; Shannon, 1989; Strain, Pincus, Gise, & Houpt, 1986). Social workers in family practice residencies also have an important role in the education of physicians (Grooper, 1992; Hess, 1985; Zayas, 1992). Social workers in one inner-city primary care program ran groups for low-income minority patients to decrease inappropriate use of medical resources (Dobrof, Umpierre, Rocha, & Silverton, 1990).

Training and Use of Social Workers

Training. Little attention has been paid to training social workers to practice in primary health care settings, despite efforts to educate them in public health concepts, with an emphasis on maternal and child health (Gitterman, Black, & Stein, 1985). Although health specializations are widespread in social work education, surveys of their content show little public health content (Black, 1985; Caroff & Mailick, 1985). Some social work education programs have integrated public health materials (Siefert, Jayaratne, & Martin, 1992) and others offer a joint master of social work–master of public health program (Coulter & Hancock, 1989).

Use. In spite of the long involvement of social work in primary health care and the compatibility of the concepts of social work and primary health care, the use of social workers in primary health care has been disappointing. For example, Hookey (1978) found that only 3 percent of primary care clinics or centers had any social work participation, and Henk's (1989) survey of federally funded primary care projects in the Midwest found that only 25 percent employed a social service director and only 19 percent had a master's-level social worker on site. Similarly, Young and Martin (1989) found that rural primary care projects were also unlikely to have a social worker on staff. Although social workers still are an important part of most family practice residencies, hospital outpatient departments, and public health programs, those in many HMOs have limited functions. As Young (1989) pointed out, "the early emphasis on social factors was given lip service only" (p. 183).

The discrepancy between the promise of social work in primary care and the low rates of its utilization is related to the economics of primary care. Funding for social work services in primary health care has been minimal. In today's cost-conscious health care system, the case management function is valued primarily as a cost-saving measure. Some primary care centers fund social work services by billing third-party payers under provisions for mental health coverage (Butterfield, 1989). However, coverage for mental health services themselves tends to be minimal in most health insurance plans, as is coverage for all preventive services. In a system where 18 percent of all Americans and 31 percent of those without either private or public health insurance have *no* source of primary health care (U.S. Public Health Service, 1991), it is hardly surprising that there is no coverage for a broad community-oriented role for social workers. Although there is little substantial support for a broad social work role in primary care, social work services have been funded for special "target populations," such as minorities, pregnant adolescents, substance abusers, people with AIDS, homeless people, and elderly people.

FUTURE TRENDS

Healthy People 2000 (U.S. Public Health Service, 1991) set the expansion of clinical preventive services as a major goal. Most proposals for health care reform also include increases in the proportion of primary care, and some propose increases in the numbers of primary care providers. In 1994, for the first time in several years, all the primary care residency slots were filled (Morgan, 1994), which suggests that physicians in training see a promising future in primary care. As the health care system becomes increasingly cost driven, primary care will receive considerably more attention. Some of the newer forms of service delivery, including HMOs, preferred provider organizations, and point-of-service plans, provide incentives, such as lower costs to patients, for using primary care practitioners, and some plans use the primary care practitioner as a gatekeeper to limit

access to specialists. Much of this increased emphasis on primary care is based more on a cost perspective than on a concern for the quality of care. The primary care that is being advocated does not necessarily fit the formal definition. It is usually not comprehensive and does not require the true application of a biopsychosocial model, in which mental health and physical health are integrated. Furthermore, community-oriented primary care is rarely mentioned.

The future of social work in primary health care remains uncertain. As the importance of social factors in disease becomes clearer, it is possible that social work skills will become increasingly valued. Whether these skills will be funded will depend, in part, on the ability of social work researchers to demonstrate social workers' effectiveness and accountability. If health care programs follow the example of Oregon's Medicaid program and ration expensive high-tech services while providing cost-effective preventive services to a wider population, it will be imperative for social workers to provide evidence of the cost-effectiveness of their services. Exciting roles in primary health care may exist for social workers in the future in the promotion of health and the prevention of disease, the reduction of the mental health effects of physical diseases, and increasing patients' compliance in treatment for chronic illnesses, as well as in the new field of psychoimmunology. Social workers in private practice may be able to build alliances with private physicians in primary care.

REFERENCES

Ader, R., Felton, D., & Cohen, N. (Eds.). (1990). *Psychoneuroimmunology* (2nd ed.). New York: Academic Press.

Adler, N. E., Boyce, T., Chesney, M. A., Folkman, S., & Syme, S. L. (1993). Socioeconomic inequalities in health: No easy solution. *Journal of the American Medical Association, 269,* 3140–3145.

Azzarto, J. (1993). The socioemotional needs of elderly family practice patients: Can social workers help? *Health & Social Work, 18,* 40–48.

Black, R. B. (1985). The state of the art in public health social work education. In A. Gitterman, R. B. Black, & F. Stein (Eds.), *Public health social work in maternal and child health: A forward plan* (pp. 159–165). Washington, DC: U.S. Department of Health and Human Services.

Butterfield, W. H. (1989). The therapist's role. In M. L. Henk (Ed.), *Social work in primary care* (pp. 67–80). Newbury Park, CA: Sage Publications.

Caroff, P., & Mailick, M. D. (1985). Health concentrations in schools of social work: The state of the art. *Health & Social Work, 10,* 5–14.

Clare, A. W. (1982). Social aspects of ill-health in general practice. In A. W. Clare & R. H. Corney (Eds.), *Social work and primary health care* (pp. 9–22). London: Academic Press.

Coulter, M. L., & Hancock, T. (1989). Integrating social work and public health education: A clinical model. *Health & Social Work, 14,* 157–164.

Diamond, E. L., Detweiller, N. L., & Noce, J. (1987). Clinical practice by behavioral scientists in family medicine programs. *Family Practice Research Journal, 7,* 96–103.

Dobrof, J., Umpierre, M., Rocha, L., & Silverton, M. (1990). Group work in a primary care medical setting. *Health & Social Work, 15,* 32–37.

Economic Opportunity Act of 1964. P.L. 88-452, 78 Stat. 508.

Ell, K., Nishimoto, R., Mediansky, L., Mantell, J., & Hamovitch, M. (1992). Social relations, social support and survival among patients with cancer. *Journal of Psychosomatic Research, 36,* 531–541.

Fawzy, F. I., Fawzy, N. W., Hyum, C. S., Elashoff, R., Guthrie, D., Fahey, J. L., & Morton, D. L. (1993). Malignant melanoma: Effects of an early structured psychiatric intervention, coping and affective state on recurrence and survival 6 years later. *Archives of General Psychiatry, 50,* 681–689.

Fawzy, F. I., Kemeny, M. E., Fawzy, N. W., Elashoff, R., Morton, D., Cousins, N., & Fahey, J. L. (1990). A structured psychiatric intervention for cancer patients II. Changes over time in immunological measures. *Archives of General Psychiatry, 47,* 729–735.

Gitterman, A., Black, R. B., & Stein, F. (Eds.). (1985). *Public health social work in maternal and child health: A forward plan.* Washington, DC: U.S. Department of Health and Human Services.

Gold, M. R. (1991). HMOs and managed care. *Health Affairs, 10,* 189–206.

Green, G. J., & Kulper, T. (1990). Autonomy and professional activities of social workers in hospital and primary health care settings. *Health & Social Work, 15,* 38–44.

Grilli, R., & Lomas, J. (1994). Evaluating the message: The relationship between compliance rate and the subject of a practice guideline. *Medical Care, 32*(3), 202–213.

Grooper, M. (1992). Lessons in caring: How social work integrates psychosocial values into family practice residency training in Israel. *Social Work in Health Care, 17,* 87–99.

Hankin, J., & Oktay, J. S. (1979). *Mental disorder and primary medical care: An analytical review of the literature.* Rockville, MD: National Institute of Mental Health.

Henk, M. L. (1989). *Social work in primary care.* Newbury Park, CA: Sage Publications.

Hess, H. (1985). Social work clinical practice in family medicine centers: The need for a practice model. *Journal of Social Work Education, 21,* 56–65.

Hill, D. R., Kelleher, K., & Shumaker, S. A. (1992). Psychosocial interventions in adult patients with coronary heart disease and cancer: A literature review. *General Hospital Psychiatry, 145,* 28S–42S.

Hookey, P. (1978). Social work in primary health care. In N. F. Bracht (Ed.), *Social work in health care: A guide to professional practice* (pp. 211–223). New York: Haworth Press.

Huxley, P., & Fitzpatrick, B. (1985). Psychiatric disorder and social work intervention in general practice social work attachments and community teams in the UK: A pilot study. *International Social Work, 28,* 29–34.

Institute of Medicine. (1978). *A manpower policy for primary health care.* Washington, DC: National Academy of Sciences.

Institute of Medicine. (1982). *Community-oriented primary care.* Washington, DC: National Academy of Sciences.

Institute of Medicine. (1989). Primary care physicians: Financing their graduate medical education in ambulatory settings. Washington, DC: National Academy Press.

Katon, W. (1987). The epidemiology of depression in primary care. *International Journal of Psychiatry in Medicine, 17,* 93–112.

Katon, W., & Schulberg, H. (1992). Epidemiology of depression in primary care. *General Hospital Psychiatry, 14,* 237–247.

Kiecolt-Glaser, J. K., & Glaser, R. (1992). Psychoneuroimmunology: Can psychological interventions modulate immunity? *Journal of Consulting and Clinical Psychology, 60,* 569–575.

Kleinman, A. (1988). *The illness narratives: Suffering, healing and the human condition.* New York: Basic Books.

Locke, S., & Colligan, D. (1986). *The healer within: The new medicine of mind and body.* New York: New American Library.

Miller, R. (1987). Primary health care. In A. Minahan (Ed.-in-Chief), *Encyclopedia of Social Work* (18th ed., Vol. 2, pp. 321–324). Silver Spring, MD: National Association of Social Workers.

Morgan, D. (1994, July 17). HMO trend squeezes big-fee medical specialists. *Washington Post,* p. A1.

Morlock, L. (1989). Recognition and treatment of mental health problems in the general health sector. In C. Taube, A. Mechanic, & A. Hohmann (Eds.), *Future of mental health services research.* Bethesda, MD: U.S. Department of Health and Human Services, National Institute of Mental Health.

Morton, C. J. (1985). Public health social work practice in maternal and child health. In A. Gitterman, R. B. Black, & F. Stein (Eds.), *Public health social work in maternal and child health: A forward plan* (pp. 41–62). Washington, DC: U.S. Department of Health and Human Services.

Moyers, W. (1993). *Healing and the mind.* New York: Doubleday.

Mrazek, P. J., & Haggerty, R. J. (1994). *Reducing risks for mental disorders: Frontiers for preventive intervention research.* Washington, DC: National Academy Press.

National Association of Community Health Centers. (1993). *National directory of community health centers, migrant health centers, health care for the homeless projects and primary care associations.* Washington, DC: Author.

National Health Service Corps Revitalization Amendments of 1990. P.L. 101-597, 104 Stat. 3013.

National Institute of Mental Health. (1993). *The prevention of mental disorders: A national research agenda.* Bethesda, MD: Author.

Oktay, J. S. (1984, March). *Social workers in primary health care: A national study of tasks and functions.* Presented at the Council on Social Work Education Annual Program Meeting, Detroit.

Pappas, G., Queen, S., Hadden, W., & Fisher, G. (1993). The increasing disparity in mortality between socioeconomic groups in the United States, 1960 and 1986. *New England Journal of Medicine, 329,* 103–109.

Parkerson, G. R. (1982). Meeting the challenge of research in family medicine: Report of the study group on family medicine research. *Journal of Family Practice, 14,* 105–113.

Pert, C., Ruff, M., Weber, R., & Herkenham, M. (1986). Neuropeptides and their receptors: A psychosomatic network. *Journal of Immunology, 135,* 820s–826s.

Public Health Service Act of 1986. P.L. 99-660, 100 Stat. 3751.

Regier, D. A., Narrow, W. E., Rae, D. S., Manderscheid, R. W., Locke, B. Z., & Goodwin, F. K. (1993). The de facto U.S. mental and addictive disorders service system: Epidemiologic catchment area prospective 1 year prevalence rates of disorders and services. *Archives of General Psychiatry, 50,* 85–94.

Rogers, D. (1973). Shattuck Lecture—the American health care scene: Views from a foundation perspective. *New England Journal of Medicine, 288,* 1377–1383.

Shannon, M. T. (1989). Health promotion and illness prevention: A biopsychosocial perspective. *Health & Social Work, 14,* 32–40.

Siefert, K. (1986). Theoretical base for social work interventions. In E. Watkins (Ed.), *Infant mortality, morbidity and childhood handicapping conditions: Biopsychosocial factors* (pp. 19–27). Washington, DC: U.S. Department of Health and Human Services.

Siefert, K., Jayaratne, S., & Martin, L. D. (1992). Implementing the public health social work forward plan: A research-based prevention curriculum for schools of social work. *Health & Social Work, 17,* 17–27.

Social Security Act of 1935. IV A U.S.C. § 401.

Strain, J., Pincus, H., Gise, L., & Houpt, J. (1986). Mental health education in three primary care specialties. *Journal of Medical Education, 61,* 958–966.

U.S. Public Health Service. (1991). *Healthy people 2000: National health promotion and disease prevention objectives.* Washington, DC: U.S. Government Printing Office.

Weiss, G. L., & Lonngvist, L. E. (1994). *The sociology of health, healing, and illness.* Englewood Cliffs, NJ: Prentice Hall.

Wells, K. B., Hays, R. D., Burnam, M. A., Rogers, A. W., Greenfield, S., & Ware, J. E. (1989). Detection of depressive disorder for patients receiving prepaid or fee for service care: Results from the medical outcomes study. *Journal of the American Medical Association, 262,* 3298–3302.

Wells, K. B., Stewart, A., Hays, R. D., Burnam, M. A., Rogers, W., Daniels, M., Berry, S., Greenfield, S., & Ware, J. (1989). The functioning and well-being of depressed patients: Results from the medical outcomes study.

Journal of the American Medical Association, 262, 914–919.

World Health Organization. (1978). *Primary health care: A joint report.* Geneva: Author.

Young, C. L. (1989). Future trends. In H. L. Henk (Ed.), *Social work in primary care.* Newbury Park, CA: Sage Publications.

Young, C. L., & Martin, L. D. (1989). Social services in rural and urban primary care projects. *Human Services in the Rural Environment, 13,* 30–35.

Zayas, D. (1992). Social workers training primary care physicians: Essential psychosocial principles. *Social Work, 37,* 247–252.

Zuvedas, A. (1990). Community and migrant health centers: An overview. *Journal of Ambulatory Care Management, 13,* 1–12.

FUTHER READING

Healthy people 2000: National health promotion and disease prevention objectives: Full report with commentary. (1992). Boston: Jones & Bartlett.

Miranda, J., Hohman A. A. , Attkisson, C., & Larson, D. B. (Eds.). (1994). *Mental disorders in primary care.* San Francisco: Jossey-Bass.

Pew Health Professions Commission. (1994). *Primary care work force 2000.* San Francisco: Center for the Health Professions, University of California.

Starfield, B. (1992). *Primary care: Concept, evaluation and policy.* New York: Oxford University Press.

Julianne S. Oktay, PhD, LCSW, is professor, University of Maryland, School of Social Work, 525 W. Redwood Street, Baltimore, MD 21201.

For further information see

Alcohol Abuse; Community Needs Assessment; Community Practice Models; Deinstitutionalization; Drug Abuse; Family Caregiving; Health Planning; Health Services Systems Policy; Hospice; Hospital Social Work; Interdisciplinary and Interorganizational Collaboration; Long-Term Care; Managed Care; Maternal and Child Health; Mental Health Overview; Natural Helping Networks; Patient Rights; Poverty; Prevention and Wellness; Primary Prevention Overview; Public Health Services; Social Security; Social Welfare Policy; Substance Abuse: Direct Practice.

Key Words	
health care	prevention
mental health	primary care

Primary Prevention Overview
Martin Bloom

Primary prevention is as ancient as the universal hope for well-being expressed in commonsense folk sayings like "an ounce of prevention is worth a pound of cure" or "a stitch in time saves nine." Yet, it is also as contemporary as the most recent recognition of the public health axiom that the most effective way to control social problems or epidemics is to prevent them, rather than treat their seemingly endless victims one by one. The astronomic costs of treatment, the suffering that attends preventable problems, and the promising results of rigorous empirical studies commend primary prevention to the present generation as never before.

DEFINITION OF TERMS

The etymology of the word *prevent* is to "come before" in the sense of taking action about some challenge before it becomes a problem. The current working definition suggests that *primary prevention* consists of those scientific practices aimed at simultaneously *preventing* predictable problems in individuals or populations at risk; *protecting* or maintaining current strengths, competencies, or levels of health and healthy functioning; and *promoting* desired goals and enhancing human potential (Hough, Gongla, Brown, & Goldston, 1985; LaLonde, 1974; Reiss, 1993).

Catalano and Dooley (1980) further categorized primary prevention into proactive forms that avoid or control the risk factors altogether, and reactive forms that prepare individuals to react appropriately to unavoidable risks. Robertson (1975) distinguished active strategies of primary prevention, which require people to perform specific actions to protect themselves, like fastening seat belts or using a fluoridated toothpaste, from passive strategies in which the protective action occurs automatically for everyone in a given context, like traveling in a car equipped with an air bag (Geller, 1990) or drinking fluoridated water (Easley, 1990).

Crisis intervention models are sometimes related to preventive thinking. In some cases the crisis describes an existing problem for which immediate treatment is needed to move the involved parties toward constructive growth and away from destructive reactions. In other cases the crisis predicts likely problems for which immediate preventive services are needed to forestall the untoward possibility and to promote positive growth (Bloom & Klein, in press; G. Caplan, 1964, 1989).

Primary prevention is an interdisciplinary science (Reiss, 1993) and a multidisciplinary practice (Buckner, Trickett, & Corse, 1985; Glanz, Lewis, & Rimer, 1990; Price, Cowen, Lorion, & Ramos-McKay, 1988). Social work's central axiom of viewing a person in the environment is well reflected in the targets of primary prevention services, including behavioral, psychological, sociocultural, and physical environmental events. These targets are generally viewed within a systems or ecological context where changes in one subsystem affect and are affected by changes in another (Benard, 1992; Hawkins & Weis, 1985; Libassi & Maluccio, 1986). In general, primary prevention practices consist of some system of actions to increase individual strengths, social supports, and resources from the physical environment while simultaneously seeking to decrease individual limitations, social stresses, and pressures from the physical environment (Albee, 1983; Albee, Bond, & Monsey, 1992).

HISTORY FROM A SOCIAL WORK PERSPECTIVE

The social work perspective is reflected in the early history of primary prevention. In 1818 the New York Society for the Prevention of Pauperism conceptualized this social problem and began gathering empirical data regarding its occurrence. The information was used to develop a system of volunteer helpers, the forerunners of today's social workers, reaching out into the community to prevent the conditions leading to pauperism (Heale, 1971). The settlement house movement, adopted from an English model in 1886, introduced community-based actions that built on the strengths of people rather than individual actions taken against weaknesses and existing problems. Jane Addams's (1910) efforts, for example, spread beyond art lessons, reading groups, and emergency shelters to concerns for child labor legislation, sanitation, and world peace.

Social workers in the early 1900s, such as Homer Folks, were directly involved in health concerns, especially with regard to contagious diseases like tuberculosis. With regard to nutrition, they helped set up depots for distributing safe milk to the poor. The Children's Bureau (1912) and the Shepard-Towner Bill of 1921 called on social workers to take the lead in addressing maternal and child health concerns. Social workers Harry Hopkins and Francis Perkins were the architects of many forward-looking social agencies that emerged during the Great Depression to prevent predictable problems such as poverty among the elderly and others (Spaulding & Balch, 1983; Trattner, 1991).

In recent years other professions have taken leading roles in new prevention initiatives, although social workers continue to make significant contributions. Social workers have clarified ways to support individuals dealing with challenging situations or to change those situations to achieve socially desired outcomes. For example, Hawkins and Weis (1985) offered a model for preventing juvenile delinquency that involved developing social bonds with units of conventional society—the family, schools, peers, and the community—by stimulating opportunities, skills, and reinforcements for appropriate social involvements. They described a wide array of ongoing projects consistent with their model; results have been encouraging (Hawkins et al., 1992; Hawkins & Lam, 1987).

GUIDING PERSPECTIVES AND PHILOSOPHIES

Three identifiable historical stages in perspectives guide primary prevention. First, reflecting a disease–pathology paradigm, primary prevention sought to identify some underlying causal condition (disease) in an individual, who was viewed essentially as a case involving pathology or weakness. For example, the Society for the Prevention of Pauperism assumed that intemperance (an individual's weakness for alcohol) was a leading cause of pauperism. Although the disease–pathology paradigm has led to important bacteriological discoveries in the field of acute physical illnesses, like smallpox, it has been unsuccessful in grasping the complexities of many chronic or social problems, such as heart disease and unwanted teenage pregnancy.

The second historical paradigm is the public health model that considers the host (would-be victim), the agent (underlying causal factor), and the environment (the context in which victim and causal factor meet). Although this paradigm includes more of the complexity of real life, especially in lifestyle problems (Coates, 1990), it still focuses on an underlying cause and tends to view the victim as limited and in need of support.

A third paradigm, which might be labeled a "stress/strens" model (Hollister, 1967) or a "competency model" (Albee, 1980, 1983), recognizes that any number of factors might combine to pro-duce a problem (dysfunction) or a strength (optimal functioning) in individuals or groups, without any one of these factors being the specific cause. Integral to this model is the recognition that people have strengths as well as limitations, both of which have to be taken into consideration for any preventive/promotive planning (Holmes & Rahe, 1967). In this approach *stress* is defined as the excess of environmental demand over the individual's capacity to respond effectively. *Strens* are defined as growth-promoting experiences that add to a person's capacity to respond to environmental demands (Hollister, 1967).

This emergent view of human behavior involves recognition of multiple risks and multiple strengths at various systems levels, which may be addressed by preventive/promotive programs that may have multiple planned effects at each of these levels. Thus, the preventive/promotive task becomes one of engaging the relevant parties, mobilizing their strengths, and acting to decrease their limitations or the environment's pressures vis-à-vis one another. (See Gullotta's, 1987, discussion of the five major technologies of primary prevention practice: education, changes in community or society, promotion of competency, promotion of natural caregiving, and consultation/collaboration.)

Another emerging aspect of the third paradigm is the need for coordinated and integrated actions involving all levels of intraindividual, interindividual, and group or organizational systems and the physical and cultural contexts involved. This integration sets rigorous requirements for the next stage of development in primary prevention: Not only must problematic factors be prevented, but promotive factors must be substituted in the system of events in their place. Furthermore, gains at one system level must not be undertaken at the expense of negative changes or losses at other system levels. Some type of overall optimization in the whole system must be sought. Probabilistic, interactive systems models await development.

LEGISLATION, POLICIES, PROGRAMS, AND GRASSROOTS EFFORTS

Primary prevention specialists pursue knowledge of the predictors of untoward events and the indicators of desired goals. This is exactly the type of information that decision makers need at all levels of government and society. At the national level, the United States is reconsidering approaches to primary prevention across the full wide spectrum of contemporary life, including the health care system, ecological policies, and educational programs. It is too early to grasp what form this new sense of national enhancement will take. Primary prevention is an idea whose time continues to come (D. C. Klein & Goldston, 1977), and it continues to speak to each generation's hopes and fears. In the American style, however, preventive legislation and programs emerge in piecemeal fashion and often change with political administrations (Goldston, 1991; Hudson & Cox, 1991).

Primary prevention is not simply a matter of governmental action. Self-help movements and public opinion play a major role in developments in primary prevention, with or without the leadership and cooperation of helping professionals. Katz (1993) estimated that there may be as many as 750,000 self-help groups of all kinds, with 10 million to 15 million members, essentially because professional helpers have failed to provide needed services sensitively delivered.

Self-help may not always be effective; consider humorist Erma Bombeck's quip that she has lost 1,000 pounds through various health food diets. But major societywide changes have taken place through mass media (DeJong & Winsten, 1990) or word of mouth, such as the reduction in smoking ("the single most preventable cause of death" [*Healthy People,* 1979, p. 7]); changes in sexual practices (Mays, Albee, & Schneider, 1989; Sepulveda, Fineberg, & Mann, 1992); and increased interest in lifetime exercise and changes in eating habits (Maccoby & Altman, 1988).

Voluntary nonprofit organizations also have made important contributions to primary prevention. For example, since the late 1960s, Action on Smoking and Health (ASH) has been active and generally successful in advocating antismoking causes, such as smoking bans on airplanes, in restaurants, in public offices, and, most recently, in the workplace. ASH has raised the consciousness of a nation concerning the effects of smoking, including secondhand smoke and chewing tobacco (the latter is a predictable epidemic in the making among young people). ASH has spawned many local and state organizations that address the particular needs of communities in ways that small self-help groups cannot and large government units will not because of vested interests.

Any major social change has innumerable repercussions, and therefore entrenched interest groups seek to modify these developments in ways favorable to themselves, often by means of lobbying in the political process. For example, the "food pyramid" is a graphic device to present information to the public on ways to promote good nutrition. The public is advised, not just in words, but also in a graphic, three-dimensional perspective, to use fats and sweets sparingly, to have two to three servings of both meat and milk products

daily, and to consume vegetables, fruits, breads, and cereals in far greater quantities. The latter are represented by the large base of the pyramid in contrast to the tiny tip given to sweets, milk, and meat. Developing this graphic illustration and getting the final version of the pyramid adopted for public presentation required the cooperation of both the U.S. Department of Agriculture and the U.S. Department of Health and Human Services and the different—and apparently opposing—constituencies they serve: producers (especially of meat and milk products) and consumers.

Prevention science exists in a political–economic matrix. A growing realization of the interdisciplinary nature of primary prevention, both in and out of government, has led to various mechanisms to integrate the flow of information and resources in this area. In 1986 the National Mental Health Association developed a constituency of sufficient strength to advocate for primary prevention at the federal, state, and local levels. The resulting organization, the National Prevention Coalition, linked together 20 national organizations, and their representatives urged the formation of the National Institute of Mental Health (NIMH) Prevention Research meetings (Reiss, 1993).

The National Association of Prevention Professionals and Advocates was formed in 1987 to define, promote, and professionalize the practice discipline of primary prevention (Mowrer & Strader, 1992). Other specialist organizations exist for similar purposes, such as SIECUS (Sex Information and Education Council of the United States) and the National Women's Health Network.

There are various prevention information centers including the National Centers for Disease Control (CDC) and state or provincial agencies, such as the Illinois Prevention Resource Center and the Ontario Prevention Clearinghouse. There are also many health and wellness newsletters produced by enterprising universities, such as the *Wellness Letter* (University of California at Berkeley), *Lifetime Health Letter* (University of Texas), *For Kids' Sake* (University of Virginia), and *Medical Letter: Health After 50* (Johns Hopkins University). Action organizations also produce informative newsletters and magazines, such as the *Nutrition Action: Health Letter* (Center for Science in the Public Interest), *Amicus Journal* (Natural Resources Defense Council), and *Sierra* (Sierra Club).

FINANCING PRIMARY PREVENTION PROGRAMS: COSTS AND BENEFITS

Funding for primary prevention is considerably lower than funding for treatment and rehabilitation. D. C. Klein and Goldston (1977) reported that median staff time devoted to primary prevention in community mental health centers was about 5 percent. The same 5 percent figure was reported with regard to the budget of the National Cancer Institute earmarked for disease prevention (Angier, 1993). About $21 million of the institute's budget was allocated for specific primary prevention activities in 1992, including about $15 million for research and about $5 million for the Prevention Intervention Research Centers.

An important development within the primary prevention field is a concern for taking cost-effectiveness data seriously. Price et al. (1988) presented exemplary programs in primary prevention with documented cost-effectiveness. Scheinhart and Weikart (1988) presented data from the Perry Preschool Project, which provided poor children with high-quality preschool training. For every $1 invested in the one-year program, there was a return of $6, and for every $1 invested in the two-year program, there was a return of $3. The Perry Preschool data included money saved in reduced special education costs, reduced crime costs, and reduced welfare assistance, but with the additional cost of more postsecondary education for project participants, who acquired more advanced education than did the control group. Viewed in a systemic and longitudinal way, quality preschool training benefits all facets of society.

PREVENTION SETTINGS AND TECHNIQUES

The major settings for primary prevention include schools from preschool through college (Elias, Gara, Schuyler, Brandon-Muller, & Sayette, 1991); workplaces, such as in employee assistance programs (Googins & Godfrey, 1987); accident prevention programs (Fox, Hopkins, & Anger, 1987); health settings, ranging from health maintenance organizations with prevention-oriented services to private settings for specialized workshops on stress reduction (Cotton, 1990; Rosen & Solomon, 1985; Smith, 1990); recreational settings, such as for lifetime sports and exercise opportunities (Haskell, 1985; McAuley & Courneya, 1993) and for regenerative recreation; and social agencies for family life education, assertiveness training, social skills training, suicide prevention, and so forth (Botvin & Tortu, 1988; Garland, Shaffer, & Whittle, 1989 [but also see Szasz, 1986]; Huey & Rank, 1984; Pill, 1981; Schinke & Gilchrist, 1984).

Minor settings for primary prevention (in the sense that only a limited number of their programs are operated by social workers) include military bases with programs to prevent family violence (Whiteman, Fanshal, & Grundy, 1987) and

substance abuse (Manger, Hawkins, Haggerty, & Catalano, 1992); religious settings to promote prosocial values and fellowship (social integration) (Hathaway & Pargament, 1991; Payne, Bergin, Bielema, & Jenkins, 1991); and sports settings that teach fair play, teamwork, and so forth (Danish, 1983).

Community health and mental health centers, health maintenance organizations (HMOs), and similar organizations may have a distinctive preventive orientation, and certain private settings, such as smoking clinics and weight loss centers, may focus exclusively on prevention as well. In social work, however, primary prevention is usually integrated with treatment and rehabilitation. Therefore, practitioners will likely see individual clients for whom preventive efforts are focused on predictable problems other than the presenting needs or problems (Ambrosino, 1979; Keefe, 1988; N. Klein, Alexander, & Parsons, 1977). As common problems emerge, agencies may address these issues collectively using a preventive orientation. For example, awareness of many clients with latchkey children may provoke an agency response to the resulting predictable problems (Peterson, 1984; Peterson, Mori, Selby, & Rosen, 1988). Once resolved (at least temporarily), a now-preventable problem becomes the target for other distinctive practices to prevent relapse. (For a general approach to relapse prevention, see Marlatt & George, 1984.)

A number of practice methods developed within primary prevention have demonstrated empirical and practical significance. These same methods may also be used in treatment and rehabilitation settings, showing that the ultimate goal of scientific practice is systemic and multimodal: Social workers should prevent predictable problems and promote desired goals as well as treat existing difficulties and rehabilitate victims to the highest levels of functioning possible. The following primary prevention methods might be selectively applicable in all forms of helping:

- problem-solving techniques (Shure & Spivack, 1988)
- social skills training (Schinke & Gilchrist, 1984)
- training to increase self-efficacy (Bandura, 1989)
- assertiveness training (L. Z. Bloom, Coburn, & Pearlman, 1975)
- cognitive reframing (Beck, 1984)
- anticipatory coping (G. Caplan, 1989)
- parent effectiveness training (T. Gordon, 1989)
- social support groups (Gottlieb, 1987)
- many others (see Buckner, Trickett, & Corse, 1985).

EPIDEMIOLOGY AS USED IN PRIMARY PREVENTION

Descriptive epidemiology refers to the description and distribution of attributes of health and illness in time and space (MacMahon, Pugh, & Ipsen, 1960); it is a basic tool used to comprehend the complex array of factors involved in human events. *Analytic epidemiology* refers to the analysis of the causes of these events from the patterns emerging in descriptive epidemiology. Such interpretations may lead to plans of action and, in effect, become hypotheses for prevention programming.

For example, adult antisocial personality characteristics, such as criminal behavior and substance abuse, may be predicted by a set of serious childhood problems termed "conduct disorder" (Kazdin, 1991; Robins & Earls, 1985). The descriptive epidemiology of conduct disorder includes behaviors that come to public attention in the early school years, such as resistance to adult authority, fighting, stealing, lying, truancy, and poor academic success relative to capability (Robins & Earls, 1985). Treatment studies regarding this pattern of events suggest that structured settings using behavioral programs attain academic and behavioral goals for young children, but these methods are not transferable to other settings (Robins & Earls, 1985). However, they cite other research that suggests a correlation between antisocial behavior of parents and that of their children, even before any signs appear in infancy. An analysis of these epidemiological patterns suggested an alternative hypothesis to Robins and Earls: that a randomly assigned group of infants at high risk for conduct disorders (as indicated by the presence of an antisocial parent) who receive structured and consistent (loving) attention in a day care situation, will be less likely to exhibit antisocial behavior within a given time period than an equivalent control group of infants left to the care of their parents. In this fashion a critical link between certain childhood experiences predictive of later adult antisocial behaviors may be broken. The epidemiological database is rich with potential hypotheses (Robins & Regier, 1991; Robins & Rutter, 1990).

SPECIAL POPULATIONS AND DIVERSITY IN PRIMARY PREVENTION

Although every group of people has ordinary life development needs, some people, particularly those from poor and oppressed groups, also have other predictable problems for which primary prevention would be appropriate. When primary prevention is used with poor and/or minority groups, it focuses on people's strengths rather than their weaknesses, as is often the case in treatment or rehabilitation services. The weakness perspective accounts for the predominant emphasis in social work education on pathology rather than health (see Saleeby, 1992). Thus, theoretically, primary prevention should empower people by motivating them, and in many cases this is accomplished. However, primary prevention may stigmatize people unintentionally by identifying them as a group thought to need services. The stigmatizing problem can be avoided by opening doors to all members of an area, even though the program is especially interested in serving certain members (Olds, 1988; Pierson, 1988).

In addition, there may be special sensitivities needed in providing primary prevention services for minority or special groups. Orlandi (1986) argued that community-based substance abuse prevention programs should take a multicultural perspective, recognizing the strengths and differences among the involved groups with regard to language, cultural values, fears about service programs as social control mechanisms, and so forth. Programs for ethnic and racial groups should employ bilingual and bicultural workers. They should emphasize culturally compatible values, such as strong family solidarity instead of double standards that give one group unfair advantages over others. Participants should be involved in developing and monitoring preventive programs, both to optimize their strengths and special knowledge and to motivate them in a program they "own" (see also Mays & Cochran, 1987; Schilling et al., 1989).

KNOWLEDGE BASE

The knowledge explosion in primary prevention is reflected in the number and diversity of specialized journals, including *AIDS Education and Prevention; Journal of Health and Safety; Journal of Health, Physical Education, and Recreation; Journal of Health Politics, Policy, and Law; Journal of Human Nutrition and Dietetics; Journal of Hygiene, Epidemiology, Microbiology, and Immunology; Journal of Peace Research; Journal of Primary Prevention; Preventing School Failure; Preventing Sexual Abuse; Prevention in Human Services; Preventive Medicine;* and *Preventive Pediatrics* (see also Bloom, 1987).

The Vermont Conferences on the Primary Prevention of Psychopathology continue to be a national forum for current theory, research, and practice. Proceedings of these conferences are major contributions to the knowledge base; recent volumes include Albee et al. (1992); Albee, Joffe, and Dusenbury (1988); Bond and Compas (1989); Bond and Wagner (1988); Burchard and Burchard (1987); Kessler and Goldston (1986); Mays, Albee, and Schneider (1989); and Rosen and Solomon (1985). (See also Bloom, 1987.)

A new conference series on primary prevention, The Hartman Conference on Children and Their Families, is located in New London, Connecticut. This biennial conference, sponsored by the Child and Family Agency of Southeastern Connecticut, also produces a book of proceedings (see Gullotta, Adams, & Montemayor, 1990; Hampton, Gullotta, Adams, Potter, & Weissberg, 1993).

A number of books on primary prevention topics also add to the literature, including Edelstein and Michelson (1986); Edwards, Tindale, Heath, & Posavac (1990); and Price et al. (1988). Specific topics in primary prevention discussed in book form include Anthony and Cohler (1987); Biegel, Farkas, Abell, Goodin, and Friendman (1989); Cummings, Greene, and Karraker (1991); Donohew, Sypher, and Bukoski (1991); Glanz et al. (1990); A. P. Goldstein (1983); T. Gordon (1989); Gore (1992); Hough et al. (1985); Insel (1980); Kelly (1988); Levenstein (1988); McAnarney and Schreider (1984); Meichenbaum (1985); Meichenbaum and Jaremko (1983); Perlmutter (1982a, 1982b); Pilisuk and Parks (1986); Price and Smith (1985); Robins and Rutter (1990); Saleeby (1992); Tzeng, Jackson, and Karlson (1991); and Weinstein and David (1987). Also adding to an important series of longitudinal studies is a book by Werner and Smith (1992). This substantial knowledge base is accessible to social work education in primary prevention. (See also Bloom, 1987.)

RESEARCH

Rigorous empirical research that reflects the multivariate nature of problems and preventive/promotive solutions is critical in the development of primary prevention. For example, the 20 longitudinal research studies on the development of psychopathology in the Robins and Rutter (1990) anthology give testimony to the enormous advances in our understanding of the childhood predictors of various adult problems. To give one instance from the anthology, Rodgers (1990) explored the complicated causal relationships in affective disorders in women. Using longitudinal data from a large sample in Britain, he identified the differential patterns of antecedents involving individual vulnerability and provoking life stresses and the interaction of these two factors. A technical analysis provides some support for the interactive hypothesis, except under the condition of long-term emotional problems. This degree of

specificity begins to provide direction for differential preventive services, which is one goal of applied social research.

Some preventive projects are directed at various childhood conditions that predict less-than-optimal life development (for example, see Heber, 1978). Project Head Start is based on the rationale that intervening in the lives of disadvantaged children will enhance their subsequent intellectual, social, and health development (Zigler & Styfco, 1993; Zigler & Valentine, 1979). There are, furthermore, specific preventive studies regarding children at high risk for antisocial behavior or emotional problems, such as children of divorce (Stolberg, Kiluk & Garrison, 1986) or those who display high levels of aggression (Goldstein, 1983) or truancy (Robins & Wish, 1977).

Yet, as Robins and Rutter (1990) noted, childhood behavior problems alone do not necessarily predict adult problems, if other resilience–promotive factors exist in the child's situation (Benard, 1992; Hauser, Vieyra, Jacobson, & Wertlieb, 1985; Luthar & Zigler, 1991; Rutter, 1987; Werner & Smith, 1992). Many of the correlates of resilience are potentially manipulatable and thus present the conceptual/empirical grounds for the next generation of enhancing or promotive research—to increase resilience in children at risk and, indeed, in all children.

The National Institute of Mental Health initiated a three-year project to comprehensively review and analyze its role in the "science of prevention" (Goodwin, 1993) in order to provide guidelines for future efforts. Major reviews of the research literature were written in the areas of conduct disorders (Kazdin, 1991), depression (Muñoz, 1991), and schizophrenia (M. J. Goldstein & Asarnow, 1991). Given this information on progress in primary prevention, the conference members made proposals for future research and support, including funding of consortia of prevention scientists and expansion of the role of the Prevention Intervention Research Centers (PIRCs).

Five national centers have been established to facilitate research in particular topic areas, such as unemployment issues and their psychosocial sequelae, that are being studied at the University of Michigan PIRC (R. D. Caplan, Vinokur, Price, & van Ryn, 1989; Vinokur, van Ryn, Gamlick, & Price, 1991). PIRCs provide rich research environments in which teams of investigators from many disciplines develop research ideas that are funded through conventional sources. PIRCs may also operate as training sites for scholars at all levels to enhance their research skills and preventive strategies. The general message of the NIMH report was one of synergistic movement across many fronts, but it highlighted the need for resources and support for PIRCs to keep up the momentum (Goodwin, 1993).

To evaluate appropriately the complexity of preventive situations, the NIMH panel called for large-scale community studies, involving multistage sampling procedures to capture the diversity of the U.S. population. Randomized, controlled trials, guided by theoretical models and their \ clearly operationalized concepts, remain the optimal testing procedures for cost-effective preventive strategies. These studies should include both risk and protective factors, so that emerging scientific information can be effectively translated into efficacious programs (Cowen, Hightower, Johnson, Sarno, & Weissberg, 1989).

FUTURE OF SOCIAL WORK AND PRIMARY PREVENTION

The prospect for dealing effectively with numerous social problems seems increasingly optimistic. This may be another instance of the triumph of hope over experience, as Sam Johnson characterized second marriage. Yet there is not only a growing rigorous research base for some well-documented practice methods, but there is also a national groundswell favoring major changes in lifestyle and of social organizations that seek to promote health and well-being. Social workers have the opportunity to renew and to participate in what looks to be the major social–educational revolution of our century: "to aid in the solution of the social and industrial problems which are engendered by the modern conditions of life" (p. 98); to arouse "a higher imagination" (p. 85); and, above all, to establish "a spot to which those who have a passion for the equalization of human joys and opportunities are early attracted" (p. 137). These are quotations from Jane Addams (1910). Social work needs to fulfill the mission we started in the 20th century before we begin the 21st.

REFERENCES

Addams, J. (1910). *Twenty years at Hull-House.* New York: Signet.

Albee, G. W. (1980). A competency model must replace the defect model. In L. A. Bond & J. C. Rosen (Eds.), *Competence and coping during adulthood* (pp. 75–104). Hanover, NH: University Press of New England.

Albee, G. W. (1983). Psychopathology, prevention, and the just society. *Journal of Primary Prevention, 4*(1), 5–40.

Albee, G. W., Bond, L. A., & Monsey, T. C. (Eds.). (1992). *Improving children's lives: Global perspectives on prevention.* Newbury Park, CA: Sage Publications.

Albee, G. W., Joffe, J. M., & Dusenbury, L. A. (Eds.). (1988). *Prevention, powerlessness, and politics: Readings on social change.* Newbury Park, CA: Sage Publications.

Ambrosino, S. (1979, December). Integrating counseling, family life education, and family advocacy. *Social Casework,* 579–585.

Angier, N. (1993, April 13). Chemists learn why vegetables are good for you. *New York Times,* pp. C1, C3.

Anthony, E. J., & Cohler, B. J. (Eds.). (1987). *The invulnerable child.* New York: Guilford Press.

Bandura, A. (1989). Human agency in social cognitive theory. *American Psychologist, 44*(9), 1175–1184.

Beck, A. T. (1984). Cognitive approaches to stress. In R. Woolfolk & P. Lehrer (Eds.), *Principles and practices of stress management* (pp. 255–305). New York: Guilford Press.

Benard, B. (1992). Fostering resiliency in kids: Protective factors in the family, school, and community. *Prevention Forum, 12*(3), 1–16.

Biegel, D., Farkas, K. J., Abell, N., Goodin, J., & Friendman, B. (1989). *Social support networks: A bibliography, 1983–1987.* Westport, CT: Greenwood Press.

Bloom, B. L. (1985). New possibilities in prevention. In R. L. Hough, P. A. Gongla, V. B. Brown, & S. E. Goldston (Eds.), *Psychiatric epidemiology and prevention: The possibilities.* Los Angeles: University of California, Neuropsychiatric Institute.

Bloom, L. Z., Coburn, K., & Pearlman, J. (1975). *The new assertive woman.* New York: Delacorte Press.

Bloom, M. (1987). Prevention. In A. Minahan (Ed.-in-Chief), *Encyclopedia of social work* (18th ed., Vol. 2, pp. 303–315). Silver Spring, MD: National Association of Social Workers.

Bloom, M., & Klein, W. (in press). Crisis prevention and crisis treatment: A critical distinction. *Crisis Intervention and Time-Limited Treatment.*

Bond, L. A., & Compas, B. E. (Eds.). (1989). *Primary prevention and promotion in the schools* (Vol. 12). Newbury Park, CA: Sage Publications.

Bond, L. A., & Wagner, B. M. (Eds.). (1988). *Families in transition* (Vol. 11). Newbury Park, CA: Sage Publications.

Botvin, G. J., & Dusenbury, L. (1989). Substance abuse prevention and the promotion of competence. In L. Bond and B. Compas (Eds.), *Primary prevention and promotion in the schools* (pp. 146–178). Newbury Park, CA: Sage Publications.

Botvin, G. J., & Tortu, S. (1988). Preventing adolescent substance abuse through life skills training. In R. H. Price, E. L. Cowen, R. P. Lorion, & J. Ramos-McKay (Eds.), *14 ounces of prevention: A casebook for practitioners* (pp. 98–110). Washington, DC: American Psychological Association.

Buckner, J. C., Trickett, E. J., & Corse, S. J. (1985). *Primary prevention in mental health: An annotated bibliography.* Washington, DC: DHHS Publication No. (ADM) 85-1405.

Burchard, J. D., & Burchard, S. N. (Eds.). (1987). *Prevention of delinquent behavior* (Vol. 10). Newbury Park, CA: Sage Publications.

Caplan, G. (1964). *Principles of preventive psychiatry.* New York: Basic Books.

Caplan, G. (1989). Recent developments in crisis intervention and the promotion of social support. *Journal of Primary Prevention, 10*(1), 3–25.

Caplan, R. D., Vinokur, A. D., Price, R., & van Ryn, M. (1989). Job-seeking, reemployment and mental health: A randomized field experiment in coping with job loss. *Journal of Applied Psychology, 74,* 759–769.

Catalano, R., & Dooley, D. (1980). Economic change in primary prevention. In R. H. Price, R. F. Ketterer, B. C. Bader, & J. Monahan, *Prevention in mental health: Research, policy and practice* (pp. 21–40). Beverly Hills, CA: Sage Publications.

Coates, T. J. (1990). Strategies for modifying sexual behavior for primary and secondary prevention of HIV disease. *Journal of Consulting and Clinical Psychology, 58*(1), 57–69.

Cormier, W. H., & Cormier, L. S. (1991). *Interviewing strategies for helpers: Fundamental skills and cognitive behavioral interventions* (2nd ed.). Pacific Grove, CA: Brooks/Cole.

Cotton, D.H.G. (1990). *Stress management: An integrated approach to therapy.* New York: Brunner/Mazel.

Cowen, E. L., Hightower, A. D., Johnson, D. B., Sarno, M., & Weissberg, R. P. (1989). State-level dissemination of a program for early detection and prevention of school maladjustment. *Professional Psychology: Research and Practice, 20*(5), 309–314.

Cummings, E. M., Greene, A. L., & Karraker, K. H. (Eds.). (1991). *Life-span developmental psychology: Perspectives on stress and coping.* Hillsdale, NJ: Lawrence Erlbaum.

Danish, S. J. (1983). Musings about personal competence: The contributions of sport, health, and fitness. *American Journal of Community Psychology, 11*(3), 221–240.

DeJong, W., & Winsten, J. A. (1990). The use of mass media in substance abuse prevention. *Health Affairs, 9*(2), 30–46.

Donohew, L., Sypher, H. E., & Bukoski, W. J. (Eds.). (1991). *Persuasive communication and drug abuse prevention.* Hillsdale, NJ: Lawrence Erlbaum.

Easley, M. W. (1990). The status of community water fluoridation in the United States. *Public Health Reports, 105*(4): 318–323.

Edelstein, B. A., & Michelson, L. (Eds.). (1986). *Handbook of prevention.* New York: Plenum Press.

Edwards, J., Tindale, R. S., Heath, L., & Posavac, E. J. (Eds.). (1990). *Social influence processes and prevention.* New York: Plenum Press.

Elias, M. J., Gara, M. A., Schuyler, T. F., Brandon-Muller, L. R., & Sayette, M. A. (1991). The promotion of social competence: Longitudinal study of a preventive school-based program. *American Journal of Orthopsychiatry, 61*(3), 409–417.

Fox, D. K., Hopkins, B. L., & Anger, W. K. (1987). The long-term effects of a token economy on safety performance in open-pit mining. *Journal of Applied Behavior Analysis, 20*(3), 215–224.

Garland, A., Shaffer, D., & Whittle, B. (1989). A national survey of school-based, adolescent suicide prevention programs. *Journal of the American Academy of Child and Adolescent Psychiatry, 28*(6), 931–934.

Geller, E. S. (1990). Preventing injuries and deaths from vehicle crashes: Encouraging belts and discouraging booze. In J. Edwards, R. S. Tindale, L. Heath, & E. J. Posavac (Eds.), *Social influence processes and prevention* (pp. 249–278). New York: Plenum.

Glanz, K., Lewis, F. M., & Rimer, B. K. (Eds.). (1990). *Health behavior and health education: Theory, research, and practice.* San Francisco: Jossey-Bass.

Goldstein, A. P. (Ed.). (1983). *Prevention and control of aggression.* New York: Pergamon.

Goldstein, M. J., & Asarnow, J. R. (1991). Prevention of schizophrenia. In *The prevention of mental disorders: Progress, problems, and prospects.* Washington, DC: National Institute of Mental Health.

Goldston, S. E. (1991). A survey of prevention activities in state mental health authorities. *Professional Psychology: Research and Practice, 22*(4), 315–321.

Goodwin, F. K. (1993). Foreword. In *The prevention of mental disorder: A national research agenda* [Mimeograph]. Washington, DC: National Institute of Mental Health.

Googins, B., & Godfrey, J. (1987). *Occupational social work.* Englewood Cliffs, NJ: Prentice Hall.

Gordon, T. (1989). *Teaching children self-discipline . . . at home and at school: New ways for parents and teachers to build self-control, self-esteem, and self-reliance.* New York: Random House.

Gore, A. (1992). *Earth in the balance: Ecology and the human spirit.* Boston: Houghton Mifflin.

Gottlieb, B. H. (1987). Using social support to protect and promote health. *Journal of Primary Prevention, 8*(1&2), 49–70.

Gullotta, T. P. (1987). Prevention's technology. *Journal of Primary Prevention, 8*(1), 4–24.

Gullotta, T. P., Adams, G. R., & Montemayor, R. (Eds.). (1990). *Developing social competency in adolescence.* Newbury Park, CA: Sage Publications.

Hampton, R. L., Gullotta, T. P., Adams, G. R., Potter, E. H., III, & Weissberg, R. P. (Eds.). (1993). *Family violence: Prevention and treatment: Issues in children's and families' lives.* (Vol. 1). Newbury Park, CA: Sage Publications.

Haskell, W. L. (1985). Exercise programs for health promotion. In J. C. Rosen & L. J. Solomon (Eds.), *Prevention in health psychology* (pp. 111–129). Hanover, NH: University Press of New England.

Hathaway, W. L., & Pargament, K. I. (1991). The religious dimensions of coping: Implications for prevention and promotion. *Prevention in Human Services, 9*(2), 65–92.

Hauser, S., Vieyra, M., Jacobson, A., & Wertlieb, D. (1985). Vulnerability and resilience in adolescence: Views from the family. *Journal of Early Adolescence, 5*(1), 81–100.

Hawkins, J. D., Catalano, R. F., Morrison, D. M., O'Donnell, J., Abbott, R. D., & Day, L. E. (1992). The Seattle Social Development Project: Effects of the first four years on protective factors and problem behaviors. In J. McCord & R. Tremblay (Eds.), *The prevention of antisocial behavior in children.* New York: Guilford Press.

Hawkins, J. D., & Lam, T. (1987). Teacher practices, social development, and delinquency. In J. D. Burchard & G. N. Burchard (Eds.), *Prevention of delinquent behavior (Vol. 10). Primary prevention of psychopathology* (pp. 241–274). Newbury Park, CA: Sage Publications.

Hawkins, J. D., & Weis, J. G. (1985). The social development model: An integrated approach to delinquency prevention. *Journal of Primary Prevention, 6*(2), 73–97.

Heale, M. J. (1971). The New York Society for the Prevention of Pauperism, 1817–1823. *New York Historical Society Quarterly, 55,* 153–172.

Healthy people: The surgeon general's report on health promotion and disease prevention (Public Health Service Publication No. 79-55071). (1979). Washington, DC: U.S. Government Printing Office.

Heber, F. R. (1978). Sociocultural mental retardation: A longitudinal study. In D. G. Forgays (Ed.), *Primary prevention of psychopathology (Vol. 2). Environmental influences* (pp. 39–62). Hanover, NH: University Press of New England.

Hollister, W. (1967). The concept of strens in education: A challenge to curriculum development. In E. Bower & W. Hollister (Eds.), *Behavioral science frontiers in education* (pp. 196–205). New York: John Wiley & Sons.

Holmes, T. H., & Rahe, R. H. (1967). The social readjustment rating scale. *Journal of Psychosomatic Research, 11*, 213–218.

Hough, R. L., Gongla, P. A., Brown, V. B., & Goldston, S. E. (Eds.). (1985). *Psychiatric epidemiology and prevention: The possibilities.* Los Angeles: University of California, Neuropsychiatric Institute.

Hudson, C. G., & Cox, A. J. (1991). *Dimensions of state mental health policy.* New York: Praeger.

Huey, W., & Rank, R. (1984). Effects of counselor and peer led assertiveness training groups for black adolescents who are aggressive. *Journal of Counseling Psychology, 31*, 193–203.

Insel, P. M. (1980). *Environmental variables and the prevention of mental illness.* Lexington, MA: Lexington Books.

Katz, A. H. (1993). *Self-help in America: A social movement perspective.* New York: Twayne.

Kazdin, A. E. (1991). Prevention of conduct disorder. In *The prevention of mental disorders: Progress, problems, and prospects.* Washington, DC: National Institute of Mental Health.

Keefe, T. (1988, October). Stress-coping skills: An ounce of prevention in direct practice. *Social Casework,* pp. 475–482.

Kelly, J. G. (1988). *A guide to conducting prevention research in the community: First steps.* New York: Haworth Press.

Kessler, M., & Goldston, S. E. (Eds.). (1986). *A decade of progress in primary prevention.* Hanover, NH: University Press of New England.

Kirk, S. A., & Kutchins, H. (1992). *The selling of DSM: The rhetoric of science in psychiatry.* New York: Aldine de Gruyter.

Klein, D. C., & Goldston, S. E. (1977). *Primary prevention: An idea whose time has come* (DHEW Publication No. (ADM) 77-447). Washington, DC: U.S. Government Printing Office.

Klein, N., Alexander, J. F., & Parsons, B. V. (1977). Impact of family system intervention on recidivism and sibling delinquency: A model of primary prevention and program evaluation. *Journal of Consulting and Clinical Psychology, 45*(3), 469–474.

LaLonde, M. (1974). *A new perspective on the health of Canadians.* Ottawa: Canadian Government Printing Office.

Levenstein, P. (1988). *Messages from home: The mother-child home program and the prevention of school disadvantage.* Columbus: Ohio State University Press.

Libassi, M. F., & Maluccio, A. (1986). Competence-centered social work: Prevention in action. *Journal of Primary Prevention, 6*(3), 168–180.

Luthar, S. S., & Zigler, E. (1991). Vulnerability and competence: A review of research on resilience in childhood. *American Journal of Orthopsychiatry, 61*(1), 6–22.

Maccoby, N., & Altman, D. G. (1988). Disease prevention in communities: The Stanford heart disease prevention project. In R. H. Price, E. L. Cowen, R. P. Lorion, & J. Ramos-McKay (Eds.), *14 ounces of prevention: A casebook for practitioners* (pp. 165–174). Washington, DC: American Psychological Association.

MacMahon, B., Pugh, T. F., & Ipsen, J. (1960). *Epidemiological methods.* Boston: Little, Brown.

Manger, T. H., Hawkins, J. D., Haggerty, K. P., & Catalano, R. F. (1992). Mobilizing communities to reduce risks for drug abuse: Lessons on using research to guide prevention practice. *Journal of Primary Prevention, 13*(1), 3–22.

Marlatt, G. A., & George, W. H. (1984). Relapse prevention: Introduction and overview of the model. *British Journal of Addiction, 79*, 261–273.

Mays, V. M., Albee, G. W., & Schneider, S. F. (Eds.). (1989). *Primary prevention of AIDS: Psychological approaches (Vol. 13). Primary prevention of psychopathology.* Newbury Park, CA: Sage Publications.

Mays, V. M., & Cochran, S. D. (1987). Acquired immunodeficiency syndrome and black Americans: Special psychosocial issues. *Public Health Reports, 102*(2), 224–231.

McAnarney, E. R., & Schreider, C. (1984). *Identifying social and psychological antecedents of adolescent pregnancy: The contribution of research to concepts of prevention.* New York: W. T. Grant Foundation.

McAuley, E., & Courneya, K. S. (1993). Adherence to exercise and physical activity as health-promoting behaviors: Attitudinal and self-efficacy influences. *Applied and Preventive Psychology, 2*, 65–77.

Meichenbaum, D. (1985). *Stress inoculation training.* New York: Pergamon Press.

Meichenbaum, D., & Jaremko, M. E. (Eds.). (1983). *Stress reduction and prevention.* New York: Plenum Press.

Mowrer, S. H., & Strader, T. N. (1992). National association addresses tough prevention issues. *Journal of Primary Prevention, 13*(1), 73–77.

Muñoz, R. F. (1991). Prevention of depression: Training issues for research and practice. In *The prevention of mental disorders: Progress, problems, and prospects.* Washington, DC: National Institute of Mental Health.

Olds, D. L. (1988). The parental/early infancy project. In R. Price, E. L. Cowen, R. P. Lorion, & J. Ramos-McKay (Eds.), *14 ounces of prevention: A casebook for practitioners* (pp. 9–23). Washington, DC: American Psychological Association.

Orlandi, M. A. (1986). Community-based substance abuse prevention: A multicultural perspective. *Journal of School Health, 56*(9), 394–401.

Payne, I. R., Bergin, A. E., Bielema, K. A., & Jenkins, P. H. (1991). Review of religion and mental health: Prevention and the enhancement of psychosocial functioning. *Prevention in the Human Services, 9*(2), 11–40.

Perlmutter, F. (1982a). *Mental health promotion and primary prevention.* San Francisco: Jossey-Bass.

Perlmutter, F. (Ed.). (1982b). *New directions for mental health services: Mental health promotion and primary prevention.* San Francisco: Jossey-Bass.

Peterson, L. (1984). Teaching home safety and survival skills to latch-key children: A comparison of two manuals and methods. *Journal of Applied Behavioral Analysis, 17*(3), 279–293.

Peterson, L., Mori, L., Selby, V., & Rosen, B. N. (1988). Community interventions in children's injury prevention: Differing costs and differing benefits. *Journal of Community Psychology, 16*, 188–204.

Pierson, D. E. (1988). The Brookline Early Education Project. In R. Price, E. L. Cowen, R. P. Lorion, & J. Ramos-McKay (Eds.), *14 ounces of prevention: A casebook for practitioners* (pp. 24–31). Washington, DC: American Psychological Association.

Pilisuk, M., & Parks, S. H. (1986). *The healing web: Social networks and human survival.* Hanover, NH: University Press of New England.

Pill, C. J. (1981). A family life education group for working with stepparents. *Social Casework, 62*(3), 159–166.

The prevention of mental disorders: A national research agenda. (1993). Washington, DC: U.S. Government Printing Office.

Price, R. H., Cowen, E. L., Lorion, R. P., & Ramos-McKay, J. (Eds.). (1988). *14 ounces of prevention: A casebook for practitioners.* Washington, DC: American Psychological Association.

Price, R. H., & Smith, S. E. (1985). *A guide to evaluating prevention programs in mental health* (Publication No. (ADM) 85–1365). Washington, DC: U.S. Government Printing Office.

Promoting health; preventing disease: Objectives for the nation. (1980). Washington, DC: U.S. Government Printing Office.

Reiss, D. (1993). Preface to *The prevention of mental disorders: A national research agenda* [Mimeograph]. Washington, DC: National Institute of Mental Health.

Robertson, L. S. (1975). Behavioral research and strategies in public health: A demur. *Social Science and Medicine, 9*(3), 165–170.

Robins, L. N., & Earls, F. (1985). A program for preventing anti-social behavior for high-risk infants and preschoolers: A research prospectus. In R. L. Hough, P. A. Gongla, V. B. Brown, & S. E. Goldston (Eds.), *Psychiatric epidemiology and prevention: The possibilities* (pp. 73–84). Los Angeles: University of California, Neuropsychiatric Institute.

Robins, L. N., & Regier, D. A. (Eds.). (1991). *Psychiatric disorders in America: The epidemiologic catchment area study.* New York: Free Press.

Robins, L. N., & Rutter, M. (Eds.). (1990). *Straight and devious pathways from childhood to adulthood.* New York: Cambridge University Press.

Robins, L. N., & Wish, E. (1977). Childhood deviance as a developmental process: A study of 223 urban black men from birth to 18. *Social Forces, 56*(2), 448–471.

Rodgers, B. (1990). Influences of early-life and recent factors on affective disorders in women: An exploration of vulnerability models. In L. N. Robins & M. Rutter (Eds.), *Straight and devious pathways from childhood to adulthood* (pp. 314–327). New York: Cambridge University Press.

Rosen, J. C., & Solomon, L. J. (Eds.). (1985). *Prevention in health psychology.* Hanover, NH: University Press of New England.

Rutter, M. (1987). Psychosocial resilience and protective mechanisms. *American Journal of Orthopsychiatry, 57*, 316–331.

Saleeby, D. (Ed.). (1992). *The strengths perspective in social work practice.* New York: Longman.

Scheinhart, L. J., & Weikart, D. B. (1988). The High/Scope Perry Preschool Program. In R. Price, E. L. Cowen, R. P. Lorion, & J. Ramos-McKay (Eds.), *14 ounces of prevention: A casebook for practitioners* (pp. 53–66). Washington, DC: American Psychological Association.

Schilling, R., Schinke, S., Nichols, S., Zayas, L., Miller, S., Orlandi, M., & Botvin, G. (1989). Developing strategies for AIDS prevention research with black and Hispanic drug users. *Public Health Reports, 104*(1), 2–10.

Schinke, S. P., & Gilchrist, L. D. (1984). *Life skills counseling with adolescents.* Baltimore: University Park Press.

Sepulveda, J., Fineberg, H., & Mann, J. (Eds.). (1992). *AIDS—Prevention through education: A world view.* New York: Oxford University Press.

Shure, M. B., & Spivack, G. (1988). Interpersonal cognitive problem-solving. In R. Price, E. L. Cowen, R. P. Lorion, & J. Ramos-McKay (Eds.), *14 ounces of prevention: A casebook for practitioners* (pp. 69–82). Washington, DC: American Psychological Association.

Smith, A. (1990). Social influence and antiprejudice training programs. In J. Edwards, R. S. Tindale, L. Heath, & E. J. Posavac (Eds.), *Social influence processes and prevention* (pp. 183–196). New York: Plenum.

Spaulding, J., & Balch, P. (1983). A brief history of primary prevention in the twentieth century: 1908–1980. *American Journal of Community Psychology, 11*(1), 59–80.

Stolberg, A., Kiluk, D., & Garrison, K. (1986). A temporal model of divorce adjustment with implications for primary prevention. In S. Auerbach & A. Stolberg (Eds.), *Crisis intervention with children and families* (pp. 105–122). Washington, DC: Hemisphere.

Szasz, T. (1986). The case against suicide prevention. *American Psychologist, 41*(7), 806–812.

Trattner, W. I. (1991). *From poor law to welfare state: A history of social welfare in America* (4th ed.). New York: Free Press.

Tzeng, O. C. S., Jackson, J. W., & Karlson, H. C. (1991). *Theories of child abuse and neglect: Differential perspectives, summaries, and evaluations.* New York: Praeger.

Vinokur, A. D., van Ryn, M., Gamlick, E., & Price, R. (1991). Long-term follow-up and benefit-cost analysis of the jobs program: A preventive intervention for the unemployed. *Journal of Applied Psychology, 76*(2), 213–219.

Wallack, L. (1984). Practice issues, ethical concerns and future directions in the prevention of alcohol-related problems. *Journal of Primary Prevention, 4*(4), 199–224.

Weinberg, J. K., & Levine, D. I. (1990). A primer on tort liability of primary prevention programs. *Prevention in Human Services, 8*(2), 65–88.

Weinstein, C. S., & David, T. G. (Eds.). (1987). *Spaces for children: The built environment and child development.* New York: Plenum.

Werner, E. E., & Smith, R. S. (1992). *Overcoming the odds: High risk children from birth to adulthood.* Ithaca, NY: Cornell University Press.

Whiteman, M., Fanshal, D., & Grundy, J. F. (1987). Cognitive-behavioral interventions aimed at anger of parents at risk of child abuse. *Social Work, 32*, 469–474.

Williams, C. L. (1989). Prevention programs for refugees: An interface for mental health and public health. *Journal of Primary Prevention, 10*(2) 167–186.

Zigler, E., & Styfco, S. J. (1993). *Head Start and beyond: A national plan for extended childhood intervention.* New Haven, CT: Yale University Press.

Zigler, E., & Valentine, J. (Eds.). (1979). *Project Head Start: A legacy of the war on poverty.* New York: Free Press.

FURTHER READING

Bloom, M. (1981). *Primary prevention: The possible science.* Englewood Cliffs, NJ: Prentice Hall.

Felner, R. D., Jason, L. A. Moritsuga, J. N., & Farber, S. S. (Eds.). (1983). *Preventive psychology: Theory, research, and practice.* New York: Pergamon Press.

McCord, J., & Tremblay, R. E. (Eds.). (1992). *Preventing anti-social behavior: Interventions from birth through adolescence.* New York: Guilford Press.

Price, R. H., Ketterer, R. F., Bader, B. C., & Monahan, J. (Eds.). (1980). *Prevention in mental health: Research, policy, and practice.* Beverly Hills: Sage Publications.

Roberts, M. C., & Peterson, L. (Eds.). (1984). *Prevention of problems in childhood: Psychological research and applications.* New York: John Wiley & Sons.

Martin Bloom, PhD, is professor, University of Connecticut, School of Social Work, 1798 Asylum Avenue, West Hartford, CT 06117.

For further information see

Advocacy; Alcohol Abuse; Cognition and Social Cognitive Theory; Community Needs Assessment; Direct Practice Overview; Drug Abuse; Ecological Perspective; Ethnic-Sensitive Practice; Families Overview; Goal Setting and Intervention Planning; Human Development; Interdisciplinary and Interorganizational Collaboration; Managed Care; Person-in-Environment; Prevention and Wellness; Primary Health Care; School-Linked Services; Self-Help Groups; Social Planning; Violence Overview.

Key Words	
health	promotion
mental health	protection
prevention	public health

Prisons

See Adult Corrections

Private Practice
Robert L. Barker

Social workers have been in private practice since the profession's earliest days, but until the 1980s their number and influence remained small. Currently, however, private practice is social work's fastest-growing employment setting (Gibelman & Schervish, 1993). In the traditional model of practice, social workers are employed in service agencies; their clients are assigned to them by their employer agencies, which also determine what types of services they are to provide. Conversely, private social work practitioners are employed by their clients, maintain their own facilities, determine their own intervention methods, and base their activities on the norms of their profession rather than the requirements of social services agencies (Barker, 1992). Although most of their time is spent in clinical work with individuals, groups, and families, private practitioners provide virtually the same range of services as those delivered by agency-based and publicly funded workers (Brown, 1989).

DEMOGRAPHICS OF PRIVATE PRACTICE

Private social work practitioners are in every state in the nation and in many of the economically developed countries of the world (Levin & Leginsky, 1989; Pinker, 1990; Rosenman, 1989). The vast majority have their offices in cities and suburbs; others are in rural settings and small towns (Cohen, 1987; Peirce, 1986). Some do not use offices, preferring to see their clients via house-calls (Whittington, 1985). Most private practitioners are engaged primarily in clinical work, such as psychotherapy, group therapy and social group work, family and marital therapy, and various forms of counseling (Brown, 1990). Others provide nonclinical services; for example, some are paid to supervise volunteer workers or consult with organizations. Some nonclinical private practice social workers conduct training groups, educational seminars, and independent research. Others establish proprietary social services—that is, for-profit, social services–related businesses such as private residential care facilities.

The number of social workers in private practice is not precisely known. NASW surveys of its members indicate that of the 134,000 members in 1991, more than 15,000 held primary jobs in solo or group private practices, and more than 40,000 were involved in some form of part-time private practice (Gibelman & Schervish, 1993). More than 4,000 social workers, most of whom have private practices, belong to the National Federation of Societies for Clinical Social Work. A similar number belong to the American Association for Marital and Family Therapy, and several hundred are members of the International Conference for the Advancement of Private Practice in Social Work. Moreover, many social workers in private practice belong to no professional association and thus remain uncounted in surveys of this type. Considering all these groups, it seems reasonable to assume that, as of 1994, approximately 20,000 social workers in the United States were primarily employed in private practice and 45,000 others were secondarily employed in private practice in addition to their primary social work jobs.

WHO ARE PRIVATE PRACTICE SOCIAL WORKERS?

One reason it is difficult to specify the precise number of private social work practitioners is that not everyone agrees who is and who is not a private practitioner. For example, are social workers considered private practitioners if they are salaried employees of others? Some salaried workers consider themselves private practitioners because their employers are private practitioners. Are social workers who provide consultation services to institutions for a fee considered private practitioners? Many of these consultants have not considered themselves to be engaged in a private practice because their services are not clinically oriented. Clearly, it is important to achieve consensus about the definition of private practice.

The Social Work Dictionary (Barker, 1995) defines *private practice* in social work as "the process in which the values, knowledge, and skills of social work, which were acquired through sufficient education and experience, are used by an autonomous professional to deliver social services autonomously to clients in exchange for mutually agreed payment."

By this definition a social worker is engaged in private social work practice only if he or she has obtained the legally or professionally prescribed education and experience and adheres to the values of the profession. It is private practice only when the specific fees for services rendered are paid to the worker by the client or the client's appointed third party. It is not private practice if the worker receives a salary from an employer, even if that employer is a private practitioner. The client may be an individual in a clinical setting but also may be an institution paying for consultation services.

EVOLUTION OF PRIVATE PRACTICE

When social work was in its infancy at the beginning of the 20th century, many of its founders advocated private practice. While Mary E. Richmond was writing social work's earliest textbooks and helping to develop its earliest social agencies, she also counseled private clients for fees. She wrote that if social work was to have value and influence, its benefits should be available to all, not only poor people. She predicted that private practice would be part of the profession (Richmond, 1922).

Until after World War II, however, only a few hundred social workers entered private practice (Smalley, 1954). Few potential clients could afford such services (Courtney, 1992). Furthermore, many social work leaders were opposed to private practice. When NASW was created in 1955, its first president thought private practitioners were not doing social work (Cohen, 1956).

Establishment of Qualifications

Eventually, more social workers entered private practice, and in 1958 NASW formally acknowledged private practice as a legitimate part of the profession. In 1962 NASW established formal qualifications for private practice: The applicant had to have a master's of social work (MSW) or equivalent degree, NASW membership, Academy of Certified Social Workers (ACSW) certification, and five years of supervised agency experience, including at least two years at one agency, practicing the methods that would be used in the private work. These requirements were modified in subsequent years as state licensing laws become more extensive. In 1964 NASW organized a national study group on private practice and later published the findings in the *Handbook on the Private Practice of Social Work* (NASW, 1974). In 1976 NASW began publishing the *Register of Clinical Social Workers* to inform the public about those qualified for private and clinical practice.

Regulation and Vendorship

The greatest growth in the number of private social work practitioners took place in the 1980s. Two factors were of special significance in this development: (1) third-party payments to social workers and (2) legal regulation (Barker, 1992). Health insurance organizations such as Blue Cross, health maintenance organizations, and managed care programs and government-financed health care programs such as the Civilian Health and Medical Program of the Uniformed Services began reimbursing social workers for their services to private clients. This trend will probably continue until health care reform modifies existing insurance programs.

Third-party funding for social workers was made possible largely because of state licensing laws. By 1994 every state in the nation licensed or certified social workers to practice. Thus, third-party payers and potential clients had greater assurance that their funds were placed with regulated professionals. As a result 33 states currently have vendor laws that require insurance reimbursement for clinical social workers' services ("Tally of 'Vendorship' Laws," 1993).

CREDENTIALS REQUIRED FOR PRIVATE PRACTICE

Licenses

In the United States the credentials required of social workers in private practice are established and enforced through the laws of all 50 states and the District of Columbia. To engage in private social work practice, a social worker must first meet the qualifications of the state in which he or she will practice and obtain a license through that state's board of professional licensing or a similar organization. The requirements for the license vary considerably. States with the most stringent rules require the applicant to have an MSW degree from an accredited school of social work, to have one or more years of relevant supervised social work experience in accredited facilities, and to pass written and oral licensing examinations. Less demanding jurisdictions require only an accredited MSW degree and some documented practice experience. (Applicants for licenses should contact their state's professional licensing board or write for further information to the American Association of State Social Work Board in Culpeper, Virginia.)

Many cities and counties also require private practice social workers to obtain local permits and registration certificates. Usually these permits are granted by local authorities when fees or taxes are paid and state licenses are obtained. (Information about local permits can be obtained by contacting the city or county executive's office.)

Certification

Professional certification is also important. Although such credentials are not necessarily required by law, private practitioners who lack professional certification find it more difficult to get third-party reimbursement and referrals from other professionals. Moreover, without the profession's credentials, a social worker is more vulnerable to malpractice suits and other legal problems.

Several professional organizations sanction private social work practitioners. These include NASW, the American Board of Examiners in Clinical Social Work, the National Federation of Societies for Clinical Social Work, and the International Committee for the Advancement of Private Practice in Social Work. Other organizations, such as the American Association for Marital and Family Therapy, that have many social work members also maintain professional sanctions for private practice. The requirements of all these organizations are similar to NASW's professional credential, the ACSW certificate. To become ACSW certified, an NASW member must have an MSW degree or doctorate from a Council on Social Work Education–accredited social work school and two subsequent years of full-time supervised practice experience or 3,000 hours of paid, part-time work. The candidate also must pass the written ACSW examination and provide three acceptable professional references, including one from a current supervisor.

BUSINESS SKILLS AND OTHER REQUIREMENTS

A private practice is, among other things, a business. Therefore, the social worker who maintains it must have knowledge and skill in business management. He or she must know and follow the regulations and standards for hiring employees and providing for their benefits, bookkeeping, paying taxes, recording all transactions with clients and third parties, obtaining and maintaining proper licenses and equipment, investing, and providing for retirement and sickness. Many social workers in private practice employ professional business managers or consultants to help with such responsibilities. The private practitioner should also have an aptitude for clientele building through such activities as networking with other professionals, meeting with community groups, advertising, and public relations.

Private practitioners pay their own overhead costs. Because these costs begin before sufficient income is generated, practitioners need adequate capital to start and maintain the practice. This amount should be at least enough to pay for three months' office rent and to purchase or rent office furniture and equipment. It should also be enough to pay the costs of building a clientele, as well as living expenses for several months.

Social work private practitioners must be internally motivated to succeed. They cannot rely on supervisors or agency chiefs for their incentives. They must be able to work in relative isolation with little daily contact with peers and to confront clients and third parties about payments.

They also must be able to promote themselves and their services to the public. Many social workers who start private practices eventually return to agency employment because they miss the collegiality of their peers and the security of organizational employment (Brown, 1990; Brown & Barker, in press).

MOTIVATIONS FOR PRIVATE PRACTICE

A number of studies have reached similar conclusions about why so many social workers enter private practice (Abell & McDonnell, 1990; Alexander, 1987; Butler, 1992; Hardcastle & Brownstein, 1989; Jayaratne, Davis-Sacks, & Chess, 1991; Morris, 1991). They find that many social workers seek more opportunity to work as professionals, independent of bureaucratic constraints. Some want a higher income or to work with more motivated clients. Others want to create their own working environments; they like the freedom to determine their own work habits and schedules, to locate and equip their offices according to their own tastes, and to choose the interventions to use with their clients. Many social workers find that independent practice is the only way they can remain in direct practice; if they stay in social agencies, they get "promoted" to administrative and supervisory positions and have no time to work directly with clients except after agency hours. (Given the low pay scales in many social agencies, "moonlighting" in private practice helps subsidize a worker's income and enables the worker to remain in social work [Goldmeier, 1990; Ozawa & Law, 1993].)

Finally, for many social workers private practice is the only practical way to remain in their chosen profession, because cutbacks in funding for social agencies have reduced the number of social work jobs.

OCCUPATIONAL HAZARDS

The attractions of private practice may be offset by unavoidable risks. Most social workers find that many of the negative aspects of agency work are also present in independent work. They still deal with bureaucracies, unmotivated clients, and excessive demands on their time. Three additional difficulties that confront social workers in private practice are financial indebtedness, burnout, and the risk of legal problems.

Financial Problems

The costs of establishing and maintaining a private organization can be heavy and the income is unpredictable. Many private practitioners collect fees of between $50 and $100 per client hour and think of this as their spendable income. Typically, less than half the money received from clients is spendable; most income goes for overhead expenses, taxes, health and other insurance, education, and retirement. When it is time to pay these costs, private practitioners are sometimes not adequately prepared, especially if their client base is smaller than they expected. To reduce financial risks, they must make realistic projections of expenses and income, make systematic budget and tax plans, and practice sound business procedures.

Burnout

Many private practitioners eventually become overworked and burned out. To make their practices succeed, they must devote as much time to practice management activities as to seeing clients. Keeping business records, filling out insurance forms, and preparing business documents and other necessary but tedious paperwork takes long hours. The private practitioner must also devote considerable unpaid time to promoting the practice and maintaining his or her skills through educational activities. An even greater source of burnout problems is the isolation of private practice. Professionals in agency work have regular access to colleagues with whom they can share case and work experience. The private worker has fewer such opportunities, and the lack of them can lead to depression and a sense of diminished well-being. Burnout is less likely when the private practitioner plans a realistic work schedule and collaborates frequently with colleagues (Arches, 1991).

Legal Problems

Legal problems, especially the omnipresent threat of malpractice litigation, are the third hazard to which private practitioners are especially vulnerable. Although the same risks may befall the agency worker, the private practitioner has no agency or supervisor to divert some of the risks or to provide emotional support. Malpractice litigation is possible when workers fail to get clients' advance consent to the methods used in the treatment, misuse the therapy relationship and exploit the client, make faulty diagnoses, provide inappropriate treatment or treatment they are unqualified to provide, prematurely terminate or abandon clients who still need service, or fail to warn others when the client has indicated a serious capacity to harm them (Barker & Branson, 1992). Workers reduce malpractice problems by understanding and avoiding these practices and by obtaining ample liability insurance.

CONTROVERSIES

As private practitioners in social work continue to grow in number and influence, so too does the debate about the extent to which private practice should be part of the profession. Many social workers continue to believe that private practice is antithetical to the values of the profession; they suggest that its existence ultimately diminishes the ability of the profession to serve its traditional clientele. Some critics of private practice say the private system discriminates against those who are unable to afford it. They believe that it encourages skilled workers to leave the public sector and that private practitioners are potentially harmful to the profession and to consumers because they are not supervised as they would be in agencies. Still other critics complain that the meager resources available to train social workers for the public sector are being diverted into training private practitioners, thus giving the traditional social work clientele even less access to social work services than before.

Specht (1992) claimed that some social workers enter private practice to avoid working with the traditional clientele of the profession—poor and truly disadvantaged people. Some also say that private practitioners are motivated primarily by the potential to make more money. Some private practitioners are even accused of having no interest in social work's goals and of having gone to a social work school as the fastest, easiest route to becoming a psychotherapist in private practice (Abell & McDonnell, 1990; Karger, 1989).

No doubt these accusations apply to some private practitioners. Private social work practitioners have higher incomes than all other social work groups except educators (Gibelman & Schervish, 1993). Some studies show that private practitioners spend less time with less affluent client groups than do agency workers (Brown, 1989), and there is probably no faster way to become a credentialed, third-party reimbursable, private counselor–therapist than by becoming an MSW social worker (Karger, 1989).

Most private practitioners claim that their values and ethics are virtually identical to those of their agency-based colleagues (Alexander, 1987; Brown, 1989). They acknowledge that they are not as well supervised as agency workers, but in the current climate of litigiousness, they are highly sensitive to the need for rigorous standards and technical practice. Furthermore, they point out that private practice is not a drain on agency staffing because agency personnel shortages no longer exist. Many schools of social work, they argue,

would experience significant cutbacks if all the students who wanted to enter private social work practice did not attend. They also contend that private social work practice is accessible to clients who are far from affluent because of widespread third-party reimbursement and their own proclivity for seeing clients pro bono or on a reduced-fee basis (Barker, 1992).

Many other questions are still being debated; they include the following:

- Should standards for private social work practice be raised to be as rigorous as those in other professions?
- Should the social work profession be more aggressive in marketing its private practitioners?
- Should accredited schools of social work provide education and encouragement to those who want to enter private practice?
- Should proof of continued education and competence be demanded of practitioners to show the public that accountability and quality assurance standards are maintained?
- Should older practitioners continue to be permitted to have licenses and certificates without passing the same competency examinations that are required of all other social workers in private practice?

The way the profession decides to answer these questions will largely determine the nature of private social work practice in the 21st century.

REFERENCES

Abell, N., & McDonnell, J. R. (1990). Preparing for practice: Motivations, expectations, and aspirations of the MSW class of 1990. *Journal of Education for Social Work, 26*(1), 57–64.

Alexander, M. P. (1987). Why social workers enter private practice: A study of motivation and attitudes. *Journal of Independent Social Work, 1*(3), 7–18.

Arches, J. (1991). Social structure, burnout, and job satisfaction. *Social Work, 36,* 203–207.

Barker, R. L. (1992). *Social work in private practice* (2nd ed.). Washington, DC: NASW Press.

Barker, R. L. (1995). *The social work dictionary* (3rd ed.). Washington, DC: NASW Press.

Barker, R. L., & Branson, D. L. (1992). *Forensic social work: Legal aspects of professional practice.* New York: Haworth Press.

Brown, P. M. (1989). Goals and goal attainment: Differences between private practice and agency workers. *Journal of Independent Social Work, 5*(1), 53–68.

Brown, P. M. (1990). Social workers in private practice: What are they really doing? *Clinical Social Work Journal, 18*(4), 56–71.

Brown, P. M., & Barker, R. L. (in press). Confronting the "threat" of private practice. *Journal of Social Work Education.*

Butler, A. C. (1992). The attractions of private practice. *Journal of Social Work Education, 28*(1), 29–34.

Cohen, D. (1987). Rural area private practice. *Psychotherapy in Private Practice, 5*(4), 41–52.

Cohen, N. E. (1956). A changing profession in a changing world. *Social Work, 1,* 12–19.

Courtney, M. (1992). Psychiatric social work and the early days of private practice. *Social Service Review, 66*(2), 199–214.

Gibelman, M., & Schervish, P. H. (1993). *Who we are: The social work labor force as reflected in the NASW membership.* Washington, DC: NASW Press.

Goldmeier, J. (1990). Combining agency and private practice: A reevaluation. *Families in Society: Journal of Contemporary Human Services, 71*(10), 614–619.

Hardcastle, D. A., & Brownstein, C. D. (1989). Private practitioners: Profile and motivations for independent practice. *Journal of Independent Social Work, 4*(1), 7–18.

Jayaratne, S., Davis-Sacks, M. L., & Chess, W. A. (1991). Private practice may be good for your health and well-being. *Social Work, 36,* 224–229.

Karger, H. J. (1989). Fast track to the shingle. *Social Work, 34,* 566–567.

Levin, R., & Leginsky, P. (1989). Independent social work practice in Canada. *The Social Worker/Le Travailleur Social, 57*(3), 155–159.

Morris, H. (1991). *Motivations for private practice: An analysis of social workers.* Unpublished doctoral dissertation, The Catholic University of America, Washington, DC.

National Association of Social Workers. (1974). *National Association of Social Workers handbook on the private practice of social work.* Washington, DC: Author.

Ozawa, M. N., & Law, S. W. (1993). Earnings history of social workers: A comparison to other professional groups. *Social Work, 38,* 542–553.

Peirce, F. J. (1986). It's scary but I have a nightlight: Private practice in a small town. *Journal of Independent Social Work, 1*(2), 45–54.

Pinker, R. (1990). *Social work in an enterprise society.* London: Routledge & Kegan Paul.

Richmond, M. (1922). *What is social case work?* New York: Russell Sage Foundation.

Rosenman, L. (1989). Privatisation of social welfare services and social work practice: An overview of the issues. *Australian Social Work, 42*(4), 5–10.

Smalley, R. (1954). Can we reconcile generic education and specialized practice? *Journal of Psychiatric Social Work, 22,* 76–68.

Specht, H. (1992). Point/counterpoint: Should the MSW curriculum include training for private practice? *Journal of Education for Social Work, 27*(2), 102–113.

Tally of "vendorship" laws rises to 32 (1993). *NASW News, 38*(10), p. 12.

Whittington, R. (1985). House calls in private practice. *Social Work, 30,* 254–259.

Robert L. Barker, DSW, ACSW, LCSW, is in private practice, 501 North Tenth Street, Tacoma, WA 98403.

For further information see

Clinical Social Work; Council on Social Work Education; Direct Practice Overview; Ethics and Values; Legal Issues: Confidentiality and Privileged Communication; Licensing, Regulation, and Certification; Management Overview; National Association of Social Workers; Professional Conduct; Professional Liability and Malpractice; Rural Social Work Overview; Social Work Education; Social Work Practice: History and Evolution; Social Work Profession Overview; Supervision and Consultation; Vendorship.

Key Words

business skills	private practice
malpractice	

Probation and Parole

G. Frederick Allen

Probation and parole in the United States refer to a class of programs used to punish adults and juveniles who have been convicted of criminal offenses. Generally, convicted offenders serve their sentences either in the community or in an institution. Offenders who are convicted of lesser crimes serve their sentences under the supervision of a probation officer and are said to be "placed on probation." Offenders who are convicted of more-serious crimes serve their sentences in an institution and are said to be "incarcerated." Offenders who have been sentenced to incarceration but are released for good behavior before serving the full term of their incarceration are said to be "granted parole."

Previously, probation officers, who usually had a social work background, participated in deciding which offenders should be placed on probation after conviction and which offenders should be granted parole after incarceration. However, as faith in rehabilitation dwindled, so did the impact of social work on the justice system. A more puni- tive, nonclinical approach to sentencing was taken. However, the dividends of this more punitive and nonclinical approach to sentencing have not been realized. The high costs of incarceration and the high crime rate in the 1990s have resulted in the reexamination of U.S. penal policy. Policymakers are again looking to rehabilitation and community-based corrections programs, such as probation and parole, to address the crisis in the criminal justice system.

PROBATION

History

John Augustus, a Boston shoemaker and philanthropist, invented a system of rehabilitating offenders that he termed probation (Augustus, 1852/1939). The word *probation* comes from the Latin *probatio,* which means a period of proving or of trial and forgiveness. In 1841 Augustus became the first probation officer by voluntarily offering to rehabilitate alcoholics. He believed that some offenders who appeared in the Boston court for alcohol-related offenses could be rehabilitated; therefore, he convinced the court to release these offenders to his care as an alternative to incarceration. It is estimated that between 1841 and 1859, Augustus saved nearly 2,000 men and women from incarceration.

Other philanthropists followed Augustus, and in 1878 Massachusetts became the first state to pass a probation statute (Augustus, 1852/1939). Several other states passed similar statutes before the 1900s. In 1899 the idea of using alternatives to incarceration for selected offenders led to the creation of the juvenile court system in Chicago. In 1901 New York passed a probation statute similar to that of Massachusetts (Lindner & Savarese, 1984), and by 1922, 22 states had provided for probation in their corrections systems (Champion, 1990). The federal government formally implemented probation on March 4, 1925. The Federal Juvenile Delinquency Act was passed on June 16, 1938, to provide for the care and treatment of juveniles and to apply probation to juveniles as well as to adults. By 1957 all states had statutes authorizing the use of probation as a sanction for adults, when appropriate.

Philosophy

Although there is still no central philosophy of probation, generally most probation jurisdictions subscribe to the original philosophy of probation: Offenders can become productive citizens through rehabilitation. The social work profession, which is committed to providing assistance to troubled people who may or may not be convicted offenders, shares this philosophy. Thus, a natural partnership between social work and corrections developed as a result of the mutuality of philosophies.

More recently, however, the philosophy of probation has been expanded to incorporate other theories—namely, punishment, deterrence, and

justice. As originally conceived, probation was the suspension of the "real sentence," contingent on good behavior. The failure of the probationer to abide by the conditions of probation could result in revocation of the probation order, leading to the imposition of the real sentence of incarceration.

However, the 1980s were a time of challenge for probation, and its proponents sought a mission (McAnany, Thomson, & Fogel, 1984). Legislatively, there was a trend toward making probation the sentence instead of a means of suspending the real sentence. The federal initiative to make probation a sentence was accomplished through the Comprehensive Crime Control Act of 1984, which attempted to improve the criminal justice system and combat crime by increasing the sanction level of probation. In so doing, Congress transformed probation from a suspended sentence to a sentence in its own right. Under this new federal law, probation is not a suspension of incarceration and the imposition of community supervision but a sentence in itself.

For probation to become a "real" sentence, however, it is necessary to incorporate into it certain sanctionlike elements of punishment, deterrence, and incapacitation (such as home confinement). If the offense is a felony and a term of probation is imposed, the court must impose at least a fine, an order of restitution, or a requirement for community service unless extraordinary circumstances exist that would make the imposition of such a condition unreasonable. A *fine* is a court-ordered assessment that requires the probationer to pay a specified sum of money to the court. *Restitution* requires the probationer to pay the victim. *Community service* requires the probationer to provide services to the community.

Fines, restitution, and community service provide the measurable outcome that has eluded social work and corrections for many years. These sanctions remedy an old dilemma of social work in corrections: the vagueness of rehabilitation as a goal. Under this explicit goal-directed probation, the probation officer is able to develop a supervision program to address the court's sanctions. The probation officer may also address the risk the offender presents to the community or the identified correctional goals of treatment: counseling, therapy, and vocational and education programs, if needed.

Goals

In the past, probation was focused on the individual offender, but the current trend is to extend this focus to the community. Generally, probation seeks to achieve four goals:

1. It keeps those convicted of nonserious crimes from the negative environment of jails and prisons. Probationers remain in the community, where they may benefit from community support of family and social services agencies.
2. It helps the offender avoid the stigma of the "criminal" label. By remaining in the community, probationers are not perceived as "ex-cons" who have been exposed to the negative impact of prison.
3. It allows offenders to integrate more easily with noncriminals. Offenders may hold jobs, earn a living for their families and themselves, and develop more positive self-concepts and conforming behavior than they probably would acquire if they were incarcerated.
4. Probation provides a practical means by which to ease the problems of prison and jail overcrowding and construction and the related burden on taxpayers.

Forms

The current trend is to use probation's underlying philosophy of rehabilitation to achieve crime control, community reintegration, punishment, and deterrence. Under this philosophical framework, probation may appear in several forms, including diversion, standard probation, intensive supervised probation, home confinement and electronic monitoring, shock probation, halfway houses, and outreach center programs.

Diversion is the official suspension of legal proceedings against a criminal defendant; the successful completion of a set of conditions usually leads to dismissal of the charges against the defendant. *Standard probation* involves the arrangement of compliance to specific conditions that are monitored by probation officers. *Intensive supervised probation* is increasingly common; it is a special form of traditional probation in which the intensity of offender monitoring is increased and the conditions of probation are considerably more stringent. In *home confinement* and *electronic surveillance,* which are designed for low-risk offenders as an alternative to incarceration in a prison or jail, offenders are restricted to their homes part or all of the time. *Shock probation* derives its name from the fact that judges initially sentence offenders to a term of incarceration. After offenders have been in prison or jail for a brief period, they are brought back before the original sentencing judge for resentencing to probation for specified terms. It is hoped that the brief application of imprisonment will shock the offender, thus deterring criminal behavior while not impeding the

readjustment of the individual on release. *Halfway houses* are community-operated homes that house probationers who require more supervision than they would otherwise receive under standard probation.

PAROLE

History

Parole is the conditional release of a prisoner from incarceration to supervision after a portion of the sentence has been served. Alexander Maconochie (1787–1860), a former Royal Navy officer and reformer, is credited with pioneering work in the early release of prisoners (see Champion, 1990). Arriving at a colony of exported prisoners, he was appalled by the conditions: Prisoners were beaten repeatedly and tortured frequently.

Maconochie believed that confinement should be rehabilitative, not punitive, and that prisoners should be granted early release if they behaved well and did good work while incarcerated. Thus, he gave prisoners "marks of commendation" and authorized the early release of some inmates who demonstrated good adjustment in the colony. Largely because of his improvements to the British penal policy and the institutionalization of early-release provisions in the English prison system, Maconochie is considered the father of parole.

Impressed with Maconochie's work, Sir Walter Crofton, a prison reformer and director of Ireland's prison system during the 1850s, copied Maconochie's three-stage intermediate system under which Irish prisoners could earn their early conditional release. Crofton is known as the father of parole in various European countries (Champion, 1990).

The U.S. link with the European use of parole was made in 1863 by Gaylord Hubbell, the warden at Sing Sing Prison in New York (Champion, 1990). By 1876, Zebulon Brockway, the superintendent of the New York State Reformatory at Elmira, was instrumental in the passage of the first intermediate sentencing law in the United States. He is also credited with introducing the first system of time off for good behavior, in which the time of an inmate's release date is reduced by the number of good marks earned.

Authorities dispute the true beginning of parole in the United States. Dressler (1969) claimed that parole was unofficially established in Boston by Samuel G. Howe in 1847. Officially, however, true parole resulted from the ticket-of-leave practice and was first adopted by Massachusetts in 1884 (Shane-DuBois, Brown, & Olson, 1985).

The U.S. Congress formally established a U.S. Board of Parole in 1930, and by 1944 all states had parole systems. By 1960 all states had some form of indeterminate sentencing.

Philosophy and Goals

The central goals of parole were to rehabilitate offenders and reintegrate them into society, alleviate overcrowding in prisons, and protect the community. Indeterminate sentencing was perceived for nearly half a century as a panacea for reforming criminals, but by the 1970s, critics were concerned about giving unlimited discretion to parole boards to regulate the process of prisoners' release. Various critics (for example, the American Friends Service Committee, 1971) argued against the state-imposed treatment of prisoners. They advocated the abolition of indeterminate sentencing in favor of determinate sentencing, which minimizes discretion in corrections and separates treatment and punishment. This separation makes therapy and counseling available to all prisoners, but on a truly voluntary basis. Later, arguments of fairness, unbridled discretion, predictability, and justice were widely heard. The scene changed rapidly toward determinate sentencing practices, culminating in the U.S. adoption of federal sentencing guidelines in 1984.

The presence of guidelines heralded determinate sentences based on just deserts punishment, general deterrence, and incapacitation. Sentencing guidelines also effectively eliminated the need for a parole system. Offenders are sentenced to what the U.S. Sentencing Commission refers to as "truth in sentencing," under which offenders serve their entire sentence without the benefit of early release. By 1985, 14 states had shifted from indeterminate to determinate sentencing. On November 1, 1987, the U.S. Sentencing Commission revamped the sentencing guidelines for federal district judges. As a result, the U.S. Parole Commission will be gradually phased out. Like probation, parole was established to rehabilitate offenders and reintegrate them into society. Therefore, social work played an important role in the process because it provided a cadre of personnel to make clinical decisions on the treatment and release of offenders.

According to U.S. Department of Justice (1994) statistics, by the end of 1993 the number of adults under correctional supervision, incarcerated, or under supervision in the community reached a new high of 4.8 million, a 165 percent increase since 1980. This figure also represents 2.8 million adults on probation and 671,000 on parole in state and federal jurisdictions in 1993.

CONTROLLING RISK AND PROVIDING CORRECTIONAL TREATMENT

Social work has shared the general approach to corrections of protecting the community by rehabilitating offenders. The trend has been to broaden this mission to emphasize protection of the community as the primary goal. For example, the new federal approach to probation and parole supervision suggests that the primary objectives of supervision are to enforce the offender's compliance with the conditions of release, minimize the risks to the public, and reintegrate the offender into a law-abiding lifestyle. In protecting the community, the probation officer may use a variety of risk-control supervision activities, including verification of employment and sources of income, financial investigation, monitoring of associates, record checks, urinalysis, and restrictions on travel.

Because of the lack of prison space and the cost of incarceration, the supervision population has changed over the years. Individuals who in the past would have been considered candidates for incarceration are routinely placed on supervision (Petersillia, Turner, Kahan, & Peterson, 1985). Therefore, the most significant change in the supervision model is the provision of effective supervision with high-risk offenders. In some departments, supervision activity is developed from the assessment of risks generated by the actuarial prediction of risk. On the basis of the actuarial prediction, offenders are classified in one of four supervision categories: high, medium, low, and nonreporting caseloads. Under this system, the higher the risk, the higher the frequency of contacts.

The federal system retains the actuarial prediction of risk as one indicator of the need for risk-control supervision, but it goes further. It explicitly recognizes both the necessity and the legitimacy of supervision activities aimed at non-risk-related concerns, such as collecting fines and restitution and meting out punishment by enforcing the conditions of confinement in the community. It also differentiates between supervision activities that are designed to monitor an offender's behavior and those that are designed to help the offender change his or her behavior.

Innovations in Probation and Parole Supervision

Correctional rehabilitation programs, including probation and parole, have not been successful in reducing recidivism with all types of offenders (Lipton, Martinson, & Wilks, 1975). However, these programs are inexpensive, and, as a result, new innovations have emerged to address the public safety concerns about supervising offenders in the community. Intensive supervision, home confinement, and goal-directed supervision are a few of these cost-effective innovations.

Intensive supervision. Intensive supervision is often described as the strictest form of probation. The high cost of incarceration means that the criminal justice system must have an intermediate sanction for those offenders who present too much of a risk for traditional supervision but not a sufficient risk to justify imprisonment. Each intensive-supervision program has its own flavor, but in general, these programs provide intensive surveillance-type supervision, including restriction of the probationer's–parolee's movements and, sometimes, mandatory or expected participation in employment, community service, counseling, and therapy programs.

The effectiveness of intensive-supervision programs has been mixed. They have shown some promise for some offenders, but research is needed to determine which characteristics of the programs are desirable and how these programs can be used effectively. In addition, these programs may achieve a balance between the public's need to be protected and the offender's need for rehabilitation services.

Home confinement. Another program, home confinement (also known as house arrest), is a sentence imposed by the court in which offenders are ordered to remain confined in their homes. Some offenders may be monitored via electronic equipment. Continued research is needed to help policymakers decide whether, when, and for whom this sanction is appropriate and the effectiveness of electronic monitoring devices in protecting the community.

Goal-directed supervision. Goal-directed, or "enhanced," supervision is a new initiative in the federal probation system. The old system defined the goal of supervision as "engaging the available community resources or providing assistance directly to aid offenders in organizing their lives to successfully meet the challenges of life in conformity with the law" (Administrative Office of the U.S. Courts, 1983, p. 2). The new system established three goals of supervision that are tied directly to the statutory responsibilities of probation officers: to ensure compliance with the conditions of release, to control risk, and to provide correctional treatment to offenders, in that order of priority.

Organization and Administration of Agencies
Probation and parole agencies, whether federal or state, serve two basic functions: (1) the investigation of offenders and (2) the supervision of offenders. State probation and parole systems are a potpourri of correctional systems that vary in organization and administration from state to state. In some states the probation and parole systems are included under the state's executive branch; in other states, such systems are under the judicial branch. All 50 state probation and parole systems are held together by the Inter-State Parole and Probation Compact, launched in 1934. This compact permits parolees and probationers to return to their home states and to remain under collateral supervision by local probation and parole authorities. For the most part, state probation and parole systems are modeled after the federal comprehensive probation and parole system.

The Division of Probation in the Administrative Office of the U.S. Courts, Washington, DC, has the responsibility for setting standards for the 95 federal district courts located in all states and U.S. territories. One aspect of the federal probation and parole agency is the Speedy Trial Act of 1974. Whereas probation and parole deal with sentencing and postsentencing services, the Speedy Trial Act of 1974 authorized the creation of pretrial services agencies.

Pretrial services agencies operate within district courts and may be a part of either the federal probation office or an independent court agency. Pretrial services began as an experiment in 1975, when most of the pretrial services agencies worked out of the federal probation office. Currently, however, most pretrial services agencies are independent agencies, except in small districts where it is economically advantageous to combine both agencies.

Pretrial services agencies generally make pre-bail investigations for judicial officers and provide supervision and supportive services to defendants who are released pending trial. The future of pretrial services has been precarious for many years. However, it appears that such agencies are well established in the courts, although the extent to which they have fulfilled their statutory mandate (that is, to reduce pretrial detention and recidivism) is at issue. Currently, states are developing their own versions of pretrial services.

Probation and Parole Staffs
The minimum requirement for consideration as a U.S. probation officer is a baccalaureate degree from an accredited college or university in one of the accepted fields of study: criminology, social

work, sociology, psychology, or law. The diagnosis-and-treatment approach of the 1960s and 1970s made social workers with master's degrees (MSWs) desirable in probation and parole agencies. However, the shift to a more punitive approach to decision making about sentencing, based on the seriousness of the offense rather than on the offender's personal characteristics, has reduced the emphasis on the MSW.

The caseloads of probation and parole officers vary among jurisdictions, from as high as 400 in some cities or counties to as low as 30 or fewer in others (Champion, 1990). As local resources for correctional programs are reduced, caseloads tend to increase. The size of caseloads remains a troublesome issue in probation and parole because caseload size is considered a critical factor in effective supervision. No ideal caseload size has been shown to be effective empirically in reducing recidivism, but recent initiatives (Petersillia & Turner, 1993) in some types of intensive caseloads appear promising. These initiatives include multiple weekly contacts with a supervising officer, random and unannounced drug testing, stringent enforcement of the conditions of release, and participation in relevant treatment.

FUTURE DEVELOPMENTS

The move to redefine probation at the federal level by making probation a sentence will influence future developments in probation. As a sentence, the mission of probation most likely will be punishment, deterrence, justice, and rehabilitation. Adapting social work practice to these multiple and often conflicting goals will redefine the role of social work in the justice system.

As most jurisdictions move toward more-determinate sentencing, parole, as it is currently practiced, will be modified considerably. A new form of the postrelease system, known as supervised release in the federal system, has the potential to make the decision-making system more rational, but may lack the focus on rehabilitation because it emphasizes protection of the community instead.

This community-protection focus, although important and politically supported, may lack the ingredients of professional status that probation and parole had in the past. To maintain and increase professional status in probation and parole, social work as a discipline may have to play its historical role in providing correctional interventions, especially because after a decade of prison construction and focused incarceration, the crime situation appears worse. According to the U.S. Department of Justice (1994), the nation's prison population has exceeded 1 million. If this incarceration rate continues, the United States would, by international standards, be among the heaviest users of prisons.

Punitive approaches to corrections have not yielded the anticipated dividends. Drug interdiction and severe penalties for drug offenses failed to win the War on Drugs. It appears that the pendulum is about to swing back and that social work will once again have an opportunity to play an important role in the criminal justice system. How this role is defined may determine the profession's impact on the justice system.

REFERENCES

Administrative Office of the U.S. Courts, Probation Division. (1983, April). *The supervision process* (Publication No. 106). Washington, DC: Author.
American Friends Service Committee. (1971). *Struggle for justice.* New York: Hill & Wang.
Augustus, J. (1939). *John Augustus: First probation officer.* New York: National Probation Association. (Originally published in Boston in 1852).
Champion, D. (1990). *Probation and parole in the United States.* New York: Macmillan.
Comprehensive Crime Control Act of 1984. P.L. 98-473, 98 Stat. 1976.
Dressler, D. (1969). *Practice and theory of probation and parole.* New York: Columbia University Press.
Federal Juvenile Delinquency Act of 1938. Ch. 486, 52 Stat. 764.
Lindner, C., & Savarese, M. (1984). The evolution of probation: University settlement and its pioneering role in probation work. *Federal Probation, 48*(4), 9.
Lipton, D., Martinson, R., & Wilks, J. (1975). *The effectiveness of correctional treatment: A survey of treatment evaluation studies.* New York: Praeger.
McAnany, P., Thomson, D., & Fogel, D. (1984). *Probation and justice: Reconsideration of mission.* Cambridge, MA: Oelgeschlager, Gunn & Hain.
Petersillia, J., & Turner, S. (1993). Evaluating intensive supervision probation/parole: Results of a nationwide experiment. Washington, DC: U.S. Department of Justice.
Petersillia, J., Turner, S., Kahan, J., & Peterson, J. (1985). Granting felons probation: Public risks and alternatives. Santa Monica, CA: Rand Corporation.
Shane-Dubois, S., Brown, A., & Olson, E. (1985). *Sentencing reform in the United States: History, content, and effects.* Washington, DC: U.S. Department of Justice.
Speedy Trial Act of 1974. P.L. 93-619, 88 Stat. 2076.
U.S. Department of Justice. (September 11, 1994). *Probation and parole populations reach new high* (Interim report). Washington, DC: Author.

FURTHER READING

Abadinsky, H. (1987). *Probation and parole: Theory and practice* (3rd ed.). Englewood Cliffs, NJ: Prentice Hall.
Andrews, D., & Bonta, J. (1994). *The psychology of criminal conduct.* Cincinnati: Anderson.

Cavender, G. (1982). *Parole: A critical analysis.* Port Washington, NY: Kennikat Press.

Clear, T., & O'Leary, V. (1983). *Controlling the offender in the community: Reforming the community-supervision function.* Lexington, MA: D.C. Heath.

Cullen, F., & Gilbert, K. (1982). *Reaffirming rehabilitation.* Cincinnati: Anderson.

Haxby, D. (1978). *Probation: A changing service.* London: Constibule.

Hussey, F., & Duffee, D. (1980). *Probation, parole and community services: Policy, structure, and process.* New York: Harper & Row.

Walker, H., & Beaumont, B. (1981). *Probation work: Critical theory and socialist practice.* Oxford, England: Basil Blackwell.

G. Frederick Allen, PhD, is deputy chief U.S. probation and parole officer, U.S. Courthouse, 219 South Dearborn Street, Room 1100, Chicago, IL 60604.

For further information see

Adult Corrections; Adult Courts; Community-Based Corrections; Criminal Behavior Overview; Criminal Justice: Class, Race, and Gender Issues; Criminal Justice: Social Work Roles; Domestic Violence: Legal Issues; Family Views in Correctional Programs; Female Criminal Offenders; Gang Violence; Homicide; Juvenile Corrections; Police Social Work; Rehabilitation of Criminal Offenders; Sentencing of Criminal Offenders; Sexual Assault; Substance Abuse: Legal Issues; Victim Services and Victim/Witness Assistance Programs; Violence Overview.

Key Words

corrections	parole
criminal justice	probation

READER'S GUIDE

Professional Associations

The following entries contain information on this general topic:

Council on Social Work Education
International Social Welfare: Organizations and Activities
National Association of Social Workers
Special-Interest Professional Associations

Professional Conduct

Ann A. Abbott

Professional conduct is behavior as defined by the ethical principles or behavioral guidelines growing out of the value base of a profession. The professional value base delineates the overall goals, objectives, and mission; the ethical principles provide a prescription for professional conduct based on those values. Values tend to provide an overview of the profession's focus, and ethics translate those values into specific guidelines for professional conduct (Abbott, 1988). As clear or deliberate as those guidelines may seem, practitioners are frequently confronted with ethical dilemmas or instances in which competing values require a personal interpretation or application of the underlying value scheme. For the most part, social workers confront those challenges, responding on the basis of professional integrity. In some instances, they may stretch the limits of ethical integrity. In rarer instances, social workers have conducted themselves in a fashion that appears to run truly counter to the value base and ethical framework. Their behavior is such that clients, peers, or co-workers question whether it conforms to the expectations of appropriate professional conduct.

Most professional associations have mechanisms for monitoring professional behavior and sanctioning members who are in violation of ethical principles or standards. Frequently these mechanisms are founded on a system of peer review. The major professional social work association—NASW—has such a system. In addition to a clearly defined value base, NASW has a *Code of Ethics* (NASW, 1994a) outlining the parameters of members' behavior, a system for reporting ethical violations, and a peer review process for evaluating alleged violations and bringing sanctions against those members whose behavior is determined to be in violation of acceptable ethical standards. This peer review activity, referred to as the adjudication process, is undertaken within NASW by means of the Committee on Inquiry (COI) structure, units of which operate in all 55 chapters of NASW.

The professional association sets standards for membership and monitors its members in light of those ethical standards. The peer review process does not preclude legal action by others or action by state regulatory bodies. However, it does identify professional misconduct and facilitate member rehabilitation. In addition to hearing complaints of alleged ethical violations by members, peers also serve important roles in educating members about the components of ethical professional practice and risk management.

PURPOSE OF ADJUDICATION

NASW promotes the "quality and effectiveness of social work practice" (NASW, 1994b, p. v). The adjudication of grievances provides a vehicle for guaranteeing that social work practice conforms to the ethical standards of the profession. The adjudication process is intended to protect the public from social work practice that violates those ethical mandates. In addition, "NASW uses the adjudication process to protect its members against exploitation and injustice in their places of employment" (NASW, 1994b, p. vi). Whenever possible, the adjudication process is "intended to be constructive and educative rather than punitive" (NASW, 1994b, p. vi). In this vein, recommendations for growth and vehicles for improvement are suggested frequently. However, consensus does not exist among members about the role of a professional association in prescribing corrective action. In some instances of professional misconduct, penalties or sanctions such as suspension from membership in NASW or notification of state regulatory boards may be necessary to carry out the professional responsibility to protect clients and peers.

In cases involving agency practices or personnel standards, the process advances the development or improvement of or adherence to personnel standards to reflect the values advanced by the profession. These personnel standards also should permit and facilitate the adherence by social work employees to ethical professional behavior.

The adjudication process advances NASW's mission, which is founded on principles of ethical conduct. The process affords a fair mechanism for examining complaints of practices that run counter to or are detrimental to the ethical mission of social work. In addition to contributing to high ethical standards of practice by both social workers and their employers, the process provides a "means of redress for aggrieved parties" (NASW, 1994b, p. v).

ADJUDICATION VERSUS JUDICIAL HEARINGS

The NASW adjudication process is not a formal legal procedure, rather it is founded on a process of peer review. Although the adjudication procedures provide for a fair hearing, legal representation is not permitted. Note that no court has found NASW's procedures insufficient to protect the rights of due process of the parties involved. Among the safeguards included in the adjudication procedures are provisions for specific written notification to the respondent of complainant's allegations and the opportunity to answer and be heard, to present witnesses and other evidence, to confront one's accusers, and to appeal an adverse decision to a higher body. Although certain components of court proceedings (for example, representation by counsel, testimony under oath, subpoena power, and transcript of the record) are not part of NASW's peer review process, clearly defined procedures, such as those outlined above, help to ensure that respondents' rights are protected and that all parties are treated equitably. An attorney may be present to serve as an advisor to a party at an adjudication hearing but only if the attorney is a social worker and is acting in the capacity of social worker and not legal counsel.

RATIONALE FOR PEER REVIEW

Social workers are best qualified to examine the behavior of other social workers. No one knows the parameters of acceptable, ethical professional behavior better than the collection of professionals educated and socialized in the behavioral expectations of that profession. These "standards for professional performance are reached by consensus within the profession" (Greenwood, 1957, pp. 49–50) and are transferred to and adopted by others as a requirement for professional membership. In joining NASW, each member, by signing the application form, agrees to abide by the *NASW Code of Ethics* and to submit to proceedings for any alleged violation of the *Code* in accordance with NASW bylaws.

In addition to a set of standards (frequently in the form of a code of ethics), a mechanism for self-regulation on the basis of those standards is typical. The adjudication process, based on peer review, guarantees compliance with ethical standards. Peers set the ethical standards for membership, and peers enforce adherence to those standards. In addition to the adjudication of alleged ethical violations, peers serve to educate other members on issues of risk management and sound professional practice.

HISTORY OF THE ADJUDICATION PROCESS

From shortly after its inception in 1955, NASW has had a code of ethics followed by a mechanism for the adjudication of complaints of ethical misconduct or violation. [The Delegate Assembly (NASW's policymaking body) approved the first *NASW Code of Ethics* in 1960, and the 1967 Assembly approved the adjudication process].

Well-defined adjudication procedures provide for three categories of complaint: (1) against NASW members for alleged unethical conduct, (2) against agencies for alleged violations of their personnel standards, and (3) against agencies for limiting or penalizing social workers for ethical professional actions taken on behalf of clients. The adjudication process has two primary purposes: (1) the protection of the public and (2) the protection of members. All three categories of complaint are heard with these two overarching purposes firmly in the foreground—the goal being a fair, thorough, and sound hearing process founded on solid guidelines for due process.

The adjudication procedures detailed in two volumes—*NASW Procedures for the Adjudication of Grievances* (NASW, 1994b) and *NASW Chapter Guide for the Adjudication of Grievances* (NASW, 1989)—put into practice the *NASW Policy Statement on Adjudication of Grievances* (amended in 1987) and reaffirm the commitment of NASW to advance the ethical practice of its members as outlined in the *NASW Code of Ethics* (most recently revised in 1993).

As with the maturation of any profession or process, the adjudication procedures and underlying code of ethics continue to be revised, with the underlying goal being the improved quality of professional practice. The most recent revision of the *NASW Procedures for the Adjudication of Grievances* occurred in 1988; the most recent revision of the Code of Ethics became effective July 1, 1994. Both continue to be reexamined to make them more explicit and useful in carrying out the mission of NASW. For example, the most recent revisions of the *NASW Code of Ethics* grew out of concern for the increased number of identified dual or multiple relationships between social workers and clients or former clients and the growing number of professionals who are impaired due to substance abuse, mental health, or physical health. (See Fewell, King, & Weinstein, 1993, and Kagle & Giebelhausen, 1994, for a discussion of behaviors and concerns resulting from these newly identified problematic behaviors.)

In 1995 a special review committee is examining the adjudication process, and a Code of Ethics Revision Committee is preparing revisions for consideration by the 1996 NASW Delegate Assembly. Both groups, in conjunction with other representative groups within NASW (for example, the Board of Directors and the National Committee on Inquiry), are working to streamline an already well-defined process.

ADJUDICATION: A PEER REVIEW PROCESS

Adjudication or peer review is carried out through COIs, which are composed of members of NASW. The size and composition of each committee varies on the basis of chapter need. The committees must reflect the diversity of membership within the chapter and have enough members to guarantee that hearings are conducted in a fair and timely fashion.

Each chapter COI has responsibility for acting on all complaints filed within its jurisdiction unless a member of the chapter staff, its Board of Directors, officers, or COI members are named as respondents, in which case jurisdiction is assumed by the National Committee on Inquiry (NCOI). In addition, a chapter COI may apply to the NCOI for a change or deferral of jurisdiction if it is convinced that judicious handling of the complaint cannot be achieved at the chapter level.

The *NASW Procedures for the Adjudication of Grievances* (NASW, 1994b) spell out in detail the process of filing a complaint, including the format for filing, time limits, acknowledgment of receipt by the chapter, and the demands or expectations of confidentiality. In addition to providing guidance on the filing of a complaint, the procedures delineate the criteria and mechanism for accepting a complaint. Responsibilities of all involved, including complainants (people filing a complaint), respondents (people being accused), chapter officers, and COI members, are explained with accompanying deadlines indicated.

Professional associations monitor and adjudicate alleged ethical violations by their members. In some instances, members who are respondents may refuse to participate in a hearing or may resign from membership. NASW takes the approach that such action does not stop the proceedings; rather the respondent's resignation or failure to cooperate is noted and the hearing commences according to plan. In cases in which a complainant wishes to withdraw his or her complaint, the respondent must grant his or her permission before the hearing or process can be terminated. Procedures governing such factors as prehearing activities; composition of the hearing panel; time frame of hearing sessions; and use of consultants, support persons, and witnesses are described in detail in the adjudication manuals (NASW, 1989, 1994b).

The hearing panel is responsible for submitting a report of its findings, conclusions, and recommendations to the chapter executive committee. This report shall state whether the alleged ethical violations are founded on fact and shall include recommendations for corrective action or penalties and sanctions.

The chapter executive committee either approves the report as presented or sends it back for reconsideration with an accompanying reason for disagreement. In most cases the reason is a procedural one. The details for such action are contained within the adjudication procedures (NASW, 1989, 1994b).

Once accepted by the chapter executive committee, copies of the report together with information about the appeals process are sent to both the complainants and respondents. The first avenue of appeal is the NCOI, with the final appellate body being the Executive Committee of the National Board of Directors.

In addition, the procedures provide guidance for the monitoring of corrective actions as well as the implementation of sanctions. Mechanisms for the removal of sanctions or for reinstatement in the association and the closing of cases also are included.

ALLEGED VIOLATIONS OF THE *NASW CODE OF ETHICS:* TRENDS AND PATTERNS

Several major studies have examined alleged violations of the *NASW Code of Ethics* and the findings of the adjudication proceedings (Berliner, 1989; Dawes, 1988; McCann & Cutler, 1979; National Center for Social Policy and Practice, 1993). McCann and Cutler, while examining the number of complaints against members for alleged unethical conduct during the first 22 years of the association (1955–1977), found that the total number of complaints accelerated or increased during the later years, with 40 percent of the cases being handled during the last two years (1976–1977). (Note that earlier violations could not be processed until 1967, the first year the adjudication process was in effect.) McCann and Cutler noted that only 15 percent of the complaints filed (154 cases) involved complaints of unethical conduct. Later findings of the National Center for Social Policy and Practice found that between 1982 and 1992, 76 percent of the cases fell in that category. The increase over time in the number of cases reported by McCann and Cutler was confirmed by later studies (Berliner, 1989; National Center for Social Policy and Practice, 1993). This increase in the number of cases parallels the growth of the association and thus should not be of concern; what should be of concern is the increase in cases involving alleged violations of the *Code of Ethics* and the increase in the number of founded allegations.

Between 1955 and 1977, one or more of the allegations in 25 percent of the 154 cases heard were upheld (McCann & Cutler, 1979). Between 1979 and 1985, 41 percent of 233 cases heard resulted in founded allegations (Berliner, 1989). Between 1982 and 1992, 42 percent of the alleged violations were founded (National Center for Social Policy and Practice, 1993).

Personnel or Collegial Interaction

Even though McCann and Cutler (1979) and Berliner (1989) examined only those cases with alleged violations of the *Code of Ethics* against individual members, they found that the majority of the cases related to personnel matters or colleagial interaction. McCann and Cutler found that between 1955 and 1977 the most frequently cited allegation involved firing (23 percent), followed by violations of personnel practices (14 percent), breach of contract (11 percent), client dissatisfaction (seven percent), confidentiality issues (six percent), sexual misconduct (five percent), social action (five percent), and discriminatory practices (three percent). It would appear that over three-quarters of the cases involved alleged actions against colleagues, supervisors, or agencies and not against social workers as direct practitioners involved with clients.

Violations Involving Clients

Over time, violations involving clients appeared to increase. Berliner (1989) found that 55 percent of the founded complaints involved ethical responsibility to colleagues or agencies; 45 percent involved direct interaction with clients. The study by the National Center for Social Policy and Practice (1993) indicated an even higher percentage of cases involving client complaints. The most frequently alleged complaints and the sections of the *Code of Ethics* that workers violated were

- II.F.5.—exploited relationship with clients for personal advantage (16 percent)
- I.A.2.—engaged in deceit, dishonesty, fraud, or misrepresentation (15 percent)

- I.D.1.—did not exercise professional discretion and impartial judgment (14 percent)
- II.F.4.—condoned or engaged in dual or multiple relationships with clients or former clients (14 percent)
- II.F.10.—withdrew services precipitously, resulting in adverse effects (13 percent)
- II.F.1.—did not serve clients with devotion, loyalty, determination, professional skill, and competence (10 percent)
- II.F.11.—did not anticipate termination adequately or interrupted service without proper notification of transfer (10 percent)
- III.J.3.—did not create and maintain conditions that facilitated ethical, competent practice by colleagues (10 percent)
- III.J.10.—did not evaluate other staff members using clear, fair evaluation standards (10 percent)
- I.D.2.—exploited professional relationships for personal gain (nine percent)
- II.H.1.—breached confidentiality (nine percent)
- III.J.4.—did not treat colleagues with respect and fairness (nine percent).

This change in type of complaint to one reflecting greater focus on unethical behavior with clients also is evident in reporting patterns over time. McCann and Cutler (1979) found clients to have assumed the role of complainant in only 13 percent of the complaints registered between 1955 and 1977, whereas the later study by the National Center for Social Policy and Practice (1993) (covering 1982 to 1992) found clients assumed reporting or filing capacity in 35 percent of the complaints. It is impossible to determine the reason for this shift: Are clients becoming more vocal, more sophisticated, more aware of their rights, more empowered? Is misconduct by social workers against their clients becoming more prevalent? Or, are these findings unique to data collection and analysis techniques? Simultaneously, reverse shifts were noted among reporting patterns of peers, supervisors, and administrators. Berliner (1989) found that 55 percent of the complaints sustained between 1979 and 1985 were generated by peers, supervisors, or administrators; the National Center for Social Policy and Practice study found that only 24 percent of the complaints between 1982 and 1992 were registered by peers, supervisors, or administrators.

Agency Violations
Until 1993 NASW published a list of agencies found to be in violation of their own personnel standards or found to have interfered with professional action of employees who were members of NASW. NASW ceased this practice of publishing agency names because the agencies are not members of NASW and the association does not have jurisdiction over them. However, NASW continues to hear cases of alleged violations involving agencies to improve quality of agency functioning and the working environment of NASW members, ultimately resulting in higher quality professional social work.

ROLES OF A PROFESSIONAL ASSOCIATION VERSUS A REGULATORY BOARD

The American Association of State Social Work Boards (AASSWB) noted that by 1988, 44 jurisdictions (states, territories, and the District of Columbia) had some form of legal regulation of the social work profession (Dawes, 1988). By 1994 all 50 states had achieved this goal. However, legal regulation takes many different forms ranging from registration to certification to licensure; the degree of control and the level of monitoring of social work practice varies considerably among jurisdictions. Although the goal of regulation is to protect the consumer from unethical practice, the degree to which this is achieved cannot be guaranteed given the current lack of uniform standards. As a result, it is important that professional associations such as NASW continue to press for a consistent format of monitoring to ensure high standards of ethical practice. Many regulatory boards are members of the AASSWB, which does provide a forum for the exchange of ideas; however, the AASSWB does not require conformity to specific regulatory standards for membership.

In many states a working relationship exists between the state social work regulatory board and the NASW chapter; in other jurisdictions, the relationship is almost negligible. Because of this lack of uniformity, it seems inevitable that NASW will find it necessary to continue an active leadership role in adjudicating alleged unethical practice to ensure high ethical standards for professional social work practice.

REFERENCES

Abbott, A. A. (1988). *Professional choices: Values at work.* Silver Spring, MD: National Association of Social Workers.

Berliner, A. K. (1989). Misconduct in social work practice. *Social Work, 34,* 69–72.

Dawes, K. J. (1988, November). *Complaints against social workers: A pilot study.* Paper presented at Social Work '88: NASW's Annual Meeting of the Profession, Philadelphia.

Fewell, C. H., King, B. L., & Weinstein, D. L. (1993). Alcohol and other drug abuse among social work colleagues and their families: Impact on practice. *Social Work, 38,* 565–570.

Greenwood, E. (1957). Attributes of a profession. *Social Work, 2,* 45–55.

Kagle, J. D., & Giebelhausen, P. N. (1994). Dual relation-ships and professional boundaries. *Social Work, 39,* 213–220.

McCann, C. W., & Cutler, J. P. (1979). Ethics and the alleged unethical. *Social Work, 24,* 5–8.

National Association of Social Workers. (1989). *NASW chapter guide for the adjudication of grievances* (rev. ed.). Silver Spring, MD: Author.

National Association of Social Workers. (1994a). *NASW code of ethics.* Washington, DC: Author.

National Association of Social Workers. (1994b). *NASW procedures for the adjudication of grievances* (3rd ed.). Washington, DC: Author.

National Center for Social Policy and Practice. (1993). *A study of the trends in adjudication of complaints con-cerning violations of NASW's code of ethics.* Unpub-lished report commissioned by the National Association of Social Workers.

FURTHER READING

Lowenberg, F., & Dolgoff, R. (1992). *Ethical decisions for social work practice* (4th ed.). Itasca, IL: F. E. Peacock.

Reamer, F. G. (1990). *Ethical dilemmas in social service: A guide for social workers* (2nd ed.). New York: Columbia University Press.

Reamer, F. G. (1994). *Social work malpractice and liabil-ity: Strategies for prevention.* New York: Columbia Uni-versity Press.

Rhodes, M. L. (1986). *Ethical dilemmas in social work practice.* Boston: Routledge & Kegan Paul.

Wells, C. C., with Masch, M. K. (1986). *Social work ethics day to day: Guidelines for professional practice.* New York: Longman.

Ann A. Abbott, PhD, ACSW, is president, National Asso-ciation of Social Workers, and associate dean, Rutgers University, School of Social Work, 327 Cooper Street, Camden, NJ 08102.

For further information see

Advocacy; Clinical Social Work; Continuing Education; Council on Social Work Education; Ethics and Values; Legal Issues: Confidentiality and Privileged Communica-tion; Licensing, Regulation, and Certification; National Association of Social Workers; Patient Rights; Private Practice; Professional Liability and Malpractice; Quality Assurance; Social Work Education; Social Work Practice: History and Evolution; Social Work Profession Overview; Supervision and Consultation; Vendorship.

Key Words	
adjudication	professional conduct
ethics	regulation
licensing	

Professional Liability and Malpractice
Paul A. Kurzman

The face of social work practice has changed over the past two decades, and so has the arena of professional liability. Liability for malpractice claims, once an issue chiefly of concern to physicians, is now a stark reality for social workers and social agencies. There are several explanations for this change in the work environment.

First, the social work profession has fought for and gained stature as the principal provider of mental health care in the United States. Both in indepen-dent and agency-based settings, clinical social workers have won recognition as fully qualified and autonomous treatment providers. In 1974 only 13 states provided for the legal regulation of social work practice; in 1994 all 50 states do. Similarly, professional social workers today enjoy vendorship privileges in 31 states, whereas such status did not exist in a single state 20 years ago (DeAngelis, 1993). Social workers now make diagnoses, furnish treatment, and authorize third-party payments with public and private carriers nationwide. How-ever, such acceptance of social work's stature by the government, insurance companies, and the public has helped create far greater risks in practice.

Second, courts and state legislatures today are much less likely to grant social agencies the veil of protection from liability that once was the

norm. The doctrines of *sovereign immunity* (shel-tering social workers who practice under public auspices) and *charitable immunity* (providing the same protection for social workers working under nonprofit auspices) have all but been abolished by judicial precedent. Hence, suing public and volun-tary agencies and their social work staff has become progressively easier and more successful (Besharov, 1985).

Third, we live and work in a more litigious environment than ever before. Clients who feel that they have been poorly served or harmed can hire negligence attorneys on a contingency basis (without an hourly fee or retainer), which makes litigation a feasible recourse for almost everyone. Such suits, for example, are being filed against NASW members insured through the association's Insurance Trust (the principal provider of cover-age for social workers) with increasing frequency. NASW data show that only one claim was filed in 1970, whereas 126 were filed in 1990. Even if they never served the aggrieved client, supervisors, partners, field instructors, and agency administrators often become codefendents in these legal proceedings through the principle of *vicarious liability*. Based on their supervisory and managerial responsibility, social work colleagues may be viewed in the role of *respondeat superior*, sharing in civil liability for wrongful acts committed solely by those under their supervision or in their employ (NASW, 1993; Watkins & Watkins, 1989).

Finally, the advent of managed care has brought new expectations and potential exposures. To receive referrals from employee assistance programs and managed care intermediaries, agencies and private practitioners usually must agree to indemnify their referral agent. In other words, social workers will be required to sign a "hold harmless" agreement whereby the provider agrees to assume all contractual liability. In this way, in an adversarial situation, potential legal exposure of one party—the employee assistance program or managed care organization—is assumed by the other party to the agreement—the social work provider—through indemnification. Generally, this is the price a social worker and a social agency must pay to become preferred providers in a managed care network.

CONCEPT OF MALPRACTICE

Simply stated, *malpractice* is professional negligence or misconduct. The social worker typically is accused of failure to exercise the degree of care that a similar professional of ordinary prudence would demonstrate under the same circumstances. *Negligence,* therefore, is conduct that "falls below the standard established by law for the protection of others against unreasonably great risk of harm" (Angell & Pfaffle, 1988, p. 59) and can become the basis for legal action. The social worker may be called on to respond to a civil suit brought by the injured party in a tort proceeding. The court then will determine if the client was damaged or injured by a breach of duty by the social worker, and if so, may assess monetary damages against the provider and others who may share a vicarious liability.

A finding of professional negligence denotes that a wrongful action has been committed, either by omission or commission. Four elements must be present to reach this conclusion: (1) The social worker incurred a professional duty, (2) the social worker was remiss or derelict in performance of that duty, (3) measurable loss or harm occurred, and (4) proximate cause can be established, on the basis of something the social worker did or did

not do, triggering the damage (Prosser & Keeton, 1984).

In addition to civil litigation to win monetary damages, social workers who have been found professionally negligent may face disciplinary action by the state that issued their license, as well as sanctions by the professional organizations to which they belong. The state social work regulatory board may call the practitioner before a disciplinary panel for a formal hearing, and the result could be a finding of "unprofessional conduct," resulting in a reprimand, public censure, fine, probation, or action to suspend or even rescind their license. Such state action could, for example, bar the social worker from practice, from use of a registered title, or from vendorship (third-party payment) privileges.

Similarly, social work malpractice may result in charges against the association member being brought before a committee on inquiry of his or her professional association, such as NASW. If the wrongful acts (represented by the discovery of malpractice) represent a violation of the association's code of ethics (NASW, 1994), a peer proceeding may result in the respondent's removal from the membership rolls and even national publication of his or her offense and the sanction.

Finally, social workers who are negligent may be denied renewal of their malpractice insurance, which is widely viewed as essential for professional practice. In fact, loss of continued eligibility for professional liability insurance may be a direct result of expulsion from the professional association that offers the coverage as a membership benefit. Furthermore, social workers who are sanctioned by their state or professional organization for negligence may find that they cannot purchase a replacement policy from other vendors.

AREAS OF LIABILITY

Experience suggests that six risks predominate for social workers, whether in independent or in agency-based practice. If these liabilities inherent in professional practice are not understood and approached from a preventive posture, they may result in litigation or claims of unethical practice.

Incorrect Diagnosis or Treatment

Providing an incorrect diagnosis or treatment is the most frequent area in which social work practitioners have been found at fault and accused of malpractice. The NASW Insurance Trust's professional liability insurance program currently covers more than 55,000 members. Claims filed between 1969 and 1990 against individual social workers who have been covered by the program show that almost one-fourth (24.3 percent) were charged with "incorrect diagnosis or treatment" (Reamer, 1994). Weak agency procedures for supervisory review and few standards to support interprofessional consultation and referral are central problems. The failure of social workers to refer a client to a physician to rule out biological, organic, or genetic conditions that may trigger psychological symptoms is perhaps the greatest arena of risk. Alexander (1983) noted that half of the claims for erroneous diagnoses by social workers covered by the NASW Insurance Trust plan were based on a charge that the clients' problems were actually medical, not psychological.

Fraud

Given the vendorship privileges that qualified social workers now enjoy in 33 states, opportunities to make false representation abound. For example, supervisors (who are eligible to activate third-party payments) cannot sign an insurance form stating that they provided treatment when the service was actually provided by a student or supervisee (who is not qualified as a vendor). Such action would qualify as an act of fraud. Similarly, clinical social workers who alter the true diagnosis to reduce the potentially adverse effects of labeling, or conversely, adjust the severity of the diagnosis so the client can qualify for third-party reimbursement, are providing a false representation. Kirk and Kutchins (1988) showed that such fraudulent conduct is more prevalent among social workers today than previously had been noted or expected.

Impairment

Social workers must ensure that they do not practice while impaired by alcohol, drugs, or mental illness, and they must not condone colleagues who do. Most state regulations consider professional practice while impaired a prima facie case of unprofessional conduct. States generally provide a professional assistance program for such providers so that their license can be placed in abeyance and protected while they remove themselves from practice and enter a supervised treatment program. A recent addition to the *NASW Code of Ethics* (1994) specifies that social workers whose personal problems interfere with their functioning are obligated "to take appropriate remedial action by seeking professional help, ... terminating practice, or taking any other steps necessary to protect clients and others" (p. 3).

Sexual Impropriety

Social workers have a duty to avoid sexual impropriety. All state codes of conduct governing the profession make this prohibition explicit. Moreover, the *NASW Code of Ethics* (1994) is unequivocal: "The social worker should under no circumstances engage in sexual activities with clients" (p. 5). Despite the clarity of the codes in this matter, accusations of sexual impropriety constitute almost one-fifth of the malpractice claims against members covered by the NASW Insurance Trust (Reamer, 1994). Sexual intimacy with clients can never be defended as beneficial to the client, supporting the transference, or acting as a sexual surrogate. Given the position of trust that the agency shares with its practitioners, courts may view employers here as having culpability as well. Agency executives and supervisors, in the role of *respondeat superior,* may share civil liability for such acts committed by practitioners under their supervision or in their employ. Furthermore, because sexual impropriety is viewed as an intentional tort (that is, gross, wanton, or willful negligence), such acts often are not covered by individual or agency professional liability insurance if damages are awarded to a plaintiff by the court.

Duty to Protect

Social workers can be liable for a negligence suit if they fail to fulfill their duty to warn the proper persons if a client discloses an intent to seriously harm himself or herself or a specific victim. Following the precedent established by a California Supreme Court decision (*Tarasoff v. Board of Regents of the University of California,* 1976), therapists have an affirmative "duty to protect" prospective victims when they conclude, through the standards of their profession, that a client presents a serious danger of violence to another person. Although the *Tarasoff* case was decided by a state, not a federal, court—following the legal doctrine of *stare decisis* (to stand by that which has previously been decided)—common law courts throughout the country usually have chosen to apply the principles of *Tarasoff* in deciding similar duty-to-protect cases. Following the standard established in *Tarasoff,* the client's disclosure of an intent to seriously harm a potential victim is (1) outside the usual boundaries of privacy and confidentiality and (2) obligates the social worker "to use reasonable care to protect the intended victim ... [and] to take whatever other steps are reasonably necessary under the circumstances" (p. 431). In an oft-quoted statement from the *Tarasoff* decision, the court (1976) stated,

> We conclude that the public policy favoring protection of the confidential character of patient–psychotherapist communications must yield to the extent to which

disclosure is essential to avert danger to others. The protective privilege ends where the public peril begins. (pp. 336–337)

Confidentiality

A final area of concern comes from the client's legitimate expectation that communications between him or her and the social worker generally will be considered private and confidential. As Reamer (1994) noted, the concept of privacy in professional practice is rooted in principles set forth by the Pythagoreans in the fourth century B.C. and later incorporated into the Hippocratic oath taken by physicians, which states, "Whatever I see or hear in the life of men, which ought not to be spoken of abroad, I will not divulge, as reckoning that all such should be kept secret." The *NASW Code of Ethics* (1994) places this principle in a social work perspective by stating that "the social worker should respect the privacy of clients and hold in confidence all information obtained in the course of professional service" (p. 6). In an era of electronic recording and communications, social workers need to understand how easy it is to compromise confidential client information inadvertently. Fax machines, cellular mobile telephones, modems, electronic mail, and computers connected to a mainframe create risks (and hence liabilities) if they are not properly used and secured.

PRIVILEGED COMMUNICATION

The concept of confidentiality is further governed for social workers in 42 states by the legal doctrine of *privileged communication*. When communications between a therapist and a client are termed "privileged," a breach of confidentiality can result in a civil suit, known as tort litigation (Gifis, 1991). Privileged communication statutes generally provide protection for social work clients similar to protection they receive in their relationships with attorneys, the clergy, and physicians. However, all states make exceptions to privilege for such disclosures as a client's intent to commit a specific crime or harmful act, or a client's knowledge of the abuse or neglect of children. (Indeed, statutes in most states proactively mandate the reporting of child abuse, and jurists would view the failure to do so as unprofessional conduct.) Hence, the concepts of confidentiality and privilege are not absolute, which is why the *NASW Code of Ethics* (1994) provides that the social worker may be expected to share confidential material when there is evidence of "compelling professional reasons" (p. 6). Practitioners should understand that there is a dynamic tension between the rules presuming confidentiality and those compelling disclosure.

Social workers also should note that the principle of privileged communication generally is in effect only when (1) it is specified in state statute and (2) the social worker is currently licensed and registered for professional practice under that statute. In a landmark 1984 decision by the U.S. Supreme Court (*United States v. Arthur Young*), Chief Justice Burger, speaking for a unanimous Court, refused to recognize the existence of a confidential accountant–client privilege, despite the argument by the accounting firm, Arthur Young, that all their professional staff engaged in the relevant case were licensed as certified public accountants and therefore their clients expected that an accountant–client privilege existed. The Court noted that there is no common law that sets a precedent or creates a presumption for granting privileged communication to any profession (including medicine and law); such privilege exists only as a specific statutory creation. Therefore, in the 42 states that provide for privileged communication between social workers and their clients, practitioners need to make sure that their license and registration are active and current. Social workers in the eight states that currently do not provide privileged communication for the social work profession by statute may need to work under the supervision of mental health practitioners whose professions do provide it (such as psychology or psychiatry), or take added precautions on both their own and their clients' behalf. Above all, in every practice situation and in all states, clients should be informed of their right to confidentiality as well as of the limits and exceptions both in case law and statute.

Because the "privilege" belongs to the client (not to the agency or the practitioner), clients in specific instances may choose to waive this right, if they feel that doing so is in their interest, giving social workers their consent to disclose otherwise confidential information. Social workers should be clear, however, that there are important differences between the concepts of "consent" and "informed consent." The latter requires full notice as to what is being consented to, generally measured by evidence that the client (1) is capable and competent to express assent (that is, he or she can read or understand the language in which the verbal or written permission is being explained), is of the age of majority, and does not suffer from dementia or a developmental disability that could impair judgment or comprehension; (2) is cognizant of the option to decline giving consent so that the disclosure will be voluntary and not coerced; and (3) is made aware of the consequences of giving or withholding consent and thus is fully informed about both the risks and the rewards implicit in this decision.

RISK MANAGEMENT

Many hazards inherent in professional practice can be mitigated by sound risk management strategies. The five recommendations that follow constitute a sound plan to reduce the perils of practice for practitioners, agencies, and the clients they serve.

Risk Management Audit

Social workers can retain a consultant to conduct a periodic risk-management audit. Such a review should ascertain the following:

- The agency's government licenses (such as those with the department of mental health, division of substance abuse services, or board of social welfare) are current and sufficient.
- The agency's papers of incorporation and current bylaws fully authorize the current scope of practice and service.
- The state license and current registration of all professional practitioners are active.
- Protocols for emergency actions (fire drills, involuntary client hospitalization, staff safety, and accident reporting) are well known and updated.
- Premiums for all forms of casualty insurance are paid and current and cover new programs, staff, and settings.
- Procedures for the maintenance and safeguard of client records are clear and are respected.
- Staff evaluations are conducted and reviewed on a scheduled basis.
- Vouchers and records for fiscal disbursements are properly authorized and filed.
- Insurance reimbursement forms are completed in a timely fashion and are authenticated in accordance with contractual requirements.

Legal Counsel

All agency and independent practitioners should establish an ongoing consultative relationship with a legal counsel, just as they would with an accountant or a psychiatrist. One should not wait until a crisis occurs and attempt to select an appropriate attorney under pressure. Counsel should review new legal documents (leases, contracts, hold-harmless agreements) before they are signed, help the practitioner and administrator put preventive risk-management strategies in place (to reduce exposure to malpractice suits), and regularly review the principal government statutes and case law that govern the agency and its professional practice.

Consultant Specialists

Consultants can ensure an availability, when needed, of (1) expertise in areas of diagnostic and treatment specialization; (2) avenues of referral for a second opinion; (3) protocols to rule out the presence of organic pathology; (4) psychological, aptitude, and projective testing; and (5) evaluation regarding the appropriateness of psychopharmacological intervention. Such consultants will reduce the common professional feeling that a social worker has to provide all the answers and also should help practitioners stay within the bounds of their training and license.

Continuing Education

Independent practitioners should return for training and engage in continuing education to expand and update their expertise. Similarly, social work administrators should schedule risk-management sessions as an integral part of in-service training for staff. Such initiatives not only ensure that experts share loss-prevention strategies with staff but also send the message that such organizational issues are everyone's concern. Training should encompass the following (Kurzman, 1994):

- state laws governing reporting procedures for child and elder abuse or neglect
- principles embodied in the *Tarasoff* decision regarding duty to protect
- current federal and state regulations on recording and maintenance of case records
- state statutes governing privileged communication and the precepts of confidentiality in the codes of ethics of the relevant professions
- proper completion and authentication of insurance forms
- additional education in areas in which social workers often are poorly trained, such as chemical dependence and learning disabilities
- state rules and standards of conduct for the licensed health professions.

In addition, special emphasis should be given to training staff to avoid even the appearance of sexual impropriety. The alarming rise in charges of professional misconduct alleging sexual intimacy being brought before licensing boards and professional associations and of malpractice suits being filed in civil courts makes this issue one of special concern and training need.

Liability Insurance

There is no substitute for adequate insurance in risk-management planning. Liability insurance in effect transfers financial risk from the social work provider, agency, or school to an insurance carrier. Because exposure to lawsuits can never be totally eliminated, even through the risk-management strategies suggested in this entry, social work practitioners need to be adequately insured. Professional liability insurance accomplishes two objectives. First, it covers the judgment for damages that a court may grant to a client. Second, it picks up the legal cost of mounting a defense against such charges, whether an award for negligence is made or whether the court finds the plaintiff's case to be without merit.

In addition to adequate individual professional liability insurance, social services agencies need to make sure their individual and organizational exposures are covered as well. Therefore, a social work manager should consider the following (Kurzman, 1991):

• *premises liability,* covering all sites at which services may be delivered, always obtaining an endorsement to cover additional program settings that may be established
• *agency professional liability insurance* that includes the activities of all staff—paid or volunteer, consultant or employee—to include contractual liability coverage
• *errors and omissions protection* for agency officers and directors, to shield members of the board of trustees and executive staff from personal liability in the performance of their administrative, managerial, and fiduciary duties
• *fidelity bonding* for all officers and staff who have the authority to manage the agency's income and assets, naming major agency funding sources as additional insured.

In sum, it is essential for individuals and agencies to obtain insurance commensurate with the organizational scope and clinical complexity of their practice.

Four criteria should be considered in the selection of an insurance company. First, does the firm hold one of the highest ratings (reflecting financial stability and adequate assets) that an independent agency, such as A. M. Best, may designate? Second, does the policy provide extended reporting and prior acts coverage? Third, does the policy guarantee coverage of the social worker for paid and volunteer professional practice at all times and in all settings? Finally, does the policy automatically indemnify independent practitioners without additional premium or fee for hold-harmless agreements they may be expected to sign under current managed care arrangements?

CONCLUSION

New opportunities for the social work profession have also brought new risks. Risk management is no longer a luxury, given (1) the enhanced status of the social work profession in recent years, (2) vendorship privileges now present in most states (as well as under federal programs such as Medicaid, Medicare, and the Civilian Health and Medical Program of the Uniformed Services [CHAMPUS]), (3) assumption by social workers of executive and broad managerial responsibility in public and private agency settings, and (4) greater numbers of clinical social workers establishing a full- or part-time private practice.

Exposure to charges of malpractice (both grounded and unfounded) have expanded, as reflected in charges being brought before administrative tribunals (such as association committees on inquiry and state disciplinary panels) as well as through civil litigation in courts of law. Social work practitioners and administrators can minimize their vulnerability by maintaining ethical professional relationships, following the canons of good practice, and practicing always within the scope of their expertise and the boundaries of their license. However, mitigating risk is better conceptualized as a proactive strategy of primary prevention than as a tertiary response to crisis. Social workers therefore must build risk management into their skills repertoire as a central, not an ancillary, function. Social workers must view education in the professional liability arena as a core activity if their response to the problem is to prove as comprehensive as the need.

REFERENCES

Alexander, C. A. (1983, November). *Professional liability insurance: Jeopardy and ethics.* Paper presented at NASW's Professional Symposium, Washington, DC.

Angell, F. J., & Pfaffle, A. E. (1988). *The whole field of insurance and risk management* (3rd ed.). Mount Vernon, NY: Roberts.

Besharov, D. J. (1985). *The vulnerable social worker.* Silver Spring, MD: National Association of Social Workers.

DeAngelis, D. (1993). *State comparison of laws governing social work.* Washington, DC: National Association of Social Workers.

Gifis, S. H. (1991). *Law dictionary* (3rd ed.). New York: Barron's.

Kirk, S. A., & Kutchins, H. (1988). Deliberate misdiagnosis in mental health. *Social Service Review, 62,* 225–237.

Kurzman, P. A. (1991). Managing risk in the workplace. In R. L. Edwards & J. A. Yankey (Eds.), *Skills for effective human services management* (pp. 267–280). Silver Spring, MD: NASW Press.

Kurzman, P. A. (1994). *Selected readings on legal and ethical issues in social work practice: Liability and risk-management for agencies, schools and practitioners.* New York: Hunter College School of Social Work.

National Association of Social Workers. (1993, May). *Vicarious liability for sexual misconduct: Social work practice update.* Washington, DC: Author.

National Association of Social Workers. (1994). *NASW code of ethics.* Washington, DC: Author.

Prosser, W. L., & Keeton, P. (Eds.). (1984). *Torts* (5th ed.). St. Paul, MN: West.

Reamer, F. G. (1994). *Social work malpractice and liability: Strategies for prevention.* New York: Columbia University Press.

Tarasoff v. Board of Regents of the University of California. 17C.3d 425 (1976).

United States v. Arthur Young. 82 S.Ct. 687 (1984).

Watkins, S. A., & Watkins, J. C. (1989). Negligent endangerment: Malpractice in the clinical context. *Journal of Independent Social Work, 3,* 35–50.

FURTHER READING

Albert, R. (1986). *Law and social work practice.* New York: Springer.

Austin, K. M., Moline, M. E., & Williams, G. T. (1990). *Confronting malpractice: Legal and ethical dilemmas in psychotherapy.* Newbury Park, CA: Sage Publications.

Brieland, D., & Lemmon, J. (1985). *Social work and the law.* St. Paul, MN: West.

Howing, P. T., & Wodarski, J. S. (1992). Legal requisites for social workers in child abuse and neglect situations. *Social Work, 37,* 330–337.

Knapp, S., & Van de Creek, L. (1987). *Privileged communication in the health professions.* New York: Van Nostrand Reinhold.

Kopels, S., & Kagle, J. D. (1993). Do social workers have a duty to warn? *Social Service Review, 67*(1), 10–26.

Maesen, W. A. (1991). Fraud in mental health practice: A risk management perspective. *Administration and Policy in Mental Health, 18*(6), 421–432.

O'Brien, J. P., Callahan, M. R., & Savaiano, J. A. (1987). A practical approach to the doctrine of informed consent. In G. R. Anderson & V. A. Glesnes-Anderson (Eds.), *Health care ethics: A guide for decision-makers.* (pp. 192–214). Rockville, MD: Aspen Publishers.

Reamer, F. G. (1987). Informed consent in social work. *Social Work, 32,* 425–429.

Reamer, F. G. (1991). AIDS, social work and the duty to protect. *Social Work, 36,* 56–60.

Saltzman, A., & Proch, K. (1990). *Law in social work practice.* Chicago: Nelson-Hall.

Siciliano, J., & Spiro, G. (1992). The unclear status of nonprofit directors: An empirical survey of director liability. *Administration in Social Work, 16*(1), 69–80.

Weil, M., & Sanchez, E. (1983). The impact of the Tarasoff decision on clinical social work practice. *Social Service Review, 57*(1), 112–124.

Wilson, S. J. (1978). *Confidentiality in social work.* New York: Free Press.

Yu, M., & O'Neal, B. (1992). Issues of confidentiality when working with persons with AIDS. *Clinical Social Work Journal, 20*(4), 421–430.

Paul A. Kurzman, PhD, ACSW, is professor, Hunter College, School of Social Work, City University of New York, 129 East 79th Street, New York, NY 10021.

For further information see

Conflict Resolution; Continuing Education; Employee Assistance Programs; Ethics and Values; Legal Issues: Confidentiality and Privileged Communication; Licensing, Regulation, and Certification; Managed Care; Management Overview; National Association of Social Workers; Occupational Social Work; Patient Rights; Private Practice; Professional Conduct; Quality Assurance; Quality Management; Social Work Profession Overview.

Key Words	
confidentiality	professional liability
malpractice	risk management
privileged communication	

Program Evaluation
Fredrick W. Seidl

Program evaluation lies in the interface between social work practice and research. Its primary purpose is to use scientific thinking, methods, measurements, and analysis to improve the efficiency and effectiveness of social programs and the quality of social work services.

The prevailing view is that program evaluation is an administrative practice method. Therefore, social workers who engage in administrative support activities should have a working familiarity with the means of evaluating programs.

DEFINITIONS AND COMPARISONS

Program evaluation differs from evaluation research, which emphasizes the results achieved by a program—its positive or negative side effects, impacts on the target audience, prediction of long-term effects, and relationship of costs to benefits (Shufflebeam, 1974). Rossi and Freeman (1985) defined evaluation research as "the systematic application of social [science] research procedures in assessing the conceptualization, design, implementation and utility of social intervention programs" (p. 19). In *program evaluation,* however, social workers primarily emphasize the formative or process aspects of programs, rather than the summative or outcome aspects (Gordon, 1991; Jones, 1980).

Evaluation research is more complex and comprehensive than program evaluation and requires extensive specialized training, even though carefully executed evaluation research usually includes program evaluation. Thus, evaluation research picks up where program evaluation leaves off.

Performance audits, accreditation reviews, and licensing procedures are also related to program evaluation, although they are derived from different intellectual roots and use different methodologies. Whereas program evaluation is a child of social science, performance audits are the progeny of accountancy, and the purpose of the review and the methods used reflects the intellectual roots of the practitioner (D. F. Davis, 1990). Program evaluations focus on improving the quality of social programs through social science research methods. *Performance audits* focus on organizational control and accountability issues through accountancy procedures.

Licensing and accrediting processes are also used to evaluate programs. Because social science methods of data collection, other than interviewing, are rarely used in licensure and accreditation reviews, such reviews are more akin to performance audits than to program evaluations. Both *licensure and accreditation reviews* evaluate programs against a predetermined, externally derived set of standards that are devised not by stakeholders in the programs, but by bodies with external authority: government agencies (in licensure) and agency and professional associations (in accreditation). These external authorities specify the criteria for the reviews, and the programs are measured against these criteria. If a program fails to "measure up," it loses its sanction to continue; to receive funds from the government or insurers; or its good standing among peer programs, colleagues, and institutions. Evaluators call this a "go/no-go" evaluation.

In contrast, program evaluations are considered developmental. Increasingly program managers view program evaluation as a data-based, problem-solving process and as a means to improve programs through informed administrative decision making.

AGENCY-BASED PROGRAM EVALUATION

Identifying Stakeholders

Essential stakeholders, with participation from evaluators, decide the problems or issues for a program evaluation. The standards of the Evaluation Research Society (1982) refer to "formulation and negotiation," during which "concerned parties should strive for a clear mutual understanding of what is to be done, how it is to be done, and why." Jones (1980) viewed program evaluation as "a political process, and researchers must build support and acceptance by recognizing the priorities of all participants with a stake in the outcome" (p. 70).

A stakeholder is anyone with an interest in the program: the sponsor, clients, social workers, the United Way, program administrators, neighborhood people, and so on. The stakeholders may change from project to project or from program to program.

Furthermore, stakeholders have different interests. For example, governmental funders may be the primary stakeholders in a cost–benefit study of a particular child abuse screening service. However, other organizational participants might not be as interested in the cost–benefit aspect. Social workers will be interested in protecting children and preserving families. The police will be interested in protecting children and punishing the abusers. Administrators will be interested in the program's ability to follow guidelines, thereby ensuring reimbursement. And, finally, clients will be interested in the services they receive and whether there are false accusations of abuse. Although the government will be interested in carrying out screening as efficiently as possible, each of the other stakeholders will have different views of which criteria are important for evaluating the program.

The social worker who is interested in conducting a program evaluation needs to perform several tasks. First is to decide who the audiences are and what they want to know. Internal audiences have different questions than do external ones. An external audience that provides funding for the program has its own agenda for the program, and conflicts with internal agendas are common. Social worker–evaluators are likely to experience pressures from various directions that may be difficult to manage. Kelly and Maynard-Moody (1993) noted that engaging stakeholders in a discussion of the problem for evaluation helps participants get past parochial views of the program and build cohesion about the program's goals. In this way, program evaluation produces desired changes even while it is under way.

It is usually best to begin with who is funding the evaluation. What do they want to know? What do they intend to do with what they know? Occasionally, program managers may want to keep the evaluation in house and not inform the funders. There may be good and sufficient reasons for this view.

Second, it is advisable to involve those who are in a position to implement recommendations that are derived from the program evaluation, usually line and staff officers. If organizational participants fail to accept the definition of the problem to be studied, they are not likely to carry out the recommendations for change.

Third, it is advisable to consult with the people who provide the program's political support—both those in positions of authority and the constituents. The reasons for their support may be a surprise to the program officers and subsequently overlooked in evaluating the program.

Finally, it is better to cast a wide net than a narrow one. It is particularly important to include minority stakeholders in the problem-development process (Madison, 1992).

Generating Problems to Study

Most commonly, evaluators solicit ideas from stakeholders through interviews or small-group meetings. Qualitative research methods, such as focus groups, which have been widely applied in recent years, and delphi and nominal-group strategies may be helpful in formulating problems for program evaluations (Kruger, 1988).

Once a list of problems is generated through the various qualitative approaches available to the social worker–evaluator, those problems that will receive attention during the evaluation must be selected. This decision requires a consideration of the costs, level of precision, time, and amount of staff attention that will be required to deal with each problem. The social worker–evaluator then renegotiates the final list of problems to be addressed in the evaluation with the stakeholders so that they understand why certain problems are to be addressed and others are not. Again, if program evaluation is viewed as a means to foster change, unless interested parties believe that their interests are represented in the evaluation process, they are not likely to support the recommendations generated during the evaluation.

Testing scientific theory is not a purpose of program evaluation, although it may be an occasional byproduct. The search for research problems in the literature of social work or in the cognate disciplines is therefore not likely to be productive. However, familiarity with relevant research can lead to useful methodological approaches and help with interpreting findings.

THE RESEARCH CYCLE

Once the problems to be evaluated are specified, the normal research cycle is initiated. This cycle includes the formulation of hypotheses, selection

of the variables of interest and their measurement, and the determination of how and by whom the data are to be collected and analyzed. Finally, the social worker–evaluator, program administrators, and staff forge agreements for making and implementing recommendations and the publication of the findings for handling (Evaluation Research Society, 1982).

Specific strategies for carrying out the program evaluation depend on the nature of the problems obtained in the negotiation–renegotiation process and the program's stage of development (Seidl & Macht, 1979; Tripodi, Fellin, & Epstein, 1978). In addition, evaluators need to consider (1) the level of technology used in the program, (2) the stability of environmental support for the program, and (3) the degree to which the program's goals are free from ambiguity, inconsistencies, and conflict in deciding specific program-evaluation strategies (Seidl & Macht). It is better to emphasize formative evaluation and qualitative methods evaluating programs in the early stages of development, programs that use complex technologies, those that have uncertain environmental support, or one just developing clear goals than to use a summative evaluation emphasizing quantification.

Formulation of Hypotheses

A hypothesis is a statement that specifies the relationship between two or more variables. Not all pieces of sought-after information must be cast as hypotheses. One gains no information, for example, by "hypothesizing" that the program "sees" 400 clients a year when the actual count is readily obtainable. Rather, evaluators need to formulate hypotheses to keep the evaluation focused on important issues and concerns so that stakeholders can follow the data collection and results regarding particular hypotheses that relate to their interests. For example, a board member in a rural agency may suspect that the level of participation by volunteers in a program is low because the volunteers have difficulty getting to the agency. The examination of the hypothesis, "the greater the difficulty in reaching the agency, the lower the participation of volunteers" will yield useful information and, if it is true, may suggest what actions an agency may take with regard to the transportation of volunteers.

Data Collection

In any evaluation, evaluators can conceptualize variables as input, throughput, or output variables, depending on the phase of the agency's program to which the variables pertain. *Input variables* describe the agency's structure and resources.

They include the program's mission, the agency context (including the program's history and auspices), the setting in which services are offered, the characteristics of the client population, the characteristics (including qualifications) of the staff, and the sources of funding and costs of the program.

Throughput variables are "process" variables. They include what happens to the client by virtue of contact with the agency; the technologies (methods) used by the professional staff; the services that are available and how they are used; and the frequency, duration, and intensity of the services provided. Concerns about cost can be both input and throughput variables because expenditures are made in establishing the infrastructure and in applying the technologies.

Output variables describe the outcomes of services. Unless these outcomes closely reflect the mission of the service, the evaluation must raise questions about why they do not and whether the agency's goals have been displaced. Typical outcomes may include improved psychological adjustment, reduced family conflict, improved personal functioning, increased self-esteem, a higher quality of life for the individual or the community, better performance in school, job placements, and ability to live independently. Program evaluations are more likely to focus on input and throughput variables than on output variables.

The scientific rigor of program evaluations may range from anecdotal accounts by the program's participants to carefully controlled experimental research designs. Evaluators, however, strive for "practical rigor" in their evaluations so that they can achieve as much validity in the design as possible against trade-offs in costs and disruption of the program. Any evaluation less rigorous than fully randomized experimental designs indicates that concessions were made to the practical issues of delivering service in vivo. Because program evaluators rarely have the opportunity to implement experimental designs fully (this is more common in evaluation research), they need to be aware of the costs in knowledge and confidence of these compromises and interpret findings and use recommendations, fully cognizant of the limits of the information they have produced.

Description of the Program

Clients are likely to describe a program differently from practitioners, administrators, or members of the board of directors. Therefore, evaluators may find it useful to understand how a program is seen to operate from these various perspectives. One common way to do so is to describe, using a set of throughput variables, what happens to a "typical" client who comes to the agency and seeks the help the agency can provide. What is the process that engages the client? Is the agency successful in engaging the client? What are the steps in that process? How are these steps likely to occur? What are the expected outcomes?

Cost–Benefit Analysis

One widely used form of program evaluation, particularly among economists, is cost–benefit analysis. Cost–benefit analysis was developed to assist in making social-investment decisions by providing information about comparative dollar-value returns of various program options (Chakravarty, 1987). In this formulation, costs are input and throughput variables and benefits are outcome variables. Programs are described in terms of their costs and expenditures for various input and throughput items. In simplistic terms, cost-benefit analysis asks whether a program's costs are greater or less than the dollar value of its benefits.

Several methodological issues immediately surface. In estimating costs, evaluators need to decide which costs they are counting: the program's sponsors, opportunity costs experienced by volunteers, or costs by government only? Because nonprofit human services agencies rarely pay property taxes, is this forgone revenue to be counted as a program cost for the municipality? Despite the conventions concerning what is an accountable cost and what is not, issues remain.

These issues loom larger in the estimation of benefits. Although the cost–benefit model was developed to capture economic benefits, most social programs do not have dollar outcomes. What is the dollar value of a happy marriage? A prevented teenage pregnancy? An integrated community? A human life? Thompson (1980), for example, spent considerable effort deciding the desirability of valuing a human life in monetary terms and how to do so. In cost–benefit studies on the delivery of health services, this is an important concern.

Furthermore, issues remain as to what is to be included as a benefit. Organizations do more than one thing. Should indirect benefits (like employed workers) be counted? If so, which ones? Both practitioners and scholars correctly complain that the results of cost–benefit studies tend to be interpreted as if only the monetized results are worth attention. In so doing, users of the evaluation may miss the whole point of the program.

Approaches to Data Collection

Patton (1986) argued that there is no best plan and no perfect design and that all designs produce errors and ambiguities. Social worker–evaluators will wish to obtain the best data they can under the realistic conditions of the naturalistic (agency) environment. What is "best" depends on more than its technical measurement properties. Other considerations include the confidence of the stakeholders, reactivity, cost, and efficiency of administration. Patton further asserted that qualitative methodologies provide fruitful approaches when there is an emphasis on individualized outcomes, or program processes, or when in-depth information is needed about certain clients. Similarly, evaluators may wish to consider qualitative approaches if there is an interest in focusing on diversity or a need for the details of how the program is implemented or if standardized tests either are not available or would be disruptive. Finally, when there may be unintended consequences of the program and when the administrators may be biased toward qualitative approaches, such methods may be indicated.

In the normal course of daily work, social agencies generate data. They have reports to prepare for governmental agencies, for boards of directors, or for the United Way. Many agencies, particularly those with large client populations, have well-organized management information systems (MIS) that routinely keep track of hundreds of elements of data. Although there was great hope in the 1970s that MIS could provide a wealth of data for social work research, these hopes have not materialized for several reasons. First, data are collected for managerial purposes, and although these purposes may overlap with those of evaluative research, they usually do not. Second, the data from MIS are not always accessible for research and evaluation purposes. If the quality of MIS data is poor, then a great deal of effort must go into "cleaning up" the data. Finally, it is usually difficult and occasionally impossible to obtain estimates of the reliability and validity of agency-collected data.

Nevertheless, program evaluators can frequently save themselves a great deal of trouble and expense using agency data. Collecting original data to answer questions using measures with known reliability and validity is usually best, provided that the social worker–evaluators can "get the data out." Obtaining cooperation from busy colleagues who have to do additional work to carry out evaluations requires a great deal of diplomacy, if not authority. Many a scientifically credible program evaluation has been planned and initiated but never finished because of the difficulties in collecting data. If the staff members consider the data being collected to be potentially

threatening in that the data may expose their poor performance and thus lead to budget cuts, they can sabotage the data collection process. In this respect, social worker–evaluators have an advantage over others in obtaining such cooperation because the staff's involvement in the evaluation process is a given: Those who are to implement the evaluation must accept it. One may expect that the social worker–evaluator is more sensitive to the subtler aspects of service delivery and can explain them to colleagues.

Reporting Results for Implementation

In good program evaluation, there are no surprises. Evaluators keep stakeholders informed about how the evaluation is proceeding. As findings emerge, evaluators apprise stakeholders of the findings and solicit the staff's, the clients', and the board's thoughts and reactions. Interim reports are useful in this respect, particularly if the findings are negative. Interim reports can also help the discussion of findings and recommendations, and meetings around their validity and potential implementation can be held. (As always, these meetings are interactive and not didactic.)

Minority Issues

Program evaluation shares many of the minority issues that have been identified for other forms of social research. For example, the tendency to use standardized test scores to determine the effectiveness of programs may contribute to further inequalities (McDowell, 1992). As in other types of research, program evaluations are remiss in using race as a variable when race becomes a proxy for understanding what the minority experience means. E. D. Davis (1992) argued that evaluators overemphasize differences between groups when they ignore or dismiss important variations within groups. In a criticism specific to program evaluation, Madison (1992) contended that evaluators are more likely to leave minority stakeholders out of the evaluation process. This problem is particularly acute because members of ethnic and racial groups have the most at stake in evaluations of human services programs.

EVALUATING PROGRAM EVALUATIONS

Referring to evaluations of human services programs, Weiss (1978) remarked: "Just as most human service programs have had indifferent success in improving the lot of clients, most program evaluations have had little impact in improving the quality of programs" (p. 113). Ten years later, Weiss (1988) observed that "the influence of evaluation on program decisions has not notably increased" (p. 7). Yet, there is cause for optimism.

Chambers, Wedel, and Rodwell (1992) projected a bright future for evaluation, based on changes that have occurred and are occurring in social work's approach to program evaluation. The trend has clearly been toward a more participatory practice model in which evaluators are less often outside authorities and more often colleagues and co-workers. Furthermore, the evaluators work to understand the complexities of "people work," value diversity, and appreciate the richness of data generated by qualitative approaches to evaluation. Although they understand the contributions that quantitative social science methods can make, as well as the limitations of these methods, evaluators bridge the gap between the social science observer–nomothetic researcher and the practicing social worker. As experience with this emerging approach accumulates, the profession will have to reevaluate evaluation.

REFERENCES

Chakravarty, S. (1987). Cost–benefit analysis. In J. Eatwell, M. Milgate, & P. Newman (Eds.), *The new Pelgrave: A dictionary of economics* (pp. 687–690). New York: Stockton Press.

Chambers, D. E., Wedel, K., & Rodwell, M. K. (1992). *Evaluating social programs.* Boston: Allyn & Bacon.

Davis, D. F. (1990). Do you want a performance audit or a program evaluation? *Public Administration Review, 50,* 35–41.

Davis, E. D. (1992, Spring). Reconsidering the use of race as an explanatory variable in program evaluation. *New Directions in Program Evaluation, 53,* 55–67.

Evaluation Research Society Standards for Program Evaluation (1982). *New Directions in Program Evaluation, 15,* 7–19.

Gordon, K. H. (1991). Improving practice through illuminative evaluation. *Social Service Review, 65,* 202–223.

Jones, W. C. (1980) Evaluation research and program evaluation: A difference without a distinction. In D. Fanshel (Ed.), *Future of social work research* (pp. 70–71). Washington, DC: National Association of Social Workers.

Kelly, M., & Maynard-Moody, S. (1993). Policy analysis in the post-positivist era: Engaging stakeholders in evaluating the economic development districts program. *Public Administration Review, 53,* 135–142.

Kruger, R. A. (1988). *Focus groups: A practical guide for applied research.* Beverly Hills, CA: Sage Publications.

Madison, A. (1992, Spring). Primary inclusion of culturally diverse minority program participants in the evaluation process. *New Directions in Program Evaluation, 53,* 35–43.

McDowell, C. (1992, Spring). Standardized test and program evaluation: Inappropriate measures in critical times. *New Directions in Program Evaluation, 53,* 45–54.

Patton, M. Q. (1986). *Utilization-focused evaluation* (2nd ed.) Beverly Hills, CA: Sage Publications.

Rossi, P. H., & Freeman, H. (1985). *Evaluation: A systematic approach.* Beverly Hills, CA: Sage Publications.

Seidl, F. W., & Macht, M. W. (1979). A contingency approach to evaluation: Manager's guidelines. In Jesse McClure (Ed.), *Managing human services* (pp. 190–200). Davis, CA: International Dialog Press.

Shufflebeam, D. L. (1974). *Meta-evaluation* (Occasional Paper No. 3). Kalamazoo: Evaluation Center, College of Education, Western Michigan University.

Thompson, M. S. (1980). *Benefit–cost analysis in program evaluation.* Beverly Hills, CA: Sage Publications.

Tripodi, T., Fellin, P., & Epstein, I. (1978). *Differential social program evaluation.* Itasca, IL: F. E. Peacock.

Weiss, C. (1978) Alternative models for program evaluation. In W. C. Sze & J. G. Hopps (Eds.) *Evaluation and accountability in human service programs* (2nd ed., pp. 113–122). Cambridge, MA: Schenkman.

Weiss, C. (1988). Evaluation for decisions. *Evaluation Practice, 9*(1), 7–9.

FURTHER READING

Berk, R. A., & Rossi, P. H. (1990). *Thinking about program evaluation.* Newbury Park, CA: Sage Publications.

Langbein, L. I. (1980). *Discovering whether programs work: A guide to statistical methods for program evaluation.* Santa Monica, CA: Goodyear.

Nowakowski, J. (Ed.). (1987). *The client perspective on evaluation* San Francisco: Jossey-Bass.

Palumbo, D. J. (Ed.). (1987). *The politics of program evaluation.* Newbury Park, CA: Sage Publications.

Posavac, E. J., & Carey, R. C. (1989). *Program evaluation methods and case studies.* Englewood Cliffs, NJ: Prentice Hall.

Riddick, W. E., & Stewart, E. (1981). *Workbook for program evaluation in the human services.* Washington, DC: University Press of America.

Rossi, P. H. (Ed.). (1982). *Standards for evaluation practice.* San Francisco: Jossey-Bass.

Royce, D. (1992). *Program evaluation: An introduction.* Chicago: Nelson Hall.

Fredrick W. Seidl, PhD, is professor and dean, University at Buffalo, State University of New York, School of Social Work, 359 Baldy Hall, Buffalo, NY 14260.

For further information see

Clinical Social Work; Computer Utilization; Direct Practice Overview; Economic Analysis; Epistemology; Expert Systems; Information Systems; Licensing, Regulation, and Certification; Management Overview; Meta-analysis; Organizations: Context for Social Services Delivery; Policy Analysis; Psychometrics; Public Social Services Management; Quality Assurance; Quality Management; Recording; Research Overview; Social Work Practice: Theoretical Base; Social Work Profession Overview; Volunteer Management.

Key Words

cost–benefit analysis   research
program evaluation

Progressive Social Work
Marti Bombyk

Progressive social work encompasses a dynamic set of theories, ideologies, values, and practice principles. Whether progressive social workers identify themselves as radicals, socialists, leftists, political practitioners, or activists, they are critical of the injustices in institutions, systems, beliefs, and social practices that cause the poorest and most-vulnerable groups to suffer. Progressive social workers articulate these social injustices into "public issues" instead of adopting a strictly case-by-case perspective that views the outcomes of social injustices as "personal troubles" that individuals must cope with or adapt to (Mills, 1959). Progressive social workers strive to alter oppressive institutions, systems, beliefs, and practices fundamentally by initiating social changes targeted at these public issues. They also work directly with individuals to help them heal from their wounds, to educate them about their life choices and strategies, and to assist them as they determine their futures.

OVERVIEW

Social change pursuits define the primary purpose of progressive social work. From agencies advocating in coalitions with other service providers and service consumers for better social policies and more funding for social services, to methods of direct practice that raise people's awareness of social forces that oppress them, social change is the essence of progressive social work. In common parlance, progressive social workers want to stop the systemic assaults on people's lives instead of merely applying a bandage to their wounds.

Progressive social workers analyze the root causes of the social problems people experience within the broad, dynamic social contexts of their lives. They critically evaluate the ways practitioners and agencies respond to the needs of communities and individuals, the social policies that structure and regulate agency behavior, and the priorities society places on meeting human needs. Progressive social workers work directly with individuals, groups, and communities to help them identify their sources of pain and to relate their problems to social, political, and economic systems. Progressive social workers assess these problems from a multidisciplinary framework that is informed by values and ideology as well as by theory and research. They respond to social problems with interventions aimed at redistributing wealth and opportunity; democratizing social institutions; guaranteeing human and civil rights for all; and promoting just, caring, humanistic societies throughout the world.

Finally, progressive social workers explore the possibilities, paradoxes, and limitations of progressive activity within social work. Can people find meaningful work as social change agents if they choose social work as a career? Social work is an occupation that is highly concerned with professionalism, prestige, and status. Can it then provide a suitable context for radical activity that is openly critical of unjust institutional arrangements (Epstein, 1970a, 1970b; Reeser & Epstein, 1991)? These questions suggest the contradictions of being simultaneously a progressive and a professional—questions that pose perennial dilemmas for activists (Wagner, 1989, 1990).

THEORETICAL BASIS

Several theories assist progressive social workers in their understanding of the root causes of social injustices and the practice implications of social change (Mullaly & Keating, 1991). One overarching theory is that of *political economy* (Corrigan & Leonard, 1978; Gough, 1979; Longres, 1986; Moscovitch & Drover, 1981), derived from Marxist theory, which analyzes how political and economic systems interact to structure and reproduce systemic inequities in the distribution of wealth and access to rights, resources, and opportunities. Power is a central concept (Hasenfeld, 1987). Questions such as "Who has the power, and why?" and "What forces are preventing powerless people from obtaining more power?" translate the theory into practice implications. Some answers point to the nature of capitalist economies that, especially when unchecked by democratic governments, enable concentrated wealth to accumulate into the hands of a small, elite group while most people receive far less (Cloward, 1993).

Racism, sexism, heterosexism, ableism, and ageism complicate the dynamics of poverty and oppression. *Theories of race, gender, and sexuality* aid in the understanding of why men of European ancestry have most of the power and wealth in U.S. society, and in the understanding of implications for sharing power and wealth among the rest of society (Andersen & Collins, 1995).

Human needs theory (Doyal & Gough, 1991) asserts that meeting human needs should supersede all other political objectives. It is a human right for people to have the means with which to satisfy human needs, and this theory presents a set of universal needs and need satisfiers that can inform a progressive social work agenda.

Structural social work theory (Carniol, 1992; Middleman & Goldberg, 1974; Moreau, 1979, 1990; Wood & Middleman, 1989) links a broader analysis of systemic oppression with direct practice methods (Middleman & Wood, 1990). *Empowerment,* a concept that is emerging into a theory, also contributes to the progressive practice paradigm. Referring to a perspective toward people who seek services, a practice methods framework, and a set of values (Simon, 1990), empowerment theory asserts that people's right to choose for themselves what they believe are their interests, what they want to do to better their condition, and what methods will work best for them is the only way they can gain control over their lives (Gutierrez, 1990, 1994; Simon, 1990, 1994).

SOCIAL CHANGE AND INDIVIDUAL CHANGE

A common concern of progressive social workers is, "How do we make social change at the same time as individual change? My clients are injured by a wide array of social problems caused by unjust social systems. My job is to work with them directly. Am I supposed to do my job and change the world at the same time?" Although they are not always easily apparent, there are natural links between progressive social change and progressive individual change that can be harnessed to work in tandem. Fortunately, the progressive vision calling for both macrosystem and microsystem change also recognizes a broad division of labor for individual social workers: They do not have to be all and do all.

Unfortunately, however, a common misunderstanding is that the only way to do progressive work is as a macrosystem practitioner organizing a community of poor people or working for alternative social policies such as universal health coverage, full employment, or children's allowances. Of course, many progressive social workers do prefer community organizing or policy practice to make structural or large-scale interventions, especially because the substantial majority of social workers work almost exclusively with individuals. However, progressive practice definitely encompasses direct practice with individuals (casework, case management, and clinical practice). Macrosystem practice also involves working with individuals: one-to-one on specific tasks or as members of groups within communities, agencies, or large institutions such as the government.

Linkages for Social Change

The placement of progressive social workers in all fields of practice and at all levels of service is an opportunity to incorporate progressive principles into all forms of social work practice. This simultaneously challenges progressives to discover ways of expanding their practice so they can create linkages and build bridges for social change activities.

Social workers also support the work of social and individual change by aligning themselves with current progressive social movements. Feminism, civil and human rights, economic justice, and other human liberation movements have already had a considerable, although uneven, effect on the education, training, and practice directions of the social work profession. Social work is a relatively liberal profession; much could be accomplished in the direction of progressive social work if social work educators, practitioners, and agencies practiced more faithfully what they preach (Hartman, 1993).

Change within Social Work

The need for individual and systemic change applies equally to social work itself. Good social work, progressive social workers assert, means examining all aspects of practice for sexist, racist, and classist assumptions and stereotypes that perpetuate the same oppressive systems we seek to change. Social workers must confront individual practitioners who are violating the ethics of the profession while also critically examining the profession's definition of ethical imperatives.

Attention also is focused on the hiring, salary, and promotion systems of agencies, as they are not immune from perpetuating institutionalized social injustices based on irrelevant demographic or status characteristics. Scrutinizing our agency's mission and relationship to the community of people it serves often will suggest needed changes (Fabricant & Burghardt, 1992; Lord & Kennedy, 1992). Finally, social workers must examine their own wages, benefits, and working conditions and advocate for themselves through unions and other forms of employee organizations against the economic exploitation of social workers by employers and society (Withorn, 1984).

PROGRESSIVE SOCIAL WORK AGENDA

The progressive social work agenda typically is aligned with those of progressive social change movements. For example, the idea of a universal, single-payer national health care system is supported by a broad coalition of citizens groups and professional associations, including NASW. Similar political objectives include the universal provision of jobs, housing, quality public education, reproductive freedom, and a children's allowance. Working for the protection of the natural environment (Goff & McNutt, 1994), for peace, and for nuclear disarmament are other obvious coalition tasks.

Social Welfare

The issue of social services and the welfare state most distinguishes social work from other progressive social movements. Although many social movements, such as feminism and civil rights, recognize the importance of welfare state provisions to meet basic human needs and to provide social security, progressive social workers are especially active against the considerable antipathy directed toward recipients of entitlements, particularly Aid to Families with Dependent Children (AFDC) benefits. Progressive social workers have formed alliances with welfare rights organizations and advocacy groups to oppose punitive, stigmatizing welfare programs and to increase the benefits allowance well above the official poverty levels that are arbitrarily set by the government.

In general, the main objective of progressive social workers is to meet human needs through an activist welfare state (Leonard, 1990). Nonetheless, some progressive social workers would prefer minimal involvement of the state in meeting human needs (Wineman, 1984). Progressive social workers tend to be averse to bureaucracy (Ferguson, 1984; Galper, 1975) because it interferes with the effective delivery of public social services. But most progressive social workers would agree that the meeting of human needs is the ultimate responsibility of the government, the form of which and quality of which are the responsibility of the people.

Human Needs and Human Potential

Therefore, it is a major priority to increase policy attention, at all levels of government, to the human needs of poor and working people, especially among the most powerless and disenfranchised groups. This requires advocacy and lobbying for alternative social policies, as well as electing public officials who will legislate those policies and uphold them. Federal, state, and local governments should also ensure economic and social justice; promote diversity and tolerance of differences among and between heterogeneous groups; work for peaceful and nonviolent solutions to international, community, and domestic conflicts; and secure human rights abroad and at home.

Finally, this institutional model of social welfare, adopted by most progressive social workers,

expects the government to not only meet basic human needs but also foster the attainment of human potential. A just, equitable, caring society can be organized to maximize the human potential of individual citizens that they may enjoy life and their roles in society and find intimacy, family, and community in satisfying and supportive relationships with one another (Reynolds, 1951/1975).

VALUES

The values of progressive social workers are humanistic. The social work profession generally is considered one of the more progressive professions; it is not always possible to distinguish the values of progressive social workers from those of social workers in general. The difference often may be of degree or emphasis as is evident in the following brief discussion of key values behind the progressive social work perspective.

Antiauthoritarianism

Progressive social workers are opposed to any form of oppression or domination of individuals or groups. They are antiauthoritarian toward those who believe it is their absolute right to subjugate others. "Question authority" is a common slogan that typifies this value stance. Because authority is not infallible or inherently judicious, abuses of power and the undemocratic, illegitimate basis of authority should be checked.

Cooperation and Collaboration

Cooperation for the common good is a value of progressive social workers that can be contrasted with the Western value of competition for individual advantages over others. The ethic of "rugged individualism," progressive social workers believe, has contributed to the corruption of the social fabric of society by promoting greed, envy, social isolation, selfishness, and a lack of compassion for oppressed and impoverished people. Progressives believe individuals can best find their fulfillment in community with others; individual and group competition tends to alienate. Therefore, the value of cooperation is fostered to improve human conditions through collaborative problem solving. Such problem-solving relationships include community-centered, democratic organizations; self-help groups; and collective action in social movements.

Equality

Equality is the cornerstone of much progressive thinking. To realize this objective, activists strive to obtain opportunities, rights, and resources for oppressed people and to eliminate unfair privileges accorded to people because of their class, sex, race, religion, age, physical or psychological ability, citizenship, marital status, sexual orientation, affectional preference, and so forth. Progressive social workers believe that inequality based on unfair or irrelevant differences among people is a major cause of social injustice and human suffering and that as these inequalities become more extreme and socially destabilizing, human suffering becomes more widespread.

Democracy

Progressives value democracy in all forms of decision making. As an ideal, democracy is inherently subversive because it is the means by which authoritarian systems can be dismantled. Progressives argue that U.S. society is not truly democratic because so many members of oppressed groups are not registered to vote and do not participate in elections. In general, U.S. political and economic institutions are not democratic because access to decision making and decision makers is limited by hierarchical forms of bureaucratic organization in which centralized decisions are made by a select few.

Even social workers' relationships with those they serve can be problematic because of the inequity produced by expertise, credentials, and power in the social services system. These differences are further exacerbated by the hierarchical power structures of social welfare bureaucracies and of many less-complex social services agencies. Progressive social workers believe that undemocratic and remote decision making is less responsive to the needs and interests of social workers and the individuals and communities they serve. More democratic and egalitarian relationships between social workers and those who seek their assistance mitigate against these inequities as do democratizing social services workplaces and leveling the agencies' bureaucratic hierarchies as much as possible.

Religion and Ethics

Finally, a discussion of values would be incomplete without acknowledging the role of religion and ethics. Progressives, who have often been stereotyped as "godless Marxists" or "secular humanists," frequently have been members of the clergy or employed by churches, or their programs have been funded by churches. In many instances, particularly in Latin America, progressives have aligned with "liberation theology" movements, finding spiritual sustenance for their struggle to help impoverished people change their circumstances. Many African American churches have been community centers for progressive social services and political organizing. In contrast, fundamentalist, right-wing Christian movements usually have been hostile to progressive values (Midgley & Sanzenbach, 1991).

Progressives' strong concern with ethics and the moral imperative to "speak truth to power" has sometimes supported stereotypes of self-righteous soapbox orators. Nonetheless, it is disconcerting among progressives that whistleblowing or otherwise enforcing the rather moderate ethics of the profession (for example, the *NASW Code of Ethics*) is often perceived to be a pursuit only for those misfits who cannot be team players and who will surely be punished for being disloyal troublemakers. It is no surprise, therefore, that a radical code of ethics that expects social workers to work for the attainment of a society committed to a more equitable distribution of wealth is not widely embraced as an ethical imperative for the profession (Galper, 1975).

PRACTICE PRINCIPLES

Whom do progressive social workers serve? Is there any group they would not serve? Populations that are considered oppressed—for example, poor people, women, people of color, immigrants, children, gay men and lesbians, and physically challenged people—are the people with whom most progressive social workers want to work. Progressive social workers usually are among the first to begin services for underserved groups, for example, people with acquired immune deficiency syndrome (AIDS), battered women, homeless people, political refugees, and migrant workers. Some progressive social workers have advocated strategic preferences for certain service consumers (Galper, 1975). Upper-income or more-privileged individuals, the so-called worried well, are less likely to receive the attention of progressive social workers. Finally, progressive social workers have favored unions, grassroots organizations, and self-help groups for their potential to facilitate social changes and empowerment.

The following conventionally defined social work practice methods apply to progressive social work: case management; clinical work with individuals, couples, and families; group work; administration; consultation; supervision; community organizing; social planning; research; and education. All social workers use assessment data and other forms of research to plan, implement, and evaluate their practice. But the practice decision-making activity of progressive social workers differs from that of other social workers by the infusion of progressive values and theories into the practice framework.

The major practice principles that guide progressives in their work include

- forming democratic, egalitarian relationships with service users and coworkers
- favoring primary prevention and education to address root causes of social problems
- assessing people's problems from their own perspective
- analyzing the oppressive systems and environmental contexts that impinge on people's lives
- intervening at both the macro and micro level in working with individuals and groups
- posing questions and raising consciousness with service providers, service consumers, and each other
- teaching and using critical thinking skills
- demystifying obscure processes that intimidate or confuse people
- doing and teaching advocacy work with service users and providers
- forgoing the technological role of expert and the cloak of professionalism
- using democratic, participatory decision-making methods
- participating with service users and coworkers in collective action
- problem solving with holistic, interdisciplinary approaches
- understanding "the personal is political" (individual concerns can often be traced to larger power systems and also have their own power issues) and "the global is local" (the world's communities are economically, politically, and socially interdependent)
- leveling hierarchical organizational structures to make decision making more participatory and services less bureaucratic.

These principles, applied to practice, are insufficient if social work practitioners do not identify themselves with progressive social work as a form of political practice (Withorn, 1984). In addition, these practice activities cannot be successfully undertaken without clear objectives in mind. The topics of contemporary radical literature and discussion forums range from ways to clarify and implement one's progressive ideals within social work (Burghardt, 1982; Wagner, 1990) to critical, historical analyses of social issues (Abramovitz, 1988; Blau, 1992; Fisher, 1984) and methods for progressive practice (Delgado, 1994; Middleman & Wood, 1990).

HISTORICAL BACKGROUND OF PROGRESSIVE SOCIAL WORK

Some roots of progressive social work originated in the Settlement House movement. At the turn of the 20th century, settlement house workers were actively engaged in social change work such as union organizing; occupational, safety, and health legislation; labor legislation; women's suffrage; and political organizing in communities. Although some of these reforms may currently seem mainstream, they often were considered revolutionary ideas in their era. Great courage and skill were required to advance these causes against powerful opposition groups.

National Health Insurance Movement

For example, social workers actively participated in a move for national health insurance in the early 1900s, taking two decades to formulate and advocate proposals. Their proposals were defeated by the now-predictable coalition composed of the health insurance companies, the American Medical Association, and business interests. Simon Nelson Patten was one of the leaders of this movement, as were Roger Baldwin, Edward Devine, Alice Hamilton, Charles Henderson, Robert Hunter, Florence Kelley, Paul Kellogg, Samuel Lindsay, James B. Reynolds, and I. M. Rubinow (Weinert, 1993).

Rank and File Movement

During the Great Depression of the 1930s, social workers were active in trade unions and in organizing unemployed people. They were critical of the government's inability to respond to the fundamental capitalist causes of the depression or to assist people most victimized by the economy's collapse. Progressive social workers rejected the moderate New Deal policies and joined the Rank and File movement by the tens of thousands (Fisher, 1980).

The Rank and File movement was committed to advancing a socialist economic program that would replace the debilitated capitalist economy. Organized within and outside social services agencies, the movement worked for the unionization of social services workers to improve wages and working conditions. One of the most influential leaders of the Rank and File movement was Mary van Kleeck, who argued, in an award-winning speech at the 1934 Conference of Social Work, that none of the government's programs were devoted to raising standards of living, but were designed to sustain the property interests of business and to maintain profits (van Kleeck, 1991).

Bertha Capen Reynolds

In the audience listening to van Kleeck's electrifying speech was a psychiatric social worker, Bertha Capen Reynolds, who converted to a more radical leftist perspective in part because of this speech (Leighninger, 1991). Reynolds has come to symbolize the historical tradition of progressive social work, although she did not stand alone in her perspectives. What distinguished Reynolds from many others was her serious and lifelong ideological commitment to understanding the forces behind oppression, war, and human degradation. She was a psychiatric social worker who had been trained in the first class at Smith College, and yet she could easily grasp and apply Marxist theories to her psychiatric social work perspective.

An author of several books (Reynolds, 1951/1975, 1934/1982, 1942/1985, 1963/1991), articles, and speeches, Reynolds was a maverick of her time (Bombyk, 1987). She was asked to resign from her position at Smith College for her unorthodox views and was eventually blacklisted from the social work profession. In her own words, "somewhere a door blew shut" (Reynolds, 1963/1991, p. 23). Thanks to the work of her former students and coworkers, especially Jack Kamaiko and Rachel Levine, her reputation and legacy have been restored to their rightful place in the history of social work. Currently Smith College houses her papers in the Sophia Smith Collection and hosted a centennial conference in her honor in 1985. NASW has reissued her books.

Decline and Rebirth

One of the consistent outlets for Reynolds and other progressive authors was a remarkable journal called *Social Work Today* (1934–1942), edited by Jacob Fisher. Working with the Rank and File movement and the discussion clubs it spawned, the journal stimulated radical critiques and wide-ranging social activism. But World War II derailed progressive social work activity, and the repression of McCarthyism led to the postwar persecution of progressive social workers. The illusively prosperous years of the 1950s were among the darkest in the history of progressivism in the United States (Withorn, 1984).

In the 1960s, in tandem with the rebirth of civil rights movements, feminism, and antiwar movements, progressive social workers again rose to the demands of the times. By organizing within and alongside these movements, progressive social workers began to direct their attention to the welfare state. They organized low-income tenants in urban communities, established new Community Action Programs throughout the country and the Mobilization for Youth in New York City, and attacked meager entitlements and repressive regulations in the welfare programs (Burghardt & Fabricant, 1987).

New Literature in 1970s

The 1970s witnessed a flourishing of progressive social work literature in the United States, Great Britain, Canada, and Australia (Bailey & Brake, 1975; Carniol, 1979; Corrigan & Leonard, 1978; Galper, 1975, 1978; Gil, 1979; Pearson, 1975; Pritchard & Taylor, 1978; Statham, 1978; Thorosell, 1975). This literature is still current in much of its analyses. Some classics, such as *Regulating the Poor* (Piven & Cloward, 1993), have been updated and revised. Occasional articles on radical social work appeared even in the mainstream professional journals (Galper, 1976; Lichtenberg, 1976; Rein, 1970) and were accompanied by a stream of books and articles on feminist social work practice, antiracism practice, and community organizing.

By 1978 progressive social workers had reestablished the tradition begun by *Social Work Today* and the activist discussion clubs of the Rank and File movement. One group in New York City established the Radical Alliance of Social Service Workers and engaged in a variety of activist projects both within and outside the profession. At roughly the same time, a collective of New York City social workers, most of them graduate students, began a discussion group. After exhausting the literature available for study and discussion, the group decided to publish *Catalyst: A Socialist Journal of the Social Services.* This journal self-consciously attempted to carry on the legacy of the progressive social workers of the 1930s, to capture the thrust of renewed activism in the 1960s and 1970s, and to clarify the theory and practice of radical social work. Like its predecessor *Social Work Today, Catalyst* made a home for progressive articles, especially those that were unlikely to be published in mainstream professional journals.

Scholarship in social work had become a more seriously contested terrain between progressive social workers and mainstream professional authorities in the late 1970s and into the 1980s. Largely inspired by feminist critiques of academe (Reinharz, Bombyk, & Wright, 1983), progressives began to question the nature of knowledge, the research process, and the limitations of relying solely on positivist research paradigms for social work research and theory (Cummerton, 1986; Karger, 1983). In the 1990s these explorations seem to have linked up with the progressive notion of *praxis* (the interactive work of creating and refining theory from practice and practice from theory, ultimately resulting in a fusion of theory and practice). Reflecting these developments, progressive researchers have engaged in action research (Wagner, 1991a, 1991b; Zuber-Skerritt, 1991) and participatory research (Sohng, 1992), or some blend of participatory–action research.

Bertha Capen Reynolds Society

At the height of the Reagan era in the mid-1980s, progressive social workers were compelled to resist the conservative drift of the social work profession and their increasing marginalization and isolation within it. Rallying around the 1985 centennial celebration of the life and legacy of Bertha Capen Reynolds, progressive social services workers formed a national organization, the Bertha Capen Reynolds Society (BCRS).

BCRS was formed around a set of 10 principles that are implemented at the national level and through the activity of local chapters in several cities throughout the country. Progressive social workers in BCRS chapters gather for presentations and discussions, study groups, and informal support. These processes typically lead to activism in local communities on wide-ranging social concerns (see *BCR Reports,* the quarterly publication of the society for chapter reports). Since 1987, BCRS has held an annual national meeting where strategies for social change are proposed and analyzed, skills for progressive practice are developed, and progressive views are affirmed and refined.

Transformed Journal

In the late 1980s *Catalyst* was pressed by the hazards of independent publishing and scarce resources to change its collective structure. The journal transformed itself by adopting a more conventional editorial staff structure, signing with an established publishing house, and renaming itself to appeal to a wider audience. With these changes, the *Journal of Progressive Human Services* resuscitated a forum for progressive writers and continued the tradition established by *Social Work Today.*

CURRENT TRENDS AND FUTURE DIRECTIONS

Promoting Study of Progressive Social Work

Contemporary progressive social workers are engaged in at least five general domains of activity. First, they are working to broaden the perception of "appropriate" social work pursuits by promoting the legitimate study and practice of progressive social work theories, values, and methods. This is largely in response to the conservative direction taken by the profession in the 1980s when, for example, community organizing and other macro level practice approaches were shunned in favor of clinical social work practice, private practice, and the quest for professional status through licensure and credentialism (Fabricant

& Burghardt, 1992; Specht & Courtney, 1994; Wenokur & Reisch, 1989). Social workers who ascribed to progressive views and practice approaches were seen as "stuck in the 1960s," and their generic methods were less valued than was specialized expertise.

Another serious obstacle was the profession's increasing responsiveness to market imperatives and the shift to privatization (Wenokur & Reisch, 1989). Agencies were defining and responding to client needs according to conservative funding mandates, and the very nature of agency practice was debased (Fabricant & Burghardt, 1992). Schools of social work were competing for a shrinking pool of students who mostly were interested in clinical social work.

In an age of cutbacks, diminishing service expectations, and restrictive social policies, progressive social workers could find few allies for political advancement of a progressive agenda. The Clinton administration has proved to progressives to be, at the least, a reprieve in the political climate of the Reagan–Bush era. Currently, progressive social workers are revitalizing the methods of community building for addressing social problems and social change through political activism.

Designing New Curricula

Social work educators are redesigning curricula and courses to better educate and train future generations. In conventional university programs, independent schools, and a variety of continuing education forums, social work trainees are being exposed to more-progressive content that expands the narrowly specialized, change-the-individual clinical focus of the 1980s. They are learning about the history of the profession and its social reform episodes. Ecological perspectives are being pushed to include the sociological as well as psychological bases of human behavior, political economy, and oppressive systems (Coates, 1992). Though far from common, empowerment practice skills, antipoverty practice, and social change practice methods are being introduced.

Improving Practice Methods

Progressives are improving on practice methods and working to discover knowledge that can serve as the basis for more-effective empowerment and social change work. The dissemination of progressive practice methods, frameworks, and techniques is a mission of educators and practitioners in a variety of professional forums. For example, in 1994 social work educators established a Progressive Practice Symposium, to be held in conjunction with the Council on Social Work Education annual program meetings, where these educators can exchange ideas and gain support for progressive teaching methods and curricula, including practice strategies, methods, and tactics for achieving the progressive social work agenda and promoting the humanistic values at its base.

Expanding Political Practice

The electoral and legislative practice of progressive social workers is expanding. Social workers have supported the electoral campaigns of progressive social workers such as Ruth Messinger, president of the borough of Manhattan in New York City; Maryann Mahaffey, president of the Detroit City Council; and U.S. Representative Ron Dellums of California. Social workers are increasingly encouraged to get involved in legislative and electoral politics at the local, state, and federal levels.

Progressive social workers are entering public debates in print and electronic media forums to advocate progressive social welfare policies and to defeat regressive proposals and are encouraging social workers to speak out as well (Stoesz, 1993). Voter registration continues to be an important electoral objective, especially the national right to register public assistance recipients in welfare centers, which has been championed by the Human Service Employees Registration and Voter Education (Human SERVE) Campaign (Cloward & Piven, 1983).

Challenging Social Work

Finally, progressive social workers are continuing to challenge, where necessary, the neglect, ignorance, and passivity in social work that are causing the profession to overlook its opportunity and responsibility to fulfill its societal function as a force for progressive social change (Newdom, 1993). A telling example is the fact that average citizens (and many social workers) cannot name a social worker with a national reputation for advocating the interests of the underdog. Is there a Ralph Nader of social work? Where are the Jane Addams, Mary van Kleeck, and Bertha Capen Reynolds of this generation? Some of the most prominent social welfare advocates, such as Marian Wright Edelman of the Children's Defense Fund or Robert Hayes of the Coalition for the Homeless, are lawyers, not social workers. What does this say about our profession and what has happened during the 1980s? Although progressive social workers are not condoning "star making" at the price of discounting the admirable work of countless unknown practitioners, the contemporary invisibility of a progressive profession is a serious concern.

Many progressive social workers believe that the success of social work in the 21st century depends on further legitimizing progressive social work, improving social work education, preparing practitioners with improved methods, becoming more deeply involved in political practice in the public domain, and asserting a greater progressive presence within and outside of the profession. Within these five domains of activity, progressive social workers will be working to create social and economic justice.

CONCLUSION

Compared with other professions such as law and medicine, social work is a progressive profession. Yet it has nonetheless been difficult, especially during the 1980s, to avoid serving a conservative, social control function for society. Progressive social workers believe it takes a strong progressive movement spanning the entire human services labor force (not just the people with a master's of social work degree) and pressuring the profession from within and without to hold social work true to its self-professed mission to serve poor and oppressed people.

Even within a liberal profession, progressive social workers are farther to the left on the political continuum than their moderate or conservative colleagues who believe that the free-market economy and the current social structures are essentially suitable forms of social organization that, at most, need some internal reforming by the process of incremental social change. Seeking both incremental and fundamental social change, progressive social workers are wary of capitalism's tendency to put profits before human needs. They look for economic, political, and social alternatives that prevent or mitigate poverty, violence, unemployment, illness, crime, and the host of other social problems affecting our society more seriously with each passing year. Progressive social workers want to foster human growth and potential within diverse and healthy families and communities. The progressive social work vision is for caring societies throughout the world to meet human needs, to guarantee and protect human rights, and to provide people with resources and opportunities they need to heal, to develop their individual potential, and to live with others responsibly and peacefully.

REFERENCES

Abramovitz, M. (1988). *Regulating the lives of women.* Boston: South End Press.

Andersen, M. L., & Collins, P. H. (Eds.). (1995). *Race, class, and gender* (2nd ed.). Belmont, CA: Wadsworth.

Bailey, R., & Brake, M. (1975). *Radical social work*. New York: Pantheon Books.

Blau, J. (1992). *The visible poor: Homelessness in the United States*. New York: Oxford University Press.

Bombyk, M. (1987). The first national meeting of the Bertha Capen Reynolds Society. *Smith College School for Social Work Journal, 5*(2), 34–35.

Burghardt, S. (1982). *The other side of organizing*. Cambridge, MA: Schenkman.

Burghardt, S., & Fabricant, M. (1987). Radical social work. In A. Minahan (Ed.-in-Chief), *Encyclopedia of social work* (18th ed., Vol. 2, pp. 455–462). Silver Spring, MD: National Association of Social Workers.

Carniol, B. (1979). A critical approach in social work. *Canadian Journal of Social Work Education, 5*(1), 95–111.

Carniol, B. (1992). Structural social work: Maurice Moreau's challenge to social work practice. *Journal of Progressive Human Services, 3*(1), 1–21.

Cloward, R. (1993). The reordered class structure. *BCR Reports, 5*(2), 1, 7.

Cloward, R., & Piven, F. F. (1983). Toward a class-based alignment: A movement strategy. *Social Policy, 13*(3), 3–15.

Coates, J. (1992). Ideology and education for social work practice. *Journal of Progressive Human Services, 3*(2), 15–30.

Corrigan, P., & Leonard, P. (1978). *Social work practice under capitalism: A Marxist approach*. New York: Macmillan.

Cummerton, J. (1986). A feminist perspective on research. In N. Van Den Bergh & L. Cooper (Eds.), *Feminist visions for social work* (pp. 80–100). Silver Spring, MD: National Association of Social Workers.

Delgado, G. (1994). *Beyond the politics of place: New directions in community organizing in the 1990s*. Oakland, CA: Applied Research Center.

Doyal, L., & Gough, I. (1991). *A theory of human need*. New York: Guilford Press.

Epstein, I. (1970a). Organizational careers, professionalization, and social work radicalism. *Social Service Review, 44*(2), 123–131.

Epstein, I. (1970b). Professionalization, professionalism, and social work radicalism. *Journal of Health and Social Behavior, 11*(1), 67–77.

Fabricant, M., & Burghardt, S. (1992). *The welfare state crisis and the transformation of social service work*. Armonk, NY: M. E. Sharpe.

Ferguson, K. (1984). *The feminist case against bureaucracy*. Philadelphia: Temple University Press.

Fisher, J. (1980). *The response of social work to the Depression*. Cambridge, MA: Schenkman.

Fisher, R. (1984). *Let the people decide: A history of neighborhood organizing*. Boston: G. K. Hall.

Galper, J. (1975). *The politics of social services*. Englewood Cliffs, NJ: Prentice Hall.

Galper, J. (1976). Introduction to radical theory and practice in social work education. *Journal of Education for Social Work, 12*(2), 10–16.

Galper, J. (1978). What are radical social services? *Social Policy, 8*(4), 37–41.

Gil, D. (1979). *Beyond the jungle: Essays on human possibilities, social alternatives, and radical practice*. Cambridge, MA: Schenkman.

Goff, M., & McNutt, J. (1994). *The global environmental crisis: Implications or social work and social welfare*. Brookfield, VT: Ashgate.

Gough, I. (1979). *The political economy of the welfare state*. New York: Macmillan.

Gutierrez, L. (1990). Working with women of color: An empowerment perspective. *Social Work, 35*(2), 149–154.

Gutierrez, L. (1994). Beyond coping: An empowerment perspective of stressful life events. *Journal of Sociology and Social Welfare, 21*(3), 201–220.

Hartman, A. (1993). The professional is political. *Social Work, 38*, 365–366, 504.

Hasenfeld, Y. (1987). Power in social work practice. *Social Service Review, 61*(3), 469–483.

Karger, H. J. (1983). Science, research, and social work: Who controls the profession? *Social Work, 28*, 200–205.

Leighninger, L. (1991). From the archives. *Journal of Progressive Human Services, 2*(1), 73–74.

Leonard, P. (1990). Contesting the welfare state in a neoconservative era. *Journal of Progressive Human Services, 1*, 11–25.

Lichtenberg, P. (1976). Introduction to radical theory and practice in social work education: Personality theory. *Journal of Education for Social Work, 12*(2), 10–16.

Longres, J. (1986). Marxian theory and social work practice. *Catalyst: A Socialist Journal of the Social Services, 5*(4), 13–34.

Lord, S., & Kennedy, E. (1992). Transforming a charity organization into a social justice community center. *Journal of Progressive Human Services, 3*(1), 21–37.

Middleman, R. R., & Goldberg, G. (1974). *Social service delivery: A structural approach to social work practice*. New York: Columbia University Press.

Middleman, R. R., & Wood, G. G. (1990). *Skills for direct practice in social work*. New York: Columbia University Press.

Midgley, J., & Sanzenbach, P. (1991). The religious right's challenge to progressive social concerns. *Journal of Progressive Human Services, 2*(1), 1–13.

Mills, C. W. (1959). *The sociological imagination*. New York: Oxford University Press.

Moreau, M. (1979). A structural approach to social work practice. *Canadian Journal of Social Work Education, 5*(1), 78–94.

Moreau, M. (1990). Empowerment through advocacy and consciousness-raising: Implications for structural social work. *Journal of Sociology and Social Welfare, 17*(2), 53–67.

Moscovitch, A., & Drover, G. (Eds.). (1981). *Inequality: Essays on the political economy of social welfare*. Toronto: University of Toronto Press.

Mullaly, R., & Keating, E. (1991). Similarities, differences, and dialectics of radical social work. *Journal of Progressive Human Services, 2*(2), 49–78.

Newdom, F. (1993). Beyond hard times. *Journal of Progressive Human Services, 4*(2), 65–77.

Pearson, G. (1975). *The deviant imagination: Psychiatry, social work, and social change*. New York: Macmillan.

Piven, F. F., & Cloward, R. (1993). *Regulating the poor: The functions of public welfare* (rev. ed.). New York: Vintage Press.

Pritchard, C., & Taylor, R. (1978). *Social work: Reform or revolution?* New York: Macmillan.

Reeser, L., & Epstein, I. (1991). *Professionalization and activism in social work: The sixties, the eighties, and the future*. New York: Columbia University Press.

Rein, M. (1970). Social work in search of a radical profession. *Social Work, 15,* 218–231.

Reinharz, S., Bombyk, M., & Wright, J. (1983). Methodological issues in feminist research: A bibliography of literature in women's studies, sociology, and psychology. *Women's Studies International Forum, 6*(4), 437–454.

Reynolds, B. C. (1975). *Social work and social living: Explorations in philosophy and practice*. Washington, DC: National Association of Social Workers. (Original work published 1951)

Reynolds, B. C. (1982). *Between client and community: A study in responsibility in social casework*. Silver Spring, MD: National Association of Social Workers. (Original work published 1934)

Reynolds, B. C. (1985). *Learning and teaching in the practice of social work*. Silver Spring, MD: National Association of Social Workers. (Original work published 1942)

Reynolds, B. C. (1991). *An uncharted journey: Fifty years in social work* (3rd ed.). Silver Spring, MD: NASW Press. (Original work published 1963)

Simon, B. (1990). Rethinking empowerment. *Journal of Progressive Human Services, 1*(1), 27–39.

Simon, B. (1994). *The empowerment tradition in American social work*. New York: Columbia University Press.

Sohng, S. L. (1992). Consumers as research partners. *Journal of Progressive Human Services, 3*(2), 1–14.

Specht, H., & Courtney, M. (1994). *Unfaithful angels: How social work abandoned its mission*. New York: Free Press.

Statham, D. (1978). *Radicals in social work*. London: Routledge & Kegan Paul.

Stoesz, D. (1993). Communicating with the public. *Social Work, 38,* 367–368.

Thorosell, H. (Ed.). (1975). *Social work: Radical essays*. St. Lucia, Australia: University of Queensland Press.

van Kleeck, M. (1991). Our illusions concerning government. *Journal of Progressive Human Services, 2*(1), 75–86.

Wagner, D. (1989). Fate of idealism in social work: Alternative experiences of professional careers. *Social Work, 34,* 389–395.

Wagner, D. (1990). *The quest for a radical profession: Social service careers in political ideology*. New York: University Press of America.

Wagner, D. (1991a). Reviving the action research model: Combining case and cause with dislocated workers. *Social Work, 36,* 477–481.

Wagner, D. (1991b). Social work and the hidden victims of deindustrialization. *Journal of Progressive Human Services, 2*(1), 15–37.

Weinert, B. (1993). The health care crisis. *BCR Reports, 5*(2), center page insert.

Wenokur, S., & Reisch, M. (1989). *From charity to enterprise: The development of American social work in a market economy*. Chicago: University of Illinois Press.

Wineman, S. (1984). *The politics of human services: A radical alternative to the welfare state*. Boston: South End Press.

Withorn, A. (1984). *Serving the people: Social services and social change*. New York: Columbia University Press.

Wood, G. G., & Middleman, R. R. (1989). *The structural approach to direct practice*. New York: Columbia University Press.

Zuber-Skerritt, O. (Ed.). (1991). *Action research for change and development*. Brookfield, VA: Gower.

For more information about the Bertha Capen Reynolds Society and its newsletter, *BCR Reports,* write to P.O. Box 20563, Columbus Circle Station, New York, NY 10023.

Marti Bombyk, PhD, is associate professor, Fordham University, Graduate School of Social Service, 113 West 60th Street, New York, NY 10023.

For further information see

Advocacy; Citizen Participation; Civil Rights; Community; Ethics and Values; Federal Social Legislation from 1961 to 1994; Human Rights; International and Comparative Social Welfare; Mass Media; Natural Helping Networks; Organizations: Context for Social Services Delivery; Peace and Social Justice; Social Planning; Social Welfare Policy; Social Work Profession Overview; Social Workers in Politics; Technology Transfer; Welfare Employment Programs: Evaluation.

Key Words	
activism	progressive social
empowerment	work
oppression	radical social work

Protective Services

See Adult Protective Services; Child Welfare Overview

Psychometrics

Kevin Corcoran

Psychometrics is the scientific study of the measurement of human behavior (Nunnally, 1978). Although its use in social work is relatively recent, it has been around since the ancient Chinese used written examinations to select people for governmental service (Sundberg, 1977). This entry discusses the use of measurement in social work practice, the essential features of quantitatively sound and qualitatively useful measurement tools, and general ways of interpreting scores.

PSYCHOMETRICS IN PRACTICE

The profession of social work has numerous needs for psychometrically sound measurement tools. The most obvious need may seem to be in research. However, practitioners of all types, from community organizers, to administrators, to clinicians, require and use measurement tools. They especially need them to prove their accountability because funding agencies, third-party payers, and consumers are increasingly demanding quality assurance before payment.

Some useful sources for locating instruments are Fischer and Corcoran (1994a, 1994b), Hudson (1992), and McCubbin and Thompson (1991). Research on measurement is frequently published in the *Journal of Behavioral Assessment and Psychopathology, Journal of Clinical Psychology, Journal of Personality Assessment, Psychological Assessment, Research on Social Work Practice,* and *Social Work Research.*

Regardless of whether social workers are doing research or practice, they frequently use measurement tools to perform a needs assessment to determine if social policies and programs are warranted, to evaluate an employee's performance, or to assess changes in a client's problem and whether a goal of an intervention has been met. Measurement tools may include a standardized intake assessment form, a mental status examination, or any one of the many rapid-assessment tools available to measure clients' problems.

QUANTIFICATION

The measurement of social work practice is a simple process that involves the application of a system of numbers to the attributes of some variables. In other words, one simply applies a number to "some thing"—most likely a person's cognition, affect, or behavior or an aspect of the environment. The assignment of the numbers is, as suggested, systematic. This process is known as quantification.

Regardless of the variable that is being quantified—whether it is a strength or a problem—measurement assesses only its *frequency, intensity,* or *duration.* For example, the measurement of Bill's love for Betty may be how often he thinks of her during the work day, how intense or passionate his feelings for her are, or how long he is in a daze. In contrast, Betty may see Bill's love as a problem and measure how often she is pestered by Bill, how angry she feels about his amorous glances, or how long she is annoyed. It really does not matter what is being measured or how it may be experienced; all quantification is limited to the frequency, intensity, and duration of a thing.

To be quantitatively sound, a measurement tool must have two essential features: reliability and validity. *Reliability* refers to the consistency of the instrument; that is, whatever the measurement ascertains, it should do so consistently. *Validity* refers to accuracy; that is, whatever the instrument is attempting to ascertain, it should do so with a high degree of accuracy.

METHODS OF ESTIMATING CONSISTENCY

There are four basic methods of estimating the reliability or consistency of an instrument. All of them are based on some form of agreement, which may be as simple as the percentage of agreements, as among different raters or different ratings, for example. Agreement is frequently estimated with a *correlation coefficient*—a statistical procedure that examines the association between two or more variables. For the purposes of reliability, the correlation coefficient produces a statistic that ranges from 0.0 to 1.0, where higher magnitudes reflect a stronger association between the variables.

Coefficient of Consistency

The first type of reliability considers the consistency of all the items of a measurement tool. It is called *internal consistency* because it is concerned with the internal structure of the instrument. For an instrument to be reliable, each item should be associated with all the other items. The conventional statistical procedure for determining internal consistency is Cronbach's alpha. If the items have dichotomous responses, such as "yes or no" or "true or false," the approach is slightly different and is based on a statistical procedure known as Kuder-Richardson Formula 20.

Both statistics produce a coefficient that ranges from being completely unreliable at 0.0— that is, not internally consistent— to completely internally consistent at 1.0. It is rare for either extreme to occur. The problem, then, is to decide what is a strong enough coefficient to determine whether an instrument is internally consistent. In part, this decision will depend on what is being assessed and why. For example, if the reason for measurement is to determine a client's eligibility or readiness for discharge, then a strong internal consistency is necessary because no one would want decisions that seriously affect clients to be based on inconsistencies. If the social worker's purpose, however, is to measure some aspect of the client, such as ego strength, to corroborate his or her clinical judgment, then less consistency may be tolerated.

Similarly, if one is measuring a well-defined construct in social work practice, such as assertiveness, then a higher internal consistency coefficient would be expected. If measurement is more nebulous, such as political empowerment, then a less-stringent internal consistency may be tolerated.

In general, instruments used in social work practice should have coefficients of consistency of at least .80. However, it may be argued that a weak measurement of something is better than no standardized measurement and, therefore, that a lower magnitude of internal consistency may be acceptable.

Coefficient of Stability

This second type of consistency, known as *test-retest reliability,* is concerned with how an instrument performs over time. The correlational procedures produce what is called a coefficient of stability. For example, if a practitioner is measuring Bill and Betty's level of marital discord during treatment, he or she does not want an instrument that is not stable, that is, one that suggests change has occurred when it has not. Coefficients of stability, then, are based on the correlation of scores between one administration of the instrument and another.

Deciding what magnitude of the correlation is acceptable is again a matter of one's purpose. If what is being measured is a flexible state of human behavior, such as situational anxiety, then lower coefficients may be acceptable. However, if the variable is a relatively enduring trait of human behavior, such as generalized anxiety, then higher coefficients of stability are needed. Coefficients of stability also depend on the length of time between one administration and the next. With less time between administrations, one would expect higher coefficients, regardless of whether a state or a trait was being measured. More time between the administrations would allow for the acceptance of lower coefficients of stability. Again, although there are no hard-and-fast rules, a coefficient of .80 tends to suggest that the instrument is stable over time.

Coefficient of Equivalence

The third type of consistency concerns the association between two forms or versions of the same instrument (called parallel forms). A coefficient of equivalence suggests that the two forms are consistent with each other. A high coefficient, say above .85, is necessary to assert that two forms of the same instrument are equivalent.

Parallel forms provide certain advantages to social workers. For the administration of an instrument in a group, respondents who are sitting next to each other may be assessed without the worry that one person's answers may inadvertently influence another's. For the practitioner who is measuring a clinical problem over the course of an intervention, parallel forms help prevent the respondent from simply remembering the earlier answers or answering an item as he or she remembers it, instead of reading it thoroughly.

Because of the difficulty and cost of developing an instrument, not many measures with parallel forms are available to social workers. When alternative forms are available, they tend to be revised versions of earlier instruments or shorter versions of the original.

Coefficients of Agreement

The fourth type of reliability concerns the agreement between ratings by one social worker who assesses a problem on two or more occasions (intrarater reliability) or by two or more raters (interrater reliability). The association between ratings reflects the agreement between them.

Both types of rater reliability are particularly important to clinical social work. For the individual social worker who is working with Bill and Betty in marital therapy, for example, it is important that his or her evaluations of different occasions agree. Similarly, in light of the need to transfer cases and because of interdisciplinary approaches to practice, it is necessary for two different professionals to agree on Bill and Betty's condition.

With rater reliability, the measurement process is not simply the administration of the tangible tool, but includes some aspect of the social worker, such as his or her clinical judgment. Because the social worker is a part of the measurement tool in some respect, it is expected that more inconsistency will occur. Coefficients of agreement, then, are acceptable at magnitudes of .75 or above.

STANDARD ERROR OF MEASUREMENT

All these procedures for determining consistency are estimates of the random error in an instrument. These estimates are highly sensitive to differences between the research samples from which the data are collected. For example, reliability estimates may be different for a sample from Canterbury, New Hampshire, than for one from Calgary, Canada. One way to minimize this potential problem is with estimates of the standard error of the measurement (SEM).

The SEM is derived by taking the square root of 1 minus the reliability coefficient (r) and multiplying that number by the standard deviation (s):

$$SEM = s\sqrt{1 - r}$$

If the SEM is small, the measurement is a consistent instrument; if it is large, it is a weaker, or inconsistent instrument. Dividing the SEM by the scale range and then multiplying by 100 determines the percentage of error in the scores. Ten percent error in an instrument is not uncommon, but 5 percent is obviously better. In general, social workers should look for measurement tools in which the reliability coefficients are high and the SEM is low.

ACCURACY

The second essential characteristic of a sound measurement tool is accuracy, or validity, and it means that a measure ascertains what it is intended to. There are a variety of ways to estimate the validity of a measurement, although they may be categorized as one of three types: content validity, criterion-referenced validity, or construct validity.

Content Validity

Content validity evaluates the substance of the items to determine if they are appropriate for assessing the domain in question, that is, if the items are a representative sample of the domain. There are two general approaches to content validity: face validity and logical content validity.

Face validity is the easier method of assessing validity. Here the user simply examines the content of the instrument's items and judges if it reflects the domain he or she wants to measure. This is one of the first steps in determining if an instrument is appropriate for one's purposes. However, it lacks any empirically based standard for reaching the decision and often results in the assertion of validity on the basis of such subjective principles as "Oh, this one will do."

Logical content validity, on the other hand, refers to a predetermined systematic procedure for developing items to be included in an instrument. The procedure assures that the content domain is thoroughly reflected in the instrument. An excellent example of logical content validity from social work is the measure of family empowerment by Koren, DeChillo, and Friesen (1992).

Criterion-Referenced Validity

Criterion-referenced validity estimates the accuracy of an instrument by determining its association with specified criteria. Because a number of methods are used to determine criterion-referenced validity, including concurrent validity, predictive validity, known-group validity, theoretical validity, empirical validity, and factorial validity, there is often quite a bit of confusion among them, especially because they are only slightly different

from each other. The first three methods capture much of what is meant by criterion-referenced validity.

Concurrent validity refers to the process of administering the instrument concurrently with another assessment of the same or similar variable and determining the association between them. Although the defining feature of concurrent validity is the time during which the instrument and the other assessment are administered, the evidence of validity is found in the association between them. For example, a new, shorter measure of marital discord should correlate positively with the reported frequency of arguments and negatively with an assessment of marital satisfaction. If the new instrument is appropriately correlated at an acceptable magnitude, the instrument is considered to have concurrent validity.

Predictive validity is somewhat more sophisticated than concurrent validity. With predictive validity, an instrument's accuracy is estimated by its correlation with future events. For example, if the same measure of marital discord was associated with future rates of marital separation and divorce, it would be seen as having predictive validity.

Known-group validity is a slightly different method of estimating an instrument's accuracy. Here scores are tested for differences on the basis of criteria for two or more groups that are known to be different on the variable. For example, separated, divorced, and newly married couples are known to differ on marital discord; if the couples in each group scored differently on the marital discord instrument, then this difference would be evidence of known-group validity.

Construct Validity

Construct validity estimates whether an instrument taps a particular theoretical construct domain. For an instrument to have construct validity, scores must converge with similar measures—much like they might with concurrent validity—*and* discriminate from nonrelevant measures. For example, if the new marital discord instrument correlated with other measures of marital discord and dissatisfaction and was concomitantly uncorrelated with such irrelevant variables as occupational or educational level, then the instrument would be considered to have construct validity.

Construct validity actually requires estimates of both convergent and discriminant validity. It is not uncommon, however, to find published reports advancing the validity of an instrument that include only convergent validity. The procedure used is most likely either concurrent or predictive validity and suggests that the instrument is an accurate assessment of the frequency, intensity, or duration of the variable.

ESSENTIAL COMPONENTS OF QUALITATIVELY SOUND MEASURES

Although the discussion of quantitative procedures may sound complex, much of it reduces to an issue of good social work judgment of what is acceptable evidence of consistency and accuracy. A measure with less-than-sterling evidence of reliability and validity may be more valuable than no empirical assessment as a guide to the social work process. And no right-minded social worker would simply rely on the score of a measurement tool if it was contrary to his or her professional judgment. Consequently, a good instrument for social work should also have certain important qualitative features. Which qualitative feature is essential depends on the social worker's purpose in doing the measurement.

Utility

Utility is probably the most important qualitative element of an instrument. It refers to the practical advantage gained from using a measurement tool. Generally, a measure should help a social worker assess a client, plan services, improve services, or evaluate services. For an instrument to have utility, it must, of course, be consistent and accurate— that is, reliable and valid. On a pragmatic level, an instrument that has utility guides practice and is relatively short, easy to score, and easy to interpret (Fischer & Corcoran, 1994b).

Sensitivity

If the social worker's purpose is to assess change over the course of an intervention, an instrument must be sensitive. Sensitivity contrasts with test–retest reliability. A sensitive instrument actually assesses the change that has occurred; test–retest reliability indicates that scores on an instrument are stable and do not change when no change has occurred. In evaluating practice, social workers need instruments that are stable and sensitive to actual change.

Directness

Directness is another qualitative feature of a sound measurement tool. A direct measure assesses the actual cognitive, affective, behavioral, or environmental variable, whereas an indirect measure assumes that the assessment reflects some underlying disposition or variable. The most obvious example of an indirect measure is a projective testing technique, such as the Rorschach test. Indirect measures often have serious problems in terms of reliability and validity, whereas direct measures are more consistent and accurate.

Suitability and Acceptability

Finally, a qualitatively sound measure must be suitable and acceptable to the situation being assessed. *Suitability* refers to the respondent's intellectual ability, emotional state, skills, and ability to discriminate among different attributes of the variable being measured. *Acceptability* means that content of the items is neither too sophisticated nor too elementary and does not offend the client because of its level or what it probes. Issues of acceptability often occur when the social worker is measuring private behaviors, such as a client's sexuality, morality, or use of alcohol and other drugs. If the content of an instrument is not acceptable to the client, the client may not answer the items truthfully or at all. There is not much practical advantage in administering an instrument that the client will not answer.

INTERPRETATION OF SCORES

Assuming that the instrument is a psychometrically sound assessment of a thing, the social worker now faces the most challenging aspect of using measurements, namely, how to make the score meaningful. After all, the score is simply a number applied to a thing, and that number, by itself, is not meaningful. The issue here is interpretation. Interpretation is based on comparing the number, known as a score, with some other number. There are two general approaches to interpreting scores: norm-referenced comparison and self-referenced comparison.

Norm-Referenced Comparison

Norm-referenced comparison makes a score meaningful by comparing it to some other group of scores, which is a norm. For example, a clinical social worker in a family service agency who is helping Bill and Betty with their marital relationship may use the new shorter instrument discussed earlier. Bill and Betty's scores alone are not meaningful. They should be interpreted in comparison to those of other couples who have completed the instruments, including couples who are divorced, separated, and newly married, to see how Bill and Betty scored in comparison to these groups.

There are, of course, some limitations to norm-referenced comparisons. First, the focus of concern is not necessarily Bill and Betty relative to others, but simply Bill and Betty as a couple who have sought services. Second, norms are difficult and expensive to collect; consequently, a norm may not be up-to-date or appropriately representative. This limitation is especially apparent in work with diverse clients, whether the diversity is racial, cultural, geographic, or based on gender or sexual orientation.

Self-Referenced Comparison

A second general method of interpreting a score is to compare it with the client's score on an earlier administration of the instrument. This method is known as *self-referenced comparison* because the point of comparison for making the score meaningful is the client. The interpretation enables the social worker to determine if the frequency, intensity, or duration of the client's behavior or another variable is more than, less than, or the same as before. Self-referenced comparison is the basis for much of the interpretation that occurs in single-subject evaluations. For example, Richy's scores on a measure of hostility over the course of treatment may suggest that he has improved (the scores are lower than they were before the intervention), worsened (the scores are higher), or not changed (the scores are about the same).

Although self-referenced comparison avoids many of the problems of norm-referenced interpretation, it is limited in that it allows for an understanding only in relation to the individual. For example, even though Richy's score may be lower after the intervention than it was before the intervention, Richy may still be so hostile that he goes to the office with a gun and shoots his boss. A representative norm, however, would allow the social worker to acknowledge Richy's improvement but see that he was still dangerous to himself and to others.

Summary

The use of standardized measurement is becoming an increasingly familiar component not only of research, but of administration, supervision, and clinical practice—in sum, of just about every domain in which social workers practice. As managed care becomes an evermore important aspect of their practice, social workers will have a greater need for instruments that are psychometrically sound.Psychometrically sound instruments are consistent (reliable) and accurate (valid) assessments of the frequency, intensity, or duration of cognitive, affective, behavioral, or environmental variables. Moreover, sound instruments must guide practice and have at least some utility.

The use of instruments, by themselves, will accomplish little. Even the most reliable, valid, and useful instrument is simply a procedure for applying a number to a thing. As such, that number must be interpreted by comparing it either to a group of other numbers (norm-referenced comparison) or to a respondent's earlier scores (self-referenced comparison). Moreover, the use of measurement tools must be put in the context of good social work practice, whether it is clinical practice, research, or whatever. That is, a score from an instrument is nothing more than a number, and that number can only supplement, but never substitute for, sound professional judgment.

REFERENCES

Fischer, J., & Corcoran, K. (1994a). *Measures for clinical practice: Vol. 2. A sourcebook for adults* (2nd ed.). New York: Free Press.
Fischer, J., & Corcoran, K. (1994b). *Measures for clinical practice: Vol. 1. A sourcebook for children, couples and families* (2nd ed.). New York: Free Press.
Hudson, W. W. (1992). *Computer assisted social services.* Tempe, AZ: Walmyr.
Koren, P. E., DeChillo, N., & Friesen, B. J. (1992). Measuring empowerment in families whose children have emotional disabilities: A brief questionnaire. *Rehabilitation Psychology, 37,* 305–321.
McCubbin, H. I., & Thompson, A. I. (1991). *Family assessment inventories for research and practice.* Madison: University of Wisconsin-Madison, Family Stress Coping and Health Project.
Nunnally, J. C. (1978). *Psychometric theory.* New York: McGraw-Hill.
Sundberg, N. D. (1977). *Assessment of persons.* Englewood Cliffs, NJ: Prentice Hall.

FURTHER READING

Allen, M. J., & Yen, W. M. (1979). *Introduction to measurement theory.* Monterey, CA: Brooks/Cole.
Anastasi, A. (1982). *Psychological testing.* New York: Macmillan.
Barlow, D. H. (Ed.). (1983). *Behavioral assessment of adult disorder.* New York: Guilford Press.
Cronbach, L. J. (1960). *Essentials of psychological testing.* New York: Harper & Brothers.
Goldstein, G., & Hersen, M. (1990). *Handbook of psychological assessment.* Elmsford, New York: Pergamon Press.
Gould, S. J. (1981). *The mismeasurement of man.* New York: Norton.
Robinson, J. P., & Shaver, P. R. (1973). *Measures for social psychological attitudes* (rev. ed.). Ann Arbor: University of Michigan, Institute for Social Research.

Kevin Corcoran, PhD, is professor, Portland State University, Graduate School of Social Work, Portland, OR 97207.

For further information see

Clinical Social Work; Intervention Research; Meta-analysis; Qualitative Research; Research Overview; Survey Research.

Key Words	
assessment	reliability
measurement	validity
psychometrics	

Psychosocial Approach

Eda G. Goldstein

Although all of social work practice embodies a psychosocial or person-in-situation perspective, the psychosocial approach is a distinctive practice model that is widely used by social work practitioners today (Mackey, Urek, & Charkoudian, 1987). It focuses on the study, diagnosis (assessment), and treatment of individuals in transaction with their social environments. Its goals are to restore, maintain, and enhance the social functioning of individuals by mobilizing strengths, supporting coping capacities, modifying dysfunctional patterns of relating and acting, linking people to necessary resources, and alleviating environmental stressors.

Contributors to the development of the psychosocial approach assigned an important role to intrapsychic factors in assessment as well as to interpersonal and environmental influences. Initially, they emphasized psychodynamically oriented techniques in the interventive process and later attempted to balance these techniques with more environmentally focused interventions.

In the 1960s, when macrosystems intervention commanded more attention and resources in the social work profession, and studies of casework effectiveness showed unexpectedly poor results (Mullen, Dumpson, & Associates, 1972), some segments of the profession criticized the psychosocial approach as being too psychodynamic, too allied with the medical model, too pathology oriented, and too lengthy and expensive (Wasserman, 1974). Nevertheless, this approach has been an open system of thought that has undergone modification over time in response to new theoretical developments and practice experience. It has shown flexibility and resilience in its responsiveness to the changing practice arena and to the needs of special populations. Today, the psychosocial approach is committed to individualized assessment within a systems perspective and tries to achieve a balance among biological, psychological, interpersonal, environmental, and cultural factors in assessment and intervention. Initially a casework model used generally with voluntary clients on an ongoing basis, the psychosocial model now encompasses individual, family, and group modalities; crisis, short-term, and extended intervention; and work with a greater range of client problems and populations.

ORIGINS AND EVOLUTION

The contemporary psychosocial approach has been associated with the work of Florence Hollis, but it evolved as part of a long and rich tradition that originated in the writings of Mary Richmond (1917). Richmond viewed environmental conditions as crucial in affecting individuals, but she saw each person as unique in the way he or she deals with these social factors. She put forth the principles of study, diagnosis, and treatment as constituting the core of social casework. The "diagnostic school" or "differential" approach emerged in the 1920s, taking its name from its emphasis on diagnosis as the foundation of all intervention. It was further developed during the period of the psychiatric deluge that followed World War I. Among the many psychologies that became popular were Sigmund Freud's views, which began to gain acceptance in certain segments of the social work profession. Freud's impact on practice was dramatic and far-reaching, particularly in the northeastern United States among diagnostic social workers. Gordon Hamilton (1958), one of the most influential members of this group, later recalled this time, describing Freud's theory as bursting into the profession "like an atom" and eventually resulting in casework becoming "so preoccupied with the inner life as almost to lose touch with outer reality and the social factors with which social workers were most familiar" (pp. 18–23).

In the 1930s, a schism developed between members of the functional school (V. P. Robinson, 1930; Taft, 1937), who adhered to the theories of Otto Rank, and those of the diagnostic school, who were followers of Freud. The functional approach linked agency function to the relationship process that it offered clients, in which they could learn to assert their will and fulfill their uniqueness by deciding whether or not to use the agency's services. Each group criticized the other for certain excesses in casework treatment (Hamilton, 1958; Yelaja, 1974). Also during this decade, the Great Depression drew attention away from people's psyches to the economic conditions that were causing extreme suffering.

At the end of the 1930s and throughout the post–World War II period, ego psychology gained recognition in the United States and had an important impact on social work practice (Goldstein, 1984). It helped bridge the psychological and social spheres and was used to help correct some of the excesses of the earlier era. In 1940 Gordon Hamilton published the widely used text *Theory and Practice of Social Casework*, which put forth the principles of the evolving diagnostic approach. Hamilton began to use the term "psychosocial," which seemed to have been initiated much earlier by Hankins (1931), of the Smith College School for Social Work. Other diagnostic social workers, such as Lucille Austin (1948), Annette Garrett (1958), and Florence Hollis (1949) tried to define the goals and techniques of social casework as differentiated from psychotherapy. Helen Perlman (1957) attempted to bridge the functional and diagnostic groups and evolved her own problem-solving approach, which drew heavily from ego psychological theory. In the latter part of the 1950s and the early 1960s, the knowledge explosion in the social sciences generated experimentation in the practice arena and resulted in new interventive models including family treatment, crisis intervention, task-centered casework, planned short-term treatment, and cognitive–behavioral intervention.

In this climate Hollis (1964) wrote the seminal text *Casework: A Psychosocial Therapy*, which reflected her effort to articulate a clear psychosocial model that was both a continuation of the diagnostic tradition and distinct from other models coming into prominence. Her thinking evolved over the years as seen in later editions of the book (Hollis, 1972; Hollis & Woods, 1981; Woods & Hollis, 1989), the last of which was published after her death in 1987.

THEORETICAL UNDERPINNINGS

The person-in-situation focus of the psychosocial approach requires the use of theories that help workers understand the person, the situation, and the interactions between them by shedding light on the nature of optimal functioning, various forms of maladaptation, economic and social deprivation, and oppression. The psychosocial model incorporates and attempts to synthesize diverse theories of human behavior and the social environment (Goldstein, 1983). Although a strength of this approach has been its practitioners' openness to new knowledge over the years and their willingness to discard ideas that are not useful, it now is more difficult to precisely delimit its knowledge base and to present a fully integrated view of its theoretical underpinnings. Consequently, one could argue that it is more accurate to describe the psychosocial approach as a perspective that

guides practice, rather than as a practice model. Nevertheless, practitioners of the psychosocial approach do rely on a main core of theoretical systems and practice principles.

To capture the person–situation gestalt, the psychosocial approach uses many concepts derived from general systems theory and the ecological point of view (Woods & Hollis, 1989). To understand personality in depth and the coping capacities that people bring to their life transactions, the psychosocial approach draws on four psychodynamic frameworks: Freudian theory, ego psychology, object relations theory, and self-psychology. It embodies new perspectives on female development; the adult life cycle; the impact of divorce and of sexual abuse; gay and lesbian development; cultural, ethnic, and racial diversity; and the effects of personality on functioning. It incorporates the findings of observational studies of infants and small children that enlarge and to some extent modify our understanding of developmental processes. Cognitive theory and new knowledge about the influence of biological factors on personality and psychopathology add an important dimension to our understanding of human functioning. Communications, family, and small group theories shed light on the nature of interpersonal interactions. Role theory provides an important link between social and environmental influences and personality development. Crisis theory focuses attention on how unusually stressful circumstances disrupt an individual's usual means of coping, precipitate a painful state that has certain characteristic stages, and result in the eventual reestablishment of the individual's equilibrium. Knowledge regarding the impact on people of organizational structure and processes, the service delivery system, the community, and society are essential to our understanding of person–environment transactions.

PRACTICE PRINCIPLES AND TECHNIQUES

Assessment

Diagnostic understanding or assessment is fundamental to the psychosocial approach (Meyer, 1993). Because each client presents with a unique constellation of needs, coping capacities, interpersonal relationships, stressors, cultural background, and environmental resources, correct assessment must be individualized and related to the development and implementation of an appropriate interventive plan. Gathering the relevant facts in a particular case may be time-consuming and may require contact with other people in the client's life. Although time constraints may require that the assessment process be abbreviated and focused, accurate understanding is just as important in crisis and short-term intervention as it is in ongoing work. Consequently, social work practitioners must develop the knowledge and skills to make accurate assessments even under difficult circumstances.

Understanding the client's perception of his or her own needs and difficulties is essential to the assessment process. The client's ability to describe and evaluate his or her situation accurately may be limited, however, by state of mind, level of awareness, personality characteristics, trust in authority, cultural background, gender, sexual orientation, and so on. The social worker must understand the factors that might be influencing the client's story.

Assessment is psychosocial in nature and focuses on the client's current and past functioning and life circumstances. It considers the client's needs, problems, gender, ethnicity, race, life stage, social roles, characteristic ego functioning and coping patterns, relationships, environmental stressors, and social supports. The use of clinical or medical diagnoses may provide important information but should be augmented by a fuller psychosocial diagnosis. Thus, concluding that a client has a learning disability, medical problem, emotional disorder, or substance abuse problem has important implications but is not sufficient for the purposes of assessment and intervention planning.

Intervention

The focus and nature of intervention follows from the assessment, and the client should be involved in establishing the treatment plan. If a recently disabled man needs help in applying for an entitlement program, intervention should focus on linking him to necessary resources. If an unemployed man has a history of poor impulse control that weakens his ability to hold jobs, intervention should be directed toward improving this ego function. If a young mother lacks knowledge about parenting, the focus should be on giving her information and helping her use it. If a depressed woman has chronic difficulties in making friends because of low self-esteem, helping her understand the origins of her poor opinion of herself and feel better about herself would be useful. If a neglectful mother is given the choice of seeking help or losing her children, intervention must focus on helping the client identify some positive value in the work and developing her positive involvement and motivation. In practice, a case often has numerous possible foci, and intervention must be partialized and prioritized.

In codifying and refining the psychosocial approach, Hollis (1964, 1972; Hollis & Woods, 1981; Woods & Hollis, 1989) described and studied a group of techniques that can be used flexibly in the interventive process. In addition to those used primarily with the individual, including sustainment, direct influence, exploration–description– ventilation, person-in-situation reflection, pattern– dynamic reflection, and developmental reflection, Hollis also discussed work with the environment. She classified environmental intervention according to the type of resource used, the type of communication used, and the type of role assumed. This last consisted of provider, locator, creator of a resource, interpreter, mediator, and aggressive intervenor.

Comparison with Psychotherapy

Whether the psychosocial approach is too much like psychotherapy is a controversial issue. Social work practitioners who wish to engage in psychotherapy are likely to find the psychosocial approach more congenial than some other models, for example, the life model (Germain & Gitterman, 1980), because it has retained its early emphasis on the personality system more than other approaches have. Psychotherapy itself has come a long way from its reliance on classical psychoanalytic techniques, although it clearly does not encompass environmental intervention. The psychosocial model, however, may include psychotherapeutic techniques, but it has a broader scope and interventive repertoire. The psychosocial model may be short term or long term in nature and involve discharge planning, case management, and linkage to community and social resources, as well as the support of functioning or modification of long-standing personality or interpersonal difficulties.

CLIENT–SOCIAL WORKER RELATIONSHIP

The relationship between the client and the social worker is a crucial element in the psychosocial approach. The social worker shows human concern for clients but disciplines his or her use of the relationship in keeping with the assessment of the client's needs and interventive goals. The social worker conveys certain key attitudes and values, irrespective of the client; these include acceptance of the client's worth, a nonjudgmental attitude toward the client, appreciation of the client's individuality or uniqueness, respect for the client's right to self-determination, and adherence to confidentiality. In contrast to earlier views that stressed the importance of social worker neutrality and objectivity, currently there is greater emphasis on the social worker's ability to show empathy for clients, to engage in controlled involvement, and to convey genuineness.

In the "engagement" phase of intervention, the social worker must recognize the factors that are influencing the client's participation in the helping relationship. These involve the client's motivation and expectations; previous experiences in getting help; values, gender, religion, sexual orientation, class, and ethnicity and race; ego functioning; current life situation; and the characteristics of the service delivery setting itself.

Two main types of responses characterize the client–social worker relationship—those that are realistic and appropriate reactions to the personalities involved, and those that are unrealistic and inappropriate responses that stem from the client's or social worker's past relationships. These latter responses are termed "transference" and "countertransference" reactions. Although many reactions are benign and may contribute positively to the work, other reactions that become disruptive must be understood and carefully monitored. Sometimes the social worker functions as a role model or provides corrective experiences for the client. The social worker, however, must guard against imposing his or her own values on the client, using the client to meet the social worker's needs, or encouraging too much client dependence on the social worker. When the social worker ends the relationship because the work is complete or the relationship is prematurely disrupted for any reason, the practitioner must consider the meaning the relationship has to the client and help the client deal with the feelings involved.

Practice Modalities

The psychosocial approach, initially developed as a casework model at a time when couples and family treatment were just emerging as specialties, now encompasses work with individuals, couples, and families (Woods & Hollis, 1989) as well as group intervention (Northen, 1988), although Hollis herself did not address the use of the group modality. The knowledge and skills necessary to use these different modalities are generic to some extent and distinctive in other respects. For this reason it is preferable to teach a multimethod approach that identifies the common core of knowledge and skills across modalities as well as their unique characteristics, rather than to teach a generalist approach that eliminates the distinctiveness of each modality.

The psychosocial approach is consistent with crisis intervention and other forms of short-term treatment. Briefer forms of intervention require somewhat different skills than do more extended forms of treatment, because time dictates faster assessments and more active and focused interventions. There are criteria for the use of these approaches (Golan, 1978; Reid & Epstein, 1972), but it seems clear that briefer forms of intervention are being used in many social work settings without proper regard for these suggested guidelines. At a time when economic and service delivery constraints dominate the practice arena, an important issue is the degree to which briefer forms of intervention are used because they are indicated or because they are less costly.

Diversity

With its early roots in psychoanalytic theory and the medical model, the psychosocial approach came under attack in the 1960s and later for being too disease oriented; for seeming to see difference as deviance; and for not being attuned to the needs, problems, and strengths of diverse and oppressed populations (Devore & Schlesinger, 1991). Since that time, the psychosocial approach has been expanded to encompass new perspectives on women's development and roles and the unique experiences, characteristics, strengths, and coping strategies of African Americans, Latinos, Asians, and other people of color and of other oppressed groups such as gay men and lesbians. The approach has attempted to incorporate many of the principles that have been suggested by more sensitive, affirmative, and empowering interventive models that have been developed for work with these populations (Collins, 1986; Falco, 1991; Gonsiorek, 1982; Greenspan, 1983; Gutierrez, 1990; Hirayama & Cetingok, 1988; Jones, 1979; Jordan, 1990; Kaplan & Surrey, 1984; Malyon, 1982; Martin, 1982; Phillips & Gonzalez-Ramos, 1989; J. B. Robinson, 1989; Ryan, 1985).

Special Populations

Changes in society and in the clients who need help have focused greater attention on the application of the psychosocial approach to special populations. For example, crisis theory has extended to almost every conceivable type of client situation, including AIDS (Lopez & Getzel, 1984), rape and other forms of violent assault (Abarbanel & Richman, 1990; Lee & Rosenthal, 1983), child abuse (Brekke, 1990), and domestic violence (Bowker, 1983). Likewise, the psychosocial approach has been used with substance abusers (Chernus, 1985; Straussner, 1993), homeless and chronically mentally ill people (Belcher & Ephross, 1989; Harris & Bergman, 1986), adult survivors of sexual abuse

(Courtois, 1990; Faria & Belohlavek, 1984), and people with AIDS (Dane & Miller, 1992).

RESEARCH BASE

Historically, the psychosocial approach has derived a great deal of its strength from the extensive experiences of social workers engaged in practice, that is, from "practice wisdom." The development and refinement of the model incorporated modifications as a result of interchanges that took place among social workers working with clients. In the late 1960s and throughout the 1970s, considerable attention was given to the disappointing results of studies of casework effectiveness. The fact that these studies were seriously flawed later came to light. The interventive goals, processes, and outcomes studied were not well selected, defined, operationalized, and measured (Perlman, 1972). Some researchers advocated more rigorous research methodology (Bloom, 1983; Blythe & Briar, 1985; Fischer & Hudson, 1983; Levy, 1983; Reid, 1983). In the years since these early studies, research on the outcomes of intervention has yielded more positive results (Rubin, 1985; Thomlison, 1984). Yet the problem of operationally defining psychosocial variables and interventive processes remains, and research on psychosocial intervention is still at an early stage. More attention has been devoted to studying behavioral, cognitive, and task-centered therapies, whose techniques and outcomes are more easily specified and measured than are those of ego-oriented or psychosocial interventions.

Outcome evaluation, although important, is not the only type of research methodology that can be used to study social work practice (Goldstein, 1983). Systematic studies of the effectiveness of intervention with specific target problems and populations are needed, and qualitative and other diverse research strategies that move beyond the current preoccupation with large experimental or single case designs are equally necessary. Furthermore, social workers involved in clinical practice must become involved in the formulation, design, and implementation of such studies either by acquiring practice research expertise themselves or through collaboration with researchers interested in and challenged by the problems inherent in conducting clinical studies.

CURRENT ISSUES

Even critics of the psychosocial approach must acknowledge that social work practitioners find it useful and that, for better or for worse, it has stood the test of time. The results of a survey of the 1982 *NASW Register of Clinical Social Workers*

(Mackey et al., 1987) showed that 51 percent of the respondents "identified ego psychology as being the most instrumental to their approach" (p. 368) and that 93 percent of those who subscribed to ego psychology chose the psychosocial approach as their orientation to practice. Although this survey was conducted more than 10 years ago, the psychosocial approach's popularity does not seem to have waned. Nevertheless, despite its person-in-situation focus, its broad interventive repertoire, its effort to be sensitive to the needs of diverse populations, and its openness to new knowledge, the psychosocial approach still is criticized for being too clinical. There is a tendency to equate the users of the psychosocial approach erroneously with those who have been criticized for abandoning the profession, who have tried to elevate their status by entering private practice and calling themselves "clinical" social workers or psychotherapists (Walz & Groze, 1991). Others argue that such stereotyping is self-serving and a form of scapegoating (Strean, 1993, p. 15).

Although some practitioners do equate clinical work with psychotherapy and do not identify with the broader mission of the social work profession, the definition of clinical social work put forth by an NASW task force reaffirmed clinical social work's person-in-situation perspective, its inclusion of a range of approaches, and the fact that psychotherapy is a part of social work but not the whole (Ewalt, 1980). Thus, clinical social work in itself is consistent with a broad psychosocial focus. The vast majority of clinical social workers continue to be identified with social work as a profession and are employed in social agencies where they use a broad repertoire of interventive modalities and skills, including advocacy and linkage to vital resources. A recent national study of graduate social work students (Abell & McDonnell, 1990) found that "students' flight from traditional social work values into entrepreneurial, private practice orientations have been overestimated" and presented evidence that "students, now as in the past, are predominantly entering social work to advance their professional skills and potential and are highly committed to the concept of involvement with the disadvantaged" (pp. 63–64).

An important issue that affects the future of the psychosocial approach involves the nature of doctoral education in social work. Doctoral programs generally do not provide opportunities for training in advanced psychosocial practice. This situation contributes to the number of clinically oriented social workers who seek training in psychotherapy institutes rather than in schools of social work. Furthermore, those who do seek doctoral education usually find that their needs for practice-oriented education are not met and are discouraged from engaging in practice in favor of research, administration, and social policy and planning. This phenomenon has led to a dearth of social workers with doctorates who are available for faculty positions and who have extensive practice experience and advanced training. Consequently, newer faculty often are not able to teach an in-depth practice approach at the master's level. How this will affect the future of the psychosocial approach is unclear. Unless doctoral programs become more responsive to the educational needs of practitioners, creative solutions such as collaboration between academic faculty and agency practitioners may be necessary to ensure a high level of practice teaching (personal communication with C. Meyer, professor, Columbia University School of Social Work, August 25, 1993).

REFERENCES

Abarbanel, G., & Richman, G. (1990). The rape victim. In H. J. Parad & L. G. Parad (Eds.), *Crisis intervention book 2: The practitioner's sourcebook for brief therapy* (pp. 93–118). Milwaukee: Family Service America.

Abell, N., & McDonnell, J. R. (1990). Preparing for practice: Motivations, expectations, and aspirations of the MSW class of 1990. *Journal of Social Work Education, 26,* 57–64.

Austin, L. (1948). Trends in differential treatment in social casework. *Social Casework, 29,* 203–211.

Belcher, J. R., & Ephross, P. H. (1989). Toward an effective practice model for the homeless mentally ill. *Social Casework, 70,* 421–427.

Bloom, M. (1983). Empirically based clinical research. In A. Rosenblatt & D. Waldfogel (Eds.), *Handbook of clinical social work* (pp. 560–582). San Francisco: Jossey-Bass.

Blythe, B. J., & Briar, S. (1985). Developing empirically based models of practice. *Social Work, 30,* 483–488.

Bowker, L. H. (1983). Marital rape: A distinct syndrome. *Social Casework, 64,* 347–352.

Brekke, J. (1990). Crisis intervention with victims and perpetrators of spouse abuse. In H. J. Parad & L. G. Parad (Eds.), *Crisis intervention book 2: The practitioner's sourcebook for brief therapy* (pp. 161–178). Milwaukee: Family Service America.

Chernus, L. A. (1985). Clinical issues in alcoholism treatment. *Social Casework, 66,* 67–75.

Collins, B. G. (1986). Defining feminist social work. *Social Work, 31,* 214–220.

Courtois, C. (1990). Adult survivors of incest and molestation. In H. J. Parad & L. G. Parad (Eds.), *Crisis intervention book 2: The practitioner's sourcebook for brief therapy* (pp. 139–160). Milwaukee, WI: Family Service America.

Dane, B. O., & Miller, S. O. (1992). *AIDS: Intervening with hidden grievers.* Westport, CT: Auburn House.

Devore, W., & Schlesinger, E. (1991). *Ethnic-sensitive social work practice* (3rd ed.). New York: Macmillan.

Ewalt, P. (1980). *Toward a definition of clinical social work.* Washington, DC: National Association of Social Workers.

Falco, K. L. (1991). *Psychotherapy with lesbian clients: Theory into practice.* New York: Brunner/Mazel.

Faria, G., & Belohlavek, N. (1984). Treating female adult survivors of childhood incest. *Social Casework, 65,* 465–471.

Fischer, J., & Hudson, W. (1983). Measurement of client problems for improved practice. In A. Rosenblatt & D. Waldfogel (Eds.), *Handbook of clinical social work* (pp. 673–693). San Francisco: Jossey-Bass.

Garrett, A. (1958). Modern casework: The contributions of ego psychology. In H. J. Parad (Ed.), *Ego psychology and dynamic casework* (pp. 38–52). New York: Family Service Association of America.

Germain, C. B., & Gitterman, A. (1980). *The life model of social work practice.* New York: Columbia University Press.

Golan, N. (1978). *Treatment in crisis situations.* New York: Free Press.

Goldstein, E. G. (1983). Issues in developing systematic research and theory. In A. Rosenblatt & D. Waldfogel (Eds.), *Handbook of clinical social work* (pp. 5–25). San Francisco: Jossey-Bass.

Goldstein, E. G. (1984). *Ego psychology and social work practice.* New York: Free Press.

Gonsiorek, J. C. (Ed.). (1982). *Homosexuality and psychotherapy: A practitioner's handbook of affirmative models.* New York: Haworth Press.

Greenspan, M. (1983). *A new approach to women in therapy.* New York: McGraw-Hill.

Gutierrez, L. M. (1990). Working with women of color: An empowerment perspective. *Social Work, 35,* 149–154.

Hamilton, G. (1940). *Theory and practice of social casework.* New York: Columbia University Press.

Hamilton, G. (1958). A theory of personality: Freud's contribution to social casework. In H. J. Parad (Ed.), *Ego psychology and dynamic casework* (pp. 11–37). New York: Family Service Association of America.

Hankins, F. (1931). The contributions of sociology to the practice of social work. In *Proceedings of the National Conference of Social Work, 1930* (pp. 528–535). Chicago: University of Chicago Press.

Harris, M., & Bergman, H. C. (1986). Case management with the chronically mentally ill: A clinical perspective. *American Journal of Orthopsychiatry, 56,* 296–302.

Hirayama, H., & Cetingok, M. (1988). Empowerment: A social work approach for Asian immigrants. *Social Casework, 69,* 41–47.

Hollis, F. (1949). The techniques of casework. *Social Casework, 30,* 235–244.

Hollis, F. (1964). *Casework: A psychosocial therapy.* New York: Random House.

Hollis, F. (1972). *Casework: A psychosocial therapy* (2nd ed.). New York: Random House.

Hollis, F., & Woods, M. E. (1981). *Casework: A psychosocial therapy* (3rd ed.). New York: Random House.

Jones, D. L. (1979). African American clients: Clinical practice issues. *Social Work, 24,* 112–118.

Jordan, J. V. (1990). Relational development through empathy: Therapeutic applications. In *Empathy revisited, work in progress* (No. 40, pp. 11–14). Wellesley, MA: Wellesley College, Stone Center.

Kaplan, A., & Surrey, J. L. (1984). The relational self in women: Developmental theory and public policy. In L. Walker (Ed.), *Women and mental health policy* (pp. 79–94). Beverly Hills, CA: Sage Publications.

Lee, J. A. B., & Rosenthal, S. A. (1983). Working with victims of violent assault. *Social Casework, 64,* 593–601.

Levy, R. L. (1983). Overview of single-case experiments. In A. Rosenblatt & D. Waldfogel (Eds.), *Handbook of clinical social work* (pp. 583–602). San Francisco: Jossey-Bass.

Lopez, D., & Getzel, G. S. (1984). Helping gay AIDS patients in crisis. *Social Casework, 65,* 387–394.

Mackey, R. A., Urek, M. B., & Charkoudian, S. (1987). The relationship of theory to clinical practice. *Clinical Social Work Journal, 15,* 368–383.

Malyon, A. K. (1982). Psychotherapeutic implications of internalized homophobia in gay men. In J. Gonsiorek (Ed.), *Homosexuality and psychotherapy: A practitioner's handbook of affirmative models* (pp. 59–70). New York: Haworth Press.

Martin, A. (1982). Some issues in the treatment of gay and lesbian patients. *Psychotherapy: Theory, Research, and Practice, 19,* 341–348.

Meyer, C. H. (1993). *Assessment in social work.* New York: Columbia University Press.

Mullen, E. J., Dumpson, J. R., & Associates. (1972). *Evaluation of social intervention.* San Francisco: Jossey-Bass.

Northen, H. (1988). *Social work with groups.* New York: Columbia University Press.

Perlman, H. H. (1957). *Social casework: A problem-solving process.* Chicago: University of Chicago Press.

Perlman, H. H. (1972). Once more with feeling. In E. J. Mullen, J. R. Dumpson, & Associates (Eds.), *Evaluation of social intervention* (pp. 191–209). San Francisco: Jossey-Bass.

Phillips, L. J., & Gonzalez-Ramos, G. (1989). Clinical social work practice with minority families. In S. M. Ehrenkranz, E. G. Goldstein, L. Goodman, & J. Seinfeld (Eds.), *Clinical social work with maltreated children and their families: An introduction to practice* (pp. 128–148). New York: New York University Press.

Reid, W. J. (1983). Developing intervention methods through experimental designs. In A. Rosenblatt & D. Waldfogel (Eds.), *Handbook of clinical social work* (pp. 650–672). San Francisco: Jossey-Bass.

Reid, W., & Epstein, L. (1972). *Task-centered casework.* New York: Columbia University Press.

Richmond, M. L. (1917). *Social diagnosis.* New York: Russell Sage Foundation.

Robinson, J. B. (1989). Clinical treatment of black families: Issues and strategies. *Social Work, 34,* 323–329.

Robinson, V. P. (1930). *A changing psychology in social casework.* Chapel Hill: University of North Carolina Press.

Rubin, A. (1985). Practice effectiveness: More grounds for optimism. *Social Work, 30,* 469–476.

Ryan, A. S. (1985). Cultural factors in casework with Chinese Americans. *Social Casework: The Journal of Contemporary Social Work, 66,* 333–340.

Straussner, S.L.A. (1993). Assessment and treatment of clients with alcohol and other drug abuse problems: An overview. In S.L.A. Straussner (Ed.), *Clinical work with substance-abusing clients* (pp. 3–32). New York: Guilford Press.

Strean, H. S. (1993). Clinical social work: An evaluative review. *Journal of Analytic Social Work, 1,* 5–23.

Taft, J. (1937). The relation of function to process in social casework. *Journal of Social Process, 1,* 1–18.

Thomlison, R. J. (1984). Something works: Evidence from practice effectiveness studies. *Social Work, 29,* 51–56.

Walz, T., & Groze, V. (1991). The mission of social work revisited: An agenda for the 1990s. *Social Work, 36,* 500–504.

Wasserman, S. L. (1974). Ego psychology. In F. J. Turner (Ed.), *Social work treatment* (pp. 42–83). New York: Free Press.

Woods, M. E., & Hollis, F. (1989). *Casework: A psychosocial therapy* (4th ed.). New York: McGraw-Hill.

Yelaja, S. A. (1974). *Authority and social work: Concept and use.* Toronto: University of Toronto Press.

FURTHER READING

Goldstein, E. G. (in press). *Ego psychology and social work practice* (2nd ed.). New York: Free Press.

Rosenblatt, A., & Waldfogel, D. (Eds.). (1983). *Handbook of clinical social work.* San Francisco: Jossey-Bass.

Strean, H. S. (1978). *Clinical social work: Theory and practice.* New York: Free Press.

Turner, F. J. (1976). *Differential diagnosis and treatment in social work.* New York: Free Press.

Turner, F. J. (1978). *Psychosocial therapy.* New York: Free Press.

Eda G. Goldstein, DSW, CSW, ACSW, is professor, New York University, Shirley M. Ehrenkranz School of Social Work, 1 Washington Square North, New York, NY 10003.

For further information see

Assessment; Case Management; Clinical Social Work; Cognitive and Social Theory; Direct Practice Overview; Ecological Perspective; Ethnic-Sensitive Practice; Interviewing; Person-in-Environment; Psychosocial Rehabilitation; Social Work Practice: Theoretical Base; Social Work Profession Overview.

Key Words

clinical practice	psychosocial
person-in-environment	assessment

Psychosocial Rehabilitation
William Patrick Sullivan

Three decades have passed since President Kennedy signed the Mental Retardation Facilities and Community Mental Health Centers Construction Act, ushering in his bold new approach to the treatment of mental illness. In the 30 years that have followed, debate has raged on the desirability of community-based treatment for those who face the most severe forms of mental illness. The experiences of offering community-based services, both positive and negative, have helped shape treatment modalities that were nonexistent in Kennedy's time. These new modalities, built on empirical analysis and guided by distinct value and philosophical orientations, fall under the rubric of psychosocial rehabilitation (PSR).

Cnaan, Blankertz, and Saunders (1992) noted that "for all its merit, PSR lacks a clear and consistent practical definition because its development as a practice modality over the past 30 years has been uncoordinated and eclectic" (pp. 95–96). In general, PSR interventions focus on consumers' living, working, and leisure environments and aim to enhance their opportunities and affirm their right to participate fully in community processes.

EVOLUTION OF COMMUNITY-BASED SERVICES

Little in the world of mental health theory and practice engenders as much debate as deinstitutionalization. Deinstitutionalization often is portrayed as a universal and coordinated public policy decision to depopulate state psychiatric institutions in favor of community-based care. In reality, a variety of forces have reduced the census of state psychiatric hospitals or eliminated them altogether. These forces, which include pharmacological breakthroughs, legal decisions, cultural values, and fiscal concerns, are guided by divergent values and act in an asynchronous fashion.

Most important, the downscaling of state psychiatric facilities has not eliminated institutionalization. Kramer (1975) offered the term "transinstitutionalization" as a better representation of reality. In fact, residential treatment programs, nursing homes, jails, and acute psychiatric wards in general hospitals are frequently used institutional options for people with severe and persistent mental illness. Families also have taken added responsibility for the care of mentally ill loved ones; this caregiver role, although accepted, is often stressful.

Much has been learned since the early days of the community mental health movement. The hope that primary prevention efforts, together with early detection and treatment of mental disorders, would halt the onset of more severe forms of mental illness has been shattered. Indeed, severe mental illness is the result of a complex mix of biophysical, psychological, and social forces that requires a multifocused helping strategy.

Severe and persistent mental illness can be described by the three-D's schema: diagnosis, duration, and disability (Farkas, Anthony, & Cohen, 1989). Current research in the area of schizophrenia, for example, illustrates the biophysical roots of mental illness while highlighting the need for psychosocial interventions. Advanced tools to study the brain, including magnetic resonance imaging and positron emission tomography, allow a glimpse of the brain's structure and information-processing capabilities. In addition, important differences are being discovered between people who face schizophrenia and those who do not, and recent studies of twins support the critical role of genetic transmission. Yet schizophrenia remains mysterious and incurable. This does not mean that people with schizophrenia do not improve or recover; in fact, many long-term outcome studies of schizophrenia suggest reason for hope (Harding, Brooks, Ashikaga, Strauss, & Breier, 1987a, 1987b; McGlashan, 1988).

Psychosocial rehabilitation aims to improve the quality of life of those afflicted with mental illness and ensure that people develop their maximum potential in spite of the illness. For many, however, the negative impact of their disorder will persist for life, thus requiring that a range of treatment options remains available on demand. The availability of community-based services also helps reduce the burden on families who have historically provided care and appropriately shifts some responsibility back to the treatment system.

The disabilities associated with severe and persistent mental illness are important areas of focus for psychosocial rehabilitation efforts and for social work. Often referred to as "negative symptoms," these disabilities impede functioning in the areas of self-care, independent living, vocational activity, and the satisfying use of leisure time. The social difficulties faced by consumers hinder their opportunity to participate fully in community life.

By the mid-1970s it was clear that traditional community-based mental health services were not adequately addressing the needs of the most severely ill. In response, the National Institute of Mental Health introduced the Community Support Program, a pilot project designed to provide comprehensive services (Turner & TenHoor, 1978). Psychosocial rehabilitation services that emphasize community-living skills, increased housing and employment options, and leisure time activities are a major component of this ongoing effort. Case management, now a popular service modality in a variety of fields, is also identified as a core element.

The Community Support Program concept reaffirmed the commitment to serve the most severely ill in community-based settings and expanded the focus of helping beyond pathology and disease. Whether through education, work opportunities, or the creation of housing options, the focus of community-based services now includes an appreciation of a person's abilities and competencies.

Since the late 1970s the field of psychosocial rehabilitation has been transformed. New programming options are available, traditional services such as case management have become more technical and specialized, and the underlying values and philosophies that guide services are being codified.

CURRENT DIRECTIONS IN PSYCHOSOCIAL REHABILITATION

A clear and consistent definition of PSR has yet to be established. However, Cnaan, Blankertz, Messinger, and Gardner (1988, 1989) and Cnaan et al. (1992) identified a set of principles that undergird the psychosocial approach in hopes of strengthening the theoretical base of this field of practice (Table 1). One step in the process of theoretical development has been to determine how these principles fit with any existing helping orientations or theories (Cnaan et al., 1989). Indeed, these principles are similar to the underlying values and theoretical perspective of social work. Therefore, it is not surprising that Cnaan and associates (1989) determined that the ecosystems perspective is most consistent with psychosocial principles. In the following sections, a host of treatment models and specialized programs are described. Two foundation interventions, case management and social skills training, are described first.

Case Management

The term "case management" has multiple meanings, and within mental health services alone many models abound. Early models focused pri-

marily on the brokerage role of the case manager. Here it was recognized that the wide range of services historically provided by state psychiatric hospitals (shelter, food, recreation, medical services, and so on) were also necessary for community living. Direct involvement in the acquisition of these resources was not a standard activity for most mental health professionals. By orchestrating the needed mix of services, case managers would become the glue in a fragmented system of care.

On the other end of the continuum, clinical models have suggested that case management activities be appended to the services provided by a primary therapist. Where clinical or therapeutic services are offered, supportive, problem-solving approaches are preferred over insight-oriented or psychodynamic strategies (Goering & Stylianos, 1988).

Case management defined exclusively as brokerage or therapeutic endeavors is too narrowly focused to qualify as psychosocial intervention. Social workers and rehabilitation specialists have broadened and synthesized these two endeavors. Rapp and Chamberlain (1985) developed a resource-acquisition model of case management that focuses on the strengths of clients and the environment. This approach is different from standard brokerage models in that it encourages the use of natural community resources as opposed to specialized and segregated services. Strengths-based models also are collaborative because they focus on consumer-directed goals. Case managers use aggressive outreach—long recognized as a critical dimension of community-based services—to advocate for consumers, provide support and information to family members, and provide situation-specific skills training. The resource-acquisition model continues to be refined, and the theoretical underpinnings of strengths-based approaches continue to be explored (Rapp, 1992; Sullivan, 1992; Weick, Rapp, Sullivan, & Kisthardt, 1989).

Libassi (1988) linked clinical practice with traditional functions of case management. Drawing from the person-in-environment approach, Libassi (1988) recognized that the case management function is not to treat or cure, but rather to support or release "the client's adaptive potential, so he or she can cope with the disability as well as improve his or her social functioning in the environment" (pp. 90–91). Rose's (1992) advocacy/empowerment model of case management also portends the possibilities for consumers' personal growth. This potential is enhanced when consumers are seen not as objects to be acted upon,

TABLE 1
Principles of Psychosocial Rehabilitation

1. All people have underutilized human capacity that should be developed.
2. All people can be equipped with skills (social, vocational, educational, interpersonal, and others).
3. People have the right and responsibility for self-determination.
4. Services should be provided in as normalized an environment as possible.
5. Assessment of needs and care should be differential (that is, based on the unique needs, abilities, deficiencies, and environments of each client).
6. Maximum commitment is required from staff members.
7. Care is provided in an intimate environment without professional authoritative shields and barriers.
8. Early intervention is preferable.
9. Environmental agencies and forces are recruited to assist in the provision of services.
10. Attempts are made to modify the environment in terms of attitudes, rights, services, and behavior (social change).
11. All clients are welcome for as long as they want to be served (with the exception of specific short-term, high-demand programs).
12. Work and vocational rehabilitation are central to the rehabilitation process.
13. There is an emphasis on a social rather than a medical model of care.
14. Emphasis is on the client's strengths rather than on pathologies.
15. Emphasis is on the here and now rather than on problems from the past.

SOURCE: Cnaan, R., Blankertz, L., & Saunders, M. (1992). Perceptions of consumers, practitioners, and experts regarding psychosocial rehabilitation principles. *Psychosocial Rehabilitation Journal, 16*(1), 97.

but as subjects who know and act. By working directly with consumers on their identified goals and taking the role of advocate seriously, case managers affirm competence. Rose noted that "people who actively participate in transforming their environments, at whatever level their capacity allows, change themselves in the process" (p. 273).

Social Skills Training
Many consumers with severe and persistent mental illness are unable to perform the roles and behaviors necessary to function adequately in the community. In instances where an illness has destroyed certain competencies, the effort to rebuild capacities is rightfully called rehabilitation. In cases where the illness has made it impossible for the individual to develop important skills and abilities, the interventions are habilitative in nature. Social skills training, drawing from social learning theory, is designed "to improve the individual's capacity to master the challenges and problems inherent in daily life" (Anthony & Liberman, 1986, p. 544). A recent extension of this service, direct skills training, draws more directly from education models (Nemac, McNamara, & Walsh, 1992).

In social skills training, individual competencies and deficits, as well as environmental resources and impediments to goal accomplish-

ment, are thoroughly assessed. An individual skill plan, often combining didactic and experiential learning exercises, is then developed. Given the impact of severe mental illness on a person's ability to process and retain information, skills must be broken down into steps that match the individual's needs and abilities. Ultimately it is hoped that consumers can master necessary skills and use them in applied settings.

Social skills training has been a stated function of many services involving day treatment, psychoeducational groups, and partial hospitalization. Skills training generally has been provided through a variety of groups or classes offered sequentially. There are difficulties with this method, a common one being that consumers have had difficulty transferring the skills learned in-house to community settings (Mueser, Liberman, & Glynn, 1990). Group modalities may also fail to address the specific competencies needed to accomplish individual goals and satisfy environmental demands.

Several important principles are basic to effective social skills training. First, skills training packages must be individually tailored to address the consumer's stated goals and needs. Second, whenever possible, training should occur where the skill is to be used. Third, consumer involvement is essential in all phases of the process, from assessment to evaluation. Skills training can be a component of outreach case management services or provided in the consumer's work, living, and leisure settings.

From Housing Programs to Homes

There is nothing so basic to human existence as adequate shelter. Concern about the prevalence of mental illness among the homeless population, as well as the burden on families who support adult relatives with severe mental illness in their homes, has focused attention on housing. From the earliest days of the community mental health center movement to the creation of the Community Support Program, the concept of a continuum of care has been trumpeted. In the area of housing it has been suggested that a range of services must be in place to match consumers' needs. Therefore, options ranging from state hospitals and nursing homes to supervised apartments and independent living opportunities have been seen as fundamental to community-based services. In theory, consumers could move back and forth from most-restrictive to least-restrictive environments as circumstances dictated. In practice, however, many community residential programs are no more than decentralized institutional services.

In recent years there has been a shift away from a continuum of housing options to a focus on the right of consumers to have a home (Posey, 1990). In continuum models the residence is a place of treatment, not a personal space of one's own. Ridgway and Zipple (1990) offered the supported housing model as an important paradigm shift in psychosocial rehabilitation. In the supported housing paradigm, "the creation of a home is the preeminent goal in serving the client, and helping people choose, acquire, and maintain a home in the community is a bona fide role and responsibility of the mental health system" (p. 17).

Basic to the supported housing approach is the affirmation of consumers' right to choose a living environment and the availability of flexible supports to help them succeed. Ridgway and Zipple (1990) contrasted supported housing with the linear continuum model. Differences include

- the notion of homeowner or tenant versus client or program resident
- shift in locus of control from staff to client
- social integration rather than homogeneous grouping by disability
- in vivo learning and support in permanent settings rather than transitional preparatory settings
- individualized flexible service and supports versus standardized levels of service. (pp. 18–24)

Clearly, the supported housing approach accents strengths rather than deficits and focuses on supporting the consumers' stated goals, in keeping with the principles of psychosocial rehabilitation. Furthermore, the emphasis is on normalcy and on helping the consumer become a full-fledged member of the community. The case management and social skills training described earlier can be tailored—*when desired by the consumer*—to support an individual's goal of independence.

Vocational Programming

The importance of vocational activity to the rehabilitation of people with mental illness has been recognized for more than 200 years. Unfortunately, the rate of competitive employment among people with severe and persistent mental illness is generally reported to be between 15 percent and 25 percent (Anthony & Blanch, 1987). Waters (1992) provided a vivid portrait of the potential restorative power of work:

> Work puts us in a unique relationship with other human beings so that the opportunity to form meaningful relationships is readily available to us. Work also allows us to feel a common bond with the larger community and gives us a better picture of what our lives will be in the future. All people benefit from work ... but in many ways, given the isolation and confusion that so often accompanies mental illness, people with psychiatric disorders may benefit most of all. (p. 41)

For much of the history of mental health treatment, work opportunities centered on consumers providing rudimentary services within the walls of an institution or toiling in a sheltered workshop. Noting her own experiences, Peckoff (1992) flatly stated, "I was sick and tired of making elephants out of clay" (p. 4). In a fashion similar to the evolution of housing programs, innovative employment programs are geared toward real work in real jobs.

Clubhouse programs. Fountain House, a psychosocial clubhouse founded in 1948, has stressed the importance of the "work-ordered day" (Propst, 1992). People are considered members, not clients, and all participate to ensure the club's smooth operation. In addition, transitional employment slots are available for everyone who desires them. These employment opportunities generally last for six months, and staff are available as job coaches and are prepared to fill in for absent members. Transitional employment placements offer members the opportunity to gain valuable work experience, earn real wages, and gain a better sense of the kind of employment they might pursue.

Supported employment. A more recent innovation, the supported employment (SE) model, is built on the partnership between mental health providers and vocational rehabilitation services. The SE approach is based on the assumption "that *all* people—regardless of the severity of their disability—can do meaningful, productive work in normal settings, if that is what they choose to do, and if they are given the necessary supports" (Anthony & Blanch, 1987, p. 7). Furthermore, failure is seen not as a function of the disability but as the result of insufficient supports or inappropriate job selection. The use of normalized settings is critical because SE attempts to move consumers beyond an endless cycle of prevocational training. As Isbister and Donaldson (1987) noted, "too often 'prevocational' has translated into 'no vocational' rehabilitation" (p. 46).

The supported employment process can be described simply as a choose, get, and keep model (Anthony & Blanch, 1987). A variety of strategies in the field of mental retardation are applicable here. *Job crews,* a common feature of many mental health centers, are specialized crews trained to perform specified tasks (for example, landscaping) that are deployed to job sites with a mental health professional as a supervisor. The *enclave* model is similar to job crews except that consumers consistently work in one setting. The *job coach* model is more individualized, with a trainer–coworker present to support the consumer for as long as it takes to learn the job.

The supported employment method eschews notions that one can predict with great certainty who will succeed or fail in naturalized work settings and that persons must be symptom-free before they can work. Again, case management and social skills training can directly support employment efforts, particularly if they are focused on the consumer's unique goals.

Leisure and Recreation Programs

Each of the program initiatives described so far embodies a basic principle of normalization. Everyone's life is enriched by friends and family and the satisfying use of leisure time. Unfortunately, many people who face severe mental illness lead very lonely lives (Sullivan & Poertner, 1989). With each illness episode, family members increasingly become the sole providers of emotional and material support. Furthermore, the lack of adequate social contacts, and thus the absence of daily structure, is not conducive to good mental health. This reality has focused professional attention on the development and maintenance of social support networks and specialized leisure and recreation programs.

An example of innovative programming in this area is the Reintegration Through Recreation (RTR) program developed at the University of North Carolina Center for Recreation and Disability Studies. This program, building from basic psychosocial principles, is dedicated to providing the necessary skills and supports consumers need to enjoy satisfying leisure and recreation activities in their chosen environment. Consistent with the principles that undergird pioneering programs in the areas of housing and vocational functioning, this model emphasizes consumer choice and involvement, the use of natural settings, individualized programming, and advocacy. The RTR process is conceptualized as following three distinct stages. The first phase involves basic assessment, data collection, and goal setting. The second phase is a period of skill acquisition and rehearsal using a cognitive–behavioral approach. The third phase attends to application and follow-through. Although these efforts tend to be discounted as secondary to other mental health services, the feeling of success that results from mastering a new skill or overcoming one's fear of social involvement can have any number of radiating positive effects on consumers' lives.

FUTURE DIRECTIONS

The trend in psychosocial programming over the past 30 years has been to emphasize community-based services in normalized settings. In addition, helping relationships have evolved from expert–client systems to an approach that affirms a collaborative posture. In the 1980s, families demanded greater participation in the care of their mentally ill loved ones and challenged the stigmatizing attitudes of professionals who had historically blamed them for the illness. In response, family support and education groups have flourished, and family members are now active participants on advisory councils and governing boards at all levels of the mental health enterprise. Professionals have been sensitized to the needs of families and recognize that families are requesting primarily support and information from them, not treatment.

The rest of the 1990s will see the continued development of consumer-driven programming and initiatives. Currently, consumer-run support groups, case management programs, and member-operated clubhouses dot the horizon. The consumer voice now joins those of the professional and family member, and the result is likely to be a healthy but sometimes painful dialogue. Issues such as hospitalization options, forced medication compliance, and commitment law reforms are all likely sources of debate.

Cnaan and associates (1988) suggested that "people are motivated by a need for mastery and competence in areas which allow them to feel more independent and self-confident" (p. 62). To satisfy this demand for mastery, people with severe and persistent mental illness will need to acquire basic skills, gain access to needed resources, and receive necessary supports. Even with the new technologies used in psychosocial rehabilitation, the base of the helping process is still the professional relationship.

Since the early 1960s, our nation's willingness to acknowledge and respect the diversity of the populace has followed an uneven course. The present challenge is to move beyond the mere recognition of our heterogeneity and view this diversity as a source of strength rather than an obstacle to progress. Central to this process are efforts to create a society that is more inclusive of previously disenfranchised groups.

Psychosocial rehabilitation requires a holistic approach to helping. Intrapersonal, interpersonal, and environmental systems are implicated in the problem and the solution. Professional social workers are versed in ecological models, systems theory, and competence–strengths models of helping. It is from this vantage point that Wintersteen (1986) noted that "the conceptual framework and nearly a century of experience in helping clients with the complexities of social interaction give social work a track record that places it in an optimal position to claim the leadership in this developing field" (p. 332).

REFERENCES

Anthony, W., & Blanch, A. (1987). Supported employment for persons who are psychiatrically disabled: An historical and conceptual perspective. *Psychosocial Rehabilitation Journal, 11*, 5–23.

Anthony, W., & Liberman, R. (1986). The practice of psychiatric rehabilitation: Historical, conceptual, and research base. *Schizophrenia Bulletin, 12*, 542–559.

Cnaan, R., Blankertz, L., Messinger, K., & Gardner, J. (1988). Psychosocial rehabilitation: Toward a definition. *Psychosocial Rehabilitation Journal, 11*, 61–77.

Cnaan, R., Blankertz, L., Messinger, K., & Gardner, J. (1989). Psychosocial rehabilitation: Towards a theoretical base. *Psychosocial Rehabilitation Journal, 13*, 33–55.

Cnaan, R., Blankertz, L., & Saunders, M. (1992). Perceptions of consumers, practitioners, and experts regarding psychosocial rehabilitation principles. *Psychosocial Rehabilitation Journal, 16*, 95–119.

Farkas, M., Anthony, W., & Cohen, M. (1989). Psychiatric rehabilitation: The approach and its programs. In M. Farkas & W. Anthony (Eds.), *Psychiatric rehabilitation programs* (pp. 1–27). Baltimore: Johns Hopkins University Press.

Goering, P., & Stylianos, S. (1988). Exploring the relationship between the schizophrenic client and the rehabilitation specialist. *American Journal of Orthopsychiatry, 58*, 271–280.

Harding, C., Brooks, G., Ashikaga, T., Strauss, J., & Breier, A. (1987a). The Vermont longitudinal study of persons with severe mental illness: I. Methodology, study sample, and overall status 32 years later. *American Journal of Psychiatry, 144*, 718–726.

Harding, C., Brooks, G., Ashikaga, T., Strauss, J., & Breier, A. (1987b). The Vermont longitudinal study of persons with severe mental illness: II. Long-term outcome of subjects who retrospectively met DSM-III criteria for schizophrenia. *American Journal of Psychiatry, 144*, 727–735.

Isbister, F., & Donaldson, G. (1987). Supported employment for individuals who are mentally ill. *Psychosocial Rehabilitation Journal, 11*, 45–54.

Kramer, M. (1975). *Psychiatric services and the changing institutional scene.* Bethesda, MD: National Institute of Mental Health.

Libassi, M. F., (1988). The chronically mentally ill: A practice approach. *Social Casework, 69*, 88–96.

McGlashan, T. (1988). A selective review of recent North American long-term followup studies of schizophrenia. *Schizophrenia Bulletin, 14*, 515–542.

Mental Retardation Facilities and Community Mental Health Centers Construction Act of 1963. P.L. 88-164, 77 Stat. 282.

Mueser, K., Liberman, R., & Glynn, S. (1990). Psychosocial interventions in schizophrenia. In A. Kales, C. N. Stefanis, & J. A. Talbott (Eds.), *Recent advances in schizophrenia* (pp. 213–235). New York: Springer-Verlag.

Nemac, P., McNamara, S., & Walsh, D. (1992). Direct skills teaching. *Psychosocial Rehabilitation Journal, 16*, 13–25.

Peckoff, J. (1992). Patienthood to personhood. *Psychosocial Rehabilitation Journal, 16*, 5–7.

Posey, T. (1990). A home, not housing *Psychosocial Rehabilitation Journal, 13*, 3–4.

Propst, R. (1992). Standards for clubhouse programs: Why and how they were developed. *Psychosocial Rehabilitation Journal, 16*, 25–30.

Rapp, C. (1992). The strengths perspective of case management with persons suffering from severe mental illness. In D. Saleebey (Ed.), *The strengths perspective in social work practice* (pp. 45–58). New York: Longman.

Rapp, C., & Chamberlain, R. (1985). Case management services to the chronically mentally ill. *Social Work, 30*, 417–422.

Ridgway, P., & Zipple, A. (1990). The paradigm shift in residential services: From the linear continuum to supported housing approaches. *Psychosocial Rehabilitation Journal, 13*, 11–31.

Rose, S. M. (1992). Case management: An advocacy/empowerment design. In S. M. Rose (Ed.), *Case management and social work practice* (pp. 271–297). New York: Longman.

Sullivan, W. P. (1992). Reconsidering the environment as a helping resource. In D. Saleebey (Ed.), *The strengths perspective in social work practice* (pp. 148–157). New York: Longman.

Sullivan, W. P., & Poertner, J. (1989). Social support and life stress: Mental health consumer's perspective. *Community Mental Health Journal, 25,* 21–32.

Turner, J., & TenHoor, W. (1978). The NIMH community support program: Pilot approach to a needed social reform. *Schizophrenia Bulletin, 4,* 319–344.

Waters, B. (1992). The work unit: The heart of the clubhouse. *Psychosocial Rehabilitation Journal, 16,* 41–48.

Weick, A., Rapp, C., Sullivan, W. P., & Kisthardt, W. (1989). A strengths perspective for social work practice. *Social Work, 34,* 350–354.

Wintersteen, R. (1986). Rehabilitating the chronically mentally ill: Social work's claim to leadership. *Social Work, 31,* 332–337.

FURTHER READING

Farkas, M., & Anthony, W. (Eds.). (1989). *Psychiatric rehabilitation programs.* Baltimore, MD: Johns Hopkins University Press.

Foley, H., & Sharfstein, S. (1983). *Madness and government.* Washington, DC: American Psychiatric Press.

Gerhart, U. (1990). *Caring for the chronic mentally ill.* Itasca, IL: F. E. Peacock.

Hatfield, A., & Lefley, H. (1987). *Families of the mentally ill.* New York: Guilford Press.

Kales, A., Stefanis, C. N., & Talbott, J. A. (Eds.). (1990). *Recent advances in schizophrenia.* New York: Springer-Verlag.

Mechanic, D. (1989). *Mental health and social policy* (3rd ed.). Englewood Cliffs, NJ: Prentice Hall.

Rose, S. (Ed.). (1992). *Case management and social work practice.* New York: Longman.

Saleebey, D. (1992) (Ed.). *The strengths perspective in social work practice.* New York: Longman.

William Patrick Sullivan, PhD, is associate professor, Indiana University, School of Social Work, Indianapolis, IN 46202, and director, Indiana Division of Mental Health.

For further information see

Adult Foster Care; Case Management; Cognition and Social Cognitive Theory; Cognitive Treatment; Community; Deinstitutionalization; Developmental Disabilities: Direct Practice; Direct Practice Overview; Family Caregiving; Goal Setting and Intervention Planning; Health Services Systems Policy; Human Development; Information and Referral Services; Mental Health Overview; Natural Helping Networks; Patient Rights; Person-in-Environment; Psychosocial Approach; Public Health Services; Self-Help Groups; Settlements and Neighborhood Centers; Social Skills Training.

Key Words	
community-based services	psychosocial rehabilitation
direct practice	social skills training
mental illness	

Psychotherapy

See Treatment Approaches *(Reader's Guide)*

Psychotropic Medications
Mary Frances Libassi

In recent years a number of factors have pushed social work practitioners and educators toward a greater recognition and awareness of the role of psychotropic medications in social work practice. First, a growing body of research documents the connections and interrelations between biological and psychological factors in the etiology of many serious mental disorders (Hogarty, Anderson, Reiss, Kornblith, Greenwald, Ulrich, & Carter, 1991; Johnson, 1988; Kaplan & Sadock, 1991; Schwartz & Schwartz, 1993; Taylor, 1987). Indeed, the plethora of research on the functioning of the brain has prompted Congress to designate the 1990s as the "Decade of the Brain" (Libassi, 1990).

Even with the mounting evidence concerning the biological component of mental illness, social work journals and the popular press continue to reflect the ongoing intense debates concerning the etiology of major mental disorders (Cohen, 1989; Gerhart, 1990; Stone, 1992; Taylor, 1987, 1989).

Some social workers focus their practice on psychosocial, interpersonal, and family dynamics. Saleebey (1985) proposed a number of reasons for this preference, including perceived lack of expertise in biological approaches, prevalence of theoretical models conceived before biological research was well developed, and a belief that incorporating biological knowledge represents a "final surrender" to the medical model (pp. 578-579). Other social workers believe that the use of interventions that flow from a biopsychosocial perspective does not diminish the importance of psychosocial interventions but rather adds another important and necessary mechanism for intervention with the whole person (Libassi, 1990).

Second, many people with serious mental disorders already receive medication (Cohen, 1988; Johnson et al., 1990). Practitioners reported in two recent surveys that the great majority of their clients had some form of psychopharmacological intervention as part of their treatment (Libassi, 1990; Johnson and Libassi, 1993). Social work students also want to know more about psychotropic medications because they encounter clients in their field placements who are receiving somatic therapy. Yet, some social workers report feeling inadequate in interdisciplinary settings because of their lack of knowledge about medications (Libassi, 1990).

Finally, surveys conducted by the National Institute of Mental Health (NIMH) indicate that social workers provide a major share of mental health treatment in the United States. In the 1980s clinical social workers outnumbered psychiatrists by 22,000, clinical psychologists by 27,000, and marriage and family counselors by 27,000 (Goleman, 1985). Social workers are taking the lead in providing mental health services to a range of individuals in a variety of settings and services.

ROLES AND RESPONSIBILITIES OF SOCIAL WORKERS

Assessment, Screening, and Referral
The role of social workers in relation to the use of psychotropic medications in treatment varies according to practice setting. For example, for those practitioners working alone in private practice, school settings, outreach programs, shelters, nursing homes, and rural areas, screening and referral are major responsibilities. Rauch, Sarno, and Simpson (1991) wrote of the tremendous responsibility of practitioners in family and children's services to assess for affective disorders and to make appropriate referrals for psychiatric evaluations. Many of these illnesses are unreported and result in needless suffering for individuals and families. Similarly, school social workers can identify children with symptoms of attention deficit disorder and refer them for psychiatric evaluation. In addition, federal regulations regarding care for elderly people in nursing homes require adequate assessment and referral for individuals who have an emotional disorder (Butler, Finkel, Lewis, Sherman, & Sunderland, 1992). Social workers in institutional settings are in key positions to screen elderly people for treatment of mental disorders.

It is important to emphasize that services provided through managed care settings sometimes rely on the use of psychotropic medications to aid in the treatment of behavioral health problems within the *community*. Professionals, including social workers, increasingly need to sharpen their skills for assessment, screening, and referral in this emerging health care environment.

Education
The role of educator is a critical one for social workers. In recent years the growth in consumer movements among client groups and families of clients has brought a greater demand for knowledge about mental illness and, in particular, the use of medication in treatment. Such organizations as the National Alliance for the Mentally Ill (NAMI) and the Association for Children with Learning Disabilities are educating their members about the biological basis of mental disorders and the use of medication in treatment. These organizations also are demanding changes in the curricula of mental health programs so that future professionals will understand mental illness and the necessary treatment components (Johnson et al., 1990).

Social workers can play a key role in educating clients and families about mental illness and the part that medications play in treatment. This educational intervention is positively associated with medication compliance and with clients' successful integration back into the family and the community (Bentley, Rosenson, & Zito, 1990). Several well-known psychoeducation programs include content on medication (see Anderson, Reiss, & Hogarty, 1986; Falloon, Boyd, & McGill, 1984).

Playing the role of educator requires an understanding of culture, race, and ethnicity. For example, the *espiritismo* model of the Puerto Rican culture sees mental illness as an imbalance between the *causas* (molesting spirits) and the *protecciones* (protecting spirits) (Gil, 1992). The Chinese attribute disease to external cosmological and internal emotional factors (Der McLeod, 1993). To "begin where the client is" means understanding these diverse cultural beliefs, meeting with folk healers when appropriate, and mediating differences in belief systems with the Western medical paradigm (Gil, 1992). Most psychoeducation programs do not reflect these alternative explanatory models when addressing mental illness and the use of psychotropic medication in treatment, but NAMI has begun to develop training materials for social workers and other mental health professionals that reflect sensitivity to cultural differences.

As educator, the social worker also empowers clients and their families to contribute to treatment planning by describing their experiences with medication. The use of medication must be highly individualized, and the client must be involved in monitoring its usefulness and side effects (Diamond, 1983). Respecting the views of clients and encouraging self-determining behaviors are core values (Bentley, 1993). Knowledge about psychotropic medications will enable social workers to educate clients in this critical area of treatment.

Case Monitoring and Advocacy
Social workers are often in a strategic position to monitor the effectiveness of medications as well as any undesirable side effects and to advocate on behalf of clients when dealing with physicians and interdisciplinary teams. For example, social workers working with elderly people often are the only members of a team who understand the total life situation of an elderly person. Through home visits and conversations with family caregivers, they understand the complexities of the environment in which the elderly person lives, his or her nutritional needs, cognitive and functional problems that may interfere with medication compliance, and the capacities of family caregivers to manage the care plan.

Cultural sensitivity is extremely important. For example, Der McLeod (1993) suggested two very important features to keep in mind when conducting home visits with Asian elders. First, elderly clients may not only be taking American medications, but also nontraditional medications such as herbal teas that could interact adversely with American medicine. Second, many elderly Asians do not read or write English, and therefore instructions for medication use must be carefully arranged and planned with the client.

The social worker becomes for the interdisciplinary team the window onto the real world in which the client lives. Information from this larger perspective can be used to influence and advocate for appropriate and individualized treatment for each client (Lewis, 1993).

As advocates, social workers must have sufficient information not only regarding mental disorders and psychotropic medications, but also about the laws regarding usage (Gerhart & Brooks, 1983). Bentley (1993) noted that for some patients side effects are the major factor in medication noncompliance. She suggested that supporting a client's right to refuse medication when the benefits do not outweigh severe side effects makes sense legally, empirically, and ethically in light of

the profession's commitment to client self-determination. In addition, consumers are pushing to become their own advocates and are requesting that social workers join them in advocacy efforts on their behalf. This joint action is the essence of client empowerment.

Interdisciplinary Collaboration
Practice that includes psychotropic medications requires social workers to establish working relationships with other disciplines. Social workers do not seek to prescribe medications but rather to establish collaborative relationships with physicians that allow for easy communication and referral so that social work clients can have access to psychotropic medications when appropriate. Social workers' knowledge of the psychosocial, environmental, legal, and cultural context of the client and of the opinions and wishes of the client and the family is invaluable. Social workers are essential members of the interdisciplinary teams and should practice as assertive collaborators and colleagues (Libassi, 1990).

PSYCHOTROPIC MEDICATIONS: CLASSES AND EFFECTS

Classes
Social workers need to know about a number of classes of psychotropic medications, including antidepressant, antipsychotic, antianxiety, mood stabilizer, and anticonvulsant medications and stimulants (particularly used with children). Within each class there are subclasses that have different mechanisms of action within the brain and different side effects. It is useful for social workers to be aware of the chemical composition and trade names of each class and subclass of drug, because psychiatrists and interdisciplinary team members use these names interchangeably. Social workers also need to know the conditions and presenting symptoms that indicate the use of a particular class of drugs in treatment. In most cases the indications are linked to a diagnostic category as described in the *Diagnostic and Statistical Manual of Mental Disorders, Fourth Edition* (American Psychiatric Association, 1994).

Mechanisms of Action
Social workers should have some knowledge about how drugs affect the chemical processes within the body. This knowledge need not be detailed or comprehensive; rather, the goal is to understand the use of drugs as a way to correct or stabilize faulty processes in brain functioning.

In many instances, clients and family members are far ahead of professionals in understanding these processes. Newsletters of the National Alliance for the Mentally Ill, for example, regularly recommend educational materials for their members that provide a comprehensive understanding of the pathophysiology of mental disorders. When clients and family members understand the disorder in brain processes, the stigma of mental illness is reduced and participation in required treatment enhanced.

Therapeutic Effects

Social workers must understand how drugs affect the symptoms and manifestations of biologically based illness and how the use of medication can help the client function better; for example, how it can make the voices stop, allow them to tune out stimulation and focus attention on the task at hand, or positively affect the neurovegetative signs of depression. This information is especially useful in motivating clients and their families to comply with the pharmacological aspects of treatment regimen.

Not all clients who have serious emotional and behavioral disorders or who are mentally ill respond to medication. For these clients, social workers must work diligently for increased use of other treatments such as psychosocial rehabilitation, skills training, and case management (Bentley, 1993).

Unwanted Side Effects

Psychotropic medications carry the risk of unpleasant or harmful side effects, both short and long term. *Tardive dyskinesia* (persistent movement disorder of the head, trunk, and neck that usually also involves an involuntary movement of the mouth and tongue), for example, is a severe and potentially irreversible effect of antipsychotic medication. Clients and family members should be made aware of potential side effects of any medication and encouraged to monitor their experience for input into treatment planning. Usually, different psychotropic medications can be tried and their dosage adjusted. The social worker and the client together can work to "personalize" the medication regimen to produce the most therapeutic effect with the fewest side effects. Information regarding side effects also is essential to social workers in their role as client advocate on the interdisciplinary team.

It is sometimes difficult to determine whether certain symptoms and behaviors are the result of medication, the illness itself, the use of over-the-counter medication, or diet. With elderly people, the physiological changes that occur as part of the aging process also affect responses to medication (Butler, Lewis, & Sunderland, 1991).

Interactions and Dosage Strategies

Social workers need some knowledge about the interactions of psychotropic medications with other substances. Substance abuse, polypharmacy, drug interactions with foods, and the use of caffeine or herbal remedies all complicate treatment. Social workers should understand indications of problems that call for a referral to a professional with expertise in this area. They should also have some knowledge of typical dosage levels, as well as what constitutes lethal doses.

Practitioners must understand research related to low-dosage strategies, drug holidays, phase of treatment, and so forth (Hogarty et al., 1988). Practice approaches that use low-dosage strategies, for example, often emphasize the use of psychosocial interventions in combination with medication therapy. These approaches provide rich opportunities for social workers to use the psychosocial and environmental interventions that are the hallmark of their profession.

Social workers also need to know how long pharmacological treatment is expected to continue. For example, antipsychotic medications and some antidepressants are taken for a long period of time, perhaps a lifetime, because of the nature of the illness and the action of the medication on the brain. But antianxiety medications can be very addictive, and their duration usually is limited.

LIMITATIONS OF MEDICATION

Treatment with psychotropic medications cannot and must not be separated from other interventions. A growing body of research indicates that medication alone does not prevent relapse and that there is, in fact, a substantial relapse rate when medication is the sole treatment. Research has indicated the necessity of combining medication with sociotherapy and family psychoeducation (see Anderson, Reiss, & Hogarty, 1986; Johnson, 1988; Klerman, 1990; Klerman, DiMascio, Weissman, Prusoff, & Paykel, 1974). By understanding the limitations of psychotropic medications in treatment, social workers can firmly integrate this somatic therapy into psychosocial and environmental interventions.

LEGAL AND ETHICAL ISSUES

In recent years the legal rights of patients regarding their medical care have expanded dramatically. Legal rights affect many issues related to psychopharmacological treatment, including mandatory and invasive assessment and treatment, the right to challenge and refuse medication, determination of competency, and determination of the need for involuntary commitment (Appelbaum, 1988;

Brooks, 1987). Bentley (1993) outlined many of the legal and ethical issues that confront social workers in considering the right of psychiatric patients to refuse medications. She emphasized the importance of proper procedures to ensure that patients have true informed consent. She also explored certain practice dilemmas that confront social workers in balancing the needs and interests of patients with what is considered to be in the best interest of the patient by other professionals and by caring family members (Rosenson, 1993; Rosenson & Kasten, 1991). Bentley concluded that "social workers must stand with the right of patients to refuse medication—even though they as individuals or the profession as a whole may experience some negative consequences for their advocacy" (p. 104).

Evidence drawn from empirical studies, judicial hearings, and the press indicates that psychotropic medications are sometimes used in a substandard manner, especially with client groups such as the elderly, children, adolescents, and adults with prolonged mental illness. There are even examples of the use of medications to punish patients (Bentley, 1993). Social workers must be at the forefront of advocacy regarding these issues. Already advocacy is credited with helping reduce dosages, polypharmacy, and inappropriate administration of drugs and with increasing patient participation in treatment (Brooks, 1987).

CONCLUSION

Social workers have vital roles to play in relation to the use of psychotropic medication in treatment. The roles of advocate and educator flow directly from social work values and practice principles, ensuring that treatment planning starts where the client is and encourages client participation and involvement every step of the way. Activities such as screening, assessment, and care monitoring ensure that clients receive proper and effective treatment, including psychotropic medications when necessary, to promote competent functioning.

REFERENCES

American Psychiatric Association. (1994). *Diagnostic and statistical manual of mental disorders* (4th ed.). Washington, DC: Author.

Anderson, C. M., Reiss, D. J., & Hogarty, G. E. (1986). *Schizophrenia and the family: A practitioner's guide to psychoeducation and management.* New York: Guilford.

Appelbaum, P. (1988). The right to refuse treatment with antipsychotic medications: Retrospect and prospect. *American Journal of Psychiatry, 145,* 413–419.

Bentley, K. (1993). The right of psychiatric patients to refuse medication: Where should social workers stand? *Social Work, 38,* 101–106.

Bentley, K., Rosenson, M., & Zito, J. (1990). Promoting medication compliance: Strategies for working with families of the mentally ill. *Social Work, 35,* 274–277.

Brooks, A. (1987). The right to refuse medications: Law and policy. *Rutgers Law Review, 39,* 339–376.

Butler, R. N., Finkel, S. I., Lewis, M. I., Sherman, F. I., & Sunderland, T. (1992). Aging and mental health: Prevention of caregiver overload, abuse and neglect. *Geriatrics, 47,* 53–58.

Butler, R. N., Lewis, M. I., & Sunderland, T. (1991). *Aging and mental health—Positive psychosocial and biomedical approaches* (4th ed.). New York: Merrill.

Cohen, D. (1988). Social work and psychotropic drug treatment. *Social Service Review, 62,* 576–599.

Cohen, D. (1989). Biological basis of schizophrenia: The evidence reconsidered. *Social Work, 34,* 255–257.

Der McLeod, D. (1993, April). [Comments during the satellite broadcast, "Psychopharmacology: Social work practice with elders"]. Alexandria, VA: Council on Social Work Education.

Diamond R. J. (1983). Enhancing medication use in schizophrenic patients. *Journal of Clinical Psychiatry, 44,*(6), 7–14.

Falloon, I., Boyd, J., & McGill, C. (1984). *Family care of schizophrenia: A problem-solving approach to the treatment of mental illness.* New York: Guilford.

Gerhart, U. C. (1990). *Caring for the chronic mentally ill.* Itasca, IL: F. E. Peacock.

Gerhart, U., & Brooks, A. (1983). The social work practitioner and antipsychotic medicine. *Social Work, 28,* 454–460.

Gil, R. (1992, April). [Comments during the satellite broadcast, "Psychopharmacology: Social work practice with adults"]. Alexandria, VA: Council on Social Work Education.

Goleman, D. (1985, April 30). Social workers vault into leading roles in psychotherapy. *New York Times,* pp. 17, 20.

Hogarty, G. E., Anderson, C. M., Reiss, D. J., Kornblith, S. J., Greenwald, D. P., Ulrich, R. F., & Carter, M. (1991). Family psychoeducation, social skills training, and maintenance chemotherapy in the aftercare treatment of schizophrenia: Two-year effects of a controlled study on relapse and adjustment. *Archives of General Psychiatry, 48,* 340–347.

Hogarty, G. E., McEvoy, J. P., Munetz, M., DiBarry, A. L., Bartone, P., Cather, R., Cooley, S. J., Ulrich, R. F., Carter, M., & Madonia, M. J. (1988). Dose of fluphenazine decanoate, familial expressed emotion and outcome in schizophrenia. *Archives of General Psychiatry, 45,* 797–805.

Johnson, H.C. (1988). Drugs, dialogue, or diet: Diagnosing and treating the hyperactive child. *Social Work, 33,* 349–355.

Johnson, H. C., Atkins, S. P., Battle, S. F., Hernandez-Arata, L., Hesselbrock, M., Libassi, M. F., & Parish, M. (1990 Spring/Summer). Strengthening the "bio" in the biopsychosocial paradigm. *Journal of Social Work Education,* pp. 109–123.

Johnson, H. C., & Libassi, M. F. (1993). *Is psychopharmacology a subject for social work?* Unpublished manuscript.

Kaplan, H., & Sadock, B. J. (1991). *Synopsis of psychiatry: Behavioral sciences clinical psychiatry* (6th ed.). Baltimore: Williams and Wilkins.

Klerman, G. L. (1990). NIMH collaborative research on treatment of depression. *Archives of General Psychiatry, 47,* 686–688.

Klerman, G. L., DiMascio, A., Weissman, M., Prusoff, B., Paykel, E. S. (1974). Treatment of depression by drugs and psychotherapy. *American Journal of Psychiatry, 131,* 186–191.

Lewis, M. (1993, April). [Comments during the satellite broadcast, "Psychopharmacology: Social work practice with elders"]. Alexandria, VA: Council on Social Work Education.

Libassi, M. F. (1990). *Psychopharmacology in social work education.* Alexandria, VA: Council on Social Work Education.

Rauch, J. F., Sarno, C., & Simpson, S. (1991). Screening for affective disorders. *Families in Society, 72,* 602–609.

Rosenson, M. (1993) Social work and the right of psychiatric patients to refuse medication: A family advocate's response. *Social Work, 38,* 107–112.

Rosenson, M., & Kasten, A. M. (1991). Another view of autonomy: Arranging for consent in advance. *Schizophrenia Bulletin, 17,* 1–7.

Saleebey, D. (1985). In clinical social work practice, is the body politic? *Social Service Review, 59,* 578–592.

Schwartz, A., & Schwartz, R. (1993). *Depression: Theories and treatments.* Irvington, NY: Columbia University Press.

Stone, E. (1992, December 6). Off the couch. *New York Times Magazine*, pp. 50, 52, 53, 78, 79.

Taylor, E. H. (1987). The biological basis of schizophrenia. *Social Work, 32,* 115–121.

Taylor, E. (1989). Schizophrenia: Fire in the brain. *Social Work, 34,* 258–261.

FURTHER READING

Beitman, B. D., & Klerman, G. L. (1991). *Integrating pharmacotherapy and psychotherapy.* Washington, DC: American Psychiatric Press.

Gitlin, M. J. (1991). *The psychotherapist's guide to psychopharmacology.* New York: Free Press.

Lawson, G. W., & Cooperrider, C. A. (1988). *Clinical psychopharmacology: A practical reference for nonmedical psychotherapists.* Rockville, MD: Aspen Publishers.

Lin, K. M., Poland, R. E., & Nakasaki, G. (1993). *Psychopharmacology and psychobiology of ethnicity.* Washington, DC: American Psychiatric Press.

Mary Frances Libassi, MSW, MRE, CISW, is associate professor, University of Connecticut, School of Social Work, 1798 Asylum Avenue, West Hartford, CT 06117.

For further information see

Aging: Direct Practice; Assessment; Bioethical Issues; Clinical Social Work; Deinstitutionalization; Developmental Disabilities: Direct Practice; Diagnostic and Statistical Manual of Mental Disorders; Direct Practice Overview; Ethics and Values; Family Caregiving; Health Care: Direct Practice; Hospice; Hospital Social Work; Interdisciplinary and Interorganizational Collaboration; Long-Term Care; Managed Care; Mental Health Overview; Patient Rights; Primary Health Care; Primary Prevention Overview; Public Health Services; Social Work Practice: Theoretical Base; Suicide.

Key Words

client rights	psychotropic
combined treatments	medication
mental illness	somatic treatment

READER'S GUIDE

Public Assistance

The following entries contain information on this general topic:

Public Health Services
Robert M. Moroney

Public health is a field of practice that is primarily concerned with the promotion of health and the prevention of illness and other disabling conditions. Although this broad definition covers public health activities over the centuries, specific interventions and programs have shifted considerably over time and between societies. These shifts have been influenced in great part not only by advances in scientific knowledge and technology but also by changes in people's mores, beliefs, attitudes and expectations, standard of living, and political economy (Vickers, 1958).

These shifts involve more than interventions and programs. The areas included under the umbrella of health promotion and illness prevention have expanded. In practice, the focus of public health has grown from a 19th-century concern with improving the sanitary conditions and physical environment in which people lived and emerging efforts to eradicate a number of infectious diseases such as cholera and typhoid fever, to a 20th-century concern with a growing number of communicable diseases (tuberculosis, acquired immune deficiency syndrome [AIDS]), chronic diseases (cancer, Alzheimer's disease), and certain social conditions (teenage pregnancy, hunger, and malnourishment).

Although public health is concerned with health promotion and illness prevention, it differs somewhat from other efforts with similar conditions. For example, although preventive medicine is also concerned with preventing diseases or the consequences of certain diseases and promoting good health behavior, its focus is the individual patient, whereas public health defines its purpose as promoting and maintaining the health of society through "collective or social actions" (Last, 1987, p. 6). The intention may be the same—in many instances both draw from the same discipline knowledge—but the methods and strategies differ considerably.

Public health, then, has evolved since the 1700s to the point that currently it is "concerned with four broad areas: (1) lifestyle and behavior, (2) the environment, (3) human biology and (4) the organization of health programs and systems" (Pickett & Hanlon, 1990, p. 8).

FIELD OF PUBLIC HEALTH

Given this broad charge, public health should be viewed as a field of practice that draws together professionals from a number of disciplines. It is not a profession in the traditional sense of the word, as this would mean that all public health workers would have the same education and experiences and would be grounded in the same theo-retical and methodological knowledge bases. It is more appropriately a field of practice in that it attracts people from different professions who are interested in solving the same problems or achieving the same goals. These professions include, among others, medicine, nursing, social work, engineering, education, public and business administration, and law.

Furthermore, as a field of practice, public health's knowledge base is as broad and comprehensive as the sum of the many professionals involved and the disciplines they draw from. In general terms these disciplines include the sanitary sciences, the biomedical sciences, and the social and behavioral sciences.

PREVENTION

A distinguishing characteristic of the public health approach is its historical emphasis on prevention. Although earlier efforts were targeted to infectious and communicable diseases, public health has expanded in a number of different directions:

> The progressive nature of public health makes any restricted definitions ... difficult. More than that—there is a real danger in attempting to narrow down a moving or growing thing. To tie public health to the concepts that answered our needs 50 years ago, or even a decade ago, can only hamstring our contribution to society in the future. (Mountin, 1952, p. 223)

In 1979 the surgeon general identified 15 major areas as appropriate for public health prevention efforts, "from accident prevention and the promotion of proper nutrition to the prevention of substance abuse and the promotion of healthful lifestyles" (Bloom, 1987, p. 306).

Prevention has a number of important dimensions and is usually discussed in terms of three levels or as a continuum. The first level, *primary prevention,* involves the prevention of the occurrence of the disease or condition. Examples include fluoridation of drinking water (to prevent cavities) and immunization against poliomyelitis and measles.

Secondary prevention efforts are usually concerned with early case findings and intervention before the condition reaches a more severe state or involves serious disability. Pap smears or colonoscopy examinations are examples of secondary prevention, as early detection of cellular changes or polyps can result in prevention of cancer.

Tertiary prevention involves treating the illness or disability once it has occurred so that the consequences of the condition can be minimized. Rehabilitation efforts for someone who has experienced a stroke would fall into this category.

Although most of the early efforts in prevention involved physical illness, these concepts have since been applied to a number of other areas. For example, the Mental Retardation Facilities and Community Mental Health Centers Construction Act of 1963 and Amendments, with its grounding in the 1961 *Action for Mental Health Report,* prepared by the Joint Commission on Mental Illness and Health, incorporated all three levels of the public health prevention model. In an attempt to move from a heavy (and to a great extent, almost sole) reliance on state hospitals (tertiary prevention), these acts provided financial incentives to develop community-based outpatient, short-term inpatient, and crisis services (secondary prevention) and educational and consultative services (primary prevention).

EPIDEMIOLOGICAL APPROACH

A second distinguishing characteristic of public health is its strong reliance on the epidemiological approach as a primary method in determining the etiology of diseases. *Epidemiology* is the study of health-related states and events in defined populations and the application of this study to the control of health problems" (Last, 1983).

The study of the distribution of these states and events is referred to as *descriptive epidemiology* and usually involves describing the characteristics of those with the condition (for example, demographics) as well as documenting trends or patterns over time. The study of the determinants of these states or events involves a search for the cause of the disease, whether this cause is a single cause, as in the case of many infectious diseases, or consists of multiple determinants, as found in the chronic diseases.

The concepts of host, agent, and environment are critical to the epidemiological approach. In early public health efforts, *host* usually referred to people—that is, those who were susceptible to a particular disease; the *agent* was the virus or the bacillus; and the *environment* consisted of the conditions that supported the agent (for example, a mosquito-infested swamp or an unhealthy water supply). The epidemiological approach hypothesizes the existence of causal chains and assumes that if a link in that chain can be altered or broken, the condition will no longer exist.

Two classic examples of the epidemiological approach are the response to a cholera outbreak in London in the 19th century and the antimalarial campaigns of the 20th century. In the former example, the investigator, Dr. John Snow, in the midst of a severe epidemic, was able to determine that those who got their water from the Broad Street Water pump had much higher mortality rates than those who obtained their water from other pumps. He then had the handle of the contaminated pump removed, which ended the epidemic. Although he was unable to determine the cause of the cholera, later scientists did isolate the cause as a microscopic organism living in the water. The epidemic abated after the water company stopped drawing water from the polluted source. In the second example, researchers found that malaria existed only when three essentials were present: a human to contract the disease, a mosquito to carry the malaria parasite, and a swamp to breed the mosquitoes. Assuming a causal chain, efforts were carried out to eliminate the breeding grounds (MacMahon, Pugh, & Ipsen, 1960).

Although the model has been less successful in dealing with multicausal problems or problems of a noninfectious nature (for example, social problems), it has demonstrated great value as a framework for thinking about problems. Cloward, Ohlin, and Piven (1959) incorporated this approach in their proposed strategy to deal with juvenile delinquency. They hypothesized that delinquent behavior resulted from "blocked opportunity"; these "blocks" or barriers included a nonresponsive educational system, an inaccessible health care system, discrimination, and substandard housing (the agents) endemic to the environment in which they lived (poverty). Their intervention, which became the overall strategy for the Ford Foundation Gray Areas Projects in 1960 and the President's Committee on Juvenile Delinquency a year later, argued for a strategy that would simultaneously attack the multiple "agents."

EMERGENCE OF MODERN PUBLIC HEALTH

Although a number of important discoveries occurred in the 18th century (for example, the control of smallpox and scurvy), modern public health emerged in the 19th century. The Age of Reason not only brought about advances in the natural sciences, it also produced significant advances in the biomedical sciences. Louis Pasteur and Robert Koch, two of the founders of bacteriology, developed vaccines for a number of infectious diseases such as anthrax, cholera, and rabies. Later in the century, others were successful in preventing such diseases as diphtheria and typhoid.

Social Reform

The 19th century also can be characterized as a period of social reform. Edwin Chadwick (cited in Flinn, 1965), concerned with substandard housing and extremely dangerous sanitary conditions, a by-product of the industrial revolution, published his famous *Report on an Enquiry into the Sanitary Conditions of the Labouring Population of Great Britain* in 1842. This report was instrumental in the passage of the Public Health Act of 1848, which created a General Board of Health and local boards of health responsible for monitoring sanitary conditions in the country. In 1875 legislation divided England into urban and rural sanitary districts. Chadwick and others such as Charles Dickens and John Stuart Mills continued these efforts and were able to demonstrate the relationship between poverty, illness, and social problems, thus bringing about reforms in working conditions, health care, and housing.

In the United States parallel efforts were carried out by individuals such as Lemuel Shattuck, who published *A Report of the Sanitary Commission of Massachusetts* in 1850 (cited in Pickett & Hanlon, 1990), detailing in broad scope the public health problems and needs of the commonwealth and the country. Although this report was initially ignored, it became a major blueprint for public health efforts in the 20th century. Massachusetts did follow one of Shattuck's recommendations, establishing the first state board of health in 1869.

Public Health and Social Welfare

By the turn of the century, local health departments had been established in most cities, and renewed efforts were being made to improve the conditions in which people lived and to control the incidence of infectious diseases. In this period, now known as the Progressive Era, reformers such as Jane Addams (Hull House), Lillian Wald (Henry House Settlement), and Edith Wood began to argue that numerous communitywide problems inevitably accompanied industrialization and urbanization. Addams, for example, used many of the evolving public health concepts and methods to improve the living and working conditions of families.

Wald, concerned with problems of maternal and infant health, was instrumental in the estab-lishment of the Children's Bureau in 1912, an agency of the federal government charged by Congress to monitor the well-being of mothers and children and to stimulate policies and programs to maintain and improve their life chances. Early efforts focused on the development of prenatal care and nutritional services, disease prevention, school health programs, and occupational health. In 1935, with the passage of the Social Security Act, the responsibilities of the Children's Bureau were increased, and the ties between public health and social welfare (recognized in the 19th century and acted on through the efforts of those working in the settlement houses) were more firmly established.

RATIONALES FOR GOVERNMENT INTERVENTION

Earlier I discussed the purpose of public health measures in terms of promoting and maintaining the health of society through collective or social actions. These collective actions have traditionally been assumed by government rather than the private sector. A major justification for government intervention in this area is the externality argument. People are forced to do something or to stop what they are doing "in the public interest" or for the good of the larger society. Government is justified in intervening even if individual members of society believe that such intervention is not in their best interest. Historically, services such as education and public health immunizations are justified on externality grounds. In both instances, individuals and society benefit from individual consumption of the service. In the first case, society as a whole achieves a high level of literacy; in the second, target diseases are eradicated, thereby improving the general health and productivity of the population:

> If the community, or at any rate, a sizable part of it has an interest in a particular utility accruing to an individual, then it would clearly be unreasonable to allow the creation of the more general utility to depend solely on that individual; he might not value the activity highly enough to make the sacrifice of paying the required fee or charge, or else ignorance may cause him or poverty force him to do without the service. Herein lies the chief justification of the modern demands for free or very cheap processes of law, education, certain public health measures, etc. (Wicksell, 1958, p. 15)

These coercive powers have come to cover a range of concerns from air and water pollution to the effects of cigarette smoking on nonsmokers, mandatory seat belt use, and more-restrictive gun control legislation. All of these have one thing in common: They are justified on the basis that they serve the public interest—that is, that society as a whole benefits when individuals are required to do something (positive externalities) or stop doing something (negative externalities).

FEDERAL EFFORTS

Until the Great Depression of the 1930s, the role of the federal government in the health and social services was virtually nonexistent. This phenomenon was deeply rooted in the historical development of this country. In the colonial period, before the advent of state and national governments, public services were the responsibility of local governments. During the 19th century, a number of these services were either assumed by or shared with state governments:

> A large part of what we do through government is done through state and local units. They are the ones to whom we usually turn when we seek to maintain or upgrade our educational efforts, improve our physical and mental health, redevelop our decaying urban areas, build better and safer highways, overcome air and water pollution and equip our suburbs with water systems, sewers, roads, parks, schools and the like. (Heller, 1967, pp. 121–122)

Major interventions at the federal level (in addition to the Children's Bureau) included the provision of medical care for merchant seamen and people with leprosy, control of infectious diseases from abroad, and control of venereal disease.

First Federal Public Health Programs

Because merchant seamen did not meet local residency requirements and therefore were not eligible for medical care, the federal government, through the Marine Hospital Service Act, in 1798 established a network of hospitals from Boston to New Orleans to serve this population group. In 1878, with the passage of the Quarantine Act, the Marine Hospital Service was given the added responsibility of "investigating the causes of epidemic diseases, especially yellow fever and cholera, and the best methods of preventing their introduction and spread" (Pickett & Hanlon, 1990, p. 34). Over the next decade the Marine Hospital Service assumed responsibility for domestic quarantine activities and inspection of all immigrants. In 1902 the Marine Hospital Service became the U.S. Public Health Service.

In 1917 the federal government established the National Leprosarium at Carville, Louisiana, with the justification that the disease was such a low-prevalence condition requiring costly and highly specialized medical services that local and state governments were inefficient providers. Finally, in 1918 the Venereal Disease Control Act was passed, establishing a Division of Venereal Diseases. During World War I, public awareness about this disease had grown, and Congress was pressured to take steps to deal with the problem.

Impact of the Great Depression

Federal involvement increased significantly after World War I, with the most momentous involvement occurring in the 1930s. During the Great Depression a dozen major grant-in-aid programs were enacted. Although the states retained a strong role in the administration of these programs, the federal government established priorities and minimum standards the states were required to meet if they were to receive federal funding. A major public health initiative during this period was the passage of Title IV-B and Title V of the Social Security Act of 1935. The former led to the creation of state-administered child welfare departments and the latter to the establishment of maternal and child health departments in each state.

Since then, the role of the federal government has continued to grow. New partnerships have been forged with the 50 state and 1,800 local health departments to expand traditional public health activities and to extend efforts in newly emerging areas of concern. Although the initial partnership involved grants-in-aid (the federal government determined what kinds of programs could be developed and supported with the funds), in the 1980s the federal government significantly redefined the nature of its relationship with the states in a number of areas, replacing categorical funding with more-flexible block grants in most areas of health and welfare (for example, mental health and social services in 1980 and health services in 1982).

National Institutes of Health

One extremely significant development was the creation in 1948 of the National Institutes of Health (NIH), whose charge was to carry U.S. research and support others to do research into the causes and treatment of various diseases. NIH initially was formed by consolidating a number of existing institutes, such as the National Cancer Institute, established by Congress in 1937. Over time, NIH grew into approximately a dozen specialized institutes concerned with such conditions as heart disease, cancer, arthritis, neurological and communicable disorders, aging, allergies, and infectious diseases. One of the institutes—the National Institute of Mental Health—assumed a service as well as a research responsibility and was later placed in a newly created umbrella agency, the Alcohol, Drug Abuse and Mental Health Administration, to better reflect its function. (It later moved back to NIH.) A parallel organization, the Centers for Disease Control and Prevention in Atlanta, was established during World War II and serves as a center for epidemiological research and training.

Expanded Program

On a programmatic level, public health services were greatly expanded (Leukefeld, 1987; U.S Public Health Service, 1984). In 1938 the first of many disease control programs was initiated with the enactment of the Venereal Disease Control Act. The 1960s, moreover, saw the federal government becoming involved in a number of areas, including the development of out-of-hospital services for chronically ill and aged persons (Community Health Services and Facilities Act of 1961); comprehensive immunization programs (Vaccination Assistance Act of 1962); mental health and mental retardation (Mental Retardation Facilities and Community Mental Health Centers Construction Act of 1963); antismoking efforts (U.S. Department of Health, Education, and Welfare, 1964); and heart disease, cancer, and stroke in 1965.

This shift from a major concern with the environment to a more balanced concern that included noninfectious diseases was in recognition of the fact that premature death was increasingly related to lifestyle problems (for example, smoking, poor nutrition, lack of exercise) rather than environmental factors (for example, unsanitary water and substandard housing). Infectious diseases were still a significant problem, but the diseases of the latter part of the 20th century saw a shift in the major causes of high morbidity and mortality from those operating at the turn of the century (for example, pneumonia, influenza, tuberculosis, diphtheria, and whooping cough) to the new infectious diseases (for example, AIDS and various sexually transmitted diseases).

EMERGING PUBLIC HEALTH AGENDA

The public health agenda for the remainder of this decade and for the foreseeable future will continue to include most, if not all, of the concerns of the previous 100 years (that is, infectious and chronic diseases) and will continue to emphasize the need for improvements in the physical environment (for example, improving the quality of our air and water), changes in individual lifestyle (cessation of smoking, exercise, and proper nutrition), and the value of prevention (for example, vaccination and early case finding).

Social Health Concerns

Public health will undoubtedly expand its agenda to include what have come to be referred to as social health concerns. Although many of the new diseases are as much attributable to social factors as they are to medical factors, they still fall under the historical definition of public health and in many ways reflect similar activities carried out by the 19th-century activists who believed it was impossible to separate social conditions from the treatment of illness and disease.

Without question a major public health concern into the early 21st century will be teenage pregnancy. Currently most teenagers (80 percent of boys and 70 percent of girls) have experienced sexual intercourse, and 11 percent of teenage girls become pregnant each year (Kettner & Moroney, 1990). Many of these teenagers do not receive adequate prenatal care, engage in a number of high-risk behaviors (for example, smoking, poor diets, substance abuse, and poverty), and are more likely to have low-birthweight infants. If these teenage mothers keep their children, they are statistically more likely to drop out of school, find marginal employment in the secondary labor market, go on welfare, and abuse their children (Kettner & Moroney).

A second emphasis for public health is mental illness. The incidence of alienation and severe depression is rising and is reflected in higher incidences of suicide and other behavioral health problems. Growing numbers of people, faced with external stressors, are experiencing problems in living. The number of individuals who are abusing drugs and alcohol or are severely mentally ill is also on the rise, and the issue of deinstitutionalization has become a major public concern.

A third emerging public health concern is violence. Although the problem of child abuse has been a public health concern since the 19th century (for example, child employment conditions, especially in workhouses, mines, and factories), spousal violence has only relatively recently been recognized as a public health problem. Homicide, gang violence, and the need for gun control have also been included as part of this agenda.

Two other concerns that are a part of the current and evolving public health agenda are the problems of hunger and malnourishment, especially among children and elderly persons, and the problems associated with an aging population (for example, Alzheimer's disease).

Finally, the greatest public health challenge is that of AIDS, which was first recognized in 1981 and had reached epidemic proportions by 1990. Technically the disease is an infection with the human immunodeficiency virus (HIV), and AIDS is the final manifestation of the disease. Although the disease was initially thought to be primarily associated with intravenous drug users and homosexual and bisexual men, it currently is found in growing numbers of women and infants of infected women. Prevention efforts are somewhat limited in terms of secondary and tertiary prevention, and most public health efforts are concerned with the prevention of new cases.

ROLE OF SOCIAL WORK IN PUBLIC HEALTH

Social workers have been involved in public health activities since the mid-19th century ushered in the modern era of public health practice. Although these individuals could not be called "professional" social workers (there was no profession at the time), their approach to dealing with the problems of their day is clearly evidenced in current professional practice. To better understand the problems they were attempting to resolve, whether these problems were related to substandard housing, employment, industrial accidents, poverty, or illness, they took a comprehensive view, searched for the interrelationship of causes, and recommended comprehensive strategies as solutions. Currently this framework is referred to as the attempt to understand the "person in environment," and the methodological approach is based on "systems theory."

Commitment to Prevention

Social workers associated with the settlement houses were not only involved in public health activities, they functioned as members of multidisciplinary teams composed of physicians, nurses, and engineers. They recognized that most of the problems they were attempting to solve—poor sanitation, substandard housing, high morbidity and mortality rates, and poverty—were multifaceted and interdependent. Simple categorical solutions were ineffective.

Since its creation in 1912, social work has been a major force in the efforts of the Children's Bureau. The bureau's first five directors (from 1912 to 1948) were social workers, and the first two (Julia Lathrop and Grace Abbott) had been residents of Hull House. Moreover, with the passage of the Social Security Act of 1935, social workers assumed important roles in child welfare programs. Both programs were philosophically grounded in the concepts of prevention (strengthening families and health promotion/disease prevention), and both recruited professionally trained social workers for positions of leadership.

Expanded Roles

Just as the field of public health expanded during the last half of the 20th century, so, too, did the roles of the social workers who worked in that field (Watkins, 1993). Initially the emphasis was on maternal and child health, with social workers functioning at federal and state levels. Their roles were primarily in program development and consultation. Over time, the federal government, in partnership with state governments, encouraged local agencies to provide prevention and treatment services to at-risk mothers and their children; programs such as the Maternal and Infant Care Programs of the early 1960s were followed by special programs dealing with family planning, neonatal care, and dental health. Social workers at this level provided both clinical services and consultation to other members of the multidisciplinary teams.

With the passage of the amendments to Title V in 1981, the existing federal categorical grants in this area were consolidated, and block grants were distributed to the states to develop maternal and child health programs. A portion of these funds was used to support training efforts at schools of social work, and by 1989, Title V monies supported 65 faculty positions and 88 graduate students.

Similar trends were taking place in other areas of public health. As program initiatives (not only in health departments but also in hospitals, long-term-care facilities, and numerous community organizations) expanded in the areas of chronic diseases (especially heart disease, cancer, and stroke), infectious diseases (sexually transmitted diseases and AIDS), and behavioral diseases (for example, drug and alcohol abuse and violence), social work involvement increased. Furthermore, these social workers provided direct services to patients and their families, consultation to other members of the team, planning and evaluation, administration, and research. Finally, the common thread that binds these social workers together is their acceptance of and commitment to the philosophy of prevention and to multidisciplinary teamwork underpinning public health in general.

REFERENCES

Bloom, M. (1987). Prevention. In A. Minahan (Ed.-in-Chief), *Encyclopedia of social work* (18th ed., Vol. 2, pp. 303–315). Silver Spring, MD: National Association of Social Workers.

Cloward, R., Ohlin, L., & Piven, F. (1959). *Delinquency and opportunity.* New York: Free Press.

Community Health Services and Facilities Act of 1961. P.L. 87-395, 75 Stat. 824.

Flinn, M. W. (1965). *Readings in economic and social history.* Edinburgh, Scotland: University of Edinburgh Press.

Heller, W. (1967). *New dimensions of political economy.* New York: W. W. Norton.

Kettner P., & Moroney, R. (1990). *Designing and managing programs: An effectiveness based approach.* Newbury Park, CA: Sage Publications.

Last, J. (1983). *A dictionary of epidemiology.* New York: Oxford University Press.

Last, J. (1987). *Public health and human ecology.* East Norwalk, CT: Appleton & Lange.

Leukefeld, L. (1987). Public health services. In A. Minahan (Ed.-in-Chief), *Encyclopedia of social work* (18th ed., Vol. 2, pp. 409–417). Silver Spring, MD: National Association of Social Workers.

MacMahon, B., Pugh, T., & Ipsen, J. (1960). *Epidemiological methods.* Boston: Little, Brown.

Mental Retardation Facilities and Community Mental Health Centers Construction Act of 1963. P.L. 88-164, 77 Stat. 282.

Mountin, J. (1952). The health department's dilemma. *Public Health Reports, 67,* 223.

Pickett, G., & Hanlon, J. (1990). *Public health: Administration and practice* (9th ed.). St. Louis: Times Mirror/Mosby.

Social Security Act of 1935. Ch. 531, 49 Stat. 620.

U.S. Department of Health, Education, and Welfare. (1964). *Smoking and health: The report of the advisory committee to the Surgeon General of the Public Health Service.* Washington, DC: U.S. Government Printing Office.

U.S. Public Health Service. (1984). *Fact sheets.* Rockville, MD: Department of Health and Human Services, Office of Public Affairs.

Vaccination Assistance Act of 1962. P.L. 87-868, 76 Stat. 1155.

Vickers, G. (1958). What sets the goals of public health? *Lancet, 1,* 599–604.

Watkins, E. (1993). The history of maternal and child health: The role of public health social workers. In *Social problems with health consequences: Program design, implementation and evaluation.* Proceedings of the Biregional Conference for Public Health Social Workers in Regions IV and V. Columbia, SC: College of Social Work.

Wicksell, K. (1958). *Selected papers on economic theory.* London: Macmillan.

Robert M. Moroney, PhD, is professor, Arizona State University, School of Social Work, Tempe, AZ 85287.

For further information see

Child Welfare Overview; Community; Disasters and Disaster Aid; Environmental Health: Race and Socioeconomic Factors; Federal Social Legislation from 1961 to 1994; Health Planning; Health Services Systems Policy; HIV/AIDS Overview; Homelessness; Housing; Hunger, Nutrition, and Food Programs; Managed Care; Maternal and Child Health; Organizations: Context for Social Services Delivery; Poverty; Primary Prevention Overview; Program Evaluation; Public Social Services; Rural Social Work; School-Linked Services; Social Planning; Social Security; Welfare Employment Programs: Evaluation.

Key Words

community health | prevention
epidemiology | public health

READER'S GUIDE

Public Policy

The following entries contain information on this general topic:

Advocacy
Aging: Public Policy Issues and Trends
Deinstitutionalization
Developmental Disabilities: Definitions and Policies
Federal Legislation and Administrative Rule Making
Federal Social Legislation from 1961 to 1994
Health Services Systems Policy

Income Security Overview
Mass Media
Policy Analysis
Public Social Services (*See Reader's Guide*)
Social Welfare Policy
Social Workers in Politics
Substance Abuse: Federal, State, and Local Policies

Public Relations

See Mass Media

Public Services Management
Leon Ginsberg

Public social services agencies play a critical role in social work. In fact, they are one of the most important elements in programming and financing for members of the social work profession. Therefore, the management of these agencies is of special interest to social workers.

Federal, state, and local expenditures for social services through public agencies constitute the largest single public expenditure in the United States. When the social security programs of Old-Age and Survivors and Disability Insurance and Medicare are included, public social services expenditures are much greater than those for public education, defense, and highways (U.S. Bureau of the Census, 1993). One survey (Meinert, Keys, & Ginsberg, 1993) found that six state agencies had budgets larger than $1 billion, which is more than the gross domestic products of many developing nations (World Bank, 1989). Fifteen agencies had staffs of over 10,000 people, and one had 32,000 employees (Meinert et al., 1993).

The magnitude of public social services expenditures results not only from the large numbers of clients who are served by the public programs but from the fact that public agencies, through a variety of contracting mechanisms, provide a large portion of the financial support for the private and volunteer agencies and organizations that deliver so many social work services and employ so many social workers. In the modern social work era, the distinction between the public and private sectors has been blurred so much that there are few exclusively private or volunteer services. Most human services that are not exclusively governmental are provided through a mixture of private and public funds. Many agencies that serve clients of public programs, including clients who receive Supplemental Security Income, Aid to Families with Dependent Children (AFDC), and mental health services, receive funds to develop and provide those services from public sources.

Social workers are heavily involved in managing public social services at all levels. One survey found that 20 percent of chief executive officers in such agencies were social workers (Meinert et al., 1993). In 1992, 22.3 percent of NASW members who responded to a national survey were involved in either supervision or management–administration (Ginsberg, 1992). In social work education, 3.9 percent of master of social work students were enrolled in administration or management concentrations in 1991, and another group of less than 10 percent combined administration or management studies with work in other practice emphases (Lennon, 1992). Many social workers who are employed in other roles in public services agencies subsequently move into supervisory and managerial positions. Therefore, a management consciousness can be beneficial to all social workers in public services.

Historically, U.S. public social services agencies are a product of the Great Depression and the New Deal of the 1930s, when the federal government, under the leadership of President Franklin Delano Roosevelt, sought to end the depression and provide assistance to the many needy Americans. When the Social Security Act of 1935 was passed, it became the cornerstone of social services planning and delivery. Social security provided, and continues to provide, direct benefits to citizens as well as assistance to states—and through them, local governments and voluntary agencies—to help ameliorate and overcome personal and social problems (Axinn & Levin, 1992; Day, 1989; Ginsberg, 1983; Jansson, 1993).

STATE SOCIAL SERVICES AGENCIES

Public social services agencies operate at the local, state, and federal levels, but most are primarily financed with federal and state dollars. Administratively, the most important level is the state government, because federal dollars that do not go directly to recipients flow through the states to recipients of federal–state entitlements and to other public and volunteer agencies.

State governments have traditionally carried the greatest responsibility for services to citizens. Federal funds go to the states to carry out the purposes of the federal programs. The states work with local agencies or subdivisions of their own agencies to provide services directly to individuals. In only a few cases is the federal government directly involved in serving people: through financial aid programs such as Supplemental Security Income; the services of the Veterans Administration; other social security programs (including Medicare); and the programs of the District of Columbia, for which the federal government has responsibility and authority (Ginsberg, 1983).

State social services agencies are usually called "departments of social services," "departments of human services," or the more historical and traditional "public welfare departments." There are other variations, such as "human resources agencies." The state social services agencies provide AFDC, food stamps, child welfare services, and a variety of combinations of services depending on the specific state. For example, some states include adult services, services to the aging, and services for disabled children. In most states, the state social services agency administers the federal social services block grant, which provides funding for such programs as homemakers, day care, and some employment placement and training. The state social services agency also usually incorporates the child support enforcement program, which works to obtain child support from noncompliant parents (Ginsberg, 1983). Many other state human services agencies, including the departments of mental health, vocational rehabilitation, public health, corrections, and juvenile services, receive some of their funds from the state social services agencies through various forms of cost-sharing and contracting.

The structures and statutes governing public social services agencies, and especially their administration, change periodically. The best current information on the administration and structure of each state's social services agency is available in the *Public Welfare Directory*, produced annually by the American Public Welfare Association (1994).

State-Administered Agencies

Public agencies are administered in various ways, according to state statute. Many agencies are directly administered by the states. In those cases, the state departments of social services operate as single units with branches in the counties or localities. Similarly, the state departments of mental health may operate the mental hospitals, the community mental health centers, and all other public mental health services at all levels.

State-Supervised Agencies

In some states, local agencies maintain control over the services provided to people at the city or county level. The state agency supervises the programs but does not administer or control them. County directors of social services in a state-supervised environment are appointed not by the state government but rather by local or county governments. However, they may operate under rules enforced by the state government, which in turn enforces federal rules. Even in state-supervised agencies, however, much of the funding comes from the state and federal governments, although the expenditure of the funds is carried out by the local government agencies.

Single-Purpose Agencies

Many state human services agencies provide only specific aid such as financial assistance, mental health services, or vocational rehabilitation. Or they provide a special combination of services expected of state departments of social services. Such single-purpose agencies are responsible only for the programs related to the specific role of the agency.

Multipurpose or Superagencies

There is a decades-long trend in the human services of organizing a group of programs into a single "superagency" or cabinet-level agency. All or most of the human services that involve social workers may be grouped into one large organization that might include the social services as well as mental health, vocational rehabilitation, juvenile and perhaps adult corrections, public health or elements of public health, and other programs in combinations particular to the state.

The "secretary" or "superdirector" of such conglomerates reports directly to the governor or the governor's staff. Heads of the specialized programs that constitute the superagency report to the secretary, rather than directly to the governor. Several states have attempted to consolidate services, avoid duplication, and improve coordination among human services programs by developing superagencies.

Local Social Services Programs

Most local government agencies (as opposed to local branches of state agencies) are parts of county government, because counties have traditionally had the greatest official status and authority in local government operations in the United States. However, many cities and towns have their own human services programs. Some cities use part of their tax revenues for the development and delivery of specialized social services programs, particularly those for which the state may not have comprehensive provisions. Local programs may include domestic violence shelters, help for people with acquired immune deficiency syndrome (AIDS), or assistance to crime victims. City governments in very large cities such as New York operate their own human services programs in cooperation with the state government. But even for a city as large as New York, federal funds for social services go to the state first, then to the city.

PUBLIC SOCIAL SERVICES MANAGERS

Managing public social services agencies requires a combination of knowledge and skills from the fields of management and the human services. Although the focus of this entry is on chief executive officers (CEOs) of public social services agencies, there are many levels of management in most such organizations. Deputy and assistant commissioners and directors, division heads, unit supervisors, local directors of statewide agencies, and many others may all be considered managers. Most of the concepts discussed in this article are applicable to all levels of management, not only the CEO.

Characteristics of State Social Services Agency CEOs

In 1990 a survey of directors of state social services, mental health, and corrections agencies was administered to determine some of their characteristics (Meinert et al., 1993). Ninety-one of the 150 subjects who were surveyed responded. Seventy-eight percent of the CEOs were men, but the 22 percent who were women exceeded, according to some sources, the proportion of women usually found in high-level managerial and administrative positions in other fields (Williams, 1985). The mean age of the managers was 47, and their average salary was $60,000 per year.

Selection Processes

There are three ways in which the CEOs of public social services agencies are designated for their positions. Most are appointed by local, state, or federal government chief executives. The U.S. government's secretary of Health and Human Services is an appointee of the president. State social services directors or commissioners in most states are appointees of governors, as are the directors or commissioners of mental health, vocational rehabilitation, and other human services agencies. In the Meinert et al. survey of state agency CEOs, 79 percent said they were appointed by a governor; only 2 percent reached their positions through merit system examinations. In 19 percent of the states, heads of social services agencies are selected by and responsible to boards or commissions that are, in turn, appointed by governors. The heads of social services agencies in such arrangements serve at the will and pleasure of the board or commission, rather than the will and pleasure of the governor.

Some CEOs of human services programs are directly elected by the voters of the state. However, most of these are heads of public education, not social services.

In local governments, there are a variety of appointment patterns. In some cases mayors or city councils appoint the heads of social services agencies. In some cases there are local boards or commissions to whom the agency managers are responsible. In other situations city managers appoint the heads of local social services programs.

AUDIENCES OF THE PUBLIC SERVICES MANAGER

Public services managers must understand and have competence in the fundamental roles of managers, which include planning, organizing, staffing, directing, and controlling organizations (Koontz & Weirich, 1988). Public social services managers must discharge these roles, just as any other manager must. However, public social services managers also are responsible to and affected by a variety of audiences that are often distinct from those encountered by the managers of other kinds of enterprises.

Appointing Authority

Managers at all levels of social services agencies respond to and are affected by the entity that appointed them or their supervisors to their positions. Whether the entity is an individual (for example, the CEO of the federal, state, or local government) or a group (for example, an appointing board or commission), the public social services manager must understand and work with the appointing authority.

When the appointing authority is an individual, public social services managers must deal effectively not only with the CEO but also with his or her staff. In most cases, social services directors report officially or in practice to an executive assistant, staff director, or another person, who then reports to the executive.

Funders and Higher Government Levels

The public social services manager must also respond to the next higher level of government. For example, in state government management, state plans must be submitted to a federal agency and approved by that agency. Therefore, the public social services manager must work directly with a regional or national counterpart who examines state plans and approves or recommends changes in them. The agency's financing depends on the actions of the higher-level agencies.

In addition, monitors who serve as auditors, evaluators, and quality control analysts in effect exercise authority over the state agency. Most managers respond to large numbers of external evaluators and monitors who determine whether the agency is complying with its requirements and, if not, whether sanctions such as withholding of funds are to be applied against it.

Legislative and Judicial Branches

Public social services managers must also respond to branches of government other than the executive branch. In the states, legislatures have control over the statutes that govern the agency, and committees of the state senate or house of representatives exercise legislative oversight over executive branch agencies. State public social services managers spend much time appearing before legislative committees, responding to requests for information and recommendations from legislators, and answering legislative critics of their activities. This is true for the federal secretary of Health and Human Services, who must respond to Congress; the county public social services manager, who must respond to the county commission or other governing body; and the city or town public social services manager, who must respond to the city or town manager or to a city council or other local legislative body.

In addition, public social services managers and their employees may find themselves in court for a number of reasons. They may be responding to accusations of failure to deliver services desired by citizens in the way those citizens wanted them delivered. In some states, portions of some public social services programs are under the supervision of the courts because the social services agency has not complied with a court ruling to the satisfaction of that court. Learning to deal with the judicial branch of government is an important responsibility for the public social services manager (Chambers, 1993).

Other Social Services Agencies

Public social services managers must also coordinate with other governmental and nongovernmental social services agencies. There are numerous examples. A manager responsible for institutions providing child care or services to children who are adjudicated delinquent may find that the licenses for such facilities are under the control of another public human services agency. The manager of a human services agency that provides Medicaid services may find that a substantial portion of the Medicaid funds are provided to the Department of Mental Health for mental health care. In some ways, agencies "subcontract" with other agencies for provision of services to clients. Voluntary agencies such as family services centers and homeless services agencies must obtain all or large portions of their funding from a public agency. Day care centers, nursing homes, hospi-

tals, medical societies, and many other recipients of public agency funds make frequent contact with and are often critics of the public social services agency.

Agency Staff

A major audience for the public social services manager is the agency's staff. A typical state agency employs thousands of people, even in small states. Almost all of the staff members are covered by a civil service or merit system plan. After a brief probationary period, they serve under carefully defined rules and regulations, not at the will and pleasure of the manager. Managers often find that they must be adept at dealing with staff discontents. Staff members in some states are organized into unions, and their manager must deal with union leadership on personnel matters.

The staff of a public social services agency is potentially capable of developing a positive reputation for the program and making the program operate effectively, or, alternatively, of sabotaging the program and the efforts of the manager. The manager must spare no effort in building effective staff support and high-quality performance, for the agency's success may depend on how the staff feel about the manager and his or her efforts.

One of the primary requirements for the public social services manager is to be sure that personnel are chosen without discrimination and to guarantee personnel diversity. The clients of social services agencies are culturally and socioeconomically diverse. The majority of the clients of many public social welfare agencies are people of color, but traditionally a minority of the staff of public social services agencies have been people of color. The public social services agency manager must take all possible steps to ensure that the diversity of its personnel is more comparable to that of its clientele than was the case when the manager assumed his or her responsibilities.

Achieving personnel diversity typically requires extensive knowledge about the ways personnel systems operate. Because personnel systems are organized around civil service and merit systems, public social services managers often find themselves frustrated in their efforts to appoint more people of color to their staffs. The manager may find it necessary to modify the personnel procedures within the agency. It is often possible, even within merit system procedures, to encourage the selection of people of color through special modifications of the selection process.

Similarly, the effective public social services manager should also work toward ethnic and gender equity in personnel evaluation, promotion, and compensation practices. Striving to increase diversity only through hiring practices may be self-defeating if individuals are not treated properly in the ongoing processes of their employment. Retention is as important as appointment in the staffing of an agency.

Many social work professional managers also provide special attention to employing and retaining staff who are professionally educated social workers. Doing so can help ensure that client-centered social work values permeate the agency and its functioning.

Media

Public attitudes about a public social services agency are strongly affected by the media. What newspapers, radio and television stations, and other outlets say about the agency has a great deal to do with the perceptions not only of the general public but also of the appointing authority about the program and its management. Legislators also form their opinions about agencies from the reputations portrayed in the media.

Because of the importance of the media audience to the success of the manager, special skills are needed in preparing media releases and in dealing directly with reporters, editors, and media executives. The importance of the media lies in the fact that its portrayals influence all of the other audiences with which the manager must deal. Brawley (1983) provided one social work text that focuses on working with the media.

Clients and Clients' Families

Perhaps the most important audience, if not always the most vocal, are clients and their families. There would be no agency and no purpose for the agency without clients. Therefore, in many ways the clients are the agency's primary "customers." Satisfactorily serving clients, within the policies established for and by the agency, is the most important indicator of sound management.

Although most public social services managers have little direct contact with clients, they are responsible for the quality of services provided to clients and their families and for responding to concerns about quality voiced by the many audiences. Dissatisfied clients or families may contact the appointing authority or legislators about their case, and the agency must courteously explain its decisions about the client. In large public social services agencies, client services units answer inquiries from members of the U.S. Congress, state legislators, governors, and other officials. Typically, inquiries are made to clarify and to provide information to the client rather than to change the agency decisions. Elected officials want to show their constituents that they care, that they have taken steps to find out more about the situation and have intervened with the public social services agency. A reputation for unresponsiveness leads to doubts about the manager's efficacy and may have an impact on appropriations or on the manager's longevity with the agency.

MANAGEMENT THEORY AND LITERATURE

There are many concepts of management and many books on the subject in the social work literature. Management is such a complex process involving so many people across such a vast variety of organizations that large numbers of managers are needed. The number of management institutes, training sessions, formal courses, books, seminars, videotapes, and the like constitute a multibillion-dollar business in the United States. Management training is also a major function in every other part of the world.

The literature on management seems limitless, perhaps because the problems of management are so complex and persistent and because so many people are involved in it. Managers of public social services agencies often find it helpful to maintain familiarity with the management literature to remain well informed about management issues and innovations. Because managers often have only minimal supervision, many find they must provide guidance to themselves to stay abreast of developments in their field.

One series of concepts that has been interestingly applied to social work management consists of the eight "principles of excellence" developed by Peters and Waterman (1982) in their book *In Search of Excellence*. The principles were based on Peters and Waterman's examination of some of America's best-run and most successful companies. The Peters and Waterman concepts were adapted to social work and other human services management by Keys and Ginsberg (1988) and by Edwards and Gummer (1988). These eight principles, which have been explicated in many books, articles, videotapes, and television programs, are stated as follows:

1. "a bias for action"—not being paralyzed by analysis
2. "close to the customer"—learning from those being served
3. "autonomy and entrepreneurship"—encouraging creativity and risk taking
4. "productivity through people"—respecting every employee
5. "hands-on, value-driven"—keeping in touch with the client and paying attention to values

6. "stick to the knitting"—doing only what you know how to do
7. "simple form, lean staff"—keeping hierarchy to a minimum and maximizing employee autonomy
8. "simultaneous loose–tight properties"—maximizing employee autonomy while promoting commitment to overarching goals.

These principles, which were and remain very popular with writers about management, help managers, particularly managers of large organizations, better understand their roles and the ways things happen in organizations.

Peters and Waterman have since written books independent of one another. Peters (1987) wrote about chaos in *Thriving on Chaos;* anyone who has been involved in large organizations, particularly large public social services organizations, recognizes the significance of chaos in organizational life. Peters (1992) also wrote *Liberation Management* about the need for organizations to accept a degree of disorganization to avoid lockstep procedures during times of rapid change. Waterman (1988) wrote *The Renewal Factor,* which extends his ideas about keeping organizations dynamic by maintaining the level of interest within the organization and building enthusiasm through techniques such as trying new things, avoiding sterility, and generally trying hard to keep the program interesting to the employees.

Crow and Odewahn (1987), Edwards and Yankey (1991), and Weinbach (1990) have applied principles from the management literature to the social services. Some popular and often enlightening management books are geared to people in business but can be readily applied to the social services. For example, Townsend's *Up the Organization* (1970) and *Further up the Organization* (1984) are lively and simplified works that help readers understand some very fundamental approaches to practical management issues. Several interesting books by Mackay (1988, 1990, 1993) have been popular with many managers. Although these books appeal mostly to those involved in the management of profit-making companies and sales, there are some parallels for public agency managers, who must obtain sufficient resources (comparable to earning a profit) and satisfy their various audiences (comparable to many of the demands of those involved in sales). Roberts's *Leadership Secrets of Attila the Hun* (1987) and *Victory Secrets of Attila the Hun* (1993) suggested that the famous conqueror, who is often perceived as brutal, had management principles at the foundation of his efforts. More than anything,

perhaps the popularity of these books reflects the massive market for books on management, one of the most successful areas of publishing.

EFFECTIVE BEHAVIOR FOR PUBLIC SERVICES MANAGERS

Public social services managers do more than direct the internal operations of their organizations. In Thompson's (1969) model, a top manager of a human services agency is more concerned with relating to the larger environment—the higher levels of government, the general public, the political structure, the top executives of other agencies—than with the internal operations of the organization itself. Internal management is typically delegated to assistants, deputies, and division heads. The results of a survey of state social services CEOs (Ginsberg & Keys, 1988) showed that Thompson's model is reflected in the real world and provides guidance for public social services executives.

Staying Visible

To relate to the larger environment, effective managers are, first of all, visible. The manager must appear at official functions, social events, legislative hearings, constituent group meetings, and other activities. Being unavailable to the broader public is viewed negatively; the CEO symbolizes the agency, and people want to know that the agency is present, active, and involved.

In addition, as Peters and Waterman (1982) put it, there is value to "managing by walking around." The manager needs to be on site, to see the people the agency works with, to talk with them, to get out into the community to see how other contract agencies are working—in short, to have a visual image of what the organization does in addition to simply understanding what the organizational chart shows.

Using National Connections

Public social services managers who are effective often are so because they are involved in national organizations. The American Public Welfare Association and its councils of state directors and local directors provide opportunities for top executives to meet one another and share ideas and information. When, from time to time, the federal government becomes overly rigid, in the opinion of the states, in its administration of its part of state–federal programs, state directors can take concerted action to overcome the problem. In many of the meetings, top federal officials attend and hear from the directors.

Individual, state, or local directors also learn new and effective strategies from their colleagues for dealing with problems. For example, attendees might learn at a meeting of the American Public Welfare Association that a new computer program can help locate absent parents who are responsible for child support. They might learn that a vendor they have been considering for a contract to process Medicaid claims is ineffective and expensive and that another vendor, less well known, is less expensive and quite effective. They may learn that groups of medical providers are collecting more money than they should through devices that are of questionable legality. Or they may learn about a new stream of federal funding that makes it possible for the state to obtain much more money at virtually no sacrifice. The most rapid way to learn about someone else's new and effective solution to an old problem is to speak with that person directly. The relationships established at national meetings often lead to further exchanges between states and localities.

In addition, it is often important for the top executives of social services agencies to remain in touch with other work possibilities. Political conflicts, reorganizations, and elections often lead to the replacement of top executives. One survey of state social services CEOs (Ginsberg & Keys, 1988) suggested that although some had served for 20 years or more, the average tenure of people in such positions is less than two years. Many people in such positions need to know about other employment options.

Inspiring Development and Change

One of the contributions of effective public social services agency managers is to examine new ways of operating. A recent article in the popular management literature (Dumaine, 1993) suggested that managers should renew their organization's functions periodically, even when times are good and when the organization appears to be operating smoothly. According to Dumaine, managers of some highly successful corporations found it effective to call their top leaders together and explain that if the organization did not change, it was doomed. Such steps often lead to redefinitions, restructuring, and other changes in the corporation. Similar steps can be greatly effective for public social services agencies, which, because of their need to conform to state law and because of the relative permanence of their employees, become inflexible and resistant to change.

Maintaining Social Work Values

There is no essential conflict between the values of public social services agency management and social work values. For reasons that are not always well understood, many social workers feel that

politics is a dirty business and that public social services agency managers are less than ethical because they serve in political positions. Careful observers of politics suggest, however, that the values of those engaged in politics are similar to those in business, education, social work, and all other employment situations: People seek to build their careers, maximize their personal situations, and otherwise pursue personal as well as organizational goals (Alexander, 1982).

Public social services agency managers are, however, subject to restrictions on their behavior that managers in other settings are not. The values of social work—the importance of the individual, the commitment to a primary emphasis on the needs of clients, the belief in democracy, the commitment to social justice—all can be carried out without conflict by social workers in public social services management. Indeed, the social services agency gives its managers special opportunities to carry out the ethical concepts of the profession.

Developing New Skills

Public social services managers often find that although they are not experts in anything but social work (or education or psychology), they must quickly become experts in accounting and law. To a lesser extent, knowledge of computer science is also a major requirement in the social services. The social services manager can learn basic accounting, legal, and computer science principles at seminars and meetings or through conversations with colleagues or employees.

CONCLUSION

The quality of the management of public social services is directly related to the quality of the direct services providers. If the service providers are not effectively deployed and supported, their personal talents and qualities will have little impact on the public that they serve. It is important that public social services employees be management conscious and skilled in working as managers in their organizations. Public social services clients, the larger public, and agency staff all benefit from effective management and suffer when it is absent from the organization.

REFERENCES

Alexander, C. A. (1982). Professional social workers and political responsibility. In M. Mahaffey & J. N. Hanks (Eds.), *Practical politics* (pp. 15–31). Silver Spring, MD: National Association of Social Work.

American Public Welfare Association. (1994). *1994/95 public welfare directory.* (Vol. 55). Washington, DC: Author.

Axinn, J., & Levin, H. (1992). *Social welfare: A history of the American response to need* (3rd ed.). New York: Longman.

Brawley, E. A. (1983). *Mass media and human services.* Beverly Hills, CA: Sage Publications.

Chambers, D. E. (1993). *Social policy and social programs: A method for the practical public policy analysis* (2nd ed.). New York: Macmillan.

Crow, R. T., & Odewahn, C. A. (1987). *Management for the human services.* Englewood Cliffs, NJ: Prentice Hall.

Day, P. J. (1989). *A new history of social welfare.* Englewood Cliffs, NJ: Prentice Hall.

Dumaine, B. (1993, June 28). Times are good? Create a crisis. *Fortune,* pp.123–130.

Edwards, R. L., & Gummer, B. (1988). Management of social services: Current perspectives and future trends. In P. Keys & L. Ginsberg (Eds.), *New management in the human services* (pp.1–29). Silver Spring, MD: National Association of Social Workers.

Edwards, R. L., & Yankey, J. A. (Eds.). (1991). *Skills for effective human services management.* Silver Spring, MD: NASW Press.

Ginsberg, L. (1983). *The practice of social work in public welfare.* New York: Free Press.

Ginsberg, L. (1992). *Social work almanac.* Washington, DC: NASW Press.

Ginsberg, L., & Keys, P. R. (1988, Summer). What will state CEOs do next? *Public Welfare,* 29–32.

Jansson, B. S. (1993). *The reluctant welfare state: A history of American social welfare policies* (2nd ed.). Pacific Grove, CA: Brooks/Cole.

Keys, P., & Ginsberg, L. (Eds.). (1988). *New management in the human services.* Silver Spring, MD: National Association of Social Workers.

Koontz, J. D., & Weirich, H. (1988). *Management* (9th ed.). New York: McGraw-Hill.

Lennon, T. M. (1992). *Statistics on social work education in the United States: 1991.* Alexandria, VA: Council on Social Work Education.

Mackay, H. (1988). *Swim with the sharks without being eaten alive: Outsell, outmanage, outmotivate, and outnegotiate your competition.* New York: Morrow.

Mackay, H. (1990). *Beware the naked man who offers you his shirt: Do what you love, love what you do, deliver more than you promise.* New York: Morrow.

Mackay, H. (1993). *Sharkproof: Get the job you want, keep the job you love—In today's frenzied job market.* New York: HarperBusiness.

Meinert, R., Keys, P., & Ginsberg, L. (1993). Performance characteristics of CEOs in state departments of social service, mental health, and corrections. *Administration in Social Work, 17*(1), 103–114.

Peters, T. J. (1987). *Thriving on chaos: Handbook for a management revolution.* New York: Random House.

Peters, T. J. (1992). *Liberation management: Necessary disorganization for the nanosecond nineties.* New York: Alfred A. Knopf.

Peters, T. J., & Waterman, R. (1982). *In search of excellence: Lessons from America's best-run companies.* New York: Harper & Row.

Roberts, W. (1987). *Leadership secrets of Attila the Hun.* New York: Peregrine.

Roberts, W. (1993). *Victory secrets of Attila the Hun.* New York: Doubleday.

Social Security Act of 1935. PL. 100-360, 49 Stat. 620.

Thompson, V. A. (1969). *Bureaucracy and innovation.* Tuscaloosa: University of Alabama Press.

Townsend, R. (1970). *Up the organization.* New York: Alfred A. Knopf.

Townsend, R. (1984). *Further up the organization.* New York: Alfred A. Knopf.

U.S. Bureau of the Census. (1993). *Statistical abstract of the United States: 1992* (112th ed.). Washington, DC: U.S. Government Printing Office.

Waterman, R. (1988). *The renewal factor: How the best get and keep the competitive edge.* New York: Bantam.

Weinbach, R. W. (1990). *The social worker as manager: Theory and practice.* New York: Longman.

Williams, M. (1985). Women and success in organization. In B. Stead (Ed.), *Women in management* (pp.333–341). Englewood Cliffs, NJ: Prentice Hall.

World Bank. (1989). *World development report.* New York: Oxford University Press.

FURTHER READING

Gates, B. L. (1980). *Social program administration: The implementation of social policy.* Englewood Cliffs, NJ: Prentice Hall.

Gilbert, N., & Gilbert, B. (1989). *The enabling state: Modern welfare capitalism in America.* New York: Oxford University Press.

Gruber, M. L. (1981). *Management systems in the human services.* Philadelphia: Temple University Press.

National Assembly of Voluntary Health and Social Welfare Organizations. (1989). *A study in excellence: Management in the non-profit sector.* Washington, DC: Author.

Neugeboren, B. (1985). *Organization, policy, and practice in the human services.* New York: Longman.

Tropman, J. E., Johnson, H. R., & Tropman, E. J. (1992). *Committee management in human services: Running effective meetings, committees, and boards* (2nd ed.). Chicago: Nelson-Hall.

Leon Ginsberg, PhD, ACSW, is Carolina Research Professor, University of South Carolina, School of Social Work, Columbia, SC 29208.

For further information see

Management Overview; National Association of Social Workers; Nonprofit Management Issues; Organizations: Contex for Social Services Delivery; Personnel Management; Planning and Management Professions; Public Social Services; Public Social Welfare Expenditures; Social Welfare History; Social Work Profession Overview; Welfare Employment Programs: Evaluation.

Key Words

administration
management

public services

Public Social Services
Michael Reisch

Social services is the area of social welfare policy that is least clear in the public mind, especially with regard to the responsibilities of government for their funding, design, implementation, and administration. In the United States the term *social services* is used quite broadly to cover nearly everything that governments (local, state, and federal); the voluntary, nonprofit sector; and the private, for-profit sector provide for people in need. One definition, which attempts to distinguish public social services from government-funded income maintenance programs, refers to those activities and resources made available at reduced or no cost to individuals and families to meet specific needs.

The public social services, therefore, consist of programs made available by other than market criteria to ensure a basic level of health, education, and welfare provision, enhance community living and individual functioning, facilitate access to services and institutions, and assist those in deficiency and need (Titmuss, 1976). In other words, it can be defined as communal provision to promote individual and group well-being. Common examples of public social services include child care, homemaker services, counseling, child protective services, transportation assistance, and information and referral programs (Kahn & Kamerman, 1976).

The presence of public social services is an implicit acknowledgment that many individual and familial problems are not created solely by a lack of income and cannot, therefore, be solved solely through the provision of financial assistance. Public social services try to protect, restore, or enhance family life; help individuals cope with external problems; enhance family and community development; and facilitate access to programs through information, guidance, advocacy, and concrete assistance. Although originally developed as complements to or substitutes for poor relief, they have evolved in the 20th century (with the forma-

tion of the modern welfare state) to the point where they are not conceived of as providing services only for low-income populations.

Nevertheless, although some public social services programs in the United States are universal (for example, protective services for children), most remain selective and are targeted to a specific portion of the population on the basis of income level or specific need. As a result, public social services in the United States are often defined by populations (that is, who is being served—for example, children or the elderly), sometimes in terms of where the services are provided (public schools or housing projects, for instance), and sometimes in terms of the nature of the problems being addressed (such as alcohol and drug abuse).

The role of government in the provision of social services in the United States has evolved to mean the use of government policy-making authority and funding to establish and maintain such services. Many public social services are connected to income maintenance programs such as Aid to Families with Dependent Children (AFDC), but this connection is not necessary for the programs to be established or implemented. Public social services, such as child welfare, services to the elderly, and counseling and other mental health programs, are often organized around a local public welfare or social services department. Other social services that are funded by the government are organized around schools, child care centers, hospitals or health clinics, community agencies that serve the elderly, community mental health centers and psychiatric hospitals, libraries, and military installations.

Throughout U.S. history, voluntary, nonprofit social services agencies have coexisted with the public social services, often performing many similar or complementary functions (Jansson, 1993). In fact, since the late 1960s many government social services agencies have contracted out for services with private, nonprofit organizations, largely for cost-cutting reasons, to provide specific services to specific populations. In the 1980s this practice of contracting expanded to include for-profit providers as well.

DEVELOPMENT OF PUBLIC SOCIAL SERVICES IN THE UNITED STATES

Unlike other Western industrialized nations, the United States lacks a national network of locally based services; an integrated national social services system; and a nationally instituted, locally based structure for providing general social services. There are several reasons for this situation, and they include the following:

- The history of social services in the United States reflects state rather than federally focused priorities in the development of social services.
- The United States has emphasized categorical programs as a solution to discrete problems.
- The voluntary, nonprofit sector has a unique role in the United States in the development and implementation of social services.
- The government has failed to create a policy or program structure that successfully combines income maintenance and social services.

The one existing structure that might have developed into a general system—the service arm of the public welfare system—almost collapsed when income maintenance and social services were separated in the early 1970s. Social services staff were either switched to eligibility tasks or were left with limited support and no clear sense of their role or function, except in the child welfare area.

In the United States the public sector began to play an active role in the field of social welfare as early as the mid-17th century, initially at the village level. Documents of town council meetings, for example, illustrate how local government intervention went beyond the provision of emergency relief to those classified as "worthy poor" to include early prototypes of foster care, home health care, and services to the aged (Pumphrey & Pumphrey, 1961).

During the 18th century, as the colonial population grew, counties began to take responsibility for the public relief of the poor and for the ancillary services that accompanied it. After the Revolutionary War and throughout the 19th century, public-sector responsibilities expanded upward to the state level (Trattner, 1980). In the 19th century, a variety of institutions focused their services on specific categories of dependent populations such as individuals who were blind, hearing impaired, orphans, aged, or developmentally disabled (Rothman, 1971, 1980). Examples include the Orphan Asylum of New York (1811), the Massachusetts School for Idiotic and Feeble-Minded Youth (1846), and private asylums for deaf and hearing-impaired persons that were built with state subsidies in Massachusetts and Connecticut (1819), New Hampshire (1821), Vermont and Maine (1825), and Kentucky (1826).

THE VOLUNTARY SECTOR AND PUBLIC SOCIAL SERVICES

Despite the growth of these institutions, funded largely by state and county governments, most social services in the United States were provided by voluntary organizations formed by family members, neighborhoods, church groups, and other public-spirited entities. In the early 19th century, these voluntary, nonprofit social services organizations emerged in the United States both to serve humanitarian ends and to increase the strength of organized churches in U.S. social life (Banner, 1973; Tocqueville, 1835/1945). However, motives other than altruism or benevolence spurred the growth of these organizations during the first half of the 19th century, even as the public sector embarked on an era of institution building.

Reasons for Growth

For women such organizations provided a means to do social good. They also served as vehicles that enhanced women's awareness of social inequality and, as such, were instruments in the early formation of the feminist movement in the United States. Many women who entered the field of community service through such organizations later formed the core of the feminist, temperance, and suffrage movements (Abramovitz, 1989).

For African Americans—both before and after Emancipation—as well as immigrant populations from Europe and, later, Asia and Mexico, voluntary social services organizations substituted in part for inadequate, insensitive, and largely inaccessible public services. By constructing their own service organizations, such groups provided a means to create their own centers of community building, which helped foster future economic and social development.

For religious humanitarians these organizations constituted "the third major ingredient of a 'Christian Republicanism'" (along with local political power and decentralized church authority) to serve as a potential deterrent to the excessive accumulation of power by the federal government and as a means for "involving citizens with their government and thus insuring that democracy would actually function in a republican framework" (Banner, 1973, p. 40; Gutman, 1976). Others saw these voluntary-sector organizations as a way to create a "harmonious community" and to protect traditional social values and social relationships in an environment of increasingly rapid economic and social change.

Consequences of Upper-Class Domination
Many of these goals were thwarted, however, as voluntary social services organizations grew in number and size. Upper-class white men quickly dominated them and shaped them to their own values and interests. This dominance of voluntary social services organizations complemented the control of public-sector services by the emerging commercial class and reflected its efforts to gain an additional means of economic control. Just as public-sector institutions provided elites with politically legitimate vehicles to control the so-called dangerous classes under the guise of humanitarian concern, voluntary-sector social services organizations freed businessmen from familial and community demands and served as a device for the concentration of diffuse investment capital (Hall, 1974–1975).

One significant consequence of this development was that the upper class strengthened its hold on the social institutions of U.S. society, including its major nongovernment social services organizations (for example, the Children's Aid Society and the Association for the Improvement of the Condition of the Poor) and the credential-granting bodies for the emerging professions. Another consequence was that the influence of the voluntary sector and its relationship to the preservation of elite power and control reduced the pressure on government to intervene in the arena of the public social services throughout the 19th and early 20th centuries. The ongoing expansion of

voluntary social services organizations provided a continuing justification for the maintenance of the precedent of government noninvolvement established by President Franklin Pierce in 1854. In fact, guided by Pierce's veto of a bill to provide federal land for the construction of asylums for indigent mentally ill people, government intervention in the field of social welfare was regarded as both unnecessary and undesirable until the 1930s.

As a result, in the half century between the end of the Civil War and the start of World War I, these voluntary organizations were the primary instruments of social services in the United States (Trolander, 1987). Leaders of such organizations as the Charities Organization Societies, the social settlements, the YMCA, and the YWCA sought to heal the intensifying wounds of social life produced by industrial growth and urbanization and to re-create a semimythic vision of an "organic community" (Bender, 1972). This notion of an organic community, however, rested on a pathological view of urban life and the urban working classes, particularly foreign-born individuals. Social services organizations established on these premises emulated "the virtues of the small town in the settings of an urban, industrial system" (Kusmer, 1973). Similarly, the location of public-sector institutions largely in isolated rural counties and their development as total institutions attempted to replicate the atmosphere of an era that was rapidly disappearing (Katz, 1986). This approach, whatever its intent, did not fundamentally alter the economic, social, or political status quo. In fact, many members of the upper class and the emerging professional class were attracted to this model of social services organization—in both the voluntary and public sectors—because it aimed to alleviate social ills without jeopardizing economic or social privileges or dominant cultural norms (Reisch & Wenocur, 1982).

Reform Movements
Experience and social research tempered the initial moralism of both voluntary and public-sector organizations and provided them with a broader understanding of the conditions of the clients they purported to serve. In the late 19th century, a moderate, reformist impulse emerged among both government officials who were responsible for the management or oversight of social services institutions and the leaders of voluntary social services organizations. Within often uneasy alliances, these reformers advocated on behalf of such measures as the eight-hour day, an end to child labor, improved public health measures and public housing reform, women's suffrage, and compulsory

public education. They also sought to end many of the abuses that had appeared in the management of state- or county-funded institutions. However, for the most part such reformers failed to engage in a rigorous analysis of the roots of poverty and chose to avoid rather than confront the issue of class conflict and social inequality (Mandler, 1990). This enabled voluntary social services organizations to retain the support of the business community throughout the heyday of organized charities and into the post–World War I era, when Community Chests and United Funds began to reshape the sector (Chambers, 1965). At the same time, local political and economic elites resisted efforts to solve the problems of government-funded institutions through closer state and local oversight, transfer of local and state government responsibility to the federal level, or construction of community-based, publicly funded services as alternatives to institutional care (Wenocur & Reisch, 1989).

THE NEW DEAL AND PUBLIC SOCIAL SERVICES

The magnitude of the social and economic problems produced by the Great Depression of the 1930s forced both the voluntary social services sector and the proponents of state-controlled social services institutions to acknowledge that they could no longer manage the burdens they had assumed. Consequently, the role of the public sector, particularly the federal government, in the provision of social services expanded enormously. In fact, the framework for the current system of public social services in the United States was created during the New Deal of the 1930s and expanded during the 1960s and 1970s, well after similar frameworks had been developed in other industrialized nations. To a considerable extent, however, the service arm of public social welfare in the United States has played a secondary role to its principal programs of income maintenance and support via old age pensions, unemployment insurance, and cash assistance to disabled and indigent individuals and families (Barak, 1992).

THE WAR ON POVERTY AND PUBLIC SOCIAL SERVICES

With the exception of child welfare services, social services were not incorporated into the original Social Security Act, despite the arguments of proponents that cash assistance alone was not adequate to meet the needs of low-income recipients. In 1956 the federal government decided to reimburse states for 50 percent of the social services provided to welfare recipients, but this matching rate was not sufficient incentive for many states,

and few chose to participate. It was not until the 1962 amendments to the Social Security Act that the federal government took major responsibility for the provision of social services to individuals and families who were receiving benefits through public welfare programs (Yankey, 1987).

1962 Social Security Amendments

The 1962 Social Security amendments sought to develop a social services strategy to address the problem of poverty in the United States. The amendments emphasized preventive and rehabilitative services, particularly family preservation (a recurring theme in the history of public social services), and provided a higher federal matching rate of 75 percent for services. The 1962 amendments also expanded eligibility for social services to former and potential welfare recipients and authorized states to contract for services with other public agencies. Significantly, no ceiling was placed on the federal expenditure level for social services.

Other key components of the 1962 amendments included the following:

- application of these services to the aged
- state maintenance of limitations on caseworkers' workloads
- counseling and information and referral services for individuals
- development of social services plans for each client
- use of home visits to determine client eligibility.

The 1962 amendments, however, failed to achieve one primary goal: to stop the rapid increase of the welfare rolls. These grew by about 50 percent between 1962 and 1967, despite the expansion of public social services in the mid-1960s. One problem was the absence of clarity regarding what constituted the social services, or even by what process they should be defined. Another problem was the lack of a sufficient corps of professionally trained social workers to implement this service strategy. A third problem was the failure of welfare grants to provide financial assistance adequate to enable clients to take advantage of social services, a critical factor that researchers discovered from data on demonstration grants (Bell, 1983).

1967 Social Security Amendments

The 1967 amendments to the Social Security Act attempted to strengthen its services provision. With the goal of moving recipients from the welfare rolls to the work force, so-called hard services such as job training and child care were authorized in addition to "soft" services such as counseling. The amendments also created the Work Incentive Program (WIN) as part of this strategy. This program made public assistance more restrictive by placing a major emphasis on the use of work incentives to reduce welfare caseloads.

The amendments also required states to establish a single organizational unit in the state agency responsible for the administration of social services and authorized the purchase of services from private as well as other public agencies. To create an added incentive for their participation, the legislation offered states an 85 percent reimbursement rate for services provided during the first year after the law took effect. The rate would be reduced to 75 percent in subsequent years.

Another important component of the 1967 law was the formal separation of the administration of federally funded social services from the administration of cash assistance. This occurred as part of a reorganization that created the Social and Rehabilitation Service within the U.S. Department of Health, Education, and Welfare (DHEW). After extensive delays the Social and Rehabilitation Service mandated the separation of services and cash assistance through 1972 regulations. Proponents of this change argued that clients could not form a trusting relationship with a caseworker if that worker also had the ability to deny cash benefits. From the federal government's perspective, separation was desirable, because it would reduce the spiraling costs that had resulted from the states' unexpected transfer of service expenditures to public welfare to take advantage of the 75 percent matching rate. Separation prevented states from claiming the 75 percent rate for services for the administration of cash assistance, which had a matching rate of only 50 percent.

Despite these legislative initiatives, AFDC rolls continued to increase, more than doubling between 1967 and 1972. Simultaneously, federal spending for social services jumped from $281.6 million in fiscal year 1967 to $1,688.4 million in fiscal year 1972. This increase occurred for several reasons:

- vagueness in the legislative language as to what constituted a "social service"
- liberal regulations regarding eligibility, which allowed such services to be provided to anyone who had received public aid within the previous two years or was likely to need aid in the next five years
- the allowance of group and neighborhood eligibility determinations, further enlarging the eligible population
- sophisticated use of the law's purchase of service (matching) authority by state governments.

This increase in spending for social services coincided with a growing demand for federal benefits and greater federal responsiveness to states (Derthick, 1975).

In 1971–1972, in response to this unprecedented growth, the Nixon administration proposed a ceiling of $2.5 billion on federal social services expenditures, effective in 1973. These funds would be divided among the states in proportion to their population. The same legislation limited to 10 percent the amount of funds available for services to former or potential welfare recipients. The secretary of DHEW was also asked to issue regulations governing the purchase of services by states from other agencies (Bixby, 1990).

TITLE XX OF THE SOCIAL SECURITY ACT AND THE NEW FEDERALISM

The two-year controversy generated by proposed DHEW regulations in this area culminated in the enactment of Title XX of the Social Security Act, signed into law on January 4, 1975. The primary political motive for this legislation was the belief of Congress that DHEW could not manage effective programs or impose controls on states. This was consistent with the political climate of the period, in which the concept of federal "revenue sharing" had become popular. Congress wanted to provide states with maximum flexibility in designing social services programs while promoting greater fiscal accountability. Title XX was the product of these distinct goals.

Development Rationale

For more than a decade, Title XX of the Social Security Act, implemented in stages in the late 1970s, in combination with Title IV-B of the same act (which provided for services to children) and the Older Americans Act (passed in 1967), provided the centerpiece of public social services in the United States. In addition to the controversy cited earlier, four critical factors shaped the development of this legislation:

1. the growing desire among policymakers to add a social services component to programs that delivered financial aid, particularly after the separation of services and income maintenance programs in local departments of social services after 1969
2. the purchase of service requirements pioneered in the late 1960s, which led to government departments contracting out for the delivery of mandated services with existing nonprofit or private-sector institutions or agencies
3. the political pressure produced by "revenue sharing," initiated by the Nixon administration

in the early 1970s, in which the federal government turned back to the states some of its tax revenues to be used at their discretion

4. the crucial role of a relatively conservative president (Nixon) in an environment of rapidly growing public welfare expenditures.

Title XX consolidated and replaced the authorizations for social services previously found in Titles IV (Grants to States for Aid to Dependent Children) and VI (Adult Services) of the Social Security Act. Although it did not create a new program, it attempted to make significant changes in the way social services were provided to low-income people. The legislation required at least 50 percent of each state's federal share of funds to be used for services to Aid to Families with Dependent Children, Supplemental Security Income, or Medicaid recipients. The remaining funds, however, could be used to provide services to anyone whose income did not exceed 115 percent of the state's median income. (Individuals with incomes between 80 percent and 115 percent of the state's median would be charged fees for services, and the states were given the discretion to charge individuals with incomes below 80 percent of the median.) Three types of services could be provided on a universal basis: (1) information and referral, (2) family planning, and (3) protective services.

In addition, Title XX established four broad goals for the design of social services:

1. the attainment or maintenance of economic self-support and self-sufficiency of recipients to prevent, reduce, or eliminate welfare dependency
2. the prevention or remediation of abuse, neglect, or exploitation of children and vulnerable adults, along with a strong emphasis on family preservation, rehabilitation, and reunification
3. the prevention or reduction of inappropriate institutional care by the provision of community-based care, home-based care, or other forms of less-intensive care
4. referral or admission for institutional care when needed.

Legislative Revisions

The Title XX program was plagued with serious problems from its inception. Expenditures increased rapidly because the availability of federal matching funds encouraged states to expand services or create new programs at little or no additional cost to the state. In addition, existing services were disorganized and marred by considerable overlap and lack of integration. The grand plan to create a national network of public social

services also suffered from a serious lack of accountability in an increasingly fiscally conscious era. In an attempt to address these problems, Congress enacted special revenue sharing in October 1975, which incorporated all the social services features of the old public welfare provisions of the Social Security Act. The significance of this legislation was that it recognized the public social services as a separate component of the social welfare system, not a mere adjunct to it.

The key feature of the new law was the authority it gave state governments to develop a unique services "package," called a Comprehensive Annual Services Plan (CASP), funded through a cost-sharing provision in which the federal government would pay 75 percent of the program costs. In return, states were required to (1) provide at least three services for Supplemental Security Income recipients; (2) provide at least one service directed at the linkage, therapeutic, or enhancement goals; (3) provide family planning services to all AFDC recipients who request them; (4) provide foster care services for certain children who were or might become clients of AFDC; and (5) develop a service plan that assesses needs and develops services to meet them in a manner involving community participation.

Shifts in Service Provision

These legislative changes led to several significant shifts in government's role in the provision of social services, which compounded the effects of the formal separation of income maintenance and social services programs in local departments of public welfare already required under law. Changes included the following:

- an increase in contracting for services with the private, not-for-profit sector to the point where most publicly funded social services programs were implemented by nongovernment organizations
- more decentralized planning, with consequent wide variations between and even within states in the scope, coverage, and quality of public social services
- more universal coverage within certain public social services programs such as family planning and child care
- the creation of so-called block grants by the Carter and Reagan administrations in the late 1970s through the 1980s, which combined formerly separate categorical programs into broad programmatic areas and established a ceiling on total state expenditures for social services in return for giving state governments more lati-

tude in how the funds provided by the federal government could be spent.

The last trend became particularly significant in the 1980s, when political leaders wanted to reduce the scope of the U.S. welfare state and were generally unsympathetic to the provision of public social services. The combination of many categorical service grants into a small number of block grants was but one short step from the reduction in the funding levels of these grants. The initial result of these fiscal cutbacks was that states had greater latitude in their use of federal dollars. Later in the 1980s the federal government gave to the states the responsibility for providing certain mandated services but did not provide the states with the additional resources they needed to implement these new mandates. Sometimes dubbed the "New Federalism," this shift in responsibility for the provision of the public social services to the states, (and, in some states, from state to county governments) without adequate resources contributed significantly to the fiscal crisis every state government and many county governments experienced and produced a sharp decline in the scope and quantity of public social services.

Failure of a National Social Services Strategy
Thus, the attempt to establish a national social services strategy through Title XX failed, largely because of a lack of political commitment and sufficient resources. Even before the retrenchment of the 1980s, however, there were signs that Title XX, the centerpiece of this national strategy, had serious flaws. The provision of comprehensive, federally funded social services did not move people off the welfare rolls and into economic self-sufficiency as intended.

One major flaw, for example, was that the spending ceiling of Title XX regulations encouraged program growth in those states that previously had been spending below the maximum allowable level and caused additional spending in other states that were already spending at that level. For the first group, this was because federal matching funds made program growth relatively inexpensive. For the second group, this was a consequence of their desire to achieve a higher level of services.

To expand or maintain existing services, therefore, states were pressured to shift funds from different spending categories to stay within the ceiling limits of the legislation. This effectively allowed states to circumvent the intent of the law. Finally, the combination of a legislatively imposed spending ceiling and the increased rate of inflation

in the mid- and late 1970s froze the Title XX budgets of many states and undermined one of the objectives of the law: to initiate innovative and comprehensive forms of public social services delivery. Other important factors that contributed to the failure of Title XX included the following:

- the existence of uneven regulations and standards, both within and between states, particularly in programs such as child care
- the disproportionate distribution of Title XX benefits to middle-income suburban families because of the power of suburban legislators in the development of state service plans, and the failure of many states to provide adequate access to these services for low-income families, despite the legislative intent to target social services programs to the inner-city poor
- the domination of mandatory participatory bodies by service providers rather than consumers
- the lack of sufficient service integration with other federally funded programs, such as services to the elderly (Gilbert, 1977).

REAGANOMICS AND PUBLIC SOCIAL SERVICES

During the 1980s the Reagan administration attempted to reduce the role of the federal government and restructure the relationship between the national and state governments. Simultaneously, President Reagan sought to stimulate the U.S. economy through a combination of tax cuts and reductions in domestic spending, particularly in the area of social welfare. A major component of this strategy was the expansion of the use of block grants, which had been initiated in the 1970s.

Block Grants
Under the Reagan administration's direction, 57 categorical health and social services grant programs were merged into nine block grants: (1) social services; (2) community development; (3) community services; (4) primary care; (5) preventive health and health services; (6) maternal and child health; (7) low-income energy assistance; (8) alcohol, drug abuse, and mental health services; and (9) elementary and secondary education. In addition to this consolidation, the Reagan administration proposed a 20 percent to 25 percent reduction in funding for these programs, believing that the reductions of costly administrative requirements at the state level would balance these funding cuts. New federal policies also restricted (through 1988) the options of local governments as to how they could spend the block grants. After 1988 local governments were free to decide which needs were greatest in their communities and shift their available resources accord-

ingly (Center on Budget and Policy Priorities, 1984).

The social services block grant combined Title XX services, including day care and Title XX training. Remaining categorical social services programs included child welfare services; child welfare services training; foster care; adoption assistance; and child abuse, runaway youth, developmental disabilities, and rehabilitation services.

Some implications of these policy shifts included the following:

- the establishment of a virtual cap on funding for social services and much greater difficulty in obtaining increases to keep pace with the inflation of program costs
- increased interagency competition for shrinking funds
- the loss of any assurance that services would be provided evenly from state to state and within states
- less accountability in the use of federal funds as a result of the elimination of regulations covering planning, standards of services delivery, resource distribution, and program evaluation
- less control over states' discriminatory practices in the delivery of services
- increased politicization of the resource allocation process at the state and county levels, with serious consequences for organizations that worked with and on behalf of low-income populations.

CLINTON ADMINISTRATION

These trends have continued into the deficit-conscious 1990s, although federal initiatives pointed to a resurgence of service strategy in the first two years of the Clinton administration to address the problems of chronic poverty, long-term welfare dependency, and family disintegration. One federal policy option currently under discussion is a welfare reform package that would include greater emphasis on job training, child care, transportation support, and other social services to enable individuals receiving public assistance to make the transition from the welfare rolls to economic self-sufficiency. This concept would expand on the requirements built into the Family Support Act of 1988, which have never been fully implemented by states because of a lack of funds. It would also build on the mixed experiences of numerous states, such as California, New York, Massachusetts, Wisconsin, and Maryland, in developing transitional "welfare-to-work" programs such as California's Greater Avenues for Independence program.

Another federal initiative was the support (through Title IV of the Social Security Act) for intensive family preservation programs delivered through child welfare services branches of local departments of social services. Other initiatives included the expansion of funding for Head Start programs; the creation of "Healthy Start" programs, which reintegrated social services and health care into the public school system; and, of enormous potential significance, the proposal to create a universal national health insurance system, which would include mental health services. This latter initiative inspired fierce congressional opposition, and the 103rd Congress failed to approve any health care reform.

ROLE OF SOCIAL WORKERS IN PUBLIC SOCIAL SERVICES

At present, social workers in the public social services serve three basic functions:

1. *Linkage function.* This function facilitates access to the programs people need. Examples of linkage activities include information and referral networks, crisis hot lines, legal services for indigent individuals, case advocacy, and community organization and development. Given the urbanization and bureaucratization of the United States during the late 20th century and the social problems resulting from profound demographic changes, these services are critical, particularly for low-income families, immigrants, and refugees. However, because of the historical role of public social services, there are many obstacles to the development of successful public social services in this category, especially in the much needed area of advocacy. Consequently, nonprofit organizations play a major role in this arena.
2. *Therapeutic and control function.* This function occurs through a variety of types of government-funded services, including probation and parole, counseling for individuals and families, foster care, and adult protective services.
3. *Enhancement function.* These services focus primarily on individual or familial growth and development. They tend to be so-called "quality-of-life" services such as developmentally oriented child care; senior citizen centers that provide cultural, educational, and social programs for the elderly; and homemaker services. They tend to substitute for the work that families and neighbors formerly provided. The five goals of such programs are (1) to help individuals achieve a better level of self-support or self-care; (2) to prevent the abuse or exploitation of

people; (3) to prevent the inappropriate institutionalization of people and to facilitate such institutionalization where appropriate; (4) to link people with other, ancillary services that they need; and (5) to help maintain family stability.

One consequence of this broad array of functions is a lack of role clarity for social workers in their implementation. This problem has been compounded since the 1970s by other environmental factors, including the following:

• the emergence and expansion of other occupations within the human services field that compete with social work and contribute to the public's confusion over the specific domain of social workers
• the growing use of voluntary, nonprofit and private, for-profit agencies to deliver publicly funded social services, which has increased the difficulty of establishing clear occupational criteria for the performance of social services tasks
• the continuing separation of service and cash assistance functions in local departments of social services, accompanied by a growing trend toward the reestablishment of integrated or consolidated services around such themes as family preservation or reducing welfare dependency
• the growing attraction of private practice as a career option for social workers, which has increased the difficulty of attracting social workers for public social services positions and has enhanced the perception that social work is no longer a profession whose primary mission is to serve low-income populations
• differential funding patterns between and within states, which have created significant regional diversity in the allocation of social services responsibilities between baccalaureate- and master's-level social workers, which, in turn, has led to the development of different patterns of educational preparation.

Currently, the only arena in which social work roles have been conceptualized with some degree of clarity is that of child welfare (Wollons, 1993). In this arena there is a strong movement toward requiring a master's degree for all social workers, particularly in those departments that have developed intensive family preservation or reunification programs. Schools of social work, in cooperation with local departments of social services, have accessed federal Title IV-E funds to create both university-based education programs and agency-based staff development programs to attract individuals to careers in the public child welfare field (Zlotnick, 1993).

FUTURE OF PUBLIC SOCIAL SERVICES

Since the late 1960s there has been an enormous transfer of the social costs of private enterprise to the public sector. This has exacerbated what O'Connor (1973) termed "the fiscal crisis of the state." Between 1981 and 1992 the fiscal and social policies of the Reagan and Bush administrations, which were designed to reduce the costs of the U.S. social welfare system and to transfer responsibilities from the federal government to the states, attempted to solve this fiscal crisis without altering existing political and economic arrangements (Midgely, 1992). Ironically, they also produced a new phase in the cost-shifting process, especially in the area of the public social services: a partial transfer of the costs of economic transformation and growth, previously borne by the federal government, to state and local governments and a "resurgent" not-for-profit sector.

This reorientation of U.S. social policy has been accompanied by a variety of political and cultural developments that have serious implications for the future of the public social services. In response to more than a decade of concerted attacks on the effectiveness of government social services programs (Murray, 1984), there has been a general decline in the public's faith in government as a vehicle for solving complex social problems, even as the decentralization of responsibility for social services programs has accelerated. A major consequence of this shift has been a rising expectation that the not-for-profit and market sectors of the economy will fill the gaps produced by government spending cutbacks in the social services, health care, and education (Rodgers, 1988). During this same period the increasing plight and powerlessness of low-income groups have weakened the potential of these groups to advocate on their own behalf (Fabricant & Burghardt, 1992). The most recent consequence of these political and cultural developments is the 1994 Republican landslide and the shift in U.S. social policies it portends.

Another consequence has been the promotion of cost–benefit efficiency in the social services, where its application not only is difficult to apply but, in many cases, is antithetical to the purposes of the activities being evaluated. A fourth effect has been the growing push to "privatize" many social services functions, without a common understanding of either the meaning or implications of such a shift (Stoesz & Karger, 1992).

Despite these trends, the persistent environment of fiscal austerity that has produced widespread cutbacks in public social services, and the resurgence of long-standing prejudices against low-income service recipients, there are signs at federal, state, and local levels that alternative visions for the public social services are being developed (Institute for Policy Studies, 1989). Key components of these conceptions of the public social services include the following:

- an emphasis on universal, integrated, noncategorical, interdisciplinary, community-based services (for example, school-linked services or the Healthy Start program)
- a proactive, prevention-focused orientation
- the use of multicultural conceptual frameworks in the design and evaluation of services, as well as in the creation of methods of service intervention.

Proponents of each of these conceptions of the public social services recognize the connection between the need for the economic supports provided by cash assistance programs and the need for the psychosocial supports provided by government-funded social services. They acknowledge that efforts to promote purposeful social change in the interests of clients—which lie at the foundation of social work practice—must be incorporated into the fabric of service design and delivery. An underlying implication of these perspectives is the potential role of the public social services in social development and societal transformation. Whether these alternative visions will be realized to meet the challenges of the 21st century remains to be seen, particularly in the turbulent political and social climate of the next decade.

REFERENCES

Abramovitz, M. (1989). *Regulating the lives of women: Social welfare policy from colonial times to the present.* Boston: South End Press.

Banner, L. (1973). Religious benevolence as social control: A critique of an interpretation. *Journal of American History, 60*(1).

Barak, G. (1992). *Gimme shelter: A social history of homelessness in contemporary America.* New York: Praeger.

Bell, W. (1983). *Contemporary social welfare.* New York: Macmillan.

Bender, T. (1972). *Towards an urban vision: Ideas and institutions in 19th century America.* Baltimore: Johns Hopkins University Press.

Bixby, A. K. (1990). Public social welfare expenditures, fiscal years 1965–1987. *Social Security Bulletin, 53*(2), 10–26.

Center on Budget and Policy Priorities. (1984). *End results: The impact of federal policies since 1980 on low income Americans.* Washington, DC: Author.

Chambers, C. (1965). *Seedtime of reform: American social service and social action, 1918–1933.* Minneapolis: University of Minnesota Press.

Derthick, M. (1975). *Uncontrollable spending for social services grants.* Washington, DC: Brookings Institution.

Fabricant, M., & Burghardt, S. (1992). *The welfare state crisis and the transformation of social service work.* Armonk, NY: M. E. Sharpe.

Gilbert, N. (1977). The transformation of social services. *Social Services Review, 53*(3), 75–91.

Gutman, H. (1976). *Work, culture and society in industrializing America.* New York: Vintage Press.

Hall, P. D. (1974–1975). The model of Boston charity: A theory of charitable benevolence and class development. *Science and Society, 38*(1), 464–477.

Institute for Policy Studies. (1989). *Women, families and poverty: An alternative policy agenda for the nineties.* Washington, DC: Author.

Jansson, B. (1993). *The reluctant welfare state: A history of American social welfare policies* (2nd ed.). Pacific Grove, CA: Brooks/Cole.

Kahn, A. J., & Kamerman, S. (1976). The course of personal social services. *Public Welfare, 34*(2), 20–32.

Katz, M. (1986). *In the shadow of the poorhouse: A social history of welfare in America.* New York: Basic Books.

Kusmer, K. (1973). The functions of organized charity in the progressive era: Chicago as a case study. *Journal of American History, 60*(3), 657–678.

Mandler, P. (Ed.). (1990). *The uses of charity: The poor on relief in the 19th century metropolis.* Princeton, NJ: Princeton University Press.

Midgely, J. (Ed.). (1992, March). The Reagan legacy and the American welfare state [Special issue]. *Journal of Sociology and Social Welfare,* 1–183.

Murray, C. (1984). *Losing ground: American social policy, 1950–1980.* New York: Basic Books.

O'Connor, J. (1973). *The fiscal crisis of the state.* New York: St. Martin's Press.

Older Americans Act Amendments of 1967. P.L. 90-42, 81 Stat. 106.

Pumphrey, R., & Pumphrey, M. (Eds.). (1961). *The heritage of American social work.* New York: Columbia University Press.

Reisch, M., & Wenocur, S. (1982). Professionalization and voluntarism in social welfare: Changing roles and functions. *Journal of Voluntary Action Research, 11*(2–3), 11–31.

Rodgers, H., Jr. (Ed.). (1988). *Beyond welfare: New approaches to the problem of poverty in America.* Armonk, NY: M. E. Sharpe.

Rothman, D. (1971). *The discovery of the asylum: Social order and disorder in the new republic.* Boston: Little, Brown.

Rothman, D. (1980). *Conscience and convenience: The asylum and its alternatives in progressive America.* Boston: Little, Brown.

Social Security Act of 1935. Ch. 531, 49 Stat. 620.

Social Security Act Amendments of 1967. P.L. 97-35, 95 Stat. 72.

Stoesz, D., & Karger, H. (1992). *Reconstructing the American welfare state.* Boston: Rowman & Littlefield.

Titmuss, R. (1976). *Essays on the welfare state.* Boston: Beacon Press.

Tocqueville, A. de (1945). *Democracy in America* (P. Bradley, Trans.). New York: Knopf. (Original work published 1835)

Trattner, W. (1980). The federal government and social welfare in early 19th century America. In F. Breul & S. Diner (Eds.), *Compassion and responsibility: Readings in the history of social welfare policy in the U.S.* (pp. 156–168). Chicago: University of Chicago Press.

Trolander, J. (1987). *Professionalism and social change: From the settlement house movement to neighborhood centers, 1886–present.* New York: Columbia University Press.

Wenocur, S., & Reisch, M. (1989). *From charity to enterprise: The development of American social work in a market economy.* Urbana: University of Illinois Press.

Wollons, R. (Ed.). (1993). *Children at risk in America: History, conceptions and public policy.* Albany: State University of New York Press.

Yankey, J. (1987). Public social services. In A. Minahan (Ed.-in-Chief), *Encyclopedia of social work* (18th ed., Vol. 2, pp. 417–426). Silver Spring, MD: National Association of Social Workers.

Zlotnick, J. L. (1993). *Social work education and public human services: Developing partnerships.* Alexandria, VA: Council on Social Work Education.

FURTHER READING

Axinn, J., & Levin, H. (1992). *Social welfare: A history of American response to need* (3rd ed.). New York: Longman.

Blau, J. (1992). *The visible poor: Homelessness in the United States.* New York: Oxford University Press.

Costin, L., Bell, C., & Downs, S. (1991). *Child welfare: Policies and practice* (4th ed.). New York: Longman.

Funicello, T. (1993). *Tyranny of kindness: Dismantling the welfare system to end poverty in America.* New York: Atlantic Monthly Press.

Hahn, A. J. (1994). *The politics of caring: Human services at the local level.* San Francisco: Westview Press.

Jencks, C. (1993). *Rethinking social policy: Race, poverty and the underclass.* New York: Harper Perennial.

Karger, H., & Stoesz, D. (1994). *American social welfare policy: A pluralist approach* (2nd ed.). New York: Longman.

Katz, M. (1989). *The undeserving poor: From the war on poverty to the war on welfare.* New York: Pantheon.

Kaus, M. (1992). *The end of equality.* New York: Basic Books.

Morris, R. (1986). *Rethinking social welfare: Why care for the stranger?* New York: Longman.

Rochefort, D. (1993). *From poorhouses to homelessness: Policy analysis and mental health care.* Westport, CT: Auburn House.

Trattner, W. (1994). *From poor law to welfare state* (5th ed.). New York: Free Press.

Wronka, J. (1992). *Human rights and social policy in the 21st century.* Lanham, MD: University Press of America.

Michael Reisch, PhD, is director, School of Social Work, and professor of social work and public administration, San Francisco State University, 1600 Holloway Avenue, San Francisco, CA 94132.

For further information see

Aging: Public Policy Issues and Trends; Aid to Families with Dependent Children; Child Welfare Overview; Community Needs Assessment; Families Overview; Federal Social Legislation from 1961 to 1994; Homelessness; Housing; Hunger, Nutrition, and Food Programs; Income Security Overview; Jobs and Earnings; Organizations: Context for Social Services Delivery; Policy Analysis; Poverty; Public Health Services; Settlements and Neighborhood Centers; Social Planning; Social Security; Social Welfare Policy; Supplemental Security Income; Welfare Employment Programs: Evaluation.

Key Words

child welfare services	social security
income maintenance	welfare
public social services	

Public Social Welfare Expenditures

Ann Kallman Bixby

From its modest beginnings in public education and local charitable endeavors, the social welfare system in the United States has come to influence nearly every aspect of modern life. Retirement programs, public assistance, health and medical care, and education at all levels are some of the areas that are now government supported. This entry describes the system and traces its growth and development over the second half of the 20th century.

Although Workers' Compensation laws began to be passed in the early 1900s, it was the passage of the Social Security Act of 1935 that laid the foundation for the modern system. It inaugurated not only Old-Age and Survivors Insurance, but Unemployment Insurance and assistance programs as well. The War on Poverty of the 1960s increased the number and scope of social welfare programs, and the maturing of the social insurance system completed the current picture. In 1990 social welfare expenditures represented 19.2 percent of the gross domestic product and accounted for nearly 59 percent of all government spending. Precisely

Note: Statistics in this entry are from the social welfare expenditures database maintained by the Office of Research and Statistics, Social Security Administration.

what is involved in these expenditures is described below.

HISTORY OF SOCIAL WELFARE SPENDING

The Great Depression brought the federal government into the social welfare field. In 1933 the Federal Emergency Relief program began to assume the burden of supporting unemployed people. As a result, 1934 was the first year in which expenditures for public aid outstripped those for education, the bulk of that aid coming from federal coffers. In 1935, the Social Security Act established a national system of old-age insurance, a federal–state system of unemployment insurance, and federal programs of grants-in-aid to develop and strengthen state public assistance and other programs. At about the same time, legislation enacted a national system of retirement and unemployment insurance for workers in the railroad industry. State workers' compensation laws had been in force since the 1920s, so with the addition of State Temporary Disability Insurance in the 1940s the social insurance system we know today was substantially complete.

By the late 1940s the federal–state system of unemployment insurance accounted for 45 percent to 60 percent of all social insurance spending. In 1951 Old-Age and Survivors Insurance (OASI) became the leading component of that category. That lead grew with the addition of Disability Insurance in 1956 and of Health Insurance for the Aged (Medicare) in 1965. By 1970 the combined Social Security programs accounted for nearly 40 percent of all social welfare expenditures. No new programs have been added to the system since 1965, but the expansion of coverage under Social Security and Medicare, the aging of the insured population, and the rapid rise in the cost of health care have kept social insurance the principal component of social welfare spending. By the 1980s the category represented half of all social welfare expenditures; social security and Medicare represented a larger share of all federal spending than any activity except national defense or debt service. More than any other social, economic, or legislative change in the past 60 years, the Social Security Act of 1935 is responsible for the course that social welfare spending has taken.

In 1965 the federal government entered into health care financing. In addition to the enactment of Medicare, that year saw the creation of the federal–state system of Grants to States for Medical Assistance, commonly known as Medicaid. Both programs rapidly became major budget items. The number of people enrolled in Medicare grew to 34.2 million by 1990, and the cost of their care reached $106.8 billion. In the same year, Medicaid provided $72 billion worth of care to 25 million people. The cost of government-financed health care has risen in part because of the increasing size and age of the covered population, and in part because of the increasing sophistication and expense of medical technology. The cost of health care has increased faster than the cost of living as a whole; since the early 1980s, the medical care component of the consumer price index has risen twice as fast as the average for all items.

Public aid spending has undergone great change since the 1930s. By the beginning of World War II, the exigencies of the Great Depression raised the cost of public aid to over 40 percent of the social welfare total. During and after the war that percentage fell sharply, and by 1960 it was only 8 percent. Then the War on Poverty began.

The Food Stamp Program began paying benefits in 1961, the Economic Opportunity Act was passed in 1964, and Medicaid was enacted in 1965. By 1970, public aid represented more than 10 percent of social welfare spending.

In 1973 the federal–state programs of Old Age Assistance, Aid to the Blind, and Aid to the Permanently and Totally Disabled were replaced by a national program of Supplemental Security Income (SSI). This program mandated uniform eligibility standards and payment levels throughout the country. In many states that level was higher than the former state level, and as a result national expenditures increased. In fact, the amount spent on such "categorical assistance" increased 80 percent between 1973 and 1975. By 1980 public aid accounted for 15 percent of all social welfare spending, a percentage that has been fairly stable ever since.

The addition of new programs was one reason that social welfare expenditures grew during the 1960s and 1970s. Another reason was the state of the economy. The expansion in spending through the early 1970s was partly a result of higher prices and partly a result of the extension of services to a larger population, but mostly it resulted from real increases in the number and scope of programs available. This expansion was reflected in the growth of social welfare expenditures in real terms. In 1965, social welfare spending represented 11.5 percent of the gross national product (GNP); by 1975 it represented 19.0 percent. However, by 1975 inflation was responsible for more than half of the annual increase in social welfare spending. At the same time, expenditures for such recession-sensitive programs as food stamps, Aid to Families with Dependent Children (AFDC), and unemployment insurance increased. Furthermore, growth in the national output of goods and services diminished, also because of the recession. As a result, social welfare programs accounted for 19.5 percent of the GNP by 1976. In that year, nearly 60 percent of all government spending went toward social welfare purposes.

Since the late 1970s, there have been few changes in the social welfare universe. Inflation continued to be a factor in the annual rise in spending, as did the general economic climate. In the recession year of 1983, for example, social welfare again reached 19.5 percent of the GNP. The programs included and the populations served remained much the same from 1976 to 1990.

DEFINITION AND SCOPE

The Social Security Administration (SSA) defines public social welfare expenditures as "the cash benefits, services, and administrative costs of all programs operating under public law that are of direct benefit to individuals and families." SSA has maintained a series of annual reports on public social welfare programs since the 1950s. The major technical characteristics of reports in this series can be summarized as follows:

1. Reports cover income maintenance, health care, education, housing, veterans' benefits, and other welfare services directed specifically toward promoting the economic and social welfare of individuals and families.
2. Data are maintained on a fiscal year basis and include expenditures from both general revenues and trust funds. The data include administrative expenditures, research and training costs, and capital outlays.
3. Loans are not included in the reports. Because loans are expected to be repaid, they are not expected to affect the net cost to government of a program or service, which is the focus of reports in the series.
4. The data are shown by source of funds, and federal, state, and local expenditures are included.
5. The economic status of the individual or family is not a criterion for including a program in the series. Rather, the requirement is that the funds be expended through the government apparatus, or in compliance with or as a result of public law.

Although the characteristics of the series have remained the same since its inception, the universe that the series describes has changed dramatically. In 1929, the first year for which data are available, social welfare expenditures accounted for less than 4 percent of the GNP. By far the largest component of expenditures was education

(60 percent), then, as now, largely a state and local responsibility. Federal spending mostly was confined to veterans' benefits and staff retirement systems and accounted for only one-fifth of the total.

In 1990 social welfare spending accounted for more than 19 percent of the GNP. The largest component of expenditures was social insurance programs (including social security and Medicare), which represented 49 percent of the total. Federal funds paid for 59 percent of total social welfare spending, and trust fund monies accounted for 64 percent of the federal amount.

SOCIAL WELFARE SPENDING MEASUREMENT

The statistical system used to measure social welfare expenditures had its beginnings in the early 1940s. The depression-driven increase in federal spending for social welfare purposes led to the need for a measurement of the programs' success in meeting the economic needs of the population and the policy objectives of the government. To this end, the Social Security Administration compiled a data series on spending for social insurance and related public programs, including the retirement, disability, and survivor programs administered by SSA, the Railroad Retirement Board, the Civil Service Commission, and the Veterans Administration, as well as the benefits paid under the unemployment insurance system. This information was first published in January 1942.

At about the same time, the proportion of national income allocated to social welfare in various countries became a topic of discussion at the United Nations. As a result, the U.S. delegation requested statistics on all U.S. social welfare spending. The first estimates were prepared by SSA during 1951. To allow international comparisons, public aid, education, and housing data were included with the social insurance figures, as well as some veterans' welfare benefits that had previously been omitted. When the data were published in October 1951, they described conceptually the same universe as data published more than 40 years later in the summer of 1992.

During the 1950s the series began to use three standard economic indicators to measure the growth and significance of the nation's investment in social welfare: (1) the relationship between social welfare expenditures and the GNP,[1]

---

[1]In 1992, the indicator was changed to the gross domestic product (GDP), in conformity with a decision by the Bureau of Economic Analysis, U.S. Department of Commerce, to use GDP as the primary measure of production. The essential difference between GNP and GDP is that GDP measures goods and services *produced by labor and property located in the United States,* regard-

TABLE 1

Social Welfare Expenditures under Public Programs as Percentage of Gross Domestic Product, Selected Fiscal Years 1965 to 1990

Program	1965	1970	1975	1980	1985	1990
Total social welfare[a]	12	15	19	19	18	19
Social insurance	4	6	8	9	9	9
Public aid	1	2	3	3	3	3
Health and medical programs	1	1	1	1	1	1
Veterans' programs	1	1	1	1	1	1
Education	4	5	5	5	4	5
Other social welfare	0	0	1	1	0	0
Total health care cost[b]	1	3	3	4	4	5

[a]Includes housing, not shown separately.
[b]Combines "health and medical programs" with medical services provided in connection with social insurance, public aid, veterans', and "other social welfare" programs.

(2) per capita expenditures expressed in constant dollars, and (3) percentage of government expenditures for all purposes that was devoted to social welfare. Later SSA found it useful also to measure the proportion of social welfare spending that came from federal funds. Tables 1 through 4 present these four measures for selected years between 1965 and 1990.

Health and medical care spending has presented a special problem in the categorization of expenditures. When the series was originally developed, it was decided that "health and medical care expenditures made as incident to other welfare programs be included in the totals for those programs." In the mid-1950s this procedure caused few problems, but the 1960s saw the enactment of two large-scale public medical programs—Medicare and Medicaid—and these too were classified "as incident to" their parent programs of Old-Age, Survivors and Disability Insurance (OASDI) and public assistance. As the programs have grown, this classification scheme has enlarged the social insurance and public aid

less of the residency status of the workers or owners, whereas GNP measures goods and services *produced by labor and property supplied by U.S. residents,* regardless of their geographic location. The GDP is, therefore, more consistent in coverage with other indicators such as employment, industry output, and capital investment, which are concerned solely with the United States. In 1990, social welfare represented 19.1 percent of both GNP and GDP.

categories to which Medicare and Medicaid have been respectively assigned. Therefore, in later years an additional exhibit category—that of "total health care costs"—was added. All functionally health- and medical-related expenses are assigned to this category, regardless of their statutory provenance. In 1990, the "health and medical care" category itself showed expenditures of $62 billion, whereas the exhibit category of "total health care costs" accounted for $272 billion. Seventy percent of the difference between the two categories is attributable to the Medicare and Medicaid programs.

TRENDS IN SOCIAL WELFARE

Before the Great Depression, state and local governments accounted for the bulk of social welfare spending and most of the money spent on education. The New Deal programs brought the federal government into the realms of relief and social insurance, culminating in the Social Security Act of 1935. That act created the architecture of the present system: The social security programs of Old-Age and Survivors Insurance, Disability Insurance, and Medicare; unemployment insurance; and AFDC were all included in the act, as was a program of Old Age Assistance that was later subsumed under Supplemental Security Income.

World War II and its aftermath expanded the system of veterans' benefits, particularly with respect to education and housing. During the 1950s and early 1960s, the social insurance programs were expanded and their coverage increased as the population grew and the programs matured.

The War on Poverty of the mid- to late 1960s, and the creation of Medicare and Medicaid, opened new vistas in the social welfare field; by the mid-1970s the current constellation of programs was virtually complete. For the next 10 years, social welfare spending responded to the cycles of inflation and recession, with no essential change in the social welfare universe itself.

Since 1984, social welfare expenditures have been essentially stable, growing annually more in response to inflation than to new populations or programs. Contributing to that annual growth are the mature social insurance programs; nearly half of all social welfare spending was in that category in 1990. Education expenditures account for one-fourth and public aid for about 15 percent of the total, and the remainder is spread out over the health, veterans', housing, and other social welfare programs. The one continuing change has been the growth in "total health care costs." This category has increased steadily, from 12 percent of all

TABLE 2

Public Social Welfare Expenditures and Expenditures per Capita, in Constant (1990) Dollars, Selected Fiscal Years 1965 to 1990

	1965	1975	1985	1990
Total social welfare	$296,880,000	$676,397,000	$903,684,000	$1,042,858,000
per capita	1,510	3,085	3,721	4,110
Social insurance	108,074,000	287,286,000	453,552,000 •	508,634,000
per capita	550	1,310	1,868	2,004
Public aid	24,266,000	97,217,000	121,176,000	145,642,000
per capita	123	443	499	574
Health and medical programs	23,770,000	39,270,000	48,113,000	62,428,000
per capita	121	179	198	246
Veterans' programs	23,018,000	39,571,000	33,068,000	30,397,000
per capita	117	180	136	120
Education	108,407,000	189,529,000	211,942,000	258,367,000
per capita	551	864	873	1,018
Housing	1,228,000	7,440,000	15,521,000	19,468,000
per capita	6	34	64	77
Other social welfare	7,977,000	16,294,000	16,696,000	17,918,000
per capita	41	74	69	71
Total health care cost[a]	36,395,000	120,566,000	211,025,000	271,530,000
per capita	185	550	869	1,070

NOTE: Data exclude expenditures in foreign countries for social security benefits, civil service retirement benefits, veterans' programs, and education.
[a]Combines "health and medical programs" with medical services provided in connection with social insurance, public aid, veterans', and "other social welfare" programs.

TABLE 3

Social Welfare Expenditures from Public Funds as Percentage of Government Expenditures for All Purposes, Selected Fiscal Years 1965 to 1990

Type of Fund	1965	1975	1985	1990
All public social welfare expenditures				
Total, as percent of all government expenditures	42.2	56.6	52.2	56.6
Federal, as percent of all federal expenditures	32.6	53.7	48.7	51.1
State and local, as percent of all state and local expenditures[a]	60.4	61.6	59.9	68.2
Trust fund social welfare expenditures				
Total, as percent of all government expenditures	14.3	22.2	25.0	26.1
Federal, as percent of all federal expenditures	17.7	29.1	31.4	33.0
State and local, as percent of all state and local expenditures[a]	7.8	10.5	10.7	11.5
Non–trust fund social welfare expenditures				
Total, as percent of all government expenditures	27.8	45.1	37.2	41.2
Federal, as percent of all federal expenditures	14.8	35.8	26.3	27.1
State and local, as percent of all state and local expenditures[a]	52.6	57.1	55.1	64.1

NOTE: Data exclude that part of workers' compensation and temporary disability insurance payments made through private carriers and self-insurers.
[a]From state and local sources only; excludes federal grants.

expenditures in 1965 to 26 percent in 1990. In spite of current efforts to contain health care costs, that percentage does not seem likely to decline in the near future.

Social welfare expenditures have represented 50 percent to 60 percent of all government spending since 1970, with the federal government spending 45 percent to 55 percent of its funds on social welfare, and the states and localities spending 60 percent to 70 percent.

CONCLUSION

The growth in social welfare spending has resulted partly from growth in population and partly from rising prices, but the major contributor has been the increase in the range of social programs. The maturing social insurance system—most notably the Social Security and Medicare programs—has made such spending a cornerstone of our domestic and political economy. More than

TABLE 4

Social Welfare Expenditures under Public Programs: Federal Funds as Percentage of Total Expenditures, Selected Fiscal Years 1965 to 1990

Program	1965	1975	1985	1990
Total social welfare	48.8	57.7	61.6	58.7
Social insurance	77.5	81.1	83.9	82.1
Public aid	57.2	65.8	64.5	63.6
Health and medical programs	43.2	47.1	6.2	44.1
Veterans' programs	99.7	97.4	98.8	98.4
Education	8.8	10.7	8.0	7.1
Housing	74.9	80.1	87.8	85.3
Other social welfare	38.9	61.4	55.7	49.7
Total health care cost[a]	47.6	65.1	71.3	69.2

[a]Combines "health and medical programs" with medical services provided in connection with social insurance, public aid, veterans', and "other social welfare" programs.

95 percent of earnings from employment are covered by a government-sponsored retirement system—federal, state, or local—and more than 90 percent are covered by Unemployment Insurance. Social welfare programs will continue to play a central role in the foreseeable future, although the system may have to be redefined somewhat in the face of growing financial constrictions.

REFERENCES

Economic Opportunity Act of 1964. PL. 88-452, 78 Stat. 508.

Elementary and Secondary Education Act of 1965. PL. 89-10, 79 Stat. 27.

Social Security Act of 1935. PL. 100-360, 49 Stat. 620.

FURTHER READING

Bixby, A. K. (1992, Summer). Public social welfare expenditures, fiscal year 1989. *Social Security Bulletin*, pp. 61–68.

Bixby, A. K. (1992, Winter). Overview of social welfare expenditures, fiscal year 1990. *Social Security Bulletin*, pp. 54–56.

Kerns, W. L. (1992, Fall). Private social welfare expenditures, 1972–90. *Social Security Bulletin*, pp. 59–66.

Lampman, R. J. (1984). *Social welfare spending: Accounting for changes from 1950 to 1978*. Orlando, FL: Academic Press.

Merriam, I. C., & Skolnik, A. M. (1968). *Social welfare expenditures under public programs in the United States, 1929–66*. Research Report No. 25, Office of Research and Statistics, Social Security Administration, U.S. Department of Health, Education and Welfare. Washington, DC: U.S. Government Printing Office.

Ann Kallman Bixby is social science research analyst, Social Security Administration, Office of Research and Statistics, 4301 Connecticut Avenue, NW, Room 203, Washington, DC 20008.

For further information see

Aid to Families with Dependent Children; Economic Analysis; Hunger, Nutrition, and Food Programs; Income Distribution; Income Security Overview; Public Social Services; Social Security; Social Welfare History; Social Welfare Policy; Veterans and Veterans Services; Welfare Employment Programs: Evaluation.

Key Words	
appropriations	social security
income security	welfare

Puerto Ricans

See Hispanics: Puerto Ricans

Purchasing Social Services
Margaret Gibelman

Government, the chief financier of human services in the United States, widely uses *purchase of service (POS)*—an organized procedure by which a government entity enters into a formal agreement with another entity to procure goods and services—at all levels. POS concerns the act of transmitting public dollars to private service providers. Inherent in this transfer are decisions about how services are best delivered. Thus, decisions about how and from whom government chooses to purchase goods and services profoundly influence the nature of the social services delivery system.

This entry provides an overview of the purchase of social services within the context of several competing social goals and values. These goals and values include the ongoing effort to limit the size and scope of the government bureaucracy; promote privatization—the shift of some functions and responsibilities from government to the private sector—of many formerly government functions; and develop and use collaborative relationships with the private sector to achieve public purposes. Perceptions about the appropriate role of government significantly affect decisions about POS. The focus of this entry is on the purchase of services that concern the prevention, amelioration, or resolution of health, mental health, social, or environmental problems that afflict individuals, families, specific groups, or communities. The entry also emphasizes those services purchased from voluntary agencies.

How POS Works

Government purchases services from nonprofit and for-profit organizations, from groups of practitioners and individual practitioners, and from other government units (Gibelman & Demone, 1989). Although for-profit organizations are relative newcomers to human services contracting, they have fast become competitors with their not-for-profit counterparts.

Government contracting for social services has traditionally been smaller in scale, both absolutely and proportionately, than contracting for other government services, such as defense. Nevertheless, POS presently is the dominant means for delivering social services. By the early 1990s, contracting for social services with nonprofit organizations had become a $15 billion-a-year business (Rathgeb Smith & Lipsey, 1993).

The use of voluntary and proprietary agencies to provide government-financed services does not alter the public nature of the service. The intent of POS is to fulfill government's responsibilities in the most cost-effective, efficient, and qualitative manner. Government pays for these services

through taxes or user fees (Ruchelman, 1989). The decision to finance a human service and the decision about how to produce or provide that service may be made on the basis of different criteria.

It is impossible to identify all human services that are purchased because of the variations in contracting across states and localities and the changes within each jurisdiction that occur over time in decision making about what should be purchased. The possibilities are as broad as the entire human services industry. Services purchased include mental health, emergency shelters for homeless people, group homes, day care, child protective services, foster care, mental health services, residential care, mental retardation services, services to pregnant and parenting teenagers, substance abuse, pupil personnel services, and psychiatric hospital care. In some instances, the decision to purchase services may be motivated by the more rapid start-up capability of the private sector and its perceived responsiveness to the need for innovative programming. In other instances, precedent may play an important role in decision making.

POS constitutes only one of several options to plan and deliver services. Government has the choice of providing a service directly, such as investigating cases of child abuse and neglect by state or local agencies, or turning to another organization—perhaps another government unit, a nonprofit agency, a proprietary organization, or an individual contractor—to provide the product or service. Government may also choose a hybrid model, in which it directly provides a service, such as child protective services, but concurrently purchases the same service from community agencies. Criticisms of this latter model, though, have concerned the potential for "creaming" the best clients by the voluntary agencies (Gibelman, 1981). (The term creaming has been associated with the selection of those clients who possess "desirable" social characteristics such as the more verbal or less disturbed [Miller, deVos van Steenwijk & Roby, 1970].) In the voucher model, the extreme form of POS, the decision about service provider is left to the individual consumer, who then purchases the service directly. That model, however, has been more widely discussed than implemented, and its immediate application has been sought mostly in housing and education.

EVOLUTION OF POS

Traditionally, state and local governments have elected to meet a part of their responsibilities through financing the provision of care and services by nongovernmental organizations. The general satisfaction with these arrangements is evident in their continued and expanded use. POS is both consistent with and an example of privatization. POS, however, is as much a practical, freestanding technology as it is an ideological preference (Gibelman & Demone, in press).

Major Alternative for Service Delivery—1960s

Although purchasing social services has been practiced in some form since the earliest days of American social welfare, it was not until the early 1960s that POS became a major alternative for service delivery. The 1962 amendments to the Social Security Act of 1935 authorized, for the first time, states to enter into agreements with other public agencies for services that the agencies could more economically provide (Slack, 1979). The 1967 amendments to the act extended the authority of states to purchase services from nonprofit or proprietary providers in addition to other state or local public agencies.

A growing disenchantment with the value of public services, as well as increased skepticism about the efficacy of public services provision, resulted in a new emphasis on private sector linkages. By 1969, nearly all restrictive language about the use of POS was dropped from regulations, with new rules promulgated to encourage states to increase their use of contracting (Gibelman & Demone, 1989). At the same time, Medicaid and Medicare were implemented through private vendors, institutionalizing the large-scale use of the private market for the delivery of publicly funded services.

Broader Statutory Authority—1970s

Broadened statutory authority for POS resulted in the escalated use of these arrangements. Such authority is found in each successive amendment to the Social Security Act and related human services legislation, such as the Comprehensive Employment and Training Act of 1973, which encouraged the use of community-based organizations to develop training and educational programs; the 1973 amendments to the Older

Americans Act of 1965, which required states to create local area agencies on aging using appropriate community providers to actually deliver services; and the Family Planning Services and Population Research Act of 1970, which authorized grants and contracts to provide voluntary family planning services (Terrell, 1987). Other stimulating factors included federal financial incentives to develop such arrangements; states' interest in maximizing federal funds; and the perceived advantages of private sector delivery, including increased flexibility, higher standards, cost-effectiveness, and control of staff size (Gibelman & Demone, in press).

Removal of Constraints—1980s

The original intent of POS was to provide an alternative means of delivering services that would better achieve public purposes. It was, in essence, a tool to achieve specific ends that was developed incrementally. As the concept and practice has evolved, however, POS for some people has become a means to further the goal of "the least government is the best government." The Reagan and Bush administrations made clear that the private sector was the provider of choice and any remaining constraints to POS were removed. In this respect, POS and privatization have been viewed as ideologically compatible, with POS representing one means to accomplish public divestiture. It represents a midpoint between predominantly government provision and total privatization (Gibelman & Demone, in press).

WHY PURCHASE SERVICES?

POS is an attractive service delivery option from the perspective of both government and the private sector. In recent years, there has been a growing body of knowledge about the process and outcome of contracting for services and the issues arising from its use. Claims and counterclaims have concerned the weaknesses and strengths of this form of service delivery based on the respective experiences of government and contracted agencies. The identified advantages of POS have included cost savings, administrative efficiency, quick program start-up and termination, program flexibility, lack of bureaucratic red tape, enhanced quality of services, higher level of professionalism, flexible use of personnel, partnership building with the private sector, promotion of innovation and competition, political climate and citizen preferences, and reduction in the size and role of government (Ferris, 1993; Gibelman & Demone, 1989; Gibelman & Demone, in press; Ruchelman, 1989). Both opponents and proponents of POS have sometimes used similar arguments. For example, proponents of POS have argued that use of POS arrangements leads to cost savings, whereas opponents have viewed the cost savings as largely illusive and unsubstantiated. When both sides lay claim to the same benefits, empirical support is typically lacking.

The identified disadvantages of POS have included the loss of public control and accountability, the lack of mechanisms to ensure standards, the increased cost of service, poorer quality services, tendency of voluntary agencies to "cream" the better clients and not service the most needy, the unreliability of contractors, and the difficulty of monitoring purchased programs and services. Arguments against POS, made from the perspective of contracted agencies, have included the potential loss of autonomy for private agencies and the problems associated with subjecting private agencies to public policy shifts (Gibelman & Demone, in press; Rathgeb Smith & Lipsey, 1993).

BOUNDARIES OF POS

The boundaries of POS arrangements are continually expanding within the broader context of the privatization movement. Several human services areas that were exclusively within the province of government, including social security, are now under reexamination to identify whether there are alternative means of delivering them (Kenworthy & Dewar, 1990).

Increased Use of Private Sector

The extent to which POS dominates a particular human services field is subject to a wide range of influences, including traditional practices, political and philosophical forces, and prevailing social and political values and preferences affecting social welfare policies and programs. Changing conceptions about the roles and functions of government and the private sector within American society affect the degree to which preference is given to alternative service delivery methods. In this regard, proponents of POS have promoted it as a means to actualize privatization (albeit, still using public funds). The use of nonprofit and for-profit human services providers as an alternative to public service delivery is consistent with current political preferences and a realistic and effective way to deal with negative public sentiment about government's perceived burgeoning role in this society.

The Reagan and Bush administrations shared a basic commitment to reducing the size and power of government, a philosophy based on the assumption that the private sector can conduct

business more efficiently and effectively than government (Rowen, 1986). Kettner and Martin (1993) summarized the various rationales used by advocates to justify privatization:

greater private sector involvement in the delivery of public programs and services would lead to: (1) more emphasis on performance and less emphasis on conducting business-as-usual; (2) more emphasis on rational decision making and less emphasis on political decision making; and (3) more emphasis on accountability and consumer preferences and less emphasis on the preferences of public administrators. (p. 90)

The use of the private sector is a strategy that has widespread political and citizen support. The ultimate goal is to have the private sector assume responsibility for both service delivery and service funding and to encourage the use of market criteria to control costs and ensure quality. The compromise, as seen during the Reagan and Bush years, is the use of the private market through the continued growth of POS, with government maintaining its role as chief financier. POS has proven to be remarkably consistent with the basic philosophical bent of the Republican domination from 1980 to 1992: the less government is the best government, government should get out of the business of direct service delivery, and formerly government functions should be relegated to the private sector (Gibelman & Demone, 1989; Palmer & Sawhill, 1982; Rathgeb Smith & Lipsey, 1993).

Impact on Voluntary Agencies

A common prediction in the early 1980s, as the blueprint for Reaganomics took shape, was that government cutbacks in human services funding would substantially curtail purchase of services and, as a result, cripple voluntary agencies that had become dependent on contracted funds. This scenario turned out to be incorrect. Voluntary agency networks found ways to cope, and many prospered (Gibelman & Demone, 1990).

The annual *profiles,* that is, fund distribution results by agency and program, published by the United Way of America (1981, 1982, 1986, 1987, 1988) revealed that agencies highly dependent on government support and most at risk for losing income with the advent of Reaganomics fared better than expected. These agencies included those that offered services to the aging, information and referral, community and neighborhood development, and day care. These agencies diversified their sources of funding; increased fees for service; raised revenues from other sources; received more help from United Way of America (if members); tightened management controls; and most important, persuaded state and local governments to compensate for federal budget reductions. Similar findings were found in regard to national voluntary health agencies, which survived and typically prospered during the Reagan years (Gibelman, 1990). POS continued to be a primary vehicle: there was a decrease in federal purchase of social services, but an increase in state and local contracting.

POS: An Alternative to Public Services Provision

POS helps to achieve practical political purposes. Dating back to the presidency of Jimmy Carter, there have been consistent efforts to trim the size of the bureaucracy. In 1993, President Clinton introduced a plan to "reinvent government," a response designed to address the negative sentiments about government. The president's plan seeks to cut 252,000 federal government positions over a five-year period, reducing the civil service by 12 percent. If achieved, this reduction in force would result in a bureaucracy smaller in size than it has been since 1966 (Barr, 1993a). This initiative is part of a systematic effort to cut costs while improving services and program effectiveness. Reducing the size and cost of government has broad-based political and popular appeal.

President Clinton's expanded domestic agenda is compatible with a decreased bureaucracy. POS offers the Clinton administration a logical alternative to accomplish both goals of reducing the size and cost of government while expanding selected social welfare programs, building on established and popular precedent. Over the past 30 years, the government's service delivery role has steadily eroded, with the gradual transfer of functions to the private sector through POS. Although it is difficult to determine exactly how much money is saved by contracting out, the appearance of substantial cost savings serves an important symbolic agenda.

The extent to which POS has already served as an alternative to public services provision is evident in the shifts that have occurred in the social work labor force. In 1961, immediately before the use of POS was legitimized as an alternative service delivery strategy in the 1962 amendments to the Social Security Act of 1935, government at the federal, state, or municipal level was the major employer of social workers. A 1960 survey of NASW members (Becker, 1961) revealed that more than 52 percent of the membership worked for federal, state, county, and municipal governmental agencies.

Over a 30-year period, this situation has significantly changed, in large part because federal, state, and local governments have come to rely on voluntary agencies to deliver the more intensive professionalized services. By 1993, only 31.1 percent of a sample of NASW members reported that they worked under government auspices, including military, federal, state, and local (Gibelman & Schervish, 1993b). A proportion of this decrease can probably be attributed to declassification, that is, the reduction in standards of professional education and work-related experience for public social service jobs. But the decrease in social services personnel in the public sector has been offset by a more than commensurate increase in the proportion of social workers employed in voluntary and for-profit organizations. Many of the positions created in the private sector are the direct result of POS contracting (Gibelman & Schervish, 1993a).

Changing Nature of Public–Private Relations

Positive Impacts

The explosion in the use of POS arrangements has permanently altered the relationship between government and the voluntary and proprietary sectors. Many of the impacts have been positive. Voluntary agencies have had to develop new management competencies, ranging from contract negotiating skills to financial accountability. POS has also resulted in the introduction of programs and services previously unavailable, as well as the start-up of new voluntary agencies or an increase in the scope of the services provided by existing voluntary agencies. For example, new authorizing legislation at the federal and state levels has resulted in the initiation or expansion of voluntary agency services to victims of crime, a category of provision that had been largely nonexistent before the early 1980s, with the exception of child abuse. From government's point of view, a key advantage in initiating services to victims of crime through contracts with voluntary agencies was the quick start-up capability of nonprofit organizations and the ease of terminating the contractual agreement when funding lagged (Rathgeb Smith, 1989). From the viewpoint of the voluntary agencies, federal funds, even when accompanied by regulations and program requirements that altered the way in which business was conducted, provided a means to expand services. The downside, of course, was the impact on these same agencies when contract funds were reduced.

The greater interaction between the public and private sectors that has been the natural consequence of POS has intensified the dialogue about the appropriate relationship between the two sectors. A component of the debate has concerned the perceived dichotomy between government's search for accountability and the desire of nonprofit organizations to preserve autonomy. As Ferris (1993) noted, voluntary agencies have always been accountable, but their primary constituency group typically comprised a board of directors, donors, and volunteers in charitable markets. Now, government has instilled its own set of accountability requirements, which may be instead of, in addition to, or in conflict with the nonprofit organizations' traditional accountability channels.

Change in Power Relationship

In the earlier days of POS, voluntary agencies were in a positive position. In the absence of precedents, the public and voluntary agencies worked together as partners to define and implement contractual arrangements. Voluntary agencies could propose and initiate the contracting process; they had the expertise that government sorely needed. In general, government funds through contracts represented only one of several diverse funding sources for voluntary agencies; whereas contracts were an attractive source of revenue to expand services or fund new services, procurement of such funds typically was an issue of augmentation rather than survival.

The power relationship has substantially changed. Goldstein (1993) has bemoaned the transformation of private charities into "agents of the state" (p. 41). POS regulations have been altered over the years to allow purchasing from proprietary agencies. Thus, voluntary agencies now compete not only with other voluntary agencies for contracts, but vie with for-profit organizations as well. The for-profit agencies generally have developed a high level of technical competence in contract writing and negotiating compared with nonprofit organizations, in large part because they have devoted personnel and resources to capacity-building in this area. Furthermore, voluntary agencies have come to depend on contract funds for many of their programs and services. The resulting financial dependence has dramatically altered the power relationship between the sectors. Moreover, bureaucratic rules and regulations governing contract negotiations, rate setting, and monitoring and evaluation have multiplied as a consequence of a new POS specialization within the public sector and implementation experience.

The rise of a contract industry within the public sector has encumbered the contracting pro-

cess, adding to the complexity of negotiations and inevitable time delays. Rules now focus not only on the outcome of POS services, but also the process in which programs and services are carried out. For example, contracting specifications may prescribe the number of social worker-client contacts or detail client eligibility criteria, allowing little room for discretion: "The effect was that a recently enlarged voluntary service sector suddenly faced the combination of fluctuating demand, declining availability of resources, and increased inter- and intra-sectoral competition for both clients and dollars" (McMurtry, Netting, & Kettner, 1990, p. 68).

The competitive advantage of nonprofit organizations thus has given way to a more defensive and reactive posture. Year-to-year funding has created a degree of financial uncertainty that taxes the ability of agencies to engage in long-range program and fiscal planning and leaves staff uncertain about their future employment. As the proportion of total agency revenues from POS increases, voluntary agencies also have found themselves resource dependent on government. The greater the dependence of an organization on resources that an outside source controls, the greater the influence of that external funding source (Hasenfeld, 1992). Resource dependence also tends to rechannel organizational time and energy to maintain interorganizational relationships that promote or enhance an agency's competitive position.

Goal Displacement

The tendency for POS to encourage, if not directly lead to, goal displacement has been one of the important unintended consequences of these arrangements, with long-term implications for voluntary social welfare agencies. With the proliferation of requests for proposals for new and expanding services, many voluntary agencies have responded by enlarging their domain. For example, a senior center may provide transportation services because public funds for planning and implementing that service are available. McMurtry et al. (1990) called this domain expansion *vertical integration,* in which the range of target groups served or type of services offered is broadened. This expansion resulted in two primary issues. First, the areas of expansion followed the money trail and were not necessarily program development priority areas determined by the agency's board of directors. Second, once the new program or service was initiated, typically with the agency assuming planning and start-up expenses, it developed a constituency of staff and clients. Thus, in the eventuality that POS funds dried up in the particular area, pressure would likely be brought to bear on the agency to continue the program or service as part of the agency's core offerings.

With varying degrees of specificity, each non-profit organization's bylaws spell out its mission, including the social problems it addresses, the programs and services it offers, and the populations it serves. For example, the purpose of a voluntary child welfare agency may be to seek permanent homes for children through adoption. The agency, however, may seek and receive a contract to provide foster care services, including home studies of potential foster parents and placement and monitoring of children in foster care. Such "opportunity-seizing" initiatives, in response to the availability of contract funds, may be only tangentially related to the organization's overall mission and goals. The board of directors may decide to modify the organization's mission to encompass its new program direction. But in most cases, the organization's mission statement will not change. The organization will hire foster care program staff under contracted funds, and the community will learn about and support the program. The contracted program is justified on the basis of its quality, the added resources it brings to the organization, and the void it fills within the community.

This example highlights a dilemma facing many nonprofit organizations engaged in contracting: the extent to which organizational maintenance and growth needs take precedence over organizational mission. The contracted foster care program in the example may become larger in scope and resources than the adoption program. Because the shifting of program resources, size, and priority may occur over time, program directions are decided by default rather than by established agency decision-making processes. When and if the contract funds are cut back or terminated, the agency faces critical issues about how it will use organizational resources. Will the foster care program be continued as part of the core agency offerings? On what basis will the agency allocate resources between the adoption and foster care programs?

When organizations seek to take advantage of available funding, they must consider the start-up costs involved in program development, as well as the potential impact on the cohesiveness and morale of staff (Edwards & Yankey, 1991). The potential of goal displacement is diminished in for-profit agencies because they operate on the basis of profitability: a program or service, at a minimum, must be self-supporting.

The environment in which nonprofit organizations function has become more turbulent as a result of POS; nonprofit agencies exert less control over decision-making processes that affect them. The advent of a contracting industry within the public sector has subjected nonprofit organizations to the schedules and bureaucratic processes of government. Delays in contract negotiations, particularly in regard to program renewals, can have devastating effects on the cash flow of the voluntary agency and can even necessitate staff layoffs or a search for other external funds to continue the program or service (McMurtry et al., 1990). The repercussions for the voluntary agencies can be long-term—overload and staff burnout, loss of valuable staff, and disruptions of operations. For example, at the national level, the Clinton administration's initial delay in appointing senior officials involved in contract decisions hampered the flow of government contracts worth hundreds of millions of dollars, thus threatening the operations and even survival of companies that depend on such funds (Southerland, 1993).

POS has also had an impact on the internal operations of voluntary agencies. Fiscal management, with multiple reporting sources and perhaps different financial monitoring procedure requirements, has complicated fiscal operations. Similarly, different funding sources may have different accountability requirements, tending to increase the time and effort professional staff must devote to paperwork. The only real power the voluntary agency can exercise over these requirements and the more general uncertainties inherent in the contract relationship is to say *no* to the contract process or product. A voluntary agency can request, negotiate, manipulate, or bargain for timely contract renewals, reasonable rate setting, less paperwork, or more discretion. Ultimately, though, the only absolute power the nonprofit agency has is to withdraw from the relationship.

OUTCOMES

How effective are POS arrangements, that is, what is their impact on quality of services, access to services, quantity of services, or cost of services? Typically, when an agency decides to contract for services, there is a concomitant decision to decrease or eliminate public provision of that same service. Alternatively, the public agency may decide to provide some components of a service, but contract out other components. For example, a public child protective services agency may maintain the investigative function, but purchase family preservation services for substantiated cases of child abuse. Because the public and contracted agencies often do not offer the same service, it is difficult to substantiate the claim that purchased services are qualitatively superior to or more cost-effective than publicly provided services. There is no basis for comparison. A complicating issue is that there is no standard or objective definition of quality; quality is more a relative than absolute measure.

There are indices of quality, however, such as professional qualifications of the staff delivering services; frequency of contacts with clients; types of services provided (concrete versus soft); and staff-client ratios. Using such indices, Gibelman (1983), in examining child protective services, found that contracted voluntary agencies offered more intense, diverse, and frequent services than did the public agency. However, replication studies using indices of quality are limited by the lack of available comparative data. Qualitative comparisons between contracted agencies providing the same or similar services to similar client populations may offer more fruitful findings than comparisons of public versus private services.

Evaluations of POS also have tended to focus more on process than outcome, largely because of the difficulty in defining specific performance standards. Judgments about the success of POS arrangements depend on the articulation of clear and measurable outcome expectations. Hence, POS suffers from the same dearth of outcome measurements that have characterized most social services interventions.

Advocates have justified and promoted POS on the basis of cost savings, a variable that may be more amenable to measurement. However, an early study of the costs of direct delivery versus purchased services (Pacific Consultants, 1979) raised questions about actual cost savings. More recently, Stein (1990) reported no significant cost savings from POS on the basis of either expenditures or labor force. Savings are more likely to accrue in regard to input costs such as capital and start-up. But such savings may be negated by the added *transactional cost*—the cost of the contracting process itself, including contractor selection, monitoring, and enforcement. POS may actually cost taxpayers more when contracted overhead rates are considered. However, POS unencumbers government, a benefit factor not easily calculated. Cost-benefits include the range of variables that motivate government to enter contractual relationships, most of which have little to do with dollars.

PROBLEMS WITH CONTRACTING

By the mid-1980s, POS had come under considerable scrutiny and attack and social services contracting has not been immune. Criticisms range from inadequate accounting procedures to ineffective services. Frequent and numerous headlines about allegations, investigations, and outright scandals concerning contracted services appear in major U.S. newspapers. For example, front-page newspaper articles about space program contractors running up a $30 million tab to produce a new space toilet resulted in perhaps understandable skepticism about contracting run amuck (Sawyer, 1993). Although the volume of defense contracting and the amount of contract dollars involved in the defense and aerospace industries make them more susceptible to public attention, a ripple effect has brought all purchase arrangements under increasing scrutiny.

President Clinton's former budget director (chief of staff in Fall 1994), Leon Panetta, has urged the administration to examine whether government contracts out services too frequently and if these contracts are cost-effective and justifiable. In a directive to federal agencies to review their contracts with outside organizations and businesses, Panetta said that "these contracts today amount to the staggering sum of $103 billion" (Barr, 1993b).

Multiple Problems

The problems with POS concern waste and fraud, cost inefficiencies, faulty contracting practices and failures in government oversight, and inadequate or ineffective service. For example, New York City awards almost half of the city's $5 billion in major government contracts without competitive bidding, according to a report by the office of the city comptroller (Baquet, 1991). That report concluded that the lack of competition encourages corruption and increases the city's cost of doing business. In addition, the New Hampshire Division of Mental Health sought an investigation of the spending practices of a contracted rehabilitation center that provided services to developmentally disabled people; the specific investigative focus was on record keeping and the manner in which the center spent public funds (Bennett, 1988). Also, the New York State Department of Social Services revoked the license of a group home for mentally ill people after an investigation revealed that, from 1985 to 1992, the managers diverted as much as $4 million in public funds for personal use (Raab, 1993). These examples illustrate that POS is susceptible to the same excesses and inefficiencies that have plagued public services delivery. Fault for the problems in purchasing services has been placed on the government agency, provider agencies, both, or the relationship between the public and private sectors. Inevitably, investigations into monitoring and accountability practices, within an environment increasingly concerned about ethics in business practices, have challenged the reputation and legitimacy of POS arrangements.

Proposals for Reform

Criticisms have led to proposals to reform the contracting system. In general, such proposals have aimed to control discretion, tighten public monitoring, encourage competitive bidding, and ensure the avoidance of conflict of interest. Recent congressional action to address procurement reform has focused on innovative procurement practices and mechanisms to streamline the way government buys goods and services (Barr, 1994). However, a frequent side effect of such reform measures is to further complicate contract management for both the already overwhelmed public agency and the contracted service providers. These sometimes burdensome requirements may serve to reduce the likelihood that purchased services will result in more efficient service delivery.

The high expectations for POS and the perception that contracting could and would solve a host of longstanding service delivery problems perhaps have made disillusionment inevitable. So, too, people have a tendency to dwell on the downside of any strategy or program, in part because of the use of public monies. Too often, POS has operated on the basis of poorly articulated assumptions about what taxpayers, clients, government, and voluntary agencies thought POS could or should achieve.

FUTURE OF POS

Several events reflect on and raise questions about the sanctity of nonprofit organizations in this society and the future relationship between government and nonprofit agencies. The nationwide publicity given to the 1992 ouster of longtime United Way of America Executive Director William Aramony and the public scrutiny of the practices of some local United Way affiliates; documented misuse of contract funds by some universities, notably Stanford University; and allegations about the excesses of nonprofit executive salaries have had the effect of opening all nonprofit organizations to public scrutiny (Eisenberg, 1993). The traditional view that nonprofit organizations are committed to high ideals and sacrifice to promote the public interest is in question. Instead, the portrait of nonprofit organizations as greedy entities that use donations inappropriately and are out of touch with the American people has created a

growing cynicism about this sector (Goss, 1993). This cynicism has led to decreases in charitable contributions. United Way of America supports, in varying amounts, more than 44,000 U.S. charities across the country; however, for some charitable organizations, their United Way of America support has decreased by 40 percent or more (Millar, 1993). The decrease in traditional sources of support places many voluntary agencies in a position of greater dependency on government sources of funding if they are to maintain their current program levels or survive. The greater dependency of the nonprofit sector, however, is matched by the need of government at all levels for a cadre of experienced service providers.

The history of American social welfare evidences many shifts in perceptions about the appropriate relationship between government and the private sector and the respective roles of each sector, including who should be responsible for delivering certain services to whom. Although the volume of contracting may be subject to political currents, the use of POS is firmly entrenched. POS arrangements are no longer idealized, but are generally considered preferable and superior to direct public sector provision. POS now constitutes a viable system of service delivery that links the public and private sectors into a more extensive and far-reaching relationship. As a result, both sectors have changed. It is unlikely that the political landscape and societal preferences will support a substantial aboutface in these arrangements.

REFERENCES

Baquet, D. (1991, February 6). Contract study faults awards without bids. *New York Times,* p. B1.

Barr, S. (1993a, September 5). Gore report targets 252,000 federal jobs. *Washington Post,* pp. A1, A18.

Barr, S. (1993b, March 17). Panetta orders review of outside contracting. *Washington Post,* p. A2.

Barr, S. (1994, June 21). House polishes procurement legislation. *Washington Post,* p. A15.

Becker, R. (1961). *Study of salaries of NASW members.* New York: National Association of Social Workers.

Bennett, S. (1988, July 10). Spending by Claremont, N.H. mental health agency is investigated. *Boston Globe,* p. 75.

Comprehensive Employment and Training Act of 1973. P.L. 93-203, 87 Stat. 839.

Edwards, R. L., & Yankey, J. A. (1991). Managing effectively in an environment of competing values. In R. L. Edwards & J. A. Yankey (Eds.), *Skills for effective human services management* (pp. 5–43). Silver Spring, MD: NASW Press.

Eisenberg, P. (1993, July 13). Press coverage sends a message to non-profits: Clean up your act. *Chronicle of Philanthropy,* p. 41.

Family Planning Services and Population Research Act of 1970. P.L. 94-63, 84 Stat. 1504.

Ferris, J. M. (1993). The double-edge sword of social service contracting: Public accountability versus nonprofit autonomy. *Nonprofit Management & Leadership, 3,* 363–376.

Gibelman, M. (1981). Are clients served better when services are purchased? *Public Welfare, 39*(4), 26–33.

Gibelman, M. (1983). Using public funds to buy private services. In M. Dinerman (Ed.), *Social work in a turbulent world* (pp. 101–113). Silver Spring, MD: National Association of Social Workers.

Gibelman, M. (1990). National voluntary health agencies in an era of change: Experiences and adaptations. *Administration in Social Work, 14*(3), 17–32.

Gibelman, M., & Demone, H. W., Jr. (1989). The evolving contract state. In H. W. Demone, Jr., & M. Gibelman (Eds.), *Services for sale: Purchasing health and human services* (pp. 17–57). New Brunswick, NJ: Rutgers University Press.

Gibelman, M., & Demone, H. W., Jr. (1990). How voluntary agency networks fared in the 1980s. *Journal of Sociology & Social Welfare, 17*(4), 3–19.

Gibelman, M., & Demone, H. W., Jr. (in press). Private solutions to public human service problems: Purchasing services to meet social need. In S. Hakim, G. W. Bowman, & P. Seidenstat (Eds.), *Privatizing government services.* New York: Praeger.

Gibelman, M., & Schervish, P. (1993a). *Who we are: The social work labor force as reflected in the NASW membership.* Washington, DC: NASW Press.

Gibelman, M., & Schervish, P. (1993b). *What we earn: 1993 NASW salary survey.* Washington, DC: NASW Press.

Goldstein, H. (1993, July 13). Government contracts are emasculating boards and turning charities into agents of the state. *Chronicle of Philanthropy,* p. 41.

Goss, K. A. (1993, June 15). A crisis of credibility for America's non-profits. *Chronicle of Philanthropy,* p. 1.

Hasenfeld, Y. (1992). Theoretical approaches to human service organizations. In Y. Hasenfeld (Ed.), *Human services as complex organizations* (pp. 24–44). Newbury Park, CA: Sage Publications.

Kenworthy, T., & Dewar, H. (1990, January 20). House Republicans push anew for privatization of social security. *Washington Post,* p. A4.

Kettner, P. M., & Martin, L. L. (1993). Purchase of service contracting in the 1990s: Have expectations been met? *Journal of Sociology & Social Welfare, 20*(2), 89–103.

McMurtry, S. L., Netting, F. E., & Kettner, P. M. (1990). Critical inputs and strategic choice in non-profit human service organizations. *Administration in Social Work, 14*(3), 67–82.

Millar, B. (1993, June 29). United Way cutbacks squeeze charities. *Chronicle of Philanthropy,* pp. 1, 22–23, 25–26.

Miller, S. M., deVos van Steenwijk, A. A., & Roby, P. (1970). Creaming the poor. *Transaction, 7,* 39–45.

Older Americans Act of 1965. P.L. 89-73, 79 Stat. 218.

Pacific Consultants. (1979). *The feasibility of comparing costs between direct delivery and purchased services.* Washington, DC: U.S. Department of Health, Education, and Welfare, Administration for Public Services.

Palmer, J. L., & Sawhill, I. V. (1982). Perspectives on the Reagan experiment. In J. L. Palmer & I. V. Sawhill (Eds), *The Reagan Experiment.* Washington, DC: Urban Institute.

Raab, S. (1993, February 4). License of home for mentally ill revoked over fiscal finding. *New York Times,* p. B3.

Rathgeb Smith, S. (1989). Federal funding, nonprofit agencies, and victim services. In H. W. Demone, Jr., & M. Gibelman (Eds.), *Services for sale: Purchasing health and human services* (pp. 215–227). New Brunswick, NJ: Rutgers University Press.

Rathgeb Smith, S., & Lipsey, M. (1993). *Nonprofits for hire: The welfare state in the age of contracting.* Cambridge, MA: Harvard University Press.

Rowen, H. (1986, February 9). Privatized priorities. *Washington Post,* pp. F1, F2.

Ruchelman, L. (1989). *Redesigning public services.* Albany: State University of New York Press.

Sawyer, K. (1993, January 5). NASA's new space toilet: $30 million up the drain? *Washington Post,* A1, A8.

Slack, I. (1979). *Title XX at the crossroads.* Washington, DC: American Public Welfare Association.

Social Security Act of 1935. Ch. 531, 49 Stat. 620.

Social Security Act Amendments of 1962. P.L. 87-543, 76 Stat. 173.

Social Security Act Amendments of 1967. P.L. 90-248, 81 Stat. 821.

Southerland, D. (1993, May 10). A trickle of U.S. contracts: Procurement process slows with delays in Clinton appointments [Business section]. *Washington Post,* p. 5.

Stein, R. M. (1990). The budgetary effects of municipal service contracting: A principle-agent explanation. *American Journal of Political Science, 34,* 471–502.

Terrell, P. (1987). Purchasing social services. In A. Minahan (Ed.-in-Chief), *Encyclopedia of Social Work* (18th ed., Vol. 2, pp. 434–442). Silver Spring, MD: National Association of Social Workers.

United Way of America. (1981). *Local United Way allocations to agencies and program services, metros I–VIII.* Alexandria, VA: Author.

United Way of America. (1982). *Profile of '82 allocations, metros I–VIII.* Alexandria, VA: Author.

United Way of America. (1986). *Profile, fund distribution results by agency, by program, metros I–VIII.* Alexandria, VA: Author.

United Way of America. (1987). *Profile, fund distribution results by agency, by program, metros I–VIII.* Alexandria, VA: Author.

United Way of America. (1988). *Profile, Fund distribution results by agency, by program, metros I–VIII.* Alexandria, VA: Author.

FURTHER READING

Bernstein, S. (1991). *Managing contracted services in the nonprofit agency: Administrative, ethical, and political issues.* Philadelphia: Temple University Press.

DeHoog, R. H. (1990). Competition, negotiation, or cooperation: Three models for service contracting. *Administration and Society, 22,* 317–340.

Demone, H. W., Jr., & Gibelman, M. (Eds.). (1989). *Services for sale: Purchasing health and human services.* New Brunswick, NJ: Rutgers University Press.

Gronbjerg, K. A. (1991). Managing grants and contracts: The case of four nonprofit organizations. *Nonprofit and Voluntary Sector Quarterly, 20,* 5–24.

Gronbjerg, K. A. (1993). *Understanding nonprofit funding: Managing revenues in social services and community development organizations.* San Francisco: Jossey-Bass.

Gutch, R. (1992). *Contracting lessons from the United States.* London: National Council for Voluntary Organisations.

Kettner, P., & Martin, L. (1987). *Purchasing of service contracting.* Beverly Hills, CA: Sage Publications.

Kramer, R. M. (1994). Voluntary agencies and the contract culture: 'Dream or nightmare'? *Social Service Review, 68,* 33–60.

Krashinsky, M. (1990). Management implications of government funding of nonprofit organizations: Views from the United States and Canada. *Nonprofit Management and Leadership, 1,* 39–53.

Salamon, L. M. (1993). The marketization of welfare: Changing nonprofit and for-profit roles in the American welfare state. *Social Service Review, 67,* 16–39.

Ware, A. (1990). *Between profit and state: Intermediary organizations in Britain and the United States.* Princeton, NJ: Princeton University Press.

Wolch, J. (1990). *The shadow state: Government and the voluntary sector in transition.* New York: Foundation Center.

Margaret Gibelman, DSW, is visiting professor, Wurzweiler School of Social Work, Yeshiva University, Belfer Hall, 500 W. 185th Street, New York, NY 10033.

For further information see

Employee Assistance Programs; Federal Social Legislation from 1961 to 1994; Health Services Systems Policy; Licensing, Regulation, and Certification; Managed Care; Mental Health Overview; Occupational Social Work; Organizations: Context for Social Services Delivery; Public Health Services; Public Social Services; Quality Assurance; Social Security; Social Welfare History; Social Welfare Policy; Social Work Profession Overview; Supervision and Consultation; Vendorship.

Key Words

contracting

privatization

purchase of services

purchasing social

services

Q

Qualitative Research
Ruth G. McRoy

Qualitative research is concerned with nonstatistical methods of inquiry and analysis of social phenomena. It draws on an inductive process in which themes and categories emerge through analysis of data collected by such techniques as interviews, observations, videotapes, and case studies. Samples are usually small and are often purposively selected. Qualitative research uses detailed descriptions from the perspective of the research participants themselves as a means of examining specific issues and problems under study.

Qualitative research differs from quantitative research in that the latter is characterized by the use of large samples, standardized measures, a deductive approach, and highly structured interview instruments to collect data for hypothesis testing (Marlow, 1993). In contrast to qualitative research, in quantitative research easily quantifiable categories are typically generated before the study and statistical techniques are used to analyze the data collected. Both qualitative and quantitative research are designed to build knowledge; they can be used as complementary strategies.

DEFINITIONS

Qualitative research is referred to by a variety of terms, reflecting several research approaches. *Field research* is often used interchangeably with qualitative research to describe systematic observations of social behavior with no preconceived hypotheses to be tested (Rubin & Babbie, 1993). Hypotheses emerge from the observation and interpretation of human behavior, leading to further observations and the generation of new hypotheses for exploration.

Qualitative research is also referred to as naturalistic research or inquiry (Taylor, 1977) into everyday living. Direct observations are made of human behavior in everyday life. Drawing on symbolic interaction theory (Blumer, 1969), naturalistic researchers believe that gaining knowledge from sources that have "intimate familiarity" (Lofland, 1976) with an issue is far better than the "objective" distancing approach that supposedly characterizes quantitative approaches (Haworth, 1984). Zurcher (1983) used this technique as he examined such common occurrences as riding on an airplane or attending a football game.

Ethnography—a term more commonly associated with anthropology and sociology than with social work—is used in qualitative research to describe a field study of a particular site or population undertaken to better understand the culture from the perspective of that population. In ethnographic studies, teams of researchers collect data by observing and interviewing participants over time. Typically, field notes are taken and life histories and case studies are derived from extensive contact with the group under study. Examples of the ethnographic approach include Rainwater (1970) and Liebow (1967). Recently, social work researchers have used participant observation and interviews in such settings as residential treatment centers (Penzerro, 1992) and housing projects (Lein, 1994) to study foster care drift and persistent poverty.

HISTORY

Although social work since its beginnings has been involved with the study of natural occurrences and the interaction between human behavior and the social context, only minor acknowledgment has been made of the contributions of qualitative methodology. Almost since 1915, when Abraham Flexner asserted that social work lacked a core of knowledge derived from the scientific process (Austin, 1978; Bruno, 1958), social work researchers have been striving to demonstrate strict adherence to the objective methods characteristic of the hard sciences, and much social work research has relied on the positivistic approach, using quantitative methods. This situation is exemplified by the Cambridge–Somerville youth delinquency prevention study, in which Powers and Witmer (1951), using traditional social science quantitative methodology, applied an innovative experimental model to assess effectiveness of social services. The study has been cited as a landmark social work research project. Although Powers and Witmer found no significant differences in terms of delinquency records and social adjustment between the treatment and control groups, Witmer, in a supplemental study, used qualitative methodology in intensive case studies and found that some children definitely benefited from the intervention (Zimbalist, 1977). Witmer's use of qualitative methods was an early indicator that qualitative techniques could be used to examine social processes that might be missed by traditional quantitative measures.

Nevertheless, social work continued to emphasize quantitative techniques. Research was heavily influenced by the methodologies of the natural sciences. Beginning in the 1950s and 1960s, numerous doctoral programs in social work were established, and formal research courses in the scientific method became a major component of the curriculum (Austin, 1978). And as social work strove for greater legitimacy through the development of empirically based theories and proof-oriented models for greater accountability and effectiveness, "discovery-oriented" qualitative research was considered to have little scientific merit (Karger, 1983).

In the late 1970s, Taylor (1977) advocated four alternative approaches to social work research, among them qualitative methods. He asserted that naturalistic inquiry is a perfect technique for a profession that deals not just with the expected and easily measurable but also with the unexpected events that are characteristic of human experiences. Taylor noted that when field researchers use quantitative methods to "increase the precision of observations" (p. 121), qualitative and quantitative approaches complement one another.

In the 1980s, debate about the use of quantitative methods as the preeminent social work strategy was ongoing (Haworth, 1984; Hudson, 1982; Karger, 1983; Reid, 1987). As social workers tried to meet the requirements of logical positivists for experimental designs with objective measures, it was found that many research questions that did not fit neatly into a quantitative research design were not investigated (Heineman, 1981). Some researchers acknowledge that qualitative strategies are appropriate for exploratory or preliminary inquiry into a topic. Others suggest that once there is an organized body of scholars who use a well-delineated qualitative methodology, more serious attention will be given to the qualitative approach (Karger, 1983).

Although debate continues in the 1990s, and the paradigm of scientific inquiry in social work is still primarily viewed to mean quantitative methodology, the merits of qualitative methods are now being acknowledged by most authors of leading social work research texts (Babbie, 1989;

Chambers, Wedel, & Rodwell, 1992; Grinnell, 1988; Marlow, 1993; Rubin & Babbie, 1993; Sherman & Reid, 1994), and some qualitative techniques are covered in the research courses of a growing number of schools of social work.

ADVANTAGES AND CONTRIBUTIONS

A number of advantages of qualitative methodologies for social work have been noted in the literature. Descriptive, inductive, and unobtrusive techniques for data collection are viewed as compatible with the knowledge and values of the social work profession (Epstein, 1988). For situations in which social workers are faced with issues and problems that are not amenable to quantitative examination, qualitative methods have been advocated (Sherman & Reid, 1994). The social-psychological bases of qualitative research suggest that it is compatible with the person-in-environment paradigm of social work practice (Epstein, 1988; Taylor, 1977).

Gilgun (1994) suggested that qualitative approaches are similar in method to clinical social work assessments. Clinicians rely on interviews to gather data on a client's issues in the context of the environment. A clinician goes over a series of hunches and working hypotheses that are based on observations made through ongoing contact with the client. Qualitative researchers, like clinicians, are trained to look at each case individually, without imposing preconceived notions or attempting to generalize to all clients having a particular problem. Qualitative researchers maintain field notes and documents on their research (Gilgun, 1994; Marlow, 1993), just as clinicians keep running accounts of contact with a client in the form of process recordings or case records.

In studies of social processes of complex human systems such as families, organizations, and communities, qualitative methodology may be the most appropriate research strategy (Reid, 1987). Scholars of the family now extol the benefits of qualitative methodologies in gaining *Verstehen* (Weber, 1947), or understanding, of the dynamic processes, meanings, communication patterns, experiences, and individual and family constructions of reality (Daly, 1992). Field settings and social service agencies provide unique opportunities for the qualitative study of social processes.

Qualitative approaches also have the advantages of flexibility, in-depth analysis, and the potential to observe a variety of aspects of a social situation (Babbie, 1986). A qualitative researcher conducting a face-to-face interview can quickly adjust the interview schedule if the interviewee's responses suggest the need for additional probes or lines of inquiry in future interviews. Moreover, by developing and using questions on the spot, a qualitative researcher can gain a more in-depth understanding of the respondent's beliefs, attitudes, or situation. During the course of an interview or observation, a researcher is able to note changes in bodily expression, mood, voice intonation, and environmental factors that might influence the interviewee's responses. Such observational data can be of particular value when a respondent's body language runs counter to the verbal response given to an interview question.

DESIGNS, PROCEDURES, AND ANALYSES

Grounded Theory

Qualitative research is theory generating. The development of theory from data is based on Glaser and Strauss's (1967) process of constant comparisons. Because theory derived from this approach is "discovered, developed, and provisionally verified through systematic data collection and analysis of data" (Strauss & Corbin, 1990, p. 23), it is known as grounded theory. Although the grounded theory approach was developed by sociologists, it is used by qualitative researchers in social work to systematically investigate an issue and to organize data.

Glaser and Strauss (1967) identified two types of grounded theory: substantive and formal. Substantive grounded theory is developed when hypotheses are based on one area of inquiry. Formal grounded theory is developed when hypotheses apply across several areas of research inquiry with different sample populations and settings (Gilgun, 1992).

Procedures

Under the grounded theory approach, cases are selected by a sampling process in which the researcher identifies new cases that are similar to previous cases. When these cases generate no new insights, the process is repeated with newly selected cases that yield different insights, again until no new insights are noted.

Gilgun (1990) suggested these steps:

1. identification of area under investigation
2. literature review
3. selection of parameters of study
4. collection of data
5. comparison of patterns of first case with those of second case
6. development of working hypothesis as common patterns emerge across interviews
7. formulation of additional questions and modification of questions, based on analysis

8. continuation of theoretical sampling
9. review of relevant literature when patterns appear to stabilize
10. linking of relevant literature to the empirically grounded hypotheses
11. testing of theoretical formulations derived from preceding step
12. revision of theoretical formulations as needed to fit empirical patterns in each subsequent step. (p. 11)

The process ends when the researcher reaches "theoretical saturation," the point at which no new data are emerging (Glaser & Strauss, 1967). Through this procedure emerging theories are grounded in data and are linked to other theories and research (Gilgun, 1992).

When cases do not fit into the common pattern ("negative" cases), researchers typically assess each to determine whether the case is a result of expected variation, the researcher's failure to consider the total range of behavior or situations that might fit a particular category, or truly exceptional (Marlow, 1993). In the presentation of findings, "negative" cases and common patterns are illustrated.

Structured interviews. Limited time and financial resources may lead some qualitative researchers to pursue other data collection techniques, such as a structured interview schedule with open-ended questions. Drawing on the theoretical and research literature, such questions may be formulated and organized in advance to address a specific research topic. Studies of adoption dissolution, for example, might include questions posed to adoptive parents that focus on such themes as parental motivation for adoption, knowledge of the child's past, initial attitudes toward the child, use of therapeutic resources, development of problematic behavior, and factors leading to dissolution. Interviewers are expected to take field notes or to keep a field diary of observations made during the interview.

Data reduction. Interview questions and responses are typically tape-recorded and then transcribed verbatim before analysis is begun. Transcription is extremely time-consuming (Marlow, 1993). Due to the large amount of data that can be generated in qualitative research, a data reduction process must be used to aid analysis. This procedure includes organizing the data; identifying emerging themes, categories, and patterns; and testing hypotheses against the data. Either "indigenous" or "analyst-constructed" typologies may be constructed. In indigenous categories, the language of respondents is used to label types of processes (Marshall & Rossman, 1989; Patton, 1990). For example, in a qualitative study of the development of emotional disturbance in adopted adolescents, researchers used "elbow babies"—the language of the participants—to classify infants who pushed away from close contact with family members. Ongoing analysis of data revealed other instances of this phenomenon (McRoy, Grotevant, & Zurcher, 1988).

In analyst-constructed categories, the researcher attaches a label to observed recurring events. For example, in Matocha's (1992) qualitative study of the needs of caregivers of acquired immune deficiency syndrome (AIDS) patients, four categories or domains of needs of caregivers were identified: physical, spiritual, social, and economic. Matocha's case study data focused on each of these identified categories.

Narrative descriptions. Narrative descriptions of data collected through interviews, observations, and case records are also used in qualitative analysis. Narrative descriptions may be developed in the form of case studies of a particular interviewee or agency for use in social work practice or program evaluation (Marlow, 1993).

Analysis

Content analysis is often used in qualitative and quantitative research methods. Some researchers view content analysis as a technique to quantify manifest (surface-level) descriptive data (Allen-Meares, 1985), in which categories are developed, content is coded, and category counts are conducted. Hollis (1972), studying communications in social work interviews, categorized specific statements according to type of communication. Qualitative content analysis typically does not transform the content into numeric patterns. Instead, recurrent themes, and typologies and illustrations of particular issues, are used.

When qualitative methods are used in evaluating the effectiveness of social work practice, a purposive sampling approach may be taken in which one or a few cases are selected for intensive interviewing and analysis. Qualitative interviews can augment single-subject studies by exploring variables other than a specific intervention that might have affected the client outcome. Similarly, in program evaluation studies, qualitative methods allow the researcher to focus on the process of "how something happens" rather than on just the "outcomes or results" that would be more characteristic of quantitative designs. Program evaluation studies involving qualitative approaches focus on participants' perceptions and their experiences in

the program (Bogdan & Taylor, 1990; Patton, 1990; Rubin & Babbie, 1993).

Naturalistic evaluation, which is now often referred to as constructivism (Chambers et al., 1992), emphasizes multiple constructions of reality in the evaluation process of social programs. It involves an interactive approach in which the "direction of inquiry is shaped through involvement with the participants" (p. 293). The research design and process emerge through interaction with participants in the setting. Although a conceptual base may guide the evaluation, grounded theory, based on the data, emerges through consideration of multiple realities and perspectives.

ISSUES IN QUALITATIVE RESEARCH

Reliability and Validity

Among the most cited criticisms of qualitative research are the presumed lack of reliability and validity of its findings. In regard to field research, critics question the ability of qualitative research to replicate observations (reliability) or to obtain correct answers or correct impressions of the phenomenon under study (validity) (Kirk & Miller, 1986). Other criticisms concern the reactive effects of the observer's or the interviewer's presence on the situation being studied and selective perception or bias on the part of the researcher. Also of concern has been the researcher's inability to observe all factors that might influence the situation under study (McCall & Simmons, 1969; Schaffir & Stebbins, 1991). For example, agency time, staff, and financial constraints may limit an agency's ability to provide the researcher with the opportunity to review the entire range of cases pertaining to a particular topic.

Qualitative researchers have addressed these issues in several ways. Purposive sampling, based on reviews of the literature and knowledge of the subject area, has been used to select cases under study, rather than as an attempt to observe or collect data from all respondents, who may be affected by the phenomena under study. Individual bias has been addressed by using teams of researchers to read cases or make observations. To ensure validity of interviews or observations, some qualitative researchers use the technique of "member validation," in which the respondent is given a copy of the observations or interview to provide feedback (Schaffir & Stebbins, 1991).

Although quantitative researchers are likely to address threats to validity through such techniques as random selection of participants and the use of controls, qualitative researchers are more likely to address validity throughout the data collection and analysis processes. As qualitative researchers review more cases, seeking common themes and patterns and testing emerging hypotheses, they are in essence working to ensure validity (Maxwell, 1992).

Qualitative researchers also confront issues of reliability and validity through *triangulation*— the use of different strategies to approach the same topic of investigation. Some researchers use multiple measures of the same phenomenon. For example, to measure self-concept, investigators may use a standardized instrument such as the Harter Self-Perception Profile (Harter, 1985) as well as the Twenty-Statements Test (Kuhn & McPartland, 1954), an open-ended measure. Observations of multiple comparison groups, cross-site analyses, and acquisition of multiple viewpoints of the sample phenomena are all techniques used to improve the reliability of findings (Jick, 1983). In data analysis, coding teams with high interrater reliability scores are used to code each interview and thus improve reliability of findings (Miles & Huberman, 1984).

Ethical Issues

Due to the subjective nature of data collection, interpretation, and analysis in qualitative research, there appear to be more ethical dilemmas and concerns with confidentiality associated with this method than with quantitative research. A qualitative researcher interviewing female-headed families on welfare, for example, may gather data on unreported financial support from fathers. Despite assurances of confidentiality, participating families may feel at risk when they reveal such support to the researcher. It is the researcher's ethical responsibility to maintain confidentiality, but there have been cases in which research data have been subpoenaed. Despite attempts to protect respondents through the use of pseudonyms, identities sometimes may be decoded.

The security of sensitive and potentially identifiable research materials contained on computer disks, in mainframes, and on paper is a persistent issue. When several people are involved in text analysis and the development of coding schemes, or in grant-funded projects that require databases to be made available to other researchers to conduct secondary analyses of computer-generated or stored data, there are risks associated with the confidentiality of data. The issue of who has rights to the data has not been resolved (Fielding & Lee, 1992).

The deception of respondents by researchers is an ethical issue in ethnographic studies. For instance, in some studies of people living in homeless shelters, a researcher has become a partici-pant, interacting with residents while giving them the impression that the researcher too is homeless. Some researchers have responded to the ethical issue in this type of data gathering by taking on the role of participant-as-observer, in which the identities of the researchers are known to the respondents (Rubin & Babbie, 1993).

Diversity

Qualitative methods are particularly appropriate for use with people who are more comfortable responding in an interview format than to a standardized survey questionnaire. Davis (1986) suggested that the gender of respondents should be a consideration in selecting a research strategy because many women may prefer qualitative research techniques to quantitative approaches because they prefer opportunities to discuss subjects in context.

Myers (1977) suggested that some members of ethnic groups, low-income populations, or others who may be socially distant from the researcher are more likely to participate in the in-depth interviews characteristic of qualitative research than to complete a structured questionnaire or survey. To enhance the validity of results in research with diverse populations, research questions must be clearly constructed and must not be subject to different cultural interpretations. Also, due to the subjective nature of qualitative research it is important for the researcher to continually engage in self-examination to be certain that his or her own biases and stereotypes are not influencing the interpretation of the findings. Conversely, because qualitative analysis allows researchers to explore in depth all factors that might affect a particular issue, this strategy permits sensitive consideration of the complexities of human diversity (Marlow, 1993).

Use of Computers

Recent advances in computer technology let qualitative researchers rapidly and efficiently gather, enter, and retrieve data. Some qualitative researchers take computer notebooks to the field, in which they enter notes directly (Babbie, 1986; Pfaffenberger, 1988). Although many word-processing packages and database managers allow for simple word or phrase searches, specific qualitative analysis programs for text retrieval, such as Ethnograph, ZyIndex, or Word Cruncher, create word lists, count frequency of occurrences, create indexes, and attach key words to words in text (Tesch, 1992).

Some qualitative researchers use computer programs to do a reliability check during data analysis. For example, after completing a personal search of a document for specific words or issues, a computer program is used to double-check the accuracy of the original analysis. Despite the advantages of computerized analysis, qualitative researchers engaged in theory construction must also undertake ongoing exploration of the data to identify patterns and categories that may be used as key words for computer searches.

FUTURE OF QUALITATIVE RESEARCH

Qualitative research methodology is receiving growing acceptance in the social work research community. Qualitative methods are becoming particularly popular among researchers working on family issues. A Qualitative Family Research Network was formed in the late 1980s, and an increasing number of social workers and family researchers exchange ideas on qualitative methodologies (Gilgun, 1990). Another indicator of the growing acceptance of qualitative research in social work practice is the recently established journal *Research on Social Work Practice*, which seeks manuscripts based on qualitative studies as well as on a combination of qualitative and quantitative research.

Clearly, quantitative and qualitative methodologies have different strengths and weaknesses, and the strategy taken should depend on the nature of the question being investigated. In many instances, both qualitative and quantitative approaches can be used in the same study. For example, standardized measures might be used to collect data in conjunction with open-ended interview questions. It is possible to code interview data using both qualitative and quantitative techniques and to report the results of both the qualitative and quantitative analyses of the same data set (McRoy et al., 1988). Qualitative strategies need not be limited to small-scale studies. Daly (1992) reported a technique for applying grounded theory principles in the design and analysis of a large national survey on adoption trends.

The close compatibility of qualitative research methods with social work practice techniques is likely to lead to greater use of qualitative strategies in practice evaluation. As more social work researchers network and refine and publish qualitative studies that clearly specify the techniques used, qualitative methodology is likely to receive even greater acceptance among social workers.

REFERENCES

Allen-Meares, P. (1985). Content analysis: It does have a place in social work research. *Journal of Social Service Research, 7*(4), 51–69.

Austin, D. (1978). Research and social work: Educational paradoxes and possibilities. *Journal of Social Service Research, 2*(4), 159–176.

Babbie, E. (1986). *Observing ourselves.* Belmont, CA: Wadsworth.

Babbie, E. (1989). *The practice of social research.* Belmont, CA: Wadsworth.

Blumer, H. (1969). *Symbolic interactionism: Perspective and method.* Englewood Cliffs, NJ: Prentice Hall.

Bogdan, R., & Taylor, S. (1990). Looking at the bright side: A positive approach to qualitative policy and evaluation research. *Qualitative Sociology, 13*(1), 183–192.

Bruno, F. (1958). *Trends in social work, 1874–1956.* New York: Columbia University Press.

Chambers, D., Wedel, K., & Rodwell, M. (1992). *Evaluating social programs.* Boston: Allyn & Bacon.

Daly, K. (1992). The fit between qualitative research and characteristics of families. In J. Gilgun, K. Daly, & G. Handel (Eds.), *Qualitative methods in family research.* Newbury Park, CA: Sage Publications.

Davis, L. V. (1986). A feminist approach to social work research. *Affilia, 1,* 32–47.

Epstein, I. (1988). Quantitative and qualitative methods. In R. Grinnell, Jr., (Ed.), *Social work research and evaluation* (pp. 185–198). Itasca, IL: F. E. Peacock.

Fielding, N. G., & Lee, R. M. (1992). *Using computers in qualitative research.* London: Sage Publications.

Gilgun, J. F. (1990). Steps in the development of theory using a grounded theory approach. *Qualitative Family Research Newsletter, 4*(2), 11–12.

Gilgun, J. (1992). Definitions, methodologies, and methods in qualitative family research. In J. Gilgun, K. Daly, & G. Handel (Eds.), *Qualitative methods in family research* (pp. 22–40). Newbury Park, CA: Sage Publications.

Gilgun, J. F. (1994). Hand into glove: The grounded theory approach and social work practice research. In E. Sherman & W. J. Reid (Eds.), *Qualitative research in social work* (pp. 115–125). New York: Columbia University Press.

Glaser, B., & Strauss, A. (1967). *The discovery of grounded theory.* Chicago: Aldine.

Grinnell, R. (1988). *Social work research and evaluation.* Itasca, IL: F. E. Peacock.

Harter, S. (1985). *Manual for the self-perception profile for children.* Denver: University of Denver.

Haworth, G. (1984). Social work research, practice, and paradigms. *Social Service Review, 58,* 343–357.

Heineman, M. B. (1981). The obsolete scientific imperative in social work research. *Social Service Review, 55,* 371–395.

Hollis, F. (1972). *Casework: A psychosocial therapy* (2nd ed.). New York: Random House.

Hudson, W. H. (1982). Scientific imperatives in social work research and practice. *Social Service Review, 56,* 246–258.

Jick, T. D. (1983). Mixing qualitative and quantitative methods: Triangulation in action. In J. Van Maanen (Ed.), *Qualitative methodology* (pp. 135–148). London: Sage Publications.

Karger, H. J. (1983). Science, research, and social work: Who controls the profession? *Social Work, 28,* 200–205.

Kirk, J., & Miller, M. (1986). *Reliability and validity in qualitative research.* London: Sage Publications.

Kuhn, M., & McPartland, T. (1954). An empirical investigation of self-attitudes. *American Sociological Review, 9*, 68–76.

Lein, L. (1994). *Children in persistent poverty.* Unpublished manuscript.

Liebow, E. (1967). *Tally's corner.* Boston: Little, Brown.

Lofland, J. (1976). *Doing social life: The qualitative study of human interaction in natural settings.* New York: John Wiley & Sons.

Marlow, C. (1993). *Research methods.* Pacific Grove, CA: Brooks/Cole.

Marshall, C., & Rossman, G. (1989). *Designing qualitative research.* Newbury Park, CA: Sage Publications.

Matocha, L. (1992). Case study interviews: Caring for persons with AIDS. In J. Gilgun, K. Daly, & G. Handel (Eds.), *Qualitative methods in family research* (pp. 66–84). Newbury Park, CA: Sage Publications.

Maxwell, J. A. (1992). Understanding and validity in qualitative research. *Harvard Educational Review, 62*(3), 279–300.

McCall, G., & Simmons, J. L. (Eds.). (1969). *Issues in participant observation.* Reading, MA: Addison-Wesley Press.

McRoy, R., Grotevant, H., & Zurcher, L. (1988). *Emotional disturbance in adopted adolescents: Origins and development.* New York: Praeger.

Miles, M., & Huberman, M. (1984). *Qualitative data analysis: A sourcebook of new methods.* Beverly Hills, CA: Sage Publications.

Myers, V. (1977). Survey methods for minority populations. *Journal of Social Issues, 33,* 11–19.

Patton, M. (1990). *Qualitative evaluation methods.* Newbury Park, CA: Sage Publications.

Penzerro, R. M. (1992). *Foster care drift: An ethnographic study of boys in residential treatment.* Unpublished doctoral dissertation.

Pfaffenberger, B. (1988). *Microcomputer applications in qualitative research.* Newbury Park, CA: Sage Publications.

Powers, E., & Witmer, H. (1951). *An experiment in the prevention of delinquency: The Cambridge-Somerville youth study.* New York: Columbia University Press.

Rainwater, L. (1970). *Behind ghetto walls.* Chicago: Aldine.

Reid, W. (1987). Research in social work. In A. Minahan (Ed.-in-Chief), *Encyclopedia of social work* (18th ed., Vol. 2, pp. 474–487). Silver Spring, MD: National Association of Social Workers.

Rubin, A., & Babbie, E. (1993). *Research methods for social work.* Pacific Grove, CA: Brooks/Cole.

Schaffir, W. B., & Stebbins, R. (1991). *Experiencing fieldwork.* Newbury Park, CA: Sage Publications.

Sherman, E., & Reid, W. J. (1994). *Qualitative research in social work.* New York: Columbia University Press.

Strauss, A., & Corbin, J. (1990). *Basics of qualitative research.* Newbury Park, CA: Sage Publications.

Taylor, J. (1977). Toward alternative forms of social work research: The case for naturalistic methods. *Journal of Social Welfare, 4*(2–3), 119–126.

Tesch, R. (1992). Software for qualitative researchers: Analysis needs and program capabilities. In N. Fielding & R. Lee (Eds.), *Using computers in qualitative research.* Newbury Park, CA: Sage Publications.

Weber, M. (1947). *The theory of social and economic organizations.* (T. Parsons, Ed.; A. M. Henderson & T. Parsons, Trans.). New York: Free Press.

Zimbalist, S. E. (1977). *Historic themes and landmarks in social welfare research.* New York: Harper & Row.

Zurcher, L. A. (1983). *Social roles: Conformity, conflict, and creativity.* Beverly Hills, CA: Sage Publications.

FURTHER READING

Berg, B. L. (1989). *Qualitative research methods for the social sciences.* Boston: Allyn & Bacon.

Crabtree, B. F., & Miller, W. L. (Eds.). (1992). *Doing qualitative research.* Newbury Park, CA: Sage Publications.

Denzin, N., & Lincoln, Y. (Eds.). (1994). *Handbook of qualitative research.* Newbury Park, CA: Sage Publications.

Fetterman, D. M. (1989). *Ethnography: Step by step.* Newbury Park, CA: Sage Publications.

Jacob, E. (1987). Qualitative research traditions: A review. *Review of Education Research, 57*(1), 1–50.

Jordan, C., & Franklin, C. (in press). *Clinical assessment: Quantitative and qualitative methods.* Chicago: Lyceum.

Lincoln, Y., & Guba, E. (1985). *Naturalistic inquiry.* Beverly Hills, CA: Sage Publications.

Moon, S. M., Dillon, D. R., & Sprenkle, D. H. (1990). Family therapy and qualitative research. *Journal of Marital and Family Therapy, 16*(4), 357–373.

Taylor, J. B. (1993). The naturalistic research approach. In R. N. Grinnell, Jr., *Social work research and evaluation* (4th ed., pp. 53–78). Itasca, IL: F. E. Peacock.

Silberman, D. (1994). *Interpreting qualitative data.* Newbury Park, CA: Sage Publications.

Taylor, S. J., & Bogdan, R. (1984). *Introduction to qualitative research: The search for meanings.* New York: John Wiley & Sons.

Van Maanen, J., Dabbs, J. M., & Faulkner, R. T. (1982). *Varieties of qualitative research.* Beverly Hills, CA: Sage Publications.

Ruth G. McRoy, PhD, CSW-ACP, is Ruby Lee Piester Centennial Professor in Services to Children and Families, University of Texas School of Social Work, Austin, TX 78712.

For further information see

Agency-Based Research; Ethical Issues in Research; Experimental and Quasi-Experimental Design; Intervention Research; Interviewing; Meta-analysis; Person-in-Environment; Program Evaluation; Psychometrics; Psychosocial Approach; Recording; Research Overview; Survey Research.

Key Words	
descriptive validity	interviewing
reliability	qualitative research

Quality Assurance
Alma T. Young

Quality assurance programs are designed to (1) systematically evaluate the effectiveness and efficiency of services provided, (2) determine whether these services comply with the expectations of adequate and complete services to consumers as mandated, and (3) correct any observed deficiencies identified in the process. Quality assurance addresses professionally determined standards of care and includes ongoing systems of monitoring, evaluation, and corrective action (Rehr, 1979).

BACKGROUND

Historically, concepts and methods of quality assurance programs have undergone many changes as health care professionals accept new ways to measure quality care. Advancements in medical technology, the emergence of new health care providers, the complexity of institutional services, and the consumer movement have all been influential with regard to changes in health care delivery. Consumerism, decision making, and choices were critical components in the determination of many health care policies in the early 1970s. This was also a time when health care professionals began to develop methods to evaluate the quality of services to patients. The Social Security Amendments of 1972 brought about the mandate calling for review and evaluation of the quality of medical care, and Professional Standards Review Organizations (PSROs) were designated throughout the nation to ensure the need for, quality of, and cost-effectiveness of care. In view of these changes, social work "anticipated the involvement of and impact on its profession and began, without mandate, evolving toward its own assessment of practice and performance within the structure of emerging requirements for quality assurance programs" (Rehr, Blumenfield, Young, & Rosenberg, 1993, p. 368).

Development of Standards and Evaluation Methods

The National Association of Social Workers and the Society for Social Work Administrators in Health Care of the American Hospital Association assumed leadership in the development of standards, methods for review, and studies to assess quality of care delivered by social workers. Eventually studies in social work departments across the country influenced the development of programs and processes regarding high-risk screening, patient classification, and patient satisfaction. Because the concept of health incorporates a comprehensive biopsychosocial approach to individuals and their families or significant others, it encompasses a wide range of physical, emotional, and environmental factors that have an impact on people's lives.

Over the years, the Joint Commission on Accreditation of Healthcare Organizations (JCAHO) has endorsed various methods for evaluating health care. The initial system of medical audits, which did not address many related activities of patient care and clinical performance, later shifted to an evaluative process that took into account all services in the hospital that contributed to patient care. By 1981 a new standard focused on the need for hospitalwide quality assurance programs that addressed the need for flexible approaches to problem identification, assessment, and resolution. It emphasized the importance of activities dealing with problems in which resolutions will have a significant impact on patient care and outcome and highlighted the need for a quality assurance program that would allow approaches to problem solving that preserve the integrity of individual disciplines and their unique quality assurance efforts while providing for appropriate sharing of information (Joint Commission on Accreditation of Hospitals, 1980).

Monitoring and Evaluation

Quality assurance activities in hospitalwide programs emphasize the importance of monitoring and evaluation. Although early attention focused more on problem identification, there was opportunity to identify areas for improvement. On the basis of direct experience, health care professionals have learned that structure, process, and outcome are three interrelated components of quality assurance and that quality assurance is achieved when the organization has appropriate resources, equipment, personnel, and other necessities to provide the care stated in its mission; when there are clearly defined policies and procedures to guide providers who are responsible for provision of care; and when there is a plan that specifies the desired expectations.

Quality assurance has been described as the "hub" of a social work program in which all services and functions provided feed into and out of the monitoring and evaluation process (JCAHO,

1992). Monitoring and evaluation of quality assurance activities is an ongoing process that begins with a well-developed plan devised with input from all levels of staff. Management and staff assume responsibility for identifying specific indicators to be monitored against established criteria or standards of performance. Although "indicators are not necessarily direct or perfect measures of quality [they] are observable signals that are sensitive to changes in quality of care" (Coulton, 1989).

QUALITY ASSURANCE IN TRANSITION

Since the 1980s, the language, mandates, and processes of quality assurance have changed considerably. In the early 1990s, the Joint Commission initiated a multiyear transition to standards in hospitals that emphasized quality improvement principles. There was a shift from quality assurance to continuous quality improvement, also known as total quality management, meaning that organizations' focus changed from retrospective reviews to prospective analyses of statistical data and trends (JCAHO, 1993). Although there has been concern that the pioneering work on quality in industry may not be applicable to health care settings, continuous quality improvement has become a way of life for health care organizations, and appropriate steps have been taken to adapt new approaches, methods, and tools to fit the characteristics of the health care environment (JCAHO, 1992).

Continuous Quality Improvement Tenets

Deming's concept of statistical control and application of methods to improve quality were developed into a 14-point program describing the implementation of continuous quality improvement (CQI) as follows (Teichholz, 1993):

1. *Create constancy of purpose for improvement of product and service.* Long-term as well as short-term goals must be established, and appropriate resources must be in place if they are to be achieved.
2. *Adopt the new philosophy.* The best way to improve quality is to improve the process and "do things right the first time" (p. 353).
3. *Cease dependence on inspection to achieve quality.* In quality assurance programs based on retrospective reviews, inspection occurs too late to improve quality. CQI attempts to look at the process prospectively.
4. *End the practice of awarding business on the basis of price.* A purchase should not be based primarily on the price; this includes products as well as personnel. "One must not look solely at the current price tag but also at long-term costs for both equipment and personnel" (p. 353).
5. *Improve constantly and forever every process for planning, production, and service.* The process must be evaluated on an ongoing basis. Reassessment and efforts to improve performance must occur constantly.
6. *Institute training on the job.* Training and continuing education are incorporated into the concepts and methods for achieving quality improvement.
7. *Institute leadership.* Leaders, managers, and others in comparable positions must help staff achieve CQI.
8. *Drive out fear.* Staff must feel sufficiently secure to make suggestions or express ideas without fear of negative reactions from people in superior positions.
9. *Break down barriers between staff areas.* Communication, cooperation, and interdepartmental activities are major components of the quality improvement process.
10. *Eliminate slogans, exhortations, and targets for the work force.* Slogans may have positive short-term effects on some members of the staff, but they do not enhance quality improvement. The primary message is improved quality as seen by the total organization.
11. *Eliminate numerical quotas for the work force and numerical goals for managers.* Although quantity is important, the emphasis is on quality.
12. *Remove barriers that rob people of the pride of workmanship.* Individual accomplishments (for example, performance appraisals) should be incorporated into group or team activities as part of the total contribution to CQI.
13. *Institute a vigorous program of education and self-improvement.* Continuing education must be an expectation for all staff and supported by leaders and management throughout the organization. Generally, advance knowledge improves overall performance and can help staff appreciate their contribution to the CQI process.
14. *Put everyone in the company to work to accomplish this transformation.* This last point summarizes many highlights from the previous points. Success depends on appropriate input by all disciplines and all levels of staff.

Basically, CQI views quality of services and products as the primary focus of all activities in the organization. With the use of statistical tools for data collection and analysis, this concept incorporates the positive aspects of quality assurance in that it searches for opportunities to improve care. Among the tools used to identify and analyze problems are flowcharts representing steps taken at various stages in the process, cause-and-effect diagrams displaying various causes that can lead to a given effect to improve quality, and a control chart determining whether the process is stable and predictable (Teichholz, 1993).

FUTURE CONCERNS

Quality assurance has changed dramatically with shifts in philosophy and new standards for health care organizations to focus on CQI. The current standards, which cut across departmental lines, recognize the interdepartmental and interdisciplinary nature of health care delivery and highlight the importance of communication and coordination of activities to achieve desired goals. Because no health care organization to date has fully integrated CQI into a hospitalwide program, the applicability of CQI principles to health care is still unknown. It is estimated that these principles will be fully adopted by health care organizations (that is, all staff on all levels will be involved in improving functions) within the next six to 10 years.

For social work, CQI means taking a closer look at the big picture. The works of many notable leaders in the profession have put social work in the position to accept the challenge of CQI. The development of instruments for high-risk population screening, measurement of patient satisfaction, data retrieval, and automatic data processing are a few of the innovative steps taken since the 1970s (Berkman, Rehr, & Rosenberg, 1980).

This challenge comes with concerns, however, as additional emphasis is placed on identifying and evaluating factors that influence outcomes. At best, outcomes are complex and continue to be one of the most difficult indicators to measure. There is no doubt that social workers as well as other health care providers will have to use all available equipment (for example, statistical tools, flowcharts, and cause-and-effect diagrams) to analyze the process.

REFERENCES

Berkman, B., Rehr, H., & Rosenberg, G. (1980). A social work department develops and tests a screening mechanism to identify high social risk situations. *Social Work in Health Care, 5*(4), 373–385.

Coulton, C. (1989). Quality care assurance. *Mount Sinai Journal of Medicine, 56*(6), 435–439.

Joint Commission on Accreditation of Healthcare Organizations. (1992). *Agenda for change, 1992 edition.* Chicago: Author.

Joint Commission on Accreditation of Healthcare Organizations. (1993). *Accreditation manual for hospitals, 1994 edition.* Chicago: Author.

Joint Commission on Accreditation of Hospitals. (1980). *The QA guide: A resource for hospital quality assurance.* Chicago: Author.

Rehr, H. (Ed.). (1979). *Professional accountability for social work practice: A search for concepts and guidelines,* New York: Prodist.

Rehr, H., Blumenfield, S., Young, A., & Rosenberg, G. (1993). Social work accountability: A key to high-quality patient care and services. *Mount Sinai Journal of Medicine, 60*(5), 368–373.

Teichholz, L. (1993). Quality, Demings' principles, and physicians. *Mount Sinai Journal of Medicine, 60*(5), 350–358.

Alma T. Young, EdD, ACSW, is director, Education and Quality Assurance, Department of Social Work Services, and assistant professor, Department of Community Medicine, Mount Sinai Medical Center, One Gustave L. Levy Place, New York, NY 10029.

For further information see

Clinical Social Work; Continuing Education; Direct Practice Overview; Ethics and Values; Health Services Systems Policy; Hospital Social Work; Interdisciplinary and Interorganizational Collaboration; Licensing, Regulation, and Certification; Managed Care; Management Overview; National Association of Social Workers; Planning and Management Professions; Professional Conduct; Professional Liability and Malpractice; Public Health Services; Public Social Services; Purchasing Social Services; Social Work Profession Overview; Supervision and Consultation; Vendorship.

Key Words	
continuous quality	quality assurance
improvement	total quality
evaluation	management
monitoring	

Quality Management
Paul R. Keys

T otal quality management (TQM), the best-known quality-management technique, is, according to the National Network for Social Work Managers (Maslyn, 1992), "a fourth generation management style, replacing the most commonly used management style of today—management by results [or management by objectives]" (p. 3). However, the network cautions, TQM should be used carefully because it may not be appropriate for all organizations or for all problems in an agency. Rather, a reformed version of TQM may be most suitable for public managers, including social work managers.

HISTORY

TQM is a derivative of Japanese management principles that were imported to the United States by American automobile manufacturers during the 1980s, with the aim of increasing the sales of American-made cars that were in competition with those imported from Japan. A specific Japanese management technique, quality circles, first caught the attention of American auto manufacturers and the American public. This technique was important because quality was the major selling point for Japanese automobiles and the major perceived drawback of American automobiles.

Quality circles, popular in Japan since the 1960s, are teams of workers, often led by line workers rather than supervisors, who meet weekly to discuss production problems and solutions. By the 1970s, these teams had become popular in U.S. businesses, having expanded beyond their use in the automobile industry. There was a modest attempt to introduce them in nonbusiness settings, usually federal and some state and local governments. In the human services, the health care system and a few major hospitals most rapidly adopted quality circles, probably because of the many oversights imposed by federal health regulations.

The use of groups to solve problems in organizations was not a new idea in the United States, however. In the 1940s, many American organizations experimented with group approaches in the workplace, as a result of the human relations movement in management, spurred by the field of industrial psychology and the work of Follett (1924), a social worker, who recognized "cross-functions" and "cumulative/collective responsibility." These group approaches were essentially the bases of new forms of organizational structures such as task forces and team or matrix management. In 1939 Kurt Lewin first used the term "group dynamics," basing it on the interdependence of individuals in organizations (Weiner, 1982). Later, numerous writers, including Lewin

(1948), Likert (1961), McGregor (1960), and Zander (1977), presented systematic theories of group dynamics in organizations.

Group approaches like quality circles did not become popular in the United States until they matured in Japan as part of Japanese management, even though quality control was introduced to Japan by two American management consultants, W. Edwards Deming and Joseph M. Juran, during the 1950s. Sashkin and Kiser (1993) noted that

> during the 1950s Japanese organizations vied with each other to see which could go the farthest in applying Deming's ideas. ... They quickly established an all-industry competition and an annual prize for the organization that displayed the most comprehensive and effective applications. (p. 21)

DEFINITIONS

According to Sashkin and Kiser (1993), "*TQM means that the organization's culture is defined by and supports the constant attainment of customer satisfaction through an integrated system of tools, techniques, and training. This involves the continuous improvement of organizational processes, resulting in high quality products and services*" (p. 39; see also Deming, 1986, p. 28). Thus, TQM is a system that becomes part of an organization's culture and continues indefinitely. In practice, it must become the *primary* philosophy of the adopting organization, which then redesigns internal procedures with the goal of continuously achieving high quality.

In TQM, *quality* is often defined as meeting the requirements of internal and external customers for error-free products, services, and business processes through continuous improvement (Kingsborough Psychiatric Center, 1993). Customers (consumers) are those who directly receive outputs of the organization. *Internal customers* are departments that receive the benefits of an output from another department in their organization. For example, various departments may need timely and efficient services from an accounting department that processes travel reimbursements. *External customers,* such as clients, receive benefits but are outside the organization. *Indirect customers* are outside the processes of an organization. They may not directly receive benefits but are affected if the output is wrong or late. For example, the management of a homeless shelter may affect the agency's neighbors (Harrington, 1991).

Meeting the requirements of internal and external customers consists of identifying customers, agreeing in advance on what they expect, and deciding how to measure their satisfaction. Customers' needs define quality; thus, for instance, after surveying the staff, an accounting department would agree to send travel-reimbursement checks within two weeks, or an adult day care center would expand its hours after surveying caregivers, many of whom work late.

The error-free goal, although not always attainable, fosters a responsible attitude within the organization. When an error or problem appears, it is the responsibility of those who oversee the service or organizational process to identify the cause of the error and to carry out corrective action; for example, an intake supervisor would assign more staff to reduce the waiting time of clients.

Managing for continuous improvement requires establishing and attaining reasonable and achievable policy goals, procedures, and technical standards while improving individual skills. Managers in a quality-focused organization are expected to evaluate policy goals, procedures, and technical standards continually and to improve them as needed to achieve the desired results. For instance, the management of a Japanese nursing home might agree that the home will be totally community based. All policies would then be changed to require a community component, and the nursing home administrator would continually review all procedures to ensure community involvement.

PRINCIPLES OF TQM

Proponents of TQM generally agree on the principles necessary to achieve it. Swiss (1992) presented seven primary tenets of TQM:

1. First and foremost, the customer is the ultimate determiner of quality.
2. Quality should be built into the product [or service] early in the production (upstream) rather than being added on at the end (downstream).
3. Preventing variability is the key to producing high quality.

4. Quality results from people working within systems, not individual efforts.
5. Quality requires continuous improvement of inputs and processes.
6. Quality improvement requires strong worker participation.
7. Quality requires total organizational commitment. (p. 357)

Thus, TQM as a process is more than a collection of tools, such as quality circles, statistical processes, and flowcharts. It includes changes in philosophy, organizational culture, and the way the organization treats people.

Deming (1986) developed the following 14 principles or obligations as a new way of explaining quality, stating that "only when these become a part of the organization's culture, can TQM work" (see also Walton, 1986):

1. Create consistency of purpose for improvement of product and service.
2. Adopt the new philosophy of doing things right the first time.
3. Cease dependence on mass inspection(s) to achieve quality.
4. End the practice of awarding business on price tag alone.
5. Improve constantly and forever the system of production and service.
6. Institute training on the job.
7. Begin leadership for system improvement.
8. Drive out fear.
9. Break down barriers between staff areas.
10. Eliminate slogans, exhortations, and targets for the work force.
11. Eliminate numerical quotas.
12. Remove barriers to pride of workmanship.
13. Institute a vigorous program of education and improvement.
14. Take action to accomplish the transformation. (p. 23)

Learning Organization

An important concept often used in the implementation of TQM is the *learning organization* (Senge, 1990a, 1990b). Although the term is still being defined, it includes the notion of

an organizational system capable of becoming smarter over time, an organization that continuously improves by anticipating and creating skills needed for future success (i.e., one that thrives on change), an organization that maximizes learning opportunities by nurturing and tapping the collective wisdom of its entire work force, a setting where people are constantly, spontaneously learning and applying their knowledge in order to improve the quality of . . . services, work, and life itself, a place, ultimately, where learning has become synonymous with working. (American Society for Training and Development, 1993, p. 3)

A learning organization is open and able to benefit from continuous self-renewal through improvement. Improvement is brought on by a continuous quality-improvement process, which renders the agency more effective. For example, an agency serving people with developmental disabilities may be recognized as anticipating and adapting to clients' future needs and well recognized for pioneering needed new programs. Internally, staff knowledge, innovation, and creativity are continually and conspicuously rewarded.

Many view TQM as an excessively technical system. In fact, human resources, defined as the human factors necessary to carry out the system, may be not only the most important part of this system, but its most difficult aspect. For example, in Japan, several practices in human resource management make TQM operations possible. First, guaranteed employment helps drive out fear and fosters a constancy of purpose in organizations. Second, lifelong training and the constant rotation of jobs help familiarize employees with other departments' problems. Third, daily recitations of an agency's philosophy ingrain in employees the agency's approach to clients. Fourth, retreats and various social events in the workplace help staff understand each other's problems in meeting clients' needs.

"TOOLS" OF TQM

Teams
Teamwork is an essential component of TQM, and the current spotlight on self-directed teams in the general management literature reflects this trend. Teams are task-oriented groups of five to 15 employees who are responsible for planning and producing an entire product or process. In so doing, they are independent (self-directed) and may manage many activities that were formerly performed only by supervisors or managers. Teams meet regularly to identify, analyze, and solve problems and may set schedules and goals, evaluate their work, and so on (Harper & Harper, 1992).

The three types of teams that make quality management work—*cross-functional improvement teams, quality circles,* and *process improvement teams*—are similar in function (although their names may differ among the various quality-management theories). These teams consist of line employees from various sections of an organization who meet regularly to solve problems. (An interdisciplinary team is an example of how these teams operate, although TQM teams work on general agency problems, rather than on the problems of clients.) A parallel TQM team is a sponsoring high-level management or *executive improvement team (EIT).* An EIT sets priorities for establishing the quality of a product or process, removing roadblocks that could impede the quality teams, and reviewing and evaluating a lower-level team's progress. (An EIT team in an agency might be composed of an associate or deputy director and various department heads.)

Other Tools
TQM features many charts to show the progress (or lack of progress) in the quality-improvement effort and hence areas that require further decision making. Some of these visual aids are *statistical process charts* (including flowcharts), which depict the timeliness and progress of improvements in quality; *Pareto charts,* which identify critical areas that need improvement; and *cause–effect analysis/diagrams,* which show the links between problems and possible causes. In addition, *control charts* show the upper and lower limits of quality performance (such as the minimum and maximum waiting time for clients), and *run charts* illustrate trends over time (for example, decreases in waiting time because of new procedures). *Scatter diagrams* and *histograms* (bar charts) show specific products or services that meet desired quality objectives.

Other tools usually include decision making based on data, perhaps *a zero defects policy,* and *benchmarking.* Benchmarking is a formal effort to compare the quality of an organization's processes and activities to the standards of recognized leaders in the field as a target for improvement. It involves surveys of and visits to these leaders, as well as surveys of internal and external customers' needs and wants, extensive training, and perhaps a revised mission statement for a better focus on quality (American Society for Training and Development, 1992).

RELATED QUALITY-MANAGEMENT TECHNIQUES

Continuous Process Improvement
By the 1980s, many American management theorists and managers had begun to use the concept of continuous process improvement (CPI) instead of TQM. Most observers credit General Electric with creating the CPI process, which is not a new system, but almost an "Americanization" of TQM in that Japanese terms are not used. The processes and techniques are similar to those of TQM, but terms and procedures differ (for exam-

ple, the names of the teams and the types of measurements that are used).

CPI focuses on examining and analyzing the various processes used in an organization and simplifying them by reducing or eliminating duplication, gaps, and time-wasting steps. Most often it examines all the work processes and activities of the various units of an organization (cross-functional) that are responsible for accomplishing them using control charts and flowcharts similar to those used in TQM to diagram the processes completely (see Robson, 1991). In a human services organization, a process, such as eligibility determination, may cut across various departments, each of which plays a role in the timeliness and effectiveness of the outcome of a client's eligibility.

Business Process Improvement

Business process improvement (BPI), also known as *business process re-engineering* (Harrington, 1991), is a related approach. Like TQM and CPI, it involves setting standards and achievable targets through benchmarking and features line and management teams, statistical process controls, and charts. It uses an appointed "quality coordinator," called a *BPI champion* or *czar*—a manager who is responsible for the total quality effort. It also uses *process coordinators,* employees who are responsible for a specific and identified process (such as intake at an agency), and *process facilitators,* frequently outside consultants, who guide the organization through the initial planning and are often responsible for team follow-up activities.

BPI looks at *macroprocesses* (major functions of an organization) and breaks them down into *subprocesses* (logically related sequential activities contributing to the mission of the macroprocess). For instance, determining eligibility (a subprocess) contributes to the function (macroprocess) of providing monetary benefits to a client in an income maintenance agency. BPI also looks at *activities* (actions in all processes that are required to produce a particular result, such as determining a client's assets during the eligibility–determination process) and *tasks* (the smallest microview of any process, usually performed by one individual, such as interviewing).

Uses of Quality Management in the Human Services

TQM and related theories are clearly business ideas. What are the advantages of using quality management concepts in social work organizations? Why have many innovative human services organizations and their managers quickly embraced these ideas as guiding principles for their agencies? One answer lies in the long-standing quest for quality and effectiveness in the delivery of human services by political bodies, boards of directors, funding sources, managers, and executives. Quality management offers yet another strategy and set of tools for attaining this sought-after goal.

What are some appropriate and practical uses of TQM and related strategies in human services organizations? The first and most sophisticated human services users of quality management, both in Japan and in the United States, have been hospitals because of their stringent external quality-control requirements (see Goldsmith, 1989). The American health care system has, in many respects, duplicated some features of the Japanese quality awards system. It offers honors and exemplars, such as the Witt Award, the National Association for Healthcare Quality, and the National Demonstration Project on Quality Improvement in Health Care.

American public-sector organizations at the federal and state levels and, to a lesser extent, the local level, have also adopted TQM ideas. In New York City, for example, the Kingsborough Psychiatric Center (1993), part of the State of New York Department of Mental Health, has an extensive TQM program and training. Few similar examples exist in general social services areas, however.

Veterans Administration

Koons (1991) described the use of TQM in reducing the time required to process insurance claims and benefits in a Veterans Administration (VA) regional office. The managers' focus on quality maximized the use of the knowledge, skills, and experience of VA employees to help improve the work processes that delivered veterans' benefits and services by teaching all employees to work on problem-solving teams. The problem began when regional officials began to question how many applications, claims, or pieces of correspondence were processed without mistakes or delays and found that the answer was uncertain. The regional office's managers did know that their efforts were frequently confusing or nonresponsive to veterans who were seeking help. Although the regional office had developed many standards based on estimates of internal work processes and procedures, these internal standards did not consider the external customers' needs. Furthermore, many services reflected paternalistic views of what regional officials thought was best for veterans, rather than the veterans' actual priorities and needs.

The regional office chose to improve the macroprocess of granting loans on a veteran's insurance policy. Although its standard required granting the loan within five days, the actual process often took up to two weeks, which was much too long because a veteran who applies for such a loan probably needs the funds immediately for an emergency. The regional office managers examined all the subprocesses and activities and then offered several options to speed up the overall process: faxing, rather than mailing, applications; retaining a special post office box for the receipt of loan applications; improving the timeliness of mail pickups; and scheduling delivery of mail by 6:00 A.M. to gain a full day's processing time. Improvements in these activities and other actions cut the processing time considerably and benefited the veterans who were the customers.

Social Services

Another example, recounted by Cupaiuolo (1987), illustrates many quality-management principles in regard to Barbara Blum's implementation of the New York State Willowbrook court decree. This decree mandated the timely placement of Willowbrook's developmentally disabled residents into appropriate community settings in New York. At the time, Blum headed the Metropolitan Unit (MPU), the agency set up to carry out the Willowbrook decree.

The principles that Blum used included developing a strategic vision and mission and espousing a commitment to good-quality community care placements for Willowbrook residents as a core value. MPU also selected contract agencies on the basis of their proved commitment to high-quality community care.

Later, as the head of the New York State Department of Social Services (DSS), Blum used similar principles: a clear commitment to the mission of providing income assistance; food stamps; Medicaid; job training; and support services, including day care and counseling, to make families and individuals as self-sufficient as possible (Cupaiuolo, 1987). Blum remained committed to the client services mission in spite of heavy political pressures to develop new computerized information systems that could have displaced this mission.

Blum's management style at the DSS included the ability to communicate the mission and her in-depth knowledge of the "product" (social services) and the ability to delegate tasks to her competent and committed staff. At the DSS, she created key planning and management teams that devised procedures and carried out mandated

programs (Cupaiuolo, 1987). In addition, the teams also framed and designed new DSS initiatives that involved setting up special housing programs for elderly people, revising foster care rates, and improving day care and other services.

Blum's style consisted of a concern for employees as people and a commitment to the "customers," in this case, the county departments of social services that provided actual services to clients using state DSS funds. As commissioner of DSS, Blum scheduled visits and public forums with county departments early in her tenure to solicit their opinions on local problems and issues to guide statewide policy-making.

School of Social Work

Another example of quality management is the experience of a large East Coast school of social work in handling increased applications for admission. The number of applicants almost doubled over a two-year period because the poor economic conditions of the recession made service occupations, such as social work, much more attractive to students. At the same time, the university administration cut back faculty and staff positions associated with admissions, so that the remaining staff and faculty had much greater demands on their time. The dean realized that normal admissions procedures were too labor intensive and not adequate to meet the challenge of the vastly increased number of applications. Consequently, the school formed a committee of faculty from all areas of the school (a cross-functional team, not limited to people in admissions).

The cross-functional committee analyzed and charted all the school's admissions processes, including the time and labor expended at each step. The faculty presented information on the types of applicants who tended to be successful in the program, including information on the characteristics of the "best" 20 percent of students who should be recruited and hence identified in admissions interviews (the Pareto principle). Then the committee reviewed the admissions process, including all subprocesses and activities, in an effort to discover duplications and gaps that wasted the faculty's and staff's time and decreased efficiency. After conducting surveys and interviews with admissions faculty and staff, the committee decided, with the faculty's approval, to retain only activities and reports that would yield the information necessary to make valid decisions on particular applicants. Reorganized staffing for the admissions function followed; quality-management changes included the greater use of the staff's,

Quality Management

rather than the faculty's; time; the elimination of some steps in the process; and an intensified review of applicants' characteristics that predicted later professional success.

ADVANTAGES AND DISADVANTAGES OF TQM IN SOCIAL WORK

A. Cupaiuolo, director of the Michaelian Center for Public Policy and Management, Pace University, White Plains, New York (personal communication, July 6, 1993), stated that in considering quality-management applications in human services agencies, it is helpful to differentiate between service management and maintenance management. The former refers to activities that are directly related to the quality, substance, and effectiveness of the agency's essential product or services, such as casework or child care, whereas the latter consists of activities such as budgeting, human resources administration, and record keeping.

According to Cupaiuolo, human services agencies that are contemplating quality management should be careful to include maintenance management and not focus solely on service management. Otherwise, there is a danger that professionally trained social work managers will not view maintenance management as being as important as service management. Employees who handle records or billing must be as sensitive to customers' or clients' needs as are the providers of direct services.

Swiss (1992) pointed out that "the 'purist' form of TQM ignores the fact that public organizations [among others] most often produce services, not products ... measuring quality for services is highly complex and difficult (though not wholly impossible)" (p. 357).

A related issue is, "Who is the customer?" In public social services and human services, multiple customers are the rule. "Since the 'customer' drives the definition of quality, it is critical to define who the customer (or client) is" (Swiss, 1992, p. 358). Swiss noted that competing interests with directly contradictory demands can be found in most government services, from education to health care, and that both the general public and funding sources are customers. He went on to say that "government organizations have obligations to more than their immediate clients. Therefore, 'quality' is often a compromise among various customers" (p. 360). To remedy this situation, Swiss recommended "reformed TQM" that would emphasize (1) providing feedback to customers, (2) tracking performance, (3) engaging in continuous improvement, and (4) including the participation of workers.

The fact that the terminology of quality management itself can be an issue for social workers is implicit in Swiss's views. Social workers, for example, generally prefer the term *client* over *customer*, the term used in quality management. Yet viewing the client as a customer suggests that the client has clear choices and decisions in the arrangement of services. Thus, viewing the client as a customer may be congruent with the principles of clients' self-determination that are basic to social work.

Some object that TQM is but the latest managerial fad and that it is only a new way of saying the same old things. Reactions such as these preclude an interest in the application of quality-management principles.

PROSPECTS FOR TQM IN SOCIAL WORK

TQM is like earlier managerial techniques, such as management by objectives, zero-based budgeting, and participatory management. If used appropriately, however, it can lead to the more effective provision of human services to social work clients by improving specific aspects of the service delivery process.

Consistent with the *NASW Code of Ethics* (NASW, 1994), TQM offers distinct techniques to operationalize clients' self-determination by more formally recognizing the needs of customers or clients. Through participation, it offers a way to include more systematically the views of all staff in the service delivery process. It also presents a means of conserving and directing more resources to actual services for clients by eliminating gaps and duplications that waste the valuable time of staff who are charged with providing direct services. In the current environment of cutbacks, TQM can allow the continuation of existing levels of service by identifying and simplifying the service delivery and administrative processes. Through its team approaches, it also offers an exciting new direction for group workers to contribute directly to the quality of the work life of organizations. Surveys (such as Walker, 1988) have shown that there is a great interest in group work and the principles of group dynamics in industry. In summary, TQM can be a useful tool if it is applied by social workers appropriately and without bias.

REFERENCES

American Society for Training and Development. (1992, June). Understanding benchmarking: The search for best practice. Issue 9207 of *Info-Line: Practical Guidelines for Training and Development*. Alexandria, VA: Author.

American Society for Training and Development. (1993, June). Learning organizations: The trainer's role. Issue 9306 of *Info-Line: Practical Guidelines for Training and Development.* Alexandria, VA: Author.

Cupaiuolo, A. (1987, March 29). *Excellence in human service management.* Paper presented at the 48th national conference of the American Society for Public Administration, Boston.

Deming, E. W. (1986). *Out of crisis.* Cambridge: Center for Advanced Engineering Study, Massachusetts Institute of Technology.

Follett, M. P. (1924). *Dynamic administration: The collected papers of Mary Parker Follett.* New York: Harper & Row.

Goldsmith, S. B. (1989). *Theory Z hospital management: Lessons from Japan.* Rockville, MD: Aspen Systems.

Harper, A., & Harper, B. (1992). *Skill-building for self-directed team members.* New York: MW Corporation.

Harrington, J. J. (1991). *Business process improvement.* New York: McGraw-Hill.

Kingsborough Psychiatric Center. (1993). *A basic CQI/TQM training module.* Queens, NY: Author.

Koons, P. F. (1991, Summer). Getting comfortable with TQM. *The Bureaucrat—the Journal for Business Managers,* pp. 35–38.

Lewin, K. (1948). *Resolving social conflicts: Selected papers on group dynamics.* New York: Harper & Row.

Likert, R. (1961). *New patterns of management.* New York: McGraw-Hill.

Maslyn, R. (1992, Summer). Social work managers: Be cautious with reinventing government and total quality management. *Social Work Executive,* pp. 3–4.

McGregor, D. (1960). *The human side of enterprise.* New York: McGraw-Hill.

National Association of Social Workers. (1994). *NASW code of ethics.* Silver Spring, MD: Author.

Robson, G. D. (1991). *Continuous process improvement: Simplifying work flow systems.* New York: Free Press.

Sashkin, M., & Kiser, K. J. (1993). *Putting total quality management to work: What TQM means, how to use it and how to sustain it over the long run.* San Francisco: Berrett-Koehler.

Senge, P. M. (1990a). *The fifth discipline: The art and practice of the learning organization.* New York: Doubleday/Currency.

Senge, P. M. (1990b, Fall). The leader's new work: Building learning organizations. *Sloan Management Review,* pp. 7–23.

Swiss, J. E. (1992). Adapting total quality management to government. *Public Administration Review, 52,* 356–362.

Walker, J. (1988). The place of social group work in organizations. In P. R. Keys & L. Ginsberg (Eds.), *New management in human services.* Silver Spring, MD: National Association of Social Workers.

Walton, M. (1986). *The Deming management method.* New York: Putnam/Perigee.

Weiner, M. E. (1982). *Human services management: Analysis and applications.* Homewood, IL: Dorsey Press.

Zander, A. (1977). *Groups at work.* San Francisco: Jossey-Bass.

FURTHER READING

Anderson, L. K. (1993). Teams: Group process, success, and barriers. *Journal of Nursing Administration, 23*(9), 9–15.

Blumenthal, D. (1993). Total quality management and physicians? Clinical decisions. *Journal of the American Medical Association, 269,* 2775–2778.

Darling, J. R. (1992). Total quality management: The key role of leadership strategies. *Leadership and Organizational Development Journal, 13*(4), 3–7.

Davis, D. S. (1992, December 7). *Total quality management: Public sector applications for training programs.* Paper presented at the American Vocational Association, St. Louis.

Hinton, J., & Stout, C. E. (1993). Patient satisfaction. In M. B. Squire, C. E. Stout, & D. H. Ruben (Eds.), *Current advances in inpatient psychiatric care: A handbook* (pp. 41–52). Westport, CT: Greenwood Press.

Raggo, W. V., & Reid, W. H. (1991). Total quality management strategies in mental health systems. *Journal of Mental Health Administration, 18*(3), 253–263.

Wakefield, D. S., & Wakefield, B. J. (1993). Overcoming the barriers to implementation of TQM/CQI in hospitals: Myths and realities. *Quality Review Bulletin, 19*(3), 83–88.

Paul R. Keys, PhD, is dean, College of Health and Human Services, Southeast Missouri State University, 1 University Plaza, Cape Girardeau, MO 63701.

For further information see

Case Management; Ethics and Values; Information Systems; Management Overview; Management: Diverse Workplaces; Organizations: Context for Social Services Delivery; Personnel Management; Planning and Management Professions; Professional Conduct; Public Services Management; Quality Assurance; Social Work Profession Overview; Supervision and Consultation; Unions; Vendorship; Voluntarism; Volunteer Management.

Key Words

management	total quality
organizations	management
quality assurance	

R

Radical Social Work

See Progressive Social Work

Rankin, Jeannette

See Biographies section, Volume 3

Rapoport, Lydia

See Biographies section, Volume 3

Rape

See Child Sexual Abuse; Sexual Assault

Recording
Jill Doner Kagle

Recording has always played a significant role in social work practice and in the administration of social services. Social workers keep records about their clients and about the purpose, process, and impact of their services. In their records, social workers identify, describe, and assess the client situation; define the purpose and describe the process of service; outline service goals, plans, and activities; and evaluate the progress and outcome of their activities with and on behalf of clients. Records are used to store information, facilitate service delivery, communicate with others inside and outside the agency, inform practice and administrative decisions, capture funding, demonstrate compliance with agency and social policies, educate and supervise practitioners, manage quality assurance, and perform research. Although records have many uses, the primary purpose for recording is accountability. Practitioners discharge an important legal and ethical responsibility to their agencies, clients, communities, and profession by documenting, explaining, and evaluating their services.

If records are to be accountable in today's complicated service environment, they must provide needed information in a usable form to a wide audience. Information from records may be used not only by the practitioner, supervisor, consultant, and other professionals in the agency, but also by the courts, other community agencies, oversight and funding organizations, managed care networks, and accrediting groups, as well as the client and the client's family, attorney, and employer. Each of these audiences has a different interest in the service relationship; each may need different information or information in a different form.

As the demand for accountability and the audience for the record have grown, so too has the need to include more detailed information in records. In preparing their records, practitioners are asked to respond to the information needs of future as well as current audiences. Agencies and practitioners are especially sensitive to the possibility of litigation and the use of the record in court. If practitioners are to meet these and other accountability demands, they need guidance and support from their agencies. They need to know what information to include in (and exclude from) their records. They need forms, formats, and guidelines for organizing information so that it is easy to find and retrieve. They need sufficient time and resources to keep their records up-to-date. They need a system that encourages them to update their records without redundancy and to correct errors and inaccuracies.

As the amount of information in the record has increased, the efficiency of record-keeping systems has deteriorated. Practitioners and administrators may spend as much as 25 percent to 50 percent of their time preparing, retrieving, and using information from records (Edwards & Reid, 1989). Although most of the statistics on the amount of time and other resources consumed by record keeping and related tasks are probably inaccurate, it is clear that the increased demand for record keeping has not been met with a commensurate investment in professional staff, clerical support, and computers or other cost-saving equipment. As a result, practitioners are finding it even more difficult to keep up with record keeping, and agency records may be out-of-date and of poor quality (Kagle, 1993).

At the same time, wider access to the record and its contents has eroded client privacy. Practitioners and their agencies seek to protect confidentiality through such mechanisms as client access, informed consent for release of information, and proper storage and handling of written and computerized records. Nonetheless, personal information that appears in a record may be disseminated within and between service organizations and may reach those who will not use the information in the client's best interests.

Recording is much more than a practice skill. It involves a series of important professional decisions at all levels of the organization. In making each entry, organizing each record, and developing each recording system, social workers constantly balance the demand for accountability against the competing and equally important goals of efficiency and client privacy.

HISTORY OF RECORD KEEPING IN SOCIAL WORK

Over the past century, records have become more diverse and complex as the demand for accountability and the audience for the record have grown and changed. New recording approaches have been introduced and have taken their place alongside existing forms. Within a single agency, practitioners with different backgrounds may use very different theories and approaches to recording. Record keeping as a whole has changed in response to changing practice theories and methods, practitioner roles and responsibilities, agency structures and interagency relationships, and recording techniques and technologies. Yet agency records are often an eclectic mix of forms and formats that originated at different points in history when different assumptions about accountability were current.

Ledgers and Narrative Records

The earliest records were simple ledgers documenting the distribution of resources to people in need (Timms, 1972). These records showed "no act of judgment" (Sheffield, 1920, p. 20), but, like today's "face sheets," stored facts about the client situation, the need, and the resources provided. By the second half of the 19th century, records had expanded to include not just who received what, but also why resources were needed and what impact they had on the client situation. For the first time, practitioners were "making a case," that is, making judgments about clients' needs, resources, and responses. The notion of accountability had broadened beyond documentation to explanation and evaluation. A new form of recording was needed; the narrative report was born.

The publication in 1920 of Sheffield's *The Social Case History: Its Construction and Content* signaled an important development in the history of social work practice and recording. Sheffield linked the three purposes of recording to those of social casework itself: "(1) the immediate purpose of furthering effective treatment of individual clients, (2) the ultimate purpose of general social betterment, and (3) the incidental purpose of establishing the caseworker herself in critical thinking" (Sheffield, 1920, pp. 5–6). In her view, the record should move beyond factual information to the "key conceptions which would give the facts significance" (p. 21). The worker should "frame a hypothesis as to what a fact means, and then search for confirmation or disproof in recurrent instances" (p. 38). These "key conceptions," a precursor of today's "assessments," focused on social rather than psychological causes of personal distress. Like Richmond (1917, 1925), Sheffield believed that the need for social casework services originated in defects in the social order. For Sheffield, accountability meant describing, evaluating, and improving social conditions as well as delivering effective services and enhancing practitioner skills.

Process Recording

During this period, records were influenced not just by developments in social casework theory, but also by developments in the social sciences and social research. In 1928, Burgess, a sociologist, suggested that social workers should make their records more useful for sociological interpretations by including verbatim accounts of what clients said. Verbatim records would reveal "the person as he really is to himself, in his own language" (Burgess, 1928, p. 527) and would therefore be useful not just in service delivery but also in research. Other sociologists and social workers argued that practitioners would find keeping such records too time-consuming and that practitioners would not be able to recall accurately what the client actually said. Further, some asked whether a caseworker could be both practitioner and researcher, a question that would again be raised in later decades. "Can one be simultaneously scientific and sympathetic? Can one simultaneously experience and reflect? Can one preserve objectivity in a subjective experience?" (Eliot, 1928, p. 540). This debate went beyond the content of the record to its ultimate purpose: Should it be accountability or research? During the 1920s, it became clear that accountability would remain the primary function of the record, with research relegated to a secondary role.

Nonetheless, by the end of the 1920s, the process record, a verbatim account of the social worker's and the client's communications during an interview, was being used in agencies to document some cases. Its purpose was twofold: to monitor service delivery and to gather information for development of practice theory. Today, process recording has been supplanted by other more-efficient approaches to accountability and other more-systematic methods of gathering information for research. However, process records are still widely used in social work education as a means of teaching and learning practice (Wilson, 1980). Students learn about their clients, the service

transaction, and themselves by preparing, recalling, documenting, and analyzing their transactions with clients and by responding to supervisory comments on the process record. Preparing for process recording means that the student must concentrate on each interaction in sessions with clients. Recalling and documenting the process of service permits the student to review and re-experience what occurred. Finally, analyzing the process and responding to supervisory comments helps students to develop a deeper understanding of self, the client, and the relationship.

Despite its widespread use, process recording has several limitations. It provides only indirect, incomplete, and distorted information about what actually occurred in the service transaction; it is time-consuming; and it does not prepare students with skills in summary recording.

Diagnostic Recording

Hamilton's *Social Case Recording* (1936) and *Principles of Social Case Recording* (1946) were the most influential books in the history and development of social work recording. Hamilton's approach to recording, the diagnostic record, was grounded in psychosocial practice theory. Like Sheffield, Hamilton (1946) believed that the record was "the writer's attempt to express, as practitioner, the meaning of the case" (p. 44). Unlike Sheffield, who believed that the record should focus on common characteristics and social causes, Hamilton believed it should focus on individual characteristics and psychosocial causes.

Hamilton's work cemented the relationship between practice, the practitioner, supervision, and the record. In her view, recording was not a skill to be learned by following guidelines; rather, the quality of a record grew out of an understanding of clients and was reflected in the practitioner's diagnostic judgment. "In the ultimate sense, only the trained diagnostician can write a good record, for only he can pluck from the unending web of social experience the thread of possible significance" (Hamilton, 1946, p. 209). To Hamilton, accountability meant documentation of the worker's evolving diagnosis of the client situation. Records were written primarily for use in supervision to develop the practitioner's diagnosis of each client situation and to build the practitioner's diagnostic skill. For subsequent generations of practitioners, recording has meant demonstrating to the supervisor the quality of one's diagnostic thinking.

The open-ended and discursive nature of the diagnostic record made it especially useful in individualizing the client situation and providing information for psychosocial supervision. However, these same qualities made it ill-suited to a wider audience and for other uses. Such records tend to be idiosyncratic, unsystematic, and inefficient. Important information may be absent or difficult to retrieve, whereas sensitive personal information and unconfirmed hypotheses may be all too accessible. As the definition of accountability broadened and agencies became more concerned with efficiency and client privacy, problems with the diagnostic record began to surface. With less time for recording and more uses for the record, agencies sought to establish guidelines and find formats that would assist practitioners in selecting information and organizing the content of the record.

CONTEMPORARY APPROACHES

The 1960s and 1970s brought major changes to social practice and to the service delivery environment. The definition of accountability had shifted: Agencies and practitioners were expected to deliver services that were demonstrably effective. During this period, three major new approaches to record keeping were introduced into the field: tape recording, problem-oriented recording, and time-series recording. These approaches took their place alongside the narrative record and process recording, which continued to have a strong influence on the field.

Tape Recording

Audiotaping and videotaping allowed the practitioner, supervisor, and classroom teacher to observe, review, and analyze individual, group, and family sessions with clients. These tapes offered a new perspective on what occurred between the worker and the client. Although such tapes might become part of the record and fulfilled most of the requirements of accountability, they supplemented but in no way replaced the need to keep other records. Rather, like process recording, audiotapes and videotapes were useful in educating students and in supervising family therapy and other process-oriented approaches to practice.

Problem-Oriented Recording

The problem-oriented record was originally developed to improve medical education and encourage interdisciplinary cooperation in health care (Weed, 1969). This approach is based on a straightforward notion of accountability. Problems are identified, services are planned and delivered, problems are resolved. Practitioners from different disciplines were to collaborate in collecting information, listing problems, formulating plans, and evaluating results. In its current use in health and

mental health settings, practitioners often work independently but record using the same format.

The problem list and progress notes are crucial to this approach. The problem list acts as a planning and accountability document; practitioners list each problem they initially identify and add new problems as they surface. Treatment is organized around solving each problem, and information in progress notes is linked by number to items on the problem list. Progress notes follow a "SOAP" format: S = subjective information (from patient and family), O = objective information (from tests and observation), A = assessment, and P = plans. At termination or discharge, problems are to be resolved or stabilized; for problems outstanding, alternative plans, such as referrals to community agencies, are to be outlined.

The problem-oriented record offers a streamlined format for organizing the record. However, it tends to partialize and oversimplify assessment, de-emphasize strengths and resources, focus on biomedical rather than psychosocial concerns, and disregard the complexity of service delivery.

Time-Series Recording

The time-series record is most closely associated with behavioral intervention, single-subject research designs, and the scientist–practitioner paradigm (Bloom & Fischer, 1982). Nonetheless, this approach may be used in records of nonbehavioral practice. Time-series records document repeated measures of the specific behaviors, attitudes, or interactions that are the focus of social work intervention. Their purpose is to provide information about movement toward achieving the goals of service. Although the selection, implementation, and interpretation of such measures are complicated and controversial, their documentation is fairly straightforward (Corcoran & Fischer, 1987; Jayaratne & Kagle, in press; Thomas, 1978). Once the goal of service and target of intervention are identified, the practitioner selects one or more measures, defines the time factors involved, and outlines a recording process. The raw data may be collected by the worker, the client, or a third party. For example, a practitioner may document observations of the client's behavior during individual or group sessions; a client may fill out a questionnaire or keep a record of his or her behaviors, feelings, or reactions; a parent, teacher, or family member may observe a client's behavior at regular intervals. Once the data are collected, the practitioner transfers the information to a chart or graph. These data can then be analyzed visually or statistically to determine whether there have been changes in target behaviors, attitudes, or interactions and whether there has been movement toward achieving treatment objectives.

Despite a decade of efforts to encourage practitioners to use this approach to practice and documentation, time-series records are being used by relatively few social work practitioners. Even behaviorists trained in the use of single-subject designs and measures do not routinely use this approach to accountability. Their reasons tend to be practical rather than conceptual: Such methods may interfere with practice; be too time-consuming; or be unsuited to the agency, clientele, or target problems (Richey, Blythe, & Berlin, 1987). For practitioners more comfortable with psychosocial, ecological, or family systems concepts, the problems may also be theoretical. This approach to record keeping tends to focus practice and the record on client behaviors rather than on other aspects of the client situation.

Computerization and Standardized Records

Some social services agencies began using computers for business and management functions during the 1960s and 1970s. Following the development of the personal computer in the 1980s, most social services agencies began using computers to support some aspects of record keeping. Automation does not necessarily change the content of the record or the functions of recording. However, it does substantially alter the process of documentation and the use of information. Today, computers are most often found on the desks of clerical workers, business managers, and agency administrators. They use computers to log appointments; perform billing, budgeting, and accounting; collect and analyze information about clients, services, and personnel; and prepare reports and other documents. Letters and records can now be routinely printed without errors. Data on client needs, caseloads, service patterns, and productivity can be quickly analyzed and used in management decisions. Archival records can be efficiently stored and retrieved. Information can be retrieved for agency-based and academic research.

Standardized forms are used in most social services agencies to collect specific information about clients, services, and workers. They are an efficient means of ensuring that particular information is systematically documented. Most forms can be completed with short answers or check marks. They simplify and routinize record keeping and permit easy access to information that is necessary for caseload, fiscal, and agency management. However, standardized forms fail to capture the unique nature of the client situation or the special qualities of the service transaction.

Agencies differ in the degree to which they balance the use of forms with the use of narrative reports. Before the widespread use of computers, standardized forms were most often used in public agencies that delivered mandated services and employed fewer professional workers. To some extent, this approach to documentation standardizes and controls not just recording but also practice decisions. Today, agencies under private auspices in which professional workers deliver services to voluntary clients are using more standardized forms in their records. Automation has affected not just those agencies that have their own computer systems but also agencies that have entered into purchase-of-service and other financial arrangements with organizations that have automated data collection and analysis.

Even in agencies with sizable computer capacity, practitioners' information needs are often neglected (Kagle, 1991). The data that practitioners supply are used to support management but not practice decisions. The next important step in the development of computerized records is to increase their use in caseload management and practice decision support. Practitioners could benefit from reports that provided them, for example, with a profile of cases they opened and closed during the previous month, a list of cases due for review, and a caseload analysis. Moreover, computers have the potential for simplifying the practitioner's record-keeping tasks; however, in most agencies computers have actually increased the demand for paperwork because practitioners are expected to fill out more forms and provide more information.

In the future, more agencies will have automated their client records so that practitioners can immediately call up current information. Social workers need direct access to these systems. Finally, practitioners need access to personal computers or workstations; to modems that permit them to call up databases with the latest information about client problems and agency resources; and to software that assists them in diagnosis, treatment, and record keeping.

CURRENT ISSUES AND FUTURE DIRECTIONS

A recent study of social services agencies and departments in 20 states found that record keeping had become a serious problem (Kagle, 1993). In many agencies, the demand for record keeping had far outstripped available resources. Record keeping had become too time-consuming and practitioners had become resistant and resentful of the task. Records were often poorly written and not up-to-date. Practitioners were preparing their records long after the events being documented and sometimes months after cases had been closed. Although some practitioners and administrators were worried about the cost of record keeping and the potential encroachments on client privacy, many were overdocumenting their cases in an effort to avoid liability.

The current challenge is to develop record-keeping systems that meet the demand for accountability at reasonable cost and without unnecessarily compromising client privacy. This means limiting the content of the record to information that is pertinent to the delivery of services: who the client is, what the client needs, what services are delivered, and how these services affect the client and the need. The record should include a description and assessment of the client situation as well as an analysis of the purpose, goals, plans, process, progress, and effect of services. Records should demonstrate a clear link between assessment of the client situation; analysis of available resources and interventions; decisions and actions regarding the purpose, goal, and plan of service; and definable and meaningful outcomes. Practitioners can best protect themselves and their agencies in situations of potential liability by following the standards for competent practice and accountability. This means conducting a careful and thorough assessment of the client situation; responding to identified problems and needs; selecting appropriate and timely interventions; and documenting all pertinent information, decisions, and actions.

As agencies respond to the various demands of accountability, they also need to establish and monitor policies to ensure that they are safeguarding information in records, informing clients of the limits of confidentiality, and providing clients with opportunities for access to their records. Agencies need procedures for professional and support staff that protect written, typed, and computerized records from unwarranted access. They also need an atmosphere in which client privacy is respected in conversation inside and outside the workplace. At the same time, clients should not be misled into believing that all information they disclose can be held confidential. The *NASW Code of Ethics* (NASW, 1994) provides excellent guidance for communicating with clients about the extent and limits of confidentiality. As an additional safeguard, clients should be given access to their records. Furthermore, if clients' consent is to be truly informed, clients should be encouraged to review records before authorizing their release to outside individuals or agencies.

The goal of accountability is best met if information in records is relevant, accurate, easy to retrieve, well written, and up-to-date. Practitioners need realistic guidelines that assist them in selecting information and preparing their records. Guidelines should suggest what information to include and how to organize content. Agencies should also formulate flexible time lines for completing each component of the record, from the opening summary to interim notes to the closing summary. Adding checklists and other forms may save time and help ensure that needed information is documented. Practitioners should not be expected to complete tasks that could be more efficiently performed by clerical staff or a computer.

Clearly, practitioners need institutional support for their record keeping. Agencies may need to redirect resources to ensure that sufficient time, time-saving equipment, and secretarial services are available and used. It may be necessary to change the agency's atmosphere so that record keeping is recognized as a meaningful practice-related responsibility rather than a burdensome task imposed by managers. Indeed, record keeping can support and enhance practice, improving clinical effectiveness. The act of recording can help the worker think through the content and meaning of the case, leading to new insights and directions. The record itself can be a valuable resource, documenting the process of service and its effect on the client situation over time. However, recording can be useful only if it is connected in time and substance with the practice it documents. If record keeping is delayed or the record's contents are not clearly linked to crucial clinical issues, recording becomes remote from practice and the record suffers. Records can further enhance clinical services if they are used as a developmental tool in supervision to demonstrate the practitioner's growth and to identify areas for further learning. In some agencies records are used only to uncover workers' weaknesses; in many, they have become a lightning rod for conflict between practitioners and managers.

Some problems in record keeping may be traced to inadequacies in education and training for recording. Most social work students are introduced to record keeping for the first time in field work and their experiences vary widely. Some spend considerable time on process recording with insufficient time spent learning to prepare narrative summary reports. Others learn to prepare the records required by their field instructors and field agencies, which may not meet the expectations of other supervisors or agencies. Some practitioners may have learned recording at a time when other theories of accountability dominated. Other practitioners may never have developed good writing and recording skills. Supervision, consultation, in-service training, and continuing education may help current practitioners improve their ability to record. Social work education may prepare future practitioners more adequately by directing classroom attention to record-keeping theories and practices and focusing field instruction on contemporary approaches and models.

Accountability is a means of demonstrating and promoting the quality of social work services. Good records can support and enhance good practice. Social work agencies and practitioners are finding it more difficult to meet increased accountability requirements while serving more and more troubled clients. Record keeping has suffered. The goal is to make records more concise and meaningful, to focus their content on service delivery and its effect on clients, and to use new and emerging technologies to simplify the record-keeping task and protect client privacy.

REFERENCES

Bloom, M., & Fischer, J. (1982). *Evaluating practice: Guidelines for the accountable professional.* Englewood Cliffs, NJ: Prentice Hall.
Burgess, E. W. (1928). What social case records should contain to be useful for sociological interpretation. *Social Forces, 6*(4), 524–532.
Corcoran, K., & Fischer, J. (1987). *Measurement in clinical practice.* New York: Free Press.
Edwards, R., & Reid, W. J. (1989). Structured case recording in child welfare: An assessment of social workers' reactions. *Social Work, 34,* 49–52.
Eliot, T. (1928). Objectivity and subjectivity in the case record. *Social Forces, 6*(4), 539–544.
Hamilton, G. (1936). *Social case recording.* New York: Columbia University Press.
Hamilton, G. (1946). *Principles of social case recording.* New York: Columbia University Press.
Jayaratne, S., & Kagle, J. (in press). Should systematic assessment, monitoring, and evaluation tools be incorporated into traditional practice as empowerment aids for clients? In W. W. Hudson & P. S. Nurius, *Controversial issues in social work research.* New York: Allyn and Bacon.
Kagle, J. (1991). *Social work records.* Belmont, CA: Wadsworth.
Kagle, J. (1993). Recordkeeping: Directions for the 1990s. *Social Work, 38,* 190–196.
National Association of Social Workers. (1994). *NASW code of ethics.* Washington, DC: Author.
Richey, C. A., Blythe, B. J., & Berlin, S. B. (1987). Do social workers evaluate their practice? *Social Work Research and Abstracts, 23*(2), 14–20.
Richmond, M. (1917). *Social diagnosis.* New York: Russell Sage Foundation.
Richmond, M. (1925). Why case records? *Family, 6,* 214–216.
Sheffield, A. E. (1920). *The social case history: Its construction and content.* New York: Russell Sage.
Thomas, E. (1978). Research and service in single-case experimentation: Conflicts and choices. *Social Work Research and Abstracts, 14*(1), 20–31.
Timms, N. (1972). *Recording in social work.* Boston: Routledge & Kegan Paul.
Weed, L. (1969). *Medical records, medical evaluation, and patient care.* Cleveland: Case Western Reserve University Press.
Wilson, S. (1980). *Recording: Guidelines for social workers.* New York: Free Press.

Jill Doner Kagle, PhD, ACSW, LCSW, is professor, School of Social Work, University of Illinois at Urbana–Champaign, 1207 W. Oregon Street, Urbana, IL 61801.

For further information see

Agency-Based Research; Assessment; Case Management; Clinical Social Work; Computer Utilization; Direct Practice Overview; Expert Systems; Goal Setting and Intervention Planning; Information Systems; Professional Conduct; Professional Liability and Malpractice; Program Evaluation; Quality Assurance; Single-System Design.

Key Words	
accountability	privacy
computer applications	records

Reform

See Health Care: Reform Initiatives

Refugees

See Displaced People

Regulation

See Licensing, Regulation, and Certification

Regulations

See Federal Legislation and Administrative Rule Making

Rehabilitation

See Psychosocial Rehabilitation; Rehabilitation of Criminal Offenders

Rehabilitation of Criminal Offenders
Paul Gendreau

This entry describes the major principles of effective intervention with offenders and presents brief explanations that illustrate the nature of each principle. The content is based on literature reviews and, to a lesser extent, on the author's clinical experience and those of colleagues who have conducted exemplary programs, such as Vicki Agee, Jim Alexander, Don Andrews, Bill Davidson, Liz Fabiano, Don Gordon, Robert E. Lee, and Robert Ross. A section on what does not "work" is also included in the belief that knowing the principles in this area is probably just as important as knowing "what works."

BACKGROUND

In the 1970s the criminal justice literature repeatedly informed criminal justice practitioners and policymakers that the rehabilitation of offenders was a failure—that, according to Martinson (1974), nothing worked. This indictment of correctional treatment programs was based on a review of 231 studies of programs from 1945 to 1967 (Lipton, Martinson, & Wilks, 1975). Various social commentators and policymakers immediately cited this evidence as justification for abandoning efforts to rehabilitate offenders.

Rationale for Antirehabilitation Sentiments

To understand why this occurred, one must recall the social context of the late 1960s and early 1970s, which was a time of considerable social upheaval and unrest in the United States. As Cullen and Gendreau (1989) pointed out, everywhere conservative sociopolitical forces looked—Attica, Kent State, Vietnam, Watergate—there were ominous signs of social chaos. Liberals, meanwhile, saw a corrupt state that could not be entrusted with the care of its citizens. The conservatives' solution was to advocate for law and order and "get-tough" policies that meant more severe sanctions and the incarceration of more offenders. Liberals, however, embraced the "justice model," which sought to limit the powers of the state—particularly to provide individualized treatment for or to process offenders by any means, including indeterminate sentencing and parole. Even though Martinson (1979) eventually changed his views, stating that some forms of rehabilitation reduced recidivism, the antirehabilitation rhetoric became firmly entrenched as many state jurisdictions embraced what Martinson (1976) called the "new epoch" of deterrence.

Evidence of Successful Rehabilitation Efforts

Despite the trend toward deterrence, rather than rehabilitation, evidence on the potency of rehabilitation programs for offenders continues to accumulate. It is found in a variety of narrative reviews and meta-analyses of the studies of treatment programs since the "nothing-works" credo was proclaimed (Andrews et al., 1990; Cullen & Gendreau, 1989; Davidson, Gottschalk, Gesheimer, & Mayer, 1984; Garrett, 1985; Gendreau, 1981, 1989; Gendreau & Andrews, 1990; Gendreau & Little, 1993; Gendreau & Ross, 1979, 1981b, 1984, 1987; Greenwood & Zimring, 1985; Izzo & Ross, 1990; Lipsey, 1992; Palmer, 1978, 1992; Ross & Fabiano, 1985; Ross & Gendreau, 1980).

What were the results of these studies? First, in Lipsey's (1992) survey of 443 treatment programs that used a control-group comparison, 64 percent of the studies reported reductions in recidivism for their treatment groups; the average reduction in recidivism for the entire sample of studies was 10 percent. Second, Lipsey found that when the results were broken down by the general types of programs, some types, for example, employment, reported reductions in recidivism that ranged from 10 percent to 18 percent.

Third, some researchers (see Andrews et al., 1990; Gendreau & Ross, 1984, 1987) began to look into the "black box" of treatment programs. They argued that it was not enough to sum across studies or break them down into general categories. Rather, it was necessary to answer the salient question, What are the characteristics that distinguish effective from ineffective programs? What does it mean that an employment program was offered; in other words, what exactly was done under the name of "employment"? With this orientation foremost, researchers discovered that programs that adhered to most of the characteristics described in this entry reduced recidivism in the range of 25 percent to 60 percent, with an average of about 50 percent. It should be noted that

approximately one-third of these studies featured random assignment and had follow-ups at one to two years. In addition, the magnitude of the results reported was greater for community-based programs and for studies conducted since the 1980s. Moreover, the quality of the research design was not a critical factor in determining the magnitude of the results (Andrews et al., 1990) if the studies in question followed the principles of effective intervention.

PRINCIPLES OF EFFECTIVE INTERVENTION

Intensive Services to High-Risk Clients

In this first principle, intensive services, behavioral in nature, are provided to high-risk clients. Intensive services occupy 40 percent to 70 percent of the offenders' time and are of three to nine months' duration. The term *behavioral* refers to programs that have been derived from the principles of learning theory (cf. Liebert & Spiegler, 1990). These programs fit into three general categories—(1) operant conditioning strategies, (2) social learning strategies, and (3) cognitive strategies—whose primary differentiation rests on the emphasis placed on changing cognitions. Radical behavioral forms of therapy are based primarily on operant conditioning strategies (classical conditioning is used occasionally) that change antisocial behaviors by prompting, shaping, fading, and stimulus-control techniques. Token economies and contingency-management programs are examples of operant strategies. Social learning and cognitive–behavioral strategies are the most commonly used; they rely on modeling, behavioral rehearsal, problem-solving, skill-building, and cognitive-restructuring techniques that explicitly reinforce alternatives to antisocial styles of thinking, feeling, and acting.

The determination of a high risk of recidivism is based on reliable, standardized, objective measures (such as the Level of Supervision Inventory, Andrews & Bonta, 1994) that sample a wide range of needs and dynamic risk factors that are predictive of recidivism. Some needs that are reliable predictors of recidivism are antisocial attitudes, values, and beliefs in the areas of school, work, and substance abuse; the rationalization of antisocial acts; and association with other criminals.

Firmness and Fairness

The second principle requires that program contingencies are enforced in a firm but fair manner. The contingencies are the rewards and punishers used to motivate changes in clients' behaviors. Examples of contingencies are praise, access to leisure activities, and money.

Staff members, with meaningful input from the offenders, design, maintain, and enforce the contingencies, which are under the control of the therapists. Positive reinforcers outnumber punishers by at least 4:1. Internal controls, for example, during treatment are used on occasion to detect antisocial activities of clientele.

Responsivity Principle
The responsivity principle is based on the concept of matching individual differences of clients and staff with each other and with the style of the program's delivery. The treatment approach is matched with the learning style and personality of the offender; for example, offenders who prefer high degrees of structure or who are impulsive are placed in a token-economy program.

The offender is matched with the therapist; for instance, offenders who are more anxious respond best to therapists who exhibit higher levels of interpersonal interaction. The therapist is matched with the type of program; for example, therapists who have a concrete conceptual style of problem solving will function best in a program that has a high degree of structure.

Skilled Therapists
It is expected that therapists relate to offenders in interpersonally sensitive and constructive ways and that they are trained and supervised appropriately. Until recently, the quality of the therapist has been neglected in the literature on rehabilitation programs for offenders. Ultimately, the quality of the service that is delivered will depend largely on the skill of the therapist.

Therapists should have at least an undergraduate degree or equivalent with training in the theories, prediction, and treatment of criminal behavior. They should receive three to six months' formal on-the-job or internship training in the application of behavioral interventions in general and those that are specific to the program. In addition, therapists should be reassessed periodically on the quality of the services they deliver.

Encouragement of Prosocial Contacts
This principle sets forth the expectation that the program's structure and activities should disrupt the criminal network. Therapists carefully monitor the offenders' social contacts at home, at work, and during leisure periods. Some programs have failed because clients found themselves in situations that encouraged antisocial behavior (O'Donnell, Lydgate, & Fo, 1979); therefore, programs should structure clients' activities to maintain contact with prosocial people and situations as much as possible.

Relapse-Prevention Services
Relapse-prevention services should be provided in the community. A concept adopted from the addictions field, relapse-prevention services are provided after the client has completed a formal treatment program. They are ideally suited to community corrections programs and are most applicable to substance abusers and sexual offenders. Relapse-prevention program activities include the following:

- planning and rehearsing alternative prosocial responses
- monitoring and anticipating problem situations that might lead to relapse
- practicing new prosocial behaviors in increasingly difficult situations and rewarding improved competencies to combat relapse
- training significant others, such as family members and friends, to provide reinforcement for prosocial behavior
- attending booster sessions, that is, returning to the formal treatment phase.

Advocacy for and Assessment of Community-Based Services
There should be a high level of advocacy for and brokerage of community-based services. Although it is fashionable and desirable to refer clients to community services, it is important to assess the appropriateness of these services for offenders. Community services should be assessed in as objective a manner as possible (for example, the Correctional Program Assessment Inventory [CPAI], Gendreau & Andrews, 1994) to ensure that high-quality services that are applicable to offenders and their problems are being provided. Frequently, such services are not provided. In a survey of 112 substance abuse programs for offenders, use of the CPAI indicated that only 10 percent had programmatic elements that would lead one to believe that an effective service was being provided (Gendreau, Goggin, & Annis, 1990).

CHARACTERISTICS OF INEFFECTIVE INTERVENTION
With few exceptions, treatment programs having any of the characteristics described in this section have failed to reduce recidivism.

Overall Intensive Approaches
These intensive strategies include the following:

- any type of program, including behavioral, that targets low-risk offenders
- any program that provides services to clients on the basis of factors that are not predictive of

criminal behavior, such as anxiety, depression, and self-esteem.

Specific Treatment Approaches

These approaches are based on therapies that are driven by distinct theoretical notions of treatment (for a complete description of the sociological approaches to intervention, including the subcultural and labeling approaches, see Andrews & Bonta, 1994):

- traditional Freudian psychodynamic and Rogerian nondirective therapies, which have been characterized, at least in the literature, as "talking" cures, being concerned primarily with the offender establishing a good relationship with a therapist; unraveling the unconscious; helping clients gain insight in an all-or-nothing fashion; helping clients resolve neurotic conflicts and self-actualize; externalizing blame to parents, staff, the victims, and society; and helping clients ventilate their anger.
- traditional medical-model approaches that involve dieting, pharmacological treatment (such as the use of Deprovera with sex offenders), and plastic surgery
- subcultural approaches in which culture is respected ("do good" for disadvantaged people; their cultures are not inferior to "ours"), the provision of legitimate opportunities is advocated, and there is a reliance on "incidental" learning (somehow, offenders will "get it" with minimal guidance)
- the labeling perspective that propounds the diversion of offenders from stigmatization by the criminal justice system and the use of alternative sanctions such as restitution in which "lower" levels of punishment are dignified, whereas treatment may do offenders an injustice
- "punishing-smarter" strategies: boot camps, drug testing, electronic monitoring, fines, confinement at home, intensive supervision of probation (including drug testing, electronic monitoring, confinement at home, restitution, and warnings or threats), scaring the offender "straight," shock incarceration, solitary confinement, and warnings or threats.

"Punishing-smarter" strategies refer to a new generation of sanctions developed in the 1980s (Gendreau, Paparozzi, Little, & Goddard, 1993). These sanctions were considered to be an alternative to the excessive use of incarceration that would still satisfy the public's need for the punishment of offenders. They have become popular in the United States but not in other Western societies, an interesting issue in itself. Gendreau and

Little (1993) conducted a preliminary meta-analysis of 174 comparisons of "punishment" groups and control groups. They found that the strategies in 13 categories of punishment produced, on average, slight *increases* in recidivism of approximately 5 percent.

Reasons for Failure

The reasons that punishment and punishing-smarter programs have been such unmitigated failures have been addressed elsewhere (Gendreau, Cullen, & Bonta, 1994; Gendreau & Ross, 1981a). The answers may be found in the literature on experimental learning in animals and humans (Walters & Grusec, 1977), the literature on punishment and behavior modification (Matson & DiLorenzo, 1984), and the social psychological literature on resistance and persistence processes in attitudinal changes (Cialdini, 1993; Eagly & Chaiken, 1993; Meichenbaum & Fong, in press).

Briefly, the reasons for the failure of these programs are as follows.

Lack of effective punishers. There is no evidence that most of the sanctions currently in use for offenders are effective punishers, that is, that they reliably suppress behavior. The only exceptions are fines and possibly some highly specialized forms of restitution, which are not easily applied to offenders. Also, the punishing-smarter programs have usually targeted behaviors that are *not* predictors of criminal behavior, such as fitness and obeisance.

Inconsistent punishers. For effective punishing stimuli to "work," the following rules must apply *without exception:*

- Escape from the punishing stimuli is impossible.
- The punishing stimulus is applied immediately (at the earliest point in the deviant-response chain) and after every occurrence of the deviant behavior and at maximum intensity.
- The punishers are not spread out and are varied.

It is virtually impossible to meet these criteria in the real world of the offender unless adherents of punishing-smarter programs envision some sort of Orwellian environment. One should also be mindful of the fact that punishment only trains a person in what *not* to do.

Negative consequences. When punishment is inappropriately applied it may result in several negative consequences, such as unwanted emotional reactions, aggression, or withdrawal or an increase in the frequency of the behavior that is to be punished.

Resistant populations. People who appear to be resistant to punishment are psychopaths, risk takers, peole under the influence of drugs or alcohol, and those who have a history of being punished. All these characteristics have been found among offenders much more than among other clinical groups.

Inoculation to coercion. The social psychology literature on attitudes and attitudinal change (see, for example, Eagly & Chaiken, 1993) has documented how many people inoculate themselves from threats and coercion by choosing to interpret "evidence" in certain ways, thinking of reasons that disregard negative consequences and have affective schema (such as free will arguments), and using ego defenses that are resistant to attitude change.

Conclusion

In conclusion, the evidence is persuasive that specific styles of service delivery can reduce offenders' criminal behavior to a degree that has meaningful policy implications for social workers. The next goal of the rehabilitation agenda is to address how social workers, as well as other treatment professionals, can overcome the sociopolitical and professional barriers to the implementation of high-quality services for offenders that have been found to work (Gendreau & Ross, 1987).

References

Andrews, D. A., & Bonta, J. (1994). *The psychology of criminal conduct.* Cincinnati: Anderson.

Andrews, D. A., Zinger, I., Hoge, R. D., Bonta, J., Gendreau, P., & Cullen, F. T. (1990). Does correctional treatment work? A clinically-relevant and psychologically-informed meta-analysis. *Criminology, 28,* 369–404.

Cialdini, R. B. (1993). *Influence: Science & practice* (3rd ed.). New York: HarperCollins.

Cullen, F., & Gendreau, P. (1989). The effectiveness of correctional rehabilitation: Reconsidering the "nothing works" doctrine. In L. Goodstein & D. L. Mackensie (Eds.), *The American prison: Issues in research policy* (pp. 23–44). New York: Plenum Press.

Davidson, W. S. III, Gottschalk, R., Gesheimer, L., & Mayer, J. (1984). *Interventions with juvenile delinquents: A meta-analysis of treatment efficacy.* Washington, DC: National Institute of Juvenile Justice and Delinquency Prevention.

Eagly, A. H., & Chaiken, S. (1993). *The psychology of attitudes.* San Diego: Harcourt Brace Jovanovich.

Garrett, C. J. (1985). Effects of residential treatment on adjudicated delinquents: A meta-analysis. *Journal of Research in Crime and Delinquency, 22,* 287–308.

Gendreau, P. (1981). Treatment in corrections: Martinson was wrong. *Canadian Psychology, 22,* 332–338.

Gendreau, P. (1989). Programs that do not work: A brief comment on Brodeur & Doob. *Canadian Journal of Criminology, 31,* 193–195.

Gendreau, P., & Andrews, D. A. (1990). Tertiary prevention: What the meta-analysis of the offender treatment literature tells us about "what works." *Canadian Journal of Criminology, 32,* 173–184.

Gendreau, P., & Andrews, D. A. (1994). *The Correctional Program Assessment Inventory* (4th ed.). Saint John, New Brunswick, Canada: University of New Brunswick, Department of Psychology.

Gendreau, P., Cullen, F., & Bonta, J. (1994). Intensive rehabilitation supervision: The next generation in community corrections. *Federal Probation, 52,* 72–78.

Gendreau, P., Goggin, C., & Annis, H. (1990). Survey of existing substance abuse programs. *Forum on Corrections Research, 2,* 6–8.

Gendreau, P., & Little, T. (1993). *A meta-analysis of the effectiveness of sanctions on offender recidivism.* Unpublished manuscript.

Gendreau, P., Paparozzi, M., Little, T., & Goddard, M. (1993). Punishing smarter: The effectiveness of the new generation of alternative sanctions. *Forum on Correctional Research, 5,* 31–34.

Gendreau, P., & Ross, R. R. (1979). Effective correctional treatment: Bibliotherapy for cynics. *Crime Delinquency, 25,* 463–489.

Gendreau, P., & Ross, R. R. (1981a). Correctional potency: Treatment and deterrence on trial. In R. Roesch & R. R. Corrado (Eds.), *Evaluation & criminal justice policy* (pp. 29–57). Beverly Hills, CA: Sage Publications.

Gendreau, P., & Ross, R. R. (1981b). Offender rehabilitation: The appeal of success. *Federal Probation, 45,* 45–48.

Gendreau, P., & Ross, R. R. (1984). Correctional treatment: Some recommendations for successful intervention. *Juvenile & Family Court Journal, 34,* 31–40.

Gendreau, P., & Ross, R. R. (1987). Revivification of rehabilitation: Evidence from the 80's. *Justice Quarterly, 4,* 349–407.

Greenwood, P. W., & Zimring, F. E. (1985). *One more chance: The pursuit of promising intervention strategies for chronic juvenile offenders.* Santa Monica, CA: Rand.

Izzo, R., & Ross, R. R. (1990). Meta-analysis of rehabilitation programs for juvenile delinquents: A brief report. *Criminal Justice & Behavior, 17,* 134–142.

Liebert, R. M., & Spiegler, M. D. (1990). *Personality: Strategies & issues.* Monterey, CA: Brooks/Cole.

Lipsey, M. W. (1992). Juvenile delinquency treatment: A meta-analytic inquiry into the variability of effects. In T. D. Cook, H. Cooper, D. S. Cordray, H. Hartmann, L. V. Hedges, R. J. Light, T. A. Louis, & F. Mosteller (Eds.), *Meta-analysis for explanation* (pp. 83–127). New York: Russell Sage Foundation.

Lipton, D., Martinson, R., & Wilks, J. (1975). *The effectiveness of correctional treatment: A survey of treatment evaluation studies.* New York: Praeger.

Martinson, R. (1974). What works? Questions and answers about prison reform. *The Public Interest, 35,* 22–54.

Martinson, R. (1976). California research at the crossroads. *Crime & Delinquency, 22,* 180–191.

Martinson, R. (1979). New findings, new views: A note of caution regarding sentencing reform. *Hofstra Law Review, 7,* 242–250.

Matson, J. L., & DiLorenzo, T. M. (1984). *Punishment and its alternatives: a new perspective for behavior modification.* New York: Springer.

Meichenbaum, D., & Fong, G. T. (in press). How individuals control their own minds: A constructive narrative perspective. In D. M. Wegner & J. W. Pennebaker (Eds.), *Handbook of mental control.* Englewood Cliffs, NJ: Prentice Hall.

O'Donnell, C. R., Lydgate, T., & Fo, W. S.O. (1979). The buddy system: Review and follow-up. *Child Behavior Therapy, 1,* 161–169.

Palmer, T. (1978). *Correctional intervention & research: Current issues and future prospects.* Lexington, MA: Lexington Books.

Palmer, T. (1992). *The re-emergence of correctional intervention.* Newbury Park, CA: Sage Publications.

Ross, R. R., & Fabiano, E. A. (1985). *Time to think: A cognitive model of delinquency prevention and offender rehabilitation.* Johnson City, TN: Institute of Social Sciences and Arts.

Ross, R. R., & Gendreau, P. (1980). *Effective correctional treatment.* Toronto: Butterworths.

Walters, G. C., & Grusec, J. E. (1977). *Punishment.* San Francisco: Freeman.

Paul Gendreau, PhD, is professor of psychology, University of New Brunswick, Saint John, NB, Canada E2L 4L5.

For further information see

Adult Corrections; Criminal Behavior Overview; Gang Violence; Homicide; Legal Issues: Low-Income and Dependent People; Probation and Parole; Runaways and Homeless Youths; Social Justice in Social Agencies; Social Welfare Policy; Substance Abuse: Legal Issues; Victim Services and Victim/Witness Assistance Programs.

Key Words	
corrections	prisons
criminal justice	rehabilitation

Religion

See Church Social Work; Sectarian Agencies

Research Overview
William J. Reid

The functions of research in social work are multifaceted. First, the perspectives and methods of science can provide a framework for practice activities. Although social work practice is indisputably an art, practitioners can make use of a scientific orientation in striving to obtain the best results possible. Such an orientation calls for the use of terms and concepts that are clearly tied to empirical events; the systematic collection of data; the cautious use of inference and the consideration of alternative explanations; the application, when possible, of research-based knowledge; and the discriminating evaluation of the outcomes of one's efforts (Reid & Smith, 1989). Although this style of practice may be thought of as simply systematic, clearheaded, or informed, a scientific orientation emphasizes such qualities and suggests how they can be put to work.

Second, research helps build knowledge for practice. It can generate and refine concepts, determine the evidence for generalizations and theories, and ascertain the effectiveness of practice methods. To be sure, most knowledge that social workers use lacks a strong empirical basis, an unavoidable limitation of a profession that deals with the elusive complexities of psychological and social phenomena. Nevertheless, empirically grounded knowledge, even if in short supply, can make a decisive difference.

Finally, research serves the practical function of providing situation-specific data to inform action, such as decisions about practice, the operations of programs, or efforts to achieve social change. Such action, or operations, research may consist of needs assessments, productivity studies, program evaluations, or the use of standardized instruments in practice contexts. Research of this type is for immediate consumption to benefit the particular activity that gave rise to it. It need not reflect a scientific practice orientation or contribute to the fund of scientific knowledge.

HISTORICAL PERSPECTIVE

These functions have been present and evolving since the beginning of the profession. A scientific orientation to social work was articulated in the late 19th century in the scientific philanthropy movement. The aim was to make the giving of relief to the poor a scientific endeavor. It was believed that science could provide the necessary understanding of pauperism and that the scientific method could be used for the systematic study and treatment of individual cases.

The subsequent evolution of this perspective can be traced most clearly in casework, whose practice, supervision, and management accounted for the bulk of professional activity in social work. In *Social Diagnosis,* Mary Richmond (1917) set forth the first major statement of the principles and methods of casework. In her formulation, a social diagnosis was made through scientific problem solving; facts were gathered to serve as the basis for hypotheses, which were then to be tested by obtaining relevant evidence.

Although the psychoanalytic movement that began in the next decade introduced radically new theories and interventions for casework, it, too, was the product of 19th-century science. Although diagnosis became more psychiatric than social in the next several decades, the paradigm of study, diagnosis, and treatment following presumed scientific principles remained intact. Hollis (1963), a leading advocate of psychoanalytically oriented casework, expressed this continuity as follows:

> Casework is a scientific art. Certainly since the days of Mary Richmond we have been committed to objective examination of the facts of each case. We draw inferences from those facts, we diagnose, we view the individual against a frame of reference which is itself the product of informal research. We constantly alert ourselves to sources of error. (p. 13)

In the years that followed, alternative conceptions of a scientific orientation emerged. Behavioral social work placed greater emphasis on measurable constructs and phenomena. Ecological social work, following the ideas of the biologist Dubos (1965), called for a shift in attention from the defects of the individual to "systems in mutual interaction" (quoted in Germain, 1970, p. 29). In casework, as well as in social work in general, the issue has not been whether a scientific or a nonscientific orientation should be the framework for practice, but rather which kind of scientific model to follow.

The role of research in building knowledge for practice also had its roots in the scientific philanthropy movement. Energies were first directed to identifying the causes of social problems—poverty, delinquency, and so on. The early studies were, by today's standards, naive and primitive, but they were the first to express the need to establish a scientific knowledge base for social work. The early leaders of the profession hoped that social work might follow the example of medicine and engineering and draw its knowledge from the physical sciences. For social work, the logical knowledge base seemed to be the social sciences, with ancillary sources in related helping disciplines.

Again, the process of evolution can be most clearly seen in casework. In 1929 the *Milford Conference Report* (American Association of Social Workers, 1929) suggested the following as a base for casework: biology, economics, law, medicine, psychiatry, sociology, and statistics. To this list Karpf (1931) added anthropology, education, and social psychology, in one of the first major works concerned with the scientific base of social work.

Despite projections of a diversified knowledge base, one discipline, psychiatry, emerged as the dominant intellectual source for casework. One school of psychiatry—psychoanalysis—not only provided most of this knowledge but molded much professional practice into a form of intra-psychically oriented personal therapy.

The knowledge base of casework became more diverse in the 1950s, when the increasing scientific output of the social sciences and the helping disciplines began to have an impact. This diversification was stimulated by criticisms of the scientific credibility of psychoanalytic knowledge, as well as by the growing awareness of the lack of fit of psychoanalysis with the types of interpersonal and social problems that were of concern to social work. It is noteworthy that the diversity in the scientific base of casework, or direct practice, to use a more inclusive and contemporary term, was realized only as practice itself became more diversified with the advent of behavioral, cognitive, family systems, ecological, and other models of intervention that first appeared in the 1950s and 1960s. Thus, other types of knowledge began to be used when views about the purposes and methods of practice began to diversify.

Another development in the scientific base of the profession has been the increased emphasis on knowledge of the processes and effects of given intervention strategies with given types of clients or problems (Fischer, 1978). Although the drive to investigate the nature of social work practice and its effects began earlier, it did not develop momentum until the late 1940s, when attempts were made to study the processes of change in clients

through content analyses of caseworkers' recordings of the processes (Dollard & Mowrer, 1947), to scale clients' progress or change while in casework (Hunt, 1948), and to classify casework methods (L. N. Austin, 1948; Hollis, 1949). The spotlight, however, fell on a series of controlled experiments that were designed to test the effectiveness of different types of direct social work practice (see Fischer, 1973; Wood, 1978). Unfortunately, most of these studies failed to provide convincing evidence that the methods tested were truly effective and thus produced little positive knowledge about intervention. With the development of new forms of practice and improvements in research designs, more recent experiments have provided support for the effectiveness of a variety of social work interventions for a range of clients and problems (Reid & Hanrahan, 1982; Rubin, 1985; Videka-Sherman, 1988).

Despite progress on this and other fronts, knowledge underlying direct practice in social work has hardly amounted to the scientific base that has been hoped for (and whose existence has often been asserted). In this regard, the observations of Briar and Miller (1971) are still pertinent; these authors described the underpinnings of casework as "a proliferation of bits and pieces of 'hard' and 'soft' knowledge—fragmented and disjointed" (p. 84).

These words could be applied as well to the foundations of knowledge of the macro level of social work practice, such as community work, administration, and social action. Throughout its history, macro social work has made use of the social sciences as sources of knowledge, but research-based knowledge that is relevant to practice at this level has been slow to accumulate and is probably even less substantial than that available for direct, or micro, practice. At all levels of social work, an unforeseen development has been the tendency of practice to outdistance its knowledge base. New forms and areas of practice have emerged at a more rapid pace than has research that might inform them. Rather than lead innovation, as is commonly the case in medicine and engineering, research in social work has tended to follow it, often at a good distance.

Thus, a hundred years of effort to construct a base of scientific knowledge for the profession has fallen far short of the enthusiastic hope of the pioneers. There is now a greater appreciation of the reality that research-based knowledge can be only a part, albeit an important one, of a vast network of information that informs practice. Newer strategies, such as those classified as intervention research, offer hope of forging more direct and solid links between research and practice.

Action, or operations, research in social work found its earliest major expression in the survey movement, which began in earnest in the 1900s. The movement, which was spurred by increasing urban problems, such as poverty, housing, working conditions, and child care, took place in a progressive political climate. There was little doubt about the intent of the surveys. As Zimbalist (1955) noted, "the social survey movement was first and foremost a means of publicizing the needs of the community in as compelling a manner as possible, so as to galvanize the populace into taking remedial action. Facts were gathered and analyzed as a means to this end" (p. 170). Following the monumental Pittsburgh survey in 1908, the movement spread rapidly throughout the country and resulted in countless applications of the method. That the leading social work journal of the time, *Charities and Commons,* was renamed *Survey* indicates how much the movement had penetrated the intellectual life of the field.

Although the survey movement was oversold by enthusiastic advocates, did not achieve its claims of being an instrument of reform, and within two decades was no longer a major force, it did lead to some instances of social change and focused attention on the ills of urbanization. Moreover, it was the predecessor of most contemporary forms of assessments of needs. Other forms of operations research, including evaluations of programs, statistical reports of services, and the construction of indexes, were all in evidence at the beginning of the century.

As these examples suggest, social work has a long tradition of using research procedures and data to inform and guide its programs and activities. Although this use of research does not produce scientific knowledge (in the sense of a body of verified propositions), it has enlightened decisions about practice and may be as important to professional practice as are knowledge-building investigations. Also, as the examples suggest, most applications have occurred at the level of macro social work. Since the 1970s, however, research procedures and tools, such as systematic observation and standardized tests, have been used increasingly at the level of direct practice with individuals, families, and groups—a development stimulated by, but not confined to, the behavioral movement in social work.

Social work research has evolved as part of the profession's more general relationship to science. Before the emergence of graduate schools of social work in the first decades of this century,

social work researchers tended to be people with training in the social or other sciences who devoted themselves to the study of social work concerns. Gradually, the profession, through its own doctoral programs, began to train a cadre of researchers who were able to bring both knowledge of social work and research methods to bear on these concerns. The activities of these researchers constitute the core of contemporary social work research, which is usually thought of as also including the investigations of scientists from allied disciplines who work under social work auspices.

INFRASTRUCTURE

The social work research enterprise depends on a complex infrastructure that consists of such elements as skilled personnel, organizational supports, financial resources, and channels for disseminating results. Over the past three decades, this infrastructure has undergone considerable change. Social work researchers have continued to move from agency to academic settings (D. Austin, 1992). Increasingly, the doctorate, with training in advanced research skills, has become a requirement for faculty positions in schools of social work.

Researchers

At present most research activity in the profession is directed by educator–researchers in schools of social work. For example, studies conducted during the 1980s found that close to three-fourths of the research articles published in social work journals were written by academics (Glisson, 1983, 1990; Grinnell & Royer, 1983). Although most social work researchers are based in academia, much of their research is conducted in agency settings in collaboration with agency personnel. In addition, agencies conduct a good deal of unpublished operations research, such as program evaluations and quality assurance studies

Most social work researchers today have doctorates in social work or related fields. Their number is difficult to determine. Only 500 members of NASW identify their primary professional activity as research (*Building Social Work Knowledge,* 1991). To be sure, the number of people engaged in social work research is much larger, when one includes social work educators and agency personnel who are involved in some form of research activity. Still, according to one analysis (*Building Social Work Knowledge,* 1991), fewer than 1,000 persons published reports of any social work research from 1985 to 1990. Moreover, the number of trained social work researchers is likely to remain small, because the profession's output of doctorates has remained fairly constant, at about 200 a year, for some time and is not expected to increase significantly in the short term (*Building Social Work Knowledge,* 1991).

In terms of its organization, the social work research enterprise is made up largely of independent researchers and research centers in academic settings and a small number of agency research departments and centers. For the profession as a whole, there have been few organizational mechanisms to facilitate the coordination or exchange of information among individual researchers or units, and those that exist, such as the NASW National Center for Social Policy and Practice, the Society for Social Work Research, and the Institute for the Advancement of Social Work Research, were recently created and have not had time to develop their roles fully.

Financial Support

Financial support for social work research is provided by a variety of sources, including universities, agencies, federal and state research funding organizations, and foundations. Support from universities, the largest source of funds, is primarily embedded in faculty salaries, office space, equipment, student assistantships, and the like. Governmental funding agencies and foundations have been important but limited sources of support. The largest source of governmental funds for social work research, the National Institute of Mental Health (NIMH), awarded just 119 grants to social work researchers during the 1980s—a small number, given the length of the period, even though social work fared as well as other disciplines in the proportion of grants that were approved (*Building Social Work Knowledge,* 1991). Green, Hutchison, and Sar (1990) found that fewer than 15 percent of the graduates of doctoral programs in social work had received more than five grants from any source during their careers. Among the reasons for the lack of success in obtaining more research grants has been "the very limited participation" of social work researchers on national research funding bodies, on grant review panels, and in multidisciplinary research centers (D. Austin, 1992, p. 313).

Outlets for Research

Social work research is disseminated through such channels as professional journals, books, conference presentations, and classrooms. Three journals—*Journal of Social Service Research, Research on Social Work Practice,* and *Social Work Research*—publish mainly research articles. For the remaining journals, the variation is consider-

able. For example, in *Social Work,* the most widely distributed professional social work journal, close to 40 percent of the articles published from 1983 through 1988 were research based (Glisson, 1990). This percentage is lower than that for several other key social work journals but higher than that for many practitioner-oriented journals (Fraser, Taylor, Jackson, & O'Jack, 1991). There does not seem to be a trend toward the publication of a higher proportion of research-based articles (Glisson, 1990). Only about 10 percent of the papers presented at major social work conferences are research based (*Building Social Work Knowledge,* 1991). It is also noteworthy that almost half the social work articles and conference papers are directed toward readers in related or multidisciplinary fields (Green, Hutchison, & Sar, 1992).

Strengthening the Infrastructure

The studies of infrastructure referred to earlier were part of a series of investigations undertaken by the Task Force on Social Work Research, an NIMH-funded body of leading social work researchers, educators, and practitioners that concluded that the infrastructure was inadequate to meet the needs of a dynamic and growing profession (*Building Social Work Knowledge,* 1991). The meager number of researchers, the failure of doctoral programs to increase their enrollments, the lack of national organizational structures, insufficient funding, and the absence of links between social work researchers and practitioners were among the shortfalls cited. Although these criticisms are well taken, they need to be seen within the historical context of the development of social work research. The cadre of researchers with social work doctorates may be insufficient for present needs, but only four decades ago they were virtually nonexistent. In short, social work research has come a long way, but it has a much longer way to go. It is also true, as the task force report made clear, that the development of social work research has not been commensurate with the growth of the profession.

Nevertheless, the work of the Task Force on Social Work Research has resulted in some tangible initiatives that should strengthen the infrastructure of social work research. For example, with regard to one recommendation—the creation of a number of social work research development centers to be located in graduate schools of social work—NIMH has committed funds, although the number of centers to be supported is still to be determined. Another result of the task force's efforts has been the creation of the Institute for the Advancement of Social Work Research, which is to be jointly sponsored by core national social work professional organizations. As currently planned, the institute will serve important facilitative, developmental, and advocacy functions in an effort to strengthen the infrastructure of social work research. Such functions may include serving as a liaison between research funding agencies and the profession and taking action to bolster research education in schools of social work.

CONTENT

What do social work researchers study? This question is of considerable importance with regard to the range of possible topics in a field as diverse as social work. It is also difficult to answer, even if one limits one's attention to published or abstracted studies. Although a good deal of the research literature of the profession can be found in such sources as *Social Work Abstracts,* major social work journals, and periodic reviews of social work research, much of it is not so readily identified—for example, the sizable number of studies published in books or in non–social work journals, as well as unpublished research reports. The interdisciplinary nature of much relevant research complicates efforts to distinguish between social work and other kinds of research, and the classification of the subject matter of any study is no simple task.

Nevertheless, a rough idea of the content of social work research can be gleaned from various studies of the social work research literature (Abbott, 1977; Hanrahan, 1978, 1984; Jenkins et al., 1982; Reid, 1978; Reid & Strother, 1986). These analyses have suggested that the literature on social work research can be divided more or less equally into four categories: studies of (1) the behavior, personality, problems, and other characteristics of individuals, families, and small groups; (2) characteristics, utilization, and outcome of services; (3) attitudes, orientations, and training of social workers, the profession, or interdisciplinary concerns; and (4) organizations, communities, and social policy.

A somewhat different, but by no means contradictory, picture of the content of social work research was obtained by Glisson (1990), who classified articles according to the practice methods with which they were concerned. Examining research articles in five major social work journals from 1983 to 1988, he found that 49 percent of the articles were related to direct practice with individuals, families, and groups. Indirect practice (social policy, social administration, and community organization) accounted for 40 percent; education for 24 percent; and research for 7 percent

(because of multiple classifications, the percentage totaled more than 100). Compared to an earlier period (1977 to 1982), Glisson found an increase in articles that were relevant to direct practice (from 34 percent to 49 percent) and that included outcome variables (from 27 percent to 52 percent).

In reviewing data on the content of published reports of social work research, one is impressed with its broad range when content areas are subdivided, for example, by the type of client or nonclient population, problem, service, and so on. That there are few concentrations of studies in any particular content area highlights the profession's dependence on research from other disciplines and the social sciences. Nevertheless, social work researchers have generated respectable bodies of knowledge in a number of areas, including child welfare services and treatment of mentally ill people in the community.

METHODOLOGY

The methods of social work research, reflecting its diverse content, run the full gamut of the methodology of the behavioral sciences. According to analyses of published research, the major strategy in social work research is to study phenomena through naturalistic methods, that is, without experimental manipulation (Fraser et al., 1991; Glisson, 1983, 1990; Tripodi, 1984). Descriptive or correlational studies using interviews, standardized instruments, questionnaires or available data, and nonrepresentative samples are dominant in research on the characteristics of client populations, practitioners, programs, and communities. Evaluation research usually includes "before-and-after" or "after-only" studies of change associated with social work programs. Controlled experimental designs account for only a small portion of social work research—apparently less than 5 percent of the published studies (Fraser et al., 1991; Glisson, 1983, 1990; Tripodi, 1984). Methods of analysis are likely to make use of descriptive statistics and simpler (bivariate) types of significance testing. Qualitative methods are used in only about 15 percent of investigations and often in combination with quantitative methods (Fraser et al., 1991; Glisson, 1990).

ISSUES AND DEVELOPMENTS

In recent years, a number of issues and developments in social work research have emerged or become salient.

Epistemological Debate

Since the early 1980s, the philosophical foundations of social work research have been questioned by a number of critics (Haworth, 1984; Heineman, 1981; Tyson, 1992; Witkin, 1989). Although these critics have not spoken with one voice, their arguments have centered on the inadequacy of the paradigm that social work researchers commonly teach, use, and accept. This paradigm, the critics say, is based on the tenets of a school of philosophy—logical positivism—that no longer has any credibility among philosophers of science. More specifically, conventional research methodology has been faulted for placing undue value on quantitative approaches, experimental designs, objective measurement, and statistical analysis. Its critics contend that social work research, as well as much social science research, has borrowed from the methods of the physical sciences that are often ill suited for studying the ever-changing and elusive complexities of social phenomena. The critics see a place for "hard-science" methods in social work but argue that these methods have been erroneously equated with "good science." Similar criticisms have been expressed about research in related professions (Fishman, Rotgers, & Franks, 1988; Gergen, 1985; Guba, 1990).

In social work the critics have proposed new paradigms, including constructivism (Rodwell & Woody, 1994) and the heuristic approach (Heineman-Piper, 1989; Tyson, 1992), which, they contend, provide more suitable frameworks for social work research than do the paradigms that are currently in use. At a methodological level, these paradigms call for greater emphasis on methods of qualitative research.

These criticisms and proposals have been challenged by a number of researchers (Fraser et al., 1991; Geismar, 1982; Hudson, 1982; Schuerman, 1982). Counterarguments by these and other authors have rejected the notions that contemporary social work research is an offspring of logical positivism or that it applies the methods of hard science inappropriately. The call for new paradigms is unnecessary, they say, because the primarily qualitative methods advocated by the paradigms are already an accepted part of the tool kit of social work research. Moreover, what is being proposed has not yet resulted in any appreciable amount of research. Products are needed to give the new paradigms tangible expression.

Although the controversy may have outlived its usefulness (Berlin, 1990; Reid, 1994), at least in the terms in which it has been cast, it has served some important functions. First, it has stimulated a much-needed examination of the rationale of the methodology of mainstream social work research. Second, it has fostered efforts to develop integra-

tive, pluralistic frameworks that may accommodate diverse epistemological viewpoints (Harrison, 1994; Orcutt, 1990; Reamer, 1992). Finally, it has provided an impetus for the application of qualitative methods. Even though qualitative methodology has long been accepted in mainstream research, it has not been widely used, in large part because it has been viewed as "second best," if not "second class," by many researchers. Regardless of their merits, the "new paradigms" have probably helped create a more favorable climate for qualitative methodology. For some researchers, they have provided the legitimation and stimulus needed to do qualitative research.

Intervention Research
Research on social work practice is central to the contribution of research to the profession. A recent development in the conceptualization of this type of research was Thomas and Rothman's (1993) formulation of intervention research. This formulation brings together three types of undertakings: (1) research on human behavior related to intervention; (2) attempts to foster the utilization of such research in practice applications; and (3) efforts to develop innovative interventions, or intervention design and development (D&D). The first two components feed into the third, D&D, which is the one with the greatest consequences for conducting practice research.

D&D is an attempt to provide a systematic approach to the creation, testing, modification, and dissemination of information on human service interventions. Its primary goal is not the generation of knowledge, as in conventional applications of research, but the building of the technology of interventions. Thus, it is essentially an engineering process. Its primary product is not a research report, but a service model delineated in such forms as practice manuals and program designs.

In creating this product, the D&D practitioner makes use of research in a series of stages. Existing research findings about target populations and methods of service are drawn on in designing the initial version of the intervention; preliminary trials of the intervention are conducted, and data on the processes and apparent outcomes of its application are collected; the data are used in the continuing task of improving the intervention; the intervention is then given more rigorous tests, such as controlled experiments to evaluate its effectiveness; and dissemination (the final stage) is guided by research on the diffusion and adoption of research findings.

D&D provides a direct link between research activity and the improvement of services. The self-corrective powers of research can be used in a systematic and efficient way in the process of constructing programs. D&D can provide at least some research input into the development of an intervention even if the more rigorous testing phase is not completed. It can also help prevent premature experiments or demonstration projects with untried interventions. Examples of studies explicitly conducted within the intervention research paradigm can be found in Reid and Bailey-Dempsey (1994); Rothman (1991); and Thomas, Santa, Bronson, and Oyersman (1987). In addition, a number of research programs that have been designed to build and test interventions have made implicit or partial use of components of the paradigm. Examples include the efforts of Hogarty, Anderson, and their colleagues (see, for example, Hogarty et al., 1986) to develop a psychoeducational approach to work with people who are mentally ill and their families and the work of Rose and his colleagues (see, for example, LeCroy & Rose, 1986) to devise social skills training programs.

Empirical Practice Movement

Empirical practice can be thought of as practice guided by a research orientation and by the application of research methods. Although social workers have long been enjoined to take a "scientific attitude" in their work, empirical practice reflects a more thorough, systematic, and technical application of a scientific approach than one finds in other forms of practice. Its development can be best understood through one of its major tools—the single-subject or single-system design (SSD).

In the late 1960s, the SSD, which had become a leading research design in behavioral psychology, began to appear in social work. SSDs were introduced as a means of assessing the effects of interventions with individual clients, usually in the context of behavioral treatment. Their use has been broadened to include larger systems, such as families, organizations, and communities (Reid, 1993; Tripodi & Harrington, 1979) as well as nonbehavioral forms of treatment (Dean & Reinherz, 1986; Nelsen, 1990).

SSDs are essentially time-series experiments. Data on a target behavior or problem collected before, during, and after intervention are used to form a profile of change over time. From this time series, one can assess if a change in the behavior or problem appears to be associated with the use of the intervention to be tested. Through various manipulations of the intervention, for example, by withdrawing it or starting it at different times with different problems or clients, it is possible to achieve a high degree of control over extraneous factors that may explain change—a degree of control comparable to what may be achieved in a classical experimental design.

SSDs were seen as a means for agency-based "practitioner–researchers" to evaluate the effectiveness of their own "methods" and hence to contribute to the knowledge base of the profession (Bloom & Fischer, 1982). To prepare social workers for this role, schools of social work developed courses featuring SSDs. The desirability of such preparation was a major factor in a decision by the Council on Social Work Education (1984) to require schools of social work to prepare students "systematically to evaluate their own practice" (p. 127).

Studies conducted during the 1980s of graduates who had taken SSD courses suggested that applications in practice were occurring, but in a limited way (Gingerich, 1984; Richey, Blythe, & Berlin, 1987). There was evidence that the graduates made appreciable use of a variety of SSD measurement techniques, including the specification of goals in measurable terms and the use of standardized instruments and self-monitoring by clients, but they appeared to make little use of full-fledged SSDs. Similarly, SSDs appeared to be seldom used in studies reported in the social work literature (Fraser et al., 1991; Glisson, 1990; Thyer & Thyer, 1992).

What seems to be taking root is not the SSD as an entity, but components of it, such as the specification of problems and goals and the use of assessment and evaluation techniques (Kirk & Penka, 1992; Penka & Kirk, 1991). Within the context of their use in regular agency programs, full-fledged SSDs are being increasingly viewed as a means of conducting relatively simple single-case evaluations (Blythe, 1990; Gingerich, 1990), that is, case outcome studies that do not use intrusive research procedures, such as the manipulation of interventions or the collection of prospective baseline data.

The SSD and its components have become identified as part of an orientation to practice, which has been described as "empirically based" (Blythe, 1990; Siegel, 1984) or "empirical" (Briar, 1990; Reid & Smith, 1989). Empirical practice has been defined as including other applications of research, such as the use of service approaches that are supported by research findings and that can be specified with enough precision to enable them to be replicated (Ivanoff, Blythe, & Briar, 1987). The notion can also encompass various frameworks that use systematic, scientific approaches and procedures to inform practice (see, for example, Berlin & Marsh, 1993; Blythe, Tripodi, & Briar, in press; Gibbs, 1991). In this larger sense, empirical practice seems to be moving forward in both social work education and practice. In addition to the growth of courses on single-case evaluation and other types of evaluation, there is evidence that curricula on direct practice are emphasizing better-specified "action-oriented" methods (LeCroy & Goodwin, 1988). There are also indications that the use of behavioral and other empirical methods is increasing at the expense of older, less research-based (and still dominant) approaches (Jayaratne, 1982; Strom, 1992).

The growing influence of research on practice is by no means confined to clinical social work. In social work administration, for example, one sees the continuing development of management information systems and an increasing emphasis on the importance of measuring outcomes for clients (Patti, Poertner, & Rapp, 1988). Contemporary texts on social administration may present the same methods for measuring clients' progress and the attainment of goals that one finds in texts on research-based clinical social work (Rapp & Poertner, 1992). Qualitative research methods, such as ethnography and grounded theory, are also being proposed as tools in administrative practice (Bernstein & Epstein, 1994; Weissman, in press).

Although the empirical practice movement has made impressive advances, it has only begun to make a significant impact on social work practice. It is certainly much more visible in social work education than in the delivery of services. However, as graduates who are trained in an empirical approach become more numerous and influential, its use should spread. At some point, the movement, with its special courses and literature, should fade into history as its contribution is fully absorbed into mainstream practice and education for practice.

Quantitative Methods
Since the 1970s, there has been an increasing use of multivariate methods of data analysis—factor analysis, multiple regression, multivariate analysis of variance, and so on. In his survey of the analytic methods discussed in research articles in core social work journals, Glisson (1990) found that multivariate techniques were used in 16 percent of the articles from 1983 to 1988, an increase of almost 100 percent from the previous five-year period. In contrast, little or no growth was seen in the use of other methods of analysis.

An organization of social work researchers, the Quantitative Methods Interest Group, was founded as a means of sharing knowledge about quantitative methods. Emerging advances in these analytic tools, including network analysis, logistic regression, log-linear analysis, and structural equation modeling, are reviewed by Gillespie and Glisson (1993).

Multivariate techniques have enabled researchers to mine their data more rapidly and thoroughly. By using these techniques, it is possible to ascertain patterns in the interrelationships among numerous variables or to build causal explanations by controlling statistically for the influences of different variables. Although these techniques have contributed enormously to the methodology of social work research, they have created problems and issues yet to be resolved. First, consumers of research—students, practitioners, managers, and so on—often cannot comprehend these more complex analytic methods. As a result, they may not be able to judge the findings of a study and instead may have to trust the researcher's conclusions. Second, many researchers who use these techniques do not understand their mathematical foundations; therefore, they are often ignorant of their pitfalls and limitations. Third, the measurements that provide the raw material for the analysis may not be sufficiently rigorous to warrant elaborate statistical manipulation; in short, the analysis may outrun the data.

Another development in quantitative methods is the emergence of meta-analysis, a tool that enables researchers to synthesize data from a large number of studies (Fischer, 1990). A well-established method in other fields, meta-analysis is relatively new to social work researchers, who thus far have produced only a few studies (see, for example, Marcus, 1992; Reid & Crisafulli, 1990; Tobler, 1992; Videka-Sherman, 1988). In meta-analysis, measures of relationships between variables (such as correlations) in different studies are combined in a unified statistical analysis. The method provides a more objective and systematic way of synthesizing the results of research related to a particular problem than do traditional reviews of the literature. The potential shortcomings of meta-analysis include its lack of sensitivity to differences among studies with respect to their quality, ways of measuring variables, and so forth— differences that may be taken into account by a scholar reviewing the same studies. Despite such limitations, meta-analysis has considerable promise for social work, which badly needs synthesizing tools to make use of the vast bodies of research relevant to its mission.

Qualitative Methods

Although the need for the greater use of qualitative methods in social work research has been long recognized, only occasional studies that have made systematic use of these methods have appeared in the social work literature. (Excluded from consideration here are impressionistic accounts that make little apparent use of any form of methodology but that could be called "qualitative" because they lack quantitative data.) Obstacles to qualitative research have been formidable—for instance, the lack of training and mentors, few models in the form of published studies, the scarcity of guidelines for doing research, and the negative attitudes toward it by mainstream researchers (Fortune, 1990).

There are signs that this situation has begun to change. Texts on qualitative methods that are written or edited by social work researchers have begun to appear (Gilgun, Daly, & Handel, 1992; Riessman, 1994; Sherman & Reid, 1994), as have reports of well-developed qualitative studies (see, for example, Belcher, Scholler-Jaquish, & Drummond, 1991; Gilgun, 1991; Mizrahi & Abramson, 1994). In addition, a major national conference on qualitative methodology was held in 1991 (Sherman & Reid), and the Task Force on Social Work Research specified that advanced research training should include qualitative methods (*Building Social Work Knowledge,* 1991).

The case for a much larger role for nonquantitative methodology in social work research is compelling. Many domains of inquiry in social work, including the processes of change in complex social systems, such as families, organizations, and communities, cannot be investigated adequately with traditional methods. Qualitative approaches may provide insights that are simply beyond the scope of standard methodology. Often, the knowledge derived may well be accepted as the best that is attainable and as the best that can be refined through further qualitative study. Finally, qualitative methods can often be used in combination with quantitative methods in the same study or in the same research program, in a mutually reinforcing manner. In fact, there have been increasing calls for the use of mixtures of the two kinds of methodologies (Sherman & Reid, 1994).

At the same time, the limitations of qualitative methods must be recognized. Imprecision and the potential biases of single investigators are among the more serious problems. Accurate and unbiased reporting is common to all research and scholarly endeavors (as well as to many others) and is not simply a demand of a particular research tradition or philosophy.

Agency-Based Research

Although most research activity in social work is now centered in academia, there have been a number of developments in agency-based research. One long-term trend has been the evolution of management information systems (MISs). With their ability to store and retrieve routinely collected information on clients and the operations, costs, and outcomes of services, MISs can provide a database for planning, developing, and monitoring programs. For some time, efforts have been made to construct systems that are more useful to line practitioners (Mutschler & Hasenfeld, 1986). An outstanding recent example is BOMIS, an MIS developed at Boysville of Michigan, a youth-serving agency. BOMIS integrates information that is useful to managers, supervisors, and clinicians (Grasso, 1992). It incorporates data on the assessment of and change in clients, as well as on interventions—data that are actively used by clinicians in the program. Other examples can be found in Durkin (1988) and Valasquez (1992).

An MIS not only can be used as a basis for research on an agency's operations but can provide databases for studies of wider interest. For example, using data generated by the MIS of the Lower East Side Family Union, a child welfare prevention agency in New York City, Fanshel, Marsters, Finch, and Grundy (1992) demonstrated how a sophisticated analysis of the distribution of a staff's time in serving families could contribute to improvements in the program's management, as well as in clinical practice. The study also added to general knowledge about preventive child welfare services. As the study illustrated, investigations drawn from information systems can amount to a new and potent form of research. Not only can large data sets be used at relatively low cost, but studies can be readily replicated or phenomena investigated over time as data continue to flow into the system.

The potential of MISs for both operations research and knowledge-building research has thus far been limited by the poor quality of the data in many systems (O'Brien, McClellan, & Alfs, 1992), difficulties encountered in developing adequate measures, concerns about the confidentiality of information on clients, the lack of appropriate data utilization, and the inability of smaller agencies or units to afford start-up costs. However, continued growth seems inevitable, especially as computers become more affordable and more MIS models and expertise become available. A likely direction for development is the greater capacity to generate operational research data to guide decision making at all levels of an agency's hierarchy.

Other types of operations research that are receiving increasing attention in agencies include quality assurance programs, needs assessments, productivity studies, and program evaluations. Research of this kind is often carried out in conjunction with accountability requirements or as part of grant-supported programs. Illustrations of them can be found in Rehr (1992) and Mizrahi (1992).

The increased emphasis on operations research in agencies does not mean that agencies are forsaking their traditional role as active contributors to knowledge building. As was noted earlier, much of the research that is based in academia is carried out in agencies in collaboration with agency staff. Often the base of such research is more in the agency than in the academy. The agency may generate the research ideas and provide the site and staff time, even though the first author of the published report may be an academic (who may have more time and a greater inclination to do the writing).

Moreover, agencies and schools of social work are searching for new kinds of partnerships that will help bridge the age-old gap between research and practice (Mattaini, 1992). An emerging trend is to institutionalize such partnerships in the form of research centers that are supported jointly by schools and agencies (Epstein, Grellong, & Kohn, 1992). A recent example is the Center for the Study of Social Work Practice, a joint undertaking by the Columbia University School of Social Work and the Jewish Board of Guardians of New York City (Jenkins, 1992).

Recent Computer-Based Advances

The developments in quantitative methods and management information systems have their origins in computer technology, which go back to the 1960s. More recent computer-based innovations include computer-assisted practice, expert systems, and the use of databases in community practice.

Computer-assisted practice involves the use of computers to perform various tasks to facilitate assessment, case monitoring and evaluation, record keeping, and the like. The most widely used programs in social work have been developed by Hudson and his associates (Hudson, 1987, 1990; Hudson, Nurius, & Reisman, 1988; Nurius & Hudson, 1993), whose most recent package of programs, Computer Assisted Social Services, or

CASS (Nurius & Hudson), contains over 20 assessment scales. Among other functions, CASS permits clients to input their responses to scales directly into the computer, scores the scales and graphs the scores over the progress of the case, and aggregates the results of single-case studies. Although the use of computer-assisted practice is not yet widespread, a significant number of practitioners are beginning to use its assessment functions (Nurius, Hooyman, & Nicoll, 1991).

"An expert system is a computer program designed to give advice on decisions" (Mullen & Schuerman, 1990, p. 67). In social work applications, the advice the program gives is derived from detailed interviews with expert practitioners concerning a particular type of problem. Using principles derived from work on artificial intelligence, the researcher uses data from the interviews to create a computer model of the experts' decision-making processes. In using an expert system, the practitioner answers questions about a case that are asked by the program, which then recommends possible actions, as in a child-placement decision. Expert systems in social work are still in an early stage of development and are not yet ready for large-scale implementation. Ultimately, they should be of considerable assistance to practitioners making decisions, especially those who lack training or experience (Schuerman, 1987).

Computer applications in community practice have taken a variety of forms, including storing and analyzing data on problem areas, organizing social action campaigns, and operating clearinghouses (Mizrahi, 1992). A particularly interesting example is MORE (Member Organized Research Exchange), a computer-run time-bartering system set up by the Grace Hill Settlement House in St. Louis. This system permits low-income residents to trade chores (measured in time units) with one another (Rogge & Smith, 1988).

Research Utilization

For social work research to have a meaningful function, it must be applied by practitioners who are responsible for planning, administering, and implementing social work programs. The utilization of research in social work has long been a source of concern, at least to researchers. As various studies have suggested, practitioners read few research articles and tend to rank research relatively low as a source of guidance in making decisions about practice, relying more frequently on knowledge derived from supervisors and on-the-job experience (Kirk, 1990; Kirk, Osmalov, & Fischer, 1976; Rosenblatt, 1968).

Among the major reasons that practitioners do not use the results of research are that most studies lack direct relevance to day-to-day practice decisions and that practitioners are unable to understand the technical language and methodology of research reports. The failure of practitioners to make use of research appears to be a problem shared by most practice professions (Kirk, 1979).

Although numerous studies have documented practitioners' failure to use research, the volume of studies continues to grow. This anomaly has focused greater attention on the problems involved in the use of research (Briar, Weissman, & Rubin, 1981; Grasso & Epstein, 1992).

Certain trends show promise of increasing practitioners' use of research. Behavioral and other empirical practice models are an important indirect means of using the products of research. In addition, research applications of agency information systems and the use of single-case studies in practice contexts are ways that managers and practitioners can directly use the research they themselves generate.

Since the 1970s, the sizable literature on the dissemination and utilization of technical innovations and scientific findings has been increasingly applied to social work (Gordon, 1984; Kirk, 1979). These efforts have resulted in dissemination and utilization methods that are appropriate for social work (Thomas & Rothman, 1994).

These developments may be helped by the increasing emphasis on research and scholarship in schools of social work. Educators who are oriented to both research and practice may lead students to the greater utilization and appreciation of practice-relevant empirical literature. At the same time, many of these academics are also opinion leaders in the world of practice and can be expected to ground their writings about practice in relevant research.

It remains to be seen how these trends affect the utilization of research in the long run, although it may be difficult to assess the various influences. There is growing recognition that direct or instrumental use—practitioners reading and applying results of studies—may be only a small piece of the pie and that there are many ways of using research besides applying findings to guide practice (Tripodi, 1992). For example, research can provide new concepts and perspectives, clarify abstractions, produce methods of measurement, challenge accepted beliefs, generate hypotheses, or just stimulate thinking.

Since the 1980s, this broader view of the use of research has received greater attention. The notion of conceptual utilization has become increasingly prominent (Beyer & Trice, 1982;

Hasenfeld & Patti, 1992; Reid & Smith, 1989; Rich, 1977; Weiss & Bucuvalas, 1980a, 1980b). In conceptual utilization, the user does not directly act on research findings; he or she adds them to his or her fund of existing knowledge, which may be derived from personal experience and other sources. As they are combined with other knowledge, research findings may exercise an indirect and delayed influence.

Moreover, there is growing recognition that the intricacies of research utilization are not just cerebral. Findings may exercise their impact through a complex knowledge-dissemination process involving multiple intermediaries and sources—researchers, educators, authors of review articles and texts on practice, workshop leaders, program directors, and so on (Reid & Fortune, 1992). For example, practitioners may turn to supervisors, rather than to the research literature, for guidance (Rosenblatt, 1968), but this does not mean that research plays no part in the practitioners' decisions because the supervisors' suggestions may have been influenced by research.

The discovery of new modes of research utilization is not equivalent, however, to documenting how and when research is put to work in social work practice. More research on the processes of utilization is needed. Meanwhile, one hopes that these new modes, especially if they are systematically cultivated, will gradually help narrow the distance between the worlds of research and practice.

REFERENCES

Abbott, A. A. (1977). *Social work doctoral dissertations (1960 to 1974): Content, method, quality and relevance for future research productivity.* Unpublished doctoral dissertation, Bryn Mawr College, Graduate School of Social Work and Social Research, Bryn Mawr, PA.

American Association of Social Workers. (1929). *The Milford Conference report: Social casework—Generic and specific.* New York: Author.

Austin, D. (1992). Findings of the NIMH task force on social work research. *Research on Social Work Practice, 2,* 311–322.

Austin, L. N. (1948). Trends in differential treatment in social casework. *Journal of Social Casework, 29,* 203–211.

Belcher, J. R., Scholler-Jaquish, A., & Drummond, M. (1991). Stages of homelessness: A conceptual model of social workers in health care. *Health & Social Work, 16,* 87–93.

Berlin, S. B. (1990). Dichotomous and complex thinking. *Social Service Review, 64,* 46–59.

Berlin, S. B., & Marsh, J. C. (1993). *Informing practice decisions.* New York: Macmillan.

Bernstein, S. R., & Epstein, I. (1994). Grounded theory meets the reflective practitioner: Integrating qualitative and quantitative methods in administrative practice. In E. Sherman and W. J. Reid (Eds.), *Qualitative research in social work* (pp. 435–444). New York: Columbia University Press.

Beyer, J. M., & Trice, H. M. (1982). The utilization process: A conceptual framework and synthesis of empirical findings. *Administrative Science Quarterly, 27,* 591–622.

Bloom, M., & Fischer, J. (1982). *Evaluating practice: Guidelines for the accountable professional.* Englewood Cliffs, NJ: Prentice Hall.

Blythe, B. J. (1990). Improving the fit between single-subject designs and practice. In L. Videka-Sherman & W. J. Reid (Eds.), *Advances in clinical social work research* (pp. 29–32). Silver Spring, MD: NASW Press.

Blythe, B. J., Tripodi, T., & Briar, S. (in press). *Direct practice research in human service agencies.* New York: Columbia University Press.

Briar, S. (1990). Empiricism in clinical practice: Present and future. In L. Videka-Sherman & W. J. Reid (Eds.), *Advances in clinical social work research* (pp. 1–7). Silver Spring, MD: NASW Press.

Briar, S., & Miller, H. (1971). *Problems and issues in social work.* New York: Columbia University Press.

Briar, S., Weissman, H., & Rubin, A. (Eds.). (1981). *Research utilization in social work education.* New York: Council on Social Work Education.

Building social work knowledge for effective services and policies: A plan for research development. A report of the task force on social work research. (1991). Washington, DC: National Institute of Mental Health.

Council on Social Work Education. (1984). *Handbook of accreditation standards and procedures.* New York: Author.

Dean, R., & Reinherz, H. (1986). Psychodynamic practice and single system design: The odd couple. *Journal of Social Work Education 22,* 71–81.

Dollard, D. J., & Mowrer, O. H. (1947). A method of measuring tension in written documents. *Journal of Abnormal and Social Psychology, 42,* 3–32.

Dubos, R. (1965). Science and man's nature. *Daedalus, 94,* 223–244.

Durkin, R. (1988). The Sage Hill behavior rating system: Some of its clinical, administrative, and research uses. *Journal of Child Care* [Spring special issue], 19–29.

Epstein, I., Grellong, B. A., & Kohn, A. (1992). Workshop 3: Models of university-agency collaborations in research. *Research on Social Work Practice, 2,* 338–349.

Fanshel, D., Marsters, P. A., Finch, S. J., & Grundy, J. F. (1992). Strategies for the analysis of databases in social service systems. In A. J. Grasso & I. Epstein (Eds.), *Research utilization in the social services* (pp. 301–323). New York: Haworth Press.

Fischer, J. (1973). Is casework effective? A review. *Social Work, 18,* 5–20.

Fischer, J. (1978). *Effective casework practice: An eclectic approach.* New York: McGraw-Hill.

Fischer, J. (1990). Problems and issues in meta-analysis. In L. Videka-Sherman & W. J. Reid (Eds.), *Advances in clinical social work research* (pp. 297–325). Silver Spring, MD: NASW Press.

Fishman, D. B., Rotgers, E., & Franks, C. M. (Eds.). (1988). *Paradigms in behavior therapy: Present and promise.* New York: Springer.

Fortune, A. E. (1990). Problems and uses of qualitative methodologies. In L. Videka-Sherman and W. J. Reid (Eds.), *Advances in clinical social work research* (pp. 194–201). Silver Spring, MD: NASW Press.

Fraser, M., Taylor, M. J., Jackson, R., & O'Jack, J. (1991). Social work and science: Many ways of knowing? *Social Work Research & Abstracts, 27*(4), 5–15.

Geismar, L. L. (1982). Comments on the "Obsolete scientific imperative in social work research." *Social Service Review, 56,* 311–312.

Gergen, K. J. (1985). The social constructionist movement in modern psychology. *American Psychologist, 40,* 260–275.

Germain, C. (1970). Casework and science: A historical encounter. In R. W. Roberts & R. H. Nee (Eds.), *Theories of social casework* (pp. 20–35). Chicago: University of Chicago Press.

Gibbs, L. E. (1991). *Scientific reasoning for social workers.* New York: Macmillan.

Gilgun, J. F. (1991). Resilience and the intergenerational transmission of child sexual abuse. In M. Q. Patton (Ed.), *Family sexual abuse: Frontline research and evaluation* (pp. 56–68). Newbury Park, CA: Sage Publications.

Gilgun J. F., Daly, G., & Handel, G. (Eds.). (1992). *Qualitative methods in family research.* Newbury Park, CA: Sage Publications.

Gillespie, D., & Glisson, C. (1993). *Quantitative methods in social work.* New York: Haworth Press.

Gingerich, W. J. (1984). Generalizing single-case evaluation from classroom to practice. *Journal of Education for Social Work, 20,* 74–82.

Gingerich, W. J. (1990). Rethinking single-case evaluation. In L. Videka-Sherman & W. J. Reid (Eds.), *Advances in clinical social work research* (pp. 11–24). Silver Spring, MD: NASW Press.

Glisson, C. (1983, October). *Trends in social work research: Substantive and methodological implications for doctoral curricula.* Paper presented at the Annual Meeting of the Group for the Advancement of Doctoral Education, University of Alabama, School of Social Work.

Glisson, C. (1990). *A systematic assessment of the social work literature: Trends in social work research, Part II.* Report submitted to the NIMH Task Force on Social Work Research. Knoxville: University of Tennessee School of Social Work.

Gordon, J. E. (1984). Creating research-based practice principles: A model. *Social Work Research & Abstracts, 20*(1), 3–6.

Grasso, A. J. (1992). Information utilization: A decade of practice. In A. J. Grasso & I. Epstein (Eds.), *Research utilization in the social services* (pp. 437–444). New York: Haworth Press.

Grasso, A. J., & Epstein, I. (Eds.). (1992). *Research utilization in the social services.* New York: Haworth Press.

Green, R. G., Hutchison, E. D., & Sar, B. K. (1990). *National survey of social work doctoral graduates: Preliminary findings* (Report to the NIMH Task Force on Social Work Research). Richmond: Virginia Commonwealth University, School of Social Work.

Green, R. G., Hutchison, E. D., & Sar, B. K. (1992). Evaluating scholarly performance: The productivity of graduates of social work doctoral programs. *Social Service Review, 66,* 442–466.

Grinnell, R. M., & Royer, M. L. (1983). Authors of articles in social work journals. *Journal of Social Service Research, 6,* 147–154.

Guba, E. C. (1990). The alternative paradigm dialog. In E. G. Guba (Ed.), *The paradigm dialog.* Newbury Park, CA: Sage Publications.

Hanrahan, P. (1978). *Trends in the subject matter of social work research.* Unpublished manuscript, University of Chicago, School of Social Service Administration.

Hanrahan, P. (1984). *Trends in the subject matter of social work research: an update.* Unpublished manuscript, University of Chicago, School of Social Service Administration.

Harrison, W. D. (1994). The inevitability of integrated methods. In E. Sherman and W. J. Reid (Eds.), *Qualitative research in social work* (pp. 409–422). New York: Columbia University Press.

Hasenfeld, Y., & Patti, R. (1992). The utilization of research in administrative practice. In A. J. Grasso & I. Epstein (Eds.), *Research utilization in the social services* (pp. 221–234). New York: Haworth Press.

Haworth, G. O. (1984). Social work research, practice, and paradigms. *Social Service Review, 58,* 343–357.

Heineman, M. B. (1981). The obsolete scientific imperative in social work research. *Social Service Review, 55,* 371–397.

Heineman-Pieper, M. (1989). The heuristic paradigm: A unifying and comprehensive approach to social work research. *Smith College Studies in Social Work, 60,* 8–34.

Hogarty, G. E., Anderson, C. M., Reiss, D. J., Kamblith, S. J., Greenwald, D. P., Javna, C. D., & Madonia, M. J. (1986). Family psychoeducation, social skills training, and maintenance chemotherapy in the aftercare treatment of schizophrenia. *Archives of General Psychiatry, 43,* 633–642.

Hollis, F. (1949). The techniques of casework, *Journal of Social Casework, 30,* 235–244.

Hollis, F. (1963). Contemporary issues for caseworkers. In H. J. Parad & R. R. Miller (Eds.), *Ego-oriented casework* (pp. 1–16). New York: Family Service Association of America.

Hudson, W. W. (1982). Scientific imperatives in social work research and practice. *Social Service Review, 56,* 246–258.

Hudson, W. W. (1987). *The clinical assessment system.* Tallahassee, FL: Walmyr.

Hudson, W. W. (1990). *Computer assisted social services.* Tempe, AZ: Walmyr.

Hudson, W. W., Nurius, P. S., & Reisman, S. (1988). Computerized assessment instruments: Their promise and problems. *Computers in Human Services, 3*(1–2), 51–70.

Hunt, J. M. C. V. (1948). Measuring movement in casework *Journal of Social Casework, 29,* 343–351.

Ivanoff, A., Blythe, B. J., & Briar, S. (1987). The empirical clinical practice debate. *Social Casework: Journal of Contemporary Social Work, 68,* 290–298.

Jayaratne, S. (1982). Characteristics and theoretical orientations of clinical social workers: A national survey. *Journal of Social Service Research, 4,* 17–29.

Jenkins, S. (1992). Research utilization in an agency-university research model: The center for the study of social work practice. In A. J. Grasso & I Epstein (Eds.), *Research utilization in the social services* (pp. 393–399). New York: Haworth Press.

Jenkins, S., Jainz, R. A., Cherry, A., Nishimoto, R., Alvedo, J., & Ockert, D. (1982). Abstracts as data: Dissertation trends, 1975–79. *Social Work Research & Abstracts, 18*(1), 29–34.

Karpf, M. J. (1931). *The scientific basis of social work.* New York: Columbia University Press.

Kirk, S. A. (1979). Understanding research utilization in social work. In A. Rubin & A. Rosenblatt (Eds.), *Sourcebook on research utilization* (pp. 3–15). New York: Council on Social Work Education.

Kirk, S. A. (1990). Research utilization: The substructure of belief. In L. Videka-Sherman & W. J. Reid (Eds.), *Advances in clinical social work research* (pp. 233–250). Silver Spring, MD: NASW Press.

Kirk, S. A., Osmalov, M., & Fischer, J. (1976). Social workers' involvement in research. *Social Work, 21,* 121–124.

Kirk, S. A., & Penka, C. E. (1992). Research utilization and MSW education: A decade of progress? In A. J. Grasso & I. Epstein (Eds.), *Research utilization in the social services* (pp. 407–419). New York: Haworth Press.

LeCroy, C. W., & Goodwin, C. C. (1988). New directions in teaching social work methods: A content analysis of course outlines. *Journal of Social Work Education, 24,* 43–49.

LeCroy, C. W., & Rose, S. D. (1986). Methodological issues in the evaluation of social work practice. *Social Service Review, 59,* 345–357.

Marcus, M. (1992). *Caregivers of dementia patients: Their burden and sources of help, a meta-analysis.* Unpublished doctoral dissertation, Columbia University.

Mattaini, M. A. (1992). Introduction to the special issue. *Research on Social Work Practice, 3,* 261.

Mizrahi, T. (1992). The future of research utilization in community practice. In A. J. Grasso & I. Epstein (Eds.), *Research utilization in the social services* (pp. 197–220). New York: Haworth Press.

Mizrahi, T., & Abramson, J. (1994). Collaboration between social workers and physicians: An emerging typology. In E. Sherman & W. J. Reid (Eds.), *Qualitative research in social work* (pp. 135–151). New York: Columbia University Press.

Mullen, E. J., & Schuerman, J. R. (1990). Expert systems and the development of knowledge in social welfare. In L. Videka-Sherman & W. J. Reid (Eds.), *Advances in clinical social work research* (pp. 67–83). Silver Spring, MD: NASW Press.

Mutschler, E., & Hasenfeld, Y. (1986). Integrated information systems for social work practice. *Social Work, 31,* 345–349.

Nelsen, J. C. (1990). Single-case research and traditional practice: Issues and possibilities. In L. Videka-Sherman & W. J. Reid (Eds.), *Advances in clinical social work research* (pp. 37–47). Silver Spring, MD: NASW Press.

Nurius, P. S., Hooyman, N., & Nicoll, A. E. (1991). Computers in agencies: A survey baseline and planning implications. *Journal of Social Service Research, 14,* 141–155.

Nurius, P. S., & Hudson, W. W. (1993). *Human services: Practice, evaluation, and computers.* Belmont, CA: Wadsworth.

O'Brien, N., McClellan, T., & Alfs, D. (1992). Data collection: Are social workers reliable? *Administration in Social Work, 16,* 89–100.

Orcutt, B. A. (1990). *Science and inquiry in social work practice.* New York: Columbia University Press.

Patti, R. J., Poertner, J., & Rapp, C. A. (Eds.). (1988). *Managing for service effectiveness in social welfare organizations.* New York: Haworth Press.

Penka, C. E., & Kirk, S. A. (1991). Practitioner involvement in clinical evaluation. *Social Work, 36,* 513–518.

Rapp, C. A., & Poertner, J. (1992). *Social administration: A client-centered approach.* New York: Longman.

Reamer, F. G. (1992). *The philosophical foundations of social work.* New York: Columbia University Press.

Rehr, H. (1992). Practice uses of accountability systems in health care settings: Social work and administrative perspectives. In A. J. Grasso & I. Epstein (Eds.), *Research utilization in the social services* (pp. 241–256). New York: Haworth Press.

Reid, W. J. (1978). The subject matter of social work research [Editorial]. *Social Work Research & Abstracts, 14*(3), 2.

Reid, W. J. (1993). Fitting the single system design to social work practice. *Journal of Social Service Research, 18,* 83–99.

Reid, W. J. (1994). Reframing the epistemological debate. In E. Sherman & W. J. Reid (Eds.), *Qualitative research in social work* (pp. 464–480). New York: Columbia University Press.

Reid, W. J., & Bailey-Dempsey, C. (1994). Content analysis in design and development. *Journal of Research on Social Work Practice, 4,* 101–114.

Reid, W. J., & Crisafulli, A. (1990). Marital discord and child behavior problems: A meta-analysis. *Journal of Abnormal Child Psychology, 18,* 105–117.

Reid, W. J., & Fortune, A. E. (1992). Research utilization in direct social work practice. In A. J. Grasso & I. Epstein (Eds.), *Research utilization in the social services* (pp. 97–116). New York: Haworth Press.

Reid, W. J., & Hanrahan, P. (1982). Recent evaluations of social work: Grounds for optimism. *Social Work, 27,* 328–340.

Reid, W. J., & Smith, A. D. (1989). *Research in social work.* New York: Columbia University Press.

Reid, W. J., & Strother, P. (1986, October 11). *The clinical study in social work doctoral dissertations.* Paper presented at the Annual Program Meeting, Group for the Advancement of Doctoral Education, Fordham University.

Rich, R. F. (1977). Uses of social science information by federal bureaucrats: Knowledge for action versus knowledge for understanding. In C. H. Weiss (Ed.), *Using social research in public policy making* (pp. 101–120). Lexington, MA: Lexington Books.

Richey, C. A., Blythe, B. J., & Berlin, S. B. (1987). Do social workers evaluate their practice? *Social Work Research & Abstracts, 23*(2), 14–20.

Richmond, M. (1917). *Social diagnosis.* New York: Russell Sage Foundation.

Riessman, C. (Ed.). (1994). *Qualitative studies in social work research.* Newbury Park, CA: Sage Publications.

Rodwell, M. K., & Woody, D. (1994). Constructivist evaluation: The policy context. In E. Sherman & W. J. Reid (Eds.), *Qualitative research in social work.* New York: Columbia University Press.

Rogge, M., & Smith, S. (1988). *MORE evaluation report.* St. Louis: Consolidated Neighborhood Services.

Rosenblatt, A. (1968). The practitioner's use and evaluation of research. *Social Work, 13,* 53–59.

Rothman, J. (1991). A model of case management: Toward empirically based practice. *Social Work, 36,* 465–560.

Rubin, A. (1985). Practice effectiveness: More grounds for optimism. *Social Work, 30,* 469–476.

Schuerman, J. R. (1982). The obsolete scientific imperative in social work research, *Social Service Review, 56,* 144–146.

Schuerman, J. R. (1987). Expert consulting systems in social welfare. *Social Work Research & Abstracts, 23*(3), 14–18.

Sherman, E., & Reid, W. J. (Eds.). (1994). *Qualitative research in social work.* New York: Columbia University Press.

Siegel, D. H. (1984). Defining empirically based practice. *Social Work, 29,* 325–331.

Strom, K. (1992). *The effect of third party reimbursement on services by social workers in private practice.* Unpublished doctoral dissertation, Case Western Reserve University, Cleveland.

Thomas, E. J., & Rothman, J. (1994). An integrative perspective on intervention research. In J. Rothman & E. J. Thomas (Eds.), *Intervention research* (pp. 1–15). New York: Haworth Press.

Thomas, E. J., Santa, C., Bronson, D., & Oyersman, D. (1987). Unilateral family therapy with the spouses of alcoholics. *Journal of Social Service Research, 10,* 145–160.

Thyer, B., & Thyer, K. (1992). Single-system research designs in social work practice: A bibliography from 1965 to 1990. *Research on Social Work Practice, 2,* 99–116.

Tobler, N. S. (1992). Drug prevention programs can work: Research findings. *Journal of Addictive Diseases, 11,* 1–27.

Tripodi, T. (1984). Trends in research publication: The study of social work journals from 1956 to 1980. *Social Work, 29,* 353–359.

Tripodi, T. (1992). Differential research utilization in macro and micro social work practice: An evolving perspective. In A. J. Grasso, & I. Epstein (Eds.), *Research utilization in the social services* (pp. 11–29). New York: Haworth Press.

Tripodi, T., & Harrington J. (1979). Use of time-series designs for formative program evaluation. *Journal of Social Service Research, 3,* 67–68.

Tyson, K. B. (1992). A new approach to relevant scientific research for practitioners: The heuristic paradigm. *Social Work, 37,* 541–556.

Valasquez, J. (1992). GAIN: A locally based computer system which successfully supports line staff. *Administration in Social Work, 16,* 41–54.

Videka-Sherman, L. (1988). Meta-analysis of research on social work practice in mental health. *Social Work, 33,* 325–338.

Weiss, C. H., & Bucuvalas, M. J. (1980a). *Social science research and decision-making.* New York: Columbia University Press.

Weiss, C. H., & Bucuvalas, M. J. (1980b). Truth tests and utility tests: Decision-makers' frames of reference for social science research. *American Sociological Review, 45,* 302–313.

Weissman, H. (in press). The administrator as ethnographer and cartographer. In E. Sherman & W. J. Reid (Eds.), *Qualitative research in social work.* New York: Columbia University Press.

Witkin, S. (1989). Towards a scientific social work. *Journal of Social Service Research, 12,* 83–98.

Wood, K. M. (1978). Casework effectiveness: A new look at the research evidence. *Social Work, 23,* 437–458.

Zimbalist, S. (1955). *Major trends in social work research: An analysis of the nature and development of research in social work, as seen in the periodical literature, 1900–1950.* Unpublished doctoral dissertation, Washington University, St. Louis.

William J. Reid, DSW, ACSW, is professor, School of Social Welfare, Rockefeller College of Public Affairs and Policy, University at Albany, State University of New York, Albany, NY 12222.

For further information see

Agency-Based Research; Assessment; Direct Practice Overview; Computer Utilization; Epistemology; Ethical Issues in Research; Experimental and Quasi-Experimental Design; Expert Systems; Information Systems; Intervention Research; Meta-analysis; Qualitative Research; Survey Research; Social Work Practice: Theoretical Base; Social Work Profession Overview.

Key Words

epistemology	practice
methods	research

Retirement and Pension Programs

Regina O'Grady-LeShane

People are living longer. As a result of longevity and the trend toward early retirement, older men and women will spend more years in retirement than did previous generations (U.S. Senate, 1991). Some individuals choose to retire, whereas others leave work involuntarily; still other people continue to work. Understanding who retires and when and under what circumstances is important for social work practice because the life circumstances of older people vary greatly.

Retirement is now a well-established stage of life (U.S. Senate, 1992), but it is not the same experience for all older people. How retirement is defined influences whether social work research and practice are limited to the fortunate few whose economic status allows them many life choices or are expanded to include the diversity of life situations facing older people today. Not everyone retires for the same reason, nor does everyone leave the labor force at the same age. Many older people are "partially" retired in that they either work at jobs that bridge the transition from a career position to full retirement or continue to work at low-wage jobs to supplement inadequate retirement income. Consequently, for some older people retirement is a welcomed stage in life when family responsibilities are lessened and they can focus on leisure activities. For others it is a time of

caring for an ill spouse or parent. Still others experience retirement as the continuation of a lifetime on the economic fringe.

RETIREMENT DECISION

Although the decision to retire is made at the end of one's work life, it often represents the culmination of a lifetime of experiences (Gibson, 1991; Szinovacz, Ekerdt, & Vinick, 1992). A person's age, sex, health status, occupation of longest job, and marital status all influence the decision to retire. Until recently the influence of the retirement decision on other family members has been minimized, but a focus on the family suggests that the retirement of one person affects many others (Szinovacz et al., 1992).

In the early stages of retirement research, retirement was not considered an important event in women's lives. Consequently, initial retirement studies were conducted on samples of men (Szinovacz, 1982). Additionally, many retirement studies have focused on men's behavior because the diversity of women's work lives and their movement in and out of the labor force result in multiple exits from the labor force and contribute to the difficulty of defining retirement for women at a single point in time (Holden, 1989). As the focus of research has shifted to include the experiences of married women, it has become clear that the decision of married women to retire is strongly influenced by their age, health, and finances. Yet they often decide to retire at the same time their husbands do (Campione, 1987). Married couples who retire at the same time are more likely to be financially better off than couples in which the wife continues to work after the husband retires or in which the wife retires first (O'Rand, Henretta, & Krecker, 1992).

A growing awareness of gender differences has also led to the recognition of differences within different racial and ethnic populations (Gibson, 1987; Jackson & Gibson, 1985). Research that simply compares white and nonwhite groups wrongly assumes that people of the same racial and ethnic background face similar life circumstances (Gibson, 1988; Jackson & Gibson, 1985). It is clear, for example, that African Americans are a diverse and heterogeneous group (Jackson, Chatters, & Taylor, 1993). Ignoring diversity within different populations may result in inappropriately designed social policies. How retirement is defined can result in either the inclusion or exclusion of experiences of racial and ethnic groups.

Definition of Retirement
The simplest definition of "retirement" is to stop working, but this is not the most accurate definition. Quinn, Burkhauser, and Myers (1990) pointed out that if a person is 45 years old and stops working, people would not consider that person retired. To distinguish between people not working at younger ages and those not working later in life, retirement is often defined as the point in time when an individual begins receiving social security benefits (Holden, 1989, p. 102). The advantage of this definition, as noted by Holden, is that receipt of social security benefits is an objective measure that can be applied to most workers. But some older people work and receive social security benefits. Are they retired? One way to answer this question would be to define retirement subjectively, that is, you are retired if you think of yourself as retired (Holden, 1989). This definition does not solve the problem of the "unretired

retired"—older individuals who are not working and yet do not define themselves as retired (Gibson, 1993). According to Gibson (1991), "the reluctance to call oneself retired is not merely a matter of working in old age, but also a matter of how little lifetime work patterns have changed" (p. S208). People who have not worked steadily throughout their adult years are less likely to think of themselves as retired when they reach age 55. If a self-reported, or subjective, definition of retirement is used, people who are not working and do not consider themselves retired will be excluded. How retirement is defined, therefore, is crucial in advancing an understanding of the experience of diverse groups of people.

Reasons for Retirement
People retire for many reasons. Whereas most people (54 percent) retire voluntarily, many (29 percent) leave work because of health reasons or because they are forced to retire by their employers (17 percent) (Sherman, 1985). In contrast to the white population, African Americans are more likely to cite health as the major reason for retirement (Gibson, 1993). Poor health as a reason for withdrawal from the labor force does not influence women's retirement decision as much as it does men's (Ruhm, 1989). Women who leave work for health reasons do so involuntarily and would prefer later retirement (Szinovacz, 1987). Yet African American women are more likely to work despite health problems (Gibson, 1987; Jackson & Gibson, 1985).

Health status is an important predictor of satisfaction with retirement. If a man or a woman feels healthy, he or she is more likely to be satisfied with retirement (Martin Matthews & Brown, 1987). Not surprisingly, choice is another important factor in determining whether a person is satisfied with retirement. Both men and women are more likely to feel good about retirement if they chose to retire (Martin Matthews & Brown, 1987).

Women are more likely to retire for family reasons than are men (Sherman, 1985). Although they were not able to measure the amount of care given, Hatch and Thompson (1992) found that women were more likely to retire if a relative who required care lived with the family rather than in a separate household. Almost one out of five women cited family reasons as to why they retired early, that is, before age 65 (Sherman, 1985).

Early versus Normal Retirement Age
Normal retirement age is commonly thought of as age 65—the age at which a person is eligible for full benefits under social security. Under provisions of the 1983 Amendments to the Social Secu-

rity Act, "normal" retirement age will rise from 65 to 67 years of age by the year 2027. Early retirement is commonly defined as exit from the labor force before age 65. If normal retirement were defined by the behavior of most people, age 62 would be "normal" because more and more people are leaving jobs before age 65 (Packard & Reno, 1989; Quinn et al., 1990).

There are important differences between individuals who retire "early" and those who retire "on time." People who have a pension are likely to leave a job early because they want to. In contrast to voluntary retirees, individuals who leave the labor force before age 62 and do not have a pension are likely to cite poor health as the reason for leaving (Packard & Reno, 1989). In terms of occupation, blue-collar workers tend to retire earlier than do white-collar workers. Although more research is necessary on this topic, it appears that blue-collar workers retire because of the physical requirements of the job and the risks associated with the work (Mitchell, Levine, & Pozzebon, 1988).

Partial Retirement
Traditionally retirement is envisioned as moving from a full-time career job to full-time retirement, but that is only one of many paths individuals may take. Not everyone leaves the world of work when they reach retirement age (Ruhm, 1989; Quinn et al., 1990). Quinn et al. studied the paths taken by individuals who reached retirement age. They found that most people (70 percent) left the labor force completely. People who stop working completely are more likely to have a pension in addition to social security benefits than are those who continue to work (Iams, 1986). However, when people continue to work, they may work at the same job but reduce their hours, or they may change jobs and work either full-time or part-time at a new job.

Whether they are working full-time or part-time, men and women work in different occupations. Iams (1987) looked at the jobs of people age 62 and older and found that men were represented across many occupational groups. Women, on the other hand, were concentrated in three job categories: clerical (25 percent), service (28 percent), and sales (18 percent). Women who were working in service occupations before age 62 were more likely to work in those jobs after age 62. Of all women who were working in service jobs after age 62, almost half (47 percent) were private household workers (Iams, 1986). Given the low wages of service occupations, and private household work in particular, it is clear that many people work

after age 62 because their retirement income from social security and other sources is too low to support them.

RETIREMENT INCOME AND PENSION PROGRAMS

Retirement income is often depicted as a three-legged stool, the legs being social security benefits, pensions, and savings. The ideal, of course, is for each leg to provide some support. Because retirement income reflects the experiences of a person's working life (Crystal & Shea, 1990), each leg of the stool provides different levels of support for different groups of older people.

Social security provides more than one-third (38 percent) of total income for people age 65 and older (U.S. Senate, 1992). The basic benefit provided under social security is Old-Age and Survivors Insurance (OASI), which is derived from the primary insurance amount (PIA), a formula designed to replace a higher percentage of preretirement earnings of low-income workers than of high-income workers. In 1993 the average monthly benefit for all retired workers was $674 (U.S. Department of Health and Human Services, 1994). The average benefit for male workers was $759, and for female workers, $581.

When all sources of income in retirement are examined, it becomes evident that the inequalities present earlier in the life course become even greater in retirement (Crystal & Shea, 1990). Pension benefits are a smaller percentage of income for more disadvantaged older people than benefits received under social security (Ozawa & Kim, 1989). Although social security and pension benefits are both important sources of income for older people, social security, in particular, contributes to greater income equality within the elderly population (Ozawa & Kim, 1989).

Historical Development of Pensions
The first private pension plan was established in 1875 by the American Express Company (Williamson, 1992). Concern for employees was one of many reasons for the establishment of pension plans. Pension plans reduced the influence of unions and were seen as a reward for long-term employees and a way to retire workers who were no longer efficient. Voluntary establishment of pension plans was also a way to avoid government requirement of pension coverage (Williamson, 1992).

The Pennsylvania Railroad pension plan, established in 1900, was the first plan to cover all workers within the company. Individuals did not have to contribute to the plan, and retirement was compulsory at age 70. To qualify for a benefit, workers had to have given 30 years of service (Williamson, 1992). Utilities, banking, and manufacturing followed the lead of the railroad industry in establishing pension plans. By 1932 only 15 percent of workers were covered by a private pension plan (Graebner, 1980). Pension plans were unregulated and generally underfunded. Coverage by a pension plan did not guarantee that the plan would still exist when an individual reached retirement age (Graebner, 1980; Williamson, 1992). Because most plans did not provide for spouse benefits, the death of the pensioner often meant a severe loss of income for the surviving spouse. It was not until pension laws were reformed in the 1970s that protection for survivors was required (Graebner, 1980).

The greatest growth in pension programs occurred between 1940 and 1970 when the percentage of full-time workers covered by a pension plan grew from 17 percent to 52 percent (Beller & Lawrence, 1992). During World War II, pension plans were a mechanism to circumvent wage and price controls (Graebner, 1980). In the post-war years, pension plans became defined as a condition of employment and consequently became part of the collective bargaining process (Beller & Lawrence, 1992; Graebner, 1980).

Another significant event in pension legislation was the passage of the Employee Retirement Income Security Act (ERISA) of 1974. An important provision of ERISA was the requirement of survivor benefits, but it was not until the Retirement Equity Act (REA) of 1984 that pension plans were required to obtain a spouse's written consent if a worker decides not to choose this benefit option (Schulz, 1992). Although ERISA did not mandate coverage of all workers by private pension, important provisions of the law were minimum vesting requirements and the establishment of an insurance fund that would protect the pension benefits of workers against the termination of the plan (Schulz, 1992). Even though ERISA contained options for various vesting provisions, most companies initiated a 10-year vesting requirement (Schulz, 1992, p. 233). This vesting provision was reduced to five years under the regulations of the Tax Reform Act of 1986.

Types of Pensions

Two types of pension plans are provided by private employers. The most common pension plan is the defined benefit plan, which yields a benefit based on a specified dollar amount times years of service, or a percentage of salary times years of service. It is possible to estimate one's future pension benefit under a defined benefit pension plan.

For example, if a pension plan specifies that a worker will receive a benefit calculated as 1 percent of the last year's salary times years of service, a worker retiring at a salary of $35,000 who worked for a company for 30 years would receive an annual pension of $10,500 (1 percent × $35,000 × 30 years) (Wiatrowski, 1991). The longer one works for a company and the higher one's salary, the higher one's pension benefit at retirement.

Since the 1970s there has been a shift to defined contribution plans (Beller & Lawrence, 1992), in which the rate of contribution (usually a percentage of earnings) is specified, and the final benefit is based on the total amount of contributions in an employee's account. Under defined contribution plans, future benefits are not known.

Pension Coverage

Close to half (48 percent) of all full-time workers were covered by a private pension plan in 1988 (Woods, 1989). Pension coverage is higher for men, 50 percent compared with 43 percent for women (Korczyk, 1992). Differences in earnings explain why women and low-wage workers are less likely to be covered by pension plans (Korczyk, 1992). In 1988, 70 percent of women earned less than $20,000, and few women workers in these income categories had pension coverage. The majority (60 percent) of male workers earned more than $20,000 and were covered by pensions (Korczyk, 1992).

In 1987 the mean pension for men was $744, and for women it was $417 (U.S. Senate, 1992). Part of the reason for the large difference is that pensions are generally related to length of service. The longer one works for an employer the greater the pension benefit, and women tend to have fewer years with an employer than men do (Korczyk, 1992).

One issue as yet unaddressed by changes in pension law is the portability of pensions, that is, the ability to carry one's pension from one employer to the next. For women and low-income workers who change jobs frequently, portable pensions would allow pension rights to accumulate over the total working career.

IMPLICATIONS FOR SOCIAL WORK PRACTICE

At each phase of the retirement decision, social workers have an opportunity to help individuals decide when to retire and adjust to life after retirement (Richardson, 1989). One critical service social workers can offer their clients, especially women, is assistance in retirement planning (Perkins, 1992). Many people do not plan for retirement because of the cost of the service

(Richardson, 1989). Women may not participate in retirement planning because they have been socialized to depend on others and not take action for themselves (Perkins, 1992). Not surprisingly, the most difficult adjustment to retirement is that made by involuntary retirees; they are far more likely to be depressed than individuals who choose to retire (Richardson, 1989).

Although married couples may anticipate and plan for a long retirement together, the reality is that many women face retirement alone—a trend that is likely to increase (Hayward & Liu, 1992). Support groups for retirees may help older women adjust to retirement by offering them opportunities to meet other people in similar circumstances (Richardson, 1989).

The adequacy of retirement income reflects the opportunities and constraints faced by individuals throughout their lives. Although social workers can be very effective in helping clients decide when to retire and in facilitating the transition from work to retirement for those who mourn the loss of a work role, interventions to ensure adequate income in retirement must begin much earlier in the client's working career and present challenges and opportunities at the level of direct and indirect practice.

In helping clients make decisions about employment, an important consideration is pension benefits. Staying at a job until one's pension is vested has consequences for economic security in retirement. As defined contribution plans increase, concern must be raised about the effect of this trend on low-wage workers. To what extent can they afford to contribute to a pension plan? Careful attention must be paid to changes in social security and pension laws, particularly the effect of such changes on vulnerable populations (Ozawa & Kim, 1989).

Retirement is a significant transition. Ideally, a person enters retirement voluntarily and in good health. For many, however, retirement represents the accumulation of a lifetime of disadvantages, and the challenge for social workers is to eliminate those disadvantages.

REFERENCES

Beller, D. J., & Lawrence, H. H. (1992). Trends in private pension plan coverage. In J. A. Turner & D. J. Beller (Eds.), *Trends in pensions, 1992* (pp. 59–96). Washington, DC: U.S. Government Printing Office.

Campione, W. A. (1987). The married woman's retirement decision: A methodological comparison. *Journal of Gerontology, 42,* 381–386.

Crystal, S., & Shea, D. (1990). Cumulative advantage, cumulative disadvantage, and inequality among elderly people. *The Gerontologist, 30,* 437–443.

Employee Retirement Income Security Act of 1974. P.L. 93-406, 88 Stat. 829.

Gibson, R. C. (1987). Reconceptualizing retirement for Black Americans. *The Gerontologist, 27,* 691–698.

Gibson, R. C. (1988). Minority aging: Opportunity and challenge. *The Gerontologist, 28,* 559–560.

Gibson, R. C. (1991). The subjective retirement of Black Americans. *Journal of Gerontology, 46,* S204–S209.

Gibson, R. C. (1993). The Black American retirement experience. In J. S. Jackson, L. M. Chatters, & R. J. Taylor (Eds.), *Aging in Black America* (pp. 277–297). Newbury Park, CA: Sage Publications.

Graebner, W. (1980). *A history of retirement.* New Haven, CT: Yale University Press.

Hatch, L. R., & Thompson, A. (1992). Family responsibilities and women's retirement. In M. Szinovacz, D. J. Ekerdt, & B. H. Vinick (Eds.), *Families and retirement* (pp. 99–113). Newbury Park, CA: Sage Publications.

Hayward, M. D., & Liu, M. (1992). Men and women in their retirement years: A demographic profile. In M. Szinovacz, D. J. Ekerdt, & B. H. Vinick (Eds.), *Families and retirement* (pp. 23–50). Newbury Park, CA: Sage Publications.

Holden, K. C. (1989). Economic status of older women: A summary of selected research issues. In A. R. Herzog, K. C. Holden, & M. M. Seltzer (Eds.), *Health & economic status of older women* (pp. 92–130). Amityville, NY: Baywood Publishing.

Iams, H. M. (1986). Employment of retired-worker women. *Social Security Bulletin, 49,* 5–13.

Iams, H. M. (1987). Jobs of persons working after receiving retired-worker benefits. *Social Security Bulletin, 50,* 4–19.

Jackson, J. S., Chatters, L. M., & Taylor, R. J. (Eds.). (1993). *Aging in Black America.* Newbury Park, CA: Sage Publications.

Jackson, J. S., & Gibson, R. C. (1985). Work and retirement among the black elderly. In Z. S. Blau (Ed.), *Current perspectives on aging and the life cycle* (pp. 193–222). Greenwich, CT: JAI Press.

Korczyk, S. M. (1992). Gender and pension coverage. In J. A. Turner & D. J. Beller (Eds.), *Trends in pensions, 1992* (pp. 119–133). Washington, DC: U.S. Government Printing Office.

Martin Matthews, A., & Brown, K. H. (1987). Retirement as a critical life event. *Research on Aging, 9,* 548–571.

Mitchell, O. S., Levine, P. B., & Pozzebon, S. (1988). Retirement differences by industry and occupation. *The Gerontologist, 28,* 545–551.

O'Rand, A. M., Henretta, J. C., & Krecker, M. L. (1992). Family pathways to retirement. In M. Szinovacz, D. J. Ekerdt, & B. H. Vinick (Eds.), *Families and retirement* (pp. 81–98). Newbury Park CA: Sage Publications.

Ozawa, M. N., & Kim, T. S. (1989). Distributive effects of social security and pension benefits. *Social Service Review, 63,* 335–358.

Packard, M. D., & Reno, V. P. (1989). A look at very early retirees. *Social Security Bulletin, 52,* 16–29.

Perkins, K. (1992). Psychosocial implications of women and retirement. *Social Work, 37,* 526–532.

Quinn, J. F., Burkhauser, R. V., & Myers, D. A. (1990). *Passing the torch: The influence of economic incentives on work and retirement.* Kalamazoo, MI: W. E. Upjohn Institute.

Retirement Equity Act of 1984. P.L. 98-397, 98 Stat. 1426.

Richardson, V. E. (1989). Social work practice and retirement. *Social Casework, 70,* 210–218.

Ruhm, C. J. (1989). Why older Americans stop working. *The Gerontoloist, 29,* 294–299.

Schulz, J. H. (1992). *The economics of aging* (5th ed.). Westport, CT: Auburn House.

Sherman, S. R. (1985). Reported reasons retired workers left their last job: Findings from the New Beneficiary Survey. *Social Security Bulletin, 48,* 22–30.

Szinovacz, M. (1982). Introduction: Research on women's retirement. In M. Szinovacz (Ed.), *Women's retirement: Policy implications of recent research* (pp. 13–21). Beverly Hills, CA: Sage Publications.

Szinovacz, M. (1987). Preferred retirement timing and retirement satisfaction in women. *International Journal of Aging and Human Development, 24,* 301–317.

Szinovacz, M., Ekerdt, D. J., & Vinick, B. H. (1992). Families and retirement: Conceptual and methodological issues. In M. Szinovacz, D. J. Ekerdt, & B. H. Vinick (Eds.), *Families and retirement* (pp. 1–19). Newbury Park, CA: Sage Publications.

Tax Reform Act of 1986. P.L. 99-509, 100 Stat. 1951.

U.S. Department of Health and Human Services. (1994). *Annual statistical supplement, 1992.* Washington, DC: Social Security Administration.

U.S. Senate. (1992). *Aging America, 1991.* Washington, DC: U.S. Department of Health and Human Services.

Wiatrowski, W. J. (1991). New survey data on pension benefits. *Monthly Labor Review, 114,* 8–22.

Williamson, S. H. (1992). U.S. and Canadian pensions before 1930: A historical perspective. In J. A. Turner & D. J. Beller (Eds.), *Trends in pensions, 1992* (pp. 35–57). Washington, DC: U.S. Government Printing Office.

Woods, J. R. (1989). Pension coverage among private wage and salary workers: Preliminary findings from the 1988 survey of employee benefits. *Social Security Bulletin, 52,* 2–19.

FURTHER READING

Burkhauser, R. V., & Salisbury, D. L. (Eds.). (1993). *Pensions in a changing economy.* Washington, DC: National Academy on Aging/Employee Benefit Research Institute.

Kingson, E. R., & Berkowitz, E. D. (1993). *Social security and Medicare: A policy primer.* Westport, CT: Auburn House.

Rapport, A. M., & Schieber, S. J. (Eds.). (1993). *Demography and retirement: The twenty-first century.* Westport, CT: Praeger.

Richardson, V. E. (1993). *Retirement counseling.* New York: Springer.

Scott, H., & Brudney, J. F. (1987). *Forced out.* New York: Simon & Schuster.

Szinovacz, M., Ekerdt, D. J., & Vinick, B. H. (1992). *Families and retirement.* Newbury Park, CA: Sage Publications.

Torres-Gil, F. M. (1992). *The new aging: Politics and change in America.* New York: Auburn House.

Regina O'Grady-LeShane, PhD, is assistant professor, Boston College, Graduate School of Social Work, Chestnut Hill, MA 02167.

For further information see

Aging: Public Policy Issues and Trends; Baby Boomers; Employment and Unemployment Measurement; Income Distribution; Income Security Overview; Jobs and Earnings; Social Security; Supplemental Security Income.

Key Words

| income inequality | pensions |
| income maintenance | retirement |

Reynolds, Bertha Capen

See Biographies section, Volume 3

Richmond, Mary Ellen

See Biographies section, Volume 3

Riis, Jacob August

See Biographies section, Volume 3

Rivera de Alvarado, Carmen

See Biographies section, Volume 3

Robison, Sophie Moses

See Biographies section, Volume 3

Rodriguez Pastor, Soledad

See Biographies section, Volume 3

Roosevelt, Eleanor

See Biographies section, Volume 3

Rothman, Beulah

See Biographies section, Volume 3

Rubinow, Isaac Max

See Biographies section, Volume 3

Runaways and Homeless Youths
Deborah Bass

There have always been young people who have left home without their parents' permission. During colonial times, many immigrants to the United States were teenagers who were placed by poor families as indentured servants. During the 18th and 19th centuries, teenagers were fleeing slavery in the South or tyranny in their native countries. Adolescents left home during the Great Depression of the 1930s to ease their parents' economic burden. And in the 1960s, rebellious youths left home to seek adventure and freedom from parental supervision.

Societal attitudes that runaways were merely rebellious youths changed in the 1960s and 1970s (Posner, 1991). Runaways were often hungry and homeless and had to resort to stealing or selling drugs or their bodies to survive. They were viewed as troubled youths, status offenders, or delinquents. In 1976 the arrest rate of juveniles exceeded that of adults (Posner, 1991).

In the 1970s clinicians divided runaways and homeless youths into two groups: (1) those who left home because they had serious psychological problems and (2) those who left to escape pathological family environments. Serious psychological problems were attributed to these youths (Pires & Silber, 1991). As the runaways were victimized, professionals began to recognize that young people often left home to escape problems that seemed insurmountable.

The Juvenile Justice and Delinquency Prevention Act of 1974 (P.L. 93-415) prohibited states from jailing youths for behavior that is not a crime if committed by adults (status offenses). Congress recognized that runaways and homeless youths come from a variety of backgrounds and environments and include those who are forced from their homes; those who frequently run away from their homes; those who run away from juvenile institutions, residential facilities, or foster homes; and those who want to escape parental control temporarily (Bass, 1992). Many run away because they have been abused by their parents or another family member or because a family member has a substance abuse problem. Often those who run away end up homeless.

SCOPE OF THE PROBLEM

The exact number of runaways and homeless youths in the United States is not known; many runaway episodes are not reported, and it is difficult to find and count all the homeless youths. A study conducted for the Office of Juvenile Justice and Delinquency Prevention of the U.S. Department of Justice estimated that in 1988, 450,700 youths ran away and 127,100 were thrown out of their homes (Finklehor, Hotaling, & Sedlak, 1990). The National Network of Runaway and Youth Services (U.S. General Accounting Office [GAO], 1989b) estimated that there are 1 million to 1.3 million runaways and homeless youths each year and that 500,000 of these youths are homeless.

GAO (1989a) estimated that 68,000 youths are homeless but projected that there may be an additional 64,000 to 208,000 homeless youths annually who are not included in this estimate, which also does not include information on unaccompanied youths served in emergency shelters. Of the runaway and homeless youths served by federally funded shelters between 1985 and 1988, 21 percent were classified as homeless by the shelter staffs (GAO, 1989b).

FACTORS THAT INFLUENCE RUNAWAY BEHAVIOR

Four key factors influence runaway and other types of damaging behavior, such as substance abuse: (1) interpersonal relationships, (2) societal influences, (3) personal factors, and (4) environmental factors.

Interpersonal Relationships
A 1991 NASW survey (Bass, 1992) of 360 agencies that provide basic shelter and crisis intervention services and transitional living services to runaway and homeless youths reported that most runaway youths leave their homes or legal residences because of severe interpersonal problems. More than two-thirds of the youths who are seen in shelters have been abused by a parent, and more

than one-fourth have been abused by other family members. Furthermore, approximately one-third of the youths have a parent who is an alcoholic, and more than one-fourth have a parent who is a drug abuser.

As youths try to cope with severe problems, many of them leave home more frequently and for longer periods and begin to lose what may remain of their interpersonal relationships with other family members (Posner, 1991). These long-term interpersonal problems are not likely to be resolved quickly, and thus, many of these youths often need longer-term help than a shelter can offer.

Societal Influences

Of the juvenile residential facilities that agreed to participate in a survey conducted for the Office of Juvenile Justice and Delinquency Prevention (Finklehor et al., 1990), group foster homes reported the most frequent runaways. Youths also ran away from other types of residential facilities.

The 1991 NASW survey (Bass, 1992) found that more than one in five youths who arrived at shelters came directly from foster care and that more than one in four had been in foster care the previous year. Other studies have reported that even higher percentages of the youths seen by shelters were "systems kids." For example, Posner (1991) reported that 50 percent to 60 percent of runaways have spent time in foster care or group homes, and a New York study (New York State Council on Children and Families, 1984) found that nearly 60 percent of the youths sampled entered shelters from foster care or from mental health or juvenile justice systems.

The fact that youths run away from foster care suggests that foster care has not met their needs. Although nationwide data are not available, Raychaba (1988), who experienced the child welfare system in Canada, suggested that systems such as the child welfare system may add to the youths' problems. He reported that many youths in foster care were maltreated by foster parents.

The NASW survey (Bass, 1992) also revealed that 83 percent of the programs responding to the survey received referrals from law enforcement agencies and that more than three-fourths received referrals from the juvenile justice system. Additionally, more than one-fourth of the clients from responding programs were in trouble with the justice system. Although shelters cultivate relationships with the justice and law enforcement systems to encourage referrals, the high percentage of referrals suggests that the youths may not have received services that could have prevented their involvement with those systems.

Personal Factors

In the NASW survey (Bass, 1992) service providers reported that more than one-fourth of the runaway and homeless youths have mental health problems and that more than one-fifth have attempted suicide. These data confirmed the serious problems noted in a GAO report (1989a) stating that about 61 percent of these youths suffer from depression and that about 10 percent are considered suicidal.

These problems are exacerbated in some instances by substance abuse and other self-damaging behaviors. The NASW survey (Bass, 1992) reported that more than one-fourth of the youths served were drug abusers and that not quite one-fifth were alcoholics. They may also be engaged in prostitution, selling drugs, and stealing (Posner, 1991). Adolescents turn to such self-damaging behavior because it is difficult to survive without support from their families.

Environmental Factors

Many of the problems of runaway and homeless youths mirror the problems faced by American society. The poor performance of the U.S. economy in the late 1980s and early 1990s and the lack of low-cost housing led to unemployment and homelessness. Shelter providers reported that 40 percent to 50 percent of their clients were from families with long-term economic problems. Half were from households with absent fathers, more than one-third had no means of support, and more than half had educational problems. Approximately 13 percent of the youths came from families that had temporarily lost their housing (Bass, 1992).

The factors that lead to runaway behavior have long-term consequences that may cause youths to face the same problems as their parents. Those who run away are less likely to complete school and are more likely to be unemployed and to have interpersonal problems such as marital conflict (Posner, 1991).

RUNAWAYS VERSUS HOMELESS YOUTHS

Definitions

The U.S. Department of Health and Human Services (DHHS) developed the following definitions to distinguish homeless youths from runaway youths (GAO, 1989b):

- A *runaway* is a youth who is away from home without the permission of his or her parents or legal guardian at least overnight.
- A *homeless youth* has no place of shelter and is in need of services, shelter, supervision, and care.

Demographics

An analysis of reports from federally funded shelters between 1985 and 1988 (GAO, 1989b) revealed that 55 percent of the homeless youths but only 35 percent of the runaways were male. Homeless youths tended to be older than runaways; 60 percent of them were 16 or older, compared with 40 percent of the runaways. Twenty-eight percent of the homeless youths were black, compared with 17 percent of the runaways. Many homeless youths did not attend school, and almost half came from broken homes. They were less likely to have spent the previous year with a parent, relative, or other adult or in a foster or group home, but they still did not go far from home; only 16 percent went to a shelter that was more than 50 miles away from home.

A high percentage of runaways and homeless youths had experienced physical and sexual abuse, drug and alcohol abuse by both parents, family violence, mental health problems, and school problems. Most of the youths did not simply enter shelters from the street but were referred to the shelters, often by child welfare and protective services agencies.

Problems Faced by Homeless Youths

Although runaways and homeless youths share many problems, homeless youths face some additional or more intense problems. Those who start as runaways and then become homeless find that their problems change.

The most serious problem faced by homeless youths is the increased risk of serious health care problems. Homeless youths have little access to health care but may be sexually active and at risk for sexually transmitted diseases, including acquired immune deficiency syndrome (AIDS). They are less likely to be treated for alcohol or drug abuse problems and are much less likely to be reunited with their families.

The results of a study of homeless youths who came to runaway shelters in the Southeast (Kurtz, Jarvis, & Kurtz, 1991) indicated that these homeless youths experienced family problems similar to those experienced by youths in the GAO study (1989b) (for example, family mental health problems, parental substance abuse, and parental unemployment) and were less likely to be in school. The study also showed that black youths were overrepresented in the homeless population.

However, a key finding of this study was that twice as many homeless youths came to agencies from foster homes or group homes than from their own families. Thus, the data from this study captured two groups of homeless youths: those who had either run away or had been pushed out by their families and those who were removed from their homes and placed in inappropriate settings from which they ran away.

FEDERAL PROGRAMS AND POLICIES

Runaway and Homeless Youth Program (Basic Center Program)

The Runaway Youth Program, established by the Juvenile Justice and Delinquency Prevention Act of 1974 and later amended to include homeless youths, was designed to respond to the increasing number of adolescents who left and remained away from home without parental permission so that the problem of finding, detaining, and returning them to their homes would not be the responsibility of law enforcement officers and juvenile justice authorities (U.S. House of Representatives, 1990). The Runaway and Homeless Youth Program, which funds short-term stays in shelters and a multitude of crisis intervention services for runaways ages 12 to 18 who have not been placed in shelters by the courts, is expected to alleviate the problems of runaways, reunite them with their families, help them resolve intrafamily problems, strengthen family relationships, and stabilize living conditions.

The age group most often served by shelters is 15- to 16-year-olds. Most shelter clients are white, but black youths are disproportionately represented, especially when shelters serve more homeless youths, 28 percent of whom are black (GAO, 1989b); the shelters serve slightly more males than females. In fiscal year 1990, 338 basic center (shelter) grantees received some support from federal funds (DHHS, 1991), but these shelters were able to serve only a small portion of the estimated population of runaways and homeless youths. For example, from October 1985 to June 1988, federally funded shelters served 44,274 youths, but the total population of runaways and homeless youths may exceed 1 million per year. Various theories have been developed to explain the poor use of facilities. Some professionals (for example, Posner, 1991; Raychaba, 1988) believe that youths have learned to distrust "the system" based on previous experiences with the juvenile justice and child welfare systems, whereas others believe that shelters must increase their outreach efforts (verbal recommendations of the NASW advisory group based on the results of Bass, 1992).

To maintain the shelters' focus on crisis intervention, DHHS has interpreted "short-term" care to mean no more than 15 days of care in a shelter setting. Shelter staff must contact each youth's

TABLE 1
Services Provided by Most Respondents to the 1991 NASW Survey

Service	Shelters Providing Service (%)
Information and referral	98
Individual counseling	98
Screening/intake	96
Temporary shelter	95
Referral to drug abuse program	95
Case management	94
Family counseling	93
Coordination with criminal/ juvenile justice	91
Meals	90
Referral for mental health services	90
Referral for health care	90
Outreach	89
Referral for treatment for suicidal behavior	89
Referral to program for alcoholics	86
Advocacy for clients	86
Recreational program	85
Referral for other living arrangements	83
Referral to educational program/ general equivalency diploma	82
Referral for individual counseling	78
AIDS/HIV education	77
Follow-up to referral	76
Aftercare services	76
Referral for family counseling	73
Transportation	73
Recreation/leisure time activities	72
Helping youths develop an independent living plan	71
Referral for employment assistance	70
Referral to transitional living beyond shelter	69
Referral to aftercare services	67

SOURCE: Bass, D. (1992). *Helping vulnerable youths: Runaway and homeless adolescents in the United States.* Washington, DC: NASW Press.
NOTE: AIDS = acquired immune deficiency syndrome; HIV = human immunodeficiency virus.

TABLE 2
Aftercare Services Offered by Two-Thirds of the Responding Providers to the 1991 NASW Survey

Aftercare Services	Providers Offering (%)
Individual counseling	89
Family counseling	86
Case management	79
Counseling for drug abuse	74
Group counseling	73
Parent counseling	71
Counseling for alcoholism	70
Mental health services	68

SOURCE: Bass, D. (1992). *Helping vulnerable youths: Runaway and homeless adolescents in the United States.* Washington, DC: NASW Press.

youth and family. The 1991 NASW survey (Bass, 1992) showed that 93 percent of the programs currently identify specific services they provide as part of aftercare. Table 2 presents the aftercare services provided by at least two-thirds of the respondents to the survey.

Transitional Living Program
Recognizing that older homeless youths are less likely to be reunited with their families and that they need more-intensive help to overcome serious problems and become independent adults, Congress amended the Juvenile Justice and Delinquency Prevention Act in 1988 (P.L. 100-690) to add the Transitional Living Program for homeless youths. All homeless youths ages 16 through 21 are eligible for the program for up to 18 months. The program serves slightly more males than females. Projects funded under this program must

- give youths an opportunity to work on a high school diploma or its equivalent or vocational training
- train youths in daily living skills, budgeting, locating and maintaining housing, and career planning
- provide individual counseling and group counseling and coordinate services for the youths
- establish outreach programs designed to attract eligible youths
- provide each youth with a written transitional independent living plan, as part of a case plan, based on an assessment of need
- provide youths with other services and assistance designed to improve their transition to independent living.

Two-thirds of the respondents to the 1991 NASW survey (Bass, 1992) said that they refer youths to transitional living services, but only one-

family to try to achieve family reunification. Despite the 15-day limitation, the shelters provide an exhaustive array of services that are designed to help youths resolve current crises and prevent future ones. The 29 services provided by at least two-thirds of the respondents to the NASW survey are identified in Table 1.

Legislation for the Runaway Youth Program required that shelters receiving federal funds develop a plan for aftercare counseling of each third actually provide such services. The number of providers offering transitional living services is growing, however; 41 respondents to the survey have added transitional living services since their programs began.

The Transitional Living Program, although relatively new, appears to have had a significant impact on the availability of services. Of the respondents to the NASW survey, more of those who received grants under this program provided extensive aftercare services than did those who received only Basic Center Program or Drug Abuse Education and Prevention Program grants.

To assess whether the availability of transitional living services affected what happened to youths after they left a program, the NASW survey asked providers about the destination of all youth clients and the destination of youth clients for whom independent or transitional living would be appropriate. The providers indicated that less than one-tenth of all runaways and homeless youths left programs for independent or transitional living, and only one-third of those whom they considered ready for independent living moved into independent or transitional living arrangements. Because of the lack of available programs in some areas, many others who were considered ready for independent living did not move into such programs but instead returned to the street or entered or returned to foster or group home care.

Unfortunately, grantees funded by the Transitional Living Program serve only 4.6 percent of the 3,137 counties in the United States. These counties, however, contain 22.5 percent of the youths in the United States. More than 59 percent of those providing services under the Transitional Living Program also run shelters for runaway and homeless youths (DHHS, 1992). Thus, providers are trying to develop a continuum of services for these youths.

Even when programs are available, most of the providers conduct a preadmission assessment to determine a youth's ability to participate in the lengthy and demanding program. Also, some of the programs do not serve certain groups of youths; for example, some will not admit substance abusers or pregnant teenagers, and others will not serve youths who are receiving services from other agencies.

Drug Abuse Education and Prevention Program
The Anti-Drug Abuse Act of 1988 (P.L. 100-690) amended the Juvenile Justice and Delinquency Prevention Act of 1974 (P.L. 93-415) by adding the Drug Abuse Education and Prevention Program for

TABLE 3
Substance Abuse Services Increased by Drug Abuse Education and Prevention Program

Service	All Responding Programs Offering (%)	Programs with Drug Abuse Funds Offering (%)
Drug abuse program	32	54
Program for alcoholics	19	37

SOURCE: Bass, D. (1992). *Helping Vulnerable Youths: Runaway and Homeless Adolescents in the United States*. Washington, DC: NASW Press.

Runaway and Homeless Youth. The purpose of the program is to fund demonstration and service delivery projects that support drug abuse education and prevention for these youths; that is, the program supplements existing programs by providing additional support to organizations that are already serving the youths, so any youth served by programs for runaways and homeless youths is eligible for this program.

The Drug Abuse Education and Prevention Program serves youths under age 12, as well as those who are served by the other programs described previously. Again, this program serves slightly more males than females. The youths served are primarily white, although black youths (24 percent) are proportionately overrepresented (unpublished data from Bass, 1992).

During its first two years of operation (fiscal years 1989 and 1990), the Drug Abuse Education and Prevention Program funded 180 providers. In 1990, approximately 6 percent of the grantees served suburban areas, 16 percent served rural areas, 25 percent served urban areas, and 43 percent served a mixed geographic area. By comparison, in 1989, a slightly higher proportion (46 percent) served urban areas (DHHS, 1990). The program has greatly expanded the availability of substance abuse education and prevention services, as shown in Table 3.

Programs for Runaways and Homeless Youths and the Child Welfare System
Research has suggested that some children first come into contact with protective services because they are abused, enter foster care, run away, and then become homeless. Risk factors for runaway behavior, placement in foster care, and substance abuse are similar. Parental neglect is a risk factor for foster care placement and runaway behavior. Parental abuse of youths and parental substance abuse are risk factors for foster care placement, runaway behavior, and substance

abuse. Mental health problems and family conflict are also risk factors for these behaviors.

These problems cannot be addressed by one service system in isolation from other systems. Runaways and homeless youths have little control over problems such as abuse, parental substance abuse, long-term economic problems, and the failure of service systems to help them resolve their problems. They have limited potential for future independence and an improved quality of life without significant support and intervention. This support must be coordinated because it is provided by a variety of systems.

Some states have recognized the overlap in the population served by programs for runaways and homeless youths and child welfare programs. For example, New York State regulations (New York State Department of Social Services, 1987) describe youths who are eligible for the foster care Independent Living Program as those who are age 16 or older and have lived in foster care for at least 12 months within the previous 36 months. During that three-year period, the youths may also have been runaways or homeless. Furthermore, because some youths who have been in foster care and in the Independent Living Program will run away or become homeless afterward, the regulations require a six-month trial discharge. If a youth becomes homeless during that six-month period, the state is responsible for helping him or her obtain housing.

KEY ROLES AND TRAINING FOR SOCIAL WORKERS

Social workers work with youths to provide protective services and oversee foster care and a foster care Independent Living Program that is designed to help youths in foster care become independent; they also work with runaways and homeless youths in shelters and other agencies serving youths. The 1991 NASW survey (Bass, 1992) showed that more than 70 percent of the respondents from shelters, transitional living programs, and drug abuse education and prevention programs employed bachelor's degree–level social workers and that close to 60 percent employed master's degree–level social workers.

Key Roles at the Local Level

Because a high proportion of runaways and homeless youths have been in the child welfare system and have had contact with the juvenile justice system, social workers in all systems must understand the needs of adolescents in general and of runaways and homeless youths in particular. Social

workers who work with runaways and homeless youths must be able to develop, manage, and practice the following essential components of service delivery:

Outreach. Social workers must be willing to contact and work with youths in areas where the youths feel comfortable. They may be able to contact youths through public and private agencies or through schools and community centers but may also have to contact them on the street or in malls and fast-food restaurants. Street outreach may be a particularly important way to reach homeless youths over age 18.

Intake and assessment. Although most providers conduct some type of intake screening to determine eligibility for services and presenting problems, the assessments needed by youths with long-term serious problems are more extensive. For example, in many of the families of these youths, the parents, the youths, or both are substance abusers. These youths and their families should be referred to treatment programs if the youth-serving agency does not offer such a program. Social workers should assess whether there has been potential abuse so that they can report it to protective services agencies for further investigation.

Case management and coordination with other service providers. Youths stay in federally funded shelters for only 15 days, but these shelters are required to develop aftercare services. Because many of the youths have serious problems and require long-term assistance, social workers should be prepared to offer case management services. It is especially essential, as part of case management, to coordinate with workers in other agencies on behalf of youths who will not be returning to their families.

Information and referral. If the agencies in which social workers are employed cannot offer long-term services to youths and their families, information and referral to agencies that can are essential.

Aftercare. Because almost half the respondents to the 1991 NASW survey (Bass, 1992) reported that they provide services for more than one month, aftercare is an important service component. Social workers must help youths develop comprehensive plans for addressing their needs as part of aftercare. Aftercare is important even after the youths complete lengthy programs, such as the Transitional Living Program. Termination of all support and concrete assistance after any program threatens the participants' continued success.

Advocacy. The provider's ability to serve youths often depends on the availability of services within the community. Social work practitioners who work with youths are in the best position to identify gaps in services and resources and to advocate for their development. Services that social workers provide to youths and their families should be designed to empower them, so they can increase their own skills and abilities to function independently.

Key Roles at the State and National Levels

Although most states consider running away an action sufficient to bring a minor into the court's jurisdiction, fewer states bring youths into the court's jurisdiction for homelessness (American Bar Association, 1993). In many cases the court ensures that youths will receive needed long-term services. Without court jurisdiction, it is up to provider agencies and individual professionals to follow up and ensure that youths receive services.

The age of majority (that is, the age at which youths are free from parental authority) is 18 in most states. Some states (almost half) allow youths early emancipation under certain conditions (American Bar Association, 1993). When youths are allowed early emancipation, programs such as the Transitional Living Program may be useful to them at an earlier age.

The existence of early-emancipation laws recognizes not only that some youths will not be able to return home but that they may be able to support themselves independently. Unfortunately, these laws do not generally address rescinding an order of emancipation. Social workers can help to develop well-thought-out emancipation laws and laws for bringing minors under court supervision. Such laws must specify under what conditions youths do not need parental consent to obtain health care, treatment for substance abuse, and other services. These laws affect social workers' abilities to meet the youths' needs.

At the national level, NASW (1993) has developed standards for the practice of social work with adolescents that guide social workers as they help adolescents become competent adults and that identify the knowledge, skills, and ethical responsibilities of social workers. Social workers should adhere to these standards and help their colleagues understand and implement them.

Staff turnover in youth-serving programs, especially shelters, is high because the pay is low and staff members work with youths and families who are always in crisis. At the state and national levels, social workers must continue to advocate for adequate pay and training to reduce staff turnover and encourage social workers to enter the field of youth services.

Training

Social work students must be trained in policy and practice issues in youth-serving agencies so that they understand the advantages and limitations of policies such as family reunification, know when specific policies and practices are appropriate, and learn about other service systems and how to work collaboratively. Furthermore, because of the increasing occurrence of substance abuse and mental health problems in response to stresses, such as long-term economic problems, social workers must be able to conduct specialized assessments and to identify potential substance abuse, possible health and mental health problems, and possible suicidal ideation.

ISSUES AND TRENDS

When Congress passed the Juvenile Justice and Delinquency Prevention Act of 1974, most runaway youths were short-term runaways who could be reunited with their families. Currently, however, shelters are seeing an increasing number of youths with long-term problems who need extensive services and may never be reunited with their families. In addition, once youths leave foster or shelter care, they are immediately without income, housing, and a social support system.

The primary issue facing social workers who work with adolescents is that although programs such as the Transitional Living Program for homeless youths and the Independent Living Program for older youths who were in foster care provide an opportunity for youths to learn to become independent, competent adults, they do not provide the long-term support youths may need as they try to succeed on their own. A few programs, such as Dale House in Colorado Springs, have recognized this problem and, through donations and private funding, allow residents to obtain silverware, dishes, and cookware upon discharge. Former residents may return for help in obtaining services when in crisis. These programs are needed throughout the United States and could become a focus of social work advocacy efforts.

A second issue is that programs are not available everywhere or for all the youths who need them. Thus, social workers must continue to advocate for the development of additional programs that are designed to meet the long-term needs of runaways and homeless youths.

REFERENCES

American Bar Association. (1993). *Final report to the Administration for Children, Youth and Families.* Washington, DC: Author.

Anti-Drug Abuse Act of 1988. P.L. 100-690, 102 Stat. 4181.

Bass, D. (1992). *Helping vulnerable youths: Runaway and homeless adolescents in the United States.* Washington, DC: NASW Press.

Finklehor, D., Hotaling, G., & Sedlak, A. (1990). *Missing, abducted, and throwaway children in America: Numbers and characteristics* (Report NCJ 123667). Washington, DC: U.S. Department of Justice, Office of Juvenile Justice and Delinquency Prevention.

Juvenile Justice and Delinquency Prevention Act of 1974. P.L. 93-415, 88 Stat. 1109.

Juvenile Justice and Deliquency Prevention Amendments of 1988. P.L. 100-690, 102 Stat. 4434.

Kurtz, P. D., Jarvis, S. V., & Kurtz, G. L. (1991). Problems of homeless youths: Empirical findings and human services issues. *Social Work, 36,* 309–314.

National Association of Social Workers. (1993). *NASW standards for the practice of social work with adolescents.* Washington, DC: Author.

New York State Council on Children and Families. (1984). *Meeting the needs of homeless youth.* New York: Author.

New York State Department of Social Services. (1987). *Notice of adoption.* Albany, NY: Author.

Pires, S. A., & Silber, J. T. (1991). *On their own: Runaway and homeless youth and programs that serve them.* Washington, DC: Children and Youth Technical Assistance Center, Georgetown University Child Development Center.

Posner, M. (1991). *Runaway youth and interagency collaboration: A review of the literature.* (Submitted to U.S. Department of Health and Human Services, Administration for Children, Youth and Families, Family and Youth Services Bureau.) Newton, MA: Project PROTECT, Education Development Center.

Raychaba, B. (1988). *To be on our own with no direction from home.* Ottawa, Ontario, Canada: National Youth in Care Network.

U.S. Department of Health and Human Services. (1990). *Report to Congress on the Drug Abuse Prevention Program for Runaway and Homeless Youth fiscal year 1990.* Washington, DC: Author.

U.S. Department of Health and Human Services. (1991). *Annual report to the Congress on the Runaway and Homeless Youth Program fiscal year 1990.* Washington, DC: Author.

U.S. Department of Health and Human Services. (1992). *Report to Congress on the Transitional Living Program fiscal year 1991.* Washington, DC: Author.

U.S. General Accounting Office. (1989a). *Children and youths: About 68,000 homeless and 186,000 in shared housing at any given time.* Washington, DC: Author.

U.S. General Accounting Office. (1989b). *Homelessness: Homeless and runaway youth receiving services at federally funded shelters.* Washington, DC: Author.

U.S. House of Representatives, Subcommittee on Human Resources of the Committee on Education and Labor. (1990). *Compilation of the Juvenile Justice and Delinquency Prevention Act of 1974 and related provisions of law as amended through December 31, 1989.* Washington, DC: U.S. Government Printing Office.

FURTHER READING

Barnes, G. M. (1990). Impact of the family on adolescent drinking patterns. In R. L. Collis, K. E. Leonard, & J. S. Searles (Eds.), *Alcohol and the family* (pp. 137–161). New York: Guilford Press.

Carbino, R. (1991). Advocacy for foster families in the United States facing child abuse allegations: How social agencies and foster parents are responding to the problem. *Child Welfare, 70*(2), 131–149.

Jarvis, S. U. (1990). *Drug use among runaway and homeless youths: A southeastern perspective.* Athens, GA: Southeastern Network of Youth and Family Services.

Kurtz, D., Jarvis, S., & Kurtz, G. (1991). Problems of homeless youths: Empirical findings and human services issues. *Social Work, 36,* 309.

Metropolitan Washington Council of Governments. (1991). *Why are kids in foster care?* Washington, DC: Author.

New York State Council on Children and Families. (1990, March). *Chemical abuse services for youth in residential care.* Albany: Author.

State Department of Social Services. (1987). *Notice of adoption.* Albany, NY: Author.

Straus, M. (1990). *Abuse and victimization across the life span.* Baltimore: Johns Hopkins University Press.

U.S. Department of Health and Human Services, Administration on Children, Youth, and Families. (1989). *Report to the Congress on independent living initiatives: Fiscal years 1987 and 1988.* Washington, DC: Author.

U.S. Department of Health and Human Services, Office of Substance Abuse Prevention. (1990). *Findings of the High-Risk Youth Demonstration Program* (Report No. 10). *Learning about the effects of substance abuse prevention: A progress report.* Rockville, MD: Author.

U.S. Department of Health and Human Services, National Center on Child Abuse and Neglect. (1981). *National incidence study.* Washington, DC: U.S. Government Printing Office.

U.S. General Accounting Office. (1990, September). *Drug abuse research on treatment may not address current needs* (Report to the Chairman, Select Committee on Narcotics Abuse and Control, U.S. House of Representatives, Report No. GAO/HRD-90-114). Washington, DC: Author.

U.S. General Accounting Office Testimony (1991, May 22). *Noncriminal juveniles: Detentions have been reduced but better monitoring is needed* (Report No. GAO/T-GGD-91-30). Washington, DC: U.S. General Accounting Office.

Van Houten, T., & Golembiewski, G. (1978). *Adolescent life stress as a predictor of alcohol abuse and/or runaway behavior.* Washington, DC: American Youth Work Center.

Deborah Bass, MSW, is a health and human services consultant, 7092 Kings Arm Drive, Manassas, VA 22111.

The author would like to acknowledge the assistance of the U.S. Department of Health and Human Services. A grant from the Family and Youth Services Bureau of the Administration on Children, Youth, and Families in DHHS funded the 1991 survey described in this entry.

For further information see

Adolescence Overview; Adoption; Alcohol Abuse; Child Abuse and Neglect Overview; Child Foster Care; Child

Labor; Childhood; Cults; Domestic Violence; Drug Abuse; Families Overview; Gang Violence; Homelessness; Juvenile Corrections; Juvenile and Family Courts; Legal Issues: Low-Income and Dependent People; Natural Helping Networks; Poverty; Primary Prevention Overview; School-Linked Services; Social Development; Social Welfare Policy; Social Work Practice: Theoretical Base; Substance Abuse: Legal Issues; Suicide; Youth Services.

Key Words

homelessness   youths

runaways

Rural Poverty

Lynne C. Morris

Millions of rural people—children, young adults, elderly people, men, women, black people, white people, Hispanics, Native Americans—are challenged each day to confront and cope with the problems of rural poverty. Rural poverty has been characterized by its persistent high rates throughout the 1980s and into the 1990s, its association with patterns of economic restructuring in rural areas in the 1990s, and its complexity resulting from the diversity of rural people and rural places.

In 1990 an estimated 9 million people lived in nonmetropolitan (rural) areas of the United States (U.S. Bureau of the Census, 1991). These small communities, located outside the census-designated boundaries of metropolitan areas, are diverse in their history, cultures, and physical environments, the features of which shape the local structure of opportunities for employment and income. However, rural areas have been experiencing forms of social and economic change similar to those associated with global economic and political restructuring that weaken the community infrastructure needed to support people in their efforts to move out of poverty. These changes include the loss of "living-wage" jobs (jobs that provide families with sufficient income to maintain themselves above the poverty level), greater social inequalities in an earnings-restricted job market, the out-migration of badly needed human resources as younger residents leave to find employment, the loss of money and credit necessary to generate local development as dollars flow out of rural communities and into global economic markets, and the reduced investment of such societal resources as government funding for public and social services. Cumulatively, these social, economic, and political processes have eroded the developmental potential of rural communities and have contributed to the persistence of rural poverty.

DEFINITIONS AND LIMITATIONS

The Census Bureau designates as nonmetropolitan all U.S. counties that are outside the boundaries of metropolitan statistical areas with populations of at least 50,000 and other surrounding counties that have commuting ties to central cities. The Census Bureau uses this metro–nonmetro classification in its analysis and reporting of poverty rates. The use of this classification scheme has two limitations. First, the scheme does not permit the analysis of problems of poverty experienced by people living in rural portions of metropolitan statistical areas. Second, the term includes counties that vary in size and concentration of population, from sparsely populated counties with central villages of fewer than 100 people to counties with large areas of wilderness or countryside and more urbanized towns and central places of fewer than 50,000 people that may fit traditional conceptions of rurality. However, the term "nonmetropolitan" includes most rural places in the United States and identifies counties outside the structure of economic opportunity and social services delivery found within metropolitan statistical areas. The dual classification encourages the examination of the different economic opportunity structures present in metropolitan and nonmetropolitan areas, which must be considered in developing policies to address rural poverty.

TRENDS

During the 1980s the poverty rate in rural areas remained consistently higher than the poverty rate in metropolitan areas (Table 1). In rural places, central cities, and the suburbs of metropolitan areas, poverty rates increased slightly from 1980 to 1990. The rise in the poverty rate was greatest for nonmetropolitan areas from 1980 to 1985, when the rural poverty rate reached 18.3 percent and exceeded the poverty rate for central cities. From 1985 to 1990, the poverty rate for nonmetropolitan areas declined slightly, but it remained higher than that in 1980 and higher than the metropolitan-area poverty rate.

TABLE 1
Poverty Rates in Metropolitan and Nonmetropolitan Areas, 1980–1990

| Year | Metropolitan Areas | | | Nonmetropolitan Areas |
	Central Cities	Outside Central Cities	Total	
1980	17.2	8.2	11.9	15.4
1985	18.0	8.4	12.7	18.3
1990	18.0	8.7	12.7	16.3

SOURCE: U.S. Bureau of the Census. (1992). Measuring the effects of benefits and taxes on income and poverty: 1979 to 1991. *Current population reports* (Series P-60, No. 192RD). Washington, DC: U.S. Government Printing Office.

This rise in the rural poverty rate reversed the trend of decreasing rural poverty that had been evident in the late 1960s and 1970s. From 1967 to 1978, the rural poverty rate declined from 20.2 percent to 13.8 percent, and the gap between the rates of poverty in metropolitan and nonmetropolitan areas narrowed (Hoppe, 1993). From 1967 to 1990, the rural poverty rate steadily decreased (1967–1979), rose sharply (1980–1985), and then declined slightly (1986–1990), whereas the poverty rate in central cities areas remained high and increased slowly. These different trends in poverty rates suggest that different variables contribute to the persistence of poverty in urban and rural places.

REASONS FOR HIGH RATES OF POVERTY

Economic Restructuring

The fluctuation in levels of rural poverty reflects the degree to which rural poverty rates are linked to economic cycles of recession and recovery, which affect unemployment rates. Throughout the 1970s the unemployment rate was higher in metropolitan areas than in nonmetropolitan areas. During the 1980s, however, this trend reversed. Since 1980 unemployment rates have been higher in nonmetropolitan areas than in rural areas. The unemployment rate, which reflects the absence of wage-earning opportunities, is a particularly significant contributor to rates of rural poverty. An analysis of changes in poverty rates between 1973 and 1987 revealed that in metropolitan areas, 37 percent of the variation in poverty rates was associated with a variation in unemployment rates, compared to 71 percent in nonmetropolitan areas (Shapiro, 1989).

High unemployment rates. In 1979 approximately 6.6 percent of the rural labor force lived in counties with an unemployment rate of 10 percent or higher. Ten years later nearly one-seventh (13.4 percent) of the rural labor force lived in counties with double-digit unemployment rates. In many of these rural counties, unemployment rates have

risen to and have remained at persistently high levels. Rural poverty is becoming more centralized in places where the lack of employment opportunities is a persistent problem. Rural residents of these communities are more likely to experience long-term rural poverty and reduced access to jobs with wages that would move them out of poverty.

The economic restructuring of business and industry that has occurred as part of the shift to a more global economy also has contributed to reduced economic opportunities, lower incomes, and higher rates of poverty in rural areas. Economic restructuring is associated with the types of jobs that have been created and lost in rural areas, particularly during the 1980s. Most rural communities have historically depended on a limited economic base. Employment has been linked to these areas' environmental resources and to jobs developed in agriculture, fishing, timber, and mining. Nationally, all these industries have experienced steady, long-term declines in employment throughout the 20th century. Although resource-based industries are no longer the primary source of employment in rural areas, the economies of many rural communities are still tied to these industries—and their declining jobs base—as a major source of local employment. In 1985, 29 percent of the nonmetropolitan counties depended on farming, and 14 percent depended on mining, energy, or forestry for 20 percent or more of their total labor and proprietor income (Flora, Flora, Spears, & Swanson, 1992).

Changes in employers. The increased movement of manufacturing industries to rural areas helped lower rural unemployment rates in the 1970s. More recently, however, many rural communities have experienced the loss of their major employers because manufacturing industries have either relocated overseas or cut back their labor force in an effort to remain globally competitive. Employment opportunities for rural residents are still heavily concentrated in manufacturing—the area of the national economy in which the loss of jobs, particularly high-wage jobs, has been the greatest. Thus, many rural areas have the potential for continued job loss, rather than growth and economic diversification. Although rural communities and some rural development agencies pursued the recruitment of manufacturing industries during the 1980s, much of the United States shifted from a goods-producing economy to a services and information economy that emphasizes investment in new technologies and specialized global markets (Tickamyer & Duncan, 1990).

Job growth in rural communities today is occurring primarily in the consumer and social services sector of the economy. Increases in employment have occurred in retail sales, food and restaurant services, and social and health services—sectors of the economy in which low wages are highly concentrated (Porterfield, 1990). By 1987 the consumer and social services sector accounted for 45 percent of all rural low-wage earners, defined as "individuals whose hourly wage and salary incomes would leave them below the official poverty line for a family of four persons, even though they worked the equivalent of a year-round, full-time job" (Gorham, 1992, p. 23).

Government Policies

Government policies can support or restrict the ability of rural residents to escape poverty. The high rates of poverty in nonmetropolitan areas have been maintained, in part, by government policies that have limited wages, reduced benefits available through income maintenance programs, and shifted government funding away from support for public services in rural communities. Government policies are not specifically targeted to the problems and needs of rural communities, and federal programs that are designed for urban areas are not easily adapted to small, diverse rural communities with low population densities.

Government funding flows to rural areas in the form of agricultural programs, primarily price supports that encourage crop production; however, less than 5 percent of the rural labor force is employed in agriculture, and less than 8 percent of rural residents live on farms. Therefore, the government's practice of equating farm policy with rural policy directs public resources toward agricultural interests, not toward the needs of most rural residents (Bonnen, 1992; Dudenhefer, 1993). During the 1980s, the number of federal government dollars allocated to rural areas, excluding military spending and farm programs, decreased 44 percent (Flora & Christenson, 1991).

Most poor rural residents live in households with at least one member who has full-time, part-time, or seasonal employment. Workers in rural areas are much more likely than are urban workers to be employed in jobs that pay at or near the minimum wage. In January 1981 the minimum wage was $3.35 an hour, an amount usually sufficient to move a family of three out of poverty if the worker had year-round, full-time employment. The minimum wage remained unchanged until legislation passed in 1989 raised it in stages to $4.25 an hour by April 1991. During the 1980s consumer prices rose, and the purchasing power of the minimum wage declined. By 1987 an hourly wage of $4.35 an hour was required to move a family of three out of poverty. During that year, 32.2 percent of the rural workers who were paid by the hour earned less than $4.35 an hour (Hendrickson & Sawhill, 1989). The failure to raise the minimum wage during most of the 1980s increased the number of rural working people who became poor even though they continued to work.

Reductions in the benefits of Aid to Families with Dependent Children (AFDC) also occurred during the 1980s. The decreases in these benefits were greater in the most rural states, which already had lower benefit levels than the most urbanized states. The Family Support Act of 1988 introduced changes in the AFDC program, extending the AFDC–Unemployed Parent (AFDC–UP) program to all states and thus making public financial assistance available to married-couple families. Because one-half of all poor rural children live in married-couple families, the AFDC–UP program may expand the use of public assistance and social services by poor rural families. However, in an analysis of the probable impacts of the 1988 act on nonmetropolitan areas, Jensen and McLaughlin (1993) concluded that

> overall, the AFDC provisions of the [Family Support Act of 1988] will have little effect on reducing poverty, or eliminating the gap in eligibility between poor families in the South [where the majority of poor rural families live] and those elsewhere. A more liberal national minimum need standard would go much further toward increasing access of the poor to AFDC benefits. (p. 98)

Historical Patterns of Oppression and Inequality

An important component of nonmetropolitan poverty is the high levels of poverty that have persisted for decades in some rural places. In 1990, 783 nonmetropolitan counties had poverty rates of 20 percent or higher. Of these counties, 546 had experienced persistent poverty rates of over 20 percent since 1960 (Beale, 1993). In these places, poverty is associated with persistently low levels of income among cultural groups that have a history and legacy of social injustice and economic oppression (Hoppe, 1985). Areas characterized by persistent rural poverty are communities in the South and West, with a high percentage of black, Hispanic, Native American, or Native Alaskan residents and communities in the Appalachian region of the South. About 30 percent of poor rural people live in these communities.

WHO ARE THE RURAL POOR?

Policies that address rural poverty must be responsive to the diversity of rural poor people and to similarities and differences in the composition of urban and rural populations living in poverty. People living in poverty vary in terms of age, gender, race, ethnicity, family and household composition, and region of residence. These differences have implications for the types of programs, services, and supports needed to help people move out of poverty.

Working Poor

Policies that target urban poverty emphasize services such as job training and time-limited child care that will help heads of households obtain employment and a greater degree of economic self-sufficiency. However, most of the rural poor live in households in which at least one member is already employed. The rural working poor are employed in full-time, low-wage jobs or on a part-time or seasonal basis. The low incomes of these poor working rural people result from the types and numbers of jobs available to the work force in rural areas. Shapiro's (1989) analysis of census data on employment patterns of poor people indicated that 24.3 percent of rural heads of families who were not ill, disabled, or retired worked full-time or year-round, and 46.2 percent worked less than full-time, year-round. According to Shapiro, in rural areas, the majority of both black and white heads of poor families are employed. Most heads of single-parent, poor rural families are employed, as are most heads of two-parent, poor rural families.

Gorham and Harrison (1990) found that the ability of rural workers to find jobs that pay wages sufficient to move them and their families out of poverty decreased from 1979 to 1987. The gap between per capita personal income in metropolitan and nonmetropolitan areas has increased continuously since 1973. Morrisey (1991) concluded that poverty rates for workers in nonmetropolitan areas were almost double the poverty rates for people in the urban work force.

Rural–Urban Differences

Three differences in the demographic characteristics of people who live in poverty suggest the need for specific rural-focused programs and services (see Table 2). Compared with urban areas, poor people in rural areas are more likely to be living in married-couple families in which at least one family member is employed, but at low wages. In the South rural poverty is much more regionally concentrated than is urban poverty. Although the South had the highest rate of economic growth in the early 1990s, it remains the region in which persistent rural poverty is the most highly concentrated and in which differences in the incomes of urban and rural residents are increasing (Applebone, 1993).

In 1990 poverty rates were higher for rural elderly people age 65 and over (14 percent) than for elderly residents in urban areas (9.6 percent). Among elderly black, Hispanic, and Native American people in rural areas, poverty rates, which have always been high, reflect the maintenance of historic patterns of social and economic inequality (Lichter, 1989). Most rural elderly people of color have spent their entire lives in poverty. More than 70 percent of the rural elderly are women. Among older women, widows in rural areas are at a particularly high risk of poverty. A lifetime of restricted opportunities to earn income and to obtain jobs with pension coverage limits the ability of rural families to plan for the financial impacts of retirement and of widowhood.

Poverty and Rural Families

Rural families with young children have high rates of poverty, and their chances of living in poverty have been increasing. In 1991, 22.5 percent of rural children under age 18 were living in poverty (U.S. Bureau of the Census, 1992). From 1979 to 1986 poverty rates for rural children and young adults rose faster than did poverty rates for their counterparts in urban areas (O'Hare, 1988).

A comparison of the 1990 rates of poverty for white, black, and Hispanic families in both metropolitan and rural areas (Table 3) shows that rural black married-couple families with young children are at the highest risk of poverty. Rural white families with young children have substantially higher poverty rates than do young urban white families, and both rural and urban Hispanic families with young children have high poverty rates. The high rates of poverty for these rural families suggest that young rural workers are not able to move out of entry-level, low-wage jobs and cannot increase their earnings when they begin to establish their families. Almost three-fourths of rural workers

TABLE 2

Percentages of People Living in Poverty in Metropolitan and Nonmetropolitan Areas, 1990

Demographic Characteristics of People Living in Poverty	Metropolitan Areas	Nonmetropolitan Areas
Living in married-couple families	31.0	44.4
65 years and older	9.6	14.0
Living in the South	34.4	55.3

SOURCE: U.S. Bureau of the Census. (1991). Poverty in the United States: 1990. *Current population reports* (Series P-60, No. 175). Washington, DC: U.S. Government Printing Office.

TABLE 3

Poverty Rates for Married-Couple Families with Children Under Age Six Years in Metropolitan and Nonmetropolitan Areas, 1990

	Metropolitan Areas	Nonmetropolitan Areas
All families with children under age six	10.0	17.4
White families with children under age six	9.4	15.5
Black families with children under age six	15.0	41.7
Hispanic families with children under age six	28.1	29.7

SOURCE: U.S. Bureau of the Census. (1991). Poverty in the United States: 1990. *Current population reports* (Series P-60, No. 175). Washington, DC: U.S. Government Printing Office.

ages 16 to 24 have hourly wage earnings that are too low to support a family of four at an income above the poverty level (Gorham, 1992).

Although as of 1990 the percentage of female-headed households was somewhat lower in rural areas than in urban areas, the proportion of poor rural people living in female-headed households rose from 23.7 percent in 1970 to 30.0 percent in 1990. Lichter and Eggebeen (1992) concluded that this change in family structure accounted for 60 percent of the increase in poverty rates for rural children during the 1980s. The poverty rates of rural female-headed households are high and are similar to those of urban female-headed families. In 1990 about two-thirds of urban female-headed families and about three-fourths of rural female-headed families with children younger than age six had incomes below the poverty level (U.S. Bureau of the Census, 1992).

Studies of the earnings of women in the rural work force have suggested that even if they are able to find employment, rural women do not work in jobs with wages that are sufficient to move them and their families out of poverty. Gorham's (1992) analysis of rural workers' earnings showed that most employed rural white, black, and Hispanic women are low-wage workers whose hourly wage earnings are too low to move a family of four out of poverty.

REGIONAL DIFFERENCES

Throughout the United States, rural communities are experiencing economic restructuring, usually in the form of the loss of jobs in traditional areas of rural employment and the growth of low-wage jobs in consumer and social services. Although individual communities have benefited economically from the relocation of small manufacturing plants, the growth of retail trade, the development of resorts, or the immigration of retirees, most rural communities have higher rates of poverty than they did in the 1970s. However, rural communities are diverse, and regional differences exist in the forms and extent of rural poverty.

Northeast

In the Northeast, because of the proximity of most rural areas to large cities with high-cost housing, poor urban people are migrating to small rural communities (Fitchen, 1991). For this reason, the Northeast is the only region of the United States in which poverty rates are lower in rural areas than in metropolitan areas. Population loss in the region's small towns has increased the supply of vacant housing that is being rented or converted into apartments. Furthermore, poor single-parent families are becoming more concentrated in trailer parks. Although moving to rural areas is an adaptive short-term strategy for poor families that seek affordable housing, the lack of living-wage employment opportunities can trap families in low-income housing that is deteriorating in quality. Or families may be forced to move again as vacancy rates decline and housing costs rise in small towns.

Midwest

In the Midwest, many of the problems of poverty are linked to changes in agriculture that occurred during the 1980s. The farm crisis forced many families, including poor families, out of farming. Although farm poverty rates have declined since 1986, small communities may have an increasing number of poor, young families, unable to enter farming or agriculture-related businesses, who work in low-wage or part-time jobs. The lack of employment opportunities has encouraged the out-migration of younger adults from small agricultural communities. As the populations of many rural towns in the Midwest are declining, essential community services are closing or consolidating. As younger people leave, the percentage of elderly residents in these communities increases. Elderly poor people are becoming more concentrated in aging communities, with reduced access to shopping, health care, social services, and informal support systems.

South

The South remains the region in which most of the rural poor population lives and in which long-term, persistent poverty is the most heavily concentrated. In the South, most poor rural people live in counties with both high rates of poverty and persistently low per capita personal income. Communities with long-term poverty are also clustered in the Appalachian region of eastern Kentucky, the upper east region of Tennessee, and West Virginia.

Long-term poverty is a particularly serious problem for rural Southern black people, most of whom live in poor counties with high poverty rates that are not adjacent to metropolitan areas. During the 1970s and 1980s, the number of poor rural families headed by black women increased; in 1990 more than half of all poor rural black people lived in female-headed households.

West

In the Western states, rural areas with high poverty rates include American Indian reservations, timber-dependent and mining-dependent communities experiencing the loss of jobs and high unemployment, and southwestern *colonias,* formed to meet the housing needs of Hispanic workers. In many of these poor rural places, low levels of per capita income are partly a result of government policies. The growth or loss of employment opportunities is linked to federal government policies that regulate the use of government-owned lands, sustainable forest management, and the availability of a low-wage agricultural labor force.

American Indian reservations, through their tribal sovereignty, maintain a unique political and legal relationship with the federal government. Although reservation communities have been pursuing many forms of economic development, including mining, tourism, and gambling, rates of unemployment and underemployment remain high. The federal government influences the availability of economic opportunities through the Bureau of Indian Affairs, which implements policies, maintains a role in the management of tribal resources, including substantial energy resources (Ambler, 1991), and is a primary source of employment on reservations.

POLICIES FOR ALLEVIATING RURAL POVERTY

Policies that have been identified as having the potential of reducing rural poverty are based on an understanding of the barriers and eligibility requirements that reduce rural people's access to social and health services, economic changes resulting in the growing number of low-wage earners in rural communities, the increasing concentration of poor people in rural areas, and the need to reduce the costs of basic living that push rural people into poverty.

Public Assistance

Poor rural people are less likely than are poor urban residents to receive public assistance (Jensen, 1988). Most poor rural people live in states where Aid to Families with Dependent Children (AFDC) and Supplemental Security Income benefits are low. Making AFDC benefits more uniform would raise the incomes of the rural poor, particularly in Southern states. The Family Support Act of 1988 allows states to set public assistance benefits and extends coverage to poor married-couple families. It also provides a federal funding match, which states can use to expand child care and transportation for poor families; this funding would benefit families in rural areas (Ginsberg, 1993).

Housing and health care consume much of the income of rural poor people. Few rural residents live in public housing or receive rental income assistance. Most of the rural work force is employed in jobs that do not offer health insurance and thus would benefit from legislation providing national health insurance.

Rural Economic Development

The federal budget for fiscal year 1994 contained expanded funding for rural economic development targeted to the needs of communities that are experiencing high rates of persistent poverty and are nominated as potential recipients by state and local governments. Economically distressed communities with high levels of poverty are eligible to apply for funding, designating them as "enterprise communities" or "empowerment zones." Ninety-five enterprise communities (65 urban, 30 rural) and nine empowerment zones (six urban, three rural) will receive Title XX social services funds to support self-sufficiency, technical assistance in using and coordinating federal programs, and tax incentives to promote economic development. Businesses in empowerment zones that employ zone residents will receive tax credits. The program is an innovative attempt to assist communities that have experienced long-term poverty by coordinated funding for both economic and social development.

Earned Income Tax Credit

State and federal tax policies can increase or reduce the net incomes of rural poor people. The earned income tax credit (EITC), which provides a tax credit refund to low-income wage earners, is of particular assistance to rural working families. Maintaining and expanding EITC benefits and extending outreach efforts to make rural workers aware of their eligibility for EITC refunds can increase the amount of actual income available to rural poor people (Greenstein & Shapiro, 1992). State income and property tax credits for low-income residents could similarly reduce the poverty of poor rural people.

The 1994 federal budget significantly expanded the EITC for families with two or more children. When the new EITC provisions have been fully phased in over a three-year period, the income credit received by a family with two or more children and full-time minimum wage earnings of $8,425 will have increased from $1,998 to $3,370 a year (Leonard & Greenstein, 1993). Families with two or more children and incomes of $8,425 to $20,000 will also receive EITC increases ranging from $800 to $1,372. Families with one child, whose incomes have already been raised above the poverty level by previous budget legislation, will receive much smaller EITC increases. In addition, the 1994 legislation extended EITC benefits to childless workers ages 25 to 64 with incomes below $9,000.

Conclusion

Public social welfare policies are usually developed with a focus on reducing poverty in urban areas and without sufficient consideration of their impact on the problems of rural poverty. At the national level, rural policy-making is directed toward developing the vast resource base of the rural United States—farmland, water resources, forests, and energy and mineral resources—in ways that enhance the perceived public national interest and the corporate and individual private interests that control, develop, sustain, or deplete rural resources. To alleviate rural poverty, rural development policies must be refocused to incorporate an ecological perspective that supports ways of working and living that enhance both the natural resource base and the well-being of rural people and rural communities.

References

Ambler, M. (1991). Indian energies devoted to self-sufficiency. *National Forum, 70*(2), 21–23.

Applebone, P. (1993, November 27). In race to outrun recession, Southeast sets dazzling pace. *New York Times*, pp. 1, 12.

Beale, C. (1993). *Persistent poverty in rural areas and small towns* (U.S. Department of Agriculture, Agriculture Information Bulletin No. 664-654). Washington, DC: U.S. Government Printing Office.

Bonnen, J. T. (1992). Why is there no coherent U.S. rural policy? *Policy Studies Journal, 20*(2), 190–201.

Dudenhefer, P. (1993). Poverty in the rural United States. *Focus, 15*(1), 37–46.

Family Support Act of 1988. P.L. 100-485, 102 Stat. 2343.

Fitchen, J. M. (1991). *Endangered spaces, enduring places: Change, identity and survival in rural America.* Boulder, CO: Westview Press.

Flora, C. B., & Christenson, J. A. (1991). Critical times for rural America: The challenge for rural policy in the 1990s. In C. B. Flora & J. A. Christenson (Eds.), *Rural policies for the 1990s* (pp. 1–7). Boulder, CO: Westview Press.

Flora, C. B., Flora, J., Spears, J. D., & Swanson, L. E. (1992). *Rural communities: Legacy and change.* Boulder, CO: Westview Press.

Ginsberg, L. (1993). Rural social services and the Family Support Act. In R. A. Hoppe (Ed.), *The Family Support Act: Will it work in rural areas?* (U.S. Department of Agriculture, Rural Development Research Report No. 83, pp. 53–78). Washington, DC: U.S. Government Printing Office.

Gorham, L. (1992). The growing problem of low earnings in rural areas. In C. Duncan (Ed.), *Rural poverty in America* (pp. 21–39). New York: Auburn House.

Gorham, L., & Harrison, B. (1990). *Working below the poverty line: The growing problem of low earnings in the United States.* Washington, DC: Aspen Institute for Humanistic Studies.

Greenstein, R., & Shapiro, I. (1992). Policies to alleviate rural poverty. In C. Duncan (Ed.), *Rural poverty in America* (pp. 249–263). New York: Auburn House.

Hendrickson, S. E., & Sawhill, I. V. (1989). *Assisting the working poor.* Washington, DC: Urban Institute.

Hoppe, R. (1985). *Economic structure and change in persistently low-income nonmetro counties* (USDA Research Report No. 55). Washington, DC: U.S. Government Printing Office.

Hoppe, R. (1993). Poverty in rural America: Trends and demographic characteristics. In the Rural Sociological Society Task Force on Persistent Rural Poverty (Ed.), *Persistent poverty in rural America* (pp. 20–38). Boulder, CO: Westview Press.

Jensen, L. (1988). Rural–urban differences in the utilization and ameliorative effects of welfare programs. *Policy Studies Review, 7*(4), 782–794.

Jensen, L., & McLaughlin, D. K. (1993). The Family Support Act and Aid to Families with Dependent Children: Implications for nonmetropolitan areas. In R. A. Hoppe (Ed.), *The Family Support Act: Will it work in rural areas?* (U.S. Department of Agriculture, Rural Development Research Report No. 83, pp. 79–105). Washington, DC: U.S. Government Printing Office.

Leonard, P., & Greenstein, R. (1993). *The new budget reconciliation law: Progressive deficit reduction and critical social investments.* Washington, DC: Center on Budget and Policy Priorities.

Lichter, D. T. (1989). Race, employment hardship, and inequality in the nonmetropolitan South. *American Sociological Review, 54*(3), 436–446.

Lichter, D. T., & Eggebeen, D. J. (1992). Child poverty and the changing rural family. *Rural Sociology, 57*(2), 151–172.

Morrisey, E. S. (1991). *Work and poverty in metro and nonmetro areas* (U.S. Department of Agriculture, Rural Development Research Report No. 81). Washington, DC: U.S. Government Printing Office.

O'Hare, W. P. (1988). *The rise of poverty in rural America.* Washington, DC: Population Reference Bureau.

Porterfield, S. (1990). Service sector offers more jobs, lower pay. *Rural Development Perspectives, 6*(3), 4.

Shapiro, I. (1989). *Laboring for less: Working but poor in rural America.* Washington, DC: Center on Budget and Policy Priorities.

Tickamyer, A. R., & Duncan, C. M. (1990). Poverty and opportunity structure in rural America. *Annual Review of Sociology, 16,* 67–86.

U.S. Bureau of the Census. (1991). Poverty in the United States: 1990. *Current population reports* (Series P-60, No. 175). Washington, DC: U.S. Government Printing Office.

U.S. Bureau of the Census. (1992). Poverty in the United States: 1991. *Current population reports* (Series P-60, No. 181). Washington, DC: U.S. Government Printing Office.

FURTHER READING

Adams, T. K., & Duncan, G. J. (1990). *Long-term poverty in nonmetropolitan areas.* Ann Arbor: University of Michigan, Survey Research Center.

Elo, I. T., & Beale, C. L. (1985). *Natural resources and rural poverty: An overview.* Washington, DC: Resources for the Future.

Fitchen, J. M. (1981). *Poverty in rural America: A case study.* Boulder, CO: Westview Press.

Harvey, D. L. (1993). *Potter Addition: Poverty, family, and kinship in a heartland community.* New York: Aldine de Gruyter.

Lyson, T., & Falk, W. (Eds.). (1993). *Forgotten places: Uneven development in rural America.* Lawrence: University of Kansas Press.

Rodgers, H., Jr., & Weiher, G. (Eds.). (1989). *Rural poverty: Special causes and policy reforms.* New York: Greenwood Press.

Sherman, A. (1992). *Falling by the wayside: Children in rural America.* Washington, DC: Children's Defense Fund.

Lynne C. Morris, PhD, is associate professor, Eastern Washington University, School of Social Work and Human Services, Senior Hall, Cheney, WA 99004.

For further information see

Aid to Families with Dependent Children; Aging Overview; Community Needs Assessment; Employment and Unemployment Measurement; Families Overview; General Assistance; Health Care: Direct Practice; Homelessness; Housing; Hunger, Nutrition, and Food Programs; Income Distribution; Income Security Overview; Jobs and Earnings; Natural Helping Networks; Poverty; Public Health Services; Public Social Services; Rural Social Work Overview; Social Planning; Social Security; Social Welfare Policy; Social Work Profession Overview; Welfare Employment Programs: Evaluation.

Key Words

earned income tax credit	poverty
	rural poverty

Rural Social Work Overview

Judith A. Davenport
Joseph Davenport III

Defining rural social work or social work in a rural community is not an easy or precise task. Each term may mean different things to different people in different circumstances. Some see rural from a romantic perspective, as an idyllic Eden inhabited by bucolic farm families possessing close family and community ties and living in harmony with the land. This view, which is often commercialized, is found in television programs, such as *The Andy Griffith Show* and *The Waltons*, and in many country music songs lamenting the loss of the good old days back on the farm (Jankovic & Edwards, 1980). Paradoxically, others see small communities as foreboding, sinister places peopled with degenerates and hiding deep and terrible secrets. Such a view would include characters from William Faulkner's novels, James Dickey's *Deliverance*, and movies such as *Mississippi Burning*. As in most cases, the truth includes both extremes and considerably more in between.

Most definitions and descriptions of "rural" begin with the U.S. Census of the Population and intervening population surveys. Traditionally, population in incorporated and unincorporated areas of 2,500 or larger was classified as urban, with the remainder defined as rural. Chicago and Detroit were urban and Ten Sleep, Wyoming, and Port Gibson, Mississippi, were rural. This rural–urban dichotomy made classification simple but of limited utility. For example, a community of 2,500 or 3,500 could be classified as urban, but most observers would define it as rural in nature. Conversely, cities and urban communities have sprawled ever farther into the countryside, making their boundaries less distinct.

In 1991, the U.S. Bureau of the Census developed a more functional definition based on a rural–urban continuum, rather than a rural–urban dichotomy. "Metropolitan" and "nonmetropolitan" became preferred terms, with a metropolitan statistical area (MSA) consisting of a central city of 50,000 population or more and the county in which it is located. The MSA also might include adjacent counties with highly urbanized populations participating in the economic complex of the central city. Nonmetropolitan or rural locales were everything lying outside of MSAs. The metropolitan counties include 77 percent of the U.S. population, and nonmetropolitan counties include 23 percent (Galbraith, 1992).

Another application of the rurality construct was used by Edwards and Minotti (1989), who defined a rural county as "one in which the largest community has a population of less than 50,000 and in which more than 50 percent of the inhabitants reside in communities of less than 2,500" (p. 324).

Such definitions include one of Deavers' (1992) three key characteristics of rurality, that is, small towns and open country are associated with small-scale, low-density settlement. Almost 90 percent of the U.S. cities and towns outside metropolitan counties have fewer than 5,000 inhabitants, and about 40 million Americans reside in these locales. Most people readily accept and understand this characteristic of rurality, even though many have not personally lived or worked in such a place.

However, after general agreement on low-population density as an explanatory factor, the discussion of what constitutes rural begins to get more tenuous, with myths and stereotypes common. Many still believe that farming is the primary occupation, with strong support from mining, fishing, and forest-products industries. Such occupations and industries are important, but they play an ever-decreasing role in the life of rural communities. In fact, manufacturing constitutes the primary source of export earnings, and services provide the greatest share of income and employment. Most growth in the rural economy has been in the service area; hence, sector definitions of rural areas are increasingly defective as a basis for social policy and social work intervention. The popular belief that farm support policies should be the foundation for rural development should be critically reexamined and, in the opinion of many experts, discarded.

Deavers' (1992) second defining characteristic of rurality is the distance to large urban centers. Sheer physical distance, social and cultural isolation, and remoteness resulting from geographic barriers such as mountains and rivers present significant obstacles to modernization and development. Rural populations tend to be peripheral to the larger society and are not fully integrated into centers of information, innovation, technology, and finance. Lack of such integration means that rural communities will fall increasingly behind in an age of national and global economic development. Conversely, locales that develop strategies for overcoming the barrier of distance may well provide an enhanced quality of life for their residents.

The third vital characteristic of rurality identified by Deavers (1992) is specialization of rural economies. Specialization may have resulted from historical competitive advantages, such as physical or natural resources (productive soil, timber, and minerals, for example), or it may have stemmed from the large size of branch-plant manufacturing firms attracted to rural areas because of inexpensive land and labor. Specialization also results from the basic fact that rural areas are too small to achieve the meaningful diversification found in most urban areas.

Specialization and dependence on a narrow economic base of natural resources can be a boon for a community when an industry prospers but a bane when that industry falters. Such communities often experience the boom–bust syndrome, with attendant social problems and human consequences. Specialization in the manufacturing arena, especially low-wage, low-skill employment in the South, may fall victim to structural changes occurring in the world economy. Although some would like to think of rural America as autonomous, independent, and self-directed, it has in fact developed a specialization of economic function that makes it increasingly interdependent with and vulnerable to outside forces.

This specialization of economic function has been examined by social scientists in the U.S. Department of Agriculture (USDA), who have engaged in a major attempt to classify nonmetropolitan counties according to the primary source of their economic base, the presence of federally owned land, and population characteristics (Bender et al., 1985). Their typology, which has value for policy and practice considerations, is as follows (Hassinger & Hobbs, 1992):

- Farming-dependent counties (702 counties, 29% of total nonmetro counties). These counties are principally located in the upper Midwest and Plains states. Most lost population in the 1980s.
- Manufacturing-dependent counties (678 counties, 28% of total nonmetro counties). These counties are concentrated in the Southeast and

Northwest. They became manufacturing counties in 1950–80, as industries relocated from cities to rural areas, largely because of cheaper labor.
- Mining-dependent counties (200 counties, 8% of total nonmetro counties). These counties are concentrated in the coal fields of Kentucky and West Virginia and in the energy producing areas of the West.
- Specialized government counties (315 counties, 13% of total nonmetro counties). These counties are generally the location of a military base, state university, or another major state or federal activity. They are quite uniformly dispersed across the nation and most have a growing population.
- Persistent poverty counties (242 counties, 10% of total nonmetro counties.) These counties are concentrated in the South, especially in the Mississippi Delta and in parts of Appalachia. They also include many Native American reservation counties. Most have a high concentration of racial and ethnic groups.
- Federal lands counties (247 counties, 10% of total nonmetro counties). These counties, all located in the West, are generally sparsely populated but grew in population during the 1980s.
- Destination retirement communities (515 counties, 21% of total nonmetro counties). These counties attract retirees, relocating because of environmental amenities or lower cost of living. Retirement counties gained population during the 1980s. (p. 180)

Although a few counties cannot be included in this typology, it covers all but 370 of the 2,443 counties in the contiguous United States. Some overlap in economic functions occurs, but 57 percent of the counties belong to one group, 22 percent are in two groups, 6 percent are in three or more, and 15 percent are ungrouped.

Typologies and classification systems such as this one emphasize the diversity of economic function and dispel the myth of one rural America. The needs, including the need for social services, of a retirement-age population would vary considerably from those of a mining-dependent population, especially a boom community with a large number of young families. Similarly, the needs of a college town with a large number of educated, affluent people might vary greatly from those of a poverty community in the Mississippi Delta. Good social policy and social work practice must be based on an understanding of such differences.

THEORETICAL PERSPECTIVES ON RURAL–URBAN DIFFERENCES

The variables of population density, distance to population centers, and regional economic variations provide a framework for discussing rural–urban distinctions. Social scientists, especially sociologists and anthropologists, have also studied the effects these and other variables have had on social institutions, processes, and relationships. In fact, sociology as a discipline essentially developed in response to changing conditions created by agrarian societies giving way to industrialization and urbanization. Sociology's theoretical perspectives on rural–urban differences are perhaps best understood in light of their evolution.

Classical Theory

The early, or classical, sociologists (for example, Tönnies, Durkheim, and Weber) wrote persuasively on the differences between rural–urban institutions and social relationships. The general tone and thrust of these writers asserted that there were distinct differences between rural and urban areas, and the urban end of the continuum was associated with social pathology. These views have influenced not only social scientists but the general public, policymakers, and related disciplines such as social work.

Ferdinand Tönnies (1957), building on the work of a variety of social philosophers, made a far-reaching and long-lasting contribution by elaborating on the concept of a societal continuum based on two ways in which people related to each other. He used the German word *gemeinschaft* (roughly, community) to refer to societal relationships rooted in a sense of mutuality, common destiny, and the resulting common bonds and obligations. These relationships characterized families, neighborhoods, and friendship groups, and were more prevalent in the small rural community. In contrast *gesellschaft* (roughly, society) referred to relationships that were formal, rational, characterized by various forms of exchange, and represented by the market. Little sentiment was involved in these relationships, which were more common in urban locales.

Emile Durkheim (1964) sought to explain differences in social organization by distinguishing between two types of social solidarity: mechanical and organic. Mechanical solidarity can be found in a society "organized by a totality of beliefs and sentiments common to all members of the group: this is the collective type (or common conscience)" (p. 129). Similar habitat and symbolic experience enhance social integration, and people cooperate with each other in a simple division of labor. Hence, as community size and density increase, the division of labor and social differentiation becomes more complex, resulting in an organic solidarity more applicable to urban areas.

Max Weber (1968) also used a polar-type concept to discuss social relationships. He maintained that the first, or pure, type of social relationship is communal, where "the orientation of social action—whether in the individual case, on the average, or in the pure type—is based on a subjective feeling of the parties—whether affectual or traditional, that they belong together" (p. 40). The second type of social relationship is associative, in which the "orientation of social action within it rests on a rationally motivated adjustment of interests or a similarly motivated agreement based on rational judgement whether it be absolute values or reasons of expediency" (p. 41). Associative relationship is more or less a feature of communities with relatively large economic marketplaces and systems. It is a relationship that is impersonal and formal as opposed to the personal and informal type found more commonly in the small community.

Georg Simmel (in Warren, 1977) focused on social–psychological factors and argued that such characteristics as intensification of nervous stimulation, intellectuality, pecuniary evolution, emphasis on a precise time schedule, a blasé attitude, individuality, division of labor, and casualness of contact are all interrelated in the life of the metropolis. He believed that urban residents had greater freedom in a spiritualized and refined sense, but that they were more likely to feel adrift in the metropolitan crowd. Urbanites experience impersonal, objective relations of the "head," whereas "ruralites" experience personal, subjective relations of the "heart."

Determinist Theory

Determinist, or Wirthian, theory, which appears to be a logical progression from the earlier classical sociologists, argues that ecological factors, such as size, diversity, and heterogeneity, contributed to major distinctions between rural and urban life. Lewis Wirth (1969) defined the city as "a relatively large, dense, and permanent settlement of socially heterogeneous individuals" (p. 166) who experience a plethora of social problems (crime and mental illness, for example) associated with social disorganization and disintegration. Subscribers to determinist theory believe that urbanization results in increased psychological pressures and social structural changes, which are major determinants of personality and behavior.

Psychological pressures result from profuse and varied stimuli (for example, horns blare, signs

flash, solicitors tug at coattails, and strange-look-
ing people distract attention), and individuals
adapt in ways that liberate them from many
demands and distractions but also insulate them
from other people. "City dwellers become aloof,
brusque, impersonal in their dealings with others,
emotionally buffered in their human relationships"
(Fischer, 1976, p. 30). Despite these protective
devices, psychic overload contributes to irritation,
anxiety, and nervous strain. The resulting interpersonal estrangement weakens bonds between people, increases the likelihood of health and mental
health problems, and ultimately results in a
decline of community cohesion. Urban residents,
therefore, face a loss of the sense of community.

Wirth's (1969) analysis of social structure led
to the belief that size, density, and heterogeneity
produce a multifaceted community with numerous
levels of differentiation. An individual's time and
attention are divided among many people and
places, thereby weakening social bonds in two
ways: (1) At the community level, people differ so
much that moral consensus is difficult to achieve;
and (2) as community cohesion is weakened, so is
the cohesion of the small, intimate, primary
groups. In line with the latter result, families and
neighbors are relatively less important than is typical in rural communities.

The end result is *anomie*, "a social condition
in which the norms—the rules and conventions of
proper and permissible behavior—are feeble"
(Fischer, 1976, p. 32). Informal and personal means
of preventing or moderating anomie give way to
formal and impersonal means (for example, police
officers and social workers, not the neighbors,
control juveniles). Because Wirth (1969) did not
believe that such formal measures could fully
replace those based on consensus and small, primary groups, he predicted that urban areas would
always have a significant number of related problems. Conversely, rural inhabitants in stable, small
communities would be less likely to experience
such problems.

Compositional Theory

Compositional (or nonecological) theory denies
such effects of urbanism and attributes rural–
urban differences to the composition of the different populations (Fischer, 1976). Compositionalists
maintain that an anti-urban bias exists and that it
can be traced back to 19th-century Romanticism.
According to the compositionalists, the portrayal
of urbanism as a debilitating and dehumanizing
way of life grew from this early reaction to urbanization and industrialization (Summers & Branch,
1982): "By implied contrast, rural existence was
portrayed as one of bucolic contentment where
people lived a happy arcadian existence in the
mainly agricultural villages and small market
towns" (p. 33).

Oscar Lewis (1965), an anthropologist, and
sociologist Herbert Gans (1962) made the first
serious attempts to refute the determinists. They
argued that social life is not a mass phenomenon
and that it occurs for the most part in small
groups within the family, the church, and both formal and informal groups. They did not believe that
urbanism weakens small, primary groups, and
they denied that ecological factors, such as size,
density, and heterogeneity, have serious consequences for personal social worlds. Instead, they
stated that nonecological factors, such as social
class, ethnicity, and stage in the life cycle, determine the dynamics of social life. Economic position, cultural characteristics, and marital–family
status are the major determinants of individuals'
behavior. Hence, rural behavior and social problems may differ from those in urban areas, but
that is not a result of ruralism per se.

Subcultural Theory

Subcultural theory draws on both determinist and
compositional theories to explain rural–urban differences. It acknowledges that "ruralites" are integrated into viable social worlds through strong
small groups and personal relationships. However,
its central thesis is that urbanism independently
affects social life, not by destroying social groups
as determinism suggests but, instead, by helping
to create and strengthen them (Fischer, 1976).

Proponents of subcultural theory argue that
urbanism promotes diverse subcultures (college
students and Chinese Americans, for example).
Like the compositionalists, subcultural adherents
believe that urbanites live in meaningful social
worlds and interact with others who share similar
traits. They do not believe, as do determinists, that
urban residents live in isolation, with little interaction with significant others.

Subculturists differ from the compositionalists in that they do think that urbanism affects
these subcultural groups. The increasing population results in a "critical mass," which creates new
subcultures, modifies existing ones, and brings
them into contact with each other. Deviance is
created because new social worlds are created,
not because old ones are damaged or destroyed.

For example, the large numbers of people in a
city would generally permit the development of
such subcultural groups as professional criminals
and delinquents. Members interact with and
receive support from their own social circles.

Thus, the behavior viewed by determinists as evidence of the failure of social groups would actually result from the opposite effect: the development of social groups (or subcultures). Concomitantly, many individuals would become members of nondeviant subcultures and find support from these groups.

IMPORTANCE OF THEORY FOR PRACTICE AND POLICY

Although the dramatic differences observed by classical sociologists may no longer exist in contemporary societies, determinists, compositionalists, and subculturalists all agree that varying levels of differences in rural–urban behavior do remain. Determinists credit these differences to ecological factors (for example, size and density), compositionalists maintain that the causative variables are nonecological (for example, class and sex), and subculturalists argue that both ecological and nonecological variables explain the dissimilarities.

A working knowledge of these theoretical explanations of rural–urban differences and how they evolved is a necessity for social scientists interested in additional research; social policymakers influencing decisions affecting large populations; and social services personnel planning, designing, administering, and evaluating service delivery systems intended for diverse groups and problems.

Social workers and service personnel should be advised to consider the implications and applications of social science research on the distinctions between rural and urban life. People who believe that such differences do not exist or are insignificant should take a thorough look at the evidence. Social behavior does vary according to locality differences; hence, social workers must be prepared for differential education and practice. Professional models, curricula, and strategies appropriate for New York City or San Francisco might not be directly transferable to Mound Bayou, Mississippi, or Hell Roaring Creek, Montana.

The social work profession does possess a long history of applying social science theory and research, but it would clearly benefit from increasing content on rural–urban differences. Material on the major, and sometimes conflicting, theories should be considered by beginning and experienced professionals, who should be acutely aware that the theory or theories they subscribe to will shape their practice decisions and social policy choices.

Consider, for example, the practice implications of a rural youth with homosexual tendencies who is leaving high school and has the option of relocating to a metropolitan environment. A practitioner influenced by determinist theory might well be concerned with the alienating forces in the city and describe positively the value of nonmetropolitan life. A social worker who subscribes to compositionalist theory would probably not consider locality differences a major issue. And another worker with a subculturalist frame of reference would likely emphasize the availability of social support and networks in the city's larger homosexual community. These professional responses to a hypothetical situation are only partial and possible approaches, but they do illustrate the impact of theory on practice.

Social policy choices and inclinations are also influenced by theoretical orientation. When faced with communities experiencing economic and population losses from agricultural decline or plant closures, determinists usually would promote fiscal and social policies targeted at enhancing rural locales and enabling people to remain in or come back to such environments. They might also promote remedial steps to lessen the dehumanizing aspects of the city for rural residents forced to move there for the sake of employment. Compositionalists probably would pay little attention to the importance of locale; instead they would support programs aimed at helping various groups of people in various places. For example, they could promote a program of general assistance for refugees and ignore or downplay rural–urban factors. Subculturalists, who usually prefer an integrated approach, would probably prefer a comprehensive strategy including both ecological and nonecological approaches in both rural and urban communities.

These practice and policy examples are hypothetical and illustrative, but they emphasize the necessity of comprehending and building on the theoretical base for rural–urban differences in social behavior. Social work educators, researchers, and policymakers now face the formidable task of defining and delineating the nature of differential practice resulting from such differences. Rural social work could be strengthened considerably in its evolutionary path if it developed a typology that focused on such components as theoretical orientation, roles of workers, tasks, strategies, and issues.

GENERAL PRACTICE CONSIDERATIONS

Although it is clear that theoretical orientation influences, if not determines, social work practice and policy, many important rural concerns could be incorporated within any one framework or combination of frameworks. The importance of diversity is one such concern. Too many urban social workers, who have no trouble understanding the importance of all kinds of urban diversity, go into rural America expecting a homogeneous client population. However, as Josephine C. Brown (1933) so astutely pointed out more than 60 years ago, rural people and communities may differ greatly. For example, consider the different ethnic, cultural, religious, racial, gender, class, and socioeconomic variables in the following rural populations: Missouri Amish, Louisiana Cajun, Wyoming Basque, New Mexico Pueblo, Alaska Aleute, North Carolina Hmong, Utah Mormon, Tennessee auto worker, Georgia poultry factory worker, California counterculture member, Atlantic Coast Gullah, Mississippi African American, Southwestern Tex-Mex, and New York migrant worker. The list could go on indefinitely; hence the social worker contemplating rural practice should be prepared to encounter and work with clients from diverse backgrounds. The large number of refugees being placed in rural locales is resulting in even more opportunities for intervention by rural social workers.

Social workers practicing with rural populations often are employed in the public sector with such agencies as public welfare, child welfare, mental health, aging, and corrections. They tend to work in relatively isolated, small local and county offices and confront a host of complex problems. Specialized services common in urban areas generally are not available. Accordingly, the generalist practice model has evolved as the one best suited for rural practice. Generalists must be highly skilled in assessing problem situations and determining where systematic intervention is necessary. Social workers rigidly oriented to practice methods (such as casework, group work, and community organization), fields of practice (such as mental health, public welfare, and corrections), or target populations (such as elderly, youths, and delinquents) are limited in their effectiveness. Organizational rules governing eligibility and forms of service cannot be ignored, but workers must use flexibility in their application. Also, statewide policies may sometimes create problems when applied to rural counties (Edwards & Minotti, 1989).

Rural people tend to evaluate social workers on the basis of help delivered or problems solved, rather than on their degrees, years of education, or areas of specialization. A mental health worker may see several survivors of sexual assault and domestic violence on an individual basis, establish a support group, organize a task force, develop a community shelter, and participate in lobbying legislators for funding these services. The same worker may also see a wide variety of clinical problems, consult with the school on behavioral problems, serve on an advisory committee for a program on aging, and coordinate an emergency food pantry.

The value of the generalist model for rural areas was initially advocated in the 1920s and 1930s by such rural pioneers as Josephine C. Brown (J. Davenport & J. A. Davenport, 1984). Brown's (1933) seminal *The Rural Community and Social Casework* seemingly emphasizes the social casework method; however, she stressed "undifferentiated practice," which required the so-called caseworker to employ both group and community approaches. Ginsberg (1976) reinforced this model when rural social work was "rediscovered" in the 1970s, and numerous authors such as Vice-Irey (1980) and Martinez-Brawley (1983) have documented its worth.

The generalist rural social worker must be adept at cultivating and maintaining horizontal and vertical ties within and outside the community. Horizontal ties include contacts and relationships with other local service providers and influential people. In rural communities where most people know each other on a personal basis, these ties are often informal and may be used to access client services more quickly or to initiate a community project. Service providers typically attend religious services together, shop at the same stores, have children who are friends, and gossip across the back fence. Newcomers from urban areas sometimes find it difficult to understand and work effectively in this environment.

Vertical ties refer to relations with the outside community: state and local organizations that have tremendous control over rural communities because of funding, rules, and regulations. Small towns prize their autonomy, independence, and self-direction, but they are more dependent on, or at least interdependent with, outside forces than ever before. For example, the county public welfare office must follow state guidelines, the hospital and nursing home must meet accreditation standards, and a grant-funded mental health program must be carried out in accord with federal mandates. Accordingly, the rural social worker with expertise in using both vertical and horizonal ties is of the most value to constituents. The worker may act as a mediator between the community and outside entities, often educating both parties and sometimes advocating for rural residents.

The generalist model appears to be uniquely suited for social workers dealing with the boom–bust problems associated with rural America's narrow specialization of economic function. These social workers often perform roles as varied as clinicians, group leaders, planners, organizers, and policy formulators. Strategies and techniques have been developed for communities experiencing rapid growth owing to energy or recreational development (J. A. Davenport & J. Davenport, 1979), for rural ghettos or declining communities with people unable to leave (Jacobsen & Sanderson-Alberson, 1987), for communities experiencing stress and mental health problems because of the farm crisis and economic dislocation (Mermelstein & Sundet, 1986), and for communities with large numbers of poor people, especially women and children (Garrett & Lennox, 1993).

Lack of anonymity may present workers, especially those with urban backgrounds, with problems. Transplanted urbanites, who sometimes accept a rural job because it is their only option, refer to "life in a goldfish bowl." Everyone seems to know what everyone else is doing, and one's personal life affects one's professional life more than it does in urban settings. Lack of attendance at religious services is apparent and may cause criticism, as would personal behavior not in accord with community norms and values. Weekend trips to the nearest city for shopping and entertainment takes money away from local merchants and may convey a message to locals that their town is deficient. A worker's desire for privacy and self-determination must be weighed against the impact these values have on clients. The same people who may be offended by a worker's personal life often sit on committees and boards that determine programs and services. Workers unwilling to consider some trade-offs for the sake of their clients might be more suited for the greater anonymity and freedom of the urban environment.

Value conflicts between rural residents, who tend to be more conservative and traditional, and social workers, who tend to be more liberal and nontraditional, must be anticipated (J. A. Davenport & J. Davenport, 1982). Again, this is especially true for social workers oriented to urban life. Social workers urging anti-gun legislation and anti-hunting rules may quickly lose community acceptance in areas where hunting is an inherent cultural tradition and where game is an important part of land subsistence (as in Native American communities). Nor do admonitions that beef is overpriced and unhealthy win many friends in rural cattle country, where attempts to help the local economy include "eat more beef" signs.

Instead, social workers may consider joining such organizations as Ducks Unlimited and fishing clubs as a means of gaining acceptance, opening doors to leaders, and securing a better position from which to promote enhanced service delivery. Although these actions may prove difficult for some, rural social workers who carefully consider such trade-offs typically obtain better client services. Workers originally from small communities usually are quite comfortable in such situations, but those from urban locales are used to more rigid boundaries between personal and professional life.

Value conflicts often are accompanied by ethical issues and dilemmas. For example a proposed change in the *NASW Code of Ethics* (NASW, 1994) would make it unethical for a social worker to employ or enter into a business endeavor with a client. This rule is obviously aimed at preventing abuse of clients, but rural advocates maintain that clients already have protection from the mandate that workers place their client's interests before their own. An overly strict code of ethics would prevent a mental health social worker from employing a client who also happened to be the only plumber or electrician in 30 miles. The variables of low population density and few skilled personnel would make such a rule onerous at best and devastating at worst for many rural communities. In addition to being inconvenient for a worker, some potential clients would forgo treatment rather than lose employment in an area where jobs are not plentiful. Additionally, the act of not using the only plumber or electrician in town would undoubtedly be noticed and questioned, thereby calling even more attention to the person.

Confidentiality may present problems if a worker adheres to an overly strict interpretation of this principle. In a small town it is easy to see who is going to social services or the mental health office, or who a worker is visiting. Concerned neighbors and friends, who are part of the all-important natural helping system, may ask the worker what is wrong. A curt reply that "professionalism precludes a breach of confidentiality" would do little to protect a client whose problem has already been noted by a neighbor, friend, or relative. It would hurt the worker's acceptance by the community, and it could prevent the client from receiving much-needed neighborly assistance. Experienced rural workers use their practice wisdom in developing strategies that do not violate confidentiality but do enlist the support of natural helpers. For example, a worker might respond: "I'm glad you're concerned about Mrs. Culpepper, but our agency rules won't really let us talk about the people we work with. However, you might just want to drop by and see how she's getting along."

RURAL SOCIAL WORK MOVEMENT

The history of rural social work, long neglected in the professional literature, was resurrected by Martinez-Brawley in *Pioneer Efforts in Rural Social Welfare: Firsthand Views Since 1909* (1980) and *Seven Decades of Rural Social Work* (1981). Stimulated by a diverse group of agriculturalists, academics, ministers, and journalists, President Theodore Roosevelt appointed a Country Life Commission in 1908 to study the problems of the countryside. This commission, headed by Lyberty Hyde Bailey, president of the New York State College of Agriculture, precipitated the Country Life Movement, which advocated for rural interests until World War II. The 1909 White House Conference on Children addressed the problems of rural children, and several states, such as Illinois and Missouri in 1911, initiated mothers' aid laws for urban and rural counties.

The period between World War I and the Great Depression saw the development of the Home Service of the American Red Cross, which began regional approaches for rural areas, employed rural specialists, and conducted rural institutes. Other voluntary organizations, especially the Child Welfare League of America and the Family Welfare Association of America (FWAA), started programs of rural social work. Josephine C. Brown gained experience with the Family Welfare Association of America, and her definitive work, *The Rural Community and Social Casework* (1933), attracted national attention.

Brown became an administrative assistant in the Federal Emergency Relief Administration and helped plan a comprehensive program of public relief administered by qualified people. Many rural people became acquainted with professional social work through the Federal Emergency Relief Administration's training program. Schools of social work stepped forward to provide both short-term and long-term training. Public programs increasingly took the place of private ones in providing rural services. Unfortunately, the onset of World War II moved rural social work to the back burner, where it attracted little attention for two decades. Rural practitioners continued their labors in the hinterlands, but professional reinforcement was lacking.

The social turmoil and increased attention to social problems in the 1960s and early 1970s brought rural social work back to life despite a distinct preoccupation with and bias toward urban

areas by federal and state governments, private organizations, and the profession of social work. Several factors contributed to this reawakening.

The Economic Opportunity Act of 1964 established the Office of Economic Opportunity to supervise a variety of antipoverty programs serving both urban and rural poor. Programs of value to rural America included Job Corps centers, community action programs, migrant services, and Volunteers In Service To America (VISTA). The Office of Economic Opportunity made special efforts to involve Native Americans, African Americans, and Hispanic Americans.

The Community Mental Health Centers Act of 1963 had a tremendous impact, and by 1973 more than 200 of the 500 funded centers (40 percent) were in nonmetropolitan locales. Social workers assumed a prominent role in administering, planning, and staffing these centers. In fact, many viewed social work as the backbone of the rural community mental health movement. In addition, many paraprofessionals, attracted by the availability of jobs at the centers, were encouraged to seek social work degrees at the bachelor's and master's levels. Furthermore, the early emphasis by community mental health centers on consultation and education resulted in social workers being actively involved all over the community, where they helped to develop new services and attracted positive visibility for social work.

Generous educational leave policies of state departments of public welfare allowed rural personnel to attain the master of social work degree and return to their agencies in small towns. The general expansion of public and child welfare services also provided employment for rural social workers. The Title XX program, in particular, funded many rural service agencies and provided significant amounts of money for educational institutions to produce social workers. Colleges and universities moved quickly to start new programs and strengthen existing ones, especially at the bachelor of social work level.

A sometimes overlooked contributor to rural social work is the federal government's provision of services to Native Americans through the U.S. Department of the Interior's Bureau of Indian Affairs and the U.S. Department of Health and Human Services' Indian Health Service. Many social workers, especially in the West, have gained valuable experience in rural environments and have pioneered creative responses to such vexing problems as alcoholism, child abuse, poverty, and suicide (Davenport, 1972).

As these developments increased the number of rural programs and personnel, a cadre of rural-oriented academics and practitioners began to emerge and coalesce. These social workers found little contemporary professional literature and few presentations at conferences and workshops. An informal group began swapping experiences, examples, and "fugitive materials" (papers that were not published or did not receive national attention).

The movement grew as Leon H. Ginsberg, then dean of the West Virginia University School of Social Work, gave his authority first to presentations on rural issues and then to an edited Council on Work Education volume, *Social Work in Rural Communities: A Book of Readings* (1976). Several graduate schools of social work (including West Virginia University, Eastern Washington University, University of Missouri–Columbia, University of Iowa, and University of Utah) began to develop rural curricula, practicum placements, and research projects. Baccalaureate-level programs also were established by several schools, including Mississippi State University, University of Wyoming, Pennsylvania State University, and University of Montana. Most institutions were public land grant schools, although smaller private colleges, such as St. Olaf (Minnesota) and Ferrum (Virginia), were active participants. These schools tended to be located in small cities and towns away from the traditional social work power centers in large cities and the East and West coasts.

In 1976, the University of Tennessee School of Social Work hosted a National Institute on Social Work in Rural Areas and published the proceedings (Green & Webster, 1977). These institutes and proceedings became annual affairs and have provided an important forum for rural social workers, an opportunity to network, and an ever-expanding knowledge base. Rotation of the institute around the country gains wide exposure for rural social work and attracts new supporters.

The Rural Social Work Caucus was formed at the first institute in Knoxville, Tennessee, and has been an important force despite a constant argument over whether it should be an informal movement or a formal organization. Although its members and followers sometimes refer to themselves as "rural caucuzoids" and their leadership process resembles a "floating crap game," the caucus has realized some major achievements: the institutionalization of annual institutes; cosponsorship of numerous rural conferences; the first National Policy Statement on Social Work in Rural Areas, passed by the NASW Delegate Assembly in 1977; formation by NASW of the first National Rural Task Force in 1979; the inclusion of rural social workers on editorial boards; and the addition of rural content at the Annual Program Meeting of the Council on Social Work Education and NASW's Annual Meeting of the Profession.

The literature has expanded greatly beyond the annual proceedings and early books by Ginsberg and Martinez-Brawley. The publication *Human Services in the Rural Environment*, which began as a newsletter at the University of Wisconsin, matured into a major refereed journal at the University of Tennessee and is now published by Eastern Washington University. Rural articles are now frequently featured in such prominent journals as *Social Work*, *Families and Society*, and the *Journal of Social Work Education*.

One final development that bodes well for the future of the rural social work movement has been the steady assumption of leadership positions by rural social workers who began their careers in the 1960s and 1970s. Several moved from practice to master's degree programs and then on to deanships and directorships. Rural social work appears to be ready for the coming challenges of the 21st century.

REFERENCES

Bender, L. D., Green, B. L., Hady, T. F., Kuehn, J. A., Nelson, M. K., Perkinson, L. B., & Ross, P. J. (1985). *The diverse social and economic structure of nonmetropolitan America*. Washington, DC: U.S. Department of Agriculture, Economic Research Service.

Brown, J. C. (1933). *The rural community and social casework*. New York: Family Welfare Association of America.

Community Mental Health Centers Act of 1963. P.L. 88-164, 77 Stat. 290.

Davenport J. (1972). *Community organization for mental health services on the Flathead Indian Reservation*. Paper presented at the Seventh Annual Meeting, Clinical Society and Commissioned Officers Association of the U.S. Public Health Service, New York.

Davenport, J., & Davenport, J. A. (1984). Josephine Brown's classic book still guides rural social work. *Social Casework, 65*(7), 413–419.

Davenport, J. A., & Davenport, J. (Eds.). (1979). *Boom towns and human services*. Laramie: University of Wyoming Press.

Davenport, J. A., & Davenport, J. (1982). Utilizing the social network in rural communities. *Social Casework, 63*(2), 106–113.

Deavers, K. (1992). What is rural? *Policy Studies Journal, 20*(2), 183–189.

Durkheim, E. (1964). *The division of labor in a society*. New York: Free Press.

Economic Opportunity Act of 1964. P.L. 88-452, 78 Stat. 508.

Edwards, R. L., & Minotti, T. (1989). Mandated case recordings: Rural and urban perspectives. *Journal of Applied Social Sciences, 13*(2), 317–342.

Fischer, C. S. (1976). *The urban experience*. New York: Harcourt Brace Jovanovich.

Galbraith, M. W. (1992). *Education in the rural American community: A lifelong process.* Malabar, FL: Kreiger.

Gans, H. (1962). *The urban villagers.* Glencoe, IL: Free Press.

Garrett, P., & Lennox, N. (1993). Rural families and children in poverty. In Task Force on Persistent Rural Poverty (Ed.), *Persistent poverty in rural America* (pp. 230–258). Boulder, CO: Westview Press.

Ginsberg, L. H. (Ed.). (1976). *Social work in rural communities: A book of readings.* New York: Council on Social Work Education.

Green, R. K., & Webster, S. A. (Eds.). (1977). *Social work in rural areas: Preparation and practice.* Knoxville: University of Tennessee School of Social Work.

Hassinger, E. W., & Hobbs, D. J. (1992). Rural society: The environment of rural health care. In L. A. Straub & N. Walzer (Eds.), *Rural health care: Innovation in a changing environment* (pp. 178–190). Westport, CT: Praeger.

Jacobsen, G. M., & Sanderson-Alberson, B. (1987). Social and economic change in rural Iowa: The development of rural ghettos. *Human Services in the Rural Environment, 11*(1), 58–65.

Jankovic, J., & Edwards, R. L. (1980). Music and the human condition: Utilizing locality-oriented music in community analyses. In J. Davenport III, J. A. Davenport, & J. R. Weibler (Eds.), *Social work in rural areas: Issues and opportunities* (pp. 1–10). Laramie: University of Wyoming Press.

Lewis, O. (1965). Further observations on the folk-urban continuum and urbanization. In P. M. Hauser & L. F. Schmore (Eds.), *The study of urbanization* (pp. 491–503). New York: John Wiley & Sons.

Martinez-Brawley, E. E. (Ed.). (1980). *Pioneer efforts in rural social welfare: Firsthand views since 1909.* University Park: Pennsylvania State University Press.

Martinez-Brawley, E. E. (1981). *Seven decades of rural social work.* New York: Praeger.

Martinez-Brawley, E. E. (1983). *Rural social work as a contextual specialty: Undergraduate focus or graduate concentration?* Paper presented at the Pre-symposium Institute, Eighth National Institute on Social Work in Rural Areas, Cheney, WA.

Mermelstein, J., & Sundet, P. A. (1986). Rural community mental health centers' responses to the farm crisis. *Human Services in the Rural Environment, 10*(1), 21–26.

National Association of Social Workers. (1994). *NASW code of ethics.* Washington, DC: Author.

Summers, G. F., & Branch, K. (1982). Human responses to energy development. In G. F. Summers & A. Selnik (Eds.), *Energy resource communities* (pp. 23–59). Bergen, Norway: MJM.

Tönnies, F. (1957). *Gemeinschaft and gesellschaft.* New York: Harper & Row.

U.S. Bureau of the Census. (1991). Poverty in the United States: 1990. *Current population reports* (Series P-60, No. 175). Washington, DC: U.S. Government Printing Office.

Vice-Irey, K. (1980). The social work generalist in a rural context: An ecological perspective. *Journal of Education for Social Work, 16*(3), 36–42.

Warren, R. (Ed.). (1977). *New perspectives on the American community.* Chicago: Rand McNally College Publishing.

Weber, M. (1968). *Economy and society.* New York: Bedminster.

Wirth, L. (1969). Urbanism as a way of life. In R. Sennet (Ed.), *Classic essays on the culture of cities* (pp. 165–169). Englewood Cliffs, NJ: Appleton-Century-Crofts.

FURTHER READING

Farley, D. W., Griffiths, K. A., Skidmore, R. A., & Thackeray, M. A. (1982). *Rural social work practice.* New York: Macmillan.

Ginsberg, L. H. (1993). *Social work in rural communities* (2nd ed.). Alexandria, VA: Council on Social Work Education.

Johnson, W. H. (Ed.). (1980). *Rural human services: A book of readings.* Itasca, IL: F. E. Peacock.

Martinez-Brawley, E. E. (1990). *Perspectives on the small community: Humanistic views for practitioners.* Silver Spring, MD: NASW Press.

Martinez-Brawley, E. E., with Delevan, S. M. (Eds.). (1993). *Transferring technology in the personal social services.* Washington, DC: NASW Press.

Watkins, J. M., & Watkins, D. A. (1984). *Social policy and the rural setting.* New York: Springer.

Judith A. Davenport, PhD, LCSW, is director and professor, University of Missouri, School of Social Work, 701 Clark Hall, Columbia, MO 65211. **Joseph Davenport III, PhD, ACSW,** is a consultant in private practice, Columbia, MO.

For further information see

Church Social Work; Community; Community Development; Community Needs Assessment; Community Practice Models; Ethnic-Sensitive Practice; Migrant Workers; Music and Social Work; Natural Helping Networks; Organizations: Context for Social Services Delivery; Rural Poverty; Sectarian Agencies; White Ethnic Groups.

Key Words	
community	networks
diversity	rural social work

Rush, Benjamin

See Biographies section, Volume 3

S

Sanders, Daniel

See Biographies section, Volume 3

Satir, Virginia

See Biographies section, Volume 3

School Social Work Overview
Edith M. Freeman

As a field of practice, school social work has expanded its scope and changed the professional identity of its practitioners since the early 1980s. Many of the economic, educational, and social changes that occurred during this period have made family life more difficult, increasing the number of at-risk children in public schools and the range of services they require. In turn, changes in the type and number of services needed by children, youths, and families have affected how school social workers practice both individually and in collaboration with other professionals in the school and community. This focus on interdisciplinary teamwork and the case management of services has profoundly affected what school social workers identify as their appropriate professional roles and tasks and the priorities among them. Radin (1989) affirmed that the roles of school social work practice—"family–school liaison, caseworker, and agent of social change intervening at larger systems levels—have reflected trends and important events in society" (p. 213).

Previously, the greatest expansion in this area of practice was in services to special education students after the passage of P.L. 94-142, the Education for All Handicapped Children Act of 1975 (Alderson, Krishef, & Spencer, 1990). This law required the educational system to provide services in the "least restrictive environment" for an increasing number of exceptional children. In addition, the system has had to meet the needs of children in regular education while responding to conflicts over professional priorities within the field of education itself (Allen-Meares, 1987; Bensky et al., 1980).

The most recent expansion in school social work, however, has been the provision of preventive interventions to high-risk children and youths supported by the Hawkins-Stafford Elementary and Secondary School Improvement Amendments of 1986 (Allen-Meares, 1990) and the Education of the Handicapped Act Amendments of 1990, as well as services to preschool children with disabilities required by P.L. 99-457, the Education of the Handicapped Act Amendments of 1986 (Radin, 1989). A review of the historical context of school social

work practice can clarify the influence of past events on these current changes.

HISTORY OF SCHOOL SOCIAL WORK

Early Period

Costin (1969) noted that "school social work began at about the same time, although independently, in three cities: New York, Boston, and Hartford during the school year 1906–07" (p. 439). These initial services were provided not in the schools, but in private agencies and civic organizations in the community. Although schools eventually agreed to administer and support some of these early efforts, the first instance of a school system establishing such services was in 1913 in Rochester, New York. As these services expanded, practitioners began to organize themselves, and the National Association of Visiting Teachers was established in 1921. The growth of the services was due to the passage of compulsory school attendance laws, which led to an early emphasis on attendance as well as the prevention of the exploitation of students through child labor. In addition, new knowledge about children's individual needs and coping abilities allowed social workers to help teachers understand how particular external factors affected children's ability to learn (Allen-Meares, 1988).

In the 1920s the focus of school social work shifted to preventing juvenile delinquency to make the work of schools more effective. The Commonwealth Fund, individual boards of education, and the National Association of Visiting Teachers were responsible for establishing many new positions in urban and rural areas in which social workers acted as home–school–community liaisons. Another influence on this practice area during the 1920s was the mental hygiene movement, which led school social workers "to assist in the diagnosis and treatment of 'nervous' and 'difficult' children" (Costin, 1969, p. 434) and to focus on understanding the relationship of students' emotional reactions to their achievement and overall performance in school. During the 1930s services emphasized the physical needs of students in response to the Great Depression and the accompanying adverse social conditions (Radin, 1989).

Middle Period

From 1940 to 1960, another shift in services occurred because of the proliferation of federal programs providing for many basic needs of families. During this period, school social work became an integral part of the school system, and its focus shifted from negative school and community conditions to a clinical orientation (Radin, 1989). This change contributed to the prestige of school social workers and removed much of the stigma attached to them as "truant officers" (Radin, 1989). Casework services were provided to individual students to help resolve their maladjustments. The refinement of practice methods and techniques became a primary goal of school social workers during this period (Costin, 1987).

Then, in response to the major social conditions that affected an increasing number of children and youths in the 1960s, the emphasis again shifted, this time to collaboration with other school personnel to change the school as a social system. However, research on practitioners' tasks indicated that some school social workers failed to make the transition to policy making and leadership that was necessary to change the system, continuing instead to focus on casework to individual students and parents. Radin (1989) stated that the further development of systems theory and the ecological perspective in the 1970s helped increase attention to the complex problems of schools and communities, including racism and students' rights.

Current Period

The focus on students' rights and cultural diversity has naturally led to a new emphasis on parental involvement and school–community–family partnerships since 1980 (Winters & Maluccio, 1988). In addition, Costin (1987) noted that school practice is involved more in "pupils' rights in relation to such matters as discipline (frequently corporal punishment), suspension and expulsion, curricular 'tracking,' placement into special education classes, and access to pupils' school records" (p. 541). P.L. 94-142 has been responsible for the active involvement of parents in the assessment and decision-making process through conferences on their children's Individualized Education Plans. It has also changed how school social workers practice by including them as a related service: as mediators in conflicts about educational decisions, as providers of information to parents about programs and services, and as presenters of mental health services in the classroom (Alderson et al., 1990).

GUIDING PHILOSOPHY AND VALUES

School social work currently emphasizes an ecological perspective and the philosophy that all aspects of a child's situation must be mobilized to facilitate his or her right to a supportive learning environment (Gailey, 1989). Freeman and Pennekamp (1988a) stated that school social work is designed to meet "the needs of children, youths, and their families by matching those needs with resources in the least restrictive environment, i.e., as close as possible to the actual place where the needs exist, surface, and can be identified" (p. 4) while in the process, facilitating "creative partnerships between all participants in this ecological field" (p. xiv).

According to this philosophy, school social workers are the primary linkers and coordinators among the home, school, and community. They are the catalysts for such partnerships from the time parents and children are introduced to the school until the students leave school to enter the world of work (Pennekamp & Freeman, 1988). This life span perspective is useful for identifying natural developmental transitions and other periods when most students may be at risk of problems and when prevention is appropriate (Freeman & Pennekamp, 1988b). Moreover, school social workers are expected to identify other students in high-risk situations that threaten the students' adjustment to and academic performance in school, so they can provide preventive services, whether at the primary, secondary, or tertiary level (Children's

Defense Fund, 1986; Committee for Economic Development, 1987; Mintzies & Hare, 1985).

Other values consistent with this philosophy pervade the field of school social work, including the self-determination of clients and beginning where the client is. These values require flexibility and judgment about how age may limit or enhance opportunities for children and youths to be involved in decisions about their educational plans and understand the consequences of those decisions. Thus, school social workers deem the input of all participants or stakeholders important, beginning with students and including family members; community leaders; other individuals who are significant to the family; teachers, principals, and other school personnel; and professionals in the community. Students' problems are viewed as having developed out of a range of interacting factors related to the various stakeholders and significant aspects of the environment. The entire ecological field must be considered in helping to create goodness of fit between the students' and families' needs and the resources available to them (Germain, 1988; Monkman, 1991).

Self-determination requires that clients have not only opportunities for meaningful input, but also the information, including key policies, staff roles, and programs or other resources, necessary for making informed decisions. The school social worker must work to enhance opportunities to provide input and must be the main conduit of important information to parents and students (Allen-Meares, Washington, & Welsh, 1986; Whittaker, Schinke, & Gilchrist, 1987; Winters & Easton, 1983).

School social workers view schools as living environments that influence the nature of the teaching–learning process as well as the quality of life of students and personnel in schools (Germain, 1988; McLaughlin & Protinksy, 1991). Because of the high value they place on the quality of life in schools, school social workers are concerned with how the changing social context impinges on quality of life, and vice versa. This philosophy provides a rationale for making each interacting system the target of intervention and for treating all systems as partners or collaborators in facilitating the intervention process when necessary. As Winters and Maluccio (1988) noted, "schools cannot alone cope with these challenges; schools, families, and communities must work together" (p. 209).

KNOWLEDGE BASE OF SCHOOL SOCIAL WORK

The knowledge base of school social work draws on theories about systems, communications,

learning, social learning, behavior modification, and human growth and development (Nelson, 1990). School social workers use these theories in various combinations in their daily practice, as well as additional ones, for example, crisis and task-centered theoretical approaches. Three models of school social work practice have been applied to services for children and families on the basis of different combinations of these theories: the traditional clinical model, the school change model, and the systems model. The models were developed to respond to historical events; shifting priorities in the field of practice for meeting the needs of children and families; and changes in policies on public education and related areas, including child welfare and mental health, which required new roles and tasks. The three models overlap in some ways, but in others, their characteristics are quite different.

Traditional Clinical Model

The focus of the traditional clinical model is largely on individual students who have been identified as having socioemotional difficulties that block their achievement in and adjustment to school. The emphasis on intrapsychic factors is consistent with psychoanalytic theory and the medical model (Freeman & Pennekamp, 1988a). The child's emotional or psychic difficulties, especially parent–child conflicts, are perceived as stemming primarily from the family, rather than from other socioenvironmental factors (Costin, 1969). Referrals come from principals and teachers in response to a perceived deviance in the student that requires tertiary prevention or rehabilitation. Individual casework, conferences with teachers and parents about the child, and referral of the child to community agencies for more in-depth counseling are the primary tasks of school social workers who use this model (Radin, 1989). The roles most often used are those of enabler, supporter, and consultant.

School Change Model

The focus of the school change model, which has also been called the "institutional change model," is on altering dysfunctional norms and conditions within a school or district that pose barriers to students' abilities to meet appropriate social and educational expectations. All individuals in a school—students, teachers, administrators, and others—are potential targets for the school social worker's interventions (Freeman & Pennekamp, 1988a; Sarri & Maple, 1972). Students who are identified as deviant may become locked into a role and have difficulty moving toward a more productive way of functioning in the school. Thus, school social workers who use this model help administrators and teachers change the school conditions that curtail learning and adjustment and provide group work services to students and families to help them eliminate dysfunctional roles (Costin, 1987; Radin, 1989). The primary roles of school social workers in this model are change agent, group facilitator, and catalyst or advocate.

Systems Model

The systems model has been linked to the ecological approach because of its focus on all aspects of the environment. The individual student's needs are addressed, but within a framework that emphasizes identifying target groups of students and the interaction of the characteristics of these students, the school, the community, and the family at points of stress in the student's life (Freeman & Pennekamp, 1988a). Preventive interventions may take the form of case finding related to students in high-risk categories, case management, family education, and work with preschool-age children and their families before the children enter school. Case finding and early intervention services in this model are designed to prevent substance abuse, child abuse, sexual abuse, teenage pregnancy, dropping out of school, and infection with human immunodeficiency virus (HIV) (Radin, 1989). This model draws on systems, communication, social learning, and organizational theories and promotes such roles as systems change agent, mediator, consultant, evaluator, educator, and member of the interdisciplinary team.

LEGISLATION, POLICIES, AND PROGRAMS

Although the philosophy and values undergirding school social work practice developed out of a professional commitment to children and their families, they have been influenced by legislation on education and formal policies. Laws and policies have also shaped the nature and quality of the educational programs available to students and their families and thus the type of related services required to supplement those programs (Allen-Meares, 1990; Bishop, 1991; Whitted, 1991). Table 1 lists some significant laws and indicates when the laws were developed or enacted and whether the laws are applicable to students with disabilities or all students. Examples of policies that affect social work practice in schools are due process procedures; policies on the disciplining, suspension, and expulsion of students; corporal punishment policies; and school dress codes.

In addition to their provisions for students and families, many of these policies and laws have defined related services and the composition of the interdisciplinary pupil personnel team. By including social work as a related service, for example, the Education for All Handicapped Children Act has increased the number of school social workers in many states and has caused them to be hired in geographic areas that did not use their services before 1975 (Alderson et al., 1990). Similarly, the Education of the Handicapped Act Amendments have strengthened the role of school social workers on the pupil personnel team by requiring them to provide many of the prescribed early intervention services for infants and toddlers. This team is also responsible for developing and monitoring the Individualized Family Service Plan as part of the preventive intervention services mandated by this law (Radin, 1989). These laws and policies not only have been instrumental in shaping education programs in this manner, but also have provided the necessary funding for such programs.

FUNDING RELATED TO SCHOOL SOCIAL WORK

Sources of Funding

The primary sources of funding for public education, and thus for school social work services, include federal, state, and local governments; private foundations and corporations; and special grants from other sources (Nelson, 1990). Thus, a combination of predictable financing and "soft money" from grants has been available for funding school social work services. Because the availability of educational programs and school social work services is linked directly to these sources of funding, school social workers should be knowledgeable about this area (Freeman & Pennekamp, 1988a).

Impact of Funding Patterns

In essence, funding patterns affect how school social work is practiced. For instance, school districts recognize the importance of average daily attendance funding, which is based on a formula allocating a set amount of money to educate each student based on mean attendance rates. For this reason, some districts expect school social workers to focus mainly on improving the attendance rates of students (Allen-Meares et al., 1986).

If funding is primarily from special education sources, then school social workers may concentrate on evaluating students for special education services and providing supportive counseling to students and families and consultation to teachers to enhance academic services. Alderson et al. (1990) found that half the 162 school social workers who responded in their study spent more than three-fourths of their time on tasks related to the

TABLE 1
Significant Laws and Policies Related to Education and Schools

Laws Directed toward Children and Youths in Schools

Applicable Only to Students with Disabilities	Applicable to All Students	Relevant Policies for Students
Section 504 of the Rehabilitation Act of 1973 (handicapped people's rights under federal law)	State compulsory attendance laws (passed between 1900 and 1918)	Due process procedures (case law)
	P.L. 93-385: Family Education Rights and Privacy Act of 1974	Policies on the disciplining, suspension, and expulsion of students
P.L. 94-142: Education for All Handicapped Children Act of 1975	P.L. 100-77: Urgent Relief for the Homeless Assistance Act of 1987	Corporal punishment policies
P.L. 99-457: Education for the Handicapped Admendments of 1986 (early intervention programs for infants and toddlers)	P.L. 100-297: School Improvement Act of 1988 (Hawkins-Stafford Elementary and Secondary Education Act)	School dress codes
P.L. 101-336: Americans with Disabilities Act of 1990	P.L. 93-247: Child Abuse and Prevention Act of 1974	
P.L. 101-476: The Education of the Handicapped Act Amendment of 1990 (Individuals with Disabilities Education Act)	Child Welfare Act of 1980	
	Mental Health Act of 1983	
	P.L. 100-485: Family Support Act of 1988	

Education for All Handicapped Children Act of 1975. Those tasks included the assessment of children who may be handicapped and implementation of Individualized Education Plans for them.

Funding also affects the position of school social work in the organizational world of the schools. When the primary source of funding is soft money, these services may occupy a relatively marginal position in the organization (Freeman & Pennekamp, 1988a). In these situations, social workers are more limited in their opportunities to influence financial and other decisions about programs and the development of relevant organizational policies (Allen-Meares et al., 1986; Winters & Easton, 1983).

Ironically, grant funds often support very important compensatory programs for high-risk and disadvantaged children, such as the Head Start Follow-Through and Chapter 1 programs. School social workers providing preventive services to the children in these programs may enable the introduction and expansion of school social work services in a district. But an administrative view that such services are marginal to the system because they are funded by soft money may limit social workers' opportunity to influence key decisions, unless they volunteer to serve on policy-making committees that are more central to the system's operations (Freeman, 1991).

Funding patterns have also affected the number of school social workers in this country and where they are located geographically. It was estimated that of the 11,000 to 14,000 school social workers in the United States in 1988–89, 8,000 to 9,000 were providing services only to special education students (Nelson, 1990). The highest num-

ber of social workers serving children with disabilities in 1988–89 tended to be concentrated in urban areas and in such states as Illinois (1,588), New Jersey (1,187), Michigan (893), Virginia (366), Massachusetts (356), Connecticut (304), and Colorado (295)—states in which the services have been mandated or have been established for many years. In comparison, such states as Nebraska, Nevada, and Ohio did not employ any school social workers to serve children with disabilities in 1988–89 (U.S. Department of Education, 1991).

SCHOOL PERSONNEL

Generally, the funding source determines who a district may place on its payroll and how, as well as the specific level of mandated services (Allen-Meares et al., 1986). The funded positions, however, must be consistent with a state's certification requirements. For this reason, staffing patterns may vary on the basis of the funding requirements in a district, but some personnel are common across all school systems.

Principals

School principals are core personnel in all districts: "Principals function at the intersection between policies and the administrative rules of the school district and the implementation of these policies and rules in their schools" (Freeman & Pennekamp, 1988a, p. 75). They also facilitate the classroom tasks of teachers by providing leadership or guidance, resources, and support. In addition, they often serve as a major source of referrals to school social workers and the locus for social workers' feedback on the resolution of problems (Freeman, 1991). In this process, school social workers use consultation to help principals enhance their managerial skills and understand the environmental and family conditions that affect the functioning of students, their parents, and personnel (Sabatino, Timberlake, & Hooper, 1991).

Classroom Teachers
Teachers and school social workers must also work collaboratively, and school social workers provide frequent consultation services to teachers. The primary focus of teachers' professional education is on content and instruction, although there has been a gradual shift to include interpersonal and social issues. Thus, teachers have been educated to believe that the main indicators of successful teaching are that most students learn appropriately and are well behaved. School social workers use consultation to help teachers learn how to adjust their expectations and methods to the needs of individual children and at-risk children, whether they teach special or regular education classes.

Support Personnel
In addition to principals and classroom teachers, the pupil personnel team usually consists of support staff: school social workers, counselors, psychologists, nurses, and specialized itinerant teaching staff and professionals in fields like speech and hearing or physical therapy. Some of these personnel are based in a particular school, whereas others typically spend a designated period in several different schools each week.

These teams are also known by the following titles: student study team, building screening team, child study team, crisis team, or high-risk team. They usually receive referrals from classroom teachers, principals, students, or parents and often facilitate the resolution of problems by developing and implementing the Individualized Family Service Plan. In other situations, the teams are expected to address crisis situations and the primary needs of high-risk students through preventive services. In addition, they may coordinate all services provided within and outside the schools through case management strategies.

Relationships with Personnel outside the School
The school social worker usually coordinates services with personnel from community organizations. Formal coordination of services may involve outposting the school social worker to a community agency for a specified period each week, assigning personnel or services from community agencies to the school site, or joint programming. Joint programming is the most complex personnel pattern (Freeman & Pennekamp, 1988a), yet it can yield the most effective and efficient use of resources because it involves the joint funding, planning, and implementation of services. Community professionals involved in formal coordination strategies include those from child welfare, mental health, juvenile justice, and vocational agencies (Brier, 1986; Freeman, Goldberg, & Sonnega, 1983).

MAJOR PRACTICE SETTINGS
Some school social workers are hired by consortia or educational cooperatives that serve several small districts, but many others are hired directly by a particular school district. Generally, most school practice takes place in public and private schools. For instance, Nelson's (1990) study of 862 NASW members who were school social workers found that 90 percent of the respondents worked in public school systems, 4 percent worked in non-public school systems, 2 percent worked in social services agencies, and 5 percent worked in "other" service sites.

This "other" category may include school practitioners who were outposted or who worked in related community settings such as specialized preschool programs, residential treatment centers for emotionally disturbed children, children's hospitals, and inpatient mental health centers with on-site educational services (Brier, 1986; Freeman et al., 1983; Gerlock, 1986). Although the primary services of these community agencies are not school-related, the school social workers are often expected to coordinate the services with the educational component. Thus, their role in these settings is similar to the one assumed by school social workers in public and private schools (Freeman & Pennekamp, 1988a).

ORGANIZATION OF SCHOOL SOCIAL WORK SERVICES
In spite of the varied sites where school social work is practiced, the services provided are typically organized in a similar manner. Currently, school social work practice tends to emphasize services that address students' educational needs in regular and special education classes and services that address other problems in adjustment that interfere with students' achievement in school. Examples of services in the first category include social assessments for evaluating the special education needs of students, participation in meetings to develop Individualized Education Plans, and implementation of due-process provisions (Alderson et al., 1990). Family counseling for

chemical dependence, a support group for bereaved students, and in-service education for teachers on cultural diversity and child abuse are examples of services in the second category (Schilling, Koh, Abramovitz, & Gilbert, 1992; Schwartz, 1988; Wykle, 1986).

The proliferation of services and diverse, often conflicting, funding requirements have contributed to the increasing fragmentation of services within and outside schools (Freeman & Pennekamp, 1988a). This fragmentation has resulted in a third way of organizing school social work services: integrating services through collaborative efforts between schools and public and private agencies in the community (Grande & Gambino, 1986; Newton-Logsdon & Armstrong, 1993; Whittaker et al., 1987). Examples of this movement include Cities in Schools, the District Service Center concept, and school-linked models of service. All these approaches have a common component: They promote comprehensive health and social services in schools through institutionalized cooperative agreements between schools and community agencies. The school social worker often serves as the vital coordinating link among these services, although in some situations this role is assumed by other human services professionals or school personnel.

PRACTICE ISSUES

Student and Family Demographics

School social work services are designed to provide early, optimal access to students who require such services. Therefore, social workers must be knowledgeable about student and family demographics and related environmental conditions that affect students' performance in school and the quality of life of students' families and communities.

In 1989, more than 59 million school-age children attended public and private schools in this country. By the year 2002, it is projected that the enrollment will be over 69 million (see Table 2). The majority of school-age children are ages 7 to 13 (U.S. Bureau of the Census, 1992).

Among 66 million families in the United States in 1991, 2.9 million were male-headed single-parent families, 11.2 million were female-headed single-parent families, and the remaining 51.9 million were two-parent families. The divorce rate rose from 3.5 per 1,000 in 1970 to 4.7 in 1988, with some sharp fluctuations in between. The unemployment rate averaged 6.6 percent per month during 1991, the highest rate since 1987 (U.S. Bureau of the Census, 1992). Increases in the numbers of school-age children and worsening social condi-

TABLE 2
U.S. School Enrollment Statistics (in thousands)

Year	Public Schools	Private Schools	Total
1983	48,935	8,497	57,432
1984	48,685	8,465	57,150
1985	48,901	8,325	57,226
1986	49,467	8,242	57,709
1987	49,980	8,272	58,252
1988	50,350	8,136	58,486
1989	51,041	8,298	59,339
1990 (estimated)	51,767	8,165	59,932
2000 (projected)	58,759	9,339	68,098
2002 (projected)	59,546	9,480	69,026

SOURCE: Extracted from the U.S. Bureau of the Census. (1992). *Statistical abstract of the United States, 1992* (112th ed., Table 210, p. 138). Washington, DC: U.S. Government Printing Office.

tions have made it likely that a growing number of these children and their families will need the services of school social workers.

Scope of Services

School practitioners use their roles and skills in the following range of services: direct practice, consultation, systems change, information and referral, collaboration, and evaluation of these services (Nelson, 1990). Furthermore, they may combine particular roles. For example, while collaborating with other members of the interdisciplinary team during meetings, they may offer consultation services as needed (Zischka & Fox, 1985). Direct practice roles in group or family counseling (facilitator or educator), based on the Individualized Family Service Plan, may lead to systems-change roles when it becomes apparent that target groups of students need similar services (Allen-Meares, 1990) or when school policies are identified as barriers to achievement in school (advocate or policy-impact analyst) (Germain, 1988). To determine whether certain environmental factors in the home, school, or community may require the adoption of a systems-change role, the practitioner must be skilled in evaluating the outcomes of intervention (Freeman & Pennekamp, 1988b).

RECENT TRENDS

Many problems and issues that affect the performance of students offer excellent opportunities for preventive intervention by school social workers. Some of these problems include the abuse of alcohol and other drugs (Priddy, 1990; Schwartz, 1988), child abuse (Darmstandt, 1990; Wodarski, Kurtz, Gaudin, & Howing, 1990), dropping out of school (Frank, 1990), teenage pregnancy (Freeman, 1988; Winter & Doty, 1985), loss and grief (Cole, 1987; Freeman, 1984), and homelessness (Fox et al., 1990). School social workers can help students normalize conditions that lead to or exacerbate such problems and prevent or resolve them. Other trends in practice include school health clinics, multicultural education, AIDS education, and sex and family life education.

Issues of Diversity

Students whose racial, ethnic, or religious backgrounds (especially African American, Asian American, Hispanic, Islamic, Jewish, or Native American students) place them at high risk for discrimination or whose culture and values may be negated by the learning process should be given priority by school social workers (Colca, Lewen, Colco, & Lord, 1982). Students of all racial, ethnic, and religious groups who live in poverty and those who are homeless may also require special services.

School social workers may provide mental health services in classrooms to all students to increase their understanding and appreciation of cultural and other differences and may provide similar services to teachers and administrators. Strategies that involve students in addressing conflicts and issues of diversity are yet another method that school social workers use to improve the climate of schools (McGary, 1991). These strategies include advocacy for students and their families who are discriminated against, for example, when culturally biased tests mislabel students who do not require special education placements or when appropriate resources such as cultural role models or practitioners are not present in a school for support, counseling, and problem solving (Brown, 1991).

Special Populations

Students with developmental disabilities and other exceptionalities, such as emotional disorders, are another important group with special needs. Facilitating early assessment and planning for the range of special education services in the least restrictive environment and assessing how the home and community environments affect students' school performance are two ways that school social workers serve these students (Alderson et al., 1990). Services may also include helping mainstream these students into regular classes and school activities and providing services to increase their self-esteem and social skills when

needed (Lee & Lee, 1989; Moroz, 1989; Raines, 1989).

RESEARCH ON SCHOOL SOCIAL WORK PRACTICE

Research applicable to school social work is needed to expand the knowledge base and skills of practitioners. Research has been applied to school social work to clarify the nature of practice, strategies for effective practice, and evaluation criteria and methods for documenting the accountability of school social work.

Nature of Practice

A number of important studies have been conducted to clarify the key roles, knowledge, tasks, and skills of school social workers. This type of research has been used to develop standards, criteria for certification, job descriptions, and qualifying examinations for school social workers (Sabatino, Timberlake, & Hooper, 1991). For example, Costin (1969) conducted the first national study on school social work tasks that also provided data on trends in practice. She found that the primary focus was on casework with individual children and that practitioners were ignoring key roles at the macro level such as leadership and policy making. Alderson and Krishef's (1973) partial replication of this seminal study indicated that school social workers in Florida were by then assuming leadership roles more frequently and using casework with individual children less frequently.

Allen-Meares's (1977) later replication of Costin's study revealed that the focus of individual counseling sessions with children and their families had shifted from emotional and intrapsychic issues to educational issues. Timberlake, Sabatino, and Hooper (1982) documented that school social workers were more frequently involved in consultation, short-term counseling, and assessment of students for special education placements because of the Education for All Handicapped Children Act. Similarly, Allen-Meares's (1987) study on educational reform determined that school social workers identified work with families, consultation, collaboration with community agencies, and interdisciplinary teamwork and assessment as their most important tasks.

In 1989–90, a more elaborate national job-analysis study was conducted, jointly sponsored by NASW and the Educational Testing Service (Nelson, 1990). This study was a replication of Allen-Meares's (1977) study. The purpose of the study was to develop certification criteria for school social workers by determining the important job responsibilities and areas of knowledge required at the entry level. The findings were expected to clarify the appropriate content for a national examination that could be used to credential beginning school practitioners. The sample of 2,257 school social workers was randomly selected from a pool of 11,285; 862 completed the mailed questionnaires (a 38 percent return rate).

The study found that the eight knowledge areas, skills, and abilities and the five job dimensions (tasks) shown in Table 3 are the most important requirements for entry-level school social workers. With regard to the dimensions of the job, leadership and policy making are addressed to some extent only in item 5—interagency collaboration, prevention, and advocacy. As Nelson (1990) observed, most of the knowledge areas, skills, and abilities are at the analytical level of cognition:

This strongly suggests that much of the knowledge required by school social workers goes beyond factual and concrete knowledge of laws, rules, and procedures. It appears that many of the knowledge areas require a clear understanding of how to break down communications, material, and processes, and the ability to express and clarify ideas and processes. (pp. 15–16)

TABLE 3
Most Important Knowledge Areas, Skills, Abilities (KSAs) and Job Dimensions for Entry-Level School Social Workers

KSAs, Listed in Order of Importance by School Social Workers (N = 862)

1. Social work ethics
2. Program development and management skills
3. Social work modalities and procedures
4. Theories of human behavior and development
5. Models of social work practice
6. Multidisciplinary activities
7. Characteristics of pupil populations
8. Public education legislation, case law, and due process

Job Dimensions (Categories of Tasks to Which KSAs Are Applied) in Order of Importance, Frequency, and Task Status

1. Relationship and services to children and families
2. Relationship and services to teachers and school staff
3. Services to other school personnel
4. Administrative and professional tasks
5. Interagency collaboration, prevention, and advocacy

SOURCE: Nelson, C. (1990). *A job analysis of school social workers.* Princeton, NJ: Educational Testing Service.

Strategies for Effective Practice

The second type of research applied to school social work documents the "best practices." Practitioners in schools have used this type of outcome research to demonstrate the effectiveness of a particular service or the relative effectiveness of alternative approaches. At a more sophisticated level, the research has been used to test new theoretically based models and programs (the latter documents how school social workers practice, in contrast to what they practice) (Weatherley, 1991). Generally, this type of research focuses on specific problem areas or populations of children and youths.

For example, research on services to high-risk youths indicates that a cognitive–behavioral prevention model is more effective when it involves psychological inoculation strategies (exposure to small doses of a problem behavior to increase resistance), pressure resistance training (ways to handle peer and media pressures), and skills interventions (teaching a broader array of skills). The effectiveness of this model is stronger in preventing a range of problems if students, their parents, and members of the community are included in the services (Schinke, Orlandi, Forgey, Rugg, & Douglas, 1992). Similar theoretical models have been used successfully in preventing such problems as infection with HIV and other sexually transmitted diseases (Green & Washington, 1991); substance abuse (Botvin, 1986; Rundall & Bruvold, 1988); dysfunctional stress (Schinke, Schilling, & Snow, 1987); and early pregnancy (Schinke, 1984).

Tests of other theoretically based practice models have been applied with equal effectiveness to school social work practice. For instance, Reid, Epstein, Brown, Tolson, and Rooney (1980) found that the use of a more detailed task-centered approach (a task-implementation sequence) was more effective in reducing school-behavior problems than was a general task-centered approach. Franklin and Streeter (1991) compared a guided group interaction model with a psychoeducational model for alternative school students from middle-income families to reduce school dropout rates. The former model focused on problem solving, feedback, support, and mutual aid, whereas the latter involved education about drugs, communication skills, social skills, problem solving, and the control of anger. The two models demonstrated similar outcomes in academic achievement: Overall, 78 percent of the dropouts showed progress; for example, they returned to traditional school, passed the test for the general equivalency diploma, or obtained a high school diploma. The psychoeducational (or positive-peer-culture) model resulted in significant increases in students' self-esteem and decreases in anxiety, and the other model led to significant decreases in the level of students' depression or potential for suicide.

Schilling et al.'s (1992) study is an example of research used by school social workers to test service delivery patterns or single strategies (rather than fully developed practice models). Its findings have implications for how school social workers can help children handle the effects of increasing violence in their communities. The 14-week group intervention involving artwork helped six- to 12-year-old Hispanic, white, and African American children who had lost a caretaker to homicide, suicide, or chronic illness, including acquired immune deficiency syndrome (AIDS), to acknowledge their loss, express their feelings, and learn factual information about death. Other examples that have tested single strategies in a group modality have effectively improved students' achievement, social skills, and problem-solving abilities (Balsanek, 1986; DeAnda, 1985; Rose, 1986).

Evaluation Criteria and Accountability Research

Evaluation criteria and accountability research has been used to establish the need for initial or additional school social work staff and related resources, to improve the relative status of school social workers compared to other school personnel, and to forestall the implementation of an undesirable policy related to the delivery of services or the deployment of school social work staff (Weatherley, 1991). Both epidemiological and action research are used for these purposes.

Epidemiological studies on the number and characteristics of certain populations are used to show that children in these families need the services provided by school social workers. For example, epidemiological studies have documented that the problems of homeless children include developmental delays and learning difficulties (Fox, Barrnett, Davies, & Bird, 1990); severe depression and anxiety (Bassuk & Rubin, 1987); inadequate health care (Miller & Lin, 1988); and an increased risk of child abuse (Wood, Valdez, Hayashi, & Shen, 1990).

Action research is an aid in decision making in school social work because of its process orientation (Flynn, 1991) and its emphasis on practical problems and innovations (Patton, 1980). For instance, action research has been used to document the types of students served and the services provided, along with feedback about their satisfaction with the services (Weatherley, 1991). It has also documented the impact of certain policies, such as suspension and expulsion policies on students, families, and school personnel (policy-impact analysis). Such data have been useful to educational administrators and school social work supervisors in improving programs and in documenting the usefulness of school social workers' data-gathering efforts in the process (Bramschreiber & Flieder, 1992).

Certain methods have been found to apply more readily than have others to the evaluation of school social work services. For example, Allen-Meares and Lane (1990) concluded that the use of qualitative evaluation methods is consistent with the ecological perspective of school social workers because these methods provide a view of the social world "as a highly complex, dynamic reality consisting of multiple layers of meanings and perspectives that are strongly influenced by the interaction between the environmental context and the subjective interpretations of situational actors" (p. 454).

A combination of qualitative and quantitative methods may be the most useful. Qualitative methods used to evaluate the work of school social workers include direct observations in a variety of school practice situations (such as counseling sessions with individual students, peer groups, or parent education services); the results of self-anchored and rating scales, self-monitoring reports, or clients' logs in various cases; tape recordings of qualitative interviews or focus groups; and changes in clients that are documented with archival records (attendance, achievement, or health records) (Allen-Meares & Lane, 1990; Freeman & Pennekamp, 1988a).

Other important criteria for evaluating the performance of school social workers include self-assessment by school social workers; feedback from the children and families served; the involvement of school administrators, such as principals, in the evaluation process; scheduled follow-ups on the results of evaluations; clarity about the purpose of evaluations; and the use of multiple sources of "natural" data (Bramschreiber & Flieder, 1992).

NASW STANDARDS AND POLICY STATEMENTS

In addition to the *NASW Code of Ethics* (1994e), which all social workers follow, school social workers adhere to relevant standards, especially the *NASW Standards for School Social Work Services* (NASW, 1992) and the *NASW Standards for the Practice of Social Work with Adolescents* (NASW, 1993). The standards for school social work services are particularly useful to practitioners because they are organized into standards of competence–practice, professional development, and administrative structure–support. In addition, the majority of school social workers must meet the requirements for certification or licensure at the state level (Nelson, 1990), often on the basis of the NASW licensure model.

NASW has also adopted a number of important policy statements that provide guidelines to school and community practitioners on needed services and policies. The most relevant policy statements for school social workers are "Adolescent Pregnancy" (NASW, 1994a), "Children and Youths: A Bill of Rights" (NASW, 1994b), "Early Childhood Care and Education" (NASW, 1994c), "Juvenile Justice and Delinquency Prevention" (1994d), and "People with Disabilities" (NASW, 1994f).

CONCLUSION

School social work is a field of practice that provides vital services to enhance the primary mission of the educational system and identifies target groups of students and families that require preventive interventions to improve students' performance in school. The traditional role of education has changed; its mission cannot be carried out in isolation from the social and economic changes that are occurring in the larger environment. The roles of school social workers have also changed. Practitioners now emphasize services to students in both special and regular education; strategies that change all interacting systems, as well as the transactions among them; school-based services and case management of community services; and both prevention and rehabilitation.

REFERENCES

Alderson, J., & Krishef, C. (1973). Another perspective on tasks in school social work. *Social Casework, 54,* 591–600.

Alderson, J., Krishef, C., & Spencer, B. (1990). School social workers' role in implementation of the Education for All Handicapped Children Act. *Social Work in Education, 12,* 221–236.

Allen-Meares, P. (1977). Analysis of tasks in school social work. *Social Work, 22,* 196–201.

Allen-Meares, P. (1987). A national study of educational reform: Implications for social work services in schools. *Children and Youth Services Review, 9,* 207–219.

Allen-Meares, P. (1988). Contribution of social workers to schooling. *Urban Education, 22,* 410–412.

Allen-Meares, P. (1990). Elementary and Secondary School Improvement Amendments of 1988. *Social Work in Education, 12,* 249–260.

Allen-Meares, P., & Lane, B. (1990). Social work practice: Integrating qualitative and quantitative data collection. *Social Work, 35,* 452–458.

Allen-Meares, P., Washington, R. O., & Welsh, B. I. (1986). *Social work services in schools.* Englewood Cliffs, NJ: Prentice Hall.

Balsanek, J. A. (1986). Group intervention for underachievers in the intermediate school. *Social Work in Education, 8,* 26–33.

Bassuk, E., & Rubin, L. (1987). Homeless children: A neglected population. *American Journal of Orthopsychiatry, 57,* 279–286.

Bensky, T., Shaw, S., Gouse, A., Bates, H., Dixon, B., & Beare, W. (1980). Public Law 94-142: Boon or bust? *Exceptional Children, 14,* 24–29.

Bishop, K. K. (1991). The early childhood amendments (P.L. 99-457) and their implementation. In R. T. Constable, J. P. Flynn, & S. McDonald (Eds.), *School social work: Practice and research perspectives* (2nd ed., pp. 127–141). Chicago: Lyceum.

Botvin, G. J. (1986). Substance abuse prevention research: Recent developments and future directions. *Journal of School Health, 56,* 369–386.

Bramschreiber, D., & Flieder, A. (1992). Best practices in evaluating school social work programs. In J. P. Clark (Ed.), *Best practices in the supervision of school social work programs* (pp. 33–44). Des Moines: State of Iowa Department of Education.

Brier, M. S. (1986). From hospital or home to school: A team approach. In M. T. Hawkins (Ed.), *Achieving educational excellence for children at risk* (pp. 56–68). Silver Spring, MD: National Association of Social Workers.

Brown, L. B. (1991). An empirical and ethnic-sensitive approach to school social work practice. In R. T. Constable, J. P. Flynn, & S. McDonald (Eds.), *School social work: Practice and research perspectives* (2nd ed., pp. 50–61). Chicago: Lyceum.

Children's Defense Fund. (1986). *Preventing children having children.* Washington, DC: Author.

Colca, C., Lowen, D., Colco, L. A., & Lord, S. A. (1982). Combating racism in the schools: A group work pilot project. *Social Work in Education, 4,* 5–16.

Cole, B. (1987). Saying good-bye: An elementary school prepares for the death of a student. *Social Work in Education, 9,* 117–123.

Committee for Economic Development. (1987). *Children in need: Investment strategies for the educationally disadvantaged.* New York: Author.

Costin, L. B. (1969). An analysis of the tasks in school social work. *Social Service Review, 43,* 274–285.

Costin, L. B. (1987). School social work. In A. Minahan (Ed.-in-Chief), *Encyclopedia of social work* (18th ed., Vol. 2, pp. 538–545). Silver Spring, MD: National Association of Social Workers.

Darmstadt, G. L. (1990). Community-based child abuse prevention. *Social Work, 35,* 487–489.

DeAnda, D. (1985). Structured vs. nonstructured groups in the teaching of problem solving. *Social Work in Education, 7,* 80–89.

Education for All Handicapped Children Act of 1975. P.L. 94-142, 89 Stat. 773.

Education of the Handicapped Act Amendments of 1986. P.L. 99-457, 100 Stat. 1145.

Education of the Handicapped Act Amendments of 1990. P.L. 101-476, 104 Stat. 1103.

Flynn, J. P. (1991). Participatory change through research and evaluation. In R. T. Constable, J. P. Flynn, & S. McDonald (Eds.), *School social work: Practice and research perspectives* (pp. 355–367). Chicago: Lyceum.

Fox, S. J., Barrnett, R. J., Davies, M., & Bird, H. R. (1990). Psychopathology and developmental delay in homeless children: A pilot study. *Journal of the American Academy of Child and Adolescent Psychiatry, 29,* 732–735.

Frank, J. (1990). High school dropout. *Social Work, 35,* 34–47.

Franklin, C., & Streeter, C. (1991). Evidence for the effectiveness of social work with high school dropout youths. *Social Work in Education, 13,* 307–327.

Freeman, E. M. (1984). Loss and grief in children: Implications for school social workers. *Social Work in Education, 6,* 241–258.

Freeman, E. M. (1988). Teenage fathers and the problem of teenage pregnancy. *Social Work in Education, 10,* 36–52.

Freeman, E. M. (1991). Analyzing the organizational context of the schools. In R. T. Constable, J. P. Flynn, & S. McDonald (Eds.), *School social work: Practice and research perspectives* (pp. 311–326). Chicago: Lyceum.

Freeman, E. M., & Pennekamp, M. (1988a). Preface. In *Social work practice: Toward a child, family, school, community perspective* (pp. xiii–xvi). Springfield, IL: Charles C Thomas.

Freeman, E. M., & Pennekamp, M. (1988b). Program planning along the life continuum: Regularities, transitions, crises, and conditions of chronicity. In *Social work practice: Toward a child, family, school, community perspective* (pp. 186–207). Springfield, IL: Charles C Thomas.

Freeman, G., Goldberg, G., & Sonnega, J. (1983). Cooperation between public schools and mental health agencies. *Social Work in Education, 5,* 178–187.

Gailey, J. A. (1989). An essay on childhood and learning. *Social Work in Education, 11,* 122–139.

Gerlock, E. F. (1986). Children with handicaps: Transition from preschool to school programs. In M. T. Hawkins (Ed.), *Achieving educational excellence for children at risk* (pp. 20–32). Silver Spring, MD: National Association of Social Workers.

Germain, C. B. (1988). School as a living environment within the community. *Social Work in Education, 10,* 260–276.

Grand, G., & Gambino, A. (1986). Parent–child centers: A preventive service in a multicultural community. In M. T. Hawkins (Ed.), *Achieving educational excellence for children at risk* (pp. 138–148). Silver Spring, MD: National Association of Social Workers.

Green, S. B., & Washington, A. E. (1991). Evaluation of behavioral interventions for prevention and control of sexually transmitted diseases. In J. N. Wasserheit, S. O. Aral, K. K. Holmes, & P. J. Hitchcock (Eds.), *Research issues in human behavior and sexually transmitted diseases in the AIDS era* (pp. 345–352). Washington, DC: American Society for Microbiology.

Hawkins-Stafford Elementary and Secondary Improvements Amendments of 1988. P.L. 100-297, 102 Stat. 140.

Lee, B., & Lee, S. (1989). Group therapy as a process to strengthen the independence of students with mental retardation. *Social Work in Education, 11,* 123–132.

McGary, R. (1991). Student forums: Addressing racial conflict in a high school. In R. T. Constable, J. P. Flynn, & S. McDonald (Eds.), *School social work: Practice and research perspectives* (2nd ed., pp. 273–280). Chicago: Lyceum.

McLaughlin, J. A., & Protinsky, R. A. (1991). Foundations for values in special education. In R. T. Constable, J. P. Flynn, & S. McDonald (Eds.), *School social work: Practice and research perspectives* (2nd ed., pp. 107–114). Chicago: Lyceum.

Miller, D. S., & Lin, E.H.B. (1988). Children in sheltered homeless families: Reported health status and use of health services. *Pediatrics, 81,* 668–673.

Mintzies, P., & Hare, I. (1985). *The human factor: A key to excellence in education.* Silver Spring, MD: National Association of Social Workers.

Monkman, M. M. (1991). The characteristic focus of the social worker in public schools. In R. T. Constable, J. P. Flynn, & S. McDonald (Eds.), *School social work: Practice and research perspectives* (2nd ed., pp. 30–49). Chicago: Lyceum.

Moroz, K. J. (1989). Educating autistic children and youths: A school–family–community partnership. *Social Work in Education, 11,* 107–122.

National Association of Social Workers. (1992). *NASW standards for school social work services.* Washington, DC: Author.

National Association of Social Workers. (1993). *NASW standards for the practice of social work with adolescents.* Washington, DC: Author.

National Association of Social Workers. (1994a). Adolescent pregnancy. In *Social work speaks: NASW policy statements* (3rd ed., pp. 8–11). Washington, DC: NASW Press.

National Association of Social Workers. (1994b). Children and youths: A bill of rights. In *Social work speaks: NASW policy statements* (3rd ed., pp. 46–48). Washington, DC: NASW Press.

National Association of Social Workers. (1994c). Early childhood care and education. In *Social work speaks: NASW policy statements* (3rd ed., pp. 88–90). Washington, DC: NASW Press.

National Association of Social Workers. (1994d). Juvenile justice and delinquency prevention. In *Social work speaks: NASW policy statements* (3rd ed., pp. 156–161). Washington, DC: NASW Press.

National Association of Social Workers. (1994e). *NASW code of ethics.* Washington, DC: Author.

National Association of Social Workers. (1994f). People with disabilities. In *Social work speaks: NASW policy statements* (3rd ed., pp. 206–210). Washington, DC: NASW Press.

Nelson, C. (1990). *A job analysis of school social workers.* Princeton, NJ: Educational Testing Service.

Newton-Logsdon, G., & Armstrong, M. I. (1993). School-based mental health services. *Social Work in Education, 15,* 187–191.

Patton, M. Q. (1980). *Qualitative evaluation methods.* Beverly Hills, CA: Sage Publications.

Pennekamp, M., & Freeman, E. M. (1988). Toward a partnership perspective: Schools, families, and school social workers. *Social Work in Education, 10,* 246–259.

Priddy, D. (1990). A social worker's agency: Working with children affected by crack/cocaine. *Social Work, 35,* 197–199.

Radin, N. (1989). School social work practice: Past, present, and future trends. *Social Work in Education, 11,* 213–225.

Raines, J. C. (1989). Social work practice with learning disabled children. *Social Work in Education, 11,* 89–105.

Reid, W. J., Epstein, L., Brown, L. B., Tolson, E., & Rooney, R. H. (1980). Task centered school social work. *Social Work in Education, 2,* 7–24.

Rose, S. R. (1986). Enhancing the social relationship skills of children: A comparative study of group approaches. *School Social Work Journal, 10,* 76–85.

Rundall, T. G., & Bruvold, W. H. (1988). A meta-analysis of school-based smoking and alcohol use prevention programs. *Health Education Quarterly, 15,* 317–334.

Sabatino, C. A., Timberlake, E., & Hooper, S. (1991). School social consultation: Theory, practice, and research. In R. T. Constable, J. P. Flynn, & S. McDonald (Eds.), *School social work: Practice and research perspectives* (2nd ed., pp. 257–272). Chicago: Lyceum.

Sarri, R. C., & Maple, F. (1972). *The school in the community.* Washington, DC: National Association of Social Workers.

Schilling, R. F., Koh, N., Abramovitz, R., & Gilbert, L. (1992). Bereavement groups for inner-city children. *Research on Social Work Practice, 2,* 405–419.

Schinke, S. P. (1984). Preventing teenage pregnancy. In M. Hersen, R. M. Eisler, & P. M. Miller (Eds.), *Progress in behavior modification* (Vol. 16, pp. 31–63). New York: Academic Press.

Schinke, S. P., Orlandi, M. A., Forgey, M. A., Rugg, D. L., & Douglas, K. A. (1992). Multicomponent, school-based strategies to prevent HIV infection and sexually transmitted diseases among adolescents: Theory and research into practice. *Research on Social Work Practice, 2,* 364–379.

Schinke, S. P., Schilling, R. F., & Snow, W. H. (1987). Stress management with adolescents at the junior high school transition: An outcome evaluation of coping skills. *Journal of Human Stress, 13,* 16–22.

Schwartz, S. (1988). School-based strategies for primary prevention of drug abuse. *Social Work in Education, 10,* 53–63.

Timberlake, E., Sabatino, C., & Hooper, S. (1982). School social work practice and P.L. 94-142. In R. T. Constable & J. P. Flynn (Eds.), *School social work: Practice and research perspectives* (pp. 49–71). Homewood, IL: Dorsey Press.

U.S. Bureau of the Census. (1992). *Statistical abstract of the United States, 1992* (112th ed.). Washington, DC: U.S. Government Printing Office.

U.S. Department of Education. (1991). *Thirteenth annual report to Congress on the implementation of the Individuals with Disabilities Education Act.* Washington, DC: U.S. Government Printing Office.

Weatherley, R. (1991). Practical approaches to conducting and using research in the schools. In R. T. Constable, J. P. Flynn, & S. McDonald (Eds.), *School social work: Practice and research perspectives* (2nd ed., pp. 368–379). Chicago: Lyceum.

Whittaker, J. K., Schinke, S. P., & Gilchrist, L. D. (1987). The ecological paradigm in child, youth, and family services: Implications for policy and practice. *Social Service Review, 61,* 355–370.

Whitted, B. R. (1991). Social work and the special education system: Overview of recent cases affecting professional decisions. In R. T. Constable, J. P. Flynn, & S. McDonald (Eds.), *School social work: Practice and research perspectives* (2nd ed., pp. 142–155). Chicago: Lyceum.

Winter, M. B., & Doty, M. K. (1985). Pregnancy prevention: A private agency's program in public schools. *Social Work in Education, 7,* 90–99.

Winters, W. G., & Easton, F. (1983). *The practice of social work in schools.* New York: Free Press.

Winters, W. G., & Maluccio, A. (1988). School, family, and community: Working together to promote social competence. *Social Work in Education, 10,* 207–217.

Wodarski, J. S., Kurtz, P. D., Gaudin, J. M., Jr., & Howing, P. T. (1990). Maltreatment and the school-age child: Major academic, socioemotional, and adaptive outcomes. *Social Work, 35,* 506–513.

Wood, D., Valdez, B., Hayashi, T., & Shen, A. (1990). Homeless and housed families in Los Angeles: A study comparing demographic, economic, and family function characteristics. *American Journal of Public Health, 80,* 1049–1052.

Wkyle, G. T. (1986). Integration is not enough. In M. T. Hawkins (Ed.), *Achieving educational excellence for children at risk* (pp. 149–160). Silver Spring, MD: National Association of Social Workers.

Zischka, P. C., & Fox, R. (1985). Consultation as a function of school social work. *Social Work in Education, 7,* 69–79.

Edith M. Freeman, PhD, ACSW, is editor of *Social Work in Education* and professor, University of Kansas, School of Social Welfare, Twente Hall, Lawrence, KS 66045.

For further information see

Adolescence Overview; Child Abuse and Neglect Overview; Child Foster Care; Childhood; Children: Mental Health; Developmental Disabilities: Definitions and Policies; Developmental Disabilities: Direct Practice; Families Overview; Families: Demographic Shifts; Family Therapy; Human Development; Interdisciplinary and Interorganizational Collaboration; Natural Helping Networks; Primary Prevention Overview; School-Based Services; Youth Services.

Key Words

adolescence
child welfare

school social work

School-Linked Services

Isadora Hare

The term "school-linked services" refers to an innovative system of delivering services in which community agencies and schools collaborate to provide a variety of health and social services to children and their families at or near school sites. When the services are located in the school building, the term "school-based" is sometimes used (Dryfoos, 1994); however, because this term may refer to the sponsorship of the service, to the employing agency of the staff who are involved, or to the location of the site at which services are delivered, the term "school-linked" is preferable. This type of service is one example of a recently developing paradigm, characterized by the integration of services by schools, public and private social services and health and mental health agencies, and the juvenile justice system. At times, businesses and foundations are also involved in funding and delivering the services. According to Kirst (1993), school-linked services are an "interagency system linking schools and local and private human service agencies with the support of business, higher education, and other community resources to meet the inter-related educational, social and psychological needs of children" (p. 11). He adds that this linkage of services empowers parents to better consume public and private services.

ORIGINS

The emergence of school-linked services was stimulated by the growing concern for the rising rates of child poverty (Johnson, Miranda, Sherman, & Weill, 1991), and other social problems, such as child abuse, homelessness, and teenage pregnancy (Schorr, 1988). Specifically, these services are derived from two separate but related movements: one from social services and the other from the educational reform movement of the mid-1980s.

Integration of services. This movement has been defined as the "systematic effort to solve problems of service fragmentation and of the lack of an exact match between an individual or family with problems and needs, and an interventive program or professional specialty" (Kahn & Kamerman, 1992, p. 5). The term "services integration" was promoted in the early 1970s by then-Secretary of the U.S. Department of Health, Education, and Welfare Elliot Richardson, but its roots go back to the late 19th century, when social work was born in Charity Organization Societies and settlement houses. In the late 1980s, the concept reemerged to counter the categorical nature, fragmentation, inaccessibility, and inadequacy of the numerous resources and services required by families with low income and multiple needs (Morrill, 1993; National Commission on Children, 1991).

School reform movement. Stimulated by the publication of *A Nation at Risk* (National Commission on Excellence in Education, 1983), this movement soon acknowledged that many nonacademic factors influenced students' ability to achieve in school (Behrman, 1992). By the mid-1980s, NASW (Mintzies & Hare, 1985); the Children's Defense Fund; and organizations, such as the Council of Chief State School Officers (CCSSO), focused on the needs of students who were at risk of failing in school because of social, economic, family, and personal factors that were barriers to the students' optimal performance in school. By 1987, CCSSO and other educational organizations, as well as public policymakers and corporate leaders, were advocating for the integration of health and social services into schools to improve educational outcomes for vulnerable students. The National Education Goals, first formulated in 1989 (National Education Goals Panel, 1991) and written into law in 1994, address this issue (Goals 2000: Educate America Act, P.L. 103-227). Four of the eight goals—readiness for school; the reduction of school dropout rates; safe, drug-free, and disciplined schools; and parental involvement—relate to nonacademic factors that influence educational outcomes. Collaboration between schools and communities is necessary to achieve these goals. Underlying the goals is the need to improve the quality of the U.S. work force, so the country can remain competitive in the emerging global economy.

GOALS AND ATTRIBUTES OF SUCCESSFUL PROGRAMS

Goals

The leaders of the services integration movement propound the development of a new paradigm of service delivery whose principal goals would include the following:

- To improve the efficiency of programs by reducing waste and duplication through the greater coordination of categorical services.
- To improve legal access to comprehensive services by modifying the rigid and exclusionary nature of the current categorical system. This change would involve modifying legislative and

regulatory requirements for eligibility through such mechanisms as waivers and pooling separate funding streams.

- To improve the quality and effectiveness of local services by providing a comprehensive array of services to meet the needs of families and children in a holistic and coordinated manner. Generally, a case manager is a key element in such a plan, as are a single point of intake, case conferences, and home visits (Ooms & Owens, 1991). Often, these programs provide a range of services in one easily accessible location—hence, the importance of the school as the site of service delivery.

Collaboration at the community level is critical, both in planning and implementing programs. Collaboration differs from cooperation. Whereas partners in an initiative that uses a cooperative strategy agree to work together to meet their individual goals, those in a project that uses a collaborative strategy "establish common goals and agree to use their personal and institutional power to achieve them" (Melaville & Blank, 1991, p.15).

Attributes

In exploring programs that produced positive outcomes for troubled families and children with seemingly intractable problems, Schorr (1993) distilled the following attributes:

- being geographically and psychologically accessible
- having a simple eligibility process and minimal barriers to participation
- providing comprehensive and responsive services with collaboration among systems and professionals of various disciplines
- offering personalized responses by encouraging flexibility and discretion in frontline workers
- responding to the concerns of the neighborhood and community culture
- providing family-centered services and supports facilitated by a partnership of parents and professionals
- being mission driven and shaped by clients' needs
- fostering an unbureaucratic climate
- manifesting the motivation and capacity to solve a wide range of problems as they arise
- having a strong orientation to outcomes, rather than to inputs
- emphasizing relationships of mutual trust
- focusing on the continuous evolution of the service.

Schorr (1993, pp. 8–10) summarized these attributes as follows:

- Successful programs are comprehensive, intensive, flexible, and responsive.
- Successful programs deal with children as parts of families and with families as parts of neighborhoods and communities.
- Staff in successful programs have the time, skills, and support to build relationships of trust and respect with children and families.
- Successful programs have a long-term, preventive orientation and continue to evolve over time.

DYNAMICS OF SCHOOL-LINKED SERVICES

One of the widely disseminated publications on this topic (Melaville & Blank, 1991) identified five variables that shape interagency partnerships:

1. the social and political *climate* in the locality
2. the communication and problem-solving *processes* used to build trust and handle conflict
3. the *people* involved in leadership, sponsorship, planning, and implementation and their vision, commitment, and competence
4. the *policies* that support or inhibit efforts to form partnerships
5. the *resources* available to enable truly collaborative initiatives to become institutionalized.

Reporting two years later on the deliberations of a study group convened by the U.S. Departments of Education and Health and Human Services, Melaville and Blank (1993) presented a model of a five-stage spiral process to build profamily, integrated services at the local level using a collaborative strategy (see Figure 1). The process is depicted as a spiral that can loop back on itself to repeat stages, if necessary. As Melaville and Blank (1993, p.19) noted, "the challenge is to develop a process of working together that is flexible enough to allow adjustments to new circumstances, while staying focused on long-term goals." Conducting a community assessment of both needs and strengths is a particularly important step (Bruner, 1991; Bruner, Bell, Brindis, Chang, & Scarborough, 1993).

EXAMPLES OF SCHOOL-LINKED SERVICES

The following categories are somewhat arbitrary and not mutually exclusive. In many cases, school-linked projects operate with a blend of public and private financing from various sources.

School-Based Health Centers

Located in or near school buildings, these centers are increasingly important examples of school-linked services. Originating in school nursing ser-

FIGURE 1

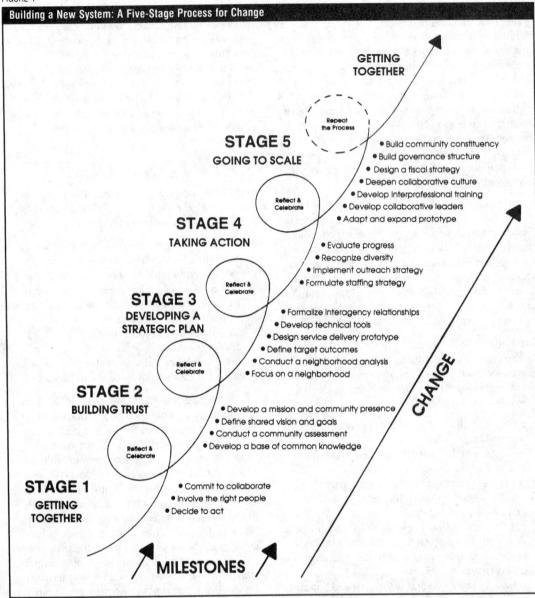

Building a New System: A Five-Stage Process for Change

GETTING
TOGETHER

Repeat
the Process

STAGE 5
GOING TO SCALE

• Build community constituency
• Build governance structure
• Design a fiscal strategy
• Deepen collaborative culture
• Develop Interprofessional training
• Develop collaborative leaders
• Adapt and expand prototype

Reflect &
Celebrate

STAGE 4
TAKING ACTION

• Evaluate progress
• Recognize diversity
• Implement outreach strategy
• Formulate staffing strategy

Reflect &
Celebrate

STAGE 3
DEVELOPING A
STRATEGIC PLAN

• Formalize interagency relationships
• Develop technical tools
• Design service delivery prototype
• Define target outcomes
• Conduct a neighborhood analysis
• Focus on a neighborhood

Reflect &
Celebrate

STAGE 2
BUILDING TRUST

• Develop a mission and community presence
• Define shared vision and goals
• Conduct a community assessment
• Develop a base of common knowledge

Reflect &
Celebrate

CHANGE

STAGE 1
GETTING
TOGETHER

• Commit to collaborate
• Involve the right people
• Decide to act

MILESTONES

SOURCE: Reprinted from Melaville, A.I., & Blank M. J., with Asayesh, G. (1993). *Together we can: A guide for crafting a profamily system of education and human services* (p. 21). Washington, DC: U.S. Government Printing Office.

vices in the early 1900s, they expanded slowly in the 1960s and 1970s.

From the late 1980s onward their number grew rapidly, from about a dozen to over 600 centers serving elementary through high school students in 42 states and Washington, DC; Puerto Rico; and Guam. Only 9 percent of the centers are sponsored by school systems; the remainder are sponsored by a variety of health institutions, such as local public health departments, federally funded community health centers, and hospitals (Advocates for Youth, 1994). The centers provide free or low-cost comprehensive health services, including medical services, counseling and mental health services, and family planning activities.

Twenty-five percent of the centers that serve middle school and high school students provide on-site contraceptive services. Although controversy has surrounded the centers' influence on teenagers' sexual behavior, support for their establishment is growing because of their accessibility and their contribution to addressing the unmet health care needs of adolescents. Furthermore, studies (Kirby, Waszak, & Ziegler, 1989; MacCord, Klein, Foy, & Fothergill, 1993) have begun to demonstrate positive health and educational outcomes.

Over 69 percent of the centers offer on-site mental health counseling on relationships, substance abuse, domestic violence, dysfunctional family systems, and family planning (Advocates for Youth, 1994). Over half the centers employ social workers, and some also use the services of school social workers (*Perspectives,* 1992; U.S. Department of Health and Human Services, 1993).

From 1987 to 1993, the Robert Wood Johnson Foundation funded centers at 23 high schools in medically underserved urban areas (Goldsmith, 1991; Robert Wood Johnson Foundation, 1993; U.S. Department of Health and Human Services, 1993). In 1993, the foundation launched a new five-year, $23.2 million program called Making the Grade. This program will fund centers in 12 states: Colorado, Connecticut, Delaware, Hawaii, Louisiana, Maryland, New York, North Carolina, Oregon, Rhode Island, Tennessee, and Vermont. Another major initiative to establish elementary school-based health centers is under way, sponsored by the National Health/Education Consortium and the Philadelphia-based Conservation Company. Furthermore, the Clinton administration is providing increased funding for centers through a variety of initiatives.

Since the late 1980s, the Centers for Disease Control and Prevention's Division of Adolescent and School Health has been vigorously promoting the concept of comprehensive school health programs to fulfill many purposes including human immunodeficiency virus and acquired immune deficiency syndrome prevention. Such programs have eight components, including counseling, psychological, and social services and parent and community involvement. The funding attached to this initiative is also used to promote the establishment of comprehensive health and social services in schools.

State-Funded Initiatives

California's Healthy Start. One of the most extensive and innovative school-linked services programs has been operating in California since 1991, when the Healthy Start Support Services for Children Act (S.B. 620) was passed. This program built on earlier California experiments with school-linked projects, such as New Beginnings at the Hamilton Elementary School in San Diego,

begun in 1988; the Focus on Youth Program, a joint venture of the Los Angeles Unified School District and the Los Angeles Education Partnership, a private-sector school-reform effort; and the Ventura County Children's Demonstration Project, established in 1984 to test the effectiveness of a community-based, culturally sensitive, interagency system of mental health services for children with severe mental disorders in four sectors, including juvenile justice, child abuse services, special education, and mental health services (Melaville & Blank, 1991; Nelson & Pearson, 1991).

S.B. 620 authorized $20 million in funding for fiscal year 1992–93 to support planning and operational grants for school-linked service sites throughout California (Carreon & Jameson, 1993). In addition, the state negotiated a public–private partnership with the Foundation Consortium for School-Linked Services whereby several foundations agreed to provide additional funds to supplement the funds provided under S.B. 620. During the first two years of implementation, $35 million was awarded to collaborative organizations of schools and community agencies for 181 planning grants and 65 operational grants. Each grantee had the freedom to select its own needs, strengths, and opportunities. For the 1993–94 grant cycle, $19 million was made available for additional grants. Evaluation is an integral part of the unfolding Healthy Start initiatives, which in time will "provide learning opportunities for many audiences" (Wagner, 1993, p. 204).

New Jersey's School-Based Youth Services Program. In 1989, the New Jersey State Department of Human Services launched the School-Based Youth Services Program in the 30 poorest school systems in the state. Called "one-stop-shopping" centers, the centers in this program link the educational and human services systems by coordinating their services at a single location. Youths aged 13 to 19 are helped to complete their education, obtain skills, and improve their physical and mental health. The patterns of service delivery vary, but all the centers must provide mental health and family counseling and health and employment services year-round during and after school and on weekends (Marzke & Both, 1994). According to Edward Tetelman (quoted in Melaville & Blank, 1993, p. 90), one of the major architects of the programs, "the idea is to wrap services around children, youth, and families that allow them to move forward and lead productive lives." Although funding for this initiative was severely curtailed by the New Jersey legislature in late 1990, the expansion continues through a process called Family Net that fosters interagency collaboration among state systems of human services, education, labor, health, corrections, the military, and veterans' affairs, as well as at the local level. The New Jersey program has been used as a model in Kentucky and Iowa.

Kentucky's integrated delivery systems. This program began in 1988 as a joint venture between the State Department of Education and the Governor's Cabinet of Human Resources, which includes the state's Departments of Social Services, Health, Mental Health and Mental Retardation, and Employment. By 1993, 134 Family and Youth Service Centers were linked to this program, providing students with comprehensive support services using an interdisciplinary approach (U.S. General Accounting Office [GAO], 1993).

Missouri's Walbridge Caring Communities. Missouri has an exemplary public–private partnership involving the collaboration among state departments of education, social services, and health and mental health; the St. Louis public schools; and the Danforth Foundation. This partnership funds the Walbridge Caring Communities project at Walbridge Elementary School, in a high-poverty community in inner-city St. Louis. The goals of the project are to keep children in school, increase their level of academic success, keep them safely in their homes and out of the juvenile justice system, and promote family preservation. The director and an interdisciplinary staff of 22 interact with the community in a wide variety of services and programs.

Other state-funded initiatives. Other state-funded initiatives include Florida's Full Service Schools (Florida Interagency Workgroup, 1991); Maryland's Family Investment Centers, based on the Family Development Center at the Lafayette Courts housing project in Baltimore; Connecticut's Family Resource Centers, modeled after the concept of Edward Zigler's Schools of the 21st Century, that provide extended day care, parent education, training for family day care providers, and services to prevent teenage pregnancy; and New York's Community Schools, begun in 1987 (Melaville & Blank, 1991). In 1994, Rhode Island announced plans to launch family centers in 20 of the state's 36 school districts (Cohen, 1994).

Foundation- and Organization-Funded Initiatives

Two foundation-funded programs are the Hogg Foundation's School of the Future project in Texas (Holtzman, 1992) and the Annie E. Casey Foundation's New Futures project. The latter allocated $5 million from 1988 to 1993 to five cities: Bridgeport, Connecticut; Dayton, Ohio; Little Rock, Arkansas; Pittsburgh, Pennsylvania; and Savannah, Georgia. Each city matched the foundation's grants in pursuit of four goals: increased school attendance by and improved academic levels of at-risk students; increased employment of youths; and reduced adolescent pregnancy and parenthood (Cohen, 1991).

In 1992, the Pew Charitable Trusts, the nation's fifth largest foundation, launched the Children's Initiative, a 10-year plan to invest $55 million to $60 million in restructuring children's services in five states. In 1994, however, Pew abandoned the project, stating that the goals could not be accomplished within the time and resources available. It is likely, however, that Georgia and Minnesota will continue to receive funds to establish school-linked family centers (Sommerfeld, 1994).

Another source of funds is national organizations, such as the Council of Chief State School Officers. This organization has produced position statements and awarded grants to states to finance school-linked integrated services (Cohen, 1989; Council of Chief State School Officers, 1991; Gerry, 1993; Joining Forces Connections, 1991; Kirst, 1993).

Federal Government Initiatives

Federal grants. Federal grants have funded several projects, including the National Center for Service Integration, which was established in 1991 with the addition of money from private foundations. The center is a collaboration among six organizations, including Mathtech, based in Princeton, New Jersey; the Child and Family Policy Center in Des Moines, Iowa; and the National Center for Children in Poverty at Columbia University, New York City, which operates the center's information clearinghouse (Chaudry, Maurer, Oshinsky, & Mackie, 1993).

Other grants from the U.S. Department of Health and Human Services and the U.S. Department of Education have provided funds for comprehensive integrated service projects that meet the goals outlined earlier. For example, a U.S. Department of Education demonstration grant funded the Linn County (Oregon) Youth Service Teams, a project school social workers designed to provide intensive case management services for students with serious emotional disturbances (U.S. GAO, 1993). Furthermore, the Office of Special Education and Rehabilitation Services of the U.S. Department of Education has selected research on school-linked services for children with disabilities as a priority for fiscal year 1994–95 (U.S. Department of Education, 1993). In 1991 the Office of the Assistant Secretary for Planning and Evaluation, U.S. Department of Health and Human Services, provided six Services Integration Facilitation Grants to diverse projects in California, Florida, Ohio, Georgia, and Washington, DC. The grant to the Institute for Educational Leadership in Washington, DC, in turn, funded projects in five different cities.

Legislation. During the 103rd Congress, a number of bills included provisions in coordinated services. Examples are the Goals 2000: Educate America Act (P.L. 103-227), signed into law on March 31, 1994, and the reauthorization of the Elementary and Secondary Education Act, now referred to as the Improving America's Schools Act of 1994 (P.L. 103-382). The Family Preservation and Family Support provisions of the Omnibus Budget Reconciliation Act of 1993 (P.L. 103-66) provide for coordinated services that integrate health, social services, and educational goals.

FUNDING FOR SCHOOL-LINKED SERVICES

Although there is as yet no definitive answer to how to finance school-linked services (Farrow & Bruner, 1993), many states and localities are experimenting with combining or pooling funding streams from various sources. Reduced budgets for education and human services pose problems, as does the categorical and crisis-oriented nature of funding, yet potential funding sources do exist, and carefully crafted fiscal strategies can result in money for school-linked services.

Major federal funds can come from educational, health, and social services. For example, in the field of education, Title 1 (formerly Chapter 1) of the reauthorization of the Elementary and Secondary Education Act (P.L. 103-382) provides dollars for educationally disadvantaged children, and Parts B (P.L. 94-142) and H (P.L. 99-457) of the Individuals with Disabilities Education Act (IDEA) (P.L. 101-476) authorize funds for disabled children, infants, and toddlers. Medicaid funding, authorized by Title XIX of the Social Security Act, provides for the Early Periodic Screening, Diagnosis, and Treatment Service (P.L. 90-248) and 31 optional benefits, including case management. Both these provisions have been used to support school-linked services.

Social services funds include Title IV-E of the Social Security Act (P.L. 96-272), the JOBS (Job Opportunities and Basic Skills Training Program) component of the Family Support Act of 1988 (P.L. 100-485), Title XX of the Social Services Block Grant (P.L. 97-35), and the Alcohol, Drug Abuse,

and Mental Health Block Grant (Omnibus Budget Reconciliation Act of 1981, P.L. 97-35, as amended by the Alcohol, Drug Abuse, and Mental Health Administration Reorganization Act of 1992, P.L. 102-321) (Melaville & Blank, 1993). In Indiana, for example, the governor and eight state agencies have submitted a Consolidated State Plan for Services for Children and Families—services that are now supported by 199 federal programs. This plan will enhance collaboration among federal, state, and local programs, as well as between the public and private sectors (State of Indiana, 1994).

Although some amount of specific core funding is required to establish a school-linked service, collaborative, long-range funding can be acquired through the redirection or redeployment of dollars (Farrow & Joe, 1992). At the simplest level, staff members can be outstationed from their employing agencies to the school site. More extensive redeployment occurs when diverse programs, such as substance abuse programs or employment services, become involved with schools in designing joint programs. The reallocation of budgets is another strategy in which money that is intended for one purpose, such as out-of-home child placements, is redirected to provide in-home services for vulnerable children and their families.

Yet another major strategy that has been used to redesign services is refinancing, through the "aggressive maximization of federal funding sources, particularly Medicaid" (Farrow & Joe, 1992, p. 66). For example, school social work services now funded by allocations from IDEA, Part B, can be reimbursed by Medicaid funds for eligible students. The savings thus generated can then be applied to school-linked integrated services. Other strategies include leveraging funds from the private sector and foundations and investing new funds, based on long-term cost-benefit analyses, into prevention-oriented services with clear accountability for outcomes (Farrow & Bruner, 1993). In the long run, the creative merging of funding streams may be partially replaced by increased funding specifically for school-linked services. It remains to be seen how financing of these new paradigms of service delivery will be affected by the Republican-controlled 104th Congress and by continuing efforts at health care reform in the United States.

The political realignment that emerged in the United States after the November 1994 elections will also undoubtedly influence the development of school-linked services. Federal funding for health and social services may well be dramatically reduced through the institution of block grants to states.

EVALUATIVE RESEARCH

A number of studies of school-based and school-linked health centers have demonstrated that such services improve adolescents' health and reduce the risk of unintended pregnancy. Some studies have shown that the use of these centers also improves school-attendance and graduation rates (Advocates for Youth, 1994). Statistical data from six centers that are associated with federally funded community health centers revealed high registration rates among the student population, indicating that the services were readily accessible. In addition, they demonstrated increasing rates of early entry into prenatal care and declining rates of teenage pregnancy and absenteeism from and dropping out of school. Interviews with students revealed that the centers also help in the early detection of medical and emotional problems and in improving self-esteem and communication skills (U.S. Department of Health and Human Services, 1993).

The U.S. GAO (1992) reported that service-oriented integration efforts that strive to link clients efficiently to existing services tend to be more successful than do system-oriented efforts, which are often unable to sustain support and resources. However, another report (U.S. GAO, 1993), based on a review of the literature and visits to 10 programs from over 200 programs identified nationwide, concluded that although school-linked comprehensive services showed promise, more rigorous impact evaluations are required.

IMPLICATIONS FOR SOCIAL WORKERS

The concept of mobilizing multiple community resources to meet the complex needs of troubled families and children is fundamental to social work. As Ooms and Owens (1991) pointed out, "much of the new technology of services integration—case management, case conferences, and outreach via home visits—represents a rediscovery of, and giving new shape to, tools that were once part of the social worker's standard repertoire" (p. 8). However, as many social workers focused more narrowly on psychotherapeutic clinical work, they became less active and less visible in the delivery of human services. Those who continue to practice in the public sector are frequently overburdened with high caseloads and inadequate resources and support. Consequently, social workers (who identify themselves as such) are underrepresented among those who have

developed and described the features of school-linked services.

Furthermore, other professions have often taken the lead in implementing, analyzing, and advocating for school-linked services. For example, in 1994, the American Academy of Pediatrics and the National Education Association formed an Ad Hoc Working Group on Integrated Services that convened the National Consensus Building Conference on School-Linked Integrated Service Systems (1994), comprising 50 organizations. This conference issued a statement of principles for such collaborative, community-based, family-centered services (National Consensus Building Conference, 1994). In some of the school-linked collaboratives, paraprofessionals from the community being served are frequently employed as caseworkers. In others, however, particularly school-based health clinics, social workers play an important role (Marks & Marzke, 1993). In addition, social workers have skills and expertise that are relevant to effective practice in these new service delivery systems (Franklin & Streeter, in press).

One of the issues that arises in developing school-linked services is the relationship between professionals who come into the schools from outside and those employed by the school system (Dryfoos, 1994). In general, providers of pupil services, both school social workers and others, have not played a major role in the new models. Their potential contribution in terms of "the glue factor," or the bridge between the school and collaborating agencies, is yet to be fully acknowledged. Progress in this area has begun (Carlson, Clark, & Marx, 1992; National Alliance of Pupil Services Organizations, 1992; Pennekamp, 1992). Yet much must still be accomplished. Process evaluations of school-based health centers have demonstrated the importance of involving school nurses and school social workers in the planning and implementation of services (Marks & Marzke, 1993).

Training for practice in school-linked projects is another issue. Interdisciplinary cross-training courses are available both inside and outside universities. Examples include the University of Washington's Training for Interprofessional Collaboration, which involves the Graduate School of Public Affairs; the College of Education; and the Schools of Public Health and Community Medicine, Nursing, and Social Work; and the School's Partnership Training Project, based at Jewish Family and Children's Services in San Francisco. Some favor educating a new category of personnel with cross-disciplinary training related to the management and coordination of "multicomponent and multi-agency programs" (Dryfoos, 1994, p. 163).

FUTURE TRENDS

Although difficulties arise in the crafting of collaborative service delivery models (National Center for Service Integration, 1994), these models are likely to proliferate in the future and to become important sites for the delivery of social work services. Both school social workers and social workers who are employed in community agencies will become increasingly involved in school-linked services. If health care reform in the United States in the future embodies the public health provisions proposed by the Clinton administration, the number of school-based health clinics will increase greatly.

Issues of role, turf, and confidentiality must be confronted in addition to the complexity and categorical nature of existing federally funded human service programs (Greenberg & Levy, 1992; National Center for Service Integration, 1994). Many barriers and challenges exist at the state and local levels as well. Problems arise in attitudes, systems, resources, and technical areas (McCart, 1994). These problems must be overcome if school-linked services are to realize their potential for the more effective delivery of services to families and children and, therefore, for improving the quality of the lives of millions of citizens.

REFERENCES

Adoption Assistance and Child Welfare Act of 1980. P.L. 96-272, 94 Stat. 500.

Advocates for Youth. (1994). *School-based and school-linked health centers: The facts.* Washington, DC: Author.

Behrman, R. (Ed.). (1992). *The Future of Children: School-Linked Services, 2*(1). [Entire issue]

Bruner, C. (1991). *Thinking collaboratively: Ten questions and answers to help policy makers improve children's services.* Washington, DC: Education and Human Services Consortium.

Bruner, C., Bell, K., Brindis, C., Chang, H., & Scarborough, W. (1993). *Charting a course: Assessing a community's strengths and needs.* New York: National Center on Service Integration, Columbia University's National Center for Children in Poverty.

Carlson, S., Clark, J. P., & Marx, D. (1992). *School and community resource collaboration* (Position paper). Des Moines, IA: Midwest School Social Work Council.

Carreon, V., & Jameson, W. J. (1993, October). *School-linked service integration in action: Lessons drawn from seven California Communities.* San Francisco: California School-Based Service Integration Project, California Research Institute, & San Francisco State University.

Chaudry, A., Maurer, K. E., Oshinsky, C. J., & Mackie, J. (1993). *Service integration: An annotated bibliography.* Falls Church, VA: National Center for Service Integration & Mathtech.

Cohen, D. L. (1989, March 15). "Joining Forces": An alliance of sectors envisioned to aid the most troubled young. *Education Week, 8*(25), 7–15.

Cohen, D. L. (1991, September 25). Reality tempers "New Futures" leaders' optimism. *Education Week, 11*(4), 1, 12, 13, 15.

Cohen, D. L. (1994, April 6). N.G.A. documents integrated services for children. *Education Week, 13*(28), 12.

Council of Chief State School Officers, Resource Center on Educational Equity. (1991, June). Promoting school-linked approaches to the delivery of effective health and social services for youth and families. *Concerns, 33,* 1–9.

Dryfoos, J. G. (1994). *Full-service schools: A revolution in health and social services for children, youth, and families.* San Francisco: Jossey-Bass.

Family Support Act of 1988. P.L. 100-485, 102 Stat. 2343.

Farrow, F., & Bruner, C. (1993). *Getting to the bottom line: State and community strategies for financing comprehensive community service systems* (Resource Brief 4). New York: National Center for Service Integration & Columbia University's National Center for Children in Poverty.

Farrow, F., & Joe, T. (1992). Financing school-linked, integrated services. *The Future of Children: School-Linked Services, 2*(1), 56–67.

Florida Interagency Workgroup on Full Service Schools. (1993). *Florida full-service schools* (Concept paper). Tallahassee: Author.

Franklin, C., & Streeter, C. L. (in press). School reform: Linking public schools with human services. *Social Work.*

Gerry, M. H. (1993). *A joint enterprise with America's families to ensure student success.* Washington, DC: Council of Chief State School Officers.

Goldsmith, M. F. (1991). School-based health clinics provide essential care. *Journal of the American Medical Association, 265,* 2458–2460.

Greenberg, M., & Levy, J. (1992). *Confidentiality and collaboration: Information sharing in interagency efforts.* Washington, DC: American Public Welfare Association, Center for Law and Social Policy, Council of Chief State School Officers, & Education Commission of the States.

Holtzman, W. H. (Ed.). (1992). *School of the future.* Austin, TX: American Psychological Association & Hogg Foundation for Mental Health, University of Texas.

Individuals with Disabilities Education Act. P.L. 101-476, 104 Stat. 1142 (1990).

Johnson, C. M., Miranda, L., Sherman, A., & Weill, J. (1991). *Child poverty in America.* Washington, DC: Children's Defense Fund.

Joining Forces Connections. (1991, Spring). Washington, DC: Joining Forces, Council of Chief State School Officers, & American Public Welfare Administration.

Kahn, A. J., & Kamerman, S. B. (1992). *Integrating services integration: An overview of initiatives, issues, and possibilities.* New York: Cross-National Studies Research Program, Columbia University School of Social Work, for the National Center for Children in Poverty, Columbia University School of Public Health.

Kirby, D., Waszak, C., & Ziegler, J. (1989). *An assessment of six school-based clinics: Services, impact and potential.* Washington, DC: Center for Population Options.

Kirst, M. W. (1993). Changing the system for children's services: Building linkages with schools. In Council of Chief State School Officers (Ed.), *Ensuring student success through collaboration: Summer institute papers and recommendations of the Council of Chief State School Officers, 1992.* Washington, DC: Council of Chief State School Officers.

MacCord, M., Klein, J., Foy, J., & Fothergill, K. (1993). School-based clinic use and school performance. *Journal of Adolescent Health, 14,* 91–98.

Marks, E. L., & Marzke, C. H. (1993). *Healthy caring: A process evaluation of the Robert Wood Johnson Foundation's school-based adolescent health care program.* Princeton, NJ: Mathtech.

Marzke, C., & Both, D. (1994). *Getting started: Planning a comprehensive services initiative.* New York: National Center for Service Integration, Columbia University's National Center for Children in Poverty.

McCart, L. (1994). *Changing systems for children and families.* Washington, DC: National Governors Association & National Center for Service Integration.

Melaville, A. I., & Blank, M. J. (1991). *What it takes: Structuring interagency partnerships to connect children and families with comprehensive services.* Washington, DC: Education and Human Services Consortium.

Melaville, A. I., & Blank, M. J. (1993). *Together we can: A guide for crafting a profamily system of education and human services.* Washington, DC: U.S. Departments of Education & Health and Human Services.

Mintzies, P., & Hare, I. (1985). *The human factor: A key to excellence in education.* Silver Spring, MD: National Association of Social Workers, Social Work Conference Planning Committee.

Morrill, W. A. (1993, Spring). Seeking better outcomes for children and families. *NCSI News,* pp. 1–2. (Available from National Center for Service Integration & Mathtech, Falls Church, VA)

National Alliance of Pupil Services Organizations. (1992). *Policy statement on school-linked integrated services.* Washington, DC: Author.

National Center for Service Integration. (1994, Winter). Providing comprehensive integrated services for children and families: Why is it so hard? *NCSI News,* pp. 1–3. (Available from National Center for Service Integration & Mathtech, Falls Church, VA)

National Commission on Children. (1991). *Beyond rhetoric: A new American agenda for children and families.* Washington, DC: National Commission on Children.

National Commission on Excellence in Education. (1983). *A nation at risk: The imperative of educational reform.* Washington, DC: U.S. Department of Education.

National Consensus Building Conference on School-Linked Integrated Service Systems. (1994). *Principles to link by: Integrated service systems that are community-based and school-linked.* Washington, DC: American Academy of Pediatrics.

National Education Goals Panel. (1991). *The national educational goals report: Building a nation of learners.* Washington, DC: Author.

Nelson, C. M., & Pearson, C. A. (1991). *Integrating services for children and youth with emotional and behavioral disorders.* Reston, VA: Council for Exceptional Children.

Omnibus Budget Reconciliation Act of 1981. P.L. 97-35, 95 Stat. 357.

Omnibus Budget Reconciliation Act of 1993. P.L. 103-66, 107 Stat. 31.

Ooms, T., & Owens, T. (1991). *Coordination, collaboration, integration: Strategies for serving families more effectively. Part one: The federal role* (Background briefing report). Washington, DC: Family Impact Seminar, American Association of Marriage and Family Therapists, & Research and Education Foundation.

Pennekamp, M. (1992, April). Toward school-linked and school-based human services for children and families. *Social Work in Education, 14*(2), 125–130.

Perspectives (Supplement to *Medicine & Health*). (1992, January 6). Washington, DC: Healthcare Information Center. (Available from Healthcare Information Center, 1133 15th Street, NW, Suite 450, Washington, DC 20005)

Robert Wood Johnson Foundation. (1993). *Making the grade: State and local partnerships to establish school-based health centers.* Princeton, NJ: Author.

Schorr, L. B. (1988). *Within our reach: Breaking the cycle of disadvantage.* New York: Doubleday Anchor Press.

Schorr, L. B. (1993). Keynote address. In *Effective strategies for increasing social program replication/adaptation.* Washington, DC: National Association of Social Workers.

Social Security Amendments of 1967. P.L. 90-248, 81 Stat. 821.

Sommerfeld, M. (1994, April 6). Pew abandons its ambitious 10-year "children's initiative." *Education Week, 13*(28), 9.

State of Indiana. (1994). *Proposal for a consolidated state plan for services to children and families.* Indianapolis: Author.

U.S. Department of Education. (1993, July 7). Research in education of individuals with disabilities program and program for children and youth with serious emotional disturbance. *Federal Register, 58*(128), 35676.

U.S. Department of Health and Human Services, Public Health Service, Bureau of Primary Health Care. (1993). *School-based clinics that work.* Washington, DC: Author.

U.S. General Accounting Office. (1992). *Integrating human services: Linking at-risk families with services more successful than system reform efforts.* Washington, DC: Author.

U.S. General Accounting Office. (1993). *School-linked human services: A comprehensive strategy for aiding students at risk of school failure.* Washington, DC: Author.

Wagner, M. (1993). School-linked services: California's healthy start. *The Future of Children, 3*(3), 201–204.

FURTHER READING

Adler, L., & Gardner, S. (1994). *The politics of linking schools and social services.* Washington, DC: Falmer Press.

Jewish Family and Children's Services of San Francisco, the Peninsula, and Marin and Sonoma Counties. (1992). *The School's Partnership Training Project: A successful model towards improving school performance.* San Francisco: Author.

Kozol, J. (1991). *Savage inequalities: Children in America's schools.* New York: Crown.

Kusserow, R. P. (1991, January). *Services integration: A twenty-year retrospective.* Washington, DC: U.S. Department of Health and Human Services, Office of Inspector General.

Schlitt, J. J., Rickett, K. D., Montgomery, L. L., & Lear, J. G. (1994, October). *State initiatives to support school-based health centers: A national survey* (A *Making the Grade* Report). Washington, DC: *Making the Grade* National Program Office.

Isadora Hare, ACSW, is director of quality assurance, National Association of Social Workers, 750 First Street, NE, Suite 700, Washington, DC 20002.

For further information see

Adolescents: Direct Practice; Children: Direct Practice; Citizen Participation; Community; Families Overview; Interdisciplinary and Interorganizational Collaboration; National Helping Networks; Organizations: Context for Social Services Delivery; Runaways and Homeless Youths; School Social Work Overview; Social Welfare Policy; Social Work Practice: History and Evolution; Social Work Profession Overview; Youth Services.

Key Words	
adolescents	school-linked services
children	social services
community	delivery

Schwartz, William

See Biographies section, Volume 3

Scott, Carl A.

See Biographies section, Volume 3

Sectarian Agencies
Larry P. Ortiz

The sectarian agencies are an integral part of the fabric used to weave together social welfare institutions in the United States. These agencies, born of religious convictions and traditions, are central to historical and contemporary social welfare. Before the government assumed much responsibility for its citizens' well-being and before the birth of the social work profession, the religiously motivated service, now called the sectarian agency, was a fixture in American society that responded to the needs of constituent populations. Patterned after European counterparts, this network of services initially sprang up in America during the 17th century but increased substantially during the 18th century.

Religiously motivated helping has been noted throughout recorded history. Even at their earliest points, societies either commanded care for the needy or regarded it as a virtue. For example, the Book of the Dead, the sacred writings of Egypt, recorded around 3500 B.C., encouraged giving aid to the poor as a means of achieving a good life after death. In Babylonia, Hammurabi incorporated care for the needy as part of the civil code. Hebrew laws and customs, written in the book of Deuteronomy around 700 B.C., required justice for the poor and needy. "Buddhism, founded in 400 B.C., taught that all other forms of righteousness 'are not worth a sixteenth part of the emancipation of the heart through love and charity'" (Trattner, 1989, p. 1). The Romans and, to a lesser extent, the Greeks also required social provisions for the poor and needy.

Christianity encouraged both charity and justice in all social interactions. There are numerous accounts in the New Testament of social benevolence and mutual support provided by the early Christian church. With the growth and spread of Christianity in the Western world, care for the needy became a responsibility of the church. Because the church had more power and wealth than the state before the Reformation and industrialization, the church and its agencies assumed the primary responsibility for the needy. As state powers grew in relation to the loss of the church's power, governments took increasing responsibility for the needy. However, they typically continued to use models of service delivery established by religious groups.

From the Reformation and Industrial Revolution through the early 20th century, the needs of poor people and needy in Western society were met primarily through a combination of state-supported and religious organization–sponsored services, although these services were often uncoordinated. It was not until after World War I in Europe and the Great Depression in the United States and other parts of the Western world that federal governments assumed more responsibility for the needs of their residents. The United States, unlike Europe, did not create a federally sponsored social welfare institution, but wove together a "safety net" of services to respond to the specific needs of particular populations. An integral part of this safety net is privately sponsored welfare services, of which sectarian agencies are a part.

SECTARIAN WELFARE IN AMERICA

The two religious groups that are most entrenched in sectarian practice in this country are Jews and Christians. Both groups have had a significant presence in American social welfare from the early days of immigration to the present. They have been especially influential in establishing the American approach to welfare and the social work profession. There is little doubt that religious motivation was the basis for social work; the markings of the Judeo–Christian perspective are evident in the values that legitimate the profession. As Leiby (1978) wrote, "Religious ideas were the most important intellectual influence on American Welfare institutions in the nineteenth century" (p. 12).

Motivation for Services

The motivation for and purpose of charitable activities were similar for both Christians and Jews, notwithstanding religious and denominational differences. The Jewish tradition for helping is founded on the communal concept of justice. Teachings from the Old Testament books of Leviticus and Deuteronomy and the Talmud and the writings of the medieval philosopher Maimonides all served to guide Jewish social welfare. Charity, the source of welfare, was interpreted as living a just and righteous life (Bernstein, 1965; Johnson & Schwartz, 1988; Macarov, 1978). To live righteously meant to love God and do justice (Micah 6:8).

Beyond the Old Testament teachings that focused on justice, the Christian motivation included the theme of love stressed in the teachings of Christ. Apostles in the early church established the structures to fulfill Christ's commands to love and care for one another. Care and love were to be administered without regard to a person's social status, ethnicity, or religious group. The parable of the Good Samaritan and the teachings of Christ, found in the book of Matthew, are the primary sources for the Christian benevolence that was later modeled in the New Testament book of Acts and in St. Paul's epistles. One of the most powerful quotes guiding Christian charity is from the book of Matthew, where Christ said,

> "For I was hungry and you gave me food, . . . thirsty and you gave me drink . . . a stranger and you welcomed me, . . . naked and you clothed me, . . . sick and you visited me, . . . in prison and you came to me. Then the righteous will answer him, "Lord when did we see thee hungry and feed thee or thirsty and give thee drink? And when did we see thee a stranger and welcome thee, nor naked and clothe thee? And when did we see thee sick or in prison and visit thee?" And the King will answer them, "Truly I say unto you, as you did it to one of the least of these my breathern, you did it to me." (Matthew 25:35–40)

Patterns of Service

Since the beginning of Christianity, the church has been active in "at least twelve areas of social ministry: care for the widows, orphans, sick, poor, disabled, prisoners, captives, slaves, victims of calamity, burial of the poor, provisions of employment services, and meals for the needy" (Popple & Leighninger, 1993, p. 97). These ministries, or services, as they have become conceptualized in modern-day welfare, have not all been simultaneously carried out. Instead, efforts emerged during different historical periods in response to prevailing needs. Furthermore, denominations have selectively implemented these services, with some denominational groups providing one service more than others. For example, Baptists have been particularly active in providing homes for children; Catholics, in health care and the needs of children, especially orphans; Episcopalians, in outreach to immigrants and residential care for the aged; and Lutherans, in overcoming language barriers and caring for their own. The Salvation Army, an international nondenominational religious organization, has provided emergency services to the poorest and most neglected people in this society.

These examples suggest that different groups vary in their preference for types of services, but in reality, most religious groups have provided a variety of services in different places at different times. However, various denominational groups have established patterns of service. These patterns are likely based on the denomination's ideological orientation, which is influenced by doctrine (Netting, 1982). Doctrine is influential in forming beliefs that lead to actions that are based on assumptions of God's teaching, human nature, social responsibility, social conditions, and the responsibility of the church. For example, a person with a doctrinal belief in the total depravity of people will view a social problem as the natural consequence of humans' fallen state. Consequently, he or she will be less likely to try to change the conditions surrounding the problem and place a greater emphasis on helping individuals through the situation and saving their souls for life hereafter. On the other hand, a person with a doctrinal belief that humans are created by God and are essentially good will be inclined to identify social structures that spawn human misery as the primary targets for change. It is important to understand doctrinal orientations in the study of sectarian agencies, for they influence the agencies' missions, programming, and staffing and motivation of their workers. Orientations also shape the types of professional dilemmas or conflicts experienced in particular agencies.

STRUCTURE OF SECTARIAN AGENCY SERVICE

Sectarian agencies in this country grew with migration and proliferated in the late 19th century, operating autonomously to meet the needs of communities. Nonsectarian groups were also operating and growing during this period, so a hodgepodge of services was created. In 1877 the Charity Organization Societies was formed, in part to coordinate private charity. Its formation made sectarian agencies permanent fixtures in American welfare and placed them in competition with each other and with nonsectarian agencies for funding, which initially consisted of private dollars and eventually of public dollars as well.

Administration

Catholic services. Structurally, Catholic social services are more centrally organized and administered than are Protestant and Jewish services. Historically, Catholic agencies have been likely to operate under the auspices of local dioceses, with local bishops assuming considerable control. These agencies are connected to a larger network known as the National Conference of Catholic Charities, a coordinating body designed to support local affiliates (Gallagher, 1965; Reid & Stimpson, 1987). Catholic religious orders have also initiated various health and welfare services, but these services tend to operate independently of the dioceses and are not affiliated with the Catholic Charities network.

Protestant services. The more autonomously operated Protestant social services have tended to be locally organized. They are provided by one of three types of agencies: church related, independent, or interdenominational (Rahn & Whiting, 1965). *Church-related agencies* are run by a particular denomination, conference, or parish. Ultimate

responsibility for administering their programs lies with these bodies, and the imprint of a group's beliefs is usually evident. For example, the Salvation Army is really a church and a social agency combined, Latter Day Saints organizations are extensions of the Mormon Church, and Lutheran synods are responsible for their agencies.

Independent Protestant organizations are administered by a board of directors that operates autonomously from a church or denomination. Board members represent the community. The boards are self-perpetuating and usually subscribe to a set of beliefs that are incorporated into the agency's bylaws, referred to as a statement of faith or purpose. This statement guides the agency's mission, programming, and staffing. These agencies might have had a denominational affiliation at one time, but for many reasons are currently only marginally linked with the group. Many Episcopal Charity agencies are examples of this type. The degree to which agencies remain true to their founding purpose varies from loose affiliation to covenantal to strict control.

Interdenominational agencies are administered by a coalition of religious groups organized to meet a particular community need. Frequently, these boards are composed of representatives from various faiths who have a commonly agreed-on ecumenical purpose. Like independent agencies, a statement of purpose guides their policies and delivery of services. Because many denominations and faith groups may be represented in these efforts, no one doctrine dominates the agencies' purpose (Rahn & Whiting, 1965).

Jewish services. Jewish agencies also operate autonomously from organized religious groups. They are not centrally funded, administered by local temples or synagogues, or tied to a national religious movement. Instead, they tend to be nationally organized by fields of service (that is, families, health care, and communal services).

The national groups do not provide fiscal support to the local affiliates, but they do regulate services through accreditation and provide information and consultation. However, the different service groups are locally organized into federations that comprise representatives from participating agencies and the Jewish community. Local federations assume different responsibilities but usually handle program planning, fundraising, and budgeting. Nationally, the Council of Jewish Federations serves as an overarching organization for local groups. Although it assumes no authoritative role, it provides a wide range of consultations for member federations (Reid & Stimpson, 1987).

Local agencies generally enjoy widespread financial support from the local Jewish community (Bernstein, 1965).

Today, sectarian agencies deliver a multitude of direct services, responding to community needs as they are able, and are no longer bound to their historic clientele or field of service. In the best-case scenario, sectarian agencies respond to community needs swiftly because they are not bound by a cumbersome legislative process that must first obtain funding for services. However, these agencies must frequently make difficult decisions about services because of limited funding, sometimes withdrawing funds from one important service to implement another.

Staffing

Paid professional staff. In the early days of sectarian agencies, staff were required to be members of the sponsoring denominations, and agency directors were often clerics. However, with the professionalization of social work, most sectarian agencies hire the most qualified staff persons available. As agencies have broadened their base of services, obtained external accreditation, and expanded their funding base to include federal money, they have developed equal opportunity practices (Reid & Stimpson, 1987).

However, some agencies may require staff to support their historical mission. Such support may take various forms, ranging from simply affirming the agency's purpose to signing statements of faith to adhering to formalized codes, such as the one developed by the National Conference of Catholic Charities (Judah, 1985). This support and endorsement of the agency's purpose is important because staff report that they feel a special sense of purpose, camaraderie with colleagues, and a sense of family, which they attribute to the common bond they share in their work (Netting, 1982). Furthermore, the agency's purpose serves to distinguish the agency and its staff and programs from secular services. This distinction is important to governing boards, contributors, and clients who share similar religious perspectives.

Paraprofessionals. In addition to paid professional staff, many religiously sponsored agencies use paraprofessionals and volunteers to deliver services. This staffing pattern has both disadvantages and advantages. On the one hand, paraprofessionals are often trained unevenly, and consequently their abilities to carry out agency services vary; on the other hand, they are frequently members of the community the agency serves and therefore facilitate a connection

between the agency and the community. Innovative agency policies frequently provide learning opportunities for these employees through in-service training and financial support to attend college and obtain degrees.

Volunteers. Volunteers present a challenge because their commitment varies and they sometimes experience boundary issues with staff and clients. Yet they, too, serve as a vital link to the local community and the sponsoring group. Retired volunteers can bring expertise in the form of consultation that the agency could not otherwise support. Agencies also benefit from the expertise of affluent, educated women who consider themselves professional volunteers and donate their time in service and governance. Historically, sectarian agencies have benefited from nationally organized volunteer groups, such as the Society of St. Vincent de Paul, for Catholic men; the Association of Ladies of Charity of the United States, for Catholic women; the National Council of Jewish Women; and Volunteers of America, an independent Protestant organization (Reid & Stimpson, 1987).

Staffing issues. Despite their creative staffing patterns, most sectarian agencies are understaffed. There is simply not enough funding to hire enough staff, and despite the staff members' commitment to service, their plight is similar to that of the typical private charity worker: They earn half of what they could be making in government or business and work many unpaid hours ("Hard Times for the Neediest," 1993). Why do many social workers choose to work in such settings? Although few studies have addressed this question, qualitative data suggest that in addition to professional commitment, staff members are dedicated to the beliefs and values of the sponsoring groups.

Funding. The funding of sectarian agencies has changed drastically since such agencies first appeared in this country. No longer are these groups solely dependent on their sponsoring denominations or constituent groups. Instead, their funding support increasingly comes from fundraising groups, such as United Way, and from government contracts (Netting, 1986). This trend toward diverse funding was first observed during the early part of this century and has accelerated since. For example, government payments to Jewish-sponsored agencies increased 20-fold from 1962 to 1973, and Catholic Charities U.S.A. estimated that government funding accounted for 44 percent of affiliate agency revenues for fiscal year 1988 (Smith & Lipsky, 1993). Clearly, the government and sectarian agencies are increasingly dependent on each other to provide both services and funding for those services.

Despite the increased government funding of sectarian agencies, religious groups still provide tremendous financial support to welfare services, second only to the government (McDonald, 1984; Rechard, 1984). In a 1983 survey conducted by the Council on Foundations (Popple & Leighninger, 1993), it was estimated that religious groups contributed $7.5 billion to social welfare concerns; if congregational giving had been included, the dollar amount would have been $8.5 billion. These contributions exceed both corporate and foundation giving.

Other trends in funding among sectarian agencies are to charge clients for services; accept third-party reimbursements, especially private insurance; and offer entrepreneurial services (that is, nursing homes, residential care facilities, and employee assistance programs). Although few agencies make large sums of money from these endeavors, such efforts often help the agencies offset programs that are underfunded and less dependent on government funds and donations. No figures are available on the amount of money agencies raise through these means, but the literature suggests that many agencies are moving in this direction.

DILEMMAS IN SECTARIAN AGENCIES

In contemporary social service there are at least two areas in which social workers in sectarian agencies experience dilemmas: personal and professional value issues and the separation of church and state.

Value Issues

Many social workers in sectarian agencies face requests for services that in some ways are in opposition to the religious traditions of the sponsoring or affiliated agencies. For many sectarian agencies that have become distant from their original missions, either through diverse funding or board decisions, this concern is not as apparent. However, in agencies that maintain a close affiliation, conflict arises with regard to clients' needs, professional values, and religious tenets.

Social workers in these agencies must grapple with conflicts between, for example, Jewish law or biblical teachings and social work education, the Catholic church's position on abortion and NASW's position, clients' sexual practices and Church teaching, civil rights of oppressed groups, and other behaviors that are viewed as morally objectionable from a religious perspective (Den-

dinger & Mathern, 1980; Howard, Lipsitz, Sheppard, & Steinitz, 1991; Lurie, 1977; Netting, 1982; Popple & Leighninger, 1993). According to Lurie (1977), "The orientation of the Jewish social worker first as a Jew and secondly as a social worker can bring ... conflict." (p. 286). Furthermore, Netting (1982) found that some church representatives feared that "spiritual values [would] be sacrificed on the altar of professional know-how" (p. 10). However, Lurie countered by stating that "the problems of the Jewish social worker are also his [her] strengths." (p. 286). Tension and conflicting values do not have to be eschewed; they can be viewed as an opportunity for dialogue. Furthermore, the worker in these situations can serve as an important link between the religious constituency and the professional community.

Resolving conflicts in values can be an arduous process and requires wide-ranging discussions among professionals, constituents, and the religious community. Although these conflicts cannot always be resolved, discussions lead to the clarification of issues and the establishment of a direction for the staff and may result in procedures that consider clients' needs, the agency's position, and the professional codes of ethics (Dendinger & Mathern, 1980; Howard et al., 1991).

Separation of Church and State

Public funding of sectarian agencies has sparked debate for many years. For some, the question is whether the government is funding religious activities, and for others, such as the administrators and boards of sectarian agencies and the sponsoring religious groups, the issue is whether public funding imposes a threat to the agency's historical mission. This concern goes back to the 1930s, when the government began to take a serious role in social welfare. The practice of government funding of sectarian agencies was debated and was the object of several legal battles from the 1930s through the 1960s. By the time the government started injecting massive funds into social welfare during the War on Poverty, the practice of purchasing services from sectarian services was well established. Despite the legal questions and fears that regulations would detract from services, government funding was welcomed. This practice was rationalized primarily through an underlying acceptance of civil religion (the transformation of sacred principles into public life) (Bellah, 1967) in American society; by the government's position that the best way to reach certain populations is through endogenous services; by the fact that the purchase of services was cost-effective; and by the notion that "private is better" (Macarov, 1978).

Sectarian agencies accepted funds because it helped them to expand their services, broaden their funding base, and reconceptualize their idea of ministry.

Although people on both sides of this issue continue to have questions and frequently disagree over regulations and the fairness of funding, sectarian agencies rely heavily on government funding. Likewise, the government relies heavily on the private sector, including sectarian agencies, to fulfill its service mandate. Since the 1980s, these agencies have served as an indispensable resource for many people as a result of attempts to decrease government-sponsored welfare. For example, the Council on Foundations reported that churches and their related agencies received "the largest volume of requests for aid in their history" in 1983 (Popple & Leighninger, 1993, p. 104), which is further evidence of the integral role these agencies play in American welfare.

FUTURE TRENDS

Many sectarian agencies have remained dynamic and have adapted to the changing needs of society while remaining loyal to their sponsoring traditions. This ability to adapt seems to be the key to existence for those agencies that have survived. What will be the complexion of these agencies in the future? It is safe to say that an agency's survival depends on the flexibility of governance, funding, staffing, and programming within the confines of the agency's tradition. Fiscal health is the major concern of all these groups. Whether they continue to provide services and maintain the quality of these services will depend on the continuation of funding from external sources, the degree to which their boards of directors are committed more to providing high-quality service than just to being cost-effective, and the degree to which committed staff are employed (Saltzman, 1987). Unless an agency can respond to these concerns within the context of its religious tradition, the distinctiveness of its services will be lost. It will become just another nonprofit agency, losing its important community function (Horowitz, 1979; Linzer, 1978; Saltzman, 1987).

Responding to Community Needs

One important function that sectarian agencies have always filled and that continues to be their distinctive characteristic is their ability to respond quickly and effectively to pressing community needs. In recent years these agencies have responded to needs in the presence of fiscal crisis in two ways: (1) by building interagency coalitions, both ecumenical and nonsectarian, and (2) by enlarging their funding base to include profitable programs that support costly ones. These coalitions have been most active in responding to "new" problems, such as homelessness, caring for persons with acquired immune deficiency syndrome (AIDS), nutritional needs of the elderly, and domestic violence.

Competition with the Private Sector

The growth of the for-profit sector in the human services has created both an opportunity and a crisis for sectarian agencies. First, because many seasoned social workers have left sectarian agencies for more lucrative opportunities in private practice, there has been a considerable decrease in the number of experienced professionals in private agencies, both sectarian and nonsectarian. Second, as entrepreneurial groups have grown, they have successfully competed with nonprofit agencies for funding from government and corporate sources (Ahmann, 1988). This new competition has placed more pressure on sectarian agencies to raise funds and deliver services. It has also created an opportunity for these agencies, in that they have followed the lead of the for-profit sector and begun to market their services to the public and to corporations, and the profits from these endeavors have offset the costs of non-income-producing services (Gibelman, 1990; Gibelman & Demone, 1991). For example, sectarian agencies have entered into contracts with corporations to provide employee assistance programs, earning a profit from this arrangement that, in turn, has been used to augment services to elderly, homeless, and drug-addicted people—services that do not have widespread financial support from either the community or the government.

New Models of Service

There is no doubt that competition will put some sectarian agencies out of service or cause them to modify their services. McDonald (1984) reported that many religious groups are altering their traditional services, opting instead to sponsor innovative grassroots, empowerment, justice-oriented services. These services are springing up within and outside traditional sectarian agencies but receive significant funding from religious groups.

Church social work. Churches and parishes have also become increasingly involved in delivering services. In social work there is the beginnings of a new field of service known as church social work. This endeavor is different from the social agency model that has been a fixture in American welfare, but it nonetheless provides many of the same services delivered by agencies and some services designed particularly for church members. Churches tend to be more doctrinaire in their practice than are sectarian agencies. Although many Protestant churches tend to separate from traditional sectarian agencies, the Catholic approach encourages greater collaboration between parishes and agencies. Joseph and Conrad (1980) proposed a model in which the neighborhood parish is a vital link between the community and the social services network. According to this model, the parish is a natural site for delivering services; identifying community needs; and using untapped resources, such as volunteers and laypersons, to meet pressing needs.

Urban theology. Since the mid-1980s, a new theological conceptualization urban theology, has emerged in Protestant seminaries. Urban ministry is the praxis of this theology, which is rooted in a rereading of individually oriented, reductionistic, systematic theology to a more contextual sociological orientation. Operationally, a goal of this approach is to relieve personal distress through changing social structures. One way to conceive of this theology is to interpret it as a North American adaptation of liberation theology, the religiopolitical approach established in Latin America and Africa. Activities associated with urban theology are reminiscent of those social workers conducted during the settlement house period of the late 19th and early 20th centuries. Endeavors to affect the welfare of communities by groups that are motivated to do so are often observed in the major urban areas of this country. Social workers are frequently employed as planners, advocates, and activists, but as a profession, social work is underrepresented in this movement. Funding for these efforts is broad based and ecumenical.

CONCLUSION

Religiously motivated systems of helping have played an integral part in the history of human helping. In the United States there is a rich tradition of this activity. It is not known how many sectarian agencies are operating in the United States because of the loose affiliation many have with religious groups and the difficulty in operationalizing the term to determine what really defines an agency as sectarian. For these reasons, it is not clear whether the number of these agencies has increased or decreased since the 1800s. Some believe that sectarian work will diminish in American society because of increased competition for funding, the scope of social problems, and increased pluralism and the subsequent need for nonsecularized services (Macarov, 1978). Challenges to the existence of sectarian agencies are not new.

Skillful adaptation has long been a trademark of these agencies. As long as people are motivated by their beliefs to serve others, there will be organized efforts to provide welfare, whether they are carried out by social workers or others.

REFERENCES

Ahmann, M. (1988). Catholic charities and pluralism: Some problems, trends and opportunities. *Social Thought, 14,* 4–12.

Bellah, R. N. (1967). *Religion in America.* Boston: American Academy of Arts and Sciences.

Bernstein, P. (1965). Jewish social services. In H. L. Lurie (Ed.-in-Chief), *Encyclopedia of social work* (15th ed., pp. 418–427). New York: National Association of Social Workers.

Dendinger, D., & Mathern, T. (1980). Abortion: Toward a policy in a Catholic social service agency. *Social Thought, 6,* 33–46.

Gallagher, R. (1965). Catholic social services. In H. L. Lurie (Ed.-in-Chief), *Encyclopedia of social work* (15th ed., pp. 130–136). New York: National Association of Social Workers.

Gibelman, M. (1990). National voluntary health agencies in an era of change: Experiences and adaptations. *Administration in Social Work, 14*(3), 17–32.

Gibelman, M., & Demone, H. (1991). How voluntary agency networks fared in the 1980s. *Journal of Sociology and Social Welfare, 17,* 3–19.

Hard times for the neediest. (1993, November 28). *New York Times,* p.142.

Horowitz, S. (1979). Issues in public funding of Jewish communal services. *Journal of Jewish Communal Services, 54*(1), 13–17.

Howard, R., Lipsitz, G., Sheppard, F., & Steinitz, L. (1991). Sexual behavior in group residence: An ethics dilemma. *Families in Society: The Journal of Contemporary Human Services, 72,* 360–365.

Johnson, L., & Schwartz, C. (1988). *Social welfare: A response to human need.* Needham Heights, MA: Allyn & Bacon.

Joseph, M. V., & Conrad, A. P. (1980). A parish neighborhood model for social work practice. *Social Casework: The Journal of Contemporary Social Work, 61,* 423–432.

Judah, E. (1985). A spirituality of professional services: A sacramental model. *Social Thought, 11,* 25–35.

Leiby, J. (1978). *A history of social welfare and social work in the United States.* New York: Columbia University Press.

Linzer, N. (1978). Synagogue, classroom and communal atmosphere for wholesome Jewish family development. *Jewish Social Work Forum, 14,* 55–70.

Lurie, A. (1977). Social work services to patients in the Jewish institution. *Journal of Jewish Communal Services, 53*(3), 232–288.

Macarov, D. (1978). *The design of social welfare.* New York: Holt, Rinehart & Winston.

McDonald, J. (1984). Survey finds religious groups strongly favor more collaboration. *Foundation News, 35,* 20–24.

Netting, F. E. (1982). Social work and religious values in church related social agencies. *Social Work and Christianity: An International Journal, 9*(1), 4–20.

Netting, F. E. (1986). The religiously affiliated agency: Implications for social work administration. *Social Work and Christianity: An International Journal, 13*(2), 50–63.

Popple, P., & Leighninger, L. (1993). *Social work, social welfare and American society.* Needham Heights, MA: Allyn & Bacon.

Rahn, S., & Whiting, N. (1965). Protestant social services. In H. L. Lurie (Ed.-in-Chief), *Encyclopedia of social work* (15th ed., pp. 567–600). New York: National Association of Social Workers.

Rechard, E. (1984). The philanthropy of organized religion: What it is, what it does, and how it relates to the work being done by private foundations and corporate grantmakers. *Foundation News, 35,* 18–19.

Reid, W., & Stimpson, W. (1987). Sectarian agencies. In A. Minahan (Ed.-in-Chief), *Encyclopedia of social work* (18th ed., Vol. 2, pp. 545–556). Silver Spring, MD: National Association of Social Workers.

Saltzman, A. (1987). The new season: Reruns and new episodes. *Journal of Jewish Communal Services, 64*(1), 77–80.

Smith, R., & Lipsky, M. (1993). *Non profits for hire: The welfare state in the age of contracting.* Cambridge, MA: Harvard University Press.

Trattner, W. (1989). *From poor law to welfare state: A history of social welfare in America* (4th ed.). New York: Free Press.

Larry P. Ortiz, PhD, LMSW-ACP, is associate professor, Worden School of Social Service, Our Lady of the Lake University, 411 SW 24th Street, San Antonio, TX 78207.

For further information see

Charitable Foundations and Social Welfare; Church Social Work; Citizen Participation; Community Needs Assessment; Community Practice Models; Deinstitutionalization; Direct Practice Overview; Disasters and Disaster Aid; Families Overview; Family Life Education; Fundraising and Philanthropy; Homelessness; International Social Welfare: Organizations and Activities; Management Overview; Mutual Aid Societies; Natural Helping Networks; Organizations: Context for Social Services Delivery; Peace and Social Justice; Poverty; Public Social Services; Self-Help Groups; Settlements and Neighborhood Centers; Social Planning; Social Welfare History; Social Work Profession Overview; Voluntarism.

Key Words

charity	religiously sponsored
nonprofit services	services
private social services	sectarian agencies

Self-Help Groups

Thomas J. Powell

Social workers and other health and human services professionals who work with clients participating in self-help groups often have an advantage in that self-help can reinforce and complement the help offered by professionals. Social workers can also play an important role in facilitating client participation in self-help groups and in helping clients benefit from the information, support, and advocacy opportunities associated with self-help.

ADVANTAGES OF SELF-HELP GROUPS

Benefits for Professionals

Self-help groups have advantages for both professionals and clients. Self-help interacts with professional help to make professional help more effective. To gain this advantage, the professional must learn something about the culture and functions of self-help and must avoid misusing it. The professional must also understand how self-help can reinforce the professional message. For example, a professional may occasionally suggest that the client check out certain ideas or feelings with other members of the self-help group, or the professional may ask the client about what is going on in the self-help group, with the intent of relating the self-help experience to the therapy.

Benefits for Participants

In addition to strengthening the relationship between professional and client, self-help can offer distinct benefits to participants. The self-help group is a resource for meeting needs that are not easily addressed in the professional relationship. For example, self-help group members may provide companionship that counteracts social isolation or stigma-driven concealment, or they may be helpful in suggesting housing, health care, and employment opportunities. National affiliates of self-help groups may provide special information in important areas. In the health care area, for example, they may provide basic scientific information about such conditions as sickle cell disease or manic–depressive illness. Critical legal information may be provided to lesbians and gay men threatened with discrimination. Special information may also be available for persons struggling with stressful situations related to divorce or unemployment.

Self-help groups can also contribute to the client's sense of empowerment when the client's desire to identify with others in the group is aroused. The client may notice how other self-help participants take responsibility for their own coping efforts. A client who stays the course will have the most empowering experience of all as a helper of others. The advantage to the professional is then twofold: The client will have discovered an important additional source of help, and as an empowered help-seeker the client will make better use of professional help.

The source of these benefits arises from the shared experience of the group members, the equality of their role relationships, and the similarity of their goals and tasks. Benefits are also generated by *referent power* (French & Raven, 1959; Janis, 1983; Litman-Adizes, Raven, & Fontaine, 1978; Raven, 1992), the power of the referent individual or group to motivate and influence the focal individual based on their understanding of and support for the individual's ongoing struggles. An excerpt from *Vital Signs* (VS), the newsletter of the National Black Women's Health Project (1987), offers a glimpse of how referent power might operate in an African American self-help group. The interview is with Zea McGaffie, the 9-year-old daughter of Sholey McGaffie, a leader of the project:

> VS: Do you have anything you would like to tell Black women?
>
> Zea: Yes, I want them to get better and stay healthy. Brush and floss every day and don't stuff food in your mouth.
>
> VS: What do you love most about Black women?
>
> Zea: I feel comfortable with them. They know what I've been through. They know what "cream your legs to get the ash off" means!

Another example is a talk I gave to mental health social workers about the potential morale-boosting referent power of ex-patients. Despite my best efforts, the audience was not engaged. Finally, one of the social workers declared that she had lupus and knew firsthand how important it was to have the understanding of others who had lupus. She made the point unforgettable for all of us with her statement, "My rheumatologist is a wonderful doctor. He's very concerned about my liver, but he could care less about how I feel about my swollen face during a flare-up." Actually, I think she meant her doctor wasn't even aware of how she felt about her swollen features, and consequently she greatly valued the instant understanding and support she received from members of her lupus group. Her story was moving, and the message was that if referent power worked for this social worker it could work for our clients as well.

MAGNITUDE OF SELF-HELP

Estimates based on recent data indicate that about 7.5 million people participate in self-help groups (Lieberman & Snowden, 1993). Self-help groups have been designed for people facing a wide variety of issues and in a variety of situations, including most chronic physical and mental illnesses. Some groups cater to people who are bereaved, disabled, or addicted; other groups are designed for people who face discrimination because of their unconventional status, such as being divorced, biracial, gay, unemployed, or adopted.

Some social workers and other health and human services professionals consider self-help groups a marginal form of help seeking. They fail to see how central self-help is in terms of the number of people involved and the number of areas it covers. Such ignorance is understandable, given the scant attention self-help usually receives in professional education programs.

Nonetheless, some professionals dealing with addictions coordinate their activities with those of self-help programs (Humphreys & Woods, 1993; Miller & Mahler, 1991). Some visionaries look to the day when all health and human services professionals will coordinate their work with self-help groups. Support for this vision is broad: The vast majority of those who go, or have gone, to self-help groups also go, or have gone, to professionals (Lieberman & Snowden, 1993).

NATURE AND CULTURE OF SELF-HELP

Two Different Perspectives

Self-help interventions or processes are based on experience with phenomena rather than on professional expertise. The perspective of self-help is phenomenological, because the emphasis is on how the experience feels to the insider rather than on how the problem or situation has been analyzed by the outside observer. The self-help perspective is subjective and committed rather than objective and neutral. The self-help and professional perspectives can be viewed as generating different truths that are fashioned into separate models, each with its own integrity.

The two perspectives can be thought of as separate cultures, each with its distinctive beliefs and language. Professionals must take it as axiomatic that one perspective is not inherently superior to the other and must be careful not to appear to be judging the truth of self-help beliefs. Professionals must restrain the impulse to translate self-help language into professional language or to otherwise colonize self-help by substituting professional concepts for those of self-help. By explicitly questioning the commonly held assumption that they have a more secure grasp of the truth, professionals can become more sensitive to the autonomy of self-help groups and the integrity of self-help beliefs and practices.

Increased Sensitivity

Professionals can increase their sensitivity by cultivating an appreciation for the language and "voice" of the particular self-help groups they are interested in. Terms such as "powerless," as used by Alcoholics Anonymous (AA); "angry temper," as used by Recovery, Inc.; or "brain disease," as used by the Alliance for the Mentally Ill, have important symbolic meanings within these organizations— meanings that must be understood by those who collaborate with them. Professionals who make the effort to understand such language send a message that they accept the self-help group on its own terms. The success of this effort can be checked by seeing if they can reconstruct a member's typical story or, even better, the prototype story or the community narrative of the membership (Rappaport, 1993).

An added benefit to understanding the "folk concepts" of self-help groups is that such concepts are often at the heart of what a group considers to be its most important problem (Antze, 1976). By demonstrating understanding, the professional acknowledges that self-help concepts are not merely thin paraphrases of superior concepts in the professional lexicon and shows an appreciation that self-help concepts enable members of the group to communicate more efficiently and precisely than they could using everyday language (Collier, 1991).

In developing an appreciation for the language, norms, rituals, and other aspects of the self-help culture, the social work field is moving beyond the well-accepted (if negative) injunction to avoid involvement in a self-help group's decision making or group leadership structure (Kurtz, 1984; Toseland & Hacker, 1982) toward a positive injunction to become conversant with the distinctive values, beliefs, and practices of self-help organizations.

A passage from the journal of Ernie K. (1984) illustrates one of the cultural norms of AA that social workers and other health and human services professionals must understand if they are to be maximally effective in facilitating client involvement in AA programs:

> We can feel at home only where we are needed. That powerful insight seems to me to capture one of the great gifts of Alcoholics Anonymous to any newcomer.

Usually, by the time most of us get to A.A., we have become so dysfunctional that it is difficult even to imagine being needed. That is probably why I found it so difficult to believe the welcome that A.A.s offered me at my first meeting. That is surely why I find it so helpful to identify with every newcomer's dawning identification as an alcoholic.

For the truth endures: what is needed in Alcoholics Anonymous is ourselves—ourselves as alcoholics. That means that what A.A. needs from any alcoholic is precisely his or her alcoholism. We are needed not for some strength or talent or ability, but precisely because of our weakness, or inability, that about us which causes us to feel worst about ourselves.

Some of us stumble on that insight. At least I did, at first, delighted in the discovery that I had finally found a place where I seemed needed, I somehow failed to realize that those recovering alcoholics needed me not for my ideas and articulateness, but for my alcoholism. I thus missed one of the main points in A.A.: we come in order to get, but we stay in order to give, and the main thing we have to give is our continuing necessity to get. We are in A.A. for our own sobriety, the moment we no longer need, we are no longer needed. (pp. 27–28)

IMPETUS FOR SELF-HELP GROUPS

Professionals are more effective collaborators with self-help groups when they understand the basic impetus to self-help. It was once fashionable to say that self-help groups came into being in reaction to the deficiencies of professional service providers. Like many generalizations, this was true in certain instances. Members of the National Alliance for the Mentally Ill, for example, felt the need to protect themselves from blaming professionals. However, it is also true that professionals were (and are) commonly in the background, nurturing self-help organizations in their formative years (Borman, 1979).

Much of the time the impetus for self-help participation is the attraction of comparing notes with like-minded people who have faced similar situations. Moreover, in self-help groups some of the talk about professional "outrageous" behavior serves to facilitate the identification of members with one another and to increase cohesion in the group.

FUNCTIONS OF SELF-HELP GROUPS

Information Dissemination

Self-help groups can be a rich source of information about a situation, condition, or illness that an individual may face. Prime mechanisms for disseminating information are literature tables at self-help meetings and national bookstores of self-help organizations through which approved publications are sold. Organizations such as the National Alliance for the Mentally Ill and the National Depressive and Manic Depressive Association offer sound, up-to-date, and practical publications from various sources about the problems the groups deal with. Other organizations, such as Recovery, Inc., and Alcoholics Anonymous, distribute only their own publications, but at their meetings other publications are talked about and may be recommended. Publications written from the perspective of consumers or family members, as well as authoritative professional publications, offer special value. Professionals could benefit from reviewing the self-help literature.

Information on the choice of professional service providers available is a frequent concern of self-help groups (Schubert & Borkman, 1994). Local self-help groups usually identify practitioners whom other members have used with good results. Self-help groups may also offer information about what to expect from a social worker or other professional, what questions to ask, and what to do to get desired services. Both local groups and the national offices of self-help organizations are valuable sources of information about entitlement programs for which members may be eligible.

Much of the information offered by self-help groups is unlikely to duplicate information offered by professionals. For example, a person affected by a long-term condition or situation may be given tips on the proper management of the myriad practical issues to be faced. Ideas may be given on how to deal with gaps in employment histories, or with specific focal problems or concerns. Relevant self-help groups can be among the best sources of information on such concerns as resisting the urge to gamble (Gamblers Anonymous), facing parental stress (Parents Anonymous), "coming out" to parents (Parents and Friends of Lesbians and Gays), explaining the genetics of illness to a son or daughter (sickle cell groups), and modifying a lifestyle to conserve energy and minimize arthritic pain (Young at Heart). Self-help groups can provide a range of examples of how others have faced difficult lifestyle issues and can respond to new ideas and strategies.

One advantage of a self-help group is that information can be gradually presented as a member is ready to take it in. The timing of the presentation of information and the amount of information presented are crucial variables in the assimilation of both printed and oral information. The self-help group also provides members with a built-in "discussion section" or "break-out group" to ponder the personal relevance and application of information.

Support

People are buoyed by information that distress has an adequate cause, that actions can be taken to reduce distress, and that highly respected individuals struggle with similar issues. When group members think of support, they think of the boost they get from close personal relationships within the self-help group. Such relationships are played out not only in the formal sessions, but also through a variety of extra-group contacts. They offer companionship, encouragement, and positive regard of a kind that social workers and other professionals tend not to provide. Social workers often help the individual to get started on the right course, but in the long run the individual is likely to benefit from the sustenance drawn from the companionship of someone who has "been there" and has experienced and overcome a similar situation. Someone who has already been through the experience is often able to offer a different kind of support than a professional can offer.

The approval of peers is different from that of professionals, and the experienced self-helper has a different potential to help people feel good about themselves. The self-helper speaks with the authentic voice of experience in the context of a relationship of equals. The approval offered by peers need not be viewed from the perspective of the supplicant's role inherent in the professional relationship.

It is also an advantage that in self-help groups approval and commendation can be expressed indirectly as the member participates in the group's ordinary activities. For example, helping with normal maintenance tasks and with setting up for and cleaning up after a meeting is a way to be appreciated without the need to ask for support. Helping to get a mailing out offers the opportunity for companionship and socially sanctioned opportunities for the expression of appreciation. It is easier for people to receive help when they also have the opportunity to give it.

Advocacy

For many individuals, the personal growth experienced in a self-help group may stimulate involvement in advocacy activities. Thus, advocacy may be part of giving help to others. Although 12-step groups do not engage in advocacy, their members do through other mechanisms, and the 12-step experience often serves to raise consciousness about the need for advocacy and through the fellowship provides ongoing support for it. Many members of Alcoholics Anonymous find the numerous local Councils on Alcoholism an important outlet for their advocacy interests.

Other organizations, such as the National Alliance for the Mentally Ill and the Lupus Foundation, make advocacy an integral part of their programs and support their members' advocacy activities. Such organizations coordinate campaigns at the national, state, and local levels, in both the public and private sectors, to fund more research and better services. Local self-help groups and their members nearly always figure prominently in the conduct of these campaigns.

Social workers and other professionals engage in advocacy on a different basis, relying on the power of information and framing their arguments in terms of science and rationality. They assume the posture of disinterested, above-the-fray experts who recommend solutions to the public. Self-help leaders, in contrast, commit themselves wholeheartedly to a campaign, neither forgoing any source of power nor overvaluing the persuasive power of rational argument.

DISTINGUISHING CHARACTERISTICS OF SELF-HELP GROUPS

Organizations that focus only on advocacy differ from self-help organizations that combine advocacy with other functions. One major difference concerns the object of the advocacy. Self-help groups advocate for themselves—"ourselves," as they put it. The pronoun is used both reflexively, as in "we work for ourselves," and emphatically, as in "we decide for *ourselves.*" Advocacy by other groups or organizations, such as mutual aid, self-care, and community development groups, is often on behalf of others and is frequently professionally directed.

The terms "mutual aid group" and "self-help group" are sometimes used synonymously. Mutual aid is an apt term in that it refers to a key quality of self-help that distinguishes it from self-care. However, the reflexive quality of self-help is compromised if the term "mutual aid" is applied so loosely as to permit professional facilitation or to include people whose issues are more heterogeneous than would be the case in a self-help group made up of people like "ourselves."

Distinctions must also be made among self-help support groups, support groups under professional auspices, and therapy groups. In general, support groups tend to favor using experiential knowledge for the purpose of ameliorating stress; therapy groups use expert knowledge in pursuit of explicit therapeutic objectives (Wasserman & Danforth, 1988). Among the distinctions between therapy groups and self-help groups, Lieberman (1990) notes self-help groups differ from therapy groups in the closeness between the experienced self-helper and the newcomer, the specificity of helping methods, and the involvement of members outside formal group meetings.

Community development groups can be distinguished from self-help groups in that community development involves a shift in focus from the personal, "ourselves" focus to a more impersonal community focus. In self-care groups the focus turns inward toward an exclusive focus on the self, rather than the self as a member of the group.

The distinctions discussed here (and others like them) and their associated consequences call for careful study to avoid suppressing the effective characteristics of self-help by inadvertently mixing them with other characteristics that might be counteractive. Through an understanding of the distinguishing qualities of self-help groups, professionals should be able to help their clients make more effective use of such groups. Greater sensitivity to terms should also clarify communication among professionals, who may not be in disagreement about a topic so much as inadvertently talking about different topics.

MISUSES AND RISKS

Avoiding Misuses

The self-help concept has been appropriated for a number of questionable practices, among them those of some professional therapists and rehabilitation centers who, for example, cloak their activities in 12-step images. Not surprisingly, such practices are probably ineffective because they do not partake of the essential culture of self-help groups. Other therapists may scheme to recruit clients from self-help groups—a practice that can be damaging if it detaches a person from a valuable source of help.

Also undermining the self-help culture is a tendency of some professionals to start their own self-help groups, if this means that the professional assumes the role of permanent decision maker or group leader. This is not to say that professionals cannot play useful behind-the-scenes roles in stimulating the development of self-help programs. In doing so, it is important that professionals take into account previous work in the field and begin by considering whether they could encourage the formation of a local chapter of a relatively well-developed self-help model (Powell, 1990) and then back off from involvement. Such models can be useful guides for developing local groups. In some organizations, national offices make available chapter start-up kits or documents.

Minimizing Risks

The misuses of self-help groups blend into the risks associated with using them. There is not likely to be much benefit derived by members of an ad hoc group of tenuously connected individuals who make up a program as they go along and as they flounder in their own problems. The proven viability of a national model can be invaluable in organizing self-help meetings and avoiding risks, but the structure of a group's program must also be actualized by experienced survivors who have struggled (and preferably are still struggling) with the focal problem. However, even among groups operating with well-structured programs and implemented by experienced survivors, the group's effectiveness for individuals will vary considerably. Thus organizations such as Alcoholics Anonymous advise newcomers to minimize the risk of a poor fit by trying out a number of groups before selecting a home group.

When newcomers do not have such choices available to them, social workers and other professionals can assist in managing the risk by helping an individual decide whether continued participation in an ill-fitting or flawed group is wise or determine what parts of a self-help experience are useful and what parts are not. However, the limits of a professional's involvement in self-help programs must be recognized (Humphreys, 1993). Social workers so engaged are empowered by having contacts within the self-help organization to turn to for information and advice, and sometimes it is appropriate for a social worker to mediate the input from the self-help leader (Powell, 1987). In other instances, a social worker might arrange direct contact between a self-help leader and the client (Kelly et al., 1990; McGill & Patterson, 1990; Sisson & Mallams, 1981).

SELF-HELP AS A SERVICE SYSTEM COMPONENT

Social workers and other professionals will be advantaged to the extent that they view the self-help sector as an integral part of the human services system and make routine use of its resources. To do so they must overcome professional-centric biases (Salzer, McFadden, & Rappaport, in press) and develop direct contacts with relevant self-help groups (Wintersteen & Young, 1988). Professionals can thus ensure that their clients have access to additional help that is complementary to professional help. Client participation in self-help can also add texture and authenticity to the professional relationship (Brown, 1985; Denzin, 1987; Miller & Mahler, 1991).

It is important for social workers to learn, as part of their professional education, how to facilitate their clients' participation in self-help groups (McCrady & Irvine, 1989; Nowinski & Baker, 1992). It is also important that members of minority populations are included in the self-help sector. There is mounting evidence that self-help groups have much to offer people of color and that, given the right circumstances, they will find self-help beneficial (Caldwell, 1983; DenHartog, Homer, & Wilson, 1986; Gutierrez, Ortega, & Suarez, 1990; Hudson, 1985; Humphreys & Woods, 1993; Martin & Martin, 1985; Neighbors, Elliott, & Gant, 1990; Snowden & Lieberman, 1994).

Professionals must also be prepared to help the client cognitively integrate the self-help and professional help experiences. Most people who have participated in self-help groups will also use professional services at some time (Lieberman & Snowden, 1993); their ability to use professional help will depend in part on an informed discussion of their effort to solve their problems by participation in a self-help program.

It should be emphasized that self-help participation should not be used as a poor person's or uninsured person's psychotherapy, although it would be proper public policy to promote self-help participation to curb inappropriate or excessive use of professional services. The self-help sector also should not be viewed as a single, homogeneous entity. Just as within a nominally well-structured organization such as Alcoholics Anonymous there is tremendous variety (Kurtz, 1993), considerable variety exists among self-help organizations (Powell, 1987; Schubert & Borkman, 1991). Practitioners must be prepared to individualize self-help organizations and to individualize local self-help groups if the full benefits are to be obtained from self-help participation. An excellent source of information about local self-help groups is available from local and state self-help clearinghouses. White and Madara's (1992) *Self-Help Sourcebook* is highly recommended for information about regional and national self-help models for any issue.

REFERENCES

Antze, P. (1976). Role of ideologies in peer psychotherapy groups. *Journal of Applied Behavioral Science, 12,* 323–346.

Borman, L. D. (1979). Characteristics of development and growth. In M. A. Lieberman & L. D. Borman (Eds.), *Self-help groups for coping with crisis* (pp. 13–42). San Francisco: Jossey-Bass.

Brown, S. (1985). *Treating the alcoholic: A developmental model of recovery.* New York: John Wiley & Sons.

Caldwell, F. J. (1983). Alcoholics Anonymous as a viable treatment resource for black alcoholics. In T. S. Watts, Jr., & R. Wright (Eds.), *Black alcoholism: Toward a comprehensive understanding* (pp. 85–99). Springfield, IL: Charles C Thomas.

Collier, G. (1991). *The essential role of language in the recovery method.* Presented at the Conference on Mental Illness, Stigma, and Self-Help: Recovery, Inc., and the Pioneering Work of Abraham A. Low, M.D. Chicago.

DenHartog, G. L., Homer, A. L., & Wilson, R. B. (1986). *Cooperation: A tradition in action: Self-help involvement of clients in Missouri alcohol and drug abuse treatment programs.* Missouri: Missouri Department of Mental Health.

Denzin, N. K. (1987). *The alcoholic self.* Beverly Hills, CA: Sage Publications.

French, J.R.P., & Raven, B. (1959). The bases of social power. In D. Cartwright (Ed.), *Studies in social power* (pp. 150–167). Ann Arbor: University of Michigan, Institute for Social Research.

Gutierrez, L., Ortega, R. M., & Suarez, Z. (1990). Self-help and the Latino community. In T. J. Powell (Ed.), *Working with self-help* (pp. 189–217, 218–236). Silver Spring, MD: NASW Press.

Hudson, H. L. (1985). How and why Alcoholics Anonymous works for blacks. *Alcoholism Treatment Quarterly, 2,* 11–29.

Humphrey, R. H., O'Malley, P. M., Johnston, L. D., & Backman, J. G. (1988). Bases of power, facilitation effects, and attitudes and behavior: Direct, indirect, and interactive determinants of drug use. *Social Psychology Quarterly, 51*(4), 329–345.

Humphreys, K. (1993). Psychotherapy and the twelve step approach for substance abusers: The limits of integration. *Psychotherapy, 30*(2), 207–213.

Humphreys, K., & Woods, M. D. (1993). Researching mutual help group participation in a segregated society. *Journal of Applied Behavioral Science, 29*(2), 181–199.

Janis, I. L. (1983). The role of social support in adherence to stressful decisions. *American Psychologist, 38,* 143–160.

K., Ernie. (1984). *90 meetings, 90 days: A journal of experience, strength and hope.* Minneapolis: Johnson Institute.

Kelly, K. M., Sautter, F., Tugrul, K., & Weaver, M. D. (1990). Fostering self-help on an inpatient unit. *Archives of Psychiatric Nursing, IV*(3), 161–165.

Kurtz, E. (1993). Research on Alcoholics Anonymous: The historical context. In B. S. McCrady & W. R. Miller (Eds.), *Research on Alcoholics Anonymous: Opportunities and alternatives* (pp. 13–26). New Brunswick, NJ: Rutgers Center of Alcohol Studies.

Kurtz, L. F. (1984). Ideological differences between professionals and A.A. members. *Alcoholism Treatment Quarterly, 1*(2), 73–85.

Lieberman, M. A. (1990). A group therapist perspective on self-help groups. *International Journal of Group Psychotherapy, 40*(3), 251–278.

Lieberman, M. A., & Snowden, L. (1993). Problems in assessing prevalence and membership characteristics of self-help group participants. *Journal of Applied Behavioral Science, 29*(2), 164–178.

Litman-Adizes, T., Raven, B. H., & Fontaine, G. (1978). Consequences of social power and causal attribution for compliance as seen by powerholder and target. *Personality and Social Psychology Bulletin, 4*(2), 260–264.

Martin, E., & Martin, J. (1985). *The helping tradition in the black family and community.* Silver Spring, MD: National Association of Social Workers.

McCrady, B. S., & Irvine, S. (1989). Self-help groups. In R. K. Hester & W. R. Miller (Eds.), *Handbook of alcoholism treatment approaches and effective alternatives* (pp. 153–169). Tarrytown, NY: Pergamon Press.

McGill, C. W., & Patterson, C. J. (1990). Former patients as peer counselors on locked psychiatric inpatient units. *Hospital and Community Psychiatry, 41*(9), 1017–1019.

Miller, N., & Mahler, J. C. (1991). Alcoholics Anonymous and the "AA" model for treatment. *Alcoholism Treatment Quarterly, 8*(1), 39–51.

National Black Women's Health Project. (1987). *Vital signs.* Atlanta: Author.

Neighbors, H. W., Elliott, K. A., & Gant, L. M. (1990). Self-help and black Americans: A strategy of empowerment. In T. J. Powell (Ed.), *Working with self-help* (pp. 189–217). Silver Spring, MD: NASW Press.

Nowinski, J., & Baker, S. (1992). *The twelve-step facilitation handbook: A systematic approach to early recovery from alcoholism and addictionism.* New York: Lexington Books.

Powell, T. J. (1987). *Self-help organizations and professional practice.* Silver Spring, MD: National Association of Social Workers.

Powell, T. J. (1990). Differences between national self-help organizations and local self-help groups: Implications for members and professionals. In T. J. Powell (Ed.), *Working with self-help* (pp. 50–70). Silver Spring, MD: NASW Press.

Rappaport, J. (1993). Narrative studies, personal stories and identity transformation in the context of mutual help. *Journal of Applied Behavioral Science, 29*(2), 237–254.

Raven, B. H. (1992). A power/interaction model of interpersonal influence: French and Raven thirty years later. *Journal of Social Behavior and Personality, 7*(2), 217–244.

Salzer, M. S., McFadden, L., & Rappaport, J. (in press). Professional views of self help groups. A comparative and contextual analysis. *Administration and Policy in Mental Health.*

Schubert, M. A., & Borkman, T. J. (1991). An organizational typology for self-help groups. *American Journal of Community Psychology, 19*(5), 769–788.

Schubert, M. A., & Borkman, T. (1994). Identifying the experiential knowledge created by a self-help group. In T. J. Powell (Ed.), *Understanding self-help organizations: Frameworks and findings* (pp. 227–246). Newbury Park, CA: Sage Publications.

Sisson, R. W., & Mallams, J. H. (1981). Use of systematic encouragement and community access procedures to increase attendance at Alcoholics Anonymous and Al-Anon meetings. *American Journal of Drug and Alcohol Abuse, 8*(3), 371–375.

Snowden, L. R., & Lieberman, M. A. (1994). African-American participation in self-help groups. In T. J. Powell (Ed.), *Understanding self-help organizations: Frameworks and findings* (pp. 50–61). Newbury Park, CA: Sage Publications.

Toseland, R. W., & Hacker, L. (1982). Self-help groups and professional involvement. *Social Work, 27,* 341–348.

Wasserman, H., & Danforth, H. E. (1988). *The human bond: Support groups and mutual aid.* New York: Springer.

White, B. J., & Madara, E. J. (Eds.). (1992). *The self-help sourcebook: Finding and forming mutual aid self-help groups* (4th ed.). Denville, NJ: American Self-Help Clearinghouse.

Wintersteen, R. T., & Young, L. (1988). Effective professional collaboration with family support groups. *Psychosocial Rehabilitation Journal, 12*(1), 19–31.

FURTHER READING

California Self-Help Center. (1990). *Resources for self-help groups: A catalog of print, audio and visual materials for starting and maintaining self-help groups.* (Available from UCLA, 2349 Franz Hall, 405 Hilgard Ave., Los Angeles, CA 90024-1453)

Chesler, M. A., & Chesney, B. K. (in press). *Self-help groups for parents of children with cancer.* Madison: University of Wisconsin.

Denzin, N. K. (1987). *The recovering alcoholic.* Newbury Park, CA: Sage Publications.

Farquharson, A. (1990). *A guide to competency profile of human service professionals working with self-help groups.* Victoria, Canada: University of Victoria.

Katz, A. H., Hedrick, H. L., Isenberg, D. H., Thompson, L. M., Goodrich, T., & Kutscher, A. H. (Eds.). (1992). *Self-help: Concepts and applications.* Philadelphia: Charles Press.

Kurtz, K. (1988). *AA: The story.* San Francisco: Harper/ Hazelden.

Lieberman, M. A., & Borman, L. D. (Eds.). (1979). *Self-help groups for coping with crisis: Origins, members, processes and impact.* San Francisco: Jossey-Bass.

McCrady, B. S., & Miller, W. R. (Eds.). (1993). *Research on Alcoholics Anonymous: Opportunities and alternatives.* New Brunswick, NJ: Rutgers Center of Alcohol Studies.

Powell, T. J. (Ed.). (1994). *Understanding self-help: Frameworks and findings.* Newbury Park, CA: Sage Publications.

Zinman, S., & Harp, H. T. (1987). *Reaching across: Mental health clients helping each other.* Riverside: California Network of Mental Health Clients.

Thomas J. Powell, PhD, is director and professor of social work, University of Michigan, Center for Self-Help Research & Knowledge Dissemination, Ann Arbor, MI 48104.

For further information see

Adolescents: Direct Practice; Advocacy; Bereavement and Loss; Child Abuse and Neglect: Direct Practice; Clinical Social Work; Community Development; Direct Practice Overview; Eating Disorders and Other Compulsive Behaviors; Ethnic-Sensitive Practice; Families: Direct Practice; Gay Men: Direct Practice; Goal Setting and Intervention Planning; Group Practice; HIV/AIDS: Direct Practice; Information and Referral Services; Lesbians: Direct Practice; Men: Direct Practice; Mutual Aid Societies; Natural Helping Networks; Social Work Practice: Theoretical Base; Substance Abuse: Direct Practice; Women: Direct Practice.

Key Words	
mutual aid groups	support groups
referent power	12-step groups
self-help	

Sentencing

See Courts and Corrections *(Reader's Guide)*

Sentencing of Criminal Offenders
Marc Mauer

Sentencing policies in the 1990s reflect the continuation of a trend from rehabilitation to punishment that dates back to the 1970s. This shift was originally the result of ideological critiques of the prison system in the late 1960s by both liberals and conservatives. However, years of steadily increasing inmate populations have created substantial fiscal and human costs for the system, leading to calls for an expansion of alternatives to incarceration and a reexamination of crime control policies. Sentencing policies into the first decade of the 21st century will be determined by the interplay of fiscal constraints, political rhetoric and leadership, and movements for reform among criminal justice professionals and others.

ROOTS OF CHANGES IN SENTENCING POLICIES

Since the birth of the penitentiary in Pennsylvania in the late 1700s, the goals of sentencing and the prison system have undergone periodic changes. The penitentiary—derived from the word "penitence"—was conceived by reformers as an institution where those who had gone astray could study the Bible, reflect on their sins, and become better citizens. Subsequent developments led to the promotion of discipline as a guiding principle, achieved through a system of prison labor. In the modern era, rehabilitation came to be viewed as the primary function of the prison. Although penal institutions rarely provided rehabilitative services of sufficient variety and intensity to accomplish their goals, significant support existed among both corrections officials and the public to make this goal a priority in corrections.

Liberal Concerns: Potential for Abuse

Beginning in the mid-1960s, however, the rehabilitative goal of prisons came under attack from two directions. Liberal groups began to question whether rehabilitation was achievable in inherently coercive institutions such as prisons and mental hospitals (American Friends Service Committee, 1971). Because prisoners were often viewed as oppressed individuals who had been denied a legitimate role in American society, this critique in its most general sense raised a fundamental challenge to the state's incarcerating powers as unnecessarily intrusive.

In the area of sentencing policy, some questioned the broad discretion and potential abuse inherent in sentencing policies of the period. At that time, almost all states used indeterminate sentencing systems. In these frameworks, prison sentences were meted out with a minimum and maximum time to be served; the actual number of years served was left to the discretion of a parole board.

The rationale for the indeterminate sentence was to support the goal of rehabilitation. A prisoner could "earn" his or her release by following prison rules and engaging in educational or vocational opportunities within the prison, with the incentive of an earlier release date. Although there was some theoretical justification for such behavioral incentives, the system also carried the potential for abuse of the broad discretion granted to judges and parole boards. Instances of sentencing disparity by race, geographic location, or sentencing judge were cited as a rationale for reducing some or all of these discretionary powers.

Conservative Concerns: Crime

Coinciding with this liberal critique of indeterminate sentencing was a conservative attack on the system. Frustrated by rising crime rates in the 1960s, the decisions of the Warren Supreme Court, and growing liberal dissent against government policies, conservatives took on the issue of crime as the centerpiece of a political program. They, too, challenged the indeterminate sentencing system. First, they asserted that indeterminate sentencing led to the early release of offenders who deserved a lengthier prison term. Second, they challenged the rehabilitative underpinnings of indeterminate sentencing, believing that a punitive response to crime, through a definite prison sentence, was more appropriate (Wilson, 1975).

Move toward Determinate Sentencing

The positions of both camps were bolstered by an influential article by Robert Martinson (1974). Based on an analysis of studies of a variety of corrections programs, Martinson concluded that there was no basis for the rehabilitative philosophy in practice. Although Martinson later reconsidered his broad conclusions, and despite critiques from other researchers, the study received broad attention and sounded the "death knell" for the rehabilitative ideal.

Thus, from both directions came support for a more fixed and determinate sentencing structure with decreased emphasis on rehabilitation. The only substantial disagreement among the contending parties regarded the length of prison terms to be imposed, with liberals arguing for shorter fixed terms and conservatives seeking longer fixed terms. The stage was set for a shift in sentencing policy.

Capital Punishment

Concurrent with these developments were changes regarding the death penalty. Although it was once widely used in the United States (there were 200 executions a year in the 1930s), by 1960 the death penalty had fallen into public disfavor. For the first time, a majority of the public indicated opposition to state-sanctioned execution; as a result, only a handful of executions were carried out in the early 1960s. At the same time, legal challenges to the arbitrary nature of the death penalty's imposition were making their way through the courts.

With the growing concern about crime and Richard Nixon's "law and order" theme in his 1968 presidential campaign came calls for stepped-up use of capital punishment. Finally, in 1972 the Supreme Court ruled in *Furman v. Georgia* that the death penalty as it was then imposed was too arbitrary. In striking down existing statutes, however, the Court provided guidance to states on a death penalty framework that it might consider acceptable. Following this, the 1976 *Gregg v. Georgia* decision delineated what the Court considered to be constitutionally permissible: statutes that allowed for the imposition of the death penalty after a consideration of aggravating and mitigating circumstances pertaining to the crime and the offender. The decision led state legislatures to draft new death penalty statutes, with 36 states doing so by the early 1990s.

CHANGES IN SENTENCING POLICIES

In response to the general dissatisfaction with indeterminate sentencing, in the late 1970s legislators began to move toward systems using more determinate, or fixed, sentencing. In keeping with the liberal and conservative forces advocating for these changes, the new sentencing policies were originally championed as meeting two primary goals: (1) to ensure a greater degree of certainty in the expected punishment for a given offense and (2) to reduce injustices caused by sentencing disparity.

Sentencing Guidelines

Determinate sentencing has taken a number of forms, with one of the most common being that of sentencing guidelines. First established in Minnesota, sentencing guideline systems establish a sentencing grid based on the seriousness of the current offense and the offender's previous record. A higher score on either axis of the grid increases the probability that the offender will serve a prison term. Judges are generally required to impose a sentence that falls within the guidelines established for each cell on the grid and can depart from this sentence only if they find compelling reason to do so according to established criteria.

A key issue in this area concerns the policy assumptions that guide a particular guideline system. In the states of Minnesota and Washington, for example, the systems were set up with the explicit purpose of attempting to control the size of the prison population. Thus, if legislators choose to increase the penalty for one offense, they must decrease sanctions for another to maintain an overall balance in the prison system. In contrast, in most state-established guideline systems, as well as in the federal guidelines that went into effect in 1987, prison population control is not an objective.

Harsher Sanctions

Beginning in the early 1980s, legislative momentum developed to adopt mandatory minimum sentences for various crimes as a response to what was characterized as judicial leniency. The premise behind mandatory minimums was that for a given crime, an offender would be required to receive a set minimum prison term regardless of any mitigating circumstances. Sponsors viewed this approach as a means of curbing the arbitrary power of judges and of sending a message to potential offenders that they could not plead their way out of a prison sentence.

By 1990 almost every state and the federal government had adopted some form of mandatory minimum sentencing (Bureau of Justice Statistics, 1992). Most often, these were imposed for drunk driving and drug and firearms offenses. The mandatory penalties for drunk driving were relatively

modest, typically a two- to seven-day jail term for a second conviction. For drug offenses, however, penalties became quite harsh. In the federal system, for example, possession of five grams of crack cocaine called for a mandatory five-year prison sentence, even for a first-time offender.

Although a number of states retained forms of indeterminate sentencing by the early 1990s, the 15-year trend of moving toward more fixed sentencing continued to gain ground. By this time, too, the original liberal–conservative coalition advocating these policies had shifted considerably. More than two decades of intolerably high levels of crime and violence, accompanied by a generally conservative shift in political attitudes across the country, had largely silenced the liberal voice on crime control policy. Increasingly, Democratic and Republican politicians alike campaigned on "get tough" platforms and moved to adopt policies calling for harsher criminal justice sanctions.

IMPACT ON THE CRIMINAL JUSTICE SYSTEM

Increased Incarceration

In the 20-year period beginning in 1973, the nation experienced an unprecedented quadrupling (from 350,000 to 1.4 million) in the number of inmates incarcerated in prisons and jails (Bureau of Justice Statistics, 1993a; Department of Justice, 1993). The magnitude of this increase can be seen in the fact that by the early 1990s, the United States was second only to Russia in its rate of incarceration. The U.S. rate of 519 inmates per 100,000 population was at least four times that of most European nations and Canada (Mauer, 1994). The number of people under probation and parole supervision also greatly increased.

During this same 20-year period, the number of prisoners on death row greatly increased, with more than 2,500 inmates awaiting execution on any given day by the early 1990s. Despite the increasing number of capital prosecutions and convictions, the number of annual executions following resumption of the practice in 1977 remained at a level of 20 to 30 a year (Bureau of Justice Statistics, 1993b); primarily owing to the lengthy appeals process and the reversal of many convictions, the average execution took place nine years after conviction. The lengthy nature of the appeals process led many death penalty proponents to advocate for more restrictive and speedier procedures, including various proposals to limit habeas corpus review.

Racial Bias

As with other aspects of the criminal justice system, imposition of the death penalty has been shown to be fraught with racial bias. A study by Baldus, Pulaski, and Woodworth (1986) clearly demonstrated that the race of both the victim and the offender is one of the key determinants in deciding which offenders receive the death penalty and which receive a life prison term. Despite this finding, the Supreme Court ruled in *McClesky v. Kemp* (1987) that unless a defendant could demonstrate racial bias in an individual case, the evidence of overall racial bias could not be used to invalidate the death penalty.

A racial and ethnic breakdown of the incarcerated population reveals particularly disturbing trends. By 1991 black Americans represented almost half of all inmates, and black males in the United States were incarcerated at a rate four times that of black males in South Africa (Mauer, 1994). Nearly one in four black males in the 20- to 29-year-old age group was under some form of supervision—prison, jail, probation, or parole (Mauer, 1990). Disparities are also found for Hispanics and Native Americans in areas of high concentration. The potential consequences of these high rates of criminal justice control for family and community stability are ominous.

The sentencing reforms introduced in noncapital cases have proved equally problematic in failing to reduce racial bias in the criminal justice system. As determinate sentencing and mandatory minimums have continued to reduce judicial discretion at sentencing, the use of discretion by prosecutors has become increasingly significant.

Studies by the U.S. Sentencing Commission (1991) and the Federal Judicial Center (Meierhoefer, 1992) have demonstrated that African American and Hispanic defendants are more likely than white defendants to be charged with mandatory penalties in similar circumstances. Thus, one of the major objectives of determinate sentencing, that of reducing sentencing disparity, proved to be as illusive as with other sentencing systems.

IMPACT ON CRIME

If this massive increase in the use of incarceration had had a significant impact on crime rates, many citizens might have believed that the fiscal and human costs associated with it were justified. However, by the early 1990s, after more than 20 years of steadily rising prison populations, few Americans perceived themselves to be safer than they had been 10 or 20 years earlier.

Crime rate data confirmed these impressions. A Federal Bureau of Investigation (1992) report on violent crime in the 1990s showed near-record levels of murder, rape, and armed robbery. Although victimization studies conducted by the Justice Department showed a declining trend for property crimes for the 20-year period beginning in 1973, there is substantial doubt as to whether the rising prison population was responsible for this trend. It is less likely that property offenses will be reduced by incarceration, as imprisonment is far more likely for violent offenders. Also, many observers (for example, Austin & Irwin, 1993) believe that the decline in property offenses was offset by the rise in drug offenses beginning in the early 1980s—that is, the teenager who was writing bad checks in 1975 was more likely to be selling cocaine in 1985, hardly a major gain for crime control.

DEVELOPMENT OF ALTERNATIVES TO INCARCERATION

Since the early 1970s there has been a substantial movement to develop a variety of sentencing policies and programs to provide alternatives to incarceration. As with the changes discussed regarding sentencing policy, the movement toward incarceration alternatives has been supported by a diverse political constituency.

The initial thrust for alternatives derived from the contention of reformers that prisons were inhumane and should be used only as a last resort. They advocated for a variety of community-based sanctions that could provide supervision of the offender along with supportive services. These alternatives included having offenders perform community service work or pay restitution to victims, partake in substance abuse programs, live in halfway houses, receive vocational training, and other methods, generally combined with a period of probation supervision.

As the cost of incarceration rose, many local and state officials became increasingly interested in nonprison sanctions. With prison costs approaching $20,000 per year per inmate, the appeal of nonresidential programming and supervision in a time of fiscal constraints became significant.

Although initially there was consensus that these alternatives could divert offenders from prison, actual implementation of this objective proved to be far more difficult in practice. The basic problem facing policymakers is that it is not simple to determine which of the offenders who might be considered good candidates for alternatives to incarceration would otherwise be likely to receive a prison sentence. For example, although a first-time shoplifter will get probation and a first-degree murderer will get a lengthy prison term, it is not always easy to predict whether burglars, low-level drug users, or car thieves will be incarcerated. Thus, the dilemma for policymakers who hope to save money through the use of alternatives is that without sophisticated screening criteria, it is quite possible that a significant portion of the offenders sentenced to an alternative would have otherwise been sentenced to probation. In these instances, the alternative program will actually increase the total cost to the system, as it involves a more intense level of services.

CURRENT SENTENCING ISSUES

Political changes have led to harsher sentencing policies since the 1970s. In particular, the advent of mandatory sentencing and the "war on drugs" have caused major changes in the use of the prison system. From 1983 to 1991 the number of drug offenders in prisons and jails increased from 57,000 to 304,000, and the African American proportion of drug possession arrests rose from 22 percent in 1981 to 37 percent in 1990 (Shine & Mauer, 1993).

More and more criminal justice leaders and state and local officials are critiquing these harsher sentencing policies. This increased scrutiny is the result of three factors: (1) the relative lack of impact of these policies on crime and drug abuse, (2) distortions produced in the system by an undue emphasis on drug abuse, and (3) the escalating costs of the system at a time of fiscal retrenchment.

Despite growing support for reform in some quarters, any substantial change in overall criminal justice and sentencing policy remains problematic. The harsh policies adopted since the 1980s—federal sentencing guidelines, mandatory sentencing, and cutbacks in parole—have created structural obstacles that will be difficult to overcome unless there is a broad commitment to new goals on the part of policymakers.

POTENTIAL DIRECTIONS

If there is to be a change in sentencing policies and direction, the following framework suggests a more rational and effective approach to dealing with criminal behavior.

Overall Approach to Crime

Establish a national crime commission. The commission should develop a long-term agenda for responding to crime, drugs, and violence. The last national commission to examine the criminal justice system, the National Advisory Commission on Criminal Justice Standards and Goals, issued its final report in 1973. Although the commission made many recommendations, its advice was largely ignored in the ensuing decades. Since that time, much has changed in the United States, including the nature of the crime problem. A national commission consisting of criminal justice experts, political leaders, representatives of civil rights and community organizations, religious leaders, and others could make a major contribution in developing public policy in this area and in overcoming the political divisions that have hindered the development of rational discourse on crime.

Establish a crime prevention action agenda. There is a need for government-supported research that aids in identifying programs and policies that can have a long-term impact on crime. Research has indicated the potential crime control impacts of programs such as Head Start and Job Corps, but the debate on effective means of crime control has been hampered by the relative lack of data from other types of interventions.

Treat drug abuse as a public health problem. The renewed "war on drugs" of the 1980s allocated 70 percent of federal funds to law enforcement agencies and just 30 percent to prevention and treatment programs. The failure of this law enforcement and corrections approach has been demonstrated by continuing high rates of drug abuse and drug-related violence despite a record number of drug offenders being incarcerated. Drug abuse should be treated like alcohol abuse, as a social problem best addressed through broad efforts aimed at prevention and treatment.

Develop "problem-solving" responses. The concept of community policing has gained popularity in many police departments. Although this reform is interpreted in varying ways, a central feature is that police effectiveness should be judged by success in resolving problems rather than making arrests. Similarly, some "neighborhood defender offices" attempt to provide legal defense services through a community-based approach. This practice might have implications for other components of the justice system, such as probation and prosecution.

Expand community-based alternatives to incarceration. Despite a mixed history of success, alternatives to incarceration offer the possibility of diverting substantial portions of prison-bound offenders into more productive and cost-effective sanctions. The federal government can play an important role in this regard by supporting research, analysis, and training designed to aid state and local communities.

Approaches to Sentencing

Repeal mandatory sentencing laws. Numerous studies have concluded that mandatory sentencing produces unjust and racially disparate results. Repealing mandatory sentencing laws would still permit judges to sentence offenders to prison but would restore appropriate judicial discretion to take into account a variety of factors regarding the offender and the offense in determining a sentence.

Abolish the death penalty. Virtually all industrialized nations except the United States have abolished the death penalty. In addition to moral concerns regarding the death penalty, there is no credible evidence that capital punishment has any impact on murder rates. States considering abolition of the death penalty may choose to adopt sentences of life without parole as an alternative. However, even this penalty should be considered judiciously, as it rules out the possibility of rehabilitation or incapacitation through a shorter prison term.

Approaches to Reducing Disparity

Reduce racial disparity. Racial disparity in the criminal justice system is a product of both high crime rates among some groups and differential treatment by the criminal justice system. Criminal justice policies that have contributed to racial disparity include law enforcement policies that unduly punish African Americans and policing practices that focus on inner-city communities. Local and state policy groups should assess these practices and recommend changes where appropriate. In addition, court systems should explore the use of increased diversion from the system or linkages with community-based organizations to provide young offenders with mentoring, training, and other services.

Reduce disparity based on economic class. The advantages accruing to wealthier defendants in the justice system include access to expert legal assistance, sentencing consultants, and treatment programs. Funding and resources should be made available so that low-income defendants have access to similar expertise and services.

CONCLUSION

Despite more than two decades of "get tough" legislation, changes in sentencing structures, and political rhetoric on crime, rates of violent crime in the 1990s have remained at near-record levels. In comparison with most other industrialized nations, three factors distinguish crime policy in the United States: (1) the proliferation of weapons among the population, with only modest gun control policies; (2) the vast disparity in wealth and poverty and the absence of a strong social welfare system; and (3) the extreme emotional nature of the crime debate in the United States and the relatively narrow range of policy options that have been considered in response to crime. Until there is a broad national commitment to address these issues, it is unlikely that changes in sentencing policy will have a substantial impact on crime.

REFERENCES

American Friends Service Committee. (1971). *Struggle for justice*. New York: Hill & Wang.

Austin, J., & Irwin, J. (1993). *Does imprisonment reduce crime? A critique of "voodoo" criminology*. San Francisco: National Council on Crime and Delinquency.

Baldus, D., Pulaski, C., & Woodworth, G. (1986). Arbitrariness and discrimination in the administration of the death penalty: A challenge to state supreme courts. *Stetson Law Review, 15*, 133–261.

Bureau of Justice Statistics. (1992). *State justice sourcebook of statistics and research*. Washington, DC: Author.

Bureau of Justice Statistics. (1993a). *Jail inmates 1992*. Washington, DC: Author.

Bureau of Justice Statistics. (1993b). *Sourcebook of criminal justice statistics*. Washington, DC: Author.

Department of Justice. (1993, October 3). *Half year increase pushes prison population to record high* (Press release). Washington, DC: Author.

Federal Bureau of Investigation. (1992). *Uniform crime reports, 1992*. Washington, DC: Author.

Furman v. Georgia, 408 U.S. 238 (1972).

Gregg v. Georgia, 428 U.S. 153 (1976).

Martinson, R. (1974). What works: Questions and answers about prison reform. *Public Interest, 35*, 22–54.

Mauer, M. (1990). *Young black men and the criminal justice system: A growing national problem*. Washington, DC: Sentencing Project.

Mauer, M. (1994). *Americans behind bars: The international use of incarceration, 1992–93*. Washington, DC: Sentencing Project.

McClesky v. Kemp, 481 U.S. 279 (1987).

Meierhoefer, B. (1992). *The general effect of mandatory minimum prison terms*. Washington, DC: Federal Judicial Center.

National Advisory Commission on Criminal Justice Standards and Goals. (1973). *Task force report on corrections*. Washington, DC: U.S. Government Printing Office.

Shine, C., & Mauer, M. (1993). *Does the punishment fit the crime? Drug users and drunk drivers, questions of race and class*. Washington, DC: Sentencing Project.

U.S. Sentencing Commission. (1991). *Mandatory minimum penalties in the federal criminal justice system*. Washington, DC: Author.

Wilson, J. (1975). *Thinking about crime*. New York: Random House.

FURTHER READING

Cullen, F., & Gilbert, K. (1982). *Reaffirming rehabilitation*. Cincinnati: Anderson.

Currie, E. (1985). *Confronting crime*. New York: Pantheon.
Currie, E. (1993). *Reckoning: Drugs, the cities, and the American future*. New York: Hill & Wang.
Friedman, L. (1993). *Crime and punishment in American history*. New York: Basic Books.
Human Rights Watch. (1993). *The Human Rights Watch global report on prisons*. New York: Author.
Prejean, H. (1993). *Dead man walking*. New York: Random House.
Reiss, A., & Roth, J. (Eds.). (1993). *Understanding and preventing violence*. Washington, DC: National Academy Press.

Marc Mauer, MSW, is assistant director, The Sentencing Project, 918 F Street, NW, Suite 501, Washington, DC 20004.

For further information see

Adult Corrections; Adult Courts; Civil Rights; Criminal Justice Overview; Criminal Justice: Class, Race, and Gender Issues; Deinstitutionalization; Family Views in Correctional Programs; Female Criminal Offenders; Homicide; Juvenile and Family Courts; Juvenile Corrections; Peace and Social Justice; Police Social Work; Probation and Parole; Program Evaluation; Rehabilitation of Criminal Offenders; Social Planning; Substance Abuse: Legal Issues; Victim Services and Victim/Witness Assistance Programs.

Key Words

capital punishment	prison
corrections	sentencing
criminal justice	

Seton, Elizabeth Ann Bayley

See Biographies section, Volume 3

Settlements and Neighborhood Centers
Rolland F. Smith

Settlement houses, which have evolved into neighborhood centers or community-based family centers, are rooted in the late 19th-century foundation of social work. The settlement house movement shares that distinction with the Charity Organization Societies movement, whose national expression was the National Conference of Charities and Correction. The settlement house movement sometimes converged with the Charity Organization Societies movement as demonstrated by prominent settlement workers in the leadership of the National Conference of Charities and Correction (Carson, 1990).

Yet settlement house leaders also felt the need to assert their own movement and expressed that sentiment in the founding of the National Federation of Settlements in 1911 as a mechanism for public policy advocacy (Carson, 1990). Charities, reformers claimed, do *for,* whereas settlements do *with* (Philpott, 1991). The reformers also contended that charities help people in the private realm and focus on personal coping. Settlements involve people in the public realm and focus on social reform (Krause, 1980). In any case, no understanding of social work is complete without identifying its roots and its present challenges in the settlement house movement.

BEGINNINGS

The settlement house movement was born as a response to industrial capitalism with its corresponding political movements of the left and right wings. It is fitting that the movement traces its origins to London, the apex of 19th century capitalism. In 1884 Samuel Barnett, a parish priest,

founded Toynbee Hall in London's East End Slum as a residence for students, a location for social services, and a place through which the poor workers of London became visible to the public (Meacham, 1987). Stanton Coit and Jane Addams, having lived and learned at Toynbee Hall, returned to their respective cities to found Neighborhood Guild (now University Settlement) on the Lower East Side of New York City in 1886 and Hull House on the Near West Side of Chicago in 1889 (Carson, 1990). Thus the settlement house movement in America was launched.

In 1891 Robert Wood founded Andover House (now South End House) in Boston. In 1893 Lillian Wald founded the Henry Street Settlement on the Lower East Side of New York. Graham Taylor founded the Chicago Commons in 1894, followed by the founding of College Settlement in Los Angeles in 1894, Hiram and Goodrich Houses in Cleveland in 1896, and settlement houses throughout the time of urbanization of and immigration to the United States. Ada McKinley, who began settlement work in the Douglas area of Chicago in 1919 and founded Southside Settlement House in 1924, began a long tradition of African American women in settlement house leadership. Even in the middle of the Pacific, Palama Settlement was organized in Honolulu by the philanthropic wives of plantation owners for poor sugar and pine workers from Japan and the Philippines.

CHARACTERISTICS OF SETTLEMENT HOUSES

Settlement houses were missions of churches intent on living out the social gospel. They were learning sites for colleges intent on applying social sciences. They also were houses of charity for philanthropists intent on reducing misery. Above all, settlements were places where ministers, students, or humanitarians "settled" (hence the name) to interact with poor slum dwellers with the purpose of alleviating the conditions of capitalism. Those conditions included a poor working class formed by the migration of people from the country to crowded cities; from agricultural Eastern Europe to an industrializing America; and from a rural, defeated South to a rapidly commercializing, urbanizing North. Depending on the character of its neighborhood, the charisma of its leader, and the source of its funding, settlement work ranged from direct aid for children and indigents to organizing people for social justice.

Social Reform

From the beginning, there was a strong social reform agenda in the settlement house movement. Barnett (cited in Bond, 1990) of Toynbee Hall "saw man as responsible, society as organized, institutions as functional and participation of persons as a duty, a privilege, and a challenge. He had a phenomenal sense for wholes—for family, neighborhood, district, city, nation, and planet" (p. 3). The first settlement house in the United States, Neighborhood Guild, was an organization of neighborhood guilds through which residents were expected to direct the settlement toward a reconstructed society based on social justice principles. Jane Addams, the patron saint of settlement houses, who did the most to articulate the mission and vision of the movement, counseled the founders of Cleveland's Alta House that the settlement "should include the family and not be confined to the children; that it should in fact stir up the adults and the leading citizens of any neighborhood to action for themselves and for their poorer neighbors" (cited in Bond, 1990, p. 12).

Settlement houses and their leaders were principal participants in the reform movement of the Progressive Era, which many historians have identified as the high point of the settlement house movement in the United States (Davis, 1984). They advocated for child labor laws, urban parks, women's suffrage, public housing, and public health. Federations of settlement houses in cities and the National Federation of Settlements were mechanisms for public policy advocacy. It has been argued that the settlement movement was a manifestation of the women's liberation movement in the United States, because so many settlements in first the ethnic European and then the African American communities were founded by women who took leadership in civic affairs (Berry, 1986).

Holistic Approach

Characteristics of the settlement house movement include having a holistic rather than a specialization approach, advocating for social reform while giving services, bridging various groups and classes of people, identifying people as neighbors rather than as needy clients, transforming people from victims of outside forces to participants who are responsible for their own lives, exercising a large and flexible range of activities that are governed by a volunteer community board, and having an orientation to family and neighborhood strengths rather than to individual pathologies.

The successes of settlement houses have been sung by their founders and by numerous historians (Krause, 1980). Indeed, many scholars have identified social settlements as the most significant institutions of social reform, that is, until they were inundated by events such as the Great Depression and the New Deal, World War II and fascism, the Cold War and Communism, the professionalization and specialization of social work, the triumph of trade unionism, the dominance of the United Way, and the civil rights movement and the War on Poverty (Trolander, 1987).

FROM SETTLEMENT HOUSES TO NEIGHBORHOOD CENTERS

As these other social movements rose in importance, the significance of the settlement house waned in the public imagination. Writers eulogized settlement houses as remnants of a rich but deceased past (Carson, 1990). During the New Deal and World War II, many of the causes for which settlement houses had been organized seemed to have been won, including child labor laws, kindergartens, recognition of unions, and social security (Carson, 1990). During the civil rights movement, the urban riots, and the War on Poverty, people created new institutions that often bypassed settlements or changed them into professionalized social services agencies. Grassroots activists trained by Saul Alinsky and his students criticized settlements for maintaining people in passive dependency under benevolent masters rather than for promoting self-determination through mass-based people's organizations (Trolander, 1987). Professional social workers criticized settlements for inadequate casework and clinical skills (Trolander, 1975). There were grounds for both critiques, because settlements (with notable exceptions), relying on funds from the corporate and governing establishment, distanced themselves from radical activists, and, employing neighborhood paraprofessionals, resisted management and program sophistication.

Now, at the end of the first decade of the second century of the settlement movement, there are many organizations that have "settlement" in their name. Few, however, have students, ministers, or social workers who have settled in the neighborhood to learn from and serve residents. The successful settlements have become large agencies run by professional staff and funded primarily through government grants and secondarily through the United Way. They provide an array of specialized social services to clients who are identified by their deficiencies: fragile elderly people, substance abusers, unruly youths, dysfunctional families, and mentally ill people. Some of the agencies have been renamed to fit with their newer siblings as neighborhood centers, community centers, or multipurpose centers. Many have merged to create a single citywide social agency with numerous branches. Success has apparently surpassed the settlement house concept.

People have argued that settlement houses, as a result of their dependence on the United Way and government for funding, have lost their independent spirit of reform (Trolander, 1975). People have also argued that the professionalization of settlement house workers through social work education has undermined the original idea of settling in to act with, rather than for, neighbors (Carson, 1990). Furthermore, some have argued that because settlement house workers see social problems as located in people, they do not attack these problems at their roots. Thus, settlement houses have failed to make lasting social change. Although there are anecdotes of individuals who have been helped, racism and poverty still divide American cities (Philpott, 1991).

By 1989 citywide and regional federations were generally disbanded or discounted because there was little agenda for social change advocacy beyond maintaining funding. The National Federation of Settlements, renamed in 1952 as the United Neighborhood Centers of America with a logo suggestive of that of the United Way, had by 1989 deni-

grated to a one-staffperson operation with a handful of members who were considering the possibility of liquidating the organization because of lack of revenue (Trolander, 1987).

ACTIVITIES AND SERVICES OF NEIGHBORHOOD CENTERS

Directors of neighborhood centers are fond of saying that they provide services from before birth to after death. Indeed, many centers offer both prenatal and funeral counseling.

Typical Center

A typical center opens early in the morning so that parents who are on their way to work or school can bring their children for day care. Later in the morning, young adults attend general education classes aimed at helping them obtain their high school diplomas. In the meantime center staff may be working in the local public schools with youths who are in danger of dropping out or acting out. A little before noon, elderly neighbors may convene for a meal and then play bingo or checkers or go on an outing. Staff and volunteers take meals to the homes of people who cannot get out, and they help them with their housecleaning. After school, younger children come to the center for a snack and some activities. Usually there is tutoring for children who need it; if the center has a gym, the reward is basketball or pool.

During the summer months, the day camp staff take youths to visit the city's museums, sports arenas, and recreation sites. The center's youth worker will be on the street talking to teenagers, recruiting them to a program or enrolling them in a youth club or leadership program, or encouraging them to drop by to play table tennis. Some of the youths will have been referred to the center by a juvenile court after or in place of detention. Local artists are employed by the center to work with the children, youths, and elderly groups, sometimes together—perhaps to do a community mural or to redecorate the park pavilion, or to create artifacts, music, and dances of their culture.

Later in the afternoon, while parents are picking up their children from day care, community organizers are working with the block or street club presidents to set up the next meeting at the center. Perhaps they are planning a voter registration drive with all the street clubs, local churches, and ethnic associations, followed by a candidates' night in which they can discuss local issues. In the evenings there are meetings: youth group meetings, block club meetings, Alcoholics Anonymous meetings, Boy and Girl Scouts meetings, board meetings, and parent meetings.

There are few "typical" neighborhood centers. The condition of a local community and the imagination of the leaders often bring a neighborhood center to emphasize certain areas. Perhaps the center has a large mental health contract through which it provides mental health services in a community setting. Perhaps it has a large drug and alcohol abuse prevention contract through which it provides special services in the schools. Perhaps the center also is a local development corporation that builds and rehabilitates housing and stimulates commercial development. Perhaps the center is a Head Start site at which children and parents are trained. Perhaps the center has an auditorium and music rooms for arts education.

Funding

Neighborhood centers today have multiple contracts with public and private agencies. Their financial reports, audited annually, may exhibit up to 30 accounts related to separate sources that fund separate programs that require separate reports. Examples of programs are Head Start, which is under the U.S. Department of Health and Human Services; food programs, which are under the U.S. Department of Agriculture; child care, which may be administered through a Social Services Block Grant (Title XX); housing services, which may be administered through the city's Community Development Block Grant; employment training and support services, which may be administered through the Job Training and Partnership Act of 1982; elderly services, administered through Title III funds of the Older Americans Act of 1965; gang-prevention activities, which may be administered through the city's department of safety; and residential services, which may be administered through the county's board of mental health. The United Way often provides matching funds, and foundations help to initiate new programs. Some centers, especially the older ones, may have an endowment to help maintain the buildings, and, periodically, centers organize capital campaigns for construction or other purposes.

Neighborhood centers greatly expanded during the 1960s and 1970s with increased federal spending in social welfare programs. During the 1980s—a time of massively increased public spending and debt for non–social welfare activities and decreasing funding from United Way (whose revenues have not kept pace with inflation and, in some cases, with previous goals)—tried to maintain services aimed at a more concentrated and increasingly poor population. Many settlements no longer deal with upwardly mobile new arrivals and work with a highly concentrated yet fragmented population of people who have been left behind, called the "underclass" or the "persistently poor" (Wilson, 1987). This concentration on poor people has led centers to use up fund balances, defer maintenance on buildings, pay salaries well below parity, scramble for funding, and often operate with a crisis mentality.

Structure

Neighborhood centers are organized as nonprofit, tax-exempt charitable organizations under Internal Revenue Code 501 c.3. They have volunteer boards of directors or trustees that are headed by a president. Many boards comprise a mixture of residents and professional specialists who are needed by the center. The executive director usually is a social worker with a master of social work degree and is responsible for hiring the other staff, usually a blend of professionals, paraprofessionals, and volunteers. Some of the larger agencies, which are less neighborhood based, have adopted the corporate model, have a chief executive officer as president of the board (in fact if not in name), and have a unionized staff.

REDISCOVERY OF THE SETTLEMENT HOUSES

Settlement houses were founded and flowered at the height of industrialization. They evolved rationally and bureaucratically into local community-based, multiservice agencies to deal with the displacement of workers, new immigration, the concentrations of poor people in depressed neighborhoods, and the resulting social problems arising through the mass-manufacturing economy. Like the social work profession, the United Way, and government welfare programs, the settlement house movement has been shaped by a wave that is now receding and is being overtaken by a third-wave information economy in which power is shifting from wealth to knowledge and from large mass-oriented organizations to small or decentralized information- and service-oriented organizations (Toffler, 1990). Although this revolution may be the ultimate challenge to the relevance of the settlement house concept, there are signs that it may indeed make the neighborhood center in the settlement house tradition more relevant than ever.

New Directions

The family resource center movement, which gained momentum throughout the nation as a means of providing multiple services in a holistic family-strengthening model, traces its roots to the settlement house movement (Weissbourd & Kagan, 1989). Family resource centers use the latest information to focus on opportunities that enable families to be in charge of their own growth and development in an extremely quickly changing society. The centers have been celebrated as the new, nonbureaucratic, high-tech, high-touch way to bring together various services for families who are considered participants or customers.

"Reinventing government" experiments, following the principles of new corporate leadership, are taking government out of administration and service delivery by using decentralized nongovernment, entrepreneurial agencies to bring services closer to citizens (Osborne & Gaebler, 1993). There is a rising clamor for service integration by ending the "stovepipe" mentality and practice in which resources flow through a narrow channel to a narrowly defined problem. Neighborhood family centers, in the settlement house tradition, are seen as capacities through which citizens can obtain access to information they need to gain income, education, and services to become more self-directing in their lives and communities.

Building New Relationships

Neighborhood revitalization and educational reform in cities in which services have largely replaced manufacturing as the economic base demand new ways of building relationships across various sectors of race, class, and social condition. Replacing the "social fabric" through information sharing in the changing yet continuing institutions of family, church, and local community is high on the agenda of progressive leaders in public and private organizations.

Neighborhood centers are still in place where many other institutions have left. They are no longer, strictly speaking, settlements where students and ministers reside to bridge various segments of society. Many of their staff, however, are residents, and so are the trustees. They are practicum sites for social work and urban planning students. Many neighborhood centers continue their affiliation with churches, the largest number being with the Methodist church (Bond, 1990). As in their origins, neighborhood centers in the settlement house tradition remain as points of contact among economic classes and groups of people.

TRENDS AND ISSUES FOR NEIGHBORHOOD CENTERS IN THE SETTLEMENT HOUSE TRADITION

Basic Premises

Neighborhood roots. A neighborhood center is distinguished by its community base, through which the neighborhood owns and operates its center. Its fundamental power comes not from people with wealth, social position, or political office but from local residents. The greatest challenge for neighborhood centers in an increasingly mobile and less geographically connected population is to strengthen their independent bases through strong neighborhood boards connected to key community networks and institutions. Once they have met this challenge, they can be leading partners in voicing a neighborhood's agenda in circles where downtown and suburban interests predominate.

Asset orientation. A neighborhood center in the settlement tradition is distinguished from a multiservice "one stop" center by its proactive, cohesive, comprehensive character. It is not a building in which many agencies provide separate programs; it is a place through which local people assemble to exchange services and act together for the good of their community. The challenge to neighborhood centers, in the current categorical funding climate, is to assess neighborhoods and families in terms of their assets and to use resources without segmenting families and neighborhoods by their deficiencies. In this way, the neighborhood center becomes a means to release the power of families and neighborhoods from within.

Interdependence. A further challenge is the renewal of citizen education and social action in ways appropriate to a social order in which there are instantaneous communications, innovations in media, and decentralized authority. As a mass economy dominated by centralized forces and counterforces passes, so does mass democracy. A neighborhood center in the settlement house tradition, therefore, must be firmly rooted in the local neighborhood as an independent voice for neighborhood people. At the same time, however, it must act with other neighborhood centers and organizations to deal from a position of strength with larger economic, social, and political systems that affect neighborhoods.

Multiple dimensions and holism. Neighborhood centers, with their strong links to other neighborhood institutions and public and private organizations, are a nexus among social services, economic development, community action, and the arts. Neighborhood centers articulate a holistic, integrated strategy that links family development to community development; job creation to artistic creation; and recreation to education, employment, and housing.

Capacity Building

Diverse and self-generating resources. As the United Way and the government reengineer themselves for the new social order, neighborhood centers are encouraged to reconsider their sources of support. Centers that manage their resources well, that have diverse sources, and that have a core of self-generated funds will be prepared to take a new position for the new millennium.

Structure for change. The organization of the future, according to management gurus (Peters, 1985; Toffler, 1990), is flexible, small, decentralized, entrepreneurial, and run by teams who can experiment, make quick decisions on their own, and focus on outcomes. This would seem to bode well for a neighborhood center with its nonbureaucratic decentralized structure, customer-directed activities, and mission-driven staff.

Wiring with information technology. Just as the freeways led to urban deterioration by dividing neighborhoods and moving investment to suburbs, so can the new electronic superhighway further hurt low-income communities by widening the gap between people with access to information and those without. In the new age, the major value-added element to goods and services is information—usually through computerized networks. The new social order requires neighborhood centers to build their management, fundraising, and program capacities through new information technology systems. More important, however, neighborhood centers can be places where neighbors can gain direct access to the information they need to manage their own lives and can learn to control rather than be controlled by the new fast-developing technology. Federations of neighborhood centers in New York, Cleveland, and St. Louis are preparing a demonstration to assure that the electronic highway supports, not bypasses, the inner cities. St. Louis's Grace Hill settlement has already shown how neighbors can use information technology to exchange services, control income, and manage their own cases.

Issues of Diversity and Justice

Cultural groundedness. Settlement houses were places to transcend ethnicity and culture into a mass American culture that supports a mass American economy. Now, however, the new information economy promotes smaller units of organization with diverse cultures. Neighborhood centers today are summoned to celebrate diversity in culture. Neighborhood centers are finding it important to explore and appreciate cultural values in specific traditions, especially in the African American community, but essentially in every community. Interaction with contemporary Indian, Hawaiian, and African societies are helping connect young and old people to their indigenous roots that unite all people. An example of this is the rites of passage program, through which young African Americans are taught traditional values by elders in a family and tribal situation (Hill, 1992). It therefore remains imperative for settlement houses in the new era to attend to the cultural and spiritual development of people, not by mainstreaming and assimilation or by segregation and conflict but by appreciation of cultural diversity and common origins.

Commitment to social justice. The independent center that is rooted in its neighborhood and allied with people who are poor or left out will, like the early settlement houses, speak and act for social justice. The task in the new social order, however, is not just the reduction of repression or the distribution of wealth; it is the access to power that comes through knowledge. The old targets of social action were the robber barons and the industrial giants who controlled markets and workers by controlling wealth. The new targets of social action are less visible: people who control markets, workers, and wealth by controlling information, people who shuffle paper to make stocks rise and fall and investment flow or stop. The social reformer of today has to advocate for and with people who have less access to employment, income, and health care in the new postindustrial economy. Education, health care, and employment reform are high priorities for settlement workers today.

FUTURE OF THE SETTLEMENT HOUSE MOVEMENT

There is evidence that settlement house people are rising to the opportunities of a radically changing era. Settlement houses are prospering throughout the country as neighborhood centers or community-based family centers. There is new recognition of neighborhood centers in the settlement house tradition as successful experiments in poverty fighting and community building (Husock, 1992). Progressive corporations and governments are courting neighborhood centers to play a role in a comprehensive urban and educational reform strategy.

Federations have been regenerated in New York, Cleveland, and Columbus, Ohio, or have been newly established in Louisville, Kentucky; Rochester, New York; and Detroit. New statewide federations are in process. In 1991 the United Neighborhood Centers of America was reorganized and revitalized and moved its headquarters to Cleveland. Its dues-paying membership of neighborhood centers and settlements has grown from 52 in 1992 to nearly 150 in 1994, with a potential of more than 800 throughout the country (Isaacs, 1994).

Social workers have sometimes said that it is their job to work themselves out of a job. Certainly the committed practitioner works for a time and place in which poverty, racism, crime, delinquency, ignorance, and other social evils are eradicated. There will always be a time, however, for strengthening families and a place for strengthening neighborhoods. Therefore, the settlement house not only has an interesting past, it has a challenging future, for a family neighborhood center in the settlement house tradition is a time-honored place for building community with families in neighborhoods. As such, social workers can find in the settlement house movement not only the roots of their yesterdays but also the blossoms of their tomorrows.

REFERENCES

Berry, M. E. (1986). *One hundred years on urban frontiers: The settlement movement 1886–1986*. New York: United Neighborhood Centers of America.
Bond, R. (1990). *Focus on neighborhoods*. Cleveland, OH: Greater Cleveland Neighborhood Centers Association.
Carson, M. (1990). *Settlement folk: Social thought and the American settlement movement, 1885–1930*. Chicago: University of Chicago Press.
Davis, A. F. (1984). *Spearheads for reform: The social settlements and the Progressive movement 1890–1914*. New Brunswick, NJ: Rutgers University Press.
Hill, P., Jr. (1992). *Coming of age*. Chicago: African American Images.
Husock, H. (1992). Bringing back the settlement house. *Public Interest, 109,* 53–72.
Isaacs, F. (1994). *UNCA annual report.* Cleveland: United Neighborhood Centers of America.
Job Training and Partnership Act of 1982. P.L. 97-300, 96 Stat. 1322.
Krause, H. P. (1980). *The settlement house movement in New York City, 1886–1914*. New York: Arno Press.
Meacham, S. (1987). *Toynbee Hall and social reform, 1880–1914: The search for community*. New Haven, CT: Yale University Press.
Older Americans Act of 1965. P.L. 89-73, 79 Stat. 218.
Osborne, D., & Gaebler, T. (1993). *Reinventing government: How the entrepreneurial spirit is transforming the public sector.* New York: Plume.
Peters, T. (1985). *A passion for excellence.* New York: Warner Books.
Philpott, T. L. (1991). *The slum and the ghetto.* Belmont, CA: Wadsworth.
Toffler, A. (1990). *Powershift: Knowledge, wealth, and violence at the edge of the 21st century.* New York: Bantam Books.
Trolander, J. A. (1975). *Settlement houses and the Great Depression.* Detroit: Wayne State University Press.
Trolander, J. A. (1987). *Professionalism and social change.* New York: Columbia University Press.
Weissbourd, B., & Kagan, S. (1989). Family support programs: Catalysts for change. *American Journal of Orthopyschiatry, 59,* 20–31.
Wilson, W. J. (1987). *The truly disadvantaged.* Chicago: University of Chicago Press.

Rolland F. Smith, MA, is executive director, Greater Cleveland Neighborhood Centers Association, 3135 Euclid Avenue, Cleveland, OH 44115.

For further information see

Advocacy; Charitable Foundations and Social Welfare; Citizen Participation; Community; Deinstitutionalization; Displaced People; Homelessness; Housing; Income Security Overview; Mutual Aid Societies; National Association of Social Workers; Natural Helping Networks; Organizations: Context for Social Services Delivery; Peace and Social Justice; Poverty; Public Social Services; Sectarian Agencies; Social Planning; Social Security; Social Welfare History; Social Work Profession Overview; Voluntarism; Volunteer Management.

Key Words

cultural diversity	settlement houses
neighborhood centers	social reform

READER'S GUIDE

Sexual Abuse

The following entries contain information on this general topic:

Child Sexual Abuse Overview
Domestic Violence
Domestic Violence: Legal Issues
Sexual Assault
Sexual Harassment

Sexual Assault

Diane B. Byington

Sexual assault is a crime of violence and power that has little in common with consensual sexual activity. It is also a major social problem. As a crime, it represents a prosecutable offense that involves individual assailants and victims. As a social problem, it has been variously conceptualized on a continuum ranging from a deviant act perpetrated by a small minority of deeply disturbed individuals to somewhat acceptable mating behavior in a patriarchal society that encompasses all acts of male aggression toward those weaker than themselves, primarily women.

SEXUAL ASSAULT AS A CRIME

Definitions

Sexual assault is defined differently depending on whether it is regarded as a crime or a sexual problem. Most state criminal justice systems distinguish between sexual assault and rape, with rape being the more serious offense and requiring forced penile penetration into a female victim's vagina. Some states also include oral or anal penetration in their definition of rape. Sexual assault involves all other types of nonconsensual sexual contact, including attempted rape, sexual molestation, criminal sexual exposure, voyeurism, and sexual coercion.

Researchers have varied widely in their use of the terms *sexual assault* and *rape* (Muehlenhard, Powch, Phelps, & Giusti, 1992). Rape, the harsher and more technical term, connotes a specific brutal act. Sexual assault is a broader and less-precise term that encompasses many types of nonconsensual behavior and may also include rape. Definitions in studies have varied and have often affected the results. The broader term *sexual assault* is used in this entry to include all forms of nonconsensual sexual behavior between individuals, including rape and the other acts previously mentioned, and is used interchangeably with the term *rape.*

Prevalence

Just as definitions of sexual assault differ, estimates of the prevalence of the crime vary widely, often according to research methodology. It has been estimated that for every reported rape, between three and 10 rapes are committed but not reported (McDermott, 1979). The primary methods for estimating prevalence involve the Federal Bureau of Investigation's (FBI's) Uniform Crime Reports (UCR) and victimization surveys.

UCR tracks rapes and attempted rapes, but not all sexual assaults, that are reported to law enforcement agencies. By definition, UCR considers rape to be an act perpetrated on women by men, so in this system no man can be considered a rape victim. Also excluded are intercourse with girls below the statutory age of consent, rapes in which the assailant was the legal or common-law spouse of the victim, and nonforcible rapes of incapacitated victims. Nevertheless, the data are widely available and frequently cited. According to UCR (FBI, 1992), an estimated 84 of every 100,000 women in the United States were reported rape victims in 1992, an increase of 14 percent since 1988. However, it is widely accepted that underreporting is a significant problem. Although a number of victimization studies have been conducted, the work of two researchers has been the most widely quoted. In Russell's (1982) study of 930 adult women living in San Francisco, 24 percent of the subjects revealed that they had experienced reported incidents of forced intercourse, and another 31 percent described incidents of forced attempts to obtain intercourse. In total, 44 percent of the women reported a rape, an attempted rape, or both. In 1987, in a nationwide sample of female college students, Koss, Gidycz, and Wisniewski (1987) found a 12-month rate of 76 per 1,000 college women who had experienced one or more attempted or completed rapes as defined by UCR. A survey by Koss, Woodruff, and Koss (1991) of working women found that 28 per 1,000 women had been victims of rape or attempted rape during the preceding year. Most rapes were perpetrated by someone the victim knew; specifically, nearly 40 percent of the rapes were perpetrated by husbands, partners, or relatives of the victims, whereas only 17 percent were committed by strangers.

It is difficult to explain the vast discrepancy between official data on rape rates and those reported by researchers, but the difference may be due largely to when and how data are collected. Whatever figure is used, however, sexual assault is a frequent crime in the United States, as well as a major social problem.

Characteristics of Victims and Assailants

Knowledge of victims and assailants is incomplete, but what is known is summarized here. Although most victims are female, a sizable percentage (an estimated 8 percent to 10 percent) are male, primarily children, prisoners, or people who are physically or mentally disabled (Kaufman, DiVastro, Jackson, Voorhees, & Christy, 1980). Researchers estimate that most sexual assaults take place within, not across, racial groups (LaFree, 1989). Although the results differ across samples, most research indicates that no significant ethnic differences exist in the prevalence of rape incidents for victims, although women of color are less likely than are white women to report the crime to law enforcement officials (Steketee & Austin, 1989; Wyatt, 1992). Victims are of all ages, but women are at the greatest risk during their adolescence and early twenties. Income is unrelated to the risk of sexual assault (Russell, 1984).

Although most rapes that are reported to law enforcement officials are perpetrated by strangers, victimization studies concur that the vast majority of rapes are perpetrated by acquaintances, especially among adolescents. Most sexual assaults involve coercion and intimidation, rather than physical violence, and only a small percentage involve a weapon. Offenders tend to be young; the largest proportion of those arrested for sexual assault are men ages 15 to 24 (Allgeier, 1986). Ageton (1983) found that approximately three-fourths of the assaults in her sample occurred in one of three locations: a vehicle, the assailant's home, or the victim's home. Clearly, sexual assault is a crime of opportunity, and the characteristics of victims particularly reflect the demographic characteristics of a locale.

CRIMINAL JUSTICE SYSTEM RESPONSE

Reasons for Low Rates of Arrest and Conviction
As a crime, sexual assault is relatively sanction-free for criminals. Few perpetrators are actually arrested and fewer still are convicted of the crime, although arrests and convictions vary widely according to a number of factors (for example, locality, assault situation, and characteristics of the victim and the assailant). There are numerous reasons for this poor outcome. First, most incidents are never reported to law enforcement officials, so convictions cannot be obtained.

Second, even if assaults are reported, the offenders may be difficult to identify and apprehend, especially if they are unknown to the victims. For example, LaFree (1989) found that only 36 percent of the rape cases reported to law enforcement officials in Indianapolis resulted in arrest. Because most offenders are known to their

victims, however, identification and apprehension are not as serious a problem as that of establishing whether the sexual act was consensual. Frequently, the case pits the testimony of the victim against that of the accused, and physical evidence may be inconclusive.

Third, the criminal justice system regards sexual assault as a crime against the state, with the victim as the main witness. Without the victim's testimony, many prosecutors consider the cases to be unwinnable, and victims may refuse to testify in court for a variety of reasons (Martin, DiNitto, Byington, & Maxwell, 1984). Among the possible reasons, victims may incorrectly believe that they were to blame for the assault, so guilt or shame may keep them from testifying. Often the trial is held many months after the actual crime, and victims do not want to dredge up unpleasant memories.

Finally, many victims are afraid of what, until recently, had amounted to virtual harassment by defense attorneys and are unwilling to be cross-examined. Therefore, most cases are plea-bargained to lesser charges to avoid forcing the victim to endure a public court trial. Lengthy prison sentences for plea bargains are relatively rare.

If cases do go to trial, juries are not likely to convict the defendants unless the evidence is overwhelming. Juries often reflect the more conservative values of a community and are slow to change. For example, LaFree (1980) found that cases involving black defendants were more likely to be tried in court than pled guilty to, regardless of the victims' race, but black defendants and white defendants were equally likely to be found guilty in trials. However, men of any race who were accused of assaulting black women were less likely to be convicted than were white men who were accused of assaulting white women. These results suggest that there is legal discrimination against black men who have assaulted white women.

Changes in the Criminal Justice System
Major modifications have been implemented in all aspects of the criminal justice system in an effort to make the system more effective and efficient in gaining convictions against people who have committed sexual assault (Byington, 1990). Currently, law enforcement agencies are likely to have units that specialize in sexual assault cases, in which the officers are trained to be sensitive to the needs of victims and to collect evidence in a manner that is likely to stand up in court. Special prosecutors are assigned to sexual assault cases,

and these attorneys are familiar with all aspects of such prosecution, as well as how to deal with victims who are frightened or ashamed. In addition, one of the responsibilities of victim/witness–assistance units, another recent innovation, is to advocate for the reasonable treatment of victims in the criminal justice system. Finally, rape laws have been amended, so that questioning a victim's past is not allowed in court and only behaviors pertinent to the crime itself are considered relevant. Because of problems with accurate data gathering and reporting, it is unclear whether these changes have resulted in a greater proportion of convictions than was previously obtained.

Needs of Victims versus the System

Difficulties abound in merging the needs of victims with the needs of the criminal justice system. One continuing issue is the treatment of victims in the criminal justice system, especially the use of the "rape kit." The sexual assault protocol, or rape kit, is a standard method for obtaining physical evidence from the person of a victim as soon as possible after a sexual assault is reported. It involves an intrusive examination, usually conducted by a physician in an emergency department of a local hospital, including impounding the victim's clothes as evidence, taking fingernail scrapings, obtaining vaginal swabs, and plucking pubic hairs, among many other procedures (Martin, DiNitto, Maxwell, & Norton [Byington], 1985). Rape kit evidence is considered to be a major tool for the prosecution of cases but is rarely used in court because of the issues already described. The plucking of pubic hairs particularly represents an additional trauma for victims, especially in light of the recent assault on their bodies.

Treatment of Offenders

Another issue is the effective treatment of assailants. Few treatment programs for sexual offenders exist in prisons, but research has found that without treatment recidivism is extremely high (Scully & Marolla, 1985). An increasing problem is the young age of many convicted assailants and the need for additional treatment options in adolescent programs. There are even fewer treatment programs outside prisons, and those that do exist are rarely attended voluntarily. Structured group treatment and self-help programs appear to be the most successful in the social rehabilitation of sex offenders (Herman, 1988). The current mood of the country, however, is more conducive to punishment and incarceration than to treatment.

Incest

Sexual assault is often differentiated from incest, primarily because of the different ways in which the cases are handled by the criminal justice system. Incest is usually defined as sexual acts performed within a family, by an adult or an older family member against a child. Although incest involves sexual assault, the criminal justice system frequently distinguishes between them. Because of the young age of the victim of incest and the family relationships involved, these cases are often handled by state departments of social services and may involve removing the victims or the offenders from their families in addition to family therapy, with prosecution waived if the assailants cooperate in treatment and cease the abuse. Other sexual assault cases involving child victims are prosecuted in the regular manner without the involvement of departments of social services and often with no mandated treatment for either the victims or the assailants.

SEXUAL ASSAULT AS A SOCIAL PROBLEM

Sexual assault has been documented throughout history but was acknowledged as a major social problem during the 1970s. One major impetus for this acknowledgment came from Brownmiller's (1975) book *Against Our Will: Men, Women, and Rape,* which depicted sexual assault historically as a hostile action by one man against another man's "property" (that is, his woman). Before that time, society had paid little attention to the emotional or physical trauma experienced by the victims. However, during the 1970s, in conjunction with other aspects of the feminist movement, more attention was paid to the needs of sexual assault victims, and the problem of sexual assault was redefined from a feminist framework as one that all women potentially face from all men as a result of the patriarchal structure of the social system.

Early Rape Crisis Centers

Specialized rape crisis centers were established in 1970 in a few cities across the United States, and by 1979 these centers could be found in at least one community in every state in the country (National Center for the Prevention and Control of Rape, NCPCR, 1981). Early rape crisis centers focused as much attention on working for social change as they did on meeting the needs of victims. Their social change efforts centered on changing values and laws that essentially blamed the victims rather than the assailants and on educating women about how to avoid rape through risk awareness and self-defense tactics. In addition, these early centers provided the first specialized services for victims of rape and sexual assault, focusing on advocacy for victims in the criminal justice system.

The early rape crisis centers were staffed by volunteers in accord with feminist principles for the provision of services and social change. The social movement that these centers represented was successful in achieving many of its social-change goals, and it was largely responsible for heightening the public's awareness of the extent of the problem and for ensuing modifications in the criminal justice system toward favorable treatment for victims. Many rape crisis centers are now affiliated with social service agencies or health care organizations (Byington, Martin, DiNitto, & Maxwell, 1991). There is much controversy about whether the professionalization represented by most of these affiliations reduces the ability of these centers to focus on social change to a greater degree than assured funding maximizes their ability to provide increased services to victims (Maxwell, Martin, Byington, & DiNitto, 1994). It is clear that most rape crisis centers are struggling to retain their dual focus on services and social change in light of reduced funding and pressure from more mainstream organizations to reduce their commitment to feminist goals (Martin, DiNitto, Byington, & Maxwell, 1992).

Rape Trauma Syndrome

The need for specialized treatment for victims was recognized as a result of the work of the rape crisis centers. Burgess and Holmstrom (1974) pioneered some of the first research that identified the common problems faced by victims of rape and sexual assault, which they called the "rape trauma syndrome." This syndrome is now considered to be a specific aspect of posttraumatic stress disorder. It involves individualized reactions, including shock and disbelief, as an immediate response to the sexual assault or rape, followed by a period of superficial adjustment (Forman, 1980). Some time later, perhaps two weeks to several months, the victims may begin to experience increased physical and emotional turmoil from the trauma, including insomnia, easy startle response, fear of crowds, unexpected crying fits, and terror of any of the circumstances that surrounded the sexual assault. Many victims experience an anger phase, in which they direct their feelings of anger at the assailant, society, the courts, the police, or men in general (Koss & Harvey, 1987). Finally, the victims begin to integrate the traumatic experience into the totality of their lives and understand that it is one experience among many and that they can be stronger than they were before the trauma. At this point, they recognize that they have become survivors of rape or sexual assault, rather than victims, a realization that can have an empowering effect on their lives and activities. Sexual assault, however, has a long-term effect on most victims; research has indicated that even years afterward, many victims still experience difficulties that they attribute to the assault (Burgess & Holmstrom, 1979; Nadelson, Notman, Zackson, & Gornich, 1982).

Treatment Services

Treatment services for victims include advocating for victims through the criminal justice system, counseling victims and their families, and teaching them strategies to avoid rape in the future.

Social workers are involved in all phases of working with both victims and the perpetrators, although it is rare for one individual to work with both. They are often associated with the hospitals where the victims are taken immediately after rape has been reported, and they stay with the victims while the rape kit examination is being conducted and other treatment is administered (Vera, 1981). Social workers may also be employed in some part of the criminal justice system to act as liaisons between the victims and the system and to advocate for the victims' needs. They are often employed as counselors who work with victims in dealing with the emotional consequences of the assault. Finally, they may work in avoidance and prevention programs to help women and men understand the scope of the problem and to develop individual and community solutions. Social workers' primary role in work with perpetrators is to provide treatment, either within or outside the criminal justice system.

Social work services for victims may be short term or long term. Short-term services include supportive counseling, concrete services (for example, notifying family members, giving assistance in moving, receiving victim-assistance funds), and advocacy for victims. Long-term services may include individual or group psychotherapy to deal with the lingering trauma, assistance in ongoing problems with romantic or familial relationships that are due to the sexual assault, and support during the court trials. In both cases, treatment involves a great deal of reassurance that the victims did not precipitate the assaults, no matter what errors in judgment they may have made.

IMPLICATIONS FOR THE FUTURE

Theories of Causation

Despite major changes in society with regard to sexual assault, one continuing issue is how to understand the causes of sexual assault, because the range of solutions is dependent on the view of the causes of the problem. Baron and Straus (1989) examined four theories of rape and compared the rates of rape among the states to test which of the theories best explains why rates vary so much across states. The four theories were as follows:

1. Rape reflects the sexist treatment of women and is a product of patriarchy.
2. Rape is a result of the prevalence of pornography.
3. Rape reflects the disorganization of society.
4. Socially approved violence spills over into less socially approved violence, such as rape.

Baron and Straus's analyses indicated that the combination of sexism, social disorganization, unemployment, economic inequality, and the alienating condition of urban life constitutes a mix of societal characteristics that precipitate rape. The two most important predictors of rape rates, however, are pornography—as indicated by the circulation of sex magazines—and level of urbanization. Prevention, according to Baron and Straus, involves eliminating inequality of income and employment, reducing sexism (including that evidenced in pornography), and ameliorating the alienating effects of urban life.

New Developments

A number of new developments are having an impact on research and society. First, several widely publicized cases of sexual assault by well-known accused assailants have drawn attention to the complexity of the issue. Second, more and more civil suits by victims against assailants are being pursued. Third, the responsibilities of each partner in dating situations are being identified, and some universities, for example, have developed agreements that both partners are supposed to share before their relationship escalates into physical intimacy. Fourth, marital rape is being recognized as a crime and is being increasingly prosecuted. Fifth, many women's groups, such as the National Organization for Women, have criticized pornography as being exploitative and degrading to women and children, and efforts are under way to identify pornographic materials and limit their availability in communities. Sixth, because it has been found that the human immunodeficiency virus (HIV) can be transmitted during sexual assaults, the rights of victims in requesting that assailants be tested are being secured. A relationship between being the victim of a previous sexual assault (or incest) and later drug addiction has been discovered. Finally, the recognition that the rape of males is more prevalent than was previously thought will have a major impact on research on and practice with victims in the future.

Research to ascertain the extent of the problem in this country and to identify methods of preventing sexual assault continues. In spite of efforts in many areas, the number of reported sexual assaults continues to increase, which may indicate either an absolute increase—reflecting a growing social problem—or an increase in reporting—reflecting a higher awareness of the crime and greater confidence in the criminal justice system. As a society, we must deal with a large number of young assailants and few options for effectively rehabilitating them. Fortunately, advances have been made in the treatment of victims and in the widespread recognition of sexual assault as a crime of violence rather than of sexuality. Social workers have an important role in instituting further advances.

REFERENCES

Ageton, S. S. (1983). *Sexual assault among adolescents.* Lexington, MA: D. C. Heath.

Allgeier, E. R. (1986). *Coercive versus consensual sexual interactions* (G. Stanley Hall Lecture). Washington, DC: American Psychological Association.

Baron, L., & Straus, M. A. (1989). *Four theories of rape in American Society: A state level analysis.* New Haven, CT: Yale University Press.

Brownmiller, S. (1975). *Against our will: Men, women and rape.* New York: Simon & Schuster.

Burgess, A. W., & Holmstrom, L. L. (1974). Rape trauma syndrome. *American Journal of Psychiatry, 113,* 981–986.

Burgess, A. W., & Holmstrom, L. L. (1979). Rape: Sexual disruption and recovery. *American Journal of Orthopsychiatry, 49,* 648–657.

Byington, D. B. (1990, March). *Rape victims and the criminal justice system: Has the system improved?* Paper presented at the annual meeting of the Academy of Criminal Justice Sciences, Denver.

Byington, D. B., Martin, P. Y., DiNitto, D. M., & Maxwell, M. S. (1991). Organizational affiliation and effectiveness: The case of rape crisis centers. *Administration in Social Work, 15*(3), 83–103.

Federal Bureau of Investigation. (1992). *Crime in the United States: Uniform crime reports.* Washington, DC: U.S. Department of Justice.

Forman, B. (1980). Psychotherapy with rape victims. *Psychotherapy: Theory, Research, and Practice, 17,* 304–311.

Herman, J. L. (1988). Considering sex offenders: A model of addiction. *Signs, 13*(4), 695–724.

Kaufman, A., DiVastro, P., Jackson, R., Voorhees, D., & Christy, J. (1980). Male rape victims: Noninstitutionalized assault. *American Journal of Psychiatry, 137,* 221–223.

Koss, M. P., Gidycz, C. A., & Wisniewski, N. (1987). The scope of rape: Incidence and prevalence of sexual aggression and victimization in a national sample of higher education students. *Journal of Consulting and Clinical Psychology, 55,* 162–170.

Koss, M. P. & Harvey, M. R. (1987). *The rape victim: Clinical and community approaches to treatment.* Lexington, MA: Stephen Greene Press.

Koss, M. P., Woodruff, W. J., & Koss, P. G. (1991). Criminal victimization among primary care medical patients: Incidence, prevalence, and physician usage. *Behavioral Sciences and the Law, 9,* 85–96.

LaFree, G. D. (1980). Variables affecting guilty pleas and convictions in rape cases: Toward a social theory of rape processing. *Social Forces, 58,* 833–850.

LaFree, G. D. (1989). *Rape and criminal justice: The social construction of sexual assault.* Belmont, CA: Wadsworth.

Martin, P. Y., DiNitto, D., Byington, D. B., & Maxwell, M. S. (1984). *Sexual assault: Services to rape victims in Florida.* Tallahassee, FL: State Department of Health and Rehabilitation Services, Health Program Office.

Martin, P. Y., DiNitto, D., Byington, D. B., & Maxwell, M. S. (1992). Organizational and community transformation: The case of a rape crisis center. *Administration in Social Work, 16*(3/4), 123–145.

Martin, P. Y., DiNitto, D., Maxwell, S., & Norton [Byington], D. B. (1985). Controversies surrounding the rape kit exam in the 1980s: Issues and alternatives. *Crime & Delinquency, 31*(2), 223–246.

Maxwell, M. S., Martin, P. Y., Byington, D. B., & DiNitto, D. (1994). Should mainstream human service organizations replace rape crisis centers as providers of specialized services for rape victims? In M. Austin & J. Lowe (Eds.), *Controversial issues in macro practice* (pp. 59–71). Needham Heights, MA: Allyn & Bacon.

McDermott, M. Y. (1979). *Rape victimization in 26 American cities.* Washington, DC: U.S. Department of Justice, Law Enforcement Assistance Administration.

Muehlenhard, C. L., Powch, I. G., Phelps, J. F., & Giusti, L. M. (1992). Definitions of rape: Scientific and political implications. *Journal of Social Issues, 48*(1), 23–44.

Nadelson, C., Notman, M., Zackson, H., & Gornich, J. (1982). A follow-up study of rape victims. *American Journal of Psychiatry, 139,* 1266–1270.

National Center for the Prevention and Control of Rape. (1981). *National directory: Rape prevention and treatment resources* (Publication No. ADM 81-1008). Washington, DC: U.S. Government Printing Office.

Russell, D.E.H. (1982). The prevalence and incidence of forcible rape and attempted rape of females. *Victimology: An International Journal, 7,* 81–93.

Russell, D.E.H. (1984). *Sexual exploitation.* Beverly Hills, CA: Sage Publications.

Scully, D., & Marolla, J. (1985). "Riding the bull at Gilley's": Convicted rapists describe the rewards of rape. *Social Problems, 31,* 251–263.

Steketee, G., & Austin, A. H. (1989). Rape victims and the justice system: Utilization and impact. *Social Service Review, 63,* 285–303.

Vera, M. I. (1981). Rape crisis intervention in the emergency room: A new challenge for social work. *Social Work in Health Care, 6,* 1–11.

Wyatt, G. E. (1992). The sociocultural context of African American and white American women's rape. *Journal of Social Issues, 48,* 77–91.

FURTHER READING

Burgess, A. W. (Ed.). (1985). *Rape and sexual assault.* New York: Garland.

Katz, J. H. (1984). *No fairy godmothers, no magic wands: The healing process after rape.* Saratoga, CA: R & E Publishers.

Parrott, A., & Bechhofer, L. (1991). *Acquaintance rape.* New York: John Wiley & Sons.

Scully, D. (1990). *Understanding sexual violence.* Boston: Unwin Hyman.

Stuart, I. R., & Greer, J. G. (1984). *Victims of sexual aggression: Treatment of children, women, and men.* New York: Van Nostrand Reinhold.

Williams, J. G., & Holmes, K. A. (1981). *The second assault: Rape and public attitudes.* Westport, CT: Greenwood Press.

Diane B. Byington, PhD, is associate professor, University of Denver, Graduate School of Social Work, Denver, CO 80208.

For further information see

Criminal Behavior; Domestic Violence; Gang Violence; Homicide; Sexual Harassment; Victim Services and Victim/Witness Assistance Programs; Women Overview.

Key Words	
rape	women
sexual assault	

Sexual Distress

Harvey L. Gochros

This entry explores the social and emotional factors contributing to common sex-related problems encountered in social work practice and suggests treatment and educational approaches to deal with them.

CULTURAL CONTEXT OF SEX-RELATED PROBLEMS

An understanding of clients' sexual choices, behaviors, and problems must be based on an understanding of their sexual attitudes as well as the sexual beliefs and values held by their reference groups at any particular time. In essence, "good sex" is culturally defined. Middle-American culture typically defines it as mutually enjoyable coitus leading to orgasm for both partners in a monogamous, loving, heterosexual relationship of white, healthy, attractive adults (Barbach 1980; Gochros, Gochros, & Fischer, 1986; Zilbergeld, 1978).

Most of the writers who have influenced the helping professions' approaches to sexuality have been white, middle-aged, well-educated, and tacitly heterosexual men. A few women who otherwise fit that category have also made contributions. There has been, therefore, a potential bias in the helping professions' work with sex-related problems, including some of the ideas described in this entry.

The concepts about problematic sexual behavior accepted by middle-American culture as well as those codified in the literature of its helping professions have also been influenced by traditional theological and medical perspectives on sexuality. In the religious model, behaviors departing from prescribed norms are labeled "sinful," and in the medical context they are seen as "diseased." Although these terms are now less frequently used, they reflect societal attitudes that affect the services provided by many within the helping professions.

The medical perception of sex is influenced by the bias that sexual behavior is basically a biological function, analogous to respiration, circulation, digestion, and elimination. Problems are defined as departures from a model of how one's body and psyche should perform sexually. Although psychological factors are seen as influencing sexual functioning (the brain has sometimes been described as the biggest and most important sex organ), thoughts and feelings are considered primarily as factors that either facilitate or interfere with the expected physiological manifestations of a healthy sex drive.

In this framework, little attention is given to ethnic–cultural differences that influence psychobiological behavior. Further, static concepts of sexual behavior fail to take into account the impact of changing social conditions on sexual behavior. The legalization of abortion, the greater availability of effective contraception, the greater sexual explicitness within the media, the women's and gay movements over the past generation—as well as the conservative backlash to these trends—and the public's awareness of the deadly presence of acquired immune deficiency syndrome (AIDS) have all had their impact on sexual norms and behavior.

Traditional medical approaches consider sexual problems as symptoms of underlying disease processes (Strean, 1983), as metaphors for other interpersonal difficulties (Glenmullen, 1993; Strean, 1983), or as anxiety-producing dysfunctional cog-

nitions that can be overcome by retraining (Kaplan, 1974; LoPiccolo & LoPiccolo, 1978; Masters & Johnson, 1970).

Other traditional medical and religious beliefs, often adopted by the lay community, have had a profound effect on sexual behavior and fulfillment. Almost every manifestation of sexual expression has at one time or another been condemned by religious or medical authorities. Masturbation, ubiquitous among all societies and age groups, has in the past been denounced as sinful by theologians and as the source of countless infirmities by medical experts (Hatfield & Rapson, 1993). Although such pronouncements have diminished in recent years, their impact remains in the belief systems of many people who experience sexual difficulties. Indeed, many sexual experts now suggest that self-pleasuring for both women and men is a first step toward overcoming many sexual concerns and is a necessary and natural precursor to coordinating and negotiating mutually satisfying sexual activities with partners (Barbach, 1975, 1980; Leiblum & Rosen, 1989; Schnarch, 1991; Zilbergeld, 1992).

Sexual repression based on what is considered "good" sex or "bad" sex derives from the cultural climate of opinion about the "true" purpose of sex. There is a reproductive bias in many beliefs about sex. Sexual activities are expected to conform to an approximation of what is required to achieve a socially approved pregnancy. Thus, sexual activities between emotionally (and preferably legally) bonded heterosexual adults who are financially comfortable, healthy, attractive, and intelligent are permitted and even culturally encouraged. However, sex involving people who are old, young, disabled, nonheterosexually oriented, poor, or people of color is generally discouraged and their sexual needs and problems relatively ignored (Gochros, 1972; Gochros, Gochros, & Fisher, 1986).

Indeed, even the choice of specific sexual activities and how they are evaluated by those engaging in them are related to reproductive potential. Thus, vaginal penetration, erection, and well-timed ejaculation in a bonded relationship are considered essential, whereas such nonreproductive activities as masturbation and oral, anal, and recreational sex are viewed less favorably.

SEXUAL DISEASE, DYSFUNCTION, AND DISTRESS

The labels given to sex-related problems reflect the approaches that have been taken in defining, treating, and preventing them.

Sexual Disease

Although this term is now usually reserved for such sexually transmitted physical diseases as AIDS, syphilis, and gonorrhea, it has been used in the past to describe atypical patterns of sexual behavior. These patterns were also sometimes referred to as *paraphilias*: literally beyond or removed from expected forms of sexual attraction. These sexual behaviors were not consistent with culturally held norms associated with the reproductive bias. Thus, the American Psychiatric Association considered homosexuality a disease until its membership voted to remove it from that category in 1973.

Sexual Dysfunction or Disorder

These terms provided a more dispassionate and pragmatic view of sexual problems as interruptions in the usual physiological processes associated with sexual arousal and satisfying culmination of intercourse. This approach to sexual problems viewed sex as basically a natural biological function generally manifested in heterosexual vaginal intercourse culminating in orgasm for both partners, thus reflecting a reproductive bias.

This view of sexual problems suggested that "natural" sexual behaviors could be impaired by anxiety stemming from faulty learning experiences or lack of adequate understanding of human sexual physiology. Retraining with a skilled therapist was used to reduce anxiety and other self-inflicted obstacles to natural sexual responses. Traditional dysfunctional and stereotypical notions of how women (Barbach, 1975, 1980) and men (Zilbergeld, 1978, 1992) should think and behave sexually, notions that often interrupted a satisfying sex life, were challenged in the literature and in sex therapists' offices. Traditional sex therapy gave little attention to the parallels and differences in homosexual and heterosexual sexual relationships and rarely extended its treatments to the range of unique problems often encountered by gay men and lesbians.

Clinicians increasingly pointed out the hazards of preoccupation with sexual technique and goal-oriented versus process-oriented sexual activities and the dysfunctional intrusion of prescribed ideas of what was needed to give a good "performance" in bed. This preoccupation often led to "performance anxiety," characterized by individuals acting as spectators rather than participants in their own sexual experiences (Masters & Johnson, 1970).

The emphasis on restoring, developing, and enhancing the general public's sex lives through overcoming sexual dysfunctions and achieving pleasurable coitus reached its zenith in the 1970s (Barbach, 1975; Kaplan, 1974; Masters & Johnson, 1970), a time of growing affluence of the upper-middle classes in American society. Along with affluence came a quest for a better sex life, including optimal sexual fulfillment, more predictable erections, better orgasms, and a demand for professional guidance in achieving these goals. This movement, part of what was called a "sexual revolution," also began to recognize the sexual uniqueness, needs, and rights of women in general and of gay men and lesbians. A significant number of sex educators and clinicians emerged to meet this demand and many schools of social work introduced elective courses on human sexuality.

This sexual renaissance dissipated in the 1980s. The association of sexual acts with AIDS, a powerful sexually conservative movement, and an economic recession contributed to a diminished quest for optimal sexual joy. AIDS was widely perceived as a warning sign about "promiscuity" and overindulgence in sex.

At the same time, a growing awareness and concern emerged about other dangers associated with sex. First, professional helpers became concerned about the victims and perpetrators of rape, then they became aware of the dimensions and consequences of child sexual abuse and incest, and most recently, they discovered sexual harassment in the workplace as well as the power of alleged "sexual addiction." In essence, the emphasis within the helping professions shifted from the task of enhancing the bright, joyful side of sex to undoing the more recently discovered destructive potential of its dark side. Meanwhile, the locus of attention in sexual counseling began to shift from the objective physical manifestations of sex to the subjective experiences associated with sexuality, especially the experience of sexual distress (Woody, 1992).

Sexual Distress

A more recent approach to sexual difficulties emphasizes clients' individual and diverse reactions to their perceived sexual difficulties. A focus on sexual distress involves the assessment, treatment, and prevention of clients' negative subjective experiences related to sexual events (Woody, 1992). It offers a perspective on sexuality that accounts for cultural variables and suggests a client-centered and holistic approach to understanding, preventing, and treating sex-related problems.

Assessment of sexual distress includes not only those biological functions that are perceived as not working properly in sexual encounters but also a search for the source of discomfort that may result from unrealistic expectations from sexual activities for oneself and one's partners. Cognitive behavior such as self-talk has been suggested as a major pathogenic factor in sexual problems (Cranston-Cuebas & Barlow, 1990). Greater emphasis is placed on viewing sexual experiences in the context of the individual's needs and capacities for intimacy, spirituality, and emotional commitment (Hatfield & Rapson, 1993).

One source of sexual distress is the terminology commonly used to describe problematic patterns of sexual behavior. Many terms reify these patterns in a pathological cast. Thomas (1951) suggested that if something is perceived as real, then it is real in its consequences. For example, if a woman has discomfort with vaginal intercourse, resulting from any of a myriad of physical and emotional factors, she might be labeled by others or herself as "frigid" (literally, cold), certainly a pejorative label. Similarly, a man who experiences occasional or frequent difficulties achieving or maintaining erections may perceive himself as "impotent" (literally, devoid of power). The difficulty might well be occasional and result from fatigue, lack of arousal, alcohol use, or a multitude of other variables. Yet the anxiety resulting from the label of impotent or frigid may well lead to subsequent related difficulties in enjoying sexual interactions. Further, the common bifurcation and reification of the concepts "gay" and "straight" may lead many people, especially youths, who have some sexual experience or attraction to people of both sexes, to feel confusion and anxiety about their sexuality.

Again, many of these societal labels reflect a reproductive bias of how sex should be experienced. Thus, a person who seemed uninterested in sexual activities was labeled as having a disorder of sexual desire (Kaplan, 1979, p. x), and a "premature ejaculator" was defined as a man who ejaculates at the wrong time or the wrong place for effective fertilization. The label is also applied if the man often ejaculates before his partner climaxes. Thus, whether or not a man has this "disorder" may be determined exclusively by the timing of his partner's orgasms (Masters & Johnson, 1970).

Different sets of descriptors are traditionally used for male and female sexual "dysfunctions." Women's problems are usually described in terms of a woman's comfort level and willingness to participate in or enjoy sexual activities (frigidity, dyspareunia, lack of desire), whereas the sexual labels used for men's difficulties (impotence and premature ejaculation) have tended to describe problems men encounter in getting their sexual work done. More recently, less pejorative and sexist labels, such as arousal concerns and inhibited orgasms, have come into use (Woody, 1992).

ASSESSMENT OF SEXUAL DISTRESS

A holistic approach to understanding the sources of sexual distress calls for an exploration of a spectrum of personal, relationship, and cultural factors. Careful exploration of a client's past experiences, current behavior, wishes, desires, fantasies, and expectations for themselves and their sexual partners is a prerequisite for an assessment of sexual distress.

Although many of the values that underlie the common assessments of sexual behavior have a white, middle-class bias, they can be modified for an understanding of the sex-related problems of other social work clients. Social workers must understand their clients' sexual lives in the context of the clients' cultural values and life situations. Distress about one's sexual interests and behavior may stem from one or a combination of influences.

Unrealistic Expectations

A major source of distress for many clients is the failure of their sexual activities to meet their expectations. U.S. media and folklore, especially pornography, tend to exaggerate the potential exhilaration of sex. Indeed, a significant proportion of traditional sex therapy has been aimed at treating those who were perceived as lacking adequate sexual desire. Such relative lack of interest has been considered pathological (Leiblum & Rosen, 1988). Many people unrealistically feel they are missing something if their sex lives are perceived as only "adequate." Others feel that there is something wrong if they and their partners do not always have the same intensity of desire, at the same time, for the same sexual activities.

Sexual activities are often used in an attempt to accomplish goals that sex alone may not achieve. Sex is often seen as a quick fix for feelings of loneliness, inadequacy, boredom, and isolation. Unsatisfying sexual patterns may reflect and be used in an attempt to resolve broader problems in relationships (Glenmullen, 1993).

Gender Stereotypes

Sex role stereotypes also provide fertile ground for sexual distress. Women are still often evaluated by many men, and each other, largely for their sexual attractiveness, desirability, and receptivity (Barbach, 1975) and men for their sexual performance, assertiveness, endurance, and prowess (Zilbergeld 1978, 1992).

Lack of Interest

It is a mistake to assume that everyone needs to be equally interested in sexual activity and that lack of such interest is necessarily pathological. Clients may be satiated after many years of sexual activity, have a basic physiological low sexual drive, or simply find their sexual practices routine and unstimulating. They may continue to enjoy physical contact of some sort but have little interest in orgasm-inducing sexual encounters.

Among adolescents, pressure for sex may present itself in a range, from the latent messages of friends' sex-related jokes and ridicule to membership requirements of adolescent sex clubs. Motion pictures, popular songs, and television programs often set sexual standards that many youths find difficult to meet.

Physical Pain for Self or Partner

Lack of sensitivity to a partner's needs and gynecological, urological, or other physical problems may contribute to painful sexual contacts. Referral to sensitive, knowledgeable, and nonjudgmental physicians may be required if no simpler explanations, such as the lack of adequate lubrication, are discovered. Homosexually active clients who experience such difficulties may hesitate to approach their physicians about these concerns for fear of a homophobic response.

Effects of Illness or Medication

Certain physical illnesses, such as diabetes, may have physiological consequences that can create sexual distress. Some medications, such as those taken for hypertension, can impede physiological processes, leading to sexual distress.

Past Sexual Trauma

Past traumatic experiences may haunt one's current attempts at sexual fulfillment. These traumas may include rape, incest, or other forms of sex abuse.

Aging

Aging may change sexual response in varying degrees at different times for different people. Although sexual contact can bring pleasure, intimacy, and a celebration of life at any age, adaptations in sexual patterns might be helpful or necessary as people age. Some people may no longer feel a need for genital sex and may be ready to reduce or even terminate their sexual activities.

Disability

Often, people around physically and mentally challenged persons ignore or even discourage their sexual interests. Disability need not signal an end to sexual enjoyment. Modifications that recognize the challenges imposed by the disability may be necessary.

Institutionalization

Living in an institution, whether in a prison, children's facility, hospital, or nursing home, greatly impedes opportunities for a satisfying sexual life. Privacy is usually a prerequisite for sexual comfort and is a need frequently overlooked in the lives of institutionalized clients.

Fear

Sexual activities frequently provoke fear for many people, who therefore either avoid opportunities for sexual fulfillment or enter into them with hesitation. Among the more common sources of fear are revealing perceived sexual inadequacy, pregnancy, and anxiety about intimacy and commitment. A growing concern for many people is the fear of contracting or transmitting the human immunodeficiency virus (HIV) (Gochros, 1992).

Guilt

There is much in middle-class American culture and some of its conservative religions that contributes to sex being closely associated with guilt. Sex and sin are often interconnected. Puritanical cultures tend to suggest that "if it feels good, it must be wrong." This message often starts with parental attitudes about self-stimulation. Sexual fantasies, even when completely separated from anticipated behavior, can also provoke guilt.

Lack of Sexual Skills

Despite commonly held notions that sexual skills are "natural" and spontaneous, mutually satisfying sex is not usually accomplished intuitively, immediately, or automatically. In both gay and straight relationships, men and women must first learn about their own minds and bodies as well as their partner's before they can communicate effectively about their sexual needs and desires. Verbal communication about sexual wishes may be relatively alien to some people.

Lack of Self-Esteem

Clients with impaired self-esteem may not feel they deserve sexual pleasure and may hesitate to satisfy their own needs in a sexual relationship. Such clients often defer to their partner's wishes while compromising or ignoring their own. Internalized homophobia may, for example, inhibit homosexually oriented individuals from negotiating their sexual activities with a partner, even precluding the negotiation of safer sex activities.

Lack of Intimacy Skills

Sexual distress is often a product of poor overall relationships. An assessment of the relationships in which sexual distress is experienced is essential. Although good sex can exist within a problematic relationship, and many otherwise good relationships experience stress because of unsatisfying sex, usually the two are synergistic.

Homosexually oriented youths do not usually have many opportunities or societal permission to explore and develop intimate same-sex relationships. This situation may affect their adult interpersonal patterns (Loulan, 1987; McWhirter & Mattison, 1984). Individuals of any sexual orientation may be either incapable of or uninterested in long-term relationships. They may prefer brief sexual contacts devoid of any explicit or implicit emotional commitment. These individuals should not be confused with those clients who desire bonded relationships but lack the skills or opportunities to seek them.

TREATMENT OF SEXUAL DISTRESS

A holistic approach to sexual distress requires that treatment be individualized and that it respect cultural and individual diversity. Such an approach is consistent with basic social work values.

When working with clients experiencing sex-related problems, the social worker must explore the physical and emotional manifestations of the client's sexuality within the context of the individual's or couple's patterns of intimacy, communication, and commitment. All this must be done with an awareness of and sensitivity to relevant cultural expectations. As a result of this assessment, the social worker can determine what and how much, or how little, the client needs from the contact.

Effective holistic treatment approaches to sexual distress combine knowledge of human sexuality, findings of traditional sex therapy, basic social work assessment, treatment and evaluation skills, behavioral technologies, and cognitive-restructuring therapies. The overall goal of interventions is to "promote new sexual learning through interventions that directly impact on thinking, feeling, sensing, imaging and behaving" (Woody, 1992, p. 73). Treatment is possible only when social workers communicate their willingness to discuss sexual matters as well as their competence to deal with such problems. Given these clinical skills and basic knowledge of human sexual behavior in its social context, the social worker may intervene with any combination of the following approaches.

Self-Understanding

Through empathy, clients are helped to understand the effect of past experiences and current beliefs on their sexual relationships. The worker may challenge clients' beliefs about themselves, their sexual patterns, and their sexual partner's behavior that impede the development, maintenance, or enhancement of intimate relationships.

Support

There are wide individual differences in the ways people choose to meet their sexual needs. Sometimes these choices depart from current cultural norms. Clients may need their social worker's support for their idiosyncratic sexual choices, including what they choose to do as well as what they choose not to do.

Client Education and Re-education

Many clients lack adequate knowledge about significant aspects of sexual anatomy, physiology, and behavior. The social worker may seek to fill these gaps. This process may involve helping clients unlearn misconceptions that interfere with their sexual fulfillment.

Intimacy Training

Many clients have never learned the requisite skills for successfully developing, maintaining, or ending intimate relationships. Role playing, cognitive restructuring, guided approximations of such basic components of intimate relationships as assertiveness and negotiation skills, and modeling elements of the client–worker relationship may help clients overcome various behavioral deficits.

Sexual Retraining

Reducing sexual distress involves unlearning old sexual habits and learning new ways to give and receive sexual pleasure. This involves the selective use of at-home behavioral or experiential assignments. Some of these assignments are aimed at remedying specific sources of sexual distress, whereas others aim to enhance the overall quality of a couple's sexual lives. The social worker can be guided in these activities by publications that describe how to help clients better express and meet their sexual needs (see Gochros & Fischer, 1992; Leiblum & Rosen, 1989; LoPiccolo & LoPiccolo, 1978; Schnarch, 1991; Woody, 1992).

PREVENTION OF SEXUAL DISTRESS

Our educational system has been uneven at best in sex education. Sexual distress could be minimized if schools and social agencies provided at least basic education about human sexuality, including sexual anatomy, physiology, and behavior.

Youths must be provided with sufficient information in a sex-positive atmosphere about sexual behavioral options, reproduction, and sexually transmitted diseases so they can make informed decisions. Diverse groups such as physically challenged, aged, and homosexually oriented people may require specialized information to avoid sexual distress common in these populations (Gochros, Gochros, & Fisher, 1986). Social workers can also work toward overturning agency policies as well as local, state, and national laws that lead to sex-related distress while at the same time supporting efforts for sex-positive policies and legislation.

IMPLICATIONS FOR SOCIAL WORK EDUCATION

Many social work students and practitioners experience discomfort in discussing sex with their clients. In a national study of social workers who counsel HIV-positive clients, the majority indicated that their social work education offered little help in dealing with sexual issues (Gochros & Gochros, 1993).

Partly because of the AIDS epidemic and other urgent priorities, a number of schools of social work have chosen to drop courses on sexuality that were initiated in the 1970s. These courses are needed now more than ever. AIDS education must be based on students' understanding of and comfort with the significant place of sexual expression in most of their clients' lives. A range of skills can help to instill in students the confidence, motivation, and ability to offer help in these areas.

Social work education should include a review of current sociosexual issues and controversies, such as the explorations of the genesis of sex-related behaviors and their associated problems (Levay, 1993; McWhirter & Mattison, 1984; Money, 1993). Interview training should teach students how to take sexual histories and procedures to overcome clients' and social workers' resistances to discussing sexual matters (Gochros, 1971).

Finally, to be true to their profession's heritage and values, social workers must try to overcome the social forces that have contributed to the sexual distress and oppression that so many of their clients experience (Gochros, Gochros, & Fischer, 1986). An awareness that all people are sexual beings, a balanced acknowledgment of both the potential joys and dangers of sexual expression, and an acceptance of sexual diversity are the basic ingredients of a humane approach to sexual distress.

REFERENCES

Barbach, L. (1975). *For yourself: The fulfillment of female sexuality.* New York: Doubleday.

Barbach, L. (1980). *Women discover orgasm.* New York: Free Press.

Cranston-Cuebas, M. A., & Barlow, D. H. (1990). Cognitive and affective contributions to sexual functioning. In J. Bancroft (Ed.), *Annual review of sex research* (Vol. 1, pp. 119–162). Mount Vernon, IA: Society for the Scientific Study of Sex.

Glenmullen, J. (1993). *The pornographer's grief and other tales of human sexuality.* New York: HarperCollins.

Gochros, H. (1971). Sexual problems in social work practice. *Social Work, 16,* 3–5.

Gochros, H. (1972). The sexually oppressed. *Social Work, 17,* 16–23.

Gochros, H. (1992). The sexuality of gay men with HIV infection. *Social Work, 37,* 105–111.

Gochros, H., & Fischer, J. (1992). *Treat yourself to a better sex life.* New York: Simon & Schuster.

Gochros, H., & Gochros, J. (1993). *Sexual counseling by social workers of people with AIDS.* Unpublished research report.

Gochros, H., Gochros, J., & Fischer, J. (1986). *Helping the sexually oppressed.* Englewood Cliffs, NJ: Prentice Hall.

Hatfield, E., & Rapson, R. L. (1993). *Love, sex, and intimacy: Their psychology, biology, and history.* New York: HarperCollins.

Kaplan, H. S. (1974). *The new sex therapy.* New York: Brunner/Mazel.

Kaplan, H. S. (1979). *Disorders of sexual desire and other new concepts in sex therapy.* New York: Brunner/Mazel.

Leiblum, S., & Rosen, R. (Eds.). (1988). *Sexual desire disorders.* New York: Guilford Press.

Leiblum, S., & Rosen, R. (Eds.). (1989). *Principles and practice of sex therapy: Update for the 90s.* New York: Guilford Press.

Levay, S. (1993). *The sexual brain.* Cambridge, MA: MIT Press.

LoPiccolo, J., & LoPiccolo, L. (1978). *Handbook of sex therapy.* New York: Plenum Press.

Loulan, J. (1987). *Lesbian passion: Loving ourselves and each other.* San Francisco: Spinsters/Aunt Lute.

Masters, W., & Johnson, V. (1970). *Human sexual inadequacy.* Boston: Little, Brown.

McWhirter, D., & Mattison, A. (1984). *The male couple: How relationships develop.* Englewood Cliffs, NJ: Prentice Hall.

Money, J. (Ed.). (1993). *The Adam principle: Genes, genitals, hormones and gender.* Buffalo, NY: Prometheus Books.

Schnarch, D. (1991). *Constructing the sexual crucible.* New York: W. W. Norton.

Strean, H. (1983). *The sexual dimension: A guide for the helping profession.* New York: Free Press.

Thomas, W. I. (1951). *Social behavior and personality.* New York: Social Science Research Council.

Woody, J. (1992). *Treating sexual distress.* Newbury Park, CA: Sage Publications.

Zilbergeld, B. (1978). *Male sexuality.* Boston: Little, Brown.

Zilbergeld, B. (1992). *The new male sexuality.* New York: Bantam Books.

FURTHER READING

Diamond, M., & Karlen, A. (1980). *Sexual decisions.* Boston: Little, Brown.

Fischer, J., & Gochros, H. (Eds.). (1977). *Handbook of behavior therapy with sexual problems.* (Vols. II–III). Elmsford, NY: Pergamon Press.

Francoeur, R. T. (1991). *Taking sides: Clashing views on controversial issues in human sexuality* (3rd ed.). Guilford, CT: Dushkin.

Gochros, H. (1988). Risks of abstinence: Sexual decision making in the AIDS era. *Social Work, 33,* 254–256.

Gordon, S., & Snyder, C. W. (1989). *Better sexual health: Personal issues in human sexuality.* Boston: Allyn & Bacon.

Kaplan, H. S. (1975). *The illustrated manual of sex therapy.* New York: Quadrangle.

Lynch, V., Lloyd, G., & Fimbres, M. F. (Eds.). (1993). *The changing face of AIDS: Implications for social work practice.* Westport, CT: Auburn House.

Pocs, O. (Ed.). (1993). *Human sexuality, 93/94: Annual editions.* Guilford, CT: Dushkin.

Schepp, K. F. (1986). *Sexuality counseling: A training program.* Muncie, IN: Accelerated Development, Inc.

Shapiro, C. H. (1993). *When part of the self is lost: Helping clients heal after sexual and reproductive losses.* San Francisco: Jossey-Bass.

Harvey L. Gochros, DSW, is professor, School of Social Work, University of Hawaii at Manoa, 2500 Campus Road, Honolulu, HI 96822.

For further information see

Adolescence Overview; Aging Overview; Assessment; Bisexuality; Childhood; Developmental Disabilities: Definitions and Policies; Disability; Ecological Perspective; Ethnic-Sensitive Practice; Gay Men Overview; HIV/AIDS Overview; Human Development; Human Sexuality; Lesbians Overview; Mental Health Overview; Primary Prevention Overview.

Key Words	
orgasmic problems	sexual dysfunction
sexual distress	sexuality

Sexual Harassment

Terry L. Singer

Social work has a long tradition of involvement with social problems of discrimination. The profession has confronted the inherent disparity of power that molds discrimination with strategies of empowerment, advocacy, and the establishment and enforcement of rights. During the 1980s and 1990s, sexual harassment became a new discriminatory concern, although it has existed since the beginning of time without a name, conceptualization, or legal opinion.

This entry examines the legal context of sexual harassment, out of which have emerged definitions that suggest a framework for understanding the concept and its evolution. It discusses the nature of sexual harassment as a social problem, along with its high costs to individuals and institutions, through the lens of the legal dilemma between the right of individual protection and the right of free speech. Policies and practice responses to eliminate sexual harassment are presented in an examination of the problem in schools of social work, social work agencies and organizations, and the larger society.

LEGAL CONTEXT

Controversies related to a hearing on a Supreme Court nominee, allegations of widespread abuse in the U.S. military, a Senate ethics committee investigation into the gross improprieties and sexual misconduct of a senator, as well as media coverage of abuse in the workplace, all seem to have propelled the concept of sexual harassment into the public dialogue in the early 1990s. This dialogue provoked disagreement among many about the nature and extent of the problem and about the mechanisms for responding to it.

It has been incumbent on the courts to define the parameters of sexual harassment and to influence the development of policies. Three major legal channels provide the basis for definition: Title VII of the Civil Rights Act of 1964, Title IX of the Higher Education Amendment of 1972, and state and local antidiscrimination laws. In addition, the Equal Employment Opportunity Commission (EEOC) (1985) established interpretive guidelines on sex discrimination to help employers understand the nature of harassment claims, remediation, and prevention. These sources have provided the groundwork for defining law and behavior, and numerous legal challenges continue to refine the social definition of sexual harassment.

Title VII of the Civil Rights Act of 1964

The congressional action embodied in Title VII of the Civil Rights Act of 1964 provides protection from harm in the workplace, which is the cornerstone of the definition of and response to sexual harassment. Title VII makes it unlawful "to discriminate against any individual with respect to his compensation, terms, conditions, or privileges of employment, because of such individual's race, color, religion, sex, or national origin" (p. 72).

Title VII was invoked in a 1986 case, *Meritor Savings Bank v. Vinson;* in a unanimous court decision, the standards of the Equal Employment Opportunity Commission (1985) were adopted for defining sexual harassment:

Unwelcome sexual advances, requests for sexual favor, and other verbal or physical conduct of a sexual nature constitute sexual harassment when

1. Submission to such conduct is made either explicitly or implicitly a term or condition of an individual's employment;
2. Submission to or rejection of such conduct by an individual is used as the basis for employment decisions affecting such individual; or
3. Such conduct has the purpose or effect of unreasonably interfering with an individual's work performance or creating an intimidating, hostile, or offensive working environment.

With this decision the Supreme Court recognized two aspects of sexual harassment: "quid pro quo," in which employment is conditioned on sexual favors, and "hostile environment," in which unwelcome sexual conduct could affect one's performance in the workplace or create an offensive working condition. Significant in this action was the prohibition against verbal conduct. Because the Court ruled that an offense of sexual harassment need not be precipitated by an assault or physical action, it granted employees the right to work in an environment that is free from insult and intimidation. This law gave form to the social definitions of acceptable and nonacceptable behavior in the workplace and held employers liable for the actions of their employees in these matters.

Quid pro quo. This form of harassment represents the most commonly held perception of the nature of sexual harassment. It involves an implicit or explicit bargain whereby the harasser promises a reward or threatens punishment, depending on the victim's response (Crocker & Simon, 1981). The legal elements of quid pro quo claims are proof of unwelcome sexual overtures or demonstration that the employee rejected overtures or was forced to suffer them to prevent a loss of an employment benefit, and proof that the refusal to cooperate caused the deprivation of a job-related benefit.

Hostile environment. The application of hostile environment broadened the definition of sexual

harassment beyond the loss of a tangible benefit to conditions in the workplace. In this context, an employee is protected from unwelcome sexual behavior or conduct that he or she did not solicit or invite and regarded as undesirable or offensive. The intent of the harasser is irrelevant, as long as the employee's ability to do her or his job was affected. It must also be demonstrated that the harassment was based on the gender of the victim; in other words, if the victim's gender had been different, she or he would not have been subject to the harassment. It is important to note here that both heterosexual and homosexual conduct may constitute sexual harassment.

Ellison v. Brady (1991), a ruling of the Ninth U.S. Circuit Court of Appeals in California, helped clarify further how unwelcome or offensive behavior is determined. In the past in U.S. law, the concept of the "reasonable man" or the "reasonable person" had directed legal doctrine. It had been common, when deciding the outcome of a case, to ask what a reasonable person would do in such a circumstance. With *Ellison v. Brady,* the concept of "reasonable woman" was developed. Presiding Judge Robert R. Beezer ruled that women, who are disproportionately victims of sexual assault, have a stronger incentive than do men to worry about sexual behavior. When perceiving risks of related violence, a reasonable woman would have a unique view of any sexual conduct and thus would respond with greater concern for protection. In this ruling, Judge Beezer validated and legitimated the need of the courts to respond to this concern of women.

After *Meritor Savings Bank v. Vinson,* the Supreme Court was silent on sexual harassment with regard to Title VII until Justice Sandra Day O'Connor wrote the leading opinion in the unanimous decision in *Harris v. Forklift Systems* (1993). She stated, "When the workplace is permeated with 'discriminatory intimidation, ridicule and insult' that is 'sufficiently severe or pervasive to alter the conditions of the victim's employment and create an abusive environment,' Title VII is violated." Thus, psychological damage or the inability to do one's job need not be demonstrated to prove sexual harassment. This decision made it easier to prove harassment, but required that factors such as the frequency, severity, and extent of a threat or humiliation and unreasonable interference with one's work be considered.

Civil Rights Act of 1991
The Civil Rights Act of 1991 provided more support to victims who had made claims of sexual harassment under Title VII. Because Title VII had

no provision for damage remedies for those who had suffered discrimination other than reimbursement of back pay and attorneys' fees, this congressional remedy provided for a jury trial to assess the possible payment of compensatory and punitive damages, back pay, front pay (the potential earnings of a litigant who is not reinstated or hired, from the time of the complaint to the projected age of retirement), reinstatement, and the recovery of fees from attorneys and expert witnesses, opening up the potential for large claims.

Title IX of the Higher Education Amendment of 1972

The Office of Civil Rights of the U.S. Department of Education is charged with enforcing Title IX of the Higher Education Amendment of 1972 to prohibit sex discrimination in higher education. Title IX states that "no person in the United States shall, on the basis of sex, be excluded from participation in, be denied the benefits of, or be subjected to discrimination under any educational program or activity receiving financial assistance" (p. 247). Institutions that violate this law could have their federal funds withdrawn, which is the major sanction of this entitlement. In addition, this amendment requires institutions that receive federal funds to have grievance procedures in place by which victims of sexual harassment may file complaints.

Title IX differs from Title VII in that it does not require complainants to seek administrative remedy before they file for relief, whereas Title VII's guidelines refer victims to the EEOC or to their state human relations commission for hearings. In *Alexander v. Yale University* (1980), a female student at Yale filed for relief under Title IX, charging a quid pro quo case in which her instructor gave her a lower grade for refusing sex. This first attempt to invoke Title IX fell short because the case was dismissed when the student graduated. In 1992 the Supreme Court heard *Franklin v. Gwinnett County Public Schools and Hill* and ruled that schools had the duty not to discriminate against students on the basis of gender. The victim was entitled to sue the school district for failing to protect her, and to sue the harasser, in a separate suit, to recover monetary compensation.

The legal arena has been the forum for debate in the evolution of the concept of sexual harassment. However, even with this development, there has been no agreement about a specific definition that would have broad-based acceptance. Much of the disagreement focuses on the right of individual protection versus the right of free speech. This dilemma can be more fully appreciated in an examination of sexual harassment as a social problem.

SEXUAL HARASSMENT AS A SOCIAL PROBLEM

For decades women have been a vital component of the workplace and currently make up about half of the work force. Before there were laws protecting women from sexual harassment, women were often left with few alternatives to suffering the abuse. The best option was the opportunity to transfer to another office or division of the workplace, but usually the woman either endured the abuse or quit her job. With legal remedies now available, more women are going to court for relief. Such active litigation has prompted social discourse and media sensationalism to debate the issues involved in sexual harassment. This section highlights the various positions in the debate and comments on the pervasiveness of the problem.

Nature of the Problem

There is disagreement about both the fundamental nature of sexual harassment and the extent of the problem. Some argue that sexual harassment is a serious problem (Clark, 1991) in the financial industry (Cohen, Power, & Siconolfi, 1991); in the U.S. Navy (Krohne, 1991); in higher education (Riggs, Murrell, & Cutting, 1993); in the church (Jordan-Lake, 1992); and in many other institutions and locations, including on the street (Bowman, 1993). Some attribute the problem to power (Stringer, Remick, Salisbury, & Ginorio, 1990), the socialization of women in American society (Dziech & Weiner, 1984), the insecurity of men (Goleman, 1991), capitalism (Onesto, 1992), the sexual revolution (Kendall, 1992), pornography (Allen, 1992), or feminism (Davidson, 1991). Still others believe that the whole problem of sexual harassment is exaggerated (McCarthy, 1991; Morgenson, 1991; Munson, 1992).

The difficulties inherent in developing a greater consensus on the nature and scope of the problem exacerbate the concern of what to do about it. It is common for a complaint of sexual harassment to consist of one person's word against another's. Yet unlike current rape laws that exclude consideration of a victim's sexual history, a case of sexual harassment may include such information, along with considerations of dress and sexually provocative conduct. Thus, what may be perceived as an innocent flirtation by one person may be viewed as harassment by another.

Forms of harassment. Sexual harassment can take several forms. It may be represented in sexually explicit graffiti, posters, or calendars; vulgar and offensive sex-related epithets; abusive language, depictions of sexually explicit behavior, and incidents of indecent exposure by coworkers; and vulgarity that interferes with the performance of one's job (Poff, 1994). Conte (1990) defined verbal (pressure for sexual activity, comments about the female body, sexual boasting, and sexist and homophobic comments), nonverbal (looking up the dresses of women or down their blouses, obscene gestures, and suggestive sounds), and physical (touching, patting, pinching, kissing, and rape, among others) aspects of harassment. The environment can also present harassing features, including sexually offensive literature, pictures, or music.

Gender base. One factor that most writers agree on is that the harassment must be based on gender, which distinguishes it from other forms of discrimination and harassment. If it were not for the gender of the person being harassed, the harassment would not occur.

Sexual harassment frequently is seen as a women's problem because of its prevalence among women. A report by the U.S. Merit Systems Protection Board (1988) suggested that more than 40 percent of female federal workers had experienced some form of unwanted and uninvited sexual attention. Likewise, women more often than men lost or quit their jobs or transferred to other positions as a result of such attention (Gutek, 1985). Little data exists on the harassment of men or on same-sex harassment, although there is some evidence of it in anecdotal material and case law. One cannot necessarily generalize, however, that women are more harassed than men because men tend to view the same behavior in a less negative light than do women (Konrad & Gutek, 1986). However, when the position of women in relation to power in institutional hierarchies is considered, it may be concluded that women are the principal victims.

Impact on victim. Like all behavior, sexual harassment can be viewed on a continuum from the least serious to the most serious. This view helps to break down the general concept into observable behaviors for identification and response. Fitzgerald (1990) provided helpful characterizations of sexually harassing behavior that include, at the lowest level, generalized sexist remarks and behavior; then, inappropriate and offensive, but essentially sanction-free sexual advances; solicitation of sexual activity or other sex-linked behavior by the promise of rewards; sexual coercion; and, finally, gross sexual imposition or assault.

The effect of such behavior on victims varies, depending on the nature of the offense, the psychological makeup of the victim, and the nature of the response to victimization. Curtis (1976) demonstrated that victims of rape by acquaintances often deny the rape, even in the presence of evidence. It is not unusual for such victims to engage in self-blame ("if only I hadn't worn that low-cut blouse") or outright denial. This dynamic, which is common in those who are victimized, complicates efforts to understand fully the extent of the problem and to formulate approaches to solve the problem. However, it is common for victims who deal with their abuse in this way to suffer similar symptoms and fates as those who do recognize their victimization.

Consensual relations. There is yet another variable that must be considered when looking at the scope of this problem: the realm of consensual relations. MacKinnon (1979) argued that the decision by women to have sexual relationships is an important way in which women exercise control over their lives. As one factors into this discussion the rights of individuals to privacy and association, it may be suggested that there is an inherent civil right for any two persons to associate for any purpose, as long as neither of them is an unwilling party. In fact, the term "unwilling" seems to be the key to establishing the legitimacy of the claim in sexual harassment litigation.

A consensual relationship in the context of the workplace and involving two persons of unequal power poses a real problem. If there is a direct line of authority between two people in a relationship, the integrity of their work may be called into question. Also, questions may arise about favoritism in employment assignments and rewards, with a concomitant negative effect on other workers. Much has been written about this phenomenon in relation to institutions of higher education, where some have argued that the combination of power, prestige, and intellect has created an atmosphere conducive to the development of consensual relationships. In fact, a number of colleges have developed policies that discourage or prohibit consensual relationships between students and faculty (National Association for Women in Education, 1992). In addition, the Supreme Court ruled in the *Meritor* case that consent is not an adequate defense. An organization, particularly a college for which a Title IX judgment may preclude federal funding for the institution, that does not stand against consensual relationships puts itself at some risk of potential litigation. Individual rights, the dynamics of organizations, and the tenuousness of human relationships complicate this issue. At the same time, organizations are reluctant to assume responsibility for the monitoring of the personal lives, decisions, and relationships of their employees.

When exploring the intricacies of the sexual harassment phenomenon, one can quickly see the complexities of the issues, even the problem of determining who is a victim and who is not. In this regard, the problem assumes another dimension of social concern; that is, the direct victims of sexual harassment are not the sole casualties of this massive social problem. Other individuals and institutions face tremendous costs as a result of this behavior (Singer, 1994).

Human and Institutional Costs

Victims. The common results of sexual harassment for victims, aside from the economic and career disruptions, are well documented in the literature; they include job dissatisfaction, stress-related distress, and mental health problems, among others (Crull, 1982; Judd, Block, & Calkin, 1985; Kissman, 1990; Maypole, 1987). These afflictions result from the double bind of abuse—giving in to the abuse to avoid penalty and facing the indignities or fighting the abuse with the resultant threat of retaliation. Some victims report symptoms characteristic of those with posttraumatic stress disorder—that is, recurring nightmares, nonspecific fears, and anger years after the event (Singer, 1994).

Fifty-two percent of the subjects in one study said they had been fired or forced to quit their jobs because of sexual harassment (Safran, 1976). It is difficult to calculate the emotional toll of sexual harassment on such victims or the economic toll because they have quit jobs or transferred to other positions to avoid continued abuse. In addition to the indignities of the abuse, victims often are revictimized through the discovery of evidence in legal or formal hearings, in which their character and sexual history may be exploited in private and public sessions.

Family members and others. The costs to other individuals and institutions are rarely discussed. For example, family members and friends of victims suffer in a parallel fashion with the victim. And although there are few data to profile this phenomenon, one may logically conclude that there is a potential for real family discord when tragedy or crisis befalls a family member.

Co-workers and other employees feel the strain of work-related problems, particularly with problems as sensitive and charged as sexual harassment. Legal and formal codes of conduct that include the necessity to remain silent during the investigations of complaints and hearings serve to confuse co-workers, who may have only partial information. If the person who is accused is well liked, feelings of betrayal or disbelief may actually cause employees to take sides according to whom they believe. This situation places increased pressure on the victim as well as co-workers, who may play out the difficulties as a dysfunctional "family" in the workplace.

Institutions. Other writers have identified the institutional and organizational costs of this social problem in terms of negative productivity, liability, employee-retention concerns, and morale (Bergmann & Darity, 1981; Klein-Freada, 1984; Ledgerwood & Johnson-Dietz, 1981; Terpstra & Baker, 1986). Clark (1991) documented the increase in complaints filed over a 10-year period (from 3,661 in 1981 to 5,557 in 1990) and related it to the broader definition of sexual harassment by the courts that included the concept of hostile environment. Some would argue that these complaints represent a small fraction of the female work force, whereas others would suggest that the problem is greatly underreported. Regardless of the position taken, it is clear that as the courts continue to broaden definitions to provide greater protection from abuse and the number of complaints continues to grow as victims are better prepared to pursue compensatory and punitive damages, the financial toll on organizations will continue to grow.

Clark (1991) pointed to some large monetary verdicts in favor of victims of sexual harassment who sought personal injury litigation: *Moore v. Cardinal Services, Inc.,* in 1986 ($3,100,000), *Bihun v. AT&T Information Systems* in 1990 ($2,000,000), *Gaffke v. U-Haul of Oregon* in 1988 ($1,448,969), *O'Connell v. Local Union 25* in 1989 ($1,100,000), and *Preston v. Douglas, Soncrant, and the city of Detroit* in 1987 ($900,000). These institutional and organizational costs can be quantified easily; however, multimillion-dollar expenditures are being made yearly for replacement costs for those involved in sexual harassment, and these costs are difficult to track systematically. Conte (1990) documented that the federal government alone spent $267 million for this problem from May 1985 to May 1987.

As one begins to calculate the personal, organizational, and social costs of sexual harassment, one can perceive the inestimable damage created by this problem. The complexity of the problem requires an equally complex and broad-based response to develop and implement effective solutions.

POLICY AND PRACTICE TO ELIMINATE SEXUAL HARASSMENT

There is considerable speculation about the reasons for sexual harassment. The following may be included in a typology of causality:

- abuse of power to obtain sexual favors
- sex used to obtain power
- power used to decrease the power of the victim
- personal crisis in the life of the harasser
- sexual attraction gone wrong
- genuine deviance related to alcohol or substance abuse, character disorders, and other socially deviant behavior patterns (Stringer et al., 1990).

Employers are compelled by law to seek solutions to such work-related abuse through programs of prevention, clear policies, and effective mediation and discipline. Social work as a profession is also expected to meet the challenge of sexual harassment in many diverse fields of practice, not only because it is the law, but because the *NASW Code of Ethics* (NASW, 1994) requires social workers to meet professional standards that reject all forms of discrimination, to disavow the exploitation of professional relationships for personal advantage, to avoid relationships that pose a conflict of interest, and to reject sexual activities with clients under all circumstances. This code provides a moral and ethical lens through which practice must be guided and evaluated and, in doing so, establishes a strong standard against which sexual harassment must be measured.

Social work must approach the problem of sexual harassment in three arenas: in the schools of social work, where it educates and develops its core of practitioners; in the workplace of professional social work practice; and, finally, in the larger arena of social and public discourse and policy.

Schools of Social Work

Singer's (1989) study of schools of social work first showed that more than half the master of social work programs in the country had experienced problems with sexual harassment during the most recent five-year period. This finding paralleled the general pervasiveness of the problem in academia, as discovered in a study that reported the sexual harassment of 32 percent of the tenured and 49 percent of the nontenured female faculty (Sandler, 1986) and in other research that documented the abuse of students (Roscoe, Goodwin,

Repp, & Rose, 1987; Schneider, 1987). In addition to the classroom environment of sexual harassment, students in professional schools such as social work are prone to another arena of abuse: the field-practicum setting (Valentine, Gandy, Burry, & Ginsberg, 1994).

The academic world poses unique challenges in this area because it combines the interests of free speech and inquiry, academic freedom, and classroom and field-practice settings. Weil, Hooyman, and Hughes (1994) addressed not only the need for, but the development of, strategies to combat sexual harassment in schools of social work. In that same work, Shank (1994) laid the groundwork for policy formulation, Hooyman and Gutierrez (1994) offered plans for prevention, and numerous examples were provided of college and school policies, along with a model policy for field settings.

Strong policies. It is clear that the most effective means of curtailing sexual harassment is through prevention. Schools and institutions must develop strong policies that prohibit harassment, both in their programs and in field placements, and should encourage field agencies to establish policies as well (Valentine et al., 1994). This information must be provided to faculty, administrators, practicum instructors, staff, and students through various means, including seminars, workshops, and continuing education programs that could provide a forum for the discussion and articulation of the problems associated with sexual harassment. Schools of social work must also consider curricular content that includes harassment to provide students with the necessary knowledge and skills to combat this form of discrimination and to prepare them for experience in the workplace.

Positive climate. Schools must have a "top-down" commitment to make prohibitions against sexual harassment work. Acts of harassment not only are acts of individuals but may reflect the organizational culture. Thus, a strong statement by an organization or institution to prevent such abuse is activated by creating a climate in which all individuals are valued and promoted for the product of their work rather than on the basis of gender, race, or other protected characteristics. Schools of social work, as well as other areas of colleges and universities that have a disproportionately smaller percentage of female deans and directors of programs, may see the rate of harassment decrease once women reach parity. Equality sends a message that discrimination will not be tolerated.

Reporting systems. Schools of social work must establish a comprehensive system of procedures for reporting complaints that is known to all employees and students. Such a system should include support for the person filing the report, including the possibility of counseling and protection from retaliation for the grievance; an assurance of confidentiality for all parties; an efficient and thorough investigation done in a timely manner; a reporting mechanism; and procedures for reconciling, mediating, or disciplining those who violate the policy.

College environments provide frequent opportunities for the development of consensual relationships, particularly between educators and students. These represent some of the most difficult cases to resolve. However, this level of difficulty should not discourage public discourse on this issue. The more individuals confront the complexities of sexual harassment, particularly consensual relationships between those with unequal power, the more likely it is that there will be a higher level of education and understanding of the dynamics involved.

It is incumbent on professional organizations, such as the Council on Social Work Education as well as other regional and professional accreditation bodies, to provide leadership in preventing sexual harassment and other forms of discrimination. The visibility of related issues helps promote greater awareness in responding to the abuses of harassment. The clout of accreditation will help ensure that policies are in place and will promote equality and nondiscrimination.

Social Work Agencies and Organizations

One might conclude that social workers would experience less sexual harassment in the workplace because of the orientation and value base of the profession that challenges discrimination and promotes the concepts of individual rights and empowerment. However, social workers do have problems with sexual harassment in their employment settings.

Kravetz and Austin (1984) first documented the accounts of sexual harassment of women in social services administration. Then Judd et al. (1985) reported the sexual harassment of social work practitioners, finding widespread abuse and resulting deleterious effects. Two other studies that followed (Dhooper, Huff, & Schultz, 1989; Maypole, 1986) documented that more than half of the social worker–respondents knew colleagues who had been sexually harassed, and approximately one-fourth had been harassed themselves. If social work as a profession is going to have an impact on larger social issues, it must first attend to affairs within the profession.

As in academic institutions, social work agencies and organizations have fewer women than men in high positions of authority. This situation is particularly disturbing, given the high percentage of women in the profession. Social work must lead by example, which requires establishing greater parity for women and other oppressed populations in positions of power. Position statements by NASW are a help in this regard.

Larger Societal Context

Concurrent with the need to address problems internal to the profession in social work schools and workplaces is the profession's obligation to work with this issue in the larger social context, in line with its commitment to social justice and human dignity. Therefore, social workers must be aware of legal definitions, interpretations, and rulings because the courts have been the most important voice in framing the public discussion. From the directions charted largely by the legal system have come new laws reflecting public policy positions against sexual harassment. The profession, in its advocacy role, must support public policies and programs that work to eliminate discrimination. Although this is no small task for social work, it is an important mandate of professional ethics that may be partially achieved by taking active roles in public discussions, education, and legislative advocacy and by modeling nondiscriminatory practices.

In the practice arena, social workers must be able to understand the complex issues of discrimination that may be complicated by issues of race, ethnicity, and sexual orientation. Thus, it is important for social workers to provide leadership in sorting out these complexities so that efforts to eliminate discrimination are not stymied by obfuscation.

In addition, social workers who are working against sexual harassment must be clear about their professional boundaries and understand that not everyone who goes over the limits of propriety in relation to clients is a harasser. Uncertainty about their roles, inexperience, and their lack of knowledge may prevent practitioners from engaging in effective, nonexploitative social work practice. Social workers who understand the dynamics of sexual harassment and monitor their own roles will also need this information to work with clients who have been victimized. Technical assistance and enhanced methods of practice are becoming more available to practitioners and administrators who work with this problem. For example, the Index of Sexual Harassment (Decker, 1993) aids in the assessment of the problems of clients or the workplace, and there are numerous professional continuing education workshops to increase one's understanding of the issues. As greater clarity and definition are given to the issues related to sexual harassment through legal rulings and public discussions, more of these types of assistance will become available.

Male administrators have a special challenge, and it is important for the disproportionate number of male managers in this predominantly female profession to consider their roles and responsibilities. As Reisch (1994) reported, male administrators tend to treat the problems of sexual harassment on a continuum from nonresponsiveness to overreaction. Their typical ineffective responses, which reflect their ignorance of the issues, include "Boys will be boys"; "Let's not get carried away with this problem"; "We'll do this strictly by the book"; and "My God, this is a crisis!" To be more responsive, male administrators must recognize what sexual harassment is and be prepared to deal with it.

CONCLUSION

By understanding the complexities of sexual harassment as embodied in concepts of power, sexual relationships, gender issues, work, and diversity, the social work profession can provide leadership and direction in the important public discourse. Social work has maintained ideals that promote diversity, inclusiveness, equality, and parity, but cultural belief systems that work against these ideals have long been held and are deeply embodied in this society and thus are difficult to change. Continuing power differentials between men and women will challenge the profession to devise creative and persistent strategies of change.

REFERENCES

Alexander v. Yale University, 631 F.2d 178 (2d Cir. 1980).
Allen, R. L. (1992, January–February). Out of the bedroom closet. *Ms.,* p. 96.
Bergmann, B. R., & Darity, W. (1981). Social relations, productivity, and employer discrimination. *Monthly Labor Review, 104*(4), 47–49.
Bowman, C. G. (1993). Street harassment and the informal ghettoization of women. *Harvard Law Review, 106*(3), 517–580.
Civil Rights Act of 1991. P.L. 102-166, 105 Stat. 1071.
Clark, C. C. (1991). Sexual harassment. *CQ Researcher, 1*(13), 537–560.
Cohen, L. P., Power, W., & Siconolfi, M. (1991, November 5). Financial firms act to curb sexism with mixed results. *Wall Street Journal,* p. 1.
Conte, A. (1990). *Sexual harassment in the workplace: Law and practice.* New York: John Wiley & Sons.
Crocker, P. L., & Simon, A. S. (1981). Sexual harassment in education. *Capital University Law Review, 10*(3), 541–584.
Crull, P. (1982). Stress effects of sexual harassment on the job: Implications for counseling. *American Journal of Orthopsychiatry, 52*(3), 539–544.

Curtis, L. A. (1976). Present and future measures of victimization in forcible rape. In M. J. Walker & S. L. Brodsky (Eds.), *Sexual assault* (pp. 61–68). Lexington, MA: D. C. Heath.
Davidson, N. (1991). Feminism and sexual harassment. *Society, 28,* 39–44.
Decker, A. L. (1993). *Index of sexual harassment.* Tempe, AZ: WALMYR Publishing.
Dhooper, S. S., Huff, M. B., & Schultz, C. M. (1989). Social work and sexual harassment. *Journal of Sociology and Social Welfare, 16*(3), 125–138.
Dziech, B. W., & Weiner, L. (1984). *The lecherous professor: Sexual harassment on campus.* Boston: Beacon Press.
Ellison v. Brady, 942 F.2d 872 (9th Cir. 1991).
Equal Employment Opportunity Commission. (1985). *Guidelines on discrimination because of sex: Sexual harassment.* §1604.11, 29 C.F.R.
Fitzgerald, L. F. (1990). Sexual harassment: The definition and measurement of a construct. In M. A. Paludi (Ed.), *Ivory power: Sexual harassment on campus* (pp. 21–44). Albany: State University of New York Press.
Franklin v. Gwinnett County Public Schools and Hill, 112 S. Ct. 1028 (1992).
Goleman, D. (1991, October 22). Sexual harassment about power, not sex. *New York Times,* pp. C1, C12.
Gutek, B. A. (1985). *Sex and the workplace: Impact of sexual behavior on women, men and organizations.* San Francisco: Jossey-Bass.
Harris v. Forklift Systems, Inc., 114 S. Ct. 367 (1993).
Hooyman, N. R., & Gutierrez, L. (1994). Planning for prevention of sexual harassment. In M. O. Weil, N. Hooyman, & M. Hughes (Eds.), *Sexual harassment and schools of social work: Issues, costs and strategic responses* (pp. 70–80). Alexandria, VA: Council on Social Work Education.
Jordan-Lake, J. (1992, February 10). Conduct unbecoming a preacher. *Christianity Today, 36,* 26–30.
Judd, P., Block, S. R., & Calkin, C. L. (1985). Sexual harassment among social workers in human service agencies. *Arete, 10*(1), 12–21.
Kendall, G. A. (1992). Sexual harassment: How not to define an issue. In C. Wekesser, K. L. Swisher, & C. Pierce (Eds.), *Sexual harassment* (pp. 77–80). San Diego: Greenhaven Press.
Kissman, K. (1990). Women in blue-collar occupations: An exploration of constraints and facilitators. *Journal of Sociology and Social Welfare, 17*(3), 139–149.
Klein-Freada, R. (1984). *Sexual harassment in federal employment: Factors affecting its incidence, severity, duration, and relationship to productivity.* Unpublished doctoral dissertation, Brandeis University, Waltham, MA.
Konrad, A. M., & Gutek, B. A. (1986). Impact of work experiences on attitudes toward sexual harassment. *Administrative Science Quarterly, 31,* 422–438.
Kravetz, D., & Austin, C. D. (1984). Women's issues in social service administration: The views and experiences of women administrators. *Administration in Social Work, 8*(4), 25–38.
Krohne, K. (1991). *The effect of sexual harassment on female navy officers: A phenomenological study.* Unpublished doctoral dissertation, University of San Diego.
Ledgerwood, D. E., & Johnson-Dietz, S. (1981). Sexual harassment: Implications for employer liability. *Monthly Labor Review, 104*(4), 45–47.

MacKinnon, C. A. (1979). *Sexual harassment of working women.* New Haven, CT: Yale University Press.

Maypole, D. E. (1986). Sexual harassment of social workers at work: Injustice within? *Social Work, 31,* 29–34.

Maypole, D. E. (1987). Sexual harassment at work: A review of research and theory. *Affilia, 2*(1), 24–38.

McCarthy, S. J. (1991, December 9). Cultural fascism. *Forbes, 148,* 116.

Meritor Savings Bank v. Vinson, 477 U.S. 57, 106 S. Ct. 2399 (1986).

Morgenson, G. (1991, November 18). May I have the pleasure. . . . *National Review, 43,* 36–37.

Munson, N. (1992, February). Harassment blues. *Commentary, 93,* 49–59.

National Association for Women in Education. (1992). Tracking sexual harassment repeat offenders. *About Women on Campus, 1*(2), 5–6.

National Association of Social Workers. (1994). *NASW code of ethics.* Washington, DC: Author.

Onesto, L. (1992). Sexual harassment: It's a bourgeois thing. In C. Wekesser, K. L. Swisher, & C. Pierce (Eds.), *Sexual harassment* (pp. 70–76). San Diego: Greenhaven Press.

Poff, P. (1994, January 11). *Sexual harassment: When sex isn't funny any more.* Paper presented at Marywood College, Scranton, PA.

Reisch, M. (1994). The role of male administrators in preventing and responding to sexual harassment. In M. O. Weil, N. Hooyman, and M. Hughes (Eds.), *Sexual harassment and schools of social work: Issues, costs and strategic responses.* Alexandria, VA: Council on Social Work Education.

Riggs, R. O., Murrell, P. H., & Cutting, J. C. (1993). *Sexual harassment in higher education: From conflict to community* (ASHE-ERIC Higher Report No. 2). Washington, DC: George Washington University, School of Education and Human Development.

Roscoe, B., Goodwin, M. P., Repp, S. E., & Rose, M. (1987). Sexual harassment of university students and student employees: Findings and implications. *College Student Journal, 21*(3), 254–273.

Safran, C. (1976, November). What men do to women on the job: A shocking look at sexual harassment. *Redbook, 148,* p. 149.

Sandler, B. (1986). *The campus revisited: Chilly climate for faculty, administrators and graduate students.* Washington, DC: Center for Women Policy Studies.

Schneider, B. E. (1987). Graduate women, sexual harassment, and university policy. *Journal of Higher Education, 58*(1), 46–65.

Shank, B. (1994). Sexual harassment: Definitions, policy frameworks, and legal issues. In M. O. Weil, N. Hooyman, & M. Hughes (Eds.), *Sexual harassment and schools of social work: Issues, costs and strategic responses* (pp. 12–24). Alexandria, VA: Council on Social Work Education.

Singer, T. L. (1989). Sexual harassment in graduate schools of social work: Provocative dilemmas. *Journal of Social Work Education, 25*(1), 68–76.

Singer, T. L. (1994). Human and institutional costs. In M. O. Weil, N. Hooyman, & M. Hughes (Eds.), *Sexual harassment and schools of social work: Issues, costs and strategic responses* (pp. 54–61). Alexandria, VA: Council on Social Work Education.

Stringer, D. M., Remick, H., Salisbury, J., & Ginorio, A. B. (1990). The power and reasons behind sexual harassment: An employer's guide to solutions. *Public Personnel Management, 19*(1), 43–52.

Terpstra, D. E., & Baker, D. D. (1986). Psychological and demographic correlates of perceptions of sexual harassment. *Genetic, Social, and General Psychology Monographs, 112*(4), 459–478.

Title VII of the Civil Rights Act of 1964. §2000e et seq., 42 U.S.C. (1988).

Title IX of the Higher Education Amendment of 1972. §1681–1686, 20 U.S.C. (1982).

U.S. Merit Systems Protection Board. (1988). *Sexual harassment in the federal government: An update.* Washington, DC: U.S. Government Printing Office.

Valentine, D., Gandy, J., Burry, C., & Ginsberg, L. (1994). Sexual harassment in social work field placements. In M. O. Weil, N. Hooyman, & M. Hughes (Eds.), *Sexual harassment and schools of social work: Issues, costs and strategic responses* (pp. 39–53). Alexandria, VA: Council on Social Work Education.

Weil, M. O., Hooyman, N., & Hughes, M. (Eds.). (1994). *Sexual harassment and schools of social work: Issues, costs and strategic responses.* Alexandria, VA: Council on Social Work Education.

FURTHER READING

American Council on Education. (1993). *Sexual harassment on campus.* Washington, DC: Author.

National Education Association. (1992). *Sexual harassment in higher education: Concepts and issues.* Washington, DC: Author.

Paludi, M. (Ed.). (1990). *Ivory power: Sexual harassment on campus.* Albany: State University of New York Press.

Paludi, M., & Berickman, B. (1991). *Academic and workplace sexual harassment: A resource manual.* Albany: State University of New York Press.

Rapoport, J., & Zevnik, B. (1989). *The employee strikes back!* New York: Macmillan.

Repa, B., & Petrocelli, W. (1992). *Sexual harassment on the job.* Berkeley, CA: Nolo Press.

Terry L. Singer, PhD, LSW, is dean, Marywood College, School of Social Work, 2900 Adams Avenue, Scranton, PA 18509.

For further information see

Civil Rights; Conflict Resolution; Employee Assistance Programs; Human Sexuality; Legal Issues: Confidentiality and Privileged Communication; Management Overview; Men Overview; Occupational Social Work; Personnel Management; Professional Conduct; Professional Liability and Malpractice; Sexual Assault; Women Overview.

Key Words	
civil rights	sexual harassment
discrimination	women
equality	

Sieder, Violet

See Biographies section, Volume 3

Simkhovitch, Mary Kingsbury

See Biographies section, Volume 3

Single Parents
Virginia C. Strand

From 1970 to 1990, the single-parent family emerged as a major family form in the United States. In 1991, 25 percent of families with children under 18 were headed by single parents, and most of these families were headed by women (Kissman, 1991). Eighty percent of children living with a single parent resided with a female head of household as opposed to a male head of household (U.S. Bureau of the Census, 1992). More than half of mothers with children under one year of age were in the work force in 1988, and it is believed that half the children born in the 1980s will spend part of their childhood with only one parent (Walters, Carter, Papp, & Silverstein, 1988). The breakdown by race and ethnicity of single-parent families in 1991 is shown in Table 1. Of particular interest to social workers is the percentage of children living with one versus two parents. Although 79 percent of children from families identified as white were living with both parents in 1991, only 36 percent of black children and 66 percent of Hispanic children were living with both parents (U.S. Bureau of the Census, 1992).

Data regarding income suggest that single-parent families have fewer financial resources than two-parent families and that single male heads-of-household fare better than their female counterparts (see Figure 1). The median income in 1990 for all married households was $39,996. The median income for all male-headed families was $31,552, whereas for black male-headed families it was $24,048 and for Hispanic male-headed households it was $25,456. Families headed by single white men had a median income of $32,869, placing them above the median for *all* male-headed households (U.S. Bureau of the Census, 1992).

The story is different for female-headed households, for which the median income was $18,069, significantly lower than that of their male counterparts and less than half the income of the typical married couple. White female heads-of-household had a median income of $20,867, whereas the median for black female heads-of-household was $12,537 and the median for Hispanic female heads-of-household was $12,603 (U.S. Bureau of the Census, 1992). No group of female single heads-of-household earned what a group of male single heads-of-household earned, regardless of race or ethnicity.

There are a number of reasons for the emergence of single-parent families. Two major ones are the rise in divorce rates and the rise in births to never-married mothers. The largest contributor to single-parent heads-of-household is the births of children to never-married mothers, with a grow-

TABLE 1
Type of Family Household by Ethnicity and Gender of Head of Household: 1991

Head of Household	Number of Family Households (in thousands)	Percentage of Total Number of Family Households
Total households	70,791	
White	56,803	80
Married couples	47,014	66
Female	7,512	11
Male	2,276	3
Black	7,471	11
Married couples	3,569	5.4
Female	3,430	5
Male	472	0.6
Asian or Pacific Islander	1,536	2
Married couples	1,230	1.64
Female	194	0.2
Male	112	0.16
Hispanic	4,981	7
Married couples	3,454	4.8
Female	1,186	1.7
Male	342	0.5

SOURCE: U.S. Bureau of the Census. (1992). *Statistical abstract of the United States: 1992* (112th ed., p. 47). Washington, DC: U.S. Government Printing Office.

ing percentage born to teenage mothers (Nichols-Casebolt, 1988). Only half of mothers giving birth before the age of 18 finish high school, and they are more likely than mothers giving birth after 18 to be dependent on welfare (Walters et al., 1988). Adoption by single parents doubled from the 1970s to the 1980s, also adding to the growth of single-parent households (Groze, 1991).

An alarming trend is that female-headed, minority households appeared to be worse off in the 1990s than they were in 1970. Adjusting for constant 1990 dollars, the median income for both male and female single heads-of-household fell from 1970 to 1990, whereas married couples, as a group, enjoyed an increase. Meanwhile, both black and Hispanic families experienced a drop in income relative to white families, while experiencing a large increase in female heads-of-household (U.S. Bureau of the Census, 1992).

In a comparison of single mothers in this country with those in eight European countries, Wong, Garfinkel, and McLanahan (1993) found that the relative economic status of single mothers is lower in the United States than in most other Western industrialized countries. This seems to be due to the heavier reliance on means-tested categorical income maintenance programs here than

elsewhere. In countries where a universal approach to benefits for families with children is in place, poor women can return to work without losing income supports for day care and medical care, for example. These findings, as well as those of Farber (1989), underscore the need for practice interventions to incorporate the social constraints faced by many single parents.

BASIC PRINCIPLES OF INTERVENTION

Incorporating the Social Context

A guiding principle underlying social work with single parents is the recognition that they are a special population with unique needs that are defined and maintained by the social context within which they live. Although individuals come to single parenthood through different routes (divorce, separation, birth outside of marriage, widowhood, and adoption), most are women, and therefore the social context of women must be taken into consideration in designing, implementing, or evaluating any approach or service. Most single mothers face the dual stresses of poverty and working outside the home (Zigler & Black, 1989). Among the most effective empowering strategies may be viewing the mother-headed family as a viable unit that can be strengthened through realignment and networking for increased use of and support from external sources (Kissman, 1991).

Until the 1980s, single-parent families were often treated indiscriminately, as if they did not differ from two-parent families. However, the single mother in particular may be more vulnerable to stress owing to limited financial resources because as a group, single-parent families are characterized by fewer financial resources (U.S. Bureau of the Census, 1992). Also typical of single parents is increased role strain, including a shortage of time for personal care activities, sleep, and rest and, if employed, less time for children and child care, household tasks, and volunteer work (D. C. Miller, 1987; Norton & Glick, 1986; Quinn & Allen, 1989; Sanik & Maudlin, 1986; U.S. Bureau of the Census, 1992; Vosler & Proctor, 1991).

Nonetheless, it has been found that if single mothers are employed, they experience lower role strain and higher overall life satisfaction than those who stay at home and receive Aid to Families with Dependent Children (Jackson, 1993). However, lower-income mothers, especially teenage mothers, are less likely than their working-class and middle-class counterparts to access the vocational and educational opportunities that would enable them to become active participants in the work force. This situation appears to be

FIGURE 1

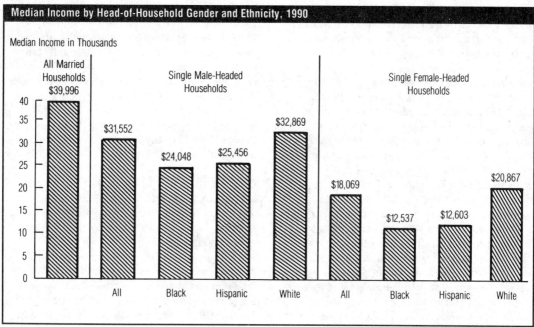

Median Income by Head-of-Household Gender and Ethnicity, 1990

Median Income in Thousands

All Married Households $39,996

Single Male-Headed Households

Single Female-Headed Households

$31,552

$24,048 $25,456

$32,869

$18,069

$12,537 $12,603

$20,867

40
35
30
25
20
15
10
5
0

All   Black   Hispanic   White   All   Black   Hispanic   White

SOURCE: U.S. Bureau of the Census. (1992). *Statistical abstract of the United States: 1992* (112th ed.). Washington, DC: U.S. Government Printing Office.

related to significant deficits in knowledge and skills, not to aspirations to employment (Farber, 1989).

Moving Away from a Deficit Model

Alternatively, single-parent families have been viewed as a deviant form of family life. Since the late 1980s, the negative outlook on single-parent families has been criticized. Researchers have found that when the effects of socioeconomic status are held constant, children in single-parent families are as well adjusted as those in two-parent families. Investigation of the effects of divorce on children has found little evidence to support the claim that negative outcomes for children are associated with divorce. More determinant are poverty and conflict between the parents (Hanson, 1986; Quinn & Allen, 1989).

In a study of healthy single-parent families, Hanson and Sporakowski (1986) found that, in general, the physical and mental health of the single parents in their study appeared to be good. Larger social support systems influenced health outcomes positively, as did good communication skills. Other studies have found that family system functioning is more important than family structure in predicting positive outcomes for children (Vosler, Green, & Kolevzon, 1987). In addition, although different family structures (biological

two-parent, single parent, or remarried) may experience varying types of stress, children in all types of families may be equally stressed (Vosler & Proctor, 1991).

The implications of these findings are critical for social work intervention. First, although single-parent families need to be conceptualized as a group with special needs, they are not by definition dysfunctional. They do, however, continue to be perceived as deficient, and this perception can have a powerful impact on the single parent. Although the greatest problem facing single mothers is economic need, negative prescriptions from society about single-parent status remain a difficulty.

Social workers serve an important function in helping single parents combat negative self-images. Individual and family counseling can help single parents counter their own and their family's negative attitudes through the implementation of peer support groups, encouragement of participation in self-help groups, and advocacy for child care and educational programs that are geared toward the single parent (Bienstock & Videka-Sherman, 1989; Schames, 1990a, 1990b; Wijnberg & Holmes, 1992).

As Walters et al. (1988) pointed out, when the single-parent family is viewed and internalized as less deviant, both parents and children have greater access to their own resources. In their interventions with single-parent families, social workers can facilitate clients' emotional availability to undertake the work associated with making their lives better.

Interventions across the Life Cycle

Interventions based on an appreciation of life-cycle development take into account the differences between single-parent and two-parent households and between single parents. For example, the crisis of the transition to single parenthood is different for every single parent (Howard & Johnson, 1986; Kalyanpur & Rao, 1991). An unplanned, out-of-wedlock birth to a teenage mother may be a very different type of crisis than a divorce for an older woman (Tracy, 1990; Wijnberg & Holmes, 1992). It is critical to recognize that most parents come to single parenthood as a result of a life crisis. The initial adjustment period is a time of high vulnerability, and there is a special need for support services (Kurdek, 1988; D. C. Miller, 1987; Schames, 1990a; Thompson & Peeble-Wilkins, 1992).

Social workers should recognize that demands on the parent will vary with the age of children. In addition, it has been found that some families experience more difficulty in the transition to single parenthood than others. Single parents with traditional sex-role orientations may experience greater difficulty as they take on new functions (Wijnberg & Holmes, 1992), and divorced women may find that the socialization that prepared them to be mothers and only secondarily wage earners has ill equipped them for the task of single head-of-household (Quinn & Allen, 1989).

According to some authors, differences between one parent and two are not found in the actual life stages, "but in the timing, number and length of the critical transitions" (Hanson & Sporakowski, 1986, p. 5), given that single-parent families lack the personnel to fulfill all the expected and necessary functions. Single working mothers experience greater role strain, with less time for personal care and time with children than married working mothers (Sanik & Maudlin, 1986).

As Hines (1989) delineated, for the poor black family the life cycle is truncated: "Family members leave home, mate, have children and become grandparents at far earlier ages than their middle-class counterparts" (p. 518). Teenagers of any racial or ethnic group who become single parents often have less time to resolve developmental tasks because they are required to assume roles and responsibilities before they are ready.

Interventions that take into account the special structure of the single-parent family, including the role strain that may make it difficult to perform all the necessary family functions, are important. Assessing the source, adequacy, and stability of income is crucial, and assistance with the development of adequate income sources is essential. This assistance may mean advocacy, establishment of community resources, and participation in legislative processes (Vosler & Proctor, 1991). Equally important is assistance with available, quality day care (Campbell, Breitmayer, & Ramey, 1986; Danziger & Farber, 1990; Quinn & Allen, 1989). Providing early intervention and outreach and offering mediation and support groups can be important for the social work practitioner in assisting with the transition to single parenthood.

Increased Salience of Social Networks

Interventions aimed at the most effective use of support from family, friends, and the father of the child positively influence the psychological well-being of mothers. Depression is often a problem for isolated women; the increase of social supports, including emotional support, feelings of value, and assistance with concrete tasks, can counter depression (Thompson & Peeble-Williams, 1992).

It is important to recognize that not all networks are inherently helpful. The young woman who is struggling with autonomy may need to postpone certain steps toward it because she needs her family's assistance. The costs and benefits for a particular woman must be part of the therapeutic assessment. The activation of intergenerational supports (Harnett, 1989) can indeed be helpful, and although engagement with social networks is usually effective in reducing isolation (Tracy, 1990), their benefits must be evaluated for each client.

Greater use of social supports may entail skills training, particularly in knowing when to ask for help, whom to ask, and how to evaluate the help that is given (Kissman, 1991). Assisting with the development of these skills may be important functions for social workers.

The immediate environment also has a mediating effect. The significance of the school setting, the workplace, the religious institution, medical facilities, and other organizations that interact with the family often gain importance for the single-parent family. The single parent's relationship to these social organizations must be explored and can often be strengthened. Efforts to improve communication between the family and school, for example, as well as efforts to facilitate engagement with entitlement programs like Medicaid, food stamps, and so forth carry special significance for single-parent families (Vosler & Proctor, 1991).

CURRENT TRENDS IN SERVICE

Over the past decade, social work services for single-parent families have begun to address the crisis of transition to parenthood as a single head-of-household, as well as the strained social circumstances under which many single-parent families, especially those that are female-headed, live. The rise in teenage pregnancy has spawned the development of school-based programs (Armstrong-Dillard, 1980; Campbell et al., 1986; Danziger & Farber, 1990; Schames, 1990a). Child welfare services have increasingly worked with single, often poor, inner-city mothers struggling to raise children in extreme situations. Foster care agencies (Fein, 1991) and residential treatment programs (Gibson & Noble, 1991) regularly encounter single parents, and services are often geared to reuniting the child with the family of origin.

Community-based agencies often serve the divorced single parent who is struggling to adjust to single parenthood while resolving the life crisis of divorce (Kurtz & Barth, 1989; Wijnberg & Holmes, 1992). Home-based services, including a range of family interventions aimed at assisting with attaining supplemental services like day care and homemaking services, are increasingly part of the social worker's repertoire in working with single parents (Harnett, 1989; Howard & Johnson, 1986; Hurn & Balgopal, 1990; Zigler & Black, 1989).

Services to Individuals

Individual counseling is still used in community-based agencies (Betchen, 1992; Kalyanpur & Rao, 1991; J. B. Miller, 1982). In terms of the psychological well-being of single mothers, research has shown that single women diversify their emotional investments as compared with married women, and a major part of this is investment in themselves (J. B. Miller, 1982). This finding points to the continued need to help women through personal counseling as they move through the psychological transition to single parenthood (Betchen, 1992). As Miller suggested, in freeing themselves from restrictions imposed by traditional values, single mothers can find inner resources to pursue goals and become successful in accomplishing things that traditional value and belief systems may have inhibited.

Individual counseling remains a major modality, and it may be most effective when intervention

proceeds from an empowerment model (Kissman, 1991). For example, Kalyanpur and Rao (1991) found that when the practitioner was perceived to be disrespectful, focused on the individual's deficits, or discounting parenting styles, the interventions were perceived as "un-empowering." An empowerment approach emphasizes a collaborative relationship in which the worker is responsive to the parent's needs by providing emotional support as well as specific services. Kalyanpur and Rao found that the important aspects of establishing rapport were being conversational, interpreting, sharing, and accepting.

Wortman (1981) pointed to the need to be sensitive to the social factors contributing to depression, dependency, and denial found particularly in poor black single parents. When the strain of living poor is incorporated into an assessment, interventions that highlight strengths rather than deficits are possible. Wortman pointed out that short-term problem-solving or solution-oriented approaches are often best, recognizing that the energy resources of the poor single parent are limited.

In terms of the population of adolescent mothers, especially those from poor inner-city communities, researchers and practitioners alike have pointed out that poor educational attainment is a problem resulting not only from adolescent childbearing but also from the negative force of extreme poverty. Adolescent mothers do best when they have support from family and peers, or, when that help is unavailable, when they have access to other people who provide individual attention and nurture their individual strengths. Establishing an environment that sets and reinforces the expectation of academic success and providing mentors or other meaningful adult relationships can be achieved through both school- and community-based programs (Danziger & Farber, 1990). If high-quality day care is available, it greatly increases the likelihood that a teenage mother will finish high school and enroll in postsecondary education and job training (Campbell et al., 1986).

Group Interventions

The emphasis on competency-based practice with single parents in groups is another important trend in service delivery. In this approach, the worker focuses on enhancing individuals' strengths as well as mobilizing resources from the environment. Results from a study of a group program for single mothers indicated that participants made significant progress in individual competencies both immediately after the program and one year later (Resnick, 1984). Other types of group interventions that have been found effective include the use of developmentally oriented groups for young mothers (Schames, 1990b) and feminist-oriented groups that reduce the isolation and emphasize the social and political factors in women's lives (Gottlieb, Burden, McCormick, & Nicarthy, 1983; Kissman, 1991; Wijnberg & Holmes, 1992).

Others who have looked at group process over time have pointed out that even mothers coming into treatment "because of the children" need help focusing on their own transitions to single parenthood before they can deal with handling the children's problematic behavior. The beneficial impact of group membership on single mothers is significant in combating negative social prescriptions. Membership in a group of single parents tends to normalize their life situation, and this has a corresponding increase on individual self-esteem (Bienstock & Videka-Sherman, 1989; Wijnberg & Holmes, 1992).

Group services for divorcing parents, parents who have neglected or abused their children, teenage mothers, and others have become an important intervention modality across settings (Bienstock & Videka-Sherman, 1989; Gottlieb et al., 1983; Howard & Johnson, 1986; Kissman, 1991; Resnick, 1984; Schames, 1990a, 1990b; Wijnberg & Holmes, 1992). Sustaining relationships with extended family and friends has been found to be of crucial support to single-parent families, and services that focus on helping parents to help themselves, through activation of self-help and mutual aid networks, have increased since the early 1980s (Harnett, 1989; Hogan, 1990; Kurdek, 1988; Quinn & Allen, 1989; Tracy, 1990; Waite, 1985).

Family Interventions

The rise of family preservation services has generated social work efforts directed at preventing placement, and the typical family served is that headed by a young single mother with more than one child and few resources (Berry, 1992; Reid, Kagan, & Schlosberg, 1988). These parents are often from lower socioeconomic groups, and the strain of single parenting coupled with environmental stresses leads some parents to conclude that putting a child in care is the only solution. Homeless women with children have also raised challenges to how services are delivered (Bassuk & Rubin, 1987). Short-term intensive services can be instrumental in linking these single parents, often mothers, to the social network resources that make a crucial difference.

School-based programs that work with parents and children (Armstrong-Dillard, 1980; Kurtz & Barth, 1989) and family approaches that incorporate an emphasis on social functioning have increased in number (Vosler et al., 1987; Vosler & Proctor, 1991). Family support services (Zigler & Black, 1989), family network therapy (Atneave & Verhulst, 1986), and multiple impact family therapy (Hines, 1989) are other innovative approaches that have been enormously successful with poor, highly stressed families, including many headed by single parents. In some instances, creative child care programs or residential institutions attuned to the special needs of single parents are successful. An example of the latter is a residential service for single parents and their families (Gibson & Noble, 1991).

SUMMARY

Single parents are best served when they are understood as a group with special needs. Single parents respond to models of intervention that capitalize on their strengths, view their family circumstances as a variant, not deviant, lifestyle, and consider the crisis of transition to single parenthood and the role strains imposed on the single parent. The overwhelming majority of single parents are women, and even working women typically earn only two-thirds as much as men do. Lack of economic resources is a major obstacle to single parents, especially women, in maximizing their potential. Strategies that mediate the negative social prescriptions of single parenthood and maximize the linkage to social supports—whether achieved through individual, group, or family interventions—work best.

REFERENCES

Armstrong-Dillard, P. (1980). Developing services for single parents and their children in the school. *Social Work in Education, 3,* 44–57.

Atneave, C. L., & Verhulst, J. (1986). Teaching mental health professionals to see family strengths. In M. A. Karpel (Ed.), *Family resources: The hidden partner in family therapy* (pp. 259–271). New York: Guilford Press.

Bassuk, E., & Rubin, L. (1987). Homeless children: A neglected population. *American Journal of Orthopsychiatry, 57*(2), 279–286.

Berry, M. (1992). An evaluation of family preservation services: Fitting agency services to family needs. *Social Work, 37,* 314–321.

Betchen, S. J. (1992). Short-term psychodynamic therapy with a divorced single mother. *Families in Society, 73*(3), 116–121.

Bienstock, C. R., & Videka-Sherman, L. (1989). Process analysis of a therapeutic support group for single parent mothers. *Social Work with Groups, 12*(2), 43–61.

Campbell, F. A., Breitmayer, B., & Ramey, C. T. (1986). Disadvantaged single teenage mothers and their children: Consequences of free educational day care. *Family Relations, 35,* 63–68.

Danziger, S. K., & Farber, N. B. (1990). Keeping inner-city youths in school: Critical experiences of young black women. *Social Work Research & Abstracts, 26*(4), 32–39.

Farber, N. B. (1989). The significance of aspirations among unmarried adolescent mothers. *Social Service Review, 63*(4), 518–532.

Fein, E. (1991). Issues in foster care: Where do we stand? *American Journal of American Orthopsychiatry, 61*(4), 578–582.

Gibson, D., & Noble, D. N. (1991). Creative permanency planning: Residential services for families. *Child Welfare, 70*(3), 371–382.

Gottlieb, N., Burden, D., McCormick, R., & Nicarthy, G. (1983). The distinctive attributes of feminist groups. *Social Work with Groups, 6*(3–4), 81–93.

Groze, V. (1991). Adoption and single parents: A review. *Child Welfare, 70*(3), 321–332.

Hanson, S.M.H. (1986). Healthy single parent families. *Family Relations, 35,* 125–132.

Hanson, S.M.H., & Sporakowski, M. J. (1986). Single parent families. *Family Relations, 35,* 3–8.

Harnett, J. (1989). An intergenerational support system for child welfare families. *Child Welfare, 68*(3), 347–353.

Hines, P. M. (1989). The family life cycle of poor Black families. In B. Carter & M. McGoldrick (Eds.), *The changing life cycle* (pp. 515–544). Needham Heights, MA: Allyn & Bacon.

Hogan, D. P. (1990). Race, kin networks, and assistance to mother-headed families. *Social Forces, 68*(3), 244–262.

Howard, T. U., & Johnson, F. C. (1986). An ecological approach to practice with single-parent families. *Social Casework, 66*(8), 482–489.

Hurn, J. J., & Balgopal, P. (1990). Child care in an age of family differences. *Child and Adolescent Social Work, 7*(3), 247–262.

Jackson, A. P. (1993). Black, single, working mothers in poverty: Preferences for employment, well-being, and perceptions of preschool-age children. *Social Work, 38,* 26–34.

Kalyanpur, M., & Rao, S. S. (1991). Empowering low-income black families of handicapped children. *American Journal of Orthopsychiatry, 61*(4), 523–532.

Kissman, K. (1991). Feminist-based social work with single-parent families. *Families in Society, 72*(1), 23–28.

Kurdek, L. A. (1988). Social support of divorced single mothers and their children. *Journal of Divorce, 11*(4), 600–613.

Kurtz, P. D., & Barth, R. P. (1989). Parent involvement: Cornerstone of school social work practice. *Social Work, 34,* 407–413.

Miller, D. C. (1987). *Helping the strong: An exploration of needs of families headed by women.* Silver Spring, MD: National Association of Social Workers.

Miller, J. B. (1982). Psychological recovery in low-income single parents. *American Journal of Orthopsychiatry, 52*(2), 346–352.

Nichols-Casebolt, A. M. (1988). Black families headed by single mothers: Growing numbers and increasing poverty. *Social Work, 33,* 306–313.

Norton, A. J., & Glick, P. C. (1986). One parent families: A social and economic profile. *Family Relations, 33,* 9–17.

Quinn, P., & Allen, K. R. (1989). Facing challenges and making compromises: How single mothers endure. *Family Relations, 38,* 300–395.

Reid, W. J., Kagan, R. M., & Schlosberg, S. B. (1988). Prevention of placement: Critical factors in program success. *Child Welfare, 67,* 25–36.

Resnick, G. (1984). The short and long-term impact of a competency-based program for disadvantaged women. *Journal of Social Service Research, 7*(4), 37–49.

Sanik, M. M., & Maudlin, T. (1986). Single versus two parent families: A comparison of mothers' time. *Family Relations, 35,* 53–56.

Schames, G. (1990a). Toward an understanding of the etiology and treatment of psychological dysfunction among single teenage mothers: Part I. A review of the literature. *Smith College Studies in Social Work, 60*(2), 153–168.

Schames, G. (1990b). Toward an understanding of the etiology and treatment of psychological dysfunction among single teenage mothers: Part II. *Smith College Studies in Social Work, 60*(3), 244–262.

Thompson, M. S., & Peeble-Wilkins, W. (1992). The impact of formal, informal, and societal support networks on the psychological well-being of black adolescent mothers. *Social Work, 37,* 322–328.

Tracy, E. M. (1990). Identifying social support resources of at-risk families. *Social Work, 35,* 252–258.

U.S. Bureau of the Census. (1992). *Statistical abstract of the United States: 1992* (112th ed.). Washington, DC: U.S. Government Printing Office.

Vosler, N. R., Green, R. G., & Kolevzon, M. S. (1987). The structure and competence of family units: Implications for social work practice with families and children. *Journal of Social Science Research, 9*(2–3), 1–17.

Vosler, N. R., & Proctor, E. K. (1991). Family structure and stressors in a child guidance clinic population. *Families in Society, 72*(3), 164–173.

Waite, M. E. (1985). Developing support services for separating families: A northern rural experience. *The Social Worker/LeTravailleur Social, 53*(1), 21–24.

Walters, M., Carter, B., Papp, P., & Silverstein, O. (1988). *The invisible web.* New York: Guilford Press.

Wijnberg, M. H., & Holmes, T. (1992). Adaptation to divorce: The impact of role orientation on family life cycle perspectives. *Families in Society, 73*(3), 159–167.

Wong, Y. I., Garfinkel, I., & McLanahan, S. M. (1993). Single mother families in eight countries: Economic status and social policy. *Social Service Review, 67*(2), 177–197.

Wortman, R. A. (1981). Depression, danger, dependency, denial: Work with poor, Black, single parents. *American Journal of Orthopsychiatry, 51*(4), 662–671.

Zigler, E., & Black, K. B. (1989). America's family support movement: Strengths and limitations. *American Journal of Orthopsychiatry, 59*(1), 6–19.

Virginia C. Strand, DSW, is assistant professor and director, Center for Training and Research in Child Abuse and Family Violence, Fordham University, Graduate School of Social Service, Neparan Road, Tarrytown, NY 10591.

For further information see
Adolescent Pregnancy; Aid to Families with Dependent Children; Child Support; Child Welfare Overview; Ethnic-Sensitive Practice; Families: Demographic Shifts; Family Planning; Family Preservation; Income Distribution; Income Security Overview; Jobs and Earnings; Poverty; School-Linked Services; Self-Help Groups; Social Security; Women Overview.

Key Words

adolescent fathers   single-parent family
adolescent mothers   single parents

Single-System Design
Betty J. Blythe

Single-system design is just one of several names for a research methodology that allows a social work practitioner to track systematically his or her progress with a client or client unit. With increasingly rigorous applications of this methodology, practitioners can also gain knowledge about effective social work interventions, although this is a less common goal.

Data collected across time allow the worker to examine the client's response to intervention. If possible, data are collected before social work intervention begins to provide an indication of the baseline level of the problem, and then one or more interventions are implemented. Continuous data collection allows the practitioner to examine the client's response to treatment and, if necessary, make modifications to the treatment plan.

Single-system design offers an alternative to the unsystematic case study as a means of documenting and evaluating a client's progress (Kazdin, 1982). Other names for this methodology include time-series research, $N = 1$, idiographic research, single-organism research, nomothetic research, single-case design, and single-subject design. Note that the "system" can be a client or a client unit.

HISTORICAL OVERVIEW

The idea of evaluating practice with single-system design is a relatively new one in social work. In the early 1970s distinguished leaders in social work noted that the profession needed to address issues related to accountability (Briar, 1973; Newman & Turem, 1974). Briar, in particular, called on social work practitioners to evaluate whether their interventions were helping clients.

Early Developments

The single-system design was essentially borrowed from psychology, where it was being applied in controlled research, often in laboratory settings or in classrooms (Campbell & Stanley, 1966; Hersen & Barlow, 1976). Psychologists studying the effects of behavioral interventions on a small number of subjects (often only one subject) frequently applied this methodology in their research. For instance, O'Brien and Azrin (1973) examined the effects of different methods of inviting family members to visit three inpatients on a mental health hospital ward. Mills, Agras, Barlow, and Mills (1973) used single-system design methods to study a behavioral intervention known as response prevention with five individuals who engaged in compulsive behaviors such as hand washing. These two examples are typical of many such studies in that they evaluated highly specified interventions that were aimed at changing discrete behaviors and in environments that afforded considerable control over extraneous factors.

At that time, psychologists were also interested in the idea of using single-system design in clinical settings. Again, they were primarily testing well-specified, circumscribed behavioral interventions. These were the models that were available when social work practitioners began to discuss evaluating direct practice with single-system designs in the 1970s.

Practitioner Concerns

In retrospect, it is not surprising that early efforts to evaluate practice with single-system designs led practitioners to voice some concerns about the appropriateness of this approach. On the basis of the standards of research in behavioral psychology, students and practitioners were taught that more-rigorous designs were more desirable without really knowing whether such designs could be implemented in routine social work practice. Unfortunately, this meant that practice was made to fit the confines of rigorous research designs and was not allowed to evolve naturally. For example, the withdrawal design, which was thought to be rigorous in demonstrating that the intervention was responsible for the observed data patterns, called for withdrawing the intervention for a period of time. This practice, however, might be unethical or impossible in practice. Similarly, students were taught that observational measures (whose reliability could be determined) or standardized measures with known reliability were preferable. However, some practitioners argued that certain client problems or situations are not easily measured by such means and may be better measured with tailor-made tools. Furthermore, the more rigorous application of single-subject design called for equal phase lengths. Thus, changes in the treatment plan were constrained by the intended length of phases, a practice that is not always in line with the treatment plan or the needs of the client.

Concerns about Validity

Over time social work practitioners came to realize that attempts to force practice and decisions about practice to fit the demands of a particular research design or measurement strategy distorted practice. As they became more flexible in their teaching of single-system designs, however, some methodologists became concerned about the extent to which research designs are adapted to fit the realities of practice, about the type of designs being used, and about the measurement tools being used in some instances. Were the findings valid and reliable? Were they generalizable? Ultimately, practitioners realized that the answers to these questions depend on the goals of the practitioner. Is the practitioner using single-system design to monitor a client's progress, inform practice decisions, and systematize her or his own thinking? Or is the practitioner attempting to document the effectiveness of a particular intervention and explore the extent to which this intervention might be effective in addressing the same concerns with other clients? If the latter is the goal, then methodological issues clearly must be examined carefully. Fortunately, most practitioners are more concerned with monitoring client progress and gathering information to inform their decision making, and most scholars and teachers are more aware of that goal as they teach and write about practice evaluation with single-system methods (Proctor, 1990).

ADVANTAGES OF SINGLE-SYSTEM DESIGNS

If practitioners accept that their objective in using single-system designs is to monitor their client's progress and to help them make practice decisions, how can these methods be helpful? Perhaps the most significant contribution of single-system designs is to provide a framework that guides the

practitioner through the assessment and specification of a client's goals, implementation of interventions, and termination and follow-up. Although these are nothing more than the phases of practice, applying the components of single-system designs to these phases provides a degree of structure and some additional tools to aid in the process.

Assessment

In the assessment phase, the information typically gathered by a social worker is enhanced by enlisting some of the measurement strategies suggested by single-system design methodology (Blythe & Tripodi, 1989). For example, obtaining multiple types of information from multiple sources helps to reduce bias and yields a more-accurate description of the client's situation. Applying principles of reliability to interviews can result in more-accurate information. The process of selecting and specifying measurement devices also helps the client and practitioner understand more fully all aspects of the presenting problem. Visually presenting the assessment data in a graph or other format, such as an ecomap, may focus the attention and increase the understanding of all the parties involved (Mattaini, 1993).

Goals and Intervention Plans

Perhaps the greatest potential for single-system designs to enhance practice is in the area of establishing goals and intervention plans, particularly with so-called multiproblem clients (Ivanoff, Blythe, & Tripodi, 1994). Because targets for intervention (that is, a client's goals) must be selected and carefully specified, goal setting receives more attention than it often does in routine practice. Goals must be clearly articulated so that appropriate dependent measures can be identified. Moreover, practitioners are less likely to lose sight of important goals when clients meet with a seemingly inevitable series of crises. Although it sometimes is necessary to rethink and revise goals, the framework imposed by single-system designs makes it more likely that the practitioner will make this decision in a thoughtful manner. Finally, the clear identification of dependent and independent (treatment) variables required by single-system designs reduces the chance that practitioners will confuse the two. Without such a structure, practitioners sometimes write treatment goals that are nothing more than a restatement of what they intend to teach clients as part of the intervention.

By examining the data patterns resulting from the ongoing collection of assessment data, the practitioner has systematic information to help him or her make decisions about treatment plans as well as about continuing, discontinuing, or revising intervention strategies (Berlin & Marsh, 1993; Rosen, 1992). Ideally, there are multiple sources of information that reflect the complexity of most client's goals. Critical incidents that may explain or be associated with extreme data points or patterns can be graphed and analyzed. When all goals have been sufficiently met, the decision is likely to be termination. Finally, follow-up is facilitated when assessment measurement strategies that were used during the initial and ongoing assessment are applied to determine whether gains have been maintained.

Another advantage, from a treatment perspective, is that applying single-case methodology in practice underscores the practitioner's responsibility for goal attainment. The practitioner is actually monitoring his or her ability to help clients achieve goals. At the same time, the client is involved in identifying target problems and goals as assessment is carried out and in evaluating progress as treatment plans are implemented. This type of collegial relationship promotes the client's engagement and involvement in treatment (Blythe, 1990).

Debates about Single-System Designs

Despite the enthusiasm about the advantages of applying single-system designs in practice, several debates about this approach have taken place. These debates can be divided into three general areas, although there is overlap in the arguments. Although some of this discussion suggests that practice simply is not improved by single-system designs and other quantitative research tools, most arguments contend that other research methods are better suited for practice.

Distortions in Practice

The first area of debate relates to the charge that single-system methods distort practice (Kagle, 1982; Thomas, 1978). To be sure, when treatment plans are dictated by the need to withhold, delay, or present treatments at certain times or for certain intervals, practice is distorted. Early teaching and writing on single-system designs presented the methodology as rigid and as making some demands on practice. Indeed, scholars such as Thomas and Kagle helped sharpen the profession's thinking about implementing single-system research methods in practice. Unfortunately, the more recent opponents of single-system design do not appear to acknowledge or perhaps understand that the methodology is now viewed as highly flexible and as unfolding as practice decisions are made. In the current view, implementing single-

case methods and applying other research tools in practice do not distort practice because it is the practice actions and needs that dictate research designs and the selection of research methods and tools (Collins, Kayser, & Platt, 1994; Corcoran, 1993; Gingerich, 1990; Proctor, 1990).

Methodology Issues

The remaining two areas of debate about implementing single-system designs in practice take issue with the methodology and suggest that other methods or worldviews are more appropriate. The arguments are based on slightly different grounds.

Male voice versus female voice. The first, posed by Davis (1985), asserts that implementing single-system methods in practice is to speak in the "male voice." Davis's premise is that the components of empirical clinical practice, such as monitoring a client's progress with quantitative indicators and objective instruments, are incompatible with the female view of the world. Davis argued that the female voice should be heard and valued in discussions of practice, especially those related to evaluating practice.

Quantitative versus qualitative methodology. At the risk of oversimplification, the other set of debates about implementing single-system methods in practice contends that practice is much too complex to be examined in cause–effect terms and with quantitative measures and single-system designs (Heineman, 1981; Ruckdeschel & Farris, 1981; Witkin, 1992). For the most part, the alternatives suggested by these critics for integrating research and social work practice are vague. For example, Witkin suggested that such integration should "include naturalistic, interpretive, and critical approaches" (p. 267).

The suggestions of these critics typically involve qualitative research methodology. Notably, some scholars have described specific means of applying qualitative methods to practice, sometimes together with single-system methods (Millstein, 1993; Rodwell, 1990). Much work remains, however, to move this line of thinking from the realm of suggestion to that of concrete proposals with procedural descriptions, case examples, and teaching materials.

OTHER ISSUES

Early in the profession's efforts to integrate practice and research, some innovative curriculum designs were developed to bring together practice, research, and field components (Downs & Robertson, 1983; Gottlieb & Richey, 1980). Rather than bolster and improve these innovations, anecdotal data suggest that these efforts have been diminished, partly because of other curriculum demands and faculty workload concerns (Blythe & Rodgers, 1993). Renewed attention and energy must be directed toward identifying creative, realistic, and flexible methods for preparing social workers to apply single-system methods to their practice. In particular, special attention must be paid to the means of involving field education in this challenge, so that students have actual experiences in evaluating their practice with single-system methods.

These proposals that other methods of research inquiry can enhance practice must be fully articulated before any suggestions can actually be implemented. Practitioners' experience in applying single-system research methods to practice is instructive. Clearly, these new initiatives will take considerable time to develop, refine, and disseminate. Ideally, the proponents of these innovations will identify and emphasize the congruency and complementarity with other forms of integrating research and practice, rather than emphasize the differences.

Finally, the profession must continue to develop institutional supports for practitioners who are attempting to integrate research and practice. Computer hardware and software technology, administrative data management systems, and peer review are just a few examples of the ways in which agency administrators can structure supports for these undertakings (Bronson & Blythe, 1987; Mattaini, 1993; Mutschler & Jayaratne, 1993; Nurius & Hudson, 1993).

CONCLUSION

The social work profession has come a long way in its understanding of how to integrate research methods, especially single-system designs, into practice. It is time to move beyond the debates and the rhetoric. Practitioners must work together to advance their understanding of and ability to apply this technology, as well as other research methods, in their work with clients. Clearly, social work practice and clients will benefit from these endeavors.

REFERENCES

Berlin, S. B., & Marsh, J. C. (1993). *Informing practice decisions.* New York: Macmillan.

Blythe, B. J. (1990). Applying practice research methods in intensive family preservation services. In J. K. Whittaker, J. Kinney, E. M. Tracy, & C. Booth (Eds.), *Reaching high-risk families: Intensive family preservation in human services* (pp. 147–164). New York: Aldine de Gruyter.

Blythe, B. J., & Rodgers, A. Y. (1993). Evaluating our own practice: Past, present, and future trends. *Journal of Social Service Research, 18,* 101–119.

Blythe, B. J., & Tripodi, T. T. (1989). *Measurement in direct social work practice.* Newbury Park, CA: Sage Publications.

Briar, S. (1973). Effective social work intervention in direct practice: Implications for education. In *Facing the challenge: Plenary session papers from the 19th Annual Program Meeting.* New York: Council on Social Work Education.

Bronson, D. E., & Blythe, B. J. (1987). Computer support for single-case evaluation of practice. *Social Work Research & Abstracts, 23*(3), 10–13.

Campbell, D. T., & Stanley, J. C. (1966). *Experimental and quasi-experimental designs for research.* Chicago: Rand McNally.

Collins, P. M., Kayser, K., & Platt, S. (1994). Conjoint marital therapy: A practitioner's approach to single-system evaluation. *Families in Society, 75,* 131–141.

Corcoran, K. J. (1993). Practice evaluation: Problems and promises of single-system designs in clinical practice. *Journal of Social Service Research, 18,* 147–159.

Davis, L. V. (1985). Female and male voices in social work. *Social Work, 30,* 106–113.

Downs, W. R., & Robertson, J. F. (1983). Preserving the social work perspective in the research sequence: State of the art and program models for the 1980s. *Journal of Education for Social Work, 19*(1), 87–95.

Gingerich, W. (1990). Rethinking single-case evaluation. In L. Videka-Sherman & W. J. Reid (Eds.), *Advances in clinical social work research* (pp. 11–24). Silver Spring, MD: NASW Press.

Gottlieb, N., & Richey, C. A. (1980). Education of human service practitioners for clinical evaluation. In R. W. Weinbach & A. Rubin (Eds.), *Teaching social work research: Alternative programs and strategies* (pp. 3–12). New York: Council on Social Work Education.

Heineman, M. (1981). The obsolete scientific imperative in social work research. *Social Service Review, 55,* 371–396.

Hersen, D. H., & Barlow, M. (1976). *Single case experimental designs.* New York: Pergamon Press.

Ivanoff, A., Blythe, B. J., & Tripodi, T. T. (1994). *Involuntary clients in social work practice: A research-based approach.* New York: Aldine de Gruyter.

Kagle, J. D. (1982). Using single-subject measures in practice decisions: Systematic documentation or distortion? *Arete, 7,* 1–9.

Kazdin, A. (1982). *Single-case research designs: Methods for clinical and applied settings.* New York: Oxford University Press.

Mattaini, M. A. (1993). *More than a thousand words: Graphics for clinical practice.* Washington, DC: NASW Press.

Mills, H. L., Agras, S., Barlow, D. H., & Mills, J. R. (1973). Compulsive rituals treated by response prevention. *Archives of General Psychiatry, 28,* 524–529.

Millstein, K. H. (1993). Building knowledge from the study of cases: A reflective model for practitioner self-evaluation. *Journal of Teaching in Social Work, 8,* 255–279.

Mutschler, E., & Jayaratne, S. (1993). Integration of information technology and single-system designs. *Journal of Social Services Research, 18,* 121–145.

Newman, E., & Turem, J. (1974). The crisis of accountability. *Social Work, 19,* 5–16.

Nurius, P. S., & Hudson, W. W. (1993). *Human services practice, evaluation, and computers: A practical guide for today and beyond.* Pacific Grove, CA: Brooks/Cole.

O'Brien, F., & Azrin, N. H. (1973). Interaction-priming: A method of reinstating patient-family relationships. *Behaviour Research & Therapy, 11,* 133–136.

Proctor, E. K. (1990). Evaluating clinical practice: Issues of purpose and design. *Social Work Research & Abstracts, 26*(1), 32–40.

Rodwell, M. K. (1990, March). *Naturalistic inquiry: The research link to social work practice?* Paper presented at the 36th Annual Program Meeting of the Council on Social Work Education, Reno, NV.

Rosen, A. (1992). Facilitating clinical decision-making and evaluation. *Families in Society, 73,* 522–530.

Ruckdeschel, R. A., & Farris, B. E. (1981). Assessing practice: A critical look at single-case design. *Social Casework, 62,* 413–419.

Thomas, E. J. (1978). Research and service in single-case experimentation: Conflicts and choices. *Social Work Research & Abstracts, 14*(4), 20–31.

Witkin, S. L. (1992). Should undergraduate and graduate social work students be taught to conduct empirically-based practice? *Journal of Social Work Education, 28,* 265–268.

FURTHER READING

Alter, C., & Evans, W. (1990). *Evaluating your practice: A guide to self-assessment.* New York: Springer.

Bloom, M., Fischer, J., & Orme, J. (1995). *Evaluating practice: Guidelines for the accountable professional* (2nd ed.). Needham Heights, MA: Allyn & Bacon.

Fischer, J., & Corcoran, K. (1994). *Measures for clinical practice.* New York: Free Press.

Betty J. Blythe, PhD, is professor, Boston College, Graduate School of Social Work, Chestnut Hill, MA 02167.

For further information see

Clinical Social Work; Direct Practice Overview; Experimental and Quasi-Experimental Design; Goal Setting and Intervention Planning; Person-in-Environment; Recording; Research Overview; Social Work Education; Social Work Practice: Theoretical Base.

Key Words

single-system design   social work research
social work practice

Smith, Zilpha Drew

See Biographies section, Volume 3

Snyder, Mitch

See Biographies section, Volume 3

Social Development
Gary R. Lowe

Social development is an encompassing concept that refers to a dual-focused, holistic, systemic–ecologically oriented approach to seeking social advancement of individuals, as well as broad-scale societal institutions. Such a dual micro–macro concern, understanding, and approach to social issues have been present throughout this century; however, theoretical and practice developments have tended to be promulgated at either end of the micro–macro continuum. Since the middle of the 20th century, particularly since the mid-1970s, a clearer theoretical and practice position has emerged in social work and other disciplines to close the gap between these ends of the conceptual continuum and to formulate an integrated understanding of the dynamics of the interrelatedness of individuals and the larger context and the interaction between the two. The articulation of this integrated approach creates the challenge for social work to view social problems as three-dimensional. Such an emerging view has come to be labeled a "social development" approach.

Khinduka (1987) cryptically captured the nature of the social development notion when he stated that it is "an incorrigibly inclusive concept" (p. 22). However, citing Meinert and Kohn (1986), he identified some common emphases: the creation of more responsive institutions or renewal of existing institutions; the recognition of both macro and micro factors and their interaction; a commitment to such values as distributive justice, cooperation, people's participation and equity; a recognition of the inadequacy of economic growth without social justice, and of the dysfunctionality of transferring, borrowing, or imposing inappropriate technology. (pp. 22–23)

As James Billups, professor of social work at Ohio State University (personal communication, May 26, 1994), observed,

Social development is a rich multidimensional concept that embraces content that is more than and different from the content ordinarily associated with the social work conception of human development. That is, the much broader concept of social development is focused not only on the well-being of individuals, but more frequently than not on the achievement of the well-being and fullest possible human realization of the potentials of individuals, groups, communities, and masses of people.

Three other authors have captured the complexity and inclusiveness of social development. Pandey (1981) stated that social development includes

improvement in the quality of life of people . . . [a more] equitable distribution of resources . . . broad-based participation . . . in the process of decision making; and special measures that will enable marginal groups and communities to move in the mainstream. (p. 33)

According to Paiva (1982), social development

has two interrelated dimensions: the first is the development of the capacity of people to work continuously for their welfare and that of society's; the second is the alteration or development of a society's institutions so that human needs are met at all levels, especially at the lowest level, through a process of improving the relationships between people and socio-economic institutions. (p. 4)

Furthermore, Maas (1986) articulated social development broadly as

the processes through which people become increasingly able to interact competently and responsibly—that is, with recognition of others' needs—in an increasing array of social contexts. The greater the number of contexts with which people can cope, the fewer the situations in which they are overwhelmed by feelings of helplessness and stress. The more often they engage in socially responsive interaction, the more likely they are to help to generate or sustain a caring and sharing society. Such a society, including its social services, reciprocally furthers the social development of its members. (p. 3)

Much of the preceding is a rhetoric that belies the real history and roots of social development as both a concept and a set of practices.

HISTORICAL DEVELOPMENT

International and Third World Roots

In Africa—particularly West Africa—in the late 1920s and during the depression years of the 1930s, the British colonial authorities began to shift their policies toward the promotion of economic development. This approach gained increased emphasis and momentum after World War II, in response to growing nationalist pressure and the beginning independence movements in those countries. The shift was a significant move away from the traditional colonial practice of the dominant power primarily removing valuable natural resources from the colony and providing only minimal welfare services designed to support and sustain the resource-extraction efforts.

British efforts. The British Colonial Office developed and promoted these efforts to benefit the indigenous colonial inhabitants through an increasing emphasis on economic development and further supported these efforts by strengthening the dual roles of education and social services. These government efforts began to supplant the other established efforts in the areas of education and social services that had historically been sponsored by missionaries. Midgley (1994a) pointed out that "the formulation of a systematic developmental perspective in social welfare emerged in West Africa in the 1940s when colonial administrators began to promote what was known as *mass literacy*" (p. 6). These efforts, particularly in the large rural areas, were more far reaching than simple literacy efforts because they incorporated instruction in numerous practical endeavors, including agriculture; crafts; and infrastructure needs, such as road building. The emphasis on literacy was soon replaced by a much broader notion of "community development," which was a new combination of words and thus a new concept. By 1954 the British authorities had adopted the term *social development* to describe these development efforts. Midgley (1994a) noted that social development incorporated "the combination of traditional social welfare and community development. The new term suggested that both elements should be linked to wider efforts to promote economic development in the colonies" (p. 5).

United Nations support. Further support from other international sources, specifically from the United Nations (UN), began to come forth for the newly emergent notion of social development. During the 1950s the UN promoted more traditional approaches to social welfare that emphasized family and child welfare services. By the beginning of the 1960s, it had redefined its earlier approach and replaced it with a broader notion that encompassed an emphasis on promotion of economic growth while simultaneously remaining concerned with families and children. It adopted the British-originated label of "social development" to describe the redefined perspective that combined an economic focus with the new emphasis on social welfare issues.

As the independent developing countries of Africa multiplied rapidly, the social development approach of striving to integrate larger societal concerns with individual needs became a hallmark of their efforts to thrive. However, the earliest postcolonial efforts were marked by centralized planning approaches, with the primary direction of intervention being from the top down. By the mid-1970s, people began to challenge this approach because it ignored the role of the local community in the development process. The result was that the UN incorporated local participation attributes into its ever-evolving social development model.

The notion of social development that grew from its original British colonial roots had matured by the 1970s into an approach promoted by major international development agencies, such as the World Bank and the International Labour Office (ILO). The World Bank, which had previously supported large-scale development projects, shifted its emphasis toward supporting human capital projects that incorporated economic development (World Bank, 1975). In essence, the foundation of the social development notion that was well established by the 1970s in the international arena, particularly in the Third World, was "a direct link between social welfare and economic development" (Midgley, 1994a, p. 8).

Industrialized Contexts

With social development's origins in the postcolonial Third World, where economic development traditionally was the purview of the government and social welfare was linked to this often centrally planned economic activity, it is not hard to see why organizations such as the UN would not promote such an approach to their industrialized Western members. In many industrialized Western countries, economic development was not the exclusive domain of the state, and social welfare activity was not seen to be linked to economic development.

Events in the United States. Midgley (1994a) noted that in the United States, proponents of the social development approach were initially "a group of social workers with prior experience of working with the international agencies" (p. 8) involved in practice based on the social development perspective. The 1970s began with the establishment of a social work program in the new School of Social Development at the University of Minnesota–Duluth, which was explicitly committed to educating social workers in a social development context. In the late 1970s, a group of social work educators from various universities who were committed to promoting the social development perspective created the Inter-University Consortium for International Social Development (IUCISD). IUCISD's establishment of the journal *Social Development Issues* was an important milestone. This journal has since provided a forum for important articles that further contribute to the development of the theory and practice of social development.

More conservative approach. As the social development perspective achieved a degree of acceptance as an organizational concept for social work practice, the political climate in the United States, as well as in other major Western industrialized countries such as England, France, and Germany, shifted to a more conservative emphasis. This shift in ideology challenged the role of government in broad areas of social development in the economic and the social spheres. With the return to laissez-faire policies that de-emphasized government intervention and promoted economic growth through efforts to maximize entrepreneurial profits on the notion of these benefits trickling down to all people, the impetus toward social development was effectively diminished, even neutralized. Thus the systemic, holistic notions of social development that had rapidly developed in the late 1960s and throughout the 1970s began to wane as an ideology and a practice.

The ascendancy of a more conservative approach toward development by the end of the 1980s accompanied a situation in the developing and industrial worlds referred to as "distorted development" (Midgley, 1994b). Because the social dimensions of development had been overlooked or neglected, many developmental gains from previous decades were lost. In two major reports, the World Bank (1990, 1992) stated that the poverty rates that had fallen during the 1970s had increased by the early 1990s: Africa's poverty rate increased from 32 percent in 1980 to 48 percent by 1989; Latin America's poverty rate fell from 18 percent in 1974 to approximately 14 percent by 1985, but rose to 25 percent by 1990. Because these indicators were somewhat matched by related factors in the industrialized world, the pendulum may move back in the direction of a reintroduction of a social development perspective in the 1990s.

DEFINITIONS AND PERSPECTIVES

Midgley (1994a) defined *social development* as "a process of planned social change designed to promote people's welfare within the context of a comprehensive process of economic development" (p. 3). This definition contains three conceptual keys that have come to mark the social development perspective as it has evolved historically: planned, comprehensive, and economic. As the preceding historical overview suggested, the separate emphases of these three elements were combined over time into a conceptual whole:

1. *Planned.* The notion of government involvement, intervention, and direction is essential to the social development perspective.
2. *Comprehensive.* Anticipating the last key of "economic," this dimension is important because it represents a stance away from ad hoc, reductionist approaches to social problem solving and recognizes the interrelatedness of social phenomena. As Midgley (1994b) noted, social development "is inclusive ... [requiring] the mobilization of all social institutions for the promotion of human welfare. Development is viewed as a comprehensive process which encompasses all citizens and fosters social solidarity" (p. 9).
3. *Economic.* The recognition of the centrality of economic variables that is present in virtually all social phenomena is a vital contribution of the social development perspective. The mutuality of the economic dimension is consistent with Titmuss's (1974) argument that social goals are equally as important as economic goals, thus removing social policy from the role of handmaiden to economic concerns.

Social Development as Synthesis

Social development has evolved into a perspective that attempts to bring together various notions of social welfare concerns that fall along the continuum of social change from individual (micro) to community (macro). In this way, it is consistent with allied views that have been developed in social work, such as the social systems perspective (Anderson & Carter, 1984) that emerged during the early to mid-1970s. The aspects of such models that are complementary are those that emphasize interdependence and the linkage of the various levels of social interaction and the need to strive for a holistic view of social phenomena to engage in lasting social change. The social development notion broadens the scope of these other views by introducing the explicit dimensions of economics and planning.

Normative Dimensions

Disciplines other than social work—specifically sociology, psychology, development studies, and political economy—have also made significant contributions to the conceptual formulation of social development. These multiple sources have lent a richness to the discourse and have produced important conceptual insights. Midgley (1994a) noted that this cacophonous discourse has "facilitated the emergence of an intellectual framework which shapes normative discussion and helps form a basis for current social development endeavors" (p. 12). The interaction between the academic and conceptual dialogues and the experiences of those practitioners in social development settings have established a basis for the emerging normative theory. Midgley (1993) presented a major initial taxonomy and identified three normative bases for social development: (1) individualist themes, (2) collectivist or statist ideas, and (3) populist or communitarian beliefs.

Individualist themes. The view that social betterment can be obtained through individual improvement and that the cumulative effect of this improvement will result in total change is a strong legacy of social work, neoclassical economics, and rational-choice theory. Currently in social work and social development, Lusk (1992) is an articulate representative of the few proponents of this theme. Basically, this view posits that "as rational actors operating in the market, [individuals] not only enhance their economic welfare, but that of the community as a whole" (Midgley, 1994a, p. 14).

Collectivist or statist ideas. At the other end of the continuum, theorists advocate strategies that involve a government's active involvement in social welfare. A major influence for these ideas has been the work of Midgley (1984a, 1984b) and his colleagues from the London School of Economics (Hardiman & Midgley, 1989; Midgley, Hall, Hardiman, & Narine, 1986). The emphasis in this view is the important role of governmentally based bureaucratic organizations.

Populist or communitarian beliefs. These views have been articulated by the famous sociologist Etzioni (1993). The more recent communitarian notion has evolved from earlier community development strategies (Brokensha & Hodge, 1969; Dore

& Mars, 1981), from advocates of popular participation (Korten, 1981; Oakley, 1991; Oakley & Marsden, 1984), and even from those who are identified as proponents of radical community action from both the developing and the industrial worlds (Alinsky, 1971; Grosser, 1973; Hollnsteiner, 1977, 1982; Marsden & Oakley, 1982). Basically, these beliefs emphasize the centrality of involving citizens and recipients of services in the process of change. This process of popular participation is promoted and guided by community workers, who may be employed either by government or private organizations.

SOCIAL DEVELOPMENT AND SOCIAL WORK

The nature—some would say, the uniqueness—of social work is its orientation to person-in-situation. As Gordon (1969) stated, "No other profession or discipline claiming any recourse to specialized science sets goals with such current breadth and temporal length" (p. 9). With the second half of the 20th century marked by the increasing complexity of social problems, both local and international, the challenge for social work to be fully engaged in the process of social change is particularly great. The social development perspective holds promise for providing social work with a basis for developing diverse practices to ensure the profession's relevance in addressing social problems.

Billups's (1994) concluding statement captures the potential and relevance of social development for social work by noting that the emergence of the social development perspective has given

the profession the prospect of a far-reaching vision and points social workers toward endorsing and adopting a set of potentially powerful ideas. The concept thereby holds much promise for occupying a central place within an integrative social development model that has evolved to a point where it may now begin to serve as a principal organizing framework for guiding social work as a practice and a profession. (p. 25)

REFERENCES

Alinsky, S. (1971). *Rules for radicals.* New York: Random House.

Anderson, R., & Carter, I. (1984). *Human behavior in the social environment: A social systems perspective.* New York: Aldine.

Billups, J. (1994). The social development model as an organizing framework for social work practice. In R. G. Meinert, T. Pardeck, & P. Sullivan (Eds.), *Issues in social work—A critical analysis* (pp. 21–37). Westport, CT: Auburn House.

Brokensha, D., & Hodge, P. (1969). *Community development: An interpretation.* San Francisco: Chandler.

Dore, R., & Mars, Z. (Eds.). (1981). *Community development.* London: Croom Helm.

Etzioni, A. (1993). *The spirit of community: Rights, responsibilities, and the communitarian agenda.* New York: Crown.

Gordon, W. E. (1969). Basic constraints for an integrative and generative conception of social work. In Gordon Hearn (Ed.), *The general systems approach: Contributions toward an holistic conception of social work* (pp. 8–13). New York: Council on Social Work Education.

Grosser, C. F. (1973). *New directions in community organizing.* New York: Praeger.

Hardiman, M., & Midgley, J. (1989). *The social dimensions of development: Social policy and planning in the Third World.* Aldershot, England: Gower.

Hollnsteiner, M. R. (1977). People power: Community participation in the planning of human settlements. *Assignment Children, 43,* 11–43.

Hollnsteiner, M. R. (1982). The participatory imperative in primary health care. *Assignment Children, 59/60,* 43–64.

Khinduka, S. K. (1987). Development and peace: The complex nexus. *Social Development Issues, 10*(3), 19–30.

Korten, D. (1981). Social development: Putting people first. In D. Korten & F. B. Alonso (Eds.), *Bureaucracy and the poor: Closing the gap* (pp. 201–221). West Hartford, CT: Kumarian Press.

Lusk, M. (1992). Social development and the state in Latin America: A new approach. *Social Development Issues, 14,* 10–21.

Maas, H. S. (1986). *From crib to crypt: Social development and responsive environments as professional focus.* New Brunswick, NJ: Rutgers University Press.

Marsden, D., & Oakley, P. (1982). Radical community development in the Third World. In G. Craig, N. Derricourt, & M. Loney (Eds.), *Community work and the state* (pp. 153–163). London: Routledge & Kegan Paul.

Meinert, R., & Kohn, E. (1986, August). *Towards operationalization of social development concepts.* Paper presented at the Fourth International Symposium on International Development, Hachioji, Tokyo.

Midgley, J. (1984a). *Social security, inequality and the Third World.* New York: John Wiley & Sons.

Midgley, J. (1984b). Social welfare implications of development paradigms. *Social Service Review, 58,* 181–198.

Midgley, J. (1993). Ideological roots of social development strategies. *Social Development Issues, 15,* 1–14.

Midgley, J. (1994a). Defining social development: Historical trends and conceptual formulations. *Social Development Issues, 16*(3), 3–16.

Midgley, J. (1994b). The challenge of social development: Their Third World and ours—1993. Daniel S. Sanders Peace and Social Justice Lecture. *Social Development Issues, 16*(2), 1–12.

Midgley, J., Hall, A., Hardiman, M., & Narine, D. (1986). *Community participation, social development and the state.* London: Methuen.

Oakley, P. (1991). *Projects with people.* Geneva: International Labour Office.

Oakley, P., & Marsden, D. (1984). *Approaches to participation in rural development.* Geneva: International Labour Office.

Paiva, F. J. (1982). The dynamics of social development and social work. In D. S. Sanders (Ed.), *The develop-*

mental perspective in social work (pp. 1–11). Manoa: University of Hawaii Press.

Pandey, R. (1981). Strategies for social development. In J. F. Jones & R. Pandey (Eds.), *Social development: Conceptual, methodological, and policy issues* (pp. 33–49). New York: St. Martin's Press.

Titmuss, R. (1974). *Social policy: An introduction.* Boston: Allen & Unwin.

World Bank. (1975). *The assault on world poverty.* Baltimore: Johns Hopkins University Press.

World Bank. (1990). *World development report 1990: Poverty.* Washington, DC: Author.

World Bank. (1992). *World development report 1992: Development and the environment.* Washington, DC: Author.

FURTHER READING

Hall, A., & Midgley, J. (1988). *Development policies: Sociological perspectives.* Manchester, England: Manchester University Press.

Korten, D. C., & Klaus, R. (1984). *People centered development: Contributions towards theory and planning frameworks.* West Hartford, CT: Kumarian Press.

MacPherson, S. (1982). *Social policy in the Third World.* Brighton, England: Wheatsheaf.

Midgley, J. (in press). *Social development: An introduction.* Thousand Oaks, CA: Sage Publications.

Moser, C. O. N. (1989). *Gender planning and development: Theory, practice and training.* London: Routledge & Kegan Paul.

Redclift, M. (1987). *Sustainable development: Exploring the contradictions.* London: Routledge & Kegan Paul.

Sanders, D. S. (Ed.). (1982). *The development perspective in social work.* Manoa: University of Hawaii Press.

United Nations Development Programme. (1990). *Human development report 1990.* New York: Author.

Gary R. Lowe, PhD, is dean and professor, East Carolina University, School of Social Work, Ragsdale Building, Greenville, NC 27858.

The author wishes to give special thanks to James Billups (Ohio State University), Roland Meinert (Southwest Missouri State University), and Jim Midgley (Louisiana State University) for their contributions and assistance in the preparation of this entry beyond their published works on the subject of social development.

For further information see

Advocacy; Charitable Foundations and Social Welfare; Citizen Participation; Civil Rights; Community Development; Community Organization; Families Overview; Federal and Administrative Rule Making; Federal Social Legislation from 1961 to 1994; Human Rights; Income Security Overview; International and Comparative Social Welfare; Organizations: Context for Social Services Delivery; Peace and Social Justice; Policy Analysis; Policy Practice; Poverty; Public Social Welfare Expenditures; Social Planning; Social Security; Social Welfare Policy; Technology Transfer.

Key Words	
international social welfare	social development
	social justice

Social Justice

See Peace and Social Justice; Social Justice in Social Agencies

Social Justice in Social Agencies
John P. Flynn

When one thinks of justice and advocacy in the social services context, it is natural first to consider strategies that are aimed at the external surroundings, such as social action, community organization, enlistment of legal counsel, and public education campaigns. However, alternatives that are easily overlooked and seldom used may be found in the immediate agency environment. The potential of this opportunity was noted in another context by Gil (1987), who suggested that social change derives not only from collective action but from "individual initiation of, and involvement in, social change oriented practice" (p. 5).

Social justice in the context of organizational structure, process, and policy can be pursued by means of constant critical thought and constructive examination of and challenges to the existing order, and these challenges need not necessarily be physically active or abrasively confrontational or perceived as "radical" behavior. Seizing the opportunity to achieve social justice goals in this organizational arena requires a style of advocacy

that must be developed over an extended period, a range of social policy practice skills (which can be developed by any practitioner), and a variety of specific tactics appropriate to social agency life. The real test of effective advocacy may be found in the extent to which the outcomes of social justice advocacy can be institutionalized or regularized in the practices or operating and governing procedures of the organization and in the consciousness of the individual practitioner. This entry explores these features of organizations as opportunities to serve the needs of both the clientele and the staff of social services agencies in pursuing their rights to social justice.

Organizational structure is a result of design decisions; the outcomes of these decisions can either enhance or impede the achievement of social justice in service delivery, both for those who provide and those who receive services. Many avenues that are based on principles of administrative law and social agency organizational structure and policy can be used to advocate effectively for social justice for clients and staff. Sound professional ethics also provide clear guideposts. Consideration of these guideposts suggests appropriate tactics of intervention and effective tools for ongoing monitoring of the desired results in achieving social justice.

RELEVANT PRINCIPLES FROM ADMINISTRATIVE LAW

There are several principles based in administrative law for achieving social justice in service delivery (see Class, 1975; Freund, 1933). The first is the principle of *due process,* according to which those who are entitled or aggrieved by the organizational system have a right to certain protection, such as the right to appeal and the right to a fair hearing. These rights need not necessarily be explicitly stated or written in agency policies or procedures; they are the foundation of modern organizational life. Consequently, it is difficult to challenge any worker's or client's claim to those rights. Although there may be some exceptions— whether such policies or procedures are available, for example, via collective bargaining agreements or client service contracts—due process and its attendant features are virtually universal entitlements. An advocate need not apologize for bringing this reality to the attention of those who are not mindful of the fact.

A second principle, one that is becoming embedded in modern organizational structure, is the *right of democratic participation* in developing agency features that have an impact on the lives of those who are affected by agency policies and procedures. In the world of social services, it is imperative that the well-being of clients and staff be considered in the formulation of both policies and procedures and how they are administered. Consequently, it is not unreasonable to provide for such participation as standard practice.

A third principle is that all constituencies of social agencies shall be treated *equitably* (that is, those in similar circumstances shall be treated

similarly). Equity is sometimes confused with the concept of equality, the latter meaning that all shall be treated the same, rather than *similarly in similar circumstances.* This is obviously a powerful principle that can provide a foil for effective advocacy for social justice. Adherence to this principle allows one to view the client simultaneously as someone who is unique and as someone who is entitled to a standard of service. The principle of equity allows the practitioner (and the organization) to avoid rigidity in dealing with human concerns. If the principle is clearly understood and appropriately applied, bureaucratic rigidity can be avoided or minimized and the impact of policies and procedures on client and staff can be humanized.

A fourth principle of administrative law useful to consider in the pursuit of social justice in social agencies is *adequate notice.* This principle provides that individuals who are affected by agency policy and procedures are accorded adequate publication of any proposed or actual changes or additions to policies and procedures that may have an impact on their lives. In fact, in administrative procedures legislation in most (if not all) states and the federal government, such notice must be followed by the explicit and systematic collection of ideas and opinions from the affected groups, and evidence must show that their input was considered. Although these provisions prevail only in state and federal agencies, the principle is firmly embedded in the culture of modern agency administration. It can be logically carried further to include the mandate that those who are affected by existing or current policies, procedures, or programs be adequately informed of their rights or entitlements and their obligations. One example is the routine of providing mental health clients with written or verbal recipients-rights statements.

OPPORTUNITIES IN ORGANIZATIONAL STRUCTURE

Chain of Command

There are opportunities for the effective pursuit of social justice in structural arrangements commonly found in social agencies (see, for example, Keys & Ginsberg, 1988). One is the organizational principle of subsidiarity and the use of the chain of command. The aggrieved client or staff person in pursuit of social justice in the agency context is well advised to honor the norm of pursuing any grievance by initially attempting to obtain his or her goal at the immediate level of supervision, responsibility, or authority. Lacking satisfaction, the grievant is then entitled to pursue the matter to the next higher level. The pursuit of justice is "gamelike" (as suggested by Lindblom, 1968) and must be played according to the rules of the constitution.

Functional Cycles
The life of social agencies, like most other organizations, marches to a cadence determined by functional cycles. Decision processes are often controlled by timing mechanisms, such as budgetary cycles (for example, first draft, first review) and timetables for reviewing programs. Informed and effective advocacy gives due consideration to when budgets are drafted or reviewed and publicly discussed, when programs are up for review, when staffing patterns are under consideration for adjustments, when opportunities for new initiatives are timely, and the like. It is imperative, then, that the practitioner in pursuit of social justice attend budget-development meetings, provide input at budgetary hearings, offer constructive criticism, and be prepared to offer assistance.

Decision Makers
Various organizational decision groups, such as standing committees, subcommittees, and task forces, have formal (and informal) charges, commissions, or prerogatives can be exploited or challenged in the interest of advocacy and justice. Informed advocates seize opportunities for membership in such groups, for timely input to key members of those groups, and for lucid critiques or evaluations beyond mere polemic. Such initiatives provide credible and helpful information in pursuit of a group's charge or agenda. Most decision makers who operate in good faith value information that enlightens the decision process; the social justice advocate becomes a resource in that regard, not just an individual pleading for special consideration or the stereotypical "thorn" in the side of the agency.

Authority Roles
Authority and power are vested in roles and positions. The task of the advocate is to identify the roles played and the positions occupied and to determine the nature of power and authority exercised. Power is the ability to control or introduce consequences in the behavior of others, authority is the right to take action in the exercise of power and is based on incumbency in a particular nominal position, and influence is the actual use of power. Authority may arise out of role, position, or even personal characteristics, the latter often being associated (even magically in the case of charisma) with a role or position. The task of the social justice advocate is to understand the differ-

ences in these characteristics, to determine how they are operationalized in agency structures, and to tailor tactics in the context of those realities.

OPPORTUNITIES IN AGENCY POLICY
Agency policy also offers opportunities for advocacy for social justice (see, for example, Flynn, 1992). These opportunities may be considered in terms of the bases of legitimacy of agency policy or the boundaries or limits placed on alternative interventive action, or they may rest in contingencies or constraints found in an agency's environment. Contingencies may be seen as boundaries that can be altered or adjusted; constraints may be seen as immutable barriers that must be considered when taking action.

Charters, Licenses, and Standards
One possibility is the legitimacy (that is, the right to take action) to be found in an agency's charter or articles of incorporation; the charter, for example, provides for the outward boundaries of legitimate action. Legitimacy may also be found in the agency's opportunities and limitations afforded or imposed by licensing requirements or accreditation standards. The effective advocate becomes familiar with the provisions of charters, licensing rules, and standards for accreditation and appropriately maximizes those features on behalf of social justice.

Formal Agency Policy
A second possibility can be found in written agency policy manuals, such as personnel policies, budgetary policies, labor agreements in collective bargaining, and the like. Agency policies are presumably written to meet expressed needs; as needs change over time, opportunities are presented to modify existing provisions that may not properly afford clients or staff the manner of social justice to which they are entitled. The effective advocate becomes well versed in those documents and seizes the opportunities afforded by impending or needed change.

Informal Policies
Practitioners may sometimes assume that the organization has no particular policy, only because some organizational principles are not committed to written statements. Although formal, written agency policy is a proper basis for action, so too is informal agency policy. Tacit approval by administrative or direct service staff for action constitutes actual or real-life policy by which agency life is guided, whether sanctioned by written policy or not. Therefore, distinctions between written, required policy and actual or informal practice

represent grist for the mill for advocacy action, as may many of the de facto past practices of agency personnel that may contradict formal agency policy. Agency staff need to be cognizant of conditions wherein such practices are not congruent with agency policy but have become the real or active policy principles by which staff members operate. Failure to attend to such incongruence may subject the individual or even the entire organization to charges of malpractice or litigation and may subvert the agency's mission.

External Influences
A factor that interconnects with agency policy is the environment external to the agency. Some examples may be found in requirements for agency practice imposed by funding bodies; local, state, or federal granting requirements; and conditions imposed by foundations or other charitable givers. Yet another example may be the standards expected or imposed by various professional cultures, such as the codes of ethics of the professional groups staffing the agency (for example, the *NASW Code of Ethics* [NASW, 1994]).

As noted earlier, these factors may be seen as either contingencies (that is, barriers impeding the achievement of goals that may be altered or removed) or constraints (that is, barriers that are not alterable). It is important for those in pursuit of social justice in the agency context to understand the differences or degrees of malleability of these barriers when pursuing advocacy goals and to tailor strategies or tactics accordingly.

CRITERIA FOR ASSESSING PROBLEMS OR OPPORTUNITIES
In considering potential avenues for intervention, it is useful to generate criteria that may be helpful in assessing features of a system that facilitate organizational and policy consciousness for social justice.

Administrative and Organizational Questions
Guidelines for assessing the nature of the problem and the opportunities for intervention can be cast as several questions. For example, to what extent have the basic principles of administrative law been honored or violated, and what, then, is suggested as a first step for advocacy? Has due process been accorded? Has staff or client participation been received appropriately? Have those who feel aggrieved been treated equitably? Has adequate notice been given? If not, how can that process be adjusted and concerns be accommodated?

In regard to organizational structure, has the chain of command been identified and appropri-

ately honored? Is there a particularly timely point to approach a specific committee or group? Has the nature of power, authority, or influence of the committee or group been adequately assessed and confirmed?

In terms of agency policy, is the relevant written policy in place to justify action, or should the focus be on informal practice, and is that behavior assailable? By whom or from what sources of legitimacy can the agency's or the grievant's actions be undertaken? Are any outside sources of influence being brought to bear? Finally, to what extent do the answers to any of these questions shed light on what can be changed and what has to be confronted, other than suggesting even more questions and recommendations for interventive tactics?

Organizational Ethics
Other criteria for assessing organizational factors are based not so much on structure but on organizational ethics for human relations. Normative standards have developed over time regarding what is appropriate ethical organizational behavior when it comes to providing services to clients, personnel management, or both. The principles enumerated earlier may be classified as values; the practitioner in pursuit of social justice must decide whether those values have been expressed in ethical behaviors (that is, the actual translation of values into action).

Definition of justice. The first issue to be considered is what constitutes justice. Social justice is defined here as the embodiment of fairness (whether people are dealt with reasonably), equity (as noted earlier, whether similar situations are dealt with similarly), and equality (whether people and situations are dealt with in the same manner). Social justice demands consideration of each criterion (see Flynn, 1992).

Respect for individuals. The second issue in examining organizational ethics, particularly for professional social workers and for members of other professions that embrace shared ethics, is whether individuals have been provided the opportunity to honor the principles of self-determination and maintenance of their own identity and sense of self, as well as the opportunity to be treated as being unique. The three principles of self-determination, identity, and individualization are central to the *NASW Code of Ethics* (NASW, 1994); therefore, they must be examined in any assessment of social justice in the context of the social services agencies.

Consideration of use of personal information.
The third set of criteria for assessment is suggested by the ever-increasing power of the role of collection, storage, and management of personal information in modern social agency life. A massive amount of information on both clients and staff has been obtained by or made available to organizations of all sizes and purposes. The social agency of today is no less charged than any other organization to ensure the maintenance of certain ethical imperatives regarding the use of personal or private information. These imperatives, then, provide another set of criteria for assessment in the pursuit of social justice. Four particularly salient imperatives are the need to give due and proper consideration to privacy, accuracy, property, and accessibility in maintaining information on individuals (Mason, 1991). Examination of these imperatives provides additional guidelines about whether social justice has been ensured or whether remedies are in order.

For example, an examination of *privacy* in this context suggests that it is necessary to decide whether it is actually essential to obtain and maintain any piece of information about a client or agency staff member and whether that information has been adequately secured. An examination of *accuracy* suggests that it would be appropriate to determine whether adequate procedures are in place to ensure the authenticity and correctness of information about clients or staff members. It also demands a clear identification of who is responsible for correcting erroneous information and some clear method of providing assurances that clarifications or corrections have been made.

The examination of the question of *property* is particularly difficult today, with the exponential growth in the quantity of electronic information storage, because the main question is "who owns this information?" The task of determining ownership of the information provides a challenge in establishing and granting staff members or clients access to information about themselves.

Accessibility is also germane to the issue of pursuing social justice after the property issue has been resolved. Effective advocates must be familiar with the personal rights and privileges available for obtaining stored information and know how to cope with the constraints that must be honored in keeping personal information inaccessible to inappropriate individuals or agencies.

INTERVENING FOR SOCIAL JUSTICE: A MATTER OF STYLE

In the pursuit of social justice in the social agency milieu, one must consider the manner or style in which such justice is pursued.

Establishmentarian Advocacy

The term advocacy generally conjures up images of individuals exhibiting highly visible and elevated levels of personal energy. The context is usually confrontational and suggests conflict. This image may be termed "radical advocacy," radical in the sense that the behavior characterized is a clear departure from the social norm of "being nice" or "playing by the social rules." This society has attached certain negative valences and biases to these words and images.

The style described in this entry may be termed *establishmentarian advocacy* in that the strategies or tactics build heavily on engaging with, and perhaps even accepting to a degree, the existing social order of today's social agency environment. This view is in contrast to the radical displacement or replacement of the existing order of things. Consequently, what follows should be seen in the context of the pursuit of social justice in the agency while acknowledging and embracing, if not necessarily accepting, the present order of agency reality.

Styles for Justice Advocacy

Effective advocacy in the social arena depends in no small part on developing credibility as a person or an agency over time with those who sit in positions of authority or who exercise influence. The early step of "getting the hearing" or "bending the ear" of the seat of power is not automatic. Some legitimacy in demanding a fair hearing is inherent in the rights of the individual; however, much is also attributed to the credibility of the advocate who demands to be heard. This credibility comes from the advocate's history of advocacy and other interactions with the social environment. The point of necessary advocacy may be considered, then, as just one of many social interactions.

The virtue of the historical track record of credibility is clear when one considers that the successful advocate for social justice has to be proactive over an extended period. Proactivity is not only essential to gathering the experience and savvy for being familiar with the issues of structure, timeliness, or ethical mandates mentioned earlier; it also puts the advocate in the position of seizing the opportunity for change before change means getting something "undone." Furthermore, it means generating a social view of oneself as someone who is prepared and has to be dealt with, rather than as someone who is reactionary and who comes to confront well after the fact of a decision having been made or an action having been taken. This style of advocacy obviously involves, then, the necessity for constant and routine consciousness in preparation and orientation to the contingencies and constraints of the system.

Justice advocacy also involves an understanding of the differences between such nuances as the authorization provided by a policy decision or a legislative mandate as opposed to the appropriation of actual financial or person–power resources to carry out the mandate of the authorization. This same level of understanding is found in being aware of the prerogatives and power of those who have the authority to make policy as opposed to those who have only the privilege to give advice.

At any rate, the central issue about style is that a mode of operation is suggested here. Success requires a consciousness for social justice advocacy that embraces the social agency organizational structure and environment as given and meets the challenge to pursue justice within set limits.

Overall Strategies for Intervention

An inclusive, practical, and functional framework for social justice advocacy in the social policy arena was suggested by Jansson (1994), who identified four policy practice skills that are necessary to an effective practitioner: (1) technical–analytic, (2) power-using–political, (3) interactional, and (4) values clarification. This list of skills suggests the following: First, social justice advocates need to be able to analyze organizational and policy issues and clearly articulate those analyses, verbally or in writing, to those who would be moved to alternative actions sympathetic to the goals of the advocate. Second, the advocate needs to know how to identify, assess, connect with, and perhaps even use power in the agency context on behalf of the staff's or the clients' interests. Third, advocacy is not only a technical task, but an interactional and interpersonal task that demands that those in pursuit of social justice acquire a range of social interactive skills, such as presentation and listening skills. Finally, Jansson's perspective suggests that strategic choices must be grounded in value and ethical bases to be considered social policy practice.

Learning How to Tinker

Whereas Jansson's work on social policy practice provides direction on the broader strategy level for social justice advocacy, Pawlak's (1976) work on organizational tinkering includes some practical suggestions at the tactical level. Three tactics that are particularly relevant for the pursuit of social justice in the social services agency are (1) capitalizing on bureaucratic succession, (2) developing

rules and guidelines, and (3) developing analyses and position papers.

The tactic of bureaucratic succession is based on the notion that the point at which individuals or positions associated with power, authority, or influence are to be replaced is an excellent time for changes in agency policy or procedures. Consequently, the effective advocate for social justice will have an ear to the ground and be prepared to take timely advantage of those opportunities.

The development of rules and guidelines should honor the principles of involving affected parties and providing adequate notice of possible or pending changes. Such instances invite the participation of the advocate and those with whom she or he is working. Because rules and guidelines provide parameters that channel and delimit alternatives over extended periods, these opportunities are particularly relevant for those who wish to institutionalize their advocacy goals over the longer term. The development of analyses and position papers is clearly consistent with the style of developing credibility over the long haul, as well as with Jansson's (1994) challenge to the practitioner to develop the technical–analytic ability for policy practice.

Ongoing Monitoring of Desired Results

Although ephemeral results may satisfy one individual or one moment from time to time, long-lasting or institutionalized effects of social justice advocacy in social services agencies must be shored by ongoing monitoring and feedback. New demands for advocacy regarding emerging issues must be continually addressed if actions are to be effective. At the least, then, ongoing vigilance is in order. The effective advocate will search for and install feedback and monitoring mechanisms that are structured into the organization, are institutionalized, and perhaps even provide for some level of automatic feedback.

One possibility for institutionalizing participatory response is to establish ad hoc or even standing committees for a specific grievance or general policy review within a social agency. Doing so legitimates those who choose to invest their time in such surveillance, provides the agency with the assistance of monitoring mechanisms outside any crisis or confrontation involving a particular grievance, and ensures ongoing attention to both old and emerging issues.

Another possibility is the establishment in agency policies of something akin to the "sunset" provision, in which the authority of the policy would expire at a future specified date. This, then, serves as a mandate for evaluation of the effectiveness of a prior policy decision and legitimates any critic who may choose to come forward to offer comments on the particular policy or its attendant procedures. A similar alternative is to build evaluation requirements into a policy decision or statement at the point of responding to a policy choice arising because of a social justice grievance. This alternative ensures continuing evaluation and monitoring of the conditions that require adjustments for social justice. It should be noted that evaluation activities and monitoring activities, although related, are separate functions. Monitoring refers generally to keeping track or observing; evaluation refers more to assessing weight and assigning value to that which is monitored. The former requires less investment; the latter requires more resources and the willingness to make value judgments on the nature and status of what is desired.

SUMMARY

Opportunities for obtaining social justice for clients and staff in social agencies may be found in common principles of administrative law and in the organizational structure and policies of the agencies themselves. The effective pursuit and achievement of social justice goals in this organizational arena require a style of advocacy that must be developed over an extended period, a range of social policy practice skills (which can be developed by any practitioner), and a variety of specific tactics appropriate to social agency life. Finally, the real test of effective advocacy may be found in the extent to which the outcomes of social justice advocacy can be institutionalized or regularized in the life of the organization.

REFERENCES

Class, N. E. (1975). Social work in the regulatory state: An inquiry into the historical dynamics of isolationism within the profession. In F. L. Feldman (Ed.), *Social work papers, XIII* (pp. 19–27). Los Angeles: University of Southern California School of Social Work.

Flynn, J. P. (1992). *Social agency policy: Analysis and presentation for community practice* (2nd ed.). Chicago: Nelson-Hall.

Freund, E. (1933). Licensing. In R. A. Seligman (Ed.), *Encyclopedia of the social sciences* (Vol. 9, pp. 447–451). New York: Macmillan.

Gil, D. (1987). Individual experience and critical consciousness: Sources of change in everyday life. *Journal of Sociology and Social Welfare, 14,* 5–20.

Jansson, B. S. (1994). *Social welfare policy: From theory to practice* (2nd ed.). Belmont, CA: Wadsworth.

Keys, P. R., & Ginsberg, L. H. (Eds.). (1988). *New management in human services.* Silver Spring, MD: National Association of Social Workers.

Lindblom, C. E. (1968). *The policy making process.* Englewood Cliffs, NJ: Prentice Hall.

Mason, R. O. (1991). Four ethical issues of the information age. In R. DeJoie, G. Fowler, & D. Paradice (Eds.), *Ethical issues in information systems* (pp. 46–55). Boston: Boyd & Fraser.

National Association of Social Workers. (1994). *NASW code of ethics.* Washington, DC: Author.

Pawlak, E. J. (1976). Organizational tinkering. *Social Work, 21,* 376–380.

FURTHER READING

Frey, G. A. (March 1990). A framework for promoting organizational change. *Families in Society, 71,* 142–147.

Galper, J. H. (1980). *Social work practice: A radical perspective.* Englewood Cliffs, NJ: Prentice Hall.

Gowdy, E. A., & Freeman, E. M. (1993). Program supervision: Facilitating staff participation in program analysis, planning and change. *Administration in Social Work, 17,* 59–79.

Kingston, E. R., & Williamson, J. B. (1993). The generational equity debate: A progressive framing of a conservative issue. *Journal of Aging and Social Policy, 5,* 31–53.

McCoin, J. M., & Miller, M. C. (1993). Quest for social justice for adult residential care. *Adult Residential Care Journal, 7,* 76–87.

Moreau, M. J. (1990). Empowerment through advocacy and consciousness-raising: Implications of a structural approach to social work. *Journal of Sociology and Social Welfare, 17,* 53–67.

Reisch, M. (1990). Organizational structure and client advocacy: Lessons from the 1980s. *Social Work, 35,* 73–74.

Simon, B. L. (1994). *The empowerment tradition in American social work.* New York: Columbia University Press.

Wilk, R. J. (1994). Are the rights of people with mental illness still important? *Social Work, 39,* 167–175.

John P. Flynn, PhD, is professor emeritus, School of Social Work, Western Michigan University, 934 Homecrest Avenue, Kalamazoo, MI 49001.

For further information see

Advocacy; Case Management; Civil Rights; Community Organization; Ethics and Values; Human Rights; International and Comparative Social Welfare; Management Overview; Peace and Social Justice; Policy Analysis; Professional Conduct; Professional Liability and Malpractice; Purchasing Social Services; Quality Assurance; Social Planning; Social Welfare Policy; Social Work Practice: History and Evolution; Social Work Profession Overview; Supervision and Consultation; Volunteer Management.

Key Words

administrative law	organizational structure
advocacy	social justice

Social Planning
Burton Gummer

The term "social planning" is often used indiscriminately to refer to a range of activities within the social welfare field. For example, social planning is frequently used to refer to activities as diverse as community organization and development, social policy analysis, program development and implementation, and strategic management planning, as well as a catchall phrase to cover all activities aimed at increasing the degree of rationality in decision making in the human services. This entry addresses the latter aspect of social planning. Specifically, *social planning* is taken here to refer to efforts to (1) improve the quality and quantity of information used to inform decisions about social policies, programs, and services and (2) increase the use of rational techniques in the decision-making process itself.

PERSPECTIVES ON RATIONAL DECISION MAKING

Before proceeding to a discussion of the history of social planning in social welfare and an assessment of its current status and techniques, it is important to clarify how the word "rational" is used here. Rational decision making is often taken to mean one specific decision model, sometimes referred to as the "goal" or "maximizing" model. In this model, goals are made explicit and quantified; all possible alternative means for attaining these goals are identified; the consequences of pursuing different alternatives are calculated; and these consequences are evaluated, according to a set of predetermined criteria, in terms of how close they are to the goals (Rothenberg, 1961). If the present discussion was confined to this definition, then this would be a very short entry. Only during one brief period—the late 1960s and early 1970s—did social planners actually use this approach on a broad scale to design, implement, and evaluate social programs (Moynihan, 1969; Novick, 1965).

Besides being rarely used, this model of social planning has come to be associated with a particular ideological orientation, often referred to as "social engineering," and usually assumed to have a decidedly left–liberal slant. In addition, this model evokes an operational philosophy of planning that places the professional planner in a key position to use his or her technical, "value-free" expertise to identify problems, assess needs, set goals, develop programs, and evaluate outcomes in terms of the degree to which they promote the public interest, which, it is assumed, can be clearly identified (Banfield, 1955). As such, this model is often contrasted with more political approaches to planning; doing so has created a false dichotomy between "rational" (technical-based) planning and "political" (value-based) planning (Baum, 1983).

Contrasts in Decision Making

Rational decision making, however, can be thought of in a broader context. Leoni (1957), for example, distinguished between rational, or logical, action and "ignorant" action decided on the basis either of mistakes about fact or of the omission of available relevant facts; "illogical" action when one confuses the possible with the necessary consequences of a decision; "blind" action when one does not consider certain important consequences; and "rash" action made after an incomplete review of the alternatives. From this perspective, planning, whether social or otherwise, can be seen as the efforts to get decision makers to replace ignorant, illogical, blind, and rash actions with knowledgeable, logical, informed, and thoughtful ones.

Simon (1989), a pioneer in promoting rationality in decision making, distinguished between rational decision making that is consciously analytic, and "nonrational" decision making that is intuitive and judgmental. Nonrational decision making can be no less logical or analytic than rational decision making; the difference is that in nonrational decision making the analytic processes are implicit and unconscious, in contrast to the consciously explicit analytic techniques in rational decision making. Intuition is not a process that operates independently of analysis: Rather, the two processes are essential complementary components of effective decision-making systems.

According to Simon,

When the expert is solving a difficult problem or making a complex decision, much conscious deliberation may be involved. But each conscious step may itself constitute a considerable leap, with a whole sequence of automated productions building the bridge from the premises to the conclusions. Hence the expert appears to take giant intuitive steps in reasoning.... It is doubtful that we will find two types of managers ..., one of whom relies almost exclusively on intuition, the other on analytic techniques. More likely, we will find a continuum of decision-making styles involving an intimate combination of the two kinds of skill. (pp. 32–33)

By using these broader definitions of rational decision making, we can examine the whole range of efforts to increase the degree of rationality in the social policy and human services arena. Even though the goal-centered planning model is of low repute, it is safe to say that rationality, more broadly defined, currently is more extensively used in policy-making, program planning, and service provision than ever before.

Social welfare often has been described as operating in an "information-poor" environment in which decisions are made on the basis of little or no reliable information. This characterization is becoming less accurate as the development of integrated information systems to serve the needs of all levels of personnel in the human services— planners, managers, supervisors, and line workers—continues to take place at a rapid pace (Grasso & Epstein, 1987; Semke & Nurius, 1991). In fact, the information base for decision making in all walks of life has been vastly improved because of the phenomenal advances in microcomputing since the 1970s; information has become readily available at rapidly decreasing costs. Although computers provide the means for improving the information base for decision making, the changing context within which social welfare programs operate makes rational, data-based decisions a necessity, whether at the policy, managerial, or service delivery level.

Changes in Resources

Since 1960 the American welfare system has gone through a "boom and bust" cycle, marked by unprecedented growth from 1960 to the late 1970s, followed by a steady attack on and reduction in the system's size and scope since then. Between 1960 and 1980, total annual public expenditures for social welfare increased from $52.3 billion to $428.3 billion, or from 10.5 percent to 18.5 percent of the gross national product (Gilbert, 1986). Beginning with the Carter administration, and significantly gaining in intensity during the Reagan and Bush administrations, there has been a steady assault on the welfare system that resulted in an 8.8 percent reduction in budget outlays for social welfare between 1981 and 1985 (Gilbert). Although this decline may be slowed down by the Clinton administration, one cannot be too sanguine about the prospects for social welfare in the next several years given the "new Democrat" positions about the central importance of "workfare" and the need

to limit the amount of time that one may receive public assistance (Chilman, 1992).

One important way in which social planners and administrators can contribute to efforts to resist further cuts in welfare programs is to provide reliable information about policy consequences. The public cannot make wise decisions without accurate information. In the words of Orfield (1991),

> Administrators should recognize a high obligation to provide valid and intelligible information on the life conditions of their clients and on the nature of the services they can or cannot provide. Information can sometimes embarrass administrators and threaten elected officials, but clear, neutral information is vital. (p. 524)

This is one important way in which planners and administrators can focus the public debate on welfare issues on the realities of program resources, capabilities, and outcomes.

When resources are declining, program planners and managers must make difficult decisions about which programs to cut back and which personnel to let go. These decisions can be made rationally only if there is an information system in place that can provide decision makers with reliable intelligence about the relative contributions and effectiveness of different programs, units, and people. Without such information, managers are constrained to use across-the-board cuts, because they will not have the data to support differential cuts that affect some programs and people but not others. Across-the-board cuts are probably the least desirable solution from a rational perspective (although not from a political perspective) because they have the same impact on efficient, high-producing programs and units as they do on inefficient, stagnant ones (Levine, 1979).

EVOLUTION OF SOCIAL PLANNING

The history of social planning in Great Britain and the United States has roughly paralleled developments in the social sciences in these countries. Although Charles Booth (1902), one of the first people to systematically analyze the causes of poverty and other social problems, was not a social scientist, the survey techniques he used to describe London's population in the late 19th century were an important tool in the evolving field of sociology. In the United States, sociologists worked side by side with social reformers in studying social conditions and making recommendations based on rational analysis and valid information. In 1907 to 1908, Pittsburgh, with funding from the

Russell Sage Foundation, carried out the first comprehensive study of social conditions in an industrial city.

Local Councils

The first council of social agencies was organized in Pittsburgh in 1908 in response to the findings of the Pittsburgh Survey. The councils, a direct descendant of the Charity Organization Societies (COS) of the post–Civil War period, continued in the "scientific philanthropy" tradition of the COS as they sought to use rational planning techniques to develop effective approaches to deal with social problems and ensure that social agencies, and the social services system in general, operated in an efficient, businesslike manner.

The plans that the councils prepared, however, were frequently ignored because the councils had little or no influence over how funds were distributed to social agencies and thus had little or no power to implement their plans. At about this time, the use of federated fundraising drives was growing in importance. These federations—the precursors of the Community Chests of the post–World War II era and the contemporary United Ways—grew out of the combined efforts of business leaders and agency executives to improve the financial base of charitable agencies through centralized fundraising drives that could be efficiently managed and that took advantage of economies of scale (Wenocur & Reisch, 1989). The role of the social planning councils gradually shifted to that of assisting federations in deciding how funds should be allocated among those social agencies requesting money. For most communities, these allocation decisions constituted the extent of their planning efforts.

Shift to Federal Government

Developments in social planning during the period 1900 to 1930 were largely confined to the voluntary, nonprofit sector because (1) this sector was where most of social services activities took place and (2) social planning in the public sector was seen as Marxist-inspired centralized control that would undermine the free-market economy and was thus anathema to both the business community and the Red-baiting politicians of the 1920s. This situation changed dramatically when the Roosevelt administration, for the first time in American history, made the federal government the primary force in addressing domestic problems, in this case those brought about by the stock market crash of 1929 and the Great Depression of the 1930s. A number of major regional and national planning efforts began during the 1930s, including the Tennessee Valley Authority and the National

Planning Board (Selznick, 1966). These efforts were curtailed or abandoned, however, with the advent of World War II.

Attention to domestic social programs in general, and social planning in particular, significantly declined after World War II and throughout the 1950s. Reich (1984) suggested that Americans tend to divide the dimensions of national life into two broad realms: (1) government and politics and (2) business and economics. Concerns about social justice are restricted to the first realm, concerns about prosperity to the second:

> Issues of participation, equality of opportunity and civil rights, public education and mass transit, social security and welfare, housing, pollution, and crime are seen as aspects of government and politics.... Issues of productivity and economic growth, inflation and unemployment, savings, investment, and trade are seen as aspects of business and economics. (p. 4)

The 1950s reflected the decline in the influence of the government realm and the ascendance of the business culture.

Renewed Focus on Cities

By 1960, however, the cycle once again moved the public's attention from the business to the civic realm. During the late 1950s, the Public Affairs Department of the Ford Foundation was interested in funding projects that would address the growing social problems of the "gray areas," the name given to the zones of deteriorating real estate that lie between downtown and the suburbs in most American cities (Marris & Rein, 1967). These projects became an important component of the President's Committee on Juvenile Delinquency and Youth Crime, the first major social policy initiative of the Kennedy administration. In addition to refocusing government's attention on the social problems of the nation's cities, the President's Committee and the gray areas projects insisted that local communities use rational planning techniques—specifically the goal model discussed earlier—in developing their proposals.

Throughout the 1960s and the early 1970s, all major social policy initiatives required that planning be integrated into the overall effort. This was the period of the greatest influence of the rational goal model of planning on social program development, management, and evaluation (Gruber, 1981). Thus, policy initiatives in community mental health, housing and community development, health, income maintenance, job training, and family and child welfare services were all required to use the rational goal–centered planning approach in the development of programs.

CHALLENGES TO THE RATIONAL MODEL OF PLANNING

Although the goal-centered planning model had considerable intellectual appeal, social planners quickly recognized a number of limitations to its implementation in the human services arena (Gummer, 1991, pp. 29–48). Primary among these is the difficulty in identifying a goal that everyone affected by a particular program could agree on and that would become the basis for choosing the best program strategy and evaluating its effectiveness. This is not to say that the individual actors and organizations involved in a particular service enterprise do not have clear, operational goals; they often do. Rationality, however, cannot be imputed to the service system as a whole because of the lack of systemwide objectives toward which all factions strive.

Nevertheless, policies and programs were able to achieve a certain degree of coherence and purposefulness through a kind of "political rationality" that Lindblom (1975) called "epiphenomenal solutions." Competition over goal setting and the diffusion of power among different stakeholders in a particular service arena "sets in motion a political interaction among individuals and groups in which no person or group analyzes the problem and arrives at a solution but in which the 'solution' nevertheless emerges from the interaction" (p. 33). From this perspective, social policy goals are best seen as an amalgam—often with major internal contradictions—of the preferences of the most powerful actors and organizations within a policy arena rather than a predetermined, unitary set of objectives.

In addition to the foregoing criticism of the rational model, which comes primarily from a political perspective, a second critique emerged from a number of scholars who were generally associated with the symbolic interaction school of social psychology (Brown, 1978). These authors attempted to demonstrate how "social actors employ rationality retrospectively as a rhetoric to account for actions that, from a rationalistic point of view, were chaotic and stumbling when performed" (p. 369). Rationality emerges in interaction and then is used retrospectively to legitimate what has already taken place or is being enacted. Because each person's behavior is contingent on another's, the interactions are more appropriately termed "double interacts" (Weick, 1979). The meaning of an activity produced through a double interact can only be established after the action has taken place, because the actual meaning is different from the individual intentions of the par-

ties to the interaction. Meaning is construed intersubjectively, after the action, through the process of "retrospective sense making." Thus, rationality, rather than being the guiding rule of policy and managerial decision making, "turns out to be an achievement—a symbolic product that is constructed through actions that in themselves are nonrational" (Brown, 1978, p. 370).

THE DEFICIT, PRIVATIZATION, AND THE FREE MARKET

The election of Ronald Reagan in 1980 brought to power a number of conservative policymakers and analysts who continued the assault on rational, centralized planning from yet another perspective: the superiority of decentralized marketplace processes for making decisions about the allocation of public goods. The belief in the power of the market for making decisions rather than any centralized planning body was combined with a growing emphasis on "privatization," the transfer of public services to the private sector (both nonprofit and for-profit), as a means of restructuring the social welfare system (Bendick, 1985).

A dramatic example of the combined use of the marketplace and privatization in providing social services is in the area of child care. Kinder-Care Learning Centers, Inc., has emerged as the largest for-profit child care corporation in the world, with estimated 1987 revenues of $26.3 million. Kinder-Care currently operates more than 1,200 centers in the United States and Canada and provides care for more than 100,000 children daily. A $100 investment in Kinder-Care stock in 1972 skyrocketed in value to approximately $7,000 by 1987. A major policy initiative in child care in the Reagan administration was the passage of the child care tax credit, currently the single largest source of federal support for child care. Of the families claiming the tax credit in 1981, the majority (64 percent) earned more than the median income. In contrast, only 7 percent of families claiming the credit earned annual incomes below $10,000 (Tuominen, 1991).

This example highlights a number of forces that are shaping the context for social welfare planning now and for the near future. First and foremost is the national debt, over $4 trillion in 1993. Because of the deficit, the federal government is unlikely to launch new programs in any area of government, including social welfare, which will have a number of consequences for the practice of social planning. For one, the primary mission of planners, whether in the government or private sector, will be to continue developing stricter management control systems for monitoring program operations, with the goal of containing or reducing program costs. Furthermore planners will be expected to stimulate agency personnel to develop program proposals that will attract funding support from nongovernmental sources.

Foremost among these sources will be the for-profit sector, as organizations like Kinder-Care capture an increasingly larger share of the social services "market." These organizations serve a predominantly middle-class clientele, with much of their income coming from the federal social welfare budget in the form of tax credits for day care and Medicare and Medicaid payments for nursing homes, to mention two of the largest categories. By 1989 the value of government spending on programs targeted to poor people remained below what it had been in 1977, whereas federal health spending grew by 81 percent throughout this period of so-called retrenchment in social welfare spending (Salamon, 1993).

Agencies in the nonprofit voluntary sector are also developing new sources of revenue through two related strategies. The first is to seek out a clientele with the ability to pay for services, either through fees or, more often, through reimbursements from third-party insurance carriers (Gronbjerg, 1990). The second is to engage in profit-making ventures, such as marketing services to industry, particularly through employment assistance programs (Perlmutter & Adams, 1990).

THE PLANNER'S DILEMMA: EXIT, VOICE, OR LOYALTY?

The new sources of funding in the nonprofit sector are likely to redirect the focus of social agencies from poor people to those able to pay for services. Similarly, the experience thus far with for-profit social services shows a strong tendency for these organizations to serve middle-class clients at the expense of poor people. Social planners, along with agency administrators, either will face this challenge by continuing to try to balance the needs of social work's traditional clientele with the conflicting pressures from government sources to curtail costs and from new funding sources to serve a more affluent clientele (Martin, 1987), or resolve the conflict by using their technical expertise to design and implement programs that will ensure agency and program solvency.

Social planners are thus faced with Hirschman's (1970) alternatives of "exit, voice, and loyalty." When faced with a difficult choice in organizations, politics, economics, or human affairs in general, people have a limited number of alternatives. They can exit the situation by simply

withdrawing from it; they can give voice by attempting to change, rather than escape, the problem; or they can accept the situation by showing loyalty. These choices pretty much cover the actions that professional social workers have taken in regard to planning practice since the 1960s.

Clearly, the most frequently used option has been exit: The number of professional social workers engaged in planning, administration, and community organization and development has steadily decreased since the 1960s. In their survey of nearly 90,000 employed NASW members, Gibelman and Schervish (1993) reported that only 350 respondents (0.4 percent) listed planning as their primary function in 1991. Although no statistics are available to compare this figure with the number of social workers in planning and executive-level positions in the 1960s, most observers note a significant decline in both the number and influence of professional social workers in policy, planning, and leadership positions in the human services (Patti, 1984). Whether social workers were forced out of these arenas by increasingly conservative national administrations, or chose to leave of their own accord as the social welfare arena became more managerial and more concerned with cost containment than with service effectiveness, the results are the same: As one looks at the top administrative and planning cadres at all levels of government, fewer and fewer social workers are to be found.

Social work has a long tradition of giving voice to the needs of clients and challenging the political wisdom of the day. But this option is increasingly difficult to exercise by the few social workers who continue to work within the system as planners and policy analysts. In a society that is strongly oriented toward seeing the private sector as productive, successful people as deserving, and welfare as dubious, "strong advocacy of adequate services will often be seen as wild-eyed and unrealistic" (Orfield, 1991, p. 528). Orfield goes on to argue that the voice option can most realistically and effectively be exercised by social work educators and researchers. Academics have the skills to do credible research that cannot be effectively challenged politically or by the bureaucracies. They are in a strong position to make research-based arguments

concerning the effectiveness of certain kinds of social policy and administrative agencies. One of the reasons why a country that is very generous on an individual level is so hostile to groups of people in need, and to those who serve them, is that there are ingrained stereotypes about recipients, in particular, and toward poor and minority people in general. Researchers need to examine carefully these stereotypes and help people better understand the social consequences of political decisions that increase inequality and diminish opportunity for the disadvantaged. (p. 528)

There will always be, I hope, that hearty band of committed and resilient social planners and policy advocates who will continue to work within the system. Social workers have a long and proud tradition of working within government and community welfare systems and balancing their bureaucratic responsibilities with efforts to protect the "precarious values" of social welfare in a society as individualistic, materialistic, and business-minded as the United States. Although it is not likely that their numbers will increase in the near future given the employment trends among professional social workers, those who do remain will continue to endeavor to maintain a social work presence in the corridors of money and power.

REFERENCES

Banfield, E. C. (1955). Note on conceptual scheme. In M. Meyerson & E. C. Banfield (Eds.), *Politics, planning and the public interest* (pp. 303–329). New York: Free Press.

Baum, H. S. (1983). Politics in planners' practice. *Journal of Planning Education, 3,* 13–22.

Bendick, M. (1985). *Privatizing the delivery of social welfare services* (Working Paper No. 6, Project on the Federal Social Role). Washington, DC: National Conference on Social Welfare.

Booth, C. (1902). *Life and labour of the people in London.* London: Macmillan.

Brown, R. H. (1978). Bureaucracy as praxis: Toward a political phenomenology of formal organizations. *Administrative Science Quarterly, 23*(3), 365–382.

Chilman, C. S. (1992). Welfare reform or revision? The Family Support Act of 1988. *Social Service Review, 66*(3), 349–377.

Gibelman, M., & Schervish, P. H. (1993). *Who we are: The social work labor force as reflected in the NASW membership.* Washington, DC: NASW Press.

Gilbert, N. (1986). The welfare state adrift. *Social Work, 31,* 251–256.

Grasso, A. J., & Epstein, I. (1987). Management by measurement: Organizational dilemmas and opportunities. *Administration in Social Work, 11*(3/4), 89–100.

Gronbjerg, K. A. (1990). Poverty and nonprofit organizational behavior. *Social Service Review, 64*(2), 208–243.

Gruber, M. L. (Ed.). (1981). *Management systems in the human services.* Philadelphia: Temple University Press.

Gummer, B. (1991). *The politics of social administration.* Englewood Cliffs, NJ: Prentice Hall.

Hirschman, A. O. (1970). *Exit, voice, and loyalty.* Cambridge, MA: Harvard University Press.

Leoni, B. (1957). The meaning of "political" in political decisions. *Political Studies, 5,* 225–239.

Levine, C. H. (1979). More on cutback management: Hard questions for hard times. *Public Administration Review, 39*(2), 179–183.

Lindblom, C. E. (1975). The sociology of planning: Thought and social interaction. In M. Bronstein (Ed.), *Planning, east and west* (pp. 23–60). Cambridge, MA: Ballinger.

Marris, P., & Rein, M. (1967). *Dilemmas of social reform.* New York: Atherton Press.

Martin, P. Y. (1987). Multiple constituencies and performance in social welfare organizations: Action strategies for directors. *Administration in Social Work, 11*(3/4), 223–239.

Moynihan, D. P. (Ed.). (1969). *On understanding poverty: Perspectives from the social sciences.* New York: Basic Books.

Novick, D. (Ed.). (1965). *Program budgeting: Program analysis and the federal budget.* Cambridge, MA: Harvard University Press.

Orfield, G. (1991). Cutback policies, declining opportunities, and the role of social service providers. *Social Service Review, 65*(4), 516–530.

Patti, R. J. (1984). Who leads the human services? The prospects for social work leadership in an age of political conservatism. *Administration in Social Work, 8*(1), 17–29.

Perlmutter, F. D., & Adams, C. T. (1990). The voluntary sector and for-profit ventures: The transformation of American social welfare? *Administration in Social Work, 14*(1), 1–13.

Reich, R. B. (1984). *The next American frontier.* New York: Penguin Books.

Rothenberg, J. (1961). *Measurement of social welfare.* Englewood Cliffs, NJ: Prentice Hall.

Salamon, L. M. (1993). The marketization of welfare: Changing nonprofit and for-profit roles in the American welfare state. *Social Service Review, 67*(1), 16–39.

Selznick, P. (1966). *TVA and the grass roots.* New York: Harper Torchbooks.

Semke, J. I., & Nurius, P. S. (1991). Information structure, information technology, and the human services organizational environment. *Social Work, 36,* 353–358.

Simon, H. (1989). Making management decisions: The role of intuition and emotion. In W. H. Agor (Ed.), *Intuition in organizations: Leading and managing productively* (pp. 23–39). Newbury Park, CA: Sage Publications.

Tuominen, M. (1991). Caring for profit: The social, economic, and political significance of for-profit child care. *Social Service Review, 65*(3), 450–467.

Weick, K. E. (1979). *The social psychology of organizing* (2nd ed.). Reading, MA: Addison-Wesley.

Wenocur, S., & Reisch, M. (1989). *From charity to enterprise: The development of American social work in a market economy.* Urbana: University of Illinois Press.

FURTHER READING

Baum, H. S. (1983). *Planners and public expectations.* Cambridge, MA: Schenkman.

Benveniste, G. (1977). *The politics of expertise* (2nd ed.). San Francisco: Boyd & Fraser.

Bryson, J. M. (1988). *Strategic planning for public and nonprofit organizations: A guide to strengthening and sustaining organizational achievement.* San Francisco: Jossey-Bass.

Checkoway, B. (Ed.). (1986). *Strategic perspectives on planning practice*. Lexington, MA: Lexington Books.

Gates, B. L. (1980). *Social program administration: The implementation of social policy*. Englewood Cliffs, NJ: Prentice Hall.

Gilbert, N., & Specht, H. (1977). *Planning for social welfare: Issues, models, and tasks*. Englewood Cliffs, NJ: Prentice Hall.

Nakamura, R. T., & Smallwood, F. (1980). *The politics of policy implementation*. New York: St. Martin's.

York, R. O. (1982). *Human service planning: Concepts, tools, and methods*. Chapel Hill: University of North Carolina Press.

Burton Gummer, PhD, is professor, School of Social Welfare, Nelson A. Rockefeller College of Public Affairs and Policy, The University at Albany, State University of New York, Albany, NY 12222.

For further information see

Advocacy; Charitable Foundations and Social Welfare; Citizen Participation; Community Organization; Federal Legislation and Administration Rule Making; Federal Social Legislation from 1961 to 1994; Health Planning; Income Distribution; International and Comparative Social Welfare; Organizations: Context for Social Service Delivery; Policy Analysis; Public Social Services; Social Welfare History; Social Welfare Policy: Strategic Planning; Welfare Employment Programs: Evaluation.

Key Words

social planning	social welfare
social policy	

Social Security

Martin B. Tracy
Martha N. Ozawa

The term *social security* is used in the United States to refer to a group of social insurance programs developed by the federal government to provide economic security for people in their old age, disabled workers, and workers' survivors in cases of a worker's death. The system provides both cash and in-kind health care benefits. Specifically, social security embraces the following three programs:

1. Old-Age and Survivors Insurance (OASI) was first established under the Social Security Act of 1935 as insurance for retired workers and expanded in 1939 to include survivors. It provides cash benefits for retired workers and their eligible family members and for survivors of insured workers.
2. Disability Insurance (DI), enacted through the 1956 amendments, provides cash benefits for disabled workers and their eligible family members.
3. Medicare, established in 1965, helps pay for the cost of hospital and medical care for eligible elderly and disabled people.

Social security coverage and benefit levels have been liberalized over the years through amendments to the original legislation. Almost all jobs are covered by social security. As of December 1992, 41.5 million people were receiving some type of social security benefit (G. Good, Social Security Administration [SSA], personal communication, March 11, 1993). Ninety-two percent of elderly people receive some form of social security benefits (Grad, 1990). At the end of 1992, an estimated 93 percent of men and 84 percent of women age 20 to 64 were fully insured for old age and survivors benefits; that is, these people are poten-

tially eligible for retirement benefits when they reach age 62 and if they die their spouses and children will be eligible for benefits. (G. Good, SSA, personal communication, March 11, 1993). In 1990, benefit expenditures for OASI and DI totaled $246 billion, or about 4.5 percent of the gross domestic product (GDP); Medicare expenditures totaled $107 billion, or about 2.0 percent of GDP (U.S. Department of Health and Human Services, 1993).

The financial impact of social security on beneficiaries, especially those who are elderly, has been phenomenal, particularly since a series of upward benefit adjustments in the 1960s. Many elderly people would have been destitute had it not been for social security. However, because of economic pressures, demographic trends, and labor force participation shifts, social security programs have been scrutinized in recent years. Policies to curb future expenditures have been adopted increasingly since the mid-1970s.

BASIC PRINCIPLES

Social security is intended to provide benefits as a matter of an earned right without means tests or income tests. Compulsory contributions by workers and their employers are pooled to help workers defray the costs of income loss and health hazards for themselves and their dependents.

Cash benefit provisions embrace two important principles: (1) individual equity, relating benefit levels directly to beneficiaries' prior earnings covered under social security, and (2) social adequacy, providing beneficiaries who had been lower-wage earners with benefits at a higher percentage of prior earnings than that received by beneficiaries who had earned higher wages. Striking a balance between these two principles is an ongoing concern of policymakers.

Social security funding is based largely on the principles of compulsory (and equal) employee and employer contributions, compulsory contributions from self-employed workers, and pay-as-you-go financing. Financing depends on the federal government's power to tax each generation of workers to pay current beneficiaries. However, in 1983 the act was amended to generate excess revenues that would build up the trust fund's assets in anticipation of the large number of baby boomers who will reach retirement age early in the next century (Dattalo, 1992). The result is a $47 billion surplus in 1992 that is projected to reach $69 billion by 1995 and $117 billion by the year 2000 (G. Good, SSA, personal communication, March 11, 1993). An amendment to the Congressional Budget Act in 1990 ended the practice of using the annual social security trust fund surpluses to reduce the federal deficit.

PROVISIONS

Old-Age and Survivors Insurance

To be eligible for OASI benefits, workers must be either fully insured or currently insured. Workers become fully insured by earning a specified amount of "work credit," calculated in quarters of coverage. In 1993, employees and self-employed workers received one quarter of credit for each $590 of covered annual earnings, with no more than four quarters credited to an individual in one year. The amount of earnings needed to gain a quarter of coverage is scaled to the national average wage and increases as the average wage increases.

The total work credit required for eligibility for retired worker benefits depends on the claimant's age. A person who reaches age 62 after 1990 needs 40 quarters of work credit to qualify for retirement benefits. The normal retirement age (NRA)—the age at which eligible persons can claim benefits without actuarial reductions—for a worker, spouse, or widow(er) is currently 65; beginning in 2000 the NRA will gradually increase to age 67 by the year 2027. The current full reduction at age 62 of 20 percent will increase to 30 percent by 2027.

Although the preceding stipulations are relatively simple, the social security regulations are highly complex, as demonstrated in the balance of this discussion of eligibility requirements. The regulations are also subject to revision, and readers should consult the SSA for the most recent provisions.

Currently insured status is achieved when a worker has acquired six quarters of coverage in the 13-quarter period ending with the calendar quarter of death, disability, or becoming age 62. This status provides benefits for a worker's surviving spouse and children, plus a lump-sum payment of $255 for the deceased worker's burial expenses. Burial expenses are paid only if a surviving spouse was living with the deceased worker at the time of death or if a spouse or child is eligible for immediate survivor benefits. Currently insured status also entitles insured workers and their auxiliaries (or eligible family members) to Medicare protection when afflicted by end-stage renal disease. In addition, divorced spouses who were married to the worker for at least 10 years can get benefits in some circumstances.

To be eligible for disability benefits, a worker must have not only fully insured status but also disability insured status. This status requires that workers earn a certain number of quarters in covered employment. People disabled by blindness need only fully insured status.

Benefits for each type of beneficiary derive from the primary insurance amount (PIA), which is obtained in a two-step process. First, the SSA calculates the worker's average indexed monthly earnings (AIME) by indexing (or adjusting) the taxable earnings for each year 1951 and after to the average wage level in the second year before age 62, disability, or death. Later earnings are not indexed. The computation period is equal to the number of years elapsed after 1950 (or age 21, if later) through age 61 (or the year before the year of prior disability or death). This number is decreased by five in claims for retirement and survivors insurance benefits. These five "dropout" years are the lowest years of contribution. (Fewer dropout years apply to workers disabled at a young age.) SSA then picks the years with the highest earnings during the computation period. If higher earnings are made in any year outside the computation period, these higher earnings can replace lower earnings made in any year during the computation period. These earnings are then summed and divided by the number of months in the computation period; the result is the AIME. The computation period for a person age 65 in

1993 is 35 years, the maximum number of years required for computation.

The primary insurance amount (PIA) is then calculated on the basis of the average indexed monthly earnings. For people retiring at age 62 in 1993, the PIA is based on the following percentages of the AIME:

PIA = 90% of the first $401 of the AIME +
32% of the next $2,019 of the AIME +
15% of the AIME in excess of $2,420

These dollar amounts (or "bend points") are adjusted each year to account for increases in average wages. Benefits for workers retiring at age 62 equal 80 percent of the PIA, or a smaller percentage as the normal retirement age (NRA) increases. Those who retire between age 62 and the NRA have a pro rata actuarial reduction. People who retire at the NRA (currently 65) will receive their primary insurance amount. The benefits for all retired workers, regardless of their age at retirement, are adjusted for cost-of-living increases occurring the year the worker reaches age 62 and after.

If a retired worker has eligible family members—an aged spouse, children, or a spouse taking care of a child under age 16 or disabled before age 22—each auxiliary receives benefits equivalent to 50 percent of the PIA. However, spouses who claim auxiliary benefits before their normal retirement age down to age 62 have an actuarial reduction unless an eligible child is present. In addition, when spouses receive a pension based on their own federal, state, or local government work not covered by social security, social security benefits are reduced by an amount equal to two-thirds of the public pension. Benefits for all eligible family members together may not exceed the maximum family benefit, which in retirement and survivor cases ranges from 1.5 to 1.87 times the primary insurance amount, depending on the amount of average indexed monthly earnings.

Widows or widowers of insured workers are entitled to 100 percent of the benefits their spouses would be receiving if they were alive, provided the benefits are claimed at the normal retirement age or later. Benefits claimed before that age are actuarially reduced with benefits being available as early as age 60 (or age 50 if the widow or widower is disabled with no further reduction for entitlement before age 60). If the deceased worker took reduced benefits, this also could result in a limit on benefits for the widow or widower.

When the insured worker dies leaving unmarried children under age 18 (or age 19 if still in secondary school), these children and the surviving spouse caring for a child who is under age 16 or disabled receive survivor benefits. Each eligible survivor is entitled to benefits equal to 75 percent of the primary insurance amount, but the maximum family benefit rule applies. When the youngest child reaches age 16, benefits for the surviving spouse cease. However, if any child has a disability that originated in childhood (before age 22), benefits for the child and caretaker parent continue without an age limit. In addition to monthly survivor benefits, a lump-sum payment of $255 is provided for burial expenses, as long as there is a person eligible for immediate survivor benefits or a spouse who was living with the deceased worker at the time of death.

Disability Insurance
To receive disability benefits, a worker must be unable to engage in any substantial gainful activity (SGA) because of a severe physical or mental impairment that is expected to last for at least 12 months or to result in death. People with human immunodeficiency virus (HIV) infection or acquired immune deficiency syndrome (AIDS) may also qualify when they are no longer able to work or when they must severely limit their work. Education, work experience, and age are taken into account in determining disability. Disability Insurance beneficiaries must accept rehabilitation services offered by state rehabilitation agencies if SSA determines that these services are likely to be successful.

Eligible disabled workers are entitled to monthly benefits equal to the PIA. Eligible children and the spouse caring for a child under age 18 or a child disabled before age 22 are each entitled to a benefit not to exceed 50 percent of the PIA. Benefits for the disabled worker and entitled family members together may not exceed the disability maximum family benefit.

Unless they recover medically from their disability, disabled people generally are allowed to continue receiving benefits for up to nine months while they test their ability to work. Benefits are not terminated until the second month following the earliest month after this trial work period in which the individual (1) engages in SGA (that is, earns more than $500 a month in 1992, or $850 if blind) or (2) is determined by SSA to be able to engage in SGA.

Although there is an earnings test for social security beneficiaries, for disabled worker beneficiaries the rule regarding SGA applies instead. Beneficiaries age 65 to 69 can earn up to a certain amount ($10,560 in 1993) without having their benefits reduced. On earnings exceeding this amount, there is a $1 reduction for each $3 earned. Beneficiaries younger than 65 have a lower exempt amount ($7,680 in 1993) and a more severe penalty (a reduction of $1 for each $2 of earnings above the exempt amount). The exempt amounts are automatically adjusted based on increases in average wages. For people age 70 and older, there are no earnings restrictions. Excess earnings by insured workers affect not only their own benefits but also their dependents' benefits, but excess earnings by auxiliaries affect only their own benefits. The earnings test is often perceived as a major work disincentive despite research that shows it plays a small role in the labor force activity of older workers (Leonesio, 1990).

Medicare

Medicare comprises two parts: Hospital Insurance (HI) and Supplementary Medical Insurance (SMI). HI represents part A of Title XVIII of the Social Security Act and SMI represents part B. The Health Care Finance Administration (HCFA) is responsible for administering both HI and SMI.

Hospital Insurance. Covered employments are the same for this program as for Old-Age and Survivors Insurance and Disability Insurance, except that all federal employees are covered. The following three categories of people are eligible for HI benefits:

1. all persons 65 and older who are eligible for cash benefits either under OASI or the Railroad Retirement system
2. all disabled beneficiaries, that is, disabled workers, disabled widows and widowers 50 and older, and insured workers' adult children 18 and older whose disability originated before age 22
3. insured workers and their families who need dialysis or a kidney transplant.

There is a 24-month waiting period for disabled beneficiaries. HI benefits may continue for three years after disability cash benefits stop in cases in which the person's medical condition has not improved but he or she has been able to engage in substantial gainful activity.

Under HI, four types of benefits are provided: hospital services, skilled nursing facility services, home health care, and hospice care. Hospital services include services and supplies normally required for inpatient hospital care, including room and board, operating facilities, laboratory tests and X rays, drugs, dressings, general nursing services, and the services of interns and residents in training. Excluded are the services of private duty nurses and personal convenience items such

as a telephone or television. Hospital insurance pays only the cost of semiprivate accommodations, unless private accommodations are warranted medically.

Hospital Insurance covers the cost of hospital care services up to 90 days in a single "spell of illness," meaning the period beginning with the first day of hospitalization and ending after the insured person has not been an inpatient in a hospital or a skilled nursing facility for 60 consecutive days. In addition, each insured person has a "lifetime reserve" of 60 additional benefit days. The patient is required to pay a deductible ($676 in 1993). Then HI pays in full for the first 60 days of hospital care. After 60 days the patient pays a coinsurance of a stipulated amount ($169 in 1993, equivalent to 25 percent of the initial deductible) for each day of hospitalization up to 30 days. A patient using part or all of the lifetime reserve pays coinsurance at the rate of 50 percent of the initial deductible. HI covers only up to 190 days of inpatient care in a psychiatric hospital during the lifetime of the beneficiary.

Low-income individuals may be entitled to have their Medicare premiums, deductibles, and coinsurance paid by state Medicaid programs under the Qualified Medical Beneficiary program. In addition, beginning in 1993, individuals with income 110 percent or less of the national poverty level will also be entitled to have their state pay the Supplementary Medical Insurance (part B) monthly premium under the Specified Low-Income Medicare Beneficiary program.

In addition to hospital care benefits, HI covers up to 100 days of services in a skilled nursing facility during a spell of illness. This care must be preceded by at least three days of hospitalization, and the admission to a skilled nursing facility must occur within 30 days of hospital discharge. There is no deductible, but there is coinsurance ($84.50 in 1993) after the first 20 days in a spell of illness.

To receive home health services, the insured person must be under the care of a physician; confined to the home; and require intermittent skilled nursing care, physical therapy, or speech therapy. Prior hospitalization is not necessary. Examples of these services are visiting nurses' care (which can include up to eight hours per day for up to 21 days under certain circumstances) and physical, occupational, or speech therapy. There is no limit on the number of home visits, nor is there a deductible or coinsurance.

Hospice services include medical and support services including the cost of outpatient drugs and respite care. Special benefit periods apply to hospice care: Hospital insurance pays for a maximum of two 90-day periods and one 30-day period for hospice care, as opposed to the single 90-day period with a 60-day reserve covered for hospital services.

Many beneficiaries purchase health insurance to supplement their Medicare coverage with so-called "Medigap" insurance. It is illegal for an insurance company to sell a policy that duplicates any Medicare coverage.

Supplementary Medical Insurance. SMI helps pay the costs of certain medical services and supplies, principally physicians' fees. All beneficiaries, regardless of whether they are covered under hospital insurance, choose whether they wish SMI coverage. Participants enroll at certain periods stipulated under the law and are required to pay a monthly premium ($36.60 in 1993).

SMI is designed to supplement HI health care services. It helps pay for physicians' services provided in the home, hospital, or office. In addition, it helps pay for diagnostic X ray or laboratory tests, surgical dressing and devices, purchase or rental of durable medical equipment (such as wheelchairs and hospital beds), ambulance services, and prosthetic devices. A 20 percent copayment applies to rental or purchase of durable medical equipment.

Under SMI, each year the beneficiary pays an initial deductible ($100 in 1993) and thereafter a coinsurance of 20 percent of the Medicare-approved amount for most services and supplies allowed under the law. SMI pays the rest. Physicians who participate in the program and take assignment are paid, through carriers, for their services according to a fee schedule based on the relative value of the resources necessary to provide the service. When the physician does not take an assignment, SMI pays the beneficiary, who must then pay the physician. Physicians who do not accept assignment can charge only 115 percent of the Medicare-approved amount.

FINANCING

To finance Old-Age and Survivors Insurance and Disability Insurance, and the Hospital Insurance component of Medicare, the federal government levies payroll taxes on employers, employees, and the self-employed. The payroll tax is authorized by the Federal Insurance Contributions Act (FICA) up to a maximum taxable earnings amount ($57,600 in 1993 for OASI and DI, and $135,000 for HI). The tax rate has been 7.65 percent since 1990, and employees and employ-

ers each pay this rate. Self-employed workers pay twice that rate (or 15.3 percent). Payroll taxes are channeled, according to a statutory allocation rate, into the OASI Trust Fund (5.60 percent), the DI Trust Fund (0.60 percent), and the HI Trust Fund (1.45 percent).

The SMI Trust Fund is maintained by monthly premiums from Supplementary Medical Insurance beneficiaries and by general revenue contributions. These separate funds pay for their respective types of benefits and related administrative costs. When SMI came into being, the premium rate and the per capita rate of the contribution from general revenue were the same. Under current law, the premium is set to cover 25 percent of program expenditures.

INCOME OF ELDERLY PEOPLE

The liberalization of coverage and benefits under social security, the spread of private pensions, and changing patterns of labor force participation have transformed the level, source, and share of income elderly people receive. At the peak of the Great Depression, as many as two-thirds of elderly people depended on public assistance, private charity, or support from friends and relatives. Those who were self-sufficient drew their income from earnings, assets, or property, or from government or private pensions (Shearon, 1938).

The picture is quite different now. The rate of labor force participation among elderly men steadily declined until the mid-1980s (Gendell & Siegel, 1992), and social security benefits are becoming increasingly significant sources of income. Public assistance and private charities are much less important sources. Personal savings are also a declining resource in old age, dropping from 8.1 percent of personal income in 1970 to 4.2 percent in 1988 (Rappaport, 1992).

Primarily because of large increases in social security benefits during the late 1960s and 1970s, the income of elderly people in relation to that of people younger than 65 improved markedly. As a result, for the last several years the official poverty rate among elderly people has been lower than the rate among younger people. In 1990, for example, the poverty rate for persons age 65 and older was 12.2 percent compared to 13.7 percent for all others (U.S. Bureau of the Census, 1991, as cited in Radner, 1992). The poverty rate for elderly people was above the rate for other adults but below the rate for children.

The impact of social security on the economic well-being of elderly people can be measured more precisely by looking at the proportion of earnings lost because of retirement, which social security benefits replace. In 1992, for workers who retired at age 65 and who had earned an average wage each year throughout their careers, benefits replaced about 42 percent of their preretirement income (Social Security Administration, January 1993).

LEGISLATIVE DEVELOPMENTS

Until the mid-1970s, decision makers for social security consistently pursued expansionary policies. However, social security's mounting financial problems caused in part by a technical error involving the benefit formula provided under the 1972 amendments and in part by unfavorable economic conditions of high unemployment and high inflation during the latter half of the 1970s and the early 1980s led policymakers to reevaluate past policies. The profound demographic shift anticipated for the early 21st century has become an added concern. Consequently, through legislation passed in 1977, 1980, 1981, and 1983, Congress adopted a policy to slow down social security's expansion. This legislation also eliminated gender-based distinctions in benefit provisions and modified provisions to discourage labor force withdrawal through incentives.

Incentive Measures

The Social Security Disability Amendments of 1980 included several measures related to work incentives for disability beneficiaries. The most notable change was the limitation on maximum family benefits for beneficiary families of disabled workers. The level was set lower than that for other types of beneficiary families so that total benefits for these families would not exceed pre-disability earnings.

Another work incentive affects people who are entitled to Old-Age and Survivors Insurance. By deferring receipt of a benefit payment beyond the normal retirement age and continuing to earn wages, these beneficiaries may substantially increase their benefit amount. This delayed retirement credit is gradually being raised from 4 percent per year for workers age 65 in 1993 to an eventual 8 percent for those who reach the normal retirement age of 66 in 2009.

Economy Measures

The movement to deliberalize benefits and curb future growth in benefit expenditures started in earnest when Congress enacted the Omnibus Budget Reconciliation Act of 1981. This act eliminated regular minimum benefits for both current and future beneficiaries. However, the minimum benefit provision for beneficiaries eligible by the end of 1981 was

restored. The 1981 legislation also phased out benefits to college students ages 18 to 22.

The movement gained momentum with the 1983 amendments to the Social Security Act. Perhaps the boldest change was the imposition of income taxes on part of the social security benefits of high-income retirees. Up to half of social security benefits are subject to federal income tax for any year in which adjusted gross income plus nontaxable interest income and one-half of the social security benefits exceed a base amount. The base amount is $32,000 for married taxpayers filing joint returns, zero for married taxpayers filing separately who lived with their spouses any time during the year, and $25,000 for all others. In another cost-cutting measure, cost-of-living adjustments were shifted to a calendar-year basis, with the increase payable in January rather than July. Increasing the normal retirement age to 67 is considered important as a long-term economy measure.

Many congressional leaders and the National Commission on Social Security Reform, who recommended most of the adopted amendments, found that cost-cutting measures alone were inadequate to balance future revenues and outlays. To strike the balance, in 1983 Congress decided to increase future revenues (National Commission on Social Security Reform, 1983). The 1983 amendments required, for the first time, compulsory coverage for newly hired federal employees and for all members of Congress, the president, the vice president, federal judges, and current employees of the legislative branch not participating in the civil service retirement system. Employees of nonprofit organizations were also brought under compulsory coverage. In addition, states may no longer terminate social security coverage of state and local employee groups. Another provision stipulates a different benefit formula for people who receive pensions from noncovered employment.

The 1983 amendments also prohibit hospitals from charging beneficiaries more than the statutory deductible and coinsurance. All hospitals that participate in Medicare are paid on a prospective payment basis, except psychiatric long-term-care hospitals and children's and rehabilitation hospitals. Under this prospective payment system, hospitals must contract for review services with a peer review organization.

Elimination of Gender-Based Distinctions

Under the 1939 amendments, only wives and widows were eligible for spouse benefits and survivor benefits. The 1950 legislation, which marked lawmakers' emerging recognition that men and women should be treated equally under social security, made husbands and widowers eligible for benefits for the first time, but only if they could prove that they were financially dependent on their wives.

The undoing of gender-based distinctions was pursued on other fronts. Legislation passed in 1961 provided that men could retire at age 62, as women could since 1956. Legislation passed in 1972 provided the same computation period for men and women; before then it had been shorter for women.

Under the 1983 amendments, aged divorced husbands and aged or disabled surviving husbands can claim benefits on their former wives' earnings records. Benefits are now provided to widowers, as they are to widows, who remarry before age 60 but who were unmarried at the time they applied for benefits. As amended previously, remarriage after age 60 does not reduce the benefits for either widows or widowers. Illegitimate children can now claim benefits based on their mothers' and fathers' earnings.

CURRENT AND FUTURE ISSUES

The future of social security will be influenced greatly by demographic, labor force, social, and economic trends. Policymakers will have to deal with the fiscal realities resulting from slowed economic growth, an aging population, early retirement patterns, and changing family configurations (especially increases in unmarried, divorced, and widowed women). Decisions will have to be responsive not only to these factors, but to increasing concerns about the income and health care needs of older women, especially lower-income women. Another issue will be the appropriate roles of private pensions and personal savings in reducing reliance on social security benefits. Perhaps the greatest challenge will be to bring the cost of health care for the elderly under control without further eroding access to quality health care.

Demographic Factors

There has been much discussion about the potentially ominous consequences that an aging population will have on the fiscal integrity of social security. Alarming projections of an increased burden on workers supporting a high proportion of older people are often cited. Although there is cause to track demographic trends to monitor their potential impact on social security, it does not necessarily follow that an older population will overwhelm the current system. Much will depend on economic growth, labor force participation, and

the total dependency ratio of the entire population (young and old), which will be no worse when the baby boomers retire than when they were children (Schulz, Borowski, & Crown, 1991).

Financing

The financing of social security is a related issue of concern, especially among many young people who question whether or not social security will still be in place when they retire (Carlson, 1991). A main source of apprehension about the fiscal viability of the system stems from negative publicity about pay-as-you-go financing in light of an aging population and erratic economic growth. Pay-as-you-go financing works well as long as the ratio of workers to beneficiaries is stable and the economy enjoys steady growth. When the baby boomers start reaching retirement age, however, an inflexible pay-as-you-go financing system would require higher tax rates, which would impose a disproportionately heavier financial burden on future generations.

The 1983 amendments to the Social Security Act raised contribution rates to build a trust fund to help offset the anticipated costs of benefits for the baby boomers. Thus, the pay-as-you-go process was replaced by what has been called a system of "partial prefunding" (Stein, 1991). The result has been that the Old-Age and Survivors Insurance and Disability Insurance trust funds are in little danger of being depleted in the foreseeable future. The Hospital Insurance component of Medicare, however, may well be exhausted by early in the next century because of escalating health costs ("Actuarial Status of the Social Security and Medicare Programs," 1992; Carlson, 1991).

Building the trust fund to forestall any undue tax burden in the future raises disagreement over the economic effects of the accumulation of funds. Some economists argue that the large accumulation of funds would deprive private-sector establishments of venture capital, because social security trust funds must be invested in federal government obligations. Other economists contend that social security savings reduce the need for federal borrowing from the private sector, thus releasing private funds for capital formation.

A related problem is that politicians have already been tempted to use the accumulated funds to raise benefits, bail out Medicare, or offset other government expenditures. It continues to be a delicate political decision to strike the balance between the advantages of adhering to pay-as-you-go financing and the advantages of accumulating a large amount of funds.

Another financing issue that will be on the agenda of policymakers is the earnings test. Controversy continues over the role of the earnings test as a necessary instrument to preserve old-age benefits as "retirement" benefits because its elimination would result in a projected annual cost of $13 billion (Social Security Administration, 1991). The opposing view is that the earnings test imposes an unacceptable tax burden on older people who want to work and discourages them from working. The consensus of mainstream economists, however, is that the earnings test has little effect on retirement patterns. In all likelihood, the test will continue to be liberalized rather than eliminated.

Income-Tested Benefits

Most policymakers traditionally have resisted increasing the prominence of income-tested benefits funded by general revenues. Income-tested benefits tend to erode the principle of individual equity, without which many beneficiaries would not feel entitled to benefits. However, as expenditures rise and payroll taxes become a more visible part of the tax structure, policymakers may be tempted to consider limiting benefits to the most needy people by imposing an income test on social security benefits.

General revenue increasingly is used to finance social security in both direct and indirect ways. The steadily increasing proportion of general revenue used to finance Supplementary Medical Insurance under Medicare is an example of direct use. Taxing part of social security benefits and crediting the proceeds to the Old-Age and Survivors Insurance and Disability Insurance trust funds, as the 1983 amendments provide, is an example of indirect use. Allowing a tax credit against income taxes for a portion of payroll taxes has the same result as an indirect use of general revenue to finance social security. There is, therefore, a clash between reality and policymakers' philosophical preferences.

There also is the question as to whether and to what extent Supplemental Security Income (SSI), a means-tested income transfer program for aged and disabled people, should be used to supplement social security benefits. There are advantages and disadvantages in relying on SSI for such purposes. The use of SSI may be an efficient way to direct government funds to the neediest groups, but it also may increase the stigma often associated with public support. Its use also may reduce some people's incentive to provide for their retirement needs. One can anticipate continuing debates on the proper role of income-tested benefits in providing retirement income to the nation's elderly population.

Retirement Policy

The main issue in retirement policy is the effect that the trend toward early labor force withdrawal will have on funding. Despite the delayed retirement credit to encourage workers to postpone retirement, about 69 percent of new awards to retired workers go to persons age 62 to 64 (Social Security Administration, January 1993), even though benefits before the normal retirement age are actuarially reduced. A fundamental question is the extent to which viable full-time work options will exist in an increasingly restricted labor market. Policy debates are also likely to focus on flexible retirement options such as phased and partial retirement.

A retirement policy issue that has received less publicity but is no less important than the early retirement issue is the relationship between involuntary retirement and the scheduled increase in the normal retirement age beginning in 2000. The higher retirement age, with a greater penalty for early pension receipt, is likely to have negative consequences for disadvantaged, lower-income workers who are often forced into involuntary retirement because of poor health and reduced work opportunities (Ozawa & Law, 1991, 1992).

Relation to Other Pensions

The latest data show that 57 percent of elderly couples and 34 percent of nonmarried elderly people receive pensions other than social security benefits (Grad, 1990). Private pensions, however, have not grown as much as was hoped, particularly for lower-income workers who are increasingly employed in the service sector or in part-time work, settings where there are few private pension options. In addition, under most private pensions, benefits are either coordinated with or offset against social security benefits. Thus, private pensions disproportionately benefit high-wage earners in the replacement of earnings lost as a result of retirement. Some policymakers consider this outcome acceptable as long as the private pension creates no unfair discrimination when considered in combination with benefits received under social security.

All these factors point to a future political challenge. Many crucial questions have to be answered as the United States faces an increasing number of elderly people, increasing demands for fairer treatment of women under social security, and extraordinarily high health care costs. How can the nation's finite resources be managed to simultaneously ensure a decent, minimum income in old age; distribute benefits equitably and efficiently; revise benefit formulas to respond to the changing roles of women in the labor force; and provide adequate and affordable health care?

Long-Term Care

Because so many more people are living into very old age, there is an increasing demand for both institutional and in-home care. In 1990, about 30 million people were age 65 and older, and 4.4 million of these had experienced limitations in activities of daily living. About 68 percent of the total elderly population were women (U.S. Senate Special Committee on Aging, American Association of Retired Persons, Federal Council on Aging, U.S. Administration on Aging, 1991). Discussion will continue on the appropriate role of social security in addressing the health care needs of this population, especially regarding the cost of medical coverage for long-term care.

Women and Social Security

Women are at the greatest risk for economic insecurity in old age, representing about 71 percent of the aged poor in 1989 despite their increased participation in the labor force (Meyer, 1990). How women should be treated under social security has become an important policy issue. Women often perceive injustice in the way they are treated under social security for three primary reasons. First, working wives who qualify as spouses may get a benefit no higher than if they had never worked for wages. Second, one-earner couples may get higher benefits than two-earner couples with the same total lifetime earnings. Third, the linking of benefits to wage levels leads to the disproportionate ratio of women among the aged poor because women's wages tend to be lower.

Many women now wish to be given credit as workers whether they work in or out of the home. Currently, the program provides relatively generous benefits for nonworking wives. However, if they are divorced after less than 10 years of marriage, women lose entitlement to their spouse's benefits. A working wife receives benefits based on her own work record if such benefits are larger than her spouse benefits based on her husband's earnings. If not, her benefits are brought up to the level of her spouse benefits; in effect, she receives either spouse benefits or her own, not both. Working wives also have added disability and survivor benefit protection that nonworking wives do not have. Unmarried working women are simply on their own. However, it is difficult for politicians to pursue greater fairness in benefits provision if it results in greatly increased expenditures.

One suggestion that received a great deal of attention in the late 1970s and early 1980s was the idea of earnings sharing (Burkhauser & Holden,

1982). Under this scheme, the annual earnings of both spouses are pooled. Half of the total pool is then credited to each spouse's account, so that each will have old-age income security independently. A commission established in 1978 by President Carter recommended earnings sharing for divorce purposes (President's Commission on Pension Policy, 1980). Through its 1983 amendments to the Social Security Act, Congress directed the secretary of Health and Human Services to study the feasibility of implementing an earnings-sharing plan. In 1992 another task force was appointed to examine these and other issues concerning women and social security. Debate on women's issues will continue, and some changes in benefits provisions for women may occur in the future.

References

Actuarial status of the Social Security and Medicare programs. (1992). *Social Security Bulletin, 55*(2), 36–42.

Burkhauser, R. V., & Holden, K. C. (Eds.). (1982) *A challenge to social security: Changing roles of women and men in American society.* New York: Academic Press.

Carlson, K. M. (1991). The future of social security: An update. *Federal Reserve Bank of St. Louis, 73*(1/2), 33–49.

Dattalo, P. (1992). Social security's surplus: An update. *Social Work, 37*(4), 377–379.

Gendell, M., & Siegel, J. (1992). Trends in retirement age by sex, 1950–2005. *Monthly Labor Review, 115*(7), 22–29.

Grad, S. (1990). Earnings replacement rates of new retired workers. *Social Security Bulletin, 53*(10), 2–19.

Leonesio, M. V. (1990). Effects of the social security earnings test on the labor-market activity of older Americans: A review of the evidence. *Social Security Bulletin, 53*(5), 2–21.

Meyer, M. H. (1990). Family status and poverty among older women: The gendered distribution of retirement income in the United States. *Social Problems, 37*(4), 551–563.

National Commission on Social Security Reform. (1983). *Report of the National Commission on Social Security Reform.* Washington, DC: U.S. Government Printing Office.

Ozawa, M. N., & Law, S. W. (1991). Health status of recently retired workers. *Social Work Research & Abstracts, 27*(4), 24–30.

Ozawa, M. N., & Law, S. W. (1992). Reported reasons for retirement: A study of recently retired workers. *Journal of Aging and Social Policy, 4*(3–4), 35–51.

President's Commission on Pension Policy. (1980). *An interim report.* Washington, DC: Author.

Radner, D. B. (1992). The economic status of the aged. *Social Security Bulletin, 55*(3), 3–23.

Rappaport, A. (1992). Retirement benefit structure in the 1990s: Defined benefit vs. defined contribution plan structures. *Employee Benefits Journal, 17*(9), 14–17.

Schulz, J. H., Borowski, A., & Crown, W. H. (1991). *Economics of population aging: The "graying" of Australia, Japan, and the United States.* New York: Auburn House.

Shearon, M. (1938). Economic status of the aged. *Social Security Bulletin, 1*(1–3), 5–16.

Social Security Administration. (1991, October). Congress focuses on social security retirement earnings test proposals. *Social Security Courier,* p. 5.

Social Security Administration. (1993, January). Government pensions may reduce social security benefits. *Social Security Courier,* pp. 3, 5.

Social Security Disability Amendments of 1980. P.L. 96-265, 94 Stat. 441.

Stein, B. (1991). Pay-as-you-go, partial prefunding, and full funding in American social security. *History of Political Economy, 23*(1), 79–83.

U.S. Bureau of the Census. (1991). Poverty in the United States: 1990. In *Current population reports* (Series P-60, No. 176-RD). Washington, DC: U.S. Government Printing Office.

U.S. Department of Health and Human Services. (1992). *Social security area population projections 1991: Actuarial study no. 106* (SSA Publication No. H-11552). Washington, DC: Author.

U.S. Department of Health and Human Services. (1993). *Social security bulletin: Annual statistical supplement, 1989* (SSA Publication No. 13-11700). Washington, DC: Social Security Administration.

U.S. Senate Special Committee on Aging, American Association of Retired Persons, Federal Council on Aging, & U.S. Administration on Aging. (1991). *Aging America: Trends and projections.* Washington, DC: U.S. Department of Health and Human Services.

FURTHER READING

Altmeyer, A. J. (1966). *Formative years of social security.* Madison: University of Wisconsin Press.

Berstein, M. C., & Berstein, J. B. (1988). *Social security: The system that works.* New York: Basic Books.

Burns, E. M. (1956). *Social security and public policy.* New York: McGraw-Hill.

Derthick, M. (1979). *Policymaking for social security.* Washington, DC: Brookings Institution.

Myers, R. J. (1985). *Social security* (3rd ed.). Homewood, IL: Richard D. Irwin.

Myers, R. J. (1991). United States. In M. B. Tracy & F. C. Pampel (Eds.), *International handbook on old-age insurance* (pp. 217–228). Westport, CT: Greenwood Press.

Pechman, J. A., Aaron, H. J., & Taussig, M. K. (1968). *Social security: Perspectives for reform.* Washington, DC: Brookings Institution.

Ross, J. A., & Upp, M. M. (1988). The treatment of women in the United States social security system, 1970-1988. In *Equal treatment in social security* (pp. 69–92, Studies and Research No. 27). Geneva, Switzerland: International Social Security Association.

Schulz, J. H. (1991). *The economics of aging* (4th ed.). Belmont, CA: Wadsworth.

Social Security Administration. (1979). *Social security and the changing roles of men and women.* Washington, DC: U.S. Department of Health, Education, and Welfare.

Witte, E. E. (1962). *The development of the Social Security Act.* Madison: University of Wisconsin Press.

Martin B. Tracy, PhD, is professor and director, Southern Illinois University, School of Social Work, Quigley Hall, Carbondale, IL 62901. **Martha N. Ozawa, PhD,** is Bettie Bofinger Brown Professor of Social Policy, George Warren Brown School of Social Work, Washington University, St. Louis, MO.

The authors would like to express their sincere appreciation to Gary Good, senior adviser, Office of Policy and External Affairs, Social Security Administration, and to Beth A. Giebelhaus, acting director, Office of the Executive Secretariat, Health Care Financing Administration, for their invaluable comments and technical assistance. We would also like to thank Harry Ballantyne, chief actuary, Social Security Administration, for his gracious help.

For further information see

Aid to Families with Dependent Children; Employment and Unemployment Measurement; General Assistance; Income Security Overview; Jobs and Earnings; Poverty; Public Social Welfare Expenditures; Retirement and Pension Programs; Social Welfare Policy; Unemployment Compensation and Workers' Compensation.

Key Words	
income security	retirement
pension	social security

Social Skills Training
Juanita B. Hepler

Social skills training is a widely used intervention model that addresses various deficits in social skills in children and adults who experience interpersonal difficulties in their social, marital, family, or job relationships. A special focus in work with children has been to work with those who are rejected or excluded from activities by their peers. Social skills training has also been successfully used with children and adults with developmental disabilities, including mental retardation and emotional, physical, and learning disabilities. Likewise, social skills programs have addressed the social skills deficits exhibited by many substance abusers.

IMPORTANCE OF PEER RELATIONSHIPS

The widespread use of social skills programs reflects the growing awareness of people in the helping professions that positive social skills and interactions play a major role in the mental health of individuals, as well as in their success in social, academic, and employment settings. The development of these skills begins at a young age and requires the assimilation of increasingly complex skills as a child moves from preschool to adolescence. Play activities and interactions with peers provide the major forum for development with children learning social, physical, and cognitive skills from one another (Fine, 1981; Gottman & Parkhurst, 1980). Peer relationships also provide much-needed support when young people are in new or stressful situations. In fact, peer support may be one of the most important resources for preventing suicide among adolescents (Seigel & Griffin, 1983). In addition, social interactions provide young people with opportunities to practice skills, develop social control, and incorporate social values (Berndt, Caparulo, McCartney, & Moore, 1980; Hartup, 1983).

CONSEQUENCES OF POOR SOCIAL SKILLS

A number of studies have indicated that the consequences of social skills deficits and poor peer relationships in childhood have long-term, pervasive negative effects. Although further research is needed to validate some of these studies, the relationship between rejection by peers and juvenile delinquency, school adjustment, and performance, including school dropout, has been well documented (Kupersmidt, 1983; Kupersmidt, Coie, & Dodge, 1990; Parker & Asher, 1987). Cowen, Pederson, Babijian, Izzo, and Troust (1973) found that the ratings of peers were a stronger predictor of adjustment in adulthood than were several other variables, including scholastic achievement and ability and self-esteem. As was previously mentioned, the lack of peer support appears to be a contributing factor in suicidal and substance

abuse behavior among adolescents (Kline, Canter, & Robin, 1987; Seigel & Griffin, 1983; Windle, 1990). Several studies have suggested long-term effects that influence emotional, mental, and employment adjustment in adulthood, although these results are tentative (Ginsberg, Gottman, & Parker, 1986; Parker & Asher, 1987). The outcomes of these and other studies validate the widespread use of social skills programs with children and adults.

DEVELOPMENTAL ISSUES

Increased knowledge of the behaviors and social interests of children has provided important information about the social development of children and the specific behaviors associated with acceptance or rejection by peers across age levels. Gottman and Mettetal (1986) postulated the following three developmental periods from preschool through adolescence:

1. *Early childhood, ages three to seven:* During this period, the major goal is coordinated play that is not disrupted by conflict. Children are emotional at this age and have difficulty controlling conflict once it begins to escalate. The important skill to be learned during this time is the ability to escalate and deescalate play activity to minimize or resolve conflict. Interaction in dyads is the predominant relationship pattern for play activities.

2. *Middle childhood, ages eight to 12:* The goal for children of this age group is inclusion in same-sex peer groups. Conformity to group norms is important; there is a strong emphasis on being rational, or maintaining emotional control. Play is predominantly with same-sex groups.

3. *Adolescence, ages 13 to 17:* The goal during this period is self-exploration and understanding, especially in relation to others. It is during this period that young people actively use cognitive skills to understand interpersonal relationships. Social activities include same- and cross-sex interactions.

Children who are accepted by their peers use positive behavioral and cognitive skills. They are able to initiate and maintain conversations with others and are friendly, outgoing, supportive, enthusiastic, self-assured, and helpful (Hartup, 1976, 1983). However, between 10 percent and 20 percent of children are rejected by their classmates, and approximately 30 percent to 35 percent of these rejected children remain in this low-status position for an extended time (Coie & Dodge, 1983; Coie, Dodge, & Coppotelli, 1982). These low-status children are noted for their use of more inappropriate, negative, aggressive behaviors and their poor problem-solving skills (Coie et al., 1982; Dodge, Pettit, McClaskey, & Brown, 1986; Hartup, 1983). However, variations in the behavioral patterns of these children have been found. Cillessen, van IJzendoorn, van Lieshout, & Hartup (1992) noted that 48 percent of the rejected children in their samples exhibited the typical inappropriate, aggressive behaviors; however, 13 percent were shy and withdrawn, and the remaining 39 percent exhibited more appropriate behaviors. As with earlier studies, Cillessen et al. found that rejected children who exhibited aggressive behaviors were more likely to maintain their low status over time. The authors' prognosis for these children was decidedly negative:

> One suspects these children are increasingly likely to receive negative treatment from other children as they grow older, as well as to experience constricted opportunities for engaging in cooperative exchanges, effective conflict management, and intimate interaction with other children. One can anticipate that they will continue to have relatively few friends and that the children who will be available to them as companions will include an ever larger proportion of unskilled, rejected and antisocial children—that is, children who are similar to themselves. (Cillessen et al., 1992, p. 903)

Several studies have verified that once children obtain a rejected status, other children tend to relate to them in a negative manner. In fact, rejected children receive fewer positive responses from peers, even when they use the appropriate or positive social behavior. Thus, on a daily basis, these children must constantly cope and respond to negative behaviors from others (Dodge, 1983; Hepler, 1990).

Apparently all children experience loneliness and have an understanding of this concept. The amount of loneliness a young person experiences seems to be associated with his or her social status. Again, it is the low-status children, especially those who use aggressive or shy behaviors, who

have the strongest feelings of loneliness (Cassidy & Asher, 1992). Even though they experience more loneliness and rejection from peers, low-status children tend to overestimate their social competence (Patterson, Kupersmidt, & Griesler, 1990). This tendency may contribute to their problems in correctly assessing social situations, which, in turn, would affect their ability to select appropriate behaviors for a particular situation.

Children learn from their experiences and interactions with peers, but it seems likely that their parents' level of social skills influences the children's social development. Few researchers have examined this concept; however, both Cohn (1990) and Hart, DeWolf, Wozniak, and Burts (1992) reported a relationship between parents' patterns of social behavior, especially those used in interactions with their children, and their children's social relationships. Cillessen et al. (1992) found that children of parents who used fewer "power assertive skills" exhibited more positive skills and experienced greater acceptance from peers than did children whose parents used more punishment-oriented methods. Cohn (1990) found that young boys who had insecure attachments with their mothers were less well liked by their peers and were described by both teachers and peers as using more aggressive behaviors than were boys who reported secure maternal attachments.

METHODS USED IN SOCIAL SKILLS TRAINING

Various assessment measures and strategies have been used in social skills programs. Assessment techniques provide information on the social competence of individuals and allow for evaluations of outcomes. Initially, most training programs focus on behavioral skills, but as the complexity of social development and interactions becomes more apparent, programs increasingly add new components, including cognitive issues.

Assessment

Sociometric ratings and nominations. These ratings are used primarily with children and youths. The rating scales allow children to indicate on a scale of 1 ("don't like to play with at all") to 5 ("like to play with a lot") how much they like to play with their fellow classmates or group members. Each child receives a mean score based on the ratings he or she receives from peers (Singleton & Asher, 1977). Children make nominations by listing up to three classmates or group members with whom they like to play or whom they view as best friends; they are also asked, but are not required, to list up to three individuals with whom they do not like to play (Moreno, 1934). The validity and reliability of these two measures have been well documented, and they yield accurate information on a child's social status in a specified group (Asher & Hymel, 1981).

Observations. Observation of children in play situations is an excellent medium for assessing the quality of a child's social interactions and skills (Furman & Masters, 1978; Gottman & Parker, 1986). Although these data are more costly and time consuming, they provide the most valid information on actual behaviors. As with sociometric measures, few observation studies are conducted with adult populations, except in institutional settings.

Role playing. Role-playing tests are used with both children and adults. With these measures, subjects typically are asked to respond to vignettes that require the use of the specific social skills that have been emphasized in the training program (Edleson & Rose, 1978; Hepler & Rose, 1988). Role-playing measures reflect subjects' knowledge of the skills and their ability to apply these skills in the appropriate situation. Consequently, they allow the group leader or researcher to assess the efficacy of the methods used in the program to teach the designated skills. This is important information because subjects cannot use new behaviors if they have not learned them. The major limitation of these tests is that knowledge concerning new skills does not mean that children or adults are actually using these behaviors in their social environment. As was previously discussed, observational data are essential for the accurate assessment of subjects' actual use of the behaviors.

Self-report measures. Self-report measures that concern the use of specific skills, including assertiveness and problem-solving steps, are easy to administer and score (Kazdin, 1992; Ladd, 1985). Although a number of these measures have been standardized, problems with internal validity continue to be an issue.

Problem-solving skills. The assessment of problem-solving skills usually includes the use of vignettes describing a problem that exists within a social situation and may be accompanied by a picture of the scene (Shure, 1982; Spivack & Shure, 1983). This measure is usually administered to children, who are asked to assess the problem, to generate alternative solutions to the problem, or both. The children may also be asked to describe the consequences of the solutions and to indicate which solution they would implement in the spe-

cific situation. As with role-playing tests, these measures assess the individual's knowledge of the problem-solving skills but do not demonstrate that the child actually uses them in his or her social environment.

Self-perception measures. Self-perception measures in social skills programs assess an individual's perception of his or her social competence in interactions with peers (Hymel & Franke, 1985). For example, the Children's Self-Efficacy for Social Interactions with Peers Scale (Wheeler & Ladd, 1982) evaluates children's perceptions of their level of confidence or ability to use prosocial verbal skills in peer interactions. On each question, the subject indicates how difficult it would be for him or her to use a specific verbal skill (for example, "A group of kids wants to play a game that you don't like. Asking them to play a game you like is _____ for you"). The subject indicates whether the skill would be very hard, hard, easy, or very easy. These kinds of measures have provided important information about children's perceptions, especially the tendency for rejected children and children with disabilities to overrate their competence in relation to their actual behaviors and social acceptance.

Strategies

Traditionally, most social skills programs have focused on specific behavioral skills or the acquisition of cognitive skills (primarily problem-solving skills). However, with more information on the social development of children and the complexity of social interactions, programs have increasingly moved toward a multicomponent format. Because children exhibit both behavioral and cognitive deficits (Coie & Kupersmidt, 1983; Dodge et al., 1986; Ladd, 1985; Putallaz & Gottman, 1981), many social skills programs that are designed for youths currently include a combined cognitive–behavioral approach. Adult training programs have shown the same trend.

Behavioral skills. The behavioral component uses modeling, role-play, feedback, and homework assignments to teach specific behaviors that have been identified as important social skills for effective, positive interactions with others. Homework assignments generally require children or adults to practice newly learned skills in their social environments. An example of an important behavioral skill for youths is the ability to enter an ongoing activity (Hartup, 1983; Putallaz, 1983). Several studies (see, for example, Dodge, 1983; Putallaz, 1983) have shown that young people must observe the activity and make positive comments about the activity or individuals participating in the activity. The goal is to be assimilated into the activity, not to disrupt the game or conversation. Disruptive techniques, including asking "Can I play?", tend to elicit negative responses from others (Putallaz, 1983).

Cognitive skills. Incorporating cognitive methods into social skills programs helps address the diverse elements that influence an individual's behavior. On the basis of Spivack and Shure's (1983) work, many children's programs have included four problem-solving steps in training sessions: (1) assessing the problem, (2) generating alternative solutions, (3) identifying consequences for each solution, and (4) selecting and implementing the most effective solution. In the program children are usually presented with a problem that occurs in a social situation and are asked to apply the problem-solving steps to resolve the conflict positively. This is an important addition because many low-status children fail to use these steps effectively. That is, they may not correctly identify the problem in their social interactions, or they may have only one or two alternative behaviors to use in a situation; when these limited solutions are not effective, low-status children tend to reapply them because they are not aware of other alternatives. When children fail to consider the consequences of their actions, they frequently use inappropriate behaviors that result in negative reactions from peers or adults, including teachers and parents (Dodge et al., 1986; Spivack & Shure, 1983). The value of including cognitive skills is apparent: Such skills enable the individual to determine when to apply the specific behavioral skills emphasized in the program and can be generalized to other behaviors and situations.

Recreation. A recreational component, including organized play activities, can improve the effectiveness of social skills programs, especially those involving children. These activities provide the opportunity for both adults and children to practice new skills in a safe environment and to develop new friendships (Rose, 1972). These activities also enhance members' enjoyment of the program and thus promote learning and participation in other aspects of the program.

Affective and somatic components. Teaching individuals to be aware of their feelings and somatic responses in difficult social situations has been integrated into many of the social skills programs. These components are especially important when the focus is on appropriate social responses when negative verbalizations or behaviors are directed at an individual (Hepler, in press). Because feelings and body responses (for example, rapid heartbeat, sweating palms, and "butterflies" in the stomach) can be important clues to the loss of self-control, both young people and adults must develop an awareness of these responses and learn to step back or temporarily leave the situation when they become stressed.

Self-perceptions. Another aspect that traditionally has not been included in social skills training is the self-perceptions of individuals concerning social interactions. For example, high- and low-status children have different perceptions of social situations. Rejected children tend to believe that social interactions are stable and cannot be changed and that they have little or no impact on the outcome of social interactions. As Sobol and Earn (1985) pointed out, three ideas must be emphasized:

1. Social interactions are not stable; they can be changed.
2. Using appropriate social behaviors results in more positive interactions with peers; thus, the individual can have an impact in these situations, which also means that the individual must assume responsibility for outcomes.
3. If someone uses appropriate social behaviors and the environment remains negative or rejecting, he or she may withdraw from the situation; in this case, the negative outcome is not caused by the individual but by the environment, which does not understand or know the individual.

These are important issues to emphasize in social skills programs; otherwise, children or adults may never be actively involved in such programs because they believe they have little power to change events.

Small-group format. The extensive use of the small-group format in social skills training reflects the social work profession's awareness of the need to work with individuals within a social context. Groups provide a safe milieu in which individuals can learn and practice new skills, and, as was previously mentioned, groups encourage the development of new friendships. However, it is the group processes themselves that provide the most powerful tool. These processes include interactions among group members and between members and the group leader and provide the impetus for change and the attainment of individual and group goals (Rose, 1972).

SOCIAL SKILLS TRAINING WITH CHILDREN AND YOUTHS

Social skills programs with children and youths are designed to improve social skills and relationships with peers. Unfortunately, no single set of skills ensures social competence. Different skills are required at various age or developmental levels, and skills become more complex as young people move from preschool through adolescence. Consequently, when developing social skills programs, social workers must be aware of the skills that are important for the particular age group with whom they will be working. For example, a program for young children could focus on how to resolve a conflict before it escalates. Brief structured activities can provide an opportunity for young children to learn to work together. Group leaders can intervene if the children are unable to prevent the escalation of a conflict and can point out to them what has happened as a result of the conflict. For preadolescents, group activities and role plays that focus on entry into an ongoing activity will provide them with a vital skill, in that studies have suggested that a child's social status can be determined by his or her competence in this skill (Putallaz, 1983). For adolescents, the major content can include learning more advanced conversation skills and increased awareness of their and others' nonverbal behaviors. These suggestions are not inclusive but serve to emphasize the importance of using the results of observational studies to determine important skills for the particular age group that will participate in a program.

It is also important to remember that one brief program (social skills programs typically include six to 10 sessions) may not be sufficient to bring about significant or clinical change. Many children need review sessions or benefit from participation in additional social skills training. Finally, although the importance of using appropriate social behaviors is the major emphasis of these programs, other factors—including intelligence, success in academics and sports, attractive physical appearance, and having a common name rather than a different or unique name (Asher, Oden, & Gottman, 1977; Hartup, 1983)—also influence social acceptance and should be addressed when possible. In particular, children who are having academic problems will benefit from support systems that are designed to improve their academic performance in the classroom.

Social Skills Training in Schools

Many social skills programs are conducted in schools because schools are one of the major environments in which children engage in social interactions with peers. In fact, in no other environment is a child's social status and its ramifications more apparent than in this setting. Principals, teachers, and helping professionals, including school social workers, are well aware of children who are rejected by their peers and must endure ridicule and isolation from other students. Most often school staff are receptive to social skills programs because they are concerned about the welfare of these children and realize that there may be long-term negative consequences for those who are not accepted by peers.

Another advantage of conducting programs in the schools is that children can be tracked over time; they can be compared with same-age peers; and outcomes, including the long-term effects of skills training programs, can be assessed.

Outcomes: Preadolescents. Most outcome studies have been conducted with elementary school children. Although working with children in self-contained classrooms simplifies logistic concerns, the need to address deficits in social skills at an early age before negative consequences, such as delinquent behavior and school dropout, occur probably accounts for the predominance of these programs in elementary schools. Social workers are also more effective and more likely to bring about change when working with younger children (Schneider & Byrne, 1985). Social skills programs have reported modest outcomes, with significant improvement on sociometric measures, role-play tests, observational data, and self-report measures (Ladd & Mize, 1983). Most studies with preadolescents have focused on the acquisition of behavioral skills (see Gresham & Nagle, 1980; Ladd, 1981; LaGreca & Santogrossi, 1980; Oden & Asher, 1977) or the effective use of problem-solving skills (Elardo & Caldwell, 1976; Shure, 1982; Spivack & Shure, 1983). Several studies have demonstrated that including popular children in the program is an effective method for improving the social skills and environment of rejected youths (Bierman & Furman, 1984; Hepler, in press; Hepler & Rose, 1988).

Outcomes: Adolescents. Programs that focus on adolescents have also used behavioral and cognitive skills and have reported success in changing behaviors and increasing the use of problem-solving skills (Filiczak, Archer, & Friedman, 1990; Foster, DeLawyer, & Guevremont, 1985; Tellado, 1984). However, as Foster et al. (1985) reported, most of these programs have worked with adolescents experiencing more severe social problems such as delinquency, learning disabilities, and the use of aggressive behaviors. This supports our earlier discussion of the negative consequences of poor peer relationships and highlights the critical need to address peer relationship problems with young children before the more severe consequences occur. Another facet of adolescent programs is that most of them work with men, whereas programs that work with younger children have been conducted with boys and girls and in some cases have included boys and girls in the same program. Because there is little empirical information concerning the behavior patterns of adolescents, social skills programs may not be addressing the skills and issues that are relevant to this age group.

In all of these programs, regardless of the age group, problems include a lack of generalization of skills outside of the program and insufficient or weak evidence that children have learned the skills or that their use of the skills has resulted in improved social interactions. Another limitation of most social skills programs is that they work with low-status children only. A number of studies (Bierman & Furman, 1984; Hepler, in press; Hepler & Rose, 1988) have shown that improving the social behaviors of low-status children is not sufficient to bring about meaningful change in their social interactions. The negative attitudes of popular children toward low-status youths must be addressed; otherwise, these children tend to continue viewing the low-status children as rejected even when the low-status children use more appropriate behaviors. Other issues are the failure of most programs to provide review sessions and the need to incorporate these programs into school curricula so that they can be offered on an ongoing basis. As was noted earlier, more information on the relationships of adolescents is needed, and the number of social skills programs available to this age group, both in clinical settings—and, more important, in school settings—should be increased.

Social Skills Training and Children with Developmental Disabilities

A number of studies (Gresham, 1982; Guralnick & Groom, 1988; Ray, 1985; Taylor, Asher, & Williams, 1987) have verified that children with developmental disabilities are not accepted by their nondisabled peers; consistently low ratings on sociometric measures reflect their low status. These studies have also found that children with disabilities receive more negative behaviors from nonhandicapped peers and are often excluded from activities. When nonhandicapped peers interact with these children, they frequently assume more adult roles, so that the interaction becomes more of an adult-to-child than a child-to-child. Therefore, the opportunities for the child with disabilities to practice critical child-to-child interactions are limited (Guralnick, 1986).

Individuals with Disabilities Education Act. With the mandate of the Individuals with Disabilities Education Act (1990) to mainstream children with disabilities, many educators, parents, and helping professionals believed that children with disabilities would enjoy improved social interactions in their new environment. However, as Gresham (1982) pointed out, this has not been the case. Children with disabilities receive low ratings on sociometric measures and are most often excluded and rejected by their nonhandicapped peers. It is clear that mainstreaming will not greatly enhance the social environment of children with disabilities; in fact, Gresham wondered if mainstreaming placed them in a more negative environment. The integration of social skills programs that work not only with children with disabilities to address their deficits in skills but also with nonhandicapped children to emphasize the replacement of negative attitudes with more positive feelings about children with disabilities is critical if the social world of disabled children is to be improved.

Learning disabled children. One group of children with developmental disabilities, those with learning disabilities, has received a great deal of attention because an increasing number of schoolchildren are being diagnosed with some form of a learning disability. These children have academic problems despite IQs of 80 to 90 or more. In addition, like other children who have disabilities, they experience problems in their social interactions with peers that may begin as early as the first months in kindergarten (Gresham, 1982; Kistner & Gatlin, 1989; Vaughn, Hogan, Kouzekanani, & Shapiro, 1990). Contrary to the negative behaviors many rejected children exhibit, learning disabled children probably use more conforming behaviors than negative behaviors, although they seem to have difficulty interpreting the social cues and nonverbal behaviors of others, which inhibits their social interactions (Bryan & Bryan, 1983).

Learning disabled children may also receive less positive reinforcement from both parents and teachers. Teachers tend to have more negative attitudes and use less-positive behaviors in their interactions with learning disabled children, especially as these children move into preadolescence (Bryan & Bryan, 1983). With negative input from several sources, learning disabled children need support systems and programs to enable them to improve their social interactions, and social skills programs can promote improved peer relations for both young children and adolescents with learning disabilities (Amerikaner & Summerlin, 1982; Straub & Roberts, 1983; Wanat, 1983).

Other developmental disabilities. Social skills programs also have been successful in working with autistic and autistic-like children and young children and adolescents with emotional disabilities (Agrin, 1987; Baum, Clark, McCarthy, Sandler, & Carpenter, 1987; Plienis, Hansen, Ford, Smith, & Kelly, 1987; Strain, 1985). An important aspect of Strain's (1985) program was the use of nonhandicapped peers who served as instructors and behavioral models for the autistic children.

These programs have reported the same weakness that other social skills programs have experienced, that is, the lack of generalization of skills and meaningful change in social environment for participants. Again, most of these programs have worked only with children who have disabilities, although positive changes in these children's social interactions can occur only if nonhandicapped peers develop more accepting attitudes toward children with disabilities. Most studies (see, for example, Guralnick & Groom, 1988; Hepler, 1994; Taylor, Asher, & Williams, 1987) have shown that children with disabilities want to interact with their nonhandicapped peers; however, it is the nonhandicapped peers who are unwilling to play or interact with developmentally delayed children.

SOCIAL SKILLS TRAINING WITH ADULTS

Social skills training with adults has included a wide array of programs, such as anger management and assertiveness training, but has primarily involved work with populations experiencing severe adjustment problems, including individuals with alcoholism problems, those with chronic mental illness (psychotic and nonpsychotic) or developmental disabilities, and chronic criminal offenders. In his meta-analysis of social skills programs for psychiatric populations, Corrigan (1991) reported that adults with developmental disabilities (mental retardation) experienced the greatest improvement, and criminal and sex offenders and individuals with drug and alcohol abuse problems showed the least improvement. However, all groups, including those with chronic mental illness, learned skills that were maintained several months after treatment. Corrigan also found that outpatient training was more effective than inpatient training.

Populations with adjustment problems. Several authors have reported similar findings for populations with adjustment problems. Dam-Baggen and Kraaimaat (1986) worked with socially anxious psychiatric inpatients and outpatients; people who participated in the program experienced a decrease in social anxiety and improved their social skills and maintained these at the three-month follow-up. Hawkins, Catalano, and Wells (1986) used a program that focused on the acquisition of behavioral and problem-solving skills designed to reduce relapse in drug abusers who were in long-term residential therapy. An important component of this program was the use of drug-free community partners who received training and worked with the participants in the community. Self-report measures revealed significant improvement for the treatment group. However, the important issue of long-term recovery had not been determined at the time the study was published.

Schizophrenic patients. Work with schizophrenic patients has yielded positive outcomes (Bellack & Morrison, 1982; Liberman, Nuechterlein, & Wallace, 1982). It is not surprising that Liberman et al. (1982) found that the interpersonal skills of schizophrenic families were one of the most significant variables that influenced patients' adjustment in the community. Families with positive social skills and interactions enhanced the patients' abilities to cope with everyday stresses and events, which thereby improved the likelihood that the patients would remain in the community. Liberman et al. viewed the use of a highly structured cognitive–behavioral approach (role-playing, modeling, homework, problem-solving skills) as essential. Bellack and Morrison (1982) and Hersen, Bellack, and Himmelhock (1982) have reported success with depression as well as with alcohol abuse.

The major problem with all these studies is the lack of evidence concerning the long-term generalization of learned skills in the community. This, along with meaningful change for individuals in their social environment, is the critical outcome for social skills programs. It also is evident, on the basis of the current knowledge of social development, that many of the problems that some individuals, particularly criminal offenders and people with substance abuse problems, exhibit as adults could have been effectively addressed in childhood. Like most programs for youths, social skills programs for adults have worked primarily with individuals who experience problems in their social environment; little emphasis has been placed on modifying the negative attitudes of others toward many of these adults who face discrimination and rejection in the community. Yet, as with children, many of these adults will not be able to improve their world substantially without the understanding and positive support of the community.

SUMMARY AND IMPLICATIONS

Social skills programs have been demonstrated to be an effective intervention model for improving the social relationships of children and adults. Given the increasing documentation of the importance of positive social interactions and the long-term negative consequences of deficits in social skills, it is imperative for social work to continue its important role in the development, implementation, and evaluation of these programs. This entry has emphasized the need to develop methods that encourage the generalization of learned skills, to promote the acquisition of relevant skills that will improve an individual's social environment, and to focus on prevention. These goals can be accomplished best by involving young children in social skills programs before their problems become severe and longstanding. In conjunction with these goals, it is essential for social work practitioners and researchers to develop programs that work not only with individuals who experience a problem, but with individuals in the school or community who have biased, negative attitudes toward youths and adults with developmental disabilities or deficits in social skills. This approach is in accordance with the profession's emphasis on bringing about change by focusing on all aspects of the environment that contribute to the problem, rather than blaming the victims.

REFERENCES

Agrin, A. R. (1987). Occupational therapy with emotionally disturbed children in a public elementary school. *Occupational Therapy in Mental Health, 1,* 105–114.

Amerikaner, M., & Summerlin, M. L. (1982). Group counseling with learning disabled children: Effects of social skills and relaxation training on self-concept and classroom behavior. *Journal of Learning Disabilities, 15*(6), 340–343.

Asher, S., & Hymel, S. (1981). Children's social competence in peer relations: Sociometric and behavioral assessment. In J. Wine & M. Smye (Eds.), *Social competence* (pp. 125–155). New York: Guilford Press.

Asher, S., Oden, S., & Gottman, J. (1977). Children's friendship in school settings. In L. G. Katz (Ed.), *Current topics in early childhood education* (Vol. 1, pp. 33–61). Norwood, NJ: Ablex.

Baum, J. G., Clark, H. B., McCarthy, W., Sandler, J., & Carpenter, R. (1987). An analysis of the acquisition and generalization of social skills in troubled youths: Combining social skills training, cognitive self-talk, and relaxation procedures. *Child and Family Behavior Therapy, 8*(4), 1–27.

Bellack, A. S., & Morrison, R. L. (1982). Interpersonal dysfunction. In A. S. Bellack, M. Hersen, & A. E. Kazdin (Eds.), *International handbook of behavior modification therapy* (pp. 717–748). New York: Plenum Press.

Berndt, T. J., Caparulo, B., McCartney, K., & Moore, A. (1980). *Processes and outcomes of social influence in children's peer groups.* Unpublished manuscript, Yale University, New Haven, CT.

Bierman, K. L., & Furman, W. (1984). The effects of social skills training and peer involvement on the social adjustment of preadolescents. *Child Development, 55,* 151–162.

Bryan, J. H., & Bryan, T. H. (1983). The social life of the learning disabled youngster. In J. D. McKinney & L. Feagans (Eds.), *Current topics in learning disabilities* (pp. 57–80). Norwood, NJ: Ablex.

Cassidy, J., & Asher, S. R. (1992). Loneliness and peer relations in young children. *Child Development, 63,* 350–365.

Cillessen, A.H.N., van IJzendoorn, H. W., van Lieshout, C.F.M., & Hartup, W. W. (1992). Heterogeneity among peer-rejected boys: Subtypes and stabilities. *Child Development, 63,* 893–905.

Cohn, D. A. (1990). Child–mother attachment of six-year-olds and social competence at school. *Child Development, 61,* 152–162.

Coie, J. D., & Dodge, K. A. (1983). Continuities and changes in children's social status: A five year longitudinal study. *Merrill Palmer Quarterly, 29,* 261–282.

Coie, J. D., Dodge, K. A., & Coppotelli, H. (1982). Dimensions and types of social status: A cross-age perspective. *Developmental Psychology, 18,* 557–570.

Coie, J. D., & Kupersmidt, J. (1983). A behavioral analysis of emerging social status in boys' groups. *Child Development, 54,* 1400–1416.

Corrigan, P. W. (1991). Social skills training in adult psychiatric populations: A meta analysis, *Journal of Behavior Therapy and Experimental Psychiatry, 22,* 203–210.

Cowen, E., Pederson, A., Babijian, H., Izzo, L., & Troust, M. (1973). Long-term follow-up of early detected vulnerable children. *Journal of Consulting and Clinical Psychology, 41,* 438–466.

Dam-Baggen, R., & Kraaimaat, F. (1986). A group social skills training program with psychiatric patients: Outcome, dropout rate, and prediction. *Behavioral Research Therapy, 24,* 161–169.

Dodge, K. (1983). Behavioral antecedents of peer social status. *Child Development, 54,* 1386–1399.

Dodge, K., Pettit, G., McClaskey, C., & Brown, M. (1986). Social competence in children. *Monographs of the Society for Research in Child Development, 51*(2, Serial No. 213).

Edleson, J., & Rose, S. (1978). *A behavioral roleplay test for assessing children's social skills.* Paper presented at the 12th annual convention of the Association for the Advancement of Behavior Therapy, Chicago.

Elardo, P., & Caldwell, B. (1976). The effects of an experimental social development program on children in the middle childhood period. *Psychology in the Schools, 16,* 93–100.

Filiczak, J., Archer, M., & Friedman, R. M. (1990). In-school social skills training. *Behavior Modification, 4*(2), 243–263.

Fine, G. (1981). Friends, impression, management, and preadolescent behavior. In S. Asher & J. Gottman (Eds.), *The development of children's friendships.* New York: Cambridge University Press.

Foster, S. L., DeLawyer, D. D., & Guevremont, D. C. (1985). Selecting targets for social skills training with children and adolescents. In K. D. Gadow (Ed.), *Advances in learning behavioral disabilities* (pp. 77–132). Greenwich, CT: JAI Press.

Furman, W., & Masters, J. (1978). *An observational system for coding reinforcing, neutral, and punishing interactions among children.* Minneapolis: University of Minnesota Press.

Ginsberg, D., Gottman, J. M., & Parker, J. G. (1986). The importance of friendship. In J. M. Gottman & J. G. Parker (Eds.), *Conversations of friends, speculations on affective development* (pp. 3–50). New York: Cambridge University Press.

Gottman, J., & Mettetal, G. (1986). Speculations about social and affective development: Friendship and acquaintanceship through adolescence. In J. M. Gottman & J. Parker (Eds.), *Conversations of friends, speculations on affective development* (pp. 192–240). New York: Cambridge University Press.

Gottman, J. M., & Parker, J. G. (1986). *Conversations of friends.* New York: Cambridge University Press.

Gottman, J. M., & Parkhurst, J. (1980). A developmental theory of friendship and acquaintanceship processes. In A. Collins (Ed.), *Minnesota symposia on child psychology* (Vol. 13). Hillsdale, NJ: Erlbaum.

Gresham, F. M. (1982). Misguided mainstreaming: The case for social skills training with handicapped children. *Exceptional Children, 49*(5), 422–431.

Gresham, F., & Nagle, R. (1980). Social skills training with children: Responsiveness to modeling and coaching as a function of peer orientation. *Journal of Consulting and Clinical Psychology, 48,* 718–729.

Guralnick, M. J. (1986). The peer relations of young handicapped and nonhandicapped children. In P. S. Strain, M. J. Guralnick, & H. M. Walker (Eds.), *Children's social behavior: Development, assessment, and modification* (pp. 93–139). San Diego: Academic Press.

Guralnick, M. J., & Groom, J. M. (1988). Friendships of preschool children in mainstreamed playgroups. *Developmental Psychology, 24*(4), 585–604.

Hart, C. H., DeWolf, D. M., Wozniak, P., & Burts, D. C. (1992). Maternal and paternal disciplinary styles: Relations with preschoolers' playground behavioral orientations and peer status. *Child Development, 63,* 879–892.

Hartup, W. (1976). Peer interaction and the behavioral development of the individual child. In E. Schopler & R. Reichler (Eds.), *Psychopathology and child development* (pp. 345–354). New York: Plenum Press.

Hartup, W. (1983). Peer relations. In E. M. Hetherington (Ed.), *Handbook of child psychology: Vol. 4. Socialization, personality and social development* (pp. 103–174). New York: John Wiley & Sons.

Hawkins, J. D., Catalano, R. F., & Wells, E. A. (1986). Measuring effects of a skills training intervention for drug abusers. *Journal of Consulting and Clinical Psychology, 51,* 661–664.

Hepler, J. B. (1990). Observing the social interactions of fifth grade children (A preliminary study). *School Social Work Journal, 15*(1), 1–13.

Hepler, J. B. (1994). Mainstreaming children with learning disabilities: Have we improved their social environment? *Social Work in Education, 16*(3), 143–154.

Hepler, J. B. (in press). Evaluating the effectiveness of a social skills program for preadolescents. *Research on Social Work Practice.*

Hepler, J. B., & Rose, S. (1988). Evaluating the effectiveness of a multicomponent group approach for improving the social skills of elementary school children. *Journal of Social Service Research, 11*(4), 1–18.

Hersen, M., Bellack, A., & Himmelhock, L. (1982). Social skills training within unipolar depressed women. In S. P. Curran & P. M. Monti (Eds.), *Social skills training: A practical handbook for assessment and treatment* (pp. 159–184). New York: Guilford Press.

Hymel, S., & Franke, S. (1985). Children's peer relations: Assessing self-perceptions. In B. H. Schneider, K. H. Rubin, & J. E. Ledingham (Eds.), *Children's peer relations: Issues in assessment and intervention* (pp. 78–92). New York: Springer-Verlag.

Individuals with Disabilities Education Act, P.L. 101-476, 104 Stat. 1142 (1990).

Kazdin, A. E. (1992). *Research design in clinical psychology* (2nd Ed.). Boston: Allyn & Bacon.

Kistner, J. A., & Gatlin, D. F. (1989). Sociometric differences between learning disabled and nonhandicapped students: Effects of sex and race. *Journal of Educational Psychology, 81,* 118–120.

Kline, R. B., Canter, W. A., & Robin, A. (1987). Parameters of teenage alcohol use: A path analytic conceptual model. *Journal of Consulting and Clinical Psychology, 55,* 521–528.

Kupersmidt, J. B. (1983, April). *Predicting delinquency and academic problems from childhood peer status.* Paper presented at the Biennial Meeting of the Society for Research in Child Development, Detroit.

Kupersmidt, J. B., Coie, J. D., & Dodge, K. A. (1990). Predicting disorder from peer social problems. In S. R. Asher & J. D. Coie (Eds.), *Peer rejection in childhood.* New York: Cambridge University Press.

Ladd, G. W. (1981). Social skills and peer acceptance: Effects of a social learning method for training verbal social skills. *Child Development, 52,* 171–178.

Ladd, G. W. (1985). Documenting the effects of social skill training with children: Process and outcome assessment. In B. H. Schneider, K. H. Rubin, J. E. Ledingham (Eds.), *Children's peer relations: Issues in assessment and intervention* (pp. 243–263). New York: Springer-Verlag.

Ladd, G. W., & Mize, J. (1983). A cognitive–social learning model of social skill training. *Psychological Review, 90*(2), 127–157.

LaGreca, M., & Santogrossi, D. (1980). Social skills training with elementary school students: A behavioral group approach. *Journal of Consulting and Clinical Psychology, 48,* 220–227.

Liberman, R. P., Nuechterlein, K. H., & Wallace, C. J. (1982). Social skills training with schizophrenics. In S. P. Curran & P. M. Monti (Eds.), *Social skills training: A practical handbook for assessment and treatment* (pp. 5–56). New York: Guilford Press.

Moreno, F. (1934). *Who shall survive? A new approach to the problem of human interrelations.* Washington, DC: Nervous and Mental Disease Publishing.

Oden, S., & Asher, S. (1977). Coaching children in social skills for friendship making. *Child Development, 48,* 495–506.

Parker, J., & Asher, S. (1987). Peer relations and later personal adjustment: Are low-accepted children at risk?, *Psychological Bulletin, 102,* 356–389.

Patterson, C. J., Kupersmidt, J. B., & Griesler, P. M. (1990). Children's perceptions of self and relationships with others as a function of sociometric status. *Child Development, 61,* 1335–1349.

Plienis, A. J., Hansen, D. J., Ford, F., Smith, S., Jr., & Kelly, J. A. (1987). Behavioral small group training to improve the social skills of emotionally-disordered adolescents. *Behavior Therapy, 18,* 17–32.

Putallaz, M. (1983). Predicting children's sociometric status from their behavior. *Child Development, 54,* 1417–1426.

Putallaz, M., & Gottman, J. (1981). Social skills and group acceptance. In S. Asher & J. Gottman (Eds.), *The development of children's friendships* (pp. 117–149). New York: Cambridge University Press.

Ray, B. M. (1985). Measuring the social position of the mainstreamed handicapped child. *Exceptional Children, 52*(1), 57–62.

Rose, S. D. (1972). *Treating children in groups.* San Francisco: Jossey-Bass.

Schneider, B. H., & Byrne, B. M. (1985). Children's social skills training: A meta-analysis. In B. H. Schneider, K. H. Rubin, & J. E. Ledingham (Eds.), *Children's peer relations: Issues in assessment and intervention* (pp. 175–190). New York: Springer-Verlag.

Seigel, L. J., & Griffin, J. J. (1983). Adolescents' concepts of depression among their peers. *Adolescence, 18*(72), 965–973.

Shure, M. (1982). Interpersonal problem-solving: A cog in the wheel of social cognition. In F. Serafica (Ed.), *Social cognitive development in context* (pp. 133–166). New York: Guilford Press.

Singleton, L., & Asher, S. (1977). Peer preferences and social interaction among third-grade children in an integrated school district. *Journal of Educational Psychology, 69,* 330–336.

Sobol, M. P., & Earn, B. M. (1985). Assessment of children's attributions for social experiences: Implications for social skills training. In B. H. Schneider, K. H. Rubin, & J. E. Ledingham (Eds.), *Children's peer relations: Issues in assessment and intervention* (pp. 93–101). New York: Springer-Verlag.

Spivack, G., & Shure, M. (1983). The cognition of social adjustment: Interpersonal cognitive–problem-solving thinking. In B. Lakey & D. Kazdin (Eds.), *Advances in clinical child psychology* (pp. 323–372). New York: Plenum Press.

Strain, P. S. (1985). Programmatic research on peers as intervention agents for socially isolated classmates. In B. H. Schneider, K. H. Rubin, & J. E. Ledingham (Eds.), *Children's peer relations: Issues in assessment and intervention.* New York: Springer-Verlag.

Straub, R. B., & Roberts, D. M. (1983). Effects of nonverbal-oriented social awareness training program on social interaction ability of learning disabled children. *Journal of Nonverbal Behavior, 7*(4), 195–201.

Taylor, A. R., Asher, S. R., & Williams, G. A. (1987). The social adaptation of mainstreamed mildly retarded children. *Child Development, 58,* 1321–1334.

Tellado, G. S. (1984). An evaluation case: The implementation and evaluation of a problem-solving training program for adolescents. *Evaluation and Program Planning, 7,* 179–188.

Vaughn, S., Hogan, A., Kouzekanani, K., & Shapiro, S. (1990). Peer acceptance, self-perceptions, and social skills of learning disabled students prior to identification. *Journal of Educational Psychology, 82,* 101–106.

Wanat, P. E. (1983). Social skills: An awareness program with learning disabled adolescents. *Journal of Learning Disabilities, 16*(1), 35–38.

Wheeler, V. A., & Ladd, G. W. (1982). Assessment of children's self-efficacy for social interactions with peers. *Developmental Psychology, 18,* 795–805.

Windle, M. (1990). A longitudinal study of antisocial behaviors in early adolescence as predictors of late adolescent substance use: Gender and ethnic group differences. *Journal of Abnormal Psychology, 99*(1), 86–91.

Juanita B. Hepler, PhD, is associate professor, Boise State University, Social Work Department, 716 Education Building, Boise, ID 83725.

For further information see

Adolescents: Direct Practice; Children: Direct Practice; Children: Mental Health; Cognition and Social Cognitive Theory; Cognitive Treatment; Developmental Disabilities: Definitions and Policies; Direct Practice Overview; Disability; Families Overview; Family Therapy; Goal Setting and Intervention Planning; Group Practice; Human Development; Mental Health Overview; Natural Helping Networks; School-Linked Services; Self-Help Groups; Social Development; Social Work Practice: Theoretical Base; Youth Services.

Key Words	
developmental disabilities	social development
peer relationships	social skills training

READER'S GUIDE

Social Supports

*The following entries contain information
on this general topic:*

Mutual Aid Societies
Natural Helping Networks
Sectarian Agencies
Self-Help Groups
Settlements and Neighborhood Centers

Social Welfare Archives

See Archives of Social Welfare

Social Welfare History
P. Nelson Reid

Social welfare is an encompassing and imprecise term, but most often it is defined in terms of "organized activities," "interventions," or some other element that suggests policy and programs to respond to recognized social problems or to improve the well-being of those at risk. To define social welfare in terms of programs or problems alone, however, is to miss a larger and more enduring element. Titmuss (1958) observed that social welfare is concerned with the "right order" of relationships in society; that is, it is some ideal of the way in which a society works and fits together to form a suitable place for human habitation and development. From a different perspective, Murray (1984) referred to social welfare as establishing the "rules of the game," with the "game" being the system of distributing valued resources, such as money; jobs; housing; and educational, health, and social services. Both Murray and Titmuss—and, therefore, both what is called the "Right" and the "Left"—have some vision of the good society. Social welfare, then, is perhaps best understood as an idea, that idea being one of a decent society that provides opportunities for work and human meaning, provides reasonable security from want and assault, promotes fairness and evaluation based on individual merit, and is economically productive and stable. This idea of social welfare is based on the assumption that human society can be organized and governed to produce and provide these things, and because it is feasible to do so, the society has a moral obligation to bring it to fruition.

This entry describes the history and development of social welfare in the United States with a focus on understanding the character and sources of the current idea of social welfare. It was written in the context of the 1990s, however, a time when much of what is commonly thought of as making up the sound welfare state is under an apparent cloud of doubt.

The beginning of the 20th century was fertile ground for the development and expansion of broad governmental responsibility for social problems in the United States. Industrialization, immigration, the growth of cities, the rapid increase in capital and wealth, and labor unrest all contributed to a dramatic change in the role of government. There was a prevailing sense that through political will, effective professional service, and adequate supports a myriad of social difficulties could be solved. Social work, born of "scientific charity" and christened in American Progressivism, reflected this nearly boundless hope and the easy acceptance of state responsibility for society and its people.

However, in the 1990s, things do not seem so clear. The century has not been altogether kind to the welfare state, and there is talk of a new paradigm. The post–World War II economic boom is long past, and postindustrial restructuring has left the welfare state vulnerable to a new conservatism that has eroded some of the programs and much of the ideology of welfare. Liberal optimism is not in vogue and seems to have given way to a less generous appraisal of human potential. What for most of this century seemed so hopeful and just two decades ago seemed inevitable currently seems to be teetering on some historical edge.

DEVELOPMENT OF STATE RESPONSIBILITY FOR SOCIAL WELFARE

The development of social welfare in the modern sense of the term depended on the assumption of state responsibility for the provision of social assistance. This assumption established a context in which policy and programs could develop in a uniform and visible fashion and in response to social and economic circumstances reflected in political pressures and processes. From the U.S. perspective, the emergence of a central role for the state in social provision had occurred before American colonization, and so the story of the transition from "private," sacred, charitable aid to "public," secular, citizenship-based aid begins in England.

Elizabethan Poor Laws

The development of a clearly defined governmental role for the provision of aid to those in need is typically associated with the Elizabethan Poor Law of 1601. As de Schweinitz (1943) observed, the statute of Elizabeth 43 represents the culmination of a two-century process of the state's progressive attempts to control aid to poor people, first through "repressive" measures and later through the establishment of a "positive obligation." This positive approach involved a system in which local parishes publicly administered locally derived tax funds that were used to provide direct grants to unemployable people, work for able-bodied individuals, and apprenticeship or some form of foster care for neglected children. The elements of the Elizabethan Poor Laws remained the basis for English and American provision to the poor for 300 years and continue to have a great influence.

Feudal system. The Poor Law statutes, beginning in 1349 with the Statutes of Laborers and culminating in Elizabeth 43, represent an effort by the state to deal with the decline and fall of the feudal system and the transition to a modern, wage-based economic and social order. The feudal system was land based, with a hereditary hierarchy controlling all property. The vast majority of people were landless serfs, who were tied to property and were required to labor for the lords in their fields or in small-scale manufacture. The serfs paid rents and taxes and were obligated to the land-controlling lords for life. In return, they were provided protection and some small measure of security. This agrarian system produced little surplus, much of which went to support the well born. Every household gave to the church (which also had a hierarchy to support), and some of the surplus was provided in the form of charitable aid. The feudal system was one of fixed social classes and minimal geographic or social mobility of individuals.

Centers of trade. By the 13th and 14th centuries, however, things began to change. Sufficient political stability gave rise to larger areas of trade, which allowed for higher degrees of specialization in agriculture and manufacturing. The result was the emergence of towns as centers of craft and trade and the beginnings of a "middle class" that was not composed of serfs, nobles, or clergy. As more and more rural agricultural workers migrated to the towns in search of greater employment opportunities, the consequent labor shortages in the countryside were a source of vexation to the landholders. The Black Plague, beginning in the mid-1300s and continuing at least 100 years, substantially reduced the population and contributed to greater labor shortages, but the underlying process was a wholesale economic and social transformation that would ultimately produce a political transformation as well. This transformation involved the emergence of large-scale markets, a surge of technology, and population shifts that would create capitalism, great cities, industrialization, and the middle classes, as well as a "working" class, and would ultimately shift democratic political power to these latter groups and away from the old aristocracy (Polyani, 1957).

State protection of public interests. At the time of the Poor Laws, the state represented the interests of powerful and landed individuals, and it could not allow the church, monasteries, and various foundations, guilds, and private donors to give aid in ways that were not consistent with what it construed to be the "public interest." The public interest, of course, was what maintained the system of economic and social relations that this landed aristocracy was used to and benefited from and that advanced the control of the government. It seemed only reasonable to have policies that would standardize aid and prevent multiple suppliers of social aid from providing benefits to whom they liked, when and where they liked, and administered by persons not accountable to public authority. So over time, starting with the Statutes of Laborers in 1349 through the acts of Henry VII, Edward VI, and Elizabeth, the government established laws determining who could be given aid, where they could be given aid, how funds were to be raised, who should administer the aid, and what punishments should befall the poor and the providers of aid for failure to comply with the demands of law. By the mid-1500s, the church had been essentially chased out of any important role in fundraising, in determining eligibility, or in administering the assistance. In its place was a system of taxes, eligibility laws, official lists of the needy, and overseers of the poor—all part of a policy designed to provide assistance to the poor in various categories while preserving local standards and ensuring no harm to the social, economic, and political order through large-scale subsidy of a begging, criminal, and dependent class.

Changes in the Poor Laws

1662 Law of Settlement. The Poor Laws were modified twice to add major features of policy. The first, the Law of Settlement of 1662, allowed the return of people to their former parish of residence if they had meager resources and appeared to be likely recipients of public aid. Thus, it clearly established a residency requirement and, not for the last time in Poor Law history, attempted to remove any incentives for geographic mobility that public aid might create.

1834 Poor Law reforms. The second major change came in the 1834 Poor Law Reforms; these measures were designed to reduce perceived work-disincentive aspects of poor relief. The reforms sought to reduce "outdoor" relief by restricting aid to able-bodied individuals to the workhouse, providing for tougher and more centralized administration, and seeking to eliminate the overlap of assistance levels and available wages. This last reform was to be accomplished through applying the principles of "less eligibility," by which benefit levels were fixed below the wages of the "laborer of the lowest class." These reforms were due, in part, but only in part, to the consequences of the Speenhamland system that was adopted in some parts of the country in 1795. Speenhamland was a system of wage subsidy that effectively created a guaranteed income of sorts for persons in some agricultural districts. It was an updated expression of the old pre–wage-relationship days of "noblesse oblige" in which workers were provided a specified level of security, regardless of employment or productivity, and were tied to a particular district. However, the days of obligation to landowners had passed, and so the predictable occurred: Wages declined because

they could be shifted to the public treasury; unemployment increased because it was "insured"; normal mobility to growing urban areas ceased; and agricultural productivity declined. The framers of Speenhamland had depended on the social forces of tradition and obligation to keep things intact, but these traditional forces had been destroyed by social and economic development. By 1834, the English government wanted nothing to do with wage subsidy and sought to extricate poor relief entirely from the labor system (de Schweinitz, 1943).

Poor Laws in American Colonies

In the American colonies, the Poor Laws became the basis for poor relief, and the same issues of indoor and outdoor relief, the centrality of administration, and problems of dependence arose. In general, however, the colonists did not pursue the administration of the Poor Laws with the same vigor or anxiety as did their English counterparts. As Rothman (1971) pointed out, the colonial pattern of poor relief was based on a fixed idea of social relations, in which the poor were seen as a permanent order, "integral" to society and not a danger to it. The probable explanation for this view was that the new world was not changing social relations or geographic mobility in ways that threatened any old order or established economy. There was no old order, and the economy was agrarian and trade based. There was no fear of migration to urban areas and no view of poor relief as a threat to the good order of society. There were certainly those who questioned whether poor relief might threaten the good character of those who got it, particularly in the more Calvinistic colonies, but in general there was toleration for the poor and no particular urge to reform them or the society in which they lived. This attitude of benign near-neglect of the poor did not survive the American Revolution and its aftermath. By the 1820s, the United States entered into the first of many episodes of searching for a solution to the problem of dependence and developing its own American version of reform.

PHILOSOPHICAL AND CULTURAL CONTEXT

To understand the particular character of social welfare development in the United States (and England) in the 19th century and much of the 20th, it is important to reflect on the ideas that guided such development and the cultural, political, and social forces that created and sustained them. These ideas have many variations, but are well represented by the works of John Locke, Adam Smith, and Jeremy Bentham. To these ideas should perhaps be added the contributions of Martin Luther, John Calvin, John Wesley, and the other Protestant reformers who sought to bring religion out of the monastery and to see God's hand in everyday work and the marketplace and who railed against elaborate and nearly royal church hierarchy. Together they, and many others, established an influential "liberal" construct involving economic liberty, political freedom, and utilitarian philosophy. These ideas have nourished and sustained the ideas of individualism, personal responsibility, the moral importance of work, and distrust of collectivism and centralized government (Leiby, 1978).

Collapse of Feudalism

All these developments in political philosophy, moral philosophy, and theology are the consequence, at least in part, of the collapse of feudalism and the emergence of a social class that was not defined by birth or knowledge or bound by law to land or master, but defined by usefulness. In short, it was not a matter of who the members of this class were, but what they did. The economic order that developed put the tradesman and the merchant in central roles, and they came to define themselves by their utility and to apply this standard to others. As the economic and social influence of this middle class increased, ideas of political liberty and equality developed, set against aristocratic claims to power and wealth. The emergence of a middle class has left a powerful cultural legacy and a political order that seeks to eliminate the useless. To some, the poor are suspect; others condemn the church or the corporation, but the basic value is the same: A person has moral worth only to the extent that he or she is identifiably useful to others and in so doing contributes to the welfare of others. This is why work is seen as a moral act, not simply as an economic act. It is the way in which an individual demonstrates his or her value to others. This system of evaluation of persons and things by their consequences has profound implications for both social welfare policy and operations.

Culture of Capitalism

In the United States, with its strong cultural commitment to individualism and personal freedom, the search for worthiness has been particularly intense. No element has contributed to the architecture of the U.S. social welfare system to an equal degree. Thus, social welfare has developed in the context of what Wilensky and Lebeaux (1965) referred to as the "culture of capitalism." That culture is not, of course, devoid of social value placed on family, community, and humanity.

Therefore, the American response to human need has been a continuous compromise between values of security and humanitarianism, on the one hand, and self-reliance and competitiveness, on the other hand. This compromise has given the system of social welfare an odd and uneven quality and has produced a patchwork of programs with little apparent coherence of articulation. However, beneath the complex program level resides perhaps a more enduring and coherent system of social thought reflecting the ideals of personal responsibility, individual utility, and equity that, combined with the U.S. multilevel government structure, gives U.S. social welfare history a consistency and character that is uniquely American.

SOCIAL WELFARE IN THE NEW REPUBLIC

The American Revolution, like many subsequent revolutions, gave rise to high social expectations. England had been blamed for many things, and once English "oppression" was lifted, the social order was expected to become more nearly perfect. America, after all, had vast and available resources and none of the burdensome elements of European social order and government. Perhaps because of these rising expectations, the new government forms in the United States, the nature of politics, or all these elements combined, the issue of poor people and dependence would become prominent. As a result, the colonial pattern of providing relief within a largely unquestioned community responsibility and with a typically casual administrative system gave way to a new and less tolerant view. This new view saw poverty as a social problem; as a potential source of crime, social unrest, and long-term dependence; and, therefore, as a proper target of reform. By the 1820s and 1830s, the social and political concern with poverty had forged a new direction for policy and a "new paradigm" for treating the problem.

Indoor Relief as Institutions of Reform

The new approach was based on the assumption that the existence of poor people was evidence that the social order needed repair. This was the age of engineering, and once the problem was identified, it was to be fixed through the application of human analytical skills and an intervention designed to fit the problem. Analysis and design often occurred through governmental commissions, such as the Yates Commission in New York and the Quincy Commission in Massachusetts. After surveying the problem and hearing much testimony, these and other similar groups came to remarkably similar conclusions: The poor have been ruined by the Poor Laws, specifically by outdoor relief, and the answer is to end these community temptations to become permanent denizens of the public dole (Rothman, 1971).

In place of the old system would be the perfect institution: a grand almshouse, where, through order, cleanliness, discipline, and routine, the poor could be transformed into useful and productive members of society. In many American communities and most large cities, almshouses of great size and expense were constructed, often becoming the most imposing public buildings in these communities. The almshouses represented not only a growing intolerance for poor people and a disregard for what would currently be considered basic civil rights, but an American optimism that anyone could be changed and reformed in the right environment. The European pessimism and belief in a fixed order had not survived the trip across the Atlantic, and the American policy was based on the belief that people are corrupted by social arrangements and can be reformed by good influence properly applied. This policy was to be applied not only to poor people, but to criminals and mentally ill individuals, and thus a similar increase in the building of asylums and penitentiaries occurred during the same period. This increase in such institutions was to work out badly, of course, and within a short time almshouses and other institutions that had been built with such pride and optimism were being described as places of routine abuse and despair. Dorothea Dix led a movement for institutional reform for mentally ill people, and by the 1850s outdoor relief for the poor was reestablished as the norm (Trattner, 1989).

Precursors of Scientific Charity

The return of relief to the poor at home was partly the result of the decline of institutions and partly the result of continued and growing immigration and periods of economic distress that made institutional relief impractical. Private organizations, such as the Society for the Prevention of Pauperism and the Association for the Improvement of the Condition of the Poor, influenced the community administration of aid and sometimes played a direct hand in such assistance. These groups generally believed that aid to the poor was the duty of society and must be provided, but that the causes of pauperism were generally personal. Therefore, it was important to provide aid cautiously and to seek to reform the individual away from intemperance, foolish spending, laziness, or whatever aspect of personal character or circumstance was believed to have led to the problem. The emphasis

on social structure as a cause of poverty was minimal and confined mainly to the community regulation of alcohol and the "ruinous" effects of outdoor relief.

This approach led, within 25 years, to the development of "scientific charity" and ultimately to the emergence of casework and the profession of social work. However, its development would be interrupted by the Civil War, which would fundamentally reorder the relations of the federal government and the states, create new agencies and new responsibilities at the national level, and raise the issue of opportunities and rights for African Americans to an enduring and high level. This latter issue would influence American social policy and social welfare in the most basic and profound way.

CIVIL WAR AND POST–CIVIL WAR ERA

The Civil War changed everything. Before the war, the United States was a collection of states; after the war, it was a genuine nation. To say that the relations between the federal government and the states would never be the same is a vast understatement. The emergence of a central government, the economic and industrial growth spurred by the war, the tremendous rate of immigration and migration west, and technological change all combined to create a new United States, with many of the social, demographic, and cultural features associated with modern times.

For social welfare, the changes came gradually but inexorably. During the Civil War, the U.S. Sanitary Commission had been organized by the War Department and, despite its quasi-voluntary character, it contributed to the later development of veterans' and public health programs. The Freedman's Bureau, established in 1865 just before the end of the war, was the first federal welfare agency. Despite its short life of four years and its limited appropriations, it managed to aid a large number of displaced people and to contribute to the establishment of a new nonslave economic role for African Americans in the South. Its promise of land reform and the spread of landownership to former slaves was never realized, but its contributions in relief and education were substantial (Trattner, 1989).

Impacts of Industrialization

The federal role began to shift in other ways as well. Land grants to states for educational and other institutions increased, creating, among other things, the current system of land-grant colleges. By the 1880s, the problems of industrial growth and labor had led to the establishment of the

Bureau of Labor Statistics, the Interstate Commerce Commission, and such legislation as the Sherman Anti-Trust Act. Labor unions were consolidating during this period; the militant Knights of Labor, for example, increased membership from 50,000 in 1880 to more than 700,000 in the mid-1880s. The Knights later gave way to the far more moderate American Federation of Labor, but organized labor would have an important political role, both in the industrial states and at the national level. It would, as Ehrenreich (1985) noted, not only have a specific political impact, but would create a climate of disorder and a sense that American industrial life must be "stabilized." In a real sense, American social policy in the 20th century was the product of this desire for an orderly and decent society. Child labor, sweatshops, miserable wages, industrial accidents, urban slums, disease, and conflict all came with the grander aspects of social change and opportunity. The streets surely were not paved with gold for most individuals, and the realities of this new industrial order were harsh, indeed. This situation would eventually offend a large number of Americans who had a different vision of the American ideal.

Charity Organization Societies and Scientific Charity

Social welfare with regard to poor people in the late 19th century was not equipped to deal with such rapid change of people and things. Charitable agencies proliferated, but with little common purpose and little ideological change from their pre-war philosophy. Many states established boards of charities, but the leadership for a new movement came from the private Charity Organization Societies (COS), first established in the United States in the late 1870s. The COS role in shaping American social welfare and the social work profession was extraordinary. This was a period of radical American labor and agrarian populists, on the one hand, and social Darwinism, laissez-faire, and the Gilded Age, on the other hand. Among most government and business leaders, the ideas of unfettered competition were in vogue, and the prevailing attitude toward social benefits for the poor was largely a hostile one until after the turn of the century. The COS, in this context, managed to organize disparate charitable groups and become a dominant presence in all the major cities of the country. Most important, the COS invented "scientific charity" and in so doing established a rationale, a method, and a system of training that would lead directly to the social work profession as it is currently known (Katz, 1986).

Social Darwinism. Scientific charity was a concept based in social Darwinism. Sociologists Herbert Spencer, in England, and William Graham Sumner, in the United States, popularized the application of Darwinistic evolutionary theory to society. Social Darwinists saw in competition and the "shouldering aside of the weak" a process of social evolution that would reward the productive and able and punish the incapable and those who lacked the virtues of thrift, hard work, and far-sightedness. This was a compelling and influential idea, but one so unfriendly to social intervention or even simple humanitarianism that it seemed to be an unlikely basis for the administration of social benefits to poor people; however, this is the remarkable feat that the COS accomplished.

Development of casework. In practice, scientific charity was a matter of creating a common registry of the needy and ensuring that the applicants for aid were both "worthy," in the sense of an absence of personal aberration or depravity, and subject to a process that would soon be called social history and casework. The emphasis was on the individual, not the social environment. The process was not simply the application of 19th-century moralism, but something closer to an assessment of potentials and barriers that would be roughly recognizable today. Josephine Shaw Lowell was the often-stern ideologue of the early COS, and her warnings about unwise philanthropy that would undermine human character and will were strong and frequent (Stewart, 1911). This was the 19th century after all, and character and will played a major role in the understanding of human life. Still, the COS provided sustained relief to poor people in an inhospitable social and political climate, consolidated many social welfare interests and organizations, pioneered in record keeping and "social research," developed training programs, and sought to establish links with the universities of the time (which were seeking a new relevance through professional education). They also created a circumstance in which the social work profession *was* social policy with regard to the poor and child welfare for nearly the first third of the 20th century. If the COS can be faulted for a lack of interest in social reform, this fault would be corrected by Jane Addams and others who were active in the settlement movement and the larger Progressive movement.

THE PROGRESSIVE ERA

Origin in Ferment

Contrary to the myth of peaceful and orderly progress, the United States has endured many periods of conflict, including the late 19th century. Between 1880 and 1900, there were more than

30,000 strikes and lockouts involving 10 million American workers. From the Molly Maguires to the Pinkerton police and many others, violence in this class warfare was a common reality. Immigration changed the demographic face of American cities, and competitive industrial capitalism was seen as having a devastating impact on traditional values, a decent standard of living, and a common American purpose. The late 19th century gave rise to utopians, such as Henry George and Edward Bellamy, and radicals like Daniel Deleon, Bill Haywood, and Eugene Debs, all searching for some new model of social and political life. Out of this social, cultural, and political ferment came a uniquely American movement known as Progressivism that would have a profound impact on politics and policies, influence the social sciences and literature, and establish much of the social welfare agenda for the remainder of the 20th century (Ehrenreich, 1985).

Multifaceted Middle-Class Movement

Oddly enough, considering the social war between labor and industrialists and the competing politics and ideologies involved, Progressivism was a middle-class movement that emphasized parks and beautification, education, the "Americanization" of new citizens, and professionalization, as well as social insurance and regulatory controls. Immigration and the complexities of urban and industrial life did drive Progressivism, but as Hofstader (1955) noted, the typical Progressive and the typical immigrant were "vastly different." Herbert Croly's (1909) *The Promise of American Life* would become a Progressive handbook, but one has the impression that the Progressives, who were mostly Anglo-Saxon, had to remind themselves constantly that the immigrant was a hard-working, brave individual with a cultural heritage and great potential as an American. Without such reminders and much mental discipline, the old prejudices might not be held at bay (Hofstader, 1955).

Influential leaders. The Progressives counted among their ranks many prominent persons, including Jane Addams, George Herbert Mead, Robert Park, Richard Ely, Paul Douglas, and John Dewey. This was a group of people, all influential within academia and politics, who shared a common commitment to an active, morally responsible government (as opposed to a laissez-faire government) and a view that economics and politics were corrupted by forces that must be constrained by rule making. They also believed that although industrial capitalism might well be a great engine of wealth and spreading prosperity, it was at best a

polluting engine that needed to be finely tuned and its waste products taken care of.

Enduring cultural impact. The Progressives gave rise to a political party that would later nominate former Republican President Theodore Roosevelt as its presidential candidate in 1912 (and come in a strong third); however, this political party was not the essence of Progressivism, and Progressivism did not die with the decline of that party. It is best to think of Progressivism as a cultural movement that would show itself in many forms and in many venues. The National Consumer League, the Urban League, the National Child Labor Committee, the American Association for Labor Legislation (AALL), and the National Association for the Advancement of Colored People were all Progressive to a large extent, and they had at least as much influence in the classroom as in the legislature and with greater and more enduring effect (Crunden, 1982).

Social Welfare Outcomes

The social welfare consequence of the Progressive movement was great in three areas: prevention through "social insurance," the use of government regulation, and the role of professions in society.

Social insurance. With regard to social insurance, the Progressives, through such organizations as AALL, sought to popularize the idea that the collectivization of the normal risks of life was a superior form of provision to charity based on need. Their basic thesis was that charity is demeaning and corrupting to both the recipient and the giver and in any case is likely to be sporadic and meager. A better system is one in which citizens "contribute" to a common fund that would provide benefits on a "membership" basis without demeaning tests of character or need and without the presumption of deviance. Addams, for one, detested charity, and this new construct, derived from Europe, seemed to fit the multiethnic American democracy. It would eliminate the charitable worker and the consequent attitude of superiority of well-to-do individuals, it would create a common bond between diverse people, and it would be regularly budgeted and administered through public auspices.

The greatest success in applying this idea was with workers' compensation, and between 1910 and 1921 the majority of states passed such provisions. Health and unemployment insurance were rejected at that time, under pressure from organized medicine and industrial interests, but old age assistance and Aid to Dependent Children (ADC) were commonplace by 1920. In the case of these last two programs, conformance to the social insurance ideal was minimal. Mother's Aid and old age "pensions" were not social insurance except, perhaps, in spirit. Both had a means test, and eligibility had nothing to do with contributions. Although old age assistance was provided on the basis of some presumed previous social role and therefore had a somewhat lower stigma (and higher benefits), ADC was, from the beginning, fraught with tests of "worthiness" of one kind or another. Nevertheless, the programs put into place through Progressive pressure established a social welfare presence in every state and set into motion the steady expansion of public welfare programs, benefits, and recipients—an expansion that would set the stage for the federal government's assumption of funding for state programs and the development of a genuine social insurance system nationally (Skocpol, 1992).

Regulations. Progressives supported the concept of regulation and spearheaded many efforts on the state and national levels to use regulation for social reform. At the federal level, these efforts included the Interstate Commerce Commission, antitrust regulation, civil service and merit system requirements for employment, the Federal Trade Commission, banking regulation, and the Food and Drug Administration. At the state and local level, regulatory advances included the areas of child and women's labor, wages, housing and fire codes, public health, food processing, merit employment requirements, property zoning, and many political reforms, including referendum and recall.

Child labor, women's suffrage, immigration, and temperance were all major national issues and attracted the involvement of many prominent social workers. The extension of suffrage to women occurred in 1919, as did the passage of another constitutional amendment to prohibit the manufacture, sale, importation, and consumption of alcohol. Prohibition was promoted by its supporters as a social welfare policy that would protect women and children and promote employment and productivity. Likewise, immigration controls passed in 1921 were promoted not as nativism, but as rational planning for improved wages and working conditions and the stabilization of cities.

Professionalization. No aspect of the Progressive mind was more important than was the strong belief in education and professionalization. The idea of a profession—a group of people with knowledge and skills dedicated to the "public interest" and to whom responsibility for major social and human problems could be delegated—was a critical part of the Progressive strategy.

Middle-class, educated individuals were rational problem solvers, planners who would harmonize and stabilize society. Medicine, by the turn of the century, was establishing itself as a model profession and successfully fighting off the efforts of the insurance industry or local governments to render them employees.

The University of Chicago and Johns Hopkins were model universities, with schools in engineering, medicine, law, education, and other professional areas. The COS had established training programs associated with universities, and by 1920 several of these programs had developed into schools of social work. By 1930, there were many more schools of social work and the beginnings of a national system of curricular standards. The COS developed into what was to become family services; the public agencies expanded, especially in child welfare areas; and the mental hygiene movement produced professional opportunities in the 1920s. These factors, combined with the founding of the American Association of Social Work in 1921, along with other more specialized associations; support from the Russell Sage Foundation and other foundations; the centrality of such books as Richmond's *Social Diagnosis* (1917); and the publication of journals like *The Compass, The Survey,* and *The Family* all combined to create an active and visible profession of social work.

This new profession was concerned mostly with individual problems and adjustment and developed as its primary method a casework method that was strongly influenced by the COS and scientific charity. Social work had been admonished by Abraham Flexner in 1915 for not being adequately professional, and it had sought diligently to heed his words and develop something equivalent to a medical model for social work (Flexner, 1915). Casework met this criterion and it reflected the American commitment to individual responsibility and practical problem solving. This is not to say that the social reform influence on the Progressives, as embodied in the settlement houses and espoused by Addams, Florence Kelley, and Lillian Wald, was chased out. Far from it, for despite the profession's method of casework and its individual orientation, social work continued to represent a Progressive-style social environmentalism, preferring explanations of human problems in terms of the deficiencies of families, communities, and social structures. The predominant professional view was that these deficiencies could be compensated for by the development of well-staffed social services, as opposed to wholesale social reform, but it is the nature of professionals to think in such terms.

Major Accomplishments

The high point of Progressivism was certainly before World War I. The war and the ensuing political and economic developments cooled the Progressive passion in the 1920s. However, Progressives had accomplished a great deal. They had put on the social policy and political agenda virtually every important social problem of the 20th century: poverty, immigration, slums, child welfare, mental health, public health, and, of course, gender and race (if not exactly class). Furthermore, they had provided the means to deal with these problems: a government concerned with social welfare; groups mobilized for social action; professionals trained to work with such problems; and model programs of social insurance, social aid, and social services. By the late 1920s, they had created a context that would serve as a vessel for federal money and federal administration efforts in the 1930s and thereafter. They established the intellectual, political, and governmental context that would allow the United States to move toward the sort of welfare-state models that would have seemed unlikely a quarter of a century earlier.

Depression and the American Welfare State

The 1920s was a period of general economic prosperity and extravagance. This prosperity had benefited the social services and social welfare generally, even though it played a role in diminishing the political demand for social reform on any scale. The Republican party, which was the original home of Progressivism, was the predominant national party, giving the country the presidencies of Warren G. Harding, Calvin Coolidge, and Herbert Hoover. These presidents were, to some degree, in a Republican tradition that had been greatly influenced by Progressivism; Hoover especially represented a commitment to what has been termed "social engineering." Social engineering, as opposed to reform, seeks to intervene in specific ways to solve particular problems. In this spirit, the 1920s saw the continued expansion of child welfare, the development of a public health service and vocational education and rehabilitation, and the continuation of White House conferences on social matters that generated and focused support for social programs. Hoover was poorly equipped to deal with a massive economic downturn, however, and despite some efforts, such as the Reconstruction Finance Corporation Act of 1932, lost to Franklin Delano Roosevelt in the election of 1932.

Roosevelt Election

The Roosevelt administration came to power promising a "New Deal." The "old" deal had surely turned sour for millions of Americans who were facing unemployment, the loss of their homes, and poverty at unprecedented levels. The Great Depression was worldwide and would cause the United States and Europe to make some fundamental reassessments of politics and economics. Some of these reassessments would have disastrous results, but in the United States, the basic elements of the economy and governmental order would remain intact. Even so, the New Deal brought to the United States a version of the welfare state and established a pattern in social welfare that is still present (Trattner, 1989).

Roosevelt had been elected in 1932 largely because he was neither a Republican nor a Hoover. Both had worn out their welcome with the majority of Americans who were desperate for a return to some measure of normalcy and security. Manufacturing output had declined nearly 40 percent by 1932, average wages were down 25 percent, unemployment was approaching 25 percent, the banking system was near collapse, and there was organized disorder in the cities and factories and on the farms. Whatever the causes of the depression, it was clearly a dangerous thing by 1932, and Roosevelt was elected to deal with it. His campaign did little to suggest much beyond business as usual (promising a balanced budget, for example), but Roosevelt had a pragmatic and authoritative character and a strong desire to succeed. He observed that if he were to fail at being president in this time of crisis, he might well be the last president.

New Legislation and Federal Agencies

Roosevelt got to a fast start with a rash of legislation and a great deal of activity and planning at the White House. To deal with the immediate effects of the crisis, he established in 1933 the Federal Emergency Relief Administration (FERA), headed by Harry Hopkins, a social worker whom he had used in New York State in a similar capacity. FERA provided funds and no small amount of administrative directive to states for the purpose of providing relief. Whatever state programs that had been in place had largely gone bankrupt, and the demand to provide aid to the unemployed had long since exceeded the capacity of private agencies. Within a short time, FERA gave rise to work programs such as the Works Progress Administration and the Civilian Conservation Corps, which became the principal means of providing assistance to unemployed poor workers in the mid-1930s. Economic reform was also part of the overall strategy; it included the National Recovery Act, with its codes for industry that sought to establish wage and price controls and to ensure labor rights in a "planned economy," and the Agricultural Adjustment Act, which sought to reform the agricultural side of the economy through allotments for farm production and the stabilization of market prices. Both acts would succumb to the Supreme Court's determination that such far-reaching legislation went beyond constitutional limits, but both would have a substantial political effect and would shape later New Deal social policies.

Social security. With the congressional elections of 1934, Roosevelt substantially increased his party's political strength. The elections brought many liberals into Congress. Outside Congress, Huey Long, Father Coughlin, and others were proposing radical solutions and gaining national attention, adding a new dimension to Roosevelt's political challenge. To these developments were added the Supreme Court decisions, the increasing militancy of labor, the sluggish economic recovery, and defections of business support. As a result, the administration moved to develop a more dramatic and long-term program for social reform, including a new program for individual economic security. The latter program was begun by the appointment of a Committee on Social Security in June 1934, and the Social Security Act became law by January 1935. The Social Security Act is the basic document of the American social welfare system, establishing a federal social insurance system for old age, unemployment, and disability and a state-federal public assistance system, including aid for dependent children and for needy elderly and disabled persons. In addition, the act established a system of federal grants to states in related social services areas. To the social security system must be added the Wagner Act, which substantially increased the rights of organized labor; the Fair Labor Standards Act, which regulated wages and hours; and a collection of programs in vocational rehabilitation, public health, housing, and child welfare.

Welfare state. More than any specific piece of legislation, the New Deal brought to American life an unprecedented federal-level focus, a new progressive coalition, and a permanent strengthening of the federal government that would place it at the center of responsibility for the character of American society and the welfare of its citizens. If the welfare state was not present in the United States

in every programmatic piece (there was no health care, for example), it was nevertheless present in spirit and intention. The welfare state idea that would be well established in England and Europe after World War II would be based on three areas of government commitment: full employment, the prevention and relief of poverty, and universal services for basic needs. Although these commitments were organized in various ways in Western countries, what emerged is often referred to as the Keynesian-Beveridge welfare state, noting the contributions of the economist John Maynard Keynes to policies of full employment and economic stabilization and of Lord Beveridge to social insurance and services. The United States lacked national health insurance, it allowed considerable variation by state in its federal system, and it did not replace all the "residual" with "institutional" social programs. However, it took its place among the welfare states, and within a few decades it would be allotting nearly 20 percent of its gross national product (GNP) to social welfare.

Separation of Insurance and Assistance

Earnings versus need. The social policies that emerged from the New Deal and were embodied in the Social Security Act contained a distinction between social insurance and public assistance that was at once practical and troublesome—practical because such a policy based on work and contribution created both a mechanism for funding and a powerful link to an important social value, but troublesome because those involved in uncovered work or who were out of the labor force had to have their needs provided otherwise, which meant the continuation of a means-tested charity-like system, albeit publicly funded and organized. This distinction created, on the one hand, a popular, politically acceptable, non-means-tested system of social insurance providing benefits to those who had "earned" them by virtue of work and, on the other hand, a much smaller, state-based system of public aid providing benefits on the basis of need. Thus, the worthiness problem was solved on the social insurance side by the device of work-based contribution, but the problem continued for those who relied on public assistance. Although other countries developed more varied means to provide nearly universal aid on a presumed worthiness basis (children's allowances, for example), the United States created a system that would prove to be a philosophical, administrative, legal, and programmatic problem. Social insurance grew in every sense to become a permanent feature of the American political and social landscape. Public assistance, particularly Aid to Families with Dependent Children, drew criticism and various welfare "reform" efforts from the beginning.

Impact on citizens. The lessons of this separation of public aid and social insurance seemed clear enough: Social policy must either effectively incorporate social and cultural values that relate to the evaluation of individuals or use programs to create common social and political interests among large groups of presumably "worthy," dissimilar people. The separation of social insurance and public aid in the American model segregated the very poor and marginal people in the labor force from mainstream social programs and created a vulnerable class that was dependent on programs that were less than generously funded and always seemed to be at the center of controversy. The losers in this American policy model, of course, were women, children, and people of color, all of whom had a lower probability of having their needs well met by work-based social insurance.

Throughout this period, women continued to play a prominent role in social welfare policy and program development. They had achieved suffrage in 1919 and had leadership roles in many organizations that promoted social services and social reform, but the policies that developed from the depression emphasized the traditional role of women in social and economic life and therefore tied the interests of women to family, specifically to maternity, child care, and marriage. Some groups, particularly African Americans, had a more visible role in the New Deal than in any previous administration, but the New Deal coalition depended heavily on southern Democrats and thus was constrained from advocating full equality. This was a time of legal segregation in the American South, and although organizations, such as the National Association for the Advancement of Colored People or the Brotherhood of Sleeping Car Porters and Maids had some visibility, civil rights gains were hard to come by. The employment programs of the New Deal did try to reduce discrimination, and Roosevelt ultimately created a Fair Employment Practices Commission in 1941, but despite these modest gains, programs like the New Deal's Agricultural Adjustment Act and later agricultural programs displaced thousands of minority farmworkers while compensating farm owners, and programs like Aid to Dependent Children would come to be seen as both inhibiting the economic participation of women and contributing to family problems.

WORLD WAR II, 1940s, AND 1950s

The New Deal lost some of its zeal with the elections of 1938 and the shift of focus to the instability of Europe. The impending war stimulated the American economy; by 1941, the unemployment rate dropped below 10 percent and by 1944, it was 1.2 percent, a low for the century. Roosevelt died just before the war ended in 1945, and he was succeeded by Vice President Harry S Truman.

Economic Concerns

The administration had been concerned that the end of the war would bring an inevitable economic downturn and a possible return to the depression. This concern had been the partial basis for the 1941 report of the National Resources Planning Board concerning the basic needs and rights of citizens—a report that was similar to the Beveridge report in England. Roosevelt had proposed the Economic Bill of Rights in 1944, seeking to establish full employment as a national goal and to engage in the sort of Keynesian fiscal policies that would support it. After much deliberation and compromise, the product of this proposal was the Full Employment Act of 1946, which specified that full employment was a primary goal of the government and established the Council of Economic Advisors and a system of economic indicators used to measure the country's national economic health. The war, and the draft used to support it, had revealed common health and mental health problems among inductees, and the administration was successful in expanding the Veterans Administration and in passing the Mental Health Act of 1946, which created the National Institute of Mental Health and ultimately ended the state institutional monopoly on public treatment programs and ushered in the era of community-based services.

The shift to the left and the reformist wave that occurred in Western Europe after the war and institutionalized much of the welfare state in Great Britain, West Germany, Belgium, and elsewhere did not occur in the United States. Despite the Truman administration's good intentions, there was little sense in the United States of a country being remade, as there was in Europe, and the continuation of the conservative Congress showed increasing divisions over civil rights. As a result, although there was no wholesale attack on the American social welfare system, there was little political support for expanding it.

Social and Cultural Developments

The 1950s was a period of little social welfare programmatic development, but of much social and cultural development that would influence the subsequent decade. The GI bill expanded opportunities for Americans to obtain a higher education, general prosperity created new economic opportunities, and mobility around the country was high. The Supreme Court ruled against segregated public education in 1954, and Little Rock, Arkansas, became the site of the test of the federal government's commitment in 1956.

President Dwight D. Eisenhower presided over an administration that witnessed the rapid rise in East–West tension that would become the full-blown cold war. Despite Eisenhower's interest in lowering military spending, cutting taxes, and allowing the economy to grow its own way, commitments to European defense, costly missile development, and threats such as Germany and Cuba frustrated his plans.

Eisenhower had few social welfare interests beyond education, but his administration had a working relationship with the Democratic leadership in Congress, especially Lyndon B. Johnson, and supported the shoring up and expansion of social security. The administration also reorganized federal programs into a new cabinet-level Department of Health, Education, and Welfare in 1953. Later, when states sought to "reform" welfare through "suitable home" or other provisions, this department intervened. The most notable of these interventions occurred in 1961, when Secretary Arthur Fleming stipulated that Louisiana could not remove 2,300 children from Aid to Dependent Children roles without making some arrangement for their welfare. The administration did support both the Federal Housing Authority and urban renewal housing programs and, however reluctantly, also supported school desegregation orders (with federal troops in the case of Little Rock) and sought the continued desegregation of the armed forces.

Structuralist Views

In the 1950s, despite what is viewed as a time of political conservatism, American academics and intellectuals who were concerned with American social life often emphasized poverty, racism, urban decay, delinquency, and the like. Social scientists, such as William Whyte, Albert Cohen, Lloyd Ohlin, Kenneth Clark, and Robert Merton, all represented a structuralist view, which emphasized that human behavior is a product of social structure and the social roles created by structure. From the structuralist perspective, juvenile delinquency, for example, was not so much a matter of pathological character, as a matter of the "structure of opportunity" that would create a "subculture" of the gang.

John Kenneth Galbraith, who wrote *The Affluent Society* in 1958, and Michael Harrington, who followed with *The Other America* in 1962, influenced a new and larger generation of college students in the 1950s and, combined with important demographic and political changes that occurred in the decades after the New Deal, produced a new politics and a new policy direction in the 1960s (Diggins, 1992).

KENNEDY, JOHNSON, AND THE NEW WELFARE

John F. Kennedy was narrowly elected president in 1960 over Richard M. Nixon, who had been Eisenhower's vice president. Kennedy, a moderate Democratic senator from Massachusetts, defeated the much more liberal Hubert H. Humphrey to gain the Democratic party nomination. He came to office promising to "get the country moving again," by which he meant a tax cut that would stimulate the economy and to close the "missile gap" with the Soviet Union. However, a movement more powerful than politics would pervade the Kennedy administration and, indeed, American politics in general and forge a new vision of American social policy. This movement was the civil rights movement.

Civil Rights Movement

The civil rights movement had been a continuous element in American life, but it took on a new character after World War II. Beginning primarily with the Montgomery bus boycott and the response to the murder of Emmett Till, it led in a few short years to widespread protests and often violent response by southern public authorities and segregationist individuals and groups. Martin Luther King, a young Baptist minister, became a national figure; the Student Non-violent Coordinating Committee brought thousands of college students to work for voter registration in the deep South; and many Americans heard of Selma, Alabama, for the first time.

The Kennedy administration was pressed to support a variety of measures that were introduced into Congress, and after some period of reluctance, the administration proposed its own civil rights bill. In June 1963, President Kennedy gave an impassioned television speech on behalf of the bill and the civil rights of African Americans, a speech that was seen as courageous and a position that came to symbolize the Kennedy presidency for many (Jansson, 1988).

That Civil Rights bill passed Congress in 1964 and became one of the hallmarks of American social policy, but not before Kennedy was murdered in Dallas and Lyndon B. Johnson, an accomplished legislator but an unhappy vice president, assumed the presidency.

Social Welfare Legislation

Shift to development. Johnson inherited from Kennedy not only the pending civil rights bill, but some notable social welfare accomplishments. Kennedy had succeeded in getting the Manpower Development and Training Act passed in 1962 and establishing the Area Redevelopment Agency in 1961. The former created the first jobs program since the New Deal, and the latter led to the Appalachian Regional Commission and other programs for "depressed areas." Both represented a shift from the "old welfare" of economic security through transfer payments to the "new welfare" of opportunity and development. This shift was accompanied by the rapid increase in public assistance roles in the early 1960s and the perceived failure of the "services strategy" of the 1962 amendments to the Social Security Act, which lowered caseloads in public welfare and increased federal support for social services. This shift also reflected a new commitment to opportunity, not the least of which was to be for people of color. The prevailing view was that economic and political opportunity structures had been closed to many Americans and that this situation had to end. Such a change could not be accomplished through a reliance on traditional social welfare programs that tended either to reflect or reinforce limitations on opportunities.

Mental health. Optimism and reformism were manifested in any number of programs, including the administration's interest in promoting alternative models of mental health care. The result was the passage of the Community Mental Health Centers Act in 1963, which emphasized a preventive public health model and created the context for rapid deinstitutionalization over the following decade.

Poverty and economic opportunity. The Johnson administration continued this expression of reformist interest and sought to expand this emphasis on opportunity and the elimination of old barriers in a number of ways. President Johnson had continued a Kennedy task force on poverty and in 1964 proposed the Economic Opportunity Act (EOA), an ambitious program that called on communities to organize themselves to fight poverty and to design programs that would be suited to their particular needs. Based on the Ford Foundation's Grey Areas project, especially Mobilization for Youth in New York City, the EOA

allowed cities to establish Community Action Boards as nonprofit agencies and allowed these boards to submit proposals that would be funded by the Office of Economic Opportunity. The innovations were numerous, but most important were the bypassing of city governments in favor of direct funding of citizens' groups and the requirements for "maximum feasible participation" of poor people, meaning representation on agency boards, the hiring of poor people for staff positions, and attempts to "mobilize" them for community action. The community action programs were controversial for all these reasons, and by 1966 were tamed by new requirements for the involvement of public officials and oversight by the state governments. Nevertheless, the idea that poverty was a product of limited opportunity and inadequate representation of poor citizens in community decision making was influential and led to requirements for citizen participation in governmental programs in many areas of public services and policy.

Other programs. In addition to the EOA, the Johnson administration successfully supported many other programs of consequence. The Food Stamps Act of 1964 and the Civil Rights Act of 1965 extended voting rights and created the Equal Opportunity Commission. Medicare and Medicaid (Titles XVIII and XIX, respectively, of the Social Security Act) passed in 1965, as did the Elementary and Secondary Education Act, which extended federal aid to schools with a high proportion of low-income children, and the Older Americans Act, which established Area Agencies on Aging. The Johnson administration was the most active in social welfare since Roosevelt's New Deal (Katz, 1986).

Income Maintenance and Work Incentives

During this time of activism and the strong interaction between the civil rights and antipoverty movements, there were those who believed in a more overt, citizens' rights-based system of income support. This belief influenced many proposals, from establishing more clearly the legal rights of welfare recipients (which the Supreme Court did by 1970, partly as a result of the Legal Services Program initiated under the EOA) to programs for a guaranteed income with few questions asked. President Johnson established a number of task forces to make recommendations on income maintenance. These task forces led both to research studies of income maintenance experiments and to the Heineman Commission in 1969, which reported on violence to the next president, Richard M. Nixon.

In 1967, Congress passed amendments to the public assistance titles of the Social Security Act, referred to as the Work Incentive Program (WIN) amendments. These amendments represented a dramatic shift in policy and a recognition that there was some overlap of public assistance benefits with low-end wages and, consequently, some work-disincentive effort of public assistance. Before 1967, there was no provision in the public assistance programs for work incentives. There were provisions for discounting work expenses, but there was no policy that held that a recipient of Aid to Families with Dependent Children (AFDC) or other public aid would be better off by working. The 1967 amendments sought to establish this very principle through a rule that allowed the setting aside of a small portion of earnings before subtracting income from needs to determine the state benefits. The WIN amendments resulted in little discernible increase in labor force participation among recipients of public welfare, but did begin a long period of search in American social policy for a "work"-based public aid system. The Johnson administration supported this reform of the "old" welfare system, but further pursuit of this idea was left to subsequent, mostly Republican, administrations.

NIXON, FORD, AND CARTER

President Johnson declined to run in 1968, chased by the Vietnam War into retirement. His vice president, Hubert Humphrey, distanced himself from the administration's war policy after the violent Democratic convention in Chicago, but lost a close election to Richard M. Nixon, who was completing a remarkable political recovery.

Nixon's Initiatives

Despite his California upbringing, Nixon was an "eastern" Republican, as opposed to the "western" Republican, Barry Goldwater, who had lost badly in 1964. Nixon always incorporated conservative political themes in his public statements, but the administration's policy positions were not typical of conservatives at the time. With its policy of "détente," determination to open relations with China, and several notable social policy proposals, the Nixon administration seemed determined to break new ground and to operate without rigid ideological constraints.

The Nixon administration came to an unhappy end over the Watergate break-in in 1973, but not before the administration had supported separation of the adult categories from public aid, creating the Supplementary Security Income program; a major expansion of the Food Stamp program; increased funding for social services under Title XX of the Social Security Act; the reinstitution of federal support for job training through the Comprehensive Employment and Training Act; establishment of the Occupational Safety and Health Administration; automatic cost-of-living adjustments in social security benefits; and the Child Abuse Prevention Act of 1973. However, the administration seemed to have little interest or faith in the social services and impounded funds for budgetary purposes that would have benefited social services, including community mental health centers. In retrospect this latter action seems especially unfortunate because it occurred in the context of court decisions that rapidly reduced the institutional population and increased demands on providers of community services.

Family Assistance Plan

The Nixon administration believed that the policies of Kennedy and Johnson in the War on Poverty had been little more than "heat and air" and had succeeded only in raising expectations and urban tempers. Nixon strongly believed in work and opposed public welfare, especially AFDC. He appointed a Democrat, Daniel Patrick Moynihan, as his urban affairs adviser, and although Moynihan had characterized the War on Poverty in a critical analysis as the *Maximum Feasible Misunderstanding* (1969), he convinced the president that a new approach to support for the poor was needed. The result was the Family Assistance Plan (FAP). FAP would have effectively nationalized the administration and benefit structure of public assistance, provided benefits to two-parent families, and incorporated work incentives. It would have subsidized poor people who were working, as well as those who were out of the labor market, simultaneously expanding eligibility and changing the mix of "welfare" recipients. However, it would have also effectively reduced benefits in some states and produced a somewhat less "eligibility-like" benefit structure. Although this plan was passed by the House of Representatives, it failed in the Senate, owing, in substantial part, to an odd coalition between conservatives who feared a major expansion of welfare provision at the federal level and Democratic liberals, who were influenced by the National Welfare Rights Organization and others, including NASW, that believed the benefits were too low and the work requirements were too stringent. Nevertheless, the FAP debate seemed to establish an enduring agenda for welfare reform and produced the concrete development of federalizing the old age assistance, aid to the blind, and aid to the disabled provisions of the public assistance titles of the Social Security Act.

Social Welfare Revolution

The years after Nixon were ones of declining federal budgetary strength and weak leadership from the White House. The administration of Gerald R. Ford exercised budgetary control through the veto, and the administration of Jimmy Carter, although a source of some interesting and comprehensive proposals, including an expanded version of FAP, was largely incapable of moving Congress and thus produced no lasting accomplishments in social welfare.

The lack of new initiatives should not suggest stagnation, however, because the 1970s witnessed what Patterson (1981) has called a social welfare "revolution." It was not a revolution of policy and program, but of the effect of past policy decisions combined with social developments. The revolution was composed of a startling decrease in the number and proportion of poor people and an equally surprising expansion of existing social welfare programs and expenditures.

Reduction in poverty. The United States had officially been counting the number of Americans in poverty since 1961, when the Social Security Administration established $3,000 as the poverty line for an urban family of four. The poverty line had been adjusted yearly for cost-of-living increases, and by 1976, the poverty standard had increased to $5,500. In 1961, nearly 40 million Americans (22 percent of the population) fell below the standard; by 1976, there were 24.6 million Americans in poverty, or about 12 percent of the total population (U.S. Bureau of the Census, 1978). Optimists also liked to point to the fact that the poverty measure did not take into account "income" from in-kind programs, such as food stamps and Medicaid, both of which grew substantially during this period. If the benefits of such programs were counted, they contended, the poverty rate could be reduced by an additional one-third or more. Such an impressive decline in poverty may have occurred earlier in the century— and there was good reason to believe it had—but there was no official census counting the number of Americans in poverty in the earlier periods. However, this apparent success of American capitalism and government policy and programs was greeted with few cheers of joy and accomplishment.

The problem was that much of the reduction in poverty was traceable to increases in social spending and consequent income transfers. The "old welfare" had finally struck, and although it was effective, it was costly and not soul satisfying. The United States wanted to reduce poverty through social opportunities and individual initiative; because of its work-ethic culture, reducing poverty through social welfare, especially public assistance, was not what its citizens had in mind. Instead, the country wanted something more akin to the "new" welfare that 1960s-era leaders had promised: a reduction in poverty through increased opportunities, education, and social services. The old welfare had reduced poverty to a level that would have been unimaginable to earlier reformers, but it submitted a sizable bill as well: Expenditures in social welfare increased at an annual rate of 7.2 percent between 1964 and 1976, a rate twice as high as that in the previous decade; social welfare as a percentage of the GNP had increased from a low (by western European standards) of 7 percent in 1960 to a more respectable 17 percent by 1976; and overall spending, which had been only $53 billion in 1960, had become $340 billion by 1976 and more than $500 billion by 1980. Much of this increase had occurred in social security and Medicare, owing to both the "graying" of the population and the expansion of benefits during the 1960s and early 1970s: Medicaid, food stamps, AFDC, and unemployment insurance all increased three to five times (in constant dollars) over the period (U.S. Social Security Administration, 1992).

Increases in active interest groups. In addition to the growth in social welfare programs and expenditures in the 1970s, there was also a dramatic increase in the number and types of active and visible interest groups that were vying for social policy consideration. President Kennedy had established the Commission on the Status of Women in 1961, Betty Friedan had published *The Feminine Mystique* in 1963, and the National Organization for Women had been established in 1966, beginning a new phase of the movement for social equality for women. Likewise a "gray" lobby was developing through such organizations as the American Association of Retired Persons, and people with disabilities, who were more visible because of the Vietnam War, were represented by organizations like the American Coalition of Citizens with Disabilities. Furthermore, the United States had come to recognize that there were Puerto Ricans in New York City, Cubans in Miami, and Mexican Americans in California, and the image of the country as a European country with an African American component was slowly giving way to a more genuinely multicultural one. In 1969 the gay rights movement in New York City was galvanized by the so-called Stonewall riot and later spread across the country to press for an end to persecution and discrimination. There emerged new conservative groups, including the "Christian Right," which were concerned with abortion, prayer in schools, and other cultural issues. In short, the 1970s was a decade of the proliferation of political and social interests and a "rights" revolution in politics and law. The context of social welfare policy-making became more complex, more participatory, and more overtly and specifically ideological. These ideologies were not the old ones of class and economic interest, but new ones of gender, ethnicity, religion, and sexual preference that diluted the politics of class and thus altered the character of support for the welfare state in its traditional form.

THE REAGAN ERA AND BUSH PRESIDENCY

Repackaging of American Conservatism
The conservative ideology that was vying for American political support was certainly not new, but it, too, would undergo something of a transformation. American conservatism had been relatively dormant for decades, and, indeed, there was much talk of the end of ideology and the irrelevance of the "Left" and "Right" in American politics. American conservatism in the 1960s and 1970s had been associated with segregationists, rabid anticommunists, isolationists, protectionists, and assorted organizations largely on the political fringe. Conservatism in the Republican party had suffered from Senator Barry Goldwater's vote against the 1963 Civil Rights Act and his poor showing in the presidential election of 1964.

However, conservatism, in the sense of a commitment to limited government, free markets, and individual responsibility, was old, and it only took some effort to repackage these ideas, dissociate them from overt racism and reactionism, and develop an effective spokesperson to give them some renewed influence. Robert Nisbet, Milton Friedman, and William Buckley had been gaining some followers on American campuses for many years, and with the decline of the Republican party under Nixon, the time was ripe for a new voice and new leadership. This leadership would be found in the person of Ronald Reagan, who won the presidential election of 1980 over a beleaguered Jimmy Carter and went on to be something of a national hero, at least for a time.

Reagan was part of what appeared to be a large-scale political phenomenon. Margaret Thatcher had been chosen as prime minister in the United Kingdom in 1978, and most European elections were showing a declining influence of leftist parties and a deterioration of the labor base on which they had been built. This decline of the Left was partly due to changing "postindustrial" economies that simply had a smaller traditional labor class and partly to the high costs of welfare state programs. High taxes, low productivity, and no-growth economies were all blamed on welfare state policies, and many electorates were convinced that something else was needed. The United States did not have European-level tax rates, but had generally higher levels of unemployment (especially before 1975) and higher rates of growth. It also had lower levels of social protection and services, but the political themes used against welfare states in Europe also worked well in the United States.

Tax Cuts and Block Grants
Public bureaucracy, economic stagnation, suffocating taxes, the undermining of self-reliance, the "starvation" of the military, and excessive regulation were the common themes of the conservative attack on social welfare as it had been defined. President Reagan came into office intent on making a difference and reordering the priorities of the U.S. government. The first of the administration's victories came in the form of the Omnibus Budget Reconciliation Act (OBRA) of 1981, a comprehensive piece of legislation that substantially cut funding for social services, generally tightened eligibility requirements to focus on the "truly needy," and created seven block-grant areas to states, greatly increasing the latitude of state governments. OBRA was an indication of things to come, in that it suggested a strategy of creating budgetary shortages that would force Congress to make cuts, rather than going after particular programs and doing battle with the often well-organized constituents of those programs. It was better to fight on the high ground of lowering taxes and controlling expenditures, things that nearly everyone claimed to support. The first of the Reagan tax cuts came shortly after OBRA was passed, and the administration made changes in the administration of taxes, regulatory processes and rules, and the enforcement of civil rights legislation. The administration appeared sympathetic to the "New Right" of the "Moral Majority," but did little substantively to implement its agenda (Anderson, 1988).

Social Security Changes
Despite the hostility expressed toward social welfare in general, the Reagan administration recognized certain realities and did not, in the end, make a frontal assault on the basic structure of social welfare, despite its opportunity to do so when the social security system was faced with dire predictions based on income and payouts to

the various trust funds in the social insurance system. Older people had increased as a percentage of the population, the post–World War II baby boom wave was still under way, and low birthrates suggested that in the future, proportionately far fewer workers would contribute to social security. The social security system was said to be facing bankruptcy, and President Reagan, who had earlier characterized social security as a "pyramid scheme," seemed to have a unique political opportunity. However, a recession was in progress, the Republican party counted on older voters, and preliminary efforts to cut benefits in social security and Medicare had been rebuffed. Therefore, in 1982, the president appointed a bipartisan commission to study social security.

The commission recommended that the retirement age should be increased gradually to 67, that the benefits of people with incomes above a certain specified level should be taxed, and that cost-of-living adjustments of social security benefits should be delayed. These changes, adopted in 1983, substantially shored up the system, producing high levels of surplus in the retirement trust account by the early 1990s. President Reagan, perhaps the most ideologically conservative president in the 20th century, had strengthened the centerpiece of the American welfare system. However, one of these reforms in social security that was adopted would prove to be the first "chink" in the social insurance armor: The taxation of benefits and the suggestion that benefits need not go to people of higher income is in effect a means test, a step toward making social security operate less "universally" and more like "welfare."

New Federalism
With regard to "welfare," which at this point consisted entirely of AFDC, President Reagan pursued a policy that, on the one hand, abandoned much of what previous Republican administrations had sought and, on the other hand, greatly expanded the role of state governments, consistent with the Republican emphasis on the "new" federalism. The White House Policy Office concluded that work incentives had little impact on labor participation of adult recipients of AFDC and thus sought to encourage the states to implement "workfare" requirements that would exchange work, however modest in hours and type, for benefits. In addition, the administration pursued a policy of "let a thousand flowers bloom" and promoted experimentation by the states by granting waivers from federal regulations. This last policy gathered momentum slowly but had an impact in the following administration of George Bush. In addition, the Reagan administration strongly supported the enforcement of child-support regulations, increasing federal support and cooperation with states in the collection of child-support payments. It also implemented a private-sector alternative to the work and training program established by the Comprehensive Education and Training Act—the Job Training Partnership Act of 1982.

Total federal outlays for social welfare continued to increase under President Reagan, but the annual rate of increase was down to 5 percent to 6 percent, as opposed to the 10 percent typical of the previous decade. As federal expenditures slowed, however, state and local government costs continued to rise at near-1970s levels. Many states and localities found that their share of spending for various social programs, often in the form of federally mandated expenditures, required substantial increases in taxes and reduced budgetary flexibility.

Privatization
The overall human and social service sector grew substantially in the 1980s, primarily in the voluntary and for-profit sectors. Title XX of the Social Security Act had allowed for the rapid expansion of contracts with private providers for services in the 1970s, and despite caps on spending and effective cuts in allocations during the Reagan era, and the number of agencies and organizations, employees, and budgets in the private sector increased. On the for-profit side, human service corporations, most evident in hospitals, nursing homes, and home health care and day care agencies, emerged as major actors in the delivery and management of services. The Reagan administration appointed a "privatization" commission and supported privatization with considerable rhetoric, as well as some operational and policy decisions. Privatization in its purest sense involves the divestment of public resources and the substitution of private ownership, management, and accountability. In the United States, however, it usually refers to the use of market forces to deliver publicly funded services in a way that provides for choice, competition, and cost constraint and diminishes the government's investment in permanent facilities, services, and personnel. The postal service, garbage collection, park management, data management, air traffic control, weather information, housing finance, and other services have all been the target of privatization plans. Conservatives, having a great deal of faith in the ability of economic markets and little faith in planning and administration, have proposed vouchers in education, health care, housing, and social services.

Such vouchers would allow individual consumers to select among competing providers. In some areas—notably food programs, special education, and housing—vouchers are more widely used, and, as was noted earlier, the private provision of health care services is the norm.

Reduced Sensitivity to Social Issues

The Reagan years, then, witnessed a political attack on the softer side of the welfare state and a significant reduction in federal and, to a degree, state funds allocated to the social services. However, the "core" of the American social welfare system not only survived, but was enhanced in some ways. In addition, there was a greater diversity in the options for funding, managing with a consequent growth in the size and importance of the voluntary and for-profit sectors. Nevertheless, the general sensitivity to social issues seemed to decline, especially in the first half of the Reagan years.

Homelessness. Perhaps no issue symbolized this decline better than homelessness. Homelessness was apparent in major American cities in the late 1970s, but the early 1980s brought reports of substantial increases in the number of homeless. The recession of the early 1980s, the cumulative effects of the deinstitutionalization of treatment for mental illness and substance abuse, the breakdown of families, and the limited supply at the lower end of the housing market all combined to contribute to the homeless stream. Estimates of the number of homeless individuals varied widely, from a few hundred thousand to many millions, and advocacy organizations gained national attention. Although it supported the McKinney Homeless Assistance Act of 1987, the Reagan administration responded with little sympathy. Its lukewarm policy proposals and the White House's observations that the homeless were mentally ill and chose to live on the street seemed to many to capture the administration's lack of heart.

Bush Presidency

George Bush became president in 1988, after eight years as vice president, promising a "kinder and gentler" America, which many understood to be a mild criticism of the previous administration. President Bush had a personal history of involvement with education and the voluntary social welfare sector that suggested a more generous role for government, but the realities of budgetary politics allowed few additional resources to be spent on domestic programs. The tax reductions of the mid-1980s, combined with Gramm–Rudman–

Hollings deficit controls and President Bush's campaign pledge of no new taxes, kept a firm grip on even the most modest of program intentions.

The administration did agree to the Civil Rights Act of 1991, which expanded the rights of those who were discriminated against to seek relief, but the legislation did not go as far as many civil rights advocates would have liked in reducing the complainant's burden of proof. The administration also supported the Americans with Disabilities Act of 1990, which dramatically increased protection from discrimination in housing, work, and public accommodation for those with disabilities. Overall, the decline of the Cold War, the collapse of the Soviet Union, and developments in Panama and Kuwait gave the Bush administration a far stronger reputation for foreign policy than for domestic policy. In the meantime, the economy slipped into a recession, and the Los Angeles riots in 1992 further reminded everyone that the problems of race and poverty were still real.

THE DEMOCRATS RETURN

President Bush was defeated after one term by Democrat Bill Clinton. Bush was regarded by many as the president of "gridlock," presiding over a divided and ineffective legislative system and incapable of controlling either the budget or the nation's economy. President Clinton promised to get the economy moving again, to end gridlock, and to address some long-neglected social issues. He also promised to reform the nation's health care system and to "end welfare as we know it." He entered the White House with an apparent personal interest in social welfare and experience with many social welfare programs as governor of Arkansas.

Emphasis on Domestic Issues

President Clinton appointed a more varied and decidedly more domestically oriented cabinet and sought to tackle a number of social matters. In the first year of the Clinton administration, he moved to support a family leave provision, reduce federal regulatory controls on abortion services, and end discrimination against gay men and lesbians in the U.S. military. The major policy thrust, however, would come in the area of health care. By appointing a task force chaired by Hillary Clinton, the White House sought both to dramatize the high costs of health care in the United States (the highest per capita in the world) and to point out the millions of citizens who do not have health coverage or who lose it because of health problems. Emphasizing basic principles, including universality of coverage and cost control, the administration proposed a far-reaching health scheme that would enroll all Americans in a "health alliance" that would seek bids from providers on a basic insurance package. Although hardly a federalized national health service plan, it would have nevertheless altered dramatically the administrative role of the federal government and created, for the first time, a genuinely national health care structure in the American government. Congress adjourned, however, without adopting any significant health care legislation. The dramatic resurgence of Republicans in the 1994 general election and the consequent control of both houses in Congress may support the passage of some sort of smaller-scale health care legislation in the next Congress.

Welfare Reform

The Clinton administration's plans in relation to welfare (that is, AFDC) remain less clear at this writing, although the basic outlines of a proposal have been drawn. President Clinton has proposed the time-limited receipt of AFDC, somewhat like unemployment insurance, that would require an individual to work or prepare for work at the end of two years. One question is, of course, where will these individuals work? Because gainful employment for people who are less skilled, less experienced, and less educated has not been easy to come by in recent decades, the administration seems to be considering various proposals for subsidizing the employment of former AFDC recipients. The cost of doing so and the associated need for child care services, as well as the feasibility and fairness of such a plan, are currently under consideration. As with health care, the Republican control of the House and Senate promises attention to welfare reform, although the character of the reform may well go beyond what the White House would prefer.

CONCLUSION

The budgetary constraints of the 1980s are still present, despite the Clinton administration's success with a budget agreement that included major tax increases. Therefore, it is too early to speculate on the administration's ultimate accomplishments in the social policy area. However, it is clear that the election of President Clinton and the simultaneous Democratic control of both houses of Congress did not unleash a wave of social reform legislation or reinvigorate the "old" welfare state idea. With Republicans in control of the Congress, the Clinton administration faces a different sort of activism, and the social policy agenda may shift dramatically to the right. There is, however,

some reason to believe that some sort of national health plan will emerge. Regardless of its form, it will represent the one element of the welfare state package of benefits and services that has been missing in the American social welfare system, but it will be organized on the basis of a public–private mix and decentralization that certainly does not reflect the welfare state tradition (Mishra, 1990).

We approach the 21st century with a social welfare system that has worked only partially well. Poverty has been substantially reduced over the century in terms of income, but the remaining poverty rate, which is still quite high for women and many racial–ethnic groups, seems particularly dangerous. Considerable income security for elderly people has been achieved, but in ways that may be difficult to sustain in the future. The U.S. system of public assistance has suffered a collapse of political support, and some sort of welfare reform that ties benefits to work seems both inevitable and long overdue. Unemployment has remained a problem even during periods of sustained economic growth, and the ability of the U.S. economy in its early postindustrial state to absorb all its people is in question. Public education, once the great pride of American public accomplishment, is widely said to be ill suited to educate the work force of the 21st century. Health care, although apparently effective, is costly and uneven and demands some sort of reorganization. In short, the five great "specters" identified by Lord Beveridge—want, disease, ignorance, squalor, and idleness—have been tamed but not eradicated by 20th-century developments (Kaus, 1992).

It is tempting to observe that the United States approaches the next century much as it approached the last: with a rapidly changing economy, a rapidly changing demography, high rates of immigration and family compositional change, challenges of urban poverty and subculture, a policy in search of a consensus, and a widespread desire for things to be made right. In the first part of this century, there emerged a major social reform movement, based in the professions and the universities, that would provide much of the social agenda for the century—social work as we know it. This movement produced a uniquely American social welfare paradigm, embodying the complexities of a federal governmental structure; a cultural emphasis on equality, individual merit, and responsibility; and a mix of private and public provision. All these elements remain. Indeed, the view that social needs are met through a multitude of sources—the state, the market, the voluntary sector, and the family—is stronger and more pertinent than ever. The vastness of these resources, combined with the largely innovative, pragmatic, and less ideological character of American social welfare development, suggests much hope for the next century of social welfare.

REFERENCES

Anderson, M. (1988). *Revolution*. San Diego: Harcourt Brace Jovanovitch.

Croly, H. (1909). *The promise of American life*. New York: Macmillan.

Crunden, R. (1982). *Ministers of reform: The progressive achievists in American civilization, 1889–1920*. New York: Basic Books.

de Schweinitz, K. (1943). *England's road to social security*. Philadelphia: University of Pennsylvania Press.

Diggins, J. (1992). *The rise and fall of the American left*. New York: W. W. Norton.

Ehrenreich, J. (1985). *The altruistic imagination: A history of social work and social policy in the U.S.* Ithaca, NY: Cornell University Press.

Flexner, A. (1915). Is social work a profession? In *Studies in social work* (Vol. 4, pp. 2–24). New York: New York School of Philanthropy.

Friedan, B. (1963). *The feminique mystique*. New York: W. W. Norton.

Galbraith, J. K. (1958). *The affluent society*. Boston: Houghton Mifflin.

Harrington, M. (1962). *The other America*. New York: Macmillan.

Hofstader, R. (1955). *The age of reform*. New York: Random House.

Jansson, B. (1988). *The reluctant welfare state: A history of American social welfare policies*. Belmont, CA: Wadsworth.

Katz, M. (1986). *In the shadow of the poorhouse: A social history of welfare in America*. New York: Basic Books.

Kaus, M. (1992). *The end of equality*. New York: Basic Books.

Leiby, J. (1978). *A history of social welfare and social work in the U.S.* New York: Columbia University Press.

Mishra, R. (1990). *The welfare state in capitalist society*. Toronto: University of Toronto Press.

Moynihan, D. P. (1969). *Maximum feasible misunderstanding: Community action in the war on poverty*. New York: Free Press.

Murray, C. (1984). *Losing ground: American social policy 1950–1980*. New York: Basic Books.

Patterson, J. (1981). *America's struggle against poverty 1900–1980*. Cambridge, MA: Harvard University Press.

Polyani, K. (1957). *The great transformation*. Boston: Beacon Press.

Richmond, M. (1917). *Social diagnosis*. New York: Russell Sage Foundation.

Rothman, D. (1971). *This discovery of the asylum: Order and disorder in the new republic*. Boston: Little, Brown.

Skocpol, T. (1992). *Protecting soldiers and mothers: The origins of social policy in the U.S.* Cambridge, MA: Harvard University Press.

Stewart, R. (1911). *The philanthropic work of J. S. Lowell*. New York: Macmillan.

Titmuss, R. M. (1958). *Essays on the welfare state*. London: Allen & Unwin.

Trattner, W. (1989). *From poor law to welfare state: A history of social welfare in America* (2nd ed.). New York: Free Press.

U.S. Bureau of the Census. (1978). *Current population reports* (Series P-23, No. 28). Washington, DC: U.S. Government Printing Office.

U.S. Social Security Administration. (1992, Winter). *Social Security Bulletin* [Entire issue].

Wilensky, H. L., & Lebeaux, C. N. (1965). *Industrial society & social welfare*. New York: Free Press.

P. Nelson Reid, PhD, is professor, North Carolina State University, Social Work Department, Raleigh, NC 27695.

For further information see

Advocacy; Archives of Social Welfare; Child Welfare Overview; Direct Practice Overview; Ethics and Values; Families Overview; Historiography; International and Comparative Social Welfare; National Association of Social Workers; Poverty; Public Social Services; Social Welfare Policy; Social Work Practice: History and Evolution; Social Work Profession: History.

Key Words

social welfare history   social work profession
social welfare policy

Social Welfare

The following entries contain information on this general topic:

Social Welfare Policy
Ronald B. Dear

As the 20th century draws to a close, U.S. social workers can take pride in the reforms of the past 65 years. Public income maintenance benefits assist nearly all retired people; large-scale medical schemes (most notably Medicare and Medicaid), financed in whole or in part by federal, state, and local governments, aid 71 million individuals; and food stamps help more than one in 10 (27.2 million) American citizens. Also, school lunch programs feed 24.8 million children each day, and cash public assistance helps to sustain 21 million disabled and elderly people, as well as children and their parents. Numerous social services, especially child care, child and adult protective services, and counseling, improve the quality of life for millions of Americans. Of major importance has been the emphasis on equity and justice and the attempt to bring women, racial and ethnic groups, and those with handicaps into the social and economic mainstream. In fact, so fast has been the growth of public and private social welfare, broadly defined, that by the early 1990s almost one-third ($1.7 trillion) of the gross domestic product was being spent on the social welfare enterprise (Bixby, 1992).

Despite these reforms, issues of tremendous magnitude remain. For example, an estimated 39.7 million citizens have no health care coverage and 39.3 million lived in poverty in 1993, more than in any year since 1962 (U.S. Bureau of the Census, 1994). Hundreds of thousands are without homes and live on the streets or in temporary shelters (Committee on Ways and Means, 1994). Furthermore, the unemployment rate, seemingly fixed at around 7 percent, has long been too high (Council of Economic Advisors, 1993); lack of universal immunization means that millions of children are at unnecessary risk of communicable disease; and, for a developed country, the United States has excessively high infant mortality rates among all low-income people, especially poverty-oppressed black people (Children's Defense Fund, 1992). Cities are afflicted with crime and senseless violence, with some having battle zones unsafe for anyone; incarceration rates are at an all-time high; and private security firms are big business. Furthermore, new problems are emerging. The human immunodeficiency virus (HIV), which leads to the acquired immune deficiency syndrome (AIDS), was first reported in the United States in 1981. Deaths resulting from this infection are climbing at an appalling rate. The 33,590 deaths caused by HIV infection in 1992 represented a 13 percent increase over such deaths in 1991. By 1992 HIV had become the eighth leading cause of death. In black men 25 to 44 years of age, it is the leading cause of death (National Center for Health Statistics, 1993).

Why does a country with the wealth of the United States tolerate so much unnecessary illness, death, pain, poverty, homelessness, violence, and despair? Perhaps more puzzling, how can the United States spend almost one-third of its gross domestic product on social welfare and yet see problems and unmet needs increase? Exactly how does social welfare policy fit into this strange equation? The answers to these questions lie in American public policy.

"Policy," "social policy," and "social welfare policy" are terms commonly used by social workers, the press, and politicians. However, these terms are highly abstract, have overlapping meanings, and are often confused with one another. Because there are no definitions on which all agree, each authority has his or her own perspective. Defining and distinguishing these terms clarifies the following discussion.

THE MEANING OF POLICY

Policy, an all-inclusive word, refers to just about anything a government does. Policies develop as "a way of dealing with problems" (Richan, 1988, p. xi); they are the end result of choices made by legislators, executives, and agency bureaucrats. Almost all such choices are the outcome of long, often tortuous debate and reflect both value preference and compromise. More concretely, policies are principles, plans, procedures, and courses of action—established in statute, interpreted in administrative code, spelled out in agency regulation, and supported by judicial decree—that direct what the government and its representatives can and cannot do. Policy, then, "is more than a single program. It is the set of principles guiding a range of actions in a particular sphere" (Richan, 1988, p. xi). Furthermore, policy "is the implicit or explicit core of principles that underlies specific programs, legislation, priorities" (Kahn, 1979, p. 67).

Most developed nations have enunciable foreign, defense, trade, environmental, tax, income support, and criminal justice policies. These policies determine specific courses of action by informing people what can and cannot be done legally in a given sphere of activity.

Social Policy

Social policies are those principles, procedures, and courses of action established in statute, administrative code, and agency regulation that affect people's social well-being. Thus, tax, transportation, public health, environmental, and social security statutes, as well as the implementation of codes and regulations that directly influence individual well-being, may be thought of as social policies. Social policy is clearly linked to economic policy and the political process; Moroney (1991) has argued that the political economy of a society determines its social policies.

Social welfare policy, in turn, is a subset or one portion of social policy. Social welfare policies may be thought of as those policies that affect the distribution of resources. According to Richan (1988),

> Social welfare policy [as opposed to social policy, which is broader, and public policy, which is broader still] is concerned mainly with the transfer of goods and services to individuals and families, either through government agencies, voluntary nonprofit organizations or profit making companies. The range of services ... included under social welfare is awesome. (p. xii)

Public social welfare policy is the mechanism used by governments to distribute limited resources. Four premises, often unarticulated, underlie this concept of social welfare policy.

Limited resources. The first premise is that resources are always limited. It is abundantly clear that no modern society has ever or likely will ever possess the means to do all that various and shifting constituents demand. For example, U.S. federal budget deficits lead to program curtailment, not expansion, and it is difficult for new, costly initiatives to gain the needed support for passage. Another excellent example is the continuous struggle to build a national health care system in the United States. State and local governments face revenue shortfalls; unlike their federal counterpart, however, they must show a balanced budget, and in most instances, they are constitutionally prohibited from running a deficit. Consequently, when state and local revenues are down, as they are in periods of recession and high unemployment—at the very time state assistance is needed most—income support and medical, education, and social services spending must be reduced to balance the budget. Furthermore, not only are public economic resources limited, but there is also a growing realization that arable land, water, and all natural resources are or will soon be in short supply.

Unmet needs. The second premise is that individuals and societies have almost unlimited needs. The lack of resources (the first premise), combined with the unmet needs of a rapidly expanding population (the second premise), means that even after 65 years of being a reluctant welfare state, the United States will end this century with an appalling litany of social ills.

How to meet apparently unlimited needs with finite resources raises difficult social policy questions. For example, 15.3 percent of the U.S. population lack access to regular medical care. Nearly everyone would agree that this is a critical issue, at best a societal embarrassment and at worst leading to unnecessary pain or death. However, should all have a right to health care? If so, who should pay? Who should be treated for what? If resources are limited, how much should be spent to keep a dying person alive? Also, the U.S. population needs more food for the hungry and better diets for all. How much food is enough? If there is a sufficient supply, how is it to be distributed? Who pays for increased food aid to low-income people and for better nutritional information for people at all income levels? As another example, the U.S. population needs more and better education and job training. In 1990 an estimated 29.8 percent of students dropped out of high school; only 21.4 percent finished four years of college (Snyder, 1992). Inadequate education keeps people out of the economic mainstream and is a recipe for a lifetime of intermittent work and poverty. Even those who have completed their education may find themselves unemployed as a result of technological advances or displaced because of shifting of the manufacturing base. Retraining displaced workers, whose education may no longer be up to date, tends to be a low priority. How can the United States remain economically competitive when many of its citizens have become economic refugees?

Unfairness. The third premise is that society has much built-in unfairness. There is unfairness inherent in the class system, growing inequality in income distribution, and gross discrimination in terms of gender, race, ethnic background, age, disabilities, and differences in sexual preference.

Lack of consensus. The fourth and final premise is that U.S. society cannot agree on how best to deal with complex problems. The United States lacks a uniform value base to guide its activities and therefore fails to act or takes only halfway measures. For instance, there may be consensus on the desirability of immunizing all children, but there is no agreement on how to implement such a policy. Publicly financed abortions, distribution of condoms in school, sex education, and affirmative action are additional examples of policies on which agreement is lacking. In summary, policies must somehow balance the tensions among limited resources, unlimited needs, extensive unfairness, and lack of value consensus.

Conflict in Allocation Process

Public social welfare policy, society's method of allocating its limited resources to meet unlimited needs, deals with society's most perplexing questions with regard to distribution, redistribution, and fairness. Such distributional decisions are usually made in local, state, and federal legislative bodies—political arenas typified by value conflict.

Public social welfare policy addresses (or fails to address) issues of inequality based on class, race, gender, age, handicap, and family size. As DiNitto (1991) emphasized, conflict is built into the policy and allocation processes. Assuming limited resources, should society pay for more services for elderly people or for extended publicly financed child care? Should there be higher salaries for professors or welfare grant increases? What is the trade-off between protecting jobs and protecting the environment? Whatever the choice, there are opportunity costs. In other words, one decision forecloses "other valued goals or claims" (Moroney, 1991, p. 2).

Public social welfare policy addresses issues of financing and administration of the programs designed to accomplish its goals. The way in which a program is financed explains much about its redistributional impact. What percentage of the cost of caring for older members of society should be covered by younger working members raising families? Should those without children, or whose children are grown, be taxed more highly to subsidize public services for those with children? What level of government should finance and administer a given program? What combination of the public and private sectors should finance and administer an agreed-on program? Such questions make policy debates complex and contentious.

Complexities in Policy Development

Newcomers to the policy arena, whether students in social work or new members of Congress, are enthusiastic to work for change. They are sometimes astonished when they learn of the complexi-

ties of the policy debate and become disheartened at the many barriers that slow down or block the change for which they had hoped to work. Complex interrelated forces can delay, make unrecognizable, or completely stop a forward-looking social agenda. These forces include shortfall of revenue; public opposition to increased taxes; strong distrust of government; impossibility of agreement on the "correct" social agenda; absence of the political vision, will, or courage to design and find funding for new initiatives; and undue influence of special interest groups, especially by well-financed political action committees. All six forces conspire to create a political gridlock that makes social change exceedingly difficult.

These six forces have worked against a coordinated development of remedies to deal with the many problems that face the United States. Nevertheless, the country has developed a broad-scale social apparatus, called by some the "welfare state." Not surprisingly, this apparatus developed with considerable wariness and "an incredible political fuss.... Our support of national welfare programs is halting; our administration of services for the less privileged is mean. We move toward the welfare state, but we do it with ill grace" (Wilensky, 1976, p. 12). If one believes that the central purpose of government is to meet the needs of its people, the welfare state would be a natural development of modern society. Indeed, the welfare state is a relatively recent phenomenon, with almost all of its growth occurring since World War II in some two dozen nations.

FORCES INFLUENCING SOCIAL WELFARE POLICY

A Changing Economy

The United States generates some $6 trillion a year in wealth and has the world's highest level of productivity. The list of millionaires and billionaires grows steadily, and the media portray America as a land of infinite wealth. From the perspective of the world community, many of whom may wish to come to America, this picture is accurate. The United States has by far the world's largest network of colleges and research institutions. Also, the U.S. per capita income, although no longer the highest in the world, is still high compared with that in almost all other countries.

However, there is a dark side to this picture: A large segment of the population does not share in this prosperity. The fundamental reason is that the United States is in the middle of a technological transformation comparable to the one that took place in the half-century after the industrial revolution began in about 1776. As Drucker (1993) has observed, "Within a few short decades, society rearranges itself— its worldview; its basic values; its social and political structure; its arts; its key institutions. Fifty years later, there is a new world" (p. 1).

Productivity issues. Several points illustrate this changing economic and production base and help explain why there are winners and losers in the transformation. First, labor productivity (output per hour in nonfarm business) has slowed dramatically; as a consequence, real earnings have declined. From 1945 to 1965, labor productivity grew at an average rate of 2.7 percent per year, but since 1973 it has grown at an annual rate of only 0.7 percent (Congressional Budget Office, 1993). Second, items once manufactured in the United States, thereby providing employment to U.S. residents, are currently manufactured abroad and imported back to this country. In both low-technology consumer items (tools, clothing, dinnerware) and high-technology items (automobiles, televisions, computer components), the United States has lost millions of jobs to low-paid workers in other countries. Third, when productivity (nonfarm and farm) is improved as a result of automation, jobs are lost because of improved efficiency. At one time, for example, one farmer could produce enough food for five people; currently, however, one farmer feeds 128 people. Fourth, although large numbers of jobs have been created (an average of 170,000 new jobs were created each month in 1993), many are low paying (Congressional Budget Office, 1993).

The 1970s and 1980s witnessed low growth in labor productivity, company downsizing, plant closures, extensive loss of well-paying manufacturing and factory jobs, sharp reductions in agricultural labor, costly health care, high inflation, and increasing taxes for all but the wealthy. These factors have conspired to stagnate the income of low- and middle-class Americans; the cost of purchasing and maintaining a home currently is beyond the reach of many families, even those with two incomes.

Technology issues. Continued technological progress can be expected; the pace of change is accelerating, and those who do not or cannot adapt will be left behind. Many jobs require computer literacy, but the United States has hardly reached the threshold of an information society that is beyond imagination. In September 1993 Commerce Secretary Ronald Brown unveiled a blueprint for an "information superhighway," a national network that would link voice, video, and computer in

every home equipped with a telephone and television. Vice President Gore said, "Make no mistake about it, [the information superhighway] is at all odds the most important and lucrative marketplace of the 21st century" (Browning, 1993, p. 675).

Drucker (1993) made a similar point when he argued that the world (not just the Western world or a few nation-states) is in the midst of a revolution similar to the industrial revolution; however, information, rather than machinery, is the driving force of this new revolution.

> The basic economic resource—"the means of production," to use the economists' term—is no longer capital, nor natural resources ... nor labor. *It is and will be knowledge.* ... The leading social groups of the knowledge society will be "knowledge workers." ... Knowledge is now fast becoming the sole factor of production, sidelining both capital and labor. (Drucker, 1993, pp. 8, 20)

Education issues. Change is everywhere, and although many can adapt to this emerging knowledge society and improve themselves economically, others cannot adapt and will fare worse. The United States seems to be moving toward two separate societies: one made up of well-trained professional, technical, and managerial workers and one consisting of low-paid workers, many of whom are service workers such as restaurant employees, custodians, security guards, secretaries, and salespeople. A bachelor's degree no longer ensures a well-paying job, and those with only a high school diploma are increasingly left behind. About 20 percent of the population competes successfully, benefits from economic growth, and obtains a high income; the remaining 80 percent finds itself losing ground (Reich, 1993). Education, especially higher education, is essential to the preparation of those about to enter the labor market; it is equally important to those older workers who find themselves reentering the market.

What does this emerging economic order, with its changing occupational requirements, suggest to policymakers? First, higher education must be made accessible. With 3,539 institutions of higher education in 1989 (including community colleges and branch campuses), the United States would seem to be positioned to become a leader in an information society (U.S. Bureau of the Census, Department of Commerce, 1992). Although a larger percentage of Americans attend college than in most other countries, low-income people and racial and ethnic groups are underrepresented on college campuses. Even for those with the ability to succeed in postsecondary education, attendance may be difficult or impossible because of inadequate preparation, lack of space in a nearby institution, high tuition, inadequate financial aid, competing family responsibilities, or lack of desire for further education. Women have overcome many of these barriers and currently constitute a larger proportion of college graduates than men. In 1991 23.4 percent of women 25 to 29 years old had completed college, compared with 22.9 percent of men (Mortenson, 1992).

In addition to expanding general access to education, the second demand for educators is to reach out to more diverse populations. Black people are only about half as likely as white people to complete college, and although the Hispanic population has made great progress since the early 1970s in obtaining college degrees, Hispanics are only about half as likely as white people to obtain a degree. The third demand for educators is to shift education to meet the needs of new careers and shape new careers to fit employment needs and national trends.

Limited Faith in Government

Many contemporary Americans, like their colonial forebears, profoundly distrust government and the bureaucrats who are elected or hired to serve. The United States was largely established by people who purposely left oppressive governments controlled by monarchs with few restrictions on their power. Currently many immigrants come for similar reasons and hold similar views. In the judgment of the early colonists, government was a necessary evil and its functions were to be confined to obvious areas such as defense, printing of money, and record keeping (Jansson, 1988). "That government is best which governs least" was the creed of founders who sought to limit the powers of all government, but especially those of the federal government.

To ensure that centralized authority was kept in bounds, the U.S. Constitution incorporated a rigid system of checks and balances, and most state constitutions closely followed the federal model. As a means of slowing the legislative process, each bill introduced into Congress (or a state legislature) must overcome numerous hurdles—several readings, committee hearings, approval of a fiscal note if money is involved, numerous amendments—and earn a majority vote. A bill must go through this process in both houses of Congress, and differences between similar bills in the two houses must be reconciled; that is, one house "checks" the action of the other. The bill can then either be signed or vetoed by the president (or governor); if it is vetoed, however,

Congress (or a state legislature) can override the veto with a two-thirds vote. A separate judicial system may, when set in action, judge the constitutionality of the law. An extreme emphasis on states' rights and individual rights has further weakened federal authority. The founders of the United States believed that most government power should reside in the states, and the Bill of Rights placed utmost emphasis on the rights of the individual.

One consequence of this diffusion of power in the U.S. government has been a slowness to develop policies and programs for the needy. Moreover, even when legislation is introduced, the process of passage is so long, complex, and difficult that social change via the legislative route is slow. In the words of Congressman Newt Gingrich, "I think the founding fathers thought the way to preserve freedom and avoid dictatorship was to build a machine so inefficient that no dictatorship could force it to work, and the corollary was you could barely get it to work voluntarily" (Benson & Baden, 1990, p. A-13).

"Demosclerosis"

As a check on government power, U.S. legislative bodies were designed to be cumbersome and to move slowly. On rare occasions the federal government has responded with relative speed, such as in times of natural disasters or wars or during uncommon periods of national social concern. Currently two additional factors are strangling the government's ability to respond quickly to the country's shifting economic and social needs.

First, demands for public programs, services, subsidies, and supports continue to outstrip revenue derived from taxes. Large annual deficits and growing national debt (discussed later) make enactment of new initiatives extraordinarily difficult. At the same time, the United States is wealthier than ever before, and the government is spending a higher proportion of the gross national product on public programs than ever. Thus, for contemporary America, the question may not be how much is spent, but how the funds collected by government are allocated. The real poverty in American government may not lie in its lack of wealth but in its inability to amend or eliminate old programs and its concomitant difficulty in agreeing on policies and finding sufficient funds for new ones.

Second, government is becoming increasingly paralyzed because of special interest groups that hamper reallocation of existing program dollars. Over time, programs that were once innovative and progressive become part of established government structure, and program employees, as well as outside interests, fight to retain programs long beyond their time of need. It is something of a truism that, once enacted, government programs are rarely eliminated. "Every program generates an entrenched lobby that never goes away" (Rauch, 1992, p. 2001).

Special interest groups working through political action committees can command huge amounts of money for election and lobbying purposes and can get thousands of letters and telephone calls to members of Congress within hours. Because most programs have more people strongly interested in retaining them than in abolishing them, few are dropped. New schemes must somehow be built on and integrated into existing policies and programs. Innovation is risky, because once changes are implemented, new supporters make program elimination unlikely. As a result of "policy gridlock," "stalemate," and "paralysis," government is becoming "frozen" at the very time it must respond quickly (Blau, 1992). One analyst called this "demosclerosis—postwar democratic government's progressive loss of the ability to adapt. Demosclerosis is the most important governmental phenomenon of our time. . . . The federal government is rusting solid and . . . nothing can be done about it" (Rauch, 1992, p. 2003).

THE REAGAN–BUSH ERA: 1981–1993

The ideas proclaimed by Ronald Reagan in his campaign for president and the legislation enacted during his presidency, especially in its early days, resulted in significant modification of programs and services for disadvantaged people. Future historians may view the 20 years from 1981 to 2001 as a turning point in social welfare, a time of increasing needs along with unmet challenges and lost opportunities.

In Reagan's view, government was not the solution to America's problems; government itself created the problems. There was too much taxation, too much spending, too much welfare, too many bureaucrats, and too many government regulations. Conservative scholars (for example, Anderson, 1978; Friedman, 1962; Gilder, 1981; Murray, 1984) and the right wing of the Republican party agreed. They challenged the liberal belief that government is the main institution responsible for the well-being of less-fortunate individuals. The New Deal and Great Society programs were declared failures. A phenomenal boost in social welfare expenditures and myriad government schemes had not extinguished poverty. Murray (1984) and Gilder (1981) contended that welfare programs actually increased poverty.

Economic Policies

Moreover, conservatives believed that the nation's economic problems—inflation, unemployment, and low productivity—were due to government interference in the marketplace. Since the 1930s both Democratic and Republican administrations had followed the Keynesian prescript that expanding the money supply (the demand side of the economy) in difficult economic times would generate employment and that contracting the supply of money would combat inflation. Furthermore, rising unemployment would decrease aggregate consumer purchasing power and thereby reduce demand, drive down prices, and decrease inflation. In the 1970s Keynesian theory seemed less applicable, as the United States experienced both high unemployment and high inflation ("stagflation"). Furthermore, increased government spending did not spur the economy to the extent expected.

Rejecting conventional Keynesian economics, Reagan and his advisors thought they knew the cause of the country's financial crisis. Inflation, unemployment, and low productivity were attributable to government intervention. The answer? Stop government intrusion. Stop meddling with private enterprise. If high taxes on business reduced incentives, then decreased taxes would expand production. In the end, as the tax base grew as a result of economic growth, government revenues would rise.

Based on the theories of Arthur Laffer, this supply-side economics emphasized the importance of a supply of capital to encourage economic growth. Large reductions in taxes, especially those levied on businesses and wealthy individuals, would provide the funds for individual and corporate investment. As businesses grew, they would hire additional employees who, in turn, would be able to purchase the items being produced. Also, government regulation was costly to implement and represented an additional drag on economic growth.

Reagan capitalized on popular opposition to an "overgenerous" welfare system. "American social policy over previous decades had harmed rather than helped the poor. The alternative, [Reagan] argued, was a radical disengagement of the state from social welfare. Unlike his conservative predecessors who sought to curtail welfare, Reagan argued for abolition" (Midgley, 1992, p. 24). Ample welfare benefits to poor people would reduce their incentive to work and increase their dependency.

To achieve his goals, Reagan introduced major modifications of the tax system; enormous budget cuts; brutal and uncompromising retrenchments in human service programs for low-income people; a massive buildup in national defense and the start of large-scale weapon systems; fundamental alterations in the nature of the welfare state, especially with regard to locus of delivery; and widespread relief from federal regulations. Included in the 1981 Omnibus Budget Reconciliation Act were cuts in personal income taxes for all groups, indexing of tax rates to avoid bracket creep, elimination of certain programs (for example, Comprehensive Employment and Training Act programs), and severe cuts in Aid to Families with Dependent Children, food stamps, housing, social services, and other programs for low-income people. Fearing a populist backlash, Reagan avoided cuts in social security (Old-Age and Survivors and Disability Insurance) and other social insurance entitlement programs.

New Federalism
The Reagan administration accented a new federalism that had begun some years earlier under President Nixon. Its essence was to get the federal government out of the human services business by returning responsibility for social programs to state and local jurisdictions, easing federal regulations, and significantly reducing federal support. Reaganites believed that both experimentation and efficiency would be encouraged by this devolution of responsibility and decentralized administration. Furthermore, the new federalism endorsed the purchase of services from the private sector and placed renewed emphasis on volunteerism.

A cornerstone of the new federalism was block grants, which were used to consolidate similar categorical programs (for example, programs in maternal and child health) into a single grant, reduce funding by 25 percent (the assumed administrative overhead), and allocate the funds to states and localities, with as few regulations as possible. Thus, although states would have fewer funds, they would have greater flexibility in the use of those funds. In Reagan's first budget of 1981, 57 categorical programs were merged into seven block grants. Each year Reagan was in office, additional attempts were made to block out categorical programs. The results were devastating for low-income discretionary programs. From fiscal year 1981 to fiscal year 1987, after inflation, the Community Development Block Grant was reduced by 39 percent, the Community Services Block Grant was reduced by 36 percent, and the Social Services Block Grant was reduced by 28 percent (Center on Budget and Policy Priorities, 1987).

Impact on Social Services
The Social Services Act was signed into law on January 4, 1975, as Title XX of the Social Security Act. It is of particular interest to social workers because it is the country's principal source of federal funding for child care, child protective services, home-based care for older people, and noninstitutional care for disabled individuals. In at least half of the states, it assists in the funding of a wide range of services that employ baccalaureate- and master's-level social workers. Prominent examples of social services are child foster care; adoption; counseling; employment, education, and training; residential care and treatment; information and referral; family planning; chore services; and adult foster care (Harris, 1987). States had broad flexibility in designing their social services programs, capped at $2.5 billion in fiscal year 1976, but there were clear federal mandates. For instance, there was a 25 percent matching requirement, services had to be targeted to low-income people, and the public had to be given the opportunity to participate in developing a statewide plan. When social services became a block grant in the Omnibus Budget Reconciliation Act of 1981, states were no longer required to match federal dollars, services did not have to be targeted to low-income individuals, citizen participation was dropped, most reporting was stopped, and funding was reduced to $2.4 billion. By 1994 the grant had grown to a modest $2.8 billion. However, over the 17 years from 1977 to 1994, federal funding for Title XX had dropped in real terms by 58 percent (Committee on Ways and Means, 1994).

Reagan was also successful in his efforts to cut back on nonblock low-income program benefits and beneficiaries. Transfer payments were sharply reduced, in-kind benefits were cut, and eligibility requirements were stiffened. In just two years, "unemployment insurance was reduced by 17.4 percent, child nutrition programs by 28 percent, food stamp expenditures by 13.8 percent, and the Community Services Block Grant program by 37.1 percent" (Midgley, 1992, p. 25). Always a popular target, Aid to Families with Dependent Children was cut by 14.3 percent in Reagan's first two years. Funding for subsidized housing assistance fell from $26.6 billion in 1980 to $7.4 billion in 1989 (Rubin, Wright, & Devine, 1992). Not surprisingly, poverty increased and that increase, coupled with a decrease in available low-income housing, led to record numbers of homeless people.

Impact on the Federal Budget
During the Reagan–Bush era, not only were large segments of the welfare state under withering attack, but defense budgets skyrocketed as a result of a philosophy that the United States can

(and should) police the world. Thus, the budget increased during a time of recession and massive tax cuts. Not surprisingly, deficits and the national debt soared. In fact, for most of Reagan's years as president, the annual federal deficit was between $200 billion and $300 billion, and it was even higher under Bush. It is projected to decline under Clinton, to $162 billion in fiscal 1995 and then, assuming discretionary caps, gradually start to rise again, reaching $231 billion in fiscal 1999. The national debt (subject to statutory limit) increased from $998 billion in 1981 to $4.3 trillion by September 30, 1993, and is projected to grow to $6 trillion by 1998 (Congressional Budget Office, 1993, 1994). With a debt and deficit of this magnitude, major new initiatives are unlikely, in spite of emerging needs such as the AIDS crisis, homelessness, single-parent families, overpopulation, rising poverty, and hunger. In fact, it has been argued that the debt and deficit run up by the Reagan administration was *intentional*. A large national debt would hamper future congresses from introducing new social programs (Block, 1987).

Under Reagan, "tax policy became social welfare policy, but in a manner antithetical to the liberal understanding, of both tax and welfare policy" (Karger, 1992, p. 49). Parts of the welfare state were dismantled, some programs for the needy were eliminated and a lack of funding starved others, states and localities were expected to assume more responsibility, regulations were dropped, accountability was lessened, the private sector grew in importance, and, possibly worst from the perspective of public welfare advocates, people lost faith in government and the political process. Americans will be less likely to look to the government, especially the federal government, as the instrument to deal with problems. Despite the attack on the comparatively small welfare programs for low-income people, expenditures for the large social insurance programs (such as social security and Medicare) continued to grow or hold steady under Reagan and Bush. Surprisingly, the welfare state remained largely intact.

POLICY RESPONSES TO TRENDS AND ISSUES

Broad social policy directions have been explored in this entry. Other *Encyclopedia* entries discuss specific social welfare and social work policy responses to the trends and issues outlined here. The purpose of this section is to distill some of these trends and to emphasize a few not discussed elsewhere. The final section highlights some unfinished portions of America's social welfare agenda and offers clues to future directions.

Disparate Treatment of Poor and Middle-Class People

Although a few programs for the poor have become larger in the 1990s (for example, Medicaid and food stamps), it is evident that, since the early 1980s, most schemes for low-income people have not expanded in relation to economic growth, inflation, or the growing numbers of the at-risk population. As has been shown, the purchasing power of Aid to Families with Dependent Children and general assistance has declined sharply. Employment and training services have been curtailed, and low-income housing has been reduced substantially. Numerous categorical line-item federal health, welfare, community, and social services schemes have been reconfigured into block grants, and funding has been reduced. General revenue sharing through the Local Fiscal Assistance Act of 1972, which allocated unrestricted billions of dollars directly to states and to thousands of local jurisdictions, was dropped entirely in 1987.

In sharp contrast to this harsh treatment of disadvantaged people, programs, services, and, especially, tax benefits for middle- and upper-income people have grown rapidly. Thus, as one group of the population experienced social program retreat, other groups saw advances. Such growth in spending for the more affluent more than offsets the funds cut from the much smaller low-income programs. This explains the apparent paradox that has so captivated Anderson, Murray, and Gilder: The country is spending more for "welfare" and yet is experiencing more poverty and homelessness.

Not discussed here are significant tax welfare benefits, referred to as "fiscal welfare" by Richard Titmuss (1965). These are special income tax deductions, exclusions, preferential tax rates, credits, and deferrals of tax liability. Combined, they are substantial and benefit individuals with sufficient income to take advantage of tax exclusion policies (that is, those in middle- and upper-income brackets).

In fiscal year 1994, tax welfare expenditures will cost the federal treasury $256.4 billion, and each year these write-offs will rise; it is estimated that they will amount to $337 billion by 1998. (To provide perspective, the federal budget deficit in fiscal year 1994 is projected to be $202 billion.) Tax expenditures related to retirement will cost the U.S. Treasury an estimated $104 billion in fiscal 1995; those related to health $63 billion; mortgage interest, $54 billion; and owner-occupied property tax, $14 billion. The poverty write-offs of $22 billion represent 7.3 percent of all personal tax welfare benefits (Committee on Ways and Means, 1994). Small wonder that Abramovitz (1983) echoed Titmuss in stating that "everyone is on welfare."

Localism versus Universalism
In times of shrinking resources and decreasing federal responsibility, a new set of social welfare policy watchwords has achieved prominence: devolution, decentralization, deinstitutionalization, declassification, reconfiguration, consolidation, privatization, and volunteerism. Most of these terms (an exception might be deinstitutionalization), with their policy and programmatic implications, have had the effect of returning the U.S. public and its decision makers to earlier times, in a simpler society, where neighbor took care of neighbor in a small community or in a rural area. Lost to many, even members of the social work profession, is a broader view of the welfare state whose benefits and services are guaranteed to all as a right and are not based on status.

Universalism has lost favor, some say, because it is too costly and relies on a national political and bureaucratic apparatus in which people have scant confidence. Big government is seen as a "big brother" to be avoided whenever possible. States and localities, not well trusted themselves, are being asked to assume more responsibility for increasing problems with fewer resources. Localities, it is argued, are better equipped to deal with local problems, and in terms of actual service delivery, this is correct. Service delivery is almost always local; a person goes to the dentist or to get counseling where he or she lives, not across the country. The local argument has appeal because it makes sense. However, there is another aspect to this question.

Advocates of localism fail to understand, or prefer not to acknowledge, that almost all major social programs and policy victories have been accomplished at the federal level. A few prominent examples are the Social Security Act, the Civil Rights Act, the Food Stamp Act, the Older Americans Act, the Housing and Urban Development Act, and the Elementary and Secondary Education Act. Contrary to popular belief, a single national administrative unit, even with numerous local offices, can be much less expensive than multiple state and local units of administration. Social Security confers benefits on 43 million people (one in six citizens) each month. The total administrative expense of Old-Age and Survivors and Disability Insurance as a proportion of benefit payments was 1 percent in 1992, and since the late 1950s, it has rarely exceeded 2 percent (Social Security

Administration, 1992, 1994). National policies can also develop agreed-on national standards and, ideally, uniform eligibility.

One of the most promising developments has been the continuing effort to bring into the mainstream people once perceived as existing on the fringes of society. The profession of social work and NASW have made significant efforts in promoting diversity and multiculturalism. Major efforts have been made to recruit members of racial minorities, gay men and lesbians, people with disabilities, and those caught in the economic underclass, especially single mothers. In fall 1992, almost one-fifth of all incoming MSW students were members of a social or ethnic minority (Council on Social Work Education, 1993). However, the social work profession is ignoring a growing gender imbalance: In the 1960s, more than 40 percent of master's-level social work students were men; currently fewer than 20 percent of such students are men.

SOCIAL WELFARE POLICY: TO THE 21ST CENTURY

Reasons for Optimism
In light of welfare policy trends and issues, it might seem difficult for social workers to be optimistic about the welfare state. However, there is cause for hope. First, public expenditures in social welfare grew from being almost nonexistent in the 1930s (aside from education) to being the single largest area of expenditure in the early 1990s. This is impressive progress in just 60 years. Second, this large-scale apparatus serves so many people and is so much a part of everyday life that it is not easy to reduce and impossible to eliminate. Third, although allocation of resources to the welfare enterprise is not likely to decrease, the public-private mix of funding could change. Fourth, in spite of cutbacks in poverty programs, a few important low-income programs continue to grow. Most schemes for poor people cost comparatively little; savings from reducing them further would be meager, and expanding them would involve relatively small amounts. For example, the Social Services Block Grant in fiscal year 1995 will cost the federal government $2.8 billion of a $1.5 trillion budget, or less than 0.2 percent. Thus, a slight reduction or increment would have scant effect on the budget.

Technological progress is a fifth reason for optimism, especially in knowledge, information, and medical realms. Sixth, U.S. society seems increasingly to tolerate (if not embrace or celebrate) growing racial and ethnic diversity and seems far more willing to accept varying lifestyles, family types, and sexual orientations. Seventh, the Clinton administration seems more inclined to address issues of social justice than any administration in recent history. Finally, during the first two years of the Clinton administration, health care was the primary issue on the national social agenda. Both Democrats and Republicans seem to agree that something must be done, but they differ greatly on how to do it.

Increasing Demands and Problems
As the 20th century nears its end, the United States and much of the world seem poised on the brink of multiple calamities. The population is growing at a rate beyond which basic needs can be met. (Currently the world's population increases as much in 12 years as it did in its first 3 million years [Zero Population Growth, 1993]). Even in America, a rapidly growing population and its burgeoning requirements collide with resource limits. Adequate supplies of affordable necessities such as food, housing, utilities, and health care are beyond the reach of millions. It may be that the resources themselves (affordable housing, arable land, water, oil) are in short supply, or it may be that funds, either individual (from employment) or public (from taxes), are in short supply. It is the job of large-scale public social welfare to see that people get the food, housing, medical care, and other services they need to survive and prosper.

Public social welfare policy determines the allocation of limited resources to meet unlimited needs. In a democratic society, such decisions are made in the political arena and presumably reflect the will of the majority. Government, then, especially the federal government, is the only viable entity equipped to redistribute taxes as transfer payments, as programs, or as services to its constituents. Yet, as mentioned earlier, faith in government, never strong in America, seems on the decline. Certainly the Reagan–Bush administrations based their policies on limited faith in government. Mounting requests for money, programs, and services and a decreasing desire and diminishing ability to respond to demands are indicated by a number of opposing forces, including the following:

- the need for more government and more centralized decision making versus less faith in government and opposition to national government
- the need for a more equitable distribution of income versus growing inequality
- the need for more higher education versus the slow, neutral, or negative growth in state funding of higher education (Lively, 1993)

- the need for a more communitarian, cohesive society versus escalating fragmentation resulting from the power of specialized interests
- the need to bring population growth in check versus individuals' rights to procreate and to decide on the size of their family
- the need for rapid public response to worsening social crises versus demosclerosis and policy gridlock.

For years to come, these and similar opposing forces will form the context of all social work practice, from direct service to planning and administration.

Changes in Policy and Planning
As the preceding discussion makes abundantly clear, the nature of public social provision in the United States continues to change. Ideologues still control the social agenda, and there is almost no forum for a balanced and evenhanded ideological debate. It is difficult to discuss issues without having a label affixed ("conservative," "liberal," "reactionary," "radical"), and discussions tend to polarize rather than draw people together. The progressive underpinnings of the 1960s seem to have vanished. Liberals have come up with no clear agenda, but conservatives have. In fact, not many liberals support the standard forward-looking positions of the 1960s. Few say, "Of course we must maintain these entitlements." More popular positions of the 1990s include "Of course all people should work" and "You must help yourself."

The centralized federal policy of the 1960s has devolved to state and local governments. Decentralization gave local governments more responsibility but not more money; it also gave them more control over quality. Conservatives have successfully dominated America's social agenda since Nixon took office in 1968. Even Carter, the only Democratic president in the quarter century spanning 1968 to 1993, was conservative in fiscal and social policies (Jansson, 1993).

If the economic trends that began in the mid-1970s continue, slow growth in public social expenditures, especially in low-income programs, will continue as well, and the rapid growth of preceding years is not likely to recur. Few people will advocate greater reliance on the federal government, and as a consequence, there will be movement away from national standards (Morris, 1987). With the possible exception of health care, it is likely that most social program changes will be incremental, with minor modifications, small additions, and slightly expanded entitlements. Serious problems, however, may lead to occasional bursts of rapid and radical change.

A number of constraints confront the progressive social planner: the apparent decline of liberalism, the devolution of responsibility to states and localities, the growing national debt and continuing high deficits, program cutbacks as a result of inadequate state and local revenues, and citizen distrust of government. Adjustments must also be made for the changing economic base and rapid movement toward international trading blocks. What can one anticipate in the future?

America will develop a reinvigorated social agenda, one that builds on the strength of successful social programs, but will drop schemes and alter policies that have not proved to be effective. Americans should not be fearful of adopting new social policies to meet the changing needs of a changing society.

This era, laden with both peril and opportunity, is no different from other eras except that the pace of change is accelerating, as are dangers and opportunities. How well the United States progresses in the coming years is linked to decisions already made, to choices currently being made, and to choices that will be made in the near future. Where does social work fit into this picture? Social workers, in addition to being direct service practitioners in every field of practice, are policymakers, planners, administrators, legislators, researchers, analysts, and teachers. With its unique values and eclectic knowledge base, the profession of social work can play a key role in this future, but only if it is able to adapt to the new world that is emerging.

REFERENCES

Abramovitz, M. (1983). Everyone is on welfare: The role of redistribution in social policy revisited. *Social Work, 28,* 440–445.

Anderson, M. (1978). *Welfare: The political economy of welfare reform in the United States.* Stanford, CA: Hoover Institution.

Benson, M., & Baden, T. (1990, December 30). *Seattle Times,* p. A-13.

Bixby, A. K. (1992, Winter). Overview of public social welfare expenditures, fiscal year 1990. *Social Security Bulletin,* pp. 54–57.

Blau, J. (1992). A paralysis of social policy? *Social Work, 37,* 558–562.

Block, F. (1987). Rethinking the political economy of the welfare state. In F. Block, R. A. Cloward, B. Ehrenreich, & F. F. Piven (Eds.), *The mean season: The attack on the welfare state* (pp. 109–160). New York: Pantheon Books.

Browning, G. (1993, March 20). Search for tomorrow. *National Journal,* p. 675.

Center on Budget and Policy Priorities. (1987). *The budget agreement: How does it compare to the Gramm–Rudman–Hollings automatic cuts?* Washington, DC: Author.

Children's Defense Fund. (1992). *The state of America's children 1992.* Washington, DC: Author.

Committee on Ways and Means, U.S. House of Representatives. (1993). *Overview of entitlement programs [The green book].* Washington, DC: U.S. Government Printing Office.

Committee on Ways and Means, U.S. House of Representatives. (1994). *Overview of entitlement programs [The green book].* Washington, DC: U.S. Government Printing Office.

Congressional Budget Office. (1993, September). *Economic and budget outlook: An update.* Washington, DC: U.S. Government Printing Office.

Congressional Budget Office. (1994, August). *Economic and budget outlook: An update.* Washington, DC: U.S. Government Printing Office.

Council of Economic Advisors. (1993). *Economic indicators April 1993.* Washington, DC: U.S. Government Printing Office.

Council on Social Work Education. (1993). *Statistics on social work education in the United States: 1992.* Alexandria, VA: Author.

DiNitto, D. M. (1991). *Social welfare: Politics and public policy* (3rd ed.). Englewood Cliffs, NJ: Prentice Hall.

Drucker, P. (1993). *Post-capitalist society.* New York: HarperBusiness.

Friedman, M. (1962). *Capitalism and freedom.* Chicago: University of Chicago Press.

Gilder, G. (1981). *Wealth and poverty.* New York: Basic Books.

Harris, S. (1987). *Investing in independence across the generations: The Title XX Social Services Block Grant.* Washington, DC: National Association of Social Workers.

Jansson, B. S. (1988). *The reluctant welfare state: A history of American social welfare policies.* Belmont, CA: Wadsworth.

Jansson, B. S. (1993). *The reluctant welfare state: A history of social welfare in America* (2nd ed.). Monterey, CA: Brooks/Cole.

Kahn, A. J. (1979). *Social policy & social services* (2nd ed.). New York: Random House.

Karger, H. (1992). Income maintenance programs and the Reagan domestic agenda. *Journal of Sociology and Social Welfare, 19*(1), 45–61.

Lively, K. (1993). State support for colleges up 2% this year. *The Chronicle of Higher Education, 40*(10), A29–A33.

Midgley, J. (1992). Introduction: American social policy and the Reagan legacy. *Journal of Sociology and Social Welfare, 19*(1), 3–28.

Moroney, R. M. (1991). *Social policy and social work: Critical essays on the welfare state.* New York: Aldine de Gruyter.

Morris, R. (1987). Social welfare policy trends and issues. In A. Minahan (Ed.-in-Chief)*Encyclopedia of social work* (18th ed., Vol. 2, pp. 664–681). Silver Spring, MD: National Association of Social Workers.

Mortenson, T. (1992). Public policy analysis of opportunity for postsecondary education. In *The Mortenson*

Report on Public Policy, no. 1. Iowa City, IA: Postsecondary Opportunity.

Murray, C. (1984). *Losing ground: America's social policy 1950–1980.* New York: Basic Books.

National Center for Health Statistics. (1993). Annual summary of births, marriages, divorces and deaths, 1992. *Monthly Vital Statistics Report, 41*(13), 6–7.

Rauch, J. (1992, September 5). Demosclerosis. *National Journal,* pp. 1998–2003.

Reich, R. (1993, January 3). American denial: Our nation must find a sense of purpose. *Seattle Times,* p. D1.

Richan, W. C. (1988). *Beyond altruism: Social policy in American society.* New York: Haworth Press.

Rubin, B., Wright, J. D., & Devine, J. A. (1992). Unhousing the urban poor: The Reagan legacy. *Journal of Sociology and Social Welfare, 19*(1), 111–197.

Snyder, T. D. (1992). *Digest of educational statistics 1992.* Washington, DC: U.S. Department of Education, National Center for Educational Statistics.

Social Security Administration. (1992). Actuarial status of the Social Security and Medicare programs. *Social Security Bulletin, 55*(2), 36–42.

Social Security Administration. (1994). *Annual statistical supplement to the Social Security Bulletin.* Washington, DC: U.S. Superintendent of Documents.

Titmuss, R. (1965). The role of redistribution in social policy. *Social Security Bulletin, 39,* 14–20.

U.S. Bureau of the Census, Department of Commerce. (1992). *Statistical abstract of the United States: 1992* (112th ed.). Washington, DC: U.S. Government Printing Office.

U.S. Bureau of the Census, Department of Commerce, Economics and Statistical Administration. (October 1994). *Income, poverty, and health insurance: 1993.* Washington, DC: U.S. Government Printing Office.

Wilensky, H. L. (1976, May/June). The welfare mess. *Society,* p. 12.

Zero Population Growth. (1993). *Update.* Washington, DC: Author.

FURTHER READING

Block, F., Cloward, R., Ehrenreich, B., & Piven, F. (Eds.). (1987). *The mean season: The attack on the welfare state.* New York: Pantheon Books.

Chambers, D. E. (1993). *Social policy and social programs: A method for the practical public policy analyst* (2nd ed.). New York: Macmillan.

Cook, F. L., & Barrett, E. J. (1992). *Support for the American welfare state: The views of Congress and the public.* New York: Columbia University Press.

Jansson, B. S. (1994). *Social policy: From theory to policy practice.* Pacific Grove, CA: Brooks/Cole.

Kennedy, P. (1993). *Preparing for the twenty-first century.* New York: Random House.

Marshall, T. H. (1965). *Social policy.* London: Hutchinson University Library.

Naisbitt, J., & Alburdene, P. (1990). *Megatrends 2000: Ten new directions for the 1990's.* New York: Avon Books.

President's Research Committee on Social Trends. (1933). *Recent social trends in the United States.* New York: McGraw-Hill.

Rein, M. (1970). *Social policy: Issues of choice and change.* New York: Random House.

Titmuss, R. M. (1959). *Essays on the welfare state.* New Haven, CT: Yale University Press.

Ronald B. Dear, DSW, is faculty senate president and associate professor of social work, School of Social Work, University of Washington, Seattle, WA 98195.

For further information see

Advocacy; Aid to Families with Dependent Children; Child Welfare Policy; Civil Rights; Community; Deinstitutionalization; Ethics and Values; Families Overview; Federal Social Legislation from 1961 to 1994; General Assistance; Homelessness; Housing; Human Rights; Hunger, Nutrition, and Food Programs; Income Distribution; Income Security Overview; Jobs and Earnings; Peace and Social Justice; Policy Analysis; Poverty; Public Social Services; Public Social Welfare Expenditures; Social Development; Social Planning; Social Security; Social Welfare History; Social Work Profession Overview; Social Workers in Politics; Supplemental Security Income; Voluntarism; Welfare Employment Programs: Evaluation.

Key Words

public welfare	welfare reform
social welfare policy	

READER'S GUIDE

Social Work Education

The following entries contain information on this general topic:

Continuing Education
Council on Social Work Education
International Social Welfare: Organizations and Activities

National Association of Social Workers
Social Work Education
Special-Interest Professional Associations

Social Work Education

Michael Frumkin

Gary A. Lloyd

Three levels of social work education are offered in colleges and universities in the 50 states and Puerto Rico: undergraduate, master's, and doctoral. Public colleges and universities are responsible for 55 percent of all programs, 49 percent of baccalaureate programs, and 78 percent of combined undergraduate–graduate programs. In 1993, 302 baccalaureate programs and 117 master's degree programs were in operation. In that same year, baccalaureate programs reporting to the Council on Social Work Education (CSWE) enrolled 36,813 students with full-time status and 6,535 part-time degree students. Another 19,827 undergraduate students were taking social work courses. At the master's level, 21,063 students were enrolled full-time and 11,132 attended part-time. Fifty-three doctoral programs were attended by 1,085 full-time and 949 part-time students (CSWE, 1994d).

EARLY HISTORY

Charity Organization Societies

Social work education developed at the end of the 19th century out of social agencies' concerns about improving the quality and consistency of services for poor and dependent people. From their founding, the Associations for Improving the Conditions of the Poor (1842) and the Charity Organization Societies (1877) had provided some form of in-service training programs for volunteers. Following the economic catastrophe of the Panic and Depression of 1893, many leaders of organized charities concluded that paid agents would have to supplant volunteers. Some formal education would be necessary to ensure an effective level of services.

The experience of the depression of the 1890s, along with observations about the interplay of individual and social causes of distress, brought about a more comprehensive view of the domain and purposes of agencies. Human problems were perceived as being more complex and malleable than had been previously believed. The moralistic approaches of earlier years gave way to an interest in finding and implementing scientific principles for assisting individuals and families with problems. By the end of the century, conviction was growing that educational programs were necessary to ensure the continuity and consistency of services, support the application and development of knowledge, and supply a cadre of trained agents.

Early Schools

The New York Charity Organization Society, acting on such interests and finding that informal agency training was inadequate, sponsored a six-week summer training program in 1898. This program, which was developed in the spirit of Mary E. Richmond's appeal in 1897 for a training school of applied philanthropy, inspired similar efforts in other cities (see Richmond, 1930). Within six years, a one-year educational program was established as the New York School of Philanthropy (later the New York School of Social Work and, since 1962, the Columbia University School of Social Work). These first programs focused attention on issues of the requisite content of the curriculum, the relationship between education and practice, and the development and application of educational standards, all of which have remained central concerns throughout the history of social work education.

Most of the early schools were independent but related to casework agencies in New York, Boston, Philadelphia, and St. Louis. Accounts differ as to when, where, and how social work progressed from independent status to affiliation with institutions of higher learning. A strong trend toward university affiliation was discernible from 1904 to 1907, when a few social work programs developed within universities; one such program was the Chicago School for Services and Philanthropy, which became part of the University of Chicago in 1907. In addition to social work programs offered independently and within universities, some education was provided through sequences of undergraduate courses, frequently offered by departments of sociology. Irrespective of the location or affiliation of these programs, casework agencies were usually influential in curricular matters related to preparing for casework practice in family welfare, child welfare, and psychiatric and medical settings.

Development of Standards

By the end of World War I, the 17 social work programs that existed were organized as the Association of Training Schools for Professional Social Work, which became the American Association of Schools of Social Work (AASSW) in 1927. The association, established primarily for communication purposes, became a forum for the development of educational standards. In 1924 it suggested standards for an organized curriculum, responsible administrative leadership, and university affiliation. In 1932 AASSW adopted a minimum one-year curriculum plan that specified certain courses and required both classroom and field instruction. It also formulated a policy that instituted standardized course work and accreditation in social work education. In 1934 AASSW formulated additional standards regarding the adequacy of program budgets, full-time faculty, library resources, and fieldwork.

The trend toward university affiliation culminated in 1937 with a policy limiting membership in AASSW to social work schools that operated in institutions of higher learning that were approved by the Association of American Universities. All university-based schools were subsequently accepted into AASSW under this standard. Another standard, issued in 1937 and implemented in 1939, required a two-year program leading to a master's degree as a condition for AASSW membership. The two-year graduate program remained the only recognized format for accredited status until 1974.

The AASSW stance on graduate-level education did not receive unanimous support. Some public institutions that were committed to preparing social workers for state-supported welfare, social insurance, and public recreation agencies offered undergraduate majors in social science and social work or master's degree programs comprising four undergraduate years and one graduate year of study. These programs, not eligible for AASSW membership after 1939, banded together in 1942 as the National Association of Schools of Social Administration (NASSA).

COUNCIL ON SOCIAL WORK EDUCATION

Standards and Policy Statements

1950s to 1970s. Both AASSW and NASSA formulated educational standards, and their versions of appropriate and necessary education for social work practice differed. By 1950, the two associations had distributed 32 conflicting standards. The National Council on Social Work Education was established in 1946 to resolve these differences and to end the resulting confusion. Membership in the council was drawn from universities, the professional associations, and voluntary and governmental agencies. *Social Work Education in the United States,* frequently referred to as the Hollis-Taylor report (Hollis & Taylor, 1951), was a landmark study of social work education. Sponsored

by the National Council on Social Work Education and supported by funds from the Carnegie Corporation, the report influenced the social work curriculum throughout the following decade and inspired the creation of the Council on Social Work Education (CSWE) in 1952. CSWE is the only national organization that represents both baccalaureate and master's level social work education.

Concerns expressed through AASSW and NASSA about standardization of the curriculum, the accreditation and evaluation of social work programs, and levels of professional preparation have continued to be important in CSWE and throughout social work education. A number of CSWE curriculum policies and formats have addressed these concerns. The so-called basic eight curriculum, advanced by AASSW in 1944, gave way to a more flexible approach in a CSWE policy statement of 1952, which required content to be organized under the rubrics of social services, human behavior, and social welfare policy and services. Whereas AASSW required that the basic eight (social casework, public welfare, social group work, community organization, administration, research, medical information, and psychiatric information) be taught in accredited programs, the 1952 policy did not specify courses.

Although this change gave schools and programs considerably more autonomy, questions persisted about the consistency of educational experiences from program to program, about the number and nature of specializations, and about the pervasive focus on social casework in most curricula. These and related curricular concerns were explored in CSWE's extensive *Social Work Curriculum Study* (Boehm, 1959, sometimes referred to as the Boehm study). The Boehm study was instrumental in refocusing attention on group work, community organization, administration, and research. It proposed theoretical frameworks from the social sciences and presented a broadened perspective on casework. The study was also a significant force in turning educators' attention to the need for formulating more specific educational objectives. Many aspects of the study were incorporated into CSWE's 1962 curriculum policy statement.

Within a short time, however, concerns arose yet again that policies were too prescriptive. The "Curriculum Policy for the Master's Degree Program in Graduate Schools of Social Work" (CSWE, 1971) allowed programs considerable latitude for designing specific courses and learning experiences. Study was required in social welfare policy and services, human behavior and the social environment, and social work practice, but organization of the curriculum was to be determined by faculty. The field practicum was presented as an essential curricular component.

1984 Curriculum Policy Statement (CPS). Programs' desires for autonomy continued to conflict with the need for consistency in the preparation of students for professional practice. Social work educators seemed to favor a middle course, expecting programs to conform to certain core content and values, while allowing them freedom to shape specific program elements. That course is reflected in the 1984 CPS (CSWE, 1984), which was adopted by the CSWE Board of Directors in 1982 for implementation in 1983 or 1984 at the option of accredited programs. This CPS succeeded the 1969 provisions for master's degree programs and provided the first curriculum policy statement for baccalaureate education. It served as the basis for the development of educational programs and the accreditation of social work programs, maintaining the prerogative of schools and programs to design curricula but requiring specific attention to the relationship between levels of social work education. For the first time, a single, binding policy statement acknowledged a situation that had existed since 1974: social work education in four-year undergraduate, as well as two-year graduate, programs leading to professional degrees.

The baccalaureate curriculum is expected to prepare students for beginning social work practice, to explicate generalist practice, and to establish the professional foundation. The CPS maintained a traditional stance on the discretion of programs to design courses while requiring that five areas be covered and designated as the professional foundation: human behavior and the social environment, social welfare policy and services, social work practice, research, and the field practicum. It was not required that the content of the professional foundation curriculum be taught in discrete courses, and integration of content was stressed.

The CPS specified that social work education at the master's level, which prepares students for advanced practice, should include the professional foundation and one or more concentrations. Each program would design its own advanced social work curriculum and concentrations, which could be organized according to fields of practice (such as services to families), problem areas (such as delinquency), population groups (such as children), or practice roles (such as practice with individuals, families, or groups). A concentration in advanced generalist practice was also supported. Concentrations were required to include

content on social policy and legislation; service strategies, from prevention through treatment; and relevant practice theories.

The CPS also clearly conveyed the view that a liberal arts perspective is a prerequisite for both undergraduate and graduate professional education. It gave unprecedented attention to values and the need for content specific to populations that have systematically experienced oppression because of ethnicity, gender, age, religion, disability, sexual orientation, or culture.

1994 CPS. The most recent versions of the baccalaureate and master's level CPSs, developed by the Commission on Educational Policy and Planning and approved by the CSWE Board of Directors in 1992 (CSWE, 1994a, 1994b) strongly emphasize social work education's commitment "to prepare competent and effective social work professionals who are committed to practice that includes services to the poor and oppressed, and who work to alleviate poverty, oppression, and discrimination" (CSWE, 1994a, p. 101; CSWE, 1994b, p. 140). They provide programs with increased freedom to design curricula while maintaining the 1984 CPS concepts of foundation and advanced content and specify, for the first time, a series of individualized student outcome measures, at both the baccalaureate and master's levels, that programs must attain.

CHANGES IN SOCIAL WORK EDUCATION

Changes in Curriculum

From the mid-1950s onward, the evolution of curricular policies and the debates concerning them took place in a climate of considerable change in social work education. Internal forces, such as the Boehm (1959) study, and external pressures coming from such arenas as the civil rights movement of the 1960s and the Reagan "revolution" of the 1980s necessitated changes in purposes and formats of the social work curriculum. In the 1960s, when social work's commitment to working with the poor was challenged, schools turned unprecedented attention to the "macro" areas of social welfare policy, administration, and planning. The "micro" practice areas of casework and group work for a time attracted fewer students, even though the interpersonal perspective of casework was enhanced by the application of systems theories and the development of ecological perspectives. Variations of combined methods and "generic" or "generalist" curricular formats emerged in the late 1950s in many programs. These variations attracted major interest by the mid-1960s because of their "person-in-environment" focus that seemed more applicable to contemporary education and practice than customary "methods-bound" approaches.

Fluctuations in Enrollment and Students' Interests

When the New Frontier and War on Poverty programs of the federal government provided scholarships and other financial assistance to students in the mid- to late 1960s, the number of undergraduate and graduate programs increased and student enrollments grew. When subsequent cuts in federal support for education and social services occurred from the mid-1970s to the mid-1980s, the decrease in admissions, number of faculty members, and experimental or innovative curricular designs was severe. The optimism and change of the 1960s gave way to retrenchment and a reassessment of professional purposes and values. Micro areas regained primacy in the curriculum, and the number of programs offering concentrations in clinical social work increased. Social work education attracted fewer students in general; there was a sharp decline in applicants, especially those who were interested in the macro areas.

The mid-1980s saw the beginning of a resurgence of interest by students in pursuing professional social work education, at both the baccalaureate and master's degree levels. From 1985 through 1993, there was continuous growth in the number of enrolled students at both levels. This renewed interest also led to a concomitant increase in the number of accredited baccalaureate and master's programs. The most common pattern of growth was the movement of baccalaureate programs to combined programs through the addition of master's degree programs. The generalist focus of undergraduate social work education led to the renewed interest in advanced generalist practice as a concentration area at the graduate level. This growth took place, however, within an environment of shrinking economic resources, so that programs were frequently placed in the situation of balancing increased demands with their ability to provide state-of-the-art social work education. In the early 1990s, there was also a reinvestment in preparing students for public sector practice, particularly in services to children and families, spurred by the availability of federal stipends and the formation of partnerships between social work programs and public human service agencies (CSWE, 1994d).

LEVELS OF SOCIAL WORK EDUCATION

Social work education encompasses undergraduate, master's, and doctoral degree programs. In the 1960s, following optimistic projections of the need for social services personnel, associate of arts or certification programs were viewed as part of the continuum of social work education. Associate of arts programs are no longer considered part of social work education, and many of the programs that are still in existence now operate under a "human services" designation.

Although social work education has a long tradition of providing courses and degrees at the undergraduate level, such endeavors were not accorded professional recognition until 1970. In that year, NASW admitted bachelor's-level practitioners to membership. The following year, CSWE—which at the time offered membership and policy guidance to undergraduate programs—established a review process whereby such programs could receive approval. As the number of baccalaureate programs increased during the late 1960s and early 1970s, concerns were expressed about the limited scope of and sanction for the approval process, quality control, and professional accountability. CSWE sought and received the authority of the U.S. Department of Education to accredit programs at the undergraduate level while maintaining the accreditation of master's degree programs.

The U.S. Department of Education granted CSWE this authority after the CSWE guidelines for reviewing programs were revised and expanded into a set of accreditation standards for undergraduate degree programs in 1974. These standards were superseded by those adopted by the CSWE Board of Directors in both 1984 and 1994.

Baccalaureate Programs

The major objective of baccalaureate programs must be to prepare students for professional practice. These programs may also prepare students for advanced study in social work and provide service courses on social work concerns and methods to students who are not seeking degrees in social work. Programs vary in format, but a program of two years of liberal arts study (with perhaps one or two introductory-level professional courses), followed by two years of study in the social work major, is typical. In addition to study in the foundation curriculum, each student must complete a field practicum of at least 400 clock hours. Programs tend to be small; for example, in 1993–94, about two-thirds of the programs enrolled fewer than 75 full-time students in the junior and senior years. In the same academic year, 10,288 students graduated from baccalaureate social work programs. Of all graduating students, 86.4 percent were female and 23.4 percent were people of color (CSWE, 1994d).

Master's Degree Programs

The chief objective of master's level education is to prepare students for advanced practice. Master's degree programs provide the professional foundation courses needed by students who enter them without baccalaureate degrees in social work and avoid the duplication of foundation content for graduates of baccalaureate social work programs. Although variations occur, the two-year format for graduate education is still typical. The first year is usually given over to the foundation curriculum and a field practicum, and the second year includes an advanced concentration and field practicum. The CPS (CSWE, 1994b) requires at least 900 hours of field practicum. In the academic year 1992–93, 12,583 students were awarded the master of social work degree. Of all graduating students, 81.8 percent were female and 20.7 percent were people of color (CSWE, 1994d).

Doctoral Programs

Doctoral programs in social work are not accredited by CSWE, but are reviewed by their respective educational institutions. They usually present a central objective of advanced preparation for research or teaching. Before 1950, doctoral education in social work was available only at Bryn Mawr College and the University of Chicago (Bernard, 1977). Advanced social work education was commonly provided through third-year programs, which have virtually disappeared because of the steady growth in the number of doctoral programs. For example, the number of doctoral programs rose from 33 in 1976 to 53 in 1993, when 229 doctoral degrees were awarded (CSWE, 1994d). Both PhD and doctor of social work degrees are offered. In recent years, interest has grown in "clinical doctorate" programs that prepare post-master's students for advanced levels of clinical social work practice.

Three national membership organizations (Association of Baccalaureate Program Directors, National Association of Deans and Directors of Graduate Social Work Education, and Group for the Advancement of Doctoral Education) have been developed by educators at the baccalaureate, masters, and doctoral levels respectively. These organizations provide a range of educational programs for their member institutions, including annual conferences, the undertaking of research projects, and activities supportive of the social work profession.

Issues of Integration

Ideally, the three levels of social work education are clearly interrelated, each being compatible with the others despite their distinct goals. In fact, however, the issue of "continuum," or "linkage," has not been resolved despite persistent efforts. The CSWE Task Force on Structure and Quality (Ripple, 1974) addressed this issue by recommending several options, including a common base of "core content" (analogous to the present professional foundation) to be completed at the undergraduate level or, for non-social work degree majors, taken before entry into an 11-month master's degree program. No consensus was reached on the issue.

The CSWE Commission on Education Policy and Planning has periodically addressed the continuum problem, but many questions remain unresolved: How well are the levels integrated? Is professional-foundation content taught at the baccalaureate level the same as that taught at the master's level? What methods can be effective for evaluating the congruence of content in master's and baccalaureate levels of professional education? How does the professional foundation support the advanced concentrations? What links the master's and doctoral levels? Although there are formal and informal programmatic linkages among the three levels, the development of a true educational continuum continues to elude social work education.

ACCREDITATION

Establishing standards and monitoring the performance of programs has been an important aspect of social work education since 1927. Accreditation is the core function of CSWE. The CSWE president appoints the Commission on Accreditation (COA), a semiautonomous unit of CSWE that succeeded AASSW in this capacity. Policies are approved by the CSWE Board of Directors. In its operations, however, COA functions independently within a framework of its own guidelines. It is empowered to accredit both baccalaureate and master's programs by the Council on Regulating Postsecondary Accreditation (CORPA). COA, the sole accrediting body in social work education, consists of educators and directors of baccalaureate programs, deans or directors and faculty of master's or combined programs, agency representatives, and two prominent members of the public who are not affiliated with social work education.

Shortly after the approval process for undergraduate programs was instituted in 1971, interest heightened in accreditation at the baccalaureate level. Standards were formulated and applied beginning in 1974, but they were not as comprehensive as those contained in the *Manual of Accrediting Standards for Graduate Professional Schools of Social Work* (see CSWE, 1971). The 1974 baccalaureate standards offered some guidelines for the development of curriculum, but did not contain a formal policy statement equal to that set forth for graduate programs.

In 1980 COA began to revise its standards for master's programs (the 1971 revised manual had governed graduate-level social work education for more than a decade) and to formulate new and complementary standards for undergraduate education. It related these standards to a unified curriculum policy statement (CSWE, 1984), which governed curricular matters and established areas for evaluation. This policy statement was adopted for both levels of social work education by the CSWE Board of Directors in May 1982, and the principle of a single curriculum policy statement (CPS) for undergraduate and graduate social work education continues as part of the 1994 CPS. Also approved by the CSWE board and implemented in July 1984 were the accreditation standards that had been developed by COA through its own working committees, consultation with CORPA, hearings with constituency groups, and presentations to the CSWE board. Following a similar process, a new set of standards was adopted by the CSWE board in 1994 for implementation in June 1995. Standards for both levels, accompanied by descriptions of statuses and procedures and the CPSs, are presented in the *Handbook of Accreditation Standards and Procedures* (CSWE, 1994c).

Eligibility versus Evaluative Standards

Unlike all previous guidelines, both the 1984 and 1994 accreditation policies clearly differentiate between eligibility and evaluative standards for baccalaureate and master's degree programs. Eligibility standards are applied to determine whether a school or program meets criteria that are prerequisite to evaluation.

Eligibility standards. For baccalaureate programs, eligibility standards require that (1) a program must be an integral part of an educational institution accredited to award the baccalaureate degree, (2) the chief executive officer of the institution must authorize COA's review of the program, and (3) the institution must indicate on its transcripts or other permanent records that the students have completed a program of preparation for beginning professional practice. Other eligibility standards require specification of social work as a major, identification of the social work program as a discrete entity in the institutional catalog, provision of a qualified director, appointment of faculty holding master's degrees in social work and having experience in professional social work

practice, and formalized affirmative action and nondiscrimination policies.

Eligibility standards for master's degree programs are similar to those for baccalaureate programs. Differences include the requirement that the master's degree program must specify that it prepares students for entry to advanced social work practice, offers two years of full-time study (at least one of which must be taken with full-time status), and has a full-time dean or director.

Evaluative standards. After schools or programs have met eligibility standards, evaluative standards guide the preparation of self-study and the conduct of on-site evaluations. The areas of evaluation mandated in the 1994 standards by COA are the same for both the undergraduate and master's levels: the rationale for and assessment, organization, governance, and resources of programs; nondiscrimination; faculty; student development; curriculum; alternative programs; and experimental programs.

Educational Issues

Liberal arts perspective. The development of accreditation standards encompasses judgments about and prescriptions for educational issues that educators have debated for a long while. For example, from the beginning of professional social work education, the relationship between professional education and liberal arts education had been examined. Some social work educators believed that the liberal arts perspective provided an essential basis for professional education, whereas others thought that content mastered at the undergraduate level was less important than motivation for graduate social work education.

This issue became more pressing when NASW and CSWE recognized the BSW as the first professional degree because a student might conceivably graduate after having taken mostly professional courses. The COA addressed this issue by requiring that baccalaureate programs have "clearly defined procedures for assuring that students have acquired the liberal arts perspective before they enter social work courses, for which such content is a prerequisite" (CSWE, 1994c, p. 90). Master's programs are required to demonstrate how they meet the expectation that graduate professional education "is built on the liberal arts perspective" (CSWE, 1994c, p. 128). Other issues that are reflected in both the 1984 and 1994 standards include renewed attention to programs' need for autonomy and the position that field instruction must be a clearly designed educational experience.

Cultural diversity. The 1994 standards reinforce social work education's commitment to including issues of nondiscrimination and cultural diversity as legitimate areas of exploration during self-study and external evaluation for accreditation. The nondiscrimination standard requires that every aspect of a program's organization and implementation shall be "conducted without discrimination on the basis of race, color, gender, age, creed, ethnic or national origin, disability, or political or sexual orientation" (CSWE, 1994c, p. 122). Programs and schools must also demonstrate that they have made "specific continuous efforts" to enrich the educational experience offered to students by reflecting racial, ethnic, and cultural diversity throughout the curriculum and in the composition of a program's faculty and students. Courses throughout the curriculum must present diverse racial, ethnic, and cultural perspectives. In addition, the standards call for special, continuous efforts to include content on women's issues and gay and lesbian issues, as well as to ensure that all courses and field practicums incorporate objectives, outcomes, and content on the role and status of women.

COA offers new programs Candidacy for Accredited Status and Initial Accreditation Review. After Initial Accreditation, accredited status lasts for eight years. The commission may then choose to defer action, extend conditional accredited status, or move to withdraw accreditation.

CONTINUING EDUCATION

The 1960s and early 1970s saw a growth in the scope of continuing education efforts in social work. Although reduced in number and attendance by the budgetary restrictions of the 1980s and 1990s, continuing education workshops, short courses, and seminars are offered by many social work programs to help practitioners refresh or refine skills or learn about developing practice methods and problem areas. The growth in state licensure of social workers, along with concomitant continuing education requirements, has provided an expanded market for continuing education activities. Social work programs and licensing boards often collaborate on designing or implementing continuing education courses to meet the specific needs of licensed social workers.

Continuing education programs are offered directly through social work programs or schools or in conjunction with university divisions of continuing education. CSWE's curriculum policy and accreditation standards do not allow social work programs to offer continuing education courses as substitutes for or equivalencies of baccalaureate or master's level courses. Content from either baccalaureate or graduate curricula may be offered in a continuing education format to paraprofessionals or people who are preparing to enter professional education. Programs may offer continuing education units that are analogous to course credits. In some states, participation in continuing education on a regular basis is tied to job promotions and salary increases.

INTERNATIONAL SOCIAL WORK EDUCATION

Biennial meetings of the International Association of Schools of Social Work (IASSW) provide the major forum for exchanging ideas and assessing the state of social work education throughout the world. Although the accreditation process is used only in North America and there is no international standard for assessing quality, IASSW has formulated criteria for including schools of social work in the *World Guide to Social Work Education* (IASSW, 1984). These criteria require an educational program to have the "objective of preparation for social work, as social work is understood within the respective country" (p. ix). Other criteria relate to the areas covered by accreditation procedures in the United States and Canada: the duration of programs (two years, including preprofessional courses), the nature of study (theoretical and applied), full-time staff, library resources, admissions policies, and so on. The duration, format, and specific objectives of programs vary according to national policies, cultural attitudes, and structure of higher education. In 1994 IASSW was supported by 433 member schools in five regional associations (Africa, 36; Asian-Pacific region, 125; Europe, 179; Latin America, 30; and the North American-Caribbean region, 63).

Using the regional associations as its main programming arm, IASSW offers special seminars, consultation, and special projects throughout the world. A number of social work programs in the United States are involved in collaborative and consultative relationships with social work programs in such countries as Mexico, China, and the republics of the former Soviet Union.

RELATIONSHIP BETWEEN EDUCATION AND PRACTICE

Social work education has developed within the context of agencies and agency practice. The application of classroom learning in agency or field practicum settings has been a characteristic of social work education throughout its history. Yet despite this long, productive, and sometimes close association, the relationship between practice and education is not an easy one to maintain.

Different Perspectives

Educators and practitioners frequently have different perspectives on establishing goals and preparing for practice. The agency must, almost by definition, provide services within a fairly specific organizational charter and context. The social work program or school is oriented toward the same service domains and value premises as an agency, but most accommodate the expectations and perspectives of higher education as well. These sometimes complementary, sometimes discrepant vantage points of agency and university probably work against a high degree of compatibility between practice and education. Nevertheless, practitioners and agencies have remained an integral part of instruction in the field practicum and sometimes in the classroom. Many schools and programs serve as resources to agencies for in-service training and continuing education.

Cooperative Ventures

CSWE and NASW. Although CSWE and NASW are separate organizations, they have engaged in cooperative ventures that have reflected both the strain and the pattern of accommodation found in practice-education relationships. NASW, for example, has consistently supported the accreditation of graduate and undergraduate programs and requires graduation from a CSWE-accredited program as a prerequisite for membership. COA site-visiting teams include a representative from practice and evaluate the field practicum curriculum, but the primary focus is on the formulation and attainment of educational objectives. For some years, a joint board committee of the two organizations has met several times a year to explore issues of mutual concern.

Field practicums. Practice and education most frequently come together in field-practicum experiences. When social work moved away from the apprenticeship model early in its history, the agency came to be viewed as a laboratory, not as an on-the-job training site. This shift greatly increased expectations that agency field instructors had to know both their own agencies and roles and the key elements of the social work program's curriculum and theoretical perspectives. Because of concern that such expectations could not be realized, some schools and programs moved in the 1960s and 1970s to develop field-practicum units that were supervised by faculty members. Whereas some educators believed that such an approach strengthened the theory-

practice connection, others argued that the units were contrived and devoid of the richness of agency practice. Although considerable assessments were made, no consensus developed. Fiscal constraints of the 1980s and 1990s not only sharply reduced the number of faculty-led practicum units, but lessened the ability of social agencies to devote declining resources to the development of field-practicum experiences for students; thus, once again, programs and agencies had to rethink their relationship.

Typically, a school or program will appoint a field-practicum coordinator who works with agency personnel to develop practicum placements, oversee the implementation of educationally focused objectives, and monitor the progress of students. Additional faculty may sometimes be appointed to serve in a field-practicum liaison capacity. Accreditation standards mandate input from field agencies and the practice community, and many schools and programs have advisory committees through which agency personnel can participate in the development of the curriculum and address mutual educational and practice concerns. The combination of shrinking resources, the increasing complexity of clients' problems, and the availability of new technologies argue for a new collaborative effort between social work education and practice that is focused on developing new models for 21st-century education and practice.

The Future

As social work education approaches the 21st century, a number of important issues require systematic thought, reflection, and action, including the need to

- identify more explicitly the domain of professional social work practice and education and to link this conceptualization to the development of a refined base of knowledge and skills in the profession
- relate the characteristics of an increasingly diverse society to the development of curricular and practice models
- reinforce the relevance of social work research as a political instrument in the definition and solution of social problems
- reconceptualize the relationship among social work programs, the academic settings in which they exist, and their commitment to involvement in the community and to social change.

Millenium Project

Recognizing the need to respond to these, as well as a number of other important concerns, the profession has responded through the creation of two exciting initiatives. The first and most inclusive initiative is the Millennium Project, established by the CSWE Board of Directors in 1994. This project was designed as an ongoing initiative to encourage the widest possible dialogue about the nature of social work education and practice through the use of such vehicles as white papers and their presentation and debate at national and regional forums, as well as the use of social work journals to report on these efforts. Its goals are to (1) identify clearly the formulations that serve as the foundation for social work education, (2) develop forums at which these formulations can be discussed and debated in a systematic and thoughtful manner, (3) encourage social work educators to develop conceptualizations of the nature of social work education that will allow for the development of effective 21st-century social work practice, and (4) foster the creation and testing of experimental program designs that are based on these conceptualizations.

Institute for the Advancement of Social Work Research

The second initiative is the result of the joint efforts of five organizations representing the social work practice and education communities (Association of Baccalaureate Program Directors, CSWE, Group for the Advancement of Doctoral Education, National Association of Deans and Directors of Social Work Education Programs, and NASW) to design an appropriate structure to meet the research-enhancement needs of the profession. The result was the creation in 1992 of a free-standing organization known as the Institute for the Advancement of Social Work Research.

The overall goal of the institute is to promote and strengthen research in the social work profession and to improve the effectiveness of services and public policies for problems of serious social concern. The specific purposes of the institute are to (1) link social work practitioners and their agencies with academic social work researchers, and social work researchers with each other and with interdisciplinary research teams; (2) provide technical assistance to increase the quantity, quality, and utility of social work research for practice and policy; (3) disseminate the findings of social work research; (4) increase public and private funding for social work research and the training of researchers; (5) collect and update data on social work researchers and research training nationally; and (6) educate the public about the contributions of social work research in addressing problems of serious public concern.

The willingness of social work educators and practitioners to follow through on these and future commitments to taking an increasingly proactive stance in systematically assessing and acting on issues that are important to both the profession and society will play a large role in shaping the nature of 21st-century social work education and practice.

REFERENCES

Bernard, L. D. (1977). Education for social work. In J. B. Turner (Ed.-in-Chief), *Encyclopedia of social work* (17th ed., Vol. 1, pp. 290–305). Washington, DC: National Association of Social Workers.

Boehm, W. M. (1959). *Social work curriculum study* (13 vols.). New York: Council on Social Work Education.

Council on Social Work Education. (1971). Curriculum policy for the master's degree program in graduate schools of social work. In *Manual of accrediting standards for graduate professional schools of social work* (Appendix I, pp. 55–60). New York: Author.

Council on Social Work Education. (1984). Curriculum policy for the master's degree and baccalaureate degree programs in social work education. In *Handbook of accreditation standards and procedures*. New York: Author.

Council on Social Work Education. (1994a). Curriculum policy statement for baccalaureate degree programs in social work education (pp. 96–104). In *Handbook of accreditation standards and procedures* (pp. 96–104). Alexandria, VA: Author.

Council on Social Work Education. (1994b). Curriculum policy statement for master's degree programs in social work education. In *Handbook of accreditation standards and procedures* (pp. 134–144). Alexandria, VA: Author.

Council on Social Work Education. (1994c). *Handbook of accreditation standards and procedures*. Alexandria, VA: Author.

Council on Social Work Education. (1994d). *Statistics on social work education in the United States: 1993*. New York: Todd M. Lennon.

Hollis, E. V., & Taylor, A. L. (1951). *Social work education in the United States*. New York: Columbia University Press.

International Association of Schools of Social Work. (1984). *World guide to social work education*. New York: Council on Social Work Education.

Lloyd, G. (1987). Social work education. In A. Minahan (Ed.-in-Chief), *Encyclopedia of social work* (18th ed., Vol. 2, pp. 695–705). Silver Spring, MD: National Association of Social Workers.

Richmond, M. E. (1930). The need of a training school in applied philanthropy. In *The long view* (pp. 99–104). New York: Russell Sage Foundation.

Ripple, L. (1974). *Report to the Task Force on Structure and Quality in Social Work Education*. New York: Council on Social Work Education.

FURTHER READING

Task Force on Social Work Research. (1991). *Task Force on Social Work Research—Building social work knowledge for effective services and policies*. Austin, TX: Author.

Zlotnik, J. L. (1993). *Social work education and public human services—Developing partnerships*. Alexandria, VA: Council on Social Work Education.

Michael Frumkin, PhD, is director, Inland Empire School of Social Work and Human Services, Eastern Washington University, MS-19, Senior Hall, 526 5th Street, Cheney, WA 99004, and president of CSWE, 1992–1995.
Gary A. Lloyd, PhD, BCSW, ACSW, BCD, is professor and coordinator, Institute for Research and Training in HIV/AIDS, Tulane University, School of Social Work, New Orleans, LA 70118.

For further information see

Clinical Social Work; Continuing Education; Council on Social Work Education; Direct Practice Overview; Ethics and Values; International Social Work Education; Licensing, Regulation, and Certification; National Association of Social Workers; Professional Conduct; Social Work Profession Overview.

Key Words

accreditation	curriculum policy
Council on Social	statement
Work Education	education
	millenium

Social Work Practice: History and Evolution
Donald Brieland

From the mid-18th century to the end of the 19th century, social work has evolved from societies organized to assist and reform poor people to a major professional discipline. Early activities were carried out by volunteers who acquired their skills and knowledge in an apprenticeship system. Over time the profession moved toward graduate education and a common framework of practice. Social work has evolved into an extraordinarily diverse profession that struggles to incorporate the theory and practice developments necessary to achieve its mission. This entry addresses the history and evolution of social work practice and reviews the political and economic developments that have affected practice.

FRIENDLY VISITORS

The organized antecedents of modern social work practice began with friendly visitors in the early 1800s—middle-class women who volunteered to visit indigent families and who eventually served Associations for Improving the Condition of the Poor that were formed in the 1840s and the Charity Organization Societies (COS) that developed later in the 1870s. Their training was based on apprenticeship.

Friendly visitors were influenced by the English Poor Laws, which were enacted from 1601 to 1834 and widely accepted in the American colonies. The Poor Laws directed local governments to take responsibility for assistance; returned needy persons to their place of birth to obtain aid; and disqualified "sturdy beggars," who were considered to be able-bodied and hence employable. The almshouse was the site of aid. The first of many American almshouses was established in 1657. The almshouse keeper had submitted the lowest bid to operate the institution and profited from the labors of the residents. The 1834 amendments to the Poor Laws established "less eligibility"; that is, the benefits provided could not exceed the lowest wage.

Outdoor Relief

In the 1800s outdoor relief—assistance to people who remained in their homes—was still considered wasteful. The needy were more likely to get advice from a friendly visitor than tangible in-kind aid, and they certainly would not qualify for cash payments. Support went to the smallest number, at the least cost, and for the shortest time.

In 1818 the New York Society for the Prevention of Pauperism described its approach to friendly visiting as follows:

> to divide the city into very small districts, and to appoint, from the members of the Society, two or three visitors for each district, whose duty it shall be to become acquainted with the inhabitants of the district, to visit frequently the families of those who are in indigent circumstances, to advise them with respect to their business, the education of their children, the economy of their houses, to administer encouragement or admonition, as they may find occasion. (Pumphrey & Pumphrey, 1961, p. 59)

The society sought to bring together all the spontaneous charities of the town into one channel, to prevent "deception and other evils" (Pumphrey & Pumphrey, 1961, p. 62).

Development of Charity Organization Societies

Associations for Improving the Conditions of the Poor were started in the 1840s and between 1877 and 1892, 92 COSs, modeled on the London Society for Organizing Charitable Relief and Repressing Mendicancy, were formed in American and Canadian cities—the first one in Buffalo, New York, in 1877. The COSs were the forerunners of modern casework. Friendly visiting was a substitute for almsgiving, using investigation, registration, cooperation, and coordination to determine adequate relief.

The COSs stressed the moral imperative for material aid only to the worthy, summarily rejecting the sturdy beggar, the alcoholic, the womanizer, and the prostitute. Only decades later would environmental conditions be recognized as causes of poverty and illness. The COSs sought to save cities from the evils of pauperism, reduce the cost of charity, and deal with antagonism created by social-class differences.

The New York COS (1888) highlighted work:

> Honest employment, the work that God means every man to do, is the truest basis of relief for every person with physical ability to work. The help which needlessly releases the poor from the necessity of providing for themselves is in violation of divine law and incurs the penalties which follow any infraction of that law. (p. 29)

As a result, the COSs developed employment and legal aid services, also offered later by family casework agencies. The societies stressed religious values based on love (Leiby, 1984). To save "the miserable from the sin of poverty" was a major goal (DeSchweinitz & DeSchweinitz, 1948, p. 109). COSs obtained "a thorough understanding of the background of each case of dependency combined with a series of preconceived moral judgments and presuppositions about the character of the poor and about human nature" (Lubove, 1965, p. 7).

Was friendly visiting really friendly?

> The relation between visitor and client may have been personal, but it was not "friendly" in the sense of the informal, natural cohesiveness of peers sharing similar social and cultural backgrounds. Consequently, the visitor saw in her client less an equal or potential equal than an object of character reformation whose unfortunate and lowly condition resulted from ignorance or deviation from middle-class values and patterns of life-organization: temperance, industriousness, family cohesiveness, frugality, foresight, and moral restraint. (Lubove, 1965, p. 16)

Smith (1892), of the Boston COS, described the apprenticeship of friendly visitors as follows:

> Life itself will still be the chief schoolmaster of the friendly visitor; and the part of the society with which he works must be to bring him into relation with new aspects of life, and to help him by contact and conferences with other workers to see them rightly, and to

use to the best advantage his opportunities for doing good. (p. 445).

Moral superiority did not provide the basis for a satisfactory relationship between volunteers and dependent citizens. Although Zilpha D. Smith visited the same family for 47 years, most friendly visitors did not volunteer for a life career and served but a short time. Consequently, paid staff replaced friendly visitors by the 1900s.

SETTLEMENT HOUSE MOVEMENT

Settlement houses, or settlements as they were also called, were so named because the staff was expected to live in and be a part of the community. Hull-House, the best-known settlement house, was established in 1889 in Chicago by Jane Addams and Ellen Gates Starr. The model was Toynbee Hall, a London settlement that Addams had visited. American settlement house workers were young, idealistic college graduates with a broad liberal education who started as apprentices. Some were volunteers, but others received modest stipends and room and board. In addition to helping individuals, the settlements emphasized solutions to such societal problems as housing, public health, and exploitation by employers.

Comparison with Charity Organization Societies

The work of the settlements provided a direct contrast to the friendly visiting of charity workers, as Addams (1902) noted:

> Let us take a neighborhood of poor people, and test their ethical standards by those of the charity visitor, who comes with the best desire in the world to help them out of their distress. A most striking incongruity, at once apparent, is the difference between the emotional kindness with which relief is given by one poor neighbor to another poor neighbor, and the guarded care with which relief is given by a charity visitor to a charity recipient. The neighborhood mind is at once confronted not only by the difference of method, but by an absolute clashing of two ethical standards.
>
> A very little familiarity with the poor districts of any city is sufficient to show how primitive and genuine are the neighborly relations. There is the greatest willingness to lend or borrow anything, and all the residents of the given tenement know the most intimate family affairs of all the others. The fact that the economic condition of all alike is on a most precarious level makes the ready outflow of sympathy and material assistance the most natural thing in the world. There are numberless instances of self-sacrifice quite unknown in the circles where greater economic advan-

tages make that kind of intimate knowledge of one's neighbors impossible. (pp. 19–20)

As to the attitudes of the COS clients, Addams (1899) wrote: "When they see the delay and caution with which relief is given, these do not appear to them conscientious scruples, but the cold and calculating action of the selfish man" (p. 165). In spite of differences, however, the settlement staff often served as friendly visitors in COS programs, and some friendly visitors volunteered and lived in settlement houses.

The COSs and the settlement houses both contributed to the legacy of social work practice. The careful assessment and accountability that characterized the COS approach laid the foundation for professional casework and were the impetus for professional education. The settlements placed a premium on thorough firsthand knowledge of the clients and their environment. Adult education was provided to empower neighborhood residents.

PROFESSIONAL EDUCATION AND FORMAL METHODS

Role models were not sufficient for friendly visitors, so manuals had to be developed to familiarize them with the basic rules. The friendly visitors clearly needed more education. Mary Richmond (1898), of the Baltimore COS, made a compelling plea for a training school in applied philanthropy at the National Conference on Charities and Correction in 1897. The New York School of Philanthropy (now the Columbia University School of Social Work) opened in 1898 with a six-week summer school. It soon offered courses over the academic year and adopted a two-year program in 1910. Richmond joined its faculty part-time.

By 1919, 17 schools of social work had been established in the United States; by 1923, 13 of them were affiliated with universities. Most students attended part-time, and separate fields of practice had separate curricula. In the 1920s, reflecting dissatisfaction with both in-service training and part-time study, schools established new master's degree programs that required a year of full-time academic study.

COS leaders guided the development of social casework. Richmond became the general secretary of the Philadelphia COS in 1900, and later joined the staff of the Russell Sage Foundation. Her first book, *Social Diagnosis* (1917), presented techniques for assessing the situation of the poor. *What Is Social Case Work?* (1922) defined the casework method as "processes which develop personality through adjustments consciously effected, individ-

ual by individual, between men and their social environment" (pp. 98–99). It presented examples of casework that resulted in "genuine growth in personality" from "strengthened and better adjusted social relations" (pp. 99–100). To Richmond, casework treatment involved the use of resources that facilitated the individual's adjustment to social living, helped clients understand their needs and possibilities, and assisted them in working out their own programs. It was the COSs, not psychiatric social work, that inaugurated the model of long-term service. Richmond's book on casework described how each family portrayed was seen over several years.

FIELDS OF PRACTICE

Medical social work, psychiatric social work, and child welfare were the first three fields to have formal courses, each with a separate curriculum. Medical and psychiatric social work had developed in host settings under physicians; social workers managed only the child welfare agencies.

Medical Social Work

Dr. Richard C. Cabot introduced medical social services at Boston's Massachusetts General Hospital in 1905. Ida M. Cannon was the first social worker. The original medical social workers were nurses who wanted a more independent status. According to Cannon (1923), social work provided "an enlarged understanding of any psychic or social conditions which may cause the patient distress of mind or body," (p. 98) and medical social workers studied "character, human relationships and community life" (p. 98) and had to put themselves in another's place and still see the situation objectively.

By 1912 the Boston School of Social Work offered a one-year course in medical social work. The New York and Philadelphia schools of social work soon followed suit.

Psychiatric Social Work

Social work was expanding to new fields of practice; at the same time, the relationship between psychiatry and casework was developing. Both psychiatrists and caseworkers came to see the individual as a product of the environment, rather than as one to be judged by fixed moral norms. Under the leadership of Adolf Meyer, psychiatry was extended from the mental hospital to the community. After 1910 the mental hygiene movement directed attention to environmental factors in the prevention and treatment of mental illness. Clinics that were established to serve juvenile courts soon provided general child guidance; research was conducted on delinquency, criminality, mental deficiency, and common behavioral problems. Casework was considered a means of solving serious problems of the general population.

The psychiatrist reached into the community, and the psychiatric social worker reached into the home to supervise the activity of the patient. Social psychiatry took into account the patient's social environment and his or her mental and physical condition. Behavior was considered to be dynamic because it responded to the pressures and tensions of the environment.

The first formal courses with psychiatric content were offered in 1908 by Dr. William Healy at the Chicago School of Civics and Philanthropy. Before World War I, training courses were inaugurated at the Boston Psychopathic Hospital, as well as at the New York, Philadelphia, and Smith College schools of social work. After the war, psychiatry become widely accepted. Skilled casework emphasized insight into emotions and psychic life and began to deal with universal problems of mental health and emotional adjustment. Child guidance clinics with grants from the Commonwealth Fund supported psychiatric social workers, who became consultants to family and child welfare agencies. Casework as a source of support and insight became attractive to middle-class people. To serve this clientele, a few social workers began limited private practice.

Child Welfare and Family Casework

In the 1900s, the community transmitted its moral, cultural, and spiritual heritage through the nuclear family. The goal of casework training was to develop skills in differential diagnosis. The distinction between the worthy and unworthy poor was gradually deemphasized, and financial aid for those who were dependent became more acceptable to society.

The insights of differential diagnosis affected the practice of child welfare. The Boston Children's Aid Society provided a two-year training program for new staff members, restricting each worker to about 40 cases. The society had access to the Judge Baker Foundation for the diagnosis and treatment of children, including clients of the newly established juvenile court.

School Social Work

School social work grew out of the teaching role, when settlement houses in New York provided visiting teachers to help improve the school performance of children who faced problematic life situations. The new field offered a broader role than that of the classroom teacher or the attendance officer. Later, school social workers also became change agents, directing their attention to barriers in the school system that affected children's learning and behavior. According to Lubove (1965),

> the visiting teacher dealt with those for whom neither the attendance officer, school nurse, nor classroom teacher was equipped. The teacher or principal referred children whose educational experience was obstructed by deficient scholarship, demoralizing home conditions, misconduct, physical defect, and similar handicaps. After an examination into the background and personality of each child, the visiting teacher used whatever personal influence or social adjustments were necessary to insure efficient performance. She relied upon casework as her major technical resource. (p. 39)

TRAINING AND EDUCATION FOR CASEWORK: TOWARD A GENERIC MODEL

The separate fields in schools of social work made it difficult to move from one field of practice to another. Therefore, caseworkers needed a unified educational model.

The Milford Conference, convened from 1923 to 1927, included both practitioners and educators who produced a single model for social work practice. The Milford report (as the conference came to be known) identified eight generic aspects of casework:

1. knowledge of typical deviations from accepted standards of social life
2. the use of norms of human life and human relationships
3. the significance of social history as the basis of particularizing the human being in need
4. established methods of study and treatment of human beings in need
5. the use of established community resources in social treatment
6. the adaptation of scientific knowledge and formulations of experience to the requirements of social casework
7. the consciousness of a philosophy which determines the purposes, ethics, and obligations of social case work
8. the blending of the foregoing into social treatment. (American Association of Social Workers, 1931, p. 15)

The Milford report defined the distinguishing concern of social casework as the capacity of individuals to structure their social activities within a given environment, a refinement of Richmond's (1922) emphasis on the reciprocal relationship between "men and their social environment" (p. 99). Social casework, the report held, could make the most significant contribution by dealing with the human being's capacity for self-maintenance when it was impaired by deviations from accepted standards of normal social life. The report helped unite practitioners and provided the needed conceptual basis for professional education in casework.

Cause and Function

The relationship between social change and social service became a primary theme in defining social work practice. As Lee (1930), a leader in the Milford Conference and director of the New York School of Social Work, stated in his address to the 1929 National Conference on "Cause and Function":

> Charity in its origin and in its finest expression represents a cause. The organized administration of relief, under whatever auspices, has become a function. The campaigns to obtain widows' pensions and workmen's compensation have many of the aspects of the cause. The administration of these benefits has become a function of organized community life in most American states. The settlement movement began as a cause, and the activities of many of its representatives still give it that character. In general, however, it has developed as a function of community life. The abolition of child labor has been, and still is, a cause. As the result of its success as a cause, it again has become a well-established function in many American states. (p. 4)

Research

Although the Milford group recognized the need to measure social services, initial research dealt with the environment or improvement of agency operations. Warner (1894) studied the causes of poverty from American, English, and German sources. Committed to the investigatory role of the COS, he used the categories *worthy* or *unworthy* in evaluating applications for relief, but he also distinguished *misconduct* from *misfortune.* According to Warner, 40 percent of those investigated in the United States needed work rather than relief. Thus, unemployment came to be seen as a cause of poverty that was not under the individual's control.

Surveys. Survey methodology was developed early in the 20th century. The pioneering survey of industrial conditions in Pittsburgh, conducted in 1909, led to social reform, including national acceptance of workers' compensation. At least a hundred cities developed plans for similar projects (Kellogg, 1914).

The second Pittsburgh survey (Klein, 1938), conducted from August 1934 to January 1936, evaluated agencies and institutions, focusing on seven social work areas: child welfare, family casework, financing, health, personnel, public relief, and recreation. Unfortunately, both surveys depended more on expert opinions than on clear standards (Zimbalist, 1977). By World War II, small specialized needs assessments had replaced the large survey.

The settlements took a different approach to research. Their prototype was *Hull-House Maps and Papers: A Presentation of Nationalities and Wages in a Congested District in Chicago* (Residents of Hull-House, 1895) which presented ethnic, racial, and sociological characteristics of the district, as well as maps that described commercial and residential properties and wage rates (the top wage was $30 per month). The development of the Social Work Research Group in 1948 stimulated the growth of systematic inquiry when it brought together researchers from public and voluntary agencies and university faculties. The group was one of the organizations that joined to form NASW. As a section of NASW, it sponsored a series of conferences on various research issues during the decade beginning in 1955.

Education. Measuring the efficacy of treatment services through social workers' ratings of change in clients came much later. Kogan, Hunt, and Bartelme (1953) and Geismar (1971) developed scales for use in evaluation. However, subjects in control groups generally functioned about as well as multiproblem families receiving experimental casework treatments. The control group model is not feasible for use outside a research project. The nine scales devised by Hudson (1982), which are filled out by the client, better meet the needs of students and practitioners for evaluating their practice. Topics include general contentment, self-esteem, marital satisfaction, sexual satisfaction, parental attitudes, child's attitude toward mother, child's attitude toward father, family relations, and peer relations.

In the single-subject approach, a practitioner may use a client's responses on the Hudson scales to assess the client's status before treatment and use this information as the baseline, readministering the scales to evaluate the client's later functioning. The client thus serves as his or her own control. The main requirement is data collection from a thorough initial assessment *before* treatment begins.

To advance the practice of other social workers, the formal evaluation of change requires not only the dissemination of results but the description of the actual treatment process in sufficient detail to permit replication.

SOCIAL WORK IN THE NEW DEAL

According to Leiby (1978), the 1920s was the seed time for New Deal reforms. But although caseworkers were developing services for the middle class, as a group they did not assume leadership in the new public agency programs for poor people that were occasioned by the Great Depression of the 1930s. There were too few social workers to meet the crisis, and many of those who were practicing were no longer involved with poor people. Public assistance programs authorized by the Social Security Act employed some social workers, especially for direct services to children. As in the COS era, cost control became a major issue. Most state officials considered people with a business background to be more efficient managers of the large relief programs. Public agencies have never placed the same value on professional social workers as have voluntary agencies.

The federal government eventually provided grants-in-aid to state agencies for social work education grants to public agency employees if these staff members agreed to come back to the agency for a specified period. The training stipends became an important source of personnel. However, many graduates moved to voluntary agencies as soon as they completed their contractual commitments.

OTHER SOCIAL WORK METHODS

Social Group Work

Group work did not join casework as a part of social work practice and education until the 1930s. Pioneer group workers in the settlement movement had no systematic training. Jane Addams did not espouse a social work identity, calling herself resident head or settlement worker (Brieland, 1990). She and her staff used apprenticeship to meet the interests and needs of neighborhood residents as they saw them.

The Salvation Army, settlement houses, and youth services agencies emphasized character building. The latter brought group work to the middle class as contributors' families benefitted directly from such programs as the Young Men's Christian Associations, the Young Women's Christian Associations, and scouting.

Although the American Association of Social Workers was formed in 1921, group workers were not admitted until 1937. Many caseworkers regarded group workers as people who played with children, led dances, went camping, or taught arts and crafts.

Coyle (1930) advanced the group work method by using John Dewey's ideas of progressive education and his definition of structure:

The structure of organized groups consists of the agreed upon instruments through which the group puts its purpose into action. They take the form sometimes of written constitutions and established precedents; sometimes of unwritten or even unspoken assumptions, commonly accepted by the organization as a permanent part of the group life. Their apparent stability is, in fact, an illusion produced by the more swiftly moving processes that go on by and through them. They too change and shift as the group creates, uses and modifies them for its purposes. (p. 79)

Group workers were influenced by the research of Lewin and his colleagues (Lewin, Lippitt, & White, 1939), which indicated that democratic leadership sustained group activities. As a result, group work placed more emphasis on the interaction of members than on direct leadership and focused more on cooperative projects than on competition.

The social work faculty at Western Reserve University first used the term *group work* to parallel casework in 1927. By 1937, 13 institutions—including 10 schools of social work—offered group work courses.

Wilson (1976) described group work's social reform goals as follows:

Workers engaged in these activities in the early part of the century ferreted out large social problems such as poverty, low wages, long working hours, poor housing and exploitation by landlords, inadequate sanitation, political corruption, and caste-class treatment of people. They provided direct service to feed the hungry and care for the sick, and created opportunities for cultural and recreational activities. They carried on programs of social action to alleviate or eliminate identified social problems through engaging the privileged and the oppressed in informational activities and by making bridges to local, state, and federal officials to secure social legislation and enforcement. (p. 7)

Wilson also summarized requisite knowledge for group workers:

When a worker undertook the responsibility of serving a group, the prime requisite was that he have knowledge about and as much understanding as possible of the dynamics of three constructs: (1) groups, (2) human beings, and (3) social situations. He had to be familiar with the range of behavior implied in all three cases. He had to be aware that all groups are different because all human beings are different, as are all social situations. He had to know that the purposes of every group differ, even if the activities are similar. (p. 16)

The group work section of the National Conference of Social Work was formed in 1935. The National Association for the Study of Group Work, which started in 1936, changed its name to the American Association of Group Workers in 1946.

Group workers gained recognition when clinics and hospitals added group work services. Neva Boyd recounted the first use of group work with mentally ill persons at the National Conference of Social Work in 1935—a program of exercise, games, and dance at the Chicago State Hospital, valuable activities used with both excitable and apathetic patients (Reid, 1981). Boyd also reported positive results with developmentally disabled patients, who quarreled less, worked more willingly, had more respect for property, and attempted fewer escapes when they received group work services.

Psychiatric group work was used with World War II veterans who were assigned to groups on the basis of similar problems. After 1945, groups developed rapidly in mental hospitals, with leadership from the Veterans Administration and the Menninger Clinic, and were used in child guidance clinics as well. By the 1950s, one-quarter of the group work graduates chose to work in hospitals or other specialized settings.

The Practice Committee of NASW stated these purposes of group work in the 1960s:

Social group work maintains or improves the personal and social functioning of group members within a range of purposes. Groups may be used for corrective purposes when the problem involves the behavior of the group member; for prevention when there is the potential danger of dysfunction; for normal growth, particularly at critical growth periods; for enhancement of the person; and for the purpose of education and citizen participation. A group may be used for any one or all of these purposes simultaneously and may change as the particular needs of the client change. (Reid, 1981, p. 185)

Euster (1980) described six levels of skill for group leaders. Paraprofessionals can usually lead groups that involve recreation, coaching activities, or teaching new skills, whereas socialization, patient governance, and therapeutic groups require professional leadership skills.

Combining Casework and Group Work
By the 1960s, caseworkers began treating family members in a group to develop social skills, improve communication and decision making, and to provide treatment. Family treatment required techniques that were already well known to group workers. Casework and group work also came together when practitioners began to serve clients in both individual and group settings. Courses and workshops were developed on casework for group workers, on group work for caseworkers, and eventually on combined individual and small-group methods, now included under micropractice.

Community Work
The terms *community organization* and *community work* are often used interchangeably to refer to planning and activity on behalf of organizations or neighborhood groups. Community work fits better with casework and group work and sometimes has broader implications than does community organization. COSs and settlement houses both engaged in what is considered community work. COSs emphasized rational order in welfare activities, requiring programs to share information about recipients. The settlements used political action and lobbied for social legislation to relieve distress among the working classes. By the middle of this century, however, many settlements had adopted the name *community center* and had lost much of their political influence. Also, staff generally were no longer required to live in the neighborhoods in which the centers were located.

Local councils of social agencies were first established in 1908 to provide planning and coordination and to set standards for the voluntary field. The Community Chest as a mechanism for federated funding was created out of fundraising for relief during World War I. Its theme of "One Gift for All" was especially attractive to businessmen and later to labor groups. Community Chests developed membership criteria for agencies that promoted both fiscal responsibility and conservative program goals.

Along with the growth of public agencies and the labor movement, the depression of the 1930s raised many public policy issues. The New Deal stimulated attention to poverty, dependence, ghettos, discrimination, and unemployment. Some people found it difficult to accept community work as part of a direct services profession, but Dunham (1958) highlighted the need in social work for direct services as well as for community planning, administration, and coordination.

The Association for the Study of Community Organization was formed in 1946 from a section of the National Conference of Social Work. At the outset, the new association had no educational requirements for membership, but by 1953, 80 percent of its members were also members of the American Association of Social Workers. Sixteen schools of social work offered at least one community organization course by 1950.

Ross (1967) classified the elements of community organization as identifying needs, ordering needs, finding the resources to meet needs, and taking action through cooperative and collaborative efforts. A successful community organization process results in increased capacity to undertake other similar projects.

Community planning in the 1960s began to include community residents, the consumers of services. The Model Cities program, the federal antipoverty effort, dealt directly with urban areas to establish neighborhood services and advocacy. Consumer participation, however, was often controlled by sophisticated bureaucrats and politicians.

Community work in the 1960s accommodated both protest and advocacy, which some social workers opposed. The civil rights movement was spurred by grassroots organizations that sought to empower minorities. Social workers, both as agency representatives and as individuals, supported freedom marches, rent strikes, protests against the Vietnam War, and demonstrations at nuclear power plants. Community work under social work auspices is now involved more in the maintenance and planning of systems than in activism. To promote service networks and advocacy for clients, major community organization concepts are now included in the curriculum for direct services students.

Toward a Common Framework

The 1950s saw the consolidation of organizations that were concerned with social work practice and education.

NASW

Seven social work membership organizations (the American Association of Group Workers, the American Association of Medical Social Workers, the American Association of Psychiatric Social Workers, the American Association of Social Workers, the Association for the Study of Community Organization, the National Association of School Social Workers, and the Social Work Research Group) came together to form NASW in 1955. NASW facilitated the development of standards and guidelines for social work practice through various commissions. It developed personnel standards, recommended minimum salary standards, and successfully promoted the legal regulation of social work practice in every state. The *NASW Code of Ethics* (NASW, 1994) makes social work values explicit. One of the association's persistent concerns has been clearer agreement on what constitutes social work.

NASW sponsored two conferences to encourage the development of a conceptual framework for social work. The first dealt with the mission of social work, its objectives, the activities of social workers, sanctions, available knowledge and skills, and implications for the profession (Conceptual Frameworks, 1977). The second conference reviewed specific fields of practice: the family, community mental health, health, schools, industry, and aging (Conceptual Frameworks II, 1981).

Recognizing that the client may be an individual, a family, a group, a community, or an organization, the second conference produced a working statement on the purposes and objectives of social work:

> The purpose of social work is to promote or restore a mutually beneficial interaction between individuals and society in order to improve the quality of life for everyone. Social workers hold the following beliefs:
> —The environment (social, physical, organizational) should provide the opportunity and resources for the maximum realization of the potential and aspirations of all individuals, and should provide for their common human needs and for the alleviation of distress and suffering.
> —Individuals should contribute as effectively as they can to their own well-being and to the social welfare of others in their immediate environment as well as to the collective society.
> —Transactions between individuals and others in their environment should enhance the dignity, individuality, and self-determination of everyone. People should be treated humanely and with justice. ("Conceptual Frameworks II," 1981, p. 6)

Council on Social Work Education

Social work education was unified in a single association, the Council on Social Work Education (CSWE) in 1952. The predecessors of CSWE were the American Association of Schools of Social Work and the National Association of Schools of Social Administration, the latter representing undergraduate schools.

In 1932, the minimum required curriculum of the American Association of Schools of Social Work included classroom and field instruction in casework, supported by medical and psychiatric information, and courses in research, social legislation, or the legal aspects of social work. By 1935, schools had to be associated with universities, and four years later, a two-year master's degree was mandated. Curriculum requirements prescribed in 1944 were casework, group work, community organization, public welfare, social administration, social research, medical information, and psychiatric information.

CSWE dealt with practice concepts in its first curriculum policy statement and accreditation standards (1952). The statement specified a framework of classroom courses, field courses, and research within which the student could test and use theoretical knowledge, acquire professional skill, achieve professional self-discipline, and develop a social philosophy rooted in an appreciation of the essential dignity of human beings.

Curriculum study. With organizational consolidation came increasing interest in the commonalities of the social work methods—casework, group work, and community work. A CSWE-sponsored curriculum study (Boehm, 1959) recommended a single goal for social work—the enhancement of social functioning, the activities that individuals must carry out as members of social groups. Social work theory was derived from the sciences and the social sciences, and research was to test these theories. The study concluded that social work education should be broad enough for all settings and yet explicate each of the three social work methods. Ethics and values were also central for the classroom and the field. Both faculty and field instructors were to serve as role models.

The curriculum study recommended education in social, biological, and psychological theory in the last two years of baccalaureate liberal arts education. The first graduate year would include social work methods, professional values, research, and concurrent field instruction. The last year would add a block field placement and integrating seminars. The profession, however, rejected both required undergraduate courses and a mandated block field placement.

Tools for unity. Two books were especially important in the search for unity. Towle's *Common Human Needs* (1945/1965), which was intended to delineate the needs that were of concern in public assistance, also identified universal needs. Bartlett's *The Common Base of Social Work Practice* (1970) explicated the "Working Definition of Social Work Practice," developed by the NASW Commission on Practice (1958). According to the working definition,

the social work method is the responsible, conscious, disciplined use of self in a relationship with an individual or group. Through this relationship the practitioner facilitates interaction between the individual and his social environment with a continuing awareness of the reciprocal effects of one upon the other. It facilitates change: (1) within the individual in relation to his social environment; (2) of the social environ-

ment in its effect upon the individual; (3) of both the individual and social environment in their interaction.

Social work method includes systematic observation and assessment of the individual or group in a situation and the formulation of an appropriate plan of action. Implicit in this is a continuing evaluation regarding the nature of the relationship between worker and client or group, and its effect on both the participant individual or group and on the worker himself. This evaluation provides the basis for the professional judgment which the worker must constantly make and which determines the direction of his activities. The method is used predominantly in interviews, group sessions, and conferences. (NASW Commission on Practice, 1958, p. 7)

In *The Common Base of Social Work Practice,* Bartlett recommended the use of practice models:

Some social workers are fearful that models are too controlling. Actually, perspectives and frames of reference are positive devices for more effective thinking. They give professions their distinctiveness; they identify what is characteristic and thus give the practitioner security; they describe what is common so that thinking can converge; they are essential for effective communication, which requires that people be in the same universe of discourse; they are essential for cumulative thinking and theory-building. (p. 206)

Consensus building. In the 1960s a consensus of practitioners and educators favored a generalist model of graduate social work education built on a base of undergraduate social science knowledge but without undergraduate professional education. The term "untrained" signified the attitude toward the caseworker who did not hold a master of social work (MSW) degree.

Consensus, however, did not last long. Federal studies predicted the need for many more social workers in the 1970s, colleges were developing undergraduate vocational and professional programs to qualify their graduates for jobs, and increasing tuition costs led to demands for a shorter degree program. As a result, NASW sanctioned a professional bachelor of social work (BSW) degree in 1970 and CSWE followed in 1974, raising the issues of redundancy and generalist versus specialized education.

Specialization on a Generalist Base

The current CSWE generalist model as the guide for the BSW degree and the MSW foundation year is based on the commonalities of systems of all sizes; the final year of the MSW emphasizes advanced practice in a concentration. This model has led schools of social work to provide separate courses for various fields of practice in the final year of the MSW concentration. However, the generalist model is hampered because single-field agencies that deal with individuals, groups, and communities are rare. Micropractice settings are easier to find.

The current Curriculum Policy Statement (CSWE, 1992) and the accompanying standards (CSWE, 1994) give added emphasis to the empowerment of groups at risk. The 1992 Curriculum Policy Statement identifies the following four purposes of social work:

1. the promotion, restoration, maintenance, or enhancement of the functioning of individuals, families, groups, organizations, and communities by helping them to accomplish life tasks, prevent and alleviate distress, and utilize resources
2. the planning, development, and implementation of social policies, services, resources, and programs needed to meet basic human needs and support the development of human capacities and abilities
3. the pursuit of such policies, services, resources, and programs through organizational or administrative advocacy and social or political action, including the empowerment of groups at risk
4. the development and testing of professional knowledge and skills related to these purposes.

Why is a consensus on the nature of social work so difficult to achieve? First, the three social work methods apparently do not lend themselves well to a single unified concept; they have different concepts of purpose, different theoretical approaches, and diverse views of both humanity and the individual. Second, the growing array of specializations within the profession detract from unitary constructs. Nonetheless, social work does involve common values and processes. Six steps that are applicable to all methods, approaches, and fields may be distilled from the vast literature:

1. the establishment of contact
2. the assessment and identification of problems
3. the identification of goals and service plans for contracts with clients
4. the provision of services
5. the evaluation of outcomes through group and single-system techniques
6. feedback and the application of results to future practice.

Development of Theory

Following the well-known rivalry between the Freudian and Rankian theories of casework, a variety of other approaches to social work have developed since 1970. They are described in separate entries in this encyclopedia. Currently, a psychodynamic, behavioral, or ecological approach may be enthusiastically embraced by practitioners or educators or distilled by them into unique eclectic combinations.

Roberts and Nee (1970) presented major theoretical approaches to casework practice written by adherents of each approach. Roberts later published similar volumes with Northen on group work (Roberts & Northen, 1976) and with Taylor on community work (Taylor & Roberts, 1985).

The profession needs similar accounts of current theories. Multicultural practice and feminist practice, which highlight oppression and empowerment, are among the newer approaches. To succeed in multicultural practice, the social worker must communicate a helping perspective that recognizes the effect of racism on clients' lives. The practitioner must also be aware of his or her attitudes regarding race and class, the different cultural customs of minorities, and the limitations of applying to minorities research findings based on samples of white people. Ho (1991) provided the Ethnic-Sensitive Inventory to enhance practitioners' skills with ethnic minorities. Bricker-Jenkins (1991) presented the following description of feminist practice:

> The purpose of feminist practice is consonant with the traditional social work practice framework: however, as a practice it has emerged from social workers' efforts to deal with the forces and consequences of sexism in people's lives. This practice has as its primary purposes healing the injuries of sexism and facilitating liberation from this particular form of oppression as well as from others. (pp. 300–301)

PUBLIC POLICY AND SOCIAL ACTION

Public policies since the beginning of the Reagan–Bush era have curtailed resources for social welfare. In addition, concern about the huge federal deficit has made conservatives out of representatives who would be expected to support social services programs. Federal concern, federal funding, and federal control have all been affected, but the effects have been less serious than predicted. Social work is still very much alive. Clearly, volunteers and self-help groups have not replaced professional practitioners.

Social workers will continue their functions and choose their causes carefully. Nevertheless, the social work profession must continue to seek both unity and diversity in its mission, in its knowledge base and principles of practice, and in its social action programs.

REFERENCES

Addams, J. (1899). The subtle problems of charity. *Atlantic Monthly, 83,* 163–168.

Addams, J. (1902). *Democracy and social ethics.* New York: Macmillan.

American Association of Social Workers. (1931). *Social case work—Generic and specific: A report of the Milford conference.* New York: Author.

Bartlett, H. M. (1970). *The common base of social work practice.* New York: National Association of Social Workers.

Boehm, W. W. (1959). *Objectives of the social work curriculum of the future.* New York: Council on Social Work Education.

Bricker-Jenkins, M. (1991). The propositions and assumptions of feminist social work practice. In M. Bricker-Jenkins, N. R. Hooyman, & N. Gottlieb (Eds.), *Feminist social work practice in clinical settings* (pp. 300–301). Newbury Park, CA: Sage Publications.

Brieland, D. (1990). The Hull-House tradition and the contemporary social worker: Was Jane Addams really a social worker? *Social Work, 35,* 134–138.

Cannon, I. M. (1923). *Social work in hospitals.* New York: Russell Sage Foundation.

Charity Organization Society of New York. (1888). *Fifth annual report.* New York: Author.

Conceptual Frameworks [Special issue]. (1977). *Social Work, 22,* 338–444.

Conceptual Frameworks II: Second Special Issue on Conceptual Frameworks. (1981). *Social Work, 26,* 5–96.

Council on Social Work Education. (1952). *Curriculum policy statement for the master's degree in social work education.* New York: Author.

Council on Social Work Education. (1992). *Curriculum policy statements.* Alexandria, VA: Author.

Council on Social Work Education. (1994). *Handbook of accreditation standards and procedures.* Alexandria, VA: Author.

Coyle, G. L. (1930). *Social process in organized groups.* New York: Richard R. Smith.

DeSchweinitz, E., & DeSchweinitz, K. (1948). The contribution of social work to the administration of public assistance. *Social Work Journal, 29*(4), 153–162.

Dunham, A. (1958). *Community welfare organization, principles and practice.* New York: Thomas Y. Crowell.

Euster, G. L. (1980). Services to groups. In D. Brieland, L. B. Costin, & C. H. Atherton (Eds.), *Contemporary social work* (2nd ed., pp. 102–106). New York: McGraw-Hill.

Geismar, L. L. (1971). *Family and community functioning: A manual of measurement for social work practice and policy.* Metuchen, NJ: Scarecrow Press.

Ho, M. K. (1991). Use of Ethnic-Sensitive Inventory (ESI) to enhance practitioner skills with minorities. *Journal of Multicultural Social Work, 1,* 57–65.

Hudson, W. W. (1982). *The clinical measurement package.* Homewood, IL: Dorsey Press.

Kellogg, P. U. (1914). *The Pittsburgh survey—Vol. 1.* New York: Survey Associates.

Klein, P. (1938). *A social study of Pittsburgh: Community problems and social services of Allegheny County.* New York: Columbia Press.

Kogan, L. S., Hunt, J. McV., & Bartelme, P. (1953). *A follow-up study of the results of social casework.* New York: Family Service Association of America.

Lee, P. R. (1930). Cause and function. In *National Conference on Social Work, Proceedings: 1929* (pp. 3–20). Chicago: University of Chicago Press.

Leiby, J. (1978). *A history of social welfare and social work in the United States.* New York: Columbia University Press.

Leiby, J. (1984). Charity organization reconsidered. *Social Service Review, 58*(4), 522–538.

Lewin, K., Lippitt, R., & White, R. K. (1939). Patterns of aggressive behavior in experimentally created social climates. *Journal of Social Psychology, 10*(2), 271–301.

Lubove, R. (1965). *The professional altruist.* Cambridge, MA: Harvard University Press.

NASW Commission on Social Work Practice. (1958). Working definition of social work practice. *Social Work, 3,* 5–8.

National Association of Social Workers. (1994). *NASW code of ethics.* Washington, DC: Author.

Pumphrey, R. E., & Pumphrey, M. W. (1961). *The heritage of American social work.* New York: Columbia University Press.

Reid, K. E. (1981). *From character building to social treatment.* Westport, CT: Greenwood Press.

Residents of Hull-House. (1895). *Hull-House maps and papers: A presentation of nationalities and wages in a congested district in Chicago.* New York: Thomas Y. Crowell.

Richmond, M. E. (1898). The need of a training school in applied philanthropy. In *National Conference on Charities and Correction, proceedings: 1897.* Boston: George H. Ellis.

Richmond, M. E. (1917). *Social diagnosis.* New York: Russell Sage Foundation.

Richmond, M. E. (1922). *What is social case work?* New York: Russell Sage Foundation.

Roberts, R. W., & Nee, R. (Eds.). (1970). *Theories of social casework.* Chicago: University of Chicago Press.

Roberts, R. W., & Northen, H. (Eds.). (1976). *Theories of social work with groups.* New York: Columbia University Press.

Ross, M. G. (1967). *Community organization.* New York: Harper & Row.

Smith, Z. D. (1892). The education of the friendly visitor. In *Proceedings of the National Conference on Charities and Correction.* Boston: George H. Ellis.

Taylor, S. H., & Roberts, R. W. (Eds.). (1985). *Theory and practice of community social work.* New York: Columbia University Press.

Towle, C. (1965). *Common human needs* (rev. ed.). New York: National Association of Social Workers. (Original work published 1945)

Warner, A. G. (1894). *American charities.* New York: Thomas Y. Crowell.

Wilson, G. (1976). From practice to theory: A personalized history. In R. W. Roberts & H. Northen (Eds.), *Theories of social work with groups* (pp. 1–44). New York: Columbia University Press.

Zimbalist, S. E. (1977). *Historical themes and landmarks in social welfare research.* New York: Harper & Row.

Donald Brieland, PhD, is professor and dean emeritus, University of Illinois at Chicago, Jane Addams College of Social Work, 1040 West Harrison, Chicago, IL 60607.

For further information see

Archives of Social Welfare; Council on Social Work Education; Direct Practice Overview; International and Comparative Social Welfare; National Association of Social Workers; Research Overview; Social Welfare History; Social Work Education; Social Work Practice: Theoretical Base; Social Work Profession Overview.

Key Words	
history	research
practice	social work education

Social Work Practice: Theoretical Base
Francis J. Turner

If any term could best describe the state of practice theory in social work at the end of the 20th century, it would be "diversity." In a remarkably short time, the social work profession has moved from a position of virtually no practice theory to the present situation in which more than 20 major theoretical systems are shaping contemporary practice (Turner, 1986). However, within this diversity has been a consistent unifying theme: The primary focus of social work theory is to seek to understand the complex reality of the person-in-situation. In this odyssey, social work theory has not only developed its own bodies of empirically tested knowledge but has drawn on bodies of knowledge from other disciplines, particularly, but not exclusively, the behavioral and social sciences. In recent years, there has been a growing awareness of the need to also include materials from the biological sciences. Theoretical concepts from other disciplines have aided social workers to better understand individual, family, group, and community systems in the same way that knowledge derived from practice has enabled the social work profession to develop its own unique bodies of theory.

In a service-oriented profession, the test of a theory is deemed to be its efficacy in helping to provide quality, effective, accountable service to some particular situations or cadre of clients in an ethical manner within the value base of the profession, as opposed to speculations whether a particular system has all the credentials of a fully developed theory. However, how one assesses the quality of efficacy is differentially viewed with ideology and personal preference at one end of the continuum and a demand for solid empirical evidence at the other end.

PLACE OF THEORY IN PRACTICE

The perceived role of a theory in social work practice is similar to that of other helping professions. *Theory* refers to an organized body of concepts that attempt to explain some aspect of reality in a manner that has been, or is capable of being, verified in an acceptable empirical manner. A theory or theories form a basis on which responsible accountable practice is built. A strong theory provides the framework in which to understand some aspect of reality in a manner that permits the taking of actions for which one is prepared to be held accountable. A theory is not a body of dogma but a body of tested knowledge (Turner, 1986).

The extent to which a profession's practice is built on theory determines whether the profession's base of legitimacy is strong or weak. However, in professions such as social work with a high service commitment, the relative importance of theories tends to be based not as much on their research base but on their perceived utility and practicality. That is, in the world of practice and within the human professions, a profession is respected from the perspective of its perceived ability to relieve suffering and bring about change, rather than on the credentials of the empirical strength or tested validity of its theory or theories. Testing of theory through research is not disparaged; rather the perception of utility and effectiveness is given more prestige, sometimes minimizing the risk of acting without the certitude of tested knowledge.

Although the social work profession has always been committed to positioning theory as the backbone of the profession, in the mores of social work, *theory* frequently takes on a range of other meanings, some of which are pejorative. The term may convey a sense of overintellectualizing, to the perceived detriment of respect and compassion for individuals. Or, the term may reflect imprecision, the opposite of its real meaning. In this way, a theory about something is equated with a hunch or a feeling, not a clear conceptualization. In addition, theory may have a connotation of impracticality: Let's forget all that theory stuff and get down to some real social work. This imprecision in terminology leads to a lack of clarity as to how the profession should view theory and plays into a lowered respect for its central position (Cocozelli & Constable, 1985; Lewis, 1982).

ROLES OF THEORY IN PRACTICE

Viewed in its most positive light, practitioners use theory to give meaning to and thus assess the strengths, weaknesses, and resources in presenting situations and to understand people and their significant environments and systems. Theory gives validity to assessment. In addition, theory helps identify differing worldviews and values in the multicultural reality in which social work practice takes place globally. Thus, theory is the basis on which diagnosis, the essential component of responsible intervention, is built, regardless of methodology.

Beyond diagnosis, theory facilitates and gives direction to the process of decision making in conjunction with the clients or situations in which the practitioner is involved, whether micro or macro. But in the current reality of a pluralistic base, practice theory not only assists in understanding presenting situations, it can aid in deciding which theory or theories will be called on as the driving force of the intervention. Theory is not only a tool for understanding, it is also an important component of a practitioner's armamentarium of techniques and methods (Turner, 1986).

Differential Use of Theory

Because of the broad spectrum of the human condition that is encompassed by social work's scope of practice, no one theory can cover everything. Different theories present different ways of viewing and understanding particular aspects of the person-in-situation continuum, such as the nature of a crisis, definition of problem, or function of task in bringing about change. Some theories strive to provide an understanding of broad aspects of reality, such as systems theory as a way of viewing interacting parts of the client's life or existential theory that helps a client develop a worldview that makes life more manageable and fulfilling. Other theories deal with specific issues, such as the nature of interpersonal interactions.

Because different theories look at different aspects of reality, these same differences can help clients achieve different goals. Hence, if a client is interested in finding an acceptable solution to a discrete problem, a problem-solving theoretical approach will be more beneficial than building an interventive strategy that focuses on the examination of the client's inner dynamics. With a wide range of theoretical perspectives available, a practitioner can tap the strengths of systems that best suit the clients and the situation being addressed.

Value Base of Theory

This concept of the differential use of theory as an aspect of intervention emerged from the growing awareness that one of the principal ways in which theories differ is the value base on which they are founded. Although the social work profession once thought theories of intervention were value free (value neutral), it has become increasingly aware that this is not so. This concept has been of considerable importance in addressing the complex issue of how to avoid a stereotypical response to clients and situations based on a unitary viewpoint and instead find appropriate ways to respond most sensitively in selecting from the diverse perspectives available in the spectrum of theories.

There are a variety of ways of looking at the value base of theories. Cultural anthropologists Kluckhohn and Strodbeck (1961) posited that, from a value orientation perspective, all people in the world need to come to terms with five major value orientations: (1) basic human nature, (2) time, (3) human activity, (4) the world of nature, and (5) human relationships. When this concept is applied to the differing theories extant in social work practice, it can be observed that such theories also vary on their perception of the rank ordering of these same orientations. If so, it appears to follow then that different theoretical approaches will better fit the worldview of some clients more than others. This important concept has considerable import for the advantages of a practice based on diversity rather than a unitary perception of theory.

For example, Kluckhohn and Strodbeck (1961) posited that all people in the world must come to terms with reality of time. For some people, the present is most important; for others, the past; and for others, the future. So too do theories differentially view time. For a developmental theory such as psychoanalysis, the past is highly important. For other theories such as problem solving, the present predominates. For still other theories such as psychosocial, the future is emphasized. It follows then that some social work theories will better fit the value set of clients than others; when social workers understand and sensitively respond to this awareness, they in turn can respond to the client in a manner that better fits the client's value set. Because a large number of combinations of value orientations exist as do a number of value sets between and among theories, the search for a proper and helpful fit between client, social worker, and theory of intervention is complex and requires a high degree of diagnostic acumen. In turn, it presents a highly exciting potential for enhancing effectiveness in a multicultural society.

Value orientation is related to human activity: doing, being, or being-in-becoming oriented (Kluckhohn & Strodbeck, 1961). Theories also are related to human activity. For example, problem solving is highly doing oriented. Gestalt theory is being oriented, and existentialism is more oriented to being-in-becoming. Apparently, a diverse theory base can provide power to a sensitive practitioner.

PRESENT SITUATION

It is difficult to find complete unanimity on how many distinct theoretical systems are extant in social work practice. This uncertainty evolves from the differential perspectives on what constitutes a practice theory and what differentiates one theory from another. There would be consensus on the principal systems, including behavioral, crisis, client-centered, cognitive, communication, existential, ego psychology, feminism, functional Gestalt, life model, Marxist, meditation, neurolinguistic programming, problem solving, psychoanalytic, psychosocial, role, systems, task-centered, and transactional analysis (Turner, 1986). All of these theoretical systems are bodies of thought, each of which meets the minimum definition of a theory, having an empirical base. The social work profession has generally acknowledged each as a practice theory. Each addresses some component of reality of significance to social work. Furthermore, each has had significant tradition and identification in the literature of social work (Turner, 1986).

Clearly, there would not be full consensus either that some of these systems would be considered theories or that some of them could stand alone. Such perceptual differences are the legitimate matter of ongoing professional dialogue and debate, processes that are essential to the development of the profession's theoretical base. Thus, even the question of how many theories are extant would receive different responses; to some people, the aforementioned list is too restrictive and to others, too expansive.

Evolution of Theory

Because of its diverse and evolutionary character, theory is always evolving and changing. Hence, an important challenge for social work is to continue to identify the process by which a new theory emerges, when it is a more updated reconceptualization of earlier knowledge, or when it is a combination of several existing theoretical systems. Hence, it is probable that a future list of distinct social work theoretical systems will add network, problem-focused therapy, radical, conflict constructivism and reconstructivism, and empowerment among others.

In addition to values, theories also vary along other lines. Turner (1986) has come to one conclusion that all theories, currently of import to social work, attempt to answer the same questions and vary on the basis of the response to them. These questions fall into five major categories: (1) values, (2) extent of specificity and empirical base, (3) nature of personality and its principal determinants, (4) nature of the therapeutic or change process, and (5) spectrum of applicability.

Plural Modalities

Another issue arising from the issue of categorizing distinct bodies of theory for social work practice relates to the spectrum of interventive modalities. As the profession has become more comfortable with the idea of a pluralistic theory base, so too has there been movement away from the idea that a practitioner is only competent in a particular method or individual group. Thus, any theory of use for social work needs to address questions of macrointervention and microintervention, including the various methods subsumed by these interventions. This issue opens discussion about whether there should be theories for various interventions, such as individual theory, group theory, family theory, or community theory, or are these interventions best viewed as emerging from the previously designated theories. Again, the literature and practice in the profession has not been consistent in applying all theories to all methods, although the trend certainly is toward an idea that each theory needs to address the full range of social work interventions. For example, crisis theory needs to address work with individuals, groups, families, and communities. Turner's (1986) book on the *interlocking approach* (each theory should be seen as a separate entity with differential uses and applications and should be respected) hedges this issue by including a chapter on family theory but not on other modalities.

Although this plurality could be viewed as a weakness—a sign of the immaturity of the profession's theory base—a more positive conclusion is that diversity reflects the growing understanding of the profession's rapidly expanding mandate in a highly complex multicultural world. Thus, as the profession's influence continues to expand on a worldwide basis, so too does the awareness of the impossibility of attempting to develop a unitary theory of person-in-situation that will comprehensively address the plethora of situations encountered in contemporary practice, wherever it takes place.

HISTORY

To fully comprehend the present situation in regard to theory and its impact on the profession, it is important to understand the historical development of this complex diversity of theory. This understanding is particularly important because the profession traditionally has not fostered diversity.

Early Dramatic Splits

Using the turn of the 19th century as a starting point, an uneven odyssey is evident. It begins from a point of virtually no theory but only commitment to change society and its conditions and to help individuals and families. Even then, this commitment was accompanied by a strong commitment to conceptualize the practice of the time, to systematize what was learned, and to seek theoretical understandings of what was being done (Richmond, 1917). The thirst for theory was great (Hamilton, 1951). Hence, when various theories of personality and society began to emerge, the profession frequently adopted them almost as bodies of dogma rather than evolving systems of thought. As a result, early dramatic splits in the profession occurred, such as the diagnostic–functional and the macro–micro dichotomies, elements of which are still observable.

This tendency to a dogmatic approach to theory greatly impeded its development because the professional mores stressed the belief that different theories, by definition, were mutually exclusive. Thus, if a person aspired to one theory, he or she had to reject all others. Such a perception of singularity also led to the search for unity, for a theory that would tie the various emerging theories together and thus better unite the profession (Hearn, 1958). It was only when the profession moved again to a much closer interest in, understanding of, and respect for the social sciences that the concept of the legitimacy of diversity emerged (Merton, 1957). In this respect, the publication of the Roberts and Nee (1970) book represented a significant turning point for the profession in that it presented an idea that, indeed, a range of legitimate theories about social work practice could be considered simultaneously.

Different Approaches

Shortly thereafter, Fischer's (1978) important book argued the case for diversity but strongly emphasized that diversity must be based on strong evidence, not authority, favoritism, or personal preference. The concept of "equifinality" from systems theory has contributed greatly to the acceptance of diversity. This concept suggests that, within systems, different inputs can result in similar outcomes.

The concept of diversity was slow to develop but presently, in some form or another, is the basis for most of social work practice. As this acceptance, begrudgingly at times, developed, its application took on a variety of forms, all of which are extant. Fischer introduced the term *eclectic practice,* a form of practice that draws on the combined strength of researched components of the various theories. A more common term in today's practice is *generalist,* a term with a variety of meanings. It is best understood as an approach to practice that avoids taking a position on the relative merits of different theories. Rather, it seeks to draw on components of most, or all, of those theories and attempts to bring the components together into a coherent approach to practice (Goldstein, 1974).

Although not as prevalent in professional vocabulary as the term *generalist,* another observable approach to diversity is a *cluster approach.* In this manner, people develop an approach to practice based on a select number of theories that have particular appeal to the practitioner and formulate the theories into a theoretical base. The conceptual basis of the cluster varies from person to person.

Furthermore, there is the interlocking approach suggested by Turner (1986). Using this approach, practice should be based on an understanding of the various strengths and limitations of each theory and how best to combine approaches to respond to particular situations, cultures, settings, and clients. At this point in the history of the social work profession, little is to be gained by attempting to clarify the distinctions between these various terms of accommodation. Rather, they are all to be viewed as responsible efforts to come to terms with diversity. Clearly, there is no final word on how to best respond to this diversity of theory. What is clear is that the search for a unitary theory has diminished. The present emphasis is on how to take advantage of the richness of diversity for the benefit of clients and the advancement of knowledge (Koglevzon & Maykrznz, 1982; Siporin, 1989).

SOCIOLOGY OF THEORIES IN SOCIAL WORK

To fully understand the state of present practice theory in addition to the history of theory in social work, it is important to understand that theory also can be viewed from a sociological perspective that extends beyond the particular empirical credentials of a theory. Several factors are related to present practice theory. As in the profession's earliest days, there presently is a strong aspect of dogmatism or cultism observable in regard to the differential importance accorded various theories. Hence, some theories of practice are espoused and promulgated based on the authority and reputation of particular people who view themselves as highly identified followers of the theory. Often, these actions are not the wish of contributors to the development of a theory who understand the need for a theory to be tested and to develop.

An opposite but equally powerful tendency is observed in the *heresy of modernism,* in which a theory is viewed as being relevant only to the extent that it is new and different. Conversely, a theory is viewed as no longer relevant to the extent that it is seen as old or traditional. The social work profession needs to take great care in deciding whether a theory being promulgated is new or is a restatement of an earlier approach to practice. However, a new viewpoint on practice that is a reconceptualization of an earlier approach should not be discounted. A restatement that makes the viewpoint more acceptable and attractive to the profession is indeed an important service. A further observable position views all new ideas as only restatements of earlier convictions. This attitude can result in the minimization of what are indeed new ideas.

An additional factor related to the present state of practice theory results from the challenge of diversity and a misunderstanding of the nature of theory and its role in practice. Thus, a frequently observed attitude to theory is that the essence of practice is the social worker's ability to respond empathically to the client or situation, rather than basing the response on a theoretically based diagnostic understanding of what is occurring. This "gut reaction" viewpoint often carries a highly negative and rejecting perception of theory. Because research to date has not demonstrated a strong connection between theory and effective intervention, this approach has considerable support in some areas of the profession, consequently diverting the search for the theory–practice relationship.

POLITICS OF THEORIES

In addition to, or complementary to, the sociological components of theories are political components that the profession needs to understand in examining the current state of practice theory. Certainly, in an era of political correctness, it is evident that some social workers view theories as

more proper than others. This viewpoint is not surprising—different value bases will have a better ideological fit than others in particular situations and for particular people. Thus, in different parts of the world, in different areas of countries, and in different practice settings, some people may view theories as much more acceptable than others. For example, in some areas, social workers would be considered politically incorrect if they stated they practiced from a psychoanalytic base, which, in other situations, would be the preferred correct theory. This kind of "in" and "out" attitudinal response has been observed in relation to theories such as psychosocial, feminism, meditation, and Marxism. Some components of the profession strongly criticized Turner's (1986) book on different theories for suggesting that meditation was an important and legitimate way of helping clients.

This interconnection between values and ideologies contributes to the phenomenon of some theories emerging as political statements and, at times, as dogmas and belief systems, rather than bodies of empirically tested concepts. From an ethical perspective, social workers who share this viewpoint may possibly deprive clients of more efficacious services or may respond to them in a nontherapeutic manner. Some theories frequently are more politically acceptable than others in social work because of the history of the theory, its conceptual sources, and its principal proponents, rather than the strength of its research base and demonstrated utility in practice, which need be the basis of the use or nonuse of a theory in practice.

A further aspect of the political correctness component of a theory is the extent to which theories go in and out of style, both from a temporal and a geographical viewpoint. This shift occurs not only on a macroscale but from a microperspective. In this regard, one finds both regional and national differences and specific services or indeed specific agencies that adapt a selected theoretical approach to practice on the basis of value fits or popularity rather than on tested evidence.

CHALLENGES

Practice

Exciting as this theoretical diversity of the 1990s is for social work, this reality creates complex challenges for contemporary practice. On the negative side, the diversity can be overwhelming for the hard-pressed line practitioner, who may feel frustrated, cynical of theories, and rejected (Curnock & Hardicker, 1979; Koglevzon & Maykrznz, 1982; Simons & Aigner, 1979). Issues concern how an individual comes to terms with such diversity.

Even when the tendency is to reject theory and to put more trust into an atheoretical approach, practitioners almost always have a sense of responsibility and lingering guilt that indeed they should be on top of this material. This situation can result in a distancing between the teachers of theory and the practitioners, as well as a distancing between researchers interested in testing theories and line workers overwhelmed by the pressures of too many demands, too serious problems, and too few resources.

On the positive side, however, is excitement for the profession. In the history of the profession, there has never been a time of more theoretical richness. To an increasing extent, thought systems are addressing the varied components of current practice, for which there was no sufficient understanding before. Because of the differential value bases of theories, there is a rich repertoire of approaches to clients of many and diverse origins and backgrounds. As each theory is translated into practice concepts and techniques, the richness of interventive strategies and comfort with the use of a much broader range of techniques, services, and resources have greatly expanded. For practitioners open to the immense potential of this theoretical bounty, practice becomes exciting and continuously enriched. However, as with all human services professions, this excitement is tempered by the limitations of knowledge and skill. An important outgrowth of this awareness of the vast and ever-expanding body of knowledge within the profession is a strong movement to commit to lifelong professional development.

Teaching

Just as this diversity has created challenges for practitioners, so too has it challenged teachers in the profession. Hence, the query "And what shall we teach?" becomes a highly challenging reality (Perlman, 1957; Woods & Hollis, 1990). This challenge becomes even more problematic because the spectrum of education for the profession ranges from community-college level to the doctorate. As yet, there is little consensus about the most effective pedagogical way to address this challenge (Stevenson, 1967). There appears to be agreement that diversity is the current reality, although less agreement as to whether diversity should or should not be the current reality. Frequently, social workers in North America meet the challenge by relying on the concept of the generalist. The difficulty, though, lies in the interpretation of what is meant by *generalist;* at times, definitions vary regarding what is generalist teaching within and between schools, faculties, and accrediting bodies.

This diversity of opinion can result in discomfort among students interested in being at the cutting edge of knowledge and feeling a sense of practice competence at graduation. Apparently, students are increasingly understanding that theory cannot be dogma, that diversity is useful in the complex realities of contemporary social work practice, that graduation is only the beginning of the learning odyssey, and that it is critically important and the students' ethical responsibility to build practice on a research base.

Research

As the profession has moved from a tradition of viewing a theory as closed and to a growing acceptance and understanding of the challenges and potential of diversity, there has been an increased understanding of the essential role of research in the development and testing of a theory. An important component of the research development is the awareness that research also has value bases so that approaches to and strategies of research are rated differently. A concomitant component of the research perspective is that research is not something to be feared. Social work practice is effective; there is much that is known (Thomlison, 1984). Unexpected findings can teach the profession much. The task now is to continuously attempt to expand the richness of social work theory and its application to practice.

Although many practitioners would verbally identify a particular theoretical orientation or perspective on diversity, there is little evidence on what is the theoretical base of much of their practice. Clearly a person could state or believe that practice is based on a particular theoretical base, when it is not. Similarly, there is little evidence on what theories drive the practice in particular situations. Do people practice from a single theoretical base, or from some amalgam of several or many? What are the differential outcomes when practitioners use different theories?

A further area of research relates to the value fit between theories and clients. Can researchers demonstrate that a theory must fit a client's value set to be effective, or is it more important that a theory fit the practitioner's value set? Should practitioners therefore use theory as a tool selected for a particular person, setting, or situation?

Perhaps the most important thing the social work profession has learned as it maturely comes to terms with the present state of theory is that advances in the understanding of the co-relation of theories and practice are not going to result from major breakthroughs or the pronouncements of individuals, regardless of those individuals' charisma. Rather, there is growing acceptance that advances in understanding will occur through the accumulated wisdom of a long series of many small but carefully constructed projects carried on in all corners of the world—projects that address specific components of the myriad of issues that are and must be raised about theory-driven practice.

CONCLUSION

As the profession continues to struggle with the excitement of diversity in practice theory, several clear trends are observable. The first is a growing humility of how, even in the face of dramatic expansion of knowledge in the profession, there is still much that is unknown. As a result of this struggle with diversity, social work has become much more accepting of the idea that we need to practice from a basis of diversity in methodology, technique, and theory. In addition, the struggle has contributed considerably to the understanding of, and commitment to, research that in itself is built on diversity. Perhaps most important, the struggle with diversity has made the profession much more open to knowledge regardless of its origins or ideologies, as long as it is applied in a responsible ethical mode.

This broadening of perspective has also helped the profession move away from a too narrow geographic approach to its own self-image. The profession increasingly is understanding that, indeed, it is worldwide; in this regard, then, the profession needs to become increasingly multicultural. In so doing, there is growing comfort with diversity and a readiness to learn from each other throughout the world.

Diversity in practice theory will be the basis on which the profession's influence will expand. However, this expanded influence will happen in a manner that reinforces an understanding that the growth of knowledge will in turn underscore the awareness of the limitations of knowledge.

REFERENCES

Cocozelli, C., & Constable, R. T. (1985). An empirical analysis of the relation between theory and practice in clinical social work. *Journal of Social Service Research, 9*(1), 47–64.
Curnock, K., & Hardicker, P. (1979). *Towards practice theory.* London: Routledge & Kegan Paul.
Fischer, J. (1978). *Effective casework practice: An eclectic approach.* New York: McGraw-Hill.
Goldstein, H. (1974). Theory development and the unitary approach to social work practice. *The Social Worker, 42,* 181–188.
Hamilton, G. (1951). *Theory and practice of social casework* (2nd ed.). New York: Columbia University Press.

Hearn, G. (1958). *Theory building in social work.* Toronto: University of Toronto Press.
Kluckhohn, F. R., & Strodbeck, F. L. (1961). *Variations in value orientations.* Evanston, IL: Row Peterson.
Koglevzon, M., & Maykrznz, J. (1982). Theoretical orientation and clinical practice: Uniformity versus eclecticism. *Social Service Review, 56*(1), 120–129.
Lewis, H. (1982). *The intellectual base of social work practice.* New York: Haworth Press.
Merton, R. K. (1957). *Social theory and social structure.* Glencoe, IL: Free Press.
Perlman, H. H. (1957). *Social casework: A problem solving process.* Chicago: University of Chicago Press.
Richmond, M. (1917). *Social diagnosis.* New York: Russell Sage Foundation.
Roberts, R. W., & Nee, R. H. (1970). *Theories of social casework.* Chicago: University of Chicago Press.
Simons, R. L., & Aigner, S. M. (1979). Facilitating an eclectic use of practice theory. *Social Casework, 60*(4), 201–208.
Siporin, M. (1989). Metamodels, models and basics: An essay review. *Social Service Review, 63*(3), 474–480.
Stevenson, O. (1967). Problems in the use of theory in social work education. *The British Journal of Psychiatric Social Work, 9*(1), 27–29.
Thomlison, R. J. (1984). Something works: Evidence from practice effectiveness studies. *Social Work, 29,* 51–56.
Turner, F. J. (Ed.). (1986). *Social work treatment: Interlocking theoretical perspectives* (3rd ed.). New York: Free Press.
Woods, M. E., & Hollis, F. (1990). *Casework: A psychosocial therapy* (4th ed.). New York: McGraw-Hill.

FURTHER READING

Duncan, B. L. (1992). Strategic therapy, eclecticism and the therapeutic relationship. *Journal of Marital and Family Therapy, 18*(1), 17–24.
Fischer, J. (1973). Is casework effective? A review. *Social Casework, 53*(1), 5–20.
Geismer, L. L., & Wood, K. M. (1982). Evaluating practice: Science as faith. *Social Casework, 63*(5), 266–271.
Germaine, C. B. (1970). Casework science: A historical encounter. In R. W. Roberts & R. H. Nee (Eds.), *Theories of social casework.* Chicago: University of Chicago Press.
Goldstein, H. (1990). The knowledge base of social work practice: Theory, wisdom, analogue, craft? *Families in Society, 71*(1), 32–43.
Gutierrey, F. R. (1978). Theory selection: Some considerations for social work. *The Journal of Applied Social Sciences, 2*(2).
Hollis, F. (1954). Casework diagnosis: What and why? *Smith College Studies in Social Work, 5*(1), 84–90.
Imre, R. W. (1984). The nature of knowledge in social work. *Social Work, 29,* 41–45.
Latting, J. K. (1990). Identifying the "isms": Enabling social work students to confront their biases. *Journal of Social Work Education, 26*(1), 36–44.
Matsushima, J. (1977). Seeking the trunk of the practice-theory tree. *Smith College Studies in Social Work, 47*(2), 181–191.
Nugent, W. R. (1987). Use and evaluation of theories. *Social Work Research & Abstracts, 23*(1), 14–19.
Paley, J. (1987). Social work and the sociology of knowledge. *The British Journal of Social Work, 17*(2), 169–186.

Payne, M. (1991). *Modern social work theory: A critical introduction.* Chicago: Lyceum Books.

Pilalls, J. (1986). The integration of theory and function: A re-examination of a paradoxical expectation. *The British Journal of Social Work, 16*(1), 79–96.

Polansky, N. A. (1986). There is nothing so practical as a good theory. *Child Welfare, 65*(1), 3–15.

Reay, R. (1986). Bridging the gap: A model for integrating theory and practice. *The British Journal of Social Work, 16*(1), 49.

Rein, M., & White, S. H. (1986). Knowledge for practice: *Social Service Review, 55*(1), 1–41.

Simon, B. K. (1970). Social casework theory: An overview. In R. W. Roberts & R. H. Nee (Eds.), *Theories of social casework* (pp. 353–396). Chicago: University of Chicago Press.

Siporin, M. (1979). Practice theory for clinical social work. *Clinical Social Work Journal, 7*(1), 75–89.

Smid, G., & Van Kreeken, R. (1984). Notes on theory and practice of social work: A comparative view. *The British Journal of Social Work, 14*(1), 11–22.

Specht, H. (1990). Social work and the popular psychotherapies. *Social Service Review, 64*(3), 345–357.

Strean, H. S. (1975). Personality theory and social work practice. In H. S. Strean (Ed.), *Personality theory and social work practice* (pp. 1–15). Metuchen, NJ: Scarecrow Press.

Turner, F. J. (Ed.). (1976). *Differential diagnosis and treatment in social work* (2nd ed.). New York: Free Press.

Turner, F. J. (Ed.). (1986). *Social work treatment: Interlocking theoretical perspectives* (3rd ed.). New York: Free Press.

Turner, F. J. (1990). *A comparative theory chart.* Kitchener, Ontario: Author.

Francis J. Turner, DSW, CSW, is dean, Faculty of Social Work, Wilfrid Laurier University, 75 University Avenue West, Waterloo, Ontario, Canada N2L 3C5.

For further information see

Clinical Social Work; Cognition and Social Cognitive Theory; Direct Practice Overview; Ecological Perspective; Epistemology; Ethics and Values; Ethnic-Sensitive Practice; Generalist and Advanced Generalist Practice; Gestalt; Goal Setting and Intervention Planning; Group Practice Overview; Intervention Research; Mental Health Overview; Person-in-Environment; Progressive Social Work; Psychosocial Approach; Qualitative Research; Research Overview; Single-System Design; Social Work Education; Social Work Practice: History and Evolution; Social Work Profession Overview; Transactional Analysis.

Key Words

practice theory · theory · social work practice

READER'S GUIDE

Social Work Profession

The following entries contain information on this general topic:

Continuing Education
Council on Social Work Education
Ethics and Values
Licensing, Regulation, and Certification
National Association of Social Workers
Professional Conduct

Professional Liability and Malpractice
Social Work Education
Social Work Profession Overview
Social Work Profession: History
Vendorship

Social Work Profession Overview
June Gary Hopps
Pauline M. Collins

As a profession social work emerged largely in response to problems associated with the industrialization and urbanization of the 20th century. Together with the unprecedented global strife of two world wars and the current instability of a changing world order, this era has witnessed extremes of economic depression and expansion; waves of immigration and in-migration; unprecedented recognition and violation of human and civil rights; control or prevention of some diseases and the resurgence of old diseases and onset of insidious new ones, such as those involving immune deficiency; and a lag in ethical and moral understanding of ways to deal with rapidly changing technological conditions. Science and engineering, for example, have produced weaponry of unsurpassed destructiveness and high-tech medicine that can prevent, prolong, or terminate life. Despite advances in agriculture that could feed the world, hunger goes unabated even in a country of surplus like the United States. In the social work sphere there is concern over whether technology will ultimately serve to enhance or diminish the human interactional dimensions of practice.

IS SOCIAL WORK A PROFESSION?

Despite historic debate and scientific inquiry, the term *profession* has not yet been clearly or consistently defined. As early as 1915 (in his paper "Is Social Work a Profession?"), Flexner concluded that the field did not qualify as a profession because it was not based on a body of scientific knowledge. Ever since, social workers have made intermittent efforts to provide information and analyses to counter Flexner's conclusions.

In 1929, Porter Lee published "Social Work As Cause and Function," in which he distinguished between the cause of social reform and service as the function of the social work profession. This dichotomization offered a choice between the option of political activism or professionalism (Lee, 1929; Specht & Courtney, 1994). In 1947 the criteria by which social work could be deemed a full-fledged profession were affirmed by Lindeman in *Social Work Matures in a Confused World* (1947), in which he stated:

> Social work may be said to be traveling towards maturity as a profession when it is capable of assimilating knowledge and skill from many sources without loss of identity; it is able to adapt itself to a variety of managerial auspices and controls without loss of integrity; it is capable of merging its methods with those of other professions dealing with related situations; it is capable and prepared to translate its technical conceptions into language comprehensible to the layman; it has achieved consistency between its goals and its methods and is willing to subject itself to self-imposed standards of conduct; it recognizes its sphere of social responsibility; it is able to adapt itself to the dynamics of society in which it operates; it evolves methods for merging its empirical and theoretical knowledge; and

> it is able to recruit its candidates from the higher levels of intelligence. (p. 51)

In "Attributes of a Profession" (1957), Greenwood noted that although social work possesses all the attributes of a profession, it is at the lower rather than the higher end of the development continuum. According to this analysis, social work has not yet attained the status of other, more accepted professions. Hall (1968), however, argued that social work had the identifying characteristics of professions: the use of professional organizations as a major reference, a belief in public service, self-regulation, a sense of calling, professional autonomy, and a specialized knowledge base.

Social work was moving toward professionalization early on when caseworkers first claimed distinctiveness through cognitive expertise. Such claims have been made repeatedly over the years, and the profession's focus on definition has also continued. Nevertheless, Flexner (1915) and others attempted to exclude social work from being categorized as a profession. This position is held by those who believe the field lacks autonomy and a theoretical knowledge base. Echoing Carr-Saunders (1965), Toren (1972) referred to social work as a "semi-profession," noting that:

> [To be] awarded an "established" position (particularly in the sense of professional autonomy), the profession must demonstrate a certain congruence between the two core elements—systematic knowledge and professional norms. If a profession ranks high only on one of these dimensions and low on the other, it will not be accredited full professional status either by the public or by social scientists. A profession may be based on a great amount of systematic knowledge but lack a col-

lectively-oriented code of ethics, as in the case of engineering specialists and other kinds of technicians. Or, it may be committed to a service ideal but lack a theoretical knowledge base, as in the case of social work, nursing and librarianship. (p. 42)

Etzioni (1969) also referred to social work as a semiprofession, noting that it could not be accorded full status for such reasons as the length of training it requires (less than for professions of law and medicine) and its failure to recognize privileged communication. Similarly, Gilbert, Miller, and Specht (1980) described the status of the field as middle range on the scale of key attributes of community sanction and authority, and they concluded that social work is still developing.

That social work is practiced primarily within a formal organization or bureaucracy has been a central issue in discussions about the profession's lack of autonomy. Max Weber characterized bureaucracies as possessing (1) a high degree of specialization; (2) a hierarchical authority structure; (3) impersonal relationships; and (4) recruitment on the basis of ability (Gerth & Mills, 1969). Although bureaucratic structures have often been seen as antithetical to the new character of a profession, some view them as complementary (C. Davis, 1983). The latter analysis seems particularly applicable to social work, which has been described as an "organizational profession." This description reflects the social reality that, in general, effective services are organized and delivered within a bureaucracy or a formal organization. In fact, the concepts of profession and bureaucracy have often been prerequisites for successful service delivery.

Although these critiques of social work as a profession differ from Flexner's (1915), most do not seem to move the dialogue substantively beyond Lindeman's (1947) view. Because social work continues to be seen as emerging and developing, it is important that the profession constantly define and clarify itself over the years. Much of the debate has stemmed from classical conceptualizations of "profession" that follow either static structural–functional approaches or process–conflictual approaches (Popple, 1985; Popple & Leighniger, 1990). Many studies of the concept of profession are based on a pragmatic perspective that takes into account political influence, perceived class stratification, and relationships with decisionmakers in the business and political–economic spheres. This approach relies more on power as a basis for analysis than on the listing of attributes by which occupational groups are measured to determine their professional ranking. The

preoccupation with control of markets (clients and consumers) and autonomy skews the debate over the concept of profession toward power, which is only one point of analysis; another that is particularly pivotal to any conception of social work as a profession is the commitment to service, particularly to the needs of poor people (Specht & Courtney, 1994).

ORIGINS

From its beginnings, social work was influenced by dual structural tensions that bore directly on how the profession viewed itself and defined its purpose and function. Early professional associations and organizations generally focused on improving and expanding their services. Reflecting the interests of individuals, however, they also functioned primarily to provide professional aid or support to them and to advocate for improved working conditions, usually on the local level.

Charity Organization Societies

During the 1800s, the Charity Organization Societies (COS) facilitated both the professionalization and bureaucratization of social work by advancing the concept of scientific charity, or philanthropy. Philanthropists combined prudence with dedication to helping and fueled the reorganization of COS. They adopted a systematic, organized approach to identify and determine needs (case evaluation) and to deliver services effectively. Their ideas about efficiency and functional specialization were based on those of the business world (Lubove, 1965).

Although the thrust toward professionalization grew out of the reorganization of COS in the context of scientific charity (Larson, 1977), the professionalization movement was aided and accelerated by caseworkers who asserted that they had the "beginnings of a scientific knowledge base, as well as specialized skill, technique and function that differentiated them from the layman or volunteer" (Larson, 1977, p. 182). In the push for professionalization, the leadership of caseworkers led to their subsequent dominance in the profession.

Professional Education

Schools and training institutions provided further impetus for the transition from craft toward profession. Developed in major urban areas, these facilities were under neither university nor college auspices until the early 1900s. Nevertheless, they proved to be vehicles for acquiring specialized knowledge and skills. Moreover, they provided an entry into the profession that in the past had been available only through membership in professional organizations. The focus of the curriculum was essentially social casework. As formal education programs improved and expanded their curricula, the drive for upgrading membership in professional associations gained momentum. The strong impetus toward training for socialization into the profession is reflected, for example, in the writings of the secretary of the Washington, DC, Associated Charities, published in the early 1900s (cited in Lubove, 1965):

> Medical science has advanced ... because of case study and professional organizations.... Similarly, charity work may be expected to become scientific ... by the development of professional skill, professional schools, and authoritative standards of entrance and excellence in the profession. (p. 124)

The approach to professional education adopted by the schools corresponded more with the apprenticeship model developed by associations than with the university-based models of other professions. The cornerstone of the apprenticeship model was a heavy reliance on agency-based supervision as a means of socialization into the profession (a pattern that is still prevalent). Although this approach to professional training has been proved effective through experience, there is growing emphasis on systematic comparative analysis of training models and evaluation of practice (Collins, Kayser, & Tourse, 1994).

HISTORICAL AND SOCIAL CONTEXT OF SOCIAL WORK

American social welfare and social work have been influenced by social and historical forces. The larger context today is shaped by fiscal constraints and related societal ills, including increases in poverty (especially as it affects children), changes in the character of urban neighborhoods, and the increase in drug use and violence. Other social forces include changes in the structure of families and the demographic transition that will result in an increase in the aged population, in addition to a people-of-color majority in the next century. Under a new administration, the country is beginning to debate a number of these social problems. Despite the enactment of new federal tax legislation in 1993, fiscal constraint is a reality that will probably continue to limit social services.

Government and Social Welfare

Historically, social welfare in the United States was based largely on the English model. The Elizabethan Poor Laws, passed in the early 17th century, are still influential. Since the 19th century, social welfare policy in this country has been driven largely by two assumptions, namely, the value of competitive individualism and the validity of market-based economics. The free enterprise-market system has been supported and encouraged by the government's laissez-faire role. The residual, noninterventionist approach was at one time dominant in other Western countries but was challenged as societal conditions deteriorated. With the full development of the secular state and industrialization in both Europe (especially Western Europe) and this country, separate philosophies for the patterns of the government's role and responsibility became clearer. In the United States the New Deal programs, initiated under President Franklin D. Roosevelt to combat the joblessness and poverty of the depression, represented a new period in social welfare. The cornerstone of these legislative programs was the Social Security Act of 1935, which distinguished between people who were considered able and unable to work. Work continues to be the focus of debate in social welfare policy for poor, vulnerable citizens (Hopps & Pinderhughes, 1992; Hopps, Pinderhughes, & Shankar, in press).

The debate and subsequent passage of the Social Security Act signified the increased recognition that poverty and other social ills were created by structural problems in the economy, not simply by individual problems and inadequacies (often perceived as sin and laziness). Similarly, it was recognized that the resolution of problems was beyond the scope of a volunteer-oriented charity system. The basic principle of government intervention to offset, moderate, or direct purely market-based economic forces and to reduce disparities in wealth and income became institutionalized and prevailed for 50 years. Although the philosophy has been challenged, particularly since the early 1980s (beginning with the agenda of the Reagan administration), the public sector continues to dominate social welfare (Hopps & Pinderhughes, 1992; Hopps, Pinderhughes, & Shankar, in press).

The philosophy of the Reagan administration in the 1980s was that the private sector, not the public sector, should carry the responsibility for planning, administering, and providing social welfare. President Reagan was a persuasive spokesperson, and under his leadership, conservative forces channeled the anxieties and dissatisfaction of middle- and working-class citizens into support of neoconservative ideals. Because of the shift in attitudes, political support for poor people declined, whereas it increased for the affluent (Edsall, 1984). The presidency of George Bush prolonged Republican control of the executive branch of government. For the first time since the depression, opponents of federal social responsibility were able to replace top-level advocates of economic reform and to dismantle the layer of mid-level public servants who had ensured its implementation.

The consecutive 12-year Republican hold on the executive branch of government ended with the defeat of President Bush in November 1992. Arkansas Governor Bill Clinton, the Democratic candidate, won the election in a three-way race against the incumbent, President Bush, and third-party candidate Ross Perot. Clinton called for greater government intervention, including major overhaul of health, welfare, and education systems, and provision of a federal jobs program. Additionally, the new administration brought to the fore violence as a public health problem. Although health and welfare reform and job programs were sidetracked in 1994, Congress enacted a new crime bill.

Poverty and Socioeconomic Ills

Structural issues in the economy, changes in taxation policy, reductions in allocations for human services, and the lack of respect for the poor evidenced under the Reagan and Bush administrations helped to increase poverty and related ills. Despite great affluence, little money was made available for efforts to improve human capital. (The total gross national product for 1990 was $5,465.1 billion, or approximately $20,000 per person; Council of Economic Advisors, 1991.) Policies reflected the historical trend of national ambivalence toward poor people, which still exists today and is reflected in the way poverty is defined and measured (Orshansky, 1978; Spade, 1994).

During the depression, at least a third of the population was poor. With the New Deal program of the 1930s and the war economy of the 1940s, poverty decreased; more Americans became middle class, and the gap between the rich and the poor classes decreased. The 1950s were harsher economically, and by the 1960s slightly more than 22 percent of the population was poor. With the War on Poverty programs of Democratic administrations in the 1960s, the poverty rate dropped below 11 percent in 1973, the lowest it has ever been. Since then, however, there has been an appreciable increase in poverty. By the late 1980s, the figure was up again to roughly 13 percent (Bloom, 1990). Despite signs that the economy is recovering, poverty is increasing. Census Bureau data indicate a rise in poverty for the third straight year, affecting 36.9 million people (14.5 percent of the population in 1992). Poverty is more concentrated than before, affecting 10.4 million in 1990, up from 5.6 million in 1980 and 3.7 million 10 years earlier in 1970 (Pear, 1993).

Children and families. The poverty of children seems particularly insidious. The numbers of poor African American, white, and Latino children increased and hit record highs in 1992. Roughly 14.6 million children (more than one in five) lived in poverty in 1992, reflecting the highest child poverty rate since 1965 (and a 276,000 increase since 1991, also reflecting rapid growth). This 21.9 percent rate of child poverty is harsh. A more striking factor is the proportion of children who are deeply mired in poverty. In 1992, 46 percent of children were in families with incomes of less than half the poverty level (in 1992 this was $5,593 for a family of three), compared with 31 percent in 1975. White children who live in poverty represented the largest group (9 million), followed by African American (4.9 million) and Latino (3.1 million) children. Another striking concern is the number of poor children under age six (5.8 million). Poverty is strongly associated with single-parent households, which are predominantly female. Slightly over 54 percent of poor families are headed by women, slightly more than 24 percent are headed by men, and nearly 11 percent are headed by both parents (Children's Defense Fund, 1993, 1994a). The poverty rate of elderly persons is lower than that of other population groups and has been since the early 1980s (due to public insurance, social security, and private sector insurance and pensions) (Pear, 1993). Both urban and rural poverty have been well documented. Over the past 20 years, the highest growth in poverty actually has occurred in the suburbs.

Contributing factors. Factors that contribute to poverty include both structural problems in the economy and deficits in human capital investments for poor families that are due largely to the lack of supportive and nurturing programs. Earnings have dropped, especially for those who are not highly skilled or professionally educated. In many cities, manufacturing and low-skill but high-paying jobs have declined. However, the relative cause and effect of the economic change in the dynamics of poverty has not been absolutely demonstrated. Most poor people work. The minimum wage ($4.25 per hour) leaves families with a single full-time minimum-wage earner with incomes that are below the poverty level.

Policy issues. Improvements in the Food Stamp Program and the expansion of the earned income credit (EIC), approved in the Omnibus Budget

Reconciliation Act of 1993 (P.L. 103-66) (which will make roughly $21 billion available to working poor families over the next five years), are the most significant efforts to provide income support to the poor in the past 20 years. For a family of two or more children the credit will increase from $1,511 in 1993 to $3,370 in 1996. This act provides up to 40 cents of credit for each $1.00 earned (Children's Defense Fund, 1994b; Saleh, 1994). These recent initiatives are important legislative achievements; so too is the allocation of $1 billion to family preservation and support programs to expand community-based services that protect children by strengthening their families (Children's Defense Fund, 1993, 1994a).

Taxation policy, insufficient allocations for the human services, and the increase in poverty and related ills such as inadequate health care and housing are only the more obvious of several contextual concerns for social work. A related problem is the downturn in the economy. Despite some signs of recovery, the recession that started earlier in the 1990s compounded the problems not only of poor people but of the cities in which many poor people live. (Although the majority of poor Americans reside in rural areas, they are not as concentrated and therefore not as visible.) Revenues are down, aid from the federal government has been severely curtailed, and all levels of government have been reluctant to raise taxes necessary to offset problems. Spending is outpacing revenues. For example, in fiscal year 1990–91 there was roughly a $500 million budget gap in New York City, and the gap was projected to reach $2.1 billion in the 1991–92 fiscal year. In Philadelphia, the deficit was $229 million; in Chicago, $75 million; and in San Francisco, $27 million. Cities are downsizing, cutting payrolls, physical services (such as the maintenance of such infrastructures as bridges, streets, and libraries), and human services programs such as food and shelter for mentally ill people, drug addicts, and homeless people (Hinds, 1991). These trends do not bode well for the future.

Demographic Changes

Yet another contextual issue is the demographic changes that have occurred from the settlement of displaced people (immigrants and refugees). This cohort has nearly doubled since 1970 (Weiss, 1990). The Center for Immigration Studies (1988) reported that the greatest immigration in U.S. history occurred between 1980 and 1990. Three acts were largely responsible for this growth and shift: the Immigration and Nationality Act of 1965 (P.L.

89-236), which facilitated the change from predominantly European to largely Third World populations; the Refugee Act of 1980 (P.L. 96-212), which identified a quota for refugees who could not return to their own countries because of potential persecution; and the Immigration Reform and Control Act of 1986 (P.L. 99-603), which gave legal status to formerly undocumented aliens. Displaced people have not been universally well received. Different regions of the country have been forced to absorb new cultures, languages, and value systems (including the concept of collective good over individualism held by many Asians) and—perhaps what is most significant—interact with people of color.

These new Americans are often viewed as siphoning off jobs, depressing wages, and consuming public assistance and social services. Actually, these attitudes are ill founded. Displaced people are not as reliant on the welfare system as are native-born people. They use kinship and informal help more than formal supports, and when they do resort to public assistance, they tend to use it to become self-sufficient, which they usually become within five years of their arrival (Ross-Sheriff, 1990). These facts notwithstanding, some new immigrant groups have been the targets of violence by those who, for various reasons, feel alienated and deprived.

Violence

Violence has also become a more serious contextual concern as reflected in the debate and passage of the 1994 Crime Bill. According to the United States Department of Justice (1993), nationwide crime decreased in the early 1990s; however, violent crimes were more troubling, owing largely to the proliferation of guns and assault weapons. The recent 3 percent decrease in the overall crime rate, which includes violence and property crimes, was reported by the Federal Bureau of Investigation (FBI) as the first since the mid-1980s. Over 14.5 million crimes were committed in 1992, which was 3 percent less than 1991. This downward movement was demonstrated in all groups in the population, and the largest decrease was in cities with populations over 1 million.

In 1992, 78 percent of murder victims were male. Juvenile violence is a major concern, with homicide ranking as the second highest cause of death among those 15 to 25 years old and death from gun wounds as the leading killer of teenage males. Domestic violence is another major concern, with husbands or boyfriends being responsible for nearly 30 percent of murders of women (U.S. Department of Justice, 1993).

Violence in the workplace is becoming a significant problem; much of it is directed toward present or former employers. Murder is now the leading cause of death for women in the workplace; for men, it is the third. Roughly 1,000 people are murdered every year at work, 6 million are threatened in some way, and 2 million are physically attacked (Toufexis, 1994).

Changes in the Family
The most basic social institution, the family, has changed dramatically. The two-parent family with two children, in which the husband is the breadwinner and the wife is the homemaker, is no longer the norm. "Alternative" or pluralistic styles dominate, including the two-parent, two-earner family; the single-parent family (due to divorce or out-of-wedlock births); and blended families, the gay or lesbian family, and informal marriage and families. These shifts indicate that individuals are less encumbered by traditional norms and social stigma and create family forms that suit their unique needs.

The role and functions of the family have also changed, and many families have less time for nurturing and caregiving. With women constituting 57.4 percent of the labor force in 1991, and predictions that they will constitute 63.5 percent of the work force by 2005 (U.S. Bureau of the Census, 1994), there will be less time for child rearing and caregiving to elderly parents, roles traditionally and currently assumed largely by women. The formal social welfare system was developed in the expectation that it would function merely to supplement strong primary informal systems, such as the family and the neighborhood. The reality is that the family, in whatever form, is becoming increasingly unable both to give the traditional range of nurturing and care and to provide for economic necessities. Compounding the situation is a government that has become less willing and less able to provide financial supports and services that many contemporary families need (Humphreys, 1989; Macarov, 1991). Families in racial and ethnic groups have experienced a particularly extensive transition from the two-parent to the single-parent family, and poverty is a major challenge for these families (L. Davis & Proctor, 1989). Recently, there has been a marked increase in the number of children born to single white women, from 14.7 percent in 1985 to 21.8 percent in 1991, resembling what occurred 30 years earlier among African Americans (spurring some concern regarding the possible emergence of a white "underclass" identified with young, welfare-dependent single parents).

PROFESSIONAL BOUNDARY: IDENTITY AND FOCUS
How is social work adjusting to these contextual changes? Given the ever-shifting context in which it is practiced, maintaining professional boundary and identity becomes a major task of social work as a "practice arm" of social welfare programs that deliver "services devised through social policy to the citizen-consumer-client-patient" (Meyer, 1976, p. 1). Like a suspension bridge, social work is sustained by its cables of respect for human dignity and the right of every individual to self-realization. The profession is anchored in service, and its goal is to empower those in acute need and to encourage those in the dominant segment of society that controls the resources and power to meet those needs (Hopps & Pinderhughes, 1987).

Societal Ambivalence
The consequences of this dual accountability have been compounded by the ambivalence of society toward social work. In its more expansive cycles, society tends to view social work benignly as a mirror of its own openhandedness and optimism. However, when times are hard and when shortages exist or conflict abounds, society regards social work as an unwelcome reflection of its own priorities and injustices.

Even in its most benign cycle, this ambivalence is characterized by a residual approach to the delivery of services. Services are delivered not to help people ensure mastery and competence in the execution of life tasks and functions, but only to help them cope with situations in which failure has occurred. Many of those helped by social work have been trapped in poverty, racism, sexism, and powerlessness, all of which breed helplessness and alienation. For them, laissez-faire and individualism have meant only abandonment and more victimization, particularly when the economy is on the downside. Thus, dual accountability and societal ambivalence, together with the constraining philosophy and the lack of a clear mandate for publicly funded services to people, have been major systemic dynamics that have hampered social work's fulfillment of its mission (Hopps & Pinderhughes, 1992).

Cause and Function Issues
The most damaging consequence of social work's boundary role is the way in which the societal inconsistency that is embodied in these dynamics has been mirrored in the function and process of social work. It is evident in the duality that has plagued the profession from the beginning.

Because social work has been responsive to the prevailing milieu, shifts in the social climate have caused it to vacillate in its emphasis on one or the other side of this duality. Throughout its history, its vulnerability to the tenor of the times has been seen in its fluctuating focus on cause or function, environmental reform or individual change, social treatment or direct service. For example, during the progressive era of the 1900s, the desperate depression of the 1930s, and the tumultuous social unrest of the 1960s, social work was preoccupied with cause, and "new" social work methods were seen as addressing noxious institutional influences, whereas the "old" methods were accused of adjusting people to them (Meyer, 1976). When times have been conservative, as in the 1920s, the 1950s, and the 1980s, the profession emphasized function and direct service and retreated from a focus on cause (Hopps & Pinderhughes, 1992).

Even in the 1990s, this context has made it difficult for social work to define itself clearly and to hone an integrated identity. Because of its state of flux and scope of practice, it continues to be viewed as having limited theory that it can claim as its own and to be accused of constructing eclectic approaches that draw on theories from other disciplines. In responding to these charges, social work has worked to define its purpose, build its knowledge base, establish high standards through self-regulation, and achieve the degree of autonomous practice that would justify its identity as a profession (Hopps & Pinderhughes, 1992). Social work's striving for recognition as a profession and its battle to gain respect for its work, its clients, and those who help them have created yet another dilemma. The demand for the empirically based knowledge, autonomy, self-regulation, and other attributes of a traditional profession can lead to a certain narrowing of social work's broad but unique commitment.

Diversity and Complexity

Yet another factor in the dilemmas inherent in the profession's boundary role has been the growing diversity and complexity of the programs in which social workers function. This growth has occurred as a result of society's efforts to meet the proliferating needs and realities emanating from urbanization, industrialization, and economic changes. It was the effort to meet these needs and realities that led to the Great Society initiatives in the 1960s and the 1962 amendments to the Social Security Act that expanded services. These programs were obtained through the efforts of activists, clients, social work students, and others, but not by professional social workers (Ehrenreich,

1985). Although social workers were swept up in the rapidly growing welfare departments, poverty agencies, community mental health centers, preschools, and other programs, at least a substantial part of the profession did not support such changes. In the battles about necessary reforms in social service delivery and social work education that ensued, "for the first time, the social work profession itself was the target rather than the ally, of a movement for social justice" (Ehrenreich, 1985, p. 205). Nevertheless, expanded roles produced a gigantic leap in the depth and breadth of the knowledge and skills that social workers needed, and the profession found itself confronted with the specters of differentiation and specialization in its various systems (Hopps & Pinderhughes, 1992).

SPECIALIZATION

The type, scope, and depth of knowledge and skills that social workers need is vast. "Whereas other professional specialists become expert by narrowing their knowledge parameters, social workers have had to increase theirs" (Meyer, 1976, p. 21). The need for social workers to broaden their horizons to cope with the range of problems that exist and to develop strategies for dealing with them has made specialization inevitable.

Specialization poses a threat to the unity of the profession because the variety of perspectives that were generated have created tension, conflict, and fragmentation. In addition, the specializations evolved in such diverse directions that there has been no coherent, orderly scheme to classify and order the categories. The lack of a scheme is evident in the following sample of a typology (Minahan & Pincus, 1977):

- Method: casework, group work, community organization
- Field of practice: schools, health care, occupational social work
- Problem areas: mental health, alcohol and drug abuse, corrections, mental retardation
- Population groups: children, adolescents, and elderly people
- Methodological function: clinical social work; social planning, development, and research; social work administration; social work education
- Geographic areas: urban, rural, neighborhoods
- Size of target: individual (micro), family group (mezzo), organization (macro)
- Specific treatment modalities: behavior modification, ego psychology, Gestalt therapy, cognitive therapy
- Advanced generalist.

CLASSIFICATION–DECLASSIFICATION

Yet another serious threat to the cohesion and unity of the profession has grown out of the effort to meet human needs in a fast-changing, complex society. Workers from various educational backgrounds were recruited to the multiplying positions (especially those in the public sector) that were created by the new Great Society programs and the Social Security Amendments of 1961 (P.L. 87-543). These new social workers were performing tasks that required them to function in difficult situations and with a range of expertise. They were identified equally in the public mind as social workers, and their inclusion in the profession meant that the profession was differentiated not only into higher levels of education and skill beyond the professional master of social work (MSW) degree but into lower levels.

Classification

In an effort to provide some order to the reigning confusion about functional parameters and to meet the demand for accountability in relation to them, in 1973 the National Association of Social Workers came up with the following classification:

Preprofessional level
• Social work aide (high school diploma)
• Social services technician (associate degree).

Professional level
• Social worker (bachelor of social work [BSW] accredited)
• Social worker (MSW accredited)
• Certified social worker or member of the Academy of Certified Social Workers (ACSW; requires two years of post-MSW experience and passage of an examination)
• Social work fellow (advanced practice).

Theoretically, each level should reflect certain responsibilities that presumably become more complex as one moves up the ladder. In practice, however, the lines of classification are not neatly drawn or clearly compartmentalized. Although some individuals without a professional education have done demonstrably well in the profession and may even control major agencies or programs, most supervisory and administrative positions require an MSW. An MSW is also required for most positions in mental health. Increasingly, a doctoral degree is required for teaching, administrative jobs, and research. These standards help clarify and differentiate the roles, responsibilities, and functions of social workers.

Declassification

Many states that have enacted legislation to regulate practice have incorporated the various levels as outlined in the 1973 NASW policy statement (NASW, 1973). However, this movement toward classification has been jeopardized by cutbacks in financial support for social services. Combined with ongoing demands for labor and rapidly rising personnel costs, budget constraints have produced a countertrend toward declassification—a move to downgrade requirements for social work positions. Under declassification, job qualifications and standards of performance were being reviewed, revised, and rewritten with the recommendation that educational requirements be lowered and the length of professional training shortened (NASW, 1981). The awareness that many of those delivering social services are not professionally trained is cause for concern. The blurring of the classification structure prompted NASW (1981) to fight the erosion of standards, to reissue its definition and classification of social work practice, and to continue to push to maintain standards.

LEGAL REGULATION OF PRACTICE

Social work educators and practitioners are not alone in their concern about quality of and standards for practice. Consumers are also aware of the need to ensure that the highest caliber of service is rendered. States are increasingly exerting more control over expert services by enacting regulatory sanctions. State regulation is in addition to the profession's self-imposed regulations and is recognized in the form of licensure, certification, or registration. The establishment of ACSW was the profession's own response to the need for professional certification.

The protection of clients through assurance of competence is a principal rationale for legal regulation in social work and in other professions. Assurance of competence also offers protection for social workers. For example, it provides a forum through which charges of malpractice and unethical conduct can be raised and addressed, thus responding to the demand that professionals be held accountable for their actions.

All 50 states and the District of Columbia now have some form of regulation. In 1934 Puerto Rico became the first territory to enact regulatory sanctions. Although 12 states followed suit over the next 35 years, the major movement toward regulation began in 1969. Each state has a regulatory board that works out administrative procedures relevant to its own needs and interests. The board is usually financed by license fees, other forms of regulation, and license renewal.

Licensure also facilitates social worker's participation in third-party payments from medical providers, such as Blue Cross and health maintenance organizations. Given the number of social workers entering private practice on either a full-time or part-time basis (nearly 60 percent of NASW membership), this benefit of licensure is significant for the profession (Gibelman & Schervish, 1993).

LIABILITY

Public demand has grown for accountability from all professionals, accompanied by a rise in malpractice actions over the past several decades. In this increasingly litigious climate, social workers are no longer insulated from liability (Sharwell, 1983). Malpractice or misconduct usually refers to negligence that has been defined as "improper treatment through carelessness, or ignorance or intentionality" (Dendinger, Hille, & Butkus, 1982, p. 76). A broad definition from Black's Law Dictionary identifies malpractice as "any professional misconduct, unreasonable lack of skill or fidelity in professional or fiduciary duties, evil practice, or illegal or immoral conduct" (cited in Sharwell, 1983, p. 71). According to this definition, social workers' liability for malpractice involves violation of the profession's ethical obligations or incompetence in the performance of a judicial or statutory duty. The Code of Ethics and the standards established by NASW serve as guidelines in criminal, civil, and ethical manners relating to social work practice.

Causes for Suits

Now more than ever social workers must be aware of legal developments, court decisions, and judicial trends relating to their practice area concerning liability. Some causes for which social workers can be sued include "breach of confidentiality, trespass, assault, battery, false imprisonment through wrongful confinement in a hospital and other actions" (Sharwell, 1983, p. 71).

Child abuse and neglect. Liability issues have become particularly complex for social workers intervening in a family to ascertain whether a child has been abused or neglected. Social workers can be sued for libel for attempting to document that a parent has been abusive or for depriving a parent of his or her child (if they remove the child from the home). Contrarily, social workers can also face criminal and civil liability for failure to take action in such cases (Alexander, 1993). Negotiating this legal conundrum will continue to be required of social workers until clearer guidelines regarding liability emerge from the courts.

Sexual relations with clients. The legal landscape regarding sexual relationships with clients has also been undergoing changes that affect the liability of social workers. The problem of sexual exploitation of clients in general and of female clients in particular has come to the fore after years of misuse of power, victim blaming, and institutional denial. Sexual intimacy between client and therapist has become grounds for legal action. In all 50 states the client may sue the practitioner under common law for battery or malpractice. In some jurisdictions the practitioner may be subject to criminal sanctions; in others, the client must initiate civil action. Complaints of sexual intimacy with a current or former client may lead to ethics sanctions against the practitioner as well as termination of membership in professional associations. The *NASW Code of Ethics* (NASW, 1994) states: "The social worker should under no circumstances engage in sexual activities with clients" (p. 5), thereby giving the client recourse in filing a complaint with the NASW Committee on Inquiry. The client (or someone acting on the client's behalf) may also lodge a complaint with the state licensing or regulatory board and all state boards (Kagle & Giebelhausen, 1994). Although relatively few clients resort to legal action or complaints of ethical impropriety, more may be expected to come forward as complaint procedures become more widely known.

Importance of Malpractice Insurance

Because of the rising concerns about malpractice and complexity of issues involving liability, social workers are becoming more aware of the importance of being adequately covered by malpractice insurance. Professionals employed in major agencies and institutions tend to have more protection than those who work in smaller programs. Private practitioners are usually responsible for arranging for their own malpractice insurance. Although schools of social work presumably cover their students under their universities' insurance plans, in the years ahead addressing students' need for professional liability insurance will become an area of concern for both the schools and agencies serving as field practicum sites. In any event, it is essential that social work students and practitioners alike become more knowledgeable about the legal protection and liability attached to performing their professional responsibilities. (NASW addresses some of these issues through the NASW Insurance Trust.)

SOCIAL WORK IN THE 1990S

Within the shifting context of practice, questions are being raised regarding the interests, commitments, and attitudes of social workers and direction of the profession. Therefore, it is important to examine demographic information about practitioners and about additional issues of significance to the profession such as practice areas, salary, supply and demand, computer technology, educational programs, and curriculum.

Demographic Trends within the Profession

In 1991 the labor force included 603,000 workers who were referred to as social workers; overall, NASW had an estimated membership of 134,200, a 15 percent rate of growth since 1988. Material presented below is based on the NASW's 1991 membership survey. Of these members, 88 percent hold the MSW degree; 7 percent hold the BSW degree; and 5 percent hold the doctoral degree (Gibelman & Schervish, 1993).

Employment. Over 75 percent of the membership reported full-time employment. Reflecting a trend that began at least in the early 1970s, employment in the public sector declined. In 1982, 45 percent worked in the public sector (Hopps & Pinderhughes, 1987), and in 1991 the figure was down to 39 percent. There has been an increase in employment under private for-profit auspices, seemingly reflecting a trend. In 1991, 24 percent of social workers identified private for-profit work as their primary source of employment, whereas even more (47 percent) reported it as a secondary source of employment. Regardless of auspices, the majority of the membership (69 percent) were employed in direct service roles, followed by 19 percent in macropractice and 5 percent in education. The overwhelming distribution in direct services has existed for some time, and we must again note the strength of the clinical sector in the profession, owing to size (Gibelman & Schervish, 1993).

Gender. Demographic data show that the profession is still predominantly female. The gender distribution was 77 percent female and 23 percent male, reflecting a 2 percent growth among female members and a corresponding decline among males. The majority of members (88 percent) are white; 6 percent are African American, 3 percent are Hispanic, 2 percent are Asian, 0.5 percent are Native American, and 1 percent are classified as "other." This is a slight growth in the percentages of African Americans and Hispanics; no change in membership of Asian, Native American, and others; and a slight decrease in the percentage of white members (Gibelman & Schervish, 1993).

Experience. The NASW membership is becoming younger and less experienced. Fifteen percent are under the age of 30, with 41 to 45 years the median age range, and 23 percent are 50 and older. Most members (93 percent) received the MSW since 1961; the largest proportion (19 percent) of workers have less than two years' experience; and 45 percent are ACSW members, a 5 percent reduction over a three-year period.

In summary, demographic data show that the profession is predominately female; workers are moving to private for-profit sources of employment away from public auspices; and the membership is younger and less experienced. Although there has been a slight rise in membership, there is still a clear need to recruit more people of color into the profession, because they represent the populations most at risk. What is at issue is the seriousness with which a "female profession" follows through in enacting its espoused values concerning diversity and equal opportunity.

Areas of Practice

For the last two decades, mental health has become an increasingly attractive area of interest and is now the lead area of employment among the NASW membership (33 percent). The second-highest ranked area was practice with children (16 percent); ranking third and fourth are medical clinics (13 percent) and family services (11 percent), respectively. No change in practice with children, at medical clinics, or with family service was noted; however, public assistance work declined. In 1972, 8 percent of the membership was employed in public assistance, and nearly 20 years later only 1 percent practiced in this area. Few members were employed in corrections (1 percent), group services (0.5 percent), and disabilities, not including mental–developmental (0.5 percent; Gibelman & Schervish, 1993).

The area of practice interest was associated with degree. For example, those with doctorates tended to work in community organization—planning, occupational, and "combined" or "other" social work as the highest areas of employment, and those with a BSW noted public assistance and work with elderly people and people with mental retardation or developmental disabilities (Gibelman & Schervish, 1993). More experienced social workers practiced in mental health, occupational social work, and medical clinics, whereas those with less experience worked with elderly people, children, the developmentally disabled, and in public assistance and substance abuse. More women than men practiced in family services, medical clinics, school social work, and with elderly people (Gibelman & Schervish, 1993).

Patterns of growth, decline, and status quo reflect not only the interest of social workers but also the weight that society places on discrete services. The profession's limited presence in public assistance, corrections, and disabilities should be of concern. Poor people and criminals are often viewed by the public as less than attractive. The profession's movement away from public assistance and the public sector may be explained in part by declassification; whatever the reason, however, it must be examined and the profession may wish to rethink the relinquishment of one of its most traditional client groups.

Salary Information
The Bureau of Labor Statistics reported that social work salaries in 1990, across settings, were between $23,000 and $36,000. For 1991, social workers employed by the federal government earned an average salary of $38,951 (U.S. Department of Labor, 1992). The NASW 1991 Membership Survey provides information on salaries, but data limitations must be noted because only 41 percent responded to questions related to salaries. The median range for full-time social workers in 1991 was $25,000 to $29,999. In a 1961 NASW salary survey, those entering practice who had earned an MSW in 1960 earned a median salary of $5,500. When that figure is adjusted for inflation, the 1991 dollar value is $25,025, meaning that the median salary merely kept up with inflation. The 1991 median earnings range was $25,000 to $29,000; however, a close examination of median salaries shows major differences in earnings. Controlling for gender, the median salary range of women is $17,500 to $19,999; for males, it is $20,000 to $24,999. At the high end of salary distribution, 2.2 percent of women received $60,000 and above, whereas 6.3 percent of men received that salary. The differential is significant and long-standing, having been reported in earlier studies (Gibelman & Schervish, 1993).

In terms of ethnicity, few differences were found in the primary income of members. For instance, 2.9 percent of those classified as "others" earned $70,000 or more (the highest income level); so did 2.3 percent of white members, 1.2 percent of Chicanos, and 1 percent of African Americans. At the other end of the income scale, 2.9 percent of other Hispanics (compared to 1.4 percent of white members and 1.2 percent of African Americans) earned in the $10,000 to $12,499 range (Gibelman & Schervish, 1993).

Earnings and social work degree are highly correlated; the higher the degree, the greater the earnings. For example, 2 percent of those with a BSW, 9 percent of those with an MSW, and 33 percent of those with a PhD or doctor of social work (DSW) degree earned $40,000 and above. Conversely, 66 percent of those with a BSW, 21 percent of those with an MSW, and 5 percent of those with a PhD or DSW earned between $10,000 and $19,999. Similarly, the date the degree was earned is correlated with salaries. Earnings tend to increase fastest during the first five years in practice, with a slower rise in income over the ensuing years. A similar pattern was discerned with time period or date that a degree was earned (Gibelman & Schervish, 1993).

Earnings were also influenced by practice area; those in mental health, group services, and community organization and planning were in the higher salary ranges, whereas those serving the aged and disabled were in the lower ranges. Social workers employed by the government earned more than others, with the exception of those in private for-profit jobs. Federal government and military employees earned more than those at other levels of government. Finally, salaries are also influenced by geography. Higher incomes were reported in New England and the mid-Atlantic and Pacific states, whereas those in the East South Central, West North Central, and U.S. territories reported lower salaries (Gibelman & Schervish, 1993).

Supply and Demand
From all indications, there will be demand for social workers in the years ahead. The Department of Labor projects a faster rate of growth than the average for all professions or occupations at least until the next decade (2005). Specifically, there is projected demand for services for elderly, mentally ill, and mentally retarded people, and for individuals and families facing crisis. Because of discharge planning, projections call for job opportunities in hospitals to grow at a faster rate than the economy, and similar projections have been made regarding employment in private social agencies. Because of the Education for All Handicapped Children Act of 1975 (P.L. 94-142), there is anticipated demand for social workers in schools, and the growing numbers of people living at home with physical disabilities suggests that home health care workers will be needed. Social workers can be expected to continue in private practice, because funding from health insurance and from employee assistance contracts is expected. Opportunities are also projected to remain strong in rural areas (U.S. Department of Labor, 1992). Cor-

rections is another area where growth for practitioners is projected. However, social work is moving away from this area; other service workers find it attractive because of the salaries (up to $40,000 for those with two-year associate degrees; Saltzman, 1993).

The projections alone could be overly optimistic. For example, it is not certain that the market will hold for private practice. Although growing numbers are attracted to it as either primary or secondary sources of employment, the prospects are shadowed by problems with vendors. Insurance companies are trying to make sure services are capped; thus, there is proliferation of managed care and "time effective" therapies.

In other fields of practice where projections are strong (for example, elderly, mentally ill, and physically disabled people) there is nothing to suggest that these fields will be staffed with social workers. Declassification, attractive as it is to government and private agencies, will continue because it saves resources, whether or not it is achieved at the sacrifice of quality services. This is one reason social workers were pushed out of public welfare. Finally, whereas average growth is anticipated in government jobs, this could shift given the hostility toward government being fanned by self-appointed media experts. They have found a following among the increasingly alienated middle class. Among the disengaged and the noisy but powerless poor, on one hand, and the well-off and powerful, on the other, it is the middle class that historically provides a reasonably benign balance.

Computer Technology

The proliferation of technology has created access to a range of computer resources that was almost unimaginable a decade ago. The increase in computerization within social services is presenting social workers with opportunities to integrate social goals with technological development for the benefit of clients. To date, however, the developing presence and function of computers in social work has followed a varied and often reactive course (Nurius, Hooyman, & Nicoll, 1991). Response to this transition has ranged from resistance to changes that the new technology may bring to enthusiastic acceptance of innovative computer applications developed by and for social workers.

Like many other professionals, social workers are finding that computer literacy is a necessary skill. Computers can be used to record, store, analyze, consolidate, and retrieve information efficiently. They save time in collecting and

processing data for use in record keeping and decision making in an increasingly complex service delivery system. Although use of computers in direct services, administration, or research may differ, social workers are becoming more aware of the potential that the new computer technology has for professional training, service delivery, quality assurance, and linkage to the larger community.

Interactive computer-assisted instructional programs are one of the innovative computer applications designed to improve social worker training in practice skills. Computer-assisted instruction has been used to teach such skills as making a diagnosis, goal-focused interviewing, crisis counseling, and group treatment. The effectiveness and potential of integrated learning programs based on videodisk applications stem from the availability of higher quality video and audio integrated with computer text and graphics (Seabury & Maple, 1993). Other applications have been designed for use by and with clients. Clients may use interactive programs to analyze their individual case history to assess their risk of human immunodeficiency virus (HIV) infection (Schneider, Taylor, Prater, & Wright, 1991). Some social workers are discovering that programs that provide rapid assessment of clients are particularly useful when using brief treatment models.

The conversion of paper records to computerized information systems creates a more serviceable work environment and improves productivity (Kagle, 1993). Centralized computer databases that allow input of data related to both direct and indirect service activities are becoming more commonplace in social services agencies. These information systems have become indispensable in maintaining individual records, describing aggregate client populations, assisting in quality assurance, and easing collection and analysis of data for basic research, program evaluation, and decisions about service delivery. Along with these innovations, serious concerns regarding the potential abuse of client confidentiality and the dehumanization of service provisions have been raised.

With growing expansion of electronic networks among people, organizations, and countries, the necessity of thinking globally and acting locally is becoming a reality. Telecomputing (using telephone lines to transmit information between computer networks) not only is improving communication within agencies, but access to such innovations as electronic bulletin boards allows social workers to participate with other network users in the larger electronic information community. As a profession, then, social work has a growing obligation to advocate that the use of the new technology be based on "democratic principles, on economic and social justice, and is accessible to all populations so as to enhance and meet human needs" (Leiderman, Guzetta, Struminger, & Monnickendam, 1993).

Educational Programs

Professionally educated social workers have earned any of four degrees: BSW, MSW, DSW, or PhD. The ranks of professional social workers have expanded greatly since 1974, when the Council on Social Work Education decided that the BSW degree represented the first professional degree in social work. Until that time, the MSW was recognized as the first professional degree and the terminal degree. The MSW is still the predominant degree, even though the doctoral degree is becoming required for tenure-track academic positions.

Increase in BSW programs. This debate notwithstanding, the number of BSW programs has grown substantially, from 142 in 1975 (CSWE, 1984) to 381 in 1993, as well as 32 programs in candidacy status for accreditation (Nancy Randolph, CSWE, personal communication, May 1994). The total number of enrollments, graduates, and faculty have increased steadily since the late 1980s (Lennon, 1993). Of the approximately 35,000 full-time students enrolled in BSW programs during 1992, the proportion of women remained steady at 85 percent whereas the proportion of ethnic minorities increased slightly to 27 percent. The proportion of women (59 percent) and ethnic minorities (27 percent) on BSW faculties also increased slightly.

Growth in graduate programs. Although there are now more than three times as many BSW as MSW programs, graduate education has also been experiencing substantial growth. In 1960 there were only 56 accredited MSW programs; by the early 1990s, the numbers increased to 116, and eight programs are candidates for accreditation (Nancy Randolph, CSWE, personal communication, May 1994). The total number of enrollments, graduates, and faculty have steadily increased since the late 1980s (Lennon, 1993). Of the approximately 20,700 full-time students enrolled in MSW programs in 1992, the proportion of women remained steady at 83 percent whereas the proportion of ethnic minorities increased slightly to 19 percent. The proportion of women (57 percent) on MSW faculties also increased, whereas ethnic minorities remained around 22 percent.

Increases in social work applicants reverses an earlier trend toward a decline in the number of people applying to social work programs. Full-time enrollments increased steadily from the mid-1950s to 1978; by 1986 they dropped to a 15-year low. Since that time programs have reported an increasing number of students. Applications to full-time and part-time MSW programs in 1992 increased by almost 19 percent over the previous year and represent an all-time high. Programs are also becoming more selective, and only 50 percent of applicants are accepted (Lennon, 1993). This represents a 20 percent decrease in the acceptance rate compared to the early 1980s (Rubin, 1983).

Doctoral programs. Enrollment in doctoral programs increased until 1980, vacillated somewhat during the next decade, then moved upward again. The number of part-time students currently remains approximately equal to that of full-time doctoral students. Of the approximately 1,000 full-time doctoral students in 1992, the proportion of women remained about 68 percent. This represents a slight decrease in the number of males enrolled in full-time doctoral study. The proportion of ethnic minorities was 22 percent. Doctorates are more likely to be held by graduate faculty than their BSW-level counterparts. However, men are more likely than women to hold a doctorate at both undergraduate and graduate faculty levels (Lennon, 1993).

Questions surrounding the continuum of social work education continue, particularly the relationship between graduate and undergraduate education and the appropriate academic level for carrying out professional training. These subjects are similar to those debated in the early 1900s and include (1) the primary focus of social work as either building the profession or providing public service; (2) the relationship of the profession to the larger social welfare system; and (3) the problem of addressing the needs of increasingly diverse populations in contemporary communities (Popple & Leighninger, 1990).

Curriculum

From the beginning, the focus on professional social reform and its emphasis on broader social approaches had its counterpart in a focus on individual change, or direct service, and both foci were reflected in the professional curriculum. These two practice models have sometimes been viewed as mutually exclusive rather than complementary, and their relative prominence over the years has depended on the times. The curriculum mirrored this duality, and variation in emphasis has reached into every area of the profession, including philosophy, purpose, organization, the role of the worker, and worker–client interactional unity. This fluctuation has been demonstrated, for example, by the primacy of casework throughout the 1950s, which yielded in the 1960s and early 1970s to the increasing popularity of community organization, planning, administration, and policy and program evaluation and, in the 1980s, to a renewed emphasis on clinical method. In the 1990s, social workers will have to draw on clinical and macropractice and research to serve effectively a population more diverse and needful than ever before. In the years ahead, the profession must embrace justice-based paradigms to be effective with this clientele (Hopps et al., in press).

Generalist practice. The historic conflict of casework versus environmental change loses importance when compared to the complexities and variations that currently characterize the profession. In education, this state of affairs is reflected in a curriculum that is structured by the levels of expertise (BSW, MSW, DSW) and by specializations (methods of practice, populations served, fields of practice, and the like). A contrasting or perhaps compensatory movement is that of generalist practice. Schools are now required to include content in generalist practice and a common core of courses that must be taught irrespective of specializations. These requirements appear to stem from efforts to unify the profession and to consolidate its identity.

Ecological theory. The introduction of systems theory and ecological concepts as an overarching perspective has advanced these efforts by helping to curb the tendency of the profession to dichotomize in response to demands for an in-depth curriculum and to expand, perhaps too quickly, in an effort to achieve breadth. Ecological theory was at once eclectic and integrative (Siporin, 1975) because it facilitated the conceptualization of human functioning on individual, interactional, familial, group, neighborhood, and community levels. According to the theory, these levels of functioning and the larger social environment are seen as interactive systems that influence each other by mutual feedback processes. On all levels, ecological theory supported the interaction of individuals with their environment as the unit of analysis. It highlighted the dual task that had been social work's historic and unique nexus—enhancing people's adaptive potential while increasing the responsive, nourishing qualities of the environment. In doing so, ecological theory compelled students once again to view themselves as part of the systemic process and to think routinely of the

multilevel context in which problems must be assessed if they are to be adequately treated.

Empirically based practice. In both education and practice, another development promises to address the call for "depth and breadth." Achievement of the profession's long-standing goal—to build knowledge in living situations that gives proper consideration to context (Rein & White, 1981)—appears imminent in view of the increased interest in empirically based practice. Empirically based practice has been given a higher priority within the profession, because of national, state, and local pressure demanding greater accountability regarding the effectiveness of social work interventions (Sze & Hopps, 1978). In line with "educating students for the new market realities" (Strom & Gingrich, 1993) of managed care systems and outcome-oriented practice, CSWE has mandated that the use of scientific inquiry be emphasized throughout the curriculum so that students develop skills that "prepare them to evaluate their own practice" (CSWE, 1984, p. 127). Practice evaluation generates documentation necessary to an assessment of the progress being made with a client system. This documentation includes quantifiable information, concerning intrapsychic or situational factors, that is systematically gathered as part of the intervention and used to assess periodically the client system's functioning level as compared to a previous level of functioning. Thus, social workers are provided with a basis useful in formulating and, if necessary, modifying interventions, and in monitoring the extent to which outcome goals are achieved (Collins, Kayser, & Platt, 1994; Collins, Kayser, & Tourse, 1994). Evidence of the importance of practice evaluation is the large number of schools that are grappling with how best to educate social work students to become more accountable practitioners.

THE FUTURE

The profession will not only continue to address issues it faced in the 1980s and early 1990s but will also be challenged with new ones. Paramount among the influences will be the shifting political and economic context. Although the former may be more subject to immediate change than the latter, some turbulence in both is anticipated. Social work must garner its resources to serve a changing, diverse clientele. The context for social work will probably be characterized by such societal trends as an increasing population of aging individuals who need services, expanding cohorts of poor people (especially children), and an electorate that is more educated or at least more schooled than in the past but less willing to commit resources to quality social services. The public's decreasing confidence in professions, its insistence on participation in the planning-helping process, the proliferation of self-help groups, and the growing emphasis on managed care will also be forces to reckon with.

Even when society was more inclined than it is today to address human needs and to support professional efforts to deal with them, resources were never infinite. Scarcity is now even more evident and is compounded by competing demands from both developed and developing countries. These demands will require that society shares more than it has in the past. To respond appropriately, the profession must aggressively recruit to its ranks a diverse and talented group of people who can think critically, deal with pressure, respond with commitment to the call for service, and appreciate difference and diversity. Coupled with this new talent, a continuation of the healthy friction that has characterized the growth and development of social work may create the synergy necessary to carry the profession to the next century.

The growth of literature on empirically based practice has given new visibility to the refinements of social work and to its contributions to the knowledge base (Hopps et al., in press). In addition, the profession has gained front-line experience in intrapersonal–environmental problem solving. These two factors, combined with its emphases on values and ethics and its assertive commitment to providing services to the less favored—regardless of the political–economic climate—place social work in a position to claim its overdue recognition as a profession.

REFERENCES

Alexander, R. (1993). The legal liability of social workers after DeShaney. *Social Work, 38*(1), 64–68.

Bloom, M. (1990). *The drama of social work*. Itasca, IL: F. E. Peacock.

Carr-Saunders, A. M. (1965). Metropolitan condition and traditional professional relationships. In R. M. Fisher (Ed.), *The metropolis in modern life* (pp. 279–287). Garden City, NY: Doubleday.

Center for Immigration Studies. (1988). 1987 Legal immigration again tops 600,000. In *CIS Announcement Series*. Washington, DC: Author.

Children's Defense Fund. (1993, November). *CDF reports, 14*(12).

Children's Defense Fund. (1994a, January). *CDF reports, 15*(2).

Children's Defense Fund. (1994b). *The state of America's children*. Washington, DC: Author.

Collins, P. M., Kayser, K., & Platt, S. (1994). Conjoint marital therapy: A practitioner's approach to single-system evaluation. *Families in Society: The Journal of Contemporary Human Services, 75*(3), 131–141.

Collins, P. M., Kayser, K., & Tourse, R. C. (1994). Bridging the gaps: An interdependent model for educating accountable practitioners. *Journal of Social Work Education, 30*(2), 241–251.

Council of Economic Advisors. (1991, April). *Economic indicators*. Washington, DC: U.S. Government Printing Office.

Council on Social Work Education (CSWE). (1984). *Handbook of accreditation standards and procedures*. Washington, DC: Author.

Council on Social Work Education. (1994). Report from the Division of Standards and Accreditation. *Social Work Education Reporter, 42*(1), 3–4.

Davis, C. (1983). Professionals in bureaucracies: The conflict thesis revisited. In R. Dingwall & P. Lewis, *The sociology of the professions* (pp. 177–194). Harrisburg, PA: St. Martin's Press.

Davis, L., & Proctor, E. (1989). *Gender, race and class*. Englewood Cliffs, NJ: Prentice Hall.

Dendinger, D. C., Hille, R., & Butkus, I. (1982). Malpractice insurance for practicum students: An emerging need? *Journal of Education for Social Work, 18*(1), 74–78.

Edsall, T. B. (1984). *The new politics of inequality*. New York: W. W. Norton.

Education for All Handicapped Children Act of 1975. P.L. 94-142, 89 Stat. 773.

Ehrenreich, J. (1985). *The altruistic imagination: A history of social work and social policy in the United States*. Ithaca, NY: Cornell University Press.

Etzioni, A. (Ed.). (1969). *The semi-professions and their organizations*. New York: Free Press.

Flexner, A. (1915). Is social work a profession? In *Proceedings of the National Conference of Charities and Correction* (pp. 576–590). Chicago: Hildman Printing.

Gerth, H. H., & Mills, C. W. (Eds.). (1969). *From Max Weber: Essays in sociology*. New York: Oxford University Press.

Gibelman, M., & Schervish, P. H. (1993). *Who we are: The social work labor force as reflected in the NASW membership*. Washington, DC: NASW Press.

Gilbert, N., Miller, H., & Specht, H. (1980). *An introduction to social work practice*. Englewood Cliffs, NJ: Prentice Hall.

Greenwood, E. (1957). Attributes of a profession. *Social Work, 2*, 44–55.

Hall, R. H. (1968). Professionalization and bureaucratization. *American Sociological Review, 33*(1), 92–104.

Hinds, M. de Courcy (1991, January 6). Strapped, big cities take painful steps. *New York Times*, section 1, p. 14.

Hopps, J., & Pinderhughes, E. (1987). Profession of social work: Contemporary characteristics. In A. Minahan (Ed.-in-Chief), *Encyclopedia of social work* (18th ed., Vol. 2, pp. 351–366). Silver Spring, MD: National Association of Social Workers.

Hopps, J., & Pinderhughes, E. (1992). Social work in the United States: History, context, and issues. In M. Hokenstad, S. Khinduka, & J. Midgley (Eds.), *Profiles in international social work* (pp. 163–179). Washington, DC: NASW Press.

Hopps, J., Pinderhughes, E., & Shankar, R. (in press). *Power to care: Clinical practice effectiveness with overwhelmed clients*. New York: Free Press.

Humphreys, N. (1989). The new demographic reality. In L. Healy & B. Pine (Eds.), *Social work leadership for human service management in the 1990's: The challenge of the new demographic reality* (pp. 8–15). West Hartford: The University of Connecticut School of Social Work.

Immigration and Nationality Act of 1965. P.L. 89-236, 79 Stat. 911.

Immigration Reform and Control Act of 1986. P.L. 99-603, 100 Stat. 3359.

Kagle, J. D. (1993). Record keeping: Directions for the 1990s. *Social Work, 38,* 190–196.

Kagle, J. D., & Giebelhausen, P. N. (1994). Dual relationships and professional boundaries. *Social Work, 39,* 213–220.

Larson, M. S. (1977). *The rise of professionalism: A sociological analysis.* Berkeley: University of California Press.

Lee, P. (1929). Social work as cause and function. *Proceedings of the National Conference of Social Work,* pp. 3–20.

Leiderman, M., Guzetta, C., Struminger, L., & Monnickendam, M. (1993). Technology in people services: Research, theory, and applications, part one. *Computers in Human Services, 9*(1/2) [entire issue].

Lindeman, E. (1947). *Social work matures in a confused world.* Albany: New York State Conference on Social Workers.

Lennon, T. M. (1993). *Statistics on social work education in the United States: 1992.* Alexandria, VA: Council on Social Work Education.

Lubove, R. (1965). *The professional altruist: The emergence of social work as a career, 1880–1930.* Cambridge, MA: Harvard University Press.

Macarov, D. (1991). *Certain change: Social work practice in the future.* Silver Spring, MD: NASW Press.

Meyer, C. (1976). *Social work practice* (2nd ed.). New York: Free Press.

Minahan, A., & Pincus, A. (1977). Conceptual frameworks for social work practice. *Social Work, 22,* 347–352.

National Association of Social Workers. (1973). *Standards for social service manpower.* Washington, DC: Author.

National Association of Social Workers. (1981). *NASW standards for the classification of social work practice.* Washington, DC: Author.

National Association of Social Workers. (1994). *NASW code of ethics.* Washington, DC: Author.

Nurius, P. S., Hooyman, N., & Nicoll, A. E. (1991). Computers in agencies: A survey baseline and planning implications. *Journal of Social Service Research, 14* (3/4), 141–155.

Omnibus Budget Reconciliation Act of 1993. P.L. 103-66, 107 Stat. 31.

Orshansky, M. (1978, June). Measuring poverty: A debate. *Public Welfare, 36*(2), 45–55.

Pear, R. (1993, October 5). Poverty in US grew faster than population last year. *New York Times,* p. 10.

Popple, P. R. (1985). The social work profession: A reconceptualization. *Social Service Review, 59,* 560–577.

Popple, P. R., & Leighninger, L. (1990). *Social work, social welfare, and American society.* Needham Heights, MA: Allyn & Bacon.

Refugee Act of 1980. P.L. 96-212, 94 Stat. 102.

Rein, M., & White, S. (1981). Knowledge for practice. *Social Service Review, 55,* 1–41.

Ross-Sheriff, F. (1990). Displaced populations. In L. Ginsberg et al. (Eds.), *Encyclopedia of social work,* (18th ed., 1990 suppl., pp. 78–93). Silver Spring, MD: NASW Press.

Rubin, A. (1983). *Statistics on social work education in the United States, 1982.* New York: Council on Social Work Education.

Saleh, C. C. (1994, March). Tax relief for working families. *Focus,* p. 5.

Saltzman, A. (1993, November 1). The changing professions. *U.S. News & World Report,* pp. 78–86.

Schneider, D. J., Taylor, E. L., Prater, L. M., & Wright, M. P. (1991). Risk assessment for HIV infection: Validation study of a computer-assisted preliminary screen. *AIDS, 3,* 215–229.

Seabury, B. A., & Maple, F. F. (1993). Using computers to teach practice skills. *Social Work, 38,* 430–439.

Sharwell, G. R. (1983). Legal issues in social work practice. In S. Briar et al. (Eds.), *1983–84 supplement to the encyclopedia of social work, 17th edition* (pp. 69–75). Washington, DC: National Association of Social Workers.

Siporin, M. (1975). *Introduction to social work practice.* New York: Macmillan.

Social Security Act, 49 Stat. 620. (1935).

Social Security Amendments of 1961. P.L. 87-543, 76 Stat. 196.

Spade, M. (1994). *Poverty measures mask the depth of poverty in America.* Boston, MA: National Consumer Law Center. Clearing House Review.

Specht, H., & Courtney, M. (1994). *Unfaithful angels: How social work has abandoned its mission.* New York: Free Press.

Strom, K., & Gingrich, W. (1993). Educating students for the new market realities. *Journal of Social Work Education, 29*(1), 78–87.

Sze, W., & Hopps, J. (1978). *Evaluation and accountability in human services programs* (2nd ed.). Cambridge, MA: Schenkman.

Toren, N. (1972). *Social work: The case of a semi-profession.* Beverly Hills, CA: Sage Publications.

Toufexis, A. (1994, April 25). Workers who fight fire with fire. *Time,* pp. 34–37.

U.S. Bureau of the Census. (1994). *Statistical abstract of the United States: 1994* (114th ed.). Washington, DC: Author.

U.S. Department of Justice, Federal Bureau of Investigation. (1993). *Crime in the United States 1992.* Washington, DC: Author.

U.S. Department of Labor, Bureau of Labor Statistics. (1992, May). *Occupational outlook handbook* (1992–1993 edition). Washington, DC: Author.

Weiss, J. (1990). Violence motivated by bigotry: Ethnoviolence. In L. Ginsberg et al. (Eds.), *Encyclopedia of social work* (18th ed., 1990 suppl., pp. 307–319). Silver Spring, MD: NASW Press.

Further Reading

Addams, J. (1992). *Twenty years at Hull-House.* Chicago: University of Illinois.

Iatridis, D. (1994). *Social policy: Context of social development and institutional human services.* Pacific Grove, CA: Brooks/Cole.

Kozol, J. (1989). *Rachel and her children—Homeless families in America.* New York: Fawcett Columbine.

Mullen, E. J., & Combre, J. (1993). *Enhancing minority recruitment & retention in graduate school work education.* New York: Columbia University School of Social Work.

Reid, N. P., & Popple, P. R. (1992). *The moral purposes of social work: The character and intentions of a profession.* Chicago: Nelson-Hall.

Wilson, W. J. (1987). *The truly disadvantaged: The inner city, the under class and public policy.* Chicago: University of Chicago Press.

June Gary Hopps, PhD, is dean and professor, and **Pauline M. Collins, PhD,** is assistant dean for field education and assistant professor, Boston College, Graduate School of Social Work, McGuinn Hall, Room 132, Chestnut Hill, MA 02167.

For further information see

Advocacy; Clinical Social Work; Direct Practice Overview; Ethics and Values; Ethnic-Sensitive Practice; Families Overview; Federal Social Legislation from 1961 to 1994; International and Comparative Social Welfare; International Social Work Education; Licensing, Regulation, and Certification; Mental Health Overview; National Association of Social Workers; Person-in-Environment; Policy Practice; Private Practice; Professional Conduct; Research Overview; Social Welfare History; Social Welfare Policy; Social Work Education; Social Work Practice: History and Evolution; Social Work Practice: Theoretical Base; Social Work Profession: History; Special-Interest Professional Associations.

Key Words	
education/training	salary information
occupational outlook	social work
profession	

Social Work Profession: History
Philip R. Popple

The history of the social work profession in the United States is embedded in the general history of social welfare, which, in turn, is related to broad patterns of economic, social, intellectual, and political history. Because this entry is brief and hence narrowly focused, it gives only scant attention to these general and broad themes. Similarly, although there is a rich literature on the sociology of the professions that is germane to the topic, this literature is touched on only lightly.

EMERGENCE OF SOCIAL WORK AS A SOCIAL FUNCTION

The emergence of social work as a profession is intertwined with the emergence of the social welfare institution during the 19th century. Before that time, there was a scattering of varied social welfare services, such as poor houses, orphanages, and mental hospitals. The scope of these services was small, and few staffing problems were encountered. The employees of these organizations tended to be members of the clergy, friends of politicians, or low-paid menial workers. Because the problems addressed by these agencies were believed to stem from the moral weakness of the clients, there was little recognition that persons who worked in the agencies had any need for specialized education or professional expertise.

Increase in Social Problems

During the last half of the 19th century, as a result of the massive growth of the population, accompanied by rapidly increasing industrialization, urbanization, and immigration, the country experienced an explosive increase in social problems. These problems were massive and were increasing at a rate that appeared to be out of control. For example, when the population of New York City was well under 1 million, the police estimated that more than 10,000 children were living on the streets; other estimates ran as high as 30,000 (Fry, 1974). In response to these problems, three social movements began that formed the basis for the development of the social work profession: the Charity Organization Societies (COS) movement, which began in 1877 in Buffalo, New York; the settlement house movement, which began in 1886 in New York City; and several loosely related developments, notably the Children's Aid Society and the Society for the Prevention of Cruelty to Children, which began in New York City in 1853 and 1875, respectively, that together formed the basic elements of a child welfare movement.

Charity Organization Societies Movement

The settlement house movement and the child welfare movement eventually made important contributions to the development of the social work profession, but it is in the COS movement that the origin of the profession is to be found. The settlements and the child welfare agencies had limited and concrete aims. The settlements wanted to be "neighbors" to the poor and to help communities solve self-identified problems, such as day care, literacy, and citizenship. The child welfare agencies were concerned with "rescuing" children from inadequate homes or from the streets and finding wholesome living situations for them. Once their goals were accomplished, the agencies considered their job to be over. The settlements rejected the idea of expertise, and the children's agencies, at least initially, rejected the idea that they were social welfare agencies, preferring to identify themselves with law enforcement.

Scientific methods. The COS movement had more ambitious goals. The COSs sought not only to assist the poor, but to understand and cure poverty and family disorganization. The name the movement quickly adopted for itself, "scientific charity," summed up this attitude. The charity organizations wanted to apply science to social welfare in the same way that it had been applied to medicine and engineering. They wanted to study the problem of dependence, gather data, test theories, systematize administration, and develop techniques that would lead to a cure.

The COS movement was a response to the rapid growth of relief-giving agencies, the lack of coordination among them, and the absence of any guiding principles for decision making about people in need. The COS leaders sought to replace the existing system of charity, which they perceived to be excessive and chaotic, with a rational system that would stress investigation, coordination, and personal service. Each case was to be considered individually; thoroughly investigated; and assigned to a "friendly visitor," who would get to know the family and would help it solve the problems that led to its dependence. The COS friendly visitors are the true forerunners of today's social workers.

Volunteer staffing. Like the majority of 19th-century social welfare agencies, the COS was originally staffed primarily by volunteers. Each COS had a few paid staff members, called "agents," who were responsible for taking applications for relief and for collecting and verifying information about each case. This information was then turned over to a board of volunteers, who made decisions about applicants' eligibility for assistance and what kind of and how much assistance was needed, and assigned the case to a volunteer friendly visitor. The friendly visitor was not concerned in any way with dispensing relief, but instead was concerned with providing treatment, or personal service as it was then called. Because the COS agencies originally thought that the causes of poverty were related to immorality (for example, vice, indolence, and intemperance), the major treatment technique was to provide a positive moral example of clean and prosperous living.

As one annual report of an early COS (cited in Lubove, 1965) stated:

> "Marvelous indeed it is to find in how many cases some cause of poverty and want exists which you can remove! ... You go in the full strength and joy and fire of life; full of cheer and courage; with a far wider knowledge of affairs; and it would be indeed a wonder if you could not often see why the needy family does not succeed, and how to help them up." (pp. 12–13)

The techniques used by the friendly visitors consisted of personal attributes such as "all possible sympathy, tact, patience, cheer, and wise advice" (Lubove, 1965, p. 13). Thus, those involved in the COS believed that it was not enough to relieve want and suffering with the provision of material assistance, but that it was possible actually to remediate the causes of dependence through the medium of personal service.

Need for expertise. Within a short time, it became obvious that there were serious problems with relying on volunteers for the provision of social services. One problem was simply that of numbers; there were never enough volunteers to meet the needs of all COS clients. An 1893 survey found that the shortage of visitors was so great that fewer than one case out of seven was ever seen by a volunteer (Lewis, 1971). The more important problem, however, was the lack of expertise. The friendly visitors initially went into the homes of the poor thinking that a cheerful nature, a willing spirit, and a good example would be sufficient to solve the families' problems. What they often found, however, was not families in need of moral example and guidance, but families of "exemplary piety" and diligence who were overwhelmed by circumstances beyond their control (Lewis, 1971). As a result of these problems, by the late 19th century the COS began to replace volunteer friendly visitors with paid staff, and the agencies and staff began to search for knowledge and techniques that would enable them to be effective in their fight against poverty and dependence.

EMERGENCE OF SOCIAL WORK AS A PROFESSION

Need for Professional Status

By the 1890s, a strong desire had developed among COS personnel to establish their work as a profession. There were several reasons for this desire. First, professionalization was a major social trend during that era. Medicine and engineering had demonstrated the wonders that could occur when science was applied to practical problems through the vehicle of a profession; as a result, the development of new professions was viewed as the answer to many modern problems. It appeared reasonable to think that the myriad and diverse social problems that were plaguing the new urban society should be the proper target for solution by a new profession.

Second, the COS workers' jobs had begun as volunteer positions, and agency boards tended to view them as volunteer positions to which a small stipend was attached. Because most charity workers were individuals who needed to earn a living, they were interested in establishing their work as deserving of a decent wage. Gaining recognition as professionals would accomplish this goal. Third, a new class of women, who were well educated and wanted careers outside of the home, was emerging. However, the traditional professions were largely closed to them, so they sought alternative avenues for success and achievement. Developing charity work into a full-fledged profession in which they would not be blocked because of their sex was a good strategy.

Fourth, paid charity workers, like the volunteers before them, were discovering the immense complexity of the task they were facing. They came to believe that helping people deal with social problems, such as poverty and family breakdown, involved tasks every bit as complicated as those performed by physicians, lawyers, and engineers. Agency administrators were finding that poorly educated persons or those with less than top-notch abilities were failures as charity workers, just as they would be failures at traditional professions. For all these reasons, by the late 1890s, a powerful movement to develop training and research centers and to demand that people doing charity work be trained and recognized as professionals was gaining momentum.

Professional Education
The first step in the effort to establish charity work as a profession was the establishment of training schools. In "The Need of Training Schools for a New Profession," Anna Dawes (1893) argued that people with experience in charity work were accumulating a good deal of knowledge and expertise and that some formal mechanism should be established to allow experienced workers to pass this knowledge along to new workers, so that these new workers would not repeat the mistakes of earlier workers. In a paper entitled "The Need of a Training School in Applied Philanthropy," COS leader Mary Richmond (1897) said of people entering charity work:

Surely, they have a right to demand from the profession of applied philanthropy (we really have not even a

name for it) that which they have a right to demand from any other profession—further opportunities for education and development and, incidentally, the opportunity to earn a living. (p. 183)

After the publication of these papers by Dawes and Richmond, along with many others, and the beginning of in-service training by organizations, such as Boston's Associated Charities, formal professional education was begun in 1898 under the sponsorship of the New York Charity Organization Society. This program, called the Summer School of Philanthropy, was six weeks long and consisted of lectures, visits to public and private charitable agencies, and supervised fieldwork. In 1903, the program was expanded to include a six-month winter course; in 1904, it was extended to one full year, and the name was changed to the New York School of Philanthropy. Other cities quickly followed New York's lead and established professional schools for the training of charity workers: the Chicago Institute of Social Science in 1903, the School for Social Workers in Boston in 1904 (the first to use the profession's new name), the Missouri School of Social Economy in 1907, and the Philadelphia Training School for Social Work in 1908.

Development of Specialties
By the early years of the 20th century, charity work had been firmly established as a full-time paid career, and training schools had been established out of the recognition that the functions performed by charity workers were complex and demanded formal training backed up by research. The new profession was rapidly beginning to be identified as social work, and the more professionally oriented segment of the profession, the COS workers, were beginning to think of their specialty as social casework, to differentiate it from the work being done by settlement house personnel, which was less professional in orientation. At this point, casework began to expand outside the traditional setting of the charity agency. As Lubove (1965, p. 22) observed, during these early years of the century, "employment in several institutions whose effectiveness had been limited by a failure to consider the social environment of clients or patients was a decisive episode in the evolution of social work as a profession."

In 1905 medical social work was established at Massachusetts General Hospital under the sponsorship of Dr. Richard C. Cabot for the purpose of studying "the conditions under which patients live and to assist those patients in carrying out the treatment recommended by the medical staff" (Trattner, 1989, p. 134). In 1906, Dr. James

Putnam, chief of Massachusetts General Hospital's neurological service, after observing the work of the social service department in the hospital, created a specialized division in the department to deal with mental patients. He hired three people to visit patients' homes, and the results provided him with a "fresh endorsement . . . of the value of skilled friendly visiting and the careful study of home conditions as a supplement to the physician's work among dispensary patients and as a means of making his directions to them effective" (Lubove, 1965, p. 63).

Starting in 1906, public schools began to use social workers to establish linkages between the schools and the students' social environments. In 1913, boards of education began to confer official recognition on school social workers, and in 1921, the prestigious Commonwealth Fund included school social work in a five-year Program for the Prevention of Delinquency (Lubove, 1965).

THE FLEXNER REPORT AND THE DRIVE FOR PROFESSIONAL STATUS

By 1915, social workers were beginning to feel confident that they were members of a new and potentially powerful profession. However, the major focus of the profession had been debated for a number of years. One faction, those with intellectual roots in the settlement house movement, believed that the new profession should focus on the social causes of dependence. Leaders of this group, including Samuel McCune Lindsey at the New York School of Social Work, Edith Abbott at the Chicago School of Civics and Philanthropy, and George Mangold at the Missouri School of Social Economy, argued for a profession based on social and economic theory and with a social reform orientation. Mangold (1914) wrote:

> The leaders of social work . . . can subordinate technique to an understanding of the social problems that are involved. . . . Fundamental principles, both in economics and in sociology, are necessary for the development of their plans of community welfare. . . .
> Courses in problems of poverty and in the method and technique of charity organizations are fundamental to our work. But the study of economics of labor is quite as important, and lies at the basis of our living and social condition. . . . The gain is but slight if our philanthropy means nothing more than relieving distress here and helping a family there; the permanent gain comes only as we are able to work out policies that mean the permanent improvement of social conditions. (p. 89)

The second faction consisted of a number of social work leaders, generally with roots in the COS and related treatment-oriented agencies, who believed that the new profession should concentrate on the development of practical knowledge related to addressing problems in individual role performance. COS leader Bruno (1928, p. 4) argued that social work should be concerned with "processes . . . with all technical methods from the activities of boards of directors to the means used by a probation officer to rectify the conduct of a delinquent child."

Flexner Conclusion: Not a Profession

In 1915 the program planning committee of the National Conference of Charities and Correction invited Abraham Flexner, an educator who had gained international renown for a study of medical education that had resulted in great improvement in the quality of medical care and, consequently, in the status of physicians, to analyze social work's progress in attaining professional status. Flexner presented his paper "Is Social Work a Profession?" at the group's 1915 meeting. His answer to the question posed in the title of his paper was an unequivocal no.

Flexner concluded that social work strongly exhibited some of the traits normally associated with professions: It was intellectual, derived its knowledge from science and learning, had a professional self-consciousness, and was altruistic. However, Flexner found social work lacking in several important areas, mainly the possession of an educationally communicable technique and practitioners' assumption of a large degree of individual responsibility. Regarding social work's lack of an educationally communicable technique, Flexner believed that the source of the deficiency was the broadness of social work's boundaries and that professions had to have definite and specific ends. However, he noted that "the high degree of specialized competency required for action and conditioned on limitation of area cannot possibly go with the width and scope characteristic of social work" (p. 585). Flexner thought that this lack of specificity seriously affected the possibility of professional training: "The occupations of social workers are so numerous and diverse that no compact, purposefully organized educational discipline is possible" (p. 588).

In the area of individual responsibility, Flexner believed that social workers were mediators, rather than responsible parties:

> The social worker takes hold of a case, that of a disintegrating family, a wrecked individual, or an unsocialized industry. Having localized his problem, having decided on its particular nature, is he not usually driven to invoke the specialized agency, professional or

other, best equipped to handle it? . . . To the extent that the social worker mediates the intervention of the particular agent or agency best fitted to deal with the specific emergency which he has encountered, is the social worker himself a professional or is he the intelligence that brings this or that profession or other activity into action? (p. 590)

Increased Training, Emphasis on Casework

Flexner's paper had a massive and immediate impact on social work. Social workers consciously set out to remedy the deficiencies Flexner identified, mainly the development of an educationally communicable technique. Social casework with individuals, families, and small groups had always been the major interest of the social workers who were most intent on professionalization, so it is no surprise that social workers emphasized this area in response to Flexner's critique. The committee that was charged with responding to Flexner's paper suggested that "the chief problem facing social work is the development of training methods which will give it [a] technical basis" (Lee, 1915, p. 598). Its members thought that the social work profession had the beginning of an educationally communicable technique in the area of social casework and that the profession should narrow its focus to emphasize this area.

In the years after Flexner's paper, social workers earnestly sought to correct the deficiencies it had identified. The number of professional schools rapidly expanded, a professional accreditation body was formed, pressure was brought to standardize curricula, training was recommended for all workers, and a series of conferences was held to develop and promote the idea that casework was a singular, generic skill, regardless of setting. Richmond's *Social Diagnosis* (1917) and *What Is Social Casework?* (1922) were seen as providing the educationally communicable technical basis for the profession that Flexner considered to be so vital.

The result of all these activities was that by 1929, social workers, following Flexner's criteria, had narrowed the definition of social work to psychiatrically oriented casework. In the process, they had all but eliminated public welfare, social and labor reform, and "less professional" techniques such as acting as liaisons between social institutions and clients and brokering resources. They had also eliminated techniques practiced by settlement workers, such as group work and community work. Lubove (1965, p. 107) observed that "like Flexner, social workers failed to realize that the opening of lines of communication between individuals, classes, and institutions, and community resource mobilization could be defended as legitimate 'professional' responsibilities."

THE GREAT DEPRESSION: A CRISIS FOR THE NEW PROFESSION

In 1929 an economic depression began that was to prove to be the longest and deepest in American history. By the end of that year, the value of securities had shrunk by $40 billion. Hundreds of thousands of families lost their homes, millions of unemployed people walked the street, and tax revenues fell to such a low level that schoolteachers could not be paid in many areas. The United States had faced depressions in 1837, 1873, and 1893, but each of them had lasted only a few years. The Great Depression of 1929 was to last a full decade (Nevins & Commager, 1966).

Expansion in the Public Sector

The Great Depression had a rapid and profound effect on social work. Before the depression, the vast majority of social welfare services, including financial assistance, were administered by private agencies. Most social workers believed that private welfare was vastly superior to public welfare because public agencies were thought to be corrupt and inefficient and therefore were not settings that were conducive to professional practice. After the election of Franklin D. Roosevelt in 1933, this situation changed rapidly. The Social Security Act, passed in 1935, moved financial assistance, as well as much of public health and child welfare, to the public sector. In response to the development of public programs and the expansion of the social welfare system, the number of social workers increased from 40,000 to 80,000; the majority of these workers were employed by public agencies.

In addition to the great increase in the number of social work positions and the change from private to public auspices, the nature of social work jobs and the characteristics of the people filling them changed during the depression. Before the depression, social work was well on its way to becoming an all-graduate degree–trained profession. Schools of social work had been steadily moving from granting certificates or baccalaureate degrees toward granting only the master's degree in social work (MSW). The nature of the social worker's task was coming to be defined as mapping and modifying the complex intrapsychic landscape of clients (that is, providing skilled casework services based on a thorough understanding of psychotherapy). The clientele of social agencies included an increasing number of nonpoor individuals. With the coming of the depression, however, this situation rapidly changed. The massive growth of jobs in social work was almost exclusively in the public sector. Most of the new jobs involved helping basically well-adjusted people deal with problems brought about by unemployment and were defined by state civil service boards as requiring only a baccalaureate degree, and often even less.

Two Professions: Graduate and Baccalaureate

In the face of this massive growth of social work jobs in the public sector, the social work profession held fast to its goal of becoming an all-graduate degree–trained profession providing skilled casework services based on psychotherapeutic theory and technique. Instead of a new social work emerging from the Great Depression, one encompassing both public and private agencies and both professionally trained and lower-level workers, two separate but overlapping professions emerged. Graduate social workers, although acknowledging that public welfare was a legitimate field of practice, were unwilling to accept people without graduate training as professional social workers. The baccalaureate-level social workers who were employed in the new public welfare programs were not allowed into professional associations, and schools offering undergraduate-level social work training were not granted accreditation or even recognition by the association of professional schools. As a result, public welfare workers generally joined unions, if they joined anything, and colleges with undergraduate social work programs formed their own association, the National Association of Schools of Social Administration, for the purpose of support and accreditation (Leighninger, 1987). Many professionally trained social workers believed that because welfare had become the responsibility of public agencies, the social work profession no longer needed to be concerned with it and could get back to what these workers perceived was the core of social work: the psychological adjustment of the individual.

RETURN TO PROSPERITY AND COMPLACENCY: 1940 TO 1960

The huge demand for goods and services caused by World War II brought an end to the Great Depression, which the Roosevelt administration's New Deal programs had succeeded in ameliorating but not ending. The war and postwar era was one of prosperity and optimism but unfortunately was accompanied by attitudes of complacency and conservatism. The prevailing attitude in the country was that the problem of poverty was rapidly disappearing in the "affluent society," so termed by

economist Galbraith (1958). To the extent that poverty still existed, most people, including many social workers, believed that it was being dealt with by the public welfare system and therefore was little cause for concern.

Mental Health Focus

Social workers once again felt free to concentrate on the individual causes of distress and on developing knowledge and techniques to deal with them. A number of developments also tended to push social work even further in this direction. The testing of millions of military recruits during the war had revealed a greater prevalence of mental health problems than anyone could have imagined. The result of these findings was a push for mental health services, which resulted in the National Mental Health Act of 1946 and the establishment of the National Institute of Mental Health in 1949. The National Mental Health Act stressed community treatment and prevention and provided new opportunities for social workers who were interested in psychopathology.

The psychotherapeutic orientation that had begun in the 1920s and been de-emphasized in the 1930s found wide acceptance in the 1940s and 1950s. This approach made sense not only to social workers but to persons who supported social agencies. The general feeling of the era could be summed up as a belief that the social system works; therefore problems are due to some defect of the individual, and the appropriate approach is to find and cure the defect. During the 1950s, 85 percent of the students in schools of social work chose casework as their major. This interest in individual counseling was reinforced by the fact that more and more persons with incomes above the poverty line were turning to social workers for help. A 1960 study of family service agencies revealed that 9 percent of the clients were upper class and 48 percent were middle class (Leiby, 1978).

Dominance of Graduate Social Workers

Accompanying the return to interest in the individual causes of social problems was a successful effort by graduate schools and MSW social workers to reassert their dominance over the profession. In the early 1940s, the social work unions died out, leaving the non-MSW social workers without an association to represent their interests. In 1955, after a lengthy negotiation, seven specialty associations (American Association of Group Workers, American Association of Medical Social Workers, American Association of Psychiatric Social Workers, American Association of Social Workers, Association for the Study of Community

Organization, National Association of School Social Workers, and Social Work Research Group) merged to form NASW. Social workers without MSWs, generally employed in the public sector, were not welcome. In a similar fashion the National Association of Schools of Social Administration, the accrediting body for undergraduate programs, and the American Association of Schools of Social Work, the graduate accrediting body, merged to form the temporary National Council on Social Work Education. The council sponsored a major study of social work education, the 1951 Hollis-Taylor report, which recommended that social work education be confined to the graduate level. As a result, the temporary association was replaced in 1952 by the Council on Social Work Education (CSWE), which accredited only graduate programs. The effect of the demise of the unions and of the National Association of Schools of Social Administration and the rise of NASW and CSWE was to eliminate undergraduate trained social workers from the profession, even though more than three-fourths of individuals occupying jobs defined by the Bureau of Labor Statistics as social work positions did not have graduate training in social work.

THE PROFESSION BROADENS: THE 1960s

Throughout the 1950s, the country had been lulled into a false sense of well-being by books, such as Galbraith's (1958) *The Affluent Society,* which argued that poverty was a small and declining problem. It was believed that, in the United States, people were poor either because they lived in areas isolated from the general economic prosperity of the country (insular poverty) or because of individual problems that prevented them from functioning as viable wage earners (case poverty). As the 1960s began, the country was shocked by a series of books, articles, and reports that demonstrated that poverty still existed in the United States on a massive scale. Notable among these publications were Harrington's (1962) *The Other America,* MacDonald's (1963) "Our Invisible Poor," and the report of the Ad Hoc Committee on Public Welfare (Wyman, 1962), appointed by the new administration of John F. Kennedy. The result of these events, along with a general feeling in the nation that change was needed, was a tremendous interest in the problem of poverty and the movement of public welfare to the forefront of policy concerns for the first time since the Great Depression.

Federal Antipoverty Programs

The new interest in poverty was demonstrated during the 1960s by major programs launched by several different administrations. Each of these programs envisioned a different role for the social work profession, but each had the effect of reaffirming the profession's commitment to public welfare and to widening the scope of social work practice well beyond the narrow intrapsychic focus of the 1950s.

The Kennedy administration successfully proposed the 1962 amendments to the Social Security Act, popularly known as the Social Service Amendments. These amendments were chiefly concerned with providing social services to welfare recipients to help them solve whatever problems were preventing them from being self-sufficient and specifically identified the social work profession as the appropriate provider of these services. The act mandated the federal government to fund 75 percent of the cost to the states of providing social services to welfare-eligible clients, allocated money for states to send welfare department personnel to school to obtain MSW degrees, and provided money for schools of social work to develop and staff curricula in public welfare.

Although successful in increasing the interest and involvement of the social work profession in public welfare, the Social Service Amendments represented an old approach—namely, providing individual services to help people lift themselves out of poverty, with little attention to altering the social conditions that caused the poverty. The approach of the administration of Lyndon B. Johnson, embodied in the Economic Opportunity Act of 1964, was different. It emphasized community organization and social action and stressed involving the poor in making decisions about programs that affected their lives. The act established the Office of Economic Opportunity, Volunteers in Service to America, the Job Corps, Upward Bound, the Neighborhood Youth Corps, Head Start, and the Community Action Program. These War on Poverty programs were concerned with empowering, rather than repairing, the poor.

Move to Policy, Planning, Administration

These antipoverty programs initially ignored professionals, including social workers, under the theory that the poor themselves were the experts in determining what they needed. However, the poor people who were involved in these programs soon brought in social workers because they perceived a need for social workers' competence in community organization, administration, and direct service with clients. The effect of these programs was to move the social work profession further from its nearly exclusive focus on the individual and his or her problems to a much wider focus on the social and economic causes of problems and on knowledge and techniques to intervene on these levels. Motivated by this policy thrust, most schools of social work added policy, planning, and administration specialties to their curricula.

The Social Service Amendments and the War on Poverty programs were not successful in stemming the rapid increases in the public welfare rolls. Faced with this apparent lack of success and with a swing of the nation's mood back toward conservatism, people quickly tired of reform. In 1967 the Social Security Act was once again amended, this time emphasizing "hard" services, such as the Work Incentive Program and day care for recipients who were employed or in job training, and instituting a formula whereby a welfare recipient's grant was reduced by only a percentage of earned income when that person became employed. Along with these programs came an interest in program management and accountability. Accountability to taxpayers was being demanded by public officials, and accountability to clients was being demanded from within the social work profession. The result was that the scope of social work continued to widen during the conservative years of the late 1960s as schools broadened their curricula to include more courses on administration, planning, and research.

SOCIAL WORK SEEKS TO FIRM UP ITS DOMAIN

In this brief survey of the history of social work as a profession, two general problems of professionalization have emerged: inclusiveness and exclusiveness. Inclusiveness refers to the fact that since the earliest years of the profession, there have always been people in social work jobs who were not accepted as social workers by the dominant professional organizations. Exclusiveness refers to the fact that the profession has had difficulty excluding people without formal social work credentials from occupying jobs that the profession argues should be restricted to persons with social work training.

Inclusiveness

When NASW was founded in 1955, it held rigidly to the standard that only those with the MSW degree were professional social workers. This requirement continued the situation, present during most of the profession's history, in which less than one-fourth of the people in social work jobs were recognized by the major professional organizations as being social workers. It is hard to defend a profession as legitimate when it represents only a minority of the people practicing in its specialty area.

Since 1970 social work has taken major steps to include more people in the definition of the profession. In 1970 NASW changed its membership requirements to allow people with bachelor's degrees in social work (BSWs) from approved programs to become full members. This change necessitated the development of some mechanism for approving undergraduate programs, and such a mechanism was instituted in 1974, when CSWE began to accredit BSW programs. In 1991 NASW developed the Academy of Certified Baccalaureate Social Workers as a method of providing recognition for exceptional competence by BSW-level workers. The certificate issued by this academy is similar to the one issued by the long-established Academy of Certified Social Workers (ACSW) and, like the ACSW, requires the demonstration of successful experience after receipt of the degree and passage of a written examination. In addition, baccalaureate social workers are included in 26 state laws regulating the practice of social work.

As a result of including baccalaureate-level social workers in the definition of the profession, nearly half the 400,000 jobs that the Bureau of Labor Statistics identifies as social work jobs are now filled with people with professional credentials, a much higher proportion than at any previous time in history (Ginsberg, 1992). However, BSWs have not taken a prominent place in the profession in any sense other than their number. Membership in NASW and offices in professional organizations continue to be held overwhelmingly by those with the MSW degree. For example, in 1994 more than 97 percent of NASW members had MSWs, and nearly all board and committee members were MSWs (NASW, 1994). This has not been the situation in social work education, however. Undergraduate programs either accredited, or in candidacy, by CSWE now number over 400, four times the number of graduate programs (CSWE, 1994). The Baccalaureate Program Directors Association, which was formed in 1982, has become an influential force within the profession. It would be an overstatement to say that undergraduate programs dominate social work education, but it can be said with some certainty that they are on an equal basis with their graduate counterparts.

Exclusiveness

The problem of exclusiveness has stemmed, in large part, from the problem of inclusiveness just discussed—namely, that social work leaders for many years held fast to the unrealistic goal that eventually all social workers would be trained at the graduate level. Because the number of social work jobs has always expanded at a rate far greater than the number of available MSWs, the profession's attempts to restrict positions to MSWs were viewed as unrealistic by those outside the professional community. The profession has come to the more realistic position that the BSW is the entry-level professional degree and that the MSW provides advanced, specialized training. Thus, since the 1970s, social work has been able to address realistically the problem of excluding unqualified people from the practice of social work.

Legal regulation. To restrict the practice of social work to qualified practitioners, the profession has followed the lead of older professions and advocated for the passage of licensing laws. Two factors have motivated the profession to seek legal regulation through licensing. The first has to do with protecting the public and consists of arguments that social work is a technical specialization that can result in great harm if practiced by people without proper qualifications. Because of this danger to the public, the government, under its mandate to ensure public safety, should assume the responsibility of regulating social work services. The second factor has to do with enhancing the status of the profession. Licensing would increase the status of the profession, protect its domain against competition, and make social workers and agencies eligible for payments as third-party vendors. This last point will become increasingly important as national health care proposals are debated. Most health benefits programs—Medicaid is a good example—will pay directly for services only if they are provided by a licensed practitioner.

In 1973 NASW developed a model licensing bill and recommended that state chapters use it to develop their own proposed statutes. The model statute recommends three levels of licensure based on educational qualifications: certified social worker (with an MSW or higher degree), social worker (with a BSW degree), and social work associate (with a junior college degree). An examination in addition to these educational criteria is recommended. As of late 1994, social work is regulated in all states and territories, licensed in 47, and registered in the other six. In 33 states and the District of Columbia, social workers are eligible to receive third-party reimbursements.

Opposition to licensing. Licensing has come under attack from persons who believe it is elitist and is being advocated to exclude people from the profession inappropriately. It has also come under attack from those who believe that it is not exclu-

sive enough, that there is no reason to include BSWs and graduates of junior colleges. The argument is that these workers provide only routine services under close supervision (that is, nonprofessional services) and that licensing should cover only those workers with MSWs who provide individual treatment. Regardless of whether licensing is a good thing, one fact is clear: In the late 20th century, licensing is the ultimate indication of whether an occupation is a profession. Without effective licensing to protect social work's domain, discussions of the professional status of social work will become moot.

Emerging Problems of Professionalization

In addition to obtaining legal regulation of social work practice in most regions of the country and extending professional education to the undergraduate level, social work has been struggling with emerging issues of inclusiveness and exclusiveness.

Competition for family services. The area of marriage and family counseling has historically been a cornerstone of the social work profession. When public welfare departments were established in every state during the Great Depression, the Charity Organization Societies shifted their focus from providing material relief to providing skilled family counseling. For many years, these agencies were the exclusive province of MSW social workers, but this situation has begun to change. The departments of family and child development and the departments of counseling psychology at a number of universities have begun to offer specializations, often at the doctoral level, in marriage and family counseling. The primary accreditation body that has emerged for family counselors is the American Association of Marriage and Family Therapists (AAMFT), whose members include a number of individuals with social work training, but the organization in no way identifies with the social work profession. Perhaps the most ominous development occurred in 1990, when *Social Casework*, one of the oldest and most prestigious professional social work journals, changed its name to *Families in Society*. The editorial introducing the new journal did not mention the social work profession, but instead talked about "creating a new journal that reflects developments in the *human services professions*" [italics added] (Burant, 1990, p. 3). In some states (for example, Michigan), social workers are not eligible for licensure as marriage and family counselors without additional training outside schools of social work. If current trends continue, marriage and family therapy will become less, rather than more, the exclusive domain of social work.

Reprofessionalization of child welfare services. A more optimistic development is social work's involvement in public child welfare services, another area that was traditionally considered to be a social work specialization. Because of a number of developments over the years, notably the drive to declassify public positions to make it easier and cheaper to staff public agencies, the traditional alliance between social work and public child welfare was weakened. In the late 1970s, the American Civil Liberties Union (ACLU) began the Children's Rights Project, which, during the 1980s and 1990s, filed a series of lawsuits representing the rights of children in foster care as a class. In these suits, ACLU argued that children in protective services caseloads have a right to professional services. ACLU won these suits in a number of states, and the judgments order the state governments to upgrade the child welfare system, typically by requiring the states to increase greatly the number of social workers in the child welfare system, hire more professionally trained (both BSW and MSW) social workers and supervisors, increase the level and quality of in-house training, and to upgrade the system in other ways.

In response to these court orders, as well as to other inputs, state social services departments and schools of social work have formed what has come to be called the New Partnerships Initiative. Supported by grants from the U.S. Children's Bureau and coordinated by the National Child Welfare Leadership Center in the Department of Social Work at Florida International University, the New Partnerships Initiative (Briar, Hansen, & Harris, 1992) has begun to hold conferences, develop curricular materials, and work with departments of social services and social work educators to improve the preparation for, and stimulate the interest in, public child welfare services.

Privatization of social work practice. Traditionally social work has been practiced in either government or private nonprofit agencies. However, a growing number of social workers are now practicing in private fee-for-service settings and in private for-profit businesses. Private fee-for-service organizations are practice organizations that are typical of those used by professionals, such as physicians and lawyers, in which social workers provide services, generally counseling or therapy, for an hourly fee. The growth of licensing laws and the corresponding expansion of many insurance and government benefit programs to include social

workers as eligible for reimbursement has greatly accelerated the expansion of social workers in private practice. Private for-profit businesses employing (or owned by) social workers that have expanded include drug and alcohol treatment programs, nursing homes, eating-disorder clinics, adult day care centers, and companion services.

Exactly how many social workers are currently practicing in private settings is difficult to determine. In 1991, 16.8 percent of the NASW members reported solo or group private practice as their primary practice setting (Gibelman & Schervish, 1993). The Bureau of Labor Statistics estimated that the number of social workers who are self-employed will increase by about 20 percent between 1990 and 2005. In any case, it is clear that this is a growing segment of the profession.

The development of private practice and for-profit social work has met with a mixed reception in the profession. A number of social workers welcome these developments as signs of the maturing of the profession and recognition of the value of social work services by segments of society other than poor people. They believe that the establishment of a private base for social work practice permits more autonomous and, hence, more professional services and that private practice creates additional career opportunities and thereby increases the attractiveness of the profession to potential social workers. However, a number of people in the profession view the development and expansion of private for-profit social work as a cause for concern. Reamer (1992) succinctly stated this view:

> In increasing numbers, social work is attracting practitioners with limited commitment to the profession's traditional concern with social justice and public welfare. Although today's social workers may be ideologically supportive of the profession's traditional values, for many this commitment is not what draws them to social work. Instead, the attractions are often professional advancement and autonomy, status and financial security. (p. 12)

REFERENCES

Briar, K. H., Hansen, V. H., & Harris, N. (1992). *New partnerships: Proceedings from the National Public Child Welfare Training Symposium, 1991.* Miami: Florida International University.

Bruno, F. (1928). The project of training for social work. *Adult Education Bulletin, 3,* 4.

Burant, R. J. (1990). Welcome to *Families in Society. Families in Society: The Journal of Contemporary Human Services, 71,* 3.

Council on Social Work Education. (1994). *Directory of colleges and universities with accredited social work degree programs* [pamphlet]. Alexandria, VA: Author.

Dawes, A. (1893). The need of training schools for a new profession. *Lend-A-Hand, 11,* 90–97.

Economic Opportunity Act of 1964. P.L. 88-452, 78 Stat. 508.

Flexner, A. (1915). Is social work a profession? In *Proceedings of the National Conference of Charities and Correction* (pp. 576–590). Baltimore: Russell Sage Foundation.

Fry, A. (1974). The children's migration. *American Heritage, 26,* 4–10, 79–81.

Galbraith, J. (1958). *The affluent society.* Boston: Houghton Mifflin.

Gibelman, M., & Schervish, P. H. (1993). *Who we are.* Washington, DC: NASW Press.

Ginsberg, L. (1992). *Social work almanac.* Washington, DC: NASW Press.

Harrington, M. (1962). *The other America: Poverty in the United States.* New York: Penguin Books.

Hollis, E., & Taylor, A. (1951). *Social work education in the U.S.* New York: Columbia University Press.

Lee, P. R. (1915). Committee report: The professional basis of social work. In *Proceedings of the National Conference of Charities and Correction* (pp. 597–600). Baltimore: Russell Sage Foundation.

Leiby, J. (1978). *A history of social work and social welfare in the United States.* New York: Columbia University Press.

Leighninger, L. (1987). *Social work: Search for identity.* Westport, CT: Greenwood Press.

Lewis, V. (1971). Charity organization society. In R. Morris (Ed.-in-Chief), *Encyclopedia of social work* (16th ed., Vol. 1, pp. 94–99). New York: National Association of Social Workers.

Lubove, R. (1965). *The professional altruist: The emergence of social work as a career.* Cambridge, MA: Harvard University Press.

MacDonald, D. (1963, January 19). Our invisible poor. *New Yorker,* pp. 82–132.

Mangold, G. (1914). The new profession of social service. In J. E. McCullock (Ed.), *Battling for social betterment* (pp. 86–90). Nashville, TN: Southern Sociological Congress.

National Association of Social Workers. (1994). *National leadership directory, October 1993–October 1994.* Washington, DC: Author.

National Mental Health Act of 1946. Ch. 538, 60 Stat. 421.

Nevins, A., & Commager, H. (1966). *A short history of the United States.* New York: Alfred A. Knopf.

Reamer, F. G. (1992). Social work and the public good: Calling or career? In P. N. Reid & P. R. Popple (Eds.), *The moral purposes of social work: The character and intentions of a profession* (pp. 11–33). Chicago: Nelson-Hall.

Richmond, M. (1897). The need of a training school in applied philanthropy. *Proceedings of the National Conference of Charities and Correction* (pp. 181–188). Boston: George H. Ellis.

Richmond, M. (1917). *Social diagnosis.* New York: Russell Sage Foundation.

Richmond, M. (1922). *What is social casework?* New York: Russell Sage Foundation.

Social Security Act of 1935. Ch. 531, 49 Stat. 620.

Social Security Act Amendments of 1962. P.L. 87-543, 76 Stat. 173.

Social Security Act Amendments of 1967. P.L. 90-248, 81 Stat. 821.

Trattner, W. (1989). *From poor law to welfare state: A history of social welfare* (4th ed.). New York: Free Press.

Whiting, L. (1992). *State comparison of laws regulating social work.* Washington, DC: NASW Press.

Wyman, G. K. (1962). A report for the secretary of health, education, and welfare. In U.S. Congress, House Committee on Ways and Means (Ed.), *Hearings on H.R. 10032, Public Welfare Amendments of 1962* (p. 78). Washington, DC: U.S. Government Printing Office.

FURTHER READING

Axinn, J., & Levin, H. (1992). *Social welfare: A history of the American response to need* (3rd ed.). New York: Longman.

Ehrenreich, J. (1985). *The altruistic imagination: A history of social work and social policy in the United States.* Ithaca, NY: Cornell University Press.

Jansson, B. (1992). *The reluctant welfare state: A history of American social welfare policy* (2nd ed.). Belmont, CA: Wadsworth.

Richan, W., & Mendelsohn, A. (1973). *Social work: The unloved profession.* New York: New Viewpoints.

Specht, H., & Courtney, M. (1994). *Unfaithful angels: How social work has abandoned its mission.* New York: Free Press.

Philip R. Popple, PhD, LCSW, is professor and director, Western Michigan University, School of Social Work, Kalamazoo, MI 49008.

For further information see

Advocacy; Archives of Social Welfare; Charitable Foundations and Social Welfare; Council on Social Work Education; Ethics and Values; Federal Social Legislation from 1961 to 1994; National Association of Social Workers; Settlements and Neighborhood Centers; Social Welfare History; Social Work Practice: History and Evolution; Social Work Profession Overview.

Key Words	
history	social work education
social welfare history	social work profession

Social Worker and Agency Safety
William V. Griffin

Social work has emerged in the late 1980s and early 1990s as a difficult area of human services. It is clear from discussions among individual professionals across the United States and from a review of national news reports that there is a heavier burden on public and private providers of social work services. High caseloads, uncooperative clients, and growing drug and crime areas—intractable problems with few solutions—complicate the tasks of professionals providing human services.

Several national and local factors have come together to create and exacerbate this situation. This entry will focus on these factors and their influence on the public agency and quasi-public agency frontline social or human services worker. Many of the points discussed herein will also have applicability to the "private" or clinical social worker who practices in the public or private setting (Newhill, 1992).

FEDERAL LAWS

In the United States several actions on the federal level have sparked a movement in the field of social work, particularly in the public realm, that has shifted social work's emphasis from the historical psychosocial program intervention to a more law enforcement–based approach. The movement started in the 1970s with passage of child abuse acts in most states and staffing of child protective services. This movement expanded child abuse intervention from an almost exclusive review by physicians to investigation by a new group of social workers: child protective workers. These acts expanded who could and should report abuse and neglect from physicians to a much wider pool of mandated reporters and, in some states, to all citizens.

Subsequently, several amendments to the Federal Child Abuse Prevention and Treatment Act resulted in an expansion of child protective services from responding to a few thousand (in the 1960s) to more than 3 million reports nationally per year estimated in 1994. In addition, new public policies in the 1980s brought in an increased number of investigations of child sexual abuse and stronger efforts to prosecute alleged perpetrators, new adult and elder protective laws, and laws designed to bring absent parents to the courts for child support.

All of these actions require greater involvement by the state and by the social worker in the normally private relationship between parent and child and adult child and parent. Supervised visitation in child custody and divorce proceedings, child and elder abuse and neglect, domestic vio-

lence, stalking, and other threatening situations currently are all within the purview of the public and private agency social worker.

When broader, more intrusive services are rendered, it may be necessary to add or adjust agency policies and procedures. In many cases this new level of involvement dictates more limits on the social worker to apply discretionary judgment. Although individual social workers currently must intervene in situations as required by the law, rarely are these situations "black and white." Instead, social workers must respond to and intervene in incidents that inevitably place them in the middle of chaotic, difficult, and often volatile and dangerous environments.

One consequence of these changes is that community receptivity to social workers has diminished. Changes that have occurred within law enforcement have carried over to social workers. Currently social workers are seen less often as helpers and more often as agents of the state's authority. A general lack of respect for such workers has become the norm rather than the exception.

PUBLIC AWARENESS

Through government effort public awareness of many issues has increased, with an attendant change in expectations. Not only are people more willing to report cases of child abuse and domestic violence, for example, than ever before, they also look for and expect solutions to problems.

Just as law enforcement officers are expected to solve violent family situations, there is a common belief that frontline social workers should be able to remedy difficult and complex emotional family problems immediately. Social workers are well aware of these increasing expectations and as a result experience increasing stress in their jobs.

The term frontline worker besides denoting an organizational line position of immediacy to a client population, may also suggest a combat perspective. The direct service worker, in some senses, may be viewed as similar to a soldier engaged in combat on the frontlines. (MacFadden, 1980, p. 1)

Overall, there is little understanding of the personal risks social workers confront as they do their work; this is particularly true in the public agency setting. Thus, it is difficult to create the broad and deep support required for establishing the personal protection systems that are a necessary part of public policy enforcement.

THE COURTS

The courts have become increasingly more involved in the resolution of cases, in part because of the changes in federal and state laws. The attitude of professionals in the legal and social work fields is that legal action is necessary in many cases to ensure compliance with treatment, protection plans, or necessary financial support.

This escalation of the court process, particularly in family or juvenile court, has led to more dramatic and adversarial hearings. It is not uncommon for case situations to lead to criminal court prosecution as well, increasing the volatility of all court sessions. It is also not uncommon to hear of an assault on a social worker in a courtroom or court building.

Protective court orders, orders for removal of children and juveniles, termination of parental rights, physical and sexual abuse hearings, and mandatory treatment participation all were virtually unheard of in the 1970s. Currently social workers must have a clear understanding of the legalities of their profession and the statutory basis for invoking their powers.

MORE–DIFFICULT CASES

Social work cases are becoming more difficult. There is greater societal violence and, consequently, often longer histories of violent client behavior and other forms of maltreatment. Many areas of the country are experiencing substantial in-migration of new residents with new cultures. This results in communities with fewer strong, extended-family networks.

Community resources and funding for outreach programs have been drastically cut. In addition, more families are living at or below poverty levels, with little hope for the future. Family stress in these new environments is often high—a contributing factor to difficulties in handling cases.

Substance abuse creates "land mines" for workers as they seek out clients. In public housing projects or crime-ridden neighborhoods, staff members are working among people who are distrustful of their efforts. The well-publicized "war on drugs" vividly points out the changes that have occurred in the United States since the mid-1980s.

Many families are living in environments where illegal drug sales are a large part of the economic base, and social work field operations are placed directly in the middle of such environments.

Currently all helping professionals are working under multidimensional hazardous conditions. Law enforcement and fire department personnel, visiting nurses and home health aides, sexually transmitted disease investigators, public health officials, and social workers all feel the drama of daily life. Assaults on agency workers are as likely to happen because of the neighborhood they enter as because of the fear and anguish of clients. Expanded coverage (the sheer number of cases), increased legal requirements, and more complex and difficult cases and environments further complicate the tasks of social workers.

SOCIAL WORKER SAFETY ISSUES

Growing concern for the critical issue of social worker safety has brought the following key issues into sharp focus:

- Application of safety procedures at all levels of an agency (management, supervision, and staff) is inconsistent.
- There is a lack of communication on safety issues among management, supervision, and staff.
- There is a lack of consideration of safety issues in the planning of operations, from configuration of offices to agency staff practices.

This entry addresses these issues and provides recommendations for improving safety in social work and related practices.

Initial Safety Programs

Developing a safety approach for social work agencies is a task that requires commitment of resources and energy. Social work agencies across the United States have made significant strides in addressing the issue of protection of staff. However, there is still more to be done and much farther to go in developing these efforts.

Since the 1980s there has been increased support for safety programming that can be used by agencies on a daily basis. Although limited, the purpose of this initial programming has been to help social workers and support staff learn how to better protect themselves. The structure has been based on four beliefs:

1. Awareness of safety issues is a primary concern for all areas of human services agency operations.
2. There must be consistency in application of safety procedures at all levels of an agency.

3. Communication on safety issues must be developed between management and staff at all levels.
4. Safety must be a part of an agency's overall planning process and included in staff orientation and training, physical plant development, and crisis response and postvictimization and trauma training.

Administrators, supervisors, and, at times, social workers often do not acknowledge the potential impact of an agency's intervention on individuals, families, and children. This intrusion into the normally private lives of individuals can and often does have emotionally charged ramifications. Not uncommonly, clients interpret professional intervention as an accusation of poor self-control or inappropriate lifestyle. They at times fear the possibility of rejection of requests for services; forced institutionalization; loss of children, elderly parents, or economic base; and other civil or criminal actions. As a consequence of the intensity of these confrontations, individuals may lash out at the agency representative. The method for venting anger may be verbal or physical and may include the use of weapons.

Communication and training about the range of possible client reactions to agency intervention is essential to prepare agency professionals, paraprofessionals, and support staff for the realities of their work. Historically, many studies have shown all too clearly that communication at all levels in human services systems breaks down with regard to safety issues (Brown, Bute, & Ford, 1986; Kaplan & Wheeler, 1983; Lanza, 1983; Lehmann, 1983; Lewis, 1980; Mace, 1989; MacFadden, 1980; Mayer & Rosenblatt, 1975; Norris, 1990; Schultz, 1985; Star, 1984; Tupin, 1983; Vandecreek & Knapp, 1984; Yelaja, 1965). There is a common desire to avoid creating an atmosphere of fear and a misconception that fear would be the outcome of dealing with safety issues in an open and forthright way. There is also a clear lack of knowledge about events occurring in and around the office space daily.

Complicating the issue is the fact that agency and individual philosophies on safety are remarkably divergent. The range embraces, at one extreme, complete support for any measure that might assist or protect the safety of social work staff, and at the other extreme, a belief that there is simply no reason to be concerned about safety—it is a nonissue.

To foster safety and enhance effectiveness, it is imperative that social workers who work with possible confrontational environments or clients have some "real" sense of control over their situation. This sense of control—grounded in the knowledge that appropriate support systems are in place for client and staff alike—starts with a planned safety program.

Safety and Risk Management
Within the context of safety, risk management involves protecting social work agency staff from the possibility of harm while they are providing services. That simple definition is grounded in the literature and is reflected in procedures established by many agencies.

Risk management is often used in relation to U.S. federal workplace safety standards and state compensation issues. It often lacks a view that includes bodily attacks from clients or others in the office or other workplace (that is, field settings). Thus, staff members are often presented with information on ventilation, carpel tunnel syndrome, and internal lighting, for example, and are given little information on protecting themselves from an aggressive and threatening client; in a dangerous neighborhood or on an unsafe street; or from an assaulting person.

Many agencies or government structures have active risk management groups. It is important in the personal safety planning process to be aware of and to keep each group informed of the other's efforts. Often there are goals that are mutually inclusive, and communicating these on a regular basis is critical to comprehensive protection.

Staff. "Staff" means all agency personnel who are vulnerable to negative client interactions. Thus, it is appropriate to make parallel connections for the social work safety methods and recommendations contained in this entry. Other professionals, paraprofessionals, aides, and clerical and other support staff are an essential part of social work practice. Safety methods are necessary and essential to these groups as well as to social workers.

This aspect of staff is a critical part of personal safety planning. Planning, staff development, and communication efforts must reflect this inclusive view. Very often nonprofessional and paraprofessional staff members are perceived and treated in a manner that leads to their exclusion from direct safety efforts. Yet these staff members are often as vulnerable, and in some instances are more so, than professional staff members. Receptionists, clerical staff, and home or community aides, particularly those who transport clients and supervise structured visitation, are all as susceptible to clients' angry outbursts.

General themes. There are many issues in the development of these safety approaches that cut across agency lines and are common throughout most field settings, whether rural or urban. These themes relate to a wide range of issues, from the physical appearance of buildings and neighborhoods to concerns raised by staff.

At first glance, several of these issues appear to go beyond variables that relate to risk management and safety of staff. On reflection, however, they are best understood as crucial concerns in the development of systematic support for job safety. Some of these themes that reflect safety areas common to most social work operations fall into four categories: (1) professional practice and training issues, (2) physical plant or office configuration, (3) inter- and intra-agency protocols, and (4) overall communications. The sections that follow describe some of the themes that are common to most agencies.

BEYOND PROFESSIONAL PRACTICE

Both clinical and general practitioners receive preparation for social work practice that emphasizes the contributions to relationships among individuals and to the relationship between individuals and social institutions. Very little attention is given to the negative effect of practitioner attempts to contribute to these complex and often difficult relationships. Professionals often enter the field missing a critical element: an open discussion of the possible dangers of social work practice.

Very few social work programs, both undergraduate and graduate, prepare students for potentially violent clients. Little supportive study has been provided for the assessment of violence in the workplace, and almost no guidelines have been developed to assist student interns and professionals on assessing risk to themselves.

Some studies, particularly in the medical community, have been undertaken to determine the correlates of violence as it relates to clinical social work practice (Newhill, 1992), but virtually no retrospective studies have been undertaken of social workers who have suffered assaults, nor has there been any attempt to develop a body of literature focused on violence and the public agency social work practitioner.

Many current public social workers are not trained in social work. Instead, overwhelming numbers are drawn from disciplines that may or may not have some relationship to social work. Agencies use a wide range of on-the-job approaches to assist staff in developing social work skills. The child welfare worker, adult protective services worker, caseworker, and income maintenance or eligibility worker are good examples of such untrained social workers.

In addition, many private agencies and their staffs have become involved in quasi-public agency social work practice through purchase-of-service contracts. The same involuntary clients are being pressured to work with these agencies, and the same safety issues exist.

ADMINISTRATIVE ISSUES

Much of the impetus for planning safety programming must come from the agency administrative structure. Administrators must recognize the vulnerability of staffs and give appropriate weight to staff concerns. Communication is a key. Administrators must communicate their willingness to discuss the nature of the work being done by the agency and simultaneously their recognition of an ever-changing outside world. Without administrative support all safety efforts are limited and not very effective. However, with support, such efforts become wide ranging, useful, and appropriate.

In general, two types of administrative profiles have evolved: administrators who in the past were frontline practitioners themselves and those who have entered the agency with little or no field experience but with strong administrative skills. The former type of administrator most likely was never assaulted or threatened or does not remember any threat and consequently plays down the idea of potential staff assaults. The latter type of administrator has similarities to the first, but has never "walked" the streets or encountered clients coming into the agency from today's more violent world. Both types of administrators have a tendency to play down safety concerns because the statistics are unavailable or not impressive. However, these same administrators will be fraught with anxiety and concern when an incident does occur, because they will have little knowledge and preparation for what can and should be done. This will lead to avoidable mistakes and severe losses of time, staff, and productivity in the recovery process.

General Guidelines

To deal realistically with the issue of safety and to maintain a healthy work environment, administrators should consider the following steps:

- forming an agency- or systemwide safety committee or appointing a key staff person to head up such an effort
- developing administrative policies and procedures that address both office and field safety
- providing training and staff development opportunities in the area of personal safety

- developing an action plan to deal with emerging safety issues, including posttrauma and victimization issues, and carefully integrate these into all agency planning.

These steps can be accomplished judiciously and with brevity. Written office policies or procedures might be one to five pages in length. Trauma plans can be dependent on internal sources or contracted out with a provider who would be available as needed. Each agency and program must be viewed individually to determine needs and appropriate level of response.

As safety planning proceeds, administrators can determine the breadth and scope of the program. Policy related to staff victimization and trauma, communicable diseases, and catastrophic leave are just a few of the more visionary additions to a safety-planning process and subsequent programming.

Ideally, agencies should attempt to develop a comprehensive safety program. The following sections discuss areas that cumulatively can provide complete safety programming.

Safety Committees

The formation of a committee to guide the development and ongoing operation of a safety program within an agency is a priority. Such a committee promotes the scope and purpose of the safety program throughout the agency. The committee can function on any of several different levels—agencywide, regionally, or at the local district or area level—as long as all levels communicate and are linked with one another.

Agencies have to determine the necessary committees based on agency size and geographic areas served. The basic structure generally consists of (1) a committee that reports to the director on a regular basis or (2) a tiered system of committees. An example of a tiered committee structure was delineated by Griffin (1990) as follows:

One state or agency wide committee would be established and have responsibility for overseeing the program across all aspects of agency work. There could also be one committee for each program, division, or region. Each local office or program would have the option of having a safety person or committee. Each local office or program would then be represented on the state or agency wide committee. (p. 17)

The committee is responsible for creating a communication "loop," communicating safety programming to all staff and being the conduit for receipt of staff needs.

Training and Staff Development

Information on personal safety must be shared with all personnel from top administration down to line and support staffs. Safety preparation should start before employment. "Before being hired, all staff candidates shall be informed of the duties and responsibilities of the positions for which they are being hired. They must know what is expected of them and what potential situations they will be expected to face" (American Probation and Parole Association, 1993, p. 36).

New staff members; administrators; supervisors; experienced staff members; student interns; volunteers; and paraprofessional, professional, and nonprofessional staff members all must be a part of training efforts and versed in agency safety procedures. When administrators, managers, supervisors, or any others are left out of training efforts, tremendous gaps in safety result.

Training and staff development are effective in dealing with both existing and emerging issues. Issues such as communicable diseases, the substance-abusing client, hostile or violent neighborhoods or housing project areas, and cultural issues are just a few of the emerging topics. A safety program should include training and staff development opportunities that provide state-of-the-art information on safety concerns, including

- recognition of unsafe situations before entering a home or neighborhood or receiving a client in the office (early warning)
- development of crisis intervention skills (managing volatile and potentially unsafe situations)
- understanding what will and should occur after an assault or life-threatening incident (follow-up).

The disseminated information must be practical and useful. Staff members should see direct gains and be able to implement many of the concepts immediately in the workplace.

Concern for staff safety. Training and staff development are key elements in supporting not only agency policy and procedures, but also a basic agency philosophy that shows concern for staff safety. This concern must be reflected in an approach that makes safety a part of everyday operations. Staff members must incorporate safety planning into all activities, and training must reinforce this idea. Training should not provide safety preparation in a vacuum but should be a part of the overall agency safety effort. Many agencies provide safety training only in response to specific incidents. When safety training is offered without being integrated into the overall agency safety planning or staff development plan, its utility and effectiveness are compromised.

Sample curriculum. A sample safety curriculum would include the following topics:

- constructive use of authority
- crisis intervention
- field safety
- office safety
- physical plant (setup)
- general prevention techniques
- predicting potential violence
- interviewing and communication
- crisis theory
- victimization and trauma
- protocols and written procedures.

All of these are elements in the development of a safety training approach. Embedded are many subtopics such as assessing personal risk, when to ask for assistance, use of teamwork and law enforcement, and cultural sensitivity.

Assessments of Risk to Staff

In most agencies there have been few efforts to assist staff members in determining their personal risk in dealing with clients. This assessment of risk is important for assisting staff members in determining the level of support they will need in working with certain clients or situations, including environments. According to Boettcher (1983), "to achieve validity for a need assessment both subjective data from the patient and objective data from several observers must be collected and synthesized for assessment" (p. 57). "Violence is a powerful way to communicate and is one of the most immediate, direct, albeit destructive, ways of communicating and intense human need. Identifying that need and addressing that need is paramount if violent behavior is to be prevented" (p. 55).

I have developed a personal safety assessment instrument (risk scale) for use in assisting agencies and staffs in assessing personal risk (Griffin, 1987). The focus is initially on the field visit, but overall the essential element is to have staff members go through a questioning mode before an impending client contact.

By starting to sensitize staff members to the need to ask themselves some very basic and simple questions about their potential risk in cases, a pattern of behavior is established. This pattern will challenge previously learned methods for viewing clients and cases. The purpose is not to create a sense of mistrust or paranoia, but to reiterate that to act in a professional manner is to gather all data, both subjective and objective, and then develop an approach that is realistic and appropriate to the situation.

Measuring risk. This risk scale was designed to achieve three goals:

1. protection of clients, by ensuring that the most serious cases receive the most prompt, intensive, and appropriate assistance
2. protection of staff, by clarifying, through prioritization, those cases that might present more potential for violence
3. development of team working relationships, by increased identification of case situations that warrant use of alternative methods to help ensure safety of clients and staff (Griffin, 1987).

The Staff Safety Risk Scale is designed to ensure the quality of office and field work. The scale is used by intake or ongoing staff members to assign an emerging situation a priority level. The risk scale identifies nine factors associated with the potential for further violence (see Figure 1, Panel A). (Boettcher, 1983, has developed an Assaultive Incident Assessment Tool for preventing violence in the nursing environment.)

Another key is that when supervisory or staff judgment clearly conflicts with these guidelines, judgment should prevail. The focus of the scale is the social worker and client and the precontact planning that is necessary to ensure the safety of each. Supervision, law enforcement, and the team concept are used to support staff safety. In addition, some agencies have determined that the risk scale (form) should become a part of the record to highlight safety issues in each case.

Flagging cases. As an agency looks at determining risk to staff, other methods can work in conjunction with personal safety assessments. "One hospital in Oregon began a program of flagging the records of patients identified as disruptive on the basis of past incidents of violence. After 12 months' experience, the hospital found that the number of visits by flagged patients had gone down somewhat, but not nearly as much as the number of violent clients, which declined by almost 90 percent" (Moss, 1994, p. 18).

One of the clearest indicators of someone's potential for violence is the history of that individual (Star, 1984). Denoting in some way that a case has a history of violence is also saying, "this case must be treated differently." If a client has a history of assaults, particularly if he or she has previously been aggressive toward an agency representative, then he or she must be treated in a different manner.

Flagging is accomplished by attaching a colorful sticker to the outside of the file, placing a copy of the risk scale inside as a cover sheet, making a notation in a special section of a hard or electronic record, or using some other identifying method. This identification allows an agency to prepare for the known aggressive client more readily and appropriately.

When flagging or assessing risk, the agency is also trying to determine what possible alternative action the agency and staff member might take. Is this a case or situation that warrants two staff members? Is law enforcement or a security guard necessary? Is there a need for an additional supervisor or worker, another man or woman, or a more culturally connected team? The result of such assessment is a response that is more appropriate for the situation.

Many situations in which a violent or aggressive history exists are missed or treated as if the information does not exist. Staff members interact in both the office and the field setting with clients who are known to be violent, and they interact with them alone. Reasons vary from lack of sufficient personnel to provide teams to the reasoning that a client would not assault a particular worker or another staff person. These responses increase the potential danger to staff members and, therefore, their safety. Furthermore, "while this position can be very compelling in informal discussion, the courts have almost always rejected it as an affirmative defense in litigation brought by an injured staff person or in a workplace safety (OSHA) suit" (Smith, 1991, p. 38).

Personal safety risk assessments and flagging alter staff perceptions and the possible methods used for client contact. They also point out the need to move ahead with the development of procedures for necessary and appropriate supports.

Obviously, if a worker is the "only" staff person in a rural area, then a team approach is not possible. Similarly, if a local law enforcement agency has only one deputy to cover 100 or more square miles and the officer is far from the place of need, there will be difficulties. However, most social workers are not in these types of situations, and even if they are, there is still a pressing need to provide better precontact safety planning. Whether the service area is rural or urban, when a situation presents serious dangers, it is foolhardy to continue without developing a plan for backup and support.

Protocols

Where appropriate, agencies must establish and maintain formal agreements with others who have responsibility for supporting their work. The purpose of the agreement is to specify, for both the social work agency and the supportive group, mutually agreed-on terms for their working relationship. These agreements can cover a wide range of items, including general communication, protocols for requesting information and receiving assistance, accompaniment, and even clarification of roles.

Protocols can be developed with agencies that can support safety efforts, such as law enforcement agencies, emergency mental health services, and local prosecuting attorneys. Regular monitoring and reworking of agreements are a necessary part of this approach. Protocols can be used to solve questions such as when to use a uniformed versus nonuniformed law enforcement officer or mental health person, the availability of such personnel, how to get priority for the prosecution of a person who assaulted a staff person, and how to receive a protective court order.

Critical Incident Reporting

What is often lost in an agency or system is the extent and magnitude of issues such as staff safety. As mentioned earlier, there have been few studies of this issue. Agencies of reasonable size and with adequate staffing should consider establishing an internal method for tracking the number and seriousness of incidents involving threats or harm to staff. Figure 2 is an example of such a process set up to assist staff in reporting incidents.

Compiling data from these reports will help social services systems more clearly define and target those areas where safety efforts are needed. Critical incident reporting will also provide current data on changing communities and trends in types of incidents.

Written Safety Procedures

In most instances agencies have not developed written guidelines for staff safety. Without such guidelines safety approaches are limited, yet many agencies have not acknowledged that these are a necessary part of office and professional practice.

In developing these procedures two broad areas must be reviewed: office and field safety. Guidelines are then developed to support agency concerns for providing for staff–client interactions in both of these arenas.

Office Safety

When developing basic safety guidelines for staff members, the focus should initially be on very practical, low-cost, easily implemented measures. More elaborate details can be added as staff members become accustomed to safety practices. Ini-

FIGURE 1

Staff Safety Risk Scale

A. STAFF SAFETY RISK SCALE

NO YES

☐ ☐ 1. Are firearms/weapons noted in the original or follow-up complaints or record?

☐ ☐ 2. Does information on the situation note the following:

   ☐ Violent to hostile client

   ☐ Domestic violence

   ☐ Mental illness (Active Phase)

   ☐ Substance abuse (Active Phase)
      ☐ Alcohol   ☐ Drugs
   ☐ Ritualistic abuse/cult practices

☐ ☐ 3. Does information note life-threatening or serious injuries to client?

☐ ☐ 4. Will client be removed from family situation on this visit? (Are we effecting a removal OR custody?)

☐ ☐ 5. Is client's geographic location potentially dangerous?
   ☐ Rural
   ☐ Drug involvement
   ☐ Isolated
   ☐ Housing or neighborhood concerns

☐ ☐ 6. Does client have previous history of violence, multiple referrals?
   (Check closed files/old records.)

☐ ☐ 7. Will field work/investigation start or continue after normal working hours?

☐ ☐ 8. Are the presence of animals noted in the complaint? Specify: _____

☐ ☐ 9. Other risk factors. Specify: _____

B. ASSIGNMENT/FIELD VISIT PRIORITY GUIDELINES

IF ONE OR MORE QUESTIONS ARE CHECKED YES, A HIGHER LEVEL OF SECURITY MAY BE NEEDED!

THE FOLLOWING ARE RANKING OPTIONS. THE OPTIONS ARE FLEXIBLE AND INHERENTLY ACKNOWLEDGE DIFFERENCES IN AVAILABILITY OF LOCAL RESOURCES NEEDED TO SUPPORT EACH PRIORITY.

IF ANY OF QUESTIONS 1–5 HAS A YES CHECKED, THIS CASE COULD BE A PRIORITY #1.

IF ANY OF QUESTIONS 6–9 HAS A YES CHECKED, THIS CASE COULD BE A PRIORITY #2.

IF NONE OF THE QUESTIONS HAS A YES CHECKED, THIS CASE COULD BE A PRIORITY #3.

PRIORITY #1
Consideration should be given to activating the protocol for use of law enforcement.

PRIORITY #2
Consideration should be given to assigning two staff members (a team) to the client contact.

PRIORITY #3
Indications are that an individual worker can make the client contact.

WHEN SUPERVISORY JUDGMENT CONFLICTS

WITH THESE GUIDELINES, JUDGMENT

SHOULD PREVAIL!

tial guidelines must deal with areas such as office access, procedures for opening and closing the building, staffing after normal office hours, wearing of identification badges, and dealing with aggressive clients.

Other, more complex procedures can be added as the concepts of safety planning progress. Procedures for signing in and out of the office, working in the evening and on weekends, control-ling visitors, and using alarm systems are appropriate and useful additions.

Building setup or configuration. In general, agencies have given little thought to development of workspace that incorporates safety features. All too often the workspace is developed to accommodate a certain number of staff and the basic tools for accomplishing agency tasks (for example, tele-

FIGURE 2

Staff Safety Incident Report

To have a more comprehensive and ongoing assessment of worker safety issues in the field and office, there is a need for cooperation on the following procedure:

1. All incidents where a staff person has been threatened or assaulted, or has been near threatening or assaultive activity must be reported to the staff person's immediate supervisor.

2. A written report signed by the staff person and his or her supervisor must be forwarded to _____ as soon as possible.

3. The written report should contain—
   a. the staff person(s) involved
   b. what they were doing at the time
   c. the time and location of the incident
   d. a description of the incident
   e. any other information that might be helpful in assessing the incident and preventing any recurrence.

4. It should be emphasized that this procedure is to collect data and in no way is meant to impede actions immediately necessary to respond to an incident.

STAFF INVOLVED

Name _____

Office Phone _____

County _____

District _____

Date of Incident _____

Time of Day _____

LOCATION OF INCIDENT
- [ ] 1. At staff's home
- [ ] 2. On client's property/residence
- [ ] 3. In DSS office
- [ ] 4. Other _____

ALLEGED PERPETRATOR
Name _____
- [ ] 1. Client
- [ ] 2. Client's spouse
- [ ] 3. Client's friend
- [ ] 4. Other _____
Narrative (What occurred—how you responded):

NATURE OF INCIDENT

PHYSICAL ATTACK
- [ ] 1. Physical harm
  - [ ] Medical attention required
- [ ] 2. Damage to property
- [ ] 3. Other

THREAT
- [ ] 1. Physical harm
- [ ] 2. Damage to property
- [ ] 3. Other
  - [ ] 1. Face to face
  - [ ] 2. Written
  - [ ] 3. Telephone
  - [ ] 4. Third party
  - [ ] 5. Other

POLICE INVOLVEMENT
- [ ] 1. Police called following incident
- [ ] 2. Police with staff at time of incident
- [ ] 3. None

phones, desks, and copy machines). Setting up a building or reconfiguring an existing structure to incorporate safety features must become a priority.

All aspects of the workspace from the waiting room or reception area to entrances and exits from staff work areas must be considered in safety planning. Many agencies have no control over clients' or the general public's access to their buildings and staff members. Most agencies complain about "client wandering," or people who are not employed by the agency moving in and around the many areas of the building, with the agency having little control over access. In many settings thefts and vandalism occur with some regularity, and these acts can lead to confrontations between staff and unknown outsiders.

Architects are often poorly prepared to define buildings for personal safety such as described herein. Exceptions are architects who have experience with the design of secured buildings such as jails and police stations. Thus, administrators must be prepared to advocate for a building configuration that provides staff with a more safe environment. Clearly defined waiting areas, work areas separated by locked doors, secure entrances and exits, separate public and employee restrooms, adequate internal and external lighting, interview rooms that are more open and easily viewed, designed "risk rooms," and other such features are a necessary part of safety planning.

Shared space and other facilities. A part of safety in the office setup is planning with other agencies that share the same buildings and workspace. Safety planning is often undermined by a lack of shared information and cooperation by agencies that occupy a common space. Program administrators and staffs of these allied agencies must be part of the safety movement.

In addition, when agency representatives are using other facilities, staff members must be aware of locations that present additional safety concerns. Courthouses and courtrooms are of particular concern, especially when protective services, custody issues, or financial hearings are involved.

Court hearings that once were nonadversarial are currently very adversarial and more explosive. Child protective cases, juvenile probation and parole, absent parent support, and other such cases are extremely authoritative and intimidating. Clients' lack of respect for legal institutions and their reactions to their personal circumstances are key elements in the creation of some very explosive situations. Many courthouses have added strong safety procedures, including more court officers, alarms, and weapons detectors.

Security measures. Because of growing public and private sector concern for safety, the security field has been developing more sophisticated alarm devices. Electronic alarms and similar surveillance gadgetry have become more refined. Such equipment can provide support for safety efforts within a wide range of budget considerations. Agencies must explore this expanding market for tools that can assist in securing the workplace and field operations more fully. Handheld and wall-mounted buzzers, alarms, cellular telephones, intercoms, pagers, and other types of warning devices are currently available to all agencies and within a wide range of budgets.

Many agencies have added electronic door openers and metal detectors to their entrances and exits. However, adding an alarm system does not necessarily mean major construction problems or costs. Newer units can be added to existing structures with minimal alteration of walls and electrical circuits. Modifications of existing equipment such as telephones or intercom systems currently are more easily accomplished than ever before.

A discussion of building safety would not be complete without a word on the use of security guards. Security guards are often criticized, largely because of misunderstandings about the types and purposes of available services. Agencies must clearly determine the level of security needed and the availability of those services in their community or from a national firm. Is it the desire of the agency to create only a psychological barrier, or to have a force that would interrupt, detain, and even take into custody disruptive persons? Each aspect demands a different level of intervention and a different approach to obtaining security guard services.

Agency staff members also must be more informed about the level and extent of services guards can provide. In most instances agencies hire very limited services. These services can range from guards who can do little more than the average citizen to those who can take a person into custody. In the former situation staff members often operate with a false sense of security, and when an incident occurs, their distress is magnified by the seemingly poor response of the guard. Having a better understanding of guard service limitations and capabilities will lead to more appropriate security in the workplace.

Field Safety
In many agencies a large percentage of staff members spend a good deal of time in the greater community or field. If field operations exist, then there

is a subsequent need for safety programming in that area. Internal policies regarding the use of teamwork, law enforcement and community personnel, and appropriate safety equipment are all essential to field safety. Some of the keys to these policies are protocols for transporting clients, use of police, working in specific geographic areas, calling in mental health authorities, and after-hours work, for example.

Pagers, cellular telephones, personal alarms, availability of and types of automobiles, and emergency safety kits are tools that staff can use during field operations. Assisting staff in understanding the impact of agency intervention, the judicious use of authority within the context of a family's environment or home, and effecting removal of a person from his or her living situation and family are just a few of the staff development issues involved in field operations.

Staff members must be more sensitive to the realities of current society and the changes that have occurred in their communities to ensure a more informed approach to field operations. Safety in field operations requires preparing staff and keeping them prepared. Many agencies are making many more home visits than ever before, and field operations should strive to maintain a certain level of awareness. Having staff "sign out and in" for field visits, leave an itinerary on their desk, and call in with any changes in plans all give safety greater visibility.

Follow-up to Victimization and Trauma

Even with the best safety planning, there may be events that are beyond an agency's control. The result can be a staff safety crisis, with staff members questioning both their role and their purpose within the agency.

Dealing effectively with postincident trauma is critical. Trauma results from crises, and fear, trepidation, and uncertainty are normal reactions to a crisis. There must be an agencywide response that gives staff members the comfort they need. As negative news unfolds, a sense of direction is the one aspect the agency can truly control.

Whether announcing a serious on-the-job injury or the death of a staff person, the agency must tell its story as positively and as powerfully as it can. The point is not to mislead, but to reassure both staff members and outsiders that those in charge have a solution to the problem and a reasonable plan for attending to everyone's needs. In practice, however, many agencies are caught with little postincident preplanning. They are forced to focus on the press release and lose sight of the process of crisis communications. Staff

members and outsiders look beyond what has happened. They look at the agency's reactions and how willing it is to deal with the pain of individuals. The agency must demonstrate that it has not been paralyzed by the incident.

It is also crucial to deliver a consistent, accurate message. The key is making sure everyone representing the agency agrees on the basic game plan. As the facts unfold, there must be agreement. Someone must ensure that actions are taken to assist everyone in a recovery process that is as healthy as possible. However, most agencies, and certainly many management staffs, have little or no training in this area. If anything, learning how to communicate in a crisis of this proportion or simply how to build trust is often a "baptism by fire." Agencies must direct the process, not let it direct them.

Developing a staff safety and support approach has many steps. Communication and staff support are the focus. What variables affect the impact of a traumatic event on staff and agency? Can these variables assist in ascertaining the impact of trauma on a victim and others? Where should an agency focus its energy in response to a traumatic event?

These critical questions recognize the stressful nature of frontline social work. They also point out the necessity of providing for an agencywide support system to assist workers with the impact of serious incidents and the postincident effects. Although every case in which a staff person intervenes may involve hostile confrontations, serious maltreatment, emotional illnesses, and public scrutiny, certain experiences evoke stronger and deeper emotions. Incidents such as a personal threat, assault, or a staff fatality are significant emotional events. These have the power, because of the circumstances in which they occur, to cause unusual psychological distress in a healthy, normal individual. Agencies must

- review the circumstances surrounding a serious incident in a nonthreatening and thoughtful manner
- support workers who are dealing with serious incidents
- build coping mechanisms for individuals who are experiencing incident-related stress and anxiety
- protect staff members from similar incidents by identifying needed supports and protective efforts.

Critical Incident Response

When an incident requiring an agency response occurs, the agency must organize and implement multiple activities. The nature of the incident will have a direct bearing on the necessary actions. However, care must be taken administratively to avoid actions that might lead to further victimization of those involved. Postincident management becomes an important aspect of intervention.

Agencies must approach critical incidents involving a staff person in a straightforward manner. Debriefing sessions are one method. Posttrauma sessions should not be intended for just fact finding. Posttrauma inquiries can be used to determine future safety needs such as actions to protect staff members from additional harm or to formulate a new or revised method for agency operations. Fact finding must be done cautiously.

A serious incident will undoubtedly trigger significant emotional reaction from the injured staff person, colleagues, and family, as well as from supervisory and administrative staff members. It is therefore critical that everyone be particularly sensitive to the needs of the people involved during this period. A very human approach to providing assistance to those who are injured in the line of duty must be in place throughout the agency. The following questions must be addressed:

• What should the agency do when an incident occurs?
• Who do staff members talk to?
• What do staff members look for?
• How do staff members minimize trauma to the injured parties?
• What supports can be offered to assist all staff in the recovery process?

The overriding emphasis throughout the process should be on sensitivity to the victim, other staff members, clients, the agency, and the community.

The importance of a cohesive and comprehensive crisis response plan is readily seen in situations where both agency and staff members are apt to lose control. An agency that mishandles bad news in the crucial early stages of crisis often does so because it is ignoring or denying the problem, maintaining that the serious incident is not an agencywide problem; lying or telling misleading half-truths; assigning blame; panicking; becoming paralyzed; or overreacting. None of these is healthy for the life and well-being of both agency and staff members.

Working with a plan, providing appropriate and clear information, explaining remedial actions, and announcing when a system is in place are all positive approaches to providing appropriate supports for the safety of staff members. Agencies

must have direction to be in position to assist everyone in a healthy recovery.

FINAL CONCERNS

In this entry I have tried to shed some light on a particularly disturbing aspect of current social work practice. There are many lessons to be learned in this area of personal and professional safety for both clinically and nonclinically trained staff people. Lessons are often learned at great expense and paid for with human turmoil and loss. The world has changed in many ways since the 1970s. All aspects of social work practice must change as well to meet the demands of this new world and the social work practitioner.

REFERENCES

American Probation and Parole Association. (1993, Spring). Staff safety standards. *Perspectives,* pp. 36–37.

Boettcher, E. G. (1983). Preventing violent behavior: An integrated theoretical model for nursing. *Perspectives in Psychiatric Care, XXI*(2), 54–58.

Brown, R., Bute, S., & Ford, P. (1986). *Social workers at risk: The prevention and management of violence.* London: Macmillan Education.

Federal Child Abuse Prevention and Treatment Act of 1993. P.L. 93-247.

Griffin, W. V. (1987). *Social worker safety—Early warning.* Durham, NC: Brendan Associates and Independent Living Resources.

Griffin, W. V. (1990). *Professionals at risk: A report to the Connecticut Department of Children and Youth Services.* Durham, NC: Brendan Associates.

Kaplan, S., & Wheeler, E. (1983). Survival skills for working with potentially violent clients. *Social Casework, 64,* 339–346.

Lanza, M. L. (1983). Reactions of nursing staff to physical assault by a patient. *Hospital and Community Psychiatry, 34*(1), 37–40.

Lehmann, L. S. (1983). Training personnel in the prevention & management of violent behavior. *Hospital and Community Psychiatry, 34*(1), 40–43.

Lewis, H. (1980). The battered helper. *Child Welfare, LIX*(4), 195–201.

Mace, P. (1989). *The effect of attitude and belief on social workers judgments concerning potentially dangerous clients.* Ann Arbor, MI: University Microfilms International.

MacFadden, R. J. (1980). *Stress, support and the frontline social worker.* Toronto: University of Toronto.

Mayer, J. E., & Rosenblatt, A. (1975). Encounters with danger: Social workers in the ghetto. *Sociology of Work and Occupations, 2*(3), 227–245.

Moss, D. (1994, January). Lawyers as targets. *The Pennsylvania Lawyer,* pp. 16–21.

Newhill, C. E. (1992, March). Assessing danger to others in clinical social work practice. *Social Service Review,* pp. 64–84.

Norris, D. (1990). *Violence against social workers: The implication for practice.* London: Jessica Kingsley Publishers.

Schultz, L. G. (1985). *Violence against social workers: Proposed interventions.* Unpublished manuscript, University of West Virginia, School of Social Work, Morgantown.

Smith, A. G. (1991, Fall). The California model: Probation and parole safety training. *Perspectives,* pp. 38–41.

Star, B. (1984). Patient violence/therapist safety. *Social Work, 29,* 225–230.

State of Connecticut, Waterbury Region. (1991). Incident reporting [administrative letter]. Hartford: Author.

Tupin, J. P. (1983). The violent patient: A strategy for management & diagnosis. *Hospital and Community Psychiatry, 34*(1), 37–40.

Vandecreek, L., & Knapp, S. (1984). Counselors, confidentiality, and life-endangering clients. *Counselor Education and Supervision, 24,* 51–57.

Yelaja, S. A. (1965). The concept of authority and its use in child protective services. *Child Welfare, 44,* 514–522.

William V. Griffin, MSW, MPA, is president, Brendan Associates, 4324 Thetford Road, Durham, NC 27707, and adjunct professor 1986–1995, University of North Carolina at Chapel Hill.

For further information see

Case Management; Clinical Social Work; Conflict Resolution; Crisis Intervention: Research Needs; Deinstitutionalization; Direct Practice Overview; Disasters and Disaster Aid; Domestic Violence; Domestic Violence: Legal Issues; Ethics and Values; Gang Violence; Homicide; Interviewing; Legal Issues: Confidentiality and Privileged Communication; Management Overview; Police Social Work; Private Practice; Professional Conduct; Professional Liability and Malpractice; Public Services Management; Quality Management; Substance Abuse: Legal Issues; Supervision and Consultation; Victim Services and Victim/Witness Assistance Programs; Violence Overview.

Key Words

risk management	victimization
safety	violence
trauma	

Social Workers in Politics
Toby Weismiller
Sunny Harris Rome

From the beginning, the experience of some social workers taught them that government action was often needed to protect and enhance the lives of people. They recognized the need to change public policies and private services delivery to meet the needs of the individuals and groups they served. Because individuals are affected by the environment in which they live, a need exists to examine social and behavioral factors in achieving change.

Such social workers as Jane Addams and Lillian Wald worked to influence government, especially at the local level, and they regarded participation in government as a part of the answer to solving individual problems. As they became involved in government, these early social workers recognized the importance of using power to enable people to develop their own abilities and resources and to create programs that meet needs other than their own. They recognized the danger of viewing the end goal as the accumulation of power to run government, a practice that too often created city bosses.

Social workers continue to be actively engaged in individual and collective political action to improve social conditions. Occupations such as coalition organizer, professional lobbyist, policy analyst, federal or state administrator, campaign manager, political party operative, and elected official are now filled by professional social workers (Haynes & Mickelson, 1991). Throughout the history of the profession social workers have been involved in action to improve social conditions.

In the 1990s major institutions representing social work education and practice are seeking to formalize and advance the role of social workers in politics. The 1992 revised Council on Social Work Education Curriculum Policy Statement (Council on Social Work Education, 1992) stated one of the four purposes of social work as, "the pursuit of policies, services, resources, and programs through organizational or administrative advocacy and social or political action, so as to empower groups at risk and promote social and economic justice" (p. 3).

NASW has recognized the importance of social workers advancing the profession's interests in public policy by adopting a formal association priority to elect more social workers to public office from 1994 to 1997. Since 1984, NASW, both at the national level and within the 55 state chapters, has expanded its program to secure a more influential role for the profession in policy development, lobbying, and electoral participation. Clearly, the profession recognizes the potential to influence public policy through a more expansive role in government and politics.

NATURE OF POLITICS

Politics involves influencing government through actions designed to make resources available. The issue is who will benefit and to what degree. Politics involves seeking power, exercising power, and achieving compromise when appropriate. Effective power is gained from serving other people's self-interest. There is no absolute power for an individual. Social workers learn early that power involves information, resources, communication, and expertise.

Social workers in politics include practitioners in both electoral politics, which Key (1964) defined as the formal and informal systems by which citizens and groups in a democracy contest for the power to run government, and government relations, which is the active intervention of citizens and groups to influence the decision making of government officials (Ornstein and Elder, 1978). Since the 19th century, social workers have been involved in political action. Social workers have developed government programs and served in government administrations at every level as consultants and staff for elected officials. They have served in appointed positions and increasingly are being elected to office.

In addition, social workers whose practice is direct service or administration frequently use various political action strategies as part of their professional work or through volunteer activities within their professional organization. Such strategies may include participating in campaigns and elections, identifying social problems that require government intervention and building public recognition of those problems, informing elected officials about alternative courses of action with their probable consequences, and actively seeking to influence their choice by providing information and political support (Patti, 1983).

Social work commitment to political action has matured as part of the profession's intellectual and experiential tradition. Political action and social reform are grounded in the profession's history, political philosophy, and value base. Although few social work educational programs provide specific preparation for careers in politics, certain skills such as organizing, political awareness, communication and public relations ability, and problem solving can be adapted from the traditional repertoire of practice skills (Kleinkauf, 1982). In fact, one study of five high-profile social worker–

politicians in British Columbia concluded that social workers have much to offer the political process (Strandberg & Marshall, 1988). Specific social work practice skills that prove useful to an elected official include empathy; analytical skill in understanding larger social problems; awareness of group dynamics; and ability to act as facilitator, educator, and advocate. Equally valuable are social workers' skills in the areas of interpersonal communication and problem solving, both essential to effective public leadership.

HISTORICAL ROOTS[1]

Since its inception, social work's engagement in political action has been part of the profession. Settlement workers of the Progressive Era like Jane Addams and Florence Kelley set out to humanize the expanding urban neighborhoods, organizing services, providing education, and building a sense of community. They quickly recognized that improving social conditions required challenging the existing power structure. Social workers mastered skills as political agents including forming coalitions, molding public opinion, lobbying government officials, and actively participating in partisan politics (Davis, 1982). Those early experiences in addressing local social problems through action campaigns soon led to crusades for change at the state and federal levels of government. Social workers have been pioneers in the movement of women into politics. Among the "firsts" noted in the following review are Jeanette Rankin, the first woman elected to the U.S. House of Representatives; Frances Perkins, the first woman appointed to the Cabinet; and Barbara Mikulski, the first Democratic woman elected to the Senate.

First Steps

In 1896, James B. Reynolds, analyzing the political process as it related to neighborhood residents' problems, urged social workers to "go into politics" (J. B. Reynolds, 1896, pp. 140–142). In the 1890s and early 1900s, settlement house workers used survey techniques to link social conditions with economic factors and legislative action. They organized neighbors to endorse candidates, organized and ran political campaigns, lobbied, and worked for reform. They initiated services such as kindergartens and playgrounds and then campaigned for city takeovers and expansion of the services. For example, Lillian Wald supported

[1]Note: Much of the history section of this entry is based on material from Mahaffey (1987).

Mayor Low's 1901 campaign in New York City. When he was elected, she then convinced him to hire school nurses (Davis, 1964). Social workers helped organize the national Child Labor Committee, National Women's Trade Union League, and the National Industrial Relations Commission.

Jane Addams (1912) enunciated the position of many during Theodore Roosevelt's Progressive Party campaign: "When the ideas and measures we have long been advocating become part of a political campaign, social workers must participate in partisan politics" (p. 12). Not everyone agreed, however. Mary Richmond believed poverty was rooted in individual and moral causes (Leiby, 1978). For her, social work began with individual diagnosis; although she believed political action for laws protecting children was appropriate, she did not seek structural change. Those who subscribed to Richmond's ideas in the 1900s thought that social workers should be nonpartisan, objective, and scientific—and act only as enablers.

In the 1920s social work focused on service to individuals and the development of proficiency in the techniques of helping individuals. The period was one of burgeoning business enterprise and hostility to social reform. During this period, many ostracized Jane Addams and Lillian Wald for their activism on behalf of unions, peace, and reform (Becker, 1987).

Like other women activists of the Progressive Era, Molly Dewson served an apprenticeship at Hull House and became the first superintendent of parole at the nation's oldest reform school for girls, the Massachusetts State Industrial School for Girls. She continued to work closely with the social reformers of the Settlement House Era to become one of the most prominent women in New Deal politics, actively promoting her colleague, Frances Perkins, for an appointment in Franklin Roosevelt's Cabinet. Dewson went on to head the Women's Division in the national Democratic Party and push for the inclusion of women in both government and politics. She was later appointed by President Roosevelt to serve on the Social Security Board (Ware, 1987).

The Critical 1930s
In the 1930s, with the turmoil and tragedies of the depression, debates on political action raged in the social work profession. Miriam Van Waters, president of the National Conference on Social Welfare, concluded that reform movements do not reflect genuine social work, which stressed personality (Van Waters, 1930). On the other hand, Harry Lurie and Katharine Lenroot of the Children's Bureau, with representatives of the American

Association of Social Workers (AASW), called for changes in the federal tax system to effect a redistribution of wealth. In 1933 AASW adopted a "radical program" that stressed the redistribution of wealth and power through reconstruction of socioeconomic institutions. AASW endorsed a permanent government welfare system and praised other New Deal programs.

Mary Van Kleeck, director of industrial studies, Russell Sage Foundation, and president of the Second International Conference of Social Welfare in Frankfurt, maintained that the resources of the nation should be used to meet the needs of all its people through a "totally planned economy under socialism" (Van Kleeck, 1934, pp. 483–484). In a presentation to the National Conference on Social Welfare in Chicago in 1934, she criticized government programs designed to protect the status quo and called on social workers to organize to effectively demand standards (Van Kleeck, 1934).

Social workers were playing key roles in national politics. Frances Perkins was secretary of labor, and Harry Hopkins, an adviser to President Roosevelt and an architect of New Deal social programs, became secretary of commerce. Social workers helped write the social security legislation.

In the 1930s Gordon Hamilton, professor at the New York School of Social Work, and Bertha Capen Reynolds, associate director of the Smith College School for Social Work, enunciated the concept that there is a close link between "casework, social welfare, and social action" (Hellenbrand, 1977, p. 517). Reynolds became a Marxist and she said, "Social work exists to help people in need. If it serves other classes who have other purposes, it becomes too dishonest to be capable of either theoretical or practical development" (B. Reynolds, 1963/1991, p. 173). She believed the primary goal of social work should be to improve economic conditions, and her writings stressed the complementarity of the scientific study of societal economic behavior and that of the "psychological and biological phenomenon in the lives of individuals" (B. Reynolds, 1940, p. 9). Reynolds eventually was forced out of her position at Smith because of her "radical" politics.

The 1940s and 1950s
During World War II, debates on the role of social work and politics were set aside, as social workers focused on winning the war against fascism. At the end of the war, many wanted a return to "normalcy" in the United States. In social work, group work focused on helping people with values clarification, working with task-oriented groups, and

participating in social action. Community organization concentrated on intergroup relations, fundraising, and planning. Many social workers served in federal and state government positions, implementing expanded public welfare programs. In the mid-1940s, Jane M. Hoey, director of the Bureau of Public Assistance, commissioned Charlotte Towle to write *Common Human Needs* as a training manual for social workers in public agencies (Towle, 1987).

Some people in the United States maintained that the nation had fought the wrong country; the real enemy was communism and the Soviet Union, not Hitler and fascism. Red baiting and McCarthyism continued into the 1950s. When California became the first state to develop a loyalty oath for all state employees, AASW opposed it. The American Medical Association declared *Common Human Needs*, first published in 1945, a treatise on socialized medicine, and in the furor the federal government burned thousands of copies. AASW immediately issued another edition. During the early 1950s, social workers opposed the war in Korea through AASW, which maintained a lobbyist in Washington.

Several prominent social workers served in key federal posts during this period. Katherine B. Oettinger was appointed head of the Children's Bureau in 1957 ("NASW Member Appointed," 1957). Charles Schottland, commissioner for Social Security; Jay Roney, director of the Bureau of Public Assistance; and Roger Cumming, director of Social Work Service of the Veteran's Administration, were other social workers serving in high federal policy-making positions during this era ("Straight from Washington," 1958).

The 1960s and 1970s
John F. Kennedy captured the imagination of many when he called for a Peace Corps and food for the hungry in the United States. The civil rights movement engaged the best humanistic instincts of many social workers, and many social workers were involved in the civil rights movement in the South. Social worker Michael Schwerner was working in the voter registration campaign when he was murdered.

In the 1960s NASW convened an urban crisis conference to respond to the demands of members who felt that NASW was not doing enough to advance civil rights and meet the needs of poor people. A study of attitudes of NASW members in the Detroit chapter revealed that members wanted a greater NASW presence in the political process, and they were prepared to pay more dues to get the work done (Boland, 1970). Throughout the association, debates occurred about the proper division of association resources among social action, professional development, and professional standards.

During the Kennedy and Johnson administrations, more resources were available to devote to the care of individuals with problems. The community mental health system was developed. Court decisions mandated the least-restrictive care for those who were mentally ill or had mental impairments. Social workers experimented with "radical social work," including community unions, and many social workers were involved in organizing welfare rights organizations. Radical social work enunciated the idea of overcoming the barriers imposed by the profit-oriented nature of society.

NASW developed the Education Legislative Action Network (ELAN) in 1971 to link education and legislation. In the beginning, ELAN was referred to as Elan Vital (Elixir of Life), for it was viewed as breathing life into the association, bringing the conflicting clinical and community action forces together. In 1972 NASW concluded that merely having a Washington office was not sufficient and moved from New York to Washington, DC: The organization had to be in the seat of power. By 1976 it had become clear that ELAN, although successful, provided limited influence on policy and on decision makers, and NASW created the Political Action and Candidate Election (PACE) to endorse candidates for office and to raise money to support their campaigns. Also in 1976 NASW held its first Social Work in Politics Conference in Washington, DC. Maryann Mahaffey, a member of the Detroit City Council and president of NASW, chaired the conference. At the conference, Ruth Messinger announced her intention to run for the New York City Council and was subsequently elected.

The 1980s and 1990s
In 1980 the White House Conference on Families (with two social workers among the five deputy chairs) publicly exposed the national swing to conservative activism. A significant number of delegates opposed using federal government resources for social programs, urging that families, churches, and local governments be the resorts for people in need. Social workers and social work programs were under pressure to eliminate fraud while the cycles of depression became more frequent and residual unemployment increased. During the Reagan and Bush administrations, more and more responsibility for meeting people's needs was pushed to lower levels of government or the private sector.

Social workers responded by intensifying their involvement in politics. The national office expanded its government relations office from one professional staff person to six lobbyists and support staff. As the capacity of the national office of NASW to wield influence over policy-making increased, so did the capacity of NASW chapters. NASW's field network—those social workers around the country who actively participate in the association's lobbying campaigns—numbered about 1,300 in 1994. The chapters, which had developed considerable political expertise in lobbying for legal regulation, also added legislative staff. Approximately one-third of NASW's chapters employed staff or consultants in 1994 to influence policy developments that affect social workers and social work clients.

In the 1992 election, more social workers worked in political campaigns and ran for office than ever before. Social workers strongly supported Governor Bill Clinton, and as result of his election as president, had closer ties than ever to a federal administration. When the first political appointments were concluded, seven social workers held undersecretary positions: (1) Ada Deer, assistant secretary for Indian Affairs; (2) Augusta Kappner, assistant secretary for vocational and adult education, Department of Education; (3) Fernando Torres-Gil, assistant secretary for aging, Department of Health and Human Services; (4) Wardell Townsend, assistant secretary for administration, Department of Agriculture; (5) Wendy Sherman, assistant secretary for legislative affairs, Department of State; (6) Thomas P. Glynn, deputy secretary, Department of Labor; and (7) Nelba Chavez, administrator, Substance Abuse and Mental Health Services Administration.

SOCIAL WORKERS IN ELECTORAL POLITICS

Social workers sought elected office in the early days of the profession. Jeffrey Richardson Brackett, a social work educator, became president of the Baltimore City Department of Charities and Corrections in 1900 and thereby obtained a seat on the city council. Zebulon Reed Brockway, a penologist, served as mayor of Elmira, New York, from 1905 to 1907. Thomas Scott Osborne, also a penologist, was elected to the Auburn, New York, Board of Education in 1885, nominated for lieutenant governor in 1888 and served as mayor in 1903.

Kate Bernard became the first elected Commissioner of Charities and Corrections in Oklahoma in 1908 and was reelected four times; she was subsequently defeated partly because she supported the Native American right to self-determination (Edmondson, 1984). T. Arnold Hill, on the

staff of the National Urban League, was an unsuccessful candidate for Chicago alderman in 1923 (Parris & Brooks, 1971).

Although lesser known than many of her famous settlement worker peers, Jeanette Rankin was the first social worker to hold high public office. Rankin was the first woman and the first social worker elected to the U.S. Congress, an extraordinary accomplishment considering the status of women in public life at the beginning of this century. Rankin completed professional studies at the New York School of Philanthropy (studying under Frances Perkins and Louis Brandeis) in the summer of 1909. Convinced she could improve social conditions she encountered as a settlement and child welfare worker by running for public office and enacting social reform legislation, she won a seat in the U.S. House of Representatives as a Republican from Montana in 1916. (Her home state had instituted women's suffrage as an enticement to bring more women to the state.) Rankin's role as a pacifist was her most notable political legacy, having cast the sole dissenting vote in Congress for the entry of the United States into World War I and against the declaration of war in 1941 (Giles, 1980). However, after her service in the House of Representatives, Jeanette Rankin continued to be an activist and spokesperson for women's rights, civil rights, election reform, and social and economic justice.

The next professional social worker (of whom there is a record) to serve in Congress was Representative Ronald Dellums, a psychiatric caseworker from Oakland, California, elected in the 1970s and re-elected every term since. He was followed by Barbara Mikulski of Baltimore, who was subsequently elected to the Senate, and by Ed Towns, of New York City.

Studies of Social Workers in Politics

Several studies have looked at the participation of social workers in politics. An early survey (Mahaffey, 1979) identified 51 people with a bachelor or master of social work degree in elected legislative office in the United States and one social worker as mayor (of San Jose, California). Of the social workers in office, 26 (51 percent) responded to Mahaffey's survey. All were either community organizers (62 percent) or clinicians (38 percent) who had administrative or large public agency expertise. In 1984 Mickelson and Haynes conducted a similar study, finding that social workers serving in elective office believe that their professional education has given them a good foundation for public service (Haynes & Mickelson, 1991).

In 1991 a national NASW PACE survey revealed 113 social workers in elected positions.

When staff conducted a similar survey in 1993, they identified 165 officeholders in 43 states, a 50 percent increase in two years (NASW, 1993).

In addition to other studies that explored the level and nature of activity of social workers in electoral politics (Epstein, 1969; Haynes & Mickelson, 1991; Mathews, 1983; Salcido, 1984; Wolk, 1981), two surveys indicate that the profession is becoming more active in campaigns and elections. To track changes in attitudes and social action behaviors, Reeser & Epstein (1990) repeated a survey of social worker activism that was conducted in 1968 and reported the same results in 1984. By comparing the findings of two large surveys of rank-and-file social workers about their level of political participation, the authors sought to capture any shifts in the political activism profile within the profession. Among the measurements of electoral participation, they found that the level of specific behaviors related to electoral participation increased, from 1968 to 1984, in categories such as contributing money to political campaigns, volunteering on behalf of a candidate, and in encouraging the political participation of clients.

In another study of electoral participation of social workers in the 1988 campaign, more than 92 percent reported voting in the presidential election, a voter turnout rate 1.62 times higher than the general public. In addition, social workers reported contributing money, attending political meetings or rallies, and working for a candidate or political party at over twice the rate of participation of the general public. The authors conclude that such high levels of electoral participation provide a foundation for the profession to exert increased political influence (Parker & Sherraden, 1991).

Other Political Action

PACE, the political action arm in NASW, has promoted efforts to build and fund an expanded political action infrastructure. A national political training institute was held in 1991, bringing together social work leaders from 46 chapters, to prepare for an associationwide campaign in the 1992 general election. By 1994 the association had 45 chapters with state political action committees, and a membership check-off system had increased funds donated to candidates for federal and state political action committees by 200 percent.

NASW expanded its involvement in the 1992 presidential campaign to include new methods of electronic communication, member education, and emphasis on social worker visibility as political agents. NASW chapters served as centers of action and mobilization for members and maintained links with the Clinton–Gore state headquarters.

In the 1992 campaign, PACE contributed over $200,000 to federal candidates, and state PACE committees contributed over $165,000 to state and local candidates. PACE supported all of the successful women U.S. Senate candidates and was the first national organization to endorse Illinois Senator Carol Moseley-Braun, the first African-American woman to be elected to the U.S. Senate. An unprecedented number of social workers ran for Congress—10 in all. However, only the three social worker incumbents were successful in their election bids: Senator Barbara Mikulski and Representatives Ronald Dellums and Ed Towns.

SOCIAL WORKERS IN ISSUE POLITICS

The influence of social work on federal and state policy-making has grown steadily since 1984. In addition to the increased involvement of social workers in electoral politics, the Clinton administration currently boasts seven social workers in high-level appointments within the executive branch. This extension of social work involvement mirrors the expansion of NASW's government relations efforts in 1992 to include not only lobbying the Congress but also promoting political appointments and conducting lobbying efforts within the administration.

Although NASW had included legislative advocacy within its mission for many years, the mid-1980s was a turning point. The profession's increased commitment to political action prompted a powerful response to the passage of the Balanced Budget and Emergency Deficit Control Act (1985) with its potential to annihilate many social programs. NASW tripled its federal lobbying staff, casting a new focus on organizing social workers throughout the country to combat threats to social services spending. NASW also won recognition of clinical social workers as independent providers under the Federal Employee Health Benefits Improvement Act of 1986, demonstrating the profession's capacity to influence legislative outcomes. The establishment of the National Center for Social Policy and Practice in 1986 reinforced this commitment to advocacy by creating a structure that would enhance the profession's capacity for policy research, information gathering, and analysis. The center was brought under NASW's auspices in 1992.

Throughout the late 1980s and the early 1990s, NASW's legislative agenda continued to grow—as did its legislative successes. NASW's role on the government relations front was further facilitated when the NASW national office relocated from the Maryland suburbs to Washington, DC, in early 1992.

After a 1979 Delegate Assembly policy that made comprehensive health care an association priority and NASW's success in winning independent provider status for clinical social workers under the Federal Employees Benefits Improvement Act in 1986, NASW won recognition of clinical social workers as reimbursable providers of mental health care services under Medicare, part B, in 1989 (Omnibus Budget Reconciliation Act of 1989). Finally, NASW's own plan for national health care reform, developed from the recommendations of social work experts and practitioners throughout the country, was introduced into Congress by Senator Daniel Inouye (D-HI) in 1992 and again in 1993. NASW continues to be an important player in the health care reform debate.

Other important victories included an increase in funding for the Title XX Social Services Block Grant (Omnibus Budget Reconciliation Act of 1989); creation of a new entitlement to fund family preservation services (Omnibus Budget Reconciliation Act of 1993); loan forgiveness under the federal Perkins program for social workers and others working with high-risk children and families in low-income communities or with disabled infants and toddlers (Higher Education Amendments of 1992); enactment of the Civil Rights Restoration Act to combat discrimination in the workplace (Civil Rights Restoration Act of 1987); and the inclusion of school social workers and other pupil services personnel in programs for disadvantaged and handicapped students (Augustus F. Hawkins–Robert T. Stafford Elementary and Secondary School Improvement Amendments of 1988). NASW also has maintained a high profile on issues including civil rights, family and medical leave, and reproductive freedom and has assumed leadership roles with national coalitions including the Coalition on Human Needs, Generations United, and the National Committee on Pay Equity. In 1993 the NASW Board of Directors approved a special project on welfare reform, through which NASW developed a set of consensus recommendations from among its members. NASW continues to devote much of its energy to ensuring that reform is both constructive and humane.

SOCIAL WORK PRACTICE AND THE GOVERNMENT'S ROLE IN SOCIAL WELFARE

Social work practice is tied to an active role in civic affairs in two ways. Because social work practice as it has evolved in this country is informed by principles of democratic thought,

social workers support the tenet that citizens must participate in the process of governmental decision making. Furthermore, the political philosophy of social work stems from the profession's long-standing interest in the role of the government in the provision of social welfare. What is the appropriate division of responsibility between the public and private spheres in regulating economic activity, or protecting and providing benefits for the vulnerable in society? These are issues of keen interest to the profession.

Among all industrialized countries, including the United States, the role of government in social provision has steadily increased. The limits of state intervention in matters of individual security and distributive justice continues to be a central theme of debate within both enduring and emerging democratic nations. Instituting regulations and providing programs that benefit disadvantaged people typically limit individual rights and private profits. Consequently, governments must seek a balance between individual self-interest and the common good. Reamer pointed to a parallel philosophical orientation in social work. For those who view professional service with the emphasis on serving the public interest, the highest obligation of the profession is the delivery of quality clinical care provided in a variety of settings. For other social workers, the central political orientation is the assumption that the well-being of individuals is inseparable from the good of the broader community (Reamer, 1993).

Social Work Values

These different approaches to social work practice reflect what some see as a conflict of values. Social work is often viewed as unique in the degree to which values are central to professional identity (Horner & Whitbeck, 1991). Despite the profession's increased sophistication in political matters, many social workers continue to be reluctant to enter into the fray because they feel ill-prepared to succeed in the political arena, are concerned that political activity would divert attention from their direct practice with clients, or believe that political activism is incongruent with fundamental social work values (Brieland, 1982). The last of these is perhaps the hardest impediment to overcome.

Haynes and Mickelson (1991) delineated a number of perceived incompatibilities between social work values and political action. "Impartiality versus partisan politics" sums up a commonly held belief that social workers must be nonjudgmental and that the political nature of the policy-making process somehow taints the purity of social work practice.

This view of social work values and politics as dichotomous has been roundly criticized by many in the profession. Haynes and Mickelson (1991) pointed out that social work is part of the political process. Many of the values articulated by the profession—for example, client empowerment and self-determination—can be attained only in the context of a system that supports individual growth and provides the resources that help individuals to thrive.

Yet another source of concern is what some believe to be the competing values of the profession. Social workers are committed, on the one hand, to helping people function effectively in society, and, on the other, to changing the society. This struggle between accommodating to and changing the status quo reflects the profession's ambivalence regarding whether improving the quality of life is best accomplished through individual intervention (micro practice) or social change (macro practice) (Alexander, 1982). Gilbert and Specht (1986) discussed the primacy of individual interests (individualist orientation) versus the common good (collectivist orientation); Richan (1988) identified the competing roles of integrator and gadfly; Miringoff and Opdycke (1986) framed the discussion in terms of traditional (human development) versus temporizing (societal resource) values. Most theorists agree, however, that both must be pursued.

The goal must be to improve interactions between people and societal institutions by mobilizing both an individual's inner capabilities and society's external resources (Alexander, 1982). The *NASW Code of Ethics* (NASW, 1994) delineates the professional social worker's ethical responsibility both to clients and to society. Both can be facilitated through the political process. Advocacy for one's client can easily find expression in political action and leadership.

Conclusion

The involvement of social work professionals in politics has varied. Despite some residual skepticism about the appropriateness of political work, there has been a resurgence in political action during recent years, manifested in the election and appointment of many social workers to high-level public office; the growth of collective political endorsements and campaign contributions through PACE, the profession's political action committee; and the profession's success in influencing policy-making through lobbying and other government relations efforts. NASW has been the primary institutional base for much of this activity.

Social work values are principles of human relationships that enable people to achieve their potential. The value of the individual is linked to the value of equality of opportunity, the right of self-determination, and the right of the individual to achieve maximum potential.

Within the profession, there is a growing recognition that the self-interest of social workers and clients can be served by effective political action. The transformation of society to meet the needs of its members can come about only through organizing and educating significant numbers of people so that they can work together. Individuals, including clients, need to see their situation within the larger context of society.

Social workers have a professional responsibility to "promote the general welfare of society" (NASW, 1994). Opportunities to improve the human condition abound. As the profession continues to mature and adapt and as poverty, crime, illness, illiteracy, and discrimination continue to assail the world community, social workers must forcefully assert themselves as legitimate participants in the politics of social decision making.

References

Addams, J. (1912). Pragmatism in politics. *Survey, 29,* 12.

Alexander, C. (1982). Professional social workers and political responsibility. In M. Mahaffey & J. Hanks (Eds.), *Practical politics: Social work and political responsibility* (pp. 15–31). Silver Spring, MD: National Association of Social Workers.

Augustus F. Hawkins–Robert T. Stafford Elementary and Secondary School Improvement Amendments of 1988. P.L. 100-297, 102 Stat. 130.

Balanced Budget and Emergency Deficit Control Act of 1985. P.L. 99-177, 99 Stat. 1038.

Becker, G. D. (1987). Wald, Lillian. In A. Minahan (Ed.-in-Chief), *Encyclopedia of social work* (18th ed., Vol. 2, p. 944). Silver Spring, MD: National Association of Social Workers.

Boland, M. (1970). *The Detroit chapter of the National Association of Social Workers: Social worker attitudes about social action.* Unpublished master's thesis, Smith College School for Social Work, Northampton, MA.

Brieland, D. (1982). Introduction. In M. Mahaffey & J. Hanks (Eds.), *Practical politics: Social work and political responsibility* (pp. 1–11). Silver Spring, MD: National Association of Social Workers.

Chambers, C. (1963). *Seedtime of reform: American social service and social action, 1918–1933.* Minneapolis: University of Minnesota Press.

Civil Rights Restoration Act of 1987. P.L. 100-259, 102 Stat. 28.

Council on Social Work Education. (1992). *Curriculum policy statement for master's degree programs in social work education.* Alexandria, VA: Author.

Davis, A. (1964). Settlement workers in politics, 1890–1914. *Review of Politics, 26*(4), 505–517.

Edmundson, L. (1984). *Kate Bernard.* Unpublished manuscript, Oklahoma University, School of Social Work, Norman.

Epstein, I. (1969). *Professionalization and social work activism.* Doctoral dissertation, Columbia University, New York.

Federal Employees Benefits Improvement Act of 1986. P.L. 99-251, 100 Stat. 14.

Gilbert, N., & Specht, H. (1986). *Dimensions of social welfare policy* (2nd ed.). Englewood Cliffs, NJ: Prentice-Hall.

Giles, K. (1980). *Flight of the dove: The story of Jeanette Rankin.* Beaverton, OR: Touchstone Press.

Haynes, K., & Mickelson, J. (1991). *Affecting change: Social workers in the political arena* (2nd ed.). New York: Longman.

Hellenbrand, S. (1977). Hamilton, Gordon. In J. B. Turner (Ed.-in-Chief), *Encyclopedia of social work* (17th ed., pp. 517–519). Washington, DC: National Association of Social Workers.

Higher Education Amendments of 1992. P.L. 102-325, 106 Stat. 448.

Horner, W., & Whitbeck, L. (1991). Personal versus professional values in social work: A methodological note. *Journal of Social Service Research, 14*(1/2), 21–40.

Key, V. O., Jr. (1964). *Politics, parties, and pressure groups* (5th ed.). New York: Thomas Y. Crowell.

Kleinkauf, C. (1982). Running for office: A social worker's experience. In M. Mahaffey & J. Hanks (Eds.), *Practical politics: Social work and political responsibility* (pp. 181–194). Silver Spring, MD: National Association of Social Workers.

Leiby, J. (1978). *History of social welfare and social work in the United States.* New York: Columbia University Press.

Mahaffey, M. (1979). *Survey of social workers in elected office.* Unpublished manuscript.

Mahaffey, M. (1987). Political action in social work. In A. Minahan (Ed.-in-Chief), *Encyclopedia of social work* (18th ed., Vol. 2, pp. 283–293). Silver Spring, MD: National Association of Social Workers.

Mathews, G. (1983). Social work PAC's and state social work associations' purpose, history and action strategies. *Journal of Sociology and Social Welfare, 10*(2), 347–354.

Miringoff, M., & Opdycke, S. (1986). *American social welfare policy: Reassessment and reform.* Englewood Cliffs, NJ: Prentice Hall.

NASW member appointed chief of Children's Bureau. (1957). *NASW News, 2*(3), 1.

National Association of Social Workers. (1993). *Social workers serving in elective offices 1993.* Washington, DC: Author.

National Association of Social Workers. (1994). *NASW code of ethics.* Washington, DC: Author.

Omnibus Budget Reconciliation Act of 1989. P.L. 101-502, 104 Stat. 1289.

Omnibus Budget Reconciliation Act of 1993. P.L. 103-66, 107 Stat. 31.

Ornstein, N., & Elder, S. (1978). *Interest groups, lobbying, and policymaking.* Washington, DC: Congressional Quarterly.

Parker, M., & Sherraden, M. (1991). Electoral participation of social workers. *New England Journal of Human Services, 11*(3), 23–28.

Parris, G., & Brooks, L. (1971). *Blacks in the city: A history of the national urban league.* Boston: Little, Brown.

Patti, R. (1983). Political action. In *Encyclopedia of Social work* (17th ed., 1983–1984 suppl., pp. 96–105). Silver Spring, MD: National Association of Social Workers.

Reamer, F. (1993). *The philosophical foundations of social work* (pp. 1–37). New York: Columbia University Press.

Reeser, L., & Epstein, I. (1990). *Professionalism and activism in social work* (pp. 70–101). New York: Columbia University Press.

Reynolds, B. (1940). Credo. *Social Work Today, 7*(2), 9–11.

Reynolds, B. C. (1963/1991). *An uncharted journey.* Silver Spring, MD: NASW Press.

Reynolds, J. B. (1896). The Settlement and Municipal Reform. In I. C. Barrows (Ed.), *Proceedings of the National Conference of Charities and Correction* (pp. 138–142). Boston: George H. Ellis.

Richan, W. (1988). *Beyond altruism: Social welfare policy in American society* (pp. 171–186). New York: Haworth Press.

Salcido, R. (1984). Social work practice in political campaigns. *Social Work, 29,* 189–191.

Straight from Washington. (1958). *NASW News, 3*(2), 5.

Strandberg, C., & Marshall G. (1988). Politics and social work: The professional interface. *The Social Worker/Le Travailleur Social, 56*(3), 112–116.

Towle, C. (1987). *Common human needs* (rev. ed.). Silver Spring, MD: National Association of Social Workers.

Van Kleeck, M. (1934). Our illusions regarding government. In *National Conference of Social Work* (pp. 476–477, 483–484). Chicago: University of Chicago Press.

Van Waters, M. (1930). Philosophical trends in modern social work. In *National Conference of Social Work* (pp. 473–485). Chicago: University of Chicago Press.

Ware, S. (1987). *Partner and I: Molly Dewson, feminism and New Deal politics.* New Haven, CT: Yale University Press.

Wolk, J. (1981). Are social workers politically active? *Social Work, 26,* 283–288.

Toby Weismiller, MSW, ACSW, is political affairs director, National Association of Social Workers, 750 First Street, NE, Washington, DC 20002. **Sunny Harris Rome, MSW, JD,** is assistant professor of social work, George Mason University, 4400 University Dr., Fairfax, VA 22030.

For further information see

Advocacy; Civil Rights; Ethics and Values; Federal and Administrative Rule Making; Federal Social Legislation from 1961 to 1994; Health Care: Reform Initiatives; Human Rights; National Association of Social Workers; Peace and Social Justice; Social Welfare History; Social Welfare Policy; Social Work Profession Overview; Special-Interest Professional Associations.

Key Words	
advocacy	politics
lobbying	public policy
political action	

Southeast Asians

See Asian Americans: Southeast Asians

Special-Interest Professional Associations
Robbie W. Christler Tourse

Social work is a profession that traverses and affects many areas of human services, including schools, hospitals, churches, mental health facilities, nursing homes, family service agencies, correctional and criminal justice settings, industrial and occupational settings, community organization and planning agencies, and rehabilitation centers. It encompasses advocacy to address the needs of clients, numerous populations, and many practice modalities. The types of modalities may vary from clinical practice to organizational practice to social action. Advocacy may exist on the micro, mezzo, or macro levels. At the macro level, the treatment focus for such practice, which can be used with various populations, may involve individual, group, or family therapies, focus or psychoeducational groups, administration, and planning.

Reflecting this wealth of practice diversity are the myriad professional associations that represent different aspects of social work. Such special-interest associations have been a part of the social work profession for more than 70 years. They stimulate the profession by providing institutional entities with which to identify and resources from which to gain knowledge and professional development. They also provide professional cohesiveness and a means by which to monitor the profession and influence social issues and policies that affect society. Special-interest associations strengthen social work, perpetuate its existence, and ensure the continuation of professionalism in the field. This entry presents some factors that have prompted the need for professional associations and a brief historical synopsis of professional social work associations, identifying certain special-interest associations within the social work profession.

NEED FOR PROFESSIONAL ASSOCIATIONS

The social work profession provides support, clinical and administrative services, and planning to individuals and organizations. It is a profession devoted to assisting and encouraging self-actualization on the individual, group, and societal levels. It is also a profession on which social welfare (Compton & Galaway, 1989) and mental health systems rely, and it is a profession in which the transactional nature of people in their environment is in the fore (Germain & Gitterman, 1980, 1987).

Many forces impinge and affect professions. To counter and regulate internal and external forces, professions must identify themselves, find ways to bring about professional cohesiveness, monitor the work of their professionals, provide professional influence, and support the development of theory and practice. Social work is no exception.

Professional Identity
What social workers do helps shape the profession's identity and forms the culture of social work. This professional cultural identity is the basis for how services are delivered to meet individual and societal needs. It helps establish the traditions, beliefs, norms, values, and attitudes on which the profession bases its work (Pinderhughes, 1989), and it provides focus, direction, continuity, cohesiveness, and purpose toward that end.

There is a general professional identity that indicates that one is a social worker, but there are also specialized identities—unique qualities and interests that define the scope of the profession and distinguish among groups of social workers. Special-interest associations are a medium through which social workers can express their differences. The more one identifies, the better one commits to the profession and its work.

Professional Cohesiveness
Associations in social work, as in other professions, help unite the profession. This unification occurs through professional identity; the establishment of organizational aims, goals, and objectives; and the structured discussion of professional and theoretical thought. The general identity, aims, goals, and objectives of a profession may conflict or, as Korr (1986) suggested in a discussion of group identity and goals, may overlap with those of special-interest associations. The general professional perspective around professional and

theoretical paradigms may also overlap with that of special-interest organizations or may proffer a divergent view in special-interest associations. This focus on and examination of the various overlapping and, at times, conflictual aspects of the profession, however, help provide direction and a cohesive structure to the profession and its special-interest associations.

Monitoring of the Profession

Standards help provide the foundation on which the profession is structured, and those such as the development of value positions and codes of ethics establish mechanisms for monitoring the profession's growth and direction. Abbott (1988) suggested that these two factors are congruent and compliment one another. Values, however, are not universal and can conflict (Jones, 1970); therefore, the profession and its associations constantly monitor and assess differences in values. The monitoring and assessment of values within and among associations provide the core for the formulation of codes of ethics, which "serve as a guide for members in their daily professional lives by ... making explicit the standards of ethical behavior held by the profession" (Kiester & Pfouts, 1985, p. 23).

Special-interest associations help with this protection through the monitoring process. "Quality control is necessary to protect the public [as well as] the profession" (Kiester & Pfouts, 1985, p. 22). Associations provide enforcement, reinforcement, and appropriate changes to standards. Such standards assist in defining professional competence, undergirding the concept of confidentiality, ensuring the integrity of social workers and the profession, and establishing guidelines for practice. The protection of the public and the profession also extends to addressing societal changes that may give impetus to professional ideological shifts. The monitoring of these shifts by associations helps ensure that the standards of the profession will be modified, when appropriate, to retain their congruence with the needs of society.

Professional Influence

The social work profession has taken numerous positions on social and mental health issues and policies. Professional influence comes from interest groups that work within the profession and sometimes with other professions and grassroots organizations. The positions taken are thought to be for the common good of society or segments of society. Many intraprofessional and interprofessional groups "focus on a narrow set of policy choices" (Reid, 1985, p. 236). Even so, to be influ-

ential means being political and establishing broad-based coalitions to effect change (Schriver, 1987). Reeser and Epstein's (1987) study suggested that the profession prefers noncontroversial change strategies. However, professional groups do face controversy and work to influence the directions that societal issues take. Professional collaborations assist social workers in regularizing and institutionalizing their contacts with other professionals, and such collaborations help secure the inclusion of social workers among professional groups (Compton & Galaway, 1989) that influence the needs of society.

Theory and Practice Development

To provide high-quality support, counsel, and assistance to those it serves, the profession must have a sound theoretical foundation as a part of the core of practice (Goldstein, 1986). Theory assists in bringing a sense of knowledge and order to a situation or problem and provides understanding of developmental, relational, and situational patterns (Turner, 1986). Practice involves problem solving and mediating the personal and environmental interface (Compton & Galaway, 1989) using various practice modalities and approaches.

Associations can help define issues and causes related to theory and practice and can provide the catalyst for research that furthers theoretical and practice knowledge. Conferences initiated by associations are a means toward this end. Through specialized interests, new theoretical concepts and approaches can emerge that then have an impact on practice. The need for professional associations are many. The preceding factors, which stand alone in importance, also impinge on one another and, therefore, are interrelated. These factors drive associations and provide the reason for their existence. Special-interest associations propel the profession into the future while understanding and acknowledging its past. In so doing, these associations are, in general, able to provide various kinds and levels of information to the profession.

HISTORY

In the second decade of the 20th century, social workers began to note and address their professional position. The impetus for this professional reflection and push toward professional credibility was an address on social work as a profession presented in 1915 by the eminent Abraham Flexner, a principal force behind the upgrading of medical education. In his address, Flexner suggested that social work did not meet the criteria that he had developed to determine whether a field of study could be properly described as a profession—that is, whether it had a unique technology, specific educational programs, a professional literature, and practice skills (DuBois & Miley, 1992; Flexner, 1961).

Two national social work organizations that emerged shortly after Flexner's pronouncement were the National Social Workers' Exchange (1917) and the American Association of Hospital Social Workers (1918; it became the American Association of Medical Social Workers in 1934). These organizations directed their attention to addressing the needs, issues, and questions that faced the profession and its members (DuBois & Miley, 1992; Pumphrey & Pumphrey, 1961). In about 1920–21, the National Social Workers' Exchange, after a year of studying the needs of the profession, was transformed into the first centrist, all-encompassing association: the American Association of Social Workers. This new organization's vision was to address "recruitment, ethics, professional standards, levels of remuneration, and means for securing better communication between branches of the profession" (Pumphrey & Pumphrey, 1961, p. 300). These beginnings led to the development of numerous organizations that have sought to address the needs of special interests within the profession.

CURRENT SPECIAL-INTEREST ASSOCIATIONS

Social work associations fit into several categories. Some associations are framed around social agencies that have common special interests, for example, the Child Welfare League of America and Family Service International. Others comprise individuals who unite and organize around a special interest (Brown, 1942), such as the National Association of Oncology Social Workers and the North American Association of Christians in Social Work. Moreover, some special-interest associations are nationally driven with state affiliates, and others are city-, metropolitan-, regional-, or state-formed associations that focus on special interests within one of these geographic areas. Special-interest associations usually complement one another, as well as supplement activities and specialized interests that are not a part of or the focus of another organization (Pharis, 1987). Even so, there are divergent views within and among groups in social work and interests sometimes do conflict or are discordant. These conflicts can be positive, however, in that they can stimulate further organizational and professional growth.

There is a plethora of special-interest associations, and the categories in which these associations may exist include the following: centrist professional organizations, organizations of color, practice-related associations, and other associations. All associations in these categories have relevant committees, conferences, or task forces.

Centrist Professional Organizations

NASW, which was founded in 1955, is the cornerstone of the social work profession. Its formation was the result of the merger of seven membership associations: the American Association of Group Workers, the American Association of Medical Social Workers, the American Association of Psychiatric Social Workers, the American Association of Social Workers, the Association for the Study of Community Organization, the National Association of School Social Workers, and the Social Work Research Group (Macht & Quam, 1986). It is the centrist association that provides focus, direction, and protection for generic interests in the profession (Pharis, 1987), and it has been at the forefront of advocating for the profession and for those served by the profession.

Only three years after its inception, NASW was viewed as a membership organization that focused on honing professional skills and knowledge and improving the quality of social services, including the social conditions under which individuals live (Adam, 1958). Today, it has the same mission, but the scope of achieving that mission has broadened. The specific purposes now are to

create professional standards for social work practice; advocate sound public social policies through political and legislative action; provide a wide range of membership services, including continuing education opportunities and an extensive professional program. (*Encyclopedia of Associations,* 1993, p. 1366)

In 1992 NASW incorporated the National Center for Social Policy and Practice, which it established in 1986 as an affiliate. The policy center was designed to collect data and conduct studies in the field of social work that would provide, at the national level, information that may influence practice by having an impact on public policy and strengthening social programs.

NASW (1994) has a code of ethics that reflects the basic values of the profession. Moreover, it has developed standards in various areas including personnel practice, clinical practice, and continuing education (Macht & Quam, 1986). It publishes the journal *Social Work* and four other practice journals with a special-interest focus, including *Health & Social Work, Social Work in Education, Social Work Research* and *Social Work Abstracts.* In addition, it publishes the *NASW News,* books, and reference works such as the *Encyclopedia of Social Work*.

Organizations of Color

These organizations formed near the end of the civil rights movement to address the needs of social workers and clients within particular racial and ethnic groups and, generally, to address the issues, policies, and research that have affected these groups. The racial and ethnic associations that were initially established were the National Association of Black Social Workers, the National Association of Puerto Rican/Hispanic Social Workers, the Asian American Social Workers, and the National Indian Social Workers Association. Only the Asian American Social Workers no longer exists.

The *National Association of Black Social Workers* emerged from the National Conference on Social Welfare held in 1968. Originally, the group was named the Black Social Workers Association. Subsequently, in 1969, the Alliance of Black Social Workers in Philadelphia sponsored a conference under the organization's current name (Macht & Quam, 1986). The conference has been an annual event, and the association has maintained its name and purpose since then. The association's objective is to influence the practice and social issues that have an impact on the lives of all black ethnic groups in the United States. The association also develops, sponsors, and supports community welfare projects (*Encyclopedia of Associations*, 1993). Currently, the organization publishes the *Black Caucus* and *Preserving Black Families: Research and Action Beyond the Rhetoric*.

The *National Association of Puerto Rican/Hispanic Social Workers* organized in 1971 as the National Association of Puerto Rican Social Workers. Following a hiatus, it reorganized in 1983 under its present name. Although the organization is headquartered in New York, it has been developing chapters beyond metropolitan New York City and New York State. The organization continues to expand its national base and currently receives inquiries from around the country about membership affiliation.

The association's mission embodies advocacy and human services issues that affect the Latino community. In addition, the organization provides training to credentialed members, serves as a resource to all levels of schools on issues affecting Latino children, and appears before legislative bodies to effect change for the good of Latino communities. A job bank is available for all credentialed social workers. Furthermore, membership is open to all human services providers regardless of race, creed, or national origin (W. Larreque, personal communication, August 17, 1993). A newsletter, *NAPR/HSW*, is provided to members.

The *National Indian Social Workers Association* was founded in 1970 as the Association of American Indian Social Workers. It was also known as the Association of American Indian and Alaskan Native Social Workers. The organization works for support and understanding of Native Americans and Alaska Natives through "training and technical assistance to tribal and nontribal organizations" (*Encyclopedia of Associations*, 1993, p. 1312) by means of counseling and administration, programming, and planning. It advocates for the rights of Native Americans and does survey research as part of its advocacy endeavors. It periodically publishes a newsletter for its members.

Practice-Related Associations

Organizations in this category focus on methodology, methodological functions, or a particular area or group in a field of practice. Educational and research associations influence practice and can be classified in this category as well. These organizations work to ensure that their practice, specific focus, or interest is addressed in the national and educational arenas, that standards are set, and that collaboration among like associations occurs.

One such organization, the *American Association of Industrial Social Workers*, was founded in 1982. This organization seeks to enlighten the social work profession and the public regarding its existence and purpose in the profession. That purpose is to educate individuals in the profession, through conferences, seminars, and research, about employee assistance and industrial social work. It also collaborates with the Organization Development Institute in trying to solve employee assistance issues that are organizationally, clinically, or environmentally based (*Encyclopedia of Associations*, 1993). The association has no publications, but does hold an annual meeting.

The *Council on Social Work Education* (CSWE) is the standard-bearer for social work education. This organization was formed in 1952 after a merger of the American Association of Schools of Social Work, which advocated for graduate social work education, and the National Association of Schools of Social Administration, which advocated for undergraduate social work education (DuBois & Miley, 1992; Macht & Quam, 1986). CSWE sets standards under which undergraduate and graduate social work educational institutions function and is the accrediting body for these institutions. With education as its focus, this association compiles data and conducts research related to education and consults with educational institutions on areas of educational interest or concern (*Encyclopedia of Associations,* 1993). CSWE's publications include the *Journal of Social Work Education,* published three times a year; the *Directory of Colleges and Universities with Accredited Social Work Degree Programs,* published annually; and *Statistics on Social Work Education,* published annually.

The *Association of Community Organization and Social Administration* (ACOSA) "is an independent organization of social work educators oriented to training students in macro aspects of part of the curriculum, including planning, policy, community organization, administration, and advocacy" (Barker, 1991, p. 17).

The *National Association of Oncology Social Workers* (NAOSW) operates to ensure the provision of high-quality oncological social work services. It also supports the professional development of oncological social work and advocates strong public policies that have an impact on this field of practice and social work in general (*Encyclopedia of Associations,* 1993). It publishes the *NAOSW News* quarterly.

The *National Federation of Societies of Clinical Social Work,* founded in 1971, is composed of state and regional societies that focus on and try to find solutions to common concerns and issues specific to clinical social work that transcend any one state society (*Encyclopedia of Associations,* 1993). In 1976 the federation developed a code of ethics for clinical social workers with periodic revisions (National Federation of Societies for Clinical Social Work, 1987). It publishes the *Clinical Social Work Journal* quarterly and a newsletter semiannually.

The objective of the *National Network for Social Work Managers,* formed in 1985, is to support, encourage, and assist social workers in managerial positions in the human services arena, thereby affecting practice. As its name implies, the organization serves "as a network to connect social work professionals in human service–related activities" (*Encyclopedia of Associations,* 1993, p. 1366) and continues its networking by conducting management institutes and developing workshops and educational programs. The journal *Administration in Social Work,* published quarterly, is a membership benefit.

The *Society for Social Work Administrators in Health Care* (formerly the Society for Hospital Social Work Directors) was founded in 1966, and its membership is composed of social work directors in health care settings. The organization's purpose is to ensure effective social work health care administration and services. This goal is carried out through work with other health care professionals and social work organizations, encouragement and sponsorship of educational programs, and written materials on social work administration (*Encyclopedia of Associations,* 1993). The society publishes *Social Work Administration* and *Discharge Planning Update* bimonthly.

Other Associations

Several other associations, and some commissions within associations, philosophically and politically influence the social work profession and the broader society. For example, the *Commission on Gay Men/Lesbian Women,* formerly the Task Force on Lesbian/Gay Issues, is a part of CSWE. Founded in 1980, its focus is to ensure that material relate and relevant to lesbians and gay men is included within the educational curriculum of social work. The commission also provides support to those within the profession who address prejudice with respect to homosexual issues (*Encyclopedia of Associations,* 1993). This commission provides pamphlets of annotated bibliographies and selected filmographies of works with gay or lesbian content.

The *North American Association of Christians in Social Work,* originally the Evangelical Social Work Conference and later the National Association of Christian Social Workers, was founded in 1954 and was established out of a series of conferences at Wheaton College (Macht & Quam, 1986). The association is an interdenominational and international organization whose mission is to assist members in developing Christian faith and values in their practice, provide a source of support and fellowship for members in their Christian practice, support and promote the interface of social work and social policy with that of a Christian worldview, and promote social reform and a commitment to love and justice within the Christian community (*Encyclopedia of Associations,* 1993; E. G. Kuhlmann, personal communication, August 9, 1993). This organization publishes the journal *Social Work and Christianity* semiannually and the newsletter *Catalyst* bimonthly. It also holds an annual convention and training conference.

REFERENCES

Abbott, A. A. (1988). *Professional choices: Values at work.* Silver Spring, MD: National Association of Social Workers.

Adam, M. E. (1958). *Social work.* Cambridge, MA: Bellman.

Barker, R. L. (1991). *The social work dictionary* (2nd ed.). Silver Spring, MD: NASW Press.

Brown, E. L. (1942). *Social work as a profession.* New York: Russell Sage Foundation.

Compton, B. R., & Galaway, B. (1989). *Social work processes.* Belmont, CA: Wadsworth.

DuBois, B., & Miley, K. K. (1992). *Social work: An empowering profession.* Needham Heights, MA: Allyn & Bacon.

Encyclopedia of associations (27th ed., Vols. 1 & 2). (1993). Detroit: Gale Research.

Flexner, A. (1961). Is social work a profession? In R. E. Pumphrey & M. W. Pumphrey (Eds.), *The heritage of American social work: Readings in its philosophical and institutional development* (pp. 301–307). New York: Columbia University Press.

Germain, C. B., & Gitterman, A. (1980). *The life model of social work practice.* New York: Columbia University Press.

Germain, C. B., & Gitterman, A. (1987). Ecological perspective. In A. Minahan (Ed.-in-Chief), *Encyclopedia of social work* (18th ed., Vol. 1, pp. 488–496). Silver Spring, MD: National Association of Social Workers.

Goldstein, H. (1986). Toward the integration of theory and practice: A humanistic approach. *Social Work, 31,* 352–357.

Jones, R. H. (1970). Social values and social work education. In K. Kendall (Ed.), *Social work values in an age of discontent* (pp. 35–45). New York: Council on Social Work Education.

Kiester, D. J., & Pfouts, J. H. (1985). Value base for social work. In A. E. Fink, J. H. Pfouts, & A. W. Dobelstein (Eds.), *The field of social work* (8th ed., pp. 19–32). Beverly Hills, CA: Sage Publications.

Korr, W. S. (1986). Exploring differences among women in social work. *Social Service Review, 60*(4), 555–567.

Macht, M., & Quam, J. (1986). *Social work: An introduction.* Columbus, OH: Charles E. Merrill.

National Federation of Societies for Clinical Social Work. (1987). National Federation of Societies for Clinical Social Work code of ethics. *Clinical Social Work, 15*(1), 81–91.

National Association of Social Workers. (1994). *NASW code of ethics.* Washington, DC: Author.

Pharis, M. E. (1987). The new old guard: Beliefs and values of members and nonmembers of societies for clinical social work. *Clinical Social Work, 15*(1), 74–80.

Pinderhughes, E. (1989). *Understanding race, ethnicity, and power.* New York: Free Press.

Pumphrey, R. E., & Pumphrey, M. W. (Eds.). (1961). *The heritage of American social work: Readings in its philosophical and institutional development.* New York: Columbia University Press.

Reeser, L. C., & Epstein, I. (1987). Social workers' attitudes toward poverty and social action: 1968–1984. *Social Service Review, 61*(4), 610–622.

Reid, P. N. (1985). Community organization. In A. E. Fink, J. H. Pfouts, & A. W. Dobelstein (Eds.), *The field of social work* (8th ed., pp. 222–243). Beverly Hills, CA: Sage Publications.

Schriver, J. M. (1987). Harry Lurie's assessment and prescription: An early view of social workers' roles and responsibilities regarding political action. *Journal of Sociology and Social Welfare, 14*(2), 111–127.

Turner, F. J. (1986). Theory in social work practice. In F. J. Turner (Ed.), *Social work treatment* (3rd ed.). New York: Free Press.

FURTHER READING

Baker, R. L. (1988). Just whose code of ethics should the independent practitioner follow? *Journal of Independent Social Work, 2*(4), 1–5.

Brown, A. W. (1991). A social work leader in the struggle for racial equality: Lester Blackwell Granger. *Social Service Review, 65,* 266–280.

Gowanlock, G. W. (1984). Perspectives on the profession. *Social Worker/Le Travailleur Social, 52*(1), 17–20.

Kutchins, H., & Kirk, S. A. (1989). DSM-III-R: The conflict over new psychiatric diagnoses. *Health & Social Work, 14,* 91–101.

Lewis, H. (1989). Ethics and the private non-profit human service organizations. *Administration in Social Work, 13*(2), 1–14.

Mandell, B. R. (1983). Blurring definitions of social services: Human services vs. social work. *Catalyst, 4*(3), 5–21.

McCullagh, J. G. (1985). School social work issues: An analysis of professional association actions. *Social Work in Education, 7,* 192–203.

Robbie W. Christler Tourse, PhD, is director of field education, Boston College, Graduate School of Social Work, McGuinn Hall, Chestnut Hill, MA 02167.

For further information see

Advocacy; Continuing Education; Council on Social Work Education; Ethics and Values; Information and Referral Services; Interdisciplinary and Interorganizational Collaboration; International Social Welfare: Organizations and Activities; Licensing, Regulation, and Certification; Management Overview; National Association of Social Workers; Organizations: Context for Social Services Delivery; Planning and Management Professions; Professional Conduct; Quality Assurance; Social Welfare Policy; Social Work Education; Social Work Profession Overview; Social Workers in Politics; Vendorship; Voluntarism; Volunteer Management.

Key Words

organizations of color
professional associations

social work associations
special-interest organizations

Spellman, Dorothea C.

See Biographies section, Volume 3

Spouse Abuse

See Domestic Violence

Starr, Ellen Gates

See Biographies section, Volume 3

Strategic Planning
John A. Yankey

During the past decade, social work organizations increasingly have engaged in strategic planning to determine their future direction. A complex, ever-changing, and competitive nonprofit environment has provided impetus for the emergence of this type of planning as a critical leadership activity. Despite its increased use, however, confusion and skepticism about the definition and value of strategic planning remain.

DEFINING STRATEGIC PLANNING

Bryson (1988) defined strategic planning as a "disciplined effort to produce fundamental decisions and actions that shape and guide what an organization (or other entity) is, what it does, and why it does it" (p. 5). Barry (1986) viewed strategic planning as the "process of determining what an organization intends to be in the future and how it will get there" (p. 10). Pfeiffer, Goodstein, and Nolan (1986) viewed such planning as the "process by which the guiding members of an organization envision its future and develop the necessary procedures and operations to achieve that future" (p. 1). In these definitions, as well as those offered by other authors, strategic planning has been viewed as a process of developing and maintaining a strategic fit among the mission of the organization, the strengths and weaknesses of the organization, and opportunities and challenges in the organization's external environment.

Other themes implicit in various definitions suggest that strategic planning be understood as a process that (1) must be embraced and supported by top volunteer and managerial leaders of the organization; (2) seeks ownership at all organizational levels; (3) requires a commitment of resources, especially time; (4) incorporates analysis, thought, judgment, and creativity; and (5) must be tailored to fit an organization's planning culture.

Some authors have distinguished between strategic planning and more-traditional long-range planning. Bryson (1988) suggested that this distinction results from strategic planning's focus on identifying and resolving issues, emphasis on assessment of environmental factors, development of an idealized version of an organization's future, and design of an action-oriented plan through consideration of a range of possible future directions. Others have incorporated strategic planning into other processes. For example, Eadie (1991),

Edwards and Eadie (in press), and the United Way of America (1986) have referred to strategic planning within the broader context of "strategic management": The entire process from development of strategies through monitoring and evaluation of their implementation.

BENEFITS AND CRITICISMS OF STRATEGIC PLANNING

Many authors (Barry, 1986; Bryson, 1988; Burkhart & Reuss, 1993; Eadie, 1991; Steiner, 1979) have pointed out strategic planning's helpfulness in (1) providing a common purpose for future organizational development, (2) stimulating forward thinking and clarifying future organizational directions, (3) improving organizational performance, (4) building teamwork and expertise, (5) developing a framework for decision making and establishing priorities, (6) promoting responsiveness to changing community needs, (7) enhancing employee morale and commitment to the organization's mission, (8) directing fundraising efforts, (9) positioning the organization to act on its strengths and opportunities; and (10) providing a mechanism for educating stakeholders about the organization.

Although these benefits are impressive, critics harbor important reservations about strategic planning. They argue that the process is too time-consuming and that the world changes too rapidly, thereby making strategic plans obsolete by the time they are developed. In addition, they point out that such planning is too abstract and will not be beneficial in day-to-day management. Many social work organizations are in "crisis situations" wherein they must address survival issues immediately; there simply is not sufficient time to conduct strategic planning. Other critics stress that social work organizations frequently do not implement the strategies they develop in the planning process, often leading to cynicism and disillusionment about the value of planning.

DESIGNING THE PLANNING PROCESS

Pfeiffer et al. (1986) referred to the initiation of the planning process as "planning to plan" and identified typical questions that require attention at the outset; for example—

- What is the level of commitment to the planning process?
- Who will lead the strategic planning effort?
- Who are the key stakeholders of the organization?
- Which of these key stakeholders will serve on the strategic planning committee?
- How will other stakeholders be involved in the planning process?
- What will be the specific steps and timetable for the planning process?

Leading the Strategic Planning Effort

A key decision in designing the planning process is to identify the desired membership of a strategic planning committee. The individual selected to chair the committee is an especially important leadership choice. This individual should be in contact with and be knowledgeable about the organization; be viewed internally and externally as an appropriate spokesperson; be able to assume a somewhat objective and facilitative role; possess strong planning, group processing, and negotiating skills; and have affluence and influence. Although the executive director or chief executive officer should also play an important role in planning, the chair of the strategic planning committee more frequently is selected from among volunteer leaders (for example, the president or vice president of the board of trustees, chair of a planning committee, or a key board member being groomed for a top leadership role). In addition to this choice of leadership, successful planning requires that the organization's volunteer leaders and top management team be enthusiastic in their support of and actively participate in the strategic planning process.

Involving Key Stakeholders of the Organization

Another important aspect of designing the planning process is to identify those individuals, organizations, coalitions, and so forth whose perceptions and support of the organization are important. These stakeholders' ownership of the strategic plan will be critical to its implementation. Stakeholders of social work organizations may include members of boards of trustees and advisory committees, management officials, staff members, volunteers, clients, former clients, funders, advocacy groups, other nonprofit (including

social work) organizations, government leaders, political leaders, religious leaders, and members of the community. The strategic planning committee should be composed of these stakeholders, although it would not be practical to have all of them serve on the committee. Thus, a decision is required regarding who will be requested to serve, with special consideration given to representation from the board of trustees, advisory committees, and top management.

Other stakeholders not serving on the strategic planning committee can and should be involved in the planning process. Although each organization engaged in strategic planning may have its own mechanisms for such involvement, stakeholders can, for example, provide their perceptions about the organization's strengths and weaknesses, serve as members of a panel providing information regarding external environmental trends, help identify or clarify issues requiring strategic consideration, participate in strategy development sessions, or act as "devil's advocates" in reviewing potential strategies.

Developing Steps and a Timetable for the Planning Process

The specific steps of the strategic planning process should reflect the planning culture of the organization. As indicated, various authors have proposed models of planning, four of which are particularly appropriate for social work organizations (Barry, 1986; Bryson, 1988; Burkhart & Reuss, 1993; Pfeiffer et al., 1986). Although these models involve some differences in emphasis, each includes steps common to most definitions of strategic planning found in the literature:

- clarifying the organization's mission
- analyzing the organization's internal strengths and weaknesses (or perceptions thereof)
- assessing the opportunities and challenges presented by current and future external environmental trends
- identifying critical issues that require strategic consideration
- developing strategic alternatives
- selecting for implementation the most appropriate alternatives
- determining how the strategic plan is to be implemented, monitored, and updated.

MISSION FORMULATION

Strategic planning involves values, beliefs, philosophy, purpose, meaning, and vision. Thus, it is both logical and necessary for the planning process to focus initially on clarification of an organization's mission. The aim of mission formulation is to determine the purpose of the organization and the values and philosophy that guide it.

Benefits and Obstacles

Clarifying its mission helps an organization have a shared set of values, define its business, determine the programs and services it wants to undertake, state its purpose clearly to all stakeholders, direct its human and financial resources, and suggest the kinds of knowledge and skills required to carry out the mission efficiently and effectively. Although the importance of mission clarification seems self-evident, the task may encounter resistance, possibly based on the notion that the organization's purpose is self-evident or the belief that the existing charter, bylaws, and mission statement are sufficient. Other resistance may stem from a concern that a discussion of values and philosophy will lead to arguments, controversy, and disagreement. Others resist this "philosophical discussion" because, in their view, it detracts from the true purpose of strategic planning, that is, developing action plans.

Visioning

It is often stated that an organization can never be greater than the vision that guides it. A vision is a description of an organization's preferred future state. In short, it is a statement of what the organization wants to be in the future. A vision emanates from deeply held values, experiences, views of the future, intuition, and dreaming. Answers to the following questions represent components of a vision:

- What will the future business of the organization be?
- What will the board composition and structure be?
- How large will the organization be?
- What programs will be conducted by the organization?
- What staff will be required?
- What volunteers will be required?
- What internal management structures will be required?
- What will the funding mix for the organization be?
- What facilities will the organization have?
- How will success be measured?

The creation of a vision for an organization necessarily deals with values and philosophy and provides the framework within which mission clarification occurs. Pfeiffer et al. (1986), in their applied strategic planning approach, offered a use-ful "values audit" element to help identify the commonly held values of an organization.

Clarification of the Mission

On the basis of the consensus reached about the values and philosophy guiding the organization, strategic planning can focus on a clear formulation of the mission. A series of questions—chosen from the following list—may be used to clarify thinking about the mission:

- Why does the organization exist?
- Who does, and who should, the organization serve?
- What are the organization's most important programs and services?
- What does the organization do best?
- What does the organization do least well?
- What makes the organization unique?
- What is the organization most noted for in the community?
- What would the community lose if the organization were to cease to exist?

Answers to these questions will provide the elements to be integrated into the statement of the organization's mission. However, it should be noted that development of this statement may represent one of the more formidable tasks in the strategic planning process. Reaching consensus on the specific language of the statement will require a tolerance of differences, a willingness to compromise, and patience. Among other things, a mission statement should be consistent with organizational values and philosophy, clear and understandable to all stakeholders, brief enough to be kept in mind and easily communicated, broad enough to allow flexibility but not so broad as to lose focus, and worded so as to serve as a motivational force and a guide to organizational decision making.

Although the aim in crafting the mission statement is to make it as succinct as possible, its length will vary among organizations. Clearly, nonprofit organizations of all kinds have moved away from mission statements exceeding one page. Such brevity often is accomplished by including a section on underpinning values and philosophy before or after the mission statement in the strategic plan. Whatever its length, the mission statement provides the reality grounding for the next step in strategic planning: assessing the organization's internal and external environments.

SWOT ANALYSIS

A frequently used tool in strategic planning is the SWOT analysis: an analysis of the internal *strengths* and *weaknesses* of the organization in relation to the *opportunities* and *threats* presented by its external environment. This step in strategic planning is important in helping position the organization to maximize its strengths and capitalize on its opportunities. A SWOT analysis will prepare an organization to respond effectively to its external environment before a crisis erupts.

Internal Analysis

Assessment of the internal environment of an organization should include attention to its resources (people, money, facilities, equipment, information, technology, and so on), present strategies, and performance (operational assessment). Any data that would help the strategic planning committee gain a comprehensive overview of the organization's strengths and weaknesses should be included in this analysis. Operational assessment is approached through an analysis of performance history or an analysis based on comparative performance. Social work organizations probably will have an extensive amount of data available regarding resources, less information available regarding current strategies, and even less data on organizational performance. In the absence of such information, the committee often must rely on self-assessment and perceptions of key stakeholders as to how well the organization is performing.

This step in the strategic planning process may involve extensive gathering of data from an organization's documents; door-to-door, mail, telephone, or shopping mall surveys; focus groups; individual interviews; and panels of experts. Information may be sought on issues such as the organization's image, program and services, governance, management, staff, volunteers, external communication, facilities, funding, and fundraising. Hard data, to the extent that they exist, should be used. However, qualitative data, especially the results of a perceptual analysis, will almost certainly represent an important element in the SWOT analysis.

External Environment Analysis

Often the external environment is not well known; however, what happens there directly affects the organization. A good strategic planning process will include information about outside forces likely to influence the future direction of the organization. Bryson (1988) and others have identified three major categories of information as important elements in any systematic approach to environmental scanning: forces and trends; clients, cus-

tomers, or payers; and actual or potential competitors.

The key forces and trends in the external environment usually will be identified in four to six broad categories. Although economic, social–demographic, political, and technological categories appear in many environmental scans, volunteerism and philanthropic categories are especially important additional categories for social work organizations involved in strategic planning. The data for this analysis of forces and trends come from literature reviews, government documents, university-produced studies and reports, nonprofit and for-profit organizations' environmental scans, public hearings, key informants, panels of experts, and so forth. These forces and trends are analyzed in terms of the potential opportunities for and threats to the organization, and they represent critical considerations in charting the organization's future course.

A thorough SWOT analysis also requires focusing on clients, customers, or payers. These groups must be given attention as to their potential positive or negative impact on an organization's future. This aspect of the SWOT analysis will identify the needs of present and potential client groups that the organization may wish to serve in the future. Equally as important, funding sources, both public and private, must be analyzed in terms of the opportunities or threats they present for the organization's future.

A final element of the SWOT analysis is a competition analysis. Although some social work organizations do not perceive themselves as being in competition with other nonprofit organizations, virtually all compete on some level (for example, clientele, public visibility and acceptance, or funding). An analysis of competition helps shape the future competitive positioning of the organization in the markets it chooses to serve. The data required for this analysis will address such issues as with whom the organization is competing, the foci of the competition, and relative competitive strengths or weaknesses. More specifically, this analysis will focus attention on competitors' current market presence; production, distribution, and promotions; competitive differences; profitability; and image in the marketplace. The results of a SWOT analysis provide a solid base from which the strategic planning committee can identify issues to be stressed.

IDENTIFICATION OF STRATEGIC ISSUES

Eadie (1991) defined a strategic issue as a "major change challenge—opportunities and problems that appear to demand an organizational response, so a successful balance can be maintained between the organization's internal and external environments" (pp. 292–293). Bryson (1988) defined such an issue as a "fundamental policy choice affecting an organization's mandates, mission, values, product or service level and mix, clients or users, cost, financing, organization, or management" (p. 56). A strategic issue may be a welcome trend, event, or development that presents an organization with an opportunity to build on its competency, or it may be an unwelcome trend, event, or development emanating from an external environmental threat or an internal shortcoming.

Determination of an Issue as Strategic

Although many issues generated by strategic planning are critical, not all are strategic. Criteria for determining whether an issue is strategic include whether it is (1) an issue that is likely to have an impact on how the organization carries out its mission, (2) one that must produce a response of organizational commitment of human and financial resources, and (3) one over which the organization may reasonably expect to have some influence.

Bryson (1988) and the United Way of America (1986) provided guidelines on the information necessary for a thorough consideration of strategic issues. This information includes a description of the issue, a discussion of the factors that make the issue strategic, and an examination of the consequences of failure to address the issue. In addition, attention must be directed toward the developmental stage of the issue (that is, emerging, developing, maturing, or declining). Further, the analysis entails consideration of such questions as, How great will the impact likely be? What will be the focus of the impact? Who are the major actors, and what positions are they likely to take on the issue? What are the options for the organization to deal effectively with the issue?

Approaches to Issue Identification

Barry (1986) suggested three approaches to the identification of strategic issues: direct, goals, and "vision of success."

Direct approach. In the direct approach, the strategic planning committee moves from a clarification of the mission and the SWOT analysis to an identification of strategic issues. Kearns (1992) presented an in-depth explanation of the way in which strategic issues can emerge from a SWOT analysis. This approach works well when there is no preexisting agreement on goals, no well-defined vision of success, and no hierarchical authority choosing to impose goals.

Goals approach. The goals approach is based on organizational objectives being agreed upon and in place. In addition to agreement on goals and objectives, there must be sufficient specificity to guide identification of issues and potential strategies. This approach then develops strategies for carrying out the mission of the organization. The approach works well in organizations with hierarchical authority that wishes to impose goals on the planning process. The approach does not work well when values are diverse, agendas are broad, and stakeholders are powerful.

"Vision of success" approach. The "vision of success" approach is similar to the visioning activities associated with mission formulation. In this approach, the organization is requested to create a "best" picture of its future as it fulfills its mission and achieves success. Strategic issues are related to how the organization should move from the way it is now to how it would behave on the basis of its vision. This approach can be especially useful when drastic change is required or when it is difficult to identify strategic issues directly.

Whatever approach is used, strategic issues are politically and technically important in the strategic planning process. Political decision making focuses on issues, and strategic planning can have a positive impact on an organization by shaping the way issues are framed and resolved. If issues are carefully framed, future decision making is likely to be both politically acceptable and technically workable.

DEVELOPING AND SELECTING STRATEGIC ALTERNATIVES

Once strategic issues have been selected, the strategic planning committee often establishes work groups to develop goals and strategies to address them. These work groups may be strengthened by the addition of key stakeholders who have expertise in specific issue areas.

Strategy Development Process

Bryson (1988) preferred a five-part strategy development process in which members of the strategic planning committee or the work groups would address the following questions about each strategic issue:

1. What are the practical alternatives that might be pursued to address this strategic issue?
2. What are the barriers precluding the realization of these alternatives?
3. What major proposals could be pursued to achieve these alternatives?
4. What major action with existing staff must be undertaken to implement these proposals?
5. What specific action steps must be taken to implement the proposals?

Various approaches to strategy development encompass similar foci of critical thinking. For example, another approach entails (1) identifying the current strategy, (2) delineating problems with that strategy, (3) pinpointing the core of the strategy problem, (4) formulating alternative strategies, (5) evaluating these strategies, and (6) choosing a new strategy. Yet other approaches highlight identification of obstacles to implementation and steps or actions to be taken to overcome such obstacles.

Evaluation of Alternative Strategies

An especially critical aspect of developing strategies is the establishment of a clear and explicit set of criteria. The United Way of America (1986) suggested a model for evaluating and selecting strategies that was adapted from business strategy within the for-profit sector. The United Way approach includes a criteria selection checklist based on the following nine issues and questions:

1. Suitability: Is there a sustainable advantage?
2. Validity: Are the assumptions realistic?
3. Feasibility: Does the organization have the necessary skills, resources, and commitment?
4. Consistency: Is the strategy externally and internally consistent?
5. Vulnerability: What are the risks and contingencies?
6. Timing: When must the organization act, and when will it benefit?
7. Adaptability: Can the organization retain its flexibility?
8. Uniqueness: What makes this strategy distinctively different from others?
9. Usability: Can the organization readily implement the strategy?

Analysis of the alternatives through this screen of nine questions represents United Way's first attempt to narrow the number of strategies. The approach also suggests a second process whereby the remaining alternatives are examined more thoroughly in regard to the support they will require for implementation. This level of consideration focuses on organizational resources, structure, and systems.

IMPLEMENTATION OF THE STRATEGIC PLAN

After selection of strategies a first draft of the strategic plan is developed. Although there can be wide content variations, many strategic plans include the following sections: introduction and background; strategic planning process and participants; environmental analyses; mission, values, and philosophy; strategic goals and strategies; strategic plan implementation; and conclusion. This initial draft of the plan is reviewed and modified by the strategic planning committee until a consensus on its content is reached. Consideration of how the plan is to be implemented, monitored, and updated is a part of this deliberation.

The strategic planning committee submits its final version of the plan to the board of trustees (or executive committee if this committee reviews matters before their submittal to the full board). Because a number of the members of the board will have been participants in the planning process, the document's review and subsequent approval will benefit from firsthand knowledge of the thinking implicit in the selected strategic alternatives. At this point, much more in-depth attention is given to the implementation challenges regarding the organization's commitment, its allocation of resources, and the required structure and process for monitoring and updating the plan. A decision also is made as to who will assume responsibility for translating the strategic plan into an operational or tactical plan. In nonprofit organizations, this responsibility is increasingly being shared in a partnership arrangement between the organization's paid staff and the appropriate board committees. The design of the operational or tactical plan should include the activities and responsibilities for monitoring and updating the strategic plan, which should be done—at a minimum—on an annual basis.

STRATEGIC PLANNING PITFALLS: A FINAL NOTE

Experience with strategic planning in the 1980s and early 1990s has resulted in important lessons about why such planning may produce less than organizations have hoped for. The following are among the practices that have led to problems:

• delegating strategic planning to other professionals in the organization
• ignoring political considerations in designing and implementing the planning process

- failing to build ownership of the plan, especially among those responsible for implementing it
- failing to allocate sufficient time for a meaningful planning process
- tending to be overly optimistic regarding an organization's capacity
- failing to plan for contingencies
- failing to plan for a transition from strategic to operational planning
- allowing the plan to become outdated
- shelving the plan after completion.

For social work organizations attentive to avoiding these pitfalls, the strategic planning process provides a powerful mechanism for making critical choices regarding their future. It is a vehicle that can take organizations beyond merely forecasting their future to envisioning the future they want and creating the road map to get there.

REFERENCES

Barry, B. W. (1986). *Strategic planning workbook for public and nonprofit organizations*. St. Paul, MN: Amherst Wilder Foundation.
Bryson, J. M. (1988). *Strategic planning for public and nonprofit organizations*. San Francisco: Jossey-Bass.
Burkhart, P. J., & Reuss, S. (1993). *Successful strategic planning: A guide for nonprofit agencies and organizations*. Newbury Park, CA: Sage Publications.
Eadie, D. C. (1991). Planning and managing strategically. In R. L. Edwards & J. A. Yankey (Eds.), *Skills for effective human services management* (pp. 285–301). Silver Spring, MD: NASW Press.
Edwards, R. L., & Eadie, D. C. (in press). Meeting the challenge: Managing growth in the nonprofit and public human services sectors. *Administration in Social Work*.
Kearns, K. P. (1992). From comparative advantage to damage control: Clarifying strategic issues using SWOT analysis. *Nonprofit Management and Leadership, 3*(1), 3–22.
Pfeiffer, J. W., Goodstein, L. D., & Nolan, T. M. (1986). *Applied strategic planning: A how to do it guide*. San Diego: University Associates.
Steiner, G. A. (1979). *Strategic planning: What every manager must know*. New York: Free Press.
United Way of America. (1986). *Strategic management and the United Way*. Alexandria, VA: Author.

FURTHER READING

Bryce, H. J. (1987). *Financial and strategic management for nonprofit organizations*. Englewood Cliffs, NJ: Prentice Hall.
Dixit, A. K. (1991). *Thinking strategically: The competitive edge in business, politics, and life*. New York: W. W. Norton.
Espy, S. N. (1986). *Handbook of strategic planning for nonprofit organizations*. New York: Praeger.
Hay, R. D. (1990). *Strategic management in non-profit organizations: An administrator's handbook*. New York: Quorum Books.
Mintzberg, H., & Quinn, J. B. (1991). *The strategy process: Concepts, contexts, cases* (2nd ed.). Englewood Cliffs, NJ: Prentice Hall.
Pattan, J. E. (1986). The strategy in strategic planning. *Training and Development Journal, 40*(3), 30–32.
Shenkman, M. H. (1992). *Values and strategies: Competing successfully in the nineties*. New York: Quorum Books.
Steiner, G. A. (1977). *Strategic managerial planning*. Oxford, OH: Planning Executives Institute.
Unterman, I., & Davis, R. (1984). *Strategic management of not-for-profit organizations: From survival to success*. New York: Praeger.
Vogel, L., & Patternson, I. (1985). Strategy and structure: A case study of the implications of strategic planning for organizational structure and management practice. *Administration in Social Work, 10*(2), 53–66.

John A. Yankey, PhD, ACSW, LISW, is Leonard W. Mayo Professor, Case Western Reserve University, Mandel School of Applied Social Sciences, 10900 Euclid Avenue, Cleveland, OH 44106.

For further information see

Boards of Directors; Management Overview; Nonprofit Management Issues; Planning and Management Professions; Quality Assurance; Quality Management; Voluntarism; Volunteer Management.

Key Words	
decision-making	planning
processes	strategic planning

Substance Abuse: Direct Practice
Nancy J. Smyth

The alcohol and other drug abuse treatment system in the United States consists of over 10,000 federal, state, local, and private programs serving approximately 812,000 active clients and over 1.8 million clients annually (National Institute on Drug Abuse & National Institute on Alcohol Abuse and Alcoholism [NIDA/NIAAA], 1993). Almost half of these treatment units provide alcohol treatment, roughly one-third provide drug treatment, and the remaining units provide combined alcohol and drug treatment. The federal treatment system consists of programs operated within federal agencies, such as the U.S. Department of Veterans Affairs, the U.S. Bureau of Prisons, the Indian Health Service, and the U.S. Department of Defense. In 1991, 3.2 percent of all treatment units were federally operated, 14.9 percent were state or locally operated, 63.4 percent were private nonprofit, and 18.5 percent were private for-profit (NIDA/NIAAA). Treatment occurs in a wide range of settings in these systems.

TREATMENT SETTINGS

Detoxification Units
The primary goal of detoxification programs is to withdraw clients safely from alcohol and other drugs. Withdrawal generally is achieved by gradually reducing the dose of the abused drug (or a drug that is pharmacologically similar and has been substituted for the abused drug because it is safer). Although many detoxification programs operate in hospitals, community-based programs also provide detoxification for inpatients and for ambulatory outpatients. Many clients do not need treatment in a detoxification unit. The need for such treatment is determined on the basis of the degree of physical dependence on the drug, the medical risk involved in withdrawal, and the presence of other associated physical or psychiatric problems (such as pregnancy, high blood pressure, and bipolar disorder).

Inpatient and Residential Settings
Live-in treatment programs are of two types: those that operate primary treatment programs in facilities and those that provide a supportive living environment while residents receive outside primary treatment. The former category includes inpatient rehabilitation programs and therapeutic communities, and the latter encompasses community residences, halfway houses, and recovery homes.

Inpatient rehabilitation programs are operated either in hospitals or in separate rehabilitation facilities. The length of stay is generally short, usually from 14 to 28 days, and treatment usually consists of group, individual, and family counseling and self-help meetings. With changes in insurance coverage and the advent of managed care, inpatient programs have been shifting to shorter lengths of stay and an increased reliance on outpatient treatment (Creager, 1991). Therapeutic communities are long-term (one to two years), structured, residential treatment programs that have been used extensively to treat streetwise drug addicts. As with inpatient rehabilitation programs, treatment is provided in the facilities and usually involves group therapy, encounter groups, training in daily living skills, and structured in-house privilege systems.

Community residences, halfway houses, and recovery homes provide supportive environments for residents to live in while they become more integrated into a recovery-oriented lifestyle. The length of stay may vary considerably; many halfway houses allow residents to stay a few months, and some recovery homes allow residents to stay indefinitely. Although some minimal programming (such as therapy groups and training in daily living skills) may be provided in community residences and halfway houses, residents most often receive their primary treatment from outpatient treatment programs and self-help meetings. Residents may also work or receive vocational training. Some halfway houses and community residences do provide extensive individual and group counseling in their facilities.

Self-run recovery homes, such as Oxford House, are operated by the members of the residence and are not part of a treatment agency. The first Oxford House was started in Maryland by residents of a halfway house that had closed because of the lack of funds (Molloy, 1990). As a result of federal legislation encouraging the development of self-run recovery homes, several states now have many Oxford House residences (Molloy, 1990).

Outpatient Settings

Outpatient treatment for alcohol and other drug problems takes many forms. Day treatment or intensive outpatient treatment provides nonresidential treatment some portion of each day, three to six days a week, generally for a specified number of weeks (for example, four to eight weeks). Group treatment, supplemented by individual counseling and self-help groups, is usually the primary treatment method. Standard outpatient treatment often involves one to two visits to a clinic each week for group or individual counseling. The length of treatment varies greatly in standard outpatient programs—generally anywhere from three to 24 months. A period of less intensive aftercare contacts often follows a course of primary treatment.

These outpatient programs are typically referred to as "drug-free" outpatient programs, to distinguish them from methadone maintenance outpatient programs. In methadone maintenance programs, methadone, a long-acting synthetic narcotic, is substituted for the other narcotics that opiate addicts have been using, and the recipients are maintained on a safe dose. In addition to providing clients with methadone, these programs monitor clients' compliance through urine tests and sometimes provide individual and group counseling and vocational services. Despite their existence since the 1960s, methadone maintenance programs remain controversial within the addictions field, with critics claiming that the programs substitute one addiction for another and do not help addicts change their drug-use behavior (Friedman, 1993).

Other Settings

Screening and treatment programs often are operated in host organizations, such as prisons, courts, schools, welfare agencies, psychiatric facilities, and businesses. These programs take many forms, from employee or student assistance programs that screen and refer people to treatment settings or to prison drug treatment programs that actually provide treatment within correctional institutions.

SCREENING

Because the abuse of alcohol and other types of drugs can create problems in any area of functioning, clients with substance abuse disorders (and their family members) usually seek services for a wide range of presenting problems, including family conflict, depression, anxiety, financial difficulties, legal problems, declining performance in school or work, and physical disorders. Because clients rarely see substance abuse as the cause of their difficulties, they usually do not volunteer information about their use of alcohol and other drugs. In addition, because the use of alcohol and other drugs can cause psychiatric symptoms, the assessment of any client with psychiatric symptoms should include the careful consideration of whether the client is abusing substances. For these reasons, it is essential for social workers in all service settings to be familiar with the ways in which substance abuse can manifest itself in an individual or a family case and to be able to screen for such problems. Information on the abuse of alcohol and other drugs should, therefore, be routinely gathered. Although specific questions can be incorporated into a social work interview (see, for example, Griffin, 1991), several brief screening tools, such as the CAGE (Mayfield, McLeod, & Hall, 1974), the Michigan Alcoholism Screening Test (Selzer, 1971), and the Drug Abuse Screening Test (Skinner, 1982), can be used.

DIAGNOSIS AND ASSESSMENT

The diagnosis and assessment of a problem with alcohol or other drugs are usually conducted through a comprehensive, focused interview with the client. Practitioners often supplement information from the interview with information from a family member, from the referral source, and from assessment instruments and medical tests, particularly because clients may deny the extent and severity of their alcohol and drug use. Diagnoses are generally determined using criteria in the fourth edition of the *Diagnostic and Statistical Manual of Mental Disorders* (American Psychiatric Association, 1994), although instruments like the Alcohol Dependence Scale (Horn, Skinner, Wanberg, & Foster, 1984) may also be used. A comprehensive assessment must include consideration of the amount and frequency of substance use, as well as the role, function, and consequences of the use of alcohol and other drugs in all domains of the client's psychosocial functioning (physical, psychological, emotional, spiritual, financial, legal, vocational and educational, leisure, family, social, cultural, and environmental). Various tools are available for use in assessments, ranging from structured interviews (such as the Addiction Severity Index, McLellan, Luborsky, & O'Brien, 1985) to self-report questionnaires (for example, the Inventory of Drinking Situations, Annis, 1986, and the Inventory of Drug-Taking Situations, Annis, 1993).

TREATMENT

Treatment Staff
Most substance abuse treatment programs use interdisciplinary teams to plan and provide treatment. Within treatment teams, social workers provide services to substance abusers and their families in individual, group, and family sessions. In addition to social workers, these teams typically consist of a variety of other health and mental health professionals, including psychiatrists and other physicians, psychologists, nurses, rehabilitation counselors, recreational therapists, art therapists, and addictions specialists. This last category of professionals is the result of the development of specialized substance abuse credentials at both the state and national levels since the 1970s (Milgram, 1990). Many treatment teams have a substantial percentage of "recovering" staff—individuals who have experienced alcohol and other drug problems in the past. Although debates about the effectiveness of recovering versus non-recovering (nonaddicted) staff members have been prominent in the treatment field for years, research on the competence of both types of counselors has yielded conflicting findings (Anderson & Wiemer, 1992). Anderson and Wiemer's (1992) survey of addictions treatment programs indicated that administrators either have no preference or prefer a balance of both types of staff in their programs.

Stages of Treatment
Substance abuse treatment is often conceptualized in three stages—stabilization, rehabilitation, and maintenance. Stabilization focuses on helping the client to establish abstinence from alcohol and other drugs, to accept his or her substance abuse problem, and to commit himself or herself to making changes. The second stage, rehabilitation or habilitation, concentrates on helping the client

establish a stable lifestyle and identity that facilitates his or her remaining drug free. This stage includes learning or strengthening skills in daily living, the management of feelings, and coping; improving interpersonal relationships and strengthening social support; grieving the loss of alcohol and other drugs; and managing high-risk relapse situations. The third stage, maintenance, centers on solidifying the gains of treatment, preventing relapse, and preparing the client for the termination of services. To minimize the risk of relapse, work on childhood trauma (such as physical or sexual abuse) is usually delayed until the client has at least reached the maintenance stage, although severely traumatized clients may need to begin this work earlier to establish a recovery program (Gorski, 1989).

Approaches to Treatment
A wide range of approaches are available for the treatment of alcohol and drug abuse. Although some research has examined the effectiveness of specific treatment approaches, agencies often do not use the treatment approaches that have been empirically demonstrated to be effective, but rely instead on approaches that either have not been effectively tested or have been found to be less effective than other methods (Miller & Hester, 1986). One proposed explanation for this discrepancy is the "near-religious acceptance" of the disease concept in the United States, as opposed to more flexible, psychosocial models of treatment (Chiauzzi & Liljegren, 1993, p. 304). Another reason suggested by Miller (1986) is that the disease concept and its accompanying treatment approaches maintain the vested interests of the medical community, the treatment industry, and the recovering community.

Self-help groups. The most widely known self-help group is Alcoholics Anonymous (AA), a fellowship of alcoholics who have dedicated themselves to helping other alcoholics (AA, 1952). Narcotics Anonymous (NA), modeled after AA, is a self-help group for drug abusers. Both AA and NA use a 12-step strategy to guide the recovery process; some of the AA and NA tenets incorporate the concept of God or a higher power. Secular Organization for Sobriety (SOS) has emerged as a self-help group for people with alcohol problems who do not want to include the concept of a higher power in their recovery (Christopher, 1992). There are also self-help groups for family members of alcoholics (Al-Anon) and other drug abusers (Nar-Anon), each of which uses the 12-step model. Al-Anon has several different types of groups, including Alateen, for teenage children of alcoholics, and Al-Anon-ACOA, for adult children of alcoholics.

Many individuals have provided testimonials that AA and NA saved their lives, and practitioners frequently refer clients to these self-help groups (McCrady & Irvine, 1989; Metzger, 1988). Research on the effectiveness of the self-help approaches has focused primarily on AA; however, all the research is hampered by the difficulties inherent in studying groups in which members maintain anonymity. To date, no study has answered the question, Does AA work?—results support both pro and con positions, and all the studies have some serious methodological problems (McCrady & Irvine, 1989).

Biological. Biological approaches to the treatment of substance abuse are either pharmacological or nonpharmacological. Pharmacological strategies include medications used in detoxification and medications used in the ongoing treatment of substance abuse. Methadone maintenance treatment is one example of an ongoing pharmacological method that is used to treat opiate addicts. Methadone programs have been evaluated more extensively than most other drug abuse treatment programs, and the findings generally are positive. Most opiate addicts experience better treatment outcomes in methadone programs than they do in nonmethadone outpatient treatment or with no treatment, although variations in specific clinical procedures appear to affect outcomes (Institute of Medicine, 1990b).

Other pharmacological methods include narcotic antagonists (drugs that block the effects of opiates) (National Institute on Drug Abuse, 1991), which have been used with opiate addicts and are being explored with alcoholics (Volpicelli, Alterman, Hayashida, & O'Brien, 1992); antidepressants, which have had promising results in reducing craving for cocaine and dropout rates from cocaine treatment (NIDA, 1991); and disulfiram (trade name: Antabuse), a drug that makes a person sick if he or she drinks alcohol (McNichol, Ewing, & Faiman, 1987). Although there is evidence that supports the efficacy of disulfiram, its potentially serious side effects (such as its toxicity to the liver and increased levels of serum cholesterol) (McNichol et al., 1987) have led many practitioners to recommend that it not be used as a regular part of treatment (Miller & Hester, 1986). The primary nonpharmacological biological treatment method currently being explored is acupuncture, which is used to manage withdrawal and the craving for drugs; to date, research on the effectiveness of acupuncture has been inconclusive (Katims, Ng, & Lowinson, 1992).

Individual. Individual treatment of substance abusers is drawn from theoretical perspectives that range from cognitive-behavioral to psychodynamic. Although almost all settings provide some type of individual counseling, many place a greater emphasis on group and self-help approaches. Although researchers have not systematically investigated the comparative effectiveness of individual versus group treatment, one study of problem drinkers found no difference between the two types of treatment, although the subjects in group therapy achieved their gains earlier in treatment than did the subjects in individual therapy (Duckert, Amundsen, & Johnsen, 1992). Research on the effectiveness of various types of individual treatment has yielded mixed results (Miller & Hester, 1986; Rounsaville & Carroll, 1992).

Brief individual treatment (one to three sessions) of clients with alcohol problems, particularly clients with low-to-moderate dependence, is receiving increased attention in the treatment literature; this type of treatment seems to be more effective for this population than no treatment and seems as effective as more extensive treatment (Heather, 1989). In addition, recent developments in substance abuse treatment have placed increasing emphasis on applying the concepts of the five stages of change (precontemplation, contemplation, preparation, action, and maintenance) to assessing individuals and selecting interventions on the basis of the stage a client is in (Prochaska, DiClemente, & Norcross, 1992). Strategies to enhance clients' motivation have been developed (Miller & Rollnick, 1991), and preliminary research has indicated that even one motivational counseling session at the beginning of an inpatient stay significantly improves treatment outcome (Miller, 1992). Finally, the application of case management to substance abuse treatment is currently being explored (Sullivan, Wolk, & Hartmann, 1992; Willenbring, Ridgely, Stinchfield, & Rose, 1991).

Group. Group treatment is the primary method used in many substance abuse treatment programs (Straussner, 1993) and is often identified by clinicians as the treatment of choice for substance abusers (Galanter, Castaneda, & Franco, 1991), although it has not been systematically evaluated against individual treatment (Cartwright, 1987) and at least one study found that problem drinkers who received individual or group treatment had similar treatment outcomes (Duckert et al., 1992). Groups are considered particularly effective in treating substance abuse because they alleviate the social stigma associated with addiction by providing social acceptance from peers and they facilitate identification with peers who are further along in recovery. Psychoeducational groups provide information on the signs and symptoms of addiction, pharmacology and the effects of alcohol and other drugs, and behavioral changes that strengthen recovery from addiction. Despite the frequent use of psychoeducational groups as part of treatment, no study has rigorously evaluated their effectiveness (Miller & Hester, 1986).

Therapy groups use feedback from peers, positive peer pressure, experiential learning, role modeling, confrontation, and support to give clients a sense of belonging and to assist them in examining and taking responsibility for their behavior. Specialized therapy groups may be offered for specific populations of substance abusers (such as women or young people) or to provide special types of therapy (such as psychodrama or feelings groups). Group treatment also can focus on teaching clients particular skills, such as how to prevent a relapse or assertiveness, or they can be activity oriented, such as a recreation group. Although some specific forms of group therapy for substance abuse (for example, coping-skills or interpersonal groups) have been associated with positive treatment outcomes (Cooney, Kadden, Litt, & Getter, 1991; Galanter et al., 1991), much of the research that has examined the effectiveness of group therapy does not support the position that group therapy is the treatment of choice for substance abuse. For example, several studies comparing group treatment with minimal (nongroup) treatment (Bruun, 1963; Zimberg, 1974), other forms of treatment (Kissin, Platz, & Su, 1970; Miller, Hersen, Eisler, & Hemphill, 1973), and control groups (Pattison, Brissenden, & Wohl, 1967) have found no alcohol-use differences favoring group treatment. One study found client-centered group therapy and psychoanalytic group therapy to be more effective than a learning-principles discussion group and a placebo discussion group (Ends & Page, 1957). Another study found that group subjects achieved their gains faster than subjects who received individual therapy, although the treatment outcomes of the two conditions were similar (Duckert et al., 1992). Much of the research (see for example, Cooney et al., 1991) on the group treatment of substance abusers has compared two types of group treatment without including control groups or nongroup comparison treatments. Unfortunately, methodological problems with many studies have made them difficult to interpret (Miller & Hester, 1986).

Family. Family treatment of substance abuse can take many forms, including couples therapy, multi-ple-family group therapy, single-family therapy, concurrent group and individual therapy with individual family members, and family therapy with a single family member. Although few studies have compared family therapy for addiction with no treatment or with nonfamily methods, the research that is available primarily supports the effectiveness of family approaches (O'Farrell, 1989; Stanton, 1979). It should be noted that these studies have not evaluated the concurrent group and individual therapy approach.

Most family treatments initially focus on making changes that will help the individual stop the substance abuse, with a subsequent emphasis on the stabilization and reorganization of the family (Heath & Stanton, 1991). Many substance abuse clinics offer specialized treatment for family members of alcoholics and drug addicts, regardless of whether the addicted family member is in treatment. Treatment programs have been developed for spouses or other partners of substance abusers (often called codependents), children of alcoholics or substance abusers (COAs or COSAs), and adult children of alcoholics (ACOAs) or others (Markowitz, 1993; Zelvin, 1993). Some treatment programs also offer family intervention, a structured process involving education, role-playing, planning, and confrontation, developed by Vernon Johnson (1986) to assist families in getting substance abusers into treatment (Casolaro & Smith, 1993).

Behavioral. Several types of cognitive and behavioral strategies have been applied to the treatment of substance abuse, including skills training (coping, craving management, refusal, assertiveness), cue exposure, aversive conditioning, self-control training, therapies that focus on changing thoughts, relapse prevention training (Mackay, Donovan, & Marlatt, 1991), and contingency management (NIDA, 1991). Several of these methods may be combined to create a comprehensive treatment package for substance abuse, such as the Community Reinforcement Approach (Sisson & Azrin, 1989) or the Coping Skills Approach (Monti, Abrams, Kadden, & Cooney, 1989).

There is some evidence supporting the efficacy of almost all these behavioral approaches, particularly with alcoholics (Mackay et al., 1991). The exceptions are relapse prevention and cue exposure, which have not yet been effectively evaluated (Mackay et al., 1991), although some research on relapse prevention with cocaine abusers has yielded positive results (Carroll, Rounsaville, & Gawin, 1991). Drinking moderation training is effective for low to moderate alcohol-dependent clients, but is not recommended for severely dependent alcoholics (Hester & Miller, 1989). There is evidence to support the efficacy of contingency management treatment with opiate addicts (NIDA, 1991).

Treatment Matching

One of the most important developments to emerge from studies of substance abuse is the treatment matching model. This model proposes that clients do not respond uniformly to all treatment methods and that positive treatment outcomes will result from matching a client to a treatment setting on the basis of key characteristics, such as the duration and intensity of treatment, goals, methods, and therapists who are best suited to the characteristics of particular clients (Gottheil, McLellan, & Druley, 1981; McLellan & Alterman, 1991). Research has identified the following characteristics of clients as significant in the matching process: demographics (marital status, social stability); the presence, type, and severity of psychiatric problems; personality factors (conceptual level, self-image, locus of control); the severity of the addiction; the antecedents to drinking (anxiety, specific situations) (Institute of Medicine, 1990a); and the severity of legal, family, and employment problems (McLellan, Woody, Luborsky, O'Brien, & Druley, 1983). For example, one study found that cocaine addicts who were more severely addicted before treatment did much better in cognitive-behavioral relapse-prevention treatment than in interpersonal therapy, whereas clients with a mild level of addiction did equally well in both types of therapy (Carroll et al., 1991).

Treatment of Special Populations

With recognition of the unique needs of particular subpopulations of substance abusers, most treatment units offer specialized treatment for at least one special population, most often women, youths, and clients who have tested positive for the human immunodeficiency virus (HIV) or acquired immune deficiency syndrome (AIDS) (NIDA/NIAAA, 1993). Specialized programs or groups are recommended for African American clients, Hispanic clients, Native American clients, women, pregnant women, elderly clients, youths, clients who have tested positive for HIV and AIDS, gay and lesbian clients, clients with multiple problems (mental health problems and substance abuse; physical disability and substance abuse), and homeless people.

Ethnic and racial minorities. Members of ethnic and racial minority groups frequently seen in treatment settings are African Americans, Hispanics, and Native Americans. Members of each of these groups may mistrust formal treatment agencies, particularly if all or most of the staff members are Caucasian. Outreach to key groups and institutions in each ethnic or racial community will facilitate the clients' access to treatment. It is also imperative that staffs be culturally sensitive. Although treatment should focus on substance abuse, not on race or ethnicity, an understanding of the culture and history of an ethnic or racial group is essential, as is the willingness to explore how the experience of oppression and the resulting racial and ethnic pain has affected an individual client (Bell & Evans, 1981). Those of lower socioeconomic status often face additional barriers to recovery, including unemployment, insufficient health care, and unsafe living conditions.

Women. Female substance abusers differ from male substance abusers in several ways that have implications for treatment, including having more frequent serious health consequences of addiction; more psychiatric problems (especially depression); and, with the exception of African American women, a higher likelihood of living with a substance-abusing partner (Blume, 1992; Turnbull, 1989). In addition, the social stigma experienced by substance-abusing women is particularly intense and results in much shame and guilt that will need to be addressed. Many other points should be considered when treating women, including the need for child care so mothers can attend treatment, careful screening for sexual and physical abuse in childhood and adulthood, the effects of alcohol and other drugs during pregnancy, and the impact of sexism (Blume, 1992). There also has been recent interest in developing specialized treatment programs for pregnant women and inpatient and residential programs for women and their children.

Elderly people. Elderly individuals are underrepresented in treatment settings, a fact that is attributed to the lack of detection of substance abuse problems by providers in the aging and medical services systems, the lack of accessible programs, the reluctance of elderly people to seek help, and the attitudes of treatment personnel (Lawson, 1989). Outpatient treatment programs for elderly people are ideally provided in settings that elderly people already frequent, and inpatient treatment programs must be equipped to handle the medical problems that members of this population often experience. Elderly clients have a great deal of grief work to do regarding losses they have experienced and can benefit from reminiscing. Treatment should be supportive and paced more slowly than for younger clients and should allow for individual differences within this population (Lawson, 1989).

Youths. Treatment of adolescent substance abusers should be adapted to incorporate the developmental tasks and level of the particular client; the needs and resources of younger and older adolescents are different from one another, as well as from those of other clients. The history of substance abuse tends to be shorter for youths than for adults. Youths are not as likely to be attracted to long-term treatment goals, and they are more susceptible to the influences of peers (Kaminer, 1991). Studies of programs to prevent substance abuse among adolescents have demonstrated that information alone is not sufficient to change adolescents' behavior and that such programs should also include skill and practice components as part of the intervention (Schinke, Botvin, & Orlandi, 1991). In addition, the need for family involvement is even more important for adolescents than for adults, particularly because adolescents often must rely on parents for transportation and finances.

Gay and lesbian clients. Gay and lesbian clients may go unrecognized in a treatment setting, particularly if questions asked during intake assume that clients are heterosexual. The successful treatment of these two groups requires that treatment staff are not homophobic, are comfortable discussing sexuality and sexual orientation, and are knowledgeable about the process of coming out and the stresses connected with being gay or lesbian in today's society. A major treatment issue for many gay and lesbian clients has been the lack of places for homosexuals to socialize that are not alcohol and drug related (Lewis & Jordan, 1989); gay and lesbian bars traditionally have served as primary locations for socializing. An increased awareness of this problem has resulted in the development of substance-free activities for lesbian and gay people in many communities. Although substance abuse, not the client's sexual orientation, will be the primary focus of treatment, clients may need to work through feelings that are the result of internalized homophobia (Lewis & Jordan, 1989). The treatment of lesbian substance abusers must also address treatment issues that are unique to women.

Clients with HIV or AIDS. Whereas the treatment of all substance abusers should include education on HIV; ways to reduce the risk of HIV infection; and, when indicated, referral for pretest counseling before obtaining an HIV test, the treatment for clients who have been diagnosed as being HIV-positive or as having AIDS must be adapted to address these clients' unique concerns. Knowledge of their positive-HIV status initially may place some individuals at risk of relapse to alcohol and drugs as they begin to question why they should bother to abstain from using substances (Schleifer, Delaney, Tross, & Keller, 1991). Substance abuse treatment units that serve clients with AIDS face more complicated medical problems than they have in the past. Treatment of clients who are both HIV-positive and who have AIDS must also address issues related to death and dying, anxiety, depression, and suicidal ideation (Schleifer et al., 1991).

Clients with multiple disabilities. Substance abusers with an additional disability are a diverse group, encompassing every possible type of developmental, physical, and psychiatric disability. Treatment must be adapted to the specific aspects of each client's condition in addition to addressing the substance abuse. The subpopulation that has received the most attention to date has been mentally ill chemical abusers, also known as clients with dual diagnoses (coexisting psychiatric and substance abuse disorders). The accurate diagnosis and assessment of clients with dual diagnoses ideally require that clients are alcohol and drug free for a sustained period; some clinicians recommend at least a month, and others recommend up to six months or more (Evans & Sullivan, 1990). The treatment of clients with dual diagnoses relies on incorporation and modification of treatment methods from both mental health and substance abuse practice and may be provided in one program or through the clients' concurrent enrollment in a mental health and a substance abuse program (Cohen & Levy, 1992), although the latter option requires that treatment in the two programs be coordinated and that at least one program takes responsibility for addressing how the two disorders interrelate.

Homeless people. Although homeless substance abusers make up only a small proportion of the population with alcohol and drug problems, it has been estimated that 35 percent to 40 percent of all homeless people have a serious alcohol problem, 10 percent to 20 percent have a serious drug problem, and 10 percent to 20 percent have substance abuse and psychiatric problems (Joseph, 1992). Given their circumstances, homeless clients have difficulty complying with scheduled appointments and committing to long-term treatment. However, concern about AIDS has resulted in the development of innovative outreach, educational, and treatment programs in jails and homeless shelters and on city streets; examples of these promising programs include needle exchanges, short-stay residential methadone programs, and therapeutic communities in homeless shelters (Joseph, 1992).

SOCIAL WORKERS' FUTURE CONTRIBUTIONS TO PRACTICE

Although the percentage of social workers who provide services in substance abuse agencies is still relatively small, it has been slowly increasing. In 1991 social workers constituted 8.5 percent of the direct care staff of alcohol and drug treatment agencies (NIDA/NIAAA, 1993), compared with the 1982 figure of 6.9 percent (NIAAA, 1983). In the future, substance abuse treatment will emphasize the development of a broader range of programs and services to meet the range of clients' needs with a concurrent emphasis on matching clients to treatment and the evaluation of treatment outcomes (Institute of Medicine, 1990a, 1990b). In light of these trends, social work has the potential to emerge as a key profession by responding to changes in the substance abuse field both in direct practice and in practice research. The emphasis in social work education on generalist practice skills, assessment of the person in the context of the environment, the individualization of intervention, and practice and program evaluation skills provides social workers with many of the necessary skills to make an important contribution to the substance abuse field. Although social work education has not included enough specialized content on the abuse of alcohol and other drugs (Van Wormer, 1987), some efforts to integrate information on alcohol and drug abuse throughout the social work curriculum are under way, as are efforts to increase social work faculty members' interest in substance abuse (Corrigan & Kola, 1993). These changes, it is hoped, will result in more interest by students in field placements, courses, concentrations, and jobs related to substance abuse and thereby increase the presence of social workers in and contributions to this important field of practice.

REFERENCES

Alcoholics Anonymous. (1952). *Twelve steps and twelve traditions.* New York: Alcoholics Anonymous World Services.

American Psychiatric Association. (1994). *Diagnostic and statistical manual of mental disorders* (4th ed.). Washington, DC: Author.

Anderson, S. C., & Wiemer, L. E. (1992). Administrators' beliefs about the relative competence of recovering and nonrecovering chemical dependency counselors. *Families in Society, 73*(10), 596–603.

Annis, H. M. (1986). A relapse prevention model for treatment of alcoholics. In W. R. Miller & N. Heather (Eds.), *Treating addictive behaviors* (pp. 407–433). New York: Plenum Press.

Annis, H. M. (1993). *The Inventory of Drug-Taking Situations.* Unpublished assessment instrument, Addiction Research Foundation, Toronto, Canada.

Bell, P., & Evans, J. (1981). *Counseling the black client: Alcohol use and abuse in black America.* Center City, MN: Hazelden.

Blume, S. B. (1992). Alcohol and other drug problems in women. In J. H. Lowinson, P. Ruiz, R. Milliman, & J. G. Langrod (Eds.), *Substance abuse: A comprehensive textbook* (2nd ed., pp. 794–807). Baltimore: Williams & Wilkins.

Bruun, K. (1963). Outcome of different types of treatment of alcoholics. *Quarterly Journal of Studies on Alcohol, 24,* 280–288.

Carroll, K. M., Rounsaville, B. J., & Gawin, F. J. (1991). A comparative trial of psychotherapies for ambulatory cocaine abusers: Relapse prevention and interpersonal psychotherapy. *American Journal of Drug and Alcohol Abuse, 17,* 221–247.

Cartwright, A. (1987). Group work with substance abusers: Basic issues and future research. *British Journal of Addiction, 82,* 951–953.

Casolaro, V., & Smith, R. J. (1993). The process of intervention: Getting alcohol and drug abusers into treatment. In S.L.A. Straussner (Ed.), *Clinical work with substance-abusing clients* (pp. 105–118). New York: Guilford Press.

Chiauzzi, E. J. & Liljegren, S. (1993). Taboo topics in addiction treatment. *Journal of Substance Abuse Treatment, 10,* 303–306.

Christopher, J. (1992). *SOS sobriety.* Buffalo, NY: Prometheus Books.

Cohen, J., & Levy, S. J. (1992). *The mentally ill chemical abuser: Whose client?* New York: Lexington Books.

Cooney, N. L., Kadden, R. M., Litt, M. D., & Getter, H. (1991). Matching alcoholics to coping skills or interactional therapies: Two-year follow-up results. *Journal of Consulting and Clinical Psychology, 59,* 598–601.

Corrigan, E., & Kola, L. A. (1993, March 1). *Alcohol and other drug abuse in the curriculum: Faculty can make the difference.* Paper presented at the Annual Program Meeting of the Council on Social Work Education, New York.

Creager, C. (1991). The treatment field meets the managed care challenge. *Professional Counselor, 5*(5), 42–49, 55.

Duckert, E., Amundsen, A., & Johnsen, J. (1992). What happens to drinking after therapeutic intervention? *British Journal of Addiction, 87,* 1457–1467.

Ends, E. J., & Page, C. W. (1957). A study of three types of group psychotherapy with hospitalized inebriates. *Quarterly Journal of Studies on Alcohol, 18,* 263–277.

Evans, K., & Sullivan, J. M. (1990). *Dual diagnosis: Counseling the mentally ill substance abuser.* New York: Guilford Press.

Friedmen, E. G. (1993). Methadone maintenance in the treatment of addiction. In S.L.A. Straussner (Ed.), *Clinical work with substance-abusing clients* (pp. 135–152). New York: Guilford Press.

Galanter, M., Castaneda, R., & Franco, H. (1991). Group therapy and self-help groups. In R. J. Frances & S. I.

Miller (Eds.), *Clinical textbook of addictive disorders* (pp. 431–451). New York: Guilford Press.

Gorski, T. T. (1989). ACA recovery: How soon is too soon? *Alcoholism & Addiction, 9*(3/4), 25.

Gottheil, E., McLellan, A. T., & Druley, K. A. (Eds.). (1981). *Matching patient needs and treatment methods in alcoholism and drug abuse.* Springfield, IL: Charles C Thomas.

Griffin, R. E. (1991). Assessing the drug-involved client. *Families in Society, 72*(2), 87–94.

Heath, A. W., & Stanton, M. D. (1991). Family therapy. In R. J. Frances & S. I. Miller (Eds.), *Clinical textbook of addictive disorders* (pp. 406-430). New York: Guilford Press.

Heather, N. (1989). Brief intervention strategies. In R. K. Hester & W. R. Miller (Eds.), *Handbook of alcoholism treatment alternatives* (pp. 93–116). New York: Pergamon Press.

Hester, R. K., & Miller, W. R. (1989). Self-control training. In R. K. Hester & W. R. Miller (Eds.), *Handbook of alcoholism treatment alternatives* (pp. 141–149). New York: Pergamon Press.

Horn, J. L., Skinner, H. A., Wanberg, K., & Foster, F. M. (1984). *Alcohol Dependence Scale (ADS).* Toronto: Addiction Research Foundation.

Institute of Medicine. (1990a). *Broadening the base of treatment for alcohol problems.* Washington, DC: National Academy Press.

Institute of Medicine. (1990b). *Treating drug problems* (Vol. 1). Washington, DC: National Academy Press.

Johnson, V. E. (1986). *Intervention.* Minneapolis: Johnson Institute Books.

Joseph, H. (1992). Substance abuse and homelessness within inner cities. In J. H. Lowinson, P. Ruiz, R. Milliman, & J. G. Langrod (Eds.), *Substance abuse: A comprehensive textbook* (2nd ed., pp. 875–889). Baltimore: Williams & Wilkins.

Kaminer, Y. (1991). Adolescent substance abuse. In R. J. Frances & S. I. Miller (Eds.), *Clinical textbook of addictive disorders* (pp. 320–346). New York: Guilford Press.

Katims, J. J., Ng, L. K. Y., & Lowinson, J. H. (1992). Acupuncture and transcutaneous electrical nerve stimulation: Afferent nerve stimulation (ANS) in the treatment of addiction. In J. H. Lowinson, P. Ruiz, R. Milliman, & J. G. Langrod (Eds.), *Substance abuse: A comprehensive textbook* (2nd ed., pp. 574–583). Baltimore: Williams & Wilkins.

Kissin, B., Platz, A., & Su, W. H. (1970). Social and psychological factors in the treatment of chronic alcoholism. *Journal of Psychiatric Research, 8,* 13–27.

Lawson, A. W. (1989). Substance abuse problems of the elderly: Considerations for treatment and prevention. In G. W. Lawson & A. W. Lawson (Eds.), *Alcoholism and substance abuse in special populations* (pp. 95–113). Rockville, MD: Aspen.

Lewis, G. R., & Jordan, S. M. (1989). Treatment of the gay or lesbian alcoholic. In G. W. Lawson & A. W. Lawson (Eds.), *Alcoholism and substance abuse in special populations* (pp. 165–203). Rockville, MD: Aspen.

Mackay, P. W., Donovan, D. M., & Marlatt, G. A. (1991). Cognitive and behavioral approaches to alcohol abuse. In R. J. Frances & S. I. Miller (Eds.), *Clinical textbook of addictive disorders* (pp. 452–481). New York: Guilford Press.

Markowitz, R. (1993). Dynamics and treatment issues with children of drug and alcohol abusers. In S. L. Straussner (Ed.), *Clinical work with substance-abusing clients* (pp. 214–229). New York: Guilford Press.

Mayfield, D., McLeod, G., & Hall, P. (1974). The CAGE questionnaire: Validation of a new alcoholism screening instrument. *American Journal of Psychiatry, 131*(10), 1121–1123.

McCrady, B. S., & Irvine, S. (1989). Self-help groups. In R. K. Hester & W. R. Miller (Eds.), *Handbook of alcoholism treatment alternatives* (pp. 153–169). New York: Pergamon Press.

McLellan, A. T., & Alterman, A. I. (1991). Patient-treatment matching: A conceptual and methodological review with suggestions for future research. In R. W. Pickens, C. G. Leukefeld, & C. R. Schuster (Eds.), *Improving drug abuse treatment* (pp. 114–135) (NIDA Research Monograph 106). Rockville, MD: National Institute on Drug Abuse.

McLellan, A. T., Luborsky, L., & O'Brien, C. P. (1985). Improved diagnostic instrument for substance abuse patients: The Addiction Severity Index. *Journal of Nervous and Mental Disorders, 168,* 26–33.

McLellan, A. T., Woody, G. E., Luborsky, L., O'Brien, C. P., & Druley, K. A. (1983). Increased effectiveness of substance abuse treatment: A prospective study of patient-treatment "matching." *Journal of Nervous Disorder and Mental Disease, 171,* 597–605.

McNichol, R. W., Ewing, J. A., & Faiman, M. D. (1987). *Disulfiram (Antabuse): A unique medical aid to sobriety.* Springfield, IL: Charles C Thomas.

Metzger, L. (1988). *From denial to recovery.* San Francisco: Jossey-Bass.

Milgram, G. G. (1990). Certification of alcoholism/drug counselors. *Psychology of Addictive Behaviors, 4,* 40–42.

Miller, P. M., Hersen, M., Eisler, R. M., & Hemphill, D. P. (1973). Electrical aversion therapy with alcoholics: An analogue study. *Behaviour Research and Therapy, 11,* 491–497.

Miller, W. (1986). Haunted by the Zietgeist: Reflections on contrasting treatment goals and concepts of alcoholism in Europe and the United States. *Annals of the New York Academy of Sciences, 472,* 110–129.

Miller, W. R. (1992, November 6). *Motivational counseling and brief interventions in the addictive behaviors.* Seminar conducted at the Research Institute on Addictions, Buffalo, New York.

Miller, W. R., & Hester, R. K. (1986). The effectiveness of alcoholism treatment: What research reveals. In W. R. Miller & N. Heather (Eds.), *Treating addictive behaviors: Processes of change* (pp. 121–174). New York: Plenum Press.

Miller, W. R., & Rollnick, S. (1991). *Motivational interviewing: Preparing people to change addictive behavior.* New York: Guilford Press.

Molloy, J. P. (1990). *Self-run, self-supported houses for more effective recovery from alcohol and drug addiction* (DHHS Publication No. ADM 90-1678). Washington, DC: U.S. Government Printing Office.

Monti, P. M., Abrams, D. B., Kadden, R. M., & Cooney, N. L. (1989). *Treating alcohol dependence: A coping skills training guide.* New York: Guilford Press.

National Institute on Alcohol Abuse and Alcoholism. (1983). *National drug and alcoholism treatment utiliza-*

tion survey: September 1983 comprehensive report. Rockville, MD: Alcohol, Drug Abuse, and Mental Health Administration.

National Institute on Drug Abuse. (1991). *Drug abuse and drug abuse research.* (DHHS Publication No. ADM 91-1704). Washington, DC: U.S. Government Printing Office.

National Institute on Drug Abuse and National Institute on Alcohol Abuse and Alcoholism. (1993). *National drug and alcoholism treatment unit survey: 1991 main findings report* (DHHS Publication No. ADM 93-2007). Washington, DC: U.S. Government Printing Office.

O'Farrell, T. (1989). Marital and family therapy in alcoholism treatment. *Journal of Substance Abuse Treatment, 6*(1), 23–29.

Pattison, E. M., Brissenden, A., & Wohl, T. (1967). Assessing specific effects of inpatient group therapy. *International Journal of Group Psychotherapy, 17,* 283–297.

Prochaska, J. O., DiClemente, C. C., & Norcross, J. C. (1992). In search of how people change: Applications to addictive behaviors. *American Psychologist, 47,* 1102–1114.

Rounsaville, B. J., & Carroll, K. M. (1992). Individual psychotherapy for drug abusers. In J. H. Lowinson, P. Ruiz, R. Milliman, & J. G. Langrod (Eds.), *Substance abuse: A comprehensive textbook* (2nd ed., pp. 496–507). Baltimore: Williams & Wilkins.

Schinke, S. P., Botvin, G. J., & Orlandi, M. A. (1991). *Substance abuse in children and adolescents: Evaluation and intervention.* Newbury Park, CA: Sage Publications.

Schleifer, S. J., Delaney, B. R., Tross, S., & Keller, S. E. (1991). AIDS and addictions. In R. J. Frances & S. I. Miller (Eds.), *Clinical textbook of addictive disorders* (pp. 299–319). New York: Guilford Press.

Selzer, M. L. (1971). The Michigan Alcoholism Screening Test: The quest for a new diagnostic instrument. *American Journal of Psychiatry, 127*(12), 1653–1658.

Sisson, R. W., & Azrin, N. H. (1989). The community reinforcement approach. In R. K. Hester & W. R. Miller (Eds.), *Handbook of alcoholism treatment alternatives* (pp. 242–258). New York: Pergamon Press.

Skinner, H. A. (1982). The Drug Abuse Screening Test. *Addictive Behaviors, 7,* 363–371.

Stanton, M. D. (1979). Family treatment approaches to drug abuse problems: A review. *Family Process, 18,* 251–280.

Straussner, S. L. (1993). Assessment and treatment of clients with alcohol and other drug problems: An overview. In S. L. Straussner (Ed.), *Clinical work with substance-abusing clients* (pp. 3–30). New York: Guilford Press.

Sullivan, W. P., Wolk, J. L., & Hartmann, D. J. (1992). Case management in alcohol and drug treatment: Improving client outcomes. *Families in Society, 73*(4), 195–204.

Turnbull, J. (1989). Treatment issues for alcoholic women. *Social Casework, 70*(6), 364–369.

Van Wormer, K. (1987). Training social work students for practice with substance abusers: An ecological approach. *Journal of Social Work Education, 23*(2), 47–56.

Volpicelli, J. R., Alterman, A. I., Hayashida, M., & O'Brien, C. P. (1992). Naltrexone in the treatment of alcohol dependence. *Archives of General Psychiatry, 49,* 876–880.

Willenbring, M. L., Ridgely, M. S., Stinchfield, R., & Rose, M. (1991). *Application of case management in alcohol and drug dependence: Matching techniques and populations* (DHHS Publication No. ADM 91-1766). Washington, DC: U.S. Government Printing Office.

Zelvin, E. (1993). Treating the partners of substance abusers. In S. L. Straussner (Ed.), *Clinical work with substance-abusing clients* (pp. 196–213). New York: Guilford Press.

Zimberg, S. (1974). Evaluation of alcoholism treatment in Harlem. *Quarterly Journal of Studies on Alcohol, 35,* 550–557.

FURTHER READING

Allen, J. P. (1991). The interrelationship of alcoholism assessment and treatment. *Alcohol Health & Research World, 15*(3), 178–185.

Brown, S. (1985). *Treating the alcoholic: A developmental model of recovery.* New York: John Wiley & Sons.

Brown, S. (1988). *Treating adult children of alcoholics: A developmental perspective.* New York: John Wiley & Sons.

Correa, E. I., & Sutker, P. B. (1986). Assessment of alcohol and drug behaviors. In A. R. Ciminmero, K. S. Calhoun, & H. E. Adams (Eds.), *Handbook of behavioral assessment* (2nd ed., pp. 446–487). New York: John Wiley & Sons.

Daley, D. C. (1989). *Relapse prevention: Treatment alternatives and counseling aids.* Blue Ridge Summit, PA: TAB Books.

Daley, D. C., & Raskin, M. S. (Eds.). (1991). *Treating the chemically dependent and their families.* Newbury Park, CA: Sage Publications.

Freeman, E. M. (1985). *Social work practice with clients who have substance abuse problems.* Springfield, IL: Charles C Thomas.

Freeman, E. M. (1992). *The addiction process: Effective social work approaches.* New York: Longman.

Jesse, R. C. (1989). *Children in recovery: Healing the parent-child relationship in addictive families.* New York: W. W. Norton.

Kurtz, E. (1979). *Not-God: A history of Alcoholics Anonymous.* Center City, MN: Hazelden.

McNeece, C. A., & DiNitto, D. M. (1994). *Chemical dependency: A systems approach.* Englewood Cliffs, NJ: Prentice Hall.

Rogers, R. L., & McMillan, C. S. (1989). *The healing bond: Treating addictions in groups.* New York: W. W. Norton.

Treadway, D. C. (1989). *Before it's too late: Working with substance abusers in the family.* New York: W. W. Norton.

Wallace, B. C. (1991). *Crack cocaine: A practical treatment approach for the chemically dependent.* New York: Brunner/Mazel.

Nancy J. Smyth, PhD, CSW, CAC, is assistant professor, the University at Buffalo, State University of New York, School of Social Work, 359 Baldy Hall, Buffalo, NY 14260, and an associate research scientist, the Research Institute on Addictions, Buffalo.

For further information see

Adolescents: Direct Practice; Alcohol Abuse; Cognitive Treatment; Crisis Intervention; Direct Practice Overview;

Drug Abuse; Employee Assistance Programs; Families: Direct Practice; Family Therapy; Goal Setting and Intervention Planning; Homelessness; Interviewing; Managed Care; Maternal and Child Health; Occupational Social Work; Primary Prevention Overview; Research Overview; Self-Help Groups; Social Work Practice: Theoretical Base; Substance Abuse: Federal, State, and Local Policies; Substance Abuse: Legal Issues.

Key Words

alcoholism

direct practice

drug abuse

substance abuse

Substance Abuse: Federal, State, and Local Policies
David N. Saunders

Substance abuse policies in the United States consist of laws and programs that control, inform, and treat people who use or misuse alcohol and other drugs. Legal and illegal drugs are approached in different ways. Illegal drugs, primarily marijuana, heroin, cocaine, and crack cocaine, are rigidly controlled. The industry that sells them is violent. Fewer people use these drugs than use legal drugs. Any use of illegal drugs is considered wrong, and drug users are viewed as deviants. Drug laws are enforced by criminal justice agencies with severe penalties. The major goals of the policy on the use of illegal drugs are deterrence and punishment. Treatment is not considered a primary goal of policy for abusers.

In contrast, legal drugs—alcohol, prescription medications, and tobacco—are loosely regulated. The industry that sells them is peaceful. More people use them than use illegal drugs. The use of legal drugs is viewed as normal, and the abuser is seen as having a disease. Administrative, rather than criminal, agencies handle the enforcement of regulations and impose mild penalties for violating these regulations. Treatment is a policy goal for abusers.

FOUNDATIONS OF PUBLIC DRUG POLICIES

Public policies in a democratic society are guided by simple yet powerful ideas that serve as ideological centers of gravity. In libertarian ideas, drug use is a private decision outside the realm of government action. In medical ideas, drug use is a medical problem arising from a search for the relief of illness or pain. In criminal ideas, drug use is a moral issue resulting from a lack of self-control (Institute of Medicine, 1990). Criminal ideas have been the foundation of drug-control policies since the 1920s and have reflected the social tensions and conflicts that exist between dominant and socially rejected groups in the United States.

National drug policies are often separated into efforts to reduce the supply of drugs, which stress law enforcement, and efforts to reduce the demand for drugs, which emphasize prevention and treatment. Current federal antidrug strategies contain a mix of supply-and-demand elements with a strong disagreement over which approach should be primary. Policies shifted sharply toward supply-side approaches in the early 1980s with the introduction of a national drug-control strategy called the War on Drugs. War is a poor metaphor for social policy because it conjures up violent images and negative consequences. Federal spending for the War on Drugs has remained at about 70 percent for supply-side programs and 30 percent for demand-side programs, although President Clinton's drug-control budget for fiscal year 1995 requested 63 percent for supply-side programs and 37 percent for demand-side programs (White House, 1994a).

CONTROLLING ILLEGAL DRUGS

Statutes or laws that define "controlled" drugs and prohibit their possession, use, manufacture, and distribution are the foundation of antidrug policies. The Comprehensive Drug Abuse Prevention and Control Act of 1970 (P.L. 91-513) separated drugs into five classes according to the potential for abusing them, their effects, and their medical usefulness. Alcohol and tobacco, although regulated, are not considered drugs under the act and may be sold legally (Abadinsky, 1989; U.S. Bureau of Justice Statistics, 1992).

Legislative bodies have also passed laws related to drug paraphernalia, money laundering, organized crime, the sale of drugs to minors, and the sale of drugs on school property. Because of the severity of penalties for drug-related offenses and the rigidity of the sentencing system, drug offenders tend to move further along the continuum in the criminal justice system that begins with arrest and prosecution and ends with conviction and incarceration than do nondrug offenders.

The criminal justice system has a pervasive influence on the lives of African Americans residing in inner-city neighborhoods. Although African

Americans represent only 12 percent of the population, they account for 41 percent of the arrests and 33 percent of the convictions for the possession of drugs (Falco, 1992). They are arrested and jailed four times as often as are white Americans in drug cases even though drug use patterns are similar. This situation causes some to argue that the War on Drugs is a war against African Americans (Mosher & Yanagisako, 1991).

Drug-related law enforcement can be subdivided into source-country programs, interdiction, high-level enforcement, and street-level enforcement. Federal agencies are solely responsible for source-country programs and interdiction and share responsibility for high-level enforcement with state and local agencies. Federal agencies have little direct involvement in street-level enforcement, which is the responsibility of local and state law agencies.

Legalizing Controlled Drugs

The failure of the War on Drugs to reduce the availability of controlled drugs, drug-related violence, and the number of hard-core drug abusers has led to calls for legalizing or decriminalizing controlled drugs. Decriminalization is a weak form of prohibition, with moderate-to-severe penalties for selling and minimal penalties for using drugs. Advocates of legalization assert that the current War on Drugs is not winnable and point to the failure to reduce the supply of drugs. They compare current antidrug efforts with efforts to prohibit alcohol during Prohibition and argue that current antidrug policies and programs have spawned a criminally controlled manufacturing and distribution system, strained the criminal justice system, promoted widespread violence, and encouraged disrespect for the law. Advocates argue that legalization would reduce drug-related crime, remove drug offenders from prisons, and free funds now spent on enforcement activities. However, there has been limited support for legalizing drugs. Legalization represents one end of a continuum that stretches from unrestricted access to complete prohibition. A middle ground would retain laws against the sale and use of psychoactive drugs, but shift the emphasis toward public health approaches that reduce harm through prevention, education, and treatment (Falco, 1992).

CONTROLLING THE USE OF ALCOHOL

Efforts to control the use of alcohol are supported by research that has found that alcohol is associated with a wide variety of social, economic, and health problems. These problems occur in many places in this society, ranging from families and workplaces to schools and highways. The consequences are borne not only by misusers but by the entire society (Jurkovich et al., 1993; Moskowitz, 1989).

Until the 19th century, heavy alcohol consumption was regarded as good and healthy. Alcoholic beverages were universally consumed, drunkenness was common, and intoxication was viewed as a harmless consequence of drinking. Beginning in the 1830s, there emerged a temperance view in which alcoholic beverages were seen as the cause of personal and social problems. Alcohol became a scapegoat for the social ills caused by broad economic and social changes that swept the United States during the 19th and early 20th centuries (Levine, 1984).

Advocates of alcohol-control policies see problems resulting from the nature of the beverage, especially the ways in which alcoholic beverages are advertised, promoted, and sold (Buchanan, no date; Jacobson, Atkins, & Hackler, 1983). Advocates want to curtail the consumption of alcohol among heavy users; limit the use of alcohol in risky situations; and reduce the use of alcohol among vulnerable groups, such as youths, pregnant women, and disadvantaged people. Opponents of alcohol-control policies consider the problem to be the irresponsible user of alcohol, and they ignore the role of promotion and advertising. They would like the use of alcoholic beverages to become a normal part of most social activities and support efforts to treat those who are addicted to alcohol, restrict inappropriate alcohol-related behaviors, and deny underage youths access to alcoholic beverages (Strickland, 1992).

Sale of Alcoholic Beverages

All levels of government are responsible for controlling the use of alcohol. The responsibility for regulating the sale and distribution of alcohol products was delegated to the states when Prohibition was repealed in 1933, but the federal government retained responsibility for content, labeling, and manufacturing. Although state governments are the primary mechanism for formulating policies that control alcohol problems, local governments have become more active in efforts to control the availability of alcoholic beverages (Gruenewald, Madden, & James, 1992).

Access controls. The availability of outlets that sell alcoholic beverages influences both the rate of alcohol consumption and the presence of alcohol-related problems. Because the number of retail alcohol outlets in states varies widely, policies that determine the structure and operation of the retail sales system are important. Critical retail distribution policies include the type of distribution system adopted, the types of alcoholic beverages that retail outlets may sell, the number and density of retail outlets that sell alcoholic beverages, the hours and days of operation, the people who are permitted to purchase alcohol, and the extent to which alcoholic beverages may be purchased for off-site consumption.

There have been few organized efforts to use alcohol-control policies to restrict sales. A major public health effort to limit access was the passage of minimum legal drinking age legislation. The 1984 act to amend the Surface Transportation Assistance Act of 1982 (P.L. 98-363) required states to raise the minimum legal drinking age to 21 to qualify for federal highway transportation funds. Communities historically limited access to alcoholic beverages by prohibiting all sales. Local prohibitions were popular at the beginning of the 20th century when almost one-third of all communities were "dry." Today, many communities use zoning powers to limit the number of locations in which alcohol can be sold or consumed.

Price controls. Another approach to reducing alcohol-related problems is to raise the price of alcoholic beverages, which discourages consumption, particularly among youths. Excise or sales taxes not only increase the price of alcoholic beverages, but raise revenue. Federal excise taxes on alcohol products are comparatively small, only four and five cents per serving of wine and beer and 12 cents per serving of liquor, representing an indirect subsidy for beer and wine sales. These taxes have been raised only once since 1951 and have had a declining impact on sales. In addition, some states and localities levy sales taxes on alcoholic beverages to support prevention and treatment services.

Another pricing policy is to ban the practice in bars and restaurants of reducing purchase prices at special times. These policies, called "happy hours," encourage the consumption of alcohol by people who are likely to misuse alcohol or to drive drunk.

Promotion of Alcoholic Beverages

The beverage industry actively promotes its products at the point of purchase, in the community, on billboards, and in the print and broadcast media. Public health advocates charge that advertising often targets vulnerable groups, glamorizes drinking, encourages the heavy consumption of alcohol, and minimizes the negative consequences of heavy consumption, especially among youths. Public health advocates have initiated several

projects to change the way alcoholic beverages are portrayed on television and in the movies.

The beverage industry also sponsors a wide variety of recreational and sporting events and distributes promotional materials. College campuses are a frequent target because college students are prone to heavy alcohol consumption. Promotions create the impression that the use of alcohol is a normal part of everyday social life. Successive U.S. surgeons general have called for the elimination of the advertising and promotion of alcoholic beverages on college campuses.

Federal controls. Federal efforts to control the advertising of alcoholic beverages are handicapped by fragmentation and blurred jurisdictional boundaries between federal agencies, such as the Bureau of Alcohol, Tobacco, and Firearms; the Food and Drug Administration; and the Federal Trade Commission (FTC) (Wilford & Morgan, 1992). Several federal efforts have influenced the promotion of alcohol products. First, the Alcoholic Beverage Labeling Act of 1988 (P.L. 100-690) requires that alcoholic beverage containers carry warning labels patterned after those on tobacco products. These warnings focus on such behaviors as using alcohol when operating motor vehicles and mixing alcohol with other drugs. A second set of federal legislative initiatives seeks to extend the product-warning labels to broadcast and print advertisements and promotional displays. Finally, public-interest groups have filed petitions requesting that the FTC expand its activities with respect to advertising of alcoholic beverages.

State and local initiatives. State and local alcohol-control initiatives address the accuracy of advertisements, advertising in public places, advertising that appeals to youths, campus promotions, advertising that discourages alcohol consumption, health-warning posters, outdoor advertising, promotional practices, and television and radio advertising. For example, some local communities have banned billboard advertising; others have limited the placement of advertisements. States have also limited such advertising near schools, residential neighborhoods, and other places where children congregate. Some cities have extended the billboard approach to public spaces and ban or restrict alcohol advertising on all forms of public transportation. Some cities and states require that posters describing the dangers of drinking be displayed where alcoholic beverages are served or sold (Wilford & Morgan, 1992).

A common feature of many state and local alcohol-control initiatives is their grassroots nature. Local groups, composed of representatives of health, professional, religious, civic, law enforcement, and anti-drunk-driving groups, have become a potent force in efforts to change the way alcoholic beverages are labeled, promoted, and advertised.

Alcohol-Impaired Behaviors

Some people who are under the influence of alcohol misbehave in public settings. Although the behavior may not be intentional, actions taken while under the influence of alcohol often have serious consequences for the users and for others who are near them. A common form of alcohol-related misbehavior is drunk driving. Alcohol-related motor vehicle fatalities are the leading cause of death for all people ages one to 34 (Randall, 1992).

Driving. The leading federal agency on drunk driving issues is the National Highway Traffic Safety Administration. Historically, states passed harsh driving-while-intoxicated laws, but were reluctant to enforce them because drunk driving was relatively commonplace and occurred among otherwise typical citizens. Beginning in the 1970s, however, communities across the United States began experimenting with comprehensive efforts to reduce drunk driving. These efforts involved a series of coordinated activities to identify and arrest drunk drivers; adjudicate those who were arrested; educate, treat, and rehabilitate those who were convicted; and educate the public. During the 1980s, most states adopted such programs.

The most effective means of reducing alcohol-related traffic problems are moderate penalties applied in a certain and swift manner. Research has shown that harsh penalties are less likely to be administered (Ross, 1992). The most effective programs for deterring and incapacitating drunk drivers are sanctions like loss of one's driver's license. Police enforcement and rehabilitation programs have more of a deterrent effect if they are linked to public information and education programs that suggest that drunk drivers will be apprehended. Rehabilitation appears to work best when it is linked to other traditional legal penalties and sanctions. Most drunk drivers who are apprehended the first time, and nearly all of those who are apprehended for repeated offenses, have serious alcohol problems. Drunk-driving programs identify persons with incipient alcohol problems and are a major source of referral to mutual support groups like Alcoholics Anonymous.

Public drunkenness. Public drunkenness is another major form of alcohol-related misbehavior. Because public inebriates are often the victims or perpetrators of criminal activities, they have traditionally been handled by the criminal justice system. Chronic public inebriates became part of a revolving-door process of repeated arrests, court hearings, and incarcerations that turned local jails into detoxification centers.

The revolving-door processing of public inebriates, coupled with the emerging view of alcoholism as a disease, led to efforts to decriminalize public drunkenness. The Uniform Alcoholism and Intoxication Treatment Act of 1971 (P.L. 92-80) provided states with a legal framework for dealing with public intoxication, and nearly two-thirds of the states have decriminalized public intoxication. Although decriminalization laws have diverted public inebriates from jails into community detoxification centers, they have failed to keep these persons in treatment (Finn, 1985).

Restrictions and liability. All state and local governments regulate who can possess or consume alcoholic beverages and where they may be consumed. The minimum legal drinking age is a familiar restriction of this type. Efforts are often made to restrict the sale of alcoholic beverages in bars and restaurants. Alcohol-control policies in public facilities range from outright prohibition to restricting the sale of alcoholic beverages before the end of events. Many states also ban the consumption of alcoholic beverages in motor vehicles.

Liability has become a key feature of efforts to influence the way alcoholic beverages are sold and consumed. By the late 1980s, more than 40 states had adopted some form of liability for servers, whether by legislative enactment or court action (Wagenaar & Holder, 1991). The fear of lawsuits and the concern about insurance rates influence servers' decisions about whom to serve. In addition, liability issues influence the decision of businesses and organizations to serve alcoholic beverages at official functions. Liability is also an issue for parties in homes because legislatures and courts have often established private-party liability, particularly if underage youths are involved.

TREATING SUBSTANCE ABUSE PROBLEMS

The War on Drugs has been shaped by the view that drug abuse is primarily a law enforcement problem. In 1994, the national drug-control budget was $12 billion, $8 billion of which was allocated for law enforcement and only $4 billion of which was allocated for prevention and research; the budgetary requests for fiscal year 1995 were $8.2 billion and $4.9 billion, respectively (White House, 1994a). This distribution reflects long-held American attitudes that addiction is a moral weakness, that addicts are throwaway people, and that treatment is a one-shot effort that depends largely on willpower (Falco, 1992). These attitudes run counter to public health views that substance abuse can be treated.

The treatment system in the United States consists of two separate sectors. The public sector includes primarily outpatient programs, often administered by not-for-profit facilities that serve mainly indigent people. The private sector consists of hospital-based and outpatient programs that serve middle- and upper-class individuals who are employed and have private health insurance. The two sectors vary by clientele, origins, services, capacity, and financing (Institute of Medicine, 1990). An unknown portion of the population is served by self-help groups, such as Alcoholics Anonymous.

Prevention services are provided by a variety of organizations, including state and local governments, not-for-profit organizations, schools, businesses, and community groups. The involvement of citizens is key to the success of prevention services, which are delivered by citizens as well as professionals.

Historically, prevention programs have addressed alcohol and other drugs as separate entities. Recently, approaches to treating the misuse of these substances have tended to merge, and tobacco has been added as an abused substance. Whereas early prevention programs focused on education and information, the prevention field now views substance abuse as one of many risk factors, including family violence, criminal activities, school problems, and suicide. However, prevention efforts tend to be underfunded and are often small programs attached to larger organizations.

Federal Efforts

The public alcohol treatment system began in the 1940s and expanded in the late 1960s and early 1970s, when federal initiatives supported community-based substance abuse treatment through grants to localities. However, federal support for substance abuse treatment was cut by 25 percent in 1981, and responsibility for the public treatment system was shifted back to the states (Institute of Medicine, 1990). This decline in federal support for treatment came at the same time as large increases in funding for law enforcement.

Early federal efforts to stimulate community prevention occurred in the 1970s, but the most innovative approach to prevention was the development of the National Prevention Network by

state prevention directors in 1983. The Anti-Drug Abuse Act of 1986 (P.L. 99-570) marked a reawakening of the federal government's interest in the treatment and prevention of substance abuse, but federal oversight of states' plans for spending in this area remained limited (Institute of Medicine, 1990).

The Anti-Drug Abuse Act of 1988 (P.L. 100-690) and an emergency supplemental appropriation for treatment and prevention in 1989 increased funding, required states to spend funds for specific populations, and mandated evaluations of how the block-grant funds were spent (U.S. Bureau of Justice Statistics, 1992). The 1988 act also created the Office of National Drug Control Policy, which was charged with developing a national drug-control strategy and a single drug-control budget. The Office of Treatment Improvement was established in 1990 to distribute basic substance-abuse block grants and to implement new treatment initiatives. Federal funding for substance abuse treatment nearly doubled from 1989 to 1993 and now represents half of all funding in the public sector (White House, 1994a).

Current federal prevention efforts date from the Anti-Drug Abuse Act of 1986. The act established the Office of Substance Abuse Prevention (OSAP) within the Alcohol, Drug Abuse and Mental Health Administration (ADAMHA). OSAP placed special emphasis on youths and families in high-risk environments, and its scope, responsibilities, and mandate were expanded by the Anti-Drug Abuse Act of 1988 and the ADAMHA Reorganization Act (P.L. 102-321) (U.S. Bureau of Justice Statistics, 1992).

In 1992 Congress consolidated existing demonstration, training, and service programs into the new Substance Abuse and Mental Health Services Administration. Separate centers for substance abuse treatment (C-SAT), substance abuse prevention (C-SAP), and mental health services were established, and the three research institutes are now part of the U.S. Public Health Service, National Institutes of Health. C-SAT is dedicated to ensuring that effective treatment and recovery services are available on demand for people with limited financial resources. C-SAP supports prevention at the local, state, and national levels and oversees the National Clearinghouse for Alcohol and Drug Information and the Regional Alcohol and Drug Awareness Resources network. The rationale for this reorganization was to develop and concentrate resources. Discussions about the further restructuring of federal treatment and prevention agencies continue.

Treatment for Selected Populations

Locking up drug offenders may keep them off the streets temporarily, but it does little to keep them off drugs, prevent drug-related crime, or protect the public. Current policies have resulted in the severe overcrowding of prisons and escalating correctional costs (Haaga & Reuter, 1990). The current system creates a vicious cycle in which untreated drug offenders are incarcerated, released, rearrested, and returned to prison.

Diversion programs. Courts are diverting drug offenders who have not been convicted into treatment programs and are sentencing convicted offenders to alternative programs, such as intensive probation, fines, and boot camps. Judges may grant conditional discharges for minor drug possession or distribution charges in return for defendants remaining drug free and attending treatment. Many cities have established special drug courts to divert nonviolent drug offenders into treatment programs and to monitor their progress. These courts have been successful because treatment is available on demand and the threat of sanctions encourages offenders to enter and remain in treatment.

Prison programs. There is increased interest in substance abuse treatment programs in prisons. Such programs complement, rather than substitute for, punitive sanctions. Successful substance abuse programs in prisons segregate participants, use motivated and well-trained staff, continue for a minimum of six months, occur before the release of prisoners, and include strong postrelease components with close supervision of parolees in the community. Well-designed therapeutic community programs in prisons appear to be more successful than are low-intensity outpatient programs.

Low-income people. Substance abuse treatment for medically indigent people is limited. More than 60 million people in the United States lack health insurance coverage for substance abuse or coverage by public programs (Institute of Medicine, 1990). The major sources of funding for substance abuse services for low-income people are the federal substance abuse block grant, state governments, Medicaid, and the Veterans Administration.

Improving Public Services

Strategies for improving public treatment include ending the delay in admissions; improving the quality and intensity of treatment; and expanding treatment services for pregnant women, young mothers, and individuals in the criminal justice system (Institute of Medicine, 1990). These strategies can be achieved, in part, by expanding the substance abuse block grant to states and including substance abuse services as a standard Medicaid benefit. Congress and state legislatures must increase funding for substance abuse treatment in prisons and jails and for other high-risk groups, especially young children. Federal agencies must develop standard guidelines for dealing with substance abuse in federal programs, such as Aid to Families with Dependent Children, Medicare, Medicaid, and Supplemental Security Income. Public treatment programs must develop a system to monitor care on a case-by-case basis. More research on treatment, especially research on treatment outcomes and matching clients to various forms of treatment, is also needed. Services for veterans must be expanded through greater outreach, easier accessibility, and referrals from other public programs.

The Private System

The private sector provides limited substance abuse services for 150 million Americans who have health insurance coverage (Institute of Medicine, 1990). Considerably smaller than its public counterpart, this sector serves approximately 25 percent of all people who receive treatment. Its clients are middle class, employed, and, until recently, were treated mostly in inpatient settings. A higher proportion of people who are employed by state and local governments have insurance coverage for substance abuse treatment than do those who work for private employers, and outlays made by private insurers are relatively small compared with public outlays.

Because businesses believed that private services were too expensive or ineffective, payers and insurers initiated efforts in the 1980s to limit the availability of services. These actions have led to an increase in outpatient treatment, sharp declines in the number of people treated in inpatient or residential settings, shorter stays for those receiving treatment, and a dramatic contraction in the private sector's capacity to provide treatment.

Government policies often work at cross purposes. Many state governments require that health insurance policies cover substance abuse problems, whereas the federal government allows companies to self-insure and thereby bypass these mandates. President Clinton's original health care reform proposal included provisions that would revolutionize the way substance abuse is handled. The initial proposal submitted to Congress would expand access to treatment for nearly 60 million Americans and would set minimum benefit standards that include services for inpatient and residential treatment, intensive nonresidential services, and outpatient services.

PREVENTING SUBSTANCE ABUSE

In the Workplace

Drug and alcohol problems impair worker productivity. Alcohol abuse is the most common problem and affects about 10 percent of the American work force. Another 2 percent to 3 percent of the work force abuses legal and illegal drugs (Institute for Health Policy, 1993; Normand, Salyards, & Mahoney, 1990). Work-related drinking is commonplace and not limited to alcohol abusers (Ames, 1990).

Drug-free programs. Public and private employers have responded by creating drug-free work programs. The components of such programs include clear policies on the use of alcohol and other drugs, employee assistance programs, supervisory training, employee education and wellness programs, drug testing, and referrals to counseling and treatment programs. Many social workers are involved in employee assistance programs and deliver assessment, referral, and short-term services to employees. Since the mid-1980s, most government employers and large businesses have established drug-free workplace programs.

The earliest federal regulation was President Reagan's Executive Order 12564 of 1986, which required federal agencies to develop workplace programs and policies and mandated drug testing for many civilian government employees (Institute of Medicine, 1994). The Drug-Free Workplace Act of 1988 required all federal grant recipients and most federal contractors to certify that they maintained drug-free workplaces (President's Drug Advisory Council, n.d.). The act also required that companies make a good-faith effort to remain drug free. Although the act stressed education and referral, it did not require employers to pay for or assist employees in obtaining services.

Testing. Two federal agencies have developed regulations aimed at nongovernment workers who are involved in the defense and transportation industries. Department of Defense regulations govern all contracts involving classified information, and Department of Transportation regulations require that workers in safety-sensitive positions be tested.

Drug testing in the private sector is used primarily to screen applicants for jobs and to test employees after accidents occur. Industries that affect public safety generally have drug-testing programs. Because drug testing represents a potential intrusion into the privacy of employees and is limited by federal and state constitutions, many states have passed laws regulating drug testing in the workplace, and several limit who

can be tested and when. The 1990 Americans with Disabilities Act prohibits employers from discriminating against people with disabilities, including substance abusers, in employment decisions provided that the job applicants do not currently use drugs.

Communities

In the late 1980s, leaders in large urban areas developed community coalitions to address substance abuse problems. Successful coalitions had small staffs, were volunteer driven, had broad community involvement, and included high-level community leaders and representatives from grassroots organizations. Coalitions assessed problems, reached out to various groups, developed comprehensive plans, and mobilized public opinion through media campaigns (Falco, 1992).

The development of community coalitions has been aided by several federal agencies. The Center for Substance Abuse Prevention funded 250 multiyear community antidrug partnerships. These grants stress the need for grassroots involvement and often target disadvantaged communities and people of color. Unlike other War on Drugs programs, these grants encourage communities to address alcohol use, especially underage drinking. Another goal of these projects is to reduce the use of tobacco.

The National Highway Traffic Safety Administration has supported community traffic safety programs to address transportation safety issues, such as drunk driving. The Department of Housing and Urban Development has supported antidrug projects in public housing communities, ranging from physical improvements to enhanced security.

Schools

"No-use" policies. Schools have developed a variety of approaches to prevent substance abuse. One is antidrug policies that identify prohibited drugs, describe the consequences of violating the policies, and explain the policy for referring students for treatment. The cornerstone of these policies is to abolish the use of any drugs, including alcohol, by students. This approach, initiated during the Reagan administration, focused on illicit drugs and stressed moral exhortations and sanctions to deter use. "No-use" policies have been criticized as intolerant and unrealistic in a culture in which there is pressure to consume alcohol and many youths drink. Critics believe that "responsible use" is a more realistic approach.

The tendency for alcohol use to precede the use of illicit drugs, the physical and emotional immaturity of youths, plus such consequences as drunk driving, support a no-use approach. However, given the level of substance use, particularly alcohol and tobacco, among youths, no-use messages are best viewed as a long-term goal. Better short-term goals are to delay and reduce the extent of use (Falco, 1992).

Antidrug and prevention programs. Antidrug curricula for students are another approach. The current curricula evolved from pre-1970 approaches that were based on scare tactics and moral exhortation. In the 1970s, the focus of programs shifted to personality issues, such as self-esteem. This approach gave way in the 1980s to a view that youths use substances not because of a lack of information or personality problems but because of their vulnerability to social pressure and a desire to model the behavior of peers. Curricula that stress knowledge have a limited effect on drug use by adolescents. As more has been learned about alcohol and drug prevention education for adolescents, school programs have become sensitive to cultural and gender differences among youths and the need to apply a variety of age-appropriate approaches.

Schools support a variety of student safety and prevention clubs, including Students Against Drunk Driving, founded in 1981, and Just Say No Clubs, founded in 1985. Many schools sponsor chaperoned graduation parties to reduce the risk of alcohol-related behavior. Prevention programs in schools seem to work best when students are involved in their development and when they are integrated into broader community efforts that target a variety of groups.

The Drug-Free Schools and Communities Act of 1986 (P.L. 99-570) authorizes grants to state and local educational agencies to develop prevention, early intervention, referral, and educational programs (Falco, 1992). Thirty percent of the funds are reserved for state governors to appropriate for programs for youths who are at risk of using drugs or have been previous users and have at least one high-risk characteristic. The act provides major funding for communication, consultation, and training.

Policy issues. School programs raise several policy issues. One is the right to confidentiality. Two key federal regulations governing confidentiality of information are in conflict. The U.S. Department of Education stipulates that parents must have access to the school records of their children, whereas the regulations of the Alcohol, Drug Abuse and Mental Health Administration restrict access to information on a student's substance abuse problems when the student has been referred for treatment. These two regulations can lead to conflict among parents, treatment agencies, and school authorities.

Other policy issues include whether teachers or specially trained school personnel should be responsible for identifying and referring students, how to separate intensive educational and treatment programs for students with incipient problems, and whether state educational programs are coordinated with those of other agencies. The unequivocal language regarding the possession and use of alcoholic beverages poses particular difficulties for colleges and universities because of the lack of adult supervision in these environments. In recent years, the Drug-Free Schools and Communities Act incorporated a focus on preventing violence, and the name was changed to the Safe and Drug-Free Schools and Communities Act.

SOCIAL WORKERS AND SUBSTANCE ABUSE POLICY

Social workers have a vital interest in public substance abuse policy. To respond appropriately, they must acquire more knowledge about substance abuse policies and programs. They must build alliances with personnel in other agencies that deal with substance abuse, especially in the criminal justice system, to promote more humane policies. Law enforcement and social agencies provide the initial point of contact with abusers and can provide legitimacy for new treatment programs.

Community coalitions and broad citizen involvement show great potential for dealing with drug problems in communities. Communities need assistance in community organization, grassroots organizing, and lobbying, areas in which social workers have knowledge and skills. Social workers must support policies to increase public understanding of the origin of substance abuse problems and the effectiveness of prevention and treatment programs. Therefore, more educational content must be included in the curricula of schools of social work and more continuing education programs must be established for social workers. The tendency to approach the use of alcohol and other drugs as separate problems and to focus on illicit drugs must be resisted. Because tobacco is a gateway drug for youths, is addicting, and has major health consequences, social workers should include tobacco as a drug of abuse.

The reduction of substance abuse problems should not be viewed as a moral crusade. The main priority should be to adopt policies that reduce the harm caused by alcohol and drugs and to eliminate policies that stress punishment to deter use. Such policies should emphasize the promotion and protection of health and the prevention of disease. Advertisements that promote the consumption of alcoholic beverages must refer to the risks of consumption. Governments at all levels should be encouraged to develop coherent and humane policies that view substance abuse programs as public health efforts to protect all citizens, not as wars aimed at particular social or ethnic groups.

Social workers must support efforts to change policies and to educate the public because public attitudes drive policies. In doing so, they must develop alliances with other professional and citizen groups that are concerned with substance abuse policies. NASW's (1994) policy statement on alcohol and other drugs can serve as the foundation for these advocacy efforts.

REFERENCES

Abadinsky, H. (1989). *Drug abuse: An introduction.* Chicago: Nelson-Hall.

ADAMHA Reorganization Act. P.L. 102–321, 106 Stat. 323.

Alcoholic Beverage Labeling Act of 1988. P.L. 100-690, 102 Stat. 4518.

Ames, G. M. (1990). The workplace as an enabling environment for alcohol problems. *Anthropology of Work Review, 11,* 12–16.

Anti-Drug Abuse Act of 1986. P.L. 99-570, 100 Stat. 3207.

Anti-Drug Abuse Act of 1988. P.L. 100-690, 102 Stat. 4181.

Buchanan, D. R., with Lev, J. (n.d.). *Beer and fast cars: How brewers target blue-collar youth through motor sport sponsorship.* Washington, DC: AAA Foundation for Traffic Safety.

Comprehensive Drug Abuse Prevention and Control Act of 1970. P.L. 91-513, 84 Stat. 1236.

Drug-Free Schools and Communities Act of 1986. P.L. 99-570, 100 Stat. 3207.

Falco, M. F. (1992). *The making of a drug-free America: Programs that work.* New York: Times Books.

Finn, P. (1985). Decriminalization of public drunkenness: Response of health system. *Journal of Studies on Alcohol, 46*(1), 7–23.

Gruenewald, P. J., Madden, P., & James, K. (1992, May–June). Alcohol availability and the formal power and resources of state alcohol beverage control agencies. *Alcoholism: Clinical and Experimental Research, 16,* 591–597.

Haaga, J. G., & Reuter, P. (1990, June). *The limits of the czar's ukase: Drug policy at the local level.* Santa Monica, CA: Rand Corporation.

Institute for Health Policy, Brandeis University. (1993). *Substance abuse: The nation's number one health problem.* Princeton, NJ: Robert Wood Johnson Foundation.

Institute of Medicine. (1990). *Treating drug problems* (Vol. 1). Washington, DC: National Academy Press.

Institute of Medicine. (1994). *Under the influence: Drugs and the American work force.* Washington, DC: National Academy Press.

Jacobson, M., Atkins, R., & Hackler, G. (1983). *The booze merchants: The inebriating of America.* Washington, DC: Center for Science in the Public Interest.

Jurkovich, G., Rivara, F., Gurney, J., Fligner, C., Ries, R., Mueller, B., & Copass, M. (1993, July). The effect of acute alcohol intoxication and chronic alcohol abuse on outcome from trauma. *Journal of the American Medical Association, 270*(1), 51–56.

Levine, H. G. (1984). The alcohol problem in America. *British Journal of Addiction, 79,* 109–119.

Mosher, J. F., & Yanagisako, K. (1991). Public health, not social welfare: A public health approach to illegal drug policy. *Journal of Public Health Policy, 12,* 278–323.

Moskowitz, J. M. (1989). The primary prevention of alcohol problems: A critical review of the research literature. *Journal of Studies on Alcohol, 50*(1), 54–87.

National Association of Social Workers. (1994). Alcoholism and other substance abuse-related problems. In *Social work speaks: NASW policy statements* (3rd ed., pp. 35–39). Washington, DC: NASW Press.

Normand, J., Salyards, S. D., & Mahoney, T. S. (1990). An evaluation of pre-employment drug testing. *Journal of Applied Psychology, 75,* 629–639.

President's Drug Advisory Council. (no date). *Drugs don't work in America.* Washington, DC: Executive Office of the President.

Randall, T. (1992). Driving while under the influence of alcohol remains a major cause of traffic violence. *Journal of the American Medical Association, 268.*

Ross, L. R. (1992). *Confronting drunk driving: Social policies for saving lives.* New Haven, CT: Yale University Press.

Strickland, D. E. (1992). Alcohol advertising orientations and influence. *Journal of Advertising, 16*(1), 307–319.

Surface Transportation Assistance Act of 1982. P.L. 98-363, 98 Stat. 435.

U.S. Bureau of Justice Statistics. (1992). *Drugs, crime and justice systems: A national report from the Bureau of Justice Statistics.* Washington, DC: Author.

Wagenaar, A. C., & Holder, H. D. (1991). Effects of alcoholic beverages server liability on traffic crashes injury. *Alcoholism: Clinical and Experimental Research, 15,* 942–947.

White House. (1994a, April). *National drug control strategy: Executive summary.* Washington, DC: Office of National Drug Control Policy.

White House. (1994b, February). *Reclaiming our communities from drugs and violence.* Washington, DC: Office of National Drug Control Policy.

Wilford, B., & Morgan, J. (1992, November). *Alcohol advertising and marketing.* Washington, DC: Georgetown University, Intergovernmental Health Policy Project.

FURTHER READING

Akers, R. L. D. (1992). *Drugs, alcohol and society.* Belmont, CA: Wadsworth.

Cahalan, D. (1991). *An ounce of prevention: Strategies for solving tobacco, alcohol and drug problems.* San Francisco: Jossey-Bass.

Clark, W. B., & Hilton, M. E. (Eds.). (1991). *Alcohol in America: Drinking practices and problems.* Albany: State University of New York Press.

Gerstein, D. R., & Harwood, H. J. (Eds.). (1990). *Treating drug problems: A study of the evolution, effectiveness and financing of public and private drug treatment systems.* Washington, DC: National Academy Press.

Holder, H. (1987). *Control issues in alcohol abuse prevention: Strategies for states and communities* (Suppl. 1). Greenwich, CT: JAI Press.

Kleiman, M.A.R. (1992). *Against excess: Drug policy for results.* New York: Basic Books.

Kraus, B. K., & Lazear, E. P. (1991). *Searching for alternatives: Drug control policy in the United States.* Stanford, CA: Hoover Institution Press.

Moore, M., & Gerstein, D. (Eds.). (1981). *Alcohol and public policy: Beyond the shadow of prohibition.* Washington, DC: National Science Foundation.

Morgan, H. W. (1981). *Drugs in America: A social history.* Syracuse, NY: Syracuse University Press.

Musto, D. F. (1987). *The American disease: Origins of narcotics control.* New York: Oxford University Press.

Ray, O., & Ksir, C. (1990). *Drugs, society and human society.* St. Louis: Times Mirror/Mosby.

Schilit, R., & Gomberg, E. S. (1991). *Drugs and behavior: A sourcebook for the helping professions.* Newbury Park, CA: Sage Publications.

Segel, B. (1988). *Drugs and behavior: Cause affects and treatment.* New York: Gardner Press.

Wright, R., & Watts, T. D. (Eds.). (1989). *Alcohol problems of minority youth in America.* Lewiston, NY: Edwin Mellen Press.

Zimbring, F. E. (1992). *The search for rational drug control.* New York: Cambridge University Press.

David N. Saunders, PhD, is associate professor, School of Social Work, Virginia Commonwealth University, 1001 West Franklin Street, Richmond, VA 23284-2027.

For further information see

Adult Corrections; Alcohol Abuse; Civil Rights; Community; Criminal Behavior Overview; Deinstitutionalization; Drug Abuse; Ethics and Values; Federal Social Legislation from 1961 to 1994; Juvenile Corrections; Policy Analysis; Primary Prevention Overview; Rehabilitation of Criminal Offenders; Research Overview; Self-Help Groups; Social Welfare Policy; Substance Abuse: Legal Issues.

Key Words

alcoholism	prevention
drug addiction	treatment policy
policy	

Substance Abuse: Legal Issues
Anna Celeste Burke

Drug policy in the last decade of the 20th century reflects a resurgence of antidrug sentiment and increased legal action aimed at limiting the availability and use of psychoactive substances. The Anti-Drug Abuse Amendments Act of 1988 counted among its hundreds of provisions a declaration to "create a drug-free America by 1995" (White House, 1989, p. 9). This goal remains elusive and has not always been the primary goal of U.S. drug policy. In the wake of a third wave of prohibition that emerged in the 1980s (Musto, 1987), antidrug efforts have increasingly taken on both the symbols and the substance of war. Like more conventional wars, the War on Drugs has involved a massive mobilization of resources deployed in the name of national security (White House, 1989). By the end of the 1980s, military and police forces had assumed a much larger role in opposing international drug production and trafficking. In addition, tighter restrictions within the United States on the production, distribution, and use of various substances have been accompanied by measures intended to increase the certainty and severity of penalties for violations of the drug law.

As in previous prohibitionist periods in the United States, the most recent battle to restrict the supply of drugs and to reduce the demand for them is bound up with fundamental concerns about the status of civil society, including concerns about the role of government, economic performance, the productivity of workers, public health, individual rights, and the control of crime and violence. As the historical record indicates, U.S. drug policy has been characterized by a longstanding ambivalence toward the use and control of psychoactive substances (Burke, 1992; Musto, 1987). This ambiguity is perhaps most apparent in the changing normative and legal status of alcohol and tobacco, but is also evident in contradictions surrounding other substances. Since the beginning of this century, legislative activity, legal proceedings, and the criminal justice system have played an integral part in the development of drug control policy.

This entry examines the legal aspects of drug use and control in detail, addressing definitional issues, the scope and aim of contemporary antidrug policy, and a number of specific developments that demonstrate how legal measures have been used to reduce the supply of and demand for drugs. It also outlines the development of care as an alternative to law enforcement and the merger of care and control through the use of "constructive coercion" and mandatory treatment (Fagan & Fagan, 1982; Smart, 1974; Soden, 1966) and concludes with a brief consideration of the debate about future U.S. drug policy.

KEY ISSUES

War on What?

The War on Drugs is aimed at controlling the production, distribution, and use of psychoactive substances—substances that induce intoxication, alter mood or thought, and significantly affect the central nervous system or other key bodily functions. The major thrust of the most recent War on Drugs has been to eliminate the availability and use of illicit substances—drugs "whose manufacture, sale, or use is prohibited by law" (Abel, 1984, p. 83). The legal status of "controlled substances" varies according to a schedule maintained by the Drug Enforcement Administration (DEA), which classifies substances from I to V on the basis of their perceived harmfulness, potential for abuse, and accepted medical usage (Abel, 1984). Schedule I substances are the most restricted; they include banned substances and those that are deemed to have no therapeutic value. Antidrug efforts have typically emphasized the control of "street drugs," which include drugs that are produced in illegal laboratories, as well as those that are manufactured legally and diverted for illicit or unauthorized use.

Current antidrug sentiment also extends to the reduction of the use, misuse, and abuse of licit substances. Alcohol and tobacco have come under renewed scrutiny, which emphasizes that both are drugs and can harm those who use them (White House, 1989). Although they retain their legal status, numerous measures have been introduced to limit their availability, restrict access to them, or impose conditions on their use (Wolfson, 1988). Much effort has been made to prevent such misuse of these substances as underage drinking, drinking while driving, or smoking in prohibited areas.

In addition, concern about alcohol, tobacco, and other drugs encompasses opposition to abuse: the "nontherapeutic use of drugs to the point where it affects the health of the individual or impacts adversely on others" (Abel, 1984, p. 53). Specifications of abuse vary but usually include notions of overuse, the loss of control, physical dependence, or psychological dependence, and substance-related problems of one kind or another. The definition, diagnosis, and assessment of drug-related problems remain the focus of much debate, which is based on subjective judgments by both users and caregivers (Lader, Griffith, & Drummond, 1992; Peele, 1989).

Drug Control Strategies

Antidrug strategy encompasses a wide range of intervention options that are usually characterized as efforts to reduce the supply of or demand for drugs. Efforts to reduce the supply of drugs include "overseas crop eradication and associated foreign policy initiatives; interdiction of foreign-manufactured drugs at our national borders" (Falco, 1989, p. 12). They also involve legislation and law enforcement that are devoted to eradicating the domestic production of and halting the traffic in illicit drugs within the United States, as well as monitoring and enforcing restrictions on psychopharmacologic agents and licit substances.

Efforts to reduce the demand for drugs primarily involve "medical or other treatment for current drug users; education about the dangers of drugs and techniques to resist them; and various interdisciplinary, community-based prevention efforts" (Falco, 1989, p. 12). Since the early 1980s, strategies to eliminate or reduce the demand for drugs have also included a greater reliance on law enforcement. These strategies include detection efforts, such as drug testing, and deterrence measures, such as incarceration for drinking while driving or the use of illicit drugs.

Status and Consequences of the U.S. Drug Policy

Expenditures for antidrug activities rose dramatically throughout the 1980s. By the beginning of the 1990s, the federal government allocated more than $10 billion annually for the control of drugs (White House, 1989, 1994). During this period, funds to reduce the supply of drugs outnumbered those spent to reduce the demand for drugs by more than 2:1. Federal authorities aimed to achieve a 70 percent to 30 percent split favoring the reduction of the supply and reflecting intentions to expand resources to enforce the drug law to their "highest levels in history" (White House, 1984, p. 9). After more than a decade of unprecedented activity to reduce the supply of drugs, the availability of illicit substances remains virtually unchanged (Belenko, 1993; White House, 1994), the potency and purity of drugs have increased, and prices in many cases have actually declined (Department of State, 1993).

Increase in expenditures. Overall expenditures for antidrug efforts grew to more than $12 billion in 1993 and will be maintained at similar levels in 1994 and 1995 (White House, 1994). In addition, the Violent Crime Control and Law Enforcement Act of 1994 (P.L. 103-322) included funding provisions intended to strengthen antidrug efforts, such as community policing, prison construction, and prison-based drug treatment. A shift in the balance between supply-reduction and demand-reduction strategies was evident in 1993, however, when 66 percent of the federal funds were allocated for the reduction of the supply and 34 percent for the reduction of the demand for drugs (White House, 1993). Lee Brown, head of the Office of National Drug Control Policy, proposed a further shift to a 60 to 40 split for fiscal years 1994 and 1995 (White House, 1994). In addition to federal funds, state and local governments allocated another $15 billion for 1994 and 1995 for antidrug efforts (White House, 1994).

Increase in arrests and imprisonment. Perhaps the most profound effect of the recent drug policy has been its impact on the criminal justice system. Both legal guidelines and practices of the justice system changed significantly during the 1980s. Since 1980 "both the number of drug arrests and the percentage of all arrestees that are charged with drug offenses have increased substantially" (Belenko, 1993, p.119). The proportion of court cases involving drug-related offenses rose along with the increase in drug-related arrests. The added burden on the courts led to larger caseloads and to longer delays in processing cases and setting court dates. The number and proportion of arrests leading to convictions rose, a larger percentage of convictions resulted in jail or prison sentences, and offenders received longer sentences for drug offenses (Belenko, 1993).

As a result of these trends, jail and prison populations grew dramatically during the 1980s. The United States has the highest per capita incarceration rate among the Western industrialized nations (Mauer, 1991). The number of inmates per 100,000 people grew from 154 in 1981 to 426 at the end of 1989 (Camp & Camp, 1990). By 1988, most federal prisons and many state prisons were at or over capacity. Many of these facilities continue to be overcrowded, despite an "unprecedented wave of prison construction at all levels of jurisdiction" in the 1980s (Belenko, 1993, p.122). From 1988 to 1994, populations in local jails and state and federal prisons increased by more than 70 percent (White House, 1994).

Changes in drug use patterns. Data from the National Household Survey of Drug Abuse and Monitoring the Future studies indicate that after increasing substantially throughout the 1970s, the use of drugs declined in the 1980s (Edwards, Strang, & Jaffe, 1993; Johnston, O'Malley, & Bachman, 1993). This decline has been attributed, in part, to the "Just Say No" campaign and to deterrence-oriented, antidrug measures. The decline in the overall use of drugs has also been attributed to the aging of the baby-boom generation and the "maturing-out" phenomenon, marked by the declining use of both licit and illicit substances as

individuals move into their 30s. Less change has occurred, however, in the small but significant proportion of individuals who are heavy or frequent users and engage in weekly or daily use. Heavy users consume a disproportionate amount of substances, are more likely than are casual users to develop alcohol- or drug-related problems, and are more likely to be involved in criminal activity (Belenko, 1993). Widespread polydrug use, human immunodeficiency virus (HIV), antibiotic-resistant tuberculosis, mental illness, poverty, and homelessness suggest that many people who develop drug or alcohol problems are at a greater risk for harm than were their counterparts in previous years. Concern about care for these individuals has escalated as treatment has taken a backseat to law enforcement (Gerstein & Harwood, 1990) and has contributed to the recent shift in funding priorities.

TRENDS IN SUPPLY-REDUCTION EFFORTS

In the 1980s, efforts to reduce the supply of drugs became the centerpiece of U.S. drug policy. A number of legislative initiatives enlarged the scope and capacity of military and law enforcement agencies to act abroad and at home to control the availability of drugs. During this period, reduction of the supply of drugs became a more integral component of foreign policy, intelligence gathering, and national-security objectives. Perhaps the most vivid images of such supply-reduction activities have been military-style interventions abroad and the interdiction of illicit drugs at U.S. borders. Since the early 1980s, however, both international and national antidrug efforts have increasingly focused on interrupting the flow of money, as well as of drugs. Crop eradication; interdiction; money laundering; and the control of pharmaceutical, alcohol, and tobacco products are all elements of these efforts.

Foreign Policy

During the 1980s, numerous federal agencies and departments, including the departments of Defense, State, Justice, and Treasury, shared responsibility for drug law enforcement activities. In 1989 the National Defense Authorization Act established the Department of Defense as the lead agency for detecting and moderating the aerial and maritime transit of illicit drugs into the United States (MacDonald & Zagaris, 1992). Supply-reduction efforts have also increasingly included attempts to stop the production of drugs at their source through overseas crop-eradication programs; the use of herbicides or manual methods, such as cutting and burning; and often the destruction of processing facilities nearby. The U.S. military has been directly engaged in such operations, but has assumed far greater responsibility for training and assisting foreign military and police forces to eradicate crops and intercept drugs before they leave their countries of origin.

Foreign assistance has also increasingly been linked to U.S. antidrug policy. Title IV of the Anti-Drug Abuse Amendments Act of 1988 amended the 1961 Foreign Assistance Act. This amendment requires certification by the president that countries with a history of involvement in the illicit drug trade demonstrate a commitment to enforcing the antidrug law before foreign aid can be released (Perl, 1992). The U.S. Agency for International Development has promoted eradication and awareness programs, disseminated antidrug information, and funded projects aimed at creating alternative sources of income for farmers who give up the cultivation of illicit substances (Perl, 1992).

Interdiction and the Control of the Domestic Supply of Drugs
Border-patrol and related efforts to interdict drugs entering the United States have been an important part of antidrug efforts since the administration of Richard M. Nixon launched Operation Intercept in 1969 along the U.S.–Mexico border. Funds for this purpose more than doubled, from $263 million in 1981 to $605 million in 1986 (Reuter, Crawford, & Cave, 1988), whereas funds for drug education and treatment were sharply reduced (Falco, 1989). In 1983, President Ronald Reagan created the National Narcotics Border Interdiction System, which expanded coordinated interdiction efforts to encompass "all borders of the United States" (White House, 1984, p. 53). Regional Operations Centers, staffed by personnel from the Coast Guard, Customs Service, Drug Enforcement Administration, the Federal Bureau of Investigation, the Immigration and Naturalization Service, the Marshals Service, military services, and the intelligence community were developed to strengthen such efforts and to intercept drugs as they move to key distribution points within the United States.

In addition, National Guard troops, the military, and police forces from various jurisdictions have conducted numerous domestic operations to search out and destroy illicit crops, such as marijuana, which is grown throughout the United States. The national Domestic Marijuana Eradication and Suppression Program, coordinated by DEA, was established to promote information sharing among various jurisdictions and to provide training, equipment, and investigative and aircraft support to state and local enforcement officers. Such efforts have been hampered by the geographic range in which marijuana grows and by the facts that marijuana is often cultivated in relatively small plots and can easily be hidden among legal crops or natural foliage.

Domestic supply-reduction activities also encompass efforts to prevent the "diversion [of drugs] from legitimate manufacturing and distribution channels, theft, and illegal dispensing by unscrupulous practitioners" (White House, 1984, p. 57). The revolution in psychopharmacology that occurred in the 1950s led to the proliferation of the number and type of drugs with mood-altering or other psychoactive properties. The list of substances controlled by DEA grew and changed as new substances were developed and as the status of substances shifted over time. Some of these substances, the benzodiazepines (such as Valium and Librium), have become the subject of lawsuits in the wake of evidence that they are habit forming and produce withdrawal symptoms even when used in prescribed doses (Lader et al., 1992). Indications that a substantial proportion of substance abuse problems are related to the use of prescription drugs (Adams, 1991; Wilford, 1991) have raised interest in curbing physicians' prescriptive authority and in scrutinizing prescribing practices (Wilford, 1991).

Illegal laboratories produce controlled substances; develop new substances, such as "designer drugs"; and refine existing substances to increase their potency. As a result, restrictions on chemical precursors—chemicals that are deemed essential to the illegal production of drugs—have been introduced. The Chemical Diversion and Trafficking Act of 1988 mandated that the U.S. attorney general "investigate and prosecute manufacturers, shippers, importers, or exporters of illegally diverted shipments" of chemical precursors (Perl, 1992, p. 76).

Disrupting the Financing and Organizing of the Drug Trade
Early in the second Reagan administration, the White House (1984) established "a high priority for pursuing the financial aspects of drug trafficking, including use of criminal and civil forfeiture laws, currency laws, tax laws and international agreements against tax evasion and money laundering" (p. 9). The vast sums of money derived from the illegal drug trade gave drug syndicates and cartels the capacity to corrupt and undermine established governments, and drug money was implicated in the financing of a variety of insurgency and counterinsurgency movements (White

House, 1984, 1989, 1994). The unregulated flow of such large sums of money, which often involved transnational currency transactions, created fears about the negative effects on financial markets (MacDonald & Zagaris, 1992). Moreover, it was clear that the illicit drug trade required the assistance of legitimate banking and business enterprises to "launder" cash accumulated from drug sales and to bring it into the mainstream economy.

Improved reporting. As early as 1970, the Bank Secrecy Act required that banks report cash transactions larger than $10,000. The Money Laundering Control Act, passed as part of the 1986 Anti-Drug Abuse Act (P.L. 99-570), made known participation in money-laundering schemes a federal offense. In 1988, the Money Laundering Prosecution Improvements Act increased the monitoring and regulatory authority of the U.S. Treasury Department and raised penalties for violating provisions of the Bank Secrecy Act. The threshold for the mandatory reporting of cash transactions was lowered to $3,000 in geographic areas that were identified as high-trafficking areas. This act also specified an exception to the Financial Right of Privacy Act, providing access to records from financial institutions when they are believed to reveal violations of the Money Laundering Control Act.

Measures to control money laundering expanded options for Treasury Department officials that had long relied on investigations by the Internal Revenue Service and prosecution for tax evasion to control the illicit drug traffic (Bakalar & Grinspoon, 1984). Early federal laws, such as the Harrison Anti-Narcotics Act (1914), were formulated as revenue measures that were based on taxing powers granted to Congress by the Constitution. These acts, which placed a nominal tax on narcotics transactions, used violations of the tax law as the basis for prosecution of illicit traffic in narcotics. Similar measures were used to enforce violations of the Volstead Act, such as the bootleg production and distribution of alcohol.

Sentencing. Other, more recent, efforts to disrupt the financing and organization of the illegal drug trade have included targeting drug kingpins—individuals who direct, control, or profit from the drug trade even when they are not directly engaged in the handling of such substances. Mandatory sentencing provisions, longer sentences, restrictions on plea bargaining, appeals processes, and parole, as well as efforts to expand the use of capital punishment for drug-related offenses, were introduced in the 1980s to punish dealers and to disrupt their

illicit operations. In addition, undercover buy-and-bust operations and mass arrests of low-level street dealers have been used to disrupt distribution networks (Belenko, 1993).

Search and seizure. Greater reliance on the search, seizure, and forfeiture of assets is also used to counteract gains from trade in illicit drugs. Seizure and forfeiture provisions were included in Racketeering Influenced and Corrupt Organizations statutes (P.L. 91-452). Drug-related forfeiture provisions were also instituted under the Controlled Substances Act. In the early 1980s, model criminal forfeiture laws produced by DEA were quickly adopted by the states (White House, 1984). Under current U.S. law, "assets may be seized prior to conviction if a police officer can obtain a warrant by showing probable cause to believe that a crime has been committed, that certain items will prove to be evidence of a crime, and that those items are located in the specific place specified by the warrant" (Kingma, 1992, p. 53). Search-and-seizure provisions do not always require that a warrant be obtained, however. Searches incident to arrest, searches that have been consented to by a proper party, automobile searches, plain-view seizures, searches of people crossing national borders, investigative stops predicated on reasonable suspicion, and searches of abandoned property can all be conducted without a warrant (Kingma, 1992).

Forfeiture. Property that has been seized can be confiscated under either civil or criminal forfeiture proceedings. Civil forfeiture is less rigorous than is criminal forfeiture, requiring only that the preponderance of evidence indicate that the property in question is associated with criminal activity. Criminal forfeiture requires conviction for a crime. Assets subject to forfeiture have traditionally been those "tainted" by their association with criminal activity, including property directly related to the commission of a crime or to proceeds from a crime. Substitute confiscation provisions now make it possible to confiscate other assets or property from a defendant if forfeitable assets from criminal activity have been "secreted or removed from the criminal jurisdiction, transferred to a third party, substantially diminished in value, or irretrievably commingled with other property" (Kingma, 1992, p. 58). Innocent third parties are protected from the forfeiture of tainted property if they unknowingly accepted as a gift or purchased such property.

These activities to enforce the antidrug law have been criticized because they have often been hampered by competing foreign policy objectives, interagency rivalries, and conflicts between agency and government jurisdictions (Belenko, 1993). Calls for the coordination of drug law enforcement led, in 1973, to the creation of DEA. In the 1980s, renewed concern resulted in the creation of the Office of National Drug Control Policy, headed by a "drug czar" who now occupies a cabinet-level post. Other mechanisms, such as multijurisdictional task forces, have also been widely used to improve drug-control efforts (Belenko, 1993; Perl, 1992). The loosening of search-and-seizure protocols, the freezing of assets before the conduct of legal proceedings, and the diminished burden of proof required for civil forfeiture have generated criticism because of the threats they pose to civil liberties (Belenko, 1993; Boaz, 1990).

Restricting the Supply of Licit Substances
Supply-reduction efforts in the 1980s were aimed not only at reducing access to illicit substances, but at limiting the availability of licit substances. The taxation of alcohol and tobacco products that generates revenue for the government is also used to reduce the supply and limit the consumption of these substances. Amid fiscal constraints and tax revolts, these "sin taxes" have taken on much greater significance. Mounting antidrug sentiment and concern about the impact of alcohol and tobacco use on health care costs have helped encourage the steady increase in such taxes.

At the state and local levels, communities restrict the sale of alcohol and tobacco in a variety of other ways. Stiffer penalties and better enforcement of restrictions on the sale of alcohol and tobacco products to minors have been pursued. Almost all communities place some limits on the hours or days of the week that alcohol can be sold, and some have chosen to be "dry," that is, to prohibit the sale of alcohol products altogether. Some states have exercised control over the supply of alcohol by restricting the sale of alcohol products, especially distilled liquor, to publicly owned and operated "state" stores. State-owned stores generally have fewer distribution points and operating hours than do private establishments. The debate continues about the relative advantages and disadvantages of public versus private sales and the implications for consumption of privatizing alcohol sales (Edwards et al., 1993).

At the state and local levels, increased interest has focused on constraining practices by bar and restaurant owners by limiting the number of liquor licenses issued and restricting the sale of "specials," including two-for-one drinks, low-cost drinks, or discounted drinks that are sold for short periods, such as "happy hours" (Wolfson, 1988). Furthermore, legislation involving third-party liability has placed greater responsibility on those who sell or otherwise supply individuals with alcohol (Wolfson, 1988). These efforts initially focused on "dram shop laws" that extended liability to owners and operators of establishments that sell drinks to patrons who subsequently become involved in driving while intoxicated (DWI) accidents. These measures were intended to discourage proprietors from selling alcohol to individuals who were obviously inebriated and to counter longstanding practices in the industry that were aimed at "pushing" drink sales to improve profitability. Shared liability has since implicated private citizens who supply alcohol to individuals who are involved in DWI accidents after leaving these persons' homes in an inebriated condition.

TRENDS IN DEMAND–REDUCTION EFFORTS

In the 1980s, an antidrug policy oriented toward law enforcement greatly influenced strategies to reduce the demand for drugs. Despite the apparent success of the medical-disease view of alcohol and drug problems, doctrines of zero tolerance and user accountability emerged, representing a resurgence of opposition to drug use on moral grounds. There was renewed enthusiasm for law enforcement initiatives to deter use by increasing the likelihood of detection and punishment. These events led to a dramatic shift of momentum from the decriminalization to the recriminalization of drug use and to drug education and treatment that were heavily influenced by control (Weisner, 1986; Weisner & Room, 1984).

Decriminalization and Publicly Funded Treatment Programs
In the post–World War II period, the medicalization of drug and alcohol problems resulted in the emergence of education and treatment as central demand-reduction efforts. The burgeoning interest in civil rights and court rulings in the 1960s led to the decriminalization of illicit drug use and to the diversion of individuals from the criminal justice system. In *Robinson v. California* (1962), the court ruled that imprisonment for being addicted to an illicit drug was cruel and unusual punishment under the Eighth amendment (Bakalar & Grinspoon, 1984). Although the court asserted that individuals can be imprisoned for actually using illicit substances, it distinguished between a "state of being" and the commission of acts that violate laws governing drug use. A similar logic prevailed in the case of *Powell v. Texas* (1968), in which the court ruled that it was not cruel and unusual pun-

ishment to jail an alcoholic for public intoxication, arguing that drunkenness in a public place is an act apart from a state of addiction to alcohol.

During the 1970s, states adopted the Uniform Alcoholism and Intoxication Treatment Act (National Conference of Commissioners on Uniform State Laws, 1973), which explicitly mandated civil commitment, rather than criminal commitment, for public drunkenness. The 1970 Comprehensive Drug Abuse Prevention and Control Act abolished mandatory minimum sentences for illicit drug use. The federally sponsored Treatment Alternative to Street Crimes, funded under the Drug Abuse Office and Treatment Act of 1972, made treatment available as an alternative to incarceration for illicit drug use. Diversion programs raise a number of concerns because civil proceedings place less emphasis on due process than do criminal proceedings and civil commitment often results in longer periods of confinement and supervision than does criminal commitment (Kittrie, 1971). By the end of the 1970s, however, care was established as an alternative to incarceration, and court-ordered clients entered treatment in large numbers (Weisner & Room, 1984).

Publicly funded, community-based programs greatly expanded in the early 1970s with increased federal financing. Federal legislation established the National Institute of Alcohol and Alcohol Abuse (NIAAA) in 1970 and the National Institute on Drug Abuse (NIDA) in 1973, placing both within the Alcohol, Drug Abuse and Mental Health Administration (ADAMHA). ADAMHA was responsible for research, training, program development, and the administration of federal funds. Controversy ensued about the mission of ADAMHA, NIAAA, and NIDA throughout the 1980s, and increasing attention was focused on their leadership role in research. Passage of the ADAMHA Reorganization Act (P.L. 102-321) in 1992 relocated NIDA and NIAAA within the National Institutes of Health (NIH), placing alcohol and drug abuse alongside health problems such as cancer and diabetes and endorsing biological research and the search for pharmacologic agents to prevent and treat drug abuse. This reorganization also created the Substance Abuse and Mental Health Services Administration (SAMHSA), whose purpose was to oversee services, research, program evaluation, the dissemination of information, and training about effective prevention and treatment strategies.

New Federalism and the Privatization of Care

In the early 1980s, the Reagan administration advocated the consolidation of alcohol and drug

services, and with passage of the 1981 Omnibus Budget Reconciliation Act of 1981 it succeeded in consolidating federal funding by creating the Alcohol, Drug and Mental Health Services block grant. The shift to block grants was accompanied by a 25 percent reduction in federal funding for treatment services (Buck, 1985; Logan, Rochefort, & Cook, 1985). Further reductions followed as federal drug policy established a preference for control over care (Falco, 1989). Although state and local jurisdictions assumed greater fiscal responsibility for such services, the number of publicly funded treatment slots declined during the 1980s (Gerstein & Harwood, 1990). In publicly funded facilities, the number of individuals on waiting lists grew and longer waiting periods ensued (Gerstein & Harwood, 1990). The rise of proprietary care, in combination with cutbacks in public funding for treatment, raised concerns about inequitable care provided in a dual-tier service system (Gerstein & Harwood, 1990).

Privatization and the greater integration of alcohol and drug services into the primary health care system were also aims of the New Federalist drug policy in the 1980s (White House, 1984). Federal alcohol and drug abuse agencies coached states about how to pass legislation mandating that insurance providers offer coverage for drug and alcohol problems and about how to encourage local programs to qualify for third-party reimbursement (NIDA, 1977, 1978, 1979). By the mid-1980s, most states had passed mandatory insurance legislation (Lang, 1986), and more providers began to rely on private insurance and fees from clients. Many of these were new providers, however, in mental health, hospital, and other health care settings, who hoped to fill empty hospital beds and raise revenues (Gerstein & Harwood, 1990). Private providers also benefitted from increases in employer-sponsored Employee Assistance Programs. The restructuring of employment in the United States has since reduced the number of individuals with coverage, and managed care practices, larger copays, restrictions on services to be reimbursed, and annual and lifetime limits on coverage have further reduced private funds, increasing competition for the remaining dollars.

Recriminalization and Deterrence

In the 1980s, the law enforcement approach to the reduction of the demand for drugs encompassed the recriminalization of illicit use; drug tests; mandatory minimum sentences; longer sentences; consecutive, rather than concurrent, sentences; and tougher parole requirements. The federal government urged state and local authorities to recriminalize drug use to demonstrate zero tolerance for such behavior (White House, 1984). Prevention programs promoting abstinence and the accountability of users emphasized that drug use is a personal choice that is negatively sanctioned by the community. Programs, such as Drug Abuse Resistance Education, warn youths about the dangers associated with drug use and get them to "say no to drugs" through "refusal skills training" (White House, 1989).

The Drug-Free Workplace Act of 1988 and the Drug-Free Schools and Communities Act of 1986 oblige employers and school officials to develop antidrug policies, provide drug education, and rid schools and workplaces of drug use. Antidrug measures include random searches of students' lockers and employees' work spaces, automobiles, and so on. Drug testing has been instituted to screen individuals when there is reason to believe that they are engaged in the illicit use of drugs, but has also been used for random or routine screening. Although courts have offered some protection to students and athletes, little opposition has emerged to the random screening of job applicants and employees.

Misuse of Licit Drugs
During the 1980s, measures were also taken to restrict alcohol and tobacco use further and to increase penalties for the misuse of these substances. States initiated numerous modifications to driving while intoxicated laws. The ".08 movement" sought to restrict the use of alcohol by lowering the blood-alcohol levels that constitute DWI to eight parts per 100 (.08), and some states decided to require an even lower blood-alcohol level for underage drivers. Sobriety checkpoints were also introduced during this period to increase the likelihood of detecting individuals who violate DWI laws. Such checkpoints are controversial because they screen drivers randomly and because they are costly but yield a small number of DWI offenders. The legality of checkpoints has been challenged, but the courts have generally upheld the right of states to carry out such activities. Supporters assert that checkpoints have a more general deterrence value and ought not to be evaluated simply on the basis of the number of offenders who are apprehended (Edwards et al., 1993).

Opposition to DWI has also involved the imposition of more severe sanctions against drinking-driver offenders, including mandatory jail terms, longer periods of confinement, revocations of driving privileges, impounding of automobiles,

higher fines, and mandatory community service. Tougher penalties have been aimed at repeat offenders, but have also been obtained for first offenders. In some cases, penalties are waived if offenders attend alcohol education or treatment programs, but participation in treatment may be mandated as an adjunct, rather than an alternative, to other penalties.

During the 1980s, states also took steps to restrict the use of alcohol by raising the legal drinking age. A lower drinking age was linked to drinking-driving accidents, and grassroots groups, such as Mothers Against Drunk Driving, mobilized to advocate that the legal drinking age be raised to 21 (Wolfson, 1988). The National Highway Traffic Safety Administration promoted such legislation, eventually threatening to withhold highway funds from states that maintained a lower drinking age. By the end of the 1980s, states had uniformly adopted 21 as the legal drinking age.

Since the 1960s, television advertisements of cigarettes and distilled spirits have been banned, and since the 1970s, tobacco and alcohol products have been required to carry warning labels alerting users to dangers associated with their use. The tobacco and alcoholic beverage industries continue to incur criticism for marketing practices that target youths or specific ethnic groups, such as African Americans; that trivialize or reinforce violence against women; and that mislead or misinform consumers, sparking interest in further restrictions on advertising (Mosher, 1994).

Despite fluctuations in antidrug sentiment, tobacco growers and distributors of tobacco products historically have enjoyed a number of government subsidies and protections. Tobacco sales helped finance the American Revolution, and many early leaders were involved in tobacco production (Walker, 1989). With evidence of the link between smoking and cancer and more health-related problems, governmental policy has begun to change. A vigorous antismoking campaign, financed, in part, by the federal government, has contributed to the declining use of tobacco in the United States. Tobacco producers have increasingly turned to markets outside the United States, making cigarettes and other tobacco products leading exports. Although subsidies for tobacco have declined, the federal government continues to subsidize export costs and administrative costs associated with a program of price supports for tobacco farmers.

Mobilization against the use of tobacco was spurred in the 1980s by evidence of the negative effects of second-hand smoke. Antismoking initiatives prohibited smoking in public areas and during commercial flights, designated smoking and nonsmoking sections in restaurants or other public facilities, and declared entire buildings as "smoke free." Support for antismoking initiatives has also stemmed from concerns about lost productivity, damage to facilities, and rising health care costs. Incentives to adopt nonsmoking policies have come from insurance carriers, who award discounts to nonsmokers and smoke-free environments.

Criminalization of Care

As antidrug policy came to regard social control and punishment as the means for reducing the demand for drugs, drug-involved offenders flooded the criminal justice system. Court-ordered care has increasingly come to be regarded as being more a part of the criminal justice system than a diversion from it. The impact on treatment programs has been profound; it has led providers of services to accept coercion as a component of care, to increase their monitoring and reporting of clients' behavior, and to refer drug-involved persons for treatment as another form of punishment (Weisner, 1986; Weisner & Room, 1984). National data on outpatient drug treatment units indicate that by the end of the 1980s, many publicly funded programs regarded courts as their most important referral source and that a substantial proportion of clients received treatment involuntarily (Burke & Rafferty, 1994).

The link between care and control is central to current efforts to address the massive growth in the number of drug-involved prisoners. The 1994 Violent Crime Control and Law Enforcement Act included more money for drug treatment and drug testing and called for the use of graduated sanctions and offender-management programs as integral components of the criminal justice system's response to drugs. "Coerced abstinence" is a proposed way to reduce the use of drugs and to reduce the burden on jails and prisons (White House, 1994). Recommendations for the further reliance on mandatory treatment are made, however, without the resolution of issues that have emerged from this blending of care and control, particularly the right of court-ordered clients to refuse certain forms of treatment such as the use of medications like disulfiram (trade name: Antabuse) or naltrexone. Ethical and legal issues also surround the reporting of confidential information by service providers to courts and the use of invasive practices, such as blood and urine tests, to monitor clients' compliance with treatment regimens.

FUTURE OF SUBSTANCE ABUSE POLICY

Indications are that a substantial investment in antidrug activity will continue throughout the 1990s. The ambiguity, conflicting aims, and competing priorities that have characterized policy in this arena are likely to remain and will no doubt shape the future debate about drug policy. This debate will also reflect issues that have arisen from more than a decade of drug policy oriented toward law enforcement and the reduction of the supply of drugs and from the relationship of drug policy to broader issues, such as health care reform and the revitalization of communities.

Proponents of legalization (Boaz, 1990), harm reduction (O'Hare, Newcomcomber, Mathews, Buning, & Drucker, 1992), or treatment on demand argue for a change in the drug policy on the basis of evidence that supply-reduction efforts have failed to limit the availability of illicit drugs. Moreover, they give priority to stopping violence that they assert is fueled, in part, by the criminalization of drug use and other punitive control measures (Belenko, 1993). Decriminalization and treatment on demand are represented as means for unclogging the courts, reducing overcrowding in prisons, and protecting citizens from invasive law enforcement practices (O'Hare et al., 1992). In addition, the continued use of mandatory treatment will inevitably provoke concern about commitment proceedings and the rights of drug-involved individuals. Much of this debate is likely to be carried out in the courts as those who are ordered to receive mandatory treatment test the use of therapeutic control.

Recognition that recovery from substance abuse is a long-term, relapse-prone process raises a number of issues about how to finance and deliver treatment, especially given the serious health problems of many individuals who pursue recovery. Access and cost are central to the debate about drug policy and health care reform and are reflected in discussions about managed care, Medicaid waivers, and specification services to be included in a standard benefit package. Arguments for the reallocation of funds from supply-reduction to demand-reduction efforts are often based on assertions that such a shift represents a more effective use of public dollars. With a broad public health approach to drug and alcohol use, savings are expected to stem from reduced drug use and the prevention of drug-related problems. Decriminalization and diversion are also deemed to be more cost-effective because they encourage early intervention. Critics argue, however, that the efficacy of prevention and treatment programs has yet to be demonstrated (Gerstein & Harwood, 1990) and that more research is needed to judge the value of these programs (White House, 1994).

Continued debate is also likely to surround community interventions that are aimed at reaching beyond conventional law enforcement, prevention, and treatment approaches, including community policing initiatives that involve the greater participation and control of law enforcement by local communities. Controversial proposals to consolidate or eliminate federal policing agencies have also been made as a way to redirect additional funds to local communities. Community partnerships have increasingly been invoked to address issues related to the use and control of drugs (White House, 1994). Such partnerships are intended to enhance leadership, promote coherent prevention efforts, and coordinate antidrug activities. Moreover, interventions that stress the revitalization of communities' social and economic development address the need to offer community members positive alternatives to drugs.

REFERENCES

Abel, E. L. (1984). *A dictionary of drug abuse terms and terminology.* Westport, CT: Greenwood Press.

ADAMHA Reorganization Act. P.L. 102-321, 106 Stat. 323.

Adams, E. H. (1991). Prevalence of prescription drug abuse: Data from the National Institute on Drug Abuse. *New York State Journal of Medicine, 91* (11, Suppl.), 32–36.

Anti-Drug Abuse Act of 1986. P.L. 99-570, 100 Stat. 3207.

Anti-Drug Abuse Amendments Act of 1988. P.L. 100-690, 102 Stat. 4181.

Bakalar, J. B., & Grinspoon, L. (1984). *Drug control in a free society.* Cambridge, England: Cambridge University Press.

Bank Secrecy Act of 1970. P.L. 91-508, 84 Stat. 1114.

Belenko, S. R. (1993). *Crack and the evolution of anti-drug policy.* Westport, CT: Greenwood Press.

Boaz, D. (Ed.). (1990). *The crisis in drug prohibition.* Washington, DC: CATO Institute.

Buck, J. A. (1985). Block grants and federal promotion of community mental health services, 1946–1965. *Community Mental Health Journal, 20,* 236–247.

Burke, A. C. (1992). Between entitlement and control: Dimensions of U.S. drug policy. *Social Service Review, 66,* 571–581.

Burke, A. C., & Rafferty, J. A. (1994). Ownership differences in outpatient substance abuse treatment units. *Administration in Social Work, 18,* 59–93.

Camp, G. M., & Camp, C. G. (1990). *The corrections yearbook—1990.* South Salem, NY: Criminal Justice Institute.

Chemical Diversion and Trafficking Act of 1988. P.L. 100-690, 102 Stat. 4181.

Comprehensive Drug Abuse Prevention and Control Act of 1970. P.L. 91-513, 84 Stat. 1236.

Controlled Substances Act. P.L. 91-513, 84 Stat. 1236.

Department of State. (1993). *International narcotics control strategy report.* Washington, DC: U.S. Government Printing Office.

Drug-Abuse Office and Treatment Act of 1972. P.L. 92-255, 86 Stat. 65.

Drug-Free Schools and Communities Act of 1986. P.L. 99-570, 100 Stat. 3207.

Drug-Free Workplace Act of 1988. P.L. 100-690, 102 Stat. 4181.

Edwards, G., Strang, J., & Jaffe, J. H. (Eds.). (1993). *Drugs, alcohol and tobacco: Making the science and policy connection.* Oxford, England: Oxford University Press.

Fagan, R. W., & Fagan, N. M. (1982). The impact of legal coercion on the treatment of alcoholism. *Journal of Drug Issues, 12,* 103–114.

Falco, M. (1989). *Winning the drug war: A national strategy.* New York: Priority Press.

Financial Right of Privacy Act. P.L. 95-630, 92 Stat. 3641.

Foreign Assistance Act. P.L. 87-195, 75 Stat. 424.

Gerstein, D. R., & Harwood, H. J. (Eds.). (1990). *Treating drug problems: Vol. 1.* Washington, DC: National Academy Press.

Harrison Anti-Narcotics Act. Ch. 1, 38 Stat. 785 (1914).

Johnston, L. D., O'Malley, P. M., & Bachman, J. G. (1993). *National survey results on drug use from the Monitoring the Future Study, 1975–1992* (2 Vols.). Rockville, MD: National Institute on Drug Abuse.

Kingma, E. (1992). The emerging regime of asset forfeiture. In S. B. MacDonald & B. Zagaris (Eds.), *International handbook on drug control* (pp. 45–67). Westport, CT: Greenwood Press.

Kittrie, N. (1971). *The right to be different: Deviance and enforced therapy.* Baltimore: Johns Hopkins University Press.

Lader, M., Griffith, E., & Drummond, D. C. (Eds.). (1992). *The nature of alcohol and drug related problems.* Oxford, England: Oxford University Press.

Lang, A. (1986). State laws mandating private health insurance benefits for mental health, alcoholism and drug abuse. *State health reports on mental health, alcoholism, and drug abuse, Special feature edition.* Washington, DC: Intergovernmental Health Policy Project.

Logan, B. M., Rochefort, D. A., & Cook, E. W. (1985, December). Block grants for mental health: Elements of the state response. *Journal of Public Health Policy, 6*(4), 476–492.

MacDonald, S. B., & Zagaris, B. (Eds.). (1992). *International handbook on drug control.* Westport, CT: Greenwood Press.

Mauer, M. (1991). *Americans behind bars: A comparison of international rates of incarceration.* Washington, DC: The Sentencing Project.

Money Laundering Control Act of 1986. P.L. 99-570, 100 Stat. 3207.

Money Laundering Prosecution Improvements Act of 1988. P.L. 100-690, 102 Stat. 4181.

Mosher, J. F. (1994). Alcohol advertising and public health: An urgent call. *American Journal of Public Health, 84,* 180–181.

Musto, D. F. (1987). *The American disease: origins of narcotic control.* New York: Oxford University Press.

National Conference of Commissioners on Uniform State Laws. (1973). *Uniform Alcoholism and Intoxication Treatment Act.* Washington, DC: U.S. Government Printing Office.

(National) Defense Authorization Act. P.L. 100-456, 102 Stat. 1933.

National Institute on Drug Abuse. (1977). *A manual of third-party reimbursement: Strategy for states and communities* (Services Research Monograph Series, DHEW Publication No. ADM 77-499). Washington, DC: U.S. Government Printing Office.

National Institute on Drug Abuse. (1978). *Utilization of third party payments for the financing of drug abuse treatment* (Services Research Report, DHEW Publication No. ADM 78-440). Rockville, MD: Alcohol, Drug Abuse and Mental Health Administration.

National Institute on Drug Abuse. (1979). *Self-sufficiency through third party reimbursements: A study of six drug treatment programs.* (Report Series 41, No. 1. National Clearinghouse for Drug Abuse Information. DHEW Publication No. ADM 80-817). Rockville, MD: ADAMHA.

O'Hare, P. A., Newcomcomber, R., Mathews, A., Buning, E. C., & Drucker, E. (Eds.). (1992). *The reduction of drug-related harm.* London: Routledge & Kegan Paul.

Omnibus Budget Reconciliation Act of 1981. P.L. 97-35, 95 Stat. 867.

Peele, S. (1989). *The diseasing of America.* Lexington, MA: Lexington Books.

Perl, R. F. (1992). The United States. In S. B. MacDonald & B. Zagaris (Eds.), *International handbook on drug control* (pp. 67–89). Westport, CT: Greenwood Press.

Powell v. Texas, 392 U.S. 514 (1968).

Racketeering Influenced and Corrupt Organizations Act. P.L. 91-452, 84 Stat. 941.

Reuter, P., Crawford, G., & Cave, J. (1988). *Sealing the borders.* Santa Monica, CA: Rand Corp.

Robinson v. California, 370 U.S. 660 (1962).

Smart, R. G. (1974). Employed alcoholics treated voluntarily and under constructive coercion. *Quarterly Journal of Studies on Alcohol, 35,* 196–209.

Soden, E. W. (1966). Constructive coercion and group counseling in the rehabilitation of alcoholics. *Federal Probation, 30,* 56–60.

Violent Crime Control and Law Enforcement Act of 1994. P.L. 103-322, 108 Stat. 1796.

Volstead Act, c. 85, 41 Stat. 305 (1919). Repealed c. 473, 45 Stat. 1446 (1929).

Walker, W. O. (1989). *Drug control in the Americas.* Albuquerque: University of New Mexico Press.

Weisner, C. M. (1986, Spring). The transformation of alcohol treatment: Access to care and the response to drinking-driving. *Journal of Public Health Policy, 7*(1), 78–92.

Weisner, C. M., & Room, R. (1984). Financing and ideology in alcohol treatment. *Social Problems, 32,* 167–184.

Wilford, B. B. (1991). Prescription drug abuse: Some considerations in evaluating policy responses [Special Issue]. *Journal of Psychoactive Drugs, 23*(4), 343–348.

White House. (1984). *National strategy for prevention of drug abuse and drug trafficking.* Washington, DC: Office of National Drug Control Policy.

White House. (1989). *National drug control strategy.* Washington, DC: Office of National Drug Control Policy.

White House. (1993). *Interim national drug control strategy.* Washington, DC: Office of National Drug Control Policy.

White House. (1994). *National drug control strategy: Reclaiming our communities from drugs and violence.* Washington, DC: Office of National Drug Control Policy.

Wolfson, M. (1988). *The consequences of a social movement: An organizational analysis of the impact of the citizens' movement against drunken driving.* Unpublished doctoral dissertation, Catholic University of America.

FURTHER READING

Carpenter, C., Glassner, B., Johnson, B. D., & Loughlin, J. (1988). *Kids, drugs, and crime.* Lexington, MA: Lexington Books.

DeLaRosa, M. R., & Adrados, J.L.R. (Eds.). (1993). *Drug abuse among minority youth: Advances in research and methodology.* NIDA Research Monograph 130. Rockville, MD: National Institute on Drug Abuse.

Hawkins, J. D., & Catalano, R. F., Jr. (1992). *Communities that care.* San Francisco: Jossey-Bass.

Inciardi, J. A. (Ed.). (1990). *Handbook of drug control in the United States.* New York: Greenwood Press.

Leukefeld, C. G., & Tims, F. M. (1988). *Compulsory treatment of drug abuse: Research and clinical practice.* NIDA Research Monograph 86. Rockville, MD: National Institute on Drug Abuse.

MacKenzie, D. L., & Uchida, C. D. (1994). *Drugs and crime: Evaluating public policy initiatives.* Thousand Oaks, CA: Sage Publications.

Richards, D. (1982). *Sex, drugs, death, and the law: An essay on human rights and overcriminalization.* Totowa, NJ: Rowman & Littlefield.

Shulgin, A. (1988). *The Controlled Substances Act: A resource manual of the current status of federal drug laws.* Berkeley, CA: Ronin Publishing.

Wiener, C. (1981). *The politics of alcoholism: Building an arena around a social problem.* New Brunswick, NJ: Transaction Books.

Wilson, J. Q., & Tonry, M. (Eds.). (1990). *Drugs and crime* (Vol. 13). Chicago: University of Chicago Press.

Anna Celeste Burke, PhD, is assistant professor, Ohio State University, College of Social Work, 1947 College Road, Columbus, OH 43210.

For further information see

Adult Corrections; Alcohol Abuse; Civil Rights; Criminal Behavior Overview; Drug Abuse; Employee Assistance Programs; Federal Social Legislation from 1961 to 1994; Juvenile Corrections; Occupational Social Work; Police Social Work; Policy Analysis; Primary Prevention Overview; Rehabilitation of Criminal Offenders; Research Overview; Social Welfare; Social Work Profession Overview; Substance Abuse: Federal, State, and Local Policies.

Key Words

criminal justice	legal issues
drug enforcement	substance abuse

Suicide

André Ivanoff
Marion Riedel

Suicide is the intentional taking of one's own life. A matter of significant interest to the social sciences and to disciplines concerned with social values, welfare, and ethics, suicide results in approximately 31,000 deaths annually in the United States (U.S. National Center for Health Statistics [USNCHS], 1993). At one time or another, most direct practitioners in the helping professions are confronted with a client who attempts or commits suicide. Those who work with clients who have multiple or chronic problems are even more likely to encounter suicidal behavior. Suicide and related suicidal behaviors constitute a public health problem with broad consequences for social policy and services delivery systems, as well as for the families and individuals who are directly involved.

Historically, suicidal behavior was judged primarily within a religious or moral context. More recently, social science findings and medical opinion have altered attitudes and legal responses to suicidal behavior. As cultural and social values have evolved, so have perspectives on suicide: Although the far-reaching social, psychological, and legal consequences of suicide are acknowledged, a consensual perspective on suicide is highly unlikely.

Attempted suicide, parasuicide (in which the intent to die cannot be judged), suicide ideation (thoughts about suicide), and suicide threats or other verbalizations are nonfatal suicidal behaviors. Traditionally, these behaviors were viewed as problems because they carried with them an increased risk of suicide. More recently, however, patterns of repeated nonfatal suicidal behavior are viewed as problems in their own right because they may signal serious mental disorder and drain helping resources, placing a chronic burden on the mental health and emergency services in the health care system.

This entry examines the study and phenomenon of suicidal behavior: definition and classification, epidemiology, social and psychological correlates, theories of causation, and the policies and programs designed to prevent or decrease suicidal behavior. In addition, it focuses on current issues in suicidology, such as technologically enhanced assessments of suicide risk and groups of individuals who are at risk, such as individuals suffering from mental disorders or aged men. Finally, the current and potential roles of social work and social workers in the development of services, programs, and policies are examined.

PROBLEMS OF DEFINITION AND CLASSIFICATION

The major obstacle to the accurate collection of suicide statistics and to the development of theory about the nature and causes of suicide is the absence of a universally agreed-on definition of suicide (Douglas, 1967). The common definition of suicide is a simple one: a "human act of self-inflicted, self-intentional cessation" (Shneidman, 1976, p. 5). It combines a wish to be dead with the action that carries out the wish. The focus is on the *intent* of the individual and the *goal* of the action. Douglas identified six criteria used to determine whether a death is a suicide: (1) the *initiation* of an act leads to the death of the initiator, (2) the *willing* of an act that leads to the death of the willer, (3) the willing of *self-destruction*, (4) the *loss of will*, (5) the *motivation* to be dead or to die, and (6) the *knowledge* by the actor that the action produces death.

Defining a death as a suicide may have negative consequences for insurance claims, for the settlement of estates, for workers' compensation benefits, and for personal reputations. Concern about accuracy in definition extends to both false-positive determinations, as when an accidentally fatal combination of drugs and alcohol is ruled a suicide, and to false-negative determinations, such as the retired police officer whose self-shooting is mistakenly ruled an accident, rather than a suicide.

Efforts have also been made to define and classify nonfatal suicidal behavior. "Suicidal" is a general term encompassing all types of suicidal behavior. The most frequently described suicidal behaviors include suicidal ideation, suicidal verbalizations, parasuicide or attempted suicide, and suicide itself. Contrary to popular belief, however, these behaviors do not constitute a continuum of lethality or seriousness: There is little evidence of predictable stagelike movement from one to the next. There is also confusion regarding the temporal aspect of suicidal acts; "suicidal" is used in the literature to describe individuals who are currently self-destructive, those who have been self-destructive in the past, and those who are likely to be self-destructive in the future. However, clinical assessments of suicidal behavior usually occur after the fact and use "suicidal" only to refer to someone who has already displayed overt suicidal behavior (Shneidman, 1979).

Intent is the "seriousness of intensity of an individual's wish to terminate his or her life" (Beck, Schuyler, & Herman, 1974, p. 45). Judgments of low intent are frequently labeled as less serious or manipulative acts and may have negative implications for treatment and prognosis. *Attempted suicide* is the term most often used to describe deliberate but nonfatal self-injurious acts and leads to the assumption that the individual intended to die but failed. The term *suicide gesture* describes an action usually of low lethality; it assumes the individual never intended the action to result in death.

There is little evidence to suggest that distinctions among levels of intent can be accurately or reliably made. It is simply too difficult to know after the fact (particularly when the act has resulted in death) whether an individual truly wanted to die. Kreitman, Philip, Greer, and Bagley (1969) coined the term "parasuicide" to replace all categories of suicide attempt without inferring intent. Parasuicide is a "non-fatal act in which an individual deliberately causes self-injury or ingests a substance in excess of any prescribed or generally recognized therapeutic dosage" (Kreitman, 1977, p. 3). In the literature, parasuicide is used synonymously with attempted suicide and deliberate self-harm (Hirsch, Walsh, & Draper, 1982). Although many medicolegal systems classifying suicidal behavior have been published, they possess little utility in clinical settings, and none is widely accepted.

EPIDEMIOLOGY

Suicide Rates

Epidemiology is the study of the occurrence and rates of a disorder or disease in a population. Published suicide rates, reported as the number of suicides per 100,000 deaths, are misleading because of errors in official reporting. The most significant reporting error is a consequence of the definitional problem described previously. Other errors concern the reporting and collection procedures used (Douglas, 1967) and misreporting of cultural variants of suicide, such as accidental deaths, drug overdoses, and "victim-precipitated" homicides (Gibbs, 1988). There are also family attitudes that create pressure to label a death by suicide as accidental or undetermined to reduce the stigma associated with suicide (Wyche & Rotheram-Borus, 1990). Together, these errors create the problem of underreporting, which is estimated to range from 10 percent (Kleck, 1988) to as high as 25 percent to 33 percent (Dublin, 1963).

Caution must be used when interpreting suicide statistics. The errors and bias reflected in reported suicide rates result from the following factors: (1) the choice of statistics used to test sociological theories of suicide, (2) subcultural differences in efforts to hide suicide, (3) the effects of different degrees of social integration on official statistics, (4) the failure to keep statistics on salient subgroups, (5) significant variations in the social imputations of suicide motives, (6) the failure to assess and record accurately certain self-annihilation behaviors as suicide, and (7) more extensive and professionalized collection of statistics among certain populations.

A comparison of suicide rates among 36 countries reveals that the United States ranks 20th with a rate of 12.2 suicides per 100,000 deaths. Countries with the highest rates of suicide are Hungary (38.2 per 100,000), Sri Lanka (36.8), Suriname (34.5), Finland (27.5), Denmark (22.4), Austria (21.7), Belgium (21.0), and Russia (20.5). Eastern European countries have a long history of high suicide rates. Countries with low suicide rates include the Bahamas (1.3), Mexico (2.9), Greece (3.6), Martinique (4.7), Barbados (4.8), Venezuela (5.9), Costa Rica (6.5), Chile (6.6), and England (7.5) (World Health Organization, 1991).

Suicide is the eighth leading cause of death in the United States. Reported rates are highest in the West (Nevada, Montana, and Idaho) and lowest in the Northeast (New Jersey, New York, and Massachusetts). White people are almost twice as likely to commit suicide as are African Americans. Suicide rates are more than four times higher for men (20.4 per 100,000) than for women (4.8 per 100,000). Although the rates for males exceed the rates for females at all ages and for all races, this difference is greatest in old age, when the risk for men is the greatest and the risk for women has passed its middle-aged peak (USNCHS, 1990). Suicide rates for men continue to rise; in the mid-1980s, the rates for males were only three times higher than those for females. This increase in the rates for males has been due largely to the staggering increase in suicide among adolescents, with the greatest increase among white males aged 15 to 24 (Garland & Zigler, 1993; Heacock, 1990). Rates are higher for men aged 65 and older, ranging from 32 per 100,000 for those aged 65 to 75 to 56 per 100,000 for those aged 75 to 84. They are highest for men aged 85 and older (65.9) than for all other groups (USNCHS, 1990).

Beginning with Durkheim's observations (1897/1952), the positive relationship between suicide and age has been the most thoroughly documented and well-established correlation in the field. It is apparent in almost every country where records are kept, although Japan is a notable exception with two peak periods: one in early adulthood and the other in old age. Among African American, Native American, and some Latino males, suicide rates peak in the teens and early adulthood, decreasing at age 40 or even sooner (Baker, 1990; Wyche & Rotheram-Borus, 1990). However, at age 40 suicide rates begin to increase among white men. For many years, these differences were obscured by the practice of comparing the total suicide rate for white people and people of color, rather than using age-specific rates. Table 1 summarizes the suicide rates from 1980 to 1990 by sex, race, and age group.

Elderly People

Elderly people made up only 12.4 percent of the U.S. population in 1988, yet they accounted for 21 percent of the suicides (U.S. Bureau of the Census, 1990). Of the 31,000 suicides reported in 1990, 6,405 were by elders (USNCHS, 1993). In spite of the high rate of completed suicides, older adults have the lowest attempt rate across the life span. Therefore, if they attempted suicide, the chance of

completing it was far greater (Lester & Yang, 1992). In 1988, the combined rates for both sexes of those over 65 were 22.4 for white people and 8.3 for people of color. This difference is magnified for men over age 65, with white people having a rate of 41.9 and people of color, a rate of only 13.9 (USNCHS, 1988).

Ethnic and Racial Groups

Suicide is the third leading cause of premature death in African American communities after homicide and accidents (Gibbs, 1988). The overall national prevalence of suicide in African American males and females is 12.0 and 2.3 per 100,000 (USNCHS, 1993), compared with 22.0 and 5.3 for white males and females; these rates are proportionately similar. The rate for African American males peaks in the 25- to 34-year-old age group (21.9), unlike the rate for white males, which peaks after age 65.

In Latino communities, there are several major barriers to analyzing the epidemiology and risk factors for suicide. First, the data are aggregated according to race, rather than ethnicity, and most suicides in these communities appear in the statistics for white people. Second, Hispanic–Latino people have been largely neglected in the suicide literature (Heacock, 1990). Finally, this is a heterogeneous population, with each subpopula-

TABLE 1
Suicide Rates by Sex, Race, and Age Group: 1980–1990

Age (yr)	White				Black			
	1980	1985	1989	1990	1980	1985	1989	1990
Males								
All ages	19.9	21.6	21.5	22.0	10.3	11.0	12.4	12.0
5–14	0.7	1.3	1.1	1.1	0.3	0.6	0.9	0.8
15–24	21.4	22.3	22.5	23.2	12.3	13.3	16.6	15.1
25–34	25.6	25.6	25.5	25.6	21.8	19.9	22.5	21.9
35–44	23.5	23.7	24.1	25.3	15.6	14.6	17.4	16.9
45–54	24.2	25.2	24.4	24.8	12.0	13.6	11.1	14.8
55–64	25.8	28.8	26.9	27.5	11.7	12.2	11.5	10.8
65–74	32.5	35.8	36.0	34.2	11.1	16.7	17.1	14.7
75–84	45.5	57.0	55.3	60.2	10.5	15.6	14.9	14.4
85+	52.8	60.9	72.9	70.3	18.9	7.7	—	—
Females								
All ages	5.9	5.6	5.3	5.3	2.2	2.1	2.4	2.3
5–14	0.2	0.5	0.3	0.4	0.1	0.2	—	—
15–24	4.6	4.7	4.3	4.2	2.3	2.0	2.9	2.3
25–34	7.5	6.4	6.0	6.0	4.1	3.0	3.8	3.7
35–44	9.1	7.7	7.2	7.4	4.6	3.6	3.8	4.0
45–54	10.2	9.1	8.1	7.5	2.8	3.3	3.2	3.2
55–64	9.1	8.4	8.0	8.0	2.3	2.2	2.6	2.6
65–74	7.0	7.3	6.4	7.2	1.7	2.0	—	2.6
75–84	5.7	7.0	6.1	6.7	1.4	4.5	—	—
85+	5.8	4.8	6.3	5.4	NA	1.4	—	—

SOURCE: U.S. National Center for Health Statistics. (1992). *Vital statistics of the United States.* Internal report, unpublished data, 1990. Hyattsville, MD: U.S. Public Health Service. These rates have been revised from previous USNCHS publications based on the 1990 census.
NOTE: Rate per 100,000 population in specified group. Excludes deaths of nonresidents of the United States. Deaths are classified according to the ninth revision of the *International Classification of Diseases.*

tion having distinct stressors, belief systems, religious affiliations, and cultural taboos. Studies that have examined specific Hispanic subgroups have found discrepant results (Wyche & Rotheram-Borus, 1990). For example, the reported rates for Mexican Americans have varied from 1.8 to 10.5 per 100,000 (Hoppe & Martin, 1986), and Puerto Rican men have been found to have rates two to three times those of African American men and white men (Monk & Warshaur, 1974). The reported rates of attempted suicide among Puerto Rican women are also three times those for African American women or white women (Heacock, 1990).

Native Americans have the highest suicide rate of any ethnic group in the United States (McIntosh, 1983–1984) with a rate of 14.1 per 100,000 (USNCHS, 1986). The highest rates are found among younger Native Americans (15 to 24 year olds); these rates are 2 1/2 times greater than those for their white counterparts (Wyche & Rotheram-Borus, 1990).

Youths

Since 1960, the suicide rate among youths ages 15 to 19 has increased from 3.6 to 11.3 per 100,000. Suicide is the third leading cause of death among youths, accounting for 14 percent of all deaths in this age group, trailing only accidents and homicide (USNCHS, 1990). This is more than a 200 percent increase for this age group and a 300 percent increase for white males ages 15 to 24 (Shaffer, Garland, Gould, Fisher, & Trautman, 1988). During this same period, rates for the general population increased by only 17 percent. This trend extends to other industrialized countries, although in a less marked fashion (Lester, 1974). The rate of suicide is accelerating especially quickly for young African American men in the United States (Baker, 1990; Gibbs, 1988). Although completed suicide in youths is still relatively rare, suicidal ideation is common, and suicide attempts are reported by 6 percent to 13 percent of the adolescent population (Garland & Zigler, 1993). The rate of childhood suicide (five- to 14-year-olds) has more than doubled since 1968 (Pfeffer et al., 1993); the 1990 rate of 0.8 per 100,000, or 264 total deaths (USNCHS, 1993), makes this the sixth leading cause of death for children this age. White boys commit suicide at rates higher than those for African American boys and girls or white girls.

Incarcerated People

Suicide is the primary cause of death in U.S. jails and detention facilities (Hayes & Rowan, 1988). Estimated rates range from 2.5 to 13 times those for the general population (Danto, 1981; Otto &

Ogloff, 1988) or as high as 144 per 100,000 in 1988 (Haycock, 1991). Reporting inconsistencies account for the widely discrepant rates: It is possible that jails neglect to report deaths that may incur liability (Hayes & Rowan, 1988) and that deaths precipitated in jails actually occur (or are reported as occurring) in local hospitals.

Early studies found state or federal prison suicide rates to be either less than or slightly more than those for similar age and ethnic groups in the general population (Rieger, 1971), but empirical studies in the 1980s reported prison suicide rates to be 1 1/2 to two times those for the general population (Anno, 1985; Lester, 1987). Parasuicide, suicide attempts, and other forms of self-harm are quite common in prison populations, however, with rates estimated at between 2,200 and 3,760 per 100,000 inmates (Toch, 1992).

Attempted Suicide and Other Behaviors

The actual rate of suicide attempts is not known because no official state or national registry exists. Some estimate the rate to be as high as 50 to 200 times that of completed suicides (Hawton, 1986; Pfeffer, 1986); using 1990 statistics, this rate would translate to more than 1.5 million attempts in the United States alone (USNCHS, 1990). Women attempt suicide at least three times as often as do men (Berman & Jobes, 1991). Suicidal ideation is common among youths; more than 50 percent of the adolescents studied have thought about suicide, and between 6 percent and 13 percent have attempted suicide at least once in their lives (Garland & Zigler, 1993), resulting in an attempt rate 50 to 200 times that of completed suicides.

Attempted suicide decreases with age; roughly 80 percent of all attempts are made by persons ages 18 to 45, and older adults have the lowest attempt rate, despite higher suicide rates. The incidence of parasuicide among African American and white gay men and lesbians has been reported to be from two to seven times higher than those for their heterosexual counterparts (Maris, Berman, Maltsberger, & Yufit, 1992). Ten percent to 20 percent of all attempters are estimated eventually to die by suicide (Lester, 1992b; Zubin, 1974).

THEORIES OF SUICIDAL BEHAVIOR

Theories about the causes of suicide extend as far back in time as the phenomenon itself. Why humans would choose to destroy themselves has been written about since the time of the Greek and Roman philosophers. Research into the explanations for suicide, however, is more recent, usually cited as formally beginning with Durkheim's

Le Suicide in 1897. Although the actual purpose of Durkheim's work was to develop the sociological method of inquiry, Durkheim's suicide classification is still taught. This classification divides suicide into three categories:

1. egoistic suicide, resulting from absent or poor social integration (family, religious, state)
2. altruistic suicide, the result of excessive integration and identification; best personified by the "honorable" suicide in Eastern culture
3. anomic suicide, the result of lost integration through trauma or catastrophe, which is accompanied by alienation, social isolation, and loneliness (Durkheim, 1897/1952).

Since Durkheim's work, there have been many attempts to categorize systematically the motives and intent of suicidal behavior. Current theories of suicide are based on sociological, psychodynamic, biological, cognitive, learning, and integrative orientations to human behavior.

Sociological theories treat suicide as a function of an individual's role and status within social systems. Social meaning, norms, and restraint and the durability and stability of social networks are factors related to suicidality, according to sociological theories. Leading theorists include Douglas (1967), Durkheim (1897/1952), Gibbs and Martin (1964), Henry and Short (1954), and Maris (1982). Braucht's (1979) ecological model suggested that suicide is promoted by an interaction between individuals and their environments, rather than by individual or situational factors alone.

Psychodynamic theories view suicide as the product of internal, largely unconscious, motives. The classic motive for suicide is an unconscious hostile impulse that is turned inward toward an introjected and ambivalently viewed love object (Litman, 1967). This hostility has three parts: the wish to kill, the wish to be killed, and the wish to die (Menninger, 1938). Reunion with one's mother, identification with a lost object, rebirth, and revenge have all been suggested as motives for suicide (Furst & Ostow, 1979). These theories suggest that if an impulse is acted out against oneself, as in the case of suicidal behavior, it will not be acted out against others. In tracing Freud's changing theory on suicide, mechanisms other than aggression also emerge as importantly related to suicide, including anxiety, guilt, dependence, and rage.

Biological theories suggest that a genetic predisposition toward suicide is inherited and that biochemical changes within the body precipitate drives toward suicide. Some research has found that reduced serotonin and dopamine metabolite levels are associated with attempted suicide (Asberg, 1991; Montgomery & Montgomery, 1982; Roy, Agren, & Pickar, in press). The methodology of these studies is problematic, however; most were conducted with small clinical populations and addressed the relationship with attempted suicide only, not with suicide. Little is understood about the genesis of these correlations or about the relationships of intervening variables to them. Although research on the biological causes of suicide has increased since the mid-1980s, strong evidence supporting biochemical precipitants remains equivocal because most studies have involved small samples and have been conducted with suicide attempters.

Cognitive theories regard suicidal behavior as an attempt to communicate or to solve problems and as the concomitant of disordered thinking and hopelessness (Beck, Resnik, & Lettieri, 1974; Kovacs, Beck, & Weissman, 1975a). *The Cry for Help,* Farberow and Shneidman's (1961) classic work, proposed this view of suicide as communication. Later work by Kreitman, Smith, and Tan (1970) suggested that attempted suicide conveys a specific message about one's difficulties. A number of theorists have suggested that both suicide and attempted suicide may be viewed as efforts to solve problems, either through death or manipulation (Kovacs, Beck, & Weissman, 1975b), that cause intense interpersonal or environmental distress (Applebaum, 1963; Levenson & Neuringer, 1971; Stengel & Cook, 1958). Hopelessness is an integral component of these theories: Only those who see no alternatives to their problems attempt to solve their problems by dying (Linehan, 1981).

Learning theories describe suicidal behavior as a function of reinforcing, environmental, and motivating conditions that created past responses in similar situations. Suicidal behaviors are acquired through socialization and are part of an individual's repertoire of responses. The probability of a suicidal response is based on expectations about the suicidal behavior that are held by the individual and others, on the availability of means to engage in suicidal behavior, and on the presence or absence of offers to intervene in the process. The expected consequences of suicide and attempted suicide are similar to those suggested by psychodynamic theorists: revenge, rest or peace, and reunion with a lost love object.

Integrative theories and models, such as Linehan's (1981) social–behavioral model, incorporate many elements of the preceding theories and conceptualize a dynamic interaction among cognitive, behavioral, and environmental domains. The primary contribution of such integrative models for social work is that they prescribe assessment and intervention based on a consideration of environmental, social, psychological, and biological factors, congruent with ecological approaches to practice.

SOCIAL AND PSYCHOLOGICAL CHARACTERISTICS ASSOCIATED WITH SUICIDAL BEHAVIOR

Mental Disorders
Several characteristics that are strongly associated with suicidal behavior transcend age (including adolescence), gender, race, sexual orientation, and geography. The single most highly correlated characteristic with suicide is a mental disorder, usually of the affective or mood-based type, including bipolar or manic–depressive disorder, and also schizophrenia (Brent et al., 1993a). Estimates suggest that two-thirds of those committing suicide suffer from a primary depressive disorder (Black & Winokur, 1986). This correlation may help explain the increased suicide rates among middle-aged men as they reach the high-risk age for depressive illness (McIntosh, 1991).

Alcoholism
Alcoholism is also consistently related to suicide; some studies report that nearly 20 percent of all alcoholics go on to commit suicide (Roy & Linnoila, 1986), perhaps because of the increased disruption of interpersonal relationships and social supports in the lives of alcoholics and alcohol abusers. Despite mixed findings on the direct relationship between suicide and the abuse of other drugs, there is evidence that suicide, affective disorders, and substance abuse frequently co-occur (Rohde, Lewinsohn, & Seeley, 1991) and that a positive relationship exists between drug abuse and the lethality (deadliness) of suicide methods (Garland & Zigler, 1993; Lester, 1992a).

Psychological Characteristics
Other psychological and interpersonal characteristics associated with suicide include apathy, indifference to treatment (Barraclough, Bunch, Nelson, & Sainsbury, 1974; Dorpat & Ripley, 1960), and low social involvement (Crook, Raskin, & Davis, 1975). Individuals who go on to suicide are less likely to ask for support or attention (Cantor, 1976; Virkkunen, 1976). Cognitively, hopelessness is the predominant feature associated with suicidality (Beck, Resnik, & Lettieri, 1974; Bedrosian & Beck, 1979; Weishar & Beck, 1992). Data also suggest that poor pain tolerance and poor health are associated with suicide (Bagley, Jacobsen, & Rehin, 1976; Farberow, McKelligott, Cohen, & Darbonne, 1970).

Social Environments
Social environments that promote suicidality are characterized by at least three factors. First, research has consistently found that a lack of adaptive social support is a contributing factor to suicide and parasuicide. Rates of suicide are higher among immigrants than among natives (Coombs & Miller, 1975), the rates for African Americans and whites are inversely proportional to their presence in the population (Davis, 1979), and individuals who commit suicide are generally unrepresentative of the populations in their neighborhoods (Braucht, 1979). With the exception of young professional women, those who commit suicide are more likely to be unemployed or retired (Kreitman et al., 1969) and may lack the support and integration that work settings provide. More than one-third of those who commit suicide live alone (Bagley et al., 1976; Maris, 1981; Shneidman, Farberow, & Litman, 1970). Female attempters who eventually commit suicide are more isolated and may receive less supportive care from professionals than may those who do not go on to suicide (Wandrei, 1985). New studies are examining the relationships between the quality (or competence) and effectiveness of social support and suicidal behavior; however, it is not yet possible to draw conclusions from this research. There is some evidence that the relatives of attempters may be hostile (Rosenbaum & Richman, 1970), whereas those who commit suicide are more likely to lack even a hostile support system.

Second, suicidal behavior is a response to stressful negative environmental events (Hankoff, 1979; Paykel, 1979). Loss, in general, and patterns of negative life events distinguish suicide attempters and completers from other psychiatric inpatients (Birtchnell, 1970; Levy, Fales, Stein, & Sharp, 1966) and may separate suicidal from nonsuicidal individuals (Humphrey, 1977). Third, exposure to others who have engaged in suicidal behavior may or may not increase risk (Dunne, 1992; Roy, 1986). Although higher rates of suicide are reported among family members of suicide victims (Moss & Hamilton, 1957; Roy, 1983), evidence linking attempters to other attempters is mixed (Chiles, Strosahl, McMurtray, & Linehan, 1985; Kreitman et al., 1970).

Risk Characteristics in Special Populations
Several populations may be at increased risk for suicide or parasuicide owing to social and cultural factors. These groups are not mutually exclusive and include racial and ethnic minorities, adolescents, elders, incarcerated people, and gay men and lesbians. Data documenting this risk, however,

exist only for some of these groups because standard reporting procedures rarely identify special populations, so it is impossible to draw conclusions.

Racial and ethnic groups. The primary characteristics associated with suicide among ethnic minorities are the same as for their white counterparts: depressive symptoms, daily drug use or alcohol abuse, conduct disorders, and previous suicide attempts (Baker, 1990; Berlin, 1987). However, the social, economic, and political factors attached to membership in minority groups differ from those for the majority culture and may exacerbate psychosocial stress. Such factors include a lack of social integration, urban stress, unsublimated anger, limited opportunities, poverty, poor health care, racism, unemployment, and relative deprivation (that is, a widening gap between aspirations and opportunities) (Baker, 1990; Berlin, 1987; Gibbs, 1988). In Latino communities, traditional sex roles, cultural identity, acculturation, and transmigration are all likely to affect the rate of suicide. There are also protective factors in some ethnic communities that may ameliorate the impact of these stressful factors and account for lower suicide rates; these factors include extended family, strong religious beliefs, alternative value systems, and alternative opportunity structures (Gibbs, 1988).

Among Native Americans, suicide rates vary widely by tribe. Suicide rates among more traditional tribes with more stable religious traditions, clan, and extended families (such as the Navajo) are close to or below the national average of eight to 12 per 100,000 (Berlin, 1987). Other tribes, such as the Apache, with suicide rates of more than 40 per 100,000 (Berlin, 1987), were moved from their traditional homelands to reservations with land incapable of producing sufficient food; lost their traditional religion, ceremonies, and leaders; and have high rates of alcoholism and family deterioration. Unfortunately, no empirical studies have contrasted members of ethnic minority groups who successfully commit suicide with those who attempt suicide or parasuicide.

Adolescents. Adolescent suicide, like that in adults, is most highly correlated with an active psychiatric episode (Garland & Zigler, 1993; Shaffer et al., 1988; Shaffi, Carrigan, Whittinghill, & Derrick, 1985), specifically depressive or bipolar disorders; estimates suggest that 90 percent of all adolescent suicides occur in psychiatrically disordered individuals (Brent et al., 1993a; Shaffer et al., 1988). Substance abuse and conduct disorder (Brent, Perper, Moritz, Baugher, & Allman, 1993b;

Ladame, 1992; Shaffi et al., 1985) are also associated with suicide by youths. A previous attempt is the best predictor of future suicide, especially for young men (Shaffer et al., 1988); 40 percent of youth attempters will make future attempts, and 10 percent to 40 percent of adolescent attempters eventually die by suicide (Spirito et al., 1992).

More than one-third of adolescents who successfully commit suicide are intoxicated at the time of death, and many more may be using other drugs; those who commit suicide via firearms are more likely to be using substances. Of the 10 percent of adolescent suicides not associated with psychiatric illness, the most distinguishing variable may be access to a loaded gun (Brent et al., 1993b). This relationship suggests a potent and pragmatic means of prevention. Suicide rates among families of adolescent suicide attempters are more than seven times greater than those for the general population. Imitative risk factors are also suggested on the basis of increased adolescent suicides in the week or two after media coverage of a suicide or a television presentation about suicide (Shaffer et al., 1988). Substance abuse and conduct disorder are also both predisposing factors for adolescent suicide (Ladame, 1992; Shaffi et al., 1985), although the interactions between these factors require further investigation.

Elderly people. Although divorced or widowed elderly white men have the highest suicide risk, rates among the elderly in general have decreased more than 50 percent since the 1930s, from 35 to 40 per 100,000 population to the current rate of approximately 21. This decrease is likely due to improved benefits (Medicare and social security), activism by elderly people, improved social services, and changed attitudes toward retirement (McIntosh, 1992). Applying such information to individual cases is problematic, however, because many general suicide risk factors, such as age, loss, and decreased social contacts, occur naturally and are an inherent part of the aged person's life. Firearms were used in 67 percent of the elderly suicides in 1988, more than in any other age group (McIntosh, 1992).

Incarcerated people. Jails contain many individuals whose characteristics place them at multiple demographic risk for suicidal behavior, primarily men who are less likely to be married, more likely to be drug or alcohol dependent and have conduct disorders, and more likely to have been physically or sexually abused. However, even when adjusted for sex, age, and socioeconomic status, jail suicide rates are still several times higher than those in the general population (Haycock, 1991). Pretrial detainees account for 89 percent of jail suicides, and 51 percent of these suicides occur in the first 24 hours of incarceration (Olivero & Roberts, 1990). The typical jail suicide victim is an individual who has not yet been convicted of a crime, has been arrested for public intoxication, and has no significant history of past arrests. Most jail suicides occur by hanging and in isolation. Estimates suggest that 60 percent to 85 percent of jail suicide victims are intoxicated (Hayes & Rowan, 1988; Rood & Faison, 1988). Other risk factors include arrest for a nonviolent offense and ideation of suicide by hanging. The rate of suicide for juveniles placed in adult correctional facilities is five times higher than the rate for unjailed juveniles (Library Information Specialists, 1983).

Higher rates in the jails than in prisons may reflect the fact that individuals at higher risk commit suicide while in jail, before entering the prison system (Haycock, 1991). In longer-term prison settings, inmates with longer sentences and those on death row may be more likely to commit suicide (Lester, 1987; Lester & Danto, 1993; Topp, 1979).

Gay men and lesbians. The high incidence of suicide attempts reported by this population is a known risk factor for completed suicides. Interrupted social ties, institutionalized homophobia, religious and cultural taboos, family rejection, and the lack of social sanctions for developing alternative families contribute to this increased risk (Starace, 1993). Gay men and lesbians have reported 30 percent more alcohol or drug use than heterosexuals (Saunders & Valente, 1987); the triad of alcoholism, depression, and previous suicide attempts was found to be associated with increased suicide risk among lesbians (Saghir & Robins, 1973). Gay and lesbian youths reportedly attempt suicide six times more than do heterosexual youths (Rotheram-Borus, Hunter, & Rosario, 1994) for reasons similar to their adult counterparts, with the added burden of deciding whether to "come out," given social stigmatization and the potential lack of family support (Hunter, 1990).

Barriers to data collection specific to gay men and lesbians may include the use of marital relationships to define social ties, the lack of gay and lesbian sampling strategies, the omission of sexual orientation on death certificates, and heterosexual bias. Until these barriers are significantly reduced, the understanding of suicide mortality in this population will continue to be largely speculative.

Parasuicide and Nonfatal Suicidal Behavior
There are some similarities but also important differences in the correlates of parasuicide or

attempted suicide and those of suicide. Although depression is still prominent in a significant proportion of both adult and adolescent cases (Ladame, 1992; Shaffer et al., 1988; Weissman, 1974), anger and hostility replace apathy (Crook et al., 1975; Lester, 1968). Alcohol and drug abuse, criminal behavior, and previous suicide attempts also characterize those who are at a higher risk for attempted suicide (Kreitman, 1977). Suicide attempters are likely to be dissatisfied with treatment, to express a high preference for affiliation and affection (Cantor, 1976; Nelson, Nielson, & Checketts, 1977), and to report discomfort when around people (Cantor, 1976). Suicide attempters report higher numbers of distressing, uncontrollable major events than do nonsuicidal depressed individuals (Paykel, 1979). From this perspective, suicidal behavior is seen as an attempt to cope with or solve these negative events.

Although data on hopelessness among attempters are equivocal (Ivanoff & Jang, 1991; Linehan & Nielson, 1981), attempters are cognitively characterized by both external attributions and a negative self-concept (Kaplan & Pokorny, 1976; Levenson & Neuringer, 1971). The cognitive style of suicide attempters is rigid (Neuringer, 1964; Neuringer & Lettieri, 1982; Patsiokas, Clum, & Luscomb, 1979), possibly impulsive (Fox & Weissman, 1975), and lacking in problem-solving ability (Levenson & Neuringer, 1971). Interpersonally, attempters have a low level of social involvement (Farberow & MacKinnon, 1974; Nelson et al., 1977), are less likely than others to ask for help, and often exhibit patterns of high friction and conflict in relationships (Greer, Gunn, & Koller, 1966; Hawton & Catalan, 1982). The expected outcomes of suicidal behavior are also important in risk assessment. Major environmental changes usually occur after an individual's suicide attempt, and these changes are frequently positive from the perspective of the attempter. The expectation of positive consequences may increase the risk of future attempts and, therefore, of suicide (McCutcheon, 1985).

The most commonly reported precipitants of parasuicide among adolescents and adults are interpersonal and may include personal rejection by a partner or parent, humiliation, and arrest (Linehan, 1981; Rotheram, 1987; Shaffer et al., 1988). Among adolescents, intrapersonal conflict about sexual orientation and school problems are linked to parasuicide (Rotheram-Borus et al., 1994; Shaffer et al., 1988). Sexual or physical abuse are also highly correlated with suicide attempts among girls (Garland & Zigler, 1993; Ladame, 1992).

POLICY

For years the problem of suicide in the United States has prompted attempts to create adequate social policy. These efforts have focused on recommendations for legal responses, preventive efforts, and research agendas. Although adolescent suicide rates continue to be lower than those of the elderly, the increase in adolescent suicide over the past several decades has prompted several policy initiatives for youths. In 1984, the leadership of the National Institute of Mental Health and the secretary of Health and Human Services jointly appointed the Task Force on Youth Suicide of the Department of Health and Human Services. The report by this task force (Alcohol, Drug Abuse and Mental Health Administration, 1989) contained policy recommendations and a proposed multidisciplinary research agenda with four goals: (1) to clarify risk and protective factors; (2) to identify biological, environmental, and psychological correlates; (3) to improve surveillance techniques; and (4) to develop more sophisticated methodologies (Pardes & Blumenthal, 1990). The task force also recommended the development of prevention and intervention programs and a community suicide response plan and broad-based education and training.

In 1987 the Youth Suicide Prevention Act (S. 1199) was introduced, calling for the establishment of a national clearinghouse to provide information, training, and funding for demonstration programs and research. Although the bill did not pass, it set a research and evaluation agenda, highlighting the need for increased empirical knowledge to inform future policy and programs. In the absence of federal policy, three states (California, Louisiana, and Wisconsin) have mandated suicide prevention programs in their schools (Garland & Zigler, 1993), and others are likely to follow. On the basis of current knowledge, widespread preventive programs and professional education should be implemented in a coherent, targeted manner. Public policy centered on the control of firearms must also be included in suicide prevention strategies.

The direction of suicide policy for adults has been less clear than that for adolescents. Historically, discussion about suicide policy centered on the legal and moral implications of the act. Legal sanctions (including threats of incarceration), involuntary hospitalizations, and threats of fines reflected this national preoccupation. More recently, however, a public health perspective has prevailed in policy efforts. The U.S. Public Health Service made suicide prevention a priority in 1980 and developed a 10-year plan to reduce the incidence of suicide (McGinnis, 1987). Mental health services, support groups, and federal coordination of services were all components of this effort. Surveillance data indicate that these efforts were not successful in reducing the incidence of completed suicides, but may have contributed to an altered perspective on suicide prevention. For example, the Centers for Disease Control and Prevention has created a Violence Epidemiology Branch (U.S. Department of Health and Human Services, 1985) to identify high-risk populations and make recommendations for preventive strategies. Continued and coordinated policy efforts focusing on preventive strategies, research and evaluation, surveillance, and public education provide promise that this public health orientation will continue.

PREVENTION AND INTERVENTION PROGRAMS

Prevention

Young people are most often the focus of preventive efforts. Over 1,000 telephone hotlines currently serve youths in the United States (Garland, Shaffer, & Whittle, 1989), although they are considered minimally effective at preventing suicide. These hotlines are used most often by young white women (Shaffer, Garland, Fisher, Bacon, & Vieland, 1990). The authors strongly support the perspective of Shaffer et al. and others (Hoberman & Garfinkle, 1988; Price, Cowen, Lorion, & Ramos-McKay, 1989), who argue that effective programs must be built on empirical findings that identify specific risks in target populations. A focus on normative stress issues and the minimization of the correlation between mental illness and suicidality (often in an attempt to reduce stigma) may undermine the effectiveness of generalized curriculum-based programs. Conversely, magnification of the problem seems unfruitful and unnecessary. Instead, preventive efforts should be aimed at those who are most at risk—namely, persons of all ages who are afflicted by mental disorders, especially depression.

There is little evidence that effective, broad-sweeping preventive programs exist, whether owing to poorly targeted prevention designs or to poorly conducted research. The development of primary prevention efforts should be targeted at the reduction of the prevalence of known risk factors (for example, affective illness or conduct disorder, substance abuse, and the accessibility of firearms).

Intervention

Intervention with those who have already been identified as at risk (for example, previous attempters and those with a family history of suicide) includes crisis intervention, followed by the use of a problem-targeted intervention protocol. Such interventions may include training in problem-solving skills and the enhancement of self-efficacy (Cole, 1989; Linehan, 1981). Unfortunately, suicidal individuals are often difficult to reach in treatment and frequently are noncompliant. Unlike broad-based preventive efforts, strategies that identify risk earlier in childhood and provide family support services have demonstrated some positive impact (Price et al., 1989).

Crisis intervention. The initial recommended response to a suicidal individual consists of crisis intervention and a functional assessment of the suicidal behavior (Doyle, 1990; Linehan, 1981). The goal is to keep the person safe from imminent harm and to implement basic crisis management principles: identifying precipitants, experiencing the related effect, and developing a plan of intervention (Parad & Caplan, 1960). It is critical to address the removal of lethal items (Linehan, 1993). A decision must also be made regarding the necessity of hospitalization. The need to balance the client's physical safety with the potential negative experience of the hospital (for example, stigma or loss of control) should be decided with the assistance of a physician or emergency department staff. Contracting with the client with regard to suicidal behavior (for example, "I will contact someone if I'm feeling suicidal"; "I will go to the emergency room if I have taken an overdose") can be effectively used as a risk-management tool for a limited time during a crisis situation (Linehan, 1981; Rotheram, 1987). The long-standing interpersonal and skills-deficit issues that contribute to suicidality should quickly become the focus of the intervention (Ivanoff & Smyth, 1992; Linehan, 1993).

Intervention for parasuicide. Recommended components of intervention for use with individuals who have engaged in parasuicide include problem-solving training, case management, other forms of behavioral skills training, and active follow-up. Because of the strong relationship between suicidal behavior and depression, a referral for the evaluation of medications is prudent (Ivanoff & Smyth, 1992). In some studies these components have been credited with improving mood and decreasing suicidal ideation and self-harm. They can be structured into an intervention that incorporates the assessment of antecedents to suicidal behavior for the client, reinforces problem-solving skills that are directly related to these antecedents, develops improved social skills, and

incorporates a strategy for emotional identification and management (Linehan, 1993). Professionals should be cautioned that this is extremely difficult work, that suicidal clients are often resistant to their efforts, and that some clients make a decision to commit suicide in spite of a professional's best efforts. This is a complex issue requiring an often arduous and complex response.

Although the preceding intervention strategies are relatively universal, there are some special considerations when working with adolescents. Identifying adolescents who are at risk is complicated by adolescents' experimentation with alcohol and drugs, which is often unanticipated by both adolescents and workers (Rotheram, 1987). Such experimentation can precipitate a suicidal crisis before the worker has time to intervene. An acute emotional reaction to rejection, humiliation, or an acute disciplinary crisis may lead a troubled adolescent to an impulsive, quickly enacted suicidal response (Shaffer et al., 1988). The onset of a mental disorder, physical and sexual abuse, accessibility to firearms, and developmentally based notions of immortality should be considered when assessing an adolescent's suicidality.

CURRENT ISSUES

Survivors

Although hampered by an accompanying lack of empirical research, the topic of suicide "survivors," or those who were involved with the victim who remain alive, is receiving increasing attention in both the popular and professional literature. Shneidman (1976) estimated that an average of six persons are directly affected by each suicide. Clinical experts who treat survivors (Dunne, 1992; McIntosh, 1987) place survivors at an increased risk of unresolved grief reactions, depression, anxiety, sleeplessness, guilt, physical symptoms, and for suicide itself (Roy, 1986). Such clinical outcomes are mediated by social supports, coping styles, and the previous relationship with the deceased (McIntosh, 1987), as well as by age, gender, and other sociocultural variables (Dunne, 1992).

A suicide survivor's experience differs from the experience that occurs after other deaths for several reasons (McIntosh, 1987):

- The method of death is often more violent or otherwise traumatic.
- Usually concerned professionals (for example, the victim's therapist or the investigating police) may be avoidant or suspicious and perhaps concerned about liability.
- Social isolation and stigma often occur.

- The survivor may be blamed, particularly if the victim was a child or a spouse.

Survivors often feel anger or unresolved guilt (Dunne, 1992), possibly as a result of conflict in their relationship with the deceased or others who were close to the deceased, which further exacerbates the risk of negative clinical states. Children may also feel guilt or responsibility after a parent commits suicide, but their response differs based on their developmental stage and how the information is communicated within the family; increased information and communication are correlated with better outcomes (McIntosh, 1987). The suicide of a spouse adds additional stigma, blame, isolation, and shame to an already significant loss. Researchers are beginning to explore what factors enable some individuals to cope with and resolve grief better than others, but to date this research has not been applied to suicide survivors.

Early intervention after suicide seems most effective in alleviating distress related to survivor status. However, it appears that psychological and suicidal risk may be longlasting for many survivors and that therapeutic intervention may continue for an extended period. Informational and problem-solving approaches can both alleviate symptoms and reduce stigma for the client, while referral to a self-help group may help the client to gain support and rebuild social ties (Dunne, 1992).

HIV/AIDS

Health care professionals express wide concern about the higher risk of suicide in people with the human immunodeficiency virus (HIV) or acquired immune deficiency syndrome (AIDS) than in other physically ill groups. Early studies reported that the suicide rate among men with AIDS ages 20 to 59 was 36 times greater than that for their noninfected counterparts (Marzuk et al., 1988). More recent studies, however, have failed to replicate these findings (Schneider, Taylor, Kemeny, & Hammen, 1991). One study found higher suicidal ideation in patients who had been recently diagnosed with HIV or AIDS-related complex than in those with full-blown AIDS, suggesting that disease crisis points, rather than simply HIV-positive status, are associated with suicidal behavior. Even among HIV-positive individuals, however, suicide attempters were more likely to have histories of previous suicide attempts, psychiatric treatment, and substance abuse, much like suicide attempters in the general population (O'Dowd, Biderman, & McKegney, 1993). Clearly, these findings indicate that the relationship between HIV–AIDS and suicide is not well understood. Furthermore, because the studies to date have been conducted with gay white men, these relationships cannot be assumed to hold true for women, children and adolescents, and people of color.

Computerized Risk Assessment

The increasing ability to define risk factors, concomitant with more sophisticated technology, has led to a variety of computerized tools for assessing the risk of suicide (Ferns, 1993; Greist et al., 1973). These programs include both statistical and knowledge-based models, frequently merging some of each (Ferns & Riedel, 1995). Such programs have a diverse audience of users: Some systems are aimed at trained professionals seeking additional consultation, others at paraprofessionals who are not trained to deal with the complexities of risk assessment, and still others at those who interact directly with clients. Some studies have indicated that such systems may provide more accurate assessments than may human clinicians (Ferns, 1993; Greist et al., 1973). Nonetheless, implementation of these systems has been slow owing to the critical nature of suicide and a reluctance to relax human oversight in the assessment process.

ROLE OF SOCIAL WORK AND SOCIAL WORKERS

Social work's person-in-situation perspective suggests that the profession is well suited to design intervention programs and policies to deal with the complex problems of suicide and attempted suicide. The subgroup of suicidal individuals that places the most stress on health and mental health resources overlaps with the multiproblem clients frequently seen in social service and community mental health agencies. When considered across all levels of service, social workers may have more contact with suicidal individuals and their families than do most other professionals. Social workers frequently coordinate and administer suicide hotlines and other preventive services; suicide education is frequently a social work task; and in emergency and crisis settings, social workers are often the first professionals to see suicidal individuals. Through hospitalization, return, and follow-up into the community, social workers may also provide the most continuous service to suicidal individuals.

Given the significance of social work's role in the provision of services, members of the profession should also take an active role in research and development of empirically based assessment and intervention models to prevent and ameliorate suicidal behavior. Social workers have contributed two known intervention studies to the literature: a home-based follow-up program after discharge from the hospital (Gibbons, Butler, Urwin, & Gibbons, 1978) and a brief intensive inpatient program comparing skills-based and desensitization interventions (Ivanoff, 1985). Both found somewhat positive but mixed results, hampered by the length of follow-up; interventions such as these should be integrated with the benefits of practice experience to develop effective models of intervention. Another social work study identified characteristics of female attempters who go on to commit suicide (Wandrei, 1985), and Shaffer's extensive work on adolescent suicidal behavior (Shaffer et al., 1988) included coauthors who were social workers.

The task of establishing priorities in suicide research is not an easy one owing to the lack of systematic intervention and innovation across practice, program, and policy levels. To serve the dual purpose of ameliorating individual suffering and improving the use of costly public health resources, social workers must attend to a broad-based goal of reducing all forms of suicidal behavior. Despite the amount written about suicide and other suicidal behaviors, there is a great deal more that must be understood and evaluated in social workers' responses to and interventions for this continuing problem.

REFERENCES

Alcohol, Drug Abuse and Mental Health Administration. (1989). *Report of the secretary's task force on youth suicide: Vol. 1. Overview and recommendations* (DHHS Publication No. ADM 89-1621). Washington, DC: U.S. Government Printing Office.

Anno, B. J. (1985). Patterns of suicide in the Texas department of corrections, 1980–1985. *Journal of Prison and Jail Health, 5,* 82–93.

Applebaum, S. A. (1963). The problem-solving aspects of suicide. *Journal of Projective Techniques, 27,* 259–268.

Asberg, M. (1991). Neurotransmitter monoamine metabolites in the cerebrospinal fluid as risk factors for suicidal behavior. In L. Davidson & M. Linnoila (Eds.), *Risk factors for youth suicide* (pp. 177–196). New York: Hemisphere.

Bagley, C., Jacobsen, S., & Rehin, A. (1976). Completed suicide: A taxonomic analysis of clinical social data. *Psychological Medicine, 6,* 429–438.

Baker, F. M. (1990). Black youth suicide: Literature review with a focus on prevention. *Journal of the National Medical Association, 82,* 495–507.

Barraclough, B., Bunch, B., Nelson, B., & Sainsbury, P. (1974). A hundred cases of suicide: Clinical aspects. *British Journal of Psychiatry, 125,* 355–373.

Beck, A. T., Resnik, H.L.P., & Lettieri, D. J. (1974). *The prediction of suicide.* Bowie, MD: Charles Press.

Beck, A. T., Schuyler, D., & Herman, I. (1974). Development of suicidal intent scales. In A. T. Beck, H.L.P. Res-

nik, & D. J. Lettieri (Eds.), *The prediction of suicide* (pp. 45–56). Bowie, MD: Charles Press.

Bedrosian, R. C., & Beck, A. T. (1979). Cognitive aspects of suicidal behavior. *Suicide and Life-Threatening Behavior, 9,* 87–96.

Berlin, I. N. (1987). Suicide among American Indian adolescents: An overview. *Suicide and Life-Threatening Behavior, 17,* 218–231.

Berman, A. L., & Jobes, D. A. (1991). *Adolescent suicide: Assessment and intervention.* Washington, DC: American Psychological Association.

Birtchnell, J. (1970). The relationship between attempted suicide, depression, and parent death. *British Journal of Psychiatry, 116,* 307–313.

Black, D. W., & Winokur, G. (1986). Prospective studies of suicide and mortality in psychiatric patients. *Annals of the New York Academy of Sciences, 487,* 106–113.

Blumenthal, S. J. (1990). An overview and synopsis of risk factors, assessment, and treatment of suicidal patients over the life cycle. In S. J. Blumenthal & D. J. Kupfer (Eds.), *Suicide over the life cycle* (pp. 685–734). Washington, DC: American Psychiatric Press.

Braucht, G. N. (1979). Interactional analysis of suicidal behavior. *Journal of Consulting and Clinical Psychology, 47,* 653–669.

Brent, D. A., Perper, J. A., Moritz, G., Allman, C., Friend, A., Rothe, C., Schweers, J., Balach, L., & Baugher, M. (1993a). Psychiatric risk factors for adolescent suicide: A case-control study. *Journal of the American Academy of Child and Adolescent Psychiatry, 32,* 521–529.

Brent, D. A., Perper, J., Moritz, G., Baugher, M., & Allman, C. (1993b). Suicide in adolescents with no apparent psychopathology. *Journal of the American Academy of Child and Adolescent Psychiatry, 32,* 494–500.

Cantor, P. C. (1976). Personality characteristics found among youthful female suicide attempters. *Journal of Abnormal Psychology, 85,* 324–329.

Chiles, J. A., Strosahl, K. D., McMurtray, L., & Linehan, M. (1985). Modeling effects on suicidal behavior. *Journal of Nervous and Mental Disease, 173,* 477–481.

Cole, D. A. (1989). Psychopathology of adolescent suicide: Hopelessness, coping beliefs, and depression. *Journal of Abnormal Psychology, 98,* 248–255.

Coombs, D., & Miller, H. (1975). The Scandinavian suicide phenomena: Fact or artifact? *Psychological Reports, 37,* 1075–1078.

Crook, T., Raskin, A., & Davis, D. (1975). Factors associated with attempted suicide among hospitalized depressed patients. *Psychological Medicine, 5,* 381–388.

Danto, B. (1981). *Crisis behind bars: The suicidal inmate.* Warren, MI: Dale Corp.

Davis, R. (1979). Black suicide in the seventies: Current trends. *Suicide and Life-Threatening Behavior, 9,* 131–140.

Dorpat, T. L., & Ripley, H. (1960). A study of suicide in the Seattle area. *Comparative Psychiatry, 1*(2), 74–79.

Douglas, J. D. (1967). *The social meanings of suicide.* Princeton, NJ: Princeton University Press.

Doyle, B. B. (1990). Crisis management of the suicidal patient. In S. J. Blumenthal & D. J. Kupfer (Eds.), *Suicide over the life cycle* (pp. 381–423). Washington, DC: American Psychiatric Press.

Dublin, L. (1963). *Suicide: A sociological and statistical study.* New York: Ronald Press.

Dunne, E. J. (1992). Following a suicide: Postvention. In B. Bongar (Ed.), *Suicide: Guidelines for assessment, management and treatment* (pp. 221–234). New York: Oxford University Press.

Durkheim, E. (1952). *Le suicide.* New York: Free Press of Glencoe. (Original work published 1897)

Farberow, N. L., & MacKinnon, D. (1974). Prediction of suicide in neuropsychiatric hospital patients. In C. Neuringer (Ed.), *Psychological assessment of suicidal risk* (pp. 186–224). Springfield, IL: Charles C Thomas.

Farberow, N., McKelligott, J. W., Cohen, S., & Darbonne, A. (1970). Suicide among cardiovascular patients. In E. S. Shneidman, N. L. Farberow, & R. E. Litman (Eds.), *The psychology of suicide* (pp. 369–384). New York: Science House.

Farberow, N. L., & Shneidman, E. S. (Eds.). (1961). *The cry for help.* New York: McGraw-Hill.

Ferns, W. J. (1993). The impact of expert system technology on the delivery of social services (Doctoral dissertation, City University of New York, 1992). *Dissertation Abstracts International, 53/10-B*, 5289.

Ferns, W. J., & Riedel, M. (1995). The expert system as a metaphor for professional knowledge development. In E. J. Mullen & P. Hess (Eds.), *Practitioner–Researcher Partnerships: Building knowledge from, in, and for practice* (pp. 229–254). Washington, DC: NASW Press.

Fox, K., & Weissman, M. (1975). Suicide attempts and drugs: Contradiction between method and intent. *Social Psychiatry, 10*(1), 31–38.

Furst, S. S., & Ostow, M. (1979). The psychodynamics of suicide. In L. G. Hankoff & B. Einsidler (Eds.), *Suicide: Theory and clinical aspects* (pp. 165–178). Littleton, MA: P.S.G. Publishing.

Garland, A., Shaffer, D., & Whittle, B. (1989). A national survey of adolescent suicide prevention programs. *Journal of the American Academy of Child and Adolescent Psychiatry, 28*, 931–934.

Garland, A. F., & Zigler, E. (1993). Adolescent suicide prevention: Current research and social policy implications. *American Psychologist, 48*, 169–182.

Gibbons, J. S., Butler, J., Urwin, P., & Gibbons, J. L. (1978). Evaluation of social work service for self-poisoning patients. *British Journal of Psychiatry, 133*, 111–118.

Gibbs, J. P., & Martin, W. L. (1964). *Status integration and suicide: A sociological study.* Eugene: University of Oregon Press.

Gibbs, J. T. (1988). Conceptual, methodological, and sociocultural issues in black youth suicide: Implications for assessment and early intervention. *Suicide and Life-Threatening Behavior, 18*, 73–89.

Greer, S., Gunn, J. C., & Koller, K. M. (1966). Aetiological factors in attempted suicide. *British Medical Journal, 2*, 1352–1355.

Greist, J., Gustafson, D., Stauss, F., Rowse, G., Laughren, T., & Chiles, J. (1973). A computer interview for suicide-risk prediction. *American Journal of Psychiatry, 130*, 1327–1332.

Hankoff, L. D. (1979). Situational categories. In L. D. Hankoff & B. Einsidler (Eds.), *Suicide: Theory and clinical aspects* (pp. 235–249). Littleton, MA: P.S.G. Publishing.

Hawton, K. (1986). *Suicide and attempted suicide among children and adolescents.* Newbury Park, CA: Sage Publications.

Hawton, K., & Catalan, J. (1982). *Attempted suicide: A practical guide to its nature and management.* New York: Oxford University Press.

Haycock, J. (1991). Crimes and misdemeanors: A review of recent research on suicides in prison. *Omega, 23*, 81–94.

Hayes, J., & Rowan, J. (1988). *National study of jail suicides: Seven years later.* Alexandria, VA: National Center on Institutions and Alternatives.

Heacock, D. R. (1990). Suicidal behavior in black and Hispanic youth. *Psychiatric Annals, 20*, 134–142.

Henry, A. F., & Short, J. F. (1954). *Suicide and homicide.* Glencoe, IL: Free Press.

Hirsch, S. R., Walsh, C., & Draper, R. (1982). Parasuicide: A review of treatment interventions. *Journal of Affective Disorders, 4*, 299–311.

Hoberman, H. M., & Garfinkle, B. D. (1988). Completed suicide in children and adolescents. *Journal of the American Academy of Child and Adolescent Psychiatry, 27*, 689–695.

Hoppe, S. K., & Martin, S. W. (1986). Patterns of suicide among Mexican-Americans and Anglos, 1960–1980. *Social Psychiatry, 21*, 83–88.

Humphrey, J. A. (1977). Social loss: A comparison of suicide victims, homicide offenders and non-violent individuals. *Diseases of the Nervous System, 38*, 157–160.

Hunter, J. (1990). Violence against lesbian and gay male youths. *Journal of Interpersonal Violence, 5*, 295–300.

Ivanoff, A. (1985). *Inpatient treatment for suicide attempters.* Unpublished doctoral dissertation, University of Washington, Seattle.

Ivanoff, A., & Jang, S. J. (1991). The role of hopelessness and social desirability in predicting suicidal behavior: A study of prison inmates. *Journal of Consulting and Clinical Psychology, 59*, 394–399.

Ivanoff, A., & Smyth, J. (1992). Intervention with suicidal individuals. In K. Corcoran (Ed.), *Structuring change: Effective practice for common client problems* (pp. 111–137). Chicago: Lyceum.

Kaplan, H. B., & Pokorny, A. D. (1976). Self-attitudes and suicidal behavior. *Suicide and Life-Threatening Behavior, 6*, 23–35.

Kleck, G. (1988). Miscounting suicides. *Suicide and Life-Threatening Behavior, 18*, 219–236.

Kovacs, M., Beck, A. T., & Weissman, A. (1975a). Hopelessness: An indicator of suicidal risk. *Suicide, 29*(5), 363–368.

Kovacs, M., Beck, A. T., & Weissman, A. (1975b). The use of suicidal motives in psycho-therapy of attempted suicides. *American Journal of Psychotherapy, 29*(3), 363–368.

Kreitman, N. (1977). *Parasuicide.* New York: John Wiley & Sons.

Kreitman, N., Philip, A. E., Greer, S., & Bagley, C. R. (1969). Parasuicide. *British Journal of Psychiatry, 115*(523), 746–747.

Kreitman, N., Smith, P., & Tan, E. (1970). Attempted suicide as a language: An empirical study. *British Journal of Psychiatry, 116*(534), 465–473.

Ladame, F. (1992). Suicide prevention in adolescence: An overview of current trends. *Journal of Adolescent Health, 13*, 406–408.

Lester, D. (1968). Suicide as an aggressive act: A replication with a control for neuroticism. *Journal of General Psychology, 79*, 83–86.

Lester, D. (1974). Effect of suicide prevention centers on suicide rates in the United States. *Health Services Reports, 89*, 37–39.

Lester, D. (1987). Suicide and homicide in the U.S.A. prisons. *Psychological Reports, 61,* 126.

Lester, D. (1992a). Alcoholism and drug abuse. In R. W. Maris, A. L. Berman, J. T. Maltsberger, & R. I. Yufit (Eds.), *Assessment and prediction of suicide.* New York: Guilford Press.

Lester, D. (1992b). *Why people kill themselves* (3rd ed.). Springfield, IL: Charles C Thomas.

Lester, D., & Danto, B. L. (1993). *Suicide behind bars: Prediction and prevention.* Philadelphia: Charles Press.

Lester, D., & Yang, B. (1992). Social and economic correlates of the elderly suicide rate. *Suicide and Life-Threatening Behavior, 22,* 36–47.

Levenson, M., & Neuringer, C. (1971). Problem-solving behavior in suicidal adolescents. *Journal of Consulting and Clinical Psychology, 37,* 433–436.

Levy, D., Fales, C. H., Stein, M., & Sharp, V. H. (1966). Separation and attempted suicide. *Archives of General Psychiatry, 15,* 158–164.

Library Information Specialists. (1983). *Corrections information series: Suicides in jails.* Boulder, CO: National Institute of Corrections.

Linehan, M. M. (1981). A social–behavioral analysis of suicide and parasuicide: Implications for assessment and treatment. In H. Glazer & J. F. Clarkin (Eds.), *Depression: Behavioral and directive intervention strategies* (pp. 147–169). New York: Garland.

Linehan, M. M. (1993). *Cognitive–behavioral treatment of borderline personality disorders.* New York: Guilford Press.

Linehan, M. M., & Nielson, S. L. (1981). Assessment of ideation and parasuicide: Hopelessness and social desirability. *Journal of Consulting and Clinical Psychology, 49,* 773–775.

Litman, R. E. (1967). Sigmund Freud on suicide. In E. S. Shneidman (Ed.), *Essays in self-destruction* (pp. 324–344). New York: Science House.

Maris, R. (1982). Rational suicide: An impoverished self-transformation. *Suicide and Life-Threatening Behavior, 12,* 4–16.

Maris, R. W., Berman, A. L., Maltsberger, J. T., & Yufit, R. I. (Eds.). (1992). *Assessment and prediction of suicide.* New York: Guilford Press.

Marzuk, P. M., Tierney, H., Tardiff, K., Gross, E. M., Morgan, E. B., Hsu, M. A., & Mann, J. J. (1988). Increased risk of suicide in persons with AIDS. *Journal of the American Medical Association, 259,* 1333–1337.

McCutcheon, S. (1985). *Behavioral decision making and the prediction of parasuicide.* Unpublished doctoral dissertation, University of Washington, Seattle.

McGinnis, J. M. (1987). Suicide in America: Moving up the public health agenda. *Suicide and Life-Threatening Behavior, 17,* 18–32.

McIntosh, J. L. (1983–1984). Suicide among Native Americans: Further tribal data and considerations. *Omega, 14,* 215–229.

McIntosh, J. L. (1987). Survivor family relationships: Literature review. In E. J. Dunne, J. L. McIntosh, & K. Dunne-Maxim (Eds.), *Suicide and its aftermath.* New York: W. W. Norton.

McIntosh, J. L. (1991). Middle-age suicide: A literature review and epidemiological study. *Death Studies, 15,* 21–37.

McIntosh, J. L. (1992). Epidemiology of suicide in the elderly. *Suicide and Life-Threatening Behavior, 22,* 15–35.

Menninger, K. (1938). *Man against himself.* New York: Harcourt, Brace.

Monk, M., & Warshaur, E. M. (1974). Completed and attempted suicide in three ethnic groups. *American Journal of Epidemiology, 100,* 333–345.

Montgomery, S. A., & Montgomery, D. (1982). Pharmacological prevention of suicidal behavior. *Journal of Affective Disorders, 4,* 291–298.

Moss, L. M., & Hamilton, D. M. (1957). Psychotherapy of the suicidal patient. In E. S. Shneidman & N. L. Farberow (Eds.), *Clues to suicide* (pp. 99–110). New York: McGraw-Hill.

Nelson, V. L., Nielson, E. D., & Checketts, K. T. (1977). Interpersonal attitudes of suicidal individuals. *Psychological Reports, 40*(3), 983–989.

Neuringer, C. (1964). Rigid thinking in suicidal individuals. *Journal of Consulting and Clinical Psychology, 28*(1), 54–58.

Neuringer, C., & Lettieri, D. J. (1982). *Suicidal women: Their thinking and feeling patterns.* New York: Gardner Press.

O'Dowd, M. A., Biderman, D. J., & McKegney, F. P. (1993). Incidence of suicidality in AIDS and HIV-positive patients attending a psychiatry outpatient program. *Psychosomatics, 34,* 33–40.

Olivero, J. M., & Roberts, J. B. (1990). Jail suicide and legal redress. *Suicide and Life-Threatening Behavior, 20,* 138–147.

Otto, R. K., & Ogloff, J.R.P. (1988). *A manual for mental health professionals working with jails.* Lincoln: Nebraska Department of Public Institutions.

Parad, H. J., & Caplan, G. (1960). A framework for studying families in crisis. *Social Work, 5,* 3–15.

Pardes, H., & Blumenthal, S. J. (1990). Youth suicide: Public policy and research issues. In S. J. Blumenthal & D. J. Kupfer (Eds.), *Suicide over the life cycle* (pp. 665–681). Washington, DC: American Psychiatric Press.

Patsiokas, A., Clum, G., & Luscomb, R. (1979). Cognitive characteristics of suicide attempters. *Journal of Consulting and Clinical Psychology, 47*(2), 478–484.

Paykel, E. S. (1979). Life stress. In L. D. Hankoff & B. Einsidler (Eds.), *Suicide: Theory and clinical aspects* (pp. 225–234). Littleton, MA: P.S.G. Publishing.

Pfeffer, C. R. (1986). *The suicidal child.* New York: Guilford Press.

Pfeffer, C. R., Klerman, G. L., Hurt, S. W., Kakuma, T., Peskin, J. R., & Siefker, C. A. (1993). Suicidal children grow up: Rates and psychosocial risk factors for suicide attempts during follow-up. *Journal of the American Academy of Child and Adolescent Psychiatry, 32,* 106–113.

Price, R. H., Cowen, E. L., Lorion, R. P., & Ramos-McKay, J. (1989). The search for effective prevention programs: What we learned along the way. *American Journal of Orthopsychiatry, 59,* 49–58.

Rieger, W. (1971). Suicide at a federal prison. *Archives of General Psychiatry, 24,* 532–535.

Rohde, P., Lewinsohn, P., & Seeley, J. R. (1991). Comorbidity of unipolar depression: Comorbidity with other mental disorders in adolescents and adults. *Journal of Abnormal Psychology, 100,* 214–222.

Rood, L. R., & Faison, K. (1988). Identifying suicidal risk in prisoners. In *Mental health basics for correctional officers* (Chap. 6). Lincoln: Nebraska Department of Public Institutions.

Rosenbaum, M., & Richman, J. (1970). Suicide: The role of hostility and death wishes from the family and significant others. *American Journal of Psychiatry,* *126*(11), 1652–1655.

Rotheram, M. J. (1987). Evaluation of imminent danger for suicide among youth. *American Journal of Orthopsychiatry, 57,* 102–110.

Rotheram-Borus, M. J., Hunter, J., & Rosario, M. (1994). Suicidal behavior and gay-related stress among gay and bisexual male adolescents. *Journal of Adolescent Research, 9,* 498–508.

Roy, A. (1983). A family history of suicide. *Archives of General Psychiatry, 40,* 971–974.

Roy, A. (1986). Genetic factors in suicide. *Psychopharmacology Bulletin, 22,* 666–668.

Roy, A., Agren, H., & Pickar, D. (in press). Reduced cerebrospinal fluid concentrations of homovanillic acid to 5-hydroxyindoleacetic acid ratios in depressed patients. *American Journal of Psychiatry.*

Roy, A., & Linnoila, M. (1986). Alcoholism and suicide. In R. W. Maris (Ed.), *Biology of suicide* (pp. 162–191). New York: Guilford Press.

Saghir, M. T., & Robins, E. (1973). *Male and female homosexuality: A comprehensive investigation.* Baltimore: Williams & Wilkins.

Saunders, J. M., & Valente, S. M. (1987). Suicide risk among gay men and lesbians: A review. *Death Studies, 11,* 1–23.

Schneider, S. G., Taylor, S. E., Kemeny, M. E., & Hammen, C. (1991). AIDS-related factors predictive of suicidal ideation of low and high intent among gay and bisexual men. *Suicide and Life-Threatening Behavior, 21,* 313–328.

Shaffer, D., Garland, A., Fisher, P., Bacon, K., & Vieland, V. (1990). Suicide crisis centers: A critical reappraisal with special reference to the prevention of youth suicide. In F. E. Goldston, C. M. Heinicke, R. S. Pynoos, & J. Yagger (Eds.), *Prevention of mental health disturbance in childhood* (pp. 135–166). Washington, DC: American Psychiatric Press.

Shaffer, D., Garland, A., Gould, M., Fisher, P., & Trautman, P. (1988). Preventing teenage suicide: A critical review. *Journal of the American Academy of Child and Adolescent Psychiatry, 27,* 675–687.

Shaffi, M., Carrigan, S., Whittinghill, J. R., & Derrick, A. (1985). Psychological autopsy of completed suicide in children and adolescents. *American Journal of Psychiatry, 142,* 1061–1064.

Shneidman, E. S. (1976). *Suicidology: Contemporary developments.* New York: Grune & Stratton.

Shneidman, E. S. (1979). An overview: Personality, motivation and behavior theories. In L. D. Hankoff & B. Einsidler (Eds.), *Suicide: Theory and clinical aspects* (pp. 143–163). Littleton, MA: P.S.G. Publishing.

Shneidman, E. S., Farberow, N. L., & Litman, R. E. (Eds.). (1970). *The psychology of suicide.* New York: Science House.

Spirito, A., Plummer, B., Gispert, M., Levy, S., Kurkjion, J., Lewander, W., Hagberg, S., & Devost, L. (1992). Adolescent suicide attempts: Outcomes at follow-up. *American Journal of Orthopsychiatry, 62,* 464–468.

Starace, F. (1993). Suicidal behavior in people infected with human immunodeficiency virus: A literature review. *International Journal of Social Psychiatry, 39,* 64–70.

Stengel, E., & Cook, N. (1958). *Attempted suicide.* New York: Oxford University Press.

Toch, H. (1992). *Mosaic of despair: Human breakdown in prison.* Washington, DC: American Psychological Association.

Topp, D. O. (1979). Suicide in prison. *British Journal of Psychiatry, 134,* 24–27.

U.S. Bureau of the Census. (1990). United States population estimates, by age, sex, race, and Hispanic origin: 1980–1988. In *Current population reports* (Series P-25, No. 1045). Washington, DC: U.S. Government Printing Office.

U.S. Department of Health and Human Services. (1985). *Prevention '84/'85.* Washington, DC: U.S. Government Printing Office.

U.S. National Center for Health Statistics. (1986). *Vital statistics of the United States, annual* (Vol. 2, *Mortality,* Part B). Hyattsville, MD: Author.

U.S. National Center for Health Statistics. (1988). *Vital statistics of the United States, annual* (Vol. 2, *Mortality,* Part B). Hyattsville, MD: Author.

U.S. National Center for Health Statistics. (1990). *Vital statistics of the United States, annual* (Vol. 2, *Mortality,* Part B). Hyattsville, MD: Author.

U.S. National Center for Health Statistics. (1992). Internal report, unpublished data, 1990. Hyattsville, MD: Author.

U.S. National Center for Health Statistics. (1993, January 7). Advance report on final mortality statistics, 1990. *Monthly Vital Statistics Report, 41,* 17–29.

Virkkunen, M. (1976). Attitude to psychiatric treatment before suicide in schizophrenia and paranoid psychoses. *British Journal of Psychiatry, 128,* 47–49.

Wandrei, K. E. (1985). Identifying potential suicides among high-risk women. *Social Work, 30,* 511–517.

Weishar, M. E., & Beck, A. T. (1992). Clinical and cognitive predictors of suicide. In R. W. Maris, A. L. Berman, J. T. Maltsberger, & R. I. Yufit (Eds.), *Assessment and prediction of suicide* (pp. 467–483). New York: Guilford Press.

Weissman, M. M. (1974). The epidemiology of suicide attempts 1960–1971. *Archives of General Psychiatry, 30,* 737–746.

World Health Organization. (1991). *World health statistics annual.* Geneva: Author.

Wyche, K. F., & Rotheram-Borus, M. J. (1990). Suicidal behavior among minority youth in the United States. In A. R. Stiffman & L. E. Davis (Eds.), *Ethnic issues in adolescent mental health* (pp. 323–338). Newbury Park, CA: Sage Publications.

Zubin, J. (1974). Observations on nosological issues in the classification of suicidal behavior. In A. T. Beck, H.L.P. Resnick, & D. J. Lettieri (Eds.), *The prediction of suicide* (pp. 3–25). Bowie, MD: Charles Press.

André Ivanoff, PhD, ACSW, is associate professor, and **Marion Riedel, CSW,** is a doctoral student, Columbia University, School of Social Work, 622 West 113th Street, New York, NY 10025.

For further information see

Adolescence Overview; Aging: Overview; Alcohol Abuse; Bereavement and Loss; Clinical Social Work; Crisis Intervention: Research Needs; Direct Practice Overview; Drug Abuse; Ethnic-Sensitive Practice; Intervention Research; Mental Health Overview; Primary Prevention Overview; Social Work Practice: Theoretical Base.

Key Words	
depression	suicide
parasuicide	suicide ideation
suicidal behavior	

Supervision and Consultation
Lawrence Shulman

Almost 60 years ago Robinson (1949) defined *supervision* in the context of social work as "an educational process in which a person with a certain equipment of knowledge and skill takes responsibility for training a person with less equipment" (p. 53). This emphasis on the educational aspect of supervision has over the years been combined with a second emphasis on administration that includes efforts to control and coordinate social workers to get the job done.

In another definition of supervision, Kadushin (1976) added to these two sets of tasks the "expressive–supportive leadership function" (p. 20) that focuses on the problem of sustaining social workers by offering emotional support and making efforts to assist them when they have "job-related discouragements and discontents." Kadushin (1976), combining these three major functions, provided a definition of supervision that serves the purposes of this entry well:

> A social work supervisor is an agency administrative staff member to whom authority is delegated to direct, coordinate, enhance, and evaluate on-the-job performance of the supervisees for whose work he [or she] is held accountable. In implementing this responsibility the supervisor performs administrative, educational, and supportive functions in interaction with the supervisee in the context of a positive relationship. The supervisor's ultimate objective is to deliver to agency clients the best possible service, both quantitative[ly] and qualitatively, in accordance with agency policies and procedures. (p. 21)

A crucial aspect of this definition is the emphasis on carrying out these tasks in interaction with the supervisee "in the context of a positive relationship." This relationship between supervisor and supervisee, which parallels the relationship between social worker and client, has been described as consisting of three elements: (1) rapport (general ability to get along); (2) trust (the ability of the social worker to be open with the supervisor and to share mistakes and failures as well as successes); and (3) caring (the communication by the supervisor of concern for the social worker as well as for the client) (Shulman, 1993).

Kaiser (1992), addressing the issue of supervisory relationship in family therapy supervision, highlighted the "phenomenon of isomorphism; what happens in supervision is reflected in the therapy" (p. 284). This is referred to later in this entry as the "parallel process," in which the interaction between supervisor and supervisee directly affects the relationship between the social worker and the client. In reviewing the literature from the fields of social work, psychology, and marriage and family therapy, Kaiser identified four consistently cited issues: "the process of accountability (maintaining objectivity), the need for promoting the supervisee's personal awareness, the importance of establishing trust, and the need to attend to power and authority issues" (p. 284).

MODELS OF SUPERVISION

Dynamic System
One descriptive model of supervision provides a dynamic system conceptualization in which staff members constantly interact with a number of systems that are directly related to their work (Shulman, 1993). A social worker in a child welfare agency, for example, must deal with clients, foster parents, the agency administrators, the supervisor, professional colleagues, clerical staff, the court system, and other agencies or institutions, such as the schools. At any moment in their work day, social workers could be called on to negotiate one or more of these systems. The relationship with each system places unique demands on the social worker and requires specific knowledge and skills if he or she is to negotiate it effectively. This model describes the supervisor's role as in the middle between the social worker and these important systems, helping the social worker to negotiate them more effectively.

This model generates four major agendas for the supervisor and the social worker. First, there is the question of job management. A social worker must be able to work within the structure of the agency in terms of time (for example, being on time for work and meetings, meeting deadlines on reports, and timely recording and developing the skills needed for effective management of caseloads). Second, the social worker must relate effectively to agency policy and procedures. Social workers must implement policies and follow established procedures while they simultaneously develop the skills necessary to influence them. Third, for effective practice, social workers must develop skills to deal with professional colleagues, support staff, and supervisors. As social workers attempt to deliver a service, their efforts must be coordinated with those of other staff members. Harmonious work relationships are required for staff members to effectively provide help to clients. When a breakdown occurs in team relationships, the outcome is an almost inevitable deterioration of client service. Fourth, social workers must also deal with supervisors—symbols of authority—and must learn how to use this relationship to their advantage.

Supervisor–Supervisee Relationship

Other models of supervision focus on the nature of the supervisor–supervisee relationship. These have been described in the literature as ranging from more traditional, authoritarian models in which the supervisor's authority emerges from agency sanction on one end, to more collaborative models in which the authority emerges essentially from the supervisor's competence on the other end.

Munson (1981, 1983) surveyed 65 supervisees and 64 supervisors. He focused on models of supervision in three areas: (1) structure (traditional–individual, group, and independent); (2) authority (sanction versus competence); and (3) teaching (Socratic, growth, and integrative). He examined the impact of the use of different models on social worker satisfaction with supervision and integration. Munson (1981) found that "The structural models did not produce significantly different outcomes regarding interaction and satisfaction, but the authority models did. The competence model of authority was the most productive in all respects" (p. 71). This was the model in which the supervisor's authority was derived from competence and skill rather than from agency sanction.

Munson's (1981) findings supported those of Kadushin (1974). Traditional supervision, in which authority for the supervisor flows from agency sanction, was questioned. Munson pointed to "the need to encourage greater independence and autonomy" (p. 296). In a study of supervision, Kadushin (1974) conducted a national survey of 750 supervisors and an equal number of supervisees. The purpose was to identify the sources of satisfaction for both supervisors and supervisees. Supervisors in the study took great satisfaction in helping supervisees grow and develop professionally; their greatest source of dissatisfaction related to dealing with administrative red tape. Supervisees identified being able to share responsibility with supervisors and being able to obtain support for difficult cases as their greatest source of satisfaction. A majority of both the supervisors and

supervisees in Kadushin's study believed that as the supervisee gained experience, the relationship became one of consultant–consultee, a form of supervision preferred by many social workers. Strong dissatisfaction with supervision was reported by many social workers, who believed the authority of the supervisor was exercised in a negative manner.

Consider that most of the research findings discussed in this entry focus on the supervisor's or the supervisee's perceptions of the process rather than on the impact of supervision on client services and the outcomes of those services. Harkness and Portner (1989) reviewed a number of these studies and examined the underlying conceptualization of social work supervision guiding research efforts in the field. They pointed out that a view of supervision as a training process shifted the research focus from the impact of supervision on client services to the impact on social workers. In 1991 Harkness and Hensley, citing Shulman et al.'s (1981) proposal for a change in the paradigm, argued for a shift back to evaluating supervision in terms of client outcomes. Their own study (1991), for example, suggested a link between a client-focused supervision and an improvement in client ratings of helpfulness and goal attainment.

Educational Function

Kadushin (1976) described educational supervision as a more specific kind of staff development in which "training is directed to the needs of a particular worker carrying a particular caseload, encountering particular problems and needing some individualized program of education" (p. 126). Four major areas of the curriculum are (1) professional practice, (2) professional impact, (3) job management, and (4) continued learning.

In one supervision study (Shulman, Robinson, & Luckyj, 1981), social workers were asked to identify what they would like to have discussed in their supervision sessions, compared with the actual content of those sessions. Their first preference was that supervisors should devote more time to teaching practice skills, followed by more time on discussing research information and providing feedback on performance. Interestingly, such supervision–consulting roles also were the favored tasks of supervisors queried in the study.

Other research has supported the idea that both supervisors and supervisees regard the educational function of supervision as important and a source of satisfaction. In Kadushin's (1974) study, two of the three strongest sources of supervisor satisfaction were found to be related to helping the supervisee grow and develop professionally and to sharing social work knowledge and skill. In the same study, social workers indicated that two of the three main sources of their satisfaction with supervision were receiving help in dealing with clients and in developing as professionals. In another study (Scott, 1969), professionally oriented social workers expressed a preference for supervisors who knew their theoretical fundamentals, were skilled in teaching, and were capable of offering professional assistance.

The notion of the parallel process is central to the educational function of supervision. There are assumed parallels between the dynamics of supervision and any other helping relationship. Therefore, the skills that are important in direct practice with clients or patients also are important to the supervisory relationship. A number of authors have identified these similarities (Arlow, 1963; Doehrman, 1972; Schwartz, 1968). Much of what is known about effective communication and relationship skills can be useful in implementing diverse aspects of the supervisory function, such as coordination, education, and evaluation.

In addition, the way the supervisor demonstrates the helping relationship with social workers will influence the manner in which staff members relate to clients. For example, when supervisors attempt to help staff members develop a greater capacity for empathy with difficult clients, they ought also to simultaneously demonstrate their own empathy for the staff. Supervisees learn what a supervisor really feels about helping by observing the supervisor in action. More is "caught" by staff than is "taught" by the supervisor.

Frankel and Piercy (1990) described the potential positive benefits of this modeling in a study of the impact of supervisory phone-ins on family therapists and the resultant therapist responses to clients. She found that effective "support" and "teach" behaviors of the supervisor were replicated by the therapists and resulted in more positive client outcomes. Jacobs (1991) discussed this process in terms of student–supervisor relationships, stressing the problem of power abuses and boundary violations in clinical supervision. She suggested that clients can become "victims of a dysfunctional supervisory system if the student replicates the harmful interaction with current or future clients" (p. 130).

ADMINISTRATIVE FUNCTION

The administrative role of the supervisor contains a number of elements, all of which are designed to aid in the implementation of the mission. These elements include coordination of activities between staff members and between one's unit or department and other parts of the organization, as well as between staff and the community (for example, other agencies). This rule also involves working with staff and administration to design and implement policies and procedures for supporting the work of the setting.

Conflict between Staff and Administration

An area of stress reported by supervisors is the feeling of being caught in the middle between staff and administration on a point of conflict. Conflicts between staff members and the administration are often the rule rather than the exception, and they make up a large part of the interaction in the formal and informal systems. Administrators may sometimes set unworkable policies, because they are too far removed from the realities of practice to understand their effect on services. New programs or procedures may be developed by study groups or outside consultants who have little understanding of the actual nature of the practice. Cost-containment and funding cutbacks can lead to organizational stress and force decisions that can affect programs and positions.

One study (Erera, 1991), which involved 62 public welfare supervisors, used qualitative and quantitative methods to examine the impact of incompatible policies as one of four examples of role conflict experienced by supervisors. Incompatible policies emerging from state, county, or public agencies were found to be associated with the supervisory role for all supervisors except for two who were involved in specialized programs guided by few policies. Erera concluded that the study supported the notion "that the middle managers are located at that critical point where the organization's structure impinges on the individual worker" (pp. 46–47).

At the same time, staff members may resist changes that are threatening to the status quo or require sacrifices such as weekend or evening work. They may be unwilling to consider the requirements of the entire institutional setting and may stubbornly resist pleas for flexibility or consideration.

Mediating Role

The "third force," or mediating role, for the supervisor is that of providing a framework in which the supervisor does not choose between identifying with either the staff or the administration. In most cases, rather than taking sides with one over the other, the supervisor can take a stand with respect to the process. Being caught in the middle can be a most effective position for stimulating change. Bunker and Wijnberg (1985) described supervisors as mediators of organizational climate who serve as a buffer between frontline staff and administration.

This role for supervisors, however, is not one in which they never take a position or are neutral on every issue. It does not mean that supervisors will shy away from conflict in attempts to smooth over real differences of interest between social workers and the administration. Just the opposite is true. Effective implementation of this role requires that conflicts smoldering beneath the surface be brought to light. There will be times when advocacy of a staff position and confrontation of the administration are essential tools for supervisors, although careful thought must be given to how these tools are used. Even in the role of advocate, supervisors must not lose sight of the essential common ground between the staff and the administration.

EXPRESSIVE–SUPPORTIVE FUNCTION

Availability to Staff

The issues of job stress and job manageability are crucial ones for both frontline social workers and supervisors. A number of studies have pointed to stress and job manageability as important factors. In a study of workloads for supervisors in a public welfare agency, Galm (1972) found that supervisors simply did not have enough time to supervise. In Kadushin's (1974) study 53 percent indicated that not having time to supervise was one of the strongest sources of their job dissatisfaction. A supervisor's stress can have a powerful impact on his or her availability to social workers as well as on the supervisor's capacity to provide support (Shulman, 1993).

Availability to social workers is a particularly important variable in those arenas of practice that generate significant stress and lead to social worker burnout. The term *burnout* has come to be used to describe a syndrome exhibited by workers who deal with intense stress over a period during which little support is available. Although most commonly noted in the child welfare literature, burnout also is seen in reference to workers in any high-stress field of practice, particularly in large government agencies (see Borland, 1981; Copans, Krell, Gundy, Rogan, & Field, 1979; Daley, 1979; Falconer, 1983; Freudenberger, 1974; Riggar, Godley, & Hafer, 1984).

Issues of Caseload Size and Trauma

Another source of stress for front-line social workers is caseload size. Social workers in both public and private agencies have increasingly been asked to do more with fewer resources. Increased caseloads, the growing complexity of the problems facing clients, and limitations on the availability of other resources combine to make social workers' jobs more difficult.

Social workers also experience high levels of burnout because of the powerful nature of the events and the emotions in the lives of their clients. The impact of the death of a child on one's caseload, the emotions associated with sexual and physical abuse, counseling a grieving family in a hospital or a suicidal client, and working with people with acquired immune deficiency syndrome are examples of work that exacts an emotional toll on the caring professional. A particularly traumatic incident—for example, a suicide on a psychiatric ward—may have effects that are felt by the social worker involved as well as by all of his or her colleagues. The impact of trauma can be exacerbated if the initial agency response is to investigate to determine blame, rather than to provide support to the helpers.

Loughlin (1991) focused on the trauma of child sexual abuse and its impact on those who work with it as well as their institutions and networks. She stressed the potential for the agency itself to become dysfunctional, responding to the social worker involved in ways that parallel the abuse in the family and for boundaries to become blurred. She suggested that "The emotional impact of such work should not be underestimated and that good supervision which considers the emotional impact of this and similar life crisis interventions is vital for everyone working in this field" (p. 111). Greene (1991) made a similar case for the importance of support for social workers in geriatric practice because they also face emotional stress and inherent value conflicts.

Kurland and Salmon (1992) argued that teachers, field instructors, consultants, and supervisors must recognize the intractability of many of the problems faced by clients and to help prepare their supervisors for the difficulty of influencing real change.

IMPACT OF DIVERSITY ON SUPERVISION

As the social work profession has increasingly turned its attention to issues of diversity in practice, similar issues have emerged in the context of supervision and management. One major issue has been the underrepresentation of women in management roles (Fanshel, 1976; Shulman, 1993; Shulman et al., 1981). Chernesky (1980), reviewing the research in this area, described how women tend to be located and to remain in direct-service positions. Similar concerns have been raised about the number of members of racial and ethnic groups who assume management roles. Affirmative action programs, designed to assure that front-line staff and management become diversified and begin to look like the clients they serve, have been initiated in federal, state, municipal, and private agencies.

As increasing numbers of women and minorities have assumed supervisory positions, interest has grown in the nature of the experience of these populations once management positions have been assumed (McNeely, 1983). Wright, King, and Berg (1985), pointing out that most studies of job satisfaction have included samples predominantly of white males, examined factors that affected job satisfaction of black females in management positions. Their tentative findings, with a few exceptions, replicated earlier findings with male populations that had pointed to organizational variables as most predictive of job satisfaction. The findings suggested that

> Black female managers who receive positive job per-
> formance evaluations, who have some degree of
> authority over their job performance, who have clearly
> specified responsibilities and functions, who are in
> positions that are commensurate with their experi-
> ence, training, and education and who occupy posi-
> tions previously occupied by females will—all other
> things being equal—be more satisfied with their jobs.
> (p. 71)

Wright et al.'s (1985) job-stress index, which included four variables that specifically identified stress related to being black and female, did not predict job satisfaction for this admittedly small sample.

Increased interest in cross-cultural supervision also has been noted in the recent literature. In their study of field supervision, McRoy, Freeman, Logan, and Blackmon (1986) noted that cross-cultural supervision was both desirable and problematic. In another study that examined the experiences of emotional support, social undermining, and criticism of African American practitioners, Jayaratne et al. (1992) found that social undermining had substantial and negative effects on the social worker, which were not significantly diminished by social support. Another report (Gant et al., 1993) on the impact of undermining an African American social worker's perceptions of coworker and supervisory relationships found a pattern of social worker perceptions that were governed by the gender and race of the supervisor. The relatively recent growth of women and minorities in supervisory positions and the tentative and exploratory nature of most of the recent studies on the effects of gender and race on supervision suggests that additional research is needed.

CONSULTATION AS A SOCIAL WORK ROLE

Consultation is an interaction between two or more people in which the consultant's special competence in a particular area is used to help the consultee with a current work problem (Caplan, 1970). Social work consultation may encompass the functions described for the supervisor; however, there is one major difference. Consultants usually do not carry administrative responsibility and accountability. Their authority is derived from their perceived expertise in a subject rather than from formal sanction by the agency or setting. Miller (1987) alluded to this difference when he suggested that consultation "consists of structured advice giving and problem clarification about clients and professional [practice; it] becomes more or less equivalent to supervision, with all the pleasures and few of the headaches" (p. 749).

Social workers have increasingly gained recognition for their knowledge in a wide range of settings; the two major areas of consultation include case consultation and program consultation. Case consultation usually involves a social work consultant's working with line staff to assist them in providing direct services to clients. Program or organizational consultation usually involves work with administrative staff and may focus on agency policies, programs, and procedures.

Drisko (1993) described one example of case consultation with special education teachers. In this model, social workers meet with teachers to detail jointly three single-spaced profiles that focus the consultation on student strengths. "The profiles aid the teacher in understanding the student from a psychological perspective while offering new knowledge and skills in assessment and self-awareness" (p. 19).

Social workers also may be consultants to teams in interdisciplinary settings (Abramson, 1989; Kadushin, 1976). Abramson pointed out that many social work skills can easily be adapted to the consultation role. These include "(1) problem assessment; (2) problem definition; (3) mediation and negotiation; and (4) contract development" (p. 57).

In a final example, periodic case consultation may be provided to private practitioners. Kaslow (1991) described general guidelines for marital therapy consultation, which, because of its private and voluntary nature, leaves the trainee "free to utilize or disregard the consultants' ideas and recommendations" (p. 133). She pointed out that clinicians may seek consultation for a number of different reasons including "licensure and/or organizational membership requirements for a certain number of documentable hours of supervision" (p. 133). They also may seek consultation because they

> "may desire supervision for a provocative professional interaction that stretches their knowledge and skills, because they are expanding their areas of therapeutic practice and want guidance and affirmation, or because they have some particularly difficult case and would like a 'second opinion' from a senior and respected colleague." (p. 132)

CONCLUSION

It is apparent that supervision and consultation in the social work profession have a number of core dynamics and processes that have persisted over the years. At the same time, both supervision and consultation are adapting to meet the new challenges facing helping professionals as client problems become more complex and organizational and social issues become more oppressive. One rarely hears a call these days for the abandonment of supervision as a process that diminishes the professional nature of practitioners. Rather, the opposite seems to be true. There is an increasing recognition of the crucial importance of providing support and accountability through the supervision process.

REFERENCES

Abramson, J. S. (1989). Making teams work. *Social Work with Groups, 12,* 45–61.

Arlow, J. A. (1963). The supervisory situation. *Journal of the American Psychoanalytic Association, 11,* 574–594.

Austin, C. D., Kravetz, D., & Pollock, K. L. (1985). Experiences of women as social welfare administrators. *Social Work, 30,* 173–179.

Borland, J. (1981). Burnout among workers and administrators. *Health & Social Work, 6,* 73–78.

Bunker, D. R., & Wijnberg, M. (1985). The supervisor as a mediator of organizational climate in public social service organizations. *Administration in Social Work, 9,* 59–72.

Caplan, G. (1970). *The theory and practice of mental health consultation.* New York: Basic Books.

Chernesky, R. H. (1980). Woman administrators in social work. In E. Norman & A. Manusco (Eds.), *Women's issues and social work practice* (pp. 241–262). Itasca, IL: F. E. Peacock.

Copans, S., Krell, H., Gundy, J. H., Rogan, J., & Field, F. (1979). The stresses of treating child abuse. *Children Today, 8,* 22–35.

Daley, M. R. (1979). Preventing worker burnout in child welfare. *Child Welfare, 58,* 443–450.

Doehrman, M. J. (1972). *Parallel processes in supervision and psychotherapy.* Unpublished doctoral dissertation, University of Michigan, East Lansing.

Drisko, J. W. (1993). Special education teacher consultation: A student-focused, skill-defining approach. *Social Work in Education, 15,* 19–28.

Erera, I. P. (1991). Role conflict among public welfare supervisors. *Administration in Social Work, 15,* 35–51.

Falconer, N. (1983). *Attack on burnout: The importance of early training.* Toronto: Children's Aid Society of Metropolitan Toronto.

Fanshel, D. (1976). Status differentials: Men and women in social work. *Social Work, 21,* 448–454.

Frankel, B. R., & Piercy, F. P. (1990). The relationship among selected supervisor, therapist, and client behaviors. *Journal of Marital and Family Therapy, 16,* 407–421.

Freudenberger, H. J. (1974). Staff burn-out. *Journal of Social Issues, 30,* 159–165.

Galm, S. (1972). *Issues in welfare administration: Welfare—An administrative nightmare* (U.S. Congress Subcommittee on Fiscal Policy of the Joint Economic Committee). Washington, DC: U.S. Government Printing Office.

Gant, L. M., Nagda, B. A., Brabson, H. V., Jayaratne, S., Chess, W. A., & Singh, A. (1993). Effects of social support and undermining on African American workers' perceptions of coworkers and supervisor relationship and psychological well-being. *Social Work, 38,* 158–164.

Greene, R. R. (1991). Supervision in social work with the aged and their families. *Journal of Gerontological Social Work, 17,* 139–144.

Harkness, D., & Hensley, H. (1991). Changing the focus of social work supervision: Effects on client satisfaction and generalized contentment. *Social Work, 36,* 506–512.

Harkness, D., & Portner, J. (1989). Research and social work supervision: A conceptual review. *Social Work, 34,* 115–118.

Jacobs, C. (1991). Violations of the supervisory relationship: An ethical and educational blind spot. *Social Work, 36,* 130–135.

Jayaratne, S., Brabson, H. V., Gant, L. M., Nagda, B. A., Singh, A. K., & Chess, W. A. (1992). African-American practitioners' perceptions of their supervisors: Emotional support, social undermining, and criticism. *Administration in Social Work, 16,* 27–43.

Kadushin, A. (1974). Supervisor–supervisee: A survey. *Social Work, 19,* 288–298.

Kadushin, A. (1976). *Supervision in social work.* New York: Columbia University Press.

Kaiser, T. L. (1992). The supervisory relationship: An identification of the primary elements in the relationship and an application of two theories of ethical relationships. *Journal of Marital and Family Therapy, 18,* 283–296.

Kaslow, F. W. (1991). Marital therapy supervision and consultation. *American Journal of Family Therapy, 19,* 129–146.

Kurland, R., & Salmon, R. (1992). When problems seem overwhelming: Emphasis in teaching, supervision, and consultation. *Social Work, 37,* 240–244.

Loughlin, B. (1991). Supervision in the face of no cure—Working on the boundary. *Journal of Social Work Practice, 6,* 111–116.

McNeely, R. L. (1983). Occupation, gender, and work satisfaction in a comprehensive human service department. *Administration in Social Work, 8,* 35–47.

McRoy, R. G., Freeman, E. M., Logan, S. L., & Blackmon, B. (1986). Cross-cultural field supervision: Implications for social work education. *Journal of Social Work Education, 1,* 50–56.

Miller, I. (1987). Supervision in social work. In A. Minahan (Ed.-in-Chief), *Encyclopedia of social work* (18th ed., Vol. 2, pp. 748–756). Silver Spring, MD: National Association of Social Workers.

Munson, C. E. (1981). Style and structure in supervision. *Journal of Education for Social Work, 17,* 65–72.

Munson, C. E. (1983). *An introduction to clinical social work supervision.* New York: Haworth Press.

Riggar, T. F., Godley, S. H., & Hafer, M. (1984). Burnout and job satisfaction in rehabilitation administrators and direct service providers. *Rehabilitation Counseling Bulletin, 27*(3), 151–160.

Robinson, V. (1949). *The dynamics of supervision under functional controls: A professional process in social casework.* Philadelphia: University of Pennsylvania Press.

Schwartz, W. (1968). Group work in public welfare. *Public Welfare, 26,* 322–368.

Scott, W. R. (1969). Professional employees in the bureaucratic structure. In A. Etzioni (Ed.), *The semi-professions and their organizations: Teacher, nurse and social worker* (pp. 82–140). New York: Free Press.

Shulman, L. (1993). *Interactional supervision.* Washington, DC: NASW Press.

Shulman, L., Robinson, E., & Luckyj, A. (1981). *A study of content, context and skills of supervision.* Vancouver: University of British Columbia.

Wright, R., Jr., King, W. S., & Berg, W. E. (1985). Job satisfaction in the workplace: A study of black females in management positions. *Journal of Social Services Research, 8,* 65–79.

FURTHER READING

Edwards, R. L., & Yankey, J. A. (Eds.). (1991). *Skills for effective human services management.* Silver Spring, MD: NASW Press.

Holloway, S., & Braeger, G. (1989). *Supervision in the human services: The politics of practice.* New York: Free Press.

Kadushin, A. (1977). *Consultation in social work.* New York: Columbia University Press.

Kadushin, A. (1992). *Supervision in social work* (3rd ed.). New York: Columbia University Press.

Keys, P. R., & Ginsberg, L. (Eds.). (1988). *New management in human services.* Silver Spring, MD: National Association of Social Workers.

Munson, C. E. (1993). *Clinical social work supervision* (2nd ed.). New York: Haworth Press.

Patti, R., Poertner, J., & Rapp, C. A. (Eds.). (1987). *Managing for service effectiveness in social welfare organizations.* New York: Haworth Press.

Perlmutter, F. D. (1990). *Changing hats.* Silver Spring, MD: NASW Press.

Rieman, D. W. (1992). *Strategies in social work consultation.* New York: Longman Publishing.

Weiner, M. E. (1990). *Human services management: Analysis and applications* (2nd ed.). Belmont, CA: Wadsworth Publishing.

Lawrence Shulman, EdD, is professor, Boston University, School of Social Work, 264 Bay State Road, Boston, MA 02215.

For further information see

Case Management; Clinical Social Work; Continuing Education; Direct Practice Overview; Ethics and Values; Interdisciplinary and Interorganizational Collaboration; Management Overview; Organizations: Context for Social Services Delivery; Planning and Management Professions; Private Practice; Professional Conduct; Professional Liability and Malpractice; Program Evaluation; Purchasing Social Services; Quality Assurance; Social Work Education; Social Work Practice: History and Evolution; Social Work Profession Overview; Volunteer Management.

Key Words

administration	supervision
consultation	teaching
field instruction	

Supplemental Security Income
Daniel R. Meyer

Supplemental Security Income (SSI) is a federal program that provides monthly cash payments to poor individuals and couples who are elderly, disabled, or blind. Because the SSI program provides benefits only to people in financial need, it is a welfare program and is similar to Aid to Families with Dependent Children (AFDC). It differs from AFDC, however, in several ways:

- SSI is for people who are elderly, have disabilities, or are blind; AFDC is for families with children (primarily single-parent families).
- SSI is administered by the federal government; AFDC is administered by the states.
- The basic SSI benefit is provided by the federal government and does not vary across states (some states supplement these federal benefits);

AFDC benefits are completely set by the states (although the federal government pays a portion), and benefit levels vary widely among the states.
- SSI benefits increase automatically with inflation; AFDC benefits do not.
- AFDC is the program most people think of as welfare and has been the subject of much

research and policy attention; SSI is less well known by the public and has been the subject of much less research and policy attention.

HISTORY

The early income support programs in the United States were based on laws of England, primarily the Elizabethan Poor Laws. (This discussion of SSI's history relies heavily on the work of Axinn & Levin, 1992; Katz, 1986; and Patterson, 1981.) Like the poor laws, early U.S. welfare programs distinguished between poor people who "deserved" assistance and those who were "undeserving." The undeserving poor were generally men of working age; provisions for them were quite minimal. The deserving poor—children and elderly and blind people—were not expected to work and were generally assisted through local programs.

In the 1800s and early 1900s, states began to offer statewide income programs for poor elderly and blind individuals. Generally only people who were quite poor, who had been residents of the state for some time, and whose relatives were unable to help them were assisted.

By the 1930s, several states had programs that provided cash assistance to poor elderly and blind individuals, but these programs were not always administered statewide. The Social Security Act of 1935 for the first time provided some federal support and guidelines to these state programs. These new federal–state programs were called Old-Age Assistance (OAA) and Aid to the Blind (AB). The federal government set minimum standards for these programs (such as requiring them to be statewide and eliminating local residence requirements) and provided part of the funding. However, each state could determine if it wanted to have a program and the level of funding it would provide. In 1950, Aid to the Permanently and Totally Disabled (APTD) was added to the list of federally supported, state-run programs for poor people.

Because benefits in these programs were determined by the states, the amount of assistance people received depended a great deal on their location. Thus, average OAA benefits in January 1972 varied from $166.73 in New Hampshire to $49.03 in South Carolina. Similar discrepancies existed in the AB program, with benefits ranging from $168.19 in Alaska to $64.41 in Kansas. Likewise, in the APTD program average benefits were $167.19 in Alaska but only $52.99 in Alabama.

During the War on Poverty in the 1960s, considerable attention and debate focused on the best way to assist poor people. One proposal that received support from both conservatives and lib-

erals was the Negative Income Tax (NIT). Under this proposal, the tax system would be used to *guarantee* a certain level of income for every family. If a family's income was below the designated amount, the family would receive income from the government; if its income was significantly above this amount, the family would have to pay taxes. The NIT would be more comprehensive than current programs, proponents argued, because there would be no complicated eligibility rules that could disqualify a needy family. Others argued that the NIT would be more administratively efficient because no determination would have to be made about whether applicants fit into particular categories. In 1969, President Nixon proposed a Family Assistance Plan that was essentially an NIT.

Although there was substantial support for reforming the welfare system, the Family Assistance Plan was the subject of a great deal of controversy and was never passed. Instead of the broad guaranteed income plan for all Americans, the proposal that came forward and was passed in 1972 was a narrower plan, one that guaranteed income for those who were elderly, disabled, or blind—the SSI program.

The SSI program became operational in 1974 when the federal government took over the state OAA, AB, and APTD programs. The federal government provided a basic cash benefit; states that were already paying recipients a higher benefit were required to pay the difference above the basic federal benefit. States were free to determine whether or not they would supplement the federal benefit for all new recipients.

Total benefits in the SSI program have increased significantly since the program began in 1974, from $14.5 billion in 1974 (in 1991 dollars) to $18 billion in 1991. The increase in total benefits is especially notable when compared to benefits in the other major cash welfare program, AFDC, in which total benefits have decreased since 1974 (Figure 1). In fact, the projected figures for 1992 show that SSI now pays more benefits than does the AFDC program.

Figure 2 shows the distribution of federal and state responsibility for SSI benefits. In 1974, when the program was federalized, federal expenditures jumped dramatically. There was little increase in benefits from 1974 through 1982, but then federal costs began to rise. State payments, in contrast, have been quite stable during this period.

PROGRAM OVERVIEW

This section describes the SSI program using the four questions Gilbert, Specht, and Terrell (1993) suggested:

FIGURE 1

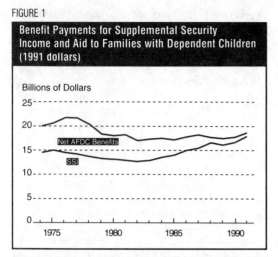

Benefit Payments for Supplemental Security Income and Aid to Families with Dependent Children (1991 dollars)

SOURCE: U.S. House of Representatives, Committee on Ways and Means. (1992). *Overview of entitlement programs*. Washington, DC: U.S. Government Printing Office.

NOTE: Net AFDC benefits include total benefits paid under the single-parent and unemployed parent programs less child support collected.

FIGURE 2

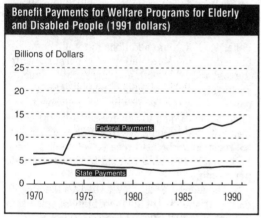

Benefit Payments for Welfare Programs for Elderly and Disabled People (1991 dollars)

SOURCE: U.S. House of Representatives, Committee on Ways and Means. (1992). *Overview of entitlement programs*. Washington, DC: U.S. Government Printing Office.

1. Who receives benefits?
2. What do they receive?
3. How do they receive benefits?
4. Who pays for these benefits?

Who Receives Benefits?

SSI is available to people who are elderly, are blind, or have disabilities and whose income and assets are below designated levels. In addition to the means test, recipients must fit into one of the three categories: Elderly recipients must be age 65 or older, and those who are blind or have disabilities must present medical verification of their disability (defined as "the inability to engage in any

FIGURE 3

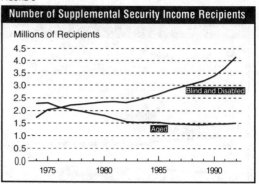

Number of Supplemental Security Income Recipients

SOURCE: U.S. House of Representatives, Committee on Ways and Means. (1992). *Overview of entitlement programs*. Washington, DC: U.S. Government Printing Office. December 1992 figures provided by the Social Security Administration.

NOTE: SSI recipients include both those who receive federal payments and those who receive state supplements only. Some people categorized as "blind and disabled" are also age 65 or over; in this figure they are included based on recipient category rather than their age. In September 1991, 592,000 of the 3,502,000 disabled recipients were age 65 and over, and 22,000 of the 85,000 blind recipients were age 65 and over.

'substantial gainful activity' by reason of any medically determinable physical or mental impairment[s] which can be expected to result in death or which has lasted or is expected to last for a continuous period of not less than 12 months") (Supplemental Security Income Modernization Project, 1992, p. 84). Children younger than 18 may also be considered disabled if their impairment is of "comparable severity" to that of an adult. Recipients of SSI can also receive social security benefits for which they are eligible, but an individual cannot get both SSI and AFDC.

SSI applicants must meet both income and asset tests. In 1992, recipients could not have countable assets of more than $2,000 ($3,000 for a couple). One's home, moderately priced automobile, household goods, and burial space are not counted among these assets. Some of the resources and income of an applicant's spouse (or of a child applicant's parents) may be counted as being available to the applicant under the "deeming" provisions.

In December 1992, more than 5.5 million people received SSI payments. The composition of SSI's recipient population has changed dramatically over the years (Figure 3). When the program began, most SSI recipients were aged rather than blind or disabled. The number of elderly recipients declined from 1974 through 1982, in spite of large increases in this population. The main reason for this change is that more and more aged people are eligible for social security benefits, and those

FIGURE 4

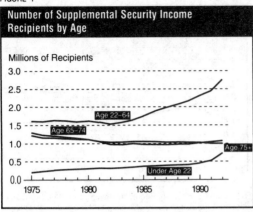

Number of Supplemental Security Income
Recipients by Age

Millions of Recipients

SOURCE: *Social Security Bulletin*, various issues. December 1992
figures provided by the Social Security Administration.

NOTE: SSI recipients do not include those who receive state supplements only.

benefits have become increasingly generous (Supplemental Security Income Modernization Project,
1992). In contrast, the number of blind or disabled
recipients has grown steadily and dramatically, so
that there are now more than twice as many blind
or disabled recipients as there were in 1974.

In Figure 4, recipients are categorized by age,
showing a dramatic increase in people under age
65. Recently there has been a sharp increase in
the number of children receiving SSI; the number
of recipients under age 22 is now more than 3½
times what it was in 1975, compared to growth
rates of 70 percent for those ages 22 to 64 and
decreases of around 15 percent for those 65 and
older. Some of this increase among children is the
result of *Sullivan v. Zebley* (1990), in which the
Supreme Court broadened the definition of disability for children and required that the Social Security Administration reevaluate any children who
had been determined not to be disabled under the
more stringent criteria.

Recipients of SSI are more likely to be women
than men, 62 percent compared to 38 percent.
This gender difference is particularly notable
among those receiving benefits because of their
age, of whom 75 percent are women. Of those for
whom race is known, there are about twice as
many whites as blacks receiving SSI.

The disabilities most frequently found among
adult disabled recipients are mental retardation
(28 percent), other mental disorders (26 percent),
and diseases of the nervous system and sense
organs (12 percent). Almost half of the child recipients (45 percent) are eligible because of mental
retardation. In 1985 acquired immune deficiency

syndrome (AIDS) was added to the list of disability
categories; since 1991 people with the human
immunodeficiency virus (HIV) have been eligible
to receive SSI benefits.

What Do They Receive?
The basic monthly SSI benefit in January 1992 was
$422 for individuals and 150 percent of this
amount, or $633, for a couple. States have the
option of increasing this basic grant amount, and
in 1992 all but nine states provided some type of
supplement, most frequently supplements to aged
individuals living independently. The amount of
the supplements for elderly people living independently varied dramatically, ranging from $2 per
month in Oregon to more than $300 per month in
Alaska and Connecticut. Almost all states provide
supplements to cover the extra costs involved for
those who cannot live alone because of mental or
physical limitations. However, the amount of the
benefit may be reduced by one-third for people
who reside in another's home, since they are
assumed to have lower expenses.

As in all welfare programs, SSI benefits are
generally reduced when the recipient has other
income. Most additional unearned income over
$20 per month reduces the SSI payment dollar for
dollar, leading to no additions in total income.
Earned income is treated more generously, with
the first $65 per month and half the remainder
excluded. Additional income may also be disre-
garded if it is received as part of a disabled or
blind person's plan to achieve self-support. Some
means-tested benefits are treated less generously:
SSI recipients who also receive veterans' pensions,
for example, are not able to keep even the first $20
per month.

The federal benefit level changes automatically with the rate of inflation. State supplements
are not automatically changed.

SSI recipients in 31 states and the District of
Columbia automatically receive Medicaid. In seven
states, SSI applicants must complete a separate
application for Medicaid but are then automatically eligible. In 12 states, SSI recipients must
complete a separate application for Medicaid, but
even then may not qualify to receive it. Most people with disabilities who now earn too much to be
eligible for SSI can continue to receive Medicaid.

SSI recipients in all states except California
and Wisconsin are eligible for food stamps. SSI
recipients in California and Wisconsin receive an
additional amount of cash each month equal to the
value of the food stamps they would receive.

How Do They Receive Benefits?
Federal Social Security offices nationwide accept
applications for SSI benefits. States that supple-

ment benefits can elect to have the federal government administer the benefits (whereby the application process would occur at the federal Social Security office) or can administer their own supplemental benefits (whereby the application process would take place at the state or county welfare office). Most states elect to have the federal government administer supplements.

The SSI application gathers thorough information about income, assets, and disability status (if applicable). There is a growing backlog of disability cases awaiting determination of eligibility; average waiting periods are up to four months before benefits begin (Supplemental Security Income Modernization Project, 1992).

Once approved, monthly checks are issued to recipients. About one-quarter of the beneficiaries are children under 18 or people who have been determined to be incapable of managing their own resources. For these individuals, payments are made to a "representative payee" who is responsible for the person's finances.

Who Pays for These Benefits?
Funding for the federal SSI benefit comes from general tax revenues. SSI is an entitlement program, so all who apply and are eligible will receive benefits. States that supplement these benefits typically do so from general tax revenues.

CONTEMPORARY PROBLEMS AND ISSUES
The most recent comprehensive analysis of the SSI program was completed by a panel of experts commissioned by the Social Security Commissioner in 1990 (Supplemental Security Income Modernization Project, 1992). The following list of contemporary issues is drawn from their work and the work of other analysts.

Benefits are inadequate. Federal maximum benefits are below the official poverty line, totaling 74 percent of the poverty line for individuals and 88 percent for couples. State supplements improve the adequacy of benefits, but all but three states still have benefits below the poverty line for individuals and 12 states have benefits below the poverty line for couples. Even in states that provide benefits that reach the poverty line, some people feel that benefits are still inadequate because the poverty line denotes an inadequate level of income (see, for example, Ruggles, 1990). Further inadequacies emerge when SSI benefits are compared to a measure of the standard of living in an area or to typical housing, food, and other costs (Bartolomei-Hill & Meyer, 1994). Nevertheless, SSI benefits are much higher than AFDC benefits—typically two to three times higher. Because of concerns

about the inadequacy of benefits, the panel of experts recommended raising the federal benefit to 120 percent of the poverty line.

Benefits vary among states. The current program structure, in which the federal government provides a basic benefit that can be supplemented by states, may create inequities. Two individuals in identical circumstances who live across a state line from each other may receive dramatically different benefits. In the most extreme example, in January 1992, aged individuals living independently who had no other income would have received $747 per month in Connecticut and $489 per month in neighboring Rhode Island.

The program has built-in disincentives to marry and to live with others. Because SSI benefits for couples are only 150 percent of the benefit for individuals, two SSI recipients who marry would receive a smaller total benefit. On the other hand, the gap between benefits and the poverty line is smaller for couples than it is for individuals. The panel of experts recommended leaving the ratio between couple and individual benefits at 150 percent.

SSI recipients who live with their families or others have their benefits reduced by one-third. Some feel this discourages recipients from living situations where they would receive more social support. The panel of experts recommended allowing those who live with others to receive full benefits.

The eligibility standards are outdated. Many of the eligibility standards have not been updated since the program's inception in 1974. The asset limits, for example, have been adjusted only once since then and are quite low, allowing individuals only $2,000 in countable assets. The general income exclusion, in which the first $20 per month of outside income does not reduce one's benefit, has never been changed, even though the basic benefit level has more than tripled.

Work incentives for disabled people are inconsistent. Currently, disabled SSI applicants must provide verification that they cannot engage in any "substantial gainful activity." Thus a condition of eligibility is to show that one cannot work. Yet there are incentives to work built into the program. Perhaps some publicly provided income support for those with temporary disabilities should be considered.

Many who appear to be eligible do not receive benefits. Social Security offices periodically have instituted a major outreach effort to those who are

Supplemental Security Income

receiving minimal social security benefits to inform them of their potential eligibility for SSI, and applications have increased somewhat. However, only about 65 percent of elderly persons who appear to be eligible for SSI report receiving benefits (Sheils, Barnow, Chaurette, & Constantine, 1990). Reasons for the lack of participation are not clear, but Sheils et al. found that those least likely to participate are people who are eligible for small benefits, are in good health or have private health insurance, or have earnings or pension income.

The program discourages savings. Asset limits are so low ($2,000 for individuals and $3,000 for couples) that many needy elderly and disabled people cannot qualify. And once an individual does qualify, he or she is unable to save for the future because of these asset limits. Not only are efforts by SSI recipients to move toward self-sufficiency by saving unrewarded; their efforts to save even a modest amount of money could result in a loss of benefits. The panel of experts recommended increasing the countable asset limits to $7,000 for individuals and $10,500 for couples.

The SSI program may not adequately provide for individual needs. Although recent programmatic changes provide different work incentives for those with disabilities from those who are aged, the bulk of the federal SSI program operates in the same basic way for all recipients. Furthermore, the program generally does not consider individual need. People with extraordinarily high shelter costs, for example, receive no additional federal benefit. People who are severely limited in their ability to complete the tasks of daily living typically receive no more in federal benefits than other recipients. In some federal programs, allowances are made for individual differences in circumstances, but SSI tends not to provide individualized help.

On a broader scale, many would argue that programs that assist poor people in this country are uncoordinated. SSI recipients in some states must complete a separate application for Medicaid. Food stamps are available to SSI recipients, but because there are different eligibility rules, more than one application (and therefore, a trip to more than one office) may be necessary. Housing benefits are not related to these other programs, necessitating yet another application. And if an individual is fortunate enough to receive all of these benefits, the combination of receiving benefits from so many programs creates problems. For example, if an individual begins to work, SSI benefits, food stamp benefits, and housing subsidies could all be reduced while work-related expenses increase, perhaps leaving the individual worse off than when he or she was not working. Most other industrialized nations have a more coordinated approach to programs for poor people.

CONCLUSION

Social workers need a basic knowledge of the SSI program for at least three reasons. First, they may be in a position to inform their clients of potential eligibility for a program that could provide an important source of income and access to medical assistance. Second, informed social workers can advocate for individual clients who may be having difficulties applying for benefits. Third, because social workers have extensive knowledge about their client's lives, they have a professional responsibility to advocate for changes in any policies that are insensitive to the needs of the less fortunate.

REFERENCES

Axinn, J., & Levin, H. (1992). *Social welfare: A history of the American response to need* (3rd ed.). New York: Longman.
Bartolomei-Hill, S., & Meyer, D. R. (1994). The adequacy of supplemental security income benefits for aged individuals and couples. *The Gerontologist, 34,* 161–172.
Gilbert, N., Specht, H., & Terrell, P. (1993). *Dimensions of social welfare policy* (3rd ed.). Englewood Cliffs, NJ: Prentice Hall.
Katz, M. B. (1986). *In the shadow of the poorhouse: A social history of welfare in America.* New York: Basic Books.
Patterson, J. T. (1981). *America's struggle against poverty 1900–1980.* Cambridge, MA: Harvard University Press.
Ruggles, P. (1990). *Drawing the line.* Washington, DC: Urban Institute Press.
Sheils, J. F., Barnow, B. S., Chaurette, K. A., & Constantine, J. M. (1990). *Elderly persons eligible for and participating in the Supplemental Security Income (SSI) program.* Available from U.S. Department of Health and Human Services/ASPE/HSP, Room 404E, HHH Building, 200 Independence Avenue, SW, Washington, DC 20201.
Social Security Act of 1935. P.L. 100-360, 49 Stat. 620.
Sullivan v. Zebley, 110 S. Ct. 885 (1990).
Supplemental Security Income Modernization Project. (1992). *Final report of the experts.* Available from SSI Modernization Project, Room 311, Altmeyer Building, P.O. Box 17052, Baltimore, MD 21235.
U.S. House of Representatives, Committee on Ways and Means. (1992). *Overview of entitlement programs.* Washington, DC: U.S. Government Printing Office.

FURTHER READING

Clark, W. F., Pelham, A. O., & Clark, M. L. (1988). *Old and poor: A critical assessment of the low-income elderly.* Lexington, MA: Lexington Books.
Danziger, S. H., & Weinberg, D. H. (Eds.). (1985). *Fighting poverty: What works and what doesn't.* Cambridge, MA: Harvard University Press.

Palmer, J. L., Smeeding, T., & Torrey, B. B. (Eds.). (1988). *The vulnerable: America's young and old*. Washington, DC: Urban Institute Press.

Patterson, J. T. (1981). *America's struggle against poverty 1900-1980*. Cambridge, MA: Harvard University Press.

U.S. House of Representatives, Committee on Ways and Means. (1993). *Overview of entitlement programs*. Washington, DC: U.S. Government Printing Office.

Zedlewski, S. R., & Meyer, J. A. (1989). *Toward ending poverty among the elderly and disabled through SSI reform* (Urban Institute Report 89-1). Washington, DC: Urban Institute Press.

Daniel R. Meyer, PhD, is assistant professor, Institute for Research on Poverty, School of Social Work, University of Wisconsin–Madison, 1180 Observatory Drive, Madison, WI 53706.

For further information see

Aid to Families with Dependent Children; Aging: Public Policy Issues and Trends; Child Welfare Overview; Disability; Hunger, Nutrition, and Food Programs; Income Security Overview; Poverty; Public Social Welfare Expenditures; Social Security; Social Welfare Policy; Unemployment Compensation and Workers' Compensation; Veterans and Veterans Services; Welfare Employment Programs: Evaluation.

Key Words	
appropriation	income security
disabilities	welfare
elderly	

Survey Research
Allen Rubin

Surveys are one of the most commonly used research methods in social work. The term *survey* typically is used to connote a data-collection method in which a sample of respondents, selected from a certain population and thought to be representative of that population, are interviewed or administered questionnaires to describe the population as a whole at a particular point in time. Surveys also can be conducted longitudinally to assess how populations change over time. Although surveys are primarily associated with descriptive research purposes, they also can be conducted for exploratory or hypothesis-testing purposes.

HISTORICAL ROOTS

Surveys have been conducted since ancient times and have held a prominent place in social work research since the birth of the profession. Polansky (1975) traced the mid-18th-century roots of survey research in social work to the efforts of Frederic Le Play, a Belgian who interviewed European workers about their budgets to establish a database for social reform. Polansky also noted that Le Play's surveys were preceded by surveys of earnings and expenditures of the working poor in Hamburg for the purpose of selecting appropriate levels of relief grants.

Booth's Study of Poverty

One prominent figure who influenced the early development and use of social survey research in social work was Charles Booth (see Zimbalist, 1977). Booth was a wealthy, conservative London shipowner who had worked his way out of poverty. In 1886 he set out to disprove, through a more scientific and objective study, an 1885 report by London Marxists claiming that one-fourth of the working class lived in severe poverty.

Funding the project himself, Booth and his assistants interviewed the residents of East London about their finances, living conditions, and

other forces bearing on their lives. Their investigation was not restricted to the survey method: They also conducted participant observation and analyzed available records. The study was reported in 17 volumes called *The Life and Labour of the People of London* (1891–1903/1970). Ironically, the conservative Booth concluded that the proportion of the population he found to be living in poverty—30.7 percent—was even higher than the estimate he had set out to debunk. This finding led him to recommend some social welfare measures that he termed "limited socialism" (Polansky, 1975; Zimbalist, 1977).

Development of Social Survey Movement

Booth's work took place during an era in which the social work profession's roots in social reform began to emerge via the settlement house movement. Settlement workers learned about the conditions of the poor and working classes by living among them and serving them in settlement houses in their neighborhoods. A few settlement workers published studies about what they learned. Most, however, lacked the time and other resources to carry out systematic research on the conditions of their target population. By the turn of the century, public receptivity to such research was being stimulated by the works of muckraking journalists and novelists writing accounts of urban squalor and exploitation. Among those aroused by the revelations was a group of social workers and civic leaders in Pittsburgh, who raised funds to conduct a study of social conditions there.

Paul Kellogg, managing editor of an early social work journal, *Charities and the Commons,* was assigned to lead the Pittsburgh study, which was inspired by Booth's work (Kellogg, 1914). It was conducted from 1909 to 1914 using social survey techniques. The study was published in a series of volumes covering a vast array of living and working conditions and eventually became known as the Pittsburgh Survey (Polansky, 1975). The major theme of the survey was "the grim omnipresence of the steel mills, whose impact on life and economy of this industrial center is seen on almost every page of the report" (Zimbalist, 1977, p. 125).

By exposing the deplorable impact of the steel mills on the lives of the mill workers, including an estimated one-fourth of the institutionalized children whose diseases or accidents were preventable (Zimbalist, 1977), the Pittsburgh Survey helped stimulate major reforms, such as the reduction of the work day to eight hours and the abolition of the seven-day work week (Polansky, 1975). Its success sparked the rapid spread during the second decade of the 20th century of what came to be known as the Social Survey Movement, as social workers in cities throughout the United States emulated the survey. (According to Zimbalist, sociologists did not take an active or leading part until 1919.) As one sign of the degree of enthusiasm for this movement, the name of Kellogg's journal, *Charities and the Commons,* was changed to *Survey.*

CHARACTERISTICS AND FATE OF EARLY SOCIAL SURVEYS

The early social surveys were extremely broad in scope. They covered all aspects of community life (industrial, economic, political, and social), reporting extensive statistics in diverse areas such as disease, crime, and income. They studied one community at a time and at one particular point in time, with no aims to generalize beyond that community at that time. Teams of outside experts were brought in to plan and conduct the surveys. Local leaders were instrumental in facilitating the implementation of the surveys and in taking action on the basis of the findings.

Social Reform Impetus

The main force driving the early social surveys was not a search for truth, but a desire to put together a compelling case that would arouse the community to take social action to achieve social reform. Conducting "applied" research as a tool to achieve noble social welfare aims, rather than conducting "pure" research in pursuit of knowledge for knowledge's sake, has always been an inescapable characteristic of research in an applied, altruisic profession such as social work. However, seeking truth and seeking to spark social reform are not mutually exclusive objectives in a survey or any other type of research. In other words, if living conditions are indeed deplorable, then research that assesses and reports that truth in a balanced and objective manner can be seen as a tool for achieving humanistic aims. But the early social surveys did not always maintain objectivity and balance. Although these surveys used research as a tool to galvanize facts, the facts sometimes were interpreted and reported in a partisan manner that struck some as propagandistic.

Reasons for Decline

Zimbalist (1977) cited the eventual perception of early social surveys as propagandistic as one factor in their fall from grace by the 1920s. Other factors included broader historical forces, such as World War I and the end of the social reform era. Also, the broad scope of the surveys made them expensive and time-consuming. During the initial overselling of social surveys as a social reform panacea that would dramatically alleviate all a city's ills, their costs seemed justified. However, these costs became less acceptable as the envisioned levels of social change were not achieved and as the profession and public began to see the surveys as biased, overambitious efforts that failed to fulfill their promise of social reform.

The decline of the social survey movement can also be attributed, in part, to its successes. One factor in the decline was the centralization of surveys in local coordinating agencies and planning organizations during the late 1920s. Rather than bring in outside experts, these agencies institutionalized survey data collection as a routine agency function, focusing the data collection more narrowly on their specialized concern with specific areas of social work needs and services. As these agencies reiterated similar descriptive data from year to year, adding little to previous knowledge, the demand for expensive surveys with a broad scope was replaced by a demand for narrower theoretical studies that attempted to answer specific research questions geared to bettering the ability to understand, explain, and alleviate specific problems in a particular area (for example, health or delinquency) (Polansky, 1975). The decline of the social survey movement did not, however, mean the decline of the use of surveys; the more narrowly focused theoretical studies that followed commonly used survey methods, and survey methods continue to be a prominent mode of inquiry for social work researchers and other social scientists.

COMMON TYPES OF SOCIAL WORK SURVEYS

Narrowly focused surveys, especially those that simply send a questionnaire for respondents to complete, are one of the least costly and least time-consuming ways to collect data. Largely because they are expedient to conduct, narrowly focused surveys are perhaps the most frequently used mode of observation in the social sciences today, including in social work. Reports of such surveys abound in social work agencies and the social work literature. Agencies survey both users and providers of services, as well as those who refuse to use or have never heard of their services; social work faculty survey their students; and national groups survey the faculty.

Although the use of self-administered questionnaires is a particularly expedient way to conduct a survey, surveys can also be conducted using face-to-face or telephone interviews. Individuals typically are the unit of analysis, and even when they are not, they are typically used as respondents or informants, such as when program directors are surveyed about the characteristics of their programs. Although some use the term *survey* in connection with studies that collect data on inanimate objects—for example, a sample of the social work literature can be surveyed to assess the characteristics of authors publishing different types of studies—most research texts do not refer to such studies as surveys and use the term only in connection with studies using individuals as respondents or informants.

Consumer Satisfaction and Needs Assessments

Surveys can be conducted for descriptive, exploratory, and explanatory purposes. For example, a new agency may conduct a descriptive telephone survey of a randomly selected sample of community residents to find out what proportion of its target population has heard of its services, what they think about the services, and whether they are likely to use them. A researcher may conduct an explanatory survey to test the hypothesis that users' satisfaction with public social services is higher in counties where all services are provided in the same centralized facility. Such a study may be conducted by mailing a brief questionnaire asking about satisfaction with services to all or a sample of users in each county. A researcher may also conduct an exploratory survey of the same users, asking them open-ended questions about what they liked and did not like about the services; and then inductively seeking statistical patterns in the data about likes and dislikes and the way those patterns differ across subgroups of clients with various demographic and other background characteristics.

The foregoing examples fall under the rubric of consumer satisfaction surveys and needs assessment surveys. These are perhaps the two most commonly used types of surveys in social work. In consumer satisfaction surveys, users of services in a particular agency can provide useful data on the need to improve service delivery in that agency and how it may be improved by reporting how satisfied or dissatisfied users are with various aspects of the agency and the services they received, why they decided to terminate treatment, and similar issues. Surveys of the satisfaction levels of current consumers can also be used to guide program planning. In needs assessment surveys, agencies survey their intended target population to gather information that will be useful in guiding program planning. What distinguishes needs assessment surveys from consumer satisfaction surveys is that needs assessment surveys focus more on potential new services being considered than on satisfaction with existing ones (although dissatisfaction with existing services may certainly be one indicator of the need for new services). Similarly, needs assessment surveys are concerned with potential users of services in the target population, not just current users.

Key informants. Needs assessment surveys are not always conducted directly on the members of the target population, the potential service users. Sometimes they are conducted on key informants, experts who are presumed to have special knowledge about gaps in service delivery, as well as about the problems and needs of the target population. Typical key informants are neighborhood leaders, public officials, law enforcement personnel, leaders of citizens' advocacy groups, and others who work in settings that put them in frequent contact with the target population. Key informant surveys tend to be less expensive and time-consuming than do direct surveys of target groups, but they yield data that could be limited by the extent of objectivity and knowledge of the presumed experts.

Consumers of services. Direct surveys of the target population—or, more commonly, of a sample selected from the target population—can be both more expensive and time-consuming, but they determine what the prospective consumers themselves have to say about their needs and likely use of the envisioned services. Of course, prospective consumers may not always respond in an unbiased fashion and what they say can over- or underestimate the degree of use that will actually occur if and when a new service is introduced. Ideally, therefore, needs assessment studies should combine target population surveys with key informant surveys and should include other, nonsurvey modalities of data collection as well (for example, examining existing records of social indicators in the target community and rates of clients under treatment in comparable communities and holding community forums).

Other Types of Surveys

Although needs assessment surveys and consumer satisfaction surveys are perhaps the most common types of surveys in social work, they are by no means the only common types. Another type of survey—one that is connected with needs assessment—assesses the incidence or prevalence of specific problems in a segment of the population. For example, a government agency concerned with substance abuse or with youth problems may commission a survey that asks adolescents about the extent and nature of their substance abuse behavior. Another common example of the use of surveys in social work is large agencies' surveys of their practitioners to assess problems in service delivery and how to alleviate them. For instance, during the 1970s and early 1980s, in the aftermath of the deinstitutionalization movement, several countywide community mental health programs authorized surveys of their clinical practitioners. The purpose of the surveys was to assess practitioners' orientation toward working with a new type of client—people who had been institutionalized and therefore were unfamiliar to community-based clinicians. The surveys identified ways in which the clinicians could improve their orientation to a chronic care model (as opposed to a treatment model for acute conditions). Some surveys also identified staffing and structural variables associated with the degree of orientation to a chronic care model (Rubin, 1978; Rubin & Johnson, 1982).

Social Action–Oriented Surveys

Finally, there is the type of survey in which scientific priorities are overridden by political or social action priorities—surveys that, like some of the surveys of the Social Survey Movement era, may seem less interested in objectively pursuing truth than in selectively galvanizing desired responses to be used as ammunition in a crusade for social reform or for a particular ideological viewpoint. One example of such surveys is a 1989 questionnaire that was published in 20 national magazines. Readers were told that the survey was being conducted to lobby President George Bush for action to improve government action on child care and were asked to respond to questions about their views on that concern and mail the questionnaire to the Child Care Action Campaign (Rubin & Babbie, 1993). Another example is a 1991 mailed survey conducted by the American Foundation for AIDS Research. After informing questionnaire recipients of the seriousness of the acquired immune deficiency syndrome (AIDS) epidemic and citing figures showing its rapid growth, the survey asked them to respond to items assessing their opinions on whether public awareness and understanding of the problem should be increased and whether politicians were providing adequate fiscal support in the fight against AIDS. The questionnaire ended with a request to enclose a check with the questionnaire for a charitable donation to the foundation (Rubin & Babbie, 1993).

METHODOLOGICAL ISSUES IN SURVEY RESEARCH

The foregoing two examples of social action–oriented surveys illustrate some critical methodological issues that influence a survey's validity. One key issue concerns the representativeness of the survey respondents. If a bias leads to overrepresentation or underrepresentation of certain segments of the population, then the survey findings will present a distorted picture of how the studied phenomena is distributed in the population. Such bias can occur in the way people are selected to be surveyed or in the way they are asked to participate. In the child care survey, for example, only people who read the selected magazines encountered the questionnaire. Those people may have differed from the rest of the population in political orientation, socioeconomic status, and—most important—opinions about government action on child care. Moreover, those who cared deeply about the issue were probably the most likely to respond. With the AIDS survey, this problem was exacerbated by asking respondents to enclose a donation along with the questionnaire. In light of this request, and assuming that the surveyors knew some of the basic fundamentals of survey methods, it seems reasonable to suppose that they "stacked the deck" in favor of obtaining data that would support their cause.

Sampling

Because the representativeness of its respondents critically affects a survey's validity, sampling procedures play a key role in survey methodology. Two broad types of sampling methods are probability sampling and nonprobability sampling.

Random sampling. Probability, or random, sampling avoids selection bias by using random numbers to give every member of a population an equal chance of being selected for the sample. The simplest form of probability sampling is aptly termed "simple random sampling." This procedure involves assigning a number to each member in a population and then using a table of random numbers to identify which numbers are chosen for a sample.

A more practical, albeit less ideal, approximation of random sampling is systematic sampling. This method does not require numbering a large list; instead, every *k*th member of the population list is selected. The reason systematic sampling is less ideal than simple random sampling is that it is possible that the list of population elements may be arranged in such a way that certain segments of the population have less chance to be selected at every *k*th interval. Typically, however, this possibility is deemed far-fetched; consequently, systematic sampling is often preferred over simple random sampling for pragmatic reasons.

Stratified sampling. A more sophisticated form of probability sampling is called "stratified sampling." This method increases the likely representativeness of the sample by grouping members of the population into relatively homogeneous strata before randomly selecting a certain proportion of members from each stratum. Doing so ensures that appropriate numbers of population subgroups are selected for the sample, a particularly important requirement when certain subgroups make up such low proportions of a population that they might be underrepresented in a simple random sample.

Multistage cluster sampling. Another sophisticated form of probability sampling is called "multistage cluster sampling." This method is most applicable when resource constraints prevent traveling to geographically diverse sites to conduct interviews or when a population is so large that obtaining or developing a list of all its members is not feasible. The first step in multistage cluster sampling is to identify clusters of population members. For example, in drawing a sample from the population of social work students in the world, a researcher may begin by developing a list of all schools of social work. The next step is to select randomly the clusters to be included in the sample. Then, the researcher obtains from each selected cluster a list of its members and randomly draws a subsample of members in each cluster.

Nonprobability sampling. Despite the superiority of the foregoing probability sampling methods for generating representative samples, many surveys do not use them. Instead, they often use nonprobability sampling procedures. Researchers often use this method because it is impossible to obtain a probability sample, for example, when attempting to survey homeless people. At other times, they may use nonprobability sampling because it is easier and cheaper than probability sampling.

Sometimes researchers use their own judgment in attempting to pick members who they think best represent a population. This is called "purposive sampling." Sometimes they simply rely on individuals who are readily available (for example, stopping people at a street corner). This risky approach is called "convenience sampling," or "relying on available subjects." In another nonprobability sampling approach, "quota sampling," the researcher attempts to improve representativeness by identifying certain characteristics (for example, gender or ethnicity) and then drawing a convenience sample in which the proportion of people with specific characteristics matches the proportion of people with those characteristics in the overall population.

Biased Wording

Another key methodological issue involves whether the questions are administered in an unbiased fashion. Respondents should not be cued as to which kinds of responses are more desirable. These cues can be conveyed in the wording of the cover letters or prefaces to questionnaires, as was blatantly done in the AIDS and child care surveys, or in the questionnaire items.

Random Measurement Error

In addition to ensuring that surveys are not administered in a biased fashion, it is important to safeguard against random measurement errors that occur when survey questionnaires or interview schedules are too complex, cumbersome, fatiguing, or boring or are asked in a language that respondents do not understand. Steps that can be taken to identify and correct these errors include obtaining ample critical feedback from colleagues about survey designs and instruments, carefully training and monitoring interviewers, translating instruments or using bilingual interviews for non–English-speaking respondents, sensitizing interviewers to cultural differences, and conducting a series of pretests and revisions to debug survey instruments.

Self-Administered Questionnaires versus Interviews

Another major methodological issue involves decisions about administering questions via self-administered questionnaires or interviews. Two prime advantages of self-administered questionnaires are that they are cheaper and less time-consuming to administer. They also provide respondents with complete anonymity, which may be an advantage when questions about sensitive topics are asked. Advantages of interviews are the decreased likelihood of obtaining incomplete questionnaires, an opportunity to explain words that respondents do not understand, avoidance of questionnaires being discarded, and the opportunity to observe and probe the unexpected.

Telephone Interviews

Researchers can decide whether to conduct interviews face to face or by telephone. In the first half of the 20th century, telephone interviews gained a bad reputation because a larger proportion of people with low incomes did not have telephones; hence, samples were biased. In 1936, for example, a notorious telephone survey predicted that Alf Landon would win a landslide victory over Franklin D. Roosevelt in the presidential election. Two weeks after the survey, Roosevelt won in a landslide, with Landon getting only 39 percent of the popular vote and only eight of 531 electoral votes. Today, however, about 97 percent of all households have telephones, so there is much less class bias in telephone surveys. Potential class biases associated with unlisted numbers can be avoided by using random-digit dialing. Consequently, telephone interviews are now much more common and acceptable than in the past. They are cheaper and quicker than face-to-face interviews because there is no travel, they avoid the problem of how to dress, and they may be safer for interviewers. Also, not having to look the interviewer in the eye may facilitate greater honesty by respondents, particularly those whose answers might meet with social disapproval. On the other hand, some respondents may be more suspicious when they cannot see the interviewer, may be alienated because of the proliferation of manipulative telephone sales solicitations, and may find it easier to abort the interview by hanging up. Ultimately, the

decision about which survey method to use will often be influenced by resource considerations (Rubin & Babbie, 1993).

CONCLUSION

Every mode of observation in social work research comes with its own special strengths and weaknesses; no one modality is inherently better than another. The decision of which modality to use will depend on the purpose and intended use of the research, the nature of the research question, and the researcher's resources. Surveys are a sensible choice when the priority is to portray a population accurately and objectively or to control statistically for a large number of variables. When these are not the major priorities, other modalities may make more sense. For example, experimentation may be used to maximize internal validity and causal inference, or qualitative methods may be used to maximize probing into the deeper meaning of a phenomenon or to observe actual behavior directly as it occurs in natural settings.

In addition to methodological weaknesses that can be minimized or avoided in a well-designed survey, there are some weaknesses that are virtually impossible to avoid in even the best surveys, just as alternative research modalities have their own inescapable weaknesses. For surveys, one such weakness is that their need for standardization can result in inflexibility, which limits the extent to which idiosyncratic probing and observation can be conducted to assess the deeper meanings and unique contexts of phenomena across diverse respondents. Therefore, survey data may appear superficial, especially when compared with qualitative studies. In addition to being vulnerable to superficiality and inflexibility, surveys are limited to assessing what people say. Individuals' words may not match their needs.

Surveys also have some special strengths that other modes of observation may lack. One strength is that they make it feasible for researchers to gather data from a large sample and generalize to a large population (assuming proper sampling and survey procedures are used). Also, by using very large samples surveys facilitate multivariate analyses in which many cases are required to control statistically for numerous extraneous or mediating variables. Finally, an inescapable weakness of surveys—their standardization and inflexibility—can also be a strength. The requirement that the same questions are asked in the same manner to all respondents and that observers do not impute the meanings of those responses can make surveys less vulnerable to biases in observation and data collection than are some other research modalities.

REFERENCES

Booth, C. (1970). *The life and labour of the people of London.* New York: AMS Press. (Original work published 1891–1903)
Kellogg, P. U. (1914). *The Pittsburgh Survey—Vol. 1.* New York: Survey Associates.
Polansky, N. A. (1975). *Social work research.* Chicago: University of Chicago Press.
Rubin, A. (1978). Commitment to community mental health aftercare services: Staffing and structural implications. *Community Mental Health Journal, 14,* 199–208.
Rubin, A., & Babbie, E. (1993). *Research methods for social work* (2nd ed.). Pacific Grove, CA: Brooks/Cole.
Rubin, A., & Johnson, P. J. (1982). Practitioner orientations toward the chronically disabled: Prospects for policy implementation. *Administration in Mental Health, 10,* 3–12.
Zimbalist, S. (1977). *Historic themes and landmarks in social welfare research.* New York: Harper & Row.

FURTHER READING

Babbie, E. (1973). *Survey research methods.* Belmont, CA: Wadsworth.
Bremner, R. H. (1956). *From the depths: The discovery of poverty in the United States.* New York: New York University Press.

Chambers, C. A. (1971). *Paul U. Kellogg and the survey: Voices for social welfare and social justice.* Minneapolis: University of Minnesota Press.
Kish, L. (1965). *Survey sampling.* New York: John Wiley & Sons.
Rossi, P. H., Wright, J., & Anderson, A. (Eds). (1983). *Handbook of survey research.* New York: Academic Press.
Rossi, P. H., & Freeman, H. E. (1983). *Evaluation: A systematic approach.* Beverly Hills, CA: Sage Publications.

Allen Rubin, PhD, LMSW-ACP, is professor, University of Texas, School of Social Work, 1925 San Jacinto Boulevard, Austin, TX 78712.

For further information see

Community Needs Assessment; Computer Utilization; Ethics and Values; Information Systems; Interviewing; Meta-analysis; Policy Analysis; Professional Conduct; Professional Liability and Malpractice; Qualitative Research; Recording; Research Overview; Social Work Practice: Theoretical Base.

Key Words	
methods	surveys
research	

Switzer, Mary Elizabeth

See Biographies section, Volume 3

T

Taft, Julia Jessie

See Biographies section, Volume 3

Taylor, Graham

See Biographies section, Volume 3

Teams

See Interdisciplinary and Interorganizational Collaboration

Technology Transfer
Pranab Chatterjee

The term "technology transfer" was first used widely during the Kennedy and Johnson administrations when the role of the United States in relation to developing countries was being formed (Heller, 1971). The assumption at the time was that the United States (and, in general, the rich countries of the West) had developed agricultural, biomedical, industrial, and social technologies that could be transferred to developing countries to foster social development. In 1966, three different conferences were held on technology transfer (see Gruber & Marquis, 1969; National Science Foundation, 1966; Spencer & Woroniak, 1967). Technology in these settings meant the application of a basic science toward one or more given ends. Technology transfer meant the passing on of such applied knowledge from one group to another.

In the social sciences, the term has been used in the discipline of economics (Mason, 1955; Salin, 1967). In anthropology, the impact of Western technology on the cultures of developing countries has been studied (Dube, 1958; Mead, 1955; Spicer, 1952). Similar studies have been conducted in sociology (Barnett, 1953; Katz, Levin, & Hamilton, 1963; Lerner, 1958; Rogers, 1962). In fact, sociology has added the idea of *diffusion of innovation* (the mass adoption of a given idea or artifact) as a related concept. However, neither anthropology nor sociology has dealt with the issue of technology transfer, and psychology has also been silent on the subject.

In social work, Rothman, Erlich, and Teresa (1977) used the concept of diffusion of innovations to understand the process of technology transfer, and they suggested the following:

Innovations which are amenable to trial on a partial basis will have a higher adoption rate than innovations which necessitate total adoption without an anticipatory trial. Practitioners wishing to promote an innovation in a general target system should attempt to have it experienced initially by a partial segment of that target system. (pp. 157–158)

APPLICATION TO SOCIAL WORK

Chatterjee (1990) proposed that the concept of technology transfer and the knowledge base developed about it are extremely relevant for social workers. Social workers need to understand the impact of agricultural, biomedical, industrial, and other technologies on the lives of human families, groups, communities, and cultures. Technology development and its transfer take place not only in the agricultural, biomedical, and industrial realms, but also in the social realm. Thus, the application of social science knowledge toward a particular end can be called *social technology*. Examples of such social technology are found in *social* intervention technology, where interventions at the direct practice level are based on a behavioral, psychodynamic, or some other paradigm; and in *social management technology*, where management of human services or other forms of goal-directed

FIGURE 1

Social Work Applications of Technology Transfer		
	Transfer	
	Within Nations	Between Nations
Technology		
1. Agricultural	_____	_____
2. Biomedical	_____	_____
3. Industrial	_____	_____
4a. Social intervention	_____	_____
4b. Social management	_____	_____

activity are based on paradigms of organizational behavior. In addition, technology transfer occurs not only between nations but also within nations.

Table 1 summarizes the various dimensions of technology transfer that are applicable to social work. Agricultural, biomedical, or industrial technology transfer can be seen to take place either within or between nations. Within nations, such a transfer may take place between interest groups, professions, organizations, regions, communities, and other macrostructures. Between nations, transfer involves a country of origin and a country of destination. Similarly, social intervention technology and social management technology may also transfer either within or between nations.

The most frequent applications of technology transfer to social work are shown in rows 4a and 4b in Figure 1. For example, how does behavior modification technology transfer from one discipline (for example, clinical psychology) to another (clinical social work), or how do techniques of group work transfer from one profession (clinical social work) to another (guidance and counseling)? Further, how do management technologies developed in profit-seeking industrial settings (time charts or zero-based budgeting, for example) transfer to nonprofit human services management either within or between nations?

MODELS OF TECHNOLOGY TRANSFER

Burton (1977) examined several ways in which industrial technologies transfer within or between nations. He suggested that importing any technology must be coupled with indigenous technology development, and that both activities must have a clear policy focus. In the case of within-nation transfer, the policy of the firm receiving or importing a technology from another firm or another sector must address ways to domesticate the imported technology. In the case of between-nation transfer, this type of policy is even more important.

Ruttan and Hayami (1973) described an example of agricultural technology transfer that supports Burton's observations. Further, Ruttan and Hayami's work has become an example of how to conceptualize the problem of technology transfer. They suggest that technology transfer involves three phases: material transfer, design transfer, and capacity transfer. Their study describes how the asexual reproductive nature of sugarcane was discovered independently in Java and Barbados during the 1880s. This discovery allowed the global export of a variety of seedlings, which, unfortunately, were highly susceptible to the diseases of the countries of destination. But experimental stations in India successfully developed interspecies hybrids that were both disease-resistant and suited to local conditions. After this breakthrough different countries began experimenting with hybrids of imported and local seedlings. Today, although relatively little actual transfer of plants occurs, a great deal of information between countries is exchanged. In this example, material transfer involved the actual transfer of the plants; design transfer involved the transfer of knowledge about breeding sugarcane under local conditions; and capacity transfer involved the actual capacity for creating different strains under local conditions.

The Ruttan and Hayami paradigm shows that the sequences of material, design, and capacity transfer are relevant in applied sciences such as social work, clinical psychology, and guidance counseling (which may correspond to social intervention technology) (Chatterjee, 1990). In these disciplines, transfers take place between teachers and students, between mentors and apprentices, and between supervisors and subordinates in the form of knowledge transfer. Foreign students studying these disciplines also become agents of such knowledge transfer from one country to another. Often in these settings, material transfer involves the "transfer, translation, or importation of vocabulary from the context of origin to context of destination" (Chatterjee, 1990, p. 170); design transfer involves transfer of the roles and values used during the service delivery; and capacity transfer involves transfer both of political support for the use of given service delivery structures and of the economic infrastructure that supports those structures (Chatterjee, 1990).

In social welfare, Martinez-Brawley and Delevan (1993) described case studies of technology transfer in the management of personal social services from the United Kingdom to Pennsylvania. These efforts represent examples of between-nation transfer of service delivery structures.

In addition to studying how a given technology transfers from a context of origin to that of destination, theory development about technology transfer addresses the following three questions: (1) Which technologies are to be chosen for transfer from a context of origin to one of destination? (2) Who decides that a given technology is "appropriate" for a given setting? (3) What are the economic and political interests of "owners" of given technologies (for example, patent or copyright holders), and how do they manifest themselves during technology transfer (for example, Lall, 1976; Patel, 1974; Penrose, 1973; Weinstein & Pillai, 1979)?

Social work can offer several examples of the politics of technology transfer. Within a given nation, if psychodynamic or ego-psychology-oriented social intervention technology is transferred from one generation of social workers to another, are the implicit biases of these theories (for example, tacit sanction of patriarchy, biological determinism, and the perception of certain groups as having deficits) transferred simultaneously? Between nations, when a developing country with massive poverty imports models of social intervention, are these models appropriate and useful, and who makes these decisions?

EXAMPLES OF WITHIN–NATION TECHNOLOGY TRANSFER

Two examples of within-nation technology transfer may be cited here. The first involves the adoption of cognitive–behavioral technologies by social workers in direct service. The second involves the adoption of time charts in human services management.

Consider the transfer of technology from the discipline of psychology to clinical social work. First, independent research and development took place within the discipline of psychology on cognition, cognitive structures, cognitive development, behaviorism, behavior modification, and cognitive–behavioral therapy (for example, Beck, 1976; Ellis, 1962; Meichenbaum & Genest, 1986; Mischel, 1973, 1979; Mischel & Baker, 1975; Thorpe, Hecker, Cavallaro, & Kulberg, 1987; Tversky, 1977). Second, a set vocabulary was transferred, translated, and imported from psychology to clinical social work (Berlin, 1982; Chatterjee, 1984; Goldstein, 1981, 1982; Hepworth & Larsen, 1990; Werner, 1982; Zastrow, 1981). Here one sees both material transfer (transfer of vocabulary) and design transfer (transfer of roles and values congruent with the vocabulary). Third, during this time, clinical social work as a special discipline gained political strength, legitimation through

licensing in most states, and support in the marketplace; inherent in these processes were political support and economic viability (leading to capacity transfer) of the use of cognitive–behavioral technology in social work.

Next consider the importation of time-management devices into social welfare administration from profit-oriented industrial product management during the 1930s. Classic administration theory, popularized by Frederick Taylor (1911), stated that "time is money" and envisioned efficient and accountable use of time by line workers as one major managerial function. That idea, imported into social welfare management, was seen as a necessity as well as a source of discomfort; in for-profit product administration, time management was a means of worker control, whereas in nonprofit social welfare administration it was a device for both worker control and worker education (for example, Abels & Murphy, 1981; Deutschberger & Spencer, 1960; DiPadova & Faerman, 1991). In this case, material and design transfer took place as early as the Milford Conference of 1929 (Deutschberger & Spencer, 1960) because social welfare administration was using the vocabulary (material transfer) and role and values (design transfer) inherent in the technology of time management. However, the conflict between norms of growing professionalism and of meeting product quotas within a particular time frame made capacity transfer difficult.

EXAMPLES OF BETWEEN–NATION TECHNOLOGY TRANSFER

Whereas the concept of technology transfer originated for understanding knowledge transfer from wealthy or developed countries to poor and developing countries, the field of social welfare saw examples of transfer from developing countries to the wealthy countries of the West. One example of such cross-national transfer was in community development technology, which had been used more extensively in the poor or developing countries (Tagore, 1906; United Nations, 1955). During the 1960s and thereafter, this model became popular in the United States as a strategy for social development (Practicing Law Institute, 1970; Twentieth Century Fund, 1971). Although it can be debated that the idea and vocabulary of community development originated independently both in the United States (Polson, 1958; Sherrard, 1962) and in India (Tagore, 1906), the roles and values (that is, Ruttan and Hayami's, 1973, design transfer concept) of community development as social technology were forged for the most part in the developing countries (Batten, 1957; United Nations,

1955). Given the changes in the United States that resulted in eroding support for community development programs during the 1970s and 1980s, one may argue that capacity transfer for such programs to the United States remained incomplete.

A second example of cross-national transfer involves exporting cognitive–behavioral technology in direct service casework as a social intervention technology to a culturally different and economically poor country—Bangladesh, for example. Some might argue that such a technology is not appropriate for Bangladesh. In that case, one would see an example of a cross-national technology transfer as well as an example of the politics of technology transfer, where the cost–benefit ratio of using a given technology in a given setting cannot be ascertained clearly, and the matter is subjected to political opinion.

A third example of cross-national transfer is a case in which the structure of delivering personal social services was transferred from the United Kingdom to Pennsylvania (Martinez-Brawley & Delevan, 1993). Material transfer occurred, but design and capacity transfer remained incomplete.

CURRENT ISSUES

The United States in 1994 does not seem to have a uniform national health or child welfare policy. If there is any effort to develop such policies, and should service delivery structures follow such an effort, then another dimension of technology transfer may unravel. Possibilities include the development of indigenous social technology (vocabulary, role and values, and capacity), or the full or partial importation of a social technology developed and tested in another country.

A current example of technology transfer may be seen in the use of computer systems. Many business ventures have developed software packages that are used to track customers, educate them about products, develop markets, or conduct billing and referral. These technologies could be imported to social work track to client progress; educate communities; reach an at-risk population; or handle billing, referral, and third-party payments. Another example of technology transfer is the use of SYMLOG techniques, developed by Bales and Cohen (1979) in the group dynamics school, to assess group behavior in family therapy, group psychotherapy, and community group work (Kutner & Kirsch, 1985).

Other examples of technology transfer may involve advocacy by social workers on behalf of vulnerable populations, both domestic and foreign, where the transfer of certain technologies may contribute to improved physical and mental health and family and community life. Such advocacy may create conflict with interest groups, such as pharmaceutical companies and business interests, both domestic and foreign.

ONGOING RELEVANCE FOR SOCIAL WORK

A major challenge for social work practitioners is to understand a client system's (an individual, family, group, or community of clients) intricate relationship with the technologies it uses and to assess both the intended and unintended consequences of introducing new technologies to this system. When such technologies are transferred to the client system by the larger political economy, the social workers' tasks are to educate the client system and assess its adaptation to the new technology. At other times (as in community development settings or newly planned national health care delivery settings), social workers may act as advocates for or against a given form of technology transfer, depending on the impact of this transfer on human lives.

REFERENCES

Abels, P., & Murphy, M. (1981). *Administration in the human services.* Englewood Cliffs, NJ: Prentice Hall.
Bales, R. F., & Cohen, S. P. (1979). *SYMLOG: A system for the multiple level observation of groups.* New York: Free Press.
Barnett, H. (1953). *Innovation: The basis of cultural change.* New York: McGraw-Hill.
Batten, T. R. (1957). *Communities and their development.* London: Oxford University Press.
Beck, A. T. (1976). *Cognitive therapy and the emotional disorders.* New York: International Universities Press.
Berlin, S. B. (1982). Cognitive behavioral interventions for social work practice. *Social Work, 27,* 218–226.
Burton, H. (1977). A note on the transfer of technology. *Economic Development and Cultural Change, 25* [supplement].
Chatterjee, P. (1984). Cognitive theories and social work practice. *Social Service Review, 58,* 63–80.
Chatterjee, P. (1990). *The transferability of social technology.* Lewiston, NY: E. Mellen.
Deutschberger, P., & Spencer, S. (1960). *Social work administration* [Mimeograph]. Nashville: University of Tennessee School of Social Work.
DiPadova, L. N., & Faerman, S. R. (1991). Managing time in the organizational setting. In R. L. Edwards & J. A. Yankey (Eds.), *Skills for effective human services management* (pp. 317–334). Silver Spring, MD: NASW Press.
Dube, S. (1958). *India's changing villages.* Ithaca, NY: Cornell University Press.
Ellis, A. (1962). *Reason and emotion in psychotherapy.* New York: Lyle Stuart.
Goldstein, H. (1981). *Social learning and change: A cognitive approach to human services.* Columbia: University of South Carolina Press.
Goldstein, H. (1982). Cognitive approaches to direct practice. *Social Service Review, 56,* 539–555.

Gruber, W., & Marquis, D. (1969). *Factors in the transfer of technology.* Cambridge, MA: MIT Press.

Heller, T. (1971). [Book review]. *Technology & Culture, 12,* 370–372.

Hepworth, D. H., & Larsen, J. A. (1990). *Direct social work practice.* Belmont, CA: Wadsworth.

Katz, E., Levin, M., & Hamilton, H. (1963). Traditions of research on the diffusion of innovation. *American Sociological Review, 28,* 237–252.

Kutner, S., & Kirsch, S. (1985). Clinical applications of SYMLOG: A graphic system of observing relationships. *Social Work, 30,* 497–503.

Lall, S. (1976). The patent system and the transfer of technology to less developed countries. *Journal of World Trade Law, 10,* 6–7.

Lerner, D. (1958). *The passing of traditional society.* New York: Free Press.

Martinez-Brawley, E. E., with Delevan, S. M. (Eds.) (1993). *Transferring technology in the personal social services.* Washington, DC: NASW Press.

Mason, E. (1955). *Promoting economic development.* Claremont, CA: Claremont College Press.

Mead, M. (1955). *Cultural patterns and technical change.* New York: UNESCO.

Meichenbaum, D., & Genest, M. (1986). Cognitive behavior modification. In F. H. Kanfer & A. P. Goldstein (Eds.), *Helping people change* (pp. 390–422). Elmsford, NY: Pergamon Press.

Mischel, W. (1973). Toward a cognitive social learning reconceptualization of personality. *Psychological Review, 80,* 252–283.

Mischel, W. (1979). On the interface of cognition and personality: Beyond the person–situation debate. *American Psychologist, 34,* 740–754.

Mischel, W., & Baker, N. (1975). Cognitive appraisals and transformation in delay behavior. *Journal of Personality and Social Psychology, 31,* 254–261.

National Science Foundation. (1966). *Proceedings of a conference on technology transfer and innovation.* Washington, DC: Author.

Patel, S. (1974). The patent system and the third world. *World Development, 2,* 3–4.

Penrose, E. T. (1973). International patenting and the less developed countries. *Economic Journal, 9,* 777–780.

Polson, R. A. (1958). Theory and methods of training for community development. *Rural Sociology, 23,* 34–42.

Practicing Law Institute. (1970). *The local economic development corporation.* Washington, DC: U.S. Department of Commerce.

Rogers, E. (1962). *Diffusion of innovations.* New York: Free Press.

Rothman, J. (1968). *Three models of community organization practice: National Conference on Social Welfare, Social Work Practice, 1968.* New York: Columbia University Press.

Rothman, J., Erlich, J. L., & Teresa, J. (1977). Adding something new: Innovation. In F. M. Cox, J. L. Erlich, J. Rothman, & J. E. Tropman (Eds.), *Tactics and techniques of community practice* (pp. 157–166). Itasca, IL: F. E. Peacock.

Ruttan, V., & Hayami, Y. (1973). Technology transfer and economic development. *Technology and Culture,* 119–150.

Salin, E. (1967). The Schumpeterin theory and continental thought. In D. Spencer & A. Woroniak (Eds.), *The transfer of technologies to developing countries* (pp. 42–51). New York: Praeger.

Sherrard, T. (1962). Community organization and community development. *Community Development Review, 7,* 11–20.

Spencer, D., & Woroniak, A. (1967). *The transfer of technology to developing countries.* New York: Praeger.

Spicer, E. (Ed.). (1952). *Human problems in technological change.* New York: Russell Sage Foundation.

Tagore, R. (1906). *Shikkha.* Republished in R. Tagore, *Collected works.* Calcutta: Viswa-Bharati University Press (1988, in Bengali).

Taylor, F. (1911). *Scientific management.* New York: Harper.

Thorpe, G. L., Hecker, J. E., Cavallaro, L. A., & Kulberg, G. E. (1987). Insight vs. rehearsal in cognitive-behaviour therapy. *Behavioural Psychotherapy, 15,* 319–336.

Tversky, A. (1977). Features of similarity. *Psychological Review, 84,* 327–352.

Twentieth Century Fund. (1971). *CDCs: New hope for the inner city.* New York: Author.

United Nations. (1955). *Social progress through community development.* New York: Author.

Weinstein, J., & Pillai, V. K. (1979). Appropriate technology versus appropriating technology. *Social Development Issues, 3,* 37–53.

Werner, H. D. (1982). *Cognitive therapy: A humanistic approach.* New York: Free Press.

Zastrow, C. (1981). Self-talk: A rational approach to understanding and treating child abuse. *Social Casework, 62,* 182–186.

FURTHER READING

Chatterjee, P., & Ireys, H. (1979). Technology transfer: Views from some social science disciplines. *Social Development Issues, 3,* 54–75.

Chatterjee, P., & Ireys, H. (1981). Technology transfer: Implications for social work practice and social work education. *International Social Work, 24,* 14–22.

Pranab Chatterjee, PhD, ACSW, is professor of social work, Mandel School of Applied Social Sciences, Case Western Reserve University, 10900 Euclid Avenue, Cleveland, OH 44106.

For further information see

Clinical Social Work; Cognition and Social Cognitive Theory; Community; Epistemology; Expert Systems; Health Services Systems Policy; Interdisciplinary and Interorganizational Collaboration; International and Comparative Social Welfare; International Social Welfare: Organizations and Activities; Planning and Management Professions; Social Development; Social Work Profession Overview; Strategic Planning.

Key Words	
community development	technology transfer
international social work	

Teenagers

See Adolescents *(Reader's Guide)*

Termination in Direct Practice
Anne E. Fortune

Sooner or later, service to individuals, families, and small groups ends. The handling of the termination phase can affect the gains that clients make in treatment and how long these gains last. The reasons for ending service influence the preparation for termination and the reactions of the client and the practitioner. Whatever the reason, however, appropriate termination includes interventions that help the client to retain and extend the gains and to make the transition out of service.

REASONS FOR ENDING SERVICE

The service plan and the reason for ending service influence the participants' expectations for termination. Common situations are (1) ending a planned, time-limited contact; (2) ending an open-ended contact by mutual agreement that the service is no longer desirable; (3) ending an open-ended contact for unplanned reasons, but with time to prepare for termination; (4) transferring to another social worker, which ends the client's relationship with one social worker but continues service with another; and (5) the client dropping out, which is a unilateral ending.

Ending planned, time-limited service. In time-limited service, the participants know how long their contact will last and use that sense of time to frame their work, to maintain a focus, and to increase motivation. Because of the short duration and the knowledge that the service will end, decisions about when and how to terminate are usually easier than in open-ended service.

Ending open-ended service by mutual agreement. If there are no time limits, termination ideally occurs when the client and the social worker agree that the service is no longer desirable or necessary. Most social workers use an eclectic cluster of indicators of success to determine when to end service. These criteria include the client's meeting of goals set by the client or practitioner, the client's improved behavior and intrapsychic functioning, and the client's readiness to terminate (Fortune, 1985; Fortune, Pearlingi, & Rochelle, 1991; Kramer, 1982). Occasionally, subtle cues to success, such as changes in the content of therapy or in the therapeutic relationship, erratic attendance, or improvements in the client's social support system, are used as criteria.

In family service, criteria for ending service also include changes in the relationships of family members: improved interaction and communication, more flexible roles for family members, and structural shifts in the expectations of authority and responsibility (Wilcoxon & Gladding, 1985). Also relevant are changes in a family's relation to others: its establishment of more appropriate boundaries; its greater ability to provide for its members' economic, socialization, and nurturing needs; and its strengthened relationship to community institutions, including schools, churches, or social service agencies.

In groups, the entire group may end when it accomplishes its purpose, for example, planning a new service for clients. Often, however, the group continues, but individuals terminate because they have met their individual goals. Then the group must deal with the disruption and emotions raised by the departure of members.

An important reason to end treatment in any modality is a lack of success, although social workers rarely report it (Fortune et al., 1991). Lack of success means either that there has been little improvement and there is no reasonable expectation of improvement if treatment continues, or that there has been some improvement but a careful assessment indicates that further gains are not worth the time and energy that are required.

Whether or not the service was successful, the client and the social worker must devote some time to prepare for ending it, often in a formal phase that includes new types of interventions for ending.

Ending open-ended service for unanticipated reasons. Open-ended treatment may also end for unanticipated reasons. As many as 40 percent to 60 percent of cases end because of situational factors (DeBerry & Baskin, 1989; Hynan, 1990). Unanticipated reasons for ending include the social worker (or social work student) leaving an agency, changes in the client's schedule, the client's move to another geographic area, agency policies about the duration of service, limits imposed by insurers, and agency constraints such as excessive caseloads (Bywaters, 1975; DeBerry & Baskin, 1989; Gould, 1978).

When the reasons for ending are unanticipated, the outcome is rarely optimal. The client and the social worker may need to deal with their disappointment or anger, and they should plan how the client can continue to progress.

Transfer to another social worker. The client may transfer elsewhere when unanticipated factors, such as the social worker leaving the agency, the client needing a service offered by another agency, or the client and the social worker being incompatible, interfere with or curtail the service. This form of ter.nination is similar to termination in other situations, but first the social worker must help establish a link between the client and the new social worker.

Dropping out. Clients may drop out of service, that is, decide to end treatment, without informing the social worker. Although dropouts are often viewed as treatment failures, two-thirds report considerable progress (Cochran & Stamler, 1989; Toseland, 1987). The drawback to dropping out is that clients miss the opportunity to assess the treatment process and to solidify their gains through planned maintenance interventions.

FACTORS THAT AFFECT REASONS FOR TERMINATION

Several factors influence social workers' choice of criteria for ending service. The first is success: If they believe a case is successful, social workers are more likely to end time-limited service. In open-ended service, they apply more criteria that signal improvement (Fortune, 1985; Fortune et al., 1991). In less successful cases, social workers cite agency policy or organizational pressures as reasons for terminating service (Bywaters, 1975; Fortune et al., 1991).

Second, the auspices of agencies also influence social workers' reasons for ending service. Social workers terminate their public mental health clients more often because of excessive caseloads, administrative reasons, and the lack of success, whereas they terminate their private clients when the clients reach their goals (DeBerry & Baskin, 1989). However, among social work agencies, auspices were not found to be related to criteria (Fortune, 1985; Fortune et al., 1991).

Third, reasons vary at different points in the service or treatment. Earlier in treatment, situational constraints, the client's discomfort with

treatment, and the client dropping out are common (Cochran & Stamler, 1989; Hynan, 1990; Toseland, 1987). Once the service gets past those initial difficulties, however, the duration of service is not related to either success or the choice of criteria to end treatment (Fortune et al., 1991).

One factor that does not affect the criteria used for termination is the social worker's theory base. Despite theory-based controversy about goals and criteria for ending treatment—ego integration, changes in the transference, the acquisition of behavioral skills, and so on—most social workers look for an eclectic combination of cues to end treatment.

CLIENTS' REACTIONS TO TERMINATION

The case literature characterizes termination as a process of mourning the loss of an intense relationship that includes stages of denial, anger and loss, depression, and finally acceptance (Fox, Nelson, & Bolman, 1969). Yet the evidence is that the reactions of most clients are more positive than negative (Fortune, 1987; Fortune, Pearlingi, & Rochelle, 1992; Marx & Gelso, 1987). Ending represents accomplishment and gain, as well as loss, and the ending of a social work relationship also represents a new beginning and independence for the client.

During the termination phase, clients typically evaluate their progress and their attainment of goals, summarize their work in treatment, and evaluate the treatment process itself (Fortune, 1987; Fortune et al., 1992; Kramer, 1982; Lewis, 1978; Marx & Gelso, 1987; Paster, 1983; Quintana & Holahan, 1992; Saad, 1984). They focus on concurrent and future outside activities, with a growing sense of autonomy. They express ambivalence about ending, but pride in their accomplishments; excitement and pleasure at ending; and feelings of health, satisfaction, and being alive.

Less often, clients reexperience previous losses, try to re-create earlier therapeutic experiences, or say they need to continue in treatment. Occasionally, they express anger about ending or experience separation anxiety.

Rare reactions include denial; regression; acting out; and extreme negative reactions like depression, feeling "destroyed," or bitterness. In general, clients' positive reactions outweigh their destructive, negative reactions to termination (Fortune, 1987; Fortune et al., 1992; Marx & Gelso, 1987; Quintana & Holahan, 1992).

Variations in Clients' Reactions

Several factors affect clients' reactions to ending treatment. The most critical factor is the reason for termination. When service ends for unexpected reasons, clients' reactions are more negative than when its ending has been anticipated; they experience more anger, mourning, mood disturbances, and a sense of unfinished business (Goldthwaite, 1986; Saad, 1984). In contrast, when the ending is mutually agreed on, clients' pride and excitement are greater. And clients who have dropped out are less satisfied than are those who have ended treatment by mutual agreement with the social worker (Cochran & Stamler, 1989).

Another important factor is the success of the treatment. The more successful the treatment, the more positive the client's reactions (Fortune et al., 1992; Quintana & Holahan, 1992).

The amount and timing of the preparation for ending are also essential. Early preparation (including setting time limits initially) allows clients time to work through their reactions, so they have less difficulty and act out less during termination (Fortune et al., 1991, 1992). Even when it is done late in treatment, systematic preparation is related to more positive reactions (Corazzini, Heppner, & Young, 1980; Fortune, 1987). The most destructive approach to termination is informing the client of an unplanned termination late in treatment, without adequate time to discuss it (Bywaters, 1975; Gould, 1978).

Another influence on clients' reactions is clients' previous losses. Many believe that termination stirs up emotions about clients' previous losses. However, clients with previous losses have less, rather than more, depression, although they appreciate discussing termination (Marx & Gelso, 1987; Saad, 1984).

The duration of treatment and the quality of the relationship may influence clients' reactions, although the evidence is equivocal. In long-term treatment, a greater number of sessions is associated with greater turmoil and mood disturbance (Saad, 1984), but in short-term treatment neither the number of sessions nor the closeness of the social worker–client relationship is relevant (Marx & Gelso, 1987). Other factors, such as the type of service, treatment modality, or cohesion in groups, which may influence clients' reactions, have not been studied carefully.

Although these factors influence clients' reactions to termination, a wide range of reactions is "normal," depending on the individual. And cultural expectations influence how clients express emotions, as well as their sense of time and attitudes toward ending (Ho, 1987; Vargas & Koss-Chioino, 1992). It is inappropriate to expect that all clients will experience the same reactions,

whether the reactions are severe loss, automatic denial, or great pride in their accomplishments.

SOCIAL WORKERS' REACTIONS TO TERMINATION

Social workers also experience a range of emotions when they end service to their clients. They must be aware of these emotions because their reactions affect their ability to recognize the time to end or to determine how to intervene. Because clients take their cues from social workers, inappropriate messages about ending may prevent further growth. Finally, termination is an opportunity for social workers to assess the therapeutic process and their skill in helping clients and to reconfirm their commitment to helping others.

Social workers' typical reactions to termination are less-intense mirrors of clients' reactions. The most common ones are pride in the client and a sense of the client's accomplishments, moderate pride in their own therapeutic skills, ambivalence, sadness at the end of a relationship, and a view of the therapeutic process as a gestalt (Fortune, 1987; Fortune et al., 1992; Kramer, 1982). Less common reactions are doubt and disappointment in the client and in oneself. Occasional reactions include feelings of guilt, helplessness, anger, and other types of emotional turmoil (Bywaters, 1975; Fair & Bressler, 1992). Many social workers report sharing more personal material (especially feelings about ending) and treating clients more as equals at this time (Kramer, 1982; Marx & Gelso, 1987; Quintana & Holahan, 1992).

Variations in Social Workers' Reactions

Social workers' reactions also vary, depending on the reason for termination, the outcome, and their expectations about termination. Like clients, social workers experience negative reactions more when the ending is unanticipated; they feel less satisfied with treatment and report more guilt, frustration, and sadness about leaving the client with unresolved issues (Bywaters, 1975; Corazzini et al., 1980; Toseland, 1987). Similarly, greater success is related to positive emotions: greater pride in the client and in one's own skills, more reminiscence about the treatment process, and less doubt or guilt about treatment and its limitations (Bywaters, 1975; Fortune, 1987; Fortune et al., 1992).

There is also some evidence of countertransference. For example, social workers who found terminating difficult reported that their clients had difficulty doing so (Fortune et al., 1992). Clinicians who have a male sex-role orientation report more hostility from clients (Paster, 1983), and social workers who are more confident about ending prepare clients for termination (Fortune, 1987; Fortune et al., 1992; Gould, 1978).

TASKS AND INTERVENTIONS FOR TERMINATION

The termination process begins when the social worker and the client agree to end treatment. In time-limited service, termination activities are built in from the beginning. In open-ended service, termination begins when the possibility of ending is raised, and there may be a distinct termination phase during which termination activities are introduced. Termination interventions are designed to help the client (1) assess his or her progress and the treatment process, (2) generalize gains to other settings and situations, (3) develop skills and strategies to maintain gains, (4) assist in the transition to no service or to another service, and (5) deal with emotional reactions to ending treatment.

Assessing Progress and the Process

In assessing a client's progress, the social worker evaluates whether goals have been achieved, the status of the client's problems, and any other major changes in the client's life (because change in one area often stimulates change in others). A systematic review, similar in scope and specificity to the initial assessment, confirms (or disconfirms) the tentative decision to terminate. The confirmation is particularly important if the social worker or the client doubts that progress has been made or if some family members are more ready to end treatment than are others (Tomm & Wright, 1979). A discussion of the specifics of what the client has learned helps solidify that learning. An assessment of the client's efforts helps increase the client's sense of mastery and ability to cope, which are important skills for maintaining gains (Karoly & Steffen, 1980). Finally, information from the assessment of progress, such as what areas need further work and what assets are available for the transition, is essential for other treatment interventions.

The client and social worker also review the treatment process, emphasizing the problem-solving steps and the skills the client can use in the future. By giving an overview of the course of treatment, the review helps bring about closure. And, for the practitioner, if not the client, the review is often reaffirming and renewing (Fortune, 1987; Kramer, 1982).

Generalizing Gains

Unless deliberate efforts are made to broaden the gains, the client's use of new skills may be limited to circumscribed areas, for example, improved communication at work but not with family members (Goldstein & Kanfer, 1979). Several interventions help extend clients' gains to other areas.

First, the client may learn the general principles about dealing with problems that underlie a coping pattern, for example, principles of self-control, parenting skills, or family communication (Northen, 1988). The review of the treatment process just mentioned, the emphasis on internalizing gains in psychosocial approaches, and the emphasis on overlearning in behavioral approaches also help clients to learn principles that generalize to other situations.

Second, clients may transfer skills into the natural environment through homework assignments or tasks, for example, trying out interpersonal skills learned in a group with acquaintances (Goldstein & Kanfer, 1979). Once the skills "work" in one social situation, clients can systematically try them in new situations or with different people.

These generalization activities may be used at any time during service. Often, however, interventions that initiate change are different from those that generalize new skills. For example, abusive parents cannot show restraint with children and spouses until they learn to control their tempers.

Maintaining Gains

Another concern is how long the client's gains endure after the service ends. Several activities that make the gains more durable are increasing the client's sense of mastery through realistic praise, highlighting the client's role in creating and maintaining change, teaching general principles, and ensuring that skills transfer to the client's normal environment.

Another maintenance activity is anticipating and planning for possible future difficulties, such as what to do if a client's welfare check is reduced (Fishman & Lubetkin, 1980). Such "fail-safe" planning is also useful in areas that need continued work.

Ensuring that supports for the new behavior are available in the client's environment is another powerful way to increase the durability of the gains. The client's support system may be brought directly into treatment; a new network may be created through the client's involvement in an organization, such as Alcoholics Anonymous; or the client may learn how to elicit support from significant others (Fortune, 1992).

Follow-up sessions may help the client maintain his or her gains. To be useful, follow-up must be more than "how are you doing?" It should include maintenance interventions, such as reinforcing what the client is doing well, reviewing principles, discussing coping strategies, or planning for the future.

Making the Transition

Whether the service is ending or the client is transferring elsewhere, the social worker must ease the transition by reducing dependence and making the new situation "real." Discussing events outside treatment sessions focuses attention on outside-service activities and supports, as do maintenance and generalization activities, such as homework assignments and fail-safe planning. In groups, the group may undertake activities in locations other than the normal meeting place. Outside activities that involve skills that the group members have been working on, such as impulse control among children, also contribute to feelings of accomplishment by allowing the members to demonstrate and celebrate their gains.

If group cohesion is so powerful that it prevents the group members from letting go, cohesion can be reduced by decreasing the levels of cooperation and interaction required during group activities (Wayne & Avery, 1979). For example, members may undertake parallel individual activities, such as sewing projects in place of cooperating on a quilt. Or they may develop homework assignments in pairs, rather than in the full group.

When the client transfers elsewhere, other activities help smooth the transition to the new agency or social worker. Linkage techniques, including making appointments, help connect the client with a referral agency (Weissman, 1987). Preparatory consultation with the provider and follow-up with the client or the provider will ensure that the client receives the appropriate service (Abramson, 1983). Because the client may feel rejected at being transferred, feelings about and expectations of the new service should be explored before the transfer. The new social worker may also need to deal with the client's reluctance and dissatisfaction (Siebold, 1992).

Dealing with Emotional Reactions

The expression of feelings is an important part of the ending phase. It makes termination "real" and, if there is ambivalence, underscores the reality of ending as a new beginning. Acknowledging the client's emotions makes them acceptable and validates the client's experience. And termination may bring up important new therapeutic material or provide a corrective emotional experience.

To help clients express emotion, social workers may model the appropriate self-disclosure of their own reactions. They may also label emotions that accompany the client's nonverbal behavior, such as angry gestures, evading discussion, or hesitant pride. Positive feelings, including the client's pride in his or her accomplishments, are important for maintaining gains. Ambivalence; sadness at saying good-bye; and other normal, mild, negative reactions should be discussed, especially when treatment has been successful. Strong negative reactions may be handled as intensive mourning and grief reactions.

Some activities permit both the discussion of a client's reactions and the achievement of other purposes. For example, a "memory book," in which children write and draw, covers the reasons for the service, issues that were dealt with, and the reasons for ending the service (Elbow, 1987). The discussion of what to include in the memory book reviews the treatment process, solidifies the gains the child has made, and brings out the child's reactions to ending treatment. In an educational or growth group, a "peak experience," such as a "toast" to each person about what members learned from them, reinforces learning and a sense of mastery (Duncan & Dorris, 1976).

Ritual markers of termination help clients deal with conflicting emotions while making the uncertainty of the transition seem like it is more under control (Gutheil, 1993). They provide a means of communication, a sense of specialness, and a connection between the past and the future. Markers may be simple, for instance, culturally defined good-byes like hugging and shaking hands, or they may be complex exchanges of mementos with special meaning or elaborate events, such as graduation ceremonies. A celebration may also demonstrate individual skills and recapitulate the group's experience, for example, a potluck supper with ethnic specialties in a group to increase self-esteem.

Timing of Termination Activities

Many activities that are typical of termination, for example, homework assignments or networking, occur throughout the service. Some, such as reviewing the client's progress, occur with the decision to end; some, like termination rituals, occur only at the end; and others are selected when and as needed. However, to aid the transition, the emphasis can shift from past activities to a present and then a future orientation (Lamb, 1985). The review of the treatment process concentrates on the past; the assessment of the client's status and generalizing gains stresses both the past and the present; and maintenance focuses on the future.

REFERENCES

Abramson, J. A. (1983). Six steps to effective referrals. In H. Weissman, I. Epstein, & A. Savage (Eds.), *Agency* based social work: Neglected aspects of clinical practice. Philadelphia: Temple University Press.

Bywaters, P. (1975). Ending casework relationships (1): The closure decision. *Social Work Today, 6,* 301–304.

Cochran, S. V., & Stamler, V. L. (1989). Differences between mutual and client-initiated non-mutual terminations in a university counseling center. *Journal of College Student Development, 30*(1), 58–61.

Corazzini, J. G., Heppner, P. P., & Young, M. D. (1980). The effects of cognitive information on termination from group counseling. *Journal of College Student Personnel, 21,* 553–557.

DeBerry, S., & Baskin, D. (1989). Termination criteria in psychotherapy: A comparison of private and public practice. *American Journal of Psychotherapy, 43,* 43–53.

Duncan, A. D., & Dorris, J. F. (1976). Symbolic toast: A closure experience. In J. W. Pfeiffer & J. E. Jones (Eds.), *Annual handbook for group facilitators, 1976* (Vol. 5, pp. 17–18). LaJolla, CA: University Associates Publishers.

Elbow, M. (1987). The memory book: Facilitating terminations with children. *Social Casework, 68,* 180–183.

Fair, S. M., & Bressler, J. M. (1992). Therapist-initiated termination of psychotherapy. *Clinical Supervisor, 10,* 171–189.

Fishman, S. F., & Lubetkin, B. S. (1980). Maintenance and generalization of individual behavior therapy programs: Clinical observations. In P. Karoly & J. J. Steffen (Eds.), *Improving the long-term effects of psychotherapy: Models of durable outcome.* New York: Gardner Press.

Fortune, A. E. (1985). Planning, duration and termination of treatment. *Social Service Review, 59,* 647–661.

Fortune, A. E. (1987). Grief only? Client and social worker reactions to termination. *Clinical Social Work Journal, 15,* 159–171.

Fortune, A. E. (1992). Inadequate resources. In W. J. Reid (Ed.), *Task strategies: An empirical approach to clinical social work* (pp. 250–279). New York: Columbia University Press.

Fortune, A. E., Pearlingi, B., & Rochelle, C. (1991). Criteria for terminating treatment. *Families in Society, 22,* 366–370.

Fortune, A. E., Pearlingi, B., & Rochelle, C. (1992). Reactions to termination of individual treatment. *Social Work, 37,* 171–178.

Fox, E., Nelson, M., & Bolman, W. (1969). The termination process: A neglected dimension in social work. *Social Work, 14,* 53–63.

Goldstein, A. P., & Kanfer, F. H. (Eds.). (1979). *Maximizing treatment gains: Transfer enhancement in psychotherapy.* New York: Academic Press.

Goldthwaite, D. E. (1986). The client's perspective on the forced termination of psychotherapy (Doctoral dissertation, Boston College, 1985). *Dissertation Abstracts International, 47,* 2164B.

Gould, R. P. (1978). Students' experience with the termination phase of individual treatment. *Smith College Studies in Social Work, 48,* 235–269.

Gutheil, I. A. (1993). Rituals and termination procedures. *Smith College Studies in Social Work, 63,* 163–176.

Ho, M. K. (1987). *Family therapy with ethnic minorities.* Newbury Park, CA: Sage Publications.

Hynan, D. J. (1990). Client reasons and experiences in treatment that influence termination of psychotherapy. *Journal of Clinical Psychology, 46,* 891–895.

Karoly, P., & Steffen, J. J. (Eds.). (1980). *Improving the long-term effects of psychotherapy: Models of durable outcome.* New York: Gardner Press.

Kramer, S. A. (1982). *The therapist's view of termination in open-ended psychotherapy.* Unpublished doctoral dissertation, University of Chicago.

Lamb, D. H. (1985). A time-frame model of termination in psychotherapy. *Psychotherapy, 22,* 604–609.

Lewis, B. F. (1978). An examination of the final phase of a group development theory. *Small Group Behavior, 9,* 507–517.

Marx, J. A., & Gelso, C. J. (1987). Termination of individual counseling in a university counseling center. *Journal of Counseling Psychology, 34,* 3–9.

Northen, H. (1988). *Social work with groups* (2nd ed.). New York: Columbia University Press.

Paster, L. F. (1983). The influence of the gender and sex role of the patient and psychotherapist on the termination of psychotherapy (Doctoral dissertation, St. John's University, Collegeville, MN, 1983). *Dissertation Abstracts International, 44,* 320B.

Quintana, S. M., & Holahan, W. (1992). Termination in short-term counseling: Comparison of successful and unsuccessful cases. *Journal of Counseling Psychology, 39,* 299–305.

Saad, J. R. (1984). After ending long-term psychotherapy: Patient reactions to planned and forced termination (Doctoral dissertation, California School of Professional Psychology, Berkeley, 1983). *Dissertation Abstracts International, 44,* 3541B.

Siebold, C. (1992). Forced termination: Reconsidering theory and technique. *Smith College Studies in Social Work, 63,* 324–341.

Tomm, K. M., & Wright, L. M. (1979). Training in family therapy: Perceptual, conceptual and executive skills. *Family Process, 18,* 227–231.

Toseland, R. W. (1987). Treatment discontinuance: Grounds for optimism. *Social Casework, 68,* 195–204.

Vargas, L. A., & Koss-Chioino, J. D. (Eds.). (1992). *Working with culture: Psychotherapeutic interventions with ethnic minority children and adolescents.* San Francisco: Jossey-Bass.

Wayne, J., & Avery, N. (1979). Activities for group termination. *Social Work, 24,* 58–62.

Weissman, A. (1987). Linkage in direct practice. In A. Minahan (Ed.-in-Chief), *Encyclopedia of social work* (18th ed., Vol. 2, pp. 47–50). Silver Spring, MD: National Association of Social Workers.

Wilcoxon, S. A., & Gladding, S. T. (1985). Engagement and termination in marital and familial therapy: Special ethical issues. *American Journal of Family Therapy, 13,* 65–71.

FURTHER READING

Brill, M., & Nahmani, N. (1993). Clients' responses to separation from social work trainees. *Journal of Teaching in Social Work, 7,* 97–111.

Johnson, C. (1974). Planning for termination of the group. In P. Glasser, R. Sarri, & R. Vinter (Ed.), *Individual change through small groups* (pp. 258–265). New York: Free Press.

Kramer, S. A. (1990). *Positive endings in psychotherapy: Bringing meaningful closure to therapeutic relationships.* San Francisco: Jossey-Bass.

Levinson, H. L. (1977). Termination of psychotherapy: Some salient issues. *Social Casework, 58,* 480–489.

Mayadas, N., & Glasser, P. (1981). Termination: A neglected aspect of social group work. *Social Work with Groups, 4,* 193–204.

McRoy, R. G., Freeman, E. M., & Logan, S. (1986). Strategies for teaching students about termination. *Clinical Supervisor, 4,* 45–56.

Palombo, J. (1982). The psychology of the self and the termination of treatment. *Clinical Social Work Journal, 10,* 15–27.

Pinkerton, R. S., & Rockwell, W. J. K. (1990). Termination in brief psychotherapy: The case for an eclectic approach. *Psychotherapy, 27,* 362–365.

Siebold, C. (1992). Forced termination: Reconsidering theory and technique. *Smith College Studies in Social Work, 63,* 324–341.

Anne E. Fortune, PhD, ACSW, is associate professor, University at Albany, State University of New York, School of Social Welfare, 135 Western Avenue, Albany, NY 12222.

For further information see

Brief Therapies; Clinical Social Work; Direct Practice Overview; Ethics and Values; Goal Setting and Intervention Planning; Interviewing; Social Work Practice: Theoretical Base.

Key Words

termination   therapeutic
                   relationship

Terrell, Mary Eliza Church

See Biographies section, Volume 3

Therapy

See Treatment Approaches *(Reader's Guide)*

READER'S GUIDE

Third-Party Payments

The following entries contain information on this general topic:

Clinical Social Work
Health Care: Financing
Licensing, Regulation, and Certification
Managed Care
Private Practice
Vendorship

Thomas, Jesse O.

See Biographies section, Volume 3

Titmuss, Richard Morris

See Biographies section, Volume 3

Total Quality Management

See Quality Management

Towle, Charlotte

See Biographies section, Volume 3

Transactional Analysis

Marlene Cooper
Sandra Turner

Transactional analysis, formulated in the early 1950s, is a treatment approach and a theory of personality development. In its optimistic conception of human growth and interaction, transactional analysis focuses and builds on people's strengths, rather than targeting deficits or weaknesses. For this reason, it is ideally suited to social work practice.

Eric Berne, the founder of transactional analysis, was trained as a physician in the early 1950s when psychoanalysis was the primary method of treating emotional problems. His teachers, Eugene Kahn and Paul Federn, were students of Sigmund Freud. Berne also was influenced by Carl Jung, Wilhelm Reik, Charles Darwin, and his analyst Erik Erikson.

Early in his training, Berne became interested in the relationship between the mind and the body and particularly in human intuition. He departed from Freudian theory initially in his conceptualization of the structure of personality. In Freudian theory, the ego, id, and superego are hypothetical constructs, whereas Berne's comparable ego states (parent, adult, and child) are observable phenomena (Berne, 1961). Although not discounting the power of the unconscious, Berne was more interested in actual happenings in his clients' lives—events that could be recalled. He conceived of the unconscious as memories of feelings and experiences that were accessible to conscious thought (Dusay, 1972). This concept was his second major departure from Freudian theory.

BASIC ASSUMPTIONS AND CONCEPTS

Assumptions

Transactional analysis is founded on the belief that people can and should take responsibility for their own destinies or life scripts and that given the proper support, encouragement, and guidance, they can lead full and productive lives. The concepts of transactional analysis are described symbolically in the form of circles, bar graphs, and arrows. In treatment, these symbols are explained to the client verbally and pictorially to further an understanding of the therapist's point of view and method of working. This serves to demystify the therapy and to build a partnership between client and worker. The following are the key assumptions of transactional analysis:

1. I'm OK, you're OK. Berne believed that people were born "OK," or in a state of health, endowed with strengths and assets rather than problems and deficits. It is the parental environment that either produces this state of health or interferes with its development.

2. People are capable of being active participants in the problem-solving process, and they should be encouraged to be active partners with their therapists. This assumption is akin to the social work principal of working with the client rather than working on the client and "starting where the client is" (Shulman, 1992). In building a therapeutic partnership, those who work within a transactional analysis framework will minimize transference reactions. A primary goal of treatment is the development of autonomous functioning within a short period (weeks or months) (Goulding, 1982). As in social work, a mutual contract is formulated at the beginning of treatment, and the client states the goals that he or she wants to accomplish (Coburn, 1986).

3. Human problems can be solved and people can be cured, given the proper approach (Steiner, 1974). The therapist, while assuming the role of partner with the client, should be caring and nurturant and have the ability and desire to give the client encouragement and support (positive strokes).

Key Concepts

The following key concepts form the basis of transactional analysis theory.

Ego states. Berne (1968) conceived of an ego state as a "system of feelings accompanied by a related set of behavior patterns" (p. 23). He believed that the personality is made up of three ego states: the parent, the adult, and the child. The parent ego state, similar to the Freudian superego, comprises a set of guidelines or rules about how one should live. These guidelines are culturally determined and come from parents or parental figures. Messages such as "work hard," "please others," "succeed at all costs," and "play fair" are examples of commands from the parent ego state. The adult ego state, most similar to the ego in psychoanalytic theory, is that part of the personality that is oriented to reality. Logical and

FIGURE 1

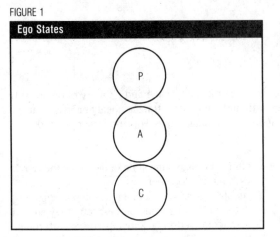

FIGURE 2

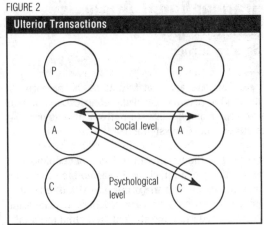

rational, it has been likened to a computer in that it takes in, stores, and processes information about oneself and the environment. Practitioners of transactional analysis assert that everyone has an adult ego state that is more or less accessible. People whose child or parent ego state is too dominant need to be helped to fully activate their adult ego state (Berne, 1968). The child ego state resembles the id and actually behaves and sounds like a child, regardless of how old a person may be. This state contains feelings, behaviors, sensations, and desires that may have been present since birth. The child either functions naturally and freely or is ruled by parental directives (Coburn, 1987).

The three ego states are symbolized by three distinct circles that represent the parent, adult, and child (see Figure 1). Affective states can be determined by observing behavior, experiencing old feelings, and cognitively experiencing the actions of the three different ego states. For example, a women who always raises her hand to speak is in a child ego state; a man who uses expressions that his mother always used (particularly if they are negative) is most likely in a parent ego state (Berne, 1968).

Interpersonal transactions. According to Berne (1961) a transaction is a social intercourse that occurs between two persons' ego states. Transactions occur on both a social level, which is overt, and on a psychological level, which is covert. Two people carry on transactions on six different levels because they each have three ego states that are interacting or transacting with each other. A parent ego state may be relating to another parent state or to a child or adult state at any given time. An example of an adult-to-adult ego state communication is two people solving a problem together.

Scripts. A script is a life plan or existential decision that one makes very early. Generally by the age of five, children have made up scripts that say that they are either basically OK and in the mainstream or not OK and on the fringes of social and emotional life (Finnegan, 1990). Transactional analysis practitioners believe that negative scripts can be converted to positive ones, because everyone is capable of being OK.

Games. This concept is best understood in terms of the graphic symbols that Berne and others developed to represent the basic transactional analysis views. (Circles represent the ego states, and arrows show the communication between them.) Because transactions between two person's ego states take place on an overt level (social) and a covert level (psychological), a game occurs when there is communication on both of these levels at the same time. Generally, these ulterior interactions that can be considered games are negative, and the people involved have bad feelings about the communication (Figure 2). An example of a game is the following: A car salesman says to a customer: "This is the best, but you can't afford it." The customer replies: "I'll take it" (Berne, 1968).

Strokes. This is a core concept in transactional analysis. A stroke is a general term describing intimate physical contact and in social and transactional analysis terms it implies the act of recognizing another's presence (Berne, 1968). People need to be told throughout their lives that they are OK and valued by receiving these strokes (Berne, 1961).

Contracting. Transactional analysis focuses on accomplishing change that is defined by the treatment contract. The contract should be an adult-to-adult interaction and an agreement between the client and the therapist about the goals and methods of treatment.

Egograms. An egogram is a bar graph that represents the amount of energy placed in each ego state. The difference between this and the three circles that show which of the three ego states are involved is that the egogram demonstrates how much energy is invested in the different ego states at any given time. Dusay (1972), who developed the egogram, conceptualized five functional ego states. The parent (P) is divided into the critical parent (CP) and nurturing parent (NP). The adult (A) is not divided, and the child (C) is divided into the free child (FC) and the adapted child (AC). Because each person's personality is unique, these five psychological forces are aligned differently in each individual (Dusay & Dusay, 1989) (Figure 3). These five ego states are interrelated so that when the time and energy is increased in one ego state, it will be diminished in another.

SIMILARITIES TO OTHER TREATMENT MODELS

Cognitive therapy, as developed by Beck (1972), incorporates many of the principles of transactional analysis. Both therapies emphasize the importance of cognition in altering one's self-image and that people do have the ability to grow and change. However, cognitive therapy does not use the same colloquial terms or symbolic representations as transactional analysis.

Gestalt therapy (Perls, 1969) is also similar to transactional analysis, but gestalt therapy places less emphasis on cognition and more on experiencing change via the emotions. These emotions are often acted out by using techniques such as the empty chair. With this exercise, the client imagines that a significant person is seated in the chair and speaks to the person in the chair as if he or she were present.

Encounter groups have much in common with transactional analysis, and both movements originated at about the same time. Both therapies primarily use the group model, along with marathon workshops. However, transactional analysis therapists tend to be more selective in their use of techniques, matching technique to ego state. A technique such as pounding a pillow, frequently used in gestalt therapy, would not be considered for all ego states in transactional analysis.

These four models are often used together in working individually and in groups.

USES OF TRANSACTIONAL ANALYSIS

Transactional analysis, because of its flexibility, is an excellent model for mental health and health care

FIGURE 3

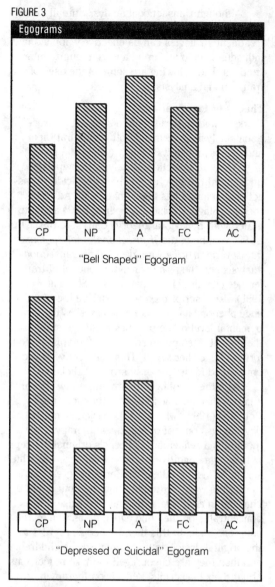

"Bell Shaped" Egogram

"Depressed or Suicidal" Egogram

SOURCE: Dusay, J., & Dusay, K. M. (1989). Transactional analysis. In R. J. Corsini (Ed.), *Current psychotherapies* (p. 410). Itasca, IL: F. E. Peacock. Copyright © 1989 by F. E. Peacock. Reprinted by permission.

professionals, educators, managers, and persons concerned with improving communication and social and interpersonal change. Settings where transactional analysis has been used include hospitals, prisons, schools, institutions, and workplaces. Because transactional analysis fosters optimism, good feeling, self-determination, and autonomy, it is harmonious with the ethics and values of the social work profession. As a theory of personality and a treatment approach, it can be employed in understanding and describing psychodynamic systems as well as interpersonal dynamics.

Although transactional analysis initially was used most widely in groups, the concepts and treatment strategies can be effectively applied in individual, conjoint, family, and community interventions. The following are some of the uses of transactional analysis.

Theory of Personality

Clarkson and Gilbert (1988) discussed transactional analysis in terms of both structural theory and ego psychology. Polansky (1991) and David (1991) used transactional analysis principles to understand the psychodynamics of suicide. Transactional analysis has been linked with Adlerian therapy (Slavik, Carlson, & Sperry, 1992) and integrated with behavioral theory (Clarkson, 1992). In a 1991 volume of the *Transactional Analysis Journal*, several articles were devoted to transactional analysis and the psychoanalytic concept of transference (Erskine, 1991; Massy, 1991; Shmukler, 1991). Using script theory to describe the transference phenomena, the therapist assesses the developmental level of the patient's child ego state as the patient attempts to set up the therapist to conform to his or her script. This perspective is recommended for fragile or unstructured clients.

As a theory of brief treatment, transactional analysis has been described in the literature by Goulding (1990), who used its basic tenants to develop his concept of redecision therapy. This method is a refinement of Berne's original concept of making a cognitive decision to change one's life script. As discussed earlier, Berne believed that life scripts were written in childhood but could be changed in adult life. Goulding's redecision work concentrates on the child ego state as well as the adult ego state. In this therapy, people regress to the original decisions that they made as children, and then they are encouraged to make redecisions about their life scripts. Redecision therapy puts more responsibility on individuals for deciding to accept or reject the directives of their parents or parental figures (Goulding, 1989). In redecision therapy, familiar bad feelings, behavior, and attitudes such as guilt, anger, discounting, cruelty, and dependency are brought to awareness by the combined use of transactional analysis, gestalt, and other behavioral techniques and discussion or group interaction.

Practice Model

Because of its versatility, transactional analysis is suited for work with groups, individuals, couples, and families. In groups, individuals often work on changing certain behaviors to obtain what they want. Members contract for specific issues to work on and often approach the therapist one-on-one within the group setting, while other group members work on scripts and redecisions. In conjoint therapy, couples experiencing poor communication can change the dynamics of their symbiotic ego states to achieve personal autonomy and independence. Within a family context, parents and children trained in transactional analysis learn to become aware of and take responsibility for their own feelings, work out decisions, and change current patterns of dysfunction, with the goal of promoting autonomy and improving communication. In individual therapy, transactional analysis helps clients to unleash the spontaneity that may have been curtailed by parents in childhood and reclaim personal control and choice. Concepts such as "script analysis" provide a simple method for reframing past experiences (Coburn, 1986).

Applying Transactional Analysis to Specific Populations

Physically ill people. Transactional analysis is effective with people who are medically ill, particularly if they have been discounted as children. People who give up childlike qualities of curiosity and creativity benefit greatly from permission to be, to think, and to feel, practicing within the therapeutic context (Coburn, 1986).

Transactional analysis has been presented as a model for the treatment of asthma and used to diminish the developmental factors that originally triggered or reinforced the asthmatic symptoms during childhood (Lammers, 1990). It has been described in physical rehabilitation as a method of conceptualizing the parent, adult, and child ego states to provide specific mechanisms by which a person with a disability, family, or health care professional can facilitate the rehabilitation process (Champeau, 1992).

Children and families. Transactional analysis is helpful to clients at all stages of the life cycle. It has been used to increase rational behavior and self-awareness in children, so that they might improve coping behaviors and increase self-awareness (Pardeck & Pardeck, 1981). It has been used with parents of handicapped children to help improve teacher–parent interactions (Grannis & Peer, 1985). Bloch and Shor (1989) demonstrated the use of transactional analysis in group work with parents of cult members. The authors discussed how the group, using transactional analysis techniques, can empower the families to reach out and assist children in crisis and work toward reunification. This has applicability to social workers dealing with the effects of externally imposed traumatic loss on the family system.

Elderly individuals have decreased anxiety and depression levels and gained more life satisfaction through transactional analysis techniques in short-term cognitive group therapy (Mills, 1986). Transactional analysis has also been used with mentally retarded individuals to help clients learn skills in problem solving and adult role behavior (Laterza, 1979).

Employees. Because transactional analysis teaches communication skills, it is well suited to the workplace. Nykodym, Longenecker, Clinton, and Ruud (1991) discussed using transactional analysis to improve the quality of one's work life. Abraham and Cunningham (1984) discussed using transactional analysis in intercultural management in developing nations, describing an experience with Saudi managers. Sethi (1979–1980, 1988–1989) demonstrated the use of transactional analysis and gestalt techniques to reduce occupational stress.

Teachers and students. Transactional analysis is widely represented in academic settings, particularly among colleges where teachers, students, and educational counselors have successfully applied the techniques to problems in the classroom. On the basis of the idea that individuals can learn to trust themselves, think for themselves, and make decisions, it has been used successfully to improve the interaction between teachers and students (Burton & Dimbleby, 1988; Champney & Schultz, 1983), increase student retention (Santa Rita, 1993), reduce math anxiety (Eisenberg, 1992), and promote discipline strategies for teachers of problem children (Ford, 1984). Leamon (1982) described how anxiety was reduced and low self-esteem was improved through transactional analysis treatment. Study participants also showed change from external to internal locus of control (the ability to attribute events to one's own effort and ability rather than to uncontrollable, external influences) and improved achievement scores.

Victims of violence, perpetrators, and those who work with them. Transactional analysis has proven successful in work within the criminal justice system. It has relevance to victims, perpetrators, and the professionals who serve them. Police officers have been trained in transactional analysis to help them to respond better to family disturbance calls, and increase their ability to guide the participants toward a nonviolent solution to their problems (Hendricks, 1977). Transactional analysis has potential in prison situations where the environment negatively reinforces angry, resentful, and depressive interactions with authority and where

feelings of low self-worth among inmates prevail (Byron, 1976). Transactional analysis is seen as a prevention technique to help defuse violent situations with clients in the mental health arena (Kaplan & Wheeler, 1983). It has also been used with women survivors of childhood sexual abuse (Apolinsky & Wilcoxon, 1991), and as a model in treatment of spouse abuse (Steinfeld, 1989).

Clayton and Dunbar (1977) advocated applying transactional analysis techniques with drunk drivers to decrease manipulative behavior and encourage more awareness of the personal responsibilities implicit in a drinking problem.

Oppressed populations. Because it can be effective in enhancing self-esteem, heightening social consciousness, and promoting personal freedom, transactional analysis is well suited for work with racial and ethnic groups and other oppressed populations.

Hlongwane and Basson (1990) demonstrated moderate support for the effectiveness of transactional analysis in improving the self-concept of African American adolescents. Chan (1991) recommended using the transactional analysis concept of script types with Chinese patients. Mohawk (1985) cited transactional analysis theory of ego states in his analysis of Native American individuals who have been dehumanized by being made to feel like children confronted by a critical parent. A study of Portuguese individuals discussed using transactional analysis strategies to raise women's self-esteem (Detry, 1986).

LIMITATIONS OF TRANSACTIONAL ANALYSIS

The limitations of transactional analysis have not been thoroughly studied. Because of the cognitive aspects of this treatment, some practitioners question its use with mentally confused or severely deprived clients. The success of the approach in clinical settings seems to hinge on the positive optimistic quality of the client–therapist relationship, which may bring some limitation for certain clients; however, no evidence exists to support this assumption (Coburn, 1986).

RESEARCH ON TRANSACTIONAL ANALYSIS: OUTCOME STUDIES

Miller and Capuzzi (1984) examined the effectiveness of transactional analysis as a method for improving interpersonal communication skills and promoting mental health by reviewing a number of studies.

Education

Instructing elementary school children in transactional analysis may result in increased self-esteem and greater acceptance of self and others (Amundson, 1975; Amundson & Sawatsky, 1976). Elementary and college students were found to exhibit an increased internal locus of control after training (Amundson, 1975; Peyton, Morris, & Beale, 1979). Middle-school students showed improved conduct after transactional analysis training (Sansaver, 1975). With high school students, transactional analysis was associated with improved attendance rates and reductions in the frequency of unacceptable behavior (Smith, 1981).

Studies have shown that transactional analysis instruction enhances self-esteem in students with learning disabilities (Golub & Guerriero, 1981), although self-esteem levels were still considerably lower than those of students of the same age without learning disabilities. Transactional analysis training has been associated with improved achievement, increased school attendance, and behavioral improvement in a group of socially maladjusted high school students (Erskine & Maisenbacherf, 1975).

Clinical Settings

College students have reported fewer negative feelings about themselves and higher achievement after participating in transactional analysis therapy (Jensen, Baker, & Koepp, 1980). Crisis intervention volunteers have reported increased service delivery and increased staff involvement after transactional analysis training (Brown, 1974).

Although transactional analysis has been found to produce greater improvements in the attitudes of juvenile delinquents than other therapies, behavior modification has been found to produce greater behavioral gains (Jesness, 1975). In comparing the effects of encounter group experiences, transactional analysis has been beneficial in some cases, but positive effects seem to be related to therapist and client characteristics, rather than to the treatment approach (Lieberman, Yalom, & Miles, 1973).

Studies of transactional analysis treatments found fewer benefits than did studies of a number of other approaches to psychotherapy. Smith and Glass (1977) reviewed over 400 studies of the effects of psychotherapy on average therapy clients, comparing the degree of therapeutic benefit of 10 types of psychotherapies. Only studies of gestalt and eclectic therapy showed fewer benefits than transactional analysis.

Miller and Capuzzi (1984) concluded that many of the studies of transactional analysis suffer from methodological shortcomings. Anecdotal reports from clients who have used transactional analysis therapy attest to personal satisfaction and benefit from the experience. Therefore, it appears that more research using vigorous methodology—perhaps single-subject design—is needed.

REFERENCES

Abraham, Y., & Cunningham, W. K. (1984, April 5–7). *Intercultural communication barriers and management education in developing nations: Problems and prospects.* Paper presented at the 31st Annual South East Convention of the American Business Communication Association, Hammond, LA.

Amundson, N. (1975). Transactional analysis with elementary school children: A pilot study. *Transactional Analysis Journal, 5,* 250–251.

Amundson, N. L., & Sawatsky, D. (1976). An educational program and transactional analysis. *Transactional Analysis Journal, 6,* 217–220.

Apolinsky, S., & Wilcoxon, S. (1991). Adult survivors of childhood sexual victimization: A group procedure for women. *Family Therapy, 18*(1), 37–45.

Beck, A. (1972). *Depression: Causes and treatment.* Philadelphia: University of Pennsylvania Press.

Berne, E. (1961). *Transactional analysis in psychotherapy.* New York: Grove Press.

Berne, E. (1968). *Games people play.* London: Penguin Books.

Bloch, A. C., & Shor, R. (1989). From consultation to therapy in group work with parents and cultists. *Social Casework 70*(4), 231–236.

Brown, M. (1974). Transactional analysis and community consultation. *Transactional Analysis Journal, 4,* 20–21.

Byron, A. J. (1976). Underworld games. *British Journal of Criminology, 16*(3), 267–274.

Burton, G., & Dimbleby, R. (1988). *Between ourselves: An introduction to interpersonal communication.* London: Edward Arnold.

Champeau, T. (1992). Transactional analysis and rehabilitation: An integrative approach to disability. *Transactional Analysis Journal, 22*(4), 234–242.

Champney, T. F., & Schultz, F. M. (1983, May 5–7). *A reassessment of the efface of psychotherapy.* Paper presented at the Annual Meeting of the Midwestern Psychological Association, Chicago.

Chan, D. W. (1991). Berne's script types and Chinese myths. *Transactional Analysis Journal, 21*(4), 220–226.

Clarkson, P. (1992). The interpersonal field in transactional analysis. *Transactional Analysis Journal, 22*(2), 89–94.

Clarkson, P., & Gilbert, M. (1988). Berne's original model of ego states: Some theoretical considerations. Special Issues, Ego States. *Transactional Analysis Journal, 18*(1), 20–29.

Clayton, S. H., & Dunbar, R. M. (1977). Transactional analysis in an alcohol safety program. *Social Work, 22,* 209–213.

Coburn, D. C. (1986). Transactional analysis: A social work treatment model. In F. J. Turner (Ed.), *Social work treatment: Interlocking theoretical approaches* (3rd ed.). New York: Free Press.

Coburn, D. C. (1987). Transactional analysis. In A. Minahan (Ed.-in-Chief), *Encyclopedia of social work* (18th ed., Vol. 2, pp. 770–777). Silver Spring, MD: National Association of Social Workers.

David, L. (1991). *Understanding the psychodynamics of suicide. Psychotherapy for suicidal clients.* Springfield, IL: Charles C Thomas.

Detry, B. (1986). Psychological intervention (for prevention) with women: Analysis of an experience realized by a delegation from the commission on the status of women in Porto: Methodological aspects. *Analise-Social, 22*(3–4), 92–93.

Dusay, J. (1972). Egograms and the constancy hypotheses. *Transactional Analysis Journal, 2*(3), 37–41.

Dusay, J., & Dusay, K. M. (1989). Transactional analysis. In R. J. Corsini (Ed.), *Current psychotherapies.* Itasca, IL: F. E. Peacock.

Eisenberg, M. (1992). Compassionate math. *Journal of Humanistic Education and Development, 30*(4), 157–166.

Erskine, R. L. (1991). Transference and transactions: Critique from an intrapsychic and integrative perspective. *Transactional Analysis Journal, 21*(2), 63–76.

Erskine, R., & Maisenbacherf, J. (1975). The effects of a transactional analysis class on socially maladjusted high school students. *Transactional Analysis Journal, 5,* 252–254.

Finnegan, W. (1990, September). Drug dealing in New Haven, part I. *New Yorker,* pp. 60–90.

Ford, R. (1984). *Discipline strategies for teachers of problem students. Washington Office of the State Superintendent of Public Instruction, Olympia KNOW-NET Dissemination Project.* Washington, DC: National Institute of Education.

Golub, S., & Guerriero, L. (1981). The effects of a transactional analysis training program on self-esteem in learning disabled boys. *Transactional Analysis Journal, 2,* 13–21.

Goulding, M. M. (1990). Getting the important work done fast: Contract plus redecision. In J. K. Zeig & S. G. Gilligan (Eds.), *Brief therapy: Myths, methods and metaphors* (pp. 303–317). New York: Brunner/Mazel.

Goulding, R. (1989). Teaching transactional and redecision therapy. *Journal of Independent Social Work, 3*(4), 71–86.

Goulding, R. L. (1982). Transactional analysis/gestalt, redecision therapy. In G. M. Gazda (Ed.), *Basic approaches to group psychotherapy and group counseling* (pp. 319–351). Springfield, IL: Charles C Thomas.

Grannis, P. D., & Peer, G. G. (1985). Using transactional analysis with parents of handicapped children. *Teaching Exceptional Children, 17*(3), 170–175.

Hendricks, J. (1977). Transactional analysis and the police: Family disputes. *Journal of Police Science and Administration, 5*(4), 416–420.

Hlongwane, M. M., & Basson, C. J. (1990). Self-concept enhancement of black adolescents using transactional analysis in a group context. *School Psychology International, 11*(2), 99–108.

Jensen, S., Baker, M., & Koepp, A. (1980). Transactional analysis in brief psychotherapy with college students. *Adolescence, 15,* 683–689.

Jesness, C. (1975). Comparative effectiveness of behavior modification and transactional analysis program for delinquents. *Journal of Consulting and Clinical Psychology, 43,* 759–779.

Kaplan, S. G., & Wheeler, E. G. (1983). Survival skill for working with potentially violent clients. *Social Casework, 64*(6), 339–346.

Lammers, W. (1990). From cure to care: Transactional analysis treatment of adult asthma. *Transactional Analysis Journal, 20*(4), 245–252.

Laterza, P. (1979). An eclectic approach to group work with the mentally retarded. *Social Work with Groups, 2*(3), 235–245.

Leamon, J. L. (1982, August). *Effects of two treatments on anxiety, self-concept, and locus of control.* Paper presented at the Annual Convention of the American Psychological Association, Washington, DC.

Lieberman, M., Yalom, I., & Miles, M. (1973). *Encounter groups: First facts.* New York: Basic Books.

Massy, R. F. (1991). The evolution of perspectives on transference in relation to transactional analysis. *Transactional Analysis Journal, 21*(3), 155–169.

Miller, C. A., & Capuzzi, D. (1984). A review of transactional analysis outcome studies. *American Mental Health Counselors Association Journal, 6*(1), 30–41.

Mills, R. (1986). *Short term cognitive group therapy with elderly clients: Training manual for mental health professionals* (Vol. 1692, pp. 132–136). Washington, DC: Denver University, Colorado Seminary, and U.S. Department of Health and Human Services.

Mohawk, J. (1985). In search of humanistic anthropology. *Dialectical Anthropology, 9*(1–4), 165–169.

Nykodym, W., Longenecker, C., Clinton, O., & Ruud, W. N. (1991). Improving quality of work life with transactional analysis as an intervention change strategy. *Applied Psychology: An International Review, 40*(4), 395–404.

Pardeck, J. A., & Pardeck, J. T. (1981). Transactional analysis as an approach to increased rational behavior and self-awareness in children. *Family Therapy, 8*(2), 113–120.

Perls, F. (1969). *Gestalt therapy verbatim.* New York: Bantam Books.

Peyton, O., Morris, R., & Beale, A. (1979). Effects of transactional analysis on empathy, self-esteem, and locus of control. *Transactional Analysis Journal, 9,* 200–203.

Polansky, N. (1991). *Integrated ego psychology.* New York: Aldine de Gruyter.

Sansaver, H. (1975). Behavior modification paired with transactional analysis. *Transactional Analysis Journal, 5,* 137–138.

Santa Rita, E. (1993). *Classroom management for student retention.* New York: Bronx Community College Department of Student Development.

Sethi, A. S. (1979–1980). Stress coping: Guidelines for executives. *Journal of Comparative Sociology and Religion, 6–7,* 87–129.

Sethi, A. S. (1988–1989). Stress coping guidelines: Strategies and their practice. *Journal of Comparative Sociology and Religion, 15–16,* 10–31.

Shmukler, D. (1991). Transference and transaction: Perspectives from developmental theory, object relations, and transformational processes. *Transactional Analysis Journal, 21*(3), 127–135.

Shulman, L. (1992). *The skills of helping.* Itasca, IL: F. E. Peacock.

Slavik, S., Carlson, J., & Sperry, L. (1992). Adlerian marital therapy with the passive aggressive partner. *American Journal of Family Therapy, 20,* 25–35.

Smith, M., & Glass, G. (1977). Meta-analysis of psychotherapy outcome studies. *American Psychologist, 32,* 752–760.

Smith, R. (1981). GEM: A goal setting, experiential, motivational program for high school students. *Transactional Analysis Journal, 11*, 256–259.

Steiner, C. M. (1974). *Scripts people live: Transactional analysis of life scripts*. New York: Grove Press.

Steinfeld, G. (1989). Spouse abuse: An integrative interactional model. *Journal of Family Violence, 4*(1), 1–23.

Marlene Cooper, PhD, ACSW, is assistant professor, and **Sandra Turner, PhD, CSW,** is assistant professor, Fordham University, School of Social Service, 113 West 60th Street, New York, NY 10023.

For further information see

Assessment; Brief Therapies; Clinical Social Work; Cognitive Treatment; Direct Practice Overview; Ecological Perspective; Gestalt; Interviewing; Psychosocial Approach; Social Work Practice: Theoretical Base.

Key Words

ego states	scripts
interpersonal transactions	transactional analysis

Truth, Sojourner

See Biographies section, Volume 3

Tubman, Harriet

See Biographies section, Volume 3

U

Undocumented Aliens

See Displaced People; Migrant Workers

Unemployment Compensation and Workers' Compensation
Linda R. Wolf Jones

Unemployment Compensation and Workers' Compensation are income security programs that provide cash benefits to workers as partial replacement of lost earnings. Unemployment Compensation covers workers who have lost their jobs, whereas Workers' Compensation covers individuals who are prevented from working as the result of a job-related disease, disability, or accident. Both programs are large: More than 100 million workers are covered under Unemployment Compensation and more than 90 million are covered by Workers' Compensation (U.S. Department of Health and Human Services, 1992).

The Unemployment Compensation program was established by the Social Security Act of 1935 and is intended to provide temporary, partial wage replacement to involuntarily unemployed workers. Unemployment Compensation operates as a federal–state program with broad federal guidelines to which all states must adhere. The specifics of each state program, however, vary widely in terms of eligibility conditions and amount and duration of benefits. Financing for the program comes from a payroll tax on employers. Two other government-financed programs—the Extended Benefits program and the Emergency Unemployment Compensation program—provide benefits to longer-term unemployed workers who have exhausted their basic Unemployment Compensation benefits.

Workers' Compensation is wholly a state program. Workers' compensation laws were enacted in some states early in the 20th century and by the 1940s had been extended to all states. These laws generally provide for benefits to individuals whose disabilities are occupation-related. As in the Unemployment Compensation program, coverage and benefit levels vary widely from state to state.

PROGRAM FINANCING

In simple terms, the Unemployment Compensation program is financed through a payroll tax. Employers are responsible for paying taxes on the amount of a worker's wages up to a specified amount per worker. The amount payable is figured as a percentage (tax rate) of the worker's wages, up to each state's specified wage minimum (tax [or wage] base).

The actual details of the financing are quite complex. Each state is responsible for determining its own method and level of taxation for its Unemployment Compensation program, resulting in considerable variation among states. In 1992, for example, the state tax base (the amount of a worker's wages on which an employer pays taxes) ranged from $7,000 to over $20,000. Further, the tax rate (the percentage the employer pays) varies not only among states but among employers within each state.

All states use experience-rating techniques to determine employer tax rates. Each state determines its own technique, but all use a formula in which the employer's tax rate depends on the degree to which the employees have used the program in the past. The experience-rating formulas "generally incorporate some combination of the employer's past tax payments, benefits used, and the size of the payroll" (Congressional Budget Office, 1983, p. 12). An individual employer may have to pay a state unemployment tax as high as 10 percent or may pay nothing at all, depending on the employer's state, the experience-rating formula used there, and the rate assigned on the basis of the employer's record of employees' use of the program.

In addition to state unemployment taxes, the federal government has established a gross federal unemployment tax equivalent to 6.2 percent of the first $7,000 of a worker's wages. If a state's Unemployment Compensation program conforms with federal rules, however, up to 5.4 percent of the tax rate paid by employers as part of their state unemployment tax obligation is credited toward their federal unemployment tax obligation. This practice reduces the unemployment tax payable to the federal government to as little as 0.8 percent of the first $7,000 of an employee's wages.

The state share of the Unemployment Compensation payroll tax is used primarily to pay cash benefits to eligible unemployed workers. It also may be used to pay the state share of the extended benefits provided to longer-term unemployed persons and to repay the federal government for program loans. The federal share of the payroll tax is used for program administration, the federal share of extended benefits, and loans to states that have exhausted their own program funds.

The financial arrangements of the Workers' Compensation program are altogether different from those of the Unemployment Compensation program. In most cases, states require employers to be insured, either through purchase of workers' compensation coverage from a private insurer or through a self-insurance plan. There is no federally mandated minimum payroll tax and no federal involvement in the financing of the program.

Financing is an important concern because both Unemployment Compensation and Workers' Compensation are major programs involving large sums of money annually. The Unemployment Compensation program in 1989 paid more than $14 billion in cash benefits to eligible claimants; the Workers' Compensation program paid over $34 billion in medical, hospitalization, and cash benefits to eligible individuals (U.S. Department of Health and Human Services, 1992). In periods of high unemployment, the Unemployment Compensation program grows commensurately; payouts increased to over $24 billion in 1991 (U.S. House of Representatives, 1992), making financing an even more critical issue than during periods of relative employment stability.

Program Eligibility

To be eligible for benefits in the Unemployment Compensation program, an individual must (1) be unemployed, (2) be covered under the program as a consequence of prior work in covered employment, and (3) meet all of the applicable program eligibility requirements. Some of the eligibility requirements are federally mandated; others vary according to the employee's state of residence.

The Bureau of Labor Statistics (U.S. Department of Labor, 1983) defined the unemployed as

> persons 16 years and over who had no job at all during the survey reference week, took some specific step to obtain a job in the 4 weeks prior to the interview

(such as applying directly to an employer or checking with a public or private employment agency), and were currently available for work (except for temporary illness). Persons expecting recall from a layoff or waiting to begin a new job within 30 days are also classified as unemployed, whether or not they actively looked for work. (p. 7)

A person with no prior attachment to the labor force is officially considered unemployed, as long as he or she is trying to find work. But someone with a past work history who is not currently employed and has given up trying to find work (sometimes referred to as a "discouraged worker") is not considered to be in the labor force and is therefore not classified as unemployed by the federal government. Jobless individuals who do not meet the definition of unemployed are not eligible to collect benefits through the Unemployment Compensation program.

The vast majority of workers meet the second requirement: that the unemployed individual must have been working in covered employment (that is, in a job for which an employer is responsible for paying applicable Unemployment Compensation payroll taxes). More than 106 million people were covered by Unemployment Compensation in 1992, representing 98 percent of all wage and salary workers and 91 percent of all employed persons (U.S. House of Representatives, 1992). Coverage under state programs is at least as broad as that under the federal system, because federal law requires that state laws cover at least the same categories of employers to qualify for the 5.4 percent federal credit. States may choose to cover additional employment categories not required by federal law, although few do so to any significant degree. Employment categories not covered under federal law include self-employment; certain agricultural labor and domestic services; services of relatives; services of patients in hospitals; and services of certain student interns, alien farmworkers, seasonal camp workers, and all railroad workers (U.S. House of Representatives, 1992).

Additional eligibility requirements vary considerably in their implementation across states. All states require that the worker be able and available to work. It is generally required that he or she have an adequate and recent work history (in covered employment), be seeking work, and be free from disqualification "for such acts as quitting without good cause or discharge for misconduct" (Congressional Budget Office, 1983, p. 5). A state's interpretation of each of these requirements is an important variable in determining who is eligible to draw benefits.

Eligibility for the Workers' Compensation program also varies greatly from state to state, but generally an individual must experience an occupation-related injury or illness leading to disability or death. Three types of disability are covered by the program: (1) temporary total disability, (2) permanent partial disability, and (3) permanent total disability. (The disability does not have to be physical; rulings in recent years have accepted work-related mental stress as a valid disability for purposes of program eligibility.) A worker may be eligible for medical, hospitalization, rehabilitation, and/or cash benefits. In the event of a work-related death, death or survivors' benefits may be payable to family members.

INTERACTION WITH SOCIAL WELFARE AND INCOME MAINTENANCE SYSTEMS

The Unemployment Compensation and Workers' Compensation programs are an important part of the overall social welfare and income maintenance systems in the United States today. Income maintenance programs are often categorized as either social insurance or public assistance. The most pronounced difference between these program categories is that social insurance programs provide benefits to eligible claimants without regard to need, whereas public assistance programs are conditioned on income and impose a means test on applicants and beneficiaries. Both Unemployment Compensation and Workers' Compensation fall into the social insurance category.

The current U.S. income maintenance system is a disparate network of both social insurance and public assistance programs. These programs extend and complement individuals' private income and resources when their income needs are not met through income from employment. Income maintenance programs in this country generally are categorical; that is, they cover a specific population and/or provide income protection against one or more specific risks.

Major cash benefit programs within the income maintenance system include Old-Age and Survivors Insurance (OASI) and Disability Insurance (DI) components of social security, Supplemental Security Income (SSI), Aid to Families with Dependent Children (AFDC), and general assistance. Whereas Unemployment Compensation provides benefits to compensate for income loss engendered by job loss, and Workers' Compensation covers income needs stemming from a job-related illness or accident, these other income maintenance programs provide benefits to cover retirement, the death of a parent or spouse, disability, impoverishment among elderly people or

dependent children, and impoverishment among people in general who have no other means of support. In addition, the food stamp, Medicare, and Medicaid programs, although they do not provide cash benefits per se, are also important sources of support for people in the income maintenance programs.

Although Unemployment Compensation and Workers' Compensation are important components of an overall income maintenance system, the system itself is not well integrated. Each program has different eligibility requirements and covers different populations; some overlap and others do not. For example, because Unemployment Compensation benefits are not means-tested and do not accrue primarily to a population in poverty, there is relatively little overlap between the Unemployment Compensation recipients and those who receive benefits from the major public assistance programs. In 1982, a time of severe economic downturn, the Congressional Budget Office (1982) estimated that only 1 percent to 3 percent of Unemployment Compensation households were receiving public assistance (either through AFDC or SSI). About 10 percent to 12 percent of Unemployment Compensation households were using food stamps, and about 10 percent (which may or may not have been the same households that used food stamps) had children who participated in various school lunch programs. More recently, a study of Unemployment Compensation recipients and exhaustees (former recipients who had exhausted their benefits) found that few participants in either group received pensions or social security benefits and even fewer received cash or in-kind public assistance (Corson & Dynarksi, 1990).

Arguments have been made both for and against closer ties between the Unemployment Compensation and Workers' Compensation programs and other income maintenance programs. On the one hand, many people oppose efforts to link social insurance programs in any way to means-tested programs such as public assistance and food stamps, fearing that this could lead to a means test for Unemployment Compensation. On the other hand, some Unemployment Compensation recipients start out poor, and a considerable number of others become poor as benefits and savings are exhausted over time. Discussions have ensued about developing new linkages in the income maintenance system so that Unemployment Compensation recipients (and other unemployed people) could retain health insurance coverage either privately or through Medicaid, meet or defer mortgage payments, and gain temporary eligibility for existing assistance programs if income and other criteria are met (but waiving the resource limits). It has been proposed that Unemployment Compensation start for each recipient as a social insurance program, leaving the basic program unchanged, but that the eligibility criteria be tightened with each subsequent benefit extension (see National Commission on Unemployment Compensation, 1981). Most of these ideas have not been enacted, but the importance of continuing medical coverage was recognized in the Comprehensive Omnibus Budget Reconciliation Act of 1986 (COBRA). Provisions in this legislation require that employers offer a continuation of health benefits to all previously covered employees who have resigned or been laid off from their positions. If an employee chooses to continue health care coverage under COBRA, the coverage generally lasts for 18 months and the employee pays all premiums, including the share previously paid by the employer.

ROLE OF SOCIAL WORKERS

Social welfare as an institution is concerned with ensuring that the entire population has access to the benefits of society and acts to mediate between the needs of individuals and those of society. Income needs are one factor, albeit an important one, in the overall social welfare sphere. Social work's involvement in the Unemployment Compensation and Workers' Compensation programs has been minimal. Both are employment-related, social insurance programs that do not concern themselves with beneficiaries' needs other than income. Issues related to recipients' personal lives are not relevant, other than for purposes of eligibility (for example, the available-to-work requirement in Unemployment Compensation) or benefit amounts (for example, dependents' benefits, where applicable). Research has shown that "job loss is strongly associated with depression, anxiety, aggression, insomnia, loss of self-esteem, and marital problems" (U.S. Congress, Joint Economic Committee, 1984). Economic losses in general are associated with increased mortality, mental health problems, and criminal activity. The Unemployment Compensation and Workers' Compensation programs help recipients meet external income needs, but they are not constructed to deal with the stresses and internal needs of recipients—needs that social workers can address. Although social workers do not generally play a direct role in Unemployment Compensation and Workers' Compensation programs, they should be aware of these programs and how they fit into the larger social welfare picture.

CURRENT ISSUES

The Unemployment Compensation and Workers' Compensation programs present many unresolved problems, both individually and in their interaction with other government programs. A nagging problem in Unemployment Compensation in recent years has been inadequate financing. During the late 1970s and early 1980s, poor economic conditions and high unemployment rates drained the program's funds in many states. The states, in turn, borrowed from the federal government in order to continue to pay benefits and several of those loans are still outstanding. Further, although the states' unemployment trust fund accounts have improved considerably since then (despite the outflow caused by the 1990–92 recession), the reserve ratios (that is, the ratio between the trust fund balance and the total wages paid in the state during the year) are still inadequate. In many states, the reserves are well below the amount needed to maintain solvency should there be another severe economic recession.

Another area of concern is that Unemployment Compensation covers only a small portion of the nonworking population and that its complex eligibility provisions exclude many individuals. Many states have rigid requirements regarding such matters as a claimant's degree of attachment to the labor force, the cause of the unemployment, and his or her subsequent availability to work and the related job search.

A third program concern is that Unemployment Compensation benefits, when available, are frequently inadequate. Benefits are limited by law in both duration and amount. The basic Unemployment Compensation program varies from state to state, but in 1991, 33 states had average weekly benefits of $160 or less and only six states had average weekly benefits of $200 or more. In seven states, the average weekly benefit was less than $120 (U.S. House of Representatives, 1992). Further, the benefit payments, regardless of amount, are only available for a specified number of weeks. The Extended Benefits and Emergency Unemployment Compensation programs provide additional benefit weeks to some recipients after basic benefits have been exhausted, but the availability of these programs depends on outside economic factors. These programs provide assistance to an even smaller proportion of the unemployed population than does the basic Unemployment Compensation program. Finally, all Unemployment Compensation is taxable, further reducing the total value of the benefits to recipients.

Major concerns regarding Workers' Compensation also focus on program adequacy and coverage. The individual state programs are tremendously varied as to populations covered and benefits available. Although there is much that could be done to strengthen the states' Workers' Compensation programs and the protections they provide, the issue of fraud and the increase in claims based on stress-related illness as a work-related disability have overtaken most other program concerns. Both of these factors are perceived as being at the root of an upsurge in the program's caseload and costs: Workers' Compensation program expenditures rose from $3 billion in 1970 to $13.5 billion in 1980 and had reached $33.8 billion by 1989 (U.S. Department of Health and Human Services, 1992).

The problems and inadequacies of the Unemployment Compensation and Workers' Compensation programs reduce their efficiency and utility as income replacement programs in different ways. Nevertheless, they remain valuable components of the income security system available to workers in the United States today.

REFERENCES

Comprehensive Omnibus Budget Reconciliation Act of 1986. P.L. 99-509, 100 Stat. 1874.

Congressional Budget Office. (1982). *Interactions among programs providing benefits to individuals: Secondary effects on the budget*. Washington, DC: U.S. Government Printing Office.

Congressional Budget Office. (1983). *Unemployment insurance: Financial condition and options for change*. Washington, DC: U.S. Government Printing Office.

Corson, W., & Dynarski, M. (1990, September). *A study of unemployment insurance recipients and exhaustees: Findings from a national survey* (Occasional Paper 90-3). Washington, DC: U.S. Department of Labor, Unemployment Insurance Service.

National Commission on Unemployment Compensation. (1981). *Unemployment compensation: Studies and research* (Vol. 1). Washington, DC: U.S. Government Printing Office.

Social Security Act of 1935. P.L. 100-360, 49 Stat. 620.

U.S. Congress, Joint Economic Committee. (1984). *Economic change, physical illness, mental illness, and social deviance* (S. Prt. 98-200). Washington, DC: U.S. Government Printing Office.

U.S. Department of Health and Human Services, Social Security Administration. (1992). *Annual statistical supplement to the Social Security Bulletin, 1991*. Washington, DC: U.S. Government Printing Office.

U.S. Department of Labor, Bureau of Labor Statistics. (1983). *Workers, jobs, and statistics* (Report 698). Washington, DC: U.S. Government Printing Office.

U.S. House of Representatives, Committee on Ways and Means. (1992). *1992 green book*. Washington, DC: U.S. Government Printing Office.

FURTHER READING

Jones, L.R.W. (1985). *Unemployment compensation and the low income worker (Working Papers in Social Policy)*. New York: Community Service Society of New York.

Nelson, W. J., Jr. (1992). Workers' compensation: 1984–88 benchmark revisions. *Social Security Bulletin, 55*, 41–58.

Price, D. N. (1985). Unemployment insurance, then and now, 1935–85. *Social Security Bulletin, 48*, 22–32.

U.S. Congress, Joint Economic Committee. (1984). *Estimating the effects of economic change on national health and social well-being* (S. Prt. 98-198). Washington, DC: U.S. Government Printing Office.

U.S. House of Representatives, Committee on Ways and Means. (1983). *Unemployment compensation issues* (Serial 98-11). Washington, DC: U.S. Government Printing Office.

Linda R. Wolf Jones, DSW, is executive director, Therapeutic Communities of America, 1818 N Street, NW, Suite 300, Washington, DC 20036.

For further information see

Aid to Families with Dependent Children; Disability; General Assistance; Hunger, Nutrition, and Food Programs; Income Security Overview; Jobs and Earnings; Poverty; Public Social Welfare Expenditures; Social Security; Social Welfare Policy; Supplemental Security Income.

Key Words	
appropriation	unemployment
disabilities	compensation
income security	workers'
	compensation

Unions
Milton Tambor

Although union membership has fallen from 34 percent of the overall labor force in 1955 to 16.4 percent in 1991 (Farber & Krueger, 1993), unionization among public employees and professionals continues to grow steadily (Goldfield, 1987). In the public sector, unions represent 44 percent of federal, state, and local government employees (Freeman, 1986), and among professional and technical workers, this figure is over 50 percent (Aronson, 1985). Professionals now constitute the third most organized occupational sector in the country (American Federation of Labor–Congress of Industrial Organizations [AFL–CIO], 1992). Reasons cited for this accelerated rate of organizing among professionals are a shift in public policy resulting in favorable legislation for collective bargaining, a changing work force of younger workers and people of color supporting a trade union orientation, and the appeal of unions to both employee and professional interests (Aronson, 1985; Burton & Thomason, 1988). Social work unionization is occurring within this context of increased labor organizing among professionals.

Collective bargaining rights for social workers are determined by state and federal statutes that cover employees in the public and private sectors. In private hospitals and voluntary agencies, depending on funding and interstate commerce, social workers likely fall under the jurisdiction of the National Labor Relations Board (NLRB). For social workers in state and local government, statutory rights to bargain are more fragmented and less uniform. Although most states have comprehensive legislation or authorize bargaining for some groups of employees, 10 states have no such statutes (Schneider, 1988). Under state statutes, the scope of bargaining is usually defined in narrower terms than in the National Labor Relations Act (NLRA) in that civil service and merit systems are exempted, and specific management rights and prerogatives are enumerated. Under bargaining laws modeled after NLRA, the process of securing union representation involves submitting a petition signed by 30 percent of the employees in an eligible unit, scheduling a hearing to determine the appropriateness of the bargaining unit, conducting a secret ballot election, and certifying the union through a majority vote.

The motives for professionals to form a union can be linked to extrinsic factors (wages, benefits, and job security) or intrinsic factors (client services, participation in decision making, organizational policies; Kleingartner & Bickner, 1977). To social work faculty, for example, collective bargaining can serve to codify participatory and governance rights (Flynn, 1980). Among state social services professionals, major reasons for joining a union were found to be similar to those of blue-collar workers—to increase wages and benefits, obtain greater job security, and reduce arbitrary management practices (Warner, Chisholm, & Munzenrider, 1978). In two other state organizing drives, caseload size, pay equity, career ladder and training, and the downgrading of classifications emerged as the major organizing issues (Karger, 1988; Tambor, 1983). In a mental health clinic in the voluntary sector, however, safer working conditions, reasonable workloads, benefits for part-time employees, and sharing in agency decision making constituted the basis for union organizing (DiBicarri, 1985).

SCOPE OF SOCIAL WORK UNION MEMBERSHIP

An estimated 125,000 social workers (Karger, 1988), or 25 percent of a 438,000-member social work labor force (Bronfenbrenner, DellaMattera, & Juravich, 1993), are union members, mostly employed in the highly organized public sector. With state and local public welfare agencies, the rate is higher—44 percent—and has remained relatively stable since 1972 (Burton & Thomason, 1988). Compared with registered nurses, the overall social work unionization percentage is about the same, but for full-time university and college faculty and secondary and high school teachers, the proportions are higher, at 40 percent and 75 percent, respectively (Aronson, 1985; Shostak, 1991). In further contrast, in Canada, 85 percent of public sector and 55 percent to 60 percent of voluntary sector social workers belong to unions (Pennell, 1987).

Most unionized social workers are members of the American Federation of State, County, and Municipal Employees (AFSCME) and the Service Employees International Union (SEIU). Social work membership in these international unions in 1993

Note: For the purpose of this entry, the terms "professional social worker" and "social worker" refer to individuals eligible for membership in the National Association of Social Workers as regular, student, or associate members.

was estimated at 55,000 for AFSCME, (J. Ponton, personal communication, September 2, 1993) and 26,000 for SEIU (S. Schwartz, personal communication, July 9, 1993). The overall national membership figures for AFSCME and SEIU are 1.2 million and 925,000, respectively (Gifford, 1990); they are among the largest and fastest-growing unions in the AFL–CIO. Major social work SEIU unions are located in the highly industrialized states of California (Local 535), Pennsylvania (Local 668), Massachusetts (Local 509), and New York (where the 50,000-member New York Public Employee Federation represents social workers and other professional, scientific, and technical personnel). Social work AFSCME unions are concentrated in councils in Illinois, Ohio, Indiana, Minnesota, and Wisconsin. In New York City, Local 371, District Council 37, represents approximately 16,000 members who are primarily classified as caseworkers and master's-level social workers, and Council 1707's 20,000 members are based in voluntary agencies. Social workers in smaller numbers belong to Local 1199 of the Drug, Hospital, and Health Care Employees Union, Communications Workers of America (CWA), American Federation of Teachers (AFT), United Automobile Workers (UAW), and faculty associations.

The impact of social work unions extends beyond membership numbers. For example, many social workers who occupy supervisory and management positions are former union members. Moreover, union contracts may directly influence the conditions and organization of the work of managers, supervisors, and other nonrepresented social workers. Complex social work and labor employment patterns have tended to discourage systematic study of unionization. Among the factors to be considered in such research are dispersion of social workers in heterogeneous bargaining units; membership in different unions; location in both public and nonprofit sectors; and employment in such diverse institutions as hospitals, clinics, welfare departments, schools, corrections facilities, and voluntary agencies.

Much of the social work union experience finds expression in labor publications at local, regional, and international levels. Progressive social workers in new-left political organizations and those writing for such journals as the *Journal of Sociology and Social Welfare, Radical America,* and *Catalyst* (now *Journal of Progressive Human Services*) have also analyzed and reported on social work unionization developments. Within the Catalyst Collective, in particular, members engaged in union organizing in their workplaces, and some served as union officials and staff (Wag-

ner, 1990). With a perspective based on a socialist critique of social services policy, the collective encouraged a strategy for action emphasizing social services workers' struggles in their own interests to better working conditions ("Why *Catalyst?*" 1978). From this more radical perspective, unions provided social workers with a strategy for confronting greater productivity demands (Tudiver, 1982); new managerial technologies (Patry, 1978); and bureaucratic constraints associated with routinization, monotony, discipline, and the loss of control over work (Arches, 1985).

However, within the professional mainstream the phenomenon of social work unionization has received scant attention (Alexander, 1987). Except for Shaffer's (1979) Unionized Social Workers Project at the University of Illinois, the study and teaching of unionism and collective bargaining have not been extensive in schools of social work. Even in social work administration, where there is interest in human resources management and new forms of decentralized and decision-making structures, labor–management relations are relatively unexplored.

EARLY HISTORY

The activist and reform traditions within the profession today owe much to social workers' participation in the labor movement in the 1930s and 1960s. Despite the gap between the two eras, social work unions had common goals—unionization, reformation of social work practices, and a commitment to broad social change.

Formative 1930s

The early history of the union movement in social work and the liberal and radical responses within the profession to the Great Depression have been well documented (Alexander & Speizman, 1980; J. Fisher, 1980; Haynes, 1975; Leighninger & Knickmeyer, 1976). For professionals facing salary cuts at the New York Federation for the Support of Jewish Philanthropic Societies, the formation of a protective association—The Association of Federation Social Workers (AFSW)—represented a necessary organizational response (Alexander & Speizman, 1980). In 1934 AFSW conducted the first strike in social work, a two-hour work stoppage (J. Fisher, 1980). Protective associations such as AFSW were supported by discussion clubs, and this network, which included activists who founded the journal *Social Work Today,* constituted the "rank-and-file movement" within social work. For the rank-and-file, interest in social action and reform encompassed domestic and policy issues, from public assistance standards to the spread of fascism in

Europe. Rank-and-filers participated in marches protesting hunger, unemployment, and racial discrimination.

The protective associations represented the major component of the rank-and-file movement, and its National Coordinating Committee considered establishing a national union of social services workers (J. Fisher, 1980). When attempts to organize under the AFL failed, these rank-and-filers joined the CIO in the United Office and Professional Workers of America (UOPWA) and the State, County, and Municipal Workers of America (SCMWA).

Prominent leaders in social work, educators, and practitioners with reputations as radicals and left-wingers advocated on behalf of social work unionization. In 1936 Mary Van Kleek argued that social workers in trade unions would not only gain a voice in determining their own working conditions, but they would also increase the effectiveness of labor movements' social programs (Galper, 1980). Bertha Capen Reynolds (1964/1991) claimed that ethical treatment of clients was inseparable from protecting one's condition as a worker.

In 1938 SCMWA membership was 35,000, including 8,500 members in 78 public welfare locals, and the membership of Social Service Employees within UOPWA during 1942 totaled 45,000, with a majority in Jewish agencies and in the larger New York City locals. In the voluntary sector, many informal agreements were reached, and by 1942, 25 written agreements were formalized (Alexander & Speizman, 1980). Being exempt from labor law coverage, UOPWA had to pressure agencies to secure voluntary recognition (Haynes, 1975).

Both UOPWA and the United Public Workers of America (UPWA)—the result of a merger between SCMWA and the United Federal Workers of America (UFWA)—were expelled from the CIO in 1950 for alleged communist domination, as were nine other unions.

Turbulent 1960s

The fusion of unionism and social reform re-emerged in new forms during the 1960s, with civil rights and antiwar movements, protests on college campuses, and the rising tide of public employee militancy setting the stage. Facing soaring caseloads, escalating demands for assistance, and inadequate public welfare funds, public welfare workers became increasingly dissatisfied. Many of these new caseworkers, radicalized on campuses and lacking special training and opportunities to realize professional aspirations, turned to social activism (Schutt, 1986). As a result, militant pro-tests accompanied the unionization of public welfare workers.

Welfare workers in New York City and surrounding Westchester County, Ohio, Los Angeles, Chicago, and Sacramento went on strike between 1965 and 1967 (Tompkins, 1967). The 28-day strike in New York City was the longest in that city's history, and the Sacramento County strike, which lasted 280 days, was the longest public employee strike in U.S. history. Several of these welfare employees' unions, distrustful of the institutional structures and goals within organized labor, opted to function as independent unions (Tambor, 1981; Transue, 1980). For a brief period they formed their own national organization, the National Federation of Social Service Employees, before affiliating with AFL–CIO international unions. These unions were characterized by a high degree of rank-and-file participation, an industrial organizational model that included employees across job classifications, and a commitment to welfare rights and reform. In two cases—the Independent Union of Public Aid Employees (IUPAE), in Chicago's Cook County, and the Social Service Employees Union (SSEU), in New York City—unionization served not only to protect traditional economic interests but also to initiate welfare policy changes and build worker–welfare recipient alliances (Maier, 1987; Schutt, 1986).

Independent Union of Public Aid Employees. In 1966, IUPAE, seeking union recognition and bargaining rights with Cook County, conducted a strike. Although union recognition remained the main objective, demands for service improvements also were made. A settlement was reached, and a fact-finding committee issued a report supporting the concept of collective bargaining. Community and civil rights organizations provided support, and the union pledged to continue its fight to improve working conditions and the quality of services (Schutt, 1986). A year later the union entered into negotiations and included among its demands the issuance of handbooks to aid recipients and the distribution of emergency checks at district offices (Weber, 1969). Despite a second strike, the county maintained its position that client service demands were outside the scope of bargaining. The union then shifted its focus to coalition work with community and welfare rights organizations. A community-relations committee was formed, and union activists participated with welfare rights groups in demonstrations and distributed welfare rights handbooks directly to clients.

Social Services Employee Union. When SSEU members in New York City walked off their jobs in

1965, their demands involved reduced caseloads; career and salary plans; training; and improved working conditions to correct overcrowding, poor ventilation, and lack of space for private interviews. Civil rights leaders and chapters of the National Association for the Advancement of Colored People (NAACP) supported the union, recognizing that welfare workers and clients alike suffered from high caseloads and inadequately paid staff (Mendes, 1974). After the strike, a mediation panel issued recommendations that incorporated union demands of caseload maximums and automatic clothing grants for aid recipients. In subsequent negotiations, the union proposed additional client service demands—budgets based on the consumer price index, automatic clothing allowances, fair housing rights, telephones, and availability of residential treatment. A second strike was unsuccessful, as the city held to its position that standards of service was a management prerogative and not subject to bargaining.

Both IUPAE and SSEU played important roles in expanding collective bargaining rights for public employees in the 1960s. Despite public policy that restricted a union's ability to negotiate client services, these unions, acting outside the collective bargaining arena, continued to advocate for welfare rights and reform. In the nonprofit sector, similar alliances between social work unions and community organizations were formed to press for greater citizen participation in decision-making policies (Tambor, 1973). These social work unions operated at the cutting edge of progressive change within the profession, the labor movement, and the larger society.

PROFESSIONALIZATION AND UNIONIZATION: COMPLEMENTARY PROCESSES

A recurring theme in the professional literature has been the compatibility of unionization with professionalization (Alexander, 1980; Karger, 1988; Lightman, 1982). Administrators have viewed collective bargaining as inappropriate for the nonprofit community service enterprise (Hush, 1969) and as inevitably promoting conflict between the agency's norm of serving the clients and the union's norm of serving the members' interests (Shulman, 1978). Unionization also has been seen as a responsible and logical means of dealing with power and decision making within the social agency workplace (Goldberg, 1960; Levine, 1975). The right to strike is considered central to the bargaining process (Levy, 1964), and NASW has consistently opposed laws or policies prohibiting strikes (NASW, 1990).

Despite the strike action's potential impact on client services (Bohr, Brenner, & Kaplan, 1971; D. Fisher, 1987; Rehr, 1960), actual strikes have been few (Shaffer & Ahearn, 1981), and provisions for providing emergency services can be maintained (Ryan & Brown, 1970). Economic disputes, unless they involve major concessions, seldom provoke a strike. Typically, issues of equity, job security, working conditions, and union survival are rooted in the labor–management conflict (Calmain, 1975; Tambor, 1979). Lightman (1983) found that social workers were more likely to consider striking to enhance the quality of client services than to improve wages and benefits. Mediation and fact-finding procedures are available for both management and union. For police and firefighters, *interest arbitration* (third-party decision making on contractual disputes) is frequently used as a means of avoiding strikes, and some social workers have supported the use of this mechanism (Alexander, Lichtenberg, & Brunn, 1980; Levy, 1964; Shaffer & Ahearn, 1981).

The consensus among researchers is that unionization and professionalization are compatible. In Shaffer and Ahearn's (1981) survey of social work trade unionists, none of the respondents considered unionization as inherently conflictual with the *NASW Code of Ethics* (NASW, 1994). Alexander (1987) concluded that the principled rejection of social work unionization is not supported by the historical record, research, and theory within the sociology of the profession, or the reality of steady union growth among professionals. However, unfavorable union stereotypes that persist within the wider society influence attitudes within the profession. For Freeman and Medoff (1984), negative attitudes toward the union are associated with its "monopoly face"—monopolistic demands for higher wages, dilution of managerial authority, decreased productivity, and promotion of the union's narrow institutional interests. In contrast, the "collective institutional response" emphasizes the union's role in providing a collective voice for workers, higher wages and benefits, lower turnover, increased productivity, and advances in industrial democracy.

In union organizing drives, social services administrators project the monopoly face of the union and are likely to conduct fierce campaigns against union representation. In the public sector, particularly in the highly organized industrialized states, employers are less apt to engage in full-fledged union-avoidance campaigns (Freeman, 1986). When these campaigns are launched, unions are portrayed as interlopers that interfere with employees' ability to discuss and resolve grievances with management and as dues-hungry organizations that promote job insecurity, strikes, and loss of job flexibility (Karger, 1988). Management may also invoke legal obstacles to divide professional and nonprofessional staff (McCormick & Mirkle, 1982) or delay certification of the union (Tambor, 1979). An alternative management strategy is to announce a salary increase and plead for another chance.

Social worker interest in professional and policy issues has been questioned as a bargaining priority. Alexander et al. (1980) found that, compared with teachers, librarians, and academicians, social workers view union representation in narrower economic terms. Shaffer (1979) suggested that social workers examine the bargaining experience of other professionals in nursing and medicine who have been more effective in negotiating provisions such as caseload size, ethical practice, and quality service.

These studies have tended to underestimate managerial opposition to an expanded scope of bargaining over matters regarded as managerial prerogatives in social services. For example, in 1991 only 28 percent of social services administrators considered workloads, job duties, employee evaluations, staff development, representation on agency board committees, and policy consultation rights as proper subjects for bargaining, compared with 78 percent of union respondents (Tambor, 1991). Case studies of teacher bargaining demonstrate a greater willingness by the public employer, despite initial resistance, to negotiate educational and public interest issues within the labor agreement (Klauss, 1969; Perry, 1979). Within social services, policy bargaining may be less developed. Although many contracts include reasonable workload standards, specific caseload size, and joint labor–management review committees, further study and research into the scope of policy bargaining clearly is warranted.

Public Policy and Union Organizing

Public policy and labor market conditions will continue to influence the course of social work unionization. Federal legislation guaranteeing bargaining rights or minimum standards for state and local employees would promote further unionization in social work, particularly in states in which no such laws have been enacted. Similarly, labor law reform could remove current obstacles to organizing by facilitating certification of the union and strengthening penalties for unfair labor practices. In *American Hospital Association v. National Labor Relations Board* (1991), the Supreme Court upheld a 1989 NLRB rule designating eight appro-

priate bargaining units in acute-care hospitals. The ruling should also improve prospects for organizing in the health care industry, the nation's most rapidly expanding employment sector.

Women and People of Color
Much of the success in public employee organizing can be attributed to the growing appeal of unions to women and people of color, who represent an expanding base within the current work force. Public-sector unions have been particularly responsive to the women's movement and gender issues—family leave, career advancement, sexual harassment remedies, job flexibility, child care, and pay equity. With AFSCME victories in Washington State and the city of San Jose, the struggle for pay equity has generated labor coalition activities. Unions representing social workers can be expected to negotiate the elimination of wage disparities, lobby for comparable worth legislation, and sue for judicial relief. More demands will also be made of unions to provide social services programs that meet the needs of working women (Martin, 1985).

Workload Standards and Caseload Size
Unions continue to pressure the courts and administrative agencies to mandate bargaining in the area of workload standards and caseload size. To change public policy, unions must file lawsuits charging employers with a failure to bargain. This litigation process may involve lengthy appeals, as in *County of Los Angeles, Los Angeles County Department of Public Social Services et al. v. Los Angeles County Employees Association, SEIU Local 660 et al.* (1973). In this case the California Supreme Court ruled that workloads were a subject of bargaining. Recognizing the link between caseloads and services, unions in Pennsylvania ("Too Many Cases," 1980) and Washington, DC ("AFSCME Members' Concern," 1991) filed suit to restore funding for child welfare services, and in Illinois ("The Child Abuse Crisis," 1988) the union has been lobbying for a statewide caseload standards bill. To gain the public's attention, unionized social workers will engage in ongoing job actions and demonstrations. Protests in New York City, Washington, DC, and California confronted issues of caseload size, staffing, worker safety, and quality of care (Hiratsuka, 1992).

The particular stresses and demands associated with human services work must also be addressed. In a survey commissioned by AFSCME, researchers found that health services professionals operate under stressful conditions resulting from excessive paperwork, crowded and noisy work environments, increased caseloads, lack of professional recognition and career advancement opportunities, and the impact of being targets of client anger. Measures proposed by the union include setting realistic limits on caseloads; allowing more time for clients; restructuring caseworker jobs to minimize paperwork; increasing autonomy; improving the work environment to allow for privacy and quiet; developing promotion, training, and career advancement opportunities; and providing counseling and referral services through joint employer and union programs ("All Stressed Out," August 1988).

In their efforts to maintain services, progressive unions are seeking to build worker–community alliances (Withorn, 1985). To cope with the lingering fiscal crises in state and local governments, unions are also participating in campaigns and educating their members in support of equitable tax reform (AFSCME, 1992).

Maintaining Public Services

The most serious threat facing unions in the public sector is *privatization*—the transfer of government services and functions to private for-profit and private nonprofit agencies. Lower wages and benefits have tended to reduce labor costs in these private-sector auspices. To defend their membership base and protect the equity in those jobs, unions have strongly opposed the contracting out of human services. Unions have contended that contracted services can result in less accountability to the citizenry, lower quality of service, a decline in public agency flexibility and expertise, increased opportunities for misuse of public funds, and higher costs (AFSCME, 1986). In Massachusetts, unions joined in a coalition to reject the administration's plan to transfer public mental health and mental retardation funds to private vendors, and instead recommended cost-saving reforms that maintained quality standards (Partnership for Quality Care & Schoen, 1991). SEIU Local 509 and members of this coalition, including consumer advocates, academicians, and other unions, have lobbied for legislation requiring the state to document the true costs of privatization and any substantive savings, to apply existing affirmative action guidelines to vendors, to qualify only companies that provide health insurance for their employees, to permit state workers to submit their own bids, and to ensure citizen rights to appeal contract decisions ("Senate Bill 1514," 1993). In Michigan, citing examples of embezzlement of state funds among group homes, a union recommended halting privatization until the proper monitoring of current contracts could be established (*Privatization*, 1992). Even with lobby-

ing and coalition building, unions may still be unable to stem the negative effects of privatization unless extensive resources are committed to organizing human services workers in the smaller agencies dispersed in the less-organized private for-profit and private nonprofit sectors.

In the public policy arena, the union and NASW share many common political objectives. Since 1968, *NASW Standards for Social Work Personnel Practice* have affirmed the right of employees to bargain collectively concerning wages and working conditions. In fact, since 1975 staff in NASW's national office, excluding those in management and supervisory positions and those deemed confidential employees, have been represented by Local 2382 of the Communications Workers of America. In the area of political action, NASW and AFSCME, in particular, have shared similar policy positions—welfare reform, pay equity, national health insurance, reduced defense expenditures, increased public spending, and more comprehensive social welfare programs. However, licensure and job classification issues (Karger, 1983; Tambor, 1983) have uncovered conflicting organizational interests. In supporting licensure, NASW contends that social work education is necessary to provide competent services and advocates that all social workers, regardless of the setting, should be licensed; in contrast, AFSCME contends that social workers and caseworkers in public agencies should be excluded from any licensure requirements. For AFSCME, restrictive education qualifications would narrow promotional opportunities, limit access to social work jobs, fail to properly credit work experience, and discount the differing demands of public service (Karger, 1988). NASW and AFSCME have maintained an open and continuing dialogue on this subject.

Future of Social Work Unionization

Social work unionization should continue to grow or, at worst, maintain current representation levels. History suggests that social work unions will continue to pursue the goals of improving wages, hours, and working conditions; enhancing services to clients; and supporting the interests of working people, including women and people of color. Although for many social workers union representation is an important aspect of their workplace and professional life, this experience has yet to be fully integrated into the core of the social work profession.

The Bertha Capen Reynolds Society, an organization of progressive social work practitioners and academicians, has begun to incorporate social work unionization into its chapter activities and national conferences. NASW and schools of social work can play a similar role in acknowledging the significance of the union experience.

REFERENCES

AFSCME members' concern leads to overhaul of D.C. child welfare system. (1991, May 13). *AFSCME Leader, 6*(19), 2.

Alexander, L. B. (1980). Professionalization and unionization: Compatible after all? *Social Work, 25,* 476–482.

Alexander, L. B. (1987). Unions: Social work. In A. Minahan (Ed.-in-Chief), *Encyclopedia of social work* (18th ed., Vol. 2, pp. 793–800). Silver Spring, MD: National Association of Social Workers.

Alexander, L. B., Lichtenberg, P., & Brunn, D. (1980). Social workers in unions: A survey. *Social Work, 25,* 476–482.

Alexander, L. B., & Speizman, M. D. (1980). The union movement in voluntary social work. In *The social welfare forum* (pp. 179–187). New York: Columbia University Press.

All stressed out and no place to go. (1988, August). *AFSCME Leader,* p. 3.

American Federation of Labor–Congress of Industrial Organizations Department for Professional Employees. (1992, July). *Current statistics on white collar employees.* Washington, DC: Author.

American Federation of State, County, and Municipal Employees. (1986). *Private profit, public risk: The contracting out of professional services.* Washington, DC: Author.

American Federation of State, County, and Municipal Employees. (1992). *The fiscal crisis in state and local governments: Causes and solutions.* Washington, DC: Author.

American Hospital Association v. National Labor Relations Board, 111 U.S. 1539 (1991).

Arches, J. (1985). Don't burn, organize: A structural analysis of burnout in the human services. *Catalyst, 5*(17–18), 15–21.

Aronson, R. L. (1985). Unionism among professional employees in the private sector. *Industrial and Labor Relations Review, 38*(3), 352–364.

Bohr, R. H., Brenner, R.H.I., & Kaplan, H. H. (1971). Value conflicts in a hospital walkout. *Social Work, 16,* 33–42.

Bronfenbrenner, K., DellaMattera, N., & Juravich, T. (1993). *Professional workers and unions: A reference manual.* Washington, DC: AFL-CIO Department for Professional Employees.

Burton, J. F., Jr., & Thomason, T. (1988). The extent of collective bargaining in the public sector. In B. Aaron, J. Najita, & J. Stern (Eds.), *Public sector bargaining* (pp. 1–52). Washington, DC: Bureau of National Affairs.

Calmain, K. E. (1975). The Big Brothers' strike and unions: A personal view. *Ontario Association of Professional Social Workers, 3*(1), 29–31.

The child abuse crisis. (1988, April 11). *AFSCME Leader,* p. 3.

County of Los Angeles, Los Angeles County Department of Public Social Services et al. v. Los Angeles County Employees Association, SEIU Local 660 et al., 33 Cal. App. 3rd 1 (1973).

DiBicarri, E. (1985). Organizing in the Massachusetts purchase of service system. *Catalyst, 5*(17–18), 45–50.

Farber, H., & Krueger, A. (1993). Union membership in the United States: The decline continues. In B. Kaufman & M. Kleiner (Eds.), *Employee representation: Alternatives and future directions* (pp. 105–134). Madison, WI: Industrial Relations Research Association.

Fisher, D. (1987). Problems for social work in a strike situation: Professional, ethical, and value considerations. *Social Work, 32,* 252–254.

Fisher, J. (1980). *The response of social work to the depression.* Cambridge, MA: Schenkman.

Flynn, J. (1980). Collective bargaining in professional social work education. *Journal of Education in Social Work, 16*(3), 101–109.

Freeman, R. B. (1986). Unionism comes to the public sector. *Journal of Economic Literature, 24,* 40–53.

Freeman, R. B., & Medoff, J. L. (1984). *What do unions do?* New York: Basic Books.

Galper, J. (1980). *Social work practice: A radical perspective.* Englewood Cliffs, NJ: Prentice Hall.

Gifford, C. D. (1990). *Directory of U.S. labor organizations.* Washington, DC: Bureau of National Affairs.

Goldberg, J. R. (1960). The professional and his union in the Jewish center. *Journal of Jewish Communal Service, 36*(3), 284–289.

Goldfield, M. (1987). *The decline of organized labor in the United States.* Chicago: University of Chicago Press.

Haynes, J. E. (1975). The rank and file movement in private social work. *Labor History, 16,* 78–98.

Hiratsuka, J. (1992, May). Social work puts it on the picket line. *NASW News,* p. 3.

Hush, H. (1969). Collective bargaining in voluntary agencies. *Social Casework, 50*(4), 210–213.

Karger, H. (1983). Reclassification: Is there a future in public welfare for the trained social worker. *Social Work, 28,* 427–433.

Karger, H. (1988). *Social workers and labor unions.* Westport, CT: Greenwood Press.

Klauss, I. (1969). The evolution of a collective bargaining relationship in public education: New York City's changing seven year history. *Michigan Law Review, 67,* 1033–1066.

Kleingartner, R. A., & Bickner, M. L. (1977). Scope of bargaining and participation in decision making by professionals. In F. Hinman (Ed.), *Professional workers and collective bargaining* (pp. 24–48). Los Angeles: University of California Institute of Industrial Relations.

Leighninger, L., & Knickmeyer, R. (1976). The rank and file movement: The relevance of radical social work tradition to modern social work practice. *Journal of Sociology and Social Welfare, 4*(2), 166–177.

Levine, G. (1975). Collective bargaining for social workers in voluntary agencies. *Ontario Association of Professional Social Workers, 3*(1), 5–8.

Levy, C. (1964). Labor–management relations in the Jewish community center. *Journal of Jewish Communal Service, 41*(1), 114–124.

Lightman, E. S. (1982). Professionalization, bureaucratization, and unionization in social work. *Social Service Review, 56*(1), 130–143.

Lightman, E. S. (1983). Social workers, strikes, and service to clients. *Social Work, 28,* 142–147.

Maier, M. (1987). *City unions.* New Brunswick, NJ: Rutgers University Press.

Martin, G. T., Jr. (1985). Union social service and women's work. *Social Service Review, 59,* 62–73.

McCormick, A. M., & Mirkle, B. (1982). Organizing workers in the contracted human services. *Catalyst, 4*(2), 59–71.

Mendes, R. (1974). *The professional union: A study of the social service employees union of the New York City Department of Social Services.* Unpublished doctoral dissertation, Columbia University, New York.

National Association of Social Workers. (1990). *NASW standards for social work personnel policies.* Washington, DC: Author.

National Association of Social Workers. (1994). *NASW code of ethics.* Washington, DC: Author.

Partnership for Quality Care & Schoen, C. (1991). Making quality the bottom line. Amherst: University of Massachusetts Press.

Patry, B. (1978). Taylorism comes to the social services. *Monthly Review, 30,* 30–37.

Pennell, J. (1987). Union participation of Canadian and American social workers: Contrasts and forecasts. *Social Service Review, 61,* 117–131.

Perry, C. (1979). Teacher bargaining: The experience in nine systems. *Industrial and Labor Relations Review, 33,* 431–453.

Privatization: The Michigan experience. (1992, December). UAW Local 6000.

Rehr, H. (1960). Problems for a profession in a strike situation. *Social Work, 5,* 22–28.

Resolutions. (1980, January). *NASW News,* p. 29.

Reynolds, B. (1991). An *uncharted journey.* Washington, DC: NASW Press. (Original work published 1964)

Ryan, T., & Brown, J. (1970). When an agency is struck. *Catholic Charities Review, 54,* 3–10.

Schneider, B.VH. (1988). Public sector labor legislation—An evolutionary analysis. In B. Aaron, J. Najita, & J. Stern (Eds.), *Public sector bargaining* (pp. 189–229). Washington, DC: Bureau of National Affairs.

Schutt, R. (1986). *Organization in a changing environment.* Albany: State University of New York.

Senate Bill 1514 is crucial legislation. (1993, April/May). *Local 509 News, SEIU,* p. 7.

Shaffer, G. (1979). Labor relations and the unionization of professional social workers. *Journal of Education for Social Work, 15,* 80–86.

Shaffer, G., & Ahearn, K. (1981). *Unionization of professional social workers: Staff development and practice implications.* Paper presented at the 7th National Association of Social Workers Professional Symposium.

Shaffer, G., & Ahearn, K. (1983). Preparation of social workers for unionization and collective bargaining practice. *Arete, 8,* 53–56.

Shostak, A. (1991). *Robust unionism.* Ithaca, NY: ILR Press.

Shulman, L. C. (1978). Unionization and the professional employee: The social service director's view. In S. Slavin (Ed.), *Social administration: The management of the social services* (pp. 460–468). New York: Haworth Press.

Tambor, M. (1973). Unions and voluntary agencies. *Social Work, 18,* 41–47.

Tambor, M. (1979). The social worker as worker: A union perspective. *Administration in Social Work, 3*(3), 289–300.

Tambor, M. (1981). Independent unionism and the politics of self-defeat. *Catalyst, 3*(3), 23–32.

Tambor, M. (1983). Declassification and divisiveness in human services. *Administration in Social Work, 7*(2), 61–68.

Tambor, M. (1991). *The scope of bargaining in labor agreements within nonprofit agencies.* Unpublished doctoral dissertation, Wayne State University, Detroit.

Tompkins, D. (1967). *Strikes by public employees and professional personnel: A bibliography.* Berkeley: University of California Institute of Governmental Studies.

Too many cases, too little service brings social work action in Pennsylvania, Rhode Island. (1980, November). *Service Employee, SEIU,* p. 3.

Transue, J. (1980). Collective bargaining on whose terms? *Catalyst, 2*(1), 25-37.

Tudiver, N. (1982). Business ideology and management in social work: The limits of cost control. *Catalyst, 4*(1), 25–48.

Wagner, D. (1990). *The quest for a radical profession.* Lanham, MD: University Press of America.

Warner, K., Chisholm, R. F., & Munzenrider, R. F. (1978). Motives for unionization among state social service employees. *Public Personnel Management, 7*(3), 181–191.

Weber, A. R. (1969). Paradise lost: Or whatever happened to the Chicago social workers. *Industrial and Labor Relations Review, 22*(3), 323–338.

Why *Catalyst?* (1978). *Catalyst, 1*(1), 2.

Withorn, A. (1985). Building democracy and working with the community: An interview with progressive trade union leaders. *Catalyst, 5*(17–18), 67–78.

FURTHER READING

Burke, D. R. (1970). *The impact of unions on social welfare agency management.* Unpublished doctoral dissertation, University of Pennsylvania, Philadelphia.

Chitnis, N., & Tigelaar, G. (1971). Impact of a strike on graduate students. *Social Work, 16,* 119–127.

Derber, C. (Ed.). (1982). *Professionals as workers: Mental labor in advanced capitalism.* Boston: G. K. Hall.

Grossman, J. (1985). Can a human service union affect clinical issues? *Catalyst, 5*(17–18), 109–114.

Karger, H. (1989). Social service administration and the challenge of unionization. *Administration in Social Work, 13,* 199–217.

Kirzner, M. L. (1985). *Public welfare unions and public assistance policy: A case study of the Pennsylvania Social Service Employees Union.* Unpublished manuscript, University of Pennsylvania, Philadelphia.

Kleingartner, A. (1973). Collective bargaining between salaried professionals and public sector management. *Public Administration Review, 33*(2), 165–172.

Lightman, E. S. (1978). An imbalance of powers: Social workers in unions. *Administration in Social Work, 2*(1), 75–84.

Nash, A. (1979). Local 1707, CSAE: Facets of a union in the nonprofit field. *Labor History, 20*(2), 256–277.

Oppenheimer, M. (1975). The unionization of the professional. *Social Policy, 5*(1), 34–40.

Pennell, J. (1990). Consensual bargaining: Labor negotiations in battered women's programs. *Journal of Progressive Human Services, 1*(1), 59–74.

Ratner, L. (1985). Understanding and moving beyond social workers' resistance to unionization. *Catalyst, 5*(17–18), 79–87.

Wagner, D., & Cohen, M. (1978). Social workers, class, and professionalism. *Catalyst, 1*(1), 25–33.

Milton Tambor, PhD, ACSW, is Michigan AFSCME Council 25 staff representative and associate member of graduate faculty, Wayne State University, 23855 Northwestern Highway, Southfield, MI 48075.

For further information see

Advocacy; Citizen Participation; Community Organization; Conflict Resolution; Ethics and Values; Health Services Systems Policy; Hospital Social Work; Jobs and Earnings; Licensing, Regulation, and Certification; Management Overview; National Association of Social Workers; Nonprofit Management Issues; Occupational Social Work; Professional Conduct; Public Social Services; Quality Assurance; Social Welfare History; Social Welfare Policy; Social Work Profession Overview; Social Workers in Politics; Vendorship.

Key Words

| collective bargaining | organizing |
| labor representation | unions |

V

Vasey, Wayne

See Biographies section, Volume 3

Vendorship
Leila Whiting

For the social work profession, vendorship, or consumer choice, legislation stipulates that the beneficiary has the freedom to choose any qualified mental health provider if his or her health insurance provides mental health coverage. Vendorship for social workers refers to the status of a group, in this case clinical social workers, in terms of eligibility for insurance and other third-party reimbursement as a qualified provider of mental health services. This legislation, usually an amendment to a state's insurance laws, refers to qualified providers as duly certified or licensed mental health practitioners in that state. As social workers have struggled for parity with other longer-established mental health professionals, they have advocated and worked for these vendorship laws that mandate their recognition as qualified mental health providers. Because legal regulation of social workers is almost always a prerequisite to a state consumer choice or vendorship law, there has been a strong movement in every state to have social workers legally regulated (NASW, 1993c).

The impetus for social workers to pass consumer choice legislation occurred before the 1960s, when most health insurers failed to recognize social workers as qualified providers of mental health services and excluded social workers from reimbursement. Some plans included reimbursement for social workers if they were supervised by a physician, a psychiatrist, or sometimes a psychologist.

SOCIAL WORKERS AS MENTAL HEALTH PROVIDERS

Since the 1960s, clinical social workers have become major providers of mental health services in the United States, and an increasing number are in solo or group private practice. Clients with health insurance that included mental health coverage became increasingly distressed when their insurance carriers would not reimburse for clinical social work services even though such reimbursement was available if the clients saw a psychiatrist for the same problems. Social workers were equally upset and indignant at what they believed was discrimination aimed at the nonmedical mental health provider. There was a groundswell among clinical social workers to achieve parity and professional recognition of their services.

Federal Legislation

At the national level, the profession has been successful in ensuring that clinical social workers are recognized as qualified mental health providers in all federal legislation that provides for mental health services. Since the early 1960s, the Civilian Health and Medical Program of the Uniformed Services, which provides medical care for military retirees, dependents of military personnel and retirees, and some other uniformed services, has reimbursed clinical social workers, although medical supervision was required. In 1983 Congress directed the U.S. Department of Defense to recognize clinical social workers as independent mental health treatment providers and regulations to that effect were published (*Federal Register,* 1984).

Furthermore, approximately 9 million federal employees currently are covered by the Federal Employees Health Benefits Act of 1959 (FEHBA) (Congressional Research Service, 1989). Before 1986, many of the plans covering federal employees voluntarily recognized social workers as reimbursable, but many also required physician supervision or referral. FEHBA was amended in 1986 to require that all plans include mental health coverage and to further provide that insurance carriers may not require that social workers be supervised by any other health professional (Federal Employees Health Benefits Improvement Act, P.L. 99-251). By 1986 all federal programs that covered mental health treatment recognized clinical social workers as independent and reimbursable providers, although reimbursement under Medicaid and Medicare, Part B Outpatient Mental Health, was limited.

State Legislation

However, states were responsible for enacting laws regulating health insurance for nonfederal programs; by 1986, only 13 states had passed vendorship laws although 36 states had some form of legal regulation of social workers (NASW, 1993b). The social work profession then engaged in vigorous legislative activity spearheaded by the NASW chapters; by 1993 some type of legal regulation had been passed in all states as well as in the District of Columbia, the Virgin Islands, and Puerto Rico. In January 1993, Hawaii repealed its weak regulation act, but Hawaii enacted a licensing law in 1994; therefore, all 50 states and the three jurisdictions have legal regulation of social work as of 1994. In addition, 30 states plus the District of Columbia had achieved mandated reimbursement for mental health treatment provided by clinical social workers (Table 1).

THE FIGHT FOR VENDORSHIP LAWS

Options

There are several ways in which clinical social workers can become recognized providers of mental health services at the local and state levels:

- consumer demand (unions negotiating for their inclusion in an employer–union contract)
- contract purchaser demand (an employer insisting that the health insurance contract include social workers as reimbursable)
- voluntary recognition by the insurance carrier
- state mandate (consumer choice laws).

It is a bread-and-butter issue for social workers to have their clients reimbursed for their services, so working for vendorship laws has great appeal for practitioners. Therefore, passage of vendorship laws is a high priority for the state NASW chapters.

Opposition to Vendorship for Social Work

However, passage of state vendorship laws has rarely been achieved without stiff opposition. In some cases, opponents to state vendorship laws perhaps have been motivated by the economics of shifting power; that is, the rewards of the mental health "business," once reaped almost solely by psychiatrists under the medical model, were now to be shared not only with psychologists but also with social workers (Fairbank, 1989). NASW chapters found that psychiatrists, psychologists, and physician-dominated insurance companies mounted organized and powerful lobbying against their social work vendorship bill, largely based on market share concerns.

The opposition also has argued that the state and the insurance industry cannot afford another "mandated benefit." This is a specious argument because a vendorship bill does not create a mandated benefit but expands the group of providers within an existing benefit. The opposition also has suggested that if the class of providers were expanded, the insurance carrier would suffer irreparable economic hardship. Research examining this issue has indicated no change in the mental health dollars expended by the insurance carriers, but a change or substitution in who received these dollars (Fairbank, 1989; Lieberman, Shatkin, & McGuire, 1988; McGuire, Gurin, Frisman, Kane, & Shatkin, 1984).

Rationale for Vendorship

NASW chapters have limited budgets and the opposition to their bills is well funded; therefore, the path to successful passage of vendorship and consumer choice legislation has been long and

TABLE 1

State Comparison of Vendorship Provisions

Jursidiction	Date Enacted	License Required	Additional Requirements	Coverage	Covered If Insurance Written in Another State	Referral
Alaska	1992	Licensed certified social worker	None	Standard	Not specific	Not required
California	1977	Licensed clinical social worker	None	Standard	Yes	By licensed physician or surgeon
Colorado	1991	Licensed clinical social worker	Additional three years of clinical experience	Standard	Yes	Not required
Connecticut	1990	Certified independent social worker	Clinical exam plus agency practice	Standard	If 51 percent of employees work in Connecticut	Not required
District of Columbia	1987	Licensed clinical social worker	None	Standard	Not specific	Not required
Florida	1983	Licensed clinical social worker	None	Coverage for licensed clinical social worker must be offered to policyholders	Not specifically but may be	Not required
Idaho	—[a]	Certified social worker–independent practice	None	Standard	Not applicable	Not required
Illinois	1990	Licensed clinical social worker	None	Standard	Not specific	Not required
Kansas	1982	Specialist clinical social worker	None	Policyholder may refuse specialist clinical social worker coverage in writing	No	Not required
Kentucky	1994	Licensed clinical social worker	None	Standard	Not specific	Not required
Louisiana	1981	Board certified social worker	Must be listed in a national clinical social work registry	Standard	Yes	Referral not required but physician consultation and collaboration required
Maine	1984	Certified social worker, clinical social worker	None	Standard	No	Not required unless a condition is diagnosed beyond the scope of clinical social worker licensure
Maryland	1978, 1992	Licensed certified social worker–clinical	None	Standard	Yes	Not required
Massachusetts	1982	Licensed independent clinical social worker	None	Standard	Yes	Not required
Minnesota	1993	Independent clinical social worker	None	Standard	Yes	Not required
Mississippi	1992	Licensed clinical social worker	None	Standard	Not specific	Not required

(continued)

TABLE 1
State Comparison of Vendorship Provisions (continued)

Jursidiction	Date Enacted	License Required	Additional Requirements	Coverage	Covered If Insurance Written in Another State	Referral
Montana	1985	Licensed social worker	None	Standard	Not specific	Not required
Nevada	1988	Licensed social worker	None	Standard	Not specific	Not required
New Hampshire	1984	Certified clinical social worker	None	Coverage must be offered for a separate and identifiable premium	Yes	Not required
New Mexico	1989	Independent social worker	None	Standard	No	Not required
New York	1985	Certified social worker	Must have "R" endorsement[b]	Standard	Yes	Not required
North Carolina	1993	Certified clinical social worker	None	Standard	Not specific	Not required
North Dakota	1989	Licensed certified social worker	Diplomate level required	Standard	Not specific	Not required
Oregon	1981	Licensed clinical social worker	None	Standard	No	Physician or psychologist
South Dakota	1988	Clinical social worker–private independent practice	None	Standard	No	Not required
Tennessee	1985	Licensed clinical social worker	None	Standard	Not specific	Not required
Texas	1987	Clinical social worker–advanced clinical practitioner	None	Standard	No	May require physician's referral unless policy does not
Utah	1986	Clinical social worker	None	Standard	No	Not required
Vermont	1989	Certified social worker	None	Standard	Not specific	Not required
Virginia	1987	Licensed clinical social worker	None	Standard	No	Not required
Wisconsin	1975	No license	Academy of certified social workers	Social workers in certified outpatient mental health clinics only	Not specific	Not required
Wyoming	1989	Licensed professional social worker	None	Standard	Not specific	Not required

NOTE: Under "Coverage," all standard policies with mental health coverage must reimburse for services provided by licensed or certified social workers.
[a]Blue Shield and Blue Cross of Idaho have contracted to reimburse social workers for mental health services.
[b]A New York State endorsement that requires a number of supervised clinical practice hours.

arduous. Successful chapters have made substantial dollar investments in professional lobbyists and grassroots networks and lobbying and have developed sophisticated campaign material to counter the opposition. Furthermore, chapters have presented arguments demonstrating why social workers should be covered:

• Social workers are cost-effective providers of mental health services.
• Social workers are often the only mental health professionals in rural and poor counties.
• The users of mental health services, like the social workers, are predominantly women and are ethnically diverse.

- The opposition to the bill is based on self-interest rather than public interest (Gibelman & Schervish, 1993; Manderscheid & Sonnenschein, 1992; NASW, 1993a).

The laws enacted to include social workers as qualified and reimbursable providers of mental health services for the most part are revisions to the state insurance code requiring that, when mental health is a covered benefit, the beneficiaries be reimbursed for mental health services delivered by a licensed or certified social worker.

CONCLUSION

Membership in a profession requires that a practitioner acquire a body of transferable knowledge and demonstrate skill in applying that knowledge. Clinical social workers have demonstrated their knowledge and skill, as witnessed by the legal regulation of social work in all 50 states. Although social workers provide the majority of outpatient mental health care in the United States, there is uneven recognition of the profession by the payer community. Social workers will undoubtedly continue to lobby successfully to change this uneven recognition and to ensure that third parties will reimburse social workers for their services. As the United States seeks major health care reform, social workers can play a vital role in delivering client-sensitive, cost-effective services.

REFERENCES

Congressional Research Service. (1989). *The federal employees' health benefits program: Possible strategies for reform* (Report prepared for the Committee on Post Office and Civil Service, U.S. House of Representatives). Washington, DC: U.S. Government Printing Office.

Fairbank, A. (1989, January 26). Expanding coverage to alternative types of psychotherapists: Demand and substitution effects of direct reimbursement to social workers. *Inquiry,* pp. 170–181.

Federal Employees Health Benefits Act of 1959. P.L. 86-382, 73 Stat. 708.

Federal Employees Health Benefits Improvement Act of 1986. P.L. 99-251, Section 105(b).

Federal Register. (1984, March 1), p. 7562, section 199.12.

Gibelman, M., & Schervish, P. H. (1993). *Who we are: The social work labor force as reflected in the NASW membership.* Washington, DC: NASW Press.

Lieberman, A. A., Shatkin, B. F., & McGuire, T. G. (1988). Assessing the effect of vendorship: A one-state case study. *Journal of Independent Social Work, 2*(4), 59–74.

Manderscheid, R. W., & Sonnenschein, M. A. (Eds.). (1992). *Mental health, United States, 1992* (DHHS Publication No. SMA 92-1942). Washington, DC: U.S. Government Printing Office.

McGuire, T., Gurin, A., Frisman, L. K., Kane, V. L., & Shatkin, B. F. (1984). Vendorship and social work in Massachusetts. *Social Service Review, 58,* 373–383.

National Association of Social Workers. (1993a). [Geographic distribution of mental health providers]. Unpublished raw data.

National Association of Social Workers. (1993b). *State comparison of laws regulating social work.* Washington, DC: Author.

National Association of Social Workers. (1993c). *Third-party reimbursement for clinical social work services.* Washington, DC: Author.

Leila Whiting, MSW, ACSW, LCSW, is a social work consultant, 401 Hinsdale Court, Silver Spring, MD 20901.

For further information see

Clinical Social Work; Council on Social Work Education; Direct Practice Overview; Ethics and Values; Licensing, Regulation, and Certification; Managed Care; Mental Health Overview; National Association of Social Workers; Private Practice; Professional Conduct; Professional Liability and Malpractice; Purchasing Social Services; Social Work Education; Social Work Practice: History and Evolution; Social Work Profession Overview.

Key Words

clinical social work	regulation
credentialing	vendorship
licensing	

Veterans and Veterans Services

Rosina M. Becerra
JoAnn Damron-Rodriguez

The United States has the most comprehensive system of services for veterans in the world (Yoshikawa, 1992). Contemporary veterans' services are grounded in a long history of national support to people who have served in the armed services.

ASSISTANCE TO VETERANS: AN AMERICAN TRADITION

Federal Government Services

As early as 1636, the Pilgrims of Plymouth Colony proclaimed in legislation that "if any man shall be sent forth as a solider and shall return maimed, he shall be maintained competently by the colony during his life" (Veterans Administration, 1984, p. v). Pensions to veterans were established by the Continental Congress in 1776 to encourage enlistments in the Revolutionary War. President Abraham Lincoln, in his second inaugural address, called on Americans "to care for him who shall have borne the battle and for his widow, and his orphan" (Veterans Administration, p. v). This phrase remains the motto for the federal agency that is responsible for veterans' services, the Department of Veterans Affairs.

Medical facilities and domiciles for veterans were first established in 1811. These facilities were expanded following the Civil War, Indian wars, Spanish–American War, and other conflicts. Medical care for veterans was federally legislated in 1878 when Congress passed an act for the relief of sick and disabled seamen. This legislation established the first U.S. Merchant Marine hospitals, which later became part of the U.S. Public Health Service (Becerra & Greenblatt, 1983).

During World War I, benefits for veterans changed with the introduction of the War Risk Insurance Act. The new provisions included compensation for war-related injuries, allotments for the support of dependents, life insurance, and vocational rehabilitation for veterans with disabilities incurred or aggravated during active military duty. Initially, the various benefits were administered by three different federal agencies: the Veterans Bureau, the Bureau of Pensions of the Interior Department, and the National Home for Disabled Volunteer Soldiers (Department of Veterans Affairs, 1993a).

In 1930 President Herbert Hoover established the Veterans Administration by consolidating the three agencies as bureaus within it. The Veterans Administration had the responsibility for coordinating all activities of the federal government related to veterans' services.

By World War II legislation was enacted to expand the Veterans Administration. These laws included the Vocational Rehabilitation Act Amendments of 1943 and the Servicemen's Readjustment Act of 1944 ("GI Bill"). The GI Bill provided education and training; allowances for unemployment; and insured loans for homes, farms, and businesses. By 1953 more than half of the nation's World War II veterans had received educational benefits (Rothman & Becerra, 1987).

In 1973, the Veterans Administration assumed the responsibility for the National Cemetery System. In 1989, the Veterans Administration was renamed the Department of Veterans Affairs and was established as a Cabinet-level position (Department of Veterans Affairs, 1993c), an action that gave the department greater stature.

Other federal agencies also offer benefits and preferences to veterans. The Department of Labor provides employment compensation and preferential job-finding assistance, the Department of Agriculture grants special farm loans, the Department of Justice gives preferential consideration for naturalization, and the Social Security Administration allows social security wage credits for military service.

Other Services
Since 1917 the American Red Cross has provided support services for people in the armed services and their families. States have also developed programs for veterans, such as special provisions for relief and preferential employment opportunities. In addition, the Federal–State Employment Service operates the Veterans Employment Service, which provides special job-placement opportunities (Rothman & Becerra, 1987). State programs, such as the Cal-Vet loan program of the California Department of Veterans Affairs, grant home and farm loans to veterans and their dependents. Some states also maintain residential care facilities for veterans.

Voluntary Organizations Representing Veterans
Over 25 voluntary veterans' organizations form a powerful advocacy network for shaping the type and range of services provided to veterans. Certain veterans' organizations, such as the Paralyzed Veterans of America and the Blinded Veterans Association, inspect and monitor Veterans Health Administration facilities and services and make recommendations for change.

In addition to lobbying for legislation affecting veterans, these organizations are formally authorized by the director of the Department of Veterans Affairs to represent veterans in the presentation and prosecution of claims under the regulations of the department (Eberhardt & McGovern, 1975). Veterans' organizations also provide valuable volunteer services at Veterans Health Administration hospitals and in other service programs.

Among the long-established veterans' organizations are the American Legion, AMVETS, Catholic War Veterans, Disabled American Veterans, Jewish War Veterans, Military Order of the Purple Heart, and Veterans of Foreign Wars. More recently established veterans' organizations, such as Vietnam Veterans of America, Vietnam Veterans Leadership Project, Vietnam Combat Veterans, the GI Forum, and the Black Veterans Organization, incorporate an identification with specific periods of military conflict, as well as with minority status.

VETERAN POPULATION

Since the nation's struggle for independence two centuries ago, more than 41 million men and women have been in military service during wartime (Department of Veterans Affairs, 1993c). The United States has been involved in 11 major armed conflicts. Most veterans (90 percent) served in one or more of the four major military conflicts during the 20th century—World War I, World War II, the Korean War, and the Vietnam War. More than 1 million Americans have died in military service. In 1992 an estimated 26.8 million veterans were living in the United States (Department of Veterans Affairs, 1993b).

World War II veterans constitute the largest period-of-service category (32 percent), followed by veterans of the Vietnam War (31 percent), Korean War (18 percent), and Persian Gulf War (2 percent). The remaining living World War I veterans number 32,000 (1 percent), and approximately 6.1 million veterans (23 percent) served only during peacetime (Department of Veterans Affairs, 1993c).

Approximately 30 percent of all civilian men over age 18 are veterans, whereas 75 percent of the total male population over age 65 are veterans (U.S. Bureau of the Census, 1989). The average age of all living veterans is 56 years. The veteran population is aging dramatically. In 1990 one in four veterans was at least 65 years old; by 2015, nearly one-half of all veterans will be age 65 (Department of Veterans Affairs, 1993d).

African Americans make up about 7.6 percent of the total population of veterans but about 12.5 percent of the civilian population (Department of Veterans Affairs, 1993c). In comparison with other veterans on several social–economic indicators, African American veterans are more in need of veterans' services. According to Dienstfrey and Byrne (1984), African American veterans had attained less education, were less likely to be in the labor force, and had the lowest income of all veteran groups.

In 1993 there were nearly 1.2 million female veterans constituting about 4.4 percent of the total veteran population (Department of Veterans Affairs, 1994). The number of women in the armed services has been increasing since 1967 legislation limiting the number of women in the armed forces was repealed (Rothman, 1984).

Of male veterans age 20 or older, approximately 62 percent were in the labor force in 1992, in contrast to 82 percent of the nonveteran male population of the same age group; this situation reflects the larger proportion of older veterans.

Female veterans do not vary significantly from their nonveteran counterparts with respect to employment. Furthermore, there is no difference between veterans and nonveterans in median years of school completed (12.9). Male veterans in general had higher incomes than did nonveterans, with a median annual income of $24,700 in 1992 compared with $21,000 for nonveterans. The difference between the incomes of veterans and nonveterans is more pronounced with advancing age; in 1992 the median income of veterans over age 65 ($16,700) was 44 percent greater than that of nonveterans ($11,600) of that age group (Department of Veterans Affairs, 1993b).

BENEFITS AND SERVICES FOR VETERANS

Benefits and services are administered by three units of the Department of Veterans Affairs: the Veterans Health Administration (VHA), the Department of Veterans Benefits (DVB), and the Department of Memorial Affairs (DMA). The VHA provides a comprehensive range of health and mental health care services; the DVB provides pension and compensation benefits to veterans and their families, including educational benefits, housing assistance, vocational rehabilitation, and counseling; and the DMA administers burial benefits.

Veterans Health Administration

The VHA is responsible for the health care of the nation's veterans (Worthen, 1984). It provides acute medical, surgical, and psychiatric inpatient and outpatient care; intermediate hospital, nursing home, and domiciliary care; noninstitutional extended care; and a range of special programs and professional services in outpatient settings (Department of Veterans Affairs, 1994).

All VHA facilities are accredited by the Joint Commission on Accreditation of Healthcare Organizations (JCAHO). In 1991 VHA facilities nationwide earned an average score of 90 on a scale of 100, compared to a national average of 80 for non-VHA facilities (Department of Veterans Affairs, 1993b). To increase compliance with JCAHO standards even further, a national training and quality assurance program is in place.

Medical services. Within the VHA system, there are 171 medical centers and 340 outpatient clinics (Yoshikawa, 1992). Each year more than 2.5 million veterans per year receive medical care in the VHA system; since 1987, the VHA has treated 6 million people (Paralyzed Veterans of America, 1993).

The VHA provides state-of-the-art, high-technology health care. The Preventive Medicine Program, begun in 1985, focuses on 11 risk factors for diseases for which veterans have high mortality and morbidity rates—such as hypertension, high cholesterol, breast cancer, and colorectal cancer—and provides screening (Department of Veterans Affairs, 1993b). In addition, 33 VHA medical centers have sickle cell screening and education programs (Department of Veterans Affairs, 1993a).

The Rehabilitation Medicine Service employs more than 4,000 physicians, rehabilitation professionals, and allied health technicians to help increase the functional capacity of veterans (Department of Veterans Affairs, 1993b). The Prosthetics and Sensory Aids Services provide extensive assistance to disabled veterans in the design and procurement of assistive devices.

Mental health services. The VHA operates one of the most comprehensive mental health services in the nation, including long-term and residential care for chronically mentally ill veterans. Its many special treatment programs include chemical dependency units, dual-diagnosis programs for cocaine-abusing schizophrenics, and posttraumatic stress disorder (PTSD) programs.

Initially for Vietnam-era veterans, outreach and counseling centers (VET centers) have extended their counseling services to veterans of the Persian Gulf War. Technically known as the Readjustment Counseling Service, this program was established under the Veterans Health Care Amendments of 1979 (Rothman & Becerra, 1987). The centers are usually small, community-based "storefront facilities" that specialize in deprogramming veterans from their war experiences and hold informal "rap groups" for participants. Outpatient treatment teams and evaluation–brief treatment units (inpatient units) provide short-term acute care for veterans with PTSD.

Psychiatric programs, in addition to acute treatment, provide vocational and supportive residential programs to promote veterans' independence. These programs include day treatment centers, day hospitals, and Compensated Work Therapy, as well as a coordinated program of residential facilities in the community.

Long-term care. The VHA provides a broad range of long-term-care services. The Office for Extended Care was established in 1975, in recognition of the need for such care by the rapidly aging veteran population. Under the Veterans Administration Health Care Amendments of 1980, geriatrics was included with extended care. Long-term care within the VHA began with institutional services (Old Soldiers' Homes) but has broadened to include a spectrum of institutional and residential care services, as well as community-based ser-

vices. The goal is to facilitate the access and flow of patients among various long-term-care alternatives for aged and disabled veterans (Damron-Rodriguez & Cantell, in press). Institutional long-term care consists of VHA nursing home units, community nursing homes, state nursing homes, and domiciliary programs. Hospital-based home care, adult day health care, community residential care, and respite care constitute noninstitutional long-term care (Department of Veterans Affairs, 1993b). Components of the long-term-care services within the VHA continuum that are not widely available in an integrated fashion in the broader health care system include the following:

Nursing home care to eligible veterans is provided at on-site units at VHA medical centers or through a network of community nursing homes that have contracted with the centers.

Domiciliary programs provide residential rehabilitation and health-maintenance services to veterans who are unable to live independently because of medical or psychiatric disabilities. The state domiciliary program serves a similar population of veterans. In 1992 the 42 state domiciles in 32 states served over 6,000 patients (Department of Veterans Affairs, 1993b).

Hospital-based home care programs provide care to homebound patients through 75 VHA medical centers. They serve 11,000 patients and make nearly 300,000 visits annually (Department of Veterans Affairs, 1993b).

Adult day health care programs provide medical, nursing, rehabilitative, and social services at 15 VHA medical centers.

Geriatric Research Education and Clinical Centers—"Centers of Excellence" for geriatrics and long-term care—develop new and innovative ways of improving health care to elderly veterans through the support of geriatric research, training, and education. In 1994, 16 such programs were operating in the nation (Department of Veterans Affairs, 1994).

Geriatric Evaluation and Management programs, both inpatient and outpatient units, provide comprehensive, multidisciplinary, health care assessments of elderly veterans. In 1992, 133 VHA medical facilities had established such programs (Department of Veterans Affairs, 1993c).

Alzheimer's disease dementia units are specialized units that function as both inpatient and outpatient evaluation and treatment programs at 56 VHA medical centers (Department of Veterans Affairs, 1993b).

Hospice units provide palliative care for terminally ill veterans and services for their families. All VHA medical centers ensure that hospice care is available to eligible veterans (Department of Veterans Affairs, 1993b).

Respite care is provided in an institutional setting for a total of 30 days per year to give caregivers of veterans periodic relief.

Department of Veterans Benefits

Compensation and pension benefits. The major responsibility of the DVB is the administration of the three types of nationally legislated benefits for eligible veterans: compensation benefits to disabled veterans and to veterans' survivors and pensions. Compensation benefits are awarded to veterans with service-connected disabilities that were incurred or aggravated during active duty; the amount of the benefit depends on the severity of the disability. In addition, dependents of a veteran who died on or after January 1, 1957, as a result of a service-connected condition are entitled to dependency and indemnity compensation. The surviving spouse and children of a veteran whose death was not service connected are eligible for death pension benefits, subject to certain income limitations. Veterans receive pension benefits if they are low income, disabled, or elderly. In 1992 entitlement appropriations for veterans' compensation and pension benefits totaled about $17 billion (Department of Veterans Affairs, 1993c).

Educational benefits. The major educational benefits include assistance to veterans and service personnel (commonly known as the GI Bill) and assistance to surviving dependents of veterans who died of service-connected causes or of veterans who were missing in action or prisoners of war for more than 90 days (Rothman & Becerra, 1987). In addition, educational assistance is given to post–Vietnam era veterans who entered active duty after December 31, 1976, and vocational rehabilitation is provided to veterans who require such services for a service-connected condition (Veterans Administration, 1984).

Housing assistance. Veterans can receive loans from private sources on terms more favorable than those generally available to nonveterans. In 1992 over 267,600 veterans were granted home-ownership loans, the second highest number in the history of the program (Department of Veterans Affairs, 1993b).

Other assistance programs. Other assistance programs inform eligible veterans of benefits to which they are entitled and help them obtain these benefits. Some special groups have been targeted for particular outreach efforts, notably elderly beneficiaries, prisoners of war, female veterans, and educationally disadvantaged veterans of the Vietnam era (Veterans Administration, 1984).

Department of Memorial Affairs

The DMA is responsible for administering programs for veterans' burial. Although DMA oversees 109 national cemeteries, in 1993 only 57 of the federal cemeteries were open (Department of Veterans Affairs, 1994). Every veteran's survivors receive a burial allowance, burial-plot allowance, and flag to drape over the veteran's casket.

SPECIAL PROGRAMS AND NEEDS

Older Veterans

The rate of growth of the population of aged veterans is exceeding the rate of growth of the older population for the nation as a whole. The older old, who require more health and social services, will have increased in number more than fourfold between 1980 and 2000 (Veterans Administration, 1984). In 1980 veterans age 85 and over constituted 7 percent of the older veterans; by the year 2020, their proportion will reach 18 percent (Department of Veterans Affairs, 1993c). Therefore, the need for long-term-care services will increase dramatically.

Older veterans are more likely to receive certain benefits, including social security and veterans' pensions, than are younger veterans and, in general, also are likely to be more financially secure (Boyle, 1983). A central concern of this population is health care. The majority of aging veterans report that because of the rising costs of medical care, in 10 years they will not be able to pay for a 30-day hospital stay or for nursing home care, despite their acknowledged economic and health coverage advantages (Bergman, Delaney, Gallagher, Atkins, & Graeber, 1987). The problem will be even more severe for the estimated 12 percent of veterans who are medically indigent and who thus limit or do not seek out needed medical care because of financial limitations.

Less than 10 percent of all veterans use VHA services for health care (Department of Veterans Affairs, 1994). Although the lack of knowledge of services is one explanation for the low use, the best predictor of the choice of VHA hospitalization is the lack of other health insurance. Veterans without other health insurance are five times more likely to go to a VHA hospital than are those who have such insurance, regardless of their age, income, or service-connected disability status. Thus VHA health services have been primarily used as the services of last resort or by those who otherwise would go without medical care.

Female Veterans

Thirty percent of female veterans are age 65 or older (Damron-Rodriguez & Cantrell, in press). It is projected that by 2020 women will constitute 11 percent of all veterans (Department of Veterans Affairs, 1993c). Age and period of service differ significantly for female veterans and male veterans. The median age of female veterans is 44.5 years, compared to 56.7 for male veterans, and nearly 29 percent of female veterans versus 11 percent of male veterans served during peacetime after the Vietnam War.

Relative to their number, women use fewer VHA services than do their male counterparts; in 1992 only 2 percent of all patients treated at VHA medical centers were women. Most of the women treated at VHA hospitals were admitted for general medicine and surgery (71 percent). Of those treated for mental illnesses, 17 percent were treated for psychoses and 11 percent for other mental disorders; the comparable figures for men were 9 percent for psychoses and 14 percent for other mental disorders (Veterans Health Services and Research Administration, 1991). However, because the life expectancy of female veterans, like women in the general population, is longer than that of male veterans, the number of female veterans receiving long-term-care services will increase.

With the increase in the number of female veterans, change will be required in VHA facilities, which are geared to serve a predominantly male population. Studies of women served by these facilities found that women veterans were as satisfied as were male veterans regarding medical care issues in which gender was irrelevant to care, but that they were dissatisfied with care involving gender-related concerns, such as the degree of privacy in hospitals and the adequacy of gynecological examinations (Rothman, 1984). It was not until 1992 that guidelines on the special treatment needs for breast diseases and gynecological disorders and for addressing privacy issues were formulated. Many VHA medical centers also established the position of women veteran coordinator to advocate for and coordinate services to female veterans (Department of Veterans Affairs, 1993b).

Chronically Mentally Ill Veterans

Mentally ill patients represent 40 percent of VHA inpatient bed-care days, and the number of mentally ill patients requiring VHA services is continuing to grow (Guggenheim & Lehman, 1991). Diagnostic categories include dementia, schizophrenia, major depression, bipolar disorder, and other psychiatric disorders, as well as substance abuse disorders. In 1990 approximately 120,000 patients with alcoholism and substance abuse problems were treated, and 19,000 of the nearly 500,000 veterans diagnosed as having PSTD received inpatient treatment for this condition. The number of veterans with severe dementia is expected to rise to 600,000 by the year 2000 (Guggenheim & Lehman).

A majority of older chronically mentally ill patients present with a significant number of coexisting medical conditions, which further complicates their care. Psychiatric staff require special education in behavioral management techniques, as well as training in the care of functionally disabled patients. Physical surroundings must include monitoring systems for wandering patients, quiet areas for a low-stimulus environment, and adequate space for individual and group treatments (Veteran Health Services and Research Administration, 1991).

Homeless Veterans

An estimated 40 percent of the more than 2 million homeless Americans are veterans (Gelberg & Linn, 1992). About half of all homeless people suffer from alcohol, drug abuse, or mental health problems (Alcohol, Drug Abuse, and Mental Health Administration, 1983), and those over age 40 are more likely to exhibit a functional disability, suffer from a chronic disease, and have a greater risk of dying than are younger homeless people (Gelberg & Linn). Because of their complex needs, homeless people require a comprehensive array of services, including medical, surgical, and mental health interventions, to help them overcome their disabilities and facilitate their reentry into society. A VHA project, the Homeless Chronically Mentally Ill program, at 45 sites, addresses many of these needs. The program offers outreach, health care, residential rehabilitation, and group-living services, with special training in social, work, and community survival skills. About 20,000 veterans received help through this program from 1988 to 1991.

Agent Orange

From 1962 to 1971 chemical herbicides were used in Vietnam to destroy ground cover and to restrict the food supplies of the enemy. The most common defoliant used was dioxin, a toxic chemical (Rothman & Becerra, 1987). Dioxin is commonly referred to as Agent Orange because of the orange stripes on the 55-gallon drums in which it was stored.

In the 1990s researchers at the National Academy of Sciences and elsewhere continue to test the risk factors from these herbicides on human beings. Although laboratory tests on animals have shown that cancer results from exposure to dioxin, the relationship between exposure to dioxin and lung cancer in veterans remains inconclusive. However, it has been verified that exposure to dioxin may cause a skin condition known as chloracne in humans (AMVETS, no date). The VA has established an Agent Orange Program that includes comprehensive medical examinations and a central registry of victims. In addition, eligible Vietnam veterans are now receiving care at VHA health care facilities for conditions that may be related to their exposure to Agent Orange (AMVETS).

Acquired Immune Deficiency Syndrome
VHA medical centers report treating more than 19,000 veterans with human immunodeficiency virus (HIV) or acquired immune deficiency syndrome (AIDS) (Department of Veterans Affairs, 1994). VHA facilities treat approximately 6 percent of the cumulative number of the reported cases of AIDS in adults in the nation (Department of Veterans Affairs, 1993c).

VA research on AIDS has received $6.6 million in VHA funds and $24.1 million in funds from other government sources to support 484 research projects, including six special AIDS Research Centers (Department of Veterans Affairs, 1993c). Computer-based information systems are being used to manage data related to clinical care and resources necessary for HIV patients through the an HIV Registry operated by the Decentralized Hospital Computer Program.

Clinical efforts to provide better services to patients and to control the spread of HIV and AIDS have included the cooperative study of the use of AZT, which found that the early use of the drug was related to delays in the progression of AIDS (Department of Veterans Affairs, 1994). Special AIDS-treatment units have been developed at both the inpatient and outpatient levels. The VHA has also developed the only dental registry in the world to document oral manifestations of HIV and AIDS. A major VHA initiative has been to institutionalize universal precaution measures to protect health care workers from contracting HIV.

Veterans with Other Special Needs
Many VA services reach out to veterans with special disabilities, such as blindness, spinal cord injury, communication disorders, speech disorders, and alcoholism (Stockford, 1983). In 1992, 17,690 paralyzed veterans were in need of comprehensive health and rehabilitation services (Paralyzed Veterans of America, 1993). Although outreach projects have been conducted with

minority veterans, such as Hispanics and African Americans (Department of Veterans Affairs, 1993a), further efforts will be needed to plan for minority veterans' use of long-term-care services and HIV/AIDS programs. Veterans in prison have also been the target of many outreach efforts.

POLICY ISSUES
The major issues affecting VA policy are the mandates to reduce the federal budget deficit and to reform the health care system. Federal health programs accounted for $310 billion of the 1994 federal budget, an 11 percent increase over the 1993 allocation (Paralyzed Veterans of America, 1993), and outlays for Medicaid and Medicare continue to demonstrate the fastest growth. Because the Department of Veterans Affairs is funded through discretionary spending accounts, its budget has been restrained to less than half the growth of Medicare and Medicaid. VA medical care represents only 5 percent of the federal health care budget (Paralyzed Veterans of America, 1993).

National health care reforms proposed during the Clinton administration contain the following major changes in access to and the delivery of health care services: mandated coverage, health care alliances, competing health plans, and a National Health Board. These changes would have a significant impact on the VHA (Office of Public and Intergovernmental Affairs, 1994). Health care alliances would offer a VA plan as one option to all veterans, and the VA could be reimbursed by veterans' employers or Medicare if the veterans had either type of coverage. A central implication of these changes for the VA is its competitive status. Because all Americans would have a choice of health care providers, VA medical centers would have to become competitive with other providers to serve veterans. Furthermore, veterans not currently eligible for VA health benefits could become eligible, as could family members of veterans. Veterans with service-connected disabilities and low-income veterans would continue to receive supplemental VA medical services. Thus, with the VA plan, there are no anticipated copayments. In addition, VA benefits are more comprehensive than those that would be provided to all Americans through a national health care plan. VA benefits include long-term care, dental services, eyeglasses and hearing aids, and extensive rehabilitation services.

In the late 1970s, critics of VA argued that VA had to become more willing to cooperate with non-VA hospitals to minimize the duplication of services. This will continue to be a major issue in a national managed care system.

The 1991 report of the Commission on the Future Structure of Veterans Health Care outlined several major policy goals for the Department of Veterans Affairs. One goal is to simplify the eligibility criteria for health care services and to provide a complete continuum of care for veterans (Department of Veterans Affairs, 1993c). Another goal is to institute total quality improvement nationally in three stages. Medical Care Cost Recovery, implemented in the 1990s to increase revenues for health care services, is another policy-level change.

Research is a major activity that has the potential for influencing both health care interventions and delivery systems. In 1992, $227 million was appropriated for VHA research and development; 2,500 researchers in 121 VHA medical centers published over 2,000 scientific papers to disseminate their findings in the areas of biomedical, clinical, and health services research. In the future, research efforts will focus more heavily on health services and clinical outcomes, areas that have a direct impact on veterans.

ROLE OF SOCIAL WORK

Social work services are an integral part of the VA system of care because veterans' services address the social, as well as physical, well-being of predominantly low-income veterans. VA is one of the largest employers of social workers in the nation, employing 4,100 graduate social workers and an additional 200 undergraduate social work assistants in 172 VA facilities (personal communication with M. Bosner, Department of Veterans Affairs Central Office of Social Work, Washington, DC, December 1993).

Social workers are key members of interdisciplinary treatment teams that include physicians, rehabilitation therapists, nurses, and psychologists. They assume clinical, community, and administrative practice roles with both individuals and groups in outpatient, hospital, and residential medical and psychiatric facilities. Clinical practice encompasses evaluation and crisis intervention through long-term treatment and case management, including discharge planning.

Macro social work practice entails the development of outreach services, programs, and working relationships with community services. For example, social workers have been engaged in screening for high-risk conditions, in computerizing management information systems in social work, and in a host of other activities that are in the forefront of the delivery of contemporary health care services. A key educational role for social workers is to serve as fieldwork instructors

and preceptors for the more than 800 social work students who are placed each year in a variety of VA settings. Approximately 50 percent of these social work interns receive stipends during their VA training. Because many VHA medical centers are closely affiliated with university medical schools, social workers also provide training in the psychosocial needs of patients to residents and medical interns. In addition, social workers provide in-service training for the VA's health professional staff.

Research is increasingly a focus of VA social work services. Clinical intervention studies, program evaluation research, and health services research are all important areas in which social workers can contribute to building improved knowledge for social work practice.

Challenges facing VA social workers include homelessness among veterans, particularly those with chronic mental illnesses; the development of effective services for veterans with HIV and AIDS; increased services for veterans with drug and alcohol problems; and innovative long-term-care services for aged veterans. Social workers will also play a major role in the implementation of new concepts of managed care and health care reform in the 1990s.

REFERENCES

Alcohol, Drug Abuse, and Mental Health Administration. (1983). *Alcohol, drug abuse and mental health problems of the homeless.* Rockville, MD: Author.

AMVETS. (no date). *The Vietnam veteran's self-help guide to agent orange.* Lanham, MD: Author.

Becerra, R. M., & Greenblat, M. (1983). *Hispanics seek health care: A study of 1,088 veterans of three war eras.* Lanham, MD: University Press of America.

Bergman, S., Delaney, N., Gallagher, D., Atkins, P., & Graeber, M. (1987). Respite care: A partnership between a Veterans Administration nursing home and families to care for frail elders at home. *The Gerontologist, 27,* 581–584.

Boyle, J. (1983). *Survey of aging veterans: A study of the means, resources, and future expectations of veterans ages 55 and over.* Washington DC: U.S. Government Printing Office.

Damron-Rodriguez, J. A., & Cantrell, M. (in press). Veterans in long term care. In Z. Harel & Dunkel (Eds.), *Long term care: People and services.* New York: Springer.

Department of Veterans Affairs. (1993a). *Chief minority affairs officer report, 1991–1993.* Washington, DC: Author.

Department of Veterans Affairs. (1993b). *Continuum of care.* Washington, DC: Author.

Department of Veterans Affairs. (1993c). *FY 1992 annual report of the Secretary of Veterans Affairs.* Washington, DC: Author.

Department of Veterans Affairs. (1993d). *Veterans population estimates, by age and period of service and by state and age.* Washington, DC: Author.

Department of Veterans Affairs (1994). *Annual report of the Secretary of Veterans Affairs: Fiscal Year 1993.* Washington, DC: Author.

Dienstfrey, S. J., & Bryne, J. J. (1984). *Veterans in the United States: A statistical portrait from the 1980 census.* Washington, DC: U.S. Government Printing Office.

Eberhardt, M., & McGovern, L. H. (1975). The veteran's right to counsel: A constitutional challenge to 38-3404. *San Fernando Valley Law Review, 4,* 121–129.

Gelberg, L., & Linn, L. (1992). Demographic differences in health status of homeless adults. *Journal of General Internal Medicine, 7,* 601–608.

Guggenheim, F. G., & Lehman, L. (1991, January). Psychiatric research in VA: Highlights from 1990. *VA Practitioner.*

Mather, J. H., & Abel, R. W. (1986). Medical care of veterans: A brief history. *Journal of the American Geriatrics Society, 34,* 757–760.

Office of Public and Intergovernmental Affairs, Health Care Reform Program Office. (1994). *The U.S. Department of Veterans Affairs and Health Care Reform.* Salt Lake City, UT: Author.

Page, W. F. (1982). Why veterans choose veterans administration hospitalization: A multivariate model. *Medical Care, 20,* 308–320.

Paralyzed Veterans of America. (1993). *The federal health budget: The veteran's perspective.* Washington, DC: Author.

Rothman, G. H. (1984). Needs of female patients in a veterans psychiatric hospital. *Social Work, 29,* 380–385.

Rothman, G., & Becerra, R. M. (1987). Veterans and Veterans' Services. In A. Minahan (Ed.-in-Chief), *Encyclopedia of social work* (18th ed., Vol. 2, pp. 809–817). Silver Spring, MD: National Association of Social Workers.

Servicemen's Readjustment Act of 1944. Ch. 268, 58 Stat. 284.

Stockford, D. (1983). Communicative disorders among patients in VA medical facilities. *Biometrics* (Monograph No. 17). Washington, DC: U.S. Government Printing Office.

U.S. Bureau of the Census. (1989). *1987 survey of veterans.* Washington, DC: U.S. Government Printing Office.

U.S. Department of Justice, Bureau of Justice Statistics. (1981). *Veterans in prison.* Washington, DC: Author.

Veterans Administration. (1984). *Annual report, 1984.* Washington, DC: U.S. Government Printing Office.

Veterans Administration, Central Office. (1984). *Caring for the older veterans.* Washington, DC: Author.

Veterans Administration, Office of Geriatrics and Extended Care. (1993). *Continuum of care.* Washington, DC: Author.

Veterans Administration Health Care Amendments of 1980. P.L. 96-330, 94 Stat. 1030 (1980).

Veterans Health Care Amendments of 1979. P.L. 96-22, 93 Stat. 2686.

Veterans Health Services and Research Administration. (1991). *Integrated psychiatric care planning guidelines, criteria and standards.* Washington, DC: Department of Veterans Affairs.

Vocational Rehabilitation Act Amendments of 1943. Ch. 190, 57 Stat. 374.

War Risk Insurance Act of 1914. Ch. 293, 38 Stat. 711.

Worthen, D. M. (1984, June). The partnership between the VA and U.S. medical schools. *VA Practitioner,* 53–58.

Yoshikawa, T. T. (1992). United States Department of Veterans Affairs: Health care for the aging veteran. *L'Année Gerontolique* (Paris), 431–437.

Rosina M. Becerra, PhD, is professor and dean, University of California, Los Angeles, School of Public Policy and Social Research, Department of Social Welfare, 247 Dodd Hall, 405 N. Hilgard Avenue, Los Angeles, CA 90024. **JoAnn Damron-Rodriguez, PhD,** is associate director of evaluation and education, Geriatric Research, Education, and Clinical Center at VA Medical Center, Los Angeles, and adjunct assistant professor, University of California, Los Angeles, School of Public Policy and Social Research, Department of Social Welfare.

For further information see

Aging: Services; Alcohol Abuse; Deinstitutionalization; Disability; Drug Abuse; Family Caregiving; Family Preservation and Home-Based Services; General Assistance; Health Services Systems Policy; Homelessness; Hospital Social Work; Income Security Overview; Mental Health; Military Social Work; Public Health Services; Public Social Services; Self-Help Groups; Social Security; Social Welfare History; Social Welfare Policy; Substance Abuse: Direct Practice; Victims of Torture and Trauma.

Key Words

Department of	Veterans
Veterans Affairs	Administration
veterans	veterans services

Victim Services and Victim/Witness Assistance Programs
Albert R. Roberts

In the 1970s advocates of victim's rights, services for victims, and victim/witness assistance programs were rarely available in the United States. In the mid-1990s, however, there are over 6,000 victim/witness assistance programs, battered women's shelters, rape crisis programs, and support groups for survivors of violent crimes nationwide. The proliferation of programs is a direct result of funding under the federal Victims of Crime Act of 1984, state and county general-revenue grants, and the earmarking of a percentage of state penalty assessments and fines levied on criminal offenders.

In cities and counties throughout the United States, victims of and witnesses to crimes are receiving help from these programs. Whether people are victimized in a small town with a population of 17,000, such as Black River Falls, Wisconsin, or in major metropolitan areas such as Chicago, New York, or Seattle, services from victim/witness assistance programs are available to them.

BACKGROUND

Emphasis on Offenders
For decades the interests of victims and witnesses were ignored by the courts. Until the mid-1970s, correctional reformers and noted authors were revered as international experts on criminology and penology. In the 1950s and 1960s, millions of dollars were spent on rehabilitation programs aimed at changing convicted felons into law-abiding citizens. The courts also spent millions of dollars on processing and protecting the best interests of defendants. Crime victims, in sharp contrast to offenders, had to wait in the halls of dreary courtrooms while defendants sometimes threatened or intimidated them. Separate waiting rooms for witnesses and their children were practically nonexistent. Although extensive correctional treatment, educational, and social services programs were available to convicted offenders (Roberts, 1971, 1974), victims and their families who had often been shattered by the victimization were given no services (McDonald, 1976).

Shift in Focus
By the mid-1970s, when the first victim/witness assistance and rape crisis programs were initiated, the pendulum began to shift toward providing critically needed services for innocent victims of crimes and fewer rehabilitation programs for convicted felons (Roberts, 1992). The changed focus was related to how the victims were treated throughout the criminal justice system, from initial contact with a police officer or detective to testimony in court. Historically, too many victims

of crime had been victimized twice: first during the actual crime and again, when insensitive and unresponsive police and prosecutors ignored their calls or requests for assistance or subjected them to harsh, repeated, and victim-blaming questions (McDonald, 1976).

The crime victims' movement has come a long way since the 1970s. From fiscal years 1973 to 1975, the Law Enforcement Assistance Administration (LEAA) spent millions of dollars for victim/witness assistance demonstration projects. During the early 1970s, a growing number of prosecutors' offices in cities and counties throughout the United States were computerized. For the first time, several systematic studies of victims were conducted. These studies indicated that "after the victim had decided to report the crime but before the problem of continuances and delays had begun to operate, many crime cases were lost because witnesses did not want to cooperate" (McDonald, 1976, p. 29).

The research documenting the noncooperation of witnesses and the insensitive and apathetic treatment of victims and witnesses by court staff led LEAA to fund 18 victim-service and victim/witness assistance programs. Ten of these programs were prosecutor-based witness-assistance programs, and four were victim-assistance programs under the direction of a nonprofit social services agency, a county probation department, and a police department. The remaining four programs focused on providing advocacy and crisis intervention to victims of rape or child abuse.

Funding Issues
In the early 1980s, with the demise of LEAA, federal grants to victim-assistance programs declined. The programs that remained tried to make up for the loss of LEAA seed grants by requesting general-revenue funds from counties or cities. At first, some local government sources were unwilling to allocate sufficient funds. However, from 1981 to 1985, 28 states enacted legisla-

tion to fund both established and new programs to aid victims and witnesses. The trend among state legislatures has been to raise the funds for these programs by earmarking a percentage of penalty assessments, fines, or both, on criminal offenders to these programs. Nineteen of the 28 states fund victim/witness assistance programs through penalty assessments and fines, and the remaining nine states fund them through general state revenues (Roberts, 1990).

Since the passage of the landmark Victims of Crime Act of 1984, responsive federal, state, and county agencies throughout the nation have allocated over $650 million to aid crime victims. A large portion of these funds has come from fines and penalty assessments on convicted felons. Unfortunately, several states are rapidly losing ground in the collection of restitution and penalty assessments. Therefore, it will be necessary for states with responsive legislators and highly organized victim compensation-and-restitution or corrections boards to hire the necessary number of accountants, fiscal monitors, and computer-literate administrators to maintain the 90 percent or higher rate of collection of fees.

Victim Service versus Victim/Witness Assistance Programs

Victim/witness assistance programs are usually located in local county prosecutors' offices, in county courthouses, or nearby the court buildings. These programs are designed to encourage witnesses to cooperate in filing criminal charges and testifying in court.

Basic Services

In general, programs include a witness-notification and case-monitoring system in which staff keep witnesses advised of indictments, continuances, and postponements; the dates of hearings and trials; negotiated pleas; and the outcomes of trials. Many of these programs also provide secure and comfortable reception rooms for witnesses who are waiting to testify in court, transportation services, and escorts who accompany the witnesses to court and remain with them to explain and interpret the court proceedings. In addition, these programs typically prepare and distribute court-orientation pamphlets about the adjudication process on topics such as "Crime Victims' Bill of Rights," "Witness Guidelines for Courtroom Testimony," "What You Should Know About Your Criminal Court and the Court Process," and "Informational Guide for Crime Victims" (Roberts, 1992).

According to the author's survey of victim service and witness assistance programs through-

out the country (Roberts, 1990), slightly less than one-third of these programs reported having some form of child care for the children of victims and witnesses while the parents testify in court. Providing responsible and structured child care for a parent while he or she is testifying in court can be an important service. Unfortunately, most criminal justice agencies do not realize that victims' and witnesses' children are affected by their parents' emotional reactions, losses, physical injuries, and disruptions that are due to being victims of crimes. Victim/witness assistance programs should be concerned with the special needs of children not only because many parent–witnesses will not be able to testify if they cannot find child care during a traumatizing court ordeal, but because it is the humane thing to do. An added benefit is that some children may have witnessed the crimes and may have noticed additional identifying characteristics of the perpetrators.

Program Objectives

The overriding objectives of victim/witness assistance programs and units are to help witnesses overcome the anxiety and trauma associated with testifying in court while encouraging them to cooperate in the prosecution of criminal cases. The primary objectives of these programs are as follows:

- to provide victims and witnesses with the message that their cooperation is essential to crime-control efforts and successful criminal prosecution
- to inform victims and witnesses of their rights to receive dignified and compassionate treatment by criminal justice authorities
- to inform witnesses of the court process, the scheduling of cases, the trials, and the disposition of cases
- to orient victims to the courts and give them tips on how best to recall the crime scene and to testify accurately (Roberts, 1990).

Crisis Intervention Programs

Victim-service or crisis intervention programs for victims of crimes are not as common as are victim/witness assistance programs. These types of programs are usually lodged in police departments, sheriffs' offices, hospitals, probation departments, or nonprofit social services agencies. Typically, they attempt to intervene within the first 24 hours after the victimization. They provide a comprehensive range of essential services for crime victims, including sending mobile response teams to the crime scene; providing crisis counseling; helping victims complete victim-compensation applications; supplying emergency financial assistance and food vouchers to local supermarkets; providing transportation to court, local battered women's shelters, hospitals, or the offices of victim-assistance programs; repairing or replacing broken locks and windows; helping to replace lost documents (for example, birth certificates, marriage licenses, and wills); and providing referrals to prosecutors' domestic violence and sexual assault intake units and to community mental health centers and social services agencies for extended counseling and psychotherapy.

LEGISLATION, FUNDING, AND STABILITY

Since the mid-1970s, the organizational stability and the number of victim/witness assistance centers and programs have varied. Most of these programs have been developed by county and city prosecutors and have received annual pass-through grants under the Victims of Crime Act of 1984 (VOCA) from their state attorney generals' offices or their state VOCA coordinators. These programs seem to be the most well established and stable in regard to their funding. In sharp contrast, police- and hospital-based victim-assistance programs often go out of business in three to five years. These temporary programs are initiated through federal or state start-up grants (seed money) and receive either no monetary match or only a 10 percent match from the budgets of their counties or municipalities. Unfortunately, without a sustained monetary commitment from local government officials or heads of agencies or hospitals, these programs are bound to fail.

The largest increase in the number of programs occurred from 1984 to 1991. For example, Massachusetts has a Victim and Witness Assistance Fund, which generates revenues through penalty assessments on convicted felons and late fees attached to civil motor vehicle violations. In Massachusetts, annual revenues soared from $137,058 in fiscal year 1984 to $2,286,512 in fiscal year 1985. During the next seven fiscal years, revenues steadily increased from $2.2 million in fiscal year 1985 to $7.9 million in fiscal year 1991—an increase of over 225 percent in the seven-year period. However, these revenues dropped by 25 percent between fiscal years 1991 and 1993. At the federal level, the funding of victims' services and domestic violence and witness-assistance programs also increased steadily, from more than $68 million in fiscal year 1985 to $115 million in fiscal year 1991.

STAFFING PATTERNS

Throughout the United States, the size and responsibilities of the staffs of these programs are similar. According to the Roberts's (1990) nationwide survey, 74 percent of the programs had five or fewer full-time employees, 13 percent had six to 10 full-time employees, approximately 10 percent had 11 or more full-time employees, and only 3 percent had 24 or more full-time staff. The predominant staffing pattern consisted of a program director–coordinator, two victim advocates–counselors, a secretary, and a data-entry clerk. The program coordinator reported directly to the county prosecutor, to the chief counsel to the prosecutor, or to a deputy prosecutor responsible for all cases of sexual assault and domestic violence.

Victim Advocate–Counselors

The sole or primary responsibility of the victim advocate–counselors is the provision of services to witnesses, particularly witnesses to violent crimes in which offenders have been charged with one or more criminal offenses. Advocate–counselors are responsible for accompanying witnesses to prefiling hearings, preliminary hearings, deposition hearings, and trials to ensure that the attorneys, court clerks, and magistrates treat them fairly and compassionately. They or the program directors accompany the victims or witnesses to all official appointments related to the filing and processing of the criminal court cases. For example, if a victim or witness has been sexually assaulted, the advocate–counselor will either accompany or meet the victim at the hospital or medical facility to make sure that the victim's rights are protected.

Volunteers

Many programs rely on volunteers to provide needed services. More than half (52 percent) of the respondents to Roberts's (1990) national survey reported that they used volunteers. Although approximately one-third of the programs used one to four volunteers, almost half had 11 or more volunteers. Programs with smaller paid staff tended to rely heavily on volunteers. The participation of volunteers enabled programs to provide services to victims and witnesses in small communities, such as Xenia, Ohio (population 130,000, four full-time staff, 25 volunteers); Sanford, Florida (population 29,000, one full-time staff, 14 volunteers); and Greensboro, North Carolina (population 360,000, two full-time staff, 12 volunteers). The programs in highly populated cities had a small number of volunteers relative to their paid staff. For example, Pittsburgh, with a population of more than 1.5 million, had a program with 14 full-time paid staff and 15 to 18 volunteers.

Staff Education

With regard to the educational background of staff, over 90 percent of the employees of these programs had bachelor's degrees; of that group, only 28 percent had graduate degrees, usually a master's degree in social work (MSW) or in sociology, counseling, or criminal justice (Roberts, 1990). Most program directors–coordinators had master's degrees in counseling, education, criminal justice, psychology, or social work. One-third had MSW degrees, and most had completed courses in social welfare policy, planning and management, administration, and crisis intervention and brief treatment.

One of the best ways to prepare for a career in this field is to complete a block field placement at a comprehensive victim/witness assistance program. Most graduate schools of social work offer opportunities for their MSW students to bridge theory and practice by placement in a prosecutor-based victim-assistance program, a rape crisis program, a battered women's shelter, or a crisis intervention unit. Graduate programs in social work are unique because of their emphasis on fieldwork, regular supervision of beginning social workers, and weekly case consultations.

PROGRAM EVALUATION

Program evaluations are useful for documenting a program's impact and value by assessing whether goals have been achieved and whether there is a need for more staff and resources to expand and improve the program's operations. According to Smith (1990), program evaluations help answer essential questions about social work programs:

- Is the program effective in reaching its intended goals?
- Does the program seem to be having the desired effect?
- Are people benefiting from the program?
- What was the outcome of the counseling that clients received?
- What are the costs of the program and the benefits to the participants?

Smith (1990) recommended that a formal evaluation process be planned and carried out annually at all local government-funded programs in cities with populations of over 100,000. These evaluations should measure selected outcomes for each major local program (Hatry, Winnie, & Fisk, 1981).

Several evaluations of victim/witness assistance programs were conducted during the late 1970s and 1980s (Bolin, 1980; Cronin & Bourque, 1981; Finn & Lee, 1987). These evaluations demonstrated the programs' effectiveness in attaining goals, success in serving target populations (for example, elderly crime victims), and cost–benefits. In addition, they indicated that the notification of witnesses reduces the amount of time that the witnesses spend while waiting to testify.

Studies have also found that victim/witness assistance programs, particularly victim-advocacy services and the accompaniment of witnesses to court, has led to the increased cooperation of witnesses (Roberts, 1990). Unfortunately, most state and county funding sources do not require annual outcome analyses and cost–benefit evaluations of these programs. As a result, thus far in the 1990s, few comprehensive evaluations of these programs have been conducted.

To date, no program evaluator or researcher has conclusively documented that victim/witness assistance or crisis intervention has been effective in reducing the suffering of crime victims. To determine the short- and long-term effects of these programs, it is necessary to plan and implement longitudinal studies using the various types of qualitative and quantitative research designs that have recently been developed. Legislators, administrators, and informed citizens should mandate the research and evaluation of victim/witness assistance programs.

FUTURE OF SOCIAL WORK IN THESE PROGRAMS

Social work has a long legacy in private philanthropy and juvenile justice. Beginning in the late 1800s, social workers volunteered to help poor, abused, or troubled children and their families. Since then, one of the primary missions of social work has been to help vulnerable populations and disenfranchised groups. Without question, victims of crime are a disenfranchised group. However, social work has had a tenuous and strained relationship with the criminal justice system. Many social workers have been reluctant to work in coercive and authoritarian agencies such as prisons and police departments. However, restitution, victim–offender mediation programs, services for victims, and battered women's shelters offer new challenges to the profession.

Gandy (1983), then associate dean at the College of Social Work at the University of South Carolina, predicted that the field of victims' services would expand and noted that because of their skills in advocacy, mediation, negotiation, and conflict resolution, social workers are ideally suited for careers this field. Although Gandy's prediction and assessment of the emerging role of social workers in this field were correct, most social workers serve as advocates–counselors, rather than as directors of these programs, because the primary sponsors of these programs are city or county prosecutors or police departments, who choose criminal justice professionals, deputy county prosecutors, or police captains or lieutenants to head the programs.

To change this situation, graduate schools of social work, state departments of personnel, assignment judges at the county level, and the state attorney general's offices need to work together to attract more qualified social workers. Specifically, schools of social work should develop courses on victimology and victim services and family violence in collaboration with educators in the field of criminal justice. To date, only seven schools of social work offer such courses (California State University at Fresno, Hunter College of the City University of New York, Indiana University at Indianapolis, Rutgers University, University of Kansas, University of South Carolina, and University of Vermont). Finally, standards for victim advocates, crisis intervenors, and victim-service workers need to be developed, field tested, and refined. These standards should be developed by a national advisory group with representatives from NASW, the Council on Social Work Education, the American Bar Association, the American Probation and Parole Association, and the National Council of Juvenile and Family Court Judges.

The special knowledge, ethics, and skills that social workers have are particularly well suited to the complex demands of a career in victim services. With the increased recognition of opportunities for victim advocates, it is hoped that more social workers will be attracted to and recruited by victim-oriented programs.

REFERENCES

Bolin, D. C. (1980). The Pima County victim/witness program—Analyzing its success. *Evaluation and Change, 7,* 120–126.
Cronin, R. C., & Bourque, B. (1981). *National Evaluation Program Phase I report: Assessment of victim/witness assistance projects.* Washington, DC: U.S. Department of Justice.
Finn, P. P., & Lee, B. (1987). *Serving crime victims and witnesses.* Washington, DC: U.S. Department of Justice.
Gandy, J. T. (1983). Social work and victim assistance programs. In A. R. Roberts (Ed.), *Social work in juvenile and criminal justice settings* (pp. 121–136). Springfield, IL: Charles C Thomas.
Hatry, H. P., Winnie, R. E., & Fisk, D. M. (1981). *Practical program evaluation for state and local governments* (2nd ed.). Washington, DC: Urban Institute.
McDonald, W. F. (Ed.). (1976). *Criminal justice and the victim.* Beverly Hills, CA: Sage Publications.
Roberts, A. R. (1971). *Sourcebook on prison education: Past, present and future.* Springfield, IL: Charles C Thomas.
Roberts, A. R. (1974). *Correctional treatment of the offender.* Springfield, IL: Charles C Thomas.
Roberts, A. R. (1990). *Helping crime victims: Research, policy and practice.* Newbury Park, CA: Sage Publications.
Roberts, A. R. (1992). Victim/witness programs: Questions and answers. *FBI Law Enforcement Bulletin, 61*(12), 12–16.
Smith, M. J. (1990). *Program evaluation in the human services.* New York: Springer.
Victims of Crime Act of 1984. P.L. 98–473, 98 Stat. 2170.

FURTHER READING

Bastion, L. D. (1993). *Criminal victimization 1992.* Washington, DC: U.S. Department of Justice, Bureau of Justice Statistics.
Bureau of Justice Statistics. (1994). *Criminal victimization in the United States: 1973–92 trends.* Washington, DC: U.S. Department of Justice.
McNeece, C. A., & Roberts, A. R. (Eds.). (1995). *Policies and practices in the justice system.* Chicago: Nelson-Hall.
President's Task Force on Victims of Crime. (1982). *Victims of crime: Final report.* Washington, DC: U.S. Government Printing Office.
Roberts, A. R. (1991). The delivery of services to crime victims: A national survey. *American Journal of Orthopsychiatry, 61,* 128–137.
Roberts, A. R. (1994). Crime in America: Trends, costs, and remedies. In A. R. Roberts (Ed.), *Critical issues in crime and justice* (pp. 3–18). Newbury Park, CA: Sage Publications.

Albert R. Roberts, DSW, is professor, Rutgers University, School of Social Work, 536 George Street, New Brunswick, NJ 08903.

For further information see

Adult Corrections; Adult Courts; Advocacy; Children's Rights; Civil Rights; Community Organization; Criminal Behavior Overview; Domestic Violence; Federal Social Legislation from 1961 to 1994; Gang Violence; Homicide; Human Rights; Juvenile Corrections; Social Planning; Social Welfare Policy; Social Work Profession Overview; Suicide; Victims of Torture and Trauma; Violence Overview.

Key Words	
advocacy	victim/witness
victim services	assistance

Victims of Torture and Trauma
Barbara Chester

> When human beings ceased to be emissaries or legatees of love and became instead agents or
> victims of power on such a massive scale, we may have witnessed a shift in civilization's priorities
> with whose psychological bequest we continue to struggle.
>
> —L. Langer, 1991

For healing professionals, working with survivors of extreme circumstances is a challenge on many levels. Extreme stress reactions epitomize the integrity of the mind–body interaction: the totality of the body's need to express psychic pain and the need of the mind to understand and comprehend overwhelming physical hardship (Chester, 1994). As clients struggle with the need to integrate the unimaginable, social workers, as partners in the healing process, often confront their own limits, both as professionals and as humans (Chester & Jaranson, 1994). It is this broader conceptualization of the impact of extreme circumstances that differentiates healers from technicians. This entry views extreme stress and attendant trauma on both a conceptual and a technical level.

VIOLENCE AND TRAUMA

Violence and attendant trauma affect millions of people. In the United States, 65 people die daily from acts of violence. During the 1980s, 20 million people suffered nonfatal physical injuries as a direct result of violence, costing an estimated $34 billion annually in direct health-related costs (Mercy, Rosenberg, Powell, Broome, & Roper, 1993). Women between the ages of 15 and 44 years lose more discounted health years of life to interpersonal violence than they do to all other causes combined, including reproductive cancers, acquired immune deficiency syndrome, and motor vehicle accidents (Heise, Pitanguy, & Germain, 1993). (Discounted health years of life are health years of life lost for a variety of causes, based on years lost as a result of premature death and fractions of years spent ill or incapacitated as a function of disability.) Presently, more children younger than age 14 years die of gunshot wounds than died from polio a generation ago (California Wellness Foundation, 1993).

Since World War II, global violence has generated 127 low-level conflicts or wars. As a result, 43 million people have fled their homes because of severe abuses of their human rights, including arbitrary arrest, unjust imprisonment, torture, and fear of extrajudicial execution (Toole & Waldman, 1993). Although the majority of those individuals migrated to developing countries, more than 2.5 million settled in countries of third asylum in Western Europe and the United States. That number does not include the undocumented but apparently large number of people who reside primarily in coastal and border areas of Arizona, California, Texas, and Florida (Kismaric, 1989). The civilian population has been affected directly by war in an increasing manner. More than 84 percent of current war casualties are civilians, a majority of whom are women and children (Amnesty International, USA, 1990).

The rapidly growing field of traumatic stress studies involves a multidisciplinary effort to understand and intervene in the lives of people as diverse as refugees, indigenous peoples, war veterans, battered women, abused children, and survivors of natural or humanmade disasters. It is important to understand the distinction between *traumatization,* which involves a severe challenge to the organism's ability to cope, and *victimization* (Ochberg, 1988), which necessitates integrating the reality of and the confrontation with deliberate acts of human cruelty into the survivor's worldview.

Surveying an international sample of 1,000 adults, the World Health Organization discovered that 69 percent ($n = 690$) of those individuals had experienced at least one severely traumatic event in their lifetimes (DiGirodamo, 1993). Studies in four southeastern U.S. communities also have indicated that large numbers of people have suffered from traumatic and violent events. For example, 30 percent of the surveyed population had experienced the unexpected and tragic death of a loved one; 25 percent had been robbed; and 15 percent had been physically assaulted (Norris, 1992). *Posttraumatic stress disorder (PTSD),* an organized and painful response to trauma found in many violence survivors, is relatively high (8 percent to 16 percent) in the general U.S. population (Davidson & Foa, 1993). Threat to life, severe harm or injury, exposure to grotesque death, and loss or injury of a loved one are strong predictors for PTSD. Researchers (Davidson & Fairbank, 1993) have found that 70 percent of rape victims, 20 percent to 40 percent of individuals who have survived terrorist attacks, 40 percent of refugees, 53 percent of combat veterans, and 24 percent of people who have witnessed the killing of another person have developed PTSD.

Trauma faced by communities displaced by war and armed conflict or disrupted by violence is severe and cumulative. For example, one study (Mollica, 1988) of refugees from Cambodia found that they suffered an average of 16 major trauma events during war, flight, and resettlement. The impact of severe trauma on the lives of individuals and communities has been likened to the "unmaking of the world" (Scarry, 1985). Clearly, the nature and scope of this problem necessitates a new paradigm for contextualization and response; one that is both multidisciplinary and multicultural in nature.

TORTURE

Torture is an extreme form of violence practiced by the governments of at least 110 countries (Basoglu, 1993b). Work with torture survivors and in their recovery is important, not only because the survivors' suffering is severe, but because the sequelae of torture involve the culmination and integration of most severe stress reactions. Understanding the nature of torture and the recovery process involved with torture survivors can promote models that are useful with survivors of other extreme circumstances.

Definition

Torture has been defined on many levels: legally by human rights groups and international lawmaking bodies, for ethical purposes by professional associations, and by survivors themselves. Most definitions include the extreme and deliberate nature of torture, and its purpose, which involves the destruction of individuals and communities. For example, the World Medical Association (1975) has defined torture as the deliberate, systematic, or wanton infliction of physical or mental suffering by one or more persons, acting alone or on the orders of any authority to force another person to yield information, to make a confession, or for any other reason.

Torture is deliberate and strategic. Everything that makes a person human and part of an integrated universe is perverted and twisted through torture (Chester, 1994). Furthermore, the torturer uses the body to access the mind and the individual to access the community (Scalpobersky, 1989); for this reason, although torture is an acute trauma, its effects are cumulative and interactive

(Chester & Jaranson, 1994). Interviews conducted in the former Yugoslavia illustrate how rape in the service of "ethnic cleansing" can be viewed as torture on the community level:

> In Bosnia-Herzegovina and Croatia, rape has been an instrument for "ethnic cleansing. . . ." The effect of rape is often to ensure that women and their families will flee and never return. . . . [and] Rapes spread fear and induce the flight of refugees; rapes humiliate, demoralize, and destroy not only the victim but also her family and community; and rapes stifle any wish to return. (Stiglmayer, 1994)

Researchers (Chester & Holtan, 1992; Christiansen & Juhl, 1990; Randall & Lutz, 1991) have reviewed and described the methods of torture. Methods involve physical insults such as beatings, whippings, suffocation, and burning with chemicals or application of electric current; psychological devastation in the form of mock executions, severe humiliation, and the forcing of people to witness the torture and execution of others; and pharmacological torture through the use of heavy doses of psychotropic medications or other mind-altering substances.

Case Study

The torturers of R, a man from a Middle Eastern country, imprisoned R with his three brothers, forced him to watch his brothers' execution by hanging, and then anally raped him. The torturers moved R to various locations to avoid detection by remaining family members or human rights groups. In one location, the torturers gave R massive doses of a substance that caused confusion, fever, and abdominal spasms. They tied R to a barrel and fired weapons continuously at him; immersed R in freezing water with electric current running to his testicles; and deprived him of food, water, and basic hygiene. After two years of maltreatment, the torturers released R, who was given asylum status in the United States.

IMPACT OF TORTURE

Humans cannot withstand such treatment without narrowing the world of pain and suffering in some appreciable manner—an adaptive response. Unfortunately, torture survivors tenaciously hold on to the survival mechanisms developed at that time, even after the danger has passed. The resultant symptoms of such a focused effort are fairly consistent across studies and include nightmares and other sleep disturbances, anxiety and panic, depression, cognitive deficits such as loss of short-term memory and concentration, and changes in identity (Somnier, Vesti, Kastrup, & Gerefke, 1993).

As well as emotional and cognitive symptoms, almost all torture victims suffer from physical symptoms including severe headaches, gastrointestinal symptoms, joint pain, dental problems, skin lesions, scars, sexual dysfunction, genital tract disorders in women, and significant changes in locomotor function (Cathcart, Berger, & Knazan, 1979; Goldfeld, Mollica, Pesavento, & Farone, 1988). In addition, dissociative reactions occur, eradicating the boundaries between past and present memories, and disconnecting the processes of the recognition of pain as an adaptive response and the ability to link emotions and feelings to memories and behaviors (Krystal, 1988). According to Carol (personal communication, 1987), recovery from torture

> is not a destination, but a journey to be experienced. The healing takes place through the re-experience of past feelings as separate from present experience. Discriminating past from present feeling is a therapeutic task. Discriminating past from present choices is a healing procedure.

Torture victims often experience the painful internal conflict between the need to remember and the need to forget that is characteristic of PTSD (Chester, 1994). At the Center for Victims of Torture in Minnesota, the first U.S.-based treatment center for political torture survivors, two-thirds of the clients served have suffered from this disorder, generally with a comorbid Axis 1 diagnosis of major depression or panic disorder (Chester, 1990). Specific aspects of an acute trauma such as physical torture, prolonged isolation, and sensory deprivation appear to be more predictive of PTSD, whereas personal losses following an acute trauma such as exile and the "disappearance" or death of loved ones are more predictive of major depression (Mollica & Caspi-Yavin, 1993). In general, PTSD as a solitary diagnosis is uncommon among traumatized populations including Vietnam veterans (Kulka et al., 1990), battered women (Kemp, Rawlings, & Greene, 1991), and refugees (Garcia-Peltoniemi, 1991). In addition, the traumatized individual's need to remember, name his or her suffering, and receive validation often conflicts with the societal need to forget (Lira, Becker, & Castillo, 1988).

The medical descriptions involved with psychiatric nomenclature, however, are inadequate to describe the lingering despair and loss of hope experienced by survivors of torture and other extreme circumstances. Freelance correspondent Alexandria Stiglmayer (1994) described the reaction of survivors of the "war on women" perpetrated in Bosnia-Herzegovina: "The amazement

remains, 'They wanted to kill us slowly, torture us to death, they wanted us to suffer ... they didn't want sex. They were gloating because they were humiliating Muslim women.' Both women look for explanations for the violence but cannot find any" (p. 121).

TREATMENT CONCEPTUALIZATION

Clarissa Pinkola Estes (1992) tells the story of *La Loba* (wolf woman) whose sole work is to collect bones. La Loba searches the desert to find the remains of animals that were destroyed and then decimated. When she has finally collected the smallest fragment that completes the skeleton or foundation of a destroyed creature, she sits, very deliberately, until she finds a song. When La Loba has found the correct song, one that is unique to that animal in that place at that time, she sings over the bones. Slowly, the bones take on substance, then form, then shape, and finally movement.

The La Loba story is a wonderful metaphor for the healing that can occur within a devastated human soul. The shattered identity, psyche, and values of the individual remain uniquely his or hers, and the treatment practitioner must find the correct "song" that will restore and remake the world of this person. For this reason, social workers or other helping professionals must work with everything an individual brings into a situation (Figure 1).

Sociocultural Aspects

Although symptoms and reactions to torture and severe trauma are generally consistent across cultures, the ways in which survivors express, understand, prioritize, and contextualize these symptoms vary considerably. For example, guilt may be an internalized and individual response to rape and humiliation in Western Cultures, whereas shame is considered an appropriate collective response to that experience in others (Skylv, 1992). The sociocultural–sociopolitical aspects of individuals also include the historical or generational components of their being. The attitudes and reactions of the various former Yugoslavian communities during the present conflict have been shaped since the 9th century, when the Serbs were converted to Eastern Orthodox Christianity and the Slovenes and Croats to Western Roman Christianity (Stiglmayer, 1994). Tribal conflicts in Ethiopia, Rwanda, Liberia, and South Africa have exacerbated the extremity of violence in these countries. The state often exploits existing racial and ethnic hatreds and tensions to exert more complete control of the population. It is essential that helping

FIGURE 1

Treatment Conceptualization

Specific traumatic event—Torture:
The strategic destruction of the
individual's physical, mental, and spiritual capacity

Trauma associated with the destruction
of the community or environment: Refugees, indigenous
people and survivors of natural disasters and war trauma

Psychological components of abuse and victimization found
in sexual assault and abuse, battering, and physical assault

Normal developmental issues presented by individuals in treatment:
The social, cultural, and political context of the survivor within his or her community

NOTE: Pyramidal shape indicates the necessity of assessing and proceeding from each preceding level of context.

professionals have a basic understanding of these conditions to work effectively with clients. Such information is often available through human rights organizations such as Amnesty International (Chester & Holtan, 1992).

Normal Developmental Issues
The age, gender, and developmental roles of the individual, both at the time of the trauma and at the time of treatment, are important considerations.

Case studies. L, a woman in her mid-forties from the Middle East who was a popular figure in the world of performing arts in her country, was detained by the secret police on several occasions as an adult in her mid-twenties and early thirties, tortured, and forced to marry against her will. Her ordeal preempted normal professional, family, and childbearing experiences in her country of origin. During treatment, L, at the time in her mid-forties, had to deal with those losses in addition to the loss of social status and culture (for example, food, language, rituals, and music), as well as the physical and emotional effects of her experience. Similarly, T, a 50-year-old former physician from Southeast Asia, had to cope with the loss of his medical career in addition to the traumatic memories associated with five years in a "re-education camp."

Psychological Components of Abuse and Victimization
Several researchers have examined the impact of a single, acute traumatic incident within the context of cumulative, multigenerational trauma. For example, Aron, Corne, Fursland, and Zelwer (1991)

described significant clinical and conceptual differences between women who were raped in the context of civil war and repression, such as found in El Salvador, as opposed to women who had experienced rape in the United States. Women raped in a political context were more likely to develop PTSD than those assaulted in the United States and less likely to report the experience to authorities. The basic components of victimization, however, exist within all individuals who confront human cruelty. Whereas victims often experience the triad of symptoms characterizing PTSD—intrusive recollections of the event, numbing or restricted range of affect, and symptoms of heightened arousal—they also may suffer from a "disorder of despair." Characteristics of this "disorder" include shame; self-blame; feelings of subjugation; morbid hatred; paradoxical gratitude toward the perpetrator; feelings of defilement; sexual inhibition or loss of sexual function; feelings of resignation; and "revictimization" as victims participate in the various "helping" systems: health and mental health systems, the criminal justice system, and immigration and naturalization services (Ochberg, 1988).

Trauma Associated with Destruction of Community and Environment
Since the classic work of Lindemann (1944) with survivors of the Coconut Grove fire, several studies have reported on the psychiatric impact of natural and humanmade disasters. Widespread impairment including psychic numbing, survivor guilt, physical illness, acute grief, anxiety, depression, despair, sleep disturbances, and nightmares were common to survivors of episodes that varied

from a destructive flash flood and volcanic eruption to the bombing of Hiroshima (Lifton, 1968; Shore, Tatum, & Vollmer, 1986; Titchener & Kapp, 1976). In addition, a progressive dose–response relationship was found to be related to the level of exposure to environmental destruction (Tatum, Vollmer, & Shore, 1986) (that is, the closer one was to the center of the disaster, the more severe the symptoms were).

Immediate rebuilding of integral support systems and techniques such as critical incident debriefing can be helpful to communities that have faced destruction of their environment. However, loss of one's country, the inability to return to one's community, or the loss of all geographic boundaries and national identity, such as the Kurdish people have experienced, makes environmental destruction particularly devastating.

Trauma Associated with Strategic Destruction of Individuals

Political torture survivors have confronted a systematic attempt to dismantle their connectedness to self, family, and community through the deliberate application of extreme physical and emotional torment. Torturers accomplish this dismantlement by breaking the body of individuals—inflicting pain and depriving individuals of basic life necessities—and breaking the will—applying psychological techniques designed to destroy the mind. In effect, "torture is a violent process that seeks to destroy all levels of meaning and replace this meaning with a state-imposed definition of reality" (Chester & Jaranson, 1994, p. 17).

Given the totality of the experience, optimal treatment involves work within the context of a multidisciplinary team. Such a format allows for recreating and reintegrating the various fragments (or bones) of the traumatized person's world. The premier center providing centralized multidisciplinary care for survivors of torture in exile is the Rehabilitation Center for Torture Victims in Copenhagen, Denmark. Created by a team of physicians from the Danish Medical Group of Amnesty International, the rehabilitation center uses core multidisciplinary teams comprising nurses, social workers, physicians, psychiatrists, psychologists, and physiotherapists. An outer network of affiliated professionals provide more specialized care including dental work, neurology, and pediatric services. Through its international branch, the rehabilitation center has aided the growth and development of almost 80 centers throughout the world. Other centers have provided or emphasized help in obtaining legal status for clients, many of whom are undocumented.

However, centralized care is expensive and labor intensive, and neither possible nor desirable in countries where torture and repression are still ongoing. In addition, some treatment teams reject the notion of "medicalizing" what is a sociopolitical phenomenon. Other treatment models include use of a widespread network of professional volunteers within the context of a small core of permanent staff, or a looser coalition of peer support groups within the community (Chester, 1990).

THERAPEUTIC ISSUES

Researchers have summarized key therapeutic issues for both treatment of PTSD in general (Davidson & Foa, 1993) and for treatment of torture survivors specifically (Basoglu, 1993a; Chester & Jaranson, 1994; Ramsay, Gorst-Unsworth, & Turner, 1993; Somnier & Genefke, 1986). These issues include the provision of meaningful assessment of trauma across cultures; the role of premorbid personality in survival and recovery; survivors' coping styles; recovery of and work with traumatic memory; cumulative trauma; complex PTSD or continuous traumatic stress syndrome; and the need to reclaim hope and meaning in a world characterized by pain, cruelty, and suffering. Because of space limitations, only two of these key issues, recovery of traumatic memory and cumulative trauma, are discussed as follows.

Traumatic Memory

Most posttraumatic therapies involve working with the trauma story using divergent techniques such as *flooding*—the practitioner, in a therapeutic setting, intensely exposes the client to the traumatic memory (Basoglu, 1993a)—to completely ignoring the content of traumatic memory and working solely with symbols and metaphors (Grove & Panzer, 1991). In addition, practitioners in Latin America have widely used the *testimony method,* a form of cognitive restructuring (Cienfuegos & Monelli, 1983).

However, some researchers have raised concerns about the need to abreact (that is, tell while accessing emotions), as well as about the veracity of past memories expressed in the context of a current life (Chester & Jaranson, 1994). Langer's (1991) comments in this regard are extremely enlightening. After reviewing several hundred testimonies of survivors of the Nazi Holocaust, Langer stated,

How credible can a reawakened memory be that tries to revive events so many decades after they occurred? I think the terminology itself is at fault here. There is no need to revive what has never died. Moreover, though slumbering memories may crave reawakening, nothing is clearer in these narratives than that Holocaust memory is an insomniac faculty, whose mental eyes have never slept. (p. xv)

The notion here is one of almost parallel lives: a current life and a Holocaust life, both of which are experienced in a nonlinear, constantly interchangeable fashion. Techniques that simply allow for telling with or without facilitating concurrent emotional reaction achieve little to enlighten "hostages to a humiliating and painful past that [a] happier future does little to curtail" (Langer, 1991, p. xi). Recovering traumatic memory, therefore, is not an end in itself but rather a therapeutic technique that must occur within the context of the entire therapy process.

Cumulative Trauma
Humanmade and other disasters have dramatically increased during the past decade, with the poorest, most disadvantaged communities suffering the greatest impact. Developing countries and U.S. communities of poverty can almost be seen as "cultures of disaster," because those communities are exposed to a multiplicity of traumatic events (DiGirodamo, 1993). When acute trauma occurs within this context, the impact can be devastating.

Indigenous people living in the Americas are an example of a population exposed to cumulative trauma. Of an estimated 12 million people who inhabited North America at the time of its "discovery" by Columbus, fewer than 270,000 remained in the early 20th century (Amnesty International, 1992). Today, although the North American Indian population stands at more than 1 million, their quality of life is inconsistent with that of other communities. The average life expectancy of American Indians is 49 years (Gunn Allen, 1989). The death rate for American Indian adolescents is twice that of youths from other racial and ethnic backgrounds, and includes death from motor vehicle injuries, suicide, as well as poor physical health (Blum & Resnick, 1992). American Indian women have a mortality rate six times higher for alcoholism, three times higher for homicide, five times higher for liver disease, and three times higher for motor vehicle accidents than women in the general U.S. population (U.S. Department of Health and Human Services, 1988).

Within this context, Amnesty International (1992) has reported on severe acute and continuous examples of human rights abuses to indigenous people in the Americas, including mass killing, extrajudicial execution, "disappearance," torture and ill treatment, arbitrary detention, and unfair trial. Treatment of acute and specific trauma must include the context of cumulative and continuous trauma to be successful. For this reason, many service providers have targeted the community as the appropriate level of intervention (Chester & Jaranson, 1994).

COUNTERTRANSFERENCE
Service providers working with survivors of extreme circumstances are vulnerable to personal reactions. These emotions of therapists toward clients during treatment are called *countertransference*. To provide competent and ethical care, therapists must recognize such reactions. Common countertransference reactions include sadness, depression, anger, irritability, overidentification, and intolerance of clients who have less stressful lives (Comas-Diaz & Padilla, 1990; Fishman, 1991). Danieli (1988) has identified 49 countertransference themes for therapists serving Nazi Holocaust survivors, including rage, bystander guilt, and privileged voyeurism.

In addition, therapists or counselors often become aware of their own sense of personal vulnerability, as well as a sense of failure with the ability of Western medicine or other therapies to cope with such overwhelming circumstances (Kinzie & Boehnlein, 1993). Ultimately, the terminal point of countertransference is burnout in both the personal and professional realms of life.

CONCLUSION
Healing professionals need more than clinical expertise to work effectively with survivors of extreme stress; they must have a deep sense of connectedness and a personal organizing philosophy. The Hopi Foundation's Center for the Resolution and Prevention of Violence (Tucson, AZ) uses the Hopi concept *qa tutsawinvu* (safety and centeredness) (E. Sekaquaptewa, personal communication, April 1994). This concept involves a state of being in which a person is not intimidated by fear from any source. The person will live a good life in any environment and will be awed by what life has to offer because he or she is not intimidated.

By addressing the person in context, social workers are in a unique position to actively create an environment both societally and within the treatment setting in which clients can be brought to the point of qa tutsawinvu. Such a guiding principle or personal philosophy can be helpful in maintaining balance when confronted by the reality of violence and extreme trauma.

REFERENCES
Amnesty International. (1992). *Human rights violations against indigenous peoples.* New York: John D. Lucas.

Amnesty International, USA. (1990). *Reasonable fear: Human rights and United States refugee policy.* New York: Author.

Aron, A., Corne, S., Fursland, A., & Zelwer, B. (1991). The gender-specific terror of El Salvador and Guatemala. *Women's Studies International Forum, 14*(1/2), 37–47.

Basoglu, M. (1993a). Behavioral and cognitive approach in the treatment of torture-related psychological problems. In M. Basoglu (Ed.), *Torture and its consequences: Current treatment approaches* (pp. 402–424). Cambridge, England: Cambridge University Press.

Basoglu, M. (1993b). The prevention of torture and the care of survivors: An integrated approach. *Journal of the American Medical Association, 270*(5), 606–611.

Blum, R., & Resnick, M. D. (1992). *The state of Native American youth health.* Minneapolis: Division of General Pediatrics and Adolescent Health, University of Minnesota Hospital and Clinic.

California Wellness Foundation. (1993, June). *Executive Summary: Violence prevention in California.* Woodland Hills, CA: Author.

Cathcart, L. M., Berger, P., & Knazan, B. (1979). Medical examination of torture victims applying for refugee status. *Canadian Medical Association Journal, 121,* 179–184.

Chester, B. (1990). Because mercy has a human heart: Centers for victims of torture. In P. Suedfeld (Ed.), *Psychology and torture* (pp. 165–184). New York: Hemisphere.

Chester, B. (1994). That which does not destroy me: Treating survivors of political torture. In J. F. Sommer & M. B. Williams (Eds.), *The handbook of posttraumatic therapy* (pp. 240–251). Westport, CT: Greenwood Press.

Chester, B., & Holtan, N. (1992). Working with refugee survivors of torture. *Western Journal of Medicine, 157*(3), 301–304.

Chester, B., & Jaranson, J. J. (1994). The context of survival and destruction: Conducting psychotherapy with survivors of torture. *Clinical Quarterly, 4*(1), 17–19.

Christiansen, J., & Juhl, E. (Eds.). (1990). Medical aspects of torture. *Danish Medical Bulletin, 37,* 1–88.

Cienfuegos, A. J., & Monelli, C. (1983). The testimony of political repression as a therapeutic instrument. *American Journal of Orthopsychiatry, 53*(1), 43–51.

Comas-Diaz, L., & Padilla, A. (1990). Countertransference in working with victims of political repression. *American Journal of Orthopsychiatry, 60,* 124–134.

Danieli, Y. (1988). On confronting the Holocaust: Psychological reactions to victim/survivors and their children. In *Remembering for the future. Theme II: The impact of the Holocaust on the contemporary world* (pp. 1257–1271). Tarrytown, NY: Pergamon Press.

Davidson, R. T., & Fairbank, J. A. (1993). The epidemiology of posttraumatic stress disorder. In R. T. Davidson & E. B. Foa (Eds.), *Posttraumatic stress disorder: DSM-IV and beyond* (pp. 147–169). Washington, DC: American Psychiatric Press.

Davidson, R. T., & Foa, E. B. (Eds.). (1993). *Posttraumatic stress disorder: DSM-IV and beyond.* Washington, DC: American Psychiatric Press.

DiGirodamo. (1993, June). *World Health Organization statistics regarding trauma.* Paper presented at the meeting on Ethnocultural Aspects of Posttraumatic Stress Disorders: Issues, Research, and Directions, Honolulu.

Estes, C. P. (1992). *Women who run with the wolves.* New York: Ballantine Books.

Fishman, Y. (1991). Interacting with trauma: Clinicians' responses to treating psychological aftereffects of political repression. *American Journal of Orthopsychiatry, 61,* 179–185.

Garcia-Peltoniemi, R. E. (1991). Clinical manifestations of psychopathology. In *Mental health services for refugees* (DHHS Publication No. APM 91-1824). Washington, DC: U.S. Government Printing Office.

Goldfield, A., Mollica, R. F., Pesavento, B. H., & Farone, S. V. (1988). The physical and psychological sequelae of torture. *Journal of the American Medical Association, 259*(18), 2725–2729.

Grove, D. J., & Panzer, B. I. (1991). *Resolving traumatic memories.* New York: Irvington.

Gunn Allen, P. (Ed.). (1989). *Spider Women's granddaughters: Traditional tales and contemporary writing by Native American women.* Boston: Beacon Press.

Heise, L., Pitanguy, J., & Germain, A. (1993). *Violence against women: The hidden health burden.* Washington, DC: The World Bank.

Kemp, A., Rawlings, E., & Greene, B. (1991). Posttraumatic stress disorder (PTSD) in battered women: A shelter sample. *Journal of Traumatic Stress, 4*(1), 137–148.

Kinzie, J. D., & Boehnlein, J. K. (1993). Psychotherapy with the victims of massive violence: Countertransference and ethical issues. *American Journal of Psychotherapy, 47*(1), 185–198.

Kismaric, C. (Ed.). (1989). *Forced out: The agony of the refugee in our time.* New York: Random House.

Krystal, H. (1988). *Integration and self-healing: Affect, trauma, alexithymia.* Hillsdale, NJ: Analytic Press.

Kulka, R. A., Schlenger, W. E., Fairbank, J. A., Hough, R. L., Jordan, B. K., Marmar, C. R., & Weiss, D. S. (1990). *Trauma and the Vietnam War generation.* New York: Brunner/Mazel.

Langer, L. (1991). *Holocaust testimonies: The ruins of memory.* New Haven, CT: Yale University Press.

Lifton, R. J. (1968). *Death in life—The survivors of Hiroshima.* London: Weidenfeld & Nicholson.

Lindemann, E. (1944). Symptomatology and management of acute grief. *American Journal of Psychiatry, 101,* 141–148.

Lira, E., Becker, D., & Castillo, M. I. (1988). *Psychotherapy with victims of political repression in Chile: A therapeutic and political challenge.* Paper presented at the meeting of the Latin American Institute of Mental Health and Human Rights, Santiago, Chile.

Mercy, J. A., Rosenberg, M. I., Powell, K. E., Broome, C. V., & Roper, W. L. (1993). Public health policy for preventing violence. *Health Affairs, 12*(4), 7–26.

Mollica, R. F. (1988). The trauma story: The psychiatric care of refugee survivors of violence and torture. In F. M. Ochberg (Ed.), *Posttraumatic therapy and victims of violence* (pp. 295–314). New York: Brunner/Mazel.

Mollica, R. F., & Caspri-Yavin, Y. (1993). Overview: The assessment and diagnosis of torture events and symptoms. In M. Basoglu (Ed.), *Torture and its consequences: Current treatment approaches* (pp. 253–273). Cambridge, England: Cambridge University Press.

Norris, F. (1992). Epidemiology of trauma, frequency and impact of different potentially traumatic events on different demographic groups. *Journal of Consulting and Clinical Psychology, 60,* 409–418.

Ochberg, F. M. (Ed.). (1988). *Posttraumatic therapy and victims of violence.* New York: Brunner/Mazel.

Ramsay, R., Gorst-Unsworth, C., & Turner, S. (1993). Psychiatric morbidity in survivors of organized state violence including torture: A retrospective series. *British Journal of Psychiatry, 162,* 55–59.

Randall, G. R., & Lutz, E. L. (1991). *Serving survivors of torture.* Washington, DC: American Association for the Advancement of Science.

Scarry, E. (1985). *The body in pain.* New York: Oxford University Press.

Scalpobersky, P. (1989). Torture as the pervision of a healing relationship. In J. Gruschow & K. Hannibal (Eds.), *Health services for the treatment of torture and trauma survivors* (pp. 51–72). Washington, DC: American Association for the Advancement of Science.

Shore, J. H., Tatum, E. L., & Vollmer, W. M. (1986). The Mount St. Helens stress response syndrome. In J. H. Shore (Ed.), *Disaster stress studies: New methods and findings* (pp. 79–97). Washington, DC: American Psychiatric Press.

Skylv, G. K. (1992, June). *Concepts of guilt and shame in the field of psychological anthropology.* Paper presented at the meeting of the Section of Psychiatry of the Royal Society of Medicine, London.

Somnier, F., & Genefke, I. K. (1986). Psychotherapy for victims of torture. *British Journal of Psychiatry, 149,* 323–329.

Somnier, F., Vesti, P., Kastrup, M., & Genefke, I. K. (1993). Psychosocial consequences of torture: Current knowledge and evidence. In M. Basoglu (Ed.), *Torture and its consequences: Current treatment approaches* (pp. 56–71). Cambridge, England: Cambridge University Press.

Stiglmayer, A. (Ed.). (1994). *Mass rape: The war against women in Bosnia-Herzegovina.* Lincoln: University of Nebraska Press.

Tatum, E. L., Vollmer, W. M., & Shore, J. H. (1986). Relationship of perception and mediating variables to the psychiatric consequences of disaster. In J. H. Shore (Ed.), *Disaster stress studies: New methods and findings* (pp. 101–121). Washington, DC: American Psychiatric Press.

Titchener, J. L., & Kapp, F. T. (1976). Family and character change at Buffalo Creek. *American Journal of Psychiatry, 133,* 295–316.

Toole, M. J., & Waldman, R. J. (1993). Refugees and displaced persons: War, hunger, and public health. *Journal of the American Medical Association, 270*(5), 600–605.

U.S. Department of Health and Human Services, Indian Health Service. (1988). *Chart series book.* Washington, DC: U.S. Government Printing Office.

World Medical Association. (1975). *Declaration of Tokyo.* Tokyo, Japan: Author.

FURTHER READING

Figley, C. R. (Ed.). (1985). *Trauma and its wake.* New York: Brunner/Mazel.

Stover, E., & Nightingale, E. O. (1985). *The breaking of bodies and minds: Torture, psychiatric abuse and the health professions.* New York: W. H. Freeman.

Terr, L. (1994). *Unchained memories.* New York: Basic Books.

Weschler, L. (1990). *A miracle, a universe: Settling accounts with torturers.* New York: Pantheon.

Wilson, J. P., Harel, Z., & Kahana, B. (Eds.). (1988). *Human adaptation to extreme stress from the Holocaust to Vietnam.* New York: Plenum.

Barbara Chester, PhD, is director, The Hopi Foundation Center for the Prevention and Resolution of Violence, P. O. Box 65720, Tucson, AZ 85728.

For further information see

Civil Rights; Direct Practice Overview; Ethnic-Sensitive Practice; Human Rights; International Social Welfare: Organizations and Activities; Mental Health Overview; Peace and Social Justice; Veterans and Veterans Services; Victim Services and Victim/Witness Assistance Programs; Violence Overview.

Key Words

post-traumatic stress disorder	trauma
torture	victimization

Violence Overview
Mark W. Fraser

Each year more than 20,000 Americans are murdered. Of these murders, approximately 4,000 involve children or teenagers (Maguire & Pastore, 1994). The American rate of about 9 murders per 100,000 people is three to four times the Canadian rate and nearly double that of Spain, which has the second highest murder rate in the industrialized world (Roth, 1994b). In addition, the United States leads other developed countries in nonfatal violent victimizations, including rapes, robberies, and aggravated assaults. These data do not include many acts of violence that occur in the privacy of the home and among people who know each other. Although no single source fully describes the extent of violence, it is clear that, directly or indirectly, violence touches many American households. America has an undeclared civil war.

DEFINITION OF VIOLENCE

Violence is difficult to define. It is not constrained to street crimes, domestic abuse, and school-related offenses. It includes child abuse, abuse of the elderly, hate crimes, suicide, terrorism, torture, and war. Both individuals and institutions (such as governments and businesses) can engage in acts that cause significant harm.

The central and defining feature of violence is that it produces injury. Historically, violence was defined as a purposeful act that "threatens, attempts, or actually inflicts physical harm" (Reiss & Roth, 1993, p. 35). However, this definition implies intent on the part of a perpetrator, and it eliminates self-destructive behaviors that may be violent in nature. The National Center for Injury Prevention and Control recently adopted a more inclusive definition: Violence is the "threatened or actual use of physical force against oneself or an individual or group that either results, or is likely to result, in injury or death" (Christoffel, 1994, p. 540). This definition does not exclude suicide; it also defines as violent the behavior of a person who consumes several drinks, chooses to drive, and has an accident that injures others. Regardless of the legal charges that might be brought or personal claims that the injury was unintentional, this act may be viewed as violent because it involves a sequence of events in which the drinker causes harm to others.

To date, no widely accepted definition of violence exists. The lack of consensus on a definition of violence reflects the fact that only recently have scholars, policymakers, advocates, and others addressed it as a serious problem. As a consequence, workers in the field of violence must take care to articulate project- or service-related definitions so as to clearly identify targeted behaviors, offenses, and populations.

It is difficult to define violence because there are different kinds of violence, and each may have different causes. Examples of types of violence are presented below.

Violent Crime

Although public fear of being victimized in a violent crime such as rape, robbery, or street assault has increased since the mid-1980s (Maguire & Pastore, 1994), overall crime rates have not increased substantially. However, the stability of aggregate crime statistics belies significant increases in violent crime victimization of teenagers. Although teenagers account for only 10 percent of the population, nearly 25 percent of all violent crimes involve a teenage victim (Moone, 1994). Each year, about 67 of every 1,000 teenagers are victims of violent crimes, compared to 26 of every 1,000 persons over the age of 20 (Allen-Hagen & Sickmund, 1993). The rate for 12- to 15-year-old victims was the highest ever in 1992, a 50 percent increase from 1980 (Bureau of Justice Statistics, 1994b). Moreover, the victimization rate for those between the ages of 16 and 19 peaked in 1991 (Bureau of Justice Statistics, 1994b). In contrast, rates of violent victimization have slightly declined or remained stable for other age groups.

African American children, youths, and young adults are more affected by violent crime than other groups. In 1992 the incidence of violent crime involving African Americans was the highest ever recorded (Bureau of Justice Statistics, 1994b). Black teenage males had the highest risk of victimization (113 per 1,000), followed by black teenage females (94 per 1,000), white teenage males (90 per 1,000), young adult black males (80 per 1,000), young adult black females (57 per 1,000), white teenage females (55 per 1,000), young adult white males (52 per 1,000), young adult white females (38 per 1,000), adult black males (35 per 1,000), and all others (Zawitz et al., 1993). Although these and related differences for other racial and ethnic groups are massive (and pose major policy challenges), they appear to be largely explained by social and economic factors such as poverty, unemployment, and exposure to drug subcultures (DuRant, Cadenhead, Pendergrast, Slavens, & Linder, 1994; Huizinga, Loeber, & Thornberry, 1994; Peoples & Loeber, in press).

The stability of overall crime rates also masks important changes affecting women. Although victimization rates are higher for men, they have fallen since 1973. In contrast, they have remained relatively stable for women (Zawitz et al., 1993). Men are more likely to be victimized by a stranger (44 percent of all male victimizations) or an acquaintance (50 percent) than by an intimate such as a spouse or relative (5 percent), whereas women are just as likely to be victimized by intimates (33 percent of all female victimizations) as by strangers (31 percent) or acquaintances (35 percent; Bachman, 1994). About two-thirds of all acts of violence against women were committed by an acquaintance or intimate. Women at greater risk of violence tend to be African American or Hispanic, under age 25, residents of central city areas, single, and to have low education and income levels (Bachman, 1994).

The consequences of violent crime pose serious health and economic problems. Approximately one in three victims of robbery and assault is injured. Over the past 20 years, the percentage of all victims of violence with minor injuries has increased, whereas those with major injuries has remained about the same. Approximately 2 million people are injured annually as a result of violent crime (Zawitz et al., 1993). Compared to younger victims of violence, violent crime victims over age 65 are nearly twice as likely to experience serious injury (Bureau of Justice Statistics, 1994a). Injuries related to violent crime lead to an average of nine days in the hospital, for a total of more than 700,000 hospital days annually. This is the equivalent of 30 percent of the hospital days for all injuries caused by traffic accidents. Cash losses and medical expenses from violent crime exceeded $1 billion in 1991; this does not include lost wages and the emotional toll of injuries (Zawitz et al., 1993).

Family Violence
Family violence is difficult to measure; it occurs within the privacy of the home, and victims are often reluctant to report incidents because they fear reprisal. Family violence includes rape, robbery, and assault among intimates such as spouses, ex-spouses, domestic partners, and friends. According to National Crime Victimization Survey data, females are three times more likely than males to be victims of family violence (Zawitz et al., 1993). Family violence holds greater potential for injury than other kinds of violence. Compared to victims of crimes committed by

strangers, victims of family violence are twice as likely to be injured (Bachman, 1994).

School Violence
Today, schools face problems that range from schoolyard bullying to drug trafficking, gang conflict, and rape (Wheeler & Baron, 1994). School violence involves attacks on students, teachers, and staff on school grounds. Overall, approximately 2 percent of students were victims of violence in 1992, but rates are higher in urban schools where gangs exist and illegal drugs are available. For youths age 12 to 15, 37 percent of all violent victimizations occurred at school or en route to or from school (Allen-Hagen & Sickmund, 1993). No consistent relationship has been demonstrated between school violence and the victim's race/ethnicity or income (Zawitz et al., 1993).

RISK FACTORS
The likelihood of a violent event is based on the presence or absence of various risk and protective factors that condition the use of physical aggression. Risk factors increase the odds of violence, whereas protective factors decrease it (Stouthamer-Loeber et al., 1993).[1] From this perspective, the probability of a violent act is determined by predisposing, situational, and activating risk and protective factors in social settings.

No social conditions and events lead inescapably to violence (Lore & Schultz, 1993; Roth, 1994b). Violence is a chance occurrence, but in some circumstances, the chances can be very high, depending on the number and nature of risk factors. If risks can be lowered or counterbalanced by strengthening protective factors, the potential for violence should go down. Intervention must be focused on and driven by strategies to alter risk factors.

Proximity to Potential Violence
Findings from the National Panel on the Understanding and Control of Violent Behavior (Reiss & Roth, 1993) suggest that risk factors for interpersonal violence (excluding institutional violence such as the dumping of highly toxic wastes, and collective acts such as terrorism or war) may be cross-classified along two dimensions. The first,

[1] In this entry, a protective factor is defined simply as the opposite of a risk factor. However, some studies suggest that protective factors may exert disproportionate or nonlinear influences on violence (that is, they operate somewhat differently from risk factors). Some life events (such as being first born or living in a neighborhood where there is strong traditional leadership) and personal attributes (such as shyness) may actually suppress the effects of exposure to high risk (see, for example, Farrington, Gallagher, Morley, St. Leger, & West, 1988; Werner & Smith, 1982).

across the top of Table 1, is the immediacy of a risk factor to an event that has the potential for violence. Social conditions that affect people at an ecological level and that "predispose" people to aggression fall in the first and most distal level of proximity. These factors are rarely contingent on the current circumstance and usually reflect long-standing discriminatory public policies or practices. They are often related to the unequal distribution of resources and opportunities by race, ethnicity, gender, class, sexual preference, religion, language, and other factors. They may heighten

TABLE 1
Risk and Protective Factors Associated with Violence

	Proximity to Violent Events		
Level	Predisposing Risks (Background Factors)	Situational Risks (Event-related Factors)	Activating Risks (Initiating Factors)
Social			
Environmental and community conditions	Poverty Low economic opportunity Decline of traditional leadership Growth of oppositional cultures and negative leadership Decline of social and community resources Exposure to violence through media	Physical structure (available cover) Routine activities (predictable) Access: weapons, emergency medical services	Catalytic social events
Interpersonal	Organized crime recruitment Illegal market recruitment Gang recruitment Family disorganization Social disorganization (low informal social control)	Proximity of responsible monitors Participants' social relationships Bystanders' activities or actions Temporary communication impairments Weapons (carrying, displaying)	Participants' communication exchange (inflammatory language, problem-solving skills, etc.)
Individual			
Psychosocial	Temperament (for example, risk taking) Learned social responses Perceptions of rewards/penalties for violence Hostile attributions Violent sexual preferences Poor information-processing skills Self-identification in social hierarchy (low status) Exposure to violence in vivo	Accumulated emotion Alcohol/drug consumption Sexual arousal Premeditation	Impulse Opportunity recognition
Biological	Neurobehavioral[a] "traits" Genetically mediated traits Chronic use of psychoactive substances or exposure to neurotoxins (for example, lead)	Transient neurobehavioral[a] "states" Acute effects of psychoactive substances	Sensory signal processing errors

Sources: Adapted from Farrington, D. P., Loeber, R., Elliott, D. S., Hawkins, J. D., Kandel, D. B., Klein, M. W., McCord, J., Rowe, D. C., & Tremblay, R. E. (1993). Advancing knowledge about the onset of delinquency and crime. In B. B. Lahey & A. E. Kazdin (Eds.), *Advances in clinical child psychology* (Vol. 13, pp. 283–342). New York: Plenum Press; Huesmann, L. R., & Miller, L. S. (1994). Long-term effects of repeated exposure to media violence in childhood. In L. R. Huesmann (Ed.), *Aggressive behavior: Current perspectives* (pp. 153–186). New York: Plenum Press; Reiss, A. J., Jr., & Roth, J. A. (Eds.). (1993). *Understanding and preventing violence.* Washington, DC: National Academy Press; Roth, J. A. (1994, February). Understanding and preventing violence. In *National Institute of Justice research in brief* (NCJ 145645). Washington, DC: U.S. Government Printing Office.
[a]Includes neuroanatomical, neurophysiological, neurochemical, and neuroendocrine. "Traits" describe capacity as determined by status at birth, trauma, and aging processes such as puberty. "States" describe temporary conditions associated with emotions, external stressors, etc.

anger in an entire neighborhood, change broad patterns of interaction and dispute resolution, or reduce access to legitimate means for achieving economic and educational goals (Bernard, 1990; Wilson, 1987).

Closer in time to violent events are situation-related conditions that provide opportunity or change the odds of apprehension. These include such factors as the availability of cover for an assailant and the nearness of police, teachers, parents, neighbors, or others who might intervene to stop a confrontation. Most proximal to an event are "activating" circumstances that often determine the extent of injurious behavior on the part of perpetrators. These include catalytic triggering events such as the 1993 Rodney King verdict in Los Angeles (in which four policemen were acquitted in the brutal beating of an unarmed black driver) or the degree to which participants control arousal at the moment of contact. Proximity, then, is used to classify research findings into predisposing, situational, and activating risk factors.

Predisposing Factors

The second way to classify risk factors is by unit of explanation. At the social level, both macrosocial environmental or community conditions and interpersonal factors affect the odds of violence. By proximity, these range from the predisposing effects of poverty and the decline of traditional leadership in neighborhoods to the activating microsocial effects of poor communication at the moment of contact between an assailant and a potential victim. At the individual level, risk factors can be classified as psychosocial or biological. Cross-classified by proximity to a violent event, they range from predisposing factors such as a risk-taking temperament or the perception that the rewards for violence outweigh the penalties, to (at the biological level) the use of psychoactive substances that impede normal cognitive processes (see also, Farrington et al., 1993; Martin, 1993).

The risk factors shown in Table 1 interact. That is, they have a multiplicative effect on the probability that violence will result from a particular set of circumstances (Rutter, 1979; Yoshikawa, 1994). Because combined risks accumulate in influence at a nonlinear rate, intervention that affects four factors may have a probability of success that is four, five, or even six times higher than intervention that focuses on two factors. Thus, comprehensive intervention that addresses comparatively more risk factors has a multiplicatively greater likelihood of success than intervention that focuses on a few risks.

CAN VIOLENCE BE PREVENTED OR CONTROLLED?

Violence is not inevitable in high-risk circumstances. Most risk factors can be changed. However, there is no single solution to the problem of violence. Changing some risk factors may involve individual-level intervention, such as cognitive behavioral training in processing social information, solving social problems, or resolving conflicts with peers. Changing other risk factors may require collective community action to strengthen protective factors. A mix of strategies tailored to the needs and risks that characterize the unique social and cultural conditions of different communities must be developed to reduce levels of violence.

Comprehensive approaches that address predisposing, situational, and activating risks are promising and warrant further investigation. No single strategy is likely to be effective in reducing community violence, and multiple activities should be considered. Each activity should be defined by identification of target risk factors, groups, and settings (National Center for Injury Prevention and Control, 1993).

Targeted Risk Factors

Targeted risk factors are the correlates and potential causes of the type of violence—street, family, school, play ground or area, gang, and so on—selected as the objective for community action. This entry briefly reviews recent research on some of the risk factors. Because risk and protective factors may differ across communities, each community should develop a framework for understanding and assessing its own needs as a preliminary step in developing strategies to control or prevent violence.

Target Groups

The target group is the population at risk. For different risk factors, different target groups will be identified. For environmental or community level risk factors, the entire population of youths may be at risk and should be designated as the target group. For other risk factors, populations within the larger population might be identified. For example, children on the verge of dropping out of school, or children who have witnessed violence in their homes or on their streets (see, for example, DuRant et al., 1994) might be targeted for special assistance. Alternatively, drug dealers and their customers at crack houses might be identified as the target group for a community activity designed to disrupt the structure of illegal drug markets.

Target Settings

Intervention must take place in the settings where the target group lives, works, learns, and plays. Usually, multiple settings will be identified, including homes, schools, churches, neighborhood centers, play grounds, day care centers, health care clinics, mental health storefronts, street corners, back alleys, social services offices, and detention or drug treatment centers. The setting should provide the target group with access to program activities, and it should be appropriate for the targeted activity. Compared to many office-centered activities, risk-focused prevention activities should be delivered where the target group lives. Selection of settings that require the generalization of knowledge or behaviors from one setting to another leaves open the possibility that unanticipated factors will complicate or prevent the transfer of program effects. Where appropriate and safe, settings should be *in vivo* to reduce the problem of generalization of the intervention effect across sites.

TYPES OF INTERVENTION

Three kinds of intervention activities are typically considered: (1) education and skills training; (2) legal and regulatory change in community law enforcement or related policies and practices; and (3) environmental modification (National Center for Injury Prevention and Control, 1993).

Education and Skills Training

Educational activities increase knowledge about risk-related subjects, teach skills for managing more successfully in the environment, and provide opportunities for practicing skills under supportive conditions. Educational strategies that have shown promise include training in conflict resolution, processing social information (including identifying attributions of intent, problem-solving, decision-making, and communication), parenting, peer mediation, and anger management (Crick & Dodge, 1994; Jenson & Howard, 1990; Kazdin, 1987; Kazdin, Siegel, & Bass, 1992; Patterson, Dishion, & Chamberlain, in press). In addition, educational strategies include, but are not limited to, programs for well-baby care, preschool readiness and early grade tutoring, cross-age tutoring, dealing with bullies, watching TV critically, and firearm safety (National Center for Injury Prevention and Control, 1993; Olweus, 1994; Roth, 1994b). In the same vein, the long-term effects of educational programs such as Head Start and other developmental enrichment activities appear to promote early academic achievement and reduce peer rejection, both of

which are predisposing risks for subsequent delinquency and violence (Zigler & Styfco, 1994). At the situation level, training to resist peer pressure to use psychoactive substances may affect levels of violence, because violence is often associated with the abuse of alcohol and drugs (De La Rosa, Lambert, & Gropper, 1990; Martin, 1993; Roth, 1994a).

Legal, Regulatory, and Law Enforcement Innovation

Legal and regulatory innovation, including changes in the enforcement of existing laws, can reduce violence and violence-related injuries. Activities focus on increasing both the effectiveness of law enforcement officers, such as police and probation officers, and on increasing collaboration among traditional community leaders in business, churches, and community organizations. Strategies of this type include enforcing limits on carrying and displaying firearms in public, ensuring that local gun dealers do not sell weapons illegally, regulating the sale of alcohol (for example, passage of keg-labeling laws to hold purchasers responsible if they supply kegs of beer to underage youths), establishing neighborhood watch-and-report programs, and ensuring that schools prohibit students from bringing weapons onto school grounds.

Some communities have made creative changes in the deployment of law enforcement resources by coupling community-oriented policing programs with specialized social and health services projects. Fulfilling a traditional peace-keeping function, officers in such programs walk a regular beat and make a point of talking with shopkeepers and residents. In Dade County, Florida, for example, neighborhood resource teams (consisting of a police officer, a public housing representative, a public health nurse, and two social workers) were formed to provide both family-centered and community-policing interventions in West Perrine, a high-crime community in metropolitan Miami (Cronin, 1994). Integrated services and partnerships between police, social service, and business leaders build economic opportunities, neighborhood cohesion, and solidarity—all protective factors—by being responsive to local law enforcement priorities and strengthening traditional leadership across the collective resources of a community (Bureau of Justice Assistance, 1994; Spergel, 1990).

Environmental Modification

Environmental modification involves making changes in the opportunity structures, service systems, and physical resources of a community.

The environment should afford community residents the means to achieve conventional educational and economic goals. For children and youths, it should provide opportunities to live in stable, safe families or in familylike settings. For teenagers and young adults, it should provide mentors and opportunities for success in conventional activities. Programs that affect opportunities, services, and resources in the environment can be classified as family, school, and community centered.

Families. At the family level, environmental modification often focuses on the concrete needs and skills of family members. Skills training is viewed as important because skills are thought to enable family members to change negative patterns of family interaction and to obtain resources within the environment. This has been one of the theoretical tenets of family preservation. Within family preservation, multisystemic family preservation programs appear quite promising in strengthening families and preventing delinquency (Henggeler, Melton, & Smith, 1992; Henggeler, Melton, Smith, Schoenwald & Hanley, 1993; Henggeler et al., 1986; Henggeler & Schoenwald, 1993; Henggeler, Smith, & Schoenwald, 1994). These programs address families' concrete needs and assist them to develop parenting, anger management, and problem-solving skills that are requisite for establishing safe, structured, and nurturing home environments.

Research on the outcome of family preservation efforts is mixed, however. Some studies show that programs have no effect on families (Schuerman, Rzepnicki, Littell, Chak, 1993; Yuan, McDonald, Wheeler, Struckman-Johnson, & Rivest, 1990). Other studies show that family preservation does indeed help to keep families together safely or to reunify children with their parents subsequent to an out-of-home placement (Feldman, 1991; University Associates, 1993; Walton, Fraser, Lewis, Pecora, & Walton, 1993). Given the research to date, family preservation programs that involve use of a multisystemic approach appear more likely to reduce delinquency and violent behavior.

Schools. Outside the home, school-related programs to increase opportunities for academic and occupational success have shown promise. Preschool programs designed to support children's cognitive, social, and emotional development, while meeting their nutritional needs and involving parents, pay long-term benefits in reduced delinquency and violence (Milton S. Eisenhower Foundation, 1990; Yoshikawa, 1994). In fact, Schweinhart, Barners, and Weikart (1993) recently

reported that, for every dollar spent on such programs, taxpayers save $7 in reduced grade retentions, welfare dependency, unemployment, and crime. Research on reforming classroom teaching practices appears also to produce changes in children's academic and social development that are related to risk factors (O'Donnell, Hawkins, Catalano, Abbott, & Day, 1994). Furthermore, efforts to increase conventional opportunities for youths by developing job training, apprenticeship, and mentoring programs appear promising in reducing gang participation and violence (Spergel, 1990).

Communities. Finally, environmental modification involves communitywide mobilization. At the macrolevel, this may include ensuring that decisions regarding the deployment of resources in law enforcement, child welfare, mental health, education, and juvenile justice involve local participation. More often than not, community mobilization begins by focusing on specific projects that can yield immediate, tangible successes, such as establishing gun-free zones, eliminating available cover for potential assailants, or attacking other conditions that favor violence. This can include the installation of better street lighting, making changes in the flow or traffic (reducing speed limits, installing circles or speed bumps), closing crack houses, opening storefront social and health services centers, installing phone systems with direct access to law enforcement (now available on many college and university campuses), and establishing mechanisms to monitor the environment through the use of uniforms, identification badges, or television. Such changes appear to deter violence in specific locations and, as projects around which a community may mobilize, they are an important element of a comprehensive approach to the control and prevention of violence (National Center for Injury Prevention and Control, 1993).

Conclusion

The central features of programs that are likely to reduce violence are quite simple. Successful programs mobilize a sufficiently large number of resources to systematically and concomitantly address many risk factors. They obtain the active support of private and public officials, who regularly attend neighborhood meetings and often share in leadership responsibilities. They involve many elements of the community—including young people—in defining the problem, establishing a vision, setting goals, marshaling resources, evaluating strategies, and refining activities. Drawing on local expertise and the experiences of successful projects in similar communities, they create a set of integrated strategies and activities that focus on immediate, tangible benefits. They hire qualified, committed staff and provide ongoing training to all who participate. They keep organizations and budgets simple and flexible (Cronin, 1994; National Crime Prevention Council, 1994). Finally, they never give in to intimidation and indifference.

REFERENCES

Allen-Hagen, B., & Sickmund, M. (1993, July). *Juveniles and violence: Juvenile offending and victimization* (Fact Sheet No. 3). Washington, DC: U.S. Department of Justice, Office of Juvenile Justice and Delinquency Prevention.

Bachman, R. (1994). *Violence against women* (NCJ 145325). Washington, DC: U.S. Government Printing Office.

Bernard, T. J. (1990). Angry aggression among the "truly disadvantaged." *Criminology, 28*(1), 73–96.

Bureau of Justice Assistance. (1994, August). *Business alliance: Planning for business and community partnerships* (NCJ 148657). Washington, DC: U.S. Department of Justice, Office of Justice Programs.

Bureau of Justice Statistics. (1994a, March). *Elderly crime victims* (NCJ 147186). Washington, DC: U.S. Government Printing Office.

Bureau of Justice Statistics. (1994b, April). *Violent crime* (NCJ 147486). Washington, DC: U.S. Government Printing Office.

Christoffel, K. K. (1994). Reducing violence—How do we proceed? *American Journal of Public Health, 84*(4), 539–541.

Crick, N. R., & Dodge, K. A. (1994). A review and reformulation of social information-processing mechanisms in children's social adjustment. *Psychological Bulletin, 115*(1), 74–101.

Cronin, R. C. (1994, May). *Innovative community partnerships: Working together for change* (NCJ 147483). Washington, DC: U.S. Department of Justice, Office of Juvenile Justice and Delinquency Prevention.

De La Rosa, M., Lambert, E. Y., & Gropper, B. (Eds.). (1990). *Drugs and violence: Causes, correlates, and consequences* (NIDA Research Monograph 103, DHHS Publication No. ADM 91-1721). Washington, DC: U.S. Government Printing Office.

DuRant, R. H., Cadenhead, C., Pendergrast, R. A., Slavens, G., & Linder, C. W. (1994). Factors associated with the use of violence among urban black adolescents. *American Journal of Public Health, 84*(4), 612–617.

Farrington, D. P., Gallagher, B., Morley, L., St. Leger, R. J., & West, D. J. (1988). Are there any successful men from criminogenic backgrounds? *Psychiatry, 51,* 116–130.

Farrington, D. P., Loeber, R., Elliott, D. S., Hawkins, J. D., Kandel, D. B., Klein, M. W., McCord, J., Rowe, D. C., & Tremblay, R. E. (1993). Advancing knowledge about the onset of delinquency and crime. In B. B. Lahey & A. E. Kazdin (Eds.), *Advances in clinical child psychology* (Vol. 13, pp. 283–342). New York: Plenum Press.

Feldman, L. H. (1991). *Assessing the effectiveness of family preservation services in New Jersey within an ecological context.* Newark: New Jersey Department of Human Services, Division of Youth and Family Services.

Henggeler, S. W., Melton, G. B., & Smith, L. A. (1992). Family preservation using multisystemic therapy: An effective alternative to incarcerating serious juvenile offenders. *Journal of Consulting and Clinical Psychology, 60*(6), 953–961.

Henggeler, S. W., Melton, G. B., Smith, L. A., Schoenwald, S. K., & Hanley, J. H. (1993). Family preservation using multisystemic treatment: Long-term follow-up to a clinical trial with serious juvenile offenders. *Journal of Child and Family Studies, 2*(2), 283–293.

Henggeler, S. W., Rodick, J. D., Borduin, C. M., Hanson, C. L., Watson, S. M., & Urey, J. R. (1986). Multisystemic treatment of juvenile offenders: Effects on adolescent behavior and family interactions. *Development Psychology, 22,* 132–141.

Henggeler, S. W., & Schoenwald, S. K. (1993). Multisystemic therapy with juvenile offenders: An effective family-based treatment. *Family Psychologist, 9,* 24–26.

Henggeler, S. W., Smith, B. H., & Schoenwald, S. K. (1994). Key theoretical and methodological issues in conducting treatment research in the juvenile justice system. *Journal of Clinical Child Psychology, 23,* 143–150.

Huesmann, L. R., & Miller, L. S. (1994). Long-term effects of repeated exposure to media violence in childhood. In L. R. Huesmann (Ed.), *Aggressive behavior: Current perspectives* (pp. 153–186). New York: Plenum Press.

Huizinga, D., Loeber, R., & Thornberry, T. P. (1994, March). *Urban delinquency and substance abuse: Initial findings* (NCJ 143454). Washington, DC: U.S. Department of Justice, Office of Juvenile Justice and Delinquency Prevention.

Jenson, J. M., & Howard, M. O. (1990). Skills deficits, skills training, and delinquency. *Children and Youth Services Review, 12*(4), 213–228.

Kazdin, A. E. (1987). Treatment of antisocial behavior in children: Current status and future directions. *Psychological Bulletin, 102,* 187–203.

Kazdin, A. E., Siegel, T. C., & Bass, D. (1992). Cognitive problem-solving skills training and parent management training in the treatment of antisocial behavior in children. *Journal of Consulting and Clinical Psychology, 60*(5), 733–747.

Lore, R. K., & Schultz, L. A. (1993). Control of human aggression: A comparative perspective. *American Psychologist, 48*(1), 16–25.

Maguire, K., & Pastore, A. L. (Eds.). (1994). *Sourcebook of criminal justice statistics—1993* (NCJ 148211). Washington, DC: U.S. Government Printing Office.

Martin, S. E. (Ed.). (1993). *Alcohol and interpersonal violence: Fostering multidisciplinary perspectives* (Research Monograph No. 24, NIH Publication No. 93-3496). Rockville, MD: National Institutes of Health, National Institute on Alcohol Abuse and Alcoholism.

Milton S. Eisenhower Foundation. (1990). *Youth investment and community reconstruction: Street lessons on drugs and crime for the nineties.* Washington, DC: Author.

Moone, J. (1994, June). *Juvenile victimization: 1987–1992* (Fact Sheet No. 17). Washington, DC: U.S. Department of Justice, Office of Juvenile Justice and Delinquency Prevention.

National Center for Injury Prevention and Control. (1993). *The prevention of youth violence: A framework for community action.* Atlanta: Centers for Disease Control and Prevention.

National Crime Prevention Council. (1994, August). *Community partnerships bulletin: Partnerships to prevent youth violence* (NCJ 148459). Washington, DC: U.S. Department of Justice, Bureau of Justice Assistance.

O'Donnell, J., Hawkins, J. D., Catalano, R. F., Abbott, R. D., & Day, L. E. (1994). *Preventing school failure, drug use, and delinquency among low-income children: Effects of a long-term prevention project in elementary schools.* Seattle: University of Washington, Social Development Research Group, School of Social Work.

Olweus, D. (1994). Bullying at school: Long-term outcomes for the victims and an effective school-based intervention program. In L. R. Huesmann (Ed.), *Aggressive behavior: Current perspectives* (pp. 97–130). New York: Plenum Press.

Patterson, G. R., Dishion, T. J., & Chamberlain, P. (in press). Outcomes and methodological issues relating to the treatment of antisocial children. In T. R. Giles (Ed.), *Effective psychotherapy: A handbook of comparative research.* New York: Plenum Press.

Peoples, F., & Loeber, R. (in press). Do individual factors and neighborhood context explain ethnic differences in juvenile delinquency? *Journal of Quantitative Criminology.*

Reiss, A. J., Jr., & Roth, J. A. (Eds.). (1993). *Understanding and preventing violence.* Washington, DC: National Academy Press.

Roth, J. A. (1994a, February). Psychoactive substances and violence. In *National Institute of Justice Research in brief* (NCJ 145534). Washington, DC: U.S. Government Printing Office.

Roth, J. A. (1994b, February). Understanding and preventing violence. In *National Institute of Justice Research in brief* (NCJ 145645). Washington, DC: U.S. Government Printing Office.

Rutter, M. (1979). Protective factors in children's responses to stress and disadvantage. In M. W. Kent & J. E. Rolf (Eds.), *Primary prevention of psychopathology: Vol. 3. Social competence in children* (pp. 49–74). Hanover, NH: University Press of New England.

Schuerman, J. R., Rzepnicki, T. L., Littell, J. H., & Chak, A. (1993). *Evaluation of the Illinois Family First placement prevention program* (Final report). Chicago: The University of Chicago, Chapin Hall Center for Children.

Schweinhart, I. J., Barnes, H. V., & Weikart, D. P. (1993). *Significant benefits: The High/Scope Perry Preschool Study through age 27* (Monographs of the High/Scope Educational Research Foundation, No. 10). Ypsilanti, MI: High/Scope Press.

Spergel, I. (1990). Youth gangs: Continuity and change. In N. Morris & M. Tonry (Eds.), *Crime and justice: An annual review of research* (pp. 171–275). Chicago: University of Chicago Press.

Stouthamer-Loeber, M., Loeber, R., Farrington, D. P., Zhang, Q., Van Kammen, W. B., & Maguin, E. (1993). The double edge of protective and risk factors for delinquency: Interrelations and developmental patterns. *Development and Psychopathology, 5,* 683–701.

University Associates. (1993). *Evaluation of Michigan's Families First program.* Lansing, MI: Author.

Walton, E., Fraser, M. W., Lewis, R. E., Pecora, P. J., & Walton, W. K. (1993). In-home family-focused reunification: An experimental study. *Child Welfare, 72*(5), 473–487.

Werner, E. E., & Smith, R. S. (1982). *Vulnerable but invincible.* New York: McGraw-Hill.

Wheeler, E. D., & Baron, S. A. (1994). *Violence in our schools, hospitals, and public places: A prevention and management guide.* Ventura, CA: Pathfinder Publishing of California.

Wilson, W. J. (1987). *The truly disadvantaged.* Chicago: University of Chicago Press.

Yoshikawa, H. (1994). Prevention as cumulative protection: Effects of early family support and education on chronic delinquency and its risks. *Psychological Bulletin, 115*(1), 28–54.

Yuan, Y. T., McDonald, W. R., Wheeler, C. E., Struckman-Johnson, D., & Rivest, M. (1990). *Evaluation of AB1562 in-home care demonstration projects: Volume 1. Final report.* Sacramento, CA: Walter R. McDonald & Associates.

Zawitz, M. W., Klaus, P. A., Bachman, R., Bastian, L. D., DeBerry, M. M., Jr., Rand, M. R., & Taylor, B. M. (1993, October). *Highlights from 20 years of surveying crime victims: The national crime victimization survey, 1973–92* (NCJ 144525). Washington, DC: U.S. Government Printing Office.

Zigler, E., & Styfco, S. J. (1994). Head Start: Criticisms in a constructive context. *American Psychologist, 49*(2), 127–132.

FURTHER READING

Spergel, I. A. (1995). *The youth gang problem: A community approach.* New York: Oxford University Press.

Mark W. Fraser, PhD, is Tate Professor for Children in Need, School of Social Work, University of North Carolina at Chapel Hill, 223 East Franklin Street, CB 3550, Chapel Hill, NC 27599.

For further information see

Adolescence Overview; Adult Corrections; Alcohol Abuse; Child Abuse and Neglect Overview; Childhood; Community-Based Corrections; Community Needs Assessment; Conflict Resolution; Criminal Behavior Overview; Domestic Violence; Drug Abuse; Elder Abuse; Environmental Health: Race and Socioeconomic Factors; Families Overview; Family Preservation and Home-Based Services; Gang Violence; Homicide; Juvenile Corrections; Peace and Social Justice; Poverty; Rehabilitation of Criminal Offenders; Runaways and Homeless Youths; Sexual Assault; Social Planning; Social Welfare Policy; Social Worker and Agency Safety; Victim Services and Victim/Witness Assistance Programs.

Key Words	
community practice	risk factors
crime	violence
delinquency	

Violence against Social Workers

See Social Worker and Agency Safety

Visual Impairment and Blindness
Adrienne Asch

A December 26, 1994, story on National Public Radio's (NPR's) "All Things Considered" vividly captured the prevailing images of blindness. The story described a 53-year-old Mexican immigrant to the United States whose work as an accordionist and singer in the New York City subways "amazes and entertains even the most cynical riders." According to the NPR reporter, "What made this so incredible was that the musician was blind. But there he was, moving slowly through the swaying and speeding car, never missing a beat in the music, never losing his balance." She reported that nickels, dimes, quarters, and dollar bills began "to fill the white plastic cup taped to his accordion." The reporter was astonished that he came from Mexico City to New York "all alone" and that "he lives in one of the poorest, highest crime areas of New York City but . . . has never been robbed or assaulted; on the contrary, strangers help him up and down the subway stairs; his neighbors . . . help him to run his errands." She closed the program by saying that the man "must have an angel looking over him."

Whereas the reporter was astonished, the musician himself was matter-of-fact. To her queries about coming from Mexico City to New York alone, he said "Yes, I was scared when I first came to New York, but now that I know my way around, I'm not afraid anymore." As to how he kept his balance in the moving subway when the reporter lost her's, he replied, "That's what you call practice." And in summing up his life, he explained, "I'm happy because I have everything I need, except that I'm blind, but that doesn't count any more. It did at the beginning, but I've been this way 33 years." And he countered the reporter's idea of a special angel by saying, "Oh I'm sure of that, not only an angel, but there's also God who looks over me and everyone else."

This story provides important clues to images and realities about visual impairment and blindness and suggests the sharply contrasting perceptions of a newcomer to blindness and of someone who has learned to live as a person with a visual impairment.

Like most people who rely on their vision, the reporter was astonished that the blind musician could make his way in the world safely and competently without it and concluded that he must have been protected by kind strangers, neighbors, and a special guardian angel. Such beliefs are not idiosyncratic, as studies of people's attitudes toward blindness and other disabilities (Makas, 1988; Siller, Chipman, Ferguson, & Vann, 1967; Siller, Ferguson, Vann, & Holland, 1967) have found and by the fact that NPR deemed the story newsworthy. Thus, although a 1991 survey by Louis Harris and Associates reported that blindness is a "more accepted" disability than is mental illness and that 47 percent of the survey population considered themselves "very comfortable" when meeting a blind person, many people equate blindness with helplessness. As Asch and Mudrick ("Disability," volume 1) explain about attitudes toward disabilities in general, people assume that life with a long-term condition, such as impaired vision, is as stressful, disorganizing, and difficult as the crisis of traumatic injury or acute illness. They imagine that if it is difficult for them to manage their lives with all their senses, then surely someone without sight would have even more trouble. Of course, the image of the blind man as a beggar, musician, or both goes back at least to the Old Testament and further enshrines the notion that those who lack vision must depend on and can make little or no positive contribution to others.

Fortunately, the facts and possibilities of life for people who are blind differ markedly from these myths. After training in managing as a blind person, and when not barred by fears of others, blind people study, hold jobs, raise families, go to restaurants, and participate in typical life roles and activities. Because blindness and visual impairment are relatively rare, because some visually impaired people may also have other social and health problems that isolate them, and because blind people have faced past and continuing patterns of discrimination, social workers may have had little contact with people who are blind and may imagine that a person's blindness precludes functioning competently in the world. Many of those with impaired vision are also over the retirement age, are new at dealing with their sight loss, and are experiencing other health problems (Ainlay, 1988). They may indeed appear frail, weak, or in need of help, but their difficulties may stem from lack of training in dealing with blindness or from these other health problems and not from blindness itself. This entry provides information on the visually impaired and blind population of the United States today, describes legislation and services of special relevance to this population, considers the significance of visual impairment at different life stages, and concludes with thoughts on the role of the social work profession in working with clients and colleagues who have visual impairments.

As will be discussed here, many people have some sort or degree of visual impairment, but if they can rely on their vision to perform tasks of daily living, reading, writing, and traveling safely, they do not have visual impairments that cause them or others to regard them as having particular problems or as requiring special services or adaptations. Thus, although some of those who have visual problems may benefit from a more accommodating environment, such as larger print on street signs or brighter lighting in buildings, they are not the focus of this entry because they do not define themselves and are not defined by others as having problems related to their vision that require services or alternative means of functioning. In fact, fewer than one-quarter of the visually impaired population are unable to see at all and would be described as totally blind (Kahn & Moorhead, 1973; personal communication with C. Kirchner, American Foundation for the Blind, 1994); the rest have some vision that may be useful and efficient for certain tasks but not for others. However, this entry uses the terms "visually impaired" and "blind" interchangeably to describe people who must rely on nonvisual methods to function.

HISTORY

The earliest approaches to helping blind and visually impaired people in the United States stressed special, separate education for blind children, sheltered or specialized noncompetitive employment for blind adults, and a specialized system of service agencies to meet the social and recreational needs of blind clients. Carroll (1961) argued that in order to adjust to the loss of vision, the newly blind person had to "mourn" the "death" of the sighted self and to work to assume a new identity.

Scott's (1969) classic study revealed that most social services agencies in "the blindness system" adhered to this philosophy and maintained that few blind or visually impaired children or adults could function in ordinary activities in school, at work, and in the community. Thus, social and educational programs for visually impaired people taught braille; travel with a long cane or a guide dog; and some methods of cooking, sewing, and maintaining daily life. However, they also engendered in their clients a belief that visual impairment prevented them from participating in their former employment or community activities and that they needed to develop new outlets and new lives as blind people. Furthermore, traditional social services agencies in the blindness system did not challenge laws that prohibited blind people from taking civil service examinations or serving as jurors, for example.

The challenge to the notion that blindness and visual impairment entail separation from ordinary activities came from blind people themselves, particularly those who founded the National Federation of the Blind (NFB)—the first major civil rights group of people with disabilities anywhere in the United States (Asch, 1985; Matson, 1990). With its civil rights, minority-group approach to blindness, NFB endorsed the need for high-quality rehabilitation training and training in alternative techniques of living for people who could not always rely on vision, but it also endorsed the right of blind people to speak for themselves and to combat laws and practices that excluded them from ordinary educational, work, civic, and leisure-time activities. This latter approach stresses learning alternative techniques of functioning, contact with other people who have mastered these techniques, involvement in consumer groups to press for public education and social change, and the application of these skills and attitudes to whichever areas of life an individual enjoyed before he or she became visually impaired. This approach wholeheartedly rejects Carroll's (1961) notion of the person's need to adopt a new identity as a blind person in favor of carrying on one's previous life and roles as a person with impaired vision (Jernigan, 1994).

PROFILE OF THE VISUALLY IMPAIRED POPULATION

Defining Visual Impairment and Legal Blindness

According to the most recent available data, 1.6 million people over age 15 are unable to see well enough to read the words and letters in ordinary print even with eyeglasses (McNeil, 1993). This figure is derived from the U.S. Bureau of the Census's 1991–92 data on the noninstitutionalized population and thus excludes about half a million people in nursing homes or other institutions from the count of those with serious visual difficulties (Nelson & Dimitrova, 1993). Furthermore, because only visual limitations with reference to reading are explored, these data do not indicate how many people cannot manage tasks that require intermediate or distance vision, such as seeing a computer screen, spotting a familiar person or building across a street, or watching television (Nelson & Dimitrova). Thus, as Kirchner (1994) pointed out, there are gaps in what is known about the status and needs of everyone in the United States with a serious visual limitation.

A number of government benefits and services are available for the approximately 1.1 million people who meet the legislative definition of "legal blindness": clinically measured visual acuity of 20/200 or less in the better eye or a visual field of 20 degrees or less after optimal correction (Chiang, Bassi, & Javitt, 1992). The person whose vision meets this definition can see at 20 feet what someone with perfect vision can see at 200 feet, and the person's width of vision is 20 degrees or less, substantially narrower than the field of vision of someone whose sight is unimpaired. Although this definition is intended to encompass people whose visual impairments may substantially hinder such daily life activities as reading, working, or traveling, it does not include all people with severe visual limitations.

Demographic Data

About 1.6 million people reported in 1991–92 that they could not see well enough to read print even with glasses, or about half a million more than the estimated population who were defined as legally blind people (McNeil, 1993). However, because visual impairment is far more prevalent in people over age 65, the omission of residents of nursing homes and other institutions from the data collection drastically understates those who could potentially benefit from vision services. Of the people who are defined as legally blind, 64 percent are over age 65, 5 percent are under age 20, and the remaining 21 percent are ages 20 to 64 (the prime working years).

Legal blindness occurs in males and females in roughly equal numbers until age 65, but because women typically live longer than do men, the elderly blind population is largely female. Blindness and visual impairment are found more often in people of color than in the white population, largely because people of color are disproportionately denied the health services that could diagnose and treat preventable blindness (Tielsch, Sommer, Witt, Katz, & Royall, 1990).

Information on the employment and income of visually impaired people also comes from the 1991–92 census data on those who reported that they were "unable to see to read," a number greater than those who are defined as legally blind. Compared to the overall working-age population, working-age men and women with visual impairments are substantially underrepresented among the employed. In 1991–92, 89 percent of all men, 73 percent of all women, and 80 percent of those ages 21 to 64 were employed. In contrast, only 31 percent of the men, 21 percent of the women, and 26 percent of the overall population of those who could not see to read were employed. These data reveal an urgent need to determine the reasons for unemployment in this population and to promote this population's entry into the world of work.

In 1991–92 the mean monthly earnings of employed people with visual impairments ($1,238), were well below those of the work force as a whole ($1,962). Perhaps the inability to read channeled some people into lower-paying jobs that did not require reading. However, many of those who were unable to read print used alternative means, such as braille, recordings, and electronic means of reading to perform their jobs; thus, not all the disparity in earnings can be attributed to the types of employment in which people were engaged.

As a whole, regardless of their employment status, people with visual impairments are far more likely to be poor than are those without visual impairments. In 1991–92, 20 percent of the total U.S. population, but 43 percent of those who reported they could not see to read, were living just above, at, or below the poverty level. Whereas 34 percent of the total population had incomes four times the poverty level or more, only 11 percent of those who could not see to read had such incomes (McNeil, 1993).

Causes of Visual Impairment

Nearly all visual impairment stems from disease; only 3 percent to 4 percent of blindness results from accidents. Although some blindness is traceable to genetic conditions, such as retinitis pigmentosa or retinoblastoma, by far the most frequent causes are associated with aging, senile degeneration, macular degeneration, cataracts, and glaucoma. Diabetic retinopathy, which can occur as the result of juvenile-onset or adult-onset diabetes, is also a significant cause of blindness.

Blindness and Other Health Impairments

Many people with visual problems, especially those over age 65, have other health problems (most commonly arthritis and back problems) in addition to blindness. However, 53 percent of those over age 65 and 63 percent of those under age 65 considered blindness to be the health condition that limited their activities the most (McNeil, 1993).

Although 60 percent of visually impaired children and young adults also have other impairments of hearing, cerebral palsy, or mental retardation (Kirchner, 1988; U.S. Department of Education, 1992), the vast majority of the reported 43,000 school-age blind students in 1993 were not listed as being served in programs for children with multiple handicaps (American Printing House, 1993). Thus, social workers who serve clients of any age with visual impairments should be aware that some of their clients' problems may be attributable to health conditions and disabilities other than blindness.

SERVICES AND LEGISLATION AFFECTING BLIND PEOPLE

People with visual impairments may obtain vision-related services from low-vision clinics, government and private agencies that serve people with many disabilities, and agencies that specialize in serving blind people. In 1993 the American Foundation for the Blind listed over 1,000 services from government, private, medical, and educational facilities in its directory of services to blind people. Some of these are schools and rehabilitation agencies that work only with the blind and visually impaired population, but many services are also located in general agencies in the medical and social welfare system that serve everyone in the community. Although two-thirds of the visually impaired population is over age 65 and the 1992 amendments (P.L. 102-569) to the Rehabilitation Act of 1973 have mandated increased services to older blind people, the blindness system still gears its services primarily to blind children and working-age adults. Some government and private agencies that specialize in serving blind people restrict their services to those who meet the definition of legal blindness, whereas others provide vision-related services to the broader visually impaired population discussed earlier. However, it is not known how many visually impaired people who do not meet the definition of legal blindness do not receive services that could restore vision or provide rehabilitation.

Blind people benefit from the legislation discussed by Asch and Mudrick ("Disability," volume 1) and Asch and Watson (1992) that is intended for all people with disabilities. Nevertheless, several pieces of legislation are of special relevance to or

have different implications for legally blind people than for people with other disabilities.

Access to the Printed Word

In 1852 the American Printing House for the Blind began producing books for blind people. The federal government began its commitment to provide blind people with literature and other educational materials in 1879 when it created legislation that enabled the American Printing House for the Blind to expand the scope of its educational work. The American Printing House continues to provide textbooks and educational materials for legally blind children and youths (from preschool through high school) and adults who require special formats for books, diagrams, and maps.

Access to literature was expanded by a 1904 law that authorized sending braille materials as "free matter for the blind," to avoid the prohibitive cost of mailing braille (and later recorded) materials that weigh much more than equivalent printed documents (Postal Reorganization Act of 1970, P.L. 91-375). In 1931 the Pratt–Smoot Act (P.L. 71-787) established the Books for the Blind program in the Library of Congress, which later became the National Library Service (NLS) for the Blind and Physically Handicapped (established under P.L. 87-765). This federal program established regional libraries to provide braille and recorded literary and music materials first to blind people and later to anyone who could not read standard print because of a visual, learning, or physical disability. Of the 765,000 NLS patrons, more than 85 percent are legally blind people who obtain books, magazines, and musical scores through the system of cooperating libraries (National Library Service, 1994).

Education and Rehabilitation

The Individuals with Disabilities Education Act of 1975 (P.L. 94-142) and its 1983 and 1990 amendments and the Rehabilitation Act of 1973 and its 1992 amendments apply to all people with disabilities, including those with visual impairments. The Rehabilitation Act authorizes payment for services to the visually impaired rendered by separate agencies that serve exclusively this population, and just over half the states have established separate agencies for such clients. Some states with separate agencies for the blind restrict their services to those who meet the definition of legal blindness discussed above, but others serve everyone with significant visual problems. For the purposes of rehabilitation, the act provides that each state may establish its own definition of legal blindness. Social workers who suspect that a client needs vision-related services should first refer clients to specialized agencies; only if a specialized agency declines service because the individual has more vision than the clients they typically work with should individuals be referred to the state's general rehabilitation agency.

Special Employment Legislation
In the 1930s the federal government passed two laws giving blind people access to sheltered and noncompetitive employment: the Wagner–O'Day Act (P.L. 75-739), which established a system of sheltered workshops, and the Randolph–Sheppard Act (P.L. 74-734), which gives blind people preference in obtaining employment as operators of vending facilities on federal properties. These laws and their subsequent amendments have provided work for thousands of blind people since that time, but because of actions of state and private rehabilitation agencies, the working conditions have not always compared favorably with those for people in the general labor force. Shop employees are considered workers under federal law, but some agencies have attempted to treat them as clients and have denied them the right to organize for improved wages and working conditions. Although the National Labor Relations Board has generally upheld the rights of shop workers to form unions and to bargain collectively to improve their working situation, some agencies continue to pay shop workers less than the minimum wage, which they are legally entitled to do so under the provisions of Section 14C of the Fair Labor Standards Act. Vendors obtain licenses to operate their facilities from the state agency that serves the blind, and the same agency supervises their work and service requirements. Despite this state agency involvement, vendors are considered self-employed entrepreneurs.

Income Support
Adults who are legally blind and have had no connection to the work force may obtain Supplemental Security Income (SSI). The federal SSI benefits for blind people are the same as those for people with other disabilities ($458 per month for individuals and $687 for couples in 1995). However, some states that supplement the federal grants choose to provide greater cash assistance for blind people than for people with other disabilities (Social Security Administration, 1994).

For legally blind people who are eligible to receive Social Security Disability Insurance (SSDI) because they have worked in the past but are not performing "substantial gainful activity," the earnings criteria for the receipt of benefits are different from those for people with other disabilities. Blind people may continue to work and receive SSDI benefits until their "substantial gainful activity" or earnings after impairment-related work expenses are deducted exceed $940 per month, or $11,280 annually (Social Security Administration, 1994).

For those with other disabilities, "substantial gainful activity" is defined as no higher than $500 per month. Social workers serving legally blind clients should be alert to this difference in entitlement and be sure that local social security offices examine work activity and earnings of their blind clients in light of this provision of the Social Security Act.

Services to Deaf–Blind and Older Blind People
Two segments of the visually impaired and blind population who have been identified as having unique and sometimes unmet needs are people with hearing as well as visual impairments and people who lose vision near the end of or after they have completed their working lives. Title VII, chapter 2 (P.L. 502-569) of the Rehabilitation Act Amendments of 1992 set up services for people over age 55 whose vision is deteriorating and who require assistance to maintain themselves in their homes, families, and communities even if they no longer expect to work in the paid labor force. Until this legislation established rehabilitation services geared to this population, hundreds of thousands of older people, the largest segment of the visually impaired population, could not always receive help because federal law tied rehabilitation services to obtaining a vocation. Similarly, with the establishment of the Helen Keller National Center for Deaf–Blind Youths and Adults under the Rehabilitation Act Amendments of 1992, Congress recognized that a portion of the visually impaired population also incur hearing loss that precludes their use of some alternative techniques and necessitates the development and teaching of new techniques at this center.

All the legislation discussed in this section provides entitlements to services and benefits that can be invaluable for blind people and their families. The distressed man or woman who assumes that loss of sight means loss of reading and independence may regain pleasure and confidence in himself or herself by discovering recorded books and tactile stove markings. Unfortunately, some people who seek vending licenses, rehabilitation services, or SSI benefits are first denied them. The legislation contains crucial appeal rights designed to protect people from the problems of bureaucracy, and social workers should alert individuals to these legislative provisions. A major function of advocacy groups like the National Federation of the Blind is to aid individuals in obtaining their rights under federal and state legislation, and social workers should urge clients to contact these these groups for their expertise and assistance.

LIFESPAN APPROACH TO BLINDNESS AND VISUAL IMPAIRMENT

Information: The Critical Factor

When individuals or family members discover that they or their loved ones are likely to have serious visual problems, it is natural for them to react with such emotions as distress, sadness, fear, and confusion. What will the fact of poor vision or total blindness mean for family life, relationships, school, work, recreation, and finances? Blind clients and their families need accurate information about laws, services, and alternative techniques for performing household tasks, reading, writing, traveling, and the like that people customarily imagine cannot be handled without vision. Although the onset of visual impairment sometimes necessitates in-depth counseling and therapy for an individual or a family, social workers should eschew the formerly common notion (Carroll, 1961) that blindness brings about a new psychology or gives rise to completely different personality problems (see Asch & Rousseau, 1985, for a critique of the psychoanalytic and social work literature on blindness).

Social workers should assume that clients need realistic information about services and possibilities for maintaining their work, school, family, and leisure roles and actively aid clients by steering them to such information as the practical guidance available from the National Center for the Blind in Baltimore, the American Foundation for the Blind (1993) directory of services, and such useful books as *If Blindness Comes* (Jernigan, 1994).

Blind Children in the Family, at School, and in the Community

How can a blind child receive a high-quality education, participate in family life, and not jeopardize the plans and goals of other family members? Social workers who deal with families of infants and toddlers who are blind can get some interesting suggestions from Fraiberg (1971), but they and the families of blind children of various ages should be referred to journals such as *Future Reflections* and to the National Organization of Parents of Blind Children, a division of the National Federation of the Blind. Along with state and private service agencies, this group can guide parents to toys and games that offer stimulation and can advise them on whether their children should learn braille and whether the children will need

assistance in learning to get around safely using the long cane.

Because many childhood eye conditions are progressive and the demands of school and social life will expand as a child grows, the blind youngster who can manage with large print and without a cane during the elementary years may be hindered later on without exposure to alternative means of reading, writing, and traveling. Social workers in school settings should aid parents to participate in meetings about their children's educational future and should help them become experts in appropriate technological devices and alternative methods that allow blind or visually impaired children to participate in sports and recreation, industrial arts, home economics, crafts, music, and extracurricular as well as academic activities in school (Willoughby & Duffy, 1989).

Blindness and Visual Impairment during the Working Years

Thirty-one percent of the legally blind population are in the prime working years, and most are unemployed. Many people who develop vision problems during these years fail to learn about available rehabilitation services from ophthalmologists or hospitals and often languish at home for months or years without obtaining information that could give them access to their valued activities. Social workers can be advocates for their clients with rehabilitation agencies, can tell clients about guide dog schools, and can convince apprehensive families that work and independent travel and family life are still feasible. They must combat the myth that the roles of spouses and parents are inevitably changed for the worse by blindness by reminding everyone of all the talents and capacities that remain despite vision loss. Similarly, there is no reason to assume that a visually impaired person cannot return to the field of work in which she or he engaged before becoming blind. Sometimes the person will not be able to do so, but the social worker should refer a client to the tools and skills that will enable her or him to continue in chosen and valued roles when possible.

Blindness in Late Life

The Rehabilitation Act Amendments of 1992 provide for increased services for the thousands of people who lose their vision after they leave the labor force. These services are intended to keep visually impaired people active in their homes and communities by providing them with tools for daily living, travel, and communication. Social workers who see clients in senior citizen centers and nursing homes should be especially alert to the clients' deteriorating vision and should link their clients with the specialized services that will enable them to continue their activities. Most people will be able to resume activities with whichever group of senior citizens they were involved before they became blind.

Blindness and Other Health Impairments

Learning the techniques to function without sight may be more difficult if individuals have manual dexterity problems that prevent them from reading braille or hearing problems that prevent their use of sound in orientation and travel. Some visually impaired people with cognitive impairments from mental disabilities or brain injuries will need services from agencies and organizations that specialize in cognitive rehabilitation. Social workers must know that a visual impairment may not be a client's chief difficulty, but they should also be aware that agencies that serve people with hearing, mobility, or cognitive impairments may fear taking on clients who have visual disabilities as well. In such circumstances, social workers can play a crucial case management and advocacy role to ensure that clients with multiple disabilities receive the services to which they are entitled.

Serving Visually Impaired Clients in General Settings

The foregoing comments were directed to social workers who meet clients or families in which visual impairment appears to be a major concern and need for service. However, visually impaired people will increasingly seek social services for marital or family problems; as part of their employment through employee assistance programs; or on behalf of other relatives, when blindness is incidental or irrelevant to the request for assistance. In the past, social workers tended to adopt the mindset that people with visual or other disabilities need services from specialists in blindness or disability in general, but such ideas were often wrong then and are now indicative of subtle prejudice and discrimination by social workers or their agencies. It is essential for a social worker whose blind client and spouse come for marital therapy, for example, to concentrate on the couple's dynamics. However, if blindness comes up repeatedly as a source of friction, the worker may properly examine whether the client and his or her spouse know the means of optimal functioning as a blind person.

Training and Working with Blind Colleagues

People with visual impairments have entered the social work profession for many decades, but schools of social work, fieldwork sites, and employing agencies sometimes still display the stereotypes and fears about blindness discussed earlier. Therefore, they, too, need to contact knowledgeable experts on blindness to ensure that blind students and practitioners are given the training, resources, and opportunities they need to function at the level of sighted students and practitioners. In addition to sources that may be obtained through the Council on Social Work Education, the National Federation of the Blind's Human Services Division maintains a list of dozens of employed social workers who can assist schools and agencies in solving problems that arise in training and working with colleagues who have visual problems.

BLINDNESS AS A SOCIAL PROBLEM

Much of the foregoing discussion has stressed serving individuals and families by linking them to people with specialized expertise and knowledge that will enable them to learn the techniques of living with reduced or no vision. Because a key approach to blindness is to recognize that it is a social as well as an individual problem, this entry concludes by commenting on how social workers can instill such notions in their clients and can link clients with consumer groups that uphold such a social-problem view.

Social workers should remember that clients and families are likely to feel overwhelmed by the challenges of managing the logistics of blindness (Ainlay, 1988) and are going to need time before they see that braille, cane or guide dog, recorded materials, live readers, adapted computers, and new ways of managing a home and work life can be as efficient as the ways that relied on sight. Not only is contact with more-experienced blind people often indispensable in convincing newly blind people of these possibilities, it is also invaluable in gaining allies with whom they can battle discrimination and exclusion when it occurs. Of the organized consumer groups of blind people, the National Federation of the Blind is the oldest and largest group committed to fighting discrimination in employment, public accommodations, and education. It has also worked to end agency custodialism and second-class treatment of visually impaired clients, and its members and leaders stand ready to help newly blind people of all ages and their families take an assertive approach to blindness as a social problem.

REFERENCES

Ainlay, S. C. (1988). Aging and new vision loss: Disruptions of the here and now. *Journal of Social Issues, 48*(1), 79–94.

All things considered. (1994, December 26). National Public Radio.

American Foundation for the Blind. (1993). *AFB directory of services for blind and visually impaired persons in the United States and Canada* (24th ed.). New York: Author.

American Printing House for the Blind. (1993). *Distribution of federal quota based on the January 4, 1993 registration of eligible students.* Louisville, KY: Author.

Asch, A. (1985). Understanding and working with disability rights groups. In H. McCarthy (Ed.), *Complete guide to employing persons with disabilities* (pp. 172–184). Albertson, NY: Human Resources Center.

Asch, A., & Rousseau, H. (1985). Therapists with disabilities: Theoretical and clinical issues. *Psychiatry, 48*(1), 1–12.

Asch, A., & Watson, S. (1992). Legislation affecting disability management practices. In S. H. Akabas, L. B. Gates, & D. E. Galvin (Eds.), *Disability management: A complete system to reduce costs, increase productivity, meet employee needs, and ensure legal compliance* (pp. 22–64). New York: Amacom.

Carroll, T. J. (1961). *Blindness: What it is, what it does, and how to live with it.* Boston: Little, Brown.

Chiang, Y., Bassi, L., & Javitt, J. (1992). Federal budgetary costs of blindness. *Milbank Quarterly, 70,* 319–340.

Fraiberg, S. (1971). *Insights from the blind.* New York: New American Library.

Jernigan, K. (Ed.). (1994). *If blindness comes.* Baltimore: National Federation of the Blind.

Kahn, H., & Moorhead, H. B. (1973). *Statistics on blindness in the model reporting area, 1969–1970.* Washington, DC: U.S. Department of Health, Education, & Welfare.

Kirchner, C. (1988). *Data on blindness and visual impairment in the U.S.* (2nd ed.). New York: American Foundation for the Blind.

Kirchner, C. (1994, May 10). *Summary of key sources re blindness and visual impairment in the USA.* Unpublished manuscript prepared for the Statistical Data Related to Visual Impairment Working Group, Baltimore.

Louis Harris & Associates. (1991). *Public attitudes toward people with disabilities.* Washington, DC: National Organization on Disability.

Makas, E. (1988). Positive attitudes toward disabled people: Disabled and non-disabled persons' perspectives. *Journal of Social Issues, 44*(1), 49–61.

Matson, F. (1990). *Walking alone and marching together: A history of the organized blind movement in the United States, 1940–1990.* Baltimore: National Federation of the Blind.

McNeil, J. M. (1993.) Americans with disabilities: 1991–1992: Data from the Survey of Income and Program Participation. In *Current population reports* (Series P-70, No. 33, pp. 70–73). Washington, DC: U.S. Government Printing Office.

National Library Service, Library of Congress. (1994, January). *Facts: Books for blind and physically handicapped individuals.* Washington, DC: Author.

Nelson, K., & Dimitrova, G. (1993). Severe visual impairment in the United States and in each state, 1990. *Journal of Visual Impairment & Blindness, 87,* 80–85.

Postal Reorganization Act of 1970. P.L. 91-375, 84 Stat. 719.

Randolph–Sheppard Act. Ch. 638, 49 Stat. 1559 (1936).

Rehabilitation Act of 1973. P.L. 102-569, Title I.

Rehabilitation Act Amendments of 1992. P.L. 102-569, 106 Stat. 4344.

Scott, R. A. (1969). *The making of blind men: A study of adult socialization.* New York: Russell Sage Foundation.

Siller, J., Chipman, A., Ferguson, L., & Vann, D. H. (1967). *Studies in reactions to disability. XI: Attitudes of the nondisabled toward the physically disabled.* New York: New York University School of Education.

Siller, J., Ferguson, L., Vann, D. H., & Holland, B. (1967). *Structure of attitudes toward the physically disabled.* New York: New York University School of Education.

Social Security Administration. (1994, October 31). 1995 cost-of-living increase and other determinations. *Federal Register, 59*(209), 54464–54469.

Social Security Disability Amendments of 1980. P.L. 96-265, 94 Stat. 441.

Tielsch, J. Sommer, A. Witt, K., Katz, J., & Royall, R. (1990). Blindness and visual impairment in an American urban population: The Baltimore eye survey. *Archives of Ophthalmology, 108,* 286–290.

U.S. Department of Education, Office of Special Education Programs. (1992). *Fourteenth annual report to Congress on the implementation of the Individuals with Disabilities Education Act.* Washington, DC: U.S. Government Printing Office.

Wagner–O'Day Act. Ch. 697, 52 Stat. 1196 (1938).

Willoughby, D. M., & Duffy, S.L.M. (1989). *Handbook for itinerant and resource teachers of blind and visually impaired students.* Baltimore: National Federation of the Blind.

RESOURCES

American Foundation for the Blind, Eleven Penn Plaza, Suite 300, New York, NY 10001.

National Center for the Blind, 1830 Johnson Street, Baltimore, MD 21230.

National Federation of the Blind Human Services Division, 1830 Johnson Street, Baltimore, MD 21230.

National Organization of Parents of Blind Children, National Federation of the Blind, 1830 Johnson Street, Baltimore, MD 21230.

Adrienne Asch, PhD, is Henry R. Luce Professor in Biology, Ethics and the Politics of Human Reproduction, Wellesley College, 106 Central Street, Wellesley, MA 02181.

For further information see

Aging Overview; Civil Rights; Deaf Community; Deafness; Developmental Disabilities: Definitions and Policies; Direct Practice Overview; Disability; Health Care: Direct Practice; Long-Term Care; Managed Care; Maternal and Child Health; Natural Helping Networks; Patient Rights; Primary Health Care; Public Health Services; Social Welfare Policy.

Key Words	
blindness	visual impairment
disability	

Voluntarism
Eleanor L. Brilliant

Voluntarism and voluntary associations have long been considered quintessential features of American life. They contribute to freedom of choice and to the U.S. economy, and they have a large, often unappreciated role in the provision of social welfare (Karger & Stoesz, 1990; Salamon, 1987; Wolch, 1990). Voluntary activity has been fundamental to American democracy since the early days of the Republic, when the rights of free speech, assembly, and religious freedom were guaranteed in the first 10 amendments to the Constitution. By 1840 Alexis de Tocqueville (1969), a French visitor to the United States, had already made his now-famous written observation about the propensity of Americans to form associations. More than 140 years later, the Commission on Private Philanthropy and Public Needs (1975), commonly called the Filer Commission, reported that "few aspects of American Society are more characteristically, more famously American than the nation's array of voluntary organizations, and the support in both time and money that is given to them by its citizens" (p. 9).

Despite cries of crises, the voluntary sector in the United States has continued to grow since the Filer Commission's report; by the early 1990s, it included more than 1 million identified formal organizations and countless other informal groups and associations (Hodgkinson, Weitzman, Toppe, & Noga, 1992; Van Til, 1990). As the century draws to a close, voluntary action and voluntary organizations are becoming more significant as the basis for a civil society in other countries as well. Thus, although the focus of this entry is on the American experience, it must be recognized that this country's experience with voluntary activity is perceived as having value for other countries throughout the world, including those in areas where democracy is reemerging, such as central and eastern Europe (Siegel & Yancey, 1992).

DEFINITIONS AND DISTINCTIONS

Although the voluntary sector has received increased scholarly attention since the mid-1970s, definitions of the sector and of its subparts remain troublesome (Hodgkinson et al., 1992; Salamon & Anheier, 1992). Conceptual ambiguity and pragmatic constraints make it difficult to map the voluntary sector (Hall, 1987; Van Til, 1988, 1990). Thus, the first step is to clarify the concepts of voluntarism, voluntary organization, voluntary agency, voluntary association, and voluntary sector.

According to Kramer (1981), *voluntarism* embodies both a set of values (known as volunteerism) and a set of voluntary structures or organizations. In this sense, voluntarism can be considered the broad philosophical underpinning for all voluntary activity, as well as an outcome of that philosophy. It is the spirit and impulses of voluntarism that historically have led to the creation of voluntary structures and that give purpose to

their continuation. These voluntary organizations, however, may take many different forms, from informal self-help groups or neighbors who come together for specific problem solving, to large, formal, bureaucratic organizations, such as hospitals and art museums, with budgets of several million dollars; they may also be social action, or social movement, organizations. Moreover, although many voluntary organizations function exclusively with volunteers, others have extensive numbers of paid staff to carry out their daily operations, and it has been suggested that the sector as a whole has become more professional (Tropman & Tropman, 1987). The immense variety of structures, purposes, and funding sources (private and public) contributes to the definitional difficulties of the field (Gronbjerg, 1993; Salamon, 1992).

Within the field of voluntary organizations, *voluntary agencies* are formal social welfare, service-related organizations that are dedicated to helping others achieve a higher quality of life and to providing resources and services for meeting crises in daily living. Therefore, they are central places for social work practice. Voluntary agency is often a shorthand term for a nonprofit, nongovernment human services agency (Tropman & Tropman, 1987). Salamon (1992) also referred to the "nonprofit public benefit-serving organization," which is close in concept to the voluntary agency, but slightly broader in scope.

Voluntary association is a term with two meanings. In its broadest sense, it relates to the entire range of voluntary organizations, from informal groups to larger professional or bureaucratic structures. In another, more delimited sense, however, it may refer to a class of organizations (for example, trade associations) that are formed specifically to benefit the members of those organizations, rather than to benefit the general public.

Voluntary sector is the term frequently used to encompass all voluntary organizations, voluntary agencies, and associations created under the rubric of voluntarism. It includes national and international groups, organizations dedicated specifically to fundraising or philanthropic giving (foundations), and both religious and secular organizations. A fundamental characteristic of the sector as a whole is the wide range of beliefs it encompasses and its essential quality of choice (Bellah, Madsen, Sullivan, Suidler, & Tipton, 1985; Douglas, 1983). Although the terms "voluntary sector" and "nonprofit sector" are generally used interchangeably, some scholars use nonprofit sector to refer specifically to the formal incorporated structures of the voluntary sector (Salamon, 1992). The term "independent sector" is more problematic. It is widely used, but questions have been raised about the degree to which organizations in the sector are independent of business or government (Brilliant, 1990; Gronbjerg, 1993; Hall, 1990; Wolch, 1990), and the term also has more specialized meanings (Hodgkinson et al., 1992).

OPERATIONAL AND LEGAL DEFINITIONS

The Filer Commission (1975) referred to the voluntary arena as "the third sector," emphasizing its difference from two other major groups of formal institutions—the business sector and government. More recently, there has been a growing acceptance of the concept of four sectors in U.S. society. The fourth sector, composed of households, is used in the United Nations economic accounts system and is recognized as being distinct from the other three more institutionalized sectors (Salamon & Anheier, 1992). Although this use complicates the delineation of some more informal groups at the margins of the voluntary sector, it does not detract from the use of the term "third sector" generally.

Master File of Tax-Exempt Organizations

The most readily identifiable universe of third-sector organizations in the United States derives from the master file of tax-exempt organizations of the U.S. Internal Revenue Service (IRS) (Table 1). Organizations on this list are explicitly excluded from paying federal income taxes under regulations of the Internal Revenue (Tax) Code and generally are exempt from local and state property taxes (Hopkins, 1991, 1992; Simon, 1987).

Smaller, more informal groups are not included in the IRS master file. With the exception of private foundations, nonprofit organizations with revenues of less than $5,000, as well as religious organizations like churches, synagogues, and mosques are not required to register with the IRS, even though they may be providing extensive amounts of concrete services, such as Meals on Wheels (Hodgkinson et al., 1992; Independent Sector, 1992). As a result, scholars believe that the IRS list actually undercounts the number of voluntary associations and organizations in the United States (Hodgkinson et al., 1992; Salamon, 1992; Weisbrod, 1988).

501(c)(3) Agencies

As Table 1 indicates, Section 501 of the Internal Revenue Code includes 25 major types of tax-exempt organizations. Within the universe of tax-exempt organizations, the 501(c)(3) category is by far the largest. It is also the one under which most voluntary human services agencies are classified and in which most social workers are employed. The 501(c)(3) organizations are commonly referred to as "charities" because of the IRS classification. In addition to benefiting from income tax exemptions under the federal tax code, charities receive an additional tax benefit through the tax deductibility of contributions made to them. The purposes of these organizations are defined as charitable, religious, scientific, testing for public safety, educational and literary activities, certain sports competitions, and prevention of cruelty to children or animals. This formulation of charitable groups is modeled on English common-law concepts and the preamble to the Elizabethan Law of Charitable Uses of 1601, which continues to influence the American legal definition of charity (Hopkins, 1991; Hopkins & Moore, 1992).

Organizations under the IRS 501(c)(3) classification share the following characteristics:

- They are created for some defined public benefit.
- They are legal entities, generally incorporated under state law and hence subject to a variety of state laws and regulations. In addition, some organizations such as the American Red Cross have national charters.
- They have their own volunteer governance structure.
- They are not expected to give profits to individual owners, but to put back into the corporation any surplus funds that may exist (Hopkins, 1992).

Indeed, in contrast with business (or for-profit) organizations, public-benefit organizations operate under a significant "distribution constraint." Surplus revenues or profits must be used to support organizational purposes and cannot be given to individuals (Douglas, 1983; Hansmann, 1980, 1987; Simon, 1987). It should be noted here that non-

TABLE 1

Number of Active Entities on Master File of Tax-Exempt Organizations, 1987–1990 and 1992–1993 (fiscal year ending September 30)

Tax Code Number	Type of Tax-Exempt Organization	1987	1988	1989	1990	1992	1993
501(c)(1)	Corporations organized under an act of Congress	24	24	9	9	9	7
501(c)(2)	Title-holding companies	5,977	6,026	6,090	6,278	6,529	6,739
501(c)(3)	Religious, charitable, etc.[a]	422,103	447,525	464,138	489,882	546,100	575,690
501(c)(4)	Social welfare	138,485	138,430	141,238	142,473	142,673	142,325
501(c)(5)	Labor, agricultural organizations	75,238	73,200	72,689	71,653	71,012	70,416
501(c)(6)	Business leagues	59,981	61,275	63,951	65,896	90,871	72,901
501(c)(7)	Social and recreational clubs	60,146	60,877	61,455	62,723	64,681	64,924
501(c)(8)	Fraternal beneficiary societies	98,979	99,568	99,621	100,321	93,544	93,728
501(c)(9)	Voluntary employees' beneficiary societies	10,979	12,360	13,228	14,210	14,986	15,048
501(c)(10)	Domestic fraternal beneficiary societies	17,813	18,574	18,432	18,350	21,415	20,827
501(c)(11)	Teachers' retirement fund	11	11	11	10	10	11
501(c)(12)	Benevolent life insurance associations	5,572	5,682	5,783	5,873	6,103	6,177
501(c)(13)	Cemetery companies	7,942	8,148	8,341	8,565	9,025	9,184
501(c)(14)	Credit unions	6,662	6,786	6,438	6,352	5,559	5,637
501(c)(15)	Mutual insurance companies	950	1,079	1,118	1,137	1,157	1,165
501(c)(16)	Corporations to finance crop operation	18	17	17	19	23	22
501(c)(17)	Supplemental unemployment benefit trusts	728	704	674	667	625	611
501(c)(18)	Employee-funded pension trust	5	9	8	8	8	4
501(c)(19)	War veterans' organizations	24,749	26,122	26,495	27,460	28,096	29,974
501(c)(20)	Legal services organizations	210	207	200	197	217	213
501(c)(21)	Black lung trusts	21	22	22	22	23	22
501(d)	Religious and apostolic organizations	88	93	94	94	92	96
501(e)	Cooperative hospital service organizations	80	79	79	76	68	69
501(f)	Cooperative service organizations of operating educational organizations	1	1	1	1	1	1
521	Farmers' cooperatives	2,405	2,347	2,279	2,372	2,086	1,954
501(c)	Holding companies for pensions, etc.					290	374
	Total	939,167	969,166	992,411	1,024,648	1,105,203	1,118,119

SOURCES: Hodgkinson, V. A., Weitzman, M. S., Toppe, C., & Noga, S. M. (1992). *Nonprofit almanac 1992–1993: Dimensions of the voluntary sector* (Table 1.2, p. 24). San Francisco: Jossey-Bass. Internal Revenue Service. (1992). *Annual report* [unpublished]. Washington DC: Author. Internal Revenue Service. (1993) *Annual report* [unpublished]. Washington, DC: Author.

NOTE: These are abbreviated descriptions only. For example, the 501(c)(3) category would include religious, educational, charitable, scientific, and literary organizations; those testing for public safety, fostering certain national or international sports competitions, or working to prevent cruelty to children or animals; and foundations.

[a] All section 501(c)(3) organizations are not included because certain organizations, such as churches, integrated auxiliaries, subordinate units, and conventions or associations of churches, need not apply for recognition of exemption unless they desire a ruling.

profit organizations are not prevented from producing surplus income or profits, only from distributing it to controlling individuals. This is one reason why people are concerned when nonprofit organizations pay executives generous salaries and perquisites, and there is an appearance of private inurement.

501(c)(4) Organizations

A smaller but significant group of tax-exempt organizations is classified as 501(c)(4) organizations in the IRS listing (see Table 1). These organizations are civic associations and other groups that serve social welfare purposes, but also engage actively in lobbying and political action. Consequently, they are not eligible for the double tax benefit of contribution deductibility that is enjoyed by 501(c)(3) organizations (Hopkins, 1991, 1992). Nonetheless, because they share essential public purposes, 501(c)(3) and 501(c)(4) organizations are often linked together by

researchers. Salamon (1992) referred to the combined 501(c)(3) and 501(c)(4) groups as "nonprofit public benefit organizations," and Hodgkinson et al. (1992) used the term "independent sector." As Table 1 shows, 501(c)(3) and 501(c)(4) organizations together make up about two-thirds of the entities in the nonprofit tax-exempt sector listed in the IRS master file.

RATIONALE FOR NONPROFIT ORGANIZATIONS

Underlying the regulatory and legal bases for favorable treatment of nonprofit public-benefit organizations in the tax code are judgments about the inability of for-profit (business) corporations to meet certain public policy objectives. Therefore, scholars have analyzed nonprofit organizations in terms of contract failure and market failure. With regard to contract failure, the distinguishing feature of nonprofit organizations is consumers' lack of information about the services that are offered

(Hansmann, 1987; Nelson, 1977). This lack of information (for example, about the quality of counseling) suggests the need to protect consumers from risks that may be associated with a profit motive. Organizations in the charitable subsector are considered to be a response to the inability of consumers to evaluate the products and services being offered. In a framework of political economy, the necessity for nonprofit charitable organizations is also explained in terms of collective needs, or public goods that the market may not provide because of high transaction costs and the "free rider" problem (in which some individuals enjoy benefits for which they do not share the cost), but that, like parks or community centers, serve a vital communal public purpose (Douglas, 1983; Hansmann, 1987; Weisbrod, 1977, 1988).

Although the market may not be able to supply enough public goods, there is theoretically no reason why the government could not satisfy these needs. Therefore, a different rationale is needed to explain why nonprofit, rather than government, organizations are called on. According to this second half of the "twin failures" concept, scholars in the nonprofit sector have concluded that nonprofit organizations have a flexibility and a capacity to move more quickly than does the government (Douglas, 1983; Wolch, 1990). Because they are incorporated for special purposes and have internal governance structures, nonprofit organizations need not fulfill universal distribution requirements, but can be selective in providing services and programs. Therefore, they can meet the needs of racial and ethnic groups or emergent interests that may not receive support through majority rule and voter preference if mandates of the majority were required to approve them (Douglas, 1983; Weisbrod, 1977, 1988). Voluntary associations can represent minority viewpoints even in the presence of government and are therefore fundamental to U.S. pluralistic society (Douglas, 1983).

HISTORICAL DEVELOPMENT

Although voluntary associations and charitable aid exist in non-Western societies, as well as in Western societies, for the most part, the American formulation of voluntarism comes from two primary Western sources: (1) Greco-Roman ideas of philanthropy providing benefits for the general welfare and love of mankind and (2) the Judeo-Christian idea of charity (for the poor) and good works as a religious duty or the path to salvation (Gurin & Van Til, 1990; Lohmann, 1992; O'Neill, 1989). This dual heritage provided both a secular and a religious tradition for voluntary and charitable activity for the early American colonists. From the

beginning, voluntary organizations, including churches, were associated with the value of freedom and choice. It has also been argued that later public social welfare structures resulted from both the innovative efforts (Bremner, 1988) and lack of adequate resources of the voluntary sector (Salamon, 1992).

The history of voluntary activity in the United States can be divided into six major periods: 1601 to 1800 (communal activity), 1800 to 1865 (expanded voluntary organizations and social action), 1865 to 1900 (rise of philanthropy and coordinating agencies), 1900 to 1932 (increased professionalism and policy reforms), 1932 to 1980 (emergent national government and voluntary partnerships), and 1980 to the present, a period of increasing privatization. In each period, voluntary-sector organizations have existed in relation to the government's provision of social welfare, but with different proportionate shares of the total mix and influence (Karger & Stoesz, 1990; Tropman & Tropman, 1987).

1601 to 1800: Communal Activity
Voluntary activity arose early in U.S. history out of necessity and philosophy, as well as religious inspiration. While sailing to New England in 1630, John Winthrop admonished the Pilgrims about the need for community support (Bremner, 1988). Often neighborly assistance proved vital for survival in the harsh conditions of the new colonies, and some self-help societies, such as the Scots Charitable Society (1657), formed quickly. When the colonists grew restive in their relations with Great Britain, revolutionary actions emerged out of community organizing actions (for example, the Boston Tea Party or the formation of the Continental Congress). Women's associations were already active in support of soldiers in Washington's army (Evans, 1989). During the 18th century, more formal institutions developed; the first orphanage was formed in 1729 in New Orleans; Pennsylvania Hospital was established as a general hospital in Philadelphia (1751); and institutions that later became influential private universities were already established by the early 18th century (Harvard, 1636; Yale, 1701).

1800 to 1865: Expansion
In the 19th century, voluntary organizations grew in strength and number, as did business and governmental organizations. So many private agencies were established in larger cities that, beginning in the 1820s, other organizations developed to coordinate charitable activities and to reform their abuses (Bremner, 1988). Early rudimentary casework activities emerged, and in 1843 the New York

Association for Improving the Condition of the Poor used "friendly visitors" to provide organized relief for the poor. By the 1840s, cause-related, or social movement, organizations had developed in connection with controversial issues of the time, including moral reform, antislavery/abolitionist organizations, and the suffrage movement.

For the most part, separate organizations existed for groups of different socioeconomic status, sex, and race (Ginzberg, 1990; Hewitt, 1984). The YMCA came to the United States in 1851, and by 1853 Charles Loring Brace had established the Children's Aid Society. A decade later the Civil War resulted in a spurt of voluntary-sector activity. The first successful national voluntary health organization (the Sanitary Commission) was formed during the war, largely to coordinate the many efforts of various women's associations (Axinn & Levin, 1982; Bremner, 1988). Initial efforts of voluntary associations led by freed slaves ("freedmen") were influential in advocating for the establishment of the national Freedmen's Bureau in 1865 (Bremner).

1865 to 1900: Rise of Philanthropy

In the period after the Civil War and through the early 1900s, voluntary agencies proliferated in cities across the country in response to increased urbanization, industrialization, and immigration. Rich industrialists such as Andrew Carnegie and John D. Rockefeller became philanthropists. In Buffalo in 1877, the precursors of current family services agencies emerged in the Charity Organization Society, which spread to other cities, attempting to institute "scientific charity" in the provision of private relief to families and deploring public charity (Lubove, 1969).

By the late 1880s, a parallel movement of community work and social reform existed in settlement houses in New York, Chicago, and elsewhere. Associations of Charities were formed in large cities, such as Pittsburgh, Cleveland, and Denver, to ensure the coordination and planning of social welfare activities. In Denver in 1887, an offshoot of the Associated Charities developed a communitywide federated fund drive in a mode that later became the United Way system of fundraising (Brilliant, 1990). State coordinating organizations developed for public and private agencies, and in 1874 the first National Conference of Charities and Correction was convened (Axinn & Levin, 1982).

1900 to 1932: Increased Professionalism

By the early 20th century, the settlement house movement was flourishing and actively involved in efforts to improve the conditions of women, children, and immigrant workers. Settlement workers influenced governmental policies at the local and national levels. The Progressive Era also saw the emergence of local youth-group activities connected to national agencies (for example, Boy Scouts, Girl Scouts, Boys Clubs) that played a large part in the americanization spirit of the time (Brilliant, 1990). During World War I, federated fundraising intensified as part of the effort to provide support for national and international service agencies, such as the YMCA and the American Red Cross, and local campaigns continued to develop after the war.

1932 to 1980: Partnerships with Government

By the mid-1930s, in response to the Great Depression, the New Deal shifted responsibility for relief of the poor from the voluntary sector to the federal government. Many voluntary family service agencies redirected their services to emphasize psychosocial intervention, and recreation and youth-group activities increased. Federated fundraising organizations, which had spread to more than 400 cities, struggled to keep their campaigns going in those years.

During World War II, national fundraising drives and war chests that were aimed at meeting the needs of service men and women flourished in various relationships with local community drives. Neighborhood organization was also strengthened in connection with civil defense and took on some attributes of community development after the war. During this period, national health agencies (for example, the American Heart Association, Tuberculosis Society, American Cancer Society) demonstrated strong fundraising activity and challenged the locally based fundraising organizations of the community chests (Brilliant, 1990). In the mid-1950s, with union and business-management support, federated fundraising spread into the workplace through payroll deductions, and community chests turned into United Funds. In the following decade the number of grant-making private foundations also expanded greatly under favorable new tax provisions.

The 1960s period was a watershed for the voluntary sector in American society, with vast increases in federal funding to new and emergent voluntary agencies. It was a time of social movement and political controversy, which spread to philanthropic actions as well, culminating in Congressman Wright Patman's criticism of the presumed abuses in the rapidly growing foundation field. Patman's populist challenge focused on two major issues: (1) the self-dealing business practices of some foundations that benefitted businesses or families that controlled them and (2) ideological questions about the supposed "leftist leanings" of many of the more powerful organizations, such as the Ford Foundation. Congressional hearings led to the Tax Reform Act of 1969, which tightened accountability requirements for foundations, including limitations on the relationships between foundations and their major donors and higher required payouts to recipients (Cuninggim, 1972).

Increased constraints on foundations after the 1969 Tax Reform Act and economic "stagflation" (recession plus inflation) during the 1970s raised concerns again about the viability of the voluntary sector. These concerns resulted in the formation of a commission to consider ways of encouraging private individual and corporate support for voluntary organizations. This commission, known as the Filer Commission because of its chairman, John Filer, was initiated by John D. Rockefeller III with support from government officials in the Treasury Department and Congress. During the commission's deliberations, charges of elitism were raised, and new questions were asked about diversity in decision making and the role of recipient groups, particularly women and people of color. By the time the commission issued its report in 1975, the issue of whose interests are served by the voluntary sector had attracted broad attention in the media and elsewhere (Brilliant, 1985; Tropman & Tropman, 1987).

The voluntary sector had, in fact, undergone significant changes in the 1960s and early 1970s. The period was marked by a groundswell of new community-based services and advocacy organizations funded first by foundations (for example, the Ford Foundation's Grey Areas project) and subsequently through the War on Poverty and Great Society programs of the administrations of John F. Kennedy and Lyndon Johnson (Gilbert & Specht, 1986; Marris and Rein, 1967). The federal government intensified the use of contracts with voluntary agencies under the 1967 amendments to the Social Security Act and later under Title XX (1974) and other federal programs (Brilliant, 1973; Kramer & Grossman, 1987; Wedel, Katz, & Weick, 1979). Although there was a cap of $2.5 billion on allocations for social services under Title XX, the principles of social planning and setting priorities were established with the mandated involvement of local nonprofit organizations.

1980 to 1990s: Increasing Privatization
By the 1980s, social action groups and community organizations had developed strength in advocating for the rights of underrepresented minorities

and disadvantaged groups and were seeking new sources for support (Brilliant, 1985). Earlier criticism about the Filer Commission's lack of attention to issues of diversity and emerging needs resulted in the creation of the alternative Donee Group (Bremner, 1988; Brilliant, 1990; Donee Group, 1977). By 1976 an offshoot of this group became the National Committee for Responsive Philanthropy (NCRP), which is still focusing the debate on problems of philanthropic giving, including the hegemony of the United Way in the workplace (NCRP, 1993).

Beginning in 1981, the conservative Republican administration of President Ronald Reagan tried unsuccessfully to limit lobbying and advocacy activities of all human services organizations through executive orders and such devices as Circular A-122 of the Office of Management and Budget (OMB) (Wolch, 1990). Part of the battle against conservative limits on advocacy groups was led by NCRP in its efforts to open up the campaign for federal government employees (known as the Combined Federal Campaign or CFC) to groups such as black people, Hispanics, and Native Americans and to social action groups of all kinds (Brilliant, 1990). By the end of the 1980s, permissible limits for lobbying activities were tied to formulaic amounts related to the agencies' operating budgets (Hopkins, 1991).

Fundraising limits for voluntary organizations were also denied by the Supreme Court (*Maryland v. Munson,* 1984; *Schaumburg v. Citizens for a Better Environment,* 1980). Finally, a combination of legal decisions in the lower courts and congressional legislative action greatly expanded choices in the federal employees campaign (Bremner, 1988; Brilliant, 1990). Consequently, by 1993, 937 organizations were represented in CFC, including additional alternative federations and funds such as the black united funds, as well as environmental advocacy federations and legal defense funds, such as the National Organization for Women Legal Defense Fund and Education Fund and the National Association for the Advancement of Colored People Legal Defense and Educational Fund. Moreover, as donor choice became a major factor in the CFC, employees in the private sector also began to want choices in the regular community-based workplace campaign, and donors' designations became more widespread.

Despite the increased number of donor-designation campaigns, in 1993 an estimated 2,300 local United Ways still were reported to be providing more than 50 percent of their funds to local affiliates of 17 national organizations, including such longtime member agencies as the Red Cross,

YMCA and YWCA, Boy Scouts and Girl Scouts, Boys Clubs and Girls Clubs, family agencies, and the Salvation Army (Sumariwalla, 1993). In addition, partnership agreements with powerful health organizations such as the American Heart Association and the American Cancer Society promised them special financial consideration. Although United Ways were trying to respond to new issues, such as acquired immune deficiency syndrome, structural unemployment, and increasing urban diversity, most donor designations were going to their own member agencies (NCRP, 1993). The United Way "pie" was not increasing fast enough to meet the new demands. United Way reported raising $3.17 billion nationwide in 1991, but contributions declined after management problems were discovered in 1992, and in 1993 receipts were only $3.05 billion (United Way of America, 1994).

DIMENSIONS AND SCOPE

Overview

The number of tax-exempt organizations in the IRS master file in 1993 was 1,118,118, up from 309,000 entities in 1967 (Weisbrod, 1988) and 939,105 entities in 1987. The sector grew rapidly starting in the late 1960s; applications for tax-exempt status averaged about 7,000 a year from the 1950s to the mid-1960s, but doubled from 7,000 to 14,000 in 1965 and reached 64,000 annually by 1984 (Weisbrod, 1988). The sector expanded thereafter but at a less accelerated rate; and from 1987 to 1989, more than 110,000 nonprofit organizations were added to the IRS list and 41,000 were removed (Hodgkinson et al., 1992).

In 1990 the 1.025 million nonprofit organizations represented about 5.9 percent of all formal entities in the United States (including businesses, farms, and government), down from 7 percent in 1970 (Hodgkinson et al., 1992); charitable organizations alone were about 4 percent of all entities. Expenditures of the nonprofit sector were estimated to be $389.1 billion in 1990, or more than double what they had been in 1982. However, these expenditures represented only $263.3 billion in 1982 dollars (Hodgkinson et al., 1992).

Variations in Scope and Size

Aggregate figures mask the considerable variation in size, purpose, and resources of organizations in the nonprofit sector. It is estimated that, excluding religious organizations and foundations, over 70 percent of 501(c)(3) organizations did not have to provide financial data to the IRS in 1989 because they had annual revenues of less than $25,000. On the other hand, of the 29 percent of the organizations that did file tax returns, 4 percent had annual expenditures of $10 million or more. According to Hodgkinson et al. (1992), this group "commanded 77 percent of total annual expenses, 75 percent of total assets, and 51 percent of total grants and contributions from government and private sources" (pp. 11–12). In contrast, 72 percent of the charitable organizations that did file annual returns had annual expenditures of less than $100,000, spent less than 4 percent of their total expenditures, received about 11 percent of total grants and contributions, and held less than 6 percent of total assets. Using different indicators, Salamon (1992) concluded that only about 164,000 nonprofit public-benefit service organizations employed one or more staff people. In short, the arena of voluntary agencies is dominated in number by many small organizations, whereas the majority of resources are commanded by a few giant organizations.

Categories and Subcategories

A variety of attempts have been made to classify subgroups of the nonprofit sector for analytic and quantitative purposes. Three major types of classification currently exist.

Donative and fee-for-service. The first (and the most inclusive and theoretical) categorization is represented by economists, such as Hansmann (1987, 1989), who are interested in differences between donative (that is, charities and foundations) and commercial or fee-for-service nonprofit organizations, such as hospitals; these differences are conceptually related to changing provisions of the tax code.

Public-serving organizations. A second related type of categorization is used by researchers who are primarily concerned with distinguishing public-benefit and social welfare organizations from other more self-serving, tax-exempt organizations. This classification system is typified by Hodgkinson et al.'s definition of the independent sector as all identified 501(c)(3) and 501(c)(4) organizations, along with 350,521 churches that are not required to register with the IRS (Hodgkinson et al., 1992). A similar concept underlies Salamon's (1992) categorization of nonprofit public-serving organizations shown in Figure 1. Salamon believes that this group is what most people mean when they refer to nonprofit organizations.

Type of focus. A third, more pragmatic categorization relates primarily to the allocation of resources among 501(c)(3) and 501(c)(4) organizations. It includes the Standard Industrial Classification (SIC) system used by the IRS (and including all business corporations) and the National Taxon-

FIGURE 1

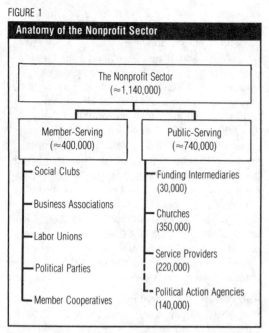

Anatomy of the Nonprofit Sector

The Nonprofit Sector
($\approx$1,140,000)

Member-Serving
($\approx$400,000)

- Social Clubs
- Business Associations
- Labor Unions
- Political Parties
- Member Cooperatives

Public-Serving
($\approx$740,000)

- Funding Intermediaries
  (30,000)
- Churches
  (350,000)
- Service Providers
  (220,000)
- Political Action Agencies
  (140,000)

SOURCE: Salamon, L. (1992). *America's nonprofit sector: A primer* (p. 13). New York: Foundation Center.

omy of Exempt Entities (NTEE), developed by the National Center on Charitable Statistics (NCCS). Although these classification systems include some easily understood categories, such as health or education, considerable inconsistency still exists among social welfare-related categories owing to variations in sources of data, the purposes for which the data were collected, and the lack of a generally accepted taxonomy. Thus, the SIC code groups social and legal services together, whereas the American Association of Fund-Raising Counsel (AAFRC) basically combines the categories of the NTEE system and reports data under the following categories: religion; education; health; human services; arts, culture, and humanities; public-society benefit; and international affairs. One additional differentiation of some significance is the distinction between national and local organizations (Tropman & Tropman, 1987).

NCCS is an affiliate of the Independent Sector, the Washington, DC–based national coordinating organization for the voluntary sector. Since 1987 the Independent Sector has been using the NTEE categories to make a complete inventory of all organizations in the sector, including those not listed with the IRS or in the SIC system (Hodgkinson et al., 1992). Also under way is the development of an international taxonomy (Salamon & Anheier, 1992).

U.S. Nonprofit Public-Benefit Organizations

Salamon (1992) analyzed data available for 1987 and 1989 on organizations with one paid staff member in the group he defined as nonprofit public-benefit service organizations. He found that social services agencies were the most numerous in this sector, encompassing more than 65,000 organizations, or almost 40 percent of the 164,360 total organizations in 1987. However, health organizations, which represented 11 percent of the total, clearly dominated financially, with expenditures of approximately $165 billion in 1989, or 56 percent of the total.

Nonprofit public-benefit organizations as a group received their largest source of income from fees and service charges (51 percent), followed by government funding (31 percent) and private giving, which had shrunk to only 15 percent of the total in 1989 (Salamon, 1992). For United Way–supported agencies, the pattern appears to be different. In 1992, these agencies received 45.4 percent of their income from government funding; 20.9 percent, from fees and dues; 10.5 percent, from fundraising; 11.6 percent from one or more United Way contributions; and 11.6 percent from other sources (United Way of America, 1992).

Charitable Contributions

Private giving to nonprofit organizations more than doubled in the period 1962 to 1993, rising from $60.93 to an estimated $126.2 billion. When these amounts are adjusted for inflation (1993 constant dollars), however, giving appears to be sensitive to difficult economic times, as well as to changes in the tax laws made in 1969, 1975, and 1981. As AAFRC (1994) reported, private giving remained at about 2 percent of the gross domestic product throughout this period, although the percentage dipped slightly in the 1970s.

Donations from living individuals remained the largest source of all gifts from 1990 to 1993. In this period, these gifts decreased slightly (from 81.47 percent to 81.25 percent) of all reported gifts. The next largest share came from bequests, which also decreased slightly, from 6.83 percent of all giving in 1990 to 6.77 percent in 1993.

Corporate and Foundation Giving

Foundation giving increased both in absolute dollars and as a percentage of the total contributions from 1990 to 1993, finally moving slightly ahead of bequests by 1993 with 7.29 percent of the total contributions. Corporation giving, which was about 4 percent of the total in 1977, rose to a high of 6.08 percent in 1987. However, after rising from $1.41 billion in 1977 to $6 billion in 1991, corporate gifts remained flat at $6 billion and declined somewhat as a share of all giving (down to 4.69 percent) in 1993. In terms of constant dollars, corporate giving decreased from 1987 to 1993. (AAFRC Trust for Philanthropy, 1994).

Distribution of Private Contributions by Subsector

As Table 2 indicates, about 45 percent of the gifts between 1990 and 1993 went to religious organizations, which consistently received the largest share of private donations. Other data reveal that more than 94 percent of the gifts to religious congregations come from individuals (AAFRC Trust for Philanthropy, 1993). Human services, which received a smaller share of individual giving, declined from 10.6 percent of all philanthropic gifts in 1990 to 9.9 percent in 1993 and had the third-largest share of all private contributions, behind education; health was a close fourth. The share of corporate gifts going to both health and human services rose from about 29.9 percent of all corporate gifts in 1988 to 31.3 percent in 1992 (Moore, 1993).

Analysis of All Revenue Sources

The picture is different when income from all revenue sources is considered, including government grants, contracts, and fees. Table 3 reveals considerable differences in the proportion of revenues received by different types of organizations in the nonprofit sector in 1989. For example, health organizations received a far larger proportion of fees for service (55 percent) than the combined SIC group of social/legal services (23 percent). Although health spending in absolute dollars (including payments to physicians and organizational costs) was much larger than spending for social services ($539.9 billion compared with $42.7 billion in 1987) (Salamon, 1992), social/legal services received a higher percentage of their

revenues directly from the government (42 percent) than did other groups, In addition, private contributions were a more significant share of their revenue support (35 percent) than for either health (9 percent) or educational organizations (19 percent).

GOVERNMENT FUNDING AND INCREASED PRIVATIZATION

By the 1980s, there had been a clear ideological move toward privatization of various kinds (Kamerman & Kahn, 1989), or what some authors (Bendick, 1989; Starr, 1991) called "load shedding" by the federal government. Moreover, cutbacks in government funding hit the social services harder than other groups (Salamon, 1993). Reduced federal expenditures for social services from 1982 to 1984 were followed by gradual shifts from 1984 to 1987 that included increased state funds, but this increase did not enable social services to make up for inflationary growths in expenditures (Gronbjerg, 1993; Hodgkinson et al., 1992; Wolch, 1990). Based on 1980 constant dollars, federal spending in budgetary areas of greatest concern to voluntary organizations (exclusive of Medicaid and Medicare) declined by $112 billion from 1982 to 1990. The largest dollar cuts were in areas close to social services: education, training, employment, and services, as well as community development and economic development assistance (Salamon, 1993).

Although public social welfare spending actually increased between 1977 and 1989, most of the growth (77 percent) was in the areas of health and social security and other insurance payments; in inflation-adjusted 1989 dollars, social services spending declined by 19 percent. Between 1977 and 1987, the number of private social services agencies grew by 66 percent (Salamon, 1993).

TABLE 2
Distribution of Philanthropic Gifts for 1990–1993 (in billions of dollars)

Category	1990 $	1990 %	1991 $	1991 %	1992 $	1992 %	1993 $	1993 %
Religion	49.79	44.6	53.92	46.1	54.91	45.0	57.15	45.3
Education	12.41	11.1	13.45	11.5	14.29	11.7	15.07	11.9
Health	9.90	8.9	9.68	8.3	10.24	8.4	10.83	8.6
Human services	11.82	10.6	11.11	9.5	11.57	9.5	12.47	9.9
Arts, culture	7.89	7.1	8.81	7.5	9.32	7.6	9.57	7.6
Public-society	4.92	4.4	4.93	4.2	5.05	4.1	5.44	4.3
Environment	2.64	2.4	2.93	2.5	3.12	2.6	3.19	2.5
International	1.50	1.4	1.75	1.8	1.71	1.4	1.86	1.5
Undesignated	10.85	9.5	10.25	9.1	11.67	9.6	10.65	8.4
Total	111.72	100.0	116.83	100.5	121.89	100.0	126.22	100.0

SOURCES: For 1990–1991 figures: AAFRC Trust for Philanthropy. (1993). *Giving USA 1993: The annual report on philanthropy for the year 1992* (pp. 22–23). New York: Author. For 1992–1993 figures: AAFRC Trust for Philanthropy. (1994). *Giving USA 1994: The annual report on philanthropy for the year 1993* (p. 11). New York: Author, and personal communication from AAFRC to E. Brilliant.

TABLE 3

Sources of Revenue for Nonprofit Organizations According to Type of Agency, 1989 (percentage)

Type	Fees	Government	Private/ giving
Health	55	36	9
Education	63	17	19
Social/legal	23	42	35
Civic	27	41	32
Arts, culture	26	11	63
All	51	31	18

SOURCE: Salamon, L. (1992). *America's nonprofit sector: A primer* (p. 27). New York: Foundation Center; based on data compiled by Hodgkinson, V. A., Weitzman, M. S., Toppe, C., & Noga, S. M. (1992). *Nonprofit almanac 1992–1993: Dimensions of the voluntary sector.* San Francisco: Jossey-Bass.

From 1977 to 1989 revenues of the nonprofit sector increased by 79 percent (after adjusting for inflation), or more than twice the increase in government spending for social welfare (Salamon, 1993). A significant share of the increases (55 percent) came from market-related activities, such as fees from clients and sales of products, reflecting the commercialization of the sector.

PERSONNEL

Although exact employment figures are hard to determine for the entire nonprofit sector, estimates suggest a range from 7.9 million to as many as 10.3 million full-time-equivalent workers. Weisbrod (1988) concluded that if the ratio of employees to revenues is assumed to be about the same as that of the federal government, the total figure would be about 9 million. The sector is labor intensive; of an estimated $357 billion in expenditures for the independent sector [501(c)(3) and 501(c)(4) organizations] in 1990, $178 billion, or approximately 50 percent, went for costs for paid personnel, including salaries and benefits (Hodgkinson et al., 1992). In 1989, employment in the nonprofit sector was estimated at 8.3 percent of all nonagricultural employment in the United States, with total earnings for the sector about 6 percent of all nonagricultural earnings (Hodgkinson et al., 1992). Average salaries are lower than in other sectors (Hodgkinson et al., 1992), and far more women than men are employed in voluntary agencies. Workers in voluntary social services agencies also appear to suffer from morale problems (Fabricant & Burghardt, 1992).

Volunteers

Volunteering remains a strong phenomenon in the United States. The 1992 Gallup Poll survey found that the percentage of respondents who had volunteered had increased from 45 percent in 1987 to 51 percent in 1991. A slightly higher proportion of female respondents (53 percent) than male respondents (49 percent) reported volunteering. Volunteers were diverse ethnically and racially: 53 percent of the white respondents, 43 percent of the black respondents, and 38 percent of the Hispanic respondents volunteered. It was also noted that black and Hispanic volunteers were asked to volunteer less frequently. Volunteers perform a variety of tasks, in addition to fundraising and sitting on boards; 8 percent of their activities overall are in human services. For agencies that are hard pressed for financial support, volunteer labor is a valued asset (Weisbrod, 1988).

The National Center for Charitable Statistics assigned dollar values to the work of volunteers based on full-time-equivalent work hours. Efforts to have these figures counted officially as part of the voluntary sector labor force have not been successful, but pressure to include them for accounting purposes continues (Greene, 1993). On the basis of the results of a 1992 Gallup Poll survey, volunteers were reported to have given 20.5 billion hours of formal and informal services in 1991, about the same as in 1989. This time was estimated to be worth $176 billion (Independent Sector, 1992).

Research has shown that volunteering has a direct effect on contributing, so it is not surprising that those who reported volunteering gave 2.6 percent of their household income, compared with 1.4 percent given by those who did not volunteer. Although higher-income respondents give large amounts in the aggregate, lower-income respondents give a higher percentage of their income (Independent Sector, 1992).

The motives for volunteering vary, from altruism to self-interest. In the 1992 Gallup Poll survey, respondents indicated the following as important reasons for volunteering: helping others (70 percent), doing something for a cause they believed in (61 percent), and compassion for people in need (58 percent) (Independent Sector, 1992). An obvious finding is that volunteers have to be asked; however, volunteering by adults is connected to other experiences in life, including voting, higher educational levels, and teenage activities. Altruism is a contestable idea that seems "impossible . . . and ubiquitous" (Schwartz, 1993). However, it is believed to be a motive for actions, including volunteering (Piliavin & Charng, 1990; Schwartz, 1993; Wakefield, 1993). Thus, although volunteers may derive personal pleasure and even personal advantage in the process (for example, contacts with other people who can be useful to their career goals), volunteering may also be done for a regard for others (Story, 1992).

Social Workers

By 1993 an NASW survey (Gibelman & Schervish, 1993a) found that nearly half (46.7 percent) the respondents were employed in the voluntary sector (see Table 4). Moreover, the data suggest that social work employment in nonprofit agencies has increased relative to the public sector. Based on reported membership data, the number of NASW members employed in nonprofit (sectarian and nonsectarian) agencies grew from 26,623 in 1988 to 32,246 in 1991 (Gibelman & Schervish, 1993b).

The decreasing proportion of public-sector employment seems congruent with cutbacks in government-funded services, as well as the preferences of social workers for moving into private mental health counseling (psychotherapy) and away from the more public-minded emphasis on serving poor people. In light of social work's historical mission of serving the most disadvantaged, the trend away from the "social" in social work and the declining government role is considered a problem (Walz & Groze, 1991; Wenocur & Reisch, 1989). However, another problem may be the lack of recognition of the reality that numerous social workers do practice in voluntary agencies and, consequently, that more attention should be paid to how these agencies influence social welfare programs and policy. Of the approximately 35 centers for the study of the nonprofit sector in the United States, only two are directly connected with schools of social work ("Academic Centers," 1993), and relatively few social work researchers focus on the sector.

EMERGING CRITICAL ISSUES

Privatization and Commercialization

By the 1990s, a trend toward commercialization in the voluntary sector had become apparent (Gaul

TABLE 4
NASW Members by Primary Auspice— 1988, 1991, 1993 (percentage)

Auspice	1988	1991	1993
Public local	18.4	18.5	14.3
Public state	17.9	15.0	13.9
Public federal	3.3	2.9	1.6
Public military	0.8	0.8	1.3
Private not-for-profit organization	39.8	38.9	46.7
Private for-profit organization			15.1
Private for-profit solo			7.0
Private proprietary	19.8	23.8	

SOURCE: Gibelman, M., & Schervish, P. H. (1993). *What we earn: 1993 NASW salary survey* (Table 6, p. 15). Washington, DC: NASW Press.

& Borowski, 1993; Salamon, 1992, 1993). A period of cutbacks in government funding for human services, coupled with the slowing of corporate support, was followed by expansion of agency entrepreneurship and fee-producing activities (Young, 1990). Despite the concern by small businesses about competition from nonprofit organizations (Bennet & DiLorenzo, 1989; U.S. Small Business Administration, 1983), the trend accelerated in the early 1990s (Salamon, 1993). Taxes paid on for-profit activities rose from $38.4 million in 1984 to $181.6 in 1992 (Gaul & Borowski, 1993). During a time of tightened federal funds for social services and a recessionary business climate, it makes sense that agencies would increase market-related efforts and that fundraising would become a more serious activity (Burlingame & Hulse, 1991). However, if the trend to additional commercial activities continues, there may also be more reluctance to continue tax deductions for organizations considered "commercial nonprofits" (Hansmann, 1987, 1989).

Who Benefits?

Despite increased need, research suggests that since the 1980s, nonprofit resources have not generally been targeted to poor and disadvantaged people (Clotfelter, 1992; Gronbjerg, 1993; Wolpert, 1993). Consequently, the debate about the purpose of the voluntary sector and the values it represents is both current and salient. The purposes of voluntary agencies are complex and perhaps best understood in the context of a reluctant American social welfare state that is facing growing social and economic problems (Fabricant & Burghardt, 1992; Gronbjerg, 1993). Although nonprofit organizations and community groups do not have the resources to deal with national poverty or the capacity to substitute for a well-defined public housing policy, nonprofit organizations can work cooperatively with the government and augment government actions in the provision of services (Gronbjerg, 1993). Grassroots organizations may also lead to community empowerment and policy changes (Wineman, 1984), although executives of nonprofit organizations who receive government money may be leery of political activism (Smith & Lipsky, 1993).

Planning and Coordination

Various studies (Brilliant, 1990; Odendahl, 1990; Wolpert, 1993) have suggested that individual choices in giving are not necessarily determined by the greatest identified community needs. In fact, individual donors are more likely to give to causes (such as health or religious causes) that affect them emotionally or from which they, more than the most needy or disadvantaged groups, may benefit (for example, the arts). The awareness of growing unmet needs in U.S. society may help refocus attention on the need for cooperation between the public and private sectors in allocation and resources planning at the community, as well as the federal, level (Wolch, 1990) and could result in the revitalization of community organization (Milofsky, 1988).

Increasing Internationalism

By the early 1990s, schools of social work and individuals from other academic disciplines (for example, economists, political scientists, sociologists, and lawyers) were showing more interest in working with their counterparts in other countries and in pursuing cross-national comparative studies. In the past, social workers paid little attention to the nonprofit sector in other countries, although a few scholars, such as Kramer (1981), pioneered studies on voluntary agencies in the early 1980s. In the 1990s, more specific attention has been paid to the role of nongovernmental (nonprofit) organizations in social welfare states of western Europe, as well as in the revitalization efforts of emerging democracies in eastern Europe and the developing nations of the "third world" (McCarthy, Hodgkinson, & Sumariwalla, 1992). Social workers are developing curricula related to community development and voluntary action in schools of social work and are active in interdisciplinary organizations, such as the International Society for Third-Sector Research.

Accountability

Although accountability has always been an issue for those who are concerned about the nonprofit sector, in February 1992 it moved dramatically to public attention. Bill Aramony, the United Way of America's national executive, was forced to resign under charges of personal excesses in his living and work styles, an excessive salary and perquisites, and poor management practices, including the abusive use of spin-off corporations (Barringer, 1992). An investigative firm hired by the United Way criticized Aramony's managerial practices and personal expenditures, but did not reach definitive conclusions about legal issues (Verner, Lipfert, Bernhard, McPherson, & Hand, 1992). He was, however, indicted in the fall of 1994. Meanwhile, in August 1992 a new national executive, Elaine Chao, was hired while the federal government was still investigating Aramony's activities. Poor results in the following United Way campaigns (in 1992 an estimated decrease of 6 percent from 1991) were at least partly due to concerns about the accountability of the organization (Millar,

1993). Moreover, by that time, the compensation of executives and the accountability of nonprofit boards of directors were high-profile issues, and congressional attention turned once again to benefits enjoyed by other nonprofit organizations. Hearings held by the Committee on Oversight of the House Ways and Means Committee in 1993 suggested that the late 1990s could see renewed attention to the privileges and responsibilities of executives and boards of directors of voluntary agencies. In light of the limited capacity of the IRS to monitor the activity of the sector (Gaul & Borowski, 1993), concern about private gain (inurement) from nonprofit organizations (Bailey, 1993) could result in pressures for new ways to ensure public accountability.

REFERENCES

Academic centers and programs focusing on the study of philanthropy, voluntarism, and nonprofit activities (list). (1993). Washington, DC: Independent Center.

American Association of Fund-Raising Counsel (AAFRC) Trust for Philanthropy. (1993). *Giving USA 1993: The annual report on philanthropy for the year 1992.* New York: Author.

American Association of Fund-Raising Counsel (AAFRC) Trust for Philanthropy. (1994). *Giving USA 1994: The annual report on philanthropy for the year 1993.* New York: Author.

Axinn, J., & Levin, H. (1982). *Social welfare: A history of the American response to need* (2nd ed.). New York: Longman.

Bailey, A. L. (1993, September 21). Poll finds widespread concern over charity spending. *Chronicle of Philanthropy, 5*(23), 27.

Barringer, F. (1992, April 4). United Way finds pattern of abuse by former chief. *New York Times.*

Bellah, R. N., et al. (1985). *Habits of the heart: Individualism and commitment in American life.* New York: Harper & Row.

Bendick, M., Jr. (1989). Privatizing the delivery of social welfare services: An idea to be taken seriously. In S. B. Kamerman & A. J. Kahn (Eds.), *Privatization and the welfare state* (pp. 97–120). Princeton, NJ: Princeton University Press.

Bennet, J. T., & DiLorenzo, T. J. (1989). *Unfair competition: The profits of nonprofits.* Lanham, MD: Hamilton Press.

Bremner, R. H. (1988). *American philanthropy* (2nd ed.). Chicago: University of Chicago Press.

Brilliant, E. L. (1973). Private or public: A model of ambiguities. *Social Service Review, 47*, 384–396.

Brilliant, E. L. (1985). United Way at the crossroads. In *The social welfare forum, 1982–83* (pp. 250–262). Washington, DC: National Conference on Social Welfare.

Brilliant, E. L. (1990). *The United Way: Dilemmas of organized charity.* New York: Columbia University Press.

Burlingame, D. F., & Hulse, L. J. (Eds.). (1991). *Taking fund raising seriously.* San Francisco: Jossey-Bass.

Clotfelter, C. T. (Ed.). (1992). *Who benefits from the non-profit sector?* Chicago: University of Chicago Press.

Commission on Private Philanthropy and Public Needs (The Filer Commission). (1975). *Giving in America: Toward a stronger voluntary sector.* Washington, DC: U.S. Government Printing Office.

Cuninggim, M. (1972). *Private money and public service: The role of foundations in American society.* New York: McGraw-Hill.

Donee Group. (1977). *Private philanthropy: Vital and innovative or passive and irrelevant?* The Donee Group Report and Recommendations (1975). (Research Papers, Vol. 1, pp. 49–85). Washington, DC: U.S. Department of the Treasury.

Douglas, J. (1983). *Why charity? The case for the third sector.* Beverly Hills, CA: Sage Publications.

Evans, S. M. (1989). *Born for liberty: A history of women in America.* New York: Free Press.

Fabricant, M. B., & Burghardt, S. (1992). *The welfare state crisis and the transformation of social service work.* Armonk, NY: M. E. Sharpe.

Gaul, G. M., & Borowski, N. A. (1993). *Free ride: The tax-exempt economy.* Kansas City, MO: Andrews & McMeel.

Gibelman, M., & Schervish, P. H. (1993a). *What we earn: 1993 NASW salary survey.* Washington, DC: NASW Press.

Gibelman, M., & Schervish, P. H. (1993b). *Who we are: The social work labor force as reflected in the NASW membership.* Washington, DC: NASW Press.

Gilbert, N., & Specht, H. (1986). *Dimensions of social welfare policy* (2nd ed.). Englewood Cliffs, NJ: Prentice Hall.

Ginzberg, L. D. (1990). *Women and the work of benevolence: Morality, politics and class in the 19th century United States.* New Haven, CT: Yale University Press.

Greene, S. G. (1993, March 9). Accounting proposals under fire. *Chronicle of Philanthropy, 5*(10), 29.

Gronbjerg, K. A. (1993). *Understanding nonprofit funding: Managing revenues in social services and community development organizations.* San Francisco: Jossey-Bass.

Gurin, M. G., & Van Til, J. (1990). Philanthropy in its historical context. In J. Van Til and Associates (Eds.), *Critical issues in American philanthropy* (pp. 3–18). San Francisco: Jossey-Bass.

Hall, P. D. (1987). Abandoning the rhetoric of independence: Reflections on the non-profit sector in the post-liberal era. *Journal of Voluntary Action Research, 16,* 11–28.

Hall, P. D. (1990). The dilemmas of research on philanthropy. In J. Van Til and Associates (Eds.), *Critical issues in American philanthropy* (pp. 242–262). San Francisco: Jossey-Bass.

Hansmann, H. B. (1980). The role of non-profit enterprise. *Yale Law Journal, 89,* 835–901.

Hansmann, H. B. (1987). Economic theories of nonprofit organizations. In W. W. Powell (Ed.), *The nonprofit sector: A research handbook* (pp. 27–42). New Haven, CT: Yale University Press.

Hansmann, H. B. (1989). The two nonprofit sectors: Fee for service versus donative organizations. In V. A. Hodgkinson, R. W. Lyman, and Associates (Eds.), *The future of the nonprofit sector* (pp. 91–102). San Francisco: Jossey-Bass.

Hewitt, N. A. (1984). *Women's activism and social change: Rochester, New York 1822–1872.* Ithaca, NY: Cornell University Press.

Hodgkinson, V. A., Weitzman, M. S., Toppe, C., & Noga, S. M. (1992). *Nonprofit almanac 1992–1993: Dimensions of the voluntary sector.* San Francisco: Jossey-Bass.

Hopkins, B. R. (1991). *The law of fund-raising.* New York: John Wiley & Sons.

Hopkins, B. R. (1992). *The law of tax-exempt organizations.* New York: John Wiley & Sons.

Hopkins, B. R., & Moore, C. L. (1992). Using the lessons learned from U.S. and English law to create a regulatory framework for charities in evolving democracies. *Voluntas, 3,* 194–219.

Independent Sector. (1992). *Giving and volunteering in the United States: Findings from a national survey, 1992 edition.* Washington, DC: Author.

Internal Revenue Service. (1992). *Annual report* [unpublished]. Washington, DC: Author.

Internal Revenue Service. (1993). *Annual report* [unpublished]. Washington, DC: Author.

Kamerman, S. B., & Kahn, A. J. (1989). *Privatization and the welfare state.* Princeton, NJ: Princeton University Press.

Karger, H. J., & Stoesz, D. (1990). *American social welfare policy: A structural approach.* New York: Longman.

Kramer, R. (1981). *Voluntary agencies in the welfare state.* Berkeley: University of California Press.

Kramer, R., & Grossman, B. (1987). Contracting for social services: Process management and resource dependencies. *Social Service Review, 61,* 32–55.

Lohmann, R. A. (1992). *The commons: New perspectives on nonprofit organizations and voluntary action.* San Francisco: Jossey-Bass.

Lubove, R. (1969). *The professional altruist: The emergence of social work as a career, 1880–1930.* New York: Atheneum.

Marris, P., & Rein, M. (1967). *Dilemmas of social reform: Poverty and community action in the United States.* New York: Atherton Press.

Maryland Secretary of State v. Joseph H. Munson Co. (1984). 467 U.S. 967.

McCarthy, K., Hodgkinson, V. A., & Sumariwalla, R. D. (1992). *The nonprofit sector in the global community: Voices from many nations.* San Francisco: Jossey-Bass.

Millar, B. (1993). Beneficiaries of a scandal. *Chronicle of Philanthropy, 5*(13), 23.

Milofsky, C. (1988). Scarcity and community: A resource allocation theory of community and mass society organizations. In C. Milofsky (Ed.), *Community organizations: Studies in resource mobilization* (pp. 16–41). New York: Oxford University Press.

Moore, J. (1993). Corporate giving to charities dropped in 1992, first decrease in 20 years. *Chronicle of Philanthropy, 5*(23), 8.

National Committee for Responsive Philanthropy. (1993, Summer). Donor choice bigger than ever for United Ways but only 2.4 percent of total pledges reach nonmembers. *Responsive Philanthropy,* p. 5.

Nelson, R. (1977). *The moon and the ghetto: An essay on public policy analysis.* New York: W. W. Norton.

Odendahl, T. (1990). *Charity begins at home: Generosity and self-interest among the philanthropic elite.* New York: Basic Books.

O'Neill, M. (1989). *The third America: The emergence of the nonprofit sector in the United States.* San Francisco: Jossey-Bass.

Piliavin, J. A., & Charng, H. W. (1990). Altruism: A review of recent theory and research. *American Review of Sociology, 16,* 27–65.

Salamon, L. M. (1987). Partners in public service: The scope and theory of government-nonprofit relations. In W. W. Powell (Ed.), *The nonprofit sector: A research handbook* (pp. 99–117). New Haven, CT: Yale University Press.

Salamon, L. M. (1992). *America's nonprofit sector: A primer.* New York: The Foundation Center.

Salamon, L. M. (1993). The marketization of welfare: Changing nonprofit and for-profit roles in the American welfare state. *Social Service Review, 67,* 16–39.

Salamon, L. M., & Anheier, H. K. (1992). In search of the voluntary non-profit sector, I.: The question of definitions. *Voluntas, 3,* 125–151.

Schaumburg v. Citizens for a Better Environment. (1980). 467 U.S. 618.

Schwartz, B. (1993). Why altruism is impossible . . . and ubiquitous. *Social Service Review, 67,* 314–343.

Siegel, D., & Yancey, J. (1992). *The rebirth of civil society: The development of the nonprofit sector in east central Europe and the role of Western assistance.* New York: Rockefeller Fund.

Simon, J. G. (1987). The tax treatment of nonprofit organizations: A review of federal and state policies. In W. W. Powell (Ed.), *The nonprofit sector: A research handbook* (pp. 67–98). New Haven, CT: Yale University Press.

Smith, S. R., & Lipsky, M. (1993). *Nonprofits for hire: The welfare state in the age of contracting.* Cambridge, MA: Harvard University Press.

Starr, P. (1991). The case for skepticism. In W. T. Gormley (Ed.), *Privatization and its alternatives* (pp. 25–38). Madison: University of Wisconsin Press.

Story, D. C. (1992). Volunteerism: The "self-regarding" and "other-regarding" aspects of the human spirit. *Nonprofit and Voluntary Sector Quarterly, 21*(1), 3–18.

Sumariwalla, R. D. (1993, September 21). Letter to the editor. *Chronicle of Philanthropy, V*(23), 42.

Tocqueville, A. de (1969). *Democracy in America* (G. Lawrence, Trans.). New York: Anchor Books.

Tropman, J., & Tropman, E. (1987). Voluntary agencies. In A. Minahan (Ed.-in-Chief), *Encyclopedia of social work.* (18th. ed., Vol. 2, pp. 825–842). Washington, DC: National Association of Social Workers.

United Way of America. (1992). *Fund distribution report.* Alexandria, VA: Author.

United Way of America. (1994, December). [Research services]. Alexandria, VA: United Way of America.

U.S. Small Business Administration. (1983). *Unfair competition by nonprofit organizations with small business: An issue for the 1990s.* Washington, DC: Author.

Van Til, J. (1988). *Mapping the third sector: Voluntarism in a changing social economy.* New York: Foundation Center.

Van Til, J. (Ed.). (1990). *Critical issues in American philanthropy.* San Francisco: Jossey-Bass.

Verner, Lipfert, Bernhard, McPherson, & Hand. (1992, April 2). *Report to the Board of Governors of United Way of America.* Washington, DC: Author.

Wakefield, J. C. (1993). Is altruism part of human nature? Toward a theoretical foundation for the helping professions. *Social Service Review, 67,* 406–458.

Walz, T., & Groze, V. (1991). The mission of social work revisited: An agenda for the 1990s. *Social Work, 36,* 500–505.

Wedel, K. R., Katz, A. J., & Weick, A. (Eds.). (1979). *Social services by government contract: A policy analysis.* New York: Praeger.

Weisbrod, B. (Ed.). (1977). *The voluntary non-profit sector: An economic analysis.* Lexington, MA: D. C. Heath.

Weisbrod, B. (1988). *The nonprofit economy.* Cambridge, MA: Harvard University Press.

Wenocur, S., & Reisch, M. (1989). *From charity to market economy.* Urbana: University of Illinois Press.

Wineman, S. (1984). *The politics of human services: Radical alternatives to the welfare state.* Boston: South End Press.

Wolch, J. R. (1990). *The shadow state: Government and voluntary sector in transmission.* New York: The Foundation Center.

Wolpert, J. (1993). Decentralization and equity in public and nonprofit sectors. *Nonprofit and Voluntary Sector Quarterly, 22*(4), 281–296.

Young, D. R. (1990). Entrepreneurship and organizational change in the human services. In D. L. Gies, J. S. Ott, & J. M. Shafritz (Eds.), *The nonprofit organization handbook: Essential readings* (pp. 301–314).

Eleanor L. Brilliant, DSW, is associate professor, Rutgers University, School of Social Work, 536 George Street, New Brunswick, NJ 08903.

For further information see

Advocacy; Boards of Directors; Charitable Foundations and Social Welfare; Citizen Participation; Community Organization; Ethics and Values; Fundraising and Philanthropy; International and Comparative Social Welfare; International Social Welfare: Organizations and Activities; National Association of Social Workers; Nonprofit Management Issues; Organizations: Context for Social Services Delivery; Planning and Management Professions; Public Services Management; Public Social Services; Quality Assurance; Quality Management; Sectarian Agencies; Social Development; Social Planning; Social Welfare History; Social Work Practice: History and Evolution; Social Work Profession Overview; Volunteer Management.

Key Words

nonprofit sector	social services
organizations	agencies
public sector	voluntarism

Volunteer Management
Patricia C. Dunn

Volunteering has always been a part of the human experience. *To volunteer* is to choose to act with an attitude of social responsibility when a need is recognized, without concern for tangible gain. To volunteer means to go beyond one's basic obligations, to go beyond what is expected or unavoidable. Ellis and Noyles (1990) emphasized the importance of the concept of volition in the definition of volunteers: The choice to act must be without coercion. People who are asked to volunteer when refusal would jeopardize their jobs or status are not volunteers. Slaves, although not paid, are obviously not volunteers. Even people who enlist in the current volunteer (nondraft) armed forces are not considered volunteers; although such enlistment is voluntary, it does not involve the choices, lack of monetary profit, and purposefulness of actions benefiting others that epitomize volunteering.

The words "volunteer" and "volunteering" have historically been a part of the American vocabulary, but the term "volunteerism" was not included in most dictionaries until the 1980s. Before that time, the term used was "voluntarism"—the "generic term for all that is done in a society voluntarily" (Ellis & Noyles, 1990, p. 5). Voluntary agencies are founded by people who recognize a need or cause and form an organization with private funds. Such agencies are nonprofit; although they may receive funds from grants or contracts from the government, they are not created by the government or law. However, volunteers are involved in voluntary agencies, government agencies, and for-profit organizations.

VOLUNTEERISM IN THE UNITED STATES

"The United States is the only country in the world where giving and volunteering are pervasive characteristics of a total society" (O'Connell & O'Connell, 1989, p. 3). The 1991 Gallup Organization survey, conducted for the Independent Sector (1992), estimated that 94.2 million Americans age 18 and older (51 percent) were involved in volunteer activities. These volunteers gave an average of 4.2 hours per week of their time, or about 20.5 billion hours, in formal and informal volunteering during 1991; the monetary value of this time was approximately $176 billion. (Formal volunteering is considered regular work with agencies and organizations, whereas informal volunteering consists of helping neighbors, friends, or organizations on an ad hoc basis, such as by baby-sitting without charge, baking cookies for a school fair, or helping a church set up its computer equipment.)

Volunteerism among People of Color
These interpretations of what constitutes formal and informal volunteering may miss important aspects of the traditions of volunteering in certain ethnic and racial segments of American society. Stanfield (1993) pointed out that when time and

volunteerism are given informal, kinship meanings, there emerge patterns and practices of civic responsibility that surveys on volunteerism have not usually captured. In his discussion of African American traditions of civic responsibility, Stanfield stated:

> The amount of time given to raising and in other ways caring for the children of others in African American communities is immeasurable. Informal adoption and child care in African American communities is a form of volunteerism that has yet to be studied as volunteerism. (p. 144)

Informal traditions and practices, such as these, may be found in other segments of society and must be identified and studied to extend the interpretation of volunteerism in such a way as to capture the richness of its meaning in the United States.

Characteristics of Volunteers
The demographic data on volunteering reported by the Independent Sector (1992) were based on the conceptualization of informal volunteering as consisting only of ad hoc activities. During the 12 months before the survey, 51 percent of the American population volunteered; 53 percent of the total female population, 49 percent of the males, 53 percent of white people, 43 percent of the African Americans, and 38 percent of the Latinos.

The three dominant reasons for volunteering cited most frequently by the respondents to the survey were the importance of helping others (70 percent), doing something for an important cause (61 percent), and compassion for people in need (58 percent). The 14 percent of the respondents who did four hours or more of volunteer work per week attended religious services regularly (63 percent), had some college education (61 percent), and belonged to a youth group or similar organization when young (66 percent). Their motives for volunteering were the importance of helping others (76 percent), admiration of people who help others (68 percent), doing something for a cause (68 percent), and exploring their strengths (64 percent).

The patterns of volunteering have changed over the years. Volunteers are more likely to be involved in more than one cause, spreading their volunteering over several different activities. Those in the health care, human services, and corrections arenas may be found on agency policy and advisory boards; on fundraising committees and groups; in advocacy and social action groups; and in various direct service settings, from nursing homes to child care centers, to crisis hot lines, to soup kitchens, to battered women's centers, to drug rehabilitation programs, to prisons. Although volunteers are the most active in direct services, there has been an increase in volunteers who are interested in advocacy and activism—who want to make a difference through petitions, testimonies, studies, and other forms of citizen participation (O'Connell & O'Connell, 1989).

IMPORTANCE OF MANAGEMENT

Types of Leadership

Competent leadership has always been necessary for volunteerism to be effective. According to Ellis and Noyles (1990), volunteer leadership has evolved along three parallel paths. Initially, volunteer leaders emerged from an all-volunteer group or were selected as leaders by group members. Such leaders were individuals who developed plans of action and around whom others rallied. Numerous examples of this type of volunteer leadership abounded in early America and still exist today. Harriet Tubman and Martin Luther King, Jr., were two such leaders of thousands.

Salaried staff who supervise volunteers as a secondary responsibility provide another form of volunteer leadership. Ministers, social workers, teachers, and physicians who are in charge of a spectrum of supplementary services for clients that are performed by volunteers are illustrative of this type of leadership.

The third type of leadership is provided by paid staff, whose primary purpose is to coordinate the work of volunteers. Hospitals, social welfare agencies, charitable organizations, and administrative offices of the courts all have directors of volunteers.

Professionalization of Leadership

There are several indications that the leadership of volunteers is evolving into a recognizable profession. In 1965 the *Dictionary of Occupational Titles*

indexed a three-tier career ladder for such leaders: supervisor of volunteers, coordinator of volunteers, and director of volunteers. The classic features that characterize a profession—a codified body of knowledge, a set of values and ethics, community sanction, self-monitoring, and commitment to service—are slowly emerging (Hoyle, 1980). Research on the nature and scope of volunteerism is becoming more prolific and sophisticated.

The establishment of standards and the development of professional values and ethics are being enhanced by professional associations and support organizations such as the Association of Volunteer Administrators, American Society for Directors of Volunteers, Directors of Volunteers in Hospitals, International Association on Justice Volunteerism, Directors of Volunteers in Agencies, the National Council on Corporate Volunteerism, VOLUNTEER: The National Center, ACTION, Voluntary Action Centers, and Retired Senior Volunteers Program.

With the professionalization of volunteer leadership has come the recognition that those who direct volunteer programs are indeed managers and must accept this responsibility. The processes of organizing and operating a volunteer program and a program involving paid staff are similar. Thus, managers of volunteers must be responsible for helping to identify suitable tasks and roles for volunteers in a community, organization, or agency; for writing job descriptions and agency policies; and for developing and monitoring budgets. They must also develop an understanding of clients, the services that clients require, and the factors that motivate people to volunteer. In addition, they must ensure that volunteers are recruited, screened, selected, and matched to jobs and be able to work with staff members to identify the services that volunteers can provide. Because volunteers are not paid for the services they render, it is necessary for volunteer managers to ensure that other reward systems are available and that special attention is paid to volunteers.

Training and Education of Directors of Volunteers

Uncertainty exists about the kind of educational preparation required for directors of volunteers. However, there is agreement that a core of general knowledge, based on a philosophy that affirms the importance of volunteering, is necessary. Few academic degree programs in volunteer administration exist; thus, continuing education departments and programs are the most common sources of educational opportunities for directors of volunteers. Many institutions offer both credit and non-credit courses that can lead to certificates (Patton, 1989). Such flexibility indicates a recognition that someone who is in or interested in the field of volunteer administration may enter the formal learning process through several entry points. The pursuit of certificates or degrees may be seen by the student or practitioner as providing both personal growth and professional status (Patton, 1989).

PLANNING AND EVALUATION OF PROGRAMS

Wilson (1976) called planning and evaluation the "Siamese twins" of management. She noted that "planning is deciding in advance what to do, how to do it, when to do it and who is to do it. It bridges the gap from where we are to where we want to go.... Evaluation is deciding if where we have gone is in fact where we intended to go" (p. 76).

Planning

The task of planning is the most basic function in the development and eventual operation of a volunteer program; without it, organizing, staffing, directing, controlling, and evaluating lose their meaning. Determining the need for creating or redesigning a volunteer program is the first step in the planning process.

When considering the creation of a volunteer program, one must ask the following basic questions regarding an organization's or community's readiness for such a program:

- What is to be achieved through a volunteer program?
- Is there a legitimate need for a volunteer staff?
- How committed are the board of directors and upper-level management to establishing and monitoring a volunteer program?
- Can the work be divided into jobs, some of which can be performed by part-time volunteers?
- What is the potential for recruiting volunteers in terms of their availability, the location of assignments, the flexibility in office hours, or other characteristics of the job?
- Can the staff provide necessary training, or are other sources readily available?
- What is the staff's attitude toward volunteers?
- How concerned are the staff about their jobs?
- Can the staff be motivated, helped, or taught to work with volunteers?
- Will paid staff time be committed to the volunteer program for defining jobs and training and supervising volunteers?

- Does the organization have (or will it have) a stated policy on volunteers?

Once a provolunteerism climate has been established and it has been decided that the time is right for starting, adjusting, or expanding a program, the planning process begins. Planning is critical not only to the initial design of a successful program, but to the ongoing evaluation that is necessary to identify possible impediments and to facilitate solutions during implementation. The planning process for volunteer programs is no different from that of any organization.

The first step is to identify clearly the purpose or mission of the program, which will form the basis for the program's goals and objectives. *Goals* are the general intents of the program and flow from the mission or purpose statement. *Objectives* are the translations of these goals into specific, measurable, achievable activities or performances. Planning addresses how goals and objectives will be accomplished through realistic budgeting, defining jobs, designing the organization's structure, and establishing timetables.

Evaluation

Evaluation—measuring what has been accomplished and how well—begins during the planning phase for new programs. For a new volunteer program, one should first evaluate the steps for establishing the program to determine how they were met. For both new and more-established programs, one should develop questions and procedures for each goal to show the extent to which it has been met.

Records of volunteer activities will provide statistics about the program's operations. Facts to be tabulated include recruitment outcomes, the types and number of volunteers, the hours of service provided by volunteers, descriptions of tasks and jobs performed by volunteers, the types of orientation and training sessions and the number of volunteers in attendance, the number of and reasons for reassignments, and the number of volunteers receiving recognition. The dollar amounts of the contributions to the community should also be computed to indicate how much the community would have had to pay for the work if it had not been done by volunteers. To calculate the dollar value, multiply the number of service hours by the minimum wage or the hourly rate paid to staff members who do similar work.

When evaluating an existing volunteer program, consider the growth of the program over the preceding years. Review the program's progress, identify its future direction, and determine how well the program fulfills its obligations to the organization, the community, and its volunteers.

DESIGNING JOBS AND RECRUITING VOLUNTEERS

The reason why volunteers are needed must be clear before volunteers are enlisted. "Recruiting before designing jobs is rather like trying to dance before the music begins" (Wilson, 1976, p. 10). The key factor in designing jobs is determining the relationship of these jobs to the organization's mission. The volunteer job should be woven into the fabric of the organization; it must be congruent with the other jobs in the organization.

Job Descriptions

The descriptions of volunteer positions should contain the following information:

- the duties the volunteer will be expected to perform
- the time requirements for the position
- the position of the person to whom the volunteer is accountable
- who assigns tasks on a regular basis
- qualifications (education and special skills)
- training (on the job or formal)
- benefits, if provided (for example, reimbursement of mileage, meal allowances, or free admission to events).

The best job descriptions are not elaborate and complicated but rather are clear and precise.

Job descriptions are important for a number of reasons. First, they provide the information volunteers need to make informed decisions. Second, they demonstrate to volunteers that their jobs are important and that the organization takes them seriously. Third, they clarify the relationship of the volunteers to the paid staff.

Recruitment of Volunteers

The best recruitment tools are an excellent volunteer program and meaningful jobs for the volunteers. Recruitment should be carefully planned and should include a determination of the best sources of volunteers, when to seek them, the message that will motivate them to join, and the easiest way to sign them up. Wilson (1976) suggested that recruiting should be targeted specifically to the appropriate audience whose interest and priorities best match the program's needs; for example, day care aides should not be sought at a club for business and professional women. Although recruitment may be specifically targeted, for it to be successful in the current environment, efforts must be directed at a broad spectrum of

geographic, gender, age, racial, and economic groups. Such efforts can be aided by organizations such as Voluntary Action Centers, Directors of Volunteers in Agencies, and Retired Seniors Volunteer Programs that recruit pools of volunteers for other organizations to use.

The Gallup poll survey (Independent Sector, 1992) found that 86 percent of the respondents who were asked actually volunteered; if people in the United States are asked to volunteer, the proportion of the population that volunteers will increase. The request to volunteer must contain a message that is developed with the audience in mind; for example, the message to an electrician's union will be different from that to retired members of NASW. The time of day, time of year, and amount of advance time needed when approaching prospective volunteers may affect the success of recruitment. For instance, the recruitment of student volunteers may be more successful in the summer than in the fall, and club members should be contacted early in the season before they commit themselves to other activities. Once a person has agreed to volunteer, the opportunity to sign up must be provided so the person can be contacted later.

SELECTION AND PLACEMENT OF VOLUNTEERS

If an organization is to benefit from the services of volunteers and the volunteers are to achieve satisfaction, the volunteers and their jobs must be well matched. Interviewing is the most commonly used method for making these judgments. The job description states the requirements of the position. The director of volunteers and the job supervisor determine how well the job description and the volunteer match.

Interviews are structured to facilitate appropriate placement, but they also give volunteers the chance to understand the job and decide whether it is something they really want and are qualified to do. The informed exchange should lead to a determination of the volunteer's motivations, aspirations, and goals for the work and should facilitate the assignments of volunteers on the basis of this information. The interview should be planned in advance and held in a comfortable setting. The interviewer must be objective, open, and friendly; establish rapport from the beginning; and record the outcome of the interview, omitting confidential information. If a volunteer cannot be placed, information about him or her may be sent, with the volunteer's approval, to a volunteer bureau. A volunteer who is not a match at one agency may nonetheless be well suited for another.

RETAINING VOLUNTEERS

Volunteers must be trained; supervised; recognized; evaluated; and, when their performance is ineffective, released with the same thoughtful planning and implementation accorded to paid staff. Orientation and ongoing training are the foundation for retaining effective volunteers.

Orientation and Training

Orientation consists of a general introduction to the organization, such as a description of the organization's mission or purpose, structure, and programs. Office tours and introductions to relevant personnel are essential; it is important for volunteers to become acquainted with the entire organization, not merely the departments in which they will work. They may become the organization's best spokespersons in the community, so they should be kept well informed.

Training is the formal learning process that may be required of volunteers through attendance at workshops, seminars, courses, or on-the-job training. If volunteers are not made aware of the requirement or expectation that they participate in formal training activities during the placement interview, then that commitment must be clearly defined during orientation. If in-service training is provided by the organization for paid staff, volunteers should also be included if the subject matter is pertinent to their assignments. Many volunteers are eager to sharpen their skills or to learn new skills. It is important to note that volunteers, although often motivated by a concern for those who are less fortunate than they, may need assistance in translating their viewpoint about people into one that is free of "isms," including paternalism. Making training available to them can result in improved services.

Recognition

To a large extent, *recognition* is the "currency" that an organization uses to express its appreciation for the work of the volunteers and is critical to the success of the program. Appreciation should be conveyed on a continuing basis. Attention can be given to volunteers in small ways and without much effort, but with a great amount of meaning to the individuals. In some instances, name tags or uniforms to wear on duty may give volunteers a sense of status and the feeling that they are members of the team. Other ways of conveying that the volunteers are valued and accepted include notes of appreciation, recognition in newsletters or on bulletin boards, positive verbal feedback, and inclusion in staff meetings. More formal recognition can be made at an annual event during National Volunteer Week, when organizations generally honor volunteers at a dinner, picnic, or special meeting. Paid staff who work with the volunteers should also be involved in the recognition.

Evaluation

Volunteers, like paid workers, should have their work evaluated. Evaluation is of value to both the organization and the volunteer. The volunteer's performance should be periodically reviewed by the director of volunteers, the job supervisor, and the volunteers. The reviewers should measure the work accomplished against the job description and the attendance record to determine whether problems must be resolved or if there is a need for training. Before a volunteer resigns, he or she should be given the opportunity to express to the director of volunteers any concerns that may require changes or adjustments. Evaluation also provides opportunities to show appreciation for the volunteer's service.

Volunteers can be ineffective in their jobs for a variety of reasons: failing health, personality problems, insufficient skills, lack of motivation, or lack of time. Many organizations and agencies have written guidelines or policies for letting volunteers go. Some policies indicate that before a volunteer is fired, certain steps should be taken, such as talking with the volunteer about his or her performance problems, retraining the volunteer, or assigning the volunteer to another position. Preventive measures such as background checks, clear job descriptions, and regular evaluations of performance can reduce the incidents of ineffective volunteering.

RECORD KEEPING

Record keeping is necessary: The organization needs it, and the volunteer has a right to expect it. The volunteer can use records for references and as permanent indicators of skills that have been learned. When treated as a managerial tool, the records of volunteer service yield information that can be used to evaluate individuals, assess programming, plan for the agency's development, and provide data to the community about the value of services (Sissel, 1989, p. 21).

There are four major steps for documenting the services of volunteers: (1) defining what is to be recorded, (2) planning how to record it, (3) collecting it, and (4) deciding what should be reported and how to report it (Sissel, 1989). Determining what is to be recorded will vary from organization to organization, but most records will document the volunteers' participation by including accurate demographic information about who the volunteers are, what jobs they perform, and how often they work. The core of a documentation system is the individual personnel file, which should include pertinent medical information, emergency numbers, evaluation forms, supervisory records, up-to-date totals of hours worked, the job description, and awards and other forms of recognition. Systems for collecting such information must be user friendly and provide the data needed by the director of volunteers. For example, a system for recording volunteers' service hours and type of work can be a simple sign-in and sign-out sheet or a more sophisticated form.

There are various ways to report the data that are collected, depending on what the director of volunteers wants to accomplish. Data may be reported in the number of hours the volunteers contributed and the dollar value of the services provided. Volunteers may be tracked by the type of services they provide, where they work, and the impact of this work on time saved by paid staff. Reports may be generated by the volunteers' age, gender, race, and work status.

STAFF–VOLUNTEER RELATIONSHIPS

In organizations that have both paid staff and volunteers, the resulting dynamics between the two groups are affected by the quality of the attention that management gives this issue. Often it is assumed that productive volunteer–paid staff relationships just happen. Actually, such relationships are forged through cooperation, consideration, and hard work; they are not merely the product of good intentions. Frequently, however, difficulties between paid staff and volunteers arise despite good intentions, especially when workloads increase, budgets decrease, and egos and tempers collide (Schroder, 1986).

In some fields or settings, labor unions have taken a strong position against what they view as volunteers' encroachment on their turf. Volunteers are viewed as contributing to unemployment by doing jobs that others can be paid to do, and it is feared that volunteers will be used as strike breakers. Paid staff may perceive volunteers as undependable or uncontrollable amateurs who cannot perform the tasks as well as they can. Other objections to volunteers are based on such grounds as insurance costs and confidentiality.

The director of volunteers has the challenge of differentiating between objections that are legitimate (for example, the amount of time it takes to train and supervise volunteers) and underlying

sources of resistance (for instance, professionals' unwillingness to share work, spend time training volunteers, or recognize the value of services that only members of the community can provide). The director must also be on guard against exploiting volunteers to the detriment of the unemployed. He or she is usually in a position to define the most appropriate roles for volunteers in such a way as to prevent exploitation.

Clear and frequent communication plays an important role in the development of productive paid staff–volunteer relationships (Schroder, 1986). Volunteers should be involved in the decision-making processes of the organization, particularly in the areas that use volunteers. Job descriptions and lines of accountability must be clear. Usually, volunteers are directly responsible to the paid staff, but the staff must be trained to use them properly, and the volunteers must be taught how to work effectively with the staff and how to be sensitive to the staff's problems.

MARKETING

Marketing is important in recruiting and retaining volunteers, establishing a climate of provolunteerism in an organization, gaining public and organizational support, and obtaining resources (goods, services, and dollars). The mastery of marketing is critical to the success of volunteer programs, particularly in times of shrinking resources and greater demands by clients.

Vineyard (1984) approached marketing as an exchange process consisting of publics, markets, and an exchange relationship. *Publics* are identifiable segments of the society that surround volunteer programs. They can be identified by title (Girl Scouts), generic quality (senior citizens), or classification (paid staff, clients, group or organizational spokespersons, regulatory bodies, and providers of goods and supplies). These segments do not have to be groups with which the volunteer program intends to interact; they simply exist. A *market* is a public with whom the volunteer director wishes to establish a trade relationship. The "bargain" that is struck between the volunteer program and the markets who have what is needed is referred to as the *exchange relationship*.

To operationalize this relationship, Vineyard (1984) suggested that directors of volunteers use the following four-stage process:

- *Stage 1:* identify the resources possessed by and available to the volunteer program (the research stage)
- *Stage 2:* identify specific needs of the volunteer program for people, goods, funds, support, and services

- *Stage 3:* discover which individuals, groups, sectors, and organizations have the resources the volunteer program needs
- *Stage 4:* establish strategies for acquiring what is needed by using data from the first three stages.

Three broad marketing strategies may be adopted—undifferentiated (treating the whole market as homogeneous), concentrated (dividing the market into segments but focusing on only one of the segments), and differentiated (focusing on two or more market segments but with different messages). Once the appropriate marketing strategy has been selected, it is important to pay careful attention to getting the message across through advertising, promotion, personal selling, and publicity.

FINANCIAL MANAGEMENT

In establishing or maintaining a volunteer program, perhaps the most crucial issue is whether the funds to be expended are justifiable. Sues and Wilson (1987) recommended a three-step approach to resolving this issue: (1) compute the costs of the program, (2) quantify the outcome of providing volunteer services, and (3) calculate the cost–benefit ratio.

The itemized budget is the usual and most effective tool for determining the costs of a volunteer program. Both direct and indirect costs are calculated and include the salaries of the director of volunteers and other paid personnel; fringe benefits; marketing costs; the cost of training materials and the trainers' time; and the cost of meals, parking, and supplies. The dollar amounts attached to these cost categories represent an estimate of the program's expenditures.

The quantification of the outcomes of volunteer services helps the director of volunteers justify the program's costs in relation to its benefits. This is not an easy task because these benefits are often intangible and do not lend themselves to quantification. They are best described in such terms as "better relations with the community" and "increased attention given to clients by volunteers" (Sues & Wilson, 1987). The number of hours of service provided by volunteers is one means of quantifying these outcomes because these hours represent the direct or more tangible benefits of the program.

The calculation of the cost–benefit ratio is computed by dividing the cost of the program by the number of volunteer hours. The resulting figure can then be compared with the costs of similar hourly services being provided by paid staff or those paid for similar services according to U.S. labor statistics. Record keeping is the indispensable key to budgeting and cost analysis. As services are provided and funds are expended, transactions must be systematically and accurately recorded and reported. Financial reports are best done on an accrual basis. *Accrual bookkeeping* involves keeping records of the income, the actual expenditure incurred, and the outstanding obligations not yet paid.

RISK AND LIABILITY

Volunteers and those who manage them must be concerned with volunteers' exposure in a litigious society. There does not appear to be a uniform answer from insurance companies about how they treat claims against a volunteer. Often underwriters do not understand volunteer organizations and have great difficulty assessing the exposure created by volunteers. Underwriters may think that an insured organization has control over when and in what manner its paid staff perform their jobs, but may view volunteers as being beyond the organization's control. Most insurance carriers, however, will defend a volunteer against liability claims on the basis that the volunteer was acting as an agent of the organization, especially when the job descriptions of volunteers and the routes of accountability are clear. The general crisis in insurance and liability has resulted in more in-depth screening of potential volunteers.

Volunteers must be placed in situations in which they feel safe. Directors of volunteers in criminal justice organizations have been leaders in providing training that includes "be wary" guidelines and discussions of realistic expectations (Arnold, 1993). Volunteers are taught, for example, not to take offenders home with them, lend them money, or provide them with alcohol or other drugs and to report irregular behavior to the program staff. Arnold found that the risks to volunteers in community corrections organizations were reduced when the emphasis was changed from providing friendship to accomplishing specific tasks, such as tutoring and developing hobbies, parenting skills, and job-search skills. Offenders often abused relationships and occasionally victimized volunteers before the focus of the volunteers' work was tightened by making it task specific.

SUMMARY

During the colonial period, when individuals and families encountered difficulties beyond their own means, friends, neighbors, or representatives of the community would often volunteer to meet their needs. Ultimately, such private attention was not sufficient to assist those who could not help themselves. Thus, out of voluntary acts of service, formal social services organizations were founded.

The social work profession has its roots in volunteerism. Social workers started as volunteers and gradually "professionalized" by becoming salaried and trained. On one level, the activities of today's volunteers are somewhat similar to those of social workers. Much of volunteer work in human services settings involves working with individuals or providing resources and support to them personally. Unlike social workers, however, volunteers frequently view problems as rooted in factors of individual motivation and inadequacies, and volunteers are generally eager to help people change (Pierce, 1989). The challenge for social workers is to transform the perspective of volunteerism, from one which focuses on help at the interpersonal level and excludes social factors in the causes of problems to one that also includes a commitment to social change and policy interventions.

REFERENCES

Arnold, C. S. (1993). Respect, recognition are keys to volunteer programs. *Corrections Today, 55*(5), 118–122.
Dictionary of occupational titles (3rd ed.). (1965). Washington, DC: U.S. Employment Security Bureau.
Ellis, S. J., & Noyles, K. H. (1990). *By the people—A history of Americans as volunteers* (rev. ed.). San Francisco: Jossey-Bass.
Hoyle, C. O. (1980). *Continuing learning in the professions.* San Francisco: Jossey-Bass.
Independent Sector. (1992). *Giving and volunteering in the United States.* Washington, DC: Author.
O'Connell, B., & O'Connell, A. B. (1989). *Volunteers in action.* New York: Foundation Center.
Patton, J. H. (1989). 1988–1989 update of programs in volunteer management in colleges and universities. *Journal of Volunteer Administration, 8*(3), 34–39.
Pierce, D. (1989). *Social work and society.* New York: Longman.
Schroder, D. (1986, Fall). Can this marriage be saved? Thoughts on making paid staff–volunteer relationships healthier. *Voluntary Action Leadership,* pp. 16–17.
Sissel, P. (1989, Spring). Documenting volunteer participation: Recording techniques. *Voluntary Action Leadership,* pp. 20–22.
Stanfield, J. H. III. (1993). African American traditions of civic responsibility. *Nonprofit & Voluntary Sector Quarterly, 22*(2), 137–153.
Sues, A. M., & Wilson, P. A. (1987). Developing a hospital's volunteer program. *Health & Social Work, 12,* 13–27.
Vineyard, S. (1984). *Marketing magic for volunteer programs.* Downers Grove, IL: Heritage Arts.
Wilson, M. (1976). *The effective management of volunteer programs.* Boulder, CO: Volunteer Management Associates.

FURTHER READING

Ellis, S. J. (1994). *The volunteer recruitment book.* Philadelphia: Energize.
Fisher, J. C., & Cole, K. M. (1993). *Leadership and management of volunteer programs: A guide for volunteer administrators.* San Francisco: Jossey-Bass.
Hall, H. (1992, July 28). How to check out the backgrounds of volunteers. *Chronicle of Philanthropy,* pp. 21–22.
Kamier, W. (1984). *Women volunteering—The pleasure, pain and politics of unpaid work from 1930 to the present.* Garden City, NY: Anchor Press.
Kipps, H. C. (1991). *Volunteerism: The directory of organizations, training programs and publications* (3rd ed.). New Providence, NJ: R. R. Bowker.
Lappe, F. M., & DuBois, P. M. (1994). *The quickening of America: Rebuilding our nation, remaking our lives.* San Francisco: Jossey-Bass.
Lopez, D., & Getzel, G. S. (1987). Strategies for volunteers caring for persons with AIDS. *Social Casework, 68,* 47–53.
Martin, M. W. (1994). *Virtuous giving: Philanthropy, voluntary service, and caring.* Bloomington: Indiana University Press.
Morrow-Howell, N., & Mui, A. (1989). Elderly volunteers: Reasons for initiating and terminating service. *Journal of Gerontological Social Work, 13*(3–4), 21–34.
Parsonnet, L., & Weinstein, L. (1987). A volunteer program for helping families in a critical care unit. *Health & Social Work, 12,* 29–38.
Peters, J. (1989, Winter). Required volunteering: Contradiction or congruity. *Voluntary Action Leadership,* p. 23.
Remington, J. (1991). *The need to thrive—Women's organization in the Twin Cities.* St. Paul: Minnesota Women's Press.
Scheier, I. H. (1993). *Building staff/volunteer relations.* Philadelphia: Energize.
Schwartz, F. S. (1984). *Voluntarism and social work practice: A growing collaboration.* New York: University Press of America.
Vosburgh, W. W. (1988). Voluntary associations, the homeless and hard-to-serve populations: Perspectives from organization theory. *Journal of Voluntary Action Research, 17*(1), 10–23.

Patricia C. Dunn, EdD, ACSW, is associate dean, Rutgers University, School of Social Work, 536 George Street, New Brunswick, NJ 08903.

For further information see

Advocacy; Charitable Foundations and Social Welfare; Citizen Participation; Community; Fundraising and Philanthropy; Information and Referral Services; International and Comparative Social Welfare; International Social Welfare: Organizations and Activities; Social Welfare: Management Overview; National Association of Social Workers; Organizations: Context for Social Services Delivery; Planning and Management Professions; Professional Conduct; Professional Liability and Malpractice; Sectarian Agencies; Social Welfare History; Social Work Profession: History; Supervision and Consultation; Vendorship; Voluntarism.

Key Words

management	volunteerism
voluntarism	volunteers

Voter Registration

Richard A. Cloward
Frances Fox Piven

The United States in the only country in the democratic West that has not developed a system of universal voter registration. Identity cards are used as proof of eligibility to vote in many West European countries. England and Canada conduct door-to-door canvasses before national elections to register voters. Historically, the United States developed a system of periodic voter registration that placed the burden on the individual of surmounting often difficult obstacles. As a result, about 37 percent of the eligible electorate is not registered to vote at any one time, roughly 65 million people (Piven & Cloward, 1988). Two of every three unregistered voters reside in households with incomes below the median—which means that many unregistered voters are beneficiaries of social welfare programs (Piven & Cloward, 1988).

NATIONAL VOTER REGISTRATION ACT

Requirements

In 1993 Congress passed a method of voter registration reform that could result in universal voter registration, and it was signed by President Clinton on May 20, 1993. The National Voter Registration Act of 1993 (NVRA) (P.L. 103-31) requires that citizens be offered the opportunity to register when they get or renew driver's licenses (popularly known as "motor voter") or when they apply for welfare, unemployment, disability, or other human services (known as "agency-based" voter registration).

The NVRA is a milestone. It enunciates the principle that state governments have an obligation to enroll the eligible electorate, and it requires that they meet this obligation by making voter registration an integral part of the application process for driver's licenses and other services. These requirements will weaken, if not eliminate, the ability of state and local election officials to circumvent constitutional guarantees of the right to vote by encumbering that right with difficult—and sometimes virtually impossible—registration procedures.

Impact

If the legislation is implemented adequately by the states—the starting date is January 1, 1995—roughly 90 percent of the eligible electorate would be registered to vote as they renew or apply for driver's licenses, although it will take a few years to reach that level because of the four-year drivers' license renewal cycle (Human SERVE, 1990). Another 5 percent—mainly nondrivers—would be registered in public assistance, food stamp, Medicaid, Special Supplemental Nutrition Program for Women, Infants, and Children (WIC), and offices serving people with disabilities. National voter registration could rise from its current level of 63 percent to 95 percent (Human SERVE, 1990).

The NVRA would reduce racial differences in registration rates because more people of color drive or receive social benefits than are currently registered to vote. Differences by income would also virtually vanish. The act would enfranchise youths: less than 40 percent of those 18 and 19 are registered to vote but 80 percent have driver's licenses; by age 21, 89 percent drive (Human SERVE, 1990). Finally, the act requires that all state-funded agencies serving citizens with disabilities offer voter registration services. The NVRA could bring to a close a long, bitter history of the use of voter registration requirements to bar people from voting.

ORIGINS OF VOTER REGISTRATION BARRIERS

Between the first decades of the 19th and 20th centuries, the legal right to vote was successively extended to unpropertied white men, then to black men after the Civil War, and finally to women in 1920. The effects on voter turnout were spectacular, at least at first. With the end of property qualifications during the administration of Andrew Jackson, turnout began a steady upward swing, reaching 80 percent of the eligible electorate in the presidential election of 1840. Moreover, stable and high levels of participation characterized elections at all levels of the federal system.

State-created Barriers

However, before this century-long process of legal enfranchisement was completed, a variety of procedural barriers were introduced by states—summed up by the term "voter registration"—that prevented many poor people and people of color from voting. These barriers included literacy tests, registration closing dates as long as one or two years before elections, and requirements that people reregister periodically. County offices were established in remote locations where citizens had to appear in person to prove that they met registration qualifications (for example, literacy or residency) to officials who could be intimidating and hostile, particularly to immigrant or working-class applicants or people of color. This system of time and place restrictions, together with the refusal of many county elections officials to deputize volunteers to register people in their neighborhoods, compelled most people to travel to a county seat or to a downtown office in a big city to register, thus imposing income and travel barriers that poor people and people of color were less able to meet. Although it was the southern states that implemented these barriers with the greatest fervor, voter registration arrangements also were also introduced in many northern states (Franklin, 1969; Kousser, 1974).

Decline in Voter Turnout
These barriers depressed voter turnout to an astonishing extent. Between the presidential elections of 1896 and 1924, national presidential turnout fell from 79 percent to 49 percent (Piven & Cloward, 1988). The decline in the South came first and was more extreme—from 57 percent in the election of 1896, to 43 percent in 1900, to 29 percent in 1904, to a low of 19 percent in 1924. Black people and most poor white people virtually disappeared from the polls. The northern voting decline was less extreme, although still considerable—from 86 percent in 1896 to 57 percent in 1924 (Piven & Cloward, 1988). The northern decline was concentrated among immigrant youths, large numbers of whom were kept from the polls as they came of age (Erikson, 1981; Glass, Squire, & Wolfinger, 1984; Powell, 1986; Rosenstone & Wolfinger, 1978).

REGISTERING THE UNREGISTERED IN THE 1970s
It took a century to overcome the early voter registration restrictions on the right to vote. It took constitutional litigation, civil disobedience, and mob violence by southern white people and riots by northern black people. Finally, Congress passed the Voting Rights Act of 1965, which removed the more-onerous barriers to voting (such as literacy tests).

Once the Voting Rights Act was passed, millions of southern black people and poorer white people became potential voters. In addition, introduction of modern techniques to southern agriculture forced millions of black and white sharecroppers off the land. Most of the white people migrated toward southern cities; so did half of the black people. Other black people went north, to the industrial cities, where they were eligible to

vote. During this period, growing numbers of Hispanic people in the North and West also became a potential untapped electoral force. The implication of these huge pools of unregistered voters was clear. A voter registration war would occur.

Registration Methods
Three basic methods existed to allow people to register to vote: (1) registering to vote on election day; (2) mail-in registration; and (3) voter registration conducted by volunteers.

Registration on election day. Four states permitted people to register to vote on election day: Maine, Minnesota, Oregon, and Wisconsin. Although election day registration worked well in these states, politicians in other states nevertheless opposed it. They claimed to fear that having two long lines, one to register and one to vote, would create logistical chaos on election day, especially in large urban centers. They also claimed that fraud would occur, because elections officials would have no time to authenticate information given on registration forms. It was doubtful that this method of reform was politically feasible.

Mail-in registration. Some states permitted people to register to vote by mail. Three states enacted mail-in registration systems in the late 1960s; 17 in the 1970s; four in the 1980s; and five in the 1990s, including South Carolina and Mississippi, the first states to adopt this reform in the deep South (Human SERVE, 1990). But reformers neglected a crucial matter. The mail-in registration laws they won from state legislatures contained no method to get the forms into people's hands so they could complete them and mail them back. As a result, most people still had to go to a county seat or downtown office in a big city to register, and that tended to discriminate against poor people, people of color, and less-educated people. The potential of this reform was thus largely vitiated and did not produce higher registration rates.

Voter registration conducted by volunteers. The most common method of raising registration levels among poor people and people of color consisted of voter registration campaigns conducted by volunteers who went out with clipboards to sign up voters, one by one. For example, various organizations assigned hundreds of volunteers to canvass for new registrants in welfare and employment office waiting rooms, on food stamp lines, in public housing projects, and in lines where mostly women (usually with children) waited for federal surplus cheese. Organizations, such as the National Association for the Advancement of Colored People and the southern-based Voter Education Project and the Southern Regional Council, greatly expanded this method of voter registration.

Voter Registration Campaigns

Outgrowth of traditional civil rights movements. In 1976 the National Coalition for Black Voter Participation was formed, with a voter registration arm called Operation Big Vote. The purpose was to stimulate and coordinate drives among existing black organizations. Similarly, the low rates of registration among Mexican American people resulted in the formation in 1974 of the Southwest Voter Education Project, which had considerable success registering Hispanic people in Texas and throughout the Southwest. The Midwest Voter Education Project was created in 1982 to reach Hispanic people who had migrated to the Midwest, and the National Puerto Rican–Hispanic Voter Participation Project was formed in 1983.

The Citizen Action Network, which grew out of the shift by some civil rights and welfare rights organizers at the end of the 1960s toward white working- and lower middle-class constituencies, was doing voter registration in about 10 states. Associated Community Organizations for Reform Now, in accord with its traditional commitments, focused more on registering poor people and people of color in the slums and ghettos of industrial cities. The Women's Vote Project was organized to stimulate and coordinate drives by a range of women's groups. A Churches' Voter Registration Project was organized (financed by a consortium of northern Protestant denominations, although not on the scale of the evangelical effort described below) to register unemployed people and welfare and food stamp recipients. Public interest research groups and the United States Student Association targeted college students. Some peace and environmental groups joined in registration drives.

Evangelical movement. A Christian Right voter registration movement was undertaken, based mainly in pentacostal and evangelical churches in the South and, to a lesser extent, in the Midwest, and led by white clergy members who were trying to reorient the Republican party. The evangelical core comprises 20 percent to 25 percent of the adult population, or roughly 30 million adults, and is defined by their belief in the literal meaning of the Bible and the divinity of Jesus, by the acceptance of Jesus as one's personal savior ("born again"), and by the importance of proselytizing (Piven & Cloward, 1988).

Before the 1960s, protestant denominations in the South were largely conversionist—believing that the multiplication of saved souls was the

means to reforming the world. One consequence of the doctrinal disdain for secular political action is that members of these denominations had extremely low voter registration levels. But after the 1960s, the leaders of this socioreligious movement adopted a more conventional theory of social change, summoning the faithful to abandon withdrawal from the world to do secular combat with the enemy forces gathering under the banners of the civil rights and sexual and gender revolutions. New religious–political organizations formed, such as the Moral Majority and the Religious Roundtable, which subsequently urged evangelical clergy members to adopt the tactics of the civil rights movement: Make the church the staging area for political education, for voter registration drives, and for mass demonstrations and civil disobedience over issues like reproductive rights (Guth, 1983; Liebman, 1983). The Moral Majority claimed that cooperating churches registered 4 million to 8 million of these white evangelical people in the pre-1980 election period. Polls reported that they registered between 1 million and 2 million people (Piven & Cloward, 1988).

CHANGES IN THE 1980s

Competition for new voters intensified after the 1980 election. Analyses appeared showing that the number of unregistered black people in some key states exceeded Ronald Reagan's margin of votes. On the other hand, opinion polls and other data showed that rates of registration were lower among evangelical than nonevangelical people and that 30 percent of all nonvoters attended church services at least three times a week (Human SERVE, 1990). Competition between activists on both sides of the political spectrum was thus spurred.

Impact of the 1982 Recession

The recession of 1982 helped to trigger the greatest voter registration drives in American history. In the 1982 midterm election, a huge surge occurred in voting by black people, blue-collar workers, and unemployed people. In response to the highest unemployment since the Great Depression, midterm turnout rose for the first time in two decades, reaching 64 million or 10 million more than in 1978, and swelling the Democratic House vote by 6 million. The additional voters were mainly black and unemployed people, and turnout was up most in the Midwest and South (Piven & Cloward, 1988).

The sharp increase in blue-collar workers helped replace retiring Republican governors with Democrats in large industrial states such as Ohio,

Michigan, New York, and Texas as well as Wisconsin and New Mexico. At the same time, Republican incumbents were ousted in a number of economically hard-hit congressional districts, contributing to the Democrat's modest victory of 26 additional House seats (Edsall, 1984). "The question [for 1984] and the rest of the decade," the *Congressional Quarterly* (Cook, 1983) editorialized, "is whether this upsurge in the 'have-not' vote will continue. Both parties are making plans for 1984 on the assumption that it is here to stay, a result of the arguments and emotions of the Reagan era" (Cook, 1983, p. 1503). Virtually every major political strategist began predicting that turnout would rise sharply in 1984, especially among "marginal groups"—poor people, people of color, and women. It was, to cite the *Congressional Quarterly* (Cook, 1983), a time of "potentially historic significance" for the Democratic Party:

> They have a large pool of potential voters to target. Following the 1982 elections, the Census Bureau reported that 7.2 million blacks, 5.4 million unemployed, and nearly 12.5 million blue-collar workers of all races were not registered to vote. There are an estimated 2.5 million unregistered Hispanic citizens. [On the other hand], with the possible exception of fundamentalist Christians, [the Republican party] has no new, reliably Republican voting bloc to mobilize. The likely GOP voters, for the most part, have already been voting. (pp. 1504, 1507)

Competition for the 1984 Election

Analysts predicted that as many as 10 million additional voters might go to the polls in 1984, most of them Democrats. "What Reagan is in the process of doing," James Reston said, "is to scare the voters and wake up the dropouts, and encourage them to register and vote. This, no doubt, is a contribution to democracy and the Democrats, but not necessarily what the President had in mind for the Republican Party" (Reston, 1984, p. A19). Republican strategists were unnerved that there might be few unregistered voters with Republican sympathies. Republican pollster Lance Terrance warned that the downward tilt of the unregistered pool meant that "[f]or every new voter the Republicans pick up, the Democrats pick up two" (Cook, 1983, p. 1503). Traditional registration methods, such as setting up tables in shopping malls, could thus boomerang, producing more Democratic than Republican registrants. Democratic strategists crowed that while the Republicans were registering the "needles," Democrats were registering the "haystack." James Kilpatrick (1983), the conservative columnist, issued the obvious warning:

> Make no mistake. Democratic leaders will go after votes from blacks, Hispanics, welfare recipients, and disenchanted women for one unimpeachable reason. That is where the votes are. If the Republicans fail to mount a massive effort to register likely new Republican voters, the Republicans will take a drubbing in 1984. A Republican registration drive must concentrate on middle-income whites and Hispanics, conservative women and young people, and non-union families. (p. 18)

Fundamentalist campaign. Christian Right leaders naturally worried that Reagan's prospects for victory in 1984 were endangered—for example, Gary Jarmin, legislative director of the Christian Voice, circulated his view among religious leaders that they would have to register 2 million fundamentalist voters in 1984 just to stay even with the Democratic Party. Consequently, a number of these leaders, including representatives of the Moral Majority and the Christian Voice, coalesced to launch a national umbrella organization, the American Coalition for Traditional Values. Its main goal was to register 2 million fundamentalist voters in 25 states.

In a word, the largest voter registration mobilization in American history was forming in advance of the 1984 presidential election, whether measured by the money that would be spent, the number of organizations engaged, the variety of innovative approaches employed, or the number of people likely to be registered. A war was on to realign the parties by bringing new groups into the electorate.

Skewed results. By election day 1984, 7 million new registrants had been added to the voter rolls. Still, more than 60 million remained unregistered (Human SERVE, 1990). This meant that the "hands-on" method of voter registration failed in two ways. On the one hand, drives were not equal to the magnitude of the problem: too few volunteer canvassers, too many unregistered voters. Millions of unregistered low-income people and people of color could not be enrolled by volunteers. On the other hand, one in three Americans moves between presidential elections and studies showed that the less time people live at the same address, the less likely they are to be registered. In effect, residential mobility created a treadmill effect, canceling the impact of drives by constantly replenishing the pool of unregistered voters (Squire, Wolfinger, & Glass, 1987). In short, a way had to be found to register people en masse and to keep them registered despite residential mobility. An institutional solution was needed.

It also is true that money and effort directed by some organizations toward raising registration rates among poor people and people of color inevitably stimulate better-funded efforts by other organizations directed at white people, including better-off white people. For example, the Republican party mounted "hi-tech" drives by merging and purging computer tapes to identify unregistered people who owned late-model cars, subscribed to financial magazines, and lived in upscale neighborhoods. If they identified themselves as Republicans during telephone surveys, paid canvassers were sent out to register them in their homes. The result was to expand the electorate while maintaining the class and racial skew.

GOVERNMENT AGENCIES AS REGISTRATION SITES

To our minds, the solution was simple. Permit people to register in a range of government agencies. Make voter registration a routine part of application procedures, whether in driver's license bureaus or food stamp offices. The growth of government social services made this solution possible, because virtually every citizen had contact with public agencies. Government agencies could cope with the huge pool of unregistered voters; they could register all citizens regardless of race or income, thus overcoming class and racial skews; and they could reregister people after they moved. In short, agencies could be the path to universal voter registration in the United States.

Human SERVE

In the fall of 1982, as ferment over voter registration spread, we created an organization to promote this idea and named it Human SERVE (for Human Service Employees Registration and Voter Education). Ten years later, the Congress enacted the core of our plan—the NVRA. Human SERVE was formed to build an electoral defense of the welfare state in the face of concerted political efforts to slash social programs. This was a time when the legitimacy of social programs—especially the income-maintenance programs—had come under insistent questioning. Powerful groups in society claimed that the income-maintenance programs undermined work and family values and that funding them drew too much money from the private sector, thus undermining capital investment and the possibilities for higher productivity and economic growth. Under the circumstances, the opinions of poor people and families of color about the social programs needed to be given full consideration in the government decision-making process, because it was they who would be hurt most by

the proposed cuts. However, their opinions were not being considered fully because of their low voting levels, which were in part a reflection of barriers to voter registration.

Governance and funding. The board of directors of Human SERVE included a number of executive directors of national human service organizations, such as NASW, the American Public Health Association, and the Planned Parenthood Federation of America. Frances Fox Piven served as secretary of the board, and Richard A. Cloward as treasurer. In addition, Cloward served as executive director for substantial periods. The national headquarters of this organization was located at the Columbia University School of Social Work, and field offices were located in a number of the larger industrial states. To fund this project, Human SERVE raised about $5 million from foundations over 11 years, mainly from the Ford, Carnegie, Rockefeller, MacArthur, Diamond, Stern, Field, Joyce, and Veatch foundations.

Lobbying efforts. For most of the 10 years between 1983 and 1993, Human SERVE field staff worked to get states to enact legislation mandating that voter registration be an integral part of application procedures in driver's license bureaus (motor voter) and in human services agencies (agency-based voter registration). This effort consisted of conventional lobbying, either directly by Human SERVE staff or by coalitions organized by Human SERVE made up of civil rights, civic, labor, and student organizations.

The outcome of these lobbying efforts was remarkable. Human SERVE found, despite the Voting Rights Act in 1965, that powerful groups still opposed providing equal access to the vote by all citizens. The evidence was unmistakable. Politicians were willing to make voter registration available in driver's license bureaus but not in public assistance offices where poor people and people of color were more likely to be found. By the late 1980s Human SERVE had succeeded in winning motor voter programs in about 30 states. Minnesota was the only state to pass legislation that included human services agencies but did not implement this provision.

Opposition. The main opposition came from Republicans. They generally went along with motor voter initiatives but were adamantly opposed to human services voter registration. Human SERVE field directors argued in state after state that significantly fewer poor people and people of color held driver's licenses, especially in big cities, so that motor voter programs should be supplemented by voter registration in human services agencies. The plea fell on deaf ears. Republicans would have none of it. The reasons were not mysterious. Public opinion surveys and exit polls strongly suggested that black people were far and away the most Democratic (and the most progressive) constituency in the electorate, with Puerto Rican and Mexican American people not far behind. It was a curious historical turnaround: The Party of Lincoln was opposing minority voting rights. However, it also must be said that many Democrats from white ethnic districts were leery of registering welfare and food stamp recipients.

Federal Legislation

Human SERVE therefore decided that the federal government was the only hope, and Human SERVE campaigned for congressional legislation incorporating both motor voter and agency-based registration. Human SERVE had a distinct advantage in mounting this effort. By this time, motor voter programs had been shown to be a cheap, efficient, and fraud-free method of registering voters and of keeping them registered after address changes when they renewed their licenses. In other words, even though Human SERVE had failed to get voter registration in human services agencies, that Human SERVE did succeed in driver's license bureaus helped to establish the precedent that government agencies should offer to register citizens to vote. Furthermore, this innovation originated at the state level, which meant that congressional opponents of reform could not argue that federal legislation would infringe on states' rights. In effect, federal legislation would simply nationalize a reform that had already spread widely among the states. Indeed, when the federal bill was enacted in 1993, *Washington Post* political columnist David Broder (1993) remarked that "by building on the State experience, its sponsors have done something that is all too rare in Washington: They allowed the design to be field-tested before taking it national" (p. 17).

Introduction and enactment. Human SERVE worked to get legislation introduced in both houses of Congress and helped mobilize a national coalition of civic, civil rights, labor, and kindred organizations, including those representing people with disabilities, to work for passage—successfully as it turned out.

Provisions for voter registration in human services agencies were the main stumbling block, and it was Republicans who were again in opposition.

The chances are that many congressional Republicans would have supported a bill that was limited to driver's license bureaus. An early version that permitted but did not mandate human services agency registration did pass the House in 1990 with Republican cosponsors and some 61 Republican votes. However, later versions that mandated agency registration provoked fierce Republican objections in both the House and Senate ("we should register those who *give* to the country, not those who *take* from the country" was a constraint refrain in these debates).

The Democrats had a majority in the House to pass a model bill. The problem was in the Senate, where the Democrats had 57 votes, three short of the 60 votes required to shut off filibusters. The Republicans did filibuster, making it difficult to round up the three Republican votes necessary to restrict debate. Three cloture motions failed to receive the necessary 60 votes: one in September 1990 and two in July 1991. Then there was the problem in the White House. When a cloture motion finally survived in the spring of 1992, President Bush vetoed the resulting bill—on the eve of Independence Day. A year later, however, after the bill survived another filibuster, this time for 11 days, there was a Democratic president in the White House to sign it.

Implementation. As of late 1994, the implementation of the NVRA is proceeding unevenly and may even be imperiled by the sweeping Republican victory in the midterm elections of 1994. The problem is that Republican governors and states with Republican legislatures are resisting provisions for registration at human services agencies. They do not want low-income people and people of color registered. It is possible that a Republican Congress will try to amend the NVRA to eliminate mandatory voter registration in human services agencies, which could lead to a new round of filibusters (this time by Democrats), to a new series of cloture votes, and even to presidential vetoes and override votes.

Consequently, Human SERVE is working closely with the civil rights community to prepare legal suits. Routine registration in driver's license bureaus but not in human services agencies would be racially discriminatory and thus in violation of Section II of the Voting Rights Act.

CONCLUSION

The NVRA encourages agencies and organizations of all kinds—whether in the public or private sectors—to offer voter registration services. This means that not-for-profit agencies can participate without risking their tax-exempt status, provided the voter registration service is nonpartisan. Day care centers, family services agencies, settlement houses, child guidance clinics, and many other agencies can help remove registration inequalities between rich and poor people and between white people and people of color.

ADDENDUM

On January 4, 1995, as the 104th Congress convened, Republicans introduced the following four bills to delay, repeal, or make the NVRA voluntary (which means that states with Republican governors or legislators would likely not institute these reforms, especially in human services agencies):

- H.R. 370, "A Bill to repeal the National Voter Registration Act of 1993," was introduced by Representative Stump (R-AZ), with 15 Republican cosponsors.
- Two bills, H.R. 326, introduced by Representative Manzullo (R-IL) and 14 cosponsors, and H.R. 60, introduced by Representative Livingston (R-LA), both consist of a single sentence: "A Bill to provide that compliance with the National Voter Registration Act of 1993 shall be voluntary."
- S. 91, "A Bill to delay enforcement of the National Voter Registration Act of 1993 until such time as Congress appropriates funds to implement such Act," was introduced by Senator Coverdell (R-GA) and six cosponsors. (If this bill were to succeed, Republicans would then vote against funding.)

Republicans are attacking voter registration reform, because it would empower the very people whose safety net the Republicans want to shred. Republicans fear that registering millions of people in food stamp, Aid to Families with Dependent Children (AFDC), Medicaid, and WIC offices just when they plan to slash these programs could produce a dangerous upsurge of voting by irate poor and minority people in 1996, even aborting their hopes for party realignment—and they could be right. Two out of three of the roughly 60 million unregistered voters in this country live in households with incomes below the median. Earlier studies show that 70 percent of people who were registered by volunteer canvassers in food stamp and AFDC centers went on to vote in presidential elections. To force minority and poor people off the social welfare rolls, the Republicans feel that they must keep them off the voter rolls. As of this

writing, there is no way of forecasting whether these efforts to gut the NVRA will succeed.

REFERENCES

Broder, D. (1993, May 25). *Washington Post*, p. 17.
Cook, R. (1983, July 23). Reagan's legacy? "Have-not" surge to polls: Major force in 1984 election. *Congressional Quarterly Weekly Report, 41*(29), 1503–1507.
Edsall, T. B. (1984). *The new politics of inequality.* New York: W. W. Norton.
Erikson, R. S. (1981, July). Why do people vote? Because they are registered. *American Politics Quarterly, 8*, 259–276.
Franklin, J. H. (1969). *From slavery to freedom: A history of Negro Americans* (3rd ed.). New York: Vintage Books.
Glass, D., Squire, P., & Wolfinger, R. (1984, December/January). Voter turnout: An international comparison. *Public Opinion, 6*, 49–55.
Guth, J. L. (1983). Southern Baptist clergy: Vanguard of the Christian Right? In R. C. Liebman & R. Wuthnow (Eds.), *The new Christian Right: Mobilization and legitimation* (pp. 117–130). New York: Aldine.
Human SERVE. (1990). *Registration and voting.* New York: Author.
Kilpatrick, J. (1983, December 6). *Staten Island Advance*, p. 18.
Kousser, J. (1974). *The shaping of southern politics: Suffrage restrictions and the establishment of the one-party South.* New Haven, CT: Yale University Press.
Liebman, R. C. (1983). The making of the new Christian Right. In R. C. Liebman & R. Wuthnow (Eds.), *The new Christian Right: Mobilization and legitimation* (pp. 227–238). New York: Aldine.
National Voter Registration Act of 1993. P.L. 103-31, 107 Stat. 77.
Piven, F. F., & Cloward, R. A. (1988). *Why Americans don't vote.* New York: Pantheon Books.
Powell, G. B., Jr. (1986, March). American voter turnout in comparative perspective. *American Political Science Review, 80*(1), 17–43.
Reston, J. (1984, January 4). The political dropouts. *New York Times*, p. A19.
Rosenstone, S. J. & Wolfinger, R. E., (1978, March). The effect of registration laws on voter turnout. *American Political Science Review, 72*(1), 22–45.
Squire, P., Wolfinger, R. E., & Glass, D. P. (1987, March). Residential mobility and voter turnout. *American Political Science Review, 81*(1), 45–65.
Voting Rights Act of 1965. P.L. 89-110, 79 Stat. 437.

FURTHER READING

Burnham, W. D. (1965). *Critical elections and the mainsprings of American politics.* New York: W. W. Norton.
Cavanaugh, T. (1981). Changes in American voter turnout, 1964–76. *Political Science Quarterly, 96*(1), 53–65.
Ferguson, T. (1983). Party realignment and American industrial structure: The investment theory of political parties in historical perspective. In P. Zarembka (Ed.), *Research in political economy* (Vol. 6, pp. 1–82). Greenwich, CT: JAI Press.
Ferguson, T., & Rogers, J. (1986). *Right turn.* New York: Hill & Wang.

Harvard/ABC Symposium. (1984). *Voting for democracy.* New York: American Broadcasting Companies.

Jackman, R. W. (1987, June). Political institutions and voter turnout in the industrial democracies. *American Political Science Review, 81,* 405–423.

Richard A. Cloward, PhD, is professor of social work, Columbia University, School of Social Work, 622 West 113th Street, New York, NY 10025, and **Frances Fox Piven, PhD,** is distinguished professor of political science, Graduate School and University Center, City University of New York, 33 West 42nd Street, New York, NY 10036.

For further information see

Citizen Participation; Civil Rights; Community Organization; Ethics and Values; Federal and Administrative Rule Making; Human Rights; Policy Practice; Social Welfare Policy; Social Workers in Politics.

Key Words

politics	voting
voter registration	

W

Wages

See Jobs and Earnings

Wald, Lillian

See Biographies section, Volume 3

Washington, Booker Taliaferro

See Biographies section, Volume 3

Washington, Forrester Blanchard

See Biographies section, Volume 3

Welfare Employment Programs: Evaluation
Dennis K. Orthner
Raymond S. Kirk

The United States does not have a long history of providing assistance to people who are out of the labor force, no matter what the reason. Until the 1930s, training and employment assistance were largely personal, family, or private-sector concerns. During the Great Depression, however, the sheer number of unemployed and displaced people gave root to an emerging set of policies that have challenged traditional assumptions of government involvement in labor force development, public assistance to those who are not employed, and the role of government in developing programs that deal with such abstract concepts as employability and self-sufficiency.

As the policies and programs that address the employment needs of people dependent on public assistance have grown, so too has the need to evaluate the effectiveness of these interventions. The expenditure of public funds requires accountability, and evaluations are the means through which public accountability is tested and potentially assured. Still, the recognized role of formal evaluations in welfare-to-work programs is relatively recent. Even more recent is the use of experimental and other systematic designs to test the effectiveness of employment and training programs.

The need for evaluation of welfare employment programs has never been more evident. The delivery of government services and support to people who are not employed has always been controversial (Goodwin & Milius, 1978). Whether the assistance was provided to out-of-work men, during the depression, or to women receiving Aid to Families with Dependent Children (AFDC), people have wanted assurance that these funds are serving as a bridge to independence and self-sufficiency. Evaluation research is the means through which this assurance is given.

This entry examines the history of evaluation research on welfare-to-work initiatives. Although evaluation efforts over the past half century have been uneven, a brief overview of early evaluations is provided as context for more recent efforts. Both implementation and outcome and impact evaluation results are examined. The entry concludes with a discussion of the implications of welfare-to-work research for social work practice.

EARLY WELFARE EMPLOYMENT PROGRAM EVALUATIONS

The focus of welfare employment programs and their evaluation has changed since the 1930s. The primary concerns of the initial programs that began during the Great Depression were (1) immediate income assistance to workers who had been displaced by unemployment and (2) protection for women and children who were widowed or deserted. Although the Social Security Act of 1935 addressed concerns of families, employment and public works programs dominated the 1930s, beginning with the Federal Emergency Relief Act of 1933. The philosophy underlying these efforts was defined by Harry Hopkins, the first administrator of social security: "Help for the unemployed meant work; public works, if no private employment could be secured; work relief, if jobs on public works projects could not be provided fast enough or in large enough numbers. Direct relief was merely a temporary, emergency expedient" (Brown, 1940, p. 150).

The operation and effectiveness of these efforts were questioned from the beginning. Initial opposition focused on the costliness of the programs, especially because these efforts represented a substantial federal expenditure in an area that had not been previously supported (Brown, 1940). A means test was instituted to control costs, to justify further congressional action, and to garner public support. The evaluation of the programs, in fact, focused on the costs of the efforts in comparison to such outcomes as the number of jobs created and the value of the public works developed. Detailed accounting of these outcomes was kept and used for further program planning (Levitan & Gallo, 1991).

Public support for depression-era work programs was divided. A 1939 public opinion poll found that the Works Progress Administration (WPA) jobs creation program was both the most and the least popular (depending on which service-receiving group was being discussed) effort developed by the Roosevelt administration (Levitan & Gallo, 1991). One historian of the period reported that support for white-collar professional work produced "more bitter criticism than any other single activity of the various federal relief agencies" (Williams, 1939, p. 133). Clearly, these evaluations were qualitative and not based on disciplined outcome studies, but the weight of

impressionistic data was so strong that President Roosevelt claimed in 1935 that "the lessons of history, *confirmed by the evidence immediately before me,* show conclusively that continued dependence upon relief induces a spiritual and moral disintegration fundamentally destructive to the national fiber" (cited in Garvin, Smith, & Reid, 1978, p. 12, italics added).

The Aid to Dependent Children component of the Social Security Act was not subjected at that time to the criticisms of the welfare employment programs (Levitan & Gallo, 1993), and the government did not undertake any formal assessments. It was generally believed that widowed mothers and their children deserved public assistance if their means were limited. This assumption was not challenged for nearly three decades. The evaluations of more modern welfare-to-work interventions are largely based on new assumptions.

EVOLUTION OF WELFARE EMPLOYMENT EVALUATIONS

Beginning with the Manpower Development and Training Act of 1962 and continuing today with the expanded Job Opportunities and Basic Skills Training (JOBS) program, new state and federal programs have been initiated to stimulate employment of economically disadvantaged people. These efforts were designed in part to stimulate the economy and to maintain full employment. More recently, programs have also targeted reductions in poverty and expenditures for welfare through increasing requirements for work among people receiving public assistance. Initially, these efforts were largely targeted to men but increasingly have encouraged or mandated women to participate. The assumption that mothers receiving AFDC could stay at home changed dramatically when the majority of other mothers, often motivated by financial necessity, moved into the labor force.

Evaluation of these increasingly complicated and diverse welfare-to-work programs became more technically sophisticated and scientific. During the 1960s, formal evaluations of program outcomes still were scarce and focused largely on implementation issues, such as the number or percent of eligible people included, or on budgetary requirements. Evaluations of welfare employment programs were more common during the 1970s, dominated by the Comprehensive Employment and Training Act of 1973 (CETA) and the Work Incentive Program (WIN). These assessments still were largely descriptive, although more sophisticated, quasi-experimental field studies of WIN were conducted (Garvin, Smith, & Reid, 1978). Not until the 1980s did more rigorous methodologies, such as experimental studies using random assignment, become more common in state and federal welfare-to-work evaluations (Gueron & Pauly, 1992). These experimental studies are now common, as are studies that use carefully controlled comparison samples, longitudinal tracking of participants, cost–benefit analyses, program model comparisons, and detailed implementation studies.

As implementation, cost, and impact evaluations have become more common, and often mandated in the enabling legislation for work programs, the role of evaluations in developing policies and programs has grown (Blum & Blank, 1990). Evaluation findings from WIN and from the state work demonstration programs of the 1980s were used to form the program elements of the Family Support Act of 1988, especially the human capital development elements of the JOBS program. Thus, even though the United States has been engaged in welfare-to-work programs for more than six decades, the more comprehensive evaluations of program components, costs, participants, and graduates are now driving program development decisions in comparison with the more purely political underpinnings of previous initiatives.

The following sections highlight some of the more important findings from state and federal welfare employment program evaluations. These are separately discussed as findings from implementation evaluations (those that focus on identifying successful program characteristics) and impact evaluations (those that focus on program and participant outcomes).

WELFARE EMPLOYMENT IMPLEMENTATION EVALUATIONS

Implementation evaluation occurs between development of the theoretical underpinnings of an intervention model and the evaluation of client outcomes and program impact. It refers to the analysis and assessment of the manner in which policy is operationalized. Examples of the kinds of questions that an implementation evaluation should be able to answer include:

- Does the basic program structure meet statutory and regulatory intent?
- Are the program goals clear, and are they understood and embraced by the program staff?
- Are staff members adequately trained and qualified to perform the required functions?
- Are resources sufficient, are program funds being spent correctly, and is there fiscal accountability?
- What are the client selection or targeting strategies, and how successful are they?

- How well do programs or agencies cooperate in cases where there is shared responsibility for service delivery or client well-being?
- Are necessary collateral services or resources in place to maximize the likelihood of client success?

The history of implementation evaluations of welfare employment programs is short. Very little was monitored or studied with regard to implementation strategies of WIN or its precursors until the 1980s (Gordon, 1978). The absence of implementation evaluations until recently seems to indicate a general attitude that the value or success of a program rests solely on the statutory or regulatory language of the program and not on the strategies used or the resources dedicated to accomplishing the goals of the program. Inadequate positive outcomes for WIN clients, however, and the frustration of legislators and administrators have led to more deliberate studies of program implementation issues. These studies have focused on client, staff, program, and fiscal issues.

Client-Related Findings

Implementation analyses have revealed that, overall, participation rates in welfare employment programs are quite modest, even when participation is "mandatory." Summary data from the numerous studies conducted between 1980 and 1989 (Gueron & Pauly, 1991) show that participation rates among mandatory clients typically are less than 50 percent; one study found mandatory participation rates as low as 24 percent for targeted AFDC applicants and recipients with children six years or older. When "voluntary" AFDC recipients were allowed to participate, however, participation rates were always above 50 percent, and in two cases they were near 90 percent.

Another finding, which represents a phenomenon that seems to have been carried over from WIN to JOBS, is high client attrition rates. Riccio, Goldman, Hamilton, Martinson, and Orenstein (1989) analyzed dropout patterns of nearly 1,000 California GAIN (Greater Avenues to Independence) participants. They reported that, among a typical 100 mandatory GAIN registrants, 29 had never gone through orientation, an additional 37 did not participate in any component after orientation, and 31 did not progress to the "assessment" phase and either left the program or remained in an initial component. This left only three participants out of 100 who obtained work experience or education and training.

Hagen and Lurie (1992) found that during the first year of JOBS, states tended to seek voluntary clients who fell into mandatory or target groups, indicating a form of "creaming" that had been relied on to meet early participation requirements. They also found that, unlike WIN, few states were aggressively using sanctions as a way to increase participation.

In North Carolina, JOBS programs have had little trouble attracting full caseloads of mandatory or target clients to date; this is due not only to client-recruitment strategies, but also to funding limitations that have effectively capped enrollments in most counties (Kirk, Orthner, Hyman, & Neenan, 1992). Focus group data gathered during this study indicate that JOBS clients generally are very pleased with the program, although many express concern over regulatory conflicts between JOBS and AFDC (such as being encouraged to work on the one hand and then on the other hand losing benefits in excess of new income). Client attrition has been higher than program managers expected, but lower than other studies predicted.

Staff-Related Findings

Trained and experienced staff members are essential to the success of any program, and implementation data from earlier studies (for example, Ball, Hamilton, & Hoerz, 1984) have credited experienced staff with smooth program implementation. An early JOBS study conducted by the Office of the Inspector General (1989) found that most states, recognizing both the complexity of the new law and the need for more of a service orientation, did not plan to train AFDC workers to be JOBS workers.

Caseload size may be a major factor, however, in the ability of employment programs to attract and retain quality staff. Kirk et al. (1992) found that in a low-caseload state (North Carolina), JOBS programs experienced little difficulty in recruiting and retaining qualified staff. AFDC workers competed for the new JOBS staff openings with social workers from elsewhere in social services, even from outside the agency. State training was found to be effective, and strong state leadership was acknowledged and applauded by the counties. This has resulted in unusually high morale and low turnover among JOBS workers in the state (Neenan, Orthner, & Pond, 1994). In contrast, Hagen (1993) found waning staff enthusiasm among large numbers of JOBS workers that was largely due to high caseloads, unfulfilled promises of increased funding, and the inability to find jobs for otherwise successful JOBS clients.

Program-Related Findings

The greatest program challenge is assembling the services and resources needed to meet programmatic and legislative intent. Hagen and Lurie (1992) pointed out that the increased complexities and multiple services required in the JOBS legislation also require different administrative structures, management strategies, and staff attitudes than those of the simpler WIN programs, even though states that ran WIN programs reported an easier transition to implementing JOBS than did states without WIN. Fortunately, the JOBS legislation provides for greater flexibility than does the WIN legislation and includes an explicit expectation that other programs (such as education and programs through the Job Training Partnership Act) will participate cooperatively with JOBS. According to the 1989 Office of the Inspector General study, most states expected to rely heavily on contracting services for training, education, job search, and job development and to use interorganizational agreements.

Interorganizational relations. Interorganizational communication and cooperation has been found in previous studies to be both necessary and difficult to achieve (Gordon, 1978). These findings have been verified in North Carolina (Kirk et al., 1992), where, in one county, a "branch office" of the employment security agency was co-located with the JOBS program and proved to be a highly effective resource for placing job-ready JOBS clients. In another county, however, the relationship was so poor that JOBS staff had to go in person to the employment office to get listings of job openings for their clients.

On-the-job training. A similar, striking finding relates to the availability of on-the-job training (OJT) for JOBS clients. Gordon (1978) observed that OJT had been perennially underused in the WIN era, reporting that less than 1 percent of WIN participants received OJT experience but that almost 13 percent of all successful WIN terminees had OJT. The Office of the Inspector General's study (1989) reported that 41 of the 42 responding states intended to use OJT as part of JOBS. All of the states Hagen and Lurie (1992) studied claimed to offer OJT. Recent data from North Carolina, where OJT was listed as a JOBS service, indicate that less than 1 percent of JOBS clients were receiving OJT, and caseworkers expressed frustration over their inability to access this service for their clients (Kirk et al., 1992).

Supportive services. Availability and use of supportive services is a complex implementation issue. Previous welfare employment evaluations very clearly supported the need for child care and transportation services, and JOBS includes greatly enhanced funding for these services. A U.S. General Accounting Office (GAO) study (1991) cited both child care and transportation as early problems for states, adding that specific kinds of shortages, such as child care for infants, may differentially affect some area clients, such as teenage mothers. More recent studies, however, have not indicated that access to child care is a serious problem for most parents, especially under the relaxed regulations that permit JOBS clients to arrange and pay for their own care, even with relatives (Hagen & Lurie, 1992; Kirk et al., 1992). Still, some child care advocates and even JOBS child care personnel oppose the relaxed rules. They cite child safety and the lack of developmental opportunities as compelling reasons for child care services, even though there is a shortage of licensed or registered child care slots.

Although funds for transportation also flow under relaxed regulations, transportation has been identified as the single biggest barrier to JOBS participation. This is largely because public transportation is not available in many communities where JOBS participants live, and JOBS participants generally do not have reliable personal transportation, even if reimbursement for personal vehicle use is permitted. The transportation shortage has led, in some cases, to very expensive services, such as taxis, to ensure the participation of some clients. In one comparatively rural state, counties spend an average of 25 percent of their JOBS budgets on transportation, and 13 percent of the counties spend more than 40 percent (Meehan & Mink, 1992).

Another important resource issue is the availability of a job for people who complete a welfare employment program. The lack of a comprehensive job development strategy to accompany employment program implementation has been cited as a major failing of WIN (Gordon, 1978). A recent GAO report (1991) stated that 75 percent of states feared there would be insufficient jobs for JOBS clients.

Fiscal Findings
If any program is to be successful, it must be adequately financed, but finances have always been a problem for welfare employment programs. Many of the welfare-to-work programs that have been implemented were intended to reduce government expenditures eventually, but states have always struggled to develop sufficient matching funds to draw down federal funds. From the very beginning, states did not believe they could raise sufficient local matching funds to fully implement JOBS programs (Office of the Inspector General, 1989). Their fear was confirmed later when it was found

that although state appropriations were increasing, there would not be sufficient funds to draw the available federal appropriation, which would most certainly limit states' abilities to provide full services (Hagen & Lurie, 1992; U.S. GAO, 1991).

At the local program level, Hagen and Lurie (1992) found that, in many cases, formal agreements were needed between agencies to ensure that funds would flow from one to another if services were provided and to ensure that funds would not be misused.

WELFARE EMPLOYMENT OUTCOME AND IMPACT EVALUATIONS
The frequency and rigor of outcome and impact evaluations of welfare-to-work programs has increased substantially over the past decade. Depression-era programs were evaluated only on broad outcomes, such as the number of people who were out of work. Great Society–era programs were evaluated more in terms of their employment influences on men or increases in labor force participation. Since the mid-1970s, however, more exacting, criteria-based evaluations have been conducted, which are largely focused on women receiving AFDC. Thus, the impact evaluations that more effectively inform the policy and program recommendations for JOBS and the Family Support Act are very recent.

Many of the evaluations conducted to date have not included randomly assigned control groups. Because these studies cannot fully control for the changes that have also occurred in nonparticipants, the results are called "outcomes" (Rossi & Freeman, 1993). Nearly all of the studies conducted up through the WIN period are of this type; they often have used carefully constructed comparison samples but not randomly assigned groups. "Impact" evaluations, which use random assignment to experimental (participant) and control (nonparticipant) groups, have become much more common and often are required in the federally sponsored evaluations of the 1990s (Gueron & Pauly, 1991).

Employment and Earnings Findings
The findings related to employment and earnings effects of welfare-to-work programs are modestly encouraging. The majority of studies WIN and JOBS have indicated higher earnings and employment rates among participants in these programs. Even though the programs themselves vary considerably in their components and target populations, reviews of multiple programs have indicated increases between 11 percent to 43 percent in earnings of participants (Gueron & Pauly, 1991).

Increases in earnings from WIN typically were lower than those from JOBS, but the services received by participants were less intensive (Gordon, 1978). Three-year follow-ups from the Massachusetts Employment and Training Program found that participants in the program were earning 18 percent to 23 percent more than people in the control group (Nightingale, Wissoker, Burbridge, Bawden, & Jeffries, 1991).

These increases, although consistent, are not the entire story. The value of the earnings increases typically were small, often not more than a few hundred dollars more per year in comparison with increases for control group nonparticipants. In all studies, both participants and nonparticipants tended to increase their earnings over time as they attempted to improve their lives. But the earnings increases were rarely high enough to move the families above the poverty line. Thus, the welfare savings rates have tended to be more limited than the earnings increases rates (Friedlander, 1988). Still, these earnings are averages across entire samples of participants, not all of whom have found jobs. Varying portions of the work program participants were able to find acceptable jobs, even though the pay rates have been modest.

On a more positive note, studies have consistently found that the greatest increases in earnings and welfare savings come from programs that focus on the most disadvantaged participants (Gueron & Pauly, 1991). Although improvements in the employment and earnings of people who are the most advantaged tend to be higher, similar increases also occur for advantaged nonparticipants, resulting in small to nonsignificant program-related gains. In contrast, people who are the least advantaged (for example, those without high school degrees, those who have spent a long time on welfare, and those with the least work experience) tend to experience the greatest earnings gains and welfare savings, but they also have the lowest employment rates (Levitan & Gallo, 1993). The effects of the program, therefore, tend to be felt by fewer people—people who face more employment barriers but for whom the employment program is more likely to be a unique means through which they can become independent.

These differential effects of employment programs have also been examined in terms of cost–benefit analyses. These analyses compare the welfare savings and taxes paid by former participants who found work with the costs incurred for all those who were assisted. Examinations of WIN generally have resulted in consistent, positive cost–benefit ratios, with rates ranging from 1.8:1

to 3.5:1 (Perry, 1975). The findings from the Work Demonstration Projects of the 1980s confirmed these ratios with estimated payback rates of two to five years (Gueron & Pauly, 1991). For example, the San Diego Saturated Work Initiative Model (SWIM) program was estimated to return approximately $3 for every $1 of initial costs (Hamilton & Friedlander, 1989). The programs with the lowest cost–benefit ratios were those that targeted higher-risk families and familes in rural areas. These programs tended to be more expensive and to result in fewer job placements.

Family Impact Findings

Until recently, little attention has been given to the noneconomic family influences of welfare employment programs. Nevertheless, Ellwood (1988) proposed that involvement in these programs could have such effects as increased personal well-being, lower subsequent fertility rates, higher levels of family adjustment, and better school performance for children. These indirect effects have become the focus of several state and federal employment program initiatives, especially those that target teenage parents or sanction parents whose children drop out of school.

Early findings from evaluations indicate mixed results on the family impacts of employment programs. In North Carolina, mothers receiving AFDC improved their personal well-being during the course of their education and training, as measured by self-esteem, coping ability, and mastery (Orthner & Neenan, 1993). They also were more likely to participate with their children in school-related activities and reported that their children received higher grades. These second-generation effects provide some hope for the future. In contrast, however, the results from Wisconsin's Learnfare program have suggested that sanctions may not be sufficient to promote positive family outcomes. Under Learnfare, AFDC grants for mothers whose children dropped out of school were reduced, but evaluation findings indicate that this consequence had no effect on school dropout rates for adolescent children (Pawasarat, Quinn, & Stetzer, 1992).

Although it may take a decade or more to adequately determine the education effects on younger children, employment programs can encourage AFDC mothers to continue in school. This effect is the result in part of the education and training activities offered under JOBS. But even pre-JOBS employment programs had some success in keeping young mothers in school (Mallar, Kerachsky, Thomston, & Long, 1982). Similarly, a JOBSTART demonstration during the 1980s found that participants were not only more likely to finish school or to earn their general equivalency diploma (GED), but they also scored higher on standardized reading tests (Auspos, Cave, & Long, 1988). Further studies are needed to assess the effects of these school outcomes on employment, earnings, and welfare savings.

Employment Program Model Findings
The strategies that have been used to assist women and men in their moves from welfare to work vary considerably. In fact, many of the debates regarding employment programs have centered around the effectiveness of selected program models for welfare recipients. For example, the role of education in building employability is still unclear. Because the educational requirements of many entry-level jobs are quite low and the dropout rates for second-chance employment and training programs have been high (SRI International, 1983), there has been a recent emphasis on education as a part of welfare employment programs. Because this emphasis is recent, there has been little research on education-intensive strategies, even though this is now a common component activity in JOBS.

Effects of education and training. Recent evidence of the effects of education and training investments provides preliminary support for the education-intensive strategy, even though it is an expensive program component. Data from the San Diego SWIM and Baltimore work demonstration programs indicate that improvements in education are linked to placements in jobs with higher potential earnings (Gueron & Pauly, 1991). These earnings increases were greatest for women who had the most severe educational deficits.

More recently, the pattern of educational and training sequencing was tested in the Minority Female Single Parent demonstration project (Gordon & Burghardt, 1990). Three of the programs used a traditional sequence of education followed by job training. The fourth program used parallel training and education centered around specific job skills. The results indicated that the participants in the parallel program experienced significantly greater earnings and welfare savings than did people in the control group and from the sequential programs. In addition, the time required to move into employment was shortened.

Effects of early job search. Early job search and placement strategies also have been evaluated. These strategies were at the heart of WIN but the amount of federal support was so low that even though modest results were demonstrated, only a small percentage of eligible people received assistance (Garvin, Smith, & Reid, 1978). Given the current desire to move larger numbers of AFDC recipients off welfare, immediate job search strategies allow broader coverage of people eligible for JOBS programs, with higher caseloads and more immediate employment of people who are job-ready. The potential for success from an immediate job search, however, has had mixed results. Several studies have found that early employment gains through a low-intensity job search led to higher job turnover and lower subsequent earnings compared with those of people who had participated in education and training components (Nightingale et al., 1991). Nevertheless, recent results from the California GAIN program are more encouraging. The higher-intensity job search strategies used in Riverside County have led to greater rates of employment and earnings compared with the strategies used in other demonstration counties (Friedlander, Riccio, & Freedman, 1993).

Evaluations of welfare employment programs to date indicate that there still is much to be learned about the effectiveness and efficiency of the strategies being used to move participants from welfare to work. Even though the JOBS program was initiated out of the most comprehensive series of employment program demonstration evaluations ever conducted, the policies and interventions used in JOBS programs are still open to some debate. In particular, the research undergirding the human capital investment focus on education and training, a hallmark of JOBS, is not yet sufficient. Gueron and Pauly (1991), in their extensive review of the employment program literature, noted that the emphasis JOBS places "on education (for those with poor basic skills) and on other intensive, usually higher-cost, services represents a very different approach—one that has not been rigorously evaluated" (p. 238).

CURRENT BARRIERS
Most employment programs have not penetrated a high percentage of people who are eligible for their services. WIN reached only a small percentage of eligible people, and the JOBS program still does not require more than a minority of the eligible people to participate. These small percentages are coupled with unusually high dropout rates for participants and high recidivism rates for graduates. Of course, the total national, state, and local allocation to these programs is relatively small, and without a heavier investment in education, training, and supportive services, impacts may not be greater.

The role of health insurance in allowing people to become economically self-sufficient is also not well integrated in the evaluations of the welfare employment programs. States that are implementing JOBS programs do not always provide transitional Medicaid assistance, and it is well known that there is a "cliff effect"—when effective earnings substantially decrease after people lose food stamps, child care, and medical benefits (Hartman, 1993). A national health policy is needed to remedy this cliff effect and to allow employment and earnings to serve more effective as a ladder to economic independence.

Similarly, the evaluations of welfare employment programs indicate that although these efforts may have some limited effect on welfare payments, they are unlikely to lead to poverty reduction in the near future. Most of the jobs acquired by graduates of welfare employment programs do not pay wages that are high enough to move them out of poverty. Thus, AFDC payments may be reduced, but other programs in public assistance, such as food stamps and Medicaid, may not experience significant declines. Likewise, state and national job development programs and policies must be more aggressively developed and accompany welfare-to-work programs. Without new and better-paying employment opportunities, welfare employment programs are hindered in their ability to move people away from public assistance and out of poverty.

Finally, for welfare-to-work programs to function more effectively, much more coordination is needed within and among agencies. Because these programs require interorganizational cooperation, welfare departments, schools, community colleges, and employment services must collaborate much more than they do at present. Similarly, coordination is needed across departments within social services agencies. All too often these departments operate autonomously and have conflicting rules and regulations that impede participants' progress toward independence.

IMPLICATIONS FOR SOCIAL WORK PRACTICE

To implement welfare employment programs more effectively, social workers need to become even more involved in the development and implementation of those programs. JOBS caseworkers frequently are involved in developing employability plans and assisting clients with decisions about their future without sufficient knowledge about the world of work in the local community. Case management services are a critical component of building an employability plan, but without an understanding of appropriate directions that these plans might take, JOBS caseworkers can, unfortunately, mislead clients or direct them down inappropriate paths.

Similarly, stronger interagency collaboration skills are needed. A JOBS worker must be an effective collaborative worker who understands the strengths and weaknesses of other agencies and is able to maximize the capabilities of available systems on behalf of his or her clients. In many ways the JOBS worker is a prototype of the more comprehensive family support specialist, who is able to work with the client on behalf of a variety of support systems to maximize opportunities for personal, family, and economic self-sufficiency.

Social workers also need better information systems to monitor their clients effectively, as well as the agencies with whom social workers must collaborate. Current inadequate information systems make it difficult to maintain appropriate records, conduct periodic assessments, and monitor progress toward employability goals. Social workers need to be prepared to assist with the design of these systems as well as to use them appropriately as tools for practice.

Finally, there is a need to increase participation of social workers in evaluations of employment programs. All too often the evaluations of social work practice are conducted by people of other professions and not by those directly involved in service delivery. Evaluation of practice, both direct and indirect, must involve social workers in the design of the evaluation instruments, collection of data, and interpretation of findings. The more involved the social work community is in evaluating its own practice, the more likely that the evaluations will reflect the needs and concerns of the people social work serves.

REFERENCES

Auspos, P., Cave, G., & Long, D. (1988). *Maine: Final report on the training opportunities in the private sector program.* New York: Manpower Demonstration Research Corporation.

Ball, J., Hamilton, G., & Hoerz, G. (1984). *Interim findings on the West Virginia community work experience demonstrations.* New York: Manpower Demonstration Research Corporation.

Blum, B., & Blank, S. (1990). Bringing administrators into the process. *Public Welfare, 48,* 4–12.

Brown, J. C. (1940). *Public relief: 1929–1939.* New York: Henry Holt.

Comprehensive Employment and Training Act of 1973. P.L. 93-203, 87 Stat. 839.

Ellwood, D. T. (1988). *Poor support: Poverty in the American family.* New York: Basic Books.

Family Support Act of 1988. P.L. 100–485, 102 Stat. 2343.

Federal Emergency Relief Act of 1933. 48 Stat. 55.

Friedlander, D. (1988). *Subgroup impact and performance indicators for selected welfare employment programs.* New York: Manpower Demonstration Research Corporation.

Friedlander, D., Riccio, J., & Freedman, S. (1993). *GAIN: Two-year impacts in six counties.* New York: Manpower Demonstration Research Corporation.

Garvin, C., Smith, A., & Reid, W. (1978). *The work incentive experience.* Montclair, NJ: Allanheld, Osmun.

Goodwin, L., & Milius, P. (1978). Forty years of work training. In C. Garwin, A. Smith, & W. Reid (Eds.), *The work incentive experience.* Montclair, NJ: Allanheld, Osmun.

Gordon, A., & Burghardt, J. (1990). *The minority female single parent demonstration: Short-term economic impacts.* New York: Rockefeller Foundation.

Gordon, J. E. (1978). WIN research: A review of the findings. In C. Garwin, A. Smith, & W. Reid (Eds.), *The work incentive experience.* Montclair, NJ: Allanheld, Osmun.

Gueron, J., & Pauly, E. (1991). *From welfare to work.* Newbury Park, CA: Sage Publications.

Hagen, J. (1993, September). Lukewarm attitudes found on the JOBS front line. *Welfare to Work,* pp. 4–5.

Hagen, J., & Lurie, I. (1992). How 10 states implemented JOBS: A study looks at states' choices during the initial stages. *Public Welfare, 50,* 13–21.

Hamilton, G., & Friedlander, D. (1989). *Final report on the saturation work initiative model in San Diego.* New York: Manpower Demonstration Research Corporation.

Hartman, K. (1993). The cliffs of self-sufficiency. In *Time for a change: Remaking the nation's welfare system* (pp. 93–104). Washington, DC: U.S. Government Printing Office.

Job Training Partnership Act. P.L. 97-300, 96 Stat. 1322. (1982).

Kirk, R., Orthner, D. K., Hyman, B., & Neenan, P. (1992). *North Carolina JOBS evaluation: Implementation evaluation report.* Raleigh, NC: Department of Human Resources.

Levitan, S., & Gallo, F. (1991). *Spending to save: Expanding employment opportunities.* Washington, DC: George Washington University Center for Social Policy Studies.

Levitan, S., & Gallo, F. (1993). *Jobs for JOBS: Toward a work-based welfare system.* Washington, DC: George Washington University Center for Social Policy Studies.

Mallar, C., Kerachsky, S., Thomston, C., & Long, D. (1982). *Project Report: Evaluation of economic impact of the Job Corps program third follow-up report.* Princeton, NJ: Mathematica Policy Research, Inc.

Manpower Development and Training Act of 1962. P.L. 87-415, 76 Stat. 23.

Meehan, T., & Mink, M. (1992). *Transportation services and JOBS success in North Carolina.* Chapel Hill, NC: Human Services Laboratory.

Neenan, P., Orthner, D. K., & Pond, S. B. (1994). *JOBS organizational climate study.* Chapel Hill, NC: Human Services Research and Design Laboratory.

Nightingale, D. S., Wissoker, D. A., Burbridge, L. C., Bawden, D., & Jeffries, N. (1991). *Evaluation of the Massachusetts employment and training program.* Washington, DC: Urban Institute Press.

Office of the Inspector General. (1989). *State implementation of the Family Support Act* (DHHS Publication No. OAI-05-90-00720). Washington, DC: U.S. Government Printing Office.

Orthner, D. K., & Neenan, P. (1993). *The JOBS evaluation: Interim report.* Chapel Hill: University of North Carolina School of Social Work.

Pawasarat, J., Quinn, L., & Stetzer, F. (1992). *Evaluation of Learnfare program in Wisconsin.* Milwaukee: Employment & Training Institute.

Perry, C. (1975). Manpower Development and Training Act. In C. Perry, B. Anderson, R. Rowan, & H. Northrup (Eds.), *The impact of government manpower programs.* Philadelphia: University of Pennsylvania Press.

Riccio, J., Goldman, B., Hamilton, G., Martinson, K., & Orenstein, A. (1989). *GAIN: Early implementation experiences and lessons.* New York: Manpower Demonstration Research Corporation.

Rossi, P. H., & Freeman, H. E. (1993). *Evaluation: A systematic approach* (5th ed.). Newbury Park, CA: Sage Publications.

Social Security Act. 49 Stat. 620 (1935).

SRI International. (1983). *Final report of the Seattle–Denver income maintenance experiment design & results* (Vol. 1). Menlo Park, CA: Author.

U.S. General Accounting Office. (1991). *Welfare to work: States begin JOBS, but fiscal and other problems may impede their progress* (GAO Publication No. HRD-91-106). Washington, DC: U.S. Government Printing Office.

Williams, E. A. (1939). *Federal aid for relief.* New York: Columbia University Press.

Dennis K. Orthner, PhD, is professor and director, and **Raymond S. Kirk, PhD,** is associate director, Human Services Research and Design Laboratory, University of North Carolina at Chapel Hill, 214 Abernathy Hall, Chapel Hill, NC 27599.

For further information see

Child Welfare Overview; Employment and Unemployment Measurement; Federal Social Legislation from 1961 to 1994; General Assistance; Homelessness; Income Distribution; Income Security Overview; Jobs and Earnings; JOBS Program; Poverty; Public Social Services; Social Security; Social Welfare History; Social Welfare Policy; Supplemental Security Income.

Key Words

| employment training | evaluation |
| programs | welfare policy |

Wells-Barnett, Ida Bell

See Biographies section, Volume 3

White, Eartha Mary Magdalene

See Biographies section, Volume 3

White Ethnic Groups

Charles Guzzetta

For generations, the many cultures represented by people who have immigrated to the United States were expected to create a "new American race," united by dedication to the democratic ideal. By the late 1800s the "new immigration" (1880–1925) shifted to poor Roman Catholic and Jewish non-English-speaking southern and eastern Europeans who faced vigorous movements of both assimilation (through public education) and exclusion (through restrictive legislation). The term "ethnic" described a supposedly unassimilable population; by 1940 the phrase "white ethnic" was introduced to distinguish the new immigrants from ethnics of color. White ethnics continued to encounter barriers of prejudice even after extensive intermarriage and success in education and income. White ethnics, feeling excluded from the benefits of the civil rights movement they supported in the 1960s, began "ethnic revival" movements, which continue today.

Social work began as a field largely devoted to concerns with respect to white ethnic groups, ranging from reduction of pauperism to social reform to societal acceptance. By advancing respect for cultural diversity, social work today supports greater sensitivity to the needs of white ethnic groups, but it might also help perpetuate ethnic stereotypes. This entry defines *ethnic* and *ethnicity* and traces the background and changing status of white ethnic groups in American society.

DEFINITIONS

"Ethnic" and "ethnicity" are unclear terms. Both are couched in ambiguity, their meanings determined by time, place, and usage. The word "ethnic" originally derived from a Greek word for "nation" and was used to distinguish particular national groups from other groups not identified by nation, such as Jews or Gypsies (Mindel & Habenstein, 1976). "Race" was a term used in a more general sense for groups now referred to as "ethnic."

Originally, ethnic implied "outsider," indicating a group identifiable by "some degree of coherence and solidarity" (Petersen, 1980, p. 2) that marked it as different from the defining group. Novak (1973) called it "a residual category, ... only used of 'the others'" (p. 5). Thus, the most consistent use of the term originally seems to have been more for exclusion than for inclusion—"ethnic" as "non-WASP" (not white Anglo-Saxon Protestant) (Stein & Hill, 1977); even with this stipulation, however, Gleason (1992) found the meanings and applications of the terms "ethnic" and "ethnicity" to be "fuzzy" and "loose" (p. ix). Novak (1980) described them as "baffling" and "elusive" (p. 29).

Although "ethnic" and "ethnicity" are commonly used today, there remains no consensus about the precise meaning of either term (Thernstrom, Orlov, & Handlin, 1980).

In current use, ethnicity tends to refer primarily to a cultural context but always with an implicit extension of meaning to include other, not necessarily stipulated, aspects. Cafferty and Chestang (1976) described ethnic identity as "more than a condition of common biological or historical origins, and of shared language, traditions, sentiments, and cultural networks. It is also a form of self-conceptualization" (pp. ix–x). This definition specifies a biological dimension; Zenner (1985) stated that the emphasis was on social and cultural features, with an implied biological kinship. As Waters (1990) put it, the terms are "historically variable." In the United States today, a common use of ethnic seeks to distinguish white from other populations (Petersen, 1980), but the divisions between them are by no means clear. For example, populations from the Middle East—or, even more commonly, Hispanics—defy easy classification on this binary scale.

At present, populations specified as ethnic tend to fall into two broad categories: (1) ascribed and (2) optional. *Ascribed ethnics* are populations to whom the designation is applied from the outside; *optional ethnics* are people who choose to so identify themselves.

The term white ethnics is a relatively recent variation. It is applied at present to descendants of southern and eastern European immigrants (Petersen, 1980) but not to people from northern European countries and "not ... British-Americans" (Novak, 1973, p. 5). The term "white ethnics" is used by some people to distinguish themselves from other ethnics, and it is used by northern European groups to distinguish themselves from ethnic Europeans. Greeley (1991) argued that "blacks and Hispanics are politically correct ethnics these days ... [but that] Irish, Poles, and Italians are not—and ... never were" (p. 754). Stein and Hill (1977), however, claimed that white ethnic means "non-black" and flatly charged that the term is "a ploy for racial exclusion" (p. 270). Lal (1983) noted that designation of ethnicity may be "a stratification phenomenon" (p. 166) aimed more at class than race. Thus, the term white ethnic appears to serve at least a double function: It is used by Americans with northern European origins to exclude people with southern and eastern European origins and by people with southern and eastern European origins to exclude people of color and those without a specific national origin.

HISTORICAL CONTEXT

Old Immigration and a New American Race

By the time of the first census in 1790, the United States already had an exceptionally diverse population (Liebman, 1982). In the early years of the republic, it was widely believed that white immigrants would blend together to create a unique American "race." This new race would be bonded together not by common heritage or culture but by a democratic ideology and the task of building a new nation.

This American experiment was described enthusiastically by the immigrant French farmer de Crevecoeur (1782/1957), who, identifying the English, Scotch, Irish, French, Dutch, German, and Swedish immigrants he knew, wrote that old and new Americans were being "melted into a new race of men" (p. 37): self-reliant, strong, and free. Fifty years later, another French visitor, Alexis de Tocqueville (1969), described the American passion for belonging to volunteer groups and for independent political activity. A leading American historian, Arthur Schlesinger (1991), expressed almost identical sentiments 160 years later; he wrote that the "American creed," which had united people of diverse ethnic origins in the past and continued to do so, was a commitment to "democratic principles" and "practical experience in civic participation" (p. 134).

Well into the 19th century, the notion of a unique American race remained firmly established, as non-English settlers continued to enter the country and pass quickly to the western frontier, which itself moved westward. The first massive influx of white immigrants who stayed in the East

Coast cities where they landed were the Irish, who spoke English but were Roman Catholic rather than Protestant. National debates were waged over whether the country could, or should, try to assimilate these newcomers. Resentment and fear were directed in particular at the Irish people, who were considered antidemocratic and clannish and were seen as instruments of the Catholic Church, bent on imposing their "popish" beliefs on the rest of Americans (Thernstrom, 1982). There was widespread question concerning whether Catholics should be allowed to vote.

Also during this period, political upheavals in Europe drove many other nationals, particularly Germans, to America. They, too, encountered strong negative reactions, but whereas the Irish worked as ordinary laborers, the Germans were considered an "aristocracy" of the trades, which they soon dominated (Kessler-Harris & Yans-McLaughlin, 1978). Both Irish and German people were resented for their opposition to compulsory, secular, public schools, which had emerged as the best hope for "making Americans" of foreigners. In about 1840, a major anti-immigrant movement began, and by the 1850s, its political arm, the American Party, had achieved considerable influence (Gleason, 1980; Thernstrom, 1982). At the same time, as the anti-immigration movement gained strength, the states and U.S. territories continued campaigns that had been initiated in colonial times to attract people from overseas. They originally sought immigrants for the East; after 1845, the main effort was to get people to settle the West (Dinnerstein & Reimer, 1982).

The dream of many diverse populations blending together into a "new American race" remained but was largely superseded by the determination that immigrants should become "American"—as defined by native-born Americans. Education was expected to be the key instrument of American assimilation.

The New Immigration: Assimilation, Exclusion, and Eugenics

After the Civil War, the stream of immigration shifted. The period of the "old immigration" of northern and western Europeans is generally considered to have ended by then. A few scholars place the cutoff at 1840, before the major Irish immigration, but the period of the "new immigration" is generally considered to have commenced in 1880. By that time, the second-generation Irish people had begun to establish themselves in jobs in the major cities. Booming industrial development required laborers, and they were actively recruited from southern and eastern Europe. This effort was buttressed by political and economic changes in Europe, a great increase in the European population, and the development of fast and convenient modes of transportation.

Several state governors met in 1870 to ask the federal government to create an office that would facilitate immigration (Dinnerstein & Reimer, 1982). Within a few years, state authority over immigration was superseded by the federal government (Abbott, 1922), but the real influence over immigration was wielded by rail and steamship lines, which steadily lowered their passage rates. By 1882 passage to the United States from England was available for as little as $12 (Dinnerstein & Reimer, 1982).

Opposition to immigration. The new immigrant wave, coming from Italy, Poland, Russia, Greece, and Slavic countries, grew from 600,000 from 1881 to 1890 to a peak of more than 4 million 20 years later (Jensen, 1989). Most of these immigrants were poor, Catholic or Jewish, and did not speak English. They were considered "inferior racial stock," and the idea of their assimilation was challenged by the notion that, like Negroes,[1] they were basically unassimilable (Pavalko, 1980). The Italians, for example, were often classified as nonwhite (Waters, 1990) and unfit for citizenship. C. D. Pott (cited in Pavalko, 1980), of the University of Pennsylvania, argued that the "southern Italian and Russian Jew [were] . . . no more desirable (possibly less) than the Chinese" (p. 63).

In 1894 the Immigration Restriction League was organized to stem the flow of immigrants that threatened to "pollute Yankee blood" (Pavalko, 1980, p. 60). Although speakers such as Philip Garrett (1900) told the 1899 meeting of social workers at the National Conference of Charities and Correction that "even the Italian and Huns" could be made fit citizens if they were "thoroughly educated in our public schools" (p. 159), the presidential address at the same meeting warned against the "degenerate blood" that, introduced through intermarriage, would be "poison in our veins" (Henderson, 1900, p. 13).

The major instrument of the assimilationists was the public school system (Rafter, 1988), following McCullough's (1888) advice to the National Conference of Charities and Correction to "get hold of the children" (p. 158). The exclusionists who opposed the assimilationists focused on legislation to bar immigrants who could not pass English literacy tests. Congress passed such laws

in 1894, 1913, and 1915; these were stopped by presidential vetoes before being passed over Woodrow Wilson's veto in 1917 (Thernstrom, 1982).

Assimilationists were beset on another front by the movement to eliminate pauperism. Pauperism was considered as resulting partly from "degenerate blood" (Henderson, 1900), which was also considered a cause of insanity and mental deficiency and which was commonly identified with the new immigrants. As early as 1884, the president of the National Conference of Charities and Correction told administrators of social agencies that "the abnormally large number of idiotic and weak-minded" among their charges was "largely attributable to unrestricted pauper immigration" (Letchworth, 1885, p. 17).

The eugenics movement provided a scientific rationale for the isolation and later sterilization of so-called "inferior" immigrant groups and also for impoverished old immigration populations. In 1912, Henry Goddard, a leading proponent of IQ testing, tested immigrants coming through Ellis Island. Goddard (cited in Pavalko, 1980) classified 87 percent of the Russians, 83 percent of the Jews, 80 percent of the Hungarians, and 79 percent of the Italians as "feeble-minded." A few years later, during World War I, Robert Yerkes (cited in Pavalko, 1980) oversaw the testing of 12,000 foreign-born men and concluded that people of English and Scandinavian ancestry were of high intelligence, whereas people of Slavic and Latin ancestry had low native intelligence.

The first scholarly analysis of ethnicity, Sumner's classic study *Folkways*, appeared in 1906. Two years later, the title of a play, Zangwill's *The Melting Pot*, provided a term that could be conveniently applied to the assimilation movement. Although the "melting pot" image came to predominate, many other descriptions of the new immigrants enjoyed periods of popularity (Gleason, 1992), ranging from "salad," "stew," and "flower garden" to "catch basin" and "dumping ground," and even Henry Pratt Fairchild's memorable 1926 characterization: "village dog pound" (cited in Gleason, 1992, p. 14).

Antecedents to cultural diversity. More complimentary terms were used by a small group that valued the diversity of the new immigrant cultures. Pitted against both the total assimilationists and the exclusionary eugenicists, Jane Addams (1909) pressed for appreciation, not obliteration, of differences. Settlement houses sponsored celebrations and exhibitions to feature crafts and customs of various cultures. Miller (1920) proposed such

---

[1]The word "Negro" is used in this entry to reflect the phrasing used in the original sources.

initiatives as native-language newspapers and education classes. However, this antecedent of the cultural diversity movement was overwhelmed by the power of the larger opposing movements.

Edith Abbott (1922) complained that federal immigration bureaucrats dealt not with difficulties faced by immigrants but "almost exclusively with problems of exclusion and deportation" (p. 463). By 1924, the exclusionists succeeded in securing passage of a law (the Johnson-Reed Act) that effectively closed U.S. borders to so-called inferior races by setting quotas on the basis of 1890 figures, before the major immigration wave from southern and eastern Europe (Thernstrom, 1982). This law ended the new immigration and began a hiatus that lasted for two generations (Waters, 1990). Typically, it was Jane Addams (1927) who spoke to the social consequences of the immigration law on ethnic minorities, but by then society had turned to other issues.

The New Immigrant Experience
With little new immigration to reinforce Old World cultures, ethnic minorities from Europe were met not only with relentless assimilation efforts but also with widespread discrimination. For example, education was the major institutional mechanism for assimilation, yet racial and ethnic groups found themselves excluded from higher education. In public grammar schools, the education of children was laden with patriotic indoctrination intended to strip away cultural identities and to "Americanize" them (Greeley, 1977), a term that John Dewey (1923) said made him "feel like blushing" because the schools were used by nativists "as a means of forcing their own conceptions of American life on other people" (p. 450). In the meantime, universities such as Columbia University and New York University had long-standing restrictions on Jewish admissions, and, according to Steinberg (1989), in 1922 Harvard openly advocated a quota system. Ability notwithstanding, ethnics did not succeed in gaining significant access to higher education throughout the 1920s and 1930s (Greeley, 1977).

The 40-year period between the quotas in the 1924 immigration law and the loosening of restrictions by the immigration laws passed in 1965 provided a vast laboratory in which assimilationists could test their theories. These theories held that ethnicity was not racial but that it represented persistent attachment to old cultures—to the detriment of acculturation to American life. These attachments could be expected to weaken with each succeeding generation (Kessler-Harris & Yans-McLaughlin, 1978), eased by education and

the acquisition of "marketable skills" (Portes & Zhou, 1992). Without the reinforcement of old cultures by new immigrants, the dilution of ethnicity would be accelerated by intermarriage, occupational and social advancement (Waters, 1990), and melding of the ethnics with mainstream American values (Portes & Zhou, 1992). With this melding there would be less prejudice and discrimination against the former ethnics, which, in turn, would enhance assimilation (Glazer, 1983). The theory never included populations of color, because an implicit expectation was that the melded (white) ethnic would not look markedly different.

According to Schlesinger (1991), the term "ethnicity" entered popular modern usage with the appearance of Warner's (1941) studies of an American city. These studies and the many other studies they spawned revealed a U.S. class structure that was considerably more fixed and resistant to penetration than had formerly been believed. Even the fully acculturated second- and third-generation descendants of ethnic immigrants were not considered to be "American." Nevertheless, optimism remained high for assimilation. Warner (as cited in Krickus, 1941/1976) predicted that the ethnics would be "absorbed" relatively soon. Times were hard for the ethnics during the Great Depression, but although their unemployment was high, they could see high unemployment all around them as well.

There were some signs that assimilation was working. An Italian–Jewish mayor was elected in New York City, thwarting the most powerful political machine. At the federal level, ethnic leadership was being recognized by the government. From 1920 to 1932, the religious avowals of 186 judges appointed to the federal bench revealed that fewer than 5 percent of them were Catholic, one of the surest indicators of ethnicity. During the subsequent Franklin D. Roosevelt administration (1933–1945), more than 25 percent of the appointed federal judges were Catholic (Krickus, 1976).

America's entry into World War II provided a new arena in which ethnics could prove their patriotism and social acceptability. They were usually confined to lower service ranks and often received the most dangerous assignments. For example, Italian Americans represented 4 percent of the U.S. population but composed 10 percent of U.S. casualties (Sowell, 1981). The postwar world was supposed to be different.

Ethnics, White Ethnics, and the Civil Rights Movement
With World War II over and the economy surging, opportunities for ethnics in expanding industries,

such as construction, seemed to assure that financial success would bring assimilation. When this did not happen, two lines of explanation appeared. One held that discrimination was "built into institutional patterns" (Yinger, 1983, p. 400), which themselves reinforced prejudices. The other explanation suggested that southern and eastern Europeans really were different, and, to denote these differences, the term "ethnic groups" was introduced in 1953 (Chapman, 1993). This new term connoted persistent attachment to Old World customs and, by inference, purposeful resistance to becoming "American," as other immigrants had done.

Yet evidence that assimilation was working came in 1960, when the United States elected as its president an Irish American who was a practicing Roman Catholic. For many Italian Americans, joy over this achievement was tempered somewhat by their memories of Irish priests calling them " 'dagoes' from the pulpit" and making them "sit in the back of the church with the Negroes" (Sowell, 1981, p. 116).

Civil rights movement. The federal government's strong commitment to civil rights initiatives was carried forward vigorously under President Lyndon B. Johnson's administration. Retention of the "Jewish seat" and appointment of the first Negro (the late Thurgood Marshall) to the Supreme Court were viewed as tangible indications of progress. In fact, the judiciary led the way. In *Brown v. Board of Education of Topeka* (1954), the Supreme Court found school segregation on the basis of race to be unconstitutional, and the Dwight D. Eisenhower administration sent troops to enforce integration of schools in the South.

By the mid-1960s, the drive for social justice for black people culminated in the passage of the most comprehensive civil rights legislation since the Reconstruction era 100 years earlier. New laws included the Civil Rights Act of 1964; the 14th amendment to the U.S. Constitution, which struck down the poll tax; and the Voting Rights Act of 1965.

The civil rights movement represented a major shift in strategy. It marked abandonment of the quest for social acceptance in favor of demanding equal legal rights for people of color. As this new strategy succeeded, it became apparent to southern and eastern European ethnics that they were to be included neither in the success of their coreligionists from Ireland nor in the progress of their fellow black and Hispanic citizens. They were left to ask, as Lewis (1991) put it: "Who are we?" One answer came in an influential book

by Glazer and Moynihan (1963), who argued that political organization, not the melting pot, was the way for ethnics to acquire power in America. That necessary organization had not been achieved by the new immigrants.

During the 1930s, the terms "ethnic" and "ethnicity" became substitutes for "race" and "racial," when events in Europe made American writers self-conscious about using those terms (Chapman, 1993). Now, "ethnic" was again applied to people of color, but primarily as a way to recognize their distinctive cultures.

Disadvantaged white ethnics. A way was needed to signify that the social justice claims of so-called ethnic people did not include southern and eastern European Americans. In ways that were both excluding and demeaning, the term "white ethnics" was applied to them. The fact that white ethnics were also disadvantaged was explained by the use of stereotypes concerning their behavior, loyalties, beliefs, and so on (Yinger, 1983), and these descriptions of how they are different were used to legitimate continued discrimination. "Some stereotypes," wrote Jones (1991) in the *Journal of Social Psychology,* "may reflect accurately the observation that certain groups occupy different social roles in society" (p. 470).

The confusion of white ethnics about their disadvantaged position was sharpened by data that showed that they seemed to have succeeded in the key areas required for assimilation. By the 1960s, white ethnics had surpassed the Irish on a combined index of income, education, and occupation (Kessler-Harris & Yans-McLaughlin, 1978).

Jiobu (1990) claimed that "without exception, analysts believe that intermarriage is the ultimate form of assimilation" (p. 65). On this scale, the white ethnics had come far, whereas the ethnics had scarcely moved at all. In the cohort born after 1950, 60 percent of people who identified themselves as Irish American married someone not from the group on either side of their parentage (Sowell, 1981), whereas for Italian Americans, the figure was 75 percent, and for Polish Americans, 82 percent (Alba, 1990).

Much the same was true for language. White ethnics tended to use their native tongues at home during the first generation, roughly before 1930, but by 1960, only 9.8 percent identified a language other than English as their primary language (Alba, 1990). Nelson and Tienda (1985) found that Hispanic people, despite a heritage of arriving before the Anglos, had not become structurally integrated into the broader society and that later generations typically continued to speak Spanish at home. Momeni (1984) asserted that Hispanics differed socioculturally from the whites of European ancestry, because their ethnic roots derived from a unique culture developed over many generations, far removed from any original Spanish immigrants.

White ethnics perceived that their achievements in assimilation were not gaining them acceptance, and they came to fear "that their heritage [was] no longer respected ..., that the rules [for] success [had] changed" (McCready, 1976, p. 24), leaving them still outsiders in a society struggling to include other groups.

As affirmative action programs for ethnics of color were enacted, many white ethnics began to believe that the price for social reform was to be extracted from them. They saw federal judges order housing and school integration in their areas, but not in affluent neighborhoods (Gesualdi, 1982). They found themselves still excluded from foundations, elite universities, and corporate boards, which actively recruited ethnics of color (Greeley, 1977). Italian Americans found themselves held responsible for crime, Polish Americans were scorned as unbright (Gans, 1979), Greek Americans were patronized as quaint, and Americans of Slavic ancestry were shunned as shifty.

White ethnics, having supported early civic rights efforts to make categorization by race, color, or national origin illegal in education, housing, employment, and elsewhere, faced the bitter irony a few years later of finding that applications for education, employment, and so on again invited such identification (Royce, 1982). The political patronage that the Irish had mastered was now, as Royce put it, "ethnic patronage," which required identification of the intended beneficiaries and did not include white ethnics. Feeling themselves victims of discrimination in policies and programs by which society alleged that it was ending discrimination, white ethnics found scant comfort in Glazer and Moynihan's (cited in Steinberg, 1963/ 1989) explanation that there is a difference between "negative discrimination," which is based on prejudice, and "positive discrimination," which is intended to achieve some social good.

White Ethnic Groups' Ascent
By the end of the 1960s, many white ethnics were turning back to their own cultural heritages. In 1970, a bill introduced by a Polish American member of Congress was passed that created ethnic heritage study centers with the aim of "letting people know about each other and recognizing their differences" (Gleason, 1992, p. 77).

Novak (1971) examined the situation of the "unmeltable ethnics." He claimed that the liberals who had helped raise Negro and Chicano consciousness had become as bigoted as WASPs when it came to white ethnics. Discriminatory practices against white ethnics had "seldom been challenged on the Left" as had been prejudice against ethnics of color (Novak, 1971, p. 7). White ethnics knew that they were unable to be WASPs, he declared, and those who succeeded in becoming professionals had lost touch with their ethnicity. The "ethnic revival" should not be lamented, he argued, but acknowledged as part of America's cultural diversity. White ethnics felt, as did ethnics of color, rejection and inferiority outside their own groups (Ryan, 1973); their ethnic revival was described as both a defense and an assertion of pride.

Ethnic pride had served other groups well. In the 1980 census, 57.8 percent of the Hispanic respondents classified themselves as white (Jiobu, 1990), even though Hispanics called themselves people of color. They had adopted ethnicity as a shield against oppression (Nelson & Tienda, 1985), and white ethnics seemed to follow their example. White ethnic identity served as a way to feel special (Hirschman, 1991) and also served "as a refuge against ... alienation" in a hostile world (Steinberg, 1989, p. 262).

Borrowing Greeley's term "ethnogenesis," Petersen (1980) described the process by which white ethnics sought to identify their cultural uniqueness. It took time for the change to occur and for white ethnic minorities to build ethnic consciousness (Kessner, 1977). Kessner, for example, quoting Max Ascoli, wrote that Italian Americans "became Americans before they became Italians" (p. 172).

By the mid-1970s, many Americans of southern and eastern European descent had adopted the condescending epithet "white ethnicity." They converted it into a "refuge for the embattled," but for much of the rest of society, it was a "reservoir of turmoil" (Nash, 1989, p. 112).

AMERICAN MOSAIC OF THEORIES

Assimilation, Cultural Diversity, and Racism
The debate over white ethnicity intensified during the 1970s and 1980s, with many theories available to explain what was happening. One theory held that the resurgence of ethnicity among white minorities was no more than dabbling with symbols by groups already essentially assimilated; a second theory considered white ethnicity a racist backlash against achievements by ethnics of color; a third held that white ethnicity represented rec-

ognition of America's cultural diversity and a positive step toward a true national identity.

Assimilation. Assimilationists, drawing on Gans's theories and adding findings from their own empirical research, explained that there was no ethnic revival at all. Gans (1979) admitted that descendants of new immigrants were engaged in some sort of ethnic involvement as part of their concern with identity but that their identity as white ethnics was only symbolic. It was a pose attractive "mainly [to] the middle class," and, because it made no real demands, did not represent a real commitment (Gans, 1992, p. 190).

Thernstrom (1982) asserted that the phenomenon actually was an ethnic revival, but he called it "the last gasp of groups nearing extinction" (p. 19). Discussing "ascribed ethnicity" and "optional ethnicity," Waters (1990) tended to confirm Thernstrom's thesis, finding that white ethnicity no longer was externally ascribed status so much as a cultural nostalgia for one's lost roots.

Alba's (1990) research led him to conclude that differences among the various European immigrant groups that compose white ethnics have faded and that such ethnicity had become subjective. He agreed with scholars who found that ethnic identities change as society changes (see, for example, Dominguez, 1986; Gleason, 1992; Lieberson, 1985) and posited that a new ethnic identity that fuses the disparate groups calling themselves white ethnics could emerge: European Americans. Alba's idea seemed consistent with what Lieberson called "unhyphenated whites," or non-WASP whites who had become assimilated. Lieberson agreed that white ethnicity was symbolic, voluntary, optional, or situational, and subject to constant new self-identification. But, he noted dryly, "Voluntary drifts in identification are never towards greater disadvantages" (Lieberson, p. 167).

Cultural pluralism. Cultural pluralists argued that white ethnics had remained distinctive in society, for a variety of reasons, and that they represented the cultural diversity that is the essence of America. Some cultural pluralists claimed that white ethnics suffered attack or rejection from both ends of the political spectrum; they were excluded from programs intended to promote social justice and accused of racism if they objected, leading to widespread disillusion among them.

The extent of white ethnic disillusion was apparent in the 1972 presidential election, in which the coalition of immigrants and minorities

of color was fractured for the first time since it had been put together by President Franklin D. Roosevelt and had subsequently helped elect Presidents Harry S. Truman, John F. Kennedy, and Lyndon B. Johnson. The 1972 Democratic presidential nominee, George McGovern, received less than 50 percent of the Catholic vote (Krickus, 1976) for the first time; in subsequent years, white ethnics continued "defecting" to the Republicans because of what they considered reverse discrimination, expressing their hostility toward "unfair rewards, not minorities, per se" (Lynch & Beer, 1990, p. 65). In explaining this shift in politics, Cornacchia and Nelson (1992) cited *strategic ethnicity,* Glazer and Moynihan's (1963) term. Greeley (1977) charged that the prejudice suffered by white ethnics was based on anti-Catholicism, permitting treatment of them that would be "a scandal" if the victims were black people or women. It was awareness of this, among other factors, that had created a serious new interest in cultural pluralism. It was a legitimate form of consciousness-raising not unlike that of other groups (Novak, 1973) and was entitled to the same respect and support.

Racism. In agreeing that an ethnic revival was occurring, Stein and Hill (1977) charged that the movement represented a racist "ideology of exclusivism" that viewed the world in "paranoid–narcissistic terms" (p. 271). Its intent was either to curtail or to capitalize on the progress of minorities of color. Olzak (1989), citing a charge common in the literature, claimed that white ethnics had historically enjoyed greater employment opportunities at the expense of Negroes. But Olzak ignored earlier research by Szymanski (1976), who also cited work by Reich (1971) that refuted the charge and noted that discrimination had hurt all workers by undermining labor solidarity, an idea akin to Gans's (1979) assertion that characteristics usually identified as white ethnic were merely working class.

One of the most forceful dissenters from the ethnic identity movement, Orlando Patterson (1977), denounced it in both whites and people of color. Although rejecting assimilationism, he stated that the new ethnicity writing was either "vulgar chauvinistic polemics" or "scientific pretensions." He was particularly concerned that the legitimation of ethnic politics could tend to make discrimination respectable again. Stein and Hill (1977) reached a similar conclusion, with a narrower focus, at the same time; they reasoned that the logical outcome of cultural and ethnic pluralism would be a revival of the doctrine of "separate but equal."

Social Work and White Ethnic Groups

Social work has a long history of relationships with the white ethnic population. In some respects, these relationships have been a major defining feature of the profession and have long been well-represented in the literature. In the 19th century, social work developed along two paths concerning its approaches to its client population, which consisted mostly of the new immigrants. One approach sought to help them leave behind their foreign ways and become Americanized, the better to begin to enjoy the many opportunities available in their adopted country. The other major approach sought to help the new immigrants find work, housing, education, and health services, and to master the challenges of adapting to the United States while simultaneously maintaining their own cultures and identities.

The extensive differences in these approaches were sharply defined among social workers: Some supported the eugenics movement; others opposed the 1924 Johnson–Reed Immigration Bill, which sharply curtailed white ethnic immigration. The differences continued through the turbulent 1930s, embodied in contrasting political activities by separate arms of the profession.

Opposition to discrimination. Since the 1960s, social work has strongly supported cultural pluralism and diversity. Social work was one of the first and most consistent supporters of civil rights activity and built the commitment to oppose prejudice and discrimination into its organizational structure and code of ethics.

Nevertheless, many people "do not seem very sure of what [cultural pluralism] is" (Glazer, 1983, p. 97), and social work may be in the same position. Alternatively, social work may share a widespread ambivalence with respect to a proper professional stance on work with and action on behalf of white ethnics. A notable early effort to define the issues was Vigilante's (1972) discussion of "ethnic affirmation," which included specific attention to appropriate strategies for professional social work. It was an exception to the rule. Although social work literature has long denounced discrimination and institutional racism, it seldom has applied sanctions specifically to prejudices against white ethnic minorities.

There is a long history of social work policy and practice literature dealing with prejudice and discrimination, intergroup relations, and social justice, both in general terms and as applied to minorities of color. NASW's 1976 publication of *The Diverse Society* (Cafferty & Chestang, 1976) was one of the first efforts by any professional organization to deal with questions related to cultural pluralism, drawing on the thinking of the most informed scholars of the time. Two years later, the Council on Social Work Education produced *The Dual Perspective* (Norton, 1978), intended to bring diversity issues into the curriculum. In 1984, the journal *Social Work with Groups* devoted a special issue to ethnicity in group work practice. By the late 1980s there existed a significant body of work that had begun to address practice issues in dealing with ethnic populations. White ethnics were included in many of these works, with descriptions of "typical" basic characteristics of each white ethnic population group.

Ethnic-sensitive practice. McGoldrick, Pearce, and Giordano (1987) applied this approach, seeking to identify unique qualities of ethnic group families and to note their implications for clinical interventions. They proposed "ethnicity training" for work with ethnic families, stating that the most important part was coming to understand one's own ethnicity. Devore and Schlesinger (1987), who sought to help practitioners understand the importance of respect for ethnic differences, used as a framework Erik Erikson's life stages of psychosocial development. Relying heavily on self-reported life experiences, Pinderhughes (1989) also emphasized the importance of mutual understanding and respect when working with ethnic populations.

Since the idea of ethnic-sensitive practice was introduced, a series of publications by and for social work practitioners has appeared, with information and guides for work in this area. Much of this literature has included work with white ethnics, but little has been specifically designed to address the immigrant experience of the offspring of the new immigrants (in contrast to a growing literature on work with post-1965 immigrants) or the professional concerns with respect to policy and practice activity with and on behalf of white ethnics with multiethnic backgrounds.

Issues to be addressed. Part of the problem in this literature is related to the difficulty in identifying unique characteristics of white ethnics without seeming to certify stereotypes. For example, literature dealing with white ethnics tends to do so in terms of "Greek families," "Polish families," and so on. With increasing numbers of white ethnic intermarriages (Alba, 1985), specification of the unique qualities of a "Greek American family," for instance, becomes more and more problematic and at risk of oversimplification. Moreover, when we can identify specific qualities that allege to distinguish white ethnic group values and beliefs as different from those of mainstream Americans, social work practitioners may have to deal with ethical problems in balancing culturally sensitive practice with responsibility for addressing socially proscribed behaviors, such as the use of physical punishment in child rearing.

At present, guidance for social work practitioners dealing with white ethnic groups tends to be generalized, emphasizing mutual understanding, empathy, and respect (Pinderhughes, 1989); advocating flexibility and adaptation (Devore & Schlesinger, 1987); or recognizing that competent practice with white ethnics requires, as does work with all ethnics, a special form of interpersonal sensitivity (Lieberman, 1990).

Despite an apparent increase in interest and a growing literature in social work with respect to white ethnics, there is little convincing evidence that the profession has reached a consensus about white ethnic groups. The profession has yet to decide whether white ethnic groups represent a legitimate manifestation of cultural diversity that is entitled to respect, service, and protection—or a retrograde and divisive effort by one portion of white society to claim a larger share of society's rewards, even at the cost of interrupting the momentum of social justice for ethnic populations of color, who historically have been the most oppressed and excluded from access to the American dream.

REFERENCES

Abbott, E. (1922). Comments. In *Proceedings of the National Conference of Social Work* (p. 463). Chicago: University of Chicago Press.

Addams, J. (1909). *The spirit of youth and the city streets.* New York: Macmillan.

Addams, J. (1927). Social consequences of the immigration law. In *Proceedings of the National Conference of Social Work* (pp. 102–106). Chicago: University of Chicago Press.

Alba, R. (1985). The twilight of ethnicity among Americans of European ancestry. *Ethnic & Racial Studies, 8*(1), 134–158.

Alba, R. (1990). *Ethnic identity: The transformation of white America.* New Haven, CT: Yale University Press.

Brown v. Board of Education of Topeka, 347 U.S. 483 (1954).

Cafferty, P., & Chestang, L. (Eds.). (1976). *The diverse society: Implications for social policy.* Washington, DC: National Association of Social Workers.

Chapman, M. (Ed.). (1993). *Social and biological aspects of ethnicity.* New York: Oxford University Press.

Civil Rights Act of 1964. P.L. 88-352, 78 Stat. 241.

Cornacchia, E., & Nelson, D. (1992). Historical differences in the political experience of American blacks and white ethnics: Revisiting an unresolved controversy. *Ethnic & Racial Studies, 15*(1), 102–124.

Crevecoeur, H. de. (1957). *Letters from an American farmer.* New York: E. P. Dutton. (Original work published 1782)

Devore, W., & Schlesinger, E. (1987). *Ethnic sensitive social work practice* (rev. ed.). Columbus, OH: Charles E. Merrill.

Dewey, J. (1923). The school as a means of developing social consciousness and social ideals in children. In *Proceedings of the National Conference of Social Work* (pp. 449–453). Chicago: University of Chicago Press.

Dinnerstein, L., & Reimer, D. (1982). *Ethnic Americans.* New York: Harper & Row.

Dominguez, V. (1986). *White by definition.* New Brunswick, NJ: Rutgers University Press.

Gans, H. (1979). Symbolic ethnicity: The future of the ethnic groups and cultures in America. *Ethnic & Racial Studies, 2*(1), 1–20.

Gans, H. (1992). Second-generation decline: Scenarios of the economic and ethnic futures of the post-1965 American immigrants. *Ethnic & Racial Studies, 15*(2), 173–192.

Garrett, P. (1900). Immigration: Its objects and objections. *Proceedings of the National Conference of Charities and Correction* (pp. 158–162). Boston: Ellis.

Gesualdi, L. (1982). A note on Boston's racial problems. *Sociological Inquiry, 52*(3), 255–257.

Glazer, N. (1983). *Ethnic dilemmas 1964–1982.* Cambridge, MA: Harvard University Press.

Glazer, N., & Moynihan, D. (1963). *Beyond the melting pot.* Cambridge, MA: MIT Press.

Gleason, P. (1980). American identity and Americanization. In W. Petersen, M. Novak, & P. Gleason (Eds.), *Concepts of ethnicity* (pp. 57–143). Cambridge, MA: Belknap.

Gleason, P. (1992). *Speaking of diversity.* Baltimore: Johns Hopkins University Press.

Greeley, A. (1977). Anti-Catholicism in the Academy. *Change, 9*(6), 40–43.

Greeley, A. (1991). Review of *Ethnic Identity* by R. Alba. *Political Science Quarterly, 106*(4), 754–756.

Henderson, C. (1900). Presidential address. In *Proceedings of the National Conference of Charities and Correction* (pp. 1–15). Boston: Ellis.

Hirschman, C. (1991). What happened to the white ethnics? *Contemporary Sociology, 20*(2), 180–183.

Jensen, L. (1989). *The new immigration.* Westport, CT: Greenwood Press.

Jiobu, R. (1990). *Ethnicity and inequality.* Albany: State University of New York Press.

Jones, M. (1991). Stereotyping Hispanics and whites: Perceived differences in social roles as a determinant of ethnic stereotypes. *Journal of Social Psychology, 131*(4), 469–476.

Kessler-Harris, A., & Yans-McLaughlin, V. (1978). European immigrant groups. In T. Sowell (Ed.), *American ethnic groups* (pp. 107–137). Washington, DC: Urban Institute.

Kessner, T. (1977). *The golden door.* New York: Oxford University Press.

Krickus, R. (1976). *Pursuing the American dream.* Bloomington: Indiana University Press.

Lal, B. (1983). Perspectives on ethnicity: Old wine in new bottles. *Ethnic & Racial Studies, 6*(2), 154–173.

Letchworth, W. (1885). Presidential address. In *Proceedings of the National Conference of Charities and Correction* (pp. 9–17). Boston: Ellis.

Lewis, S. (1991). Who are we? *Ethnos, 56*(3–4), 3–4.

Lieberman, A. (1990). Culturally sensitive intervention with children and families. *Child and Adolescent Social Work, 7*(2), 101–120.

Lieberson, S. (1985). Unhyphenated whites in the United States. *Ethnic & Racial Studies, 8*(1), 159–180.

Liebman, L. (Ed.). (1982). *Ethnic relations in America.* Englewood Cliffs, NJ: Prentice Hall.

Lynch, F., & Beer, W. (1990). You ain't the right color, pal. *Policy Review, 51,* 64–67.

McCready, W. (1976). Social utilities in a pluralistic society. In P. Cafferty & L. Chestang (Eds.), *The diverse society: Implications for social policy* (pp. 13–25). Washington, DC: National Association of Social Workers.

McCullough, O. (1888). The tribe of Ishmael. In I. C. Barrows (Ed.), *Proceedings of the National Conference of Charities and Correction* (pp. 154–159). Boston: Ellis.

McGoldrick, M., Pearce, J., & Giordano, J. (Eds.). (1987). *Ethnicity and family therapy.* New York: Guilford Press.

Miller, H. (1920). Treatment of immigrant heritages. In *Proceedings of the National Conference of Social Work* (pp. 730–738). Chicago: Rogers & Hall.

Mindel, C., & Habenstein, R. (Eds.). (1976). *Ethnic families in America.* New York: Elsevier–North Holland.

Momeni, J. (1984). *Demography of racial and ethnic minorities in the United States.* Westport, CT: Greenwood Press.

Nash, M. (1989). *The cauldron of ethnicity in the modern world.* Chicago: University of Chicago Press.

Nelson, C., & Tienda, M. (1985). The structuring of Hispanic ethnicity: Historical and contemporary perspectives. *Ethnic & Racial Studies, 8*(1), 49–74.

Norton, D. (1978). *The dual perspective: Inclusion of ethnic minority content in the social work curriculum.* New York: Council on Social Work Education.

Novak, M. (1971). *The rise of the unmeltable ethnics.* New York: Macmillan.

Novak, M. (1973). How American are you if your grandparents came from Serbia in 1888? In S. TeSelle (Ed.), *The rediscovery of ethnicity* (pp. 1–20). New York: Harper & Row.

Novak, M. (1980). Pluralism in humanistic perspective. In W. Petersen, M. Novak, & P. Gleason (Eds.), *Concepts of ethnicity* (pp. 27–56). Cambridge, MA: Belknap.

Olzak, S. (1989). Causes of shifts in occupational segregation of the foreign-born: Evidence from American cities, 1870–1880. *Social Forces, 68*(2), 593–620.

Patterson, O. (1977). *Ethnic chauvinism.* New York: Stein & Day.

Pavalko, R. (1980). Racism and the new immigration: A reinterpretation of the assimilation of white ethnics in American society. *Sociology and Social Research, 65*(1), 56–77.

Petersen, W. (1980). Concepts of ethnicity. In W. Petersen, M. Novak, & P. Gleason (Eds.), *Concepts of ethnicity* (pp. 1–26). Cambridge, MA: Belknap.

Pinderhughes, E. (1989). *Understanding race, ethnicity & power.* New York: Macmillan.

Portes, A., & Zhou, M. (1992). Gaining the upper hand: Economic mobility among immigrant and domestic minorities. *Ethnic & Racial Studies, 15*(4), 491–522.

Rafter, N. (1988). *White trash.* Boston: Northeastern University Press.

Reich, M. (1971). The economics of racism. In D. Gordon (Ed.), *Problems in political economy* (pp. 107–113). Lexington, MA: D.C. Heath.

Royce, A. (1982). *Ethnic identity.* Bloomington: Indiana University Press.

Ryan, J. (Ed.). (1973). *White ethnics.* Englewood Cliffs, NJ: Prentice Hall.

Schlesinger, A. (1991). *The disuniting of America.* New York: W. W. Norton.

Sowell, T. (1981). *Ethnic America.* New York: Basic Books.

Stein, H., & Hill, R. (1977). *The ethnic imperative.* University Park: Pennsylvania State University Press.

Steinberg, S. (1989). *The ethnic myth.* Boston: Beacon Press.

Sumner, W. G. (1906). *Folkways.* Boston: Ginn.

Szymanski, A. (1976). Racial discrimination and white gain. *American Sociological Review, 41*(3), 403–414.

Thernstrom, S. (1982). Ethnic groups in American history. In L. Liebman (Ed.), *Ethnic relations in America* (pp. 3–27). Englewood Cliffs, NJ: Prentice Hall.

Thernstrom, S., Orlov, A., & Handlin, O. (Eds.). (1980). *Harvard encyclopedia of American ethnic groups.* Cambridge, MA: Belknap.

Tocqueville, A. de. (1969). *Democracy in America.* Garden City, NY: Doubleday.

Vigilante, J. (1972). Ethnic affirmation, or kiss me, I'm Italian. *Social Work, 17,* 10–20.

Voting Rights Act of 1965. P.L. 89-110, 79 Stat. 437.

Warner, W. L. (1941). *The social life of a modern community.* New Haven, CT: Yale University Press.

Waters, M. (1990). *Ethnic options.* Berkeley: University of California Press.

Yinger, J. (1983). Ethnicity and social change: The interaction of structural, cultural, and personality factors. *Ethnic & Racial Studies, 6*(4), 395–409.

Zenner, W. (1985). Jewishness in America: Ascription and choice. *Ethnic & Racial Studies, 8*(1), 117–133.

Charles Guzzetta, EdD, is professor, Hunter College, School of Social Work, 129 East 79th Street, New York, NY 10021.

For further information see

Citizen Participation; Civil Rights; Community; Displaced People; Ethics and Values; Ethnic-Sensitive Practice; Families Overview; Homelessness; Housing; Human Rights; Income Distribution; Mutual Aid Societies; Natural Helping Networks; Peace and Social Justice; Policy Analysis; Poverty; Rural Social Work; Social Development; Social Planning; Social Welfare Policy; Social Work Practice: History and Evolution.

Key Words

assimilation	exclusion
diversity	white ethnics

Wiley, George

See Biographies section, Volume 3

Wilkins, Roy

See Biographies section, Volume 3

Witte, Ernest Frederic

See Biographies section, Volume 3

Williams, Anita Rose

See Biographies section, Volume 3

Wittman, Milton

See Biographies section, Volume 3

READER'S GUIDE

Women

The following entries contain information on this general topic:

Adolescent Pregnancy
Domestic Violence
Domestic Violence: Legal Issues
Gay and Lesbian Adolescents
Lesbians Overview
Lesbians: Direct Practice
Lesbians: Parenting

Sexual Assault
Sexual Harassment
Women Overview
Women: Direct Practice
Women and Health Care
Women in Social Policy

Women Overview
Naomi Gottlieb

The role of women in professional social work has an ironic history. Women were the pioneers in establishing the profession and both its practice and educational missions. However, as the 20th century proceeded, social work came to reflect the widespread societal dominance of men. Men, mainly white men, became the educational leaders and agency administrators. Knowledge for social work practice developed within that institutional context, and the particular issues for women in society were largely ignored. Since the 1960s many social work scholars, practitioners, and grassroots activists have challenged that dominant view. They have demonstrated that women in American society experience the world differently than do men, often to women's detriment. The byword of the feminist movement—that the personal is political—has been applied increasingly to the personal problems that women bring to social workers. Scholars and activists alike maintain that women's individual problems can never be wholly separated from the negative aspects of women's societal roles. This perspective enables social workers to understand how an individual woman's problem may be related to, or created by, the social circumstances she shares with many other women.

Social work has always promoted the connection between the social and individual, but until recently that connection for women in a sexist society has not been clear. In clarifying that connection, social work is taking part in an extensive reexamination of knowledge about women occurring in most academic disciplines and professional schools. In those areas most relevant to social work—law, medicine, psychology, sociology, and anthropology, for example—researchers and practitioners have questioned biased practices and developed gender-fair knowledge of great utility to social work.

To serve women clients effectively, social workers need to know about and evaluate the extensive new knowledge about women. Several entries about women in this encyclopedia indicate the range of that knowledge. This entry outlines some major aspects of women's lives and has two main purposes: (1) to present basic data about women's current status in society and (2) to illustrate, when appropriate, the manner in which discrimination and stereotypes are reflected in women's circumstances.

A major result of bias in considering women in American society is the frequent lack of information about women of all races, of different sexual orientations, and of all ages. To the extent that such information is available, this entry attempts to address the condition of all women. Only recently have some national statistics reflected the range of data on racial and ethnic groups. Inconsistencies remain in the completeness of the collection and reporting of national data. In particular, data concerning Asian American and Native American women are often conspicuously lacking.

The aggregate data presented, although important in revealing overall trends, conceal individual differences. Most women do not identify themselves by a single characteristic such as race or educational level, but by their unique combination of many traits.

WOMEN IN THE U.S. POPULATION

Of the 245 million people in the United States in 1989, 126 million (51 percent) were female. Of the female population, approximately 97 million (77 percent) were white, 16 million (13 percent) were African American, 9 million (7 percent) were of Hispanic origin, and the 4 million women of other races and ethnicities constituted 3 percent of all women. From 1980 to 1989, the populations of racial and ethnic groups, encompassing both men and women, increased: African Americans from 11.8 percent to 12.4 percent of the population; Asian and Pacific Islanders from 1.6 percent to 2.8 percent; American Indians, Eskimos, and Aleuts from 0.6 percent to 0.7 percent; and people of Hispanic origin from 6.4 percent to 8.3 percent (U.S. Bureau of the Census, 1990).

For many years more boys have been born each year than girls—in 1989 there were 105 male live births to 100 female (U.S. Bureau of the Census, 1992a). Through the life span, however, the gender balance moves toward a greater proportion of women in the population. In the over-65 age group in 1988, there were 68 men for every 100 women (U.S. Bureau of the Census, 1989). The proportion of men to women among people over age 65 differs somewhat by race and ethnicity. For every 100 African American women over age 65 there are 67 African American men, for every 100 older women of Hispanic origin there are 71 men, and for every 100 older women of other races there are 77 men (U.S. Bureau of the Census, 1990).

HEALTH

Life expectancy has been used as a major criterion of health. In all societies, women have a greater life expectancy; in 1990, U.S. women's life expectancy was seven years longer than that of men. On the average, white men born in 1990 are expected to live 72.6 years and white women 79.3 years. For African Americans, those expectancies are 66 years for men and 74.5 years for women (U.S. Public Health Service, 1992). By the year 2010, the average life expectancy is expected to be 86.1 years for women (Older Women's League, 1989).

Although women live longer than men, they experience more chronic illnesses and, even taking reproductive needs into account, use health care facilities more than men do. In 1990 women had an average of 6.1 physician contacts, compared with 4.7 for men. African American women consulted doctors less frequently than did white women, with an average of 4.9 contacts in 1990 (U.S. Public Health Service, 1992).

The disparity between the longevity figures for men and women has critical social consequences for women. Because they live longer, women need retirement income for longer periods than do men. Women's economic status in society leaves many women poor in their old age. Society's failure to provide long-term care for the frail elderly population also has a greater impact on women than it does on men.

The two leading causes of death—heart disease and cancer—are the same for men and women. The third leading cause for men (both white and African American) is accidental death; for women (again both white and African American) it is cerebrovascular illness. The three most frequent causes of death for Native American women are similar to those for men. However, among Asian women, the ranking is somewhat different from that for men and non-Asian women—cancer leads the list, followed by heart disease and cerebrovascular illness (U.S. Public Health Service, 1992).

In recent years feminist health care activists and others have exerted strong pressure for health research that acknowledges gender differences. Research has ignored the gender factor in heart disease, for example, the leading cause of death for both women and men. The most prominent long-term study of aging to include studies of heart disease, the Baltimore Longitudinal Study of Aging, did not include women as research subjects until 1978, 20 years after the study's inception (Older Women's League, 1989). Currently, the medical profession is giving long-overdue attention to this issue. The March 1993 meetings of the American College of Cardiology paid considerable attention to the fact that therapies that work well for men may be less successful for women and that women often receive less aggressive treatment for heart attacks ("Asking Why," 1993).

Lifetime health concerns for women also must be understood in the context of their economic circumstances. Considerable evidence exists for the connection between poverty and poor physical health (Brenner, 1984). Improvement in women's health conditions cannot be considered separately from their economic circumstances.

BIRTH AND PREGNANCY RATES

The fertility rate for American women increased somewhat in the 1980s, from 67.4 live births per 1,000 women ages 15 to 64 in 1981 to 69.2 for the same group in 1989. The rate for white women was 64.7 births; for African American women it was 85.8 (U.S. Public Health Service, 1992).

The infant mortality rate continues to be higher in the United States than in many industrialized countries. In 1988 there were 10 infant deaths for every 1,000 live births in the United States, compared with 4.8 in Japan, 7.5 in Germany, and 8.7 in Australia (U.S. Public Health Service, 1992).

In 1991 there was a small drop in the U.S. infant mortality rate to 9.8 deaths for every 1,000 live births, but the racial difference was marked. For white infants the figure was 8.1, for African American infants it was 18.6. The considerable difference was also true for maternal mortality. In 1989, for every 1,000 births 7.3 women died in childbirth, but the rate for white women was 5.4 and for African American women was 18.6 (U.S. Public Health Service, 1992).

Patterns of childbearing have altered considerably in recent years. Women are entering marriage later and are postponing childbearing. Their educational advancement and the growth in workplace opportunities appear to be the main determining factors for these changes. Data are not available to indicate whether these trends are consistent across racial and ethnic groups.

Racial differences also exist in the proportion of unmarried mothers (Figure 1). In 1989, 27 percent of live births were to white unmarried mothers, whereas 66 percent of African American, 55 percent of Puerto Rican, and 53 percent of Native American live births were to unmarried women (U.S. Public Health Service, 1992).

Pregnancies among young women ages 15 to 19 have increased since the 1970s. In 1973 the teenage pregnancy rate was 96.2 per 1,000 young women; in 1988 the rate was 112.7. However, the rate of live births for this group declined in those same years, from 59.3 per 1,000 to 53.6. Correspondingly, and related to this decline, the abortion rate for that same age group increased from 22.8 per 1,000 in 1973 to 44.0 in 1988 (Henshaw, 1992).

The pregnancy rate of teenagers of color is more than twice that of white teenagers. In 1988 the rates were 197 per 1,000 for young women of color and 93 per 1,000 for white teenagers. The proportion of live births among teenagers also differed considerably by racial group. In 1990 the fertility rate for young white women ages 15 to 17 was 27.5 per 1,000; for the same age group among African Americans the rate was 82.4 (U.S. Public Health Service, 1991). Other data about these racial differences show that by the age of 18, 21 percent of white teenagers and 40 percent of minority teenagers will become pregnant (Alan Guttmacher Institute, 1993).

Teenage pregnancies are more likely to occur in poor families and among teenagers with less education (Chilman, 1988). Young women who anticipate a more encouraging future through education and better employment may be less likely to risk pregnancy that would endanger that potential. The future for teenage mothers is not bright: Throughout their lives they are at greater risk for poverty and welfare dependency (Alan Guttmacher Institute, 1993).

The average number of children per mother in 1991 was 2.1, but many women were having their children later (U.S. Bureau of the Census, 1992b). In 1990, 65 percent of childless women under the age of 30 said they expected to have children. However, in looking at older cohorts of childless women that proportion decreases: Among women ages 30 to 35, 41 percent still expected to have a child; among those 35 to 39, only 16 percent still had that expectation (U.S. Bureau of the Census, 1991a).

Other demographic changes have influenced these fertility patterns. More women are college educated now, and there appears to be a relationship between higher education, later marriages, and fewer children. In 1976, 61.9 percent of women in the age range of 20 to 24 were never married; in 1990, that proportion had risen to 76.9 percent (U.S. Bureau of the Census, 1991a).

The duration of marriages has also changed. In 1976, among women ages 25 to 29, 43.1 percent had been married more than two years. By 1990 the proportion of marriages lasting more than two

FIGURE 1

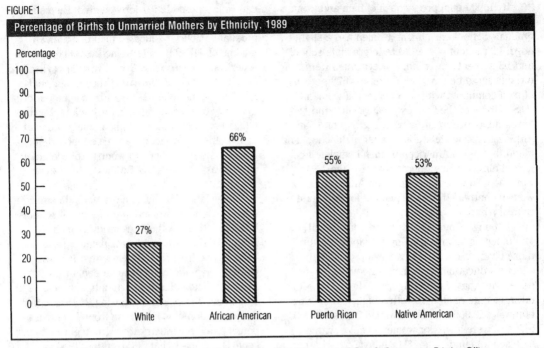

Percentage of Births to Unmarried Mothers by Ethnicity, 1989

SOURCE: U.S. Public Health Service. (1992). *Health United States, 1991*. Washington, DC: U.S. Government Printing Office.

years among people in the 25 to 29 age group had decreased to 27.1 percent. Even in families with a child, marriages of longer duration had decreased in number. In 1976, 80.1 percent of women ages 25 to 29 with one child reported marriages of more than two years; by 1990 only 65.6 percent of that group reported similar marriage longevity (U.S. Bureau of the Census, 1991a). In 1988 the median duration of all marriages was 7.1 years, only a small change from the figure of 6.7 years reported for 1970 (U.S. Bureau of the Census, 1992a).

Legal abortions have increased considerably in recent years. In 1973, the year of the *Roe v. Wade* decision, the rate of legal abortions was 19.6 per 1,000 live births. By 1989 that proportion had increased to 34.6. The rates varied considerably by race and age. For white women, the rate was 24.8 per 1,000 in 1990; for all women of color it was 46.1. Young women under the age of 15 had the highest abortion rate in 1990, 83.5 per 1,000. For young women ages 15 to 19, the rate was 54.8. Although the rates fell for women of more mature years (for example, the rate was 26.8 per 1,000 for women ages 35 to 39), the rate increased to 49.4 for women age 40 and older (U.S. Public Health Service, 1992).

EDUCATION

In 1991 white men and women were about equal in the average number of years of schooling com-

pleted—12.8 years for men, 12.7 years for women. Racial groups differed somewhat. African Americans, both men and women, completed 12.4 years on the average; Hispanic men, 12.1 years; and Hispanic women, 12 years (U.S. Bureau of the Census, 1992a).

Since 1950 the percentage of women among high school graduates—51 percent—has mirrored women's proportion in the population. However, not until 1981 did women constitute one-half of all college graduates (U.S. Bureau of the Census, 1985).

By 1990 high school and college attendance reached all-time national highs. Seventy-eight percent of all people over the age of 25 had completed high school, and 21.4 percent had completed four or more years of college. There were no gender differences in high school completion rates but some in college completion—24.3 percent of men finished college, whereas 18.8 percent of women did. However, the college completion rate was only 11.5 percent for African American women and 9.7 percent for Hispanic women (U.S. Bureau of the Census, 1992a). Similar marked differences were evident among women with a graduate education (that is, five or more years of college). Although 6.1 percent of white women had such education, only 3 percent of African American women and 2.9 percent of women of Hispanic origin had had similar education (U.S. Bureau of the Census, 1992d).

By 1990 equal proportions of men and women were enrolled in college—3.7 percent—and for graduate school enrollment, women had a slight edge: 1.2 percent of men were in graduate school and 1.3 percent of women. However, men were more likely to be enrolled full-time—67.8 percent of men compared with 60.5 percent of women (U.S. Bureau of the Census, 1992e). One study followed the educational paths of a group of Asian American and white students after high school and found that Asian American women completed college at almost twice the rate of the white women—33 percent for the Asian American women contrasted with 18 percent for the white women (Brandon, 1991).

Although women's increased educational attainment is an encouraging sign for the future, those changes have yet to alter appreciably the effect of education on women's income as compared with that of men (Figure 2). In 1993 the mean income of all men with a high school education was $22,966; for white women it was $13,003. Incomes were lower for women of color with a high school education—$11,944 for African American women and $12,107 for women of Hispanic origin. The contrasts were similar among college graduates: College-educated men had a mean income of $41,402; white women, $23,600; African American women, $23,823; and women of Hispanic origin, $21,425 (U.S. Bureau of the Census, 1994).

The gender difference can be seen most dramatically by comparing men having a high school education with women having a college education. In 1993 the mean income for male high school graduates was $22,966; for women college graduates it was $22,949. (U.S. Bureau of the Census, 1994).

Legislation has made a dramatic difference in the enrollment of women in professional schools. In 1972, Title IX of the Education Act made it illegal to discriminate in educational programs on the basis of sex. In 1971, just before that law was passed, 9 percent of medical students were women; by 1989 that proportion had increased to 33 percent. In law schools during that same period the proportion of women rose from 7 percent to 40 percent and in dentistry from 1 percent to 26 percent (U.S. Department of Education, 1990).

FIGURE 2

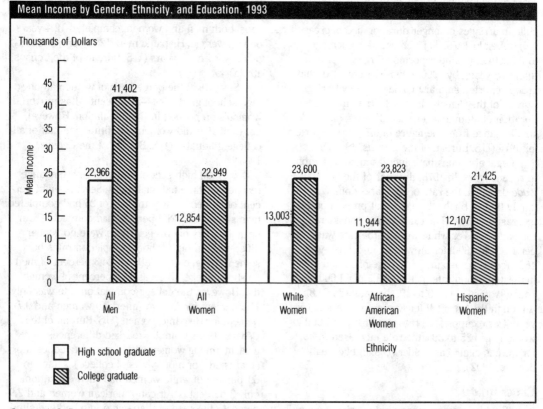

Mean Income by Gender, Ethnicity, and Education, 1993

SOURCE: U.S. Bureau of the Census. (1994). Educational attainment in the United States—March 1993. *Current population reports* (Series P-20, No. 476). Washington, DC: U.S. Government Printing Office.

Although more and more women are working in professions previously dominated by men, most women still work in low-paying jobs.

EMPLOYMENT

Women's increased participation in the labor force is one of the most important demographic trends affecting women's lives in recent years. In 1970, 42.6 percent of the civilian labor force were women; by 1991 that proportion had increased to 57.4 percent, and it is predicted to increase to 63.5 percent by the year 2005. African American women traditionally have had higher labor-force participation than have white women, and from 1970 to 1991 their proportion in the work force increased from 49.5 percent to 62.6 percent. The data for Hispanic women were available only for 1991, at which time their proportion in the work force was 53 percent. Men's labor-force participation decreased somewhat in the period from 1970 to 1991, from 80 percent to 76.4 percent (U.S. Bureau of the Census, 1992a).

The proportion of married women in the work force also has increased dramatically from previous generations. In 1950, 24.8 percent of married women were in the work force; in 1991 that proportion was 58.5. Similar changes have occurred for women with children. In 1960, 39 percent of women with children ages six to 17 were in the labor force; by 1991 that percentage increased to 73.6 percent. Even mothers with children under the age of six were joining the work force in increasing numbers, from 18.6 percent in 1960 to 59.9 percent in 1991 (U.S. Bureau of the Census, 1992a).

The changes are also noteworthy for women with infants. In 1976, 31 percent of such women were in the work force; by 1990, that proportion had increased to 56 percent and, for women with a college education, to 68 percent. For women of color with children less than a year old, the picture is somewhat different. Among African American women with infants, the proportion in the work force had remained fairly steady over a decade—47 percent in 1980 and 46 percent in 1990. Among Hispanic women, the percentage had increased from 33 percent in 1980 to 44 percent in 1990. Although no data are available about Asian American women in 1980, in 1990 49 percent of Asian American women with infants were in the labor force (U.S. Bureau of the Census, 1991b).

Notwithstanding the advancement of many women in the professions and the increased proportion of women in the total work force, most women continue to work in sex-segregated occupations. Millions of women still perform low-paying jobs and work at occupations in which women are the majority:

- secretaries (99 percent are women)
- child care workers (97 percent)
- licensed practical nurses (96 percent) and registered nurses (94 percent)
- sales and retail service workers (68 percent)
- social workers (68 percent) (U.S. Bureau of the Census, 1991b).

Comparable Worth

Ample evidence indicates that the more an occupation is dominated by women, the lower its wages are (Tomaskovie-Devey, 1995). Comparable worth is an economic strategy designed to correct that injustice. In contrast to the concept of "equal pay for equal work"—which mandates that people doing the same work, regardless of gender, should be paid similarly—comparable worth maintains that very different jobs can be equated and paid comparable wages. Using such criteria as the amount of training needed and the extent of the employee's responsibilities, people doing very different jobs can be evaluated and earn similar pay, regardless of gender.

The advantage of the comparable-worth strategy is that it recognizes that most women are crowded into a small number of low-paying jobs. Comparable-worth proponents recognize that most women work at low-wage jobs, and they maintain that the status of women in those occupations can be improved considerably by implementing comparable-worth procedures. In jurisdictions where these mechanisms have been put into place, women's wages have increased (Ehrenberg, 1989). As of 1991, 20 state governments had made some salary adjustments to correct sex bias, up from just five states in 1984.

Seven of these states have fully implemented a pay-equity plan. In addition, as of 1991, 22 other states and the District of Columbia had completed or were conducting studies on sex discrimination in salaries (National Committee on Pay Equity, 1992).

The economic benefits of comparable-worth implementation have a positive impact on many other aspects of women's lives. And just as important, comparable-worth policies result in a fuller appreciation of "women's work" in U.S. society.

SEXUAL HARASSMENT

Sexual harassment in the workplace has received some long-overdue public attention in recent years. But the impact of this abuse on women's longevity on the job remains an unrecognized negative outcome. Study results vary in terms of prevalence rates, but nine surveys conducted between 1976 and 1991 found that between 30 percent and 90 percent of working women had reported sexual harassment (Kaplan, 1991; Maypole & Skaine, 1983; U.S. Merit System Personnel Board, 1988). Thus, on average it appears that 60 percent of working women report being sexually harassed. Studies also show that about 70 percent of women who experience sexual harassment leave their jobs: They either quit or are fired in retaliation for refusing sexual advances (Coles, 1986; Jones, Remland, & Brunner, 1987). Aside from the debilitating effect on women of what courts have called a "hostile environment" on the job, these study results suggest that sexual harassment forces millions of women to leave their jobs, with possibly important consequences on their earnings and promotional potential.

INCOME AND POVERTY

In view of social work's commitment to societally oppressed people, the economic condition of women is of special importance to the profession. Women are economically disadvantaged in many ways throughout their lifetimes, for example, by earning lower salaries than men, by the special economic hardships of single parenthood, and by a gender-biased social security system. They are overrepresented among those living below the poverty level, and their poorer economic conditions lead in turn to poorer physical and mental health.

The wage gap between men and women continues to be a problem for women, although there has been a recent narrowing of the difference. In 1990, women still earned only 71 percent of what men earn. Although this constituted an increase from 60 percent in 1980, greater wage equity exists in a number of other industrialized countries. For example, in Italy and Denmark, women earn 86 percent of what men earn (Hewlett, 1986).

Young women in the United States are gaining ground. Women between the ages of 24 and 35 now earn 80 cents for every dollar earned by men of the same age (Nasar, 1992a). Economists noted in 1992 that the new generation of working women secures better jobs with higher salaries by working more continuously and obtaining more education than had previous generations of women (Nasar, 1992b).

The effects of race on women's income become more evident when considering the proportions of people with low earnings and the changes in those proportions during the 1980s. The threshold for low earnings (that is, household income less than the poverty level for a family of four) was determined to be an annual income of $6,905 in 1979 and $12,195 in 1990. In 1979, 8 percent of men and 20 percent of women had low earnings; by 1990, these proportions had increased to 14 percent for men and 24.3 percent for women. But the percentages of those with low earnings were greater for women of color. In 1979, 24 percent of African American women had low earnings, and by 1990 that proportion had reached 28 percent. The comparable data for Hispanic women were 32 percent in 1979 and 37 percent in 1990 (U.S. Bureau of the Census, 1992c).

The proportion of people who live below the poverty level is another way to look at the phenomenon of low income, especially when comparing the overall rate of households headed by women. In 1990, 13.5 percent of the U.S. population lived below the poverty level, but among single-mother households that proportion was 44.5 percent (Figure 3). Racial differences also were considerable. The percentage of white men and women living below the poverty level in 1991 was 10.7; for female-headed households, it was 37.9 percent. The comparable figure for African Americans was 31.9 percent as compared with 56.1 percent and for Hispanics 28.1 percent as compared with 58.2 percent (U.S. Public Health Service, 1992).

Poverty rates increase as women age. In 1990 the median income for full-time, year-round workers ages 45 to 64 was about $12,000 less for women than it was for men (U.S. Bureau of Census, 1991c). In addition, 75 percent of people receiving Supplementary Security Income (SSI) that year on the basis of age were women (U.S. Department of Health and Human Services, 1991).

Many women age 65 and older, especially women of color and unmarried women, fare badly. In 1989, the median income for men over the age of 65 was $13,107; for women it was $7,635 (U.S. Bureau of the Census, 1992f). The median income of African American women age 65 and older in 1990 was $5,617—$651 below the poverty level. The poverty rate of elderly African American women was 38 percent and for Hispanic women 25 percent, compared with 13 percent for white women (U.S. Bureau of the Census, 1991c). If an elderly woman is unmarried, her chances of being poor increase considerably. In 1990 only 5 percent of married women age 65 and older were poor, but for older unmarried women that proportion was 27 percent (U.S. Bureau of the Census, 1991d).

Many women depend on social security for at least 90 percent of their income—in 1988 this was true for about one-third of elderly unmarried women. Yet, in 1991 the average monthly social security benefit for retired women workers was

FIGURE 3

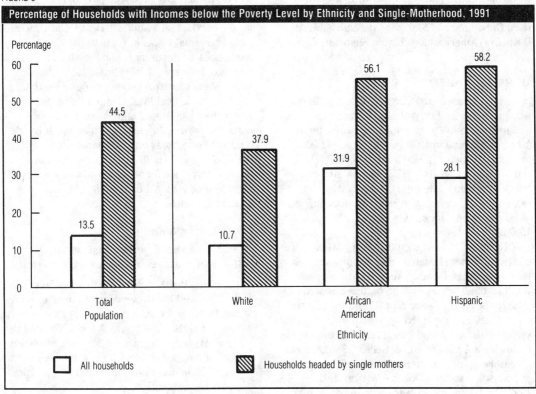

Percentage of Households with Incomes below the Poverty Level by Ethnicity and Single-Motherhood, 1991

Percentage

Ethnicity

☐ All households   ▨ Households headed by single mothers

SOURCE: U.S. Public Health Service. (1992). *Health United States, 1991*. Washington, DC: U.S. Government Printing Office.

$520, compared with $681 for men (U.S. Department of Health and Human Services, 1991).

MENTAL HEALTH

Recent surveys (Robins & Regier, 1991) confirm previous findings that men and women differ in the prevalence of certain mental problems. For example, men are more likely to have problems with alcohol and drugs and to exhibit antisocial personality traits. Women are more likely to be diagnosed with somatization syndrome (that is, multiple physical complaints without organic cause) and to have affective disorders such as depression. Somatization is more likely among African American women than among white women, but the rate of affective disorders is similar among African American, Hispanic, and white women.

The Robins and Regier (1991) study questioned the stereotype of the psychiatric patient as a middle-age anxious or depressed woman, finding that, overall, disorders in men occur as frequently or somewhat more frequently than they do in women and that recovery in middle age is common (Robins & Regier, 1991). Other research on

depression in women (Wetzel, 1984) has found that young, poor women with children are more likely to be depressed than are older women.

Embedded in these overall figures are special issues for women. Epidemiologists have known for years that the rate of depression for women is two to three times that of men. Yet, with only some exceptions, those data have not called forth further examination of why this is so. One possible explanation is the connection between women's "learned helplessness" syndrome—women's relative powerlessness in society—and the incidence of depression (Bromberger & Costello, 1992). Others make the connection between social factors and psychiatric problems. Bruce, Takeuchi, and Leaf (1991) noted that poverty may be a clear predictor of mental illness, which relates to gender in that women are more likely than men to be poor. Researchers and practitioners note that the progress of alcoholism and drug abuse in women differs from that of men and that interventions need to be responsive to women's special needs (Van den Bergh, 1991).

Concerning both interventions for mental health problems and the study of their prevalence, feminist scholars (Brown & Balou, 1992) have challenged the sexist biases present in the widely used *Diagnostic and Statistical Manual of Mental Disorders* (American Psychiatric Association, 1994).

DOMESTIC VIOLENCE

Physical and emotional violence affects millions of women each year. Recognizing that reported rapes underestimate the total number of rapes, the rate for reported rape in 1990 was 102.6 per 1,000 women, a 23 percent increase since 1980 (U.S. Bureau of the Census, 1992a). Recent attention to marital rape and date rape demonstrates that women's experiences with rape are not confined to strangers on dark streets (Levy, 1991; Russell, 1982).

Definitive statistics on domestic violence are difficult to obtain because many women are reluctant to report it. However, researchers estimate that half of all women will be battered at some time in their lives (Walker, 1989) and that 1.5 million women are assaulted by their partners each year (Fagan, 1988). Some maintain that even these estimates are low (Straus & Gelles, 1988). Women constitute 90 percent to 95 percent of the victims of domestic assaults (Dobash, Wilson, & Daly, 1992), and domestic violence is found among all religious, ethnic, racial, economic, and educational groups. Thirty-one percent of all women killed in America are murdered by their husbands, ex-husbands, or boyfriends (Rose & Goss, 1989). Lesbian battering has only recently received public attention, and in New York, for example, a 180 percent increase in reported cases of such violence was noted between 1900 and 1991 (National Clearing House for the Defense of Battered Women, 1992). In a dramatic comparison, Jaffe, Wolfe, and Wilson (1990) noted that 39,000 soldiers died during the Vietnam War; in that same period, 1967 to 1973, 17,500 women and children were killed by family members.

Even if women leave abusive partners, they still are not safe because they often are followed and harassed by their abusers for months or years. One study found that 30 percent of assaulted women separated from their partners when they were battered (Browne, 1987). And most battered women—72 percent in one study (Follingstad, Rutledge, Berg, Hause, & Polek 1990)—asserted that the emotional abuse they experienced was far worse than the physical abuse.

SEXUAL ORIENTATION

National data do not reflect the experiences of lesbians in the United States because homophobia

and discriminatory practices have made it unsafe for many lesbian women to self-identify. Nonetheless, we know that lesbians have special concerns, including equal rights in such areas as employment, housing, insurance, and health care (Hidalgo, Peterson, & Woodman, 1985; Pharr, 1988). Many closeted lesbians experience the constant psychological impact of not being open about their identities. Some states have enacted domestic-partnership legislation in which the definition of households includes same-sex couples. Perhaps as more rights are afforded lesbians, future encyclopedia entries about women may include solid national data similar to data for heterosexual women.

POLITICAL CHANGES

Women have won important legal and political battles in the last several decades. For example,

- The Equal Pay Act of 1963 states that women must be paid the same salary as men for doing substantially the same work.
- Title VII of the Civil Rights Act of 1964 bans discrimination on the basis of sex, race, color, religion, and national origin. This act serves as the basis for claims of sexual harassment and sex-based harassment.
- The Age Discrimination in Employment Act of 1967 bans discrimination against anyone in the workplace on the basis of age.
- Title IX of the 1972 Education Amendments Act prohibits sex discrimination in educational programs that receive federal funds.
- The Pregnancy Discrimination Act of 1978 states that pregnant women must have the same rights as other workers on the job.
- The 1973 *Roe v. Wade* Supreme Court decision ensured women the right to have an abortion. Although other court decisions, federal laws, and separate state actions have whittled away at that right, so far the Supreme Court has reaffirmed the essential right to privacy and abortion.

The number of women elected to government positions has increased dramatically in the past 20 years. After the November 1992 elections, there were six women senators, 47 representatives, three governors, 11 lieutenant governors, nine attorneys general, 16 state treasurers, and many more women in state legislatures. President Clinton appointed seven women to cabinet and subcabinet posts in his new administration (Center for the American Woman and Politics, 1992).

Women's political clout is also evidenced in the proliferation of women's political organizations in recent years. For example, the National Women's Political Caucus, Women's Campaign Fund, Fund for the Feminist Majority, and National Political Congress of Black Women operate throughout the nation. Emily's List provides funding for women candidates and contributed the most money to those candidates in 1992 (Center for the American Woman and Politics, 1993). Women's political organizations are also in place in many states, some of them focused on issues for women of color. For example, California has the Latina Political Action Committee and the Los Angeles African American Women's Political Action Committee. Because political decisions about government programs and policies affect so many of the problems women bring to social workers, the increase in women in government and in women's political organizations offers promise for a better future.

ROLE OF SOCIAL WORK

Social workers have contributed to the understanding of societal problems experienced by women. Social workers also have been part of the efforts, initiated by many grassroots groups in the 1970s, to provide services that recognize the effects of sexism. A growing literature on feminist practice (for example, Bricker-Jenkins, Hooyman, & Gottlieb, 1991) describes interventions aimed at empowering women and counteracting the effects of bias and discrimination against them. Many feminist agencies provide models of intervention based on feminist values and principles. These principles fit into and enlarge on social work's commitment to correct injustice and to understand the impact of society on individual women.

REFERENCES

Age Discrimination in Employment Act of 1967. P.L. 90-202, 81 Stat. 602.

Alan Guttmacher Institute. (1993). *Facts in brief.* New York: Author.

American Psychiatric Association. (1994). *Diagnostic and statistical manual of mental disorders* (4th ed.). Washington, DC: Author.

Asking why heart treatments fail more often for women. (1993, March 18). *New York Times,* p. A-8.

Brandon, P. (1991). Gender differences in young Asian Americans' educational achievement. *Sex Roles, 25,* 45–60.

Brenner, M. H. (1984). *Estimating the effects of economic change on national health and social well-being.* Report prepared for the U.S. Congress Joint Economic Committee. Washington, DC: U.S. Government Printing Office.

Bricker-Jenkins, M., Hooyman, N., & Gottlieb N. (1991). *Feminist social work practice in critical settings.* Newbury Park, CA: Sage Publications.

Bromberger, J. T., & Costello, E. J. (1992). Epidemiology of depression for clinicians. *Social Work, 37,* 120–125.

Brown, L.S., & Balou, M. (1992). *Personality and psychopathology: Feminist reappraisals.* New York: Guilford Press.

Browne, A. (1987). *When battered women kill.* New York: Free Press.

Bruce, M. L., Takeuchi, D. T., & Leaf, P. J. (1991). Poverty and psychiatric status: Longitudinal evidence from the New Haven ECA Study. *Archives of General Psychiatry, 48,* 470–474.

Center for the American Woman and Politics. (1992). *Women candidates and winners in 1992.* New Brunswick, NJ: Author.

Center for the American Woman and Politics. (1993, Winter). Women's PACs dramatically increase their support in 1992: An overview. *News and Notes,* p. 10.

Chilman, C. S. (1988). Never-married, single, adolescent parents. In C. S. Chilman, E. W. Nunnally, F. M. Cox (Eds.), *Variant family forms* (pp. 17–38). Newbury Park, CA: Sage Publications.

Civil Rights Act of 1964. P.L. 88-352, 78 Stat. 241.

Coles, F. S. (1986). Forced to quit: Sexual harassment complaints and agency response. *Sex Roles, 4,* 81–95.

Dobash, R. E., Wilson, M., & Daly, M. (1992). The myth of sexual symmetry in marital violence. *Social Problems, 39,* 71–91.

Education Amendments Act of 1972. P.L. 92-318, 86 Stat. 235.

Ehrenberg, R. (1989). Empirical consequences of comparable worth. In M. A. Hill & M. R. Killingsworth (Eds.), *Comparable worth: Analysis and evidence* (pp. 90–106). Ithaca, NY: Cornell University Press.

Equal Pay Act of 1963. P.L. 88-38, 77 Stat. 56.

Fagan, J. (1988). Contributions of family violence research to criminal justice policy on wife assault. *Violence and Victims, 3,* 159–186.

Follingstad, D. R., Rutledge, L., Berg, B. J., Hause, E. S., & Polek, D. S. (1990). The role of emotional abuse in physically abusive relationships. *Journal of Family Violence, 5,* 107–120.

Henshaw, S. (1992). *U.S. teenage pregnancy statistics.* New York: Guttmacher Institute.

Hewlett, S. A. (1986). *A lesser life: The myth of women's liberation in America.* New York: William Morrow.

Hidalgo, H., Peterson, T., & Woodman, N. (Eds.). (1985). *Lesbian and gay issues.* Silver Spring, MD: National Association of Social Workers.

Jaffe, P. G., Wolfe, D. A., & Wilson, S. K. (Eds.). (1990). *Children of battered women.* Newbury Park, CA: Sage Publications.

Jones, T. S., Remland, M. S., & Brunner, C. C. (1987). Effects of employment relationship, response of recipient and sex of rater in perceptions of sexual harassment. *Perceptual and Motor Skills, 65,* 55–63.

Kaplan, S. (1991). Consequences of sexual harassment in the workplace. *Affilia, 6,* 50–65.

Levy, B. (Ed.). (1991). *Dating violence: Young women in danger.* Seattle: Seal Press.

Maypole, D., & Skaine, R. (1983). Sexual harassment in the workplace. *Social Work, 28,* 385–386.

Nasar, S. (1992a, October 26). Women are outgaining men in wage rage, new data show. *Seattle Post-Intelligencer,* p. B-1.

Nasar, S. (1992b, October 18). Women's progress stalled? Just not so. *New York Times,* pp. 3-1, 3-10.

National Clearing House for the Defense of Battered Women. (1992). Report of the New York City Gay and Lesbian Anti-Violence Project. In *Statistics—Domestic violence* (p. 9). Philadelphia: Author.

National Committee on Pay Equity. (1992). *Questions and answers on pay equity.* Washington, DC: Author.

Older Women's League. (1989). The picture of health in mid-life and older women in America. In L. Grau. (Ed.), *Women in the later years* (pp. 53–74). New York: Harrington Park Press.

Pharr, S. (1988). *Homophobia: A weapon of sexism.* Inverness, CA: Chardon.

Pregnancy Discrimination Act of 1978. P.L. 95-555, 92 Stat. 2076.

Robins, L., & Regier D. (Eds.). (1991). *Psychiatric disorders in America.* New York: Free Press.

Rose, K., & Goss, J. (1989). *Domestic violence statistics.* Washington, DC: U.S. Department of Justice, Bureau of Justice Statistics.

Russell, D.E.H. (1982). *Marital rape.* New York: Macmillan.

Straus, M., & Gelles, R. (1988). How violent are American families? In G. Hotaling (Ed.), *Family abuse and its consequences* (pp. 14–36). Newbury Park, CA: Sage Publications.

Tomaskovie-Devey, D. (1995). Sex composition and gendered earnings inequality: A comparison of job and occupational models. In J. A. Jacobs (Ed.), *Gender inequality at work* (pp. 23–56). Thousand Oaks, CA: Sage Publications.

U.S. Bureau of the Census. (1985). *Statistical abstract of the United States.* Washington, DC: U.S. Government Printing Office.

U.S. Bureau of the Census. (1989). *United States population estimates by age, sex, race and Hispanic origin, 1980–1988* (Current Population Reports, Series P-25, No. 145). Washington, DC: U.S. Government Printing Office.

U.S. Bureau of the Census. (1990). *U.S. population estimates by age, sex, race, and Hispanic origin* (Current Population Reports, Series P-25, No. 145). Washington, DC: U.S. Government Printing Office.

U.S. Bureau of the Census. (1991a). *Studies in American fertility* (Current Population Reports, Series P-23, No. 176). Washington, DC: U.S. Government Printing Office.

U.S. Bureau of the Census. (1991b). *Statistical abstract of the United States.* Washington, DC: U.S. Government Printing Office.

U.S. Bureau of the Census. (1991c). *Money income of households, families and persons in the United States: 1990* (Current Population Reports, Series P-60, No. 174). Washington, DC: U.S. Government Printing Office.

U.S. Bureau of the Census. (1991d). *Poverty in the United States* (Current Population Reports, Series P-60, No. 175). Washington, DC: U.S. Government Printing Office.

U.S. Bureau of the Census. (1992a). *Statistical abstract of the United States.* Washington, DC: U.S. Government Printing Office.

U.S. Bureau of the Census. (1992b) *Trends in the 1980s* (Current Population Reports, Series P-23, No. 175). Washington, DC: U.S. Government Printing Office.

U.S. Bureau of the Census. (1992c). *Consumer income* (Current Population Reports, Series P-60, No. 178). Washington, DC: U.S. Government Printing Office.

U.S. Bureau of the Census. (1992d). *Educational attainment in the United States—March 1991 and 1990* (Current Population Reports, Series P-20, No. 462). Washington, DC: U.S. Government Printing Office.

U.S. Bureau of the Census. (1992e). *School enrollment—Social and economic characteristics of students* (Current Population Reports, Series P-20, No. 460). Washington, DC: U.S. Government Printing office.

U.S. Bureau of the Census. (1992f). *Studies in the distribution of income* (Current Population Reports, Series P-60, No. 183). Washington, DC: U.S. Government Printing Office.

U.S. Bureau of the Census. (1994). *Educational attainment in the United States—March 1993* (Current Population Reports, Series P-20, No. 476). Washington, DC: U.S. Government Printing Office.

U.S. Department of Education. (1990). *Digest of educational statistics.* Washington, DC: U.S. Government Printing Office.

U.S. Department of Health and Human Services, Social Security Administration. (1991). *Social Security Bulletin, 54,* 9.

U.S. Merit System Personnel Board. (1988). *Sexual harassment in the federal government: An update.* Washington, DC: U.S. Government Printing Office.

U.S. Public Health Service. (1992). *Health United States, 1991.* Washington DC: U.S. Government Printing Office.

Van den Bergh, N. (Ed.). (1991). *Feminist perspectives on addictions.* New York: Springer.

Walker, L. (1989). *Terrifying love: Why battered women kill and how society responds.* New York: Harper & Row.

Wetzel, J. W. (1984). *Clinical handbook of depression.* New York: Gardner.

FURTHER READING

Abramovitz, M. (1988). *Regulating the lives of women: Social welfare policy from colonial times to the present.* Boston: South End Press.

Acker, J. (1989). *Doing comparable worth.* Philadelphia: Temple University Press.

Amott, T., & Matthaei, J. (1991). *Race, gender and work: A multicultural economic history of women in the United States.* Boston: South End Press.

Buechler, S. (1990). *Women's movements in the United States.* New Brunswick, NJ: Rutgers University Press.

Dobash, R. E., & Dobash, R. P. (1992). *Women, violence and social change.* London: Routledge.

Garner, J. D., & Mercer, S. (1989). *Women as they age.* New York: Haworth Press.

Goldberg, G. S., & Kremen, E. (1990). *The feminization of poverty: Only in America?* New York: Praeger.

Moen, P. (1992). *Women's two roles: A contemporary dilemma.* Westport, CT: Auburn House.

Nolen-Hoeksema, S. (1990). *Sex differences in depression.* Stanford, CA: Stanford University Press.

Rix, S. (Ed.). (1990). *The American woman: 1990–1991: A status report.* New York: W. W. Norton.

Naomi Gottlieb, PhD, is professor, University of Washington, School of Social Work, 4101 15th Avenue NE, Seattle, WA 98195.

For further information see

Abortion; Adolescent Pregnancy; Direct Practice Overview; Families Overview; Family Planning; Jobs and Earnings; Lesbians Overview; Marriage/Partners; Maternal and Child Health; Men Overview; Poverty; Single Parents; Women: Direct Practice; Women and Health Care.

Key Words	
equality	gender issues
feminism	women

Women: Direct Practice

Mary Bricker-Jenkins
Patricia W. Lockett

The worldwide emergence in the late 1960s of the "second wave" of the women's liberation movement has resulted in dramatic and continuing changes in the language, focus, and methods of practice with women. It has also stimulated the development of a distinguishable approach to practice—feminist social work practice—with all populations. We examine the reconceptualization of womanhood that has taken place, distinguish among several social work practice responses to this reconceptualization, and provide an overview of the development of feminist social work practice. (Although the feminist movement is global, this entry focuses primarily on women and practice developments in North America.)

RECONCEPTUALIZING "WOMAN"

The early influences of the grassroots feminist movement on social work led to a reconceptualization of "woman" as well as her contexts and conditions. By the time of the first NASW-sponsored National Conference on Women's Issues (NCOWI) in 1980, the terms "sexism"—gender-based oppression—and "patriarchy"—the institutionalized system of male privilege—had entered the social work vocabulary as relevant concepts. The primary focus of the literature of the late 1970s and early 1980s, however, was on establishing the unique qualities of women's developmental experiences and the existence of "women's issues." This literature called vigorously for a reexamination of practice with women. During this period, some social workers began to incorporate the analysis and empirical work of feminist psychologists that repudiated developmental and behavioral theories derived primarily from studies of white men. These researchers argued that women were different from men but that most of these differences were rooted in the sociopolitical construction of gender rather than in biologically based sex differences (Chesler, 1972; Chodorow, 1978; Gilligan, 1982; Miller, 1976).

Concomitantly, feminist-influenced social workers began to examine the sociopolitical contexts of women as a "special population" and to define women's issues. An analysis of the literature on feminist social work from 1975 to 1985 (Deanow, 1986) documented this work. Empirical studies had revealed significant gender-based differences in such areas as poverty, depression, health care, employment, and education. Violence against women had become a major focus of research and action. Articles had appeared on practice in battered women's shelters, with rape and sex abuse survivors, and with women in prison. In fact, in virtually every area of concern to social workers, work was being done that revealed the differential experiences of women and men in "shared arenas" of our culture. Moreover, the roles ascribed to women had generated issues specific to those roles, including a lifetime of caregiving and the other uncompensated reproduction and maintenance work that women do for communities, the state, and the culture (Abromovitz, 1988; Miller, 1990).

Although these efforts to reconceptualize "woman" and her gender-nuanced experiences continue today, attention has expanded since the mid-1980s to (1) the diversity of women's experiences and (2) a more complex analysis of the concept of patriarchy. Just as feminists had critiqued scholarship that generalized from male experience two decades earlier, they began in the mid-1980s to challenge the extension of white women's experiences to all women (Gould, 1987; Gutierrez, 1990, 1991; Joseph & Lewis, 1986; Wyatt, 1985). Similarly, feminist scholars in such foundation disciplines as anthropology, history, economics, political science, and linguistics challenged universal and unitary notions of patriarchy, pointing out that systems of privilege are variously constructed and experienced in different cultures and historical periods (Tong, 1989).

These conceptual refinements also have had significant implications for practice. First, the contours of identity, development, and experience are influenced not only by gender but also by multiple intersecting factors and social locations (Swigonski, 1993). Thus, it is necessary but insufficient to ask "what difference does gender make?" One must also examine the influences of race and ethnicity, class, sexual orientation, age, "ablement," and other factors that are historically associated with stereotyping, discrimination, and oppression. Second, when we analyze the ways that patriarchal privilege is both maintained and resisted, we see patterns of women's victimization and exploitation, but we also can see patterns of creativity, strength, and agency.

GENDER–SENSITIVE, NONSEXIST, AND FEMINIST PRACTICE

These efforts to reconceptualize and reframe the experiences and conditions of women have influenced practice with and for women and with men and children as well. Three related trends can be identified: (1) gender-sensitive, (2) nonsexist, and (3) feminist practice approaches.

Gender-sensitive practice attempts to incorporate the new scholarship on differential male and female development and life experiences. Practitioners recognize, for example, that self-image and self-esteem in our culture may have different meanings and require different practice experiences for male and female adolescents or that one must screen for a history of childhood sex abuse, especially among pregnant adolescents, or that a lesbian woman may have a lifelong history of and interest in positive nonsexual relationships with men. *Women-centered practice,* a form of gender-sensitive practice, approaches practice from the standpoint of women and often incorporates aspects of "women's culture," including women's poetry, music, and art, into practice techniques.

Nonsexist practice goes a step further than gender-sensitive practice. Incorporating an analysis of gender-based power relations as well as culturally defined gender roles and issues, the nonsexist practitioner attempts to eliminate sexist dynamics in practice and, more proactively, to advocate for the elimination of sexism in all social relations. She or he may, for example, use inclusive language in practice, help adolescent men rethink the sources of their power and pride with women, or develop female leadership in a group or organization to achieve gender balance.

Feminist social work practice and its subset, feminist therapy, have emerged in the last three decades as distinguishable approaches to practice rooted in multidisciplinary feminist scholarship and experience-based theory. Feminist practice is a multicultural, multimodal, liberatory practice that attempts in its theory and methods to address simultaneously the content and conditions, consciousness, and contexts of people's lives. Feminist practitioners, who work with both women and men in all social work practice settings and roles, assume that the transformation of sociopolitical structures is necessary for the meeting of human needs and for healing the multiple injuries of sexism and other forms of domination and exploitation. Although nonsexist and gender-sensitive practices attempt to modify and reform conventional practice, feminist practitioners attempt an alternative model of practice. The remainder of this entry focuses on this, the most innovative of the social work responses to the women's liberation movement.

ORIGINS AND PHASES OF FEMINIST SOCIAL WORK PRACTICE

The development of feminist social work practice can be traced through three overlapping phases: (1) the "alternative services" phase, at its height in the mid-1970s; (2) the "worldview" definitional phase, which peaked in the mid-1980s; and (3) the contemporary "integrative methods development" phase (Walker, 1990). Although activities in theory, method, and services development have occurred in each phase, each has had a different emphasis.

Alternative Services for Women

Beginning in the mid-1960s, the grassroots feminist movement generated new analyses and awareness of women's needs and issues that were not addressed in conventional social work settings. During this period, many feminist social workers formed collectives or attempted to use private practice less for entrepreneurial motives than as a way to develop feminist-based theory and practice. This trend, although limiting opportunities for work with low-income and working class women, contributed significantly to practice model development.

The themes of sisterhood, self-help, and political activism were also infused into "alternative" community-based organizations and services for women such as battered women's shelters, rape survivors' programs, strengths-based counseling for lesbians, women's health centers, "displaced homemaker" services, and training and advocacy for the nontraditional employment sector (Gottlieb, 1980; Masi, 1981; Norman & Mancuso, 1980). Because they were organized as collectives and staffed primarily by nonprofessional activists, these programs often had difficulty finding stable funding until they were "mainstreamed" and non-professional staff was replaced by professional staff. With the professional staff and bureaucracy came greater stability, but "depoliticization" and pathologizing of women's conditions were scored by feminist critics as the (perhaps inevitable) result (Aherns, 1980; Kravetz & Jones, 1991; Sullivan, 1982). Similarly, the period from 1970 to 1985 marked an increase in attention to women's issues in the social work literature but a decrease in the proportion of those articles written from a feminist perspective (Bricker-Jenkins, 1989; Deanow, 1986).

Alternative Worldview
Efforts continued, however, to develop and make legitimate a politicized feminist practice within the profession and in conventional agencies. The emphasis of the second phase of feminist practice development was on defining the "alternative worldview" or conceptual framework from which feminist practice derived and that it attempted to advance. Several books and articles, some published by NASW, made distinctions between a narrowly defined "women's issues" orientation and an explicitly feminist perspective that was "not for women only" and that challenged all forms of institutionalized oppression (Bricker-Jenkins & Hooyman, 1986; B. G. Collins, 1986; Morrell, 1987; Valentich, 1986; Van Den Bergh & Cooper, 1986; Wetzel & The Feminist World View Educators, 1986). These works shared a conviction that a simultaneous focus on the personal and the political was necessary and methodologically possible; thus, feminist practice held the promise of achieving the profession's espoused purpose of integrating "cause and function" in a unitary method of practice. These works also espoused an explicitly ideological practice. To define the core concepts of a feminist ideology, they described and prescribed methods and techniques that were compatible with that orientation (see Table 1).

Attempts were made to refine the conceptual framework by distinguishing among liberal–reformist, cultural–radical, and Marxist–socialist feminists (Bricker-Jenkins & Hooyman, 1986; Nes & Iadicola, 1989); however, later studies indicate that the influence and espousal of these political theories do not translate into actual differences in methods and techniques used by most feminist social workers studied (Bricker-Jenkins, 1989; Freeman, 1990; Sandell, 1993). A more predictive distinction among feminist social workers appears to be their epistemological and ontological stances—that is, their beliefs about the nature of

TABLE 1
Feminist Ideological Themes

End of Patriarchy

Demystify and demythicize; reclaim history
Meet human needs; respect life
Transform personal and social relationships; end all systems of subordination and privilege
Value women's perspectives and experiences

Empowerment

"Power" reconceptualized as limitless, collective, and transactive
Implies individual responsibility, not individual property
Egalitarianism; no "power over"
Enabling, nonviolent problem solving
Inclusiveness; making common cause

Process

Process as product; ends in the means
Must be prefigurative, culture building, nonoppressive
Must educate, democratize, enable leadership and responsibility
"We're all in process"; nonjudgmental
Nonlinear, dynamic; consciousness and conditions are ever changing
Developmental; effectiveness, as well as efficiency

The Personal Is Political

Personal problems and conditions have historical, material, and cultural bases and dimensions
We are all connected; there are no personal private solutions
Failure to act is to act
Achieve personal growth through political action, "taking charge"
Change selves, change the world
Orientation to fundamental structural change

Unity–Diversity

None is free until all are free
Sisterhood, solidarity
Respect differences, preserve uniqueness; diversity as a source of strength and growth
Conflict is inevitable; peace is achievable
Elimination of false dichotomies and artificial separations
Synthesis and wholeness

Validation of the Nonrational

Healing
Spirituality
Nonlinear, multidimensional thinking
Reintegrating public and private spheres
Process of defining problems is recognized as subjective
Multiple competing definitions of problems; many "truths"

Consciousness Raising/Praxis

Renaming = re-creating reality
Liberation through one's own actions; self-reliance
"Rugged collectivism"
Infusion of consciousness and values in material world
Revolution as process, not event

SOURCE: Bricker-Jenkins, M., & Hooyman, N. (Eds.). (1986). *Not for women only: Social work practice for a feminist future* (pp. 10–11). Silver Spring, MD: National Association of Social Workers.

reality and what constitutes legitimate knowledge of reality (Bricker-Jenkins, 1989).

Creating Methods for Personal–Political Transformation

The ontological and epistemological debates that have engaged feminist theorists since the mid-1980s have stimulated considerable innovation in both feminist social work practice and research (Maguire, 1987; Reinharz, 1992; Stanley & Wise, 1993). Viewing reality and truth as dynamic, multidimensional, situated, and politically shaped has invigorated a search for methods and techniques for political–personal transformation, which is the goal of feminist work. Particularly influential have been feminist postmodernism and standpoint epistemologies, which have helped to expand the feminist practitioner's repertoire beyond group-based consciousness raising and grassroots organizing methods (P. H. Collins, 1990; Haraway, 1988; Harding, 1987, 1991). Figure 1 depicts a convergence of feminist practice and research from which methodological advances are emerging. Social workers also are continuing to incorporate the theoretical and empirical work on women's realities and development being done in the sister disciplines, particularly that of the Stone Center for Research on Women at Wellesley College (Jordan, Kaplan, Miller, Stiver, & Surrey, 1991).

This phase of practice model development also has been supported by the establishment of alternative publications and organizations within

the profession. The feminist Association for Women in Social Work was established in 1984 to supplement the more narrowly focused NASW NCOWI and the Commission on the Status of Women of the Council on Social Work Education. *Affilia—The Journal of Social Work with Women* began publication in 1986 with an explicitly feminist editorial mission to supplement the limited feminist scholarship available in the mainstream social work journals. With this infrastructure in place, feminist practice has moved from the definition of concepts to an exploration of methods and techniques with specific populations; this development, in turn, is likely to stimulate an increasing number of research efforts in the next decade to examine the effectiveness and impact of feminist practice.

NASW NCOWI Feminist Practice Project

The first national study of feminist practitioners and their work documented the trends and phases described above in its attempt to define and describe this emergent practice model (Bricker-Jenkins, 1989, 1991). In this project sponsored by NASW NCOWI, staff adapted grounded-theory methods (Chenitz & Swanson, 1986; Glaser, 1978; Glaser & Strauss, 1967; Strauss, 1986; Strauss & Corbin, 1990) to conduct and analyze over 100 hours of in-depth, semistructured interviews of 23 feminist practitioners and educators and 10 years of feminist social work literature. Because most of the literature available at the time was by and about white middle-class clinical practice with women, the purposive sample of 23 included 12 people of color and three men, and it was drawn from direct practitioners and administrators in both agency-based and private practice.

Tables 2 and 3 list the findings of the study. The 10 principles derived from the data analysis are organized under the categories that comprise the elements of a practice model: basic philosophy, values, and goals; human behavior and the social environment; and practice methods and relationships.

Table 3 illustrates the methods and techniques that participants were attempting to use in their daily practice. The list is suggestive, not exhaustive, of feminist practice, which is becoming increasingly diverse and refined as it is becoming accepted as a worthy focus of doctoral and other research work.

Although feminist practitioners are different from one another, differentially nuancing and applying the practice principles, review of Tables 2

FIGURE 1

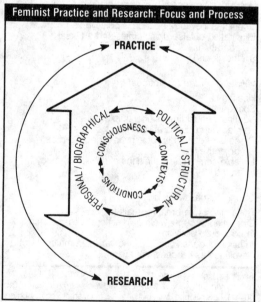

Feminist Practice and Research: Focus and Process

TABLE 2
Ten Propositions and Assumptions of Feminist Practice

Basic Philosophy, Values, and Goals

1. Collectivism/conditions: The inherent purpose and goal of human existence is self-actualization; however, self-actualization is a collective endeavor involving the creation of material and ideological conditions that facilitate it.
2. Politicization: The purpose of social work practice is to support collective self-actualization. Given structural and ideological barriers to self-actualization, practice must address itself explicitly to them. All practice is inherently political in consequence; feminist practice is explicitly political in intent.
3. Pro-woman stance: Feminist practice is pro-woman; women have unique histories, conditions, developmental patterns, and strengths that must be discovered and engaged by social workers.

Human Behavior and the Social Environment

4. Strengths/health: Since human beings strive in community for safety, health, and self-actualization, it is possible to identify and mobilize individual and collective capacities for healing, growth, and personal/political transformation.
5. Diversity: Diversity creates choices for all and is thus a source of strength, growth, and health.
6. Interdependence: All things are connected.
7. Constructivism: Reality is an unfolding, multidimensional, politically shaped process.

Practice Methods and Relationships

8. Personal is political: Individual and collective pain and problems of living always have a cultural and/or political dimension.
9. Nonviolent relationships and structures: All systems and ideologies of domination, exploitation, and supremacy are inherently violent and inimical to well-being; they can be resisted and replaced in our practice with social forms, relations, and processes that are democratic, egalitarian, synergetic, and nonviolent.
10. Transformation: Healing, health, and growth are functions of validation, consciousness, and collective transformative action; these, in turn, must be supported and sustained through resources to meet basic human needs, relationships that preserve and nurture uniqueness and wholeness as well as connectedness, and the creation of validating environments.

SOURCE: Bricker-Jenkins, M. (1989). Foundations of feminist social practice: The changes and the changed are one. *Dissertation Abstracts International*, 5104A. (University Microfilms No. 9015943)

and 3 and the following discussion of the last three propositions and assumptions (those related primarily to practice methods and techniques) will suggest their common ground.

Assessment

Individual collective pain and problems of living always have a cultural or political dimension. The primary application of this proposition is in assessment. Regardless of the practice setting or primary modality being used, assessment focused simultaneously on consciousness, conditions of concern, and contexts. *Consciousness* refers to both critical awareness of the cultural and political factors that shape identity, personal and social realities, and relationships and to one's stance toward those factors. *Conditions of concern* include those presented both by the client and by the worker, but the beginning place for work is the set of meanings ascribed to those conditions by the client. Contexts include both the material and ideological factors that constitute the challenges and possibilities for work together. For example, contexts may include both the material and emotional effects of racist, classist, and sexist dynamics that an African American woman faces on her job that contribute to her depression and to the

natural healing and helping resources of her African American community, culture, and spiritual traditions. It is the simultaneous focus on the interaction of consciousness, conditions, and contexts—the personal–political nexus where personal biography and social structures intersect—that typifies a feminist assessment.

Evolving from this focus is a *power analysis*—an examination of who has material and symbolic power in a situation and how it is overtly and covertly exercised. These analyses serve the depathologizing/politicizing agenda of feminist practice and are a bridge to the strengths assessment, in which one identifies patterns of both individual and cultural resources and opportunities that can be mobilized. Here the practitioner will draw heavily from the recent literature of women's history and development to correct the conventional literature.

Relationships

All systems and ideologies of domination, exploitation, and supremacy are inherently violent and inimical to well-being; they can be resisted and replaced in our practice with social forms, relations, and processes that

TABLE 3
Preferred Methods and Techniques in Feminist Practice

Engagement/Relationship Building

Encourage clients to express their personalized experiences and tell their own stories
Secure concrete needs and safety first and throughout work
Use language that reflects desired realities
Really begin where the client is
Reduce actual and symbolic status differential between worker and client
Identify specific client expertise
Establish collaborative relationship with client as partner
Acknowledge mutuality and reciprocity in relationship
Respect defenses/"denial"; identify their function in preserving psychic safety
Engage all dimensions: physical, intellectual, emotional, social, spiritual, and cultural
Promote sense of entitlement

Exploration/Assessment

Begin with a fluid examination of women's experiences rather than existing conceptualizations and abstract variables
Ask client to write own social history
Believe women's stories
Focus on conditions and environment
Explore client's meanings of words and events
Explore ideological and material barriers and opportunities
Search for alliances with people's innate health-seeking aspirations and efforts
Identify individual and cultural patterns of strength
Analyze power dimension in worker–client relationships
Analyze power dimension in client–context relationships
Use dreams, fantasies, and stories to surface strengths and perceptions of power
Analyze and address desires for change in power relations and ascribed role behaviors
Identify consequences of internalized "isms" (e.g., "de-selfing," silencing, judgmentality)
Acknowledge the connectedness of all things; think systems
Use symbols, myths, and rituals grounded in clients' actual and desired realities

Action/Ongoing Work

Teach interactional skills, including confrontation
Encourage woman-affirming reading in professional and popular literature
Use client journals, creative writing, art, dance, play, and theatre
Use natural or constructed support and action groups
Combine task-centered methods for resource acquisition/concrete goal achievement with expressive, nurturing
    processes
Teach consensual decision making
Identify and structure practice around existing healing and helping patterns
Create opportunities for self-definition and exercise of personal power
Encourage and teach individual responsibility and collective action
Create choices as practice goal
Value and analyze process: "Preserve the ends in the means"
Reach for political power through collaboration and collective action to change oppressive structures
Teach self-advocacy
Create or strengthen connections that work for people and confront those that do not
Challenge men to analyze and share power and privilege
Make women's strengths and culture visible in environment
Focus on accessibility (economic, cultural, physical) of programs and services
Practice in teams and collectives
Reflect practice principles in organizational structure, processes, and program design
Incorporate diversity into practice processes and environment

SOURCE: Bricker-Jenkins, M. (1989). Foundations of feminist social practice: The changes and the changed are one. *Dissertation Abstracts International*, 5104A. (University Microfilms No. 9015943)

are democratic, egalitarian, synergetic, and nonviolent. Assessment, ongoing work, and evaluation are viewed in feminist practice as dialogical processes in which client and worker share their perspectives, meanings (belief systems), and analyses. In this open, dialogical process the practitioner recognizes her power but strives for egalitarian, symmetrical partnerships in which both client and worker are presumed to have different but equally valued expertise. The worker has specialized knowledge and skill, but the client is the expert on her own story. Through this process, the social work relationship becomes a template and training ground for transformations of consciousness, conditions, and contexts.

Personal–Political Transformation

Healing, health, and growth are functions of validation, consciousness, and collective transformative action; these, in turn, must be supported and sustained through resources to meet basic human needs, relationships that preserve and nurture uniqueness and whole- ness as well as connectedness, and the crea- tion of validating environments. Implicit in the final proposition is a theory of transformation based on linking and integrating personal and sociocultural change processes. Although still evolving and untested, the proposition is an attempt to challenge the conventional macro– micro bifurcation in social work theory and prac- tice. We consider each of the elements of the prop- osition; however, it is important to bear in mind that they are related.

Validation refers primarily to actions taken to affirm that a person's subjective experience of reality is believed in, important, and valuable. It is achieved through such techniques as encouraging the "telling of one's story" in journals, pictures, or drama; "active listening"; reflecting back the per- son's reality in her or his own words; sharing information from the worker's own direct and indi- rect experience that conforms to a person's expe- rience; creating and working with people who have similar concrete realities, issues, and experiences; and encouraging the client to "set the agenda," whether in a clinical setting, research, or the com- munity. An essential first step in validation is "believing the client"—working from within her definition of realities, concerns, and issues.

Consciousness raising is "the process by which [people], not as recipients, but as knowing subjects, achieve a deepening awareness both of the sociocultural reality, which shapes their lives and of their capacity to transform that reality by acting upon it" (Freire, 1970, p. 205). It begins with an examination and affirmation of one's reality (validation) and then moves to an exploration of the forces and factors that contribute to that real- ity and to one's experience of it. It is a search for meanings and how those meanings were derived. The basic technique for consciousness raising is problem-posing dialogue, which involves an explo- ration of a series of questions that can be summa- rized as follows:

- "Who am I?" What are my needs, my desires, my visions of a life that is safe, healthy, and fulfilling?
- "Who says?" What is the source of my self- definition and that of my reality? Does it con- form to my experience of self and the world?
- "Who benefits from this definition?" Does it conform to my needs, my "truths?" Is it possible for me to live by these definitions? If not . . .

- "What must change, and how?"

The last question in this dialogical process is the bridge to transformative action. It is the point at which one begins to formulate a vision of the possible in concrete terms and to experience one- self as an actor in the world. The worker infuses her or his analysis, however tentatively, to chal- lenge the authority of those in the person's life who have imposed definitions and recipes for liv- ing that are not working for the person.

Consciousness raising is not simply providing information and analysis, although these can help. Rather, it evolves from a process in which the practitioner creates the conditions for others to develop their own analyses. It is most fully accom- plished in groups. In a group, it is possible to experience a sense of belonging and the potential for social power and to develop the bonds and skills needed to claim that power. Having posed the question "What must change?," the next ques- tions are "What can I do to effect the change?" and "What are the sources of power for effecting change?" These questions are central to transfor- mative action.

Transformative action is rooted in an analysis of the network of social, historical, and material realities that both impede and compel action. It evolves from a vision of oneself as co-creator of those realities and therefore responsible for them; it contributes, however minutely, to the restructur- ing of relationships and processes to augment self- definition and choices for self and others. As a participant in the Feminist Practice Project said, "Transformative action is self-healing that becomes actualized in the world" (Bricker-Jenkins, 1989, p. 247).

The practitioner's role is to assist in the artic- ulation of a vision of the possible; identify or cre- ate the opportunities for the person to actualize it in the social, historical, and material context of her life; teach the skills and mobilize the resources needed; and put forth and reinforce the notion that each of us is, in community, capable of and responsible for the creation of reality. The practi- tioner's knowledge of action and lifestyle alterna- tives and skill in teaching people how to take action in complex and entrenched environments are called on in this process, during which consul- tation and partnership become the prevailing means of work.

Mobilizing resources to meet basic human needs, providing for safety, and building skills—all traditionally concerns of social work—have a spe- cial significance in feminist work. Attention to peo- ple's basic, concrete, material needs—food, clothing, shelter, health care, and physical safety—is the necessary beginning place in any practice system, but a feminist conceptualization of need also includes the people's social, cultural, and spiritual lives. Physical and psychic safety are of particular concern in working with women, whose concrete realities often render them unsafe. The creation and exercise of choices—which may be seen as a common purpose in all practice—cannot happen without establishing this foundation.

Methods and techniques for mobilizing social resources include such common social work approaches as teaching problem-solving skills; assertiveness (or, more precisely, self-confidence); "life skills" for such tasks as parenting, employment, and self-defense; group communication skills—especially learning to hear and reflect other people's meanings; and skills to identify and engage resources in one's formal and informal networks.

Creation of relationships that nurture and sustain uniqueness and wholeness as well as connectedness is, as noted above, critical in feminist practice. By participating in the creation of practice relationships that are open, egalitarian, mutual, and reciprocal, people can begin to formulate a vision of these becoming the norm in their families, workplace, and communities. "Macro" systems can then be experienced not as inevitable and immutable "facts of life," but as resulting from people's choices of how to structure social, political, and economic relations. Much effort is focused on searching out and building a network of affirming and nonexploitative relationships, and the worker also may teach the process of evaluating the dynamics and structures of new relationships.

The creation of validating environments is an integral component of a practice of transformation. Alternative values and visions must be validated in the environment if they are to be sustained. Therefore, feminist practice emphasizes the need to identify the strengths of groups of people that are ignored or trivialized in the dominant culture and infuse alternative values into the structures and processes of agencies and organizations.

Practitioners attempt to incorporate in their work rituals and symbols that reflect the strengths of clients' cultural heritage, such as feminist and culture-specific music, poetry, graphic arts, and literature. The implicit message in the use of cultural symbols is that choices can be and are created by people who value their own experience and commit to actualizing it in the world. The use of culture becomes a metaphor for and means to discover the pathways available for healing, health, and growth. The metaphor becomes concrete through action to expand the repertoire of cultural choices available to clients in their own environments.

The second application of the concept of creating validating environments entails the restructuring of organizations. Feminist practitioners tend to view the organizational context of practice as a component of the practice system. Although most feminist practitioners would agree that their approach to practice can be developed best in feminist organizations, most feminists work in conventional, hierarchically organized agencies and struggle with ways to incorporate feminist structures and decision-making processes in the workplace.

Feminist practitioners use other conventional and nonconventional methods and techniques in their work but tend to use the following four criteria for selecting and using them as follows:

1. process orientation—that is, does the approach "preserve the ends in the means"
2. congruence with the values of both practitioner and client
3. potential for self-empowerment in the sense of helping people to act out of their inner knowledge and repertoire of skills
4. potential for transformation of the realities that people are experiencing as injurious, whether the reality is a bad marriage, an unfulfilling job, a chemical dependency, or a negative evaluation of oneself and one's group based on an internalization of somebody else's definition of their worth, capabilities, or health.

RESEARCH ISSUES IN FEMINIST PRACTICE

The propositions and assumptions presented above, although grounded in research on practitioner experience, are global and tentative. As a new approach, feminist social work practice has only recently begun to create a body of literature, and much of that is conceptual and descriptive. Out of necessity and ethical commitments, however, feminist activists have been creators and consumers of research since the early days of the movement, and feminists have been at the center of the contemporary dialogue about research methods and their underpinning ontologies and epistemologies.

Refining Constructs

Appropriate to the current stage of development of feminist practice are efforts to refine its constituent constructs. For example, Freeman (1990) examined the relationship between feminist identities and problem definitions; Calame (1992) examined her practice to see if and how her feminism was reflected in her work with women with eating disorders; Lazzari (1991) used a feminist framework to ground a definition of empowerment; and Sandell (1993) studied the application of feminist beliefs and values in an intensive analysis of the practice of seven practitioners. These kinds of "definitional" studies are laying the foundation for the validation and comparative studies of the future.

Although definitions, outcomes, and comparisons are a focus of feminist social work research, however, related epistemological issues have generated much more debate and development (Hartman, 1990, 1991, 1992; Nuccio & Sands, 1992; Scott, 1990; Swigonski, 1994; Weick, 1986, 1987). Because feminist practitioners tend to view life as process and in multidimensional terms, they tend to use knowledge derived from positivist research with caution. In particular, feminist practitioners will be wary of linear, unicausal models of behavior constructed from such research efforts. In addition to the issues that feminists have raised about the invisibility and distortions of women's experience in positivist research, the use of the paradigm itself is being subject to scrutiny as potentially inadequate to the social and behavioral dynamics it attempts to elucidate. Aware that epistemologies are tools, not truths, and are themselves politically shaped, feminist researchers are attempting to find and create research paradigms and methods that can accommodate the multidimensional processes of social life (Dean, 1989; Laird, 1989; Maguire, 1987; Millstein, 1993; Rodwell, 1987; Scott, 1989).

Using a Multidimensional Process

Research methods that begin with a fluid examination of practice processes and women's experiences, rather than existing conceptualizations and abstract variables, are generally preferred (Gottlieb & Bombyk, 1987; Reinharz, 1992). Oral history, linguistic analysis, ethnography, and grounded-theory protocols provide useful existing approaches to the study of practice processes (Millstein, 1993). Also highly congruent with feminist practice are action and participatory research in which research "subjects" set the agenda, pose the questions, and function as coinvestigators (Maguire, 1987; Yeich & Levine, 1992). The protocols and purposes of such research advance the mutual political interests of participants and researchers and their need for knowledge of effective practice.

In sum, viewing reality in multidimensional–process terms has enormous implications for the way knowledge of it is understood, developed, and used in feminist practice. In contrast to the positivist assumptions that research can be value free and "controlled" in relation to a presumably static "truth," feminists assume that all knowledge is infused with values and that we are constantly creating reality. Thus, knowledge is always contextualized and tentative. Moreover, an ethical responsibility is implied in the notions that there are many truths and that people create truths and realities. These notions compel not only an active posture in the world but also a profoundly humble one. Like any other form of feminist practice, feminist research is political in purpose and method. In fact, research becomes a method of practice. The challenge of feminist social work practice research today is to develop an epistemology and methods that incorporate the empirical rigor of positivism, the politicized subjectivism of postmodern constructivism, and the liberatory empowerment agenda of critical theory and standpoint epistemologies.

Conclusion

Social work practice with women has developed in the last two decades from a concern about sexism and women's issues to an emerging model of practice grounded in feminist theory, scholarship, and action. Like the broader feminist movement, the analytical focus of feminist social work has expanded from circumscribed gender issues to the intersection of gender with race, class, and other factors that shape identity and experience. Although its primary applications have been in such "woman centered" practice areas as rape, domestic violence, sexual abuse, and families, the purview of feminist practice is expanding to include addictions, health care, child welfare, and poverty—all of which are areas of concern to social workers.

Like other emerging models of practice, feminist practice is developing an array of methods and techniques that express and apply its assumptions about the interactions among conditions of concern, critical consciousness, and political–cultural contexts (Saleebey, 1992; Simon, 1994). These efforts are being aided by corresponding advances in feminist concerns about prevailing paradigms of epistemology and research methods in social work. As institutional supports for feminist practice and scholarship continue to develop, we can expect feminist social workers to meet the challenge of conceptual refinement and evaluation of its effectiveness as a distinctive approach to practice.

REFERENCES

Abramovitz, M. (1988). *Regulating the lives of women: Social welfare policy from colonial times to the present.* Boston: South End Press.

Aherns, L. (1980). Battered women's refuges: Feminist cooperatives vs. social service institutions. *Radical America, 14*(3), 41–47.

Bricker-Jenkins, M. (1989). Foundations of feminist social work practice: The changes and the changed are one. *Dissertation Abstracts International,* 5104A. (University Microfilms No. 9015943)

Bricker-Jenkins, M. (1991). The propositions and assumptions of feminist social work practice. In N. Hooyman, M. Bricker-Jenkins, & N. Gottlieb (Eds.), *Feminist social work practice in clinical settings* (pp. 271–303). Newbury Park, CA: Sage Publications.

Bricker-Jenkins, M., & Hooyman, N. (Eds.). (1986). *Not for women only: Social work practice for a feminist future.* Silver Spring, MD: National Association of Social Workers.

Calame, C. (1992). *The politics of feminist therapy as a construct: A therapist's self-evaluation of work with young women who have eating disorders.* Unpublished masters thesis, Simmons College School of Social Work, Boston.

Chenitz, W. C., & Swanson, J. M. (Eds.). (1986). *From practice to grounded theory: Qualitative research in nursing.* Menlo Park, CA: Addison-Wesley.

Chesler, P. (1972). *Women and madness.* New York: Doubleday.

Chodorow, N. (1978). *The reproduction of mothering: Psychoanalysis and the sociology of gender.* Berkeley: University of California Press.

Collins, B. G. (1986). Defining feminist social work. *Social Work, 31,* 214–219.

Collins, P. H. (1990). *Black feminist thought: Knowledge, consciousness, and the politics of empowerment.* Boston: Unwin Hyman.

Dean, R. (1989). Ways of knowing in clinical practice. *Clinical Social Work Journal, 17,* 116–127.

Deanow, C. (1986, May). *From mother-blaming to women's issues and back? Trends in journal articles on women: 1970–1985.* Paper presented at the National Association of Social Workers Conference on Women's Issues, Atlanta.

Freeman, M. L. (1990). Beyond women's issues: Feminism and social work. *Affilia, 5,* 72–89.

Freire, P. (1970). The adult literacy process as cultural action for freedom. *Harvard Educational Review, 40,* 205–225.

Gilligan, C. (1982). *In a different voice.* Cambridge, MA: Harvard University Press.

Glaser, B. G. (1978). *Theoretical sensitivity: Advances in the methodology of grounded theory.* Mill Valley, CA: Sociology Press.

Glaser, B. G., & Strauss, A. (1967). *The discovery of grounded theory.* New York: Aldine.

Gottlieb, N. (Ed.). (1980). *Alternative social services for women.* New York: Columbia University Press.

Gottlieb, N., & Bombyk, M. (1987). Strategies for strengthening feminist research. *Affilia, 2,* 23–35.

Gould, K. (1987). Feminist principles and minority concerns: Contributions, problems, and solutions. *Affilia, 3,* 6–19.

Gutierrez, L. M. (1990). Working with women of color: An empowerment perspective. *Social Work, 35,* 97–192.

Gutierrez, L. M. (1991). Empowering women of color: A feminist model. In M. Bricker-Jenkins, N. Hooyman, & N. Gottlieb (Eds.), *Feminist social work practice in clinical settings* (pp. 199–214). Newbury Park, CA: Sage Publications.

Haraway, D. (1988). Situated knowledges: The science question in feminism and the privilege of partial perspective. *Feminist Studies, 14,* 575–599.

Harding, S. (1987). *Feminism and methodology: Social science issues.* Bloomington: Indiana University Press.

Harding, S. (1991). *Whose science? Whose knowledge? Thinking from women's lives.* Ithaca, NY: Cornell University Press.

Hartman, A. (1990). Many ways of knowing. *Social Work, 35,* 3–4.

Hartman, A. (1991). Words create worlds. *Social Work, 36,* 275–276.

Hartman, A. (1992). In search of subjugated knowledge. *Social Work, 37,* 483–484.

Jordan, J. V., Kaplan, A. G., Miller, J. B., Stiver, I. P., & Surrey, J. L. (1991). *Women's growth in connection: Writings from the Stone Center.* New York: Guilford Press.

Joseph, G. I., & Lewis, J. (1986). *Common differences: Conflicts in black and white feminist perspectives.* Boston: South End Press.

Kravetz, D., & Jones, L. E. (1991). Supporting practice in feminist service agencies. In M. Bricker-Jenkins, N. Hooyman, & N. Gottlieb (Eds.), *Feminist social work practice in clinical settings* (pp. 233–240). Newbury Park, CA: Sage Publications.

Laird, J. (1989). Women and stories: Restorying women's self-constructions. In M. McGoldrick, C. Anderson, & F. Walsh (Eds.), *Women in families: A framework for family therapy* (pp. 428–449). New York: W. W. Norton.

Lazzari, M. (1991). Feminism, empowerment, and field education. *Affilia, 6,* 71–87.

Maguire, P. (1987). *Doing participatory research: A feminist approach.* Amherst: University of Massachusetts, School of Education, Center for International Education.

Masi, D. A. (Ed.). (1981). *Organizing for women: Issues, strategies, and services.* Lexington, MA: Lexington Books.

Miller, D. C. (1990). *Women and social welfare: A feminist analysis.* New York: Praeger.

Miller, J. B. (1976). *Toward a new psychology of women.* Boston: Beacon Press.

Millstein, K. (1993, March). *Building knowledge from the study of cases: The challenges of practice evaluation.* Paper presented at the Annual Program Meeting of the Council on Social Work Education, New York.

Morell, C. (1987). Cause *is* function: Toward a feminist model of integration for social work. *Social Service Review, 61,* 144–155.

Nes, J., & Iadicola, P. (1989). Toward a definition of feminist social work: A comparison of liberal, radical, and socialist models. *Social Work, 34,* 12–21.

Norman, E., & Mancuso, A. (Eds.). (1980). *Women's issues and social work practice.* Itasca, IL: F. E. Peacock.

Nuccio, K. E., & Sands, R. G. (1992). Using postmodern feminist theory to deconstruct "phallacies" of poverty. *Affilia, 7,* 26–48.

Reinharz, S. (1992). *Feminist methods in social research.* New York: Oxford University Press.

Rodwell, M. (1987). Naturalistic inquiry: An alternative model for social work assessment. *Social Service Review, 61,* 232–242.

Saleeby, D. (Ed.). (1992). *The strengths perspective in social work practice.* White Plains, NY: Longman.

Sandell, K. S. (1993). *Different voices: Articulating feminist social work.* Unpublished doctoral dissertation, Case Western Reserve University, Mandel School of Applied Social Sciences, Cleveland.

Scott, D. (1989). Meaning construction and social work practice. *Social Service Review, 63,* 39–51.

Scott, D. (1990). Practice wisdom: The neglected source of practice research. *Social Work, 35,* 364–368.

Simon, B. L. (1994). *The empowerment tradition in American social work: A history.* New York: Columbia University Press.

Stanley, L., & Wise, S. (1993). *Breaking out again: Feminist ontology and epistemology.* New York: Routledge.

Strauss, A. L. (1986). *Qualitative analysis.* Cambridge, England: Cambridge University Press.

Strauss, A. L., & Corbin, J. (1990). *Basics of qualitative research: Grounded theory procedures and techniques.* Newbury Park, CA: Sage Publications.

Sullivan, G. (1982). Cooptation of alternative services: The battered women's movement as a case study. *Catalyst, 4,* 39–56.

Swigonski, M. E. (1993). Feminist standpoint theory and the questions of social work research. *Affilia, 8,* 171–183.

Swigonski, M. E. (1994). The logic of feminist standpoint theory for social work research. *Social Work, 39,* 387–395.

Tong, R. (1989). *Feminist thought: A comprehensive introduction.* Boulder, CO: Westview Press.

Valentich, M. (1986). Feminism and social work practice. In F. Turner (Ed.), *Social work treatment: Interlocking theoretical frameworks* (3rd ed., pp. 564–589). New York: Free Press.

Van Den Bergh, N., & Cooper, L. B. (Eds.). (1986). *Feminist visions for social work.* Silver Spring, MD: National Association of Social Workers.

Walker, L. (1990). A feminist therapist views the case. In D. Cantor (Ed.), *Women as therapists: A multitheoretical casebook* (pp. 78–95). New York: Springer.

Weick, A. (1986). The philosophical context of a health model of social work. *Social Casework, 67,* 551–559.

Weick, A. (1987). Reconceptualizing the philosophical perspective of social work. *Social Service Review, 61,* 218–230.

Wetzel, J. W., & The Feminist World View Educators. (1986). A feminist world view conceptual framework. *Social Casework, 67,* 166–173.

Wyatt, G. (1985). The sexual abuse of Afro-American and white women in childhood. *Child Abuse and Neglect, 9,* 507–519.

Yeich, S., & Levine, R. (1992). Participatory research's contribution to a conceptualization of empowerment. *Journal of Applied Social Psychology, 22,* 1894–1908.

Mary Bricker-Jenkins, DSW, is associate professor, and **Patricia W. Lockett, MSW,** is assistant professor, Social Work Program, Western Kentucky University, Bowling Green, KY 42101.

For further information see

Abortion; Adolescents: Direct Practice; Civil Rights; Direct Practice Overview; Domestic Violence; Ethics and Values; Families Overview; Families: Direct Practice; Human Rights; Lesbians: Direct Practice; Progressive Social Work; Social Welfare Policy; Social Work Practice: Theoretical Base; Women Overview; Women and Health Care; Women in Social Policy.

Key Words	
feminist	sexism
feminist practice	women
feminist research	

Women and Health Care

Marian A. Aguilar

Although various aspects of women's health, such as teenage pregnancy, breast cancer, menopause, the health behavior of various groups of women, and issues of aging, have been discussed in the literature, research has dissected women into many pieces, and the literature reflects this fact. Little coordination has been done to create a profile of the health care needs of and services for women. Even the social work profession has been remiss in this regard. As limiting as it may be, the country's early record on women's health, viewed in the context of children's health, is the only one that exists. Although the sociopolitical and medical history of women's health care services has been dismal, the efforts of women to promote health services for children have been impressive.

HISTORICAL CONTEXT

The initiation of social policy for women and children, including efforts to improve health care, paralleled the development of social work as a profession. In 1879 the Conference of Boards of Public Charities broke away from the American Social Science Association to become the National Conference of Charities and Correction because of conflicting philosophical and social concerns. In 1898 the Charity Organization Society of New York established a professional school (the New York School of Philanthropy, now the Columbia University School of Social Work), as Mary Richmond had suggested in 1897 at the National Conference of Charities and Correction. In 1904 a similar effort took place in Boston, where a training center affiliated with Simmons College and Harvard University was established. Medical social work as a field of practice came into existence in 1905, when Dr. Richard C. Cabot introduced social services into Massachusetts General Hospital in Boston. It was the women at Hull House, however, who promoted and developed legislation related to women's and children's health and worked to ensure the professionalization of social work by placing the program under the auspices of the University of Chicago, where a Hull House resident, Edith Abbott, became its first director (Costin, 1983a).

The political, cultural, social, and economic conditions that brought women's health to the forefront occurred during the Progressive Era of the early 1900s, along with a variety of issues like women's suffrage, child labor, the rights of women in industry, and the problems of immigrants (Costin, 1983a, p. 41). Even though it was a time not of reform, but of planting the seeds of reform that would take place in the 1930s, social programs were expanded and maintained because of social reformers' efforts to agitate and educate. The Children's Bureau was established in 1912, with the mandate to investigate and report on the status of children. The appointment of Julia Lathrop as its first chief marked the commencement of a lifelong collaboration of pioneers, such as Jane Addams, Lillian Wald, Florence Kelley, Edward T. Devine, Grace and Edith Abbott, and Grace Meigs, in fighting for the causes of children and women. The work of these pioneers in the name of justice allied them to social causes.

The passage of the Maternity Act of 1921 (popularly called the Sheppard–Towner Act), whose goal was to reduce the incidence of maternal and infant mortality and to promote maternal and child health, signaled the beginning of a federal–state matching program modeled after the Smith–Lever Act of 1914 for agricultural collaboratives (Costin, Bell, & Downs, 1991). The Sheppard–Towner Act was significant because it not only created an avenue to address the injustices done to women and children but demonstrated the potential power and value of the vote that women had just obtained (Costin, 1983a).

Grace Abbott, the chief of the Children's Bureau at that time, was charged with administering the Sheppard–Towner Act. The act provided federal matching grants to states that developed plans to improve the care of infants and women through education, individual care, and the exten-

sion of facilities to outlying and remote areas. Social research conducted by the Children's Bureau made a strong case for the need for legislation on maternal and child health. The Sheppard–Towner Act provided funding for five years. Although the program was extended for two more years, the struggle to get it extended was relentless because of strong opposition from at least three groups with different philosophical points of view: antisuffrage groups, patriotic organizations, and the American Medical Association (AMA). The antisuffrage groups were concerned that if women knew more about health care, they would reject their proper roles as wife and mother; the patriotic organizations argued that such interference of the federal government in family life constituted communism; and AMA expressed the fear that the government would try to interfere with medical practice and that the medical profession would lose its autonomy (Costin, 1983b).

The greatest controversy arose between the Children's Bureau and the Public Health Service over where jurisdiction for maternal and child health services should be placed. The Surgeon General believed that health programs belonged under the Department of Health, whereas the reformers and founders of the Children's Bureau thought that a unified social, health, economic, and industrial approach was needed and that the problems of women and children could not be viewed solely from a medical perspective (Costin, 1983b). When the Sheppard–Towner Act was allowed to lapse, some physicians, led by Robert L. De Normandies of Harvard Medical School and the bureau's Obstetric Advisory Committee, along with Grace Abbott, designed a comprehensive study that investigated the deaths of 7,537 mothers. The study revealed that the lack of adequate prenatal care and puerperal septicemia resulted in the enormous loss of life. The study further noted that surgical techniques performed by untrained physicians and the use of pituitrin, which was associated with sepsis, hemorrhage, and rupture of the uterus, had led to the women's deaths. There were many stillbirths and infant deaths, and many infants were born with physical or mental disabilities. At least a quarter of the maternal deaths were a result of illegal abortions. Twenty years later in the late 1940s, a physician testifying before a Senate committee referred to this study when maternal and child health legislation was again pending (Costin, 1983a).

Social workers were deeply involved in the passage of the Social Security Act of 1935, which included the Maternal and Child Health program Crippled Children's program. These programs were administered by the Children's Bureau until 1969, when they were transferred to the newly created Office of Maternal and Child Health in the Health Services and Mental Health Administration of the Pubic Health Service (Kumabe, Nishida, O'Hara, & Woodruff, 1977). Under Title V, Part 1, of the Social Security Act, funds were granted to states to improve the health of mothers and children, especially those in rural, underserved, or economically strained areas. With respect to women's health care, funds were provided to preserve and promote maternal health throughout the woman's reproductive cycle (Davis & Schoen, 1978). The appropriations further provided for the development of a central medical social work section at the federal level. Social workers served as consultants to this section, and their efforts on behalf of maternal and child health were widely recognized.

In 1963 the Maternal and Child Health Act provided for prenatal care for high-risk women. The maternal and infancy projects reached a large number of minority women, 60 percent of whom were black. Some support for family planning services was provided under the Social Security Act of 1967, and in 1970 the Family Planning and Population Research Act further expanded such services. According to Davis and Schoen (1978), it is difficult to estimate the costs and extent of services for pregnant women, because no historical information exists on either the total costs or the services that were delivered. However, the records reveal that those programs have served an increasing number of women since 1963. Although some of the maternal and infancy projects provided comprehensive health care to pregnant women, with the passage of Medicaid and Medicare in 1965, some form of comprehensive health care was made available for the first time to poor women and to elderly women.

GUIDING PHILOSOPHICAL PERSPECTIVES

Social policies to improve women's work lives or to maintain their health have been historically interrelated with the preservation of the woman's place within the family and the preservation of the family. As Abramovitz (1991) aptly noted, "Like most ideologies, the ideology of women's roles represents dominant interests and explains reality in ways that create social cohesion and maintain the status quo" (p. 37). According to Miller (1987), "protective legislation for women workers was justified on the grounds that it would protect motherhood" (p. 289). A classic example of this belief was the statement by Dr. M. L. Holbrook in 1882 in *Parturition without Pain: A Code of Directions for*

Escaping from the Primal Curse (quoted in Mahowald, 1993), that "the Almighty, in creating the female sex, had taken the uterus and built up a woman around it" (p. viii). Childbearing was seen as women's contribution to society, and women's health was considered in relation to that contribution.

The ideology surrounding the term *equality* has assumed that it means "sameness" and having access to the same arenas as do men. The women's health movement, however, does not seek liberation for women so they can be free to be like men. Rather, it acknowledges that there are differences in the bodies of males and females and hence that each gender has specific health needs. As a consequence, women have a distinct perspective about medicine that largely has not been recognized by the medical community (Broom, 1991). Since the 1960s, as women have become visible in the workplace, the association of women's health only with reproductive health has begun to diminish. However, medical research about women's health is still limited (Clancy & Massion, 1992; Mahowald, 1993) as are national studies on health issues of people of color. Protests about the exclusion of women in clinical trials in the early 1990s led to the creation of the Office of Research on Women's Health at the National Institutes of Health (Clancy & Massion, 1992; Mahowald, 1993), so that women's health would be given fair consideration.

Historically, health care has never been considered a "right" or a matter of justice, except by the women of the Children's Bureau and their allies. In the late 1980s, the "unequal majority" initiated a movement that refuses to recognize a woman's worth solely by her reproductive capacity. According to Mahowald (1993), this new philosophy is based on the recognition of respect for individual and group differences and choices and does not require women's health to be appended to children's health as a basis for funding and legislation.

This movement has been hindered by its ideological conflicts with the medical profession. According to Inlander (1992), women are the "cash cows of medicine" because they generate billions of dollars for the medical system. Thus, the medical profession would rather keep women ignorant of medical matters so as to benefit financially from their lack of knowledge.

FINANCING

Early funding was provided for health care to reduce infant mortality and only indirectly benefited pregnant women who were at risk. Expenditures for Maternity and Infancy Projects rose from $5 million in 1965 to $73 million in 1972. The Projects served 141,000 women, most of whom resided in urban areas. That same year, state and local health departments served 335,000 women through maternity medical clinic services and 624,000 women in maternity nursing services. In the Maternity and Infancy Projects the cost per maternity admission was $500, and in state and local health department maternity clinic programs it was $250. In 1973 the average cost per woman was $114 (Davis & Schoen, 1978). Although Medicaid and Medicare have expanded health services for needy and elderly women, the bulk of the funding is still designated for maternal and child health. However, none of the programs offers comprehensive health care.

In their 10-year assessment of the health care programs of the War on Poverty, Davis and Schoen (1978) reported that one out of every five Americans benefited from Medicaid and that Medicare reached one in nine Americans during that period. With the passage of these two programs, health care expenditures quadrupled between 1968 and 1976 and have continued to rise (Jencks & Schieber, 1991). Of the Medicaid recipients in 1972, almost two-thirds were female, and three out of every five people covered were white (Davis & Schoen, 1978). The total federal and state payments for Medicaid recipients increased from $3.45 billion in 1968 to $17.16 billion in 1977. However, the costs for the program did not rise much faster than did governmental expenditures in general and accounted for an average of 2 percent of both the federal and the state budgets. The average expenditures per Medicaid recipient were $338 in 1969 and $361 in 1977, most of the increase in cost being attributed to the increased cost of medical care. In 1977, $3 of every $5 was used for services for elderly or disabled adults, with 38 percent of the payments going for services provided by nursing homes. In that year, expenditures per Medicaid recipient varied greatly by state, ranging from an average of $214 in Missouri to an average of $911 in Minnesota (Davis & Schoen, 1978).

Notable differences in care and expenditures were seen in the Medicaid program in 1974. For example, 74 percent of white people and 67 percent of black people had private physicians as their primary caregivers. In Georgia the average Medicaid payment for white recipients was $587, compared to $271 for black recipients. Government data indicated that white people covered by Medicaid had higher hospitalization rates, whereas black people tended to have longer stays and therefore incurred greater expenses.

From 1975 to 1984, funding under the Maternal and Child Health program (Title V) and health departments for prenatal care and related services increased substantially even though there was a sharp decline in Medicaid and health insurance coverage for poor pregnant women. Although state-funded initiatives were responsible for the rise in services to pregnant women, they had little effect on comprehensive health care (Strobino, Kane, Frank, & Decoster, 1992).

In 1989 the expenditures for Medicaid totaled $59.3 billion, 43.1 percent of which was for long-term care. Medicaid pays for basic health care for needy women. The type of care provided to these women is limited because providers must elect to participate, and those who do so accept Medicaid reimbursement levels as payment in full. Recipients of Aid to Families with Dependent Children (AFDC) consume only one-fourth of the benefits; the adults in AFDC families (who are mostly women of childbearing age) account for 12.1 percent of the Medicaid payments, whereas elderly recipients account for 35.2 percent and blind and disabled recipients account for 38.2 percent. Medicaid is the largest third-party payer for long-term care (Lazenby & Letsch, 1990; Office of National Cost Estimates, 1990). Medicare represents the largest health care expenditure of the federal government. It pays at least 80 percent of the allowable costs, but it does not cover medication or long-term care. In 1987 the average cost per person for individuals ages 65 to 74 was $2,017, and for those 85 and over it was $3,215 (Schneider & Guralnik, 1990). In 1991, 24.3 million people were served by the Medicaid program (Levit, Olin, & Letsch, 1992). Table 1 illustrates the differences in coverage for men and women aged 19 to 44.

It is difficult to assess the expenditures dedicated to women's health because most public dollars under Medicaid and maternal and child health programs are earmarked for both children and women. In 1970, $190 million in federal funds and $260 million in state and local funds were spent on maternal and child health services, and in 1989, the figures were $494 million and $260 million, respectively. In 1970, $2.6 billion in federal funds and $2.6 billion in state and local funds were spent for Medicaid and general assistance recipients, compared with $34.9 billion and $30.3 billion, respectively, in 1989. Obstetrical care expenditures were 85 percent higher in 1987 than in 1982, having risen from $8.2 billion to $15.2 billion (Bixby, 1992). Individuals ages 19 to 64 accounted for 22 percent of public expenditures for health care services in 1987 (Lefkowitz & Monheit, 1991; Monheit & Schur, 1989).

TABLE 1

Comparison of Medicaid and Insurance Coverage of Men and Women Ages 19–44 Who Were Living in Poverty in 1991

	Women	Men
Number living below poverty	7.4 million	4.5 million
Percentage covered by Medicaid	46.0	19.6
Percentage insured	21.4	25.9
Percentage uninsured	33.1	54.5

SOURCE: Levit, K., Olin, G., & Letsch, S. (1992). Americans' health insurance coverage, 1980–91. *Health Care Financing Review, 14,* 31–47.

Levit et al. (1992) found that women ages 19 to 44 who were living in families whose incomes were below the poverty level were less likely than men to be uninsured. Of the 7.4 million women in this age group, 46 percent were covered by Medicaid, 21.4 percent had private insurance, and 33.1 percent were uninsured in 1991. Levit et al. (1992) found that 95.7 percent of the elderly were covered by Medicare and that less than 1 percent were uninsured. People of color, especially Hispanic and, to a large extent, black people, were the least likely to have health insurance even when employed (Short, Cornelius, & Goldstone, 1990).

HEALTH STATUS OF WOMEN

Overview

The health care industry is heavily dependent on women, who constitute the majority of consumers or patients, as well as providers of health care services. Women make more office visits, have more surgical procedures, and consume more medications than do men (Collins & Thornberry, 1989; Inlander, 1992). Yet there have been major problems in measuring the health status of women. First, historically, health care researchers have not made gender distinctions when reporting data. When they have presented data on women separately, they have not usually considered the differential impact of race, ethnicity, age, education, economic status, sexual orientation, marital status, or employment status.

Second, data on health status have generally been reported on the basis of the practices of the heads of households, as well as their educational and economic status. Therefore, the health status of women is not sufficiently reflected in these data (Pinn, 1992).

Third, reports indicate that women tend to respond to surveys more readily than do men and that it is more socially acceptable for women than for men to report illness. Thus, men tend to under-report illness. Reports that have relied on male respondents have had to minimize the extent of various health problems that may be of greater concern to women.

Fourth, the data collected through employment-related health insurance plans may also be gender biased because women are less likely to be employed in companies that offer this benefit (Collins & Thornberry, 1989).

Finally, the assumption that women's illnesses are psychological, rather than physiological, may deter many women from reporting some conditions. In addition, because women delay reporting alcoholism and may not report attempted suicide, venereal disease, rape, or abortion, it is difficult to establish accurate morbidity rates for them (Clancy & Massion, 1992; Marieskind, 1980; Pinn, 1992; Weisner & Schmidt, 1992).

Health and well-being are generally measured by researching biological inheritance, lifestyle, environment, and the receipt of health care services. Health status that is defined as the absence of disease or the presence of feelings of well-being is an elusive term. Nonetheless, it is this measure, along with its indicators—mortality rate, morbidity rate, occupational injuries, and immunization statistics—that is used in reporting data on health care. Factors that are related to, but are not traditionally considered indicative of, a community's health status are being studied more frequently today because of the direct impact they have on the well-being of individuals. These factors include sociodemographic, lifestyle, and environmental factors; age; race; income; education; marital status; and residence, as well as personal lifestyle habits and health behavior, including diet, exercise, eating habits, smoking, drinking, and type of work. Several of these factors are noted in the following subsections to profile women's health.

Mortality

The leading causes of death for both men and women ages 25 to 64 are cancer, heart disease, and stroke. There has been an increase in lung cancer in women primarily because a greater number of women are smoking. For all persons 65 and over, the leading causes of death are heart disease, malignant neoplasms, cerebrovascular diseases, chronic obstructive lung disease, pneumonia, and influenza (Pinn, 1992). Lung, breast, colon–rectal, and stomach cancer are the leading causes of death in women, although the ranks vary by race and ethnicity (American Cancer Society, 1991).

Morbidity

Women live an average of 78.9 years, and they outlive men by an average of 6.9 years. White people are expected to outlive black people by an average of 7 years; the life expectancy for black females is 73.9 years and for black males, 64.6 years (Caserta, 1990; Connell, 1993; Pinn, 1992). According to Lemrow, Adams, Coffey, and Farley (1990), the most prevalent reported chronic conditions of women in 1987 were chronic sinusitis, arthritis, and hypertension. Furthermore, of the 10 most frequent diagnoses made of women admitted to hospitals, eight were associated with reproductive problems; benign uterine tumors and gallbladder disorders were the ninth and tenth diagnoses. Seven of the 10 procedures most often performed on women in hospitals were also associated with reproduction. Hysterectomy, mastectomy, and cholecystectomy were the other three. "Medicare provides better coverage for those illnesses more common to men than those more prevalent in women" (Lemrow et al., p. 1918) because the acute diseases associated with men, such as lung cancer, pneumonia, prostate disorders, and myocardial infarction, have lower out-of-pocket costs than do breast cancer, depression, hypertension, and arthritis, the chronic diseases of women (see Table 2). Not only is there a difference in coverage, but older women are less likely to receive recommended preventive services than are younger women (Clancy & Massion, 1992). Women also have significantly higher rates of use of prescribed medicine within most age groups. In 1987 they used 18 percent more medicines and spent 10 percent more to obtain them than did men ($272 and $247, respectively) (Moeller & Mathiowetz, 1989).

USE OF HEALTH CARE SERVICES

Studies reveal that a number of variables contribute to the use and type of use of health care services. In general, the average number of visits to physicians per person in 1989 was 5.4. Women visit medical offices and are hospitalized and undergo surgery 25 percent more often than men ("Washington Focus," 1992).

Age and Gender

According to the 1987 National Medical Expenditure Survey (NMES) (Cornelius, Beauregard, & Cohen, 1991), about 84 percent of all women versus 77.7 percent of men had a usual source of health care. Adults aged 55 and older were the most likely of all age brackets to have a source of health care. The physician's office was the usual source of health care for about 85 percent of both men and women. The remaining 15 percent almost evenly identified hospital outpatient clinics, emergency rooms, community health centers, or other medical facilities as their usual source of health care. Nonetheless, women were more likely to use more sources of care than were men.

Family Income

The NMES respondents with high incomes identified physicians' offices as their usual source of health care. In contrast, those who were poor were three times more likely than were those with high incomes to identify their usual source of care as outpatient hospital clinics or community health centers (Cornelius et al., 1991).

Residence

The NMES respondents who lived outside metropolitan statistical areas were more likely than were the residents of these areas to have a usual source of health care and to report physicians' offices as their usual source of health care (Cornelius et al., 1991).

Coverage

According to Clancy and Massion (1992), 14 million women of childbearing age do not have health insurance and another 5 million have insurance that does not cover prenatal care and delivery. Women traditionally use health care services more frequently than do men but encounter more financial barriers to care. Although women are more likely to have some form of insurance than are men, they are also twice as likely to be underinsured. Most women have lower incomes than men because they constitute the majority of part-time and service workers, and their employers are not obligated to provide health insurance. If married, many women are insured through their husbands, and if their marriages dissolve, they lose their health insurance.

WOMEN OF COLOR AND HEALTH STATUS

Few reports include the health status of women of color even when their primary focus is women's health. Yet, the information that is available points to disparities in the access to services, health status, and health practices of minority and other women. In

TABLE 2
The Ten Most Frequent Diagnosis Related Groups (DRGs), Diagnoses, and Procedures Performed on Women in Hospitals, by DRG Rank

DRG Rank	Description	Diagnoses	Procedure
2	Vaginal delivery without complications	Delivery in a completely normal case	Episiotomy
4	Cesarean section without complications	Fetal distress xxxxx	Cesarean section
10	Nonradical hysterectomy	Vacuum abstractor delivery	Manually assisted delivery
36	Other antepartum diagnoses	First-degree perineal laceration	Abdominal hysterectomy
38	Vaginal delivery with complicating diagnosis	Cord entanglement	Repair obstetric laceration
42	Uterus and adnexa procedures for nonmalignancy	Second-degree perineal laceration	Dilation and curettage
43	Abortion with dilation and curettage, aspiration, curettage, or hysterotomy	Threatened premature labor	Vaginal hysterectomy
39	Total cholecystectomy (excision of a gallbladder) without common bile duct exploration, without complication and/or comorbidity, age under 70	Spontaneous abortion	Mastectomy
41	Total cholecystectomy without common bile duct exploration, age over 70	Benign leiomyoma of the uterus, unspecified	Cholecystectomy
23	Major joint and limb reattachment	Gallbladder	Diagnostic ultrasound
29	Kidney–urinary-tract infections		

SOURCE: Lemrow, N., Adams, D., Coffey, R., & Farley, D. (1990). *The 50 most frequent diagnosis related groups (DRGs), diagnoses, and procedures: Statistics by hospital size and location* (Publication No. 90-3465). Washington, DC: U.S. Department of Health and Human Services.

addition, three major factors place women of color at a greater risk for developing chronic illnesses than white women: poverty, unemployment, and lack of insurance coverage.

Use of Selected Services

Having a specific physician as one's usual source of care is indicative of continuity of care. A greater percentage of white people than of black or Hispanic people report a usual source of care. Both blacks and Hispanics who identify a usual source of care are twice as likely to use hospital outpatient departments, emergency rooms, health centers, or other nonhospital facilities as their usual source of care. Black people are more likely than whites to report a greater use of ambulatory care services and to be admitted to hospitals. Mexican Americans are least likely to have contacts with physicians. They average 3.7 visits per year, compared to 4.8 for whites, 4.6 for blacks, 6.0 for Puerto Ricans, and 6.2 for Cuban Americans (Cornelius, 1991; Cornelius et al., 1991; Gardocki, 1987). According to Cornelius, the utilization of ambulatory care services appears to be a function of health status, income, a usual source of care, and age. Differences in the use of health care services are not a function of race or ethnicity but result

from being poor, uninsured, or without a usual source of care.

Health Status and Risk Factors

Black people have a higher infant mortality rate, a lower life expectancy, and a higher rate of lung cancer and are 10 times more likely to die from hypertension than are white people (Council on Ethical and Judicial Affairs, 1990). Hispanics also have a higher prevalence of hypertension than do whites, and both Hispanic and black people have a higher incidence of diabetes and obesity than do white people (Caralis, 1990).

The incidence of cancer by site varies in different ethnic–racial groups. Although the incidence of breast cancer ranks number one for white, black, Chinese, Japanese, Filipino, Mexican American, and Native American women, it is highest among Native American women. The incidence of lung cancer is next in these groups followed by colon–rectal cancer. The greatest variation among different ethnic–racial groups occurs in the mortality rates. Although the mortality rate from lung cancer is high for all ethnic–racial groups, it is highest for black people. Breast and colon–rectal cancer are the second and third leading causes of death from cancer for all ethnic–racial groups except Japanese and Native Americans, who have a higher mortality rate from stomach cancer.

Whites are the most likely of all the groups to exceed the five-year survival rate for cancer of the uterus, blacks for breast cancer, and Mexican Americans for skin cancer. Native Americans have the highest mortality rates from infectious diseases (Becker, Wiggins, Peek, Key, & Samet, 1990).

Hispanic women visit physicians primarily for prenatal care, general medical examinations, and fever. Their principal diagnoses are diseases of the respiratory system, injury and poisoning, diseases of the musculoskeletal system, and diseases of the genitourinary system (Gardocki, 1987). The most prevalent chronic conditions of black women are hypertension, arthritis, respiratory disease, and diabetes, and for white women, arthritis, hypertension, respiratory disease, and diabetes. In most surveys people of color are more likely to report being in fair or poor health than are whites (Cornelius, 1991).

Disparities in Treatment

Some studies have found that black and white people receive different treatment in cardiology, cardiac surgery, internal medicine, kidney transplants, and obstetrics. A greater percentage of people of color who are discharged from hospitals have not undergone the same procedures compared to white people who were admitted for the same diagnoses. People of color are more likely to require health care because they are more likely to report being in fair or poor health, but they are less likely to receive adequate health care services. These racial disparities in the quality of health care are the result of differences in both the need for and access to health care (Council on Ethical and Judicial Affairs, 1990). In a study on acculturation and access to care, Solis, Marks, Garcia, and Shelton (1990) found that language, but not ethnic identification, predicted the use of health care services. They suggested that the "effect of language on screening practices should not be interpreted as a cultural factor, but as an access factor, i.e., use of English favors access to services" (p. 11). Despite the myth, the majority of Hispanics do *not* use indigenous health providers, and those who do eventually use both indigenous and mainstream systems simultaneously. However, studies have found that Hispanics delay using mainstream health care services and do so for the following reasons: lack of health insurance, use of indigenous providers, poverty, and low educational levels.

Finally, the majority of elderly people in the United States are women. As health care costs and expenditures have risen and the elderly continue to use a higher percentage of health care dollars, there has been a concomitant tendency to reduce care and services to this population. The denial of certain services and treatment to the elderly, especially to elderly women, is one option that is chosen to reduce costs (Diekema, 1992). However, this option unfairly discriminates against elderly people and can lead to gender-based euthanasia (Schneider & Guralnik, 1990).

Dementia, hip fracture, and nursing home placements are major concerns because of their particular impact on older women. The prevention and treatment of diseases that cause disabilities in old age help reduce the costs of long-term care.

Access to Services

Although black women are more likely than white women to have a usual source of care, they are less likely to optimize that use and are more likely to use hospital outpatient clinics or emergency rooms as their usual source of care. They are also more likely to be admitted to hospitals, to be unemployed, and to have a disability that prevents them from working than are white women. These factors, in addition to lower levels of education, higher levels of unemployment and poverty, and the lack of private or public health insurance coverage, create barriers to the receipt of services. Medicaid recipients encounter barriers to access because providers are reluctant to accept the lower reimbursement rates for services (Cornelius, 1991). Furthermore, the findings from the Hispanic Health and Nutrition Examination Survey suggest that those with low incomes, those who lack health insurance, the less acculturated, those with functional limitations, and those who are perceived to be in poor health encounter more barriers to obtaining health care (Estrada, Trevino, & Ray, 1990). Marks et al. (1987) found that cultural factors may not have the impact on the health behavior of Hispanics that has often been suggested. Rather, they found that access to and the availability of services, emotional reactions to screening, and sociodemographic factors are stronger determinants of Hispanic health practices than are cultural factors.

Coverage

Cornelius et al. (1991) reported that of the 44.3 million Americans who were without a usual source of care in 1987, 38 million were uninsured, poor, relatively poor, Hispanic, or black. Furthermore, Short et al. (1990) noted that the number of uninsured white people rose 4 percent, the number of uninsured black people rose by 17 percent, and the number of uninsured Hispanic people increased by 65 percent. The decline in coverage among black people was caused by the reduction in private insurance, and among Hispanic people, the decline was the result of the rapid increase in the Hispanic population. Furthermore, in 1987 employment did not guarantee coverage; 60 percent of black families with an adult worker and 77 percent of Hispanics with an adult worker were uninsured.

OTHER CURRENT HEALTH ISSUES

Drugs and Alcohol

Although little data are available on the prevalence of drug and alcohol use among women of color, there is some indication of the existence of a problem from three sources: (1) reports of the impact of drugs and alcohol on fetuses and infants, (2) statistics on the high percentage who are incarcerated for drug- or alcohol-related incidents, and (3) the prevalence of acquired immune deficiency syndrome (AIDS).

It has been estimated that about 6 million women are either drug abusers (2.5 million) or alcohol abusers (over 3.3 million) (Blume, 1988). Women are the most frequent users of prescribed drugs and the primary abusers of therapeutic drugs, whether prescribed or sold over the counter. The highest proportion of heavier drinkers is found among women age 34 to 49, whereas 30 percent of women of childbearing age (ages 18 to 34) report the use of illicit drugs (Blume). Mexican Americans appear to have more alcohol-related problems, and Puerto Rican and black people appear to have more drug-related problems. According to Kasper (1989), 70 percent of intravenous drug users are either black or Hispanic. Seventy-two percent of human immunodeficiency virus (HIV)–positive women are black or Hispanic. These women are more likely to have been intravenous drug users or to have been infected by men who are intravenous drug users (Kasper).

In 1989 only 30 percent of clients in substance abuse treatment programs were women. White people constituted 63 percent of those in treatment, black people 20 percent, and Hispanic people 14 percent (*Challenges in Health Care*, 1991). Furthermore, Weisner and Schmidt (1992) found that although the rates of problem drinking were higher for men, women were at greater risk for problem drinking because they were less likely to have reported seeking services and their symptoms were more severe.

AIDS

In 1987, 52 percent of the women with AIDS were black and 20 percent were Hispanic; they were infected through the two primary modes of transmission: intravenous drug use and heterosexual

contact (Kasper, 1989; Mays & Cochran, 1988). Poor women of color, who are socially, educationally, and economically disadvantaged, are most at risk of being infected with HIV. For some of these women, drug dealing provides an economic base for their families.

A number of sociopolitical factors continue to influence the extent to which HIV infection and AIDS are recognized in women. The first has to do with the evolution of the epidemic, which appeared first in gay men, toward whom most of the funding was directed. Other factors are the lack of recognition of differences in the health status of men and women and the lack of research on women's health; the double bind of sexism and racism; the role expectation of women as sexual partners, caregivers, and parents; the unconscious relegation of women to the role of mere channels of transmission to children and partners; and the fear that a requirement of testing and treatment may be misconstrued as coercion (Smeltzer, 1991).

Because funding for treatment and services was based on the Centers for Disease Control's (CDC's) definition of AIDS, women were consistently denied treatment and services. Furthermore, because the symptoms of the disease differ in men and women, CDC's inclusion of esophageal candidiasis as the initial opportunistic infection, along with cervical abnormalities, in the definition of AIDS would reduce the denial of and delay in treatment for women. In addition, women would be eligible for social services that they had been previously denied (Smeltzer, 1991). Timely intervention is critical because it has been found that many women do not survive long enough to be diagnosed with the disease; the average survival rate of women is 6.6 months (Kasper, 1989).

There is a high cost to ignoring the needs of women who are infected with AIDS. Counseling, treatment, advocacy, education, encouraging behavior that reduces the risk of infection, using existing cultural and social norms, establishing social networks, and including women in drug trials will both enhance the quality of life and reduce the mortality rate of women with AIDS. The fact that most of the women are caregivers to many people with AIDS and also the bearers of children with HIV cannot be ignored in terms of both risk and new treatment forms.

Health Care for Lesbians

Few studies have documented the health status of lesbians and their needs. However, it is known that there is a low incidence of sexually transmitted diseases within the lesbian population, which has been attributed to the fact that 80 percent of these women are in relationships, 60 percent of which are monogamous.

Lesbians were at the forefront of the AIDS cause. Many of them in the professions of nursing and social work have worked to promote changes in policies (Salholz et al., 1993).

From all appearances, the physical problems experienced by lesbian women are minor: vaginitis, weight problems, and irregular menses. However, these problems can lead to more chronic illnesses such as chronic yeast infections, arthritis, hypertension, and heart disease. Lesbians fall in the at-risk category for breast cancer and have taken the initiative in requesting funding for research in this area and other areas of women's health (Salholz et al., 1993). Furthermore, there is some indication that emotional and mental health problems, such as depression, alcoholism, and suicide, may be more pervasive than health problems (Trippet & Bain, 1990).

Most lesbians seek care only when there is a problem, although most can identify a source of health care and prefer female physicians and therapists. Furthermore, many experience discrimination based on their sexual orientation.

A number of health-related issues affect lesbians today. One significant problem is that a lesbian partner is not recognized as the next of kin by the health care system or in most health insurance policies, and thus decision making and support are hampered when one woman in the relationship becomes ill. Two other issues—reproductive freedom and artificial insemination—are of particular concern for lesbians of childbearing age who want children (Salholz et al., 1993).

HEALTH CARE FOR YOUNG WOMEN

The information available on the health care of young women appears to be a patchwork quilt. Two factors influence this type of scenario: (1) the assumption that adolescents are healthy and (2) the tendency to report statistics only for young men.

Adolescents often act on the assumption that they are invincible because they are young. As a result, they often take unnecessary risks, and mortality statistics confirm this fact. In 1990 the leading causes of death among young people between the ages of 15 and 24 were accidents, homicide, suicide, cancer, heart disease, AIDS, congenital anomalies, cerebrovascular disease, and pulmonary disease (National Center for Health Statistics, 1991).

Nelson (1991) found that adolescents represented 9 percent of all patient visits and that the purpose of these visits could be categorized into four areas: general care, gynecological or routine prenatal care, dermatological care, and throat infections. The typical patient in this age bracket was a non-Hispanic white female. However, because an adolescent does not use the health care system does not mean that he or she exercises good health practices. The focus on more recent adolescent research has been to examine risk behaviors: use of alcohol and other drugs; smoking; unprotected sex and the resultant exposure to sexually transmitted diseases and HIV; sporadic use of contraceptives, leading to pregnancy; accidents; and suicide. Homicide, AIDS, and pregnancy have a disproportionate adverse effect on adolescent females of color. Suicide and homicide are two of the leading causes of death among white females between the ages of 15 and 19. Cancer of the breast and uterus, leukemia, diabetes, anemia, and other diseases also threaten adolescent health (American Cancer Society, 1991; Marieskind, 1980).

According to most reports pregnancy among adolescents has reached epidemic proportions. Of major concern to health professionals is the impact of drugs and alcohol on pregnant adolescents. The rate of AIDS among women of color and their low use of contraceptives place younger females at a high risk of HIV infection (Mays & Cochran, 1988).

According to a poll on eating disorders, 2 million women aged 19 to 39 and about a million teenagers are affected by bulimia or anorexia nervosa (Farley, 1991). Although neither new nor rare, anorexia nervosa has come to be associated with adolescents who have a false feminine ideal of thinness (Mahowald, 1993). Farley estimated that bulimia, a binge–purge eating disorder, is found in 4.5 percent to 18 percent of female high school and college students.

Young women are able to receive only a few services when they have been physically or sexually abused. They are too young for women's shelters and are ignored by child protective agencies because they are old enough to run away from abuse.

Adolescent females experience patchwork care more than any other group. They are cared for by a variety of providers, including pediatricians, internists, family physicians, gynecologists, nurse practitioners, and family planning clinics. Most of the care is limited to the presenting problem.

OCCUPATIONAL HEALTH AND WOMEN

There is little in the literature on women and health that relates to the hazards women face in the workplace and the home. Women who work in industry, in offices, in medical settings, and in schools are all exposed to risks to their health and safety. The diversity of women's work in these settings makes it difficult to develop adequate safety policies. The women's movement has examined issues related to women's health, such as birth control, sterilization, abortion, pregnancy, childbirth, gynecological care, surgery, and menopause, but, according to Chavkin (1984), the women's movement and the occupational health and safety movement have seldom overlapped. In addition, although the impact of stress on the job has been recognized as a major health hazard, it has not been satisfactorily considered. Exclusionary policies, including those related to reproduction, have delayed analysis of the risks to reproductive health in the workplace. For example, pregnancy and parenting are often considered activities of the home, so their impact on work is not considered. Furthermore, a hazard that affects only a small number of women is the risks to which female migrant farmworkers are exposed. Besides the workplace, the home environment contains its own health hazards, along with stress and household pollutants.

Women of color have encountered special problems not only because of their exposure to more dangerous jobs and environments but because of low wages; the denial of their legal and civil rights; and their exclusion from social services and organizations such as trade unions. Their exploitation has been justified and rationalized on the basis of biological and cultural inferiority. Finally, Chavkin noted that the issues of harassment of women in the workplace were ignored as an issue of health and safety until the 1980s.

To highlight the impact of the work environment on women, Collins and Thornberry (1989) provided strong evidence of health and safety issues. Women still constitute 94 percent of the labor force in the home and 84 percent of administrative support occupations in the labor force. Women in the labor force, especially women in transportation and material-moving occupations, report not only more restricted activity and work-loss days than do men but more visits to physicians per year. This same group of women report 47 percent higher discharge rates and double the incidence of acute conditions than do men. In addition, one in five women in private household occupations assesses her health as fair or poor.

Complicating the discussion of issues of health and safety in the workplace are variations in the prevalence rates of chronic conditions in women in diverse occupations. Collins and Thornberry (1989) found that women in household occupations reported a much higher rate of hypertension than did women in executive, administrative, or managerial occupations. They also found that the incidence of hay fever was higher among women working as technicians, in support occupations, professional specialty occupations, and executive and administrative occupations than among those working as machine operators, assemblers, and inspectors and that there was a higher rate of chronic sinusitis in women in transportation and material-moving occupations, precision production craft, repair occupations, farming, forestry, and fishing occupations than in women machine operators, assemblers, and inspectors. Women reported a 40 percent higher prevalence rate of arthritis than did men, and women in private household occupations reported a much higher rate than did women in farming, forestry, and fishing occupations and women in professional and executive occupations. Furthermore, a higher incidence of orthopedic impairments of the back was found in women than in men, with the highest incidence occurring in women in private household occupations.

ISSUES FOR THE FUTURE

A number of issues related to female reproduction will continue to confront women and the health care professions. First, according to Mahowald (1993), abortion, the curtailment and enhancement of fertility, the right to have a baby, in vitro development and childbirth, coercive treatment after fetal viability, fetal tissue transplantation, and decisions regarding disabled newborns are issues that affect women and require ethical and moral reasoning and decision making based on a model of care.

Second, neither the health problems of poor women and women of color nor the psychosocial issues of women that are outside the scope of medical specialties can be ignored. According to Clancy and Massion (1992), the "failure to recognize the psychosocial factors precipitating women's use of health services and their health-related behaviors may lead to inappropriate diagnosis and treatment" (p. 1919).

Third, attempts must be made to protect elderly women from policies that reduce their care. Research on the prevention and treatment of the disabling diseases of elderly women will reduce both health care costs and the costs of long-term care. Aging is not a disease, and social workers can be real advocates for this population (Inlander, 1992).

Fourth, more individuals should conduct gender-specific biomedical research and promote policies that reflect the intent of the Women's Health Equity Act of 1990. Efforts have to be made to eliminate discrepancies in women's health care; to reduce the fragmentation of women's care that has resulted from the lack of integration of women's social, mental, and physical health; and to address gender disparities in the treatment of alcohol problems such as lack of access to treatment and inequitable treatment. These goals can be achieved through the efforts of social workers and other providers of care.

Fifth, the encouragement of early prenatal care, breast self-examinations, mammograms, home and environmental safety techniques, control of infection, education in parenting skills, stress management and relaxation techniques, and exercise and nutritional programs, as well as knowledge of community resources, are all within the domain of social work intervention in health care settings.

Finally, all social workers in medical and mental health settings need to join the profession in the national movement toward health care reform to provide basic health care, including psychosocial services, for all Americans. Social workers need to join with women to create a model of caring in the provision of health care services.

REFERENCES

Abramovitz, M. (1991). *Regulating the lives of women.* Boston: South End Press.

American Cancer Society. (1991). *Cancer facts and figures for minority Americans, 1991.* Atlanta: Author.

Becker, T., Wiggins, C., Peek, C., Key, C., & Samet, J. (1990). Mortality from infectious diseases among New Mexico's American Indians, Hispanic whites, and other whites, 1958–87. *American Journal of Pubic Health, 80,* 320–323.

Bixby, A. (1992). Pubic social welfare expenditures, fiscal year 1989. *Social Security Bulletin, 55,* 61–65.

Blume, S. (1988). *Alcohol/drug dependent women: New insights into their special problems, treatment, recovery.* Edina, MN: Johnson Institute.

Broom, D. (1991). *Damned if we do: Contradictions in women's health care.* Sydney, Australia: Allen & Unwin.

Caralis, P. (1990). Hypertension in the Hispanic American population. *American Journal of Medicine, 88,* 3b-9s–3b-16s.

Caserta, J. (1990). Women of the 1990's. *Home Healthcare Nurse, 8,* 4.

Challenges in health care: A chartbook perspective, 1991. (1991). Princeton, NJ: Robert Wood Johnson Foundation.

Chavkin, W. (1984). *Double exposure: Women's health hazards on the job and at home.* New York: Monthly Review Press.

Clancy, C., & Massion, C. (1992). American women's health care: A patchwork quilt with gaps. *Journal of the American Medical Association, 268,* 1918–1920.

Collins, J., & Thornberry, I. (1989). *Health characteristics of workers by occupation and sex: United States, 1983–85* (Publication No. 89–1250). Hyattsville, MD: U.S. Department of Health and Human Services.

Connell, C. (1993, September 2). 1991: A record year for deaths in America. *Austin American-Statesman,* p. A30.

Cornelius, L. (1991). Access to medical care for black Americans with an episode of illness. *Journal of the National Medical Association, 83,* 617–626.

Cornelius, L., Beauregard, K., & Cohen, J. (1991). *Usual sources of medical care and their characteristics* (Publication No. 91-0042). Rockville, MD: U.S. Public Health Service, Agency for Health Care Policy and Research.

Costin, L. (1983a). *Two sisters for social justice.* Chicago: University of Illinois Press.

Costin, L. (1983b). Women and physicians: The 1930 White House Conference on Children. *Social Work, 28,* 108–115.

Costin, L., Bell, C., & Downs, S. (1991). *Child welfare: Policies and practice* (4th ed.). New York: Longman.

Council on Ethical and Judicial Affairs. (1990). Black–white disparities in health care. *Journal of the American Medical Association, 263,* 2344–2346.

Davis, K., & Schoen, C. (1978). *Health and the war on poverty.* Washington, DC: Brookings Institution.

Diekema, D. (1992). Age-based rationing and women. *Journal of the American Medical Association, 167,* 1612.

Estrada, A., Trevino, F., & Ray, L. (1990). Health care utilization barriers among Mexican Americans. *American Journal of Public Health, 80,* 27–31.

Farley, D. (1991). Eating disorders when thinness becomes an obsession. In *Current issues in women's health* (Report No. 91-1181). Rockville, MD: U.S. Department of Health and Human Services, Public Health Service, and the Food and Drug Administration.

Gardocki, G. (1987). *Visits to office-based physicians by Hispanic persons: United States, 1980–81.* Rockville, MD: U.S. Department of Health and Human Services, National Center for Health Statistics.

Inlander, C. (1992). Making women a disease. *Nursing Economics, 10,* 146.

Jencks, S., & Schieber, G. (1991). Containing U.S. health care costs: What bullet to bite? *Health Care Financing Review* (Annual Suppl.), 1–3.

Kasper, B. (1989). Women and AIDS: A psychosocial perspective. *Affilia, 4*(4), 7–22.

Kumabe, K., Nishida, C., O'Hara, D., & Woodruff, C. (1977). *A handbook for social work education and practice in community health settings.* Honolulu: University of Hawaii School of Social Work.

Lazenby, H., & Letsch, S. (1990). National health care expenditures, 1989. *Health Care Financing Review, 12,* 1–11.

Lefkowitz, D., & Monheit, A. (1991). *Health insurance, use of health services, and health care expenditures* (Publication No. 92-0017). Rockville, MD: U.S. Public Health Service, Agency for Health Care Policy and Research.

Lemrow, N., Adams, D., Coffey, R., & Farley, D. (1990). *The 50 most frequent diagnosis-related groups (DRGs), diagnoses, and procedures: Statistics by hospital size and location* (Publication No. PHS 90-3465). Washington, DC: U.S. Department of Health and Human Services.

Levit, K., Olin, G., & Letsch, S. (1992). Americans' health insurance coverage, 1980–91. *Health Care Financing Review, 14,* 31–47.

Mahowald, M. (1993). *Women and children in health care.* New York: Oxford University Press.

Marieskind, H. (1980). *Women in the health care system.* St. Louis: C. V. Mosby.

Marks, G., Solis, J., Richardson, J., Collins, L., Birba, L., & Hisserich, J. (1987). Health behavior of elderly Hispanic women: Does cultural assimilation make a difference? *American Journal of Public Health, 77,* 1315–1319.

Mays, V., & Cochran, S. (1988). Issues in the perception of AIDS risk and risk reduction activities by black and Hispanic/Latina women. *American Psychologist, 43,* 949–957.

Miller, D. (1987). Children's policy and women's policy: Congruence or conflict? *Social Work, 32,* 289–292.

Moeller, J., & Mathiowetz, N. (1989). *Prescribed medicines: A summary of use and expenditures by Medicare beneficiaries* (Publication No. 89-3448). Rockville, MD: U.S. Public Health Service, National Center for Health Services Research and Health Care Technology Assessment.

Monheit, A., & Schur, C. (1989). *Health insurance coverage of retired persons* (Publication No. 89-3444). Rockville, MD: U.S. Public Health Service, National Center for Health Services Research and Health Care Technology Assessment.

National Center for Health Statistics. (1993). *Advance report of the final mortality statistics, 1990.* Hyattsville, MD: U.S. Public Health Service.

Nelson, C. (1991). Office visits by adolescents. *Advance data from vital and health statistics* (No. 196). Hyattsville, MD: National Center for Health Statistics.

Office of National Cost Estimates. (1990, Summer). National health expenditures, 1988. *Health Care Financing Review, 11,* 1–40.

Pinn, V. (1992). Women's health research. *Journal of the American Medical Association, 268,* 1921–1922.

Salholz, E., Glick, D., Beachy, L., Monserrate, C., King, P., Gordon, J., & Barrett, T. (1993, June 21). The power and the pride. *Newsweek,* pp. 54–60.

Schneider, E., & Guralnik, J. (1990). The aging of America. *Journal of the American Medical Association, 263,* 2335–2340.

Short, P., Cornelius, L., & Goldstone, D. (1990). Health insurance of minorities in the United States. *Journal of Health Care for the Poor and Underserved, 1,* 9–24.

Smeltzer, S. (1991). Women and AIDS: Sociopolitical issues. *Nursing Outlook, 40,* 152–156.

Solis, J., Marks, G., Garcia, M., & Shelton, D. (1990). Acculturation, access to care, and use of preventive services by Hispanics: Findings from HHANES 1982–1984. *American Journal of Public Health, 80,* 11–17.

Strobino, D., Kane, L., Frank, R., & Decoster, E. (1992). Trends in publicly financed prenatal and related services, 1975–1984. *Journal of Public Health Policy, 13,* 277–290.

Trippet, S., & Bain, J. (1990). Preliminary study of lesbian health concerns. *Health Values, 14,* 30–36.

Washington focus: Women's health—Its time has come again. (1992). *Nursing & Health Care, 12,* p. 176.

Weisner, C., & Schmidt, L. (1992). Gender disparities in treatment for alcohol problems. *Journal of the American Medical Association, 268,* 1872–1876.

FURTHER READING

Draper, E. (1993). Fetal exclusion policies and gendered constructions of suitable work. *Social Problems, 40,* 90–98.

Garfinkel, L. (1993). Current trends in breast cancer. *CA, 43,* 5–6.

LaRosa, J. (1990). Executive women and health: Perceptions and practices. *American Journal of Public Health, 80,* 1450–1453.

Malterud, K. (1993). Strategies for empowering women's voices in the medical culture. *Health Care Women International, 14,* 365–373.

Sidel, R. (1992). Women's health, women's lives, women's rights. *American Journal of Public Health, 82,* 663–665.

Thomas, T., Kang, H., & Dalager, N. (1991). Mortality among women Vietnam veterans, 1973–1987. *American Journal of Epidemiology, 134,* 973–979.

Turshen, M. (1993). The impact of sexism on women's health and health care. *Journal of Public Health Policy, 14,* 164–173.

Marian A. Aguilar, PhD, LMSW-AP, is assistant professor, University of Texas at Austin, School of Social Work, 1925 San Jacinto Boulevard, Austin, TX 78712.

For further information see

Adolescence Overview; Adolescent Pregnancy; Domestic Violence; Eating Disorders and Other Compulsive Behaviors; Family Planning; Health Care: Reform Initiatives; HIV/AIDS Overview; Lesbians Overview; Managed Care; Poverty; Primary Health Care; Primary Prevention Overview; Public Health Services; Social Security; Substance Abuse: Direct Practice; Suicide; Women Overview; Women: Direct Practice; Women in Social Policy.

Key Words	
health	women

Women in Social Policy
Ruth A. Brandwein

Social policy has been intrinsic to social work since the profession's inception. According to Gil (1990), who reviewed definitions of social policy in his book *Unravelling Social Policy,* Freeman and Sherwood distinguished *social policy* as a philosophical concept, a product, a process, or a framework for action. Burns viewed it as "the organized efforts of society to meet identifiable personal needs of, or social problems presented by, groups or individuals" (pp. 4–5). In addition, Baumheier and Schorr (1977) defined social policy as "a settled course of action with respect to selected social phenomena that govern social relationships and the distribution of resources in a society" (p. 1453). Put succinctly, social policy is a set of procedures and principles that distributes rewards and punishments (Brandwein, 1986).

Many social policies have been considered "women's issues," that is, issues that intrinsically affect women, such as marriage and divorce, child welfare, women's health issues, domestic violence, and rape. However, because women constitute more than half the U.S. population, all policy issues are of concern to women. Women have played key roles in the policy arena; however, they also have generally been viewed as recipients of social services rather than as creators and decision makers of social policy. Recently, though, changing gender roles in society have brought larger numbers of women into prominence in decision-making roles.

This entry reviews historical trends in women's roles in social policy from the beginning of the social work profession, through the Progressive Era and the New Deal, to the present. The discussion is not limited to traditionally defined areas of "women's" policy; rather, the entry examines the proactive role women have played in all areas of social policy. Finally, it explores how the recent changes in the political arena of policy-making could affect the process and outcomes of social policy.

HISTORICAL TRENDS

One view of social work is that women have replicated their traditionally accepted nurturing, caring roles by becoming direct practitioners and helping individuals. Conversely, this view assumes that men have been drawn to the macro practice areas of planning, administration, and policy, which supposedly require more-masculine roles. Traditionally, casework services have been seen as the province of women, whereas men have dominated administration, planning, and social policy.

Over the years the absolute numbers in each of these areas have supported this traditional bifurcation of the social work profession (Bakke & Edson, 1977; Brandwein, 1982, 1984, 1987; Ezell & Odewahn, 1980; Fanshel, 1976; Fortune & Hanks, 1988; Gibelman & Schervish, 1993; Jennings & Daley, 1979; Kadushin, 1976; Kravetz, 1976; Munson, 1982; Rubenstein, 1981; Scotch, 1971; Sutton, 1982). On closer inspection of the historical data, however, it is clear that this stereotypical gender breakdown is inaccurate. Many women have been drawn to social work as social reformers rather than as caseworkers, or have started as caseworkers and then have become involved in policy issues.

Progressive Era through the New Deal
Social work as a profession was born out of the social reform movement of the Progressive Era. Many of the early pioneers of social work, predominantly women, were drawn to social welfare as an extension of their role as nurturers who were concerned with the plight of women and children. The Victorian dichotomy of a woman's place in the home and a man's place in the world accommodated the exception of women expanding their family concerns to the public sector to improve conditions for women and children. Such early leaders as Dorothea Dix, Jane Addams, Grace and Edith Abbott, and Julia Lathrop quickly expanded their concerns for women and children from the private to the public spheres. This limited role for women is exemplified by the fact that although women advocates provided key leadership in policies for women and children, men dominated corrections policy.

Dorothea Dix, who preceded the settlement house movement, was not, strictly speaking, a social worker, because the social work profession did not develop until after her death in 1887. Her policy activism for federal and state support for more-humane treatment of mentally ill people, as well as her international work on their behalf, however, serves as an early example of the leadership of women in the social policy arena. She was successful in establishing more than 30 public and private institutions.

The Charity Organization Societies movement, with its friendly visitors, was the forerunner of casework, direct practice, or micro practice. The branch of social work that developed during the Progressive Era was that of the settlement house, which was the incubator for community organization, policy analysis and development, and other forms of macro practice. Settlement house leaders often spearheaded legislative lobbying and social reform campaigns to end child labor, to lower hours, and to initiate a minimum wage and suffrage for women. Most of these social reformers, who lived and worked in the settlement houses, were women.

Of these, Jane Addams is best known as the founder of Hull-House in Chicago in 1889, one of the first settlement houses in the United States. She was also the first female president of the National Conference of Charities and Corrections and the first head of the National Federation of Settlements. She spoke out vociferously against America's entrance into World War I, was a founder of the Women's International League of Peace and Freedom, and in 1931 was the first female recipient of the Nobel prize for peace. She also played a prominent part in the founding of the Progressive Party, whose presidential candidate was Theodore Roosevelt (Addams, 1910/1960; Quam, 1987).

Other residents of Hull-House also were social policy activists. Sophonisba Breckenridge, who later became dean of the University of Chicago School of Civics and Philanthropy (precursor to the current School of Social Service Administration) was active in the women's trade union movement and conducted research on the legal aspects of women's employment. Julia Lathrop, a cofounder of the school, became the first head of the U.S. Children's Bureau. She was active in the reform of poorhouses and mental institutions and the care of delinquents. She also became president of the National Conference of Social Work. Florence Kelley, another early Hull-House resident, was appointed chief factory inspector in Illinois, where she helped reform working conditions, especially for women and children. She was instrumental in introducing minimum-wage legislation in nine states. As secretary of the National Consumers League, she organized 60 leagues in 20 states. She was also a cofounder of the national Child Labor Committee and was an active proponent of legislation regarding women's and children's labor.

Two other residents of Hull-House who were active in social policy were the Abbott sisters. Grace Abbott, who followed Lathrop as the director of the U.S. Children's Bureau, was responsible for establishing 3,000 child health and prenatal care centers throughout the United States. She organized the first White House Conference on Children and was a professor of public welfare at the University of Chicago School of Social Service Administration. Edith Abbott was the dean of the School of Social Service Administration and published many studies on the condition of women in industry. In 1934 she was named to President Franklin D. Roosevelt's Commission on Economic Security, which drafted the Social Security Act.

Josephine Goldmark worked for Florence Kelley at the National Consumers League, where she researched the working conditions of women. Her research formed the basis of the "Brandeis Briefs." This documentation of women's working conditions, which she prepared for Louis Brandeis, helped him win his case, *Muller v. Oregon* (1908), before the Supreme Court. She also drafted legislation for Senator Robert LaFollette of Wisconsin for the protection of working women (Blumberg, 1971; Goldmark, 1912).

Edith Abbott was not the only female social worker who was active in social policy areas during the New Deal era. Frances Perkins, another Hull-House resident, earned a master's degree from Columbia University and went on to become executive of the New York Consumers' League and the New York State Factory Commission. She was appointed chair of the New York State Industrial Commission in 1929 by then-governor Roosevelt and in 1933 was appointed secretary of labor by the new president. As such, she was the first woman to hold a Cabinet position. In that capacity, she also served on the Commission on Economic Security and was instrumental in developing the new social security legislation. As secretary, she advocated for minimum wages, maximum hours, child labor legislation, and unemployment compensation. Many of her goals were implemented in the National Labor Relations Act of 1935 and other New Deal legislation.

Women of color. Among the female leaders were a number of women of color who made outstanding contributions to social policy. Mary McLeod Bethune, who founded what is now Bethune–Cookman College in Daytona Beach, Florida, and the National Council of Negro Women, is perhaps the best known of these women. In 1936 she was appointed head of Negro Affairs for the National Youth Administration and was influential in promoting policies that led to a more equitable distribution of resources in the African American community.

Less well known is Sara Fernandis, founder of the first African American settlement house in the United States. She organized social welfare and public health activities in African American communities and during World War I founded the Women's Cooperative Civic League, which worked for improved sanitation and health conditions in African American neighborhoods (Peebles-Wilkins, 1987). Another little-known policy leader was Beatriz Lassalle, who coordinated the first Child Congress ever held, which took place in Puerto Rico in 1922. During the Great Depression of the 1930s, she headed programs in the Puerto Rico Emergency Reconstruction Administration. In that role, she helped integrate social services within the Puerto Rico Department of Health. She also headed the first suffrage organization in Puerto Rico (Longres, 1987b).

New Deal. Other social policy leaders began their careers serving in the New Deal era. Eveline Burns, who moved from England and joined the Columbia University faculty in 1928, also served on Roosevelt's Committee on Economic Security and continued her national work in economic and employment policy through the 1940s. Mary Switzer began her career in 1934 as assistant secretary of the Minimum Wage Board; her career culminated in 1967 when she was named head of the new Social and Rehabilitation Services, a position in which she was responsible for social security and federal welfare programs. Until the advent of the Clinton administration, she had the greatest administrative responsibility of any woman in U.S. government.

Mary Van Kleek, another social work educator and researcher who advocated for the rights of working women, criticized New Deal legislation for not going far enough to promote social justice. She expressed her criticisms of Roosevelt's reform plan in a historic speech at the 1934 annual meeting of the National Conference of Social Work (Ehrenreich, 1985).

The most outstanding female leader in social policy during the New Deal and through the 1940s was Eleanor Roosevelt. Although she was not a professional social worker, she had a profound influence on social welfare legislation and was an advocate and mentor for women. In 1933 she convened a White House Conference on the Emergency Needs of Women (Scharf, 1983). Through her travels, her daily syndicated newspaper column "My Day," and her influence over President Roosevelt by inviting labor leaders and leaders of civil rights organizations and social work to the White House, she helped shape the national debate on human rights, social justice, and social programs (Cook, 1992).

Even those social work leaders such as Mary Richmond and Gordon Hamilton (Longres, 1987a,

1987c), who are known primarily for their contributions to direct practice, became active in social policy. Richmond fought for legislation for deserted wives and founded the Pennsylvania Child Labor Committee, the Public Charities Association, the juvenile court, and the Housing Association. Hamilton, in a 1962 editorial in *Social Work,* advocated the separation of social services from income-maintenance programs. A decade later this culminated in a major change in public assistance policy and practice that is still in effect today. Germain and Hartman (1980), in their study of four social work leaders, found that although these women began their careers as caseworkers, they eventually turned to working for social change.

In the 17th edition of the NASW *Encyclopedia of Social Work* (Turner, 1977), women were the subjects of only one-third of the biographical entries, yet almost 80 percent were involved in organizing and policy-making activities at the local, state, or national level. In the 18th edition of the *Encyclopedia* (Minahan, 1987), women constituted slightly more than half of the biographical entries and about 80 percent were involved in social policy endeavors.

Nevertheless, throughout the history of social work, men have been overrepresented in positions of leadership at the policy-making level. The proportion and visibility of women in these positions have fluctuated. From the early period of the social work profession through the New Deal, women played a central and visible role. Between 1935 and 1945 women authored approximately half of the articles in *Social Welfare Forum,* the proceedings of the annual conference of the National Conference of Social Work.

The 1950s and 1960s
A dramatic shift in the participation of women in social policy began in the 1950s and culminated in the 1960s, which was the nadir of women's social work leadership in the policy arena. In an effort to "upgrade" the profession and raise salaries, an aggressive effort was made to recruit men into social work in the post–World War II era. This was facilitated by the G.I. Bill of Rights, which provided educational payments for men who had served in the U.S. Army. Social work leaders and educators felt that because men enjoyed a higher social status than women, social work's image would be enhanced by recruiting men. Men were actively recruited into the profession and were promoted over women into positions of leadership and high visibility (Brager & Michael, 1969; Brandwein, 1982; Ehrenreich, 1985; Giovannoni & Purvine, 1973; Kadushin, 1976; Kravetz, 1976; West, 1933).

This development mirrored what was occurring in the broader social context. After World War II, women who had been working in the war industry and in other jobs that had been abandoned by men in uniform were induced to go back to the home and resume more-traditional roles. This was done both subtly—through massive propaganda efforts in the popular media—and overtly—through the closure of child care centers that had been established throughout the country during the war. Much of the popular media, as well as professional publications, reflecting a popularization and distortion of Freudian psychology, broadcast the message that women's place was in the home and that women in leadership positions were denying their feminine roles, demonstrating "penis envy," and "castrating" men (see, for example, Lundberg & Farnham, 1947; Wylie, 1942). The growth of suburban living and nuclear families reinforced women's roles as mothers, wives, and consumers. Strong women in public policy positions were contrary to the cultural norms of the day.

Publications. Publication in *Social Welfare Forum* is a good indicator of who was recognized as a policy leader in the social work profession. Some authors were invited to present papers at the National Conference on Social Welfare, then the most prestigious national conference of the profession, and after 1950 only selected papers among all of those delivered were published. Although in 1945, 16 of the 39 entries in *Social Welfare Forum* were written by women, by 1950 only two of 18 were written by women (National Conference on Social Welfare, 1935–1981). This low representation of female authors continued throughout the 1950s and 1960s (National Conference on Social Welfare, 1958–1961).

Other indicators of women's declining role in policy leadership during this period were the dramatic decreases of female authors in policy and planning publications, conferences, and organizational leadership. During the 1930s and 1940s, women had held the presidency of the National Conference on Social Welfare. Beginning in the 1950s, men held this office. The National Conference on Social Welfare published an annual volume of selected papers in community organization in the 1950s and 1960s. In the early 1950s, about half of these entries were written by women, but by 1958 only one of the 13 entries was written by a woman. This pattern continued until publication ceased in the 1960s. Similarly, a widely used reader in community organization practice that was published in 1969 included only two women among 42 authors (Kramer & Specht, 1969).

People who hold doctorates are more likely to exert leadership positions in the policy arena. Between the mid-1930s and the 1950s, more women received doctorates than men in every year but one. Then a shift occurred: By the mid-1950s, men held a small majority, and by the early 1960s—with a large increase in the total number of social work doctoral degrees—men maintained the majority.

Policy trends. Although the 1960s was a time of great social ferment and change, in general, the position of women did not improve. Stokely Carmichael's response to the question, "What is the position of women in the civil rights movement?" was apocryphal: "Prone" was his answer. Some people claim that this comment was the catalyst for the reemergence of the women's liberation movement in the late 1960s and early 1970s.

In the social work profession, the adversarial approach to community organization, which became more acceptable in the late 1960s, was considered a more "macho" approach than the earlier emphasis on collaboration and cooperation (Brandwein, 1981). The dichotomy between casework on the one hand and community organization, administration, and policy on the other hand, was gender related. Women were tracked into casework and direct practice specializations in schools of social work, and men were groomed for agency administration and policy leadership.

The 1970s and 1980s

These trends continued in the 1970s. By 1971 women had earned only 30 percent of all the doctorates awarded in social work. Women held only 9 percent of social work deanships in 1970, indicating a steady decline since the mid-1940s, when almost 50 percent of deans were women. At "Centrally Planned Change," a prestigious national conference on social planning held in 1972, none of the 33 invited participants was a woman (Mayer, Moroney, & Morris, 1974).

Women's movement. Women have reemerged from this low point in the early 1970s as leaders in social policy. Much of this can be attributed to the pressures from the women's liberation movement. Some trace its beginnings to Betty Friedan's 1963 book *The Feminine Mystique,* but it was not until the end of the 1960s and the early 1970s that the women's liberation movement and feminism began to pervade the national consciousness. Women began to seek political office to influence social policies affecting women. Most prominent among these were members of Congress Bella Abzug, from New York, and Patricia Schroeder, of Colorado.

Social work, a profession dominated numerically by women, was influenced by the women's liberation movement. By 1973 NASW had established the National Committee on Women's Issues, and in 1974 the Council on Social Work Education (CSWE) established the Commission on the Role and Status of Women in Social Work Education. In 1977 the CSWE Standards for Accreditation of Social Work Programs was expanded to add an affirmative action standard that pertained to female students, faculty, and curriculum content (CSWE, 1977).

Education. In the 1970s the number of women in the macro practice track in master's programs increased, as did the proportion of women in doctoral degree programs. In 1975, 35 percent of all doctoral degrees in social work were awarded to women. By 1980 this figure had grown to 49 percent. In 1983 more than 60 percent of all enrolled doctoral students were women, and by the end of the 1980s, this figure was 65 percent. That trend has continued into the 1990s. Similarly, the proportion of female deans increased from the 9 percent low in 1970 to 26 percent by 1984 and to 38 percent at the end of the 1980s. Significantly, one-fourth of those were women of color. That trend has also continued into the 1990s (CSWE, 1991).

Administrative leadership. Another indicator of women in social policy is the number of those who hold administrative leadership positions. Frequently, and particularly in larger agencies, people in top positions are involved in policy development, policy analysis, and legislative advocacy for the adoption of policies and programs. Unlike the gender shifts in deanships, doctoral programs, and master's degree programs, the 1970s saw a backward movement for women in executive positions. In the 1970s not only did fewer women hold leadership positions than in past decades, but also their proportions decreased while salary differentials increased (Brandwein, 1984; Knapman, 1977; Szakacs, 1977; Weiner & Engel, 1977). This phenomenon can be explained by examining age cohorts. The World War II era provided an opportunity for women to enter positions that had previously been held by men. By the 1960s most of these women had retired, and they tended to be replaced by men because the 1960s was not a positive period for female leadership. The 1970s saw a continuation of these older men holding the top leadership positions in the social work profession.

In the 1980s, as these men began to retire, fewer men were drawn into the social work profession because of the tightening of budgets and opportunities (the proportion of male graduate students in social work reached a high of about 40 percent in the late 1960s and then declined to fewer than 20 percent by the 1980s) (CSWE, 1978/1984/1989/1991). Both of these factors—male retirement and fewer men entering the profession—opened up more opportunities to women, who began to move not only into leadership positions as deans but also into other leadership roles. The establishment of *Affilia: The Journal of Women and Social Work* in 1986 provided an outlet for the publication of social policy articles with feminist content.

Policy trends. Once again, larger social forces interacted with and had a profound effect on the social work profession. After the strides of the women's liberation movement in the early 1970s, the Reagan era saw a backsliding of and a reduction of emphasis on women's issues at the national level. The failure to pass the Equal Rights Amendment after years of mobilization and legislative advocacy was symbolic. The Supreme Court, with the appointments of conservative justices by Presidents Reagan and Bush, was beginning to chip away at the *Roe v. Wade* (1973) decision, which protects a woman's right to choose whether to have an abortion.

At the grassroots level, however, women were continuing to work on the issues of reproductive rights, domestic violence, rape, and other issues of vital importance to women. Women were also becoming more politically sophisticated. A watershed event in 1985 was the establishment of Emily's List—*E*arly *M*oney *I*s *L*ike *Y*east—a national political action committee that raises money for the election of women to national office. At its inception, Emily's List endorsed Barbara Mikulski, a social worker, who was elected as a Democratic senator from Maryland. She joined Senator Nancy Kassebaum from Kansas, who until then had been the only woman in the U.S. Senate. By the 1992 election cycle, Emily's List raised over $6.2 million and supported 55 prochoice women. Of these, five were elected to the U.S. Senate and 21 to the House (Emily's List, no date).

CURRENT EVENTS—THE 1990s

Electoral Politics

These efforts culminated in the 1992 elections; that year was proclaimed the Year of the Woman. Perhaps as a consequence of the nation's viewing a panel of white male senators deliberating the Anita Hill case, women swept into office in unprecedented numbers. In 1992 the number of women in the Senate tripled to six, including the first African American female senator (Carol Moseley-Braun) and two female senators from the same state (Barbara Boxer and Dianne Feinstein from California). In the same election, the number of women in the House of Representatives increased greatly, from 28 to 47, including 13 women of color. Recently, a seventh woman (Kay Bailey Hutchinson) was elected to the Senate. Still, women make up only 7 percent of the Senate and less than 11 percent of the House membership.

Perhaps even more significant, more women are serving in elected positions in state and local offices, which serve as a pipeline for national office. Since 1969 the number of women in state legislatures has increased fivefold, to 1,517 in 1993, so that women now constitute more than 20 percent of the membership of all state legislatures. Similarly, 19 of the 100 largest cities in the country have female mayors, and in cities with populations of more than 30,000, the number of female mayors increased 16 percent just in the last election cycle (Center for the American Woman and Politics, 1993).

In addition to Emily's List, which is now one of the largest political action committees in the nation, there are 10 other national women's political action committees and 42 women's political action committees in 16 states, which have raised nearly $12 million (Weismiller & Dempsey, 1993). Recently, Political Action for Candidate Election (PACE), the political action committee of NASW, which is in the top 5 percent of all political action committees, compiled a national directory listing 104 women social workers in elected positions. These included, in addition to Senator Mikulski, 31 members of state legislatures, 18 on county or borough boards, 21 on city councils, and 32 on school boards, as well as two mayors, a judge, and an attorney general (NASW, 1993).

PACE has supported large numbers of progressive women, as well as men who support NASW's positions, and has been of particular assistance to NASW members who have run for office. One of the practice advancement priorities of the 1993 NASW Delegate Assembly is to recruit, train, and promote social workers for elective and appointive office. Given that 75 percent to 80 percent of NASW's membership is women, this means the promotion of more social work women to policy positions in government.

Clinton Administration

Some people attribute the changes that have been occurring since the November 1992 election to the "Hillary Syndrome." Although other presidents' wives had been involved in particular projects, not since the time of Eleanor Roosevelt has any president's wife taken on the breadth and depth of policy issues as her central role. In appointing his wife to oversee health reform, President Clinton broke with tradition. The First Lady was not to be engaged in some peripheral activity but was to have a full-time, albeit unpaid, position of leadership in the most significant policy change attempted by the federal government since the establishment of social security in 1935. Hillary Clinton provides a role model of an intelligent, effective, knowledgeable, and successful female policy leader.

The president also broke with tradition by appointing more women, including women of color, to top-ranking positions in the Cabinet. Not surprisingly, all these women are in positions that affect domestic social and health policy. They include Donna Shalala, secretary of health and human services—the largest agency in the federal government—who has responsibility for Medicare, Medicaid, and social security, as well as public assistance and child welfare programs; Hazel O'Leary, secretary of energy; Janet Reno, the first female attorney general, who was lambasted as sounding more like a social worker than a prosecutor in her approach to juvenile crime (Johnston, 1993); and Joycelyn Elders, the daughter of a sharecropper, surgeon general of the United States (who was forced to resign in December 1994). Clinton's first Supreme Court appointment was Ruth Bader Ginsburg, who joined Justice Sandra Day O'Connor (who had been appointed by President Reagan), assuring that from now on there will no longer be one "token" woman's seat on the bench.

Many other women, among them leaders in social work, have been appointed to subcabinet positions. Ada Deer, a Native American social worker; Augusta Kappner, an African American social worker; and Wendy Sherman, who previously served as an aide to Senator Mikulski, were named, respectively, assistant secretary for Indian Affairs, U.S. Department of the Interior; assistant secretary for vocational and adult education, U.S. Department of Education; and assistant secretary, Office of Legislative Affairs, U.S. Department of State.

IMPACT OF GENDER ON PUBLIC POLICY

Following the demise of the Soviet Union and the end of the Cold War, coupled with the residue of a dozen years of neglect and cutbacks in domestic inner-city programs, the 1992 national elections refocused the nation's attention on a domestic agenda. President Clinton proposed major changes in both health and welfare policy. Issues of teenage pregnancy, child care, family leave, birth control, and abortion, which were previously considered peripheral women's issues, took front and center stage on the national agenda.

The Center for the American Woman in Politics at Rutgers University has found that gender does make a difference in politics and political issues. When researchers asked female and male state legislators to prioritize issues, almost three times as many women (11 percent) as men (3 percent) gave children and families top priority; more than twice as many women (14 percent) as men (6 percent) listed health care; and more than twice as many women (10 percent) as men (4 percent) named women's rights (Center for the American Woman and Politics, 1991). Conversely, issues that have traditionally been the province of men— such as military expenditures—are now being addressed by women, such as Representative Patricia Schroeder. Moreover, women in these leadership positions are redefining the policy agenda. An example has been the leadership of women in Congress in forcing the armed services to address the issue of sexual harassment in the military.

Not only are the national issues different, but how women conduct business also is different. The same study of state legislators found that almost twice as many female (57 percent) as male (32 percent) legislators favored conducting business in public view; 50 percent of female legislators as opposed to 36 percent of male legislators cited citizens as very helpful sources of support, and 79 percent of female legislators versus 59 percent of male legislators valued access of economically disadvantaged people to the legislature (Center for the American Woman and Politics, 1991). The study also found that women are more responsive to groups that have previously been denied full access to the policy-making process and are more likely to seek governmental solutions to implement policy goals when money is involved.

These findings seem to support the work of Gilligan (1982) and other feminist theorists who contend that women and men have different ways of approaching decision making and leadership. They operationalize this feminist approach as more inclusive; less hierarchical; more prone to sharing power; and more concerned with social justice, empowerment, and choice, particularly for women and people of color (Brandwein, 1985, 1986; Gilligan, 1982; Jagger & Struhl, 1978).

CONCLUSION

Clearly, women, and particularly female social workers, have been involved in and have pro-
foundly affected social policy. Nevertheless, their proportions and influences have waxed and waned over the years as a reflection of what was occurring in the larger social context. In times when women's rights and equality were in the forefront, women were more prominent in social policy leadership. In more-traditional and regressive periods, women's influence and strength ebbed.

We are at present seeing a revitalization of women in leadership positions in society, a greater societal emphasis on social policy issues that were once considered women's issues, and the emergence of an alternative approach to policy-making that some people have styled feminist or gender related. Concurrently, NASW, whose membership is more than three-quarters female, is now actively promoting women for political leadership. Whether this is another turn of the cycle, or whether this is a trend that will continue to increase, is yet to be known.

REFERENCES

Addams, J. (1960). *Twenty years at Hull-House.* New York: New American Library. (Original work published 1910)
Bakke, L., & Edson, J. (1977). Women in management: Moving up. *Social Work, 22,* 512–514.
Baumheier, E., & Schorr, A. (1977). Social policy. In J. B. Turner (Ed.-in-Chief), *Encyclopedia of social work* (17th ed., Vol. 2, pp. 1453–1462). Washington, DC: National Association of Social Workers.
Blumberg, D. (1971). Goldmark, Josephine Clara. In R. Morris (Ed.-in-Chief), *Encyclopedia of social work* (16th ed., Vol. 1, pp. 478–479). New York: National Association of Social Workers.
Brager, G., & Michael, J. (1969). The sex distribution in social welfare: Causes and consequences. *Social Casework, 50*(10), 595–601.
Brandwein, R. (1981). Toward the feminization of community and organization practice. *Social Development Issues, 5*(2–3), 180–193.
Brandwein, R. (1982). Toward androgyny in community and organizational practice. In A. Weick & S. T. Vandiver (Eds.), *Women, power and change* (pp. 158–170). Washington, DC: National Association of Social Workers.
Brandwein, R. (1984). Where are the women—And why: An analysis of women administrators in Jewish communal services. *Journal of Jewish Communal Service, 60*(3), 204–213.
Brandwein, R. (1985). Feminist thought structure: An alternative paradigm of social change for social justice. In D. Gil & E. Gil (Eds.), *Toward social and economic justice* (pp. 169–181). New York: Schocken Books.
Brandwein, R. (1986). A feminist approach to social policy. In N. Van Den Bergh & L. B. Cooper (Eds.), *Feminist visions for social work* (pp. 250–261). Silver Spring, MD: National Association of Social Workers.
Brandwein, R. (1987). Women in macropractice. In A. Minahan (Ed.-in-Chief), *Encyclopedia of social work* (18th ed., Vol. 2, pp. 881–892). Silver Spring, MD: National Association of Social Workers.

Center for the American Woman and Politics. (1991). *Impact of women in public office*. New Brunswick, NJ: Rutgers University Press.

Center for the American Woman and Politics. (1993). *Women in elective office*. New Brunswick, NJ: Rutgers University Press.

Cook, B. (1992). *Eleanor Roosevelt, volume one*. New York: Viking Press.

Council on Social Work Education. (1977). *Manual of accrediting standards for graduate professional schools of social work*. New York: Author.

Council on Social Work Education. (1978/1984/1989/1991). *Statistics on social work education in the United States*. Alexandria, VA: Author.

Council on Social Work Education. (1993). *Directory of colleges and universities with accredited social work degree programs*. New York and Alexandria, VA: Author.

Ehrenreich, J. (1985). *The altruistic imagination*. Ithaca, NY: Cornell University Press.

Emily's List. (no date). *Emily's List: The facts*. Washington, DC: Author.

Ezell, H., & Odewahn, C. (1980). An empirical inquiry of variables impacting women in management in public social service organizations. *Administration in Social Work, 4*(4), 53–70.

Fanshel, D. (1976). Status differentials: Men and women in social work. *Social Work, 21*, 448–454.

Fortune, A., & Hanks, L. (1988). Gender inequalities in early social work careers. *Social Work, 33*, 221–226.

Friedan, B. (1963). *The feminine mystique*. New York: Dell.

Germain, C., & Hartman, A. (1980). People and ideas in the history of social work practice. *Social Casework, 61*(6), 323–331.

Gibelman, M., & Schervish, P. (1993). *Who we are: The social work labor force as reflected in the NASW membership*. Washington, DC: NASW Press.

Gil, D. (1990). *Unravelling social policy* (4th ed.). Cambridge, MA: Schenkman.

Gilligan, C. (1982). *In a different voice: Psychological theory and women's development*. Cambridge, MA: Harvard University Press.

Giovannoni, J., & Purvine, M. (1973). The myth of the social work matriarchy. In *Social welfare forum* (pp. 166-195). New York: Columbia University Press.

Goldmark, J. (1912). *Fatigue and efficiency: A study in industry*. New York: Charities Publications Committee.

Hamilton, G. (1962). Editor's page. *Social Work, 7*(2), 128.

Jagger, A., & Struhl, P. (1978). *Feminist frameworks*. New York: McGraw-Hill.

Jennings, P., & Daley, M. (1979). Sex discrimination in social work careers. *Social Work Research & Abstracts, 15*(2), 17–21.

Johnston, D. (1993, May 1). Washington at work: Reno's popularity rises from ashes of disaster. *New York Times*, p. 9.

Kadushin, A. (1976). Men in a women's profession. *Social Work, 21*, 440–447.

Knapman, S. (1977). Sexual discrimination in family agencies. *Social Work, 22*, 461–465.

Kramer, R., & Specht, H. (Eds.). (1969). *Readings in community organization practice*. Englewood Cliffs, NJ: Prentice Hall.

Kravetz, D. (1976). Sexism in a women's profession. *Social Work, 21*, 421–426.

Longres, J. (1987a). Hamilton, Gordon. In A. Minahan (Ed.-in-Chief), *Encyclopedia of social work* (18th ed., Vol. 2, pp. 926–927). Silver Spring, MD: National Association of Social Workers.

Longres, J. (1987b). Lassalle, Beatriz. In A. Minahan (Ed.-in-Chief), *Encyclopedia of social work* (18th ed., Vol. 2, p. 931). Silver Spring, MD: National Association of Social Workers.

Longres, J. (1987c). Richmond, Mary Ellen. In A. Minahan (Ed.-in-Chief), *Encyclopedia of social work* (18th ed., Vol. 2, p. 937). Silver Spring, MD: National Association of Social Workers.

Lundberg, F., & Farnham, M. (1947). *Modern woman: The lost sex*. New York: Grosset & Dunlap.

Mayer, R., Moroney, R., & Morris, R. (Eds.). (1974). *Centrally planned change*. Urbana: University of Illinois Press.

Minahan, A. (Ed.-in-Chief). (1987). *Encyclopedia of social work* (18th ed.). Silver Spring, MD: National Association of Social Workers.

Muller v. Oregon, 208 U.S. 412 (1908).

Munson, E. (1982). Perceptions of female social workers toward administrative positions. *Social Casework, 631*, 54–59.

National Association of Social Workers. (1993). *Social workers serving in elective offices 1993*. Washington, DC: Author.

National Conference on Social Welfare. (1935–1981). *Social welfare forum*. New York: Columbia University Press.

National Conference on Social Welfare. (1958–1961). *Community organization: Selected papers from annual NCSW forums*. New York: Columbia University Press.

National Labor Relations Act of 1935. Ch. 372, 49 Stat. 499.

Peebles-Wilkins, W. (1987). Fernandis, Sarah A. Collins. In A. Minahan (Ed.-in-Chief), *Encyclopedia of social work* (18th ed., Vol. 2, p. 923). Silver Spring, MD: National Association of Social Workers.

Quam, J. (1987). Addams, Jane. In A. Minahan (Ed.-in-Chief), *Encyclopedia of social work* (18th ed., Vol. 2, p. 913). Silver Spring, MD: National Association of Social Workers.

Roe v. Wade, 410 U.S. 113 (1973).

Rubenstein, H. (1981). Women in organizations: A review of research and some implications for teaching social work practice. *Journal of Education for Social Work, 17*(3), 20–27.

Scharf, L. (1983). "The forgotten woman": Working women, the New Deal, and women's organizations. In L. Scharf & J. Jensen (Eds.), *Decades of discontent: The women's movement, 1920–1940* (pp. 243–259). Boston: Northeastern University Press.

Scotch, C. (1971). Sex status in social work: Grist for women's liberation. *Social Work, 16*, 5–11.

Sutton, J. (1982). Sex discrimination among social workers. *Social Work, 27*, 211–217.

Szakacs, J. (1977, February). Is social work a women's profession? *Womenpower*, pp. 1–4.

Turner, J. B. (Ed.-in-Chief). (1977). *Encyclopedia of social work* (17th ed.). Washington, DC: National Association of Social Workers.

Weiner, R., & Engel, S. (1977, June). *The status of women in Jewish communal services*. Paper presented at the National Conference of Jewish Communal Service.

Weismiller, T., & Dempsey, D. (1993). *Women in politics: Will social workers convert activism into leadership?* Unpublished manuscript. Washington, DC: National Association of Social Workers.

West, W. (1933). Social work as a profession. In *Social work yearbook, 1933* (pp. 492–496). New York: Russell Sage Foundation.

Wylie, P. (1942). *A generation of vipers.* New York: Rinehart.

FURTHER READING

Chafetz, J. (1974). *Masculine/feminine or human.* Itasca, IL: F. E. Peacock.

Cook, B. (1992). *Eleanor Roosevelt.* New York: Viking.

DuBois, E. (Ed.). (1981). *Elizabeth Cady Stanton/Susan B. Anthony: Correspondence, writings, speeches.* New York: Schocken Books.

Helgesen, S. (1990). *The female advantage: Women's ways of leadership.* New York: Doubleday.

Horner, M. (1972). Toward an understanding of achievement related conflicts in women. *Journal of Social Issues, 28*(2), 157–175.

Kanter, R. (1977). *Men and women of the corporation.* New York: Basic Books.

Martin, P., & Chernesky, R. (1989). Women's prospects for leadership in social welfare: A political economy perspective. *Administration in Social Work, 113*(3/4), 117–143.

Nes, J., & Iadicola, P. (1989). Toward a definition of feminist social work: A comparison of liberal, radical, and socialist models. *Social Work, 34*, 12–21.

Padgett, D. (1993). Women and management: A conceptual framework. *Administration in Social Work, 17*(4), 57–75.

Yasas, F., & Mehta, V. (1991). *Exploring feminist visions: Case studies on social justice issues.* Pune, India, and Vienna, Austria: Streevani & International Association of Schools of Social Work.

Ruth A. Brandwein, PhD, is professor of social policy, School of Social Welfare, Health Science Center, University at Stony Brook, State University of New York, Stony Brook, NY 11794.

For further information see

Advocacy; Citizen Participation; Community Organization; Ethics and Values; International and Comparitive Social Welfare; National Association of Social Workers; Planning and Management Professions; Policy Analysis; Social Development; Social Planning; Social Welfare Policy; Social Work Profession Overview; Supervision and Consultation; Women Overview.

Key Words	
leadership	social welfare
politics	women
social policy	

Workers' Compensation

See Unemployment Compensation and Workers' Compensation

Y

Young, Whitney Moore, Jr.

See Biographies section, Volume 3

Youngdahl, Benjamin Emanuel

See Biographies section, Volume 3

Younghusband, Dame Eileen

See Biographies section, Volume 3

Youth Services

Fernando J. Galan

Youth services agencies are social services organizations that are designed and established to provide a broad array of services to meet the needs of young people. A wide variety of programs and activities in these agencies are aimed at helping youths meet specific developmental needs, ranging from educational and recreational needs to character building and adjustment. Youth services agencies are structured as groups of institutional and residual programs to provide specific activities to meet particular objectives.

As society has become more urbanized and youths have become a larger sector of the population, public and private resources have been extended to address the development of youths and the prevention of delinquency. Newer efforts have incorporated youth services as part of an overall strategy aimed at family preservation and moral welfare. Youth services agencies exist because there is a recognized need for programs to assist youths in developing a sense of competence for responsible adulthood and to provide training for work-related roles. Also, through prevention activities, youth services agencies help young people address the challenges of peer pressure, drugs, crime, violence, and family disruption, while also providing more in-depth intervention services to youths who are afflicted by the stresses and consequences of family crises and social disorganization (Brandeis University, 1989).

Youth services agencies are designed to provide support for youths throughout the developmental life cycle. This support includes services for infants and children, older children, early adolescents, adolescents, and early adults. Youth services agencies usually address various themes of service. Services designed for infants and children, including day care and after-school services, focus primarily on healthy human and personality development, parental relationships, and adjustments of children to their families and communities. Services designed for adolescents focus mainly on friendship groups, special interests, and organized, adult-supervised educational and recreational activities. An increased number of special youth services for young people with disabilities, alternative lifestyles, or different cultural backgrounds have added to the repertoire of resources available to adolescents who wrestle with identity-formation issues and emerging relationships with other youths. Services designed for older adolescents focus mostly on developing competencies—educational or social—that help facilitate the transition into early adulthood. Services range from job training programs, leadership development programs, and sexual education and relationship training programs to mental health counseling or rehabilitation, custodial, correctional, or treatment programs. Counseling and individual guidance characterize many youth services agencies, and adults are usually involved in leadership roles to influence the character and human development process.

BACKGROUND

The concept of the youth services agency developed during the growth of volunteerism in the American social welfare system between the Civil War and the passage of the Social Security Act of 1935. Youth services agencies have used the services of parent volunteers and older youths at all levels of policy and planning. The basic programs of these agencies paralleled social reform efforts of the settlement house movement in the mid- to late 1800s. Programs were designed to prevent dependence and to provide various services to help youths develop. These activities focused on youths' moral, religious, and social welfare.

Much of the origins of youth services agencies were influenced by the recreation movement. Traditional youth services agencies included recreational and leisure-time programs, even though remediation and rehabilitation programs were central.

Definitions

Over the years, eligibility requirements for many youth services programs have been determined on the basis of their definitions of "youth" and "adolescence." In the early 1970s the Panel of Youth of the President's Science Advisory Committee chose the arbitrary age range of 14 to 24 years as constituting adulthood. Even though the terms youth and adolescence are used for different ages and with various meanings, youth generally encompasses the traditional teenage years, from 13 to 19. Standard definitions of youth use this age range and describe youth as the actual physiological process separating childhood from adulthood; young people in this age range constitute an ambiguous social and economic group that has moved beyond childhood but has yet to assume adult roles and responsibilities. Still other agencies incorporate more expanded definitions of youth in their eligibility requirements and include latency-age children. Child guidance centers or clinics, often supported by private funds or governmental entities, may also offer services to children.

Types of Services

Youth services agencies offer various types of services and provide a wide range of benefits, including general guidance and counseling, recreational and leisure activities, information and referral, prevention and developmental activities, clinical treatment and intervention, networking, and political consciousness-raising. Although they typically involve day and early-evening formats, these agencies also provide various weekend and extended-period services delivered in different arrangements, including youth-to-youth, adult-and-youth-to-youth, and adult-to-youth services (Conrad & Hedin, 1987). Feldman (1987) stated that youth services agencies are basically designed around four basic objectives: (1) goal attainment programs that help young people develop skills, values, and behavioral patterns to facilitate their transition to responsible adulthood; (2) adaptation programs that help youths adjust to changes in their immediate social systems, such as families, neighborhoods, or communities; (3) integrative programs that help youths establish connections with other youths; (4) tension-management programs that assist troubled young people through services designed to provide guidance and social control. Feldman noted that these objectives create the types of programs and benefits that characterize youth services.

OPERATIONS OF AGENCIES

Developmental and Inspirational

Youth services agencies reflect variations in ideology and are designed to provide a network of benefits to youths who are dependent on an agency's purpose or mandate. Agencies whose broad purposes are for recreation and character development are typically governed by a local board of directors that oversees the policy and planning functions of the organization. Such agencies derive their support from memberships that are open to families. Examples of such agencies are the YMCA and the Boy Scouts of America.

Other youth agencies are local or regional chapters of national organizations and are formed by professional and civic activists who strive to bring a fuller range of specialized services related to educational advancement and the development of personal leadership among youths. Their purpose is to inspire young people and to offer training in personal problem solving, cultural awareness, and community citizenship. Examples of these types of organizations are the Mexican American Youth Organization, Aspira, and League of United Latin American Citizens Youth Councils.

Religious

Another type of youth services agency is founded on religious or spiritual bases and is usually sponsored by an organized religion or a denominational entity of a religious organization. These agencies encourage either specialized or ecumenical services that are designed to develop in youths a stronger traditional religious affiliation while providing an array of educational, developmental, and recreational activities to preserve the family, develop social competencies in youths, and instill a pride in traditional cultural values and beliefs. Youths served by these organizations are exposed to encounter and sensitivity training, race relations and cultural appreciation training, and specialized encounters on youth relationships, the world of work, and reconciliation and management of differences in families. Examples of these organizations include Roman Catholic youth organizations, B'nai B'rith youth organizations, Jewish community centers, and United Methodist youth organizations.

School-Related
Other youth services agencies are school-related and offer youths a series of options. Some provide after-school extracurricular activities that are centered on cultural, social, or civic orientations. These programs are often operated under the auspices of local independent school districts and provide a series of activities for youths to practice citizenship, engage in dialogue, or promote their own ethnic or cultural backgrounds. Other school-related programs are designed to provide options for students who are identified as being at high risk for expulsion. These programs offer problem solving, emotional, individual, and family counseling, and information and referral. They also offer personal leadership skill training to help youths deal with a myriad of social issues, such as their parents' divorce or alcohol and drug use, gang pressure, violence, and crime. These types of programs provide support services in an attempt to help youths develop the skills necessary to confront issues that identify them as being at high risk. They have emerged as a result of newer community-school partnerships and can be structured as off-campus programs or as on-campus services. Examples include Communities-In-Schools and various high-risk programs funded by school districts.

Community Services
Service activities form the central objective of other youth services agencies that attempt to mobilize youths to provide various kinds of community services to needy people as a way of developing citizenship. School-based voluntary programs are designed to create opportunities for youths to contribute labor and talent. The service ethic is instilled incrementally, with experiences appropriate to the developmental age of young people, in an effort to promote adolescent development. Individual- and group-service learning projects create one-to-one service experiences that encourage close relationships between adults and youths, and foster intergenerational understanding.

Youths contribute millions of hours of service annually through state, federal, and local programs. Youth Service America (1988) estimated that the monetary value of high school students' annual contribution of 17 million hours of unpaid service is $59.5 million. Examples of these types of programs include Fresh Force of Minneapolis, Pittsburgh's Oasis Program, and Indianapolis's Dropouts in Touch program.

Youth Community Service, a joint project of the Constitutional Rights Foundation and the Los Angeles Unified School District, is the largest program. It operates in more than 22 Los Angeles high schools and involves more than 5,000 students—largely racial and ethnic group membership—in service. Youth Service America, a national information clearinghouse, reports on more than 50 state and local full-time youth corps, nearly 500 campus-based service programs, and more than 3,000 school-based programs, and offers technical assistance to start youth services programs. Youth volunteer corps are a means by which young adults can develop and provide service. The Peace Corps, Volunteers in Service to America (VISTA), and the National Health Service Corps are examples of such service at the national level.

The City Volunteer Corps of New York City has advanced volunteer youth efforts in the delivery of human services. The New York City model spawned Youth Volunteer Corps of greater Kansas City. Various kinds of youth services agencies exist under public and private auspices, including many residual and institutional efforts. Collaborations with various youth networks nationwide have created a new form of youth services. This resulted in using modern-day technology and combinations of designs in service delivery to create multiple kinds of services networks.

HISTORICAL DEVELOPMENT

Late 19th Century
Much of what is known about the historical development of youth services agencies can be traced to the late 19th century, when many organizations that were concerned with the welfare of young people created such programs to help youths develop morally. In 1851 the YMCA was organized to help provide moral guidance to boys away from home and to instill in youths an identification with traditional Protestantism. A few years later, in 1866, the YWCA was formed to provide similar guidance to young women who were members in good standing of any evangelical church. As newly formed youth organizations of the industrial period, the YMCA and the YWCA created programs

for youths that served the social, spiritual, intellectual, and physical needs of young people. Papell (1977) noted that the YMCA was a forerunner of the classical conceptualization of the function of social work: remediation or treatment, prevention, and provision.

As Roman Catholic and Jewish agencies were created along similar themes, they became part of a settlement house movement that helped immigrants deal with issues of acculturation and assimilation during the Americanization process. According to Papell (1977), these services helped stabilize youths in their homes and gave them opportunities for education and healthy expressive leisure time in their neighborhoods.

1900 to 1930
The combined theme of youth services agencies—to provide leisure-time programs and to engage in social reform—marked the period of 1900 to 1930. Jane Addams was one of the first to bring attention to the need for actions to strengthen the family and to provide educational opportunities, and recreational resources for adolescents. Youth services that were aimed at providing leisure-time services and educational supports began to form part of the emerging social welfare system during this era of social reform.

New youth organizations were founded during the first part of the 20th century. These included the YWCA, which became a national organization in 1906, the Boys Scouts of America (1910), the Camp Fire Girls (1910), and the Girl Scouts of America (1912). The National Federation of Settlements was created in 1911 as one of the first networks in youth services, and the National Jewish Welfare Board was formed in 1917. The federal government contributed to the emerging youth services agency field when in 1914 Congress, under the auspices of the Cooperative Extension Service established to train youths in farming and homemaking, authorized the 4-H (Head, Heart, Hands, and Health) program for youths ages nine to 19.

New Deal to Post–World War II
In the 1930s the federal government began funding the expansion of youth services under President Franklin D. Roosevelt's New Deal. Both the Civilian Conservation Corps and the National Youth Administration provided employment opportunities for youths to alleviate the unemployment, demoralization, and social chaos of the Great Depression. These government programs provided youths with part-time employment and addressed their vocational, educational, and leisure-time needs.

Youth services developed more fully after World War II and during the mid-20th century. In 1961 the Juvenile Delinquency and Youth Offenses Control Act provided funding for many demonstration projects in disadvantaged urban areas in an attempt to curb juvenile delinquency. Traditional youth services agencies and programs funded during this period provided recreational opportunities for youths, but new policies in youth services now sought to use federal funds to equip youths with skills and resources to facilitate their full participation in the community. Youth services programs began to address issues of unemployment, family breakdown, urban crisis, racism, and teenage pregnancy.

Late 1960s to 1980s
In 1967 the President's Commission on Law Enforcement and Administration of Justice recommended the establishment of youth services bureaus to provide a viable alternative to official juvenile court proceedings at the local level. Accepting referrals of youths in trouble from agencies, schools, and police, youth services bureaus, in addition to the traditional recreational and leisure-time activities, provided individual, family, and group counseling; job referral; drug treatment; and legal services. The advocacy role in behalf of youths was developed as an important function of agencies. Financed by a combination of federal, state, and local funds, youth services bureaus began to stimulate community involvement, but found themselves in situations in which they alienated agencies that attempted to take action against youths. The later local juvenile conference committees provide a more collaborative form of involvement of the community with the government.

When 18-year-olds won the right to vote, in 1971, traditional youth services agencies had the new pressure of responding to youths' desire to enter the policy-making process. With the advent of young people's assumption of a more pronounced voice in decision making, youth services agencies began to expand their programming. With the passage of the Juvenile Justice and Delinquency Prevention Act of 1974, the federal government began to fund new youth services to help youths become more productive citizens, and the Administration of Children, Youth, and Families became a strong promoter of youth services.

The role of the federal government since the 1970s has been to finance the development of youth-serving agencies. Feldman (1987) noted that in the early 1970s and 1980s, many youth services agencies addressed such concerns as parental separation and divorce, sex-role development, substance abuse, environmental stress, racism, teenage parenting, and neighborhood development. Organizations, such as the National Collaboration for Youth, began to coordinate the efforts of various youth agencies in 1973.

MODERNIZATION OF YOUTH SERVICES AGENCIES

The youth services agencies of today are influenced by geography, structure, mandate, funding constraints, and programming. They are also affected by whom they serve, what benefits they can provide, their organization for delivering services, and their modes of finance. Because the population of young people includes more and more members of ethnic minority groups, an increasing number of programs are being reconceptualized to be appropriate, adequate, and relevant for the youths they serve. These demographic considerations are critical when youth policy must consider the nature of programming and the provision of services, the multicultural aspects of benefits, and the developing cross-cultural scientific knowledge base that undergirds services. With the advent of multiple nontraditional approaches to service delivery, many existing youth services agencies have responded to the needs of modern-day youths who live in a menacing urban and violent postindustrial information society. New challenges and new problems have created new mandates for youth services agencies, and traditional agencies have redirected their programming to respond appropriately (Sherraden, 1992).

Increase in Serious Problems

The mandates for youth services at the end of the 20th century appear to be grounded in disturbing trends among youths. According to Feldman (1987), the literature in the mid-1980s revealed an increasing emphasis on research on and direct services for youths and those who were at risk for running away, committing suicide, and developing depression, and that rehabilitation and prevention programs expanded from the traditional social services or psychiatric settings to schools and recreational centers. With the acknowledgment that schools were social institutions that could provide a multitude of after-school programs, youth services quickly expanded during the 1990s to incorporate new approaches to address the problems of young people in classrooms during evening hours through the joint efforts of community laypeople and professional social workers.

Youth services agencies have expanded their sources of financing to include innovative arrangements with the private sector like community-corporate partnerships. One such partnership is the Basic Employment Skills Training program in Houston, which provides specialized training for young mothers who have dropped out of school, applied for welfare, and attempted to reenter the mainstream. In this type of agency, community professionals and social workers collaborate to provide vocational training and employment skills training, individual and family counseling, and grooming and personal leadership classes (National Service Secretariat, 1988).

Mental Health Factors

Social and mental health issues that create a demand for youth services with a markedly mental health focus also characterize modern-day youth services agencies. With the increase in addictive behaviors and the abuse of cocaine, crack, and "ice," as well as the abuse of synthetic pleasure drugs, such as "MDMA," "ecstasy," and "bliss," the incidence of adolescent suicide and homicide, premarital sex, eating disorders, and alcohol abuse has also increased. Such behaviors have given rise to new problems among youths, such as acquired immune deficiency syndrome (AIDS), drug-induced paranoias, high-risk pregnancies, and hypertension. The rise in drug abuse; dropout and expulsion rates from schools; and youth crime, gang violence, and the use of handguns are new areas that youth services agencies have been asked to address in the 1990s (Center for Population Options, 1990).

Attention to Diversity

Youth services agencies have developed to respond to these social and mental health issues within a specialized organizational structure and format aimed at increasing sensitivity and respect for diversity. Youth services for different racial and ethnic groups were created during the 1990s to address the needs of African American youths, Chicano and Mexican American youths, Asian and Pacific Islander youths, and American Indian youths.

Other youth programs have designed relevant and appropriate services to assist gay and lesbian youths. Services for young women, as well as programs for disabled youths, recognize the different needs of a diverse population of young people who seek services throughout their developmental years. An example of such agencies is Jack and Jill of America, a nationwide nonprofit youth services organization founded in the 1930s that serves African American youths. Originally formed by mothers to combat their children's problems in school, Jack and Jill of America has grown to more than

200 chapters nationwide and serves youths of various ethnic backgrounds.

YOUTH SERVICES AS PART OF THE TOTAL SERVICE NETWORK

New partnerships among community agencies, schools, and private businesses are providing multiple services to youths who are challenged by social, educational, economic, and psychological needs. These collaborative efforts are designed to reach a broader youth audience, provide multiple benefits and services, and deliver after-school services during the late-afternoon and evening hours (Ianni, 1993). These types of programs incorporate creative modes of financing and use contributions, grants, and in-kind services (National Service Secretariat, 1988). An example is the Students Identified as High Risk for Expulsion Support Program in Edinburg, Texas. This program, funded by the local independent school district, receives contributions from a local university and from various corporations. It uses professional social workers, student interns, community counselors, and citizens to provide an array of services to help youths remain in school.

Examples of Youth Organizations

Various youth services organizations have been developed to serve various aspects of youths' needs. Some provide specialized services, such as policy analysis, for youths, and others provide services for special populations, including youths from ethnic and racial groups, gay and lesbian youths, and youths with disabilities.

ARROW Incorporated. Founded in 1949, ARROW (Americans for Restitution and Righting of Old Wrongs) is an agency, based in Washington, DC, that is dedicated to the advancement of American Indians and seeks to help them achieve a better educational, cultural, and economic standard and provide needy individuals with health care and drug and child abuse prevention. The agency also provides scholarships for American Indian youths.

Covenant House. One of the most visible youth services agencies in the United States, Covenant House was founded in 1972 to provide crisis counseling and immediate, short-term care for youths up to the age of 21. Its services include food, shelter, clothing, medical treatment, and legal assistance.

Hetrick–Martin Institute. Founded in 1981, this agency informs and educates the public and youth services agencies about the needs of gay and lesbian youths, including group and individual counseling and referral, outreach services, and

education on human sexuality and AIDS. Based in New York City, it helped established and sponsors the Harvey Milk School, a New York City high school for gay and lesbian students.

Indian Youth of America. Founded in 1978, this youth organization is dedicated to improving the lives of American Indian children and works to provide opportunities and experiences that will aid their educational, career, cultural, and personal growth. The organization also provides career-awareness and placement services, parenting classes, and athletic clinics.

National Black Youth Leadership Council. Founded in 1983, this organization conducts workshops for groups involved with African American youths and the academic and leadership development of ethnic-minority students. The council advises educators and parents on their role and responsibility to display leadership and success skills to youths with whom they come into contact. In addition, it conducts training workshops for educators and parents on cultural diversity, multiculturalism, and problems of bigotry and racism.

National Center for Youth Law. Founded in 1978, this agency employs attorneys full time to provide assistance to legal services programs and private attorneys throughout the country who represent poor youths, especially adolescents from poor families who may be involved in issues of abuse and neglect, termination of parental rights, foster care, health, and housing discrimination.

National Network of Runaway and Youth Services. This network of youth services agencies, based in Washington, DC, addresses the concerns of runaway, homeless, and other at-risk youths and promotes the development of responsive local services for them and their families. It acts as a clearinghouse and sponsors educational programs for policymakers and the public.

Teenage Assembly of America. The members of this Honolulu-based organization are elementary school through college students. The purpose of the organization is to involve young people in constructive community activities to overcome juvenile delinquency through their own efforts.

Youth Counseling League. Based in New York City, this outpatient psychiatric clinic serves emotionally disturbed adolescents and young adults ages 12 to 25.

Youth for Understanding. Founded in 1951, this agency provides educational opportunities for young people who want to learn more about people, languages, and cultures through international student exchanges. It administers scholarship programs for students in cooperation with other governments, the U.S. Senate, professional associations, and youth groups.

Youth Policy Institute. Based in Washington, DC, this organization monitors federal youth policy and provides comprehensive updates to youth-serving agencies on the development of policy by the federal government, Congress, and public-interest groups.

Youth Resources. Founded in 1961, this agency creates, authorizes, registers, and sponsors institutes that use an interdisciplinary approach to conduct investigative studies in specialized fields, such as educational and occupational therapy and the teaching of business management and the free enterprise system.

Youth Service America. Founded in 1985, this organization promotes and develops youth services programs in schools, colleges, and community-based agencies and seeks to organize and mobilize youths for community service.

Youth Suicide National Center. Established in 1985, this national agency coordinates and supports efforts to reduce youth suicide and develops and disseminates educational materials, programs, and services to the public. One of its purposes is to establish model programs for the prevention of youth suicide.

As youth services continue to be conceptualized as part of family services and as more youths become involved in social welfare policy, collaborative efforts are expected to increase and provide direction for the development of cross-cultural programs for youths.

REFERENCES

Brandeis University, Center for Human Resources. (1989). *Working it out: Performance management strategies for increasing services to at-risk youth.* Waltham, MA: Author.
Center for Population Options. (1990). *Reaching high-risk youth through model AIDS education programs: A case-by-case study.* Washington, DC: Author.
Conrad, D., & Hedin, D. (1987). *Youth service: A guidebook for developing and operating effective programs.* Washington, DC: Independent Sector.
Feldman, R. A. (1987). Youth service agencies. In A. Minahan (Ed.-in-Chief), *Encyclopedia of social work* (18th ed., Vol. 2, pp. 901–906). Silver Spring, MD: National Association of Social Workers.
Ianni, F.A.J. (1993). *Joining youth needs and program services: Urban diversity series no. 104.* New York: ERIC Clearinghouse on Urban Education.
Juvenile Delinquency and Youth Offenses Control Act of 1961. P.L. 87-274, 75 Stat. 572.
Juvenile Justice and Delinquency Prevention Act of 1974. P.L. 93-415, 88 Stat. 1109.
National Service Secretariat. (1988). *National service: An action agenda for the 1990's: Coalition for national service.* Washington, DC: Author.
Papell, C. P. (1977). Youth service agencies. In J. B. Turner (Ed.-in-Chief), *Encyclopedia of social work* (17th ed., pp. 1598–1608). Washington, DC: National Association of Social Workers.
Sherraden, M. (1992). *Community-based youth services in international perspective.* Washington, DC: Carnegie Council on Adolescent Development.
Social Security Act. Ch. 531, 49 Stat. 620 (1935).
Youth Service America. (1988). Pathways to success: Citizenship through service. In *The forgotten half: Pathways to success for America's youth and young families* (pp. 79–90). Washington, DC: Youth and America's Future: The William T. Grant Foundation Commission.

FURTHER READING

Carnegie Council on Adolescent Development. (1989). *Turning points: Preparing youth for the 21st century.* Waldorf, MD: Author.
Dryfoos, J. G. (1990). *Adolescents at risk.* New York: Oxford University Press.
Henriksson, B. (1991). Youth as a resource. *Future Choices, 2*(3), 73–75.
Maunders, D. (1990). Youth work as a response to social values. *Youth Studies, 9*(2), 42–50.
Reingold, J. R., & Frank, B. R. (1994). *Targeting youth: The source book for federal policies and programs.* Washington, DC: Institute for Educational Leadership.
Schine, J. (1989). *Young adolescents and community service.* Washington, DC: Carnegie Council on Adolescent Development.
Wehlage, G. G., Rutter, R. A., Smith, G. A., Lesko, N., & Fernandez, R. R. (1990). *Reducing the risk: Schools as communities of support.* New York: Falmer Press.

Fernando J. Galan, PhD, ACSW, LMSW-ACP, is associate professor, University of Texas–Pan American, Department of Social Work, 1201 W. University Drive, Edinburg, TX 78539.

For further information see

Adolescence Overview; Child Foster Care; Child Welfare Overview; Community; Direct Practice Overview; Families Overview; Family Life Education; Gay and Lesbian Adolescents; Homelessness; Human Development; Information and Referral Services; Juvenile Corrections; Legal Issues: Low-Income and Dependent People; Natural Helping Networks; Runaways and Homeless Youths; School-Linked Services; School Social Work Overview; Social Welfare Policy; Social Work Profession Overview; Substance Abuse: Legal Issues; Suicide.

Key Words	
adolescent services	diversity
developmental services	youth services

Biographies

In addition to soliciting expository entries that would describe and define the social work profession as it exists in the 1990s, the editorial board also wished to pay tribute to the people who have influenced its development. The board, therefore, elected to continue the tradition of publishing biographical sketches, which was begun when NASW published the 15th edition of the *Encyclopedia of Social Work* in 1957. In selecting names for this section, the board sought to identify those people who had made important and outstanding contributions to the profession through their leadership, inspiration, focus, and courage. Because men whose heritage was Northern or Western European and whose careers were spent largely in the Northeast and Midwest dominated the entries in earlier editions, board members paid special attention to generating nominations of women and members of other racial and ethnic groups.

After reviewing the sketches in the 18th edition, the editorial board agreed to include all 99 from that edition. They then sought additional names from the NASW membership and advertised the following criteria for inclusion:

- The person must be deceased.
- The person must have contributed significantly to the general social welfare in the United States.

- Priority is given to people who made lasting contributions in social work practice and practice theory, advancement of social work, advancement of special populations, and development or implementation of programs of national importance.

Although contribution to social work was an essential criterion, the board determined that the person being profiled need not be a social worker; therefore, the list of additional names includes such people as Martin Luther King, Jr., and Thurgood Marshall. In the end, an additional 43 people were added to the 99 people profiled in the 18th edition of the *Encyclopedia of Social Work*.

Board members selected authors for the biographical sketches on the basis of their familiarity with the people being sketched. In addition, as much as possible, we selected social workers as authors, following our general criterion for authorship of the main entries. We also decided to continue the precedent set in the 18th edition of separating the biographies from the other entries, instead of interspersing them as had been done in the 15th, 16th, and 17th editions.

The 142 people in the following biographical sketches represent much of the greatness of the profession—the heros, both sung and unsung, the giants upon whose shoulders we stand.

Fredrick Seidl

Abbott, Edith (1876–1957)

Edith Abbott, dean of the School of Social Service Administration at the University of Chicago from 1924 to 1942, was one of the chief architects of a new model of social work education. Abbott was born in Grand Island, Nebraska, daughter of Elizabeth Griffin Abbott, a high school principal and a women's suffrage leader, and Othman Abbott, first lieutenant governor of Nebraska. Her sister, Grace Abbott, was born two years later. Edith Abbott graduated from the University of Nebraska in 1901, received her PhD in economics from the University of Chicago in 1905, and studied at the London School of Economics. In 1908, after teaching economics at Wellesley, she became assistant director of the research department of the Chicago School of Civics and Philanthropy (later incorporated as part of the University of Chicago).

Abbott emphasized the state's responsibility in social problems, the importance of public welfare administration, the social aspects of legislation, and the need for a more humane social welfare system. She was president of the National Conference of Social Work and the American Association of Schools of Social Work and was a founder of and frequent contributor to the *Social Service Review*. Abbott participated in establishing the Cook County Bureau of Public Welfare in 1926 and in drafting the Social Security Act of 1935. At the 1951 National Conference of Social Work, accepting an award for her contributions to social work, she gave a fiery speech demanding abolishment of means tests and establishment of children's allowances. Her books include *Immigration: Selected Documents and Case Records* (1924), *The Tenements of Chicago, 1908–1935* (1936), *Public Assistance* (1941), and *Social Welfare and Professional Education* (1942). See also *Two Sisters for Social Justice: A Biography of Grace and Edith Abbott* (1983), by Lela B. Costin.

Jean K. Quam

Abbott, Grace (1878–1939)

Grace Abbott, dynamic director of the U.S. Children's Bureau, was most influential in her work with child labor legislation, immigrants, and social security. Born in Grand Island, Nebraska, two years after her sister, Edith Abbott, she graduated from Grand Island College in 1898 and became a teacher. From 1908 to 1917, she was director of the Immigrants Protective League of Chicago and a resident of Hull-House. Julia Lathrop, first director of the U.S. Children's Bureau and a former resident of Hull-House, encouraged Abbott to become interested in child labor problems. In 1917, at President Wilson's invitation, Abbott moved to Washington to administer the child labor law. She helped to organize the 1919 White House Conference on Children, succeeded Lathrop as director of the U.S. Children's Bureau in 1921, and edited numerous U.S. Children's Bureau publications on infant and child care and training. Abbott served as president of the National Conference of Social Work in 1924.

In 1934 she returned to Chicago as professor of public welfare at the University of Chicago's School of Social Service Administration. Abbott was also a member of the Advisory Council (1934–1935) that contributed to the establishment of the Social Security Act. Grace Abbott's writings, which reflect her professional experiences, include *The Immigrant and the Community* (1917); *From Relief to Social Security* (1941); and the two-volume classic, *The Child and the State* (1945). See also *Two Sisters for Social Justice: A Biography of Grace and Edith Abbott* (1983), by Lela B. Costin.

Jean K. Quam

Abernathy, Ralph David (1926–1980)

Ralph David Abernathy, second only to his co-worker, Dr. Martin Luther King, Jr., as champion of the civil rights movement, was born in Linden, Alabama. The grandson of slaves, he was the 10th of 12 children. He was drafted into the U.S. Army and completed the general equivalency diploma on discharge. Dr. Abernathy was a graduate of Alabama State University where he majored in mathematics. He completed one year of course work at Atlanta University and returned to Alabama State University, where he served as director of personnel, dean of men, and professor of social studies.

Dr. Abernathy was raised in the Baptist Church and announced his call to the ministry at the age of 22. He pastored two churches in Alabama. Dr. Abernathy met Dr. King in 1955 and helped to found the Southern Christian Leadership Conference (SCLC) in 1957 after the arrest of Rosa Parks. He and Dr. King led the Montgomery Bus Boycott for 381 days during which time his church and his home were bombed, he was wrongfully sued for $3 million, and he was severely beaten. Dr. Abernathy and Dr. King were jailed 44 times as a result of their civil rights activities, and they shared the victories (the passage of the Civil Rights Act of 1964, the Voting Rights Act of 1965, and the Fair Housing Act of 1968). It was King and Abernathy, through the SCLC, who ended de jure segregation in the south, thereby changing the course of history.

Having completed a master's degree of sociology at Atlanta University in 1958, Dr. Abernathy assumed the pastorate of the historic West Hunter

Street Baptist Church in Atlanta. In 1961 he intensified his efforts in the civil rights movement. Dr. Abernathy was at Dr. King's side when King was assassinated on April 4, 1968. He succeeded Dr. King as president of the SCLC and was diligent in working to help poor and downtrodden people. He was responsible for the Poor People's Campaign that culminated in Resurrection City, addressed in the United Nations in 1971, and was granted many awards and accolades, including 27 honorary doctoral degrees from some of the nation's most prestigious colleges and universities. In 1989 Harper & Row published Dr. Abernathy's autobiography, *And the Walls Came Tumbling Down,* a detailed account of his life and the nonviolent human and civil rights movement.

Lou M. Beasley

Adams, Frankie Victoria (1902–1979)

Frankie Victoria Adams, prominent social worker, author, educator, and community organizer in social work, was born in Danville, Kentucky. She attended Knoxville College and earned her master's degree from the New York School of Social Research. After she left graduate school, she worked for the YWCA in Chicago.

In 1931 Adams joined the faculty of the Atlanta University School of Social Work, where she was assigned to teach community organization and develop courses in group work. She developed the Group Work and Community Organization concentrations at Atlanta University, served as administrative advisor to three deans, and performed as acting dean during two interims. Although she retired from Atlanta University in 1964, she continued to serve as a consultant to the school until three weeks before her death in 1979.

Adams wrote *A History of the Atlanta University School of Social Work: Reflections.* In addition, she was the author of *The Negro Woman in Industry: Sketches on Race Relations*, and she published in many scholarly social work journals on the topics of social work education and juvenile delinquency as well as group work. She also published in general interest publications such as *Phylon* and the *YMCA Magazine.* She was a member of the Committee on Group Work of the American Association of Social Workers and influenced curriculum developments in group work at the national level.

During her tenure at Atlanta University, she influenced the lives of over 2,500 students. Each year the Georgia chapter of NASW presents the Frankie V. Adams Award to outstanding social workers in community organization as a lasting memorial to an outstanding black social worker who influenced the development of social work education and of professional social work in the South.

Lou M. Beasley

Addams, Jane (1860–1935)

Jane Addams—organizer, settlement house leader, and peace activist—is probably best remembered as the founder of Hull-House and the winner of the 1931 Nobel Peace Prize. Addams was the youngest of eight children born to John Huy Addams, an Illinois state senator from 1854 to 1870. Senator Addams, a Quaker and an abolitionist, influenced his daughter's political views.

Addams was educated at Rockford Female Seminary, Women's Medical College, in Philadelphia and in Europe. In London she visited Toynbee Hall, the first settlement house, and was inspired to open Hull-House in Chicago with Ellen Gates Starr, an art teacher. Programs at Hull-House, which became models for other settlements, included children's clubs; nurseries; an art gallery; a circulating library; an employment bureau; a lunchroom; and classes in history, music, languages, painting, dancing, and mathematics. Addams fought corrupt aldermen and was appointed neighborhood sanitation inspector, seeking to gain more services. Francis Hackett, William Lyon Mackenzie King (later prime minister of Canada), John Dewey, Julia Lathrop, Florence Kelley, Alice Hamilton, Edith and Grace Abbott, Sophonisba Breckinridge, Jessie Binford, and many others came to live and work at Hull-House to learn more about social welfare.

Addams's efforts to advocate nationally for improved social conditions led her to the presidency of the National Conference of Charities and Correction and memberships in the National Child Labor Committee, the National Recreation Association, the National Association for the Promotion of Industrial Education, and the National Conference of Social Work.

Concerned about the effects of war on social progress, Addams played a prominent part in the formation of both the National Progressive Party in 1912 and the Women's Peace Party, the latter of which she became president in 1915. She was also elected president of the Women's International Peace Congress at The Hague (later named the Women's International League for Peace and Freedom) in 1915. She was a delegate to similar congresses in Zurich (1919), Vienna (1921), The Hague (1922), Washington, DC (1924), Dublin (1926), and Prague (1929). Despite public opposition to her pacifist views, she continued in her efforts to condemn war and later urged the United States to join the League of Nations and the World Court. She won the Nobel Peace Prize in 1931, sharing the award with the American educator Nicholas Murray Butler. Among her books are *Democracy and Social Ethics* (1902), *Newer Ideals of Peace* (1907), *The Long Road of Woman's Memory* (1916), *Peace and Bread in Time of War* (1922), and two autobiographical pieces, *Twenty Years at Hull-House* (1910) and *The Second Twenty Years at Hull-House: September 1909 to September 1929* (1930). The many biographies of Jane Addams include *American Heroine* (1973), by Allen F. Davis; *Jane Addams: A Biography* (1937), by James Weber Linn; and *Jane Addams of Hull-House, 1860–1935* (1961), by Margaret Tims.

Jean K. Quam

Altmeyer, Arthur J. (1891–1972)
A recognized leader of social welfare policy, Arthur J. Altmeyer helped design and implement the most far-reaching social reform in American history— the Social Security Act of 1935. Born and educated in Wisconsin, Altmeyer taught briefly, became a school principal, and then took a position in Wisconsin state government. In 1931 he earned a PhD in economics at the University of Wisconsin, studying under Professor John R. Commons, a pioneer in the development of workers' compensation, unemployment insurance, health insurance, and other social legislation. As an administrator in Washington, DC (1934–1953), he helped put into practice the merit system for federal and state personnel programs (1939), survivor's insurance (1939), variable federal grants in relation to state per capita income (1939–1946), disability insurance (1939–1953), and federal financing of social work education (1939–1953). He also initiated and encouraged the movement for national health insurance from 1935 to 1953.

Altmeyer designed the social security program to be responsive to changes over time, making the Social Security Board one of the outstanding research units in the federal government. His appointment as social security commissioner was terminated by the Republicans in 1953. In *The Formative Years of Social Security: A Chronicle of Social Security Legislation and Administration, 1934–1954* (1966), Altmeyer described the early years of the Social Security program.

Jean K. Quam

Barrett, Janie Porter (1865–1948)
Janie Porter Barrett was a social welfare leader who founded the first social settlement in Virginia. She was born to emancipated slaves in Athens, Georgia. In 1894 Barrett began teaching after graduating from Hampton Institute in Virginia. She

taught for five years before becoming involved in social welfare activities. In 1902, with the help of northern philanthropists, Barrett founded the Locust Street Social Settlement. This settlement was the first of its kind in Virginia and one of the first settlements for black people in the United States. In 1908 she helped organize the Virginia State Federation of Colored Women's Clubs. As first president of the organization, she led the federation in the establishment of the Virginia Industrial School for Colored Girls, a rehabilitation facility. Barrett later became the superintendent of the school. By 1920, with help from child welfare leaders such as Hastings Hart, the institution had achieved national recognition. The William E. Harmon Award for Distinguished Achievement Among Negroes was presented to her in 1929. In 1950 the Virginia Industrial School was renamed the Janie Porter Barrett School for Girls. See *Notable American Women* (1971), by Edward T. Jones, Janet W. James, and Paul S. Boyer, and *Dictionary of American Negro Biography* (1982), by Rayford W. Logan and Michael Winston.

Wilma Peebles-Wilkins

Bartlett, Harriett M. (1897–1987)
Harriett Bartlett acted as the social work profession's theoretician, an intellectual giant despite being inarticulate, rigid, and inexperienced in the rigors of life. Educated at Vassar College, the London School of Economics, and the University of Chicago, she took what she called an unorthodox route to social work. Physically she was very tall, very thin, and very ascetic. As a social worker, she was compassionate, loving, and concerned about clients and their welfare. Through early acquaintance with Dr. Richard Cabot, and later with his protégé Ida Cannon, she became a caseworker at Massachusetts General Hospital. She became heavily involved with the American Association of Medical Social Workers (AAMSW, formerly the American Association of Hospital Social Workers, the earliest association of professional social workers, organized in 1918). She wrote often for the association, acted as its president from 1942 to 1944, and was a spokesperson for medical social workers.

Bartlett's work appears in 20 journal articles and particularly in two monographs: *Some Aspects of Social Casework in a Medical Setting* and *Fifty Years of Social Work in the Medical Setting*. She described minutely what medical social workers do in NASW's *Social Work Practice in the Health Field*. As a caseworker at Massachusetts General Hospital and a writer and active member of AAMSW, Bartlett sought to apply what she had

learned to what she called "the whole profession."
Her objective was to identify the distinguishing
characteristics of social work, an endeavor that
was captured in *Analyzing Social Work Practice by
Fields* and eventually in *The Common Base of
Social Work Practice,* in which she highlighted
social functioning as a central focus of social work
practice. She believed in *all* social workers using
shared values and knowledge and the same range
of interventive measures. Her work as chair of the
first Commission on Practice of NASW and its subcommittee on the Working Definition of Social
Work led to the article entitled "Toward Clarification and Improvement of Social Work Practice"
(*Social Work,* April 1958) and led her to think
about social work as a whole.

Bartlett's feelings about her contribution to
social work are revealed in her oral history, part of
a project of the NASW Publications Department.
The history, available to qualified researchers at
the Social Work Archives of the University of Minnesota, Twin Cities, contains a list of her seven
monographs and 40 journal articles as well other
biographical data. Besides her work at Massachusetts General Hospital, Bartlett was a consultant
at the Children's Bureau and a member of the faculty at Simmons College for 10 years. She said, "As
social work grew and changed from 1934 to 1970,
during these 36 years my own thinking and writing moved and expanded with it, from the beginning in the hospital to the perspective of the
whole profession."

Beatrice N. Saunders

Barton, Clarissa (Clara) Harlowe (1821–1912)

Founder of the American Red Cross and its president from 1881 to 1904, Clara Harlowe Barton
worked nationally and internationally to aid disaster victims. Born in Oxford, Massachusetts, she
was educated at home. She began teaching in 1839
and established many free schools in New Jersey.
After several years as a clerk in the Patent Office in
Washington, DC, she became a volunteer nurse
during the Civil War, distributing supplies to
wounded soldiers. Appointed by President Lincoln,
she supervised a systematic postwar search for
missing prisoners.

In 1870 Barton worked at the front with the
German Red Cross during the Franco–Prussian
War and was awarded the Iron Cross. Returning to
the United States, she organized the American
National Committee of the Red Cross (later the
American National Red Cross) and became its
president. In 1884, as U.S. delegate to the Red
Cross Conference in Geneva, she introduced the
"American Amendment," establishing that the Red

Cross was to provide relief in peacetime as well as
in war.

She supervised relief work after the yellow
fever epidemic in Florida (1887), the Johnstown
flood (1889), the Russian famine (1891), the Arme-
nian massacres in Turkey (1896), the Spanish–
American War (1898), the Boer War (1899–1902),
and the Galveston, Texas, flood in 1900. Barton
retired in 1904 after colleagues criticized her leadership. Her books include *The Red Cross in Peace
and War* (1899), *A Story of the Red Cross: Glimpses
of Field Work* (1904), and *The Story of My Childhood* (1907). See also *Life of Clara Barton, Founder
of the American Red Cross* (1922), by William E.
Barton, and *Angel of the Battlefield: The Life of
Clara Barton* (1956), by Ishbel Ross.

Jean K. Quam

Beers, Clifford Whittingham (1876–1943)

Clifford Whittingham Beers devoted his life to the
study and advancement of mental hygiene. Born in
New Haven, Connecticut, Beers graduated from
Yale in 1897. After a mental breakdown, he spent
three years in mental institutions: a private asylum
run for profit, a private nonprofit asylum, and a
state hospital. In *A Mind That Found Itself* (1908),
Beers described the inhumane treatment he
received from untrained staff and his efforts to
persuade the governor of Connecticut to investigate conditions in the state hospital. William
James wrote the introduction for the book, which
aroused intense public interest and the attention
of psychiatrists and psychologists.

Beers founded the Connecticut Society for
Mental Hygiene (1908), served as the first secretary of the National Committee for Mental Hygiene
(1909), helped establish the American Foundation
for Mental Hygiene (1928) and the International
Foundation for Mental Hygiene (1931), and was the
first secretary of the International Congress on
Mental Health (1931), which he organized. For his
work in broadening knowledge of the causes,
treatment, and prevention of mental illness, Beers
received the Legion of Honor from the French government and the gold medal of the National Institute of Social Sciences in 1933.

Jean K. Quam

Bethune, Mary McLeod (1875–1955)

Mary McLeod Bethune was influential for 30 years
in encouraging black women to develop pride, self-
respect, and self-control. She was born to emancipated slaves in Maysville, South Carolina. In 1894
she graduated from Scotia Seminary (now Barber-
Scotia College), a religious and industrial school
with an interracial faculty. Her courses there prepared her for teaching. For two years, she trained

for missionary work at the Moody Bible Institute in Chicago, but because black people were not accepted for missionary positions, she began a teaching career. The education and development of black women was one of her deepest commitments. In 1904 Bethune founded the Daytona Normal and Industrial Institute for Women (now Bethune–Cookman College) in Florida. Her role as president of the National Association of Colored Women led to the founding of the National Council of Negro Women in 1935. In 1936 she became head of Negro Affairs in the National Youth Administration. During the New Deal, Bethune influenced policies that led to a more equitable distribution of resources within the black community. Her leadership style of negotiation and interracial cooperation gave her national recognition among both black and white people. When the Daytona Institute merged with the Cookman Institute for Boys, Bethune was named president of the college. She held this position until 1942. See *Mary McLeod Bethune: A Biography* (1964), by R. Holt; *Mary McLeod Bethune* (1951), by C. O. Peare; and *Mary McLeod Bethune* (1959), by E. M. Sterne.

Wilma Peebles-Wilkins

Beveridge, Lord William (1879–1963)

William Beveridge was one of the founders of the British welfare state. During World War II, he chaired an important committee responsible for planning the reorganization of government social programs. The committee's recommendations facilitated a massive expansion of social services in Britain when the war ended, and Beveridge earned an international reputation for his advocacy of the welfare state.

Educated in the law at Oxford University, he abandoned his legal studies and went to work at Toynbee Hall, the famous settlement house in the East End of London. In 1905 he joined the *Morning Post* as a journalist, and his articles on social conditions attracted widespread attention. Beveridge, who was particularly concerned about unemployment, recommended the creation of employment exchanges to help unemployed workers find jobs. In 1909, when his ideas were accepted by the British government, Beveridge was put in charge of establishing employment exchanges.

Beveridge's reputation grew, and he became widely recognized as an authority on social problems. During World War I he helped plan a system of food rationing. In 1919 he was appointed director of the London School of Economics, a position he held until 1937. Although he was a friend of the Webbs and the other Fabians, he did not join the Fabian Society and identified himself as a liberal rather than a socialist.

When Prime Minister Winston Churchill named a committee in 1941 to plan the reorganization of Britain's social programs, he appointed Beveridge as the chairperson. The committee's report, *Social Insurance and Allied Services: A Report by Sir William Beveridge,* was published at the end of 1942 and soon became a best-seller. The report formed the basis for the Labour Government's social policies between 1945 and 1950 and fostered the creation of Britain's national health services; the introduction of comprehensive social security; and the expansion of public education, housing, and other social programs.

Beveridge, who earned an international reputation for his contribution to the postwar expansion of social services in Britain, was knighted in 1919; he became a peer, entitled to a seat in the House of Lords, in 1946. He wrote numerous books, including *Unemployment: A Problem of Industry* (1909), *Pillars of Security and Other Wartime Essays and Addresses* (1943), *Full Employment in a Free Society* (1944), *Why I Am a Liberal* (1945), *Voluntary Action: A Report on Methods of Social Advance* (1948), and *Power and Influence* (1953). See also *William Beveridge: A Biography* (1977), by Jose Harris.

James Midgley

Blackey, Eileen (1902–1979)

Eileen Blackey made a significant contribution to the field of social work as a practitioner, an educator, an administrator, and a consultant. Born of Irish parents in Blackpool, England, as the family was on its way to the United States, Blackey grew up in the Midwest and received a bachelor's degree from the University of Wisconsin in 1925. In 1930 she returned to school and received a master's degree from the Smith College School for Social Work. After the war Blackey entered the doctoral program at Case Western Reserve University. Her dissertation, "Group Leadership in Staff Training," was published by the U.S. Department of Health, Education, and Welfare and is considered a classic.

Blackey's professional career coincided with national and international events that offered her the opportunity to use her considerable talents. During the Great Depression, when emergency relief programs across the country were desperate for trained professionals, she established programs for inservice staff development in West Virginia and Florida. After World War II Blackey became director of staff development for social work service in the Veterans Administration, charged with training staff for positions in the administration's hospitals and clinics across the United States.

Blackey also made an important contribution to social work education in the United States and abroad. Before the war she taught at the Smith School and helped lay the groundwork for a school of social work in Hawaii. After the war she was asked to establish a school of social work at Hebrew University in Israel, and her reputation earned her consulting assignments throughout the Middle East. When she returned to the United States, she became dean of the School of Social Work at the University of California, Los Angeles. After her retirement, she continued to consult with national and international schools of social work.

Blackey's death made impossible her plans to publish her experience with the United Nations Relief and Rehabilitation Agency as director of the Child Search and Repatriation Program in Germany. Her many articles on social work appeared in national and international journals, and her unpublished papers are in the Social Welfare History Archives Center of the University of Minnesota's Walter Library.

Margaret Daniel

Brace, Charles Loring (1826–1890)

Writer, minister, and social reformer, Charles Loring Brace was one of the organizers of the Children's Aid Society of New York City. As its executive director for almost 40 years, Brace chronicled the problems of destitute, vagrant, and homeless children and initiated many child welfare services. After graduating from Yale University in 1846, Brace taught briefly and then entered Yale Divinity School. As a minister he preached to prisoners of Blackwell's Island in New York City. Frequently described as an independent thinker, Brace was an abolitionist and accepted Darwin's theory of evolution.

After traveling through Europe, Brace served as a city missionary in New York, becoming aware of the many homeless children roaming the streets. In 1853, when a group of influential citizens encouraged him to establish a mission for children, he founded the Children's Aid Society. Among its programs were industrial schools, reading rooms, newsboys' lodging houses, night schools, summer camps, sanatoriums, children's shelters, special classes for children with disabilities, and dental clinics.

Brace's most controversial program was sending some 50,000 to 100,000 homeless children on "orphan trains" to be adopted by farmers in the West. Although placements were made with little investigation, most children successfully adjusted to their new homes. Brace's writings, especially his popular book *The Dangerous Classes of New York and Twenty Years' Work among Them* (1872), crystallized public sentiment on behalf of the needs of children. *Hungary in 1851* (1852) is Brace's account of a trip to that country, where he was imprisoned for criticizing the country's autocratic regime. His accomplishments are reviewed in *The Life of Charles Loring Brace Chiefly Told in His Own Letters* (1894), edited by Emma Brace.

Jean K. Quam

Breckinridge, Sophonisba Preston (1866–1948)

Sophonisba Preston Breckinridge was an educator and social activist who taught the first course of public welfare administration and strongly advocated for a rigorous postgraduate curriculum in social work education. Born in Lexington, Kentucky, into a family noted for public service, she was a brilliant student. A graduate of Wellesley College in 1888, she became the first woman to graduate from the University of Chicago Law School, to be admitted to the bar in Kentucky, and to earn a PhD in political science and economics from the University of Chicago (1901). In 1902 she joined the faculty of the University of Chicago and helped develop the Chicago School of Civics and Philanthropy. As its dean from 1908 to 1920, she convinced the university to accept the pioneering school of social work as a graduate professional school and designed two unique courses, "Social Work and the Courts" and "The Family and the State." She introduced the case method as the mode of instruction, publishing the first volume of edited case records for students' use. She remained at the university until 1933.

Breckinridge was a charter member of the American Association of Social Workers and president of its Chicago chapter, twice president of the Illinois Conference on Social Welfare, and one of the organizers and the president (1933–1935) of the American Association of Schools of Social Work. For 14 years she was a resident of Hull-House during her annual vacation quarter from the university. She also championed unions, collective bargaining, better working conditions for women, and fair treatment for immigrants and black people, and she was one of the first members of the Chicago branch of the National Association for the Advancement of Colored People. A managing editor of and contributor to the *Social Service Review,* she wrote a number of books,

Biographies

including *Women in the Twentieth Century* (1933),
Social Work and the Courts (1934), and *Public Welfare Administration in the United States* (1938).

Jean K. Quam

Brockway, Zebulon Reed (1827–1902)

Zebulon Reed Brockway, whose lifelong work in
prison service included 25 years as superintendent
of the New York State Reformatory in Elmira, was a
reformer who believed in rehabilitation rather than
punishment. Born in Lyme, Connecticut, Brockway
began his career as a clerk at the Connecticut
State Prison in Wethersfield, where his father had
been a director. His early positions included deputy to the warden at the Albany County Penitentiary (1851–1853), director of the Albany
Municipal and County Almshouse (1853–1861),
head of the Monroe County Penitentiary at Rochester (1861–1864), and superintendent of the
Detroit House of Correction. He resigned in 1872
when his reforms were not fully accepted.

In 1875 Brockway became warden at the New
York State Reformatory of Elmira, establishing
reforms that applied advanced principles of penology. He initiated a program of physical and manual
training for prisoners to prepare them for release
and advocated inclusion of indeterminate sentencing and parole in state statutes. Although the New
York State Board of Charities, concerned about his
innovations, recommended his dismissal in 1894,
he was retained. During this period he also served
as president of the National Prison Association
(1897–1898). In 1905 he was elected mayor of
Elmira, serving for two years. Brockway's history
of the changes he observed in penal reform during
his work in the field, *Fifty Years of Prison Service,*
was published in 1912.

Jean K. Quam

Bruno, Frank John (1874–1955)

Frank John Bruno was an administrator and educator whose expertise and leadership were influential in American social work. After graduating from
Williams College (1899) and Yale Divinity School
(1902), he spent five years as a Congregational
minister. In 1907 he became a general agent of the
Associated Charities in Colorado, moving to the
staff of the New York Charity Organization Society
in 1911. In New York he studied at the New York
School of Philanthropy (now the Columbia University School of Social Work), where he was greatly
influenced by Mary Richmond. From 1914 to 1925,
Bruno was general secretary of the Associated
Charities of Minneapolis (later the Family Welfare
Association).

Bruno was acting chair of the Department of
Sociology and Social Work at the University of

Minnesota (1912–1922) and professor of applied
sociology and head of the Social Work Department
(later the George Warren Brown School of Social
Work) at Washington University in St. Louis. As a
civil rights advocate, Bruno created opportunities
for black students to receive social work training.
As president of the National Conference of Social
Work from 1932 to 1933 and president of the American Association of Social Workers from 1928 to
1930 and again during a period of turmoil in the
organization in 1942, Bruno promoted the expansion of the profession. Bruno wrote *The Theory of
Social Work* (1936) and *Trends in Social Work,
1874–1956* (1957). In 1955 the George Warren
Brown School of Social Work published a monograph on Bruno, *Frank John Bruno, 1874–1955.*

Jean K. Quam

Buell, Bradley (1893–1976)

Bradley Buell, community organizer and planner,
consulted on and conducted research projects in
156 communities in the United States. Born in Chicago, Buell was educated at Oberlin College and
the New York School of Philanthropy (now the
Columbia University School of Social Work). As a
result of work by Buell and others on the problems
of the National Social Workers Exchange, the
American Association of Social Workers evolved as
the major professional social work association.
Until 1923 Buell served the organization, first as its
secretary and then as its associate executive.

His community organization activities
included service as director of the New Orleans
Community Chest and Council; field director of
Community Chests and Councils, Inc.; and founder
and executive director of Community Research
Associates. From 1943 to 1947 Buell edited *Survey
Midmonthly,* writing extensively on community
planning. In 1952 he published *Community Planning for Human Services,* in which he analyzed the
work of more than 100 agencies in St. Paul, Minnesota, during a one-year period, finding that multiproblem families used almost 50 percent of all
services. Another book, *Solving Community Problems,* was published in 1973.

Jean K. Quam

Burns, Eveline Mabel (1900–1985)

Eveline M. Burns was a social economist and educator who helped formulate the original Social
Security Act. Born in London, she was educated at
the London School of Economics. She moved to
the United States in 1926 and joined the faculty of
Columbia University in 1928, where she taught
until her retirement in 1967. She served as a consultant to many government and private agencies;
it was as a member of the President's Committee

on Economic Security in 1934 that she helped develop the specifics of the Social Security Act. She later became director of research for the Committee on Long-Range Work and Relief Policies of the National Resources Planning Board, which shaped public assistance and work programs through the 1940s. In addition to more than 100 articles, Burns wrote nine books, including *Social Security and Public Policy* (1956), which is the basic textbook on analysis of the social security program, and *Social Welfare in the Nineteen Eighties and Beyond* (1978). See also *Social Security in International Perspective: Essays in Honor of Eveline M. Burns* (1969), edited by Shirley Jenkins.

John F. Longres

Cabot, Richard Clarke (1865–1939)

A well-known physician and educator, Richard Clarke Cabot initiated the first medical social work department in the United States at Massachusetts General Hospital in 1905. Born in Brookline, Massachusetts, Cabot graduated from Harvard University (1889) and Harvard Medical School (1892). His association with Harvard continued as a member of the medical school faculty from 1899 to 1933 and as a professor of social ethics from 1920 to 1934. He began as a physician at Massachusetts General Hospital in 1898 and became chief of staff in 1912.

As director of the Boston Children's Aid Society, Cabot saw the need to understand family relationships and environmental factors in diagnosing children more effectively. The use of home visits by social workers to gain more information about patients became a model for social work practice in other hospitals. In 1930 he served as president of the National Conference of Social Work and received the National Institute of Social Science gold medal in 1931. An outspoken critic of the expense and inefficiency of medicine and an advocate for social work services, Cabot wrote extensively; his works include *Social Service and the Art of Healing* (1915), *Social Work: Essays on the Meeting Ground of Doctor and Social Worker* (1919), and *The Meaning of Right and Wrong* (1936).

Jean K. Quam

Cannon, Ida Maud (1877–1960)

As director of the Social Service Department at Massachusetts General Hospital in Boston (1906–1946), Ida Maud Cannon defined and developed medical social work. Cannon attended the City and County Hospital Training School for Nurses in St. Paul, Minnesota, and the Boston School for Social Workers (now Simmons College School for Social Work). Although medical social work was growing as a field of practice in New York and Bal-

timore, Cannon became its nationally recognized symbol through her activities at Massachusetts General Hospital in the department created by Dr. Richard Cabot.

Cannon's conception of medical social work involved moving beyond the hospital into community health and welfare agencies. She also advocated for the establishment of psychiatric clinics staffed by social workers in general hospitals. She held that social workers needed specialized medical knowledge but that a strong social work base and knowledge of casework techniques were the foundation of medical social work. A founder of the American Association of Hospital Social Workers (later the American Association of Medical Social Workers), Cannon served as its president and vice president. She also led the first committee on social work in a medical school. In 1923 she wrote *Social Work in Hospitals,* and in 1952 she published *On the Social Frontiers of Medicine: Pioneering in Medical Social Service.*

Jean K. Quam

Cannon, Mary Antoinette (1884–1962)

During her long career as a social worker and educator, Mary Antoinette Cannon helped develop medical social work. She graduated from Bryn Mawr in 1907 and joined Dr. Richard Cabot's pioneering medical social work department at Massachusetts General Hospital. Continuing her career at the Boston Consumptives Hospital (1909–1910) and teaching high school, she received an MA from Columbia University in 1916. As director of social work at University Hospital of Philadelphia (1916–1921), she became the first secretary of the American Association of Medical Social Workers.

Cannon's experiences led her to see the value of courses in psychiatry and medicine in schools of social work, an idea she put into practice at the New York School of Social Work, where she taught from 1921 to 1945. During this period she helped establish the Social Services Employees Union and served on its board of directors. She served as director of social work at the University of Puerto Rico (1941–1942), consultant to the New York office of the Commonwealth of Puerto Rico Department of Labor (1948–1952), and organizer of the first social workers' workshop in Puerto Rico in 1953. At her death, she was volunteer director at the James Weldon Johnson Community Center in Harlem. Her writings include *Outline for a Course in Planned Parenthood* (1944) and *Social Casework: An Outline for Teaching* (1933), edited with Philip Klein.

Jean K. Quam

Carlton, Thomas Owen (1937–1992)

Thomas Owen Carlton was an expert in curriculum development in social work education as well as an author, an editor, and a scholar in health social work and social policy. Born in Quincy, Illinois, he received a PhD in social work from the University of Pennsylvania, a master's degree in social work from the University of Southern California, a master's degree in government from California State University, and a bachelor's degree in international relations from the University of California, Los Angeles. From 1961 to 1963 he served in the U.S. Peace Corps in the Philippines, where he met his future wife.

Carlton left early employment in banking to become a social worker. His first love was teaching and writing in social policy, especially as it affected health social work. Carlton's approach to policy had a strong historical bent. He believed that profound and powerful themes in American history worked their way into social welfare and social welfare planning in the colonial period and well into the 20th century. He expressed his views during his long-term teaching and scholarly tenure at the School of Social Work of Virginia Commonwealth University, where he began in 1973 as an assistant professor and then became full professor, associate dean, and for 18 months in 1990–1991, acting dean. The founding chair of the school's health specialization program, Carlton wrote extensively on the school's history as the oldest school of social work in the South.

Carlton's writings were central to his career. He believed that scholarship in social work education should be a central characteristic of the professional role. In 1984 he published *Clinical Social Work in Health Settings—A Guide to Professorial Practice with Exemplars,* in which he demonstrated the application of (Falck's) membership theory to health social work. He served as editor-in-chief of *Health & Social Work* from 1986 to 1990. His editorials, which were enthusiastic, pointed, and thoroughly researched, became the subject of much discussion in the health social work field.

In 1990 Carlton was recognized by the Society of Hospital Social Work Directors of the American Hospital Association, which gave him the Hyman J. Weiner award for "leadership, scholarship, teaching ability, compassion, and commitment to values." In the final years of his career, Carlton often served as an educational consultant to hospitals and agencies. As part of one such assignment, he taught in Cyprus at a training program in rehabilitation sponsored by the World Rehabilitation Fund.

Hans S. Falck

Cassidy, Harry (1900–1951)

Harry Cassidy was a prominent Canadian social scientist, social welfare reformer, and social work educator during the 1930s and 1940s. He was a tireless crusader for public social welfare services in Canada and the United States. In 1926 he obtained a PhD in economics from the Robert Brookings Graduate School of Economics and Government, where the basis was laid for his lifelong interest in problems of poverty, living standards, industrial relations, and social legislation. Cassidy's social welfare studies of the early 1930s were among the first Canadian reports on unemployment, housing needs, and labor conditions. His two books, *Social Security and Reconstruction in Canada* (1943) and *Public Health and Welfare Reorganization* (1945), were the first to examine in detail Canadian social welfare programs at both the federal and provincial levels.

Cassidy taught social welfare at the University of Toronto from 1929 to 1934 and was director of social welfare for the province of British Columbia from 1934 to 1939. In this position he was instrumental in developing the province's public social services and in preparing a comprehensive scheme of public state health insurance. Had Cassidy's scheme been implemented, it would have been the first such insurance program in Canada. As a social scientist, Cassidy viewed his task as director of social welfare for British Columbia as being largely one of social engineering. He saw himself as a technical expert who would restructure the province's social services according to modern methods of management. He favored practical, efficient solutions to social problems, in accordance with the best tenets of social science, and he displayed an enormous interest in collecting social facts that were largely detached from theoretical considerations. Social progress for Cassidy depended on technology and bureaucracy.

Cassidy developed important schools of social work at the University of California, Berkeley, and at the University of Toronto, both of which are leading schools today largely as a result of his work. His plans for both schools were tremendously ambitious. He wanted to broaden the base of university education for social workers by placing much greater emphasis on the social sciences, social research, and the legal and administrative features of social welfare. Only then, he believed, could high standards be demanded, which would attract the best students and ultimately result in an increased status for professional social work. Even more important for Cassidy was that graduates of these improved educational programs would be able to assume leadership roles to ensure that public welfare was administered more efficiently and humanely.

Allan Irving

Chavez, Cesar (1927–1993)

Cesar Chavez was born in the North Gila Valley of Arizona, 20 miles outside Yuma. His family owned a ranch and a grocery store, which it lost during the Great Depression. His father's search for work led them to the Central Valley of California, where his parents became migrant farmworkers. Chavez left school after finishing the eighth grade and joined the Marines at the age of 16. In 1948 he married Helen Fabela, and they worked together in the fields of the large ranches.

In 1952 Chavez was hired to chair a voter registration drive for Saul Alinsky's Community Service Organization. He registered more than 4,000 people in two months and became the general director of the national organization in 1958.

In 1962 Chavez returned to the work that he loved: organizing farmworkers. Chavez began a different kind of social movement, fighting to establish farmworkers' rights and access to services. He established cooperative organizations whose membership benefits were paid for by dues and contributions. The nonprofit corporations he established began with a burial fund, followed by a credit union, and then a health care system, which today covers the Central and Imperial valleys in California.

Delano was the site of Chavez's greatest victories in his efforts to gain respect and better working conditions for farmworkers. The Delano area was the headquarters of the union's strike of growers begun in 1965. A pilgrimage of 67 strikers left Delano on March 17, 1966, with the theme of "penitence, pilgrimage, and revolution." By the time the strikers arrived at the state capitol in Sacramento, they had been joined by 10,000 supporters. The strike and the five-year boycott of California table grapes brought international prominence to the United Farm Workers and Chavez and led Delano-area growers to agree to a contract in 1970.

Chavez's advocacy went beyond social work in the conventional sense, finally focusing on the issue of birth defects and diseases caused by the application of fumigants, insecticides, and defoliants by agribusiness corporations. Before the U.S. government succeeded in banning the use of the insecticide DDT, the United Farm Workers won this ban in its first labor contracts with Californian agribusinesses. To achieve his successes, Chavez emulated his hero, Mahatma Gandhi, by relying on nonviolent methods and hunger strikes. See *Cesar Chavez: Autobiography of La Causa* (1975), by

Jacques Levy, and *Sal Si Puedes* (1969), by Peter Matthiessen.

Juan Paz

Cohen, Wilbur (1913–1987)

Wilbur Cohen, a leading figure in the history of social security and secretary of the U.S. Department of Health, Education, and Welfare (DHEW) under Lyndon B. Johnson, was born in Milwaukee, Wisconsin. After attending Alexander Meiklejohn's Experimental College at the University of Wisconsin, he accompanied Edwin E. Witte to Washington, DC, in 1934 and helped draft the original Social Security Act. As a staff member in the Social Security Administration (1935–1956), Cohen developed legislative proposals and successfully promoted amendments to broaden coverage and increase benefits.

In 1956 Cohen became professor of public welfare administration at the University of Michigan and chaired the governor's Public Health Advisory Committee when Michigan became the first state to establish medical assistance for the elderly. In 1960 he led President John F. Kennedy's Task Force on Health and Social Security and in 1961 became DHEW's assistant secretary for legislation. Cohen was the chief architect of the 1965 amendments that inaugurated Medicare and Medicaid. Following passage of this legislation, President Johnson named Cohen undersecretary and, in 1968, secretary of DHEW.

Cohen became dean of the School of Education at the University of Michigan in 1969 and 10 years later the Sid W. Richardson professor of public affairs at the Lyndon Baines Johnson School of Public Affairs in Austin, Texas. In 1979 Cohen founded Save Our Security (SOS), an umbrella organization representing more than 100 groups, to oppose reductions in disability and welfare programs. During the 1980s Cohen energetically defended social security against cutbacks proposed by the Reagan administration.

A visionary as well as a legislative technician, Cohen wrote and lectured widely on public welfare policy issues. He received more than 30 awards and honorary degrees. Cohen's career is detailed in the Wilbur J. Cohen papers at the State Historical Society of Wisconsin.

Roland L. Guyotte

Coyle, Grace Longwell (1892–1962)

Grace Longwell Coyle was the first social work educator to develop a scientific approach to group work practice. Born in North Adams, Massachusetts, Coyle received a BA from Wellesley College (1914), a certificate from the New York School of Philanthropy (1915), and an MA in economics

(1928) and a doctorate in sociology from Columbia University (1931). Her early activities included work in settlement houses and the YWCA. From 1934 to 1962, she taught at the School of Applied Social Sciences at Western Reserve University in Cleveland, developing the first group work course to be taught at that university.

Coyle was president of the National Conference of Social Work (1940), the American Association of Social Workers (1942–1944), and the Council on Social Work Education (1958–1960). Her many writings—such as *Social Process in Organized Groups* (1930), *Studies in Group Behavior* (1937), *Group Experiences and Democratic Values* (1947), *Group Work with American Youth* (1948), and *Social Science in the Professional Education of Social Workers* (1958)—contributed to the acceptance of group work as a social work method.

Jean K. Quam

Day, Dorothy (1897–1980)

Dorothy Day—social activist, journalist, and publisher—was cofounder of the Catholic Worker Movement and edited the *Catholic Worker* for more than 40 years. Born in Brooklyn, Day attended the University of Illinois (1914–1916), leaving to begin writing for *Socialist Call, The Masses*, the *Liberator*, and Pathé Films. In 1928, seeing the Catholic Church as a church of immigrants and the laboring class, she converted to Catholicism. With Peter Maurin, a teacher, she began publishing the *Catholic Worker* in 1933. Her column "Day after Day" (later "On Pilgrimage") expressed prounion and pacifist views and opposition to racism. In 1934 she and Maurin opened St. Joseph's House of Hospitality in New York City. Many other farms and houses of hospitality for poor and homeless people were based on their model.

A lifelong activist, Day traveled extensively on public speaking engagements. She was first arrested in 1917 during a Washington, DC, march for women's suffrage. At age 76 she was arrested for demonstrating in support of Cesar Chavez's United Farm Workers. Her books include *The Eleventh Virgin* (1924), *House of Hospitality* (1939), *On Pilgrimage* (1948), *Therese* (1960), and *On Pilgrimage: The Sixties* (1972). See also *Dorothy Day: A Biography* (1982), by William D. Miller.

Jean K. Quam

De Forest, Robert Weeks (1848–1931)

Robert Weeks De Forest, president of the New York Charity Organization Society from 1888 to 1931, was a lawyer, philanthropist, and social reformer. A native New Yorker, he was often referred to as "New York's first citizen" because of his efforts on the city's behalf. He received an LLB from Columbia University Law School in 1872 and an MA from Yale University in 1873. For more than 50 years he served as general counsel of the Central Railroad of New Jersey. He helped draft New York's first tenement house law in 1901, fought the activities of loan sharks who took advantage of poor people, and helped found a national association to combat tuberculosis.

De Forest is credited with developing the New York School of Philanthropy—the first training school for social workers—and the Russell Sage Foundation, a model for other philanthropic foundations. He supported such projects as the Metropolitan Museum of Art, Survey Associates, the National Housing Association, the Prison Association of New York, and the State Charities Aid Association. De Forest also helped establish the disaster relief program of the American Red Cross and the Welfare Council of New York. His writings include *The Tenement-House Problem* (1903).

Jean K. Quam

Devine, Edward Thomas (1867–1948)

Edward T. Devine, trained as an economist, was an outstanding educator, writer, and administrator. Born near Union, Iowa, Devine graduated in 1887 from Cornell College in Iowa. He studied economics at the University of Halle–Wittenberg in Germany and received his PhD from the University of Pennsylvania in 1895. During this period he lectured for the American Society for the Expansion of University Teaching, a pioneer adult education project, and at Oxford and Edinburgh. In 1896 he became general secretary of the New York Charity Organization Society. During his 20-year leadership, he formed the Wayfarer's Lodge and the Tenement House Committee (later the Committee on Housing), and he expanded the in-house magazine *Charities* to produce the leading social work journal of its day, *Survey*.

Devine helped found the National Association for the Study and Prevention of Tuberculosis and the National Child Labor Committee in 1904. That same year, he was named director of the New York School of Philanthropy, which he had helped found in 1898. As director (1904–1907, 1912–1917), he worked to establish a strong relationship between the school and Columbia University, where he was a professor of social economy. He was American Red Cross special representative in San Francisco in 1906 after the earthquake and was in charge of flood relief in Dayton, Ohio, in 1913. During World War I, he headed American Red Cross relief work in France. He also directed the Graduate School of American University in Washington, DC, the Bellevue–Yorkville Health Demonstration in New York City, and the Nassau County Emergency Work and Emergency Relief Bureau in New York. His writings documenting the history of the profession include *Misery and Its Causes* (1909), *Social Work* (1928), *Progressive Social Action* (1933), and *When Social Work Was Young* (1939).

Jean K. Quam

Dix, Dorothea Lynde (1802–1887)

Dorothea Lynde Dix, whose reporting of the neglect, suffering, and abuse of the insane prepared the way for the mental health movement, was born in Hampden, Maine. In 1841, after working as a schoolteacher, she became concerned about the conditions in prisons and almshouses for the insane. Despite her recurring bouts of tuberculosis and malaria, she encouraged state legislatures to support better institutions and finally persuaded Congress to appropriate public land for hospitals for the deaf and the insane. Although President Franklin Pierce vetoed this bill in 1854 and federal assistance was not given to state welfare programs until the 1930s, Dix lobbied nationally and internationally on behalf of the mentally ill and was personally responsible for the establishment of 32 public and private institutions. During the Civil War she served the Union as superintendent of army nurses. Her writings include an encyclopedia, a number of hymns and moral stories for children, *Remarks on Prisons and Prison Discipline in the United States* (1845), and *The Garland of Flora* (1829). See also *Dorothea Dix, Forgotten Samaritan* (1937), by Helen E. Marshall; *Life of Dorothea L. Dix* (1892), by Francis Tiffany; and *Stranger and Traveler: The Story of Dorothea Dix, American Reformer* (1975), by Dorothy Clarke Wilson.

Jean K. Quam

DuBois, William Edward Burghardt (1868–1963)

W.E.B. DuBois was an outstanding black scholar and militant civil rights activist for five decades. He was born of African, Dutch, and French ancestry in Great Barrington, Massachusetts. DuBois earned two bachelor's degrees, one from Fisk University in 1888 and another from Harvard University in 1890. Prior to earning a doctorate from Harvard University in 1896, he studied at the University of Berlin. DuBois began a career in university teaching and spent three years as a professor in the Department of History and Economics at Atlanta University. He headed the University's

Department of Sociology from 1932 to 1944. There, he organized efforts to begin a scientific study of the problems of the black community. DuBois promoted higher education for the "talented tenth," or leadership class, within the black population. Actively fighting discrimination in all aspects of American life, DuBois organized the Niagara Movement in 1905. This group was absorbed into the organization of the National Association for the Advancement of Colored People in 1909. DuBois served on the NAACP Board of Directors from 1910 to 1934 and edited *The Crisis,* the organizational magazine he founded in 1910. A prolific writer, DuBois wrote numerous articles and books on black people in America and Africa. Notable among his works are *The Philadelphia Negro, A Social Study* (1899), *The Souls of Black Folk* (1903), and *The Autobiography of W.E.B. DuBois* (1968). See also *W.E.B. DuBois, Negro Leader in a Time of Crisis* (1959), by Francis L. Broderick.

Wilma Peebles-Wilkins

Dunham, Arthur (1893–1980)

Arthur Dunham, pacifist and social work educator, wrote extensively about community development and social welfare administration. Born in St. Louis, Missouri, Dunham earned an AB from Washington University in St. Louis (1914) and an MA in political science from the University of Illinois (1917). He began his social work career as assistant director of a neighborhood center and as a family caseworker. A member of the Society of Friends (Quakers), Dunham refused to enter the service during World War I and was sentenced to 25 years' hard labor. However, in 1919, his sentence was overturned after only a few months.

Dunham was secretary of the Philadelphia Social Service Exchange (1919–1923), secretary of the Newton, Massachusetts, Central Council (1923–1925), and secretary of the Child Welfare Division of the Public Charities Association of Pennsylvania (1925–1935). In 1935 he became a professor at the University of Michigan's Institute of Health and Social Sciences (later the School of Social Work), serving as its acting director from 1949 to 1951. During his retirement he held various visiting professorships; studied community development programs in India in 1956; and wrote a history of the Quakers, *The Ann Arbor Friends Meeting 1935–1975: A History of Its First Forty Years* (1976). His other books—such as *Community Welfare Organization: Principles and Practice* (1958) and *Community Organization in Action* (1959), edited with Ernest B. Harper—contributed to the evolution of community organization as a social work method.

Jean K. Quam

Dybwad, Rosemary Ferguson (1910–1992)
Rosemary Ferguson Dybwad, born in Howe, Indiana, gained international recognition for her pioneering efforts in bringing together nationally organized groups of parents of children with intellectual limitations into a worldwide movement. Following her graduation from Western College for Women, she received from the Institute of International Education a two-year exchange fellowship in sociology at the University of Leipzig and later returned to Germany to complete her PhD in sociology at the University of Hamburg. Her dissertation topic was "Social Work in American Reformatories for Women." She worked in correctional institutions in New Jersey and New York, resigning in 1939 prior to the birth of her first child.

In 1958 Dybwad was asked by her husband, Dr. Gunnar Dybwad, then executive director of the National Association for Retarded Children, to assist with a rapidly growing correspondence from parents around the world. She soon developed and edited an international newsletter that connected parent groups in Europe, North and South America, Asia, and the Pacific Rim. This effort led to the founding of the International League of Societies for Persons with Mental Handicap and the development of her most outstanding achievement, the *International Directory of Mental Retardation Resources.* The third edition of this compendium was published in 1989 by the President's Committee on Mental Retardation. A year later, on the occasion of Dybwad's 80th birthday, Brookline Press published a collection of her presentations at national and international conferences under the title *Perspectives on a Parent Movement—The Revolt of Parents of Children with Intellectual Limitations.* An early supporter of the self-advocacy movement, she participated actively in the first International People First Conference in Tacoma, Washington, in 1984.

Constance W. Williams

Egypt, Ophelia Settle (1903–1984)
Ophelia Settle Egypt, a pioneer in family planning among economically disadvantaged African Americans, also made significant contributions in the areas of historical social research and social work education. Born in a small town near Clarksville, Texas, Egypt received a BA degree from Howard University in 1925 and obtained an MA in sociology from the University of Pennsylvania in 1928. In 1944 she was awarded an MS from the New York School of Social Work. She later received an advanced certificate for work toward a PhD at the Pennsylvania School of Social Work.

In 1929, while serving as a research assistant to Dr. Charles S. Johnson, director of the Social Science Department at Fisk University in Nashville, Tennessee, Egypt conducted original research on the conditions of slavery among African Americans. Her personal interviews with more than 100 former slaves in Tennessee and Kentucky are contained in *Unwritten History of Slavery: Autobiographical Accounts of Negro Ex-Slaves,* which was published by Fisk University in 1968. The original historical research conducted by Johnson and Egypt was one of the earliest uses of oral history documentation in the United States, predating the Works Progress Administration 1936–1938 study, the largest collection of ex-slave interviews available in this country.

Egypt served as director of the medical social work program of Flint Goodridge Hospital in New Orleans (1935–1939) and assisted in the development of the program of studies at the Howard University School of Social Work (1939–1951). In 1952 Egypt became executive director of the Ionia R. Whipper Home, one of the only homes for unwed African American teenage mothers in the Washington, DC, area. Egypt is best known for her pioneering work in the area of planned parenthood through her efforts at the Parklands Planned Parenthood Clinic in Washington, DC, from 1956 to 1968. On October 15, 1981, the clinic was renamed the Ophelia Egypt Clinic, and Mayor Marion Barry proclaimed October 17, 1981, as Ophelia Settle Egypt day.

Carrie J. Smith

Eliot, Martha May (1891–1978)
Martha May Eliot, educator and public health official, was associated for more than 30 years with the U.S. Children's Bureau. Born in Dorchester, Massachusetts, Eliot graduated from Radcliffe College in 1913 and received her MD in 1918 from Johns Hopkins University. She began her work with the Children's Bureau as director of the Division of Maternal and Child Health (1924–1934), becoming assistant chief (1934–1941), associate chief (1941–1949), and chief (1951). As administrator of the federal grants-in-aid program to help states develop health services for mothers and children, she introduced the idea of allotting some money for innovative programs designed by individual states. Eliot also introduced the use of social workers in public health programs and drew attention to the problems of juvenile delinquency and high infant mortality resulting from fetal damage and genetic defects.

In 1946 she was vice chair of the U.S. delegation to the international health conference that drafted the constitution of the World Health Organization (WHO), and she was the only woman to sign the document. She was named chief medical consultant to the United Nations International Children's Emergency Fund (UNICEF) in 1947. From 1949 to 1951, she was assistant director general of WHO, and from 1952 to 1957 she was the U.S. representative to the executive board of UNICEF. Eliot taught at Yale University School of Medicine (1921–1949) and was professor of maternal and child health at the Harvard School of Public Health, chairing the department from 1957 to 1960. She served as president of the National Conference of Social Work in 1949 and became the first woman president of the American Public Health Association in 1947. Her writings include articles on her studies of rickets and on maternal and child health care.

Jean K. Quam

Epstein, Abraham (1892–1942)

Abraham Epstein, a Russian immigrant who came to the United States in 1910, was a leader in the post–World War I movement for passage of social security legislation. A graduate of the University of Pittsburgh, Epstein was research director of the Pennsylvania Commission on Old Age Pensions (1918–1927) and helped draft Pennsylvania's first old age pension bill. During this time he also organized and served as secretary–treasurer of the Workers Education Bureau of America. In 1927 he founded the American Association for Old Age Security (later the American Association for Social Security). As its executive secretary, he was instrumental in building public support for the subsequent passage of social security legislation.

Epstein served as U.S. representative to the Social Insurance Commission of the International Labour Office (1934–1937), as a consulting economist to the Social Security Board, and as executive board member of the New York City Affairs Committee. He lectured on social insurance at New York University and Brooklyn College and edited the official publication of the American Association of Social Security, *Social Security.* Epstein wrote *Facing Old Age* (1922); *The Challenge of the Aged* (1928); and *Insecurity: A Challenge to America* (1938), a primary sourcebook in the field of social insurance.

Maryann Syers

Fauri, Fedele Frederick (1909–1981)

Fedele Frederick Fauri, dean of the University of Michigan School of Social Work for almost 20 years, was one of the foremost experts on public welfare in the United States. Trained as an attorney, Fauri received his BA in 1930 and his JD in 1933 from the University of Michigan. His interest in public welfare began in 1934, when he became adviser and general assistant to a county relief administration in his home state.

Fauri served as legal advisor to the Old Age Assistance Bureau in Lansing (1937) and supervisor of the Michigan Bureau of Social Security (1941). In 1943 he became director of the Michigan Department of Social Welfare, and from 1947 to 1951, he worked in Washington, DC, as a senior specialist in social legislation for the Library of Congress as a social security adviser to the House Ways and Means Committee.

Invited to be dean of the newly established School of Social Work at the University of Michigan in 1951, Fauri was instrumental in the establishment of the school's innovative doctoral program, combining social work and the social sciences. Fauri continued to act as a consultant on public welfare to various congressional committees, study commissions, and panels. After leaving the deanship in 1970, he became vice president for State Relations and Planning at the University of Michigan. After his retirement in 1975, he was Michigan state racing commissioner from 1975 to 1980. Fauri wrote many articles on public welfare and served as president of the Council on Social Work Education (1954–1956), the American Public Welfare Association (1967), and the National Conference on Social Welfare (1961–1962).

Maryann Syers

Federico, Ronald Charles (1941–1992)

Ronald Federico was a leader in the development of undergraduate social work education. As a teacher, program administrator, and scholar, he helped shape social work education at the baccalaureate level. A native of the Bronx, New York, he received an undergraduate degree from Yale University, an MSW from the University of Michigan, and a PhD from Northwestern University.

Federico served as director of three undergraduate social work programs. He also served on the board of directors of the Council on Social Work Education, was instrumental in the development of the Association of Baccalaureate Social Work Program Directors, and was a member of the BSW Task Force of NASW. Federico provided curriculum consultation to countless social work education programs and served as mentor to a generation of undergraduate social work educators. He is coauthor of *Educating the Baccalaureate Social Worker* (Vols. 1 and 2; 1978 and 1979) and *Human Behavior: A Perspective for the Helping*

Professions (1982; revised 1985 and 1991) and author of many other books, including *Social Welfare in Today's World* (1990).

Dean Pierce

Fernandis, Sarah A. Collins (1863–1951)

Sarah Fernandis was a civic leader and founder of the first black social settlement in the United States. She was born in Port Deposit, Maryland. Her undergraduate degree was from Hampton Institute in Virginia, and her master's degree in social work was from New York University. After three years of teaching in the Baltimore public schools, she began a lifelong career of organizing social welfare and public health activities in black communities. Fernandis established the first American settlement for blacks in the District of Columbia and a second settlement in Rhode Island. Between 1913 and 1917 she organized the Women's Cooperative Civic League and became its first president. The league worked for improved sanitation and health conditions in black neighborhoods. During World War I she moved to Pennsylvania and organized a War Camp Community Center. In 1920 Fernandis became the first black social worker employed in the City Venereal Disease Clinic of the Baltimore Health Department. In this position she continued to work for improved health conditions in the black community. See *Notable Maryland Women* (1977), edited by Winifred G. Helmes.

Wilma Peebles-Wilkins

Fizdale, Ruth (1908–1994)

Ruth Fizdale, a caseworker and administrator in health care, was a pioneer in professionalizing social work. Early in her career, she was a psychiatric caseworker at the Mandel Clinic of the Michael Reese Hospital in Chicago. She later worked at Jewish Family Services in Brooklyn and at the New York Association for New Americans, where she used counseling and job training to help immigrants become self-sustaining within a year of arriving in the United States.

As chief of social services staff development for the Veterans Administration following World War II, she created an innovative structure for staff and student training, which later served as the basis for continuing education of social workers in other health settings. Her work resulted in enhanced curricula in the schools of social work and had a positive impact on the quality of social work services in health care. In addition, she developed competitive stipends for students who would enter Veterans Administration and other health care services.

For 19 years Fizdale was executive director of the Arthur Lehman Counseling Service (ALCS), where she developed the fee-for-services system in for-profit agencies. ALCS, which had been established to serve middle-class and upper-income clients, was known for charging reasonable fees and paying attractive salaries. Fizdale's work helped remove the "charitable institution" label from voluntary organizations and influenced the acceptance of work with people from all socioeconomic groups. Her book *Social Agency Structure and Accountability* (Burdick, 1974) was used in graduate schools, agencies, and private practice to standardize quality fee-paid social work services.

Fizdale actively worked with many professional social work organizations to improve the professional standing of social work, including the American Association of Psychiatric Social Workers, NASW, and the National Conference on Social Welfare. She was a founding member of NASW's Competence Certification Board, which was responsible for overseeing the Academy of Certified Social Workers, the profession's first national credential.

She received her professional education at the University of Chicago, the Smith College School for Social Work, and the University of Pennsylvania. She served as adjunct associate professor emerita at the Mount Sinai School of Medicine. She was named a fellow of the Brookdale Center on Aging of Hunter College for her service to elderly people, and in 1994 Columbia University established the Helen Rehr and Ruth Fizdale Professorship of Health and Mental Health.

Linda Beebe

Flexner, Abraham (1866–1959)

Abraham Flexner was an educator and educational reformer who influenced social work through his challenge to the professional status of the field. Of immigrant background, Flexner graduated from Johns Hopkins University in 1886 and spent his early career in secondary education as a teacher and a school principal. After a period of study at Harvard University and in Berlin, Flexner began his work in educational reform. His 1910 report to the Carnegie Foundation for the Advancement of Teaching, *Medical Education in the United States and Canada,* had tremendous impact on the development of medical education. He was a member and secretary of the General Education Board of the Rockefeller Foundation (1917–1925) and later became director of the Institute for Advanced Study at Princeton University (1930–1939).

At the 1915 National Conference of Charities and Correction, Flexner raised the question, "Is social work a profession?," listing six essential criteria for a profession. Although social work met four—a learned character, practicality, a tendency toward self-organization, and altruistic motivation—Flexner concluded that social work did not qualify as a profession because it lacked individual responsibility and educationally communicable techniques. His writings include *Abraham Flexner: An Autobiography* (1960).

Maryann Syers

Folks, Homer (1867–1963)

Homer Folks was a social pioneer during the early years of the social work profession whose views were sought, respected, and acted on by legislators, governors, presidents, and foreign governments. Born in Hanover, Michigan, he graduated from Albion College in 1889 and from Harvard University in 1890. Folks served as general superintendent of the Children's Aid Society of Pennsylvania (1890–1893), executive director of the State Charities Aid Association of New York (1893–1947), commissioner of Public Charities of New York City (1902–1903), president of the National Conference on Social Welfare (1911 and again in 1923), and president of the board of directors of the National Tuberculosis Association (1912–1913). Folks also worked abroad with the American Red Cross from 1917 to 1919.

Folks was among the first to recognize illness as a major cause of poverty and to emphasize the importance of preventive public health measures. He played a leading role in the organization and administration of movements for the improvement of health and welfare. Both the New York State Public Health Law and the Public Welfare Act are credited to Folk's skill as a bill drafter. His public service activities included the care of dependent children, mental hygiene, tuberculosis control, public assistance programs, social research, and corrections and parole. In 1940 Folks was awarded the Distinguished Services Medal by the Theodore Roosevelt Memorial Association for his promotion of social justice, and in 1952 he became the first recipient of the National Tuberculosis Association's Will Ross Medal for his outstanding contributions toward the control of tuberculosis.

Folks is the author of *The Care of Destitute, Neglected and Delinquent Children* (1902) and *The Human Costs of the War* (1920). See also *Public Health and Welfare: The Citizen's Responsibility* (1958).

Sara Harmon

Follett, Mary Parker (1868–1933)

Mary Parker Follett, a native of Quincy, Massachusetts, and an 1898 graduate of Radcliffe College, was active in vocational guidance, industrial relations, civic education, and settlement work. As a vocational counselor for Boston's Roxbury Neighborhood House, Follett became aware that poor working families needed social, recreational, and educational facilities. In 1909 her lobbying resulted in legislation that allowed her to open the Boston School Centers for after-school recreation and education programs.

As a member of the vocational guidance board of the Boston School Board and the Minimum Wage Board of the Women's Municipal League, Follett was active in the business community and addressed groups of businesspeople. She continued her interest in industrial relations after moving to England in 1924, serving as vice president of the National Community Center Association and as a member of the Taylor Society, an organization concerned with scientific management and efficiency in industry.

Follett's interest in the concept of "psychological interpenetration"—that is, a plan to get people of different socioeconomic and occupational backgrounds to understand one another's viewpoints—is described in her 1924 book, *Creative Experience.* See also *Dynamic Administration: The Collected Papers of Mary Parker Follett* (1941), edited by Henry C. Metcalf and L. Urick.

Maryann Syers

Frankel, Lee Kaufer (1867–1931)

Lee Kaufer Frankel, originally trained as a chemist, is best known for his contributions to health insurance, family services, and Jewish welfare. Frankel received a BS (1887) and PhD (1888) from the University of Pennsylvania and taught chemistry there until 1893. After six years as a consulting chemist in Philadelphia, Frankel became manager of the United Hebrew Charities in New York City. An outstanding leader in the family service field and one of the early developers of family casework practice, he was also one of the first instructors at the New York School of Philanthropy and was instrumental in establishing the Training School for Jewish Social Work.

As president of the National Conference of Jewish Charities in 1912, Frankel was active in Jewish relief efforts during and after World War I. With a grant from the Russell Sage Foundation he conducted a two-year study of various forms of health insurance. This led to a position as manager of the Metropolitan Life Insurance Company's industrial department and then as a second vice president. Frankel continued his interest in social welfare, initiating social programs within the company. Frankel served as director and vice president of the National Association for the Study and Prevention of Tuberculosis (1914), treasurer of the American Public Health Association (1919), president of the New York State Conference of Charities and Correction (1917), welfare director of the Post Office Department (1921–1922), chairperson of the National Health Council (1923–1925), and vice president of the National Conference of Social Work (1923–1924). His books include *Cost of Medical Care* (1929) and *The Health of the Worker* (1924). See also *Half a Century in Community Service* (1948), by Charles Bernheimer.

Maryann Syers

Frazier, Edward Franklin (1894–1962)

E. Franklin Frazier is noted for his studies of the black family and the black middle class. He was born in Baltimore, Maryland. Frazier received a bachelor of arts degree from Howard University in 1916. He studied sociology at Clark University where he earned a master's degree in 1920 and a doctorate in 1931. In 1922 Frazier became director of the Atlanta University School of Social Work. He remained in this position for five years before leaving Atlanta as a result of controversy created in the white community by his article in *Forum Magazine* on racial prejudice. For three years Frazier served as a research sociologist at Fisk University. In 1934 he became head of the Department of Sociology at Howard University and remained in this position until his retirement in 1959. Prior to the establishment of a separate School of Social Work at Howard, Frazier directed a social work program there for eight years. Frazier's career as an educator included precollegiate teaching as well as national and international university teaching. As a sociologist Frazier contributed widely to the knowledge of black families through his research studies and publications. His works include *The Negro Family in Chicago* (1932), *The Negro Family in the United States* (1939), *Black Bourgeoisie* (1955), and *Race and Culture Contacts in the Modern World* (1957). See also R. W. Logan and M. Winston, *Dictionary of American Negro Biography* (1982).

Wilma Peebles-Wilkins

Galarza, Ernesto (1905–1984)

Ernesto Galarza was a pioneer, an advocate, and a scholar whose commitment to social justice, especially through the power of his convictions conveyed by the written word, triggered a number of significant policies on behalf of individuals and families without power in American democracy. His report, which was later published in a book entitled *Merchants of Labor,* is credited with ending the Bracero program and its exploitative characteristics. His careful documentation of unjust treatment of farmworkers in the Southwest and the deep South directly contributed to major policy changes. His report "Tragedy at Chualar," which was published as a book, led to the uncovering of unsafe conditions for farmworkers and specifically the death of 32 farmworkers as the result of unsafe practices in the transportation of farmworkers, resulting in compensation for the families of the 32 men who were killed. Overall he directly contributed to policy changes in the health and safety of farmworkers.

Social workers, and especially the School of Social Work at San Jose State University, benefited tremendously from Dr. Galarza's dispassionate analysis of social injustice; his advocacy/scholarly approach to controversial social policy issues; and his careful and thorough documentation of celebrated cases that led to much-needed policy changes. A social worker close to Dr. Galarza characterized him as "Don Quixote with a pen." The School of Social Work honors him annually through a symposium and the Ernesto Galarza Scholarship Fund. In addition, the School of Social Work and a high school district created the Ernesto Galarza Institute for Community Development and established it in the Eastside Union High School District in San Jose, California. His delightful and thought-provoking stories for children in both English and Spanish are a testimony to the importance that he and his family placed on education, which led Galarza to earn a PhD in history from Columbia University. His contribution to social work and social work education was through the power of his ideas, which he committed to writing and developed therein. The products of his labor are built into the various annual and established activities in social work education and social work services and remain a testimony to a man who contributed his life for the cause of social justice. Thus, social work honors him and is honored by his lifetime of achievements and the power of his ideas, which live on.

Juan Ramos

Gallaudet, Edward Miner (1837–1917)

Like his father and older brother, Edward Miner Gallaudet devoted his life to working with deaf people. Born in Hartford, Connecticut, near his father's school, he attended Trinity College. After graduating in 1856 he taught at the Gallaudet School for a period of time and then moved to Washington, DC, where he founded the Columbia Institute for the Deaf and Dumb. This school (renamed Gallaudet College in 1893 in honor of his father) was the first institution to provide college-level education for deaf people.

In addition to his work with deaf people, Gallaudet wrote extensively on methods of education for deaf people and was president of the Convention of American Instructors of the Deaf from 1895 until 1917.

Maryann Syers

Gallaudet, Thomas (1822–1902)

Thomas Gallaudet was the oldest son of Thomas Hopkins Gallaudet and Sophia Fowler, a deaf woman who had been a pupil at the Gallaudet School. Growing up near the school founded by his father, he learned sign language at an early age and eventually devoted his life to ministering to deaf people. Gallaudet graduated from Washington College in 1842 and began his career teaching at the New York Institution for the Deaf. Later he converted to the Episcopal Church and was ordained a priest in 1851. In 1850, while studying for the priesthood, he began a Bible class for deaf people at St. Stephen's Church in New York City, and in 1852 he established St. Ann's Church for Deaf Mutes, conducting regular services in sign language. In addition to his parish duties, Gallaudet founded the Gallaudet Home for aged and infirm deaf–mutes near Poughkeepsie, New York.

Maryann Syers

Gallaudet, Thomas Hopkins (1787–1851)

Thomas Hopkins Gallaudet and his two sons, Thomas and Edward Miner, are renowned for their commitment to the education of deaf people. Born in Philadelphia, Gallaudet moved to Hartford, Connecticut, at the age of 13. After graduation from Yale University, poor health forced him to give up law school. Subsequently, he worked as a traveling salesperson and entered Andover Theological Seminary, graduating in 1814. During this time, the father of a deaf girl who was impressed with Gallaudet's ability to communicate with his daughter raised money to send him to Europe to study methods for educating deaf people. In 1816 Gallaudet returned to the United States accompanied by Laurent Franc, one of the outstanding teachers at the Institute Royal des Sourds-Muets in Paris. In 1817 Gallaudet established the first free American school for the deaf in Hartford. The school taught deaf students and trained teachers of the deaf; Gallaudet remained its principal until 1830.

Gallaudet was instrumental in the establishment of public normal schools in Connecticut and worked to promote manual training programs in the schools. He was also interested in the education of black people and advocated for higher education for women. See *Gallaudet: Friend of the Deaf* (1964), by Etta Degering.

Maryann Syers

Garrett, Annette Marie (1898–1957)

Annette Marie Garrett was a social worker and social work educator whose main contribution was in the development of casework practice. A native of Kansas, Garrett received her BA from the University of Kansas, did graduate work at the University of Chicago, and received an MSS from Smith College School for Social Work in 1928. After several years in casework practice, she was appointed chief of social service at the Judge Baker Guidance Center in Boston. In 1935 she became associate director of Smith College School for Social Work, remaining there until her death.

As an instructor and director of field operations, Garrett believed that students should have a wide range of firsthand field experience. Out of just such an experience, working with a troubled child in foster placement, she wrote *Casework Treatment of a Child* (1942). Her contributions to social work education include *Learning through Supervision* (1954). Garrett's influential book, *Interviewing, Its Principles and Methods* (1942), was translated into 12 languages, and her *Counseling Methods for Personnel Workers* (1945) helped to extend the use of casework principles to the new field of industrial counseling.

Maryann Syers

Gonzalez Molina de la Caro, Dolores (1910–1979)

Dolores Gonzalez Molina de la Caro was a pioneer in mental health training, public welfare, public health, school health, and university counseling in Puerto Rico. Born in a rural community where her father was a leader in local politics, she received social work training at the age of 19. At the rural vocational school to which she was assigned, her leadership abilities quickly emerged. She also studied at the New York School of Social Work and earned her master's degree in medical social work at the University of Chicago.

Caro's long career in public service included appointments as director of the Bureau of Medical Social Work and director of the Mental Health Program, both in the Department of Health in Puerto Rico. In her work she gave special emphasis to the development of training programs and to the integration of state and local services. She was also dean of students at Lesley College in Massachusetts and associate dean of students at the University of Puerto Rico, where she developed innovative support programs incorporating mental health and group dynamics. Her published works include *Human Relations in the Public Service* (1956) and the two-volume *Manual in Human Relations Training for Student Orientors* (1970).

John F. Longres

Granger, Lester Blackwell (1896–1976)

Lester Blackwell Granger, an outspoken advocate for interracial cooperation and equal opportunity for black people, was best known for his leadership of the Urban League and for his efforts to desegregate the U.S. armed forces after World War II. Born in Newport News, Virginia, Granger was the son of a physician and a schoolteacher. After graduating from Dartmouth College in 1917, Granger served for two years in France during World War I. Returning to civilian life, he worked for the New Jersey Urban League but soon left to teach at Winston–Salem State University and St. Augustine's College in Raleigh, North Carolina. In 1922 he became an extension worker at the Manual Training School for Colored Youth in Bordentown, New Jersey. He reorganized the Los Angeles affiliate of the Urban League in 1930, worked briefly at Bordentown, and returned to the Urban League in 1934.

Thus began Granger's 27-year association with the agency—uninterrupted except for the period from 1938 to 1940, when he established the Standing Committee on Negro Welfare of the Welfare Council of New York City, which attempted to obtain equality of social and welfare services for black people. As leader of the Urban League (1940–1961), Granger worked to gain employment for blacks and garner support for equal opportunity from industrial and community leaders. At the end of World War II—when the return of white veterans threatened the advances made by black people—Granger initiated a community relations project aimed at abating racial tensions.

In 1945, after Granger was commissioned by the secretary of the U.S. Navy to study the serious racial tensions plaguing the Navy, his recommendations became implemented throughout the armed services. He also served as president of the National Conference of Social Work (1951–1952) and as president of the International Conference on Social Welfare (1961).

Maryann Syers

Gurin, Arnold (1917–1991)

Arnold Gurin was a leader in advancing community organization, social work policies and practices, planning and research, education, and administration in voluntary, government, and Jewish services. He served as caseworker in the Chicago Relief Administration; as a caseworker, employment interviewer, and migration worker to resettle victims of Nazi persecution in the National Refugee Service; and as director of budget research and director of field services for the Council of Jewish Federation. In the last capacity he was involved in a broad spectrum of social, health, and educational services of Jewish communities across the United States and Canada and in other countries. He then turned to social work education, teaching at Michigan State, Columbia, and Brandeis universities. At Brandeis he became professor and dean of the Florence Heller Graduate School for Advanced Studies in Social Welfare.

Gurin's guidance was sought by many organizations. He directed a landmark study of teaching community organization for the Council on Social Work Education as well as the evaluation of Project Renewal in Israel, an innovative program to help lift scores of deprived neighborhoods out of poverty. Gurin advised Israel on the development of social work education and the Jewish community of France on the professional education of staffs of communal agencies. He also assisted state and federal government agencies in addressing public–private agency relationships, the organization of social services, and other critical issues.

Those who sought Gurin's advice and assistance relied on the excellence of his standards, his balance of vision and realism, the depth and clarity of his thinking, his objectivity, and his skill in resolving conflicts and achieving consensus. He was an officer of NASW and was honored by the Massachusetts chapter as its Man of the Year. His books include *Community Organizations and Social Planning* (with Robert Perlman, 1972) and *Community Organization Curriculum in Graduate Social Work Education* (1970). His other works include numerous articles, monographs, chapters in books, and papers.

Philip Bernstein

Gurin, Helen (1918–1991)

Helen Gurin was a leading teacher, supervisor, and guide for a generation of professionals in social work and other fields and an outstanding therapist, planner, clinician, and administrator. After graduating from Hunter College, she earned a master's degree in educational psychology at City College of New York and an MSW at the Columbia School of Social Work.

In addition to teaching social work students at the master's and doctoral levels, Gurin trained psychiatrists, psychiatric nurses, psychologists, and child care workers. Many in other professions sought her for training because of her depth of knowledge and insights in social work, coupled with her background in psychological thought and practice. Committed to ensuring that disadvantaged children would have the same quality of service that other children received, she was at the forefront of planning and establishment of clinical programs to serve the child welfare system. Clinicians referred parents and children to her for therapy because of her exceptional skill in analyzing and treating complex social problems of families and especially children.

Gurin had a keen commitment to the institutional setting in which she worked and was a constructive institution builder. She practiced at the New York City Department of Social Welfare, the United Service for New Americans, the South Shore Children Guidance Service, the South Shore Planned Parenthood Center, the Lansing Child Guidance Clinic, and the Tavistock Clinic (London). Gurin also taught at the schools of social work of Simmons College, Michigan and Michigan State universities, and Smith College. In recognition of her unique leadership and service, the Massachusetts chapter of NASW named her Social Worker of the Year in 1983.

Philip Bernstein

Gurteen, Stephen Humphreys (1836–1898)

Stephen Humphreys Gurteen, founder of the first Charity Organization Society in the United States, was born near Canterbury, England. After graduating from Cambridge University in 1863, he emigrated to the United States and worked as a lawyer and a teacher of Latin. In 1875 he was ordained as an Episcopal priest and appointed assistant minister of St. Paul's Church, Buffalo, New York. Buffalo was in the midst of the depression of 1873–1878, and Gurteen was put in charge of the church's relief work. He spent the summer of 1877 in England observing efforts to assist the poor, including the London Charity Organisation Society, and on his return proposed a Charity Organization Society (COS) for Buffalo that would involve prominent businessmen representing a variety of religious faiths. The Buffalo COS, launched in December 1877, differed little from the English model except for its policy of strict nonsectarianism, on which Gurteen had insisted.

Following a congregational rift, Gurteen left St. Paul's in 1880. He wrote about the COS movement and served for a year as director of the Chicago COS. From 1884 to 1886 he served as rector of a church in Springfield, Illinois. In 1886 he retired to New York City, where he pursued an interest in early English literature. Gurteen wrote *A Handbook of Charity Organization* (1882) and "Beginning of Charity Organizations in America" in *Lend a Hand* (1894). See also "Stephen Humphreys Gurteen and the American Origins of Charity Organization," *Social Service Review* (1966), by Verl S. Lewis.

Paul H. Stuart

Hale, Clara (1905–1992)

Clara Hale was the first proprietor of a not-for-profit child care agency serving children born addicted to drugs or alcohol or with acquired immune deficiency syndrome (AIDS). Born in Philadelphia, Hale migrated to New York City after her marriage to Thomas Hale, who died prematurely. From 1941 to 1968, to care for her three young children as a young, single parent, she became a foster parent for more than 40 children. She was praised for her parenting skills, which she credited to her strict black Baptist code of discipline.

"Mother," as she was called, started Hale House in her home in 1969 to care for addicted babies. In 1975 Hale House, now a licensed child care facility, became a residential center for children exposed in utero to addictive drugs and whose parents were temporarily unable to care for them.

Hale's work attracted national attention. In his 1985 State of the Union address, President Reagan called her an "American heroine." In the same year, at the age of 80, she was appointed to President Reagan's American Commission on Drug-Free Schools and was made an honorary "soror" of Delta Sigma Theta Sorority. Hale's unfinished dream was to develop a hospice for terminally ill children. A biography of her life and work—written by her daughter, Dr. Lorraine Hale, the current proprietor of Hale House—is in progress.

Yvonne Asamoah

Hamilton, Gordon (1892–1967)

Gordon Hamilton was a practitioner, an educator, a consultant, and a writer whose works profoundly influenced the development of casework theory. Born into an upper-class family, she received her early education at home and obtained a BA from Bryn Mawr in 1914.

During World War I she did war work in England. Later she worked in Denver, Colorado, for the American Red Cross, meeting Mary Richmond, who recommended her to the New York City Charity Organization Society. After three years as a caseworker and a research secretary for the society, in 1923 she began her career with the New York School of Social Work. As an educator Hamilton was closely involved with consultation and administration in various fields of practice. She worked with the Social Service Department of Presbyterian Hospital in New York City (1925–1932) and served as director of Social Service in the Temporary Emergency Relief Administration (1935–1936), research consultant to the Committee on Social Issues of the Group for the Advancement of Psychiatry (1949–1953), and consultant for such international organizations as Church World Service and UNRRA (1944–1952).

Perhaps Hamilton's greatest contributions were as a teacher and a writer. A leading expression of the "diagnostic" school of thought, her enormously influential *Theory and Practice of Social Casework* (1940/1951) was widely translated and used as a training text for at least two decades. The book dealt with the philosophy and values underlying service provision and with such considerations as the professional relationship, the use of community resources, and the relationship among social agencies, problem diagnosis, and casework intervention. Hamilton also argued that social workers should be interested in work with poor people and in the economic hardships that disrupt family life.

As a teacher she believed that knowledge of and ability to organize content were the keys to precise yet imaginative thinking in students. She worked with Eveline Burns and Philip Klein to develop a doctoral program in social work at Columbia University—efforts that led to the development of doctoral programs in other universities.

After her retirement from Columbia she served as editor-in-chief of *Social Work* (1956–1962), putting forth ideas about method specializations and the unity of social work goals and values. In a famous 1962 editorial, she proposed that the administration of income maintenance grants be separated from social service programs. Her works include *Principles of Social Case Recording, Psycho-therapy in Child Guidance,* and *Theory and Practice of Social Case Work.*

John F. Longres

Haynes, Elizabeth Ross (1883–1953)
Elizabeth Ross Haynes (wife of George Edmund Haynes) is noted for her organizational work to improve the quality of life in the black community. She was born in Mount Willing, Alabama. In 1903 Haynes received a bachelor of arts degree from Fisk University, and 20 years later she earned a master's degree in sociology from Columbia University. She taught for four years, then turned to volunteer work and paid employment in social services. In 1918 Haynes became the assistant director of the Negro Economics Division in the U.S. Department of Labor (George E. Haynes was director). She spent two years as a consultant with the Domestic Service Section of the U.S. Employment Service. During her 10 years with the national board of the Young Women's Christian Association, she helped develop the association's Industrial Division. Her efforts to better the economic circumstances of black people continued as she worked to improve state employment policies while serving on the New York State Temporary Commission of the Urban Colored Population. Her philosophy of black upward mobility is communicated in her publications *Unsung Heroes* (1921) and *The Black Boy of Atlanta* (1952). See also *Notable American Women: The Modern Period* (1980), by B. Sicherman et al.

Wilma Peebles-Wilkins

Haynes, George Edmund (1880–1960)
George Haynes (husband of Elizabeth Ross Haynes) was a social scientist who was recognized as cofounder of the National Urban League. Born in Pine Bluff, Arkansas, he received a bachelor's degree from Fisk University and a master's degree from Yale University. In 1910 Haynes became the first black graduate of the New York School of Philanthropy. He received a PhD in economics in 1912 and was the first black person to earn a doctorate from Columbia University. He was the director of Negro Economics for the U.S. Department of Labor and director of the Department of Social Sciences at Fisk University. Haynes was a social activist during a period of great concern over the living conditions of black people migrating to urban centers. While serving as a research fellow for the Bureau of Social Research of the Charity Organization Societies, he began doing research on migration. His research activities generated active involvement in associations to improve the working conditions of black people. These reform efforts led to the 1911 founding, with Ruth Standish Baldwin, of the Committee on Urban Conditions Among Negroes. In 1920 this committee became the National Urban League. He published many articles in addition to his research on the effects of migration on black people, *The Negro at Work in New York City* (1912). See also "Notes on a Forgotten Black Social Worker and Sociologist: George Edmund Haynes," *Journal of Sociology and Social Welfare* (1983), by I. Carlton-LaNey, and *Dictionary of American Negro Biography* (1982), by R. W. Logan and M. Winston.

Wilma Peebles-Wilkins

Hearn, Gordon (1914–1979)
Gordon Hearn was an influential theoretician and group worker who introduced general systems theory into social work. Born in Canada, where his father was an educator, he received his early education and professional experience there, working with boys in the Young Men's Christian Association. He earned a master's degree from George Williams College in Chicago in 1939 and was a member of the first doctoral class in group psy-

chology organized and directed by Kurt Lewin at the Massachusetts Institute of Technology.

As a professor at Berkeley and as the first dean of the School of Social Work at Portland State University, Hearn taught and wrote in the field of human relations training. For many years, too, he was a staff associate of the National Training Laboratories. Gordon Hearn will also be remembered as a humanist who, in addition to his interests in group theory, was an accomplished painter. Among his published works are *Theory Building in Social Work* (1958) and *The General Systems Approach to the Understanding of Groups* (1962).

John F. Longres

Hoey, Jane M. (1892–1968)

Jane M. Hoey's major contribution to social work was in the establishment and enforcement of standards in public welfare administration. The daughter of Irish immigrants, she was born in Greeley County, Nebraska. After receiving an MA in political science from Columbia University and a diploma from the New York School of Philanthropy in 1916, she began working for Harry Hopkins at the New York Board of Child Welfare. Employed by the American Red Cross, she later became secretary of the Bronx Committee of the New York Tuberculosis and Health Association. She helped organize the Health Division of the New York Welfare Council and became its assistant director in 1926. A combination of family and administrative experiences helped acquaint her with the political world. Her political skills were helpful in negotiations with government officials and in program interpretation when she served as a delegate to the United Nations.

Hoey later became director of social research for the National Tuberculosis Association and served as president of the National Conference of Social Work, the Council on Social Work Education, and the William J. Kerby Foundation. The Jane M. Hoey Chair in Social Policy was established by the Columbia University School of Social Work in 1967. Between 1931 and 1953, Hoey published a number of articles related to government policy and welfare.

Larraine M. Edwards

Hopkins, Harry Lloyd (1890–1946)

Harry Hopkins became a national leader during the Great Depression as the administrator of the Federal Emergency Relief Administration (FERA), the country's first federal relief program. Born in Sioux City, Iowa, he graduated from Iowa's Grinnell College in 1912. He began his social work career as director of a boys' camp run by New York's Christodora House Settlement. While living at the

house, Hopkins joined the staff of the Association for Improving the Condition of the Poor and served two years as an agent for its Bureau of Family Rehabilitation and Relief. In 1924 he was appointed executive director of New York's Temporary Emergency Relief Administration by Governor Franklin D. Roosevelt. Under Roosevelt's presidential administration, Hopkins headed the federal relief program for two years. He then became administrator of the Works Progress Administration, which replaced FERA, and he became secretary of commerce in 1938. Hopkins wrote *Spending to Save: The Complete Story of Relief* (1936). See also *Minister of Relief: Harry Hopkins and the Depression* (1963), by Searle F. Charles; *Harry Hopkins and the New Deal* (1974), by Paul A. Kurzman; and *Roosevelt and Hopkins* (1948), by Robert E. Sherwood.

John F. Longres

Howard, Donald S. (1902–1982)

Donald S. Howard, an eminent social work educator and administrator, was born in Tokyo, the son of missionaries. A 1925 graduate of Otterbein College, he earned his PhD in 1971 from the School of Social Service Administration at the University of Chicago. He was director of research and statistics for the Colorado Emergency Relief Administration and Works Progress Administration (1934–1936) and then became research assistant and director of the Department of Social Work Administration of the Russell Sage Foundation, where he remained until 1948. During this time he also taught part-time at Hunter College, Rutgers University, and Columbia University. In 1948 Howard was appointed first dean of the School of Social Welfare at the University of California, Los Angeles. He remained in that position until 1960 and remained on the faculty until his retirement in 1970. Howard believed deeply in the goal of improving the world for all people. As an educator, he emphasized the importance of social work's underlying values.

After his retirement he became chairperson of the Los Angeles County Mental Health Board, on which he had served since 1958. Active in many professional organizations, he served as president of the American Association of Social Workers. The author of numerous articles, Howard also wrote *The WPA and Federal Relief Policy* (1942) and *Social Welfare: Values, Means and Ends* (1969).

Maryann Syers

Howe, Samuel Gridley (1801–1876)

Samuel Gridley Howe was a noted philanthropist, educator, and advocate for the physically and mentally handicapped. A native Bostonian, Howe graduated from Brown University in 1821 and from Harvard Medical School in 1824. In 1831 he became director of the New England Asylum for the Blind (later renamed the Perkins Institute), which became internationally known under his leadership. In addition to his pioneering educational efforts for blind, deaf, and retarded people, Howe supported reform for mentally ill people, prisoners, and juvenile offenders. He encouraged investigation and supervision of state charitable and correctional systems. As a result the Massachusetts State Board of Charities was established in 1863. Under Howe's 10-year term as chairperson of the board, conditions in state institutions were studied and reforms were initiated to improve the quality of life for poor children, people with disabilities, and prison inmates.

Howe's writings include *Insanity in Massachusetts* (1843), *An Essay on Separate and Congregate Systems of Prison Discipline* (1846), and *The Refugee from Slavery in Canada West* (1864). See also *Samuel Gridley Howe* (1935), by Laura E. Richards, and *Samuel Gridley Howe, Social Reformer, 1801–1876* (1956), by Harold Schwartz.

Larraine M. Edwards

Huantes, Margarita R. (1914–1994)

Margarita R. Huantes was a social worker and an adult educator. She was a pioneer in the adult literacy movement. As founder and first executive director of the San Antonio Literacy Council, she worked tirelessly to combat adult illiteracy for more than three decades. Since its founding in 1960, the San Antonio Literacy Council has taught more than 60,000 adults how to read and write.

Born in Nueva Rosita, Coahuila, Mexico, Huantes immigrated with her family to San Antonio, Texas, when she was three months old. She received a bachelor of arts degree from the University of Texas in 1939 and a master of social work degree from Case Western Reserve University in 1948.

In her early career Huantes was a schoolteacher and later a social group worker in youth programs and community center settings. In the early 1970s she served on the faculty of the Worden School of Social Service at Our Lady of the Lake University. It was during her work in the community center that Huantes recognized the high rate of functional illiteracy, particularly among Mexican Americans, and worked to establish literacy programs and subsequently the San Antonio Literacy Council. She saw the council grow from a single class with a handful of students in a community center to more than 1,500 students in 20 centers.

Huantes received numerous local, state, and national honors and recognitions for her work on behalf of literacy. She was a member of the Academy of Certified Social Workers, NASW, the National Association of Public School Educators, and the Adult Education Association among others.

Huantes published *Manual de Ciudadania* (1963, 1987), *First Lessons in English, Books I and II* (1965, 1980), *I Want to Learn English and Spanish* (1980), and several articles on adult basic education and women. She is one of 23 Hispanic people featured in *Spanish-Speaking Heroes* (1973) by Roger W. Axford, where she is described as "San Antonio's fighter against illiteracy."

Santos H. Hernández

Jarrett, Mary Cromwell (1876–1961)

Mary Cromwell Jarrett delineated the specialty of psychiatric social work in mental hospitals. After graduating from Goucher College in 1900, she worked for the Boston Children's Aid Society. In 1913 Jarrett organized and headed the social services department of the Boston Psychopathic Hospital, and in 1918 she developed an eight-week course to help prepare social workers to meet the emergency psychiatric needs of patients. The Smith College School for Social Work was an outgrowth of this training course, and Jarrett was associate director there for five years. In 1923 she founded the Psychiatric Social Workers' Club (later the American Association of Psychiatric Social Workers).

As a staff member of the Welfare Council of New York City, Jarrett worked to alleviate the problems associated with chronic illness. From 1927 to 1943 she supported efforts to increase public awareness of chronic illness. Her books include *The Kingdom of Evils* (1922), with Elmer E. Southard; *Chronic Illness in New York City* (1933); and *Housekeeping Service for Home Care of Chronic Patients* (1938).

Larraine M. Edwards

Johnson, Campbell Carrington (1895–1968)

Johnson spent most of his life working to improve military services and social conditions for the black population. A native of Washington, DC, he was educated at Howard University, where he earned a bachelor's degree in 1920 and a law degree in 1922. Johnson spent 17 years as executive secretary of the Twelfth Street Branch of the Washington Young Men's Cristian Association, a position he assumed in 1923. Camp Lichtman, which he helped establish in 1932 for the recreation of black youths, was one of his many community contributions. Beginning in 1932 Johnson taught social science at the Howard University School of Religion for 15 years. During this time he helped organize the Washington Housing Association. In 1940 he was appointed executive assistant to the director of the national Selective Services by President Franklin D. Roosevelt. Recalled to duty from the Army Reserve, Johnson remained with the Selective Service system for 28 years, attaining the rank of full colonel. He worked actively for the equitable treatment of black men and women in the services. In 1946 Johnson was awarded the Army Commendation Ribbon and the Army Distinguished Service Medal. A posthumous award of the Legion of Merit and Distinguished Service Award was made to his family in 1968. See *Dictionary of American Negro Biography* (1982), by R. W. Logan and M. Winston.

Wilma Peebles-Wilkins

Jones, Mary Harris "Mother" (1830–1930)

Mary Harris "Mother" Jones, known as the "white-haired miner's angel" to those who loved her and "the most dangerous woman in America" to those who feared her, was a union organizer for the United Mine Workers of America and was known for her tireless efforts to improve the lives of working people; her courage in facing armed guards, angry mine owners, U.S. senators, or union presidents if they stood in her way; her willingness to go to jail for her beliefs; and her dramatic flair.

Jones was born on May 1, 1830, in Ireland and immigrated to the United States at age seven, according to her autobiography, which was published in 1925 when she was 95 years old. Her "Irish agitator" father, Richard Harris, worked as a laborer on railroad construction and ended up in Toronto where Mary Harris studied elementary education and dressmaking. As a young woman she taught at a convent school in Michigan and worked as a seamstress in Chicago. In 1861 she took a teaching job in Memphis, Tennessee, and married George Jones, a member of the Iron Moulders' Union and an organizer for the Knights of Labor. In 1867 a yellow fever epidemic hit Memphis, and in one week she lost her husband and their four children. In 1871 her dressmaking shop burned to the ground in the Chicago fire. She was in her late forties when she joined the Knights of Labor. In the early 1890s she began organizing coal miners.

With her motto, "Pray for the dead, and fight like hell for the living," Mother Jones participated in the 1892 Homestead strike against Carnegie Steel; the 1894 railman's strike; the anthracite strike of 1900; the Paint and Cabin Creek strike of 1913 in West Virginia; and the Colorado Fuel and Iron strike of 1913–1914, in which seven men, two women, and 11 children died in one of the most

brutal attacks on workers in American history, known as the Ludlow Massacre.

Understanding that "no strike was ever won that did not have the support of the womenfolk," one of Mother Jones's successful strike tactics was the invention of "bucket and broom brigade." In this show of protest, wives of striking miners would march with pots, pans, mops, and brooms to mine entrances dressed in a wild assortment of rags with "loose-flying hair," scaring strikebreakers, mules, and mine owners and confusing company gunmen by banging loudly on pots and pans.

In 1903 Mother Jones sought to dramatize the evils of child labor by leading a march of small children from the striking textile mills of Philadelphia to Oyster Bay, Long Island, where President Theodore Roosevelt lived. When her band of child laborers, many of whom were victims of industrial accidents, reached the president's home, he declined to meet with them. The incident brought much-needed public attention to the issue, although it would be another 13 years before child labor was abolished legally.

Her successful tactics engaged the foes of labor. In 1902, when she was called into a West Virginia courtroom after being arrested for ignoring an injunction banning meetings of striking miners, a prosecuting attorney turned to Mother Jones and stated, "There sits the most dangerous woman in America. She comes into a state where peace and prosperity reign. She crooks her finger—20,000 contented men lay down their tools and walk out."

Coal companies hired the Pinkerton Detective Agency to discredit her, calling her a "vulgar, heartless, vicious creature with a fiery temper and a cold-blooded brutality rare even in the slums."

A U.S. senator trying to denigrate her efforts on behalf of working people, asked her, "Do you think the things you do are ladylike?" "It's the last thing on earth I want to be," she replied.

Mother Jones was a strong critic of the capitalist system: "I asked a man in prison once how he happened to be there and he said he had stolen a pair of shoes. I told him if he had stolen a railroad he would be a United States senator." She also agitated for the release of Mexican revolutionaries jailed in U.S. prisons.

Although she held many old-fashioned views on the roles of women, she herself lived nontraditionally and was fond of saying, "No matter what your fight, don't be ladylike!" and "God almightly made women, and the Rockefeller gang of thieves made the ladies."

Mary Harris Jones died on November 30, 1930, and was buried in the miners' cemetery in Mount

Olive, Illinois.

Joanne "Rocky" Delaplaine

Kelley, Florence (1859–1932)

Florence Kelley was a lifelong advocate for government protection of women and children in the labor force. Born in Philadelphia, where her father was in politics, she earned her undergraduate degree from Cornell University. With credit for graduate studies at the University of Zurich, she obtained a law degree from Northwestern University. As an agent of the U.S. Bureau of Labor Statistics, Kelley investigated sweatshops before being appointed head of the Factory Inspection Department in 1892. In 1899 her work enforcing labor laws earned her the directorate of the National Consumer League, an organization founded by Josephine Shaw Lowell.

As a member of the New York Child Labor Committee in 1902 and of the National Child Labor Committee in 1904, Kelley crusaded against child labor. She and Lillian Wald advocated for government protection of children, leading to the establishment of the U.S. Children's Bureau in 1912. Her published works include *Some Ethical Gains through Legislation* (1905) and *Modern Industry in Relation to the Family, Health, Education, Morality* (1914). See also *Florence Kelley: The Making of a Social Pioneer* (1966), by Dorothy Blumberg, and *Impatient Crusader: Florence Kelley's Life Story* (1953), by Josephine Goldmark.

Larraine M. Edwards

Kellogg, Paul Underwood (1879–1958)

Paul Underwood Kellogg's career as a journalist led him to actively support social welfare projects. Born in Kalamazoo, Michigan, Kellogg took special courses at Columbia University from 1901 to 1906 in addition to attending the New York School of Philanthropy in 1902. He received a LittD from Wesleyan University in 1937. Kellogg worked as a reporter in Michigan for two years before becoming editor of the New York magazine *Charities*. In 1901 he went to Pittsburgh and conducted the first social survey of labor conditions in the steel industry. The findings of his study were published in *The Pittsburgh Survey,* and as a result this approach was used in other cities. From 1912 until his retirement in 1952, Kellogg served as editor of *Survey.* His support for controversial causes earned him a medal for "courageous journalism" from the New York *Evening Post.*

In 1934 Kellogg was appointed vice chairman of the President's Committee on Economic Security by President Franklin D. Roosevelt. In the mid-1930s, Kellogg also served on the Federal Action Committee of the American Association of Social Workers. He was president of the National Conference of Social Work in 1939. With Arthur Gleason, he coauthored *British Labor and the War* (1919). See also *The Pittsburgh Survey* (1909–1914), edited by Paul Underwood Kellogg.

Larraine M. Edwards

Kenworthy, Marion Edwena (1891–1980)

Marion Edwena Kenworthy was a pioneer in introducing psychoanalytic concepts into a social work curriculum. She was influential in the professionalization of social work, playing a role in heightening the profile of social workers both in the World War II military and in the juvenile justice system in New York City. A nationally renowned psychiatrist, Kenworthy increased the recognition of the value of the social work profession within her own discipline as she helped define roles for both professions and fostered interdisciplinary teamwork in various mental health forums throughout her career.

Born in Hampden, Massachusetts, Kenworthy graduated from Tufts University School of Medicine in 1913. After working in the Massachusetts state hospital system and at the Boston Psychopathic Hospital, she moved to New York City in 1919 and taught mental hygiene at the Central School of Hygiene at the Young Women's Christian Association. Through her work at the Vanderbilt Clinic, she met Dr. Bernard Glueck, who invited her to lecture at the New York School of Social Work in 1920. Kenworthy succeeded Dr. Glueck as medical director of the Bureau of Children's Guidance in 1924. After her own analysis by Otto Rank in 1921, Kenworthy began her psychoanalytic practice, which she maintained long after her retirement from teaching. One of the first psychiatrists in New York City to specialize in child psychiatry, she was an active participant in the child guidance movement.

Kenworthy taught full-time at the New York School of Social Work from 1921 until her retirement in 1956. She developed a conceptual framework, the "ego–libido method," which she used to help students understand psychodynamic concepts and apply their understanding to work with individuals and families. On her retirement from the Columbia University School of Social Work, a chair in psychiatry was established in her name.

As a consultant, Kenworthy was instrumental in focusing attention on mental health services in the armed forces in the early 1940s. She advocated for the establishment of mental hygiene units in basic training camps and supported the creation of a distinct status for social workers in the service. In 1944 Kenworthy was appointed to the

National Civilian Advisory Committee to the Women's Army Corps. Among her many elected positions, Kenworthy was the first woman president of the American Psychoanalytic Association (1958–1959), the American Academy of Child Psychiatry (1959–1961), and The Group for the Advancement of Psychiatry (GAP) (1959–1961). She was also the first chairperson of GAP's Committee on Psychiatric Social Work (1943–1949). Her many published works on mental hygiene and children's mental health include her coauthored (with Porter Lee) *Mental Hygiene and Social Work,* a summary of the work of the Bureau of Children's Guidance.

Rebecca L. Sperling

King, Martin Luther, Jr. (1929–1968)

Martin Luther King, Jr., was a civil rights leader, an author, a minister, and an orator. Born in Atlanta, Georgia, to a middle-class family, King spent most of his career advocating for civil rights and protesting American social injustices. King entered Morehouse College at the age of 15 and graduated with a BA degree in sociology in 1948. Ordained as a minister, King graduated from Crozer Theological Seminary in Pennsylvania in 1951 with a BD degree. In 1955 he received a PhD from Boston University's School of Theology.

King's involvement with the Montgomery Bus Boycott helped to catapult him to national and international prominence. He soon became the voice of the nonviolent civil rights movement. King helped organize the Southern Christian Leadership Conference in 1957, and within a month he was elected president of the organization. King also gave moral and financial support to the Student Nonviolent Coordinating Committee, which was also headquartered in Atlanta. King's "Letter from the Birmingham Jail" has become a classic statement about African American–organized aggression for equal access to opportunity. While King systematically confronted social injustices, he was constantly harassed by the FBI and a target of personal and professional attacks.

King's "I Have a Dream" speech was the highlight of the 1963 March on Washington, where he spoke to the crowd of more than 200,000 people of his dream of justice and peace for all Americans. King was invited to Sweden in 1963 to receive the Nobel Peace Prize, and in 1964 he was selected by *Time* magazine as Man of the Year, the first African American to be so honored. King was assassinated in Memphis, Tennessee, in 1968. In 1977 President Jimmy Carter posthumously awarded him the Medal of Freedom. King wrote numerous articles and several books, including *Stride Toward Freedom* (1958), *Why We Can't Wait* (1964), and *Where*

Do We Go From Here? (1967).

Iris Carlton-LaNey

Kuralt, Wallace H., Sr. (1908–1994)

Wallace H. Kuralt, Sr., father of noted journalist Charles Kuralt, was a lifelong social work practitioner and administrator. Throughout his career, Kuralt was distinguished by his innovative spirit and deeply held convictions about helping children and families. From 1945 until his retirement in 1972, Kuralt directed the Mecklenburg County Department of Social Services (Charlotte, North Carolina). He pioneered efforts to implement child care and child development centers and is credited for instituting family planning services long before such programs were nationally accepted. Many of his innovative ideas served as models for public welfare programs throughout North Carolina and the nation. Kuralt was highly regarded as an imaginative administrator who was at the forefront of efforts to implement programs to enable welfare recipients to escape poverty and dependence. He also was a strong advocate of the value of early childhood education and stressed the importance of giving children a sense of their own worth and ability even before their kindergarten years. Kuralt's advocacy efforts to improve public welfare programs included frequent testimony before government bodies, including the North Carolina general assembly, the U.S. Congress, and the United Nations. Numerous foreign countries sent social services officials from the public and private sectors to visit Mecklenburg County to learn about innovative programs implemented by Kuralt. Kuralt was a skilled teacher and mentor, and many of those he influenced became successful directors of social services agencies throughout North Carolina. Kuralt was a 1931 graduate of the University of North Carolina at Chapel Hill and attended the university's School of Social Work from 1937 to 1938. In 1991 the Wallace H. Kuralt, Sr., Professorship in Public Welfare Policy and Administration was established at the University of North Carolina at Chapel Hill School of Social Work. In 1994 the Department of Social Services building in Charlotte was named in his honor.

Elizabeth A. S. Benefield

Lassalle, Beatriz (1882–1965)

Beatriz Lassalle is recognized as the most important pioneer of social work practice in Puerto Rico. Beginning her career at the age of 17, she dedicated herself to the needs of children and families, especially those affected by blindness and other disabilities. She studied at the New York School of Social Work from 1920 to 1921 and shortly afterward was named executive secretary of the Juvenile Red Cross of Puerto Rico, for which she established the first Department of Social Work. In 1922 she coordinated the first Child Congress ever held in Puerto Rico. During the Great Depression she headed programs in the Puerto Rico Emergency Reconstruction Administration, making social services an integral component of the Department of Health. She was a leader in the development of the first laws regulating social work practice in Puerto Rico.

Both before and after retirement Lassalle promoted social action and participated actively in civic affairs. She was president of the first suffragist organization in Puerto Rico, established the Home for Tubercular Children, and cofounded the Society for the Welfare of the Blind. In 1946 the College of Social Workers of Puerto Rico named her its honorary president and dedicated its sixth annual meeting to her as "testimony of profound admiration." After her death the Graduate School of Social Work at the University of Puerto Rico was named in her honor. See "Semblanza de la Srta. Beatriz Lassalle: Servia, Devisa de Una Vida," *Revista de Servicio Social* (1946), by Julia Denoyers.

John F. Longres

Lathrop, Julia Clifford (1858–1932)

Julia Clifford Lathrop was a well-known advocate for the welfare of children and mentally ill people. The daughter of abolitionists, she was born in Rockford, Illinois. Her social work career began at Hull-House after she graduated from Vassar College in 1880. As a resident of Hull-House, Lathrop was involved in the establishment of the Chicago United Charities and other activities to help poor people. In 1899 the establishment of the first juvenile court in the United States resulted from her work with Illinois law. After a European study tour of methods of caring for mentally ill people, Lathrop became involved in the founding efforts of the national mental hygiene movement. In addition, she helped found the country's first mental hygiene clinic for children, the Juvenile Psychopathic Institute, in 1909.

In 1912, Lathrop, an activist in the mothers' pension movement, became the first director of the U.S. Children's Bureau. During her 12 years as director, maternal and infant problems as well as the social, economic, and health problems of children were studied, investigated, and analyzed. After leaving the bureau, she became active in the women's suffrage movement. From 1925 to 1931 she served as an advisor to the Child Welfare Committee of the League of Nations. See *My Friend, Julia Lathrop* (1935), by Jane Addams; and

Unto the Least of These: Social Services for Children (1947), by Emma O. Lundberg.

Larraine M. Edwards

Lee, Porter Raymond (1879–1939)

Porter Raymond Lee was a pioneer in the development of social work education. Born in Buffalo, New York, he graduated from Cornell University in 1903. He developed an interest in social work as an undergraduate student and later attended the summer institute of the New York School of Philanthropy. In 1909, after serving as assistant secretary of the Charity Organization Society of Buffalo, he succeeded Mary Richmond as general secretary of the Philadelphia Society for Organizing Charity. Lee joined the faculty of the New York School of Philanthropy as a social casework instructor in 1912. Recognizing the need for differential training in social work, he became instrumental in organizing the American Association of Schools of Social Work in 1919.

As a teacher and philosopher, Lee integrated ideas from other fields such as psychiatry, economics, and political science to help formulate a generic social casework theory. He served on a number of professional boards and was elected president of the National Conference of Social Work in 1929. Lee's published works include *Social Salvage* (1924), coauthored with Walter Pettit; *Mental Hygiene and Social Work* (1929), coauthored with Marion Kenworthy; and *Social Work: Cause and Function* (1937).

Larraine M. Edwards

Lenroot, Katharine Fredrica (1891–1982)

Associated with the U.S. Children's Bureau for 37 years, Katharine Fredrica Lenroot became its chief in 1934. Lenroot was born and raised in Superior, Wisconsin, the daughter of Swedish immigrants. Influenced by her father—he was a congressional representative, senator, and a judge of the U.S. Court of Customs and Patent Appeals—Lenroot's interest in public affairs began early. In 1911, just two years out of high school, she spoke before a committee of the state legislature for a minimum wage law. Lenroot graduated from the University of Wisconsin in 1912 and in 1913 became a deputy of the Wisconsin Industrial Commission.

Lenroot's career with the Children's Bureau began in 1914 when she became a special agent. In 1915 she attended the New York School of Social Work and also became assistant director of the Social Service Division of the Children's Bureau. In 1922 she was made assistant chief, and in 1934 President Roosevelt appointed her chief. As the bureau's third chief, Lenroot represented the United States on the executive board of UNICEF, served as secretary of the 1950 White House Conference on Children and Youth, and testified frequently before Senate and House committees on juvenile delinquency, child labor laws, and federal aid for maternal and child welfare and school health services. Widely praised for her contributions to child welfare and for her skillful administration, Lenroot was also president of the National Conference of Social Work (1935) and a member of the board of the Child Welfare League of America. Her writings include *Juvenile Delinquency, a Summary of Available Material on Extent, Causes, Treatment, and Prevention* (1929).

Maryann Syers

Lindeman, Eduard Christian (1885–1953)

Eduard Christian Lindeman's participation in community and professional organizations and his teaching and writings on social philosophy and group methods earned him the respect of the social work profession. One of 10 children of Danish immigrants, he studied on his own to qualify for college admission and graduated from Michigan Agricultural College in 1911. He edited an agricultural journal and became assistant to the minister of a Congregational church. A desire to combine teaching with religious activity resulted in his appointment to George Williams College in Chicago. In 1920 he became professor of sociology at North Carolina College for Women but was asked to resign because his opposition to segregation antagonized the local community.

Lindeman subsequently joined the faculty of the New York School of Social Work, where he remained until his retirement in 1950. In 1952 he became president of the National Conference of Social Work. His books include *Social Discovery: An Approach to the Study of Functional Groups* (1936) and *Wealth and Culture* (1936). See also *Eduard C. Lindeman and Social Work Philosophy* (1958), by Gisela Konopka.

John F. Longres

Lindsay, Inabel Burns (1900–1983)

Inabel Lindsay was the first dean of the Howard University School of Social Work. Born in St. Joseph, Missouri, she prepared for a teaching career during her college education. After receiving her undergraduate degree, she entered the New York School of Social Work as an Urban League Fellow from 1920 to 1921. Sixteen years later she completed a master's degree at the University of Chicago, School of Social Service Administration. In 1952 Lindsay earned a doctorate in social work from the University of Pittsburgh. She taught a few years before beginning her social work experiences as a family welfare practitioner, agency administrator, and social researcher. In 1937 Lindsay joined the Department of Sociology at Howard University as an instructor and assistant in charge of social work under E. Franklin Frazier. In 1945 a School of Social Work was established at Howard University and Lindsay became dean. When she retired in 1967, Lindsay was the only female university academic dean in the Washington, DC, area. Committed to principles of social justice, she maintained a strong role in professional leadership while promoting the growth of the School of Social Work. Under Lindsay's leadership, the Howard University School of Social Work became the second accredited school in the country serving black students. She published a number of survey papers and articles on community leadership, elderly people, and black participation in social welfare. See "Portrait of a Dean: A Biography of Inabel Burns Lindsay, First Dean of the Howard University School of Social Work" (dissertation by LayMoyne Mason Matthews, University of Maryland, 1976).

Wilma Peebles-Wilkins

Lodge, Richard (1921–1981)

A social work educator and administrator, Richard Lodge was a strong advocate for the essential role of theory in social work. Born in Ohio, Lodge graduated from the Carnegie Institute of Technology in 1943. He received his MSW from the University of Pittsburgh School of Social Work in 1950 and became a worker, supervisor, and administrator of group work agencies. In 1955 he joined the faculty of the University of Pennsylvania School of Social Work, receiving his DSW in 1958. In 1966 he was appointed dean of the School of Social Work at Virginia Commonwealth University, and in 1972 he became executive director of the Council on Social Work Education (CSWE).

As director of CSWE, Lodge implemented accreditation of baccalaureate social work programs, acted on proposals to bring practice and education into closer correspondence, and helped establish the Commission on the Role and Status of Women in Social Work Education and on Educational Planning. He was also active in maintaining threatened federal funding for social work education. Lodge left CSWE in 1978 to join the doctoral faculty at Adelphi University School of Social Work. At Adelphi, he taught courses in theory building in social work and cofounded a faculty study group researching new means of generating social work theory. Lodge was the author of numerous journal articles on social group work and social work education.

Maryann Syers

Loeb, Martin B. (1913–1983)

Martin Loeb was a leader in both social work education and gerontology in higher education. Educated in Toronto, he received a PhD in human development from the University of Chicago in 1957. Loeb was director of the School of Social Work at the University of Wisconsin from 1965 to 1973 and director of the McBeath Institute on Aging and Adult Life, which he founded, from 1973 to 1980. Following his retirement in 1980, he remained active in university life, continuing to teach, conducting research, and participating in faculty governance. He presented his final paper, "Toward a Technology of Caring," just five days before his death.

Prior to joining the Wisconsin faculty, Loeb served on the faculties of the University of California, Los Angeles; the University of Kansas City; the University of Chicago; and the University of California, Berkeley. While on faculty, he directed several major research projects, including the Santa Monica Teen-Age Study and the Kansas City Study of Adult Life. His first book, coauthored with W. Lloyd Warner and Robert Havighurst, *Who Shall Be Educated? The Challenge of Unequal Opportunities* (1941), is regarded as a classic. He also wrote six other books, monographs, and some 30 articles and book chapters on a wide range of topics.

A member of many professional organizations, Loeb was a fellow of the Gerontological Society, the American Anthropological Society, the American Sociological Association, and the American Association for the Advancement of Science as well as a member of NASW, CSWE, the Academy of Certified Social Workers, and the Society for the Study of Social Gerontology in Higher Education, for which he served as president in 1975–1976.

In addition to his professional academic career, Loeb was a professional dancer, a figure skater, an actor, a consulting editor for the *Toronto Star,* a sailor, an international traveler, and a maker of pewterware. Among the most important of his accomplishments was the contribution he made to the lives and careers of his students and colleagues. A dedicated mentor of many, he had the ability to identify talent and to find ways to develop that talent. Through Loeb's stimulation, vision, and leadership, the University of Wisconsin School of Social Work experienced significant growth and attained national prominence during his years as a faculty member and director.

Mona Wasow

Love, Maria Maltby (1840–1931)

Maria Maltby Love, born in 1840 near Buffalo, New York, was a social architect and humanitarian who crusaded for education, health, and tenement reform. She pioneered two projects to help women and their families achieve better lives: the Fitch Crèche (1881)—the first day nursery for the children of working women in the United States—and the Church District Plan (1896), a citywide, interdenominational program designed to provide neighborhood-based community services. Love was involved in the formation of the Charity Organization Society in Buffalo (1877) and organized its first Provident Scheme, the Fitch Crèche. Besides being a day nursery, it offered health care programs and the city's first kindergarten to children of poor working women. An on-site nursemaids training school for young women was the first in the nation. Crèche staff provided family services outreach through home visitation, and a system of convalescent care boarding homes was created for ill women and children. The Crèche and its innovative programs gained widespread national recognition at the Chicago World's Fair in 1893 and the Pan American Exposition in 1901. Internationally, Denmark and Siam adopted the Crèche model.

Love also was the originator of the Church District Plan, which, by sectoring the entire city and placing each district in the care of a cooperating church, promoted the development of neighborhood outreach efforts within the community. The plan's first decade saw an enhancement of social work activities through the cooperative efforts of 122 interfaith congregations. The Church District Plan was presented at the National Conference on Charities and Correction in May 1896 and was copied in Brooklyn, New York; Seattle, Washington; and Cambridge, Massachusetts. Following her death, Love was honored in 1932 by the Charity Organization Society, which called her "a moving and guiding spirit in the development of social work."

Renee Bowman Daniel
Karen Berner Little

Lowell, Josephine Shaw (1843–1905)

Josephine Shaw Lowell, a leader in the "scientific philanthropy movement," helped to promote the reorganization of public and private charities in the United States. Born in West Roxbury, Massachusetts, she was educated in private schools around the country. Her volunteer service began at the start of the Civil War when she worked with a forerunner of the American Red Cross—the United States Sanitary Commission. She joined the New York State Charities Aid Association in 1873 and became the first female member of the New York State Board of Charities in 1876. Lowell spent 13 years with the board and succeeded in providing more institutions for mentally ill people and more correctional facilities for women. In 1882 she helped found the New York Charity Organization Society. Her concern for women in the labor force led her to become the first president of the Consumers League, an organization founded in 1891 to protect shopgirls from exploitation in New York City. Lowell's published works include *Public Relief and Preventive Charity* (1884) and *Industrial Arbitration and Conciliation* (1893). See also *The Philanthropic Work of Josephine Shaw Lowell* (1911), by W. R. Stewart.

Larraine M. Edwards

Lowy, Louis (1920–1991)

Louis Lowy was a scholar, a teacher, a leader in the fields of gerontology and social work education, and a pioneer in advancing international social work education. Born in Munich, Germany, he was studying philosophy at Charles University in Prague when World War II broke out. From 1941 to 1945 Lowy was imprisoned by the Nazis in concentration camps, and at the war's end he was the sole survivor of his family. After working as a welfare worker in a displaced persons camp in Deggendorf, Bavaria, Lowy emigrated with his wife to Boston, Massachusetts, in 1946. While employed as a social group worker, he earned a BS from Boston University and an MSW from its Graduate School of Social Work. Following graduation he served at the Jewish Community Center in Bridgeport, Connecticut, as activities director for adults and older adults, beginning a lifelong connection to the emerging field of gerontology. He returned to Boston in 1955 as assistant executive director of the Jewish Centers Association and in 1957 joined the faculty of the Boston University School of Social Work. He earned an EdD from the Harvard University Graduate School of Education in 1966.

In 1974 Lowy cofounded the Boston University Gerontology Center and became its codirector. His talent and skill as a great teacher and lecturer were recognized in 1979 when the trustees of Boston University awarded him the Metcalf Award for Excellence in Teaching. He retired from Boston University in 1985, having served as chair of the social welfare policy sequence for 16 years, associate dean for curriculum, and director of the joint doctoral program in sociology and social work. In 1988 Lowy was awarded an honorary doctoral degree by Wheelock College, and in 1990 he was honored with a Life Achievement Award by the Eastern Massachusetts chapter of NASW in recognition of his contributions to gerontology, social work education, and the profession of social work. Lowy's published works include *The Challenge and Promise of the Later Years: Social Work with the*

Aging (1985), *Social Policies and Programs on Aging: What Is and What Should Be in the Later Years* (1986), and *Why Education in the Later Years* (coauthored with Darlene O'Connor, 1986). He also contributed chapters to numerous books, wrote many monographs, and authored more than 40 journal articles.

Leonard Bloksberg

Lucas, Elizabeth Jessemine Kauikeolani Low (1895–1986)

Elizabeth (also known as Clorinda) Low Lucas was an advocate for children and the first Hawaiian woman to receive a professional education in social work. Lucas was the daughter of Elizabeth Napoleon, a descendant of Hawaiian and Tahitian royalty, and Ebenezer Parker Law, great grandson of John Palmer Parker, owner of the Parker Ranch and a direct descendant of King Kamehameha I. She married Charles W. Lucas. They had a daughter, Laura.

Lucas was born just after the Hawaiian monarchy was overthrown and three years before Hawaii was annexed by the United States. The Caucasians formed their own government and their own society. Socially ostracized, deprived of their language, their land, their government, their culture, and their religion, the Hawaiian people had been taught by the Christian missionaries to feel shame for what they were and what their parents and heroic ancestors were. By the time of annexation, they had lost their sense of worth and self-respect—in effect, their identity.

Lucas learned early the meaning, to children and adults, of the fundamental difference between basic values of her Hawaiian heritage—caring, sharing, trusting relationships, and cooperation in work and in play—and the values of competition and achievement as the measure of success held by the Caucasians. Guiding her wide-ranging professional activity was the long-term goal of a community, a society that would value and respect its people and would be socially just for all—a philosophy that is critical for humanity's survival today. Permeating all that she did was the concern that all children have the opportunity to develop understanding, attitudes, and strengths within themselves for daily living and problem solving that would enable them to take social responsibility as citizens for maintaining a humane and just society in the future. Lucas was accepted and respected in her own right in both Hawaiian and Caucasian cultures.

She became involved in community activity during her high school years when she worked as a volunteer with children in an impoverished neighborhood. Guiding her in this early community involvement and in her later professional efforts was a concern that all children have the opportunity to develop the necessary skills and attitudes for daily living and problem solving to become responsible citizens. Following her graduation from Smith College in 1917, Lucas worked in New York City for the national board of the Young Women's Christian Association in the Division of Education for Foreign-Born Women. On her return to Hawaii in 1921, she served as assistant director of the Strong Foundation Dental Clinic for underprivileged children and as executive secretary of the Hawaiian Humane Society, which then was concerned about abused children as well as abused animals.

Lucas received a diploma, the equivalent of an MSW degree, from the New York School (now Columbia University School of Social Work) in 1937 and returned to Hawaii to be the Oahu County chief of the Department of Social Welfare. She later was director of the Division of Child Welfare. In 1943 Lucas accepted the position of director of pupil guidance in the Department of Public Instruction, which she held until retirement in 1960. Lucas believed that the schools offered a natural opportunity for a team approach to the problems experienced by children. A team approach could bring the teacher, pupil, parent, community, and school into a trusting relationship that could create a better environment as well as new attitudes of acceptance and respect.

Lucas was the first woman to be selected as a member and rotating chair of the board of trustees of the Queen Liliuokalani Trust, which served orphaned and destitute Hawaiian children. Under her leadership, units of the Queen Liliuokalani Children's Center were established on the main islands. Lucas also served as president of the board of directors of the Kapiolani Children's and Maternity Hospital, chair of the State Commission on Children and Youth and in 1970 its delegate to the White House Conference, chair of the Kamehameha Schools Advisory Council, president of the 4-H Foundation board of directors, and president of the Pan-Pacific and Southeast Asian Women's Association. The breadth of Lucas's contribution to the community is partly reflected by some of the many awards she received: the Smith College Distinguished Alumni Award; the David Malo Award of the West Honolulu Rotary Club; the Distinguished Service Award for Home, School, and Community Services of the Hawaiian Congress of the PTA; and the Francis E. Clark Award of the Hawaii Personnel and Guidance Association. In 1979 she was named a Living Trustee of Hawaii by

the Buddhist Honpa Hongwanji Mission in Hawaii.

Patricia L. Ewalt

Lurie, Harry Lawrence (1892–1973)

During his 60-year professional career, Harry Lawrence Lurie became a leader in the establishment and proliferation of Jewish charities. A native of Latvia, he earned both his bachelor's and master's degrees from the University of Michigan. His career began in 1913 as an agent for Buffalo's Federated Jewish Charities. Among Lurie's leadership positions, he served as director of research for the Associated Jewish Charities of Detroit, superintendent of the Jewish Social Service Bureau of Chicago, and executive director of the National Bureau of Jewish Social Research. In 1932 Lurie became executive director of the newly created Council of Jewish Federations and Welfare Funds, remaining there until his retirement in 1954.

In addition to establishing several national and international Jewish philanthropic organizations, Lurie lectured at universities around the United States. He formulated basic curriculum guidelines for community organization for the Council on Social Work Education. Between 1937 and 1955 Lurie published a number of articles on social welfare, and in 1965 he became the first editor of the *Encyclopedia of Social Work*. He was the author of *A Heritage Affirmed: The Jewish Federation Movement in America* (1961).

Larraine M. Edwards

Manning, Leah Katherine Hicks (1917–1979)

Leah Katherine Hicks Manning was instrumental in the development and passage of the Indian Child Welfare Act. Manning, a Shoshone-Paiute, was born in Reno, Nevada, and attended high school in Oklahoma. She was educated at Bacone Indian Junior College at Muskogee, Oklahoma, and Keuka College for Women in New York, becoming a fourth-grade teacher at an American Indian school. She studied social work at the University of Chicago, practiced in Los Angeles after World War II, and became a part-time social worker with the United Presbyterian Church.

In the early 1960s, Manning began working for the Bureau of Indian Affairs (BIA). In 1968 she earned an MSW from the University of Utah School of Social Work and was honored as the year's outstanding social work student. In 1971 she took a two-year leave of absence to set up and direct the first social services program for the Inter-Tribal Council of Nevada. This contracted program, run entirely by American Indian professionals, served the Indian population of member tribes. As a BIA staff development specialist, Manning promoted better understanding of Indian families and culture for social workers who worked with American Indians. She favored keeping Indian children on reservations or near their families to promote healthy development, a key component of the Indian Child Welfare Act. In 1974 the Nevada chapter of NASW named her Social Worker of the Year. She served on the National American Indian Graduate Scholarship Board, the executive board of the National American Indian Women's Association, and the National Indian Presbyterian Advisory Committee and was a lifetime member of the National Congress of American Indians.

Jean K. Quam

Marín, Rosa C. (1912–1989)

Rosa C. Marín was a prominent social worker, educator, and research consultant. She was born in Arecibo, Puerto Rico, and received a bachelor of science degree from the University of Puerto Rico in 1933; she received a master of science degree in 1944 and a doctorate in social work in 1953, both from the University of Pittsburgh. She worked with the Puerto Rico Emergency Relief Administration from 1933 to 1940 as "town head," junior social worker, director, social supervisor, and chief researcher. From 1940 to 1944 she worked as supervisor of special projects and was chief of scientific research and statistics at the Health Department. From 1944 to 1974 she worked as professor, director of the research unit, and director of the School of Social Work of the University of Puerto Rico. In 1980 she received the professor emeritus distinction from the University of Puerto Rico. Dr. Marín founded *Revista Humanidad* in 1967, a social welfare journal well known in Latin America. She was a visiting professor of social work and social research in Colombia (1965), Peru (1965–1966), Bolivia (1966), Chile (1966), and Panama (1968) through the U.S. State Department. She was president of the Puerto Rican College of Social Work from 1943 to 1945 and president of the Puerto Rican chapter of NASW. She was a member of the Council on Human Resources, Association of Teachers of Puerto Rico, National Conference on Social Welfare, Social Newspaperwomen, American Academy of Politics and Social Sciences, American Association of Statisticians, and the Association of Research Centers Administration. She was a prolific researcher and writer and well known for studies on dependent multiproblem families in Puerto Rico, the female drug addict in Puerto Rico, and fraudulent medical prescriptions of controlled substances in Puerto Rico. Marín coauthored *Manpower Resources Projections* and was a key researcher for "La Vida." In 1987 she received the Bicentennial Medal of the University of Pittsburgh for lifetime achievement.

During the latter part of her career, Dr. Marín participated actively as a member of boards and as a researcher. Known as a humanist, she believed that "Compassion is the supreme value. Everything is subordinated to that." She made a strong impact among Puerto Rican social workers with her expertise as a social scientific researcher.

Victor I. García Toro

Marshall, Thurgood (1908–1993)

Thurgood Marshall, the first African American U.S. Supreme Court Justice, was born in Baltimore, Maryland, and is credited with ending American apartheid. Marshall was the great grandson of a former slave and of a Union soldier and was the son of a Pullman porter and schoolteacher. Marshall graduated from Howard University Law School after having been denied admission to the University of Maryland's law school because of his race.

Beginning in 1936, Marshall, as legal counsel for the National Association for the Advancement of Colored People, investigated lynchings, staged boycotts, won salary equalization for African American teachers, and obtained voting rights for African American southerners (*Smith v. Allwright*). Marshall also successfully challenged the legality of racially restrictive housing covenants (*Shelly v. Kraemer*). In 1954, Marshall successfully argued *Brown v. Board of Education of Topeka*, striking down segregation in public education in the United States.

President Kennedy appointed Marshall to the U.S. Court of Appeals in 1961. In 1965 President Johnson named Marshall as U.S. solicitor general. Marshall was the first African American to hold the post of solicitor general and in 1967 became the first African American Supreme Court Justice, a post he held until 1991. Although Marshall's career as an attorney included an array of "firsts," he was best known as a jurist who fought for the rights of the oppressed: civil and equal rights for ethnic minorities, women's rights, prisoner rights, and rights of poor people. Marshall was well known for his opposition to the death penalty, believing it to be cruel and unusual punishment.

In 1992 NASW honored Justice Marshall with the first National Social Justice Award. NASW President Barbara White noted that NASW honors Marshall "because we recognize there are few individuals who can look back on a lifetime of work and know that the world is a different place because of their wisdom and courage."

Karen D. Stout

Matthews, Victoria Earle (1861–1907)

Victoria Earle Matthews was a civic leader and activist in the black women's club movement. She was born to a slave mother in Fort Valley, Georgia. Her formal education consisted of only brief public school attendance. She taught herself by using the library in a home in New York City, where she was a domestic worker. After writing for local literary publications, Matthews became involved in women's activities. In 1892 she became the first president of the Woman's Loyal Union of New York and Brooklyn. She participated with Josephine St. Pierre Ruffin in the founding of the National Federation of Afro-American Women. The federation was renamed the National Association of Colored Women after merging with the National Colored Women's League. Matthews worked as a national organizer for the league for two years and subsequently became concerned about young black girls arriving in the city with no support. On tours of the south, Matthews investigated the circumstances related to prostitution among young black girls. In 1897 she organized the White Rose Industrial Association for young black women working in New York City. See *Notable American Women* (1971), by Edward T. James, Janet Wilson James, and Paul S. Boyer.

Wilma Peebles-Wilkins

Mayo, Leonard Withington (1899–1993)

Leonard Mayo was born at the Berkshire Industrial Farm, in Canaan, New York, where his father was director. He graduated from Colby College in Maine and from 1922 to 1930 worked as an administrator in children's institutions. For the next five years, he did graduate work in sociology and social work at New York University and the New York School of Social Work, where he also was an instructor. From 1935 to 1941 Mayo was an administrator at the Welfare Council of New York City. He then served as dean of the School of Applied Social Sciences, Western Reserve University, in Cleveland, from 1941 to 1948. He left Cleveland in 1949 to become director of the Association for the Aid of Crippled Children (later renamed the Foundation for Child Development) in New York City. He returned to Colby College, as a professor, from 1966 to 1971, developing a major that combined the social and natural sciences. In 1981 Mayo accepted a second post at Western Reserve University as vice president and development officer for the school he had formerly headed.

Mayo's influence spanned the areas of child welfare, mental retardation, and public health. In the course of a long career, he had an impact on social services for children and for disabled people in the United States and abroad. During World War II Mayo was chairperson of the Federal Commission on Children in Wartime. He served on four White House Conferences on Children and Youth and was an advisor to five presidents, from Truman to Ford. He also served as chairperson of President Kennedy's Committee on Mental Retardation, which produced recommendations that modernized care and services for mentally retarded people. Mayo served as president of the National Conference of Social Work, chairperson of the Social Welfare Department of the National Council of Churches, and chairperson of the Board of the Child Welfare League of America. He was president of the International Union for Child Welfare from 1957 to 1973.

Mayo was awarded honorary doctorates by Colby College and Case Western Reserve University. He also was awarded the Albert Lasker Award in World Rehabilitation and a presidential citation for his work on employing people with disabilities. In 1978 a chair was established in his name at the school he had headed. He produced hundreds of speeches and published papers but only one book, *From Service to Research* (1965). In his last years, he worked on a book about children and families, which is unpublished.

Mayo's investment in children never flagged. When, in his 90s, Mayo read that a child had died in a county foster home, he sent me the clipping with a message: "Do something about this!" Yes, sir! Leonard, wherever you are.

Alvin L. Schorr

Miller, Samuel O. (1931–1994)

Samuel O. Miller was a social work educator, scholar, and practitioner. Born in Panama, he earned a BA (cum laude) in sociology and education from Dakota Wesleyan University, an MSW (with honors) in casework from Boston University, and a PhD in social work practice from the University of Chicago School of Social Service Administration. From 1970 through 1973 he was an associate professor at the Western Michigan University School of Social Work. From 1973 until his death Miller was a faculty member at the Columbia University School of Social Work (associate professor, 1973–1989; professor, 1989–1994). Miller's teaching and scholarly contributions were complemented by an active private social work practice.

Miller was a member of the House of Delegates of the Council on Social Work Education (1982–1984) and a member of the board of directors of the Manhattan Country School, the James Weldon Johnson Counseling Center, and the New York City chapter of NASW. He was a recipient of a Career Teacher Award from the National Institute of Mental Health (NIMH), a Whitney Young Academic and Internship Award, and an NIMH National Research Service Award. Listed in *Who's Who among Blacks* and *Who's Who in the East,* Miller had wide-ranging scholarly interests. Among the topics examined in his published articles and books are racial barriers in schools of social work, Hispanic social workers, clinical social work in cross-cultural contexts, primary prevention for ethnic minorities, maternity homes, long-term care facilities, and social work interventions for acquired immune deficiency syndrome (AIDS). With Barbara Dane, he coauthored *AIDS: Intervening with Hidden Grievers* (1993).

Ronald A. Feldman

Newstetter, Wilber I. (1896–1972)

Wilber I. Newstetter encouraged the development of specialized training for social workers in youth and group leadership. Born in Massillon, Ohio, he served in World War I and graduated from the University of Pennsylvania in 1919. Newstetter later received a master's degree in sociology from Western Reserve University. His career began with a position as head worker at the Woodland Center and directorship of Harkness Camp in Cleveland, Ohio. In 1926 he helped develop a two-year group work program at the School of Applied Social Sciences at Western Reserve University. During the 1930s, Newstetter established Cleveland's University Settlement—the first university-operated social work training center—which served families and youths and provided neighborhood outreach services. His recommendations helped establish a school of social work at the University of Pittsburgh, and he served as its first dean in 1938.

In the course of Newstetter's professional career, he served as an officer of the Cleveland Welfare Federation, the National Federation of Settlements, and the American Camping Association. He was also president of the American Association of Social Workers, the American Association of Schools of Social Work, and the National Conference on Social Welfare. With Marc Feldstein and Theodore Newcomb, he coauthored *Group Adjustment* (1938).

Larraine M. Edwards

Pagan de Colon, Petroamerica (1911–1980)

Petroamerica Pagan de Colon championed the causes of employment security, safe working conditions, and workers' rights throughout her public career. Born in the mountains of Puerto Rico, she studied social work at the University of Puerto Rico and human resources development at Columbia University. Her career began in rural vocational education, but her commitment to employment issues led to executive appointments

with the Departments of Education and of Labor in Puerto Rico. In the course of her work, she introduced programs benefiting migrant workers, people with disabilities, and other disadvantaged groups. Her pioneering work in vocational rehabilitation continues to be the base around which these services are offered. She helped draft original legislation for the protection and security of Puerto Rican migrant workers in the United States and developed employment services during Operation Bootstrap.

As increasing numbers of Puerto Ricans took industrial jobs in the United States, Pagan de Colon worked tirelessly, through program development and voter registration drives, to ensure that migration to the United States would not produce disillusionment. After 1960 she headed programs and departments in the U.S. Department of Labor and for the Organization of American States. She was honored as Woman of the Year by the Commonwealth of Puerto Rico in 1978, and in 1985, the Foundation for Workers' Homes named its home for retired workers in her honor. Similarly, the main meeting hall of the Puerto Rican Department of Labor was named in her honor. Her published speeches include "The Status of the Migrant: The Migrant and the Affluent Society" (1962) and "Migration: Dream or Disillusionment?" (1964).

John F. Longres

Perkins, Frances (1882–1965)

Best known as the first woman member of a U.S. Cabinet, Frances Perkins was appointed secretary of labor in 1933 by President Franklin D. Roosevelt. Born in Boston, Perkins was raised in Worcester, Massachusetts, in a conservative Republican family. Trained as a chemist, she graduated from Mount Holyoke in 1902. She did social work for the Episcopal Church for two years, lived at Hull-House for six months to learn more about social work, and earned a master's degree from Columbia University in 1910. As secretary of the New York Consumer's League (1910–1912), executive secretary of the New York Committee on Safety (1912–1917), and director of investigations for the New York State Factory Commission (1912–1913), she earned a reputation as an authority on industrial conditions and hazards.

Perkins became executive director of the New York Council of Organizations for War Services (1919–1921), director of the Council on Immigrant Education (1921–1923), and member (1922–1926) and chair (1926–1929) of the New York State Industrial Board. There was criticism when Governor Roosevelt appointed her New York State Industrial Commissioner in 1929 and much greater outcry, when—as president—he appointed her secretary of labor.

As secretary, Perkins instituted a fact-finding system on employment and unemployment statistics, helped standardize state industrial legislation, and promoted the adoption of the social security system. Her social work background led her to advocate for improving workers' conditions, including minimum wages, maximum hours, child labor legislation, and unemployment compensation. In 1945 she resigned and was appointed to the U.S. Civil Service Commission, where she remained until 1953. She wrote a memoir of Roosevelt and many books and articles on labor issues. See also *Madam Secretary, Frances Perkins* (1976), by George Whitney Martin.

Jean K. Quam

Pray, Kenneth (1882–1948)
Kenneth Pray was a leader in social work education. A native of Whitewater, Wisconsin, he graduated from the University of Wisconsin and moved to Philadelphia where he worked as a reporter for the city's *Record*. Pray left journalism to become executive secretary of social planning and administration for the Public Charities Association. He was also interested in prison reform and served as a member of the boards of the Pennsylvania Prison Society, the Pennsylvania State Industrial School at Huntington, and the Pennsylvania State Industrial Home for Women at Muncy. Leadership roles in the American Association of Social Workers and the National Conference of Social Work were among his other professional activities. For 26 years, Pray served as director and professor of social planning and administration at the School of Social Work at the University of Pennsylvania.

During the latter part of his career, Pray chaired the National Council on Social Work Education committee that conducted the first major comprehensive study of social work education. He outlined the activities of the community organization social work method and was the author of *Social Work in a Revolutionary Age and Other Papers* (1949).

Larraine M. Edwards

Rankin, Jeannette (1880–1973)
Jeanette Rankin, the first woman elected to the U.S. Congress and the only member of Congress to vote against U.S. participation in both world wars, was born near Missoula, Montana, and graduated from the University of Montana in 1902. After spending several years caring for her parents and younger siblings, she enrolled in 1908 at the New York School of Philanthropy, receiving her diploma the following year. After a brief career in social

work, Rankin became active in successful campaigns for women's suffrage in Washington and Montana. In 1916 Rankin ran for Congress from her home state as a progressive Republican, favoring women's suffrage, protective legislation for children, prohibition, and peace. Her election made her the first female member of the House of Representatives. She was one of 56 members of Congress who voted against President Wilson's declaration of war against Germany. During the remainder of her term, Rankin worked on legislation to aid women and children and on a women's suffrage amendment to the Constitution. In 1918 she was defeated in her bid for the Republican nomination for the Senate from Montana.

During the 1920s and 1930s, Rankin lobbied for social welfare legislation and peace. In 1940 she was again elected to the House of Representatives. She was the only member of Congress to vote against the declaration of war against Japan in 1941. Defeated for re-election, she spent the next decade in obscurity. During the late 1960s and early 1970s, she campaigned against the Vietnam War, again becoming nationally prominent. Rankin is the subject of two biographies: *Jeannette Rankin: First Lady in Congress* (1974), by Hannah Josephson, and *Flight of the Dove: The Story of Jeannette Rankin* (1980), by Kevin S. Giles. See also the biographical essay by Joan Hoff Wilson in *Notable American Women: The Modern Period* (1980).

Paul H. Stuart

Rapoport, Lydia (1923–1971)
Lydia Rapoport, a prominent social work educator, theorist, and practitioner, was born in Vienna, Austria, and came to the United States with her parents in 1932. A graduate of Hunter College (1943), she received her MSS in psychiatric social work from Smith College School for Social Work in 1944 and became a psychiatric social worker in Chicago at the Michael Reese Hospital, University of Chicago hospitals, and the Jewish Children's Bureau. She also took a three-year training course in childhood psychoanalysis at the Chicago Institute for Psychoanalysis, becoming a specialist in treating emotionally disturbed children.

As a Fulbright scholar in the Social Sciences Department of the London School of Economics (1952–1954), Rapoport was instrumental in strengthening British training for social workers. In 1954 she joined the faculty of the School of Social Welfare at the University of California, Berkeley, directing its psychiatric social work programs and establishing an advanced training program in community mental health. On leave,

Rapoport worked at Harvard University's Laboratory of Community Psychiatry, which led to her most important contribution to social work practice: crisis intervention and short-term therapy. Rapoport also served as the first United Nations interregional family welfare and family planning advisor in the Middle East.

Rapoport wrote numerous articles and two books, *Consultation in Social Work Practice* (1963) and *The Role of Supervision in Professional Education* (1963). See also *Creativity in Social Work, Selected Writings of Lydia Rapoport* (1975), edited by Sanford N. Katz.

Maryann Syers

Reynolds, Bertha Capen (1885–1978)

Bertha Capen Reynolds, social worker, educator, and activist, advocated for the working class and oppressed groups and stressed the importance of working together for a more humane world. Born and raised in Stoughton, Massachusetts, she graduated from the Boston School of Social Work in 1914. She participated in the first course in psychiatry ever offered to social workers at Smith College in 1918 and in the historic Milford Conference in 1923. In 1925 she was appointed associate director of Smith College School for Social Work. She remained there until 1938 when she was asked to leave because she wanted rank-and-file workers to unionize to improve their working conditions and the lives of their clients. An acknowledged Marxist, she wrote extensively in *Social Work Today* (the journal of the rank-and-file movement) on the need for social workers to become more politically active and concerned about the civil rights of their clients.

Finding it difficult to obtain employment in schools of social work or social agencies, she believed she had been blacklisted for her union activities but in 1943 she was hired by the National Maritime Union, where she stayed until 1948. She taught and wrote, publishing *Between Client and Community* (1934), *Learning and Teaching in the Practice of Social Work* (1942), *Social Work and Social Living* (1951), *McCarthyism versus Social Work* (1954), and an autobiography, *An Uncharted Journey* (1963).

Jean K. Quam

Richmond, Mary Ellen (1861–1928)

Mary Richmond was an outstanding practitioner, teacher, and theoretician who formulated the first comprehensive statement of principles of direct social work practice. Born in Belleville, Illinois, she joined the Baltimore Charity Organization as an assistant treasurer at the age of 28. In 1891 her administrative abilities led to her appointment as general secretary. In addition to her assigned duties, she volunteered as a friendly visitor.

Concerned about the frequent failures of cases to respond to service, in 1897 she delivered her historic speech at the National Conference of Charities and Correction, calling for schools to train professional social workers. In 1899 she published the first comprehensive presentation of practical suggestions, *Friendly Visiting Among the Poor.*

In 1900 Richmond became general secretary of the Philadelphia Society for Organizing Charity. During her tenure she emphasized the need for volunteer effort. She also fought to obtain legislation for deserted wives and founded the Pennsylvania Child Labor Committee, the Public Charities Association, the juvenile court, and the Housing Association.

Between 1905 and 1909, Richmond was associated with *Charities,* which developed teaching materials for Charity Organization Societies nationwide. She then became director of the Russell Sage Foundation's Charity Organization Department in New York City. She also taught and did research at the New York School of Philanthropy.

From 1910 through 1922 she developed and headed summer institutes attended by secretaries of charity organization societies from all parts of the country. Her most celebrated book, *Social Diagnosis,* was based on her lectures and on her wide readings in history, law, logic, medical social work, psychology, and psychiatry. Widely hailed as evidence of the professionalization of social work, it was the first formulation of theory and method in identifying the problems of clients. In 1922 she defined social casework as "those processes which develop personality through adjustments consciously effected, individual by individual, between men and their social environment."

Richmond's other publications include *The Good Neighbor in the Modern City* (1907) and *What Is Social Case Work? An Introductory Description* (1922).

John F. Longres

Riis, Jacob August (1848–1914)

The writings and lectures of Jacob August Riis on slum conditions had a profound effect on social reform for poor people at the turn of the century. Educated in Denmark by his father before coming to America in 1870, Riis worked as a police reporter in New York City for 22 years—first at the *Tribune* and then at the *Evening Sun.* In addition to his realistic descriptions of slum conditions, Riis recommended health, educational, and environmental reform. His work inspired other writers to give humanistic accounts of the harsh realities of slum life. As a result of the influence of Riis's writings, he developed a personal relationship with Theodore Roosevelt. To Riis's satisfaction, during Roosevelt's term as police commissioner, police lodging houses and the Mulberry Bend tenements were eliminated. Riis also worked to establish parks, playgrounds, and school facilities for children's clubs. In 1889 a settlement house in Mulberry Bend Park was renamed for him. His works include *How the Other Half Lives* (1890), *The Children of the Poor* (1892), *The Making of an American* (1901), and *The Battle with the Slum* (1902). See also *Jacob A. Riis, Police Reporter, Reformer, Useful Citizen* (1938), by Louise Ware.

Larraine M. Edwards

Rivera de Alvarado, Carmen (1910–1973)

Carmen Rivera de Alvarado had a distinguished career as a pioneer in social work practice and education in Puerto Rico and the United States. She graduated magna cum laude and received an award for excellence from the University of Puerto Rico. In 1935 she founded the first professional association of Puerto Rican social workers—the Insular Society of Social Workers—and served two terms as its president. One of the founders of the College of Social Workers of Puerto Rico (1940), which remains the island's foremost association of social workers, she also served as its first president. She received a social work master's degree from Washington University and a doctorate from the University of Pennsylvania.

Rivera de Alvarado's career included administrative and consultative positions in research, in-service training, maternal health, and medical and psychiatric social work. She served as member of, consultant to, and principal speaker for numerous Latin American bodies, commissions, and congresses and was an outspoken champion of Puerto Rican independence. She was a revered professor at the Universities of Puerto Rico and Pennsylvania and at Hunter College, where she was named distinguished visiting professor. Among her writings are *The Social Worker Confronting the Dilemma of the Times* (1951), *Changing Values of the Puerto Rican Culture* (1967), and *Social Work at the Crossroads* (1973).

John F. Longres

Robison, Sophie Moses (1888–1969)

Sophie Moses Robison's multifaceted roles of social worker, educator, and researcher helped create social policy changes for juvenile delinquents. A Phi Beta Kappa graduate of Wellesley College in 1909, she received a master's degree in German literature from Columbia University in 1913 and a graduate certificate from the New York School of Social Work in 1928. In 1936 she earned a PhD in sociology from Columbia University.

Believing that research methods were slanted against minorities and poor people, Robison challenged the differential treatment and outcomes for youths based on sociocultural factors. Her research efforts and recommendations resulted in urban educational reform. Robison held that research should be socially relevant and serve human needs. As an educator, she attempted to integrate theory and practice. Throughout her life, Robison was an activist in the civil rights and women's movements. In 1963 the Leah Rudas Memorial Fund was established in her daughter's memory at the Columbia University School of Social Work. Her works include *Can Delinquency Be Measured?* (1936), *Juvenile Delinquency: Its Nature and Control* (1936), and *Refugees at Work* (1942).

Larraine M. Edwards

Rodriguez Pastor, Soledad (1897–1958)

Soledad Rodriguez Pastor was a pioneer in services for deaf and blind people, an active social reformer, and a leader in the development of professional social work in Puerto Rico. She was raised in a family of modest means by her father after the death of her mother. At the age of 17 she became a rural teacher, later working with the Insular Home for Girls and doing volunteer work with blind children. She studied at the Perkins Institute and became director of the Institute for Blind Children in 1936. In 1943 she organized and directed the Office of Services for the Handicapped for the Department of Health of Puerto Rico. She received a certificate in social work in 1946 from the University of Puerto Rico. Her wide range of activities included the organization of the first islandwide survey of the feebleminded and the creation of the first home-based classes for blind adults.

A leader in professional activities, she also served as editor of the *Journal of Public Welfare* of the Department of Health of Puerto Rico from 1945 to 1952. Poor health forced her to retire in 1950, but she continued to do volunteer work with tuberculosis patients and to hold conferences on the prevention of blindness and deafness. She was posthumously awarded the Citizen of the Year Award by the governor of Puerto Rico.

John F. Longres

Roosevelt, Eleanor (1884–1962)

Sometimes called "First Lady of the World," Eleanor Roosevelt broke the mold for the role of the modern presidential spouse. She brought her own strong political and professional identity to the public life she shared with her husband, Franklin Delano Roosevelt. Though born into a family of wealth and privilege, she consciously sought to broaden her outlook. Eventually, she became a strong advocate for women, workers, minority groups, children, and poor people. Working in settlement houses on New York's Lower East Side brought her, as it did so many other women of her class, a first awareness of the reality of the lives of people living in poverty. She joined Florence Kelley's National Consumers League, and later the Women's Trade Union League, to improve the wages and working conditions of women workers.

As First Lady, Roosevelt represented the president in a variety of capacities. As his health deteriorated, she increasingly served as his eyes and ears. Her own independent work continued as she investigated social conditions and the effectiveness of programs to address them. Her investigations influenced many of the New Deal programs of her husband's administration. It was she who became the embodiment of the president's sympathy for the masses of the American people. After her husband's death, Roosevelt served as the U.S. representative to the general assembly of the newly formed United Nations. She chaired the Commission on Human Rights and crafted its ambitious Universal Declaration of Human Rights, which the full body ratified in 1948. Roosevelt earned the respect and admiration of millions of common people worldwide through her work for civil rights and world peace. Upon her death, she was compared to Jane Addams—an acknowledgment of the range of her interests and commitments, her many talents, and the depth of her compassion.

Fred Newdom

Rothman, Beulah (1924–1990)

Beulah Rothman dedicated most of her life to the education, research, practice, and expansion of social work with groups. A native of New York City, she graduated from Long Island University (1945) and received MSW and DSW degrees from Columbia University School of Social Work (1947 and 1963, respectively). In 1957 Adelphi University School of Social Work employed Rothman as the first chairperson of its group work sequence. She subsequently became associate dean and director of the doctoral program until her retirement in 1981. Moving to Florida in 1981, she became Distinguished Professor at Barry University School of Social Work where she developed and served as director of the PhD program. One of the three

founders of the Association for the Advancement of Social Work with Groups (AASWG), Rothman served on its board. In 1983 she founded the Center for Group Work Studies, which became the Florida chapter of AASWG in 1988. Rothman served as its executive director and cochaired AASWG's 12th Annual Symposium in Miami.

With Catherine Papell, Rothman coedited the quarterly publication *Social Work with Groups: A Journal of Community and Clinical Practice* from 1978 to 1990. Two of her numerous articles have become basic readings in group work education: "Social Group Work Models—Possession and Heritage" (1966) and "Group Work's Contribution to a Common Method" (1966). A respected leader in the field of group work, she was curriculum consultant to many national and international schools of social work and received numerous honors, including Master Teacher by the Council of Social Work Education, the Distinguished Leadership Award of the National Committee for the Advancement of Group Work, and Outstanding Editor of the *Journal of Teaching in Social Work.* Her greatest achievement was her generous gift of time and energy and her dedication to her students, whom she encouraged and supported in their growth and development as social group workers.

Linda Adler

Rubinow, Isaac Max (1875–1936)

Isaac Max Rubinow used his knowledge of medicine, economics, and social work to lead the American social insurance movement and to contribute to Jewish American welfare programs. Born in Russia, Rubinow came to America in 1893 and graduated from Columbia University in 1895. He received a medical degree from New York University in 1898 and a PhD in political science from Columbia University in 1914. Between 1904 and 1911, Rubinow's major activities were in the field of economics. He worked with the Bureau of Statistics of the U.S. Department of Agriculture, the U.S. Bureau of Labor, and the Bureau of Statistics of the U.S. Department of Commerce and Labor. From 1912 to 1915, he lectured on social insurance at the New York School of Philanthropy. As one of the nation's experts on social insurance, Rubinow often testified at congressional hearings on unemployment.

Rubinow was a consultant to the President's Committee on Economic Security, which drafted federal social security legislation. From 1923 to 1928, he directed the Jewish Welfare Society of Philadelphia, and from 1925 to 1929 he edited the *Jewish Social Service Quarterly.* He was instrumental in the founding of the Anti-Defamation League of B'nai B'rith in 1934. Rubinow was the author of *Social Insurance* (1913), *The Care of the Aged* (1931), and *The Quest for Social Security* (1934).

Larraine M. Edwards

Rush, Benjamin (1746–1813)

Benjamin Rush was a political activist who worked to improve the quality of life in colonial America. Born in Byberry, Pennsylvania, he received a bachelor's degree from the College of New Jersey (later Princeton University) and a medical degree in 1768 from the University of Edinburgh in Scotland. He was a member of the Continental Congress and a signer of the Declaration of Independence. Throughout his career he was an advocate for free public education, adequate sanitation laws, prison reform, and abolition of slavery. Rush became a teaching physician at the University of Pennsylvania in 1780 and three years later was appointed to the staff at Pennsylvania Hospital. As a result of his concern, better accommodations were built for mentally ill people. In addition, he insisted that mentally ill people be treated with dignity and respect.

Rush's book *Medical Inquiries and Observations upon Diseases of the Mind* (1812) greatly influenced the development of psychiatric treatment. His works include *The Autobiography of Benjamin Rush* (1948), edited by G. W. Corner, and *Letters* (1951), edited by L. H. Butterfield. See also *Benjamin Rush* (1934), by Nathan Goodman, and *The Selected Writings of Benjamin Rush*, edited by Dagobert Runes.

Larraine M. Edwards

Sanders, Daniel (1928–1989)

Daniel Sanders was an educator and leader in the field of international social work and social welfare. Sanders spent the first part of his life and career in Sri Lanka, where he served first as associate director of the Ceylon Institute of Social Work (1955–1961) and then as executive director and research associate at the Institute of Social Studies (1961–1965). A graduate of the University of Ceylon, he also received a diploma in social welfare from the University of Wales, Swansca. He continued his education in the United States, receiving both an MSW and a PhD in social work from the University of Minnesota. Sanders held the positions of associate professor (1971–1974) and then dean and professor (1974–1986). In both universities he developed a program emphasis on international social work. He was responsible for the establishment of the Center for the Study of International Social Welfare Policies and Services in Illinois. He also was a founder of the Inter-University Consortium for International Social Devel-

opment and served as the organization's first president.

Sanders was the author or editor of six books, including *The Development Perspective in Social Work* (1982), *Education for International Social Welfare* (1983), *Visions of the Future: Social and Pacific Asian Perspectives* (1988), and *Peace and Development: An Interdisciplinary Perspective* (1989). He also authored numerous articles, monographs, and book chapters and served on several editorial boards. He wrote widely on the themes of peace, social development, and the international context of social work practice and education.

M. C. Hokenstad

Satir, Virginia (1916–1988)

Virginia Satir, pioneer family therapist, author, consultant, and teacher, was born Virginia Mildred Pagenkopf on June 26, 1916, on a farm in Neillsville, Wisconsin, the eldest of five children. After earning a degree in education and teaching for several years, she entered the School of Social Service Administration at the University of Chicago, where she received her master's degree in social work in 1948. In recognition of her distinguished career, she was awarded an honorary Doctor of Social Sciences degree from the University of Wisconsin in 1973, and in 1976 she received a special alumni medal from the University of Chicago for her outstanding work in family therapy and human relationships.

Her early agency work included working with families at the Dallas Child Guidance Center (1949–1950). Returning to the Chicago area, she consulted for various social services agencies, conducted a private practice, and taught at the Illinois State Psychiatric Institute. In 1959 she moved to California, joining with Gregory Bateson, Don Jackson, and Jules Riskin in developing basic principles of human interaction and communication that have continued to serve as the theoretical foundation guiding the practice of family therapy. That collaboration led to the creation of one of the first and foremost formal training programs in family therapy at the Mental Research Institute in Palo Alto, California. As her vision broadened, she became a leading force in the human growth potential movement, serving as director of training at the Eselen Institute in the mid-1960s.

Satir's book *Conjoint Family Therapy*, published in 1964, remains a classic in the field and has been translated into a number of foreign languages. She published 11 other books in her lifetime, among them *Peoplemaking*, in 1972, and *New Peoplemaking*, in 1988, reaching a large international audience. Among her many honors, she was named a Fellow of the American Association of Marriage and Family Therapy in 1973, elected President of the Association for Humanistic Psychology, 1982–1983, and in 1983 named one of the 100 most influential women in America by the *Ladies Home Journal*. From 1986 to 1988 she was a member of the California Task Force to Promote Self-Esteem and Personal and Social Responsibility. During her lifetime she conducted hundreds of workshops around the world, presenting her "human validation process model." Creator of a number of innovative experiential techniques, such as "family sculpting" and "family reconstruction," her work emphasized health rather than pathology and focused on coping rather than problems, thereby enabling people to experience personal growth through self-affirmation and direct relationship change. Research studies have found her work to have greatly influenced the clinical practice of many social workers and other mental health professionals.

Michele Baldwin
Froma Walsh

Schwartz, William (1916–1982)

William Schwartz, social work educator and theorist, played a major role in improving the standards of practice, supervision, and teaching and contributed to the theory and practice of group social work. Born and raised in New York City, Schwartz was active in youth group work throughout his early career. After graduating from Brooklyn College in 1939, Schwartz served as youth director at the Young Men's Hebrew Association (YMHA) Community Center in Lynn, Massachusetts (1943–1944); director of activities for the Jewish Community Center in Bridgeport, Connecticut (1944–1945); and supervisor of the senior division of Bronx House.

Schwartz earned an MS in 1948 from the New York School of Social Work at Columbia University and was employed as director of the Horace Mann-Lincoln Neighborhood Center (1946–1947) and assistant director of the Manhattanville Neighborhood Center, an interracial settlement house in New York. He spent the summertime (1938–1957) directing summer camping programs for the YMHA, Educational Alliance of New York City, the Jewish Community Center, and other organizations. Schwartz was on the faculty of the School of Social Administration at Ohio State University (1950–1955), the School of Social Work at the University of Illinois in Chicago (1955–1962), and the New York School of Social Work at Columbia University (1962–1977); he was a distinguished visiting professor at Fordham University (1977–1982).

Schwartz wrote on group work as a developmental and rehabilitative force for mutual aid, and his text, *The Practice of Group Work* (1971), coedited with Serapio Zalba, became required reading in many graduate schools of social work.

Maryann Syers

Scott, Carl A. (1928–1986)

Carl A. Scott, a champion of equity and social justice in social work education, was born in Battle Creek, Michigan. He received a BA in psychology (1950) and an MSW (1954) from Howard University. Early in his career, Scott held practice and administrative positions in children and family services agencies and was director of admissions and assistant professor at the New York University School of Social Work. In 1968 he joined the staff of the Council on Social Work Education (CSWE) as a senior consultant on minority groups. Scott was at the helm of CSWE's early efforts to foster diversity in social work education. He secured funding from government and private sources to recruit students and faculty from minority groups to schools of social work and guided five minority task forces in developing programs directed toward enhancing minority presence in curricula. He also designed minority fellowship programs to prepare mental health researchers and clinicians. Through these programs, which are among CSWE's most highly regarded activities, African Americans, Asian Americans, Native Americans, Mexican Americans, and Puerto Ricans have received stipend support for doctoral study.

Scott wrote or edited a number of CSWE publications, including *Ethnic Minorities in Social Work Education* (1970), *The Current Scene in Social Work Education* (with Arnulf Pins, Frank Loewenberg, and Alfred Stamm; 1971), and *Primary Prevention Approaches to the Development of Mental Health Services for Ethnic Minorities* (with Samuel O. Miller and G. M. Styles O'Neal; 1982). See also *Perspective on Equity and Justice in Social Work: The Carl A. Scott Memorial Lecture Series, 1988–1992,* edited by Dorothy M. Pearson.

Dorothy M. Pearson

Seton, Elizabeth Ann Bayley (Mother Seton) (1774–1821)

Elizabeth Ann Bayley Seton founded the religious order of the Sisters of Charity and was among the first leaders in parochial education and Catholic social services in the United States. Early in her married life she was one of the founders of the Society for the Relief of Poor Widows with Small Children. After the death of her husband in 1803, she converted to Catholicism. In 1809 she became a nun and took the name Mother Seton. A few years later she was selected to head a new girls' academy near Baltimore. In 1812 she was joined by a community of religious women who became known as the American Sisters of Charity of St. Joseph. Mother Seton later established free schools for poor children in Philadelphia, forming the core of the parochial school system. The first Catholic orphanage, the first Catholic hospital, and the first Catholic maternity hospital were operated by Mother Seton and the Sisters of Charity. On September 14, 1975, she became the first American to be canonized by the Church. See *Mother Seton and American Women* (1947), by L. Feeney, and *Elizabeth Bayley Seton—1774–1821* (1951), by A. Melville.

Larraine M. Edwards

Sieder, Violet M. (1909–1988)

Violet Sieder was a distinguished social welfare educator and leader. Her major professional interests and contributions were in community organization, rehabilitation, and volunteerism. She received her undergraduate education at Douglass College, Rutgers University; a master's degree from the University of Chicago School of Social Service Administration; and a PhD from the Florence Heller Graduate School for Advanced Studies in Social Welfare, Brandeis University. Sieder's career in social services began during the Great Depression. From 1931 to 1944 she held positions as investigator for the New Jersey Department of Labor; supervisor for the New Jersey Emergency Relief Administration; executive secretary for the Allegany County, Maryland, Welfare Board; research assistant for the Maryland Board of State Aid and Charities; consultant to the U.S. Children's Bureau; and executive secretary for the Bronx, New York, Council for Social Welfare. From 1944 to 1954 she served as associate director, Health and Welfare Planning Department, Community Chest and Councils of America. In 1954 she was appointed professor and chair of community organization at the New York School of Social Work, Columbia University.

In 1959 Sieder enrolled in the first class of the newly established doctoral program in social policy at the Florence Heller Graduate School, Brandeis University. Within two years she was invited to join that school's faculty to teach social planning, community organization, and rehabilitation. After her retirement from Brandeis in 1974, she remained active as a volunteer organizer. Her major achievement during the final phase of her career was organizing the Massachusetts Human Services Coalition, a statewide advocacy agency, and serving as its first president from 1975 to 1981.

Sieder served NASW as a member of the Commission on Social Work Practice, the Committee on Community Organization, and the Central Review Committee. She also chaired the Committee on Community Organization of the Council on Social Work Education and served on the Executive and Nominating Committees of the National Conference on Social Welfare.

Sieder was also active on the international scene. After World War II, she served as a consultant on community organization to the U.S. State Department High Commission on Germany and to the London and National Councils of Social Services in England. She later was chair of the NASW Committee on International Social Work, a member of the Executive Committee of the International Federation of Social Workers, and secretary of the Editorial Committee of the International Conference of Social Work. She traveled widely to maintain contacts with social workers and their professional schools and organizations and undertook teaching assignments for schools of social work in Zagreb, Yugoslavia, and Rio de Janeiro, Brazil. Sieder was named Social Worker of the Year by NASW's Massachusetts chapter in 1976 and was honored by the national organization with a citation for service.

David G. Gil

Simkhovitch, Mary Kingsbury (1867–1951)

Mary Kingsbury Simkhovitch achieved international recognition as the founder of the Greenwich House social settlement in New York City. A native of Chestnut Hill, Massachusetts, she received an undergraduate degree from Boston University in 1890. Later she did graduate work at Radcliffe College and the University of Berlin. Simkhovitch began her social work career working with immigrants at the College Settlement and Friendly Aid House in New York. In 1902 she founded Greenwich House, remaining there until her retirement in 1946. The settlement met the needs of the community by providing such services as a day care center, a family counseling service, and cultural activities. In addition to her pioneering work in public housing, Simkhovitch was a professor of social economy at Barnard College for three years and an associate in social economy at Teachers College of Columbia University for three years.

Simkhovitch's other professional activities included membership in the New York City Housing Authority, the New York State Board of Social Welfare, and the National Public Housing Conference. Simkhovitch wrote *The City Worker's World in America* (1917), *Neighborhood: My Story of Greenwich House* (1938), *Group Life* (1940), and

Here Is God's Plenty: Reflections on American Social Advance (1949).

Larraine M. Edwards

Smith, Zilpha Drew (1852–1926)

Zilpha Drew Smith developed the method of friendly visiting in the charity organization movement. Born in Pembroke, Massachusetts, she was trained as a telegraph operator at Boston Normal School. She began her career as head of office staff with Associated Charities of Boston in 1879, and in 1886 was appointed general secretary. Smith devised a systematic approach to screening and investigating relief applications by using friendly visitors. She later helped Mary Richmond develop a similar program in Baltimore. In 1888 Smith founded the Monday Evening Club, the country's first social workers' discussion group. A strong advocate for trained charity workers, she left direct service to help develop a school of social work. Smith became associate director of the Boston School of Social Work in 1904 and remained there until her retirement in 1918. In later years, she became convinced of the necessity for public assistance and helped shape the legislation for mothers' aid in Massachusetts. She wrote *Deserted Wives and Deserting Husbands* (1901).

Larraine M. Edwards

Snyder, Mitchell "Mitch" (1943–1990)

Mitch Snyder left the comforts of a well-paying job as a management consultant at the age of 26 because he believed that there was something more meaningful in life to accomplish. He took to the streets and eventually was arrested for car theft. He was sentenced to Danbury Prison where he spent three years with Daniel and Philip Berigan, radical Catholic antiwar protestors. While in prison Snyder organized a work strike that shut down the prison for eight days because inexpensive inmate labor was being used to make parts for the Polaris submarine. It was in prison that Snyder found the value of working together in a community for social change.

After leaving prison in 1972, he helped form the Prisoners Strike for Peace in New York. Later in 1973 he relocated to Washington, DC, and joined the Creative Community for Non-Violence (CCNV), a nonhierarchical religious community of 50 to 60 people who provide food, shelter, medical care, and clothing to approximately 2,000 people each day. CCNV also is deeply involved in political activities intended to change violent and unjust programs, policies, and values. Snyder committed numerous acts of nonviolent civil disobedience. He fasted, lived on the streets for extended periods, and demonstrated in a variety of ways.

Snyder received no salary. He lived in the CCNV-operated 1,400-bed Second Street Shelter for the homeless, the largest and most-comprehensive facility of its kind in the nation. The Second Street Shelter was the object of a two-year struggle with the Reagan administration. For example, in November 1984 Snyder completed a 51-day hunger strike that almost cost him his life. He was successful in getting President Reagan to agree to provide funds for repair to the shelter run by CCNV. The struggle has been documented in a made-for-television movie, "Samaritan: The Mitch Snyder Story"; an Academy Award–nominated documentary, "Promises to Keep"; and a book, *Signal through the Flames: Mitch Snyder and America's Homeless* (1986). Snyder recorded his ideas about homelessness in a book with coauthor Mary Ellen Holmes entitled *Homelessness in America: A Forced March to Nowhere* (1983).

Snyder spent considerable time traveling around the country and speaking to a variety of organizations about poverty and homelessness. He and other CCNV members also provided support to cities that needed help in creating emergency facilities for poor and homeless people or in combating local efforts against them.

Frederick A. DiBlasio
John R. Belcher

Spellman, Dorothea C. (1907–1979)

A distinguished social work educator and practitioner, Dorothea C. Spellman made her primary contributions in group work and as an advocate for a unified profession during the years before the formation of the National Association of Social Workers. Born in St. Louis, Missouri, Spellman received a BA in 1928 from Washington University. After teaching for a year, she entered the School of Applied Social Sciences of Western Reserve University to study group work and subsequently worked for Young Women's Christian Associations (YWCAs) in Cleveland and Honolulu and at the Brashear Settlement in Pittsburgh. In 1944 she joined the faculty of the Graduate School of Social Work at the University of Denver, heading the group work specialization until 1977.

As a member of the Temporary Inter-Association Council of Social Work Membership Organization and an early board member of NASW, Spellman fought to unite the many specializations in the field of social work. She also demonstrated the important role of group work. In the profession and the community, she was a strong advocate of social change to achieve social justice, helping to establish the Social Services Employees Union and the American Civil Liberties Union in the 1930s and 1940s and later joining the civil rights movement. Spellman was a long-time member of the National Board of the YWCA and consultant to the Southern Ute Tribal Council and the Navajo Tribal Council.

Maryann Syers

Starr, Ellen Gates (1859–1940)

Ellen Gates Starr is best known for cofounding Hull-House with Jane Addams. Born on a farm in rural Illinois, she attended Rockford Seminary for Women where she met Jane Addams and the two began a lifetime relationship. After Starr taught at a prominent girls' school in Chicago, and following a long and intense correspondence with Jane Addams, Starr and Addams traveled together in Europe. It was during this trip that they shared with each other their concern with the lack of meaningful options for women, particularly educated women. Although they were influenced by the social and cultural goals of Toynbee Hall in England, the goal of both women in starting Hull-House was to provide for themselves and for other women a new avenue for living independently and giving meaning to life.

Hull-House opened in 1889. Aesthetic, artistic, and eventually religious values were for Starr the key to human liberation. This belief system shaped almost all of the contributions she made to Hull-House. It was she who established reading clubs, cultural and language classes, and skilled crafts at Hull-House. She learned the craft of bookbinding in England and established a bookbindery within Hull-House, though it proved quite impractical.

The condition of the poor population, particularly the immigrant poor people who lived in the neighborhood around Hull-House, led Starr to become active in the labor movement in Chicago. Industrial society offended her not only because of the social conditions it spawned but also because she saw it dampening the aesthetic and spiritual lives of its participants. A frequent figure on the picket lines during the strikes of the garment and textile workers, Starr often used her influence to complain about the brutal treatment of strikers by the police force. While at Hull-House, she also helped organize against child labor, was a charter member of the Illinois branch of the National Women's Trade Union, and ran in local elections as a socialist.

Starr's life at Hull-House took a somewhat different direction than that followed by many of the women who came to live there and who became prominent social reformers. She had an intense personality and was prone to sudden outbursts of temper. Moreover, she was set apart by her growing interest in religion, and as an older woman she devoted more and more time to her own spiritual quest. Although born a Unitarian, Starr converted to Catholicism later in life. Starr's active association with Hull-House ended in 1929 when she became paralyzed below the waist following an operation for a tubercular tumor. Until her death at age 80, she lived at the Convent of the Holy Child in Suffern, New York, and at the time of her death was an obviate of the Third Order of St. Bernadet.

Starr wrote editorials and newspaper and magazine articles dealing primarily with labor issues, her reasons for becoming a socialist, and eventually her religious conversion. Among these are "The Chicago Clothing Strike," *New Review,* March 1916; "Hull House Bookbinding," *Commons,* June 30, 1900; and "A Bypath into the Great Roadway," *Catholic World,* May/June 1924. Her papers and letters are in the Sophia Smith Collection at Smith College.

Susan Donner

Switzer, Mary Elizabeth (1900–1971)

Mary Elizabeth Switzer's 20-year administration of major federal social agencies influenced the evolution and expansion of federally funded services to those in need. Born in Newton, Massachusetts, she graduated from Radcliffe College in 1921. Her federal career began as an assistant secretary with the Minimum Wage Board in Washington, DC. In 1934 she worked with the assistant secretary of the treasury, who supervised the U.S. Public Health Service. Here Switzer developed a concern for the delivery of health, medical, and social services and served in several administrative positions over a 16-year period. In 1950 she was named director of the Office of Vocational Rehabilitation (OVR) in the Federal Security Agency (later the U.S. Department of Health, Education, and Welfare). For the next few years she was successful in increasing and improving services to people with disabilities.

When she became head of the new Social and Rehabilitation Service in 1967, Switzer acquired the greatest administrative responsibility of any woman in U.S. government history. The budget of this service for disabled people, elderly people, and mothers and children exceeded $8 billion. After Switzer's federal career ended in 1970, she continued to support efforts to enhance the quality of life for those in need. Between 1955 and 1969, she published several articles on disability and rehabilitation.

Larraine M. Edwards

Taft, Julia Jessie (1882–1960)

Julia Jessie Taft founded the "functional" school of social casework practice, which was based on the psychoanalytic approach of Otto Rank. She received a master's degree from Drake University in 1904 and a doctorate in psychology from the University of Chicago in 1913. After practicing psychology for four years, she became director of the Child Study Department of the Children's Aid Society in Pennsylvania. In addition to gaining recognition as a therapist and mental health consultant, Taft became a social work instructor. With the help of Virginia Robinson, she developed a psychologically oriented curriculum at the Pennsylvania School of Social Work, where she taught until her retirement in 1952. In 1959 the school awarded her a citation for her contributions to social work. Taft was the author of *The Dynamics of Therapy in a Controlled Relationship* (1933) and the editor of *A Functional Approach to Family Casework* (1944). See also *Jessie Taft, Therapist and Social Work Educator* (1962), by Virginia Robinson.

Larraine M. Edwards

Taylor, Graham (1851–1938)
The Chicago Commons settlement house founded by Graham Taylor in 1894 helped to improve slum conditions in Chicago. Born in Schenectady, New York, Taylor was educated at Rutgers College and at the Theological Seminary of the Reformed Church at New Brunswick, New Jersey. Ordained a minister in 1873, Taylor became interested in applied religion. In 1892 he began teaching social economics at the Chicago Theological Seminary and while there encouraged his students to assume responsibility for solving social problems. Modeling his activities at Chicago Commons on the work of Jane Addams, Taylor initiated such projects as drafting protective labor legislation, promoting better housing conditions, developing playground facilities, and publishing the charity periodical *Commons* (later *Survey*).

Among Taylor's other contributions were the 12-week training courses he established for social workers. These courses were incorporated as the Chicago School of Civics and Philanthropy in 1908, with Taylor serving as president of the Board of Trustees. Taylor's published works include *Religion in Social Action* (1913), *Pioneering on Social Frontiers* (1930), and *Chicago Commons through Forty Years* (1936). See also *Graham Taylor, Pioneer for Political Justice, 1851–1938* (1964), by Louise Wade.

Larraine M. Edwards

Terrell, Mary Eliza Church (1863–1954)
Mary Church Terrell was a leading educator, social reformer, and participant in the international women's movement. Born in Memphis, Tennessee, she was educated in classical studies at Oberlin College. She received her BA in 1884 and her MA in

1888. Her mastery of foreign languages was achieved through a study tour of France, Germany, and Italy. A lecturer at Wilberforce University for two years, she later taught Latin in the District of Columbia secondary schools.

Terrell is best known for her professional lecture tours and writings on race relations and women's rights. In 1904 she represented black women at the International Congress of Women in Berlin, delivering her address in three languages. She participated in the 1919 International League for Peace and Freedom in Zurich, under the presidency of Jane Addams. A lifelong social activist, Terrell was also involved in the organizing meetings of the National Association for the Advancement of Colored People, was a member of the National American Women's Suffrage Association, and demonstrated actively against segregation until the time of her death. Her ideals and activities are expressed in her autobiography, *A Colored Woman in a White World* (1940). See also *Mary Church Terrell—Respectable Person* (1959), by Gladys B. Shepperd.

Wilma Peebles-Wilkins

Thomas, Jesse O. (1883–1972)
Jesse O. Thomas was one of the founders of the Atlanta University School of Social Work. Born in McComb, Mississippi, Thomas studied at Tuskegee Institute in Alabama, the New York School, and the Chicago School of Research. Before joining the Urban League in 1919 as field secretary for the Southern states, he held leadership positions in industrial education. In 1928 he served on the Mississippi Flood Relief Committee.

During his term as Urban League field secretary, in Atlanta, Thomas substituted for the national executive secretary, Eugene Kinckle Jones, at the 1920 National Conference of Social Work in New Orleans. It was at this meeting that he called attention to the shortage of trained black social workers—a call that brought recognition of the need for a school to educate black professionals. With the help of Robert Cloutman Dexter, Thomas subsequently organized a group that led to the founding in 1920 of the Atlanta University School of Social Services (later the School of Social Work). Details of these organizing efforts appear in Thomas's autobiography, *My Story in Black and White* (1967). See also *Black Heritage in Social Welfare, 1860–1930* (1978), by E. L. Ross.

Wilma Peebles-Wilkins

Titmuss, Richard Morris (1907–1973)
Richard Morris Titmuss, scholar, author, and educator, made great contributions to social policy and administration. The son of a farmer in Great

Britain, Titmuss left school at 15. After a few years as an office boy, he began work at the county fire insurance office, achieving success rapidly. As family breadwinner, he had firsthand experience of dependency, and as a company inspector, he learned more from company statistics and client records.

In the late 1930s, Titmuss began to write on such questions as poverty, migration, social class, and public health. His early books, such as *Poverty and Population* (1938) and *Birth, Poverty and Wealth* (1943), reflected his growing interest in the socioeconomic origins of poverty and the relationship between inequality and dependency and are examples of well-conceived, impartial scientific investigation. During these years Titmuss also became a fellow of the Royal Statistical Society and the Royal Economic Society.

In 1950 his widely acclaimed book, *Problems of Social Policy,* a study of the British social services during World War II, led to his appointment as chair of Social Administration at the London School of Economics although he had no university degree or even a secondary school equivalency certificate. As an educator and administrator, Titmuss developed the new subject area of social policy and administration as a legitimate, intellectually respectable field of inquiry and demonstrated a strong commitment to vocational social work education. Through his writings, Titmuss had worldwide influence on issues of social welfare and its underlying philosophy. His other works include *The Irresponsible Society* (1960), *Income Distribution and Social Change* (1962), *Commitment to Welfare* (1968), and *The Gift Relationship* (1973). See also *Richard Titmuss: Welfare and Society*, by David A. Reisman.

Maryann Syers

Towle, Charlotte (1896–1966)

Charlotte Towle was born and grew up in Butte, Montana. She graduated from Goucher College in Maryland in 1919 with a BA in education. After graduation she did volunteer work with the American Red Cross and worked for the Veterans Bureau in San Francisco and as a psychiatric caseworker in Tacoma, Washington. She attended the New York School of Social Work on a Commonwealth Fellowship and completed her degree in 1926. Following this, she served as director of the Home Finding Department of the Children's Aid Society in Philadelphia, where she was influenced by the "functional" approach to casework. From 1928 to 1932 she was a field work supervisor at the Institute for Child Guidance in New York. She joined the School of Social Service Administration at the University

of Chicago in 1932 and remained there until her retirement.

Towle's major accomplishments include her work in creating a generic casework curriculum, her study of the educational process of training social workers, and her attempts to link the understanding of human behavior and needs with the administration of public assistance programs. Among her works are *Common Human Needs* (1965), *The Learner in Education for the Professions* (1954), and *Social Case Records from Psychiatric Clinics* (1941). See also *Helping: Charlotte Towle on Social Work and Social Casework* (1969), by Helen Harris Perlman.

John F. Longres

Truth, Sojourner (1797–1883)

Sojourner Truth was a reformer and evangelist before and during the Civil War. Born into slavery in Ulster County, New York, she was named Isabella (Bell) Baumfree by her Dutch owner. As a fugitive slave in 1826, she was given refuge in New York City by the Van Wagener family and later took that surname. Influenced by the negative experiences of slavery and inspired by religious enthusiasts, she became an evangelist. In 1843 she took the name Sojourner Truth and began speaking tours to advocate for the abolition of slavery and for women's suffrage. With men such as Frederick Douglas and with suffrage leaders Elizabeth Cady Stanton and others, she was active in the abolitionist movement.

During the Civil War, Truth helped Union soldiers, and in 1864 she served as "counselor to the freed people" at the National Freedmen's Relief Association. Truth supported herself by selling an autobiography written for her by Olive Gilbert, *The Narrative of Sojourner Truth, A Northern Slave* (1850). See also *Journey Toward Freedom: The Story of Sojourner Truth* (1967), by Jacqueline Bernard; *Sojourner Truth: God's Faithful Pilgrim* (1938), by Arthur H. Fauset; and *Her Name Was Sojourner Truth* (1962), by Hertha Pauli.

Wilma Peebles-Wilkins

Tubman, Harriet (1820–1913)

Harriet Tubman became known as the Moses of black people for her leadership in the Underground Railroad movement. Born a slave in Dorchester County, Maryland, she was given the name Araminta Ross. She later took her mother's first name, Harriet. Escaping from bondage in 1849, Tubman fled to Philadelphia. She returned to Maryland some 19 times to rescue her family and the other slaves she had left behind and is thought to have rescued as many as 300 slaves before the Civil War. She worked with such individuals as the

Quaker Thomas Garrett and the black Philadelphia leader William Still. During the Civil War, Tubman served three years as a cook, nurse, spy, and scout. After the war, she set up the Harriet Tubman Home for Indigent Aged Negroes. After years of struggling with red tape, Tubman was given a $20-per-month government pension for her military service, which she used to help support her Harriet Tubman Home. Near the end of her life, she supported education for freedmen in the South and women's suffrage. Tubman was also involved in the organization of the National Federation of Afro-American Women. See *Harriet Tubman: The Moses of Her People* (1886), by S. H. Bradford; *Harriet Tubman: Negro Soldier and Abolitionist* (1943), by E. Conrad; *Harriet Tubman* (1955), by A. Petry; and *Freedom Train, The Story of Harriet Tubman* (1954), by D. Sterling.

Wilma Peebles-Wilkins

Vasey, Wayne (1910–1992)

Wayne Vasey was a gifted educator and prominent leader in the fields of social policy and social welfare. A native of Iowa, he was educated at William Penn College and the University of Denver. He served as director or dean of social work schools at the University of Iowa (1948–1952), Rutgers University (1954–1962), and Washington University (1962–1968) and founding executive of the first two. In subsequent years he was a professor at the University of Michigan School of Social Work (1968–1975), codirector of the University of Michigan–Wayne State University Institute of Gerontology, and visiting distinguished professor at San Diego State University and the University of South Florida. His many board memberships and offices included the presidencies of the National Conference on Social Welfare and the Association for Gerontology in Higher Education.

At a time when social work's dominant perspective in practice as well as education was shifting from the social to the clinical, Vasey was an influential voice in charting a course toward a more balanced emphasis. His book, *Government and Social Welfare* (1958), spelled out the tasks and goals of the profession in the context of multilevel welfare systems and a changing philosophy of government responsibility. He stressed the need for social work involvement in the social and political arena and, during the latter part of his career through his teaching, administrative work, and writing, addressed the problems of elderly people and the need for communitywide planning on their behalf.

Vasey's professional perspective, as reflected in some 30 published writings, visualized the developments of fields such as public welfare, gerontology, and the social work profession as intricately bound up with the functioning of the basic societal institutions and the process of social change. This orientation furnished him with a useful platform for his consultations to the secretary of health, education, and welfare and to other key organizations involved in American social welfare.

Ludwig L. Geismar

Wald, Lillian (1867–1940)

Lillian Wald was a pioneer in public health nursing. A native of Cincinnati, Ohio, she enrolled at New York Hospital for nurses' training, graduating in 1891. Wald decided to live among New York City's poor immigrants to provide them with nursing care. In 1893 she and a colleague, Mary Brewster, founded the Henry Street Settlement (originally called the Nurses Settlement). During her 40 years as its director, professional nursing care and visiting nurse services were provided to poor people at little or no cost. In addition to nursing, Wald had a strong interest in child welfare problems and was one of the founders of the New York Child Labor Committee. In association with Florence Kelley, Wald is credited with the proposal that led to the establishment of the Children's Bureau in 1912. Her works include *The House on Henry Street* (1915) and *Windows on Henry Street* (1934). See also *Lillian Wald, Neighbor and Crusader* (1938), by R. L. Duffus, and *Lillian Wald, Angel of Henry Street* (1948), by Beryl Williams.

Larraine M. Edwards

Washington, Booker Taliaferro (1856–1915)

Booker T. Washington, an outstanding proponent of industrial education for blacks, was also known for his accommodationist approach to race relations in the segregated South. Born into slavery on a plantation in Franklin County, Virginia, Washington graduated from Hampton Normal and Agricultural Institute in Virginia in 1875 and began a teaching career. He became head of Tuskegee Normal and Industrial Institute in 1881 where he remained for more than 20 years. Under Washington's leadership, Tuskegee developed into an endowed institution with expanded faculty and facilities. With support from fellow blacks and concerned whites, Washington promoted economic advancement through racial pride and individual industry. This approach to racial inequality was expressed in an address at the Atlanta Cotton States and International Exposition in 1895. Also known as the Atlanta Compromise, the speech drew criticism from more politically active black intellectuals. Washington's many accomplishments in the black community included the founding of the Negro

Business League. Among his writings are publications on industrial education and economic development and the autobiographical works *The Story of My Life and Work* (1900), *Up from Slavery* (1901), and *My Larger Education* (1911). See also *Booker T. Washington Papers* (Vols. 1–4, 1972–1975), edited by Louis R. Harlan; and *Booker T. Washington Papers* (Vols. 5–13, 1976–1984), edited by L. R. Harlan and R. W. Smock.

Wilma Peebles-Wilkins

Washington, Forrester Blanchard (1887–1963)
Forrester B. Washington, an Urban League Fellow and director of the Atlanta University School of Social Work for 27 years, was born in Salem, Massachusetts. Washington graduated from Tufts College in 1909 and received a master's degree from Columbia University in 1917. Before becoming a social work educator, he served in leadership positions with such black social welfare agencies as the Armstrong Association in Philadelphia (forerunner of the Urban League) and the Urban League in Detroit and at the national level.

A strong proponent of the scientific method for professional training of social workers, Washington used his knowledge and understanding of the needs of black people to broaden the curriculum at the Atlanta University School of Social Work. Under Washington's leadership (1927–1954), the school underwent tremendous growth—faculty size increased and the school was accredited and gained national recognition. Social research and community projects sponsored by the Atlanta University School of Social Work supported social work in the black community. See *The Legacy of Forrester B. Washington: Black Social Work Educator and Nation Builder* (1970), by the Atlanta University School of Social Work, and *Black Heritage in Social Welfare* (1978), by E. L. Ross.

Wilma Peebles-Wilkins

Wells-Barnett, Ida Bell (1862–1931)
Ida Wells-Barnett was a journalist, civil rights spokeswoman, and civic organizer. Born to slave parents in Holly Springs, Mississippi, she received a high school education at Rust College—a freedmen's school—and studied at Fisk University in 1884. After seven years as a teacher, Barnett was fired for giving newspaper exposure to the poor educational provisions for black children in Memphis, Tennessee. Her journalism career began in 1892, and she was co-owner of the Memphis *Free Speech* until the offices were destroyed by a mob in 1892. Despite this, she continued to write and lecture about the plight of blacks in the South, particularly the lynching of black men.

Barnett's activity in the women's club movement led to the organization of a Negro women's club in Chicago. A settlement house was maintained by the Negro Fellowship League—another organization that she founded in Chicago in 1908. As chairperson of the Anti-Lynching Bureau of the National Afro-American Council—a forerunner of the National Association for the Advancement of Colored People (NAACP)—she participated in the founding meeting of the NAACP. Another of her great concerns was women's suffrage, and Barnett founded the Alpha Suffrage Club of Chicago, the first black women's organization of its kind. Barnett's *A Red Record* (1895), includes autobiographical material and data on lynching. See also *Crusade for Justice: The Autobiography of Ida B. Wells* (1970), edited by Alfreda Wells Duster.

Wilma Peebles-Wilkins

White, Eartha Mary Magdalene (1876–1974)
Eartha White, a civic-minded black businesswoman, organized health and welfare services for the black community in Jacksonville, Florida, the place of her birth. After studying at Madame Thurber's National Conservatory of Music in New York, she spent a year on tour with an opera company. White returned to Jacksonville to study and teach before initiating her lifelong community service activities, which were supported by profits from buying and selling small businesses and other real estate. Before World War I, White was involved in organizing and fundraising activities for elderly people and children, and during the war she coordinated war camp services. In 1928 she founded the Clara White Mission for the homeless, named in honor of her mother. This mission, which served as a relief center for black people during the Great Depression, expanded after World War II to include other services, such as care for dependent children and unwed mothers.

While serving in the Women's National Defense Program during World War II, White donated a building and provided American Red Cross services to enlisted men, and in 1967 she established a 120-bed facility for welfare patients, the Eartha M. M. White Nursing Home. Among the honors she received for her public service contributions were the Better Life Award of the American Nursing Home Association and the Booker T. Washington Symbol of Service Award from the National Negro Business League. See *Notable American Women: The Modern Period* (1980), by B. Sicherman et al.

Wilma Peebles-Wilkins

Wiley, George (1931–1973)
George Wiley is credited with organizing poor people into a significant political force in the

United States during the late 1960s and early 1970s. Educated as a chemist, he graduated from the University of Rhode Island in 1953 and received his PhD from Cornell University. In 1960, he became associate professor of chemistry at Syracuse University and also began his work as a reformer, organizer, and social activist, founding a local chapter of the Congress of Racial Equality (CORE) at Syracuse and serving on the National Action Council of CORE.

Wiley left Syracuse in 1966 to found the Poverty/Rights Action Center in Washington, DC, a central communications link for groups of poor people trying to work together. Representatives of the groups involved established the National Welfare Rights Organization (NWRO) in 1967 and appointed Wiley its first executive director. NWRO, the largest poor people's membership organization in the United States, lobbied for a guaranteed adequate income for all and for improved welfare services at the state and local levels. Wiley resigned in 1973 to organize a broader-based organization devoted to tax reform and national health insurance.

A brilliant community organizer, Wiley had begun to found the Movement for Economic Justice when he drowned in a boating accident at age 42. See *A Passion for Equality: George A. Wiley and the Movement* (1977), by Nick Kratz.

Jean K. Quam

Wilkins, Roy (1901–1981)
Roy Wilkins became a national civil rights spokesperson during his 46 years of leadership of the National Association for the Advancement of Colored People (NAACP). He was born in St. Louis, Missouri, and earned a BA degree from the University of Minnesota in 1923. Wilkins subsequently took a job in journalism at the *Kansas City Call*. His concern about segregation caused him to resume activities he had begun in college with the NAACP. In 1931, Wilkins became the assistant executive secretary of the NAACP. From 1934 to 1949, he served as editor of *Crisis* magazine, succeeding W. E. B. DuBois. As chairperson of the National Emergency Civil Rights Mobilization in 1949, he worked for fair employment and other civil rights legislation.

In 1955 Wilkins was named executive director of the NAACP, and during his 22 years in that position he struggled for justice and civil rights in all aspects of American life. Among the numerous awards he received were the Roosevelt Distinguished Service Medal in 1968 and the presidential Medal of Freedom in 1969. His books include an autobiography (with Tom Mathews), *Standing Fast*

(1982), and a book of public speeches compiled by Helen Solomon and Aminda Wilkins, *Talking It Over* (1977).

Wilma Peebles-Wilkins

Williams, Anita Rose (1891–1983)
Anita Rose Williams was the first black Catholic social worker in the United States and the first black supervisor employed by a Baltimore, Maryland, agency. Born in Baltimore, she had no formal education beyond high school, although she attended sociology lectures at Johns Hopkins University. During the early 1900s, she did volunteer work in family and child welfare agencies. In 1921 she restructured the city's four black parishes as the Bernard Atkins Organization, which promoted the economic and social assistance of Catholic youths. In 1923, after a year of employment with the Vincent de Paul Society, she began working for the Bureau of Catholic Charities of Baltimore. With the help of four other social workers, she organized District Eleven of the Baltimore Emergency Relief Commission. Before returning to Catholic Charities in 1936, she worked as a supervisor for the commission for three years. She retired from Catholic Charities in 1958. Williams also served on a number of health, welfare, and human relations boards. A building at the Barrett School for Girls in Glen Burnie, Maryland, was named in her honor. See *Notable Maryland Women* (1977), edited by Winifred G. Helmes.

Wilma Peebles-Wilkins

Witte, Ernest Frederic (1904–1986)
Ernest Frederic Witte was an educator and administrator whose work in the social welfare field was influential both in the United States and internationally. Born in Swanton, Nebraska, he graduated from the University of Nebraska, received his PhD from the University of Chicago in 1932, and taught economics at Ohio Wesleyan University. During the Great Depression, Witte served on various federal relief commissions and as a field representative of the Social Security Board. From 1937 to 1939, he was director of the University of Nebraska Graduate School of Social Work and, for the next four years, of the Graduate School of Social Work at the University of Washington.

During World War II, Witte coordinated welfare services in Allied-occupied Italy and was subsequently in charge of the welfare section of Supreme Headquarters in France. He continued his work with refugees and displaced persons in occupied Germany, where he was among the first to deal with survivors of the Nazi death camps.

Decorated by the French, Dutch, and U.S. governments for his war efforts, Witte returned to the

United States to head the social services division of the Veterans Administration. In 1963, after 10 years as executive director of the Council on Social Work Education (CSWE), Witte was appointed by the State of California to set up graduate schools of social work at California State University at Fresno, California State University at Sacramento, and San Diego State University, where he served as dean until 1968. He held the deanship of the University of Kentucky's School of Social Professions from 1969 to 1974 and then headed the Institute for Graduate Social Work at the University of Trondheim in Norway. He returned to the United States in 1979. Although retired, Witte remained active as a consultant, continuing his work in such organizations as CSWE, NASW, and the Unitarian Universalist Church and maintaining his lifelong commitment to improve conditions for those groups most at risk in society. Witte contributed articles to numerous professional journals and reference books, including the 16th edition of the *Encyclopedia of Social Work*.

John F. Longres

Wittman, Milton (1915–1994)

Milton Wittman played a key role in the expansion of opportunities for social work education and for the involvement of social workers in the provision of mental health services. Born in New York City, his social work education and career began in the Midwest. He received a BA degree from the University of Nebraska and an MA degree from the University of Chicago School of Social Service Administration. He later received a doctorate in social work from the Columbia University School of Social Work, where he taught for a year after his retirement, and completed a year of postdoctoral study at the London School of Economics.

After holding caseworker positions in Lincoln, Nebraska; Chicago; and St. Louis, Wittman spent four years in the U.S. Army during World War II, rising to the rank of major as chief of rehabilitation programs at a base in New Guinea. He was chief social worker for the Veterans Administration facility in Milwaukee before joining the newly formed National Institute of Mental Health (NIMH) in 1947. At NIMH Wittman administered a unique social work training grant program and also worked to find ways of meeting the social work manpower requirements of the national community mental health program. During his 32-year career at NIMH, Wittman worked on these objectives with schools of social work; the Council on Social Work Education, NASW, and other professional organizations; and federal, state, and local mental health, public health, and social welfare

programs. An effective administrator, he succeeded in broadening the scope, priorities, and funding of the NIMH social work training grant program. His efforts contributed to the incorporation of mental health content as an integral part of the education of all social workers and to the emergence of new roles for social workers in mental health. He also helped to support curriculum revisions, scholarship aid, and practice innovations that reflected cultural and racial diversities and balanced inequities and promoted public health principles and the importance of prevention in social work practice and education.

In the 1960s he was appointed chairperson of the Federal Task Force on Social Work Education and Manpower. The task force report, "Closing the Gap in Social Work Manpower," resulted in the funding of social work education for welfare programs. In 1977 Wittman was named social work's first Professional Liaison Officer in the Public Health Service Commissioned Corps. His appointment gave a new level of visibility to social work in the public health service and provided an opportunity to coordinate standards across health programs.

A leader in social work as well as public health and mental health organizations, Wittman served on numerous national, state, and local boards and committees. He was a frequent speaker at conferences and seminars and a prolific writer who published more than 30 articles and chapters in books and monographs. His optimism and courage in coping with multiple disabilities during the last decade of his life, as well as his interest in and dedication to the field of social work, were a great source of inspiration for many.

Ruth Irelan Knee

Young, Whitney Moore, Jr. (1921–1971)

Whitney Moore Young, Jr., was the son of a Kentucky educator. He graduated from Kentucky State College at 18 and became a high school teacher and coach. From 1942 to 1944, while in the U.S. Army, he studied engineering at the Massachusetts Institute of Technology. After his discharge, he received an MSW from the University of Minnesota (1947) and began to work with the Urban League in Minnesota. He became executive secretary of the Urban League in Omaha, Nebraska (1950), taught social work at the University of Nebraska and Creighton University, and became dean of the Atlanta University School of Social Work (1954).

In 1961 Young was appointed executive director of the National Urban League, remaining there until his death. (He drowned during a visit to Nigeria.) He became president of the National Conference on Social Welfare in 1965 and president of NASW in 1966. A noted civil rights leader and statesman, he worked to eradicate discrimination against blacks and poor people. He served on numerous national boards and advisory committees and received many honorary degrees and awards—including the Medal of Freedom (1969), presented by President Lyndon Johnson—for his outstanding civil rights accomplishments. Young's books include *Beyond Racism: Building an Open Society* (1969).

Wilma Peebles-Wilkins

Youngdahl, Benjamin Emanuel (1897–1970)

Benjamin Emanuel Youngdahl, public welfare administrator, educator, and lecturer, influenced the social work profession as president of the American Association of Schools of Social Work (1947–1948), the American Association of Social Workers (1951–1953), and the National Conference on Social Welfare (1955–1956). Born in Minneapolis, Minnesota, Youngdahl grew up in a prominent Swedish Lutheran family. He graduated from Gustavus Adolphus College in 1920, earned an MA from Columbia University, and returned to Gustavus Adolphus as a professor of sociology and economics. A passionate New Dealer, during the Great Depression Youngdahl worked in various Minnesota welfare programs, becoming director of social services for the State Emergency Relief Administration (1933) and director of public assistance under the State Board of Control (1937).

In 1939 Youngdahl joined the faculty of Washington University's George Warren Brown School of Social Work, St. Louis, Missouri. As dean of the school (1945–1962), Youngdahl upgraded training standards, developed a more integrated curriculum, doubled the school's enrollment, and established a doctoral program. In 1947 the school was the first division of Washington University to admit black students. For his concern for civil liberties, he received the Florina Lasker Award in Social Work in 1963. Youngdahl's writings on social action and social work education appear in his book *Social Action and Social Work* (1966).

Jean K. Quam

Younghusband, Dame Eileen (1902–1981)

Dame Eileen Younghusband, international educator and scholar, influenced the development of social work education around the world. Born in London, she was the daughter of mountaineer and explorer Sir Francis Younghusband. She earned a certificate of social studies and a diploma in sociology at the London School of Economics and then joined the faculty (1929–1957). During World War II she set up one of the first Citizen's Advice Bureaus, worked with the Service of Youth Program and the United Nations Relief and Rehabilitation Administration, and conducted a national survey of welfare functions.

Younghusband taught the first generic casework courses in Great Britain and advocated the expansion of university-based training for social workers. After several years as presiding magistrate of the Hammersmith Juvenile Court in London, she was recruited by the Council on Social Work Education in 1960 to design a project to strengthen American social work education in the field of corrections. She helped transform the International Association of Schools of Social Work from a predominantly Western organization into a worldwide, United Nations–linked body to establish schools of social work in developing countries. She served on the executive board (1950), as vice president (1954–1961), and as president (1961–1968) and was named honorary president for life.

Younghusband chaired the British Committee on Social Workers of the Local Authority Health and Welfare Services, which organized and developed extra university social work training, and helped initiate the Council for Training in Social Work and the National Institute of Social Work. She received many honorary degrees and honors, and in 1964 Queen Elizabeth II conferred on her the Order of Dame Commander of the British Empire. Her writings include *Third International Survey of Training for Social Work* (1959), *Social Work and Social Change* (1964), *Casework with Families and Children* (1965), *Social Work and Social Values* (1967), *Education for Social Work* (1968), and *Social Work in Britain, 1950–1975* (1978).

Jean K. Quam

Contributors to the Biographies

Linda Adler, MSW, LCSW
Psychotherapist
Private Practice
South Miami, FL

Yvonne Asamoah, PhD, ACSW
Associate Professor
Hunter College
New York, NY

Michele Baldwin
Assistant Professor
Family Institute
Northwestern University
Evanston, IL

Lou M. Beasley, PhD
Dean, School of Social Work
Clark Atlanta University
Atlanta, GA

John R. Belcher, PhD
Associate Professor
School of Social Work
University of Maryland at Baltimore
Baltimore, MD

Elizabeth A. S. Benefield, BA
Director of Development
School of Social Work
University of North Carolina at Chapel Hill
Chapel Hill, NC

Philip Bernstein, BA, MSSA
Executive Vice President Emeritus
Council of Jewish Federations
New York, NY

Leonard M. Bloksberg, PhD
Professor
School of Social Work
Boston University
Boston, MA

Iris Carlton-LaNey, PhD
Associate Professor
School of Social Work
University of North Carolina at Chapel Hill
Chapel Hill, NC

Margaret Daniel, MSW (retired)
Training Specialist
Social Work Education Division of Manpower Training
  Program
National Institute of Mental Health
New York, NY

Renee Bowman Daniel, PhD, CSW
Dean
Department of Sociology and Social Work
Daemen College
Amherst, NY

Joanne "Rocky" Delaplaine
Co-Director, Labor Heritage Foundation
Washington, DC

Frederick A. DiBlasio, PhD
Associate Professor
School of Social Work
University of Maryland at Baltimore
Baltimore, MD

Susan Donner, PhD
Associate Dean
School for Social Work
Smith College
Northampton, MA

Larraine M. Edwards, MSW
Practitioner
Winston-Salem, NC

Patricia L. Ewalt, PhD, ACSW
Dean, School of Social Work
University of Hawaii at Manoa
Honolulu, HI
(with the assistance of Laura L. Thompson and Mildred
  Sikkema)

Hans S. Falck, PhD, ACSW
Professor Emeritus
School of Social Work
Virginia Commonwealth University
Richmond, VA

Ronald A. Feldman, PhD
Dean, School of Social Work
Columbia University
New York, NY

Ludwig L. Geismar, PhD
Professor Emeritus
School of Social Work
Rutgers University
New Brunswick, NJ

David G. Gil, DSW, ACSW, LICSW
Professor and Director of Center for Social Change
Heller Graduate School for Advanced Studies in Social
  Welfare
Brandeis University
Waltham, MA

Roland L. Guyotte, PhD
Associate Professor of History
University of Minnesota
Morris, MN

Sara Harmon, MSW
Development Associate
State Communities Aid Association
Albany, NY

Santos H. Hernández, PhD
Dean, Worden School of Social Work
Our Lady of the Lake University
San Antonio, TX

Merl C. Hokenstad, PhD
Professor
Mandel School of Applied Social Sciences
Case Western Reserve University
Cleveland, OH

Allan Irving, PhD
Associate Professor
Faculty of Social Work
University of Toronto
Toronto, Ontario, Canada

Ruth I. Knee, MSSA, ACSW
Consultant in Long-Term/Mental Health Care
Fairfax, VA

Karen Berner Little, CSW
Professor
Department of Sociology and Social Work
Daemen College
Amherst, NY

John F. Longres, PhD
Professor
School of Social Work
University of Washington
Seattle, WA

James Midgley, PhD
Associate Vice Chancellor
Louisiana State University
Baton Rouge, LA

Fred Newdom, ACSW
President
ProAct Consulting Services
Albany, NY

Juan Paz, PhD
Assistant Professor
School of Social Work
Arizona State University
Tucson, AZ

Dorothy M. Pearson, PhD, ACSW, LICSW
Professor, School of Social Work
Howard University
Washington, DC

Wilma Peebles-Wilkins, PhD
Dean
School of Social Work
Boston University
Boston, MA

Dean Pierce, PhD
Director
School of Social Work
University of Nevada, Reno
Reno, NV

Jean K. Quam, PhD, ACSW
Director, School of Social Work
University of Minnesota
Minneapolis, MN

Juan Ramos, PhD
Associate Director for Prevention
National Institute of Mental Health
Rockville, MD

Beatrice N. Saunders, BA
Editor-in-Residence
Graduate School of Social Services
Fordham University
New York, NY

Alvin L. Schorr, MSW, LHD, ACSW
Leonard W. Mayo Professor Emeritus
Mandel School of Applied Social Sciences
Case Western Reserve University
Cleveland, OH

Carrie J. Smith, MSW, ACSW
Teaching Assistant
Howard University
Washington, DC

Rebecca L. Sperling, MSW
Lecturer
School of Social Work
Columbia University
New York, NY

Karen D. Stout, PhD
Associate Professor
Graduate School of Social Work
University of Houston
Houston, TX

Paul H. Stuart, PhD, ACSW
Professor
Chair, BSW Program
School of Social Work
University of Alabama
Tuscaloosa, AL

Maryann Syers, PhD
Practitioner
Private Practice
Minneapolis, MN

Victor I. García Toro, PhD
Director
College of Social Sciences
University of Puerto Rico
San Juan, PR

Froma Walsh, PhD
Co-director
Center for Family Health
University of Chicago
Chicago, IL

Mona Wasow, MSW
Clinical Professor
School of Social Work
University of Wisconsin–Madison
Madison, WI

Constance W. Williams, PhD
Associate Professor
Florence Heller School for Advanced Studies in Social
  Policy
Brandeis University
Waltham, MA

Appendixes

1. NASW Code of Ethics

PREAMBLE

This code is intended to serve as a guide to the everyday conduct of members of the social work profession and as a basis for the adjudication of issues in ethics when the conduct of social workers is alleged to deviate from the standards expressed or implied in this code. It represents standards of ethical behavior for social workers in professional relationships with those served, with colleagues, with employers, with other individuals and professions, and with the community and society as a whole. It also embodies standards of ethical behavior governing individual conduct to the extent that such conduct is associated with an individual's status and identity as a social worker.

This code is based on the fundamental values of the social work profession that include the worth, dignity, and uniqueness of all persons as well as their rights and opportunities. It is also based on the nature of social work, which fosters conditions that promote these values.

In subscribing to and abiding by this code, the social worker is expected to view ethical responsibility in as inclusive a context as each situation demands and within which ethical judgment is required. The social worker is expected to take into consideration all the principles in this code that have a bearing upon any situation in which ethical judgment is to be exercised and professional intervention or conduct is planned. The course of action that the social worker chooses is expected to be consistent with the spirit as well as the letter of this code.

In itself, this code does not represent a set of rules that will prescribe all the behaviors of social workers in all the complexities of professional life. Rather, it offers general principles to guide conduct, and the judicious appraisal of conduct, in situations that have ethical implications. It provides the basis for making judgments about ethical actions before or after they occur. Frequently, the particular situation determines the ethical principles that apply and the manner of their application. In such cases, not only the particular ethical principles are taken into immediate consideration, but also the entire code and its spirit. Specific applications of ethical principles must be judged within the context in which they are being considered. Ethical behavior in a given situation must satisfy not only the judgment of the individual social worker, but also the judgment of an unbiased jury of professional peers.

This code should not be used as an instrument to deprive any social worker of the opportunity or freedom to practice with complete professional integrity; nor should any disciplinary action be taken on the basis of this code without maximum provision for safeguarding the rights of the social worker affected.

The ethical behavior of social workers results not from edict, but from a personal commitment of the individual. This code is offered to affirm the will and zeal of all social workers to be ethical and to act ethically in all that they do as social workers.

The following codified ethical principles should guide social workers in the various roles and relationships and at the various levels of responsibility in which they function professionally. These principles also serve as a basis for the adjudication by the National Association of Social Workers of issues in ethics.

In subscribing to this code, social workers are required to cooperate in its implementation and abide by any disciplinary rulings based on it. They should also take adequate measures to discourage, prevent, expose, and correct the unethical conduct of colleagues. Finally, social workers should be equally ready to defend and assist colleagues unjustly charged with unethical conduct.

NASW CODE OF ETHICS

I. THE SOCIAL WORKER'S CONDUCT AND COMPORTMENT AS A SOCIAL WORKER

    A. *Propriety*—The social worker should maintain high standards of personal conduct in the capacity or identity as social worker.

        1. The private conduct of the social worker is a personal matter to the same degree as is any other person's, except when such conduct compromises the fulfillment of professional responsibilities.

        2. The social worker should not participate in, condone, or be associated with dishonesty, fraud, deceit, or misrepresentation.

3. The social worker should distinguish clearly between statements and actions made as a private individual and as a representative of the social work profession or an organization or group.

B. *Competence and Professional Development*—The social worker should strive to become and remain proficient in professional practice and the performance of professional functions.
 1. The social worker should accept responsibility or employment only on thebasis of existing competence or the intention to acquire the necessary competence.
 2. The social worker should not misrepresent professional qualifications, education, experience, or affiliations.
 3. The social worker should not allow his or her own personal problems, psychosocial distress, substance abuse, or mental health difficulties to interfere with professional judgment and performance or jeopardize the best interests of those for whom the social worker has a professional responsibility.
 4. The social worker whose personal problems, psychosocial distress, substance abuse, or mental health difficulties interfere with professional judgment and performance should immediately seek consultation and take appropriate remedial action by seeking professional help, making adjustments in workload, terminating practice, or taking any other steps necessary to protect clients an others.

C. *Service*—The social worker should regard as primary the service obligation of the social work profession.
 1. The social worker should retain ultimate responsibility for the quality and extent of the service that individual assumes, assigns, or performs.
 2. The social worker should act to prevent practices that are inhumane or discriminatory against any person or group of persons.

D. *Integrity*—The social worker should act in accordance with the highest standards of professional integrity and impartiality.
 1. The social worker should be alert to and resist the influences and pressures that interfere with the exercise of professional discretion and impartial judgment required for the performance of professional functions.
 2. The social worker should not exploit professional relationships for personal gain.

E. *Scholarship and Research*—The social worker engaged in study and research should be guided by the conventions of scholarly inquiry.
 1. The social worker engaged in research should consider carefully its possible consequences for human beings.
 2. The social worker engaged in research should ascertain that the consent of the participants in the research is voluntary and informed, without any implied deprivation or penalty for refusal to participate, and with due regard for the participants' privacy and dignity.
 3. The social worker engaged in research should protect participants from unwarranted physical or mental discomfort, distress, harm, danger, or deprivation.
 4. The social worker who engages in the evaluation of services or cases should discuss them only for professional purposes and only with persons directly and professionally concerned with them.
 5. Information obtained about participants in research should be treated as confidential.
 6. The social worker should take credit only for work actually done in connection with scholarly and research endeavors and credit contributions made by others.

II. THE SOCIAL WORKER'S ETHICAL RESPONSIBILITY TO CLIENTS

F. *Primacy of Clients' Interests*—The social worker's primary responsibility is to clients.
 1. The social worker should serve clients with devotion, loyalty, determination, and the maximum application of professional skill and competence.
 2. The social worker should not exploit relationships with clients for personal advantage.
 3. The social worker should not practice, condone, facilitate, or collaborate with any form of discrimination on the basis of race, color, sex, sexual orientation, age, religion, national origin, marital status, political belief, mental or physical handicap, or any other preference or personal characteristic, condition, or status.

4. The social worker should not condone or engage in any dual or multiple relationships with clients or former clients in which there is a risk of exploitation of or potential harm to the client. The social worker is responsible for setting clear, appropriate, and culturally sensitive boundaries.

5. The social worker should under no circumstances engage in sexual activities with clients.

6. The social worker should provide clients with accurate and complete information regarding the extent and nature of the services available to them.

7. The social worker should apprise clients of their risks, rights, opportunities, and obligations associated with social service to them.

8. The social worker should seek advice and counsel of colleagues and supervisors whenever such consultation is in the best interest of clients.

9. The social worker should terminate service to clients, and professional relationships with them, when such service and relationships are no longer required or no longer serve the clients' needs or interests.

10. The social worker should withdraw services precipitously only under unusual circumstances, giving careful consideration to all factors in the situation and taking care to minimize possible adverse effects.

11. The social worker who anticipates the termination or interruption of service to clients should notify clients promptly and seek the transfer, referral, or continuation of service in relation to the clients' needs and preferences.

G. *Rights and Prerogatives of Clients*—The social worker should make every effort to foster maximum self-determination on the part of clients.

1. When the social worker must act on behalf of a client who has been adjudged legally incompetent, the social worker should safeguard the interests and rights of that client.

2. When another individual has been legally authorized to act on behalf of a client, the social worker should deal with that person always with the client's best interest in mind.

3. The social worker should not engage in any action that violates or diminishes the civil or legal rights of clients.

H. *Confidentiality and Privacy*—The social worker should respect the privacy of clients and hold in confidence all information obtained in the course of professional service.

1. The social worker should share with others confidences revealed by clients, without their consent, only for compelling professional reasons.

2. The social worker should inform clients fully about the limits of confidentiality in a given situation, the purposes for which information is obtained, and how it may be used.

3. The social worker should afford clients reasonable access to any official social work records concerning them.

4. When providing clients with access to records, the social worker should take due care to protect the confidences of others contained in those records.

5. The social worker should obtain informed consent of clients before taping, recording, or permitting third-party observation of their activities.

I. *Fees*—When setting fees, the social worker should ensure that they are fair, reasonable, considerate, and commensurate with the service performed and with due regard for the clients' ability to pay.

1. The social worker should not accept anything of value for making a referral.

III. THE SOCIAL WORKER'S ETHICAL RESPONSIBILITY TO COLLEAGUES

J. *Respect, Fairness, and Courtesy*—The social worker should treat colleagues with respect, courtesy, fairness, and good faith.

1. The social worker should cooperate with colleagues to promote professional interests and concerns.

2. The social worker should respect confidences shared by colleagues in the course of their professional relationships and transactions.

3. The social worker should create and maintain conditions of practice that facilitate ethical and competent professional performance by colleagues.

4. The social worker should treat with respect, and represent accurately and fairly, the qualifications, views, and findings of colleagues and use appropriate channels to express judgments on these matters.
5. The social worker who replaces or is replaced by a colleague in professional practice should act with consideration for the interest, character, and reputation of that colleague.
6. The social worker should not exploit a dispute between a colleague and employers to obtain a position or otherwise advance the social worker's interest.
7. The social worker should seek arbitration or mediation when conflicts with colleagues require resolution for compelling professional reasons.
8. The social worker should extend to colleagues of other professions the same respect and cooperation that is extended to social work colleagues.
9. The social worker who serves as an employer, supervisor, or mentor to colleagues should make orderly and explicit arrangements regarding the conditions of their continuing professional relationship.
10. The social worker who has the responsibility for employing and evaluating the performance of other staff members should fulfill such responsibility in a fair, considerate, and equitable manner, on the basis of clearly enunciated criteria.
11. The social worker who has the responsibility for evaluating the performance of employees, supervisees, or students should share evaluations with them.
12. The social worker should not use a professional position vested with power, such as that of employer, supervisor, teacher, or consultant, to his or her advantage or to exploit others.
13. The social worker who has direct knowledge of a social work colleague's impairment due to personal problems, psychosocial distress, substance abuse, or mental health difficulties should consult with that colleague and assist the colleague in taking remedial action.

K. *Dealing with Colleagues' Clients*—The social worker has the responsibility to relate to the clients of colleagues with full professional consideration.
1. The social worker should not assume professional responsibility for the clients of another agency or a colleague without appropriate communication with that agency or colleague.
2. The social worker who serves the clients of colleagues, during a temporary absence or emergency, should serve those clients with the same consideration as that afforded any client.

IV. THE SOCIAL WORKER'S RESPONSIBILITY TO EMPLOYERS AND EMPLOYING ORGANIZATIONS

L. *Commitments to Employing Organization*—The social worker should adhere to commitments made to the employing organization.
1. The social worker should work to improve the employing agency's policies and procedures, and the efficiency and effectiveness of its services.
2. The social worker should not accept employment or arrange student field placements in an organization which is currently under public sanction by NASW for violating personnel standards, or imposing limitations on or penalties for professional actions on behalf of clients.
3. The social worker should act to prevent and eliminate discrimination in the employing organization's work assignments and in its employment policies and practices.
4. The social worker should use with scrupulous regard, and only for the purpose for which they are intended, the resources of the employing organization.

V. THE SOCIAL WORKER'S ETHICAL RESPONSIBILITY TO THE SOCIAL WORK PROFESSION

M. *Maintaining the Integrity of the Profession*—The social worker should uphold and advance the values, ethics, knowledge, and mission of the profession.
1. The social worker should protect and enhance the dignity and integrity of the profession and should be responsible and vigorous in discussion and criticism of the profession.

2. The social worker should take action through appropriate channels against unethical conduct by any other member of the profession.
3. The social worker should act to prevent the unauthorized and unqualified practice of social work.
4. The social worker should make no misrepresentations in advertising as to qualifications, competence, service, or results to be achieved.

N. *Community Service*—The social worker should assist the profession in making social services available to the general public.
   1. The social worker should contribute time and professional expertise to activities that promote respect for the utility, the integrity, and the competence of the social work profession.
   2. The social worker should support the formulation, development, enactment, and implementation of social policies of concern to the profession.

O. *Development of Knowledge*—The social worker should take responsibility for identifying, developing, and fully utilizing knowledge for professional practice.
   1. The social worker should base practice upon recognized knowledge relevant to social work.
   2. The social worker should critically examine and keep current with emerging knowledge relevant to social work.
   3. The social worker should contribute to the knowledge base of social work and share research knowledge and practice wisdom with colleagues.

VI. THE SOCIAL WORKER'S ETHICAL RESPONSIBILITY TO SOCIETY

P. *Promoting the General Welfare*—The social worker should promote the general welfare of society.
   1. The social worker should act to prevent and eliminate discrimination against any person or group on the basis of race, color, sex, sexual orientation, age, religion, national origin, marital status, political belief, mental or physical handicap, or any other preference or personal characteristic, condition, or status.
   2. The social worker should act to ensure that all persons have access to the resources, services, and opportunities which they require.
   3. The social worker should act to expand choice and opportunity for all persons, with special regard for disadvantaged or oppressed groups and persons.
   4. The social worker should promote conditions that encourage respect for the diversity of cultures which constitute American society.
   5. The social worker should provide appropriate professional services in public emergencies.
   6. The social worker should advocate changes in policy and legislation to improve social conditions and to promote social justice.
   7. The social worker should encourage informed participation by the public in shaping social policies and institutions.

As adopted by the 1979 NASW Delegate Assembly and revised by the 1990 and 1993 NASW Delegate Assemblies.

2. Distinctive Dates in Social Welfare History

Chauncey A. Alexander

B.C.

1792–1750 King Hammurabi of Babylon issues the Code of Hammurabi, which creates the first code of laws: 3,600 lines of cuneiform, written on a diorite column, include protection of widows, orphans, and the weak against the strong.

600–500 Buddhism, founded by Siddhartha Gautama (Buddha), teaches that all other forms of righteousness "are not worth the sixteenth part of the emancipation of the heart through love and charity."

500–400 The Talmud, a vast compilation of Oral Laws of Jews, prescribes exactly how charitable funds are collected and distributed, including the appointment of tax collectors to administer the system.

386–322 Aristotle recognizes man as a social animal who necessarily must cooperate with and assist his fellow man.

A.D.

30 Christianity, a martyr's church during its first 250 years, in its religious writings cites Jesus Christ as teaching people's love for one another as God's will. The writings emphasize sympathy for poor, disabled, and dispossessed people. Recognized in law in the 4th century, the Canon Law was codified in the 12th century to provide an elaborate discussion of the theory and practice of charity.

622 The Koran, the book considered to be the revelation of God to Muhammad and the foundation of the religion Islam, sets forth five duties, the third of which is to give prescribed alms generously and also to give some alms beyond the minimum.

1215 King John of England signs the Magna Carta, forerunner of modern civil rights documents.

1349 The Statute of Labourers, the first national-level English law to control the movement of laborers, fixes a maximum wage and treats poor people as criminals, thus influencing colonial poor laws.

1536 The Act for the Punishment of Sturdy Vagabonds and Beggars, enacted in England, increases penalties for begging and makes the parish the local government unit for poor relief, requiring local officials to provide resources by making voluntary contributions in churches.

17TH CENTURY

1601 The Elizabethan Poor Law is enacted by the English Parliament, establishing three categories of people eligible for relief: (1) able-bodied poor people; (2) "impotent poor" people (that is, "unemployables"—aged, blind, and disabled people); and (3) dependent children. This law, on which colonial poor laws were based, became a fundamental concept in U.S. public welfare.

1624 Virginia Colony passes the first legislation recognizing services and needs of disabled soldiers and sailors based on "special work" contributions to society.

1642 Plymouth Colony enacts a poor law that directs that relief cases be discussed at town meetings.

1647 The first colonial Poor Law enacted by Rhode Island emphasizes public responsibility for "relief of the poor, to maintain the impotent, and to employ the able, and shall appoint an overseer for the same purpose. Sec. 43 Eliz. 2."

1657 Scots' Charitable Society, the first American "friendly society," founded in Boston, represents the starts of voluntary societies to meet special welfare needs.

The first almshouse is established in Rensselaerswyck, New York, followed by one in Plymouth in 1658 and another in Boston in 1660.

1662 The Settlement Act (Law of Settlement and Removal) is passed by the English Parliament to prevent movement of indigent groups from parish to parish in search of relief. The law makes residence a requirement for assistance, thus influencing American colonies.

1692 The Province of Massachusetts Bay Acts establish indenture contracting or "binding out" for poor children so they will live "under some orderly family government."

1697 The Workhouse Test Act is passed by the English Parliament as a means of forcing unemployed people to work for relief; the act is copied by the colonies.

18TH CENTURY

1703 The New Plymouth Colony Acts establish systems of indenture and apprenticeships for children.

1729   The Ursuline Sisters of New Orleans establish a private home to care for mothers and children who are survivors of Indian massacres and a smallpox epidemic.

1773   The first public mental hospital, Williamsburg Asylum, is established in Williamsburg, Virginia. It is later renamed Eastern Hospital.

1776   The Declaration of Independence is adopted on July 4 by action of the Second Continental Congress.

1777   John Howard completes his study of English prison life and inhumane treatment of prisoners; his study influences reform efforts in the United States.

1787   The U.S. Constitution is completed in Convention on September 17.

1790   The first state public orphanage is founded in Charleston, South Carolina.

1791   The Bill of Rights is ratified on December 15 by Virginia; 10 of the 12 proposed amendments became part of the U.S. Constitution.

1797   Massachusetts enacts the first law regarding insane people as a special group of dependents.

1798   The U.S. Public Health Service is established following severe epidemics in Eastern seaboard cities, which were caused by diseases brought into the country as a result of increased shipping and immigration.

19TH CENTURY

1812   The first American textbook on psychiatry, *Medical Inquiries and Observations upon the Diseases of the Mind,* by Dr. Benjamin Rush, is published.

1813   Connecticut enacts the first labor legislation to require mill owners to have children in factories taught reading, writing, and arithmetic.

1817   The first free U.S. school for the deaf—the Gallaudet School—is founded in Hartford, Connecticut.

1818   New York, Baltimore, and Philadelphia Societies for the Prevention of Pauperism are established to help victims of the depression following the War of 1812.

1819   The U.S. House of Representatives passes a bill that grants the Connecticut Asylum for the Deaf and Dumb six sections of public land.

1822   The first state institution for deaf people is established in Kentucky.

1824   The House of Refuge, the first state-funded institution for juvenile delinquents, is founded in New York.

The Bureau of Indian Affairs is organized in the War Department. It is later (1849) moved to the Department of the Interior.

1829   The New England Asylum for the Blind (later the Perkins Institution), the first such private institution, is founded.

1834   The Poor Law Reform Act, the first major poor law legislation in England since the Elizabethan Poor Law of 1601, influences American social welfare with its emphasis on complete assumption by able-bodied people of responsibility for their own economic security.

1836   The first restrictive child labor law is enacted in Massachusetts (at the time, two-fifths of all employees in New England factories were aged 7 to 16 years).

1837   The first state institution for blind people is established in Ohio.

1841   Dorothea Dix investigates the care provided to insane people. She ultimately is responsible for establishing 41 state hospitals and the federal St. Elizabeth's Hospital in Washington, DC.

1843   Robert Hartley and associates organize the New York Association for Improving the Condition of the Poor, which later merges with the Charity Organization Society of New York to form the present Community Service Society.

1844   Drapery clerk George Williams organizes the first Young Men's Christian Association (YMCA) in London.

1846   John Augustus, a shoemaker in Boston, gives up his work as a shoemaker to devote time to taking people on probation from the courts; from 1841 to 1858, Augustus took 1,152 men and 794 women on probation.

1848   Pennsylvania establishes the first minimum wage law in the United States.

The *Communist Manifesto,* published by Karl Marx and Friedrich Engels, influences worker demands in the United States for labor and social welfare reforms.

1850   The first school for "idiotic and feebleminded" youths is incorporated in Massachusetts.

1851   The YMCA is founded in North America (Montreal). Traveler's Aid (now Traveler's Aid International) is founded by Bryan Mullanphy in St. Louis, Missouri.

1853 The Children's Aid Society of New York—the first child placement agency separate from an institutional program—is founded by the Reverend Charles Loring Brace.

1854 A bill that authorized grants of public land to establish hospitals for insane people and that was initiated by Dorothea Dix and passed unanimously by Congress is vetoed by President Franklin Pierce. The rationale for the veto is that the general welfare clause in the U.S. Constitution reserves such care to the states, not to the federal government, an interpretation that establishes federal welfare policy until the Social Security Act of 1935.

The first day nursery in the United States opens in New York City.

1855 The first Young Men's Hebrew Association is organized in Baltimore. The YMCA is organized in Boston by retired sea captain Thomas C. Sullivan.

1859 The *Origin of Species,* published by Charles Darwin, sets forth the theory of evolution, which provides a scientific approach to the understanding of plant and animal development.

1861 The U.S. Sanitary Commission, a forerunner of the American Red Cross, is established by the Secretary of War to encourage women's volunteer service during the Civil War.

1862 Freedmen's Aid Societies are established in the North to send teachers and relief supplies to former slaves in the South.

The Port Royal Experiment, a precursor to the Freedmen's Bureau, is begun. It is a presidentially authorized but voluntarily funded relief and rehabilitation program to relieve the destitution of 10,000 slaves who have been abandoned on island plantations.

1863 The New York Catholic Protectory is established. It eventually becomes the largest single institution for children in the country.

The first State Board of Charities is established in Massachusetts to supervise the administration of state charitable, medical, and penal institutions.

1865 The Freedmen's Bureau (Bureau of Refugees, Freedmen and Abandoned Lands) is founded as a joint effort of the federal government with private and philanthropic organizations. The bureau provides food, clothing, and shelter for freedmen and refugees; administers justice to protect the rights of black men; protects freedmen and refugees from physical violence and fraud; and provides education.

Slavery is abolished by the 13th amendment, which is ratified on December 6.

1866 The first municipal Board of Health is created by the New York Metropolitan Health Law.

The Young Women's Christian Association (YWCA), which originated in England in 1855, is founded in Boston by Grace Dodge. The YWCA establishes the first boarding house for female students, teachers, and factory workers in 1860 and the first child care facility in 1864. It initiates a history of "firsts" for helping women.

1867 The state of Ohio authorizes county homes for children.

1868 The Massachusetts Board of State Charities begins payments for orphans to board in private family homes.

The 14th amendment is ratified on July 9; it provides that all people born or naturalized in the United States are U.S. citizens and have rights no state can abridge or deny.

1869 The first permanent state board of health and vital statistics is founded in Massachusetts.

1870 The Massachusetts Board of State Charities appoints the first "agent" to visit children in foster homes.

The National Prison Association is founded in Cincinnati; it is renamed American Prison Association in 1954 and is now called the American Correctional Association.

The Home for Aged and Infirm Hebrews of New York City opens; it is the first Jewish institutional home in the United States.

Ratification on February 3 of the 15th amendment to the U.S. Constitution establishes the right of citizens (except women) to vote, regardless of race, color, or previous servitude.

1871 *The Descent of Man,* published by Charles Darwin, applies the theory of evolution to the human species, thus breaking the authority of theologians in the life sciences and providing a basis for a scientific approach to humans and their social relationships.

1872 The American Public Health Association is founded (the Social Work Section is later formed in 1976).

The Dangerous Classes of New York and Twenty Years' Work among Them, by Charles Loring Brace, exposes the conditions of immigrants and children and helps initiate the adoption movement in the United States.

1874 Representatives of the State Boards of Charities of Massachusetts, Connecticut, New York, and Wisconsin organize the Conference of Boards of Public Charities within the American Social Science Association on May 20. An annual conference, in 1879 it became the National Conference of Charities and Correction in a takeover by the voluntary agencies. It was a precursor to the National Conference of Social Work, renamed in 1917. The organization became the National Council on Social Welfare in July 1956.

1875 New York State grants per capita subsidies to the New York Catholic Protectory for the care of children who would otherwise be public charges.

The New York Society for the Prevention of Cruelty to Children is incorporated.

1876 The New York State Reformatory at Elmira is founded; it is a model penal institution for children. Zebulon K. Brockway, a noted corrections reformer and founder of the National Prison Association, is appointed as the first warden.

The American Association for the Study of the Feeble-Minded is organized. (The name is changed to the American Association on Mental Deficiency in 1933 and to the American Association on Mental Retardation in 1987.)

1877 The first Charity Organization Society is founded in December in Buffalo by the Reverend S. Humphreys Gurteen. The society operates on four principles: (1) detailed investigation of applicants, (2) a central system of registration to avoid duplication, (3) cooperation between the various relief agencies, and (4) extensive use of the volunteers in the role of "friendly visitors."

1879 Franklin B. Sanborn, chair of the Massachusetts State Board of Charities, advocates use of foster homes for delinquent and dependent children.

The Conference of Boards of Public Charities is renamed the National Conference of Charities and Correction in the first session, independent of the American Social Science Association (1865).

1880 The Salvation Army is founded in the United States after William Booth established it in London in 1878.

1881 Clara Barton organizes the American Association of the Red Cross, which is renamed the American National Red Cross in 1893 and the American Red Cross in 1978.

Booker T. Washington founds the Tuskegee Normal and Industrial Institute, a leading black educational institution that emphasizes industrial training as a means to self-respect and economic independence for African Americans.

1883 The Federal Civil Service Commission is established.

1884 Germany, under Bismarck, inaugurates accident, sickness, and old age insurance for workers, influencing future U.S. worker demands for social welfare measures.

Toynbee Hall, the first social settlement, is opened in East London by Samuel A. Barnett, vicar of St. Jude's Parish. Visited by many Americans, it became a model for American settlement houses.

1885 The first course on social reform is initiated by Dr. Francis G. Peabody at Harvard University. It is Philosophy II, described as "The Ethics of Social Reform: The Questions of Charity, Divorce, the Indians, Labor, Prisons, Temperance, Etc., as Problems of Practical Ethics—Lectures, Essays and Practical Observations."

1886 The first settlement house in the United States, the Neighborhood Guild (now the University Settlement), is founded on New York City's Lower East Side.

1887 The only 19th century National Conference of Charities and Correction "dealing with indians and Negroes" is organized in 1887 and 1892 by Phillip C. Garrett, who states that the society had a special responsibility toward "the Indian because of being displaced and toward the Negro because of being here through no wish of their own."

The first attempt at cooperative financing is made in Denver.

1889 Hull House, the most famous settlement house, is opened on September 14 by Jane Addams and Ellen Gates Starr on Chicago's West Side.

1890 *How the Other Half Lives,* by Jacob A. Riis, is published. A documentary and photographic account of housing conditions in New York City slums, it helps initiate the U.S. public housing movement.

1893 In September, Lillian Wald founds the Nurses Settlement, a private nonsectarian home nursing service. In 1895 it moved to become the famous Henry Street Settlement.

1894 *American Charities,* by Amos G. Warner, is published. A social work classic, it is the first systematic attempt to describe the field of charities in the United States and to formulate the principles of relief.

1895   The first Federation of Jewish Charities is established in Boston.

1896   The first special class for "mentally deficient" people in an American public school is established in Providence, Rhode Island.

Volunteers of America is founded.

1897   The first state hospital for crippled children is founded in Minnesota.

1898   The first social work training school is established as an annual summer course for agency workers by the New York Charity Organization Society, which in 1904 becomes the New York School of Philanthropy (and later the Columbia University School of Social Work).

The National Federation of Day Nurseries is organized.

1899   The first U.S. juvenile court is established in June as part of the Circuit Court of Chicago.

Florence Kelley, who initiated fact-finding as a basic approach to social action, organizes the National Consumers League in New York City. The league is a combination of several local leagues, the earliest of which was formed in New York by Josephine Shaw Lowell to campaign against sweatshops and to obtain limits on hours of work for girls.

Friendly Visiting Among the Poor, by Mary E. Richmond, is published in January as "A Handbook of Charity Workers."

The National Conference of Jewish Charities is established in New York to coordinate the developing network of private Jewish social services.

20TH CENTURY

1902   Maryland enacts the first U.S. worker's compensation law, which is declared unconstitutional in 1904.

Care of Destitute, Neglected and Delinquent Children, by Homer Folks, founder of the New York State Charities Aid Association, is a major influence on service directions in child welfare.

Goodwill Industries of America is founded.

1903   The Chicago School of Civics and Philanthropy (now the University of Chicago School of Social Service Administration) is founded by Graham Taylor.

1904   The National Child Labor Committee, which is organized by a combination of New York and Chicago settlement groups, becomes primarily responsible for the 1909 White House Conference on Children.

The New York School of Philanthropy (now the Columbia University School of Social Work) is founded, with a one-year educational program.

The National Association for the Study and Prevention of Tuberculosis (later the National Tuberculosis Association and now the American Lung Association) is founded on March 28.

Poverty, the classic work by Robert Hunter, is published; it states that at least 10 million Americans, or one out of every eight, are poor.

1905   Medical social work is initiated with the employment of Garnet I. Pelton by Richard L. Cabot, MD, at Massachusetts General Hospital in Boston.

1906   The National Recreation Association is organized, later becoming the National Recreation and Park Association following a 1965 merger of the American Institute of Park Executives, American Recreation Society, National Conference on State Parks, and National Recreation Association.

The Boys Clubs of America is founded in Boston.

The first school social workers' programs are introduced in Boston, Hartford, and New York under private agencies.

1907   The Russell Sage Foundation is incorporated "to improve the social and living conditions in the United States"; it later financed publication of the *Social Work Year Book* (now the *Encyclopedia of Social Work*, published by the NASW Press).

Psychiatric social work is initiated with the employment of Edith Burleigh and M. Antoinette Cannon by James J. Putnam, MD, to work with mental patients in the neurological clinic of Massachusetts General Hospital in Boston.

The National Probation Association is founded (renamed the National Probation and Parole Association in 1947 and the National Council on Crime and Delinquency in 1960).

1908   The first community welfare council is organized in Pittsburgh as the Pittsburgh Associated Charities.

A Mind That Found Itself, by Clifford Beers, is published. An exposé of the inadequacies of mental hospitals, it initiates the mental health movement.

The Federal Council of Churches of Christ in America begins to coordinate its network of social services.

Workers' compensation is enacted by the federal government; it represents the earliest form of social insurance in the United States.

1909 The National Committee for Mental Hygiene (now the National Mental Health Association) is founded by Clifford Beers.

Jane Addams is elected as the first woman president of the National Conference of Charities and Correction (later the National Council on Social Welfare).

England's Royal Poor Law Commission majority report seeks to modify the Poor Law as "the principle of 1834," defining the relationship of private, voluntary welfare organizations to the public assistance system. The minority recommends breaking up the Poor Law and transferring responsibility to divisions of local government, implying the creation of universal services and anticipating features of a 20th-century welfare state.

The Juvenile Psychopathic Institute is established in Chicago by Dr. William Healy, on the initiative of Julia Lathrop, to study offenders brought to the juvenile court. The institute initiates delinquency research and examination of children by a professional team.

The first White House Conference on Children (concerned with the care of dependent children) is initiated under the sponsorship of President Theodore Roosevelt on the suggestion of James E. West, who later heads the Boy Scouts of America.

The Pittsburgh Survey, the first exhaustive description and analysis of a substantial modern city, is begun.

The Niagara Movement stimulates the formation of the National Association for the Advancement of Colored People (NAACP) in May. The NAACP is a broad-based organization with interracial membership.

1910 The Boy Scouts of America is founded by William D. Boyce. It originally was started in England by Lord Baden Powell.

The American Camping Association is founded to research, develop, and implement a program of inspection and accreditation of camps.

Camp Fire Girls (now Camp Fire Boys and Girls) is founded.

Catholic Charities is founded.

The first social work training program for black workers is started by Dr. George Edmund Haynes at Fisk University in Nashville. The National League on Urban Conditions Among Negroes (now the National Urban League) is organized by Dr. George E. Haynes and Eugene Kinckle Jones through a union of the Committee for Improving the Industrial Conditions of Negroes in New York (formed in 1907); the National League for the Protection of Colored Women (formed in 1906); and the Committee on Urban Conditions Among Negroes (formed in 1910).

1911 The First Mother's Aid Law is enacted in Illinois.

The first state workers' compensation law that was not later declared unconstitutional is enacted by the state of Washington.

The American Association for Organizing Family Social Work is formed to promote the development of family social work. (In 1930 the organization becomes the Family Welfare Association of America and in 1946 the Family Service Association of America. In 1983 the name is changed to Family Service America; in 1995 it is Families International, Inc.)

Catholic Big Brothers is founded.

Social workers are placed on payrolls of New York's mental hospitals. Aftercare work soon becomes an integral part of the services of such institutions throughout the United States.

The National Federation of Settlements is founded. (It became the National Federation of Settlements & Neighborhood Centers in 1959 and the United Neighborhood Centers of America in 1979.)

1912 The Children's Bureau Act (ch. 73, 37 Stat. 79) is passed on April 9. It establishes the U.S. Children's Bureau as a separate government agency, based on an idea initiated by Florence Kelley and Lillian Wald. Julia C. Lathrop is appointed the first chief.

Girl Scouts of the United States of America is founded.

Survey Associates, Inc., a membership society combining research and journalism methods for the advancement of general welfare, is founded. Publications are used as "shuttles of understanding"; Paul Kellogg is editor. *Survey Midmonthly* spans the fields of social work, and *Survey Graphic*, which is addressed to lay readers, swings wider arcs of social and economic concern. Discontinued.

1913 *Social Insurance,* by I. M. Rubinow, advocates a comprehensive social insurance system to protect against sickness, old age, industrial accidents, invalidism, death, and unemployment.

The Modern Community Chest movement is begun with the organization of the Cleveland Federation for Charity and Philanthropy as an experiment in federated financing, after a first trial in Denver in 1888. The Community Chests and Councils of America is organized in 1918.

The U.S. Department of Labor and Department of Commerce are established on March 4.

1914 National Negro Health Week, the first health program for Negroes inaugurated by a Negro, is begun by Booker T. Washington.

The Joint Distribution Committee for Relief of Jewish War Sufferers (now American Jewish Joint Distribution Committee) is founded.

1915 The Bureau for the Exchange of Information Among Child-Helping Organizations is founded.

Abraham Flexner in his address to the National Conference of Charities and Correction on "Is Social Work a Profession?" states social work does not qualify as a bona fide profession, consequently stimulating continual definition efforts by social workers.

1916 National health insurance is advocated by I. M. Rubinow, executive secretary of the American Medical Association Social Insurance Commission.

The American Birth Control League is founded (becoming the Planned Parenthood Federation of America in 1939).

The first birth control clinic is opened by Margaret Sanger in Brooklyn, New York.

The Child Labor Act (ch. 676, 520 Stat. 1060) is passed by Congress on June 25; the act forbids interstate commerce of goods manufactured by child labor and is declared unconstitutional by the Supreme Court in 1918.

1917 *Social Diagnosis,* by Mary Richmond, is published in May. It is the first textbook on social casework, marking the development of a body of social work knowledge and techniques.

The first state department of public welfare is established in Illinois.

The National Conference of Charities and Correction becomes the National Conference of Social Work.

The National Social Workers Exchange (becoming, in 1921, the American Association of Social Workers and merging with other organizations to form NASW in 1955) is organized as "the only social work organization with specific concern for matters of personnel [and] additional functions pertaining to professional standards."

The National Jewish Welfare Board is established (becoming the Jewish Welfare Board in 1977 and the Jewish Community Centers Association of North America in 1990).

1918 The American Association of Hospital Social Workers is organized. (It becomes the American Association of Medical Social Workers in 1934 and merges with other organizations to form NASW in 1955.)

The National Association of Jewish Center Workers is organized. (In 1970 it becomes the Association of Jewish Center Workers and in 1989 the Association of Jewish Center Professionals.)

The first formal training program for psychiatric social workers is instituted at Smith College in Northampton, Massachusetts.

The Vocational Rehabilitation Act of 1918 (ch. 107, 40 Stat. 617) is passed on June 27. It establishes the first national program that provides physically handicapped veterans with occupational training and prostheses and, in 1920, is extended to provide rehabilitation in civilian life.

The Community Chests and Councils of America is founded. (In 1956 it becomes the United Community Funds and Councils of America and in 1970 the United Way.)

1919 The National Association of Visiting Teachers is formed. (It later becomes the National Association of School Social Workers, which subsequently merges with other organizations to form NASW in 1955.)

The Association of Training Schools for Professional Social Work (a forerunner of the American Association of Schools of Social Work, now the Council on Social Work Education) is formed by leaders of 15 schools of social work. It is the first organization concerned exclusively with social work education and educational standards in Canada and the United States.

1920 The Chicago School of Civics and Philanthropy becomes the Graduate School of Social Service Administration, University of Chicago.

The Atlanta School of Social Service (now the Atlanta School of Social Work) opens in September, originating from Institutes of Social Service sponsored by the Neighborhood Union of Morehouse College from 1919 to 1920. Complete professionalization comes under the directorship of E. Franklin Frazier in 1922. The school is incorporated and chartered on March 22, 1924.

The National Conference of Catholic Charities is founded to coordinate a network of sectarian social services.

The right of women to vote is passed on August 18 as the 19th amendment.

The Child Welfare League of America (CWLA) is founded. (In 1976 CWLA absorbs the Florence Crittendon Association.)

1921 The National Social Workers Exchange becomes the American Association of Social Workers (which later merges into NASW), the first national professional association of all social workers.

The Social Work Publicity Council is founded as the primary agency for interpreting social problems and social work. The council served as clearinghouse for ideas and materials on public relations and published *Channels* periodical and special bulletins.

The Maternity and Infancy Hygiene Act (Sheppard-Towner Act) (ch. 135, 42 Stat. 224), which provides for the first national maternal and child health program, is passed by Congress on November 23. The Commonwealth Fund establishes demonstration clinics for child guidance, initiating the child guidance clinic movement and establishing the essential role of social workers.

The Association of Junior Leagues of America is founded. (It becomes the Association of Junior Leagues in 1971 and the Association of Junior Leagues International in 1990.)

1923 The Jewish Welfare Society of Philadelphia establishes the first organized homemaker service.

The first course in group work in a school of social work is introduced at Western Reserve University in Cleveland, Ohio, by Clara Kaiser.

Education and Training for Social Work is published, detailing the first major study of social work education conducted by James H. Tufts, professor of philosophy at the University of Chicago.

1924 The Atlanta School of Social Work is incorporated on March 22 as the first Negro school.

1926 The American Association of Psychiatric Social Workers, originally a section of the American Association of Hospital Social Workers, is organized. (It later merges into NASW.)

1927 The first school of social work is professionally certified by the American Association of Schools of Social Work.

The American Association for Old Age Security is organized to further national interest in legislation for aged people; Abraham Epstein is appointed as the director.

1928 The Milford Conference on November 9 and 10 accepts a committee report defining generic social casework and promulgating the principle that process in social casework and the equipment of the social worker should be basically the same for all fields of practice.

The International Conference of Social Work (ICSW) is formed during the first international conference of philanthropists, charity organizers, social workers, government officials, and others in Paris. The organization later became the International Council on Social Welfare.

1929 The *Social Work Year Book* (now the *Encyclopedia of Social Work*) is initiated under the auspices of the Russell Sage Foundation. (Publication is transferred to AASW in 1951 and to NASW in 1955.)

The International Committee of Schools of Social Work (ICSSW) is formed by 46 schools in 10 countries. The impetus for the new organization came from the 1928 international conference, in which participants called for social work education as a means of professionalizing social work and improving services. (ICSSW later became the International Association of Schools of Social Work, IASSW).

1930 The American Public Welfare Association is founded.

1931 The Nobel Peace Prize is awarded to renowned social worker Jane Addams.

The Temporary Emergency Relief Administration is established in New York State by Governor Franklin Delano Roosevelt as a prototype of federal public relief to unemployed people.

1932 President Herbert Hoover signs the Emergency Relief and Construction Act (ch. 520, 47 Stat. 709) into law on July 21; a provision of the act enables the Reconstruction Finance Corporation to lend money to states for relief purposes, moving federal government into the field of public relief.

Formal accreditation is initiated by the American Association of Schools of Social Work with development of a minimum curriculum requiring at least one academic year of professional education encompassing both classroom and field instruction.

The Council of Jewish Federations and Welfare Funds is founded. (In 1978 it becomes the Council of Jewish Federations.)

1933 The Civilian Conservation Corps Act (ch. 17, 48 Stat. 22) is passed by Congress on March 31. The act is established to meet part of the need caused by the Great Depression by providing work and education programs for unemployed and unmarried young men ages 17 to 23 years.

The Federal Emergency Relief Act (ch. 30, 48 Stat. 55) is passed on May 12. It creates the Federal Emergency Relief Administration (FERA), which provides 25 percent matching and direct grants to states for public distribution for relief. Social worker Harry Hopkins becomes the director on May 22. (On April 8, 1935, the Federal Emergency Relief Administration is superseded by the Works Progress Administration, which is phased out in 1943.)

1934   The first licensing law for social workers is passed in Puerto Rico and is a precursor to later state laws.

The National Housing Act (ch. 847, 48 Stat. 1246) is enacted by Congress on June 27. It is the first law in U.S. history designed to promote housing construction.

The National Foundation for Infantile Paralysis is initiated by President Franklin D. Roosevelt to raise funds for a Warm Springs Foundation, Georgia, treatment center. It becomes the successful Annual March of Dimes under Basil O'Connor.

Social Work Today, progressive publication of 1930s depression period, is begun by Social Work Today, Inc. This individual and organizational membership group also published professional pamphlets and conducted educational activities; it was discontinued in 1942.

1935   The Health, Education and Welfare Act (Social Security Act; ch. 531, 49 Stat. 620) is passed by Congress on August 14, providing old-age assistance benefits, a Social Security Board, grants to states for unemployment compensation administration, aid to dependent children, maternal and child welfare, public health work, and aid to blind people. Social worker Jane M. Hoey is appointed as the first director of the Federal Bureau of Public Assistance, which administers federal–state aid to aged people, blind people, and dependent children under the provisions of the act.

The National Conference on Social Work, in its reorganization, recognizes group work as a major function of social work along with social casework, community organization, and social action.

The Works Progress Administration is created by presidential executive order on May 6—and the Federal Emergency Relief Administration is terminated—to shift the federal government from home relief to work relief. The administration is committed to provide work "for able-bodied but destitute workers."

The National Youth Administration is created by presidential executive order on June 26 as a division of the Works Progress Administration to provide work and school aid under direction of social worker Aubrey Williams.

1936   The American Association for the Study of Group Work is organized. (In 1946 it becomes the American Association of Group Workers and merges into NASW in 1955.)

1937   A state-administered program in North Carolina pioneers the development of family planning as part of maternal and child health services.

The Housing Act (ch. 896, 50 Stat. 885) is passed by Congress on September 1 to provide subsidies and credit to states and local governments. It is the first attempt to finance residential accommodations for tenants not exclusively federal employees.

1938   The Works Progress Administration Act (ch. 554, 52 Stat. 809) is passed by Congress on June 21.

The National Association of Day Nurseries, formerly the National Federation of Day Nurseries founded in 1898, is established. (The organization becomes the National Association for the Education of Young Children in 1964.)

1939   A food stamp plan to dispose of agricultural commodities is begun in Rochester, New York.

1941   The United Service Organization is incorporated in February to coordinate services provided to armed forces and defense workers by six voluntary agencies: (1) National Jewish Welfare Board, (2) National Catholic Community Service, (3) National Traveler's Aid Association, (4) Salvation Army, (5) YMCA, and (6) YWCA.

1942   The first U.S. responsibility to provide day care for children of working mothers is initiated through the Lanham Act (ch. 260, 55 Stat. 361), providing 50 percent matching grants to local communities for use in operation of day care centers and family day care homes.

The United Seaman's Service is established in the National Maritime Union in September to provide medical, social work, and other services to merchant seamen; Bertha C. Reynolds is named the director.

The National Association of Schools of Social Administration (now the Council on Social Work Education) is formed by 34 land grant college undergraduate social work programs.

1943   The United Nations Relief and Rehabilitation Administration is established by 44 nations for postwar relief and refugee settlement.

The American Council of Voluntary Agencies for Foreign Service is established "to promote joint program planning and coordination of national voluntary agency activities on foreign relief and rehabilitation."

1944 The Servicemen's Readjustment Act (ch. 268, 58 Stat. 284), the "G.I. Bill of Rights," provides education and training through state-administered payments to educational units; subsistence allowance; loans for purchase or construction of homes, farms, or business property; job counseling and employment placement; and 52 weeks of adjustment allowances. It is liberalized by Amendment 12/21/45 (ch. 588, P.L. 268). It initiated many men into the social work profession.

1945 The National Social Welfare Assembly, formerly the National Social Work Council formed in 1923, is organized. (It is now the National Assembly of National Voluntary Health and Social Welfare Organizations.)

The United Nations is chartered in April, including the Economic and Social Council, to provide "international machinery for the promotion and social advancement of all peoples" and coordinate agencies dealing with social welfare problems, such as the World Health Organization, United Nations International Children's Emergency Fund, International Labor Office, and International Refugee Organization.

Common Human Needs, by Charlotte Towle and published by the Federal Security Agency, reaffirms the principle of public assistance services as a right and the need for public assistance staffs to understand psychological needs and forces and their relationship to social forces and experiences. (Banned by the federal government in 1951, it is then distributed by the American Association of Social Workers.)

The Girls Clubs of America is founded. (The organization becomes Girls, Inc., in 1990.)

1946 The Hospital Survey and Construction Act (ch. 958, 60 Stat. 1040), or Hill-Burton Act (P.L. 79-725), is passed by Congress, initiating massive construction and expansion of inpatient hospital facilities with significant standards requirements for community participation.

The National Mental Health Act (ch. 538, 60 Stat. 421), passed on July 3, recognizes mental illness as a national public health problem.

The Association for the Study of Community Organization is formed. (It merges into NASW in 1955.)

The Full Employment Act (ch. 33, 60 Stat. 23) is passed by Congress on February 20. It establishes a policy of federal responsibility for employment and is not yet implemented.

Big Brothers of America is founded. (In 1977 it merges with Big Sisters to form Big Brothers/Big Sisters of America.)

1948 The American Association of Social Workers and School of Applied Social Sciences of Western Reserve University (now Case Western Reserve University) sponsors a conference that helps define the identity and function of research in social work as distinguished from social research.

1949 The Social Work Research Group is organized. (It merges into NASW in 1955.)

1950 *Social Workers in 1950,* published by the Bureau of Labor Statistics, is the first survey of 75,000 social workers, with 50,000 replies.

The Social Security Act Amendments (ch. 809, 64 Stat. 477) are passed on August 28. The amendments establish a program of aid to permanently and totally disabled people and broaden Aid to Dependent Children (later Aid to Families with Dependent Children) to include relatives with whom a child is living. The amendments extend Old-Age and Survivors' Insurance and liberalize other programs.

The National Council on Aging is founded.

1951 *Social Work Education in the United States,* by Ernest V. Hollis and Alice L. Taylor, is published. Generally known as the Hollis–Taylor Report, it is a comprehensive study of social work education "in relation to the responsibility of social work in the broad field of social welfare."

The American Association of Social Workers reissues *Common Human Needs* after the federal government burns its stock in response to pressure from the American Medical Association.

The American Association of Social Workers publishes the 11th edition of the *Social Work Year Book,* following 10 editions published by the Russell Sage Foundation.

1952 The U.S. Children's Bureau grants funds for special projects to develop and coordinate statewide programs for medical and social services to unwed mothers.

The Council on Social Work Education is created from temporary study and a coordinating body, the National Council on Social Work Education (in 1946), to unite the school accrediting responsibility of the National Association of Schools of Social Administration and the American Association of Schools of Social Work. The council includes board representatives of schools, faculty, agencies, and the public for educational policy and decisions.

The U.S. Committee of the International Conference on Social Welfare is formed.

1953 The U.S. Department of Health, Education and Welfare is established on April 11.

1954   Rutland Corner House in Brookline, Massachusetts, is established as the first urban transitional residence (halfway house) for mental patients.

Brown v. Board of Education of Topeka, Shawnee County, Kansas, (347 U.S. 483) eliminates the "separate but equal" doctrine in educational facilities.

1955   NASW commences operation on October 1 through a merger of five professional membership associations—(1) American Association of Group Workers, (2) American Association of Medical Social Workers, (3) American Association of Psychiatric Social Workers, (4) American Association of Social Workers, and (5) National Association of School Social Workers—and two study groups— (1) Association for the Study of Community Organization and (2) Social Work Research Group.

The National Association of Puerto Rican Hispanic Social Workers is organized.

1957   The Civil Rights Act (P.L. 85-315, 71 Stat. 634) is passed by Congress on September 9. It is the first such act since 1875; it establishes the Commission on Civil Rights and strengthens federal enforcement powers.

NASW publishes the 13th edition of the *Social Work Year Book.*

1958   *A Working Definition of Social Work Practice,* developed by the National Commission on Practice headed by Harriett Bartlett, is published by NASW. It establishes the basic constellation of elements of social work practice: values, purpose, sanction, knowledge, and method.

1959   The *Social Work Curriculum Study,* by Werner W. Boehm, director and coordinator, is published by the Council on Social Work Education. The 13-volume study is a "milestone in the development of effective educational programs for professions."

1960   The National Committee for Day Care is established to promote day care as an essential part of child welfare services and to develop standards of care.

Newburgh, New York, legislates 13 restrictive work requirements for welfare recipients, precipitating a nationwide retrogression in public welfare.

1961   The Juvenile Delinquency and Youth Offenses Control Act (P.L. 87-274, 75 Stat. 572), which recognizes economic and social factors leading to crime, is passed by Congress. The act authorizes grant funds for demonstration projects for comprehensive delinquency programs in ghettos.

The Academy of Certified Social Workers is incorporated by NASW to promote standards for professional social work practice and the protection of social welfare clients. It requires a master of social work degree and two years of supervised practice by an Academy of Certified Social Workers member.

1962   *The Other America,* by Michael Harrington, is published, awakening the United States to the problem of poverty.

The Manpower Development and Training Act (P.L. 87-415) is passed by Congress to provide government financing of training to move unemployed and displaced workers into new fields.

1963   The Mental Retardation Facilities and Community Mental Health Centers Construction Act (P.L. 88-164, 77 Stat. 282) is passed on October 31, authorizing appropriations to states that started significant development of community health and retardation services with single state agency administration and advisory committees with consumer representation.

The Civil Rights March on Washington is held at the peak of the civil rights coalition movement.

1964   The Civil Rights Act (P.L. 88-352, 78 Stat. 241) is passed by Congress on July 2 and results in significant changes for racial and ethnic groups in institutional health care programs and procedures to ensure equal treatment, in policies to eliminate discrimination in employment and pre-employment, and in policies to open entry opportunities in particular occupations.

The Food Stamp Act (P.L. 88-525, 785 Stat. 703) is passed on August 31 to provide cooperative federal–state food assistance programs for improved levels of nutrition in low-income households.

The Economic Opportunity Act (P.L. 88-452, 78 Stat. 5088) is passed by Congress on August 20, establishing the Office of Economic Opportunity and calling for the creation of Volunteers in Service to America, Job Corps, Upward Bound, Neighborhood Youth Corps, Operation Head Start, and Community Action programs.

1965   The Elementary and Secondary Education Act (P.L. 89-10, 79 Stat. 27) is passed on April 11, initiating the first major infusion of federal funds into the U.S. educational system. The act provides aid to economically disadvantaged children, counseling and guidance services, community education, and planning.

The Older Americans Act (P.L. 89-73, 79 Stat. 218) is passed by Congress on July 14, creating the Administration on Aging, the first central body within the federal government dealing with aging.

The Social Security Amendments ("Medicare Act"; P.L. 89-97, 79 Stat. 286) are enacted on July 30 as Title XVIII of the Security Act. The amendments provide federal health insurance benefits for aged (older than 65 years) and entitled people to benefits under Title II. The amendments establish a compulsory hospital-based program for aged people; a voluntary supplemental plan to provide physicians and other health services; and an expanded medical assistance program (Medicaid) for needy and medically needy aged, blind, and disabled people and their families.

Medicaid, enacted on July 30 as Title XIX of the Social Security Act, provides federal grants to match state programs of hospital and medical services for welfare recipients and medically indigent populations.

Abstracts for Social Workers is initiated by NASW under contract with the National Institute for Mental Health. (The journal is subsequently titled *Social Work Research & Abstracts* when a primary research journal is added in 1977 and re-titled *Social Work Abstracts* when the two journals are separated in 1994.)

Heart Disease, Cancer and Stroke Amendments (P.L. 89-239, 79 Stat. 926), or Regional Medical Programs, provide grants for planning to establish regular cooperative arrangements among medical schools, research institutions, and hospitals to meet local health needs. The amendments require broadly representative advisory committees and involve key social worker leadership.

The Academy of Certified Social Workers is promoted by NASW as a national standard-setting body for social work practice.

Closing the Gap in Social Work Manpower is published by the U.S. Department of Health, Education and Welfare in November; it projects escalating demands for social workers and delineates the master of social work and bachelor of social work classifications. It also plays an exceptional role in focusing labor force problems and advocating for the bachelor of social work as an entry professional classification.

Griswold v. State of Connecticut (381 U.S. 479) holds against state fine of Planned Parenthood for providing contraceptive information to married people. It initiates a constitutional concept of privacy formulated by Thomas I. Emerson, which later leads to the *Roe v. Wade* decision in 1973.

NASW publishes the 15th edition of the *Encyclopedia of Social Work,* as a follow-on to the 14 editions of the *Social Work Year Book.*

1966 The Narcotic Addict Rehabilitation Act (P.L. 89-793, 80 Stat. 1438), passed by Congress on November 8, emphasizes total treatment and aftercare rather than criminal prosecution and fragmented efforts, providing pretrial civil commitment in the custody of the Surgeon General for treatment.

The Comprehensive Health Planning and Public Health Services Amendments of 1966 (P.L. 89-749, 80 Stat. 1180), passed by Congress on November 3, authorizes grants to support comprehensive state planning for health services, labor, and facilities. The Veteran's Readjustment Benefits Act (P.L. 89-358, 80 Stat. 12) enhances service in the armed forces, extending higher education and providing vocational readjustment. It also emphasizes programs requiring veterans to make contributions to their own educational programs.

The Society for Hospital Social Work Directors is formed under the auspices of the American Hospital Association. (In 1993 the society changes its name to the Society for Social Work Administrators in Health Care to reflect changes in health care.)

1967 In May, the U.S. Supreme Court in the *In re Gault* decision rules that timely notice of all charges against a juvenile must be given and that a child has the right to be represented by legal counsel, to confront and cross-examine complainants, and to be protected against self-incrimination in juvenile delinquency proceedings.

The Child Health Act (P.L. 90-248, 81 Stat. 821), passed by Congress on January 2, adds three new types of medical care project grants—(1) infant care, (2) family planning, and (3) dental care to social security.

1968 The National Association of Black Social Workers, the National Association of Puerto Rican Social Service Workers, and the Asian American Social Workers are established.

The Southwest Council of La Raza is organized. (In 1973 it becomes the National Council of La Raza, a major national coalition.)

1969 Richard M. Nixon proposes the Family Assistance Plan in a historic message to Congress. He asserts the welfare system has failed and recommends a federal welfare system with a virtually guaranteed annual income. The House, but not the Senate, passes the plan, which is subsequently reintroduced in 1971. After two years of negotiation with welfare groups, the plan is withdrawn.

The bachelor of social work degree is recognized for NASW membership as a result of a national membership referendum and is implemented in 1970.

The Social Worker's Professional Liability Insurance program is started by the NASW administration; it is transferred to the NASW Insurance Trust in 1985.

The Association of American Indian Social Workers is founded. (In 1981 it becomes the Association of Indian and Alaskan Native Social Workers, and in 1984, the National Indian Social Workers Association.)

1971 The ACTION agency is formed through President Nixon's reorganization plan, centralizing direction of volunteer agencies, including Volunteers in Service to America, Peace Corps, and others, and beginning a pattern of reductions.

Congress passes the Comprehensive Child Development Act to provide comprehensive high-quality day care and support services to all children. President Nixon vetoes the act.

The Educational Legislative Action Network (ELAN) is initiated by NASW as a national congressional district legislative structure; ELAN commits the social work profession to legislative advocacy as a professional responsibility.

NASW initiates the objective examination, the first national testing of social work knowledge and practice, for the Academy of Certified Social Workers.

The National Federation of Clinical Social Workers is established. (In 1976 it becomes the National Federation of Societies for Clinical Social Work.)

1972 Community-based work and education programs for juvenile delinquents are established by the Massachusetts Youth Services Department to replace juvenile reformatories.

Supplemental Security Income (P.L. 92-603, 86 Stat. 1328) establishes a separate program administration for aged, blind, and disabled populations in the Social Security Amendments of 1972, (P.L. 92-603, 86 Stat. 1329), which are passed on October 30 and become effective on January 1, 1974.

The State and Local Fiscal Act (P.L. 92-512, 86 Stat. 919), "Revenue Sharing," becomes a landmark in the federal–state–local relationship, providing states and localities with specified portions of federal individual income tax collections to be used for nine specific priority expenditures.

The Equal Employment Opportunity Act (P.L. 92-261, 86 Stat. 103) is passed to grant the Equal Employment Opportunity Commission authority to issue judicially enforceable cease-and-desist orders. The act establishes a quasijudicial agency to implement national policy of employment opportunity without discrimination of race, color, religion, national origin, or gender.

The landmark legal principle of "right to treatment" is established in *Wyatt v. Stickney* (344 F. Supp. 387, M.D. Ala., N.D. 1972) by Frank M. Johnson, Jr., chief judge of the U.S. Middle District Court in Montgomery, Alabama. The ruling sets forth minimal constitutional standards of care, treatment, and habilitation for patients involuntarily confined to public mental hospitals in Alabama.

The National Institute on Drug Abuse is established on March 21 by the Drug Abuse Office and Treatment Act (P.L. 92-255, 86 Stat. 65) to provide leadership, policies, and goals for the total federal effort to prevent, control, and treat narcotic addiction and drug abuse.

Professional Standards Review Organizations are initiated on October 30 as part of the Social Security Amendments. This national program of local and state organizations establishes service standards and reviews quality and costs of health services provided to beneficiaries of Medicare, Medicaid, and maternal and child health programs. Through NASW intervention, the program includes social workers in all phases.

1973 The Health Maintenance Organization Act (P.L. 93-222, 87 Stat. 914) is enacted on December 29, authorizing federal aid to support and stimulate group medical practice. Through NASW intervention, the act includes social services components and standards.

Roe v. Wade (410 U.S. 179) determines that a Texas statute prohibiting abortion violates the due process clause of the 14th amendment. The decision establishes that trimester stages of pregnancy determine state's limits on regulation of abortions. It also affirms the right of privacy.

The Children's Defense Fund is founded by Marian Wright Edelman to "provide long-range advocacy on behalf of nation's children."

1974 The Council on Social Work Education offers accreditation to bachelor of social work programs.

The Child Abuse Prevention and Treatment Act (P.L. 93-247, 88 Stat. 4), passed by Congress on January 31, initiates financial assistance for demonstration programs for prevention, identification, and treatment of child abuse and neglect and establishes the National Center on Child Abuse and Neglect.

The Comprehensive Employment and Training Act (CETA; P.L. 92-603) initiates extensive job education and experience opportunities for unemployed people.

1975   The National Health Planning and Resources Development Act of 1974 (P.L. 93-641, 88 Stat. 2225) is enacted on January 4, combining regional medical programs, comprehensive health planning, and Hill–Burton programs to establish an integrated system of national, state, and area planning agencies with consumer majorities on policy bodies.

The Social Service Amendments of 1974 (P.L. 93-647, 88 Stat. 2337), Title XX of the Social Security Act, are enacted on January 3, initiating comprehensive social services programs directed toward achieving economic self-support and preventing dependence. Five levels of services, meeting federal standards, are implemented by states with 75 percent federal subsidy. The amendments were initiated and planned as a result of NASW opposition and coalition-building against the Nixon administration's attempt to misuse regulations to reduce social services expenditures.

The Education for All Handicapped Children Act (P.L. 94-142, 89 Stat. 773), enacted on November 29, extends national public education policy to mandate free public education for all handicapped people. The provision for social work services in the public schools by 1978 is included through NASW intervention.

1976   The Political Action for Candidate Election in initiated as a political action committee of NASW, committing the social work profession to political action as a professional responsibility.

In a class action suit, Judge Frank M. Johnson, Jr. of the U.S. Middle District Court in Montgomery Alabama, rules on January 13 that conditions of confinement in the Alabama penal system constitute cruel and unusual punishment where they bear no reasonable relationship to legitimate institutional goals.

The Health Professional Educational Assistance Act (P.L. 94-484, 90 Stat. 2243), enacted on October 12, applies to all health professions and authorizes funding to train social workers in health care, including administration, policy analysis, and social work. This is the first mention of schools of social work in national health legislation.

The *International Code of Ethics for Professional Social Workers,* written by Chauncey A. Alexander, is adopted at the Puerto Rico Assembly by the International Federation of Social Workers, which consists of 52 national professional social worker organizations.

NASW endorses Carter and Mondale, the Democratic Party candidates for president and vice president, initiating the NASW Political Action for Candidate Election program to raise funds for political action, the first such political effort for a professional social work organization.

The Rural Social Work Caucus is initiated to aid rural social workers.

Health & Social Work, the first health specialty journal, is published by NASW.

1977   NASW's journal *Abstracts for Social Workers* is expanded to *Social Work Research & Abstracts.*

1978   The Child Abuse Prevention and Treatment and Adoption Reform Act (P.L. 95-266, 92 Stat. 205) is passed on April 24, extending the 1974 act and initiating new programs to encourage and improve adoptions.

The Full Employment and Balanced Growth Act (P.L. 95-523, 68 Stat. 590) is passed on October 27 by Congress through the tenacity of Congressman Augustus Hawkins (D–CA). The act reaffirms the right of all Americans to employment and asserts the federal government responsibility to promote full employment, production and real income, balanced growth, and better economic policy planning and coordination.

Social Work in Education, a journal for school social workers, is published by NASW.

1979   The American Association of State Social Work Boards is initiated by NASW; the association consists of state boards and authorities empowered to regulate the practice of social work within their own jurisdictions.

1980   The Adoption Assistance and Child Welfare Act (P.L. 96-272) restructures child welfare services, mandating reasonable efforts to prevent out-of-home placement.

1981   The Omnibus Budget Reconciliation Act (P.L. 97-35, 95 Stat. 357), passed by Congress on August 13, initiates a federal policy reversal of "general welfare" responsibility for human services, reducing federal programs (including food stamps, child nutrition, comprehensive employment and training, mental health, and community development) by means of block grants under the guise of decentralization to states.

The Social Service Block Grant Act (P.L. 97-35, 95 Stat. 357), passed by Congress on August 13, and part of the Omnibus Budget Reconciliation Act of 1981, amends Title XX of the Social Security Act to consolidate social services programs and to decentralize responsibility to the states.

Human immunodeficiency virus (HIV) and acquired immune deficiency syndrome (AIDS) are first identified in the United States and soon are defined as an epidemic. New requirements of social workers are initiated: They must further their knowledge of transmission and prevention of the virus, adapt practice techniques, and act on civil rights and service policies.

1982   The Tax Equity and Fiscal Responsibility Act (P.L. 97-248, 96 Stat. 324), passed by Congress on September 3, initiates severe reductions in service provisions of Medicare, Medicaid, Utilization and Quality Control Peer Review, Aid to Families with Dependent Children, child support enforcement, supplemental security income, and unemployment compensation. The legislation provides the "largest tax increase ever recommended in a single piece of legislation." It gives Medicare beneficiaries the option to enroll in health maintenance organizations.

1983   The Social Security Amendments (P.L. 98-81, 97 Stat. 65), passed on April 20, secure the program, providing mandatory coverage of federal employees and employees of nonprofit organizations, withdrawing and reducing benefits such as cost of living delay to calendar year, increasing retirement age, and reducing initial benefits.

The Hospital Prospective Payment System replaces Medicare cost reimbursement systems with predetermined payment rates for 468 diagnosis related groups, initiating significant role changes for social workers in discharge planning and increased service coordination requirements.

1985   The Consolidated Omnibus Budget Reconciliation Act (COBRA) encourages states to provide case management as an optional medicaid service.

The National Network for Social Work Managers is formed as a professional society by Robert Maslyn to advance knowledge, theory, and practice of management and administration in social services and the social work profession and to obtain recognition of social work managers.

1986   The Immigration Reform and Control Act (P.L. 99-603) provides temporary resident status for undocumented workers who have continuously resided in the United States since before January 1, 1982. The act allows them to become permanent residents after an additional 18-month period. Provisions make it unlawful for any person to knowingly employ undocumented workers. The objectives of the act are to decrease the number of illegal aliens as current residents, regain control of U.S. borders, and increase the number of legal migrant workers.

The Tax Reform Act (P.L. 99-514) reduces and consolidates tax brackets into two basic rates: (1) 15 percent and (2) 28 percent. The law increases the standard deduction for all taxpayers, with the largest increases for heads of households, single parents, and others who maintain households for dependent children. The Earned Income Tax Credit provision significantly increases the credit and raises the income levels at which the credit begins to be reduced and eliminated.

NASW establishes the National Center for Social Policy and Practice to analyze practice data and make recommendations on social policy, including information, policy, and education services.

The Anti-Drug Abuse Act (P.L. 99-570) creates the Office for Substance Abuse Prevention in the Alcohol, Drug Abuse, and Mental Health Administration. It also includes funding for a White House Conference for a Drug-Free America in fiscal year 1988 and authorizes funding of $450 million over three years to develop drug education and prevention programs through a new Drug-Free Schools and Communities Act.

The Education of the Handicapped Act Amendments (P.L. 99-457) establish a new federal discretionary program to assist states to develop and implement early intervention services for handicapped infants and toddlers (birth through age two) and their families. Seven criteria for "early intervention services" include provisions for qualified personnel, including social workers, and individualized family service plans; the states must serve all children.

1987   *The Social Work Dictionary* (1st edition), the first compilation of terms related to social work, is published by NASW.

The Stewart B. McKinney Homeless Assistance Act (P.L. 100-77) establishes the Interagency Council on Homeless to use public resources and programs in a more coordinated manner and to provide funds to assist homeless people, especially elderly people, people with disabilities, families with children, Native Americans, and veterans.

1988   The Family Support Act (P.L. 100-485) alters welfare provisions in critical ways. The act includes provisions for improved child support enforcement; state-run education, training, and employment programs for recipients of Aid to Families with Dependent Children; and supportive services for families during and after participation in employment and training. The act also establishes the Job Opportunities in the Business Sector program. Other provisions include guaranteed child care, transitional benefits, and reimbursement for work-related expenses.

The Hunger Prevention Act (P.L. 100-435) expands the federal food stamp program and initiates state outreach, employment, and training programs.

The Adoption Assistance and Child Welfare Act (P.L. 96-272) requires states to offer prevention services before removing a child from a home.

The NASW Communications Network is established by Suzanne Dworak-Peck as an affiliate group to encourage socially conscious media programming and accurate portrayal of social issues and professional social work. The network uses a computerized network of several hundred social workers for technical medial assistance.

The Medicare Catastrophic Coverage Act (P.L. 100-360) limits yearly out-of-pocket expenses for beneficiaries; adds a prescription drug benefit; extends hospice, respite, and home health benefits; adds a Medicaid buy-in provision; and offers some protection of a couple's assets for nursing home care. The act later is rescinded by Congress as a result of senior citizen protests about added premium requirements.

The Augustus F. Hawkins/Robert T. Stafford Elementary and Secondary School Improvement Amendments (P.L. 100-297) authorize funding for elementary and secondary education, including Chapter I—Financial Assistance; Chapter II—Federal; State & Local Partnership for Educational Improvement; dropout prevention; suicide prevention; and other programs. For the first time, use of pupil service personnel (including social workers and other professionals) is promoted and, in some cases, required.

The Civil Rights Restoration Act (P.L. 100-259) overturns the 1984 Supreme Court *Grove City College v. Bell* decision and clarifies that four major civil rights laws pertaining to gender, disability, age, and race must be interpreted to prohibit discrimination throughout entire organizations if any program received federal funds.

1989 Appropriations legislation for fiscal year 1990 for the departments of Labor, Health and Human Services, and Education (P.L. 101-166) include requirements that the National Institute of Mental Health (NIMH) distribute clinical training funds equitably among five core mental health professions, increasing social work's share. Other provisions include encouraging scholarships for people with master of social work degrees to provide case management to people with AIDS, commending the NIMH Task Force on Social Work

Research and Support for "services research," and providing appropriations for research on rural mental health.

1990 The social work profession is legally regulated in 50 states and jurisdictions as of January 1.

The Americans with Disabilities Act (42 U.S.C. 1210) is signed into law July 26 and becomes effective in 1992. This comprehensive civil rights law for people with disabilities prohibits employment discrimination (Title I); discrimination in state and local government services (Title II); and discrimination in public accommodations and commercial facilities (Title III).

The Education of the Handicapped Act Amendments (P.L. 101-476) increase access for students and their families to needed social work services.

The Ryan White Comprehensive AIDS Resources Emergency Act (P.L. 101-381) authorizes $880 million annually to provide emergency relief to metropolitan areas hardest hit by the AIDS epidemic. Other provisions address comprehensive planning, early intervention, treatment of children, and AIDS in rural areas.

The NASW School Social Work Specialist Credential is created to provide objective testing and certification of school social workers.

NASW transforms its publications department into the NASW Press.

1991 The NASW Academy of Certified Baccalaureate Social Workers is established to provide objective testing and certification of social workers with a bachelor of social work degree.

The Civil Rights Act (S. 1745, P.L. 102-166) amends the Civil Rights Act of 1964 to reverse a set of Supreme Court decisions that eroded protection of women and people of color in the workplace. Victims of intentional discrimination based on gender, disability, or religion, but not age, can obtain monetary damages.

1992 The Alcohol, Drug Abuse, and Mental Health Administration (ADAMHA) Reorganization Act (P.L. 102-321) transfers the research function in mental health, alcohol, and other substance abuse to the National Institutes of Health and establishes separate state block grants for mental health and substance abuse services. The National Institute of Mental Health, the National Institute of Drug Abuse, and the National Institute on Alcohol Abuse and Alcoholism are moved from ADAMHA to the National Institutes of Health. ADAMHA, renamed the Substance Abuse and Mental Health Services Administration, includes the Center for

Substance Abuse Treatment, the Center for Substance Abuse Prevention, and the Center for Mental Health Services.

On June 9, Senator Daniel K. Inouye (D–HI) introduces the NASW National Health Care Proposal as S. 2817, the National Health Care Act. Based on NASW universal health care policies, it is the only bill to price out the costs of a new health care system.

The Preventive Health Amendments (P.L. 102-531) include a new Office of Adolescent Health in the Department of Health and Human Services. Among the responsibilities of the new office is the coordination of training for health providers, including social workers, who work with adolescents.

The Older Americans Act Amendments (P.L. 102-375) reauthorizes Older American Act programs for four years and include provisions for long-term care ombudsmen, legal assistance, outreach, counseling, and abuse and neglect prevention programs. The amendments authorize a White House Conference on Aging by the end of 1994; grants for training in gerontology in schools of social work; and counseling, training, and support services for caregivers.

The Higher Education Amendments (P.L. 102-325) create new opportunities for reduction and cancellation of federal Perkins loan indebtedness for social work students who seek employment in child welfare, mental health, juvenile justice, or other agencies serving high-risk children and families from low-income communities, as well as those who provide early intervention services to infants and toddlers with disabilities.

The NASW Press publishes the *Social Work Almanac,* the first stand-alone compilation of statistics related to social work content.

1993 The National and Community Service Trust Act (P.L. 103-82) provides funds for community services, further institutionalizing the federal responsibility for meeting unmet social needs, including educational awards and living allowances for full-time community service.

The Family and Medical Leave Act (P.L. 103-3, 107 Stat. 6), passed on February 5, balances demands of workplace and family needs by requiring that employers of 50 or more employees allow up to 12 weeks of unpaid leave annually for a child's birth or adoption, the care of a spouse or immediate family member, or the employee's "serious health condition"—one requiring either inpatient care or ongoing treatment by a health provider.

The Family Preservation and Support Services Provisions (P.L. 103-66), part of the Omnibus Budget Reconciliation Act, provide $1 billion for a comprehensive approach to improving the child welfare system, emphasizing prevention and early intervention to maintain a natural care system.

The Brady Handgun Violence Prevention Act (P.L. 103-159) is signed by President Clinton on November 24. The bill institutes a five-day waiting period for handgun purchase, to be replaced in five years by a nationwide "instant check" system to ensure that guns are not being sold to criminals.

1994 The Improving America's Schools Act of 1994 (P.L. 103-382) reauthorizes the Elementary and Secondary Education Act for five years. Provisions include the Elementary School Counseling Demonstration Act; Title I, Helping Disadvantaged Children Meet High Standards; Title II, the Dwight D. Eisenhower Professional Development Program; Title IV, Safe and Drug-Free Schools and Communities; Families of Children with Disabilities Support Act; Urban and Rural Education Assistance; Multi-Ethnic Placement Act; and many others.

The Violent Crime Control and Law Enforcement Act (P.L. 103-322) is signed by President Clinton on September 13. In addition to authorizing new prisons and other punishment provisions, the law includes 16 prevention programs, among them grants to combat violence against women, drug treatment programs, and a local crime prevention block grant program. The Violence Against Women Act of 1993, which increases penalties for offenders, authorizes funding for prevention and training, and provides protection for victims, is incorporated into P.L. 103-322.

The Freedom of Access to Clinic Entrances Act (P.L. 103-259) is enacted on May 26 to combat violence against "abortion clinics." The act makes it a federal offense to restrict access to reproductive health services or to destroy the property of reproductive health services facilities.

The NASW Press separates *Social Work Research & Abstracts* and creates *Social Work Abstracts*, which publishes abstracts of previously published materials, and *Social Work Research*, which publishes primary research articles.

Person-in-Environment (PIE) System is published by the NASW Press to enable social workers to describe, classify, and code the problems of adult clients.

Chauncey A. Alexander, ACSW, LCSW, CAE, is president, Alexander Associates, 8072 Driftwood Drive, Huntington Beach, CA 92646.

3. Council on Social Work Education Curriculum Policy Statements

MASTER'S DEGREE PROGRAMS IN SOCIAL WORK EDUCATION

M1.0 SCOPE AND INTENT OF THE CURRICULUM POLICY STATEMENT

M1.1 This document sets forth the official curriculum policy for the accreditation of master's (MSW) programs of social work education by the Council on Social Work Education (CSWE). It supersedes all prior statements of curriculum policy for the master's program level.

M1.2 The curriculum policy statement establishes mandates for minimum requirements for the curricula of master's programs to be accredited by CSWE. The policy statement specifies certain content areas and requires that they be logically related to each other, to the purposes and values of social work as set forth in this document, and to the purposes, mission, resources, and educational context of each professional program. The statement does not prescribe any particular curriculum design.

M1.3 Each program is responsible for making every faculty member, student, field instructor, and administrator associated with the program aware of the content of the Curriculum Policy Statement.

M2.0 RELATIONSHIP TO ACCREDITATION STANDARDS

M2.1 The Commission on Accreditation of CSWE develops standards by which social work education programs are evaluated for accreditation. These standards pertain to the organization, administration, and curriculum implementation of programs of social work education. Curriculum standards are derived from and must conform with this Curriculum Policy Statement.

M3.0 PREMISES UNDERLYING SOCIAL WORK EDUCATION

M3.1 The purpose of social work education is to prepare competent and effective social work professionals who are committed to practice that includes services to the poor and oppressed, and who work to alleviate poverty, oppression, and discrimination.

M3.2 Social work education is based upon a specific body of knowledge, values, and professional skills. It is grounded in the profession's history and philosophy. Education for the profession promotes the development and advancement of knowledge, practice skills, and services that further the well being of people and promote social and economic justice. Social work education is responsible for the production and application of research and scholarship aimed at advancing social work practice.

M3.3 Programs of social work education are offered at the baccalaureate, master's, and doctoral levels. Doctoral programs are not accredited by CSWE.

M3.4 Programs of social work education maintain close, reciprocal, and ongoing relationships with social work practitioners and with groups and organizations that promote, provide, or seek to influence social policies and social work services. Responsibility for initiating these relationships rests with social work education programs. Effective programs develop and maintain a systematic process of communication with these individuals and groups.

M3.5 The effectiveness of any profession depends on the active engagement of its members in continuous learning. Programs of social work education strive to promote continuing professional development of students and faculty. Programs seek to teach students how to become lifelong learners who are motivated to continue the development of knowledge and skills throughout their careers.

M3.6 Effective social work education programs recognize the interdependence of nations and the need for worldwide professional cooperation.

M3.7 Social work education programs must assume a leadership role within the profession by offering curricula that are at the forefront of the new and changing knowledge base of social work and its supporting disciplines.

M4.0 PURPOSE OF SOCIAL WORK

M4.1 The profession of social work is committed to the enhancement of human well-being and to the alleviation of poverty and oppression. The social work profession receives its sanction from public and private auspices and is the primary profession in the provision of social services. Within its general scope of concern, professional social work is practiced in a wide variety of settings and has four related purposes:

M4.1.1 The promotion, restoration, maintenance, and enhancement of the social functioning of individuals, families, groups, organizations, and communities by helping them to accomplish tasks, prevent and alleviate distress, and use resources.

M4.1.2 The planning, formulation, and implementation of social policies, services, resources, and programs needed to meet basic human needs and support the development of human capacities.

M4.1.3 The pursuit of policies, services, resources, and programs through organizational or administrative advocacy and social or political action, so as to empower groups at risk and promote social and economic justice.

M4.1.4 The development and testing of professional knowledge and skills related to these purposes.

M5.0 PURPOSE AND STRUCTURE OF MASTER'S SOCIAL WORK EDUCATION

M5.1 The purpose of professional social work education is to enable students to integrate the knowledge, values, and skills of the social work profession into competent practice. The achievement of this purpose requires clarity about learning objectives and expected student outcomes, flexibility in programming and teaching to accommodate a diverse student population, and commitment of sufficient time and resources to the educational process.

M5.2 Two levels of social work education are accredited by the Council on Social Work Education: the baccalaureate and the master's. The baccalaureate level prepares students for generalist social work practice, and the master's level prepares students for advanced social work practice in an area of concentration. These levels of education differ from each other in the depth, breadth, and specificity of knowledge and skill that students are expected to synthesize and apply in practice.

Both levels of social work education must provide the professional foundation curriculum which contains the common body of knowledge, values, and skills of the profession. This common base is transferable among settings, population groups, and problem areas. The master's level of social work education must include the professional foundation content and concentration content for advanced practice in an identifiable area.

M5.3 Professional social work education at the master's level takes place in accredited colleges and universities. It requires the equivalent of two academic years of full-time study and leads to a professional degree at the master's level. Entry into the MSW program does not require completion of the BSW degree.

M5.4 All master's social work programs must:

M5.4.1 Provide content about social work practice with client systems of various sizes and types.

M5.4.2 Prepare graduates to practice with diverse populations.

M5.4.3 Provide content about the social contexts of social work practice, the changing nature of those contexts, the behavior of organizations, and the dynamics of change.

M5.4.4 Infuse throughout the curriculum the values and ethics that guide professional social workers in their practice.

M5.4.5 Prepare graduates who are aware of their responsibility to continue their professional growth and development.

M5.5 The master's curriculum must be based upon a liberal arts perspective and must include the professional foundation and one or more concentrations.

M5.6 The master's curriculum must be developed and organized as a coherent and integrated whole.

M5.7 Graduates of a master's social work program are advanced practitioners who can analyze, intervene, and evaluate in ways that are highly differentiated, discriminating, and self-critical. They must synthesize and apply a broad range of knowledge as well as practice with a high degree of autonomy and skill. They must be able to refine and advance the quality of their practice as well as that of the larger social work profession. These advanced competencies must be appropriately integrated and reflected in all aspects of their social work practice, including their ability to:

M5.7.1 Apply critical thinking skills within professional contexts, including synthesizing and applying appropriate theories and knowledge to practice interventions.

M5.7.2 Practice within the values and ethics of the social work profession and with an understanding of and respect for the positive value of diversity.

M5.7.3 Demonstrate the professional use of self.

M5.7.4 Understand the forms and mechanisms of oppression and discrimination and the strategies and skills of change that advance social and economic justice.

M5.7.5 Understand and interpret the history of the social work profession and its current structures and issues.

M5.7.6 Apply the knowledge and skills of a

generalist social work perspective to practice with systems of all sizes.

M5.7.7 Apply the knowledge and skills of advanced social work practice in an area of concentration.

M5.7.8 Critically analyze and apply knowledge of bio-psycho-social variables that affect individual development and behavior, and use theoretical frameworks to understand the interactions among individuals and between individuals and social systems (i.e., families, groups, organizations, and communities).

M5.7.9 Analyze the impact of social policies on client systems, workers, and agencies and demonstrate skills for influencing policy formulation and change.

M5.7.10 Evaluate relevant research studies and apply findings to practice, and demonstrate skills in quantitative and qualitative research design, data analysis, and knowledge dissemination.

M5.7.11 Conduct empirical evaluations of their own practice interventions and those of other relevant systems.

M5.7.12 Use communication skills differentially with a variety of client populations, colleagues, and members of the community.

M5.7.13 Use supervision and consultation appropriate to advanced practice in an area of concentration.

M5.7.14 Function within the structure of organizations and service delivery systems and seek necessary organizational change.

M5.8 Duplication and redundancy of content mastered at the baccalaureate level must be avoided in master's programs. Specifically, BSW graduates who enter MSW programs are not to repeat professional foundation content in the Master's program that has been mastered in the BSW program. In order to verify mastery and to prevent unproductive repetition, master's programs must develop explicit policies and procedures relevant to admission, course waivers, substitutions, exemptions, or advanced placement. Credit for advanced placement can be granted only for content in the professional foundation. Advanced placement signifies mastery of required content but does not necessarily signify exemption of credit hours. Specific policies and procedures for providing advanced placement must be clearly explicated by the program.

Liberal Arts Perspective

M5.9 A liberal arts perspective enriches understanding of the person-environment context of professional social work practice and is integrally related to the mastery of social work content. This perspective is prerequisite for the master's professional program in social work.

M5.10 A liberal arts perspective provides an understanding of one's cultural heritage in the context of other cultures; the methods and limitations of various systems of inquiry; and the knowledge, attitudes, ways of thinking, and means of communication that are characteristic of a broadly educated person. Students entering the professional curriculum must be capable of thinking critically about society, about people and their problems, and about expressions of culture such as art, literature, science, history, and philosophy. Students must have knowledge about social, psychological, and biological determinants of human behavior and of diverse cultures, social conditions, and social problems.

M5.11 Determination of whether students have acquired a liberal arts perspective is left to the judgment of the faculty of each social work program. Each program must clearly explicate the requirements for attaining a liberal arts perspective and the rationale for those requirements.

M6.0 MASTER'S CURRICULUM CONTENT

M6.1 The curriculum at the master's level must include both foundation and concentration content. The professional foundation includes content on social work values and ethics, diversity, social and economic justice, populations-at-risk, human behavior and the social environment, social welfare policy and services, social work practice, research, and field practicum. Concentration content includes knowledge, values, and skills for advanced practice in an identifiable area. Master's programs must achieve integration among these content areas. Curriculum areas do not need to be taught in discrete courses, but mastery of the curriculum must occur through classroom experiences and field practica. The master's social work curriculum must cover but is not necessarily limited to the professional foundation and the concentration content.

M6.2 The curriculum design of each program must identify a coherent approach for the selection of research and theories offered. Every part of the master's curriculum must strengthen the student's understanding and appreciation of a scientific, analytic approach to building knowledge for the delivery and evaluation of practice. Content provided in each curricular area must be relevant to the objectives, philosophy, and mission of the individual program and must facilitate the student's understanding of how the knowledge relates to social work practice.

M6.3 The Professional Foundation

M6.4 New advances in practice knowledge, as well as the accumulated knowledge of social work education and the social work profession, determine the specific content required for the professional foundation. The professional foundation curriculum must include content on social work values and ethics, diversity, social and economic justice, populations-at-risk, human behavior and the social environment, social welfare policy and services, social work practice, research, and field practicum.

Social Work Values and Ethics

M6.5 Programs of social work education must provide specific knowledge about social work values and their ethical implications, and must provide opportunities for students to demonstrate their application in professional practice. Students must be assisted to develop an awareness of their personal values and to clarify conflicting values and ethical dilemmas. Among the values and principles that must be infused throughout every social work curriculum are the following:

M6.5.1 Social workers' professional relationships are built on regard for individual worth and dignity and are furthered by mutual participation, acceptance, confidentiality, honesty, and responsible handling of conflict.

M6.5.2 Social workers respect people's right to make independent decisions and to participate actively in the helping process.

M6.5.3 Social workers are committed to assisting client systems to obtain needed resources.

M6.5.4 Social workers strive to make social institutions more humane and responsive to human needs.

M6.5.5 Social workers demonstrate respect for and acceptance of the unique characteristics of diverse populations.

M6.5.6 Social workers are responsible for their own ethical conduct, the quality of their practice, and seeking continuous growth in the knowledge and skills of their profession.

Diversity

M6.6 Professional social work education is committed to preparing students to understand and appreciate human diversity. Programs must provide curriculum content about differences and similarities in the experiences, needs, and beliefs of people. The curriculum must include content about differential assessment and intervention skills that will enable practitioners to serve diverse populations.

Each program is required to include content about population groups that are particularly relevant to the program's mission. These include, but are not limited to, groups distinguished by race, ethnicity, culture, class, gender, sexual orientation, religion, physical or mental disability, age, and national origin.

Promotion of Social and Economic Justice

M6.7 Programs of social work education must provide an understanding of the dynamics and consequences of social and economic injustice, including all forms of human oppression and discrimination. They must provide students with the skills to promote social change and to implement a wide range of interventions that further the achievement of individual and collective social and economic justice. Theoretical and practice content must be provided about strategies of intervention for achieving social and economic justice and for combatting the causes and effects of institutionalized forms of oppression.

Populations-at-Risk

M6.8 Programs of social work education must present theoretical and practice content about patterns, dynamics, and consequences of discrimination, economic deprivation, and oppression. The curriculum must provide content about people of color, women, and gay and lesbian persons. Such content must emphasize the impact of discrimination, economic deprivation, and oppression upon these groups.

Each program must include content about populations-at-risk that are particularly relevant to its mission. In addition to those mandated above, such groups include, but are not limited to, those distinguished by age, ethnicity, culture, class, religion and physical or mental disability.

Human Behavior and the Social Environment

M6.9 The professional foundation must provide content about theories and knowledge of human bio-psycho-social development, including theories and knowledge about the range of social systems in which individuals live (families, groups, organizations, institutions, and communities). The human behavior and social environment curriculum must provide an understanding of the interactions between and among human biological, social, psychological, and cultural systems as they affect and are affected by human behavior. The impact of social and economic forces on individuals and social systems must be presented. Content must be provided about the ways in which systems promote or deter people in the maintenance or attainment of optimal health and well-being.

Content about values and ethical issues related to bio-psycho-social theories must be included. Students must be taught to evaluate theory and apply theory to client situations.

Social Welfare Policy and Services

M6.10 The foundation social welfare policy and services content must include the history, mission, and philosophy of the social work profession. Content must be presented about the history and current patterns of provision of social welfare services, the role of social policy in helping or deterring people in the maintenance or attainment of optimal health and well-being, and the effect of policy on social work practice. Students must be taught to analyze current social policy within the context of historical and contemporary factors that shape policy. Content must be presented about the political and organizational processes used to influence policy, the process of policy formulation, and the frameworks for analyzing social policies in light of the principles of social and economic justice.

Social Work Practice

M6.11 The professional foundation prepares students to apply a generalist perspective to social work practice with systems of all sizes. Foundation practice content emphasizes professional relationships that are characterized by mutuality, collaboration, and respect for the client system. Content on practice assessment focuses on the examination of client strengths and problems in the interactions among individuals and between people and their environments.

Foundation practice content must include knowledge, values, and skills to enhance the well-being of people and to help ameliorate the environmental conditions that affect people adversely. Practice content must include the following skills: defining issues; collecting and assessing data; planning and contracting; identifying alternative interventions; selecting and implementing appropriate courses of action; using appropriate research to monitor and evaluate outcomes; applying appropriate research-based knowledge and technological advances; and termination. Practice content also includes approaches and skills for practice with clients from differing social, cultural, racial, religious, spiritual, and class backgrounds and with systems of all sizes.

Research

M6.12 The foundation research curriculum must provide an understanding and appreciation of a scientific, analytic approach to building knowledge for practice and for evaluating service delivery in all areas of practice. Ethical standards of scientific inquiry must be included in the research content.

The research content must include qualitative and quantitative research methodologies; analysis of data, including statistical procedures; systematic evaluation of practice; analysis and evaluation of theoretical bases, research questions, methodologies, statistical procedures, and conclusions of research reports; and relevant technological advances.

M6.13 Each program must identify how the research curriculum contributes to the student's use of scientific knowledge for practice.

Field Practicum

M6.14 The field practicum is an integral component of the curriculum in social work education. It engages the student in supervised social work practice and provides opportunities to apply classroom learning in the field setting.

M6.15 Field education at the master's level requires a minimum of 900 hours in field practicum.

M6.16 Each educational program must establish standards for field practicum settings that define their social work services and practices, field instructor assignments and activities, and student learning expectations and responsibilities. Individual programs may organize their practica in different ways but must insure educationally directed, coordinated, and monitored practicum experiences for all students. All programs must provide:

a. A placement that is based upon the objectives of the educational program and the learning needs of each student.

b. Structured learning opportunities that enable students to compare their practice experiences, integrate knowledge acquired in the classroom, and expand knowledge beyond the scope of the practicum setting.

c. Support for field practicum instructors by:

1. Sharing pertinent information about practicum students.

2. Providing information about the organization and content of the educational curriculum, emphasizing the interrelationships among human behavior, social policy, research, and practice content.

3. Providing information about the sequencing of course content.

4. Articulating clear practice and evaluation goals for the field practicum and for each individual student.

5. Offering orientation and training programs.

Foundation Practicum

M6.17 The purpose of the foundation practicum is for the student to apply foundation knowledge, skills, values and ethics to practice.

M6.18 The foundation practicum must provide the student with opportunities for:

a. The development of an awareness of self in the process of intervention.
b. Supervised practice experience in the application of knowledge, values and ethics, and practice skills to enhance the well-being of people and to work toward the amelioration of environmental conditions that affect people adversely.
c. Use of oral and written professional communications which are consistent with the language of the practicum setting and the profession.
d. Use of professional supervision to enhance learning.
e. Critical assessment, implementation, and evaluation of agency policy within ethical guidelines.

M6.19 Concentration Curriculum

M6.20 The central purpose of the master's curriculum is to prepare students for advanced social work practice in an identifiable concentration area. Each program must clearly explicate for each concentration the: 1) conceptualization and design, 2) expected educational outcomes, and 3) content.

Conceptualization and Design

M6.21 A concentration provides a context within which advanced practice skills and knowledge are acquired. A conceptual framework, built upon relevant theories, shapes the breadth and depth of knowledge and practice skills to be acquired.

Programs have the freedom to establish concentrations within an organizing framework that is consistent with the purpose of social work and its traditional values. The organizing framework for concentrations must have curricular coherence and logic, and must be anchored in the liberal arts and the professional foundation. The program must have sufficient resources to support the concentrations offered. Frameworks and perspectives for concentrations that are frequently offered by programs include fields of practice, problem areas, populations-at-risk, intervention methods or roles, and practice contexts and perspectives. Combinations of concentrations are permitted.

Concentration Outcomes

M6.22 Each master's program must apply foundation content to the central issues relevant to the areas of concentration. Programs must determine educational outcomes for each concentration offered.

Concentration Content

M6.23 Concentration content must be designed to prepare students for advanced practice. The emphasis of content areas must be relevant to the concentration and may vary across concentrations.

Concentration Practicum

M6.24 The concentration practicum for master's social work education must clearly support the student's area(s) of concentration.

M7.0 AVENUES OF RENEWAL

M7.1 Programs of social work education must remain vital and progressive by actively pursuing ongoing exchanges with the practice community and other essential groups, and by developing and assessing new knowledge and technology.

M7.1.1 Programs must establish and maintain close, reciprocal and ongoing relationships with social work practitioners, and use those relationships to continuously evaluate the total curriculum.

M7.1.2 Programs must establish and maintain relationships with groups that develop, implement, and benefit from social policies and services.

M7.1.3 Programs must establish and maintain involvement with the professional associations and with disciplines and departments in the academic community.

M7.1.4 Programs must assume responsibility for systematic and high quality scholarship that assesses social work practice and develops new knowledge.

Approved by Board of Directors July 19, 1992
Revised June 24, 1994

BACCALAUREATE DEGREE PROGRAMS IN SOCIAL WORK EDUCATION

B1.0 SCOPE AND INTENT OF THE CURRICULUM POLICY STATEMENT

B1.1 This document sets forth the official curriculum policy for the accreditation of baccalaureate (BSW) programs of social work education by the Council on Social Work Education (CSWE). It supersedes all prior statements of curriculum policy for the baccalaureate program level.

B1.2 The curriculum policy statement establishes mandates for minimum requirements for the curricula of baccalaureate programs to be accredited by CSWE. The policy statement specifies certain content areas and requires that they be logically related to each other, to the purposes and values of social work as set forth in this document, and to the purposes, mission, resources, and educational context of each professional program. The statement does not prescribe any particular curriculum design.

B1.3 Each program is responsible for making every faculty member, student, field instructor, and administrator associated with the program aware of the content of the Curriculum Policy Statement.

B2.0 RELATIONSHIP TO ACCREDITATION STANDARDS

B2.1 The Commission on Accreditation of CSWE develops standards by which social work education programs are evaluated for accreditation. These standards pertain to the organization, administration, and curriculum implementation of programs of social work education. Curriculum standards are derived from and must conform with this Curriculum Policy Statement.

B3.0 PREMISES UNDERLYING SOCIAL WORK EDUCATION

B3.1 The purpose of social work education is to prepare competent and effective social work professionals who are committed to practice that includes services to the poor and oppressed, and who work to alleviate poverty, oppression, and discrimination.

B3.2 Social work education is based upon a specific body of knowledge, values, and professional skills. It is grounded in the profession's history and philosophy. Education for the profession promotes the development and advancement of knowledge, practice skills, and services that further the well-being of people and promote social and economic justice. Social work education is responsible for the production and application of research and scholarship aimed at advancing social work practice.

B3.3 Programs of social work education are offered at the baccalaureate, master's, and doctoral levels. Doctoral programs are not accredited by CSWE.

B3.4 Programs of social work education maintain close, reciprocal, and ongoing relationships with social work practitioners and with groups and organizations that promote, provide, or seek to influence social policies and social work services. Responsibility for initiating these relationships rests with social work education programs. Effective programs develop and maintain a systematic process of communication with these individuals and groups.

B3.5 The effectiveness of any profession depends on the active engagement of its members in continuous learning. Programs of social work education strive to promote continuing professional development of students and faculty. Programs seek to teach students how to become lifelong learners who are motivated to continue the development of knowledge and skills throughout their careers.

B3.6 Effective social work education programs recognize the interdependence of nations and the need for worldwide professional cooperation.

B3.7 Social work education programs assume a leadership role within the profession by offering curricula that are at the forefront of the new and changing knowledge base of social work and its supporting disciplines.

B4.0 PURPOSE OF SOCIAL WORK

B4.1 The profession of social work is committed to the enhancement of human well-being and to the alleviation of poverty and oppression. The social work profession receives its sanction from public and private auspices and is the primary profession in the provision of social services. Within its general scope of concern, professional social work is practiced in a wide variety of settings and has four related purposes:

B4.1.1 The promotion, restoration, maintenance, and enhancement of the functioning of individuals, families, groups, organizations, and communities by helping them to accomplish tasks, prevent and alleviate distress, and use resources.

B4.1.2 The planning, formulation, and implementation of social policies, services, resources, and programs needed to meet basic human needs and support the development of human capacities.

B4.1.3 The pursuit of policies, services, resources and programs through organizational or administrative advocacy and social or political action, so as to empower groups at risk and promote social and economic justice.

B4.1.4 The development and testing of professional knowledge and skills related to these purposes.

B5.0 PURPOSE AND STRUCTURE OF BACCALAUREATE SOCIAL WORK EDUCATION

B5.1 The purpose of professional social work education is to enable students to integrate the knowledge, values, and skills of the social work profession into competent practice. The achievement of this purpose requires clarity about learning objectives and expected student outcomes, flexibility in programming and teaching to accommodate a diverse student population, and commitment of sufficient time and resources to the educational process.

B5.2 Two levels of social work education are accredited by the Council on Social Work Education: the baccalaureate and the master's. The baccalaureate level prepares students for generalist social work practice, and the master's level prepares students for advanced social work practice in an area of concentration. These levels of education differ from each other in the depth, breadth, and specificity of knowledge and skill that students are expected to synthesize and apply in practice.

Both levels of social work education must provide a professional foundation curriculum which contains the common body of knowledge, values, and skills of the profession. This common base is transferable among settings, population groups, and problem areas. The baccalaureate level of social work education must include a liberal arts perspective and the professional foundation content, which prepares students for direct services with client systems of various sizes and types.

B5.3 Professional social work education at the baccalaureate level takes place in accredited baccalaureate degree granting colleges and universities.

B5.4 All baccalaureate social work programs must:

B5.4.1 Provide content about social work practice with client systems of various sizes and types.

B5.4.2 Prepare graduates to practice with diverse populations.

B5.4.3 Provide content about the social contexts of social work practice, the changing nature of those contexts, the behavior of organizations, and the dynamics of change.

B5.4.4 Infuse throughout the curriculum the values and ethics that guide professional social workers in their practice.

B5.4.5 Prepare graduates who are aware of their responsibility to continue their professional growth and development.

B5.5 The baccalaureate curriculum must be based upon a liberal arts perspective and must include the professional foundation.

B5.6 The baccalaureate curriculum must be developed and organized as a coherent and integrated whole.

B5.7 Graduates of a baccalaureate social work program will be able to:

B5.7.1 Apply critical thinking skills within the context of professional social work practice.

B5.7.2 Practice within the values and ethics of the social work profession and with an understanding of and respect for the positive value of diversity.

B5.7.3 Demonstrate the professional use of self.

B5.7.4 Understand the forms and mechanisms of oppression and discrimination and the strategies of change that advance social and economic justice.

B5.7.5 Understand the history of the social work profession and its current structures and issues.

B5.7.6 Apply the knowledge and skills of generalist social work to practice with systems of all sizes.

B5.7.7 Apply knowledge of bio-psycho-social variables that affect individual development and behavior, and use theoretical frameworks to understand the interactions among individuals and between individuals and social systems (i.e., families, groups, organizations, and communities).

B5.7.8 Analyze the impact of social policies on client systems, workers, and agencies.

B5.7.9 Evaluate research studies and apply findings to practice, and, under supervision, evaluate their own practice interventions and those of other relevant systems.

B5.7.10 Use communication skills differentially with a variety of client populations, colleagues, and members of the community.

B5.7.11 Use supervision appropriate to generalist practice.

B5.7.12 Function within the structure of organizations and service delivery systems and, under supervision, seek necessary organizational change.

B5.8 LIBERAL ARTS PERSPECTIVE

B5.9 A liberal arts perspective enriches understanding of the person-environment context of professional social work practice and is integrally related to the mastery of social work content. The baccalaureate professional program in social work is built upon a liberal arts perspective.

B5.10 A liberal arts perspective provides an understanding of one's cultural heritage in the context of other cultures; the methods and limitations of various systems of inquiry; and the knowledge, attitudes, ways of thinking, and means of communication that are characteristic of a broadly educated person. Students must be capable of thinking critically about society, about people and their problems, and about such expressions of culture as art, literature, science, history, and philosophy. Students must have direct knowledge about social, psychological, and biological determinants of human behavior and of diverse cultures, social conditions, and social problems.

B5.11 Determination of whether students have acquired a liberal arts perspective is left to the judgment of the faculty of each social work program. Each program must clearly explicate the requirements for attaining a liberal arts perspective and the rationale for those requirements.

B6.0 BACCALAUREATE CURRICULUM CONTENT

B6.1 The baccalaureate curriculum must include a liberal arts perspective and the professional foundation. The professional foundation includes content on social work values and ethics, diversity, social and economic justice, populations-at-risk, human behavior and the social environment, social welfare policy and services, social work practice, research, and field practicum. Baccalaureate programs must achieve integration among these professional content areas. Curriculum areas do not need to be taught in discrete courses, but mastery of the professional curriculum must occur through classroom experiences and field practica. The baccalaureate social work curriculum must cover but is not necessarily limited to the professional foundation.

B6.2 The curriculum design of each program must identify a coherent approach for the selection of research and theories offered. Every part of the baccalaureate curriculum must strengthen the student's understanding and appreciation of a scientific, analytic approach to building knowledge for the delivery and evaluation of practice. Content provided in each curricular area must be relevant to the objectives, philosophy, and mission of the individual program and must facilitate the student's understanding of how the knowledge relates to social work practice.

Social Work Values and Ethics

B6.3 Programs of social work education must provide specific knowledge about social work values and their ethical implications and must provide opportunities for students to demonstrate their application in professional practice. Students must be assisted to develop an awareness of their personal values and to clarify conflicting values and ethical dilemmas. Among the values and principles that must be infused throughout every social work curriculum are the following:

B6.3.1 Social workers' professional relationships are built on regard for individual worth and dignity and are furthered by mutual participation, acceptance, confidentiality, honesty, and responsible handling of conflict.

B6.3.2 Social workers respect people's right to make independent decisions and to participate actively in the helping process.

B6.3.3 Social workers are committed to assisting client systems to obtain needed resources.

B6.3.4 Social workers strive to make social institutions more humane and responsive to human needs.

B6.3.5 Social workers demonstrate respect for and acceptance of the unique characteristics of diverse populations.

B6.3.6 Social workers are responsible for their own ethical conduct, the quality of their practice, and seeking continuous growth in the knowledge and skills of their profession.

Diversity

B6.4 Professional social work education is committed to preparing students to understand and appreciate human diversity. Programs must provide curriculum content about differences and similarities in the experiences, needs, and beliefs of people. The curriculum must include content about differential assessment and intervention skills that will enable practitioners to serve diverse populations.

Each program is required to include content about population groups that are particularly relevant to the program's mission. These include, but are not limited to groups distinguished by race, ethnicity, culture, class, gender, sexual orientation, religion, physical or mental disability, age, and national origin.

Promotion of Social and Economic Justice

B6.5 Programs of social work education must provide an understanding of the dynamics and consequences of social and economic injustice, including all forms of human oppression and discrimination. They must provide students with the skills to promote social change and to implement a wide range of interventions that further the achievement of individual and collective social and economic justice. Theoretical and practice content must be provided about strategies of intervention for achieving social and economic justice and for combatting the causes and effects of institutionalized forms of oppression.

Populations-at-Risk

B6.6 Programs of social work education must present theoretical and practice content about patterns, dynamics, and consequences of discrimination, economic deprivation, and oppression. The curriculum must provide content about people of color, women, and gay and lesbian persons. Such content must emphasize the impact of discrimination, economic deprivation, and oppression upon these groups.

Each program must include content about populations-at-risk that are particularly relevant to its mission. In addition to those mandated above, such groups include, but are not limited to, those distinguished by age, ethnicity, culture, class, religion, and physical or mental disability.

Human Behavior and the Social Environment

B6.7 Programs of social work education must provide content about theories and knowledge of human bio-psycho-social development, including theories and knowledge about the range of social systems in which individuals live (families, groups, organizations, institutions, and communities). The human behavior and the social environment curriculum must provide an understanding of the interactions between and among human biological, social, psychological, and cultural systems as they affect and are affected by human behavior. The impact of social and economic forces on individuals and social systems must be presented. Content must be provided about the ways in which systems promote or deter people in the maintenance or attainment of optimal health and well-being. Content about values and ethical issues related to bio-psycho-social theories must be included. Students must be taught to evaluate theory and apply theory to client situations.

Social Welfare Policy and Services

B6.8 Social welfare policy and services content must include the history, mission, and philosophy of the social work profession. Content must be presented about the history and current patterns of provision of social welfare services, the role of social policy in helping or deterring people in the maintenance or attainment of optimal health and well-being, and the effect of policy on social work practice. Students must be taught to analyze current social policy within the context of historical and contemporary factors that shape policy. Content must be presented about the political and organizational processes used to influence policy, the process of policy formulation, and the frameworks for analyzing social policies in light of the principles of social and economic justice.

Social Work Practice

B6.9 At the baccalaureate level, professional social work education prepares students for generalist practice with systems of all sizes. Practice content emphasizes professional relationships that are characterized by mutuality, collaboration, and respect for the client system. Content on practice assessment focuses on the examination of client strengths and problems in the interactions among individuals and between people and their environments.

Social work practice content must include knowledge, values, and skills to enhance the well-being of people and to help ameliorate the environmental conditions that affect people adversely. Practice content must include the following skills: defining issues; collecting and assessing data; planning and contracting; identifying alternative interventions; selecting and implementing appropriate courses of action; using appropriate research to monitor and evaluate outcomes; applying appropriate research-based knowledge and technological advances; and termination. Practice content also includes approaches and skills for practice with clients from differing social, cultural, racial, religious, spiritual, and class backgrounds and with systems of all sizes.

B6.10 Each program must explicate the ways in which students are prepared for generalist practice.

Research

B6.11 The research curriculum must provide an understanding and appreciation of a scientific, analytic approach to building knowledge for practice and for evaluating service delivery in all areas of practice. Ethical standards of scientific inquiry must be included in the research content.

The research content must include quantitative and qualitative research methodologies; analysis of data, including statistical procedures; systematic evaluation of practice; analysis and evaluation of theoretical bases, research questions, methodologies, statistical procedures, and conclusions of research reports; and relevant technological advances.

B6.12 Each program must identify how the research curriculum contributes to the student's use of scientific knowledge for practice.

Field Practicum

B6.13 The field practicum is an integral component of the curriculum in social work education. It engages the student in supervised social work practice and provides opportunities to apply classroom learning in the field setting.

B6.14 Field education at the baccalaureate level requires a minimum of 400 hours in field practicum.

B6.15 Each educational program must establish standards for field practicum settings that define their social work services and practices, field instructor assignments and activities, and student learning expectations and responsibilities. Individual programs may organize their practica in different ways but must insure educationally directed, coordinated, and monitored practicum experiences for all students. All programs must provide:

a. A placement that is based upon the objectives of the educational program and the learning needs of each student.
b. Structured learning opportunities that enable students to compare their practice experiences, integrate knowledge acquired in the classroom, and expand knowledge beyond the scope of the practicum setting.
c. Support for field practicum instructors by:
1. Sharing pertinent information about practicum students.
2. Providing information about the organization and content of the educational curriculum, emphasizing the interrelationships among human behavior, social policy, research, and practice content.
3. Providing information about the sequencing of course content.
4. Articulating clear practice and evaluation goals for the field practicum and for each student.

5. Offering orientation and training programs.

B6.16 The baccalaureate practicum must provide the student with opportunities for:

a. The development of an awareness of self in the process of intervention.
b. Supervised practice experience in the application of knowledge, values and ethics, and practice skills to enhance the well-being of people and to work toward the amelioration of environmental conditions that affect people adversely.
c. Use of oral and written professional communications which are consistent with the language of the practicum setting and of the profession.
d. Use of professional supervision to enhance learning.
e. Critical assessment, implementation, and evaluation of agency policy within ethical guidelines.

B7.0 AVENUES OF RENEWAL

B7.1 Programs of social work education must remain vital and progressive by actively pursuing ongoing exchanges with the practice community and other essential groups, and by developing and assessing new knowledge and technology.

B7.1.1 Programs must establish and maintain close, reciprocal and ongoing relationships with social work practitioners, and use those relationships to continuously evaluate the total curriculum.

B7.1.2 Programs must establish and maintain relationships with groups that develop, implement, and benefit from social policies and services.

B7.1.3 Programs must establish and maintain involvement with the professional associations and with disciplines and departments in the academic community.

B7.1.4 Programs must assume responsibility for systematic and high quality scholarship that assesses social work practice and develops new knowledge.

Approved by Board of Directors July 19, 1992
Revised June 24, 1994

4. International Federation of Social Workers

ETHICS OF SOCIAL WORK—PRINCIPLES AND STANDARDS

1. BACKGROUND

Ethical awareness is a necessary part of the professional practice of any social worker. His or her ability to act ethically is an essential aspect of the quality of the service offered to clients.

The purpose of IFSW's work on ethics is to promote ethical debate and reflection in the member associations and among the providers of social work in member countries.

The basis for the further development of IFSW's work on ethics is to be found in *"Ethics of Social Work—Principles and Standards,"* which consists of two documents, *"International Declaration of Ethical Principles of Social Work"* and *"International Ethical Standards for Social Workers."* These documents present the basic ethical principles of the social work profession, recommend procedure when the work presents ethical dilemmas, and deal with the profession's and the individual social worker's relation to clients, colleagues, and others in the field. The documents are components in a continuing process of use, review and revision.

2. INTERNATIONAL DECLARATION OF ETHICAL PRINCIPLES OF SOCIAL WORK

2.1 Introduction

The IFSW recognises the need for a declaration of ethical principles for guidance in dealing with ethical problems in social work.

The purposes of the **International Declaration of Ethical Principles** ***are:***

1. to formulate a set of basic principles for social work, which can be adapted to cultural and social settings.
2. to identify ethical problem areas in the practice of social work (below referred to as 'problem areas'), and
3. to provide guidance as to the choice of methods for dealing with ethical issues/problems (below referred to as 'methods for addressing ethical issues/problems').

Compliance

The *International Declaration of Ethical Principles* assumes that both member associations of the IFSW and their constituent members adhere to the principles formulated therein. The IFSW expects each member association to assist its members in identifying and dealing with ethical issues/problems in the practice of their profession.

Member associations of the IFSW and individual members of these can report any member association to the Executive Committee of the IFSW should it neglect to adhere to these principles. National Associations who experience difficulties adopting these principles should notify the Executive Committee of IFSW. The Executive Committee may impose the stipulations and intentions of the Declaration of Ethical Principles on an association which neglects to comply. Should this not be sufficient the Executive Committee can, as a following measure, suggest suspension or exclusion of the association.

The *International Declaration of Ethical Principles* should be made publicly known. This would enable clients, employers, professionals from other disciplines, and the general public to have expectations in accordance with the ethical foundations of social work.

We acknowledge that a detailed set of ethical standards for the member associations would be unrealistic due to legal, cultural and government differences among the member countries.

2.2 The Principles

Social workers serve the development of human beings through adherence to the following basic principles:

2.2.1. Every human being has a unique value, which justifies moral consideration for that person.

2.2.2. Each individual has the right to self-fulfilment to the extent that it does not encroach upon the same right of others, and has an obligation to contribute to the well-being of society.

2.2.3. Each society, regardless of its form, should function to provide the maximum benefits for all of its members.

2.2.4. Social workers have a commitment to principles of social justice.

2.2.5. Social workers have the responsibility to devote objective and disciplined knowledge and skill to aid individuals, groups, communities, and societies in their development and resolution of personal-societal conflicts and their consequences.

2.2.6. Social workers are expected to provide the best possible assistance to anybody seeking their help and advice, without unfair discrimination on the basis of gender, age, disability, colour, social class, race, religion, language, political beliefs, or sexual orientation.

2.2.7. Social workers respect the basic human rights of individuals and groups as expressed in the *United States Universal Declaration of Human Rights* and other international conventions derived from that Declaration.

2.2.8. Social workers pay regard to the principles of privacy, confidentiality, and responsible use of information in their professional work. Social workers respect justified confidentiality even when their country's legislation is in conflict with this demand.

2.2.9. Social workers are expected to work in full collaboration with their clients, working for the best interests of the clients but paying due regard to the interests of others involved. Clients are encouraged to participate as much as possible, and should be informed of risks and likely benefits of proposed courses of action.

2.2.10. Social workers generally expect clients to take responsibility in collaboration with them, for determining courses of action affecting their lives. Compulsion which might be necessary to solve one party's problems at the expense of the interests of others involved should only take place after careful explicit evaluation of the claims of the conflicting parties. Social workers should minimise the use of legal compulsion.

2.2.11. Social work is inconsistent with direct or indirect support of individuals, groups, political forces or power-structures suppressing their fellow human beings by employing terrorism, torture or similar brutal means.

2.2.12. Social workers make ethically justified decisions, and stand by them, paying due regard to the *IFSW International Declaration of Ethical Principles*, and to the *"International Ethical Standards for Social Workers"* adopted by their national professional association.

2.3 Problem Areas

2.3.1. The problem areas raising ethical issues directly are not necessarily universal due to cultural and governmental differences. Each national association is encouraged to promote discussion and clarification of important issues and problems particularly relevant to its country. The following problem areas are, however, widely recognized:

1) *when the loyalty of the social worker is in the middle of conflicting interests*

- between those of the social worker's own and the client's
- between conflicting interests of individual clients and other individuals
- between the conflicting interests of groups of clients
- between groups of clients and the rest of the population
- between systems/institutions and groups of clients
- between system/institution/employer and social workers
- between different groups of professionals

2) *the fact that the social worker functions both as a helper and controller*

The relation between these two opposite aspects of social work demands a clarification based on an explicit choice of values in order to avoid a mixing-up of motives or the lack of clarity in motives, actions and consequences of actions. When social workers are expected to play a role in the state control of citizens they are obliged to clarify the ethical implications of this role and to what extent this role is acceptable in relation to the basic ethical principles of social work.

3) *the duty of the social worker to protect the interests of the client will easily come into conflict with demands for efficiency and utility*

This problem is becoming important with the introduction and use of information technology within the fields of social work.

2.3.3. The principles declared in section 2.2 should always be at the base of any consideration given or choice made by social workers in dealing with issues/problems within these areas.

2.4. Methods for the Solution of Issues/Problems

2.4.1. The various national associations of social workers are obliged to treat matters in such a way that ethical issues/problems may be considered and tried to be solved in collective forums within the organization. Such forums should enable the individual social worker to discuss, analyse and consider ethical issues/problems in collaboration with colleagues, other expert groups and parties affected by the matter under discussion. In addition such forums should give the social worker opportunity to receive advice from colleagues and others. Ethical analysis and discussion should always seek to create possibilities and options.

2.4.2. The member associations are required to produce and/or adapt ethical standards for the different fields of work, especially for those fields where there are complicated ethical issues/problems as well as areas where the ethical principles of social work may come into conflict with the respective country's legal system or the policy of the authorities.

2.4.3. When ethical foundations are laid down as guidelines for actions within the practice of social work, it is the duty of the associations to aid the individual social worker in analysing and considering ethical issues/problems on the basis of:

1) The basic *principles* of the Declaration (section 2.2)
2) The ethical/moral and political *context* of the actions, i.e. an analysis of the values and forces constituting the framing conditions of the action.
3) The *motives* of the action, i.e. to advocate a higher level of consciousness of the aims and intentions the individual social worker might have regarding a course of action.
4) The *nature* of the action, i.e. help in providing an analysis of the moral content of the action, e.g. the use of compulsion as opposed to voluntary co-operation, guardianship vs participation, etc.
5) The *consequences* the action might have for different groups, i.e. an analysis of the consequences of different ways of action for all involved parties in both the short and long term.

2.4.4. The member associations are responsible for promoting debate, education and research regarding ethical questions.

3. INTERNATIONAL ETHICAL STANDARDS FOR SOCIAL WORKERS

(This section is based on the *"International Code of Ethics for the Professional Social Worker"* adopted by the IFSW in 1976, but does not include ethical principles since these are now contained in the new separate *International Declaration of Ethi-*

cal Principles of Social Work in section 2.2 of the present document.)

3.1. Preamble

Social work originates variously from humanitarian, religious and democratic ideals and philosophies and has universal application to meet human needs arising from personal-societal interactions and to develop human potential. Professional social workers are dedicated to service for the welfare and self-fulfilment of human beings; to the development and disciplined use of validated knowledge regarding human and societal behaviour; to the development of resources to meet individual, group, national and international needs and aspirations; and to the achievement of social justice. On the basis of the *International Declaration of Ethical Principles of Social Work*, the social worker is obliged to recognize these standards of ethical conduct.

3.2. General Standards of Ethical Conduct

3.2.1. Seek to understand each individual client and the client system, and the elements which affect behaviour and the service required.
3.2.2. Uphold and advance the values, knowledge and methodology of the profession, refraining from any behaviour which damages the functioning of the profession.
3.2.3. Recognise professional and personal limitations.
3.2.4. Encourage the utilisation of all relevant knowledge and skills.
3.2.5. Apply relevant methods in the development and validation of knowledge.
3.2.6. Contribute professional expertise to the development of policies and programs which improve the quality of life in society.
3.2.7. Identify and interpret social needs.
3.2.8. Identify and interpret the basis and nature of individual, group, community, national, and international social problems.
3.2.9. Identify and interpret the work of the social work profession.
3.2.10. Clarify whether public statements are made or actions performed on an individual basis or as representative of a professional association, agency or organization, or other group.

3.3. Social Work Standards Relative to Clients

3.3.1. Accept primary responsibility to identified clients, but within limitations set by the ethical claims of others.

3.3.2. Maintain the client's right to a relationship of trust, to privacy and confidentiality, and to responsible use of information. The collection and sharing of information or data is related to the professional service function with the client informed as to its necessity and use. No information is released without prior knowledge and informed consent of the client, except where the client cannot be responsible or others may be seriously jeopardized. A client has access to social work records concerning them.

3.3.3. Recognise and respect the individual goals, responsibilities, and differences of clients. Within the scope of the agency and the client's social milieu, the professional service shall assist clients to take responsibility for personal actions and help all clients with equal willingness. Where the professional service cannot be provided under such conditions the clients shall be so informed in such a way as to leave the clients free to act.

3.3.4. Help the client—individual, group, community, or society—to achieve self-fulfilment and maximum potential within the limits of the respective rights of others. The service shall be based upon helping the client to understand and use the professional relationship, in furtherance of the client's legitimate desires and interests.

3.4. Social Work Standards Relative to Agencies and Organizations

3.4.1. Work and/or cooperate with those agencies and organizations whose policies, procedures, and operations are directed toward adequate service delivery and encouragement of professional practice consistent with the ethical principles of the IFSW.

3.4.2. Responsibly execute the stated aims and functions of the agency or organizations, contributing to the development of sound policies, procedures, and practice in order to obtain the best possible standards or practice.

3.4.3. Sustain ultimate responsibility to the client, initiating desirable alterations of policies, procedures, and practice, through appropriate agency and organization channels. If necessary remedies are not achieved after channels have been exhausted, initiate appropriate appeals to higher authorities or the wider community of interest.

3.4.4. Ensure professional accountability to client and community for efficiency and effectiveness through periodic review of the process of service provision.

3.4.5. Use all possible ethical means to bring unethical practice to an end when policies, procedures and practices are in direct conflict with the ethical principles of social work.

3.5. Social Work Standards Relative to Colleagues

3.5.1. Acknowledge the education, training and performance of social work colleagues and professionals from other disciplines, extending all necessary cooperation that will enhance effective services.

3.5.2. Recognise differences of opinion and practice of social work colleagues and other professionals, expressing criticism through channels in a responsible manner.

3.5.3. Promote and share opportunities for knowledge, experience, and ideas with all social work colleagues, professionals from other disciplines and volunteers for the purpose of mutual improvement.

3.5.4. Bring any violations of professional ethics and standards to the attention of the appropriate bodies inside and outside the profession, and ensure that relevant clients are properly involved.

3.5.5. Defend colleagues against unjust actions.

3.6. Standards Relative to the Profession

3.6.1. Maintain the values, ethical principles, knowledge and methodology of the profession and contribute to their clarification and improvement.

3.6.2. Uphold the professional standards of practice and work for their advancement.

3.6.3. Defend the profession against unjust criticism and work to increase confidence in the necessity for professional practice.

3.6.4. Present constructive criticism of the profession, its theories, methods and practices.

3.6.5. Encourage new approaches and methodologies needed to meet new and existing needs.

Adopted by the IFSW General Meeting, Colombo, Sri Lanka, July 6–8, 1994.

5. National Association of Social Workers

PRESIDENTS

Nathan E. Cohen	1955–1957
John McDowell*	1957–1959
John C. Kidneigh*	1959–1961
Norman V. Lourie	1961–1963
Kurt Reichert	1963–1965
Howard Gustafson*	1965–1966
Helen Cassidy-McGrail*	1966–1967
Charles I. Schottland	1967–1969
Whitney M. Young*	1969–1971
Alan D. Wade	1971
Mitchell I. Ginsberg	1971–1973
Lorenzo H. Traylor	1973–1975
Maryann Mahaffey	1975–1977
Arthur J. Katz	1977–1979
Nancy A. Humphreys	1979–1981
Maryann Quaranta	1981–1983
Robert P. Stewart	1983–1985
Dorothy V. Harris	1985–1987
Suzanne Dworak-Peck	1987–1989
Richard L. Edwards	1989–1991
Barbara W. White	1991–1993
Ann A. Abbott	1993–1995
Jay J. Cayner	1995–1997

* Deceased

EXECUTIVE DIRECTORS

Joseph P. Anderson*	1955–1969
Chauncey A. Alexander	1970–1982
Annette C. Maxey	1982–1983
John E. Hansan	1983–1984
Mark G. Battle	1984–1992
Sheldon R. Goldstein	1992–present

* Deceased

6. Council on Social Work Education

PRESIDENTS

Helen R. Wright	1952–1954
Fedele F. Fauri	1954–1956
Jane M. Hoey	1956–1958
Grace L. Coyle	1958–1960
Ruth E. Smalley	1960–1963
Roger Cumming	1963–1966
Herman D. Stein	1966–1969
Alton A. Linford	1969–1972
James R. Dumpson	1972–1978
Dorothy Bird Daly	1978–1981
Richard A. English	1981–1984
Bradford W. Sheafor	1984–1986
M. C. "Terry" Hokenstad	1986–1989
Julia M. Norlin	1989–1992
Michael L. Frumkin	1992–1995
Moses Newsome, Jr.	1995–1998

EXECUTIVE DIRECTORS

Ernest F. Witte	1952–1963
Katherine A. Kendall	1963–1966
Arnulf M. Pins	1966–1971
Lilian Ripple, Acting Director	1971–1972
Richard Lodge	1972–1978
Gary A. Lloyd	1978–1980
Arthur J. Katz	1980–1985
Diane Bernard, Interim Executive Director	1985–1986
Eunice O. Shatz	1986–1988
Donald W. Beless	1988–present

7. Social Work Year Books and Encyclopedias

Edition	Title	Editors	Publisher
1st	SOCIAL WORK YEAR BOOK 1929 A Description of Organized Activities in Social Work and Related Fields	Fred S. Hall, Editor David H. Holbrook, Chair	Russell Sage Foundation
2nd	SOCIAL WORK YEAR BOOK 1933 A Description of Organized Activities in Social Work and Related Fields	Fred S. Hall, Editor David H. Holbrook, Chair	Russell Sage Foundation
3rd	SOCIAL WORK YEAR BOOK 1935 A Description of Organized Activities in Social Work and Related Fields	Fred S. Hall, Editor David H. Holbrook, Chair	Russell Sage Foundation
4th	SOCIAL WORK YEAR BOOK 1937 A Description of Organized Activities in Social Work and Related Fields	Russell H. Kurz, Editor David H. Holbrook, Chair	Russell Sage Foundation
5th	SOCIAL WORK YEAR BOOK 1939 A Description of Organized Activities in Social Work and Related Fields	Russell H. Kurz, Editor David H. Holbrook, Chair	Russell Sage Foundation
6th	SOCIAL WORK YEAR BOOK 1941 A Description of Organized Activities in Social Work and Related Fields	Russell H. Kurz, Editor David H. Holbrook, Chair	Russell Sage Foundation
7th	SOCIAL WORK YEAR BOOK 1943 A Description of Organized Activities in Social Work and Related Fields	Russell H. Kurz, Editor David H. Holbrook, Chair	Russell Sage Foundation
8th	SOCIAL WORK YEAR BOOK 1945 A Description of Organized Activities in Social Work and Related Fields	Russell H. Kurz, Editor David H. Holbrook, Chair	Russell Sage Foundation
9th	SOCIAL WORK YEAR BOOK 1947 A Description of Organized Activities in Social Work and Related Fields	Russell H. Kurz, Editor David H. Holbrook, Chair	Russell Sage Foundation
10th	SOCIAL WORK YEAR BOOK 1949 A Description of Organized Activities in Social Work and Related Fields	Margaret B. Hodges, Editor Russell H. Kurz, Chair	Russell Sage Foundation
11th	SOCIAL WORK YEAR BOOK 1951 A Description of Organized Activities in Social Work and Related Fields	Margaret B. Hodges, Editor Russell H. Kurz, Chair	American Association of Social Workers
12th	SOCIAL WORK YEAR BOOK 1954 A Description of Organized Activities in Social Work and Related Fields	Russell H. Kurtz, Editor Arthur Dunham, Chair	American Association of Social Workers
13th	SOCIAL WORK YEAR BOOK 1957 A Description of Organized Activities in Social Work and Related Fields	Russell H. Kurtz, Editor Arthur Dunham, Chair	National Association of Social Workers
14th	SOCIAL WORK YEAR BOOK 1960 A Description of Organized Activities in Social Work and Related Fields	Russell H. Kurtz, Editor Arthur Dunham, Chair	National Association of Social Workers
15th	ENCYCLOPEDIA OF SOCIAL WORK 1965 Successor to the Social Work Year Book (two volumes)	Harry L. Lurie, Editor Fedele F. Fauri, Chair	National Association of Social Workers

16th	ENCYCLOPEDIA OF SOCIAL WORK 1971 (two volumes)	Robert Morris, Editor-in-Chief Beatrice N. Saunders, Staff Editor-in-Chief	National Association of Social Workers
17th	ENCYCLOPEDIA OF SOCIAL WORK 1977 (two volumes)	John B. Turner, Editor-in-Chief Beatrice N. Saunders, Staff Editor-in-Chief	National Association of Social Workers
18th	ENCYCLOPEDIA OF SOCIAL WORK 1987 (two volumes)	Anne Minahan, Editor-in-Chief Jacqueline M. Atkins, Executive Editor	National Association of Social Workers
19th	ENCYCLOPEDIA OF SOCIAL WORK 1995 (three volumes)	Richard L. Edwards, Editor-in-Chief Linda Beebe, Executive Editor	NASW Press

8. Acronyms

AA	Alcoholics Anonymous
AAFP	American Academy of Family Practice
AAFRC	American Association of Fund-Raising Counsel
AAGW	American Association of Group Workers
AALL	American Association for Labor Legislation
AAMD	American Association on Mental Deficiency
AAMFT	American Association of Marriage and Family Therapists
AAMR	American Association on Mental Retardation
AAMSW	American Association of Medical Social Workers
AAP	affirmative action program
AAPSW	American Association of Psychiatric Social Workers
AARP	American Association of Retired Persons
AASSW	American Association of Schools of Social Work
AASSWB	American Association of State Social Work Boards
AASW	American Association of Social Workers
AB	Aid to the Blind
ABE	American Board of Examiners in Clinical Social Work
ABW	average body weight
ACEHSA	Accrediting Commission on Education for Health Services Administration
ACLU	American Civil Liberties Union
ACM	anticult movement
ACOAs	adult children of alcoholics
ACOSA	Association of Community Organization and Social Administration
ACSUS	AIDS Cost and Service Utilization Survey
ACSW	Academy of Certified Social Workers
ACT-UP	AIDS Coalition to Unleash Power
ADA	Americans with Disabilities Act of 1990
ADAMHA	Alcohol, Drug Abuse, and Mental Health Administration
ADC	Aid to Dependent Children
ADC	adult day care
ADHD	attention-deficit hyperactivity disorder
AFAR	American Foundation for AIDS Research
AFDC	Aid to Families with Dependent Children
AFDC-UP	Aid to Families with Dependent Children—Unemployed Parent program
AFL–CIO	American Federation of Labor–Congress of Industrial Organizations
AFRAIDS	fear of AIDS
AFSCME	American Federation of State, County, and Municipal Employees
AFSW	Association of Federation Social Workers
AFT	American Federation of Teachers
AGI	adjusted gross income
AHA	American Hospital Association
AID	Agency for International Development
AIDS	acquired immune deficiency syndrome
AIM	Aid to Imprisoned Mothers
AIME	average indexed monthly earnings
AIRS	Alliance of Information and Referral Systems
ALMACA	Association of Labor and Management Consultants on Alcoholism
AMA	American Medical Association
AMFAR	American Foundation for AIDS Research
ANCSA	Alaska Native Claims Settlement Act
AoA	Administration on Aging
APA	American Psychiatric Association
APMs	annual program meetings

APS	adult protective services
APTD	Aid to the Permanently and Totally Disabled
APWA	American Public Welfare Association
ARC	AIDS-related complex
ARROW	Americans for Restitution and Righting of Old Wrongs
ASAP	Automated Screening and Assessment Package
ASCO	Association for the Study of Community Organizations
ASH	Action on Smoking and Health
ASL	American Sign Language
ASO	AIDS services organizations
ASPA	American Society for Personnel Administrators
ASSIST	American Stop Smoking Trial
AUPHA	Association of University Programs in Health Administration
AZT	azidothymidine
BCRS	Bertha Capen Reynolds Society
BLS	Bureau of Labor Statistics
BSW	bachelor of social work
CAB	Citizens Advice Bureau (British)
CAP	Community Action Program
CAPTA	Child Abuse Prevention and Treatment Act
CARE	Community and Resource Exchange
CARE	Comprehensive AIDS Resources Emergency
CARE	Cooperative for American Relief Everywhere, Inc.
CASA	court-appointed special advocate
CASP	Comprehensive Annual Services Plan
CASS	computer-assisted social services
CASSP	Child and Adolescent Services Programs
CCC	Competence Certification Commission
CCDBG	Child Care and Development Block Grant
CCETSW	Council of Education and Training in Social Work
CCIP	Center for Children of Incarcerated Parents
CCMC	Committee on the Costs of Medical Care
CCMS	Child Care Management Service
CCS	Crippled Children's Services
CCSSO	Council of Chief State School Officers
CDC	Centers for Disease Control and Prevention
CDF	Chapter Development Fund
CD-I	compact disk—interactive
CD-ROM	compact disk—read-only memory
CEOs	chief executive officers
CES	Current Employment Statistics
CETA	Comprehensive Employment and Training Act
CEUs/CECs	continuing education units/credits
CFC	Combined Federal Campaign
CHAMPUS	Civilian Health and Medical Program of the Uniformed Services
CHAP	Children Have a Potential
CHAP	Comprehensive Homeless Assistance Plan
CHAS	Comprehensive Housing Affordability Strategy
CHIP	Comprehensive Health Insurance Plan
CHP	Comprehensive Health Planning and Public Health Services Amendments
CIA	Central Intelligence Agency
CIAS	Committee on Inter-Association Structure
CIP	Council of International Programs
CLAIM	Chicago Legal Aid for Imprisoned Mothers

CMHC	commuinity mental health centers
CMHCA	Community Mental Health Centers Act
CMHS	Center for Mental Health Services
CMHSA	Community Mental Health Services Act
CMV	cytomegalovirus
CNHI	Committee of One Hundred for National Health Insurance
COA	Commission on Accreditation
COAs	children of alcoholics
COBRA	Comprehensive Omnibus Budget Reconciliation Act
CODAs	children of deaf adults
COI	Committee on Inquiry
COMPSYCH	computerized software service for psychologists
CON	certificate of need
COPA	community-oriented primary care
CORE	Congress of Racial Equality
CORPA	Council on Regulating Post-Secondary Education
COS	Charity Organization Societies
COSAs	children of substance abusers
COSSMHO	Coalition of Spanish-Speaking Mental Health Organizations
CPAI	Correctional Program Assessment Inventory
CPC	child protective services
CPI	consumer price index
CPS	Child Protective Services
CPS	Current Population Survey
CPS	curriculum policy statement
CRA	Community Reinvestment Act
CREP	Cuban Refugee Emergency Program
CSA	Child Support Assurance
C-SAP	Centers for Substance Abuse Prevention
C-SAT	Centers for Substance Abuse Treatment
CSCE	Commission on Security and Cooperation in Europe
CSFII	Continuing Survey of Food Intakes by Individuals
CSHCN	children with special health care needs
CSOs	Community Service Organizations
CSWE	Council on Social Work Education
CVS	chorionic villus sampling
CWA	Communications Workers of America
CWEP	Community Work Experience Program
CWLA	Child Welfare League of America
CWS	Child Welfare Services
D&D	design and development
DAWN	Drug Abuse Warning Network
dB	decibels
DBMS	database management system
DD	design and development (of interventions)
ddC	dideoxycytidine
ddI	dideoxyinosine
DEA	Drug Enforcement Administration
DHEW	Department of Health, Education, and Welfare
DHHS	U.S. Department of Health and Human Services
DI	Disability Insurance
DipSW	Diploma in Social Work
DMA	Department of Memorial Affairs
DNA	deoxyribonucleic acid
DNR	Do Not Resuscitate

DoD	U.S. Department of Defense
DRG	diagnosis related group
DSM	*Diagnostic and Statistical Manual of Mental Disorders*
DSS	decision support system
DSW	doctor of social work
DUI	driving under the influence
DVB	Department of Veterans Benefits
DVI	digital video interactive
DWI	driving while intoxicated
EAP	employee assistance program
EAPA	Employee Assistance Professionals Association
EBRI	Employee Benefit Research Institute
EBT	electronic benefits transfer
ECA	Epidemiologic Catchment Area
ECOSOC	Economic and Social Council
EEO	equal employment opportunity
EEOC	Equal Employment Opportunity Commission
EIC	earned income credit
EITC	earned income tax credit
ELAN	Education Legislative Action Network
ELISA	enzyme-linked immunosorbent assay
E-Mail	electronic mail
EMSC	emergency medical services for children
ENIAC	Electronic Numerical Integrator and Computer
EOA	Economic Opportunity Act
EPA	Environmental Protection Agency
EPO	exclusive provider organization
EPSS	electronic performance support system
ERISA	Employee Retirement Income Security Act of 1974
ES	effective size
ESL	English as a Second Language
FAO	Food and Agriculture Organization
FAP	Family Assistance Program
FAS	fetal alcohol syndrome
FBI	Federal Bureau of Investigation
FDA	Food and Drug Administration
FEHPA	Federal Employees Health Benefits Act
FEMA	Federal Emergency Management Agency
FERA	Federal Emergency Relief Administration
FHA	Federal Housing Administration
FICA	Federal Insurance Contributions Act
FIDCR	Federal Interagency Day Care Requirements
FLE	Family Life Education
FLSA	Fair Labor Standards Act
FmHA	Farmers Home Administration
FMLA	Family and Medical Leave Act
FNS	Food and Nutrition Service
FOSR	Function, Organization, and Structure Review
FPAs	Family Program Administrators
FSA	Federal Security Administration
FSAA	Family Service Association of America
FTC	Federal Trade Commission
FWAA	Family Welfare Association of America
FY	fiscal year
FYSB	Family and Youth Services Bureau

GA	General Assistance
GAI	guaranteed annual income
GAIN	Greater Avenues to Independence
GAO	U.S. General Accounting Office
GARF	Global Assessment of Relational Functioning
GDP	gross domestic product
GED	general equivalency diploma
GEM	Geriatric Evaluation and Management
GNP	gross national product
GRECC	Geriatric Research Education and Clinical Centers
GRID	gay-related immune disorder
4-H	Head, Heart, Hands, and Health
HCFA	Health Care Financing Administration
HI	Hospital Insurance
HIP	Helping Incarcerated Parents
HIV	human immunodeficiency virus
HIV/AIDS	HIV disease
HMO	health maintenance organization
HRD	(National) Health, Planning, and Resources Development Act
HRR	Human Rights Report
HRSA	Health Resources and Services Administration
HSAs	health system agencies
HUD	U.S. Department of Housing and Urban Development
Human SERVE	Human Service Employees Registration and Voter Education
Hz	hertz
I&R	information and referral
IASSW	International Association of Schools of Social Work
ICD	International Classification of Diseases
ICSSW	International Committee of Schools of Social Work
ICSW	International Congress of Social Welfare
ICWA	Indian Child Welfare Act
IDA	injection drug abusers
IDEA	Individuals with Disabilities Education Act
IDU	injecting drug use
IEP	individualized educational program
IFSW	International Federation of Social Workers
IHHS	In-Home Health Services
IHS	Indian Health Service
ILO	International Labour Organization
INS	Immigration and Naturalization Service
IPEC	International Programme on the Elimination of Child Labour
IPO	independent practice organization
IQ	intelligence quotient
IRCA	Immigration Reform and Control Act of 1986
IRS	Internal Revenue Service
IS	information system
ITV	interactive television
IUCISD	Interuniversity Consortium on International Social Development
IUD	intrauterine devices
IUPAE	Independent Union of Public Aid Employees
IV	intravenous
IVD	interactive video disk
JCAHO	Joint Commission on Accreditation of Healthcare Organizations
JJDPA	Juvenile Justice and Delinquency Prevention Act

JOBS	Job Opportunities and Basic Skills Training
JTPA	Job Training and Partnership Act
LAN	local area network
LEAA	Law Enforcement Assistance Administration
LRU	La Raza Unida
LULAC	League of United Latin American Citizens
LULU	locally unwanted land uses
MADD	Mothers Against Drunk Driving
MAG	Mothers Against Gangs
MAGIC	Merced Automated Global Information Control
MALDEF	Mexican American Legal Defense and Education Fund
MAP	membership assistance program
MAPA	Mexican American Political Association
MASH	Make Something Happen
MCC	Metropolitan Community Church
MCH	maternal and child health
MCHS	Maternal and Child Health Services
MDRC	Manpower Development Research Corporation
MIS	management information system
MORE	Member-Organized Resource Exchange
MPSW	military psychiatric social worker
MRI	magnetic resonance imaging
MSA	metropolitan statistical area
MSSP	Multipurpose Senior Services Project
MSW	master of social work
NA	Narcotics Anonymous
NAACP	National Association for the Advancement of Colored People
NABSW	National Association of Black Social Workers
NACW	National Association of Colored Women
NAEYC	National Association for the Education of Young Children
NAMI	National Alliance for the Mentally Ill
NAOSW	National Association of Oncology Social Workers
NAPWA	National Association of People with AIDS
NARCEA	National Aging Resource Center on Elder Abuse
NASHP	National Academy for State Health Policy
NASPAA	National Association of Schools of Public Affairs and Administration
NASSA	National Association of Schools of Social Administration
NASSW	National Association of School Social Workers
NASUA	National Association of State Units on Aging
NASW	National Association of Social Workers
NCATE	National Council for Accreditation of Teacher Education
NCCC	National Conference of Charities and Correction
NCCS	National Center on Charitable Statistics
NCF	National Civic Federation
NCFA	National Council for Children
NCHS	National Center for Health Statistics
NCLC	National Child Labor Committee
NCN	NASW Communications Network
NCOI	National Committee on Inquiry
NCOLGI	National Committee on Lesbian and Gay Issues
NCOMA	National Committee on Minority Affairs
NCORED	National Committee on Racial and Ethnic Diversity
NCOWI	National Committee on Women's Issues

NCPCR	National Center for the Prevention and Control of Rape
NCRP	National Committee for Responsive Philanthropy
NCSPP	National Center for Social Policy and Practice
NCSW	National Conference of Social Work
NCSWE	National Council on Social Work Education
NCVS	National Crime Victimization Survey
NFB	National Federation of the Blind
NGO	nongovernmental organization
NGT	nominal group technique
NHIP	National Health Insurance Program
NHIS	National Health Interview Survey
NHO	National Hospice Organization
NIAAA	National Institute on Alcoholism and Alcohol Abuse
NIADC	National Institute on Adult Day Care
NIDA	National Institute on Drug Abuse
NIDS	National Inventory of Documentary Sources
NIH	National Institutes of Health
NIMH	National Institute of Mental Health
NIT	negative income tax
NLRA	National Labor Relations Act
NLRB	National Labor Relations Board
NLS	National Library Service
NLS	national longitudinal survey
NMES	National Medical Expenditure Survey
NMHA	National Mental Health Association
NPR	national public radio
NRA	normal retirement age
NRM	new religious movement
NSFG	national surveys of family growth
NTEE	National Taxonomy of Exempt Entities
NVRA	National Voter Registration Act of 1993
O&M	orientation and mobility
OAA	Old-Age Assistance
OAA	Older Americans Act of 1965
OASDI	Old-Age and Survivors and Disability Insurance
OASI	Old-Age and Survivors Insurance
OBRA	Omnibus Budget Reconciliation Act
ODP	Orderly Departure Program
OJJDP	Office of Juvenile Justice and Delinquency Prevention
OJT	on-the-job training
OMB	Office of Management and Budget
OSAP	Office of Substance Abuse Prevention
OSIQ	Offer Self-Image Questionnaire for Adolescents
OXFAM	Oxford Committee on Famine
PACE	Political Action for Candidate Election
PAR	population-attributed risk
PASSO	Political Association of Spanish-Speaking Organizations
PATCH	Planned Approach to Community Health
PCP	*pneumocystis carinii* pneumonia
PET	positron emission tomography
PIA	primary insurance amount
PIE	person-in-environment
PIN	personal identification number
PIRC	Prevention Intervention Research Center

PKU	phenylketonuria
POS	purchase of service
PPO	preferred provider organization
PSID	Panel Study of Income Dynamics
PSIR	presentence investigation report
PSR	psychosocial rehabilitation
PTSD	posttraumatic stress disorder
PVO	private voluntary organization
PVS	persistent vegetative state
PWA	people with AIDS
QMB	qualified medical beneficiary
RDA	recommended dietary allowance
REA	Retirement Equity Act of 1984
RFP	Request for Proposal
RICO	Racketeer Influenced and Corrupt Organization (1970 statute)
RLIN	research libraries information network
RMP	regional medical program
RMP Act	Regional Medical Programs Act
RR	risk ratio
RTR	Reintegration Through Recreation
SAMHSA	Substance Abuse and Mental Health Services Administration
SCLC	Southern Christian Leadership Conference
SCMWA	State, County, and Municipal Workers of America
SDI	strategic defense initiative
SE	supported employment
SEIU	Service Employees International Union
SEM	standard error of measurement
SERVE	Service Employees Registration and Voter Education
SES	socioeconomic status
SGA	substantial gainful activity
SHARE	Source of Help in Airing and Resolving Experiences
SHPDA	state health planning and development agency
SIC	Standard Industrial Classification
SIECUS	Sex Information and Education Council of the United States
SIPP	Survey of Income and Program Participation
SMHAs	State Mental Health Authorities
SMI	Supplementary Medical Insurance
SNCC	Student Non-Violent Coordinating Committee
SOFAS	Social & Occupational Functioning Assessment Scale
SOS	Secular Organization for Sobriety
SOSAD	Save Our Sons and Daughters
SPL	sound pressure level
SPRANS	Special Programs of Regional and National Significance
SRO	single-room occupancy
SSA	Social Security Administration
SSD	single-subject (or -system) design
SSDI	Social Security Disability Insurance
SSEU	Social Service Employees Union
SSI	Supplemental Security Income
STD	sexually transmitted disease
STEPA	Street Terrorism Enforcement Prevention Act
SVREP	Southwest Voter Registration Education Project

SWIM	Saturated Work Initiative Model
SWOT	Strenghts, Weaknesses, Opportunities, and Threats
SWRG	Social Work Research Group
TB	tuberculosis
TDHS	Texas Department of Human Services
TFP	Thrifty Food Plan
TIAC	Temporary Inter-Association Council of Social Work Membership
TVA	Tennessee Valley Authority
UAW	United Automobile Workers
UCR	Uniform Crime Reports
UFWA	United Federal Workers of America
UN	United Nations
UNDP	United Nations Development Program
UNESCO	United Nations Education, Scientific, and Cultural Organization
UNHCR	United Nations High Commission for Refugees
UNICEF	United Nations Children's Fund (formerly United Nations International Children's Emergency Fund)
UNRRA	United Nations Relief and Rehabilitation Agency
UOPWA	United Office and Professional Workers of America
UPWA	United Public Workers of America
USCC	U.S. Catholic Conference
USCRA	U.S. Coordinator for Refugee Affairs
USDA	U.S. Department of Agriculture
USINS	U.S. Immigration and Naturalization Service
USNCHS	U.S. National Center for Health Statistics
UWASIS	United Way of America Services Identification System
UWI	University of the West Indies
VA	Veterans Administration
VCR	videocassette recorder
VET Centers	Vietnam-era Veterans Outreach and Counseling Centers
VHA	Veterans Health Administration
VISTA	Volunteers in Service to America
VOCA	Victims of Crime Act
VS	vital signs
VSC	voluntary surgical contraception
VSIS	Voluntary Cooperative Information System
WAN	wide area network
WASP	white Anglo-Saxon Protestant
WHO	World Health Organization
WHO/GPA	World Health Organization Global Programme on AIDS
WHO/SPA	World Health Organization/Special Programme on AIDS
WIC	Special Supplemental Nutrition Program for Women, Infants, and Children
WIN	Work Incentive Program
WPA	Works Progress Administration
YMCA	Young Men's Christian Association
YWCA	Young Women's Christian Association

9. Evolution of Selected Organizations

	Pre-1900	1901–1910	1911–1920	1921–1930	1931–1940	1941–1950	1951–1960	1961–1970	1971–1980	1981–1990	1991–1995
CHILDREN											
	National Federation of Day Nurseries—1898		Child Welfare League of America—1920	National Committee on Nursery Schools—1926	National Assn of Day Nurseries—1938	National Assn for Nursery Education—1946		National Assn for the Education of Young Children—1964	CWLA absorbs Florence Crittenton Assn of America—1976		
FAMILIES											
			American Assn for Organizing Family Social Work—1911	Family Welfare Assn of America—1930		Family Service Assn of America—1946				Family Service America—1983	Families International, Inc.—1993
SOCIAL WELFARE											
	Conference of Boards of Public Charities—1874 National Conference of Charities and Correction—1879		National Conference of Social Work—1917				National Conference on Social Welfare—1956			Last NCSW proceedings of National Social Welfare Forum (1982) published—1985	
SOCIAL WORK EDUCATION											
			Assn of Training Schools for Professional Social Work—1919		American Assn of Schools of Professional Social Work—1931 American Assn of Schools of Social Work—1933	National Assn of Schools of Social Administration—1942 National Council on Social Work Education—1946	American Assn of Schools of Social Work and National Council on Social Work Education merged into Council on Social Work Education—1952				

American Assn of Hospital Social Workers—1918		American Assn of Medical Social Workers—1934	American Assn of Medical Social Workers merged into NASW—1955
National Social Workers' Exchange—1919	American Assn of Social Workers—1921		American Assn of Social Workers merged into NASW—1955
National Assn of Visiting Teachers—1919		National Assn of School Social Workers—1945	National Assn of School Social Workers merged into NASW—1955
	American Assn of Psychiatric Social Workers—1926		American Assn of Psychiatric Social Workers merged into NASW—1955
	American Assn for the Study of Group Work—1936	American Assn of Group Workers—1946	Assn of Group Workers merged into NASW—1955
		Assn for the Study of Community Organization—1946	Assn for the Study of Community Organization merged into NASW—1955
		Social Work Research Group—1949	Social Work Research Group merged into NASW—1955

Sources: *Encyclopedia of associations* (27th ed.). (1993). Detroit: Gale Research. *Proceedings of first Conference of Charities and Correction.* (1885). Boston: George H. Ellis; *Proceedings of the Conferences of Charities and Correction, 1877/1878/1879.* (1880). Chicago: American Social Science Association; *Proceedings of the National Conference of Social Work.* (1917). Chicago: Author; *Social work year book.* (1929/1933/1935/1947). New York: Russell Sage Foundation; *Social work year book.* (1954). New York: American Association of Social Workers.

10. Contributors

Ann A. Abbott
Professional Conduct

Mimi Abramovitz
Aid to Families with Dependent Children

Julie S. Abramson
Interdisciplinary and Interorganizational
   Collaboration (with Beth B. Rosenthal)

Marian A. Aguilar
Women and Health Care

Frederick L. Ahearn, Jr.
Displaced People

Sheila H. Akabas
Occupational Social Work

Chauncey A. Alexander
Appendix 2: Distinctive Dates in Social Welfare
   History

Josephine A. Allen
African Americans: Caribbean

G. Frederick Allen
Probabation and Parole

Paula Allen-Meares
Children: Mental Health

Sandra C. Anderson
Alcohol Abuse

Bruce Armstrong
Family Planning

Adrienne Asch
Disability (with Nancy R. Mudrick); Visual
   Impairment and Blindness

Carol D. Austin
Adult Protective Services

David M. Austin
Management Overview

Darlyne Bailey
Management: Diverse Workplaces

Pallassana R. Balgopal
Asian Americans Overview; Asian Indians

Robert L. Barker
Private Practice

Richard P. Barth
Adoption

William H. Barton
Juvenile Corrections

Deborah Bass
Runaways and Homeless Youths

Marleine Bastien
Haitian Americans

Marion L. Beaver
Adult Foster Care

Rosina M. Becerra
Veterans and Veterans Services (with JoAnn
   Damron-Rodriguez)

Joyce O. Beckett
Human Development (with Harriette C. Johnson)

Linda Beebe
National Association of Social Workers (with
   Sheldon R. Goldstein)

John R. Belcher
Health Care: Homeless People (with Frederick A.
   DiBlasio)

Donald W. Beless
Council on Social Work Education

Neal S. Bellos
Aging: Services (with Mary Carmel Ruffolo)

Raymond M. Berger
Gay Men Overview (with James J. Kelly)

Sharon B. Berlin
Cognition and Social Cognitive Theory
   (with Paula S. Nurius)

Lucy Berliner
Child Sexual Abuse: Direct Practice

Marilyn A. Biggerstaff
Licensing, Regulation, and Certification

Ann Kallman Bixby
Public Social Welfare Expenditures

Rita Beck Black
Genetics (with Julia B. Rauch)

Martin Bloom
Primary Prevention Overview

Betty J. Blythe
Single-System Design

Marti Bombyk
Progressive Social Work

Gary L. Bowen
Marriage/Partners (with Allie C. Kilpatrick)

Neil Bracht
Prevention and Wellness

Ruth A. Brandwein
Women in Social Policy

Edward Allan Brawley
Mass Media

Mary Bricker-Jenkins
Women: Direct Practice (with Patricia W. Lockett)

Donald Brieland
Social Work Practice: History and Evolution

Eleanor L. Brilliant
Voluntarism

Sheryl Brissett-Chapman
Child Abuse and Neglect: Direct Practice

Anna Celeste Burke
Substance Abuse: Legal Issues

William H. Butterfield
Computer Utilization

Jeffrey A. Butts
Community-Based Corrections

Diane B. Byington
Sexual Assault

Angel P. Campos
Hispanics: Puerto Ricans

Donald E. Chambers
Economic Analysis

Pranab Chatterjee
Technology Transfer

Leon W. Chestang
Men: Direct Practice

Barbara Chester
Victims of Torture and Trauma

Julian Chow
Poverty (with Claudia J. Coulton)

Richard A. Cloward
Voter Registration (with Frances Fox Piven)

Pauline M. Collins
Social Work Profession Overview (with June Gary Hopps)

Elaine P. Congress
Gestalt

Jon R. Conte
Child Sexual Abuse Overview

Joan M. Cottler
Managed Care (with Golda M. Edinburg)

Marlene Cooper
Transactional Analysis (with Sandra Turner)

Kevin Corcoran
Psychometrics

Claudia J. Coulton
Poverty (with Julian Chow)

Richard T. Crow
Planning and Management Professions

Herman Curiel
Hispanics: Mexican Americans

JoAnn Damron-Rodriguez
Veterans and Veterans Services (with Rosina M. Becerra)

Joseph Davenport III
Rural Social Work Overview (with Judith A. Davenport)

Judith A. Davenport
Rural Social Work Overview (with Joseph Davenport)

Larry E. Davis
Families: Direct Practice (with Enola K. Proctor and Nancy R. Vosler)

Liane V. Davis
Domestic Violence

Diane de Anda
Adolescence Overview

Ronald B. Dear
Social Welfare Policy

Wynetta Devore
Ethnic-Sensitive Practice (with Elfriede G. Schlesinger)

Kevin L. DeWeaver
Developmental Disabilities: Definitions and Policies

Frederick A. DiBlasio
Health Care: Homeless People (with John R. Belcher)

Nancy S. Dickinson
Federal Social Legislation from 1961 to 1994

Diana M. DiNitto
Hunger, Nutrition, and Food Programs

Andrew W. Dobelstein
Federal Legislation and Administrative Rule Making

Ruth E. Dunkle
Aging Overview (with Theresa Norgard)

Patricia C. Dunn
Volunteer Management

Quang DuongTran
Asian Americans: Southeast Asians (with Jon S. Matsuoka)

Golda M. Edinburg
Managed Care (with Joan M. Cottler)

Richard L. Edwards
Introduction

Susan D. Einbinder
Policy Analysis

Kathleen Ell
Crisis Intervention: Research Needs

Laura Epstein
Brief Task-Centered Practice

Juanita C. Evans
Maternal and Child Health (with Kenneth J. Jaros)

Joyce E. Everett
Child Foster Care

Mark Ezell
Juvenile and Family Courts

Cynthia DeVane Fair
HIV/AIDS: Pediatric (with Lori Wiener and Anna Garcia)

Margot Taylor Fanger
Brief Therapies

Josefina Figueira-McDonough
Abortion

Richard J. First
Homeless Families (with John C. Rife and Beverly G. Toomey)

John P. Flynn
Social Justice in Social Agencies

Anne E. Fortune
Termination in Direct Practice

Larry W. Foster
Bioethical Issues

Mark W. Fraser
Violence Overview

Ruth I. Freedman
Developmental Disabilities: Direct Practice

Edith M. Freeman
School Social Work Overview

Michael Frumkin
Social Work Education (with Gary A. Lloyd)

Katherine Gabel
Female Criminal Offenders (with Denise Johnston)

Fernando J. Galan
Youth Services

Maeda J. Galinsky
Group Practice Overview (with Janice H. Schopler)

Dorothy N. Gamble
Citizen Participation (with Marie Overby Weil); Community Practice Models (with Marie Overby Weil)

Larry M. Gant
HIV/AIDS: Men

David L. Garber
Miliary Social Work (with Peter J. McNelis)

Anna Garcia
HIV/AIDS: Pediatric (with Lori Wiener and Cynthia DeVane Fair)

Irwin Garfinkel
Child Support

Diana R. Garland
Church Social Work

J. Dianne Garner
Long-Term Care

Sheldon R. Gelman
Boards of Directors

Paul Gendreau
Rehabilitation of Criminal Offenders

Carel B. Germain
Ecological Perspective (with Alex Gitterman)

Margaret Gibelman
Purchasing Social Services

David F. Gillespie
Ethical Issues in Research

Wallace J. Gingerich
Expert Systems

Leon Ginsberg
Public Services Management

Jeanne M. Giovannoni
Childhood

Alex Gitterman
Ecological Perspective (with Carel B. Germain)

Harvey L. Gochros
Sexual Distress

Jean S. Gochros
Bisexuality

Eda G. Goldstein
Psychosocial Approach

Sheldon R. Goldstein
National Association of Social Workers (with Linda Beebe)

Judith G. Gonyea
Family Caregiving (with Nancy R. Hooyman)

Natalie Gordon
Adult Day Care

Kevin M. Gorey
Environmental Health: Race and Socioeconomic Factors

Sol Gothard
Legal Issues: Confidentiality and Privileged Communication

Naomi Gottlieb
Women Overview

Donald K. Granvold
Cognitive Treatment

Muriel C. Gray
Drug Abuse

Ronald Green
Continuing Education (with Kimberly Strom)

William V. Griffin
Social Worker and Agency Safety

Burton Gummer
Social Planning

Charles Guzzetta
White Ethnic Groups

Jan L. Hagen
JOBS Program

Creasie Finney Hairston
Family Views in Correctional Programs

Dianne M. Hampton
African American Pioneers in Social Work
(with Barbara W. White)

Isadora Hare
School-Linked Services

Dianne F. Harrison
Human Sexuality

W. David Harrison
Community Development

Ann Hartman
Family Therapy

Helen Andon Haynes
Alaska Natives (with Eileen M. Lally)

Karen S. Haynes
Information and Referral Services

Lynne M. Healy
International Social Welfare: Organizations and
Activities

Juanita B. Hepler
Social Skills Training

Santos H. Hernández
Mutual Aid Societies

Merl C. Hokenstad
International Social Work Education (with
Katherine A. Kendall)

Thomas P. Holland
Organizations: Context for Social Services Delivery

Katharine Hooper-Briar
Jobs and Earnings (with Essie Tramel Seck)

Nancy R. Hooyman
Family Caregiving

June Gary Hopps
Social Work Profession Overview (with Pauline M.
Collins)

Joyce Hunter
Gay and Lesbian Adolescents (with Robert
Schaecher)

David L. Hussey
Adolescents: Direct Practice (with Mark I. Singer)

Demetrius S. Iatridis
Policy Practice

Alfreda P. Iglehart
Criminal Justice: Class, Race, and Gender Issues

Paul M. Isenstadt
Adult Courts

André Ivanoff
Suicide (with Marion Riedel)

Kenneth J. Jaros
Maternal and Child Health (with Juanita C. Evans)

Rosa Jimenez-Vazquez
Hispanics: Cubans

Alice K. Johnson
Homelessness

Geneva B. Johnson
Families: Demographic Shifts (with Maureen Wahl)

Harriette C. Johnson
Human Development (with Joyce O. Beckett)

Denise Johnston
Female Criminal Offenders (with Katherine Gabel)

Linda R. Wolf Jones
Unemployment Compensation and Workers'
Compensation

Alfred Kadushin
Interviewing

Jill Doner Kagle
Recording

Si Kahn
Community Organization

Sheila B. Kamerman
Families Overview

Karen Orloff Kaplan
End-of-Life Decisions

James M. Karls
Person-in-Environment (with Karin E. Wandrei)

James J. Kelly
Gay Men Overview (with Raymond M. Berger)

Katherine A. Kendall
International Social Work Education (with Merl C.
Hokenstad)

Paul R. Keys
Quality Management

Allie C. Kilpatrick
Marriage/Partners (with Gary L. Bowen)

Eric Kingson
Baby Boomers

Raymond S. Kirk
Welfare Employment Programs: Evaluation
(with Dennis K. Orthner)

David J. Klaassen
Archives of Social Welfare

Ruth Irelan Knee
Patient Rights (with Betsy S. Vourlekis)

Paul A. Kurzman
Professional Liability and Malpractice

Joan Laird
Lesbians: Parenting

Eileen M. Lally
Alaska Natives (with Helen Andon Haynes)

Pamela S. Landon
Generalist and Advanced Generalist Practice

Thomas R. Lawson
Music and Social Work

Bogart R. Leashore
African Americans Overview

Leslie Leighninger
Historiography

Carl G. Leukefeld
Health Services Systems Policy (with Richard Welsh)

Sar A. Levitan
Employment and Unemployment Measurement

Edith A. Lewis
Natural Helping Networks (with Zulema E. Suarez)

Ronald G. Lewis
American Indians

Mary Frances Libassi
Psychotropic Medications

Philip Lichtenberg
Men Overview

David S. Liederman
Child Welfare Overview

Alice Mu-jung P. Lin
Mental Health Overview

Gary A. Lloyd
HIV/AIDS: Overview; Social Work Education (with Michael Frumkin)

Patricia W. Lockett
Women: Direct Practice (with Mary Bricker-Jenkins)

Sadye L. Logan
Eating Disorders and Other Compulsive Behaviors

Roger A. Lohmann
Financial Management

John F. Longres
Hispanics Overview

Gary R. Lowe
Social Development

Doman Lum
Asian Americans: Chinese

Ann E. MacEachron
Experimental and Quasi-Experimental Design

Anthony N. Maluccio
Children: Direct Practice

Emilia E. Martinez-Brawley
Community

Jon K. Matsuoka
Asian Americans: Southeast Asians (with Quang DuongTran)

Marc Mauer
Sentencing of Criminal Offenders

Bernard S. Mayer
Conflict Resolution

Edward A. McKinney
Health Planning

C. Aaron McNeece
Adult Corrections

John S. McNeil
Bereavement and Loss

Peter J. McNelis
Military Social Work (with David L. Garber)

Ruth G. McRoy
Qualitative Research

Carol H. Meyer
Assessment

Daniel R. Meyer
Supplemental Security Income

James S. Mickelson
Advocacy

James Midgley
International and Comparative Social Welfare

Jerome G. Miller
Criminal Justice: Social Work Roles

Terry Mizrahi
Health Care: Reform Initiatives

Noreen Mokuau
Pacific Islanders

Ernestine Moore
Legal Issues: Low-Income and Dependent People

Vernon L. Moore
Case Management (with Stephen M. Rose)

Armando Morales
Homicide

Julio Morales
Gay Men: Parenting

Robert M. Moroney
Public Health Services

Lynne C. Morris
Rural Poverty

Elizabeth A. Mulroy
Housing

Kenji Murase
Asian Americans: Japanese

Theresa Norgard
Aging Overview (with Ruth E. Dunkle)

Paul S. Nurius
Cognition and Social Cognitive Theory (with Sharon B. Berlin)

Regina O'Grady-LeShane
Retirement and Pension Programs

Julianne S. Oktay
Primary Health Care

Dennis K. Orthner
Welfare Employment Programs: Evaluation
(with Raymond S. Kirk)

Larry P. Ortiz
Sectarian Agencies

Jack Otis
Child Labor

Martha N. Ozawa
Income Security Overview; Social Security
(with Martin B. Tracy)

Peter J. Pecora
Personnel Management

Felice Davidson Perlmutter
Nonprofit Management Issues

K. Jean Peterson
HIV/AIDS: Women

Elaine Pinderhughes
Direct Practice Overview

Frances Fox Piven
Voter Registration (with Richard A. Cloward)

Robert D. Plotnick
Income Distribution

William L. Pollard
Civil Rights

Dennis L. Poole
Health Care: Direct Practice

Philip R. Popple
Social Work Profession: History

Thomas J. Powell
Self-Help Groups

Enola K. Proctor
Families: Direct Practice (with Larry E. Davis and
Nancy R. Vosler)

Michele A. Puccinelli
Aging: Public Policy Issues and Trends (with
Fernando M. Torres-Gil)

Juan Ramos
Migrant Workers

Eloise Rathbone-McCuan
Agency-Based Research

Julia B. Rauch
Genetics (with Rita Beck Black)

Frederic G. Reamer
Ethics and Values

Thomas A. Regulus
Gang Violence

P. Nelson Reid
Social Welfare History

William J. Reid
Research Overview

Mildred Rein
General Assistance

Michael Reisch
Public Social Services

Dorothy P. Rice
Health Care: Financing

Jack M. Richman
Hospice

Marion Riedel
Suicide (with André Ivanoff)

John C. Rife
Homeless Families (with Richard J. First and
Beverly G. Toomey)

Donald P. Riley
Family Life Education

Susan P. Robbins
Cults

Albert R. Roberts
Victim Services and Victim/Witness Assistance
Programs

Sunny Harris Rome
Social Workers in Politics (with Toby Weismiller)

Sheldon D. Rose
Goal Setting and Intervention Planning

Stephen M. Rose
Case Management (with Vernon L. Moore)

Beth B. Rosenthal
Interdisciplinary and Interorganizational Collaboration (with Julie S. Abramson)

Judith W. Ross
Hospital Social Work

Fariyal Ross-Sheriff
African Americans: Immigrants

Jack Rothman
Intervention Research

Joseph R. Rowan
Health Care: Jails and Prisons

Allen Rubin
Survey Research

Mary Carmel Ruffolo
Aging: Services (with Neal S. Bellos)

K. Dean Santos
Deafnesss

Rosemary C. Sarri
Criminal Behavior Overview

Daniel G. Saunders
Domestic Violence: Legal Issues

David N. Saunders
Substance Abuse: Federal, State, and Local Policies

Robert Schaecher
Gay and Lesbian Adolescents (with Joyce Hunter)

Elfriede G. Schlesinger
Ethnic-Sensitive Practice (with Wynetta Devore)

Dick Schoech
Information Systems

Janice H. Schopler
Group Practice Overview (with Maeda J. Galinsky)

Essie Tramel Seck
Jobs and Earnings (with Katharine Hooper-Briar)

Steven P. Segal
Deinstitutionalization

Fredrick W. Seidl
Program Evaluation

Michael Shernoff
Gay Men: Direct Practice

Lawrence Shulman
Supervision and Consultation

Mark I. Singer
Adolescents: Direct Practice (with David L. Hussey)

Terry L. Singer
Sexual Harassment

Rolland F. Smith
Settlements and Neighborhood Centers

Nancy J. Smyth
Substance Abuse: Direct Practice

Virginia C. Strand
Single Parents

Kimberly Strom
Continuing Education (with Ronald Green)

Zulema E. Suarez
Natural Helping Networks (with Edith A. Lewis)

William Patrick Sullivan
Psychosocial Rehabilitation

Carol R. Swenson
Clinical Social Work

Milton Tambor
Unions

Toshio Tatara
Elder Abuse

Susan Taylor-Brown
HIV/AIDS: Direct Practice

Beverly G. Toomey
Homeless Families (with Richard J. First and John C. Rife)

Fernando M. Torres-Gil
Aging: Public Policy Issues and Trends (with Michele A. Puccinelli)

Ronald W. Toseland
Aging: Direct Parctice

Robbie W. Christler Tourse
Special-Interest Professional Associations

Elizabeth M. Tracy
Family Preservation and Home-Based Services

Martin B. Tracy
Social Security (with Martha N. Ozawa)

Harvey Treger
Police Social Work

John E. Tropman
Community Needs Assessment

Carol Thorpe Tully
Lesbians Overview

Francis J. Turner
Social Work Practice: Theoretical Base

John B. Turner
Fundraising and Philanthropy

Sandra Turner
Transactional Analysis (with Marlene Cooper)

Nan Van Den Bergh
Employee Assistance Programs

Dorothy Van Soest
Peace and Social Justice

Ione D. Vargus
Charitable Foundations and Social Welfare

Lynn Videka-Sherman
Meta-analysis

Michele J. Vinet
Child Care Services

Nancy R. Vosler
Families: Direct Practice (with Enola K. Proctor and Larry E. Davis)

Betsy S. Vourlekis
Patient Rights (with Ruth Irelan Knee)

Maureen Wahl
Families: Demographic Shifts (with Geneva B. Johnson)

Karin E. Wandrei
Person-in-Environment (with James M. Karls)

Tovah M. Wax
Deaf Community

Stephen A. Webster
Disasters and Disaster Aid

Marie Overby Weil
Citizen Participation (with Dorothy N. Gamble);
  Community Practice Models (with Dorothy N.
  Gamble)

Richard Welsh
Health Services Systems Policy (with Carl G.
  Leukefeld)

Toby Weismiller
Social Workers in Politics (with Sunny Harris
  Rome)

Susan J. Wells
Child Abuse and Neglect Overview

Barbara W. White
African American Pioneers in Social Work (with
  Dianne M. Hampton)

Leila Whiting
Vendorship

James K. Whittaker
Children: Group Care

Lori Wiener
HIV/AIDS: Pediatric (with Cynthia DeVane Fair and
  Anna Garcia)

Constance W. Williams
Adolescent Pregnancy

Janet B. W. Williams
Diagnostic and Statistical Manual of Mental
  Disorders

Leon F. Williams
Epistemology

David Wineman
Children's Rights

Natalie Jane Woodman
Lesbians: Direct Practice

Joseph Wronka
Human Rights

John A. Yankey
Strategic Planning

Alma T. Young
Quality Assurance

Maria E. Zuniga
Aging: Social Work Practice

Index

(Note: References to entire entries are in **boldface**)

A

Abandonment, 470–471
Abbott, Ann A., 1916
Abbott, Edith, 2553, 2570
Abbott, Grace, 393, 2570
Abernathy, Ralph David, 2570–2571
Abortion, **7–14**
    access to, 36, 969
    bioethics and, 293
    conclusions regarding, 13–14
    historical background of, 7–9, 969
    for HIV-infected women, 1327
    implications for social work, 11–13
    public opinion on, 10–11
    right of adolescents to obtain, 470
    Roe v. Wade and, 9–10, 498–499, 1803
Abramovitz, Mimi, 183, 785–786
Abramson, Julie S., 1479
Abstinence syndrome, 796
Abuse. *See* Child abuse/neglect; Elder abuse;
    Family violence; Sexual abuse
Academic achievement. *See* Educational attain-
    ment
Academy of Certified Social Workers (ACSW), 1617,
    1623
Accountability
    changing mechanisms of, 507
    in nonprofit organizations, 2480
    shifts in, 940
Accreditation, 633, 2242–2243
Acculturation, 253
Acquired immune deficiency syndrome (AIDS),
    1257–1283. *See also* Human immunodefi-
    ciency virus (HIV)
    adult day care for people with, 76
    advocacy for people with, 1302–1303, 1308–
        1313, 1322–1323
    in African Americans, 110, 1309–1311, 1316,
        1325
    behavior change in people with, 1273–1274
    bioethics and, 294–295
    caregivers and, 1300, 1318
    case management and, 1296–1298, 1306, 1321–
        1322
    challenges of working with people with, 1302–
        1303
    child welfare and, 431
    in children and adolescents, 23–24, 42, 438,
        1059–1060, 1280–1281, **1314–1323,** 1688
    confidentiality issues and, 885
    in correctional institutions, 1184, 1310
    counseling and psychotherapy for, 1298–1299
    definitions of, 1257–1259, 1315–1316, 1325–1326

direct practice for people with, 1081–1082,
    1291–1303
drug therapies for, 1266–1268, 1308–1309
duty to treat, 1804
duty-to-warn laws and, 1582–1583
epidemiology of, 1291–1292, 1310–1311, 1315–
    1316
in females, 1279–1280, 1316, **1325–1329,** 2547
in gay men, 1072
in Hispanics, 1241, 1310, 1316, 1325
impact on families, 1092, 1299, 1308, 1314–1323
in men, **1306–1313**
in parents, 1092, 1316–1318
peer supports for, 1299–1300
practice interventions for, 1295–1296
practice issues related to, 1292–1295
psychosocial issues related to, 1268–1272
rewards for working with, 1300–1302
service delivery and, 1277–1278, 1306–1307
sexual orientation and, 301, 303
social workers and, 1276–1277, 1281–1283,
    1312–1313, 1329
substance abuse and, 206, 1080, 1307–1308
substance abuse treatment and, 2334
suicide and, 2368
terminal care and death from, 289, 1317–1318,
    1363
transmission of, 1257, 1259–1261, 1272–1273,
    1279, 1325–1327
U.S. responses to, 1274–1277, 1688
in veterans, 2437
Acute care
    explanation of, 1162
    financing for, 1162
    for homeless people, 1176
    social workers and, 1162–1163
Adams, Frankie Victoria, 2571
Adaptations, 817
Addams, Jane, 487, 500, 577, 2248–2249, 2307, 2553,
    2571–2572
Addiction, 796, 801. *See also* Alcoholism; Drug use/
    abuse; Substance abuse
Adequate notice principle, 2174
Adjudication, 1917–1920
Adler, A., 1389
Administration for Children and Families (DHHS),
    1504
Administrative rules, 996
Administrative tribunals, 1587–1588
Adolescence, **16–29, 40–46**
    biological development in, 16–18, 40–41
    cognitive development in, 20
    definition of, 16, 40

Bowen, Gary L., 1663
Bowlby, John, 286
Brace, Charles Loring, 376, 2575
Bracht, Neil, 1879
Brain neurochemistry, 798–799
Brandwein, Ruth A., 2552
Brawley, Edward Allan, 1674
Breckinridge, Sophonisba Preston, 2575–2576
Bricker-Jenkins, Mary, 2529
Brief contact therapy, 329–330
Brief counseling, 1371
Brief task-centered practice, **313–322**
Brief therapies, **323–331**
  approaches used in, 327–330
  client selection for, 326
  future of, 330–331
  history of, 325–326
  outcome studies of, 326–327
  overview of, 323–325
Brieland, Donald, 2247
Brilliant, Eleanor L., 2469
Brissett-Chapman, Sheryl, 353
Brockway, Zebulon Reed, 2576
Brookins, G. K., 904
Brown v. Board of Education, 107, 467, 498, 902
Bruno, Frank John, 2576
Bryce-Laporte, R., 124
Buddhism, 235, 251
Budman, S. H., 329
Buell, Bradley, 2576
Bulimia nervosa. *See also* Eating disorders
  biological factors of, 810
  demographic and family characteristics of, 808, 809
  explanation of, 805–806
  psychodynamic explanations for, 811
  treatment and management of, 812
Bulletin boards, computerized, 599–600
Bureau of Indian Affairs, 220, 222, 224
Burke, Anna Celeste, 2347
Burnout, 1277, 1908
Burns, Eveline Mabel, 2576–2577
Bush administration
  campaign to recruit volunteers by, 486
  health policy of, 1194, 1203
  social policy of, 2, 1010, 2223
Business administration, 1837–1838
Business process improvement (BPI), 2022
Butler, R. N., 867
Butterfield, William H., 594
Butts, Jeffrey A., 549
Byington, Diane B., 2136

C
Cabot, Richard Clarke, 2577
Cambodians

immigration of, 233, 250
  social and cultural profile of, 251
Campos, Angel P., 1245
Canada, social work education in, 1518
Cannon, Ida Maud, 2577
Cannon, Mary Antoinette, 2577
Capital punishment
  efforts to abolish, 2128
  as negative model, 1353
  racial bias and, 2125–2126
  trends in, 2124
Capitation financing, 1639
Caregivers
  collaboration between social workers and, 956–957
  elder abuse by, 837
  for elderly relatives, 1627–1628
  growth in need for, 951–952
  of HIV/AIDS patients, 1300, 1318
  policy issues affecting, 955–957
Caregiving
  baby boomers involved in, 278–279
  changing needs for, 937
  community and institutional, for elderly people, 149
  consequences of, 954–955
  by employed women, 954
  by family, 148–149
  future directions for, 957
  gender issues in, 952
  nature of, 952–953
  policy issues related to, 955–956
  reduced capacity for, 192
  social context of, 953–954
Caribbean Americans, **121–128**
  differences between African Americans and, 124
  economic and social conditions of, 122–123
  Haitian and Cuban, 125
  historical overview of, 121–122
  migration patterns of, 123–124
  naturalization and citizenship for, 125–126
  racism and racial distribution in United States and, 124–125
  social workers and, 126–128
  stages of adaptation for, 126
Caribbean region, social work education in, 1518
Carlton, Thomas Owen, 2578
Carrier screening, 1111
Carter administration
  health care policy of, 1193–1194
  social policy of, 1008, 1009
Case law, 69, 996
Case management, **335–339**
  approaches to, 742–743
  coordination issues in, 336–337
  criticisms of, 505–506

Encyclopedia of Social Work, 19th Edition
Designed by Quinn Information Design
Composed by Harlowe Typography, Inc., in Cheltenham Book and Helvetica
Printed by United Book Press on 40# Woodlawn

ISBN 0-87101-255-3

90000>

EAN

9 780871 012555